Warman's®

Antiques and Collectibles

Price Guide

36th Edition

Edited by Ellen T. Schroy

Published by

krause publications

700 E. State Street • Iola, WI 54990-0001
Telephone: 715/445-2214
Web: www.krause.com

Please call or write for our free catalog.

Please call or write for our free catalog of publications.
Our toll-free number to place an order or obtain a free catalog is 800-258-0929
or please use our regular business telephone 715-445-2214.

Library of Congress Catalog Number: 82-643543
ISBN: 0-87341-975-8

Printed in the United States of America

INTRODUCTION

Warman's: Serving the trade for more than 40 years

Individuals in the trade refer to this book simply as *Warman's*, a fitting tribute to E. G. Warman and the product he created. *Warman's* has been around for more than 40 years. We are proud as peacocks that *Warman's* continues to establish the standards for general antiques and collectibles price guides in 2002, just as it did in 1972, when its first rival appeared on the scene.

Warman's, the antiques and collectibles "bible," covers objects made between 1700 and the present. Because it reflects market trends, *Warman's* has added more and more 20th-century material to each edition. Remember, 1900 was more than 100 years ago—the distant past to the new generation of 20-something and 30-something collectors.

The general "antiques" market consists of antiques (for the purposes of this book, objects made before 1945), collectibles (objects of the post-World War II era that enjoy an established secondary market), and desirables (contemporary objects that are collected, but speculative in price). Although *Warman's* contains information on all three market segments, its greatest emphasis is on antiques and collectibles. In fact, this book is the essential field guide to the antiques and collectibles marketplace, which indicates that *Warman's* is much more than a list of object descriptions and prices. It is a basic guide to the field as a whole, providing you with the key information you need every time you encounter a new object or collecting category.

'Warman's is the Key'

Warman's provides the keys needed by auctioneers, collectors, dealers, and others to understand and deal with the complexities of the antiques and collectibles market. A price list is only one of many keys needed today. *Warman's* 36th edition contains many additional keys including: histories, marks, reference books, periodicals, collectors' clubs, museums, reproductions, videotapes, and special auctions. Useful buying and collecting hints also are provided. Used properly, there are few doors these keys will not open.

Organization

Listings: Objects are listed alphabetically by category, beginning with ABC Plates and ending with Zsolnay Pottery. If you have trouble identifying the category to which your object belongs, use the extensive index in the back of the book. It will guide you to the proper category. We have made the listings descriptive enough so that specific objects can be identified.

We also emphasize items that are actively being sold in the marketplace. Some harder-to-find objects are included to demonstrate market spread—useful information worth considering when you have not traded actively in a category recently.

Each year as the market changes, we carefully review our categories—adding, dropping, and combining to provide the most comprehensive coverage possible. *Warman's* quick response to developing trends in the marketplace is one of the prime reasons for its continued leadership in the field.

Krause Publications also publishes other *Warman's* titles. Each utilizes the *Warman's* format and concentrates on a specific collecting group, e.g., American pottery and porcelain; Americana and collectibles; coins and currency; country, English, and continental pottery and porcelain; glass; and jewelry. Most are subsequent editions. Their expanded coverage compliments the information found in *Warman's Antiques and Collectibles Price Guide*.

History: Collectors and dealers enhance their appreciation of objects by knowing something about their history. We present a capsule history for each category. In many cases, this history contains collecting hints or other useful information.

References: Books are listed in most categories to help you learn more about the objects. Included are author, title, publisher, and date of publication or most recent edition. If a book has been published by a small firm or individual, we have indicated (published by author). To assist in finding these sometimes hard-to-locate authors, we have included the address.

Many of the books included in the lists are hard to find. The antiques and collectibles field is blessed with a dedicated core of book dealers who stock these specialized publications. You will find them at flea markets and antiques shows and through their advertisements in trade publications. Books go out of print quickly, yet many books printed more than 25 years ago remain the standard work in a category. Used book dealers often can locate many of these valuable reference sources. Many dealers publish annual or semi-annual catalogs. Ask to be put on their mailing lists.

Periodicals: The newsletter or bulletin of a collectors' club usually provides the concentrated focus sought by specialty collectors and dealers. However, there are publications not associated with collectors' clubs that collectors and dealers should be aware of. These are listed in their appropriate category introductions. In addition, there are several general interest newspapers and magazines which deserve to be brought to our users' attention. These are:

- *Antique & The Arts Weekly*, Bee Publishing Company, 5 Church Hill Road, Newton, CT 06470; http://www.thebee.com/aweb

- *Antique Review*, P.O. Box 538, Worthington, OH 43085

- *Antique Trader Weekly*, P.O. Box 1050, Dubuque, IA 52001; http://www.csmonline.com

- *AntiqueWeek*, P.O. Box 90, Knightstown, IN 46148; http://www.antiqueweek.com

- *Antiques* (The Magazine Antiques), 551 Fifth Avenue, New York, NY 10017

- *Antiques & Collecting*, 1006 South Michigan Avenue, Chicago, IL 60605

- *Maine Antique Digest*, P.O. Box 358, Waldoboro, ME 04572; http://www.maineantiquedigest.com

- *MidAtlantic Monthly Antiques Magazine*, P.O. Box 908, Henderson, NC 27536
- *New England Antiques Journal*, 4 Church St., Ware, MA 01082
- *New York-Pennsylvania Collector*, Drawer C, Fishers, NY 14453

Space does not permit listing all of the national and regional publications in the antiques and collectibles field. The ones listed are just a sampling. Their publications and conventions produce knowledge which often cannot be found elsewhere. Many of these clubs are short-lived; others are so strong, they have regional and local chapters.

Museums: The best way to study a specific field is to see as many documented examples as possible. For this reason, we have listed museums where significant collections in that category are on display. Special attention must be directed to the complex of museums which make up the Smithsonian Institution in Washington, D.C.

Reproductions: Reproductions are a major concern to all collectors and dealers. Throughout this edition, we alert you to known reproductions and keys to recognizing them. Most reproductions are unmarked; the newness of their appearance is often the best clue to uncovering them. Specific objects known to be reproduced are marked within the listings with an asterisk (*). The information is designed to serve as a reminder of past reproductions and prevent you from buying them, believing them to be period.

We strongly recommend subscribing to *Antique & Collectors Reproduction News*, a monthly newsletter that reports on past and present reproductions, copycats, fantasies, and fakes. Send $32 for 12 issues to: ACRN, Box 12130, Des Moines, IA 50312-9403 (www.repronews.com). This newsletter has been published for years. Consider buying all available back issues. The information they contain will be of service long into the future.

Special Auctions: In the 36th edition, we have chosen to again feature boxes highlighting auction houses. To qualify for placement in one of these boxes, auction houses have to meet specific requirements: They must actively hold auctions solely devoted to that specialty, and they must provide a catalog and prices realized. Often the catalogs become an important part of a collection, serving as reference and identification guides. Many of the auction companies featured have more than one auction annually; some work with a particular collectors' club or society. It is our hope that these boxes will give collectors and those searching for specific objects a better idea of who to contact. *Warman's* is designed to give collectors and dealers a lot of clues to find out what they have, what it is worth, and where to sell it.

These special auction boxes are not intended, however, to diminish the outstanding work done by the generalists, those auctioneers who handle all types of material. The fine auctions like Garth's, Jackson's, Joy Luke, Skinner's, Sloan's, and Swann's provide us with excellent catalogs all through the year covering many aspects of the antiques and collectibles marketplace. Several categories had too many auction houses to list. For example, most auctioneers sell furniture, clocks, and fine arts. We just couldn't list them all. In addition to these auction-house boxes, we hope you will consult the master list of auction houses included in this edition. We are sure that any one of them will be eager to assist in consigning or selling antiques and collectibles.

Index: A great deal of effort has been expended to make our index useful. Always begin by looking for the most specific reference. Remember, many objects can be classified in three or more categories. If at first you don't succeed, try, try again.

Black-and-white photographs: You may encounter a piece you cannot identify well enough to use the index. Consult the photographs and manufacturers' marks. If you own several editions of *Warman's*, you have a valuable photographic reference to the antiques and collectibles field. Learn to use it.

Price notes

In assigning prices, we assume the object is in very good condition. If otherwise, we note this in our description. It would be ideal to suggest that mint, or unused, examples of all objects exist. The reality is that objects from the past were used, whether they be glass, china, dolls, or toys. Because of this, some normal wear must be expected. In fact, if an object such as a piece of furniture does not show wear, its origins may be more suspect than if it does show wear.

Whenever possible, we have tried to provide a broad listing of prices within a category so you have a "feel" for the market. We emphasize the middle range of prices within a category, while also listing some objects of high and low value to show market spread. We do not use ranges because they tend to confuse, rather than help, collectors and dealers. How do you determine if your object is at the high or low end of the range? There is a high degree of flexibility in pricing in the antiques field. If you want to set ranges, add or subtract 10 percent from our prices.

One of the hardest variants with which to deal is the regional fluctuations of prices. Victorian furniture brings widely differing prices in New York, Chicago, New Orleans, or San Francisco. We have tried to strike a balance. Know your region and subject before investing heavily. If the best buys for cameo glass are in Montreal or Toronto, then be prepared to go there if you want to save money or add choice pieces to your collection. Research and patience are key factors to building a collection of merit. Another factor that affects prices is a sale by a leading dealer or private collector. We temper both dealer and auction house figures.

Price research

Everyone asks, "Where do you get your prices?"

They come from many sources. First, we rely on auctions. Auction houses and auctioneers do not always command the highest prices. If they did, why do so many dealers buy from them? The key to understanding auction prices is to know when a price is high or low in the range. We think we do this and do it well. The 36th edition represents a concentrated effort to contact more regional auction houses, both large and small. The cooperation has been outstanding and has resulted in an ever-growing pool of auction prices and trends to help us determine the most up-to-date auction prices.

Second, we work closely with dealers. We screen our contacts to make certain they have full knowledge of the market. Dealers make their living from selling antiques, so they cannot afford to have a price guide which is not in touch with the market.

More than 50 antiques and collectibles magazines, newspapers, and journals come into our office regularly. They are excellent barometers of what is moving and what is not. We don't hesitate to call an advertiser and ask if his listed merchandise sold.

Our conversations with dealers and collectors around the country have enhanced this book. and we are in the field at antiques shows, malls, flea markets, and auctions recording prices and taking photographs.

Collectors work closely with us. They are specialists whose devotion to research and accurate information is inspiring. Generally, they are not dealers, but whenever we have asked them for help, they have responded willingly and admirably.

Board of advisers

Our Board of Advisers is made up of specialists, both dealers and collectors, who have a commitment to accurate information. You'll find their names listed in the front of the book. Many have authored a major reference work on their subject.

Our esteemed Board of Advisers has increased in number and scope. Participants have all provided detailed information regarding the history and reference section of their particular area of expertise, as well as preparing price listings. Many furnished excellent photographs and even shared their thoughts on the state of the market.

We are delighted to include those who are valuable members, officers, and founders of collectors' clubs. They are authors of books and articles, and many frequently lecture to groups about their specialties. Most of our advisers have been involved with antiques and collectibles for more than 20 years. Many are retired and the antiques and collectibles business is a hobby which encompasses most of their free time. Others either work full time or part time in the antiques and collectibles profession. We asked them about their favorite publications, and most responded with the names of specialized trade papers. Many told us they are regular readers of *AntiqueWeek* and the *Maine Antique Digest*.

One thing they all have in common is their enthusiasm for the antiques and collectibles marketplace. They are eager to share their knowledge with collectors. Many have developed wonderful friendships through their efforts and are enriched by them. If you wish to buy or sell an object in the field of expertise of any of our advisers, drop them a note along with a SASE. If time permits, they will respond.

Buyer's guide, not seller's guide

Warman's is designed to be a buyer's guide, suggesting what you would have to pay to purchase an object on the open market from a dealer or collector. It is not a seller's guide to prices. People frequently make this mistake. In doing so, they deceive themselves. If you have an object listed in this book and wish to sell it to a dealer, you should expect to receive approximately 50 percent of the listed value. If the object will not resell quickly, expect to receive even less.

Private collectors may pay more, perhaps 70 to 80 percent of our listed price, if your object is something needed for their collection. If you have an extremely rare object or an object of exceptionally high value, these guidelines do not apply.

Examine your piece as objectively as possible. As an antiques and collectibles appraiser, I spend a great deal of time telling people their treasures are not "rare" at all, but items readily available in the marketplace.

In respect to buying and selling, a simple philosophy is that a good purchase occurs when the buyer and seller are happy with the price. Don't look back. Hindsight has little value in the antiques and collectibles field. Given time, things tend to balance out.

Always improving

Warman's is always trying to improve. Space is freely given to long price descriptions to help you understand what the piece looks like and perhaps what's special about it. With this edition, we've arranged the design into a three-column format, using more bold words to help you find what you're looking for more easily. Also new to this edition is an eight-page color section.

Some categories have been arranged so that if the only thing you know is how high, you can start there. Many times, identifying what you've got is the hardest part, so the first place to start is how big the object is—grab that ruler and see what you can find that's a comparable size. You are still going to have to make a determination about what the object is made of, be it china, glass, porcelain, wood, or other materials. Use all your senses to discover what you've got. Ask questions about your object—who made it, and why, how was it used, where, and when. As you find answers to these questions, you'll be helping yourself figure out just what the treasure is all about. Now take that information and you'll be able to look it up and discover the value.

Eager to hear from readers

We're always eager to hear what you think about *Warman's* and how we can improve it. Write to either Ellen Schroy, *Warman's* editor, P.O. Box 392, Quakertown, PA 18951-0392 or e-mail at schroy@voicenet.com. The fine staff at Krause Publications can be reached at 700 E. State St., Iola, WI 54990. It's our goal to continue in the *Warman's* tradition and make it the best price guide available.

STATE OF THE MARKET

The state of antiques and collectibles in spring of 2002 has shown real signs of improvement, with collectors and dealers enjoying the new collecting climate together. Last fall, some segments of the antiques and collectibles marketplace were soft; signs of an overall recession were weakening collectors' desire and their financial ability to add to their collections. However, after weathering the turmoil of last September 11, many collectors and dealers are starting to see that antiques and collectibles may represent a certain stability in their lives, perhaps a better way to connect with their roots and expand interests that they have been nurturing for years.

There were many reasons for the uncertain period in the marketplace last fall. Many folks were finding less discretionary money in their pockets, so less was spent on antiques and collectibles. But, when stocks started to fail, some folks felt they needed a safer place to invest in. Some turned to the antiques market, finding bargains at auctions in fine arts, furniture, and high-end antiques. The plus side to this is that a lovely painting can hang on the wall and give pleasure to the viewer, probably more pleasure than the equivalent to its purchase price sitting in some floundering stock. There will always be people with more money than they need to live on (don't we all wish that was us!) and when those people enjoy antiques and collectibles, they can buy what tickles their fancy. How they go about doing that directly affects the antiques and collectibles marketplace.

Some of the highlights of this past year's antiques marketplace include several areas. One that shines with a renewed interest is the area of art glass lamps. Names such as Handel, Tiffany, and Pairpoint are commanding more interest than ever. When a lamp is all original—meaning the base and shade match, both are in pristine condition, and signed, the prices soared.

Another area where prices seemed to be soaring again is paintings. Every auction house can claim some outstanding results in this area. For example, Jackson's International Auctioneers & Appraisers in Cedar Falls, Iowa, sold a fresh-to-the-market 20" x 12" unidentified landscape, oil on canvas by American artist Albert Bierstadt (1830-1902). The painting attracted many bidders from coast to coast and sold for an impressive $78,200 (including premium), which was slightly over the high estimate.

Good American furniture was also strong this past auction season. As in the past, original condition, hardware, and good provenance helped keep prices strong. Skinner, Inc., Auctions and Appraisers of Antiques and Fine Arts in Boston, Massachusetts, sold a Federal mahogany inlaid serpentine sideboard for $74,000. This fine piece was made by John Shaw of Annapolis, Maryland, with the Eastern shore provenance and a named cabinet maker adding to the value of the sideboard. Following the current decorator trends, painted furniture also did quite well. Made in the Concord, New Hampshire area, a Queen Anne looking glass with an olive-green painted and parcel gilt frame sold for $16,100.

Several other areas that saw increased collector interest were silver and jewelry. Last June, a 15-ct cushion-cut Kashmir sapphire, flanked by diamonds and set as a ring, sold for $206,000 at Skinner's auction. What helped make this ring so special, besides its great beauty and color, was that it was signed "Yard," indicating it had been crafted by jeweler Raymond Yard. Bidding was fierce for that ring, from bidders at the Boston gallery, as well as telephone bidders.

Telephone bidders also secured a valuable piece of Americana when they purchased a 108-inch long piece of veiling worn by Martha Washington. When Alderfer Auction Company sold this fragment for $27,500 (plus 10 percent commission), it included documentation that it had been worn by Martha when she sat for the portrait that Gilbert Stuart painted of her. Again, it was provenance and documentation that helped add value to the antique.

Some areas of the antiques and collectibles market that seemed to soften this past season were ones where more items were suddenly available to collectors, either through auction or on-line. Mechanical banks are a great example of where increased supply has caused collector interest to actually lower prices on some items. Rare examples in pristine condition are still commanding high prices, but collectors are not paying as much for lesser quality or more common banks. The market for Oriental-type rugs is also somewhat soft as collectors demand higher-quality rugs than those that have entered the marketplace recently. Collectors interested in purchasing rugs that will retain their investment quality value now demand handmade examples with few, if any, repairs and little wear.

As we emerge from our cocoons this spring, we are seeing record attendance at antiques and collectibles shows, fierce bidding at auctions, and parking lots full at antiques malls and shops.

When buyers decide to shop at antiques malls, shows, and shops, the local dealer benefits. When buyers decide to visit and bid at antiques auctions, the auctioneer and his consignors benefit. When buyers decide to use their time to seek out antiques and collectibles on-line, the seller benefits. Where the grumbling sets in, is that the on-line buyer probably is not spending as much time visiting shops, shows, malls, and flea markets, which causes dealers to see less traffic and less revenue. Many savvy dealers are turning to the Internet to create virtual stores to supplement their bricks and mortar establishments, trying to display their merchandise in as many venues as possible. Bet we can all remember when the thought of selling antiques via the computer was pretty foreign—we wanted to see and touch everything before we purchased it. Perhaps it's the big on-line auctions and the ease of bidding on-line that has changed our collective minds. Perhaps it's also the ability to find objects that aren't usually within our usual travel distances. Add to that the ability to control what we can afford to pay, and the ease of finding another similar object if the first gets too pricey for our grasp.

There has never been a better time when buyers should know their collecting area more than the dealers and other collectors might know it. Buyers should also know and trust the dealers and auctioneers they are buying from and trust them well. Education, knowledge, and perseverance are the keys to finding the best you can for your collections.

Remember when you, as the buyer, went to an auction? You could walk around and preview the items to be sold, make notes about what you were interested in, grab a chair and sit down, and wait for the item to come up. Today, auctions are getting as sophisticated as their buyers. Previews are now often held days before, and through catalogs and on-line listings, more individuals are now viewing the objects for sale. This should be good news for the auctioneers and consignors. But what about the buyers? Are they still coming to the auction hall? Or are they choosing to sit at home and bid via their computers? Sure, it might be more convenient, but does it give that same adrenaline rush? And what about the buyers sitting in the auction hall? Are they becoming frustrated by not only bidding against the other bidders in the hall, but also trying to stare down the competition? Now they are often competing with absentee bids, phone bidders, and Internet bidders, all for the same object.

Some of the many auctions I visited in the past year have tried this method and it seems to be working for them. However, it's not a perfect world either. Many lots fail to reach a satisfactory minimum, having phone and Internet bidding causes the auction house to hire more staff to handle all the technology and, I've got a hunch, some are a bit nervous until the objects are paid for and delivered to the new owners. Plus, someone has got to smile and try to soothe the feathers of the on-the-floor bidders who constantly lose to the unseen phone bidder. One auctioneer I visited was visibly shaken by the lack of bidders in the hall when a catalog auction began. The seats never were filled, but fairly stable prices were achieved, thanks to a dedicated core of interested bidders, and a few phone bids. The level of trust between the buyer and seller is constantly tested with this absentee bidding, since who can be sure that the auctioneer really has a buyer and is not just bouncing bids off the wall to raise the price? It's certainly a time in our history for auctioneers to practice the highest standards and be responsible for checking references, credit, and other security issues.

The other issue that greatly affects the state of the antiques and collectibles marketplace is the type of goods coming into it to be sold. Now that the Baby Boomers are becoming grayer and many are starting to downsize, some interesting objects are coming to auction. Many of the generation before the Baby Boomers are also starting to sell off collections for many reasons: downsizing, needing to supplement their income, being tired of maintaining a collection, or the real human desire to see someone else enjoy the objects. Wouldn't it be wonderful to think that all these objects are great, first-rate condition? The trouble is, they aren't—many have condition problems and as the buyers are offered more and more examples, they can (and should) become choosier. The trouble with that concept is that the damaged (or second rate) goods are still around, filling up the back shelves at antiques shops and malls.

Time will tell if the Generation X'ers will be interested in decorating their homes and apartments with antiques and collectibles. They might be more than willing to take the cast-offs from Dad's or Grandma's, but how many are going out searching for more? How the antiques and collectibles marketplace learns to attract those buyers will determine how well it moves forward.

A long line of people waiting to get into the spring 2002 Atlantique City show.

Ellen Ruck of Chester, New Jersey, dressed in period costume, stands next to a selection of items from her booth. The chest of drawers is a circa 1820 Chester maple with sandwich glass pulls and was tagged at $2,750. The apothecary chest above the drawers is Scottish and was offered for $1,765.

Throughout the show, Florida dealers Jinx and Dann Perszyk had numerous vintage advertising and ephemera seekers at their booth.

At the Atlantique City Antiques Show in March 2002, I was asked by the promoter, Ted Jones, to walk around and see what was offered for sale. Was the merchandise tagged well, were the goods presented in a pleasing manner, etc. While taking this tour, I spoke to many dealers and also shoppers and tried to gauge their reaction. The March show was a real contrast to the October 2001 show held only a few weeks after September 11, where many dealers felt privileged to be able to show their wares and that they could carry on the tradition of a fine antiques show like Atlantique City. Many felt it was time for Americans to start to get on with their lives again, but feared it would take some time for this collective healing to begin.

The October show went well, but was a bit quiet, with collectors somewhat reserved. The attendance at the March 2002 show was enthusiastic and great numbers of collectors came to view the vast array of antiques and collectibles offered. The dedicated collectors were there, scouting with their telephones, pagers, and other electronic devices, hoping to find that wonderful treasure. Many shoppers left clutching objects to add to their collections and were glad for the opportunity to participate in such a lively antiques show experience.

In general, shoppers found a virtual feast of interesting objects. Many dealers sported a spring or patriotic theme to their booths, giving visual appeal and/or decorating insights to the shoppers. Most dealers told me at the end of the show that they had a good experience, while a few were not quite as optimistic and had hoped for more sales. But, that's the usual response and is nothing really new. Where is that crystal ball we're all looking for to see what the future will hold?

What is certain is that the future will brighten and that antiques and collectibles will always remain the intriguing hobby it has been for decades.

BOARD OF ADVISERS

Dale Abrams
Tea Leaf Antiques
960 Bryden Road
Columbus, OH 43205
(614) 258-5258
e-mail:
70003.2061@compuserve.com
Tea Leaf Ironstone

John and Alice Ahlfeld
2634 Royal Road
Lancaster, PA 17603
(717) 397-7313
e-mail: AHFELDS@aol.com
Pattern Glass

Bob Armstrong
15 Monadnock Road
Worcester, MA 01609
(508) 799-0644
Puzzles

Susan and Al Bagdade
The Country Peasants
1325 N. State Parkway, Apt 15A
Chicago, IL 60610
(312) 397-1321
Quimper

Tina M. Carter
882 S. Mollison Ave.
El Cajon, CA 92020
(619) 440-5043
e-mail: premos2@aol.com
Teapots

Craig Dinner
P.O. Box 4399
Sunnyside, NY 11104
(718) 729-3850
Doorstops

Roselyn Gerson
P.O. Box 100
Malverne, NY 11565
(516) 593-6746
Compacts

Ted Hake
Hake's Americana & Collectibles
Auctions
P.O. Box 1444
York, PA 17405
(717) 848-1333
e-mail: auction@hakes.com
Disneyana, Political

Mary Harris
221 Scarborough Lane
Millersville, PA 17551
(717) 872-8288
e-mail: marymaj@dejazzd.com
Majolica

Tom Hoepf
P.O. Box 90, 27 Jefferson St.
Knightstown, IN 46148
(800) 876-5135
e-mail: antiqueth@aol.com
Cameras

Joan Hull
1376 Nevada
Huron, SD 57350
(605) 352-1685
Hull Pottery

David Irons
Irons Antiques
223 Covered Bridge Road
Northampton PA 18067
(610) 262-9335
e-mail: Dave@ironsantiques.com
Irons

Michael Ivankovich
P.O. Box 2458
Doylestown, PA 18901
(215) 345-6094
e-mail: Wnutting@comcat.com
*Wallace Nutting, Wallace
Nutting Look-Alikes*

Dorothy Kamm
P.O. Box 7460
Port St. Lucie, FL 34985-7470
(561) 465-4008
e-mail: dorothy.kamm@usa.net
*American Hand-Painted
Porcelain, American
Hand-Painted Jewelry*

James D. Kaufman
248 Highland St.
Dedham, MA 2026
(800) 283-8070
Dedham Pottery

W.D. and M. J. Keagy
P.O. Box 106
Bloomfield, IN 47424
(812) 384-3471
Yard-Long Prints

Ellen G. King
King's Antiques
102 N. Main St.
Butler, PA 16001
(724) 894-2596
e-mail: egking@attglobal.net
Flow Blue, Mulberry China

Samuel Kissee
P.O. Box 3762
Chico, CA 95927-2763
e-mail: skissee@cschico.edu
Pattern Glass

Michael Krumme
P.O. Box 48225
Los Angeles, CA 90048-0225
Paden City

Elizabeth M. Kurella
2133 Davis Ave.
Whiting, IN 46396
(219) 659-1124
Lace and Linens

Mel and Roberta Lader
8212 Glyn St.
Alexandria, VA 22309
(703) 360-6078
e-mail: lader@gwu.edu
Pattern Glass

Robert Levy
The Unique One
2802 Centre St.
Pennsauken, NJ 08109
(856) 663-2554
e-mail:
theuniqueone@worldnet.att.net
Coin-Operated Items

Clarence and Betty Maier
The Burmese Cruet
P.O. Box 432
Montgomeryville, PA 18936
(215) 855-5388
e-mail: burmesecruet@erols.com
*Burmese Glass, Crown
Milano, Royal Flemish*

James S. Maxwell, Jr.
P.O. Box 367
Lampeter, PA 17537
(717) 464-5573
Banks, Mechanical

Bob Perzel
4 Mine St.
P.O. Box 1057
Flemington, NJ 8822
(908) 782-9361
Stangl Birds

Evalene Pulati
National Valentine Collectors Assoc.
P.O. Box 1404
Santa Ana, CA 92702
Valentines

John D. Querry
RD 2, Box 1378
Martinsburg, PA 16662
(814) 793-3185
Gaudy Dutch

David Rago
David Rago Auctions, Inc.
333 N. Main St.
Lambertville, NJ 8530
(609) 397-9374
e-mail: http://www.ragoarts.com
*Art Pottery, Arts & Crafts,
Fulper, Grueby, Newcomb*

Charles and Joan Rhoden
8693 N. 1950 East Road
Georgetown, IL 61846-6254
(217) 662-8046
e-mail: rhoden@soltec.net
Yard-Long Prints

Julie P. Robinson
P.O. Box 117
Upper Jay, NY 12987
(518) 946-7753
Celluloid

Kenneth E. Schneringer
271 Sabrina Ct
Woodstock, GA 30188
(707) 926-9083
e-mail: trademan68@aol.com
Catalogs

Susan Scott
882 Queen Street West
Toronto, Ontario Canada M6K 1Q3
e-mail:
Susan@collecting20thcentury.com
Chintz

Judy Smith
1702 Lamont St. NW
Washington, DC 20010-2602
(202) 332-3020
e-mail: judy@bau-
ble-and-bibebs.com, judy@quilt.net
Lea Stein Jewelry

**Richard M. Smith
Lissa Bryan-Smith**
17 Market St.
Lewisburg, PA 17837
e-mail: lbs8253@ptdprolog.net
Christmas Items

George Sparacio
P.O. Box 791
Malaga, NJ 08328-0791
(856) 694-4167
e-mail: mrvesta1@aol.com
Match Safes

Louis G. Jr. St. Aubin
44 North Water St.
New Bedford ,MA 2740
(508) 993-4944
Mount Washington

Henry A. Taron
Tradewinds Antiques
P.O. Box 249
Manchester By-The-Sea, MA
01944-0249
(978)526-4085
e-mail:
taron@tradewindsantiques.com
Canes

George Theofiles
Miscellaneous Man
P.O. Box 1776
New Freedom, PA 17349
(717) 235-4766
Posters

Clifford Wallach
81 Washington St., #7J
Brooklyn, NY 11201
(718) 596-5325
e-mail: info@trampart.com
Tramp Art

Lewis S. Walters
143 Lincoln Lane
Berlin, NJ 08008
(856) 719-1513
e-mail: lew69@erols.com
Phonographs, Radios

AUCTION HOUSES

The following auction houses cooperate with *Warman's* by providing catalogs of their auctions and price lists. This information is used to prepare *Warman's Antiques and Collectibles Price Guide*, volumes in the Warman's Encyclopedia of Antiques and Collectibles. This support is truly appreciated.

Albrecht & Cooper Auction Services
3884 Saginaw Road
Vassar, MI 48768
(517) 823-8835

Sanford Alderfer Auction Company
501 Fairgrounds Road
Hatfield, PA 19440
(215) 393-3000
Web site:
http://www.alderfercompany.com

American Social History and Social Movements
4025 Saline St.
Pittsburgh, PA 15217
(412) 421-5230

Andre Ammelounx
The Stein Auction Company
P.O. Box 136
Palatine, IL 60078
(847) 991-5927

Antique Bottle Connection
147 Reserve Road
Libby, MT 59923
(406) 293-8442

Apple Tree Auction Center
1616 W. Church St.
Newark, OH 43055
(614) 344-4282

Arthur Auctioneering
RD 2, P.O. Box 155
Hughesville, PA 17737
(717) 584-3697

Auction Team Köln
Jane Herz
6731 Ashley Court
Sarasota, FL 34241
(941) 925-0385

Auction Team Köln
Postfach 501168 D 5000
Köln 50, W. Germany

Noel Barrett Antiques & Auctions, Ltd.
P.O. Box 1001
Carversville, PA 18913
(610) 297-5109

Robert F. Batchelder
1 W. Butler Ave.
Ambler, PA 19002
(610) 643-1430

Bear Pen Antiques
2318 Bear Pen Hollow Road
Lock Haven, PA 17745
(717) 769-6655

Beverly Hills Auctioneers
9454 Wilshire Blvd., Suite 202
Beverly Hills, CA 90212
(310) 278-8115

Bill Bertoia Auctions
1881 Spring Road
Vineland, NJ 08360
(609) 692-1881

Biders Antiques Inc.
241 S. Union St.
Lawrence, MA 01843
(508) 688-4347

Brown Auction & Real Estate
900 East Kansas
Greensburg, KS 67054
(316) 723-2111

Buffalo Bay Auction Co.
5244 Quam Circle
Rogers, MN 55374
(612) 428-8440
Web site:
www.buffalobayauction.com

Butterfield, Butterfield & Dunning
755 Church Road
Elgin, IL 60123
(847) 741-3483
Web site: http://www:butterfields.com

Butterfield, Butterfield & Dunning
7601 Sunset Blvd.
Los Angeles, CA 90046
(213) 850-7500
Web site: http://www:butterfields.com

Butterfield, Butterfield & Dunning
220 San Bruno Ave.
San Francisco, CA 94103
    (415) 861-7500
Web site: http://www:butterfields.com

C. C. Auction Gallery
416 Court
Clay Center, KS 67432
(913) 632-6021

Cerebro
P.O. Box 327
East Prospect, PA 17317
(717) 252-3685

W. E. Channing & Co., Inc.
53 Old Santa Fe Trail
Santa Fe, NM 87501
(505) 988-1078

Chicago Art Galleries
5039 Oakton St.
Skokie, IL 60077
(847) 677-6080

Childers & Smith
1415 Horseshoe Pike
Glenmoore, PA 19343
(610) 269-1036
e-mail: harold@smithautionco.com

Christie's
502 Park Ave.
New York, NY 10022
(212) 546-1000
Web site: http://www.christies.com

Christie's East
219 E. 67th St.
New York, NY 10021
(212) 606-0400
Web site: http://www.christies.com

Cincinnati Art Galleries
635 Main St.
Cincinnati, OH 45202
(513) 381-2128
Web site:
http://www.cincinnatiartgalleries.com

Mike Clum, Inc.
P.O. Box 2
Rushville, OH 43150
(614) 536-9220

Cobb's Doll Auctions
1909 Harrison Road
Johnstown, OH 43031-9539
(740) 964-0444

Cohasco Inc.
Postal 821
Yonkers, NY 10702
(914) 476-8500

Collection Liquidators Auction Service
341 Lafayette St.
New York, NY 10012
(212) 505-2455
Web site:
http://www.rtam.com/coliq/bid.html
e-mail: coliq@erols.com

Collectors Auction Services
RR 2, Box 431 Oakwood Road
Oil City, PA 16301
(814) 677-6070
Web site: http://www.caswel.com

Collector's Sales and Service
P.O. Box 4037
Middletown, RI 02842
(401) 849-5012
Web site:
http://www.antiquechina.com

Coole Park Books and Autographs
P.O. Box 199049
Indianapolis, IN 46219
(317) 351-8495
e-mail: cooleprk@indy.net

Copeke Auction
226 Route 7A
Cokepe, NY 12516
(518) 329-1142

Samuel J. Cottonne
15 Genesee St.
Mt. Morris, NY 14510
(716) 583-3119

C. Wesley Cowan Historic Americana
673 Wilmer Ave.
Cincinnati, OH 45226
e-mail: info@HistoricAmericana.com
Phone: (513) 871-1670
Fax: (513) 871-8670

Craftsman Auctions
1485 W. Housatoric
Pittsfield, MA 01202
(413) 442-7003
Web site: http://www.artsncrafts.com

Dawson's
128 American Road
Morris Plains, NJ 07950
(973) 984-6900
Web site: http://www.idt.net/-dawson1

Decoys Unlimited, Inc.
P.O. Box 206
West Barnstable, MA 02608
(508) 362-2766
http://www.decoysunlimited.inc.com

DeWolfe & Wood
P.O. Box 425
Alfred, ME 04002
(207) 490-5572

Marlin G. Denlinger
RR3, Box 3775
Morrisville, VT 05661
(802) 888-2775

Dixie Sporting Collectibles
1206 Rama Road
Charlotte, NC 28211
(704) 364-2900
Web site: http://www.sportauc-tion.com

Dorothy Dous, Inc.
1261 University Drive
Yardley, PA 19067-2857
(888) 548-6635

William Doyle Galleries, Inc.
175 E. 87th St.
New York, NY 10128
(212) 427-2730
Web site:
http://www.doylegalleries.com

Dunbar Gallery
76 Haven St.
Milford, MA 01757
(508) 634-8697

Early Auction Co.
123 Main St.
Milford, OH 45150
(513) 831-4833

Fain & Co.
P.O. Box 1330
Grants Pass, OR 97526
(888) 324-6726

Ken Farmer Realty & Auction Co.
105A Harrison St.
Radford, VA 24141
(703) 639-0939
Web site: http://kenfarmer.com

Fine Tool Journal
27 Fickett Road
Pownal, ME 04069
(207) 688-4962
Web site:
http://www.wowpages.com/FTJ/

Steve Finer Rare Books
P.O. Box 758
Greenfield, MA 01302
(413) 773-5811

Fink's Off The Wall Auctions
108 E. 7th St.
Lansdale, PA 19446
(215) 855-9732
Web site: www.finksauctions.com

Flomaton Antique Auction
P.O. Box 1017
320 Palafox St.
Flomaton, AL 36441
(334) 296-3059

Fontaine's Auction Gallery
1485 W. Housatonic St.
Pittsfield, MA 01201
(413) 488-8922

William A. Fox Auctions Inc.
676 Morris Ave.
Springfield, NJ 07081
(201) 467-2366

Freeman\Fine Arts Co. of Philadelphia, Inc.
1808 Chestnut St.
Philadelphia, PA 19103
(215) 563-9275

Garth' Auction, Inc.
2690 Stratford Road
P.O. Box 369
Delaware, OH 43015
(740) 362-4771

Greenberg Auctions
7566 Main St.
Skysville, MD 21784
(410) 795-7447

Green Valley Auction Inc.
Route 2, Box 434
Mt. Crawford, VA 22841
(540) 434-4260

Guerney's
136 E. 73rd St.
New York, NY 10021
(212) 794-2280

Hake's Americana & Collectibles
P.O. Box 1444
York, PA 17405
(717) 848-1333

Gene Harris Antique Auction Center, Inc.
203 South 18th Ave.
P.O. Box 476
Marshalltown, IA 50158
(515) 752-0600
Web site:
www.harrisantiqueauction.com

Norman C. Heckler & Company
Bradford Corner Road
Woodstock Valley, CT 06282
(203) 974-1634

High Noon
9929 Venice Blvd.
Los Angeles, CA 90034
(310) 202-9010
Web site: www.High Noon.com

Randy Inman Auctions, Inc.
P.O. Box 726
Waterville, ME 04903
(207) 872-6900
Web site: www.inmanauctions.com

Michael Ivankovich Antiques & Auction Co., Inc.
P.O. Box 2458
Doylestown, PA 18901
(215) 345-6094
Web site: http://www.nutting.com

Jackson's Auctioneers & Appraisers
2229 Lincoln St.
Cedar Falls, IA 50613
(319) 277-2256
Web site:
http://www.jacksonauction.com

James D. Julia Inc.
Rt. 201 Skowhegan Road
P.O. Box 830
Fairfield, ME 04937
(207) 453-7125
Web site: www.juliaauctions.com

J. W. Auction Co.
54 Rochester Hill Road
Rochester, NH 03867
(603) 332-0192

Lang's Sporting Collectables, Inc.
31 R Turthle Cove
Raymond, ME 04071
(207) 655-4265

La Rue Auction Service
201 S. Miller St.
Sweet Springs, MO 65351
(816) 335-4538

Leonard's Auction Company
1631 State Road
Duncannon, PA 17020
(717) 957-3324

Howard Lowery
3818 W Magnolia Blvd.
Burbank, CA 91505
(818) 972-9080

Joy Luke
The Gallery
300 E. Grove St.
Bloomington, IL 61701
(309) 828-5533
Web site: http://www.joyluke.com

Mapes Auctioneers & Appraisers
1729 Vestal Pkwy
Vestal, NY 13850
(607) 754-9193

Martin Auctioneers Inc.
P.O. Box 477
Intercourse, PA 17534
(717) 768-8108

McMasters Doll Auctions
P.O. Box 1755
Cambridge, OH 43725
(614) 432-4419

McMurray Antiques & Auctions
P.O. Box 393
Kirkwood, NY 13795
(607) 775-2321

Metropolitan Book Auction
123 W. 18th St., 4th Floor
New York, NY 10011
(212) 929-7099

Gary Metz's Muddy River Trading Company
P.O. Box 1430
Salem, VA 24135
(540) 387-5070

William Frost Mobley
P.O. Box 10
Schoharie, NY 12157
(518) 295-7978

William Morford
RD #2
Cazenovia, NY 13035
(315) 662-7625

Neal Auction Company
4038 Magazine St.
New Orleans, LA 7015
(504) 899-5329
Web site: http://www.nealauction.com

New England Auction Gallery
P.O. Box 2273
W Peabody, MA 01960
(508) 535-3140

New Orleans Auction St. Charles Auction Gallery, Inc.
1330 St. Charles Ave.
New Orleans, LA 70130
(504) 586-8733
Web site:
http://www.neworleansauction.com

New Hampshire Book Auctions
P.O. Box 460
92 Woodbury Road
Weare, NH 03281
(603) 529-7432

Norton Auctioneers of Michigan Inc.
50 West Pearl at Monroe
Coldwater, MI 49036
(517) 279-9063

Nostalgia Publications, Inc.
21 S. Lake Dr.
Hackensack, NJ 07601
(201) 488-4536
Web site: www.nostalgiapubls.com

Old Barn Auction
10040 St. Rt. 224 West
Findlay, OH 45840
(419) 422-8531
Web site: http://www.oldbarn.com

Ohio Cola Traders
4411 Bazetta Road
Cortland, OH 44410
(330) 637-0357

Richard Opfer Auctioneering Inc.
1919 Greenspring Dr.
Timonium, MD 21093
(410) 252-5035
Web site: www.opferauction.com

Pacific Book Auction Galleries
133 Kerney St., 4th Floor
San Francisco, CA 94108
(415) 989-2665
Web site: http://www.nbn.com/~pba/

Past Tyme Pleasures
PMB #204, 2491 San Ramon Valley Blvd., #1
San Ramon, CA 94583
(925) 484-6442
Fax: (925) 484-2551
Web site: http://www.pastyme.com
e-mail: Pasttyme@excite.com

Phillips Ltd.
406 E. 79th St.
New York, NY 10021
(212) 570-4830
Web site:
http://www.phillips-auction.com

Postcards International
2321 Whitney Ave., Suite 102
P.O. Box 5398
Hamden, CT 06518
(203) 248-6621
Web site:
http://www.csmonline.com/
postcardsint/

Poster Auctions International
601 W. 26th St.
New York, NY 10001
(212) 787-4000
Web site: www.posterauction.com

Profitt Auction Company
684 Middlebrook Road
Staunton, VA 24401
(540) 885-7369

Provenance
P.O. Box 3487
Wallington, NJ 07057
(201) 779-8725

David Rago Auctions, Inc.
333 S. Main St.
Lambertville, NJ 08530
(609) 397-9374
Web site: http://www.ragoarts.com

Lloyd Ralston Toy Auction
350 Long Beach Blvd.
Stratford, CT 06615
(203) 375-9399
Web site: www.lloydralstontoys.com

James J. Reeves
P.O. Box 219
Huntingdon, PA 16652-0219
(814) 643-5497
Web site: www.JamesJReeves.com

Mickey Reichel Auctioneer
1440 Ashley Road
Boonville, MO 65233
(816) 882-5292

Sandy Rosnick Auctions
15 Front St.
Salem, MA 01970
(508) 741-1130

Thomas Schmidt
7099 McKean Road
Ypsilanti, MI 48197
(313) 485-8606

Seeck Auctions
P.O. Box 377
Mason City, IA 50402
(515) 424-1116
Web site:
www.willowtree.com/~seeckauctions

L. H. Selman Ltd.
761 Chestnut St.
Santa Cruz, CA 95060
(408) 427-1177
Web site: http://www.selman.com

Sentry Auction
113 School St.
Apollo, PA 15613
(412) 478-1989

Skinner Inc.
Bolton Gallery
357 Main St.
Bolton, MA 01740
(978) 779-6241
Web site: http://www.skinnerinc.com

Skinner, Inc.
The Heritage on the Garden
63 Park Plaza
Boston, MA 02116
(978) 350-5429
Web site: http://www.skinnerinc.com

C. G. Sloan & Company Inc.
4920 Wyaconda Road
North Bethesda, MD 20852
(301) 468-4911
Web site: http://www.cgsloan.com

Smith & Jones, Inc., Auctions
12 Clark Lane
Sudbury, MA 01776
(508) 443-5517

Smith House Toy Sales
26 Adlington Road
Eliot, ME 03903
(207) 439-4614

R. M. Smythe & Co.
26 Broadway
New York, NY 10004-1710
(212) 943-1880
Web site: http://www.rm-smythe.com

Sotheby's
1334 York Ave.
New York, NY 10021
(212) 606-7000
Web site: http://www.sothebys.com

Southern Folk Pottery Collectors Society
220 Washington St.
Bennett, NC 27208
(336) 581-4246

Stanton's Auctioneers
P.O. Box 146
144 South Main St.
Vermontville, MI 49096
(517) 726-0181

Stout Auctions
11 W. Third St.
Williamsport, IN 47993-1119
(765) 764-6901

Michael Strawser
200 N. Main St.
P.O. Box 332
Wolcottville, IN 46795
(219) 854-2859
Web site: www.majolicaauctions.com

Swann Galleries Inc.
104 E. 25th St.
New York, NY 10010
(212) 254-4710
Web site: www.swanngalleries.com

Swartz Auction Services
2404 N. Mattis Ave.
Champaign, IL 61826-7166
(217) 357-0197
Web site:
http://www/SwartzAuction.com

The House In The Woods
S91 W37851 Antique Lane
Eagle, WI 53119
(414) 594-2334

Theriault's
P.O. Box 151
Annapolis, MD 21401
(301) 224-3655
Web site: http://www.theriaults.com

Toy Scouts
137 Casterton Ave.
Akron, OH 44303
(216) 836-0668
e-mail: toyscout@salamander.net

Treadway Gallery, Inc.
2029 Madison Road
Cincinnati, OH 45208
(513) 321-6742
Web site:
http://www.a3c2net.com/
treadwaygallery

Unique Antiques & Auction Gallery
449 Highway 72 West
Collierville, TN 38017
(901) 854-1141

Venable Estate Auction
423 West Fayette St.
Pittsfield, IL 62363
(217) 285-2560
e-mail: sandiv@msn.com

Victorian Images
P.O. Box 284
Marlton, NJ 08053
(609) 985-7711
Web site: www.tradecards.com/vi

Victorian Lady
P.O. Box 424
Waxhaw, NC 28173
(704) 843-4467

Vintage Cover Story
P.O. Box 975
Burlington, NC 27215
(919) 584-6900

Bruce and Vicki Waasdorp
P.O. Box 434
10931 Main St.
Clarence, NY 14031
(716) 759-2361
Web site:
http://www.antiques-stoneware.com

Web Wilson Antiques
P.O. Box 506
Portsmouth, RI 02871
1-800-508-0022

Winter Associates
21 Cooke St. Box 823
Plainville, CT 06062
(203) 793-0288

Wolf's Auctioneers
1239 W. 6th St.
Cleveland, OH 44113
(614) 362-4711

Woody Auction
Douglass, KS 67039
(316) 746-2694

York Town Auction, Inc.
1625 Haviland Road
York, PA 17404
(717) 751-0211
e-mail:
yorktownauction@cyberia.com

ABBREVIATIONS

The following are standard abbreviations, which we have used throughout this edition of *Warman's*.

4to = 8" x 10"
8vo = 5" x 7"
12mo = 3" x 5"
ABP = American Brilliant Period
ADS = Autograph Document Signed
adv = advertising
ah = applied handle
ALS = Autograph Letter Signed
AQS = Autograph Quotation Signed
C = century
c = circa
Cal. = caliber
circ = circular
cyl. = cylinder
cov = cover
CS = Card Signed
d = diameter or depth
dec = decorated
dj = dust jacket
DQ = Diamond Quilted
DS = Document Signed
ed = edition
emb = embossed
ext. = exterior
eyep. = eyepiece
Folio = 12" x 16"
ftd = footed
ga = gauge
gal = gallon

ground = background
h = height
horiz. = horizontal
hp = hand painted
hs = high standard
HT = hard top
illus = illustrated, illustration
imp = impressed
int. = interior
irid = iridescent
IVT = inverted thumbprint
j = jewels
K = karat
l = length
lb = pound
litho = lithograph
ll = lower left
lr = lower right
ls = low standard
LS = Letter Signed
mfg = manufactured
MIB = mint in box
MOP = mother-of-pearl
n/c = no closure
ND = no date
NE = New England
No. = number
ns = no stopper
r/c = reproduction closure

o/c = original closure
opal = opalescent
orig = original
os = orig stopper
oz = ounce
pat = patent
pcs = pieces
pgs = pages
PUG = printed under the glaze
pr = pair
PS = Photograph Signed
pt = pint
qt = quart
rds = roadster
RM = red mark
rect = rectangular
sgd = signed
S. N. = Serial Number
sngl = single
SP = silver plated
SS = Sterling silver
sq = square
TLS = Typed Letter Signed
unp = unpaged
vert. = vertical
vol = volume
w = width
yg = yellow gold
# = numbered

Grading Condition

The following numbers represent the standard grading system used by dealers, collectors, and auctioneers:

C.10 = Mint
C. 9 = Near mint
C.8.5 = Outstanding
C.8 = Excellent
C.7.5 = Fine +
C.7 = Fine
C. 6.5 = Fine – (good)
C. 6 = Poor

ABC PLATES

History: The majority of early ABC plates were manufactured in England and imported into the United States. They achieved their greatest popularity from 1780 to 1860. Since a formal education was uncommon in the early 19th century, the ABC plate was a method of educating the poor for a few pennies.

ABC plates were made of glass, pewter, porcelain, pottery, or tin. Porcelain plates range in diameter from 4-3/8 inches to slightly over 9-1/2 inches. The rim usually contains the alphabet and/or numbers; the center features animals, great men, maxims, or nursery rhymes.

References: Susan and Al Bagdade, *Warman's English & Continental Pottery & Porcelain*, 3rd edition, Krause Publications, 1998; Mildred L. and Joseph P. Chalala, *A Collector's Guide to ABC Plates, Mugs and Things*, Pridemark Press, 1980; Irene and Ralph Lindsey, *ABC Plates & Mugs*, Collector Books, 1998; Noel Riley, *Gifts for Good Children*, Richard Dennis Publications, 1991.

Collectors' Club: ABC Plate/Mug Collector's Circle, 67 Stevens Ave., Old Bridge, NJ 08857.

Glass

6" d, amber, duck **48.00**
6" d, clear

Christmas Eve, Santa on
chimney **75.00**
Elephant with howdah, three waving
Brownies, Ripley & Co. **135.00**
Little Bo Peep, center scene, raised
alphabet border **50.00**
Plain center, white scalloped
edge **65.00**
Young Girl, portrait **65.00**
7" d, frosted and clear, clock face center, Arabic and Roman numerals, alphabet center **75.00**

Pottery or porcelain

5" d, Franklin value of money
maxim **110.00**
6" d

Gathering Cotton **425.00**
Take Your Time Miss Lucy, black transfer of money and cat, polychrome enamel, titled, molded hops rim, red trim, ironstone, imp "Meakin" **125.00**
6-3/4" d, Horses for Hire or Sale, brown transfer and polychrome dec . . . **145.00**
7" d, brown transfer of fox
hunt **125.00**
7-1/4" d, boy, stringed instrument, bird on fence, brown transfer, emb alphabet border, marked "Adams" **80.00**
7-1/2" d

Crusoe Finding the
Footprints **80.00**

Tin, Liberty ABCs, 5-1/2" d, **$75.**

Old Mother Hubbard, brown transfer, polychrome enamel trim, alphabet border, marked "Tunstall" . . **200.00**

Tin

3-1/2" d, girl on swing, lithographed center, printed alphabet border . **60.00**
4-1/2" d, two kittens playing with basket of wood **80.00**
6-1/8" d, Washington profile, rust spot, minor wear **200.00**
7-3/4" d, Who Killed Cock
Robin **120.00**
8" d, Mary Had A Little Lamb, rust spot, minor wear **175.00**

ADVERTISING

History: Before the days of mass media, advertisers relied on colorful product labels and advertising giveaways to promote their products. Containers were made to appeal to the buyer through the use of stylish lithographs and bright colors. Many of the illustrations used the product in the advertisement so that even an illiterate buyer could identify a product.

Advertisements were put on almost every household object imaginable and were constant reminders to use the product or visit a certain establishment.

References: *Advertising & Figural Tape Measures*, L-W Book Sales, 1995; Pamela E. Apkarian-Russell, *Washday Collectibles*, Schiffer Publishing, 2000; Donna S. Baker, *Chocolate Memorabilia*, Schiffer Publishing, 2000; Steve Batson, *Country Store Counter Jars and Tins*, Schiffer Publishing, 1997; Michael Bruner, *Advertising Clocks*, Schiffer Publishing, 1995; ——, *Encyclopedia of Porcelain Enamel Advertising*, 2nd ed., Schiffer Publishing, 1999; ——, *More Porcelain Enamel Advertising*, Schiffer Publishing, 1997; Donald A. Bull, *Beer Advertising*, Schiffer Publishing, 2000; *Collector's Digest Letter Openers: Advertising & Figural*, L-W Book Sales, 1996; Albert and Shelly Coito, *Elsie the Cow and Borden's Collectibles*, Schiffer Publishing, 2000; Fred Dodge, *Antique Tins*, Collector Books, Book I (1995, 1999 value update,) Book II, (1998),

Book III (1999); Warren Dotz, *Advertising Character Collectibles*, Collector Books, 1993, 1997 values updated; ——, *What a Character! 20th Century American Advertising Icons*, Chronicle Books, 1996; Robert Forbes and Terrence Mitchell, *American Tobacco Cards: Price Guide and Checklist*, Tuff Stuff Books, 1999; Bob and Sharon Huxford, *Huxford's Collectible Advertising*, 4th ed., Collector Books, 1999; Don and Elizabeth Johnson, *Warman's Advertising*, Krause Publications, 2000; Ray Klug, *Antique Advertising Encyclopedia*, Vol. 1 (1978, 1993 value update) and Vol. 2 (1985), L-W Promotions; Rex Miller, *The Investor's Guide to Vintage Character Collectibles*, Krause Publications, 1999; Richard A. Penn, *Mom and Pop Stores*, Schiffer Publishing, 1998; Robert Reed, *Bears and Dolls in Advertising*, Antique Trader Books, 1998; ——, *Paper Advertising Collectibles: Treasures from Almanacs to Window Signs*, Antique Trader Books, 1998; Loretta Metzger Rieger and Lagretta Metzger Bajorek, *Children's Paper Premiums in American Advertising 1890-1990s*, Schiffer Publishing, 2000; Bob Sloan and Steve Guarnaccia, *A Stiff Drink and a Close Shave*, Chronicle Books, 1995; Tom Webster, edited by David

D. Kowalski, *Winchester Rarities*, Krause Publications, 2000; Richard White, *Advertising Cutlery*, Schiffer Publishing, 1999; David L. Wilson, *General Store Collectibles*, Collector Books, Vol. 1, 1994, Vol. 2, 1998; Neil Wood, *Smoking Collectibles*, L-W Book Sales, 1994; David and Micki Young, *Campbell's Soup Collectibles from A to Z*, Krause Publications, 1998; David Zimmerman, *The Encyclopedia of Advertising Tins, Vol. 1 (*1994) and *Vol. II* (1999), Collector Books.

Periodicals and Internet Resources: *Advertising Collectors Express*, P.O. Box 221, Mayview, MO 64071; *Advertising Trade Card Quarterly*, 3706 Acoma St., Englewood, CO 80110, www.tradecardcollectors.com; *Paper Collectors' Marketplace*, P.O. Box 128, Scandinavia, WI 54917; *Paper & Advertising Collector (PAC)* P.O. Box 500, Mount Joy, PA 17552; *Past Times*, P.O. Box 1121, Morton Grove, IL 60053, www.pastimes.org; *The Magazine, Ephemera News*, P.O. Box 95, Cazenovia, NY 13055-0095, www.ephemerasociety.org.

Collectors' Clubs: Antique Advertising Association of America, P.O. Box 1121, Morton Grove, IL 60053, www.pastimes.org; Ephemera Society of America, P.O. Box 95, Cazenovia, NY 13035, www.ephemerasociety.org; Farm Machinery Advertising Collectors, 1018 Tamarack Drive, Vienna, VA 22182-1843; Inner Seal Collectors Club, 6609 Billtown Road, Louisville, KY 40209; National Association of Paper and Advertising Collectibles, P.O. Box 500, Mount Joy, PA 17552; Porcelain Advertising Collectors Club, P.O. Box 381, Marshfield Hills, MA 02051; Trade Card Collector's Assoc., 3706 S. Acoma St., Englewood, CO 80110, www.tradecardcollectors.com.

Museums: American Advertising Museum, Portland, OR; American Sign Museum, Cincinnati, OH; Creatability Toys Museum of Advertising Icons, Miami, FL; Museum of Beverage Containers & Advertising, Goodlettsville, TN; Museum of Transportation, Brookline, MA; National Museum of American History, Archives Center, Smithsonian Institution, Washington, DC; U. S. Patent & Trademark Museum, Arlington, VA.

Almanac, Dr. Kilmer & Co., Binghamton, NY, Swamp-Root, 1926, 32 pages, **$15.**

Blotter, Great American Insurance Co., NY, 1929, red printing on white, 9" l, 4" h, **$7.50**

Additional Listings: See *Warman's Americana & Collectibles* for more examples.

Ashtray, tin
- Green River Whiskey, match holder, c1900 . . . . **25.00**
- Kellogg Telephone Co., emb telephone, 50th anniversary . **38.00**

Bean pot, Heinz 57, brown glazed ceramic, emb letters **115.00**

Bill hook, "Don't Forget to Order J. G. Davis Co.'s Granite Flour," gray and dark blue, 5-1/2" x 3-5/8" **210.00**

Biscuit jar, 10-1/2" h, glass jar, glass lid, "Sunshine Biscuits" emb on front, "Loose-Wiles Biscuit Company" on back **350.00**

Blotter, unused
- Culliman Shoe Hospital, J. L. Vick, Prop., 1930s, 3" x 6" **4.00**
- Fairbanks Portable Pumping Outfit, graphics of metal vehicle, road paving machinery, 7-1/4" x 9-1/2" **10.00**
- Gordon Keith Studio, Oakland, CA, elegant couple dancing, "For a rhythmic thrill learn the new Latin American Dances! Conga! Tango! Rhumba! And the season's newest - Samba," black and white, 4" x 9" **10.00**
- I. Tucker Shoe Repair, Moultrie, GA, 1930s, 3" x 5" **3.50**
- Reichert Miling Co., girl wearing wooden shoes, boy playing accordion, multicolored, c1910, 3-1/4" x 6" **7.50**

Booklet
- Crocker Fertilizer & Chemical Company, bluetone engravings of Buffalo, NY, plant, 62 pgs, c1891, 3-1/2" x 6-1/2" **10.00**
- Dutch Boy Paint, 20 pgs, 5" x 6" **12.00**
- Moxie Menu, 12 pgs, color art on front and back cover, Moxie recipes and illus, c1920, 4-3/4" x 7" **35.00**

Bookmark
- Cruver Co., diecut thin celluloid topped by red and yellow roses,

green rose bud and leafy stems, lower half black and white text, 1912 Newark Industrial Exposition. **35.00**
- F. F. Pulver Co., diecut thin celluloid, topped by multicolored turkey, lower half black and white Thanksgiving verse by sponsor, early 1900s. **80.00**
- Geneva National Mineral Water, celluloid, diecut water fountain, adv on back, c1905 . . . . **35.00**

Box, cardboard
- Adams Sappota Chewing Gum, 7-1/2" x 8-1/2", two Victorian ladies, graphic labels **90.00**
- Andy Gump Sunshine Biscuits, cardboard, 5" x 3" x 2" **425.00**
- Fairbank's Gold Dust Washing Powder, tri-panel, three printed panels on front and back, 19" x 9-1/4" **1,000.00**
- Williams Brothers Valvriggans, men's long underwear **15.00**

Calendar
- DeLaval Cream Separator, 1909, full pad, 19-1/2" x 12-1/2" **475.00**
- Houghton, Mifflin & Co. 1887, Whittier, calendar in center, girl raking field at left labeled Maude Muller, poet Whittier in center, Marble Martin image of Pilgrim girl in snow on right, Armstrong & Co. Litho, Boston, 8-3/4" x 12-1/4", some creasing, wear **12.00**
- L. L. Ferriss, Boots, Shoes, and Rubbers, 1885, framed, 6" x 8-1/2" **70.00**
- M. A. Theoford's Black Draught Liver Medicine and McElree's Wine of Cardui Woman's Relief Medicine, 1911, metal edge. **40.00**
- Nestle's Food, "Give the Babies Nestle's Food," ©1894, starts with May 1894, ends April 1895, framed to show both sides, 5-1/2" x 11-3/4" x 35-1/2" **50.00**

Swift's Premium, 1913, four pages, each with different scene, 17" x 9" **20.00**

Candy dispenser, Hershey, one-cent, Moderne Vendor, glazed front with Hershey placard, c1930, 18" h. .**490.00**

Candy pail

Lovell & Covel, Queen of Hearts design, 3" x 2-7/8", 3 oz, slot added later to lid **110.00**

Riley's Rum & Butter Toffee, Halifax, England, 7-1/4" x·7", emb name, silhouettes of children playing with kite, slip lid **50.00**

Sharps' Toffee, 10" x 3-1/4", colorful parrot **55.00**

Cartoon book, Borden's Compliments of Elsie, 16 pgs, 14 color cartoons with captions describing various Borden products, c1945, 3-1/4" x 4" **35.00**

Cereal bowl, Vita B, white china, blue accent rim, 2" h full-color image of soldier lad standing at attention in military parade outfit, 1930s-40s, 6" x 6" x 1-1/2" h. **20.00**

Chair, wooden, folding, adv on both sides of backrest

Cross-Cut Cigarettes, Victorian Lady, slogan, and illus of package, 30-1/2" h **200.00**

Duke's Cigarettes, Victorian Lady and slogan, 32" h **150.00**

Cigar can, Home Run Stogies, tin litho, baseball players on both sides, 5-3/4" x 4-1/4", C.8+ **2,800.00**

Cigar display, Poppers Cigars, slant front glass, 10" h. **175.00**

Cigar lighter, hotel lobby type

Midland Spark, wood base, Model L, c1920, 15" x 7-1/4" x 7" **400.00**

Clock, Chew Friendship Cut Plug, metal, animated movement, $475. Photo courtesy of Joy Luke Auctions.

Rising Sun Stove Polish, oak, lighter and cigar cutter, 23" x 9" . **1,600.00**

Clock, International Tailoring, Chicago, cast iron, emb design, bronzed, orig working clock, 12" w, 2-1/2" d, 16" h, C.8+ **1,000.00**

Coffee can

Blanke's Portonilla Coffee, green and gold, bail handle, dome lid, c1900, 10" h, some losses **60.00**

Elmwood Coffee, tin top and bottom, paper label with country club image, three-pound size, 5-1/2" d, 9-5/8" h **190.00**

Gillies Coffee, pail type, salmon ground, detailed graphic of Victorian children playing at seashore on one side, playing football on other, one-pound size, 4-3/4" d, 4-5/8" h, some scattered areas of chipping and litho loss, C.7.5+ **450.00**

Honeymoon Coffee, paper label over tin, image of couple cuddling on crescent moon, red ground, one-pound size, 3-5/8" x 5-3/8", C.8+ **275.00**

King Cole, tin litho, shows king and servant, one-pound size, 5-3/4" x 4-1/4" **300.00**

Yale Coffee, Steinwender Stoffregen, St. Louis, MO, tin litho, navy, red, white, and gold, one-pound size, 5-7/8" x 4-1/8" **200.00**

Welcome Guest Coffee, tin litho, black butler carrying serving tray on both sides, red ground, 2-1/2 pound size, 5-1/2" d, 7-5/8" h, C.7.5 . . . .**625.00**

Counter display

Bicycle Playing Cards, tin display, front shows royal flush, sides simulated wood grain, 12-1/2" x 4-1/2" x 8" **100.00**

Ever-ready Shaving Brushes, tin, oversized shaving brush on left side, right side with bald man shaves "trademark" face, shaving brushes displayed behind window, 12" h, 15" w. **450.00**

Horseshoe Tobacco, wood, hinged display box, decal on glass lid, orig tax stamp, 13" x 13" x 4". . .**200.00**

Regal Elastic Web, slanted oak case, int. compartmentalized for corset supplies, 7" x 6" x 18" **400.00**

Sir Walter Raleigh Tin, six orig pocket tins **130.00**

Counter jar

Chicos Spanish Peanuts, glass, tin litho lid and base, minor losses, 12" h **230.00**

Planters Peanuts, 7" dia glass jar with lid, yellow and blue Mr. Peanut image, orig 8" x 8" x 9-1/2" corrugated cardboard shipping carton **90.00**

Cup, Manhattan Oil Co. Trop-Artic Auto Oil, tin litho, multicolored motoring image, 5" w, 2-3/4" h, C.8.5+ . . .**425.00**

Dispenser, Karo Tape, porcelain. **25.00**

Door push

Fleischmann's Yeast, 4" x 2-3/4", C.8+ **210.00**

Vicks Cold Medicine, porcelain, red, blue, and white, 3-3/4" w, 7-7/8" h, C.8+ **350.00**

Dye cabinet, Putnam, tin litho lid with General Putnam, 36 divided compartments, c1920, 19" x 14" . **200.00**

Figure

Esquire, Esky, 5-1/2" h jigsawed wood, painted **70.00**

Hallmark, Scribbles, painted plaster, blond boy, broad brimmed hat, long neck scarf, bib overalls, hands clasped at waist, title on base front, copyright Hall Brothers, Inc., 1940s, 4-3/4" h, 2-1/2" d base **50.00**

Heinz 57, painted hard rubber image of Aristocrat Tomato, red tomato head with green leaf sprigs, black top hat, black and white base, c1940, 2-1/2" x 2-1/2" x 5-3/4" **185.00**

RCA Nipper, chalkware, textured finish, light scattered stains and age toning, 9-3/4" h. **525.00**

Snap, Crackle, Pop, vinyl, Kellogg's copyright on each, 3" h, price for set **70.00**

Reddy Kilowatt, stuffed felt, c1950, 5" h **120.00**

Gum display, counter top

Beech-Nut Gum, back of tin display shows little girl with package of gum, mounted on metal pedestal, 14-3/4" h **1,450.00**

Smith Bros., cardboard, 17 packs of gum with 1915 copyright, 6" l, 4-1/4" w, 4-1/8" h **5,500.00**

Wrigleys Gum, green figural spearmint, celluloid face, 1920s, 13" h **1,495.00**

Gum dispenser, Adams One-Cent, stainless steel, divided racks for four varieties of Chiclets and Dentyne, 10" x 16" **435.00**

Gum tin, Frozen Mints, hinged, satin pebbly finish litho, 1-3/8" x 4" x 2-5/8", C.8 . . . . **150.00**

Gum wrapper, Pulver's Yellow Kid Chewing Gum, paper litho, 15/16" x 2-3/4" **160.00**

Lamp shade, Eat L. V. Orsinger's Ice Cream, red, two white opaque glass panels, metal frame, six colored jewels, 6" h **750.00**

Magazine ad

American Clover Blossom Co., black and white, copyright 1890, 16" x 20" period mahogany ogee frame **50.00**

Queen City Printing Ink Company, yellow, blue, and purple profile of woman holding flowers, September 1907 issue of *The Inland Printer* magazine, double matted, 5-3/4" x 9" **8.00**

Mask, diecut stiff paper, Good Humor man, black and white hat, red, white, and blue wings symbol, fleshtone face with diecut eye openings, back text describes ice cream varieties, c1940, 9" x 11" **45.00**

Mirror, pocket, celluloid

Adam's Pepsin Gum, oval, pretty girl holding basket of gum packs **475.00**

Angelus Marshmallows, multicolored, brunette and blond cherub angels resting on box, tiny lettering "A Message of Purity" **75.00**

Berry Brothers, Apex Varnish and Paint Remover, red and gold, dark olive green ground **30.00**

Boston Varnish Company, multicolored, child wearing dark blue outfit, glasses, red hair, carrying product box, captioned "Take A Tip From Winthrop Wise-Invest On The Varnish Called Kyanize," blue and red lettering **60.00**

Buster Brown Shoes, portrait of Buster and Tige, shades of fleshtone, brown, crisp red hat and neck bow, white background, black lettering, 1930s **50.00**

Carlson Currier Silks, multicolored Art Nouveau profile portrait of Dutch lady **125.00**

Checkers Popcorn Confection, A Nice Prize in Every Package, red, white, and blue design, box in center, Shotwell Mfg. Co., Chicago **135.00**

Harry Mitchell Fine Tailoring, sepiatone real photo, dark brown border, white lettering **40.00**

Hotel Tuller, In The Heart of Detroit, multicolored image of 13-story hotel **115.00**

Johnstons-The Appreciated Chocolates, Clark Drug Co., Northfork, WV, black and white fabric covering, photo of pretty young hostess displaying three boxed products, c1920 . . . . . **55.00**

Liberal Life Assurance Co., multicolored, portrait of mother and infant dressed in white, gray rim inscribed "If The Man On the Other Side Should Die Would His Family By Provided For," Anderson, IN, sponsor **145.00**

Litz & Dunn, multicolored crest logo, gold lettering "Ladies Fine Shoes" **55.00**

Meet Me at the Eagle Hotel, Slatington, PA, nude standing on rock ledge, breaking waves, 2-3/4" x 1-3/4" **475.00**

Occident Flour, red, white, and blue logo, mellowed white ground **30.00**

Old Reliable Coffee, multicolored Dutch gentleman putting clay pile, resting elbow on package . . . **65.00**

Pacific Shoe, red lettering outlined in black, black and white lady's ankle shoe, lower half has logo for Friedman-Shelby Shoe Co. in two shades of blue outlined in gold **80.00**

RCA Victrola, detailed image of early floor model, 1-3/4" w, 2-3/4" h **300.00**

Staples the Jewelry, brown and white center, real photo of smiling Portland, Oregon, watchmaker and optician, 1920s **40.00**

Strawbridge & Clothier Co., Philadelphia, Whitehead & Hoag, Santa at chimney, 2-1/8" dia. **850.00**

The Bar-Keepers Friend, multicolored art of nude woman posed at beverage bar, displaying product package, gold rim lettered in black "George Wm. Hoffman Co., Indianapolis, Indiana" . **245.00**

Travelers Insurance, blue letters, white ground **15.00**

Union Made Cigars, pale blue Union labor label, buff tan background, black lettering, complimentary

sponsor Cigar Makes Union No. 393, early 1900s **75.00**

Yellow Cab, 1920s, combination pocket mirror and paperweight, 3-1/2" d **700.00**

Wilbur's Cocoa, Whitehead & Hoag, detailed color graphic of early cocoa box, 1-3/4" d **400.00**

Paperweight, National Lead Co., emb Dutch Boy logo, c1925, 4" d **15.00**

Peanut-butter pail, tin litho, one-pound size

Golden Nut Brand Peanut Butter, C. J. Jones, Winnipeg, 3-1/2" x 3-5/8", C.8+ **120.00**

Jumbo Peanut Butter, Frank Tea & Spice Co., elephant graphic, 3-3/8" x 3-7/8", C.7.5, some light scattered surface scuffing and wear **775.00**

Monarch Peanut Butter, Teenie Weenie, bail handle, 4" h . . . **85.00**

Planters, circus images with Mr. Peanut, orig marked lid with heavy wear, 4" x 3-5/8", C.8+ **925.00**

Pencil clip

Morton's Salt, It Pours, blue and white celluloid, silvered tin clip, c1930-40 . . . . **15.00**

Pepsi, red, white, and blue celluloid, silvered tin clip, c1950 . . . . . . **5.00**

Starrett Tools, silvered litho tin, silvered tin clip **7.00**

Pinback button, Fleischmann's Yeast, multicolored, **$125.** *Photo courtesy of Hake's Americana & Collectibles.*

Pinback button

Armour Star America's Most Delicious Ham, black and white text, yellow star designs, white background, c1930 . . . . **10.00**

Ask Me About Wilson's Certified Ham, It's New, Tender, Tasty, Ready to Serve, black and white text, orange background, company logo in center, c1940 . . . . **10.00**

Churngood Employees Picnic, margarine box at top, c1930 . . **8.00**

Cupid Brand Pickles and Preserves, multicolored Cupid in center with bow and arrow, deep blue background, white text, gold rim, Dodson-Braun Co., St. Louis . **35.00**

Eat More Natural Cheese, black text, gold map of Wisconsin, white background, c1950 . . . . **8.00**

Elsie Three Ring Circus, red text, circus theme **24.00**

Fox's Is Good Bread, red and white, c1940 . . . . **8.00**

Old Smuggler The Fashionable Scotch, black on gold shield center design, white text, black background, c1940 . . . . **8.00**

Oven Ready Buttermilk Biscuits, red, white, and blue can image, 1940s **12.00**

RCA Micro Mike, ivory-white celluloid, crisp red image and title, 1940s-50s, 3" d **40.00**

Reddy Killowatt, celluloid, Ohio Edison Co., large image of Reddy, 3-1/4" d **95.00**

Stroehmann's, full color, blonde haired girl eating slice of buttered bread, c1958 . . . . **24.00**

Take Home a Quart of Purity Ice Cream, black, white, and red image, Art-Deco background, c1930 . . . . **35.00**

White House Coffee, The Flavor Is Roasted In, c1930 . . . . **7.50**

Playing cards

Edison-Mazda, Maxfield Parrish illus, orig box, c1920 . . . . **150.00**

Kelly Springfield, girl with watermelon, orig box, c1930 . **25.00**

Pot scraper, tin litho, 2-7/8" x 3-3/8"

Fairmont Creamery, red ground, white, black, and gold lettering, C.8.5 . . . . **275.00**

Henkel's Flour Co., C.8+ **220.00**

Nye's Wholesome Bread, blue and white, 2-7/8" x 3-3/8", C.8 . . **250.00**

Salt and pepper shakers, pr

RCA Nipper, white china, black ears, eye dots, one with black collar, other with brown collar, base inscription "His Master's Voice/RCA Victor," cork stoppers, c1930, 3" h **30.00**

Tappan Kitchen Ranges, heavy glass with glossy yellow or pale blue finish, baker figure on one panel, black plastic threaded cap, 1940s **20.00**

Sample

Amaml Talc, Pritchard & Constance, New York & London, tin litho, 2-1/8" x 1-1/4" x 3/4", C.8 . . . . . . **220.00**

American Can Co., American Meat Packers Association, Chicago, October 1910 Convention, Lard and Meat Can, red ground, black and gold lettering, 1-5/8" d, 1-3/4" h, C.8- **240.00**

Donald Duck Coffee, Goyer Coffee Co., Greenville, Miss, tin litho, 3 oz, coin slot in lid, 2-3/8" x 3", C.8+ **325.00**

Heinz Malt Vinegar, miniature glass bottle, orig label, stopper, and contents, 1-1/2" d, 4-5/8" h, C.8+ **180.00**

Mulford Talc, tin litho, color image of pretty woman in center, 2-1/8" x 1-1/4" x 3/4", C.8.5 . . . . . . **210.00**

Par Shaving Talc, image of 1920s golfer, green, orange, black, and white, some fading, light denting, wear to back, 5-3/4" x 2-1/4" x 1-1/8", C.7+ **250.00**

Seed box, Rice's Seeds, dovetailed wood box, color graphic label on inside, brass closure, 11" l, 9" w, 11-3/4" h, C.8.5+ **375.00**

Sheet music, The Campbells Are Comin' Varnish Stain, color cover with camel, red blanket with "The Name of the Only Real Varnish Stain," back cover with graphics of family members using varnish, four pages, 10-1/2" x 13-3/4", heavy wear around edges **5.00**

Sign, J & P Coats Spool Cotton, coated card stock, gilt emb British lion, eagle, shield, and weapons in center, hand-colored emb roses, women with floral sprays in hair, c1850, 11-1/4" x 13-3/4", $400. Photo courtesy of Cowan Historic Americana Auctions.

Sign

Atlas Cement, heavy porcelain enamel, cement bag design in center, 14-3/4" x 10" **550.00**

Beauty Shoppe, porcelain, lightly emb lettering and oval portrait of woman, 9" x 18", C.8+ **375.00**

Carnation Fresh Milk, porcelain, red and white, center milk bottle, 15" x 14-1/4", C.8" **600.00**

Castle Gate Washed Duspruf Stoker Coal, porcelain, orange, blue, and white, 12" x 30", C.8.5+ **300.00**

Cherry Blush, Cherries Only Rival, beveled tin over cardboard, dark background, 6-1/2" x 9-1/4", C.8+ **550.00**

Dupont Defender Photographic Products, buff gray wooden frames, black and white semi-gloss photo enlargements on cardboard of scenic mountain view with three posed young ladies, slogan "Better Things For Better Living Through Chemistry" on bottom, orig wire hanger, 1940s, 15" x 18" **30.00**

Eddie's Everlasting Black Dye, diecut hanger, lightly emb tin litho, E-Jay-R Mfg Co., Baltimore, illus of products, c1920, 6-1/2" x 8-1/2" **70.00**

Eureka Vacuum Cleaners, litho beveled tin over cardboard, detailed interior image with lady using cleaner, blue background, 19" x 13", C.8.5+ **1,100.00**

Franklin Mills, Lockport, NY, diecut cardboard, easel back, little girl holding boxes of Wheatlet Cereal and Franklin Flour, 4-3/4" w, 9" h, C.8.5+ **250.00**

Hudepohl Brewery, Cincinnati, tin litho, self framed, 19-1/4" x 15-1/4", C.8+ **275.00**

Kellogg's Corn Flakes with Bananas, cardboard stand-up, easel back, 30" x 20", C.8+ **275.00**

King Quality Shoes for Men, diecut tin litho shield, light emb royalty crown in center, chain hanger, 9-1/2" x 12" **60.00**

Mayo's Plug, Smoking Cock O' The Walk, porcelain, large color image of crowing rooster, 6-1/2" w, 13" h **1,250.00**

Phez Loganberry Juice, litho tin, c1920, 9" x 6-1/2" **575.00**

Red Goose Shoes, light-up neon, diecut porcelain back, 24" x 12" x 5" **2,100.00**

Ronson Table Lighters, molded hard plastic, 1" recess to hold lighter, 1950s, 7" x 8" **20.00**

Shield Lighters, rigid cardboard easel, holding 12 identical gold luster finish metal lighters, c1950, 9-1/2" x 12-1/2" **60.00**

Snow Drift Fancy Patent Flour, Imperial Enamel Co., NY, heavy porcelain, two-sided flange type, 14" x 18-5/8", C.8+ **300.00**

Stone Hill Wine, litho tin, allegory of white, nude woman titled "Autumn," molded wood grain self framed border printed "Compliments of Stone Hill Wine Co., Hermann, MO, U.S.A.," c1910 . . . . **635.00**

Sunoco Motor Oil, porcelain, yellow ground, black letters, C.8- **350.00**

Waterman's Fountain Pen, porcelain, orig wood frame, dark blue, white lettering, 30" l, 8" h **300.00**

Waterman's Ideal Fountain Pen, diecut cardboard litho, Santa with arms extended around large glove, 15" x 14", C.8.5+ **600.00**

Wings Cigarettes, high gloss paper, model in negligée glamour pose, c1940, 12" x 18", some archival tape repairs on back **70.00**

Wrigley's Double Mint Gum, litho tin, red ground, c1930, 13" x 6" **865.00**

Yeast Foam Is The Best, We Sell Only the Best Goods, heavy porcelain, white lettering, blue ground, 20" l, 4-1/4" h, C.8+ **425.00**

Stickpin

Grand Andes Range, diecut thin celluloid red, white, and blue U.S. flag, brass stickpin, made by Whitehead & Hoag, June 6, 1905 patent date **10.00**

Old Dutch Cleanser, miniature brass replica of trademark cleaning woman, blue and white porcelain enamels, tiny slogan "Old Dutch Cleanser Chases Dirt" on reverse, 1920s **20.00**

Store display, Borden's Fine Cheese, copyright 1944, 11-1/2" x 18" cardboard, mechanical wheel with ration points **195.00**

Talc can, tin litho

American Baby, before and after images of naked baby, 2-5/8" w, 1-3/8" d, 4-3/4" h, C.8 . . . . . **550.00**

Frescodor, Sidney Ross Co., New York, multicolor graphic image of woman on both sides, orig contents, 3-1/8" w, 1" d, 5-1/2" h, C.8.5+ **725.00**

Mother Goose, nursery rhyme images on both sides, 2-1/2" w, 1-3/4" d, 6-3/8" h, C.8.5+ . . **1,150.00**

Royal Violet Talc, image of young girl, 1-3/4" w, 4-1/8" h, some spots and small dent **90.00**

Violet Talc, image of young Victorian children, 4-5/8" x 2-1/2" x 1-3/8", C.8 . . . . **425.00**

Thermometer

Pepsi, metal, oversize dot logo bottle, c1930, 15-3/8" x 6-1/4" x 3/4", C.8+ **525.00**

White House Coffee, wooden, white ground, black image of man drinking coffee, 4" w, 15" h, light overall wear, C.8- **275.00**

Tin, Buffalo Bill Saddle Soap, made by Geo. J. Kelly, Inc., Lynn, Mass, chromolithograph on tin, 5" d, **$360.** *Photo courtesy of Cowan Historic Americana Auctions.*

Tin, miscellaneous, tin litho

Crispo Biscuits, c1900, 5" h . . . **60.00**

Donald Duck Pop Corn, Disney cartoon characters on both sides, unopened, 2-7/8" w, 4-7/8" h, C.7.5+ **300.00**

Drug-Pak Condoms, navy blue and white, orig contents, 1-5/8" x 2-1/8", C.8.5+ **400.00**

Henalfa Hair Restorer, girl with long hair on both sides, 4" x 2-5/8" x 1-1/2", light scuffing, C.7.5 . **400.00**

Imperial Shaving Stick, Talcum Puff Co., New York, image of man lathering face, 3-3/8" l, C.8+ **325.00**

Lauderdale Red Pepper Spice, Oppenheim & McEwan Co., Albany, NY, multicolored flowers on both sides, 2-1/4" l, 1-14" w, 3-1/4" h **210.00**

Novia Kiddie Pops, pail shape, image of pops and children and dog on both sides, 3-3/4" d, 3-1/4" h, C.7.5+ **675.00**

Professor Searele's Veterinary Blood Purifier Medicinal, Sommers Bros., litho of barnyard animals, 3-1/4" x 2-7/8" x 1-3/4", C.8.5+ **450.00**

Tom Thumb Crescent Crackers, blue and silver litho, red ground, two pound size, 7" h **60.00**

Velvet Tread Foot Powder, green, black, and brown, winged foot and giant winged insect, 4-3/4" x 2-1/4" x 1-3/8", C.8 . . . . **400.00**

Tobacco bin, Game Cut Tobacco, Jon Babley Co., held forty-eight 5 cent packs of tobacco, litho on tin, 11-1/2" w, 7-3/4" d, 7" h **850.00**

Tobacco can, tin litho

Dixie Kid Cut Plug, Nall & Williams, lunch pail type, white kid, 7-3/4" l, 5-1/4" d, 3-3/4" h, C.8.5+ . **1,600.00**

Mayo's Inspector, roly poly, 7" x 5-1/4", C.8+ **1,450.00**

Uniform Cut Plug, early sailor on both sides, 6-1/4" x 4-7/8", C.8.5 . . . . **1,250.00**

U. S. Marine, lunch pail type, colorful graphics on four sides, 4-3/4" x 7-3/8" x 4-3/8", C.8.5 . . . . . **525.00**

Tobacco tin, pocket, tin litho

Black and White, vertical, 4-1/2" x 3" x 7/8", C.8 . . . . **375.00**

Century, Ginna type lithography, references to 1878 tobacco sales on base, horizontal, 1-1/4" x 2-1/8" x 3/8", C.8 . . . . **170.00**

Charm of the West, Spaulding & Merrick, horizontal, graphics on both sides, 2-3/8" x 3-3/4" x 5/8" **300.00**

Checkers, vertical, red and black checkerboard pattern, 4-1/2" x 3" x 7/8", C.8.5 . . . . **625.00**

Ensign Perfection Cut Tobacco, vertical, Missouri flag on back, 4-1/2" x 3" x 7/8", C.8+, minor wear, litho chip on back **900.00**

Ehrlich Plug Crumb Cut, Boston, vertical, 4-1/4" x 3-3/8" x 1", C.8+ **550.00**

Forest and Stream, Canadian, vertical, 4-1/4" x 3" x 7/8", C.8+ **425.00**

King George, Frishmuth Bros., vertical, 4-1/4" x 3-1/8" x 1", C.8 .... **425.00**

Lord Kenyon, vertical, dark blue and white, 3" x 3-1/2" x 1", C.8 .. **375.00**

North Star, Cotterill Fenner & Co., vertical, Ginna graphics, 2-3/8" x 3-3/4" x 5/8", C.8+ **325.00**

Old Glory, Spaulding & Merrick, horizontal, red ground, detailed graphics on both sides, 2-3/8" x 3-3/4" x 5/8", C.8.5 .... **325.00**

Palmy Days Tobacco, vertical, green ground, 4-1/2" x 3" x 7/8", C.8+ **475.00**

Paul Jones Clean Cut Tobacco, vertical, teal ground, multicolored image of Jones on front, sea battle on back, 4-1/2" x 3" x 7/8", C.8.5+ **2,900.00**

Perfect Pipe Tobacco, Cobb, Bates & Yerxa Co., vertical, 4-3/8" x 3-3/8" x 1", C.8- **300.00**

Prexy Plug Cut Tobacco, vertical, red ground, scholar in center, 4-1/2" x 3" x 7/8", C.8+ **2,700.00**

Qboid Cube Cut, vertical, plantation illus, 4" x 3-1/2" x 1", C.8+ .. **190.00**

Red Jacket Smoking Tobacco, vertical, red ground, white horse with jockey in red jacket, 4-1/2" x 3" x 7/8", C.8.5 .... **1,000.00**

Trout-Line Smoking Tobacco, vertical, dark green ground, image of trout fisherman on both sides, 3-3/4" x 3-1/4" x 1-1/8", C.8+ **775.00**

Tray, Stegmaier Brewing Co., Wilkes-Barre, PA, 12" d, **$30.**

Tray, tin litho

Anheuser-Busch, Bevo wagon, team of horses, c1910, 13" x 10-1/2" **115.00**

Beer Drivers Union, 14th anniversary, dogs in stable, horse,

and colt, 1908, 10-1/2" x 13-1/2" **195.00**

Cunningham Ice Cream, image of early factory and delivery trucks, 15-1/4" x 18-1/2", C.8 ..... **450.00**

Edelweiss Beer, young lady, 1913, 13" d **130.00**

Falstaff Brewing, merry group of cavaliers, c1920, 24" d **75.00**

Fan Tan Gum, Oriental beauty, 13" x 10-1/2", c1920 .... **130.00**

Success Manure Spreader, side margins name sponsor Kemp & Burpee Mfg. Co., Syracuse, early 1900s, 3-1/4" x 4-3/4" **140.00**

Trolley sign, Planters Cocktail Peanuts, cardboard, 1930s, 21" l, 11" h, slight water staining and some mildew on back **550.00**

Watch fob

Lions Live Stock Remedy Co., oval celluloid and metal, barnyard animals and product box, 1-3/4" l, 1-3/4" h, C.8.5+ **425.00**

Savage Arms, emb metal, pointing Indian chief, painted head band, orig patina, 1-5/8" d **325.00**

ADVERTISING TRADE CARDS

History: Advertising trade cards are small, thin cardboard cards made to advertise the merits of a product. They usually bear the name and address of a merchant.

With the invention of lithography, colorful trade cards became a popular way to advertise in the late 19th and early 20th centuries. They were made to appeal especially to children. Young and old alike collected and treasured them in albums and scrapbooks. Very few are dated; the prime years for trade card production were 1880 to 1893; cards made between 1810 and 1850 can be found, but rarely. By 1900, trade cards were rapidly losing their popularity, and by 1910, they had all but vanished.

References: Kit Barry, *Advertising Trade Card*, Book 1, published by author, 1981; Dave Cheadle, *Victorian Trade Cards*, Collector Books, 1996, 1998 value update; Robert Forbes and Terrence Mitchell, *American Tobacco Cards: Price Guide and Checklist*, Tuff Stuff Books, 1999; Robert Jay, *Trade Card in Nineteenth-Century America*, University of Missouri Press, 1987; Murray Cards (International) Ltd. (comp.), *Cigarette Card Values*, Murray Cards (International) Ltd., 1994.

Periodicals and Internet Resources: *Card Times*, 70 Winified Lane, Aughton, Ormskirk, Lancashire L38 5DL England, Cigarette Cards Central, 555 W. Dryden St., #1, Montrose, CA 91020, www.cigcards.com.

Collectors' Clubs: Cartophillic Society of Great Britain, 63 Ferndale Road, Church Crookham, Fleet,

Hants, GU13 0LN UK, www.cardclubs.ndirect.co.uk; Trade Card Collector's Association, 3706 S. Acoma St., Englewood, CO 80110, www.tradecardcollectors.com.

Beverages

Arbuckle Brothers Coffee

Eskimos, seals, Alaska scenery, adv and Alaska history on back, 3" x 5" **10.00**

Indians, miners, Montana scenery, 1892, 3" x 5" **15.00**

Ayer's Sarsaparilla

"Ayer's Sarsaparilla Makes the Weak Strong," two gentlemen **18.00**

"The Old Folks at Home," 8" x 12", bottle of tonic **325.00**

Duff's Malt Whiskey, man in red jacket working on formula **30.00**

Hermitage Sour Mash Whiskey, two rats and bottle **30.00**

Lion Coffee, canaries and parakeets **12.00**

Gibson's Pure Rye Whiskey **35.00**

Mayer Brewing, Palest Brewery, New York, diecut **65.00**

Union Pacific Tea, young lad sailors with American flag, includes Easter greeting **8.00**

Clothing

A. S. Shaw Footwear, floral chromo, c1885, 4-1/2" x 7" **12.00**

Ball's Corsets, center corset illus, child and mother holding baby **25.00**

Child's & Staples, Gilbertsville, ME, young girl chasing butterfly, 2-3/4" x 4-1/2" **12.00**

Hapke Knit Goods, 1876 Centennial, light green knitting machine vignette **45.00**

Honest Abe Work Shirts-Overalls, black and white, Abe Lincoln type with text, sgd by Abe N. Cohen, diecut hole for hanging, c1910, 2-1/2" x 4-1/2" ... **8.00**

Mattmueller, C., Boots, Shoes and Rubbers, Cleveland, floral designs, 1880s, 4-1/2" x 2-1/2" **9.00**

Solar Tip Shoes, Girard College, Philadelphia, Where Boys Wear our Solar Tip Shoes **20.00**

Strauss, Levi & Co., multi-fold, multiple images of children and adults wearing jeans, when folded it's shape of pair of Levi Strauss jeans showing both front and back pockets **275.00**

Thompson's Glove Fitting Corsets, lady and cupids **35.00**

Farm machinery and supplies

Gale Mfg. Co., Daisy Sulky Hay Rake, folder type, four panels, field scene. **75.00**

Keystone Agricultural Implements, Uncle Sam talking to world representatives, metamorphic. . . **75.00**

Mast & Foos Columbia Steel Wind Mill, folder type, child with pump **45.00**

New Essay Lawn Mower, scene of Statue of Liberty, New York harbor **35.00**

Reid's Flower Seeds, two high wheeled bicyclers admiring flowers held by three ladies. **15.00**

Sheridan's, To Make Hens Lay, Use Sheridan's Condition Powder, before and after views of farmer in chicken house. **25.00**

Food

Bardenwerper, C. E., Dealer in Choice Meats & Poultry, NY, front adv, floral dec, c1880, 2" x 3-1/2" **7.50**

Batsford, W. A., Dealer in Milk in Orange Co., NY, floral motif, c1880, 2" x 3-1/2". **6.00**

Chocolat du Planteur, woman in green dress, reading **20.00**

Czar Baking Powder, black woman and boy with giant biscuit. **25.00**

Enterprise Meat and Food Chopper **45.00**

Heinz Apple Butter, diecut, pickle shape. **45.00**

Hornby's Oats, diecut of girl peeking out of box. **35.00**

Pearl Baking Powder, light blue and sepia, reverse with order blank, c1890. . . . . **35.00**

Royal Hams, Chief Joseph & His Tribe examining barrel of hams **48.00**

Thurber Connoisseur Ketchup, product label illus **70.00**

E. Tunison Grocer, elf standing next to pansies **15.00**

Woolson Spice, Lion Coffee, young children portraying Cinderella. . . **25.00**

Health and beauty

Ayer's Hair Vigor, four mermaids, ship in background. **7.00**

Golf Queen Perfume, Ricksecker Co., c1895, blotter type **12.00**

Hill's Hair and Whisker Dye, New York proprietor **40.00**

Hoyt's German Cologne, E. M. Hoyt & Co., mother cat and kittens **25.00**

Ray Hubbell's Oil Cloths, 3-1/4" x 5-1/2", $8.

Laundry and soaps

Empire Wringer Co., Auburn, NY, child helping "I Can Help Mama" **35.00**

Higgin's Soap, comical black scene showing various uses for soap, set of seven cards, framed, 29-1/2" x 8" **150.00**

Ivorine Cleanser, lettering on side of elephant, other animals **15.00**

Mrs. Potts' Sad Irons, sign painters. **35.00**

Sapolio Soap, young black face peering out of watermelon center **18.00**

Soapine, Kendall Mfg. Co., Providence, RI Carriage. **15.00**

Soapine on mantle, product box plus name spelled out over mantle . . . **15.00**

Steam Engine **10.00**

Street Scene **10.00**

Wizard, lady talking to wizard. . . . **10.00**

The Fort Wayne Improved Western Washer, Horton Manufacturing Co., Fort Wayne, Ind, one lady watching as other works new machine **35.00**

Medicine

Dr. Kilmer & Co., Binghamton, NY, 36" x 60", Standard Herbal Remedies, detailed graphics **395.00**

King of the Blood Medicine, Automation Musical Band, Barnum's Traveling Museum **45.00**

Perry Davis, Pain Killer for Wounds, armored man of war ships battle scene **25.00**

Quaker Bitters, Standard Family Medicine, child in barrel. **17.50**

Scott's Emulsion of Cod Liver Oil, man with large fish over back, vertical format **20.00**

Shaker Family Pills, little girl in white bonnet **38.00**

Miscellaneous

Agate Iron Ware, Father Time at stove, 3-7/8" x 2-3/4" **45.00**

Drew's Good Singing Canaries Only, NY, fox and hounds racing on front, 2" x 3-1/2" **7.50**

Emerson Piano Co., black and white illus **40.00**

Forbes, C. P., Jewelry, Greenfield, MA, Santa in front of fireplace, toys on table **15.00**

Granite Iron Ware, three ladies gossiping over tea. **25.00**

Middleton, Walter, Photographer, floral insert, baby face, gold trim, c1880, NH, 2-3/4" x 4" **6.00**

Read McCraney, Sonora, Tuolumne Co., CA, Diamonds and Watches, Jewelry & Optical Goods, 1890s, 2-1/2" x 4" **10.00**

The American Machine Co., Manufacturers of Hardware Specialties, three women ironing, vertical format **40.00**

Two Headed Lady, 8th Wonder of the World. **150.00**

Wells Portrait & Landscape Photographer, Sonora, CA, adv on front, ship motif, gold and silver trim, 4-1/4" x 6" **35.00**

Stoves and ranges

Andes Stove, black children. . . . **15.00**

Dixon's Stove Polish, Brownies illus **20.00**

Enamieline Stove Polish, paper-doll type, distributed by J. L. Prescott & Co., 11 Jay St., 1900s

    Pansy, 5" h **30.00**
    Poppy, 5-1/2" h **30.00**
    Rose, 5" h **30.00**

Florence Oil Stove, colorful illus of two women and two children. **40.00**

Rising Sun Stove Polish, folder type, "The Modern Cinderella". **50.00**

Rutland Stove Lining, child talking to parrot. **115.00**

Thread and sewing

Brooks' Spool Cotton, three kittens playing instruments made from spools **25.00**

Corticelli Spool Silks, Nonotuck Silk Co., diecut leaf shape with silkworm, green and white, c1888, 2" **10.00**

J. & P. Coats, Best Silk Thread, "We Never Fade," black youngster straddling spool, hot sun in corner **12.00**

Singer Manufacturing Co., choir of children singing as birds listen . . **20.00**

White Sewing Machine Co., elves working at sewing machine. **15.00**

Tobacco

Capadura Cigar, two baseball players, "Judgment, Judgment is always decided in favor of the Capadura Cigar" 30.00

49 Cut Plug, miners' scene 225.00

Horsehead Tobacco, Dansman Tobacco Co., horse head illus ...15.00

AGATA GLASS

History: Agata glass was invented in 1887 by Joseph Locke of the New England Glass Company, Cambridge, Massachusetts.

Agata glass was produced by coating a piece of peachblow glass with metallic stain, spattering the surface with alcohol, and firing. The resulting high-gloss, mottled finish looked like oil droplets floating on a watery surface. Shading usually ranged from opaque pink to dark rose, although pieces in a pastel opaque green also exist. A few pieces have been found in a satin finish.

Bowl, 8" d, 4" h, green opaque body, staining and gold trim....... **1,150.00**

Celery vase, 7" h, sq, fluted top **685.00**

Creamer................. **1,200.00**

Finger bowl

5-1/4" d, 2-1/2" h, shiny, ruffled, peachblow opaque body, large areas of black mottling, lace-like gold tracery.............**685.00**

5-1/4" d, 2-5/8" h, crushed raspberry shading to creamy pink, all over gold mottling, blue accents **995.00**

5-1/4" d, 3" h, ruffled, peachblow opaque body, all over bright blue staining spots **750.00**

Pitcher, 6-3/8" h, crimped rim **1,750.00**

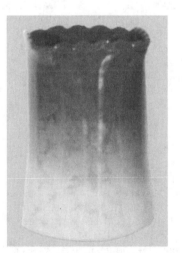

Vase, crimson New England peachblow ground, gold tracery, 4-1/2" h, $685. Photo courtesy of Clarence and Betty Maier.

Spooner, 4-1/2" h, 2-1/2" w, sq top, wild rose peachblow ground, small areas of wear..................... **400.00**

Toothpick holder, 2-1/4" h, flared, green opaque, orig blue oil spots, green trim **795.00**

Tumbler, 3-7/8" h, peachblow ground, gold tracery, bold black splotches.................. **785.00**

Vase

4-1/2" h, square scalloped top, gold tracery, crimson peachblow ground **685.00**

6" h, lily, crimson peachblow ground, large black splotches..... **885.00**

8" h, lily, shiny surface, crimson peachblow ground, large black splotches **1,085.00**

AMBERINA GLASS

History: Joseph Locke developed Amberina glass in 1883 for the New England Glass Works. "Amberina," a trade name, describes a transparent glass which shades from deep ruby to amber. It was made by adding powdered gold to the ingredients for an amber-glass batch. A portion of the glass was reheated later to produce the shading effect. Usually it was the bottom which was reheated to form the deep red; however, reverse examples have been found.

Most early Amberina is flint-quality glass, blown or pattern molded. Patterns include Diamond Quilted, Daisy and Button, Venetian Diamond, Diamond and Star, and Thumbprint.

In addition to the New England Glass Works, the Mount Washington Glass Company of New Bedford, Massachusetts, copied the glass in the 1880s and sold it at first under the Amberina trade name and later as "Rose Amber." It is difficult to distinguish pieces from these two New England factories. Boston and Sandwich Glass Works never produced the glass.

Amberina glass also was made in the 1890s by several Midwest factories, among which was Hobbs, Brockunier & Co. Trade names included "Ruby Amber Ware" and "Watermelon." The Midwest glass shaded from cranberry to amber, and the color resulted from the application of a thin flashing of cranberry to the reheated portion. This created a sharp demarcation between the two colors. This less-expensive version was the death knell for the New England variety.

In 1884, Edward D. Libbey was given the use of the trade name "Amberina" by the New England Glass Works. Production took place during 1900, but ceased shortly thereafter. In the 1920s, Edward Libbey renewed production at his Toledo, Ohio, plant for a short period. The glass was of high quality.

Marks: Amberina made by Edward Libbey in the 1920s is marked "Libbey" in script on the pontil.

References: Gary Baker et al., *Wheeling Glass 1829-1939*, Oglebay Institute, 1994 (distributed by Antique Publications); Neila and Tom Bredehoft, *Hobbs, Brockunier & Co. Glass*, Collector Books,

1997; Kenneth Wilson, *American Glass 1760-1930*, 2 vols., Hudson Hill Press and The Toledo Museum of Art, 1994.

Reproduction Alert: Reproductions abound.

Additional Listings: Mount Washington.

Beverage set, Optic Diamond Quilted pattern, 7" h pitcher, three punch cups, two tumblers, New England, six pcs **825.00**

Bonbon, 7" d, 1-1/2" h, wavy six pointed 1-1/2" w rim, fuchsia shading to pale amber, sgd "Libbey" **625.00**

Bowl

4-1/2" d, 2-1/4" h, tricorn, fuchsia shading to amber, Venetian Diamond design **325.00**

4-1/2" d, 2-1/2" h, Optic Diamond Quilted pattern **125.00**

Butter pat, 2-3/4 d, Daisy and Button pattern, sq, notched corners, pr **250.00**

Celery boat, 14" l, 5" w, 2-1/2" h, Daisy and Button pattern, Hobbs, Brockunier, minute roughness on bow **750.00**

Celery vase

Diamond Quilted pattern, sq scalloped rim, 6-1/8" h **275.00**

Inverted Thumbprint pattern . **145.00**

Optic Expanded Diamond pattern, New England Glass Works, 6-1/2" h **345.00**

Centerpiece, 14" l, canoe, Daisy and Button pattern, Hobbs Brockunier **950.00**

Cordial, 4-1/2" h, trumpet shape **225.00**

Cracker jar, cov, 8" h, 5-3/4" d, Inverted Thumbprint pattern, barrel shape, rare glass cov, applied amber knob finial, attributed to Hobbs, c1885 ....**785.00**

Cruet, 5-1/2" h, Inverted Thumbprint pattern, fuchsia trefoil spout, neck, and shoulder, Mt. Washington......**435.00**

Juice Glass, New England, eight optic panels, ribbed handle, 3-1/4" h, $185. Photo courtesy of Clarence and Betty Maier.

Decanter, 12" h, Optic Diamond Quilted pattern, solid amber faceted stopper **475.00**

Juice tumbler, 3-1/4" h, tapered cylindrical, applied ribbed handle **185.00**

Lemonade glass, 4-7/8" h, 16 optic ribs, upper 2" blushed with color **215.00**

Pickle castor insert, 4-1/4" h, 4" d, Inverted Thumbprint pattern, Mt. Washington **425.00**

Pitcher
> 4-1/2" h, sq top, Inverted Thumbprint pattern, applied amber reeded handle **325.00**
> 5" h, Daisy and Button pattern, Hobbs Brockunier **425.00**
> 8" h, 5" d, amberina-opalescent, clear reeded handle, ruffled top, wide flange petticoat shape **650.00**
> 10" h, 4-3/4" d, Optic Diamond Quilted pattern, applied amber handle, ground pontil **235.00**

Punch cup, 2" h, applied reeded handle, 16 optic panels **185.00**

Sauce dish, Daisy and Button, scalloped, set of six **450.00**

Spooner, 4-1/2" h, Inverted Thumbprint pattern, New England Glass Works **100.00**

Syrup pitcher, Hobnail pattern, orig pewter top std "Pat. Jan 29 84," Hobbs, Brockunier & Co., three hobs chipped **300.00**

Tankard
> 6-5/8" h, 10 paneled cylinder, applied reeded handle **395.00**
> 7" h, flared cylinder, Diamond Quilted pattern, applied handle **450.00**

Toothpick holder
> 2-1/4" h, 1-1/2" w, Inverted Thumbprint pattern, sq top **295.00**
> 2-1/2" h, Optic Diamond Quilted pattern, sq, shape #8, Mt. Washington **285.00**

Tumbler, fuchsia shading to rich honey-amber, slight rim flake . . . **50.00**

Vase
> 6-3/4" h, roll down lip, optic diamond body **300.00**
> 9-1/2" h, lily, ribbed trumpet form, tricorn rim, disk base **400.00**
> 10-1/4" h, lily, ribbed trumpet form, tricorn rim, round disk base **350.00**
> 15" h, lily shape, deep red shading to amber, large lily top, flint, c1880 . . . . **825.00**

AMBERINA GLASS, PLATED

History: The New England Glass Company, Cambridge, Massachusetts, first made Plated Amberina in 1886; Edward Libbey patented the process for the company in 1889.

Plated Amberina was made by taking a gather of chartreuse or cream opalescent glass, dipping it in Amberina, and working the two, often utilizing a mold. The finished product had a deep amber to deep ruby red shading, a fiery opalescent lining, and often vertical ribbing for enhancement. Designs ranged from simple forms to complex pieces with collars, feet, gilding, and etching.

A cased Wheeling glass of similar appearance had an opaque white lining but is not opalescent and does not have a ribbed body.

Bowl, 8" w, 3-1/2" h, border of deep dark mahogany, 12 vertical stripes alternating with 12 vertical opalescent fuchsia stripes, off-white casing **7,500.00**

Celery vase **2,750.00**

Cruet, 6-1/2" h, 12 ribs, orig faceted amber stopper **7,500.00**

Lamp shade, 14" d, hanging, swirled, ribbed **4,750.00**

Milk pitcher, applied amber handle, orig "Aurora" label **7,500.00**

Punch cup, vertical ribs, applied handle **1,500.00**

Salt shaker, vertical ribs, orig top **1,200.00**

Tumbler, 2-1/2" d, 3-3/4" h, vertical ribbed cylinder, deep fuchsia-red at top shading to golden yellow base, creamy opal lining **1,750.00**

Vase, 7-1/4" h, lily shape, raspberry red shading to bright amber, opal white casing **2,750.00**

AMERICAN HAND-PAINTED CHINA

History: The American china painting movement began in 1876 and remained popular over the next 50 years. Thousands of artisans—professionals and amateur—decorated tableware, desk accessories, dresser sets, and many other items with floral, fruits and conventional geometric designs and occasionally with portraits, birds, and landscapes. Some American firms, such as Lenox and Willetts Manufacturing Co. of Trenton, New Jersey, produced Belleek, a special type of porcelain that china painters decorated, but a majority of porcelain was imported from France, Germany, Austria, Czechoslovakia, and Japan.

References: Dorothy Kamm, *American Painted Porcelain: Collector's Identification & Value Guide,* Collector Books, 1999; —, *Comprehensive Guide to American Painted Porcelain,* Antique Trader Books, 1999; —, *Painted Porcelain Jewelry and Buttons: Identification & Value Guide,* Collector Books, 2001.

Periodical: *Dorothy Kamm's Porcelain Collector's Companion Newsletter,* P.O. Box 7460, Port St. Lucie, FL 34985-7460; Dorothy.kamm@usa.net.

Museums: Museum of Porcelain Art, International Porcelain Artists & Teachers, Inc., Grapevine, Texas; World Organization of China Painters Foundation Center & Museum, Oklahoma City, Oklahoma.

Marks: American painted porcelains bear foreign factory marks. However, the American style was distinctive, whether naturalistic or conventional (geometric). Some pieces were signed and dated by the artist.

Notes: The quality of the artwork, the amount of detail, and technical excellence—not the amount of gilding or the manufacturer of the porcelain itself—are key pricing factors. Unusual subjects and uncommon forms also influence value.

Adviser: Dorothy Kamm.

Creamer and sugar, decorated with conventional floral border design in blue and soft green on burnished gold band, burnished gold lips, spout, rims, and handles, ivory ground, signed "Helen Hurley,", **$55.** *Photo courtesy of Dorothy Kamm.*

Berry bowl, 7" d, decorated with cherry clusters, sgd "W.Beville," c1900-1915 . . . . **50.00**

Bowl, 6" d, 3-15/16" h, pedestal base, decorated with conventional butterfly design, tan luster and burnished gold, burnished gold rim and foot, sgd "E. T. Low, Dec. 1909," marked "O.& E.G., Royal, Austria" **60.00**

Bread and butter plate, 6" d
> Coupe, decorated with violets, burnished gold rim, sgd "WANDS," marked "Favorite, Bavaria," c1910-1916 . . . . **20.00**
> Round, decorated with border design of pink roses, burnished gold rim and band borders, marked "Haviland, Limoges, France," c1894-1918 . . . . . . **15.00**

Cake plate, individual, double-handled
> 7" d, decorated with central conventional floral bouquet, sgd "IFP," marked "Schumann, Bavaria" **20.00**

7-1/8" d, decorated with conventional border design, burnished gold rim and handles, sgd "LMC," marked "MADE IN JAPAN," c1925 . . . . **22.00**

Celery dish, 12-3/4" l, 5-3/4" w, decorated with border of daisies and leaves on pastel polychrome ground; ivory center, sgd "Weiler," illegible backstamp, 1900-20 . . . . **65.00**

Coffee pot, decorated with conventional design in enamel, outline in raised paste covered with burnished gold, burnished gold finial and base, marked "CAC, BELLEEK," 1889-1906 . . . . **600.00**

Comb and brush tray, 10-1/4" l, 7" w, decorated with pink roses, sgd "to Isabelle Moore from C. B. Tompson, Christmas, 1889" **75.00**

Compote, ftd, 8-7/8 "dia., 4-1/4" h, interior decorated with cluster of pink and white morning glories and pink butterfly, rim and foot decorated with bands of conventional pink butterflies, burnished gold rim and foot, sgd and dated "CL, April 13th, 1881," marked "CFH" **200.00**

Cracker and cheese dish, 9-3/8" d, decorated with conventional border design of primrose, burnished gold borders and trim, sgd "E.S.P., I. M. P.," marked "T & V, Limoges, France," c1891-1907 . . . . **125.00**

Cream soup cup, 4-3/8" d, double handled, decorated with conventional border, burnished gold handles and rim, marked "Bavaria," c1900-1915 . . . . **25.00**

Creamer, decorated with conventional design of pink and lavender flowers on yellow ground, burnished gold handle, foot and rim, marked "MA, Austria," with crown and double-headed bird, 1884-1909 . . . . **10.00**

Creamer and sugar, decorated with conventional floral border design in blue and soft green on burnished gold band, burnished gold lips, spout, rims, and handles, ivory ground, sgd "Helen Hurley" **55.00**

Cup and saucer
Decorated with conventional Celtic border design in celadon, light blue border, ivory center, cup bottom and interiors, burnished gold rims and handle, sgd "L.E.S.," marked with crown in double circle, "Victoria, Austria," 1900-20 . . **30.00**
Decorated with conventional swag design of blue flowers, burnished

gold rims and handle, sgd "Jane Bent Telin," marked "Favorite Bavaria," 1910-25 . . . . **45.00**

Demitasse cup and saucer, decorated with border design of forget-me-nots, burnished gold rims and handle, sgd "KEW," marked "W. G. & Co., Limoges, France," c1901-20 . . . . **25.00**

Dessert set, three pieces, 7-7/16" d plate, decorated with forget-me-not clusters, cup and saucer, opal luster on cup interior, burnished gold rims and handle, plate marked with shield, "Thomas, Bavaria," cup and saucer marked "JAPAN," c1925-30 . . . . **40.00**

Humidor, cov, 3-1/4" d, 5-1/4" h, decorated with pipe and swirling smoke on a light green luster ground burnished gold knob, marked "NIPPON," c1891-1920 . . . . **65.00**

Milk pitcher and plate set, 5-11/16" h pitcher, 7-3/8" d plate, decorated with conventional design of yellow wild roses on yellow ground, burnished gold rims, handle, and trim, sgd "M.S.C. '90," pitcher marked "H & Co., Limoges," plate marked "CFH/GDM" **75.00**

Olive or bonbon dish, 6" d, ring-handles, decorated with conventional border motif in matte antique green, sgd "M.H.Butler," marked "Thomas Bavaria," c1908-15 . . . . **35.00**

Orange cups, 3-1/4" d, 2-3/4" h, ftd, decorated with orange blossoms, white and yellow enamel embellishments, burnished gold rims and interior prongs, sgd "CKI," marked "T & V," c1900-15, price for pr **100.00**

Perfume bottle, flower-shaped stopper, 5-1/4" h, decorated with yellow roses on polychrome ground, burnished gold handle, lip and stopper, sgd "LAIRD" **75.00**

Pin tray and vase, 5-3/16" l, 3-13/16" w tray, 2-3/8" h vase, decorated in an Arabic-style design in blues, burnished gold rims, sgd "FCS," tray marked "W.G. & Co., Limoges," vase marked "ADK, France," 1890-1910 . . . . . **60.00**

Plate
6-3/4" d, decorated with border of pink roses in burnished gold cornucopias, interspesed on pink band, ivory center and rim, burnished gold edge and banding, marked with crown and scepter, Silesia, 1900-20 . . . . **25.00**
7-3/4" d, decorated with multicolored pansies, ivory center, lavender rim,

burnished gold scrolling and rim, sgd "BS," marked J & C, "Louise," Bavaria, 1902+ **45.00**

Powder box, cov, 3" h, decorated with four panels of monochromatic blue landscapes, green gold borders, feet and knob, marked "Bavaria," c1900-20 . . . . **65.00**

Rose bowl, 2-7/8" h, decorated with band of conventional-style violets and bands in burnished gold, marked "O. & E.G., Royal, Austria," c1898-1918 . . . . **30.00**

Salt and pepper shakers, pr, 3" h, decorated with conventional blue-winged insects, burnished gold tops, 1905-20 . . . . **35.00**

Talcum powder shaker, 4-1/2" h, decorated with pink roses, burnished gold top, marked "O. & E. G., Royal, Austria," 1898-1918 . . . . **85.00**

Tea pot stand, 6-3/8" d, decorated with border design of forget-me-not clusters, burnished gold rim, c1900-1920 . . . . **45.00**

Tumbler, 3-3/4" h, decorated in conventional Japanese design, bluebirds on flowering branches, burnished gold rims, sgd "MERRY man," marked "Victoria, Austria," c1904-1915, price for pr **30.00**

Vase 7-7/8" h, decorated with two Art Deco-style floral panels in various lusters and burnished gold, signed "M.D.P. 1920," **$85.** *Photo courtesy of Dorothy Kamm.*

Vase, 7-7/8" h, decorated with two Art Deco-style floral panels in various lusters and burnished gold, sgd "M.D.P. 1920" **85.00**

AMERICAN HAND-PAINTED CHINA JEWELRY AND BUTTONS

History: The American china painting movement began in 1876, about the time the mass production of jewelry also occurred. Porcelain manufacturers and distributors offered a variety of porcelain shapes and settings for brooches, pendants, cuff links, and shirt-waist buttons. Thousands of artisans painted flowers, people, landscapes, and conventions (geometric) motifs. The category of hand-painted porcelain jewelry comprises a unique category, separate from costume and fine jewelry. While the materials were inexpensive to produce, the painted decoration was a work of fine art.

References: Dorothy Kamm, *American Painted Porcelain: Collector's Identification & Value Guide*, Collector Books, 1999; —, *Comprehensive Guide to American Painted Porcelain*, Antique Trader Books, 1999; —, Painted Porcelain Jewelry and Buttons: Identification & Value Guide, Collector Books, 2001.

Periodical: *Dorothy Kamm's Porcelain Collector's Companion Newsletter*, P.O. Box 7460, Port St. Lucie, FL 34985-7460; Dorothy.kamm@usa.net.

Museums: Museum of Florida History, Tallahassee, Florida, has a collection of hand-painted porcelain jewelry by Olive Commons.

Marks: American painted porcelain jewelry bears no factory marks, and is usually unsigned.

Notes: The quality of the artwork, the amount of detail, and technical excellence—not the amount of gilding—are the key pricing factors. Uncommon shapes also influence value.

Adviser: Dorothy Kamm.

Bar pin, 2" w, decorated with forget-me-nots, burnished gold rim, brass bezel, 1880-1920 . . . . **40.00**

Belt buckle brooch

1-7/8" x 2-3/8" oval, decorated with bachelor buttons on a polychrome ground, irregular burnished gold border outlined in black, gold-plated bezel, 1900-17 . **85.00**

1-7/8" x 2-5/8" oval decorated with Art Nouveau-style water lily design outline with raised paste, lavender enamel petals, burnished green gold background, gold-plated bezel, 1900-17 . . . . **110.00**

Brooch

7/8" d, decorated with Colonial man, white enamel on lace, raised paste scrolled border covered with burnished gold brass bezel, c1890-1910 . . . . **40.00**

7/8" sq, diamond shape, decorated with waterscape with water lilies,

white enamel highlights, burnished with gold border, brass bezel, c1920-40 . . . . **35.00**

1" d, decorated with Colonial dame, burnished gold rim, brass bezel, c1890-1910 . . . . **40.00**

1" d, decorated with white pansy on a matte black background, brass bezel, 1890-1910 . . . . **30.00**

1" x 3/4" rectangle, Florida landscape in white on platinum ground, sterling silver bezel, c1920-40 . . . . **75.00**

1-1/8" x 1-3/8" oval, decorated with forget-me-nots, sgd "A. Jibbing," brass bezel, c1900-20 . . . . . **80.00**

1-3/8" x 1-1/4" oval, decorated with tropical river scene, sgd "OC" (Olive Commons, Cocoanut Grove, FL, 1920s), gold-plated bezel **75.00**

1-7/16" x 1-7/8" oval, decorated with pink roses, burnished gold border, sgd "Albrecht," brass bezel **65.00**

1-1/2" x 2" oval, decorated in Native American-inspired geometric design, brass bezel, 1915-1935 . . . . **75.00**

1-1/2" x 2" oval, decorated with stained glass-like conventional design in polychrome colors and burnished gold, gold-plated bezel, 1905-15 . . . . **65.00**

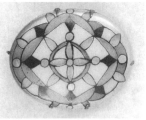

Top: Brooch, decorated with tropical river scene, signed "OC," gold-plated bezel, 1-3/8" x 1-1/4" oval, **$75.** *Bottom: Brooch, decorated with stained glass-like conventional design in polychrome colors and burnished gold, 1-1/2" w x 2" oval,* **$65.** *Photos courtesy of Dorothy Kamm.*

1-3/4" d, decorated with daisy, burnished gold border, brass bezel, c1900-10 . . . . **45.00**

1-7/8" w, crescent shape, decorated with dark pink roses, burnished gold tips, brass bezel, 1900-20 . . . . **45.00**

1-9/16" x 1-7/8" oval, decorated with pink roses and greenery on light blue and yellow, burnished gold ground, scrolls, and dots, sgd "E. GARDE," 1920s, gold-plated setting **50.00**

1-9/16" x 1-7/8 " oval, decorated with blackberries on polychrome ground, sgd "E. GARDE," gold-plated setting, 1920s . . **75.00**

1-11/16" x 2-1/8" oval, decorated with a tropical landscape, burnished gold rim, sgd "OC" (Olive Commons, St. John's Island, FL, 1908-1920), gold-plated bezel **105.00**

2" x 1-5/8" oval, decorated with Art Nouveau-style poppies, burnished gold border, brass bezel, 1856-1915 . . . . **75.00**

2" x 1-1/2" oval, decorated with pink and ruby roses, solid dark blue ground, white enamel highlights, burnished gold border, brass bezel, c1940 . . . . **65.00**

2-1/16" d, decorated with violets, burnished gold rim, brass bezel, 1900-1920 . . . . **65.00**

2-1/8" w, crescent shape, decorated with forget-me-nots, burnished gold rim, brass bezel **40.00**

2-1/2" l, horseshoe shape, decorated with violets, burnished gold tips, brass bezel **100.00**

Cuff buttons, pr, 3/4" x 1" ovals, decorated with lavender flowers, border of burnished gold dots and apple green jewels, burnished gold rims, c1890-1920 . . . . **40.00**

Cuff links, pr, 3/4" x 1" ovals, decorated with forget-me-nots, white enamel highlights, burnished gold borders, gold-plated bezel, c1900-10 . . . . **80.00**

Dress set

Five pieces: 2" x 2-5/8" belt buckle brooch, oval brass bezel, pr 1" d shirt waist buttons with shanks, pr 1" d shirt waist buttons with sew-through backs; decorated with forget-me-nots, black green scalloped borders rimmed in burnished gold, c1900-17 . . . . **400.00**

Four pieces: 3/4" d shirt waist collar button, three 5/8" d shirt waist buttons, decorated with pink roses, white enamel highlights, burnished gold rims, shank backs **60.00**

Flapper pin, 1-5/8" x 2-1/8" oval, decorated with stylized woman, burnished gold border, brass bezel, 1924-28 . . . .**75.00**

Hat pin, 3/4" wide by 1" oval medallion, 6" l shaft, decorated with four-leaf clover on burnished gold ground, brass bezel, 1900-20 . . . .**115.00**

Pendant

1-5/8" x 2-1/8" oval, decorated with violets, burnished gold border, brass bezel, c1880-1914 . . .**60.00**

1-3/4" x 1-3/4" oval, decorated with forget-me-nots, white enamel highlights, burnished gold rim, brass bezel, c1900-20 . . . . .**50.00**

Shirt waist button, 1" d, decorated with pink and ruby roses, burnished gold stippled border, c1900-20 . .**20.00**

AMPHORA

History: The Amphora Porcelain Works was one of several pottery companies located in the Teplitz-Turn region of Bohemia in the late 19th and early 20th centuries. It is best known for art pottery, especially Art Nouveau and Art-Deco pieces.

Marks: Several markings were used, including the name and location of the pottery and the Imperial mark, which included a crown. Prior to World War I, Bohemia was part of the Austro-Hungarian Empire, so the word "Austria" may appear as part of the mark. After World War I, the word "Czechoslovakia" may be part of the mark.

Additional Listings: Teplitz.

Basket, decorated in cuerda seca, butterfly, band of flowers and leaves, pink textured ground, ink stamp mark, 4-1/2" x 5", $115. Photo courtesy of David Rago Auctions.

Center bowl, 2-1/8" h, incised dec outlined in black, enameled blue-green and pink cabochons, mottled tan matte ground, four legs, circular base **200.00**

Creamer, 5-1/4" h, gold trim, raised flowers, sgd "Turin, Teplitz, Amphora" **215.00**

Ewer, 14-1/2" h, pink, gold, and green floral dec, gold accents, salamander entwined handle, c1900 . . . . . . **575.00**

Figure

16-1/4" h, peasant woman carries basket on back, reaching for another basket at feet, tan clothes, gold highlights, crown mark and "Austria" **550.00**

18-1/2" h, peasant woman empties apron of greens into basket, tan, gold highlights, crown mark and "Austria" **550.00**

Pitcher, 11" h, emb owl sitting on branch **165.00**

Sugar bowl, cov, 6-1/4" d, 4-1/2" h, Art Deco enamel dec, polychrome birds and leaves, stamped mark "15449/30" **280.00**

Vase

5-1/4" h, three buttressed handles dec with naturalistic leafy rose vines, rose hip clusters, matte green rose on mottled brown round, gilt highlights, imp mark and stamp on base **250.00**

5-1/2" h, 3-3/4" d, bottle shape, portrait of Art Nouveau style woman, enameled flowers in her hair, imp "Amphora/492" . . **400.00**

6" h, flattened spherical form, shoulder dec with alternating large and small moths in shades of blue, pink, and yellow, raised gilt outline, relief spider webs and enameled disk centers, gilt highlights on green and blue ground, imp "Amphora" in oval, printed "R. S. & K. Turn-Teplitz Bohemia" with maker's device on base . . . **900.00**

8-1/2" h, 5" d, bulbous, four sided, Art-Nouveau profile of woman against blooming forest glaze, umber, gilded details, stamp mark "Teplitz" **1,200.00**

10" h, shouldered form, textured green and blue glaze, gilt accents **650.00**

11-1/8" h, pear shape, extended neck, two tri-part handles, mottled matte green and brown glaze, inscribed cipher, R. S. & K, Teplitz, Bohemia, c1900, crazing, base chip **1,035.00**

ANIMAL COLLECTIBLES

History: The representation of animals in fine arts, decorative arts, and on utilitarian products dates back to antiquity. Some religions endowed certain animals with mystical properties. Authors throughout written history used human characteristics when portraying animals.

The formation of collectors' clubs and marketing crazes, e.g., flamingo, pig, and penguin, during the 1970s increased the popularity of this collecting field.

References: Felicia Browell, *Breyer Animal Collector's Guide*, 2nd ed., Collector Books, 1999; Elaine Butler, *Poodle Collectibles of the 50s & 60s*, L-W Book Sales, 1995; Candace Sten Davis and Patricia Baugh, *A Treasury of Scottie Dog Collectibles*, Collector Books, Volume I (1998), Volume II (2000); John Edwards, *The Charlton Standard Catalogue of Royal Worcester Animals*, Charlton Press, 2001; Marbena Jean Fyke, *Collectible Cats*, Book I (1993, 1995 value update), Book II (1996), Collector Books; Deborah Rashkin, *Horse Antiques and Collectibles*, Schiffer Publishing, 2001; Patricia Robak, *Dog Antiques and Collectibles*, Schiffer Publishing, 1999.

Periodicals: *Jumbo Jargon*, 1002 West 25th St., Erie, PA 16502; *Scottie Sampler*, P.O. Box 450, Danielson, CT 06239-0450; *Western Mule Magazine*, P.O. Box 46, Marshfield, MO 65706, www.westernmulemagazine.com.

Collectors' Clubs: Breyers Collectors Club, 14 Industrial Road, Pequannock, NJ 07440, www.breyerhorses.com; Cat Collectors, P.O. Box 150784, Nashville, TN 37215-0784, www.catcollectors.com; Folk Art Society of America, P.O. Box 17041, Richmond, VA 23226; Frog Pond, P.O. Box 193, Beech Grove, IN 46107; International Owl Collectors Club, 54 Triverton Road, Edgware, Middlesex HA8 6BE UK; National Elephant Collector's Society, 380 Medford St., Somerville, MA 02145; The Happy Pig Collectors Club, 4542 N. Western Ave., Chicago, IL 60625-2117; Wee Scots, Inc., P.O. Box 450, Danielson, CT 06239-0450, www.campbellscotties.com.

Museums: American Kennel Club, New York, NY; American Kennel Club Museum of the Dog, St. Louis, MO; American Saddlebred Museum, Lexington, KY; American Saddle Horse Museum Association, Lexington, KY; Antiquibles Mall Dog Museum, Waco, TX; International Museum of the Horse, Lexington, KY; Stradling Museum of the Horse, Patagonia, AZ, The Frog Fantasies Museum, Eureka Springs, AR.

Additional Listings: See specific animal collectible categories in *Warman's Americana & Collectibles*.

Barnyard

Carving, folk art, wood

7" l, peep, painted, c1900, with stand **9,545.00**

9-1/2" l, 2-1/2" w, 8" h, rooster, polychrome red, mustard yellow, and brown, base with indistinct pencil inscription, PA, c1840 . . . . **4,320.00**

17" l, 15" h, rooster, old cream-colored paint, 3/4 flat body, stand **460.00**

Chopper, 12" l, 7-1/2" d, 7-1/4" h, rooster, iron, fanciful silhouette, incised feather detail, mounted on wooden fragment, with stand, late 18th/early 19th C, lacks wooden handle . **1,035.00**

Figure, pearlware, 3-1/2" l, 2-1/4" h, lamb, reclining, white, brown legs, ears, tail, and facial features, light green base, hairlines in base **165.00**

Figure, sewer tile

5-1/4" l, 5" h, frog on log, hand modeled, tooled bark, inscribed initials "H.S." on base, dark brown, slightly metallic glaze, traces of gold on one end of log **425.00**

7-7/8" h, pig, standing, wearing pants, vest, and bow tie, reddish-brown glaze, few spots of wear **320.00**

Mirror, pocket, Cow-Ease, Carpenter Morton Co., Boston, farmer spraying cow, celluloid, 2-3/4" l, 1-3/4" h oval **575.00**

Sign, International Milk and Cream, molded head of brown cow in center, cast aluminum, maroon rim, silver lettering, scalloped border, c1920, 14" d **635.00**

Tin, Dr. Daniels' Cow Invigorator, 18 oz pry lid tin litho, image of cow on each side, C-8+ **275.00**

Toy, stuffed

Cow, 11-1/2" l, 8-1/2" h, brown, felt covering, glass eyes, black painted nostrils and mouth, fur tip of tail, tin wheels attached to wooden hooves, early 20th C, some soil and wear, break to top of leg **230.00**

Painting, oil on canvas, rural farmyard scene with cattle, chickens, ducks, pigs, and figures, signed lower left "C. Shayer" (Charles Waller Shayer), plate on carved and gold painted wood and gesso frame titled "Farm at Alton, Hants," 43" w, 31" h, $4,400. Photo courtesy of Joy Luke Auctions.

Goat, 4-3/4" h, black mohair legs and face, long white mohair body, felt horns, green glass eyes . **60.00**

Birds

Architectural element, 18-1/2" h, owl, pottery, unglazed, traces of old silver paint, base imp "Owens and Howard, St. Louis, MO," minor hairlines . . **550.00**

Carving

10" l, 12-1/4" h, carved wood, painted brown and white, shore birds, New England, c1910, stands, price for pr **1,725.00**

12-1/2" w, 6-3/4" h, marble, attributed to Midwest America, 19th C **690.00**

Eagle, cast iron, painted, black with white spots, America, late 19th C, 11" l, 5-1/2" d, 3-1/2" h **250.00**

Figure, sewer tile, 10-1/2" h, horned owl, perched on round pedestal base, orange glaze **450.00**

Lamp base, 16" h, owl perched on stump, sewer pipe, hollow body, good detail, dark brown glaze, shallow edge chips **385.00**

Painting on velvet, 25" w, 29" h, painted heron with cat tails, wide walnut frame with molded edge, chevron inlay around outer edges, checkered inlay around inside, gilt liner **775.00**

Pitcher, 6-1/2" d, 8" h, figural, owl, pewter, jade cabochon eyes, stamped "Tudric/5/055" **900.00**

Tobacco container, Bob White Tobacco, paper label on cloth pouch, multicolored Bob White on both sides, 1910 tax stamp, 2-3/4" w, 1-1/4" d, 4" h **400.00**

Towel rack, 13-1/2" w, 45" h, wood, parrot form, perched on turned towel holder, round turned base painted with stylized persimmons, c1930 . . . . **325.00**

Trivet, parrot, pastel central figure with intricate flower and vine pattern, eight triangular feet, Rookwood marks, 1929, 5-3/4" sq **325.00**

Cats

Bas relief

6-1/2" w, 6-3/4" h, carved marble, inscribed "May 1943," with stand **425.00**

8" w, 8" h, patinated cast iron, face with whiskers, America, late 19th C, with stand **1,495.00**

13" w, 8" h, carved granite, 19th C **420.00**

Figure

2-5/8" h, carved marble or alabaster, sitting, glass eyes, America, 19th C, chip on base corner . . **1,035.00**

9" l, sewer tile, reclining, hand tooled eye lashes, white glazed eyes **360.00**

9-1/2" w, 7" d, 17-1/4" h, carved pine, fat cat, incised "E. Sweet," 20th C, cracks **435.00**

13-1/4" h, sewer tile, elongated form, head cocked to one side, curious look, hand tooled eyelashes, metallic glaze, Ohio **660.00**

Jewelry, bar pin, reverse painted crystal, hand engraved 14kt gold bar surmounted by white cat in round frame, ropetwist dec, orig a locket **1,380.00**

Needlework picture, 19-1/4" w, 15-3/4" h, woolen needlepoint and petit point background, central stumpwork tabby cat, giltwood frame, Victorian, late 19th C **175.00**

Pillow, 13" w, 14-1/2" h, central image of kitten's head printed on silk, wide brocade border, pink and teal fringe border, teal velvet backing **125.00**

Smoker toy, 3-1/8" l, carved wood, standing cat, brass collar, PA, 19th C, one leg repaired **230.00**

Wall pocket, 10-3/4" l, all over polychrome floral sprigs, inset glass eyes, French Faience, late 19th/early 20th C, price for pr **350.00**

Dogs

Candlesticks, pr, 7-1/2" h, brass, figural, cup shaped sconce, slender standard, round socle base set with three figures of seated hounds joined by chains at collars, blue cabochon stone eyes, French, late 19th C **650.00**

Carving, folk art, wood

Chow, standing, open mouth, showing teeth, early 20th C, 12" l, 10" h **1,265.00**

Standing dog, white, black markings, curly tail, integral carved base, 8" l, 9-1/2" h **6,900.00**

Figure

2-7/8" l, 3-1/4" h, pearlware, long hair seated dog, white, brown and gold spots, minor flakes on base, short hairline **520.00**

7" w, 3-1/2" d, 9-1/2" h, seated, freestanding front legs, yellow Ohio clay, mottled green glaze on base, brown dec on dog, black eyes, blue ink stamp label "E. Houghton

& Co. Dalton, Ohio, 1928," hairline in base **1,450.00**

7-1/4" l, 9-1/4" h, seated, freestanding front legs, gray clay, cream colored glaze, brown and blue polka dots, long tail with brown, one ear brown, other blue, chips on base **6,270.00**

7-1/2" h, sewer tile, seated, hand modeled, tooled fur and facial features, matte glaze with metallic speckles, traces of white paint **110.00**

8-1/8" h, Ohio white clay, seated, short ears and tail, long jowls, grown glaze, chip on back of base, small flake on ear **110.00**

10" h, Newcomerstown, Ohio, pottery, seated, unglazed clay, good detail, shallow front chip **3,750.00**

10-1/4" h, white clay, seated, dark brown glaze, free standing front legs, molded fur, collar, facial features, high base with invected corners, molded shells, and rosettes, base chips **750.00**

10-1/2" l, 5-1/2" w, 11-1/2" h, Collie, sewer tile, standing, reddish brown glaze, rect molded base, firing separations, small chips on ears **935.00**

26-1/4" l, 16" d, 19" h, Hound, molded lead, full bodied, recumbent, Fiske Foundry, NY, c1880, on cast iron base, weathered surface, repair, imperfections **7,475.00**

Compote, pattern glass, frosted reclining dog finial, 6-1/4" d, 8-1/2" h, $275. Photo courtesy of Joy Luke Auctions.

Hooked rug, 26" x 43-1/2", black dog, dark green detail, black ground, multicolored borders, wear, holes **360.00**

Inkwell, 4-1/4" d, 4-5/8" h, brass, orb inkwell opening to glass liner, raised on three silvered seated hound figures joined by chains at collars, set with marcasite eyes, round socle base, French, late 19th C **375.00**

Jewelry, brooch

Micromosaic, recumbent King Charles spaniel, gold ropetwist frame, minor lead solder on verso **900.00**

Platinum and diamond, terrier, pave setting, green stone eyes. **1,725.00**

Reverse painted crystal, standing boxer, oval 14kt gold frame, sgd "W. F. Marcus" **920.00**

Sculpture, 13" l, 14" h, carved limestone, Ohio, c1920-30, repair to right ear **1,150.00**

Sign, Glovers Dog Remedies, litho tin, bull dog, green ground, c1900, 13" d **1,210.00**

Snuff mull, 3" l, carved horn, curved and carved dog's head, bone detailed eyes, gilt-metal neck rim etched with initials, Scottish, first half 19th C. **520.00**

Watch fob, four graduated round 14kt gold plaques depicting dog's heads in repoussé, suspended by trace link chains, monogrammed, swivel clasp, 15.0 dwt **575.00**

Horses

Calligraphy, 15-3/4" x 22-1/2", pen and ink on paper, horse and dog, unsigned American School, 19th C, framed, puncture, minor staining, creases **460.00**

Cane, 3-1/2" l handle, carved ivory horse head, grain painted wood stick, late 19th C **230.00**

Center bowl, 18-1/4" d, sterling silver, Black, Starr & Frost, New York, late 19th/early 20th C, circular, everted down-spreading openwork rim, molded saddles interspersed with foliage, eight protruding horse heads set within horseshoes surmounted by riding crops and bits, edge shaped as vine, four beaded scroll and foliate feet, 155 troy oz **29,900.00**

Cigar tin, 6" l, 4-1/8" w, 5-1/4" h, Sunset Trail, litho tin, cowboy and cowgirl riding into sunset on both sides, C-8+ **700.00**

Clothes brush and holder, 10" w, 11" l, carved wood, realistically modeled

ebonized horse head, glass eyes, leather bridle, felt-lined compartment at top for carved ebony clothes brush, wall mounted, England, early 20th C **460.00**

Condiment set, 5" l, 3-5/8" h, electroplate, base formed as horseshoe, spur-form handle, toothpick holder flanked by boot form castor, mustard pot with whip-form spoon, central jockey cap open salt, Elkington & Co., England, late 19th C **175.00**

Figure, carved and painted wood

7-1/2" h, laminated, stylized form, grommet eyes, orig glossy black paint, America, late 19th C, losses to tail **1,610.00**

7-3/4" l, laminated and polychrome, standing, red, grommet eyes, horsehair tail, attributed to New York State, late 19th/early 20th C **2,185.00**

10-1/2" l, 14-1/2" h, articulated circus figure with red textile shoulder girth, riding horse with glass bead eyes, attributed to Connecticut, c1900-10, stand, minor wear, paint imperfections **2,530.00**

Mirror, pocket, Kaffo, Anheuser Busch, 2-3/4" l, 1-3/4" h, oval **240.00**

Pull toy

11-1/4" l, painted and laminated carved pine, full stride, horsehair tail, wheeled platform base, America, early 20th C **635.00**

14" l, 12" h, brown burlap covering, leather bridle and collar, bentwood brace, traces of horsehair mane, make-do straw tail, traces of red paint on base, wear, ears missing, poorly replaced hoof **350.00**

Walking stick, 3-3/8" l handle, cylindrical ivory band topped by brass jockey's cap, faux bamboo stick, late 19th/early 20th C **350.00**

Weathervane, 26-1/2" l, 16-1/2" h, full-bodied trotting horse, copper, verdigris surface, black metal stand, America, late 19th C, minor dents **4,325.00**

Wild animals

Bookends, pr, fox head, 4-3/8" w, 6-5/8" h, carved wood, mahogany backplate mounted with realistically carved and painted head, stepped base, early 20th C **320.00**

Bottle opener, 3-1/2" h, elephant, cast iron, glossy pink enamel, scattered paint nicks, c1960 . . . . **40.00**

*Figure, bisque, elephant and young, Italian, 21" l, 15-1/2" h, **$595**. Photo courtesy of Joy Luke Auctions.*

Door stop, bear, cast iron, painted brown, America, late 19th/early 20th C, 2-1/2" w, 5-1/4" l, 4-1/2" h..... **1,130.00**

Figure, carved alabaster, reclining rabbit, full relief, rect base, 9" l, 5" d, 6" h...................... **2,185.00**

Figure, ceramic, white elephant figures, gray and pink enamel detailing, sq bronze bases with gilt rocaille scrollwork to sides, early 20th C, 10" w, 5-3/4" d, 10-1/2" h, price for pr...................... **2,760.00**

Figure, clay, reclining lion, scalloped base, dark brown shiny glaze, Ohio, in-the-making hairlines **250.00**

Figure, polychromed carved wood

Deer, worn brown paint, white accents on nose and underbelly, green ground stand, America, 19th C, missing one antler and part of right foreleg, 18" l, 3-1/4" d, 17-3/4" h............. **3,450.00**

Kangaroo, Fred Alten, (1872-1945, Wyandotte, MI), body with traces of brown stain, red glass eyes, shaped base, 3-1/4" w, 7-1/4" h, with stand............. **575.00**

Leopard, Fred Alten, (1872-1945, Wyandotte, MI), yellow-brown paint with black spots, 12" l, 1-3/4" w, 6" h, minor paint loss, with stand............ **1,265.00**

Shooting gallery target, 21" w, 7" d, 31-1/2" h, rabbit, MA, c1940, some paint remaining, with stand **815.00**

Sign, Royal Stag Whiskey, tin litho, multicolored center with large antlered stag, 14-1/2" w, 14-1/2" h...... **525.00**

Tin, litho

Green Turtle Cigars, Gordon Cigar Co., hinged lid, color image of turtle on rock smoking cigar, 6" l, 3-7/8" d, 4-1/2" h........ **1,000.00**

Jumbo Peanut Butter, Frank Tea & Spice Co., one-lb size, 3-3/8" x 3-7/8"................. **775.00**

Red Wolf Coffee, Ridenour-Baker Co., Kansas City, one-lb size, vacuum pack, trademark wolf, 5" d, 4" h **575.00**

Squirrel Brand Salted Jumbo Peanuts, diecut, gray squirrel holding nut, red oval with white and yellow slogans and peanuts as base, 8-1/2" w, 9-1/2" h **325.00**

Tiger Bright Sweet Chewing Tobacco, P. Lorillard Co., vertical pocket size, 3" w, 7/8" d, 2-7/8" h **275.00**

ARCHITECTURAL ELEMENTS

History: Architectural elements, many of which are handcrafted, are those items which have been removed or salvaged from buildings, ships, or gardens. Part of their desirability is due to the fact that it would be extremely costly to duplicate the items today.

Beginning about 1840, decorative building styles began to feature carved wood and stone, stained glass, and ornate ironwork. At the same time, builders and manufacturers also began to use fancy doorknobs, doorplates, hinges, bells, window locks, shutter pulls, and other decorative hardware as finishing touches to elaborate new homes and commercial buildings.

Hardware was primarily produced from bronze, brass, and iron, and doorknobs also were made from clear, colored, and cut glass. Highly ornate hardware began appearing in the late 1860s and remained popular through the early 1900s. Figural pieces that featured animals, birds, and heroic and mythological images were very popular, as were ornate and very graphic designs that complimented the many architectural styles that emerged in the late 19th century.

Fraternal groups, government and educational institutions, and individual businesses all ordered special hardware for their buildings. Catalogs from the era show hundreds of patterns, often with a dozen different pieces available in each design.

The current trends of preservation and recycling of architectural elements has led to the establishment and growth of organized salvage operations that specialize in removal and resale of elements. Special auctions are now held to sell architectural elements from churches, mansions, office buildings, etc. Today's decorators often design an entire room around one architectural element, such as a Victorian marble bar or mural, or use several as key accent pieces.

References: Bakewell & Mullins, *Victorian Architectural Sheet-Metal Ornaments,* Dover Publications, 1999; Ronald S. Barlow (comp.), *Victorian Houseware, Hardware and Kitchenware,* Windmill Publishing, 1991; Margarete Baur-Heinhold, *Decorative Ironwork,* Schiffer Publishing, 1996; Louis

Blanc, *Decorative French Ironwork Designs,* Dover, 1999; Len Blumin, *Victorian Decorative Art,* available from ADCA (P.O. Box 126, Eola, IL 60519), n.d.; David A. Hanks, *The Decorative Designs of Frank Lloyd Wright,* Dover Publications, 1999; Barbara Israel, *Antique Garden Ornaments: Two Centuries of American Taste,* Harry N. Abrams, 1999; Joan Kahr, *Edgar Brandt: Master of Art Deco Ironwork,* Harry N. Abrams, 1999; Dona Z. Meilach, *Architectural Ironwork,* Schiffer Publishing, 2001; Alistair Morris, *Antiques from the Garden,* Antique Collectors' Club, 1999; Web Wilson, *Great Glass in American Architecture,* E. P. Dutton, New York, 1986; — *Antique Hardware Price Guide,* Krause Publications, 1999; Myra Yellin and Eric B. Outwater, *Garden Ornaments and Antiques,* Schiffer Publishing, 2000.

Periodicals: *Old House Journal Restoration Directory,* 2 Main St., Gloucester, MA 01930; *The Old House Journal,* 2 Main St., Gloucester, MA 01930; *Traditional Building,* 69A Seventh Ave., Brooklyn, NY 11217-3618.

Collectors' Clubs: Antique Doorknob Collectors of America, Inc., P.O. Box 31, Chatham, NJ 07928-0031, www.members.aol@knobnews; International Brick Collectors Assoc., 80 E. 106th Terrace, Kansas City, MO 64114-5080.

Museum: American Sanitary Plumbing Museum, Worcester, MA; The Museum of the American Architectural Foundation, Washington, DC.

Architectural

Bird bath, 19" d, 33-1/2" h, cast iron, shallow basin, gadrooned rim mounted by two doves, fluted baluster form standard on circular base cast with pierced rose design **300.00**

Bird cage, 21" x 19-1/2" x 18", house form, grand entrance, front porch, bay windows, dormers, cupola, painted green, trimmed with red painted wooden buttons, knobs, and perches, some paint loss................... **230.00**

Catalog

Arkansas Soft Pine Bureau, Little Rock, AR, 36 pgs, 8-1/4" x 11", 1918, loose sheets in company folder **32.00**

Burhans & Black, Inc., Syracuse, NY, 42 pgs, c1923, spring and summer hardware **32.00**

Janusch Manuf Co., NY, 152 pgs, 9" x 12", 1922, Cat. No. 33, fireplace implements, bathroom cabinets, electrical grates, screens, hoods, etc. **55.00**

National Trade Journals, NY, 368 pgs, 8-1/2" x 11-1/4", 1931, Home Builders Catalog, 5th ed., contractor's reference work . . **36.00**

Sears, Roebuck & Co., Chicago, IL, 78 pgs, 8-1/2" x 11-1/2", 1930, "Honor Bilt," building materials, doors, moldings, cabinets, etc. **50.00**

Webber Lumber & Supply Co., Fitchburg, MA, 48 pgs, 7" x 10", c1930, Cat. No. 95, The Home from Cellar to Shingles **35.00**

Carving, wood, Renaissance-style dolphin with upturned tail, dark stained finish, 20th C, 11-1/4" l, 13-1/4" h, price for pair **575.00**

Column

25-1/2" h, green marble, black marble base, Italian, pr . . **1,500.00**

86" h, Baroque-style giltwood, spiraled form, trailing vines, grape clusters, and putti, Spanish, 19th C, minor losses, flaking . . **5,750.00**

Cornice board, 41-1/2" l, 8-1/4" h, green painted boards, gilt foliage flanking pictorial central reserves outlined with gilt banding, house portraits and fencing similar on both, orig painted and gilt surfaces, New England, 1830s, price for pr. . **4,025.00**

Door

27-1/4" w, 69-1/2" h, raised panel, pegged construction, orig red paint, wrought iron thumb latch, old corner chip **580.00**

31-1/2" w, 78-1/2" h, two molded recessed panels, grain painted to resemble exotic wood, attributed to Maine, early 19th C, very minor surface imperfections **920.00**

Door knocker, 4" w, 11-1/4" h, wrought and hammered copper, tulip shape, monogrammed "IGW," orig dark patina **175.00**

Eagle, carved wood, America, 19th C

19" l, 9-1/2" h, oak, half figure, outstretched wings, perched on branch, glass eye **490.00**

22-1/2" l, 16-1/2" h, gilt, full bodied, outstretched wings, mounted on wooden bracket, minor imperfections **690.00**

Fern stand, 25" d, 57-1/2" h, wire-work, three graduated scrollwork baskets with everted rims, tripod base with scroll feet, 19th C **375.00**

Finial, 13" d, 24" h, figural, pineapple, carved and painted white, attributed to

Portsmouth, NH, early 19th C, mounted on base, some loss at base, imperfections, price for pr **4,315.00**

Fountain, 24" d, 50" h, cast iron, enameled gray paint, detailed casting, two graduated urn-shaped bowls with scalloped edges, lobed bottoms, ivy leaves on center column with reeding, flower bud finial, base missing . **690.00**

Fragment, 11" w, 7" d, 15" h, cast iron, lion's head, old weathered surface, America, late 19th C, with stand **1,725.00**

Garden basin

15" w, 17" l, cast iron, heart-shape, sides with continuous scene of putti cavorting with puppies, bird mounted on one side, late 19th C. **550.00**

25" w, 25" h, cast concrete, Neoclassical-style, sq, cast with scenes of birds and beasts on ribbon-tied fruit swags, 20th C **445.00**

Garden bench, cast iron

36" w, 13-1/2" d, 28" h, openwork vintage design, scrolled seat, worn white paint, price for pr . . . **350.00**

43-1/2" w, 15" d, 31" h, openwork fern design on back and legs, geometric cast designs on seat, old white repaint, two hairlines, chip near front corner **325.00**

Garden chair, 21-1/2" w, 26-1/2" h, cast iron, openwork vintage design, scrolled seat, worn white paint **200.00**

Garden figure, 13" h, cast spelter, late 19th/early 20th C, classical-style seated young woman feeding bird from tazza, lacking base **150.00**

Garden ornament

10" l, 11-5/8" h, rabbit, cast iron, seated figure, traces of white, green, and red paint, late 19th C, wear **345.00**

16-1/2" l, 29-1/2" h, carved and painted wood and gesso, urn with flame, painted tan, putty, and white, traces of gilt, 19th C **2,185.00**

Gas post light, 18-1/4" w, 42" h, copper, dark patina, four cased glass panes, peaked top, sgd "Foster & Pullen, Avil Works, Bradford" . . . **990.00**

Gate latch, 7" l, 3-3/4" d, 3-1/2" h, duck's head, sand cast iron, attributed to California, late 19th C, weathered surface, with stand **230.00**

Gate weight, 9" d, cast iron, sun face, MA, late 18th C, with stand . . **10,925.00**

Hitching post, cast iron

3-1/2" w, 6" h, fist holds stationary ring, cylindrical shaft, old weathered surface, New England, 19th C **1,495.00**

4-1/4" h, 9-1/2" d, 11-1/2" h, horse's head, molded features, stationary ring, old weathered surface, America, 19th C, with stand **635.00**

4-1/2" h, 9-7/8" h, horse's head, oval ring, cast iron, traces of black paint, Rochester, NY, forge, c1850, with stand **1,850.00**

5-1/2" w, 6" d, 9-1/2" h, face of African-American man, holding ring and chain in mouth, 19th C, with stand **2,300.00**

7" w, 5" h, nodding horse's head, traces of black paint, W. H. Vaughn, Quincy, Illinois, Pat. 1889, losses **320.00**

11" l, 12" h, dog's head, ring in mouth, cast iron, traces of black paint, America, 19th C, minor surface rust, with stand . . **4,025.00**

Lectern, 27" h, figural eagle, pine, old mellow finishing **3,100.00**

Lock, 8-1/2" w, 11" h, iron, rect plate with male and female silhouettes, key with quatrefoil terminal, 19th C, stand, minor surface corrosion **650.00**

Marble reclining lion, replicas of lions at the tomb of Clementi XIII, reputed to have been purchased by Dr. J.T.B. Strapp of Decatur, IL, who purchased the pair from the Crystal Palace, New York, for $800. Sold as a pair in 2001 for **$9,900**. *Photo courtesy of Joy Luke Auctions.*

Mantle

Carved Carerra marble, Empire, stepped molded rect top, over carved pilasters with acanthus leaf carved molding, paw feet, molded block plinth base, 55" w, 16" d, 40" h **2,000.00**

Poplar, old worn finish, applied moldings, face turned circular medallions, 33" h x 35" w opening, 63" h shelf, 52-1/4" w, 52" h waist, found in OH **110.00**

Obelisk, 31-1/2" h, faux grained wood and composition, raised on four gold

painted supports, plinth base, 20th C,
pr **460.00**
Overmantel element, 49-3/4" w, 5-1/4"
d, 67-7/8" h, French, molded top,
reeded panels and mirror surround, rect
mirror plate flanked by Corinthian
topped reeded pilasters **1,150.00**
Painted wood panel, Victorian, late
19th C, 23-1/2" w, 23-3/4" h, rect,
japanned ground, printed sepia toned
border of flowers and anthemion,
central roundel painted with Venetian
scene of Canal and Piazza San Marco,
panel veneered onto pine back board
. . . . **250.00**
Pedestal
5-1/2" w, 5-3/4" l, 42" h, smoke dec,
recessed top, sq flaring column,
stepped base with ogee molding,
America, 20th C, wear,
separations, price for pr . . . **650.00**
11" w, 30-1/4" h, faux marble painted
wood, sq oak cornice, sq column,
applied moldings, America, 19th C,
chips, abrasions **650.00**
15-1/4" d, 16-1/4" h, painted red,
white, and blue, double tapering
sq form, recessed panels,
applied moldings, America, early
20th C **1,150.00**
16" w, 28" h, carved marble, stepped
top, tapered sq sides carved in
high relief with foliage, America,
20th C, price for pr **1,500.00**
Planter, stump type, sewer tile
10-1/2" l, 15" w, 12" h, textured
surface, stamped medallion
"Cambria-Co., C. e. Blackfork,
Ohio," few chips **385.00**
18" h, three branches, hand tooled
bark, carved "Gram" plaque,
crack **110.00**
22" h, emb oval signature for
"Superior Clay Co., Uhrichsville,
Ohio, Handcrafted by Water
Smith," sq molded base, round
stump, three open branches, one
raccoon on branch, another on
edge of top, minor firing
separations **220.00**
28" h, 32" d, three branches, edge
chips, repairs **330.00**
Podium, pine, rect plank top, two
faceted columns joined by sq panel,
old finish, painted white, attributed to
New York state, c1860-70, 33" w,
17-3/4" d, 33" h **635.00**
Roof finial, 46-1/2" h, zinc, light gray
and white oxidized surface, top column
tapering down to point, flower petals at
center, square to round formed base,

removable flag and scrolled wire arrow,
19th C, soldered restorations, late
enameled steel stand **1,320.00**
Slide bolt, 14-1/8" l, wrought iron,
human head bolt knob **980.00**
Suite, settee, pair of arm chairs, cast
iron, curved vintage backs and legs,
scrollwork seats, white repaint, 60" l,
29-1/2" h settee, 14-1/4" h seat,
24-7/8" h chairs **495.00**
Sundial, 17" d, 34" h, lead, circular,
alpha numerics, terra cotta base
shaped like three gargoyles, shaped
plinth **850.00**
Suspension pulley, 12-1/2" l, 6-1/2" w,
pine, heart-shape, dual wooden
wheels over pierced end, decorative
central heart-shaped cut-out, America,
19th C, black wood stand, missing
wheel **490.00**
Tie rod bolt plate, cast iron, weathered
surface, America, 19th C
Flower petal **95.00**
Letter "M" **100.00**
Star **125.00**
Topiary form, 13-1/2" w, 24" h,
lyre-shape, wire, conical base,
painted green, America, late 19th/early
20th C **150.00**
Well weight, 7" w, 5-1/2" d, 9-3/8" h,
carved granite, oviform, pierced for
rope, 19th C, stand **550.00**

ART DECO

History: The Art-Deco period was named after an
exhibition, "l'Exposition Internationale des Arts
Décorative et Industriels Modernes," held in Paris in
1927. Its beginnings succeed those of the
Art-Nouveau period, but the two overlap in time, as
well as in style.

Art-Deco designs are angular with simple lines.
This was the period of skyscrapers, movie idols, and
the Cubist works of Picasso and Legras. Art Deco
motifs were used for every conceivable object being
produced in the 1920s and 1930s (ceramics, furniture,
glass, and metals) not only in Europe but in America
as well.

References: Victor Arwas, *Glass: Art Nouveau to Art
Deco*, Rizzoli, 1977; Bryan Catley, *Art Deco and Other
Figures*, Antique Collectors' Club, 1999; Alastair
Duncan, *American Art Deco*, Thames and Hudston,
1999; Mary Gaston, *Collector's Guide to Art Deco*, 2nd
ed., Collector Books, 1997, 2000 value update; Colin
Mawston, *British Art Deco Ceramics*, Schiffer
Publishing, 2000; Herb Millman and John Dwyer, *Art
Deco Lighting*, Schiffer Publishing, 2001; Betty Ward
and Nancy Schiffer, *Weller, Roseville, and Related
Zanesville Art Pottery and Tiles*, Schiffer Publishing,
2000; Joan Kahr, *Edgar Brandt: Master of Art Deco
Ironwork*, Harry N. Abrams, 1999; Wolf Uecker, *Art
Nouveau and Art Deco Lamps and Candlesticks*,
Abbeville Press, 1986.

Periodicals and Internet Resources:
ArtDeco.com, www.ArtDeco.com; *Chicago Art Deco
Society Magazine*, Chicago Art Deco Society, 950
Stonegate Drive, Highland Park, IL 60035-5147;
Impressions, Miami Design Preservation League, P.O.
Box 190180, Miami Beach, FL 33119, www.mdlp.org;
Modernist Newsletter, Art Deco Society of New York,
P.O. Box 160, Planetarium Station, New York, NY
10024, www.artdeco.org; *Modern Times Newsletter*,
Sacramento Art Deco Society, P.O. Box 162836,
Sacramento, CA 95816-2836; *Newsreel*, Art Deco
Society of Cleveland, P.O. Box 210134, Cleveland, OH
44121; *Streamline*, Art Deco Society of the Palm
Beaches, 325 SW 29th Ave., Delray Beach, FL 33445;
The Exposition Newsletter, Art Deco Society of Los
Angeles, P.O. Box 972, Los Angeles, CA 90078-0972,
www.adsla.org; *The Modern Newsletter*, Detroit Area
Art Deco Society, P.O. Box 1393, Royal Oak, MI
48068-1393; *The Sophisticate Magazine*, Art Deco
Society of California, 100 Bush St., Suite 511, San
Francisco, CA 94104-3908, www.art-deco.org;
Translux, Art Deco Society of Washington, P.O. Box
11090, Washington, DC 20008-0290, www.adsw.org.

Collectors' Clubs: Art Deco Society of Boston, One
Murdock Terrace, Brighton, MA 02135-2817; Art Deco
Society of New York, P.O. Box 160, Planetarium
Station, New York, NY 10024, Art Deco Society of
Washington, P.O. Box 11090, Washington, DC
20008-0290, www.adsw.org; Art Deco Society of the
Palm Beaches, 325 SW 29th Ave., Delray Beach, FL
33445; Art Deco Society of Cleveland, P.O. Box
210134, Cleveland, OH 44121; Art Deco Society of
Louisiana, P.O. Box 1326, Baton Rouge, LA
70821-6367; Art Deco Society of Los Angeles, P.O.
Box 972, Los Angeles, CA 90078-0972; Art Deco
Society of California, 100 Bush St., Suite 511, San
Francisco, CA 94104-3908; Canadian Art Deco
Society, #626 Pender St., #800, Vancouver, British
Columbia V6B 1V9 Canada; Carlton Ware
International, P.O. Box 161, Sevenoaks, Kent TN15
6GA England; Chase Collectors Society, 2149 W.,
Jibsail Loop, Mesa, AZ 85202-5524,
www.publich.aus.edu/~icblv/chase.html; Chicago Art
Deco Society, 950 Stonegate Drive, Highland Park, IL
60035-5147; Detroit Area Art Deco Society, P.O. Box
1393, Royal Oak, MI 48068-1393; International
Coalition of Art Deco Societies, One Murdock Terrace,
Brighton, MA 02135; Miami Design Preservation
League, P.O. Box 190180, Miami Beach, FL 33119,
www.mdlp.org; Sacramento Art Deco Society, P.O. Box
162836, Sacramento, CA 95816-2836; Twentieth
Century Society, 70 Cowcross St., London EC1M 6DR
England.

Museums: Art Institute of Chicago, Chicago, IL;
Copper-Hewitt Museum, National Museum of Design,
Smithsonian Institution, New York, NY; Corning
Museum of Glass, Corning, NY; Jones Museum of
Glass and Ceramics, Sebago, ME; Virginia Museum of
Fine Arts, Richmond, VA.

Additional Listings: Furniture and Jewelry. Also
check glass, pottery, and metal categories.

Andirons, pr, 15-7/8" h, figural owls,
angled geometric features, "P" at lower
center, c1930 . . . . **115.00**
Architectural panels, pr, 29" x 98",
plaster, frieze of reclining woman

surrounded by flower and fruit
motifs **1,000.00**

Bookends, pr

4-4/8" h, cast bronze, stepped base
supports two columns joined by
pediment, green patina, center
medallion of Katarina Elizabeth
Geothe, brown patina, sgd "E.
Stelzer, Frankfurt" **400.00**

6-1/2" h, patinated metal figures,
nude dancing maidens, felted
half-oval base, imp "203" near
base **230.00**

Books, Arts et Metiers Graphiques,
Volumes 1 to 68, Paris, 1927-39, 4to,
orig wrappers, some spines worn, very
good condition covers and spines,
each volume with color and black and
white tipped in plates **1,955.00**

Box, 2-7/8" d, mother-of-pearl and
brass inlaid Bakelite, circular,
grasshopper with one antennae inlaid in
lid, French. **175.00**

Bust, 8-3/4" h, woman, wearing turban,
white marble, gray-veined marble
bodice, Continental **500.00**

Cane, 35-3/4" l overall, 4-7/8" h, 1-1/8" d
elephant ivory handle, octo-carved with
two horizontal and eight vertical
tortoiseshell string inlay highlights,
octo-carved black enameled hardwood
shaft, 3/4" black horn ferrule, probably
English, 1920s **1,800.00**

Centerpiece bowl, 5-1/2" h, gray glass
bowl cut with foliage and geometric
details, stepped chrome foot . . . **100.00**

Chandelier

15" w, 34" l, press-molded yellow
frosted glass plaffonier light bowl,
five matching shades mounted on
cast iron frame, chain and ceiling
mount with floral and geometric
dec, America, c1930, corrosion to
metal **350.00**

17-1/2" w, 21" h, five press-molded
frosted amber shades with floral
dec, suspended from gilt and
enameled metal mount with linear
and floral dec, imp and raised
marks "Halcolite Co. P750 Pat
Pend" on ceiling mount, wear to
gilt, minor chips. **520.00**

23-1/2" d, 28-1/2" h, gilt metal and
frosted glass, seven-light,
triangular, rope-twist basket
supporting conforming glass
inverted shade, six foliate candle
branches **600.00**

Cigarette case, Cartier, 18kt gold, all
over engraved geometric motif, int. with
engraved signatures of orig presenters,

dated Paris, Nov. 15, 1934, thumbpiece
set with row of buff-top sapphires, orig
box, 114.7 dwt. **1,495.00**

Compact and cigarette case, 5" x
2-3/4", sterling silver, top enameled in
green over scalloped ground, opening
off-center to reveal cigarette
compartment and mirrored compact,
engine turning on underside,
Birmingham, England, c1913 . . **650.00**

Console set, 12" d bowl, four 3-3/4" h
candleholders, shallow center bowl,
crystal, cut sq foot, bases stamped
"Libby," 1939-42 . . . . **290.00**

Desk set, comb, mirror, cov etched
glass jar, two brushes, enamel dec with
fan motif in black and creamy white,
lavender engine-turned ground, sterling
silver mounts, imp "F & B sterling,"
attributed to Theodore W. Foster and
Bros. Co., Providence, RI, c1930, five
pcs, some enamel loss **800.00**

Display cabinet, 43" w, 12-3/4" d,
54-3/4" h, walnut veneer, c1920-30,
arch form widening at base, ogee
molded bracket feet, two glass
fronted doors with stylized shell form
astragal detailing, enclosing three glass
shelves **450.00**

Dress clips, pr, platinum and
diamonds, chevron design, set with
round and emerald cut diamonds
. . . . **21,850.00**

Dressing mirror, 27" l, 14-3/4" h,
bronze, after Erté, by R. K. Parker,
numbered 2/25, formed as head of
woman, face obscured by large feather
held in her hand, mold signature
"Erté," mirrored kidney-shaped base,
revolving platform, gold and bronze
patination. **750.00**

Furniture

Bed, brass, stylized sunburst
design on headboard and
footboard, side rails, c1930, 48-3/4"
w, 42-1/2" h. **300.00**

Cabinet, step-back, veneered wood,
chrome pulls, rect single door
compartment on setback
conforming top, two long drawers
over two cabinet doors in base,
c1935, 29-3/8" w, 60" h, nicks, wear
to veneer **800.00**

Canapé, c1920, carved walnut,
slightly arched padded back,
leaf-carved frame surmounted
by leaf-carved crest, continuing
into similarly padded curved
arms, loose cushion seat raised
on carved block feet, 77-1/2" l
. . . . **700.00**

Chair, rattan, Heywood Wakefield,
c1935, curvilinear arms, gold
Naugahyde seats, one with arm for
newspaper, one 40" d, 30" h, other
31" d, 30-1/2" h, pr **800.00**

Desk, lady's, French, c1920, molded
rect top, leather-lined writing slide
opening, lidded compartments,
superstructure with two hinged
banks of drawers opening to int.
with two open shelves flanked by
tambour-fronted end sections,
turned, tapered and reeded legs,
24-3/4" w, 16-3/4" d, 38-1/4" h
. . . . **550.00**

Dining table, walnut, rect expanded
top, plain frieze, rhomboidal
support, plinth base, stepped
feet, 58-1/2" l, 36-1/2" d,
29-3/4" h **700.00**

Sideboard, Chinoiserie eglomise,
shaped mirrored top, two doors
with polychromed and gilt dec
exotic birds and flowering trees
flanking four drawers, peach and
white flora with gilt highlights, plinth
base, 72" l, 15" d, 34" h. . **1,200.00**

Vitrine, ebonized and teak,
breakfront form top, ebonized trim
over three doors, trapezoidal
glazed panels above three
drawers, reeded and ebonized bun
feet, 67" w, 19-3/4" d, 79" h . **800.00**

Lamp

Boudoir, 10-1/4" h, chrome,
cylindrical base, shaped shade
depicting woman's head, imp linear
facial features, America, c1930
. . . . **230.00**

Desk, 11-1/4" l, 7-5/8" h, figural,
airplane, frosted colorless glass
body, silver paint accents, nickel
plated wings, tail, and base,
looped metal support on flat rect
base with rolled ends, c1935
. . . . **375.00**

Floor, 71" h, 22" w, torch, bronze,
alabaster bowl, reeded and
pierced shaft, gilt-toned arrow
motifs, pierced and shaped round
base, pr. **275.00**

Table, 16-1/2" h, metal figure of
woman in architectural setting,
green patina, backlit by frosted
glass panel, black marble base,
emb "Fayral" at side, "Made in
France, Ovington New York" at
back, wear to patina **2,300.00**

Mantel garniture, pink and Verte Antico
marble, 14-1/2" shaped angular clock
case, inlaid marble forming "X" across

front, pair of tapered vases, French, c1930 . . . . **400.00**

Pedestal, 18-3/4" w, 14" d, 31" h, rect marble top inset within carved frieze, tapering sq supports resting on plinth base **200.00**

Perfume atomizer, 6" h, shaped sq with pulls at shoulders, blue glass body with uniform bubbles, remnants of orig paper label **45.00**

Perfume bottle

4-7/8" h, tapered sq form, molded geometric pattern, transparent smoky amethyst glass, gilt-metal screw cap **190.00**

6" h, sq prismatic shape, teardrop shaped stopper, cut colorless to ruby, stylized flowers **225.00**

Purse

Leather, front set with silver plate mount with basse tailed enamel plaques with bat's wings fluted engine turned ground, offset by vertical bands of fine floral filigree, opening to mirror and faille-lined compartments with coin purse, Continental, 3-3/4" w, 6-3/8" h **525.00**

Tri-color 18kt gold mesh, harlequin pattern, ruby and diamond padlock highlight, clasp with acorn terminals, partially obliterated European hallmark, 145.0 dwt, minor discoloration to gold **2,650.00**

Sauce boat, 8-7/8" l, English silver, Birmingham, 1934, Wilson & Gill makers, paneled boat shape, stepped foot, two cylindrical ivory handles, one side engraved and dated 1936, 8 troy oz **750.00**

Snuff box, 3" x 2" x 1/2", .935 fine silver and enamel, rect, black enamel sides within chased silver borders, hinged lid with central red enamel, bordered by black, engine turned bottom and gilt int. **410.00**

Tea cart, 31-1/2" l, 18-1/2" w, 25-3/4" h, oval chromed metal curvilinear framework, oblong smoky glass top and shelf **800.00**

Tea set, 5-1/2" h teapot, 3-1/4" h creamer, 3-1/4" h sugar, chrome over cream glazed ceramic body, Bakelite finial, marked "Ellgrave . . . Co. Ltd., Burslem England," matching tea cozy, c1930 . . . . **250.00**

Vanity case, Cartier, London, gold and diamond, rect, textured woven pattern, surmounted by diamond-set initial "C"

and thumbpiece, powder compartment and mirror, fitted leather box . . . **750.00**

Vase

8-3/4" h, foil under opalescent white, copper, gold, yellow, and black, gilt sgd "C. Faure Limoges" **3,450.00**

11-1/2" h, tapered oval, flared rim, geometric shapes in foil under shades of blue, black, and opalescent white enamel, gilt "C. Faure Limoges" signature near base, some corrosion to metal on base, minor stress crack below surface **3,565.00**

ART NOUVEAU

History: Art Nouveau is the French term for the "new art," which had its beginning in the early 1890s and continued for the next 40 years. The flowing and sensuous female forms used in this period were popular in Europe and America. Among the most recognized artists of this period were Gallé, Lalique, and Tiffany.

The Art-Nouveau style can be identified by flowing, sensuous lines, florals, insects, and the feminine form. These designs were incorporated into almost everything produced during the period, from art glass to furniture, silver, and personal objects. Later wares demonstrate some of the characteristics of the evolving Art-Deco style.

References: Victor Arwas, *Glass: Art Nouveau to Art Deco,* Rizzoli, 1977; Graham Dry, *Art Nouveau Domestic Metalwork,* Antique Collectors' Club, 1999; Alastair Duncan, *The Paris Salons 1895-1914, Vol. IV, Ceramics and Glass,* Antique Collectors' Club, 1998; Albert Christian Revi, *American Art Nouveau Glass,* reprint, Schiffer Publishing, 1981; Wolf Uecker, *Art Nouveau and Art Deco Lamps and Candlesticks,* Abbeville Press, 1986; Kenneth Wilson, *American Glass 1760-1930,* 2 vols., Hudson Hill Press and The Toledo Museum of Art, 1994.

Museum: Virginia Museum of Fine Arts, Richmond, VA.

Additional Listings: Furniture and Jewelry. Also check glass, pottery, and metal categories.

Advertising counter display, 5-1/2" x 10" x 10", Dana's Sarsaparilla, metal rim and glass, fancy Art Nouveau filigree on all corners, etched glass **50.00**

Belt buckle, sterling silver, two repoussé plaques of female faces with flowing hair and flower blossoms, hallmark for William B. Kerr & Co. **300.00**

Candlesticks, pr

8" h, gilt metal, foliate and floral dec, c1900, minor scratches **345.00**

10-1/2" h, gilt metal, partially clad maidens carrying vessels on heads, oval base, imp "MP," and

"D. P. Muller" around base, patina and gilt loss **375.00**

Cane, 34-3/4" l overall, 4-3/4" l, 2-3/4" h silver handle shaped as peacock, faceted sapphire eyes, tail with 20 larger faceted sapphires and single small diamond, highly figured snakewood shaft, 1-7/8" light horn ferrule, handle designed by French artist Edouard de Martily, c1904 . . . . **3,900.00**

Chandelier, 15" d, 32" h, brass, four flame-shaped citrine glass shades with opalescent flower dec, larger center shade drops below others, branching arms, ceiling plate, unmarked . **3,105.00**

Charger, 14-3/4" d, porcelain, circular, molded open handles, central painting of black, blue, and red parrot on perch, yellow ground, Limoges **225.00**

Cigarette case, 2-1/4" x 3", silver, rect, repoussé of maiden, hair issuing flowers and scrolls, Mauser, 3.64 troy oz **375.00**

Clock

Desk, 3-3/4" w, 4-3/8" h, bronze, Chelsea Clock movement, gilt-metal and glass mount, red enamel dec devices, ftd base, circular face with Arabic chapters, imp "Chelsea Clock Co., Boston, USA, 155252" on inside clock works, worn patina **460.00**

Figural, 12-1/2" h, enameled cast white metal, relief of woman's head, flowing hair, leaves, thistles, Seth Thomas movement, circular dial with Roman numerals, c1900, minor wear **300.00**

Wall, 24-1/2" w, 10" d, 38" h, carved walnut, two train movement, floral etched gilt metal dial sgd "Trilla, Barcelona," case topped by bust of young beauty on rocaille shell above iris flower, flanked by poppy roundels, case further carved with stylized florets, writing flower buds at corners, Spanish, early 20th C **490.00**

Door pulls, 3" w, 15" h, bronze, whiplash handles, orig patina, Belgian, price for pr **1,050.00**

Ewer, 11" h, cylindrical Serves body with sgrafitto dec of cosmos flowers, .950 fine silver mounts, similar boldly molded florals, sinuous loop handle, domed lid with flowerbud finial, short stippled spout, French, early 20th C **3,335.00**

Fire fender, 52-1/2" l, brass, sq section rail raised at each end by architectural plinth, stylized plant motif, molded base with rounded corners, c1900 . . . **225.00**

Floor vase, cov, 38" h, Serves-style, figural panels with cherubs framed within stylized floral designs, France, c1900 . . . . **6,900.00**

Garniture, centerpiece with bronze patina, female spelter figure of "L. Historie," flanked by spelter plinth with clock, enameled dial with painted Arabic numbers, sgd "L. Satre-A Pont. Aven," rect molded marble base with center bronze gilt neoclassical mounting, bronze gilded bun feet, pr of bronze patina spelter Louis XVI style urns, ribbons and swags centering figural medallion, sq marble base, bronze gilded feet **950.00**

High chair, 15" w, 13-1/2" d, 38" h, walnut, straight backrest with shaped and floral carved top rail, spindle-turned gallery, emb leather panel, flanked by downswept armrests, emb leather seat, sq legs joined by turned stretchers, c1900 . . . . **200.00**

Inkstand, 12" l, gilt metal, stylized shell form base, four flattened ball feet, chased and emb with bird on branch of stippled ground, stylized shell-form inkwell with removable liner, two scrolled pen supports **150.00**

Jardiniere, 14-1/2" d, 9-1/2" h, flowing handles, olive-green majolica glaze, designed by Hector Guimard, made by Gustav de Bruyn Fils, raised "BD" with anchor, several hairlines **1,150.00**

Lamp, table, 16" h, 8" d abalone shell shade, hammered brass water lily shape, natural patina, imp "Charles Frederick Eaton/Santa Barbara, Ca" **2,100.00**

Lorgnette

Gold, 14kt, repoussé iris handle, collet-set diamond highlights, monogrammed **990.00**
Sterling silver, handle stylized as repoussé iris flower **350.00**

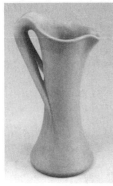

Pitcher, Teco Pottery, double whiplash handle, covered in smooth matte green glaze, stamped "Teco," minor fleck to base, 9" x 5", **$980.** *Photo courtesy of David Rago Auctions.*

Perfume bottle, 4-1/4" h, paneled slender baluster form bottle painted with blue and gold flowers, gilt-metal hinged lid enclosing glass stopper, lid with short chain **520.00**

Picture frame

4-7/8" h, sterling silver, oval, emb flowers and maiden, Unger Bros., Newark **175.00**
8-1/2" w, 11-3/8" h, wood, penwork and colored stained dec of stylized fruiting flowers, easel back **100.00**
10-1/4" w, 13-3/8" h, brass, organic shaped wood frame applied with sheet of brass beaten with sinuous stylized water lilies, easel back **290.00**

Plant stand, 67-1/2" h, wrought iron, each foot of trifid base rising to scrolling vine topped by leaf-form surface at stepped intervals, central stem continuing to vine-form book . . . **400.00**

Plate, 7-1/4" d, silver, chased and emb with profile of woman with flowing tresses, background of reeded formed as stylized sun's rays, shaped edge, Gorham, 1883, 6 troy oz **1,150.00**

Stove, coal, 28-1/2" w, 22" d, 36" h, bronze and iron, shaped structure, pierced bronze plaque with "S" scroll motifs centering pineapple, applied bronze medallions with female profiles, stamped "Deville Pailliette Forest, No. 17, Charlesville, Ardennes," c1900 . . . . **375.00**

Table, side, 24" w, 17" d, 30" h, scallop-edge rect top inlaid with poppies in exotic woods, fluted legs, cabriole feet, lower shelf with variation of poppy motif, orig finish, inlaid "Galle" signature **2,100.00**

Umbrella, 36" l, 7-1/4" h cylindrical ivory handle applied with two bands of woven silver gilt hammered wire, ivory tip, leather wrist strap with carved ivory acorn, Continental, early 20th C **265.00**

Vanity set, sterling, mirror, three brushes, comb, emb lilies and maidens, America, early 20th C, price for five-pc set **375.00**

ART POTTERY (GENERAL)

History: America's interest in art pottery can be traced to the Centennial Exposition in Philadelphia, Pennsylvania, in 1877, where Europe's finest producers of decorative art displayed an impressive selection of their wares. Our young artists rose to the challenge immediately, and by 1900, native artisans were winning gold medals for decorative ceramics here and abroad.

The Art Pottery "Movement" in America lasted from about 1880 until the first World War. During this time, more than 200 companies, in most states, produced decorative ceramics ranging from borderline production ware to intricately decorated, labor intensive artware establishing America as a decorative art powerhouse.

Below is a listing of the work by various factories and studios, with pricing, from a number of these companies. The location of these outlets are included to give the reader a sense of how nationally-based the industry was.

References: Susan and Al Bagdade, *Warman's Americana Pottery and Porcelain,* 2nd ed., Krause Publications, 2000; Paul Evans, *Art Pottery of the United States,* 2nd ed., Feingold & Lewis Publishing, 1987; Lucile Henzke, *Art Pottery of America,* revised ed., Schiffer Publishing, 1996; Norman Karlson, *American Art Tile, 1876-1941,* Rizzoli Publications, 1998; Ralph and Terry Kovel, *Kovels' American Art Pottery,* Crown Publishers, 1993; Richard and Hilary Myers, *William Morris Tiles,* Richard Dennis (distributed by Antique Collectors' Club), 1996; David Rago, *American Art Pottery,* Knickerbocker Press, 1997; Dick Sigafoose, *American Art Pottery,* Collector Books, 2001.

Periodicals: *Style 1900,* 17 S. Main St., Lambertville, NJ 08530.

Collectors' Clubs: American Art Pottery Association, P.O. Box 834, Westport, MA 02790-0697, http://www.amartpot.org; Pottery Lovers Reunion, 4969 Hudson Dr., Stow, OH 44224.

Museums: Cincinnati Art Museum, Cincinnati, OH; Everson Museum of Art of Syracuse and Onondaga County, Syracuse, NY; Los Angeles County Museum of Art, Los Angeles, CA; Metropolitan Museum of Art, New York, NY; Newcomb College Art Gallery, New Orleans, LA; Zanesville Art Center, Zanesville, OH.

Additional Listings: See Clewell, Clifton, Cowan, Dedham, Fulper, Grueby, Jugtown, Marblehead, Moorcroft, Newcomb, North Dakota School of Mines, Ohr, Paul Revere, Peters and Reed, Rookwood, Roseville, Van Briggle, Weller, and Zanesville.

Notes: Condition, design, size, execution, and glaze quality are the key considerations when buying art pottery. This category includes only companies not found elsewhere in this book.

Adviser: David Rago.

Arequipa

Bowl, 6-1/2" d, 2-1/4" h, closed-in, emb eucalyptus branches, matte green and dark blue glaze, stamped mark, incised "KH/11" **800.00**

Vase, 7" h, 4" d, bulbous, squeezebag wreath of heart-shaped leaves, frothy matte green glaze, Rhead period blue and white enamel mark . . **4,250.00**

Vase, 10" x 5", squeezebag dec, stylized yellow-orange irises and green leaves, deep purple ground, cobalt blue mark on white "670 Arequipa/California," c1912, small bruise to base **74,750.00**

Avon, Vance, vase, 5" d, 5-1/2" h, designed by Frederick Rhead, squeezebag stylized trees, orange and green ground, incised "Avon/WPTS.CO./174-1241" . . . **920.00**

Bachelder, O. L., vase, 5" h, 3-3/4" d, bulbous, cobalt blue and teal sheer glossy glaze, incised "OLB/R," ink cipher **500.00**

Bennett, John, vase, 3-3/4" d, 7-1/2" h, bulbous, painted burgundy phlox and honeybee, ivory ground, minute rim fleck, marked "BENNETT/W2E24/NJ/ artist's cipher" **2,870.00**

Brouwer, vase, 12" x 7-1/4", baluster, flame-painted, orange, yellow, and brown lustered glaze, thick bronze glaze dripping on neck and shoulder, incised wishbone mark and flame, remnants of paper label, firing line and flat chip under base, minor scratches to body, glaze flakes on rim **8,575.00**

Cole, A. R., urn, 18-1/2" h, 9-1/2" d, hand-thrown, three fanciful twisted handles, mirror black glaze, unmarked, shallow scratches **400.00**

Crook, Russel, urn, 16-1/2" h, 10" d, wax-resist, cowboys on horseback, brown clay under glossy, mottled dark blue glaze, incised "John Lampus/potter/RCrook/92," 1892, restored small rim chip, larger chip at base **3,750.00**

Denaura, Denver

Vase, 6-3/4' h, 3-1/4' d, ovoid, emb mistletoe, semi-matte Robin's egg blue glaze, stamped "Denver," stilt pull **1,200.00**

Vase, 9" h, 5' d, ovoid, emb tulips and leaves, matte green glaze, "Denaura U.S.A 1903." written on base, stamped "Denver," and ink stamp **2,600.00**

Graham, Charles, Pottery, Brooklyn, NY, floor urn, 27' d, 32-3/4' h, stoneware, stylized floral motif, decorative bands in matte umber and ivory, rich brown ground, two inset pottery stamp wafers, sgd in umber "C. Benham, NY" for Charles Benham, Brooklyn, NY, 1882-1899 . . . . **5,750.00**

Jervis/Briarcliff, vessel, 3-3/4' d, 3-1/2' h, hand carved, stylized trees in dead matte blue and green glazes, probably dec by F. H. Rhead, incised "Briarcliff/Jervis," few minute flecks **1,355.00**

Merrimac

Jar, cov, 5-1/4" h, 3-1/4" d, glossy speckled brown glaze, paper label, stilt-pulls to int. rim of lid . . . **450.00**

Umbrella stand, 22-3/4" h, 8-1/2' d, tolled and applied leaves, leathery matte green glaze, paper label, base crack, few small chips to dec, some glaze pooling **3,750.00**

Vase, 10" h, 5' d, bulbous, cylindrical neck, green and mirrored black mottled glaze, unmarked **1,500.00**

Vessel, 4" h, 9" l, broad squat, matte green glaze, imp mark, minute fleck to rim **1,200.00**

Pewabic, bulbous vase with flaring rim, covered in blue, green, and purple lustered glaze, imp circular mark, small glaze chip to base, 8" x 8", $1,150. Photo courtesy of David Rago Auctions.

Pewabic

Plate, 10-3/4" d, blue slip dragonflies, white crackled ground, stamped "PEWABIC," several glaze flakes and chips to foot ring **1,000.00**

Vase, 4-3/4" h, 3-1/2" d, ovoid, gold and mauve lustered glaze, circular stamp **650.00**

Vase, 8" d, 8" h, bulbous, flaring rim, blue, green, and purple lustered glaze, imp circular mark, small glaze chip to base **1,150.00**

Pisgah Forest

Tea set, Cameo Ware, wagon and landscape dec, dark matte green ground, raised mark and date 1943, 5-1/4" h teapot **950.00**

Vase, 4-3/4" d, 6-1/4" h, bulbous, white, blue, and yellow crystalline glaze, unmarked **460.00**

Vase, 4-3/4" d, 8" h, classic shape, white, gold, and blue crystalline glaze, raised mark **490.00**

Vessel, 3-3/4" h, 5-3/4" d, spherical, white glaze, white crystals, raised "Cameo/Stephen" mark and date 1951 . . . . **275.00**

Vessel, 5" h, 5-3/4" d, spherical, amber glaze, white and blue crystals, raised potter's mark and date 1947 . . . . **350.00**

Rhead, Frederick, University City, jardinière, 9-3/4" d, 8-3/4" h, incised with clusters of light blue trees, green field and yucca plants, ivory clouds, white semi-matte ground, incised "HR/UC/ 1911/JUNE," 1911, some burst bubbles **21,850.00**

Robineau, Adelaide, vase, 4" d, 3-3/4" h, spherical, bright cobalt blue glaze with blooming crystals, incised "AR," hairline to base **6,300.00**

Teco

Low bowl, 9-1/2" d, 2-1/2" h, organic, smooth matte green glaze, stamped "Teco 450," restoration to hairline, several small chips **200.00**

Pitcher, 5" d, 9" h, Art Nouveau style, double whiplash handle, smooth matte green glaze, stamped "Teco," minor base fleck . . **980.00**

Vase, 2-1/2" d, 5-3/4" h, four full-height buttresses, smooth matte green and gunmetal glaze, stamped "Teco," small grinding chip on base, minute fleck to top **1,495.00**

Vase, 4-1/2" d, 9" h, ovoid, emb tall leaves and daffodils, matte green glaze with charcoaling, stamped "TECO" **980.00**

Vase, 5-1/2" d, 6-3/4" h, double gourd shape, four buttressed handles, smooth matte green glaze with charcoaling, stamped "TECO/237," two small glaze flakes **4,600.00**

Vase, 5-1/2" d, 6" h, bulbous, smooth matte green glaze with charcoaling, stamped "TECO/76," restoration to rim chip **630.00**

Vase, 5-1/2" d, 7" h, beaker shape, smooth matte green glaze, stamped "TECO" **1,725.00**

Vase, 7" d, 7" h, bulbous, collar rim, smooth matte green glaze, stamped "TECO" **2,070.00**

Vase, 7-1/2" d, 15-1/2" h, gourd shape, curdled matte green glaze with charcoaling, stamped "TECO/182" **1,840.00**

Vase, 8" d, 5-1/2" h, two handles, smooth matte green glaze with charcoaling, stamped "TECO/297" **1,955.00**

Vase, 9-3/4" d, 16" h, tapering, ftd, emb broad leaves, sq buttressed handles, smooth matte green glaze with charcoaling, stamped "TECO," restoration to three small nicks on edges and handles **16,100.00**

Volkmar

Vase, 12-1/4" h, 7-3/4" w, 3-3/4" d, pillow shape, painted barotine, sepia scenes of horses pulling carts, sgd "Chas. Volkmar," pr **5,000.00**

*Teco, bulbous vase with collar rim, covered in smooth matte green glaze. Stamped "TECO," 7" x 7", **$2,100**. Photo courtesy of David Rago Auctions.*

Vessel, 5-1/2" h, 5-3/4" d, spherical, mottled Robin's egg blue vellum glaze, incised "Volkmar" and dated **650.00**

Walrath

Cider pitcher, 7" d, 5" h, matte, yellow fruit, green leaves, brown ground, marked "Walrath Pottery/MI" **1,495.00**

Sculpture, 4" h, 6" l, kneeling nude picking rose, sheer matte green glaze, yellow details, incised "Walrath" **300.00**

Vase, 5-1/4" h, 3-3/4" d, bell shape, ochre and red painted landscape of cypress trees, blue-gray ground, incised "Walrath Pottery" . **5,000.00**

Vase, 6-1/4" h, 4" d, painted stylized purple and dark green flowers, light gray-green ground, incised "Walrath Pottery" **4,000.00**

Wheatley

Lamp base, 14" d, 23" h, emb poppy pods, frothy matte green glaze, new hammered copper fittings, Japanese split-bamboo shade lined with new coral silk, stamped mark **1,380.00**

Sand jar, 15" d, 24" h, high relief sculpted grape leaves and vines from rim, feathered medium green matte glaze, incised mark/722, several glaze nicks restored **2,415.00**

Vase, 6-3/4" d, 12-1/4" h, bulbous, three climbing lizards, feathered medium matte green glaze, remnant of paper label, restoration to drill hole on side **1,380.00**

Vase, 7-1/4" d, 11-1/2" h, closed-in buttressed rim, stylized flowers, broad leaves, charcoaled green matte glaze, incised "WP/613," several short, tight lines, small restored rim chip, stilt-pull chip **1,380.00**

Zark, pitcher, 8-1/4" d, 7-1/2" h, squatty, textured turquoise glaze, several base chips **145.00**

ARTS AND CRAFTS MOVEMENT

History: The Arts and Crafts Movement in American decorative arts took place between 1895 and 1920. Leading proponents of the movement were Elbert Hubbard and his Roycrofters, the brothers Stickley, Frank Lloyd Wright, Charles and Henry Greene, George Niedecken, and Lucia and Arthur Mathews.

The movement was marked by individualistic design (although the movement was national in scope) and re-emphasis on handcraftsmanship and appearance. A reform of industrial Society was part of the long-range goal. Most pieces of furniture favored a rectilinear approach and were made of oak.

The Arts and Crafts Movement embraced all aspects of the decorative arts, including metalwork, ceramics, embroidery, woodblock printing, and the crafting of jewelry.

References: Steven Adams, *Arts & Crafts Movement,* Chartwell Books, 1987; *Arts and Crafts Furniture: The Complete Brooks Catalog of 1912,* Dover Publications, 1996; Annette Carruthers and Mary Greensted, eds., *Simplicity of Splendour Arts and Crafts Living,* Lund Humphries, distributed by Antique Collectors' Club, 1999; David Cathers, *Furniture of the American Arts and Crafts Movement: Revised Edition,* Turn of the Century Editions, 1996; —, *Stickley Style: Arts and Crafts Homes in the Craftsman Tradition,* Simon & Schuster, 1999; Douglas Congdon-Martin, *Arts & Crafts Designs for the Home,* Schiffer Publishing, 2000; Paul Evans, *Art Pottery of the United States,* 2nd ed., Feingold & Lewis Publishing, 1987; *Furniture of the Arts & Crafts Period With Prices,* L-W Book Sales, 1992, 1995 value update; Charlotte Gere and Geoffrey Munn, *Pre-Raphaelite to Arts & Crafts Jewelry,* Antique Collectors' Club, 1999; Bruce Johnson, *Pegged Joint,* Knock on Wood Publications, 1995; Elyse Zorn Karlin, *Jewelry and Metalwork in the Arts and Crafts Tradition,* Schiffer Publishing, 1993; *Limbert Arts and Crafts Furniture: The Complete 1903 Catalog,* Dover Publications, n.d.; Thomas K. Maher, *The Jarvie Shop: The Candlesticks and Metalwork of Robert R. Jarvie,* Turn of the Century Editions, 1997; James Massey and Shirley Maxwell, *Arts & Crafts,* Abbeville Press, 1995; ——, *Arts & Crafts Design in America: A State-By-State Guide,* Chronicle Books, 1998; Kevin McConnell, *More Roycroft Art Metal,* Schiffer Publishing, 1995; Richard and Hilary Myers, *William Morris Tiles,* Richard Dennis (distributed by Antique Collectors' Club), 1996; David Rago, *American Art Pottery,* Knickerbocker Press, 1997; Roycrofters, *Roycroft Furniture Catalog, 1906,* Dover Publications, 1994; Joanna Wissinger, *Arts and Crafts: Metalwork and Silver* and *Pottery and Ceramics,* Chronicle Books, 1994.

Periodicals and Internet Resources: *American Bungalow,* P.O. Box 756, Sierra Madre, CA 91204; *Style 1900,* 333 N. Main St., Lambertville, NJ 08530. *American Bungalow* focuses on the contemporary owner of period homes and the refurbishing of same. *Style 1900* has a more historically oriented approach to the turn of the century artisans. The Arts & Crafts Society, www.arts-crafts.com; On-Line Arts & Crafts Resource Directory, www.sni.net/tagtime; Roycroft Copper Online Price Guide, www.roycroftcopper.com; The Movement, http://members.aol.com/TheMvmt.

Collectors' Clubs: Foundation for the Study of the Arts & Crafts Movement, Roycroft Campus, 31 S. Grove St., East Aurora, NY 14052, www.roycroftshops.com; Roycrofters-At-Large Association, P.O. Box 417, East Aurora, NY 14052, www.roycrofter.com/talia/talia.html; William Morris Society of Canada, 52 Berkeley Court, Unionville,

Ontario, LeR 6LP, Canada, www.hedgerowhouse.net/wmsc.html; William Morris Society UK, Kemscot House, 26 Upper Mall, Hemmersmith, London, W6 9TA UK, uk@morrissociety.org; William Morris Society US, P.O. Box 53263, Washington, DC 20009, www.morrissociety.org. Students of the Arts and Crafts Movement are encouraged to participate in the two major conferences now available. The Grove Park Inn Conference is held annually in Ashville, NC, in February, by Bruce Johnson.

Museums: Cooper Hewitt Museum, Manhattan, NY; Elbert Hubbard Library-Museum, East Aurora, NY; Los Angeles County Museum of Art, Los Angeles, CA; Metropolitan Museum of Art, Manhattan, NY; Museum of Modern Art, New York, NY; Richmond Museum of Art, Richmond, VA.

Adviser: David Rago.

Additional Listings: Roycroft, Stickleys, and art pottery categories.

Bookcase
36" w, 10-1/2" d, 47" h, open, gallery top, three adjustable shelves, orig finish, missing shelf clips, Liberty & Co. tag, c1900 . . . . **2,615.00**
37" w, 10-1/4" d, 47" h, gallery top, adjustable shelves, small cabinet with leaded glass door, orig finish, Liberty & Co. tag, c1900 . . . . **3,105.00**
56-1/2" w, 13-1/4" d, 55" h, three-door, gallery top, faux mullions, hammered copper pulls, Lifetime paper label, refinished, new back **2,875.00**

Box, cov, 4-1/2" l, 2-3/4" d, 2" h, hammered copper, cloisonné enamel with pink flower and cabochon on lid, scrolling sterling feet, natural patina **345.00**
Cabinet, corner, hanging, 20" w, 13" d, 34-1/2" h, attributed to Heal & Son, English, oak, backsplash, carved door inlaid with marquetry, good orig finish, door knob missing **475.00**
Candlestick, 5-1/2" d, 15" h, Delta, brass, sgd "Jarvie," bobeche missing, cleaned patina **690.00**
Carpet runner, 12' 13" x 3', silk, Wilton style, acanthus leaves, stylized blossoms, gold, teal, and brick, William Morris, c1890 . . . . **5,350.00**
Chair and rocker set, vertical slats, replaced upholstered drop-in seats, refinished, unmarked Harden, 28" w, 22-1/2" d, 38" h arm chair, 29" w, 22-1/2" d, 36-1/2" h rocker . . . **1,045.00**
Chair, café, Limbert, sloped arms, cut-out sides, plank back with cut-out tree, very good orig finish, seat needs rewebbing, branded mark . . . **3,335.00**
Chair, dining, Limbert, five side, one arm chair, each with three vertical slats, arched crest rail, fabric upholstered seat, cleaned orig finish, branded marks, orig retail labels, 36" x 18" x 17", price for six-pc set **2,530.00**
China cabinet, 61-3/4" x 46" x 17", Limbert, plate rail and corbels, glass panel doors with strap hinges over one drawer with hammered copper pulls, very good orig finish, missing door pull, branded mark, retail label . . . **5,175.00**
Clock, 14" w, 4-3/4" d, 21-3/4" h, New Haven, Japanese-style, brass hands, keyed through-tenon sides, amber ripple glass, orig ebonized finish, paper label **490.00**
Coffee and tea service, coffeepot, teapot, creamer, sugar, and tray, pewter, wicker handles, by Archibald Knox, stamped "Liberty/Tudric," price for five-pc set **3,105.00**
Coffee service, coffeepot, creamer, sugar, tongs, hand hammered polished brass, riveted spouts, boars tusk handles, monogrammed "LPH," marked "Jarvie," price for four-pc set **23,000.00**
Compote, 8" d, 6-3/4" h, pewter, cluthra green glass liner with opalescent and gold swirls, Liberty Tudric, Archibald Knox **3,105.00**
Cuff link box, 6-1/2" l, 3-1/4" w, 2" h, hammered copper, emb quatrefoil, leather lining, marked "K. K." for Karl Kipp, old cleaning to patina . . **2,530.00**
Curtains, 44-1/2" w, 104" l, linen, stenciled stylized brown and beige poppies, green leaves, red ground, three panels **230.00**
Desk set, sterling on bronze, clematis overlay, helmet-shade lamp, desk blotter, letter holder, perpetual calendar, inkwell, stamp box, letter opener, pen gray, match holder, orig patina, stamped "HAMS," Heintz, price for nine-pc set **2,530.00**
Foot stool, 18" w, 11-1/2" d, 9" h, sq posts, drop-in leather cov cushion, one peg missing. **460.00**
Humidor, 7-1/2" w, 7" h, hammered copper, four riveted handles, emb stylized flowers, natural medium patina, unmarked, English **630.00**
Inkwell, 5-1/4" sq, 3-1/2" h, faceted copper, curled, riveted feet, enameled green, red, and black, spade pattern, orig patina, unmarked Arts & Crafts Shop, couple of nicks to dec . . **250.00**
Lamp, ceiling, 8-1/2" d, 11" h, polished hammered brass, four arms, flame-shaped opalescent glass shade with green pulled feather pattern, English. **1,355.00**
Lamp, table
20" h, 13" d, canister shaped copper or bronze base with four flaring legs, two-toned mica shade, orig dark patina. **1,840.00**
20" h, 13" w copper and shellacked canvas faceted shade, heavy pottery base with four buttressed handles, matte green and gunmetal glaze, unmarked, attributed to Philadelphia School of Applied Arts, some burnt spots to canvas, minor nicks to base **1,725.00**
21" h, 13-1/2" w sq flaring caramel glass shade, orig cap, flaring four-sided oak base, orig finish, unmarked. **990.00**
23-1/2" h, 20" d, Dirk Van Erp, hammered copper, shouldered base mounted on carved wooden Chinese base, early conical three panel orange mica shade, pristine orig patina, closed box mark **30,575.00**
29" h, 8" d flaring opalescent ripple leaded glass shade, shaft of four polished hammered brass bands, wood base, unmarked, English **690.00**
Lamp, student, 16" h, 13" d, Roycroft brass washed hammered copper base, Stickley Bros. copper and mica shades with silhouetted trees, orig finish, replaced mica, orb and cross mark **1,840.00**

Lantern, hanging

7" d, 9-1/2" h, patinated cast brass, rustic branch pattern, orig white frosted glass panels, orig patina, hanging chains, replaced ceiling plate, price for pr........**630.00**

12-1/2" d, 20-1/2" h, hammered brass and copper, emb spade pattern, opalescent blown-glass shade with flowers and arabesques, shade attributed to Powell, English, stamped numbers **1,650.00**

13" d, 28" h, polished hammered copper, octagonal, clear hammered glass panels, English **800.00**

Library table

41-3/4" l, 26" d, 29-1/2" h, Ebon-Oak, flush top, single drawer, sides and legs inlaid with dark wood squares, good refinished condition, branded Limbert mark.........**2,070.00**

47-1/2" l, 36-1/4" w, 28-1/2" h, double oval, flaring legs, cut-out stretchers, orig finish, branded Limbert mark, 1" cut off legs **7,475.00**

52" l, 24" w, 29-1/2" h, two arched drawers, corbels, one shelf, orig finish, Lifetime Paine Furniture Co. metal tag.............**2,300.00**

Magazine stand

18-1/4" w, 14" d, 50-1/2" h, gallery top, vertical slats all around, five tiers, fine orig dark finish, branded "CPM" **2,415.00**

24" w, 12" d, 41-1/2" h, three shelf, two short drawers, arched side rails over slatted sides, light finish, loose joints.............**630.00**

Mirror, 16-3/4" w, 27-3/4" l, two carved peacocks, glass gemstone tails, beveled edge mirror, round armorial shield, traces of polychrome staining, branded label "H. H. Bennett, Chillicothe, Ohio, June 1903," some wear, missing stones........**550.00**

Morris chair, 31" w, 36" d, 38" h, flat arm, slats to floor, long corbels, leather back and seat cushions, orig finish, remnants of J. M. Young paper label, wear to top of arms........**2,760.00**

Music cabinet, 21-1/2" w, 17" d, 42" h, attributed to G. M. Ellwood for J. S. Henry, c1900, English, mahogany, beveled top, paneled door inlaid with fruitwoods and mother-of-pearl, two drawers, brass hardware, good new finish.................**2,870.00**

Occasional table, 30" d, 29-1/2" h, circular top over flaring legs joined by cut-out stretchers, orig finish, branded Limbert mark, wear and stains to top **2,070.00**

Parlor set, cube style, chair, settle, and rocker, broad vertical slats, orig drop-in spring seats covered in new green leather, also new green leather on top back rails, enhanced orig finish with waxed overcoat, 78" l, 25" w, 31-1/2" h settle, price for three-pc set ..**5,175.00**

Picture frame, hammered sterling silver, English hallmarks

6" w, 8" h, emb morning glories.................**630.00**

6" w, 9" h, emb daisies.....**750.00**

Pitcher, owl shape, pewter, jade cabochon eyes, stamped "TUDRIC/5/055," 8" x 6-1/2", $1,150. Photo courtesy of David Rago Auctions.

Pillow

16" x 25", embroidered stylized orange and green poppies, beige linen ground............**490.00**

17" x 23", embroidered stylized blue, gold, and green flowers, silky linen beige ground, minor staining **175.00**

23" x 21", embroidered ovals and crescents, shades of green silk, beige linen ground.......**115.00**

Room divider, three panel, unmarked

67-1/2" h, mahogany, Japan leather panels stenciled with white clematis, green leaves, orig finish,

small tear to cloth on back center panel **520.00**

68" h, oak, grid-like top, each panel cut-out with fern design, replaced linen panels, orig finish, some minor chipping to edges.**1,045.00**

Settee, two seat, carved floral motif on crest rail and posts, reupholstered drop-in seats, worn orig finish, unmarked David Kendall (Phoenix) **2,185.00**

Settle

69-1/2" l, 25-1/2" d, 29-3/4" h, vertical slats all around, drop-in seat cov in green canvas, worn orig condition, branded Limbert mark ..**3,450.00**

78" l, 29-3/4" d, 29-1/2" h, cube, vertical slats all around, straight rail, drop-in spring seat recovered in fabric, orig finish, J.M. Young paper label, separation to posts, chips **2,530.00**

Server, 42" x 42" x 18", Limbert, plate rail, corbels, two short drawers over long drawer, hammered copper pulls, lower shelf, very good orig finish, branded mark.............**3,450.00**

Sewing table, 18" l, 18" w closed, 29" h, drop leaf, two drawers with wooden pulls, tapering legs, orig finish, two splits to top.................**350.00**

Sideboard, Limbert, large backsplash with plate-rail and shelf, two long drawers flanked by two shorter ones and two doors, open shelf over linen drawer, all with hammered copper pulls, knobs and strap hinges, very good original finish and condition, branded mark, 51" x 60" x 23", $5,350. Photo courtesy of David Rago Auctions.

Sideboard, 51" x 60" x 23", Limbert, large backsplash with plate rail and shelf, two long drawers flanked by two shorter ones and two doors, open shelf over linen drawer,

hammered copper pulls, knobs, and strap hinges, good orig finish, branded mark **5,350.00**
String holder, 3-3/4" d, 3-1/2" h, sterling on bronze, bell shape, applied silver leaves and vines, orig patina, stamped "HAMS," Heintz **535.00**
Tablecloth

27-1/2" sq, white linen, embroidered white Glasgow roses **115.00**
39" d, circular, linen, embroidered red poppies, green leaves **860.00**

Table runner, 53" l, 19-1/2" w

Embroidered amber cornflowers, beige linen ground, few minor stains **115.00**
Embroidered geometric red, blue, yellow, and green flowers and leaves, buff linen, crocheted ends **415.00**

Table, trestle, 60" l, 33-1/2" w, 28-1/2" h, Robert "Mouseman" Thompson, oak, rough-hewn top, turned legs, shoe feet, signature carved mouse, orig finish, wear to top. **4,600.00**
Vice cabinet, Limbert

29" w, 18-1/2" d, 36-1/4" h, pull-out copper tray, small drawer, two cabinet doors with pipe racks, new dark finish, copper hardware with patina, branded Limbert mark **2,185.00**
31" w, 19" d, 36" h, pull-out bar shelf inset with hammered glass, single drawer, two cabinet doors, sq brass pans, cleaned finish and hardware, branded Limbert mark **2,300.00**

Wall cabinet, 30-1/2" l, 9" d, 22-1/2" h, hanging, two drawers, pierced through-tenons, gallery top, faceted wooden pulls, refinished, stamped "R 1903" for Charles Rohlfs, chip in drawer, small section of left side replaced **2,870.00**
Wall sconce

6" d shade, 14-1/2" h, brass, emb stylized poppies, leaded glass period shades, English, price for pr **2,530.00**
9" w, 15" l, Jarvie, brass, double, tooled back plate, two riveted candleholders, each with scrolled braces and flaring bobeche, orig patina, stamped "Made By The Jarvie Shop" **5,750.00**
11" l, 3" d, 10" h, brass washed, irid amber "hammered" glass shade, shade marked "HANDEL" **460.00**

AUSTRIAN WARE

History: More than 100 potteries were located in the Austro-Hungarian Empire in the late 19th and early 20th centuries. Although Carlsbad was the center of the industry, the factories spread as far as the modern-day Czech Republic.

Many of the factories were either owned or supported by Americans; hence, their wares were produced mainly for export to the United States.

Marks: Many wares do not have a factory mark but only the word "Austrian" in response to the 1891 law specifying that the country of origin had to be marked on imported products.

Additional Listings: Amphora, Carlsbad, Royal Dux, and Royal Vienna.

Bowl, 10-1/2" d, glazed pottery, gnarled branch section, grape bunch at one end, incised mark, c1900 . . . . . . **325.00**
Celery tray, 12" l, scalloped border, pink roses, green leaves, gold trim . . . **75.00**
Ewer

5-5/8" h, 2-7/8" d, dark green, maroon, tan, and cream, gold trim, Alhambra pattern **90.00**
11-3/4" h, 6" d, rococo gold scroll, hp pink and yellow wild roses, gold outlines, four ftd. **125.00**

Figural group, bronze, cold painted, late 19th/early 20th C

7" w, 8-3/4" h, Moroccan man with turban, standing by monkey playing cymbals, seated on donkey, Franz Bergman . **2,100.00**
13-1/2" w, 14-1/2" h, realistically modeled as small songbird perched on wide leaf in front of tall iris flowers, twig base . . . **1,840.00**
14" l, 6-1/2" h, realistically modeled as two white and pink parakeets perched on leafless tree branch **1,380.00**

Figure, 7" h, frog musician playing clarinet, bronze, cold painted brilliant green, 20th C **245.00**
Inkstand, 12-3/8" l, bronze, horse head within horseshoe to left, oblong pen tray, sq lidded inkwell with glass liner, traces of brown painted finish, early 20th C **290.00**
Lamp, 15-1/2" h, 9" d metal shade dec with three red glass inserts, three foliate stem arms, reticulated bronzed Secessionist-inspired base **750.00**
Oyster plate, 9-7/8" d, shell shaped wells, scalloped rim with blue and gilt enamel flora, fish, and birds dec, 19th C **175.00**
Pitcher, light green ground shaded to brown, purple grapes with white and

green leaves, brown handle, gold rim, marked "Vienna, Austria" **200.00**
Portrait vase, 34-1/2" h, cov, oval cartouche, polychrome enameled female portrait, burgundy luster ground, raised gilt scrolled foliate design, sgd "Rosley," beehive mark, early 20th C, rim repair, lines to handles . . . **2,875.00**
Potpourri vase, pierced cov, 16-1/2" h, urn shape, two short gilt griffin handles, maroon and pink ground over-painted with gilt vines and scrolls, body painted to one side with allegorical figure of Music, Hector on other side, sgd "A. Hoijer" on trumpet foot, stepped rect base, titled to underside, late 19th C **1,265.00**

Punch bowl, porcelain, central scenic panel, green border with gilt trim, base with gilded claw feet, 14-3/4" d, 6-1/2" h, $550. Photo courtesy of Joy Luke Auctions.

Salt, 3" h, figural, donkey, two dish-shaped baskets on back, c1915 . . . . **265.00**
Stamp box, cov, 4-1/4" x 3-1/8", ftd, two compartments, hp, roses, gold trim **50.00**
Tankard, 14" h, hp Dutch scene, marked "Made in Austria, 159 Haag" **400.00**
Tray, 7" h, two bronze dancers, round green and white marble base, imp mark, c1925, abrasions. **175.00**
Vase

10" h, divided rim forms two spouts, large dolphin handles, gold scales, raised gold florals, cream ground **125.00**
10-1/2" h, 4-1/2" w, pedestal, reticulated handles, peacock on balcony scene, aqua, roses, green, brown, marked "Carlsbad, Austria". **265.00**
13-3/8" h, 6-1/2" d, hp florals and holly, shaded ground, raised enameling, marked "Carlsbad," pr **320.00**

Wine glass, 4-1/4" h, blown and etched glass, conical, cobalt blue rim, short stem, single trapped air bubble, plain foot, etched with monogram and date "1797" in wheat roundel, price for pr **225.00**

AUTOGRAPHS

History: Autographs appear on a wide variety of formats—letters, documents, photographs, books, cards, etc. Most collectors focus on a particular person, country, or category, e.g., signers of the Declaration of Independence.

References: Mark Allen Baker, *All-Sport Autographs,* Krause Publications, 1995; ——, *Advanced Autograph Collecting,* Krause Publications, 2000; ——, *Collector's Guide to Celebrity Autographs,* 2nd ed., Krause Publications, 2000; *Standard Guide to Collecting Autographs,* Krause Publications, 1999; Kevin Keating and Michael Kolleth, *The Negro Leagues Autograph Guide,* Tuff Stuff Books, 1999; Kevin Martin, *Signatures of the Stars,* Antique Trader Books, 1998; Tom Mortenson, *Standard Catalog of Sports Autographs,* Krause Publications, 2000; Kenneth W. Rendell, *Forging History: The Detection of Fake Letters & Documents,* University of Oklahoma Press, 1994; ——, *History Comes to Life,* University of Oklahoma Press, 1996; George Sanders, Helen Sanders and Ralph Roberts, *Sanders Price Guide to Sports Autographs,* 2nd ed., Alexander Books, 1997; ——, *Sanders Price Guide to Autographs,* 5th ed., Alexander Books, 2000.

Periodicals: *Autograph Collector,* 510-A S Corona Mall, Corona, CA 91720-1420, www.autographs.com/acm.html; *Autograph News,* P.O. Box 580450, Modesto, CA 95358, www.autographnews.com; *Autograph Review,* 305 Carlton Road, Syracuse, NY 13207; *Autograph Times,* P.O. Box 5790, Peoria, AZ 85385, www.autographtimes.net; *Autographs & Memorabilia,* P.O. Box 224, Coffeyville, KS 67337; *Pop Culture Collecting,* 510-A S Corona Mall, Corona, CA 91720-1420, www.autographcs.com/collect.html; *The Collector,* P.O. Box 255, Hunter, NY 12442-0255, www.benjaminautographs.com; *Celebrity Access,* 20 Sunnyside Ave., Suite A241, Mill Valley, CA 94941-1928; *V.I.P. Autogramm-Magazine,* 3000 W. Olympic Blvd., Blvd. 3, Suite 2415, Santa Monica, CA 90404, http://www.vip-entertainment.com.

Collectors' Clubs: International Autograph Collectors Club & Dealers Alliance, P.O. Box 848486, Hollywood, FL 33084, www.iacc-da.com; Manuscript Society, 350 N. Niagara St., Burbank, CA 95105-3648, www.manuscript.org; Professional Autograph Dealers Assoc., P.O. Box 1729, Murray Hill Station, New York, NY 10156; Universal Autograph Collectors Club, P.O. Box 6181, Washington, DC 20044, www.nacc.org; Washington Historical Autograph & Certificate Organization, P.O. Box 2428, Springfield, VA 22152-2428, www.whaco.com.

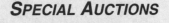

SPECIAL AUCTIONS

Christie's
20 Rockefeller Plaza
New York, NY 10020
(212) 636-2000

Cohasco, Inc.
P.O. Box 821
Yonkers, NY 10702-0821
(914) 476-8500

Swann Galleries, Inc.
104 E. 25th St.
New York, NY 10010
(212) 254-4710

Additional Listings: See *Warman's Americana & Collectibles* for more examples.

Notes: The condition and content of letters and documents bear significantly on value. Collectors should know their source, since forgeries abound and copy machines compound the problem. Further, some signatures of recent presidents and movie stars were done by machine rather than by the persons themselves. A good dealer or advanced collector can help spot the differences.

Abbreviations: The following are used to describe autograph materials and their sizes.

Materials:

ADS	Autograph Document Signed
ALS	Autograph Letter Signed
AQS	Autograph Quotation Signed
CS	Card Signed
DS	Document Signed
FDC	First Day Cover
LS	Letter Signed
PS	Photograph Signed
TLS	Typed Letter Signed

Sizes (approximate):

Folio	12 x 16 inches
4to	8 x 10 inches
8vo	7 x 7 inches
12mo	3 x 5 inches

Colonial America

Butcher, John, ALS, Alexandria, VA, Jan. 4, 1800, to daughter, giving lengthy comments on last will and testament of George Washington, whereby he wills 130 Negroes free after Martha's death, two pgs, folio, integral address leaf..............**1,035.00**

Laird, David, DS, Nov. 2, 1779, as commander of British prison ship, HMS Jersey, ordering officer to proceed to Sea Brook to seize an American vessel, one page, folded tall 4to sheet, light dampstaining, minor separation at folds **980.00**

Pickering, Timothy, LS, Department of State, Jan. 11, 1799, as Secretary of State, to Valck and Company, regarding incident between their ship Aurora and British Frigate Latona, early

---

bibliographic note written on verso by B. Mayer, one page, single 4to, offsetting from portrait engraving, hinged to larger sheet **230.00**

Steuben, Baron Von, March 1782, clipped partly-printed DS, sgd "Steuben Maj General," certifying contents of shipment, one page, 2" x 7-1/2", silked, partially mounted to larger sheet with portrait engraving **750.00**

Foreign

Cuvier, Georges L. C., Baron, signature on ticket for free admission to Museum d'Historie Naturelle, Paris, 2-1/4" x 3-3/4", mounted at edged to larger sheet.....................**115.00**

Disraeli, Benjamin, envelope, sgd "Disraeli," addressed to Lady Corneila Guest, 3" x 4" inches, matted and framed **80.00**

Eiffel, Gustave, TLS, Paris, April 19, 1889, sgd "G. Eissel" to E. Hippeau, in French, one page, single 4to sheet, business stationery, folds.....**375.00**

Humboldt, Alexander Von, ALS, sgd "Humboldt," to Monsieur Tomard of the Bibliotheque Royale, in French, about mapping of the interior of Africa, inquiring about 15th C Catalan atlas, one page, folded 8vo sheet, integral address leaf, hinged to larger sheet **320.00**

Peron, Eva, PS, Buenos Aires, Oct. 10, 1950, bust portrait, sgd on mount beneath calligraphic inscription, 9" x 6-1/2" photo on 13-1/2" x 9-1/2" mount, signature light, framed **620.00**

General

Bell, Alexander Melville, ALS, Washington, Sept. 30, 1891, to Mrs. Bingham regarding gramphone matters, one page, 8vo sheet, framed **130.00**

Benjamin, Judah, ALS, Piccadilly, Feb. 22, 1874, sgd "J. P. Benjamin" to his friend Judge Robert Fowler, regarding meeting with Sir H. James, arranging visit, three pgs, folded 8vo sheet, Junior Athenaeum Club stationery **750.00**

Clark, William, DS, partially printed, St. Louis, June 6, 1820, sgd "Wm Clark" as Governor of Territory of Missouri, appointing Abraham McClellan as Justice of the Peace in Cooper County, one page, 10" x 16", browning, some separations along holds, docketed on verso **1,320.00**

Dallas, Alexander James, printed LS, Washington, Aug. 25, 1815, sgd "A. J.

Dallas" as Secretary to the Treasure, to the Collector of New York, informing him that the Russian government is sending ship on voyage of discovery, and it should be received at any U. S. ports, one page, folded 4to, franking signature on address leaf **115.00**

Edison, Thomas, PS, sgd "Thos A. Edison," c1904, seated portrait, real photo postcard by Pach Brothers, sgd on mount below, 5" x 3", silvered, corner mounted **1,610.00**

Einstein, Albert, TLS, Princeton, June 10, 1939, sgd "A. Einstein," to Michael Schaap of Bloomingdale's, congratulating him on his work on behalf of the refugees, one page, single 4to, blind-stamped Princeton stationery, folds....................**4,370.00**

Kennedy, Robert, TLS, US Senate stationery, Washington, April 5, 1967, sgd "Bob," additionally sgd "My Best, Bob," to Judge Frances Biddle, concerning Choate Academy, one page, single 4to sheet....... **550.00**

Lindbergh, Charles A., TDS, Cuba, Nov. 19, 1932, sgd "C. A. Lindbergh," as Pan American Airways pilot, passenger list for flight from Cuba to Miami, one page, single 4to sheet, Republica de Cuba Secretaria de Hacienda letterhead, minor chips at edges, corner mounted **1,495.00**

Lister, Joseph, ALS, Portland Place, May 25, 1898, sgd "Lister" to Martin Conway, regarding Anglo-American Committee, one page, folded 8vo, mourning stationery, mat burn, remnants of tape on verso of blank **350.00**

Morse, Samuel F. B., ALS, Auburn, July 10, 1847, sgd "Sam. F. B. Morse," to T. R. Walker, regarding visit to Utica, one page, folded 8vo sheet **1,150.00**

Muir, John, ALS, Martinez, Sept. 12, 1902, to H. C. Bridgman, regarding visit, one page, single 4to sheet **1,265.00**

Russell, Bertrand, ALS, Malvern, Sept. 21, 1942, to George Chatalin, regarding his views dealing with causes of World War II, speculating on aftermath, role of capitalism, two pgs, single 4to sheet, folds, minor toning, orig envelope **1,380.00**

Seton, Ernest Thompson, book signed, New York, 1910, Boy Scouts of America, *A Handbook of Woodcraft, Scouting, and Life-Craft*, inscribed and signed twice by Ernest Thompson Seton to Charles Horton, additionally

signed by Dan Beard, and nine members of first Boy Scout troop, 8vo, publisher's cloth, worn, hinges cracked, Charles Horton bookplate on front pastedown, sgd on front free endpaper, inscription on half-title **2,760.00**

Story, Joseph, ALS, Cambridge, May 8, 1843, to John McDonough, concerning African colonization, one page, folded 4to sheet with integral address leaf, light toning, mounted to larger sheet **1,265.00**

Literature

Anderson, Sherwood, TLS, Oct. 14, 1939, to Ralph Hartman, regarding autographing books, one pg, oblong 8vo sheet, folds, framed with photograph..................**220.00**

Blunden, Edmund, ALS, Kent, Aug. 7, 1931, to bookseller D Schwartz, detailed critique and suggestions for forthcoming bibliography to Charles Lamb, commenting on Havelock Ellis, five pgs, small 8vo **425.00**

Cooper, James Fenimore, ALS, Cooperstown, Sept. 2, 1845, sgd "J. Fenimore Cooper" to Elliot Cowdin, chair of lecture committee of the Merchantile Library Assoc. of Boston, agreeing to lecture, one page, folded 4to sheet **635.00**

Emerson, Ralph Waldo, ALS, Concord, Sept. 22, 1846, sgd "R. W. Emerson" to Elliot Cowdin, President of Merchantile Library Assoc., agreeing to give lecture, one page, folded 4to sheet with integral address leaf, usual folds **575.00**

Frost, Robert, inscribed book, A Cabin in the Clearing, Spiral Press, 1951, inscribed "To Edmund Randolph Biddle from Robert Frost, Washington, 1669 31st St., March 21, 1952" on the half title, 16 mo, publisher's wrappers, small tear to rear wrappers **260.00**

Hemingway, Ernest, ALS, Key West, March 31, 1936, sgd "Ernesto" to Miami Herald fishing columnist Ed Roman, about broadbill swordfish, four pgs, two 4vo sheets, folds, orig holograph mailing envelope **3,450.00**

Holmes, Oliver Wendell, ALS, Boston, March 8, 1866, sgd "O. W. Holmes," addressed to Gentlemen, thanking them for sending Jean Ingelow's Stories Told to A Child, two pages, single 8vo sheet....................**260.00**

Hughes, Langston, book signed, Fields of Wonder, New York, 1947, first edition, inscribed "For Kurt and Lenya," (Kurt

Weill and Lotte Lenya), thin 8vo, publisher's cloth, dust jacket.. **1,150.00**

Machen, Arthur, ALS, Amersham, Feb. 19, 1934, to Munson Havens, commenting on his work, schooling, Greek theater, four pgs, two 8vo sheets, folds, mounted into first edition of Machen's Things Near and Far, orig envelope **210.00**

Prescott, William H., ALS, Pepperill, Sept. 30, sgd "Wm H. Prescott" regarding portraits of Cortez, four pages, folded 8vo sheet, hinged to larger sheet **260.00**

Sandburg, Carl, ALS, Chicago Daily News letterhead, Chicago, Dec. 12, 1926, to poet Sara Teasdale, concerning poetry, one page, single oblong 8vo sheet, folds, holograph mailing envelope, framed **490.00**

Shaw, George Bernard, ALS, Ayot St, Lawrence, July 2, 1923, sgd "G.B.S." to Ben Turner, thanking him for sending books, criticizing Dialect Societies, one page, 8vo postcard addressed and postmarked on verso, minor soiling **980.00**

Steinbeck, John, ALS, Siasonset, July 30, 1951, sgd "John," to William Beecher, concerning wife's birthday, his progress on *East of Eden*, two pgs, single tall 4to sheet, ruled yellow paper, written in pencil, minor browning, orig holograph mailing envelope .. **2,990.00**

Williams, William Carlos, personal stationery, Rutherford, Dec. 14, 1959, TLS, to Henry Sturtz, praising Albert Einstein, one page, single 8vo . **635.00**

Military

Corbett, Boston, 3-1/2" x 8" ruled paper, sgd "Boston Corbett/Sergt Co. L. 16th NY Cav." **635.00**

Cornwallis, Charles, Earl, ALS, Calcutta, Sept. 17, 1786, sgd as Governor General of the British Indian Government, to Lord Sydney (Thomas Townsend), Home Secretary under William Pitt, concerning arrival in Calcutta, 2-1/2 pgs, folded 4to sheet **1,495.00**

Farragut, David G., LS, New York, Dec. 14, 1863, sgd "D. G. Farragut" to Elliot Cowden, regarding department for station, one page, folded 4to, integral blank, blue-ruled paper, folds.. **350.00**

Ingraham, Duncan, sgd "Dn Ingraham" at top of 8vo sheet, faded, mat burn, framed with medal commemorating his naval achievements **175.00**

James "Jimmy" Harold Doolittle, black and white photo distributed by Mutual of Omaha, inscribed and signed "J. H. Doolittle," 8" x 10", **$110**. Photo courtesy of Cowan Historic Americana Auctions.

Mussolini, Benito, PS, close-up bust portrait, looking downward, sgd on sheet below image, red wax seal affixed to lower left corner, 11" x 7-1/2", minor creases in image, emb stamp on lower right corner of image, framed **. . . 520.00**

Napoleon, I., LS, Palais des Tuileries, Jan. 11, 1808, sgd "Napoi," to his cousin, Cardinal Castiglione, in French, thanking him for letter, wishing him well **. 865.00**

Sherman, William T, PS, sgd "W. T. Sherman, General, New York, Feb. 8, 1889," standing 3/4 portrait, in uniform, 11-1/2" x 7" image size, matted, framed **. 2,300.00**

Spotswood, M. L., ALS, Richmond, July 19, 1888, to unnamed Captain, sending small piece of lining of George Lee's coat, worn at the surrender, 2-1/2" x 2-3/4" piece of lining mounted to bottom of letter, 1-1/2 pgs, single 4to sheet, quite dampstained **. 920.00**

Thomas, Lorenzo, PS, "Brig Genl I. Thomas, Adj. Genl U.S.A.," bust portrait carte-de-visite by Frederick Gutekunst, orig photographer's mount, sgd on recto at bottom of image, bit yellowed and soiled, revenue stamp affixed on verso **. 260.00**

Yamaashita, Tomoyki, Phillippine one peso banknote, Victory issue, boldly signed in Japanese and English, plus signatures of two of his aides, 2-1/2" x 6-1/4", folds **. 920.00**

Music

Bruckner, Anton, ALS, Vienna, June 26, 1891, to Carl Ludwig Edlen von Schwarzbek-Waran, government official, in German, extending condolences, 1-1/2 pgs, folded 8vo sheet with integral blank, folds touching signature, even toning, orig envelope **. 3,450.00**

Caruso, Enrico, souvenir illus menu for dinner in his honor, sgd by Caruso and other attendees, including Otto Kahn, Victor Herbert, Winston O. Lord, David Bispham, and Melville E. Stone, New York, Feb. 5, 1916 **. 290.00**

Holst, Gustav, partially printed DS, London, April 19, 1923, signed and initialed five times, contract for publication of opera Savitri, manuscript changes to terms, countersigned by publisher and witness, two pgs, folio sheet, folds, bit toned, signed over revenue stamp **. 320.00**

Melba, Nellie, PS, inscribed "To darling Mr. Shaw with love from Nellie Melba 1917," full-length portrait of soprano standing beside piano, sgd below image, 8-1/2" x 6" image on 14" x 9-1/2" in sheet, minor staining in upper right corner **. 460.00**

Paganini, Niccolo, ALS, London, July 1, 1831, in Italian, agreeing to take part in benefit for poor musicians, one page 7-1/2" x 7-1/4" sheet, trimmed, minor browning **. 2,300.00**

Presidents

Adams, John Quincy, sgd endorsement, Boston, June 11, 1793, sgd "J. Q. Adams" on verso of partly-printed writ for arrest of debtor, two pgs, single sheet, 6-1/2" x 8", expert restoration closing separations at folds, reinforced corners **. 260.00**

Coolidge, Calvin, book signed, The Autobiography of Calvin Coolidge, New York, 1929, illus, 8vo, publisher's cloth, dust jacket, inscribed and sgd to Emory G. Van Loan on front blank, chipped with loss, separations repaired **. 350.00**

Eisenhower, Dwight D, ALS, Jan. 27, 1944, to General Lee at bottom of typed note signed from Lee to Eisenhower, replying to question about transfer of officer, one page, 7-1/2" x 3-1/2" sheet, Headquarters stationery, reply written in pencil **. 200.00**

Grant, Ulysses, ALS, Long Branch, June 28, 1875, sgd as President to Senator Matthew Carpenter, regarding

remarks about recent speech, emb personal stationery **. 1,380.00**

Hayes, Rutherford B., DS, Camp Hastings, Feb. 19, 1865, sgd as Brigadier General, endorsement on verse of partly-printed Civil War furlough pass issued to Oscar Crall, one page, multiple endorsements on verso, single 4to sheet, separated at folds **. 865.00**

Hoover, Herbert, ALS, Feb 1940, to Lewis Strass, sending him corrected typescript of speech given at the Jewish Welfare Fund of Chicago, ALS is one page, single 4to sheet, written in pencil, paper quite toned, received stamp in upper right corner, typescript if five pages, single 4to sheets, with 10 holograph corrections in pencil, first page toned, last page with minor chipping along left edge **. . . 10,350.00**

Johnson, Andrew, check signed, as President, Washington, June 1869, on First National Bank of Washington, endorsed on verso, 3-1/2" x 8", contemporary stamp affixed in the upper right corner **. 2,100.00**

Johnson, Lyndon, B., TLS, Washington, Jan. 29, 1958, U.S. Senate stationery, sgd "Lyndon" to Admiral Lewis Strauss, regarding co-signing of note to Walter Winchell, single 8vo sheet **. 230.00**

Kennedy, John F., TLS, as President, White House stationery, Feb. 9, 1962, to Secretary of Labor Arthur Goldberg, thanking him for his role in White House Regional Conference, one page, single tall 8vo sheet **. 1,725.00**

Lincoln, Abraham, ALS, as President, Washington, Sept. 11, 1861, sgd "A. Lincoln," presumably to Secretary of War Cameron, asking him to provide General Sigel's brother with a railroad pass, one page, 4" x 5-1/4", folds, very minor offsetting, minor restoration on verso **. 5,290.00**

Monroe, James, ALS, Washington, June 14, 1811, sgd "Jas Monroe" as Secretary of State, enclosing letters to be forwarded, one page, oblong 8vo sheet, trimmed, archivally mounted to larger sheet **. 865.00**

Nixon, Richard, TLS, personal stationery, New York, Sept. 9, 1963, sgd "Dick" to Admiral Lewis Strauss regarding nuclear test ban treaty, Cold War, and Khrushchev, one page, single tall 8vo, ink notation in left margin highlight paragraph **. 1,380.00**

Roosevelt, Franklin D., TLS, White House stationery, Washington, Sept. 14,

1936, as President, to Governor Tom Terral, appreciating Terral's efforts, one page, folded 8vo sheet, integral blank, minor browning **460.00**

Taft, William H., ALS, New Haven, Oct. 25, 1919, sgd "Wm H Taft" to Colonel Meekins, apologizing for abrupt end to their visit, four pgs, folded 8vo sheet, minor soiling and fading **290.00**

Taylor, Zachary, signature lower right on printed document, handwritten information "In consideration of service performed by James Conway, a Lieutenant" for land "Northwest of the River Ohio, between the Little Miami and Scioto," given to his son, dated 1850, fold lines, 22-1/2" x 19-1/2" Victorian shadow box frame . . . **200.00**

Van Buren, Martin, ALS, Lindenwald, Aug. 1, 1858, sgd "M. Van Buren" to Miss Silvester, concerning her admittance into a society of women, discussing attributes of her grand father as member of first Congress, 3-1/2 pgs, folded 8vo sheet, mat burn on first and last page, very minor chips at edges, text from verso visible on recto . **460.00**

Show business

Crawford, Joan, PS, inscribed "To Maria from Joan Crawford," 14" x 11" portrait by Hurrell, his emb stamp in lower right corner, minor damage at edges, framed **320.00**

Gielgud, John, PS, captioned, dated, youthful 3/4 pose as Hamlet, 10" x 8", signature, date, and caption in light area, 1936 . . . . **230.00**

Grant, Cary, PS, inscribed "To Arnold, with all good wishes, Cary Grant," 13" x 10" portrait by Clarence Bull, MGM stamp on verso, minor creasing, framed **580.00**

Harrison, George, signed book, *I Me Mine*, Guildford, Surrey, Genesis Publications, Ltd., 1980, 8vo, publisher's slipcase, one of 2,000 numbered copies **1,150.00**

Holiday, Billie, PS, inscribed "To Norman Stay Happy," souvenir group photo taken in Chicago, showing "Lady Day" with five other people, sgd on mat above image, 5" x 7", presentation folder of Garrick Stage Bar, also inscribed by another, inscriptions in pencil **980.00**

Monroe, Marilyn, check signed, Bankers Trust Co., New York, Oct. 6, 1961, to Hedda Rosten, 3" x 7-1/2", cancellation stamp and perforations, nicely framed **1,955.00**

Statesmen

Anthony, Susan B, ALS, Rochester, Dec. 1, 1872, sgd "S. B. Anthony" to Isabella Beecher Hooker, concerning trial in Rochester for voting, written on the conjugate leaf of an autograph letter, unsigned, by Hooker to Anthony, concerning Woodhull's "obscene" accusation that Reverend Henry Ward Beecher (Hooker's half brother) committed adultery, each two pgs, folded 8vo sheet. **4,850.00**

Catt, Carrie Chapman, New York, 1917, book, *Woman Suffrage* by Federal Constitutional Amendment, inscribed to Congressman Frederick C. Hicks on front free endpaper **1,495.00**

Semple, James, ADS, Williamsburg, July 29, 1809, detailed description of lot of land for sale, one page, single tall 4to sheet, minor browning **1,610.00**

Webster, Daniel, ALS, March 1, 1842, sgd "D. Webster" to C. F. Mayer, dismissing rumor about Brantz Mayer, one page, folded 8vo sheet **460.00**

AUTOMOBILES

History: Automobiles are generally classified into two categories: prewar, those manufactured before World War II; and those manufactured after the conflict. The Antique Automobile Club of America, the world's oldest and largest automobile historical society, considers motor vehicles, including cars, buses, motorcycles, and trucks, manufactured prior to 1930, "antique." The Contemporary Historical Vehicle Society, however, accepts automobiles that are at least 25 years old. There are also specific clubs dedicated to specific marques, like the Wills/Kaiser/AMC Jeep Club, and the Edsel Owners Club.

Some states, such as Pennsylvania, have devised a dual registration system for older cars—antique and classic. Models from the 1960s and 1970s, especially convertibles and limited-production models, fall into the "classic" designation if they are not used as daily transportation. Many states have also allowed collectible vehicles to sport "year of issue" license plates, thus allowing an owner of a 1964-1/2 Mustang to register a 1964 license plate from their home state.

References: Robert C. Ackerson, *Standard Catalog of 4x4s, 1945-2000,* Krause Publications, 2000; Dennis A. Adler, *Corvettes,* Krause Publications, 1996; John Chevedden & Ron Kowalke, *Standard Catalog of Oldsmobile, 1897-1997,* Krause Publications, 1997; James M. Flammang, *Standard Catalog of American Cars, 1976-1999,* 3rd ed., Krause Publications, 1999; —, *Standard Catalog of Imported Cars, 1946-1990,* 2nd ed., Krause Publications, 2000; —, *Volkswagen Beetles, Buses and Beyond,* Krause Publications, 1996; Patrick R. Foster, *American Motors, The Last Independent,* Krause Publications, 1993; *The Metropolitan Story,* Krause Publications, 1996; Gordon Gardner and Alistair Morris, *Automobilia, 20th Century International Reference with Price Guide,*

3rd ed., Antique Collectors' Club, 1999; Robert Genat, *The American Car Dealership,* MBI Publishing, 1999; John Gunnell, *American Work Trucks,* Krause Publications, 1994; —, *Marques of America,* Krause Publications, 1994; — (ed.), *100 Years of American Cars,* Krause Publications, 1993; —, *Standard Catalog of American Light Duty Trucks, 1896-1986,* 2nd ed., Krause Publications, 1993; —, *Standard Catalog of Chevrolet Trucks, Pickups & Other Light Duty Trucks, 1918-1995,* Krause Publications, 1995; Beverly Kimes and Henry Austin Clark, Jr., *Standard Catalog of American Cars, 1805–1942,* 3rd ed., Krause Publications, 1996; Ron Kowalke, *Old Car Wrecks,* Krause Publications, 1997; —, *Standard Guide to American Cars, 1946-1975,* 3rd ed., Krause Publications, 1997; —, *Standard Guide to American Muscle Cars, 1949-1995,* 2nd ed., Krause Publications, 1996; —, *2001 Standard Guide to Cars & Prices, Prices for Collector Vehicles, 1901-1993,* 13th ed., Krause Publications, 2000; James T. Lenzke, *Standard Catalog of American Light-Duty Trucks, 1896-2000,* 3rd ed., Krause Publications, 2000; —, *Standard Catalog of Cadillac, 1903-2000,* 2nd ed., Krause Publications, 2000; Jim Lenzke and Ken Buttolph, *Standard Guide to Cars & Prices,* 12th ed., Krause Publications, 1999; Albert Mroz, *The Illustrated Encyclopedia of American Trucks & Commercial Vehicles,* Krause Publications, 1996; Robert Murfin (ed.), *Miller's Collectors Cars Price Guide,* Reed International Books (distributed by Antique Collectors' Club), 1996; Gerald Perschbacher, *Wheels in Motion,* Krause Publications, 1996; Edwin J. Sanow, *Chevrolet Police Cars,* Krause Publications, 1997; Ed Lindley Peterson, *First to the Flames,* Krause Publications, 1999; Donald F. Wood and Wayne Sorensen, *Big City Fire Trucks, 1951-1997,* Krause Publications, Volume I, 1996, Volume II, 1997; Peter Winnewisser, *The Legendary Model A Ford,* Krause Publications, 1999. Krause Publications' *Standard Catalog* series includes special marque volumes, including *Standard Catalog of Cadillac, 1903-1990; Standard Catalog of Chrysler, 1925-1990; Standard Catalog of Pontiac, 1926-1995; Standard Catalog of Ford, 1903-1990; Standard Catalog of Chevrolet, 1912-1990; Standard Catalog of American Motors, 1902-1987; Standard Catalog of Oldsmobile, 1897-1997; Standard Catalog of Buick, 1903-1990.*

Periodicals and Internet Resources: *American Rodder,* 28210 Dorothy Drive, Suite 400, Agoura Hills, CA 91301-2605; *Automobile Quarterly,* 115 E. Spring St., New Albany, IN 47150, www.autoquarterly.com; *Black Book Official Auction Report,* P.O. Box 758, Gainesville, GA 30503, www.blackbookguides.com; *Cars & Parts,* P.O. Box 482, Sydney, OH 45365; *Car Collector,* 5211 S. Washington Ave., Titusville, FL 32780, www.carcollector.com; *Classic Car Source,* http://www.classicar.com; *Classic Motor* Monthly, P.O. Box 129, Bolton, Lancashire BL3 4YQ UK, www.classicmotor.demon.co.uk; *Citroen Quarterly,* P.O. Box 30, Boston, MA 02113; *Corvette & Chevy Trader,* P.O. Box 9059, Clearwater, FL 345618-9059; *Corvette Fever,* 6420 Wilshire Blvd., Los Angeles, CA 90048; *DuPont Registry,* 3051 Tech Drive, St. Petersburg, FL 33716, www.dupontregistry.com; *Hemmings Motor News,* P.O. Box 256, Bennington, VT 05201, www.hemmings.com; *Maserati Resource Center,* www.maserati-rc.org; *Muscle Car Review,* 6420 Wilshire Blvd., Los Angeles, CA 90048;

Mustang GT Registry, www.mustanggt.org; *Mustang Monthly,* 6420 Wilshire Blvd., Los Angeles, CA 90048; *National Automobile Dealers Assoc. Price Guide,* www.nada.org; *Old Cars* and *Old Cars Price Guide,* 700 E. State St., Iola, WI 54990; *Old Car Trader,* P.O. Box 9059, Clearwater, FL 34618-9059; *Old Cars Weekly, News & Markeplace,* 700 E. State St., Iola, WI 54990; *Skinned Knuckles,* 175 May Ave., Monrovia, CA 91016-2227, www.skinnedknuckles.com; *Special Car Journal,* www.specialcar.com; *Thunderbird Scoop,* P.O. Box 2250, Dearborn, MI 48123; *Thunderbird Script,* 20 Northview Dr., Hanover, PA 17331, www.intl-tbirdclub.com; *Vintage Mustang.com,* www.vintage-mustang.com

Collectors' Clubs: Alberta Antique & Classic Automobile Clubs, 14621 103rd Ave., Lethbridge, Alberta, T5N OT6 Canada, http://clubs.hemmings.com/aaac; Antique Automobile Club of America, 501 West Governor Road, P.O. Box 417, Hershey, PA 17033, www.aaca.org; Classic Car Club of America, 1645 Des Plaines River Road, Suite 7, Des Plaines, IL 60018, www.classiccarclub.org; Contemporary Historical Vehicle Assoc., P.O. Box 98, Tecumseh, KS 66542; Council of Vehicle Assoc./Classic Vehicle Advocate Group, Inc., P.O. Box 2136, Little Falls, NJ 07424-3311, www.covacvag.org; Fifties Automobile Club of America, 1114 Furman Drive, Linwood, NJ 08234, www.classiccar.com/clubs/gardenstate50%27s/home.html; Horseless Carriage Club of America, 128 S. Cypress St., Orange, CA 92866, www.horseless.com; Inliners International, 14408 SE. 169th, Renton, WA 98058, www.inliners.org; International Hot Rod Assoc., 9-1/2 E. Main St., Norwalk, OH 44857; Mid-America Old Time Automobile Assoc., 8 Jones Lane, Petit Jean Mountain, Morrilton, AR 72110, www.motaa.com; Milestone Car Society, P.O. Box 24612, Indianapolis, IN 46224, http://clubs.hemmings.com; National Auto Racing Historical Society, 121 Mount Vernon St., Boston, MA 02018; National Motorists Assoc., 402 W. Second St., Waunakee, WI 53597, www.motorists.org; Perfect 10 Motor Vehicle Society, P.O. Box 1890, St Paul, MN 55101; Society of Automative Historians, Inc., 1102 Long Cove Road, Gales Ferry, CT 06335-1812, www.autohistory.org; Sportscar Vintage Racing Association, 257 Dekalb Industrial Way, Decatur, GA 30030; Sports Car Club of America, Inc., 9033 E. Easter Place, Englewood, CO 80112, www.scca.org; Veteran Motor Car Club of America, P.O. Box 360788, Strongsville, OH 44136; Vintage Auto Racing Assoc., 1442 E. Lincoln Ave., #367, Los Angeles, CA 92865; Vintage Sports Car Club of America, 155 Post Road East, Suite 12, Westport, CT 06880-3412, www.vacca.org; Vintage Sports Car Drivers Assoc., 3160 Thornapple River Drive, Grand Rapids, MI 49546, www.vacda.org. See *Maloney's Antiques & Collectibles Resource Directory, 6th Edition,* Krause Publications, for car clubs relating to specific automobile makes.

Museums: Alfred P. Sloan Museum, Flint, MI; Auto Museum at Wells, Wells, ME; Auburn-Cord-Duesenberg Museum, Auburn, IN; Bulgari Trust, Cheltenham, Gloucestershire, UK; Detroit Historical Museum, Detroit, MI; Dixie Gun Works Old Car & Steam Engine Museum, Union City, TN 32861; Gast Classic Motorcars Exhibit, Strasburg, PA; Gilmore Classic Car Club Museum,

Hickory Corners, MI; Hartford Heritage Auto Museum, Hartford, WI; J. K. Lilly III Automobile Museum at Heritage Plantation, Sandwich, MA; Museum of Science & Industry, Chicago, IL; Museum of Automobile History, Syracuse, NY; Museum of the Automobile, Morrilton, AR; National Automobile Museum, Reno, NV; National Corvette Museum, Bowling Green, KY; Peterson Automotive Museum, Los Angeles, CA; Sarasota Classic Car Museum, Sarasota, FL; Studebaker National Museum, South Bend, IN; Towe Auto Museum, Sacramento, CA; Volo Auto Museum, Round Lake, IL.

Notes: The prices below are for cars in running condition, with a high proportion of original parts and somewhere between 60 percent and 80 percent restoration. *Prices can vary by as much as 30 percent in either direction.* Prices of unrestored automobiles, or those not running, or missing original parts can be 50 percent to 75 percent below prices listed.

Many older cars, especially if restored, are now worth more than $15,000. Their limited availability makes them difficult to price. Auctions, more than any other source, are the true determinant of value at this level.

Prices of high-powered 1964 to 1972 "muscle cars" will continue to escalate, while the value of pre-war cars will remain steady for all but unique custom-built roadsters and limousines. There is renewed interest in the original Volkswagen Beetle since the introduction of the updated 1990s version. Look for prices of these economical little cars to climb as well.

AMC

1960 Rambler Station Wagon **5,500.00**

1968 AMX Fastback coupe **8,500.00**

Amphicar, 1962 conv **19,500.00**

Auburn, 1935, Model 6-653, four-door sedan, 6 cyl **23,000.00**

Bricklin, 1975, Model SV-1, gullwing coupe **12,500.00**

Buick

1941 Roadmaster, four-door sedan, 8 cyl **17,500.00**

1986 Regal, Grand National **10,500.00**

Checker, 1963, Aerobus **6,500.00**

Chevrolet

1932 Model AE, two-door sedan, 6 cyl **12,000.00**

1955 Cameo Pickup Truck **19,500.00**

1964 Chevelle Super Sport, coupe **15,000.00**

1969 Camaro Convertible **18,000.00**

Chrysler

1932 Imperial Sedan, 6 cyl **18,000.00**

1956 New Yorker, Hemi engine, two-door hardtop **15,000.00**

1970 300, two-door "Hurst" edition **9,500.00**

Crosley, 1950 "Hot Shot" Roadster **8,900.00**

Dodge

1915, two-door roadster . **14,500.00**

1948 Power Wagon **9,500.00**

Essex, 1929 Challenger Series, four-door Town Sedan **9,500.00**

Edsel, 1958 Ranger two-door HT **12,000.00**

Ford

1924 Model T coupe **8,500.00**

1931 Model A rds **18,500.00**

1956 F-100 pickup **7,500.00**

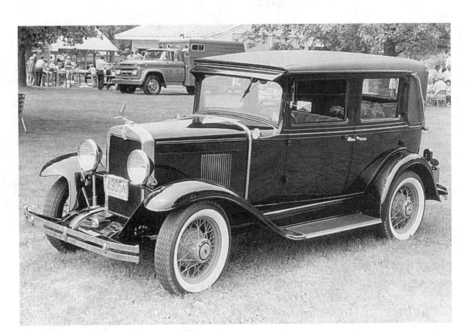

Chevrolet, 1930, **$8,000.**

1959 Thunderbird two-door HT
.................**19,500.00**
Henry J, 1953, Allstate **8,500.00**
Hudson, 1951 Hudson Hornet
.................**18,000.00**
Hummer, 1985, government sale, served in Desert Storm **21,500.00**
International Scout, 4x4, 1966
.................**6,500.00**
Jeep, 1966 Wagoneer, four-door, 4x4
.................**8,500.00**
Julian, 1922 Model 60 coupe, 6 cyl
.................**9,500.00**
Kaiser, 1953 Manhattan, four-door sedan.................**12,000.00**
Lambert, 1909, roadster, 6 cyl
.................**12,500.00**
Mercury
   1966 Comet Cyclone GT .**12,000.00**
   1969 Cougar XR-7 HT.....**7,500.00**
Nash
   Ambassador, 1954, two-door HT
   ....**4,500.00**
   Metropolitan, 1956, conv ..**8,500.00**
Oakland, 1930 sedan **7,500.00**
Oldsmobile
   1934 Business coupe....**11,000.00**
   1967 Toronado **9,500.00**
   1970 Vista Cruiser Station Wagon
   ....**6,500.00**
Packard, 1946 Clipper, sedan.................**12,000.00**
Plymouth
   1942 Model P14S, two-door sedan, 6 cyl.................**6,500.00**
   1970 Barracuda, one of 1,554
   ....**11,000.00**
Pontiac
   1934 two-door sedan **9,500.00**
   1955 Star Chief custom Safari
   ....**19,500.00**
   1966 2+2 convertible **13,500.00**
   1970 GTO two-door HT...**15,000.00**
Rolls Royce, 1951 Silver Wraith
   ....**49,000.00**
Studebaker
   1932 Rockne, two-passenger coupe.............**12,500.00**
   1962 Lark **4,500.00**
Volkswagen
   1949 sedan...........**10,500.00**
   1974 Super Beetle **6,500.00**
Willys, 1954, Eagle........**8,500.00**

AUTOMOBILIA

History: Automobilia is a wide-ranging category. It includes just about anything that represents a vehicle, from cookie jars to toys. Car parts are not usually considered automobilia, although there are a few

exceptions, like the Lalique radiator ornaments. Most sought after are automobile advertising, especially signs and deal promotional models. The number of items related to the automobile are endless. Even collectors who do not own an antique car are interested in automobile, bus, truck, and motorcycle advertising memorabilia. Many people collect only items from a certain marque, like Hupmobiles or Mustangs, while others may collect all advertising, like matchbooks or color brochures showing the new models for a certain year. Most material changes hands at automobile swap meets, and specialty auctions held throughout the year. Notably "hot" items on the market are service station and trucking company hat badges.

References: Mark Anderton, *Encyclopedia of Petroliana, Identification and Price Guide*, Krause Publications, 1999; Mark Allen Baker, *Auto Racing Memorabilia and Price Guide*, Krause Publications, 1996; Leila Dunbar, *Automobilia*, Schiffer Publishing, 1998; Scott Benjamin and Wayne Henderson, *Gas Pump Globes*, Motorbooks International, 1993; Mike Bruner, *Gasoline Treasures*, Schiffer Publishing, 1996; Bob and Chuck Crisler, *License Plates of the United States*, Interstate Directory Publishing Co. (420 Jericho Tpk., Jericho, NY 11753), 1997; Leila Dunbar, *Motorcycle Collectibles*, Schiffer Publishing, 1996; James K. Fox, *License Plates of the United States, A Pictorial History 1903 to the Present*, Interstate Directory Publishing Co., 1996; Ron Kowalke and Ken Buttolph, *Car Memorabilia Price Guide*, 2nd ed., Krause Publications, 1997; Rick Pease, *A Tour With Texaco*, Schiffer Publishing, 1997; Jim and Nancy Schaut, *American Automobilia*, Wallace-Homestead, 1994.

Periodicals: *Hemmings Motor News*, P.O. Box 256, Bennington, VT 05201; *Mobilia*, P.O. Box 575, Middlebury, VT 05753; *Petroleum Collectibles Monthly*, 411 Forest St., LaGrange, OH 44050; *PL8S*, P.O. Box 222, East Texas, PA 18046; *WOCCO*, 36100 Chardon Road, Willoughby, OH 44094.

Collectors' Clubs: Automobile Objects D'Art Club, 252 N. 7th St., Allentown, PA 18102; Classic Gauge & Oiler Hounds, Rte 1, Box 9, Farview, SD 57027; Hubcap Collectors Club, P.O. Box 54, Buckley, MI 49620; International Petroliana Collectors Association, P.O. Box 937, Powell, OH 43065; Spark Plug Collectors of America, 14018 NE. 85th St., Elk River, MN 55330.

Ashtray

   Figural pot bellied stove, orange and black ceramic, decal says "'49 Nash, hotter than a depot stove"
   ....**75.00**

   Tire, green Depression glass insert, 1936 Texas exposition.....**125.00**

Auto clock, 3" d, brass, Chalmers, eight day, black dial, second hand, dated 1912.................**48.00**

Auto lamps

   11" h, Ford, beveled glass lenses, marked "Ford Motor Lamp #2," price for pair **80.00**

   11-1/2" h, brass, two beveled glass lens, red bull's eyes, marked "Solar" **70.00**
   12-1/2" h, brass, Westchester #8, two beveled glass lenses, red bulls eyes, price for pair........**60.00**
Badge, attendant's hat
   Sinclair Grease, celluloid, 3" d
   ....**350.00**
   Texaco, 1930s era, with Scottie dogs
   ....**750.00**
Badge, driver's hat, Trailways Bus Lines, enamel **225.00**
Bank, shaggy dog, "Ford" on collar, marked "Florence Ceramics" ...**65.00**
Blotter, Sunoco advertising, Disney's Goofy character, near mint **60.00**
Box, Mobil oil "Gargoyle" logo, designed to hold lubrication charts
   ....**45.00**
Bud vase, Fostoria glass, hard-to-find mounting bracket, unusual pattern
   ....**150.00**
Calendar, 1940, Norem Buick Co., Ottawa, Ill, 8" x 6"............**45.00**
Can, motor oil
   D-A Speed Sport, racing oil, yellow tin with black & white checkered flags, near mint, full quart ..**50.00**
   Duplex, 8 oz. tin, Outboard Motor Oil, Quaker State, near mint.**60.00**
   Ronson, Wayne Oil Company, Philadelphia, racing streamlined car, airplane and car, full quart
   ....**900.00**
Catalog
   Durant Motors of Canada, Toronto, Canada, c1929, six pgs, 5" x 9-1/2", Quality Motor Cars ..**50.00**
   Ford Motor Co., Detroit, MI, 1950, 12 pgs, 8-1/2" x 11", 22" x 25-1/2" sheet folded, as issued, presented "Better Than Ever 1950 Mercury in Sport Sedan" **18.00**
   General Motors Corp., Detroit, MI, 1954, 16 pgs, 6" x 9", "Things You'll Want To Know About Our New 1954 GM Cars," cuts of Chevrolet sedan and convertible, Pontiac Star Chief and Silver Streak Chieftan, Oldsmobile sedan and convertible, Buicks, Cadillacs**16.00**
   Nash Motors Co., 1930, 16 pgs, 5-1/4" x 8-1/2", 16-1/2" x 21-1/2" sheet folded as issued, Nash 400 Twin Ignition Eight, Twin Ignition Six, Single Six, 24 cuts of models
   ....**45.00**
   North East Electric Co., Rochester, NY, 1925, 72 pgs, 4" x 9", North

East Equipment on Dodge Brothers Motor Equipment **22.00**

Plymouth Motor Corp., Detroit, MI, eight pcs, 6" x 7", 14" x 15-1/2" sheet folded as issued, color, Division of Chrysler Corp., Plymouth with silver dome engine, cuts of engine, two interviews, six models, specifications **40.00**

Clock

Atlas Tires and Batteries, wall clock, 1950s **175.00**

Pontiac Service, glass front, dark blue painted rim **300.00**

Studebaker, 15" h, gold metal rim, red/blue emblem, electric . . **400.00**

Compression tester, Hasting's Piston Ring advertising on dial, orig metal storage box **45.00**

Credit card, Husky, 1961, fair to good condition **25.00**

Decanter, figural race car, Lionstone, Al Unser's Johnny Lightning Special, 1970 and 1972 Indianapolis 500 Winner **75.00**

Display

Champion Spark Plugs, 12" h, 19" w, 5 1/2" d, tin, yellow with black lettering **200.00**

Exide battery, 40" high, tin and metal, black with orange lettering . **150.00**

Display cabinet

Gates fan belts, hangers inside for various sizes, painted tin front, 15" l, 30" w, 24" h **75.00**

Auto Lite Spark Plug, 18 1/2" h, 13" w, painted metal cabinet, glass front **125.00**

Schrader tire gauge cabinet, figural tire gauge, opens to reveal parts **350.00**

Emblem, Wolverine, model made only a few years by Reo **50.00**

Gas pump globe

Mobilgas Special, red Pegasus logo **275.00**

Shell, figural white Shell **450.00**

Thoroughbred, horse head **2,800.00**

Gas pump salt and pepper set, plastic, decals crazed, Phillips 66 . . . . **45.00**

Grease can, Texaco, red and green, one-lb size, 3-1/2" h **130.00**

Grill badge, Sports Car Club of America, black and red wire wheel logo, cloisonné, early 1960s' era . **50.00**

Hood ornament, 1955 Chevrolet, mint, unused **275.00**

Key fob

1960 Oldsmobile, color print in clear Lucite **10.00**

Esso Tiger logo, 1960s, engraved serial number for lost key return **10.00**

Knife, Cadillac Crest, 1958 Certified Mechanic, orig box **80.00**

License plate, porcelain on iron, black and white, New Jersey, 1909, minor losses, 13" x 6" **135.00**

Light, red bubble light for roof, 6 volts, early 1950s emergency vehicle **225.00**

Lighter, Zippo, 1953 Buick Suggestion Winner, Buick Crest engraved, mint and unused in orig box **125.00**

Map

1938 Standard Oil Map of Idaho **25.00**

1967 Texaco, map of Texas . . . **5.00**

Map rack, gas station display, Conoco, "branding iron" logo **95.00**

Motometer, Boyce, unpitted chrome, working condition **135.00**

Nodder, Chrysler advertising, "Little Profit" **60.00**

Paperweight

1938 Pontiac, cast pot metal car on base, probably by Banthrico **95.00**

Laughing Bear cast metal on base, advertising Bear Wheel Alignment, 4" h **200.00**

Pencil, mechanical, "floating" 1953 Cadillac in clear top, dealer advertising on side **45.00**

Pin, "Chevrolet Corvette Owner," 10K, makers' mark on reverse **300.00**

Plate, Ford Rotunda logo, 10" d **125.00**

Playing cards, AMC Pacer Wagon, still sealed, dealer giveaway **25.00**

Service pin

Buick, 25 years, screwback, 10K gold, 1930s logo **50.00**

Lincoln-Mercury Registered Mechanic, 10K gold filled . . **25.00**

Shell Oil 15-year tie bar, 10K gold, dated 1944 . . . . **75.00**

Sign, gas price type, yellow lettering, matte black, 11" x 6" **100.00**

Sign

Illinois Farm Supply Company, two sided, reverse-painted convex glass, lighted, minor losses, 44" d **635.00**

Oilzum, 10" by 15 1/2", double sided, few chips **450.00**

Reo Sales & Service, 18" by 24" **1,000.00**

Triple X Trucking, Phoenix, Arizona, porcelain over steel **250.00**

Speedometer

4" d, Cadillac, c1910, nickel plate brass, trip and total miles odometer, lighted dial, up to 60 mph **48.00**

4-1/2" d, brass, cylinder dial indicator up to 60 mph, trip odometer **130.00**

Thermometer

Buick Motor Cars, 27" h, porcelain, blue, c1918 . . . . **300.00**

Texaco, Plastic Pole Thermometer, 6" h **75.00**

Tin

American Motors, one quart all season coolant **20.00**

Cadillac, Blue Coral Wax, light scratches **25.00**

Mopar, polishing cloth, red, yellow, blue tin, 1950s Chrysler Corp. logo **35.00**

Tie bar, replica of 1950s Ford truck grill **60.00**

Tire patch repair kit, Belnord/Cornell Tires, (Pep Boys), tin, orig contents **25.00**

Tissue dispenser, chrome, Buick logo affixed, mounts under dash and swivels out for access, mint, orig box **40.00**

Watch fob

"Good Roads," celluloid logo affixed to metal fob **75.00**

Thomas Flyer, cloisonné, reverse unmarked **250.00**

Weathervane, 27" by 32", Mobil service station, double sided, porcelain, flying red horse **1,500.00**

Watch, Elgin, eight-day movement, 3" d, **$135.**

BACCARAT GLASS

History: The Sainte-Anne glassworks at Baccarat in Voges, France, was founded in 1764 and produced utilitarian soda glass. In 1816, Aime-Gabriel d'Artiques purchased the glassworks, and a Royal Warrant was issued in 1817 for the opening of Verrerie de Vonâoche éa Baccarat. The firm concentrated on lead-crystal glass products. In 1824, a limited company was created.

From 1823 to 1857, Baccarat and Saint-Louis glassworks had a commercial agreement and used the same outlets. No merger occurred. Baccarat began the production of paperweights in 1846. In the late 19th century, the firm achieved an international reputation for cut glass table services, chandeliers, display vases, centerpieces, and sculptures. Products eventually included all forms of glassware. The firm still is active today.

References: Jean-Louis Curtis, *Baccarat*, Harry N. Abrams, 1992; Paul Jokelson and Dena Tarshis, *Baccarat Paperweights and Related Glass*, Paperweight Press, 1990.

Additional Listings: Paperweights.

Bowl, 14" d, 3-1/2" h, wide flattened rim, narrow knopped foot, etched "Baccarat, France" **500.00**

Box, cov, 2-3/4" d, 2-1/4" h, white airplane design on sides, etched mark **125.00**

Candelabra, pr, crystal, 32" h, four light, diamond-cut baluster standard, four scrolling candle arms terminating urn-form sockets, etched glass globes hung with prisms **2,000.00**

Chandelier, 42" h, 29" w, 12 scrolling candle arms, foliate crown surmounting figures, prisms **12,365.00**

Carafe, Rose Tiente swirl, **$100.**

Cigar lighter, Rose Tiente, SP top **150.00**

Cologne bottle, 7" h, crystal, frosted rosette ground, gold floral swags and bows, cut faceted stopper, pr . . **335.00**

Decanter, 11-5/8" h, flattened ovoid, scalloped edge, etched flat sides with hunter on horseback, forest animals, scrolling vine, neck with vine etching, similarly shaped and etched stopper, 20th C, price for pr **550.00**

Epergne, 10-3/4" h, four cranberry overlay cut to clear vases, gilt metal holder **550.00**

Finger bowl, 4-3/4" d, 6-3/4" d underplate, ruby ground, gold medallions and flowers dec **350.00**

Jar, cov, 7" d, cameo cut, gilt metal mounts, imp "Baccarat" **350.00**

Lamp, 19-1/2" l, 24-1/2" h, central cut glass urn on short brass stem, two horizontal reeded candle arms, fan cut drip pans suspending cut prisms, ovoid glass knop stem, paneled trumpet foot cut with roundels, brass flat leaf base, one with collar at urn for further prisms, other with collars for two etched-glass shades, electrified, early 20th C, price for pr **2,875.00**

Pitcher, 9-1/4" h, Rose Tiente, Helical Twist pattern **295.00**

Paperweight, Zodiac, sulfide, Libra, c1955 . . . . **165.00**

Rose bowl, 5-1/2" h, 2-1/4" d opening, Cuir, round seal mark **400.00**

Toothpick holder, 2-1/2" h, Rose Tiente **110.00**

Vase, 9-3/4" h, colorless, tapered cylindrical, slightly everted rim, vertical tapered flutes on body, press-cut, 20th C **165.00**

BANKS, MECHANICAL

History: Banks which display some form of action while accepting a coin are considered mechanical banks. Mechanical banks date back to ancient Greece and Rome, but the majority of collectors are interested in those made between 1867 and 1928 in Germany, England, and the United States.

Initial research suggested that approximately 250 to 300 different or variant designs of banks were made in the early period. Today that number has been revised to 2,000-3,000 types and varieties. The field remains ripe for discovery and research.

More than 80 percent of all cast-iron mechanical banks produced between 1869 and 1928 were made by J. E. Stevens Co., Cromwell, Connecticut. Tin banks are usually of German origin.

References: *Collectors Encyclopedia of Toys and Banks*, L-W Book Sales, 1986, 1993 value update; Al Davidson, Penny Lane, *A History of Antique Mechanical Toy Banks*, Long's Americana, 1987; Don Duer, *A Penny Saved: Still and Mechanical Banks*, Schiffer Publishing, 1993; Bill Norman, *The Bank Book: The Encyclopedia of Mechanical Bank Collecting*, Collectors' Showcase, 1984.

Collectors' Club: Mechanical Bank Collectors of America, P.O. Box 128, Allegan, MI 49010.

Reproduction Alert: Reproductions, fakes, and forgeries exist for many banks. Forgeries of some mechanical banks were made as early as 1937, so age alone is not a guarantee of authenticity. In the following price listing, two asterisks indicate banks for which serious forgeries exist, and one asterisk indicates banks for which casual reproductions have been made.

Notes: While rarity is a factor in value, appeal of design, action, quality of manufacture, country of origin, and history of collector interest also are important. Radical price fluctuations may occur when there is an imbalance in these factors. Rare banks may sell for a few hundred dollars, while one of more common design with greater appeal will sell in the thousands.

The mechanical bank market is being greatly affected by the on-line auctions found on the Internet. This past year has seen more examples of banks being offered for sale than has been seen in decades. Many of these previously unavailable examples are being eagerly purchased by collectors. However, because of large numbers of more common banks also coming into the market, this past year represents a drop in the price of many banks, especially those in the under $3,500 range.

The values in the list below accurately represent the selling prices of mechanical banks in the specialized collectors' market. As some banks are hard to find, and the market is quite volatile both up and down in price structure, consultation of a competent specialist in mechanical banks, with up-to-the-moment information, is advised prior to selling any mechanical bank.

The prices listed are for original old mechanical banks with no repairs, in sound operating condition, and with at least 90 percent of the original paint intact.

Adviser: James S. Maxwell, Jr.

Note: Prices quoted are for 100 percent original examples, no repairs, no repaint, and which have at least 90 percent bright original paint. A * indicates casual reproductions; † denotes examples where casual reproductions and serious fakes exist.

†Acrobat **900.00**
†Afghanistan **465.00**
African Bank, black bust, back emb "African Bank" **450.00**
American Bank, sewing machine. **650.00**
*Artillery. **900.00**
Atlas, iron, steel, wood, paper . **525.00**
Automatic Chocolate Vending, tin. **450.00**
Automatic Coin Savings, predicts future, tin **150.00**

Automatic Fortune Bank, tin . . **3,700.00**
Automatic Savings Bank, tin,
soldier. **270.00**
Automatic Savings Bank, tin,
sailor. **170.00**
Automatic Surprise Money Box,
wood. **7,500.00**
†Baby Elephant X-O'clock, lead and
wood. **1,200.00**
*Bad Accident **1,920.00**
Bambula, black bust, back emb
"Bambula" **3,200.00**
Bank Teller, man behind three-sided
fancy grillwork **5,500.00**
Bank of Education and Economy, must
have orig paper reel **1,200.00**
Barking Dog, wood. **200.00**
Bear, tin. **220.00**
†Bear and Tree Stump **3,500.00**
†Bear, slot in chest **240.00**
†Bill E. Grin. **400.00**
†Billy Goat Bank. **230.00**
Bird In Cage, tin **200.00**
†Bird on Roof **575.00**
†Bismark Bank **15,000.00**
Bonzo, tin **300.00**
Book-Keepers Magic Bank,
tin **20,000.00**
Bow-ery Bank, iron, paper,
wood. **1,850.00**
Bowing Man in Cupola **1,920.00**
†Bowling Alley **4,500.00**
†Boy Robbing Birds Nest **950.00**
*Boy Scout Camp. **1,200.00**
†Boy and bull dog **4,500.00**
†Boy on trapeze **3,500.00**
†Boys stealing watermelons. . . . **750.00**
Bread Winners **1,800.00**
British Clown, tin. **12,000.00**
†Bucking Mule **1,500.00**
*Bull Dog, place coin on nose **1,800.00**
†Bull and Bear **75,000.00**
Bull Dog Savings, clockwork . . . **750.00**
†Bull Dog, standing **950.00**
Bureau, wood, Serrill patent . . **5,500.00**
Bureau, Lewando's, wood . . **28,000.00**
Bureau, wood, John R. Jennings
Patent **9,500.00**
Burnett Postman, tin man with
tray **3,500.00**
†Butting Buffalo **510.00**
†Butting Goat **1,200.00**
†Butting Ram **225.00**
*Cabin, black man flips **720.00**
Caller Vending, tin **3,500.00**
†Calamity **2,800.00**
†Called Out **1,500.00**
Calumet, tin and cardboard, with
Calumet kid **180.00**

Calumet, tin and cardboard,
with sailor. **18,000.00**
Calumet, tin and Cardboard, with
soldier **20,000.00**
†Camera **750.00**
*Cat and Mouse. **875.00**
†Cat and Mouse, giant cat standing on
top **45,000.00**
Chandlers **550.00**
Chandlers with clock. **210.00**
*Chief Big Moon **1,080.00**
Child's Bank, wood **510.00**
Chinaman in Boat, lead. **2,500.00**
Chinaman with queue, tin **200.00**
Chocolate Menier, tin. **950.00**
†Chrysler Pig. **750.00**
Cigarette Vending, tin **420.00**
Cigarette Vending, lead. **1,200.00**
Circus, clown on cart in circular
ring **1,200.00**
†Circus, ticket collector. **300.00**
Clever Dick, tin **170.00**
Clown Bust, iron **750.00**
Clown, Chein, tin **45.00**
†Clown on Bar, tin and iron . . . **1,200.00**
*Clown on Globe **3,000.00**
Clown and Dog, tin **150.00**
Clown with arched top, tin. **150.00**
Clown with black face, tin **800.00**
Clown with white face, tin **125.00**
Clown with white face, round,
tin. **3,700.00**
Cockatoo Pelican, tin. **120.00**
Coin Registering, many
variants **25-1,000.00**
Columbian Magic Savings, iron **150.00**
Columbian magic Savings, wood and
paper. **12,000.00**
Confectionery **1,500.00**
Coolie Bust, lead. **240.00**
Cowboy with tray, tin **210.00**
†Creedmoor **750.00**
Crescent Cash Register **3,700.00**
Cross Legged Minstrel, tin **250.00**
Crowing Rooster, circular base,
tin. **6,500.00**
Cupid at Piano, pot metal,
musical **450.00**
†Cupola. **750.00**
Dapper Dan, tin. **950.00**
*Darktown Battery **2,200.00**
†Darky Fisherman, lead **6,000.00**
†Darky Watermelon, man kicks football
at watermelon **7,500.00**
†Dentist. **2,200.00**
Dinah, iron **300.00**
Dinah, aluminum **150.00**
Ding Dong Bell, tin, windup. . . **2,000.00**
Dog on turntable **400.00**

Speaking Dog, Norman 5170A, "Pat. July 14, 1885 and Oct. 20, 1885," wear to polychrome, trap missing, 7" h, $715. Photo courtesy of Garth's Auction, Inc.

†Dog with tray **300.00**
Domed vending, tin **4,000.00**
Driver's Service Vending, tin . **1,500.00**
Droste Chocolate **900.00**
*Eagle and Eaglettes **450.00**
Electric Safe, steel **1,200.00**
*Elephant and Three Clowns . . . **850.00**
*Elephant, locked howdah **220.00**
Elephant, made in Canada . . **9,500.00**
Elephant, man pops out, wood, cloth,
iron **330.00**
†Elephant, no stars **3,700.00**
*Elephant, pull tail **60.00**
Elephant, three stars **400.00**
*Elephant, trunk swings, large . . **210.00**
*Elephant, trunk swings, small . . **150.00**
Elephant, trunk swings, raised coin
slot **900.00**
†Elephant with tusks, on wheels **300.00**
Empire Cinema, tin. **350.00**
English Bulldog, tin **220.00**
Feed the Goose, pot metal. **480.00**
5 cents Adding. **150.00**
Flip the Frog, tin **270.00**
Football, English football **1,200.00**
Fortune Savings, tin, horse race **575.00**
Fortune Teller, Savings, safe . **1,320.00**
†Fowler. **1,200.00**
†Freedman's Bank, wood, lead, brass,
tin, paper, etc. **75,000.00**
Frog on arched track, tin **575.00**
Frog on rock **575.00**
*Frog on round base **570.00**
†Frogs, two frogs **650.00**
Fun Producing Savings, tin . . **1,920.00**
*Gem, dog with building **1,700.00**
German Sportsman, lead and
iron **900.00**
German Vending, tin **1,200.00**
†Germania Exchange, iron, lead,
tin **1,200.00**
†Giant in Tower. **750.00**

†Giant, standing by rock **1,200.00**
Girl Feeding Geese, tin, paper,
lead **24,000.00**
†Girl Skipping Rope **8,500.00**
†Girl in Victorian chair **1,200.00**
Give Me A Penny, wood **8,000.00**
Grenadier **1,125.00**
Guessing, man's figure, lead, steel,
iron **8,800.00**
Guessing, woman's figure,
iron **1,320.00**
Guessing, woman's figure,
lead **900.00**
Gwenda Money Box, tin **3,500.00**
Hall's Excelsior, iron, wood **450.00**
Hall's Liliput, no tray **240.00**
Hall's Liliput, with tray **150.00**
†Harlequin **7,500.00**
Harold Lloyd, tin **220.00**
Hartwig and Vogel, vending, tin **900.00**
Hen and Chick **990.00**
Highwayman, tin **380.00**
Hillman Coin Target **900.00**
*Hindu, bust **450.00**
†Hold the Fort, two varieties,
each **650.00**
Home, tin building **570.00**
*Home, iron **300.00**
Hoop-La **5,500.00**
*Horse Race, two varieties,
each **1,200.00**
†Humpty Dumpty, bust of clown with
name on back, iron **1,680.00**
Humpty Dumpty, aluminum,
English **210.00**
Huntley and Palmers, tin,
vending **1,080.00**
*I Always Did 'spise a Mule, black man
on bench **600.00**
*I Always Did 'spise a Mule, black man
on mule **750.00**
Ideal Bureau, tin **3,700.00**
*Indian and Bear **875.00**
†Indian Chief, black man bust with
Indian feathered headdress,
aluminum **450.00**
Indiana Paddlewheel Boat **950.00**
†Initiating Bank, first degree . . . **600.00**
Initiating Bank, second degree . **720.00**
Japanese Ball Tosser, tin, wood,
paper **900.00**
Joe Socko Novelty Bank, tin . . . **270.00**
John Bull's Money Box **1,200.00**
John R. Jennings Trick Drawer Money
Box, wood **16,500.00**
Jolly Joe Clown, tin **1,920.00**
*Jolly Nigger, American **390.00**
*Jolly Nigger, English **210.00**
Jolly Nigger, lettering in Greek . **225.00**

Jolly Nigger, lettering in Arabic **1,200.00**
*Jolly Nigger, raises hat, lead . . . **900.00**
*Jolly Nigger, raises hat, iron . **1,320.00**
*Jolly Nigger, stationary ears . . . **150.00**
*Jolly Nigger, stationary eyes . . . **270.00**
*Jolly Nigger, with fez, aluminum **450.00**
Jolly Sambo Bank **1,680.00**
*Jonah and The Whale Bank, large
rectangular base **1,200.00**
†Jonah and The Whale Bank, stands on
two ornate legs with rectangular coin
box at center **5,500.00**
†Jumbo, elephant on wheels . . . **300.00**
Kick Inn Bank, wood **1,500.00**
Kiltie **390.00**
Lawrence Steinberg's Bureau Bank,
wood **15,000.00**
†Leap Frog **1,320.00**
Lehmann Berlin Tower, tin **230.00**
Lehmann,. London Tower, tin . . . **270.00**
†Light of Asia **270.00**
†Lighthouse Bank **300.00**
Lion, tin **345.00**
Lion Hunter **875.00**
†Lion and Two Monkeys **1,110.00**
*Little High Hat **900.00**
Little Jocko, tin **390.00**
*Little Joe Bank **570.00**
Little Moe Bank **210.00**
Lucky wheel Money Box, tin . . **3,500.00**
*Magic Bank, iron house **400.00**
Magic Bank, tin **200.00**
Magic, safe, tin **270.00**
†Magician **950.00**
†Mama Katzenjammer **900.00**
†Mammy and Child **900.00**
*Mason **1,500.00**
Memorial Money Box **240.00**
*Merry-Go-Round, mechanical,
coin activates **1,400.00**
†Merry-Go-Round, semi-mechanical,
spin by hand **510.00**
Mickey Mouse, tin **1,450.00**
Mikado Bank **5,000.00**
†Milking Cow **2,200.00**
Minstrel, tin **2,500.00**
Model Railroad Drink Dispenser,
tin **15,500.00**
Model Savings Bank, tin, cash
register **4,120.00**
*Monkey and Coconut **900.00**
Monkey and Parrot, tin **850.00**
†Monkey Bank **650.00**
Monkey, chimpanzee in ornate circular
bldg, iron **575.00**
Monkey Face, tin with arched
top **1,920.00**
Monkey, pot metal, nods head . . **450.00**
†Monkey, slot in stomach **225.00**

Monkey, tin, tips hat **270.00**
Monkey with Tray, tin **570.00**
Mosque **270.00**
Motor Bank, coin activates
trolley **950.00**
Mule Entering Barn **775.00**
Music Bank, tin **225.00**
Musical Church, wood **345.00**
Musical Savings Bank, Regina **1,500.00**
Musical Savings, tin **195.00**
Musical Savings, velvet covered
easel **270.00**
Musical Savings, velvet covered
frame **300.00**
Musical Savings, wood house . . **570.00**
National Bank **570.00**
National, Your Savings, cash
register **1,680.00**
Nestle's Automatic Chocolate,
cardboard, vending **1,200.00**
*New Bank, lever at center **240.00**
*New Bank, lever at left **180.00**
†New Creedmoor Bank **200.00**
Nodding Clown, pewter and
brass **350.00**
Nodding Dog, painted tin **225.00**
†North Pole Bank **1,200.00**
*Novelty Bank **650.00**
Octagonal Fort Bank **700.00**
Old Mother Hubbard, tin **400.00**
*Organ Bank, boy and girl **570.00**
*Organ Bank, cat and dog **450.00**
*Organ Bank, medium, only monkey
figure **270.00**
*Organ Bank, tiny, only monkey
figure **210.00**
Organ Grinder and Dancing
Bear **410.00**
Owl, slot in book **200.00**
Owl, slot in head **220.00**
*Owl, turns head **260.00**
*Paddy and the Pig **950.00**
Panorama Bank **1,050.00**
Pascal Chocolate Cigarettes, vending,
tin **1,080.00**
Patronize the Blind Man **675.00**
Pay Phone Bank, iron **1,680.00**
Pay Phone Bank, tin **510.00**
†Peg-Leg Beggar **410.00**
*Pelican, Arab head pops out . . **345.00**
*Pelican, Mammy head pops
out **315.00**
*Pelican, man thumbs nose . . . **300.00**
*Pelican, rabbit pops out **270.00**
†Perfection Registering, girl and dog at
blackboard **950.00**
Piano, musical **450.00**
*Picture Gallery **1,400.00**
Pig in High Chair **270.00**

Pinball Vending, tin......... **1,320.00**
Pistol Bank, iron **275.00**
Pistol Bank, iron, Uncle Sam figure
pops out **1,320.00**
Pistol Bank, litho, tin **3,700.00**
Pistol Bank, sheet steel **1,120.00**
Policeman, tin............... **300.00**
Popeye Knockout, tin **950.00**
Post Office Savings, steel.... **1,200.00**
†Preacher in the Pulpit **7,500.00**
†Presto, iron building **570.00**
Presto, mouse on roof, wood and
paper **570.00**
*Presto, penny changes optically
to quarter **575.00**
*Professor Pug Frog **2,800.00**
Pump and Bucket.......... **2,000.00**
*Punch and Judy, iron **1,570.00**
Punch and Judy, iron front, tin
back **450.00**
Punch and Judy, litho tin, circa
1910 .... **275.00**
Punch and Judy, litho tin, circa
1930 .... **165.00**
†Queen Victoria, bust, brass . **1,500.00**
†Queen Victoria, bust, iron... **2,800.00**
Rabbit in Cabbage........... **210.00**
†Rabbit Standing, large **410.00**
†Rabbit Standing, small...... **225.00**
Reclining Chinaman with
cards...................... **1,200.00**
Record Money Box, tin scales **6,700.00**
†Red Riding Hood, iron **1,650.00**
Red Riding Hood, tin, vending.. **700.00**
†Rival Bank................ **1,950.00**
Robot Bank, aluminum **390.00**
Robot Bank, iron............. **620.00**
Roller-Skating Bank **1,200.00**
Rooster **1,200.00**
Royal Trick Elephant, tin **5,500.00**
Safe Deposit Bank, tin,
elephant **990.00**
Safety Locomotive, semi **500.00**
Sailor Face, tin, pointed top .. **1,920.00**
Sailor Money Box, wood....... **270.00**
Saluting Sailor, tin............ **300.00**
Sam Segal's Aim to Save, brass and
wood...................... **780.00**
Sam Segal's Aim to Save, iron **1,080.00**
*Santa Claus................ **750.00**
Savo, circular, tin **200.00**
Savo, rectangular, tin **200.00**
†Schley Bottling Up Cevera.... **585.00**
Schokolade Automat, tin,
vending.................. **1,200.00**
School Teacher, tin and wood,
American **750.00**
School Teacher, tin, German ... **410.00**
Scotchman, tin **650.00**

Seek Him Frisk............. **1,700.00**
Sentry Bank, tin............. **375.00**
Sentry Bugler, tin............ **165.00**
†Shoot That Hat Bank **1,600.00**
†Shoot the Chute Bank **1,200.00**
Signal Cabin, tin **750.00**
†Smith X-ray Bank........... **675.00**
Snake and Frog in Pond, tin .. **2,000.00**
*Snap-It Bank **840.00**
Snow White, tin and lead...... **525.00**
*Speaking Dog **1,125.00**
Spring Jawed Alligator, pot
metal **120.00**
Spring Jawed Bonzo, pot metal **120.00**
Spring Jawed Bulldog, pot
metal **120.00**
Spring Jawed Cat, pot metal... **120.00**
Spring Jawed Chinaman, pot
metal **550.00**
Spring Jawed Donkey, pot metal **120.00**
Spring Jawed Felix the Cat, pot
metal **3,700.00**
Spring Jawed Mickey Mouse,
pot metal **13,500.00**
Spring Jawed Monkey, pot
metal **120.00**
Spring Jawed Parrot, pot metal. **120.00**
Spring Jawed Penguin, pot
metal **120.00**
Springing Cat **2,820.00**
†Squirrel and Tree Stump **410.00**
Starkies Aeroplane, aluminum,
cardboard **9,500.00**
Starkies Aeroplane, aluminum,
steel...................... **14,000.00**
Stollwerk Bros., vending, tin ... **650.00**
Stollwerk Bros., two penny, vending,
tin........................ **840.00**
Stollwerk Bros., Progressive Sampler,
tin........................ **330.00**
Stollwerk Bros., Victoria, spar-automat,
tin........................ **570.00**
Stollwerk Bros., large vending,
tin........................ **960.00**
*Stump Speaker Bank....... **1,200.00**
Sweet Thrift, tin, vending...... **345.00**
Symphonium Musical Savings,
wood..................... **1,200.00**
†Tabby.................... **225.00**
*Tammany Bank............. **225.00**
Tank and Cannon, aluminum.. **1,200.00**
Tank and Cannon, iron **1,680.00**
†Target Bank **252.00**
†Target In Vestibule.......... **570.00**
*Teddy and The Bear........ **990.00**
Ten Cent Adding Bank **950.00**
Thrifty Animal Bank, tin **300.00**
Thrift Scotchman, wood,
paper..................... **4,500.00**

Thrifty Tom's Jigger, tin...... **1,500.00**
Tid-Bits Money Box, tin **210.00**
Tiger, tin **270.00**
Time Is Money **750.00**
Time Lock Savings........... **345.00**
Time Registering Bank........ **350.00**
*Toad on Stump **400.00**
Toilet Bank, tin **300.00**
Tommy Bank................. **500.00**
Treasure Chest Music Bank **150.00**
*Trick Dog, six-part base **950.00**
*Trick Dog, solid base **400.00**
*Trick Pony Bank **750.00**
Trick Savings, wood, end
drawer **400.00**
Trick Savings, wood, side
drawer **400.00**
Tropical Chocolate Vending,
tin........................ **1,800.00**
Try your Weight, tin, semi...... **570.00**
Try Your Weight, tin,
mechanical................. **1,560.00**
†Turtle Bank **1,200.00**
Twentieth Century Savings Bank **300.00**
Two Ducks Bank, lead **2,000.00**
U.S. Bank, Building **510.00**
†U.S. and Spain **720.00**
†Uncle Remus Bank.......... **765.00**
†Uncle Sam Bank, standing figure with
satchel **1,125.00**
†Uncle Sam, bust........... **240.00**
†Uncle Tom, no lapels, with star **255.00**
†Uncle Tom, lapels, with star ... **240.00**
†Uncle Tom, no star.......... **210.00**
United States Bank, safe **330.00**
Viennese soldier............. **750.00**
Volunteer bank **570.00**
Watch Bank, blank face, tin **120.00**
Watch Bank, dime disappears,
tin........................ **165.00**
Watch Bank, stamped face, tin .. **90.00**
Watchdog Safe.............. **390.00**
Weeden's Plantation, tin, wood . **510.00**
Weight Lifter, tin **350.00**

*William Tell, patent June 23, 1896,
cast iron, no paint, 10-1/2" l,
6-1/2" h, **$750**. Photo courtesy of Joy
Luke Auctions.*

Whale Bank, pot metal	300.00
*William Tell, iron	775.00
William Tell, crossbow, Australian, sheet steel, aluminum	950.00
Wimbledon Bank	750.00
Winner Savings Bank, tin	575.00
Wireless Bank, tin, wood, iron	300.00
Woodpecker Bank, large, tin, c1910	450.00
Woodpecker Bank, small, tin, c1930-1960	50.00
World's Banker, tin	500.00
*World's Fair Bank	720.00
Zentral Sparkasse, steel	750.00
Zig Zag Bank, iron, tin, papier-mâché	4,120.00
*Zoo	900.00

BANKS, STILL

History: Banks with no mechanical action are known as still banks. The first still banks were made of wood or pottery or from gourds. Redware and stoneware banks, made by America's early potters, are prized possessions of today's collectors.

Still banks reached a golden age with the arrival of the cast-iron bank. Leading manufacturing companies include Arcade Mfg. Co., J. Chein & Co., Hubley, J. & E. Stevens, and A. C. Williams. The banks often were ornately painted to enhance their appeal. During the cast-iron era, banks and other businesses used the still bank as a form of advertising.

The tin lithograph bank, again frequently a tool for advertising, reached its zenith from 1930 to 1955. The tin bank was an important premium, whether a Pabst Blue Ribbon beer can bank or a Gerber's Orange Juice bank. Most tin advertising banks resembled the packaging of the product.

Almost every substance has been used to make a still bank—die-cast white metal, aluminum, brass, plastic, glass, etc. Many of the early glass candy containers also converted to a bank after the candy was eaten. Thousands of varieties of still banks were made, and hundreds of new varieties appear on the market each year.

References: *Collector's Encyclopedia of Toys and Banks,* L-W Book Sales, 1986, 1993 value update; Don Duer, *Penny Banks Around the World,* Schiffer Publishing, 1997; Richard L. Heuser, *Heuser's Price Guide to Official Collectible Banks,* Heuser Publishing, 2001; Earnest Ida and Jane Pitman, *Dictionary of Still Banks,* Long's Americana, 1980; Beverly and Jim Mangus, *Collector's Guide to Banks,* Collector Books, 1998; Andy and Susan Moore, *Penny Bank Book, Collecting Still Banks,* 3rd ed., Schiffer Publishing, 2000; Tom and Loretta Stoddard, *Ceramic Coin Banks,* Collector Books, 1997.

Periodical: *Glass Bank Collector,* P.O. Box 155, Poland, NY 13431.

Collectors' Club: Still Bank Collectors Club of America, 4175 Millersville Road, Indianapolis, IN 46205, www.stillbankclub.com.

Museum: Margaret Woodbury Strong Museum, Rochester, NY.

Brass, beehive, 4" h, 4-1/2" d, EOS, well detailed, base marked "A. B. Dalames Bank" 385.00

Cast iron, left: clown with crooked hat, M210, worn gold repaint, glued feet, 6-7/8" h, $360; right: Billiken, M73, gold and red, minor wear, 6-1/2" h, $55. Photo courtesy of Garth's Auction, Inc.

Cast iron

Bear with honey pot, 6-1/2" h, Hubley, painted brown, white and yellow coin pot 595.00

Boston Bull Terrier, 5-1/4" x 5-3/4", Vindex, painted brown and white 415.00

Buffalo, 5-1/4" x 8", detailed fur, emb "Amherst Stoves" 310.00

Building

2-1/2" h, 2" w, John Brown's Fort, slotted sides 1,100.00

2-3/4" to 4-3/4" h, Kyser & Rex, Town Hall and Log Cabin, chimney on left side, "Town Hall Bank" painted yellow, c1882 .... 260.00

3-1/4" h, Kenton, State, japanned, gold and bronze highlights . 180.00

3-3/4" h, Grey Iron Ceiling Co., bungalow, porch, painted 470.00

Cab, Arcade

7-3/4" l, Yellow Cab, painted orange and black, stenciling on doors, seated driver, rubber tires, painted metal wheels, coin slot in roof 935.00

8" l, Yellow Cab, painted orange and black, iron wheels, rubber tires, stenciled "Yellow Cab Main 4321" on door, spare tire missing 3,575.00

8-1/4" l, Green Cab, painted green, white, and black, coin slot in front hood, head lamps, seated figure, disc wheels, new license plate, spare tire attached to rear 1,870.00

Cat with ball, 2-1/2" x 5-11/16", A. C. Williams, painted gray, gold ball 190.00

Circus elephant, 3-7/8" h, Hubley, colorfully painted, seated position 180.00

Coronation, 6-5/8" h, Syndeham & McOustra, England, ornately detained, emb busts in center, England, c1911 .... 200.00

Duck, 4-3/4" h, Hubley, colorfully painted, outstretched wings, slot on back 165.00

Dutch boy and girl, 5-1/4" and 5-1/8" h, Hubley, colorfully painted, boy on barrel, girl holding flowers, c1930, price for pr 260.00

Egyptian tomb, 6-1/4" x 5-1/4", green finish, pharaoh's tomb entrance, hieroglyphics on front panel 275.00

Elk, 9-1/2" h, painted gold, full antlers 154.00

Globe safe, 5" h, Kenton, round sphere, claw feet, nickeled combination lock on front hinged door 80.00

Hall clock, 5-3/4" h, swinging pendulum visible through panel...110.00

Horseshoe, 4-1/4" x 4-3/4", Arcade, Buster Brown and Tige with horse, painted black and gold ... 125.00

Husky, 5" h, Grey Iron Casting Co., painted brown, black eyes, yellow box, repaired 365.00

Jewel chest, 6-1/8" x 4-5/8", ornate casting, ftd bank, brass combination lock on front, top lifts for coin retrieval, crack at corner ... 90.00

Kodak, 4-1/4" x 5" w, J & E Stevens, nickeled, highly detailed casting, intricate pattern, emb "Kodak Bank" on front opening panel, c1905 .... 225.00

Merry-go-round, 4-5/8" x 4-3/8", nickeled, Grey Iron Casting Co., ornate, round merry-go-round mounted on pedestal for spinning, replaced shaft 105.00

North Pole, 4-1/4" h, nickeled, Grey Iron Casting Co., depicts wooden pole with handle, emb lettering 415.00

Mailbox, 5-1/2" h, Hubley, painted green, emb "Air Mail," with eagle, standing type **220.00**

Maine, 4-5/8" l, Grey Iron Casting Co., japanned, gold highlights, c1900 . . . . **660.00**

Mammy, 5-1/4" h, Hubley, hands on hips, colorfully painted **300.00**

Pagoda, 5" x 3" x 3", England, gold trim, c1889 . . . . **245.00**

Pershing, General, 7-3/4" h, Grey Iron Casting Co., full bust, detailed casting **65.00**

Pig, 2-1/2" h, 5-1/4" l, Hubley, laughing, painted brown, trap on bottom **120.00**

Professor Pug Frog, 3-1/4" h, A.C. Williams, painted gold, blue jacket, new twist pin **195.00**

Radio, Kenton

2-7/8" h, 4-1/2" w, painted red, nickeled combination on front panel, three dial style, orig Kenton tag **440.00**

4-1/2" h, metal sides and back, painted green, nickeled front panel in Art-Deco style **435.00**

Reindeer, 9-1/2" h, 5-1/4" l, A. C. Williams, painted gold, full rack of antlers, replaced screw **55.00**

Rumplestiltskin, 6" h, painted gold, long red hat, base and feet, marked "Do You Know Me," c1910 . . . . **210.00**

Safe

3-9/16" h, 2-5/8" w, painted black, nickeled scroll design, key lock on front door, factory flaw **190.00**

4-3/8" h, Kyser & Rex, Young America, japanned, intricate casting, emb at top, c1882 . . . . **275.00**

4-3/16" h, IXL, Kyser & Rex, vault safe shape, painted green, gold highlights, emb front door, c1881 . . . . **140.00**

4-1/2" h, 3-1/4" w, Junior, painted black, gold highlights, emb floral casting, combination lock on front, c1892 . . . . **220.00**

5-3/8" h, Kyser & Rex, Japanese-style, japanned, cast Oriental designs, c1882 . . . . **85.00**

5-3/4" h, 4-3/16" w, cast iron and metal, National Safe Deposit, ornate emb, combo lock on front, black, gold highlights **190.00**

5-11/16" h, 4-1/4" w, J & E Stevens, Burglar Proof House, scalloped edges, combination lock, promising phrase **160.00**

6" h, 6-3/8" w, Kenton Hardware, Chicago & NY Bank, double vault, two separate combination locks **385.00**

6-1/2" h, 4-11/16" w, Mud Mfg. Co., Liberatas, copper electroplated, emb eagle and combination lock on front door **605.00**

6-3/4" h, 4-7/8" w, Kenton, Bank of Commerce, nickeled, vault safe, heavily emb with Miss Liberty, scroll work, lettering **550.00**

8" h, 5-3/4" w, nickeled, Coin Deposit, heavily emb, handle on top, front combo **150.00**

Sharecropper, 5-1/2" h, A. C. Williams, painted black, gold, and red, toes visible on one foot . . . **240.00**

Spitz, 4-1/4" x 4-1/2" h, Grey Iron Casting Co., painted gold, repaired **165.00**

Steamboat, 7-1/2" l, Arcade, painted gold **190.00**

Stove

4-3/4" h, Gem, Abendroth Bros., traces of bronzing, back marked "Gem Heaters Save Money" **275.00**

5-1/2 x 4", gas, Berstein Co., NY, cast iron and sheet metal, metallic scale version of early stove, railed handle on top **150.00**

5-3/4" h, upright, enameled violet color, marked "Tiger" on back, removable base plate **360.00**

6-7/8" h, parlor, nickeled finial and center bands, ornately cast, free standing **360.00**

Tank, 9-1/2" l, 4" w, Ferrosteel, side mounted guns, rear spoke wheels, emb on sides, c1919 . . . . . **385.00**

U.S. Mail, 4-3/4" h, Kenton, painted silver, red highlights on lettering, small combo trap on back panel **195.00**

5-1/8" h, Kenton, painted silver, gold painted emb eagle, red lettering large trap on back panel . . **180.00**

6-7/8" h, 4-3/8" w, D.B. Fish, painted silver, red emb lettering, nickeled combination lock on front panel, c1903 . . . . **130.00**

World Time, 4-1/8" x 2-5/8", Arcade, paper time-tables of various cities around the world **315.00**

Yellow Cab, 7-3/4" l, Arcade, painted yellow and black, slot on door, stenciled on doors **2,970.00**

Chalk, Winston Churchill, 5-1/4" h, bust, painted green, back etched "Save for Victory," wood base **55.00**

Glass, Charles Chaplin, 3-3/4" h, Geo Borgfeldt & Co., painted figure standing next to barrel slotted on lid, name emb on base **220.00**

Lead

Boxer, 2-5/8" h, Germany, head, painted brown, black facial details, lock on collar, bent in back . **130.00**

Burro, 3-1/2" x 3-1/2", Japan, lock on saddle marked "Plymouth, VT" **125.00**

Ocean liner, 2-3/4" x 7-5/8" l, bronze electroplated, three smoking stacks, hinged trap on deck, small hole **180.00**

Pug, 2-3/4" h, Germany, painted, stenciled "Hershey Park" on side, lock on collar **300.00**

Pottery

Cat, 3" h, head, white clay, green glaze **275.00**

Dog, 2-1/2" h, head, white clay, dark green glaze, flake at coin slot **110.00**

Pig, Germany, two pigs on seesaw on top of money bag **120.00**

Steel

Life boat, 14" l, pressed, painted yellow and blue, boat length decal marked "Contributions for Royal National Life Boat Institution," deck lifts for coin removal, over painted **360.00**

Piano, 5-1/8" x 5-7/8", Lyon & Healy's, free standing, etched wording on cabinet panel . . **380.00**

Postal savings, 4-5/8" h, 5-3/8" w, copper finish, glass view front panel, paper registering strips, emb "U.S. Mail" on sides, top lifts to reveal four coin slots, patent 1902 . . . . **95.00**

Stoneware

Dog's head, white clay, yellow glaze, two-tone brown sponging, 4" h, shallow flakes **175.00**

Ovoid, brushed cobalt blue flowers, leaves, and finial, minor flakes at coin slot, 6" h **6,875.00**

White metal

Amish Boy, seated on bale of straw, 4-3/4" x 3-3/8", U.S., painted in bright colors, key lock trap on bottom **55.00**

Cat with bow, 4-1/8" h, painted white, blue bow **155.00**

Gorilla, colorfully painted in brown hues, seated position, trap on bottom **165.00**

Pig, 4-3/8" h, painted white, decal marked "West Point, N.Y." on belly **30.00**

Rabbit, 4-1/2" h, seated, painted brown, painted eyes, trap on bottom, crack in ear **30.00**

Santa, 5-7/8" l, colorfully painted, full figure of standing Santa, holding toy bag, book and box marked "York National Trust Co." . . **165.00**

Spaniel, seated, 4-1/2" h, painted white, black highlights **470.00**

Uncle Sam Hat, 3-1/2" h, painted red, white, and blue, stars on brim, slot on top, trap on bottom **135.00**

Wood, burlwood inlaid with exotic woods, top dec with geometric banding, front with sailing vessels, end panels with flags, Prisoner of War, late 19th C, 5" x 8" x 5-1/4", imperfections **1,150.00**

BARBER BOTTLES

History: Barber bottles, colorful glass bottles found on shelves and counters in barber shops, held the liquids barbers used daily. A specific liquid was kept in a specific bottle, which the barber knew by color, design, or lettering. The bulk liquids were kept in utilitarian containers under the counter or in a storage room.

Barber bottles are found in many types of glass—art glass with various decorations, pattern glass, and commercially prepared and labeled bottles.

References: *Barbershop Collectibles*, L-W Book Sales, 1996; Keith E. Estep, *Shaving Mug & Barber Bottle Book*, Schiffer Publishing, 1995; Richard Holiner, *Collecting Barber Bottles*, Collector Books, 1986; Ralph & Terry Kovel, *Kovels' Bottles Price List*, 11th ed., Three Rivers Press, 1999.

Collectors' Club: National Shaving Mug Collectors Assoc., 320 S. Glenwood St., Allentown, PA 19104-6529; www.nsmca.org.

Museums: Atwater Kent History Museum, Philadelphia, PA; Barber Museum, Canal Winchester, OH; Lightner Museum, Saint Augustine, FL; National Shaving & Barbershop Museum, Meriden, CT; The Barber Museum, Canal Winchester, OH; The Barber Shop Museum, Hamilton Square, NJ.

Note: Prices are for bottles without original stoppers unless otherwise noted.

Advertising

Klorofil Dandruff Cure, glass label, 2-1/2" d, 7-1/2" h **170.00**

Koken's Quinine Tonic for the Hair, 7-1/2" h, clear, label under glass **195.00**

Clear, pink flowers, green leaves, outlined in gold, white porcelain stopper, 8" h, $175. Photo courtesy of Joy Luke Auctions.

Lucky tiger, red, green, yellow, black, and gilt label under glass, emb on reverse **85.00**

Vegederma, cylindrical, bulbous, long neck, amethyst, white enamel dec of bust of woman with long flower hair, tooled mouth, pontil scar, 8" h **130.00**

Amber, Hobb's Hobnail **250.00**

Amethyst, Mary Gregory type dec, white enameled child and flowers, 8" h **200.00**

Cobalt blue, cylindrical, bulbous body, long neck, white enamel, traces of gold dec, tooled mouth, pontil scar, 7-1/4" h **100.00**

Emerald green, cylindrical bell form, long neck, orange and white enameled floral dec, sheared mouth, pontil scar, some int. haze, 8-1/2" h **210.00**

Latticino, cylindrical, bulbous, long neck, clear frosted glass, white, red, and pale green vertical stripes, tooled mouth, pontil scar, 8-1/4" h **200.00**

Lime green, Amethyst, cylindrical, bulbous bodies, long necks, profuse floral gilt dec, tooled mouth, pontil scar, 8" h, matched pr **350.00**

Lime green, satin glass, classical bird claw grasping ball, ground mouth, smooth base, 7" h, pr **100.00**

Milk glass, Witch Hazel, painted letters and flowers, 9" h **115.00**

Opalescent

Coin Spot, blue **300.00**

Seaweed, cranberry, bulbous **465.00**

Spanish Lace, electric blue ground, sq, long neck, tooled mouth, smooth base, 7-7/8" h, pr . . **250.00**

Stars and Stripes, cranberry, pale blue, tooled mouth, smooth base, 7-1/4" h, pr **575.00**

Sapphire blue

Enameled white and yellow daisies, green leaves, 8-5/8" h **125.00**

Mary Gregory type dec, white enamel dec of girl playing tennis, cylindrical bulbous form, long neck, tooled mouth, pontil scar, 8" h **150.00**

BAROMETERS

History: A barometer is an instrument that measures atmospheric pressure, which, in turn, aids weather forecasting. Low pressure indicates the coming of rain, snow, or storm; high pressure signifies fair weather.

Most barometers use an evacuated and graduated glass tube which contains a column of mercury. These are classified by the shape of the case. An aneroid barometer has no liquid and works by a needle connected to the top of a metal box in which a partial vacuum is maintained. The movement of the top moves the needle.

Reference: Nicholas Goodison, *English Barometers, 1680-1860*, Antique Collectors' Club, 1999.

Banjo, Short & Mason, London, #2468, mahogany, inlaid decoration, Fahrenheit and centigrade scales, 33-1/2" l, 12-1/2" w, $1,400.

4-1/2" h, aneroid, Taylor, circular mahogany frame **75.00**

31-1/2" h, wheel, aneroid, oak case topped by carved bellflower on stippled ground, thermometer, barometer dial with further single bellflower below, English, late 19th/early 20th C . . **350.00**

26-1/2" h, wheel, Georgian, mahogany, dial sgd "Dolland, London," rounded pediment over thermometer, urn inlaid central roundel line inlay throughout, early 19th C **1,840.00**

33" d, wheel, carved oak, foliage and C-scrolls, English, late 19th C . . **230.00**

34" l, stick, sgd E. Kendall, N. Lebanon, mahogany, etched steel face, mirrored well cov. **550.00**

37" h, stick, Central Scientific Co., Chicago, IL, engraved silver brass scale, ebonized backboard **200.00**

37-1/2" h, wheel, Sheraton-style, mahogany and inlay, antique elements, embellished with shell and bellflower inlay, broken pediment top, barometer face sgd "A. Torone, Dundee," thermometer **700.00**

38-1/2" h, wheel, George III style, dial sgd "J. Poltil," broken pediment top over inlaid patera roundel, later thermometer flanked by inlaid shells, steel dial, further patera roundel. **920.00**

38-3/4" h, banjo, mahogany, dial engraved "P. Nossi & Co. Boston," broken pediment cresting above shaped case with thermometer, circular barometer dial flanked by inlaid patera **690.00**

39" h, wall, pierced crest above paper dial in rect frame, scrolling brackets continuing to shaped base with applied boss, painted black, Thomas Shaw, England, early 19th C, minor imperfections **690.00**

39-1/2" h, stick, Georgian style, mahogany, swan's neck cresting, carved well cov, engraved steel face, 20th C. **290.00**

39-3/4" h, banjo, shell inlaid, painted black, Kirner Bros., Oxford, Victorian, mid-19th C **460.00**

40" l, wheel, rosewood veneer, onion top cornice with hygrometer dial over thermometer over convex mirror, large barometric dial, small level at base, English, mid-19th C **350.00**

41" h, stick, retailer plaque Williams, Page & Co., Boston, paper labels, two thermometers, Victorian, c1850, losses **290.00**

42" h, wheel, L. Solomons, Bath Warantes, Regency period, early 19th C, shaped case **850.00**

44" l, Fortin Pattern, by Henry J. Green, Brooklyn, c1900, oxidized brass, lacquered scale and vernier, body tube engraved "C. B. Robinson, Georges Mills, NH," mahogany cabinet, milk glass reflectors **750.00**

BASKETS

History: Baskets were invented when man first required containers to gather, store, and transport goods. Today's collectors, influenced by the country look, focus on baskets made of splint, rye straw, or willow. Emphasis is placed on handmade examples. Nails or staples, wide splints which are thin and evenly cut, or a wire bail handle denote factory construction which can date back to the mid-19th century. Decorated painted or woven baskets rarely are handmade, unless they are American Indian in origin.

Baskets are collected by (a) type—berry, egg, or field, (b) region—Nantucket or Shaker, and (c) composition—splint, rye, or willow.

References: Don and Carol Raycraft, *Collector's Guide to Country Baskets*, Collector Books, 1985, 1994 value update; Nancy Schiffer, *Baskets,* 3rd ed., Schiffer Publishing, 2001.

Museums: Heard Museum, Phoenix, AZ; Old Salem, Inc., Winston-Salem, NC.

Reproduction Alert: Modern reproductions abound, made by diverse groups ranging from craft revivalists to foreign manufacturers.

Note: Limit purchases to baskets in very good condition; damaged ones are a poor investment even at a low price.

Half buttocks, woven splint, thick brown paint, bentwood handle, 8" w, 5" h. **200.00**

Miniature

Bushel, painted cream-white over red, America, 19th C, 5-3/4" d, 3-1/4" h **760.00**

Melon ribbed, woven splint, 12 ribs, wide bentwood handle forms central rib, 3-1/2" d, 2" h plus handle, some minor wear **150.00**

Woven splint, single handle, painted blue, 1-3/4" d, 2" h **550.00**

Nantucket Light Ship, America

Oval, cov, swing handle, purse, carved ivory whale mounted on walnut oval lid medallion, carved ivory pins and peg, base inscribed "Made in Nantucket Jose Formoso Reyes" with rending of island, 20th C, 8" l, 6-1/4" w, 7" h **3,115.00**

Oval, open, two carved handles, 10" l, 7-1/2" w, 3-3/4" h, handle repaired, late 19th/early 20th C **575.00**

Round, swing handle, 7-1/2" d, 9-5/8" h **1,725.00**

Round, swing handle, inscribed note on base states "Light Boat Baskets made by Joseph G. Fisher, Nantucket, 1893," 7-1/2" d, 7-1/2" h **1,840.00**

Splint, gathering, 14" d, 8-1/4" h, **$45.**

Native American

Splint, old patina, black painted fern design, 19th C, 8" w, 4-1/4" d, 4" h **350.00**

Splint, Schaticoke Tribe, CT, 19th C, rect, two carved handles, decorative bands, polychrome blue, orange, green, and brown splints, 13" l, 10-1/4" w, 7" h **1,725.00**

Oak, 11-1/2" h, 14" d top, peach basket shape, initials "CMT" **235.00**

Painted

Fixed handle, twisted rim, painted orange, America, late 19th C **60.00**

Miniature, tapering cylindrical form, loop handles, old taupe paint, America, 19th C, 5" d, 3" h **1,150.00**

Splint, round shape, sq bottom, old dark red paint over white, New England, mid-19th C, minor paint wear, 12" d, 3-3/4" h **200.00**

Vertical shaped wooden slats joined by twisted wire banding, wooden circular base, old painted surface, America, early 19th C, 12-1/2" d, 18" h **865.00**

Rye Straw

23" d, dough rising, shallow, hickory splint binding, PA, late 19th C **125.00**

24" d, domed lid, wear, edge damage, one bentwood rim handle missing **300.00**

Splint and cane, Guilford, CT, late 19th C, fixed bale handle, circular rim and sq base, old natural color, 3-1/2" d, 4-3/4" h **100.00**

Stave Construction, vertical wood staves taper down at base, fixed with wire, dark orig finish over varnish, 13" d, 17" h. **250.00**

Storage, cov, splint, painted blue, attributed to New England, late 19th C, 17" d, 24" h **1,380.00**

Woven splint

7-1/4" x 7-1/4" x 4-1/4" h, buttocks, 26 ribs, natural patina, faded red and green **220.00**

10-1/2" d, 5-1/2" h, round, good patina **275.00**

10-1/2 x 13" x 5-3/4", rect, courses of splint have unfaded dyed color, red, blue, yellow, and brown **385.00**

11-1/2" d round, 8" h plus bentwood swivel handle, kick-up in base **275.00**

12-1/2" x 12-1/2" x 6-1/2" h, buttocks, 58 ribs, old orange-tan pigmented varnish, twisted detail at handle **550.00**

13" x 16-1/2" x 9" h, buttocks, 44 ribs, scrubbed finish, some exposure damage **110.00**

13-1/4" d, 7" h, old green paint **440.00**

13-1/2" x 14" x 7" h, buttocks, 40 ribs, old gray paint **60.00**

13-1/2" x 16-1/2" x 8-1/2" h, buttocks, 22 ribs, blue and black stripes. **140.00**

14" d, buttocks, single handle **160.00**

16" d, market type, single handle **90.00**

BATTERSEA ENAMELS

History: Battersea enamel is a generic term for English enamel-on-copper objects of the 18th century.

In 1753, Stephen Theodore Janssen established a factory to produce "Trinkets and Curiosities Enameled on Copper" at York House, Battersea, London. Here the new invention of transfer printing developed to a high degree of excellence, and the resulting trifles delighted fashionable Georgian society.

Recent research has shown that enamels actually were being produced in London and the Midlands several years before York House was established. However, most enamel trinkets still are referred to as

"Battersea Enamels," even though they were probably made in other workshops in London, Birmingham, Bilston, Wednesbury, or Liverpool.

All manner of charming items were made, including snuff and patch boxes bearing mottos and memory gems. (By adding a mirror inside the lid, a snuff box became a patch box). Many figural whimsies, called "toys," were created to amuse a gay and fashionable world. Many other elaborate articles, e.g., candlesticks, salts, tea caddies, and bonbonnières, were made for the tables of the newly rich middle classes.

Reference: Susan Benjamin, *English Enamel Boxes*, Merrimack Publishers Circle, 1978.

Bonbonniere, reclining cow, natural colors, grassy mound, floral lid, Bilston, c1770 . . . . **3,750.00**

Box, 1-3/4" l, oval, white beaded lid edge, polychrome scene of bird's nest, black border, gilt "Trifles shew (sic) Respect," molded aqua base, hinge break, hairlines in base **165.00**

Candlesticks, pr, 6" h, pink ground, all over nosegays, pastels, Bilston, 1770 . . . . **3,500.00**

Etui, white tapered column, pastoral scenes within reserves, gilt scrolling and diaper work, int. fitted with perfume bottle, writing slide, pencil, and bodkin, Bilston, c1770. . . . . **3,400.00**

Mirror knobs, 2-7/8" d, rural genre scenes, woman on shore, two restored, three-pc set **300.00**

Patch box, oval

1-1/2" l, pastoral riverside scene, full color, pale green top and base, Bilston, c1780 . . . . **650.00**

2-1/2" x 1-3/4" x 1-1/2", black and white King Charles Spaniel, pink ground, floral dec, around sides **2,750.00**

Portrait medallion, 4" l, oval, enameled portrait of George II, third quarter 18th C, painted en grisaille **1,265.00**

Snuff box, 3" l, molded spaniel cover, landscape painted base, lines **1,265.00**

Trinket box, May Nature Pain the Cheek and Virtue the Mind, oval, 1-7/8" l, **$425.**

Tiebacks, 2-1/2" d, enamel and brass, Cupid dec, pr **150.00**

Topsy-turvy box, 2-3/4" l, oval, white, Before and After Marriage, humorous drawing of couple whose smiles turn into frowns with box is turned upside down, Bilston, c1780 . . . . **1,500.00**

BAVARIAN CHINA

History: Bavaria, Germany, was an important porcelain production center, similar to the Staffordshire district in England. The phrase "Bavarian China" refers to the products of companies operating in Bavaria, among which were Hutschenreuther, Thomas, and Zeh, Scherzer & Co. (Z. S. & Co.). Very little of the production from this area was imported into the United States prior to 1870.

Schaumann, orange, cream, and plum service plates, reticulated rims, central panels, 11" d price for set of 12, **$150.** *Photo courtesy of Joy Luke Auctions.*

Bowl, 7-3/8" l, 6" w, ovoid, reticulated sides, beaded rim, center and sides painted with scenic roundels en grisaille, blue ribbon cartouches with gilt detailing, scenes titled on underside "Badenburg," "Apolloscumpeil," and "Schloss Nymphenburg," late 19th C **325.00**

Cabinet plate, 9-1/4" d, central painted portrait of Empress Louise, indistinctly titled and sgd "L. Dgt" in gilt surround, paneled rim with scrolls, urns, and griffins, attributed to Hutschenreuther, late 19th/early 20th C. **125.00**

Celery tray, 11" l, center with basket of fruit, luster edge, c1900 . . . . **45.00**

Charger, scalloped rim, game bird in woodland scene, bunches of pink and yellow roses, connecting garlands **95.00**

Chocolate set, cov chocolate pot, six cups and saucers, shaded blue and white, large white leaves, pink, red, and white roses, crown mark **295.00**

Creamer and sugar, purple and white pansy dec, marked "Meschendorf, Bavaria" **65.00**

Cup and saucer, roses and foliage, gold handle **25.00**

Figure, 10-1/2" h, dark blue and pale orange marabou standing beside tan and navy cactus, marked "Hutschenreuther Selb-Bavaria, K. Tutter" **285.00**

Fish set, 13 plates, matching sauce boat, artist sgd **295.00**

Hair receiver, 3-1/2" x 2-1/", apple blossom dec, marked "T. S. & Co." . . **60.00**

Pitcher, 9" h, bulbous, blackberry dec, shaded ground, burnished gold lizard handle, sgd "D. Churchill" **125.00**

Plate

8-1/2" d, hp, poinsettia dec . . . **50.00**

9-1/2" d, red berries, green leaves, white ground, scalloped border **35.00**

Portrait plate, 16" l, side view of lady, sgd "L. B. Chaffee, R. C. Bavaria" **95.00**

Ramekin, underplate, ruffled, small red roses with green foliage, gold rim **45.00**

Salt and pepper shakers, pr, pink apple blossom sprays, white ground, reticulated gold tops, pr **35.00**

Shaving mug, pink carnations, marked "Royal Bavarian" **65.00**

Sugar shaker, hp, pastel pansies **60.00**

Vase, 4-3/4" h, hp, florals, sgd . . . **40.00**

BELLEEK

History: Belleek, a thin, ivory-colored, almost-iridescent porcelain, was first made in 1857 in county Fermanagh, Ireland. Production continued until World War I, was discontinued for a period of time, and then resumed. The Shamrock pattern is most familiar, but many patterns were made, including Limpet, Tridacna, and Grasses.

There is an Irish saying: If a newly married couple receives a gift of Belleek, their marriage will be blessed with lasting happiness.

Several American firms made a Belleek-type porcelain. The first was Ott and Brewer Co. of Trenton, New Jersey, in 1884, followed by Willets. Other firms producing this ware included The Ceramic Art Co. (1889), American Art China Works (1892), Columbian Art Co. (1893), and Lenox, Inc. (1904).

Marks: The European Belleek company used specific marks during given time periods, which makes it relatively easy to date a piece of Irish Belleek. Variations in mark color are important, as well as the symbols and words.

First mark	Black	Harp, Hound, and Castle 1863-1890
Second mark	Black	Harp, Hound, and Castle and the words "Co. Fermanagh, Ireland" 1891-1826
Third mark	Black	"Deanta in Eirinn" added 1926-1946
Fourth mark	Green	same as third mark except for color 1946-1955
Fifth mark	Green	"R" inside a circle added 1955-1965
Sixth mark	Green	"Co. Fermanagh" omitted 1965-March 1980
Seventh mark	Gold	"Deanta in Eirinn" omitted April 1980-Dec. 1992
Eighth mark	Blue	Blue version of the second mark with "R" inside a circle added January 1993-present

References: Susan and Al Bagdade, *Warman's English & Continental Pottery & Porcelain*, 3rd Edition, Krause Publications, 1998; Richard K. Degenhardt, *Belleek*, 2nd ed., Wallace-Homestead, 1993.

Collectors' Club: The Belleek Collectors' Society, 144 W. Britannia St., Taunton, MA 02780.

Museum: Museum of Ceramics at East Liverpool, East Liverpool, OH.

Additional Listings: Lenox.

Bowl, band of fern fronds, scalloped rim and prunted porcelain body, Trenton stamp mark, 9-3/4" d, 4" h, $230. Photo courtesy of David Rago Auctions.

American

Bowl, 9-3/4" d, 4" h, painted band of fern fronds, scalloped rim, prunted porcelain body, Trenton stamp mark **230.00**

Cup and saucer, 6" h, sq pedestal base, undecorated, Willets brown mark **45.00**

Dresser set, cov powder box, pink tray, buffer and container, nail brush, pin cushion, hp violets, artist sgd "M. R.," Willets brown mark **600.00**

Figure, 4" h, Lenox green wreath mark

Elephant, white **325.00**

Swan, green **75.00**

Loving cup, three handles, wine keeper in wine cellar dec, artist sgd, SS repoussé collar, CAC mark **195.00**

Mustache cup, gold leaves, butterflies **100.00**

Perfume bottle, figural, rabbit, white, Lenox green wreath mark **550.00**

Powder box, 4" x 6", pink, gold wheat on lid, Lenox green wreath mark . **60.00**

Punch set, 15-1/2" d, 13" h pedestal bowl, 11 cups, painted stylized purple grape clusters, green leaves, gilded rim, Lenox stamp mark **575.00**

Salt, 2" d, gold ftd, green ground, pink roses, Lenox green palette mark . **40.00**

Thimble, hand painted

Border of flowers and foliate, very worn thin gilt rim, squatty, late 19th C **245.00**

Border painted with roses, forget-me-nots, and foliage, gilt rim, late 19th C **295.00**

Vase

5" h, 5" d, tree trunk shape, transfer printed flowers, polychrome dec, red Ott & Brewer stamp . . . **450.00**

18-1/2" h, enamel and gilt dec, female within landscape, floral bouquet, artist sgd "J. Wallbridge," printed "Ceramic Art Co." NJ mark, c1900, restoration **320.00**

Irish

Basket, 8" d, Melvin, sq, decorative border, twig handles, turquoise-blue, four applied violet floral sprays, green leaves **625.00**

Box, cov, 3" h, Forget-Me-Not, globular, ftd, applied flowerheads, conical knob, pearl luster glaze, 3BM **395.00**

Butter dish, cov, figural, cottage, 6th mark **160.00**

Cake plate, Limpet pattern, 2BM **195.00**

Creamer, Lotus pattern, green handle, 2BM **95.00**

Cup and saucer, Shamrock pattern, 2BM **200.00**

Demitasse cup and saucer, Shamrock pattern, 6th mark **55.00**

Dish, coral and shell, 6th mark . . **35.00**

Figure

3-1/2" h, terrier, 4GM **45.00**

5-1/2" h, fish on rocky pedestal, 7th mark **75.00**

Mustache cup, Tridacna pattern, first black mark **125.00**

Plate, 9" d, Harp and Shamrock pattern, 5th mark **60.00**

Sandwich tray, Mask pattern,
2BM **285.00**
Spill jug, 7" h, Limerick pattern,
5th mark **60.00**
Tea and toast set, Tridacna pattern,
6th mark **90.00**
Tub, 3-1/4" d, Shamrock pattern,
3BM **65.00**
Vase, 6-1/2" h, Harp and Shamrock pattern, 5GM **60.00**

BELLS

History: Bells have been used for centuries for many different purposes. They have been traced as far back as 2697 B.C., though at that time they did not have any true tone. One of the oldest bells is the "crotal," a tiny sphere with small holes, a ball, and a stone or metal interior. This type now appears as sleigh bells.

True bell making began when bronze, a mixture of tin and copper, was invented. Bells are now made out of many types of materials—almost as many materials as there are uses for them.

Bells of the late 19th century show a high degree of workmanship and artistic style. Glass bells from this period are examples of the glassblower's talent and the glass manufacturer's product.

Collectors' Club: American Bell Association, P.O. Box 19443, Indianapolis, IN 46219-0443, www.collectoronline.com/club~ABA.html.

Bicycle, cast brass, nickel plated,
eagle **90.00**
Brass, hand held
Jacobean, head handle, cast figures on sides, emb inscription, 3-1/4" d, 4" h **95.00**
School, turned hardwood handle, late 19th C **70.00**
Ceramic, figural
Anniversary, Florence Ceramics, applied pink Dresden-style flowers, white ground, gold trim, 4-1/2" h **80.00**
Belle, Royal Doulton, HN2340, green dress, 1968-88 . . . . **85.00**
Belle O' the Ball, Royal Doulton, HN1997, red and white dress, 1947-79 . . . . **400.00**
Lillibelle, Ceramic Arts Studio, 6-1/2" h **45.00**
Southern Belle, Royal Doulton, HN2229, red and cream dress, 1958-97 . . . . **250.00**
Sovereign Bonnet Lady, Gonder, Mold No. 800, 3-1/2" h **60.00**
Desk type, 4-3/8" h, bell enclosed in five polished mother-of-pearl shells, gilt metal surrounds, small mother-of-pearl mounted striker, round alabaster base, late 19th C **185.00**

Dinner, china
Figural, Chinaman, Noritake, 3-1/2" h **210.00**
Franciscan Ware **150.00**
Rose Tapestry, Royal Bayreuth, three color roses, gold handle, 3-1/4" h **400.00**

Glass, amber, etched floral dec, 5" h, $28.

Glass
Bryce, No. 1, beaded rope handle **38.00**
Burmese, Thomas Webb, flaring base, applied amber handle, glossy finish, 6-3/4" h **750.00**
Cambridge, Rose Point pattern **150.00**
Cameo, DeVez, amber overlaid with red, cut daisy flowers and leaves, metal handle, tassel shaped clapper on chain, 8-1/4" h . . . **8,025.00**
Carnival, BPOE Elks, Atlantic City, 1911, blue **2,200.00**
Cranberry, applied clear handle, English, late 19th C, 11" h . . . **95.00**
Fostoria, American pattern . . **290.00**
Fostoria, Chintz pattern, orig label **135.00**
Imperial, Candlewick pattern, No. 400/108, 5" h **95.00**
Mount Washington, white satin, pink floral dec, gold trim, 5" h . . . **150.00**
Nickel-plated, railroad engine, arched yoke with U-shaped support, pedestal base, 25" h **2,145.00**
School, 10-1/4" h, turned curly maple handle **385.00**

Sleigh, 55" l, fifteen graduated brass bells on leather strap, wear **200.00**
Sterling silver, 4-5/8" h, cupid blowing horn, figural handle, foliate strap work border, frosted finish, Gorham, c1870 . . . . **750.00**

BENNINGTON AND BENNINGTON-TYPE POTTERY

History: In 1845, Christopher Webber Fenton joined Julius Norton, his brother-in-law, in

the manufacturing of stoneware pottery in Bennington, Vermont. Fenton sought to expand the company's products and glazes; Norton wanted to concentrate solely on stoneware. In 1847, Fenton broke away and established his own factory.

Fenton introduced to America the famous Rockingham glaze, developed in England and named after the Marquis of Rockingham. In 1849, he patented a flint enamel glaze, "Fenton's Enamel," which added flecks, spots, or streaks of color (usually blues, greens, yellows, and oranges) to the brown Rockingham glaze. Forms included candlesticks, coachman bottles, cow creamers, poodles, sugar bowls, and toby pitchers.

Fenton produced the little-known scroddled ware, commonly called lava or agate ware. Scroddled ware is composed of differently colored clays, which are mixed with cream-colored clay, molded, turned on a potter's wheel, coated with feldspar and flint, and fired. It was not produced in quantity, as there was little demand for it.

Fenton also introduced Parian ware to America. Parian was developed in England in 1842 and known as "Statuary ware." Parian is translucent porcelain that has no glaze and resembles marble. Bennington made the blue and white variety in the form of vases, cologne bottles, and trinkets.

The hound-handled pitcher is probably the best-known Bennington piece. Hound-handled pitchers were made by about 30 different potteries in more than 55 variations. Rockingham glaze was used by more than 150 potteries in 11 states, mainly in the Midwest, between 1830 and 1900.

Marks: Five different marks were used, with many variations. Only about 20 percent of the pieces carried any mark; some forms were almost always marked, others never. Marks include:

1849 mark (four variations) for flint enamel and Rockingham

E. Fenton's Works, 1845-1847, on Parian and occasionally on scroddled ware

U. S. Pottery Co., ribbon mark, 1852-1858, on Parian and blue and white porcelain

U. S. Pottery Co., lozenge mark, 1852-1858, on Parian

U. S. Pottery, oval mark, 1853-1858, mainly on scroddled ware.

References: Richard Carter Barret, *How to Identify Bennington Pottery*, Stephen Greene Press, 1964; William C. Ketchum, Jr., *American Pottery and Porcelain*, Avon Books, 1994.

Museums: Bennington Museum, Bennington, VT; East Liverpool Museum of Ceramics, East Liverpool, OH.

Additional Listings: Stoneware.

SPECIAL AUCTION

**The Armans Collector's
Sales and Services**
P.O. Box 4037
Middletown, RI 02842
(401) 849-5012

Bank, 6-1/2" h, flint enamel,
c1850-60 . . . . **865.00**

Bowl, 7-1/8" d, shallow, brown and yellow Rockingham glaze, Fenton's 1849
mark **775.00**

Candlestick, 8-1/4" h, flint enamel
glaze. **875.00**

Churn, stoneware, six gallon, cobalt
blue cornucopia of flowers, orig dasher,
marked "A. J. Norton & Co.". . **8,800.00**

Curtain tiebacks, 4-1/2" l, 1849-58,
Barrett plate 200, one chipped,
pr **175.00**

Figure
  7-1/2" h, 10" l, lion, facing left,
  coleslaw mane, tongue up, flint
  enamel, Barrett plate 377, minor
  repair to tail, repaired on chip on
  paw **4,315.00**
  8-1/2" h, 9" l, poodle, standing,
  basket in mouth, Barrett plate
  367, repairs to tail and hind
  quarters **2,500.00**

Flask, book, flint enamel, title imp on
spine, 1849-58, Barrett plate 411
  5-3/4" w, 2-5/8" d, 7-3/4" h, brown
  and blue flint enamel glaze, "Bennington Battle" on spine . **3,300.00**

Bottles, boot-shaped stoneware, brown glaze, one on left with darker glaze, white auctioneer's label, price for pair, $200. Photo courtesy of Joy Luke Auctions.

6" h, titled "Hermit's Life &
  Suffering" **980.00**
7" h, titled "Ladies
  Companion" **690.00**
8" h, titled "Bennington Companion
  G" **750.00**
Foot warmer, 11-1/2" h, molded feet on
one side, molded face just below spout,
flint enamel, green splotches, restoration on face, firing separations . **175.00**
Jar, 4-3/8" h, 4-1/4" d, Parian, blue and
white, Acanthus Leaf pattern, lid missing **85.00**
Jug, 10-3/4" h, stoneware, strap
handle, imp label "F. B. Norton & Co.,
Worcester, Mass," cobalt blue slip floral
design **220.00**
Marble, 1-1/2" d, blue, some wear
. . . . **90.00**
Nameplate, 8" l, Rockingham
glaze **145.00**
Paperweight, 3" h, 4-1/2" h, spaniel,
1849-58, Barrett plate 407 . . . . . **815.00**
Picture frame, 9-1/2" h, oval, 1948-58,
Barrett plate VIII, chips and repairs,
pr **230.00**
Pie plate, 9" d, brown and yellow Rockingham glaze, Fenton's 1949 mark,
minor wear. **925.00**
Pitcher
  8" h, hunting scene, Barrett pate 26,
  chips. **175.00**
  9-1/2" h, hound handle, 1852-67,
  Barrett plate 32, crack and repair to
  spout **345.00**
Planter, 11" h, stump form, stoneware,
base marked "F. B. Norton & Co.,
Worcester," minor chips **320.00**
Spittoon, 9-1/2" d, flint enamel glaze,
rare 1849 mark **450.00**
Sugar bowl, cov, 3-3/4" h, Parian,
blue and white, Repeated Oak
Leaves pattern, raised grapevine dec
on lid **150.00**
Teapot, cov, flint enamel, Alternate Rib
pattern, pierced pouring spout . **425.00**
Toby bottle, 10-1/2" h, Barrett plate
421, marked on base, mold cracks,
top of foot repaired, other foot
chipped **550.00**
Wash bowl and pitcher, flint enamel
glaze **1,100.00**

Bennington-Type

Bank, 3-1/4" h, 3-3/4" h, chest of
drawers shape, Rockingham glaze,
Barrett plate 428, small chip to front top
edge **150.00**
Creamer, 5-1/2" h, 6-3/4" l, figural, cow,
Rockingham glaze, Barrett plate 378,
chipped cov, repairs **115.00**

*Cake crock, J. & E., Bennington, VT, 1-1/2 gallon, brilliant cobalt blue thistle design, c1855, 7-1/2" h, **$715**. Photo courtesy of Bruce & Vicki Waasdorp.*

Flask, book
  7" h, titled "Spiritual Manifestations
  By" imp on spine, Rockingham
  glaze, mid-19th C, crack. . . **260.00**
  7-3/4" h, untitled, Rockingham glaze,
  roughness to top edge **175.00**
Spittoon, 8-1/2" d, scallop shell form,
Rockingham glaze, 19th C. **175.00**
Toby bottle, 9" h, barrel, Rockingham
glaze, mid-19th C, rim and base
chips. **175.00**

BISCUIT JARS

History: The biscuit or cracker jar was the forerunner of the cookie jar. Biscuit jars were made of various materials by leading glassworks and potteries of the late 19th and early 20th centuries.

Note: All items listed have silver-plated mountings unless otherwise noted.

Bristol glass, 6-1/2" h, all over enameled pink, blue, white and yellow floral dec, green leaves, SP top, rim, and handle **125.00**
Cased glass, 6-1/4" h, blue, enameled pink roses and green leaves, SP top, rim and handle **145.00**
Cranberry glass, 9" h, 6-1/4" d, two applied clear ring handles, applied clear feet and flower prunt pontil, ribbed finial knob **195.00**
Jasperware, 6" h, white classical cameos, black ground, SP handle, rim, and lid, imp "Wedgwood" **450.00**
Milk glass, barrel shape, multicolored glass beaded flowers and butterfly, silver plate neck and foot mounts, flat engraved lid, swing handle, English, late 19th C. 9-3/4" h **230.00**

New England Glass Co., melon ribbed, pink floral dec, lid and bail missing **60.00**

Nippon China, 7-1/2" h, 4-1/2" w, sq, white, multicolored floral bands, gold outlines and trim **110.00**

Pairpoint, 9-1/2' h, burnt orange, floral dec, blown-out floral base, sgd **350.00**

Royal Bayreuth, Poppy, blue mark. **650.00**

Satin glass, 7-1/4" h, pink, molded shell base, enameled floral dec, SP lid and handle **315.00**

Turquoise, 8" h, hand applied white and coral dot flowers connected by network of squiggly gold lines, white casing, thick base with pontil mark, bright metal fittings **485.00**

Vaseline glass, 7" h, threaded, SP rim, lid, and handle. **160.00**

Wave Crest, 9" h, yellow roses, molded multicolored swirl ground, incised floral and leaf dec on lid, marked "Quadruple Plate" **410.00**

Wavecrest, green shading to white body with two horizontal wavy lines, painted floral design, silver plated lid, $245.

BISQUE

History: Bisque or biscuit china is the name given to wares that have been fired once and have not been glazed.

Bisque figurines and busts, which were popular during the Victorian era, were used on fireplace mantels, dining room buffets, and end tables. Manufacturing was centered in the United States and Europe. By the mid-20th century, Japan was the principal source of bisque items, especially character-related items.

Reference: Susan and Al Bagdade, *Warman's English & Continental Pottery & Porcelain*, 3rd Edition, Krause Publications, 1998.

Hen on Nest, hand painted, minor nicks on inside of basket, 8-1/2" l, $225. Photo courtesy of Joy Luke Auctions.

Center bowl, 8-3/4" h, figural, pierced bowl supported by tripod feet modeled as cherubs, white, France, 19th C. **575.00**

Dish, cov, 9" x 6-1/2" x 5-1/2", dog, brown, and white, green blanket, white and gilt basketweave base **500.00**

Doll, 15" h, tinted bisque shoulder head, painted blue eyes, single stroke brows, closed mouth, molded and painted blond hair, cloth body with bisque lower arms and lower legs with molded socks and shoes, dressed in orig Scottish lad outfit. **225.00**

Figural group, 19-1/2" l, 9" w, 13" h, Napoleon and Josephine playing with their daughters, alfresco setting, oval base, flat leaf gilt-metal bands, gilt-metal base mounted with mythic beasts and Napoleon's cipher, Continental, early 20th C **1,725.00**

Figure

12" h, 3-3/8" d, young boy, dressed in pastel blue, carries blue hat and flower, gold and lavender floral trim, gold dot trim on suit . . **155.00**

17-3/4" h, snowy egret, amidst cattails, naturalistic base, Cybis, numbered "12," 20th C **290.00**

20-3/4" h, man offering lady a rose, Victorian costumes, polychrome dec, German, 19th C, pr . . **325.00**

Match holder, figural, Dutch girl, copper and gold trim. **45.00**

Nodder, 2-1/2" x 3-1/2", jester, seated holding pipe, pastel peach and white, gold trim **85.00**

Piano baby

Crawling, crying, marked "Made in Japan" **20.00**

Lying on stomach, wearing bib, dog, and cat, 6-3/4" l, German. . **100.00**

Planter, carriage, four wheels, pale blue and pink, white ground, gold dots, royal markings. **165.00**

Salt, 3" d, figural, walnut, cream, branch base, matching spoon . . **75.00**

Wall plaque, 10-1/4" d, light green, scrolled and pierced scallop, white relief figures in center, man playing mandolin, lady wearing hat, c1900, pr. **275.00**

BITTERS BOTTLES

History: Bitters, a "remedy" made from natural herbs and other mixtures with an alcohol base, often was viewed as the universal cure-all. The names given to various bitter mixtures were imaginative, though the bitters seldom cured what their makers claimed.

The manufacturers of bitters needed a way to sell and advertise their products. They designed bottles in many shapes, sizes, and colors to attract the buyer. Many forms of advertising, including trade cards, billboards, signs, almanacs, and novelties, proclaimed the virtues of a specific bitter.

During the Civil War, a tax was levied on alcoholic beverages. Since bitters were identified as medicines, they were exempt from this tax. The alcoholic content was never mentioned. In 1926, when the Pure Foods Regulations went into effect, "an honest statement of content on every label" put most of the manufacturers out of business.

References: Ralph and Terry Kovel, *Kovels' Bottles Price List,* 11th ed., Three Rivers Press, 1999; John Odell, *Digger Odell's Official Antique Bottle and Glass Collector Magazine Price Guide Series,* Vol. 2, published by author (1910 Shawhan Road, Morrow, OH 45152), 1995; Carlyn Ring, *For Bitters Only,* published by author 203 Kensington Road, Hampton Falls, NH 03844), 1980; J. H. Thompson, *Bitters Bottles,* Century House, 1947; Richard Watson, *Bitters Bottles,* Thomas Nelson and Sons, 1965; Jeff Wichmann, *Antique Western Bitter Bottles,* Pacific Glass Books, 1999; —, *The Best of the West Antique Western Bitters Bottles,* Pacific Glass Books, 1999.

Periodicals: *Antique Bottle and Glass Collector,* P.O. Box 180, East Greenville, PA 18041, www.glswrk-auctions.com; The *Bitters Report,* P.O. Box 1253, Bunnell, FL 32110.

A. S. Hopkins Union Stomach Bitters, greenish-yellow, applied tapered collar lip, smooth base, 9-1/4" h **265.00**

Alpine Herb Bitters, amber, sq, smooth base, tooled lip, 9-5/8" h **175.00**

Baker's Orange Grove Bitters, yellowish-amber, smooth base, applied mouth, 90-1/2" h **185.00**

Bell's Cocktail Bitters, Jas. M. Bell & Co., New York, amber, applied ring, smooth base, 10-1/2" h **450.00**

Browns Celebrated Indian Herb Bitters/Patented Feb. 11, 1868, figural, emb, golden amber, ground lip, smooth base, 12-1/4" h **350.00**

Bourbon Whiskey Bitters, barrel shape, cherry puce, applied sq collar, smooth base, 9-3/4" h **500.00**

Caldwell's Herb Bitters/The Great Tonic, triangular, beveled and lattice work panels, yellowish-amber, applied tapered lip, iron pontil **395.00**

Clarke's Vegetable Sherry Wine Bitters, aqua, smooth base, applied mouth, 14" h **575.00**

Dr. Loew's Celebrated Stomach Bitters & Nerve Tonic, green, smooth base, tooled lip, 9-1/4" h **150.00**

Drake's Plantation Bitters, puce, Arabaseque design, tapered lip, smooth base, 9-3/4" h **295.00**

Godfrey's Celebrated Cordial Bitters, NY, aqua, pontil, applied mouth, 10" h **1,225.00**

Greeley's Bourbon Bitters, barrel shape, smoky gray-brown, sq collared lip, smooth base, 9-1/4" h **225.00**

Doyles 1872, amber, raised fruit design, 9-3/4" h, $115.

Hibernia Bitters, amber, sq, smooth base, tooled lip, 9-1/4" h **125.00**

Hops & Malt Bitters, golden amber, tapered collar lip, smooth base, 9-1/8" h **250.00**

J. C.& Co., molded pineapple form, deep golden amber, blown molded, 19th C, 8-1/2" h **460.00**

Kelly's Old Cabin Bitters, cabin shape, amber, sloping collar lip, smooth base, 9" h **725.00**

Keystone Bitters, barrel shape, golden amber, applied tapered collar, sq lip, smooth base, 9-3/4" h **175.00**

McKeever's Army Bitters, amber, sloping collared lip, smooth base, 10-5/8" h **1,700.00**

Mist of the Morning Sole Agents Barnett & Lumley, golden amber, sloping collar lip, smooth base, 9-3/4" h **300.00**

National Bitters, corn-cob shape, puce amber, applied ring lip, smooth base, 12-5/8" h **350.00**

Red Jacket Bitters, Monheimer & Co., sq, amber, tooled lip, smooth base, 9-1/2" h **100.00**

Schroeder's Bitters, Louisville, KY, amber, tooled lip, smooth base, 11-3/4" h **350.00**

Simon's Centennial Bitters, George Washington bust shape, aqua, applied mouth, smooth base, 9-1/8" h . . **650.00**

Suffolk Bitters, Philbrook & Tucker, Boston, pig shape, amber, applied mouth, smooth base, 10-1/8" l . . **600.00**

Sunny Castle Stomach Bitters, Jos. Dudenhoefer, Milwaukee, sq, amber, tooled lip, smooth base, 9" h . . . **125.00**

Tippecanoe, Warner & Co., amber, applied mushroom lip, 9" h **95.00**

Warner's Safe Bitters, amber, applied mouth, smooth base, 8-1/2" h . . **265.00**

Zingan Bitters, amber, applied mouth, smooth base, 11-7/8" h **150.00**

BLACK MEMORABILIA

History: The term "Black memorabilia" refers to a broad range of collectibles that often overlap other collecting fields, e.g., toys and postcards. It also encompasses African artifacts, items created by slaves or related to the slavery era, modern Black cultural contributions to literature, art, etc., and material associated with the Civil Rights Movement and the Black experience throughout history.

The earliest known examples of Black memorabilia include primitive African designs and tribal artifacts. Black Americana dates back to the arrival of African natives upon American shores.

The advent of the 1900s saw an incredible amount and variety of material depicting Blacks, most often in a derogatory and dehumanizing manner that clearly reflected the stereotypical attitude held toward the Black race during this period. The popularity of Black portrayals in this unflattering fashion flourished as the century wore on.

As the growth of the Civil Rights Movement escalated and aroused public awareness to the Black plight, attitudes changed. Public outrage and pressure during the early 1950s eventually put a halt to these offensive stereotypes.

Black representations are still being produced in many forms, but no longer in the demoralizing designs of the past. These modern objects, while not as historically significant as earlier examples, will become the Black memorabilia of tomorrow.

References: Douglas Congdon-Martin, *Images in Black: 150 Years of Black Collectibles,* 2nd ed., Schiffer, 1999; Kyle Husfloen (ed.), *Black Americana Price Guide,* Antique Trader Books, 1997; Kevin Keating and Michael Kolleth, *The Negro Leagues Autograph Guide,* Tuff Stuff Books, 1999; Jan Lindenberger, *Black Memorabilia for the Kitchen: A Handbook and Price Guide,* 2nd ed., Schiffer, 1999; —, *More Black Memorabilia,* 2nd ed., Schiffer Publishing, 1999; J. L. Mashburn, *Black Postcard Price Guide* 2nd ed., Colonial House, 1999; Dawn Reno, *Encyclopedia of Black Collectibles,* Wallace-Homestead/Krause, 1996; J. P. Thompson, *Collecting Black Memorabilia,* L-W Book Sales, 1996; Jean Williams Turner, *Collectible Aunt Jemima,* Schiffer Publishing, 1994.

Periodical: *Blackin,* 559 22nd Ave., Rock Island, IL 61201.

Collectors' Club: Black Memorabilia Collector's Association, 2482 Devoe Ter, Bronx, NY 10468.

Museums: African American Museum, Cleveland, OH; Great Plains Black Museum, Omaha, NE 68110; Museum of African American History, Detroit, MI; National Afro-American Museum & Culture Center, Wilberforce, OH; Orans' Black Americana Historical Museum, Omaha, NE.

Reproduction Alert: Reproductions are becoming an increasing problem, from advertising signs (Bull Durham tobacco) to mechanical banks (Jolly Nigger). If the object looks new to you, chances are that it is new.

Andirons, 12-1/2" w, 16-1/2" d, 19-1/2" h, cast iron and polychrome, figural man, white shirts, red pants, c1870, paint imperfections, minor corrosion **1,880.00**

Animation, minstrel group, 17 animated carved gesso and polychrome figures, late 19th/early 20th C **29,325.00**

Autograph, ALS

Burleigh, Charles Calistus, addressed to Francis Gannon, son of William Lloyd Garrison, Boston, September 1860, one pg, 8vo, "May you live to see the last fetter broken from the limbs of the slave in this pretended land of freedom; & meanwhile may you so live as to earn a full right to join in the song of jubilee at the triumph of liberty" **690.00**

Crawford, A. M. F., to Messrs Dickenson & Hill, Richmond slave dealers, Charlottesville, VA, April 1854, notifying them that slave bearing letter is to be sold on Crawford's behalf, one pg, 4to, some staining **4,170.00**

Badge, 3-1/2" x 7-1/2", rect, card stock, black letters, brown ground, "Marching for Equal Rights Now! To Be Free by 1963-Emancipation 100 Years," GOP Convention, July 1960 . . . . **215.00**

Bank, mechanical, Jolly Nigger, cast iron, 6-1/4" h, $775. Photo courtesy of Joy Luke Auctions.

Banner, 40" x 48", Martin Luther King Jr., 1929-1968, black printing on white, center bust of King, slogan "Make His Dream a Reality," grommets in corners **440.00**

Baseball cap, Kansas City Black Royals Negro League, white, gray pinstripes, worn black visor, large black "KC" stitched on front, c1920 . . **930.00**

Book

Argument Before the Supreme Court, Appellants vs Cinque, and

Others, Africans, Captured in the Schooner Amistad, John Quincy Adams, New York, 1841, 135 pgs, 8vo, orig shelf wrappers, covers lightly soiled, scattered minor foxing **1,840.00**

A Report of the Decision of the Supreme Court of the United States and the Opinions of the Judges Thereof, in the case of Dred Scott versus John F. A. Sandford, Benjamin C. Howard, New York, 1857, 8vo, first edition, publisher's wrappers, minor foxing and wear **2,300.00**

A Sketch of Henry Franklin and Family, Henry Franklin, Collins Printing House, Philadelphia, 1887, 5 pgs, 8vo, orig lettered wrappers, inscribed and sgd on front cover, ex-library, inked marks **350.00**

Our World: or, The Slaveholder's Daughter, Francis Coburn Adams, Orton, Miller & Mulligan, 1855, first edition, engraved frontispiece, 9 plates, 8vo, publisher's cloth, worn, corners bumped, foxing . . . **115.00**

The Work of Colored Women-YMCA-1919, War Work Council of the YMCA, photos, chart, worn, small spine tear **425.00**

Who's Who in Colored America, Volume I, J. Joseph Boris, ed., New York, 1927, first edition, portrait plates, small 4to, orig cloth **375.00**

Women of Achievement, Benjamin Brawley, Woman's American Baptist Home Mission Society, 1919, portrait plates, small 8vo, orig cloth **375.00**

Carte-de-Visite

Colored Baptist Church, Petersburg, VA, Lazell & McMillin, Petersburg, photographers, 1966, ext. view, men and women sitting on front fence, pencil inscription "Church of Petersburg Negroes burned by rebels, given by Lottie, Feb 9th, 1868," soil, wear, slight crimp **345.00**

Frederick Douglas, full-length portrait, c1860, erased pencil marks on top border **550.00**

Runaway Slave-60 Mile Marcher, seated black barefoot man, McPhearson & Oliver, Baton Rouge, LA, photographer, back marked "Contraband that marched 60 miles to get in our lines," c1862 . . . . **1,030.00**

Sojourner Truth, 3/4 view, seated at table, knitting, "I Sell the Shadow to Support the Substance," 1864, corners clipped, toning, light browning **660.00**

Cigar box label, 6-1/4" x 10", glossy paper label, Booker T., Perfecto Cigars, black and white portrait of Booker T. Washington, red, pale blue, and dark blue border, white stars, c1930s, unused **20.00**

Cigarette lighter, 6" l, 3" d, 6-3/4" h, figural metal, cast metal black bartender mixing cocktail behind fully stocked bar, flanking side compartments open to hold cigarettes, center panel lighter, striated wood grain brown and black enameled bar, black painted base, marked "Ronson Touch-Tip, Art Metal Works, Incentury, Newark, New Jersey," c1936, one shaker replaced . . **1,475.00**

Coffee can, Welcome Guest Coffee, tin litho, black butler carrying serving tray on both sides, red ground, 2-1/2" pound size, 5-1/2" d, 7-5/8" h, C.7.5 . . . **625.00**

Doll

8-3/4" h, papier-mâché shoulder head, black painted head and features, short curly hair, red lips, painted goldtone necklace, milliner's model style brown cloth body, wood lower limbs, pink cotton dress overlaid with tiers of lace, mid-19th C, fine crack on shoulder head **750.00**

9" to 30" h, Golliwogg, painted and applied features, black plush strip hair, bodies formed by clothing, blue jackets, red plaid or striped pants, English, c1950, set of six graduated sizes, minor wear and damage **300.00**

12" h, Mammy, nut head, painted features, looped plush hair, whisk broom body, orig commercial assemblage, pink print dress, twin black babies in green print organdy outfits, early 20th C **635.00**

15-1/2" h, painted oil cloth, dark brown painted head, shoulders, and lower arms, flat face, black painted eyes and nose, white accents, no wig, sewn-on red print bandanna, blue cloth legs, red painted shoes, print dress, American, early 20th C **750.00**

Figure, Eva and Uncle Tom, Staffordshire, 8-1/4" h, $475. Photo courtesy of Joy Luke Auctions.

16" h, handmade stuffed cloth, stockinette head, needle sculptured nose, ears, and chin, painted eyes and mouth, wire earrings, yard braids, black cloth body **600.00**

18" h, Mammy, stuffed cloth, hand embroidered features, red trimmed dress, blue and white cap, wear, damage **220.00**

20" h, Golliwog, velveteen face, hands, and feet, applied felt eyes and mouth, inked nose, yellow checked shirt, golden crepe pants, red braid trim, removable gray and white checked wool jacket, c1930, some wear and soil **460.00**

27-1/2" h, topsy-turvy type, painted black and white faces, calico and chintz clothing, c1860, some soil and wear on white doll, black doll clean and bright **1,320.00**

Paper ephemera

Bill of Sale, mother and daughter, recording payment of $500, Amherst County, VA, October 1812, one pg, folio, docketed on verso **690.00**

Certificate of Freedom, for Thomas Chambers, resident of New York City, September 1814, partly printed document, sgd, small folio, docketed on verso **920.00**

Deed of Sale, male slave for 90 pounds current money, Frederick County, MD, November 1768, two pgs, single folio sheet, red wax seal partially destroyed ... **750.00**

Document of Emancipation, for Negro girl slave, 14 years old, Halifax County, VA, June 1793, one pg, oblong 8vo, 5-3/4" x 7-3/4", trimmed along bottom edge with loss of signature **375.00**

Graduation Certificate, Indianapolis, 1915, partially printed, Lelia College, made out to Mary E. Moody, for completion of course work, sgd by C. J. Walker, browned, horizontal separation, mounted to stiff board, framed, 10-3/4" x 11-1/2" **420.00**

Handbill, 5-1/2" x 8-1/2", "Save Our Lives," photos of Clarence Norris and Hayward Patterson, "They Must Not Burn Dec 7-Join the Fight to Free Them," fold in center **245.00**

Letter, three pgs, folio, handwritten, Detroit, Michigan Territory, May 1829, to ex-master stating he ran away because he was to be sold, lamenting treatment of his wife **1,265.00**

Letter, 7-3/4" x 9-3/4", handwritten, Paris, TN, Oct. 27, 1833, apology concern proposed sale of married slaves, slight soiling **200.00**

Manuscript, unpublished, Hannah Crafts, *The Bondswoman's Narrative by Hannah Crafts, a Fugitive Slave, recently Escaped from North Carolina,* New Jersey, c1850, 301 pgs, 4to, cloth, extremities worn **9,775.00**

Minutes, Proceedings of the Committee appointed by the Committee of the Pennsylvania Abolition Society, for the improving the Condition of Free Blacks, to take charge of those sent from Jamaica by David Barclay & Others, Philadelphia, June 1795 to March 1796, 49 pgs, small 4to, contemporary wrappers, detached, dampstained, ex-library **7,475.00**

Pamphlet, *Slavery as It Is: Testimony of a Thousand Witnesses,* Theodore Weld, New York, 1839, 8vo, orig lettered wrappers, nicks, rear cover missing, few pencil markings on title page **290.00**

Pamphlet, *The Gospel to be Given to Our Servants, A Sermon,* Rev.

Paul Trapier, Charleston, 1847, 24 pgs, 8vo, disbound, scattered foxing **690.00**

Seaman's passport, Philadelphia, April 1834, partly printed, for Robert Barnaby, "black complexion, black eyes, wooly hair," one pg, oblong 4to, emb seal of Customs Office of Philadelphia **520.00**

Stock certificate, *Black Star Line,* Garvey Marcus, company president, one share, 1919, 8-3/4" x 10-3/4" **4,600.00**

Poster

5-1/2" x 14", Corning, Look for Date, Satchel Paige, at Holding, Mo, Thurs, June 22, 8:30 PM, Holden Chiefs vs. Hilton Smith's Eagles, full-length portrait of Satchel Paige, white ground, red and black lettering, some toning **2,630.00**

Painting, oil on board, African American man with basket of cotton, signed "W. A. Walker," 6" w, 12" h, modern frame, $7,700. Photo courtesy of Garth's Auction, Inc.

9" x 11", Negro Woman for Sale, Jackson, May 1852, to settle estate, terms specified, framed **2,530.00**

11-3/4" x 6-1/2", Topsy or Slave Girl's Appeal to the Visitors and Patrons of the Anti-Slavery Bazaar, held in Boston, December 1852, letterpress, ornamental border, lightly toned **1,035.00**

12" x 8-1/2", broadside selling gang of 101 Negroes by John B. Habersham & Co., Macon, GA, 1863, letterpress, listing names with spaces to add prices realized, some browning and folds **27,600.00**

20" x 16", Emancipation Proclamation, R. A. Dimmick, New York, 1864, engraved, text surrounded by oval vignette of Lincoln draped in two American flags, American eagle above with dates 1861-1863 on either side, three engraved vignettes of slavery scenes, scenes of freedom, signatures in print of Lincoln and Seward at bottom of text, some chipping to edge **2,530.00**

28" x 42", The Flaming Crisis, multi-colored, black man in jail cell, ghost of another man pointing to him "with a Notable Cast of Colored Artists," Monarch Production, c1920, archival backing . . . **825.00**

Print

12-3/4" x 14-3/4", litho, *The Resurrection of Henry Box Brown at Philadelphia,* Kramer, Rosenthal, Philadelphia, c1850, browned, few repaired tears, some damp-staining, matted, archivally conserved **2,990.00**

13-1/4" x 9-3/4", litho, *I'm Not to Blame for Being White Sir,* young white child holding out her hand for coins while passing stranger places coins in hands of black child, c1850, heavily toned **290.00**

Roly poly, Mayo's Roly Poly Tobacco, Mammy, litho tin, 7" x 5-1/4", two pcs, C-8+ **825.00**

Tintype, man wearing vest coat, hat, sixth plate, liner and gutta-percha case damaged **110.00**

Ventriloquist's figure, 30" h, polychrome carved wood, man, head with horsehair, glass eyes, leather jar, cloth body, period clothing, America, late 19th C, stand **5,060.00**

BLOWN THREE MOLD

History: The Jamestown colony in Virginia introduced glassmaking into America. The artisans used a "free-blown" method.

Blowing molten glass into molds was not introduced into America until the early 1800s. Blown three-mold glass used a pre-designed mold that consisted of two, three, or more hinged parts. The glassmaker placed a quantity of molten glass on the tip of a rod or tube, inserted it into the mold, blew air into the tube, waited until the glass cooled, and removed the finished product. The three-part mold is the most common and lends its name to this entire category.

The impressed decorations on blown-mold glass usually are reversed, i.e., what is raised or convex on the outside will be concave on the inside. This is useful in identifying the blown form.

By 1850, American-made glassware was relatively common. Increased demand led to large factories and the creation of a technology which eliminated the smaller companies.

Reference: George S. and Helen McKearin, *American Glass*, reprint, Crown Publishers, 1941, 1948.

Collectors' Club: Early American Pattern Glass Society, P.O. Box 266, Colesburg, IA 52035; National Early American Glass Club, P.O. Box 8489, Silver Spring, MD 20907.

Museum: Sandwich Glass Museum, Sandwich, MA.

Toilet water bottle, medium blue, 12 panels, Boston & Sandwich Glass, McKearin GI-7, type 5, 6" h, **$195.**

Bottle, 7-1/4" h, olive green, McKearin GIII-16 . . . . **330.00**

Bowl, 5-3/8" d, colorless, folded rim, pontil, 12-diamond base, McKearin GII-6 . . . . **125.00**

Celery vase, colorless, Pittsburgh, McKearin GV-21 . . . . **650.00**

Cordial, 2-7/8" h, colorless, ringed base, pontil, heavy circular foot, free-hand formed, McKearin GII-18 . **550.00**

Creamer, 3-1/2" h, colorless, applied handle **125.00**

Cruet, 7-3/4" h, cobalt blue, scroll scale pattern, ribbed base, pontil, applied handle, French **265.00**

Decanter

6-3/4" h, olive-amber, pint, attributed to Marlboro Street Glass Works, Keene, NH, some abrasions **460.00**

8" h, colorless, three applied rings, McKearin GII-18, replaced wheel stopper **110.00**

8-1/4" h, colorless, McKearin GII-19, replaced wheel stopper **115.00**

8-1/2" h, light sea green, Kent-Ohio pattern, McKearin GII-6 . . **2,415.00**

10" h, colorless, arch and fern design, snake medallion, McKearin GIV-7, minor chips, mold imperfections **165.00**

11" h, colorless, sunburst in square, minor chips, mold imperfections **150.00**

Dish, colorless

5-1/4" d, McKearin GII-16 . . . . **65.00**

5-1/2" d, McKearin GII-18 . . . . **50.00**

Flip glass, colorless

5-1/2" h, McKearin GII-18 . . . **165.00**

6" h, McKearin GII-18 . . . . . . **125.00**

Ink bottle, 2-1/4" d, deep olive green, McKearin GII-2 . . . . **195.00**

Miniature, 2-5/8" h decanter, colorless, McKearin GIII-12 . . . . **165.00**

Mustard, 4-1/4" h, colorless, pontil, cork stopper, orig paper label, McKearin GI-15 . . . . **85.00**

Pitcher, 7" h, colorless, base of handle reglued, McKearin GIII-5 . . . . . **145.00**

Salt, basket shape, colorless . . **120.00**

Toilet water bottle, 5-3/4" h, cobalt blue, tam-o-shanter cap **300.00**

Tumbler, 6-1/4" h, colorless, McKearin GII-19 . . . . **155.00**

Vinegar bottle, cobalt blue, ribbed, orig stopper, McKearin GI-7 . . . **285.00**

Whiskey glass, 2-3/8" h, colorless, applied handle, McKearin GII-18 . . . . **285.00**

BOHEMIAN GLASS

History: The once independent country of Bohemia, now a part of the Czech Republic, produced a variety of fine glassware: etched, cut, overlay, and colored. Its glassware, which first appeared in America in the early 1820s, continues to be exported to the U.S. today.

Bohemia is known for its "flashed" glass that was produced in the familiar ruby color, as well as in amber, green, blue, and black. Common patterns include Deer and Castle, Deer and Pine Tree, and Vintage.

Most of the Bohemian glass encountered in today's market is from 1875 to 1900. Bohemian-type glass also was made in England, Switzerland, and Germany.

References: Dr. James D. Henderson, *Bohemian Decorated Porcelain,* Schiffer Publishing, 1999; Sylvia Petrova and Jean-Luc Olivie (eds.), *Bohemian Glass,* Abrams, 1990; Robert and Deborah Truitt, *Collectible Bohemian Glass, 1880-1940,* R & D Glass, 1995; —, *Collectible Bohemian Glass, Volume II, 1915-1945,* R & D Glass, 1998; —, *Mary Gregory Glassware, 1880-1990,* R & D Glass, 1992, 1998 value update.

Reproduction Alert.

Berry set, 10-5/8" d bowl, five 6" d bowls, blue overlay cut with crenelated edge, shaped flutes, etched with roses, gilt enamel detailing, late 19th C **1,150.00**

Box, cov, 5-1/8" l, 4" d, 4" h, blue and white cased cut to clear, rect, clipped corners, oval and star cut panels, brass-hinged lid and escutcheon, late 19th C **635.00**

Cologne bottle, 5" h, cobalt blue, tiered body dec, white and gold flowers and scrolls **175.00**

Compote, 7" d, amber flashed, cut leaf and floral dec, green band at top, pedestal base **125.00**

Cruet, amber cut to clear, floral arrangement intaglio carved on ruby flashed ground of three oval panels with carved frames of floral swags, five cut-to-clear panels at neck, three embellished with gold scrolls, all edged in brilliant gold, 16 decorative panels edged in gold, base and stopper both sgd "4" **750.00**

Decanter set, 10-1/4" w, 20-1/2" h, three 14" h shouldered decanters, flashed blue, green, and cranberry, cut with circles, etched Greek key band, silver plated stand with tall central handle above three cylindrical wells, with geometric engine turning, borders with fruiting grapevine, three grapevine feet, late 19th C **865.00**

Goblet, 6-3/4" h, white and cranberry overlay, thistle form bowl, six teardrop panels alternately enameled with floral

bouquets and cut with blocks of diamonds, faceted knob and spreading scalloped foot, gilt trim **600.00**

Jar, 6" h, quatraform, green, maroon-red threading, metal rim, swing bail handle and cover **250.00**

Jewel box, 5-1/8" w, 4" d, 4-3/8" h, white overlay cut to cranberry, oblong, gilt-metal hinge mount, cut with roundels and leaves, roundels enamel dec with floral bouquets, gilt details, late 19th C **1,035.00**

Mantel lusters, pair, hand painted floral decoration, white cased over pink, cut prisms, 9" h, **$425.** *Photo courtesy of Alderfer Auction.*

Mantel lusters, pr, 11-1/2" h, white cased cut to green, trumpet shaped body, scalloped edge, pillar flutes, lozenge cuts, gilt edging, stippled roundels, hung with faceted cut glass drops, spreading foot, late 19th C **700.00**

Perfume bottle, 7" h, ruby flashed, Deer and Castle, clear and frosted, gold dec **120.00**

Powder box, 4-1/4" d, round, straight sides, flat top, ruby flashed, etched cov with leaping stag, forest setting, landscape and birds on sides, clear base **120.00**

Tazza, 8-3/8" h, white cased cut to clear, bowl with circular cuts and serpentine edge, lobed silver plate foot, late 19th C **175.00**

Urn, cov, 15-3/4" h, colorless, paneled bell-shaped body, tapered octagonal lid with stepped octagonal finial, short baluster stem on octagonal foot, star cut base, late 19th C, price for pr **750.00**

Vase

6-1/4" h, beaker form, blue cased cut to clear, pattern of grape clusters

and leaves, etched tendril detailing, early 20th C **75.00**
12-5/8" h, cranberry flashed conical body, long pillar flutes, scalloped edge, classical-style ormolu tripod base, three pendant rings suspending from flat leaf scrolls, flat leaf and anthemion legs, late 19th/early 20th C, price for pr **1,380.00**

Wine goblet, 7-1/8" h, cup-shaped bowl, decorated with C-scrolls and floral swags, twisted baluster stem between flattened knops, stem with further C-scrolls, quatrefoil pincer-molded foot with diapered C-scroll cartouches, late 19th C, set of 17 goblets, two damaged **3,910.00**

BOOKS, GENEALOGY

History: Finding one's roots has always been an interesting hobby. Some families have taken the information gathered and created wonderful books detailing the lives and genealogical lines of ancestors. As today's researchers dig into their backgrounds, many of these older genealogical books are eagerly sought after.

Today the Internet and computer programs have also become tools for researchers. Many early records have been microfilmed during the years and now these microfilm records are being converted to CD-roms, etc. When researching family roots, be sure to check out old church records, deeds, wills, and other types of personal papers. Many small libraries have excellent collections of materials relating to their geographical area.

References: *American Book Prices Current,* Bancroft Parkman, published annually; Sharon and Bob Huxford, *Huxford's Old Book Value Guide,* 12th ed., Collector Books, 2001; Ian C. Ellis, *Book Finds,* Berkley Publishing, 1996; Norma Levarie, *Art & History of Books,* available from Spoon River Press, 1995; Catherine Porter, *Collecting Books,* available from Spoon River Press, 1995; Caroline Seebohm, Estelle Ellis, and Christopher Simon Sykes, *At Home with Books: How Book Lovers Live with and Care for Their Libraries,* available from Spoon River Press, 1996; Edward N. Zempel and Linda A. Verkler (eds.), *Book Prices: Used and Rare 1996,* Spoon River Press, 1996; —, *First Editions: A Guide to Identification,* 3rd ed., Spoon River Press, (2319C W Rohmann, Peoria, IL 61604) 1995.

Periodicals: *ABBA Newsletter,* 20 W. 44th St., 4th Floor, New York, NY, 10036-6604, www.abaa.org; *AB Bookman's Weekly,* P.O. Box AB, Clifton, NJ 07015; *Book Source Monthly,* 2007 Syosett Dr., P.O. Box 567, Cazenovia, NY 13035, www.booksourcemonthly.com; *Dime Novel Round-Up,* P.O. Box 226, Dundas, MN 55019-0226; *Firsts, The Book Collector's Magazine,* P.O. Box 65166, Tucson, AZ 85728, www.firsts.com; *Modern Library Collector,* 340 Warren Ave., Cincinnati, OH 45220-1135; *Mystery & Adventure Series Review,* P.O. Box 3488, Tucson, AZ 85772-3488;

Paperback Parade, P.O. Box 209, Brooklyn, NY 11228-0209, www.grphonbooks.com; *Paper Collectors' Marketplace,* P.O. Box 128, Scandinavia, WI 54977, www.pcmpaper.com; *are Book Bulletin,* P.O. Box 201, Peoria, IL 61650; *Used Book Lover's Guides,* Book Hunter Press, P.O. Box 193, Yorktown Heights, NY 10598, www.bookhunterpress.com; *Yellowback Library,* P.O. Box 36172, Des Moines, IA 50315-0310.

Collectors' Clubs: Antiquarian Booksellers Association of America, 20 West 44th St., 4th Floor, New York, NY 10036-6604, www.abaa.org; Antiquarian Booksellers' Assoc., Sackville House, 40 Piccadilly, London W1J 0DR UK, www.ABAinternational.com; Big Little Book Collectors Club of America, P.O. Box 1242, Dansville, CA 94526-8242, www.biglittle-books.com; Florida Bibliophile Society, 1908 Deagull Drive, Clearwater, FL 34624; Illustrator Collector's News, P.O. Box 1958, Sequim, WA 98382, www.olypen.com/ticn; International Book Collectors Assoc., P.O. Box 947, Mechanicsville, MD 20659, www.rarebooks.org; Lewis Carroll Society of North America, 18 Fitzharding Place, Owings Mills, MD 21117, www.lewiscarroll.org; Long Island Antiquarian Book Dealers Assoc., P.O. Box 42, Manhasset, NY 11030, www.liabda@usa.net; North American Jules Verne Society, 539 Verde Drive, Schaumburg, IL 60173-2041, www.interlog.com/~amash/najvs.html

Museums: American Antiquarian Society, Worcester, MA; Consortium of Popular Culture Collection, Popular Culture Library, Bowling Green State University, Bowling Green, OH; Free Library of Philadelphia, Philadelphia, PA; Library of Congress, Washington, DC; Toledo Museum of Art, Toledo, OH.

A Genea-Biographical History of the Rittenhouse Family, David Cassel, Volume 1, Philadelphia, 1933, 1st edition **150.00**

A History of the Descendants of John Lawless II and Margaret Skirvin Lawless, 1968 rev ed. **80.00**

Among The Scotch-Iris...History of Dinemoor Family, Leonard Allison Morrison, Boston Damrills Upham, 1891 . . . . **50.00**

A Stewart Family, W. B. Stewart, Cleveland, OH, 1947, 1st edition, sgd **60.00**

Banks Family, The, Jane Pritchett Banks, 1908 . . . . **80.00**

Boydstun Family, The, Gustaine C. Weaver, Powell & White, 1921, 1st ed **50.00**

Braithwaite, J. Bevan, A Friend of the Nineteenth Century, By His Children, J. Bevan Braithwaite, Hodder, 1909, slight foxing **25.00**

Chronological History of William and Harriet Moore and Their Relatives and Descendants, U. S. Moore, 1904 . . . . **48.00**

Colonial Families of the Southern States of America, Sheila Pickett Hardy, Baltimore, 1958, 2nd ed. **25.00**

Descendants of George Fowle, 1610-1682, Charlestown, Mass, E. C. Fowle, 1990, color illus. **13.00**

Descendants of Michael Moulton Harrison and Related Pioneer Families of the Republic of Texas, privately printed, 1972, 249 pgs **40.00**

Early Friends Families of Upper Bucks, Clarence V. Roberts, 1925, published by the compiler, solid blue cover, 680 pages, **$65**

Family Memorials, Antoinette Bradshaw Shattuck and John Herman Bradshaw, Chicago, 1890, 1st ed. **65.00**

Family Portrait, The Drinker Family of Philadelphia, Catherine Drinker Bowen, Little Brown, 1970, 3rd ed., 301 pgs **16.00**

Friends and Relations, Three Centuries of Quaker Families, Verily Anderson, Hodder and Stoughton, 1980, 1st ed., dj **25.00**

From Mill Wheel to Plowshare, Story of the Contributors of the Christian Orndorff Family to the Social and Industrial History of the United States, Julie Angeline Drake and James Ridgely Orndorff, Torch Press, 1938, 1st ed. **75.00**

Genealogical Gleanings of Siggins and Other Pennsylvania Families, Emma Siggins White, Kansas City, MO, 1st ed., sgd **75.00**

Genealogy Monograph of Edward Dyer Peters, privately printed, 61 pgs. **65.00**

Genealogy of Gallemore, Bullen, McAnulty, Pierce, MacFarland, and Dunlap Families, Esther Gallemore Hold, 1922 . . . . **68.00**

Handy Book for Genealogists, George B. Everton Sr., ed., Everton Pub., 1971, 6th ed. **10.00**

History and Reunion Fally Seminary, Fulton, NY, Morrill Bros., 1890, 1st edition, hard cover **35.00**

History of Peter Parker and Sarah Ruggles of Roxbury, Mass, and Their Ancestors and Descendants, The, John William Litzee, 1913 . . . . **127.50**

History of the Family of Dallas, The, James Dallas, Edinburgh, 1921, 1st edition. **75.00**

Indian Eve and Her Descendants, History, Genealogy, Bradford County, PA, E. Replodge, 1966, reprint of 1911 orig **20.00**

Levering Family, The, Migard and Gerhard Levering, 1958, 1st edition . **50.00**

Manual for the Members of the Old Briery Presbyterian Church of Prince Edward County, Virginia, James W. Douglas, first published 1828, republished 1907 . . . . **48.00**

Memories of Jordans and the Chalfonts, and the Early Friends of The Chiltern Hundreds, W. H. Summers, Headley Brothers, 1895, 1st ed. **30.00**

Notable Men of Illinois & Their State, Chicago, IL, 1912 . . . . **50.00**

Origin, History & Genealogy of the Buck Family, S. Buck, 1917, 215 pgs, illus, ex-library **30.00**

Proceedings of the Reunion of Apples Church & the Boehm Family, Rev. A. Horn, Hellertown, PA, 1902 . . . . . **40.00**

Parr Family History, The, 1968 . . . **11.00**

Research in American Genealogy, E. Kay Kirkham, Descret Book CO., 1956, 447 pgs **12.00**

Riley Smith Emons & Priscilla Eleanor Howard, Their Ancestors & Descendents, Katherina Jane Emmons Taylor, Baltimore, 1965 . . . . **30.00**

Roots in Virginia, Acct of Capt. Thos Hale by Nathaniel Claborne, 1938 . . . . **50.00**

Salisburian, The, history, biography, and genealogical record of the House of Salisbury, Phelps, NY, 1921, 1st ed. **30.00**

Spelman Genealogy, Fannie Cooley, Williams Barbour, NY, 1910 . . . . . **60.00**

Without Drums, Three Generations of the Widener Family, P. A. B. Widener,

G P Putnam Sons, 1940, 279 pgs, worn dj 16.00

BOOTJACKS

History: Bootjacks are metal or wooden devices that facilitate the removal of boots. Bootjacks are used by placing the heel of the boot in the U-shaped opening, putting the other foot on the back of the bootjack, and pulling the boot off the front foot.

Reproduction Alert.

Cast iron, John Van Buren, filigree base, wrench sockets at end, 15-1/4" l, $50.

Brass, 10" l, beetle 95.00

Cast iron

9-3/4" l, Naughty Nellie, painted blond hair, blue ribboned white lingerie, minor wear 150.00

10" l, Naughty Nellie, unpainted, minor wear 100.00

10-1/4" l, lyre shape 50.00

11-1/2" l, intertwined scrolls form letter "M" 35.00

11-3/4" l, crick, emb lacy design 30.00

12" l, tree center 35.00

12-1/2" l, 4-1/2" w, 1-3/4" h, heart-shaped cut-out, America, 19th C, slight corrosion, with stand 220.00

Wood

10" l, tiger stripe maple 25.00

13" l, maple, hand hewn 20.00

15" l, folk art, monkey, painted suit, c1900 .... 35.00

22" l, walnut, heart and diamond openwork 40.00

24" l, pine, rose head nails, pierced for hanging 40.00

25" l, pine, oval ends, sq nails . 30.00

BOTTLES, GENERAL

History: Cosmetic bottles held special creams, oils, and cosmetics designed to enhance the beauty of the user. Some also claimed, especially on their colorful labels, to cure or provide relief from common ailments.

A number of household items, e.g., cleaning fluids and polishes, required glass storage containers. Many are collected for their fine lithographed labels.

Mineral water bottles contained water from a natural spring. Spring water was favored by health-conscious people between the 1850s and 1900s.

Nursing bottles, used to feed the young and sickly, were a great help to the housewife because of their graduated measure markings, replaceable nipples, and the ease with which they could be cleaned, sterilized, and reused.

References: Hugh Cleveland, *Bottle Pricing Guide,* 3rd ed., Collector Books, 1999 value update; Kyle Husfloen, *Antique Trader's American Pressed Glass & Bottles Price Guide,* 2nd ed., Krause Publications, 2000; Ralph & Terry Kovel, *Kovels' Bottles Price List,* 11th ed., Three Rivers Press, 1999; Peck and Audie Markota, *Western Blob Top Soda and Mineral Bottles,* 2nd ed., published by authors, 1994; John Odell, *Digger Odell's Official Antique Bottle and Glass Collector Magazine Price Guide Series,* Vols. 1 through 8, published by author (1910 Shawhan Road, Morrow, OH 45152), 1995; Diane Ostrander, *Guide to American Nursing Bottles,* 1984, revised ed. by American Collectors of Infant Feeders, 1992; Michael Polak, *Bottles,* 3rd ed., Quill, 2000; Dick Roller (comp.), *Indiana Glass Factories Notes,* Acorn Press, 1994; Jeff Wichmann, *Antique Western Bitter Bottles,* Pacific Glass Books, 1999; —, *The Best of the West Antique Western Bitters Bottles,* Pacific Glass Books, 1999.

Periodicals and Internet Resources: *Antique Bottle and Glass Collector,* P.O. Box 180, East Greenville, PA 18041, www.glswrk-auction.com; *Antique Bottle Collectors Haven,* www.antiquebottles.com; *Bottles & Extras,* 2230 Toub St., Ramona, CA 92065, www.fchbc.com; *Canadian Bottle and Stoneware Collector,* 179D Woodridge Crescent, Nepean, Ontario K2B 7T2 Canada; *Glen Poch's Bottle Collecting Newsletter,* 1537 Silver Strand, Palatine, IL 60074; *Miniature Bottle Collector,* P.O. Box 2161, Palos Verdes Peninsula, CA 90274, www.bottlecollecting.com; *World of Bottles & Bygones,* www.members.tripod.co.uk/~MikeSheridan.

Collectors' Clubs: American Collectors of Infant Feeders, 5161 W. 59th St., Indianapolis, IN 46254; Antique Bottle Club of Northern Illinois, 1537 Silver Strand, Palatine, IL 60074; Antique Poison Bottle Collectors Assoc., 312 Summer Lane, Huddlestown, VA 24104; Apple Valley Bottle Collectors Club, 3015 Northwestern Pike, Winchester, VA 22603-3825; Baltimore Antique Bottle Club, P.O. Box 36031, Townson, MD 21296-6061; Capital Region Antique Bottle & Insulator Club, 3363 Guilderland Ave., Apt 3, Schenectady, NY 12306-1820; Del Val Miniature Bottle Club, 57104 Del Aire Landing Road, Philadelphia, PA 19114; East Tennessee Antique Bottle & Collectibles Society, 220 N. Carter School Road, Straw Plains, TN 37871-1237; Empire State Bottle Collectors Assoc., 115 Marshia Ave., North Syracuse, NY 13212; Federation of Historical Bottle Collectors, Inc., 2230 Toub St., Ramona, CA 92065, www.fchbc.com; First Chicago Bottle Club, P.O. Box A3382, Chicago, IL 60690; Forks of the Delaware Bottle Collectors Assoc., 20 Cambridge Place, Catasauqua, PA 18032; Genessee Valley Bottle Collectors Assoc., 17 Fifth Ave., Fairport, NY 14450-1311; Great Lakes Miniature Bottle Club, 19734 Woodmont, Harper Woods, MI 48225; Historical Bottle Diggers of Virginia, 242 E. Grattan St., Harrisonburg, VA 22801; Hudson Valley Antique Bottle Club, 6 Columbian Ave., Cornwall on Hudson,

NY 12520; Huron Valley Antique Bottle & Insulator Club, 2475 W. Walton Blvd., Waterford, MI 48329-4435; Las Vegas Antique Bottle & Collectibles Club, 5895 Dunesville St., Las Vegas, NV 89118; Lilliputian Bottle Club, 54 Village Circle, Manhattan Beach, CA 90366; Midwest Antique Fruit Jar & Bottle Club, P.O. Box 38, Flat Rock, IN 47234; Midwest Miniature Bottle Collector, P.O. Box 240388, Apple Valley, MN 55124-0388; Middle Tennessee Bottle & Collector's Club, 1750 Keyes Road, Greenbrier, TN 37073; Milk Route, 4 Ox Bow Road, Westport, CT 06880-2602; New England Antique Bottle Club, 120 Commonwealth Road, Lynn, MA 01904; North Jersey Antique Bottle Collectors Assoc., 117 Lincoln Place, Waldwick, NJ 07463-2114; North Star Historical Bottle Assoc., 3308 32nd Ave. South, Minneapolis, MN 55406-2015; Ohio Bottle Club, 7126 12th St., Minerva, OH 44657; Pennsylvania Bottle Collector's Assoc., 251 Eastland Ave., York, PA 17402-1105; Pittsburgh Antique Bottle Club, 650 Hood School Road, Indiana, PA 15701; Potomac Bottle Collectors, 4028 Williamsburg Court, Fairfax, VA 22032-1139; Raleigh Bottle Club, P.O. Box 13736, Durham, NC 27709; Richmond Area Bottle Collectors Assoc., 4718 Kyloe Lane, Moseley, VA 23210; San Bernardino County Historical Bottle and Collectible Club, 22853 DeBerry, Grand Terrace, CA 92313; San Jose Antique Bottle Collectors Assoc., P.O. Box 5432, San Jose, CA 95150-5432; Sarasota-Manatee Antique Bottle Collectors Assoc., P.O. Box 3105, Sarasota, FL 34230-3105; Southeastern Antique Bottle Club, 143 Scatterfoot Dr., Peachtree City, GA 30269-1853; Violin Bottle Collectors Assoc., 158 Rosamond St., Carleton Place, Ontario, K7C 1V2, Canada; Western New York Miniature Bottle Club, P.O. Box 182, Cheekwaga, NY 14225; Yankee Bottle Club, 382 Court St., Keene, NH 03431; 49er Historical Bottle Club, P.O. Box 561, Penryn, CA 95663.

Museums: Hawaii Bottle Museum, Honolulu, Hawaii; National Bottle Museum, Ballston Spa, New York, www.family.knick.net/nbm; National Bottle Museum, Nr. Barnsley, South Yorks, UK; Old Bottle Museum, Salem, New Jersey.

Additional Listings: Barber Bottles, Bitter Bottles, Figural Bottles, Food Bottles, Ink Bottles, Medicine Bottles, Poison Bottles, Sarsaparilla Bottles, and Snuff Bottles. Also see the bottle categories in *Warman's Americana & Collectibles* for more examples.

Beverage

Arny & Shinn, Georgetown, D. C., "This Bottle Is Never Sold," soda water, squat cylindrical, yellow ground, applied heavy collared mouth, smooth base, half pink, professionally cleaned **150.00**

Bay Rum, 11-1/4" h, amethyst, blown molded, paneled body, partial label, burst bubble, mold imperfections **375.00**

Cole & Southey Washington DC, soda water, squat cylindrical, aquamarine, applied sloping collared mouth with ring, smooth base, half pint, professionally cleaned **110.00**

M. Flanagan Petersburg Va, Philadelphia XXX Porter & Ale, squat cylindrical, green with olive tone, heavy applied collared mouth, iron pontil mark, half pint, overall ext. wear **230.00**

Cosmetic

De Vry's Dandero-Off Hair Tonic, clear, paper label, 6-1/2" h **15.00**

Kickapoo Sage Hair Tonic, cylindrical, cobalt blue, tooled mouth, matching stopper, smooth base, 5" h **160.00**

Kranks Cold Cream, milk glass, 2-3/4" h **6.50**

Pompeian Massage Cream, amethyst, 2-3/4" h **9.00**

Violet Dulce Vanishing Cream, eight panels, 2-1/2" h **7.50**

Household

Demijohn, 18-3/4" h, olive, blown, straight sides, long neck, applied lip, whittled mold, attributed to Vermont **115.00**

Ink, Waterman's, paper label with bottle of ink, wooden bullet shaped case, orig paper label, 4-1/4" h **10.00**

Sewing Machine Oil, Sperm Brand, clear, 5-1/2" h **5.00**

Shoe Polish, Everett & Barron Co., oval, clear, 4-3/4" **5.00**

Mineral or spring water

Albergh A. Spring, VT, cylindrical, apricot amber, applied sloping collared mouth with ring, smooth base, quart, rare with misspelling **1,000.00**

Alburgh A. Spring, VT, cylindrical, golden yellow, applied sloping collared mouth with ring, smooth base, quart **800.00**

Caladonia Spring Wheelock VT, cylindrical, golden amber, applied sloping collared mouth with ring, smooth base, quart **130.00**

Chalybeate Water of the American Spa Spring Co., N. J., cylindrical, light to medium blue green, olive green slag striation neck, applied heavy collared mouth, smooth base, pint **400.00**

Champlain Spring, Alkaline Chalybeate, Highgate, VT, cylindrical, emerald green, applied sloping collared mouth with ring, smooth base, quart. . . **200.00**

Gettysburgh Katalysine Water, yellow olive, applied sloping collared mouth with ring, smooth base, quart. . . **200.00**

Guilford Mineral Spring Water, Guilford VT, cylindrical, yellow-olive, applied sloping collard mouth with ring, smooth base, quart **475.00**

Hopkins Chalybeate Baltimore, cylindrical, dense amber, applied double collared mouth, iron pontil mark, pint **130.00**

Middletown Healing Springs, Grays & Clark, Middletown, VT, cylindrical, yellow apricot amber, applied sloping collared mouth with ring, smooth base, quart **1,200.00**

Missiquoi, A. Springs, cylindrical, apricot amber, applied sloping collared mouth with ring, smooth base, quart **150.00**

Saratoga (star) Springs, cylindrical, dark olive green, applied sloping collared mouth with ring, smooth base, quart **300.00**

Vermont Spring, Saxe & Co., Sheldon, VT, cylindrical, citron, applied sloping collared mouth with ring, smooth base, quart **600.00**

Nursing

Acme, clear, lay-down, emb. **65.00**

Cala Nurser, oval, clear, emb, ring on neck, 7-1/8" h **8.00**

Empire Nursing Bottle, bent neck, 6-1/2" h **50.00**

Mother's Comfort, clear, turtle type. **25.00**

BRASS

History: Brass is a durable, malleable, and ductile metal alloy consisting mainly of copper and zinc. The height of its popularity for utilitarian and decorative art items occurred in the 18th and 19th centuries.

References: Mary Frank Gaston, *Antique Brass & Copper*, Collector Books, 1992, 1998 value update; Rupert Gentle and Rachael Feild, *Domestic Metalwork 1640-1820*, Revised, Antique Collectors' Club, 1994; Henry J. Kaufmann, *Early American Copper, Tin & Brass*, Astragal Press, 1995.

> **Reproduction Alert:** Many modern reproductions are being made of earlier brass forms, especially such items as buckets, fireplace equipment, and kettles.

Heibluft Ventilator, hot air fan, c1900, $4,000. Photo courtesy of Auction Team Breker.

Additional Listings: Bells, Candlesticks, Fireplace Equipment, and Scientific Instruments.

Andirons, pr

16-1/2" h, 5-3/4" w, Louis XVI style, flame top over scroll tripod base centered by female mask, late 19th/early 20th C **250.00**

17-1/2" h, acorn tops, seamed columns, cabriole legs, ball feet. **220.00**

17-3/4" h, cast turned columns with pagoda tops, scalloped legs, ball feet. **220.00**

18" h, ring-turned columns, scalloped cabriole legs, ball feet. **360.00**

Bed warmer

40-1/2" l, spun brass, foliage and flower detail, turned wooden handle, minor age splints in handle, soldered repairs on rim . . . **150.00**

44-1/2" l, brass pan with engraved scroll work lid, turned wooden handle **250.00**

Book stand, 9" h, folding, pierced and scrolled, rect base, English. **17.00**

Boot scraper, 12" h, 15" d, brass lyre, cast iron pan **315.00**

Brochure holder, Elevated News-Take One, 5-1/2" sq, 15" h **35.00**

Bucket, 22-1/2" d, tapered cylinder, rolled rim, iron bail handle, 19th C **350.00**

Candlestick

4-3/4" d, Capstan, raised rings around socket, extracting hole on either side **495.00**

5-3/8" d, three knob stem, octagonal base, minor wear **350.00**

5-1/2" d, 6-1/8" h, incised lines on socket and base, spiral twist stem, saucer base with few dents **110.00**

Chandelier, 10-1/2" h, three scrolled branches, turned candle sockets and pans, turned ball drop, early 20th C **175.00**

Chestnut roaster

18-3/4" l, oval, pierced hinged lid, long handle **120.00**

20-7/8" l, triangular roasting box, pierced hinged lid, long handle **115.00**

Coal bin, 18" w, 16" h, hand hammered, polished, Ruskin ceramic cabochons, emb, riveted legs, tulip-shaped finial, orig lacquered finish, unmarked, English **2,100.00**

Coal grate, 19-1/2" l, 10-1/4" d, 27" h, Neoclassical-style, late 19th C, back plate cast with scene of figures in revelry, grate with central horizontal bar over guillouche band, uprights with brass urn finials, rear plinth base, front tapered legs **175.00**

Coal hood

14-1/8" w, 12-3/4" d, 19-1/8" h, Neoclassical-style, 19th C, bowed front, slanted hinged lid with applied patera, band of emb scrolls, two pendant handles, three paw feet topped by flat leaves, removable tin liner **425.00**

16-3/4" l, 13-1/8" w, 20" h, Neoclassical-style, late 19th C, rect, two cornucopia handles, lid with mushroom finial, front set with bellflower and paterae pilasters, central urn, pointed feet . . . **375.00**

Easel, late 19th/early 20th C

61-5/8" h, A-frame topped by girdled round finial **500.00**

65-3/8" h reeded uprights, lyre top **500.00**

72-3/4" h, slender uprights, cast cartouche below flower urn flanked by herms **725.00**

Fireplace fender, 54-3/4" l, Rococo-style, 19th C, pierced center

with tree flanked by rocaille follies, cartouches engraved with helmets on diapered ground, flanked by leaf scrolls **4,600.00**

Letter opener, 6-1/2" l, Union Station, St. Louis **25.00**

Mitten warmer, 9-1/2" d, emb lid with vining flowers and star, delicate turned wooden handle **585.00**

Mortar and pestle, 3-3/4" h ovoid mortar cast in low relief with figures at prayer, everted rim, 10" l pestle with beaded end **175.00**

Steam whistle, 2-1/2" d, 12" h, single chime, lever control **150.00**

Tobacco box, Dutch

4-3/4" l, 2-1/2" w, 1" h, engraved scenes of couple and cherub on each side, Dutch script, resoldered hinge **110.00**

7" l, 2" w, 3/8" h, copper body with brass lid and base, engraved floral designs, scenes of three wise men at manger on lid and base, Dutch script **440.00**

Wood box, 19" l, 12-3/8" w, 13-3/8" h, Neoclassical-style, late 19th C, rect, hinged lid with flat leaf finial, front with band of vertical pierced flutes with three applied rosettes, two pendant handles, four flattened ball feet **325.00**

BREAD PLATES

History: Beginning in the mid-1880s, special trays or platters were made for serving bread and rolls. Designated "bread plates" by collectors, these small trays or platters can be found in porcelain, glass (especially pattern glass), and metals.

Bread plates often were part of a china or glass set. However, many glass companies made special plates which honored national heroes, commemorated historical or special events, offered a moral maxim, or supported a religious attitude. The subject matter

appears either horizontally or vertically. Most of these plates are oval and 10 inches in length.

Reference: Anna Maude Stuart, *Bread Plates and Platters*, published by author, 1965.

Additional Listings: Pattern Glass.

Majolica

Apple and Pear, brown ground, minor wear rim **385.00**

Bamboo and Fern, cobalt blue, Wardles **395.00**

Corn, yellow center, minor rim chip on back **440.00**

Give Us This Day Our Daily Bread, cobalt border and basket center, wheat handles **360.00**

Picket Fence and Floral, cobalt blue **385.00**

Pineapple, cobalt blue center **440.00**

Pond Lily, very minor rim repair **440.00**

Water Lily, 12" l, surface wear. **110.00**

Milk glass, Wheat & Barley **65.00**

Mottos, pressed glass, clear

Be Industrious, handles, oval . **50.00**

Give Us this Day, round, rosette center and border **65.00**

Rock of Ages, 12-7/8" l **175.00**

Waste Not Want Not **35.00**

Pattern glass, clear unless otherwise noted

Actress, Miss Nielson **80.00**

Beaded Grape, sq **35.00**

Butterfly & Fan **40.00**

Canadian, 10" d **45.00**

Cupid and Venus, amber **85.00**

Deer and Pine Tree, amber . . **110.00**

Egyptian, Cleopatra center . . . **60.00**

Frosted Lion **95.00**

Good Luck **45.00**

Iowa, motto **80.00**

Lion, amber, lion handles, motto **135.00**

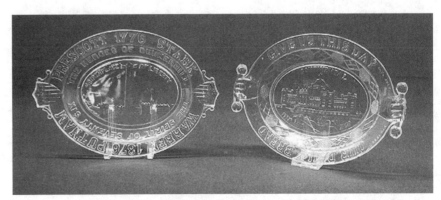

Pattern glass, left: Prescott and Stark, right: Continental, each, **$60.** *Photo courtesy of Joy Luke Auctions.*

Scroll and Flowers, 12" d **40.00**
Tennessee, colored jewels ... **75.00**
Train **75.00**

Souvenir and Commemorative

Old State House, sapphire
blue **185.00**
Three Presidents, frosted
center **95.00**
Virginia Dare **135.00**
William J. Bryan, milk glass .. **45.00**

Silver, sterling, American

12" l, oval, four claw feet, Francis I
pattern, acanthus dec, applied foliage and scrolls on sides, Reed &
Barton, 16 oz, 8 dwt **400.00**
12-1/2" d, oval, partly fluted sides,
reeded rim, Gorham, 10 oz,
6 dwt **100.00**
14-1/2" l, oval, applied scroll border
rim, marked "E. P. Roberts & Sons,"
14 oz, 6 dwt **250.00**

BRIDE'S BASKETS

History: A ruffled-edge glass bowl in a metal holder
was a popular wedding gift between 1880 and 1910,
hence the name "bride's basket." These bowls can be
found in most glass types of the period. The metal
holder was generally silver plated with a bail handle,
thus enhancing the basket image.

Over the years, bowls and bases became separated and married pieces resulted. If the base has been
lost, the bowl should be sold separately.

Reference: John Mebane, *Collecting Bride's Baskets
and Other Glass Fancies*, Wallace-Homestead, 1976.

Reproduction Alert: The glass bowls have been
reproduced.

Note: Items listed below have a silver-plated holder
unless otherwise noted.

8" d, 2-1/8" h, bowl only, satin overlay,
shaded pink, clear edging on base,
gold and silver sanded flowers and
leaves dec, ruffled, off-white lining,
ground pontil **145.00**
8-1/4" w, sq, cased, deep rose and
white ext., whit int., dragon, floral,
and leaf dec, ruffled edge, Mt.
Washington **675.00**
8-1/2" d, 12" h, amber, enameled berries and buds, SP holder..... **1,195.00**
9-1/4" d, Peachblow, yellow flowers
dec, orig SP holder **225.00**
9-1/2" d, 12" h, satin, deep pink ruffled
bowl, white ext., marked "Nemasket Silver Co." SP holder **275.00**
9-3/4" d, 2-3/4" h, 3" d, base, bowl only,
shaded pink overlay, ruffled edge, white
underside, colored enameled flowers
and foliage dec, clear and opaque ribbon applied edge **220.00**

9-7/8" d, 3" h, 3-3/4" base, bowl only,
peachblow, glossy finish, deep pink
shading to pale.............. **250.00**
10" d, 11" h, Vasa Murrhina, outer
amber layer, center layer with hundreds
of cream colored spots, random toffee
colored spots, dark veins, gold mica
flakes, mulberry pink lining, crossed rod
thorn handles **635.00**
10" w, sq, custard, melon ribbed,
enameled daisies, applied Rubena
crystal rim, twisted and beaded
handle, ftd, emb SP frame, marked
"Wilcox" **450.00**
10-1/2" d, Hobnail, pink, enameled
flowers, ruffled rim, reticulated SP
frame **250.00**
10-3/4" d, 3-1/2" h, bowl only

Overlay, heavenly blue, enameled
white flowers, green leaves, white
underside, ruffled **215.00**
Satin, shaded purple, white underside, dainty purple and white flowers, lacy foliage dec **225.00**

11" d, 7-1/2" h, satin, light beige shading to orange ruffled bowl, hp pink, purple and yellow flowers, green leaves,
raised gold outlines, blue int., sgd "Simpson, Hall, Miller Co. Quad Plate" SP
holder **895.00**
11-1/8" d, 3-3/4" h, bowl only, satin,
brown shaded to cream overlay, raised
dots, dainty gold and silver flowers and
leaves dec, ruffled **250.00**
11-3/8" d, 3-1/4" h, 2-7/8" d base, bowl
only, maroon shaded to cream overlay,
fancy leaf edges with circle and slot
emb designs, dainty enameled pink
flowers, gold leaves, white
underside................. **215.00**

Bride's basket, bowl, 10" d, **$275.**

11-1/2" d, 3-5/8" h, bowl only, shaded
green overlay satin, ruffled emb lattice
edge, white underside **210.00**
12-1/2" d, 12" h, maize, amber and
crystal crest, hp roses, SP frame,
Fenton **275.00**

BRISTOL GLASS

History: Bristol glass is a designation given to a
semi-opaque glass, usually decorated with enamel
and cased with another color.

Initially, the term referred only to glass made in
Bristol, England, in the 17th and 18th centuries. By the
Victorian era, firms on the Continent and in America
were copying the glass and its forms.

Biscuit jar, 6-1/2" h, white, brown
leaves and white flowers...... **165.00**
Bowl, light blue, Cupid playing mandolin, gold trim................. **40.00**
Box, cov, 4-1/8" l, 2-3/4" d, 3-1/2" h,
oblong, blue, gilt-metal mounts and
escutcheon **550.00**
Cake stand, celadon green, enameled
herons in flight, gold trim...... **135.00**
Candlesticks, pr, 7" h, soft green, gold
band **75.00**
Decanter, 11-1/2" h, ruffled stopper,
enameled flowers and butterfly.. **75.00**
Dresser set, two cologne bottles, cov
powder jar, white, gilt butterflies dec,
clear stoppers **75.00**
Ewer, 6-3/8" h, 2-5/8" d, pink ground,
fancy gold designs, bands, and leaves,
applied handle with gold trim .. **135.00**
Finger bowl, 4-3/8" d, blue, faceted
sides, early 20th C, eight-pc
set **500.00**
Hatpin holder, 6-1/8" h, ftd, blue,
enameled jewels, gold dec.... **100.00**
Mug, 5" h, white, eagle and
"Liberty"................... **375.00**
Perfume bottle, 3-1/4" h, squatty, blue,
gold band, white enameled flowers and
leaves, matching stopper **100.00**
Puff box, cov, round, blue, gold
dec **35.00**
Stein, 10-1/4" h, cylindrical body
painted with polychrome flowers and
sprigs, pump handle, mounted with
pewter foot band, domed pewter lid
with ball thumbpiece, early
19th C **175.00**
Sugar shaker, 4-3/4" h, white, hp
flowers.................... **60.00**
Sweetmeat jar, 3" x 5-1/2", deep pink,
enameled flying duck, leaves, blue
flower dec, white lining, SP rim, lid, and
bail handle.................. **110.00**

Vase, hand-painted birds, 6-3/4" h, price for pair, **$220.** *Photo courtesy of Joy Luke Auctions.*

Urn, 18" h, pink, boy and girl with lamp **550.00**
Vase, 8-1/2" h, light pink shading to dark pink, hp enameled design . . **65.00**

BRITISH ROYALTY COMMEMORATIVES

History: British commemorative china, souvenirs to commemorate coronations and other royal events, dates from the 1600s, with the early pieces being rather crude in design and form. With the development of transfer printing, c1780, the images on the wares more closely resembled the monarchs.

Few commemorative pieces predating Queen Victoria's reign are found today at popular prices. Items associated with Queen Elizabeth II and her children, e.g., the wedding of HRH Prince Andrew and Miss Sarah Ferguson and the subsequent birth of their daughter HRH Princess Beatrice, are very common.

Some British Royalty commemoratives are easily recognized by their portraits of past or present monarchs. Some may be in silhouette profile. Royal symbols include crowns, dragons, royal coats of arms, national flowers, swords, scepters, dates, messages, and monograms.

References: Susan and Al Bagdade, *Warman's English & Continental Pottery & Porcelain*, 3rd Edition, Krause Publications, 1998; Douglas H. Flynn and Alan H. Bolton, *British Royalty Commemoratives*, Schiffer Publishing, 1994; Lincoln Hallinan, *British Commemoratives*, Antique Collectors' Club, 1999.

Collectors' Club: Commemorative Collector's Society, The Gardens, Gainsborough Road, Winthrope, New Newark, Nottingham NG24 2NR England.

Periodical: *The Commemorative Collector Newsletter,* Douglas H. Flynn, P.O. Box 294, Lititz, PA 17543-0294.

Additional Listings: See *Warman's Americana & Collectibles* for more examples.

Autograph
Edward VII, letter, sgd "Albert Edward," three pages, 8vo, Abergeldie Castle, Sept. 1, to Choimsedale, relating to grouse hunting **250.00**
Elizabeth I, letter, sgd as Queen, one page, oblong folio, London, Jan. 21, 1592, "Our Trustie and well beloved William Colles," concerning money to be paid toward "...the defense of our Realms...," striking signature, upper right corner of letter missing, integral address intact. **7,900.00**
George I, broadside, sgd as Elector of Hanover, in German, one page, small folio, Hanover, Dec. 31, 1701, approves request by the Duchy of Catenberg that year's tithe be paid entirely in corn, with complete translation, chip in left margin **900.00**
George II, letter, sgd as Prince of Wales, in French, two pages, 4to, Leicester House, Jan. 11/22, 1723, to Madame Marygrove, sympathies over loss of relation **1,200.00**

Henry VII, document, sgd with wood-cut stamped signature, one page irregularly cut, 8" x 9", Greenwich, Feb. 14 (c1509), to Sir Edward Poynings, Comptroller of the Household and Lord Warden of the Cinque Ports, regarding seven lasts and eight barrels of herring to be sold without delay, torn on right edge **3,500.00**
James II, document, sgd as Duke of York and Lord High Admiral, one page, 4to, Whitehall, June 25, 1660, concerning payment for bill **975.00**
William IV, document, sgd as king, one page 4to, Bushby House, Sept. 18, 1827, appoints David Davis as his personal surgeon, red wax seal next to signature **350.00**

Book
The Life and Reign of His Majesty King George V, 64 pgs, 1935 . . . . **18.00**
The Little Princesses, Marion Crawford, Governess to Elizabeth & Margaret, Harcourt Brace, 1950, 1st ed. **10.00**
The Princess Elizabeth Gift Book, Cynthia Asquith and Eileen Bigland, wear to cover **10.00**

Bottle opener, King Edward, brass, coronation souvenir **8.50**

Bowl
Charles, 1969 Investiture, Aynsley, 50-1/2" d **60.00**
Edward VII, 1937 Coronation, profile in well, pressed glass, 10 d . **70.00**
Elizabeth II, 1953 Coronation, pressed glass, 4-3/4" h **60.00**
George VI and Elizabeth, 1937 Coronation, coat of arms, Paragon, 5-1/2" d **55.00**

Box, cov, Elizabeth the Queen Mother, 1980, 80th birthday, color portrait, Crown Staffordshire, 4" d **75.00**

Brochure, Canadian Visit, 1959, Queen Elizabeth II and Prince Philip, opening of St. Lawrence Seaway, 8-1/2" x 11" **15.00**

Cup and saucer
Andrew and Sarah, 1986 Wedding, Colclough **30.00**
Edward VII and Alexandra, 1888 Silver Wedding Anniversary, coat of arms **185.00**
Elizabeth II, portrait flanked by flags, coronation, pairs of flags inside cup and on saucer, marked "Alfred

Meakin England," 3" h x 3-1/4" d cup, 6" d saucer **45.00**
George V and Mary, 1911 Coronation, color portraits **60.00**

Drinking glass

3-3/4" h, clear, red and blue illus of George VI and Elizabeth I, 1939 Canadian visit. **18.00**
4" h, Queen Elizabeth II, color profile, Coronation, June 2, 1953, porcelain, 4" **60.00**

Figure, 5-1/4" h, Elizabeth I, carved ivory, lower section of skirt hinged to reveal triptych of Queen and Sir Walter Raleigh, Continental, 19th C, hairlines **550.00**

Handkerchief, white fabric, small red, white, and blue stitched British flag above printed full-color view across Thames toward Buckingham Palace, Westminster Abbey, rural countryside scenes on border, May, 1937, orig small cardboard price tag, 10-1/2" x 11". **20.00**

Jug

Elizabeth II, 1953 Coronation, emb crowning scene, Burleigh Ware, 8-1/4" h. **250.00**
Victoria, 1887 Gold Jubilee, black and white portraits, 5" h . . . **145.00**

Lithophane, cup, crown, and cypher, 2-3/4" h

Alexandra, 1902 . . . . **195.00**
George V, 1911 . . . . **165.00**

Loving cup

Elizabeth II and Philip, 1972 Silver Wedding Anniversary, Paragon, 3" h **175.00**
George VI and Elizabeth, 1937 Coronation, brown Marcus Adams portraits, 3-1/4" h **145.00**

Mug, Edward VIII Coronation, decal decoration, dated May 1937, Minton, **$40.**

Magic Lantern Slide, Victoria and Albert **15.00**
Medallion, Anne and Mark, 1973 Wedding, molded pale pink portraits, pink frame, Hutchenreuther 3-1/4" d . . **60.00**

Mug

Edward VIII, Coronation, 1937, sepia portrait of king flanked by multicolored flags, reverse with Union Jack and Flag of commonwealth, flanking names of some of the nations, topped by crown, gold trim, 2-1/2" h, 2-1/2" d, crest mark and "Empire England" **50.00**
Elizabeth II

Coronation, portrait of Queen facing left, "Coronation of Her Majesty Queen Elizabeth" on reverse, gold trim, 3" h, 3" d, crown and "Radfords Bone China Made in England" mark **45.00**
Silver Jubilee, Queen in circle flanked by flags, topped by crown, 3-1/2" h, 3" d, royal crest on back, marked "Made in England" in raised letters, red and yellow crown mark. . . **35.00**

Paperweight

Charles and Diana, 1981 Wedding, white sulfide portraits, cobalt blue ground, CR Albret, France, 2-3/4" d **175.00**
Edward VIII, 1937 Coronation, black and white portrait, 4-1/4" d . . **50.00**

Pinback button

Edward VIII, multicolored, for 1937 coronation, 7/8" d **15.00**
George V and Queen Mary Silver Jubilee, black and white oval portraits, pale turquoise ground, full-color British flags, 1" d. . . **20.00**
George VI and Elizabeth, black and white, May 2, 1937, coronation, 1-1/4" **20.00**
Prince of Wales, c1910 portrait, 7/8" d. **30.00**
Prince of Wales, 1920, Australian-made, celluloid, inscribed "Souvenir Adelaide 1920," color portrait captioned "H.R.H. The Prince Of Wales Australian Tour," 1-1/4" **20.00**
Victoria, Queen of England, multicolored, from 1900 series, 1-1/4" d **35.00**

Pin tray, Elizabeth II, 1977 Silver Jubilee, black silhouette, Coalport, 3-3/4" d. **35.00**

Pitcher, 8-3/4" h, marriage of Princess Charlotte and Prince Leopold, c1816, relief dec, double scroll handle, Pratt ware, minor enamel loss **1,265.00**

Plate

Edward VII and Alexandra, 1902 Coronation, blue and white, Royal Copenhagen, 7" d **200.00**
George VI and Elizabeth, Canadian visit, 1939, word "Canada" in relief under portraits in center, "King George IV, Queen Elizabeth, 1939" in relief on rim. **65.00**
Princess Elizabeth and Duke of Edinburgh, visit to Canada, October 1951, maroon colored portraits flanked by flags of Great Britain and Canada, gold trim, marked "Casidian Guaranteed 22K Gold," 10" d, some crazing **60.00**

Postcard, Royal Visit to New Zealand, 1953-54, 39" x 29", creased on folds, small tears. **20.00**

Program

Prince of Wales Royal Investiture, July 1, 1969, glossy paper, 6-1/2" x 9" **12.00**
Queen Elizabeth II, Silver Jubilee, 1977, 42 pgs, glossy paper, 8-1/4" x 11-3/4" **10.00**

Snuff box, 3" d, round, bronze, round, dark patina, angel riding lion with "Regent," reverse emb inscription "In record of the reign of George III" covered by sunburst and cross, visible on int., engraved paper bust and "H.R.H. George Augustus Frederick Prince Regent...Feb 1811". **2,100.00**

Teapot

Charlotte, 1817 In Memoriam, black and white dec, 6" h **275.00**
Victoria, 1897 Diamond Jubilee, color coat of arms, Aynsley. **225.00**

Tea set, 8-3/4" l cov teapot, creamer, cov sugar, manufactured for the coronation of Elizabeth II, 1953, applied white relief, solid royal blue ground, Wedgwood imp marks, chip on teapot finial. **230.00**

Tin

Queen Elizabeth II, coronation, sq, Queen Elizabeth II on horseback, full view, marked "Sharp Assorted Toffee," stamped "Made In England by Edward Sharp & Sons Ltd. Of Maidstone Kent," 7" x 6" x 2", minor scratches and edge rubbing. **40.00**
Queen Elizabeth II and Prince Philip, round, coats of arms of the com-

monwealth nations on sides alternating with pictures of Buckingham Palace, Westminster Abbey, Windsor Castle, and Palace of Holyrood, marked "Huntley & Palmer Biscuits Reading & London, England," 7-1/2" d 30.00

Prince of Wales, Yardley Invisible Talc for Men, Prince of Wales crest, "By Appointment to HM Queen Elizabeth II Purveyors of Soap Yardley and Co. Ltd.," 5" h ..15.00

BRONZE

History: Bronze is an alloy of copper, tin, and traces of other metals. It has been used since Biblical times not only for art objects, but also for utilitarian wares. After a slump in the Middle Ages, the use of bronze was revived in the 17th century and continued to be popular until the early 20th century.

References: Harold Berman, *Bronzes: Sculptors & Founders 1800-1930*, Vols. 1–4 and Index, distributed by Schiffer Publishing, 1996; James Mackay, *The Dictionary of Sculptors in Bronze*, Antique Collectors' Club, 1999; Christopher Payne, *Animals in Bronze, Reference and Price Guide*, Antique Collectors' Club, 1999; Stuart Pivar, *The Bayre Bronzes, A Catalogue Raisonné*, Antique Collectors' Club, 1999.

Notes: Do not confuse a "bronzed" object with a true bronze. A bronzed item usually is made of white metal and then coated with a reddish-brown material to give it a bronze appearance. A magnet will stick to it but not to anything made of true bronze.

A signed bronze commands a higher market price than an unsigned one. There also are "signed" reproductions on the market. It is very important to know the history of the mold and the background of the foundry.

Bookends, pr

6-3/4" h, cupid, swathed in swirl of fabric, tip-toeing with bow in hand, other young girl with flowing hair and bouquet in hand, inscribed "Cast by Griffoul, Newark, NJ," early 20th C............420.00

9" h, daffodil silhouette, imp mark of G. Thew, 1928...........225.00

Cake basket, 9-1/2" d, 7-5/8" h, circular bowl, molded pedestal, flat arch handle with enameled mottled red, pink, and amber enamel, imp "Favrile, Louis C. Tiffany Furnaces, IN 511," monogram, c1918 .... 1,300.00

Candelabra, 24-5/8" h, Rococo-Revival, late 19th C, six-light, central sconce with gilt drip pan, flanked by five serpentine candle arms with vines and beaded roundels, parcel gilt tripartite foot, white marble and parcel gilt trefoil base, price for pr 1,725.00

Figure

2-1/2" x 2-1/4", Babylonian bull, standing, Mesopotamia, 1800-1700 BC **600.00**

3-1/4" x 3", prancing bull, tail curled over back, curly hair between horns, Roman, first center A.D. **700.00**

5" l, 4" h, bear lying on back, dark brown patination, mold signature of Antoine-Louis Barye...... **490.00**

6" h, boy with turtle, early 20th C, wooden base **290.00**

7-5/8" l, 7-5/8" h, stag, walking down grade, naturalistic base, signature on front of Jules Moigniez, dark greenish-brown patination **1,380.00**

7-3/4" h, owl, realistically modeled, glass eyes, standing on stack of small books with trailing ties, one tie is latch, opens to gilt bronze standing female nude, cold painted, Austria **3,450.00**

10" l, 6" h, young lion, realistically modeled in recumbent pose, brown patination, 20th C .. **460.00**

11-1/2" h, soldier, raised pistol, tattered flag at side, waisted socle with title plaque, "La Défense du Drapeau," C. Anfrie, reddish-brown patina **650.00**

12" h, standing man, one arm at waist, other extended behind him, C. Höland, round base with foundry mark for Gladenbek & Son, tapered and beveled marble base **575.00**

13" h, female harvester, carved ivory face and arms, carrying sack of wheat, rocky base, doré, circular marble plinth, mold signature and mark for "Salon 1908," Henry Kossowski, Jr.............. **1,265.00**

13-3/4" h, molded grouse, naturalistic ovoid base with oat stalks, doré, Ferdinand Pautrot........ **950.00**

15-3/4" h, sower, standing male figure, dark brown patina, oval black marble base, Bruno Zach . **700.00**

16" h, standing male laborer with scythe, dark brown patina, oval black marble base, Bruno Zach.................. **550.00**

24-12" h, young Dionysius, standing, white skin, round leaf top socle, oxidized green patination. **1,035.00**

27" h, standing woman with ewer, headscarf, bib necklace, diaphanous dress, naturalistic ovoid base,

medium greenish-gold patina, I. Chilmany **1,100.00**

32" h, La Baigneuse, c1900, female bather, marked for "I. Marchand," after Etienne Falconet, oval foundry mark, brown patina **2,760.00**

Lamp base, 20" h, figural, cherub seated on parcel-gilt fluted column hooding reeded cornucopia, white marble base with clipped corners, applied beaded panels, Louis XV style, late 19th C, electrified.......... **2,450.00**

Posset pot, 17-5/8" l, 7-1/4" h, long handle, tripod feet, imp "J. Davis Boston" on handle, c1800, two small rim cracks................... **2,530.00**

Snuff box, cov, 3" l, round, dark patina, angel riding lion with "Regent," reverse emb inscription "In record of the reign of George III" covered by sunburst and cross, visible on int., engraved paper bust and "H.R.H. George Augustus Frederick Prince Regent…Feb 1811" **2,100.00**

Sculpture, Wood-Music, deep olive green patina, inscribed "Beatrice Fenton," c1920, 29" h, **$3,475.** *Photo courtesy of Freeman\Fine Arts of Philadelphia, Inc.*

Standish, 16" l, retriever flanked by pair of foliate molded inkwells, oval verte antico marble base, French, early 20th C **435.00**

Statue, 38-1/2" h, Caesar Augustus, after antique, standing figure with one outstretched arm, small cherub supporter, round base, 20th C ...**4,315.00**

Trophy, 5-1/2" d, 10" h, sterling on bronze, cylindrical, two handles, applied silver clematis and winning boar prize at Michigan State Fair, orig patina, stamped "HAMS," Heintz **490.00**

Urn, 11-3/8" h, cast, black patinated, everted reeded rim, central band of classical figures, two short handles with male masks, fluted foot, sq black marble base, Classical-style, late 19th/early 20th C, price for pr **2,530.00**

Vase

15" h, Neoclassical style, after Clodion, baluster form, continuous bacchanalian scene of infant satyrs, putti, and goats, light brown patina **345.00**

17-1/2" h, Neoclassical style, Barbedienne, Bacchantes picking grapes, late 19th C, pr...**3,110.00**

Wall plaque, 21-1/4" d, shield-form, Classical Revival, raised and pointed center section, continuous battle scene, Continental, late 19th C **500.00**

BUFFALO POTTERY

History: Buffalo Pottery Co., Buffalo, New York, was chartered in 1901. The first kiln was fired in October 1903. Larkin Soap Company established Buffalo Pottery to produce premiums for its extensive mail-order business. Wares also were sold to the public by better department and jewelry stores. Elbert Hubbard and Frank Lloyd Wright, who designed the Larkin Administration Building in Buffalo in 1904, were two prominent names associated with the Larkin Company.

Early Buffalo Pottery production consisted mainly of semi-vitreous china dinner sets. Buffalo was the first pottery in the United States to produce successfully the Blue Willow pattern. Buffalo also made a line of hand-decorated, multicolored willow ware, called Gaudy Willow. Other early items include a series of game, fowl, and fish sets, pitchers, jugs, and a line of commemorative, historical, and advertising plates and mugs.

From 1908 to 1909 and again from 1921 to 1923, Buffalo Pottery produced the line for which it is most famous—Deldare Ware. The earliest of this olive green, semi-vitreous china displays hand-decorated

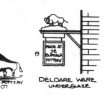

scenes from English artist Cecil Aldin's *Fallowfield Hunt.* Hunt scenes were done only from 1908 to 1909. English village scenes also were characteristic of the ware and were used during both periods. Most pieces are artist signed.

In 1911, Buffalo Pottery produced Emerald Deldare, which used scenes from Goldsmith's *The Three Tours of Dr. Syntax* and an Art Nouveau-type border. Completely decorated Art Nouveau pieces also were made.

Abino, which was introduced in 1912, had a Deldare body and displayed scenes of sailboats, windmills, or the sea. Rust was the main color used, and all pieces were signed by the artist and numbered.

In 1915, the manufacturing process was modernized, giving the company the ability to produce vitrified china. Consequently, hotel and institutional ware became the main production items, with hand-decorated ware de-emphasized. The Buffalo firm became a leader in producing and designing the most-famous railroad, hotel, and restaurant patterns. These wares, especially railroad items, are eagerly sought by collectors.

In the early 1920s, fine china was made for home use. Bluebird is one of the patterns from this era. In 1950, Buffalo made its first Christmas plate. These were given away to customers and employees primarily from 1950 to 1960. However, it is known that Hample Equipment Co. ordered some as late as 1962. The Christmas plates are very scarce in today's resale market.

The Buffalo China Company made "Buffalo Pottery" and "Buffalo China"—the difference being that one is semi-vitreous ware and the other vitrified. In 1956, the company was reorganized, and Buffalo China became the corporate name. Today, Buffalo China is owned by Oneida Silver Company. The Larkin family no longer is involved.

Marks: Blue Willow pattern is marked "First Old Willow Ware Mfg. in America."

Reference: Seymour and Violet Altman, *Book of Buffalo Pottery,* reprinted by Schiffer Publishing, 1987.

Gravy boat, Willow Ware, blue decoration, buffalo mark, dated 1911, **$40.**

Abino Ware

Candlestick, 9" h, sailing ships, 1913 .... **475.00**

Pitcher, 7" h, Portland Head Light **700.00**

Tankard, 10-1/2" h, sailing scene **900.00**

Advertising Ware

Mug, 4-1/2" h, Calumet Club ... **110.00**

Plate

9-3/4" d, Indian Head Pontiac **45.00**

10-1/2" d, Stuyvesant Hotel . **145.00**

Platter, 13-1/2" l, US Army Medical Dept., 1943 .... **25.00**

Deldare

Calling card tray

Street scene **395.00**

Three Pigeons **450.00**

Candlesticks, pr, street scene.. **895.00**

Cereal bowl, Fallowfield Hunt

6" d **295.00**

9" d **495.00**

Chop plate, 14" d

Fallowfield Hunt **795.00**

Street scene **695.00**

Cup and saucer, street scene.. **225.00**

Fruit bowl, street scene....... **575.00**

Hair receiver, street scene **495.00**

Jardiniere, street scene....... **995.00**

Mug

Fallowfield Hunt, 3-1/2" h ... **395.00**

Street Scene, 4-1/2" h...... **395.00**

Three Pigeons, 4-1/2" h **350.00**

Pin tray, street scene........ **325.00**

Pitcher

8" h, street scene **700.00**

12" h, 7" w, The Great Controversy, sgd "W. Fozter," stamped mark.................. **290.00**

Plate, 10" d, Fallowfield Hunt... **295.00**

Powder jar, street scene **395.00**

Punch cup, Fallowfield Hunt ... **375.00**

Soup plate, 9" d, street scene.. **425.00**

Tankard, Three Pigeons...... **1,175.00**

Teapot, cov, large, street scene **395.00**

Tea tile

Fallowfield Hunt **395.00**

Street scene **395.00**

Tea tray, street scene **650.00**

Vase

7" h, street scene **450.00**

7-3/4" h, 6-1/2" d, King Fisher, green and white dec, olive ground, stamped mark, artist signature **1,380.00**

Emerald Deldare

Creamer **450.00**

Fruit bowl................. **1,450.00**

Mug, 4-1/2" h............... **475.00**

Vase, 8-1/2" h, 6-1/2" h, stylized foliate motif, shades of green and white, olive ground, stamp mark **810.00**

Miscellaneous

Jug

Chrysanthemum **495.00**

Robin Hood **550.00**

Roger Williams **595.00**

Plate, Willow, 9" d **20.00**

BURMESE GLASS

History: Burmese glass is a translucent art glass originated by Frederick Shirley and manufactured by the Mt. Washington Glass Co., New Bedford, Massachusetts, from 1885 to c1891.

Burmese glass colors shade from a soft lemon to a salmon pink. Uranium was used to attain the yellow color, and gold was added to the batch so that on reheating, one end turned pink. Upon reheating again, the edges would revert to the yellow coloring. The blending of the colors was so gradual that it is difficult to determine where one color ends and the other begins.

Although some of the glass has a glossy surface, most pieces were acid finished. The majority of the items were free blown, but some were blown molded in a ribbed, hobnail, or diamond-quilted design.

American-made Burmese is quite thin and, therefore, is fragile, and brittle. English Burmese was made by Thos. Webb & Sons. Out of deference to Queen Victoria, they called their wares "Queen's Burmese Ware."

Reference: Kyle Husfloen, *Antique Trader's American & European Decorative and Art Glass Price Guide*, 2nd ed., Krause Publications, 2000.

Collectors Club: Mount Washington Art Glass Society, P.O. Box 24094, Fort Worth, TX 76124-1094.

Reproduction Alert: Reproductions abound in almost every form. Since uranium can no longer be used, some of the reproductions are easy to spot. In the 1950s, Gundersen produced many pieces in imitation of Burmese.

Abbreviations:

MW	Mount Washington
Wb	Webb
a.f.	acid finish
s.f.	shiny finish

Advisers: Clarence and Betty Maier.

Bonbon bowl, 6-1/2" l, 4-3/4" w, 2-3/8" h, Mt. Washington, shiny finish, heart shaped, applied ring handle, three applied prunts 835.00
Charger, 10" d, shallow, disk shape 365.00
Cream pitcher, 5-1/2" h, Mt. Washington, Shape #154, crimped edge with re-fired yellow border 485.00
Cruet
6-1/2" h, three striking chrysanthemum blossoms, two white and one yellow, coral colored detail stripes mushroom stopper, signed "88" in enamel. 2,950.00
7" h, shiny finish, mushroom stopper, each of 30 ribs has hint of pink 1,250.00
Epergne, 14" h, 8" center floriform vase, Webb, satin finish, pastel yellow stripes,

unique pink blush borders, undecorated, shallow bowl-shaped base with muted Burmese color, cone-shaped center rising to support brass fittings that hold three petite Burmese bud vases 1,950.00
Fairy lamp, Webb
3-3/4" h, pyramid, Burmese shade, clear glass base sgd "S. Clarke's Pyramid Fairy" 335.00
4" h, pyramid, pressed glass base has molded-in "S. Clarke Fairy Pyramid" and dancing fairy logo signature 335.00
5-1/2" h, Cricklite, satin, dome shade, 6" sq base with fold-in sides, impressed signature "Thos. Webb & Sons Queens Burmeseware Patented," clear glass candle cup signed, "S Clarke Fairy Trade Mark Patent" 985.00
6" h, 7-1/2" d spreading, skirt-like, pleated base, two acid etched signatures, "Thos Webb & Sons Queen's Burmeseware Patented" and "S. Clarke's Fairy Patent Trade Mark," clear glass candle cup signed, "Clarke's Criklite Trade Mark" 950.00
Finger bowl, 2-3/4" d, Mt. Washington, shiny finish, refired crimped rim 435.00
Milk pitcher, 5" w handle to spout, 4" h, Mt. Washington, satin 850.00
Nut dish, 4" d, coral and gray fronds laden with tiny bittersweet colored blossoms, slightly upward draped sides 345.00
Rose bowl, 3-1/4" h, Webb, prunus blossom dec, sq top 285.00
Salt shaker, 4-1/4" h, Mt. Washington, lemon-yellow lower half, intense color on upper half, two part metal top 265.00
Toothpick holder, 2" h, Mt. Washington, satin, tricorn folded in rim, optic diamond quilt design. 385.00
Tumbler, Mt. Washington
Pastel salmon shading to a creamy-yellow 285.00
Shiny finish, egg-shell thin satin body 375.00
Vase
7" h, Mt. Washington, lily, delicate blush to the mouth of the "lily," refired yellow rim 285.00
8" h, gourd shape, roses and forget-me-nots, three lovely peach-colored rose blossoms cling to leaved branch which swirl down rim, around body and down to the base, entwining strands of

turquoise-colored forget-me-not blossoms, double gourd shaped, 8" tall 1,250.00
10" h, Mt. Washington, lily, flesh tone blush, well defined re-fired yellow border 385.00
11" h, 6" d base, white daisies with distinctive yellow-dot centers 1,750.00
23-1/2" h, circa 1890 . . . . . 1,250.00
Whiskey taster, 2-3/4" tall, molded-in elongated diamond quilted design 285.00

Vase, Mt. Washington, Shape 52-1/2 C, satin, 4-5/8" h, **$465.** *Photo courtesy of Clarence and Betty Maier.*

BUSTS

History: The portrait bust has its origins in pagan and Christian traditions. Greek and Roman heroes dominate the earliest examples. Later, images of Christian saints were used. Busts of the "ordinary man" first appeared during the Renaissance.

During the 18th and 19th centuries, nobility, poets, and other notable people were the most frequent subjects, especially on those busts designed for use in a home library. Because of the large number of these library busts, excellent examples can be found at reasonable prices, depending on artist, subject, and material.

Additional Listings: Ivory, Parian Ware, Soapstone, and Wedgwood.

5-1/2" w, 13" h, carved wood, young man, furrowed brown, inlaid eyes, old dark patina, America, early 20th C, minor losses and imperfections 575.00

7-1/2" h, bronze, Nubian Princess, Edrmann Encke, Gladenbeck foundry mark, short socle, marble base. **415.00**

8-3/4" h, bronze, Voltaire, bronze socle, green marble plinth, medium-dark brown patina, late 19th/early 20th C **290.00**

9" h, bronze, winged cherub, seated on broken column, playing hornpipe, pair of doves perched opposite, after Mathurin Moreau, dark brown patination, green marble socle **250.00**

9" h, carved stone, Boddhiharma, traces of red lacquer, China, 19th C or earlier. **990.00**

9" w, 3-1/2" d, 11-1/4" h, carved wood, young man, black, brown, white, and red polychrome, stand, paint imperfections. **17,250.00**

10" h, black basalt, Cicero, waisted circular socle, imp title and Wedgwood & Bentley mark, c1775, chips to socle rim **2,300.00**

10-1/2" h, bronze, young woman, hair pulled back in kerchief, half mask by her side, George (Joris) Van Der Straeten, Paris Bronze Society foundry mark, fluted marble socle, reddish brown and black patination. . . . **375.00**

10-7/8" h, bronze, Watteau-style woman, tricorn hat, low décolletage, George (Joris) Van Der Straeten, Paris Bronze Society foundry mark, fluted marble socle, reddish brown and black patination. **460.00**

11-1/4" h, bronze and marble, medieval woman, after Patricia by Roger Hart, young woman, sheer headdress, marked "Mino di Tiesole" on ovoid white marble base, 20th C **575.00**

11-1/2" h, bronze, Mercury, after the antique, chocolate brown and parcel-gilt patina, short socle, sq base, 20th C **415.00**

12-1/2" h, bronze, young child, curly hair, cylindrical stone base, 20th C **650.00**

13-3/4" w, 9-3/4" d, 26" h, carved marble, Pharaoh's Daughter, John Adams-Acton, snake headdress, beaded necklace, tapered sq section base, carved on front with scene of the discovery of Moses and title, 13-3/8" w, 10-3/4" d, 39" h breche d'alep marble tapered sq section pedestal, England, late 19th C **16,100.00**

15-1/4" w, 6-3/4" d, 15" h, carved marble, Jeanne D'Arc, white marble face and base, pink marble bodice, incised title on front, early 20th C. **700.00**

Marble, lady with flowers, signed "G. Bessi," small wooden stand, 14-3/4" h, $1,750. Photo courtesy of Joy Luke Auctions.

16-1/4" h, bronze, Ajax, after the antique, helmet, beard, parcel gilt toga, sq base, dark green patination, 20th C **865.00**

17-1/4" h, alabaster, woman in lace headdress and bodice, tapered alabaster socle, early 20th C **450.00**

19" h, carved marble, Venus, classical-style nude goddess, trumpet socle, early 20th C **635.00**

19-1/2" w, 11" d, 24" h, carved marble, elegant woman, Kentucky, c1870 . . . . **8,625.00**

20" h, marble, lady with rose, incised "A. Testi," associated partial alabaster pedestal with spiral fluted stem **2,645.00**

20-1/2" h, bronze, Rembrandt, Albert-Ernest Carrier-Belleuse, silvered patination, bronze socle, marble plinth. **2,300.00**

24-1/2" h, white marble, young lady, powdered wig, lace edged bodice, turned socle, French, third/fourth quarter 18th C **3,450.00**

26" h, marble, young pious woman, lace and flower bodice, hair in long braid,

matching 6" h marble socle, Italian, late 19th C **7,475.00**

BUTTER PRINTS

History: There are two types of butter prints: butter molds and butter stamps. Butter molds are generally of three-piece construction—the design, the screw-in handle, and the case. Molds both shape and stamp the butter at the same time. Butter stamps are generally of one-piece construction, but can be of two-piece construction if the handle is from a separate piece of wood. Stamps decorate the top of butter after it is molded.

The earliest prints are one piece and were hand carved, often heavily and deeply. Later prints were factory made with the design forced into the wood by a metal die.

Some of the most common designs are sheaves of wheat, leaves, flowers, and pineapples. Animal designs and Germanic tulips are difficult to find. Prints with designs on both sides are rare, as are those in unusual shapes, such as half-rounded or lollipop.

Reference: Paul E. Kindig, *Butter Prints and Molds*, Schiffer Publishing, 1986.

Reproduction Alert: Reproductions of butter prints were made as early as the 1940s.

Butter mold

2" l, oval, warbonnet with feathers, vine border, good patina, handle with age crack, some edge damage to case. **200.00**

2-3/4" d, anchor, carved wood . **185.00**

3-1/2" d, sunflower, carved wood **85.00**

4-3/8" d, pineapple, carved wood **325.00**

5" x 8", roses, carved maple, serrated edges **165.00**

Butter stamp

1-7/8" d, round, carved flower, one piece handle, 1-7/8" d **175.00**

2-3/8" x 1-3/4", rectangular, backward looking crested peafowl-type bird, sitting on flowering branch, turned inset handle, dark stains **250.00**

2-1/2" d, round, carved thistle, turned handle **50.00**

2-7/8" d, 4-1/2" l, carved fruitwood, strawberry **50.00**

3-1/4" d, round, carved wide-eyed cow and fence, threaded insert handle with chip on end **200.00**

3-5/8" d, 2-1/4" l, fruitwood, leaf and branch. **65.00**

3-3/4" d, pinwheel, four teardrop and triangular arms form design, old dark finish **115.00**

3-7/8" d, round, stylized tulip, one-piece turned handle **175.00**

4-1/8" d x 4-1/2", star design, similar carving on handle **145.00**

4-1/4" d, round, cow, turned
handle **150.00**
4-1/4" d, round, sunflower, feather
leaves, old dark finish, turned
handle **435.00**
4-1/4" d, round, swan, turned
handle **125.00**
4-3/8" d, round, carved primitive eagle,
rayed sunbursts, dark patina, worn finish, large one piece handle,
4-3/8" d **330.00**
4-1/2" d, round, carved strawberries
and leaf, threaded handle, age
cracks. **110.00**
4-5/8" d, round, carved pineapple,
turned handle, wear, cracks. **95.00**
4-3/4" d, round, carved tulip with buds,
deeply carved, PA, age cracks, inset
handle missing. **1,485.00**
4-3/4" d, 5-1/2" l, walnut, foliage and
flowers **115.00**
5" d, round, carved tulip, good patina,
PA, age cracks, 5" d. **665.00**
5-7/8" l, lollipop, carved rosette, hardwood. **110.00**
6-1/2" l, lollipop, carved heart and
leaves, chip carved stars, soft worn fin-

ish, hold through handle for cord to
hang **1,375.00**
6-3/4" l, sheaf of wheat, stylized design,
notched rim band **200.00**

7" l, lollipop style, star, zig-zag
band rim, flared end handle, old
patina. **300.00**

Double heart with flower, crimped stylized edges, oval, 5-1/2" x 3-1/2", **$425.**

CALENDAR PLATES

History: Calendar plates were first made in England in the late 1880s. They became popular in the United States after 1900, the peak years being 1909 to 1915. The majority of the advertising plates were made of porcelain or pottery and the design included a calendar, the name of a store or business, and either a scene, portrait, animal, or flowers. Some also were made of glass or tin.

Periodical: *The Calendar*, 710 N. Lake Shore Drive, Tower Lakes, IL 60010-1277.

Collector Club: Calendar Plate Collectors Club, 710 N. Lake Shore Drive, Tower Lakes, IL 60010-1277.

Additional Listings: See *Warman's Americana & Collectibles* for more examples.

1915, Panama Canal, marked "O. E. McMoob Pottery Co., East Liverpool, Oh," 7-1/4" d, $32.

1906, holly and roses, 9" d 40.00
1907, Santa and holly, 9-1/2" d .. 80.00
1908, hunting dog, Pittstown, PA. 40.00
1908, roses center............ 55.00
1909, woman and man in patio garden, 9" d 35.00
1910, Buffalo Pottery, Deldare, sgd "L. Anna," 9-1/2" d 2,750.00
1910, Homer Laughlin, Hudson, "Compliments of Crivest Bros., 96 Lincoln," four scenes, 9-1/4" d .. 50.00
1911, Souvenir of Detroit, MI, months in center, hen and yellow chicks, gold edge 28.00
1912, Martha Washington 40.00
1912, Milford Square, PA, floral center 35.00
1913, roses and holly 30.00
1914, Point Arena, CA, 6-3/4" d.. 30.00
1915, black boy eating watermelon, 9" d 60.00
1916, man in canoe, IA, 7-1/2" d
.... 35.00

1916, eagle with shield, American flag, 8-1/4" d..................... 40.00
1917, cat center 35.00
1919, ship center 30.00
1920, The Great War, MO...... 30.00
1921, bluebirds and fruit, 9" d .. 35.00
1922, dog watching rabbit..... 35.00
1957, Homer Laughlin, Skytone, blue, Zodiac signs in gold.......... 18.00
1969, Royal China, Currier & Ives, green, 10" d 40.00
1972, Alfred Meakin, Staffordshire, England, engraved pattern, "God Bless Our Home," farm scene, 9" d 18.00
1990, Wedgwood, British Birds, marked "Wedgwood of Etruria & Barlaston," 10" d 12.00

CALLING CARD CASES AND RECEIVERS

History: Calling cards, usually carried in specially designed cases, played an important social role in the United States from the Civil War until the end of World War I. When making formal visits, callers left their card in a receiver (card dish) in the front hall. Strict rules of etiquette developed. For example, the lady in a family was expected to make calls of congratulations and condolence and visits to the ill.

The cards themselves were small, embossed or engraved with the caller's name, and often decorated with a floral design. Many handmade examples, especially in Spencerian script, can be found. The cards themselves are considered collectible and range in price from a few cents to several dollars.

Note: Don't confuse a calling card case with a match safe.

Case
2-7/8" x 3-7/8", Chinese Export silver, rect, all over hammered appearance, central monogrammed roundel, attributed to Tuck Chang & Co., late 19th/early 20th C, approx four troy oz..................... 200.00
3" l, burl wood, Victorian 95.00
3" w x 4", mother-of-pearl, Victorian 180.00
3" x 4-1/2", Chinese-Export silver, rect, obverse with emb genre scenes and central cartouche, reverse with emb bamboo shoots, maker's mark "SM," late 19th/early 20th C, approx two troy oz...................... 300.00
3" x 4-3/8", Mauchline Ware, White-Fern pattern.................... 225.00
3-3/8" x 3", white-metal case, enamel dec of harem girl disrobing in exotic int., late 19th/early 20th C, giltwood frame..................... 800.00
3-1/2" x 3-3/4", quadruple silver plate, orig chain, Victorian 125.00
3-3/4" x 2-3/4", sterling silver, engine turned spiral dec, dark green emerald moiré silk concertina int., hallmarked Birmingham, England 175.00
4" l, rect, ivory, wood inlay, block rows, center framed with diamond design rim band 175.00

Bronze, hammered, ovoid, emb comedy and tragedy masks, Gorham, original dark patina, stamp mark, 9-1/2" x 6", $750. Photo courtesy of David Rago Auctions.

4" x 1-1/2", porcelain, hand painted violets, artist's signature **25.00**

4" x 3", tortoiseshell with stylized floral plique, hinged metal lid, 19th C . **110.00**

4-1/8" x 3-1/8", ivory inlay with lines of plique, hinged metal lid, 19th C . **115.00**

Receiver

5" l, figural, majolica, duck and bird, Continental, minor rim nicks **90.00**

7" l, figural, bronze, monkey, Victorian **135.00**

7-1/4" l, 5-1/2" h, silver plate, marked "Meriden," wear to plating **60.00**

9-1/2" l, 6" w, hammered bronze, ovoid, emb comedy and tragedy masks, orig dark patina, crisp details, Gorham stamp mark **650.00**

10" l, porcelain, hand painted, roses, foliage, gold handles **45.00**

CAMBRIDGE GLASS

History: Cambridge Glass Company, Cambridge, Ohio, was incorporated in 1901. Initially, the company made clear tableware, later expanding into colored, etched, and engraved glass. More than 40 different hues were produced in blown and pressed glass.

The plant closed in 1954 and some of the molds were later sold to the Imperial Glass Company, Bellaire, Ohio.

Marks: Five different marks were employed during the production years, but not every piece was marked.

References: Tom and Neila Bredehoft, *Fifty Years of Collectible Glass, 1920-1970, Volume 1, Volume II,* Antique Trader Books, 2000; Gene Florence, *Elegant Glassware of the Depression Era,* 8th ed., Collector Books, 1998; ——, *Glass Candlesticks of the Depression Era,* Collector Books, 1999; National Cambridge Collectors, Inc., *Cambridge Glass Co., Cambridge, Ohio* (reprint of 1930 catalog and supplements through 1934), Collector Books, 1976, 1998 value update; ——, *Cambridge Glass Co., Cambridge, Ohio, 1949 through 1953* (catalog reprint), Collector Books, 1976, 1996 value update; ——, *Colors in Cambridge Glass,* Collector Books, 1984, 1999 value update; ——, *"Nearcut"* (reprint of 1910 catalog), 1997; Naomi L. Over, *Ruby Glass of the 20th Century,* Antique Publications, 1990, 1993-94 value update; Miami Valley (Ohio) Study Group, *Etchings by Cambridge, Volume 1,* Brookville Publishing, 1997; Bill and Phyllis Smith, *Cambridge Glass 1927-1929* (1986) and *Identification Guide to Cambridge Glass 1927-1929* (updated prices 1996), published by authors (4003 Old Columbus Rd., Springfield, OH 45502).

Periodical: *The Daze,* P.O. Box 57, Otisville, MI 48463.

Collectors' Club: National Cambridge Collectors, Inc., P.O. Box 416, Cambridge, OH 43725, www.cambridgeglass.org.

Museums: Cambridge Glass Museum, Cambridge, OH; Museum of the National Cambridge Collectors, Inc., Cambridge, OH.

Banana bowl, Inverted Thistle, 7" l, radium green, marked "Near-cut" **95.00**

Basket

Apple Blossom, crystal 7" . . . **475.00**
Hunts Scene, pink, 11" h . . . **215.00**

Bell, Rose Point **150.00**

Bonbon, Diane, crystal, 8-1/2" . . **25.00**

Bookends, pr, eagle, crystal . . . **65.00**

Bowl

10" d, Wildflower, crystal, gold krystol, matching 12-1/2" d plate, sgd **375.00**
15" d, Rose Point, crystal . . . **100.00**

Butter dish, cov

Gadroon, crystal **45.00**
Rose Point, crystal, quarter pound **750.00**

Candlestick

Caprice, blue, three lite, #1338 . . . . **75.00**
Cascade, crystal, 1-lite, pr . . . **47.50**
Doric, black, 9-1/2" h, pr **160.00**
Rose Point, crystal, two lite, keyhole, pr **95.00**

Candy dish, cov, three ftd

Caprice, Alpine Blue **130.00**
Wildflower, crystal, 8" d, three part **75.00**

Goblet, Rose Point, 8-1/2" h, **$40.**

Champagne, Wildflower, crystal, 6 oz **20.00**

Cigarette box, Caprice, blue, 3-1/2" x 4-1/2" **70.00**

Claret, Wildflower, crystal, 4-1/2 oz **42.00**

Cocktail

Caprice, blue **45.00**
Rose Point, crystal, 3 oz **35.00**
Stradivary **50.00**

Comport

Honeycomb, rubena, 9" d, 4-3/4" h, ftd **150.00**
Nude Stem, #3011, Heatherbloom, cupped bowl, 6-1/2" w bowl, 8" h **1,260.00**
Rose Point, amber, 7-1/4" d, 7" h **2,035.00**

Condiment set, Pristine, crystal, five pc **98.50**

Cordial

Caprice, blue **120.00**
Chantilly, crystal **55.00**
Stradivary **65.00**
Wildflower, crystal, 1 oz **60.00**

Corn dish, Portia, crystal **50.00**

Creamer

Inverted Thistle, dark marigold, marked "Near-cut," slight rim damage **65.00**
Martha Washington, amber, clear stick handle **15.00**

Creamer and sugar, Cascade, emerald green **35.00**

Creamer and sugar, tray, Caprice, crystal **40.00**

Cream soup, orig liner

Decagon, green **35.00**
Willow Blue, #3400/55 . . . . . . **25.00**

Cup and saucer

Caprice, crystal **14.00**
Decagon, pink **10.00**
Martha Washington, amber . . . **12.00**

Decanter, Nautilus, #84482, crystal **45.00**

Decanter set, decanter, stopper, six handled 2-1/2 oz tumblers, Tally Ho, amethyst **185.00**

Dressing bottle, Chantilly, crystal, silver base **150.00**

Finger bowl, Adam, yellow **25.00**

Flower frog

Draped Lady, dark pink, 8-1/2" h **165.00**
Draped Lady, green, oval base, Pat. No. 1645577 imp inside of base, 9" h **325.00**
Eagle, pink **365.00**
Jay, green **365.00**
Nude, 6-1/2" h, 3-1/4" d, clear . **95.00**

Rose Lady, amber, 8-1/2" h. . **350.00**
Rose Lady, crystal, 9-3/4" h . **350.00**
Seagull **65.00**
Two Kids, clear **155.00**
Fruit Bowl, Decagon, pink, 5-1/2" **5.50**
Goblet
Caprice, blue **40.00**
Diane, crystal **25.00**
Nude Stem, smoke crackle, orig
sticker. **1,200.00**
Portia, Carmen (red), etched-basket
design with flowers and foliage,
c1930, 7-5/8" h **1,575.00**
Rose Point, crystal, 10 oz **30.00**
Ice bucket
Blossom Time, crystal. **125.00**
Chrysanthemum, pink, silver
handle **85.00**
Tally Ho, cobalt blue **175.00**
Iced tea tumbler, ftd, Wildflower,
crystal, 12 oz. **28.00**
Ivy ball
Japonica dec, #3400/92,
5-1/2" **3,450.00**
Nude Stem, Statuesque #3011/2,
9-1/2" h, 4-1/4" h d ruby ball, 4" d
base **500.00**
Juice tumbler, ftd
Candlelight etch, 5 oz, #3114. **35.00**
Diane, crystal, ftd **15.00**
Lemon plate, Caprice, blue, 5" d **15.00**
Martini pitcher, Rose Point,
crystal **700.00**
Mustard, cov, Farber Brothers, cobalt
blue **50.00**
Oil cruet, Chantilly etch, 4 oz . . . **95.00**
Oyster cocktail, Portia, crystal. . **40.00**
Pitcher
Mt. Vernon, forest green **300.00**
Tally Ho, crystal, metal spout and
lid **105.00**
Plate
Apple Blossom, pink, 8-1/2" d **20.00**
Caprice, crystal, 9-1/2" d **38.00**
Crown Tuscan, 7" d. **45.00**
Decagon, pink, 8" **8.00**
Martha Washington, amber,
lunch. **15.00**
Rose Point, crystal, 8" d, ftd . . **70.00**
Platter, Caprice, crystal, 14" l,
ftd **30.00**
Relish
Mt. Vernon, crystal, 5 part. . . . **35.00**
Rose Point, crystal, 12" l, 5
part. **100.00**
Tally Ho, blue, 8-1/4" l, 3 part,
handle **25.00**
Salad bowl, Caprice, blue,
10" d **250.00**

*Water or lemonade set, with pitcher and
six tumblers. Pitcher is 10" h; tumblers
are 3-3/4" h,* **$275.**

Salt and pepper shakers, Rose Point,
ball-shaped, silver base, marked
"Wallace Sterling 100" **550.00**
Sauce dish, Inverted Strawberry, 5" d,
marigold **25.00**
Seafood cocktail, Seashell, #110,
Crown Tuscan, 4-1/2" oz. **95.00**
Server, center handle
Apple Blossom, amber **30.00**
Decagon, blue. **16.00**
Sherbet
Diane, crystal, low **20.00**
Regency, low **22.00**
Rose Point, crystal, 7 oz **24.00**
Sherry, Portia, gold encrusted. . . **60.00**
Sugar, Martha Washington,
crystal. **25.00**
Torte plate, Rose Point, crystal, 13" d, 3
ftd **95.00**
Tray, #3500/112, 3 part, 15". **35.00**
Tumbler
Adam, yellow, ftd. **25.00**
Caprice, blue, 12 oz, ftd **40.00**
Carmine, crystal, 12 oz **25.00**
Decagon, blue, 8 oz, ftd **12.00**
Vase
Diane, crystal, keyhole,
12" h **110.00**
Rose Point, 3-1/4" d, 10" h, black
amethyst **665.00**
Songbird and Butterfly, #402, 12" h,
blue **375.00**
Tall Flat Panel, swung, 19-1/4" h,
sgd **100.00**
Wildflower, 12" h, flip **800.00**
Whiskey, Caprice, blue,
2-1/2" oz. **225.00**
Wine
Caprice, crystal **24.00**
Diane, crystal, 2-1/2 oz **30.00**

CAMEO GLASS

History: Cameo glass is a form of cased glass. A shell of glass was prepared, then one or more layers of glass of a different color(s) was faced to the first. A design was then cut through the outer layer(s), leaving the inner layer(s) exposed.

This type of art glass originated in Alexandria, Egypt, between 100 and 200 A.D. The oldest and most famous example of cameo glass is the Barberini or Portland vase found near Rome in 1582. It contained the ashes of Emperor Alexander Serverus, who was assassinated in 235 A.D.

Emile Gallé is probably one of the best-known cameo-glass artists. He established a factory at Nancy, France, in 1884. Although much of the glass bears his signature, he was primarily the designer. Assistants did the actual work on many pieces, even signing Gallé's name. Other makers of French-cameo glass include D'Argental, Daum Nancy, LeGras, and Delatte.

English-cameo pieces do not have as many layers of glass (colors) and cuttings as do French pieces. The outer layer is usually white, and cuttings are very fine and delicate. Most pieces are not signed. The best-known makers are Thomas Webb & Sons and Stevens and Williams.

Marks: A star before the name Gallé on a piece by that company indicates that it was made after Gallé's death in 1904.

References: Victor Arwas, *Glass Art Nouveau to Art Deco*, Rizzoli International Publications, 1977; Alastair Duncan and George DeBartha, *Glass by Gallé*, Harry N. Abrams, 1984; Ray and Lee Grover, *English Cameo Glass*, Crown Publishers, 1980; Kyle Husfloen, *Antique Trader's American & European Decorative and Art Glass Price Guide*, 2nd ed., Krause Publications, 2000; Albert C. Revi, *Nineteenth Century Glass*, reprint, Schiffer Publishing, 1981; John A. Shuman, III, *Collector's Encyclopedia of American Art Glass*, Collector Books, 1988, 1999 value update.

Reproduction Alert.

American
Harrach, vase, 8" h, 4" d, bright white carved daffodils, leaves, and stems, frosted and green ground **950.00**
Honesdale Glass, vase, 12" h, green etched to clear, gold dec trim **1,295.00**
Mount Washington
Bowl, 8" d, 4" h, sq, ruffled edge, two winged Griffins holding up scroll and spray of flowers design, blue over white ground **1,475.00**
Lamp, 17" h, 10" d shade, fluid font and shade composed of opal white opaque glass overlaid in bright rose pink, acid-etched butterflies, ribbons, and bouquets centering cameo-portrait medallions in classical manner, mounted on silver-plated metal fittings, imp "Pairpoint Mfg. Co. 3013," electrified **3,200.00**

English

Florentine Art, cruet, 6-1/2" h, ruby-red body, textured white enamel meadowland scene, Meadowlark on tall plant stalk, smaller scene on reverse, white rim, trefoil spout, clear frosted handle, teardrop shaped stopper, pontil mark sgd "59" **750.00**

Stevens and Williams

Vase, 4-1/2" h, broad bright blue oval, overlaid in opaque white glass, cameo etched and cut clusters of cherries on leafy boughs, circular mark on base "Stevens & Williams Art Glass Stourbridge" **1,265.00**

Vase, 6-1/4" h, Rose du Barry, lush pink-rose oval body, etched with white six-petaled blossoms and buds, intricate leaves, butterfly at reverse, linear border . . . **1,610.00**

Unknown maker

Plaque, 5-1/2" l, 3-1/2" w, citron yellow, five white, carved carnation flowers, leaf **1,275.00**

Vase, 7" h, 5" w, corset shape, cranberry, white overlay, carved sprays of sweet peas, leaves, branches, butterfly in flight **1,750.00**

Webb

Bonbon, 7-1/2" h, 5" d, morning glory blossoms, white on red on citron, deep yellow base layer, creamy white lining, hammered sterling-silver standard and lid, lid stamped "800," silversmith's mark obscured by finial, attributed to Webb **1,950.00**

Vase, Richardson, golden amber lily blossoms, shiny golden foliage, signed pontil, 8" h, $1,350. Photo courtesy of Clarence and Betty Maier.

Cup and saucer, handleless, 2-3/4" h, 5" d, cranberry over crystal, prunous blossom carving, leaves, and branches, 10 blossoms on cup with large butterfly and 25 buds **550.00**

Perfume bottle, 3-3/4" l, flattened-teardrop shape, bright blue, etched forget-me-nots all around, two butterflies on shoulder, one chip on surface flower, wear to gilt-metal screw cap **435.00**

Scent bottle, 4" l, flattened-teardrop shape, sapphire blue, white ferns and grasses dec, butterfly at side, gilt-metal hinged cover . . . **920.00**

Vase, 7-1/2" h, bulbous baluster, gold ground, carved white geraniums, carved white coral bells on reverse, sgd "Webb" **1,750.00**

French

Arsall, vase, 5" h, flared, pink mottled yellow overlaid ground, green layer etched as decumbent blossoms, buds, and leafy stems, sgd "Arsall" in design **325.00**

Burgen, Schverer, and Cie, Alsace-Lorraine, vase, ftd broad ovoid, frosted colorless glass, amethyst overlay etched and engraved trailing nasturtium blossom, gilt highlights, elaborate gold enamel trademark on base, c1900, enamel wear . . . **2,760.00**

D'Argental

Atomizer, 4" h, cylindrical amber perfume bottle, green and brown overlay, etched landscape of leafy trees, wild geese in flight, sgd "D'Argental" on side, gilt-metal fittings marked "Le Parisien Made in France," "BTE, S.G.D.G." **825.00**

Vase, 10-1/2" h, 4-1/2" d, three acid cuttings, brown cut to tan to gold, forest scene, mountains, castle on hill, sgd **1,300.00**

Daum Nancy

Bowl, 7-3/4" d, 3" h, pinched rim, mottled white, pink, purple, and yellow, etched and intricately enameled Coreopsis daisies in shaded yellows, green foliage, sgd in enamel "Daum Nancy France" on side, c1910, burst int. bubble **2,100.00**

Lamp base, 23-1/4" h, elongated body, mottled orange overlaid in dark orange and brown, cameo-etched trumpet flowers

rising from broad leaves, engraved "Daum (cross) Nancy" at side, metal lamp fittings **1,380.00**

Night light, 8-3/4" h, slender tapered form, frosted pale pink and green, cameo etched and enameled black trees in rain, illuminated patinated metal stand . . . **3,450.00**

Perfume bottle, 5" h, ovoid red body, acid etched and enameled spray of daisies, gold-enamel highlights, chased silver base and stopper, sgd "Daum (cross) Nancy" in gold enamel **1,035.00**

Salt, 1-3/8" h, bucket form, two upright handles, frosted colorless ground, cameo etched and enameled black tree lined shore, distant ruins, gilt rim, sgd "Daum (cross) Nancy" in gilt on base, small rim chips **575.00**

Vase, 4-1/4" h, two handles, light green and pale red, etched Japanese-style scene of herons and water plants, gilded trailing vines, mounted in finely cast and chased silver mounts with roses and foliage on rim and base, French hallmarks 925 fine, etched and gilt signature "Daum Nancy" on base **3,100.00**

Vase, 4-1/2" h, flattened oval, gray ground, overlaid in vitrified yellows, light greens, and rose pink, etched rose hips among leaves, polished to enhance design, sgd "Daum Nancy (cross)," c1910 . . **1,150.00**

Vase, 15-1/2" h, oval body with raised rim, shaded gray to sky yellow to gray, vitrified autumn colors on falling leaves above and below landscape scene, medial cameo mark "Daum Nancy (cross)" **3,750.00**

Wine glass, 7-3/4" h, slender, opalescent and frosted sea green, etched and enameled violets in pale rose and green, gilded rims, base inscribed and enameled "Daum Nancy Rube 62 B2 Haussmann Paris," light wear to gilding and enameling, pr **2,185.00**

Degue, vase, 5-1/2" h, cylindrical, tapered raised rim, mottled shades of frosted orange, layered in dark brown, etched desert oasis scene, camels and palm trees, side cameo sgd, small inside rim chip **750.00**

Delatte, vase, 6-1/8" h, flared cylindrical form, frosted colorless ground, brown enamel and etched tree lined shore and rocky outcropping, distant hills, gilt metal pedestal, raised leaf pattern, sgd "A. Delatte Nancy" on lower side 520.00

De Vez

Bell, 8-1/4" h, amber overlaid with red, cut daisy flowers and leaves, metal handle, tassel-shaped clapper on chain **8,025.00**

Rose bowl, 3-1/2" d, cobalt blue foliated trees and mountains, pink to yellow sky and water, scalloped rim, sgd 500.00

Vase, 6" h, maroon and fiery amber oval body, etched cottages, mother, child, under tall trees, sgd "de Vez" at side, polished rim 900.00

Vase, 8" h, tubular, three-color scenic brown castle and trees, blue mountains, frosted ground, sgd **1,400.00**

Galle

Bowl, 6" d, tricorn, frosted colorless and pale yellow pinched bowl, lavender and blue layers, etched flowering myrtle vines, sgd "Galle" on side, nick at base 800.00

Bowl, 7-3/4" d, 4-1/4" h, ftd, four pulled points, pale pink ground, light yellow-green and amber overlay, etched clusters of blossoms on leafy branches, sgd "H Galle" among leaves, several bubble bursts and int. wear 690.00

Decanter, 10-1/4" h, flattened oval body, upturned rim, conical stopper, frosted colorless and purple ground, overlaid in deep purple, etched iris, engraved "Cristallerie de Galle Nancy modele et decor deposes" on base **2,530.00**

Tazza, 10-3/4" d, amber-yellow ground, maroon layer etched as flowering clematis vines, short maroon foot, sgd "Galle" on underside, light wear, matte surface to rim, two bubble bursts on top **1,150.00**

Vase, 3-1/2" h, bulbous, raised neck, opaque pink cased to colorless ext., olive green layer etched as round berries among leaves, sgd "Galle" on side, black inclusion 460.00

Vase, 4-3/4" h, broad ovoid body, raised rim, frosted colorless ground, yellow, orange, and green

layers, etched daffodils in meadow, flowers polished, sgd "Galle" near base, nick near base 980.00

Vase, 6-3/4" h, flattened-spherical form, elongated neck, pale yellow cased to colorless, brown layer, etched woodland orchids, sgd "Galle" among leaves 525.00

Vase, 7-7/8" h, ovoid, elongated neck, frosted colorless and pink ground, periwinkle and green layer, etched flowering hydrangea branches, sgd "H Galle" near base 750.00

Vase, 8" h, bulbous, elongated neck, gray with pink streaked ground, periwinkle and green layers, acid-etched stalk of stylized flowers, sgd "Galle" near base 875.00

Vase, 8" h, bulbous, flared neck, pink layered with olive green, etched spray of berries among leaves, sgd "Galle" on side, bubble bursts 400.00

Vase, 8" h, stepped cylindrical, colorless ground, overlaid in pink and purple etched crocus in field, sgd "Galle" near base. . . 1,265.00

Vase, 8-1/2" h, barrel form, transparent topaz colored ground, etched and naturalistic colored enameled grains of barley, sgd "Galle" near base, some wear to enamel. 865.00

Vase, 11" h, brown berry and vine dec, clambroth ground, fire polished, mounted as lamp. 400.00

Vase, 13" h, ovoid, amber and frosted colorless ground, light green and olive layers etched as leafy maple branch, sgd "Galle" near base 920.00

Vase, LeGras, rust cut to orange to gray to green, black sunset scene, 5" x 3-1/2" x 4-3/4", **$500.**

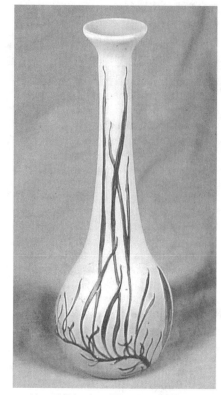

Vase, 10" h, signed "Legras," $350.

LeGras

Bowl, 10" d, 3-3/4" h, olive-green body, heavily etched and engraved Art-Deco swag and drapery design, fire polished, acid-etched "Legras" near base 825.00

Vase, 4-3/4" h, spherical body, quatreform rim, colorless ground, enameled bare trees in snow at sunset, yellow, orange, brown, black, and white, sgd "Legras" near base. 410.00

Vase, 5-5/8" h, pinched rim, swollen and waisted vessel, colorless body, etched and enameled dark fuchsia ivy on textured and frosted surface, sgd "Legras" on side, light scratches to enameled surface. 350.00

Vase, 8-3/4" h, scalloped-oval shape, landscape scene, green, brown, peach, and frosty white. 50.00

Michel

Vase, 7-1/2" h, 4-3/4" d, maroon overlay, yellow opaque satin ground, sailboats, branches, and leaves frame border, sgd "Michel, Paris" 725.00

Vase, 14-1/8" h, baluster, frosted cream overlaid yellow, orange,

brown, and dark blue,
cameo-etched bayou scene at
sunset, "Michel" at lower side,
burst bubbles **990.00**

Richard

Bowl, 6" l, 2-3/4" h, brilliant cased
poppy red, brown overlay,
acid-etched stylized foliate motif,
sgd "Richard" at side **460.00**

Vase, 7-1/4" h, yellow-cased oval,
layered in brown, cameo-etched
mountainous village waterfront
scene, applied brown-black
handles at each side, sgd
"Richard" at side **825.00**

Wine, 7-3/4" h, cobalt-blue scenic
water and sailboats, frosted
ground, notched stem **400.00**

CAMERAS

History: Photography became a viable enterprise in
the 1840s, but few early cameras have survived.
Cameras made before the 1880s are seldom available
on the market, and when found, their prices are
prohibitive for most collectors.

George Eastman's introduction of the Kodak
camera in 1888, the first commercially marketed
roll-film camera, put photography in the hands of the
public.

Most collectors start with a general interest that
becomes more defined. After collecting a broad range
of Kodak cameras, a collector may decide to specialize
in Retina models. Camera collectors tend to prefer
unusual and scarce cameras to the most common
models, which were mass-produced by the millions.

Because a surplus exists for many common
cameras, such as most Kodak box and folding models,
collectors are wise to acquire only examples in
excellent condition. Shutters should function properly.
Minimal wear is generally acceptable. Avoid cameras
that have missing parts, damaged bellows, and major
cosmetic problems.

References: Brian Coe and Paul Gates, *The
Snapshot Photograph,* Ash and Grant Ltd., 1977;
Rudolpf Hillebrand and Gunther Kadlubek,
*Photographica: The Fascination with Classic
Cameras,* Schiffer Publishing, 2000; John F. Maloney,
Vintage Cameras and Images, Books Americana,
1981; James and Joan McKeown, *McKeown's Price
Guide to Antique & Classic Cameras, 1997-1998,*
Centennial Photo Service, 1996; Beaumont Newhall,
The History of Photography, The Museum of Modern
Art, 1982.

Periodicals: *Camera Shopper,* P.O. Box 1086, New
Cannan, CT 06840; *Classic Camera,* P.O. Box 1270,
New York, NY 10157-2078; *Shutterbug,* 5211 S.
Washington Ave., Titusville, FL 32780.

Collectors' Clubs: American Photographic
Historical Society, Inc., 1150 Avenue of the Americas,
New York, NY 10036; American Society of Camera
Collectors, 4918 Alcove Ave., North Hollywood, CA
91607; International Kodak Historical Society, P.O.
Box 21, Flourtown, PA 19301; Leica Historical Society

of America, 7611 Dornoch Lane, Dallas, TX 75248;
National Stereoscopic Association, P.O. Box 14801,
Columbus, OH 43214; Nikon Historical Society, P.O.
Box 3213, Munster, IN 46321; Photographic Historical
Society, P.O. Box 39563, Rochester, NY 14604; The
Movie Machine Society, 50 Old Country Rd, Hudson,
MA 01749; Zeiss Historical Society, 300 Waxwing
Drive, Cranbury, NJ 08512.

Museums: Cameras & Images International, Boston,
MA; Fleetwood Museum, North Plainfield, NJ; George
Eastman Museum, Rochester, NY; International
Cinema Museum, Chicago, IL; Smithsonian
Institution, Washington, DC.

Additional Listings: See *Warman's Americana &
Collectibles* for more examples.

Adviser: Tom Hoepf.

*Perfex, One-O-One Camera Corp. of
America, Wollensak lens, Alphox shutter, F4 5/50 mm, 1947-50, $35.*

Adams & Westlak Co., Chicago, IL,
Adlake Repeater, c1897, box camera
with fixed-focus lens, crank on side
advances, 12 plates **75.00**

American Camera Mfg. Co.,
Northboro, MA, No. 1 Tourist Buckeye,
c1895, folding roll-film camera in two
sizes: 3-1/2" x 3-1/2" or 3-1/4" x 4-1/2"
exposures, maroon bellows . . . **150.00**

Ansco, Binghamton, NY

Ansco Special, c1925, simple box
camera, red leather covered,
No. 2 for 120 film, No. 2A for 116
film **30.00**

Anscoflex, c1957, metal twin-lens
reflex, gray finish, front panel slides
up and opens, finder hood . . **15.00**

Automatic Reflex, c1947,
high-quality twin-lens reflex,
Ansco anastigmat f3.5 83mm
lens, ground-glass focusing
screen **200.00**

Bingo No. 2, c1925 black-box
camera, 120 film, leather strap
handle **20.00**

Anthony Camera Co., New York, NY,
Climax Imperial, 1890s, 8" x 10"
studio camera, single extension
bellows **300.00**

Bell & Howell, Chicago, IL, Electric Eye
127, c1960, all-metal box camera with
large eye-level viewfinder on top and
automatic diaphragm lens **15.00**

Blair Camera Co., Rochester, NY, Baby
Hawk Eye, c1896, small, lightweight
box camera, 2" x 2-1/2" exposures on
roll film **200.00**

Bolsey Corp. of America, New York,
NY

Bolsey B, c1950, small 35-mm
camera with coupled range finder,
f3.2 44mm anastigmat lens,
inoperative shutter **25.00**

Bolsey Jubilee, c1955, 35-mm
camera with coupled range finder,
Steinhill f2.8 45mm, Gauthier leaf
shutter **35.00**

Burke & James Inc., Chicago, IL,
Cub, c1915, series of box cameras
that load from the side, models 2A,
3 and 3A **20.00**

Chicago Ferrotype Co., Mandelette,
1929, street-box camera,
leather-covered wooden camera body
measures 4" x 4-1/2" x 6", black-cloth
sleeve at rear with metal tank attached
below camera body **60.00**

Eastman Kodak, Rochester, NY

Disney Mickey-Matic Camera Outfit,
1988, new on card in plastic blister
pack, with 110 film **15.00**

Kodak disc camera, model 4000,
c1985, brushed stainless-steel
front, chain wrist strap **5.00**

Kodak Six-20, 1930s folding
camera using 620 film, Art-Deco
silver trim on black-enamel side
panels **25.00**

Kodak Stereo Hawk-Eye, c1915,
folding-stereo camera with
horizontal side-by-side lenses,
polished wood interior, red
bellows **400.00**

Vigilant Six-16, 1940s folding
camera using 616 film **25.00**

C.F. Foth & Co., Berlin, Germany,
Derby, 1930s miniature camera using
127 film, flip-up tube viewfinder, Foth
anastigmat f3.5 50mm lens **40.00**

Hanna-Barbera, novelty cameras using
127 roll film and 126 cartridges, plastic
bodies with face of cartoon character
on the front, e.g., Fred Flintstone, Yogi
Bear **15.00**

Remco, Teenage Mutant Ninja Turtles
Signature Camera, 1990, plastic 110
camera, new on card in plastic blister
pack **15.00**

Rolls Camera Manufacturing Co.,
Chicago, IL, Rolls, c1939, Bakelite

novelty mini camera, metal
nameplate **10.00**
Sears, Chicago, IL, Tower Reflex,
1950s twin-lens reflex, f9 85mm
Roeschlein Kreuznach lens, 30-100
shutter **40.00**
Zeiss Ikon, Jena, Germany, Ikoflex I,
1940s twin-lens reflex, f3.5 7.5-cm
Novar anastigmat taking lens, 1-250
shutter **50.00**

CANDLESTICKS

History: The domestic use of candlesticks is traced to the 14th century. The earliest was a picket type, named for the sharp point used to hold the candle. The socket type was established by the mid-1660s.

From 1700 to the present, candlestick design mirrored furniture design. By the late 17th century, a baluster stem was introduced, replacing the earlier Doric or clustered column stem. After 1730, candlesticks reflected rococo ornateness. Neoclassic styles followed in the 1760s. Each new era produced a new style of candlesticks; however, some styles became universal and remained in production for centuries. Therefore, when attempting to date a candlestick, it is important to try to determine the techniques used to manufacture the piece.

References: Margaret and Douglas Archer, *Collector's Encyclopedia of Glass Candlesticks,* Collector Books, 1983; Veronika Baur, *Metal Candlesticks,* Schiffer Publishing, 1996; Gene Florence, *Glass Candlesticks of the Depression Era,* Collector Books, 1999; Ronald F. Michaels, *Old Domestic Base-Metal Candlesticks,* Antique Collectors' Club, 1999; Sherry Riggs and Paul Pendergrass, *Glass Candle Holders of the Depression Era, and Beyond,* Schiffer Publishing, 2001; Kenneth Wilson, *American Glass 1760-1930,* 2 vols., Hudson Hills Press and The Toledo Museum of Art, 1994.

Brass

5" d, 5-1/2" h, brass, kingfisher figures perched on standard, orig patina, stamped "W. T. & S.," English, price for pr **1,495.00**

6-3/4" h, short prickets over baluster, flattened and ball-knopped stem, tiered spreading base, Continental, late 19th/early 20th C **125.00**

7-5/8" h, Queen Anne, push-up, scalloped bases, burnished finish, one has solder underneath at seam, price for pr **770.00**

8-3/4" h, turned stems of solid stock, threaded into bases, base with six semicircular feet, scalloped edges, domed tops, price for pr . . **200.00**

9-3/8" h, well-turned stems of solid stock, threaded into bases, heavy cast sq bases with semicircular feet, domed tops, price for pr **275.00**

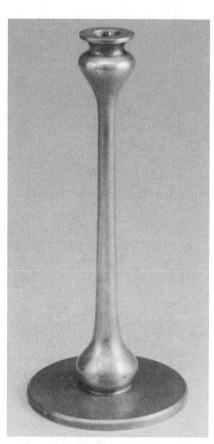

Brass, Arts & Crafts, in the style of Jarvie's Kappa, medium patina, bobeche missing, unmarked, 5" d, 11-1/2" h, **$460.** *Photo courtesy of David Rago Auctions.*

11-3/8" h, Neoclassical-style, 18th/19th C, push-up, nozzles engraved with drapery swags, tapered sq section stems with stylized stippled branches, tapered sq section bases, price for pr **290.00**

Bronze, 9-1/2" d, 15" h, triple, ribbed shaft and collar bobeche, dark patina, E. T. Hurley, marked "918," price for pr **920.00**

Cast brass and wrought iron, Gothic Revival, late 19th C, pricket, trefoil-edged drip pan, girdled multi-knopped cast brass standard, wrought-iron trefoil base with serpentine legs, acanthus knees and flowerhead scrolls, 61" h, price for pr **1,610.00**

Glass

Clambroth, 9-7/8" h, dolphins, paneled tulip-shaped socket, stepped base, roughness and one corner chip, price for pr . . . **330.00**

Vaseline, 9-3/4" h, dolphins, paneled floriform candle cups, sq stepped

bases, America, 19th C, chips, price for pr **1,380.00**

Hogscraper

6-3/8" h, push-up knob replaced, lip hanger, single **115.00**

8-1/4" h, push-up, marked "Shaw's Brim," lip repair, hanger missing, single **90.00**

Marble, 8" h, Empire-style, late 19th C, engine turned and beaded ormolu nozzles, gray marble columns hung with gilt-metal chains suspending acorns, stepped white marble base with flat leaf and beaded mounts, flattened ball feet, price for pr **350.00**

Metal, cast, 16" h, Renaissance Revival-style, 20th C, wide drip pan over flower-form knop, beaded baluster stem, trefoil scrolled base, reddish-black patination, price for pr **150.00**

Pewter, 22-3/4" h, pricket, wide drip pan, double-baluster stem, shaped-tripartite base, three ball feet, Continental, 18th C **700.00**

Porcelain, 10-5/8" h, figural, male and female flower gatherers, against brocage, rocaille base, attributed to Samson, France, late 19th C, price for pr **425.00**

Silver gilt, gessoed and turned wood, 5-3/4" w base, 8" h, base incised "Coro 1725," Europe, repairs, wear, minor losses, price for pr **460.00**

Silver plate

6-3/4" h, Neoclassical-style, England, early to mid-19th C, columnar, nozzles with acanthus dec, emb foliate spirals on stems, stepped sq bases, sides festooned, price for set of four **425.00**

11-1/2" h, Neoclassical-style, England, 19th C, campana-shape sockets fitted with beaded nozzles, reeded tapering stems, circular banded and beaded bases, engraved crests on bases, price for pr **175.00**

Silver, sterling, 5-1/2" h, Neoclassical, England, first half 19th C, emb gadrooned nozzle, campana-shape stems, foliate festoons and acanthus dec, waisted pedestal base, emb arms and beaded rims, price for pr . . **230.00**

Tin, 7-1/4" h, round weighted base, single **460.00**

Wrought iron, 11-1/2" h, scrolled handle and feet, lip handle, notched push-up, price for pr **550.00**

CANDY CONTAINERS

History: In 1876, Croft, Wilbur, and Co. filled small glass Liberty Bells with candy and sold them at the Centennial Exposition in Philadelphia. From that date until the 1960s, glass candy containers remained popular. They reflect historical changes, particularly in transportation.

Jeannette, Pennsylvania, a center for the packaging of candy in containers, was home for J. C. Crosetti, J. H. Millstein, T. H. Stough, and Victory Glass. Other early manufacturers included: George Borgfeldt, New York, New York; Cambridge Glass, Cambridge, Ohio; Eagle Glass, Wheeling, West Virginia; L. E. Smith, Mt. Pleasant, Pennsylvania; and West Brothers, Grapeville, Pennsylvania.

References: *Candy Containers*, L-W Book Sales, 1996; Douglas M. Dezso, J. Lion Poirier & Rose D. Poirier, *Collector's Guide to Candy Containers*, Collector Books, 1998, 2001 value update; George Eikelberner and Serge Agadjanian, *Complete American Glass Candy Containers Handbook*, revised and published by Adele L. Bowden, 1986; Jennie Long, *Album of Candy Containers*, published by author, Vol. I (1978), Vol. II (1983).

Collectors' Club: Candy Container Collectors of America, 2711 De La Rosa St., The Villages, FL 32159, www.candycontainers.org.

Museums: Cambridge Glass Museum, Cambridge, OH; L. E. Smith Glass, Mt. Pleasant, PA.

Additional Listings: See *Warman's Americana & Collectibles* for more examples.

Notes: Candy containers with original paint, candy, and closures command a high premium, but beware of reproduced parts and repainting. The closure is a critical part of each container; if it is missing, the value of the container drops considerably. Small figural perfumes and other miniatures often are sold as candy containers.

Airplane, P-38 Lightning, orig wire clip, motors, and ground, no closure . **200.00**
Amos & Andy, glass, car, 2-3/4" x 4-1/2" x 1-1/2" **525.00**
Auto, couple, long hood, orig tan snap-on strip, orig gold stamped tin wheels, orig closure **120.00**
Barney Google and bank
    Orig paint, orig closure **650.00**
    Repainted, orig closure **450.00**
Barney Google and bell, 70% orig paint, orig closure **350.00**
Baseball player with bat, 50% orig paint, orig closure **500.00**

Bear on circus tub, orig tin, orig closure **500.00**
Begging dog, 3-1/2" h, pressed glass, clear, no closure **150.00**
Bird on mount, orig whistle, 80% orig paint, orig closure, some chips . **550.00**
Boat, USN *Dreadnaught*, orig closure **350.00**
Boot, 3" h, clear glass, etched "Rick I Love You Penny" **35.00**
Bulldog, 4-1/4" h, screw closure. **60.00**
Bus
    Chicago, replaced closure . . **270.00**
    Jitney, orig tin, imperfect paint on top, crack to one wheel, orig closure **220.00**
    New York-San Francisco, orig closure **375.00**
    Victory Glass Co., replaced closure **300.00**
Camera on tripod, 80% paint, all paints replaced **200.00**
Cannon
    Cannon #1, orig carriage, orig closure **375.00**
    Rapid Fire Gun, orig closure **425.00**
    U. S. Defense Field Gun #17, orig closure **380.00**
    Two-Wheel Mount #1, orig carriage, orig closure **220.00**
    Two-Wheel Mount #2, orig carriage, orig closure, one replaced wheel **260.00**
Cash register, orig paint, orig closure **600.00**
Cat, papier-mâché
    3-3/4" h, seated, gray and white paint, pink ribbon, glass eyes, touch up and repairs **375.00**
    5" h, polychrome paint, glass eyes, boy's outfit **275.00**

Chick, composition
    3" h, painted, orange, yellow, and white, lead legs **65.00**
    5" h, cardboard, base, Germany **20.00**
Clarinet, musical, tin whistle, cardboard tube **35.00**
Coach, Esther Overland Limited, chipped glass coupler projections, replaced wheels **175.00**
Dog by barrel, 90% paint, chip on base, orig closure **220.00**
Elf on rocking horse, 3-1/2" h, pressed glass, no closure **160.00**
Felix the Cat, repainted, replaced closure **550.00**
Fire truck, with ladders **25.00**
Football, tin, Germany **20.00**
Gentleman, 6" h, papier-mâché head and hollow body, large pink nose, closed smiling mouth, painted brown eyes, molded and painted yellow vest, black jacket, gray pants with black stripe, black shoes, green bow tie, brown cane in left hand **210.00**
George Washington, 3" h, papier-mâché, with tricorn hat, white ponytail and blue coat, standing beside cardboard cabin with deep roof and chimney, unmarked **165.00**
Ghost head, 3-1/2" h, papier-mâché, flannel shroud **150.00**
Girl, celluloid, crepe-paper dress **30.00**
Goblin head, 60% orig paint, orig closure **625.00**
Green taxi, orig wheels, orig closure, small chip **600.00**
Gun, 5-3/4" l, West Specialty Co. . **20.00**
Hanging basket, flashed ruby glass, orig chain, no closure **70.00**

Left: train, right: fire engine with driver, metal wheels, clear glass, sold as pair, **$220.**
Photo courtesy of Joy Luke Auctions.

Hearse #2, replaced closure.... **80.00**
Horse and wagon, pressed glass **35.00**
Hot doggie, traces of paint, orig closure.................... **525.00**
House, all glass, 95% paint, orig closure.................... **250.00**
Independence Hall, corner steeple chip, orig closure............ **250.00**
Indian, 5" l, pressed glass, riding motorcycle with sidecar, no closure.................... **350.00**
Jack-o-lantern
    Open top, 95% orig paint, no closure **350.00**
    Pop eyed, 75% orig paint, orig closure, orig bail........ **475.00**
    Screw on lid, 95% orig paint. **360.00**
Kettle, 2" h, 2-1/4" d, pressed glass, clear, T. H. Stough, cardboard closure..................... **50.00**
Kewpie on radio, orig paint, orig closure.................... **650.00**
Lantern, 3-3/4" h, marked "Pat. Dec. 20, '04" **35.00**
Lawn swing, orig red-and-white tin canopy, orig closure **650.00**
Learned fox bottle, large chips on closure threads, orig closure.... **35.00**
Limousine, orig wheels, orig closure, small chip **600.00**
Little boy, 6" h, papier-mâché head and hollow body, large pink nose, closed smiling mouth, painted brown eyes, molded and painted red vest, green jacket, yellow short pants, purple socks, black shoes, brown tie........ **210.00**
Locomotive, Mapother's 1892, orig closure.................... **125.00**
Lynne clock bank. **750.00**
Man on motorcycle, side car, repainted, replaced closure ... **525.00**
Mule, pulling two-wheeled barrel with driver, 95% paint, orig closure... **80.00**
Nursing bottle, pressed glass, clear, natural wood nipple closure, T. H. Stough, 1940-50 .... **20.00**
Powder horn, orig closure **30.00**
Pumper, 5" l, pressed glass, tin wheels and bottom **110.00**
Pump for candy, yellow, both labels complete **235.00**
Pumpkin-head witch, 50% orig paint, orig closure **650.00**
Puppy, 2-1/2" h, papier-mâché, painted, white, black muzzle, glass eyes..................... **35.00**
Rabbit, glass
    Rabbit pushing chick in shell cart, orig closure............. **500.00**

Rabbit wearing hat, 90% orig paint above waist, repainted below waist, orig closure **900.00**
Rabbit with basket on arm, no paint, orig closure **120.00**
Rabbit, papier-mâché, 10" l, glass eyes, removable head, hollow body, four wood legs, stamped "Germany" on base of body, pulling wooden cart with wood-and-cardboard wheels, tin egg in cart, some orig dec, light wear. . **225.00**
Record player with horn **200.00**
Rocking horse, small chips on rockers, no closure.................. **180.00**
Rolling pin, orig handles, orig closure **250.00**
Rooster, 6-1/2" h, papier-mâché, pewter feet, orig polychrome paint, marked "Germany".......... **225.00**
Sailor, 6" h, papier-mâché head and hollow body, large pink nose, closed smiling mouth, protruding lower lip, molded and painted sideburns and hair, molded gray fez, painted blue eyes, molded and painted blue sailor uniform, black belt with knife case and sword, black shoes, unmarked . **265.00**
Santa Claus
    By sq chimney, 60% paint, replaced closure................. **180.00**
    Double cuff, repainted, orig closure................. **75.00**
    Paneled coat, orig closure... **140.00**
Spark plug, no paint, roughness in front, replaced closure **45.00**
Stop and Go, replaced switch handle, orig closure................. **440.00**
Submarine F6, no periscope or flat, orig super structure, orig closure **250.00**
Suitcase, milk glass, orig handle, traces of bear decal, orig closure **30.00**
Swan boat with rabbit and chick, repainted, replaced closure.... **650.00**
Tank, World War I, traces of orig paint, no closure................... **90.00**
Telephone, small glass receiver . **55.00**
Toonerville Depot Line, orig paint, orig closure **575.00**
Turkey, gobbler, small chip under orig closure **100.00**
Village bank, with insert, log-cabin roof...................... **110.00**
Wagon, orig closure.......... **90.00**
Wheelbarrow, orig wheel, no closure **35.00**
Windmill
    Dutch windmill, orig blades, chip on back, no closure **220.00**
    Five windows, ruby-flashed orig blades, orig closure **475.00**

CANES

History: Canes or walking sticks have existed through the ages, first as staffs or symbols of authority, to religious ceremonial pieces. They eventually evolved to the fashion accessory that is the highly desirable antique prized by today's collector for it's beauty and lasting qualities. The best were created with rare materials such as carved ivory, precious metals, jewels, porcelain, and enamel, with many being very high-quality works of art. They were also fashioned of more mundane materials, with some displaying the skill of individual folk artists. Another category of interest to collectors is the gadget canes that contained a myriad of hidden utilitarian objects, from weapons to drinking flasks, telescopes, compasses, and even musical instruments, to cite just some.

References: Catherine Dike, *Cane Curiosa*, Cane Curiosa Press (250 Dielman Rd, Ladue, MO 63124), 1983; ——, *Canes in the United States*, Cane Curiosa Press (250 Dielman Rd, Ladue, MO 63124), 1994; ——, *La Cane Object díArt;* Cane Curiosa Press (250 Dielman Rd, Ladue, MO 63124), 1988; Ulrich Klever, *Walkingsticks*, Schiffer Publishing, 1996; George H. Meyer, *American Folk Art Canes*, Sandringham Press, 1992; Francis H. Honer, *Canes Through the Ages*, Schiffer Publishing, 1995; Jeffrey Snyder, *Canes From the 17th to the 20th Century*, Schiffer Publishing, 1993.

Museums: Museum of American Folk Art, New York, NY; Museum of Fine Arts, Boston; Peabody Essex Museum, Salem, MA; Remington Gun Museum, Ilion, NY; Valley Forge Historical Society, Valley Forge, PA.

Adviser: Henry A. Taron.

Civil War, 3-1/3" l, 2-3/4" h "L" polished bone handle, scrimshaw dec on top with spread-winged eagle, American shield, olive branch, and arrows, shaft portion with scrimshaw "Co. H. 86th Ohio, Vol's," 1/2" silver collar marked "Sergt. John Laver," black painted hardwood shaft, 1" white metal-and-iron ferrule, 34-1/4" l, accompanied by framed roster of Company H, 86th Ohio Volunteer Infantry **1,300.00**
Folk art, American, made from single piece of straight hickory, 1" d, tapers to 7/8" replaced brass ferrule, entire length relief carved, begins with American eagle, followed by text and other randomly placed animals, "Thos. Jefferson of Va., born Apr 13, 1743, was

President USA 1801 to 1809, Wrote Declaration of Independence, Founder of Univ. of VA, Died July 4, 1821, Jefferson's Dying Words Were I Resign My Spirit to God, My Daughter to My Country, This Cane was Cut Near Jefferson's Tomb, 1911," 36" l overall **700.00**

Gadget, Cheese sampling, America, c1840, 1-1/2" d, 1-1/4" h elephant ivory handle, inlaid top with round 2/3" ebony circle centered with ivory dot, 1/4" narrow coin silver collar, heavy ebony shaft, 4-1/2" below handle is 1/2" coin silver band inscribed, "Austin Belknap, Boston," (orig owner), 17" l scoop device can be withdrawn, 2-1/8" l brass-and-iron ferrule, 35-1/2" l overall **1,300.00**

Cigarette lighter, Ronson, 1930s, large thick Malacca crook shaft, 3-3/4" down there is a 4" dec chromium-hinged compartment with small u-marked cartouche, slide catch to open door, chromium-plated cigarette lighter inscribed, "Ronson De-Light," 1-1/2" horn ferrule, 35-1/2" l overall, flint loaded, no fluid, unused condition **4,750.00**

Gun, Remington, c1860, 3" l half-crock handle-molded gutta percha hound-dog head, 1/4" lined nickel-silver collar, 5" down-shaft piece unscrews to insert 22-caliber shell, gun cocked with straight pull that allows notched sight to pop up, another sight at bottom of cane, fired by round trigger below collar, entire piece veneered in gutta percha, three silver rings have been added to prevent cracking and/or lifting at the breech, 1-1/3" removable hollow steel ferrule marked "75" for the 75th of the 22-cartridge model made, 35" l overall, thin 3/4" crack at bottom of handle in-filled, working order **5,500.00**

Hearing aid, French, c1860, 3-1/2" l, 6-3/4" h black-enameled metal handle, end of horn-shaped handle with opening for sound, decorative lattice openwork dec, below horn is movable ear piece that pivots, gutta percha mount for insertion into ear, 1/4" gold collar, bamboo shaft, worked under finish with dark stained bands, 3/4" brass-and-iron ferrule, 35" l overall, minor denting in top of handle, working condition **2,500.00**

Gold, Tiffany, c1900, 1-1/8" d, 2-1/2" h handle, elaborately initialed on top for orig owner, overlaid with 20 1/3" long platinum fleur-de-lis around entire circumference, marked "Tiffany & Co. makers, 18 ct, solid gold and platinum," cherrywood shaft, 1-1/3" white metal-and-iron ferrule, 34-1/4" l overall **6,750.00**

Ivory, carved, figural handle

Mother Goose, Continental, c1880, 4-1/4" l, 1-2/3" h elephant-ivory handle, Mother Goose with glass eyes, frilled bonnet, mouth agape, glasses resting on her beak, 1" silver collar, Malacca shaft, 1" metal ferrule, 35-1/2" l overall **1,200.00**

Nude Maiden, Continental, c1880, 2-1/2" w, 4-1/2" h elephant-ivory handle, damsel bending over spring and filling jug with water, ebony shaft, 7/8" replaced-brass ferrule, 35-3/4" l overall, some loss of shaft finish **2,850.00**

Rabbit, American, c1860, 5" l, 2" h elephant-ivory handle, well-carved rabbit, amber-glass eyes, long ears held straight back, 1/2" coin silver collar inscribed for the orig owner, honey-toned full-bark Malacca shaft, 1-1/2" white-metal ferrule, 35-3/4" l overall . . **1,700.00**

Ram, 5-3/4" l, 1-2/3" h "L"-shaped elephant-ivory handle, carved ram's head, brown-glass eyes, horns curled right around its cheeks, 1-1/2" highly dec sterling collar with initials and London hallmarks for 1885, ebony shaft, 1-1/2" brass-and-iron ferrule, 36" l overall, some wear to shaft finish **1,500.00**

Setter, English, c1890, 4-1/2" l, 2" h elephant ivory, running setter, clear-glass eyes, tongue tip protruding, 7/8" worn sterling collar, fashioned as buckle, with unreadable hallmarks, ebony shaft, 7/8" replaced-brass ferrule, 35-1/2" l overall, some wear to shaft finish **1,500.00**

Shakespeare, English, c1890, 1-1/2" w, 4-1/3" h elephant ivory, bust in Elizabethan costume, detailed carving with ferns and beading, Malacca shaft, 7/8" brass ferrule, 35" l overall **1,000.00**

Ivory, 4-2/3" l, 1-1/3" h carved elephant ivory handle, one end carved with two screaming monkeys, mouths open, glass eyes, looking for their baby who is carved on other end, hiding in a nook, 1/4" collar marked "Sterling," cocobolo rosewood shaft, 7/8" white metal and iron ferrule, 37-1/8" l, $375. Photo courtesy of Tradewinds Antiques & Auctions.

Ivory, knop style handle

America, c1820, whale ivory and rosewood, whale ivory flat knob, 1-3/4" w across top, 1-3/4" h, yellow patina, inscribed "W'm Meldrum, 1820" across top, octo-carved, decorative lines and eight inlaid baleen dots, very dark exotic Chinese rosewood shaft carved with deep fluting and rings for 6-1/2" followed by 18" of rope-twist carving ending with small taper, 2-1/4" whalebone ferrule, 35" l overall **5,500.00**

America, c1850, 1-3/4" w, 3-3/4" h whale-ivory ball in hand, 1/2" coin silver collar, thick white tapered whalebone shaft, 38-1/4" l overall **4,250.00**

Musical

Flute, Viennese, c1840, 1-1/4" h silver handle, round-raised nub, playing area with large oval mouthpiece, six small finger holes, larger raised hole to emit sound, dark rosewood, small area of lighter heartwood showing through, tapers gently to additional silver dec 7/8" w silver band, stamped "Hamig, Wien," (maker), 1-1/8" white metal-and-iron ferrule, 36-1/4" l overall **4,500.00**

Harmonica, Continental, c1890, mahogany, 1-3/4" w, 6" h bec de corbin handle, multiple round inlay ivory dots of varied sizes spill down from top, harmonica hidden inside handle, played from the side, holes for mouth on one side, four decorative "S"-cut sound holes on opposite side, carved rings on shaft, 7/8" dark-metal ferrule, 35" l overall **2,200.00**

Pique, English, c1692, 1-1/3" d, 3-1/2" h elephant-ivory handle, elaborately dec in scrolls, swirls, and other patterns, dated "92," typical dec eyelets pierce ivory, 7/8" scalloped silver collar punch dec, worn Malacca shaft, 7-1/2" l brass-and-iron ferrule, 35-1/2" l overall, age lines **4,000.00**

Porcelain and silver, English, 2" w, 2-1/8" h handle, three hand-painted balls, one with putti and ball, other with two lovers, gilt trim, hammered and blown-out sterling base hallmarked for London 1893, dark cherrywood shaft, 7/8" white metal and iron ferrule, 34" l, $980. Photo courtesy of Tradewinds Antiques & Auctions.

Porcelain

German, c1860, 3" w, 2-1/2" h cockerel handle, young male bird with immature orange combs, orange eyes, reddish-brown feathers, 1/2" fancy brass openwork collar, thick Malacca shaft, undecorated eyelets, 1-3/4" horn ferrule, 37" l overall **1,600.00**

Japanese Imari, probably English, c1880, 1-1/2" d ball handle, painted in shades of faded blue, terra cotta, and white, random circular shapes painted with chrysanthemums, mounted on 1/3" gold-plated cap collar, 36" l overall **1,700.00**

Tau, lady, Berlin Factory, c1880, 4-1/2" l, 3" h figural handle, flesh tones, gold beading, black hair ribbon, matching black-ruffled collar, hand-painted top, with scene of courting 18th C couple on garden bench, gentleman holding sweetheart's hand, mother sitting in chair, gold "C" scrolls and painted flowers, 1/2" vermeil silver collar, Malacca shaft, 1" replaced-brass ferrule, 37-1/2" l overall . . **1,000.00**

Wedgwood, English, late 1920s or early 1930s, 1-1/8" w, 3" h slightly curved handle, matte finished pale blue, four 1-1/4" l applied white leaves, imp "Wedgwood, England," 1/2" silver collar, thin smooth partidgewood shaft, 1-1/3" white metal-and-iron ferrule, 34-3/4" l overall **2,600.00**

Presentation, California, c1875, solid gold, 4" l, 4" h, 1" thick tau handle, inlaid on each end is 1" x 3/4" oval beveled and polished gold-quartz stone, each matrix with gold flecking on gray/white background, gold handle inscribed on inside "From H.P.B.," shaft portion inscribed "To Owen Perry, Esq.," finely dec in swirls of foliage and linear design, dark exotic tropical wood, perhaps padauk, shaft, 1" white metal-and-iron ferrule, 36-1/4" l overall **4,750.00**

Semi-precious, knop

Bloodstone, 2-3/4" l, 1" h, 1/3" d "L" bloodstone with tones of green, red-flecks handle, dec gold endcap with silver overlay, central piece of highly dec gold with silver highlights and four tiny cabochon rubies, 7/8" gold collar matches endcab, black hardwood shaft, 1-1/8" horn ferrule, 36" l overall **1,200.00**

Lapis, 1-1/2" d ball handle, overlaid with finely dec "C" scrolls and foliage patterns, 1/3" double-ring silver collar fashioned to simulate leather, ebonized hardwood shaft, 7/8" black-horn ferrule, 36-1/2" l overall **1,500.00**

Rose Quartz, French, c1900, 1-1/4" d, 2" h, pale pink stone with natural internal fissures, overlaid with 10 clusters, each cluster with four-faceted amethysts with central seed pearl, all set in silver, clusters connected by thin bright copper wire that has been recessed into

the quartz, 3/8" silver collar, black painted hardwood shaft, 7/8" horn ferrule, 36" l overall **3,750.00**

Silver

Gorham, lady's, c1890, 3-1/3" l, 1-1/2" h "L" silver handle, dec on each end with wavy lines of applied silver and name "Marguerite" encircles smooth top, initials on end cap, Gorham hallmarks, marked "Sterling," de-barked natural hardwood shaft with protruding knots decoratively polished, narrow 1/2" replaced-brass ferrule, 33" l overall **300.00**

Japanese, Tako the Octopus, probably made in America, c1880, 1-1/3" d, 4" l handle of finely fashioned octopus, long tentacles extending down shaft, red-glass eyes, faint traces of gold gilt around eyes, dark Malacca shaft, 1-1/4" horn ferrule, 35-1/4" l overall **3,500.00**

Russian, c1896-1908, 3/4" d, 5-1/4" l crook handle, cloisonné enamel dec in tones of light and dark blue, dark red, and white, hallmarked for "84 zolotnicks (875/1000)" and "Kokoshnik" for 1896-1908, Kiev, stepped partridge-wood shaft, 1" replaced brass ferrule, 35-1/4" l overall, small, shallow depression on top **2,500.00**

Tiffany, c1900, 2-2/3" l 1-3/4" h eagle handle, long beak, marked "Tiffany & Co. Makers, Sterling," faint initials scratched in, debarked natural hardwood shaft with polished branch nubs, 1-1/4" horn ferrule, 35" l overall **7,000.00**

Unger Brothers, America, c1890, Indian, 1-1/2" d, 4" h handle, ducal crown on smooth top, three matching Indian chiefs each 2-3/4" l fashioned on sides, detailed facial features, feathered headdresses, medallions, and beading, base stamped with two round Unger Brothers makers' marks, and "Sterling, 925/fine," smooth partidgewood shaft, 1-1/4" white metal-and-iron ferrule, 36" l overall **3,300.00**

Sword, Continental, c1840, carved-ivory handle of hand, 1-1/8" d, 2-3/4" h carved-elephant ivory, separate knob top dec with gadrooning, stem with well patinated delicate hand, rope turned cuff, holding thick rod, 1/4" brass

collar, two silver oval eyelets, brass fitting 2-3/4" down, straight pull reveals 12-1/2" triangular sword, two blood grooves, minimal pitting, whangee bamboo shaft, 7/8" brass-and-iron ferrule, 34-1/4" l overall. **1,200.00**
Tortoiseshell and silver, Continental, c1890, 2-1/2" w, 2/3" h pistol handle, checkered tortoiseshell with silver diamond and square inlay, hallmarks, honey-toned Malacca shaft, 1-1/4" horn ferrule, 36" l overall. **750.00**
Wood, carved

English, 1861, 3" l, 2" h handle, face of pig carved at end of handle, just below handle is fancy silver plate inscribed "Edward Nesbitt, 1/61," shaft with brown background, octo-caved with eight sections that are inlaid with ivory, boxwood, ebony, and mother-of-pearl, tools of workers, snakes, crescent moon, star, chicken, spade, pitchfork, shovel, draftsmen's tools, boots, shoes, hearts, diamonds, etc., 1" brass ferrule, 36" l overall . . **400.00**
English, c1895, carved Airedale, 3" l, 1-1/2" w handle, well-carved brown-and-black Airedale, amber-glass eyes, thong hole present, 1-1/2" smooth-silver collar, stepped-Malacca shaft painted brown to match handle, 1" brass-and-iron ferrule, 35" l overall **500.00**
European, carved from one piece of tan hardwood, 2" w, 1-3/4" h satyr's head handle, porcelain eyes, curved horns covering long pointed ears, holding pointed metal object in his mouth, leaves carved down shaft for 4", then 14" of carved "chain" extending down to fluted carved remainder, 1/2" metal ferrule, 34" l overall . . **325.00**

CANTON CHINA

History: Canton china is a type of Oriental porcelain made in the Canton region of China from the late 18th century to the present. It was produced largely for export. Canton china has a hand-decorated light- to dark-blue underglaze-on-white ground. Design motifs include houses, mountains, trees, boats, and bridges. A design similar to willow pattern is the most common.

Borders on early Canton feature a rain-and-cloud motif (a thick band of diagonal lines with a scalloped bottom). Later pieces usually have a straight-line border.

Early, c1790-1840, plates are very heavy and often have an unfinished bottom, while serving pieces have an overall "orange-peel" bottom. Early covered pieces, such as tureens, vegetable dishes, and sugars, have strawberry finials and twisted handles. Later ones have round finials and a straight, single handle.

Marks: The markings "Made in China" and "China" indicate wares that date after 1891.

Reproduction Alert: Several museum gift shops and private manufacturers are issuing reproductions of Canton china.

Bowl, 9-1/2" d, cut corner, minor int. glaze imperfections, 19th C . . . **920.00**
Box, cov, sq, domed top, cloud-and-rain border on lids, early 19th C, pr. **6,270.00**
Cider pitcher, cov, 8-1/4" h, double-woven strap handle with flower impressed ends, cover with fu-dog finial, chips on base, 19th C . . **1,955.00**
Coffeepot, 7-1/4" h, mismatched cover **750.00**
Cup and underplates, handleless, 1-3/4" h, 5-1/2" d, Chinese Imperial, set of eight. **300.00**
Dish, 8-7/8" d, scalloped rim, blue and white, 1/4" glued rim chip **300.00**
Egg cup, 2-1/4" h, chips, cracked, nine-pc set. **345.00**
Fish platter, 13-1/2" l, glaze roughness **1,265.00**
Fruit basket

9-1/4" d, minor chips. **690.00**
10-1/2" l, reticulated, undertray **1,100.00**
11" l, reticulated, mismatched undertray, star crack, minor chips. **345.00**
Ginger jar, cov **230.00**
Milk pitcher, 6-1/8" h, very minor chips **575.00**
Pitcher, 3" to 6-1/2" h, chips, four-pc set **2,760.00**
Plate, early, c1820-30

6" d, bread and butter **65.00**
7-1/2" d, salad. **85.00**
8" d, dessert **95.00**
9" d, lunch. **115.00**
10" d, dinner **150.00**
Platter

10-1/2" x 13-1/4", octagonal, 19th C. **650.00**
11-1/4", 13", 16" d, graduated, octagonal, well and tree platter, two deep platters, rim chips . . **1,035.00**
12-1/4" x 9-3/8", octagonal, unglazed bottom **200.00**

12-1/2" x 15-5/8", blue dec of pagoda, bridge, and canal scene, geometric line borders within octagonal shape, white ground, few shallow edge flakes . . . **800.00**
Pot de creme, 4" h, three-pc set **325.00**
Salt, 3-3/4" l, trench, chips, three-pc set. **550.00**
Sauce tureen

6" l, minor chips. **245.00**
8-1/2" l, mismatched cover . . **865.00**
Serving dish

8-3/4" sq, 19th C, cracks, price for pr. **460.00**
13-1/2" w, 10-3/4" d, 2-1/2" h, oblong, octagonal rim, deep blue dec of pagodas, boats, and bridge, white ground. **110.00**
15-1/4" x 18-1/4", octagonal, 19th C **650.00**
15-3/8" x 18-3/4", octagonal, 19th C **865.00**
Shrimp dish, 10-1/4" d, minor edge roughness, pr. **690.00**
Syllabub, 3" h, imperfections, 16-pc set **850.00**
Tea caddy, cov, 5-1/2" h, octagonal, 19th C. **2,645.00**
Tea canister, cov, 11-1/2" h, restoration to lids, damage to one base, pr **3,336.00**
Tureen, cov, 14" l, 9-3/4" w, 7-3/4" h, stem finial, oval, ftd, hog snout handles. **1,265.00**
Vegetable dish, cov, 9-1/2" w, 8" d, 3-1/4" h, diamond shape, scalloped edges, fruit finial, orange peel glaze, unglazed bottom **220.00**

Cup and saucer, loop handle, **$70.**

CAPO-DI-MONTE

History: In 1743, King Charles of Naples established a soft-paste porcelain factory near Naples. The firm made figurines and dinnerware. In 1760, many of the workmen and most of the molds were moved to Buen Retiro, near Madrid, Spain. A new factory, which also made hard-paste porcelains, opened in Naples in 1771. In 1834, the Doccia factory in Florence purchased the molds and continued production in Italy.

Capo-di-Monte was copied heavily by other factories in Hungary, Germany, France, and Italy.

Museums: Metropolitan Museum of Art, New York, NY; Museo of Capodimonte, Naples, Italy; Woodmere Art Museum, Philadelphia, PA.

> **Reproduction Alert:** Many of the pieces in today's market are of recent vintage. Do not be fooled by the crown over the "N" mark; it also was copied.

Figurines, pair, 6" h, from left: boy with garland, yellow coat, pink garments; girl reading, blue coat and yellow pants. Marked Italy, **$525.**

Box, cov, 8" d, 4-1/4" h, round, domed lid molded with low relief figures of cherubs with flower baskets, sides similarly molded with cherubs at various artistic pursuits, gilt-metal rim mounts, int. painted with floral sprigs, late 19th C **490.00**

Creamer and sugar, mythological raised scene, dragon handles, claw feet, lion finial, 5-1/2" x 6" creamer, 6-1/4" x 6" cov sugar **250.00**

Demitasse cup and caddy, 14" shaped frame with upright metal handle, central cov sugar bowl, surrounded by platforms for six 3" h cups and saucers, each with low relief scenes of children, gilt int. with polychrome enamel detailing, 20th C **375.00**

Dresser set, mythological raised scene, pair of 4" d, 7" h perfume bottles with figural stoppers, 5" d, 4" h cov powder jar, 30" l x 15" w tray . . . **500.00**

Ferner, 11" l, oval, relief molded and enameled allegorical figures, full relief female mask at each end **110.00**

Figure

7-1/2" l, 6-1/2" h, mare and foal, sgd "G. Armani" **210.00**

14" l, 10" h, pair of white Arabian stallions at play, sgd "G. Armani" **275.00**

Lamp, table

25" h, figural Bacchus, female, and grapes **1,300.00**

35" h, white base with dec, green custom-made shade, c1940 . . . . **400.00**

Plate, 8-3/8" d, each with Capo-di-Monte crest at top, pair of swans, pair of cranes, crimson, blue, yellow, and burnt-orange flowers on border, gold trim, minor wear, price for eight-pc set **1,050.00**

Snuff box, 3-1/4" d, hinged lid, cartouche shape, molded basketweave and flowerhead ext., painted int. with court lady and page examining portrait of gentlemen, gold mountings, c1740, minor restoration **1,650.00**

Stein, 7-1/2" h, lion-hunt scene, lion on lid, elephant-trunk handle **400.00**

Urn, cov, 21-1/8" h, ovoid, central-molded frieze of Nerieds and putti, molded floral garlands, gadroon upper section, acanthus-molded lower section, socle foot with putti, sq plinth base, applied ram's-head handles, domed cov, acorn finial, underglaze crowned "N" mark, minor chips and losses, pr **1,650.00**

CARLSBAD CHINA

History: Because of changing European boundaries during the last 100 years, German-speaking Carlsbad has found itself located first in the Austro-Hungarian Empire, then in Germany, and currently in the Czech Republic. Carlsbad was one of the leading pottery manufacturing centers in Bohemia.

Wares from the numerous Carlsbad potteries are lumped together under the term "Carlsbad China." Most pieces on the market are post-1891, although several potteries date to the early 19th century.

Bone dish, crescent shape, hp pink flowers **15.00**

Bowl, 14" d, handles, marked "Imperial H&C Carlsbad Austria," numbers "2552" and "18," wear to gold edge, repaired chip **50.00**

Butter dish, cov, 7-1/4" d, pink flowers, green leaves, wavy gold lines, white ground **65.00**

Chocolate pot, cov, 10" h, blue, scenic portrait, marked "Carlsbad Victoria" **115.00**

Creamer and sugar, Bluebird pattern, marked "Victoria Carlsbad" **70.00**

Boot, black, white auctioneer label, $110.
Photo courtesy of Joy Luke Auctions.

Ewer, 14" h, handles, light green, floral dec, gold trim, marked "Carlsbad Victoria" **85.00**

Fish platter, 19-3/4" l, 8-3/4" w, center fish design, wear to gold edges.**165.00**

Game plates, 8" sq, each hand painted with gold trim, light and dark gray corners, center with game birds, gold outlines, mauve circular mark "Carlsbad Mark & Gutherz," price for 11-pc set **700.00**

Hair receiver, 4" d, cobalt-blue flowers, emb basketweave at top, gold trim, white ground. **45.00**

Oyster plate
8-1/4" d, five wells plus center well, stylized pink-and-blue peonies, green leaves, gold accents, marked "Marx & Gutherz" . .**120.00**
9-3/4" d, lavender flowers, gold outlining, white ground **125.00**

Pin tray, 8-1/2" l, irregular scalloped shape, roses, green leaves, white ground, marked "Victoria Carlsbad Austria". **40.00**

Plate, 9" d, hp cherries, artist sgd **35.00**

Platter, 13" x 18", hand-painted pink-and-blue flowers, marked "Mark & Gutherz, Carlsbad," imp "LS&S," early 1900s **60.00**

Rose bowl, 4-3/4" x 5", cream ground, yellow flowers, brown leaves, gold accents, marked "Carlsbad" with crown mark, numbered "23" and "2240". **95.00**

Sugar shaker, 5-1/2" h, egg shape, floral dec **70.00**

Urn, 14-1/2" h, rose bouquet, shaded ivory ground, marked "Carlsbad Austria" **155.00**

Vase, 5" d, 9" h, applied brown dragon, pale-yellow ground, pink flowers, blue-and-yellow leaves, gold accents, marked "Victoria, Carlsbad China" **60.00**

CARNIVAL GLASS

History: Carnival glass, an American invention, is colored-pressed glass with a fired-on iridescent finish. It was first manufactured about 1905 and was immensely popular both in America and abroad. More than 1,000 different patterns have been identified. Production of old carnival-glass patterns ended in 1930.

Most of the popular patterns of carnival glass were produced by five companies: Dugan, Fenton, Imperial, Millersburg, and Northwood.

Marks: Northwood patterns frequently are found with the "N" trademark. Dugan used a diamond trademark on several patterns.

References: Elaine and Fred Blair, *Carnival Hunter's Companion: A Guide to Pattern Recognition*, published by authors (P.O. Box 116335, Carrolton, TX 75011), 1995; Carl O. Burns, *Collector's Guide to Northwood Carnival Glass*, L-W Book Sales, 1994; ——, *Dugan and Diamond Carnival Glass, 1909-1931;* Collector Books, 1998; ——, *Imperial Carnival Glass,* Collector Books, 1996, 1999 value update; Dave Doty, *A Field Guide to Carnival Glass*, Antique Trader Publications, 1998; Bill Edwards and Mike Carwile, *Standard Encyclopedia of Carnival Glass*, 7th ed., Collector Books, 2000; ——, *Standard Encyclopedia of Carnival Glass Price Guide*, 12th ed., Collector Books, 2000; Marion T. Hartung, *First Book of Carnival Glass to Tenth Book of Carnival Glass* (series of 10 books), published by author, 1968 to 1982; published by authors (36 N. Mernitz, Freeport, IL 61032), 1996; Diane C. Rosington, *Carnival Glass Club Commemoratives, 1964-1999*, published by author (P.O. Box 348, North Greece, NY 14515-0348), 2000; Glen and Steven Thistlewood, *Carnival Glass, The Magic & The Mystery*, Schiffer Publishing, 1998; Margaret and Ken Whitmyer, *Fenton Art Glass: 1907-1939*, Collector Books, 1996, 1999 value update.

Periodicals and Internet Resources: *Network*, PageWorks, P.O. Box 2385, Mt. Pleasant, SC 29465; *WWW.CGA*, www.woodsland.com.

Collectors' Clubs: American Carnival Glass Assoc., 44 Water St., Poland, OH 44514; Canadian Carnival Glass Assoc., 34 Bellholme Ave., Brantford, Ontario N3T 1S1 Canada; Carnival Glass Society (UK), P.O. Box 14, Hayes, Middlesex UB3 5NU UK; Collectible Carnival Glass Assoc., 3103 Brentwood Circle, Grand Island, NE 68801; Gateway Carnival Glass Club, 108 Riverwoods Cove, East Alton, IL 62024; Heart of America Carnival Glass Assoc., P.O. Box 4361, Topeka, KS 66604; International Carnival Glass Assoc., P.O. Box 306, Mentone, IN 46539; Lincoln Land Carnival Glass Club, N951, Hwy 27,

Conrath, WI 54731; National Duncan Glass Society, P.O. Box 965, Washington, PA 15301; National Imperial Glass Collectors Society, P.O. Box 534, Bellaire, OH 43906; New England Carnival Glass Club, 12 Sherwood Rd, West Hartford, CT 06117-2736; Pacific Northwest Carnival Glass Club, 17625 S. W. Frederick Lane, Sherwood, OR 97140; Sunshine State Carnival Glass Assoc., 9087 Baywood Drive, Seminole, FL 33777; Tampa Bay Carnival Glass Club, 5501 101st Ave. N., Pinellas Park, FL 34666; Texas Carnival Glass Club, 611 W. Main, Tomball, TX 77375.

Museums: National Duncan Glass Society, Washington, PA; Fenton Art Glass Co., Williamstown, WV.

Notes: Color is the most important factor in pricing carnival glass. The color of a piece is determined by holding it to the light and looking through it.

Acorn Burrs, Northwood
Bowl, 4-3/4" d, marigold **30.00**
Tumbler, marigold **60.00**

Acorns, Millersburg, compote, six ruffles, marigold and vaseline **3,750.00**

Apple Blossom Twigs, Dugan
Bowl, 9-1/2" d, low, ruffled, white, irid pink and green **130.00**
Plate, low, ruffled, purple, electric purple-and-blue highlights .**225.00**

Basket of Roses, Northwood, bonbon, stippled, amethyst **475.00**

Beaded Cable, Northwood
   Candy dish, ftd, amethyst **70.00**
   Rose bowl, ice blue **410.00**
Big Fish, Millersburg, bowl, 8-1/4" d, six ruffles, marigold, radium finish
. . . . **550.00**
Blackberry, Fenton, miniature compote
   Green **65.00**
   Marigold **40.00**
Blackberry Block, Fenton, tumbler, blue **45.00**
Blackberry Spray, Fenton, hat, 6-1/2" h
   Green, two sides up **95.00**
   Red, small flake **365.00**
   Vaseline, sq, four sides up . . . **40.00**
Blackberry Wreath, Millersburg
   Bowl, 7-1/2" d, six ruffles,
     green **65.00**
   Bowl, 10-1/4" d, six ruffles,
     amethyst **250.00**
   Bowl, 10-1/2" d, three-in-one edge,
     green **155.00**
   Ice cream bowl, 8" d, green, some
     wear to berries **85.00**
   Ice cream sauce, 5-1/2" d, dark
     marigold **110.00**
   Sauce, 6" d, six ruffles,
     marigold **60.00**
   Sauce, 6-1/4" d, six ruffles, green,
     satiny finish **65.00**
Blossomtime, Northwood, compote, marigold **200.00**
Boggy Bayou, Fenton, vase, 9" h, black amethyst **75.00**
Border Plants, Dugan, bowl, 7" d, 10 ruffles edge, peach opalescent **225.00**
Bouquet, Fenton
   Tumbler, blue **55.00**
   Tumbler, marigold **15.00**
   Water pitcher, marigold **150.00**
Bull's Eye & Beads, Imperial, vase, 7" h, flared, dark marigold **40.00**
Bushel Basket, Northwood, aqua opalescent, light opalescence . **195.00**

Butterflies, bonbon dish, two handles, purple, 7-1/4" w, 3-1/8" h, $60.

Butterfly & Fern, Fenton
   Tumbler,
     blue **115.00**
   Tumbler, green **55.00**
   Water pitcher, blue, radium
     finish **800.00**
Butterfly & Tulip, Dugan, bowl, sq, purple, satin irid **1,400.00**
Captive Rose, Fenton, marigold, compote, crimped edge **42.00**
Cherries, Dugan
   Banana boat, electric blue, purple
     highlights, three ftd **275.00**
   Sauce, low, ruffled, 6" d,
     purple **120.00**
Cherries, Fenton, banana boat, blue, satin irid, cracked **250.00**
Concave Diamond, Northwood
   Tumbler, celeste blue **30.00**
   Tumbler, vaseline **95.00**
   Tumble-up, russet green **900.00**
   Vase, 6" h, celeste blue **175.00**
Concord, Fenton, bowl, three-in-one edge, green **245.00**
Cosmos, Millersburg, ice cream bowl, green, radium irid **115.00**
Courthouse, Millersburg, ice cream bowl, 7-1/2" d, amethyst, lettered example **900.00**
Daisy Wreath, Westmoreland, 8-1/2" d, ice cream bowl, moonstone **110.00**
Dandelion, Northwood, tumbler, purple **55.00**
Diamond Points, Northwood, vase, 10-1/4" h, aqua opalescent, iridescent and opalescent from top to base **1,650.00**
Diamond Rib, Fenton, vase, 9" h, purple **40.00**
Diving Dolphins, Millersburg, compote, Rosiland int., green **1,700.00**
Drapery, Northwood
   Rose bowl, aqua opalescent , light
     butterscotch overlay **250.00**
   Vase, 8-3/4" h, aqua
     opalescent **575.00**
Drapery Variant, Northwood, dark marigold, radium finish **375.00**
Embossed Scroll
   Bowl, 7" d, Hobstar & Tassel exterior,
     electric purple **400.00**
   Sauce, 5" d, purple **45.00**
Embroidered Mums, Northwood
   Bowl, 9" d, ruffled, electric-blue
     border, bronze highlighted
     center **475.00**
   Plate, 9" d, ice green **1,100.00**
Enameled Grape, Northwood, water set, six pcs, blue, enamel dec . . **800.00**

Fanciful, Dugan
   Bowl, low, ruffled, frosty white, pink,
     blue, and green highlights . . **115.00**
   Plate, 9" d, blue, basketweave back,
     multicolored highlights **350.00**
Fashion, Imperial
   Punch cup,
     marigold **24.00**
   Tumbler, marigold **90.00**
   Water set, marigold, seven-pc
     matched set **150.00**
Fentonia, Fenton, tumbler, marigold **45.00**
Fine Cut & Roses, Northwood, rose bowl
   Dark Ice Blue, fancy feet, slight
     damage to feet **265.00**
   Purple **135.00**
Fine Rib, Fenton, vase
   10" h, powder blue **60.00**
   10-1/2" h, blue **85.00**
   10-1/2" h, cherry red **225.00**
   10-1/2" h, marigold **40.00**
   11-3/4" h, vaseline, marigold
     overlay **70.00**
Fishscale & Beads, Dugan
   Plate, 7" d, electric purple . . **575.00**
   Plate, 7" d, marigold, satin irid **45.00**
   Plate, 7-1/2" d, low, ruffled,
     purple **325.00**
Fleur-De-Lis, Millersburg, bowl, 10" d, six ruffle crimped edge, collar base, amethyst, radium finish **525.00**
Floral & Optic, Imperial, bowl, 9" d, electric purple, electric blue irid **775.00**
Flowers, Fenton, rose bowl
   Blue, multicolored irid **110.00**
   Blue, flake on foot **45.00**
Flute, Imperial, toothpick holder, blue **925.00**
Frosted Block, Imperial, rose bowl, deep marigold **30.00**
Fruits & Flowers, Northwood
   Bonbon, handled, lavender . **200.00**
   Sauce, 5-1/2" d, ruffled, purple **55.00**
Good Luck, Northwood
   Bowl, 9" d, ruffled, ribbed ext.,
     marigold **175.00**
   Bowl, pie crust edge, blue . . **350.00**
   Bowl, ruffled, electric blue . . **435.00**
   Bowl, ruffled, purple **300.00**
Grape, Imperial
   Bowl, ruffled, 8-1/2" d, electric
     purple **135.00**
   Decanter, electric purple, stopper
     missing **85.00**
   Punch set, marigold **300.00**
   Water carafe, emerald
     green **4,300.00**

Water pitcher, electric
purple **600.00**
Grape & Cable, Fenton
Bowl, 6-1/2" d, smoky blue . . . **40.00**
Bowl, 7-3/4" d, eight ruffles, brick
red, satiny iridescence **300.00**
Grape and Cable, Northwood
Banana boat, purple **185.00**
Berry bowl, master, emerald
green **145.00**
Bonbon, two handles, marigold
. . . . **50.00**
Bowl, 8-1/2" d, ruffled, stippled,
ribbed back, pumpkin
marigold **255.00**
Butter dish, cov, green **175.00**
Hatpin holder, purple **175.00**
Sweetmeat compote, cov,
purple **170.00**
Grape & Gothic Arches, Northwood,
tumbler, electric blue **45.00**
Grape Arbor, Northwood
Tankard pitcher, dark marigold,
radium finish **575.00**
Tankard pitcher, purple, blue irid
highlights, bronze highlights at
base **400.00**
Grapevine & Lattice, Dugan, tumbler,
white **225.00**
Grape Wreath, Millersburg
Bowl, 8-1/2" d, three-in-one-edge,
green, radium finish **135.00**
Bowl, 9" d, six ruffles, marigold, blue
radium finish **65.00**
Ice cream bowl, 8" d, amethyst,
radium finish **155.00**
Grape Wreath Variant, Millersburg,
bowl, 7" d, three-in-one edge, Feather
center, purple, radium finish **115.00**
Greek Key, Northwood, tumbler,
purple **150.00**
Hanging Cherries, Millersburg,
compote, stemmed, round
Amethyst **2,100.00**
Green **1,600.00**
Marigold **700.00**
Hearts & Flowers, Northwood
Bowl, ruffled, frosty white,
multicolored pastel
highlights **165.00**
Compote, aqua opalescent , pastel,
small flake on base **800.00**
Heavy Grape, Imperial
Chop plate, 11" d, electric
purple **400.00**
Chop plate, 11" d, helios green, flat,
wear on high points **135.00**
Nappy, 5" d, electric purple . . **110.00**
Plate, 8" d, electric purple . . . **165.00**
Plate, 8" d, violet, minor wear on
grapes **85.00**

Heavy Iris, water pitcher, marigold, **$325.**

Heavy Iris, Dugan, tumbler,
amethyst **75.00**
Heavy Pineapple, Fenton, bowl, ftd,
10" d, amber, satiny iridescence **500.00**
Hobnail, Millersburg
Rose Bowl, purple **220.00**
Spittoon, marigold **700.00**
Hobnail Swirl, Millersburg, vase, 11" h,
amethyst, radium iridescence . . **250.00**
Hobstar & Feather, Millersburg
Compote, round, clear **75.00**
Compote, round, frosted . . . **135.00**
Punch cup, crystal **25.00**
Tumbler, crystal, clear **65.00**
Tumbler, crystal, frosted **125.00**
Holly, Fenton
Bowl, 9" d, ruffled, light
amethyst **130.00**
Compote, ruffled, lime green,
marigold overlay **100.00**
Jack-in-the-pulpit hat, crimped
edge, marigold **50.00**
Plate, 9" d, marigold **155.00**
Holly Sprig, Millersburg
Bowl, 6-1/2" d, deep, tight crimped
edge, amethyst **120.00**
Bowl, 8-1/2" d, six ruffles,
amethyst **150.00**
Nappy, tri-corn, handle,
green **160.00**
Holly Sprig Variant, Millersburg, bowl,
8-1/2" d, Star center, ruffled and

crimped edge, amethyst, blue radium
finish **465.00**
Holly Whirl, Millersburg
Bonbon, Issac Benesch 54th
Anniversary adv, marigold . **150.00**
Bowl, 9-1/2" d, ruffled, marigold,
radium finish **85.00**
Nappy, two handles, deep, flared,
amethyst, radium finish **100.00**
Nappy, two handles, deep, flared,
green, satin finish **110.00**
Horse Head Medallion, Fenton
Jack-in-the-pulpit bowl, ftd,
marigold **75.00**
Plate, 7-1/2" d, crystal **105.00**
Plate, 7-1/2" d, marigold **175.00**
Inverted Strawberry, Cambridge,
sauce dish, 5" d, marigold **25.00**
Kittens, Fenton
Bowl, six ruffles, marigold . . . **135.00**
Cup and saucer, marigold . . . **245.00**
Toothpick holder, ruffled, marigold,
radium finish **115.00**
Lattice Hearts, Dugan, plate, 8-1/2" d,
electric purple **115.00**
Leaf & Beads, Northwood
Nut bowl, ftd, aqua opalescent,
butterscotch irid **1,525.00**
Rose bowl, marigold **50.00**
Leaf and Little Flowers, Millersburg
Compote, flared, deep, green,
radium finish with bright blue
highlights **500.00**
Compote, flared, deep, marigold,
radium finish **225.00**
Compote, six ruffles,
amethyst **475.00**
Compote, six ruffles, dark
marigold **300.00**
Compote, six ruffles, purple, radium
finish **325.00**
Leaf Columns, Northwood, vase,
10-1/2" h
Radium green, multicolored irid,
slightly flared top **135.00**
Sapphire blue, small flake on
base **135.00**
Leaf Swirl, Westmoreland, compote
Purple **65.00**
Yellow **30.00**
Leaf Tiers, Fenton, tumbler, ftd,
marigold **80.00**
Lotus & Poinsettia, Fenton, bowl, 10"
d, ruffled, ftd, dark marigold **75.00**
Many Stars, Millersburg
Bowl, 10" d, six ruffles, green,
five-pointed star **650.00**
Bowl, 10" d, three-in-one edge,
amethyst, five-point star and Trefoil
Fine Cut exterior **775.00**

Bowl, 10-1/2" d, six ruffles, amethyst, five-pointed star **525.00**

Mayan, Millersburg, ice cream bowl, green, radium irid **120.00**

Memphis, Northwood

Punch bowl and base, adv for Shannon's Furniture-Carpets, crystal, one small flake.... **125.00**

Punch bowl base, purple **45.00**

Milady, Fenton, tumbler, blue ... **75.00**

Morning Glory, Imperial

Funeral vase, 16-1/2" h, 4-3/4" d base, purple **250.00**

Vase, 6-1/2" h, olive green ... **60.00**

Night Stars, Millersburg, bonbon, two handles, two sides, olive green, blue radium finish **800.00**

Ohio Star, Millersburg

Cider pitcher, 11" h tankard, crystal................ **250.00**

Cider set, six pcs, 10" h tankard, crystal, chip on one tumbler **625.00**

Compote, 4-1/2" d, crystal ... **35.00**

Creamer and sugar, open, crystal.................. **45.00**

Punch set, 10 pcs, crystal .**1,550.00**

Toothpick holder, crystal.... **115.00**

Water carafe, crystal....... **255.00**

Open Rose, Imperial

Bowl, 8-1/2" d, electric purple. **85.00**

Plate, 9" d, marigold **45.00**

Rose bowl, electric purple int. and ext. **625.00**

Sauce, 5" d, electric purple . **105.00**

Optic & Buttons, Imperial, rose bowl, marigold **30.00**

Orange Tree, Fenton

Bowl, 9" d, ruffled, Tree Trunk center, white, blue irid **90.00**

Mug, standard size, amber, weak impression **55.00**

Plate, 9" d, frosty white, blue-and-pink highlights... **155.00**

Plate, 9" d, marigold, radium finish................... **255.00**

Plate, 9-1/2" d, Tree Trunk center, white, frosty irid **185.00**

Powder box, cov, blue **115.00**

Punch set, punch bowl, stand, 12 cups, marigold........ **395.00**

Tumbler, blue **60.00**

Wine, blue................ **60.00**

Oriental Poppy, Northwood, tumbler

Light Marigold............. **25.00**

Purple **40.00**

Peacock, Millersburg

Berry bowl, individual, 5" d, purple, radium finish............ **115.00**

Berry bowl, master, 9" d, purple, radium finish, small nick ... **225.00**

Bowl, 9" d, ruffled, with bee and beads, amethyst, radium finish **650.00**

Bowl, 10" d, three-in-one edge, green, radium finish, blue highlights.............. **425.00**

Ice cream bowl, 5" d, marigold, satiny irid.............. **200.00**

Peacock at Fountain, Dugan, tumbler, blue...................... **35.00**

Peacock at Fountain, Northwood

Berry bowl, 5" d, purple...... **35.00**

Punch cup, white.......... **20.00**

Tumbler, amethyst **25.00**

Water pitcher, amethyst..... **250.00**

Peacock at Urn, Fenton

Compote, stemmed, celeste blue, marigold overlay **150.00**

Plate, 9" d, blue, bright red, blue, and green highlights **500.00**

Peacock at Urn, Millersburg

Berry bowl, individual, 5" d, flared, marigold, radium irid with blue highlights.............. **225.00**

Berry bowl, master, 9" d, flared, marigold, radium irid with blue highlights.............. **275.00**

Bowl, 9" d, green, satin irid .. **700.00**

Bowl, 10-1/2" d, six ruffles, green, satin finish, bee, no beading................ **250.00**

Compote, stemmed, ruffled, large, amethyst **1,600.00**

Compote, stemmed, ruffled, large, green................ **1,500.00**

Compote, stemmed, ruffled, large, marigold **2,300.00**

Ice cream bowl, 9-3/4" d, amethyst, radium finish, bee, no beading **225.00**

Plate, 6" d, amethyst, satin finish, no bee, no beading **1,200.00**

Sauce, 6" d, ruffled, blue, no bee, no beading.............. **1,050.00**

Peacock Tail Variant, Millersburg, compote, stemmed, ruffled

Green.................... **55.00**

Marigold.................. **85.00**

Purple **115.00**

Peacocks, Northwood

Bowl, pie-crust edge, clambroth, multicolored irid.......... **325.00**

Bowl, ruffled, aqua opalescent........... **1,650.00**

Persian Garden, Dugan, plate, 6-1/2" d, marigold............. **40.00**

Persian Medallion, Fenton

Bonbon, two handles, vaseline, marigold overlay **140.00**

Hair receiver, frosty white ... **130.00**

Plate, 6" d, marigold........ **25.00**

Rose bowl, deep marigold .. **120.00**

Petals, Northwood, compote, 7", marigold **30.00**

Pinecone, Fenton, plate, 6" d, marigold **40.00**

Plume Panels, Fenton, vase, 11" h, green..................... **95.00**

Pond Lily, Fenton, calling card tray, two handles, white, weak irid....... **25.00**

Poppy, Millersburg, compote, flared, dark marigold **475.00**

Poppy, Northwood, pickle dish, blue..................... **55.00**

Poppy Show, Northwood, bowl, ruffled, marigold **400.00**

Primrose, Millersburg, bowl, 9-1/2" d, ruffled, Fine Cut Heart exterior, marigold, radium finish with blue highlights.................. **95.00**

Rays & Ribbons, Millersburg

Bowl, 9-1/2" d, ruffled, crimped edge, Cactus exterior, purple, blue radium irid **175.00**

Bowl, 9-3/4" d, three-in-one edge, marigold............... **140.00**

Ribbon Tie, Fenton, bowl, three-in-one edge, low, blue **160.00**

Ripple, Imperial, funeral vase, 17" h, marigold **115.00**

Rosalind, Millersburg

Bowl, 10-1/2" d, six ruffles, amethyst................ **225.00**

Bowl, 10-1/2" d, marigold satin **125.00**

Jelly, stemmed, flared, deep, 8-1/2" h, amethyst **3,500.00**

Rose Columns, Millersburg, vase, green.................... **3,000.00**

Roses and Fruit, Millersburg, bonbon

Green, two handles **600.00**

Marigold, stemmed, handles **550.00**

Rose Show, Northwood, bowl, ruffled, aqua opalescent, light-butterscotch overlay, opalescent highlights.. **775.00**

Rose Spray, Fenton

Goblet, marigold.......... **30.00**

Jack-in-the-pulpit, celeste blue **65.00**

Round-Up, Dugan

Bowl, low, ruffled, peach opalescent **250.00**

Plate, 9" d, blue, basketweave back, blue-and-pink highlights .. **275.00**

Rustic, Fenton
Funeral vase, 18-1/2" h, blue, electric-blue highlights **675.00**
Swung vase, 15" h, 4-1/4" d base, green, radium multicolored irid **110.00**

Seacoast, Millersburg, pin tray, marigold **1,000.00**

Seaweed, Millersburg
Bowl, 10-1/4" d, three-in-one edge, amethyst **525.00**
Bowl, 10-1/4" d, three-in-one edge, marigold, satiny irid **350.00**
Plate, 9" d, flared, green, satiny irid **1,900.00**
Plate, 9" d, flared, marigold **1,600.00**
Sauce, 5-1/2" d, ice-cream shape, dark marigold **850.00**

Ski Star, Dugan, plate, 6-1/2" d, tightly crimped edge, Compass ext., peach opalescent **135.00**

Smooth Rays, Dugan, berry, ruffled, Jeweled Heart ext., amethyst **35.00**

Squatty Thin Rib, Northwood, vase, 7" h, purple **60.00**

Stag and Holly, bowl, blue, 11" d, $200.

Stag & Holly, Fenton
Bowl, 10" d, ruffled, ftd, powder blue, marigold overlay **200.00**
Bowl, 10-1/2" d, crimped edge, ftd, marigold **125.00**
Bowl, 11-1/4" d, ruffled, ftd, light-blue aqua base, marigold overlay **200.00**

Stippled Petals, Dugan, plate, purple, dome ftd, tightly crimped edge . **750.00**

Stippled Rays, Fenton
Ice cream bowl, 6" d, cherry red **450.00**
Plate, 7" d, Scale Band back, marigold **25.00**

Strawberry, Northwood
Bowl, 8" d, pie crust edge, purple **90.00**
Plate, 9" d, basketweave back, dark marigold, etched "St. Joe, Mich" **155.00**

Plate, 9-1/4" d, basketweave back, green **235.00**

Strawberry Wreath, Millersburg
Bowl, 9" d, low-crimped ruffled, purple **185.00**
Compote, six ruffles, amethyst **375.00**
Compote, six ruffles, dark marigold **175.00**
Compote, six ruffles, green . **400.00**
Sauce, 5" sq, crimped edge, green **650.00**

Swirl Hobnail, Millersburg, rose bowl, purple **275.00**

Ten Mums, Fenton
Bowl, 9" d, three-in-one edge, green **100.00**
Bowl, 10" d, six ruffles edge, emerald-green base, multicolored irid **350.00**

Thin Rib, Fenton, vase, 10" h, blue **60.00**

Thin Rib, Northwood, vase, 10" h, blue, multicolored irid **55.00**

Three Fruits, Northwood
Bowl, eight ruffles, stippled, green **300.00**
Plate, 9" d, basketweave back, dark marigold **225.00**
Plate, 9" d, stippled, amethyst **300.00**

Tiger Lily, Imperial, tumbler, marigold **75.00**

Tree Trunk, Northwood
Funeral vase, 10-1/2" h, aqua opalescent, butterscotch overlay, opalescence extending to base **950.00**
Funeral vase, 12-1/2" h at back, 10-1/2" h at front, green, radium finish **425.00**
Swung vase, 11" h, blue, radium electric blue highlights **225.00**

Trout and Fly, Millersburg
Bowl, 9" d, three-in-one edge, light amethyst **700.00**
Ice cream bowl, 8-1/4" l, marigold, satiny finish **525.00**
Ice cream bowl, 8-1/2" l, green, satiny finish, bruise on base **625.00**

Two Flowers, Fenton
Bowl, 9" d, ftd, emerald green **275.00**
Bowl, 11" d, ruffled, ftd, blue, small flake on foot **95.00**

Vintage, Fenton, jack-in-the-pulpit vase, marigold **1,400.00**

Whirling Leaves, Millersburg
Bowl, 9-1/2" d, six ruffles, amethyst **215.00**

Bowl, tri-corn, crimped edge, amethyst **475.00**

Wide Panel, Northwood, sherbet, russet green **20.00**

Wild Berry, Westmoreland, powder jar, cov, marigold **210.00**

Wild Flower, Northwood, compote, stemmed, light marigold **65.00**

Wild Rose, Northwood, rose bowl, ftd, stippled rays int., electric purple **650.00**

Wild Strawberry, Northwood, plate, 8" d, hand grip, basketweave back, electric purple **325.00**

Windmill, Imperial
Pitcher, marigold **65.00**
Sauce, 5" d, purple **55.00**
Tumbler, purple **75.00**

Wishbone & Spades, Dugan, chop plate, 10-3/4" d, plain back, purple, with electric purple and blue highlights **900.00**

Wreath of Roses, Fenton, punch cups, Vintage interior
Blue **40.00**
Green. **40.00**

Zig-Zag, Millersburg
Bowl, 10" d, three-in-one edge, amethyst **400.00**
Bowl, tri-corn, crimped edge, amethyst **1,050.00**

CAROUSEL FIGURES

History: By the late 17th century, carousels were found in most capital cities of Europe. In 1867, Gustav Dentzel carved America's first carousel. Other leading American firms include Charles I. D. Looff, Allan Herschell, Charles Parker, and William F. Mangels.

References: Charlotte Dinger, *Art of the Carousel,* Carousel Art, 1983; Tobin Fraley, *The Carousel Animal,* Tobin Fraley Studios, 1983; Frederick Fried, *Pictorial History of the Carrousel,* Vestal Press, 1964; William Manns, Peggy Shank, and Marianne Stevens, *Painted Ponies,* Zon International Publishing, 1986.

Periodicals and Internet Resources: *Carousel,* www.carousel.org; *Carousels.com,* www.carousels.com; *Carousel News & Trader,* Suite 206, 87 Park Ave. West, Mansfield, OH 44902, www.carousel.net/trader; *Carousel Shopper,* Zon International Publishing, P.O. Box 6459, Santa Fe, NM 87502.

Collectors' Clubs: American Carousel Society, 3845 Telegraph Road, Elkton, MD 21921, www.carousel.org/acs; National Amusement Park Historical Assoc., P.O. Box 83, Mount Prospect, IL 60056; National Carousel Assoc., P.O. Box 4333, Evansville, IN 47724, www.carousel.org/nca; National Carousel Assoc., P.O. Box 4165, Salisbury, NC 28145-4165, www.carouselmagazine.com; National Wood Carvers Assoc., P.O. Box 43218, Cincinnati, OH 45243, www.chipchats.org.

Museums: Carousel Museum of America, San Francisco, CA; Children's Museum of Indianapolis, Indianapolis, IN; Heritage Plantation of Sandwich, Sandwich, MA; Herschell Carrousel Factory Museum, North Tonawanda, NY; International Museum of Carousel Art, Hood River, OR; Merry-Go-Round Museum, Sandusky, OH; New England Carousel Museum, Inc., Bristol, CT.

Notes: Since carousel figures were repainted annually, original paint is not a critical factor to collectors. "Park paint" indicates layers of accumulated paint; "stripped" means paint has been removed to show carving; "restored" involves stripping and repainting in the original colors.

Camel
European, 1890 . . . . **2,400.00**
Loeff **7,000.00**
Morris, E. Joy **8,000.00**

Chariot Bench
Loeff, gilded **625.00**
Parker, C. W. **12,500.00**
Spillman, with flowers **300.00**
Unknown maker, one panel having applied carved flowers, other side with applied carved eagle and horse, 52" x 29" **800.00**

Cow, Bayol, France **5,000.00**
Elephant, fiberglass **600.00**
Donkey, Illions, from Willow Grove Amusement Park, Willow Grove, PA **17,000.00**

Giraffe, old mottled painted surface, carved mane, attributed to Ohio, c1880-90, some losses, saddle and tail missing, 39" l, 10" d, 53" h . . . **6,325.00**
Goat, Loeff **7,500.00**

Horse, jumper
Anderson, J. R. **5,000.00**
Bayol, France **3,000.00**
Carmel **3,700.00**
Dare, Charles W. F., New York Carousel Manufacturing Company, Brooklyn, NY, orig paint, 60" l, 39" h, very minor losses, paint wear and loss **8,625.00**
Dentzel, top knot **5,000.00**
Herschell, Allen, all wood, 1920 . . . . **2,000.00**
Herschell, Allen, metal, restored **800.00**
Herschell-Spillman, North Tonawanda, NY, orange, green, and blue, 60" x 56" x 12" cast iron stand **2,750.00**
Illions, from Willow Grove Amusement Park, Willow Grove, PA **4,750.00**
Ortega, jumper **300.00**
Parker, C. W., inside jumper, carved, sgd on shoes "C. W. Parker, Leavenworth, Kansas," early worn paint, brown body, black mane and

tail, relief-carved saddle blanket, green, yellow, and red saddle, incised stars, red-and-yellow bridle, glass eyes, black-enameled steel base with pole with brass-spiral casing, 62" w, 36" h horse, 101" h pole **5,500.00**
P.T.C. **3,250.00**
Spillman, restored **3,300.00**
Stein & Goldstein **2,750.00**

Horse, prancer
Dentzel, orig paint **8,000.00**
Hubner, fully restored **4,250.00**
Loeff, Charles, attributed to, outside prancer, carved, repainted in white, carved black mane, horsehair tail, blue-and-gray relief-carved straps and saddle, plaid saddle blanket, red-and-gold detailing, cobalt-blue faceted jewel on outside, glass eyes, 57" w, 55-1/2" h, enameled steel base and pole with brass-spiral casing, 90" h pole . . **2,750.00**

Horse, stander
Illions, from Willow Grove Amusement Park, Willow Grove, PA **12,500.00**
Morris, E. J. **10,500.00**
Spillman, animal pelt **4,600.00**
Stein & Goldstein **10,500.00**

Indian Pony
Parker, C. W., pelt saddle . . **9,000.00**
Spillman **4,500.00**

Panel, carved wood
37-1/2" x 45", cowboy on bucking bronco in panoramic view . **200.00**
63" x 13", cherub at top, carved leaves overall **450.00**

Pig
Dentzel, restored **12,000.00**
Spillman, with pear **5,000.00**

Horse, Philadelphia Toboggan Co., carved and painted, C1918, 70" l, 65" h, **$11,000.**

CASTLEFORD

History: Castleford is a soft-paste porcelain made in Yorkshire, England, in the 1800s for the American trade. The wares have a warm, white ground, scalloped rims (resembling castle tops), and are trimmed in deep blue. Occasionally, pieces are decorated further with a coat of arms, eagles, or Lady Liberty.

Creamer, 3-1/4" d base, 4-3/4" h, white, blue trim, c1805 . . . . **175.00**
Milk jug, 4-3/4" h, oval, relief of American eagle on one side, Liberty and cap on reverse, acanthus-leaf border **195.00**
Sugar, cov, relief of classical figure leaning on urn, acanthus-leaf panel, blue-enamel border, scalloped edge, three enameled bands on cov . **250.00**

Sugar bowl, cov, $250.

Teapot, cov

9-1/2" w, 5" h, white, blue trim, c1800, slight wear to blue on handle **475.00**

9-3/4" w, 5-1/2" h, white, classical mourning scene, hinged lid, wooden-hinge pin, c1790-1820, small nick to spout **750.00**

CASTOR SETS

History: A castor set consists of matched condiment bottles held within a frame or holder. The bottles are for condiments such as salt, pepper, oil, vinegar, and mustard. The most commonly found castor sets consist of three, four, or five glass bottles in a silver-plated frame.

Although castor sets were made as early as the 1700s, most of the sets encountered today date from 1870 to 1915, the period when they enjoyed their greatest popularity.

2-bottle, English, two cut-glass condiment jars, rect oak caddy mounted with silver-plate frame, upright handle, decorative strapwork and plain central shield, four ball feet, late 19th C, 7-7/8" l, 4-3/8" d, 10-5/8" h **500.00**

3-bottle, Bohemian, three shouldered 14" h decanters, flashed blue, green, and cranberry, cut with circles, etched Greek key band, silver-plated stand with tall central handle above three cylindrical wells, with geometric engine turning, borders with fruiting grapevine, three grapevine feet, late 19th C, 10-1/4" w, 20-1/2" h **865.00**

3-bottle, clear, Daisy-and-Button pattern, toothpick holder center, matching glass holder **125.00**

3-bottle, clear, Ribbed-Palm pattern, pewter tops and frame **185.00**

4-bottle, clear, mold blown, pewter lids and frame, domed based, loop handle, marked "I. Trask," early 19th C, 8" h. **320.00**

4-bottle, cranberry bottles and jars, clear pressed-glass frame, silver-plated look handle, two brass caps, one pewter, 9-1/2" h **275.00**

4-bottle, green cut to clear, sq bottles, SP frame **340.00**

4-bottle, rubena, Venecia pattern, glass frame **200.00**

4-bottle, ruby stained, Ruby-Thumbprint pattern, glass frame **360.00**

5-bottle, clear, Bellflower pattern, pressed stoppers, pewter frame with pedestal. **295.00**

5-bottle, clear, all over cut linear and geometric design, SS mounts and frame, shell-shaped foot, English hallmarks, c1750, 8-1-2/" h **625.00**

5-bottle, clear, Honeycomb pattern, ornate Wilcox frame **265.00**

5-bottle, cut glass, ornate Rogers & Bros. frame **295.00**

5-bottle, etched, wreath-and-polka-dots pattern, rib-trimmed frame **195.00**

6-bottle, china, Willow ware, matching frame **150.00**

Pattern glass, Jumbo pattern, pair of salt and pepper shakers, mustard bottle, metal center handle, three elephant head supports, **$775.** *Photo courtesy of Joy Luke Auctions.*

6-bottle, clear, pressed bottles, SP Simpson Hall & Miller frame. . . .**150.00**

6-bottle, cut, diamond-point panels, rotating sterling-silver frame, all-over flowers, paw feet, loop handle, Gorham Mfg. Co., c1880, 11-1/2" h . . .**2,500.00**

CATALOGS

History: The first American mail-order catalog was issued by Benjamin Franklin in 1744. This popular advertising tool helped to spread inventions, innovations, fashions, and necessities of life to rural America. Catalogs were profusely illustrated and are studied today to date an object, identify its manufacturer, study its distribution, and determine its historical importance.

References: Ron Barlow and Ray Reynolds, *Insider's Guide to Old Books, Magazines, Newspapers, Trade Catalogs*, Windmill Publishing (2147 Windmill View Rd, Cajon, CA 92020), 1995; Lawrence B. Romaine, *Guide to American Trade Catalogs 1744-1900*, Dover Publications, n.d.

Museums: Grand Rapids Public Museum, Grand Rapids, MI; National Museum of Health and Medicine, Walter Reed Medical Center, Washington, DC.

Additional Listings: See *Warman's Americana & Collectibles* for more examples.

Adviser: Kenneth Schneringer.

Acme Chair Co., Reading, MI, 1925, 24 pgs, 7-3/4" x 10-1/2", Catalog No. 40, *Acme Quality Folding Chairs of Hard Maple Stock* **40.00**

American Cabinet Co., Two Rivers, WI, 1930, 64 pgs, 6" x 9", Illus price list, loose color flyers laid in, dental-office furniture, color illus. **100.00**

Amtorg Trading Corp., New York, NY, c1932, 31 pgs, 6" x 7-3/4", *Rubs of the Cacasus & Turkestan Areas*, pictures of rooms and rugs **25.00**

Bachman Bros., Inc., Philadelphia, PA, 1969, 26 pgs, 8-1/2" x 11", *"N" Gauge Trains and Accessories* **20.00**

Baird-North Co., Providence, RI, 1927, 162 pgs, 6-3/4" x 10-1/2", *Jewelry Year Book*, slight damage to cover . . .**42.00**

Bamford, Ltd., Uttoxeter, Great Britain, 1924, 36 pgs, 4-1/2" x 5-1/2", *Bamfords' Harvesting Implements*, cuts of mowers and reapers **25.00**

Boy Scouts of America, LaSalle, IL, 1962, 24 pgs, 5-1/2" x 8-1/2", *Spring & Summer Catalogue of Boy Scout Equipment and Uniforms* **24.00**

Bradley Fertilizer Co., Boston, MA, 1892, 50 pgs, 7" x 7", cuts and views of lawns, crop fields, fertilizers. **20.00**

Brown Bros. Supply Co., Maplesville, AL, 1956, 32 pgs, 8-1/2" x 11", *Christmas Time Toys* **50.00**

Burgess Seed & Plant Co., Galesburg, MI, 1936, 130 pgs, 6-1/2" x 9-1/2", *Burgess Guaranteed Seeds & Plants for 1936*, colorful wraps **10.00**

Butler Brothers, New York, NY, 1927, 436 pgs, 9-1/4" x 13-1/2", *Our Drummer, Mid Winter, 50th Anniversary*, spine reinforced with tape, some tears on wraps **55.00**

Central States Fire Apparatus, Lyons, SD, six pgs, 8-1/2" x 11", color, complete line of tankers and pumpers, 10 models **12.00**

Chase Brothers Co., Rochester, NY, 1922, 139 pgs, 7-1/2" x 10-1/2", *Chase Fruit & Flowers*, natural colors, hard cover with some roughness..... **38.00**

Chicago Flag & Decorating, Chicago, IL, c1928, 32 pgs, 6" x 9", Catalog No. 30, *Catalog of Flags, Canvas Goods, etc.*................ **27.00**

Corbin, P & F., New Britain, CT, 1896, 289 pgs, 4-1/4" x 6-1/4", Volume A, *Hardware*, cuts, hard cover..... **80.00**

Central Scientific Co., Chicago, IL, 1923, 428 pgs, 8" x 10-3/4", Catalog No. 123, physical apparatus, instruments, tools, hard cover **95.00**

Chandler & Pease, Springfield, MA, 24 pgs, 4-1/4" x 5-3/4", *Catalog of Steel Stamps, Letters & Figures*...... **30.00**

Curtis Co. Service Bureau, Clinton, IA, 1923, 48 pgs, 5-1/4" x 7", *Permanent Furniture for Better Built Homes* . **22.00**

Davis Sewing Machine Co., Watertown, NY, 1881, 64 pgs, 5-1/2" x 8-3/4" **24.00**

Eagle Magic Co., Minneapolis, MN, c1927, 46 pgs, 5" x 7", Catalog No. 26, *Apparatus That Works, Magic Tricks, Card Tricks, etc.* **10.00**

Eclipse Machine Co., Elmira, NY, 1903, 32 pgs, 6" x 8-1/2", *The Morrow Has Circled the Globe* **50.00**

Ehrich Brothers, New York, NY, 1894, 32 pgs, 8" x 10-1/2", *Holiday Bulletin of Special Values*............... **45.00**

Enterprise Mfg Co., Columbiana, OH, 1888, 14 pgs, 6" x 8-3/4", *Catalogue & Price List of the Young America Improved No. 1 Feed Mill* **38.00**

Eureka Mower Co., Towanda, PA 1883, 144 pgs, 5-3/4" x 8-3/4", *Testimonial Circular of new model* **24.00**

Forsland, Carl, Grand Rapids, MI, 48 pgs, 7" x 10", *Quaint American Furniture* **24.00**

Four Winds Farm Nursery, Williamsville, NY, c1932, six pgs, color, hyacinths................... **4.00**

Freeland Steel Tank Co., Portage, WI, 1912, 32 pgs, 6" x 9", Catalog No. 21, *Galvanized Steel Storage Tanks, etc.* **16.00**

General Electric Co., Schnectady NY, 1910, 212 pgs, 4" x 6-1/2", No. 3915, *G. E. Specialties*, cuts of sockets, receptacles, fuses, boxes, electrical supplies **20.00**

Gilbert, B. L., Magic Co., Chicago, IL, 1924, 48 pgs, 5-3/4" x 8-1/2", Catalog 33, *Magical Effects Par Excellence* **20.00**

Gordon-Van Tine Co., Davenport, IA, 1917, 72 pgs, 8-1/2" x 11-1/2", *Catalogue of Farm Buildings*, barns with plant frame trussed-roof style, self-supporting or braced-rafter roof or Gothic-roof style, gambrel-roof bank barns, hog houses, poultry houses, etc. **46.00**

Graves & Son, L. S., Rochester, NY, 1883, 34 pgs, 4" x 5-3/4", pulleys, freight-and-passenger elevators, equipment **15.00**

Hamilton Piano Co., Chicago Heights, IL, 31 pgs, 8" x 10-1/2", cuts of factory **45.00**

Hanson, Van Winkle & Co., Newark, NJ 1890, 64 pgs, 6" x 9", *Catalogue of Nickel Electro Plating & Polishing Material*.................... **100.00**

Hesse, Henry, Importer, New York, NY, 1914, 64 pgs, 5" x 6-3/4", *Catalog of Wollen, Worsted, Cotton Yarns, Art Embroiders, Textiles, etc.*........ **15.00**

Horrocks-Ibbotson Co., Utica, NY, 1940, 30 pgs, 5-1/4" x 6-1/4", *Fishing Tackle & Tackling Fish* **36.00**

Howe Scale Co., St. Louis, MO, 1926, 153 pgs, 4-1/4" x 7-1/2", Catalog No. 61, *Special Mercantile & Industrial Equipment*, 16-pg price list laid in **85.00**

Hudson Equipment Co., Chicago, IL, 1940, 256 pgs, 6-1/2" x 9-3/4", Hudson Barn Equipment Catalog No. B-31, *Stalls, Stanchions, Bull Stall, etc.*....................... **30.00**

Hutcher Bros. Saw Mfg Co., Rochester, NY, 1940, 119 pgs, 5" x 6-1/2", Catalog No. 60 of *Saws*... **18.00**

Ideal Dairy Supplies, Chicago, IL, 1953, 4-3/4" x 9", *Price List of Dairy Supplies for Spring and Summer*. **15.00**

Iver Joynson's Arms, Fitchburg, MA, c1930, 28 pgs, 6" x 9", shotguns, rifles, revolvers, etc.................. **48.00**

Keith Brothers, Chicago, IL, 1871, 20 pgs, 3" x 5-1/4", *Importers and Mfgrs of Buffalo and Fancy Robes, Millinery and Straw Goods*, 45 cuts......... **220.00**

Keuffel & Esser Co., Hoboken, NJ, 1936, *Catalogue of Drawing Materials, Surveying Instruments & Measuring Tapes*, price list laid-in, hard cover.................. **60.00**

Kochs, Theo. A., Co., Chicago, IL, 1930, 48 pgs, 9" x 12", Catalog No. 40, *Barber & Beauty Shop Fixtures*, price list laid-in.................. **285.00**

Lane Bryant, New York, NY, 1930, 24 pgs, 7-1/2" x 10", July and August sale of bargains for children........ **10.00**

Lauriat Co., The, Boston, MA, 1925, 36 pgs, 6-1/2" x 9-1/4", *Summer Catalogue of Book Bargains for the 1925 Season*................ **10.00**

Little Tree Farm, Framingham Center, MA, 1927, 48 pgs, 8-1/2" x 11-1/2", Section II Year Book, No. 37, *Complete Catalog of Evergreens, Shrubs, Trees, Vines, Annuals, Perennials, Landscaping Accessories, etc.* . **15.00**

Maher & Grosh Cutlery Co., Toledo, OH, 1895, 80 pgs, 5-3/4" x 8-3/4", hand-forged cutlery, razors, shears, pocket knives, etc. **85.00**

Mantle Lamp Co. of America, Chicago, IL, 1928, 12 pgs, 8" x 9-3/4", orig envelope, letter on Christmas letterhead, price and order forms, six double-page sheets of Aladdin supplies and parts **40.00**

Marble & Shattuck Chair, Cleveland, OH, c1923, 64 pgs, 7-3/4" x 10-3/4", Catalog No. 50, *Dining, Café & Bedroom Chairs* **50.00**

Truman & Shaw, Market Street, Philadelphia, general and hardware goods, 6" h, **$35.** *Photo courtesy of Sanford Alderfer Auction Co.*

Massey-Harris Harvester, Batavia, NY, 1920, 18 pgs, 6" x 9"..........**32.00**

Melrose Boat Works, Melrose Park, IL, c1930, 19 pgs, 5-1/2" x 7-1/2", *You Won't Go Wrong With the Melrose Boat Way! Build Your Own Boat with Our Blue Prints*, cuts of cabin cruisers, sail boat, etc. **40.00**

Meneely Bell Co., Troy, NY, 1912, 46 pgs, 6-1/4" x 9-1/2", *Manufacturers of Bells for Church, Chime, Academy, Tower-Clock, Court House, etc.* ...**75.00**

Miller Stockman Supply Co., Denver, CO, 1957, 64 pgs, 8" x 10-1/2", Catalog No. 109, *Western Wear*.........**40.00**

Milton Bradley Co., Springfield, MA, 1913, 108 pgs, 6" x 9", kindergarten materials, school supplies **42.00**

Milwaukee Harvester Co., Milwaukee, WI, 1900, 16 pgs, 4" x 5", in color, given out at the Universal Exposition, Paris, small map of Paris grounds, guide to grounds and buildings **100.00**

Mohawk Carpet Mills, Amsterdam, NY, 1946, 169 pgs, 6" x 9", *Woven Floor Covering Retail Sales Manual*, hardcover **20.00**

Moline Plow Co., Moline, IL, c1908, 32 pgs, 6" x 8-3/4", *Flying Dutchman Souvenir Song Book*, songs, articles, and pictures of sulky plow, cultivator, corn planter, disc harrow, etc. ...**32.00**

Montgomery Ward & Co., Chicago, IL, 1,016 pgs, 9-1/2" x 13", Catalog & Buyers Guide No. 89, *Clothing for the Family, Furniture, Farm Supplies & Implements, Household*, parted at binding, some sheets have tears **85.00**

Morgan Sash & Door Co., Chicago, IL, c1953, 180 pgs, 8-1/2" x 11", Catalog & Price List No. 553, *Morgan-Anderson Woodwork*...................**35.00**

Moulton Ladder Mfg. Co., Somerville, MA, 1946, 7" x 10", *Catalog of Ladders*, color laid-in.................**35.00**

Nash & Bro., Millington, NJ, c1886, 48 pgs, 5" x 8-1/2", *Acme Pulverizing Harrow*, etc. **36.00**

National Carbon Co., Inc., 1952, 16 pgs, 8-1/2" x 10", Catalog No. A1352, *Eveready Flashlights & Batteries* .**38.00**

Navigator Instruments, Inc., San Francisco, CA, 1924, 22 pgs, 6-1/4" x 9-1/4", *Paulin System* **24.00**

New Jersey Fireworks Mfg., Elkton, MD, c1948, 18 pgs, 7-1/4" x 11", *Fireworks Display Catalogue*, red-and-blue inks, lists open stock, fireworks and aerial displays **55.00**

New Moline Plow Co., Moline, IL, 1924, 34 pgs, 5-3/4" x 8-3/4", *Farmer's Catalog* **32.00**

Old Town Canoe Co., Old Town, ME, 1973, 28 pgs, 8-1/2" x 11", *Old Town Discovery, The Finest in Canoes, Kayaks & Power Boats* **35.00**

Oriental Process Rug Renovating Co., Boston, MA, 1901, 48 pgs, 4-3/4" x 6", discusses methods of preservation, cuts of weaving, spinning wool, etc. **25.00**

Penn Metal Co., Boston, MA, 1912, 94 pgs, 8-3/4" x 11", 41st *Catalog of Metal Ceilings and Accessories for Banks, Hotels, Theaters, Churches and Auditoriums*.................**45.00**

Peter Paul & Son, Buffalo, NY, 1915, 80 pgs, 6" x 9", *Pauls' Gift Guide for the Whole Year* **28.00**

Police Equipment Supply, Chicago, IL, 1939, 12 pgs, 8" x 11", equipment, uniforms...................**40.00**

Porter, H. K., & Co., Pittsburgh, PA, c1900, 216 pgs, 6" x 9", *Builders of Light Locomotives*...........**90.00**

Port Huron Engine & Thresher Co., Port Huron, MI, 1908, 82 pgs, 5-3/4" x 8-1/4", Catalog No. 15, leather belting for machinery, canvas covers, tank pumps, specialized tools **18.00**

Pratt Food Co., Philadelphia, PA, 1906, 48 pgs, 5" x 8", animal-and-poultry regulators **18.00**

Printz-Biederman Co., Cleveland, OH, 1923, 8-1/4" x 11-1/2", *The Identification of a Smart Garment*, cuts of three-piece suits.......................**28.00**

Pullman Mfg. Corp., Rochester, NY, 1939, 32 pgs, 8-1/2" x 11", Pullman unit sash balances..............**14.00**

Read & Dahir, Chicago, IL, 1915, 128 pgs, 8-3/4" x 11-1/2", Wholesale Catalog No. 27, *Watches, Jewelry, Clocks* **82.00**

Revere Copper & Brass Co., Rome, NY, c1936, 8 pgs, 3" x 6", 6" x 12" sheet folded as issued, retail price list .**15.00**

Rice & Hutchins, Boston, MA, c1918, 16 pgs, 4" x 6-3/4", *A Treat for the Feet, All American Shoes for Men*, large cuts of shoes...................**12.00**

Richard's, New York, NY, c1900, 26 pcs, 8" x 11-1/4", *Richard's Fashion Album of Tailor Made Costumes for Women*..................**45.00**

Rich Brothers, Sioux Falls, SD, 1968, 38 pgs, 8-1/2" x 11", *Interstate Display Fireworks Co.*................**40.00**

Rochester Fur Dressing Co., Rochester, NY, c1924, 18 pgs, 8-1/4" x 11", *We Tan Them You Wear Them*, tanning and leather supplies **20.00**

Rochester Stamping Co., Rochester, NY, 64 pgs, 4-1/2" x 7", chafing-dish suggestions **26.00**

Sanders Manufacturing Co., Nashville, TN, 1937, 34 pgs, 3-3/4" x 8-1/2", Catalog No. S-8-37, *Advertising Specialties* **21.00**

Schmidt, Oscar, Jersey City, NY, 16 pgs, 4-3/4" x 12-1/2", *Catalogue of Music for the Menzenhauer Guitar Zither and the American Mandolin Harp*......................**15.00**

Scully Steel & Iron Co., Chicago, IL, 1900, 120 pgs, 4-1/2" x 7", *September and October Illustrated Stock List*, steel floor plates, corrugated sheets, pressed-brick siding, roofing, etc........................**36.00**

Sears, Roebuck & Co., Chicago, IL

16 pgs, 8-1/2" x 10-1/2", 1925, *Fall & Winter Made-To-Order Clothing for Men & Boys*, cloth swatches...............**32.00**

114 pgs, 9-1/2" x 11-3/4", *Catalog of Cameras, Platesfilms, Papers, Developing and Finishing Equipment*..............**135.00**

Shear Packard Co., Albany, NY, 1869, 15 pgs, 5-1/4" x 8-1/2", *Magic Light Direct Draft Self-Feeding Gas Burner*.....................**50.00**

Starrett Precision Tools, Atol, MA, Catalog 26, copyright 1938, 4-7/8" x 7" h, $35.

Silver Truss Corp., Coudersport, PA, 1940, 66 pgs, 6-1/2" x 9", Catalog No. 43, *Trusses, Abdominal Supporters, etc.*, price list laid-in **21.00**
Simmons Hardware Co., St. Louis, MO, 1921, 2,736 pgs, 8-1/2" x 10-3/4", *Keen Kutter Cutlery, Tools & Farming Implements* **275.00**
Sohmer & Co., New York, NY, c1930, 20 pgs, 6" x 7-3/4", *Piano Makers Catalog* **35.00**
Spaulding, A. G., & Bros., Chicopee, MA, 1911, 52 pgs, 9-1/4" x 12", *Catalog X*, steel playground apparatus . . **55.00**
Spirella Companies, Niagara Falls, NY, c1915, eight pgs, 3-1/2" x 6-1/4", showing posture correction, etc. using Spirella Corsets **12.00**
Sterling Magic Co., Royal Oak, MI, 1947, 26 pgs, 5-1/2" x 8-1/2", *Catalog of Selected Magic*, cuts of billiard ball holder, silk winder, fanning powder, card tricks, stage money, etc. . . . **20.00**
Stewart-Warner Co., 1939, 12 pgs, 3-1/2" x 6-1/4", 10-1/2" x 12-1/2" sheet folded as issued in tinted colors, AC-DC radios for 1929, cuts of AC receivers, floor models **22.00**
Stover Mfg. & Eng. Co., Freeport, IL, c1927, 16 pgs, 8" x 9", Catalog No. 85, *Stover Feed Mills*, folded in center as issued **30.00**
Thayer & Chandler, Chicago, IL, 1922, 64 pgs, 8-1/2" x 11", Catalog No. 51, *Artists' China Parchment Shades* **15.00**
Universal Fashion Co., New York, NY, 1883, 14 pgs, 6-3/4" x 10-1/4", *Autumn & Winter Catalog of Perfect Fitting Patterns for Women and Girls* . . . **20.00**
Victor Talking Machine Co., Camden, NJ, 1921, 32 pgs, 5-3/4" x 8", line drawings **20.00**
Vulcan Copper Works, Co., Cincinnati, OH, 1904, 149 pgs, 7-3/4" x 10-1/2", *Catalog of Products*, written in Spanish **45.00**
Warner, W. E., & Co., New York, NY, 94 pgs, 4-3/4" x 8", *Catalog "B" of Brushes* **21.00**
Weir Stove Co., Taunton, MA, six pgs, 5-3/8" x 8-1/2", *Manufacturers of the Glenwood C Range* **25.00**
Wells & Edwards, Chicago, IL, 1922, 40 pgs, 3-1/4" x 6", *Catalogue of Latest & Best Practical, Mechanical & Automobile Books* **9.00**
Western Land Roller Co., Hastings, NE, 20 pgs, 7-3/4" x 9", *Western Bear-Cat Feed Grinder*, folded in center as issued for mail-out **21.00**

Westinghouse Electric Mfg., c1929, 21 pgs, 8-1/4" x 10-1/2", marine equipment **40.00**
Widow Jones, Boston, MA, 1905, 8 pgs, 4" x 10", *Widow Jones Fall & Winter Style for Young Men* **26.00**
World Air Brush Mfg Co., Chicago, IL, c1949, two pgs, 8-1/2" x 11" **24.00**
Yale & Towne Mfg Co., New York, NY, 1918, 51 pgs, 6" x 9", *Catalog & Price List of Keys and Blanks* **55.00**

CELADON

History: The term "celadon," meaning a pale grayish-green color, is derived from the theatrical character Celadon, who wore costumes of varying shades of grayish green in Honore d'Urfe's 17th-century pastoral romance, *L'Astree*. French Jesuits living in China used the name to refer to a specific type of Chinese porcelain.

Celadon divides into two types. Northern celadon, made during the Sung Dynasty up to the 1120s, has a gray-to-brownish body, relief decoration, and monochromatic olive-green glaze. Southern (Lung-ch'uan) celadon, made during the Sung Dynasty and much later, is paint-decorated with floral and other scenic designs and is found in forms that appeal to the European- and American-export market. Many of the southern pieces date from 1825 to 1885. A blue square with Chinese or pseudo-Chinese characters appears on pieces after 1850. Later pieces also have a larger and sparser decorative patterning.

Reproduction Alert.

Vase, Lung-Chuan, deep sea green, China, Ming Dynasty, **$375.**

Bowl, 14-3/4" d, deep rounded sides, waisted rim, everted lip, ext. with interwoven bands of flowering magnolias, three cylindrical-applied monster-head feet, pale gray-green glaze, unglazed base, Chinese **975.00**
Censor, 10-3/4" d, compressed-globular form, three monster-head supports, carved with eight Trigrams, thick gray-green crackle glaze, int. central portion and glaze unglazed, kiln flaws, Lonquan, Ming Dynasty . **675.00**
Garden seat, 17" h, sea green, sgraffito carving, China, Ming dynasty, 1368-1644 . . . . **2,530.00**
Incense burner, 12" d, Lung-Chuan ware, sgraffito-carved star dec, cracked kiln flow, China, Ming dynasty **400.00**
Libation cup, 3-3/4" h, steep tapering sides, foliate rim, dragon and clouds, blue-green glaze, 19th C **250.00**
Plate, 7-3/8" d, polychrome flowers, birds, and butterflies, pr, one with chip on table ring **200.00**
Umbrella stand, 24-3/4" h, blue-glazed dec, Chinese **275.00**
Vase
 8-1/2" h, Lung-Chuan ware, deep sea green, sgraffito dec, China, Ming dynasty, 1368-1644 . . **375.00**
 16-1/2" h, Rouleau form, front with blue-and-white scene of dancing figures, crackled, Chinese, Ming style, second half 19th C, sgd **700.00**

CELLULOID ITEMS

History: In 1869, an Albany, NY, printer named John W. Hyatt developed and patented the world's first commercially successful semi-synthetic thermoplastic. The moldable material was made from a combination of camphor, the crystalline resin from the heart of a particular evergreen tree, and collodion, a type of nitrated-cellulose substance (also called Pyroxylin), which was extremely flammable. Hyatt and his brother, Isaiah, called their invention Celluloid, a name they made up by combining the words cellulose and colloid.

By 1873, the Hyatts were successfully producing raw pyroxylin plastic material at the Celluloid Manufacturing Company of Newark, NJ. In the early days of its commercial development, Celluloid was produced exclusively in two colors: flesh tone, for the manufacture of denture-base material, and off white, which was primarily used for utilitarian applications like harness trimmings and knife handles.

However, during the late 1870s, advances in plastics technology brought about a shift in the ways Celluloid could be used. Beautiful imitations of amber, ivory, tortoise shell, jet, and coral were being produced and used in the fabrication of jewelry, fashion accessories, and hair ornaments. Because the faux-luxury materials were so realistic and affordable, Celluloid quickly advanced to the forefront of consumerism by the working and middle classes.

Throughout the 1880s and 1890s, competition in the infant plastics industry was rampant and a number of newly organized fabricating companies were aggressively molding their brands of pyroxylin plastic into a variety of consumer products. However, since there was such limited knowledge about the nature of the material, many companies failed due to inferior products or devastating fires.

By the early 20th century, there were four major American manufacturers firmly established as producers of quality pyroxylin plastics. In addition to the Celluloid Company of Newark, NJ, there was the Arlington Manufacturing Company of Arlington, NJ, which produced Pyralin; Fiberloid Corporation of Indian Orchard, MA, makers of Fiberloid; and the Viscoloid Company of Leominster, MA. Even though these companies branded their plastic products with their registered trade names, today the word "celluloid" is used in a general sense for all forms of this early plastic.

Celluloid-type plastic became increasingly popular as an alternative for costly and elusive natural substances. Within the fashion industry alone, it gained acceptance as a beautiful and affordable substitute for increasingly dwindling supplies of ivory and tortoise shell. However, it should be noted that celluloid's most successful application during the late 19th century was realized in the clothing industry; sheet stock in imitation of fine-grade linen was fashioned into stylish waterproof cuffs and collars.

In sheet form, Celluloid found other successful applications as well. Printed political and advertising premiums, pin-back buttons, pocket mirrors, and keepsake items from 1890-1920 were turned out by the thousands. In addition, transparent-sheet celluloid was ornately decorated by embossing, reverse painting, and lamination, then used in the production of decorative boxes, booklets, and albums. The toy industry also capitalized on the used of thin-celluloid sheet for the production of blow-molded dolls, animal toys, and figural novelties.

The development of the motion-picture industry helped celluloid fulfill a unique identity all its own; it was used for reels of camera film, as well as in sheet form by animation artists who drew cartoons. Known as animation cels, these are still readily available to the collector for a costly sum, but because of the depredation of old celluloid, many early movies and cels have been lost forever.

By 1930, and the advent of the modern-plastics age, the use of celluloid began to decline dramatically. The introduction of cellulose-acetate plastic replaced the flammable pyroxylin plastic in jewelry and toys, and the development of non-flammable safety film eventually put an end to its use in movies. By 1950, the major manufacturers of celluloid in the United States had ceased production; however, many foreign companies continued manufacture. Today, Japan, France, Italy, and Korea continue to manufacture cellulose-nitrate plastics in small amounts for specialty items such as musical-instrument inlay, ping-pong balls, and designer fountain pens.

Beware of celluloid items that show signs of deterioration: oily residue, cracking, discoloration, and crystallization. Take care when cleaning celluloid items; it is best to use mild soap and water, avoiding alcohol- or acetone-based cleansers. Keep celluloid from excessive heat or flame and avoid direct sunlight.

References: Shirley Dunn, *Celluloid Collectibles*, Collector Books, 1999, 2001 value update; Keith Lauer and Julie Robinson, *Celluloid, A Collector's Reference and Value Guide*, Collector Books, 1999, 2001 value update; Karima Parry, *Bakelite Bangles, Price & Identification Guide*, Krause Publications, 1999; Joan Van Patten and Elmer and Peggy Williams, *Celluloid Treasures of the Victorian Era*, Collector Books, 1999.

Collectors' Club: American Plastics History Association, 534 Stublyn Road, Granville, OH 43023-9554.

Museum: National Plastics Center & Museum, Leominster, MA 01453.

Marks: Viscoloid Co. manufactured a large variety of small hollow animals that ranged in size from two to eight inches. Most of these toys are embossed with one of three trademarks: "Made in USA," an intertwined "VCO," or an eagle with a shield.

Adviser: Julie P. Robinson.

Advertising letter opener, ivory grained, sickle-shaped, advertising for Zylonite Novelties, $85. Photo courtesy of Julie Robinson.

Advertising and souvenir-keepsake items

Badge, 2" d, printed with "P H" and two intertwined American flags, fraternal organization for Patrons of Husbandry—The Grange, Whitehead & Hoag Co., early 1900s, shaped metal pin-back frame **20.00**

Booklet, 4-3/4" x 3", memo, celluloid cover printed with lovely lady by Whitehead & Hoag, ad for Alphonse Judas Co., Season's Greetings 1906. . . . . **45.00**

Bookmark
3 1/4" l, 1/4" w, folded top for slipping over a page, violets dec, "Greetings" on the long flat surface **20.00**
4 3/4" l, diecut ivory-grained celluloid, poinsettia motif with "Footpath to Peace by Henry Van Dyke" **25.00**

Card
3-1/16" x 2", engraved "Baldwin & Gleason With Best Wishes," ivory-grained sheet cream-colored celluloid, deep-blue floral motif **30.00**
4" x 3" folding-paper card, emb-celluloid front showing gold cornucopia with flowers and "Remembrance," unused . . . **12.00**

Clothing brush, 3-1/2" d, celluloid-laminated printed paper showing Parisian Novelty Company of Chicago, USA—"Supplies for Making Fiberloid Novelties and Advertising Specialties," rare **175.00**

Comb, case, 4-1/2" x 7/8" ivory-grained comb, case with blue and black graphics, "New England Made Cigars" **35.00**

Compact, 1-3/4" d, imitation ivory-grained celluloid with gold Elk motif and "Third Annual Ball, BPOE, Leominster Lodge No. 1237, Jan. 26, 1917," produced by the Viscoloid Co. of Leominster, MA. **55.00**

Fan, 4" tall when closed, mottled turquoise-and-cream celluloid Brise fan, light-blue ribbon, shows the Washington Monument and words, "Washington D.C." in gold-tone paint **15.00**

Game counter, 2-3/4" x 1" ivory-grained celluloid, disks turn to keep baseball score, "Peter Doelger Bottled Beer—Expressly for the Home" **55.00**

Ink blotter
2-1/2" x 6" rect booklet of blotters with holiday-lantern motif, "May this be your Merriest Christmas and 1929 your Happiest Year," The Charis Corp. of Allentown, PA **45.00**
4 1/8" x 2 7/8" ivory-grained celluloid, front and back covers w/ blotters inside, engraved scene of Black Diamond File Works, Philadelphia, PA, 1890 calendar, Baldwin & Gleason Co. **45.00**

Match safe, 2-1/2" x 1-1/2"
Ivory-grained safety-match holder, red outline, blue lettering, "Joseph's Economy Store, 406 Penn St. Reading, PA" **18.00**
Sepia-celluloid photo dec of historical scenes from Gettysburg, PA **20.00**

Pencil clip, 5/8" d, celluloid disc, red, white, and yellow graphics, image of pretty maiden in center diamond, "Diamond Crystal Shaker Salt". . . **20.00**

Pinback button

3/4" d, red celluloid, white lettering "I'm the Guy that put the oysters in Oyster Bay" **18.00**

1-1/4" d, bird series, cardinal, blue jay, robin, goldfinch, Whitehead & Hoag Co., Newark, NJ, each . **7.50**

1-1/2" d, "Erin Go Braugh," crossed American and Irish flags, center shamrock and lyre motif **25.00**

Pin holder, 1-3/4" d, celluloid disc, metal framework, "F Krupps Steel Works, Thomas Prosser & Son, NY," front shows advertising, back shows small child, engraved ivory-grained celluloid **40.00**

Pocket mirror

1-3/4" d, topsy-turvy image of a smiling man, "This man trades at Hager's Store, Frostburg, MD," turned upside down, the man is frowning and caption reads, "This man does not. For a satisfied customer see other side" . . **110.00**

2-1/4" d, beautiful woman with long red hair, wearing teal-blue dress and cloche, holding a bouquet of roses. **45.00**

2-3/4" x 1-3/4," oval, pink-rose motif, "Use Mennen's Flesh Tint Talcum Powder," information on curl, "Duplicate mirror 5 cents postage, Gerhard Mennen Co., Newark **60.00**

Postcard, 5-1/2" x 3-1/2", emb-fan motif with applied fabric and metal-script words, "Many Happy Returns," applied over fabric, circa 1908. . . . . **10.00**

Tape measure

1-1/4" d, pull-out tape, colorful pretty girl with flowers, adv for "The First National Bank of Boswell, The Same Old Bank in its New Home," printed by P.N. Co. (Parisian Novelty Co. of Chicago), Patent 7-10-17, emb in the side . . . **65.00**

3" d, center winding key, cream-colored celluloid, blue printing, "The GM Parks Co. Fitchburg, Mass, The Measure of Good Piping is Results," printed by Whitehead & Hoag **45.00**

Template, 3-7/16" x 1-13/16", Remtico Typewriter Supplies, Remington Typewriter Co., printed by Whitehead & Hoag **25.00**

Animals

Viscoloid Co. of Leominster, MA, manufactured a variety of small hollow toy animals, birds, and marine creatures, most of which are embossed with one of these three trade marks: "Made In USA," an intertwined "VCO," or an eagle with shield. A host of foreign countries also mass produced celluloid toys for export into the United States. Among the most prolific manufacturers were Ando Togoro of Japan, whose toys bear the crossed-circle trademark, and Sekiguchi Co., which used a three-petal flower motif as its logo. Paul Haneaus of Germany used an intertwined PH trademark, and Petticolin of France branded its toys with an eagle head. Japanese- and American-made toys are plentiful, while those manufactured in Germany, England, and France, are more difficult to find.

Alligator

3", green, white-tail tip, VCO/USA. **18.00**

5-3/4", tan, brown highlights, VCO/USA trademark **25.00**

Animal set, six circus animals, garish bright colors, marked "Made In Occupied Japan," elephant, gorilla, giraffe, tiger, lion, and hippo, set . **85.00**

Bear

4" l, peach bear, purple highlights, poor details, Japan **15.00**

5" w, cream bear, pink and gray highlights, VCO/USA. **20.00**

Bison, 3-1/4" l, dark brown, eagle-and-shield trademark. . . . **18.00**

Boar, 3-1/4" l, brown, Paul Haneaus of Germany/PH trademark **75.00**

Camel

2-1/4" l, cream, light-brown highlights, Made in USA trademark **15.00**

3-1/2" x 2-1/2", peach celluloid, pink and black highlights, marked with crossed circle and Made in Japan **15.00**

Cat

3" l, 2-1/4" h, cream or peach celluloid, black spots, pink bows, ears and mouth, floral trademark, JAPAN, and Made in Occupied Japan **25.00**

5-1/4", cream, pink and black highlights, molded collar and bell, Made in USA trademark **60.00**

Chick, 7/8", yellow, black eyes and beak, no trademark **8.00**

Chicken (hen)

2-3/4" h, metal feet, Double Diamond, Made In Japan . . . **18.00**

3" h, standing in grass, cream, gray, yellow feet, VCO/USA trademark **22.00**

Cow

4-1/2", cream-and-orange cow; intertwined VCO/USA **18.00**

5-1/2", purple and cream, red-rhinestone eyes, crossed circle, Made In Japan **25.00**

7-1/2", cream, orange and black highlights, hand-painted facial features, eagle mark **45.00**

Dog

Airedale, 3" w, 2-1/2" h, white with pink and dark purple highlights, hand-painted collar, plaster filled, nice detailing; Made In Japan trademark. **18.00**

Bulldog, 4-3/4" l, 2-1/2" h, spiked neck collar, translucent-green color, rhinestone eyes, intertwined VCO/USA **30.00**

Hound, 5", long tail, peach celluloid, gray highlights, crossed-circle Japan **18.00**

Scottie, 3-1/4" l, plaster-filled cream-colored celluloid, no detailing, marked JAPAN . . . **15.00**

St. Bernard, 3-1/4" , tan, black highlights, intertwined VCO/USA **18.00**

Donkey

2-1/4", dark gray, Made in USA **18.00**

4" l, 3-3/4" h, molded harnesses, saddles and blankets, grayish brown, red, and orange highlights, intertwined VCO/USA. **35.00**

Swan, cobalt blue, magenta, and teal feathers, red feet and beak, marked "USA," 4" l, 3-1/2" h, **$18,**

Duck

2-1/4", standing, cream-colored celluloid, hand-painted eyes and bills, original paper label, Made In Japan. **18.00**

3-1/2", yellow, green highlights, VCO/USA, circle. **12.00**

4", glossy surface, red and green, VCO/USA **15.00**

4", yellow, applied green and orange, PH (Paul Hunaeus), "25 cents" on bottom **25.00**

Elephant

2-3/8" x 1-1/2", white, gray highlights, VCO/USA **8.00**

3", white and gray, purple ears, Made in Occupied Japan . . . **20.00**

3-1/2" x 2", peach, gray highlights, poor detailing, no trademark . . **5.00**

6-3/4" x 4-3/4", gray elephant, tusks, Made In USA **35.00**

Fish

2-1/2", medium-reddish pink, molded scales and fins, nicely detailed, Japan **12.00**

2-7/8", yellow, brown highlights, molded scales, intertwined VCO, circle **10.00**

4-1/2", yellow and red, molded scales, Made in USA **12.00**

6", red, rattle, sharp fin, molded scales, gold eyes, intertwined YM trademark and Japan **22.00**

6-3/4", white and red, smooth-shiny surface, molded fin, VCO/USA **15.00**

Frog

1-1/4", green or yellow, stripe on back, intertwined VCO/USA . **12.00**

2-3/8", painted green, molded from white or yellow celluloid, spotted back, Made in USA inside circle or VCO in circle over USA **15.00**

2-3/4", white, painted green- and black-striped back, Made in Japan **15.00**

Giraffe, 10" h, cream, beaded neck alternating brown and cream, brown- and yellow-painted highlights, detailed face, crossed-circle mark of Ando Togoro, Made In Japan **110.00**

Goat

2-1/8", white, hand-painted facial features, poor detail, no trademark **15.00**

3", white, curled horns, flower, "N" in circle, Japan **18.00**

3-1/2", white, gray, beard & horns, VCO/USA **22.00**

Hippopotamus, 3-3/4", pink, closed mouth, crossed circle, Japan **15.00**

Horse

2-1/4" x 2", cream, brown highlights, Made in USA **10.00**

4", yellow, rattle, orange highlights, painted reins and saddle, Made in USA **22.00**

5-1/4", pink, black highlights, crossed circle, Japan **20.00**

7", cream, purple and pink highlights, Made in USA **22.00**

9-1/4" x 7-3/4", cream, grayish-brown highlights, Made In USA **45.00**

Leopard, 4-1/2", white, orange highlights, black spots, Made in Occupied Japan **25.00**

Lion

3", orange, black highlights, Made in USA **15.00**

3-3/4", tan, brown highlights, TS Made in Japan **20.00**

4", rattle, tan, brown, black, VCO/USA trademark on belly **20.00**

Lobster

1-3/4", bright red, detailed shell, no trademark **55.00**

3-1/4", shiny, red lobster, smooth surface, intertwined VCO/USA **85.00**

Parakeet, 6-3/8" l, cream colored, yellow and black highlights, marked "Germany" **40.00**

Parrot, 4", white, bright pink, green and yellow highlights, fine detailing, CT— Made In JAPAN **20.00**

Pig

1-1/8", cream, pink highlights, VCO **30.00**

4-1/2", pink, painted eyes, Made in USA **35.00**

Polar Bear, 2-1/4" l, white, USA . **10.00**

Ram

2-1/2", cream, poor detailing, Japan **10.00**

4-1/2", cream, gray highlights, Made in USA **18.00**

Rhino

4", white, gray, smiling, double horn, Made in Occupied Japan . . **22.00**

5", gray, fine detail, PH trademark, Paul Haneaus **55.00**

Seal, 4-1/2", gray, balancing red ball, VCO/USA **70.00**

Sparrow

3-1/4", balancing, yellow teal, tail weighted, oval Made in USA trademark near talon **18.00**

4-1/2", yellow, red highlights, Made in Japan **20.00**

Squirrel, 2-7/8", brown celluloid, holding a nut, Made in USA **40.00**

Stork, 6-3/4", standing, white, pink legs, flower mark and Japan **22.00**

Swan, 3-3/8", multicolored purple, pink, yellow, crossed circle **15.00**

Turtle

1-3/8", two tone, brown top, yellow bottom, USA on foot **15.00**

3", cream, brown highlights, VCO/USA with circle **18.00**

4", cream, brownish-gray highlights, CC in diamond and Made in Japan **20.00**

Whale, 4-1/2", curled tail, smooth-molded tails, cream, green, red, and yellow highlights **45.00**

Autograph album, celluloid cover, ocean scene with seagulls, c1907, 5-1/2" x 4", $75. Photo courtesy of Julie Robinson.

Decorative albums and boxes

Autograph album

4" x 5-1/2", printed pastoral scene of a couple giving thanks in a garden, celluloid front, paper-covered back **75.00**

6" x 4", silver and violet clear celluloid-coated paper, central emb oval with beautiful lady in wide-brimmed hat, white dress and fur, maroon-velvet back and binding **85.00**

Collar box, 6" h, 6" d, covered in gold paper with pink, green, and yellow flowers, clear-celluloid overlay, central image of a pretty woman wearing ruffled dress with corsage **175.00**

Dresser-set box, 8" x 6-1/4" x 3-1/2" d, emb-white celluloid, cornflower motif in two strips across top, blue-satin lining, fitted with brush, mirror, salve box, file and nail cleaner, all original, pieces individually marked "Celluloid" **250.00**

Hankie box, 7" sq, 3" h, center vignette of pretty girl in hat and gown picking pink flowers, emb Greek-key design on sides, overall pale yellow, green, and blue grapevine with leaf design . **165.00**

Manicure box, 5" x 7" x 2" h, cream-colored emb celluloid, snowy-house scene, puffed-satin lining, manicure implements **125.00**

Necktie box, 12-1/2" x 4", emb script "Neckties," cream-colored celluloid, emb-circular design on sides . . **145.00**

Photograph album

8" x 11", celluloid-covered photo album, Gibson girl, lavender dress, hat with lavender plumes, emb corners, applied-gilt paint **195.00**

18" l, 6" w, standing lady in flowing, red-draped dress **275.00**

Dolls and toys

Baby rattle

2-1/4", peach horse on cream-colored 4-1/2" d ring, two pink and white balls attached to ring, "Japan" on horse **45.00**

4-1/2", bright-red celluloid, clown playing lute, intertwined "VCO/USA" trademark on back, unusual color **55.00**

4-3/4", cream, bell-shaped, blue-triangular painted dec, no trademark **35.00**

6-1/4", yellow pear, orange-red highlights, brown-twig handle, finely detailed and realistic, no trademark **75.00**

Doll

3-1/4" black baby, strung arms and legs, unidentified lantern trademark, Made in Japan . . **50.00**

3-3/4", toddler, pink snowsuit, yellow and red trim, F in diamond, Made In JAPAN **22.00**

5-3/4" Dutch girl, green, pink, yellow, and black details, butterfly trademark—Made In JAPAN, mfg. by Yoshino Sangyo Co. **35.00**

6" girl and boy dressed in ethnic costumes, turtle in diamond trademark, Rheinische Gummiund Celluloid Fabrik Co. of Germany, pr **125.00**

7" all celluloid, molded, moving arms, molded bracelet on right wrist, mermaid in shield trademark on back, DRP Germany, mfg. by Cellba, Celluloidwarenfabrik Co. **95.00**

8-1/2" side-glancing googlie-eyed, blue and white printed dress and kerchief trimmed in rick rack, trademarked with unidentified-lantern trademark, "Made in Japan" **55.00**

16-1/2" realistic baby, movable arms and legs, bright-blue eyes, red hair, smiling face, made in USA by Viscoloid **175.00**

18" realistic baby doll, stuffed-textile body, beautifully molded-celluloid head, blond, blue eyes, mfg.

by Minerva, Buschow & Beck, helmet trademark, No.7-42, German **250.00**

Roly Poly

2-1/2", Buster Brown winking, cream, brown and black highlights, PH, Paul Hunaeus, Germany **225.00**

2-1/2", duckling, peach hat trimmed in flowers, jacket, necktie, green trim, cream celluloid, VCO trademark **75.00**

3-1/2", gray man, spectacles; black and white highlights on pink base, emb "Palitoy, Made In England" **85.00**

4-1/2", baby face, green and white base, orange bow tie, sticker on bottom, lacking detail, Made In China **40.00**

Toy

4", Bathing Beauty, double figural showing two little girls, pink and green bathing suit, umbrella, floral trademark, Made In Japan, mfg. by Sekiguchi Co. **75.00**

5", steamer, gray and red, flag, intertwined PH **55.00**

Whistle

3-1/4" l, 2-1/4" h, Nightingale bird, yellow celluloid, green and red highlights, VCO/USA **22.00**

4-1/2" l, 1-1/2" w, 3-1/4" w at ends, black and cream graduated pipe, "Baby Grand" **28.00**

Fashion accessories

Bar pin

2-1/2" l, ivory-grained rect shape, orange-brown swirled-pearlescent laminate, center hp florals . . . **18.00**

2-3/4" l, elongated oval, black-imitation jet, molded-cameo motif, C-clasp, on orig card that states "Persian Ivory collar or jabot pin" **85.00**

Belt, 22" l, 3/4" x 1-1/2" rect mottled-green celluloid slabs linked by chain, applied silver-tone filigree dec **35.00**

Bracelet, bangle

Ivory colored, embedded with center row of red rhinestones and flanked by outside rows of clear rhinestones **75.00**

Molded imitation coral, imitation ivory, or imitation jade, all-over floral dec, blue-ink stamp "Made in Japan," 3" d, each **40.00**

Translucent amber, single row of alternating red and amber

rhinestones, further decorated with scored white painted scallop edging around stones **95.00**

Translucent green, 1/2" wide, studded with three rows of aqua-blue rhinestones **85.00**

Bracelet, link, 3" d, 4 oblong two-tone cream and ivory links, attached by smaller round cream links **50.00**

Brooch

1-1/4" d thin gold-tint metal frame, blue and white enamel floral embellishment, clear celluloid, designed to hold photo, safety clasp **25.00**

1-3/4" x 3/4", rect pearlized cream celluloid, black stencil silhouette of man and woman conversing over picket fence **30.00**

Comb and case

2-1/4" l, folding molded case, emb-rose motif, imitation ivory **25.00**

3" l cream-colored celluloid comb, 3-1/4" x 1" pearlized amber and gray rhinestone-studded case **15.00**

Cuff links, pr

Separable "Kum-a-part" Baer & Wilde Co., 1/4" sq shape divided by purple and black triangular shapes of celluloid, center diamond shape, Art Deco, mid-1920s, orig card **55.00**

Toggle back, realistic molded-celluloid lion heads, c1896 . . . . **95.00**

Cuff links, pr, matching stickpin, lever-back links of silver-tone metal, octagonal framework with circular imitation ivory set with rhinestone **75.00**

Dress clips, pr, molded-floral motif, semi-translucent cream celluloid, marked "Japan" **35.00**

Eyeglasses, Harold-Lloyd type, black frames **20.00**

Fan

Brise style, diecut and emb-imitation ivory, silk ribbon, mirrored heart on end stick, pink-floral motif, tassel **45.00**

Cockade style, cream celluloid handles, bottom link clasp, pleated linen body, opens to full circle **55.00**

Hair comb, 4" x 5-1/4", imitation tortoiseshell, 24 teeth, applied-metal trim studded with rhinestones and brad-fastened Egyptian-Revival pink and gold metal floral and beetle dec **145.00**

Dresser set, Fiberloid Fairfax, mottled brown and gold celluloid, floral trim, nine pieces, $85. *Photo courtesy of Julie Robinson.*

Hair pin container, 2-1/2" holder, ivory, bird motif; dark-gray lid **35.00**

Hat pin
4" l elephant head, tusks, black-glass eyes, imitation ivory **95.00**
10" l, diecut 1" filigree-hollow egg, pale-green paint applied over grained celluloid **45.00**
12" l, conical, imitation tortoiseshell **20.00**

Hat ornament
3-1/2" h, Art Deco, pearlized red and cream half circles, rhinestone trim **45.00**
4" l, amber feather, red rhinestones **18.00**
4-1/2" h, calla lily, cream-pearlized celluloid, white rhinestones, 1-1/2" l threaded pin with screw-on celluloid point **25.00**

Necklace, 2" elegant Art Nouveau-filigree pendant, cream celluloid, oval cameo, profile of a beautiful woman, suspended from 20" cream celluloid-beaded necklace **110.00**

Purse frame
4" l, black pointed-horseshoe shape, rhinestones, white-molded cameo clasp **95.00**
6" l, imitation tortoiseshell, crescent shape, molded filigree and center cameo, celluloid push-button latch and linked chain **110.00**

Purse
4" d clasp, red rose, dangling leaves, green-velvet bag, velvet handle, marked "#35" on fame **1,250.00**
4" d, round clam shell, imitation tortoiseshell and ivory, leather strap, celluloid findings and finger ring, applied celluloid-leaf decoration **125.00**

4-1/2" x 4-1/2", basketweave, link-celluloid chain, mottled grain ivory and green **185.00**

Holiday items

Angels, 1-1/2" h, set of three, one holding cross, star, or lantern, Japan, Mt. Fuji trademark **25.00**

Christmas decoration, roly poly-type house, opening in back for a small bulb, shows Santa approaching door, red and white, intertwined VCO/USA trademark **125.00**

Christmas ornament
3-3/4" little boy on swing, all celluloid, dark-green highlights, holding onto string "ropes" for hanging on tree **145.00**
3-3/4", Santa, horn and sack, hole in back for light bulb, trademarked "S" in circle, Japan **100.00**
4" l, stripped green and white Christmas stocking filled with gifts including duck and kitten, crossed-circle trademark, Ando Togoro **145.00**
6-1/2", horn, red, pink, and yellow **80.00**
7-1/2", Santa holding gift box in arm, cream, red-painted detailing, marked with oval Made in USA **125.00**

Figure
3" x 3-1/2", bunny, dressed in top hat and tails, in teal shoes, crossed-circle mark, Japan . **85.00**
3-3/4", Swan Boat, Easter rabbit and chick in eggshell, intertwined VCO/USA **145.00**
5-1/4", Uncle Sam, white celluloid, painted red, white, and blue patriotic clothing **175.00**
7-3/4" h, Easter Rabbit, dressed in tails and top hat, holding chicken under arm, cream, pink, and blue highlights, VCO **125.00**

Halloween favor, 4" l, orange horn, black witch and trim, intertwined VCO/USA **110.00**

Rattle, 3-3/4" l, standing black cat, orange bow, intertwined VCO/USA **175.00**

Reindeer, 3-1/2", white deer, gold glitter, red eyes and mouth, molded ears and antlers, USA **18.00**

Roly poly, 3-1/2", black cat on orange pumpkin, intertwined VCO/USA **200.00**

Santa
4", yellow or mint-green translucent celluloid, holding lantern and

sack, Japanese, Mt. in circle trademark **40.00**
5" h, basket of flowers, fur-trimmed suit, nice detail, VCO/USA trademark **75.00**

Toy
2-7/8" l, Easter rabbit in harness, attached to cart full of eggs, "Made in Japan" on cart, "Pat.15735" on rabbit **85.00**
3-3/8" x 2", Santa driving house-shaped automobile, white, applied red-, yellow-, and green-painted highlights, VCO/USA trademark **125.00**
3-1/2", black Halloween cat pushing a witch in a pumpkin carriage, intertwined VCO/USA **245.00**
4" x 2-1/8", reindeer pulling sleigh, Santa, sack and packages, red and white, VCO/USA trademark **125.00**
4-3/4" h, Paddy, riding pig, movable legs, little boy with dunce cap riding on back, Japan **185.00**
5-3/8" x 2", Santa riding on a train laden with holiday decorations and gifts including doll, puppy, and rocking horse, cream, red, and green highlights, VCO/USA on Santa **165.00**

Novelty items

Letter opener
7" l, celluloid-paper knife, bronze Art Nouveau-cupid handle **95.00**
7 3/8" l, ivory grained, magnifying glass in top, coiled-metal snake, red-glass eyes around the handle **85.00**
8" l, solid celluloid, blade top by intricately detailed full-figure lady holding a flask **80.00**
9 5/8" l, solid celluloid, handle molded with lighthouse and filigree **95.00**

Pin cushion
2" h, rabbit with pin cushion baskets, marked "Germany" **130.00**
2-1/4" h, straight pin holder, brown hen on base **65.00**

Tape measure
1" h, strawberry with pull-tab tape measure **200.00**
1-1/4" d, basket of fruit, marked "Made in Germany" **145.00**
1-3/4" h, chariot, horse, and driver, imitation bronze **225.00**
2" h, handled basket, flowers, marked "Made in Japan" . . **125.00**

2" h, Swashbuckler, ivory, ivory and tan highlights **250.00**

2-1/2" h, Billiken, cream celluloid, applied-brown highlights, marked "Japan". **185.00**

Utilitarian and household items

Bookends, pr, 4-1/4" h, 3-1/4" w, 2-1/4" d, mottled-pink celluloid, emb ornamental gold neoclassic drape, plaster weighted, no trademark, c1930. . . . . **35.00**

Candle holders, pr, 5-1/4" h, cylindrical, round flared-weighted bases, unmarked. **60.00**

Clock

3" sq, New Haven Clock Co., alarm, folding travel case, pearlescent pink laminated over amber celluloid **30.00**

5-1/2" x 3", classical Gothic cathedral design, round face, dark-yellow ivory-grained celluloid, Germany. **45.00**

9" x 6-1/2", mantle clock, neoclassical design, front molded pearlized gray columns, imitation-ivory weighted base and top, marked "Made in USA," patented clockworks, Apr. 27, 1920 . . . . **65.00**

Crumb tray set, two dust pan-shaped trays

Ivory celluloid, one large and one small, unadorned, Fuller trademark. **22.00**

Ivory celluloid, dark-blue dec border, monogrammed "T" in center of each tray **55.00**

Cutlery, solid imitation ivory grained-handle utensils, eight forks, eight knives in orig box, Standard Mfg. Co. **30.00**

Frame

4" d, round, ivory grained, easel back **18.00**

5-1/2" x 7", pearlized-amber celluloid, diecut floral motif, attached over wood frame, celluloid butterflies in each corner. **35.00**

6" x 8", plain oval frame, imitation ivory-grained celluloid, glass, easel back **30.00**

Napkin ring

1" w, basketweave strips of celluloid **12.00**

1" w, ivory grained, monogram name "Agnes" **6.00**

1-1/2" w, plain, pale-green celluloid **4.00**

Pen holder, 3" sq, black base, laminated pearlized top, conical holder attached in center **20.00**

Stamp box, 2-1/2" x 1-1/2", ivory-grained box, hinged lid, two int. stamp-sized compartments separated by a center divider **20.00**

String holder, round sphere on a weighted base, twist apart, center hole in top for string, imitation-ivory grain, no trademark. **65.00**

Vase

6" h, imitation ivory, conical, fluted weighted base, flange around top. **15.00**

7" h, yellow, bulbous bottom, narrow opening, fluted top, painted pink and blue floral motif, no trademark **25.00**

8" h, imitation tortoiseshell, weighted-scalloped base . . . **45.00**

Watch holder, 6-1/2" l, pearlescent blue, green, and amber, wall-hanging banjo-clock style, Wilcox trademark, late 1920s. **22.00**

Vanity items

Dresser boxes, pr, oval-shaped pearlized peach boxes, dec-shaped lids, marked "Amerith," Lotus Pattern, c1929 . . . . **25.00**

Dresser set

Three-piece, mirror, brush and comb, green-pearlized celluloid, emb gold-flower motif in center of each item, plaster-filled mirror, orig cardboard box, poor-quality unmarked set **15.00**

Eight-piece, pearlized yellow-laminated amber celluloid, black trim, mirror, brush, shoe horn, button hook, soap box, nail buffer, toothbrush holder, hair-pin holder, marked "Arch Amereth, Windsor," c1928, orig box. **65.00**

Seventeen-piece, Fairfax pattern, Fiberloid Company, mottled brown and gold, carved floral trim, comb, brush, mirror, powder box, hair receiver, nail file, scissors, button hook, and clothing brush, c1924 . . . . **125.00**

Dresser tray, 7-1/2" l, 5" w, oval, pearlized cream color and amber framework, Normandy lace inserted between double-glass bottom, c1925 . . . . **30.00**

Hair receiver/powder box set

3-1/2" d, pearlized-gray containers, octagonal lids, no trademark. **25.00**

4" d, ivory-grained set, scalloped lids laminated in Goldaleur, marked "The Celluloid Co.". **45.00**

Hat-pin holder, weighted base

5" h center post, round circular disc on top, circular base, cream celluloid, cranberry-colored velvet cushion. **90.00**

5" h, pale-green celluloid, triangular shape, painted flower **20.00**

Manicure set, rolled-up leather pouch fitted with six imitation-tortoiseshell celluloid manicure tools, gold trim, pink-velvet lining **30.00**

Powder box, 4" d, flared round box, fitted lid, imitation ivory-grained celluloid, hand-applied floral swag and ribbon dec in pink, white, and blue, includes down puff with blue satin and celluloid handle. **65.00**

Trinket box, 5" l, 2" h, oval, amber, butterfly, grass and milkweed silk under clear-celluloid lid. **35.00**

Vanity set, amber, teal-green pearlescent laminate surface, dresser tray, octagonal amber hair-receiver box with pearlized lid, nail buffer, scissors, and button hook, hp-rose motif on all pcs, unmarked, c1930 . . . . **45.00**

CHALKWARE

History: William Hutchinson, an Englishman, invented chalkware in 1848. It was a substance used by sculptors to imitate marble and also was used to harden plaster of paris, creating confusion between the two products.

Chalkware pieces, which often copied many of the popular Staffordshire items made between 1820 and 1870, was cheap, gaily decorated, and sold by vendors. The Pennsylvania German folk-art pieces are from this period.

Carnivals, circuses, fairs, and amusement parks gave away chalkware prizes during the late 19th and 20th centuries. These pieces often were poorly made and gaudy.

Additional Listings: See Carnival Chalkware in *Warman's Americana & Collectibles.*

Notes: Don't confuse the carnival-chalkware giveaways with the earlier pieces.

Animal

Cat, 5-1/4" h, seated, gray, black spots, ears, and tail, yellow eyes and base, red collar, repaired, some wear, base chips . . . **330.00**

Deer, 5-1/2" h, red, black, and yellow, old worn paint, pr . . **935.00**

*Dachshund, black-brown glaze,
5-1/2" l, 4-3/4" h, $35.*

Dog, 5-1/2" h, molded detail, painted
brown, black spots, red collar, PA,
19th C, pr **375.00**
Hen and rooster, 15" h hen, 20" h
rooster, full bodied, comb, wattle,
and feather detail, inset glass eyes,
quatrefoil base, scrolled acanthus
support, repairs, pr **1,495.00**
Lion, 7" l, 4-3/4" h **315.00**
Ram, 2-1/8" l, 2-1/8" h, worn
paint **45.00**
Ram, 6" w, 3-3/4" d, 8-7/8" d, raised
dots on coat, black eyes,
red-accented ears and horns,
reattached to base **250.00**
Squirrel, worn red and green, base
flakes **250.00**

Bank, 11" h, dove, worn orig
polychrome paint **350.00**

Bust

10" h, lady, elegant green and gold
costume, red beads, raised-letters
"Maria" on her shoulders, early
19th C, paint loss **1,495.00**
18" h, Native American, wear,
chips **75.00**

Mantel ornament

12-1/2" h, fruit and foliage design,
American, 19th C, restoration, paint
wear, pr **460.00**
16" l, 15-1/2" h, reclining stag,
polychrome dec, minor paint
loss **300.00**

Match holder, 6" h, figural, man
with long nose and beard, Northwestern
National Insurance Co. adv,
c1890 . . . . **110.00**

Nodder, 8-1/2" l, cat, white, black spots,
late 19th C **1,495.00**

Plaque, 9" h, horse head,
orig-polychrome paint **100.00**

Wall pocket, basket shape **35.00**

CHARACTER AND PERSONALITY ITEMS

History: In many cases, toys and other products
using the images of fictional comic, movie, and radio
characters occur simultaneously with the origin of the
character. The first Dick Tracy toy was manufactured
within less than a year after the strip first appeared.

The golden age of character material is the TV era
of the mid-1950s through the late 1960s; however,
some radio-premium collectors might argue this
point. Today, television and movie producers often
have their product licensing arranged well in advance
of the initial release.

Do not overlook characters created by advertising
agencies, e.g., Tony the Tiger. They represent a major
collecting sub-category.

References: Bill Blackbeard (ed.), *R. F. Outcault's
The Yellow Kid*, Kitchen Sink Press, 1995; Bill
Bruegman, *Cartoon Friends of the Baby Boom Era*,
Cap'n Penny Productions, 1993; ——, *Superhero
Collectibles*, Toy Scouts, 1996; *Cartoon & Character
Toys of the 50s, 60s, & 70s*, L-W Book Sales, 1995;
Albert and Shelly Coito, *Elsie the Cow and Borden's
Collectibles*, Schiffer Publishing, 2000; James D.
Davis, *Collectible Novelty Phones*, Schiffer, 1998;
Warren Dotz, *Advertising Character Collectibles*,
Collector Books, 1993; ——, *What a Character! 20th
Century American Advertising Icons*, Chronicle
Books, 1996; Ted Hake, *Hake's Guide to Cowboy
Character Collectibles*, Wallace-Homestead, 1994;
——, *Hake's Price Guide to Character Toys*, 3rd ed.,
Gemstone Publishing, 2000; Jim Harmon, *Radio & TV
Premiums*, Krause Publications, 1997; Clark Kidder,
Marilyn Monroe: Cover to Cover, Krause Publications,
1999; Jack Koch, *Howdy Doody*, Collector Books,
1996; Mary Jane Lamphier, *Zany Characters of the Ad
World*, Collector Books, 1995; Cynthia Boris Liljeblad,
TV Toys and the Shows That Inspired Them, Krause
Publications, 1996; Jan Lindenberger with Cher
Porges, *Peanuts Gang Collectibles; An Unauthorized
Handbook and Price Guide*, Schiffer, 1998; David
Longest, *Character Toys and Collectibles* (1984, 1992
value update), 2nd Series (1987, 1990 value update),
Collector Books; Rex Miller, *The Investor's Guide To
Vintage Collectibles*, Krause Publications, 1999;
Andrea Podley with Derrick Bang, *Peanuts
Collectibles, Identification and Value Guide*, Collector
Books, 1999; Jon R. Warren, *Collecting Hollywood:
The Movie Poster Price Guide*, 3rd ed., American
Collectors Exchange, 1994; David and Micki Young,
Campbell's Soup Collectibles from A to Z, Krause
Publications, 1998.

Periodicals: *Autograph Times*, 2303 N. 44th St.,
#225, Phoenix, AZ 85008; *Baby Boomer*, P.O. Box
1050, Dubuque, IA 52004; *Big Reel*, P.O. Box 1050,
Dubuque, IA 52004; *Button Pusher*, P.O. Box 4,
Coopersburg, PA 18036; *Celebrity Collector*, P.O. Box
1115, Boston, MA 02117; *Classic Images*, P.O. Box
809, Muscatine, IA 52761; *Collecting Hollywood*,
American Collectors Exchange, 2401 Broad St.,
Chattanooga, TN 37408; *Cowboy Collector Newsletter*,
P.O. Box 7486, Long Beach, CA 90807; *Frostbite Falls
Far-Flung Flier*, P.O. Box 39, Macedonia, OH 44056;
Hollywood & Vine, Box 717, Madison, NC 27025;

Hollywood Collectibles, 4099 McEwen Drive, Suite
350, Dallas, TX 75224; *Movie Advertising Collector*,
P.O. Box 28587, Philadelphia, PA 19149; *Movie
Collector's World*, 17230 13 Mile Rd, Roseville, MI
48066; *Television History Magazine*, 700 E. Macoupin
St., Staunton, IL 62088; *TV Collector Magazine*, P.O.
Box 1088, Easton, MA 02334.

Collectors' Clubs: All About Marilyn, P.O. Box
291176, Hollywood, CA 90029; Beatles Fan Club, 397
Edgewood Ave., New Haven, CT 06511; Betty Boop
Fan Club, P.O. Box 42, Moorhead, MN 56561;
C.A.L./N-X-211 Collectors Society, 2820 Echo Way,
Sacramento, CA 95821; Camel Joe & Friends, 2205
Hess Drive, Cresthill, IL 60435; Charlie Tuna
Collectors Club, 7812 NW. Hampton Road, Kansas
City, MO 64152; Dagwood-Blondie Fan Club, 541 El
Paso, Jacksonville, TX 75766; Dick Tracy Fan Club,
P.O. Box 632, Manitou Springs, CO 80829; Dionne
Quint Collectors, P.O. Box 2527, Woburn, MA 01888;
Howdy Doody Memorabilia Collectors Club, 8 Hunt
Ct., Flemington, NJ 08822; Official Popeye Fan Club,
1001 State St., Chester, IL 62233; R. F. Outcault
Society, 103 Doubloon Drive, Slidell, LA 70461; Three
Stooges Fan Club, P.O. Box 747, Gwynedd Valley, PA
19437.

Additional Listings: See *Warman's Americana &
Collectibles* for expanded listings in Cartoon
Characters, Cowboy Collectibles, Movie Personalities
and Memorabilia, Shirley Temple, Space Adventurers,
and TV Personalities and Memorabilia.

Character

Andy Gump, pinback button

7/8" d, Andy Gump/The Gumps by
Syndey Smith, black, white, and
red, issued by Western Theatre
Premium Co., 1930s **24.00**
1-1/4" d, "Andy Gump For President/I
Endorse The Atwater Kent
Receiving Set," red, white, blue,
and fleshtone **40.00**

Betty Boop

Book, *Betty Boop Cartoon Lessons*,
Fleischer Studios, 1935,
12" x 9" **500.00**
Handkerchiefs, set of four cotton
handkerchiefs in orig 8-1/2" sq
cardboard box, c1931 . . . . **775.00**
Marble, 11/16", Peltier Glass Co.,
black and white swirl, black
transfer of Betty, c1932 . . . . **175.00**

Pinback button, 1-1/4" d, celluloid on tin, black and white Betty in front of yellow curtains, copyright Fleischer Studios, c1941 . . . . **850.00**

Pocket-watch box, cardboard, issued by Fleischer Studios, 1932, 2-1/4" sq **195.00**

String holder, 6-1/2" w, 7-1/2" h, chalk, head and shoulders, orig paint **625.00**

Brownies, Palmer Cox

Book, *The Brownies, Their Book,* Palmer Cox, NY, 1887, first edition, second issue, illus by Cox, 4to, pictorial glazed boards . . . **230.00**

Child's fork and spoon, emb Brownies on handles **15.00**

Doll, set of 8" dolls, stuffed cloth, Uncle Sam, Indian, Highlander, Chinaman, German, Sailor, Soldier, Canadian, Irishman, Policeman, John-Bull, and Dude, each has name stitched on back, colorful-printed outfits, marked "Copyright 1892 by Palmer Cox" on back of each, "Brownie's" on right foot of each, set of 12 . . . . . **760.00**

Ice-cream tray, colorful tin litho, 10-1/2" w, 13-1/4"l **280.00**

Photograph mat, images of Dutchman, Dude, and Policeman, 2-1/4" x 3" **18.00**

Pinback button, 1-1/4" d, blue on white, eight Brownies around board fence imprinted with calendar page for January, 1897, Whitehead & Hoag **20.00**

Plate, 7" d, octagonal, china, full-color illus of three Brownies, dressed as Uncle Sam, Scotsman, and golfer, soft-blue ground, gold trim, sgd "La Francaise Porcelain" **95.00**

Buster Brown, pinback button, multicolored, original back paper text reads "Look for Buster's Picture on the Sole of Every Shoe," 1-1/2" d, $195. *Photo courtesy of Hake's Americana & Collectibles.*

Buster Brown

Button, 1/2" d, two pieces, metal, loop shank, price for pr **15.00**

Children's feeding dish, Buster and Tige, wear to gold trim **115.00**

Figure, 2" h, bisque, red hat and suit, blue bow tie, black shoes, c1920 . . . . **100.00**

Magazine tear sheet, *Ladies Home Journal*, April, 1924, Buster Brown shoes adv, wood frame **25.00**

Pencil case, 10-1/2" l, Buster Brown Powers Mercantile Co., Minneapolis, MN, wood, cardboard, and tin, orig label **85.00**

Record, 5" x 4-1/4" orig sleeve, "Happy Birthday from Captain Kangaroo and Buster Brown" **15.00**

Shaving mug, 3-1/2" d, 2-1/2" h, white porcelain, gold trim, Buster Brown with blue and white teapot, filling cup, Tige standing on his hind feet holding blue cup, "Buster Brown" printed near left, marked "Made in Germany" **295.00**

Sunday comics, 1914, St. Paul Daily News, full section **20.00**

Teacup, white porcelain, illus of Buster on side, copyright 1910 . . . . **75.00**

Campbell's Kids

Children's dishes, "Campbell's Lunch Time," 4" x 14" x 17-1/2" unopened display carton, service for six, child's hard-plastic soup bowls and coaster plates, cups, saucers, spoons, and forks, prominent Campbell's marking, sealed in orig clear shrink wrap, six miniature placements on back, ©1984 . . . . **45.00**

Doll, 16" h, boy, orig clothing, 1970 . . . . **35.00**

Menu book, 5-1/2" x 7-1/2", softcover, ©1910, 48 pgs, menus for 30 days of the month, full-color Campbell's Kids art on cov **20.00**

Salt and pepper shakers, pr, 4-1/2" h, painted hard plastic, red and white outfits, yellow-molded hair, ©Campbell Soup **40.00**

Sign, 11-1/2" x 17-1/2", tin, Kid holding spoon, red, white, and yellow **250.00**

String holder, 6-3/4" h, chalk, incised "Copyright Campbell" **395.00**

Charlie the Tuna

Animation cel, 10-1/2" x 12" clear acetate sheet, centered smiling full-figured 4" image of Charlie gesturing toward 4" image of goldfish holding scissors, 10-1/2" x 12-1/2" white paper sheet with matching blue/lead pencil, 4" tall image of Charlie, c1960 . . . **150.00**

Figure, 7-1/2" h, soft vinyl, blue, dark pink-opened mouth, black-rimmed eyeglasses, orange cap inscribed "Charlie," ©1973 . . . . **30.00**

Wristwatch, 1-1/2" d bright gold luster bezel, full-color image of Charlie on silver background, ©1971 Star-Kist Foods, grained purple leather band **60.00**

Dutch Boy, string holder, 14-1/2" x 30", diecut tin, Dutch Boy sitting on swing painting the sign for this product, White Lead Paint Bucket houses ball of string **300.00**

Elsie the Cow, Borden

Display, mechanical milk carton, cardboard and papier-mâché, figural milk carton rocks back and forth, eyes and mouth move from side to side, made for MN state-fair circuit, 1940s **500.00**

Lamp, 4" x 4" x 10", Elsie and Baby, hollow ceramic figure base, Elsie reading to baby nestled on her lap, brass socket, c1950 . . . . . . **125.00**

Mug, 3-1/4" h, white china, full-color image of Elmer, gold-accent line, orig sq box with image of child's alphabet block including panels "E for Elsie" and "B for Borden," Elmer pictured on one side panel, ©1950 . . . . **95.00**

Felix the Cat

Figure, 1" h, dark copper-colored plastic, loop at top, 1950s . . **10.00**

Pinback button, 1" d, Herald and Examiner, c1930s **45.00**

Place-card holder, 1-3/4" h celluloid Felix, arched-back black cat, base, glossy black holder, Japanese, 1930s **85.00**

Valentine, diecut, jointed cardboard, full color, "Purr Around If You Want To Be My Valentine" inscription, ©Pat Sullivan, c1920 . . . . . . **20.00**

Vending label, 3" x 3", red, white, blue, black, and fleshtone, Little King and Felix the Cat illus, for Popeye "Kid Kartoon Komics" button, King Features ©, mid-1940s **15.00**

Yarn holder, 6-1/2", diecut wood, black images, inscription "Felix Keeps On Knitting, Pathe Presents" symbol in center, c1930 . . . . **38.00**

Happy Hooligan

Figure, 8-1/4" h, bisque, worried expression, tin-can hat, orange, black, blue, and yellow **75.00**

Pinback button, 11-16" d, brown and cream, profile, inscribed, "Son of Rest," initials below "G.T.A.T.," c1910 . . . . **30.00**

Stickpin, 2-1/4" l, brass **25.00**

Howdy Doody

Bank, 6-1/2" x 5", ceramic, riding pig **65.00**

Belt, suede, emb face **35.00**

Cake-decorating set, unused . **40.00**

Handkerchief, 8" x 8-1/4", cotton **20.00**

Pencil case, vinyl, red **25.00**

Jiggs and Maggie, chalkware afigures, multicolored; Jiggs 8-1/2" h, Maggie 9-3/4" h, pair, **$225.**

Jiggs and Maggie

Paperweight glass **40.00**

Pinback button, 3/4" d, *The Knoxville Sentinel,* black and white image of Jiggs, red bow tie, c1920 . . . **15.00**

Salt and pepper shakers, pr, ceramic **48.00**

Katzenjammer Kids

Christmas card, 4-1/4" x 4-1/2", 1951, copyright King Features Syndicate **15.00**

Comic strip, Ovaltine ad on back **10.00**

Krazy Kat, pinback button

7/8" d, full color, cigarette premium, c1912, Tokio back paper **20.00**

1-3/8" d, "Cash Prices See Comic Pages Daily," Los Angeles Evening Herald & Express, black-on-green litho, 1930s **30.00**

Li'l Abner

Bank, Schmoo, blue plastic . . **50.00**

Magazine tear sheet, Cream of Wheat Breakfast Food, Rastus on front of box illus, 5" w, 11" h . **20.00**

Pin, 1-1/2" l, figural, Schmoo, brass tone **15.00**

Pinback button, 13/16", Li'l Abner, *Saturday Daily News,* black litho, cream ground, newspaper name in red **20.00**

Little Annie Rooney, pinback button,

1-1/4" d, comic-strip contest button, serial-number type, c1930 . . . . . **25.00**

Little Orphan Annie

Big Little Book, Whitman, *Little Orphan Annie Goonesville Mystery,* No. 1435 . . . . **65.00**

Big Little Book, *Little Orphan Annie Secret of the Well,* No. 1417 . **85.00**

Child's Book, *Little Orphan Annie and the Gila Monster Gang,* Harold Gray, Whitman Publishing, copyright 1944, licensed by Famous Artists Syndicate, 248 pgs, 5" x 8" **10.00**

Nodder, bisque, marked "Little Orphan Annie" and "Germany" **150.00**

Toothbrush holder, 4" h, bisque, back inscribed "Orphan Annie & Sandy, Copyright F.A.S., #1565," bottom stamped "Japan," some wear to paint **145.00**

Mr. Peanut

Ashtray, Golden Jubilee, 50th Anniversary, gold-plated metal, figural, orig attached booklet, orig box, 5" h, 5-3/4" h **130.00**

Bank, 8-1/2" x 4", full figure, orange plastic **725.00**

Booklet, *Mr. Peanuts Guide to Tennis,* 6" x 9", ©1960, 24 illus pgs **20.00**

Box, Planters Chocolate Covered Nut Assortment, silver-alligator texture, two early Mr. Peanut figures, 8-1/4" sq **350.00**

Case, salesman's sample, attaché, nine different unopened vacuum-pack display cans, orig promotional divider **475.00**

Paint book, *Planter's Paint Book No. 2,* 7-1/4" x 10-1/2", © 1929, 32 pgs **35.00**

Salad set, ceramic tops, wooden fork and spoon, rhinestone monocle, 10" h **170.00**

Shipping box, corrugated cardboard, adv for Planters Salted Peanut 5¢ cellophane bags, 1950s, 17" x 14" x 11" **140.00**

Toy, trailer truck, red cab, yellow and blue plastic trailer, 5-1/2" l . . **275.00**

Mr. Zip

Bank, 2-1/4" x 4" x 5-3/4", tin litho, mail box, red, white, and blue, photos of coins, chart on back, trap missing **15.00**

Decal, 6" d, red, white, and blue glossy paper, May, 1963, unused **5.00**

First-day cover, 3-1/2" x 6-1/2", with zip-code commemorative stamp, "Saluting the U.S. Postal Service Zip Code System 1974" **10.00**

Mutt & Jeff

Bank, 4-7/8" h, cast iron, orig paint **125.00**

Book, *The Mutt & Jeff Cartoon Book,* Bud Fisher, black and white illus by author, Ball Pub. Co., 1911 . **100.00**

Sheet music, "Moonlight," 1911 . . . . **12.00**

Popeye

Charm, 1" h, bright copper-luster plastic figure of Olive Oyl, 1930s **10.00**

Children's book, *Popeye Borrows A Baby Nurse,* Whitman, #712 . **45.00**

Figure, 14" h, chalkware **140.00**

Mug, 4" h, Olive Oyl, figural . . . **20.00**

Pencil sharpener, figural, Catalin plastic, dark yellow, multicolored decal, 1930s **60.00**

Sticker book, Lowe #2631 . . . . **40.00**

Tie bar, 2-1/2" l, 3/4" h enameled figure of Popeye, 1930s **45.00**

Reddy Kilowatt

Bib, 10" x 10" fabric, printed nursery rhyme and Reddy, c1950 . . . **65.00**

Employee cap, white-canvas fabric, 2" bright red, white, blue, and yellow fabric patch for PA Power and Light Co., 1920-1996 commemorative date **10.00**

Hot pad, 6" d, laminated heat-resistant cardboard, textured top surface with art and verse inscription, "My name is Reddy Kilowatt-I keep things cold. I make things hot. I'm your cheap electric servant. Always ready on the spot," c1940 . . . . **40.00**

Pinback button, "Please Don't Litter," blue and white, 1950s **15.00**

Pocket knife, metal cast, red-figure image and title on one side, single-knife blade, Zippo, c1950 . . . . **60.00**

Statuette, 5" h, 1-1/2" x 3" black-plastic base, ivory white-glow plastic head, gloves, and boots, translucent-red body, c1950 . . . . **195.00**

Stickpin, red enamel and silvered-metal miniature diecut figure, c1950 . . . . **30.00**

Rocky Jones, Space Ranger

Coloring book, Whitman, cockpit cov, 1951 . . . . **40.00**

Pinback button, membership type **45.00**

Wings, pin **40.00**

Smokey Bear

Ashtray, 4" d, tin **55.00**

Coloring book, 1971, 126 pgs, unused **8.00**

Doll, 22" h, stuffed, Knickerbocker **75.00**

Hand puppet, 9" h, head incised "1965 Ideal Toy Corp." **195.00**

Little Golden Book, *Smokey Bear and the Campers*, 1971 . . . . . **5.00**

Neck scarf, 22" sq, official Forest Service logo **65.00**

Salt and pepper shakers, pr, 3-7/8" h, marked "Made in Japan," c1960 . . . . **95.00**

Soaky, 7-3/4" h **50.00**

Tab, 2" d, metal, Smokey in center, marked "Green Duck Co., Chicago," unused **15.00**

Tom & Jerry, cookie-cutter set, Quaker Oats MGM Carton Cookie Cutter Set, orig box, red plastic cookie cutters, copyright Loew's Inc., 1956 . . . . **185.00**

Yellow Kid

Cap bomb, 1-1/2" h, cast iron, c1898 . . . . **185.00**

Cigar box, 3-1/2" x 4-1/4" x 9", wood, illus and name inscription in bright gold, brass hinges, label inside says, "Smoke Yellow Kid Cigars/Manuf'd by B. R. Fleming, Curwesville, Pa," tax label strips on back, c1896 . . . . **225.00**

Fireworks, 5" l, 5/8" d, "Yellow Kid Salute," orig cartoon illus of Kid holding lit firecracker under his arm, "Don't touch me when I'se Lit," fuse missing **850.00**

Pinback button, #2, 1894, orig paper label **55.00**

Yellow Kid, pin cushion, silvered metal, "I'm Weightin For Yer 'See'," 4-5/8" h, $145.

Personality

Amos and Andy

Ashtray and match holder, plaster **30.00**

Diecut, 3" x 5", cardboard, Amos, Andy, and Kingfish, 1931 . . . **22.00**

Poster, 13" x 29", multicolored, Campbell's Soup ad, radio show listings, framed **145.00**

Toy, Fresh Air Taxi, litho tin wind-up, Marx, 1929 . . . . **425.00**

Autry, Gene

Badge, 1-1/4" d, Gene Autry Official Club Badge, black and white, bright orange top rim, c1940 . . . . **50.00**

Child's book, *Gene Autry Makes a New Friend*, Elizabeth Beecher, color illus by Richard Case, Whitman Tell A Tale, 1952 . . . **12.00**

Watch, orig band **145.00**

Ball, Lucille

Magazine, *Life*, April 6, 1953, five-pg article, full-color cover of Lucy, Desi Arnaz, Desi IV, and Lucy Desiree **30.00**

Movie-lobby card, 11" x 14", full color, 1949 Columbia Picture "Miss Grant Takes Richmond" **40.00**

Captain Kangaroo

Badge, 2-1/4" h, emb-tin shield, came on 1960's doll **15.00**

Puzzle, 10" x 14", frame tray, Captain and nursery-rhyme characters, 1956, Milton Bradley **20.00**

Whisk broom, 7" h, wood handle, blue and fleshtones, black, white, red, and yellow accents, ©R.K.A., 1960 . . . . **40.00**

Cassidy, Hopalong

Badge, silvered metal, star shape, raised center portrait, c1950 . **25.00**

Coloring book, 1950, large size **30.00**

Rug, chenille **100.00**

Tablet, 8" x 10", color-photo cov, facsimile signature, unused . **24.00**

Wallet, leather, metal fringe, multicolored cover, made by Top Secret **35.00**

Chaplin, Charlie

Candy container, 3-3/4" h, glass, Charlie and barrel, small chip **100.00**

Magazine, *Life*, April 1, 1966, Chaplin and Sophia Loren . . **10.00**

Pencil box, 7-3/4" l, Henry Cline design, tin litho **75.00**

Thimble, pewter, hand painted, black hat, navy jacket, cane raised in left hand, English **30.00**

Crosby, Bing, songbook, *Bing Crosby's Pick of Popular Songs*, 1946, 33 pgs **80.00**

Dionne Quintuplets

Advertisement, 5" x 7", Quintuplet Bread, Schultz Baking Co., diecut cardboard, loaf of bread, brown crust, bright red and blue letters, named silhouette portraits, text on reverse **70.00**

Book, *Now We Are Five*, Jas Brough, 256 pgs, dj **7.50**

Dolls in Ferris wheel, 18-5/8" h, five 6-1/2" h composition Madame Alexander dolls with brown-painted eyes, closed mouth, orig white organdy dresses, lawn bibs, blue accented yellow and green wooden Ferris wheel, some paint loss, c1936 . . . . **1,035.00**

Fan, 8-1/4" x 8-3/4", diecut cardboard, titled, "Sweethearts of the World," full-color-tinted portraits, light-blue ground, ©1936, funeral director name on reverse **35.00**

Garland, Judy, Pinback button

1" h, "Judy Garland Doll," black and white photo, used on c1930 Ideal doll, name appears on curl, also "Metro-Goldwyn-Mayer Star" in tiny letters **125.00**

1-1/4" d, "Oz/Your Dollars Will Work Magic in Hecht Month,"

Baltimore department store,
multicolored............**275.00**
Sheet music, "On the Atchison,
Topeka, and the Sante Fe," 1945
MGM movie, "The Harvey Girls,"
sepia photo, purple, light pink, and
brown cov...............**35.00**

Gleason, Jackie
Coloring book, *Jackie Gleason's Dan
Dan Dandy Color Book*, Abbott,
©1956, unused...........**25.00**
Magazine, *TV Guide*, May 21, 1955,
Philadelphia edition, three-pg
article on the Honeymooners **18.00**
Pinback button, 1-5/8" d, "Jackie
Gleason Fan Club/And Awa-a-ay
We Go!," blue on cream litho,
checkered suit, 1950s......**65.00**

Houdini, Harry, Big Little Book,
Houdini's Big Little Book of Magic,
Whitman, 1927, premium or American
Oil and Amoco Gas, 192 pgs....**35.00**

Henie, Sonja
Pinback button, 1-3/4" d, "Sonja
Henie Ice Review," orange on blue,
illus of skater, c1940s......**20.00**
Portrait art, 15-1/2" x 19-1/2", rigid
white art board, 12-1/2" x 16-1/2"
paint and ink portrait by John
Cullen Murphy, figure skater
wearing cap with Olympic-rings
symbols, bottom margin with title in
red pencil, "Once in a Lifetime," for
nostalgia feature in January 1948
Sports Magazine........**300.00**

Laurel & Hardy
Bank, plastic, 14" h........**45.00**
Movie poster, "Laurel and Hardy in
the Big Noise," Fox, 1944, Tooker
Litho..................**300.00**
Salt and pepper shakers, pr .**230.00**

Lindberg, Charles
Book, *Lindberg, The Lone Eagle, His
Epochmaking Flight*, George Fife,
A. L. Burt, 299 pgs, ex-lib copy,
1930 ....**10.00**
Book, *Of Flight and Life*, Charles
A. Lindberg, Scribners, 1948,
56 pgs..................**20.00**
Book, *We*, Charles A. Lindberg,
Grosset & Dunlap, 1927,
318 pgs.................**25.00**
Notepad, child's, Lindy on cover
with airplane, 5" x 8", one blank
page **7.00**

Lone Ranger
Coloring book, unused **50.00**
Game board, target bull's
eye...................**185.00**
Ring, Cheerios premium, saddle
type, filmstrip missing **225.00**

Tom Mix, pinback button, Ralston
Straight Shooters, Mike Shaw, black on
white ground, red checkerboard, 1" d,
$20.

Mix, Tom
Big Little Book, Whitman, *Tom Mix
and The Stranger from the Sea*,
Pete Daryll, 1936, #1183 ...**75.00**
Big Little Book, Whitman, *Tom Mix
Rides to the Rescue*, 2-1/16" x
3-3/4" **250.00**
Periscope, cardboard, Ralston
Straight Shooters on ends,
1930s **95.00**
Premium, Tom Mix Ralston Telegraph
Set, 1940 ....**95.00**
Ring, magnet, 1946 ....**145.00**
Scarf, reads, "Tom Mix Ralston
Straight Shooters," stained, small
hole...................**145.00**
Trading cards, unopened pack of
eight, 2-1/2" x 3-1/2" **10.00**

Rogers, Roy
Bank, Roy on Trigger, porcelain, sgd
"Roy Rogers" and "Trigger" **200.00**
Bedspread **115.00**
Camera.................**110.00**
Charm, 1" h, blue plastic frame,
black and white glossy paper
photo **35.00**
Comic book, April, 1958.....**60.00**
Guitar, orig box, 1950s **140.00**
Ring, litho tin, Post's Raisin Bran
premium, Dale Evans, ©1942
.......................**45.00**
Toy, Roy Fit It Stagecoach, figure,
Bullet, 2 horses, complete
accessories **95.00**
Yo-Yo, orig display box with 12
yo-yos.................**250.00**
Watch, Roy and Dale **120.00**

Temple, Shirley
Children's book, *Shirley Temple's
Birthday Book*, Dell Publishing Co.,
c1934, soft cover, 24 pgs ..**100.00**
Figure, 6-1/2" h, salt-glazed ..**85.00**
Handkerchief, Little Colonel, boxed
set of three **200.00**
Magazine advertisement, Lane Hope
Chests, 1945..............**8.00**
Magazine, *Parade*, Oct. 20,
1957, Shirley and her children
on cov..................**22.00**
Pin-back button, 1-1/4" d,
brown-tone photo, light-pink rim,
Ideal Dolls, 1930s **75.00**

Three Stooges
Autograph, letter, 4-1/2" x 5-1/2"
mailing envelope, two folded 6" x 8"
sheets of "Three Stooges"
letterhead, personally inked
response to fan, sgd "Moe
Howard," March 10, 1964 Los
Angeles postmark........**200.00**
Badge, 4" d, cello, black and white
upper face image of Curly-Joe on
purple background, Clark Oil
employee type **20.00**
Movie poster, 14" x 36", "The Three
Stooges Meet Hercules," paper
insert for 1961 Columbia Pictures
movie, folded **60.00**
Photo, 4" x 5" glossy black and white,
facsimile signatures of Curly-Joe,
Larry, and Moe, plus personal
inscription in blue ink by
Moe....................**95.00**
Pinback button, 7/8" d, black
and white photo of Moe, series
issued by "Button-Up Co." on
the curl **8.00**

Wayne, John
Doll, 18-1/2" h, Effanbee, Calvary
uniform, copyright 1982 ...**225.00**
Magazine, *Life*, Jan. 29, 1972.**25.00**
Magazine tear sheet, 10" x 13",
"Back to Bataan," black and white,
1945 ....**15.00**
Movie poster, "McLintock,"
1963 ....**250.00**

Wynn, Ed
Oil can, 2-1/8" d, 2-7/8" h, Wynn's
Top Oil, condition 8.5 ......**30.00**
Sheet music, "You're My Everything,"
Laugh Parade, 1931........**6.00**

CHILDREN'S BOOKS

History: Because there is a bit of the child in all of us,
collectors always have been attracted to children's
books. In the 19th century, books were popular gifts
for children, with many of the children's classics

written and published during this time. These books were treasured and often kept throughout a lifetime.

Developments in printing made it possible to include more attractive black and white illustrations and color plates. The work of artists and illustrators has added value beyond the text itself.

References: E. Lee Baumgarten, *Price Guide for Children's & Illustrated Books for the Years 1880-1960 Sorted by Artist* and *Sorted by Author,* published by author, 1996; David & Virginia Brown, *Whitman Juvenile Books,* Collector Books, 1997, 1999 value update; Richard E. Dickerson, *Brownie Bibliography,* 2nd ed., Golden Pippin Press, 1995; Glenn Erardi, *Collecting Edgar Rice Burroughs,* Schiffer Publishing, 2000; Virginia Haviland, *Children's Literature, a Guide to Reference Sources* (1966), first supplement (1972), second supplement (1977), third supplement (1982), Library of Congress; John Henty, *The Collectable World of Mabel Lucie Attwell,* Richard Dennis Publications, distributed by Antique Collectors' Club, 1999; Alan Horne, *Dictionary of 20th Century British Book Illustrators,* available from Spoon River Press, 1994; Simon Houfe, *Dictionary of 19th Century British Book Illustrators,* revised ed., available from Spoon River Press, 1996; E. Christian Mattson and Thomas B. Davis, *A Collector's Guide to Hardcover Boys' Series Books,* published by authors, 1996; Diane McClure Jones and Rosemary Jones, *Collector's Guide to Children's Books, 1850 to 1950,* Vol. I and II, Collector Books, 2001 value update; —, *Collector's Guide to Children's Books, 1950-1975,* Vol. III, Collector Books, 2000; Jack Matthews, *Toys Go to War,* Pictorial Histories Publishing, 1994; Edward S. Postal, *Price Guide & Bibliography to Children's & Illustrated Books,* M & P Press (available from Spoon River Press, 2319C W. Rohmann, Peoria, IL 61604), 1995; *Price Guide to Big Little Books & Better Little, Jumbo Tiny Tales, A Fast Action Story, etc.,* L-W Book Sales, 1995; Steve Santi, *Collecting Little Golden Books,* 4th ed., Krause Publications, 2000; Albert Tillman, *Pop-Up! Pop-Up,* Whalesworth Farm Publishing, 1997.

Periodicals: *Book Source Monthly,* 2007 Syosset Drive, P.O. Box 567, Cazenovia, NY 13035; *Firsts: The Book Collector's Magazine,* P.O. Box 65166, Tucson, AZ 85728, http://www.firsts.com; *Martha's KidLit Newsletter,* P.O. Box 1488, Ames, IA 50010, http://www.kidlitonline.com; *Mystery & Adventure Series Review,* P.O. Box 3488, Tucson, AZ 85722; *The Authorized Edition Newsletter,* RR1, Box 73, Machias, ME 04654; *Yellowback Library,* P.O. Box 36172, Des Moines, IA 50315.

Collectors' Clubs: Horatio Alger Society, 4907 Allison Drive, Lansing, MI 48910; Movable Book Society, P.O. Box 11645, New Brunswick, NJ 08906; Society of Phantom Friends, P.O. Box 1437 North Highlands, CA 95660.

Libraries: American Antiquarian Society, Worcester, MA; Free Library of Philadelphia, Philadelphia, PA; Library of Congress, Washington, DC; Lucile Clark Memorial Children's Library, Central Michigan University, Mount Pleasant, MI; Pierpont Morgan Library, New York, NY; Toronto Public Library, Toronto, Ontario, Canada.

Additional Listings: See *Warman's Americana & Collectibles* for more examples and an extensive listing of collectors' clubs.

Abbreviations:

dj	dust jacket
n.d.	no date
pgs	pages
teg	top edges gilt
unp	unpaged
wraps	paper covers

Aladdin and the Wonderful Lamp, Charles E. Graham & Co., New York, made in USA, **$7.50.**

Abe Lincoln Kentucky Boy, Raymond Warren, Reilly & Lee Publishers . . **10.00**
A Child's Garden of Verses, color illus by Jessie Wilcox Smith, Scribners, 1905, 1st ed., one illus missing . . **17.50**
A Day With Our Gang, Eleanor Lewis Packer, color and black and white illus by Stax, Whitman Pub Co., 1929 . . . . **15.00**
Adventures of Huckleberry Finn, The, Mark Twain, eight color illus by N. Rockwell, Pub Heritage, 1936, 6" x 9", emb red cover **37.50**
Adventures of Tom Sawyer, The, Mark Twain, eight color illus by N. Rockwell, Pub Heritage, 1936, 6" x 9", emb green cover. **37.50**
Alice in Wonderland, Macmillan, 1877, red-cloth cover with gold Alice, some wear **12.50**
Alice's Adventures in Wonderland & Through the Looking-Glass, Lewis

Carroll, color illus by John Tanniel, Macmillan, 1966, orig dg **12.00**
All About Peter Pan, retold by Sir J. M. Barrie's Stories, Emma Gelders Sterne, published by Cupples Leon, 1924, 49 pgs, 4-1/4" x 5-1/2" **85.00**
Andersen's Fairy Tales, color illus by Arthur Szyk, Grosset & Dunlap Pub Co., 1945 . . . . **15.00**
An Alphabet of Animals, Carton Moore Park, Blackie and Son, London, 1899, black and white plates by Park, 4to, pictorial green boards, spine ends, bottom edge, and tips rubbed . **100.00**
Anything Can Happen, Alice and Jerry reader, 1940 . . . . **15.00**
Around the Rocking Chair, Kate Tannatt Woods, 1870 . . . . **30.00**
Aunt Jaunty's Tales: Dame Brown's Visit to London, Marks & Son publisher, London, six hand-colored plates, 8vo, pictorial wrappers, list of books on rear cover **80.00**
Babar and His Children, Jean De Brunhoff, first edition, illus, 4to, pictorial boards. **150.00**
Billy Whiskers At the Circus, F. G. Wheeler, color frontispiece, black and white illus by Arthur DeBebian, Saalfield Pub Co., 1908, pages yellowed . **15.00**
Black Arrow, The, Robert Louis Stevenson, color illus by N. C. Wyeth, Charles Schribner's Sons, 1929 . **30.00**
Black Beauty, Anna Sewell, color plates by Fritz Eichenberg, 1945 . . . . . **15.00**
Boys Story of Lindberg, The Long Eagle, Richard Beamish, John C. Winston, 320 pgs **20.00**
Burgess Bird Book for Children, The, Thorton Burgess, illus in color by L. A. Fuertes, Little Brown & Co., 1919, 1st ed, water marks along top of pages last quarter of book **40.00**
Burgess Seashore Book for Children, The, Thornton Burgess, Little Brown & Co., black and white illus, 1929 . **40.00**
Captain June, Alice Hegan Rice, black and white illus by C. D. Wheldon, The Century Co., 1909. . . . . **15.00**
Chaga, William Lipkind, illus by Nicolas Mordvinoff, Harcourt, Brace & Co., New York, 1955, 1st ed, 40 pgs, hardcover **7.50**
Chaucer for Children: A Golden Key, Mrs. H. R. Hawies, London, 1877, first edition, eight color plates, numerous woodcut illus, 4to, gilt pictorial cloth. **130.00**
Cherry Ames, Dude Ranch Nurse, 1953, some light coloring **10.00**

Child's Geography of the World, V. M. Hillyer, Appleton Century Vrofts, Inc., c1951, red-cloth cover, hardbound **7.00**

Cowboys and the Songs They Sang, S. J. Sackett, Wm R. Scott, 1967, 72 pcs, ex-school copy **16.00**

Do Not Disturb, The Adventures of M'm and Teddy, Elizabeth Luling, illus by George Salter, 1937, 1st ed., 96 pgs, hardbound, 6" x 5" **60.00**

Five Little Peppers and How They Grew, The, Margaret Sidney, color illus by Elizabeth Tedder, Whitman Pub Co., 1938 .... **10.00**

Gigi & GoGo, Edgard Liger-Belair, illus by Luiz Sa, 1943, 15 pgs, written in four languages, 8-3/4" x 6-1/4" **90.00**

Golden Book of Flowers, The, Simon & Schuster, 1943, 1st printing, blue spine **17.50**

Gulliver's Travels, Jonathan Swift, color and black illus by Willy Pogny, George Harrap & Co., 1922 .... **15.00**

Hardy Boys, Hunting For Hidden Gold, Franklin Dixon, illus by Walter Rogers, Grosset & Dunlap , 1928, 1st ed. . **25.00**

Hardy Boys, The Shore Road Mystery, Franklin Dixon, illus by Walter Rogers, Grosset & Dunlap , 1928, 1st ed. . **25.00**

Honey Bunch Her First Visit to the City, Helen Louise Thorndyke, black and white illus by Walter Rogers, G &D Pub, 1923 .... **10.00**

I Wonder Why, Elizabeth Gordon, color and black and white illus by M. T. Penny Ross, Rand McNally Co., 1938 . . **15.00**

Kipling's Stories for Boys, Rudyard Kipling, illus by H. Hastings, Cupples & Leon Co., 1931, 499 pgs **10.00**

Light Princess and Other Fairy Stories, The, George MacDonald, black and white illus by Maud Humphrey, G. P. Putnam's Sons, 1893 .... **90.00**

Little Alexander, Besse Schiff, copyright 1955, 30 pgs, 8" x 10-3/4" **90.00**

Little Black Sambo, Helen Bannermann, illus in color and black and white by Eulalie, Platt & Munk Co., 1955, dj........................ **125.00**

Little Brown Koko, Blanche Seale Hunt, illus by Dorothy Wagstaff, 1940, 1st ed., hard cover, 8" x 11" **70.00**

Little Colonels' Holidays, The, Annie Fellows Johnston, black and white illus by L. J. Bridgeman, The Page Co., 1914 .... **10.00**

Little Folks Delight, illus by I. A. Tomkins, H. W. Cutts, Butterworth & Heath, Pesoa, McLoughlin Bros., New York, nine full-page black and white illus, four partial-page illus, stories and poems, 8" x 6-1/2", some wear, stain on spine **20.00**

Little Orphan Annie and the Haunted House, Harold Gray, black and white illus by author, Cupples & Leon, 1928...................... **45.00**

Little Red Riding Hood, color illus by Eulalie, Platt & Munk Co., 1934 . **10.00**

Little Washingtons' Holidays, The, Lilly Elizabeth Roy, frontispiece and colorful end papers illus by Paul Spener Johst, 1925, 1st ed. **60.00**

Mama's Helpers, Maud Humphrey cover, c1900, 160 pgs, 7-3/4" x 10" **40.00**

Man From Bar 20, The, Clarence Mulford, black and white frontispiece by Frank Schoonover, A. L. Burt Co......................... **10.00**

Marcella Stories, Johnny Gruelle, M. A. Donohue Co., 1930s, color and black and white illus, dj............. **95.00**

Mary Poppins, P. L. Travers, black and white illus by Mary Shepard, Reynal and Hitchcock, 1934.......... **35.00**

Master Key, The, L. Frank Baum, color illus by F. Y. Cory, Bown, Merill Co., 1901, 1st ed. **275.00**

Mother Goose, Simon & Schuster, Little Golden Book, 1944 .... **8.50**

Mother West Wind Where Stories, Thornton Burgess, black and white illus by Harrison Cady, G& D Pub., 1940s..................... **15.00**

My Very Own Fairy Stories, Johnny Grulle, P. F. Volland CO., 1917, 30th ed, color illus **65.00**

Nancy Drew, The Password to Larkspur Lane, illus by Russell Tandy, Grosset & Dunlap , 1933, some fading to blue cover **65.00**

Now We Are Six, Miline Pub., Dutton, November 1927, orange cover . . **17.50**

On a Torn Away World or the Captives of the Great Earthquake, Roy Rookwood, black and white illus, Cupples and Leon Co., 1913 . . . **20.00**

Pirate's Apprentice, The, Peter Wells, John C. Winston, Philadelphia, Toronto, 1943, 1st ed., 7-1/4" x 9-3/4" **50.00**

Raggedy Ann's Wishing Pebble, Johnny Gruelle, M. A. Donohue Co., 1930s, color and black and white illus, dj **85.00**

Riley Songs O'Cheer, James Whitcomb, six color plates, black and white illus by Will Vawler, 1905............. **35.00**

Seven Lady Godivas, The, Dr. Seuss, color illus by author, Random House, 1939, 1st ed, some fading to cover **275.00**

Seven Little Monsters, Maurice Sendak, color illus by author, Harper & Row, 1977, 1st ed., dj **25.00**

Story of Babar, The Little Elephant, The, Jean De Brunoff, Random House, c1960, 48 pgs **8.00**

Sunshine Corner Picture and Story Book, Violet Harford, Juvenile Prod. Lt., color illus by author **65.00**

Tarzan and City of the Gold, Edgar Rice Burroughs, Whitman, 1952, dj . . . **15.00**

Uncle Remus His Songs and Sayings, Joel Chandler Harris, 112 illus by A. B. Frost, D. Appleton & Co., 1916 . . **75.00**

Uncle Wiggily and the Runaway Cheese, Howard R. Garis, color illus by A. Watson, Platt & Munk, 1977, oversize **12.50**

Young Salesman, The, Horatio Alger Jr., A. L. Burt, hardbound........... **6.50**

CHILDREN'S FEEDING DISHES

History: Unlike toy dishes meant for play, children's feeding dishes are the items actually used in the feeding of a child. Their colorful designs of animals, nursery rhymes, and children's activities are meant to appeal to the child and make mealtimes fun. Many plates have a unit to hold hot water, thus keeping the food warm.

Although glass and porcelain examples from the late 19th and early 20th centuries are most popular, collectors are beginning to seek some of the plastic examples from the 1920s to 1940s, especially those with Disney designs on them.

References: Maureen Batkin, *Gifts for Good Children, Part II, 1890-1990,* Antique Collectors' Club, 1996; Doris Lechler, *Children's Glass Dishes, China and Furniture,* Vol. I (1983), Vol. II (1986, 1993 value update), Collector Books; Noel Riley, *Gifts for Good Children: The History of Children's China, Part I, 1790-1890,* Richard Dennis Publications, 1991; Margaret and Kenn Whitmyer, *Collector's Encyclopedia of Children's Dishes: An Illustrated Value Guide,* Collector Books, 1993.

Bowl, Little Red Riding Hood . . . **95.00**
Butter pat, 3-1/4" d, "A Present For Ann," blue transfer medallion. . . **125.00**
Cereal set, Nursery Rhyme, amber, divided plate, Humpty Dumpty on mug and bowl, Tiara. **125.00**
Cup, Raggedy Ann, Johnny Gruelle, 1941, Crooksville China **65.00**

Divided, decal of cat, dog, and cock, marked "Roma," 7-3/8" d, **$50.**

CHILDREN'S NURSERY ITEMS

History: The nursery is a place where children live in a miniature world. Things come in two sizes. Child scale designates items actually used for the care, housing, and feeding of the child. Toy or doll scale denotes items used by the child in play and for creating a fantasy environment which copies that of an adult or his own.

Cheap labor and building costs during the Victorian era encouraged the popularity of the nursery. Most collectors focus on items from 1880 to 1930.

References: Marguerite Fawdry, *International Survey of Rocking Horse Manufacture*, New Cavendish Books, 1992; Marcia Hersey, *Collecting Baby Rattles and Teethers: Identification and Value Guide*, Krause Publications, 1998; Sally Kevill-Davies, *Yesterday's Children, The Antiques and History of Childcare*, Antique Collectors' Club, 1999; Elizabeth Kurella, *The Complete Guide to Vintage Textiles*, Krause Publications, 1999; Doris Lechler, *Children's Glass Dishes, China and Furniture*, Vol. I (1983), Vol. II (1986, 1993 value update), Collector Books; Patricia Mullins, *Rocking Horse: A History of Moving Toy Horses*, New Cavendish Books, 1992; Lorraine May Punchard, *Playtime Kitchen Items and Table Accessories*, published by author, 1993; Herbert F. Schiffer and Peter B. Schiffer, *Miniature Antique Furniture: Doll House and Children's Furniture from the United States & Europe*, Schiffer Publishing, 1995; Tony Stevenson and Eva Marsden, *Rocking Horses: The Collector's Guide to Selecting, Restoring, and Enjoying New and Vintage Rocking Horses*, Courage Books, 1993.

Museum: The Victorian Perambulator Museum of Jefferson, Jefferson, OH.

Additional Listings: Children's Books, Children's Feeding Dishes, Children's Toy Dishes, Dolls, Games, Miniatures, and Toys.

Cup plate, 4-5/8" d, "Constant dropping wears away stones and little strokes fell great oaks," green transfer, polychrome enamel dec **90.00**

Feeding dish
Bunnies, puppies, Nippon . . . **45.00**
Kiddieware, pink, Stangl. **75.00**
Little Bo Peep, glass, divided, white, red trim **45.00**
Nursery Rhyme, green enamelware, marked "Made in Germany" . **40.00**
Raggedy Ann, Johnny Gruelle, 1941, Crooksville China, 8-3/4" d . . **85.00**
Sunbonnet babies, sweeping, 7-1/4" d **400.00**

Mug
2-1/8" h, two sheep reserve, luster rim, yellow glazed, transfer print, England, c1850, glaze and transfer wear **220.00**
2-3/8" h, "A new doll for Margaret," yellow glazed, transfer print, England, c1850, glaze and transfer wear, very minor chips **490.00**
3-3/4" h, Little Red Riding Hood, white, red animation **32.00**

Plate
6" d, Buster Brown, 1910, mint center image **135.00**
8" d, nursery rhymes, glass, green **30.00**
8" d, "Where Are You Going My Pretty Maid, See Saw Margery Daw," three parts, transparent-green Depression-era glass **35.00**

Sherbet, white Depression-era glass, red dec of Three Little Pigs **12.00**
Saucer, 3-3/8" d, white, lacy gold trim at end, floral trim **2.00**

Blocks
Boxed set, ABC's, animals, litho of Noah and ark on cov, Victorian **185.00**
Twenty-three wooden blocks, colored litho dec of sailors, letters, etc. **250.00**

Boat, play, ice, 24" l, wood with iron runners, c1900 . . . . **460.00**
Bucket, 5-1/2" d, 4-1/4" h, wooden-stave construction, orig yellow paint, blue-painted tin bands, stenciled stars, chick, and eagle, wood and wire bale handle, int. has some crayon marks, bottom band replaced . . **660.00**
Carriage, 53" l, 37" h, wicker, brown and white hide-covered horse with glass eyes, leather tack, hair mane, horse-hair tail, two-wheeled vehicle pushed by handle, horse sets between shafts on three-wheeled frame, wire wheels with rubber tread, late 19th/early

20th C, some damage to hide, wear to paint **1,380.00**
Chair, child size
English, yew wood, old dark finish, one board sides, wing back, and seat, shaped arms, rosehead nail construction, pierced handle at top, warped sides with insect damage and restoration, 7" h seat, 20-1/2" h back **350.00**
Windsor, arm, quality reproduction by "David T. Smith & Co., New Morrow, Ohio," red paint, green "D"-shaped seat, nine spindle back, scroll carved ears on crest, shaped arms, well-turned legs with blunt-arrow feet, 11" h seat, 31-1/4" h **330.00**
Windsor, birdcage, orange paint over earlier green, shield-shaped seat, bamboo turned base, late 19th/early 20th C, wear on one seat, 10-1/4" h seat, 20-3/4" h, price for pr **650.00**

Chest of drawers, child-size, Hepplewhite-style, curly maple, pine secondary wood, banded inlay around two-board top and base, four graduated dovetailed drawers with dark line inlay, and fans at corners, well-scalloped base, French feet, diamond-shaped escutcheons, emb brasses with cornucopia designs, 27" w, 17" d, 28" h **1,320.00**
Clothes form, 34" h, wood form cov in black-fabric padding, black stockings, leather shoes, stenciled label on front for Ourman, Paris, late 19th C. . **175.00**
Crib, 38-3/4" d, 69-1/2" h, orig 48" l rails, refinished bird, tapered high posts with incised line beading along edges, urn-shaped supports on all sides, narrow vertical slats added for stability **220.00**
Cupboard, child-size, step-back
24" w, 11" d, 37-1/4" h, middle Atlantic States, mid-19th C, cherry, flat-molded cornice above cock-beaded case, two cupboard doors with raised panels, two shelves int., arched opening over projecting case with two short drawers with applied molding, two raised-panel cupboard doors, old red-stained surface **1,725.00**
24-1/2" w, 8-1/8" d, 33" h, New England, early 19th C, stained, molded top overhangs case of two drawers opening to two-shelved int., stepped out board overhangs two drawers on legs, side shaping, orig surface **1,265.00**

Baby carriage, dapple gray painted horse, worn harness, wood frame with old cream-colored paint, red and black striping, old yellow paint with green trim on wicker seat, wire wheels, horse rocks back and forth when pushed, 70" l, $650. Photo courtesy of Garth's Auction, Inc.

Doll carriage
   30" l, 28" h, Heywood Wakefield, woven wicker, natural finish, diamond pattern weave, steel wheels, rubber tires, clamshell hood, maker's label on underside, early 20th C **150.00**
   30" l, 28" h, natural wicker wooden spoked wheels, original button-upholstered back, red cotton parasol on wire hook, late 19th C **230.00**
   32" l, 28" h, American, fringed top surrey, original dark green paint, gold stenciling, wooden wheels, platform top, fringe replaced, c1870 . . . .**350.00**
Doll cradle, 15" l, 8-1/4" w, 13" h, pine, sq and "T" head nails, footboard and part of hood are dovetailed, scrolled end rockers, layers of red paint, age cracks, wear, one rocker glued **150.00**
Doll crib, 16-1/2" l, 11-1/2" d, 11" h, poplar, orig reddish-brown painted dec, shaped head and footboards, rockers, turned posts with ball finials, edge wear, finial chips **320.00**

Game, ring toss, 16" d, green painted wood backplate set with small hooks, each with gold transfer printed number, four leather tossing rings, England, first quarter 20th C **175.00**
Needlework picture, silk threads and watercolor on silk, titled "The Mother's Hope," young girl in landscape setting, MA, early 19th C, framed in oval format, minor scattered staining, small areas of fabric loss, replaced tablet **1,725.00**

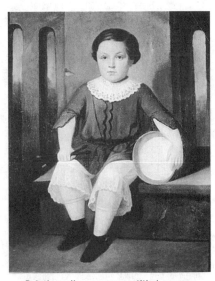

Painting, oil on canvas, untitled, young boy holding drum, blue costume, white lace and pantaloons, 39-1/4" h, 32" w, $2,200. Photo courtesy of Jackson's Auctioneers & Appraisers.

Noah's Ark, 18-1/2" l, 5" d, 11-1/2" h, painted red, blue, orange, white, and green wood, roof and one side of base open to inner compartments, six carved and painted animals, Noah, two ladies, one glued leg, some edge wear **750.00**
Quilt, 32-1/2" x 32", printed center fabric with four playful kittens, surrounded by appliquéd parrots, crazy quilt borders, highlighted with decorative embroidery, initials "SBW," imperfections **125.00**
Pram coverlet, quilted silk, satin rosebud dec. **60.00**
Rattle, 4" l, sterling silver, pink coral handle below knopped body with emb dec, five silver bells, whistle, maker's mark "E.S.B.," Birmingham, England, 19th C. **475.00**
Riding horse, 34-1/2" l, 13" d, 38-3/8" h, painted wood pinto horse, muslin saddle blanket, painted with initials, leather saddle, bucking motion, American, 20th C **320.00**
Rocking Horse, 40-1/2" l, 14-1/2" w, 21-1/2" h, painted and carved, leather and green velvet saddle, America, mid-19th C, ears, bridle, one stirrup and stirrup leather missing **1,150.00**
Sled, 37" l, 12-1/4" w, 20" h, carved oak and wrought iron, carved horse head, traces of polychrome dec, PA, 19th C. **3,110.00**
Sleigh, 19" l, 13-1/2" w, 18" h, high sides, wooden runners, old repaint with scrollwork and foliage, red ground, yellow line borders, blue int., edge wear **385.00**
Tricycle horse, 39" l, 22-1/2" w, 33" h, painted wood horse model, glass eyes, suede saddle, velvet saddle blanket, single front wheel, two rear wheels, chain-driven mechanism, by Jugnet, Lyon, repainted **850.00**

CHILDREN'S TOY DISHES

History: Dishes made for children often served a dual purpose—playthings and a means of learning social graces. Dish sets came in two sizes. The first was for actual use by the child when entertaining friends. The second, a smaller size, was for use with dolls.

Children's dish sets often were made as a sideline to a major manufacturing line, either as a complement to the family service or as a way to use up the last of the day's batch of materials. The artwork of famous illustrators, such as Palmer Cox, Kate Greenaway, and Rose O'Neill, can be found on porcelain children's sets.

Teether and rattle, Santa Claus head, bag of toys on back, sterling silver, English, , mother-of-pearl teether, 5-1/4" l, $275.

References: Doris Lechler, *Children's Glass Dishes, China and Furniture*, Vol. I (1983), Vol. II (1986, 1993 value update), Collector Books; Lorraine May Punchard, *Playtime Kitchen Items and Table Accessories*, published by author, 1993; ——, *Playtime Pottery & Porcelain from Europe and Asia*, Schiffer Publishing, 1996; ——, *Playtime Pottery and Porcelain from the United Kingdom and the United States*, Schiffer Publishing, 1996; Margaret and Kenn Whitmyer, *Collector's Encyclopedia of Children's Dishes*, Collector Books, 1993.

Collectors' Club: Toy Dish Collectors, P.O. Box 159, Bethlehem, CT 06751.

Candle holder, Jack-Be-Nimble, moongleam, c1908-44, Heisey diamond H mark, **$300.**

Akro Agate

Tea set, octagonal, large, green and white, Little American Maid, orig box, 17 pcs **225.00**
Water set, Play Time, pink and blue, orig box, seven pcs **125.00**

Bohemian glass, decanter set, ruby flashed, Vintage dec, five pcs **. . 135.00**

China

Cheese dish, cov, hunting scene, Royal Bayreuth **65.00**
Chocolate pot, Model-T car with passengers **90.00**
Creamer, Phoenix Bird **20.00**
Cup and saucer, Phoenix Bird. **15.00**
Dinner set, Willow Ware, blue and white, Japanese **200.00**
Tea set, Children playing, cov teapot, creamer, cov sugar, six cups, saucers, and tea plates, German, Victorian. **285.00**
Tureen, cov, Blue Willow, 3-1/2" w, marked "Made in China" . . . **60.00**

Depression glass, 14-pc set

Cherry Blossom, pink **390.00**
Laurel, McKee, red trim **355.00**
Moderntone, turquoise, gold **210.00**

Milk glass

Cheese dish, blue opaque, McKee **65.00**
Creamer, Wild Rose **65.00**
Cup, Nursery Rhyme **24.00**
Ice-cream platter, Wild Rose **. . 60.00**

Pattern glass

Berry set, Wheat Sheaf, seven pcs **85.00**
Butter, cov, Hobnail with Thumbprint base, blue **95.00**
Cake stand, Palm Leaf Fan . . . **35.00**
Creamer, Lamb **75.00**
Cup and saucer, Lion **50.00**
Pitcher, Oval Star, clear **20.00**
Punch set, Wheat Sheaf, seven pcs **75.00**
Spooner, Tulip and Honeycomb. **24.00**
Sugar, cov, Beaded Swirl. **40.00**
Water set, Nursery Rhyme, pitcher, six tumblers. **225.00**

CHINESE CERAMICS

History: The Chinese pottery tradition has existed for thousands of years. By the 16th century, Chinese ceramic wares were being exported to India, Persia, and Egypt. During the Ming dynasty (1368-1643), earthenwares became more highly developed. The Ch'ien Lung period (1736-1795) of the Ch'ing dynasty marked the golden age of interchange with the West.

Trade between China and the West began in the 16th century, when the Portuguese established Macao. The Dutch entered the trade early in the 17th century. With the establishment of the English East India Company, all of Europe sought Chinese-made pottery and porcelain. Styles, shapes, and colors were developed to suit Western tastes, a tradition which continued until the late 19th century.

Fine Oriental ceramics continued to be made into the 20th century, and modern artists enjoy equal fame with older counterparts.

References: Carl L. Crossman, *The Decorative Arts of the China Trade*, Antique Collectors' Club, 1999; Gloria and Robert Mascarelli, *Warman's Oriental Antiques*, Wallace-Homestead, 1992; Nancy N. Schiffer, *Imari, Satsuma, and Other Japanese Export Ceramics*, Schiffer Publishing, 1997.

Periodical: *Orientalia Journal*, P.O. Box 94, Flushing, NY 11363-0094, http://members.aol.com/Orientalia/index.html.

Collectors' Club: China Student's Club, 59 Standish Rd, Wellesley, MA 02181.

Museums: Art Institute of Chicago, Chicago, IL; Asian Art Museum of San Francisco, San Francisco, CA; George Walter Vincent Smith Art Museum, Springfield, MA; Morikami Museum & Japanese Gardens, Delray Beach, FL; Pacific Asia Museum, Pasadena, CA.

Additional Listings: Canton, Fitzhugh, Imari, Kutani, Nanking, Rose Medallion, and Satsuma.

Chinese

Bowl, 6-3/4" d, flared sides, cut foot, molded int. with twin fish medallion at well, pale crackled blue-green glaze, Song Dynasty **265.00**
Brush washer, 4-3/4" d, compressed circular form, splayed base, incurved rim, thick bluish-gray crackle glaze **175.00**
Censer, 3-1/2" h, compressed globular form, splayed raised foot, everted rim, countersunk band dec, two scroll handles, white glaze, 19th C. . . **395.00**
Cup, 2-1/4" h, Blanc-De-Chine, molded animal and foliate dec, Qing dynasty, 18th C **100.00**

Dish

9-1/4" d, blue and white porcelain, scalloped, central figural scene surrounded by shaped panels alternating with figures and flowering prunus branches, price for pr. **450.00**
11" d, shaped rim, incised floral dec, celadon glaze, Ming dynasty. **1,200.00**

Figure, 16" h, horse, standing, draped trappings and saddle, green, chestnut, and honey glaze, Tang style . . . **650.00**
Garden set, blue and white, 18-1/2" h **635.00**
Ginger jar, cov, 3-1/2" h, blue and white porcelain, figural procession dec, wood cover **300.00**

Jar, cov, blue and white porcelain

3-3/4" h, petal-shaped panels, figures and flower-filled jardinieres, Kangxi **225.00**
8" h, shaped panels with kylins on blue ground, floral dec, carved wood lid, Kangxi **425.00**
11" h, flowering prunus branch dec, crackled ice ground, fu dog finials, Qing dynasty, 19th C, price for pr. **275.00**

Jardiniere, 14" d, iron red and white, dragon chasing flaming pearl of wisdom dec. **150.00**
Lamp base, 16" h vase, celadon and blue ovoid form, warriors in landscape dec **150.00**
Moon flask, 8-1/4" h, blue and white porcelain, two central bird- and flower-filled panels, all over scrolling floral and foliate dec, c1830 . . . **425.00**

Plate

8-1/2" d, blue and white, Ming Dynasty **395.00**
9-3/8" d, Cabbage Leaf and Butterfly, 19th C, minor chips, gilt

and enamel wear, cracks, 9-pc set **345.00**

Soup plate, 9-5/8" d, Cabbage Leaf and Butterfly, 19th C, minor chips, gilt and enamel wear, four-pc set ... **175.00**

Urn, 17" h, baluster, blue and white, scrolling foliate, floral dec, pr ... **450.00**

Vase

2-3/4" l, globular, underglaze blue and celadon, two handles, molded fluting, Yuan dynasty **200.00**

5" h, ovoid, blue and white porcelain, all-over floral and foliate dec, Kangxi **175.00**

8-3/4" h, gu form, raised mid-section, two countersunk bands, thick ivory-colored glaze, 18th C. **800.00**

12" h, baluster body, flared neck, fluted rim, incised scroll and applied Imperial dragon dec, Sing Dynasty **600.00**

16-1/2" h, club form, celadon and blue glazed, figures in landscape dec **150.00**

Chinese Export, salt, 5-1/2" h, **$350.**

Chinese export

Basin, 16" d, 5" h, extended rim dec with figures in garden, alternating with reserve of bird on branch surrounded by a border of overlapping blue fans, int. with figures in a garden, 19th C **750.00**

Bough pot, 8-1/2" h, 8-1/4" w, 5-1/4" w base, 7-7/8" d, octagonal, applied dec of squirrels among grapes on canted corners which flank shaped lanes, central floral sprays, gilt-dec base, Famille Rose palette, gilt rope-twist handles, inserts with five circular apertures, gilt edges, Chinese Export for European market, c1775-85, gilt wear, three insert handles missing, pr **13,800.00**

Bowl, 11-1/4" d, children and adults flying kites, surrounded by wide red, white, and blue geometric border with four reserves dec with flowers and birds, 18th C, glaze wear **260.00**

Dinner plate, 9-5/8" d, Red Bird and Sacred Flower, 19th C, set of six, imperfections **950.00**

Dinner service, cobalt-blue and gilt-diaper border, cavetto with band of cobalt-blue star and gilt scallop, 19 dinner plates, 10 soup bowls, 8 salad plates, 9 saucers, 17 small sauce bowls, 11 tea cups, 7 cov syllabubs, rect cov tureen with undertray, 2 sq trays, sq bowl, 2 cov serving dishes, 1 open serving dish, large round bowl, large mug, round cov sauce bowl, gravy boat, 3 shaped serving dishes, oval veg dish cov, late 18th/early 19th C, imperfections, price for 100 pcs **2,875.00**

Dinner service, partial, dec with two birds perched above monogram "EB" in oval cartouche, teapot, cov sugar, cream jug, eight tea cups and saucers, late 18th/early 19th C, imperfections, price for 19 pcs **865.00**

Games table, 13" w, 18" d, 29" h, black lacquer, reversible top, turned standard, dragon-form feet, gilt Chinese scenes, third quarter 19th C **3,175.00**

Luncheon plate, 8" d, Red Bird and Sacred Flower, 19th C, set of six, imperfections **850.00**

Mustard pot, cov, 2" d, 3-1/4" h, red floral pattern, 19th C **400.00**

Platter and drainer, 16-3/4" l, oval, Red Bird and Sacred Flower, 19th C **920.00**

Punch bowl, 9-1/4" d, Famille Rose palette, 19th C, minor glaze loss **375.00**

Tureen, cov, undertray, Red Bird and Sacred Flower, 19th C, minor imperfections **2,650.00**

Japanese

Bowl, cov, 11" d, iron red and white, fish dec, Qing dynasty, 19th C . **200.00**

Brush washer, 4-3/4" d, compressed circular form, splayed base, incurved rim, thick bluish-gray crackle glaze **175.00**

Censer, 3-1/2" h, compressed globular form, splayed raised foot, everted rim, countersunk band dec, two scroll handles, white glaze, 19th C ... **395.00**

Charger, 18" d, iron red, fish dec, Qing dynasty, 19th C **175.00**

Plate, 8-1/4" d, Kakiemon, lobed form, straw rope edge, relief dec of three friends, pine, bamboo, and prunus, center with pair of pheasants and flowers, red, yellow, blue, turquoise, and black enamel, gilt accents, three spur marks on base, late 19th/early 19th C, small chip and hairline .. **520.00**

Vase, 7-1/2" h, celadon glaze with band of peach blooms across boy and mouth, sgd in underglaze blue "Tai Nihon Kozan Sei" within square for Makuzu Kozan, c1900 .... **575.00**

CHINTZ CHINA

History: Chintz china has been produced since the 17th century. The brightly colored exotic patterns produced on fabric imported from India to England during this century was then recreated on ceramics. Early chintz patterns were hand painted and featured large flowers, fantastical birds, and widely spaced patterns. The advent of transfer printing resulted in the development of chintz dishes, which could be produced cheaply enough to sell to the masses. By the 1830s, a number of Staffordshire potteries were producing chintzware for everyday use. These early patterns have not yet attracted the interest of most chintz collectors.

Collectors typically want the patterns dating from roughly 1920 until the 1950s. In 1920, A.G. Richardson "Crown Ducal" produced a range of all-over-transfer chintz patterns which were very popular in North America, particularly the East Coast. Patterns such as Florida, Festival, and Blue Chintz were originally introduced as tea sets and then expanded to full dinner services. Florida is the most popular of the Crown Ducal patterns in North America, but Peony has become increasingly popular in the past year or two.

What most collectors consider the first modern chintz was designed by Leonard Grimwade in 1928 and named Marguerite. This pattern was very successful for many years, but has never been highly regarded by collectors. Every year at the British Industries Fair, factories vied with each other to introduce new patterns which would catch the buyers' eye. From the late 1920s until the mid-1950s, Royal Winton produced more than 80 chintz patterns. In some cases, the background color was varied and the name changed: Hazel, Spring, and Welbeck is the same pattern in different colors. After the second world war, Royal Winton created more than 15 new patterns, many of which were more modern looking with large flowers and rich dark burgundy, blue, or black backgrounds—patterns such as May Festival, Spring Glory, and Peony. These patterns have not been very popular with collectors, although other 1950s patterns such as Florence and Stratford have become almost as popular as Julia and Welbeck in the past year.

The 1930s were hard times in the potteries and factories struggled to survive. They copied any successful patterns from any other factories. James Kent Ltd. produced chintzes such as DuBarry, Apple Blossom, and Rosalynde. These patterns were sold widely in North America and complete dinner sets still occasionally turn up. The most popular pattern for collectors is the white Hydrangea, although Apple Blossom seems to be more and more sought after. Elijah Cotton "Lord Nelson" was another factory which produced large amounts of chintz. Cotton had always been known for the hundreds of utilitarian jugs it produced and it continued to be great producers of institutional ware. The workers at Elijah Cotton were never as skilled as the Grimwades' workers, and usually the handles and spouts of teapots and coffeepots were left undecorated. The shapes are chunky and the pottery thicker than the other factories. Collectors, however, love the Nelson Ware jugs and stacking teapots, especially in Black Beauty and Green Tulip.

Although a number of factories produced bone china after World War II, only Shelley Pottery seems to be highly desired by today's collector.

By the late 1950s, young brides didn't want the dishes of their mothers and grandmothers, and preferred the clean lines of modern Scandinavian furniture and dishes. Chintz gradually died out by the early 1960s, and it was not until the 1990s that

collectors began to search for the dishes their mothers had scorned.

References: Eileen Busby, *Royal Winton Porcelain*, The Glass Press Inc., 1998; Susan Scott, *Charlton Standard Catalogue of Chintz*, 3rd edition, Charlton Press, 1999; Heller/Feljoy, *Chintz by Design*, Chintz International, 1997; Muriel Miller, *Collecting Royal Winton Chintz,* Francis Joseph Publications, 1996, Jo Anne Welch, *Chintz Ceramics*, 2nd edition, Schiffer Publishing 1998.

Collectors' Clubs: North American Chintz Newsletter, 882 Queen Street West, Toronto, Ontario M6J 1G3, Chintzclub@aol.com; Royal Winton Collectors' Club, 2 Kareela Road, Baulkham Hills, Australia 2153 sherylwinton@optushome.com.au; Free Chintz Discussion Group: www.chintz.net/mail.list

Reproduction Alert: In the last couple of years, with the rising prices of chintz, both Royal Winton and James Kent have started to reproduce some of their more popular patterns. Royal Winton is reproducing Welbeck, Florence, Summertime, and Julia, while James Kent has so far reproduced Du Barry and Hydrangea. The Old Chintz Company has bought the Lord Nelson backstamp and there are plans to reproduce some of the Elijah Cotton patterns as well. The new Royal Winton backstamp has a black circle around the original deco backtamp; the new James Kent backstamp includes 100-year anniversary. Contact the factories for current production lists to avoid confusing old and new chintz.

Warning: Ask before you buy chintz whether it is new or vintage. Ask to see a photograph of the backstamps. Compare old and new backstamps on www.chintz.net/backstamps or in the Charlton 3rd edition new chintz section. Contact the factories for current production lists to avoid confusing old and new chintz.

Adviser: Susan Scott.

Elijah Cotton "Lord Nelson"

Cream and sugar on tray, Skylark pattern 95.00
Cup and saucer, Heather pattern 65.00
Mustard pot with lid and underplate, Rosetime pattern 85.00
Plate, 8-1/2" sq, Rosetime pattern 125.00
Salt and pepper on tray, Pansy pattern 150.00
Stacking teapot, totally patterned Anemone pattern 850.00

Grimwades "Royal Winton"

Biscuit barrel, Royalty pattern . 485.00
Bowl, Corfe shape, Sunshine pattern 295.00
Breakfast set, Triumph pattern . 750.00
Bud vase, Wild Flowers pattern . 141.00
Butter dish, Square Ascot, Hazel pattern 200.00
Candlestick, Beeston pattern . . 300.00

Hazel, footed compote, Royal Winton, $175. Photo courtesy of Susan Scott.

Cup and saucer trio, Estelle pattern 125.00
Eggcup, footed, Eleanor pattern 105.00
Jampot with liner and silver lid, Kinver pattern 175.00
Mayonnaise bowl, underplate and spoon, Julia pattern 500.00
Plate, 9" sq Ascot, Nantwich pattern 135.00
Sugar shaker, Julia pattern . . . 500.00
Teapot, stacking Julia pattern 1,500.00
Toast rack, Five Bar, Royalty . . 250.00

James Kent Ltd.

Bowl, 5-1/2 ruffled, Florita pattern 75.00
Coffee pot, Granville Shape, Du Barry 200.00
Compote, footed, Du Barry . . . 150.00
Celery dish, 13" x 6-1/2", Hydrangea 125.00
Cream and sugar, Rapture pattern 75.00
Cup and saucer, Crazy Paving pattern 45.00
Jampot, Du Barry pattern 125.00
Nut dish, 3" sq, Apple Blossom pattern 45.00
Plate, 7" round, Rosalynde pattern 95.00
Tennis set, Du Barry pattern . . 100.00

Midwinter Ltd.

Biscuit barrel, chrome lid, Coral Chintz pattern 150.00
Three tier cake plate, Brama pattern 95.00

A.G. Richardson "Crown Ducal"

Bowl, 9-1/2" round, Roseland pattern 300.00
Cake plate, 8", metal handle, Primula pattern 95.00
Comport, 7", Spring Blossom pattern 325.00

Crown Ducal, vase, pierced cover, purple, A. G. Richardson, $275. Photo courtesy of Susan Scott.

Cup and saucer, demitasse, Pink
Chintz **125.00**

Jug, 3" cream, Pink Chintz
pattern **160.00**

Plate, 9", Spring Blossom
pattern **95.00**

Teapot, four cup, Priscilla
pattern **295.00**

Vase, 6-1/4", Purple Chintz
pattern **200.00**

Vase, 4-1/2, Pink Chintz
pattern **350.00**

Shelley Potteries Ltd.

Dish, pin, 4-1/2", Green Daisy
pattern **50.00**

Cake plate, Summer Glory Chintz
pattern **175.00**

Cup and saucer, Henley shape,
Countryside pattern **175.00**

Cup and saucer, Oleander shape,
Summer Glory pattern **135.00**

Jug, Maytime Chintz pattern . . . **210.00**

Reamer, Maytime Chintz
pattern **375.00**

Teapot, six cup, Summer Glory
pattern **600.00**

Toast rack, Three Bar, Melody Chintz
pattern **175.00**

CHRISTMAS ITEMS

History: The celebration of Christmas dates back to Roman times. Several customs associated with modern Christmas celebrations are traced back to early pagan rituals.

Father Christmas, believed to have evolved in Europe in the 7th century, was a combination of the pagan god Thor, who judged and punished the good and bad, and St. Nicholas, the generous Bishop of Myra. Kris Kringle originated in Germany and was brought to America by the Germans and Swiss who settled in Pennsylvania in the late 18th century.

In 1822, Clement C. Moore wrote, "A Visit From St. Nicholas" and developed the character of Santa Claus into the one we know today. Thomas Nast did a series of drawings for *Harper's Weekly* from 1863 until 1886 and further solidified the character and appearance of Santa Claus.

References: Robert Brenner, *Christmas Past*, 3rd ed., Schiffer Publishing, 1996; ——, *Christmas Through the Decades*, Schiffer Publishing, 1993, 2000 price update; ——, *Christmas Revised*, 2nd ed., Schiffer Publishing, 1997; Beth Dees, *Santa's Guide to Contemporary Christmas Collectibles*, Krause Publications, 1997; Jill Gallina, *Christmas Pins Past and Present*, Collector Books, 1996; George Johnson, *Christmas Ornaments, Lights & Decorations* Vol. I, (1987, 1998 value update), Vol. II (1996, 1997 value update), Vol. III (1996, 1997 value update), Collector Books; Constance King, *Christmas Customs, Antiques, Decorations & Traditions*, Antique Collectors' Club, 1999; Chris Kirk, *Joy of Christmas Collecting*, L-W Book Sales,

1994; James S. Morrison, *Vintage View of Christmas Past*, Shuman Heritage Press, 1995; Mary Morrison, *Snow Babies, Santas and Elves: Collecting Christmas Bisque Figures*, Schiffer Publishing, 1993; ——, *Christmas Jewelry,* Schiffer Publishing, 2000; Leslie Pina and Lorita Winfield, *Nativity, Crèches of the World*, Schiffer Publishing, 2000; Charlene Pinkerton, *Holiday Plastic Novelties*, Schiffer Publishing, 1999; Margaret Schiffer, *Christmas Ornaments: A Festive Study*, Schiffer Publisher, 1984, 1995 value update; ——, *Holidays: Toys and Decorations*, Schiffer Publishing, 1985; Clara Johnson Scroggins, *Silver Christmas Ornaments*, Krause Publications, 1997; Lissa Bryan-Smith and Richard Smith, *Holiday Collectibles, Vintage Flea Market Treasures Price Guide*, Krause Publications, 1998.

Collectors' Club: Golden Glow of Christmas Past, 6401 Winsdale St., Golden Valley, MN 55427.

Museum: National Christmas Center, Paradise, PA.

Reproduction Alert: Almost all holiday decorations, including Christmas, are now being skillfully reproduced. Only by knowing the source of a possible purchase, trusting the dealer, and careful observation can you be sure you are obtaining an antique.

Additional Listings: See *Warman's Americana & Collectibles* for more examples.

Advisers: Lissa Bryan-Smith and Richard M. Smith.

Advertising

Bank, molded rubber, Santa Clause holding a coin, toys in pack, marked "Christmas Club A. Corp, N.Y. 1972" **6.00**

Postcard, Santa Claus and little girl, artist A. Tekauz, **$100.** *Photo courtesy of Postcards International.*

Booklet, "When All The World Is Kin," 5" x 4", collection of Christmas stories, Christmas giveaway, Fowler, Dick, and Walker, The Boston Store, Wilkes-Barre, PA **7.00**

Calendar, 3" h, 7" l, celluloid, Christmas scene with holly border and 1929 calendar, giveaway from the Penny Specialty Shop, Selinsgrove, PA . **15.00**

Candy tin, 9" l, rect, red and green holly on white ground, marked "Satin Finish, hard candies, div. of Luden's Inc., Reading, PA" **18.00**

Catalog, Boston Store, Milwaukee, WI, 1945, 48 pgs, 8-1/2" x 11", "For An American Christmas" **20.00**

Coin, Johnson's Book Store, Santa Lucky Coin, metal, gold-luster finish, detailed Santa head above "Merry Christmas," reverse inscribed, "Lucky Coin from Santa at Johnson's Book Store," c1940 . . . . **6.00**

Dexterity puzzle, Santa face, cardboard rim holding Plexiglas over green and flesh-tone paper portrait, red cap, four balls, cardboard insert inscribed for Oklahoma merchant, marked "Made in USA," c1940 . . **18.00**

Matches, 4" x 2", "Season's Greetings," winter scene on cover, intact matches create Christmas scene, Boehmer's Garage, Milton, MA **15.00**

Pinback button

Boston Store, full-color Santa with holly accents on his hat, toy pack on back, black text "Meet Me At The Boston Store," early 1940s **35.00**

Grand Rapids, The Christmas Store, multicolored portrait of Santa on pastel-blue ground, red lettering, c1930 . . . . **40.00**

Santa's Visitor North Pole, NY, red and green on white ground, Santa gesturing toward reindeer, 1955 . . . . **10.00**

Touring with Talmage, multicolored portrait of Santa, black lettering, curl imprint and back paper for Philadelphia button maker, c1940 . . . . **25.00**

Tuberculosis Association, diamond-shaped replica of Christmas seal, centered by red double-barred cross symbol of American TB Association, Santa head and two children at chimney top, border inscribed, "Merry Christmas-Happy New Year," 1921 . . . . **40.00**

Stickpin, diecut thin cello multicolored portrait of Santa on short hanger stickpin, back inscribed, "Meet Me At Bowman's," c1920............ **45.00**

Trade card, child holding snowballs, "The White is King of all Sewing Machines, 80,000 now in use," reverse reads "J. Saltzer, Pianos, Organs, and Sewing Machines, Bloomsburg, Pa." **10.00**

Book, *The Miracle of Christmas, Beautiful Words by Billy Graham,* Hallmark, 1972, color illus, hardbound **7.00**

Candy box, cardboard

4-1/2" l, 3" h, Christmas Greetings, three carolers, USA................. **4.00**

6" x 5", pocketbook style, tuck-in flap, Merry Christmas, Santa in store window with children outside, marked "USA".................... **15.00**

8" h, four-sided cornucopia, Merry Christmas, Santa, sleigh, and reindeer over village rooftops, string bail, USA **35.00**

Children's books

How Santa Filled the Christmas Stockings, Carolyn Hodman, color illus by F. W. Stecher, Stecher Litho Co., 1916, 13" x 71".............. **85.00**

Santa Claus in Santa Claus Land, Dr. Harold Trott, color illus by Ben Rueby and Spence Easton, Crosset & Williams, 1943.............. **20.00**

The Night Before Christmas, Clement C. Moore, Corrine Malvern illustrator, A Golden Book, Golden Press, 1975...................... **8.00**

Rudolph the Red-Nosed Reindeer, Robert I. May, Maxton Publishers, Inc., 1939...................... **12.00**

The Littlest Snowman, Charles Tazewell, Grosset Dunlap, NY, 1958 ..... **18.00**

Christmas card list box, tin, Santa illus, marked "Mayfair Co. Chicago 6, Ill.," index cards and dividers, 1940-50 .... **24.00**

Feather tree, 4' h, green goose feather-wrapped branches with metal candleholders, painted white with green trim round wooden base, marked "Germany"................. **400.00**

Figures

Belsnickle

5-1/8" h, chalk, green-hooded coat with clear mica flecks, painted black base, feather tree missing, minor damage to base.... **275.00**

Viscoloid Santa Express, blow-molded holiday toy, Santa engineer on train, celluloid, **$125.** *Photo courtesy of Julie Robinson.*

13-1/2" h, cardboard, red-hooded coat with gold specks, realistic face, painted black base, damage................. **75.00**

Father Christmas

7" h, composition, pink face, red-cloth coat, painted blue pants, black boots, mounted on mica-covered cardboard base, marked "Japan" **90.00**

8" h, papier-mâché, hollow molded, plaster covered, white coat, black boots, sprinkled with mica . **300.00**

Nativity, 7" h, composition, shepherd holding lamb, marked "Germany" **12.00**

Reindeer

1" h, pot metal, marked "Germany".............. **18.00**

4" h, celluloid, white......... **7.00**

Santa Claus

3" h, bisque, long red coat, marked "Japan" **25.00**

3" h, cotton batting, red, attached to cardboard house, marked "Japan" **48.00**

3" l, celluloid, molded, one-piece Santa, sleigh, and reindeer.. **35.00**

5" h, hard plastic, Santa on green plastic skis, USA **120.00**

10" h, pressed cardboard, red hat and jacket, black boots.... **90.00**

14" h, pressed cardboard, head, store display **95.00**

Sheep, 3" h, composition body, carved wooden legs, covered with cloth or wool, glass eyes.............. **40.00**

Greeting cards

1892, "Sincere Good Wishes," purple pansy with green leaves, greeting inside, Raphael Tuck & Sons.... **12.00**

1910, "Loving Greetings," flat card, two girls pictured hanging garland, marked "Germany".................... **8.00**

1933, "Merry Christmas," series of six envelopes, decreasing in size, small card in last envelope, American Greeting Publishers, Cleveland, USA **12.00**

1943, Strand Baking Co., Marshalltown, IA, holiday scene, wish for "peace and victory in the coming year" **5.00**

1954, Mickey and Minnie Mouse, 25th Anniversary Disney Corporate card, 1954 calendar, Jiminy Cricket on back, "Copyright Walt Disney Productions World Rights Reserved," 7" x 7"..................... **250.00**

House, cardboard

2" x 2", mica covered, wire loop on top, marked "Czechoslovakia"....... **7.00**

4" x 5", house and fence, sponge trees, marked "USA" **10.00**

Lantern, 8" h, four sided, peaked top, wire bail, metal candleholder in base, black cardboard, colored tissue paper scenes, 1940s............... **25.00**

Magazine, *St. Nicholas,* bound edition of 1915 and 1916, color covers, ads, illus, story **15.00**

Ornaments

Angel, 4" h, wax over composition, human-hair wig, spun-glass wings, cloth dress, Germany **60.00**

Ball, 2" d, silvered glass, any color
. . . .**3.00**

Beads, 72" l, glass, half-inch multicolored beads, paper label marked "Japan" **8.00**

Bulldog, 3" h, Dresden, three-dimensional, marked "Germany" **250.00**

Camel, 4" h, cotton batting, Germany **160.00**

Cross, 4" h, beaded, two-sided, silvered, wire hanger, paper label marked "Czechoslovakia" **18.00**

Drummer boy, 3" h, wax, hollow, metal-ring hanger, USA **5.00**

Father Christmas on donkey, 10" h, chromolithograph, blue robe, tinsel trim **25.00**

Kugel, 4-1/2" d, round, deep sapphire blue, brass hanger **110.00**

Kugel, 5-3/4" l, bunch of grapes, deep blue, brass hanger, little silvering left **800.00**

Mandolin, 5" h, unsilvered glass, wrapped in lametta and tinsel . . .**45.00**

Parakeet, 5" h, multicolored glass, spun glass tail, mounted on metal clip **23.00**

Pear, 3" h, cotton batting, mica highlights, paper leaf, wire hanger, Japan **12.00**

Santa Claus in chimney, 4" h, glass, Germany **75.00**

Swan, 5" x 6", Dresden, flat, gold with silver, green, and red highlights .**150.00**

Tree top, 11" h, three spheres stacked with small clear glass balls, silvered, lametta and tinsel trim, attached to blown glass hooks **90.00**

Postcards, Germany
Christmas bells and snow scene, marked "Made in Germany," used, one cent stamp, 1911 . . . .**20.00**

"Happy Christmas Wishes," Santa steering ship **10.00**

"May Your Christmas Be Merry and Gay," photo card, sepia tones, Father Christmas peeking between two large wooden doors, wearing fur cap . . .**18.00**

Putz
Brush tree, 6" h, green, mica-covered branches, wooden base **8.00**

Christmas-tree fence
Cast iron, silver, ornate gold trim, fifteen 10" l segments with posts, Germany **600.00**
Wood, folding red and green sections, 48" l, USA **35.00**

Choir boy, 3" h, hard plastic, red and white **4.00**

Penny wooden, two children on seesaw, hand-carved wood, multicolored, Nurenberg or Erzgebrige **32.00**

Toys
Jack-in-the-box, 9-1/2" h, "Santa Pops," hard plastic, red-felt hat, orig box, Tigrette Industries, 1956 . . .**30.00**

Merry-go-round, wind-up, celluloid, green and red base, four white reindeer heads, Santa sitting under umbrella, Santa spins around, stars hanging from umbrella bounce of bobbing deer heads, orig box, Japan **65.00**

Santa, 10" h, battery operated, metal covered with red and white plush suit and hat, soft-plastic face, holding metal wand with white star light, wand moves up and down and lights up while Santa turns head **90.00**

Tree stand, 9-3/4" sq, 4" h, cast iron, old worn green, gold, white, and red paint, relief tree trunk, foliage, and stairway design **90.00**

CIGAR CUTTERS

History: Counter and pocket cigar cutters were used at the end of the 19th and beginning of the 20th centuries. They were a popular form of advertising. Pocket-type cigar cutters often were a fine piece of jewelry that attached to a watch chain.

Reference: Jerry Terranova and Douglas Congdon-Martin, *Antique Cigar Cutters and Lighters*, Schiffer Publishing, 1996; —, *Great Cigar Stuff for Collectors*, Schiffer Publishing, 1997.

Advertising

Betsy Ross 5¢ Cigars, nickel-plated placard with paper image of Betsy surrounded by emb wording, cast-iron base, lever on base pushed to expose cigar cutter, damage to adv . . .**310.00**

Brunhoff Manufacturing Co., framed Havana Cigar adv on top, 1906, cast iron, counter type **400.00**

Pistol, nickel plate, gutta-percha handle, English, 3-3/8" l, **$160**

Country Gentleman 5c, chrome plated, ornate counter-top plate **110.00**

El Commercio Havana Cigars, c1906, 9" l **675.00**

Fifth Avenue Cigar, key-wind pocket type **45.00**

Home Run Cigars, reverse painted on glass, key-wind mechanism, H. F. Kohler Cigar Manufacturer, Nashville, Pa., late 19th/early 20th C baseball game vignette on front, similar scenes on side, 8-1/4" w, 6-1/2" d, 4-1/2" h, some paint chipped off **1,600.00**

Hotel Sherman, figural street light, red globe, ornate base, marked "Reed & Barton" **250.00**

Lillian Russell Cigar Five Cents, cast metal, countertop, emb red letters, 8-1/2" l, 6-3/4" h **275.00**

Louis Bergdull Brewing Co., Philadelphia, china, patent 1904, cigar cutter and ashtray, wording around match holder on top, 5" w, 4" h. .**165.00**

Tutt's Liver Pills, captain's wheel, cast metal, adv on reverse, wheel spins to expose cigar cutters, 6" w, 6" h, some surface rust **550.00**

Charm/fob, lady's cheroot cutter, 10K yg, figural bird, ruby eyes, diamond nose, monogrammed on back, Victorian, c1900, 1-1/2" l **695.00**

Counter

Enterprise Mfg. Co., #19, star, emb "Save the Tags" **95.00**

Griffin Goodness Grocer Co., Tulsa, OK, stamped "Patent Dec. 1, 1914," 12-3/4" l, 4-1/4" d, 8-1/2" h **195.00**

Master Workman, decal, long handle **85.00**

Silhouette, wooden handle joining iron blade centering silhouetted head, pivoting on post in form of full silhouetted figure, 16" l, 9-1/2" w, 6-1/2" h, mounted on woodblock, 19th C, cracks in block, surface rust on blade **920.00**

Three Bros. Cigars, 7-7/8" w, 5-7/8" d, 4-1/2" h, reverse-glass dec, slight wear, C.8+ **650.00**

Yankee, Union Shield, cast iron with nickel plate, match dispenser, c1900, 7" h **750.00**

Figural

Arrowhead, SP, enamel dec, pocket-knife type **125.00**

Boy sitting on ornate rock, metal, 7" h **400.00**

Burro, heavy cast iron, base lever pushed to operate cigar cutter, ears and tail move, cigar snuffer on saddle

with emb pots and pans, minor paint
loss **525.00**
Crying child, cast iron, painted black,
gray base, cigar in mouth, 4-3/4" h,
4-1/2" l **415.00**
Man wearing fez, cast metal, right hand
lowered to activate cutter, shield dated
"1881," wood base, 7" h **250.00**
Ship's wheel, brass-plated tin, handle
revolves to expose cigar cutter, 5" h,
minor surface rust **65.00**
Trumpet, brass, pocket knife
type **50.00**

Pocket

Shagreen and silver, 7" l,
English. **895.00**
Sterling silver, 6" l, cutter on one end,
small hammer on other end, marked "S
& S, Sterling" **195.00**

CIGAR STORE FIGURES

History: Cigar store figures were familiar sights in
front of cigar shops and tobacco shops starting about
1840. Figural themes included Sir Walter Raleigh,
sailors, Punch figures, and ladies, with Indians being
the most popular.

Most figures were carved in wood, although some
also were made in metal and papier-mâché for a short
time. Most carvings were life size or slightly smaller
and brightly painted. A coating of tar acted as a
preservative against the weather. Of the few surviving
figures, only a small number have their original bases.
Most replacements were necessary because of years
of wear and usage by dogs.

Use of figures declined when local ordinances
were passed requiring shopkeepers to move the
figures inside at night. This soon became too much
trouble, and other forms of advertising developed.

References: Edwin O. Christensen, *Early
American Wood Carvings*, Dover Publications, out
of print; A.W. Pendergast and W. Porter Ware, *Cigar
Store Figures*, The Lightner Publishing Corp., out of
print.

Blackamore, 27" h, carved wood, old
polychrome dec, 19th C, minor damage
to right hand **4,750.00**
Indian Brave, 17-1/2" h, carved wood,
orig polychrome over green, 19th C,
damage to right shoulder and chip from
base. **2,000.00**
Indian Chief
27-1/2" h, counter type, pine, holding
bunch of cigars in raised right hand,
feathered headdress, orange
costume, green cloak, leather-
fringed leggings, mounted on
sq-painted base, 19th C . . **8,250.00**

88" h, pine, arm raised shielding
eyes, bunch of cigars in other
hand, one foot resting on rock,
wearing feathered headdress,
feather-trimmed costume with
leggings, painted green, red, and
yellow, orig base inscribed "Ed A
Feltham, Cigars and Tobacco,"
orig bars surround top of base,
c1880 . . . . **36,500.00**

*Indian maiden, carved polychrome,
brown and gray fringed dress wtih
beaded necklace, fringed leggings, black
moccasins, holding cigars in right hand,
rectangular plinth base, right arm
restored, 69" h.* **$4,675.**

Indian Princess, 61" h, carved wood,
gold over polychrome, weathered,
age cracks, loose three-feather
headdress **1,575.00**
Indian Squaw, 45-1/2" h, carrying box
quiver, applied carved and
polychromed arrows, circular bosses
and tomahawk, painted, mounted on
metal base, left arm missing, American,
c1870 . . . . **26,000.00**
Punch, 50" h, pine, carved and
painted, holding bunch of cigars in one
hand, other hand raised, circular base,
early 20th C **3,000.00**
Scotchman, 34-1/2" h, wearing plumed
head dress, costume, right arm
extended and carved to hold cigars,
carved oak, polychrome, and gilt,
America or British Isles, 19th C,
imperfections. **6,325.00**
Turk
19" h, carved wood, orig
polychrome, smoking pipe, 19th C
. . . . **2,000.00**
27" h, carved wood, orig polychrome
over gesso, 19th C, two chips off
base, missing chip from
turban. **2,800.00**

CINNABAR

History: Cinnabar, a ware made of numerous layers
of a heavy mercuric sulfide, often is referred to as
vermilion because of the red hue of most pieces. It
was carved into boxes, buttons, snuff bottles, and
vases. The best examples were made in China.

Bowl, 8" d, garden scene, blue enamel
int. **225.00**
Box, 3-3/4" x 5-3/8", Chinese figures in
garden setting **95.00**
Cup, 4-1/2" d, dragon handles,
c1900 . . . . **225.00**
Dish, 10-3/4" d, deeply carved,
leafy melon vines, black lacquer
base **900.00**
Ginger jar, 12" h, figural landscape
dec, Chinese, mounted as lamp **425.00**
Incense burner, pagoda type, Taoist
mask design, c1900 . . . . **1,300.00**
Jar, 4" h, flowering plants, carved
floral scrolls, diaper ground, domed
cov, gilt metal rim and finial, price for
pr. **150.00**
Plate, 12-3/4" d, double dragon
design **375.00**
Tray, 15" l, bird and flower scene,
reddish brown **625.00**
Vase, 10" h, carved continuous scenic
dec, Chinese, pr **120.00**

CLEWELL POTTERY

History: Charles Walter Clewell was first a metal worker and secondarily a potter. In the early 1900s, he opened a small shop in Canton, Ohio, to produce metal-overlay pottery.

Metal on pottery was not a new idea, but Clewell was perhaps the first to completely mask the ceramic body with copper, brass or "silvered" or "bronzed" metals. One result was a product whose patina added to the character of the piece over time.

Since Clewell operated on a small scale with little outside assistance, only a limited quantity of his artwork exists. He retired at the age of 79 in 1955, choosing not to reveal his technique to anyone else.

Marks: Most of the wares are marked with a simple incised "Clewell," along with a code number. Because Clewell used pottery blanks from other firms, the names "Owens" or "Weller" are sometimes found.

References: Paul Evans, *Art Pottery of the United States*, 2nd ed., Feingold & Lewis Publishing Corp., 1987; Ralph and Terry Kovel, *Kovels' American Art Pottery*, Crown Publishers, 1993.

Museum: John Besser Museum, Alpena, MI.

Vase, classic shape, good bronze and verdigris patina, marked "Clewell 288-256," some scarring to surface, 3-1/2" x 8-1/2", $815. Photo courtesy of David Rago Auctions.

Candlesticks, pr, 7" h, 3-1/2" d, copper clad, four sided, dark bronzed patina, unmarked **1,300.00**
Jardiniere, 14" h, ovoid, matte finish **130.00**

Mug, 4-1/2" h, copper clad, riveted design, applied monogram, relief signature **65.00**
Vase
3-1/2" d, 8-1/2" h, copper-clad, classical shape, bronze and verdigris patina, marked "Clewell 288-256," some surface scarring **800.00**
5" d, 11" h, copper-clad, baluster, verdigris patina, incised "Clewell 315-2-6," surface scratches **980.00**
7-1/2" h, 4" d, ovoid, copper clad, verdigris to bronze patina, incised "Clewell/351-25" **1,000.00**
11" h, 5" d, bulbous, copper clad, bronzed finish, incised "Clewell/357-5," cleaned some time ago **500.00**
Vessel, 7-1/2" w, 11" h, copper-clad, verdigris patina, incised "Clewell 72-26" **1,725.00**

CLIFTON POTTERY

History: The Clifton Art Pottery, Newark, New Jersey, was established by William A. Long, once associated with Lonhuda Pottery, and Fred Tschirner, a chemist.

Production consisted of two major lines: Crystal Patina, which resembled true porcelain with a subdued crystal-like glaze, and Indian Ware or Western Influence, an adaptation of the American Indians' unglazed and decorated pottery with a high-glazed black interior. Other lines included Robin's-Egg Blue and Tirrube. Robin's-Egg Blue is a variation of the crystal patina line, but in blue-green instead of straw-colored hues and with a less-prominent crushed-crystal effect in the glaze. Tirrube, which is often artist signed, features brightly colored, slip-decorated flowers on a terra-cotta ground.

Marks: Marks are incised or impressed. Early pieces may be dated and impressed with a shape number. Indian wares are identified by tribes.

References: Paul Evans, *Art Pottery of the United States*, 2nd ed., Feingold & Lewis Publishing Corp., 1987; Ralph and Terry Kovel, *Kovels' American Art Pottery*, Crown Publishers, 1993.

Biscuit jar, cov, 7" h, 4-1/4" d, gray-brown ground, enameled running ostrich and stork, florals, bail handle **300.00**
Creamer, Crystal Patina, incised "Clifton," dated **225.00**
Decanter, 11-1/2" h, rose shading to deep rose, purple flowers, gilt butterfly on neck, applied handle, marbleized rose and white stopper **150.00**

Vase, spherical, Crystal Patina, unusual green and mirrored caramel glaze, signed and dated 1906, 5-1/2" x 6-1/2", $575. Photo courtesy of David Rago Auctions.

Jardiniere, 8-1/2" h, 11" d, Four Mile Ruin, Arizona, incised and painted motif, buff and black on brown ground, imp mark and incised inscription, hairline to rim **400.00**
Sweetmeat jar, 4" h, hp ducks and cranes, robin's egg blue ground, cow finial **375.00**
Teapot, 6" h, brown and black geometric design **200.00**
Vase
6-1/2" d, 5-1/2" h, spherical, Crystal Patina, green and mirrored caramel glaze, sgd and dated 1906 . . . . **575.00**
9-1/2" h, 4-1/2" d, bottle shape, Crystal Patina, incised "Clifton/158" **350.00**
10" h, 7" d, angular handles, Crystal Patina, incised "Clifton" . . . **450.00**
Vessel
4-1/2" h, ovoid, two handles, Crystal Patina, incised "Clifton," dated, firing line to base **65.00**
8" h, 11" d, squat, Homolobi, bands of geometric umber designs, terra-cotta ground, incised "Clifton/233," titled, flaking of glaze **450.00**

CLOCKS

History: The sundial was the first man-made device for measuring time. Its basic disadvantage is well expressed by the saying: "Do like the sundial, count only the sunny days."

Needing greater dependability, man developed the water clock, oil clock, and sand clock, respectively. All these clocks worked on the same principle—time was measured by the amount of material passing from one container to another.

The wheel clock was the next major step. These clocks can be traced back to the 13th century. Many improvements on the basic wheel clock were made and continue to be made. In 1934, the quartz-crystal movement was introduced.

The first carriage clock was made about 1800 by Abraham Louis Breguet as he tried to develop a clock that would keep accurate time for Napoleon's officers. One special feature of a carriage clock was a device that allowed it to withstand the bumpy ride of a stagecoach. These small clocks usually are easy to carry with their own handle built into a rectangular case.

The recently invented atomic clock, which measures time by radiation frequency, only varies one second in a thousand years.

References: Robert W. D. Ball, *American Shelf and Wall Clocks*, Schiffer Publishing, 1992; F. J. Britten, *Old Clocks and Watches & Their Makers*, Antique Collectors' Club, 1999; Cesinsky & Webster, *English Domestic Clocks*, Antique Collectors' Club, 1999; J. E. Connell, *The Charlton Standard Catalogue of Canadian Clocks*, 2nd ed., Charlton Press, 1999; Brian Loomes, *Brass Dial Clocks*, Antique Collectors' Club, 1999; —, *Painted Dial Clocks*, Antique Collector's Club, 1994; Tran Duy Ly, *Seth Thomas Clocks & Movements*, Arlington Book Co., 1996; Derek Roberts, *Skeleton Clocks*, Antique Collectors' Club, 1999; Tom Robinson, *The Longcase Clock*, Antique Collectors' Club, 1999; Ronald Rose, *English Dial Clocks*, Antique Collectors' Club, 1999; Robert and Harriet Swedberg, *Price Guide to Antique Clocks*, Krause Publications, 1998; John Ware Willard, *Simon Willard and His Clocks*, Dover Publications, n.d.

Periodicals: *Clocks*, 4314 W. 238th St., Torrance, CA 90505.

Collectors' Club: National Association of Watch and Clock Collectors, Inc., 514 Poplar St., Columbia, PA 17512.

Museums: American Clock & Watch Museum, Bristol, CT; Greensboro Clock Museum, Greensboro, NC; National Association of Watch and Clock Collectors Museum, Columbia, PA; National Museum of American History, Washington, DC; Old Clock Museum, Pharr, TX; The Time Museum, Rockford, IL; Willard House & Clock Museum, Grafton, MA.

Notes: Identifying the proper model name for a clock is critical in establishing price. Condition of the works also is a critical factor. Examine the works to see how many original parts remain. If repairs are needed, try to include this in your estimate of purchase price. Few clocks are purchased purely for decorative value.

Advertising

Chew Friendship Cub Plug, face of man with moving mouth chewing Friendship Tobacco to the tic of the clock, pat'd March 2, 1886, 4" h **900.00**
Coca-Cola, neon, light-up type, metal frame, some weathering to case, does not run, c1942, 15-1/2" w, 4-3/4" d, 15-1/2" h **400.00**
Electric Ad Clock Co., Chicago, cathedral-shaped clock, drum in lower window rotates to promote advertising,

wood front, rest sheet metal, c1933, 21-1/2" x 13", some chipping to veneer **200.00**
Gruen Watch, Williams Jewelry Co. on marquee at bottom, blue neon around perimeter, 15" x 15" **600.00**
Hire's Root Beer, "Drink Hires Root Beer with Root Barks, Herbs," 15" d . . **250.00**
International Tailoring, Chicago, cast iron, emb design, bronzed, orig working clock, 12" w, 2-1/2" d, 16" h, C.8+ **1,000.00**
Longine's Watches, "The World's Most Honored Watch," brass, 18-1/2" d **300.00**
None Such Mincemeat, pumpkin face, 8-1/2" w, some wear **300.00**
Pepsi-Cola, metal and glass double bubble electric type, c1950, 16" d **625.00**
Reddy Kilowatt, compliments of Philadelphia Light and Electric, Westclox alarm clock, 5" h **350.00**
Victrola Records, orig pendulum **2,100.00**

Alarm

Attleboro, 36 hours, nickel-plated case, owl dec, 9" h **75.00**
Bradley, brass, double bells, Germany **40.00**
Champion, 30 hours, American movement, metal frame, ornamental feet, 9" h **75.00**
New Haven, c1900, 30 hours, SP case, perfume-bottle shape, beveled-glass mirror, removable cut-glass scent bottle, beaded handle **185.00**
Search Light, patent 1910, wind-up clock mechanism attached to battery box with bells, lights, 8" l **70.00**
Western, wind-up, oak battery base with bells, c1900, 8-1/2" l **45.00**

Bracket

Parke, Solomon, Federal case, mahogany veneer, old finish, brass feet, brass hands, brass fusee works, painted steel face with "Strike" and "Silent," labeled "Solomon Parke, Philadelphia," some veneer damage, old veneer repair, pendulum and keys, 17-3/4" h plus top handle **9,350.00**
Regency, Bennett & Co., Norwich, c1810, brass inlaid and gilt bronze mounted mahogany, dial and backplate sgd, oak leaf spandrels, case inlaid with scrolls, gadrooned bun feet, 17" h, chips **4,325.00**
Tiffany & Co., bronze, stepped rect-shaped top, four acorn finials, cast

foliate frieze, four capitals with reeded columns, shaped and foliate cast base, beveled glass door and panels, circular face dial with Roman numerals, marked "Famiel Marti Medaille…Paris 1900, Tiffany & Co."13" h **600.00**

Carriage

French, early 20th C, brass, retailed by Tiffany & Co., subsidiary seconds dial, beveled-glass panels, morocco traveling case, 5-3/4" h **350.00**
French, oval, brass, four beveled glass panels, fine cut flowers in border to sides, top oval glass panels initialed "M.E.H.," dial painted with woman and cupid, decorative D-shaped handle on top, 5-1/2" h **1,150.00**
New Haven Clock Co., gilded brass case, beveled glass, gold repaint to case, orig pendulum and key, 11-1/2" h **315.00**
Tiffany & Co., early 20th C, brass and glass, French half strike repeater movement marked for Souaillet Freres, enamel dial with Arabic numerals and subsidiary seconds dial, 3-3/8" w, 3" d, 7" h **950.00**

Desk, American, shaped rect, brass case, white enamel bordering cobalt blue, stylized applied monogram, decorative brass corners, central dial with Arabic numerals, 4-3/4" h . **150.00**

Garniture, Napoleon III, black marble, clock with central dial, painted Roman numerals, flanked by marble scrolls, supported on rect base with motifs, short round feet, pr black marble tazza on plinth base, gilded floral highlights **500.00**

Half, Aaron Willard Jr., Hepplewhite case, figured mahogany with inlay, old finish, French feet, shaped apron, molding at base of hood with molded and fretwork cornice, brass finials, brass banjo works with hourly strike, weight, and pendulum, painted face labeled "Aaron Willard Junior, Washington Street Boston," orig paper label on back of case "directions for putting up the time piece," repairs to case, some old veneer repair, minor touch-up to face, 35-1/2" h . . **27,500.00**

Mantel
America

Aaron Willard, Boston, c1800, Federal, mahogany inlaid, molded scrolled cornice with inlaid terminals centering plinth above inlaid oval and glazed door, enclosing painted iron kidney-shaped dial inscribed

"Aaron Willard Boston" within gilt cartouche and eight-day weight-driven movement, lower case with cock-beaded door inlaid with stringing and cross banding joining ovolo corners, cut-out feet with diagonal inlaid banding, old finish, restoration, 36-1/2" h **8,050.00**

Folk Art, c1900, carved walnut, eight-day spring-driven movement, symmetrically carved case of oak trees flanking bezel and dial above two elk, 18" w, 5" d, 22" h **1,265.00**

Seth Thomas, Plymouth, CT, pillar and scroll, curly maple, curly veneer with golden refinish, orig floral painting on face, wooden works, orig printed label on int., early brass finials, free-standing pillars on either side of two-part door, old pane of glass at top, 20th C reverse painting on lower panel of eagle with flag, scalloped base, delicate feet, weights missing, some restorations, 17-1/2" w, 31" h **2,425.00**

Seth Thomas, Plymouth, CT, c1816-17, pillar and scroll, Federal,

Bracket, late 18th C, ebony case, loop brass bail handle, four metal urn finials, arched door, conforming steel face, marked "Edwd. Stevens Boston," four gilt metal cast winged claw and ball feet, 19-1/2" h, **$3,700.** *Photo courtesy of Freeman/Fine Arts.*

scrolled cornice, maple plinths, brass urn finials above glazed door, painted dial, 30 hour weight-driven wooden strap movement of second type, eglomise glass tablet, flanked by free-standing columns, cut-out feet, restorations, 30-1/4" h **1,955.00**

Seth Thomas, Plymouth, CT, pillar and scroll, refinished mahogany and flame veneer, reverse-painted panel, orig painted pendulum, orig label, restorations and missing finials, 29" h **1,375.00**

Continental, late 19th C

Bronze and marble, clock mechanism with demilune magnifier at back, flat gilt dial with colorless paste-set bezel, raised on bronze figure of cherub, fluted marble columns with beaded-ormolu band, oak-leaf ormolu feet, rect-marble base with concave corners, 17" h **650.00**

Faience, blue-glazed elephant, rococo-ormolu mount, center enamel dial, rococo-style naturalistic base, 14" w, 16-1/4" h **865.00**

English

Late Regency, London, second quarter 19th C, two-train bell-striking movement, dial sgd "Brandreth & Walker," mahogany case with cornice inlaid with brass scroll, sides with two brass handles above sound dampeners, dial flanked by gilt-metal spandrels, plinth base, applied gilt-metal detail on front, ball feet, 11-3/4" w, 6-3/4" deep, 19" h **1,610.00**

Shagreen and silver plate, first half 20th C, single-train non-chiming movement by Abec, corniced case set to front with panel of green shagreen, two short plinth supports, 5-1/4" w, 2-1/8" d, 6-1/2" h **700.00**

French

Black marble, late 19th C, two-train chiming movement, round hood flanked by roundels at base, rect case with glass panel on front, pendulum with enamel roundel with arrow and finials, "RA" on plinth base, 9-1/4" w, 6" d, 17" h **400.00**

Empire-Style, gilt bronze, two-train half-strike movement, urn-form body set to corner with enamel dial sgd "Michelez," high loop

handles ending in deer's heads, applied grapevines and husk swags, trumpet foot on sq section base with clipped corners, applied wreaths and anthemia, 18-1/4" h **4,600.00**

Figural, late 19th C, ormolu, two-train half-strike movement, engine-turned dial with enamel chapter ring, pedestal with rose spandrels, topped by basket of doves, flanked by figure of classical woman, column topped by urn, plinth base with classical motifs, flat-leaf band, tulip-shaped feet, 12" w, 4-1/2" d, 16-1/2" h . **1,850.00**

Louis XVI Style, 19th C, enamel and ormolu, two-train half-strike movement, round dial centered by glass, white enamel bezel bordered by gold stars on cobalt-blue ground, topped by eagle holding fruit swag, white marble base, ormolu demilune legs with blue enameling, rect marble plinth, four pointed pad ormolu feet, 8-1/2" w, 4-3/8" d, 15-3/8" h **8,050.00**

Louis XVI Style, 20th C, brass, two-grain half-strike movement, engraved dial set into rect case with domed cornice topped by husk garland, berry-form finials on four corners, dial with cherub head and flat-leaf spandrels, sides of case with pierced strapwork panels with red sound dampening, front of base set with large cherub herm, concave bracket feet, 15-1/2" w, 13" d, 28" h **1,955.00**

Louis XVI Style, gilt bronze and enamel, early 20th C, two-train chiming movement, enamel dial with delicate floral garlands, flanked by flat leaves, shaped case topped by torch and rose wreath, blue basse taille enamel plaque, over enameled with scene of courting couple, three flat leaf and hoof feet, 9-1/4" w, 4-1/2" d, 16" h . . **1,100.00**

Louis XVI Style, gilt-metal and enamel, two-train half-strike movement, round bezel with enamel chapter ring accented with blue band with gold stars, sgd "Chopin a Paris," pierced scroll surround, raised on four round section supports topped by urn finials, base with flat-leaf band, flattened stippled feet, marble socle and glass dome, 15-5/8" h **2,415.00**

French Empire, ormolu, young woman at well holding staff, pitcher on one side, sheep on other, brass works, enameled face labeled "Dubois fils, a Paris," minor damage, no pendulum, back cover missing, 17-1/4" h, **$1,980.** *Photo courtesy of Garth's Auction, Inc.*

Louis XVI Style, late 19th C, onyx and ormolu mounts, two-train half-striking movement, case topped by bust of worman, domed case with beading, plaque of classical figures, flat-leaf band on spreading base, 13-1/2" w, 7-5/8" d, 24" h **550.00**

German, Jugendstil, oak, retailed by Liberty & Co., exposed bell on top, open sides, copper face emb with violets, purple and yellow slag glass window, orig finish, working condition, unmarked, 9-3/4" w, 14-1/4" h **1,840.00**

Victorian, late 19th C, black, rect, two-train strike and bell movement, front with breche d'alep marble pilasters flanking round dial, plinth base with breche d'alep band and diamond inlay, gilt incised line dec, 9-3/4" w, 5-3/4" d, 10-3/4" h **425.00**

Mirror, attributed to Benjamin Morrill, Boscawen, NH, c1830, rect case with hinged split baluster framed gilt and black-painted door, enclosing stenciled tablet framing white painted iron dial and brass wheelbarrow weight-driven movement above mirror plate, minor imperfections, 15" w, 4" d, 30" h **5,175.00**

Novelty, figural

American, c1880, three stacked rifles supporting drum form pendant housing movement, brass and copper, 10-3/4" h **345.00**

French, 19th C, sedan shape, bronze dore, body with low relief depicting cherubs within low relief within scrolling foliate borders, central enamel dial with Arabic numerals over applied ivory panel depicting cherub, each side with miniature portrait of elegant lady, one sgd "r. peter," other "Renner," 11-1/4" h **1,500.00**

Pillar and scroll

Downes, Ephraim, Bristol, CT, 1825, mahogany, 30-hour wooden-weight movement, old finish, imperfections, 31" h **950.00**

Leavenworth and Son, Mark, Waterbury, CT, c1825, mahogany, 30-hour wooden movement, imperfections, 16-1/2" w, 4-1/2" d, 29-3/4" h **950.00**

Thomas, Seth, c1825, Federal, mahogany, scrolled cresting joining three brass urn finials above glazed door, 30-hour wooden weight-driven movement, polychrome and gilt dec dial, landscape tablet, flanked by freestanding columns on cut bracket feet, old refinish, minor imperfections, 17-1/4" w, 4-1/2" d, 32" h **2,185.00**

Shelf

Ansonia, gingerbread, carved and pressed walnut case, paper on zinc dial, silver dec glass, eight-day time and strike movement with pendulum, 22" h **185.00**

Atkins and Downs, eight-day triple, reverse-painted glass with buildings, pendulum window, and split columns, middle section with mirror and full columns, top section with dec dial, split columns, top crest with spread eagle, most of orig label remains, 38" h, 17" w, 6" d **450.00**

Botsford's Improved Patent Timepiece, Coe & Co. 52 Dey St., New York, papier-mâché, scrolled front, gilt, polychrome embellishments, mother-of-pearl floral designs, circular enamel dial inscribed "Saml. S. Spencer," lever spring-driven movement, mounted on dec oval base, brass ball feet, glass dome, 11" h **1,265.00**

Brown, J. C. and Forestville Mfg Co., laminated rosewood veneered case, painted tablet with floral dec and geometric designs, painted zinc dial,

eight-day time and strike double-fusee movement with pendulum, 19" h **5,000.00**

Classical, Norris North, Torrington, CT, c1825, mahogany, flat cornice above glazed door, eglomise tablet of young woman flanked by engaged black paint stenciled columns, polychrome and gilt white painted dial, 30-hour wooden weight-driven movement, 23-3/4" h, 13-1/2" w, 5-1/4" d **4,900.00**

Empire, mahogany veneer, ebonized and stencil-gilded pilasters and crest, wooden works with weights, key, and pendulum, very worn paper label "William Orion & Co.," door with mirror in base, replaced reverse-painted glass in middle section, finials missing, some veneer damage and repair **350.00**

Federal, New England, early 19th C, mahogany and mahogany veneer, shaped fretwork joining three plinths and brass urn finials, flat cornice, glazed veneer door, white painted wood dial with red painted drapery, lower projecting base with cross-banded frame and flame mahogany panel pierced for viewing pendulum, slightly flaring French feet, 39" h, 13-3/4" w, 5-1/2" d, imperfections, replaced old movement **1,500.00**

Tiffany & Company, walnut case, worn finish, traces of gilding in incised carved detail, brass works, blue and white enameled face, marked "Tiffany & Comp. New York," orig pendulum and key, 20" h **935.00**

Willard, Aaron, Boston, c1825, Federal, mahogany, molded plinth above glazed door, eglomise tablet of lyre spandrels and foliate designs, oval inscribed "Aaron Willard Boston," wooden framed white painted concave iron dial, eight-day weight-drive brass movement, lower section with mirror, framed by rounded moldings, ball feet, refinished, imperfections, 31" h **7,500.00**

Skeleton, French, by Brocot, Rue D'Oleans 15 (Maris), brass, arch form, shaped sides, enamel face, two-train chiming movement with pull repeater, mounted to felt lined giltwood base with bun feet, 10-1/2" h brass and bound glass cover, 7-3/8" h **650.00**

Tall case

American, cherry, wag on wall works, orig painted dec, dovetailed hood with freestanding columns, broken arch top with turned finials, chamfered quarter columns, molded waist, rounded platform base with beveled feet, old mellow varnished refinish, weights, pendulum, some repairs to case, 98" h **2,750.00**

Chippendale

I. Bailey, N Yarmouth, Maine, late 18th C, birch, arch molded crest with pierced fretwork, three plinths surmounted by wood finish above glazed tombstone door flanked by freestanding turned columns enclosing painted iron dial with Arabic and Roman numeral chapter ring, silver and gilt vine and geometric designs in arch and spandrels, waist with arched thumb-molded door with flanking molded corners, boxed base, ogee bracket feet, eight-day brass and bell metal time and strike movement, refinished, fretwork restored, other imperfections, 17-1/4" w, 9-1/2" d, 88" h **17,250.00**

Issac Grotz, Easton, PA, 1810-35, curly maple, mellow old refinishing, bonnet with freestanding columns, fluted and dentilated moldings, broken-arch pediment with inlaid rosettes and turned finials, molded edge waist door with carved fan, fluted quarter columns, molded edge panel in base, moldings between sections, ogee feet, brass works with second hand and calendar movement, painted sheet face with phases of the moon dial, cornucopias in the spandrels and labeled "Issac Grotz, Easton," weights, pendulum, and key, finials and plinths replaced, minor repairs to case, calendar dial repainted or replaced, 103" h **28,600.00**

Jacob Hostetter, York County, PA, cherry, old finish, bonnet with four fluted freestanding columns with brass fittings and Corinthian capitals on front columns, broken-arch pediment with Greek-key molding, carved floral rosettes and flame-carved finials on reeded and fluted plinths, molded-edge door with double-arch top, molding between sections with fluted quarter columns in waist, fluted quarter columns and molded panel in base, ogee feet, brass works with second hand and calendar movement, pained steel face with spandrels, labeled "Jacob Hostetter," weights, pendulum, and

key, touch-up and repair to face, feet replaced, minor repairs, 99-3/4" h **14,300.00**

Benjamin Willard, cherry, old mellow refinishing, arched top, bonnet with freestanding fluted columns with brass trim and stop fluting, molded curved cornice with fretwork and brass finials on plinths, overlapping door, moldings between sections, scrolled apron, bracket feet with replaced foot pads, brass works, brass face with engraved eagle and cast floral scroll-work detail, engraved "Benja. Willard, Grafton" and "Tempus Fugit" under eagle and "No. 114" on second-hand dial, calendar movement with weights, key, and cast-lead pendulum with "Willard" label, 89" h **38,500.00**

Connecticut, early 19th C, grain painted, pine case, shaped scrolled crest over glazed tombstone door, painted wooden dial, Arabic and Roman numeral chapter ring, gilt and red spandrels below arch with gilt Masonic symbols over the waist with arched door, boxed base with cut-out feet joined by scrolled skirt, allover red and black graining simulating rosewood, wooden 30-hour movement, some paint loss to dial, 15" w, 10" d, 84" h **2,990.00**

Federal, Elisha Smith, Sanbornton, NH, early 19th C, birch inlaid, hood with flat cornice molding door above two quarter-fan inlays, glazed tombstone door enclosing pained iron moon phase dial with seconds hand, calendar aperture, inscribed "Elisha Smith Sanbornton," flanked by freestanding columns, rect molded waist door with bird's eye maple veneer and mahogany cross-banded border flanked by reeded quarter columns on base with cut-out fee over which cast brass hairy paw feet have been added, old finish, dial repainted, lacks fretwork, 83" h **2,990.00**

George III

English, late 18th C, unsigned works, two-train movement, subsidiary seconds dial, date aperture and moon phrases in arch, dentil-molded swan's neck cresting, mahogany case inlaid with checkered banding, freestanding ebonized column form supports, gilt bronze mounts, 94" h **7,500.00**

English, William Nash, Bridge, works signed, brass and steel face with

date aperture and seconds dial, inlaid mahogany case with swan's neck cresting, columnar supports, cross-banded door inlaid with shell, bracket feet, 85" h **6,900.00**

Provincial, works signed by Benjamin Smith, Leeds, brass face, steel chapter ring, two-train movement, lunar arch, date dial and subsidiary seconds hand, pierced spandrels, inlaid oak case with broken arch cresting, checkered banding, inlaid with shell and fans, bracket feet, 96" h **7,495.00**

Polyphon No. 63, unusual coin-operated tall case clock, uses 11-1/4" metal discs to produce music, c1900, **$13,300.** *Photo courtesy of Auction Team Breker.*

Scottish, mahogany and gilt bronze mounted, dial sgd "Alexander Farquharson, Edinburgh," steel-etched face with date aperture and seconds dial, case with broken pediment cresting, dentil mounting, two columnar supports with gilt capitals, shaped long door, bracket feet, 89" h **2,800.00**

Hepplewhite

A. Read, country, cherry with old mellow refinishing, bonnet with turned front columns and reeded pilasters in back, broken arch pediment and chip carving on arch, waist with chamfered corners, lamb's tongues and molded edge door, molding between sections, cutout feet and apron, painted wood face labeled "A. Read & Co. Xenia, Ohio," polychrome flowers and vintage dec, wooden works replaced with electric movement, age crack in base, minor pierced repairs, 94-1/2" h **4,400.00**

Ephraim Willard, mahogany with inlay, bonnet with freestanding front columns with brass stop fluting, molded curved cornice with fretwork and brass finials on fluted plinths, fluted quarter columns with brass fittings and brass stop fluting and molded edge door in base, molding between sections, base molding, ogee feet, stringing inlay with invected corners, brass works with second hand and calendar movements, painted steel face with polychrome flowers and birds, labeled "Warranted by Em. Willard," weights, pendulum, and key, repairs to feet, pierced repair where lock was removed on waist door, minor repairs to bonnet, 93-3/4" h **33,000.00**

Simon Willard, mahogany with stringing and fans inlay, old finish, bonnet with fluted quarter columns, molded-arch cornice and fretwork with fluted plinths, brass trim and stop fluting, eagle finials, molded edge door and fluted quarter columns, base moldings and moldings between sections, ogee feet, brass works with calendar movement, second hand and painted steel face with rocking ship with American flag, face labeled "S. Willard," weights, pendulum,

and key, center plinth and fretwork restored, minor repairs to feet and age cracks in base, 94" h **55,000.00**

Queen Anne, Rhode Island, c1785-1810, mahogany, block and shell carved case, dial engraved "Caleb Wheaton Providence," arched molded cornice capped by three gilded carved urn and flame finials above glazed door, silver-plate brass dial with second and date hands, eight-day time and strike movement, dial engraved with maker's name, location centered in arch below bird flanked by engraved scythe and hour glass on left, indistrince profile of Chronos on right, surmounted by Latin "Ab hoc memento pendet aeternitas" (translates to "Eternity depends on this moment"), bonnet flanked by two sets of fluted columns above shell carved and blocked waist door, paneled base, ogee bracket feet, old surface, 91-3/4" h case, minor imperfections **266,500.00**

Victorian, English works, c1900, retailed by Tiffany & Co., three-train movement, quarter strike, lunar phrases in arch, mahogany case with ogee molded cresting, glass door, stepped plinth, 91" h, missing four tubes **2,300.00**

Travel, Elgin, 20th C, 2-1/2" sq, Stratford movement, sq sterling-silver case, black-enameled lid with central rose spray, engine-turned face, octagonal bezel, leaf engraved spandrels **150.00**

Wall

America

E. Howard & Co., Boston, c1870, banjo, rosewood grained, molded wooden bezel, white painted metal dial inscribed "E. Howard & Co., Boston," number 3 weight-driven movement, tapering maroon and black eglomise throat glass and lower tablet with rounded sides framed by half-round moldings, orig label, movement stamped by maker, very minor imperfections, 28-3/4" h **3,750.00**

E. Ingraham & Co., Bristol, CT, c1870, gilt gesso, molded circular glazed frame, white painted metal dial, eight-day spring driven movement, minor imperfections, 20" d **1,955.00**

Massachusetts, c1815, Federal, banjo, mahogany, case with brass

bevel, iron painted dial, eight-day brass weight driven movement, "I" bridge escapement above tapering throat, pendulum box with eglomise tablets with navel battle with *Constitution* and *Guerriere*, flanking gilt reserve titled "Hull," (for Issac Hull) framed by cross-banded moldings, flanked by pierced-brass side pieces, restorations, 33-1/4" h . . . **1,955.00**

Tall case, Chester County, PA, 18th C, walnut, double scroll top, rosettes, three-flame urn finials, arched brass face with moon phases, engraved leaves and flowers, sweep second hand, signed "Eli Bentley, West Whiteland," rectangular lip molded waist door, recessed panel below, quarter round fluted corners, ogival bracket feet, 96" h, $15,000. Photo courtesy of Freeman/Fine Arts.

English, W. Morrison, London, mahogany regulator, 19th C, 66-1/2" h **1,955.00**

French, mid-19th C

Derval, two-train weight-driven moment, enamel dial sgd "Felix Loudiere a Derval," large pressed metal surround with flower basket, diapered C-scroll and paterae, later bracket, oversized pressed metal pendulum with similar detailing, 12-3/8" w, 17" h clock, 39" l pendulum **690.00**

Mobilier, 19th C, enamel dial sgd "Antoine Fournier à Mèneton," gold-painted pressed tin surround, weighted two-train movement, large banjo-shaped tin pendulum pressed with flowers above floral basket, 16" l clock, 43-1/2" l pendulum **500.00**

Piradelles, two-train weight-driven movement, enamel dial sgd "J. Belin a Piradelles," center of dial with floral spray, large pressed metal surround, with urn, wheat shaves, and grape vines, later bracket, oversized pressed-metal pendulum with similar detailing, 13-3/4" w, 18-1/4" clock, 44" l pendulum **460.00**

CLOISONNÉ

History: Cloisonné is the art of enameling on metal. The design is drawn on the metal body, then wires, which follow the design, are glued or soldered on. The cells thus created are packed with enamel and fired; this step is repeated several times until the level of enamel is higher than the wires. A buffing and polishing process brings the level of enamels flush to the surface of the wires.

This art form has been practiced in various countries since 1300 B.C. and in the Orient since the early 15th century. Most cloisonné found today is from the late Victorian era, 1870-1900, and was made in China or Japan.

Reference: Lawrence A. Cohen and Dorothy C. Ferster, *Japanese Cloisonné*, Charles E. Tuttle Co., 1990.

Collectors' Club: Cloisonné Collectors Club, P.O. Box 96, Rockport, MA 01966.

Periodical: *Orientalia Journal*, P.O. Box 94, Flushing, NY 11363-0094, http://members.aol.com/Orientalia/index.html.

Museum: George Walter Vincent Smith Art Museum, Springfield, MA.

Box, cov

4-3/4" d, 2-3/4" h, rounded form, butterflies among flowering

branches, turquoise ground, Chinese, 19th C **345.00**

6" l, rect, rounded corners, wisteria, pines, scrolls, and birds of paradise, Japanese, inner flange separated, slight fracture to lid **325.00**

Charger, 14-1/4" d, central phoenix, red ground, lotus and dragon panels on cream ground, late 19th or early 20th C **150.00**

Cup, 4" h, ftd, butterflies and flowers, lappet borders, Chinese, 19th C **100.00**

Desk set, brush pot, pen, pen tray, blotter, and paper holder, Japanese, price for set **130.00**

Figure

7-1/4" h, prancing horse, left front leg raised, neck curved, mouth open, all over tightly scrolled lotus, Chinese, 18th/19th C, damage **320.00**

9" h, bird chariot, bronze base, Chinese **100.00**

12" h, horse head, Chinese, Qing dynasty **250.00**

21" h, prancing deer carrying two-handled vase on its back, two dragons chasing flaming pearl on rect base, Chinese, 19th/20th, losses **575.00**

Garniture, 9" h, gilt bronze urn, multicolored cloisonné foliage design, two bronze putti, onyx base, French, early 20th C **865.00**

Incense burner, 19-3/4" h, globular, three dragon-head feet, high curving handles, scrolling lotus and ancient bronzes motif, openwork lid, dragon finial, raised Quinlong six-character mark, damage **815.00**

Jar, cov, 6" h, ovoid, even green over central band of scrolling flowers, dome lid, ovoid finial, marked "Ando Jubei," 20th C **230.00**

Planter, 11" l, quatralobe, classical symbol and scroll dec, blue ground, Chinese, pr **200.00**

Scepter, 22" l, three cloisonné plaques inset with wooden cloud-carved frame, China, early 20th C **125.00**

Tea kettle, 10-1/2" h, multicolored scrolling lotus, medium-blue ground, lappets border, waisted neck with band of raised auspicious symbols between key-fret borders, floral form finial, double handles, Chinese, 19th C **690.00**

Teapot, 4-3/4" d, 3-1/4" h, central band of flowering chrysanthemums on pink

ground, shoulder with shaped cartouches of phoenix and dragon on floral and patterned ground, lower border with chrysanthemum blossom on swirling ground, flat base with three small raised feet, single chrysanthemum design, spout and handle with floral design, lid with two writhing dragons on peach-colored ground, Japanese, late 19th/early 20th C **4,025.00**

Urn, 23-3/4" h, ovoid, slightly waisted neck, peony dec, black ground, base plaque marked "Takeuchi Chubei," Japanese, late-19th C, Shichi Ho Company, Owari **690.00**

Button, red ground, 1-1/4" d, **$25.**

Vase

3 5/8" h, shouldered form, long slender neck flaring at rim, colored enamels, spider chrysanthemums and songbirds, midnight-blue ground, Japanese, Meiji period, pr **550.00**

4-3/4" h, ovoid, continual scene of geese on riverbank, flowering bushes and mountains in distance, Japanese **2,875.00**

6" h, six sided, each side with shield below floral band, alternating dragon and phoenix motif, flecked-blue ground, Japanese, early 20th C **460.00**

7-1/4" h, blood red ground, pink and white apple blossoms **145.00**

7-1/4" h, partially wireless, crane looking at reflection, mountain in background, celadon ground, Japanese **225.00**

8-1/2" h, 3-1/8" d, dark colors, wide rust band, small colored flowers, bird in flight, goldstone in band, other bands of dainty flowers, pr **425.00**

8 7/8" h, flattened ovoid, large cartouches of dragon with serpent and phoenix flying among vines, surrounded by flowering vines, black ground, Japanese, Meiji period **8,350.00**

9 1/8" h, angled shoulder, ovoid, waisted neck, multicolored flowering chrysanthemum, bright blue ground, Meiji period, Ota, minor crazing **1,380.00**

9 5/8" h Angular baluster, single naturalistic scene of songbirds among flowering trees and bushes, midnight-blue ground, lappet foot and rim borders, Japanese, early 20th C **1,725.00**

High-angled shoulder, straight sides, short-waisted neck, eagle perched on flowering cherry tree, wisteria and bamboo below, dark-blue ground, lappet borders above and below, late 19th C, pr **2,300.00**

10" h, silver wire dec, slender iris, deep-blue ground, Japanese, base sgd "Obei Tsukuru," scratches, fracture **375.00**

12" h, slender ovoid, waisted neck and foot, beetle and cricket resting on flowering branches, midnight-blue ground, Japanese, early 20th C **1,955.00**

12-1/4" h, ovoid, waisted neck, inverted rim, two songbirds among prunus and bamboo, colored enamels with silver wire, dark-blue ground, stamped silver rim, wire Ando Jubei mark on base, Meiji period, orig fitted box **4,975.00**

CLOTHING AND CLOTHING ACCESSORIES

History: While museums and a few private individuals have collected clothing for decades, it is only recently that collecting clothing has achieved a widespread popularity. Clothing reflects the social attitudes of a historical period.

Christening and wedding gowns abound and, hence, are not in large demand. Among the hardest items to find are men's clothing from the 19th and early 20th centuries. The most sought after clothing is by designers, such as Fortuny, Poirret, and Vionnet.

References: LaRue Johnson Bruton, *Ladies' Vintage Accessories*, Collector Books, 2000; Blanche Cirker (ed.), *1920s Fashions From B. Altman & Company*, Dover, 1999; Paula Jean Darnell, *Victorian to Vamp, Women's Clothing 1900-1929*, Fabric Fancies, 2000; Roseann Ettinger, *Handbags*, 3rd ed., Schiffer

Publishing, 1999; Roselyn Gerson, *Vintage & Contemporary Purse Accessories*, Collector Books, 1997; —, *The Estée Lauder Solid Perfume Compact Collection, 1967 to 2001*, Collector Books, 2001; —, *Vintage & Vogue Ladies Compacts*, 2nd ed., Collector Books, 2000; —, *Vintage Vanity Bags and Purses*, Collector Books, 1994, 1997 value update; Michael Jay Goldberg, *The Ties That Blind*, Schiffer Publishing, 1997; Carol Belanger Grafton, *Fashions of the Thirties*, Dover Publications, 1993; —, *Shoes, Hats and Fashion Accessories*, Dover Publications, 1998; —, *Victorian Fashion: A Pictorial Archive*, Dover Publications, 1999; Helenka Gulshan, *Vintage Luggage*, Phillip Wilson Publishers, 1998; Kristina Harris, *Authentic Victorian Dressmaking Techniques*, Dover Publications, 1999; —, *Collector's Guide to Vintage Fashions*, Collector Books, 1999; —, *Victorian & Edwardian Fashions for Women*, Schiffer Publishing, 1995; —, *Vintage Fashions for Women*, Schiffer Publishing, 1996; Richard Holiner, *Antique Purses*, Collector Books, 1999 value update; Erhard Klepper, *Costume Through the Ages*, Dover Publications, 1999; Elizabeth Kurella, *The Complete Guide to Vintage Textiles*, Krause Publications, 1999; Susan Langley, *Vintage Hats & Bonnets, 1770-1970*, Collector Books, 1997, 1999 value update; Ellie Laubner, *Fashions of the Roaring '20s*, Schiffer Publishing, 1996; —, *Fashions of the Turbulent 1930s*, Schiffer Publishing, 2000; Jan Lindenberger, *Clothing & Accessories from the '40s, '50s, & '60s*, Schiffer Publishing, 1996; Sally C. Luscomb, *The Collector's Encyclopedia of Buttons*, Schiffer Publishing, 1997; Roseanna Mihalick, *Collecting Handkerchiefs*, Schiffer Publishing, 2000; Laura M. Mueller, *Collector's Encyclopedia of Compacts, Carryalls & Face Powder Boxes*, Collector Books, Vol. I (1999 values), Vol. II (1997 values); Herbert Norris, *Ancient European Costume and Fashion*, Dover Publications, 1999; Mary Brooks Picken, *A Dictionary of Costume and Fashion: Historic and Modern*, Dover, 1999; Leslie Piña, Lorita Winfield, and Constance Korosec, *Beads in Fashion, 1900-2000*, Schiffer Publishing, 1999; Maureen Reilly, *California Couture*, Schiffer Publishing, 2000; —, *Hot Shoes, 100 Years*, Schiffer Publishing, 1998; Desire Smith, Desire Smith, *Fashion Footwear, 1800-1970*, Schiffer Publishing, 2000; —, *Hats*, Schiffer Publishing, 1996; —, *Vintage Styles: 1920-1960*, Schiffer Publishing, 1997; Pamela Smith, *Vintage Fashion & Fabrics*, Alliance Publishers, 1995; Jeffrey B. Snyder, *Stetson Hats & The John B. Stetson Company 1865-1970*, Schiffer Publishing, 1997; Diane Snyder-Haug, *Antique & Vintage Clothing*, Collector Books, 1996; Geoffrey Warren, *Fashion & Accessories, 1840-1980*, Schiffer Publishing, 1997; Lorita Winfield, Leslie Pina, and Constance Korosec, *Beads on Bags, 1880s to 2000*, Schiffer Publishing, 2000; Debra Wisniewski, *Antique and Collectible Buttons*, Collector Books, 1997.

Periodicals: *Glass Slipper*, 653 S. Orange Ave., Sarasota, FL 34236; *Lady's Gallery*, P.O. Box 1761, Independence, MO 64055; *Lill's Vintage Clothing Newsletter*, 19 Jamestown Drive, Cincinnati, OH 45241; *Vintage Clothing Newsletter*, P.O. Box 88892, Seattle, WA 98138; *Vintage Connection*, 904 N. 65th St., Springfield, OR 97478; *Vintage Gazette*, 194 Amity St., Amherst, MA 01002.

Collectors' Clubs: Textile Group of Los Angeles, Inc., 894 S. Bronson Ave., Los Angeles CA 9005-3605; The Costume Society of America, P.O. Box 73, Earleville, MD 21919, http://www.costumesocietyamerica.com; Vintage Fashion and Costume Jewelry Club, P.O. Box 265, Glen Oaks, NY 11004.

Museums: Bata Shoe Museum, Toronto, Canada; Fashion Institute of Technology, New York, NY; Los Angeles County Museum (Costume and Textile Dept.), Los Angeles, CA; Metropolitan Museum of Art, New York, NY; Museum of Costume, Bath, England; Philadelphia Museum of Art, Philadelphia, PA; Smithsonian Institution (Inaugural Gown Collection), Washington, DC; Wadsworth Atheneum, Hartford, CT; Whiting and Davis Handbag Museum, Attleboro Falls, MA.

Additional Listings: See *Warman's Americana & Collectibles* for more examples.

Note: Condition, size, age, and completeness are critical factors in purchasing clothing. Collectors divide into two groups: those collecting for aesthetic and historic value and those desiring to wear the garment. Prices are higher on the West coast; major auction houses focus on designer clothes and high-fashion items.

Bed jacket, peach silk, lace trim **40.00**

Bodice, green and lilac floral silk print on black ground, stays, cream linen lining, black glass beading, trimmed in front with panel of green silk, c1890, damage to green silk panel **45.00**

Bonnet, white lawn, lace and embroidery, pink silk ribbon, white organdy lining, wire frame, c1890 . . . . **45.00**

Braces (suspenders), needlepoint on canvas, floral rose, lilac, tangerine, and green pattern, ivory silk lining, 26" l **275.00**

Cape

Black silk crepe, lined with gray silk crepe, black fur collar, black braided satin alternating with black fur trim, c1900 . . . . **145.00**

Etched silk velvet, black floral pattern, tan and black silk faille ground, long black chenille fringe trim at sleeves and back, soutache at cuffs, silk velvet lining, c1850, some fringe loose. **200.00**

Capelet, cream lace over pink silk chiffon, tie at neckline, c1900 . . . **45.00**

Coat, woman's

Black silk crepe, embroidered with irid black glass beads, labeled "Ray Morris, New York," c1925 . . . . **90.00**

Black velvet, raglan sleeves, tangerine and gray satin lining, c1950 . . . . **70.00**

Crinoline, wire, tan and brown tapes, c1870, some rust **60.00**

Dress, afternoon

One piece, brown silk brocade, glass beading on bodice, stays, brown polished cotton lining, c1890 . . . . **195.00**

One piece, cream linen, hand-made lace insert, eyelet lace with embroidery, 18 cream crocheted buttons up front, c1900 . . . . **140.00**

One piece, navy blue silk, cream pin stripes, cream lace yoke, bright green silk trim, green silk covered buttons, detailing on bodice, navy blue knotted string fringe on skirt, c1900 . . . . **185.00**

One piece, white dotted swiss, white lawn and ruffles trim, drawn work on bodice and skirt, c1900 . . **90.00**

One piece, white lawn, embroidery and lace trim, white cotton petticoat with ruffles and crocheted lace, c1900, small holes on skirt **85.00**

Two piece rose and cream silk, lace, pleated ruffle on bodice, elaborate ruching on skirt and train, pleated hem, lined with light tan polished cotton, c1870, some fading **350.00**

Two piece sailor blue wool twill, trimmed with cream wool challis, pleated hem, cream tulle cuffs, bow trim, blue and cream polished cotton lining, c1890, some facing, small holes **225.00**

Dress, bustle, two piece, slate gray silk, steel beading on shoulders, cut steel buttons up the front of bodice, fully lined in tan linen and cotton, full bustle skirt, pleated hem, c1870, some buttons missing **375.00**

Dress, day, crepe, lilac, wrap step, lilac silk satin trim, floral pattern satin embroidery with pale yellow and lilac, c1925 . . . . **45.00**

Dress, evening, golden silk chiffon, crocheted lace, white glass beading, tiers of smocked ruffles of silk chiffon on skirt, dropped waistline, c1925, some damage, discoloration **85.00**

Etui, 4-5/8" l, serpentine oblong form, vertical panels of incised mother-of-pearl offset by ormolu bands engraved with cartouches, florals, and masks, incised mother-of-pearl mounts to base and lid with ball finials, bale handle, interior fitted with utensils and pistol grip pen knife, Continental, mid-19th C **1,150.00**

Suit, blouse, jacket, and bustle skirt, brown and cream floral print silk skirt, lined with brown cotton with bustle inside lining, sleeveless blouse with lace, brown velvet jacket with tan and brown embroidery, c1870 . . . . . **150.00**

Dress, visiting

One piece, white organdy, black floral pattern embroidery, decorative stitching on bodice, tiered and ruffled skirt, wide black silk sash, c1900 . . . . **90.00**

Two piece, light brown silk faille, copper glass beading, brown soutache on bodice, leg-of-mutton sleeves, stays, brown cotton lining, hem ruffle, c1890 . . . . **250.00**

Gown

Lawn, cream, drawn work, embroidered zigzag and geometric patterns in white glass beads, pin tucks, sleeves open at the shoulder, c1915 . . . . **145.00**

Satin, black, gold embroidered tulle overlay on skirt, embroidered tulle covered bodice, c1940, some damage, loose threads **85.00**

Silk, black silk chiffon, elaborately embroidered with black glass beads, c1915, braided glass belt **125.00**

Silk, light tan, leg-of-mutton sleeves, blue and green satin embroidery, gold metallic lace yoke, c1890, small hole in skirt **75.00**

Silk, mauve sleeveless silk chiffon, heavily beaded floral design with silver and rose bubble and round glass beads, tunic style, mauve silk chiffon underpinnings, heavily beaded hem, c1930, some discoloration, wear **465.00**

Silk, two piece, cream silk, ruching and tucks on bodice, large puff sleeves, boned and lined with cream polished cotton, skirt lined with stiffened gauze, c1865, two small holes on skirt **60.00**

Silk velvet, purple, smocking at neckline, long sleeves, rhinestone dec buttons partially up back, on cuffs, c1935 . . . . **225.00**

Gown, tea

Floral embroidered tulle, lace insertion, lace sleeves, pin tucks on bodice, asymmetrical hem, c1915 . . . . **195.00**

Pale gray silk chiffon, elaborately embroidered with clear glass beads, long sleeves, sash with fringe, underpinnings of pale gray silk, c1910 . . . . **65.00**

White tulle, embroidered lace insertion, ruffles, fabric cov buttons on front of bodice, c1910 . . **140.00**

Purse, beadwork, dated 1837, inscription with spread-winged eagle, opalescent white ground, green grass, red and pink design, wreath of flowers on opposite side, green and gold bead fringe, 8" x 8", $525. Photo courtesy of Sanford Alderfer Auction Co.

Handbag

Alligator, brown, brass clasp, brown leather lining, c1945 . . . . **45.00**

Black silk faille, embroidered with black glass beads, matching fringe, c1900 . . . . **95.00**

Black velvet, lined with cream silk with rosettes, pierced ivory frame, c1930 . . . . **45.00**

Cream satin lace reticule, blue silk ribbon drawstring, c1910 . . . **80.00**

Floral tapestry, rose, green, and blue on cream ground, black border, brass frame with chain handle, c1940, 8-1/2" x 5-1/2" **30.00**

Leather, plastic frame molded with harlequin playing mandolin, musical instruments to one side, moon and pair of owls on other, modern red snakeskin bag, black beaded cord strap, French, 20th C, 6" w **825.00**

Microbead, oblong, beaded biblical scene of the Gleaners, beaded fringe, satin-lined interior, flat leaf cast gilt-metal frame, round link double strap, French, first half 20th C, 7-3/4" l, 18" chain **200.00**

Petit Point, floral design, rose, gold, pale tangerine, cream ground, black border, elaborate brass frame, chain handle, gray silk lining, c1920 . . . . **35.00**

Petit Point, rose, gold, mauve, lilac, and green, cream ground, tan silk lining, labeled "Jolles, Made in Austria," elaborate brass frame, clasp, and chain handle, c1940, some discoloration near frame **65.00**

Silver and enamel, Birmingham, England, 1938, maker's mark "EJH," oval, lid with lavender basse taille enamel, leather lined interior, silver link chain, monogrammed, 6-1/4" l, 3-7/8" d **250.00**

Silver and enamel mesh, R. Blackington & Co., mesh link bag, frame enameled with white geometric pattern, green squares, lavender border, interior engraved with name, silk cord strap, early 20th C, 6" w **250.00**

Suede, oblong black suede bag with engraved sterling frame set to front with rect plaques of carnelian offset by X-patterned marcasite, matching clasp above, faille lined int., suede strap, German, 20th C, 7" l, 6" w **425.00**

Hat

Chinese, black silk, red satin topknot, tangerine cotton lining, 20th C **15.00**

Fashion, aqua silk pillbox, aqua veil, colorful beads embroidery, c1960 .... **50.00**

Fashion, black velour, wide brim, black feathers, black and white ostrich plumes, c1910 ..... **95.00**

Fashion, navy blue and tan cloche, blue silk embroidered with stripes of natural straw, band of navy blue grosgrain ribbon, labeled "Gloria Hats, Paris, New York," c1920, hatbox marked "Hochschild Kohn" **55.00**

Fashion, wide-brimmed black beaver, felt base, black silk lining, elaborately trimmed with ostrich feathers, stamped "H. Leh & Co., Allentown, PA," c1910, brown hatbox **215.00**

Fashion, wide-brimmed black velvet, under brim of blue velvet, blue ostrich plume, silver stamped on the black silk lining "Dives Pomeroy & Stewart," c1910....... **150.00**

Fashion, wide-brimmed natural straw, gold grosgrain ribbon, white cotton daisies, labeled "Jean Allen," c1945 .... **35.00**

Top hat, orig box.......... **75.00**

Jacket

Silk, mauve, blue silk brocade trim, embroidered with silk satin, metallic threads in floral design, frog closures, blue silk lining, early 20th C, some fading and discoloration **50.00**

Silk velvet, purple, lined with purple silk, fabric covered buttons, patch pockets, c1890 .... **120.00**

Wool flannel, black, bolero, black taffeta lining, black fur trim, c1955 .... **65.00**

Wool, skating, navy blue, gray mother-of-pearl carved buttons, partially lined with red silk, c1890 .... **65.00**

Mantle, black silk faille and beaded net, floral embroidery with black glass beads, black glass beads, black silk lining, c1890................ **225.00**

Nightgown, blue floral print silk, c1935 .... **45.00**

Pocketbook, canvas work, Irish stitch, wool yarn, flame stitch pattern, wool lining, two double pockets bound with woven twill tape, America, late 18th C, wear, some losses **865.00**

Robe, Chinese, red wool crepe, black silk elaborately embroidered with gold metallic threads, color satin dragon and flaming pearl motif, Chinese figures and geometric shapes, lined in copper silk, c1900, some damage on yoke and shoulders **215.00**

*Shawl, paisley, allover design in vibrant colors, 131" x 61", **$325.** Photo courtesy of Sanford Alderfer Auction Co.*

Shawl

Cream silk, floral cream satin embroidery, knotted fringe, braided dec, back tassel, c1890... **150.00**

Embroidered and woven wool, paisley, plain red body embroidered in one corner with single boteh and stylized signature, border with applied band of woven scroll pattern, followed by embroidered Middle Eastern patterns, 62-1/2" x 59-1/2" . **250.00**

Ivory silk, floral ivory satin embroidery, knotted satin fringe, Spanish, c1900, 44" sq **75.00**

Woven silk taffeta, light gray plaid, rose and green satin flowers, long knotted silk fringe, c1900, 70" sq................. **125.00**

Skirt

Lace alternating with voile, black, train, underpinnings of cream silk taffeta, pinking and ruffles, c1870, some minor damage on tulle and lining.................. **150.00**

Wool, black, brown polished cotton waistband, tan printed cotton and linen lining, c1860 .... **45.00**

Sports outfit, woman's, black wool twill pants with pleats at waistline, matching middy blouse, partially lined with black cotton, c1890 .... **125.00**

Suit, gray wool tweed, fabric cov buttons, button detailing on jacket pockets, lined with pale gray crepe, flared skirt with gores, "Freiss Orig" label, c1945.................**110.00**

Umbrella

Black silk, sterling silver oblong handle with central carved ivory plaque of cavorting elephants, silver panels above and below chased and emb with navettes, engraved detailing, 11" l handle **375.00**

Black silk, silver handle formed as looped snake, Continental, English import hallmarks for London, 1904, 7-1/8" l handle, 36" l overall................. **150.00**

Gold, brown, orange, and yellow paisley ruffle, unused, orig gold and black hang tag for "Made in U.S.A., 100% Nylon," orig Strawbridge & Clothier box, c1955.................. **45.00**

Round tapered handle with stamped and engraved vertical bands of leafy scrolls and flowerheads, mother-of-pearl

central band, 7-5/8" l handle, 31" l
overall **230.00**

Vest

Black silk satin, chenille flower,
leaves, and clover embroidery,
plaid silk and polished cotton
lining, c1890 . . . . **175.00**

White cotton, mother-of-pearl
buttons, c1910 . . . . **65.00**

Waistcoat, gentleman's, silk,
embroidered with floral vines and
sprigs, two covered pockets, applied
cherub-printed roundels below,
England or France, late 18th C,
restorations **250.00**

Wedding gown

Satin, ivory, sleeveless, cut on bias,
ivory lace long sleeved jacket with
train, detailed ivory satin bows,
c1935 . . . . **375.00**

Silk, purple, long sleeves, hand
sewing, bodice lined with cream
linen, worn in 1796 by Mehitable
Lawrence, when wed to Captain
James Lawrence, Burlington
County, NJ, War of 1812 naval
hero **1,575.00**

COALPORT

History: In the mid-1750s,
Ambrose Gallimore established a
pottery at Caughley in the Severn
Gorge, Shropshire, England.
Several other potteries, including
Jackfield, developed in the area.

About 1795, John Rose and Edward Blakeway
built a pottery at Coalport, a new town founded along
the right-of-way of the Shropshire Canal. Other
potteries located adjacent to the canal were those of
Walter Bradley and Anstice, Horton, and Rose. In

1799, Rose and Blakeway bought the Royal Salopian
China Manufactory at Caughley. In 1814, this
operation was moved to Coalport.

A bankruptcy in 1803 led to refinancing and a new
name—John Rose and Company. In 1814, Anstice,
Horton, and Rose was acquired. The South Wales
potteries at Swansea and Nantgarw were added. The
expanded firm made fine-quality, highly decorated
ware. The plant enjoyed a renaissance from 1888 to
1900.

World War I, decline in trade, and shift of the
pottery industry away from the Severn Gorge brought
hard times to Coalport. In 1926, the firm, now owned
by Cauldon Potteries, moved from Coalport to
Shelton. Later owners included Crescent Potteries,
Brain & Co., Ltd., and finally, in 1967, Wedgwood.

References: Susan and Al Bagdade, *Warman's
English & Continental Pottery & Porcelain*, 3rd
Edition, Krause Publications, 1998; Michael
Messenger, *Coalport 1795-1926*, Antique Collectors'
Club, 1995; Tom Power, *The Charlton Standard
Catalogue of Coalport Figures*, 2nd Edition, Charlton
Press, 1999; —, *The Charlton Standard Catalogue of
Coalport Figures, Millennium Edition*, Charlton Press,
1999; Alf Willis, *The Charlton Standard Catalogue of
Coalport Collectables*, Charlton Press, 2000.

Collectors' Club: Coalport Collector Society, P.O.
Box 99, Sudbury, CO10 6SN England.

Museums: Cincinnati Museum of Art, Cincinnati,
OH; Coalport China Works Museum, Ironbridge Gorge
Museum Trust, Shropshire, England; Victoria & Albert
Museum, London, England.

Additional Listings: Indian Tree Pattern.

Creamer, Athione, blue **375.00**
Cream soup bowl, two handles,
Athione, blue **330.00**
Demitasse cup and saucer, quatrefoil
shape, 2-1/4" x 1-1/2" cup with ring
handle, 3-1/8" d saucer, pink, gilt
trim **350.00**
Dessert plate, 9-3/8" d, central gilt
flowerhead in holly vine roundel,
molded rim with further flowerheads

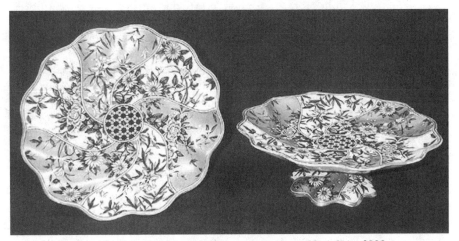

Dish, blue and white, dec with flowers and gilding, pedestal base, 10" d, 3" h, **$330.**
Photo courtesy of Joy Luke Auctions.

and rocaille, late 19th/early 20th C, set
of 12, one damaged **920.00**
Gravy boat with underplate, Indian
Tree **480.00**
Place setting, five pcs
Athione, blue **360.00**
Hazelton, white **315.00**
Indian Tree **450.00**
Platter
Athione, blue, 15-3/8" l **750.00**
Hazelton, white, round **360.00**
Indian Tree, small **450.00**
Rosalinda, large **360.00**
Sugar bowl, cov, Athione, blue . **385.00**
Vegetable dish, open, Athione, blue,
9-3/4" l, oval **470.00**
Vegetable dish, cov, Rosalinda . **435.00**

COCA-COLA ITEMS

History: The originator of Coca-Cola was John
Pemberton, a pharmacist from Atlanta, Georgia. In
1886, Dr. Pemberton introduced a patent medicine to
relieve headaches, stomach disorders, and other
minor maladies. Unfortunately, his failing health and
meager finances forced him to sell his interest.

In 1888, Asa G. Candler became the sole owner of
Coca-Cola. Candler improved the formula, increased
the advertising budget, and widened the distribution.
A "patient" was accidentally given a dose of the syrup
mixed with carbonated water instead of still water. The
result was a tastier, more refreshing drink.

As sales increased in the 1890s, Candler
recognized that the product was more suitable for the
soft-drink market and began advertising it as such.
From these beginnings, a myriad of advertising items
have been issued to invite all to "Drink Coca-Cola."

References: Chris H. Beyer, *Coca-Cola Girls*,
Collectors Press, 2000; Gael de Courtivron,
Collectible Coca-Cola Toy Trucks, Collector Books,
1995; Steve Ebner, *Vintage Coca-Cola Machines*, Vol.
II, published by author (available from FunTronics,
Inc., P.O. Box 448, Middletown, MD 21769; Bob and
Debra Henrich, *Coca-Cola Commemorative Bottles*,
2nd ed., Collector Books, 2000; Deborah Goldstein
Hill, *Price Guide to Vintage Coca-Cola® Collectibles:
1896-1965*, Krause Publications, 1999; Allan Petretti,
Classic Coca-Cola Calendars, Antique Trader Books,
1999; —, *Classic Coca-Cola Collectibles Cardboard
& Paper Signs*, Krause Publications, 2000; —,
Petretti's Coca-Cola Collectibles Price Guide, 10th
ed., Antique Trader Books, 1997; —, *Petretti's Soda
Pop Collectibles Price Guide*, 2nd ed., Antique Trader
Books, 1998; Allan Petretti and Chris Beyer, *Classic
Coca-Cola Serving Trays*, Antique Trader Books,
1999; B. J. Summers, *B. J. Summers' Guide to
Coca-Cola*, 3rd ed., Collector Books, 2000; Jeff
Walters, *Complete Guide to Collectible Picnic Coolers
& Ice Chests*, Memory Lane Publishing, 1994; Helen
and Al Wilson, *Wilson's Coca-Cola Price Guide*, 3rd
ed., Schiffer Publishing, 2000.

Collectors' Club: Cavanagh's Coca-Cola Christmas
Collector's Society, 1000 Holcomb Woods Parkway,
Suite 440B, Roswell, GA 30076; Coca-Cola Collectors

Club, 400 Monemar Ave., Baltimore, MD 21228-5213; Coca-Cola Collectors Club International, P.O. Box 49166, Atlanta, GA 30359-1166; The Coca-Cola Club, P.O. Box 158715, Nashville, TN 32715.

Museums: Coca-Cola Memorabilia Museum of Elizabethtown, Inc., Elizabethtown, KY; World of Coca-Cola Pavilion, Atlanta, GA.

Additional Listings: See *Warman's Americana & Collectibles* for more examples.

Notes: Dates of interest: "Coke" was first used in advertising in 1941. The distinctively shaped bottle was registered as a trademark on April 12, 1960.

SPECIAL AUCTIONS

Nostalgia Publications, Inc.
21 S. Lake Dr.
Hackensack, NJ 07601

Ohio Cola Traders
4411 Bazetta Rd.
Cortland, OH 44410

Badge, Bottlers Convention, 1930. . . . . **65.00**
Binder, 13" x 15-1/2", rigid cardboard, red oilcloth cover, four-ring metal binder to hold advertising sales sheets, c1950, no contents **48.00**
Blotter, 3-1/2" x 7-1/2", cardboard, full-color ski scene, copyright 1947, unused. **20.00**
Bolo tie, 14-1/2" l copper-colored thick cord, metal accent tips, relief metal center piece with smiling Kit Carson as portrayed by Bill Williams, flanked by single Coke bottle on each side, c1951. **100.00**
Bookmark, Romance of Coca-Cola, 1916. . . . . **30.00**
Bottle
  Amber, marked "Lewisburg". . **30.00**
  Christmas, Williamstown, WV . **15.00**
  Commemorative, Nascar Series, Bill Elliott, Dale Earnhardt, or Bobby Labonte **5.00**
Bottle opener, bottle shape, Glascock Mfg Co., Muncie, IN c1930 . . . . . **48.00**
Calendar, 1913, 13-1/2" x 22-1/2", Hamilton King illus. **900.00**
Change tray
  1914, Betty **150.00**
  1941, girl with skates **45.00**
  1970, Santa Claus **85.00**
Charm bracelet, 6" l, gold finished metal-link bracelet, metal miniature charms of green and white Philadelphia Eagles pennant, gold football, NHL blue and red image on gold shield, red on gold "Drink Coca-Cola" disk **20.00**

Diecut counter display, Santa with bundle of toys, holding Coke bottle, copyright 1938, 9-1/2" w, 18" h, slight water damage, some blue spotting, **$110.** *Photo courtesy of Sanford Alderfer Auction Co.*

Clock, neon, light-up type, metal frame, some weathering to case, does not run, c1942, 15-1/2" w, 4-3/4" d, 15-1/2" h. **400.00**
Door push bar, porcelain, 1960 . **85.00**
Game board
  11-1/4" x 26-1/2", Steps to Health, prepared and distributed by Coca-Cola Co. of Canada, Ltd., copyright 1938, orig unmarked brown paper envelope **60.00**
  18-1/2" x 19", India, Milton Bradley, corners with images of Coca-Cola bottle cap kid, early 1950s . . **35.00**
Magazine advertisement tear sheet
  National Geographic, Santa, c1942 . . . . **25.00**
  Success Magazine, lady driving carriage, being served Coca-Cola in glass, 1906 . . . . **65.00**
Mirror, pocket, 1-3/4" w, 2-3/4" h oval, celluloid, 1914, pretty girl, dark green ground, white and red lettering. **400.00**
Paperweight, girl in white swimsuit **80.00**
Service pin, 10 Years, 10K gold, raised image of bottle, c1930 . . . . **65.00**
Sign, round, Enjoy Coca-Cola in Bottles, metal, 1954 . . . . **4,950.00**
Thermometer, 16", "Trade Mark Registered, Bottle Pat Dec. 25, 1 923" **120.00**

Toy
  Coca-Cola dispenser, 5-1/2" x 8" x 11" hard plastic, red and white, 8" x 9-1/2" x 12-1/2" corrugated cardboard box, early 1960s. **75.00**
  Van, Corgi, 5" l diecast metal and plastic replica, copyright 1978, 2-3/4" x 6" x 3-1/2" color box with display window **35.00**
Tray
  1909, World's Fair, young lady **3,000.00**
  1917, Elaine **200.00**
  1925, girl with fur **185.00**
  1930, bathing beauty **195.00**
  1935, Madge Evans **165.00**
  1938, girl in large brimmed hat **125.00**
Vending machine
  23-5/8" x 21-5/8" x 64" h, Select-O-Matic, Westinghouse, six dial selector, bottle opener set into front, c1960 . . . . **3,200.00**
  34" x 24-1/2" x 25" h, Cooler, Beverageair, top loader, sliding glass top, chrome shelf . . **1,200.00**

COFFEE MILLS

History: Coffee mills or grinders are utilitarian objects designed to grind fresh coffee beans. Before the advent of stay-fresh packaging, coffee mills were a necessity.

The first home-size coffee grinders were introduced about 1890. The large commercial grinders designed for use in stores, restaurants, and hotels often bear an earlier patent date.

References: Edward C. Kvetko and Douglas Congdon-Martin, *Coffee Antiques,* Schiffer Publishing, 2000; Joseph Edward MacMillan, *MacMillan Index of Antique Coffee Mills,* Cherokee Publishing (657 Old Mountain Road, Marietta, GA 30064), 1995; Michael L. White and Judith A. Sivonda, *Antique Coffee Grinders: American, English and European,* Schiffer Publishing, 2001.

Collectors' Club: Association of Coffee Mill Enthusiasts, 5941 Wilkerson Road, Rex, GA 30273.

Arcade, 17" h, wall type, crystal jar, emb design, marked "Crystal" and "Arcade" orig lid rusted. **185.00**
Crown Coffee Mill, cast iron, mounted on wood base, decal "Crown Coffee Mill Made By Landers, Frary, & Clark, New Britain, Conn, U.S.A.," number 11 emb on top lid **525.00**
Enterprise, 00, 12-1/2" x 7-1/2" x 8-3/4", two wheel, store type, orig paint, orig decals, C8+. **1,450.00**
Imperial No. 705, long cast iron crank handle, domed cast iron top, molded scrolls above dovetailed case, small

Enterprise No. 1, painted black cast iron, marked "Philadelphia 1876 Exposition," $245.

drawers, remnants label above drawer, 11" h **65.00**

"J. P.," dovetailed walnut, molded edges around top, beveled edges around base, small drawer with brass pull, wrought-iron crank and plates engraved "J. P.," 7-3/4" w, 7-3/4" d, 9-1/2" h **650.00**

Pine, fingered joints, one drawer, iron pull, iron top cup and handle, wooden knob, c1880, 5-3/4" sq, 6" h **90.00**

Sun Manufacturing, Greenfield, Ohio, worn orig label, round wooden sides, cast iron hardware, directions for use, 12" h **300.00**

Tin, tole dec of tulip and stars, 12" h **250.00**

X-R, cast iron, mounted on oval board, early 1900s **250.00**

WHC emb on handle, cast iron top with handle, wooden base with drawer **95.00**

Woodruff Edwards, Elgin, IL, 66" h, store type, 28" d wheels, eagle finial, repainted **1,800.00**

COIN-OPERATED ITEMS

History: Coin-operated items include amusement games, pinball machines, jukeboxes, slot machines, vending machines, cash registers, and other items operated by coins.

The first jukebox was developed about 1934 and played 78-RPM records. Jukeboxes were important to teen-agers before the advent of portable radios and television.

The first pinball machine was introduced in 1931 by Gottlieb. Pinball machines continued to be popular until the advent of solid-state games in 1977 and advanced electronic video games after that.

The first three-reel slot machine, the Liberty Bell, was invented in 1905 by Charles Fey in San Francisco. In 1910, Mills Novelty Company copyrighted the classic fruit symbols. Improvements and advancements have led to the sophisticated machines of today.

Vending machines for candy, gum, and peanuts were popular from 1910 until 1940 and can be found in a wide range of sizes and shapes.

References: Michael Adams, Jurgen Lukas, and Thomas Maschke, *Jukeboxes*, Schiffer Publishing, 1995; Michael F. Baute, *Always Jukin' Official Guide to Collectible Jukeboxes*, published by author (221 Yesler Way, Seattle, WA 98104), 1996; Richard M. Bueschel, *Collector's Guide to Vintage Coin Machines*, Schiffer Publishing, 1995; —, *Guide to Vintage Trade Stimulators & Counter Games*, Schiffer Publishing, 1997; —, *Lemons, Cherries and Bell-Fruit-Gum*, Royal Bell Books, 1995; —, *Pinball 1*, Hoflin Publishing, 1988; —, *Slots 1*, Hoflin Publishing, 1989; Richard Bueschel and Steve Gronowski, *Arcade 1*, Hoflin Publishing, 1993; Herbert Eiden and Jurgen Lukas, *Pinball Machines*, Schiffer Publishing, 1992, values updated 1997; Bill Enes, *Silent Salesmen Too, The Encyclopedia of Collectible Vending Machines*, published by author (8520 Lewis Drive, Lenexa, KS 66227), 1995; Eric Hatchell and Dick Bueschel, *Coin-Ops on Location*, published by authors, 1993; Bill Kurtz, *Arcade Treasures*, Schiffer Publishing, 1994; Joseph E. Meyer, *Protection: The Sealed Book*, 10th ed., Mead Publishing Co., 1999.

Periodicals: *Antique Amusements Slot Machines & Jukebox Gazette*, 909 26th St. NW, Washington, DC 20037; *C.O.C.A. Times*, 3712 W. Scenic Ave., Mequon, WI 539092; *Co-Op Newsletter*, 909 26th St., NW, Washington, DC 20037.

Museum: Liberty Belle Saloon and Slot Machine Collection, Reno, NV.

Additional Listings: See *Warman's Americana & Collectibles* for separate categories for Jukeboxes, Pinball Machines, Slot Machines, and Vending Machines.

Adviser: Bob Levy.

Notes: Because of the heavy usage these coin-operated items received, many are restored or, at the very least, have been repainted by either the operator or manufacturer. Using reproduced mechanisms to restore pieces is acceptable in many cases, especially when the restored piece will then perform as originally intended.

Arcade

Fortune Teller, Princess Doraldina, Rochester, NY, c1928, 5 cent, lifelike, gives fortune **13,000.00**

Grip Tester, Shake with Your Uncle Sam, Howard, c1904, 1 cent, 66" h **17,250.00**

Photo Viewing Machine, American Mutoscope, NY, c1920, 1 cent, metal, orig photos and paper marquee **1,100.00**

Gum machines

Adams, c1934, four column, tab gum vendor, chrome, decal, 22" h . . . **100.00**

Ford, c1950, round globe, gum balls, large, organizational use, 12" h . . **75.00**

Master, c1923, 1 cent, confection, 16" h **200.00**

Penny King, c1935, four in one, rotates, Art-Deco style, four glass compartments **500.00**

Pulver, c1930, 1 cent, two-column, porcelain, stick dispenser, policeman figure rotates, 21" h **600.00**

Juke boxes

Seeburg, Model 100R, c1954, high fidelity, classic style, plays 45s **2,000.00**

Wurlitzer, Model 1015, c1946, The Bubbler **7,500.00**

Miscellaneous

Cash register, National Brass, Model 317, c1910, barber shop size, orig marquee **800.00**

Scale, American Scale, Fortune Model, c1937, 1 cent, health chart **200.00**

Slot machines

Caille, Superior, c1929, three reels, fancy design, 5 cent **1,400.00**

Groetchen, Columbia, c1936, three reels, high maintenance, 25 cent **500.00**

Jennings, Standard Chief, c1947, three reels, classic design, 10 cent **1,400.00**

Mills

    Jewel Hightop, c1948, three reels, rugged and popular style, 5 cent **1,400.00**

    Puritan Bell, c1925, cash-register design, 5 cent, 8" h, 8" w . . . **700.00**

Pace, All Star Comet, c1936, three reels, side mint vendor, 5 cent **1,400.00**

Watling, Rolatop, c1935, three reels, gold coins on front, 25 cent . . **3,200.00**

Vending machines

Card, slot dispenser, various subjects, exhibit supply, c1930, table top, 12" h, 10" w **225.00**

Cigarettes, Advance, c1930, 15 cent, 30" h, 14" w **100.00**

Schokoladen-Fabrik, German chocolate vending machine, c1900, $3,150. Photo courtesy of Auction Team Breker.

Coke, Vendo V81, c1955, 6-1/2, 8- or 10-oz bottles, orig condition . . **1,200.00**

Food, Horn and Hardart Automat Dispenser, c1902, four-item unit **1,200.00**

Matches, Edwards Mfg Co., c1930, Diamond, one to four books, 13-1/2" h **225.00**

Nut, Ajax, Newark, NH, c1947, three-unit vendor, serves hot nuts, 21-1/2" h **300.00**

Pen, Vendorama, Victor Corp, c1962, oak case, 20" h, 14" w **100.00**

Perfume, Perfumatic, c1950, four fragrances, 10 cent spray, pink, 16" h, 18" w **325.00**

Stamp, Dillion Mfg, c1930, two selections, 12" x 12" **75.00**

COMIC BOOKS

History: Shortly after comics first appeared in newspapers of the 1890s, they were reprinted in book format and often used as promotional giveaways by manufacturers, movie theaters, and candy and stationery stores. The first modern-format comic was issued in 1933.

The magic date in comic collecting is June 1938, when DC issued Action Comics No. 1, marking the first appearance of Superman. Thus began the Golden Age of comics, which lasted until the mid-1950s and witnessed the birth of the major comic-book publishers, titles, and characters.

In 1954, Fredric Wertham authored *Seduction of the Innocent*, a book which pointed a guilt-laden finger at the comics industry for corrupting youth, causing juvenile delinquency, and undermining American values. Many publishers were forced out of business, while others established a "comics code" to assure parents that their comics were compliant with morality and decency standards upheld by the code authority.

The silver age of comics, mid-1950s through the end of the 1960s, witnessed the revival of many of the characters from the Golden Age in new comic formats. The era began with Showcase No. 4 in October 1956, which marked the origin and first appearance of the Silver-Age Flash.

While comics survived into the 1970s, it was a low point for the genre; but in the early 1980s, a revival occurred. In 1983, comic-book publishers, other than Marvel and DC, issued more titles than had existed in total during the previous 40 years. The mid- and late-1980s were a boom time, a trend which appears to be continuing.

References: *Comic Buyer's Guide Annual*, Krause Publications, issued annually; Ron Goulart, *Comic Book Culture: An Illustrated History*, Collectors Press, 2000; Alex G. Malloy, *Comics Values Annual 1999*, 6th ed., Antique Trader Books, 1998, and *Comics Values Annual 2002*, Krause Publications, 2002; John Jackson Miller, Brent Frankenhoff, Maggie Thompson, and Peter Bickford, *Standard Catalog of Comic Books*, Krause Publications, 2002; Robert M. Overstreet, *Overstreet Comic Book Price Guide*, 29th ed., Avon Books, 1999; —, *The Overstreet Comic Grading Guide*, published by author, 1999; Don and Maggie Thompson (eds.), *Comic Book Superstars*, Krause Publications, 1993; —— (eds.), *Marvel Comics Checklist & Price Guide*, Krause Publications, 1993; Maggie Thompson and Brent Frankenhoff, *2001 Comic Book Checklist & Price Guide*, 7th ed., Krause Publications, 2000; Maggie Thompson and John Jackson Miller, *Comic Buyer's Guide 1997 Annual*, 6th ed., Krause Publications, 1996; Stuart W. Wells, III, *Science Fiction Collectibles: Identification & Price Guide*, Krause Publications, 1999; *X-Men—Collector Handbook and Price Guide*, Checkerboard Publishing.

Periodicals: *Archie Fan Magazine*, 185 Ashland St., Holliston, MA 01746; *Comic Book Market Place*, P.O. Box 180900, Coronado, CA 92178; *Comics Buyer's Guide*, 700 E. State St., Iola, WI 54990, http://www.krause.com; *Comics Interview*, 234 Fifth Ave., New York, NY 10001; *Comics Journal*, 7563 Lake City Way, Seattle, WA 98115, http://www.tcj.com; *Comics Source*, P.O. Box 2512, Chattanooga, TN 37409; *Duckburg Times*, 3010 Wilshire Blvd. #362, Los Angeles, CA 90010; *Overstreet Comic Book Marketplace*, 1996 Greenspring Drive, Suite 405, Timonium, MD 21093-4117; *Overstreet's Advanced Collector*, 1996 Greenspring Drive, Suite 405, Timonium, MD 21093-4117; *Western Comics Journal*, 1703 N. Aster Place, Broken Arrow, OK 74012; *Wizard: The Guide To Comics*, 151 Wells Ave., Congers, NY 10920.

Collectors' Clubs: American Comics Exchange, 351-T Baldwin Rd, Hempstead, NY 11550; Fawcett Collectors of America, P.O. Box 24751, Minneapolis, MN 55424-0751, http://shazam.imginc.com/fca.

Museums: International Museum of Cartoon Art, 300 SE 5th Ave., #5150, Boca Raton, FL 33432; Museum of Cartoon Art, Rye, NY.

Reproduction Alert: Publishers frequently reprint popular stories, even complete books, so the buyer must pay strict attention to the title, not just the portion printed in oversized letters on the front cover. If there is any doubt, look inside at the fine print on the bottom of the inside cover or first page. The correct title will be printed there in capital letters.

Also pay attention to the dimensions of the comic book. Reprints often differ in size from the original.

Note: The comics listed below are in near-mint condition, meaning they have a flat, clean, shiny cover that has no wear other than tiny corner creases; no subscription creases, writing, yellowing at margins, or tape repairs; staples are straight and rust free; pages are supple and like new; generally just-off-the-shelf quality.

Tarzan #137, August 1963, Edgar Rice Burrough, K. K. Publications, $8.

Action, #298	200.00
Adventures Into the Unknown, #30	145.00
Adventures of Rex the Wonder Dog, #5	500.00
Amazing Tales, #2	275.00
Amazing Detective Stories, #13	425.00
Amazing Spider-Man, #22	325.00
Atom, #35	26.00
Atomic Mouse, #2	115.00
Avengers, #24	200.00
Daredevil, #9	340.00
DC Super Spectacular, #20	80.00
Diary Loves, #2	85.00
Durango Kid, #7	150.00
Famous Crimes, #4	100.00
Fantastic Four, #20	200.00
Fighting Americans, #1, 1996	100.00
Flame, #5	400.00
Flash Gordon, #16	18.00
Forbidden Love, #2	325.00
Forbidden Worlds, #8	450.00
Four Color, #324	90.00
GI Joe I Battle, #1	60.00
Green Lantern, #27	125.00
Justice League of America, #14	150.00
Leave It To Beaver, #1285	320.00
Little Orphan Annie, #1	90.00
Mad, #20	1,500.00
Marvel Premiere, #1	160.00
Modern Comics, #98	200.00
My Greatest Adventure, #24	195.00
Mystery in Space, #66	410.00
Mystic, #54	185.00
Our Army At War, #21	135.00

Rawhide Kid, #49	100.00
Rip Hunter, #13	65.00
Sea Devils, #54	125.00
Six Gun Heroes, #81	12.00
Space Squadron, #5	395.00
Spellbound, #33	165.00
Strange Adventures, #7	45.00
Strange Tales, #57	265.00
Super Boy, #88	100.00
Superman, #109	410.00
X-Men-14, #18	560.00
X-Men-24, #60	74.00

COMPACTS

History: In the first quarter of the 20th century, attitudes regarding cosmetics changed drastically. The use of make-up during the day was no longer looked upon with disdain. As women became "liberated," and as more and more of them entered the business world, the use of cosmetics became a routine and necessary part of a woman's grooming. Portable containers for cosmetics became a necessity.

Compacts were made in myriad shapes, styles, combinations and motifs, all reflecting the mood of the times. Every conceivable natural or man-made material was used in the manufacture of compacts. Commemorative, premium, souvenir, patriotic, figural, Art Deco, and enamel compacts are a few examples of the types of compacts that were made in the United States and abroad. Compacts combined with other forms, such as cigarette cases, music boxes, watches, hatpins, canes, and lighters, also were very popular.

Compacts were made and used until the late 1950s, when women opted for the "au naturel" look. The term "vintage" is used to describe the compacts from the first half of the 20th century as distinguished from contemporary examples.

References: Juliette Edwards, *Compacts*, published by author, 1994; Roselyn Gerson, *Ladies Compacts*, Wallace-Homestead, 1996; —, *The Estée Lauder Solid Perfume Compact Collection, 1967 to 2001*, Collector Books, 2001; ——, *Vintage and Contemporary Purse Accessories, Solid Perfumes, Lipsticks, & Mirrors*, Collector Books, 1997; ——, *Vintage Ladies Compacts*, Collector Books, 1996; ——, *Vintage Vanity Bags and Purses: An Identification and Value Guide*, 1994, 1997 value update, Collector Books; Frances Johnson, *Compacts, Powder and Paint*, Schiffer Publishing, 1996; Laura M. Mueller, *Collector's Encyclopedia of Compacts, Carryalls & Face Powder Boxes* (1994, 1999 value update), Vol. II (1997), Collector Books.

Collectors' Club: Compact Collectors Club, P.O. Box 40, Lynbrook, NY 11563.

Additional Listings: See *Warman's Americana & Collectibles* for more examples.

Adviser: Roselyn Gerson.

Art Deco, 15-1/4" l, rect black plastic case, lid engraved with roses, set with colorless faceted pastes, center green chrysophrase roundel, opening to int. fitted with compact and two smaller

Walt Disney's Comics & Stories, Dell, #131, **$4.50.**

lipsticks, one bearing paper label, acanthus-shaped open work and paste set clasp, black cord handle, large black tassel enclosing cylindrical perfume case with small glass flask, French, 1930s **650.00**
Austrian, vanity bag, 3-3/4" x 2", silver and enamel, sectioned rect, ext. with cobalt blue enamel on sunburst ground flanked by enameled on engine-turning, central medallion of bird in star and swag circle, amethyst-colored cabochon thumbpiece, int. with two small sections, larger mirrored section, Austrian **650.00**
BOAC, British Overseas Airways Corp, 3" d, gold, black leatherette, gold metal logo, framed mirror, BOAC puff, royal blue felt cover **65.00**
Celluloid, unknown maker
> 1-1/2" d, 1-1/2" h, powder box, ornate wreath and fleur-de-lis motif, pink and white cameo lid ... **40.00**
> 2" sq, metal compact, celluloid top showing pastoral scene with lovers, c1940 .... **45.00**
> 3" d, orange compact studded with floral rhinestone motif **45.00**
> 5" celluloid diamond shaped purse, 2" tassel and silk cord, mottled cream, green and brown with oval cameo attached to center top, mirror, powder puff and chrome scent vial **275.00**
Coty, #405, envelope box **65.00**
Daniel, black leather, portrait of lady encased in plastic dome, Paris .. **90.00**
Djer Kiss, with fairy **95.00**
Estee Lauder, compact necklace, oval silvertone engraved pendant suspended from ornate silvertone ball and tube chain, orig solid fragrance **45.00**
Evans, goldtone, heart shape, black twisted carrying cord, lipstick concealed in black tassel suspended from bottom **250.00**
Fifth Avenue, vanity case "Cosmetist," aquamarine enamel, powder, rouge, lipstick, cleansing cream, and mascara, England **175.00**
Flato, 2-1/2" x 2-1/4" x 1/2", goldtone, faux emerald fir tree bijoux, framed mirror, marked "Flato" inside **95.00**
Foster & Bailey, Providence, anity case
> Blue cloisonné suspended from enameled perfume container, powder and rouge compartments, lipstick attached at base, tassel and black enameled finger carrying ring **950.00**

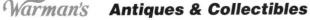

Sterling silver and enamel, 3-1/2" x 2", rect, canted corners, lid enameled in center over diamond-shaped starburst ground, vase of roses on white ground, bordered by turquoise enamel cornered by roses, green cabochon thumbpiece open to hinged mirror, off-center hinged double compartment each with cabochon thumbpiece, braided wrist chain, c1880 . **800.00**

Gray, Dorothy, engine turned goldtone, hat shape, ribbon and fruit dec. . **80.00**

Halston, SP, name on puff, used **150.00**

Italian, hand-mirror shape, SS, stylized floral engraving, lipstick concealed in handle, coral cabochon thumb piece **325.00**

Kigu, lady swinging **45.00**

Lampi, light blue enamel, five colorful three-dimensional scenes from *Alice in Wonderland* enclosed in plastic domes on lid **180.00**

Lucite, sq, colorless, sterling silver roundel, two Jensen-style doves . **95.00**

Marin, Paris, .800 silver, sq, obverse with engraved figure of Orion, faceted red and orange stones in pattern of constellation, reverse with engine turned dec, 3-1/8" l, early 20th C **150.00**

Max Factor, 2-1/4" d, solid perfume, round faux jade pendant, goldtone twisted braided wire disk, orig Khara fragrance **35.00**

Norida, emb lady, silver tone . . . **75.00**

Rex Fifth Avenue, vanity-pochette, navy blue, gold polka dots, taffeta drawstring, mirror on outside base **90.00**

R. G. & Co., vanity case, SS, yellow cloisonné enamel, finger chain, painted flowers on lid, chain, perfume tube suspended from enameled and silver finger ring chain **290.00**

Schildraut, seed-pearl design . . **55.00**

Sterling silver, 2-18" d round compact with lid enameled to center with 18th C lady, white basse taille surrounded with black border, opening to mirror and makeup compartment, strung with white chord suspending 2-1/8" l white basse taille lipstick case, American, 20th C **175.00**

Tiffany & Co., Art Deco, sterling silver, gold, and sapphire, sq engraved lineal design, surmounted by gold and sapphire crescent, mirror and powder compartment, sgd **450.00**

Enamel, hexagonal-shaped case made of .935 silver, chased dec, luminous enamel panel with woman, putti, doves, flowers, and cloudy sky, 3-1/2" x 3". $1,550. Photo courtesy of Sanford Alderfer Auction Co.

Unknown maker, compact
Castanets shape, ebony wood, metal Paris insignia centered on lid, orange tasseled carrying cord **220.00**
Flamingo motif **90.00**
Sterling silver, chain handle . . . **90.00**
Telephone-dial shape, red, white, and blue, slogan "I Like Ike" imprinted on lid, red map of USA on lid center **225.00**
Wagon wheel, 4-1/2" d, goldtone, framed mirror, powder screen, orig puff, felt cover **55.00**

Unknown maker, compact, English, Birmingham, sterling silver and enamel
2-1/8" x 3", rect, enameled pale green over scalloped sunburst ground stemming from thumbpiece **250.00**
2-1/2" sq, canted corners, green enamel over "L"-shaped engine-turning, scalloped sunray issuing from scrolls, c1940 . . . . **225.00**
2-7/8" sq, canted corners, blue enamel over spiraling engine-turning, central nautical flag with crown **250.00**

Unknown maker, compact, Europe, early 20th C, silver, 800 silver
Oval, enameled violet on lid, int. mounted with mirrors, 2-3/8" l, 1-1/2" w, losses to int. **290.00**

Quadrangular with shaped edges, engraved lid with polychrome enamel genre scene, underside with engraved foliates, gilt interior with mirror mounted to lid, 3" l **300.00**

Unknown maker, powder tier, silvertone triple tier vanity case, swivel compartments for powder, rouge, and lipstick **195.00**

Unknown maker, vanity bag, SS mesh, hallmarked, octagonal, goldtone int. and finger ring carrying chain . . **500.00**

Unknown maker, vanity case, antique goldtone, two sided filigree, red stones set in lids, powder and rouge compartments, lipstick concealed in tassel, carrying chain **245.00**

CONSOLIDATED GLASS COMPANY

History: The Consolidated Lamp and Glass Company was formed as a result of the 1893 merger of the Wallace and McAfee Company, glass and lamp jobbers of Pittsburgh, and the Fostoria Shade & Lamp Company of Fostoria, Ohio. When the Fostoria, Ohio, plant burned down in 1895, Corapolis, Pennsylvania, donated a seven-acre tract of land near the center of town for a new factory. In 1911, the company was the largest lamp, globe, and shade works in the United States, employing more than 400 workers.

In 1925, Reuben Haley, owner of an independent-design firm, convinced John Lewis, president of Consolidated, to enter the giftware field utilizing a series of designs inspired by the 1925 Paris Exposition (l'Exposition Internationale des Arts Décorative et Industriels Modernes) and the work of René Lalique. Initially, the glass was marketed by Howard Selden through his showroom at 225 Fifth Avenue in New York City. The first two lines were Catalonian and Martele.

Additional patterns were added in the late 1920s: Florentine (January 1927), Chintz (January 1927), Ruba Rombic (January 1928), and Line 700 (January 1929). On April 2, 1932, Consolidated closed it doors. Kenneth Harley moved about 40 molds to Phoenix. In March 1936, Consolidated reopened under new management, and the "Harley" molds were returned. During this period, the famous Dancing Nymph line, based on an eight-inch salad plate in the 1926 Martele series, was introduced.

In August 1962, Consolidated was sold to Dietz Brothers. A major fire damaged the plant during a 1963 labor dispute and in 1964, the company permanently closed its doors.

References: Tom and Neila Bredehoft, *Fifty Years of Collectible Glass, 1920-1970,* Volume 1, Volume II, Antique Trader Books, 2000; Ann Gilbert McDonald, *Evolution of the Night Lamp,* Wallace-Homestead, 1979; Jack D. Wilson, *Phoenix & Consolidated Art Glass, 1926-1980,* Antique Publications, 1989.

Collectors' Club: Phoenix and Consolidated Glass Collectors, 41 River View Drive, Essex Junction, VT 05452, http://www.collectoronline.com/club-PCGCC-wp.html.

Berry bowl, master, Criss-Cross, cranberry opalescent, 8" d **175.00**

Bonbon, cov, 8" d, Ruba Rhombic, faceted, smoky topaz, catalog #832, c1931 . . . . **325.00**

Bowl
   5-1/2" d, Coronation, Martelé, flared, blue **75.00**
   8" d, Dancing Nymph, dark blue wash **365.00**

Box, cov, 7" l, 5" w, Martelé line, **Fruit and Leaf pattern,** scalloped edge **85.00**

Butter dish, cov, Cosmos, pink band **200.00**

Candlesticks, pr
   Hummingbird, Martelé line, oval body, jade green, 6-3/4" h . . **245.00**
   Ruba Rhombic, smoky topaz **215.00**

Cocktail, Dancing Nymph, French Crystal **90.00**

Cologne bottle, orig stopper, 4-1/2" h, Cosmos **120.00**

Cookie jar, 6-1/2" h, Regent Line, #3758, Florette, rose pink over white opal casing **370.00**

Lamp, blown-out floral shade, silvered base, 10" h. **$660.** *Photo courtesy of Jackson's Auctioneers & Appraisers.*

Creamer and sugar, pink, florals, emb shells, ornate finial, silver plated fittings **995.00**

Cruet, orig stopper, Florette, pink satin **225.00**

Cup and saucer, Dancing Nymph, ruby flashed **265.00**

Dinner service, Five Fruits, service for six, goblet, plate, sherbet, one large serving plate, purple wash, mold imperfections, wear **375.00**

Goblet, Dancing Nymph, French Crystal **90.00**

Humidor, Florette, pink satin . . . **225.00**

Jar, cov, Con-Cora, #3758-9, pine cone dec, irid **165.00**

Jug, Spanish Knobs, 5-1/2" h, handle, pink **125.00**

Lamp
   Cockatoo, 13" h, figural, orange and blue, black beak, brown stump, black base **450.00**
   Elk, 13" h, chocolate brown, blue clock mounted between horns, black bass base, shallow annealing mark **1,000.00**
   Flower basket, 8" h, bouquet of roses and poppies, yellows, pinks, green leaves, brown basketweave, black glass base **300.00**

Mayonnaise comport, Martelé Iris, green wash **55.00**

Miniature lamp, 10" h, opalescent blue **400.00**

Night light, Santa Maria, block base **450.00**

Old-fashioned tumbler, 3-7/8" h, Catalonian, yellow **20.00**

Perfume bottle, 5-1/2" h, Ruba **Rombic,** gray frosted body, nick on stopper **1,400.00**

Pitcher, water, Florette, pink satin **200.00**

Plate
   7" d, Catalonian, green **25.00**
   8-1/4" d, Bird of Paradise, amber wash **40.00**
   8-1/4" d, Dancing Nymph, French Crystal **85.00**
   8-1/2" d, Five Fruits, green . . . **40.00**
   10-1/4" d, Catalonian, yellow . **40.00**
   12" d, Five Fruits, white **65.00**
   12" d, Martelé, Orchid, pink, birds and flowers **115.00**

Platter, Dancing Nymph, Palace, dark-blue wash **1,000.00**

Puff box, cov
   Hummingbirds, milk glass **75.00**
   Lovebirds, blue **95.00**

Salt and pepper shakers, pr
   Cone, pink **75.00**
   Cosmos **185.00**
   Guttate, green **85.00**

Sauce dish, Criss-Cross, cranberry opalescent **55.00**

Sherbet, ftd
   Catalonian, green **20.00**
   Dancing Nymph, French Crystal **80.00**

Snack set, Martelé Fruits, pink . . **45.00**

Spooner, Criss-Cross, cranberry opalescent **75.00**

Sugar bowl, cov, Guttate, cased pink **120.00**

Sugar shaker, 3-1/2" d, puff quilted body, pink, brass lid **150.00**

Sundae, Martelé Russet Yellow Fruits **35.00**

Syrup
   Cone, squatty, pink **295.00**
   Cosmos, SP top **275.00**

Toilet bottle, Ruba Rombic, dark Jungle green **875.00**

Toothpick holder
   Florette, cased pink **75.00**
   Guttate, cranberry **185.00**

Tumbler
   Catalonian, ftd, green, 5-1/4" h **30.00**
   Cosmos **85.00**
   Dancing Nymph, frosted pink, 6" h **175.00**
   Guttate, pink satin **60.00**
   Katydid, clambroth **165.00**
   Martelé Russet Yellow Fruits, ftd, 5-3/4" h **5.00**
   Ruba Rhombic, faceted, ftd, silver gray, 6" h **200.00**

Umbrella vase, Blackberry **550.00**

Vase
   5" h, Dancing Nymph, crimped, ruby stain, reverse French Crystal highlights, 5" h **145.00**
   6" h, Regent Line, #3758, cased blue stretch over white opal, pinched **175.00**
   6-1/2" h, sea foam green, lavender, and tan, floral pattern **150.00**
   8-1/2" h, Katydid, blue wash, fan shaped top **300.00**
   10-1/2" h, Love Bird pattern, golden birds, custard ground **600.00**
   10-3/4" h, Dogwood, green ground **600.00**

Whiskey glass, 2-5/8" h, Ruba Rhombic, faceted, transparent jungle green, catalog #823 . . . . **250.00**

CONTINENTAL CHINA AND PORCELAIN (GENERAL)

History: By 1700, porcelain factories existed in large numbers throughout Europe. In the mid-18th century, the German factories at Meissen and Nymphenburg were dominant. As the century ended, French potteries assumed the leadership role. The 1740s to the 1840s were the golden age of Continental china and porcelains.

Americans living in the last half of the 19th century eagerly sought the masterpieces of the European porcelain factories. In the early 20th century, this style of china and porcelain was considered "blue chip" by antiques collectors.

References: Susan and Al Bagdade, *Warman's English & Continental Pottery & Porcelain*, 3rd Edition, Krause Publications, 1998; Rachael Feild, *Macdonald Guide to Buying Antique Pottery & Porcelain*, Wallace-Homestead, 1987; Geoffrey Godden, *Godden's Guide to European Porcelain*, Random House, 1993.

Additional Listings: French—Haviland, Limoges, Old Paris, Sarreguemines, and Sevres; German—Austrian Ware, Bavarian China, Carlsbad China, Dresden/Meissen, Rosenthal, Royal Bayreuth, Royal Bonn, Royal Rudolstadt, Royal Vienna, Schlegelmilch, and Villeroy and Boch; Italian—Capo-di-Monte.

French

Choisy, plate, 8-1/4" d, earthenware transfer printed and hand enameled, each with different numbered scene relating to story of soldier's courtship and military life, naïve enamel accenting, mid-19th C, price for set of 12 .. **500.00**
Faience
　Bulb pot, 3-1/8" d, sq, molded acanthus-capped scroll feet, conforming handles, front with scene of courting couple, verso landscape, each side with floral sprays, sq form insert, gilt highlights, attributed to Marseilles, last quarter 18th C, pr **900.00**
　Inkstand, 13-1/2" l, figural, cartouche-shaped base molded with scrolls, front painted with harbor scene flanked by tower and knight-shaped inkpots, back sections support large figure of lion with raised paw resting on shield with armorial **650.00**
　Plate, 9" d, blue and white floral dec, foliate border **115.00**
　Plate, 9" d, central vase and large floral blossoms, stylized garland border, yellow rim **150.00**
　Sugar caster, 8-1/2" h, brightly polychrome scene of courting

French Faience, inkwell, Oriental florals yellow ground, marked "Aladin, France,", 5" l, 3" h, **$95.**

couple in landscape, floral sprays borders, dec band of fleur-de-lis border, pierced cov with conforming dec, early 19th C **450.00**
Paris
　Cache pot, 6" h, ovoid, apple-green ground, floral roundels in leaf surround, two gilt lion's head masks on sides, narrow undertray, late 19th C **115.00**
　Candlesticks, pr, 9" h, everted sconce, column form standard, shaped base with figural man and woman among rocaille leaves, late 19th C **175.00**
　Dessert dish, 8-5/8" w, 11" l, oblong, pheasant and scroll-molded edge, enamel dec center with fruit, cobalt-blue border, gilt details, late 19th C, price for pr **750.00**
　Dessert plate, 9-1/8"d, hand painted, four with flower centers, two with fruit centers, all with peach borders, gilt scrolls, maroon band at molded rim, late 19th C.. **750.00**
　Vase garniture, 8" h, 8-1/4"h, 9-1/2" h, three vases, each with aqua ground, floral bouquet roundels in gilt surrounds, short scroll handles, domed foot molded with scallop shells, late 19th C **500.00**
　Veilleuse, 4-1/2" h pot, 9" h overall, hand painted, small pot with black and pink bands, over enameled with gilt scrolls, short gilt spout, angular handle, octagonal

pagoda-form stand hp with scenes titled "acqueduque de Buc," showing elevated aqueduct, and "a Bonnebose (Calvados)," showing village, 20th C, base missing **475.00**
Samson & Co.
　Character figure, 6-3/8" to 7-5/8" h, three figures in masks and caps, two wielding swords, other dagger, bearded figure with guitar, each by vine-covered tree trunk, rect base, guilloche borders, 20th C, price for four-pc set **450.00**
　Figure, 12-1/4" h, Neptune, upraised hands standing on scallop shell, dolphin at feet, rocaille base encrusted with shells and seaweed, gilt accents, late 19th C **230.00**
　Perfume bottle, 2-7/8" l, figural, boy with vessel seated on dolphin, enamel detailing, boy's head as stopper, late 19th C **230.00**
　Tea service, Chinese Export, 6-1/4" h teapot, 5" h cov cream jug, 4-3/4" h cov sugar, six 2-3/8" h cups, six saucers, white reeded body, enamel dec with central heraldic mottoed crest, floral sprays, white slip scroll and chrysanthemum dec, early 20th C **980.00**
Saint Cloud
　Bonbonniere, cov, cat form, SS mountings, late 19th C.... **295.00**
　Cup and saucer, pr, tremleuse, c1750 .... **650.00**

Germany

Hutschenreuther

Plaque, 5-1/8" x 6-7/8", oval, Madonna and Child, giltwood frame, late 19th C **600.00**

Service plate, 10-7/8" d, central dec, summer flowers within heavily gilt cavetto, rim worked with scrolling acanthus, textured ground, underglaze green factory marks, minor rubbing, 12 pc set . **1,600.00**

Ludwigsburg, bowl, cov, underplate, 6-1/4" h, molded vine handles, applied pink flowers, scenes of putti at play, cobalt blue and gilt reserves, underplate with scalloped rim, conforming reserves, large floral sprays, c1800 . . . . **1,000.00**

Tirschenreuth, service plate, 10-3/4" d, gold inner band of Egyptian Revival lotus and roundel, dark apple green edge, gilt rim, price for set of eight **225.00**

Von Schierholz's Porcelain Manufactory, Plaue, Turingia, urn on stand, 11-1/2" w, 22-1/2" h, domed-pierced cover, large floral finial, two loop handles, each side painted with floral spray in floral-encrusted surround, rococo foot, oblong base with further floral sprays, floral encrusting **500.00**

Portuguese, unknown maker, shaving bowl, 3-5/8" h, molded indention in rim, central dec, blue, yellow, and green floral border **100.00**

COOKIE JARS

History: Cookie jars, colorful and often whimsical, are now an established collecting category. Do not be misled by the high prices realized at the 1988 Andy Warhol auction. Many of the same cookie jars that sold for more than $1,000 each can be found in the field for less than $100.

Cookie jars often were redesigned to reflect newer tastes. Hence, the same jar may be found in several different variations.

Marks: Many cookie-jar shapes were manufactured by more than one company and, as a result, can be found with different marks. This often happened because of mergers or separations, e.g., Brush-McCoy, which became Nelson McCoy. Molds also were traded and sold among companies.

References: Fred and Joyce Roerig, *Collector's Encyclopedia of Cookie Jars*, Book I (1991, 1997 value update), Book II (1994, 1999 value update), Book III (1998), Collector Books; Mike Schneider, *The Complete Cookie Jar Book*, 3rd ed., Schiffer, 2001; Mark and Ellen Supnick, *Wonderful World of Cookie Jars*, L-W Book Sales, 1995, 1998 value update; Ermagene Westfall, *Illustrated Value Guide to Cookie Jars*, Book I (1983, 1997 value update), Book II (1993, 1997 value update), Collector Books.

Periodical: *Cookie Jarrin'*, RR 2, Box 504, Walterboro, SC 29488-9278.

Collectors' Club: American Cookie Jar Association, 1600 Navajo Road; Norman, OK 73026, http://cookiejarclub.com.

Museum: The Cookie Jar Museum, Lemont, IL.

Apple, Watt Pottery, No. 21, 7-1/2" h **400.00**

Baby, No. 561, Abingdon Pottery, 11" h **850.00**

Ballerina Bear, Metlox Pottery . . **110.00**

Barefoot Boy, Hull Pottery **320.00**

Basketweave and Morning Glory, marked "Put Your Fist In," blue and white stoneware, 7-1/2" h **625.00**

Bear, blue sweater, Metlox Pottery **105.00**

Bo Peep, No. 694D, Abingdon Pottery, 12" h **425.00**

Brickers, blue and white stoneware, 8" h **475.00**

Chef Pierre, Metlox Pottery . . . **100.00**

Choo Choo, No. 561D, Abingdon Pottery, 7-1/2" h **100.00**

Cinderella, Shawnee Pottery, unmarked **125.00**

Clock, No. 563, Abingdon Pottery, 9" h **100.00**

Cookie Barrel, Watt Pottery, wood grain, 10-1/2" h **50.00**

Cottage, Shawnee Pottery, marked "USA 6," 7" h **900.00**

Daisy, No. 677, Abingdon Pottery, 8" h **50.00**

Desert Rose, Franciscan Ware . **325.00**

Drum Major, Shawnee Pottery, marked "USA 10," 10" h **295.00**

Drummer Boy, Metlox Pottery . **750.00**

Duck, Hull Pottery **50.00**

Dutch Boy, Shawnee Pottery, striped pants, under glaze dec, marked "USA," 11" h **150.00**

Dutch Girl, Shawnee Pottery, under glaze dec, marked "USA," 11-1/2" h **150.00**

Fat Boy, No. 495, Abingdon Pottery, 8-1/4" h **650.00**

Flying Bird, blue and white stoneware, 9" h **1,250.00**

French Chef, Red Wing Pottery, blue glaze **250.00**

Gingerbread Boy, Hull Pottery, blue and white trim **400.00**

Gingerbread Man, Hull Pottery, 12" h **550.00**

Goodies, Watt Pottery, No. 76, 6-1/2" h **150.00**

Grapes, Red Wing Pottery, yellow, marked "Red Wing USA," 10" h . . **85.00**

Great Northern Boy, Shawnee Pottery, marked "Great Northern USA 1025," 9-3/4" h **375.00**

Happy/Sad Face, Watt Pottery, No. 34, wooden lid **150.00**

Indiana State Fair 1940, miniature, globe shape, Uhl Pottery, pink ground, 4" h **625.00**

Jo-Jo the Clown, Shawnee Pottery, marked "Shawnee USA, 12," 9" h **300.00**

Little Chef, Shawnee Pottery **75.00**

Little Red Riding Hood, open basket, gold stars on apron, Hull Pottery **400.00**

Mammy, Brayton Laguna Pottery, turquoise bandanna, burgundy base **1,300.00**

Monterey Moderne, chartreuse, Bauer Pottery **100.00**

Morning Glory, Watt Pottery, No. 95, 10" h **600.00**

Mother Goose, No. 695D, Abingdon Pottery, 12" h **550.00**

Muggsy Dog, Shawnee Pottery, blue bow, gold trim and decals, marked "Patented Muggsy U.S.A.," 11-3/4" h **900.00**

Owl, Shawnee Pottery **110.00**

Panda Bear, black and white, Morton Pottery **95.00**

Parrot, tree stump, green and yellow, Metlox Pottery, Model No. 555 . . **425.00**

Partridges, pale blue, yellow, and orange dec, dark brown branches, light brown matte honeycomb textured ground, pale blue lid, glossy white int., Brayton Laguna Pottery, Model No. V-12, 7-1/4" h **195.00**

Pine Cone, gray squirrel finial, Metlox Pottery, Model NO. 509, 11" h . . **115.00**

Pirate, Gonder Pottery, 8" h **225.00**

Nippon Type, green ground, purple and yellow flowers, gilt border, green mark "IC Japan-Hand Painted," 5" h, **$225.** *Photo courtesy of Sanford Alderfer Auction Co.*

Policeman, Watt Pottery,
10-1/2" h **1,100.00**
Provincial Blue, Metlox Pottery **225.00**
Provincial Lady, textured wood-tone
base, high-gloss white apron and scarf,
red, green, and yellow flowers and
hearts, marked "Brayton Laguna Calif.
K-27," 13" h **465.00**
Pumpkin, No. 674D, Abingdon Pottery,
8" h. **550.00**
Rex Dinosaur, Metlox Pottery,
white **110.00**
Ring Ware, Bauer Pottery
   Red **995.00**
   Yellow **995.00**
Rooster, Red Wing Pottery, green
glaze **145.00**
Rose Blossom, Metlox Pottery, pale
pink, green leaves, Model No.
513. **380.00**
Sheriff, Gonder Pottery, Mold No. 950,
12" h. **1,100.00**
Smiley Pig, Shawnee Pottery, clover
blossom dec, marked "Patented Smiley
USA," 11-1/2" h **550.00**
Starflower, Watt Pottery, No. 503,
8" h. **350.00**
Swedish Maid, Brayton Laguna Pottery,
1941, incised mark, 11" h **600.00**
Three Bears, No. 696D, Abingdon
Pottery, 8-3/4" h **95.00**
Tulip
   Metlox Pottery, yellow and
      green **425.00**
   Watt Pottery, No. 503, 8" h . . **350.00**
Turkey, poultry finial, Morton Pottery,
brown. **150.00**
Windmill, No. 678, Abingdon Pottery,
10-1/2" h **500.00**
Winnie Pig, Shawnee Pottery, clover
blossom dec, marked "Patented Winnie
USA," 12" h **575.00**
Witch, No. 692, Abingdon Pottery,
11-1/2" h **1,000.00**

COPELAND AND SPODE

History: In 1749, Josiah Spode was apprenticed to
Thomas Whieldon and in 1754 worked for William
Banks in Stoke-on-Trent. In the early 1760s, Spode
started his own pottery, making cream-colored
earthenware and blue-printed whiteware. In 1770, he
returned to Banks' factory as master, purchasing it in
1776.

Spode pioneered the use of steam-powered
pottery-making machinery and mastered the art of
transfer printing from copper plates. Spode opened a

London shop in 1778 and sent William Copeland
there about 1784. A number of larger London
locations followed. At the turn of the century, Spode
introduced bone china. In 1805, Josiah Spode II and
William Copeland entered into a partnership for the
London business. A series of partnerships between
Josiah Spode II, Josiah Spode III, and William Taylor
Copeland resulted.

In 1833, Copeland acquired Spode's London
operations and seven years later, the Stoke plants.
William Taylor Copeland managed the business until
his death in 1868. The firm remained in the hands of
Copeland heirs. In 1923, the plant was electrified;
other modernization followed.

In 1976, Spode merged with Worcester Royal
Porcelain to become Royal Worcester Spode, Ltd.

References: Susan and Al Bagdade, *Warman's
English & Continental Pottery & Porcelain, 3rd
Edition*, Krause Publications, 1998; Robert Copeland,
Spode & Copeland Marks, Cassell Academic, 1993;
—, *Spode's Willow Pattern & Other Designs After the
Chinese*, Blanford Press, 1990; D. Drakard & P.
Holdway, *Spode Printed Wares*, Longmans, 1983; L.
Whiter, *Spode: A History of the Family, Factory, and
Wares, 1733-1833*, Random Century, 1989; Sydney B.
Williams, *Antique Blue & White Spode*, David &
Charles, 1988.

Museums: Cincinnati Art Museum, Cincinnati, OH;
City of Stoke-On-Trent Museum, Hanley, England;
Jones Museum of Glass & Ceramics, Sebago, ME;
Spode Museum, Stoke-on-Trent, UK; Victoria & Albert
Museum, London, England.

*Plaque, bust of man with beard, titled
Shylock, floral border, artist signed "L.
Besche," framed, 22-1/2" d, $475.
Photo courtesy of Joy Luke Auctions.*

Cabinet plate
   8-1/4" d, jeweled border, with coral
      and pearls, dark green ground,
      c1883 . . . . **600.00**
   9-1/2" d, artist sgd "Samuel Alcock,"
      1-3/4" jeweled border, intricate
      gold, beading, pearl and turquoise
      jeweling, c1889. . . . . **750.00**
Coffee cup and saucer, 2-1/4" h
cylindrical cup with all over maroon and

gilt scrolled dec, 5" d saucer, retained
by Tiffany & Co., late 19th C, price for
set of twelve **325.00**
Demitasse cup and saucer, Heather
Rose, marked "Spode's Jewel,
Copeland Spode, England,"
registration, patent numbers, pattern
name **25.00**
Fish plate, 9-3/4" d, artist sgd "H. C.
Lea," four-part gold-swirled design, hp
fly in each section, c1891 . . . . . **175.00**
Jar, cov, 10" h, globular, handles,
Oriental style, apple green, birds on
flowering peony branches, iron-red,
pink, and gilt dec, gilt knob finial,
Spode mark, Pat. #3086, c1820
. . . . **725.00**
Jug, orange, teal green, and gold dec,
matte cream ground, ornate handle
with two mythological characters,
c1847 . . . . **450.00**
Pitcher, 7-1/2" h, deep-blue glaze,
raised white figures, tavern scenes and
berries **225.00**
Plate, 9-1/2" d, blue and white, hunting
scenes. **225.00**
Platter, 17" l, Wicker Lane. **150.00**
Service plate, 10" d, central gilt
roundel, slightly serpentine rim with
raised gilt scrolling cartouches,
diapered reserved offset by foliage
swags, retailed by Gilman Collamore &
Co., late 19th C, price for set of 12
. . . . **2,100.00**
Serving bowl, 10" d, 7" h, floral
dec **325.00**
Spill vase, 4-3/4" h, flared rim, pale
lilac, gilt octagonal panels with portrait
of bearded man, band of pearls on rims
and bases, Spode, c1920. . . . . **425.00**
Tea set, Blue Willow, retailed by Tiffany
& Co., pattern registered January 1879,
printed at rim with quotation from
Robert Burns "Auld Lang Syne," 5" h
cov hexagonal teapot, creamer, cov
sugar, seven cups, six saucers,
20-3/4" d round tray with scalloped gilt
rim, gilt handles, gilt foo dog lid finials,
price for 17-pc set. **950.00**
Tray, 8-1/2" l, black transfer, passion
flowers, grape vines border, emb
grapes, vines, and leaves on tab
handles, c1900 . . . . **200.00**
Tureen, cov, 13" w, 11" h, white, gold
and blue accents, marked "Spode New
Stone" **1,470.00**
Urn, cov, 15" h, Louis XVI style, cobalt
blue ground, medallions on each side
with bouquet of roses, majolica, repair to
one handle, nick to one lid, pr . . **900.00**

Water pitcher, 8-1/4" h, bulbous, tan acanthus leaf handle and spout, green field dec with white relief classical figures of dancing women, white relief banded floral garland dec at neck, marked "Rd. No. 180288" **250.00**

COPPER

History: Copper objects, such as kettles, teakettles, warming pans, and measures, played an important part in the 19th-century household. Outdoors, the apple-butter kettle and still were the two principal copper items. Copper culinary objects were lined with a thin protective coating of tin to prevent poisoning. They were relined as needed.

References: Mary Frank Gaston, *Antique Brass & Copper*, Collector Books, 1992, 1998 value update; Henry J. Kauffman, *Early American Copper, Tin, and Brass: Handcrafted Metalware from Colonial Times*, Astragal Press, 1995.

Reproduction Alert: Many modern reproductions exist.

Additional Listings: Arts and Crafts Movement and Roycroft.

Notes: Collectors place great emphasis on signed pieces, especially those by American craftsmen. Since copper objects were made abroad as well, it is hard to identify unsigned examples.

Boiler, $30. *Photo courtesy of Joy Luke Auctions.*

Bookends, pr, 6" w, 5-1/2" h, Dirk Van Erp, repoussé stylized floral design, D'Arcy Gaw box mark, old cleaning to orig patina **2,300.00**
Charger, 29-1/2" d, hand hammered, emb high relief of owl on branch, naturally-forming patina, Liberty paper label **3,105.00**
Cistern, 25" l, 14" w, Neoclassical, 19th C, bombe ovoid form, front with applied heraldic shield, two lion's head pendant handles. **350.00**
Coal hood, 13-5/8" w, 13-5/8" d, 16" h, Gothic Revival, late 19th C, rect, swollen sides, hinged lid, cast brass

loop handle, two similar handles on sides, openwork brass base, pointed feet, int. with removable tin liner **195.00**
Desk set, hammered blotter, letter holder, bookends, stamp box, each with bone carved cabochon, branch and berry motif, Potter Studio, fine orig patina, die-stamp mark **750.00**
Fire screen, 18-1/2" w, 32-1/2" h, copper fire screen emb with owl flanked by fruit, iron framework with whiplash feet, cleaned patina, unmarked, English. **2,185.00**
Fish poacher, cov, 20-1/2" l, oval, rolled rim, iron swing ball handle, 19th C **350.00**
Inglenook hood, 30" w, 8" d, 34-1/2" h, hammered, emb Glasgow roses, English, small tear at bottom . . **1,610.00**
Inkwell, 3" sq, 2-1/2" h, hammered copper, overhanging top, liner, Dirk Van Erp open box mark, some cleaning to orig patina **520.00**
Rain collection box, 26" w, 8" d, 19-1/2" h, eagle, three stars, two attached scrolled wings with stars, thick layer of old flaking light gray paint, rust, some damage **175.00**
Store sign, 28" l, 24" h, hammered surface, The British Gallery, emb name in elaborate font, flanked by knights, fine orig patina, made by A. A. Simpson Fine Arts (London). **1,495.00**
Tea kettle
11-1/2" h, curved spout, upright swing handle, brass lid knob, imp "G. Tyron" on handle, dents, wear, PA, 19th C **690.00**
12-1/2" h, curved spout, upright swing handle, brass lid knob, imp "H. Dehuff" on handle, dents, wear, PA, 19th C **800.00**
Tray, 13-1/2" d, circular, hammered copper, emb handles, Dirk Van Erp open box mark with "San Francisco," orig patina on front, cleaned on back. **920.00**
Umbrella stand, 25" h, hand hammered, flared rim, cylindrical body, two-strap work-loop handles, repoussé medallion, riveted flared foot, c1910
. . . . **650.00**
Vase
4" d, 11" h, hammered, tapering, angular brass handles continue to band at base, emb Glasgow roses, German Jugendstil, cleaned patina, price for pr **980.00**
5-1/2" d, 7" h, hammered, ovoid, Dirk Van Erp, fine orig mottled patina, D'Arcy Gaw box mark, small shallow dent on rim **8,050.00**

10" d, 10" h, flaring, two riveted handles, emb with green enameled flower, unmarked, English, lacquered finish, some shallow dents **366.00**
Vessel, 4" d, 3-1/4" h, hammered, ovoid, closed-in rim, orig dark patina, Dirk Van Erp closed box mark **2,300.00**
Wall sconce, 4-1/2" w, 11" h, hammered, flame head, riveted Arts & Crafts details, attributed to Dirk Van Erp, cleaned patina **425.00**

CORALENE

History: Coralene refers to glass or china objects which have the design painted on the surface of the piece along with tiny colorless glass beads which were applied with a fixative. The piece was placed in a muffle to fix the enamel and set the beads.

Several American and English companies made glass coralene in the 1880s. Seaweed or coral were the most common design. Other motifs were Wheat Sheaf and Fleur-de-Lis. Most of the base glass was satin finished.

China and pottery coralene, made from the late 1890s until after World War II, is referred to as Japanese coralene. The beading is opaque and inserted into the soft clay. Hence, it is only one-half to three-quarters visible.

Reproduction Alert: Reproductions are on the market, some using an old glass base. The beaded decoration on new coralene has been glued and can be scraped off.

China
Condiment set, open salt, cov mustard, pepper shaker, white opaque ground, floral coralene dec, SP stand
. . . . **250.00**
Pitcher, 4-1/2" h, 1909 pattern, red and brown ground, beaded yellow daffodil dec. **950.00**
Vase, 8" h, 6-3/4"w, melon ribbed, sq top, yellow drape coralene, rose shaded to pink ground, white int. **850.00**

Glass
Cruet, pink satin, yellow coralene, orig stopper. **420.00**
Fairy lamp, 7" h, six rows of yellow coralene, white opaque shade with yellow tinting, brass colored metal holder. **375.00**
Lamp shade, 4-1/2" h, egg shape, scalloped tops, coral pink with yellow beaded wheat design, pr. **350.00**
Lamp, table, 16-1/2" h, 5-1/2" d, green glass, pink, white, and yellow coralene flowers and leaves, coralene branch at top, white enameled dot dec, frosted shade with birds and bows **325.00**

Muffineer, royal blue ground, pink seaweed coralene, steeple shaped metal fittings, signed "Patent," 6" h, $985. Photo courtesy of Clarence and Betty Maier.

Mug, 3-5/8" h, light blue shading to white satin body, DQ, MOP, yellow coralline, gold rim, applied frosted reeded handle **525.00**
Vase

5-1/2" h, 4" d, butterscotch MOP, Coinspot pattern, heavy coralene beading, pink and white flowers, yellow centers, green leaves **525.00**
7" h, pink shaded and cased to white, DQ pattern, gold beading within design, pr **450.00**

CORKSCREWS

History: The corkscrew is composed of three parts: handle, shaft, and worm or screw. The earliest known reference to "a Steele Worme used for drawing corks out of bottles" is 1681. Samuel Henshall, an Englishman, was granted the first patent in 1795.

Elaborate mechanisms were invented and patented from the early 1800s onward, especially in England. However, three basic types emerged: T handle (the most basic, simple form), lever, and mechanism. Variations on these three types run into the hundreds. Miniature corkscrews, employed for drawing corks from perfume and medicine bottles between 1750 and 1920, are among those most eagerly sought by collectors.

Corkscrew styles tend to reflect the preferences of specific nationalities. The English favored the helix worm and often coppertoned their steel products. By the mid-18th century, English and Irish silversmiths were making handles noted for their clean lines and practicality. Most English silver handles were hallmarked.

The Germans preferred the center worm and nickel plate. The Italians used chrome plate or massive solid brass. In the early 1800s, the Dutch and French developed elaborately artistic silver handles.

Americans did not begin to manufacture quality corkscrews until the late 19th century. They favored the center worm and specialized in silver-mounted tusks and carved stag horn for handles.

References: Donald A. Bull, *Bull's Pocket Guide to Corkscrews*, Schiffer Publishing, 1999; Fred O'Leary, *Corkscrews*, Schiffer Publishing, 1996.

Collectors' Clubs: Canadian Corkscrew Collectors Club, 670 Meadow Wood Road, Mississauga, Ontario, L5J 2S6 Canada; Just For Openers, 3712 Sunningdale Way, Durham, NC 27707.

Bone handle

Mechanism type, English rack and pinion corkscrew, polished, brush and hanging ring, four plain post open barrel, narrow rack, long wire helix, side handle, sgd "Verinder" **410.00**
T-handle, Henshall, incised button, helical worm, c1820 . . . . . . **125.00**

Brass

5" l, leering Bacchante, two herm figures, Victorian **420.00**
15-3/4" l, Publican's, steel mounted large vice for placement over bar, steel and wood plunger handle, late 19th C **490.00**

Bronzed steel, lever, Heeley A1, double-lever patent, helical worm **65.00**

Cast iron, clamp on mechanism type, lacy openwork, emb "Phoenix," patented 1887 . . . . **200.00**

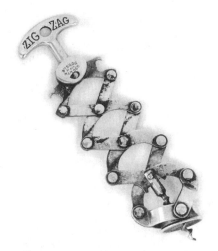

Zig-zag, marked "S.G.D.G. Fr. & E. T. M & M Dep," $75.

Celluloid, novelty type, figural mermaid, bends at waist, marked "Geschutz" **275.00**
Chrome, lever, zig-zag design, French, 10 1/2" l extended **65.00**
Ebony handle, mechanism type, steel frame, foliate scrolling raised arm, steel ciphered worm, marked "Champion, Made in USA" **110.00**
Ivory handle, miniature, crescent shape, chromed turned steel shaft wire helix, c1790-1820 . . . . **75.00**
Palmette handle, miniature, carved handle with MOP, helical worm . . **30.00**
Silver, novelty type, gaucho and horse, oblong platform handle, Archimedian screw **775.00**
Staghorn handle, T-handle, ornate SS cap **100.00**
Wood handle, duck bill cap, simple Archimedean screw, German . . . **85.00**

COWAN POTTERY

History: R. Guy Cowan founded the Cowan Pottery in 1913 in Cleveland, Ohio. The establishment remained in almost continuous operation until 1931, when financial difficulties forced closure.

Early production was redware pottery. Later a porcelain-like finish was perfected with special emphasis placed on glazes, with lusterware being one of the most common types. Commercial wares marked "Lakeware" were produced from 1927 to 1931.

Marks: Early marks include an incised "Cowan Pottery" on the redware (1913-1917), an impressed "Cowan," and an impressed "Lakewood." The imprinted stylized semicircle, with or without the initials "R. G.," came later.

References: Mark Bassett and Victorian Naumann, *Cowan Pottery and the Cleveland School*, Schiffer Publishing, 1997; Leslie Piña, *Pottery, Modern Wares 1920-1960*, Schiffer Publishing, 1994; Tim and Jamie Saloff, *Collector's Encyclopedia of Cowan Pottery: Identification and Values*, Collector Books, 1994.

Museums: Cowan Pottery Museum, Rocky River Public Library, Rocky River, OH; Everson Museum of Art, Syracuse, NY.

Bookends, pr

6-1/4" h, 4" d, boy and girl, special-ivory glaze, stamped "Cowan" **350.00**
7-1/2" h, 5" w, elephant, semi-matte green glaze, stamped "Cowan," minor nick to base of one . . **700.00**
8-1/2" h, 6" d, flying fish, antique-green glaze, stamped "Cowan," restored point on each **600.00**

Candlesticks, pr, 3-1/2" d, 4" h, pearlized blue. **150.00**
Charger, 11-1/4" d, emb undersea motif, light green fish and plants, blue-green ground, imp "Cowan"
. . . .**500.00**
Demitasse cup and saucer, 2-1/2" h cup, 4" saucer, block letter logo . .**30.00**
Figure
    8" h, Pierrette, old-ivory glaze, stamped "Cowan" **250.00**
    9-1/2" x 9", horse, mahogany and gold flambé glaze, imp mark
    . . . .**1,500.00**
Flower frog
    7" h, figural nude, #698, original-ivory glaze **250.00**
    7-3/4" h, 4-1/4" d, Heavenward, original-ivory glaze, stamped "Cowan" **175.00**
    7-3/4" h, 6-1/4" d, Duet, original-ivory glaze, stamped "Cowan," small shallow chip to base **450.00**
    10" h, 5-1/4" d, Pan, special-ivory glaze, stamped "Cowan," minor base nick. **250.00**
    10-1/4" h, Debutante, special-ivory glaze, stamped "Cowan/S" **850.00**
    10-3/4" h, 4" d, Swirl Dancer, original-ivory glaze, stamped "Cowan" **850.00**
    11-3/4" h, Loveliness, original-ivory glaze, incised "B," crack to wrist. **400.00**
Lamp base, 11-1/2" h, 9-1/2" d, bulbous, Oriental-red glaze, stamp mark, drilled at side and bottom
. . . .**300.00**
Match holder, 3-1/2" h, cream color **60.00**
Paperweight, 4-1/2" h, 3-1/4" l, elephant, special-ivory glaze, stamped "Cowan" **300.00**

Trivet, bust of woman, blue ground, rose and yellow flowers, green and aqua leaves, Louis Mora, 6-1/2" d, **$220.**

Snack set, hexagon-shaped plate, solid light blue **115.00**
Trivet, 6-1/2" d, woman's head and flowers, blue, cream, yellow, and pink, die-stamped mark, minor scratches. **450.00**
Vase
    5" d, 7-1/4" h, classical shape, dripping brown crystalline glaze, mirrored orange glaze, ink mark **300.00**
    5" d, 8-1/2" h, blue, emb flowers and leaves. **225.00**
    10" d, 10" h, spherical, ribbed, leathery vermillion glaze, stamped "Cowan," two hairlines to rim **125.00**

CRANBERRY GLASS

History: Cranberry glass is transparent and named for its color, achieved by adding powdered gold to a molten batch of amber glass and reheating at a low temperature to develop the cranberry or ruby color. The glass color first appeared in the last half of the 17th century, but was not made in American glass factories until the last half of the 19th century.

Cranberry glass was blown, mold blown, or pressed. Examples often are decorated with gold or enamel. Less-expensive cranberry glass, made by substituting copper for gold, can be identified by its bluish-purple tint.

Reference: William Heacock and William Gamble, *Encyclopedia of Victorian Colored Pattern Glass: Book 9, Cranberry Opalescent from A to Z,* Antique Publications, 1987.

Reproduction Alert: Reproductions abound. These pieces are heavier, off-color, and lack the quality of older examples.

Additional Listings: See specific categories, such as Bride's Baskets, Cruets, Jack-in-the-Pulpit Vases, etc.

Basket, 7" h, 5" w, ruffled edge, petticoat shape, crystal loop handle, c1890. . . . .**250.00**
Bottle, 8" h, 3" d, gold mid-band, white-enameled trim, clear-faceted stopper **150.00**
Bride's basket, 5" h, 3-1/2" d bowl, German silver-filigree frame, plain cranberry bowl **115.00**
Centerpiece, 19-1/2" h, central trumpet-form vase, shallow dish, pedestal foot, gilt Greek-key dec, Victorian. **300.00**
Condiment dish and underplate, 6-1/2" h, cranberry, scrolling vines and grapes dec, Continental **175.00**
Creamer, 5" h, 2-3/4" d, Optic pattern, fluted to, applied clear handle . .**95.00**

Cruet, 6-3/4" h, 4" d, white-enameled flowers and leaves, applied clear handle, cut clear stopper **225.00**
Epergne, 19" h, 11" d, five pcs, large ruffled bowl, tall center lily, three jack-in-the-pulpit vases **1,200.00**
Finger bowl, Inverted Thumbprint pattern, deep color. **200.00**
Garniture, 14" d bowl, pr 11" h candlesticks, cranberry overlay cut to clear, faceted cut dec, Continental **450.00**
Lamp, 10" h, 5" d, peg, silver-plated base, ruffled-Rubena shade, emb daisies, chimney **265.00**
Pipe, 18" l, hand blown, tapering-bent neck, bulbous bowl, three bulbs at base, white-enamel dec at outer rim of bowl **250.00**
Pitcher
    6-1/2" h, 4-1/8" d, Ripple and Thumbprint pattern, bulbous, round mouth, applied clear handle **175.00**
    10" h, 5" d, bulbous, ice bladder int., applied clear handle. **250.00**
    11-3/8" h, 9" w, bulbous, internal vertical ribs, white and blue enameled floral dec, applied clear loop handle, c1895. . . . . . .**300.00**
Plate, 6" w, ruffled edge, air bubbles **15.00**
Rose bowl, 5" h, heart shaped, Raindrop pattern, marked "Rd 81051," attributed to Stevens & Williams .**300.00**
Salt, master, ftd, enameled floral dec. **200.00**
Tumble-up, Inverted Thumbprint pattern **195.00**

Lamps, table, glass fonts and shades with ruffled rims, 14-1/2", price for pair, **$175.** *Photo courtesy of Joy Luke Auctions.*

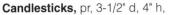

Tumbler, Inverted Thumbprint pattern **65.00**

Vase

7-1/2" h, emb ribs, applied clear feet, three swirled applied clear leaves around base **120.00**

8-7/8" h, bulbous, white-enameled lilies of the valley dec, cylindrical neck **150.00**

Wine decanter, 11" h, 5" d, heavy-cut clear base, gold trim, clear-cut faceted stopper, wear to gold trim **195.00**

CROWN MILANO

History: Crown Milano is an American art glass produced by the Mt. Washington Glass Works, New Bedford, Massachusetts. The original patent was issued in 1886 to Frederick Shirley and Albert Steffin.

Normally, it is an opaque-white satin glass finished with light-beige or ivory-colored ground embellished with fancy florals, decorations, and elaborate and thick raised gold. The same glass in shiny finish is Colonial Ware.

Collectors' Club: Mount Washington Art Glass Society, P.O. Box 24094, Fort Worth, TX 76124-1094

Marks: Marked pieces have a purple enamel entwined "CM" with a crown on the base. Sometimes paper labels were used. Since both Mount Washington and Pairpoint supplied mountings, the silver-plated mounts often have "MW" impressed or a Pairpoint mark.

Advisers: Clarence and Betty Maier.

Creamer and sugar, melon-ribbed bodies which shade from pale pink to natural white to pale green at base, blue cornflowers and green foliage, silver-plated fittings, sgd "3905/201" **1,500.00**

Demitasse cup and saucer, raised golden vine laden with single-petaled blossoms, buds, and tiny leaves meander around satin white ext., raised gold borders, coral-colored ring of dots centers in four blossoms, black rings in other three blossoms, sepia-colored rococo scrolls entwine floral dec, pale pink tint, sgd with logo, 2" h cup, 5" d saucer **1,750.00**

Ewer, 7-1/2" d, 6-1/2" h, Colonial Ware, shiny white body, two reserves of colorful blossoms framed by rococo borders of raised gold scrolls, gold cross-hatching across cream colored shoulder, some loss to wash of color around rope handle, sgd "0100" **1,250.00**

Lamp, banquet, 23" h, 9" d, Colonial Ware, shiny ground, base and globe-shaped shade dec with sprays of golden

roes and blossoms, touches of gold accent molded-in dec of florals, swags, and geometric designs, opaque white chimney, brass burner sgd "Made in United States of America" **2,950.00**

Muffineer, melon ribbed, butter yellow tint, swags of dainty powder blue and cream daisies, metal collar, lid emb with butterfly, dragonfly, and blossoms **535.00**

Syrup pitcher, 4" h, white body with six panels, each dec with sprays of pink single-petaled summer roses, framed by gold tinted molded-in ribbed columns, dark patina on shaped silver-plated spout and lid, numbered "744 230" on base **485.00**

Tumbler, Colonial Ware, shiny body, shades of raised gold, swags of finely detailed roses and daisies descend from free-flowing ribbon, numbered "1026" **585.00**

Vase

4-1/2" h, white satin body with tint of lilac at neck, three fully opened chrysanthemum blossoms, two partially opened buds, raised gold borders, rich gold rim, raised DQ design, sgd **685.00**

6" h, 5-3/4" d, butter yellow neck and mouth, four fold-down sides, twenty-four swirling molded-in ribs, cream-colored body, blue and white forget-me-nots, leaves, and foliage **1,350.00**

8" h, huge mauve, creamy white, and peach-yellow peony blossoms, soft lemon ground, green and sepia foliage, gold dec around neck. **765.00**

Vase, spring floral bouquet, pastel hues, reverse with white flowering dogwood branches, 6" h, $1,950. Photo courtesy of Clarence and Betty Maier.

9" h, Colonial Ware, sprays of colorful enamel blossoms, shadow foliate branches of single-petaled roses and buds, neck with gold embellishments, sgd logo and "0615" **945.00**

10-12" h, petticoat shape, white body, pastel pansies, freeform gold accents **750.00**

CRUETS

History: Cruets are small glass bottles used on the table and holding condiments such as oil, vinegar, and wine. The pinnacle of cruet use occurred during the Victorian era, when a myriad of glass manufacturers made cruets in a wide assortment of patterns, colors, and sizes. All cruets had stoppers; most had handles.

References: Elaine Ezell and George Newhouse, *Cruets, Cruets, Cruets,* Vol. I, Antique Publications, 1991; William Heacock, *Encyclopedia of Victorian Colored Pattern Glass: Book 6, Oil Cruets from A to Z,* Antique Publications, 1981.

Additional Listings: Pattern Glass and specific glass categories such as Amberina, Cranberry, and Satin.

Amberina, 5-1/2" h, Inverted Thumbprint, trefoil spout, attributed to Mt. Washington Glass **385.00**

Bluerina, 7-1/4" h, deep royal blue neck fades to clear at shoulder, optic inverted thumbprint design in body, applied clear glass handle, teardrop shaped airtrap stopper, in-the-making thin elongated bubble in neck . **500.00**

Bohemian, amber cut to clear, floral arrangement intaglio carved on ruby flashed ground of three oval panels with carved frames of floral swags, five cut-to-clear panels at neck, three embellished with gold scrolls, all edged in brilliant gold, 16 decorative panels edged in gold, base and stopper both sgd "4" **750.00**

Burmese, 6-1/2" h, three striking chrysanthemum blossoms, two white and one yellow, coral-colored detail, striped mushroom stopper, signed "88" in enamel. **2,950.00**

Cranberry Opalescent, Hobnail, Hobbs, Brockunier & Co., Wheeling, WV, 7-1/2" h **485.00**

Custard Glass, Wild Bouquet pattern, fired-on dec. **500.00**

Frosted Blue, 12" h, 3" d, enameled large pink and white flower, green leaves, applied blue handle, matching blue frosted bubble stopper, gold trim **165.00**

Green, 9-1/4" h, 3-1/8" d,
white-enameled dec, applied green
handle, green bubble stopper **..165.00**

Greentown

Cactus, chocolate, ns **125.00**

Leaf Bracket, chocolate, os..**265.00**

Pattern Glass

Amazon, orig bar-in-hand stopper,
8-1/2" h **185.00**

Beveled Star, green, os **225.00**

Big Button, ruby stained, os ..**250.00**

Croesus, large, green, gold trim,
os.....................**395.00**

Cut Log, os **60.00**

Daisy and Button with Crossbars,
os.....................**75.00**

Dakota, etched, ns **55.00**

Delaware, cranberry, gold trim,
os.....................**295.00**

Esther, green, gold trim, os ..**465.00**

Fandago, ns...............**85.00**

Fluted Scrolls, blue dec, os..**265.00**

Louise, os **70.00**

Mardi Gras, ns.............**35.00**

Millard, amber stain, os.....**345.00**

Riverside's Ransom, vaseline,
os.....................**225.00**

Shoshone, os.............**55.00**

Tiny Optic, green, dec, os...**150.00**

Peachblow, 6-1/2" h, petticoat shape,
orig cut amber stopper,
Wheeling................**1,750.00**

*Cranberry, bulbous base,
applied clear handle, clear faceted stopper, 6-1/2" h,* **$70.**

Rubena Verde, 7" h, IVT, Tee Pee
shape, trefoil top, vaseline handle
and faceted stopper, Hobbs,
Brockunier & Co.............**550.00**

Sapphire Blue

7-1/4" h, Hobnail, faceted stopper,
applied blue handle, damage to
three hobs **385.00**

7-1/2" h, hp bridal white-leafed
branches, orig stopper with
teardrop-shaped airtrap... **185.00**

7-1/2" h, 3-1/4" d, enameled pink,
yellow, and blue flowers, green
leaves, applied clear handle and
foot, cut clear stopper **165.00**

Satin, 8-1/4" h, DQ, white shaded to
gold, clear-frosted handle, orig frosted
clear knobby stopper **595.00**

CUP PLATES

History: Many early cups were handleless and came
with deep saucers. The hot liquid was poured into the
saucer and sipped from it. This necessitated another
plate for the cup, hence the "cup plate."

The first cup plates made of pottery were of the
Staffordshire variety. From the mid-1830s to 1840s,
glass cup plates were favored. The Boston and
Sandwich Glass Company was one of the main
manufacturers of the lacy-glass type.

References: Ruth Webb Lee and James H. Rose,
American Glass Cup Plates, published by author,
1948, Charles E. Tuttle Co. reprint, 1985; Kenneth
Wilson, *American Glass 1760-1930*, 2 vols., Hudson
Hills Press and The Toledo Museum of Art, 1994.

Collectors' Club: Pairpoint Cup Plate Collectors of
America, P.O. Box 52D, East Weymouth, MA 02189.

Notes: It is extremely difficult to find glass cup plates
in outstanding (mint) condition. Collectors expect
some signs of use, such as slight rim roughness,
minor chipping (best if under the rim), and, in rarer
patterns, portions of scallops missing.

The numbers used are from the Lee-Rose book in
which all plates are illustrated.

Prices are based on plates in average condition.

Glass

LR 26, 3-9/16" d, colorless, attributed
to Sandwich or New England Glass
Co....................... **160.00**

LR 37, 3-1/4" d, opalescent, attributed
to Sandwich or New England Glass
Co....................... **200.00**

LR 61, 3-3/8" d, opalescent, attributed
to Sandwich or New England Glass
Co....................... **250.00**

LR 75-A, 3-13/16" d, colorless,
attributed to New England Glass
Co....................... **120.00**

LR 81, 3-3/4" d, fiery-red opalescent,
New England origin......... **350.00**

Glass, log cabin with flag in center, **$65.**

LR 88, 3-11/16" d, deep opalescent
opaque, attributed to Sandwich or New
England Glass Co............**300.00**

LR 100, 3-1/4" d, colorless, attributed to
Philadelphia area, normal mold
roughness **115.00**

LR 121, colorless, lacy, Midwestern
.........................**150.00**

LR 242-A, 3-1/2" d, black amethyst,
lacy, Eastern origin, mold underfill and
overfill......................**600.00**

LR 247, 3-7/16" d, emerald green, lacy,
attributed to Sandwich or New England
Glass Co. **775.00**

LR 319, 3-5/16" d, colorless **120.00**

LR 433, 4-1/8" d, colorless, mold
roughness **95.00**

LR 459-E, 3-7/16" d, colorless, hearts,
43 even scallops, attributed to
Sandwich **75.00**

LR 476, 3-5/16" d, colorless, hearts,
12 plain sides, attributed to
Sandwich **75.00**

Glass, historical

LR 568, 3-7/16" d, colorless, attributed
to Sandwich **165.00**

LR 586-B, colorless, Ringgold, Palo
Alto, stippled ground, small letters,
attributed to Philadelphia area,
1847-48 ....**665.00**

LR695, 3" d, colorless, Midwestern
origin, normal mold roughness .**145.00**

Pottery or porcelain

Gaudy Dutch, Butterfly pattern ..**750.00**

Leeds, 3-3/4" d, soft paste, gaudy blue
and white floral dec, very minor pinpoint
edge flakes..................**250.00**

Majolica, leaf motif **250.00**

Mulberry, cabbage roses, wheat
border.....................**175.00**

Staffordshire, Historical
3-1/4" d, Woodlands Estate near
Philadelphia, dark blue....**475.00**

3-1/2" d, Franklin Tomb, dark blue,
Wood **650.00**
4" d, The Tyrants Foe, light blue,
unknown maker **295.00**

CUSTARD GLASS

History: Custard glass was developed in England in the early 1880s. Harry Northwood made the first American custard glass at his Indiana, Pennsylvania, factory in 1898.

From 1898 until 1915, many manufacturers produced custard-glass patterns, e.g., Dugan Glass, Fenton, A. H. Heisey Glass Co., Jefferson Glass, Northwood, Tarentum Glass, and U.S. Glass. Cambridge and McKee continued the production of custard glass into the Depression.

The ivory or creamy yellow-custard color is achieved by adding uranium salts to the molten hot glass. The chemical content makes the glass glow when held under a black light. The more uranium, the more luminous the color. Northwood's custard glass has the smallest amount of uranium, creating an ivory color; Heisey used more, creating a deep yellow color.

Custard glass was made in patterned tableware pieces. It also was made as souvenir items and novelty pieces. Souvenir pieces include a place name or hand-painted decorations, e.g., flowers. Patterns of custard glass often were highlighted in gold, enameled colors, and stains.

> **Reproduction Alert:** L. G. Wright Glass Co. has reproduced pieces in the Argonaut Shell and Grape and Cable patterns. It also introduced new patterns, such as Floral and Grape and Vintage Band. Mosser reproduced toothpicks in Argonaut Shell, Chrysanthemum Sprig, and Inverted Fan & Feather.

References: Gary E. Baker et al., *Wheeling Glass 1829-1939*, Oglebay Institute, 1994, distributed by Antique Publications; William Heacock, *Encyclopedia of Victorian Colored Pattern Glass, Book IV: Custard Glass from A to Z*, Peacock Publications, 1980; William Heacock, James Measell and Berry Wiggins, *Harry Northwood: The Early Years 1881-1900*, Antique Publications, 1990.

Additional Listing: Pattern Glass.

Banana stand, Grape and Cable, Northwood, nutmeg stain **315.00**
Berry bowl, individual size
Fan **45.00**
Ring Band, gold and rose dec **48.00**
Berry set, master
Diamond with Peg **225.00**
Louis XV, gold trim **165.00**
Berry set, Intaglio, 7" master berry, six sauces **375.00**
Bonbon, Fruits and Flowers, Northwood, nutmeg stain **225.00**

Bonbon, Scroll, green, embossed maple leaf with chrysanthemum decoration, signed "Northwood," 5-7/8" l, 3-1/3" w, 2-5/8" h, **$45.**

Bowl, Grape and Cable, Northwood, 7-1/2" d, basketweave ext., nutmeg stain **65.00**
Butter dish, cov
Everglades **375.00**
Grape and Cable, Northwood, nutmeg stain **450.00**
Tiny Thumbprint, Tarentum, dec **300.00**
Victoria **300.00**
Celery, Ring Band **300.00**
Compote
Argonaut Shell **85.00**
Geneva **65.00**
Creamer
Fluted Scrolls **90.00**
Heart with Thumbprint **80.00**
Cruet, Chrysanthemum Sprig, 7" h, gold dec **485.00**
Goblet, Grape and Gothic Arches, nutmeg stain **80.00**
Hair receiver, Winged Scroll . . . **125.00**
Nappy
Northwood Grape **60.00**
Prayer Rug **65.00**
Pitcher, Argonaut Shell **325.00**
Plate, Grape and Cable, Northwood **55.00**
Punch cup
Diamond with Peg **60.00**
Louis XV **55.00**
Salt and pepper shakers, pr, Chrysanthemum Sprig **175.00**
Sauce
Cane Insert **35.00**
Intaglio **35.00**
Spooner
Grape and Gothic Arches **95.00**
Intaglio **115.00**

Sugar, cov
Georgia Gem, pink floral dec **185.00**
Tiny Thumbprint, rose dec . . **185.00**
Table set, cov butter, creamer, spooner, cov sugar
Argonaut Shell **450.00**
Intaglio **500.00**
Tankard pitcher, Diamond with Peg **275.00**
Toothpick holder, Louis XV . . . **200.00**
Tumbler
Cherry Scale **50.00**
Geneva, green and red enamel dec **60.00**
Inverted Fan and Feather **80.00**
Vermont **90.00**
Wild Bouquet **45.00**
Water Set, Ring Band, Heisey, blue floral dec, pitcher, six tumblers . **695.00**

CUT GLASS, AMERICAN

History: Glass is cut by grinding decorations into the glass by means of abrasive-carrying metal or stone wheels. A very ancient craft, it was revived in 1600 by

Bohemians and spread through Europe to Great Britain and America.

American cut glass came of age at the Centennial Exposition in 1876 and the World Columbian Exposition in 1893. The American public recognized American cut glass to be exceptional in quality and workmanship. America's most significant output of this high-quality glass occurred from 1880 to 1917, a period now known as the Brilliant Period.

Marks: Around 1890, some companies began adding an acid-etched "signature" to their glass. This signature may be the actual company name, its logo, or a chosen symbol. Today, signed pieces command a premium over unsigned pieces since the signature clearly establishes the origin. However, signatures should be carefully verified for authenticity since objects with forged signatures have been in existence for some time. One way to check is to run a finger tip or fingernail lightly over the signature area. As a general rule, a genuine signature cannot be felt; a forged signature has a raised surface.

Many companies never used the acid-etched signature on their glass and may or may not have affixed paper labels to the items originally. Dorflinger Glass and the Meriden Glass Co. made cut glass of the highest quality, yet never used an acid-etched signature. Furthermore, cut glass made before the 1890s was not signed. Many of these wood-polished items, cut on blown blanks, were of excellent quality and often won awards at exhibitions.

References: Bill and Louis Boggess, *Identifying American Brilliant Cut Glass*, 3rd ed., Schiffer Publishing, 1996; ——, *Reflections on American Brilliant Cut Glass*, Schiffer Publishing, 1995; Jo Evers, *Evers' Standard Cut Glass Value Guide*, Collector Books, 1975, 2000 value update; Kyle Husfloen, *Antique Trader's American & European Decorative and Art Glass Price Guide*, 2nd ed., Krause Publications, 2000; Bob Page and Dale Fredericksen, *A Collection of American Crystal*, Page-Fredericksen Publishing, 1995; ——, *Seneca Glass Company 1891-1983*, Page-Fredericksen Publishing, 1995; J. Michael Pearson, *Encyclopedia of American Cut & Engraved Glass*, Vols. I to III, published by author, 1975; Albert C. Revi, *Encyclopedia of American Cut & Engraved Glass*, Schiffer Publishing, 2000; Jane Shadel Spillman, *American Cut Glass, T. G. Hawkes and His Competitors*, Antique Collectors' Club, 1999; Martha Louise Swan, *American Cut and Engraved Glass*, Krause Publications, 1998. Kenneth Wilson, *American Glass 1760-1930*, 2 vols., Hudson Hills Press and The Toledo Museum of Art, 1994.

Collectors' Club: American Cut Glass Association, P.O. Box 482, Ramona, CA 92065.

Museums: Corning Museum of Glass, Corning, NY; High Museum of Art, Atlanta, GA; Huntington Galleries, Huntington, WV; Lightner Museum, St. Augustine, FL; Toledo Museum of Art, Toledo, OH.

Banana bowl, 11" d, 6-1/2" d, Harvard pattern, hobstar bottom **210.00**

Basket

6" l, 5-1/2" w, rect, applied clear glass handle, Visica miter cuts, hobstars, diamonds, and sunbursts **190.00**

7-1/2" h, 8-1/2" d, four large hobstars, two fans applied crystal rope-twisted handle **350.00**

8-1/2" h, 6-1/2" w, square-shaped, three large cut hobstars with panels of floral cut-leaf design, double notched handle . . . **300.00**

9-1/2" h, 11-1/2" d, five large hobstars, fancy emb floral silver handle and rim **225.00**

Bonbon, 8" d, 2" h, Broadway pattern, Huntly, minor flakes **135.00**

Bowl

8" d, Checker Board pattern **250.00**

8" d, Heart pattern **250.00**

9" d, deep cut, medallions, large pointed ovals, arches, and base **110.00**

10" d, deep-cut buttons, stars, and fans **220.00**

12" d, 4-1/2" h, rolled-down edge, cut and engraved flowers, leaves, and center thistle, notched-serrated edge **275.00**

Box, cov

5" d, 2-3/4" h, cut-paneled base, cover cut with large eight-pointed star with hobstar center surrounded by fans, C. F. Monroe **275.00**

6-1/2" d, hinged, hobstars, cross hatching, fan, Hawkes **400.00**

Bread tray, 8" x 12", Anita, Libbey in circle mark **535.00**

Butter dish, cov, Hobstar **250.00**

Candlesticks, pr

9-1/2" h, hobstars, teardrop stem, hobstar base **250.00**

10" h, faceted cut knobs, large teardrop stems, ray base . . **425.00**

12" h, Adelaide pattern, amber, Pairpoint **250.00**

American Brilliant Period examples, left: dish, 10" d, $90; front: oblong dish, 12-1/4" l, $50; right: water pitcher, 10-1/2" h, $115. Photo courtesy of Joy Luke Auctions.

Celery vase, 9-3/4" h, fan and linear cuts **95.00**

Centerpiece, 10-3/4" d, wheel cut and etched, molded, fruiting foliage, chips **490.00**

Champagne

Kalana Lily, pattern, Dorflinger **75.00**

Stone engraved rock crystal, Dorflinger, c1890 . . . . **85.00**

Champagne bucket, 7" h, 7" d, sgd "Hoare" **400.00**

Champagne pitcher

10" h, hobstars and cane, double thumbprint handle **210.00**

11" h, Prism pattern, triple notch handle, monogram sterling silver top **425.00**

Cheese dish, cov, 6" h dome, 9" d, plate, cobalt blue cut to clear, bull's eye and panel, large miter splints on bottom of plate **250.00**

Cider pitcher, 7" h, hobstars, zippers, fine diamonds, honeycomb-cut handle, 7" h **175.00**

Cocktail shaker, 12-1/2" h, 5-1/2" w, mallard duck in flight over marsh, fancy sterling silver rim and cover, both glass and sterling rim sgd "Hawkes" . . **210.00**

Cologne bottle

6" h, Hob and Lace pattern, green cased to clear, pattern-cut stopper, Dorflinger **625.00**

7-1/2" h, Holland pattern, faceted-cut stopper **275.00**

7-1/2" h, 2-3/4" d, Parisian pattern, sq shape, Dorflinger, pr . . . **700.00**

Compote

6" h, hobstar and arches, flared pedestal **150.00**

8" d, 5-5/8" h, bowl cut with floral sprays offset by cross cup lappets joined by beaded garlands, Hawkes sterling trumpet foot **230.00**

9" h, deep cut sunburst, arches and buttons, zippered stem, starcut petal base **150.00**

Console set, 12" d ftd bowl with wide flat rim, 9-1/8" h baluster form candlesticks, cross-hatched diamond and flute cutting **750.00**

Creamer and sugar, pr

4-1/2" h, pedestal, geometric cuttings, zippered handles, teardrop full length of handle, sgd "Hawkes" **750.00**

5-1/2" h, pedestal, Carolyn variation, notched handles **895.00**

Decanter, orig stopper

11-1/2" h, stars, arches, fans, cut neck, star cut mushroom stopper **95.00**

14" d, eight panels, hollow pointed stopper, sgd "Hawkes" **220.00**

Dish

5" d, hobstar, pineapple, palm leaf **45.00**

8" d, scalloped edge, all over hobstar medallions and hobs **175.00**

Dresser box, cov, 7" h, 7" w, Harvard pattern variation, three-ftd, silver-plated fittings, orig beveled mirror on swivel hinge under lid, cut by Bergen Glass Co., couple of minute flakes . . . **750.00**

Fern dish, 3-3/4" h, 8" w, round, silver-plate rim, C. F. Monroe, minor roughness to cut pattern, normal wear on base, no liner **200.00**

Flower center

5" h, 6" d, hobstars, flashed fans, hobstar chain and base . . **325.00**

7-3/4" h, 12" d, etched and wheel cut motif, honeycomb flared neck, some wear **500.00**

Goblet

7" h, Buzzstar, pineapple, marked "B & B" **40.00**

8-1/2" h, intaglio vintage cut, 8-1/2" h, sgd "Sinclaire" **80.00**

Hair receiver, 4-1/4" d, deep cut arches, diamonds, engraved florals **60.00**

Humidor, cov

7-1/2" d, Middlesex, hollow stopper, sponge holder in lid, Dorflinger **490.00**

9" h, hobstars, beaded split vesicas, hobstar base, matching cut glass lid with hollow for sponge . . **575.00**

Ice bucket

6-1/2" h, 7" w, Harvard pattern, floral cutting, eight sided form , minor edge flaking on handles . . . **100.00**

7" h, hobstars and notched prisms, 8" d underplate, double handles **940.00**

Ice cream set, Russian pattern, eight 7" d dishes, 8-1/2" d serving bowl, 11" d cake plate, some chips to edges , price for 10-pc set **500.00**

Knife rest, 4" l **90.00**

Lamp, 21-3/4" h, standard with egg-shaped knop over flattened knop, two further egg knops, round knop, each cut with diagonal floral bands, bronzed metal leaf end caps, round spreading foot, bronzed metal base **490.00**

Lamp, mushroom shade, hobstars, prism, strawberry diamond, feathered fan, $3,000. Photo courtesy of Woody Auction.

Loving cup, three handles, sterling top **350.00**

Nappy, two handles

6" d, hobstar center, intaglio floral, strawberry diamond button border, 6" d **45.00**

9" d, deep-cut arches, pointed sunbursts and medallions . . **135.00**

Orange bowl, 9-3/4" x 6-3/4" x 3-3/4" h, hobstars and strawberry diamond **200.00**

Perfume bottle

3-1/2" l, cranberry overlay, shaped sides, notched cuts, S. Mordan & Co., silver-mounted cap . . . **325.00**

5-1/2" h, 3" d, six-sided, alternating panels of Harvard pattern and engraved florals, rayed base, matching faceted stopper . . **175.00**

6-1/2" h, bulbous, all over cutting, orig stopper **220.00**

Pickle tray, 7 x 3", checkerboard, hobstar **45.00**

Pitcher

8-7/8" h, baluster form body, upper section vertically ribbed and cut, lower section with stylized flowerheads, facet cut handle, silver-plated rim mount with

beaded edging, monogrammed, marked "Wilcox Silver Plate Co." **750.00**

14-1/8" h, baluster, vertical flutes with bead and lozenge cuts, crosshatched and diamond-cut diamonds at base, mounted with sterling bead-edged spout, monogrammed **250.00**

Powder jar, cov, 2-1/2" h, circular, body wheel cut with ribboned garland, pink enamel over sunbursts ground on cov, unmarked, attributed to Hawkes **275.00**

Plate

10" d, Carolyn pattern, J. Hoare **525.00**

12" d, alternating hobstar and pinwheel **100.00**

Punch bowl

11" h, 10" w, two pc, Elgin pattern, Quaker City **600.00**

14" d, 7" h, five large hobstars, central large hobstar **550.00**

Punch ladle, 11-1/2" l, silver plated emb shell bowl, cut and notched prism handle **165.00**

Relish

8" l, two handles, divided, Jupiter pattern, Meriden **120.00**

13" l, leaf shape, Clear Button Russian pattern **375.00**

Salad serving fork and spoon, silver plated, cross-cut diamond glass handles **300.00**

Salt shaker, prism columns **30.00**

Spooner, 5" h, hobstar and arches **90.00**

Tankard pitcher

10-1/4" h, Harvard cut sides, pinwheel top, mini hobnails, thumbprint notched handle **200.00**

11" h, hobstar, strawberry diamond, notched prism and fan, flared base with bull's eye, double thumbprint handle **275.00**

Tray

12" d, round, Monarch, sgd "Hoare" **975.00**

12" d, round, Wilhelm, Fry . . **850.00**

14" x 7-1/2", Sillsbee pattern, Pairpoint **335.00**

Tumbler

Clear Button Russian pattern . **95.00**

Harvard, rayed base **45.00**

Hobstars **40.00**

Vase

8" h, 11" d, squatty body, short flaring neck, scalloped rim . **550.00**

11" h, fan, amber, engraved grape leaves and vines, round disk base, acid-etched Hawkes mark, small chip on base **300.00**

12" h, three cartouches of roses, star and hobstar cut ground. . . . **225.00**

12" h, 5-1/2" w, triangular, three large and three small hobstars, double notched pedestal and flaring base **150.00**

12-1/2" h, 6-1/2" d, floral and diamond point engraving, sgd "Hawkes" **250.00**

14" h, club form **300.00**

14" h, pedestal, Florentine pattern, Higgins & Seiter **775.00**

16" h, corset shape, well-cut hobstar, strawberry diamond, prism, flashed star and fan **300.00**

Water carafe

Harvard pattern **185.00**

Hobstars and notched prisms **125.00**

Pinwheel and Fan cutting, notched neck, 8" h, 4" w **125.00**

Water pitcher

9-1/2" h, Harvard pattern panels and intaglio cut sprays of flowers and foliage **300.00**

10" h, Keystone Rose pattern **190.00**

Whiskey jug, 6-1/4" h, bulbous, thistle and grape cutting, orig stopper, sgd "Sinclaire" **295.00**

Wine

4" h, flint, cut panels, strawberry diamonds, and fans, Pittsburgh **60.00**

4-1/8" h, flint, Gothic Arch, sheaf like ferns, Pittsburgh **75.00**

CZECHOSLOVAKIAN ITEMS

History: Objects marked "Made in Czechoslovakia" were produced after 1918 when the country claimed its independence from the Austro-Hungarian Empire. The people became more cosmopolitan and liberated and expanded the scope of their lives. Their porcelains, pottery, and glassware reflect many influences.

Marks: A specific manufacturer's mark may include a date which precedes 1918, but this only indicates the factory existed during the years of the Bohemian or Austro-Hungarian Empire.

References: Dale and Diane Barta and Helen M. Rose, *Czechoslovakian Glass & Collectibles* (1992, 1995 values), Book II (1997) Collector Books; *Bohemian Glass*, n.d., distributed by Antique Publications; Ruth A. Forsythe, *Made in Czechoslovakia*, Antique Publications, 1995 value update; Jacquelyne Y. Jones-North, et. al., *Czechoslovakian Perfume Bottles and Boudoir Accessories, Revised Ed.*, Antique Publications, 1999.

Periodical: *New Glass Review*, Bardounova 2140 149 00 Praha 4, Prague, Czech Republic.

Collectors' Club: Czechoslovakian Collectors Guild International, P.O. Box 901395, Kansas City, MO 64190.

Museum: Friends of the Glass Museum of Novy Bor, Kensington, MD.

Rose bowl, mauve exterior, white interior, scalloped gold rimmed top, Crown, T. K. Thiemy mark, 3-1/4" h, **$20.**

Cologne bottle, 4" h, porcelain, glossy blue, bow front. **40.00**

Decanter set, 7-3/4" h decanter, seven 6" h wine glasses, Moorish style, heavily dec gold borders, red enamel, multicolored glass jewels **800.00**

Demitasse service, partial, hp, red Geisha tea house scene, five cups and saucers, cov sugar, 19-1/2" x 9-1/2" oval tray. **120.00**

Figure

6" h, white horse **28.00**

8-1/2" h, doctor, orig label, set of three **450.00**

Flower frog, bird on stump, pottery **35.00**

Goblet, 6-1/2" h, mold blown, cobalt blue, strong oil spot irid ext.,

acid-etched stamp "Czechoslovakia" **375.00**

Lamp

Boudoir, 13" h, enamel dec shade with raised enamel castle, mountainous landscape, sunset orange ground, baluster form glass base with similar dec, base stamped "Made in Czechoslovakia" **400.00**

Table, 14-1/2" h, 13-1/4" d conical shade, spherical base, frosted dark amber glass, acid etched and enameled Art Deco-style geometric diamond and triangle patterns in orange and green, silver stamp "Bulova Czechoslovakia" on base, c1930 . . . . **2,645.00**

Perfume bottle

8-1/4" h, colorless, wide-stepped design, elaborate oval stopper engraved and etched as kneeling woman gathering flowers . . **350.00**

9-3/4" h, mold blown red glass, figural woman with butterfly wings, some frosting, colorless glass lily stopper frosted and polished **750.00**

Pitcher, 6" h crackled, irid marigold flashing, hp underwater scene of fish and coral, polished pontil. **150.00**

Powder box, cov, glass, round, yellow, black knob top **75.00**

Stemware

Goblet, red bowls with silver overlay, vignettes of deer surrounded by floral ground, black stems, 10 pcs **325.00**

Sherbet, red bowl, silver trim, black stem, acid stamp mark, 12 pcs **350.00**

Vase

6-1/4" h, cylindrical, mottled white and purple, cased to colorless, enameled stylized vignette of woman fishing, silver mounted rim with English hallmarks, c1930 . . . . **275.00**

7-1/2" h, mold-blown ovoid, tapered neck, flared mouth, black glass, furnace dec winding ribbons of yellow-green to dark green, acid mark, c1930 . . . . **320.00**

8" h, crystal, red threading, cut to clear spots, flared rim, sgd **250.00**

DAVENPORT

History: John Davenport opened a pottery in Longport, Staffordshire, England, in 1793. His high-quality light-weight wares are cream colored with a beautiful velvety texture.

The firm's output included soft-paste (Old Blue) products, luster-trimmed pieces, and pink luster wares with black transfer. Pieces of Gaudy Dutch and Spatterware also have been found with the Davenport mark. Davenport later became a leading maker of ironstone and early flow blue. His famous Cyprus pattern in mulberry became very popular. His heirs continued the business until the factory closed in 1886.

Reference: T. A. Lockett and Geoffrey A. Godden, *China, Earthenware & Glass, 1794-1884,* Random Century, 1990.

Museums: British Museum, London, England; Cincinnati Art Museum, Cincinnati, OH; Hanley Museum, Stoke-on-Trent, England; Liverpool Museum, Liverpool, England; Victoria & Albert Museum, London, England.

Cup and saucer, Amoy pattern, flow blue on white, incised anchor mark, 3-3/4" cup, 6" saucer, $150.

Charger, 17-1/2" l, oval, Venetian harbor scene, light-blue transfer **80.00**

Compote, 2-1/2" h, 8-1/2" d, turquoise and gold band, tiny raised flowers, hp scene with man fishing, cows at edge of lake, c1860, pr **225.00**

Creamer, tan, jasperware, basketweave, incised anchor mark **60.00**

Cup plate, Teaberry pattern, pink luster **40.00**

Dish, ftd, tricorn, Belvoir Castle dec **90.00**

Ewer, 9" h, floral dec, multicolored, c1930. . . . . **190.00**

Jug, 5-1/2" h, Jardiniere pattern, blue, orange, green, peach, and gold, peach luster rim, c1805-20 . . . . **450.00**

Plate

7" d, Chinese River Scene, reticulated, medium to dark blue **310.00**

8" d, Imari, orange, blue, purple, and gold, wear **165.00**

9-1/4" d, Peony & Pheasant . . **185.00**

9-1/2" d, Flying Bird, blue, orange, pink, yellow, and green **250.00**

Platter

18-1/4", stone china, polychrome dec blue transfer print bird and floral pattern, printed mark, c1810, glaze wear **230.00**

19-1/8" l, purple transfer, idyllic scene, boat and church, marked "Davenport" **440.00**

Sauce tureen, cov, ladle, creamware, molded leaves, lime green veining, early **450.00**

Serving bowl, cov, 7" w, 9-3/4" l, Chinoiserie Bridgeless pattern, internal bowl with steam holes, c1810 . . **700.00**

Soup tureen, matching stand, 13-1/4" l, stone china, polychrome dec blue transfer printed bird and floral patter, gilded lion mask handles, printed marks, c1810, large hairline on stand, glaze wear **1,610.00**

Tea service, Imari pattern, 18" l tray, teapot, creamer, cov sugar, four cups and saucers **850.00**

DECOYS

History: During the past several years, carved wooden decoys, used to lure ducks and geese to the hunter, have become widely recognized as an indigenous American folk-art form. Many decoys are from 1880 to 1930, when commercial gunners commonly hunted and used rigs of several hundred decoys. Many fine carvers also worked through the 1930s and 1940s. Fish decoys were also carved by individuals and commercial decoy makers.

Because decoys were both hand made and machine made, and many examples exist, firm pricing is difficult to establish. The skill of the carver, rarity, type of bird, and age all effect the value.

References: Joel Barber, *Wild Fowl Decoys*, Dover Publications, n.d.; Russell J. Goldberger and Alan G. Haid, *Mason Decoys—A Complete Pictorial Guide*, Decoy Magazine, 1993; Loy S. Harrell, Jr., *Decoys: North America's One Hundred Greatest*, Krause Publications, 2000; Carl F. Luckey, *Collecting Antique Bird Decoys and Duck Calls: An Identification & Value Guide*, 2nd ed., Books Americana, 1992; Donald J. Peterson, *Folk Art Fish Decoys*, Schiffer Publishing, 1996.

Periodicals and Internet Resources: *Decoy Magazine*, P.O. Box 787, Lewes, DE, 19558, http://www.DecoyMag.com; *E-Decoy Online Magazine*, http://www.edecoy.com; *North America*

Decoys, P.O. Box 246, Spanish Fork, UT 84660; *Sporting Collector's Monthly*, RW Publishing, P.O. Box 305, Camden, DE 19934; *Wildfowl Art*, Ward Foundation, 909 South Schumaker Dr., Salisbury, MD 21801; *Wildfowl Carving & Collecting*, 1300 Market St., Suite 202, Lemoyne, PA 17043, http://www.wildfowl-carving.com

Collectors' Clubs: American Fish Decoy Assoc., 624 Merritt St., Fife Lake, MI 49633-9142; Carolina Decoy Collectors Assoc., 4 St. Mary's Place, Wilmington, NC 28403; East Coast Decoy Collectors Assoc., P.O. Box 305, Camden, DE 19934; Great Lakes Fish Decoy Collectors & Carvers Assoc., 35824 W. Chicago, Livonia, MI 48150-2522; Long Island Decoy Collectors Assoc., P.O. Box 807, Smithtown, NY 11787; Midwest Collectors Assoc., 6 E. Scott St., Chicago, IL 60610, http://www.midwesterndecoy.org; New England Decoy Collectors Assoc., P.O. Box 206, West Barnstable, MA 02668, http://www.decoysunlimitedinc.com; New Jersey Decoy Collectors Assoc., 1745 Silverton Rd, Toms River, NJ 08753; Ohio Decoy Collectors & Carvers Assoc., P.O. Box 499, Richfield, OH 44286, http:www.odcca.org; Potomac Decoy Collectors Assoc., 6813 Moon Rock Court, Alexandria, VA 22306.

Museums: Chesapeake Bay Maritime Museum; Saint Michaels, MD; Havre de Grace Decoy Museum, Havre de Grace, MD; Heritage Plantation, Sandwich, MA; Long Island Museum of American Art, Stony Brook, NY; Peabody Essex Museum, Salem, MA; Refuge Waterfowl Museum, Chincoteague, VA; Shelburne Museum, Inc., Shelburne, VT; Ward Museum of Wildfowl Art, Salisbury, MD.

Reproduction Alert.

Notes: A decoy's value is based on several factors: (1) fame of the carver, (2) quality of the carving, (3) species of wild fowl—the most desirable are herons, swans, mergansers, and shorebirds—and (4) condition of the original paint.

The inexperienced collector should be aware of several facts. The age of a decoy, per se, is usually of no importance in determining value. However, age does have some influence when it comes to a rare or important example. Since very few decoys were ever signed, it is quite difficult to attribute most decoys to known carvers. Anyone who has not examined a known carver's work will be hard pressed to determine if the paint on one of his decoys is indeed original. Repainting severely decreases a decoy's value. In addition, there are many fakes and reproductions on the market and even experienced collectors are occasionally fooled. Decoys represent a subject where dealing with a reputable dealer or auction house is important, especially those who offer a guarantee as to authenticity.

Decoys listed below are of average wear, unless otherwise noted.

American Bittern Drake, miniature, H. Gibbs, sgd and identified in ink on base, 2-3/4" x 2-1/2" **375.00**

Baldgate Wigeon Drake, miniature
A. Elmer, Crowell, East Harwich, MA, identified in ink, rect stamp on base, 2-1/2" x 4" **635.00**
James Lapham, Dennisport, MA, sgd in ink, oval stamp, natural wood base, 3-3/4" x 5-3/4" . **230.00**

Black Bellied Bustard, miniature, H. Gills, initialed "H. G. 1957," identified in pencil, natural wood base, 3-1/2" x 4" **230.00**

Black Bellied Plover, unknown American 20th C maker, orig paint, glass eyes, mounted on stick on lead base
12-1/2" h, minor paint loss, small chips to beak **2,530.00**
13-1/2" h, minor paint loss, beak repair **1,725.00**

Black Breasted Plover
A. E. Crowell, oval brand on bottom **2,750.00**
Harry C. Shourds, orig paint **2,650.00**

Black Duck
A. Elmer Crowell, East Harwich, MA, orig paint, glass eyes, stamped mark in oval on base, sleeping, wear, crack, 5-1/4" h **520.00**
A. Elmer Crowell, East Harwich, MA, orig paint, glass eyes, stamped mark in oval on base, minor paint wear and wear to tip of beak, 7" h **460.00**
Ira Hudson, preening, raised wings, outstretched neck, scratch feather paint **8,500.00**
Mason Factory, challenge grade, snakey head, orig grade stamp on bottom **1,700.00**
Charles Thomas, MA, glass eyes, orig paint **365.00**
Unknown maker, carved balsa body, wood head, glass eyes, orig pant, 15-1/2" l **150.00**
Wildfowler, CT, inlet head, glass eyes, worn orig paint, green overpaint on bottom on sides, 13" l, c1900 . . . . **220.00**

Black Drake, miniature
A. Elmer Crowell, East Harwich, MA, identified in ink, rect stamp on base, break at neck, reglued, minor paint loss, 3-1/2" x 4-3/4" . . . **635.00**

James Lapham, Dennisport, MA, identified in black ink, oval stamp, minor imperfections, 2-1/2" x 4" **290.00**

Bluebill Drake, Rozell Bliss, Stratford, CT, c1910, **$290.**

Bluebill Drake
Jim Kelson, Mt. Clemens, MI, carved wing detail, feather stamping, glass eyes, orig paint, orig keep and weight, 13-1/2" l, c1930 . . . . **295.00**
Sandusky, well-shaped head, tack eyes, orig paint traces, 19th C **350.00**

Bluebill Hen
Irving Miller, Monroe, MI, carved wood, glass eyes, orig paint, 11-1/2" l **165.00**
Thomas Chambers, Canada Club, hollow body, glass eyes, old repaint, 15-3/4" l, c1900 . . . **550.00**

Bluebill, mated pair, Maryland, worn orig paint, 14" l, price for pair . . **225.00**

Blue-Wing Teal Drake, Mason Factory, premier grade, replaced eyes . . **850.00**

Brant, Ward Brothers, MD, carved, hollow body, head turned left, sgd "Lem and Steve," dated 1917 . . . . . . **1,650.00**

Bufflehead Drake
Bob Kerr, carved detail, glass eyes, orig paint, scratch carved signature, 10-1/2" l, c1980 . **250.00**
James Lagham, Dennisport, MA, identified in ink, oval stamp on base, 3" x 4-1/2" **345.00**
Harry M. Shrouds, carved, hollow body, painted eyes **1,800.00**

Canada Goose
Hurley Conklin, carved, hollow body, swimming position, branded "H. Conklin" on bottom **600.00**
H. Gibbs, identified and initialed "HG 1957" on natural wood base, 2-1/2" x 4-1/2" **290.00**
Unsigned, attributed to Harry Ackerman, MI, old black, gray, and white repaint, glass eyes, incised detail, wear to paint, chips on bill, 11-1/2" h, 23" l **450.00**

Canvasback Drake, attributed to VA, stamped "W. O & G. H.," old worn working repaint, glass eyes, 14-1/2" l, 7-1/2" h **300.00**

Canvasback Hen
Charles Bean, carved wood, glass eyes, orig paint, 14-3/4" l . . **250.00**
Frank Schmidt, orig paint, glass eyes, relief carved wing tips, 16-1/4" l **165.00**

Common Golden Eye Drake, miniature, A. Elmer Crowell, East Harwich, MA, identified in ink, rect stamp on base, minor paint imperfections, 2-1/2" x 4" **825.00**

Curlew
A. E. Crowell, hollow carved, orig paint **850.00**
Dan Leeds, Pleasantville, NJ, 1880-1900, carved and painted brown, stand, 13" l **2,415.00**
Harry V. Shrouds, orig paint **2,000.00**

Curlew Oyster Eater, Samuel Jester, Tennessee, c1920, carved and painted, slight paint wear, age crack in body, stand, 16" l, 9" h **1,035.00**

Eider Duck, polychrome-carved wood
America, early 19th C, cracks, 15" l **400.00**
Attributed to Maine maritime region, early 20th C, on stand, 19" l **550.00**

Eider Hen, attributed to Amos Wallace, Harpswell, Maine, 19th C, traces of paint and horseshoe keel weight, 18" l **1,495.00**

Flying Duck, glass-bead eyes, old natural surface, carved pine, attributed to Maine, c1930, 16" l, 11" h . . **2,300.00**

Goldeneye Duck, New England, c1900, minor paint wear, 12" l **2,300.00**

Great Northern Pike, attributed to Menomene Indian, WI, c1900, painted green, glass eyes, ribbed sheet metal fin, tall stand, 36" l, 9" h **3,450.00**

Green Wing Teal Duck, miniature, A. Elmer Crowell, East Harwich, MA, identified in ink, rect stamp on base, 2-1/2" x 4" **865.00**

Heron, unknown maker, carved wig and tail, wrought iron legs **900.00**

Herring Gull, attributed to Gus Wilson, c1910-20, used as weathervane, traces of old paint, metal feet, weathered and worn, 18-3/4" l **3,110.00**

Hooded Merganser Drake, miniature, H. Gibbs, 1965, sgd in pencil on base, 2-1/2" x 2-3/4" **290.00**

Loon, carved and painted, wooden rudder, America, 19th C, stand, paint wear, 27" l **9,200.00**

Mallard Drake

Ben Schmidt, Detroit, relief carved, feather stamping, glass eyes, orig paint, orig keep, marked "Mallard drake Benj Schmidt, Detroit 1960," 15-1/4" l **450.00**

Bert Graves, carved, hollow body, orig weighted bottom, branded "E. I. Rogers" and "Cleary" . . . **900.00**

James Lapham, Dennisport, MA, sgd and identified in ink on bottom, 4" x 5" **435.00**

Mason Factory, standard grand, carved wood, glass eyes, orig paint, 15-3/4" l **225.00**

Mallard Hen

Ralph Johnston, Detroit, MI, high head, glass eyes, orig paint marked "R. D. Johnston orig keel 1948" in pencil, 17-1/2" l . . **250.00**

Robert Elliston, carved, hollow body, orig paint **1,800.00**

Top: Golden Eye or Whistler, Joe Wooster, signed "Good Hunting, Josef Wooster, '70," original paint, glass eyes, very good detail, 14-1/2" l, $360; middle: Merganser Hen, Joe Wooster, signed "Good Hunting Joseph 'Buckeye Joe' Wooster," original paint, glass eyes, very good detail, minor paint separation, 21-1/2" l, $200; bottom: Merganser Drake, Joe Wooster, mate to one above, signed the same, minor wear edge, $385. Photo courtesy of Garth's Auctions.

Merganser

Attributed to George Hye, c1900, carved head on streamlined body, painted shades of brown with white, brick red bill, wear, minor losses, 19" l, 6-1/2" h **2,415.00**

Attributed to Massachusetts, 19th C, 17" l **460.00**

Attributed to New Jersey, 19th C, 20" l **4,485.00**

Attributed to New York state, late 19th C, 14" l **2,185.00**

Pigeon, carved and painted wood, America, late 19th/early 20th C, 12-1/4" l **575.00**

Pintail Drake

America, c1930, carved head, glass eyes, hollow body, painted brown, black and white, green bill, wear, minor losses, body cracks, 15" l, 7-1/4" h **2,185.00**

Mason Factory, premier grade, sloping breast, orig paint . . **750.00**

Zeke McDonald, MI, high head, hollow body, glass eyes, orig paint, c1910 . . . . **550.00**

Pintail Hen, Mason Factory, premier grade, sloping breast, orig paint, marked "Big Point Co. Pathcourt, Ont. James S. Meredith, member 1900-1920" **2,400.00**

Pintail Hen, miniature, sgd "Cleon" in ink on bottom, 2-3/4" x 3-1/2" . . . **250.00**

Plover, Joe Lincoln, winter plumage, feather painting, orig paint **800.00**

Red Breasted Merganser Drake

George Boyd, NH, carved, orig paint **8,000.00**

Amos Wallace, ME, inlet neck, carved crest, detailed feathered paint **2,000.00**

Red Breasted Merganser Drake, miniature, A. Elmer Crowell, East Harwich, MA, identified in ink, rect stamp on base, minor paint imperfections, 2-1/2" x 6" **980.00**

Redhead Drake

R Madison Mitchell, carved wood, orig paint, unused, 13" l . . . **300.00**

Frank Schmidt, Detroit, MI, orig paint, glass eyes, relief carved wing tips, 15-1/2" l **250.00**

Redhead Drake, miniature

Crowell, A. Elmer, East Harwich, MA, identified in ink, rect stamp on base, minor paint imperfections, 2-1/2" x 4" **550.00**

Gibbs, H., sgd in pencil on natural wood base, 2-1/4" x 3-1/4" . . **230.00**

Robin Snipe, Obediah Verity, carved wings and eyes, orig paint . . . **4,400.00**

Ruddy Duck, miniature, maker unknown, identified in ink on base, paint loss to bill, 2" x 2-3/4" **690.00**

Ruddy Duck Drake, Len Carmeghi, Mt. Clemens, MI, hollow body, glass eyes, orig paint, sgd and dated, 10-3/4" l **250.00**

Ruffled Grouse, miniature, A. Elmer Crowell, East Harwich, MA, rect stamp, mounted on natural wood base, 3-1/2" x 4-1/2" **865.00**

Sea Gull

14" l, weathered surface, used as weathervane, attributed to WI, late 19th/early 20th C **1,840.00**

17" l, carved pine, studded with nails, old natural surface, America, c1900, stand **2,415.00**

Shore Bird, carved

11" l, attributed to David Goodspeed, America, c1900, stand **1,150.00**

11-1/2" l, traces of orig paint, weathered surface, America, early 20th C **350.00**

Sickle Bill Curlew, unknown maker, carved wood, glass eyes, pitchfork tine beak, orig paint, 22" l **150.00**

Swan, unknown Chesapeake Bay, MD, maker, carved wood, braced neck, white paint, 30" l **900.00**

Widgeon, matted pair, Charlie Joiner, MD, sgd on bottom **800.00**

Wood Duck Drake, miniature, A. Elmer Crowell, East Harwich, MA, identified in ink, rect stamp on base, 3" x 4-1/2" **1,150.00**

Yellowlegs, carved and painted, New Jersey, c1890, stand, 11" l . . . **2,185.00**

DEDHAM POTTERY

History: Alexander W. Robertson established a pottery in Chelsea, Massachusetts, about 1866. After his brother, Hugh Cornwall Robertson, joined him in 1868, the firm was called A. W. & H. C. Robertson. Their father, James Robertson, joined his sons in 1872, and the name Chelsea Keramic Art Works Robertson and Sons was used.

The pottery's initial products were simple flower and bean pots, but the firm quickly expanded its output to include a wide variety of artistic pottery. It produced a very fine redware body used in classical forms, some with black backgrounds imitating ancient Greek and Apulian works. It experimented with underglaze slip decoration on vases. The Chelsea Keramic Art Works Pottery also produced high-glazed vases, pitchers, and plaques with a buff clay body, with either sculpted or molded applied decoration.

James Robertson died in 1880 and Alexander moved to California in 1884, leaving Hugh C. Robertson alone in Chelsea, where his tireless experiments eventually yielded a stunning imitation of the prized Chinese Ming-era blood-red glaze. Hugh's vases with that glaze were marked with an impressed "CKAW." Creating these red-glazed vases was very expensive, and even though they received great critical acclaim, the company declared bankruptcy in 1889.

Recapitalized by a circle of Boston art patrons in 1891, Hugh started the Chelsea Pottery U.S., which produced gray crackle-glazed dinnerware with cobalt-blue decorations, the rabbit pattern being the most popular.

The business moved to new facilities in Dedham, Massachusetts, and began production in 1896 under the name Dedham Pottery. Hugh's son and grandson operated the business until it closed in 1943, by which time between 50 and 80 patterns had been produced, some very briefly.

Marks: The following marks help determine the approximate age of items:

- "Chelsea Keramic Art Works Robertson and Sons," impressed, 1874-1880
- "CKAW," impressed, 1875-1889
- "CPUS," impressed in a cloverleaf, 1891-1895
- Foreshortened rabbit only, impressed, 1894-1896
- Conventional rabbit with "Dedham Pottery" in square blue stamped mark along with one impressed foreshortened rabbit, 1896-1928
- Blue rabbit stamped mark with "registered" beneath, along with two impressed foreshortened rabbit marks, 1929-1943

References: Lloyd E. Hawes, *Dedham Pottery and the Earlier Robertson's Chelsea Potteries*, Dedham Historical Society, 1968; Paul Evans, *Art Pottery of the United States*, Feingold & Lewis, 1974; Ralph and Terry Kovel, *Kovels' American Art Pottery*, Crown Publishers, 1993.

Collectors' Club: Dedham Pottery Collectors Society, 248 Highland St., Dedham, MA 02026, http://www.dedhampottery.com.

Museum: Dedham Historical Society, Dedham, MA.

Adviser: James D. Kaufman.

Reproduction Alert: Two companies make Dedham-like reproductions primarily utilizing the rabbit pattern, but always mark their work very differently from the original.

Bowl, 8-1/2" sq
    Rabbit pattern, reg. stamp .. **600.00**
    Rabbit pattern, reg. stamp, hairline crack **275.00**
    Swan pattern, reg. stamp ... **725.00**
Candlesticks, pr
    Elephant pattern, reg. blue stamp **525.00**
    Rabbit pattern, reg. blue stamp **325.00**
Creamer and sugar, type #1, 3-1/4" h, Duck pattern, blue stamp **650.00**
Demitasse cup and saucer, Rabbit pattern, blue stamp **320.00**

Plate, Rabbit pattern, crackleware, impressed rabbit mark, couple of minor flecks around edges, 8-1/2" d, **$215.** *Photo courtesy of David Rago Auctions.*

Knife rest, Rabbit form, blue reg. stamp **575.00**
Paperweight, Rabbit form, blue reg. stamp **495.00**
Pickle dish, 10-1/2" l, Elephant pattern, blue reg. stamp **750.00**
Pitcher
    5" h, Rabbit pattern, blue stamp **325.00**
    5-1/8" h, Chickens pattern, blue stamp **2,300.00**
    7" h, Turkey pattern, blue stamp **585.00**
    9" h, Rabbit pattern, blue stamp **700.00**
    Style of 1850, blue reg. stamp **975.00**
Plate, 6" d
    Clover pattern, reg. stamp .. **625.00**
    Dolphin pattern, blue reg. stamp, chip **225.00**
    Iris pattern, blue stamp, Maude Davenport's "O" rebus **280.00**
    Rabbit pattern, blue stamp.. **145.00**
Plate, 8" d, Iris pattern, reg. stamp..................... **230.00**
Plate, 8-1/2" d
    Crab central design, blue stamp **550.00**
    Duck pattern, blue stamp, Maude Davenport's "O" rebus **375.00**
    Elephant pattern, blue reg. stamp **650.00**
    Rabbit pattern, blue stamp.. **175.00**
    Rabbit pattern, blue stamp, Maude Davenport's "O" rebus **235.00**
    Snow Tree pattern, blue stamp **210.00**
    Upside down dolphin, CPUS **900.00**

Plate, 10" d
    Clover pattern, blue stamp .. **825.00**
    Dolphin pattern, blue reg. stamp **875.00**
    Elephant pattern, blue reg. stamp **900.00**
    Pine Apple pattern, CPUS... **775.00**
    Turkey pattern, blue stamp, Maude Davenport's "O" rebus **475.00**
Platter, 14" x 8", oval, steak platter, Rabbit pattern, blue reg. stamp. **825.00**
Sherbet, two handles, Rabbit pattern, blue stamp **350.00**
Tea cup and saucer
    Azalea pattern, reg. stamp .. **130.00**
    Butterfly pattern, blue stamp. **345.00**
    Duck pattern, reg. stamp ... **190.00**
    Iris pattern, reg. stamp **155.00**
    Rabbit pattern, reg. stamp .. **155.00**
    Turtle pattern, reg. stamp ... **680.00**
    Water Lily pattern, reg. stamp **130.00**
Teapot, 6-1/8" h, Rabbit pattern, blue stamp **875.00**
Vase, 4" d, 8" h, experimental, by Hugh Robertson, brown and green flambé glaze, incised "DEDHAM POTTERY/HCR" **980.00**

Vase, experimental, by Hugh Robertson, brown and green flambé glaze, incised "Dedham Pottery/HCR," 4" d, 8" h, **$980.** *Photo courtesy of David Rago Auctions.*

DELFTWARE

History: Delftware is pottery with a soft, red-clay body and tin-enamel glaze. The white, dense, opaque color came from adding tin ash to lead glaze. The first examples had blue designs on a white ground. Polychrome examples followed.

The name originally applied to pottery made in the region around Delft, Holland, beginning in the 16th century and ending in the late 18th century. The tin used came from the Cornish mines in England. By the 17th and 18th centuries, English potters in London, Bristol, and Liverpool were copying the glaze and designs. Some designs unique to English potters also developed.

In Germany and France, the ware is known as Faience, and in Italy as Majolica.

Collectors' Club: Delftware Collectors Assoc., P.O. Box 670673, Marietta, GA 30066, http://www.delftware.org.

> **Reproduction Alert:** Since the late 19th century, much Delft-type souvenir material has been produced to appeal to the foreign traveler. Don't confuse these modern pieces with the older examples.

Bowl
8-3/4" d, shallow, blue and white, figure of young woman with bough **475.00**
12" d, shallow, blue and white, landscape with figure, edge chips **550.00**
12-1/2" d, 6-1/2" h, blue and white, broken, poorly repaired . . **1,155.00**
13" d, shallow, polychrome dec, minor edge wear, English . . **715.00**
Bowl, attached strainer, 8-3/4" d, 3-1/2" h, blue and white floral dec, hairlines and deteriorating old repair
. . . . **470.00**

Plaque, pottery, blue and white harbor scene, 18" x 21-1/2", $420. Photo courtesy of Joy Luke Auctions.

Charger
12" d, blue and white, floral rim, landscape, edge chips **200.00**
13" d, floral design, building scene, manganese and blue, edge chips **615.00**
13-1/8" d, blue and white, foliate devices, Dutch, 19th C, chips, glaze wear **410.00**
13-1/4" d, polychrome floral design, blue, red, yellow, green, and black, edge chips **880.00**
13-5/8" d, blue and white, foliate devices, 19th C, chips, glass wear, restoration **320.00**
14" d, polychrome floral dec, tree, edge chips **550.00**
16 1/2" d, center branch with fruiting blossoms, two birds, conforming florals on wide rim, sgd "G. A. Kleynoven," c1655 . . . . . **2,250.00**

Dish
8-1/4" d, molded rim, blue and white, stylized landscape and floral design, edge chips **315.00**
12-3/8" l, fluted oval, blue and white floral design, attributed to Lambeth, chips **440.00**
Flower brick, 4-5/8" l, 2-1/2" h, blue and white, Chinese figures in landscape, Dutch, 18th C, chips, cracks . . . **375.00**
Garniture, three bulbous 17-1/4" h cov urns, two octagonal tapered 12-3/4" h vases, polychrome dec foliage surrounding central blue figural panels, Dutch, late 18th/early 19th C . **8,625.00**
Inkwell, 4-1/2" h, heart shape, blue and white floral dec, wear and edge chips **495.00**
Jar, 5" h, blue and white, chips, pr **715.00**
Model, 17-1/2" h, tall case clock, blue dec white ground, panels of figural and architectural landscapes between scrolled foliate borders, 19th C, slight glaze wear **320.00**
Mug, 6-3/8" h, blue and white, armorial surrounded by exotic landscape, palm trees, marked on base, Dutch, 19th C, minor chips, glaze wear **490.00**

Plate
8-1/2" d, blue and white, floral, pots of flowers and insects, small edge chips, five-pc set **825.00**
8-5/8" d, blue and white, central reserves of foliate devices, neoclassical urn, Continental, 18th C **175.00**
8-3/4" d, manganese, iron red, yellow, and underglaze blue floral design, chips **200.00**
9" d, blue and white floral dec, Dutch inscription on front, another on back, edge chips **200.00**
9" d, tin glaze, flowering branch behind fence, blue, yellow, green, and pale purple, English, rim chips **550.00**
10-1/4" d, blue and white Bible illustration, small over reserve with bible reference and date "MAT 2:IV.00, 1752," small edge chips **770.00**

Posset pot
4-3/4" h, blue and white, birds among foliage, England, 19th C, minor chips and cracks . . . **920.00**
7-1/4" h, blue and white floral dec with bird, attributed to Lambeth, mismatched lid, base hairlines, minor edge chips **1,650.00**
Sauce boat, 8-1/4" l, applied scrolled handles, fluted flaring lip, blue and white Oriental design, edge chips and hairline, later added yellow enamel rim **440.00**
Saucer, 8-3/4" d, table ring, blue, iron-red, yellow, and manganese bowl of flowers dec **825.00**
Strainer bowl, 9-1/8" d, blue and white floral design, three short feet, chips **520.00**
Tea caddy, 5-7/8" h, blue and white floral dec, scalloped bottom edge, marked "MVS 1750," cork closure, wear, edge flakes, old filled in chip on lid **550.00**
Tile picture, 12 5-1/8" x 5-1/2" blue and white tiles, scene of windmills and figures by canal, 20-3/4" w x 30-1/4" h oak frame, Netherlands, late 19th/early 20th C **500.00**
Tobacco jar, 10" h, blue and white, Indians and "Siville," older brass stepped lid, chips **1,870.00**
Vase, 19" h, tapering octagonal, molded lobes, blue, green, and red polychromed continuous band of birds of paradise within foliage, marked "J.V.D.H.," late 19th C, pr **1,200.00**
Vase, cov, 18-3/4" h, baluster, body with three cartouches depicting courting couple, sailing ships bordered by molded diaper work, foliate cast ormolu base with conforming dec cov, Holland, late 19th C, pr **3,000.00**
Wall pocket, 6-1/4" w, 4-1/2" d, 7" h, vasiform, ogee backplate, pierced grillwork, blue and white scenes of figures at harbor, scrollwork borders, applied flower buds on sides, 20th C, price for pr **350.00**

DEPRESSION GLASS

History: Depression glass was made from 1920 to 1940. It was an inexpensive machine-made glass and produced by several companies in various patterns and colors. The number of forms made in different patterns also varied.

Depression glass was sold through variety stores, given away as premiums, or packaged with certain products. Movie houses gave it away from 1935 until well into the 1940s.

Like pattern glass, knowing the proper name of a pattern is the key to collecting. Collectors should be prepared to do research.

References: Tom and Neila Bredehoft, *Fifty Years of Collectible Glass, 1920-1970, Volume 1, Volume II*, Antique Trader Books, 2000; Debbie and Randy Coe, *Elegant Glass: Early, Depression & Beyond*, Schiffer Publishing, 2001; Shirley Dunbar, *Heisey Glass, The Early Years, 1896-1924*, Krause Publications, 2000; Gene Florence, *Anchor Hocking's Fire-King & More*, 2nd ed., Collector Books, 2000; ——, *Collectible Glassware from the '40s, '50s, '60s*, 5th ed., Collector Books, 2000; ——, *Collector's Encyclopedia of Depression Glass*, 14th ed., Collector Books, 2000; ——, *Elegant Glassware of the Depression Era*, 9th ed., Collector Books, 2000; ——, *Florence's Glassware Pattern Identification Guide*, Collector Books, Vol. I,

1998, Vol. II, 1999; ——, *Glass Candlesticks of the Depression Era*, Collector Books, 2000; ——, *Pocket Guide to Depression Glass & More, 1920-1960s*, 12th ed., Collector Books, 2000; ——, *Stemware Identification Featuring Cordials with Values, 1920s-1960s*, Collector Books, 1997; ——, *Very Rare Glassware of the Depression Era*, 1st Series (1988, 1991 value update), 2nd Series (1991), 3rd Series (1993, 1995 value update), 4th Series (1996, 1997 value update), 5th Series (1996, 1999 value update), Collector Books; Philip Hopper, *Forest Green Glass*, Schiffer Publishing, 2000; Ralph and Terry Kovel, *Kovels' Depression Glass & American Dinnerware Price List*, 5th ed., Crown, 1995; Carl F. Luckey and Mary Burris, *Identification & Value Guide to Depression Era Glassware*, 3rd ed., Books Americana, 1994; Jim and Barbara Mauzy, *Mauzy's Depression Glass*, 3rd ed., Schiffer, 2001; James Measell and Berry Wiggins, *Great American Glass of the Roaring 20s & Depression Era, Book 2*, Antique Publications, 2000; Leslie Piña and Paula Ockner, *Depression Era Art Deco Glass*, Schiffer Publishing, 1999; Leslie Piña, *Fifties Glass*, 2nd ed., Schiffer Publishing, 2000; Sherry Riggs and Paula Pendergrass, *Glass Candle Holders of the Depression Era and Beyond*, Schiffer Publishing, 2001; Ellen T. Schroy, *Warman's Depression Glass*, 2nd ed., Krause Publications, 2000; Kent G. Washburn, *Price Survey*, 4th ed., published by author, 1994; Hazel Marie Weatherman,

Colored Glassware of the Depression Era, Book 2, published by author 1974, available in reprint; ——, *1984 Supplement & Price Trends for Colored Glassware of the Depression Era, Book 1*, published by author, 1984.

Periodical and Internet Resource: Depression Glass Shopper Online, http://www.dgshopper.com.

Collectors' Clubs: Canadian Depression Glass Assn., 119 Wexford Road, Brampton, Ontario L6Z 2T5, Canada; National Depression Glass Assoc., Inc., P.O. Box 8264, Wichita, KS 67209, http://www.glassshow.com/NDGA; 20-30-40 Society, Inc., P.O. Box 856, LaGrange, IL 60525; plus many local and regional clubs.

Reproduction Alert: The number of Depression Glass patterns that have been reproduced continues to grow. Reproductions exist in many patterns, forms, and colors. Beware of colors and forms that were not made in the original production of the pattern. Carefully examine every piece that seems questionable and look for loss of details, poor impressions, and slight differences in sizes.

Additional Listings: See *Warman's Americana & Collectibles* for more examples.

AMERICAN SWEETHEART

Manufactured by MacBeth-Evans Glass Company, Charleroi, Pennsylvania, from 1930 to1936. Made in blue, Monax, pink, and red. Limited production in Cremax and color-trimmed Monax.

American Sweetheart Monax large plate.

Item	Blue	Cremax	Monax	Monax w/color trim	Pink	Red
Berry bowl, 3-1/4"d, flat	—	—	—	—	60.00	—
Berry bowl, 9" d....................	—	36.00	60.00	150.00	65.00	—
Cereal bowl, 6" d	—	19.50	15.00	37.50	20.00	—
Chop plate, 11" d	—	—	15.00	—	—	—
Console bowl, 18" d..............	1,000.00	—	375.00	—	—	850.00
Cream soup, 4-1/2" d...............	—	—	135.00	—	85.00	—
Creamer, ftd	115.00	—	11.50	85.00	12.00	110.00
Cup........................	100.00	75.00	15.00	70.00	18.00	75.00
Lamp shade	—	450.00	400.00	—	—	—
Pitcher, 60 oz, 7-1/2" h.............	—	—	—	—	675.00	—
Pitcher, 80 oz, 8" h.................	—	—	—	—	575.00	—
Plate, 6" d, bread & butter	—	—	5.50	15.00	7.00	—

AMERICAN SWEETHEART (cont.)

Item	Blue	Cremax	Monax	Monax w/color trim	Pink	Red
Plate, 8" d, salad	75.00	25.00	10.00	—	11.00	75.00
Plate, 9" d, luncheon	—	—	14.00	35.00	—	—
Plate, 9-3/4" d, dinner	—	—	25.00	70.00	38.00	—
Plate, 10-1/4" d, dinner	—	—	30.00	—	45.00	—
Platter, 13" l, oval	—	—	85.00	—	70.00	—
Salt and pepper shakers, pr, ftd	—	—	325.00	—	425.00	—
Salver plate, 12" d	180.00	—	24.00	—	30.00	125.00
Saucer	25.00	—	4.00	15.00	5.75	20.00
Serving plate, 15-1/2" d	450.00	—	250.00	—	—	350.00
Sherbet, 3-3/4" h, ftd	—	—	10.50	—	22.00	—
Sherbet, 4-1/4" h, ftd	—	—	25.00	70.00	17.00	—
Soup bowl, flat, 9-1/2" d	—	—	95.00	90.00	85.00	—
Sugar lid	—	—	300.00	—	—	—
Sugar, open, ftd	115.00	—	15.00	85.00	15.00	100.00
Tidbit, two tiers	250.00	—	95.00	—	—	200.00
Tidbit, three tiers	650.00	—	275.00	—	—	575.00
Tumbler, 5 oz, 3-1/2" h	—	—	—	—	110.00	—
Tumbler, 9 oz, 4-1/4" h	—	—	—	—	85.00	—
Tumbler, 10 oz, 4-3/4" h	—	—	—	—	185.00	—
Vegetable bowl, 11"	—	—	90.00	—	80.00	—

AUNT POLLY

Manufactured by U.S. Glass Company, Pittsburgh, PA, in the late 1920s. Made in blue, green, and iridescent.

Aunt Polly blue sherbet.

Item	Blue	Green	Iridescent
Berry bowl, 4-3/4" d, individual	18.50	9.00	9.00
Berry bowl, 7-1/8" d, master	45.00	22.00	22.00
Bowl, 4-3/4" d, 2" h	—	15.00	15.00
Bowl, 5-1/2" d, one handle	25.00	15.00	15.00
Bowl, 8-3/8" l, oval	100.00	42.00	42.00
Butter dish, cov	215.00	200.00	200.00
Candy jar, cov, two handles	42.00	30.00	30.00
Candy jar, ftd, two handles	—	27.50	27.50
Creamer	48.00	32.00	32.00
Pickle, 7-1/4" l, oval, handle	42.00	17.50	17.50
Pitcher, 48 oz, 8" h	175.00	—	—
Plate, 6" d, sherbet	12.00	6.00	6.00
Plate, 8" d, luncheon	20.00	—	—
Salt and pepper shakers, pr	220.00	—	—
Sherbet	15.00	12.00	12.00
Sugar	48.00	32.00	32.00
Tumbler, 8 oz, 3-5/8" h	30.00	—	—
Vase, 6-1/2" h, ftd	48.00	30.00	30.00

BOWKNOT

Unknown maker, late 1920s.
Made in green.

*Bowknot green tumbler
and footed berry bowl.*

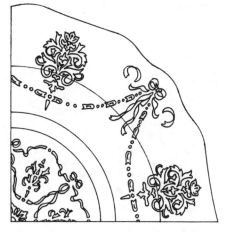

Item	Green
Berry bowl, 4-1/2" d	18.00
Cereal bowl, 5-1/2" d	20.00

Item	Green
Cup	15.00
Plate, 7" d, salad	12.50

Item	Green
Sherbet, low, ftd	24.00
Tumbler, 10 oz, 5" h, flat	15.00
Tumbler, 10 oz, 5" h, ftd	15.00

CAMEO

Ballerina, Dancing Girl

Manufactured by Hocking Glass Company, Lancaster, Ohio, from 1930 to 1934. Made in crystal, green, pink, and yellow. Only the crystal has a platinum rim.

Reproductions: † Salt shakers made in blue, green, and pink. Children's dishes have been made in green and pink, but were never part of the original pattern. Recently a squatty candy dish in cobalt blue has also been made. Again, this was not an original color.

Cameo clear tumbler.

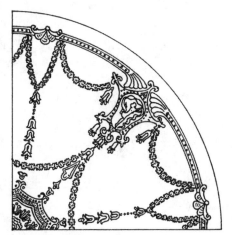

Item	Crystal	Green	Pink	Yellow
Berry bowl, 4-1/4" d	15.00	—	—	—
Berry bowl, 8-1/4" d	—	45.00	175.00	—
Butter dish, cov	—	245.00	—	1,500.00
Cake plate, 10" d, three legs	—	22.00	—	—
Cake plate, 10-1/2" d, flat	—	115.00	165.00	—
Candlesticks, pr, 4" h	—	85.00	—	—
Candy jar, cov, 4" h	—	90.00	495.00	120.00
Candy jar, cov, 6-1/2" h	—	195.00	—	—
Cereal bowl, 5-1/2" d	8.50	35.00	160.00	35.00
Cocktail shaker	600.00	—	—	—
Comport, 5" w	—	42.00	200.00	—
Console bowl, three legs, 11" d	—	75.00	45.00	95.00
Cookie jar, cov	—	60.00	—	—
Cream soup, 4-3/4" d	—	175.00	—	—
Creamer, 3-1/4" h	—	30.00	110.00	25.00
Creamer, 4-1/4" h	—	30.00	115.00	—
Cup	10.00	19.00	85.00	8.50
Decanter, 10" h	225.00	195.00	—	—
Domino tray, 7" l	150.00	165.00	250.00	—
Goblet, 6" h, water	—	65.00	175.00	—
Ice bowl, 3" h, 5-1/2" d	265.00	190.00	700.00	—

CAMEO (cont.)

Item	Crystal	Green	Pink	Yellow
Jam jar, cov, 2" h	175.00	185.00	—	—
Juice pitcher, 6" h, 36 oz	—	65.00	—	—
Juice tumbler, 3 oz, ftd	—	55.00	90.00	—
Juice tumbler, 5 oz, 3-3/4" h	—	25.00	—	—
Pitcher, 8-1/2" h, 56 oz	550.00	65.00	1,450.00	—
Plate, 6" d, sherbet	6.00	9.00	90.00	4.00
Plate, 7" d, salad	12.00	—	—	—
Plate, 8" d, luncheon	8.00	14.00	36.00	12.50
Plate, 8-1/2", luncheon, sq	—	50.00	—	250.00
Plate, 9-1/2" d, dinner	—	24.00	85.00	12.00
Plate, 10-1/2" d, dinner, rimmed	—	115.00	175.00	—
Plate, 10-1/2" d, grill	—	12.00	55.00	10.00
Platter, 12" l	—	30.00	—	42.00
Relish, 7-1/2" l, ftd, three parts	175.00	35.00	—	—
Salad bowl, 7-1/4" d	—	60.00	—	—
Salt and pepper shakers, pr, ftd †	—	70.00	900.00	—
Sandwich plate, 10" d	—	18.00	45.00	37.00
Saucer	4.00	4.00	90.00	4.50
Sherbet, 3-1/8" h, blown	—	17.50	75.00	—
Sherbet, 3-1/8" h, molded	—	16.00	75.00	40.00
Sherbet, 4-7/8" h	—	40.00	100.00	45.00
Soup bowl, rimmed, 9" d	—	75.00	135.00	—
Sugar, 3-1/4" h	—	21.00	—	20.00
Sugar, 4-1/4" h	—	30.00	125.00	—
Syrup pitcher, 20 oz, 5-3/4" h	—	250.00	—	1,950.00
Tumbler, 9 oz, 4" h, 9 oz	16.00	30.00	80.00	—
Tumbler, 9 oz, 5"h, ftd	—	29.00	115.00	14.00
Tumbler, 10 oz, 4-3/4" h, flat	—	35.00	95.00	—
Tumbler, 11" oz, 5" h, flat	—	30.00	90.00	48.00
Tumbler, 11 oz, 5-3/4" h, ftd	—	70.00	135.00	—
Tumbler, 15 oz, 5-1/4" h	—	80.00	145.00	—
Tumbler, 15 oz, 6-3/8" h, ftd	—	495.00	—	—
Vase, 5-3/4" h	—	245.00	—	—
Vase, 8" h	—	65.00	—	—
Vegetable, oval, 10" l	—	50.00	—	45.00
Wine, 3-1/2" h	—	1,200.00	950.00	—
Wine, 4" h	—	95.00	250.00	—

COLONIAL

Knife and Fork

Manufactured by Hocking Glass Company, Lancaster, Ohio, from 1934 to 1938. Made in crystal, green, and pink.

Colonial crystal wine and cocktail.

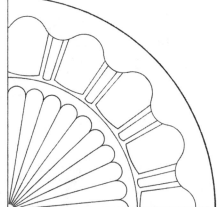

Item	Crystal	Green	Pink
Berry bowl, 3-3/4" d	—	—	45.00
Berry bowl, 4-1/2"	12.00	22.00	18.00
Berry bowl, 9" d	24.00	55.00	35.00
Butter dish, cov	40.00	60.00	625.00

COLONIAL (cont.)

Item	Crystal	Green	Pink
Cereal bowl, 5-1/2" d	32.00	85.00	60.00
Claret, 4 oz, 5-1/4" h,	20.00	25.00	—
Cocktail, 3 oz, 4" h	15.00	25.00	—
Cordial, 1 oz, 3-3/4" h	20.00	30.00	—
Cream soup bowl, 4-1/2" d	70.00	85.00	72.00
Creamer, 8 oz, 5" h	17.00	25.00	60.00
Cup	8.00	15.00	12.00
Goblet, 8-1/2 oz, 5-3/4 h	25.00	35.00	40.00
Ice-tea tumbler, 12 oz.,	28.00	55.00	45.00
Juice tumbler, 5 oz, 3" h	17.50	27.50	22.00
Lemonade tumbler, 15 oz.	47.50	75.00	65.00
Milk pitcher, 8 oz, 5" h	17.00	25.00	60.00
Mug, 12 oz, 5-1/2" h	—	825.00	500.00
Pitcher, 54 oz, 7" h, ice lip	40.00	45.00	48.00
Pitcher, 54 oz, 7" h, no lip	40.00	45.00	48.00
Pitcher, 68 oz, 7-3/4" h, ice lip	35.00	72.00	65.00
Pitcher, 68 oz, 7-3/4" h, no lip	35.00	72.00	65.00
Plate, 6" d, sherbet	4.50	7.50	7.00
Plate, 8-1/2" d, luncheon	6.00	8.00	10.00
Plate, 10" d, dinner	32.00	45.00	46.00
Plate, 10"d, grill	17.50	27.00	27.50
Plate, 12" d, oval	17.50	25.00	30.00
Platter, 12" l, oval	17.50	25.00	35.00
Salt and pepper shakers, pr.	65.00	140.00	148.00
Saucer	4.50	7.50	6.50
Sherbet, 3" h	—	—	24.00
Sherbet, 3-3/8" h	10.00	15.00	12.50
Soup bowl, 7" d	30.00	85.00	82.00
Spoon holder or celery vase	80.00	125.00	135.00
Sugar, cov	35.00	45.00	42.00
Sugar, 5", open	10.00	12.00	15.00
Tumbler, 3 oz, 3-1/4" h, ftd	11.00	15.00	16.50
Tumbler, 5 oz, 4" h, ftd	15.00	35.00	27.50
Tumbler, 9 oz, 4" h	15.00	20.00	25.00
Tumbler, 10 oz, 5-1/4" h, ftd	30.00	46.50	50.00
Tumbler, 11 oz, 5-1/8" h	25.00	37.00	40.00
Vegetable bowl, 10" l, oval	18.00	25.00	45.00
Whiskey, 2-1/2" h, 1-1/2 oz.	10.00	20.00	15.00
Wine, 4-1/2" h, 2-1/2 oz.	17.00	30.00	14.00

DIAMOND QUILTED

Flat Diamond

Manufactured by Imperial Glass Company, Bellaire, Ohio, from late 1920 to early 1930s. Made in amber, black, blue, crystal, green, pink, and red.*

Diamond Quilted pink sugar and creamer.

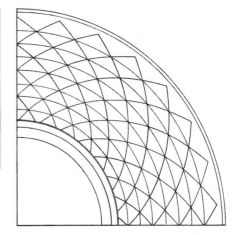

Item	Black	Blue	Crystal	Green	Pink
Bowl, 5-1/2" d, one handle	20.00	—	—	15.00	18.00
Bowl, 7" d, crimped edge	22.00	—	—	18.00	20.00
Cake salver, 10" d, tall	—	—	—	60.00	65.00

DIAMOND QUILTED (cont.)

Item	Black	Blue	Crystal	Green	Pink
Candlesticks, pr.	60.00	—	50.00	32.00	28.00
Candy jar, cov, ftd	—	—	25.00	65.00	65.00
Cereal bowl, 5" d	15.00	—	8.00	9.00	8.50
Champagne, 9 oz, 6" h	—	—	—	12.00	—
Compote, 6" h, 7-1/4" w	—	—	—	45.00	48.00
Compote, cov, 11-1/2" d	—	—	—	80.00	75.00
Console bowl, 10-1/2" d, rolled edge	65.00	60.00	15.00	20.00	24.00
Cordial, 1 oz	—	—	—	12.00	15.00
Cream soup bowl, 4-3/4" d	22.00	20.00	20.00	12.00	14.00
Creamer	18.50	20.00	15.00	12.00	12.00
Cup	18.00	18.50	7.00	10.00	12.00
Ice bucket	90.00	90.00	—	50.00	50.00
Iced-tea tumbler, 12 oz	—	—	—	10.00	10.00
Mayonnaise set, comport, plate, ladle	60.00	65.00	25.00	37.50	40.00
Pitcher, 64 oz.	—	—	—	50.00	55.00
Plate, 6" d, sherbet	10.00	8.50	7.50	7.00	7.50
Plate, 7" d, salad	10.00	10.00	8.00	8.50	8.50
Plate, 8" d, luncheon	12.00	12.00	9.00	6.50	8.50
Punch bowl and stand	—	—	—	450.00	450.00
Sandwich plate, 14" d	—	—	—	15.00	15.00
Sandwich server, center handle	50.00	50.00	20.00	25.00	25.00
Saucer	5.00	5.00	2.00	4.00	4.00
Sherbet	16.00	16.00	14.00	6.00	5.00
Sugar	20.00	25.00	12.00	15.00	13.50
Tumbler, 6 oz, ftd	—	—	—	9.00	10.00
Tumbler, 9 oz	—	—	—	14.00	16.00
Tumbler, 9 oz, ftd	—	—	—	14.00	16.00
Tumbler, 12 oz, ftd	—	—	—	15.00	15.00
Vase, fan	80.00	75.00	—	50.00	50.00
Whiskey, 1-1/2" oz	—	—	—	10.00	12.00
Wine, 2 oz	—	—	—	12.50	12.50
Wine, 3 oz	—	—	—	15.00	15.00

*Amber and red prices would be valued slightly higher than black.

FLORAL AND DIAMOND BAND

Manufactured by U.S. Glass Company, Pittsburgh, PA, late 1920s. Made in pink and green with limited production in black, crystal, and iridescent.

Floral and Diamond Band green plate.

Item	Green	Pink
Berry bowl, 4-1/2" d	10.00	12.00
Berry bowl, 8" d	15.00	18.00
Butter dish, cov	140.00	175.00
Compote, 5-1/2" h	18.00	17.50
Creamer, 4-3/4"	20.00	17.50
Iced-tea tumbler, 5" h	38.00	32.50
Nappy, 5-3/4" d, handle	12.00	11.00
Pitcher, 42 oz, 8" h	95.00	90.00
Plate, 8" d, luncheon	40.00	40.00
Sherbet	8.00	9.50
Sugar, 5-1/4"	15.00	15.00
Tumbler, 4" h, water	25.00	25.00

FOREST GREEN

Manufactured by Anchor Hocking Glass Company, Lancaster, Ohio, and Long Island City, New York, from 1950 to 1957. Made only in forest green.

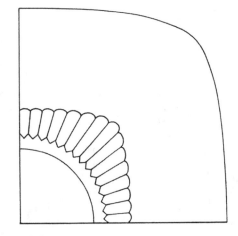

Item	Forest Green
Ashtray, 3-1/2" sq.	3.50
Ashtray, 4-5/8" sq.	5.50
Ashtray, 5-3/4" hexagon	8.00
Ashtray, 5-3/4" sq.	7.50
Batter bowl, spout	25.00
Berry bowl, large	15.00
Berry bowl, small	5.50
Bonbon, 6-1/4" w, tricorn	12.00
Bowl, 4-1/2" w, sq	5.50
Bowl, 5-1/4" deep	8.50
Bowl, 6" w, sq	18.00
Bowl, 6-1/2" d, scalloped	9.00
Bowl, 6-3/8" d, 3 toes	15.00
Bowl, 7-3/8" w, sq	30.00
Bowl, 7-1/2" d, crimped	10.00
Cocktail, 3-1/2 oz.	12.00
Cocktail, 4-1/2 oz.	14.00
Creamer, flat	7.50
Cup, sq	7.00
Dessert bowl, 4-3/4" d	7.00
Goblet, 9 oz	10.00
Goblet, 9-1/2 oz	14.00
Iced-tea tumbler, 13 oz.	8.00

Item	Forest Green
Iced-tea tumbler, 14 oz, Boopie	8.00
Iced-tea tumbler, 15 oz, tall	10.00
Iced-tea tumbler, 32 oz, giant	18.00
Ivy ball, 4" h	5.00
Juice tumbler, 4 oz	10.00
Juice tumbler, 5-1/2 oz	12.50
Juice roly-poly tumbler, 3-3/8" h	6.00
Ladle, all-green glass	80.00
Mixing bowl, 6" d	9.50
Pitcher, 22 oz	22.50
Pitcher, 36 oz	25.00
Pitcher, 86 oz, round	45.00
Plate, 6-3/4" d, salad	7.50
Plate, 7" w, sq	6.75
Plate, 8-3/8" d, luncheon	9.00
Plate, 9-1/4" d, dinner	33.50
Platter, 11" l, rect	22.00
Popcorn bowl, 5-1/4" d	10.00
Punch bowl	25.00
Punch bowl and stand	60.00
Punch cup	4.25
Relish tray, 4-3/4" x 6-3/4" l, two handles	25.00

Item	Forest Green
Roly-poly tumbler, 5 1/8" h	7.50
Salad bowl, 7-3/8" d	15.00
Sandwich plate, 13-3/4" d	45.00
Saucer, 5-3/8" w	3.00
Sherbet, 6 oz	9.00
Sherbet, 6 oz, Boopie	7.00
Sherbet, flat	7.50
Soup bowl, 6" d	17.00
Sugar, flat	7.00
Tray, 6" x 10", two handles	30.00
Tumbler, 5 oz, 3-1/2" h	4.00
Tumbler, 7 oz	4.50
Tumbler, 5-1/4" h	4.00
Tumbler, 9-1/2 oz, tall	8.00
Tumbler, 9 oz, fancy	7.00
Tumbler, 9 oz, table	5.00
Tumbler, 10 oz, 4-1/2" h, ftd	7.50
Tumbler, 11 oz	7.00
Tumbler, 14 oz, 5" h	8.00
Tumbler, 15 oz, long boy	10.00
Vase, 6-3/8" h, Harding	10.00
Vase, 7" h, crimped	15.00
Vase, 9" h	8.00
Vegetable bowl, 8-1/2" l, oval	24.00

HORSESHOE
No. 612

Manufactured by Indiana Glass Company, Dunkirk, Indiana, from 1930 to 1933. Made in crystal, green, pink, and yellow.

Horseshoe, No. 612 yellow cup.

HORSESHOE (cont.)

Item	Green	Yellow
Berry bowl, 4-1/2" d	30.00	25.00
Berry bowl, 9-1/2" d	40.00	35.00
Butter dish, cov	750.00	—
Candy dish, metal holder	175.00	—
Cereal bowl, 6-1/2" d	25.00	35.00
Creamer, ftd	18.00	20.00
Cup and saucer	18.50	17.50
Pitcher, 64 oz, 8-1/2" h	250.00	295.00
Plate, 6" d, sherbet	9.00	9.00
Plate, 8-3/8" d, salad	10.00	10.00
Plate, 9-3/8" d, luncheon	13.00	17.50
Plate, 10-3/8" d, grill	85.00	85.00
Platter, 10-3/4" l, oval	25.00	25.00

Item	Green	Yellow
Relish, three part ftd	20.00	24.00
Salad Bowl, 7-1/2" d	24.00	24.00
Sandwich Plate, 11-1/2" d	24.00	27.50
Saucer	6.00	6.50
Sherbet	16.00	18.50
Sugar, open	16.50	17.00
Tumbler, 9 oz, ftd	25.00	28.00
Tumbler, 9 oz, 4-1/4" h	150.00	—
Tumbler, 12 oz, ftd	140.00	150.00
Tumbler, 12 oz, 4-3/4" h	150.00	—
Vegetable bowl, 8-1/2" d	30.00	30.00
Vegetable bowl, 10-1/2" d, oval . .	25.00	28.50

LINCOLN INN

Manufactured by Fenton Art Glass Company, Williamstown, West Virginia, late 1920s. Made in amber, amethyst, black*, cobalt blue, crystal, green, green opalescent, light blue, opaque jade, pink, and red.

Lincoln Inn pink plate.

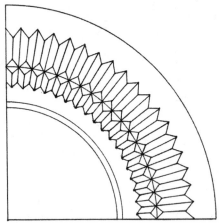

Item	Cobalt Blue	Crystal	Other colors	Red
Ashtray	17.50	12.00	12.00	17.50
Bonbon, oval, handle	17.50	12.00	14.00	18.00
Bonbon, sq, handle	15.00	12.00	14.00	15.00
Bowl, 6" d, crimped	14.50	7.50	10.00	14.50
Bowl, 9" d, shallow	—	9.00	—	—
Bowl, 9-1/4" d, ftd	42.00	18.00	20.00	45.00
Bowl, 10-1/2" d, ftd	50.00	28.00	30.00	50.00
Candy dish, ftd, oval	24.00	14.50	14.50	24.00
Cereal bowl, 6" d	12.50	7.50	9.50	12.50
Comport	25.00	14.00	15.00	25.00
Creamer	24.00	12.00	15.00	24.00
Cup	17.50	8.50	9.50	18.00
Finger bowl	20.00	14.00	14.50	20.00
Fruit bowl, 5" d	14.00	7.00	9.00	14.00
Goblet, 6" h	30.00	18.50	16.00	30.00
Iced-tea tumbler, 12 oz, ftd	40.00	22.00	24.00	40.00
Juice tumbler, 4 oz, flat	27.50	9.00	14.00	27.50
Nut dish, ftd	20.00	14.50	16.00	20.00
Olive bowl, handle	15.00	8.50	12.00	15.00
Pitcher, 46 oz, 7-1/4" h	812.00	700.00	715.00	820.00
Plate, 6" d	19.50	12.00	12.50	19.50
Plate, 8" d	27.50	15.00	14.00	27.50
Plate, 9-1/4" d	30.00	15.00	16.50	30.00
Plate, 12" d	35.00	16.00	18.00	35.00
Salt and pepper shakers, pr	215.00	175.00	175.00	225.00
Sandwich server, center handle	115.00	95.00	100.00	115.00
Saucer	5.00	4.00	4.50	5.00
Sherbet, 4-1/2" h, cone shape	18.00	12.00	14.00	18.00

LINCOLN INN (cont.)

Item	Cobalt Blue	Crystal	Other colors	Red
Sherbet, 4-3/4" h	20.00	14.00	14.50	20.00
Sugar	24.00	12.00	15.00	24.00
Tumbler, 5 oz, ftd	24.00	14.00	14.50	24.00
Tumbler, 9 oz, flat	—	14.00	15.00	15.00
Tumbler, 9 oz, ftd	28.00	32.00	35.00	30.00
Vase, 9-3/4" h	150.00	85.00	95.00	145.00
Vase, 12" h, ftd	185.00	115.00	125.00	175.00
Wine	35.00	20.00	24.00	40.00

*Production in black was limited to salt and pepper shakers, valued at $325. Some rare pieces have been identified in several other colors.

MOONDROPS

Manufactured by New Martinsville Glass Company, New Martinsville, West Virginia, from 1932 to 1940. Made in amber, amethyst, black, cobalt blue, crystal, dark green, green, ice blue, jadeite, light green, pink, red, and smoke.

Moondrops ruby sugar and creamer.

Item	Cobalt Blue	Crystal	Other colors	Red
Ashtray	30.00	—	18.00	30.00
Berry bowl, 5-1/4" d	20.00	—	12.00	20.00
Bowl, 8-1/2" d, ftd, concave top	40.00	—	25.00	40.00
Bowl, 9-1/2" d, three legs, ruffled	60.00	—	—	60.00
Bowl, 9-3/4" l, oval, handles	50.00	—	30.00	50.00
Butter dish, cov	425.00	—	275.00	295.00
Candlesticks, pr, 2" h, ruffled	40.00	—	25.00	40.00
Candlesticks, pr, 4" h, sherbet style	30.00	—	18.00	30.00
Candlesticks, pr, 5" h, ruffled	32.00	—	22.00	32.00
Candlesticks, pr, 5" h, wings	90.00	—	60.00	90.00
Candlesticks, pr, 5-1/4" h, triple light	100.00	65.00	65.00	100.00
Candlesticks, pr, 8-1/2" h, metal stem	40.00	—	32.00	40.00
Candy dish, 8" d, ruffled	40.00	—	20.00	40.00
Casserole, cov, 9-3/4" d	185.00	—	100.00	185.00
Celery bowl, 11" l, boat-shape	30.00	—	24.00	30.00
Cocktail shaker, metal top	60.00	—	35.00	60.00
Comport, 4" d	25.00	—	15.00	25.00
Comport, 11-1/2" d	60.00	—	30.00	60.00
Console bowl, 12" d, round, three ftd	—	—	40.00	
Console bowl, 13" d, wings	—	—	80.00	120.00
Cordial, 3/4 oz, 2-7/8" h	—	—	25.00	48.00
Cream soup, 4-1/4" d	90.00	—	35.00	90.00
Creamer, 2-3/4" h	15.00	—	10.00	18.00
Creamer, 3-3/4" h	12.00	—	12.00	16.00
Cup	14.00	8.00	10.00	16.00
Decanter, 7-3/4" h	70.00	—	40.00	70.00
Decanter, 8-1/2" h	72.00	—	45.00	72.00
Decanter, 10-1/4" h, rocket-shape	425.00	—	375.00	425.00
Decanter, 11-1/4" h	100.00	—	50.00	110.00
Goblet, 5 oz, 4-3/4" h	25.00	—	15.00	22.00
Goblet, 8 oz, 5-3/4" h	35.00	—	20.00	33.00

MOONDROPS (cont.)

Item	Cobalt Blue	Crystal	Other colors	Red
Goblet, 9 oz, 6-1/4" h, metal stem	15.00	—	17.50	15.00
Gravy boat	120.00	—	90.00	125.00
Juice tumbler, 3 oz, 3-1/4" h, ftd	15.00	—	10.00	15.00
Mayonnaise, 5-1/4" h	32.50	—	30.00	32.50
Mug, 12 oz, 5-1/8" h	40.00	—	24.00	42.00
Perfume bottle, rocket-shape	200.00	—	150.00	210.00
Pickle, 7-1/2" d	25.00	—	15.00	25.00
Pitcher, 22 oz, 6-7/8" h	175.00	—	90.00	175.00
Pitcher, 32 oz, 8-1/8" h	195.00	—	110.00	195.00
Pitcher, 50 oz, 8" h, lip	200.00	—	115.00	200.00
Pitcher, 53 oz, 8-1/8" h	195.00	—	120.00	195.00
Plate, 5-7/8" d	12.00	—	7.50	12.00
Plate, 6" d, round, off-center indent	12.50	—	10.00	12.50
Plate, 6-1/8" d, sherbet	8.00	—	6.00	8.00
Plate, 7-1/8" d, salad	12.00	—	10.00	12.00
Plate, 8-1/2" d, luncheon	15.00	—	12.00	15.00
Plate, 9-1/2" d, dinner	25.00	—	15.00	25.00
Platter, 12" l, oval	35.00	—	20.00	35.00
Powder jar, three ftd	175.00	—	100.00	185.00
Relish , 8-1/2" d, three ftd, divided	30.00	—	20.00	30.00
Sandwich plate, 14" d	40.00	—	20.00	40.00
Sandwich plate, 14" d, w handles	44.00	—	24.00	45.00
Saucer	6.00	2.00	4.00	6.50
Sherbet, 2-5/8" h	15.00	10.00	11.00	20.00
Sherbet, 3-1/2" h	25.00	—	15.00	25.00
Shot Glass, 2 oz, 2-3/4" h	17.50	—	12.00	17.50
Shot Glass, 2 oz, 2-3/4" h, handle	17.50	—	15.00	17.50
Soup bowl, 6-3/4" d	80.00	—	—	80.00
Sugar, 2-3/4" h	10.00	—	10.00	18.00
Tray, 7-1/2" l	15.00	—	20.00	16.00
Tumbler, 5 oz, 3-5/8" h	15.00	—	10.00	15.00
Tumbler, 7 oz, 4-3/8" h	17.50	—	10.00	18.00
Tumbler, 8 oz, 4-3/8" h	17.50	—	12.00	22.00
Tumbler, 9 oz, 4-7/8" h, handle	30.00	—	15.00	28.00
Tumbler, 9 oz, 4-7/8" h	20.00	—	15.00	19.00
Tumbler, 12 oz, 5-1/8" h	30.00	—	15.00	33.00
Vase, 7-1/4" h, flat, ruffled	60.00	—	60.00	60.00
Vase, 8-1/2" h, bud, rocket-shape	245.00	—	185.00	245.00
Vase, 9-1/4" h, rocket-shape	240.00	—	125.00	240.00
Vegetable bowl, 9-3/4" l, oval	48.00	—	24.00	48.00
Wine, 3 oz, 5-1/2" h, metal stem	17.50	—	12.00	16.00
Wine, 4-3/4" h, rocket-shape	27.50	—	30.00	85.00
Wine, 4 oz, 4" h	24.00	—	12.00	24.00
Wine, 4 oz, 5-1/2" h, metal stem	20.00	—	12.00	18.00

OYSTER AND PEARL

Manufactured by Anchor Hocking Glass Corporation, from 1938 to 1940. Made in crystal, pink, royal ruby, and white, with fired-on green or pink.

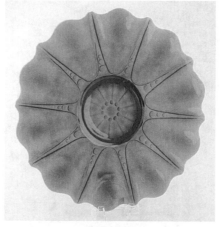

Oyster and Pearls ruby plate.

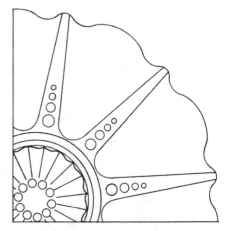

OYSTER AND PEARL (cont.)

Item	Crystal	Pink	Royal Ruby	White, fired-on green	White, fired-on red
Bowl, 5-1/2" d, handle	8.00	15.00	15.00	—	—
Bowl, 5-1/4" w, handle, heart-shape	12.00	21.00	21.00	10.00	—
Bowl, 6-1/2" d, handle	12.00	15.00	22.50	—	—
Candleholders, pr, 3-1/2" h	24.00	45.00	48.00	15.00	15.00
Fruit bowl, 10-1/2" d, deep	20.00	25.00	50.00	15.00	15.00
Relish dish, 10-1/4" l, divided	10.00	12.00	—	—	—
Sandwich plate, 13-1/2" d	20.00	34.00	50.00	—	—

PRINCESS

Manufactured by Hocking Glass Company, Lancaster, Ohio, from 1931 to 1935. Made in apricot yellow, blue, green, pink, and topaz yellow.

Reproductions: † The candy dish and salt and pepper shakers have been reproduced in blue, green, and pink.

Princess green cookie jar and vegetable bowl.

Item	Apricot Yellow	Blue	Green	Pink	Topaz Yellow
Ashtray, 4-1/2" d	100.00	—	70.00	80.00	100.00
Berry bowl, 4-1/2" d	55.00	—	30.00	32.00	55.00
Butter dish, cov	650.00	—	110.00	95.00	650.00
Cake plate, 10" d, ftd	—	—	37.50	100.00	—
Candy dish, cov †	—	—	70.00	85.00	—
Cereal bowl, 5" d	—	—	40.00	35.00	—
Coaster	100.00	—	35.00	65.00	100.00
Cookie jar, cov	—	875.00	65.00	75.00	—
Creamer, oval	25.00	—	15.00	17.50	22.50
Cup	7.50	115.00	14.00	15.50	10.00
Hat-shaped bowl, 9-1/2" d	125.00	—	45.00	50.00	125.00
Iced-tea tumbler, 13 oz, 5-1/2" h	45.00	—	125.00	115.00	40.00
Juice tumbler, 5 oz, 3" h	28.00	—	25.00	28.00	28.00
Pitcher, 24 oz, 7-3/8" h, ftd	—	—	550.00	75.00	—
Pitcher, 37 oz, 6" h	565.00	—	55.00	62.00	565.00
Pitcher, 60 oz, 8" h	95.00	—	65.00	80.00	95.00
Plate, 5-1/2" d, sherbet	4.75	65.00	12.00	12.00	4.75
Plate, 8" d, salad	10.00	—	15.00	15.00	10.00
Plate, 9-1/2" d, dinner	25.00	—	33.50	45.00	25.00
Plate, 9-1/2" d, grill	10.00	115.00	15.00	15.00	10.00
Plate, 10-1/2" d, grill, closed handles	10.00	—	15.00	15.00	10.00
Platter, 12" l, closed handles	60.00	—	25.00	25.00	60.00
Relish, 7-1/2" l, divided, 4 part	100.00	—	35.00	30.00	100.00
Relish, 7-1/2" l, plain	160.00	—	115.00	175.00	160.00
Salad bowl, 9" d, octagonal	125.00	—	46.00	40.00	125.00
Salt and pepper shakers, pr, 4-1/2" h †	75.00	—	60.00	65.00	85.00
Sandwich plate, 10-1/4" d, two closed handles	165.00	—	20.00	35.00	165.00
Saucer, 6" sq	2.75	65.00	10.00	10.00	3.75
Sherbet, ftd	40.00	—	28.00	25.00	40.00
Spice shakers, pr, 5-1/2" h	—	—	20.00	—	—
Sugar, cov	30.00	—	35.00	45.00	30.00
Tumbler, 9 oz, 4" h	25.00	—	28.00	25.00	25.00

PRINCESS (cont.)

Item	Apricot Yellow	Blue	Green	Pink	Topaz Yellow
Tumbler, 9 oz, 4-3/4" h, sq, ftd	—	—	65.00	25.00	—
Tumbler, 10 oz, 5-1/4" h, ftd	28.00	—	35.00	32.00	28.00
Tumbler, 12-1/2 oz, 6-1/2" h, ftd	25.00	—	115.00	95.00	25.00
Vase, 8" h	—	—	45.00	50.00	—
Vegetable bowl, 10" l, oval	60.00	—	30.00	30.00	65.00

ROYAL LACE

Manufactured by Hazel Atlas Glass Company, Clarksburg, West Virginia, and Zanesville, Ohio, from 1934 to 1941. Made in cobalt (Ritz) blue, crystal, green, pink, and some amethyst.

Reproductions: † Reproductions include a 5-ounce, 3 1/2-inch high tumbler, found in a darker cobalt blue. A cookie jar has also been reproduced in cobalt blue.

Royal Lace clear plate.

Item	Cobalt Blue	Crystal	Green	Pink
Berry bowl, 5" d	35.00	18.00	30.00	35.00
Berry bowl, 10" d	60.00	20.00	35.00	45.00
Bowl, 10" d, three legs, rolled edge	650.00	225.00	125.00	100.00
Bowl, 10" d, three legs, ruffled edge.	675.00	45.00	125.00	100.00
Bowl, 10" d, three legs, straight edge	—	24.00	45.00	40.00
Butter dish, cov	650.00	75.00	275.00	200.00
Candlesticks, pr, rolled edge	—	45.00	85.00	60.00
Candlesticks, pr, ruffled edge	—	28.00	70.00	60.00
Candlesticks, pr, straight edge	—	35.00	75.00	55.00
Cookie jar, cov †	495.00	45.00	75.00	55.00
Cream soup, 4-3/4" d	48.00	18.00	35.00	30.00
Creamer, ftd	60.00	15.00	25.00	20.00
Cup and saucer	45.00	16.00	25.00	18.00
Nut bowl	1,500.00	200.00	395.00	395.00
Pitcher, 48 oz, straight sides	150.00	40.00	110.00	85.00
Pitcher, 64 oz, 8" h	225.00	45.00	110.00	120.00
Pitcher, 68 oz, 8" h, ice lip	240.00	50.00	—	95.00
Pitcher, 86 oz, 8" h	—	60.00	135.00	95.00
Pitcher, 96 oz, 9-1/2" h, ice lip	265.00	69.00	140.00	100.00
Plate, 6" d, sherbet	16.50	7.50	12.00	18.00
Plate, 8-1/2" d, luncheon.	40.00	12.00	18.00	24.00
Plate, 9-7/8" d, dinner.	42.00	24.00	30.00	27.50
Plate, 9-7/8" d, grill.	40.00	20.00	25.00	22.50
Platter, 13" l, oval	60.00	42.00	45.00	48.00
Salt and pepper shakers, pr	250.00	65.00	130.00	80.00
Sherbet, ftd	50.00	20.00	25.00	18.00
Sherbet, metal holder	45.00	18.00		
Sugar, cov	45.00	35.00	40.00	50.00
Sugar, open	—	12.50	25.00	22.00
Toddy or cider set	275.00	—	—	—
Tumbler, 5 oz, 3-1/2" h †	65.00	15.00	35.00	35.00
Tumbler, 9 oz, 4-1/8" h †	45.00	20.00	35.00	28.00
Tumbler, 10 oz, 4-7/8" h	100.00	25.00	60.00	60.00
Tumbler, 12 oz, 5-3/8" h	125.00	25.00	50.00	55.00
Vegetable bowl, 11" l, oval	60.00	25.00	35.00	35.00

SANDWICH

Manufactured by Hocking Glass Company, and later Anchor Hocking Corporation, from 1939 to 1964. Made in crystal, Desert Gold, 1961-64; Forest Green, 1956-1960s; pink, 1939-1940; Royal Ruby, 1938-1939; white/ivory (opaque), 1957-1960s.

Reproductions: † The cookie jar has been reproduced in crystal.

Sandwich, Hocking crystal oval bowl.

Item	Crystal	Desert Gold	Forest Green	Pink	Royal Ruby
Bowl, 4-5/16" d, smooth	5.00	—	4.00	—	—
Bowl, 4-7/8" d, smooth	5.00	6.00	—	7.00	17.50
Bowl, 4-7/8" d, crimped	20.00	—	—	—	25.00
Bowl, 5-1/4" d, scalloped	5.00	6.00	—	—	25.00
Bowl, 5-1/4" d, smooth	—	—	—	7.00	35.00
Bowl, 6-1/2" d, scalloped	7.50	9.00	60.00	—	35.00
Bowl, 6-1/2" d, smooth	7.50	9.00	—	—	—
Bowl, 7-1/4" d, scalloped	8.00	—	—	—	—
Bowl, 8-1/4" d, oval	10.00	—	—	—	—
Bowl, 8-1/4" d, scalloped	10.00	—	80.00	20.00	35.00
Butter dish, cov	45.00	—	—	—	—
Cereal bowl, 6-3/4" d	32.00	12.00	—	—	—
Cookie jar, cov † *	40.00	45.00	20.00	—	—
Creamer	6.50	—	30.00	—	—
Cup, coffee	2.00	12.00	24.00	—	—
Cup, tea	3.00	14.00	24.00	—	—
Custard cup	7.00	—	4.00	—	—
Custard cup liner	5.50	—	1.50	—	—
Custard cup, crimped	12.50	—	—	—	—
Dessert bowl, 5" d, crimped	18.50	—	—	—	—
Juice pitcher, 6" h	115.00	—	145.00	—	—
Juice tumbler, 3 oz, 3-3/8" h	12.00	—	6.00	—	—
Juice tumbler, 5 oz, 3-9/16" h	7.50	—	4.50	—	—
Pitcher, half gallon, ice lip	85.00	—	550.00	—	—
Plate, 6" d	5.00	—	—	—	—
Plate, 7" d, dessert	25.00	—	—	—	—
Plate, 8" d, luncheon	18.00	—	—	—	—
Plate, 9" d, dinner	20.00	10.00	125.00	10.00	—
Plate, 9" d, indent for punch cup	12.00	—	—	—	—
Punch bowl, 9-3/4" d	18.00	—	—	—	—
Punch bowl and stand	32.00	—	—	—	—
Punch bowl Set, bowl, base, 12 cups	60.00	—	—	—	—
Punch cup	3.00	—	—	—	—
Salad bowl, 7" d	8.00	25.00	—	—	—
Salad bowl, 7-5/8" d	—	—	60.00	—	—
Salad bowl, 9" d	24.00	20.00	—	—	—
Sandwich plate, 12" d	14.00	17.50	—	—	—
Saucer	3.50	5.00	15.00	—	—
Sherbet, ftd	8.00	8.00	—	—	—
Snack set, plate and cup	9.00	—	—	—	—
Sugar, cov	30.00	—	—	—	—
Sugar, no cover	6.00	—	30.00	—	—
Tumbler, 9 oz, ftd	32.50	125.00	—	—	—
Tumbler, 9 oz, water	9.00	—	7.00	—	—
Vase	—	—	27.50	—	—
Vegetable, 8-1/2" l, oval	10.00	—	—	—	—

*No cover is known for cookie jar in Forest Green.

TEA ROOM

Manufactured by Indiana Glass Company, Dunkirk, Indiana, from 1926 to 1931. Made in amber, crystal, green, and pink.

Tea Room pink sugar and creamer.

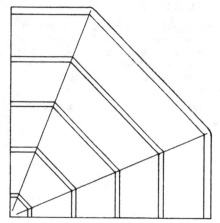

Item	Amber	Crystal	Green	Pink
Banana-split bowl, 7-1/2" l	—	75.00	100.00	145.00
Candlesticks, pr, low	—	—	48.00	85.00
Celery bowl, 8-1/2"d	—	—	35.00	27.50
Creamer, 3-1/4" h	—	—	30.00	28.00
Creamer, 4-1/2" h, ftd	80.00	—	20.00	18.00
Creamer and sugar on tray	—	—	180.00	75.00
Cup	—	—	65.00	60.00
Finger bowl	—	79.00	50.00	40.00
Goblet, 9 oz.	—	—	75.00	65.00
Ice bucket	—	—	85.00	80.00
Lamp, electric	—	140.00	175.00	145.00
Mustard, cov	—	—	160.00	140.00
Parfait	—	—	72.00	65.00
Pitcher, 64 oz.	425.00	400.00	150.00	135.00
Plate, 6-1/2" d, sherbet	—	—	35.00	32.00
Plate, 8-1/4" d, luncheon	—	—	37.50	35.00
Plates, 10-1/2" d, two handles	—	—	50.00	45.00
Relish, divided	—	—	30.00	25.00
Salad bowl, 8-3/4" d, deep	—	—	150.00	135.00
Salt and pepper shakers, pr, ftd	—	—	60.00	55.00
Saucer	—	—	30.00	25.00
Sherbet	—	—	39.50	35.00
Sugar, 3" h, cov	—	—	115.00	100.00
Sugar, 4-1/2" h, ftd	80.00	—	20.00	18.00
Sugar, cov, flat	—	—	200.00	170.00
Sundae, ftd, ruffled	—	—	85.00	70.00
Tumbler, 6 oz., ftd	—	—	35.00	32.00
Tumbler, 8 oz, 5-1/4" h, ftd	75.00	—	35.00	32.00
Tumbler, 11 oz., ftd	—	—	45.00	40.00
Tumbler, 12 oz., ftd	—	—	60.00	55.00
Vase, 6-1/2" h, ruffled edge	—	—	145.00	125.00
Vase, 9-1/2" h, ruffled	—	50.00	175.00	100.00
Vase, 9-1/2"h, straight	—	175.00	95.00	225.00
Vase, 11" h, ruffled edge	—	—	350.00	395.00
Vase, 11" h, straight	—	—	200.00	395.00
Vegetable bowl, 9-1/2" l, oval	—	—	75.00	65.00

TULIP

Manufactured by Dell Glass Company, Millville, New Jersey, early 1930s. Made in amber, amethyst, blue, crystal, and green.

Tulip green creamer.

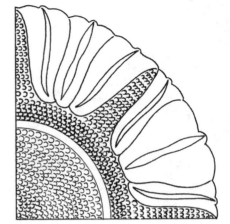

Item	Amber	Amethyst	Blue	Crystal	Green
Bowl, 6" d	20.00	18.00	18.00	20.00	20.00
Bowl, 13-1/4" l, oblong oval	40.00	50.00	50.00	40.00	40.00
Candleholders, pr, 3-3/4" h	24.50	30.00	30.00	24.50	24.50
Candy, cov	32.00	45.00	45.00	32.00	32.00
Creamer	15.00	20.00	25.00	20.00	25.00
Cup	12.00	18.00	18.00	12.00	16.00
Decanter, orig stopper	42.00	50.00	50.00	42.00	42.00
Ice tub, 4-7/8" wide, 3" deep	24.00	35.00	35.00	24.00	24.00
Juice tumbler	15.00	17.50	40.00	15.00	15.00
Plate, 6" d	10.00	12.00	22.00	9.50	10.00
Plate, 7-1/4" d	12.00	24.00	14.00	13.50	24.00
Plate, 10-1/4" d	35.00	40.00	35.00	20.00	35.00
Saucer	10.00	8.50	10.00	5.00	7.50
Sherbet, 3-3/4" h, flat	8.50	12.00	12.00	8.00	20.00
Sugar	15.00	20.00	20.00	15.00	15.00
Whiskey	19.50	20.00	25.00	18.50	20.00

WINDSOR

Windsor Diamond

Manufactured by Jeannette Glass Company, Jeannette, Pennsylvania, from 1936 to 1946. Made in crystal, green, and pink, with limited production in amberina red, Delphite, and ice blue.

Windsor crystal plate and pink pitcher.

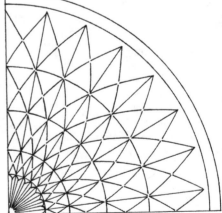

Item	Crystal	Green	Pink
Ashtray, 5-3/4" d	15.00	45.00	45.00
Berry bowl, 4-3/4" d	5.00	12.00	10.00
Berry bowl, 8-1/2" d	7.50	18.50	22.00
Bowl, 5" l, pointed edge	10.00	—	25.00
Bowl, 7" x 11-3/4", boat shape	18.00	35.00	32.00

WINDSOR (cont.)

Item	Crystal	Green	Pink
Bowl, 7-1/2" d, three legs	8.00	—	24.00
Bowl, 8" d, 2 handles	9.00	24.00	20.00
Bowl, 8" l, pointed edge	10.00	—	48.00
Bowl, 10-1/2" l, pointed edge	25.00	—	32.00
Butter dish, cov	27.50	95.00	60.00
Cake plate, 10-3/4" d, ftd	12.00	22.00	20.00
Candlesticks, pr, 3" h	22.00	—	85.00
Candy jar, cov	18.00	—	—
Cereal bowl, 5-3/8" d	10.00	32.50	25.00
Chop plate, 13-5/8" d	24.00	42.00	50.00
Coaster, 3-1/4" d	8.50	18.00	25.00
Comport	9.00	—	—
Cream soup, 5" d	6.00	30.00	25.00
Creamer	5.00	15.00	20.00
Creamer, Holiday shape	7.50	—	—
Cup	7.00	22.00	12.00
Fruit console, 12-1/2" d	45.00	—	115.00
Pitcher, 16 oz, 4-1/2" h	25.00	—	115.00
Pitcher, 52 oz, 6-3/4" h	20.00	55.00	35.00
Plate, 6" d, sherbet	3.75	8.00	5.00
Plate, 7" d, salad	4.50	20.00	18.00
Plate, 9" d, dinner	9.00	25.00	25.00
Platter, 11-1/2" l, oval	7.00	25.00	25.00
Powder jar	15.00	—	55.00
Relish platter, 11-1/2" l, divided	10.00	—	200.00
Salad bowl, 10-1/2" d	12.00	—	—
Salt and pepper shakers, pr	20.00	48.00	42.00
Sandwich plate, 10" d, closed handles	10.00	—	24.00
Sandwich plate, 10" d, open handles	12.50	18.00	20.00
Saucer	2.50	5.00	4.50
Sherbet, ftd	3.50	15.00	13.00
Sugar, cov	10.00	40.00	30.00
Sugar, cov, Holiday shape	12.00	—	100.00
Tray, 4" sq	5.00	12.00	10.00
Tray, 4" sq, handles	6.00	—	40.00
Tray, 4-1/8" x 9"	5.00	16.00	10.00
Tray, 4-1/8" x 9", handles	9.00	—	50.00
Tray, 8-1/2" x 9-3/4"	7.00	35.00	25.00
Tray, 8-1/2" x 9-3/4", handles	14.00	45.00	85.00
Tumbler, 4" h, ftd	7.00	—	—
Tumbler, 5 oz, 3-1/4" h	9.00	42.00	25.00
Tumbler, 7-1/4" h, ftd	19.00	—	—
Tumbler, 9 oz, 4" h	7.50	38.00	22.00
Tumbler, 11 oz, 4-5/8" h	8.00	—	—
Tumbler, 12 oz, 5" h	11.00	55.00	32.50
Tumbler, 11 oz, 5" h, ftd	12.00	—	—
Vegetable bowl, 9-1/2" l, oval	7.50	29.00	25.00

DISNEYANA

History: Walt Disney and the creations of the famous Disney Studios hold a place of fondness and enchantment in the hearts of people throughout the world. The 1928 release of "Steamboat Willie," featuring Mickey Mouse, heralded an entertainment empire.

Walt and his brother, Roy, were shrewd businessmen. From the beginning, they licensed the reproduction of Disney characters on products ranging from wristwatches to clothing.

In 1984, Donald Duck celebrated his 50th birthday, and collectors took a renewed interest in material related to him.

References: Ted Hake, *Hake's Guide to Character Toys*, 3rd ed., Gemstone Publishing (1966 Greenspring, Ste. 405, Timonium, MD 21093), 2000; Robert Heide and John Gilman, *Disneyana*, Hyperion, 1994; Maxine A. Pinsky, *Marx Toys: Robots, Space, Comic, Disney & TV Characters*, Schiffer Publishing, 1996; Rex Miller, *The Investor's Guide to Vintage Character Collectibles*, Krause Publications, 1999; Carol J. Smith, *Identification & Price Guide to Winnie the Pooh Collectibles*, Hobby House Press, 1994.

Periodicals: *Mouse Rap Monthly*, P.O. Box 1064, Ojai, CA 93024; *Tomart's Disneyana Digest*, 3300 Encrete Lane, Dayton, OH 45439; *Tomart's Disneyana Update*, 3300 Encrete Lane, Dayton, OH 45439.

Collectors' Clubs: Imagination Guild, P.O. Box 907, Boulder Creek, CA 95006; Mouse Club East, P.O. Box 3195, Wakefield, MA 01880; National Fantasy Fan Club for Disneyana Collectors and Enthusiasts, P.O. Box 19212, Irvine, CA 92713.

Archives/Museum: Walt Disney Archives, Burbank, CA 91521.

Additional Listings: See *Warman's Americana & Collectibles* for more examples.

Adviser: Theodore L. Hake.

SPECIAL AUCTION

**Hake's Americana
& Collectibles Auctions**
P.O. Box 1444, Dept. 344
York, PA 17405
(717) 848-1333

Bambi

Book, *Bambi*, D. C. Heath & Co., from educational "Walt Disney Storybooks" series, copyright 1944, 102 story pages, full color illus, brown and green cover. **40.00**

Charm bracelet, 6" l gold luster metal link bracelet, five figural gold luster charms of red/brown Bambi and Faline, blue Thumper, black and white Flower, yellow/green Friend Owl. 1950s **. . 20.00**

Figure

3" x 7" x 8", painted and glazed ceramic, Bambi looking at blue butterfly on his tail, 1940s **. . 65.00**
4" x 6" x 7-1/2" h, painted and glazed ceramic, Bambi with head tilted upward, 1940s **65.00**
Studio fan card, 7" x 9", stiff buff paper, brown design, Walt Disney facsimile signature, small copyright, 1940s **35.00**

Disneyland

Flicker, I'm Goofy About Disneyland, red-metal case, Disneyland logo-type face, c1961 Productions copyright on back. **28.00**
Guide book, 10-1/2" x 10-1/2", 32 pgs, copyright 1965 . . . . **20.00**
Locket, 1-1/8" h brass, heart shape, raised image of castle on front, pink and blue enamel paint, opens to hold photos, c1956 . . . . **12.00**
Paint set, Disneyland Color by Number Oil Set, 10-1/4" x 14-1/4" x 1" box, illus of Tinkerbell using paint brush as magic wand to paint portrait of Pluto on cover, pair of unused pictures, 12 vials of paint, Hassenfield Brothers, Inc., c1950, unused set. **45.00**
Puzzle, Disneyland Christmas, 11-1/4" x 14-3/4", Whitman, frame tray, Santa checking extremely long list with Mickey's nephews on his lap, other characters, around him are Mickey, Minnie, Donald, Daisy, Goofy, and Pluto, Sleeping Beauty castle in background, copyright 1955, crayoned birthday message on back **25.00**
View-Master reel, Tomorrowland, copyright 1956 . . . . **20.00**

Disney World

Convention badge, 4" d, black printing, gold background, "110 Club '79/Disney World" **10.00**
Dish, 7" x 7" x 1-1/2" box with 7" d glass dish, fluted edge, gold foil sticker "A Gift of Glass From Walt Disney World," black, white, blue, and green design with center castle, surrounded by six park scenes, early 1970s **20.00**
Flicker, I Like Walt Disney World, red-metal case, text on reverse including "Vari-Vue" and Walt Disney World logo, black, white, and red image of Mickey wearing blue bow tie, changes to slogan in white on red background. **15.00**

Donald Duck

Animation cel, 10-1/2" x 12-1/2" acetate sheet, nicely centered 6" x 7"

color portrait, from 1980s TV show, "57" of numbered sequence **100.00**
Bank, 3" x 6" x 5-1/2" h, glazed and painted, blue TV set, brown accent around screen and on raised buttons, screen with full color decal of Donald and nephews having picnic, missing rubber plug and foil sticker, c1960. . . . . **60.00**
Blotter, 3-3/4" x 6-1/8", color illus of Donald wearing suit of armor, driving jeep, Sunoco Oil, 1934, unused. **. . 45.00**
Book, hardcover
Donald Duck, Grosset & Dunlap, copyright 1936, 36 pgs, 9-1/2" x 10-1/2". **200.00**
Donald Duck and His Cat Troubles, same as Whitman #845 series as #2445, tanned margins. **50.00**
Donald Duck and His Friends, D. C. Heath & Co., from educational "Walt Disney Storybooks" series, copyright 1939, 102 story pages, full-color illus **40.00**
Donald Duck and His Nephews, D. C. Heath & Co., from educational "Walt Disney Storybooks" series, copyright 1940, 66 story pages, full-color illus, blue and orange cover. **40.00**
Cereal bowl, 5-1/2" d, 1-1/5" h, yellow hard plastic, black and red Donald image on inside bottom, raised alphabet and numerals on rim, underside marked "Beetleware/Post's 40% Bran Flakes, Grape Nut Flakes," 1930s **35.00**
Doll, 6" x 8" x 13-1/2" h, stuffed fabric body, oilcloth head and legs, painted eyes, attached hat, separate collar piece tied around neck, four felt buttons on jacket, unmarked, 1930s. . . . **400.00**
Figure

2" h, painted and glazed ceramic of Donald waving, small black on yellow copyright sticker, Shaw **110.00**
4" h, bisque, with violin, incised "S1130" **265.00**
Handkerchief, 8-1/4" x 8-1/2", black, white, and green cotton, musical notes each containing character illus, long-billed Donald, Clara Cluck, Peter, and Polly Penguin, c1934 . . . . . . **65.00**
Little Golden Book, *Donald Duck and the Witch*, Simon & Schuster, copyright 1953, 28 pgs, title page with light penciled name at top margin. . . . **20.00**
Planter, 4" x 6" x 6-1/2" h, painted and glazed ceramic, Donald holding flower in air, standing next to basket planter,

pastel blue, yellow, and pink, Leeds China Co., c1949 . . . . **35.00**

Dumbo

Premium button, 1-1/4" d, black, white, red, and gray, "D-X" printed on platform, reverse Kay Kamen back paper includes small image of running Mickey, 1942 . . . . **24.00**

Toothbrush holder, 3-1/2" x 5-1/2" x 3-3/4", painted ceramic, matte finish, three openings for toothbrushes, incised 1942 copyright **150.00**

Jungle Book

Movie poster, 27" x 41", full-color glossy paper, one sheet for orig 1967 release, folded to 10" x 13-1/2" . . **40.00**

Record/book set, 12-1/4" x 12-1/2", gatefold cardboard album, 33-1/3 rpm record, Disneyland label, copyright 1967, 12-page story booklet **12.00**

Stuffed toy, Mickey Mouse, red paints, yellow shoes, 17" l, $40.

Mickey Mouse

Bar pin, brass, undecorated, full luster, center 1-1/2" h silver-plated diecut image of Mickey, hands on hips, English, 1930s **65.00**

Big Little Book, *Mickey Mouse the Mail Pilot,* Whitman #731, hardcover, 1933, 300 pgs, missing few pgs **25.00**

Book, *The Adventures of Mickey Mouse,* David McKay Co., softcover

version, full-color art on front and back covers, minor wear **140.00**

Charm

Celluloid, flat, cream, black accents on body, deep pink coloring on shorts, one leg crossed, holding guitar in arms, elongated nose, attributed to Japan, 1930s . . **12.00**

Flicker, red plastic frame, black and white flicker alternates between Mickey and name, Disney copyright below, female cameo image on back, c1960 . . . . . **10.00**

Sterling silver, classic pose, small loop at top, reverse with circular and rect panels reading "Walt Disney Productions/Sterling/Made in U.S.A.," c1960 . . . . **5.00**

Child's book, *Mickey Mouse and His Friend,* Whitman #904, copyright 1936, 12 pgs, linen-like pages with full-color art **125.00**

Egg cup, 2-1/2" x 3-1/4" x 3-1/2", china, Mickey riding scooter, side car serves as egg cup, yellow shirt, brown scooter, irid tan egg cup, marked "copyright, Made in Japan" **125.00**

Figure, 2" x 3-1/2" x 4-1/2" h, jointed wood, flat-disk hands, orig ears, long string tail, replaced nose, most of copyright decal missing, decal on chest with scattered flakes **325.00**

Magazine, *Mickey Mouse Magazine,* Vol. 2, #1, November 1934, 16 pgs, imprint of St. Louis Dairy, Thanksgiving Day cover, crossword neatly done in pencil **175.00**

Mirror, 1-7/8" x 2-1/2" paper covered mirror, large black, white, and red image of Mickey along with copyright symbol, text "By Special Permission Walt Disney Enterprises," 1930s **85.00**

Necklace, brass-link chain, diecut silvered-brass figure of Mickey in classic pose, black enamel and silver luster body, green-enamel pants and tips of shoes, 1930s **85.00**

Paint book, *Mickey Mouse Pictures to Paint,* Saalfield No. 210, copyright 1931, 9" x 10-1/2", 48 pages, well-used copy with defects **135.00**

Patch, fabric, red rim, white background, center Mickey in black and fleshtone, black and white eyes, red accent tongue, c1950 . . . . **5.00**

Pencil holder, 3-3/4" x 4-1/4" x 1-1/2", painted jig sawed wood, Mickey holding club, unmarked, Spanish, 1930s **145.00**

Pin

Diecut brass, vertical pin fastener on back, English, 1930s **70.00**

White metal, Mickey as Sorcerer's Apprentice, 1-3/4" h, enamel accents, copyright on reverse and "WDP," vertical bar pin, c1940 . . . . **48.00**

Pinback button

Boston Comics, 1-1/8" d, bright yellow litho, black and red lettering, black and yellow image of Mickey's head, advertises the "20-Page Comic Section in Colors-Boston Sunday Advertiser," maker's name "Geraghty/Chicago," 1930s, some loss to silver luster **85.00**

Emerson radio, black, white, and red, used to promote electric radio dec with Mickey images, curl with copyright symbol and "By Special Permission Walt Disney Ent.," orig back paper by Offset Gravure Corp., 1930s **145.00**

JC Penney, 7/8" d, black, white, and orange, text "Penney's For Back to School Needs," center image of Mickey, 1930s, orig back paper **55.00**

Mickey Mouse Good Teeth, 1-1/4" d, black, white, and red, Mickey standing next to molar, holding toothbrush aimed at mouth of Big Bad Wolf, inscribed "Walt Disney Enterprises," back paper or American Dental Association, Chicago **125.00**

Mickey Mouse Undies, 3-3/4" d, black and faded red image and type, cream background, copyright symbol below and "1928-1930 W. E. Disney" **25.00**

Publicity glossy, 7-1/2" x 10" glossy black and white, "Mickey Mouse in Mickey's Trailer" **20.00**

Sand pail

5" h, tin litho, 5-1/4" d opening at top, Mickey's Garden, wrap-around gardening scene with Mickey, Minnie, Pluto, Goofy, Horace, and Clarabell, Ohio Art Co., 1930s, heavy int. wear **295.00**

8" h, 8" d, tin litho, wrap-around beach scene with Mickey, Minnie, Pluto, Horace, Clarabell, and Goofy, int. with wear, Ohio Art Co., 1930s **525.00**

Sheet music, "The Wedding Party of Mickey Mouse," music by Stasny Music Corp., copyright 1931, cover art of wedding procession with Mickey and Minnie.....................**90.00**

Tab, 1-1/4" h, diecut tin, Mickey in classic pose, hands on hips, black body and face, gloves, shoes, and background areas dark gray finish that originally had been silver luster, bright red remnants, unbent, Australian, 1930s......................**85.00**

Whisk broom, 3-1/2" h painted white metal three-dimensional Mickey Mouse figure serves as handle, 1930s, marked with English registration number, spring tail......................**400.00**

Wrist watch, Ingersoll, 1-1/4" d metal case, metal link band, each link with image of Mickey, replaced crystal, recently cleaned, works, but runs sporadically **375.00**

Mickey Mouse Club
Club Member button, black and white Mickey, bright-orange background, curl reads "Copyright 1928-1930 by W. E. Disney," no back paper **125.00**

Magazine, *Walt Disney's Mickey Mouse Club Magazine*, Vol. 1, #4, Fall 1956, 8-1/2" x 11-1/2", 44 pgs **25.00**

Paperdolls, *Mouseketeers Cut-Outs*, Whitman, copyright 1963, 9-1/4" x 12", full-color cover, punch-out Karen, Cheryl, Bobby, and Cubby, six pages of outfits, unused **60.00**

Minnie Mouse
Candy dish, 5-3/4" d, 1" deep, china dish, orig attached curved wood handle, Mickey serving Minnie, black, red, green, and brown, light yellow tinted background, irid blue rim, 1930s, marked "Made in Japan" **175.00**

Child's feeding dish, 7-1/2" d, 1" deep, glazed white ceramic, black image in each of three divided sections, two with Mickey walking, other with Minnie pointing, copyright and "Mickey Mouse" on back, 1930s **95.00**

Figure
   1" h, diecut white metal, silver luster, three-dimensional miniature bench, marked "Japan" on back top edge of bench **10.00**
   7-1/2" h, composition, body, coil spring arms and legs, separate composition hands and feet, fringe fabric skirt attachment, missing spring tail and small flower hat attachment, 1930s.......**265.00**

Serigraph, 10-3/4" x 14" acetate sheet, 5-1/2" x 7" cel image of Mickey and Minnie skating, based on 1935 "On Ice" short, color laser background of frozen

lake, issued in early 1990s, Walt Disney Company seal at bottom **100.00**

Tin, 5" x 5-3/4" x 1", tin litho, emb Minnie holding flowers, marked "W. D. Ent.," Australian, 1930s...........**225.00**

Toothbrush holder, 2-1/2" x 3-1/4" x 5" h, movable right arm, orig string tail, marked "Japan," paper label under base, 1930s...............**175.00**

Pinback button, Good Teeth, Pinocchio and Jiminy Cricket, pair marching down road past "Good Teeth" sign, copyright initials "W.D.P." on bottom edge, backpaper "Distributed by The Bureau of Public Relations American Dental Assoc., Chicago," 1-1/4" d, $300. Photo courtesy of Hake's Americana & Collectibles.

Pinocchio
Charm, Gideon, sterling silver, three dimensional, by Delta & Cleon, Hollywood, CA, tiny copyright symbol on reverse **18.00**

Drinking glass, 3-3/4" h, clear, scalloped bottom, color image of Jiminy Cricket....................**25.00**

Figure
   2-1/2" x 2-3/4" x 7", Honest John, wood composition, painted features, Multi Products, 1940..................**195.00**
   3" h, Gideon, bisque, painted, dark gray/blue outfit, yellow accents on cape, marked "Japan," c1940 ....**35.00**

Hand puppet
   Jiminy Cricket, 11" h, fabric body, soft vinyl head, non-working squeaker, stitched Gund tag, c1960 ....**18.00**
   Pinocchio, 10-1/2" h, fabric body, soft vinyl head, working squeaker, attached copyright tag, c1970 ....**20.00**

Paint book, *Pinocchio Story Paint Book*, set of six Whitman books, each #1059, copyright 1940, 24 black and white pages, stiff color covers, some pages colored, price for six books **95.00**

Photo, 8" x 10" full-color glossy photo of orig lobby card, black Sharpie pen autograph "Ward Kimball" in blue background area just above Jiminy Cricket who is standing on Pinocchio's shoe **30.00**

Pinback button, 1-1/8" d, Jiminy Cricket, blue, bright yellow litho, slogan "You Help More the United Way," curl has Productions copyright, c1950....................**10.00**

Premium button, 1-1/4" d, "Walt Disney's Pinocchio," large portrait in black, white, and bright red, store giveaway type, 1940 ....**24.00**

Toy, 2-1/2" x 3-1/2" x 7-1/2" h, wind-up, built-in key, painted composition body and legs, metal wind-up mechanism on inside of body, painted hollow cast metal head, paper label eyes, holding apple and books, French, c1940..................**650.00**

Valentine, mechanical, 3" x 5-3/4", Cleo, diecut stiff paper, black, white, red, and orange, copyright 1939 ....**20.00**

Pluto
Big Little Book, *Pluto the Pup*, Whitman #1467, copyright 1938, full-color art on front and back covers.....................**45.00**

Decal, 2-3/4" x 3-1/4", brown, yellow, and white, insignia for 37th Recon Co., Pluto holding machine gun, ears up listening to radio signature being emitted from his tail, Disney copyright, 1940s, reverse with instructions and "Columbia Supply Company," unused....................**20.00**

Pencil drawing, 9-1/2" x 12" sheet of animation paper, nicely centered 3-1/2" x 4" image of Pluto as devil with horns, tail, holding pitchfork, from 1933 short, "13," from numbered sequence......**300.00**

Tru-View film card, Pluto as baseball catcher, 3-3/4" x 5-1/2" black and white card, color photos of studio models, red and white envelope, copyright 1953......................**15.00**

Silly Symphony
Big Little Book, *Silly Symphony Featuring Donald Duck and His (Mis)Adventures*, Whitman #1441, published 1937, error book, pages bound upside down as published, color

front and back art with Donald as angel and devil **125.00**

Sheet music, "Silly Symphony Grasshopper and the Ants," Irving Berlin, eight pgs, copyright 1934, black, white, orange, and green cover art, glued repair, scattered light dust soiling **25.00**

Snow White, alarm clock, Bayard, marked "Made in France, Par Autorisation Walt Disney," $120.

Snow White

Baby rattle, 6" l, 2-1/4" d, celluloid, cylindrical top, wrap around design of Snow White and Dwarfs in row holding hands, copyright 1938 **195.00**

Big Little Book, *Snow White and the Seven Dwarfs,* Whitman #1460, copyright 1938 **45.00**

Night light, 3-1/2" d painted tin base, tin litho battery compartment cylinder with wrap around scene of Snow White in bed surrounded by Dwarfs, thick diecut cardboard Dopey figure, Micro-Light Co., Inc., copyright 1938 **300.00**

Pencil drawing, 10" x 12" sheet of animation paper, nicely centered 4" x 4-1/4" image in lead pencil of Happy, head turned to one side, pointing finger, 1937, "54" from numbered sequence **200.00**

Press kit, 9" x 12", glossy folder, full-color illus on cover, 8-1/2" x 11" 24-page booklet, set of six 8" x 10" glossy black and white publicity photos issued for 1987 50th anniversary re-release **25.00**

Record, 6-3/4" x 7-1/2", colorful paper sleeve, yellow vinyl 78 rpm record, Simon & Schuster, 1950s **15.00**

Three Little Pigs

Pencil holder, set of three painted jig-sawed wood pencil holders, each 1-1/2" x 4" x 4" h, attachment on back to hold pencils, Fiddler Pig has one row for placement of six pencils, other two have two rows for placement of 12 pencils, unmarked, but Spanish **275.00**

Plate, 7" d, china, Little Red Riding Hood and Three Pigs dancing and playing instruments as Grandmother knits, gold imprint for Salem China Co., 1930s **60.00**

Sand pail, 5-1/2" h, 5-1/4" d top opening, tin litho, wrap-around scene of Practical Pig outside his house, being passed by Little Red Riding Hood, Fiddler, and Fifer Pigs, unmarked by attributed to Ohio Art, 1930s, wear and defects **350.00**

DOLLHOUSES

History: Dollhouses date from the 18th century to modern times. Early dollhouses often were handmade, sometimes with only one room. The most common type was made for a young girl to fill with replicas of furniture scaled especially to fit into a dollhouse. Specially sized dolls also were made for dollhouses. All types of accessories in all types of styles were available, and dollhouses could portray any historical period.

References: Evelyn Ackerman, *Genius of Moritz Gottschalk*, Gold House Publishing, 1994; Mary Brett, *Tomart's Price Guide to Tin Litho Doll Houses and Plastic Doll House Furnishings*, Tomart Publications, 1997; Nora Earnshaw, *Collecting Dolls' Houses and Miniatures*, Pincushion Press, 1993; Charles F. Donovan Jr., *Renwal-World's Finest Toys, Dollhouse Furniture*, L-W Book Sales, 1999; Flora Bill Jacobs, *Dolls' Houses in America: Historic Preservation in Miniature*, Charles Scribner's Sons, 1974; Margaret Towner, *Dollhouse Furniture*, Courage Books, 1993; Dian Zillner, *American Dollhouses and Furniture from the 20th Century*, Schiffer Publishing, 1995.

Periodicals: *Doll Castle News*, P.O. Box 247, Washington, NJ 07882, http://www.dollcastlenews.com; *International Dolls' House News*, P.O. Box 79, Southampton S09 7EZ England; *Miniature Collector*, 30595 Eight Mill, Livonia, MI 48152.

Museums: Art Institute of Chicago, Chicago, IL; Margaret Woodbury Strong Museum, Rochester, NY; Peabody Essex Museum, Salem, PA; Washington Dolls' House and Toy Museum, Washington, DC.

American

12-1/4" w, 13" d, 11" h, painted wood and board, bungalow style, blue building, cream and orange trim, red roof, one room with orig wall covering, 1920s, some paint wear, side door warped **300.00**

21" w, 43" h, ivory-painted gable and center hallway, five large rooms and attic bedroom, attached garage, separate blue shutters and window boxes, most furnishings from same period as house,

McLoughlin folding dollhouse, two rooms, highly decorated interiors, original box, 16" h, 17" l, 12" d, $950.

approx. 40 items, made by John Leonard Plock, NY architect, c1932 . . . . **250.00**

21-1/4" l, 28-3/4" h, Victorian, last quarter 19th C, two-story house, modified Federal style, mansard roof with widow's walk, fenced-in front garden, simulated grass and fountains, polychrome details **400.00**

28-1/4" w, 17-1/4" d, 32-1/2" h, gambrel roof, painted off-white, red paste board scalloped shingles, front opening half doors, six rooms, original paper wall and floor coverings, hinged door in rear roof, front steps, orig furniture, bisque dolls, accessories, and rugs, some paint and paper wear **920.00**

Bliss, chromolithograph paper on wood

13" h, two story, litho blue roof, red wood base, two opening windows, working front door, orig litho walls and floors, marked "R. Bliss" on front door, some wear, stains, and discoloration **900.00**

14" h, two story, blue litho paper on roof, blue wood on back, red wood chimney and base, two open lower windows and two upper windows, house opens in front, litho wall and floor coverings inside, marked "R. Bliss" on door, some wear, one wall slightly warped **575.00**

14" h, two story, stable, red shingle roof, painted green roof and red spire on cupola, painted red base and side poles of stable, single opening door on second floor, brown papier-mâché horse, marked "R. Bliss" **900.00**

16-1/2" h, two story, front porch with turned columns, working front door, overhanging roof with lattice-work balcony, blue-gray roof with dormer windows, hinged front, int. with two rooms, printed carpeting and wallpaper, celluloid windows with later lace curtains, electric lights, two scratch-built chairs . . **1,725.00**

19" h, two story, front porch with balcony, two real windows, working front door, litho windows on 2nd floor and sides, red litho shingles on roof, blue litho shingles on porch roof, litho wall and floor coverings inside, wood chimney, marked "R. Bliss" on porch balcony, some general soil and discoloration **1,200.00**

Elastolin, Germany, 29" w, farmyard, house, barn, fencing, trees, and various figures **1,150.00**

German, 35" w, 11-1/4" d, 17" h, Nuremberg Kitchen, dark yellow walls with deep red trim, red and black checkerboard floor, cream stove hood, green furniture, tin stove, tin and copper pots, set of scales, wash boiler, baking pans, utensils, pottery, porcelain, and pewter tableware, late 19th C, some paint wear and imperfections . **2,300.00**

McLoughlin, 12" x 17" x 16", folding house, two rooms, dec int., orig box. **950.00**

Schoenhut, 20" x 26" x 30", mansion, two story, eight rooms, attic, tan brick design, red roof, large dormer, 20 glass windows, orig decal, 1923 . . . **1,750.00**

Tootsietoy, 21" w, 10-1/8" d, 16" h, house, furniture, and accessories, printed Masonite, half-timbered style, two rooms down, two up, removable roof, open back, orchid and pink bedroom sets, orchid bathroom, brown dining room set, flocked sofa and chairs, green and white kitchen pcs, piano, bench, lamps, telephone, cane-back sofa, rocker, some damage and wear to 3/4 scale furniture . **525.00**

DOLLS

History: Dolls have been children's play toys for centuries. Dolls also have served other functions. From the 14th through 18th centuries, doll making was centered in Europe, mainly in Germany and France. The French dolls produced in this era were representations of adults and dressed in the latest couturier designs. They were not children's toys.

During the mid-19th century, child and baby dolls, made in wax, cloth, bisque, and porcelain, were introduced. Facial features were hand painted, wigs were made of mohair and human hair, and the dolls were dressed in the current fashions for babies or children.

Doll making in the United States began to flourish in the 1900s with companies such as Effanbee, Madame Alexander, and Ideal.

Marks: Marks of the various manufacturers are found on the back of the head or neck or on the doll's back. These marks are very important in identifying a doll and its date of manufacture.

References: J. Michael Augustyniak, *Thirty Years of Mattel Fashion Dolls, 1967 Through 1997: Identification and Value Guide,* Collector Books, 1998; Kim Avery, *The World of Raggedy Ann Collectibles,* Collector Books, 1997, 2000 value update; John Axe, *Encyclopedia of Celebrity Dolls,* Hobby House Press, 1983; Mary Caruso, *Care of Favorite Dolls, Antique Bisque Conservation,* Hobby House Press, 1999; Jurgin and Marianne Cieslik, *German Doll Studies,* Gold Horse Publishing, 1999; Carol Corson,

Schoenhut Dolls, Hobby House Press, 1993; Carla Marie Cross, *Modern Doll Rarities,* Antique Trader Books, 1997; Linda Crowsey, *Madame Alexander Collector's Dolls Price Guide #25,* Collector Books, 2000; —, *Madame Alexander Store Exclusives & Limited Editions,* Collector Books, 2000; Maryanne Dolan, *The World of Dolls, A Collector's Identification and Value Guide,* Krause Publications, 1998; Stephanie Finnegan, *The Robert Tonner Story: Dreams and Dolls,* Portfolio Press, 2000; Jan Foulke, *Doll Classics,* Hobby House Press, 1997; —, *Insider's Guide to China Doll Collecting,* Hobby House Press, 1995; —, *Insider's Guide to Doll Buying and Selling,* Hobby House Press, 1995; —, *Insider's Guide to Germany "Dolly" Collecting,* Hobby House Press, 1995; —, *14th Blue Book Dolls and Values,* Hobby House Press, 2000; Sandra Ann Garrison, *The Raggedy Ann and Andy Family Album,* 2nd ed., Schiffer Publishing, 1999; Cynthia Gaskill, *Legendary Dolls of Madame Alexander,* Theriault's, 1995; Patricia Hall, *Johnny Gruelle: Creator of Raggedy Ann and Andy,* Pelican Publishing (1101 Monroe St., Gretna, LA 70053), 1993; Dawn Herlocher, *Antique Trader's Doll Makers & Marks,* Antique Trader Books, 1999; —, *200 Years of Dolls,* Antique Trader Books, 1996; R. Lane Herron, *Warman's Dolls,* Krause Publications, 1998; Judith Izen, *Collector's Guide to Ideal Dolls,* 2nd ed., Collector Books, 1998; Judith Izen and Carol Stover, *Collector's Guide to Vogue Dolls,* Collector Books, 1998, 2000 value update; Polly Judd, *African and Asian Costumed Dolls,* Hobby House Press, 1995; —, *Cloth Dolls,* Hobby House Press, 1990; Polly and Pam Judd, *Composition Dolls, Vol. I* (1991), *Vol. II* (1994), Hobby House Press; —, *European Costume Dolls,* Hobby House Press, 1994; —, *Glamour Dolls of the 1950s & 1960s,* revised ed., Hobby House Press, 1993; —, *Hard Plastic Dolls,* 3rd ed. (1993), Book II (1994), Hobby House Press; Michele Karl, *Composition & Wood Dolls and Toys: A Collector's Reference Guide,* Antique Trader Books, 1998; Kathy and Don Lewis, *Talking Toys of the 20th Century,* Collector Books, 1999; A. Glenn Mandeville, *Glenn Mandeville's Madame Alexander Dolls, 3rd Collector's Price Guide,* Hobby House Press, 2000; —, *Ginny,* 3rd ed., Hobby House Press, 1998; Marcie Melilo, *The Ultimate Barbie Doll Book,* Krause Publications, 1997; Ursula R. Mertz, *Collector's Encyclopedia of American Composition Dolls, 1900 to 1950,* Collector Books, 1999; Patsy Moyer, *Doll Values, Antique to Modern,* 4th ed., Collector Books, 2000; —, *Modern Collectible Dolls,* Collector Books, 1997, *Vol. II.* (1997, 1998 value update), *Vol. III* (1999), *Vol. IV* (2000); Myra Yellin Outwater, *Advertising Dolls,* Schiffer Publishing, 1997; Edward R. Pardella, *Shirley Temple Dolls and Fashion,* Schiffer Publishing, 1992; Sabine Reinelt, *Magic of Character Dolls,* Hobby House Press, 1993.

Lydia Richter, *China, Parian, and Bisque German Dolls,* Hobby House Press, 1993; Lydia and Joachim F. Richter, *Bru Dolls,* Hobby House Press, 1989; Lydia Richter and Karin Schmelcher, *Heubach Character Dolls and Figurines,* Hobby House Press, 1992; Joyce Rinehart, *Wonderful Raggedy Anns,* Schiffer Publishing, 1997; Cindy Cabulis, *Collector's Guide to Dolls of the 1960s and 1970s,* Collector Books, 2000; Jane Sarasohn-Kahn, *Contemporary Barbie,* Antique Trader Books, 1997; Patricia N. Schoonmaker, *Patsy Doll Family Encyclopedia, Vol. II,* Hobby House Press,

1998; Patricia R. Smith, *Antique Collector's Dolls*, Vol. I (1975, 1991 value update), Vol. II (1976, 1991 Value update), Collector Books; ——, *Collector's Encyclopedia of Madame Alexander Dolls, 1965-1990*, Collector Books, 1999; ——, *Effanbee Dolls*, Collector Books, 1998 values update; ——, *Madame Alexander Dolls 1965-1990*, 1991, 1997 values update, Collector Books; ——, *Modern Collector's Dolls*, Series I through VIII (1973-1996 value updates), Collector Books; ——, *Patricia Smith's Doll Values Antique to Modern*, Eleventh Series, Collector Books, 1995; ——, *Shirley Temple Dolls and Collectibles*, Vol. I (1977, 1992 value update), Vol. II (1979, 1992 value update), Collector Books; Evelyn Robson Stahlendorf, *Charlton Standard Catalogue of Canadian Dolls*, 3rd ed., Charlton Press, 1997; Carl P. Stirn, *Turn-of-the-Century Dolls, Toys, and Games* (1893 catalog reprint), Dover Publications, 1990; Florence Theriault, *The Beautiful Jumeau*, Gold Horse Publishing, 1997; Marci Van Ausdall, *Betsy McCall*, Hobby House Press, 2000.

Periodicals and Internet Resources: *Antique & Collectables*, P.O. Box 12589, El Cajon, CA 92002, http://www.collect.com/antiquesandcollectables; *Antique & Collectible Dolls*, 218 W. Woodin Blvd., Dallas, TX 75224; *Antique Doll Collector*, 6 Woodside Ave., Suite 300, Northport, NY 11768, http://www.antiqueDollCollector.com; *Doll Castle News*, P.O. Box 247, Washington, NJ 07882-0247, http://www.dollcastlenews.com; DollFinder, http://www.dollfinder.com; *Doll Magazine*, Avalon Court, Star Road, Patridge Green, West Sussex RH13 BRY +44(0) 1403 711511, http://www.dollmagazine.com; *Doll Reader*, 6405 Flank Drive, Harrisburg, PA 17112, http://www.dollreader.com; *Doll World*, 306 East Parr Road, Berne, IN 46711, http://www.whitebirches.com; *Dollmasters*, P.O. Box 151, Annapolis, MD 21404; *Dolls In Print*, P.O. Box 95116, Lake Mary, FL 32795-1116, http://www.dollsinprint.com; *Dolls—The Collector's Magazine*, 170 Fifth Ave., 12th Floor, New York, NY 10010; Master Collector, 225 Cattle Barron Parc Drive, Fort Worth, TX 76108, http://www.mastercollector.com; *Patsy & Friends*, 12415 W. Monte Vista Road, Avondale, AZ 85323; *Rags*, P.O. Box 0130, Arcola, IL 61910-0130.

Collectors' Clubs: Doll Club of Great Britain, 16E Chalwin Industrian Estate St., Clements Road, Parkstone Poole, Dorset BH15 3PE UK; Doll Doctor's Assoc., 6204 Ocean Front Ave., Virginia Beach, VA 23451, http://www.gndollseminar.com; Fashion Doll Collector's Club of S. E. Georgia, P.O. Box 115, Pembroke, GA 31321; Ginny Doll Club, P.O. Box 338, Oakdale, CA 95361; Modern Doll Collectors, Inc., 12415 W. Monte Vista Road, Avondale, AZ 8533323; United Federation of Doll Clubs, 10920 N. Ambassador Drive, Suite 130, Kansas City, MO 64153, http://www.ufdc.org.

Museums: Aunt Len's Doll House, Inc., New York, NY; Children's Museum, Detroit, MI; Doll Castle Doll Museum, Washington, NJ; Doll Museum, Newport, RI; Toy and Miniature Museum of Kansas City, Kansas City, MO; Gay Nineties Button & Doll Museum, Eureka Springs, AR; Margaret Woodbury Strong Museum, Rochester, NY; Mary Merritt Doll Museum, Douglassville, PA; Mary Miller Doll Museum, Brunswick, GA; Prairie Museum of Art & History,

Colby, KS; Washington Dolls' House & Toy Museum, Washington, DC; Yesteryears Museum, Sandwich, MA.

Additional Listings: See *Warman's Americana & Collectibles* for more examples.

SPECIAL AUCTIONS

Cobb's Doll Auctions
1909 Harrison Road North
Johnstown, OH 43031-9539
(740) 964-0444
http://www.cobbsdolls.com

McMasters Doll Auctions
P.O. Box 1755
Cambridge, OH 43725
(614) 432-4419
http://www.mcmastersauctions.com

Skinner Inc.
Bolton Gallery
357 Main St.
Boston, MA 01740
(508) 779-6241
http://www.skinnerinc.com

Theriault's Auction
P.O. Box 151
Annapolis, MD 21404-0151
(800) 638-0422
http://www.theriaults.com

A.M., 310 Just Me, 9" h, **$1,050.**
Photo courtesy of McMasters.

Amberg

12-1/2" h, Bottle Babe Twins, solid-dome bisque heads, light blue sleep eyes, blue brows, painted upper and lower lashes, open mouths, molded tongues, lightly molded and painted hair, cloth bodies with non-working criers, composition arms, right arms molded to hold celluloid bottles, orig white lace-trimmed baby dresses, slips, crocheted bonnets, diapers, and socks, hold orig celluloid baby bottle, blue and white celluloid rattle, marked "A.M./Germany/341/3" on back of heads, "Amberg's/Bottle Babe/Pat. Pending/Amberg Dolls/The World Standard" on dress, both dolls have light rubs on cheeks or hair, cloth bodies are aged, some flaking on arms, paint flaked off right arm of one, price for pr
. . . . **500.00**

15" h, New Born Babe, solid dome bisque head, blue sleep eyes, softly blushed brown, painted upper and lower lashes, closed mouth, lightly molded and painted hair, cloth body with composition hands, white lace-trimmed antique baby dress, slip and diaper, light dust in bisque, tiny run on upper lip, left side seam split near bottom of torso **315.00**

Armand Marseille

8-1/2" h, Googlie, bisque head, closed smiling mouth, dimples, blue glass sleep eyes to right, wisp of brown mohair peeking from black felt hat, composition five-pc toddler body, Tyrolean outfit, imp "Armand Marseille Germany 323," c1920 . . . . **1,035.00**

10" h, character baby, bisque socket head, blue sleep eyes, open mouth, two upper teeth, blond mohair wig, bent-limb composition body, orig gauze shift, imp "251 GB, Armand Marseille for George Borgfeldt," 1920s **415.00**

10" h, character toddler, bisque head, blue sleep eyes, open smiling mouth, dimples, blond mohair wig, chunky composition straight-limb doll, white pique jacket and pants, knit tam, white scalloped socks, imp "A.M. 560 a. DRMR 232," c1920, some repaint **750.00**

10" l, 9" d head circumference, Dream Baby, brown bisque socket head, brown sleep eyes, closed mouth, black painted hair, brown bent limb composition baby body, fine lawn christening gown with tucks, ruffles, and lace trim, c1920 . . . .**300.00**

11" h, 1894, bisque socket head, set blue eyes, single stroke brows, painted upper and lower lashes, open mouth, four upper teeth, orig mohair wig, jointed wood and composition body with well-modeled parts, orig clothing, light blue lace-trimmed print dress, lace-trimmed bonnet, orig underclothing, black cotton socks with garters attached to chemise, orig handmade shoes, marked "1894/A.M. 3/0 DEP" on back of head **400.00**

16" h, 351 baby, solid dome bisque socket head, blue sleep eyes, softly blushed brows, painted upper and lower lashes, open mouth, two lower teeth, lightly molded and painted hair, composition bent-limb baby body, antique baby gown and slip, diaper, new sweater and bonnet, marked "A.M./Germany/351/4 K" on back of head, body has excellent orig finish with normal wear at joints, cracks in finish and flaking around neck socket .**200.00**

23" h, 990 baby, bisque socket head, brown sleep eyes, feathered brows, painted upper and lower lashes, open mouth, well-accented lips, two upper teeth, antique human hair wig, composition bent-limb baby body, antique baby dress, slip, diaper, new crocheted sweater, cap and booties, marked "Armand Marseille/Germany/990/A 12 M" on back of head, heavy French-style body, arms repainted and have rough finish, right big toe missing, other toes repaired and repainted, normal wear at joints **275.00**

24" h, bisque head, blue sleep eyes, open mouth, dark blond mohair wig, fully articulated composition body, unsullied, orig white cotton cutwork dress, imp "AM 390," early 20th C, chip on inner edge of mouth rim, orig stringing loose **230.00**

Arranbee

17" h, Nancy Lee, composition head, brown sleep eyes with real lashes, painted lower lashes, single stroke brows, closed mouth, orig human-hair wig in orig set, five-pc

composition body, orig brown-flannel belted dress, white ruffle trim, orig underwear combination, orig socks and brown-suede shoes with fringe tongue, marked "R & B" on back of head, unplayed with condition. **300.00**

21" h, Nanette, hard plastic head, blue sleep eyes with real lashes, single-stroke brows, painted lower lashes, closed mouth, saran wig, five-pc hard-plastic walking body, orig red and white striped dress with red organdy sleeves and apron, blue vinyl wide belt with charms attached, wrist tag, curlers on card, comb, marked "R & B" on head, "Nanette/An R & B Quality Doll/R & B Dolly Company New York 3, NY" on label on end of box, "R & B/Nanette/Walks/Sits/Stands/ Turns Her Head/R & B Doll Company New York City" on wrist tag, near mint in aged box, lid damaged and repaired . . . **700.00**

Averill, Georgene, 6-3/4" h, Bonnie Babe, all bisque, brown sleep eyes, open mouth, two lower teeth, molded painted hair, flange jointed neck imp "17" on rim, jointed limbs, pink molded and painted shoes, white socks, c1926, small chip on torso at neck edge **920.00**

Bahr & Proschild, 11" l, character baby, bisque head, brown sleep eyes, open mouth, two upper teeth, old blond mohair wig, bent-limb composition baby body, cream-colored crocheted baby suit and booties, fabric hat, imp "BP 585 2/0 Germany," early 20th C, scratch line on bisque to back of head, darkened mold line above ear . **300.00**

Bisque, unmarked, 19-1/2" h, bisque shoulder head, very light tint, painted blue eyes, red accent line, single stroke brows, closed mouth, accent line between lips, pierced ears, molded blond hair, black bead dec, molded blouse on shoulder plate with pink accents, black cross necklace, replaced cloth body, bisque lower arms and lower legs, two-pc black velvet outfit with flower design, underclothing **450.00**

Bru Jne, 23" h, walking, bisque socket head mounted on base for mechanism, brown paperweight eyes with blush above, feathered brows, painted upper and lower lashes, closed mouth with accent lines and shading, pierced ears,

orig human hair wig over cork pate, wood and composition body with un-jointed legs, leather shoes with metal soles, rollers for "walking," turns head, swings arms, rolls on rollers on bottom of feet, dressed in possibly orig clothing, underclothing, marked "Bru Jne/9" on back of head, flaking off both arms and hands, opening in front of torso for missing crier, mechanism works slowly **7,100.00**

Century Doll Co., Kestner, Character Baby, c1920

17" l, 12-1/2" d bisque head, brown sleep eyes, open/closed smiling mouth with two upper molded teeth and tongue, deep modeling across bridge of nose, light dimples, flange neck on cloth body with side-swivel cloth legs, non-working squeaker, mechanism in body waves composition hands, long white lawn baby gown, imp mark "Century Doll Co Kestner Germany" **550.00**

19" l, 13" d bisque head, blue sleep eyes, closed pursed pouty mouth, light painted molded hair, deep modeling on bridge of nose, flange neck on cloth body with side-swivel cloth legs, composition arms, white cotton baby dress, pink knit sweater and hat with moth damage, imp mark "Century Doll Co. Kestner Germany" **815.00**

Chase, Martha, 13" h, baby, oil-painted stockinette head, painted brown eyes, single-stroke brows, painted upper lashes, closed mouth, applied ears, oil-painted hair, cloth body with sateen-covered torso, antique white baby dress, slip and diaper, marked "Chase/Stockinet Doll/Trade Mark" in round stamp on left hip, "Feb. 20, 1912/Polly" hand written on front of torso, some wear **325.00**

China, unmarked

11-1/2" h, Frozen Charlie, pink tint, painted blue eyes with blue accent line, single-stroke brows, closed mouth, accent line between lips, painted blond hair with brush strokes around face, un-jointed body with arms extended, hands held with fingers curled, finger nails and toe nails outlined, color flaw on right side of forehead at edge of hair, couple spots of inherent roughness on right back of head and right shoulder, light color wear on edges of feet and hands, small flake off right finger. **450.00**

18" h, open mouth, low brow, china shoulder head with turned head, painted blue eyes, red accent line, single-stroke brows, open mouth, molded teeth, molded and painted wavy hair, cloth body, china lower arms and lower legs, painted garters, molded and painted brown shoes with heels, possibly orig beige print dress, underclothing **850.00**

Cloth, 21" h, Philadelphia Baby, painted head and shoulders, heavily lidded brown painted eyes, deeply modeled mouth, brown hair, cloth body, painted lower limbs, gray and white striped cotton shift, white undergarments, c1900, overall wear, paint rubs and loss **1,100.00**

Cuno & Otto Dressel

14" h, bisque head, blue sleep eyes with lashes, open mouth, two upper teeth, replaced auburn mohair wig, fully articulated composition body, blue dress, imp "Cuno & Otto Dressel," early 20th C, some repair to body **200.00**

15-1/2" h, girl, painted bisque socket head, blue sleep eyes with real lashes, feathered brows, shading around eyes, open mouth, four upper teeth, orig human hair wig, jointed wood and composition teen-age body with high knee joints, orig clothing, short dress, slip, teddy, socks, and leather shoes, marked "Cuno & Otto Dressel/Germany" on back of head **450.00**

Demalcol, 9-1/2" h, Googlie, bisque socket head, blue eyes set to side, single-stroke brows, painted upper and lower lashes, closed smiling mouth, human-hair wig, new jointed-composition body, blue and white flowered dress, matching bonnet, new underclothing, socks and shoes, marked "Demalcol/5/0/Germany" on back of head **525.00**

Eden Bebe, 16-1/2" h, bisque socket head, blue paperweight eyes, feathered brows, painted upper and lower lashes, open mouth, six upper teeth, pierced ears, replaced mohair wig, jointed wood and composition French body, redressed, pale blue and ecru outfit, blue and beige jacket, antique underclothing, new stockings, and old shoes, marked "Eden

Bebe/Paris/7/Depose" on back of neck, "7" on front of neck, light kiln dust on left cheek, flaking at neck socket of body and on both lower legs, normal wear at joints and on hands **1,200.00**

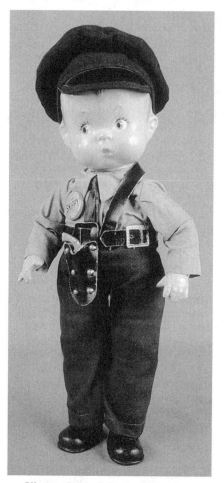

Effanbee, Skippy Policeman, rare original outfit and accessories, 14" h, $1,950. Photo courtesy of McMasters.

Effanbee

11" h, Grumpy Cowboy, composition shoulder head, painted blue eyes to side, single-stroke brows, closed pouty mouth, molded and painted hair, cloth body, composition arms and feet, cowboy outfit with plaid shirt, gold pants, green bandanna, imitation-leather chaps, holster with gun, replaced felt hat, marked "Effanbee/Dolls/Walk Talk Sleep" on back of shoulder plate, light crazing, light wear back of head, few flakes off shoulder plate, wear on edges of feet **475.00**

14" h, Skippy Policeman, composition head, molded and painted hair, painted blue eyes to

side, peaked brows, painted upper lashes, closed mouth, cloth body with composition arms and legs, rare policeman outfit, dark blue cap with black oilcloth bill, light-blue shirt, black ribbon tie, tagged dark-blue pants, black belt with holster and orig gun, molded and painted black socks and shoes, orig pinback button, marked "Effanbee Skippy © P. L. Crosby" on back of head "Effanbee Durable Dolls Made In USA" on tag on pants **1,950.00**

17" h, American Child Boy, composition head, painted blue eyes, multi-stroke brows, tiny painted upper and lower lashes, closed smiling mouth, orig human-hair wig, five-pc composition child body, orig blue wool two-pc suit, jacket and shorts, white shirt, multicolored tie, orig socks and black leatherette shoes, unmarked, light facial crazing, few light lines of crazing on legs **1,050.00**

19-1/2" h, American Child, composition head, blue sleep eyes with real lashes, multi-stroke brows, painted lower lashes, closed mouth, orig human hair wig with orig curlers, five-pc composition child body, orig blue and white striped zippered dress, nylon panties, orig white socks with blue trim, blue leatherette tie shoes, marked "Effanbee/American Children" on back of head, "Effanbee/Anne-Shirley" on back, unplayed with condition. . **1,500.00**

Gaultier, Francois

21" h, Bebe, bisque socket head, large blue paperweight eyes, feathered brows, painted upper and lower lashes, full-closed mouth, molded tongue, pierced ears, replaced mohair wig, jointed wood and composition body with straight wrists, new blue silk dress with matching bonnet, new underclothing, socks and lace-up boots, marked "F. G. (in scroll)/8" on back of head, fingers touched up, minor repairs **2,200.00**

24" h, Bebe, bisque socket head, large brown paperweight eyes, feathered brows, painted upper and lower lashes, closed mouth, accent between lips, pierced ears, synthetic wig, jointed wood and composition body with overall orig finish, jointed wrists, straight legs, antique white dress with ruffle, underclothing, socks and shoes, marked "9/F.G." in scroll on back of head, "9" on front of neck, three repaired hairlines, minor rubs on right cheek and nose, touch-up at shoulders, hips, and bottoms of feet **700.00**

Gebruden Heubach, walking doll, 11" h, $2,000. Photo courtesy of McMasters.

Halbig, Simon

7" h, Oriental, bisque, medium skin tone, dark pupil-less stationary eyes, closed mouth orig black mohair Oriental-style wig, swivel neck, kid-lined neck socket and legs, long black stockings, brick red one-strap shoes, imp "852 3," late 19th C, some mottling/soil to bisque **920.00**

8" h, bisque head, blue sleep eyes, open mouth, four molded teeth, pierced ears, blond mohair wig, chunky straight wrist articulated composition body, orig finish and stringing, new red faille dress, imp "1079 DEP," c1900, tiny chip to right ear hole **550.00**

21" h, C M Bergmann bisque head, brown sleep eyes with lashes, open mouth, synthetic auburn wig, jointed composition body, period white lawn dress with lace insertion, sprinkling of pepper spots primarily to the right cheek, early 20th C **260.00**

27" h, CM Bergmann bisque head, blue sleep eyes, open mouth, pierced ears, orig blond mohair wig, fully articulated composition body, period white lawn dress with lace insertion and ruffled lace hemline, imp mark "SH CM Bergmann 12," late 19th/early 20th C **575.00**

28" h, 949, bisque head, late 19th century, brown stationary eyes, closed mouth, pierced ears, blond mohair wig, fully articulated composition body stamped "Made in Germany," yellow cotton faille dress, imp "949," late 19th C **2,530.00**

Hamburger & Co., 22-1/2" h, Viola, bisque socket head, blue sleep eyes, feathered brows, painted upper and lower lashes, open mouth, four upper teeth, synthetic wig, jointed wood and composition body, antique dress with lace trim, underclothing, new socks and leather shoes, marked "Made in/Germany/Viola/H & Co./7" on back of head, several wig pulls on right side of forehead, light rub on nose, small inherent cut on H in back of head, repairs at neck socket of body, bottom of torso and left upper arm, normal wear at joints, finish of legs slightly different color than rest of body **300.00**

Handwerck, 16" h, bisque head, blue sleep eyes, open mouth, pierced ears, orig blond mohair wig, fully articulated composition body, Alice in Wonderland blue dress and white pinafore, dark brown shoes, imp "109-6 Germany Handwerck" **460.00**

Handwerck, Heinrich

25" h, bisque socket head, brown sleep eyes with real lashes, molded and feathered brows, painted lower lashes, open mouth with accented and well-modeled lips, four upper teeth, pierced ears, orig human-hair wig, jointed wood and composition body, possibly orig white lace-trimmed dress, underclothing, white cotton socks, marked Handwerck shoes, marked "Germany/Heinrich/Handwearck/H

albig/4-1/2" on back of head, "Heinrich Handwerch/Germany/4-1/2" stamped on back of left hip, "4-1/2 /HH" in heart on shoes, light rubs on cheeks, touch-up around neck socket of body and on right side seam of torso, normal wear at joints, sole of left shoe damaged **450.00**

32-1/2" h, bisque socket head, blue sleep eyes, molded and feathered brows, painted upper and lower lashes, open mouth, accented lips, four upper teeth, pierced ears, orig human-hair wig, jointed wood and composition Handwerck body with orig finish, antique white child's dress, antique underclothing, cotton socks, black patent leather shoes, marked "Germany/Handwerck/Simon & Halbig/7" on back of head, "Heinrich Handwerck/Germany/7" stamped in red on lower back, finish flaking on lower left arm and knees, left knee ball replaced **1,025.00**

33" h, 99, bisque socket head, brown sleep eyes, painted brown sleep eyes, molded and feathered brows, painted upper and lower lashes, open mouth, accented lips, four upper teeth, pierced ears, orig human-hair wig, jointed wood and composition Handwerck body, antique white dress trimmed with tucks and eyelet, underclothing, socks and antique shoes, marked "16/99/DEP/Germany/Handwerck/7 " on back of head, "Heinrich Handwerck/Germany" on faint stamp on back of right hip, minor firing lines behind right ear, body has excellent orig finish with minimal wear, normal wear at joints **950.00**

Handwerck, Max, 21" h, bisque head, blue sleep eyes, open mouth, inset teeth, pierced ears, jointed-composition body, orig finish, newly made pink linen dress and hat, imp "421 10 Germany M HANDWERCK 2-1/2," bisque speckling, small chin pit **320.00**

Harmann, Kurt, 26" h, bisque head, brown sleep eyes, open mouth, replaced blond mohair wig, fully articulated composition body, new blue satin and lace dress, worn period blue leather shoes, imp mark "30 5 K (over script H) 4," early 20th C, white scratch line each cheek **230.00**

Hertel, Schwab & Co., Patsy Baby, bisque head, five-piece composition body, 18" h, $1,400. Photo courtesy of McMasters.

Hertel, Schwab & Co.

9" l, 7" d head circumference, twin character babies, blue sleep eyes, open mouths, two upper teeth, wispy blond tufts of hair, composition bent-limb bodies, matching period long white baby gown, one with pink, one blue ribbon trim, imp marks "152/2/0," early 20th C, price for pair **635.00**

11" l, 8" d head circumference, Character Baby, bisque head, gray-blue sleep eyes, open/closed mouth, two molded upper teeth and tongue, newer auburn mohair wig, bent-limb composition baby body, period white baby slip, dress, knit sweater, and booties with pompoms, imp "152," early 20th C, paint chips to legs, fingers with repainted areas...... **200.00**

15" h, 140 character, bisque socket head, painted brown eyes, red accent line, feathered brows, closed mouth, accented lips, mohair wig, jointed wood and composition body, straight wrists, white factory chemise, dark green pants, matching cap, cotton socks, and new leather shoes, marked "140/4" on back of head, light rub on right cheek, minor repair at neck

socket of body, light flaking on right upper leg............ **4,200.00**

18" h, Patsy Baby, solid dome bisque head, molded and painted baby-type hair, brown sleep eyes with real lashes, soft brows to match hair, closed rosebud mouth, five-pc composition toddler body, no visible marks, body repainted............ **1,400.00**

20" h, bisque socket head, blue paperweight eyes, feathered brows, painted upper and lower lashes, open mouth with accented lips and six upper teeth, pierced ears, replaced human-hair wig, jointed composition body with straight wrists, separate balls at shoulders, elbows, hips and knees, nicely redressed in pale pink French-style dress, new underclothing, socks and shoes, marks "8/0" on back of head and "Jumeau Medaille d'Or Paris" stamped in blue on lower back, replaced antique paperweight eyes, tiny flake at each earring hole, tiny fleck on upper rim at inside corner of right eye, body has good orig finish with wear at all joints, on toes and heels . **1,100.00**

Heubach, Ernest

12-1/2" h, 399 baby, solid dome painted bisque socket head, brown sleep eyes, single stroke brows, painted upper and lower lashes, closed mouth, lightly molded and painted hair, composition bent-limb baby body, orig multicolored "grass" skirt, marked "Heubach*Koppelsdorf/399*9/0/Germany" on back of head ... **350.00**

21" h, 300 baby, bisque socket head, set brown eyes, feathered brows, painted upper and lower lashes, open mouth, accented lips, four upper teeth, replaced wig, composition bent-limb baby body, antique white long baby dress, lace-trimmed antique baby bonnet, underclothing, diaper, and booties, marked "Heubach * Koppelsdorf/ 300 * 6/Germany" on back of head, arms and legs repainted, cracks in finish under repaint, neck socket touched up, repair on right arm joint and right wrist **275.00**

Heubach, Gebruder, 17" h character, bisque head and shoulder plate, blue intaglio eyes, single stroke brows, open-closed mouth with accent colors, two painted lower

teeth, molded and lightly painted hair, kid body with gussets at hips and knees, bisque lower arms, cloth lower legs, antique two-pc boy's outfit with belt, new socks and shoes, marked "5/Germany" on back of shoulder plate, arms replaced, repairs on upper legs **475.00**

Heubach, Koppelsdorf

10-1/2" h, Screamer, bisque head, painted hair, painted blue intaglio eyes, open-closed screaming mouth, furrowed brow, straight-limb composition toddler body, maroon velvet short overalls, white shirt, imp "7684," sunburst mark **690.00**

24" h, bisque head, blue sleep eyes with lashes, open mouth, brown human-hair wig, fully jointed wood and composition body, period underwear, new print cotton dress, imp mark "312," early 20th C, rub on cheek **220.00**

Horsman, 15" h, toddler, composition socket head, brown sleep eyes, single stroke brows, painted upper and lower lashes, mohair wig, jointed composition toddler body, straight wrists, diagonal hip joints, old white organdy dress with lace trim, underclothing, socks, high button boots, marked "E.I.H./Co." on back **650.00**

Ideal

13" h, Shirley Temple, composition head, hazel sleep eyes with real lashes, painted lower lashes, feathered brows, open mouth, six upper teeth, orig mohair wig in orig set, five-pc composition body, orig plaid "Bright Eyes" dress, underwear combination, replaced socks, orig shoes, marked "13/Shirley Temple" on head, "Shirley Temple/13" on back................. **700.00**

20" h, Shirley Temple, composition head, hazel sleep eyes, real lashes, painted lower lashes, feathered brows, open mouth, six upper teeth, molded tongue, orig mohair wig in orig set, five-pc composition child body, orig dotted organdy dress with pleats from "Curly Top" movie, orig underwear, combination socks and shoes, marks: "20/Shirley Temple/Co. Ideal/N & T Co." on back of head, "Shirley Temple/20*" on back, and "Genuine/Shirley Temple/registered U.S. Pat. Off/Ideal Nov & Toy

Co./ Made in U.S.A." on dress
tag....................**500.00**

25" h, Deanna Durbin, composition
socket head, hazel sleep eyes with
remnants of real lashes, painted
lower lashes, single-stroke brows,
open mouth, six upper teeth, orig
human-hair wig, five-pc
composition body, orig flower print
dress, orig underclothing, replaced
socks and shoes, marked "Deanna
Durbin/Ideal Doll" on back of head,
"Ideal Doll/25" on back **400.00**

28" h, Lori Martin, vinyl socket head,
blue sleep eyes with real lashes,
painted lower lashes, feathered
brows, closed smiling mouth,
rooted hair vinyl body jointed at
waist, shoulders, hips, and ankles,
orig tagged clothing, plaid shirt,
jeans, vinyl boots with horses,
marked "© Metro Goldwyn Mayer
Inc./Mfg by/Ideal Toy Corp/80" on
back of head, "© Ideal Toy
Corp./6-30-5" on back, "National
Velvet's/Lori Martin/© Metro
Goldwyn Mayer, Inc./All Rights
Reserved" on shirt tag.....**550.00**

*Jumeau, 31" h, bisque head, brown
sleep eyes, open mouth, human-hair
wig, $2,900. Photo courtesy of
McMasters.*

Jumeau

9-1/2" h, Bebe, bisque head, blue
paperweight eyes, closed mouth,
pierced ears, blue earrings, orig
cork pate and blond mohair wig,
fully articulated wood and

composition body, orig stringing,
undressed, orig Jumeau Bebe
marked brown leather shoes,
France, c1890, string loose, paint
flaking on lower leg **6,325.00**

14-1/2" h, Portrait Jumeau, bisque
socket head, dark brown almond
paperweight eyes, multi-stroke
brows, painted upper and lower
lashes, closed mouth with
accented lips, pierced ears,
replaced human-hair wig, jointed
wood and composition body with
separate balls at shoulders and
elbows, hips, and knees, straight
wrists, well redressed in turquoise
silk dress with ecru silk and lace
trim, matching bonnet, antique
underclothing, new socks and
shoes, marked "2/0" on back of
head, "Jumeau Medaille d'Or
Paris" stamped in blue on lower
back, head has been broken and
repaired, crack on right forehead to
eye, at corner of right eye to below
ear, on left forehead down to ear
and to crown in back, body finish
worn on arms, hands, lower legs,
and around neck socket .. **800.00**

17-1/2" h, lady, bisque swivel head,
cobalt blue glass eyes, mauve
shadow, lightly feathered
eyebrows, closed mouth,
pierced-in ears, light brown
human-hair wig, cloth body, kid
arms, period dark green silk taffeta
dress, black lace trim, straw hat,
additional brown crepe wrapper
and lace hat, blue leather
high-button boots, 1870s,
unmarked shoulder plate has
discoloration line in making, front
corner and across back, break at
wrist **2,070.00**

18" h, 1907, bisque socket head,
blue paperweight eyes, long
painted upper and lower lashes,
open mouth, accented lips, six
upper teeth, pierced ears,
replaced mohair wig, jointed wood
and composition late-French body,
redressed in peach silk
French-style dress, white silk
bonnet, antique underclothing, old
socks and white leather shoes,
marked "1907/7" on back of head,
light nose rub, small flakes at each
earring hole, hands repainted,
repairs and wear at knees touched
up, right upper arm has paint
flaked to wood **1,700.00**

20" h, Bebe, bisque head, brown
paperweight eyes, mauve eye
shadow, closed mouth, pierced
applied ears, orig red Jumeau
earrings, imp DEPOSE E.9J, cork
pate, orig blond mohair wig, jointed
straight wrist, eight-ball composition
body marked "Jumeau Medaille
d'Or," vintage commercial dress of
aqua satin and ecru silk faille,
brown leather shoes, marked "E.J.,
France," c1885, tiny red age line
side of nose...........**5,475.00**

20" h, bisque socket head, blue
paperweight eyes, feathered brows,
painted upper and lower lashes,
open mouth with accented lips and
six upper teeth, pierced ears,
replaced human-hair wig, jointed
composition body with straight
wrists, separate balls at shoulders,
elbows, hips, and knees, nicely
redressed in pale pink French-style
dress, new underclothing, socks
and shoes, marked "8/0" on back of
head, "Jumeau Medaille d'Or Paris"
stamped in blue on lower back,
replaced antique paperweight
eyes, tiny flake at each earring hole,
tiny fleck on upper rim at inside
corner of right eye, body has good
orig finish with wear at all joints, on
toes and heels........**1,100.00**

20" h, DEP Tete, bisque socket head,
set blue eyes with real lashes,
painted lower lashes, molded and
painted brows, open mouth,
accented lips, four upper teeth,
pierced ears, replaced human-hair
wig, jointed wood and composition
Jumeau body with jointed wrists,
orig (fragile, repaired) red silk and
lace dress with remnants of orig
"Bebe Jumeau" label stitched onto
red grosgrain ribbon, orig
underclothing, socks, marked
shoes, elaborate red velvet hat
trimmed with ribbon and feathers,
incised "DEP/9," "Tete Jumeau"
stamped in red on back of head,
"Bebe Jumeau/Diplome d'Honneur"
on oval label on back, "9/Paris/
(bee)/ Depose" on soles of shoes,
eyes broken off rocker and set, few
kiln specks on right side of nose
and bridge of nose, very light rub
on right cheek, inherent red
discoloration on back of right ear
lobe, touch-up or repaint on arms,
hands, upper legs and feet, flaking
on hands, feet and arms, minor

Jumeau, bisque head, blue glass sleep eyes, closed mouth, brunette wig, pierced ears, 16-1/2" h, marked "E.D.," $2,600. Photo courtesy of McMasters.

flaking on upper legs, polish on fingers and toes **1,500.00**

23" h Jumeau, Bebe Soleil box, bisque socket head, blue paperweight eyes, feathered brows, painted upper and lower lashes, open mouth, accented lips, six upper teeth, human-hair wig, jointed wood and composition French body, dressed in factory chemise pants, "Tete Jumeau" stamped in red, "9" incised on back of head, "Bebe due Bon Marche" partial paper label on lower back, "10700" written upside down on upper back, "S.F.B. J. Paris Bebe Soleil Yeux Mobiles Formes Naturelles Entierement Articule" on label on end of box, 2" hairline on right side of forehead, body finish flaking or loose in places, wear on edges of feet, at joints and on hands, box bottom repaired, lid missing **1,400.00**

23" h, 1907, bisque socket head, blue paperweight eyes, feathered brows, painted upper and lower lashes, open mouth with accented lips and six upper teeth, pierced ears,

antique mohair wig, jointed wood and composition body, redressed in copy of factory Jumeau dress, underclothing, cotton socks, and old leather shoes, marked "1907/10" on back of head, antique wig is sparse on wig cap, body has excellent orig finish with normal wear at joints, hands repainted, toe repair **1,800.00**

24" h, bisque socket head, brown paperweight eyes, feathered brows, painted upper and lower lashes, open mouth, accented lips, six upper teeth, pierced ears, replaced human-hair wig, jointed wood and composition French body, redressed in brown velvet and beige dress with lace trim, straw bonnet trimmed with flowers, antique underclothing, and antique high-button baby shoes, marked "X/9 on back of head," V-shaped hairline on back of head above mark, small repair on right knee and left toes, hands repainted, finish of right hand rough, neck socket of body lined with kid, normal wear to joints of body **1,100.00**

26" h, Tete Jumeau, bisque socket head, large blue paperweight eyes, heavy feathered brows, painted upper and lower lashes, closed mouth, accented lips, pierced ears, human-hair wig, jointed wood and composition body, nicely redressed in new turquoise French-style outfit with matching bonnet, new underclothing, old socks and shoes, marked "Depose Tete Jumeau 2" as partial red stamp, red and black artist marks, "Bebe Jumeau//Bte S.G.D.G. Depose" on body, inherent 5/8" firing separation at crown in right front, 1" horizontal hairline at right front splits in two, several fingers and feet, normal wear at joints, composition and finish damaged on toes. . **2,100.00**

Kamkins, 19" h, girl, cloth, molded face with painted features, blue eyes, orig brown mohair wig, cloth body and limbs, blue cotton dress, orig undergarments, purple Kamkins stamp mark on back of head, early 20th C, some soil and wear on face . . **1,150.00**

Kammer & Reinhardt

10" h, 115A baby, bisque socket head, blue sleep eyes, feathered brows, painted upper and lower lashes, closed mouth, orig mohair

wig, five-pc composition baby body, antique-style white baby dress, slip, lace-trimmed panties, eyelet bonnet, marked "1/K*R/Simon & Halbig/115A/30" on back of head, wear to orig finish, arms mostly repainted, touch-up around neck socket, on toes, and feet **1,300.00**

11" h, baby, bisque socket head, brown sleep eyes, feathered brows, painted upper and lower lashes, open mouth, two upper teeth, spring tongue, orig mohair wig, bent limb composition baby body, antique white baby dress, underclothing, marked "K*R/28" on back of head, "W" at crown in front, few flakes off body on lower front of torso and back of neck socket, normal wear at joints, light wear on fingers and toes, arms repainted **350.00**

17" h, character baby, blue glass sleep eyes, open mouth, tongue, dark brown mohair wig, jointed bent limb baby body, period long white baby dress, imp "K*R Simon & Halbig 126 42, W" on forehead at crown, early 20th C, repairs to fingers, voice box functions intermittently **325.00**

17-1/2" h, 1728 toddler, celluloid socket head, blue sleep eyes, remnants of real lashes, single-stroke brows, open mouth, two upper teeth, molded tongue, orig mohair wig, five-pc composition toddler body, pale pink dress tagged Alexander, slip, diaper, new socks and shoes, marked "K*R/1728/7/Germany/ turtle mark" on back of head, cheek and lip colors faded, small rub on nose and right cheek, areas of celluloid lightly discolored, body has good orig finish, surface cracks at elbows, normal wear on hands **315.00**

19" h, 115/A character toddler, bisque head, brown sleep eyes, closed pouty mouth, reddish-blond caracul wig, side-jointed composition toddler body, red and green plush jester's costume, also orig pink gingham outfit, imp "K*R Simon & Halbig 115/A, 48," c1910 . . . . **4,320.00**

Kestner

12" h, pouty child, bisque head, brown sleep eyes, closed mouth, characteristic fat roll on back of neck, no pate, new strawberry-blond human-hair wig, early classic straight wrist mitt-fingered body, pink china silk dress, imp "7," late 19th C, cinder to left of mouth **2,070.00**

13" h, 211 Toddle, bisque socket head, brown sleep eyes, feathered brows, painted upper and lower lashes, open-closed mouth, accented lips, molded tongue, orig mohair wig over plaster pate, jointed composition body with stubby toddler proportions, well redressed, beige wool jacket, brown tweed pants, underclothing, new socks and shoes, "C made in Germany 7/211,211" incised on pate, "Germany" stamped in red on lower back, light touch-up on body, normal wear at joints **675.00**

13-1/2" h, character, bisque head, blue sleep eyes, open mouth, two upper teeth, replaced blond mohair wig, fully articulated Kestner body, pink cotton print dress, extra green print dress, imp "143," red stamp "Germany," one finger broken **635.00**

14" h, bisque shoulder head, brown sleep eyes, open mouth, orig brown mohair wig, kid body, bisque lower arms, off-white cotton dress, imp "154," some mending to body, chips on fingers **175.00**

14-1/2" h, 257 baby, bisque socket head, blue sleep eyes, feathered brows, painted upper and lower lashes, open mouth, accented lips, two upper teeth, spring tongue, synthetic wig, composition Kestner baby body, antique-style long baby dress and bonnet, slip, diaper and new booties, marked "Made in/ Germany/J.D.K./257/Germany/35" on back of head, "Made in Germany" stamped in red on upper back, real lashes missing, worn body finish, moisture damage on lower right near torso and back of right arm **600.00**

15" h, 154, bisque shoulder head, brown sleep eyes, feathered brows, painted upper and lower lashes, open mouth, four molded upper teeth, orig human-hair wig over plaster pate, kid body, bisque lower arms, gussets at elbows, pin joints at hips and knees, possibly orig dress with embroidered

design, underclothing, socks and shoes, marked "154 dep. 5" on back of head, minor inherent firing lines on side seams of head, soiled body shows general wear, repair at right shoulder of body **375.00**

23" h, Hilda, solid dome bisque socket head, blue sleep eyes, feathered brows, painted upper and lower lashes, open mouth, accented lips, two upper teeth, lightly molded and painted blond hair composition bent-limb Kestner baby body, antique white baby dress, matching slip, diaper, new pink knit booties, antique baby bonnet, marked "Hilda/C/J.D.K. Jr. 1914/ges.gesch.N. 1070/made in 18 Germany" on back of head **4,000.00**

32" h, 164, bisque socket head, blue sleep eyes, molded and feathered brows, painted upper and lower lashes, open mouth, shapely accented lips, four upper teeth, skin wig, jointed wood and composition Kestner body, faded dark blue velvet sailor suit, white shirt, old socks and shoes, marked "M1/2 made in Germany 16 1/2/164" on back of head, "Excelsior/ Germany/7" stamped in red on right lower back, body has orig finish with light wear, normal wear at joints, right finger repaired **1,200.00**

Kley & Hahn, 11-1/2" h, 160 Baby, bisque socket head, brown sleep eyes, remnants of real lashes, painted upper and lower lashes, feathered brows, open mouth, wobble tongue, antique human-hair wig, five-pc bent-limb composition baby body, new pink baby dress, panties, new socks, old leatherette shoes, marked "Germany/K & H (in banner)/160-4" on head, light rub on left cheek, minor firing lines on both ears, small inherent discoloration high on right side of forehead; body has light general wear, normal wear at joints, on fingers and toes, cracks in finish of both lower arms **235.00**

Knickerbocker, 11" h, Mickey Mouse, cloth swivel head, white facial, black oilcloth pie eyes, large black nose, painted open/closed smiling mouth with accent lines, black felt ears, un-jointed black cloth body, orange hands with three fingers and a thumb, red oversized composition feet, black rubber tail, orig shorts with two buttons on front and back, some fading **650.00**

Konig & Wernicke, Germany, early 20th C

17" h, character toddler, bisque head, brown sleep eyes, open mouth, two upper teeth, tongue, orig dark brown mohair wig, fully articulated side hip-joint composition toddler body marked "Made in Germany," period cotton sailor outfit, blue pants, white overblouse, white fabric shoes, imp "Made in Germany 99/7," some wear to finish of limbs, repaint to hands **750.00**

27" l, 16-1/2" d head circumference, character baby, bisque head, early 20th century, blue sleep eyes, open mouth, two upper teeth, wobble tongue, orig brown mohair wig, bent limb composition baby body, red circle stamp "K & W," minor wear **815.00**

Kathe Kruse, Rose X, painted facial features, original clothing and tags, 14" h, $1,050. Photo courtesy of McMasters.

Kruse, Kathe

13" h, Schlenkerchen, all-stockinette, pressed and oil-painted double-seam head, painted features, brown hair, shaded brown painted eyes with eyeliner, light upper lashes, closed mouth in smiling expression, cloth neck ring, stockinette covered, padded armature frame body, mitten hands, rounded feet, unlaundered off-white undergarments, soles stamped "Kathe Kruse, Germany," c1922, paint rub tip of nose, soil. **5,475.00**

14" h, Rose X, oil-painted swivel head with single seam in back, painted hair, painted brown eyes with highlights, single-stroke brows, closed mouth, cloth body, stitched fingers, jointed hips, orig pink linen dress and kerchief, blue print jacket, nylon teddy, orig socks and shoes, marked "Kathe Kruse 1687" on left foot, "Made in Germany US Zone Original gekleidet, Kathe Kruse Rose X Original gekleidet" on paper tag around neck, "Kathe Kruse Germany Art Dolls Unique" on paper wrist tag. **1,050.00**

Lenci

8" h, Mascotte, pressed felt swivel head, painted brown "surprise" eyes to side, single-stroke brows, painted upper lashes, open-closed two-tone mouth, orig red mohair wig in braids, cloth body with felt arms and legs, orig blue and white polka dot nylon dress, white felt collar, red felt belt, orig one-pc underwear, red felt sandals, light display soil, front of dress faded. **150.00**

21" h, child, all-felt construction, painted blue side-glancing eyes, blond mohair, swivel head, jointed limbs, blue felt and organdy dress and shoes, organdy underwear, c1930 **575.00**

28" h, lady, "Mary Pickford" felt face, light gray-blue painted eyes to right, long nose, closed mouth, long bare felt arms, classic Lenci fingers, white and green organdy summer frock, felt wide-brimmed bonnet, all trimmed with felt flowers and ruffles, silk stockings, pale green felt shoes with felt flowers, orig Lenci tag sewn to dress, c1930, small stain back of skirt. **1,840.00**

Limbach

Limbach, 23" h, character, bisque socket head, blue sleep eyes with real lashes, painted upper and lower lashes, open mouth, accented lips, six upper teeth, human-hair wig, jointed wood and composition body, new white lacy dress, underclothing, new socks and shoes, marked "W/crown/17 72 in shamrock/Limbach" on back of head,

two right fingers and three left fingers repaired, finish flaking around neck socket of body, cracks in finish on side seams of torso, wear at all sockets on torso **625.00**

Madame Alexander

13" h, Princess Elizabeth, closed mouth, dimples, blue sleep eyes, blond side-part human-hair wig, unmarked composition body and head, good blushing, silver tiara, pink rayon dress (washed), tagged "Princess Elizabeth Madame Alexander," c1937 **230.00**

14" h, Marme from the *Little Women* Series, hard plastic head and body, gray sleep eyes, closed mouth, dark brown wig in snood, gray and pink print dress with orig tags, organdy shawl, shoes and socks, c1955 **200.00**

17" h, Maggie Walker, hard plastic head, blue sleep eyes with real lashes, painted lower lashes, feathered brows, closed mouth, orig wig, five-pc hard plastic body with walking mechanism, orig blue and white taffeta dress, white collar and cuffs, white taffeta slip and panties, orig stockings, black center snap shoes, marked "Madame Alexander/All Rights Reserved/New York U.S.A." on dress tag **700.00**

18" h, Sweet Violet, hard plastic head, blue sleep eyes with real lashes, painted lower lashes, feathered brows, closed mouth, orig synthetic wig, hard plastic body jointed at shoulders, elbows, wrists, hips, and knees, walking mechanism, orig tagged blue cotton dress, underclothing, flowered bonnet, white gloves, black side-snap shoes, carrying orig pink Alexander hat box, marked "Alexander" on back of head, "Madame Alexander/All Rights Reserved/New York, U.S.A.," c1954, unplayed-with condition comb and curlers missing **1,700.00**

21" h, Cissy, hard plastic, blue sleep eyes, closed mouth, golden blond hair, tiara, vinyl body and limbs, orig white damask Queen gown, jeweled bracelets, blue-diagonal sash, stockings, high-heeled shoes, orig box (some damage), labeled "Cissy, style 2042," c1955 **1,495.00**

21" h, Jacqueline, vinyl head, brown sleep eyes with blue shadow, real lashes, painted upper corner and lower lashes, feathered brows, closed mouth, pierced ears, rooted hair, hard plastic body jointed at hips and knees, vinyl arms with jointed elbows, adult figure, high-heel feet, orig white satin gown, matching cape, taffeta slip and panties, stockings, high heels, "diamond" bracelet and ring, pearl necklace, purse and earrings with pearls and "diamond," marked "Alexander/19 C 61" on back of head, "Jacqueline by Madame Alexander" on tag on slip seam, hair lightly mussed, small split on outside of left knee, light rust-colored stains lower part of cape, one pearl missing from right earring **450.00**

23" h, Special Girl, composition head, composition shoulder plate, blue sleep eyes with real lashes, painted lower lashes, feathered brows, closed mouth, orig human-hair wig in orig set, cloth torso with composition arms and legs, orig pale blue taffeta dress with lace and ribbon trim, attached blue panties, orig socks and center snap shoes, "Madame/Alexander/New York U.S.A." on dress tag **750.00**

Menjou, Adolph, 32" h, composition shoulder head, painted brown eyes with accent line, molded monocle on right eye, feathered brows, molded and painted mustache, open-closed mouth, seven upper teeth, molded white shirt collar with hole, presumably for a tie, molded and painted hair, excelsior-stuffed cloth body with long limbs, composition white hands as gloves, composition lower legs as socks and shoes, orig black two-pc suit with satin lapels. **725.00**

Parian, unmarked, untinted bisque shoulder head, painted blue eyes, red accent line, molded lids, single stroke brows, closed mouth

14" h, man, molded and painted café au lait hair brushed back behind ears, molded shirt and striped tie on shoulder plate, new cloth body with old china lower arms and new bisque lower legs, two-pc men's wool suit, gold trim on decorated shoulder, plate is worn. **250.00**

15" h, lady, pierced ears, molded and painted café au lait hair with curls and waves around face, molded curls in back, elaborately decorated shoulder plate with glazed pink ribbon around her neck, blue and white ruffle with gold trim, cloth body with kid lower arms, striped lower legs with brown cloth boots for feet, beautiful pin-striped dress made with antique silk, underclothing, small chip on left earlobe; body is lightly aged with a few stains, arms replaced, cloth boots are worn and have some cotton stuffing showing on heels and toes **620.00**

Petzold, Dora, 16-1/2" h, composition head, painted blue eyes with eye shadow, single-stroke brows, accented nostrils, closed mouth, orig mohair wig, stockinette body stitch-jointed at shoulders and hips, mitten-type hands with stitched fingers, possibly orig white velvet dress with embroidery and lace trim, white teddy, orig socks and marked shoes, marked with girl in circle, "D P/7/7/0" on back of head, girl in circle with "D P" on bottom of shoes **275.00**

Poupee Peau, 11" h, pale cup-and-saucer swivel bisque head, bisque shoulder plate, set cobalt blue eyes, fine multi-stroke brows, painted

upper and lower lashes, closed mouth, accented lips, mohair wig, kid fashion body with gussets at hips, individually stitched fingers, antique brown print dressing gown, underclothing, new mesh stockings, antique paper shoes, repair on left side of forehead at crown, pate is glued to head and head is strung through pate, body is aged and worn with several repairs **750.00**

Poupee Raynal, 19" h, pressed felt swivel head, painted blue eyes, single-stroke brows, painted upper lashes, closed mouth with three-tone lips, orig mohair wig in orig set, five-pc cloth body with stitched fingers, orig light blue organdy dress with pink flower appliqués, matching hat, orig teddy, blue organdy slip, socks, white leather shoes, "Paris" typed on piece of paper pinned to back, unplayed with condition **725.00**

Putnam, Grace

8" h, Bye-Lo Baby, solid dome bisque swivel head, tiny blue sleep eyes, softly blushed brows, painted upper and lower lashes, closed mouth, lightly molded and painted hair, all bisque baby body jointed at shoulders and hips, orig knit pink and white two-pc baby outfit with matching cap, marked "Bye-Lo Baby/©/Germany/G.S. Putnam" on label on chest,

"6-20/Copr. By/Grace S. Putnam/Germany" incised on back, "6-20" on hips and right arms, "20" on left arm, chip on right back of neck edge of head, minor firing line behind left ear **525.00**

11" h, 10-1/2" d head circumference Bye-Lo Baby, solid dome bisque head, brown sleep eyes, softly blushed brows, painted upper and lower lashes, closed mouth, lightly molded and painted hair, cloth body with celluloid hands and "frog" legs, redressed in white lace-trimmed baby dress, old baby sweater, slip, diaper, socks, marked "Copr. by/Grace S. Putnam/Made in Germany" on back of head, illegible faint stamp on body, rubs on cheeks, nose, and back of head, light kiln dust on head **425.00**

21" h, 17" d head circumference, Bye-Lo Baby, solid dome bisque head, blue sleep eyes, softly blushed brows, painted upper and lower lashes, closed mouth, lightly molded and painted hair, cloth body with "frog" legs, celluloid hands, orig white Bye-Lo dress, slip, and flannel diaper, marked "Copr. By/Grace S. Putnam/Made in Germany" on back of head, turtle mark on wrists of celluloid hands, light bur on right cheek, body lightly soiled and aged **600.00**

Recknagel, 9" h, character, bisque socket head, tiny painted blue squinty eyes, single-stroke brows, open-closed mouth, five painted upper teeth, four lower teeth, molded tongue, molded and painted short hair with molded pink bow, five-pc chubby composition body, crude unpainted torso, molded and painted socks and shoes, redressed in pink lace-trimmed dress, matching hair ribbon, lace pants, marked "R 57 A/8/0" on back of head, light dust in bisque, light wear on orig body finish . . . **675.00**

Schmidt, Bruno, 22" h, 2042, solid dome bisque socket head, painted brown eyes, two-tone single-stroke brows, open-closed mouth, accented lips, brush-stroked hair, jointed composition body, redressed in maroon velour two-pc suit, ecru satin shirt with lace trim, black cotton socks, new black shoes, marked "5/B.S.W. in heart/2042" on back of head, "Handwerck" stamped in red in middle of lower back **1,500.00**

Grace Putnam Storey, Bye-Lo, toddler, 12" h, 10" circ, original layette box and contents, **$2,500.** *Photo courtesy of McMasters.*

Schmidt, Franz, 33-1/2" h, child, bisque head, open mouth, brown glass eyes set stationary, pierced ears, replaced long blond human-hair wig, chunky fully jointed composition body, period undergarments, strong blue silk twill dress, imp "S & C 7 1/2 85," late 19th/early 20th C, light soil, repairs, some repaint **1,035.00**

Schoenhut

12" h, composition head, painted blue eyes, lightly molded and single-stroke brows, closed mouth, molded and painted hair, five-pc composition body with bent right arm, pale pink dotted Swiss dress, panties, replaced socks and shoes, marked "Schoenhut/ Toys/Made in/U.S.A." on label on back, light wear on fingers, chipped left first finger . . . **1,300.00**

15" h, Tootsie Wootsie, wooden character socket head, brown intaglio eyes, feathered brows, open-closed mouth, two upper teeth, molded tongue, old mohair wig, spring-jointed wooden body with joints at shoulders, elbows, wrists, hips, knees, and ankles, redressed in copy of Schoenhut two-pc sailor suit, new socks and tie shoes, illegible partial imp mark on head, "Schoenhut Doll/Pat. Jan 17, '11, U.S.A. & Foreign Countries" imp on back, repaint on face, touch up, normal wear at points, paint worn and flaking on legs and feet, hands repainted **1,500.00**

19" h, 19/308 girl, wooden socket head, brown intaglio eyes, feathered brow, closed mouth with excellent modeling, orig mohair wig, spring-jointed wooden body jointed at shoulders, elbows, wrists, hips, knees, and ankles, white dress with red dots in Schoenhut style, slip, knit union suit, replaced cotton socks and red flocked shoes, marked "Schoenhut Doll/Pat. Jan 17th 1911/U.S.A." on oval label on back, very light touch up on left cheek, nose, edge of lips, craze lines on front of lower neck, light crazing on right cheek and outer corner of left eye, body has "suntan" color with normal wear at joints and light overall soil, few flakes off ankles **450.00**

Schoenhut & Hoffmeister, 20" h, 13-1/2" d head circumference, character

baby, bisque head, blue sleep eyes with lashes, hint of smile, open mouth, two upper teeth, pointy chin, orig dark brown mohair wig, bent-limb composition baby body, white cotton slip, imp "SHPB" in a star, "5, Germany," early 20th C, white spot back of head at rim **325.00**

S.F.B.J.

12" h, 236 baby, bisque socket head, blue sleep eyes, feathered brows, painted upper and lower lashes, open/closed mouth, two painted upper teeth, human-hair wig, composition bent-limb French baby body, yellow organdy dress with matching bonnet, underwear combination, rayon socks tied with ribbons, marked "21/S.F.B.J./236/ Paris/4" on back of head, light wear at joints, fingers and toes, few spots of light touch-up on body **365.00**

17" h, 226, solid dome bisque socket head, blue "jewel" eyes, single-stroke brows, painted upper and lower lashes, open-closed mouth, molded and painted hair, orig finish wood and composition French toddler body with diagonal hip joints, old white top, sweater, maroon velvet pants, new black socks and shoes, marked "S.F.B.J./226/Paris/6" on back of head, flaking, normal wear at joints **1,100.00**

Simon & Halbig, 1078, bisque, paperweight eyes, open mouth, 11-1/2" h, $875. *Photo courtesy of McMasters.*

Steiner

17-1/2" h, Gigoteur, bisque head, blue threaded paperweight eyes with blush over eyes, delicate feathered brows, painted upper and lower lashes, open mouth and accented lips, four upper and three lower teeth, orig blond mohair wig, papier-mâché torso with walking and crying mechanism, kid covering on lower torso, replaced composition arms, kid-covered upper legs, wax-over composition lower legs, possibly orig white openwork and lace dress, antique underclothing, socks and white leather shoes, unmarked, worn torso, seams taped, kid covering on lower torso and upper legs is deteriorating on left leg, arms replaced, limited movement in legs **1,050.00**

18" h, Figure B, bisque socket head, blue eyes made to sleep with lever left back of head, feathered brows, painted upper and lower lashes, blush over eyes, open smiling mouth, seven upper and seven lower teeth, pierced ears, human-hair wig, jointed composition Steiner body with jointed wrists, torso cut for (non-working) crier, pale blue silk dress with lace trim, matching hat, underclothing, socks and old shoes, marked "Figure B No 2/Steiner Bte S.G.D.G./Paris" on back of head, "Bebe Steiner/Le Petit Parisien" purple stamp on left hip, orig body finish has light wear on lower arms and hands and lower legs, normal wear at joints. **2,900.00**

23" h, Figure A, bisque socket head, large blue paperweight eyes, feathered brows, painted upper and lower lashes, closed mouth, pierced ears, orig mohair wig, orig cardboard pate, jointed composition body, jointed wrists, dark brown and beige French-style dress made with antique fabric, antique underclothing, beige/ black-striped bonnet, brown cotton socks, brown shoes, marked "J. Steiner/Bte S.G.D.G./Paris/Fire A 15" on back of head, small triangular piece broken out at rim on left front and repaired, hairline to corner of left eye, body repainted, right thumb repaired **2,000.00**

24" h, Figure C, bisque socket head, blue paperweight eyes, blush over eyes, feathered brows, painted upper and lower lashes, closed mouth with accented lips, pierced ears, antique human hair wig, jointed wood and composition French body, jointed wrists, pink silk dress made of antique fabric, underclothing, and straw bonnet with flower trim, new socks and shoes, marked "Figure C No. 3/J. Steiner Bte SGDG/Paris" on back of head, rub on nose, few small flakes at each earring hole, couple small flakes edge of left ear, small flake at edge of cut for eye mechanism, replaced antique paperweight eyes **1,600.00**

Terri Lee

12" h, Buddy Lee, hard plastic head with stiff neck, eyes painted to side, single-stroke brows, painted upper lashes, closed mouth, molded and painted hair, hard plastic body jointed at shoulders only, molded and painted black boots, orig Phillips 66 suit with labeled shirt and pants, black imitation-leather belt, marked "Buddy Lee" on back, "Union Made/Lee/Sanforized" on label on back of pants, "Phillips/66" on label on front of shirt. . . . **215.00**

16" h, bride, hard plastic head, painted brown eyes, single-stroke brows, painted upper and lower lashes, closed mouth, orig brunette wig, five-pc hard plastic body, orig tagged bride dress, matching veil, panties, satin shoes, marked "Terri Lee" on back and dress tag, accompanied by nine orig outfits in a trunk, including yellow Southern Belle with black shoes, Girl Scout uniform with brown and white shoes, nurse uniform with white shoes, tagged pants outfit with shirt, tagged pajamas with rabbit slippers, sweater, beret, shirt, blouse; school dress with pinafore, cowgirl costume with gauntlets and boots, hat missing, also booklets and papers, as well as extra accessories, unplayed with condition **2,400.00**

16" h, Terri Lee, hard plastic head, painted brown eyes, single-stroke brows, painted upper and lower lashes, closed mouth, orig skin wig, five-pc hard plastic body, blue and white check western-style shift, blue pants, orig socks and shoes, includes extra Roundup

Costume #4450 from 1954, missing hat and gun, marked "Terri Lee Pat. Pending" on back, Terri Lee tag on shirt **650.00**

16" Terri Lee, hard plastic head, painted brown eyes, single-stroke brows, painted upper and lower lashes, closed mouth, saran wig, five-pc hard plastic body, yellow organdy tagged dress, orig nylon slip and panties, socks and shoes, marked "Terri Lee"" on head and back, and dress tag **425.00**

18" Connie Lynn, hard plastic head, blue sleep eyes with real lashes, single-stroke brows, painted lower lashes at corners of eyes, closed mouth, orig skin wig, hard plastic baby body, orig two-pc pink baby outfit, plastic panties, orig socks and white baby shoes, Terri Lee Nursery Registration Form and three Admission Cards to Terri Lee Hospital, Connie Lynn tag on clothing, orig box, unplayed with condition **625.00**

Vogue, Ginny, Red Riding Hood, hard plastic, elastic strung, painted lashes, blue eyes in downcast position, strong cheek color, side-part blond hair, red polka dot dress, red suede-like cape and hat, red straw basket, red shoes, white socks, orig hinged lid pink box #52, illegible Gilchrest's price tag, c1952. **490.00**

Walker, Izannah, 18" h, oil cloth, painted features, brown eyes with highlights, pink mouth and cheek coloring, brown hair, two long curls in front of applied ears, four curls down her back onto shoulders, cloth body, oil-painted hands, stockings stitched on, gray-green plaid silk taffeta dress, blue leather shoes, carries period red leather strap slip-on ice skates, Rhode Island, c1870, some paint wear, rubs **24,150.00**

Wax, unmarked, 18" h, reinforced poured-wax shoulder head, set blue glass eyes, multi-stroke brows, painted upper and lower lashes, closed smiling mouth, pierced ears, orig mohair wig, cloth body, wax-over composition lower arms and lower legs, antique red/white gingham dress, orig underclothing, socks and leather shoes, color worn on lips, eyelashes and brows, minor crack in wax on right front of shoulder plate, cracks on right leg, body is aged, soiled, and repaired **475.00**

Wislizenus, Adolph, 18" h, girl, bisque socket head, brown sleep eyes,

feathered brows, painted upper and lower lashes, open mouth, accented lips, pierced ears, replaced human-hair wig, jointed composition body with orig finish, possibly orig clothing, white low-waisted dress, antique underclothing, socks and shoes marked "8," blue velvet coat and matching hat with ribbon trim, marked "8/A.W./Germany/6" on back of head, "46" stamped in red on bottom of feet **550.00**

DOORSTOPS

History: Doorstops became popular in the late 19th century. They are either flat or three dimensional and were made out of a variety of different materials, such as cast iron, bronze, or wood. Hubley, a leading toy manufacturer, made many examples.

All prices listed are for excellent original paint unless otherwise noted. Original paint and condition greatly influence the price of a doorstop. To get top money, the original paint on a piece must be close to mint condition. Chipping of paint, paint loss, and wear reduce the value. Repainting severely reduces value and eliminates a good deal of the piece's market value. A broken piece has little value to none.

References: Jeanne Bertoia, *Doorstops*, Collector Books, 1985, 1996 value update; Douglas Congdon-Martin, *Figurative Cast Iron*, Schiffer Publishing, 1994.

Adviser: Craig Dinner.

Reproduction Alert: Reproductions are proliferating as prices on genuine doorstops continue to rise. A reproduced piece generally is slightly smaller than the original unless an original mold is used. The overall casting of reproductions is not as smooth as on the originals. Reproductions also lack the detail apparent in originals, including the appearance of the painted areas. Any bright orange rusting is strongly indicative of a new piece. Beware. If it looks too good to be true, it usually is.

Notes: Pieces described contain at least 80 percent or more of the original paint and are in very good condition. Repainting drastically reduces price and desirability. Poor original paint is preferred over repaint.

All listings are cast-iron and flat-back castings, unless otherwise noted.

Doorstops marked with an asterisk are currently being reproduced.

Basket, 11" h, rose, ivory wicker basket, natural flowers, handle with bow, sgd "Hubley 121" **165.00**

Bear, 15" h, holding and looking at honey pot, brown fur, black highlights **1,500.00**

Bellhop

7-1/2" h, carrying satchel, facing sideways, orange-red uniform and cap **425.00**

8-7/8" h, blue uniform, with orange markings, brown base, hands at side **300.00**

Bobby Blake, 9-1/2" h, boy holding teddy bear, blue shirt, pink socks, black pants, blond hair, Hubley **350.00**

Bowl, 7" x 7", green-blue, natural colored fruit, sgd "Hubley 456" . **125.00**

Boy, 10-5/8" h, wearing diapers, directing traffic, police hat, red scarf, brown dog at side **665.00**

Caddie, 8" h, carrying brown and tan bag, white, brown, knickers, red jacket* **725.00**

Cat, reaching, full figure, two-piece hollow casting, green eyes, off-white body, 13-5/8" h, $675. Photos courtesy of Craig Dinner.

Cat

8" h, black, red ribbon and bow around neck, on pillow* . . . **155.00**

10-3/4" h, licking paw, white cat with black markings, marked "Sculpture Metal Studios" **425.00**

13-5/8" h, reaching, full figure, two-piece hollow casting, green eyes, off-white body **675.00**

Cat Scratch Fever, 8-3/4" h, girl in blue dress, blond hair, black cat at side, scratches on arm, marked "CJO 1271" **875.00**

Child, 17" h, reaching, naked, short brown curly hair, flesh color . . **1,375.00**

Clipper ship, 5-1/4" h, full sails, American flag on top mast, wave base, two rubber stoppers, sgd "CJO" . **65.00**

Clown, 10" h, full figure, two sided, red suit, white collar, blue hat, black shoes **875.00**

Cosmos Flower Basket, 17-3/4" h, blue and pink flowers, white vase, black base, Hubley **1,350.00**

Cottage, 8-5/8" l, 5-3/4" h, Cape type, blue roof, flowers, fenced garden, bath, sgd "Eastern Specialty Mfg Co. 14" **150.00**

Dancer, 8-7/8" h, Art Deco couple doing Charleston, pink dress, black tux, red and black base, "FISH" on front, sgd "Hubley 270" **1,475.00**

Dog

7" h, three puppies in basket, natural colors, sgd "Copyright 1932 M. Rosenstein, Lancaster, PA, USA" **350.00**

8" x 7-1/2", Beagle pup, full figure, cream with darker markings **685.00**

9" h, Boston Bull, full figure, facing left, black, tan markings . . . **175.00**

10-1/2" x 3-1/2", St. Bernard, lying down, full figure, cream with brown markings, Hubley **775.00**

14" x 9", Sealyham, full figure, Hubley, cream and tan dog, red collar **675.00**

Dolly, 9-1/2" h, pink bow in blond hair, holding doll in blue dress, white apron, yellow dress, Hubley **365.00**

Doorman in Livery, 12" h, twin men, worn orig paint, marked "Fish," Hubley **1,760.00**

Drum major, 12-5/8" h, full figure, ivory pants, red hat with feather, yellow baton in right hand, left hand on waist, sq base **225.00**

Duck, 7-1/2" h, white, green bush and grass **335.00**

Dutch Boy, 11" h, full figure, hands in pockets, blue suit and hat, red belt and collar, brown shoes, blond hair . **425.00**

Elephant, 14" h, palm trees, early 20th C, very minor paint wear **335.00**

Fisherman, 6-1/4" h, standing at wheel, hand over eyes, rain gear **185.00**

Dutch Boy, full figure, hands in pockets, blue suit and hat, red belt and collar, brown shoes, blond hair, 11" h, $425.

Frog, 3" h, full figure, sitting, yellow and green **50.00**

Giraffe, 20-1/4" h, tan, brown spots, squared off lines to casting . . . **2,850.00**

Girl, 8-3/4" h, dark blue outfit and beanie, high white collar, black shoes, red hair, incised "663" **475.00**

Golfer, 10" h, overhand swing, hat and ball on ground, Hubley* **475.00**

Halloween Girl, 13-3/4" h, 9-3/4" l, white hat, flowing cape, holding orange jack-o-lantern with red cutout eyes, nose, and mouth* **2,000.00**

Indian Chief, 9-3/4" h, orange and tan headdress, yellow pants, and blue stripes, red patches at ankles, green grass, sgd "A. A. Richardson," copyright 1928 . . . . **295.00**

Lighthouse, 14" h, green rocks, black path, white lighthouse, red window and door trim **385.00**

Mammy

8-1/2" h, full figure, Hubley, red dress, white apron, polka-dot bandanna on head **225.00**

Mammy, full figure, one-piece hollow casting, white scarf and apron, dark blue dress, red kerchief on head, 10" h, $325.

10" h, full figure, one piece hollow casting, white scarf and apron, dark blue dress, red kerchief on head*.................**325.00**

Monkey
8-1/2" h, 4 5/8" w wrap-around tail, full figure, brown and tan...**265.00**
14-3/8" h, hand reaching up, brown, tan, and white **650.00**

Old Mill, 6-1/4" h, brown log mill, tan roof, white patch, green shrubs....................**425.00**

Owl, 9-1/2" h, sits on books, sgd "Eastern Spec Co" **285.00**

Pan, 7" h, with flute, sitting on mushroom, green outfit, red hat and sleeves, green grass base.....**165.00**

Parrot, 13-3/4" h, in ring, two sided, heavy gold base, sgd "B & H" ..**250.00**

Peasant woman, 8-3/4" h, blue dress, black hair, fruit basket on head .**250.00**

Penguin, 10" h, full figure, facing sideways, black, white chest, top hat and bow tie, yellow feet and beak, unsgd Hubley..............**435.00**

Policeman, 9-1/2" h, leaning on red fire hydrant, blue uniform and titled hat, comic character face, tan base, "Safety First" on front **725.00**

Prancing horse, 11" h, scrolled and molded base, "Greenlees Glasgow" imp on base, cast iron........**175.00**

Quail, 7-1/4" h, two brown, tan, and yellow birds, green, white, and yellow grass, "Fred Everett" on front, sgd "Hubley 459" *..............**365.00**

Rabbit, 8-1/8" h, eating carrot, red sweater, brown pants **350.00**

Rooster, 13" h, red comb, black and brown tail.................**360.00**

Squirrel, 9" h, sitting on stump eating nut, brown and tan **275.00**

Storybook
4-1/2" h, Humpty Dumpty, full figure, sgd "661" **375.00**
7-3/4" h, Little Miss Muffett, sitting on mushroom, blue dress, blond hair..................**175.00**
9-1/2" h, Little Red Riding Hood, basket at side, red cape, tan dress with blue pattern, blond hair, sgd "Hubley" **450.00**
12-1/2" h, Huckleberry Finn, floppy hat, pail, stick, Littco Products label **475.00**

Sunbonnet Girl, 9" h, pink dress.....................**235.00**

Whistler, 20-1/4" h, boy, hands in tan knickers, yellow striped baggy shirt, sgd "B & H"..............**2,750.00**

Windmill, 6-3/4" h, ivory, red roof, house at side, green base*.....**115.00**

Woman, 11" h, flowers and shawl* **285.00**

Zinnias, 11-5/8" h, multicolored flowers, blue and black vase, sgd "B & H" **185.00**

DRESDEN/MEISSEN

History:
Augustus II, Elector of Saxony and King of Poland, founded the Royal Saxon Porcelain Manufactory in the Albrechtsburg, Meissen, in 1710. Johann Frederick Boettger, an alchemist, and Tschirnhaus, a nobleman, experimented with kaolin from the Dresden area to produce porcelain. By 1720, the factory produced a whiter hard-paste porcelain than that from the Far East. The factory experienced its golden age from the 1730s to the 1750s under the leadership of Samuel Stolzel, kiln master, and Johann Gregor Herold, enameler.

The Meissen factory was destroyed and looted by forces of Frederick the Great during the Seven Years'

War (1756-1763). It was reopened, but never achieved its former greatness.

In the 19th century, the factory reissued some of its earlier forms. These later wares are called "Dresden" to differentiate them from the earlier examples. Further, there were several other porcelain factories in the Dresden region and their products also are grouped under the "Dresden" designation.

Marks: Many marks were used by the Meissen factory. The first was a pseudo-Oriental mark in a square. The famous crossed swords mark was adopted in 1724. A small dot between the hilts was used from 1763 to 1774, and a star between the hilts from 1774 to 1814. Two modern marks are swords with a hammer and sickle and swords with a crown.

References: Yvonne Adams, *Meissen Figures 1730-1775, The Kaendler Period*, Schiffer Publishing, 2001; Susan and Al Bagdade, *Warman's English & Continental Pottery & Porcelain*, 3rd edition, Krause Publications, 1998; Robert E. Röntgen, *The Book of Meissen*, revised ed., Schiffer Publishing, 1996.

Museums: Art Institute of Chicago, Chicago, IL; Cincinnati Art Museum, Cincinnati, OH; Dresden Museum of Art & History, Dresden, Germany; Gardiner Museum of Ceramic Art, Toronto, Canada; Meissen Porcelain Museum, Meissen, Germany; Metropolitan Museum of Art, New York, NY; National Museum of American History, Smithsonian Institution, Washington, DC; Robertson Center for the Arts and Sciences, Binghamton, NY; Schlossmuseum, Berlin, Germany; Stadtmuseum, Cologne, Germany; Wadsoworth Atheneum, Hartford, Ct; Woodmere Art Museum, Philadelphia, PA; Zwinger Museum, Dresden, Germany.

Dresden

Compote, 14-1/4" h, figural, shaped pierced oval bowl with applied florets, support stems mounted with two figures of children, printed marks, late 19th/early 20th C, pr..........**350.00**

Cup, 3-1/2" d, white, relief prunus dec, two handles, attributed to Boettger, unmarked, 1715.............**265.00**

Demitasse cup and saucer, blue ground, floral reserves........**275.00**

Dessert plate in frame, 8" d printed and tinted plate, scenes of courting couples, insets, and floral sprigs, gilt details, 15-3/4" sq giltwood shadowbox frame, early 20th C, set of four..**175.00**

Figure, 8-1/4" h, spaniel, seated, scratching chin with back leg ..**520.00**

Loving cup, 6-1/2" h, three handles, woodland scene with nymph, gold trim......................**475.00**

Perfume bottle, 3-3/8" l, cylindrical, enamel dec with scene of courting couple, floral sprays, gilt-metal lid enclosing cut glass stopper, early 20th C.....................**115.00**

Compote on base, blue and white floral design with insects, separate base with water spout stem and two figures, reticulated bowl with shell base, crossed swords mark and numbers, some edge damage, 22" h, **$2,420.** *Photo courtesy of Garth's Auction, Inc.*

Portrait vase, 6" h, front with oval roundel printed with portrait bust of 18th C lady, gilt floral surround, central band of beaded landscape cartouches and foliate scrolls, faux jeweled diapered ground, two short gilt flying-loop handles **635.00**

Urn, cov, 14-1/2" h, domed lid with fruit finial, body with two gilt flying-loop handles, trumpet foot on sq base, rose Pompadour ground, painted scenes of courting couples and floral bouquets, late 19th/early 20th C, price for pr, one damaged **700.00**

Vase, 13-1/4" h, alternating panels of figures and yellow floral bouquets, Thieme factory, late 19th C **115.00**

Vase, cov, 14" h, alternating panels of flowers and turquoise ground floral bouquets, c1900, minor damage, pr **375.00**

Whatnot shelf, 13-1/2" w, 13-1/3" h, figural and foliate porcelain posts,

mirrored back, shaped ebonized wood tiers, 20th C **200.00**

Meissen

Basket, 12" l, shaped oval, molded rococo cartouches, scrolling foliage, heavy gilt highlights, gilt bronze swing handles, late 19th/early 20th C, pr **850.00**

Cabinet plate, 9-5/8" d, enameled center with cupid and female in wooded landscape, gilt dec pink and burgundy border, titled on reverse "Lei Wiedergut" **490.00**

Cake basket, 12-3/8" l, oval, open lattice work body, applied flower and rococo cartouches, painted Deutsche Blumen, molded vine handles, gilt highlights, c1910 . . . . **650.00**

Chandelier, 23" h, baluster-form shaft with hand-painted flower and leaf motifs, similar applied motifs on white ground, six S-scroll arms with conforming applied floral dec, candle cups, suspending tassels with applied floral bouquets **900.00**

Clock, 18-3/4" h, Rococo style, clock face surrounded by applied floral dec, four fully molded figures representing four seasons **3,400.00**

Cup and saucer, flower-filled basket dec **90.00**

Dessert service, partial, pink floral dec, gilt trim, five 8" d plates with pierced rims, two 11-1/2" h compotes with figures of boy and girl flower sellers in center of dish, pierced rims, 20th C **1,850.00**

Dinner service, partial, Deutsche Blumen, molded New Dulong border, gilt highlights, two oval serving platters, circular platter, fish platter, 8-1/2" cov tureen with figural finial, two sauce boats with attached underplates, two serving spoons, sq serving dish, two small oval dishes, cov jam pot with attached underplate and spoon, 20 dinner plates, 11 teacups and saucers, nine salad plates, 10 bread plates, 10 soups, 74-pc set **8,500.00**

Dish, cov, 6-5/8" h, female blackamoor, beside covered dish with molded basketweave and rope edge, modeled on freeform oval base with applied florets, incised #328, 20th C **575.00**

Figure

4-1/4" cherub making hot chocolate over brazier **750.00**

4-1/2" figural group of female putto crowning cherub with wreath **600.00**

Figures, shepherd and shepherdess, multicolored and interlocking mark, 8" h, **$250.**

5" h, cherub motto figure, bows and arrows, titled "Las de vainere je me repose" **1,500.00**

5" l, 5" h, courting couple, seated man looking at woman in side chair, both in 18th C dress, ovoid base, gilt rocaille to sides, early 20th C **980.00**

5-1/4" h and 5-1/8" h, boy preparing to throw snowball, girl preparing to be hit, 20th C **1,850.00**

5-1/2" h, cherub motto figure, bows and arrows, titled "Coup sur coup" **1,200.00**

14-1/4" h, cockatoo, perched on tree stump, flower and leaves at base, early 20th C **2,300.00**

Plate, 9" d, molded with four cartouches of bunches of fruit, shaped edge with C-scroll and wings, gilt dec, late 19th C, price for pr **250.00**

Tea set, partial, brown, pink, green, blue, gray, purple, and orange enameled birds in center, dragons on rim, gilt accents, seven teacups, seven 6" d saucers, nine 7" plates, 23 pcs. **700.00**

Tray, 17-3/8" l, oval, enameled floral sprays, gilt trim, 20th C **400.00**

Urn on pedestal, 21" h, figural cartouches, scattered floral dec, two handles in form of pair of entwined snakes, mounted as lamps, pr **4,000.00**

Vase

10-1/2" h, floral dec, bands of molded gilt dec, each handle molded as two entwined snakes, gilt highlights **475.00**

15-1/2" h, scrolled snake handles, cobalt blue ground, gold and silver floral dec, 19th C, new gold trim to handles **2,300.00**

Wall garniture, 12-5/8" w, 19" l two-light girandole in rococo-style frame topped by putto figure, two figures of children among flowers on sides, brackets for two serpentine candle arms, two 15-1/2" w, 15-3/4" h scenic plaques with center painted scenes of bustling harbor, similar styled frames, sockets for candle arms, two 15-3/4" w, 15-3/4" h rococo-style three-light wall sconces, framed as rocaille scroll with three floral-encrusted serpentine candle arms, 19th C **3,100.00**

DUNCAN AND MILLER

History: George Duncan, and Harry B. and James B., his sons, and Augustus Heisey, his son-in-law, formed George Duncan & Sons in Pittsburgh, Pennsylvania, in 1865. The factory was located just two blocks from the Monongahela River, providing easy and inexpensive access by barge for materials needed to produce glass. The men, from Pittsburgh's south side, were descendants of generations of skilled glassmakers.

The plant burned to the ground in 1892. James E. Duncan Sr. selected a site for a new factory in Washington, Pennsylvania, where operations began on February 9, 1893. The plant prospered, producing fine glassware and table services for many years.

John E. Miller, one of the stockholders, was responsible for designing many fine patterns, the most famous being Three Face. The firm incorporated and used the name The Duncan and Miller Glass Company until the plant closed in 1955. The company's slogan was, "The Loveliest Glassware in America." The U.S. Glass Co. purchased the molds, equipment, and machinery in 1956.

References: Tom and Neila Bredehoft, *Fifty Years of Collectible Glass, 1920-1970, Volume 1, Volume II*, Antique Trader Books, 2000; Gene Florence, *Elegant Glassware of the Depression Era*, 8th ed., Collector Books, 1998; Naomi L. Over, *Ruby Glass of the 20th Century*, Antique Publications, 1990, 1993-94 value update, *Book II*, 1999.

Collectors' Club: National Duncan Glass Society, P.O. Box 965, Washington, PA 15301, http://www.duncan-glass.com

Museum: Duncan Miller Glass Museum, Washington, PA.

Additional Listing: Pattern Glass.

Animal
Goose, fat, crystal **275.00**
Heron, crystal **125.00**
Swan, 6-1/2" h, opal pink **115.00**

Ashtray, Terrace, red, sq **35.00**

Bowl, First Love, crystal, 11" d, scalloped **72.00**

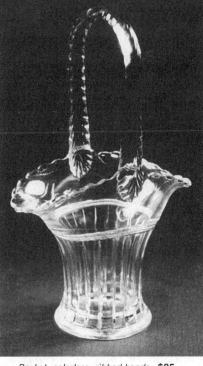
Basket, colorless, ribbed bands, **$85.**

Bud vase, First Love, crystal, 9" h **75.00**

Candleholder, Canterbury, #115-121, price for pr **55.50**

Candy box, cov, Canterbury, crystal, three parts, 6" d **70.00**

Champagne, Tear Drop, 5 oz . . . **10.00**

Coaster, Sandwich, crystal **15.00**

Cocktail
Caribbean, blue, 3-3/4 oz **45.00**
Sandwich, crystal , 3 oz **14.00**

Compote, Spiral Flutes, amber, 6" d **20.00**

Console bowl, 11" d, Rose etch, crystal **37.50**

Cornucopia, #121, Swirl, blue opalescent, shape #2, upswept tail **75.00**

Creamer and sugar, Passion Flower, crystal **42.00**

Cup
Sandwich, crystal **9.00**
Tear Drop, crystal, 6 oz **6.50**

Finger bowl, Astaire, red **65.00**

Goblet, water
First Love, crystal, 10 oz **32.00**
Plaza, cobalt blue **40.00**
Sandwich, crystal, 9 oz **19.00**

Ice cream dish, Sandwich, crystal, 4-1/4" d **12.00**

Juice tumbler, Sandwich, crystal, 3-3/4" h, ftd **12.00**

Mint tray, Sylvan, 7-1/2" l, crystal, ruby handle **35.00**

Nappy, Sandwich, crystal, two parts, divided, handle **14.00**

Oyster Cocktail, Canterbury, citrone **18.00**

Floating garden bowl, candlestick holders at ends, Sanibel, pink opalescent, 13-1/2" l, **$45.**

Plate
Astaire, red, 7-1/2" d **15.00**
Canterbury, 8" d, crystal **8.00**
Radiance, light blue, 8-1/2" d . **17.50**
Spiral Flute, crystal, 10-3/8" d . **15.00**
Terrace, cobalt blue, 7-1/2" d . **30.00**

Relish
First Love, three parts, #115, two handles, 10-1/2" x 1-1/4", minor wear **60.00**
Language of Flowers, three parts, three handles, #115 . . . . **37.50**
Terrace, four parts, 9" d, crystal **55.00**
Tear Drop, three parts, applied handle, crystal **24.00**
Terrace, five parts, hammered-aluminum center lid, 12" w . . **50.00**

Seafood-sauce cup, Spiral Flutes, green, 2-3/8" h **20.00**

Sherbet
Canterbury, chartreuse **15.00**
Sandwich, crystal **20.00**

Sugar
Caribbean, crystal **12.00**
Tear Drop, crystal, 8 oz **10.00**

Sugar shaker, Duncan Block, crystal **42.00**

Tray, Sandwich, crystal, 8" l, two handles **18.50**

Whiskey, sea horse, etch #502, red and crystal **48.00**

Wine, Sandwich, crystal , 3 oz . . . **20.00**

DURAND

History: Victor Durand (1870-1931), born in Baccarat, France, apprenticed at the Baccarat glassworks, where several generations of his family had worked. In 1884, Victor came to America to join his father at Whitall-Tatum & Co. in New Jersey. In 1897, father and son leased the Vineland Glass Manufacturing Company in Vineland, New Jersey. Products included inexpensive bottles, jars, and glass for scientific and medical purposes. By 1920, four separate companies existed.

When Quezal Art Glass and Decorating Company failed, Victor Durand recruited Martin Bach Jr., Emil J. Larsen, William Wiedebine, and other Quezal men and opened an art-glass shop at Vineland in December 1924. Quezal-style iridescent pieces were made. New innovations included cameo and intaglio designs, geometric Art-Deco shapes, Venetian Lace, and Oriental-style pieces. In 1928, crackled glass, called Moorish Crackle and Egyptian Crackle, was made.

Durand died in 1931. The Vineland Flint Glass Works was merged with Kimble Glass Company a year later, and the art glass line was discontinued.

Reference: Edward J. Meschi, *Durand: The Man and His Glass,* Glass Press, 1998.

Marks: Many Durand glass pieces are not marked. Some have a sticker with the words "Durand Art Glass," others have the name "Durand" scratched on the pontil or "Durand" inside a large V. Etched numbers may be part of the marking.

Bowl, 9-3/4" d, butterscotch, partial silver sgd **345.00**

Candlesticks, pr, mushroom, red, opal pulled florals, pale yellow base. **725.00**

Decanter, 12" h, blue cut to clear, mushroom shaped stopper, unsigned **600.00**

Jar, cov, 7-1/4" h, ginger jar form, King Tut, green, irid gold dec, applied amber glass dec on cov **3,100.00**

Lamp base, Moorish crackle, orange, greenish highlights, 9-1/4" l, **$125.**

Lamp shade, 6-3/4" h, spherical, blue and white craquelle, replacement single brass hanging fixture **625.00**

Table torchieres, pr, 15-1/2" h, Egyptian crackle, trumpet form, green and white striated glass with irid gold crackle dec, bronze acanthus leaf electrified bases, c1926, pr . . **1,725.00**

Vase

6" h, blue Aurene, pontil sgd "Durand 1964-6" in silver script **1,675.00**

6-3/8" h, broad ovoid, ambergris with peach-gold irid, applied gold spider-web thread dec, cased to white flashed gold int., polished pontil, minor loss to threading **500.00**

7" h, ovoid, flared rim, light-blue ground with strong overall blue irid, polished pontil, sgd in silver "Durand 1710-7," c1925, scratches to irid surface **435.00**

7-1/4" h, ovoid, wide flared rim, irid blue, silvery blue threaded spider web glass overlay, unmarked, some loss to threading. . . . **635.00**

7-3/4" h, Cluthra, ovoid, colorless ground with trapped bubbles and mottled blue and green rising to yellow at flared neck, obscured silver signature in polished pontil, c1930 . . . . **635.00**

8-1/2" h, vasiform, red, white, and gold craquelle **2,250.00**

9-1/2" h, vasiform, irid dark cobalt blue ground, silver heart and vine motif, silver-blue irid int. of flared mouth, polished pontil inscribed "Durand 1707" in silver . . **1,955.00**

12" h, green, white pulled feather pattern at base, Shape 1978, sgd **1,500.00**

12-1/2" h, Lady Gray Rose, elongated neck, bulbous and ftd body, rose pink, coiled irid, cased to white-yellow flared int., silver enamel "Durand" over polished pontil. **2,875.00**

EARLY AMERICAN GLASS

History: The term "Early American glass" covers glass made in America from the colonial period through the mid-19th century. As such, it includes the early pressed glass and lacy glass made between 1827 and 1840.

Major glass-producing centers prior to 1850 were Massachusetts (New England Glass Company and the Boston and Sandwich Glass Company), South Jersey, Pennsylvania (Stiegel's Manheim factory and many Pittsburgh-area firms), and Ohio (several different companies in Kent, Mantua, and Zanesville).

Early American glass was popular with collectors from 1920 to 1950. It has now regained some of its earlier prominence. Leading auction sources for early American glass include Garth's, Heckler & Company, James D. Julia, and Skinner, Inc.

References: William E. Covill, *Ink Bottles and Inkwells*, William S. Sullwold Publishing, out of print; George and Helen McKearin, American Glass, Crown, 1975; ——, *Two Hundred Years of American Blown Glass*, Doubleday and Company, 1950; Helen McKearin and Kenneth Wilson, *American Bottles and Flasks*, Crown, 1978; Dick Roller (comp.), *Indiana Glass Factories Notes*, Acorn Press, 1994; Jane S. Spillman, *American and European Pressed Glass*, Corning Museum of Glass, 1981; Kenneth Wilson, *American Glass 1760-1930*, 2 vols., Hudson Hills Press and The Toledo Museum of Art, 1994; ——, *New England Glass and Glassmaking*, Crowell, 1972.

Periodicals: *Antique Bottle & Glass Collector*, P.O. Box 187, East Greenville, PA 18041.

Collectors' Clubs: Early American Glass Traders, RD 5, Box 638, Milford, DE 19963; Early American Pattern Glass Society, P.O. Box 266, Colesburg, IA 52035; National Early American Glass Club, P.O. Box 8489, Silver Spring, MD 20907.

Museums: Bennington Museum, Bennington, VT; Chrysler Museum, Norfolk, VA; Corning Museum of Glass, Corning, NY; Glass Museum, Dunkirk, IN; New Bedford Glass Museum, New Bedford, MA; Sandwich Glass Museum, Sandwich, MA; Toledo Museum of Art, Toledo, OH; Wheaton Historical Village Association Museum of Glass, Millville, NJ.

Additional Listings: Blown Three Mold; Cup Plates; Flasks; Sandwich Glass; Stiegel-Type Glass.

Blown

Bottle, globular

3-1/8" h, Zanesville, dark amber **1,320.00**

3-1/8" h, Zanesville, light aqua **325.00**

5" h, Midwestern, aqua, 22 swirled ribs, pontil, flared lip **550.00**

5-7/8" h, Zanesville, dark amber, 24 vertical ribs, small burst blister, in-the-making imperfections in neck. **800.00**

Bottle, colorless, pontil mark, 6-3/4" h, $45.

6" h, Kent/Mantua, aqua, 16 slightly swirled ribs, flattened lip, tiny pot stones. **200.00**

7-3/8" h, Zanesville, olive green, applied lip, few pot stones. **385.00**

7-1/2" h, Zanesville, aqua, 24 swirled ribs, pot stones and scratches **330.00**

7-1/2" h, Zanesville, brilliant golden amber, 24 swirled ribs, small pot stones. **2,200.00**

7-1/2" h, Zanesville, citron, 24 tightly swirled ribs, one pot stone. **4,500.00**

7-5/8" h, Zanesville, aqua, 24 melon ribs, few pot stones **285.00**

7-3/4" h, Zanesville, brilliant aqua, 24 broken-swirl ribs, high kick-up, applied collar lip, broken blister on base, slight residue in neck **5,500.00**

8" h, attributed to Kent, brilliant aqua, three-mold, applied collar lip **3,200.00**

8" h, Zanesville, dark amber, 24 swirled ribs, tiny pot stones, broken blister **770.00**

8-1/2" h, Zanesville, aqua, high kick up, small broken blister on base **200.00**

8-1/2" h, Zanesville, olive green, tiny pot stones, overall wear . . . **825.00**

Bowl

4-1/4" d, 2-7/8" h, brilliant amethyst, 16 ribs, flared rim with folded lip, applied foot **550.00**

4-3/4" d, 3-1/2" h, deep violet, 16 prominent ribs, ground pontil **990.00**

Canister, 4" d, 9-1/4" h, Pittsburgh, cobalt wafer finial, two applied cobalt blue rings on base, one on lid . . **625.00**

Compote, cov, 6-1/4" d, 10-1/4" h, Pittsburgh, clear, prominent swirled ribs on bowl and lid, applied foot and wafer finial, McKearin Plate 55-2 . . **10,175.00**

Compote, open, 8-1/4" d, 8-1/2" h, Ribbon, brilliant amethyst, sawtooth edge, reticulated flared sides, hexagonal base with rayed bottom, straw marks, Lee 153 . . . . . . **22,000.00**

Creamer

3-7/8" h, brilliant cobalt blue, 20-diamond, applied foot and handle **550.00**

4" h, brilliant cobalt blue, 21 slightly swirled ribs, applied handle **450.00**

4-1/2" h, Pittsburgh, sapphire blue, applied handle with crimped base **495.00**

4-1/2" h, Zanesville, brilliant violet blue, applied handle **2,650.00**

4-3/4" h, brilliant peacock blue, applied foot and handle . . . **450.00**

4-3/4" h, cobalt blue, 10 diamond quilted, applied handle **250.00**

Cruet, 7-1/4" h, cobalt blue, 16 vertical ribs, Pittsburgh stopper, applied handle, tiny pot stone **800.00**

Flask

3" h, chestnut, cobalt blue, 18 swirled ribs, pontil, sheared and fire polished lip **425.00**

3-3/8" h, Mantua, sea green, 16 swirled ribs, few pot stones and residue **500.00**

5" h, Zanesville, brilliant pale green, chestnut, 24 swirled ribs, pontil, sheared and fire polished lip, minor scratches **450.00**

5" h, Zanesville, deep amber, chestnut, 10 diamond . . . **3,960.00**

5-3/4" h, amber, pint, scroll . . **635.00**

5-3/4" h, Midwestern, light green, chestnut, 16 vertical melon ribs, flared lip, minor scratches, trace of residue **275.00**

6-3/4" h, dark amber, 24 vertical ribs, wear, pot stones **1,265.00**

Flip glass, cov, 11-3/4" h, cone shaped finial applied to lid, three rows of way lines etched dec on lid, tapering body

dec with two sprays of stylized flowers, minor imperfections......... **550.00**
Mug, 4" h, brilliant cobalt blue, applied handle **1,155.00**
Pan

5-3/8" d, 2" h, Zanesville, aqua, 10 diamond, flared sides, folded-in rim **8,470.00**

5-3/4" d, 2" h, Pittsburgh, amethyst, 12 ribbed-panel bowl, applied foot, folded rim **4,400.00**

6-1/4" d, 1-1/4" h, Zanesville, dark amber, 24 ribs, folded-in rim, very minor scratches **4,850.00**

8-7/8" d, 2-1/8" h, Zanesville, golden, flared sides, fold-out rim, pot stone................ **1,045.00**

10-3/8" d, 2" h, Pittsburgh, pale amethyst, eight panels, folded out lip, in-the-making imperfection in one panel **1,750.00**

Pitcher, 6" h, Zanesville, pale green, 24 swirled ribs, applied ribbed handle **21,725.00**
Salt, master

2-1/2" d, 3" h, dark cobalt blue, diamond quilted pattern **250.00**

2-5/8" d, cobalt blue, 14 diamond pattern, applied foot, rim roughness............. **200.00**

Sugar, cov

4" d, 6-1/4" h, brilliant dark cobalt blue, diamond quilted, applied ribbed foot with 14 ribs, folded rim, swirled finial, small rim chip **825.00**

4-1/4" d, 6-1/2" h, dark cobalt blue, diamond quilted, applied foot, cone-shaped finial **1,925.00**

Wine glass, 7-1/4" h, clear, cotton stem, early 19th C, price for pr **1,380.00**

Lacy

Bowl, 7-3/8" d, 1-5/8" h, Nectarine, chips **100.00**
Candlesticks, pr, 6" h, reeded and ribbed socket attached with wafer, reeded stem, sq stepped base, chips, checks in socket **450.00**
Compote, cov, 9-1/2" h, 8-1/4" d, Sawtooth, flint, chips **155.00**
Miniature lamp, 4" h, lacy cup-plate base, blown spherical font, knob stem, chips on base **385.00**
Plate, 7" d, eagle, chips **175.00**
Toddy, 5-3/8" d, brilliant dark amethyst, lacy, Roman Rosette, Sandwich, edge chips **330.00**

Pillar mold

Candlestick, 7-5/8" h, teal green, hexagonal, center wafer, small flake on socket, base flakes, chipped corner **1,925.00**
Cologne bottle, 5-5/8" h, cobalt blue, eight ribs, two applied rings, flared lip, mushroom stopper, stopper base shipped **400.00**
Decanter, 9-3/4" h, cobalt blue, applied handle and collar, pewter jigger cap **7,950.00**
Pitcher, 5-5/8" h, colorless, applied handle, Pittsburgh, bottom ground flat, minor wear **275.00**
Vase

9-5/8" h, 5-3/4" d, Pittsburgh, clear, applied stem and foot **660.00**

10" h, Pittsburgh, brilliant amethyst, white edging applied on ribs, baluster stem, applied foot **4,750.00**

ENGLISH CHINA AND PORCELAIN (GENERAL)

History: By the 19th century, more than 1,000 china and porcelain manufacturers were scattered throughout England, with the majority of the factories located in the Staffordshire district.

By the 19th century, English china and porcelain had achieved a worldwide reputation for excellence. American stores imported large quantities for their customers. The special-production English pieces of the 18th and early 19th centuries held a position of great importance among early American antiques collectors.

References: Susan and Al Bagdade, *Warman's English & Continental Pottery & Porcelain*, 3rd edition, Krause Publications, 1998; John A. Bartlett, *British Ceramic Art: 1870-1940*, Schiffer Publishing, 1993; Peter Bradshaw, *English Eighteenth Century Porcelain Figures, 1745-1795*, Antiques Collectors' Club, 1980; John and Margaret Cushion, *Collector's History of British Porcelain*, Antique Collectors' Club, 1992; Rachael Field, *Macdonald Guide to Buying Antique Pottery & Porcelain*, Wallace-Homestead, 1987; Geoffrey A. Godden, *Godden's Guide to Mason's China and the Ironstone Wares*, Antique Collectors' Club, out of print; —, *Godden's Guide to English Porcelain*, Wallace-Homestead, 1992; Pat Halfpenny, *English Earthenware Figures 1740-1840*, Antique Collectors' Club, 1992; R. K. Henrywood, *Relief Molded Jugs, 1820-1900*, Antique Collectors' Club; Llewellyn Jewitt, *Ceramic Art of Great Britain*, Sterling Publishing, 1985 (reprint of 1883 classic); Griselda Lewis, *Collector's History of English Pottery*, 5th ed., Antique Collectors' Club, 1999.

Additional Listings: Castleford, Chelsea, Coalport, Copeland and Spode, Liverpool, Royal Crown Derby, Royal Doulton, Royal Worcester, Staffordshire, Historical; Staffordshire, Romantic; Wedgwood, Whieldon.

Bow

Bowl, 4-1/2" d, blue trailing vine, white ground, c1770.............. **175.00**
Candlesticks, pr, two birds on flowering branches, dog and sheep on grassy base, wood stand, c1755 .... **1,200.00**
Egg cup, 2-1/2" h, two half-flower panels, powder blue ground, pseudo Oriental mark, c1760......... **900.00**
Plate, 9" d, Turk's Cap Lily, dragonfly and moths, c1755 .... **850.00**

Chelsea

Bowl, 8-3/4" d, swirled ribs, scalloped, foliage and floral dec **75.00**
Candlesticks, pr, 7-1/2" h, figural, draped putti, sitting on tree stump holding flower, scroll-molded base, encircled in puce, gilt, wax pan
.... **850.00**
Cup and saucer, multicolored exotic birds, white ground, gold anchor mark, c1765 .... **750.00**
Plate, 8-1/2" d, multicolored floral design, scalloped rim, gold anchor mark **475.00**

Derby

Figure, 8" h, 8-1/2" h, pastoral, boy resting against tree stump playing bagpipe, black hat, bleu-do-roi jacket, gilt trim, yellow breeches, girl with green hat, bleu-du-roi bodice, pink skirt, white apron with iron-red flowerheads, gilt centers, leaves, scroll molded mound base, crown and incised iron-red D mark, pr ... **2,200.00**
Jar, cov, 22" h, octagonal, iron-red, bottle green and leaf green, alternating cobalt blue and white grounds, gilding, grotesque sea-serpent handles, now fitted as lamp with carved base, 19th C, pr...................... **10,000.00**
Plate, 10-1/8" d, enamel dec, stylized Imari-type designs of birds in three, shaped molded rim, Bloor mark, second quarter 19th C, price for set of seven..................... **300.00**

Flight, Barr & Barr

Crocus pot, 9" w, 4" d, 6-1/4" h, D-form, molded columns and architrave, peach-ground panels, ruined abbey landscape reserve, gilding ... **2,400.00**
Pastille burner, 3-1/2" h, cottage, four open chimneys, marked, c1815 .... **425.00**

Jackfield

Creamer, 4-1/4" h, bulbous, emb grapes design, leaves, and tendrils, gilt highlights, three pr paw feet, ear-shape handle **185.00**

Pitcher, 6-1/2" h, applied handle, black, traces of enameling, bird, initials and "1763," wear, small flakes......**125.00**

Sugar bowl, cov, 4-1/2" h, 3-3/4" d, scalloped SS rims, SS-mounted cov and ornate pierced finial **250.00**

Lowestoft

Coffeepot, cov, 9" h, dark blue, underglaze river scene, Chinese man fishing, trellis diaper border, c1770-75 ....**950.00**

Demitasse cup and saucer, blue underglaze dec **150.00**

Milk jug, 3-1/4" h, dark blue underglaze, Chinese river scene, diaper border, brown rim, c1775 ....**210.00**

Masons

Creamer, 4" h, Oriental-style shape, marked "Mason's Patent Ironstone" **85.00**

Jug, 8" h, octagonal, Hydra pattern, waisted straight neck, green-enameled handle, lion-head terminal, underglaze blue and iron-red flowers and vase, two imp marks and printed rounded crown mark, c1813-30 ....**320.00**

Platter, 13-1/2" x 10-3/4", Double-Landscape pattern, Oriental motif, deep green and brick red, c1883 ....**265.00**

Potpourri vase, cov, 25-1/4" h, hexagonal body, cobalt blue, large gold

stylized peony blossom, chrysanthemums, prunus, and butterflies, gold and blue dragon handles, and knobs, trellis diaper-rim border, c1820-25...........**1,750.00**

New Hall

Creamer, Chinese figure on terrace, c1790....................**190.00**

Dessert set, two oval dishes, eight plates, printed and colored named views, lavender-blue borders, light-blue ground, c1815..............**450.00**

Tea set, interwoven ribbon and leaf trails, blue and gilt oval-medallion border, c1790, minor repairs, 44 pcs **1,500.00**

Woods

Cup and saucer, handleless, Woods Rose **65.00**

Dish, 8" l, 6" w, dark blue transfer of castle, imp "Wood" **165.00**

Jug, 5-3/4" h, ovoid, cameos of Queen Caroline, pink luster ground, beaded edge, molded and painted floral border, c1820....................**425.00**

Plate, 9" d, Woods Rose, scalloped edge **125.00**

Stirrup cup, 5-1/2" l, modeled hound's head, translucent shades of brown, c1760....................**2,200.00**

Whistle, 3-7/8" h, modeled as seated sphinx, blue accents, oval green base, c1770.....................**600.00**

Worcester

Cream jug, cov, 5" h, floral finial, underglaze blue floral and insect dec, shaded crescent mark, 18th C, cover possibly married, slight finial chips, shallow flake to cover.........**175.00**

Deep dish, 9-1/2" l, oval, underglaze blue Chantilly sprig pattern, shaded crescent mark, 18th C, foot-rim chips......................**320.00**

Miniature, cup and saucer, handleless

Blue and white fence design, Dr. Wall underglaze blue crescent mark, paper label "John Williams Collection," filled in rim flake on saucer...................**85.00**

Blue and white three-flower and butterfly design, Dr. Wall underglaze blue crescent mark **150.00**

Sauce boat, 5-1/4" l, molded body, panels of underglaze blue flowers, cell border, open crescent mark, 18th C.....................**300.00**

Teapot, cov, globular, 5-5/8" h, underglaze blue dec of Waiting Chinaman, floral finial, open crescent mark, 18th C, slight spout nick, chips to finial **865.00**

Tureen, cov, 10-1/2" l, oval, underglaze blue pine cone pattern, artichoke finial, shell handles, shaded crescent mark, 18th C, one handle restored, int. rim flake **800.00**

ENGLISH SOFT PASTE

History: Between 1820 and 1860, a large number of potteries in England's Staffordshire district produced decorative wares with a soft earthenware (creamware) base and a plain white or yellow glazed ground.

Design or "stick" spatterware was created by a cut sponge (stamp), hand painting, or transfers. Blue was the predominant color. The earliest patterns were carefully arranged geometrics which generally covered the entire piece. Later pieces had a decorative border with a central motif, usually a tulip. In the 1850s, Elsmore and Foster developed the Holly Leaf pattern.

King's Rose features a large, cabbage-type rose in red, pale red, or pink. The pink rose often is called "Queen's Rose." Secondary colors are pastels— yellow, pink, and, occasionally, green. The borders vary: a solid band, vined, lined, or sectional. The King's Rose exists in an oyster motif.

Strawberry China ware comes in three types: strawberries and strawberry leaves (often called strawberry luster), green featherlike leaves with pink flowers (often called cut-strawberry, primrose, or old strawberry), and relief decoration. The first two types are characterized by rust-red moldings. Most pieces have a cream ground. Davenport was only one of the many potteries which made this ware.

New Hall, teapot, silver shape, red and pink trim, pastel flowers, vase finial, marked "No. 594," c1790-1805, **$400.**

Yellow-glazed earthenware (canary luster) has a canary yellow ground, a transfer design which is usually in black, and occasional luster decoration. The earliest pieces date from the 1780s and have a fine creamware base. A few hand-painted pieces are known. Not every piece has luster decoration.

Because the base material is soft paste, the ware is subject to cracking and chipping. Enamel colors and other types of decoration do not hold well. It is not unusual to see a piece with the decoration worn off.

Marks: Marked pieces are uncommon.

Additional Listings: Gaudy Dutch, Salopian Ware, Staffordshire Items.

Creamware

Coffeepot, cov, 10" h, pear shape, polychrome dec black transfer of Tea Party and Shepherd prints, leaf-molded spout, chips, restoration to body, attributed to Wedgwood, c1775 . . . . **350.00**

Cup and saucer, handleless, blue bands, gaudy foliage dec, minor wear, pinpoint flake on cup rim **175.00**

Jug, 5-1/8" h, reeded lapped handle, emb floral applications, sides dec with red and green floral sprays, 19th C, glaze wear, small rim nicks **260.00**

Plate

6-1/2" d, Leeds-type colors, blue and gold leaf border, green and yellow pineapple center, hairline, small rim flakes **550.00**

8-7/8" d, dark purple grape-vine border, shades of green, yellow, and red, floral center with red rose, dark purple columbine, yellow and blue flowers, minor stains **110.00**

Platter, 18" l, 14-1/2" w, oval, scallop dec rim, chips, restorations **300.00**

Sugar bowl, 5-1/8" d, 2-3/4" h, int. with red and green enamel floral dec, purple luster and underglaze blue, ext. marked "Be Canny with the Sugar" flanked by small flowers **385.00**

Teapot

4" h, floral dec, early 19th C, hairline along spout and handle . . . **115.00**

4-3/4" h, molded acanthus spout, ribbed handle, small flakes **385.00**

6-1/2" h, flower knop, floral dec entwined reeded handle with touches of gilt, rim chip, restored spout, gilt loss, 19th C **230.00**

Design Spatterware

Bowl, 7-1/2" d, 4" h, polychrome stripes **95.00**

Creamer, 4-3/8" h, gaudy floral dec, red, green, blue, and black, marked "Baker & Co., England" **75.00**

Cup, oversize, gaudy floral dec, red, blue, and green, 6-1/8" d **200.00**

Jug, 7" h, barrel shape, blue, rosettes and fern prongs **185.00**

Miniature

Cup and saucer, green and black, polychrome center flower **75.00**

Tea set, five pieces, 5-3/4" h teapot, creamer, sugar, two handleless cups and saucers, blue and white design spatter, teapot finial restored, chips **440.00**

Mug, 4" h, octagonal, red, blue, and green stripes **135.00**

Plate, 8-5/8" d, red, blue, green, and black, imp "Elsmore & Foster," minor wear and scratches, price for set of six **385.00**

Sugar bowl, cov, 5" h, white, blue, and red flowers, green leaves, closed ring and shell handles **120.00**

King's Rose

Bowl, 7-3/4" d, Rose, broken solid border, flakes **55.00**

Cup and saucer, handleless

Oyster pattern, hairline cracks **40.00**

Rose, solid border **100.00**

Rose, vine border **150.00**

Plate

5-5/8" d, pink border, wear . . . **55.00**

6-1/2" d, broken solid border, flakes **55.00**

6-1/2" d, vine border, wear **80.00**

7-3/8" d, some flaking **90.00**

8-1/4" d, scalloped borders and edges, some flakes, six pcs **275.00**

8-1/4" d, pink border, wear . . . **70.00**

8-1/4" d, vine border, three pcs **255.00**

9-3/4" d, scalloped border, four pcs **220.00**

Pitcher, 5-5/8" h, dark red rose, blue and yellow flowers, green leaves, some wear **220.00**

Soup plate, 9-1/2" d, broken solid border, scalloped edges, some flakes, three pcs **360.00**

Teapot, 5-3/4" h, broken solid border, some flakes **140.00**

Pearlware

Bowl

8-3/4" d, 3-7/8" h, blue and white Oriental transfer, yellow rim, wear and stains, chip on foot . . . **145.00**

10-3/8" d, 4-1/8" h, interior with pink, green, red, and black floral enameled rim, mahogany stripes, minor wear **250.00**

10-3/4" d, 4" h, polychrome enamel Oriental dec, minor wear and scratches **440.00**

Coffeepot, cov, 13" h, baluster form, dome lid, ochre, green, brown, and blue floral dec, early 19th C, imperfections **200.00**

Creamer, cup shape, straight sides, applied handle, light brown stripes, yellow band, gilt and light brown foliage

Queen's Rose, teapot, covered, squatty shell form, pink rose decoration, extra lid with matching decoration, loss to teapot, $200. Photo courtesy of Sanford Alderfer Auction Co.

band, slight bubbles to yellow, minor spout rim flake **125.00**
Cup and saucer, handleless, 3-1/2" d cup, 5" d saucer, black transfer scene of horse-drawn chariot, flying putti set of six **525.00**
Figure
   3" l, sheep, brown, blue, and yellow ochre sponging, small edge flakes **275.00**
   3-1/4" h, squirrel, nut and collar with ring, polychrome, orange coat, attributed to Derby, minor wear and small flakes on base **635.00**
   3-7/8" h, cat, seated, green base, yellow and brown polka dots, attributed to Wood, repairs, hairline in base, small flakes **550.00**
   6-3/4" h, Autumn, molded base, green, brown, yellow, orange, black, and pink flesh tones, chips on base, old repair **330.00**
Jar, cov, 12-1/4" h, blue transfer, willow pattern, gilt highlights, c1830 . . **550.00**
Pitcher
   6-5/8" h, gaudy floral dec, red, blue, green, and black, minor enamel wear, deteriorating professional repair **110.00**
   8-5/8" h, Leeds floral dec, green, brown, blue, and tan, later added row of peacocks, very flaked, stains, chips on spout **275.00**
Plate
   5-3/4" d, rose dec, molded luster rim, wear **85.00**
   7-3/4" d, blue and white Oriental dec, imp "Turner," minor wear **165.00**
Platter, 20-3/4" l, blue feather edge, Leeds blue and white Oriental dec, wear, scratches, edge chips, old puttied repair **500.00**
Punch bowl, 9-5/8" d, 4-3/8" h, stylized floral bands on int., floral bands and central medallion on ext., polychrome enamel dec, late 19th C **1,265.00**
Teapot, 5-3/4" h, octagonal, molded designs, swan finial, Oriental transfer, polychrome enamel, attributed to T. Harley, some edge flakes and professional repair **425.00**
Vase, 7" h, five-finger type, underglaze blue, enameled birds and foliage, yellow ochre, brown, and green,

Yellow glazed earthenware, bowl, 7-1/4" d, 3-1/4" h, $400.

silver-luster highlights, chips and crazing, pr **500.00**
Wall plaque, 8-1/2" w, 12-1/4" l, oval, molded, polychrome dec, female Harvest figure, late 18th C, minor chip **435.00**

Queen's Rose
Cream pitcher and sugar, cov, vine border, some flakes **250.00**
Cup and saucer, handleless, broken solid border **495.00**
Plate
   6-1/2" d, broken solid border . . **50.00**
   7-1/2" d, solid border **75.00**
   8-1/4" d, vine border, scalloped edge **85.00**
   10" d, vine border **110.00**
Tea set, assembled, Strawberry and Queen's Rose, 7" h teapot, creamer, cov sugar, handleless cup and saucer, waste bowl, professional repairs **550.00**

Strawberry China
Bowl, 4" d **165.00**
Cup and saucer, pink border, scalloped edge **225.00**
Plate, 8-1/2" d, Cut Strawberry . . **200.00**
Soup bowl, 8-1/4" d, red, green, pink, and yellow flower and strawberry border, basket of strawberries and roses in center **880.00**

Sugar bowl, cov, raised strawberries, strawberry knob **175.00**
Tea bowl and saucer, vine border **250.00**

Yellow Glazed
Child's mug
   Floral leaf and vine dec **195.00**
   Pious verse, "My son if sinners entice thee consent thou not disgrace come upon thee" **250.00**
   Silver luster foliate band **185.00**
Pitcher, 4-3/4" h, transfer dec of foliate devices, reserve of shepherd with milk maid, hand-painted dec, c1850 . . . . **635.00**
Plate, 8-1/4" d, brown transfer print, Wild Rose pattern, imp "Montread" **250.00**
Soup bowl, 8-1/4" d, molded border, Cabbage Rose pattern, iron-red and green dec **400.00**
Sugar bowl, cov, 5-1/2" h, printed transfer of The Tea Party, fishing scene, iron-red painted rims **1,250.00**
Tea bowl and saucer, iron-red print of two cupids, marked "Sewell" . . . **250.00**
Teapot, 5-1/2" h, printed transfer of The Party, iron-red painted rims, minor hairline, spout damage **850.00**

FAIRINGS, MATCH-STRIKERS, AND TRINKET BOXES

History: Fairings are small, charming china objects which were purchased or given away as prizes at English fairs in the 19th century. Although fairings are generally identified with England, they actually were manufactured in Germany by Conte and Boehme of Possneck.

Fairings depict an amusing scene, either of courtship and marriage, politics, war, children, or animals behaving as children. More than 400 varieties have been identified. Most fairings include a caption. Early examples, from 1860-1870, were of better quality than later ones. After 1890, the colors became more garish, and gilding was introduced.

The manufacturers of fairings also made match safes and trinket boxes. Some of these were also captioned. The figures on the lids were identical to those on fairings. The market for the match safes and trinket boxes was the same as that for the fairings.

Reference: Janice and Richard Vogel, *Victorian Trinket Boxes*, published by authors (4720 S.E. Ft. King St., Ocala, FL 34470), 1996.

Figure

After The Race, cats in a
basket **215.00**
Begging Terrier, white, touches of pink,
4" h. **60.00**
Bicycle Rider, 2-1/2" l, 3" h, head broken
and reglued, few old hairlines . . . **15.00**
Elephants, one with boy rider, facing
with girl rider, painted faces, wear to
gilding, small chip on one, price for
pr **75.00**
Five O'Clock Tea, group of
cats **225.00**
Girl with flowers, 3-3/4" h **40.00**
God Save the Queen, children singing
around piano **350.00**
Let Us Do Business Together . . . **95.00**
Peep Through A Telescope, sailor and
child **175.00**
Retiring Couple, 3" h, wear on
trim **60.00**
Stag, seated, white, gold antlers, 3" l,
3" h **40.00**
Swan, girl, and clock, 2" w, 3" h, gilding
worn **35.00**
The Entertainer, playing wind
instrument, puppet in basket,
3-1/2" h **40.00**
The Welsh Tea Party, magenta dresses,
striped aprons, black hats, gilt trim,
c1870. . . . . **95.00**
Who Said Rats **95.00**

Trinket box, blue and white, girl putting on stockings, base impressed with shield and "3572 I76," 3-1/2" x 4" x 2", $145.

Box

Commode, bowl and pitcher and
tumbler on top with mirror frame,
1-5/8" d, 2" h **75.00**
Crown, cross, and sword on lid, flowers
around edge, band of flowers on base,
3" l, 2" h, large chip on lid **65.00**
Red Riding Hood and Wolf, 2-1/4" w,
2-1/2" h, imp "37" on inside of lid, lid
chipped **45.00**
Swan, round base, 2-1/2" d,
2" h **75.00**

FAIRY LAMPS

History: Fairy lamps, which originated in England in the 1840s, are candle-burning night lamps. They were used in nurseries, hallways, and dim corners of the home.

Two leading candle manufacturers, the Price Candle Company and the Samuel Clarke Company, promoted fairy lamps as a means to sell candles. Both contracted with glass, porcelain, and metal manufacturers to produce the needed shades and cups. For example, Clarke used Worcester Royal Porcelain Company, Stuart & Sons, and Red House Glass Works in England, plus firms in France and Germany.

Fittings were produced in a wide variety of styles. Shades ranged from pressed to cut glass, from Burmese to Nailsea. Cups are found in glass, porcelain, brass, nickel, and silver plate.

American firms selling fairy lamps included Diamond Candle Company of Brooklyn, Blue Cross Safety Candle Co., and Hobbs-Brockunier of Wheeling, West Virginia.

Two-piece (cup and shade) and three-piece (cup with matching shade and saucer) fairy lamps can be found. Married pieces are common.

Marks: Clarke's trademark was a small fairy with a wand surrounded by the words "Clarke Fairy Pyramid, Trade Mark."

References: Bob and Pat Ruf Pullin, *Fairy Lamps*, Schiffer Publishing, 1996; John F. Solverson (comp.), *Those Fascinating Little Lamps: Miniature Lamps Value Guide*, Antique Publications, 1988.

Periodical: *Fairy Lamp Newsletter*, 6422 Haystack Road, Alexandria, VA 22310-3308.

Collectors' Club: Fairy Lamp Club, 6422 Haystack Road, Alexandria, VA 22310-3308.

Reproduction Alert: Reproductions abound.

Burmese Cricklite, pleated skirt, signed "Thomas Webb & Sons Queens Burmese-Ware," clear candle cup signed "Clarke," 5-3/4" d, 5-3/4" h, $985. Photo courtesy of Clarence and Betty Maier.

3-1/2" h, overshot, yellow swirl, cased,
clear marked Clarke candle
cup **125.00**
3-7/8" h, peachblow, cream lining,
acid-finished rose-shaded pink, black
lacy flower and leaf dec, clear marked
Clarke candle cup, gold washed metal
stand, attributed to Thomas
Webb **350.00**
4" h, bisque, figural, owl, cat, and dog,
glass eyes, clear marked Clarke candle
cup **265.00**
4-1/4" h, colored lithophane, dome
shade, gold accents, boy and girl in
garden, girl peering from window,
another girl carrying basket and pole,
boy and dog, clear candle cup holder
marked "S. Clarke Patent Trade Mark
Fairy" **1,485.00**
4-1/2" h, cranberry, crown shape,
overshot shade, clear base, clear

marked Clarke candle cup,
c1887 . . . . **220.00**
4-3/4" h, 6" d, Burmese, Webb,
pyramid, garland of stylized purple
blossoms and green leaves on
cream-colored porcelain base, int. of
base sgd "S. Clarke's Fairy Pyramid
Patent Trade Mark," base marked
"Tunnicliffe 1444A" **1,250.00**
5" h, 5-1/2" d, ruby red Verre Moiré,
bowl-shaped base with fluted edge,
clear-glass candle cup holder marked
"S. Clarke Patent Trade
Mark" **1,035.00**
5-1/2" h, white spatter, chartreuse
cased in crystal ground, swirled rib
mold, heavy applied crystal feet and
base trim, clear marked Clarke candle
cup **550.00**
5-1/2" h, 7-1/2" d, Burmese, Cricklite,
pleated base, clear candle cup sgd
"Clarke's Cricklite Trade
Mark" **1,350.00**
5-1/2" h, 7-1/2" d pleated skirt, Burmese
Criklite, clear candle cup marked
"Clarke's Criklite Trade Mark" . **1,085.00**
5-3/4" h, 5-3/4" d, Burmese, Webb,
Cricklite, intense blush, lemon-yellow
pedestal base, 1-1/2" w pleated skirt,
clear candle cup sgd "Clarke," sgd
"Thomas Webb & Sons Queens
Burmese-Ware" **985.00**
5-3/4" h, 8-1/2" d, ruby red, profuse
white loopings, bowl-shaped base with
eight turned-up scallops, clear-glass
candle cup holder marked "S. Clarke
Patent Trade Mark Fairy" **1,250.00**

*Ribbed Drape shade, vaseline shade,
green Clarke base, $195.*

6" d, lavender satin ruffled dome top,
three gold inset jeweled medallions,
ruffled base **350.00**
6" h, blue and white frosted ribbon
glass dome top shade, ruffled base,
clear marked "S. Clarke" insert, flakes
on shade **490.00**
6" h, 7" d, Cricklite, ruby red, profuse
white loopings, base with 26 evenly
spaced pleats, dome-shaped shade,
clear-glass candle cup sgd "S. Clarke
Patent Trade Mark Fairy" **875.00**
6-1/2" h, 8" w, Verre Moiré, sweeping
white loopings blend into delicate blue
background, dome-shaped shade,
triangular-shaped base with pinch-in
folds, clear-glass cup holder with ruffled
edge, marked "S. Clarke Patent Trade
Mark Fairy" **950.00**

FAMILLE ROSE

History: Famille Rose is Chinese export enameled
porcelain on which the pink color predominates. It was
made primarily in the 18th and 19th centuries. Other
porcelains in the same group are Famille Jaune
(yellow), Famille Noire (black), and Famille Verte
(green).

Decorations include courtyard and home scenes,
birds, and insects. Secondary colors are yellow, green,
blue, aubergine, and black.

Rose Canton, Rose Mandarin, and Rose
Medallion are mid- to late- 19th century
Chinese-export wares which are similar to Famille
Rose.

*Plate, set of 10" d plates and five
9-1/2" d plates, all with Famille Rose
decoration, imperfections,* **$360.** *Photo
courtesy of Sanford Alderfer Auction Co.*

Bowl, 12" d, int. dec with alternating
floral and figural reserves against foliate
pattern ground, floral dec ext., Ch'ing
Dynasty **400.00**
Box, cov, 4-1/2" d, figural and floral
dec **90.00**

Bride's lamp, 14" h, hexagonal form,
reticulated panels, electrified . . . **345.00**
Charger, 12" d, central figural dec,
brocade border **265.00**
Dish, 10-3/4" d, figural dec, Qing
dynasty **65.00**
Dish, cov, 11" d, figural dec, Qing
dynasty **200.00**
Figure
6-1/2" h, Ho Ho erh hsien, China,
c1800, price for pr **450.00**
13" h, peacocks, pr **275.00**
16" h, cockerels, pr **550.00**
Garden set, 18-1/2" h, hexagonal,
pictorial double panels, flanked and
bordered by floral devices, blue
ground, 19th C, minor glaze
loss **1,100.00**
Ginger jar, cov, 10-1/2" h, ovoid, foo
dog beside sea reserve, floral and
butterfly patterned ground, Famille
Verte, Kangxi **420.00**
Jar, cov, 18" h, baluster, dec with
female-sprite figure emerging from
flower blossom, surrounded by floral
devices, minor base chips,
19th C **750.00**
Jardiniere, 9-3/4" h, flowering branches
dec, Jiaqing **700.00**
Lamp base, 17" h, figural and crane
dec, molded fu-dog mask and ring
handles **175.00**
Mug, 5" h, Mandarin palette, Qianlong,
1790 . . . . **425.00**
Pillow, 15-1/4", Phoenix and floral
dec **225.00**
Plate, 10" d, floral dec, ribbed body,
Tongzhi mark, pr **275.00**
Platter, 16-3/4" l, chamfered corners,
floral dec **150.00**
Tea caddy, 5-1/2" h, Mandarin palette,
arched rect form, painted front, figures
and pavilion reserve, c1780 . . . . **550.00**
Tray, 8" l, oval, multicolored center
armorial crest, underglaze blue diaper
and trefoil borders, reticulated rim, late
18th C **550.00**
Vase, 17-1/2" h, Rouleau form, molded
fu-dog handles, scene of figures
picking fruit from large vines, verso with
butterflies, traditional borders, late
19th C **250.00**
Vase, cov, 26" h, shouldered ovoid,
large cartouches with scenes of
warriors on horseback, dignitaries
holding court, molded fu-dog handles,
conforming cartouches on lid, fu-dog
finial, c1850-70, pr **2,400.00**

FENTON GLASS

History: The Fenton Art Glass Company began as a cutting shop in Martins Ferry, Ohio, in 1905. In 1906, Frank L. Fenton started to build a plant in Williamstown, West Virginia, and produced the first piece of glass there in 1907. Early production included carnival, chocolate, custard, and pressed glass, plus mold-blown opalescent glass. In the 1920s, stretch glass, Fenton dolphins, jade green, ruby, and art glass were added.

In the 1930s, boudoir lamps, Dancing Ladies, and slag glass in various colors were produced. The 1940s saw crests of different colors being added to each piece by hand. Hobnail, opalescent, and two-color overlay pieces were popular items. Handles were added to different shapes, making the baskets they created as popular then as they are today.

Through the years, Fenton has beautified its glass by decorating it with hand painting, acid etching, and copper-wheel cutting.

Marks: Several different paper labels have been used. In 1970, an oval-raised trademark also was adopted.

References: Tom and Neila Bredehoft, *Fifty Years of Collectible Glass, 1920-1970, Volumes I and II*, Antique Trader Books, 2000; Robert E. Eaton, Jr., (comp.), *Fenton Glass: The First Twenty-Five Years Comprehensive Price Guide 1998*, Glass Press, 1998; —, *Fenton Glass: The Second Twenty-Five Years Comprehensive Price Guide 1998*, Glass Press, 1998; *Fenton Glass: The Third Twenty-Five Years Comprehensive Price Guide 1998*, Glass Press, 1998; William Heacock, *Fenton Glass: The First Twenty-Five Years* (1978), *The Second Twenty-Five Years* (1980), *The Third Twenty-Five Years* (1989), available from Antique Publications; Alan Linn, *Fenton Story of Glass Making*, Antique Publications, 1996; James Measell (ed.), *Fenton Glass: The 1980s Decade*, Antique Publications, 1996; —, *Fenton Glass: The 1990s Decade*, Antique Publications, 2000; Naomi L. Over, *Ruby Glass of the 20th Century*, Antique Publications, 1990, 1993-94 value update, —, *Book II*, Antique Publications, 1999; Ferill J. Rice (ed.), *Caught in the Butterfly Net*, Fenton Art Glass Collectors of America, Inc., 1991; John Walk, *Fenton Glass Compendium, 1940-1970*, Schiffer Publishing, 2001; — *Fenton Glass Compendium, 1970-1985*, Schiffer Publishing, 2001; Margaret and Kenn Whitmyer, *Fenton Art Glass 1907-1939*, Collector Books, 1996, 1999 value update; —, *Fenton Art Glass, 1939-1980*, Collector Books, 1996, 2000 value update; —, *Fenton Art Glass Patterns 1939-1980*, Collector Books, 1999.

Periodical: *Butterfly Net*, 302 Pheasant Run, Kaukauna, WI 54130.

Collectors' Clubs: Fenton Art Glass Collectors of America, Inc., P.O. Box 384, Williamstown, WV 26187; National Fenton Glass Society, P.O. Box 4008, Marietta, OH 45750; Pacific Northwest Fenton Association, 8225 Kilchis River Road, Tillamook, OR 97141.

Videotape: *Making Fenton Glass, 1992*, Fenton Art Glass Co. Museum, 1992.

Museum: Fenton Art Glass Co., Williamstown, WV.

Additional Listing: Carnival Glass.

Ashtray, #848 2 Ruby, three feet **20.00**
Basket, Cranberry Opalescent Swirl, 6" w, 10" l, 12-1/4" h, applied handle, orig label. **800.00**

Bell
  #7466 CV hp Christmas Morn **45.00**
  #8466 OI Faberge, Teal Marigold **55.00**
  #9463WS Nativity. **55.00**

Bonbon
  #1621 Dolphin Handled, Green **32.50**
  #8230 Rosalene Butterfly, two handles **35.00**

Bowl
  Gold Crest, 8" d **40.00**
  Peach Crest, Charleton dec . **105.00**
  #846 Pekin Blue, cupped **40.00**
  #848 8 Petal, Chinese Yellow . **45.00**
  #1562 Satin Etched Silvertone, oblong bowl. **55.00**
  #7423 Milk Glass bowl, hp Yellow roses **65.00**
  #8222 Rosalene, Basketweave. **30.00**

Bride's basket
  Cranberry Opalescent Hobnail, 10-1/2" d bowl, 11-1/2" h SP frame **300.00**
  Maize, amber and crystal crest, hp roses, 12-1/2" d bowl, 12" h, SP frame. **275.00**

Candlestick, single
  #318 Pekin Blue, 3" h **40.00**
  #951 Silvercrest Cornucopia . . **37.50**
  #7272 Silver Crest **17.50**

Candy box, cov
  Hobnail, 6-1/2" sq, white, ... **40.00**
  Ruby Iridized, Butterfly, for FAGCA **100.00**
  #1980CG Daisy and Button. . . **45.00**
  #7380 Custard hp Pink Daffodils Louise Piper, dated March 1975 . . . . **160.00**
  #9394 UE three pcs, Ogee, Blue Burmese **110.00**
  #9394 RE three pcs, Ogee, Rosalene **100.00**

Compote
  #3728 PO Plum Opal Hobnail 5-1/2". **75.00**
  #8422 Waterlily ftd, Rosalene . **30.00**
Cocktail shaker, #6120 Plymouth, Crystal **55.00**
Cracker jar
  Lilac Big Cookies, no lid, handle **250.00**
  #1681 Big Cookies, Jade . . . **125.00**

Creamer
  #1502 Diamond Optic, Black . **35.00**
  #1502 Diamond Optic, Ruby . **30.00**
  #6464 RG Aventurine Green w/Pink, Vasa Murrhina **45.00**

Creatures (Animals and Birds)
  #5174 Springtime Green Iridized Blown Rabbit **45.00**
  #5178 Springtime Green Iridized Blown Owl **45.00**
  #5193 RE Rosalene Fish, paperweight. **25.00**
  #5197 Happiness Bird, Cardinals in Winter. **32.50**
  #5197 Happiness Bird, Rosalene **40.00**
Cruet, #7701 QJ, 7" Burmese, Petite Floral **175.00**
Cup and saucer, #7208 Aqua Crest **35.00**
Epergne
  #3902 Petite Blue Opal, 4" h. **125.00**
  #3902 Petite French Opal, 4" h. **40.00**
  #7308 SC Silvercrest, three horn **125.00**

Butterfly, #5170, chocolate, FAGCA, $55. Photo courtesy of Ferill Rice.

Fairy light
  #1167 RV Rose Magnolia Hobnail three pcs, Persian Pearl Crest, sgd "Shelly Fenton". **80.00**
  #3380 CR Hobnail, three pcs, Cranberry Opal **75.00**
  #3680 RU Hobnail, three pcs . **55.00**
  #3804 CA Hobnail three pcs, Colonial Amber **25.00**
  #3804 CG Hobnail three pcs, Colonial Green **20.00**
  #8406 WT Heart, Wisteria. . . . **65.00**
  #8406 PE Heart, Shell Pink. . . **25.50**
  #8408 VR Persian Medallion, three pcs, Velva Rose-75th Anniv. **75.00**

#8408 BA Persian Medallion three
pcs, Blue Satin **35.00**
Ginger jar, #893 Persian Pearl w/base
and top **150.00**
Goblet, #1942 Flower Windows
Blue **55.00**
Hat, #1922 Swirl Optic, French
Opal **110.00**
Jug, #6068 Cased Lilac, handled,
6-1/2" **50.00**
Lamp, Blue Coin Dot, Gone with the
Wind, 31" h **300.00**
Liquor set, #1934 Flower Stopper, floral
silver overlay, eight-pc set **250.00**
Lotus bowl, #849 Red **25.00**
Miniature lamp, Cranberry Coin Spot,
4-5/8" d, 11" h **600.00**
Nut bowl, Sailboats, Marigold
Carnival **50.00**
Pitcher
    Amber Crest. **115.00**
    Christmas Snowflake, Cranberry
        Opal, water (L.G. Wright) . . **350.00**
    Daisy & Fern, Topaz Opal, water
        (L.G. Wright) **200.00**
    Plum Opal, Hobnail, water,
        80 oz. **190.00**
Powder box, #6080, Wave Crest, blue
overlay **95.00**
Plate
    Lafayette & Washington, Light Blue
        Iridized, sample **80.00**
    #107 Ming Rose, 8" **30.00**
    #1614 9-1/2" Green Opal w/Label
        New World **65.00**
    #1621 Dolphin Handled, Fenton
        Rose, 6" **25.00**
    #5118 Leaf, 11" Rosalene,
        sample **120.00**
Punch bowl set, Silver Crest, 15" d,
7-5/8" h ftd punch bowl, 12 4" d, 2-3/4" h
cups, 12-3/4" l handle. **800.00**
Rose bowl, #8954TH hanging
heart **95.00**
Salt and pepper shakers, pr, #3806
Cranberry Opal, Hobnail, flat **47.50**
Sauce, Pinecone, 5" d, red. **35.00**
Sherbet
    #1942 Flower Windows,
        Crystal **35.00**
    #4441 Small, Thumbprint, Colonial
        Blue **35.00**
    #4443 Thumbprint, Colonial
        Blue **20.00**
Sugar and creamer, #9103 Fine Cut &
Block (OVG) **20.00**
Temple jar, #7488 Chocolate Roses on
Cameo Satin. **25.00**

Tumbler
    #1611 Georgian, Royal Blue, 5-1/2",
        ftd, 9 oz **18.00**
    #1634 Diamond Optic, Aqua . . **6.00**
    #3700, Grecian Gold, grape
        cut **15.00**
    #3945MI Hobnail, 5 oz **10.00**
    #3945FO Hobnail, 2 oz. **15.00**
Tumble-up, Blue Swirl, 8" h, 5-1/2" w,
applied handle, c1939 . . . . **900.00**
Vanity bottle, #3965MI **75.00**

*Happiness Birds, #5197, ruby, hand
painted by Louis Piper,* **$85 each.**
Photo courtesy of Ferill Rice.

Vase
    Aristocrat Bud Vase, #98 cutting,
        Fenton Rose **45.00**
    Butterfly & Berry, red, tightly crimped
        edge, 7" h **65.00**
    Ivory Crest, 10" **65.00**
    #847 Periwinkle Blue, Fan . . **62.50**
    #3759 Plum Opal, Hobnail,
        swung. **150.00**
    #4454OR Thumbprint, swung. **45.00**
    #5858 Wild Rose, wheat. **85.00**
    #6457 GA Vasa Murrhina, fan. **85.00**
    #7460 Amberina Overlay crimped,
        6-1/2" h **80.00**
    #7547 Burmese, hp Pink Dogwood,
        5-1/2" h **75.00**
    #8457VE Grape, three toed . . **35.00**
Water pitcher, 8-1/2" h, custard,
hand-painted fall scene with red barn,
chickens, rooster, birds flying, sgd "Jan
Curtis," applied ribbed
handle **395.00**
Water set, Blue Opalescent, 8-1/4" h
cannonball-shaped pitcher, six 5" h
tumblers. **550.00**

FIESTA

History: The
Homer Laughlin
China Company
introduced Fiesta
dinnerware in
January 1936 at the
Pottery and Glass Show in Pittsburgh, Pennsylvania.

Frederick Rhead designed the pattern; Arthur Kraft and
Bill Bensford molded it. Dr. A. V. Bleininger and H. W.
Thiemecke developed the glazes.

The original five colors were red, dark blue, light
green (with a trace of blue), brilliant yellow, and ivory.
A vigorous marketing campaign took place between
1939 and 1943. In mid-1937, turquoise was added.
Red was removed in 1943 because some of the
chemicals used to produce it were essential to the war
effort; it did not reappear until 1959. In 1951, light
green, dark blue, and ivory were retired and forest
green, rose, chartreuse, and gray were added to the
line. Other color changes took place in the late 1950s,
including the addition of a medium green.

Fiesta ware was redesigned in 1969 and
discontinued about 1972. In 1986, Fiesta was
reintroduced by Homer Laughlin China Company. The
new china body shrinks more than the old
semi-vitreous and ironstone pieces, thus making the
new pieces slightly smaller than the earlier pieces. The
modern colors are also different in tone or hue, e.g.,
the cobalt blue is darker than the old blue. Other
modern colors are black, white, apricot, and rose.

References: Susan and Al Bagdade, *Warman's
American Pottery and Porcelain*, 2nd ed., Krause
Publications, 2000; Mark Gonzalez, *Collecting Fiesta,
Lu-Ray & Other Colorware*, L-W Books Sales, 2000;
Homer Laughlin China Collectors Association, *Fiesta,
Harlequin, Kitchen Kraft Tablewares*, Schiffer
Publishing, 2000; Sharon and Bob Huxford,
Collector's Encyclopedia of Fiesta, 8th ed., Collector
Books, 1998; Ronald E. Kay and Kathleen M. Taylor,
Finding Fiesta: A Comprehensive Price Guide, Fiesta
Club of America, Inc., 1998 (P.O. Box 15383, Loves
Park, IL 61132-5383; Richard Racheter, *Post 86 Fiesta
Identification and Value Guide*, Collector Books, 2000;
Jeffrey B. Snyder, *Fiesta, Homer Laughlin China
Company's Colorful Dinnerware*, 3rd ed., Schiffer
Publishing, 2000.

Periodicals and Internet Resources: *Fiesta
Collector's Quarterly*, P.O. Box 471, Valley City, OH
44280; *Homer's Hunting*, 7314 134th St. Ct. E.,
Puyallup, WA 98373; *The Dish*, P.O. Box 26021,
Crystal City, VA 22215-6021, http://www.hlcca.org;
http://www.chinaspecialities.com;
http://www.digdesign.com/fiestaware;
http://www.fiestafanatic.com; http://www.hlcca.org;
http://www.ohioriverpottery.com.

Collectors' Clubs: Fiesta Collector's Quarterly, P.O.
Box 471, Valley City, OH 44280; Homer Laughlin
China Collectors Association, P.O. Box 26021, Crystal
City, VA 22215-6021, http://www.hlcca.org

Reproduction Alert.

Additional Listings: See *Warman's Americana &
Collectibles* for more examples.

After Dinner coffeepot, cov, cobalt
blue **550.00**
After Dinner cup and saucer
    Charcoal **550.00**
    Chartreuse. **495.00**
    Cobalt blue **95.00**
    Gray. **550.00**
    Green. **85.00**
    Ivory. **25.00**
Ashtray, red. **50.00**

Bowl, 5-1/2" d
   Green 60.00
   Red 34.00
Cake plate, green 1,950.00
Candlesticks, pr
   Bulb, ivory 125.00
   Tripod, yellow 550.00
Carafe
   Turquoise 380.00
   Yellow 275.00
Casserole, cov
   Red 275.00
   Turquoise 135.00
Casserole, French, yellow 275.00
Chop Plate, 13" d
   Gray 95.00
   Ivory 45.00

Coffeepot, green, 10-1/2" h, $50.

Coffeepot, turquoise 235.00
Comport, 12" d, Ivory, marked . 225.00
Creamer, stick handle
   Ivory 75.00
   Red 75.00
   Turquoise 115.00
   Yellow 45.00
Cream soup
   Gray 60.00
   Ivory 60.00
   Rose 95.00
Cup
   Cobalt blue 35.00
   Dark green 45.00
   Light green 25.00
   Medium green 70.00
   Turquoise 25.00
   Yellow 25.00
Dessert bowl, 6" d
   Red 45.00
   Rose 45.00

Fruit bowl, cobalt blue, 11-5/8" d, 2-3/4" h, **$485.**

Egg cup
   Green 50.00
   Red 70.00
Fruit bowl, 4-3/4" d
   Cobalt blue 25.00
   Medium green 550.00
Fruit bowl, 11-3/4" d, cobalt
blue 485.00
Gravy boat
   Ivory 20.00
   Turquoise 30.00
Juice pitcher, ivory 20.00
Juice tumbler
   Cobalt blue 40.00
   Rose 65.00
   Yellow 40.00
Marmalade
   Turquoise 325.00
   Yellow 360.00
Mixing bowl
   #1, cobalt blue 375.00
   #2, cobalt blue 195.00
   #2, yellow 140.00
   #4, green 195.00
   #5, ivory 275.00
   #7, ivory 580.00
Mixing-bowl lid, #1, red 1,100.00
Mug
   Dark green 90.00
   Ivory, marked 125.00
   Rose 95.00
Mustard, cov
   Cobalt blue 325.00
   Turquoise 275.00
Nappy, 5-1/2" d, turquoise 25.00
Onion soup, cov
   Green 895.00
   Ivory 950.00
Pitcher, disk
   Chartreuse 275.00
   Turquoise 110.00

Water pitcher, orange, **$325.**

Pitcher, ice lip
   Green 135.00
   Turquoise 195.00
Plate, deep
   Gray 42.00
   Rose 42.00
Plate, 6" d
   Dark green 15.00
   Ivory 7.00
   Light green 9.00
   Turquoise 8.00
   Yellow 5.00
Plate, 7" d
   Chartreuse 12.00
   Ivory 10.00
   Light green 8.50
   Medium green 30.00
   Rose 14.00
   Turquoise 8.50
Plate, 9" d
   Cobalt blue 15.00
   Ivory 14.00
   Red 15.00
   Yellow 8.00
Plate, 10" d, dinner
   Gray 42.00
   Light green 28.00
   Medium green 125.00
   Red 35.00
   Turquoise 30.00
Plate, 15" d, cobalt blue 62.00
Platter, oval
   Gray 35.00
   Ivory 25.00
   Red 45.00
   Yellow 22.00
Relish
   Ivory base and center, turquoise
     inserts 285.00
   Red, base and inserts 425.00
Salt and pepper shakers, pr
   Red 24.00
   Turquoise 135.00

Vegetable dish, turquoise, 11" d, **$45.**

Saucer

Light green **5.00**
Turquoise **5.00**

Soup plate

Ivory **36.00**
Turquoise **29.00**

Sugar bowl, cov

Chartreuse **65.00**
Gray **75.00**
Rose **75.00**

Syrup

Green **450.00**
Ivory **600.00**
Red **695.00**

Sweets compote, yellow **65.00**

Tea cup, flat bottom, cobalt
blue **100.00**

Teapot, light gray, medium, **$295.**

Teapot, cov

Cobalt blue, large **335.00**
Green, medium, 9" spout to handle,
　7" h, chip on spout **600.00**
Red, large **245.00**
Rose, medium **350.00**

Tumbler, cobalt blue **75.00**

Utility tray, red **55.00**
Vase

8" h, green **825.00**
8" h, ivory, c1936-42 . . . . . . **550.00**
12" h, cobalt blue,
　c1936-42 . . . . **1,275.00**
12" h, light green,
　c1937-42 . . . . **1,195.00**

FIGURAL BOTTLES

History: Porcelain figural bottles, which have an average height of three to eight inches and were made either in a glazed or bisque finish, achieved popularity in the late 1800s and remained popular into the 1930s. The majority of figural bottles were made in Germany, with Austria and Japan accounting for the balance.

Empty figural bottles were shipped to the United States and filled upon arrival. They were then given away to customers by brothels, dance halls, hotels, liquor stores, and taverns. Some were lettered with the names and addresses of the establishment, others had paper labels. Many were used for holidays, e.g., Christmas and New Year's.

Figural bottles also were made in glass and other materials. The glass bottles held perfumes, food, or beverages.

References: Ralph & Terry Kovel, *Kovels' Bottles Price List, 11th ed.,* Three Rivers Press, 1999; Kenneth Wilson, *American Glass 1760-1930,* 2 vols., Hudson Hills Press and The Toledo Museum of Art, 1994.

Periodical: *Antique Bottle and Glass Collector,* P.O. Box 187, East Greenville, PA 18041.

Collectors' Clubs: Federation of Historical Bottle Collectors, Inc., 2230 Toub St., Ramona, CA 92065; New England Antique Bottle Club, 120 Commonwealth Rd, Lynn, MA 01904.

Museums: National Bottle Museum, Ballston Spa, NY; National Bottle Museum, Barnsley, S. Yorkshire, England; Old Bottle Museum, Salem, NJ.

Bisque

Cowboy, 7-1/2" h, little black boy dressed in cowboy hat, vest, chaps, marked "Made in Japan" **125.00**

Farmer's Relief, 5-1/2" h, marked "Made in Japan," wear to paint . . **45.00**

Man, 4-1/" h, "Toasting Your Health," flask style, tree bark back **85.00**

Sailor, 6-1/2" h, white pants, blue blouse, hat, high-gloss front, marked "Made in Germany" **115.00**

Turkey Trot, 6-3/4" h, tree trunk back, marked "Made in Germany" . . . **150.00**

Glass

Bear, 10-5/8" h, dense yellow amber, sheared mouth, applied face, Russia, 1860-80, flat chip on back **400.00**

Big Stick, Teddy Roosevelt's, 7-1/2" h, golden amber, sheared mouth, smooth base, flat flake at mouth **170.00**

Boot, clear glass, 12" h, **$150.** *Photo courtesy of Joy Luke Auctions.*

Bull, John, 11-3/4" h, bright orange amber, tooled mouth, smooth base, attributed to England, 1870-1900 . . . . **160.00**

Cabin, 9" h, two stories, Kelly's Old Cabin Bitters, dark olive green **5,675.00**

Chinaman, 5-3/4" h, seated form, milk glass, ground mouth, orig painted metal atomizer head, smooth base, America, 1860-90 . . . . **120.00**

Fish, 11-1/2" h, Doctor Fisch's Bitters, golden amber, applied small round collared mouth, smooth base, America, 1860-80, some ext. high point wear, burst bubble on base **160.00**

Garfield, James, President, 8" h, colorless-glass bust set in turned-wood base, ground mouth, smooth base, America, 1880-1900 . . . . **80.00**

Indian Maiden, 12-1/4" h, Brown's Celebrated Indian Herb Bitters, yellow amber, inward rolled mouth, smooth base, America, 1860-80 . . . . **600.00**

Monkey, 4-1/2" h, sitting, opaque white milk glass **200.00**

Pig, 10-3/8" l, Berkshire Bitters, golden amber **1,200.00**

Queen Mary, ocean liner, c1936 . . . . **155.00**

Shoe, dark amethyst, ground mouth, smooth base **125.00**
Washington, George, 10" h, Simon's Centennial Bitters, aquamarine, applied double-collared mouth, smooth base, America, 1860-80 .... **650.00**
Woman, 13-1/2" h, Victorian, frosted, painted head **900.00**

Fish, Bennington-type pottery, brown glaze, 9" l, $495.

Pottery and porcelain

Book, 10-1/2" h, *Bennington Battle*, brown, tan, cream, and green flint enamel, minor chips **850.00**
Camel, 4" h, mother of pearl glaze, os....................... **45.00**
Canteen, painted bust of Lincoln, Garfield, and McKinley, half pint....................... **375.00**
Cucumber, 11-3/4" l, stoneware, green and cream mottled glaze...... **100.00**
Fox, reading book, beige, brown mottled dec **85.00**
Mermaid, 7-1/4" h, brown and tan Rockingham-type glaze....... **125.00**
Pig, 8-1/2" l, gray salt glaze, tan highlights, one ear chipped, other ear missing **470.00**
Pretzel, brown.............. **75.00**

FINDLAY ONYX GLASS

History: Findlay onyx glass, produced by Dalzell, Gilmore & Leighton Company, Findlay, Ohio, was patented for the firm in 1889 by George W. Leighton. Due to high production costs resulting from a complex manufacturing process, the glass was made only for a short time.

Layers of glass were plated to a bulb of opalescent glass through repeated dippings into a glass pot. Each layer was cooled and reheated to develop opalescent qualities. A pattern mold then was used to produce raised decorations of flowers and leaves. A second mold gave the glass bulb its full shape and form.

A platinum luster paint, producing pieces identified as silver or platinum onyx, was applied to the raised decorations. The color was fixed in a muffle kiln. Other colors such as cinnamon, cranberry, cream, raspberry, and rose were achieved by using an outer glass plating, which reacted strongly to reheating. For example, a purple or orchid color came from the addition of manganese and cobalt to the glass mixture.

References: Neila and Tom Bredenhoft, *Findlay Toothpick Holders*, Cherry Hill Publications, 1995; James Measell and Don E. Smith, *Findlay Glass: The Glass Tableware Manufacturers, 1886-1902*, Antique Publications, 1986.

Collectors' Club: Collectors of Findlay Glass, P.O. Box 256, Findlay, OH 45839.

Tumbler, platinum floral decoration, 3-5/8" h, $375.

Celery vase, cream **450.00**
Cream pitcher, platinum-colored blossoms, creamy-white background, opalescent clear-glass handle.. **435.00**
Dresser box, cov, 5" d, cream.. **675.00**

Mustard jar, covered, raspberry, SP cover, 3-3/8" h, $1,350.

Pitcher, 7-1/2" h, cream, applied opalescent handle, polished rim chip **800.00**
Spooner, 4-1/2" h, satin surface, bright silver dec, few small rim flakes . **485.00**
Sugar, cov, 6" h, Onyx, platinum blossoms, cream-white ground, silver medallion on base of bowl, rim chip and roughness to cover **485.00**
Sugar shaker, raspberry **495.00**
Syrup, 7" h, 4" w, silver dec, applied opalescent handle.......... **1,150.00**
Toothpick holder, cream **375.00**

FINE ARTS

History: Before the invention of cameras and other ways to mechanically capture an image, paintings, known as portraits, served to capture the likeness of an individual. Paintings have been done in a variety of mediums and on varying canvases, boards, etc. Often it was what was available in a particular area or time that influenced the materials. Having one's portrait painted was often a sign of wealth and many artists found themselves in demand once their reputations became established. Today art historians, curators, dealers, and collectors study portraits to determine the age of the painting and often use clues found in the backgrounds or clothing of the sitter to determine age, if no identification is available. Many portraits have a detailed provenance that allows the sitters, and often the artists, to be identified.

In any calendar year, tens, if not hundreds of thousands, of paintings are sold. Prices range from a few dollars to millions. Since each painting is essentially a unique creation, it is difficult to compare prices.

Since an essential purpose of *Warman's Antiques and Collectibles Price Guide* is to assist its users in finding information about a category, this Fine Arts introduction has been written primarily to identify the reference books you will need to find out more about a painting in your possession. The listings below of portraits will give a general idea of what portraits sold for in the auction year of 2001.

Artist Dictionaries: *2000 ADEC International Art Price Annual*, ADEC, 2000; E. H. Russell Ash, *Impressionists' Seasons*, Pavilion, 1999; Emmanuel Benezit, *Dictionnaire Critique et Documentaire des Peintres, Sculpteurs, Dessinateurs et Graveurs*, 10 volumes, Grund, 1999; John Castagno, *Old Masters: Signatures and Monograms*, Scarecrow Press, 1996; Ian Chilvers, *Concise Oxford Dictionary of Arts & Artists*, 2nd ed., Oxford University Press, 1996; Peter Hastings Falk, *Dictionary of Signatures & Monograms of American Artists*, Sound View Press, 1998; Mantle Fielding, *Dictionary of American Painters, Sculptors and Engravers*, Apollo Books, 1983; Franklin & James, *1988-1998 Decade Review of American Artists at Auction*, Franklin & James, 1999; J. Johnson and A. Greutzner, *Dictionary of British Artists, 1880-1940: An Antique Collector's Club Research Project Listing 41,000 Artists*, Antique Collector's Club, 1976; Blake McKendry, *A to Z of Canadian Artists & Art Terms*, published by author, 1997.

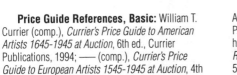

Price Guide References, Basic: William T. Currier (comp.), *Currier's Price Guide to American Artists 1645-1945 at Auction*, 6th ed., Currier Publications, 1994; —— (comp.), *Currier's Price Guide to European Artists 1545-1945 at Auction*, 4th ed., Currier Publications, 1994.

Price Guide References, Advanced: R. J. Davenport, *1999-2000 Davenport's Art Reference & Price Guide*, Davenport Publishing, 1998; Peter Hastings Falk (ed.), *Art Price Index International 2000*, Sound View Press, 2000; Enrique Mayer, *International Auction Record*, Paris, Editions Enrique Mayer, since 1967; Susan Theran (ed.), *Leonard's Price Index of Art Auctions*, Auction Index, since 1980.

Museum Directories: *American Art Directory*, R. R. Bowker, 1995; American Association of Museums, *Official Museum Directory: United States and Canada*, R. R. Bowker, updated periodically.

Collectors' Clubs: American Art Collectors, 610 N. Delaware Ave., Roswell, NM 88201; Art Dealers Assoc. of America, 575 Madison Ave., New York, NY 10022-2511; International Foundation for Art Research, 500 Fifth Ave., Suite 1234, New York, NY 10110; National Antique & Art Dealers Assoc. of America, 220 East 57th St., New York, NY, 10022.

Periodicals and Internet Resources: *American Art Review*, 12230 State Line Road, Shawnee Mission, KS 66209; *Art & Auction*, 11 E. 36th St., 9th Floor, New York, NY 10016, http://www.artandauction.com; Art.com, http://www.art.com; Artcyclopedia, Inc., http://www.artcyclopedia.com; ArtDirectory, http://www.artframing.com; ArtFact, Inc., http://www.artfact.com; Art Library Online, http://www.artlibrary.com; Artnet.com, http://www.artnet.com; *Art Newspaper*, 80 E. 11th St., Rooms 224 & 26, New York, NY 10003; http://www.theartnewspaper.com; *Art On Paper*, 39 E. 78th St., #501, New York, NY 10021-0213, http://www.artonpaper.com; Art Resource on the Web, http://www.witcombe.sbc.edu/ARTHLinks.html;

AskArt.com, http://www.askart.com; *Fine Arts Trader*, P.O. Box 1273, Randolph, MA 02368, http://www.fineartstrader.com; *Westbridge Art Market Report*, 1737 Fir St., Vancouver, British Columbia, V6J 5J9, Canada, http://www.westbridge-fineart.com; World Wide Arts Resource, http://www.wwar.com.

Goache and watercolor on paper, gentleman writing letters at lap desk, unsigned American School, 19th C, molded gilt frame, abrasions and small losses, 17-1/2" w, 20-1/2" h ... **3,750.00**

Oil on academy board
Gentleman, wearing evening dress, oval format with drapery at top, unsigned American School, 19th C, 10-1/2" w, 13" h, framed as rect, scattered retouch, abrasions **980.00**
Pair, Prior School, man and woman, minor edge damage, some touch up, 12" w, 15" h, modern 17-1/2" w, 20-1/2" h frames **4,400.00**
Woman, wearing high lacy collar, white dress, bright red shawl, green drape and pillar in background with clouds, old typewritten label "Elsie Ray," "Delvecchio's Looking Glass and Picture Frame Manufactory (New York)" label on back, 20-1/4" w, 27" h, cleaned, revarnished, 25" w, 41" h period gilt frame with edge chips **2,750.00**

Oil on canvas
Boy with basket of fruit, heavily alligatored surface, cut down and replaced stretcher, 22-1/2" w,

30-1/2" h, modern gilt 25-1/2" w, 33-1/2" h frame **990.00**
Coffin, William James, young boy in blue off-shoulder dress, small white dog at side, straw hat with blue ribbons in background, unsigned but attributed to Joseph Whiting Stock, shaped elaborate gilt gesso frame, accompanied by copies of Coffin family Bible records, handwritten codicil referring to Stock in family will **42,550.00**
Currier, Edward Albert and Sarah, unsigned American School, 19th C, unframed, lined, minor retouch, craquelure, children of Albert Currier, Newburyport, MA, genealogical information included, price for two portraits ... **5,465.00**
Frontiersman, fur-trimmed overcoat, black slouch hat, smoking clay pipe, rebacked on canvas, restoration, 25-1/4" w, 32" h, dark gray painted 32-1/2" w, 39-1/2" h frame **1,155.00**
Gentleman and Wife, orig sgd "H. Bundy, Claremont, May 1846" on reverse of one, lined, scattered re-touch, framed, price for pr **2,530.00**
Gentleman, black cat, white vest, white high collar, black and red tie, signature "B. Landsman, 1851," scratched into paint before dry, canvas crazed, cleaned, some areas of touchup, 25" w, 31" h, repainted period frame with reeding, raised corner blocks **770.00**
Gentleman, dapper looking, graying blond hair and beard, tuxedo, pince nez, later label on back "Adolph Haberl in his 60th year, 1899, by J. Steiner," orig signature and date attached to back of stretcher, cut down and rebacked on masonite with restoration, 16" w, 21-1/4" h, ornate gilt 28" w, 32" h two-tone frame with some gold repaint **250.00**
Gentleman, white wig, rebacked and restored, 25-1/2" w, 30" h, 30-1/2" w, 36-1/2" h frame .. **825.00**
Girl, pink dress, roses and apple, unsigned American School, 19th C, framed, lined, retouched, craquelure, 23-1/4" w, 28-1/2" h **5,175.00**
Holmes, Henry, as a child, holding riding crop, (Marshfield, MA, 1841-1909), unsigned American School, molded gilt frame, full

Prior School, pair, man and woman, oil on academy board, minor edge damage, some touch up, 12" w, 15" h, **$4,400.** *Photo courtesy of Garth Auctions, Inc.*

genealogy included, minor punctures, losses, scattered retouch **4,320.00**

Hudson, Mr., gentleman sitter identified in inscription as "Mr. Hudson, a Southerner" on reverse, Prior Hamblen School, 19th C, framed, repaired punctures, retouched, craquelure, 21" w, 26-1/4" h **5,465.00**

Old Woman, attributed to Sheldon Peck, drapery, book, black dress, white bonnet, replaced on canvas with repairs, more recent splint in center, 24-3/4" w, 29-1/2" h **11,500.00**

Powell, James, unsigned American School, 19th C, cove molded gilt composite frame, lined, minor retouch, craquelure, 20" w, 23-1/2" h **1,495.00**

Ralli, John, Esq., US Consul to the Port of Odessa, unsigned American School, 19th C, carved gilt frame, lined, retouched, small repaired puncture, craquelure, 32" w, 38" h **2,990.00**

Regal Lady, blue lace trimmed satin dress, pearls, other jewelry, holding sprig of red flowers, rebacked, new stretcher, restored, 27" w, 31-3/4" h, gilt frame **550.00**

Stone Fruit, oil on canvas by Martin Cone (1891-1964, Iowa), $57,750. Photo courtesy of Jackson's Auctioneers & Appraisers.

Young Woman, dark eyes, brown hair parted in middle, black dress, fancy lace shawl, long gold chain necklace, orig condition, couple of touch-ups, 25-1/4" w, 30" h, gilt 30-1/2" w, 35-3/4" h frame with edge damage **1,320.00**

Young Woman, floral fichu, laced bonnet, seated on sofa, unsigned,

American School, 19th C, grain painted frame, 23-1/2" w, 28-1/2" h, minor retouch **1,380.00**

Washington, George, 19th C copy of Gilbert Stuart's portrait, some paint crazing, old patched repair, 24" w, 36" h, old 29-1/2" w, 41-1/2" h frame with gilding and black repaint **825.00**

Woman, brown hair, blue eyes, black dress, white lace collar and cuffs, coral drop earrings, professional rebacked on canvas, new stretcher, some restoration, 24" w, 30-1/2" h, minor wear to 26-5/8" w, 32-1/2" h gilt frame **990.00**

Pastel on paper

Man, American School, 19th C, laid down onto canvas, repair, crease, small tears, losses to margins, scattered flaking and stains, 11-1/2" w, 15-1/2" h, framed **2,185.00**

Reverend Seth Storer, Minister of Watertown, MA, identified in inscriptions and on labels on reverse, oval format, matted, 10-1/4" x 8-1/4", repaired tears and losses, pigment loss **980.00**

Watercolor on paper, young girl seated on rock beneath tree, flower dec bonnet nearby, pink dress, American School, 19th C, framed, 5-3/4" x 7", minor staining **1,150.00**

FIREARM ACCESSORIES

History: Muzzle-loading weapons of the 18th and early 19th centuries varied in caliber and required the owner to carry a variety of equipment, including a powder horn or flask, patches, flints or percussion caps, bullets, and bullet molds. In addition, military personnel were responsible for bayonets, slings, and miscellaneous cleaning equipment and spare parts.

During the French and Indian War, soldiers began to personalize their powder horns with intricate engraving, in addition to the usual name or initial used for identification. Sometimes professional hornsmiths were employed to customize these objects, which have been elevated to a form of folk art by some collectors.

In the mid-19th century, cartridge weapons replaced their black-powder ancestors. Collectors seek anything associated with early ammunition—from the cartridges themselves to advertising material. Handling old ammunition can be extremely dangerous because of decomposition of compounds. Seek advice from an experienced collector before becoming involved in this area.

References: Ted and David Bacyk, *The Encyclopedia of Shotgun Shell Boxes*, SoldUSA, 2000; Ralf Coykendall Jr., *Coykendall's Complete Guide to*

Sporting Collectibles, Wallace-Homestead, 1996; Jim Dresslar, *Folk Art of Early America—The Engraved Powder Horn*, Dresslar Publishing (P.O. Box 635, Bargersville, IN 46106), 1996; John Ogle, *Colt Memorabilia Price Guide*, Krause Publications, 1998; Nick Stroebel, *Old Gunsights, A Collector's Guide, 1850-1965*, Krause Publications, 1999.

Periodical: Military Trader, P.O. Box 1050, Dubuque, IA 52004.

Museums: Fort Ticonderoga Museum, Ticonderoga, NY; Huntington Museum of Art, Huntington, WV.

Reproduction Alert: There are a large number of reproduction and fake powder horns. Be very cautious!

Notes: Military-related firearm accessories generally are worth more than their civilian counterparts.

Additional Listing: Militaria.

Belt, 36" l, 2" w, 30 nickel metal clips for holding shot shells, canvas shoulder straps, nickel-plated buckle with Savage-Arms logo cast into it, nickel-plated hook **350.00**

Canteen, 7" d, 2-5/8" deep, painted, cheese-box style, dark red paint overall, one side painted gold with a large primitive eagle with shield breast, the top of the shield red with cream lettering "No. 37," other side painted in gold letters, "Lt. Rufus Cook," pewter nozzle, sq nail construction, strap loops missing **1,650.00**

Cartridge box

3-7/8" x 2" x 1", Hall and Hubbard, .22 caliber, green and black label "100 No. 1/22-100/Pistol Cartridges," cov with molded cream and black paper, empty, missing about half green side label **300.00**

3-7/8" x 2-1/8" x 1-1/4", Phoenix Metallic Cartridge Co., early green and black label, "50 Cartridges/32-100 Caliber Long," opened, but full **250.00**

4" x 2-1/8" x 1-1/4", Union Metallic Cartridge Co., .32 caliber, cream and black label "Fifth .32 caliber/No. 2/Pistol Cartridges," engraving of Smith & Wesson 1st Model 3rd Issue, checked covering, orange and black side labels, unopened **210.00**

Catalog

Colt's Patent Fire Arms, Hartford, CT, 1933, 40 pgs, 6-3/4" x 9-1/4" **85.00**

J. W. Fecker, Pittsburgh, PA, c1929, 22 pgs, 3-1/2" x 8", *Fecker Precision Telescopic Signs* . **15.00**

J. Stevens Arms & Tool Co., Chicopee Falls, MA, c1916, 136 pgs, 5-1/4" x 8", Catalog No. 51 . . . .**110.00**

Bowie knife, stag grip, blade marked "Kingman & Hassam Boston," some chips, few nicks,
$4,670. *Photo courtesy of Jackson's Auctioneers & Appraisers.*

Savage Arms Corp., Chicopee Falls, MA, 1951, 52 pgs, 8-1/2" x 11", No. 51, *Component Parts Price List for Savage, Stevens, Fox Shotguns & Rifles* **35.00**

Winchester Repeating Arms, New Haven, CT, 1918, 215 pgs, 5-1/2" x 8-1/2", Cat No. 81, illus of repeating and single-shot rifles, repeating shotguns, cartridges, shells, primers, percussions caps, shot **250.00**

Powder horn

6-1/2" h, "E. K. B. 1831 Horn NH," dec foliate border, hearts, star, and patriotic banner, rounded plug dec with hearts, centers inset brass button depicting eagle surrounded by stars **1,955.00**

9" l, whale's tooth, engraved ship under sail, crosshatched diamond design, losses, cracks **350.00**

10-1/2" l, buffalo horn, sterling silver bands and cap, silver panel on either side with engraving, "The horn of the buffalo killed by Col. John Darrington on the upper Brassos, 1835," and "Presented by J. Darrington to Col. Wade Hampton," engraved scene on end cap shows hunter perched on limb, long rifle aimed at two buffalo, few insect holes, brass end may be later **9,900.00**

12-1/2" l, engraved foliage detail, old dark finish, pine plug, shaped flats **385.00**

13" l, engraved, initialed, and dated "AB 1807," floral and geometric motifs **980.00**

18-1/2" l, engraved coat of arms with dragons and crowns, soldier with kilt and feathers on helmet, officer tipping his hat, good patina, plug missing **660.00**

Puzzle game, J. Stevens Arms, cardboard litho, shows three factories, eight different rifles, 7" sq **750.00**

Shot flask, leather, 7" l, black pigskin body stamped "Sykes/Extra/lb/1," fitted with carrying ring, 2" German silver top with bright steel dispenser stamped "Skyes Extra" **85.00**

Target ball, 2-3/4" d, Bogardus, molded, amber glass, surface with overall net patter, bottom with raised sunburst pattern, middle with 1/2" band "Bogardus Glass Ball Patd April 18 1877," chips at neck **200.00**

Tinder box, 4-3/8" d, tin, candle socket, inside damper, flint, and steel . . **330.00**

Tinder lighter, flintlock

5-1/2" l, rosewood pistol grip, tooled brass fittings **750.00**

6-1/2" l, compartment for extra flint, taper holder **550.00**

Uniform button mold, 9" l, brass, American, 18th C, casts six round buttons with central raised letter "I" for infantry, one 25 mm, one 18 mm, four 14.5 mm, each with eyelet, wooden handles missing **625.00**

Water keg, 9" x 7-1/2" x 9", wooden, American, late 18th/early 19th C, oval, flattened bottom, two Shaker-style wide-tongued wooden straps, large hand-forged nail on each end for carrying cord, orig wood stopper **400.00**

FIREARMS

History: The 15th-century Matchlock Arquebus was the forerunner of the modern firearm. The Germans refined the wheelock firing mechanism during the 16th and 17th centuries. English settlers arrived in America with the smoothbore musket; German settlers had rifled arms. Both used the new flintlock firing mechanism.

A major advance was achieved when Whitney introduced interchangeable parts into the manufacturing of rifles. Continued refinements in firearms continued in the 19th century. The percussion ignition system was developed by the 1840s. Minie, a French military officer, produced a viable projectile. By the end of the 19th century, cartridge weapons dominated the field.

References: Robert W. D. Ball, *Mauser Military Rifles of the World*, Krause Publications, 1996; Robert W. D. Ball, *Mauser Military Rifles of the World*, 2nd ed., Krause Publications, 2001; Robert W. D. Ball, *Remington Firearms*, Krause Publications; ——, *Springfield Armory Shoulder Weapons, 1795-1968*, Antique Trader Books, 1997; Ralf Coykendall, Jr., *Coykendall's Complete Guide to Sporting Collectibles*, Wallace-Homestead, 1996; Norman Flayderman, *Flayderman's Guide to Antique American Firearms and Their Values*, 7th ed., Krause Publications, 1998; *Gun Trader's Guide*, 15th ed., Stoeger Publishing, 1992; Herbert G. Houze, *Colt Rifles and Muskets from 1847-1870*, Krause Publications, 1996; ——, *History of Winchester Repeating Arms Company*, Krause Publications, 1994; David D. Kowalski, *Standard Catalog of Winchester*, Krause Publications, 2000; Harold A. Murtz, *Guns Illustrated 2000*, 32nd ed., Krause Publications, 1999; John Ogle, *Colt Memorabilia Price Guide*, Krause Publications, 1998; Russell and Steve Quertermous, *Modern Guns Identification & Values*, 13th ed., Collector Books, 2000; Ken Ramage, ed., *Gun Digest 2001*, 55th ed., Krause Publications, 2000; Ken Ramage, ed., *Gun Digest 2002*, 56th ed., Krause Publications, 2001; Ken Ramage, ed., *Guns Illustrated 2001*, 33rd ed., Krause Publications, 2000; Ken Ramage, ed., *Guns Illustrated 2002*, 34th ed., Krause Publications, 2001; Ken Ramage, ed., *Handguns 2000*, 12th ed., Krause Publications, 1999; Ken Ramage, ed., *Handguns 2001*, 13th ed., Krause Publications, 2000; Ken Ramage, ed., *Handguns 2002*, 14th ed., Krause Publications, 2001; Ned Schwing, *Browning Superposed*, Krause Publications, 1996; Ned Schwing, *Standard Catalog of Firearms*, 9th ed., Krause Publications, 1999; Ned Schwing, *2002 Standard Catalog of Firearms*, 12th ed., Krause Publications, 2002; Jim Supica and Richard Nahas, *Standard Catalog of Smith & Wesson*, Krause Publications, 1996; John Taffin, *Action Shooting: Cowboy Style*, Krause Publications, 1999; John Taffin, *Big Bore Sixguns*, Krause Publications, 1997; Tom Turpin, *Modern Custom Guns*, Krause Publications, 1997; Tom Turpin, *Custom Firearms Engraving*, Krause Publications, 1999; John Walter, *Rifles of the World*, Krause Publications, 1998; Ken Warner, ed., *Gun Digest 2000*, 54th ed., Krause Publications, 1999; Tom Webster, edited by David D. Kowalski, *Winchester Rarities*, Krause Publications, 2000.

Periodicals: *Grand Times*, P.O. Box 1592, Rocky Point, NY 11778; *Gun List*, 700 E. State St., Iola, WI 54990; *Gun Report*, P.O. Box 38, Aledo, IL 61231; *Historic Weapons & Relics*, 2650 Palmyra Road, Palmyra, TN 37142; *Man at Arms*, P.O. Box 460, Lincoln, RI 02865; *Single Shot Exchange*, P.O. Box 1055, York, SC 29745-1055.

Collectors' Clubs: American Single Shot Rifle Assoc., 625 Pine St., Marquette, MI 49855-3723, http://www.assra.com; Arizona Arms Assoc., P.O. Box 46464, Phoenix, AZ 85063-6464, http://www.azarms.com; Browning Collectors Assoc., 5603-B W. Friendly Ave., Suite 166, Greensboro, NC 27410; Colt Collectors Assoc., P.O. Box 2241, Los Gatos, CA 95031-2241, http://www.coltcollectorsassoc.com; Dallas Arms Collectors Assoc., Inc., P.O. Box 704, DeSoto, TX 75123, http://www.dallasarms.com; Garand Collectors Assoc., P.O. Box 181, Richmond, KY 40476-0181, http://www.garandcollector.org; German Gun

Collectors Assoc., P.O. Box 385, Meriden, NH 03770-0385, http://www.germanguns.com; Mannlicher Collectors Assoc., P.O. Box 7144, Salem, OR, 97303; National Mossberg Collectors Assoc., P.O. Box 487, Festus, MO 63028-0487; National Automatic Pistol Collectors Assoc., P.O. Box 15738, St. Louis, MO 63163; National Rifle Assoc., 11250 Waples Mill Road, Fairfax, VA 22030, http://www.nrahq.org; New York State Arms Collectors Assoc., 24 S. Montain Terrace, Binghamton, NY 13902-3128; Potomac Arms & Collectors Assoc., P.O. Box 6641, Silver Spring, MD 20916-6641; Ontario Arms Collectors' Assoc., P.O. Box 477, Richmond Hill, Ontario L4C 4&8 Canada; Winchester Arms Collectors Association, Inc., P.O. Box 230, Brownsboro, TX 75756-0230.

Museums: Battlefield Military Museum, Gettysburg, PA; Museum of Weapons & Early American History, Saint Augustine, FL 32084; National Firearms Museum, Washington, DC; Remington Gun Museum, Ilion, NY; Springfield Armory National Historic Site, Springfield, MA; Winchester Mystery House, Historic Firearms Museum, San Jose, CA.

Notes: Two factors control the pricing of firearms—condition and rarity. Variations in these factors can cause a wide range in the value of antique firearms. For instance, a Colt 1849 pocket-model revolver with a 5-inch barrel can be priced from $100 to $700, depending on whether all the component parts are original, some are missing, how much of the original finish (bluing) remains on the barrel and frame, how much silver plating remains on the brass trigger guard and back strap, and the condition and finish of the walnut grips.

Be careful to note a weapon's negative qualities. A Colt Peterson belt revolver in fair condition will command a much higher price than the Colt pocket model in very fine condition. Know the production run of a firearm before buying it.

Laws regarding the sale of firearms have gotten more strict. Be sure to sell and buy firearms through auction houses and dealers properly licensed to transact business in this highly regulated area.

Carbine

Burnside Precision, 21" round barrel, orig dark finish, bold inspectors' marks and signatures, 39-1/2" l, as found condition **1,320.00**

Hall-North, Model 1843, percussion, .52 caliber, rifled 21" barrel, bold metal stampings, signature and 1849 on receiver, traces of old brown finish, walnut stock with old split between trigger guard and barrel, small repairs near breech, 40" l **935.00**

Maynard Percussion, Civil-War era, orig dark finish, inspector's markings on walnut stock, areas of faint case coloring on receiver, bold stampings, 20" blued barrel, 36-3/4" l **1,450.00**

Joslyn Model 1862, .52 caliber, 22" round barrel, walnut stock, clear inspector's markings, brass buttplate, trigger guard and barrel band, stamped signatures on lock and breech block, 38-5/8" l **650.00**

C. S. Richmond, .58 caliber, 25" barrel, all-steel hardware, brass nose cap, buttplate stamped "U.S.," Type 3, humpback lock, "C. S. Richmond, 1864" mark, no sling swivels, 43" l **3,300.00**

Sharp's New Model 1863, breech loading, walnut stock and forearm, double inspectors markings, 22" blued barrel, areas of very light case coloring on lock, buttplate, hammer, barrel band, and receiver, clear stampings on lock, 34" l **1,980.00**

Spencer

Civil War Model, .52 caliber rimfire, 22" round barrel, overall brown finish on all metal surfaces, worn walnut stick, faint inspector's mark, forearm with additional coat of varnish, 39" l **2,100.00**

Contract Model 1865, Burnside Rifle Co., unusual stamping on buttstock "U. S. Col. Ter.," .50 caliber, 20" round barrel, good inspector's markings on stock, overall chocolate brown patina on metal surfaces, old split on one side of buttstock, one early cartridge, 37" l **2,650.00**

Springfield, Model 1884 Trapdoor, saddle ring, mint bore, Buffington sight, stamped "C. Proper," range with inspector's cartouche **825.00**

Wesson, Frank, 28" octagonal barrel, folding rear peep sight, walnut stock with orig dark finish, rear open sight missing, 43" l overall **275.00**

Colt model 1851 Navy, engraved to corporal in 15th Kansas Cavalry, **$2,750.**

Dueling pistols, percussion lock

English, London, second quarter 19th C, dolphin hammer, belt clip, engraved scrollwork on frame, checkered burl-wood grip, barrel engraved "London," 8-1/2" l, price for pr . . **650.00**

English, Queen-Anne style, London, for J. Wilson, late 18th C, scrolled mask butt, grip set with small monogrammed cartouche, plain stylized dolphin hammer, cannon barrel engraved with cartouches, and maker's mark on underside, 8" l, price for pr **500.00**

Flintlock long arms

French, Model 1766 Charlesville Musket, 44-3/4" l orig barrel length, lockplate only partially legible, matching ramrod, top jaw and top screw period replacements . . . **1,250.00**

Kentucky, N. Beyer, .50 caliber, orig smooth bore, 58-1/2" overall, 42-1/2" part rounded barrel, orig front sight mounted on light engraved brass oval, sgd in script "N. Beyer" on top flat and secured to stock with incise carving on the fore end to the faceted brass tailpipe, two faceted brass ramrod pipes and brass fore-end cap, beveled brass sideplate, raised scroll carving about tang with lightly engraved silver oval wrist escutcheon, incise carving at wrist on right side, left side with raised carved scrolls, a large raised carved scroll to rear of cheek piece, engraved brass patch box with bird finial, typical Beyer beveled brass trigger guard, reconverted barrel and lock . . **3,650.00**

Pennsylvania, attributed to W. Haga, Reading School, 50-1/2" l octagon to round barrel, maple stock, relief carving, incised details, brass hardware with flintlock, some age cracks, glued repair, good patina, replaced patch box lid **1,760.00**

U. S. Model 1808, Thomas French, Canton, MA, Contract Musket, Harpers Ferry pattern, tail of lock stamped "Canton/1810," below the pan with the eagle and "US" over "FRENCH"

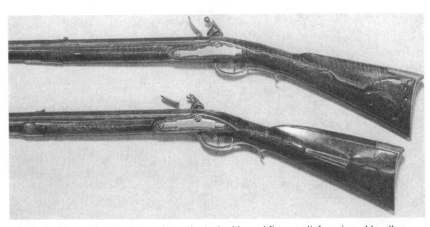

Flintlock long rifles, top: VA, curly maple stock with good figure, relief carving, old mellow varnished finish, brass hardware includes engraved and pierced patch box, "Ketland" lock skillfully converted back to flint, silver thumb piece inlay, 41-1/2" l barrel and forend shortened slightly, top flat engraved "H.B.," $3,300. Bottom: PA, attributed to W. Haga of the Reading school, 50-1/2" octagon to round barrrel, maple stock with relief carving and incised detail, brass hardware with a flintlock, some age cracks, glued repair, patch box lid replaced, $1,760. Photo courtesy of Garth's Auctions.

(well struck with no trace of "T"), barrel stamped "US/V," with sunken eagle head CT proof (Flayderman 9A-131)................. **1,200.00**

U. S. Model 1819, Hall, breech loading, second-production type, Harpers Ferry Armory, John Hall's patents, .52 caliber, single shot, 32-5/8" round barrel, three barrel bands, brechblock deeply stamped................. **1,200.00**

Virginia, curly-maple stock with good figure, relief carving, old mellow varnished finish, brass hardware, engraved and pierced patch box, Ketland lock reconverted back to flint, silver thumb piece inlay, 41-1/2" l barrel and fore-end shortened slightly, small pierced repair at breech area, top flat engraved "H. B." **3,300.00**

Flintlock pistols-single shot
English

Blunderbuss, 29-1/2" overall, 14" round iron barrel with Birmingham proofs, fitted with 12-1/2" triangular snap bayonet, walnut full stock with lightly engraved brass furniture, two ramrod pipes, buttplate, trigger guard, small shield-shaped wrist plate, two lock-plate screw escutcheons, attributed to John Whitehouse, early 19th C, metal parts complete and orig throughout, missing sliver of wood along right side at muzzle.............. **1,500.00**

Tower, .60 caliber, 12" round barrel, full-length military stock, brass

trigger guard, butt cap and sidelined, lockplate marked "Tower" behind hammer and crown over "GR" forward of hammer, proofed on left side of barrel at breech, crown on tang behind tang screw, good condition, re-browned and cleaned, replaced front sight, working order.......... **700.00**

European, blunderbuss, .70 caliber, 16" brass barrel, brass trigger guard and buttplate, full stock, lock plate marked with crown over "R" under pan, good condition, mellow brass patina, working order, all orig **750.00**

French, military, 16" overall length, 9" round iron barrel, flat beveled lockplate with faceted pan fitted with flat beveled reinforced hammer, brass furniture, unmarked **800.00**

Halsbach & Sons, Baltimore, MD, holster pistol, c1785 to early 1800s, 9" brass part round, part octagon barrel, .65 caliber, lock marked "Halsbach & Sons," large brass butt cap with massive spread wing eagle (primitive) in high relief surrounded by cluster of 13 stars, large relief shell carving around tang of barrel, full walnut stock, pin-fastened **1,750.00**

Kentucky, T. B. Cherington, 12-1/2" octagonal smoothbore barrel, stamped "T. P. Cherington" on barrel and lockplate, .45 caliber, brightly polished iron parts, walnut stock **2,500.00**

Middle Eastern, 9" tapered barrel with several touch marks, relief carved stock

with ornate brass butt cap, 16-1/2" l
.... **175.00**

U. S. Model 1805, 10" round iron barrel with iron rib underneath holding ramrod pipe, lockplate marked with spread eagle and shield over "US" and vertically at rear "Harper's Ferry" over "1808," .54 caliber, walnut half stock with brass buttplate and trigger guard, Flayderman 6A-008 .... **3,000.00**

Musket

Colt, Model 1861, .58 caliber, 39" barrel, "17th N.Y.V." beneath stock, good signature, date, and stampings on metal, inspector's cartouche on stock, bright gray metal, areas of pitting around bolster and lock..... **1,375.00**

Harper's Ferry, browned lock stamped with eagle, signature, and 1851, trumpet head ramrod, walnut stock stamped "Ohio," small pierced repair near tang of buttplate, 57-1/2" l . **770.00**

Parker Snow & Co., Miller conversion, 40" round barrel, bold stampings include signature, eagle, and 1864 on lock, 56" overall **1,375.00**

Tower, percussion, sling, triangular bayonet, orig browned surfaces on barrel, lock, and barrel bands, signature with 1862 and crown on lock plate, walnut stock stamped "Birmingham small arms trade" with stamped crown, brass buttplate, trigger guard, 55-1/4" l........... **2,100.00**

U.S. Moro, large bore, 31-1/2" round barrel, single shot, center fire, may have been made to shoot shot shells, pulls apart at center for loading, walnut stock with fine figure, 45" l.......... **250.00**

Percussion pistol
English

Folding bayonet, simple engraving on frame, stands of flags and "Lenning," old hairlines in grip, 4" l barrel, 8-1/2" l **250.00**

Single shot, sgd "W. Parker" on lock, "Maker to His Majesty, London" on barrel, finely checkered bag grip, narrow pierced repair just below lock, 8-1/4" l............. **715.00**

I. N. Johnson 1842, Navy Model, anchor mark on breech, inspectors initials, .54 caliber, 8-1/2" barrel, brass hardware, walnut stock, faint inspector's cartouche, areas of light pitting, 14" l....................... **770.00**

U. S. Springfield, lock stamped with signature and 1856, eagle on Maynard primer door, 12" barrel dated 1855, brass hardware with iron backstrap, walnut shoulder stock, brass hardware, few hairlines, pierced repair on hammer, 28-1/2" l **1,750.00**

Waters, 8-1/2" round barrel, bright metal, stamped address and "1838" on lock, double inspector markings on stock, 14" l **660.00**

Pistol

Colt, Model 1911 Army, .45 caliber auto, orig blued finish, checkered walnut grips, good signature and other stampings, 8-1/2" l **825.00**

Sharp's Pepperbox, four shot, .22 caliber, 3" barrels, traces of orig bluing, stamped signature, patent information around hammer screw, gutta percha grips with checkered design, 5-1/2" l **220.00**

Volcanic Lever Action, Navy, .38 caliber, 8" barrel, signature "The Volcanic Repeating Arms Co." on top, walnut grips, brass frame with old patina, minor pitting on one side, tab for magazine tube broken, spring missing, 14-1/2" l **9,900.00**

Revolver

Colt

Model 1849 Pocket, 4" barrel, .31 caliber, faint New York address, all serial numbers matching, replaced catch **495.00**

Model 1849 Pocket, 5" barrel, silver plate remaining on trigger guard, good cylinder scene, all serials numbers matching **715.00**

Model 1851 Navy, all serial numbers matching, .36 caliber, 7-1/2" octagon barrel, cylinder scene remaining, "U.S." and "Colts Patent" stamped on frame, New York address, old replaced grips, 13-3/8" l **1,850.00**

Model 1851, Navy, .36 caliber, 7-1/2" barrel, faint New York address on barrel, brass trigger guard and grip straps, orig walnut grips, 13-1/2" l **495.00**

Model 1851 Navy, .36 caliber, percussion, all serial numbers matching, Hartford address on barrel, one screwhead damaged below barrel, grip chips, 13" l **1,320.00**

Model 1851 Navy, stainless steel model, 7-1/2" barrel, overall bright finish, New York address, Colt's patent, all serial numbers match, small pieced repair on grip, sold with orig Colt mold, screwdriver,

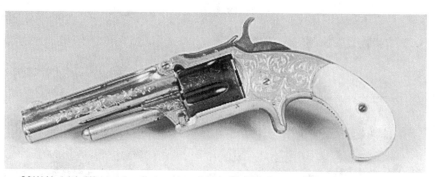

S&W Model 1-1/2 ivory-handled revolver, 7.5" l, **$1,320.** *Photo courtesy of Jackson's Auctioneers & Appraisers.*

and caps, old but not orig case **1,320.00**

Model 1860 Army, matching serial numbers, butt signature, New York address, overall light brown to gray surface on metal, brass trigger guard, iron grip straps, 8" barrel, 14" overall, old corner chips on grips, period black leather holster with raised "U. S." design and eight or three over stamped "G" on front flap, worn to grain, 13" l **675.00**

Lefaucheux Pin Rimfire, old bright surface on barrel, frame, and cylinder, bold signature and proofmarks, walnut grips finely alligatored varnish, 6-3/8" octagon to round barrel, one Lefaucheux cartridge on mount, 12-1/2" l **450.00**

Remington

Beals, 7-3/4" barrel, 13-1/2" l, old dark finish **825.00**

Model 1858, .44 caliber, 8" octagonal barrel, good signature with faint inspector's stamp on grips, 14" l **880.00**

Model 1861 Navy, 7-3/8" octagon barrel, all over matte gray finish, signature stamp **990.00**

Rifle

Allin Conversion Model 1866, 40" round barrel, worn browned finish, three bands, "U. S. Springfield" lock with eagle and 1865 date, walnut stock, in-the-making file marks, 56" l . . **250.00**

Percussion, half stock

Partial stamped signatures on lock and barrel for J. Henry & Son, 36-3/8" octagon barrel with browned surface, walnut stock, stepped beaver tail, steel buttplate, brass trigger guard, nickel silver inlays, small "U. S." stamp just below trigger guard,

52-1/2" l, orig 8-1/2" l powder horn **950.00**

Very faint signature possibly J. Henry & Son, 37 octagon barrel with browned surface, curly-maple stock, engraved brass hardware, engraved cap box, beavertail cheek piece, hammer restoration, some deterioration behind bolster, 54" l **220.00**

Remington, rolling block

Military, approx .45 caliber, full stock, three barrel bands, 35" tapered round barrel with adjustable rear sight, clear signature on tag, ramrod missing, 50-1/2" l **220.00**

Remington signature and address on tang, crown proofs, "G" stamp on buttstock, old dark finish, brass handle bayonet, dents, one band spring mission, 50" l **330.00**

Spencer Repeating, 30" round barrel with three bands, walnut stock, old refinish, traces of inspector's stamp, brass inlay added to top of comb, few chips, 47" l **2,310.00**

Springfield, Model 1873 Trapdoor, 45-70 caliber, cadet model, 29-1/2" round blued barrel, three click tumbler, eagle mark and signature on lock with eagle's head and "V. P." on breech area, minor dents on stock, ramrod, 48-3/4" l **450.00**

Shotgun

European, double barrel, 12 gauge, 30-1/2" Damascus barrels, silver band overlay, sgd "R. Baumgarter in Bernburg" on barrel, engraved stag on tang, "Hubertus Geweher," figured walnut stock, horn trigger guard, 47" l **275.00**

Fox Sterlingworth, 16 gauge, double barrel, 26" barrel, top lever break-open, hammerless, double trigger, blued, checkered walnut pistol grip stock and forearm **400.00**

Ithaca, Grade 2E NID, four-barrel set, cal. 10 gauge, 32, 30, and two 28" barrels, all numbered to receiver and all fitted with ejectors and marked 3-1/2" chambers, one set of 28" barrels appears to be of later origin (marked SB & Co.), all four sets marked with Grade 2 designation, double beads, received fitted with single trigger and cocked indicators, typical Grade 2 engraved with standing quail on left side and woodcock on right with light coarse floral engraving to back and bottom, professional replacement wood with wide carved and checkered beavertail forearm, heavy carved and checkered cheek piece buttstock, 14-7/8" over an Ithaca recoil pad, refinished trigger guard **2,000.00**

Parker GHE, double barrel, cal. 28 gauge, standard Parker configuration, 26" barrels on double "O" frame, double triggers and ejectors, splinter forearm, pistol grip stock, 14-3/8" over an ancient leather faced pad, receiver is game scene engraved with flying mallards, quail, and pheasants, surrounded by Arabesque patterns, 96% orig bright barrel blue, numerous small handing marks **6,250.00**

Savage Model 720, 12 gauge, 4-shot tubular, 30" cylinder bore, Browning patent, semi-automatic, hammerless, blued, checkered walnut pistol grip stock and forearm, plain receiver **200.00**

Stevens, Model 970, 12 gauge, single shot, 32" l round barrel with octagonal breech, top lever break-open, hammerless, automatic shell ejector, automatic safety, blued, case hardened frame, checkered walnut pistol grip stock and forearm **95.00**

FIREHOUSE COLLECTIBLES

History: The volunteer fire company has played a vital role in the protection and social growth of many towns and rural areas. Paid professional firemen usually are found only in large metropolitan areas. Each fire company prided itself on equipment and uniforms. Conventions and parades gave the fire companies a chance to show off their equipment. These events produced a wealth of firehouse-related memorabilia.

References: Andrew G. Gurka, *Hot Stuff! Firefighting Collectibles,* L-W Book Sales, 1994; Ed Lindley Peterson, *First to the Flames: The History of Fire Chief*

Vehicles, Krause Publications, 1999; Sandra Frost Piatti and James G. Piatti, *Firefighting Antiques & Memorabilia,* Schiffer Publishing, 2001; Donald F. Wood and Wayne Sorensen, *Big City Fire Trucks, 1900-1950,* Krause Publications, 1996 (Volume I), 1997 (Volume II).

Periodicals: *Fire Apparatus Journal,* P.O. Box 141295, Staten Island, NY 10314, http://fireapparatusjournal.com; *Fire Collector News,* P.O. Box 2393, Conroe, TX 77305-2393, http://www.firecollector.com; *Fire Patch Collector,* P.O. Box 2393, Conroe, TX 77305-2393, http://www.firecollector.com.

Collectors' Clubs: Fire Collectors Club, P.O. Box 992, Milwaukee, WI 53201; Fire Mark Circle of the Americas, 2859 Marlin Dr., Chamblee, GA 30341, http://www.firemarkcircle.org; Gibson Road Antique Fire Association, 1545 Gibson Road, Bensalem, PA 19020, http://www.grafa.org; Great Lakes International Antique Fire Apparatus Association, P.O. Box 2519, Detroit, MI 48231; Society for the Preservation & Appreciation of Motor Fire Apparatus in America, 5420 S. Kedvale Ave., Chicago, IL 60632, http://www.spaamfaa.org.

Museums: American Museum of Fire Fighting, Hudson, NY, http://www.firemumsumnetwork.org; Fire Museum of Maryland, Lutherville, MD; Hall of Flame, Phoenix AZ, http://www.halloflame.org; Insurance Company of North America (INA) Museum, Philadelphia, PA; New England Fire & History Museum, Brewster, MA; New York City Fire Museum, New York, NY, http://nyfd.com/museum.html; Oklahoma State Fireman's Association Museum, Oklahoma City, OK, http://tulsaweb.com/FIREMUS.HTML; San Francisco Fire Dept. Memorial Museum, San Francisco, CA; Smokey's Fire Museum, Chamblee, GA; Toledo Firefighters Museum, Toledo, OH, http://www.toledolink.com/~matgerke/~thm.

Additional Listings: See *Warman's Americana & Collectibles* for more examples.

Advertising

Calendar, Quincy Mutual Fire Insurance Co., 1889, three rats playing with box of stick matches, burnt claws, coming to cat holding Quincy fire policy, 9-3/4" x 6-1/2" **575.00**

Ink blotter, Fireman's Fund 75th Year, Allendale, CA, fireman with little child, 1938, 4" x 9" **7.50**

Ledger marker, Caisse General Fire Insurance, statue of Liberty illus, multicolored, tin litho, 12-1/4" l, 3" w **275.00**

Alarm call box, Gamewell Fire Alarm Tel. Co., cast iron, 12" h **115.00**

Badge, brass

Allison H. & L. Co., No. 2, pendant with 1" gray/black cello insert picture PA State Capitol Bldg, inscribed, "Harrisburg, PA, State Fireman's Convention, PA, Oct. 3-4-5, 1923" **15.00**

Engine lamp, left: six-sided main engine lamp, ruby, cobalt blue, and clear panels, wheel cut scrolling vines and "H&L 1," front-hinged panel with city seal of Manchester, New Hampshire, one H&L panel cracked, **$8,625;** *center: brass main engine lamp, Brookline, MA, c1873, by "Devoursney Bros NY," with twin cobalt blue shield-shaped panels etched with name "Thomas Parson," crossed axes, trumpet and foliate decoration, single ruby panel with American eagle and shield on smoky ground, clear panel (cracked) with shield and foliate etching, original burner and shell finial, double chimney, 19-1/2" h,* **$6,900;** *right: main engine lamp, two blue etched beveled glass panels "American 5," one clear beveled panel with floral, foliate, and geometric etching, one plain red panel, Devoursney Bros. Maker, 19" h,* **$2,300.** *Photo courtesy of Skinner Auctions.*

C.B.F.D. No. 1/Cresson, PA, silvered, pale bronze luster over raised center relief image of fire fighting symbols, 1930s **20.00**

Bell, 11", brass, iron back **125.00**

Belt, red, black, and white, 43" l, marked "Hampden" **85.00**

Book, *Fireground Tactics,* Emanuel Fried, Ginn Publishing, 1972, 1st ed., 372 pgs **25.00**

Fire bucket, painted leather

12-1/2" h, green body, leaf dec banner "E. Sargent 1827," black painted rim and handle, some minor cracking to paint, pr **3,500.00**

13" h, inscribed "Garibaldi" in scrolled banner in gold, green, and black, red ground, leather handle, minor wear **3,080.00**

13" h, inscribed "Waltham Fire Club 1824 J. Hastings" in gilt on dark green ground, red band and int., handle missing, paint loss and abrasion **460.00**

Fire engine cart, 48" l, wooden, iron frame, hand lever propelled **750.00**

Fire extinguisher

Babcock, American La France Fire Engine Co., Elmire, NY, grenade, amber glass **500.00**

Hayward's Hand Fire Grenade, yellow, ground mouth, smooth base, 6-1/4" h, c1870 ...... **85.00**

Red Comet, red metal canister, red glass bulb **50.00**

Fire mark, cast iron, oval

8" x 11-1/2", relief molded design, pumper framed by "Fire Department Insurance," polychrome paint **495.00**

8" x 12", black, gold eagle and banner dec, marked "Eagle Ins. Co. Cin O" **950.00**

Helmet

Leather, four-comb type, painted red, black brim, gilt inscribed shield, "o. 3-EBD," orig padded straw liner, early 19th C . . **1,800.00**

Oil cloth, blue, tin shield inscribed "Niagara 3 Brunswick," red under brim, early 19th C **1,200.00**

Lantern, Dietz, King Fire Dept., copper bottom **150.00**

Magazine, *Blazes,* March-June issue, American-Lafrance-Foamite, Elmira, NY, 1950, 28 pgs, 8-1/2" x 11", articles and illus relating to fires, fire fighting **18.00**

Medal, Jacksonville Fire Co., silvered brass, firefighting symbols circled by "I.A.F.E.-1917-Jaconsville, Fla.," reverse "Compliments of N. Snellenburg & Co. Uniforms, Philadelphia, Pa," looped ring **15.00**

Nozzle, hose, 16" l, brass, double handle, marked "Akron Brass Mfg. Co., Inc." **165.00**

Parade hat, 6-1/2" h, painted leather, polychrome dec, green ground, front with eagle and harp, banner above "Hibernia," back inscribed "1752" in gilt, "1" on top, red brim underside, some age cracks, small losses to brim edge **3,335.00**

Pinback button

Fairfax Fire Department, blue and white, pink tint on engine of cartoon fire vehicle, inscribed for July 4th celebration, attached red, white, and blue ribbon, c1920, ribbon badly faded **15.00**

Myerstown Fire Co., blue and white, real photo of motorized fire engine linked to primitive pumper, early 1900s **15.00**

Presentation trumpet, 16-1/4" h, coin silver, derby-style bell, inscribed "Presented by the City of Lowell to Mazeppa Engine Company No. 10 for the Third Best Horizontal Playing July 4, 1856" **1,500.00**

Print, 9-1/2" x 13-1/2", hand colored lithograph, "Prairie Fires of the Great West," Currier and Ives, publishers, identified in inscriptions in matrix, period frame **320.00**

Stickpin, Firemen's Celebration, celluloid, multicolored portrait, brass stickpin, early 1900s **12.00**

Toy

Arcade, fire chief car, cast iron, painted red, cast bell on hood, emb "Chief" on doors, orig decal on front hood, rubber tires, 5" l **1,650.00**

Arcade, fire pumper, 1941 Ford, cast iron, painted red, emb sides, cast fireman, hose reel on bed, rubber tires, repaired fender, 13" l . **440.00**

Arcade, ladder truck, cast iron, painted red, two cast fireman, rubber tires, bed contains ladder supports, open frame design, 9-1/4" l **440.00**

Hubley, Ahrens Fox fire engine, cast iron, rubber tires, 7-1/2" l ... **475.00**

Hubley, Hubley Fire Dept., cast iron pumper, fire chief's car, hose reel truck, Harley Davidson with police driver, painted red, silver highlights, 9-1/2" x 14", orig box **2,750.00**

Kenton, fire pumper, cast iron, painted red, gold highlights on boiler, and ball, emb sides, disc wheels with spoke centers **615.00**

Kingsbury, horse-drawn ladder wagon, sheet metal, pained red, wire supports, holding yellow wooden ladders, two seated drivers, pulled by two black horses, yellow spoke wheels, bell on frame rings as toy is pulled, 26" l **2,150.00**

Williams, A. C., fire pumper, cast iron, painted red, gold highlights, cast driver, bell, and boiler, rear platform with railing, rubber tires, 7-1/2" l **315.00**

FIREPLACE EQUIPMENT

History: In the colonial home, the fireplace was the gathering point for heat, meals, and social interaction. It maintained its dominant position until the introduction of central heating in the mid-19th century.

Because of the continued popularity of the fireplace, accessories still are manufactured, usually in an early-American motif.

References: John Campbell, *Fire & Light in the Home Pre-1820,* Antique Collectors' Club, 1999; Rupert Gentle and Rachael Feild, *Domestic Metalwork 1640-1820,* revised, Antique Collectors' Club, 1994; George C. Neumann, *Early American Antique Country Furnishings,* L-W Book Sales, 1984, 1993 reprint.

Reproduction Alert: Modern blacksmiths are reproducing many old iron implements.

Additional Listings: Brass and Ironware.

Andirons, pair, bronze, top surmounted by full-length putti, tripod plinth, ram's head and satyr supports, base with inverted griffin supports, center allegorical figure flanked by putti, mid-19th C, 36" h, **$4,375.** *Photo courtesy of Freeman/Fine Arts of Philadelphia, Inc.*

Andirons, pr

8-3/4" w, 21-1/2" d, 19-3/4" h, iron, snake-form, heads with open mouths, projecting tongues on S-form bodies ending in coiled tails, bolted to log supports, 19th C, surface rust **5,465.00**

9-3/4" w, 16" d, 16" h, iron, ball tops, vase and ring-form shafts joining short curved legs, penny feet, straight log supports, ball top log stops, old surface, Rhode Island, mid-18th C, some surface corrosion **1,495.00**

9-3/4" w, 18" d, 18" h, brass and iron, flame over faceted ball brass finials, baluster form iron shafts, arched legs, penny feet, attributed to PA, mid to late 18th C, imperfections **635.00**

10-3/4" w, 20-1/2" d, 21-1/2" h, brass and iron, belted lemon tops, conforming finials over ring turned and faceted shafts, cabriole legs with spurred knees and ankles, ball feet, stepped leg supports, old surface, America, c1800, minor imperfections **825.00**

11-3/4" w, 24" d, 16-3/4" h, brass, belted ball top with finials, ring-form shafts, cabriole legs, spurred knees, arris slipper feet, conforming stops, straight log supports, sgd "Davis Boston," c1801, old surface, minor imperfections **690.00**

16" h, brass, Louis XIV-style, guilloche-molded urn on trefoil-diapered base centered by husk swags, rect bow front base, 20th C **300.00**

Andirons, pair, brass plated, black metal ball and finial, 20-1/2" h, **$145.**

Bellows, turtleback

12" w, 20-1/4" d, 26-3/4" h, engraved metal and iron, Chippendale, urn-on-urn finials, engraved tassel bows an swags over turned columns, sq plinth, engraved edges, spurred cabriole legs ending with ball and claw feet, urn top, turned column and plinth log stops, attributed to Philadelphia, c1775 . . . . **6,900.00**

17-1/4" l, orig yellow paint, green edging, red, green, and copper colored fruit, brass nozzle, leather has wear, some damage, minor wear to paint **615.00**

17-1/2" l, orig red paint, dark green (black) and copper colored fruit, yellow accents, smoked black and copper edging, brass nozzle, releathered, some wear, some alligatoring **360.00**

18-1/4" l, orig black over cream smoke dec on both sides, fruit and foliage on front, gold and black

stenciled border, touch-up on green leaves and handle, expertly restored leather **385.00**

Bench, 29-5/8" l, 9" w, 9-1/4" h, seat with openwork slats, six turned and tapered brass legs, tufted white vinyl cushion, early 20th C **360.00**

Coal hood, 16-1/2" w, 13" d, 19-3/4" h, Neoclassical-style, late 19th C, brass, rect, serpentine sloped hinged lid set with husk swag, two reeded handles on side, front hammered with stylized floral motif, hoof feet, removable tin liner **325.00**

Additional Listings: Brass and Ironware.

Fender

39-1/2" w, 13" d, 10-1/4" h, brass and wire, D-form, brass top rail over wirework screen with scroll motifs, England or America, c1800, minor imperfections **815.00**

39-1/2" w, 14" d, 24" h, brass and wire, D-form, brass top rail over conforming wirework screen with swag and scroll work, England or America, late 18th/early 19th C, minor imperfections **1,840.00**

52-1/2" l, brass, pierced and engraved pairs of lions among scrolling leaves **400.00**

55-1/2" w, 23" d, 24" h, wire and brass, bowed front, vertical wire rods and decorative wire weaving, unraveling of wire at base . . **495.00**

Fireboard, 31-1/2" w, 10" d, 32" h, attributed to Northeast, c1840, sq mitered shadowbox frame with faux marble paint, central portion with large chained dog, small seated man with hat at base of post, old surface, losses **4,600.00**

Fire dogs, pr

7-1/2" w, 6-1/2" h, brass, central horizontal reeded orb raised on three reeded legs, reeded horizontal bar on top, Aesthetic Movement, English, third quarter 19th C **150.00**

15" h, cast iron, rampant lion bearing twisted horizontal bars, seated on ropetwist rounded and octagonal base, late 19th/early 20th C **700.00**

Fireplace surround, 29-1/2" l, Renaissance-Revival style, 20th C, brass, two seated 6-1/2" w x 16" h griffins on teardrop and paterae bordered base, figures joined by fluted and flat leaf bar, single loop handle **1,725.00**

Fire screen, Arts and Crafts copper and iron, embossed owl flanked by fruit, whiplash feet, unmarked, English, cleaned patina, 32-1/2" x 18-1/2", **$2,185.** *Photo courtesy of David Rago Auctions.*

Fire screen

25" w, 36" h, Renaissance Revival, late 19th C, patinated brass frame, center grotesque mask at top and bottom, enclosing 16 caned beveled colorless glass panels, flat leaf and anthemion tripod base **375.00**

28-1/2" w, 44" h, mahogany frame carved with ginko leaves, leaded cameo glass insert center, etched with tall purple trees, sgd "Jacques Grueber," orig finish, Arts & Crafts styling **6,900.00**

Fire tools, brass

3-1/8" to 26-3/8" l, poker, tongs, and shovel, paneled handles ending in urns with horizontal reeding and stylized leaf engraving **175.00**

30" h, poker, tongs, and shovel, reeded knop handles, faceted knop terminals, late 19th/early 20th C **225.00**

Hearth broom, 28" l, orig red paint, black, yellow, and gold striping, stenciled and free hand dec in bronze powder and black, horse hair bristles, wear and flaking **250.00**

Kettle stand, 12" h, wrought iron, twisted iron cross member, ring top, smaller inner ring, penny feet . . . **200.00**

Log holder, 19-3/4" w, 18-3/4" d, 20" h, Arts & Crafts, L. and J. G. Stickley, slatted sides and foundation, cut-out handles, tapering posts, arched toe boards, orig finish, unmarked, minor scrapes and nicks **3,335.00**

Pole screen

English, Chippendale-style, mahogany, early petit point panel of urn with flowers, urn turned column, high tripod base with cabriole legs, scroll feet, relief rococo carving at knees, late 19th or 20th C, 54" h **440.00**

English, 1760-80, mahogany, pole with shaped top, turned tapering urn shaped pillar, cabriole leg base ending in arris pad feet on platforms, orig needlework panel, gold and blue floral pattern, brown ground, outlined with applied wood moldings, old surface, imperfections **5,175.00**

Irish, Chippendale, inlaid walnut and fruitwood veneers, oblong panel with scalloped edges, orig silk needlework of a dragon, saber legs with line border inlay graduate into triangular block with three turned supports, tripod base, short turned feet below applied blocks, some stains on fabric, few veneer chips missing, 53-1/2" h **470.00**

Tiles, pr, rect, each urn filled with lemon or tiger lilies, guilloche border, black ground, 9-1/2" w, 37-1/2" h ebonized frame, attributed to England, late 19th/early 20th C **1,035.00**

Trivet, 10-1/2" l, 4-3/4" d, 3-1/4" h, wrought iron, coiled snake form, incised underside, tripod base, 19th C, minor surface corrosion **980.00**

FISCHER CHINA

FISCHER J.
BUDAPEST.

History: In 1893, Moritz Fischer founded his factory in Herend, Hungary, a center of porcelain production since the 1790s.

Confusion exists about Fischer china because of its resemblance to Meissen, Sevres, and Oriental export wares. It often was bought and sold as the product of these firms.

Fischer's Herend is hard-paste ware with luminosity and exquisite decoration. Pieces are designated by pattern names, the best known being Chantilly Fruit, Rothschild Bird, Chinese Bouquet, Victoria Butterfly, and Parsley.

Fischer also made figural birds and animal groups, Magyar figures (individually and in groups), and Herend eagles poised for flight.

Museum: Victoria & Albert Museum, London, England.

Marks: Forged marks of other potteries are found on Herend pieces. The initials "MF," often joined together, is the mark of Moritz Fischer's pottery.

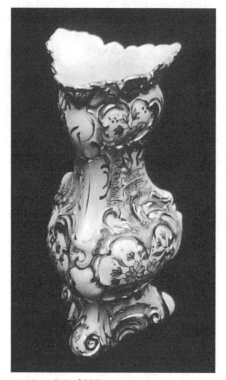

Vase, 9" h, **$295.**

Box, cov, 7-3/4" w, 4-3/8" h, delicate flowers on lattice, firing imperfections **195.00**

Bowl, 10" w, 5-1/2" h, leaf shape, reticulated, multicolored, marked "J. Fischer, Budapest" **750.00**

Cache pot, 5" h, Rothchild Bird pattern, handled **175.00**

Charger, 13" d, multicolored enameled floral dec, gold trim **350.00**

Ewer, 16-1/2" h, reticulated body, roe, blue, green, and gold enameled floral dec **295.00**

Jar, cov, 7-1/4" h, multicolored floral motif, raised relief medallions with reticulated fleur-de-lis, white ground, matching oval reticulated finial. . **275.00**

Jug, 10-3/4" h, Persian-style flowers and leaves, putty ground, gilt tracery, blue underglaze mark "Patent, J. Fischer Budapest," incised "575" **600.00**

Nappy, 4-1/2", triangular shape, Victoria Butterfly pattern, gold trim **150.00**

Pitcher, 12" h, reticulated, multicolored floral dec **350.00**

Plate, 7-1/2" d, Chantilly Fruit pattern **90.00**

Sauce boat, underplate, matching ladle, Parsley pattern **250.00**

Tureen, cov, 8-1/2" l, Chantilly Fruit pattern, natural molded fruit finial, handles **350.00**

Urn, 12" h, reticulated, blue floral dec, shield mark **250.00**

Vase, 15" h, signed "Fischer J. Budapest," **$750.**

Vase

13" h, 8" w, reticulated body, base, and neck, two winged serpent handles, blue, pink, and gold bands and accents, stamped in blue "Fischer J. Budapest" **395.00**

15-1/4" h, 7-1/2" w, wide flaring shaped top, gold dec vine and fruit handles, turquoise background, front panel with pear-shaped painting of birds in flowery landscape, back panel with flower spray on white ground, imp mark "C. F. 728," some loss to ruffled edge rim, pr **950.00**

FITZHUGH

History: Fitzhugh, one of the most recognized Chinese Export porcelain patterns, was named for the Fitzhugh family for whom the first dinner service was made. The peak years of production were 1780 to 1850.

Fitzhugh features an oval center medallion or monogram surrounded by four groups of flowers or emblems. The border is similar to that on Nanking china. Occasional border variations are found. Butterfly and honeycomb are among the rarest.

Reproduction Alert: Spode Porcelain Company, England, and Vista Alegre, Portugal, currently are producing copies of the Fitzhugh pattern. Oriental copies also are available.

Notes: Color is a key factor in pricing. Blue is the most common color; rarer colors are ranked in the following ascending order: orange, green, sepia, mulberry, yellow, black, and gold. Combinations of colors are scarce.

Platter, blue and white, 15-3/4" l, **$475.**

Basket, oval, reticulated, blue
   10-7/8" l **500.00**
   11" l, matching undertray,
     handles **1,500.00**
Bowl
   6-1/4" d, blue **220.00**
   9-3/4" d, shallow, scalloped rim,
     blue **125.00**
   10" w, sq, blue **325.00**
Brush box, cov, 7" w, 3-1/2" l, 2-1/4" h, blue, Nanking border, China, 19th C, minor cracks **575.00**
Creamer, 5-1/2" h, helmet shape, blue. **450.00**
Cup and saucer, blue, set of six **395.00**
Dish, 5-1/8" l, 5-1/4" w, scallop shell shape, c1770 . . . .**295.00**
Gravy boat, plain sides, blue . .**125.00**
Jug, 12-1/2" h, blue **800.00**

Warming dish, 9-1/2" d, 2-1/2" h, **$495.**

Pitcher
   6-7/8" h, blue. **850.00**
   7-1/2" h, blue. **850.00**
Platter, 16" l, oval, well and tree, blue and white, China, 19th C, minor glaze imperfections. **750.00**
Rice bowl, blue, pr **90.00**
Soap dish, 5-1/2" l, drain, blue **375.00**
Sugar bowl, cov, 5-1/4" h, blue **565.00**
Teapot, cov, 5-1/2" h, drum shape, blue **1,200.00**
Tureen, cov, undertray, blue, pr. **2,750.00**
Vase, 13-1/4" h, beaker shape, blue, teakwood stand. **1,250.00**
Vegetable dish, cov, 13" l, oval, liner **1,750.00**
Wine bottle, 10-3/4" h, blue . . . **900.00**

FLASKS

History: A flask, which usually has a narrow neck, is a container for liquids. Early American glass companies frequently formed them in molds which left a relief design on the front and/or back. Historical flasks with a portrait, building, scene, or name are the most desirable.

A chestnut is hand-blown, small, and has a flattened bulbous body. The pitkin has a blown globular body with a spiral rib overlay on vertical ribs. Teardrop flasks are generally fiddle shaped and have a scroll or geometric design.

References: Gary Baker et al., *Wheeling Glass 1829-1939*, Oglebay Institute, 1994, distributed by Antique Publications; Ralph and Terry Kovel, *Kovels' Bottles Price List*, 11th ed., Three River Press, 1999; George L. and Helen McKearin, *American Glass*, Crown Publishers, 1941 and 1948; John Odell, *Digger Odell's Official Antique Bottle and Glass Collector Magazine Price Guide Series*, Vol. 3, published by author (1910 Shawhan Road, Morrow, OH 45152), 1995; Michael Polak, *Bottles Identification and Price Guide*, 3rd ed., Quill, 2000; Kenneth Wilson, *American Glass 1760-1930*, 2 vols., Hudson Hills Press and The Toledo Museum of Art, 1994.

Periodical: *Antique Bottle & Glass Collector*, P.O. Box 187, East Greenville, PA 18041.

Collectors' Clubs: Federation of Historical Bottle Clubs, 88 Sweetbriar Branch, Longwood, FL 32750; The National Early American Glass Club, P.O. Box 8489, Silver Spring, MD 20907.

Notes: Dimensions can differ for the same flask because of variations in the molding process. Color is important in determining value—aqua and amber are the most common colors; scarcer colors demand more money. Bottles with "sickness," an opalescent scaling which eliminates clarity, are worth much less.

SPECIAL AUCTION

Norman C. Heckler & Company
Bradford Corner Road
Woodstock Valley, CT 06282

Glass
Chestnut, 4-3/4" h, Zanesville, OH, blown, 24 vertical ribs, amber, half pint, minor wear **250.00**
Historical
   Eagle-Cornucopia, early Pittsburgh district, 1820-40, light greenish-aquamarine, sheared mouth, pontil scar, pint, McKearin GII-6 . . . .**475.00**
   Eagle-Stag, Coffin and Hay Manufacturers, Hammonton, NJ, 1836-47, aquamarine with pale yellowish green tint. Sheared mouth, pontil scar, half pint, McKearin GII-50 . . . .**325.00**
   Eagle-Willington/Glass Co., Willington Glass Works, West Willington, CT, 1860-72, bright medium yellowish-olive, applied double-collared mouth, smooth base, half pint, McKearin GII-63 . . . .**210.00**

Scroll and two stars, green, pontil mark, **$75.**

For Pike's Peak Prospector-Hunter Shooting Deer, attributed to Ravenna Glass Works, Ravenna, OH, 1860-80, aquamarine, applied mouth with ring, smooth base, quart, McKearin GXI-47, 1/4" shallow flake............ **325.00**

Masonic-Eagle, Keene Marlboro Street Glassworks, Keene, NH, 1815-30, pale bluish-green, tooled collared mouth, pontil scar, pint, McKearin GIV-7a **950.00**

Masonic-Eagle, Zanesville, emb "Zanesville, J. Sheppard & Co.," golden amber, pint, McKearin GIV-32 .... **2,975.00**

Success to the Railroad, Keene Marlboro Street Glassworks, Keene, NH, 1830-50, light yellow amber with olive tone, sheared mouth, pontil scar, pint, McKearin GV-3 .... **250.00**

Pattern molded

4-5/8" l, Midwest, 1800-30, 24 ribs swirled to the right, golden amber, sheared mouth, pontil scar **190.00**

7-3/8" l, Emil Larson, NJ, c1930, swirled to the right, amethyst, sheared mouth, pontil scar, some exterior high point wear ... **250.00**

Pictorial

Cornucopia-Urn, Lancaster Glass Works, NY, 1849-60, blue green, applied sloping collared mouth, pontil scar, pint, McKearin GIII-17, some minor stain **350.00**

Flora Temple/Horse, Whitney Glass Works, Glassboro, NJ, 1860-80, cherry puce, applied collared mouth with ring, smooth base, pint, handle, McKearin GXIII-21 .... **170.00**

Monument-Sloop, Baltimore Glass Works, Baltimore, MD, 1840-60, medium variegated yellow green, sheared mouth, pontil scar, half pint, McKearin GVI-2, some exterior high point wear, overall dullness **1,100.00**

Pitkin type

Midwest, 1800-30, 6-1/4" l, ribbed and swirled to the right, 16 ribs, olive green with yellow tone, sheared mouth, pontil scar, some int. stain **300.00**

New England, 1783-30, sheared mouth, pontil scar, 5-1/4" l, ribbed and swirled to the left, 36 ribs, light olive yellow............. **375.00**

Pitkin, medium green, 14 right swirls, pontil mark, $195.

Portrait

Adams-Jefferson, New England, 1830-50, yellow amber, sheared mouth, pontil scar, half pint, McKearin GI-114........ **325.00**

General Jackson, Pittsburgh district, 1820-40, bluish-aquamarine, sheared mouth, pontil scar, pint, McKearin GI-68........ **1,500.00**

Lafayette-DeWitt Clinton, Coventry Glass Works, Coventry, CT, 1824-25, yellowish-olive, sheared mouth, pontil scar, half pint, 1/2" vertical crack, weakened impression, McKearin GI-82................ **2,100.00**

Rough and Ready Taylor-Eagle, Midwest, 1830-40, aquamarine, sheared mouth, pontil scar, pint, McKearin GI-77........ **1,200.00**

Washington, Albany Glass Works, sailing ship, deep green, pint, McKearin GI-28, 5-7/8" h... **110.00**

Washington-Eagle, Kensington Glass Works, Philadelphia, PA, 1820-38, bright aquamarine, sheared mouth, pontil scar, pint, McKearin GI-14......... **375.00**

Washington-Sheaf of Wheat, Dyottville Glass Works, Philadelphia, PA 1840-60, medium yellow-olive, inward rolled mouth,

pontil scar, half pint, McKearin GI-59 .... **9,000.00**

Washington-Taylor, Dyottville Glass Works, Philadelphia, PA 1840-60, bright bluish-green, applied double collared mouth, pontil scar, quart, McKearin GI-42 .... **400.00**

Majolica, 4-1/2" h, polychrome dec bulldog, landscape, and crest design, Italy, 19th C **200.00**

Pewter, 14" h, Pilgrim, shaped figural handles, moon-shaped body, molded foliage, pierced base, losses, 16th C **345.00**

Pottery, 3-1/2" h, shield shaped, eagle, brown glaze, "McKearin Collection of American Pottery" paper sticker, threaded neck repaired, screw cap missing **550.00**

Silver, sterling

4-1/4" l, America, late 19th/early 20th C, ovoid, emb foliates on textured ground, domed lid with attached chain, approx two troy oz.. **175.00**

9" h, Clarence Vanderbilt, New York, c1909-35, rect, overall textured finish, reeded circular screw cap, approx 10 troy oz........ **260.00**

FLOW BLUE

History: Flow blue, or flown blue, is the name applied to china of cobalt and white china whose color, when fired in a kiln, produced a flowing or blurred effect. The blue varies from dark royal cobalt to a navy or steel blue. The flow may be very slight to a heavy blur, where the pattern cannot be easily recognized. The blue color does not permeate through the body of the china. The amount of flow on the back of a piece is determined by the position of the piece in the sagger during firing.

Flow blue was first produced around 1830 in the Staffordshire area of England and credit is generally given to Josiah Wedgwood, who worked in that area. Many other potters followed, including Alcock, Davenport, Grindley, Johnson Brothers, Meakin, and New Wharf. Early flow blue, 1830s to 1870s, was usually of the ironstone variety. The later patterns, 1880s to 1900s, and modern patterns, after 1910, usually were made of the more delicate semi-porcelain. Approximately 90 percent of the flow blue was made in England, with the remainder made in Germany, Holland, France, Belgium, Wales, and Scotland. A few patterns were also made in the United States by Mercer, Warwick, and the Wheeling Pottery companies.

References: Susan and Al Bagdade, *Warman's English & Continental Pottery & Porcelain*, 3rd ed., Krause Publications, 1998; Mary F. Gaston, *Collector's Encyclopedia of Flow Blue China*, Collector Books, 1983, 1993 value update; ——, *Collector's Encyclopedia of Flow Blue China*, 2nd Series, Collector Books, 1994; Ellen R. Hill, *Mulberry*

Ironstone: Flow Blue's Best Kept Little Secret, published by author, 1993; Norma Jean Hoener, *Flow Blue China, Additional Patterns and New Information*, Flow Blue International Collectors' Club, Inc. (P.O. Box 1526, Dickensen, TX 77539), 1996; Jeffrey Snyder, *Fascinating Flow Blue*, Schiffer Publishing, 1997; —, *Flow Blue, A Collector's Guide to Pattern, History, and Values*, Schiffer, 1992; —, *Historic Flow Blue*, Schiffer Publishing, 1994; Petra Williams, *Flow Blue China: An Aid to Identification*, revised ed. (1981), *Flow Blue China II* (1981), *Flow Blue China and Mulberry Ware: Similarity and Value Guide*, revised ed. (1993), Fountain House East (P.O. Box 99298, Jeffersontown, KY 40269).

Collectors' Club: Flow Blue International Collectors' Club, Inc., 9412 High Drive, Leawood, KS 66206.

Museum: The Margaret Woodbury Strong Museum, Rochester, New York.

Adviser: Ellen G. King.

> **Reproduction Alert:** There are reproductions in flow blue and have been made since the mid-1950s. Many of these patterns look sloppy and blotched, with light blue all over background color. Some are plainly marked "flo blue" or "romantic flow blue," so the novice collector needs to be aware.

Abbey, G. Jones
  Cheese dish, cov **355.00**
  Inkwell, single, glass insert . . **175.00**
Alaska, Grindley
  Butter dish, cov, insert **365.00**
  Plate, 10" d **95.00**
  Tea cup and saucer **110.00**
  Teapot, cov **495.00**
Albany, Grindley
  Egg cup **165.00**
  Platter, 14" l **180.00**
  Vegetable tureen, cov **205.00**
Albany, Johnson Bros.
  Plate, 9" d **60.00**
  Tea cup and saucer **85.00**
Alton, Grindley
  Soup ladle, handle professionally
    restored **425.00**
  Soup tureen, cov **395.00**
Amoy, Davenport
  Cup and saucer, child's **800.00**
  Plate, 10-1/2" d **225.00**
  Platter, 19-1/2" l **600.00**
  Sauce tureen, two pcs **500.00**
  Soup bowl, 9" d **110.00**
  Soup bowl, 10-1/" d **175.00**
Ancient Ruins, Ashworth, hot water pitcher, small **375.00**
Anemone, S. F. & J., sugar bowl, cov **250.00**
Arabesque, Mayer
  Teapot, cov **750.00**

Vegetable bowl, open, 11" d,
    round **300.00**
  Vegetable tureen, cov **385.00**
Argyle, Grindley
  Creamer **325.00**
  Platter, 17" l **450.00**
  Platter, 19-1/2" l **850.00**
  Vegetable bowl, open, 10-1/8" l,
    oval **155.00**
Arundle, Doulton, tankard, three handles **275.00**
Astor & Grapeshot, unknown, teapot, cov, professional restoration to lid **675.00**
Bamboo, Alcock
  Compote, polychrome **425.00**
  Creamer **350.00**
  Platter, 16-3/4" l **550.00**
Batavia, Alcock, foot bath **3,500.00**
Beaufort, Grindley
  Butter pat **35.00**
  Dessert/individual vegetable
    bowl **40.00**
  Plate, 9" d **60.00**
Belmont, Ford & Sons, soup tureen, cov **355.00**
Bluebell, Dillwyn-Swansea
  Pitcher, small, rim restoration **250.00**
  Syrup pitcher, pewter lid **795.00**
Bluebell, Ridgway, sauce tureen, cov, undertray, ladle **900.00**
Blueboy, unknown, pitcher, copper luster, small **250.00**
Boston, Grindley, toothbrush vase **175.00**
Bryonia, Utzscheider
  Sugar bowl, cov **355.00**
  Teapot, cov **575.00**
Calico, Warwick, pitcher, pinched **375.00**
California, Podmore, Walker, teapot, cov, restoration to finial **300.00**
Canton, W. R., vegetable tureen, cov **285.00**
Cashmere, Morley
  Creamer **650.00**
  Jam dish, attached undertray,
    open **995.00**
  Platter, 14-3/4" l **1,100.00**
Chapoo, Wedgwood
  Cake/fruit server, ftd **1,200.00**
  Creamer **450.00**
  Sugar bowl, cov **550.00**
  Teapot, cov **2,500.00**
  Wash set, pitcher and wash
    bowl **3,200.00**
  Waste bowl **275.00**

Cashmere, wash pitcher, green polychrome decoration, gilt highlights, $1,000. Photos courtesy of Ellen King.

Chen Si, Maddock, teacup and saucer **195.00**
Chinese, Dimmock
  Coffee mug **295.00**
  Mush cup **275.00**
  Teapot, cov **650.00**
Chusan, Clementson
  Creamer **450.00**
  Platter, 13-3/4" l **750.00**
  Soup ladle **500.00**
  Sugar bowl, cov **475.00**
Clayton, Johnson Bros., platter, 14" l **290.00**
Cracked Ice, Warwick
  Plate, 9" d **80.00**
  Syrup pitcher, pewter lid **455.00**
Dahlia, Challinor
  Teapot, cov **575.00**
  Vegetable tureen, cov **625.00**
Derby, E. B., teapot, cov, restoration to spout **320.00**
Delft, Warwick, tea caddy, cov . **250.00**
Dresden, C & H, chamber pot . . **525.00**
Dudley, Ford & Sons, milk pitcher, 8-1/2" h **250.00**
Eton, Till & Sons, platter, 16" l . . **275.00**
Excelsior/Eagle, Furnival, teapot, cov **450.00**
Fairy Villas, Adams
  Creamer **255.00**
  Vegetable bowl, open, 10" d . **175.00**
Fern & Bar, unknown, sugar bowl, cov, restoration to handle **200.00**

Festoon, Grindley, wash set, pitcher
and wash bowl 625.00

Floral, Doulton

    Biscuit jar, cov. 550.00

    Teapot, cov 425.00

Floral, Forester & Sons, vase,
8" h. 275.00

Gainesborough, Ridgway

    Berry set, master bowl, six individual

      bowls 350.00

    Gravy boat 110.00

    Plate, 9" d 55.00

    Platter, 16" l 250.00

    Sauce tureen, cov, ladle. . . . 450.00

    Soup bowl. 55.00

    Tea cup and saucer 95.00

Geisha, Ford & Sons

    Creamer 185.00

    Dessert set, cake plate, six

      individual plates 350.00

    Teapot, cov, oversized 450.00

Grace, Grindley

    Butter dish, cov. 375.00

    Creamer and sugar bowl, cov

    . . . . 550.00

    Gravy boat, with tray. 195.00

    Plate, 9" d 65.00

Haddon, Grindley

    Plate, 10" d 110.00

    Platter, 20" l 350.00

Hawthrone, Mercer, ice-cream set,
tray/dish, 12 individual serving dishes
. . . . 675.00

Heath's Flower, Heath, creamer and
sugar bowl, cov 575.00

Hindustan, W & B, platter, with well and
tree. 750.00

Hong Kong, Meigh

    Cake plate 200.00

    Sauce tureen, cov. 425.00

    Sugar bowl, cov 350.00

    Syrup pitcher, pewter lid. . . . 650.00

    Tea cup and saucer, handleless

      cup 225.00

India, Villeroy & Boch, teapot,
cov. 875.00

Indian, Pratt

    Dessert/sauce dish. 45.00

    Tea cup and saucer 135.00

Irene, Adams, gravy boat 125.00

Jenny Lind, Wilkinson, humidor and
ashtray. 275.00

Kaolin, Podmore, Walker

    Creamer 325.00

    Soup bowl. 110.00

Kin Shan, Challinor

    Platter, 16-1/2" l 550.00

    Teapot, cov 675.00

Kirkee, Meir, creamer 285.00

Kremlin, S. Alcock, creamer. . . 275.00

LaBelle, pitcher with ice strainer, **$1,400.**

LaBelle, Wheeling Pottery

    Biscuit jar, cov 550.00

    Butter pat. 110.00

    Bone dish. 125.00

    Bowl, 10" d, shell shape, one

      handle 350.00

    Chamber pot 375.00

    Chocolate pot, cov 950.00

    Creamer. 275.00

    Demitasse cup and saucer . . 400.00

    Jardiniere, hairline 375.00

    Jardiniere stand. 1,800.00

    Pitcher, ice strainer 1,400.00

    Punch cup 525.00

    Syrup pitcher, pewter lid,

      undertray 550.00

Lakewood, Wood & Sons

    Gravy boat. 185.00

    Vegetable tureen, cov 325.00

Lancaster, New Wharf Pottery

    Plate, 9" d. 60.00

    Platter, 12-1/2" l 225.00

    Soup bowl 55.00

    Tea cup and saucer. 85.00

Lily, mug, **$250.**

Lily, Morley, mug 250.00

Maltese, Cotton & Barlow, cake plate,
tab handles 255.00

Manhattan, Alcock

    Gravy boat 135.00

    Plate, 9" d 80.00

    Soup bowl, rimmed 85.00

    Tea cup and saucer 125.00

    Waste bowl 130.00

Manilla, Podmore, Walker

    Cup plate 185.00

    Pitcher, 7-1/2" h. 450.00

    Plate, 10" d 125.00

    Sauce tureen, cov, base,

      tray 675.00

    Sauce tureen ladle 1,100.00

    Tea cup and saucer 150.00

Marguerite, Grindley

    Plate, 10" d 95.00

    Vegetable bowl, open, 10" d,

      round 200.00

Melbourne, Grindley

    Butter dish, cov, liner 450.00

    Comport 375.00

    Soup tureen, cov 650.00

    Tazza (sweetmeats dish) . . . 325.00

    Tea cup and saucer 125.00

Minerva, unknown, pitcher,
small 350.00

Moderna, Meakin, toothbrush
holder 250.00

Nankin, lemonade pitcher, **$275.**

Nankin, Doulton, lemonade
pitcher 275.00

Nankin, Pratt, toast pitcher,
cov. 1,200.00

Nautilus Shell, Ponder, Bourne,
vase/spoon holder, shell shape
. . . . 750.00

Ning Po, Hall, teapot, cov. 850.00

Non Pariel, Burgess & Leigh
  Creamer 265.00
  Hot water pitcher 550.00
  Soup bowl 110.00
  Vegetable tureen, cov, rect . . 350.00
Orchid, Maddock, teapot, cov,
matching trivet 450.00
Oregon, Mayer
  Butter dish, cov 395.00
  Tea cup and saucer 185.00
  Vegetable tureen, cov 500.00
Oriental, S. Alcock
  Platter, 10-1/2" l, polychrome
  . . . . 450.00
  Soup ladle 1,350.00
  Tea cup and saucer 155.00
Ornithology, Adams, wash set, pitcher
and wash bowl 1,200.00
Paisley, Doulton, commode/toilet
. . . . 1,500.00
Pansy, Warwick
  Syrup pitcher, undertray 245.00
  Tray, 6" x 9", rect 125.00

Paris, butter dish, covered, $255.

Paris, New Wharf Pottery
  Butter dish, cov 255.00
  Platter, 14-1/2" l 165.00
  Soup bowl 50.00
  Tea cup and saucer 95.00
Peach, Johnson Bros.
  Dessert/sauce dish,
  individual 40.00
  Sauce tureen, cov, base,
  tray 350.00
Peacock, Forester & Co., umbrella
stand, 22" 1,250.00
Pelew, Challinor
  Plate, 8-1/2" d 90.00
  Punch cup 110.00
  Sugar bowl, cov 485.00
  Teapot, cov 775.00
Princess, Wood & Son
  Chamber pot 325.00
  Wash set, pitcher and wash
  bowl 700.00
Portsmouth, New Wharf Pottery
  Dessert/sauce dish,
  individual 35.00

Plate, 9" d 60.00
Tea cup and saucer 85.00
Progress, Grindley, creamer and sugar
bowl, cov 250.00
Raleigh, Burgess & Leigh,
egg cup 95.00
Rose, Humphreys Bros., pitcher,
11" h 500.00
Rose, Ridgway, sauce tureen, cov,
base, tray 325.00
Scinde, Alcock
  Compote undertray 900.00
  Creamer 450.00
  Gravy boat 325.00
  Plate, 8-1/2" d 175.00
  Plate, 10-1/2" d 225.00
  Platter, 18" d 750.00
  Sauce tureen, cov, base,
  tray 775.00
  Sugar bowl, cov, 12-panel shape,
  rose finial 395.00
Shanghai, Grindley
  Butter dish, cov 295.00
  Creamer 250.00
  Gravy boat 175.00
  Plate, 7-7/8" d 80.00
  Platter, 16" l 350.00
  Vegetable tureen, cov 290.00
Shapoo, Boote, sauce boat . . . 165.00
Simla, Elsmore & Foster, sugar bowl,
cov 300.00

Sloe Blossom, pitcher, 4-1/2" h, $500.

Sloe Blossom, Ridgway pitcher,
4-1/2" h 500.00
Sobraon, S. Alcock
  Platter, well and tree 900.00
  Sauce tureen, cov, base, tray,
  ladle 1,150.00
Steers, Doulton, meat set, platter,
12 10" d plates 2,400.00

St. Regis, Wood & Son
  Pitcher, 7" h 75.00
  Toothbrush holder 125.00
  Wash basin 295.00
Sutherland, Doulton, sauce tureen,
cov, base, tray 300.00
Teaberry, Edge, Malkin, teapot, cov
. . . . 325.00
Tivoli, Furnival, punch cup 55.00
Tonquin, Adams
  Cup plate 145.00
  Pitcher, 6-1/2" h 375.00
  Soap dish, cov, base,
  drainer 500.00
  Tea cup and saucer 225.00
Touraine, Stanley
  Bowl, 9" l, oval 85.00
  Coffee cup and saucer 125.00
  Plate, 9" d 60.00
  Soup bowl 85.00
  Tea cup and saucer 110.00
Tulip and Sprig, unknown, tea cup and
saucer 225.00
Turkey, Salem Pottery
  Plate, 10" d 90.00
  Platter, 22" l 250.00
Venetia, Barker Ltd. Bros., vase,
9" h 200.00
Vermont, Burgess & Leigh
  Gravy boat, undertray 135.00
  Plate, 10" d 90.00
  Soup bowl, 9" d 55.00
  Tea cup and saucer 115.00
Waldorf, New Wharf Pottery
  Creamer 225.00
  Platter, 11" l 150.00
  Vegetable bowl, open, 9" d,
  round 110.00
Watteau, Doulton
  Crepe/pancake dish, cov, ftd
  . . . . 375.00
  Platter, 20" l, well and tree . . . 450.00
  Underplate for sauce tureen . 100.00
York, Cauldon, tea cup and
saucer 65.00

FOLK ART

History: Exactly what constitutes folk art is a question still being vigorously debated among collectors, dealers, museum curators, and scholars. Some want to confine folk art to non-academic, handmade objects. Others are willing to include manufactured material. In truth, the term is used to cover objects ranging from crude drawings by obviously untalented children to academically trained artists' paintings of "common" people and scenery.

References: Edwin O. Christensen, *Early American Wood Carvings*, Dover Publications, n.d.; Country Living Magazine, *Living with Folk Art*, Hearst Books, 1994; Catherine Dike, *Canes in the United States*, Cane Curiosa Press, 1995; Jim Dresslar, *Folk Art of*

Early America—The Engraved Powder Horn, Dresslar Publishing (P.O. Box 635, Bargersville, IN 46106), 1996; Wendy Lavitt, *Animals in American Folk Art*, Knopf, 1990; Jack L. Lindsey, *Worldly Goods, The Arts of Early Pennsylvania, 1680-1758*, Pennsylvania Museum of Art, distributed by Antique Collectors' Club, 1999; Jean Lipman, *American Folk Art in Wood, Metal, and Stone*, Dover Publications, n.d. George H. Meyer, *American Folk Art Canes*, Sandringham Press, Museum of American Folk Art, and University of Washington Press, 1992; Donald J. Petersen, *Folk Art Fish Decoys*, Schiffer Publishing, 1996; Beatrix Rumford and Carolyn Weekly, *Treasures in American Folk Art from the Abby Aldrich Rockefeller Folk Art Center*, Little Brown, 1989.

Periodical and Internet Resource: *Folk Art Magazine,* Museum of American Folk Art, Columbus Ave. at 66th St., New York, NY 10023-6214, http://folkartmuseum.org; http://www.folkart.org.

Collectors' Clubs: Folk Art Assoc. of the Southwest, 3993 Old Santa Fe Trail, Santa Fe, NM 87501; Folk Art Society of America, P.O. Box 17041, Richmond, VA 23226-7041, http://www.folkart.org.

Museums: Abby Aldrich Rockefeller Folk Art Center, Williamsburg, VA; Albany Institute of History & Art, Albany, NY; Bayou Bend Collection & Gardens, Houston, TX, http://www.mfah.org/bayou.html; Daughters of the American Revolution Museum, Washington, DC; Fruitlands Museums, Inc., Harvard, MA; Landis Valley Farm Museum, Lancaster, PA; Library of Congress American Folklife Center, Washington, DC; Mercer Museum, Doylestown, PA; Museum of American Folk Art, New York, NY, http://www.folkartmuseum.org; Museum of Early Southern Decorative Arts, http://www.mesda.org; Winston-Salem, NC; Museum of Fine Arts, Boston, MA; Museum of International Folk Art, Sante Fe, NM; National Museum of American History, Washington, DC; New York Historical Society, New York, NY; New York State Historical Assoc. & The Farmers' Museum, Inc., Cooperstown, NY; Pennsylvania Academy of Fine Arts, Philadelphia, PA; Yale University Art Gallery, New Haven, CT.

Cameo carved conch shell, relief carved foliate around rim, three portrait busts of America, Lady Liberty, and Washington, eagle with E. Pluribus Unum, garland of roses and other flowers, dated 1885, initials "A" and "W," some edge roughness, 8-1/2" l, **$990.** *Photo courtesy of Garth's Auction, Inc.*

Bird tree, carved and painted wood

9" h, America, c1900, mother robin with nest, two chicks perched on tree branch, imperfections **1,380.00**

12-3/4" w, 9" d, 10" h, carved mahogany, attributed to Midwest America, late 19th C, seated figure of hunter and his dog at base of tree, birds in branches above, flanked by two rabbits, three roosters, large bird on log in foreground, integral rect base, dark varnished surface **2,300.00**

20" h, PA, c1900, seven assorted birds perched on branch, tree root, and sq wooden base . . . **3,910.00**

Box, cov, 6" w, 3-1/2" d, 4-1/2" h, carved oak, America, late 19th/early 20th C, figure of man wearing cap with visor, sitting cross-legged on large dog, both have tails, border of turned finials joined by spiral rails, dovetailed box, leaf-carved drawer, paneled sides, old variegated varnish finish **1,265.00**

Candlestand, make-do, 18-3/4" w, 18" d, 26" h, New England, early 19th C, sq top, pedestal fashioned from parts of a yarn winder, tripod cabriole leg base on pads, old cream-colored paint, minor surface imperfections. . **1,150.00**

Decoy, 11" l, carved root head, old paint and natural surface, America, late 19th C **2,070.00**

Figure

4-3/4" w, 2" d, 12-3/4" h, Indian Warrior, carved pine and gilt gesso, hand raised, armed with arrows, America, 19th C, losses and gilt gesso wear. **1,035.00**

6" l, 2" d, 9-1/4" h, fan-tail rooster, yellow, brown, and red polychrome, PA, c1800-20, one feather repaired **5,175.00**

6-1/4" w, 7-1/2" d, 30" h, carved walnut, Lady Liberty, attributed to Edgar Alexander McKillop (1879-1950, Balifour, NC,) pearly bead eyes, stand **29,900.00**

13" l, 2-1/4" w, 10-1/4" h, carved and polychrome, horse and groom, leather Western saddle, America, early 20th C **5,175.00**

Clown, wooden, polychrome decoration, from Dunn's Toy Land, 14-1/2" h, **$200.** *Photo courtesy of Garth's Auction, Inc.*

9-3/4" h, Union Soldier, carved and gilded, figure standing at parade rest, "Lincoln's Boy, 61-65" carved on base, stand **550.00**

19-3/4" l, 3-1/2" w, 14" h, trotting horse, polychrome-molded copper over wood, attributed to Louis Jobin (1870-90, Quebec City,) twilled mane and tail, worn red paint, black hooves, stand, losses **11,500.00**

20-1/2" l, 6-1/2" w, 21-3/4" h, horse, carved and painted, ivory body, black-tipped nose and hooves, America, early 20th C, stand **4,600.00**

26" h, root, glass eyes, applied shell and minerals dec, attributed to Moses Ogden (1844-1919, Angelica, NY,) stand **1,495.00**

Grotesque face jug, stoneware, 5-1/2" h, brown-speckled glaze, found in Ohio, 19th C, imperfections **14,950.00**

Hammer, 13" l, oak and iron, figural, handle surmounted by carved man's head and upper torso, found in PA, 19th C **1,955.00**

Immigrants totem, 2-1/2" w, 3" d, 26" h, attributed to Canada, late 19th/early 20th C, polychrome, carved pine, four seated male figures all wearing hats, one cross-legged, one in kilt, lowest with head of dog at his feet, stand. **815.00**

Picture frame

12-5/8" w, 15-3/4" h, painted and incised wood, meandering vine and dot border, corner bosses, one corner boss missing **920.00**

19-1/4" w, 22" h, cherry, both sides carved with relief eagle, "US" within star and acorns on one side, incised geometric line detail on other, 11-1/8" x 8-1/2" opening **800.00**

Plaque, 14" d, sun face, carved polychrome, molded edge, America, early 19th C, minor imperfections, stand. **16,100.00**

Schierschnitt, 12-7/8" x 13-7/8", bouquet in vase, bright green, c1840, framed **350.00**

Sculpture, 8-1/2" l, carved mahogany, "When God took a Rib from Adam to Make Eve," Ulysses Davis (1914-1992), underside inscribed "King of Egypt Rameses Ulysses Davis, 15 W. 45th St., Savanah (sic) GA" **3,750.00**

Stand, 7-1/4" d top, 13" d base, 33" h, carved and turned wood, telemon, one

arm extended, legs crossed at knees, balancing dish top on head, old red-brown varnish, America, late 19th/early 20th C **17,250.00**

Theorem, 16" w, 13-1/2" h, watercolor on silk, blue, yellow, and cream-colored flowers, green foliage, blue, yellow, and white-striped bowl, framed, American School, 19th C, minor staining, creases **690.00**

Tinsel picture, 16-1/4" w, 11-1/2" h, double panel, polychrome tulips and carnations in ribbed bowls, painted pine frame **630.00**

Tower, carved wood

2-1/4" w, 11-1/4" h, carved and incised wood, surmounted by carved bust of George Washington over tier enclosing sphere and two-legged base, old natural surface, stand, c1876, found in Ohio, chip at base **4,900.00**

3" d, 18-1/2" h, tapered finial over six tiers enclosing spheres, integral base with heart motif, old dark stained surface, America, 19th C, minor losses **1,035.00**

Watercolor, two birds sitting on tulip branch potted in heart, David Y. Ellinger, signed "D.Y. Ellinger" on left corner, 11-1/2" h, 9-1/2" w, **$880.** *Photo courtesy of Alderfer Auction Company, Inc.*

Watercolor, pen and ink, on paper

4-1/2" w, 4-1/2" h, still life, basket of daisies, roses, and carnations, yellow, pink, green, and blue, light foxing, wear to gilt frame . . **650.00**

6" w, 7" h, mermaid holding book and comb, figures written on page of account book, Hiram Hayes,

Warwick, Maine, 1815, antique black frame **4,890.00**

7" w, 7-1/4" h, naïve, Brazilian Humming Bird, on thorny flowering branch, green, blues, red, pink, and tan, inked title, cross corner frame, minor damage **495.00**

8" d, compass, indistinctly inscribed on revere "L. Schultz, Solomon School," attributed to PA, 19th C, repairs, flaking, toning **320.00**

8-1/2" w, 9-1/2" h, fruit in basket, grassy, leafy ground, label "The Old Print Shop, New York" on revere, scattered stains and foxing **5,750.00**

11-7/8" w, 14-3/4" h, Mariner's Compass, America, mid-19th C, framed, fading, foxing, tears, and creases **2,185.00**

Whimsey, wood, 2-5/8" sq base, 20-1/8" h, polychrome carved, gray, blue, and salmon paint, sgd "M. M. Watts, 1881," found in New York state, some wear to paint. **2,760.00**

FOOD BOTTLES

History: Food bottles were made in many sizes, shapes, and colors. Manufacturers tried to make an attractive bottle that would ship well and allow the purchaser to see the product, thus giving assurance that the product was as good and as well made as home preserves.

References: Ralph & Terry Kovel, *Kovels' Bottle Price List*, 11th ed., Three Rivers Press, 1999; John Odell, *Digger Odell's Official Antique Bottle and Glass Collector Magazine Price Guide Series*, Vol. 6, published by author (1910 Shawhan Road, Morrow, OH 45152), 1995.

Periodical: *Antique Bottle and Glass Collector*, P.O. Box 187, East Greenville, PA 18041.

Collectors' Club: Federation of Historical Bottle Collectors, Inc., 2230 Toub St., Ramona, CA 92065.

Catsup, 10" h, Cuyuga County Tomato Catsup, aqua, swirl design **65.00**

Celery salt, 8" h, Crown Celery Salt, Horton Cato & Co., Detroit, yellow amber, smooth base, ground lip, orig shaker type cap **175.00**

Codd, Lehigh & Sons, Salford, olive-amber, emb globe **50.00**

Extract

Baker's Flavoring Extracts, 4-3/4" h, aqua, sq ring lip **15.00**

L. C. Extract, label, orig box . **180.00**

Red Dragon Extract, emb dragon. **20.00**

Ginger, Sanford's orig label **12.00**

Horseradish, dark green, $8.

Horseradish

As You Like It, pottery, clamp . **25.00**
Bunker Hill, aqua, label **24.00**
Lime juice, 10-1/4" h, arrow motif, olive amber, smooth base, applied mouth **85.00**
Maraschino cherries, orig tin lid, red and white dec, reads "Packed by Pacific Cherry Fruit Corp., Los Angeles" **15.00**

Milk

Cloverleaf Creamery Co., quart **85.00**
Dellinger Dairy Farm, Jefferson, IN **25.00**
Holsgern Farms Dairy, quart, tin top and closure **90.00**
Purity Dairy, pint **60.00**
Scott's Dairy, quart, emb **30.00**
Wonsidlers Dairy, quart **25.00**

Mustard

Blossom Brand Prepared Mustard, wire bale, orig label **22.00**
Giessen's Union Mustard, 4-3/8" h, clear, eagle **85.00**

Olive oil

7-1/2" h, Bertin Brand Pure Olive Oil, dark green **18.00**
11" h, Elwood Cooper Pure Olive Oil, aqua **45.00**
Peanut butter, 5" h, Bennett Hubba **20.00**

Pepper sauce

8" h, S & P Pat. Appl. For, teal blue, smooth base, tooled lip **50.00**
8-7/8" h, W & E Peppersauce, sq, aqua **165.00**

Pickle, cathedral, America, 1845-80, sq, beveled corners
11-1/2" h, three fancy cathedral designs, greenish-aqua, tooled rolled mouth, smooth base . **150.00**
11-3/4" h, four different fancy cathedral arch designs, protruding irregular panels, aquamarine, tooled sq mouth, iron pontil mark **170.00**
13-5/8" h, sq, medium green, tooled collared mouth, pontil scar, Willington Glass Works, CT **2,200.00**
Syrup, 12-1/4" h, Boston Cooler, clear, blue and gold label, tooled mouth, metal cap, smooth base, c1900. **350.00**
Vinegar, Weso Biko Co. Cider Vinegar, jug shape **45.00**

FOOD MOLDS

History: Food molds were used both commercially and in the home. Generally, pewter ice-cream molds and candy molds were used commercially; pottery and copper molds were used in homes. Today, both types are collected largely for decorative purposes.

The majority of pewter ice-cream molds are individual-serving molds. One quart of ice cream would make eight to 10 pieces. Scarcer, but still available, are banquet molds which used two to four pints of ice cream. European-made pewter molds are available.

Marks: Pewter ice-cream molds were made primarily by two American companies: Eppelsheimer & Co. (molds marked "E & Co., N.Y.") and Schall & Co. (marked "S & Co."). Both companies used a numbering system for their molds. The Krauss Co. bought out Schall & Co., removed the "S & Co." from some, but not all, of the molds, and added more designs (pieces marked "K" or "Krauss"). "CC" is a French mold mark.

Manufacturers of chocolate molds are more difficult to determine. Unlike the pewter ice-cream molds, makers' marks were not always used or were covered by frames. Eppelsheimer & Co. of New York marked many of their molds, either with their name or with a design resembling a child's toy top and the words "Trade Mark" and "NY." Many chocolate molds were imported from Germany and Holland and were marked with the country of origin and, in some cases, the mold-maker's name.

Reference: Judene Divone, *Chocolate Moulds*, Oakton Hills Publications, 1987.

Museum: Wilbur's American Candy Museum, Lititz, PA.

Additional Listing: Butter Prints.

Chocolate mold

Basket, 3-1/2" x 6", one cavity . . . **50.00**
Boy on bicycle, 8-1/4" h, two parts **395.00**

Catalog, Anton Reich, 13" x 17", 86 pgs **2,420.00**
Chick and egg, 3-1/2" h, two parts, folding, marked "Allemagne," Germany **65.00**
Easter Rabbit, 18-1/2" h, standing, two-part mold, separate two-part molds for ears and front legs, "Anton Reiche, Dresden, Germany" **220.00**
Elephant, tin, three cavities **95.00**
Fish **95.00**
Heart, 6-1/2" x 6", two cavities . . **70.00**
Hen on basket, two pcs, clamp type, marked "E. & Co./Toy" **60.00**
Pig **95.00**
Rabbits, 10-1/2" l, three cavities, sitting, tin-plated steel, folding, two-part mold **70.00**
Skeleton, 5-1/2" h, pressed tin . . **60.00**
Teddy Bear, two pcs, clamp type, marked "Reiche" **295.00**
Turkey, 14" x 10", tray type, eight cavities **65.00**
Witch, 4-1/2" x 2", four cavities . . **75.00**

Cake mold, lamb, No. 866, #2 size, $80.

Food mold

Cake mold, 9-3/4" l, 11-1/2" h, cast iron, two-part full-figure seated rabbit, Griswold, Erie, PA, late 19th C . **260.00**
Cheese, 5" x 13", wood, relief-carved design and "Bid," pinned, branded "Los," carved scratch date 1893 **60.00**
Pudding, tin and copper
4-1/2" d, round, star, ribbed sides **175.00**
5" x 5" x 6-1/2", oval, pineapple **95.00**
6" l, oval, trimmed copper eagle **195.00**
6-1/4" w, 8" l, tin, melon shape, marked "Kreamer #3," c1930 . . . . **35.00**
6-1/2" d, round, fruit design . **125.00**
8" l, oval, lion **220.00**
9" l, rect, oval sheaf **175.00**

Ice-cream mold, pewter

Asparagus, 3-5/8" h **35.00**
Basket, replaced hinge pins . . . **25.00**

Camel, pewter, marked "E & Co. NY, #681" **75.00**
Cherub riding Easter Bunny, 4" h. **45.00**
Circle, marked "Kiwanis Club" and "E & Co. NY" **25.00**
Easter Lily, three part **75.00**
Egg, 2-3/4" d, marked "E & Co. NY" **35.00**

Ice cream, flag, pewter, marked "Krauss NY 292," $95.

Flag, 13 stars **95.00**
Fruit, 2-3/4" d, marked "E & Co. NY" **30.00**
Heart with Cupid, 4" h. **65.00**
Man in the Moon, 5-1/2" h, marked "E & Co. copyright 1888" **95.00**
Naked lady with drape, three parts, 5-1/4" h **275.00**
Owl, banquet size, four pints, marked "S & Co. 7" **600.00**
Pear, banquet size, marked "S & Co. 17" **325.00**
Potato, 4" h, pewter **70.00**
Rose, two parts, 3-1/2" d **125.00**
Ship, banquet size, two quarts . **265.00**
Steamboat **115.00**
Tulip, 4-1/8" h, marked "E. & Co. NY" **45.00**
Wedding Bells, 3" h. **45.00**

FOSTORIA GLASS

History: Fostoria Glass Co. began operations at Fostoria, Ohio, in 1887, and moved to Moundsville, West Virginia, its present location, in 1891. By 1925, Fostoria had five furnaces and a variety of special shops. In 1924, a line of colored tableware was introduced. Fostoria was purchased by Lancaster Colony in 1983 and continues to operate under the Fostoria name.

References: Frances Bones, *Fostoria Glassware; 1887-1982,* Collector Books, 1999; Tom and Neila Bredehoft, *Fifty Years of Collectible Glass, 1920-1970, Volume 1, Volume II,* Antique Trader Books, 2000; Gene Florence, *Elegant Glassware of the Depression Era,* 8th ed., Collector Books, 1998; —, *Glass Candlesticks of the Depression Era,* Collector Books, 1999; Ann Kerr, *Fostoria: An Identification and Value Guide of Pressed, Blown, & Hand Molded Shapes* (1994, 1997 values), *Etched, Carved & Cut Designs* (1996, 1997 values) Collector Books; Milbra Long and Emily Seate, *Fostoria Stemware,* Collector Books, 1995, 1998 value update, —, *Fostoria Tableware, 1924-1943,* Collector Books, 1999; —, *Fostoria Tableware 1944-1986,* Collector Books, 1999, —, *Fostoria, Useful and Ornamental: The Crystal for America,* Collector Books, 2000; L-W Book Sales, *Fostoria: Fine Crystal & Colored Glassware, Cut, Etched, and Pain,* L-W Book Sales, 2000; Gary Schneider, Melanie Hildreth, Therese Ujfalusi and Irene Gardner, *Navarre by Fostoria,* Past Reflections, 1998; Sidney P. Seligson, *Fostoria American, A Complete Guide,* printed by author, 1999.

Periodical: *The Daze,* P.O. Box 57, Otisville, MI 48463.

Collectors' Clubs: Fostoria Glass Collectors, Inc., P.O. Box 1625, Orange, CA 92856; Fostoria Glass Society of America, P.O. Box 826, Moundsville, WV 26041.

Museums: Fostoria Glass Museum, Moundsville, WV; Huntington Galleries, Huntington, WV.

Ashtray
    Century, individual size. **12.00**
    Coin, crystal **30.00**
    June, blue. **75.00**
Basket, American, reeded handle **210.00**
Bell
    American **290.00**
    Chintz, orig label. **130.00**
Berry bowl, June, blue, 5" d. . . . **50.00**
Biscuit jar, American, c1915-28, electro plated nickel silver top, 4" d, 6" h. **850.00**
Bowl
    Baroque, blue, 4" sq, one handle **22.00**
    Century, 10-1/2" d **35.00**
    Coin, emerald, 8" d **110.00**
    June, 12" d, blue. **125.00**
Bud vase, Coin, crystal, 8" h . . . **17.00**
Cake salver
    Century, crystal. **60.00**
    Coin, crystal **98.00**
    Corsage, 10-1/2" d **32.00**
Candleholders, pr
    Baroque, 4" h, 1-lite, silver deposit Vintage dec on base, #2496 **75.00**
    Baroque, 8-1/2" h, 10" w, 2-lite, removable bobeche and prisms, #2484 . . . . **375.00**
    Buttercup, 8" h, 8" w **150.00**
    Coin, red, tall **150.00**
    Meadow Rose. **185.00**
    Midnight Rose, #2472, etched, 5" h, 8" w. **150.00**
    Navarre, #2496. . . . . **185.00**
    Trindle, #2594, 3-lite, Buttercup etch, 8" h, 6-1/2" w **250.00**

Candy dish, cov
    Baroque, crystal **40.00**
    Coin, amber, 6-1/2" d. **20.00**
    June, yellow. **370.00**
    Navarre, three parts **175.00**
    Versailles, blue, three parts. . **345.00**
Card tray, Brocaded Daffodil, two handles, pink, gold trim **40.00**
Celery tray, five parts
    Lido **100.00**
    Navarre **175.00**
Champagne
    Chintz **20.00**
    Navarre **22.00**
Cheese and cracker
    Chintz **70.00**
    Colony **55.00**
Cigarette box, cov
    Morning Glory etching. **65.00**
    Oriental **170.00**
Claret
    Camelia **30.00**
    June, pink **175.00**
    Navarre **80.00**
    Trojan, yellow, 6" h. **100.00**
Cocktail, Baroque, yellow **15.00**
Compote
    Baroque, crystal, 6" **18.00**
    Century, 4-1/2". **20.00**
Condiment set, American, salt and pepper shakers, pr, cloverleaf tray, pr cruets **200.00**

Console set, Royal Amber, #273, c1925, $150.

Console set
    Brocaded Palms, 14" oval console bowl, pr candlesticks, white . **70.00**
    Chintz, 12" oval flame bowl, pr double candlesticks **185.00**
Cookie jar, American, orig red, white, and blue label "Fostoria, Made in U.S.A.," 5-3/4" d, 9" h **285.00**
Cordial, Holly. **30.00**
Cosmetic box, cov, American, 2-1/2" d, flake on bottom. **900.00**
Courting lamp, Coin, amber . . . **150.00**

Creamer, individual size

Century 9.00
Raleigh 8.00

Creamer, table size

American, hexagon, 4-3/4" w, rare
form 1,400.00
Chintz 20.00
Raleigh 10.00

Creamer, sugar, tray, individual size

Camelia 45.00
Century 30.00

Cream soup

Colony 95.00
Versailles, pink 65.00
Vesper, amber 30.00

Cruet, June, yellow 700.00

Crushed fruit jar, cov, America,
c1915-25, 5-7/8" d, 6" h 1,600.00

Cup and saucer

Baroque, blue 35.00
Buttercup 21.00
Camelia 20.00
Fairfax, crystal 7.00
Raleigh 6.50
Rose 25.00

Dinner plate

American 20.00
Colony, slight use 18.00
June, pink, 10-1/4" d 160.00
Lido 45.00

Ewer, hand-painted florals, red ground,
pot metal fittings, 6-1/2" w, 16" h, price
for matched pr 345.00

Figure, Lute and Lotus, black,
gold highlights, 12-1/2" h, price for pr
. . . . 675.00

Float bowl, Century, 8-1/2" d . . . 35.00

Goblet, Colonial Mirror, c1930, **$45.**

Goblet, water

Baroque, crystal 12.00
Captiva, light blue 12.00
Century 22.00
Chintz 33.00
Coin, red 105.00
Jamestown, blue 20.00
June, yellow 55.00
Meadow Rose 30.00

Navarre 40.00

Grapefruit, Coronet 9.00

Gravy boat, liner, Kasmir, blue . 180.00

Handkerchief box, cov, American,
blue, 5-1/2" l, 4-5/8" d, 2-1/2" h . . 830.00

Ice bucket

Brocaded Palms, ice green, irid,
gold trim 110.00
Shirley 50.00
Sunray 50.00

Iced-tea tumbler, Jamestown,
brown 10.00

Jelly, cov

Coin, amber 30.00
Meadow Rose, 7-1/2" d 90.00

Juice tumbler

Captiva, light blue 12.00
Jamestown, blue 25.00
Navarre 27.00

Lily pond, Buttercup, 12" d 55.00

Marmalade, cov, American 125.00

Mayonnaise, liner, Navarre 90.00

Milk pitcher, Century 60.00

Muffin plate, Century, 9-1/2" d . . 30.00

Nappy, handle

Century, 4-1/2" d 12.00
Coin, blue, 5-3/8" d 30.00

Nut cup, Fairfax, amber 15.00

Oil cruet

Century 50.00
Versailles, yellow 550.00

Old-fashioned tumbler, Coin,
crystal 30.00

Oyster cocktail

Colony 12.00
Holly 15.00

Parfait, June, pink 180.00

Pickle castor, American, ornate silver
plated frame, 11" h 900.00

Pickle tray

Century, 8-3/4" 15.00
Colony, two parts 16.00

Pitcher, Lido, ftd 225.00

Plate

Baroque, blue, 7-1/2" d 15.00
Century, 9-1/2" d 30.00
Rose, 9" d 15.00

Platter, Versailles, pink, 15" l,
oval 350.00

Punch bowl, ftd, Baroque, crystal, orig
label 425.00

Relish dish, cov, Brocaded Summer
Gardens, three sections, white . . 75.00

Relish dish, open

American, divided, small 18.00
Baroque, blue, four parts . . . 225.00
Corsage, five parts 58.00
Fairfax, yellow, three parts,
11-1/2" l 15.00
Romance, two parts, 8-1/2" l . 25.00

Ring holder, American, 4-1/2" l,
3" h 800.00

Rose bowl, American, small 18.00

Salad plate

Buttercup 12.00
June 14.00

Salt and pepper shakers, pr

Century 20.00
Coin, red 60.00
Coronet 15.00
Virginia, amber 20.00

*Sandwich server, Trojan, yellow, center
handle,* **$40.**

Sauce boat, Versailles, green . . 240.00

Sherbet

Baroque, blue 25.00
Buttercup, low 18.00
Chintz 22.00
Holly, tall 12.00
Jamestown, amber 6.00
Seville, amber, high 10.00
Sunray, blue 19.00

Snack plate, Century, 8" d 25.00

Sugar, individual size

Baroque, blue 4.00
Raleigh 8.00

Sugar, cov, table size

American, hexagon, 5" w, 2-3/8" h,
rare form 950.00
Chintz 20.00
Fairfax, orchid, ftd 10.00
Lido 9.00

Syrup, American, Bakelite handle
.............................**200.00**
Tidbit, 12" d, six-sided, Brocaded
Summer Garden, white.........**45.00**
Torte plate
   Century, 14" d **30.00**
   Colony, 15" d **80.00**
   Heather, 13" d **45.00**
Tray, Navarre, 8" l...........**100.00**
Tumbler, water
   Chintz...................**33.00**
   Colony **18.00**
Urn, cov, Coin, amber, 12-3/4" h .**68.00**
Vanity set, #2276, pink **125.00**
Vase
   Century, 8-1/2" h **125.00**
   June, yellow, 8" h.........**575.00**
   Meadow Rose, 9-1/2" h **260.00**
   Minuet, yellow, 6-3/4" h **250.00**
   Oak Leaf Brocade, c1929-31,
     8" h **240.00**
   Versailles, yellow, 8" h, flip...**395.00**
Whipped-cream pail, Versailles,
blue......................**270.00**
Whiskey, June, yellow **85.00**
Wine
   Chintz...................**40.00**
   Coin, red **90.00**
   Jamestown, green **20.00**
   June, pink **118.00**

FRAKTUR

History: Fraktur, the calligraphy associated with the Pennsylvania Germans, is named for the elaborate first letter found in many of the hand-drawn examples. Throughout its history, printed, partially printed/partially hand-drawn, and fully hand-drawn works existed side by side. Frakturs often were made by schoolteachers or ministers living in rural areas of Pennsylvania, Maryland, and Virginia. Many artists are unknown.

Fraktur exists in several forms—geburts and taufschein (birth and baptismal certificates), vorschrift (writing examples, often with alphabet), haus sagen (house blessings), bookplates and bookmarks, rewards of merit, illuminated religious texts, valentines, and drawings. Although collected for decoration, the key element in fraktur is the text.

SPECIAL AUCTION

Sanford Alderfer Auction Company
501 Fairgrounds Road
Hatfield, PA 19440
(610) 368-5477

References: Corinne and Russell Earnest, *Fraktur: Folk Art and Family,* Schiffer Publishing, 2000; Donald A. Shelley, *Fraktur-Writings or Illuminated*

Manuscripts of the Pennsylvania Germans, Pennsylvania German Society, 1961; Frederick S. Weiser and Howell J. Heaney (comps.), *Pennsylvania German Fraktur of the Free Library of Philadelphia,* 2 vols., Pennsylvania German Society, 1976.

Museum: The Free Library of Philadelphia, Philadelphia, PA.

Notes: Fraktur prices rise and fall along with the American folk-art market. The key marketplaces are Pennsylvania and the Middle Atlantic states.

Birth certificate
  (Geburts and Taufschein)
  5" h, 8-1/4" w, pen and ink, wove paper, brown, black, and green flourishes and German inscription, "Marie Grager, 1850, born June 4th, AD 1833 in State of Ohio," minor paper damage, 6-1/2" x 9-1/2" w frame **825.00**
  6-3/8" h, 8" w, watercolor, pen and ink on paper, sgd "Martin Brechall," Linn Township, Northampton County, PA, paired tulips, red and yellow blossoms, for Lea Claus, dated March 7, 1808 .... **1,035.00**
  7-1/2" h, 8" w, Jesse Snyder, Towamencin Twp, PA, born in 1812, Schwenkfelder, 1873, orange, yellow, and green, two birds on branches **275.00**
  9" h, 11" w, watercolor, pen and ink on paper, heart with vintage, birds, flowers, orange, green, blue, black, and yellow, penciled birth entries for 1878 and 1886, edge sgd

"Henry E. Witmer," stains and minor edge damage, framed **220.00**
11-3/4" w, 7-3/4" h, attributed to Fredrich Krebs, scalloped heart, flowers, and two long necked birds, shades of brown, red, yellow/tan, records birth of Anna Barbara Huinelsin, Bethlehem Tow ship, PA, 1805, fold lines, stains, damage.............. **1,155.00**
12" h, 15"w, hand-colored printed form, Frederick Krebs, watercolor elements, red and green parrots, tulips, sun faces and crown, for Henrich Ott, Bucks County, Bedminster Township, PA, dated Oct. 29, 1800 .... **990.00**
12" h, 15-1/2" w, hand-colored printed form, S. Baumann, for Joseph Raub, Berks County, Bern Township, PA, dated July 8, 1809 .... **460.00**
12-1/4" h, 15-1/2" w, watercolor, pen, and ink on paper, Berks County artist, winged angels, paired birds, and mermaids, for Frederick Heverling, dated 1784 .. **2,100.00**
12-3/4" h, 15-1/2" w, watercolor, pen, and ink on paper, Flat Parrot artist, for Susana Gensemer, dated 1811 .... **1,265.00**
13" h, 15-7/8" w, hand-colored printed form, printed by Gottleib Jungmann, Reading, 1795, Friedrich Krebs imprint, paired

Birth and baptismal certificates for brothers Daniel Raup (1784) and Peter Raup (1791), by Frederick Krebs, Adam and Eve, Apple Tree and Serpent in Garden of Eden, printed cut-out birds, watercolor, pen, and ink on paper, gilded decoupage elements, 15-1/2" h, 12-1/4" w, pair, **$3,740.** *Photo courtesy of Southeby's.*

parrots, blossoms, and sun faces, for Johannes Ries, Paxton Township, Dauphin County, PA, dated Aug. 28, 1799 . . . . **2,185.00**

13" h, 16" w, hand-colored printed form, watercolor elements, Frederick Speyer, paired angels, parrots, blossoms, and mermaids, for Sarra Grill, Lehigh County, PA, dated April 18, 1789. . . . . **1,380.00**

13" h, 17" h, watercolor, pen and ink on wove paper, heart with parrots, tulips, corner fans, crown and birds, red, blue, brown-yellow, and green, 1820 Columbia County, OH, birth, worn and wrinkled, edge damage, old newspaper backed repair along one tear, framed **2,530.00**

15-1/2" h, 12-1/4" w, watercolor, pen and ink on paper, gilded decoupage elements, Frederick Krebs, pair of certificates for brothers Daniel Raup (1784) and Peter Raup (1791), pr. . . . **3,800.00**

Bookplate

2-1/4" w, 4-1/2" h, red and green watercolor German verse, crown, heart, and red, green, and yellow bird with flower, German New Testament, published 1796, gold tooling on cover "J. G. St. 1807," loose from book, few stains **220.00**

3-5/8" w, 6-1/2" h, for Peter Springer (Jr.), dated 1815, red inked title lines, brown ink German verse, marbleized paper bound German book, published in Harrisburg, 1814, worn book, some stains, minor edge wear **220.00**

3-3/4" w, 4-5/8" h, red, yellow, dark blue, and teal green crested exotic bird sitting on flowering branch, minor stain and foxing, some damage in lower right, black painted frame. **660.00**

3-7/8" w, 6-3/4" h, for Jacob Hekler, calligraphy, verse, and pot of flowers, red, yellow, blue, shades of green watercolor, brown ink, leather bound German New Testament book, published in Philadelphia, 1813, stains, some damage to both bookplate and book **110.00**

4-1/8" w, 7-1/8" h, for Anna Borpholder, born 1798, colorful watercolor, red, yellow, blue, and green tulips, daisy, and grapes, yellow heart, leather bound

German Psalm book, published in Lancaster 1820, minor wear, leather book straps missing **1,375.00**

4-1/4" w, 3-3/4" h, pen and ink inscription, "Catharina Barbara Heinlenin," watercolor floral garland below in red and yellow, black ink, light foxing, 5-7/8" w x 5-1/2" h burl frame. **360.00**

4-3/8" w, 5-7/8" h, watercolor red, yellow, and dark green flower, paid paper, date appears to be 1800, stains, light wear, taped split in middle, black painted frame with minor wear. **615.00**

4-5/8" w, 5-5/8" h, red and yellow bird on flowering branch, red and yellow watercolor, blue ink, yellow and blue borders, wooden frame with light wear **440.00**

5-5/8" w, 6-7/8" h, ink and watercolor on laid paper, two long necked blue birds with red wings, yellow and red tulip with green leaves, German script, later frame with some curl. **2,475.00**

5-7/8" w, 4-1/2" h, inked German script, blue and red watercolor flowers, blue and yellow foliage wreath, some foxing and stains, wear to some of the red flowers, bird's eye maple veneered frame. **385.00**

Child's Book of Moral Instruction (Metamorphis), watercolor, pen and ink on paper

5-3/4" x 7-1/2", dec on both sides of four leaves, each with upper and lower flaps showing different versus and color illus, unknown illustrator **345.00**

6" x 7", printed form on paper, hand colored elements, The Great American Metamorphosis, Philadelphia, printed by Benjamin Sands, 1805-06, printed on both sides of four leaves, each with upper and lower flaps, engraved collar illus by Poupard. **420.00**

6-1/4" x 7", dec on both sides of four leaves, when folded reveals different versus and full-page color illus, executed by Sarah Ann Siger, Nazareth, PA, orig string hinges **575.00**

Confirmation certificate, 6" x 7-3/4", watercolor, pen and ink on paper, David Schumacher, paired tulips and hearts, for Maria Magdalena Spengler, dated 1780 . . . . **4,600.00**

Daniel Peterman, Manheim Township, York County, PA, wove paper, watermark, colored decoration, bird, distelfink, and floral motifs, two women, 15-3/4" x 12-1/2", **$1,750.**

Copybook, Vorschrift, 8" w, 5-5/8" h, pen and ink, red watercolor, laid paper, German text with ornate Gothic letters in heading, blocked cut area in lower left unfinished, minor edge damage, 11-3/8" w, 9-1/2" h yellow and red leather covered frame. **250.00**

Drawing, watercolor, pen and ink

4" h, 2-3/4" w, red yellow and blue rooster with bushy tail, American School, 19th C **865.00**

5-3/8" h, 7-3/4" w, pen and ink and watercolor on heavy paper, Daniel Sehaey, Smithville, Wayne County, OH, Oct. 11th, A.D. 1854, written by T.H.C.B., black, red, and greenish yellow, 8-3/4" h, 10-3/4" w walnut beveled frame. **590.00**

15-3/8" w, 12-1/2" h, central heart bordered in blue, orange, and light brown, flowering tulip plant with four buds in blue, red, black, and light brown, compass star flowers, brown and white foliate at upper corners, six pointed starts in lower corners, colors similar to those found on Shenandoah Valley, VA, examples, foxing, stains, and tears, contemporary frame. **495.00**

Family register, 19-3/4" w, 16" h, hand drawn, blue-green and red border with stars and flowers in corners, hearts, cherubs, and cross hatch work at center, German names, written in old brown ink, dates from 1814 to 1870, heart and hand medallion with inscription "Orphans Home and Ft. Wayne Hospital, Allen Co., Ind," sgd "John Cornelius Martin," old taped tear near top margin, small piece of corner missing **1,100.00**

House blessing (Haus Segen)

15-1/2" h, 11-3/4" w, printed by Johann Ritter, Reading, hand colored, orange, green, blue, yellow, brown, and black, professionally repaired and rebacked on cloth, 18-1/4" h, 14-3/8" w old stenciled dec frame **500.00**

16-1/2" h, 13" w, printed and hand-colored, red, blue, green, and yellow, dated 1785, damage and portions missing, framed **385.00**

Marriage certificate, 8" x 12-1/2", watercolor, pen and ink on paper, Daniel Schumacher, paired red, yellow and green birds flanking an arch with crown, for Johannes Haber and Elisabeth Stimmess, Windsor Township, Berks County, PA, dated 1777 **1,035.00**

Reward of merit, American School, early 19th C, watercolor, pen, and ink on paper

3-5/8" x 3-1/8", red, yellow, and blue-tailed bird perched on flowering branch **1,092.00**

4-1/8" x 3-1/4", red and yellow birds, green and yellow pinwheel flower **345.00**

Song book, 4-1/8" x 6-3/4", watercolor, pen, and ink on paper, marbled covers, leather binding, several handwritten and calligraphy pages, illuminated bookplate, David Hiestand, dated Feb. 8, 1823, Macungie Township, Lehigh County, PA **1,380.00**

FRANKART

History: Arthur Von Frankenberg, artist and sculptor, founded Frankart, Inc., in New York City in the mid-1920s. Frankart, Inc., mass produced practical "art objects" in the Art-Deco style into the 1930s. Pieces include aquariums, ashtrays, bookends, flower vases, and lamps. Although Von Frankenberg used live female models as his subjects, his figures are characterized by their form and style rather than specific features. Nudes are the most collectible; caricatures of animals and human figures were also produced, no doubt, to increase sales.

Pieces were cast in white metal in one of the following finishes: cream—a pale iridescent white; bronzoid—oxidized copper, silver, or gold; french—medium brown with green in the crevices; gunmetal—iridescent gray; jap—very dark brown, almost black, with green in the crevices; pearl green—pale iridescent green; and verde—dull light green. Cream and bronzoid were used primarily in the 1930s.

Marks: With few exceptions, pieces were marked "Frankart, Inc.," with a patent number or "pat. appl. for."

Note: All pieces listed have totally original parts and are in very good condition unless otherwise indicated.

Ashtray

5" h, stylized duck with outstretched wings supports green glass ash receiver **120.00**

6" h, nude figure kneels on cushion, holding 3" d removable pottery ashtray **225.00**

Bookends, pr

Cocker spaniel, 6-1/2" h, c1934, some corrosion on top of base **165.00**

Gazelle, 7-1/4" l, 6-1/4" h, marked "Frankart Inc. Pat Appld For," bronze finish, orig felt bottom **155.00**

Owl, 6" h, gray metal, c1920. **225.00**

Candlesticks, pr, 12-1/2" h, nude figures standing on tiptoes, holding candle cup over head **395.00**

Cigarette box, 8" h, back to back nudes supporting removable green glass box **450.00**

Figure, 7" h, waving boy, raised ring near right foot **75.00**

Lamp

11" h, 8-1/4" w, 4" d, frosted amber crackle glass shade, metal base, worn patina **345.00**

13" h, two back to back dancing nude figures support 11" sq glass cylinder satin finished shade **775.00**

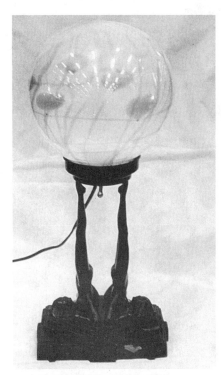

Lamp, No. L220X, two inverted figures balance 8" ball of glass with gold iridescent decoration, green leaves, marked "Patented design No. D77202," 1928, 17" h, $900.

18" h, standing nude figure holds 6" d round crackled rose glass globe **425.00**

Wall pocket, 12" h, seated nude figure supported by wrought iron metal frame work, metal pan for flowers **350.00**

FRATERNAL ORGANIZATIONS

History: Benevolent and secret societies played an important part in America from the late 18th to the mid-20th centuries. Initially, the societies were organized to aid members and their families in times of distress. They evolved from this purpose into important social clubs by the late 19th century.

In the 1950s, with the arrival of the civil rights movement, an attack occurred on the secretiveness and often discriminatory practices of these societies. Membership in fraternal organizations, with the exception of the Masonic group, dropped significantly. Many local chapters closed and sold their lodge halls. This resulted in the appearance of many fraternal items in the antiques market.

Museums: Iowa Masonic Library & Museum, Cedar Rapids, IA, http://www.gl-ia.org/museums.html; Knights of Columbus Headquarters Museum, New Haven, CT, http://www.kofc-supreme-council.org; Masonic Grand Lodge Library & Museum of Texas,

Figure, elk, bronze finish, 6-1/4" l, $135.

Waco, TX, http://www.gltexas.org; Museum of Our National Heritage, Lexington, MA, http://www.mnh.org; Odd Fellows Historical Society, Caldwell, ID.

Additional Listings: See *Warman's Americana & Collectibles* for more examples.

Pinback button, Elks Congress of Nations, 1908, multicolored, $120. Photo courtesy of Hake's Americana & Collectibles.

Benevolent & Protective Order of the Elks, (BPOE)

Badge, 1920 Chicago 56th Annual Reunion 20.00

Beaker, 5" h, cream, black elk head, marked "Mettlach, Villeroy & Boch" 110.00

Book, *National Memorial*, 1931, color illus 35.00

Bookends, pr, bronzed cast iron, elk in high relief 75.00

Shaving mug, pink and white, gold elk head, crossed American flags and floral dec, marked "Germany" on bottom 90.00

Tip tray, Philadelphia, 21st Annual Reunion, July 1907, rect, 4-7/8" x 3-1/4" 135.00

Eastern Star

Demitasse cup and saucer, porcelain 25.00

Pendant, SP, rhinestones and rubies 45.00

Ring, gold, Past Matron, star-shape stone with diamond in center . . 150.00

Independent Order of Odd Fellows (I.O.O.F)

Ceremonial staff, 3" w, 1-1/2" d, 64" h, polychrome carved wood, reverse tapering staff surmounted by carved open hand in cuffed sleeve holding heart in palm, old red, gold, and black painted surface, mounted on iron base, minor surface imperfections. . 2,300.00

Gameboard, reverse painted black and gold metallic squares bordered by "I.O.O.F" chain links and other symbols, areas of flaking, 20-1/2" x 20-1/2" black oak frame 350.00

Shaving mug, 3-3/4" h, B. F. Smith, insignia, gold trim, wear 165.00

Tintype, seated gentleman, wearing white fringed lodge vest, late 1800s, 2-1/4" x 3-3/4" 15.00

Vignette, 7-3/4" x 14-1/2", oil on board, hand beneath three links holding heart and card bearing archery scene, molded gilt gesso frame, flaking, subtle surface grime 920.00

Wall hanging, 75" l, 47-1/2" h, painted canvas, from Odd Fellows Lodge #4 in Whitehall, NY, 19th C, several symbols reflecting high ideals, imperfections 2,990.00

Watch fob, 94th Anniversary, April 12, 1913 . . . . 30.00

Knights Templar

Business card, Reynolds, J. P., Columbia Commandery No. 18 (K of P) Sturgis, MI, color logo, c1890 . . . . 6.00

Plate, 9" d, Pittsburgh Commandry, 1903, china 50.00

Tumbler, 4" h, 36th Conclave, glass 75.00

Masonic
Apron

14" x 12", leather, white, blue silk trim, white embroidery, silver fringe 35.00

18" x 17", satin, ivory, red fringe, polychrome painted insignia 65.00

Book, *Morals & Dogma of the Ancient & Accepted Scottish Rite of Freemasonry*, Albert Pike, L. H.. Jenkins, 1949, 861 pgs 20.00

Bookends, pr, patinated metal, "appl'd for" on back 200.00

Box, cov, 5" x 16-1/4" x 12-1/2", Chinese Export black lacquer, molded top with mother-of-pearl and lacquer Masonic devices, sides with floral dec, top loose, lock mechanism missing, minor lacquer loss 920.00

Ceremonial cane, 33-1/2" l, carved lizards, rounded top knop with emblem and eagle, metal top, several age cracks 350.00

Cufflinks and tie bar, carved bone, detailed, patent number on back 150.00

Doorstop, cast iron, red base, white bird, gold chain, $125.

Gavel, 11-3/4" l, oak handle, walnut head, boxwood, tip and back of head, two engraved silver fittings, some splits and wear 170.00

Goblet, St. Paul, 1908 . . . . 70.00

Ice-cream mold, 3-3/4" d, pewter, symbol, marked "E & Co., NY" . . 30.00

Jug, 5-5/8" h, lusterware, transfer printed and painted polychrome enamels, horseman, inscribed "James Hardman 1823," Masonic dec, royal coat of arms, minor wear 410.00

Match holder, 11" h, wall type, walnut, pierce carved symbols 75.00

Medal, Amarillo, Texas 90.00

Painting, 23-1/4" h, 20" w, oil on canvas, "Our Motto," framed, retouched, craquelure 2,645.00

Pendant, 1" l, 14K rose gold, enameled blue and white 110.00

Pinback button, 6" d, photos of members, 1940 . . . . 75.00

Ring, 14K rose gold, enameled cross on one side, enameled 32 degrees on other, double eagle head set with 10-point diamond, hand engraved 1900-20 . . . . 175.00

Shield, 19-1/2" x 17-1/2", carved walnut, figural, square and compass framing arm and gavel, mounted on shield, upper end of rim incised "March 6, 1902" 230.00

Patriotic Order Sons of America, top pin printed celluloid, center portrait of George Washington, gold trim, center medallion with image of Washington kneeling in prayer, made by Whitehead & Hoag, 7" l, $125. Photo courtesy of Julie Robinson.

Watch fob, 10K yg, raised emblem, chain and ring **90.00**

Shriner

Cup and saucer, Los Angeles, 1906 .... **70.00**

Dinnerware, Rajah, partial set, various marks, 52 pcs **150.00**

Goblet, St. Paul, 1908, ruby stained, pedestal foot **70.00**

Ice-cream mold, 4-1/4" d, pewter, crescent with Egyptian head, marked "E & Co., NY" **30.00**

Mug, Syria Temple, Pittsburgh, 1895, Nantasket Beach, gold figures.. **125.00**

Shot glass, cranberry and clear, symbols and officers' names, St. Louis, 1909 .... **300.00**

FRUIT JARS

History: Fruit jars are canning jars used to preserve food. Thomas W. Dyott, one of Philadelphia's earliest and most innovative glassmakers, was promoting his glass canning jars in 1829. John Landis Mason patented his screw-type canning jar on November 30, 1858. This date refers to the patent date, not the age of the jar. There are thousands of different jars and a variety of colors, types of closures, sizes, and embossings.

References: Tom Caniff, *The Label Space*, printed by author (1223 Oak Grove Ave., Steubenville, OH 43925); Douglas M. Leybourne, Jr., *Red Book No. 7*, published by author (P.O. Box 5417, N. Muskegon, MI 49445), 1993; Dick Roller (comp.), *Indiana Glass Factories Notes*, Acorn Press, 1994; Bill Schroeder, *1000 Fruit Jars*, 5th ed., Collector Books, 1987, 1995 value update; Betty Zumwalt, *Ketchup Pickles Sauces,* Mark West Publishers (P.O. Box 1914, Sand Point, ID 83864).

Periodicals: *Antique Bottle & Glass Collector*, P.O. Box 180, East Greenville, PA 18041; *Bottles & Extras,* 2230 Toub St., Ramona, CA 92065, http://www.fohbc.com; *Fruit Jar News*, 1223 Oak Grove Ave., Steubenville, OH 43952.

Collectors' Clubs: Ball Collectors Club, 497 Fox Drive, Monroe, MI 48161; Federation of Historical Bottle Collectors, Inc., 2230 Toub St., Ramona, CA 92065; Midwest Antique Fruit Jar & Bottle Club, P.O. Box 38, Flat Rock, IN 47234, http://www.fruitjar.org.

Additional Listings: See *Warman's Americana & Collectibles* for more examples.

Dray Mason, square, embossed, zinc lid, half pint, $20.

Advance, Pat. Appl'd For, aqua, ground lip, qt **95.00**

A. Stone & Co./Philada, aquamarine, applied collared mouth, glass lid, smooth base, half gallon, two mouth chips, L #2747 .... **175.00**

Atlas Mason's Patent, medium yellow green, ABM lip, qt **50.00**

Ball, Ideal, colorless, bottom emb "Pat'd July 14, 1908," wire closure. **7.50**

Ball, mason, yellow green, amber striations, qt **75.00**

B. B. Wilcox, aquamarine, ground mouth, glass lid, wire bale, smooth base, half gallon, L #3000 ..... **100.00**

Belle, Pat. Dec. 14th 1869, aqua, three raised feet, ground lip, metal neck band, wire bail, qt **75.00**

Canton Domestic, Patent 1889, clear **85.00**

Clarke Fruit Jar Co., Cleveland, OH, aqua, ground lip, lid, metal cam lever closure, 1-1/2 pt **165.00**

Crystal Jar, Patd Dec. 17, 1878, clear, ground lip **70.00**

Dillion G. Co., Fairmont, IN, green, quart, wax seal, long crack **12.50**

Dodge Sweeney & Co.'s California, aqua, ground lip, glass insert, zinc band, 1-1-2 qt **425.00**

Eagle, deep aquamarine, applied collared mouth, glass lid, iron yoke, smooth base, half gallon, #872 . **160.00**

Excelsior, aqua, ground lip, insert, zinc band, qt **575.00**

Fahnestock Albree & Co., aqua, applied mouth, qt **35.00**

Franklin Fruit Jar, aqua, ground lip, zinc lid, qt **225.00**

Friedley & Cornman's Patent Oct. 25th 1958, Ladies Choice, aquamarine, ground mouth, iron rim, gutta percha or leather insert, smooth base, half gallon, iron rim lid rusty, L #1039 .... **1,200.00**

Gilberds Improved Jar, aqua, ground lip, wire band, qt **160.00**

Good Luck, Hazel Atlas, four-leaf clover on front, glass lid, half gal . **50.00**

Green Mountain, CA, clear **10.00**

Helmen's Railroad Mills, amber, ground lip, insert, zinc band, pt.. **70.00**

High Grade, aqua, ground lip, zinc lid, qt **150.00**

H & R, #2, half moon, aqua, 7" h . **45.00**

Johnson & Johnson, New York, cobalt blue, ground lip, orig insert, screw band, qt **325.00**

Keystone Mason, Patent Nov. 3, 1858, quart, aqua................. **50.00**

Lafayette, aqua, tooled lip, orig three-pc glass and metal stopper, qt **200.00**

Mason Crystal Jar, clear, ground lip, zinc lid **65.00**

Mason's Kempton, 1858........ **4.25**

Mason jar with 1858 patent date,
$4.25.

Mason's Patent Nov. 30th, 1858, light green, profuse amber striations, machined mouth, zinc lid, smooth base, half gallon, some int. stain, L#1787
. . . . **325.00**

Midget, T. M. Improved, pint, green-aqua **20.00**

Moore's Patent Dec. 3 1861, aquamarine, applied collared mouth, glass lid, iron yoke clamp, smooth base, qt, L #2204 . . . . **120.00**

Peerless, aqua, applied mouth, iron yoke, half gallon **85.00**

Pet, aqua, applied mouth, qt. . . . **55.00**

Presto Wide Mouth, patent date and opening instructions, metal ring marked "Tested and Approved By The Good Housekeeping Institute," Serial No. 2285 Conducted by Good Housekeeping Magazine, pint. . . **12.00**

Protector, aquamarine, ground mouth, unmarked tin lid, smooth base, qt, L #2420. . . . . **70.00**

Star, aqua, emb star, ground lip, zinc insert and screw band, qt **300.00**

Sun, aquamarine, ground mouth, glass lid, iron clamp, smooth base, qt **130.00**

The Magic (star) Fruit Jar, greenish-aqua, ground mouth, glass lid, iron clamp, smooth base, half gallon, chips to mouth, L #1606 . . . . . . **180.00**

The Pearl, aqua, ground lip, screw band, qt. **40.00**

The Van Vilet Jar of 1881, aqua, ground lip, orig wire and iron yoke, qt **365.00**

Union N1, Beaver Falls Glass Co., Beaver Falls, PA, aqua, applied wax seal ring, half gallon **45.00**

Woodbury Improved (monogram), aquamarine, ground mouth, quart, L #3029. **40.00**

FRY GLASS

History: The H. C. Fry Glass Co. of Rochester, Pennsylvania, began operating in 1901 and continued in business until 1933. Its first products were brilliant-period cut glass. It later produced Depression glass tablewares. In 1922, the company patented heat-resisting ovenware in an opalescent color. This "Pearl Oven Glass," produced in a variety of pieces for oven and table, included casseroles, meat trays, and pie and cake pans.

Fry's beautiful art line, Foval, was produced only in 1926 and 1927. It is pearly opalescent, with jade green or delft blue trim. It is always evenly opalescent and never striped like Fenton's opalescent line.

Marks: Most pieces of the oven glass are marked "Fry," with model numbers and sizes. Foval examples are rarely signed, except for occasional silver-overlay pieces marked "Rockwell."

Reference: Fry Glass Society, *Collector's Encyclopedia of Fry Glass,* Collector Books, 1989, 1998 value update.

Collectors' Club: H. C. Fry Glass Society, P.O. Box 41, Beaver, PA 15009.

Reproduction Alert: In the 1970s, reproductions of Foval were made in abundance in Murano, Italy. These pieces, including items such as candlesticks and toothpicks, have teal blue transparent trim.

Fry-Foval, lemonade set, pitcher and six glasses, vaseline with cobalt handles, **$700.**

Goblet, three-Buttress, open stem, quilted optic, emerald, rare, **$275.**

Bowl, 8" d, cut glass, pineapple design, wheel cutting, sgd **120.00**

Butter dish, cov, Pearl Oven Ware **75.00**

Canapé plate, 6-1/4" d, 4" h, cobalt blue center handle, Foval **165.00**

Candlesticks, pr, 12" h, Foval, pearl white candlesticks, jade green threading and trim. **1,380.00**

Child's baking set, two 3-1/8" d cake pans, 3-3/8" d pie dish, 4-3/4" x 2-3/4" loaf pan, 4-1/2" cov casserole, small rim flake on one cake pan. **325.00**

Compote, 6" d, 6-7/8" h, Foval, jade green foot **450.00**

Creamer and sugar, Set 200, Foval, delft blue handles **175.00**

Cruet, Foval, cobalt blue handle, orig stopper **125.00**

Cup and saucer, Foval, blue handles **65.00**

Decanter, 9" h, ftd, Foval, applied Delft blue handle **195.00**

Fruit bowl, 9-7/8" d, 5-1/4" h, Foval, pearl white, ridged, delft blue foot **520.00**

Ice-cream tray, 14" l, 7" w, cut glass, Nelson pattern variation, all over cutting, sgd "Fry" **290.00**

Ivy ball, 3-7/8" d, 7" h, amethyst **180.00**

Lamp base, 10-1/2" h, bottle shape, jade green, some wear on base. **165.00**

Lamp shade, 6" h, 2" d fitter ring, Foval, blue trim **95.00**

Nappy, 6" d, cut glass, pinwheel and fan with hobstar center, sgd **60.00**

Pitcher, cov, 7" w, 9-1/4" h, colorless crackle glass body, green handle and knob **230.00**

Platter, 17" l, Oven Ware **65.00**

Punch cup, Crackle, clear, cobalt blue ring handle **45.00**

Sherbet, 4" h, cut glass, Chicago pattern **75.00**

Sugar bowl, 5" w, 3" h, Foval, jade green handles. **230.00**

Teacup and saucer, Foval, delft blue handles. **95.00**

Teapot, 10" w, 6" h, Foval, jade green spout, handle, and finial, two small chips. **330.00**

Trivet, 8", Oven Ware **20.00**

Tumbler, cut glass, pinwheel, zipper, and fan motifs, sgd, six-pc set . . **280.00**

Vase, 7-1/2" h, Foval, jade green, rolled rim and foot **200.00**

Water set, 10" h cov pitcher, six 5-3/8" tumblers, crackle glass, white knob and applied handle **195.00**

FULPER POTTERY

History: The Fulper Pottery Company of Flemington, New Jersey, made stoneware pottery and utilitarian ware beginning in the early 1800s. It switched to the production of art pottery in 1909 and continued until about 1935.

The company's earliest artware was called the Vasekraft line (1910-1915), featuring intense glazine and rectilinear, Germanic forms. Its middle period (1915-1925) included some of the earlier shapes, but they also incorporated Oriental forms. Their glazing at this time was less consistent but more diverse. The last period (1925-1935) was characterized by water-down Art-Deco forms with relatively weak glazing.

Pieces were almost always molded, though careful hand-glazing distinguished this pottery as one of the premier semi-commercial producers. Pieces from all periods are almost always marked.

Marks: A rectangular mark, FULPER, in a rectangle is known as the "ink mark" and dates from 1910-1915. The second mark, as shown, dates from 1915-1925; it was incised or in black ink. The final mark, FULPER, die-stamped, dates from about 1925 to 1935.

References: Susan and Al Bagdade, *Warman's American Pottery and Porcelain*, 2nd ed., Krause Publications, 2000; Ralph and Terry Kovel, *Kovels' American Art Pottery*, Crown Publishers, 1993; David Rago, *American Art Pottery*, Knickerbocker Press,
1977; —, *Fulper Pottery*, Arts & Crafts Quarterly Press, n.d.

Collectors' Clubs: American Art Pottery Assoc., P.O. Box 834, Westport, MA 02790-0697, http://www.amartpot.org; Stangl/Fulper Collectors Club, P.O. Box 538, Flemington, NJ 08822, http://www.stanglfulper.com.

Adviser: David Rago.

Bowl, 8" d, 5" h, flower holder, blue-green crystalline glaze, rect ink mark. **110.00**

Bud vase, 9" h, baluster, Butterscotch flambé glaze, ink racetrack mark **275.00**

Center bowl, 11" d, 5" h, Chinese-form, ftd, ivory crystalline int., Chinese Blue flambé ext., imp racetrack mark **435.00**

Effigy bowl, cat's eye flambé glaze interior, mustard matte flambé exterior, rectangular ink mark, 7-1/2" x 10-1/2", $1,200. Photo courtesy of David Rago Auctions.

Effigy bowl, 10" d, 8" h, blue, ivory, and green flambé int., matte blue glaze base, rect ink mark **8,050.00**

Ibis bowl, 10-1/2" d, 5-1/2" h, green and blue flambé over Copperdust Crystalline, ink racetrack mark . **815.00**

Lamp base

7" d, 13" h, tear-shape, built-in glazed cap, orig fittings, acorn pulls, Cucumber Matte glaze, mark under Chinese wooden stand, rewired **920.00**

8-1/2" d, 11-3/4" h, post-factory, Vasekraft, amber crystalline glaze over matte mustard base, label "425/jardinière/mustard matte/brown flambé," rect ink mark **1,610.00**

Roman urn, 6" d, 11" h, blue and green flambé glaze over cobalt matte, rect ink mark, small flake to one handle **365.00**

Lamp, flaring base, mushroom shade, green and ivory leaded glass pieces, Cat's Eye flambe glaze, rectangular ink mark, rare, $11,000. Photo courtesy of David Rago Auctions, Inc.

Urn

6" d, 7-3/4" h, turquoise crystalline glaze, ink racetrack mark . . **435.00**

7-1/2" d, 12" h, two handles, fine Mirrored Green, Mahogany, and Ivory flambé glazes, rect ink mark **1,200.00**

Vase

3" d, 10-3/4" h, cylindrical, Leopard Skin Crystalline glaze, early rect ink stamp, small stilt-pull or grinding chip **860.00**

3-1/4" d, 5" h, shouldered, Chinese Blue flambé glaze, speckled blue glaze, rect ink mark. **230.00**

4-3/4" d, 7" h, bullet, frothy Leopard Skin Crystalline glaze, ink racetrack mark, two small opposing bursts at rim, grinding chips on base **520.00**

5" d, 5-1/2" h, bulbous, brown and Chinese Blue glaze, raised racetrack mark **290.00**

5" d, 7" h, classic shape, blue-green mirrored glaze, raised racetrack mark **490.00**

5" d, 11" h, hexagonal, frothy Wisteria glaze, imp racetrack mark, fleck to shoulder, several glaze bubbles on rim **350.00**

6" d, 7" h, bulbous, flaring rim, blue and green mirror glaze, raised racetrack mark **290.00**

6" d, 8-1/2" h, bulbous, closed-in rim, Elephant's Breath flambé glaze dripping over frothy green and

ochre matte glaze, rect Prang
mark, hairline to rim **1,150.00**

6-3/4" d, 8" h, gourd-shape,
two buttressed handles, Cucumber
Matte and Leopard Skin
crystalline glaze, imp racetrack
mark **1,045.00**

7" d, 12" h, classic shape,
Copperdust Crystalline glaze,
incised racetrack mark, restored
drill-hole in bottom **7,475.00**

Vessel

4" l, 3" h, squatty, two handles,
amber and Chinese Blue glaze,
stamped horizontal mark . . **175.00**

8" l, 6-1/2" h, squatty, buttressed
handles, Chinese Blue crystalline
glaze, ink racetrack mark . . **460.00**

8-1/2" l, 14" h, three handled, Art
Deco, emb tulips, stylized flowers,
amber and blue flame glaze,
stamped "FULPER/895" . . . **980.00**

FURNITURE

History: Two major currents dominate the American
furniture marketplace—furniture made in Great Britain
and furniture made in the United States. American
buyers continue to show a strong prejudice for objects
manufactured in the United States. They will pay a
premium for such pieces and accept them above
technically superior and more aesthetically appealing
English examples.

Until the last half of the 19th century, formal
American styles were dictated by English examples
and design books. Regional furniture, such as the
Hudson River Valley (Dutch) and the Pennsylvania
German styles, did develop. A less-formal furniture,
often designated as "country" or vernacular style,
developed throughout the 19th and early 20th
centuries. These country pieces deviated from the
accepted formal styles and have a charm that many
collectors find irresistible.

America did contribute a number of unique
decorative elements to English styles. The American
Federal period is a reaction to the English Hepplewhite
period. American designers created furniture which
influenced, rather than reacted to, world taste in the
Gothic-Revival style and Arts and Crafts, Art Deco, and
Modern International movements.

Reproduction Alert: Beware of the large
number of reproductions. During the 25 years
following the American Centennial of 1876, there
was a great revival in copying furniture styles and
manufacturing techniques of earlier eras. These
centennial pieces now are more than 100 years
old. They confuse many dealers, as well as
collectors.

FURNITURE STYLES APPROX. DATES	
William and Mary	1690-1730
Queen Anne	1720-1760
Chippendale	1755-1790
Federal (Hepplewhite)	1790-1815
Sheraton	1790-1810
Empire (Classical)	1805-1830
Victorian	
French Restauration	1830-1850
Gothic Revival	1840-1860
Rococo Revival	1845-1870
Elizabethan	1850-1915
Louis XIV	1850-1914
Naturalistic	1850-1914
Renaissance Revival	1850-1880
Néo-Greek	1855-1885
Eastlake	1870-1890
Art Furniture	1880-1914
Arts and Crafts	1895-1915
Art Nouveau	1896-1914
Art Deco	1920-1945
International Movement	1940-Present

References: *Antique Wicker from the
Heywood-Wakefield Catalog*, Schiffer Publishing,
1994; Edward Deming Andrews and Faith Andrews,
Masterpieces of Shaker Furniture, Dover Publications,
1999; John Andrews, *British Antique Furniture Price
Guide and Reasons for Values*, Antique Collectors'
Club, 1999; —, *Victorian and Edwardian Furniture
Price Guide and Reasons for Values*, Antique
Collectors' Club, 1999; Luke Beckerdite (ed.),
American Furniture 1998, Chipstone Foundation,
University Press of New England, 1998; Joseph T.
Butler, *Field Guide to American Furniture*, Facts on
File Publications, 1985; David Cathers, *Furniture of
the American Arts and Crafts Movement: Revised
Edition*, Turn of the Century Editions, 1996; —,
*Stickley Style: Arts and Crafts Homes in the Craftsman
Tradition*, Simon & Schuster, 1999; Victor Chimnery,
Oak Furniture, The British Tradition, Antique
Collectors' Club, 1999; Frances Collard, *Regency
Furniture*, Antique Collectors' Club, 1999; Douglas
Congdon-Martin, *Arts & Crafts Designs for the Home*,
Schiffer Publishing, 2000; Bernard D. Cotton, *The
English Regional Chair*, Antique Collectors' Club,
1999; Anna Tobin D'Ambrosio, (ed.), *Masterpieces of
American Furniture from the
Munson-Williams-Proctor Institute*, Syracuse
University Press, 1999; Joseph Downs, *American
Furniture: Queen Anne and Chippendale Periods,
1725-1788*, Schiffer Publishing, 2001; Eileen and
Richard Dubrow, *American Furniture of the 19th
Century: 1840-1880*, 2nd ed., Schiffer Publishing,
2000; —, *Styles of American Furniture, 1860-1960*,
Schiffer Publishing, 1997; Nancy Goyne Evans,
American Windsor Chairs, Hudson Hills Press, 1996;
—, *American Windsor Furniture: Specialized Forms*,
Hudson House Press, 1997; *Fine Furniture
Reproductions*, Schiffer Publishing, 1996; Helaine
Fendleman and Jonathan Taylor, *Tramp Art: A Folk Art
Phenomenon*, Stewart, Tabori & Chang, 1999; Oscar
P. Fitzgerald, *Four Centuries of American Furniture*,
Wallace-Homestead, (Krause Publications,) 1995; Tim
Forrest, *Bulfinch Anatomy of Antique Furniture*,
Bulfinch Press, 1996; Don Fredgant, *American
Manufactured Furniture*, revised and updated ed.,

Schiffer Publishing, 1996; Phillipe Garner,
Twentieth-Century Furniture, Van Nostrand Reinhold,
1980; Harris Gertz, *Heywood-Wakefield*, Schiffer
Publishing, 2001; Cara Greenberg, *Op To Pop:
Furniture of the 1960s*, Bulfinch Press, 1999; David
Hawkins, *Close Encounters with American Furniture:
A Restorer's Story*, Sage Crest Press, 1999; Clarke
Hess, *Mennonite Arts*, Schiffer Publishing, 2001;
Barbara Israel, *Antique Garden Ornament: Two
Centuries of American Taste*, Harry N. Abrams, 1999;
Bruce Johnson, *The Pegged Joint*, Knock on Wood
Publications, 1995; Edward Joy, *Pictorial Dictionary of
British 19th Century Furniture Design*, Antique
Collectors' Club, 1999; John Kassay, *The Book of
American Windsor Furniture: Styles and Technologies*,
University of Massachusetts Press, 1998;

Myrna Kaye, *Fake, Fraud, or Genuine*, New York
Graphic Society Book, 1987; —, *There's a Bed in the
Piano: The Inside Story of the American Home*,
Bulfinch Press, 1998; Leigh and Leslie Keno, *Hidden
Treasures: Searching for the Masterpieces of American
Furniture*, Warner Books, 2000; William C. Ketchum,
Jr., *American Cabinetmakers*, Crown, 1995; Ralph
Kylloe, *History of the Old Hickory Chair Company and
the Indiana Hickory Furniture Movement*, published by
author, 1995; —, *Rustic Traditions*, Gibbs-Smith,
1993; David P. Lindquist and Caroline C. Warren,
Colonial Revival Furniture with Prices,
Wallace-Homestead, 1993; —, *English &
Continental Furniture with Prices*,
Wallace-Homestead, 1994; —, *Victorian Furniture
with Prices*, Wallace-Homestead, 1995, distributed by
Krause Publications; Jack L. Lindsey, *Worldly Goods,
The Arts of Early Pennsylvania, 1680-1758*,
Pennsylvania Museum of Art, distributed by Antique
Collectors' Club, 1999; Paul McCobb, *Fifties
Furniture*, Schiffer Publishing, 2000; Robert F.
McGiffin, *Furniture Care and Conservation*, revised
3rd ed., American Association for State and Local
History Press, 1992; *Herman Miller 1939 Catalog,
Gilbert Rohde Modern Design*, Schiffer Publishing,
1998; Charles Montgomery, *American Furniture, The
Federal Period, 1788-1825*, Schiffer Publishing, 2001;
John Morley, *The History of Furniture: Twenty-Five
Centuries of Style and Design in the Western
Tradition*, Bulfinch Press, 1999; Marie Purnell Musser,
Country Chairs of Central Pennsylvania, published by
author, 1990; Milo M. Naeve, *Identifying American
Furniture*, W. W. Norton, 1998; John Obbard, *Early
American Furniture, A Practical Guide for Collectors*,
Collector Books, 1999; Peter Philip, Gillian Walkling,
and John Bly, *Field Guide to Antique Furniture*,
Houghton Mifflin, 1992; Leslie Piña, *Dunbar: Fine
Furniture of the 1950s*, Schiffer Publishing, 2000; —,
Fifties Furniture, Schiffer Publishing, 1996; Rudolf
Pressler and Robin Staub, *Biedermeier Furniture*,
Schiffer Publishing, 1996; Don and Carol Raycraft,
*Wallace-Homestead Price Guide To American Country
Antiques, 16th Edition*, Krause Publications, 1999;
Steve and Linda Rouland, *Knoll Furniture, 1938-1960*,
Schiffer Publishing, 1999; Steve and Roger W.
Rouland, *Heywood-Wakefield Modern Furniture*,
1995, 2001 value update, Collector Books; Paul
Royka, *Mission Furniture, from the American Arts &
Crafts Movement*, Schiffer Publishing, 1997.

Albert Sack, *New Fine Points of Furniture*, Crown,
1993; Nancy N. Schiffer, *The Best of Golden Oak
Furniture*, Schiffer Publishing, 2000; Ellen T. Schroy,
Warman's American Furniture, Krause Publications,

2000; Harvey Schwartz, *Rattan Furniture,* Schiffer Publishing, 1999; Marvin D. Schwartz, Edward J. Stanek and Douglas K. True, *The Furniture of John Henry Belter and the Rococo Revival,* Antiques and Books by Lise Bohm, 2000; Klaus-Jurgen Sembach, *Modern Furniture Designs, 1950-1980s,* Schiffer Publishing, 1997; Nancy A. Smith, *Old Furniture,* 2nd ed., Dover Publications, 1990; Robert W. and Harriett Swedberg, *Collector's Encyclopedia of American Furniture,* Vol. 1 (1990, 1998 value update), Vol. 2 (1992, 1999 value update), Vol. 3 (1998, 2000 value update), Collector Books; ——, *Encyclopedia of American Oak Furniture,* Krause Publications, 2000; ——, *Furniture of the Depression Era,* Collector Books, 1987, 1999 value update; ——, Thonet Co., *Thonet Bentwood and Other Furniture* (1904 catalog reprint), Dover Publications, 1980; Treadway Gallery, Inc., *The 1950's/Modern Price Guide: Furniture, Volumes 1 and 2,* Treadway Gallery, Inc., 1999; Clifford A. Wallach and Michael Cornish, *Tramp Art, One Notch At A Time,* Wallach-Irons Publishing, (277 W. 10th St., NY, NY 10014) 1998; Elizabeth White, ed., *Pictorial Dictionary of British 18th Century Furniture Design,* Antique Collectors' Club, 1999; S. Whittington & C. Claxton Stevens, *18th Century Furniture,* Antique Collectors' Club, 1999; Eli Wilner, *Antique American Frames: Identification and Price Guide,* Avon Books, 1999; Ghenete Zelleke, Eva B. Ottillinger, and Nina Stritzler, *Against the Grain,* The Art Institute of Chicago, 1993.

There are hundreds of specialized books on individual furniture forms and styles. Two of note are: Monroe H. Fabian, *Pennsylvania-German Decorated Chest,* Universe Books, 1978, and Charles Santore, *Windsor Style In America,* Revised, Vols. I and II, Dover Publications, n.d.

Additional Listings: Arts and Craft Movement, Art Deco, Art Nouveau, Children's Nursery Items, Orientalia, Shaker Items, and Stickley.

Notes: Furniture is one of the types of antiques for which regional preferences are a factor in pricing. Victorian furniture is popular in New Orleans and unpopular in New England. Oak is in demand in the Northwest, but not as much so in the middle Atlantic states.

Prices vary considerably on furniture. Shop around. Furniture is plentiful unless you are after a truly rare example. Examine all pieces thoroughly—avoid buying on impulse. Turn items upside down; take them apart. Price is heavily influenced by the amount of repairs and restoration. Make certain you know if any such work has been done to a piece before buying it.

The prices listed below are "average" prices. They are only a guide. High and low prices are given to show market range.

Beds
Arts and Crafts
American, attributed to Stickley Bros., double, oak, headboard with narrow vertical slats and panels, tapered feet, orig side rails, orig finish, minor scratches, stenciled "9001-1/2," 80-1/2" l, 56-1/2" w, 30" h **1,355.00**

Bed, double, Arts & Crafts, attributed to Stickley Brothers, headboard with narrow vertical slats and panels, tapered feet, side rails, stenciled "9001-1/2," good original finish, minor scratches, 40" x 56-1/2" x 80-1/2", **$1,355.** *Photo courtesy of David Rago Auctions.*

Limbert, #651, daybed, angled headrest with spade cut-out, orig finish, recovered cushions, branded, numbered, 74" w, 25" d, 23" h **650.00**
Scottish, attributed to E. A. Taylor, oak, slatted head and footboards, inlaid with mother-of-pearl and fruitwood Glasgow roses, orig finish, 79-3/4" l, 55" w, 56-1/2" h **2,185.00**

Arts and Crafts-Style, quarter-sawn oak, three vertical panels in head and foot board, 42" x 53" h headboard, 34-1/2" h footboard **375.00**

Baroque, Italian, simulated marble high scrolling headboard dec in patiglia with vacant cartouches and foliage, carved scrolling feet, painted, green and blue marbleized dec, losses to paint and gilt, pr, 45-3/4" w, 84" h.......... **3,750.00**

Biedermeier, figured mahogany veneer, octagonal posts, turned feet and finials, paneled head and footboards, orig rails, some veneer damage, 38" w, 72" l, 45" h, pr.. **750.00**

Chippendale, tall post, curly maple, turned posts, scrolled headboard with poplar panel, orig side rails, old mellow refinishing, minor repairs to posts, 60" w, 72" l, 80" h **3,000.00**

Classical
Massachusetts, c1825-35, carved mahogany, tall post, scrolled mahogany headboard flanked by reeded, carved, and ring-turned posts, acanthus leaf, beading, gothic arches, and foliage carving, reeded and turned feet, orig rails later fitted for angle irons and bed bolts, orig surface, central finial

missing, 59" w, 81" d, 98" h **6,900.00**
Middle Atlantic States, 1835-45, carved mahogany veneer
Low post, scrolled and paneled headboard, leaf-carved finials flanked by posts with pineapple finials, acanthus leaves above spiral carved and ring-turned posts, orig rails, bed bolts, and covers, refinished, imperfections, 58-1/2" w, 78" d, 56-1/2" h **1,100.00**
Tall post, four turned, carved, and reeded posts continuing to turned feet on casters, flanked by scrolled recessed panel headboard with rolled veneered crest, shaped footboard, joined by flat tester, rails with added angle irons, old refinish, height loss, 61-1/2" w, 72" d, 77-1/2" h **2,550.00**
New England, c1820, painted, turned tall post, turned and tapering headposts flanking shaped headboard, spiral-carved footpost joined by rails fitted for roping, accompanying tester, old red paint, restored, 54" w, 79" l, 60-1/2" h **1,400.00**

Country, American, rope, high post
Curly maple, areas of tight curl, evidence of old red wash, turned and tapered legs, boldly turned posts taper toward the top, paneled headboard with scrolled crest, turned top finial, 53-1/2" w, 70" l rails with orig bolts, pierced restorations **1,890.00**
Poplar, scalloped walnut headboard with arched crest, well turned legs and posts, old dark finish, converted from larger size, had canopy at one time, 40" d, 76" l rails **525.00**

Country, American, trundle, southwestern PA, walnut, mortised joints, turned posts, and finials, shaped corners along top edge of head, foot, and sideboards, refinished, 71-1/2" l, 44" d..................... **125.00**

Empire, American
Single, fitted as daybed or sofa, mahogany and mahogany figured veneer, turned and acanthus carved posts, upholstered cushion, 31-1/2" x 80" x 43-3/4" h ... **825.00**
Tall Post, curly maple posts, poplar scrolled headboard with old soft finish, turned detail, acorn finials, rails and headboard replaced, 57-1/4" w, 72-1/2" l rails, 89" h **1,650.00**

Empire-Style

Cannonball, mahogany, bold detail, replaced headboard with carved eagle, originally rope bed, side rails changed, other repairs, replaced rails, 78" l, 54" w, 59" h
. . . .**1,200.00**
Sleigh, red painted, scrolled ends, bronze mounted foliate and mask mounts, 20th C, price for pr
. . . .**1,650.00**

Federal

American, first half 19th C, cherry, tester, three-quarter, rect headboard with concave side edges, footboard lower, baluster-turned posts continuing to turned legs, rails with rope pegs, 81-1/2" l, 53-1/2" w, 78-1/4" h
. . . . **500.00**
New England, c1820, painted red, tall post, vase and ring turned and reeded foot posts joined to turned head posts and shaped pine headboard, arched canopy frame, old red stain, minor imperfections, 48" w, 69" l, 75" h **2,750.00**
New England, early 19th C, painted low post, folding, turned headposts planking shaped headboard, joined to footposts by joined rails fitted for roping and folding, old Spanish brown paint, 52-3/4" w, 77-1/2" d, 33-1/2" h. **700.00**
Salem, MA, c1810-30, carved mahogany, tall post, flat tester frame joining vase and ring reeded and swelled acanthus leaf carved footposts, sq tapering legs, molded spade feet, leaf-carved vase and ring reeded and swelled head posts, shaped headboard, old finish, 62" w, 78-1/2" d, 87" h
. . . . **10,925.00**
George III, four poster, carved walnut, brass mounted, circular tapered head posts, shaped mahogany headboard, reeded and acanthus-carved footposts, ring-turned feet, casters, 9-1/2" h
. . . .**10,000.00**
Gothic Revival, American, c1850, carved mahogany, tall headboard with three Gothic arch panels, leaf-carved crest rail, flanked by heavy round ribbed posts topped by ring-turned finials, arched and paneled footboard flanked by lower footposts, heavy bun feet. **4,750.00**
Modern, Ludwig Mies van der Rohr, made by Knoll, daybed, tufted leather cushion and bolster supported by

leather straps, rosewood and steel frame, 78" w, 40" d, 18" h **5,450.00**
Queen Anne, Pennsylvania, early 19th C, low poster, turned and painted pine, head and footposts with flattened ball finials, shaped head and footboards, tapered feet, orig rope rails, orig green paint, 48-1/2" w, 74-3/4" h. . . . **3,600.00**

Hepplewhite style, mahogany, satinwood inlay, c1920-30, **$300.**

Sheraton

Canopy

Carved mahogany, headboard posts simple turned with ring and block turnings, simple headboard, heavily carved footboard posts with spiral turnings and acanthus leaf bell, sq tester with curtains, 58" w, 73-1/2" l, 88" without finials
. . . . **3,200.00**
Painted, headboard with D-type cut outs on side, footboard with reeded and turned posts, canopy frame,

painted red, 52" w, 76" l, 68" h
. . . . **750.00**
Tall post, refinished maple and birch, pine headboard, turned posts with reeded detail on foot posts, rope end rails, replaced side rails, curved canopy frame covered in white cotton with floral embroidery, matching bed clothes included, 55" w, 78" l, 66-3/4" h **1,550.00**

Victorian

American, refinished walnut, paneled head and footboards with applied scroll and fruit detail, matching crest, orig 73" l side rails, 54" w, 71-1/2" h. **450.00**
Brass, c1900, straight top rail, curved corners, ring shaped capitals, cast iron side rails, 55" w, 61" h. **1,200.00**
Chaise, c1845, carved oak, one end carved with foliage and gadrooning, circular gadrooned legs, casters, 64" l **1,380.00**
Half Tester, attributed to Prudent Mallard, New Orleans, LA, c1850, carved rosewood, tall arched headboard, shell carved crest, fruit and nuts, scroll carved borders, shaped bordered panels flanked by tall tapering turned headposts supporting upholstered half tester, scroll carved crest, turned finials, paneled sideboards and footboard, turned and carved details, scroll carved corner braces . .**15,000.00**

Benches

Arts & Crafts, oak, rect top with raised edge, pierced and arched apron supported by side slabs, scrolled cut-outs at base, refinished top, orig

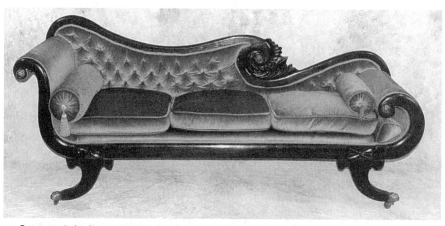

Regency, chaise lounge, rosewood, tufted shaped back, over-scrolled head and end, brass rosettes, three bolsters, three loose cushions, splayed legs, brass paw feet, 83" l, 25" d, **$2,400.**
Photo courtesy of Alderfer Auction Company, Inc.

finish to base, 42" w, 14" d, 18" h
.... **1,600.00**

Bucket, pine, old worn green paint, sq nail construction, bootjack cut outs on ends, two shelves, shaped tops, 41-1/2" w, 12-1/2" d, 30-3/4" h ..**660.00**

Classical, window

Boston, 1835-45, carved mahogany veneer, upholstered seat, veneered rail, leaf-carved cyma curved ends, joined by ring-turned medial stretcher, 48" w, 16-1/4" d, 17-1/2" h
.... **2,185.00**

New York, 1815-25, mahogany veneer, curving upholstered seat flanked by scrolled ends, scrolled base, old refinish, some veneer cracking and loss, 20th C olive green velvet upholstery, 39-1/2" w, 14" d, 23-5/8" h **3,500.00**

New York, c1820, mahogany and mahogany veneer, upholstered slip seat, veneered rect frame, beaded curule legs joined by vase and ring-turned stretcher, old finish, 24-1/4" w, 15" d, 19" h ... **1,035.00**

Classical Revival, mahogany, carved paw feet and lion's heads, maroon velvet cushion, old finish, 16-1/2" l, 29-1/4" w, 23" h............**600.00**

Country

68-1/2" l, Canadian, settle, pine, paneled construction, shaped arms, turned spindles, shaped crest, folds open into bed, old worn finish, traces of paint......**600.00**

96" l, 18-1/4" w, 13" h, pine, orig red paint, PA, early 19th C.....**750.00**

104" l, 13-1/2" w, pine, old worn and weathered green repaint, one board top with rounded front corners, beaded edge apron, cut-out feet mortised through top, age crack in one end of top
.................**325.00**

Decorated, orig dark green with reddish brown paint, yellow line dec, mortised construction, some sq nails, arched end panels, replaced shoe feet, some later nails added, 33" w, 14" d, 23-1/4" h.................**275.00**

Federal

New England, c1810, window, mahogany, upholstered seat and rolled arms, sq tapering legs, H-form stretchers, refinished, minor repair to one leg, 39-1/2" l, 16" d, 29" h **900.00**

New York, c1825, window, figured mahogany, each end with rect crotch-figured crest centering

removable slip seat, matching seat rail, saber legs, 40-1/2" l..**3,500.00**

George III, English, mid-18th C, window, mahogany, rect seat, scrolling arms, later velvet cov, straight legs, blind fret craved, H-form stretcher, pr, 38" l **4,750.00**

Gothic Revival, American, c1820-40, carved mahogany, angled over-upholstered seat, carved seat rails centering quatrefoil, facet lancet-carved legs, molded faceted feet, 65" l, 20" d, 15-1/2" h **1,750.00**

Louis XVI-Style, window

Carved cherry, overstuffed seat, channeled rails, flanked by molded, overscroll arms carved with be-ribboned foliate sprays, turned, tapered, and leaf-capped legs.................**200.00**

Mahogany, out-curved overscroll arms with X-splats, close-nailed, horsehair upholstered seat, sabre legs with casters, frame reeded and carved with paterae, brass plaque reading, "...Colonial Mft Co., Zeeland, Michigan" ..**550.00**

Bench, modern, George Nelson For Herman Miller, slatted, original ebonized finish with some flaking, unmarked, 14" x 72" x 18-1/2", $690. Photo courtesy of David Rago Auctions.

Settle

Arrowback, cream-colored repaint, green tulips and foliage on crest, three-section slat back, scrolled arms, rabbit ear posts, incised detail around back of seat, ring turned legs, stretcher base, restorations, 80" w, 20" d, 37" h
.................**800.00**

Arts & Crafts, J. M. Young, cube, capped top rail, vertical slats all around, fabric cov drop-in spring seat, refinished, unmarked, 78" l, 29-1/2" h, 34" h........**2,870.00**

Country, curly maple and poplar, shaped crest and slats, scrolled

arms with four turned spindles, one support, matching spindles across back, seat frame with old leather insert with brass tacks, turned legs and cross stretchers, old dry refinish, pierced restoration to one arm, small repair to seat, 71-3/4" w, 27" d, 36" h............**800.00**

Windsor, 20th C green paint, yellow in turnings, 29 spindles with bamboo turnings across back with turned arms, well-shaped seat with incised rain gutter around back, eight splayed legs joined by cross stretchers, splits in seat, old iron braces added underneath for support, 77-1/2" w, 22" d, 36-3/4" h
.................**2,100.00**

Victorian-Style, chaise lounge, Chesterfield, early 20th C, tufted brown leather, adjustable backrest, casters, 62" l.................**3,000.00**

Wagon seat, New England, late 18th C, painted, two pairs of arched slats joining three turned stiles, double rush seat flanked by turned arms ending in turned hand-holds, tapering legs, old brown paint over earlier gray, 15" h seat, 30" h.................**1,200.00**

Wicker, painted white, hooped crest rail flanked by rows of dec curlicues, spiral wrapped posts and six spindles, pressed-in oval seat, dec curlicue apron, wrapped cabriole legs, X-form stretcher, 35" w, 31" h........**500.00**

Windsor

Country, kneeling, gray over olive green and red paint, reeded edge top, bamboo-turned legs, splayed base, 36-3/4" l, 6-3/4" d, 6" h
.................**350.00**

Mammy, painted black over red, gold stenciling, back crest with stenciled flowers, removable front gate, bench fitted with orig rockers, light brown painted scrolled arms, 48" w, 29-1/4" h........**1,000.00**

Bentwood

In 1856, Michael Thonet of Vienna perfected the process of bending wood using steam. Shortly afterward, Bentwood furniture became popular. Other manufacturers of Bentwood furniture were Jacob and Joseph Kohn, Philip Strobel and Son, Sheboygan Chair Co., and Tidoute Chair Co. Bentwood furniture is still being produced today by the Thonet firm and others.

Box

5-3/4" w, 4-1/4" d, 2-3/16" h, attributed to C. Hersey, Higham, MA, oval, single finger construction on lid and base, old green paint, traces of earlier green underneath **475.00**

8" d, 7" h, round, worn orig paint resembles wallpaper, yellow and black foliage scrolls on blue ground, some edge damage to lid **750.00**

14-3/4" l, oblong, pine, laced seams, old blue paint, edge damage **250.00**

17-1/4" l, band, pine, orig blue paint, unusual decoupage paper scene of black man, woman, and child, foreign inscription, wear and loose bottom board **550.00**

Chair

Austrian, Vienna Secession-style, c1910, side, back splat with three circular perforations, three slender spindles, painted black, set of eight **5,500.00**

Thonet, arm, c1935, lacquered, pine frame, upholstered back and seat, 43" h **600.00**

Cradle, 41" l, 39" h, ivory fittings **440.00**

Hall tree, Thonet, c1910, bentwood frame, contrasting striped wood inlay, coat hooks with central beveled mirror above one door, metal drip pan, orig label, 57" w, 13" d, 76" h **2,750.00**

Rocker, Thonet, arched twined top rail, cut-velvet fabric fitted back, armrests, and seat, elaborate scrolling frame, curved runners, 53" l **750.00**

Stool, Thonet, attributed to Marcel Kammerer, Austria, 1901, beech, sq seat, four legs, U-shaped braces forming spandrels, shaped bronze sabot feet, 14-1/4" sq, 18-1/2" h **1,500.00**

Table, Josef Hoffman, c1905, circular top, wooden spheres dec below rim, 21-1/4" h **500.00**

Blanket chests

Chippendale, country, pine, molded rect and hinged top, storage well, front with two simulated drawer fronts over two drawers, molded surrounds, outset molded base with bracket feet, 37-1/2" w, 20" d, 41" h **750.00**

Decorated

American, pine, orig red and mustard grain dec, high bracket feet, inset panels on front and sides have mustard graining, surrounded by red brushed borders, splits in high bracket feet, scalloped returns, semicircular drop at center,

applied reeded molding around base, int. till fitted with unusual pigeon holes with scalloped tops, edge wear, small piece of reeding missing from base...... **2,200.00**

American, poplar, orig black over red sponge dec, one board top, molded trim, arched cut-outs on end aprons, scalloped front apron, int. fitted with covered till, dovetailed drawer, cast iron hinges, minor touch-up, later coat of varnish, 43-1/4" w, 17" d, 21-1/4" h **495.00**

New York, Schohaire County, early 19th C, six board, painted blue, molded top, dovetailed constructed base with painted diamond and draped frieze with Chinese export punchbowl and ladle, dotted, banded, vine, and diamond border flanked by enamel Stiegel flip glasses with circular borders, minor imperfections, 37" w, 17" d, 15" h **6,900.00**

Ohio, c1820-40, pine and poplar, six-board construction, eagle dec, cover with considerable paint wear, restoration, 49-1/2" w, 21" d, 23-3/4" h **2,300.00**

Ohio, attributed to Knox County, dovetailed poplar, orig sponged circles and meandering borders, two board top with molding, scalloped base painted black, beveled aprons, fitted int. with covered till, early iron casters, 39" w, 29-1/2" d **825.00**

Ohio, found in Smithville, Wayne County, poplar, orig reddish-brown paint, scribed geometric designs, one board top with applied molding, dovetailed case and bracket feet, arched sides, well scalloped front aprons, cov till fitted into int., 44" w, 25" h, 22" d **1,650.00**

Pennsylvania, attributed to Somerset County, poplar, green stenciled signature for "Hiram Gardner, 1852," salmon, light and dark green, stenciled foliage and scroll detail, freehand heart just below keyhole, green trim on lid and base, dovetailed case and feet, molded apron and scrolling, int. till, replaced hinges, restorations, split in lid, corner chips, 43-1/2" w, 18" d **825.00**

Pennsylvania, Mahatonga Valley, early 19th C, pine and poplar,

molded lift top painted with American flag, lattice and banded border above recessed paneled sides with banded borders, joined by stiles continuing to feet, dec attributed to third quarter 19th C, 33" w, 19" d, 21" h **17,250.00**

Dowry, Mahantango Valley, Pennsylvania, "Samuel Grebiel 1799," orig paint dec, red, blue, mustard, black, and white, two shaped polygons painted in blue grain painting, identical polygons on each side, two in front with banner above with name and date, int. lidded till, black painted dovetailed bracket base, off-set strap hinges, orig lock, 48-1/2" w, 21" d, 23-1/2" h **3,000.00**

Grain Painted, New York state, c1830, molded hinged lift top, lidded till, molded bracket black painted base, orig fanciful ochre and raw umber graining, 48" w, 22" d, 29" h... **1,265.00**

Jacobean, oak, paneled construction with relief carving, drawer and feet replaced, repairs to lid and molding, old dark finish, 44-1/2" w, 19-1/2" d, 31-3/4" h **825.00**

Miniature, England, early 19th C, mahogany, molded lift-top with wire hinges, dovetail constructed box base, mid molding trim, heavy molded bracket base, worm holes, wear, 14-1/4" l, 6-3/4" h **1,035.00**

Mule, America, pine, thumb-molded top, two overlapping dovetailed drawers, bracket feet, old dark finishing, int. lined with 1875 Boston newspaper, pierced repairs to feet and drawer fronts, 40" w, 18" d, 34-3/4" h **700.00**

Painted

Massachusetts, western, 18th C, pine, hinged top with molded edge, lidded molded till, single base drawer, molded bracket feet, old green paint over red, old replaced glass pulls, paint wear on top, 45" w, 17" d, 31-5/8" h **2,650.00**

Milford, Connecticut, early 18th C, yellow pine, six-board construction, vestiges of painted dec, replaced ball feet, imperfections, 42-1/2" w, 20" d, 26-1/2" h.......... **950.00**

New England, c1780, six-board, molded hinged top, dovetail constructed base, bracket feet, orig red paint, minor imperfections, 43-3/4" w, 19" d, 26" h **700.00**

New England, late 18th C, molded lift top, two thumb-molded drawers on bracket base, old blue paint, brasses and hinges replaced, 36" w, 19" d, 44" h **1,955.00**

New England, late 18th C, pine, hinged molded lid, dovetailed box, applied carved ropetwist beading, applied molded base, orig blue paint, 43-1/2" w, 18" d, 17" h **2,645.00**

Pennsylvania, c1780, pine, green and blue paint, one board top with bread-board ends, applied lower molding, dovetailed case, strap hinges, till with molded lid, ogee feet, 45" w, 19" d, 25-1/4" h **1,500.00**

Pennsylvania, poplar, old brownish-red finish, dovetailed case, hinged lid, three dovetailed drawers, dovetailed bracket feet, applied moldings, till with lid, tattered printed Haus Segen fraktur on int. of lid, bear trap lock, 50-1/4" w, 23" d, 30" h . . . **2,100.00**

Pennsylvania or Ohio, attributed to, early 19th C, six-board, molded and beaded top, four stiles continuing to feet, old brilliant blue paint, 40" w, 22-3/4" d, 25-3/4" h **3,450.00**

Queen Anne, New England, c1750, marriage chest, pine, hinged rect lift lid, upper half faced with faux drawer fronts, brown paint, 35" **4,000.00**

Sheraton, country, pine and poplar, orig red paint, molded edge top, paneled front and ends, sq corner posts, mortised and pinned frame, scalloped apron, turned feet, 44" w, 19-1/2" d, 25-1/2" h **900.00**

William and Mary, New England, c1700, oak and yellow pine, joined, drawer base, old finish, minor imperfections, 48-1/2" w, 22" d, 32-3/4" h **4,500.00**

Bookcases
Arts & Crafts

English, double door, corbelled overhanging top, inlaid pewter, ebony, and fruitwood tulips, leaded glass panels with green tear-shaped inserts, curvilinear backsplash, emb strap handles, orig finish, unmarked, some corbels loose, 46" w, 12-1/2" d, 52-1/2" h **2,615.00**

Limbert, attributed to, single door, corbelled gallery top, three small glass panes over one pane, three

adjustable shelves, good orig dark finish, unmarked, needs regluing, 28" w, 12" d, 55" h **1,610.00**

Paine Furniture Co., three sliding doors, arched leaded glass panel at top with organic design over single pane of glass, eight adjustable shelves, missing backsplash, orig dark finish, sgd with metal tag, 60" w, 14" d, 59" h **2,200.00**

Stickley Brothers, oak, three door form, arched gallery top, leaded stained glass at top above two vertical panes on each door, orig copper hardware, orig finish, unsigned, 59" w, 12" d, 60" h **4,750.00**

Stickley, L. & J. G., double door, gallery top, eight panes per door, through tenons, copper pulls,

cleaned orig finish, "The Work of L. & J. G. Stickley" decal, 39-1/2" w, 12-3/4" d, 36" h **5,750.00**

Biedermeier-Style

Inlaid cherry, outset molded cornice with ebonized bead, front with two recessed glazed doors, four shelves, outset molded base raised on black feet, burr poplar panels, ebonized stringing, 53-1/2" w, 21" d, 72" h **700.00**

Mahogany, outset molded top, front with two glazed doors, three shelves, sq section stile feet, 35-3/4" w, 15" d, 52" h **375.00**

Chippendale, Maryland or Pennsylvania, 1765-65, mahogany, three sections, upper: dentiled triangular pediment, plinth with contemporary bust of William Shakespeare, plain veneered frieze;

Renaissance Revival, walnut, three sections, **$11,500.** *Photo courtesy of Jackson's Auctioneers & Appraisers.*

center: bookcase with double glazed cupboard doors, astragal mullions, Chinoiserie pattern, molded base; lower: chest with short thumb-molded central drawer flanked by two similar box drawers, two graduated long box drawers, two graduated long drawers, flanked by fluted quarter columns, ogee bracket feet, 44-3/4" d, 25-1/4" d, 106-1/4" h **18,500.00**

Chippendale-Style, New England, mahogany, broken arch pedestal over two arched-paneled doors, fitted secretary int. with pigeonholes, six small drawers, lower section with fall front, stepped fitted int., straight front, two small and two wide drawers, brass bail handle, escutcheons, lock plates, straight bracket feet, 42" w, 24" d 93-3/4" h **3,200.00**

Classical, Boston, 1830s, carved mahogany veneer, cove molded cornice above two glazed doors flanked by columns with leaf carved tops and turned bases, fold-out felt lined writing surface, sectioned for writing implements, two small cock-beaded drawers over two long drawers, flanked by similar columns with carved tops, four reeded and carved bulbous feet, glazed doors open to bird's eye maple veneered int. with two adjustable shelves, valanced open compartments, five small drawers, brasses and wooden pulls appear to be orig, old refinish, imperfections, 44-3/4" w, 22-1/4" d, 88" h **11,500.00**

Eastlake, America, c1880, cherry, rect top, flaring bead trimmed cornice, pair of single-pan glazed cupboard doors, carved oval paterae and scrolls across top, adjustable shelved int., stepped base with line-incised drawers, bail handles, 47-1/2" w, 15-1/4" d, 69-1/4" h **1,200.00**

Empire, crotch mahogany veneers, top section: large architectural type cornice, two large glass doors with cathedral top muttons, three adjustable shelves; base: 11 drawers, oval brass knobs, applied base molding, two panes of glass cracked, 66" w, 83" h **5,500.00**

Empire-Style, mahogany, two-door bookcase top with cathedral-type door, base with one top drawer over two doors, three smaller drawers under doors, shelved int., 43-1/2" w, 83-1/2" h **1,700.00**

Federal, Philadelphia, 1790-1810, mahogany veneered, four-part

construction: long rect top with detachable molded cornice; two bookcase sections each with pairs of glazed cupboard doors, 12 rect panes below top row of arched panes, adjustable shelves int.; lower: center butler's fall-front desk drawer, kneehole area flanked by bands of three cock-beaded short drawers, large paneled cupboard doors, molded base, 119" w, 17-1/2" d, 105-3/4" h **27,500.00**

George III, third quarter 18th C, inlaid mahogany, dentil-molded cornice above two paneled doors, shelved interior, two candle slides, slant front enclosing fitted interior, two short and three graduated drawers, bracket feet, 37" w, 22" d, 85-1/2" h **4,600.00**

George III-Style

   Breakfront, mahogany, upper section fitted with four glazed doors, int. section fitted with sliding secretary drawer, long drawers, cabinet doors, 85" l, 18" d, 91" h . **8,050.00**

   Bureau, 18th C elements, mahogany, later swan's neck cresting, pair of paneled doors opening to shelves, candle rests, lower section with slant lid enclosing fitted int., above three long drawers, ogee bracket feet, 35" w, 20" d, 95" h . . **2,650.00**

Louis XVI-Style, 19th C, inlaid mahogany, parquetry top, low three-quarter gallery and center oval panel inlaid with fleur-de-lis, open shelf raised on sq-section tapered legs, conforming sabots, 24" w, 8-1/4" d, 27-1/4" h, pr **900.00**

Regency, mahogany, projecting molded cornice over two mullion-glazed doors, two lower cupboard doors, int. shelves, bracket feet, 56" w, 22" d, 89" h **9,000.00**

Revolving, American, second half 19th C, oak, molded rect top, five compartmentalized shelves with slatted ends, quadruped base with casters, stamped "Danners Revolving Book Case...Ohio," 24" w, 24" d, 68-1/4" h **1,200.00**

Rococo-Style, Italian, late 19th C, serpentine front with three shelves, cabriole legs, dec with Chinoiserie scenes, green ground, 38" w, 14" d, 49" h **690.00**

Victorian

   Globe-Wernicke, barrister type, stacking, three sections, oak, glass fronted drawers, drawer in base, metal bands, orig finish. . . . **900.00**

Bookcase, Victorian, walnut, carved crest and gallery with sunburst, two carved panels decorated with owls, acorns, oak leaves, and berries, three glass doors, small central cupboard, two base drawers, 56" w, 19" h, 84" h, photo also shows various china pieces, not sold with bookcase, **$9,350.**

   Macey, barrister type, stacking, oak, leaded glass door, drawer in base, three sections of varying height, needs regluing, 34" w, 11" d **400.00**

Boxes

Band, 23" l, oval, wallpaper covering, cardboard, scene of Castle Garden, red, brown, white, and green, blue ground, wear, bottom loose, bottom sgd in ink "Joel Post" **3,300.00**

Bible, chestnut, some curl in lid, molded edges, front panel with punched design, initials and date "L. T. 1705," int. with cov till and single drawer, wrought-iron lock, old dark patina, hasp missing, some edge damage, pulls added to drawer, 27" l **650.00**

Book, Maine, carved spruce gum, sliding lids, carved rosette and triangle motifs, chip-carved embellishments, gilt highlights, minor wear, late 19th/early 20th C, 4-3/4" w, 6" h **420.00**

Bride's, oval, bentwood

   Bright orig floral dec and 1854, blue ground, laced seams, few areas of wear, short split on lid, 15-1/4" w, 9-1/8" d, 5-3/4" h **990.00**

Overlapping laced scenes, orig painted dec, couple in colonial dress, white, red, brown, and black on brown stained ground, German inscription and 1796 in white, edge damage, 15-7/8" l, 10" w, 6-1/2" h **495.00**

Candle

12" l, 8-1/4" w, 4-3/8" h, hanging, sq nail construction, slightly curved sides, divided int., worn gray paint over red, hanging piece inset on back **525.00**

14" l, 20" h, hanging, pine, two compartments, old red repaint, minor wear.............**625.00**

22" l, 10" d, 6-3/8" h, pine, slide top, painted red, America, early 19th C **425.00**

Cheese, 6-1/2" h, 12-1/8" d, pine, circular, incised "E. Temple" on lid, painted blue, America, 19th C, cracks, paint wear, minor losses.......**175.00**

Collar, 13" l, 5" h, wallpaper covering, oval, marked "E. Stone no. 116 1/2 William Street, New York" **575.00**

Cutlery, Victorian, 19th C, mahogany, brass lifting handle, three divisions, later sq tapered legs, 11" w, 14" d, 23" h **260.00**

Decorated, dovetailed, pine

Orig grain painting, rect, dovetailed, conforming hinged lid, ochre ground paint with red putty or vinegar painted seaweed-like designs, orig lock, wallpaper lined int., New England, 1820s, missing top bail handle, later waxing of surface, 14-5/8" w, 7-1/8" d, 6-3/4" h **690.00**

Orig black wavy line dec over brown, applied iron lock, hasp missing, minor wear and touch-up, 27" w, 14-3/4" d, 12-1/4" h **475.00**

Orig red grain paint dec, internal lock, minor wear, 24" w, 12" d, 8-1/4" h **250.00**

Document

10-1/4" w, 10-1/4" d, 13-1/4" h, Federal, Southern states, early 19th C, walnut and yellow pine, hinged top outlined with ovolo corners, centers with inlaid star above dovetailed case with applied moldings, stringing, and fan inlays on front and sides, refinished, repairs **4,830.00**

18" l, 9-1/2" d, 8-1/4" h, paint dec poplar, lidded till, ochre paint on red ground, gilt lettering "G.W.S.,"

brass bail handle, America, 19th C **1,150.00**

Dome Top

America, 19th C, hinged lid, mottled brown grain painted ext, bun feet, int. fitted with two compartments, minor wear, 6-1/2" w, 6-5/8" h **490.00**

Vermont, Shaftsbury, 1820s, attributed to Matteson family, whitewood, green and yellow vinegar painted central dec surrounded by simulated inlaid quarter round fans, cross banded tiger maple veneers and circles, repeated on four areas of six board form, orig surface, varnished, imperfections, 24" w, 12-1/2" d, 12" h **5,465.00**

Pennsylvania, Lancaster County, decorated, orig blue paint, incised compass start designs painted red and white, orig punched tin latch, tin and wire hinges, some damage, few holes where hinges attach, 5-1/2" w, 3-7/8" d, 4-3/4" h **11,550.00**

Pennsylvania, pine, dovetailed and nail construction, white and red compass star flowers and vines, pale blue ground faded to soft gray, tin hinges, incomplete hasp with diamond escutcheon, minor damage, age cracks, few places where newspaper print and other paper transferred to box, 12-1/4" w, 7-3/4" d, 8-7/8" h........**5,775.00**

Dough, pine and poplar, rect removable top, tapering well, splayed ring-turned legs, ball feet, Pennsylvania, 19th C, 38" w, 19-3/4" w, 29-1/2" h **500.00**

Hatbox, wallpaper covered

10-3/4" h, 16-3/4" l, birds among foliage, architectural view, imperfections **500.00**

11" h, 17-3/4" l, scene of stagecoach among hunters, imperfections **150.00**

12-1/4" h, 17-3/4" l, 12-1/2" d, Clayton's Ascent, showing hot air balloons in flight, labeled on underside of lid "From J. M. Hulbert's paste board band box manufactory no. 25 Court Street, Boston," imperfections....**980.00**

Knife

9" w, 10" d, 15-3/4" h, English, inlaid flame mahogany veneer over pine, bow front, scalloped corners with banded inlay, brass handles on both sides, star inlay on int. of lid,

old refinish, contemporary, dovetailed int. lifts out, slotted for letters, hidden compartment below, some sections of inlay missing, age splits in veneer **550.00**

14-1/2" h, mahogany veneer with inlay, edge veneer damage, int. incomplete, inlaid oval on inside of lid **225.00**

14-1/2" h, mahogany veneer with inlay, short feet, banded corner inlay, inlaid star on lid and also inside lid, edge and veneer damage, int. incomplete...**425.00**

16" h, 9-3/4" w, 14-1/2" d, Federal, flamed grained mahogany, serpentine and block front, reeded front columns, fitted int., orig keys, pr...................**2,500.00**

Letter, Gothic Revival, English, late 19th/early 20th C, oak, sloped lid with brass trefoil strapwork, two handles on sides, front doors opening to fitted int., single drawer in base, maker's tag for "Lechars," London and Paris, 16" w, 12-1/4" d, 15-1/4" h..........**635.00**

Pantry, circular, nailed construction, swing handle

7-1/2" d, 3-1/2" h, green, two-finger construction, orig paint....**250.00**

10-7/8" d, 7" h, orig red painted surface, 19th C, chip to top and bottom, paint wear **550.00**

12" d, 6-3/4" h, orig green painted surface, 19th C, minor surface abrasion **550.00**

Pencil, 10-1/2" l, swivel lid, carved from one piece of pine, old red paint **175.00**

Pipe

16-3/4" h, pine, red stain, molded bottom edge, one dovetailed drawer, two compartments with later, but finely cut, scalloped edges, three cut-out hearts and elaborately scrolled crest, back of drawer with scratch carved inscription "January 13, 1813, John _," minor repairs and small hole added for hanging **1,320.00**

17-1/8" h, 7-1/2" w, 5-1/4" d, red painted poplar and yellow pine, reverse sgd "Emma E. Robbins," southern New England, early 19th C, minor loss on molded edge **1,200.00**

19-1/2" h, 8-3/8" w, 5-1/4" d, carved cherry, painted red, metal lined int., old finish, CT River Valley, late 18th/early 19th C.......**6,000.00**

21-1/4" h, 6" w, 4-1/4" d, yellow pine, traces of red paint, old finish, southern New England, early 19th C, very minor losses, crack, minor insect damage to base. . . **2,650.00**

Salt, 11-1/2" w, 7-1/4" d, 9" h, oak, dovetailed, lift lid, crest, divided int., old finish **120.00**

Sewing, 9-1/2" l, 6-3/4" w, 7-3/4" h, bird's eye maple and inlaid walnut, tiered, one drawer, America, mid-19th C, very minor losses to finials . . **375.00**

Spice, 9-3/8" d, circular, maple, eight spice containers with stenciled names, America, late 19th C **450.00**

Spill, 10-1/8" h, 3" w, 2-3/4" d, hanging, walnut and poplar, New England, late 18th/early 19th C, old refinish, front molding replaced **550.00**

Storage

8-1/2" l, 6-1/2" w, 3-1/2" h, America, late 19th C, pine, painted red, floral and linear dec, int. paper lined **635.00**

11-1/2" w, 8" d, 7" h, Northern Europe, late 19th C, polychrome dec, sliding rect box, scenes with red and yellow buildings, green trees, brown ground **350.00**

18-7/8" l, 8-3/4" h, Massachusetts, early 19th C, ochre-painted pine, six board, dovetailed, thumb molded lid dec with flags, shield, and banner inscribed "Mass. Militia 2nd Regt. 1st B. 2nd D," partial paper tag tacked to lid inscribed "…K Rogers Boston," minor imperfections **1,150.00**

Tea bin, 24-1/8" h, 17-1/2" w, 25" d, dec of gentleman toasting lady, dec by Ralph Cahoon, oil on wood, with certificate of authenticity from Cahoon Museum of American Art. **2,530.00**

Wall

7-7/8" w, 3-1/4" d, 15" h, attributed to New York State, early 19th C, painted, shaped top, open rect compartment with worn dark gray patina **2,760.00**

13-1/4" w, 8-1/2" d, 14-3/8" h, attributed to Oxford, Ohio, poplar case, old brick red paint, sq nail construction, two drawers with solid walnut fronts, walnut hinged slant lid, storage compartment below lid, mellow finish. . . **1,265.00**

Work, 12" w, 10-1/2" d, 7-1/4" h, European, marquetry inlaid mahogany veneer, pine secondary wood, slant top lid with pincushion covered in old burgundy velvet, paper lined int., till with lid, engraved strap hinges, old finish, repairs **275.00**

Cabinets

Apothecary, attributed to New Hampshire, c1900, miniature, butternut, case with 24 drawers, turned wooden pulls, old variegated finish, 8-3/4" w, 5-1/2" d, 18" h **2,100.00**

Bar, Art Deco, walnut, sarcophagus form, two doors, sq top with drop-front cabinet on left, mirrored bar, small drawer on right between two open bays, 48" w, 21" d, 54-1/2" d. . . . **600.00**

China

Art Moderne, mahogany, double doors, floral-carved relief panels, int. shelves, two drawers below, 45" w, 17" d, 62" h **2,000.00**

Arts & Crafts

Limbert, #428, trapezoidal form, two doors, each with four windows at top over one large window, orig copper pulls, sides with two windows over one, refinished, branded, 40" w, 19" d, 63" h **4,250.00**

Secessionist style, gallery top set on pillars around mirror, two glass panel doors over open shelf, inlaid ebony and MOP detail, orig mahogany finish, orig hardware, 42" w, 15" d, 72" h **3,500.00**

Biedermeier, highly figured and burl olive wood veneer, ebonized trim, classical-style details, architectural cornice, single glass door, two dovetailed drawers, refinished, 52" w, 32" d, 58" h **1,200.00**

Edwardian-Style, curved glass sides, single flat glazed door, illuminated int., mirrored back, 42" w, 16" d, 64" h, pr . . . **1,675.00**

International Movement, Gilbert Rhode, manufactured by Herman Miller, glass-sided china cabinet top over two doors with burled fronts, brushed steel pulls, refinished, glass doors and shelves missing, 36" w, 17" d, 58" h **800.00**

Victorian, American, c1900, shaped crest with lion's head and carved foliage, curved central door flanked by curved glass to either side, four ball and claw feet, 48" w, 16" d, 72" h **1,500.00**

Chinoiserie, two drawers, double doors, two adjustable int. shelves, walnut veneer with inlay and black lacquer, gilded detail, attached base with turned legs, 20th C, 43" w, 15-1/2" d, 63" h. **625.00**

Cabinet, vice, Arts & Crafts, Limbert, pull-out bar shelf inset with hammered glass, single drawer, two cabinet doors, and square brass pulls, branded mark, leaned finish and hardware, 36" x 31" x 19", $2,300. Photo courtesy of David Rago Auctions.

Corner display, Georgian-Style, c1880, mahogany and inlay, swan's crest, pair of glazed mullioned doors, int. shelves, pair of cabinet doors with marquetry, bracket feet. **2,415.00**

Curio, Louis XV, French, mahogany and mahogany veneer, well detailed ormolu with cherubs, marble top, beveled glass panel in door and plain glass in sides, lighted int., lined with very worn silk moiré, 20th C, 28" w, 14" d, 65" h **3,410.00**

Display

Biedermeier-style, poplar and burr-poplar, single door, outset molded cornice, three-pane glazed door flanked by similar stiles and sides, three mirror-backed shelves supporting shaped half shelves, block feet, 41" w, 16" d, 68" h **800.00**

Dutch, late 19th C, fruitwood marquetry inlaid walnut, pair of glass doors, case inlaid with scrolling leafy vines, 36" w, 14" d, 54" h **1,150.00**

Edwardian, c1900, paint dec, satinwood, breakfront top, glazed doors, int. shelves, splayed legs, 42" w, 15" d, 4-1/2" h **900.00**

Empire-style, gilt metal mounted mahogany, rect case fitted with arched glass door, stemmed bun feet, foliate cast mounts, 33" w, 16" d, 68" h. **1,975.00**

Rococo, South Germany, 18th C, walnut, scrolling heavily molded open pediment, center gilt-bronze cartouche plate, two arched doors of fielded panels, mahogany figures of court ladies, basal-molded and conforming stand, shaped apron, cabriole legs, 46" w, 19-1/2" d, 71-1/2" h **4,750.00**

Filing, American, c1910, golden oak, plain vertical stack, five drawers, orig brass nameplates and pulls **650.00**

Ledger, American, 19th C, walnut and mixed hardwoods, poplar secondary wood, dovetailed case, single paneled door, int. with divided compartments, later salmon paint, pr, 15-1/2" w, 12" d, 24" h **600.00**

Music, walnut, two dovetailed drawers, two paneled doors, molded and punched designs, four adjustable shelves, old varnish finish, orig casters, 22" w, 16-1/4" d, 37-1/2" h **450.00**

Side

Arts & Crafts, oak, single door, orig sq copper pull, notched toe-board, refinished, 22" w, 22" d, 38" h **700.00**

Baroque, Dutch, oak, rect case fitted with three paneled doors, borders carved in shallow relief with scrolling tulip vines, stemmed bun feet, 82" w, 20" d, 53" h . . **1,380.00**

Biedermeier, late 19th C

Fruitwood parquetry, rect top, canted corners, pr of cabinet doors enclosing shelves, bracket feet, 55-1/4" w, 24-3/4" d, 40-1/2" h . . . **1,725.00**

Inlaid walnut, single door, outset molded cornice, door with arched, sunken panel, flanked by bowed stiles continuing to molded stile feet, three int. shelves, 39-1/2" w, 19" d, 65-1/4" h **1,500.00**

Empire-Style, late 19th/early 20th C, gilt bronze mounted mahogany, rect marble top, conforming case fitted with cabinet door, pull-out shelves, plinth base, 20-3/4" w, 16-1/4" d, 52-1/4" h **750.00**

Louis XVI, Provincial, late 18th/early 19th C, oak, paneled door carved with urns, 41" w, 18-1/2" d, 73" h **1,380.00**

Napoleon III, c1850-70, brass and mother-of-pearl inlaid, ormolu mounts, white serpentine marble top, conforming case, fitted with

door, bracket feet, 35-1/2" w, 16" d, 41" h **2,645.00**

Renaissance Revival, attributed to New York, c1865-75, ebonized, marquetry, and parcel-gilt, central elevated cupboard flanked by two similar cupboards, 75" w, 15" d, 64" h **4,900.00**

Spice, poplar, old brown sponge dec, vertical stack with four sq nailed drawers with beveled edges, turned wooden pulls, chamfered side moldings, tongue and groove boards on sides of case, one drawer front split, 8-3/8" w, 17-1/2" d, 19-5/8" h . . . **495.00**

Vitrine

Edwardian, c1900, mahogany and boxwood inlay, rect, Gothic-style mullioned glazed doors, sq tapering legs, spade feet, 41-1/2" w, 14-1/4" d, 63-1/4" h **1,200.00**

George III-Style, early 20th C, mahogany, open swan's neck cresting, glazed doors, lower section with glass top shelf, sq legs joined by stretchers, 22" w, 18-1/2" d, 68" h **1,495.00**

Louis XV-Style, late 19th/early 20th C, giltwood, boxed glass on each side, cabriole legs, 19" w, 17" d, 38" h **800.00**

Louis XVI-Style, c1850, giltwood, outset molded rect top, frieze with beribboned floral garlands, front with glazed door with inset corners, flanked by fluted stiles, opening to two shelves, glazed sides, paneled skirt with swags, turned, tapered, and fluted legs with paterae, 27-1/4" w, 16" d, 61-1/2" h **1,200.00**

Wall, hanging, Arts & Crafts, Liberty, softwood, overhanging top, side shelves, door stenciled with panel titled "Spring," pre-Raphaelite maiden with irises, refinished, some breaks to back panel, ivorine Liberty tag, 22" w, 8" d, 23" h **1,610.00**

Candlestands
Chippendale

Connecticut River Valley, late 18th C, cherry, old refinish, minor imperfections, 17" w, 16-1/2" d, 25-1/2" h **16,100.00**

New England, late 18th C

Dish-top, cherry, turned pedestal, cabriole legs, pad feet, refinished, 18-1/4" d, 26-3/4" h **2,185.00**

Candlestand, Chippendale, American, mahogany, serpent feet, 18" d, 27-1/2" h, **$1,850.**

Tilt top, refinished walnut, one board dish turned top, turned column, tripod base, snake feet, hinge block and latch are old replacements, pieced repairs on top, minor age cracks, 21-3/4" d, 29" h **935.00**

New Hampshire, attributed to Lt. Samuel Dunlap, old refinish, birch, painted red, imperfections, 16-1/2" w, 16-1/8" d, 26-1/2" h . . . **2,950.00**

Pennsylvania, late 18th C, walnut, circular molded top, turned birdcage support, vase and ring-turned post, tripod cabriole leg base, pad feet on platforms, old refinish, 20-1/2" d, 29" h **3,450.00**

Country

Cherry and Maple, southeastern New England, late 18th C, circular top, vase and ring turned post and tripod base, three tapering legs, remnants of old dark green paint, imperfections, 12" d, 25" h **1,150.00**

Stained cherry, Connecticut, late 18th C, tilt-top, dished top, ring-turned swelled pedestal, cabriole lets, pad feet, old surface, 20-1/4" d, 28-3/4" h **3,220.00**

Federal

Massachusetts, c1800, mahogany, octagonal tilt-top, vase and ring-turned post, tripod spider leg base, spade feet, refinished, 21-1/4" w, 15-3/4" d, 29-1/2" h **1,500.00**

New England, early 19th C, black painted birch, old surface, repair, 16-1/4" x 15-3/8" top, 27-1/2" h **2,070.00**

New Hampshire, c1810, painted, sq top, canted corners, urn-shaped pedestal, chip carving, exaggerated cabriole legs terminating in human feet, old brown paint, minor imperfections, 15-3/4" w, 16-1/2" d, 27" h **11,500.00**

New Hampshire, early 19th C, birch, painted, sq top with rounded corners, urn shaped turned pedestal, high arched cabriole tripod base, pad feet, old red paint, imperfections, 13-3/4" w, 13-1/4" d, 26-1/4" h **7,475.00**

Hepplewhite, American

Cherry, one-board octagonal top, turned column with chip carving, tripod base, spider legs, old refinishing, minor damage, old repair, 17-1/4" x 18-1/8" top, 27" h **500.00**

Cherry and birch, one board top with rounded corners, boldly turned columns, tapered legs, high spider base, old alligatored varnish finish, small burns on top, 19" w, 18" d, 28-1/2" h **495.00**

Painted and decorated, Connecticut, late 19th C, cherry, octagonal top with molded edge, turned pedestal with urn shaping over high-arched cabriole leg base ending in pad feet, early black paint with 19th C yellow striping on pedestal and legs, minor imperfections, 15-1/4" w, 15-3/4" d, 29-1/2" h . **4,025.00**

Primitive, 40" h, wooden, adjustable candle arm, dark brown patina, early 19th C **715.00**

Queen Anne

Attributed to Vermont, 18th C, cherry, circular top, vase and ring turned post, tripod cabriole leg base ending in arris pad feet on platforms, old refinish, 15-1/4" d top, 25-3/4" h **1,150.00**

Country, mahogany, piecrust tilt top, center turned pedestal, graceful legs, pad feet, 20" d, 28-1/2" h **275.00**

Windsor

Hardwoods, acorn finial, dish top slightly warped, tapered and threaded column, high tripod base,

candleholder with replaced tin sockets, refinished, 39" h . **1,100.00**

Pine, one board top with old patina and traces of finish on underside, circular platform at center, tapered column, old gold and dark brown repaint on tripod base, 16" x 16-3/4" top, 27-1/2" h **725.00**

Chair, arm, transitional, attributed to Zoar, Ohio, cherry, serpentine crest with beaded detail, vase splat, scrolled arms, turned arm posts, slip seat, turned legs, mortised and pinned stretchers, refinished, 16" h seat, 43" h, $3,450. Photo courtesy of Garth's Auction, Inc.

Chairs
Arm

Aesthetic Movement, after Philip Webb's Sussex chair for Morris & Co., c1885, new natural rush seat, turned spindles, orig black paint, unmarked, 21-1/4" w, 19" d, 36-1/4" h.... **1,045.00**

Art Deco, France, c1925, giltwood, sloping U-form back rail ending in gently swollen reeded arm supports, D-shaped seat upholstered seat cushion, pr **15,750.00**

Art Nouveau, L. Majorelle, France, c1900, carved mahogany, horseshoe-shaped back rail, upholstered back, front of arm supports carved with pine cones and needles, continuing to form molded front legs with similar carving, dark green leather upholstery............... **7,000.00**

Arts & Crafts

Indiana Hickory, twig construction, orig hickory splint seat, weathered finish, branded signature, 26" w, 17" d, 37" h............. **50.00**

Limbert, #931, three vertical back slats, recovered drop-in leather cushion, orig finish, branded, 28" w, 24" d, 37" h....... **800.00**

Olbrich, Joseph Marie, Jugendstil, mahogany, small back panel inlaid with fruitwood floral pattern, inset upholstered seat, unmarked, good old refinish, 23-1/2" w, 19" d, 41-1/2" h............. **1,840.00**

Stickley, Charles, four back slats, recovered spring cushion seat, orig finish, remnant of decal, 26" w, 22" d, 41" h............. **230.00**

Stickley, Gustav, V-back, five vertical slats, corbels, replaced tacked-on leather seat, unmarked, refinished, 25-1/2" w, 21" d, 37-1/2" h . **690.00**

Stickley, Gustav, V-back, five vertical slats, corbels, tacked on orig leather seat, early box mark, orig dark finish, normal wear to arms, 26" w, 20" d, 36" h...... **1,050.00**

Baroque, Flemish, 17th C elements, walnut, needlework backrest and seat, foliate carved arms, block and ring turned legs, faceted ball feet . **2,530.00**

Centennial, Colonial Revival, Queen-Anne Style, wing back, hardwood cabriole legs, turned stretcher, upholstery removed, old dark finish, 46" h **900.00**

Chippendale, Hartford, CT, area, late 18th C, painted, scrolling crest above pierced splat with center urn, old black paint with traces of yellow striping, 14-3/4" h seat, 40" h, minor paint wear **2,100.00**

Egyptian Revival, American, c1865, ebonized and parcel-gilt, upholstered scrolling back and seat, matching upholstered arm pads, sphinx head arm supports, claw feet, 39-1/2" h **8,050.00**

Empire-Style, mahogany, rect padded back, padded arms, ormolu-mounted classical busts, bowed padded seat, sq tapering legs with brass caps, white striped upholstery **850.00**

George III, late 18th C, in the French taste, giltwood, beaded oval backrest carved with anthemion, scrolled arms similarly beaded, serpentine seat raised on circular reeded legs **8,100.00**

Gothic Revival, America, walnut, old finish, reupholstered in damask, age cracks, 52-1/2" h **200.00**

Louis XIV, early 18th C, fauteuil, giltwood, serpentine cresting, scrolled and reeded arms, over upholstered seat, scrolled legs joined by stretchers **2,990.00**

Louis XIV-Style, Baroque, late 19th C, walnut, rect backrest, foliate carved arms and legs, X-form stretcher, price for pr **2,650.00**

Modern

Hardoy, Bonet and Kurchan, for Knoll, butterfly sling, brown leather seat cov, tubular black metal base, unmarked, 30-3/4" w, 28-1/2" d, 35" h **300.00**

Verner Panton, heart chair, by Plus-Linji, orig red fabric upholstery over metal frame, swivel chrome base, 40" w, 24" d, 36" h **10,350.00**

Neoclassical, Italian, late 18th/early 19th C, walnut, urn and wheat carved splat, downswept arms, raised sq tapering legs, 34-1/4" h **1,100.00**

Queen Anne

Country, banister back, old black repaint, gold leaf on crest, shaped arms, turned legs, posts, and stretchers, replaced rush seat, mortised joints redoweled, wear and some edge damage, 16" seat, 45" h **500.00**

New Hampshire, hardwood with old black repaint, molded and curved back posts with vase splat and carved crest, turned posts support molded and scrolled arms, turned legs, Spanish feet, turned rungs with bulbous front stretcher, old rush seat, some loss of height to feet, 15-3/8" seat, 41" h . . **4,125.00**

New Hampshire, maple and other hardwood, old worn brown finish, molded arms, vase splat, shaped back posts with crest, turned legs, Spanish feet, bulbous front stretcher, old rush seat, 16-1/2" seat, 41-1/2" h **2,475.00**

Renaissance Revival, attributed to Pottier & Stymus, New York, 1865, walnut, scrolled arms, upholstered back and seed, spherules on seat rail, 38" h **1,100.00**

Rococo Revival

John H. Belter, rosewood, Rosalie pattern, laminated, solid back, crest carved with large rose, fruit, and grape clusters, yellow silk upholstery, tufted back, 42-1/2" h **3,500.00**

J. & J. Meeks, rosewood, Stanton Hall pattern, laminated curved back, tufted gold velvet brocade reupholstery, minor age cracks, 43" h **3,400.00**

Rococo-Style, Italian, late 19th/early 20th C, grotto, scallop shell seat, dolphin-shaped arms, rusticated legs **1,725.00**

Victorian, George Huntzinger, NY, patent March 30, 1869, walnut, pierce carved crest, rect upholstered back panel flanked by turned and curved slats and stiles, low upholstered barrel-back, arm frame carved with classical heads, upholstered seat, pierced and scroll-carved front drop under seat connected to turned rung joining carved and turned front legs, ball feet, front leg stamped . . . **2,100.00**

Windsor

Brace Back, Rhode Island or Connecticut, late 18th C, painted, continuous arm, maple and ash, incised bowed crest over 13 turned spindles, two braces, arms with shaped terminals on vase and ring turned supports, incised saddle seat, similar legs joined by ring turned bulbous H-form stretchers, remains of old red over green paint, minor repairs, 17" h seat, 35" h **3,105.00**

Comb Back, New England, c1810, serpentine cresting, bamboo turnings, painted black, 17" h seat, 46-1/2" h **4,025.00**

Sack Back, New England, c1790, bowed crest rail above seven spindles and arms, vine and ring-turned supports, saddle seat, splayed legs joined by stretchers, painted yellow, later coat of salmon paint and green, 17-1/2" h seat, 40-1/2" h, price for pr . . .**72,900.00**

Corner

Chippendale, walnut, rolled back rest with stepped detail, pierced harp shape splats, serpentine arm supports, scrolled handholds, molded seal frame, slip seat covered in worn upholstery, scalloped aprons, cabriole legs with relief carved shells on knees, claw and ball feet, old dark surface, restorations and replacements **1,870.00**

Chippendale-Style, 20th C, mahogany, shaped arms, openwork splats, rush slip seat raised on cabriole legs, claw and ball feet. **575.00**

Country, New England, late 18th/early 19th C, maple, arms with scrolled terminals, shaped crest, scrolled horizontal splats attached to swelled and turned baluster forms continuing to turned legs, joined to similar stretchers, old surface, replaced rush seat, minor imperfections, 16-3/8" h seat, 30-1/2" h back **1,610.00**

Queen Anne, New England, maple, commode, shaped crest, scrolled arm, shaped splat, molded seat, frontal cabriole leg ending in pad foot, old refinish, minor imperfections, 16-1/2" h, 31" h **2,100.00**

William and Mary

New England, 18th C, shaped backrest and chamfered crest, scrolled handholds, three vase and ring-turned stiles continuing to turned legs, joined to front leg by turned double stretchers, old dark brown paint, replaced wood seat, 30" h **1,380.00**

Southern New England, late 17th C, roundabout, maple, shaped crest above scrolled arms, turned arm supports joining shaped horizontal splats over replaced rush seat, turned stretchers, old refinish, 16" h, 28" h **1,100.00**

Dining

Arts & Crafts, Limbert, #1825, five #1821, dining, one armchair, two horizontal slats over three vertical slats, orig leather and tacks, orig finish, branded, #1825: 24" w, 18" d, 38" h, #1821 17" w, 17" d, 38" h **2,900.00**

Biedermeier, fruitwood and part ebonized, black faux-leather upholstery, restorations, set of four, 36" h **2,500.00**

Centennial, Colonial Revival, Sheraton-style, mahogany, two arm, eight side, shield back, reeded front legs, corner posts with carving of urns, needlepoint slip seats, 19-1/2" w, 17-1/4" d, 37-1/2" h **3,000.00**

Chippendale-Style, English, early 20th C, refinished mahogany, one arm and five side chairs, pierced splat, hand carving, slip seat, ball and claw feet, 18" h seat, 38" h, price for set of six **2,400.00**

Classical, New England, c1830, tiger maple, concave crests, horizontal splat, turned raked stiles, caned seat, rein-turned legs, joined by stretchers, old finish, minor imperfections, 33-1/2" h, price for set of eight **2,500.00**

Eastlake, American, c1870, mahogany, one armchair, six side chairs, fan-carved crest rail, reeded stiles and stretchers, block-carved front legs, minor damage, seven-piece set, 35" h **850.00**

Federal, Rhode Island or Salem, MA, c1795, mahogany carved, set of four side and matching arm chair, shield back with molded crest and stiles above carved kylix with festoons draped from flanking carved rosettes, pierced splat terminating in carved lunette at base above molded rear seat rail, seat with serpentine front rail, sq tapering legs joined by stretchers, over-upholstered seats covered in old black horsehair with scalloped trim, old surface, 16-1/2" h seat, 37-3/4" h **23,000.00**

George III, c1800, carved mahogany, yoke back, upswept reeded terminals, carved openwork vasiform splat with center pendant tassels over three flowerheads, green leather over upholstered seat, nailhead trim, fluted, molded, and chamfered front supports, H-form stretchers, swept rear supports, six-piece set **5,500.00**

George III-Style, late 19th C, mahogany, anthemion pierced backrest, over upholstered seat, cabriole legs, claw and ball feet, price for set of six side chairs, associated arm chair **2,100.00**

Regency-Style, late 19th/early 20th C, mahogany and inlay

    Two armchairs, four side chairs, back splats with dark and light veneer inlays, carved lyre form supports with rosettes, reeded arms terminating in turned supports, crimson red floral upholstered seat, 36-1/2" h **3,900.00**

    Two armchairs, six side chairs, curved inlaid crest rail, dec horizontal splats, pale blue silk upholstery, Greek key design, 33-3/4" h **10,350.00**

Renaissance Revival, America, c1870, oak, two arm and eight side chairs, each with foliate and beast carved cresting, paneled seat rail and turned legs, price for set of 10 ...... **3,105.00**

Sheraton, Hitchcock type, two arm chairs, six side chairs, old red and black repaint, yellow striping, stenciled and freehand dec, replaced rush seats, 18" h seat, 33-1/2" h **2,500.00**

High, child's

Ladderback, early dark green paint with traces of earlier green beneath, well-defined turnings on arms, three slat back, turned legs with blunt arrow feet on front, tapered rear feet, old worn woven tape seat, 20-1/2" h seat, 38-1/" h **3,850.00**

Windsor, rod-back, New England, early 19th C, painted, incised tapering spindles, 21-3/4" h seat, 33-1/2" h **980.00**

Library

George III, c1800, mahogany and caned, pink upholstered loose cushion, 33-1/2" h **2,070.00**

Potty

Queen Anne, country, corner, maple and pine, old red repaint, shaped crest and arms, three turned posts, heart-shaped pierced splats, slip seat with base recovered in green leather upholstery, turned legs, button feet, deep aprons, 16" h, 31" h **770.00**

Side

Arrowback, 19th C mustard paint, tan, brown, red, and black dec of cornucopias on crest, leaves on back and front stretcher, incising around seat, brushed detain between, evidence of earlier green, bamboo turned base, 15-3/4" h, 32" h ... **935.00**

Art Deco, Europe, wooden gondola backs, ivory sabots on front legs, cream striped fabric upholstery, pr, 25" h **2,000.00**

Arts & Crafts, Gustav Stickley, H-back, drop-in seat recovered in burgundy leather, red decal, over-coated orig dark finish, roughness to leg edges, 17" w, 16" d, 40" h **690.00**

Banister Back, Massachusetts or Hudson River Valley, 18th C, scrolled crest with pierced heart flanked by block, vase, and reel stiles, similar front legs which join swelled and ring turned medial stretcher, carved feet, old red paint, 19" h, 45-1/2" h **14,950.00**

Centennial, Colonial Revival, Chippendale-Style, carved mahogany, shaped shell-carved crest rail, pierced vasiform back splat, balloon slip seat, shell-carved apron, cabriole legs, leaf-carved knees, claw and ball feet, pr **850.00**

Chippendale

    Boston or North Shore, c1760-80, carved mahogany, leaf carved lunettes and C-scrolls centered in shaped crests, raked molded

terminals above pierced splats and over-upholstered seats, cabriole front legs terminating in scratch carved high pad feet, old refinish, 18" h seat, 37-1/4" h, price for pair **13,800.00**

    Boston or Salem, MA, 1760-80, carved walnut, raked terminals of crest above pierced splat with C-scrolls, compass slip seat, cabriole legs, high pad feet, old refinish, restoration to stiles, 16-1/2" h seat, 38-1/2" h .. **2,185.00**

    Connecticut River Valley, tiger maple, serpentine crest with raked molded terminals above pierced splat, old rush seat, block and vase turned front legs joined by turned stretcher, old refinish, 17-1/4" h seat, 39" h **900.00**

    Country, maple with some curl, pierced spat and shaped crest with carved ears, sq legs, mortised and pinned stretchers, old mellow refinishing, damage to paper rush seat because of breaks in front seal rail, 39" h **110.00**

    Country, refinished birch, pierced splat and crest with carved ears, replaced paper rush seat, sq legs with molded corners, 15-3/4" seat, 36-1/2" h.............. **450.00**

Chair, Transitional, Philadelphia, c1760, walnut, serpentine crest rail, urn back splat, flaring arm, spooned supports, scroll and scroll-carved grips, slip seat with straight seat rail, shell-carved cabriole legs, claw and ball feet, **$8,500.** *Photo courtesy of Freeman/Fine Arts.*

Massachusetts, attributed to Salem, mahogany, arched crest, pierced and scroll carved splat with heart design, tapered rear stiles with molded ears, tan silk upholstered seat with floral pattern, brass tacks around lower edge, front cabriole legs, well carved claw and ball feet, turned stretcher base, old dark refinish, restorations and replacements, 17" h seat, 36" h **1,550.00**

New London, CT, 1760-95, carved cherry, serpentine crest rails, pierced splats with C-scrolls and beaded edges, molded shoes, flanked by stiles and rounded backs, molded seat frames and straight legs with beaded edges, pierced brackets joined by sq stretchers, old refinish, set of five, 17" h seat, 39" h...... **10,350.00**

New York, 1755-65, carved mahogany, carved crest ending in raked molded terminals above pierced splat with C-scrolls, slip seat, molded seat frame, front carved cabriole legs ending in ball and claw feet, rear raked legs, old surface, imperfections, 18" h seat, 39-1/2" h **2,990.00**

Chippendale-Style, late 19th C, carved mahogany, foliate and C-scroll carved baluster splat, over upholstered seat, cabriole legs ending in scrolled toes, price for set of six **2,990.00**

Classical

Baltimore, painted and dec, scrolled crest above inverted vase-shaped splat, cane seat, dec front legs joined by medial stretcher, stencil dec, orig gilt classical motifs on black ground, 34-1/2" h.... **750.00**

Connecticut, 1830-50, tiger maple, curving shaped crests, curving front rail, Grecian legs, branded "A. G. Case," refinished, seats missing caning, other imperfections, 17-3/4" h seat, 33-1/2" h, set of six **3,200.00**

Middle Atlantic States, 1830s, mahogany veneer, curving veneered crests, similar horizontal splats, upholstered seats, Klismos-type legs, old refinish, 17-3/4" h seat, 33-1/2" h, set of seven............... **1,850.00**

New York, 1810-20, carved mahogany veneer, scroll back, beaded edges, horizontal splats carved with leafage and other

classical motifs, slip seat, curving legs, old surface, 16-1/2" h, 32" h, set of six............. **5,200.00**

Decorated, attributed to Carlisle, PA, plank seat, orig black over red dec, floral panels surrounded by gold stencils, bordered with salmon and yellow line border dec, carefully cleaned, applied coat of protective varnish, professionally executed slight touch-up, 17" h seat, 31" h, price for set of six **3,650.00**

Federal

Massachusetts, early 19th C, carved mahogany, shaped crests and stiles above stay rails, beaded edges, seat with serpentine front, sq tapering molded legs, beaded edges, joined by sq stretchers, old surface, over-upholstered needlepoint seats, 17" h seat, 36" h, set of three **1,150.00**

Massachusetts or Rhode Island, c1780, mahogany inlaid, shield back, arched molded crest above five molded spindles and inlaid quarter fan, over-upholstered seats with serpentine fronts, molded tapering legs joined by stretchers, 17-1/2" h seat, 37" h, pr .. **5,475.00**

New Hampshire, Portsmouth, attributed to Langley Boardman, 1774-1833, mahogany, sq back, reeded on rest rail, stiles, and stay rail, over upholstered serpentine seat, molded sq tapering front legs, sq stretchers and rakes rear legs, refinish, minor imperfections, 18" h seat, 36" h **1,035.00**

Gothic Revival, New York City, 1850s, mahogany veneer, trefoil pierced splats, curved stay rails, veneered seal rails, curving rococo legs, old refinish, 20th C upholstery, 16-1/2" h seat, 33-1/2" h, set of eight.................. **6,900.00**

Hepplewhite, American, mahogany, shield back, rush seat **325.00**

Hitchcock, Hitchcocksville, CT, 1825-32

Painted and dec, crown tops, wide horizontal splats, cane seats, turned gold leaf dec legs, orig graining and gilt dec, red-brown ground, 36" h, price for set of six **1,000.00**

Rosewood grained surface, orig gilt dec, urn centering cornucopia splat, old rush seats, ring-turned legs, orig surface, 35-1/2" h, price for set of four **1,265.00**

Neoclassical

American, attributed to workshop of Duncan Phyfe, New York City, 1810-15, carved mahogany and tiger maple veneer, spiral carved crest rail flanked by curving beaded stiles, flanking carved scrolls above horizontal splat with oval tiger maple veneer reserve flanked by carving, beaded seat rail, klismos-type molded legs, 17" h seat, 32-1/4" h, price for set of three **4,900.00**

Italian, early 19th C, fruitwood, shaped trapezoidal backrest, serpentine over-upholstered seat, flared legs, price for set of four **1,275.00**

Plank, northern New England, 1830s, side, arrow-back, yellow ground, stencil dec with dark green and blue leafage and fruit, gold accents, shaped plank seat, splayed bamboo turned legs, paint loss, minor imperfections, 17-3/4" h seat, 35" h, set of five **1,725.00**

Queen Anne

American, early 18th C, burl walnut, shaped cresting, serpentine slat, slip-seat raised on shell carved cabriole legs, hoof feet, price for pr **1,650.00**

Country, maple, arched crest, vase splat, replaced paper rush seat, turned front legs, bulbous turned front stretcher (partially worn), tapered rear posts, refinished, restorations, 16-1/4" h seat, 39-1/2" h **225.00**

Country, maple, scalloped crest, graceful urn-shaped splat with tapered stiles, replaced paper rush seat, boldly turned front legs and stretchers, front Spanish feet, old refinishing, evidence of thin red wash, feet ended out, other old restorations, 17" h seat, 41" h **325.00**

Massachusetts or New Hampshire, c1740 painted, carved crest continues to spooned stiles with molded edges, vasiform and spooned splat, molded stay rail over black and baluster form front legs, carved Spanish feet, old brown paint with black paint in outline, imperfections, 17" h seat, 40-1/2" h **1,495.00**

Newport, RI, 1750-75, black walnut, curving crest above vase-shaped pierced splat, compass seat, front and side rail shaping, cabriole front legs joined to rear sq tapering legs by block and vase-swelled side stretchers, swelled and turned medial stretchers, rear feet without chamfering, old refinish, minor repairs, affixed brass plaque reads "Ebenezer Storer 1730-1807," 17" h seat, 38-1/4" h **2,990.00**

Rococo Revival

John H. Belter, rosewood, Rosalie without the Grapes pattern, laminated, solid back, crest carved with large rose and fruit, red silk upholstery, casters, pr, 37-1/2" h **2,550.00**

J. & J. Meeks, rosewood, Stanton Hall pattern, laminated curved back, floral brocade reupholstery, minor age cracks, 40-1/2" h **1,870.00**

William IV, England

Carved mahogany, foliate carved cresting, slip seat, split baluster seat rail, saber legs, c1830, price for pr **2,185.00**

Carved rosewood, foliate carved backrest with central diamond shaped upholstered panel, slip seat, leaf carved circular legs, c1835, price for pr **700.00**

Windsor

Birdcage, branded signature "S. H. Horton," (Samuel H. Horton, Boston, 1804-10), seven spindled back, well-shaped seat, molded edge, splayed bamboo turned legs, refinished, one rear leg replaced, 17-1/2" h seat, 34" h **385.00**

Birdcage, Jonathon Tyson, Philadelphia, 1808-18, curving birdcage crests centering octagonal panels over seven turned spindles flanked by bamboo turned stiles over incised shaped seats, four bamboo turned legs joined by stretchers, old brown paint with gilt accents, paint wear, 17-1/4" h seat, 34" h, price for pr **865.00**

Birdcage, small ink signature on bottoms of seat for "Fitch," one has later painted name, seven spindle back, bamboo turnings, shield shaped seat with incised detail, refinished, small corner chip on one crest, edge of seat chip on other, 17" h, 33-1/2" h, price for pr **750.00**

Brace Back, nine spindles bowback, well shaped seat with incised detail around spindles, vase and ring

turned legs, turned "H" stretcher, old mellow refinish, restorations, 17-1/2" h, seat, 36-3/4" h . . . **385.00**

Comb Back, mixed woods, arched crest with flared ears, seven-splindle back, turned arms, bentwood arm rail, shield shaped seat, vase and ring turned legs, stretcher base, light refinish, 17" h seat, 38-1/4" h **800.00**

Fan Back, old dry red paint with evidence of earlier colors beneath, arched crest, shield shaped seat, incised rain gutter around seven spindles back, faint bamboo turnings on rear posts, turned legs, repegged ring turned "H" stretcher, 17-1/2" h seat, 35-1/2" h . . . **880.00**

Rod Back, New England, early 19th C, painted and dec, curving crest above bamboo-turned spindles, incised similarly turned shaped seat, similarly turned splayed legs, old polychrome painted red, green, and yellow dec with black highlights, restoration, paint imperfections, 18-1/2" h seat, 53-3/4" h **9,545.00**

Slipper

Arts & Crafts, Gustav Stickley, spindled back, drop-in spring seat recovered in brown leather, orig finish, black decal, 17-3/4" w, 16" d, 37" h **1,150.00**

Victorian, c1875, rosewood, angular foliate carved backrest with urn form splat, over upholstered seat and circular turned legs **300.00**

Victorian, late, c1880, ebonized and bobbin turned needlepoint upholstery, foliate dec seat **175.00**

Wingback

Chippendale, country, birch base, old dark finish, sq slightly tapered legs with molded corners, H stretcher, reupholstered, glued split on one foot, 47-1/2" h **1,650.00**

Chests of drawers

Art Deco, Quigley, France, c1925, parchment covered, rect top, three tapering drawers, pyramid mirrored stiles, bracket feet, back branded, 44-1/2" x 35" **2,750.00**

Arts & Crafts, English, dresser, orig pivoting mirror with chamberstick shelves, glove boxes, copper repoussé panels, two drawers over one long drawer, orig medium-dark finish, unmarked, split to side, 42-3/4" w, 21-1/2" d, 64" h **1,725.00**

Chest of drawers, Philadelphia, c1765, cherry, rectangular-molded top, notched front corners, graduated molded drawers, openwork brasses, quarter round fluted corners, ogival bracket feet, 30-1/2" w, 32" d, 32" h, $29,000. Photo courtesy of Freeman/Fine Arts.

Biedermeier, c1820, maple, rect case fitted with two drawers, splayed sq legs, 36" w, 19" d, 31" h **1,725.00**

Chippendale

Boston, 1750-90, mahogany, block front, thumb-molded shaped top, conforming case, four graduated drawers, molded base, bracket feet, old refinish, replaced brass, rear foot missing, backboard inscribed "G. Russell" (George Russell, 1800-1866, born in Providence, RI, married Sarah Shaw, and died in Manchester, MA,) 33" w, 19-1/4" w, 29-1/4" h **46,000.00**

Chester County, PA, late 18th C, high, cherry, cornice cove molding above single drawer, visually divided into three, over split drawer, four graduated drawers below, flanked by quarter engaged fluted columns with capitals and bases, molded base, four bracket on platforms characteristic of Octorara, (area between Chester and Lancaster counties), imp "T. Stock-ton" on backboard, old surface, casters added, minor imperfections, 38" w, 21-3/8" d, 66-3/4" h **19,550.00**

Country, curly maple, four dovetailed drawers, bracket feet, refinished, bottom backboard and feet replaced, brasses replaced, 41-1/4" w, 19-1/2" d, 37-1/2" h **2,450.00**

Massachusetts, c1720, wavy birch, overhanging molded top, cock-beaded case, four graduated drawers, bracket feet, replaced brasses, old refinish, 35-1/4" w, 19" d, 32-3/4" h **2,990.00**

Massachusetts, 1770-80, oxbow, mahogany, overhanging reverse serpentine top with end blocking and molded edge, conforming case with four graduated drawers with beaded edges, similar end blocking, heavy molded base, ogee bracket feet, old refinish, replaced brasses, restored, 35" w, 19-3/4" d, 32-1/4" h **10,350.00**

New England, southeastern, c1770, maple, flat molded cornice, case with two thumb-molded short drawers over five long drawers, tall bracket feet, old brasses, old refinish, 35" w, 17-1/8" d, 62" h **4,900.00**

New England, southeastern, late 18th C, maple, molded cornice, case with six thumb-molded drawers, top one visually divided into thirds, central fan carving, bracket base, replaced brasses, refinished, 37" w, 17-1/2" d, 57" h **4,900.00**

Rhode Island, late 18th C, carved tiger maple, tall, cornice with dentil molding, case of seven graduated thumb-molded drawers, molded tall bracket base with central drop, top drawer with fan-carving, orig brasses, early surface, 38" w, 18-3/4" d, 63-3/4" h **27,600.00**

Chippendale to Hepplewhite Transitional, attributed to the Chapius family, CT, cherry, bowfront, line inlay around two-board top, four dovetailed drawers with beaded edging, reeded quarter columns, ogee feet with boldly scalloped returns, molded base, orig oval emb brasses, drawer glides fitted through the backboards and pegged, restorations to feet **17,160.00**

Classical

Boston, 1820-30, dressing, mahogany veneer, veneered mirror flanked by scrolled supports, ormolu mounts, two small drawers, stepped out case with blind convex drawer, two flat front drawers, flanked by columns, frontal bulbous carved and reeded feet, orig finish, old surface, minor imperfections, 38" w, 20-7/8" d, 58" h **980.00**

Vermont, 1820-30, bureau, mahogany and tiger maple, upper section with three glove drawers over projecting case of one long cock-beaded drawer flanked by veneered shaped panels over three recessed long cock-beaded graduated drawers, applied ring turned half columns, leaf carved legs, claw feet, old opalescent glass pulls, old finish, imperfections, 46-1/4" w, 22-1/2" d, 53-1/4" h **1,150.00**

Eastlake, curly walnut, burl veneer, carved detail, scrolled crest, four dovetailed drawers, two handkerchief drawers, well detailed molded panel fronts, refinished, 39" w, 17-1/2" d, 46" h **750.00**

Empire

America, birch and mahogany flame veneer, scrolled crest, raised center block, two small bonnet drawers on top, four (top drawer overhanging) dovetailed drawers with flame veneer and turned pulls, freestanding rope twist pilasters, turned feet, refinished, restorations, replacements, 42" w, 19" d, 47-3/4" h **500.00**

America, decorated, dark over light green dec, orig red undercoat, top with beveled trim around top edge, two drawers above with beveled edges, right one with wooden spring lock, three dovetailed drawers flanked by half turned pilasters, boldly scalloped front apron, inset panels on ends, high turned feet, clear blown glass pulls with polished pontil tops, edge wear to paint, one pull cracked, 44-1/4" w, 22-1/4" d, 47-1/4" h **600.00**

America, mahogany and mahogany veneer, gadrooned edging around top drawer opening and base, free standing pilasters with scrolled capitals and acanthus carving, four graduated drawers with book page flame veneer, front paw feet topped with acanthus leaves, turned rear feet, old dark finish, old replaced Chinese Chippendale style brasses, veneer splits in top, pierced repair along back at top, 43-1/4" w, 22-1/4" d, 42" h . **700.00**

Maine, attributed to, cherry, mahogany veneer, pine secondary wood, two board top with shaped back splash, four dovetailed

drawers with orig brass pulls and key escutcheons, high crisply turned feet, refinished, veneer repairs, pulls cleaned with minor dents, 41-1/4" w, 20" d, 41-1/2" h **1,100.00**

Federal

America, bowfront, mahogany, flame mahogany veneer, pine secondary wood, old replaced top with biscuit corners, four dovetailed drawers with applied beading, replaced brass pulls, rope twist carvings on front pilasters, high boldly turned feet, refinished, pierced restorations, one rear foot replaced, 40-1/2" w, 19" d, 36-3/4" h **770.00**

Country, mahogany and satin wood veneer, biscuit corners, "D"-shaped facade, four dovetailed drawers with applied edge beading and inlay, turned and reeded feet and pilasters, ring turned posts, turned wooden pulls, backboards marked "J. J. Drew, Norwalk, O," repairs, some veneer and edge damage, age cracks in top and side panels, 45-1/2" w, 23-5/8" d, 37-3/4" h **2,000.00**

Massachusetts, Boston area, early 19th C, bowfront, mahogany veneer, figured mahogany top with lunette inlaid edge overhangs case of four cock-beaded veneered graduated drawers, serpentine veneered skirt flanked by flaring French feet, drawers include cross banded mahogany veneer bone inlaid escutcheons, orig brasses, old refinish, veneer losses, 41-1/2" w, 22-1/2" d, 35-3/4" h . . **24,150.00**

Massachusetts, c1815-20, mahogany inlaid, rect top with ovolo corners, inlaid edge, case with four cock-beaded drawers bordered with tiger maple cross-banding, flanked by quarter engaged ring-turned reeded posts continuing to vase and ring turned legs and joined by shaped apron with tiger maple banding continuing around legs to sides, replaced old brasses, old refinish, veneer losses, 43" w, 20" d, 41-1/4" h **1,610.00**

New England, c1820, maple, rect top with ovolo corners, ring-turned columns ending in turned tapering legs, flanking four reverse graduated drawers, refinished, replaced brasses, 41" w, 18-1/2" d, 41" h **900.00**

New Hampshire, c1800, bowfront, maple and mahogany veneer, rect top with swelled front, conforming case, four graduated drawers with inlaid edges, shaped inlaid skirt, French feet, old drawers, refinished, imperfections, 40-1/2" w, 21-1/2" d, 38-1/2" h **3,450.00**

Portsmouth or Greenland, New Hampshire, 1810-14, bowfront, mahogany and flame birch veneer, bowfront mahogany top with inlaid edge overhanging conforming case, four cock-beaded three paneled drawers, divisions outlined with mahogany cross banded veneer and stringing above skirt, central veneered rect drop panel, high bracket feet joined by shaped side skirts, similar rear feet, turned pulls appear to be orig, old refinish, minor repairs, 40-1/4" w, 21-1/4" d, 39" h **28,750.00**

George III, 19th C, cross-banded mahogany, serpentine, four graduated drawers, bracket feet, 36" w, 22-1/2" d, 31-1/2" h **3750.00**

Hepplewhite

American, bowfront, refinished cherry, facade of curly maple and mahogany veneer and inlay, four dovetailed drawers, banding around base, drawer edges, and top, inlaid diamond escutcheons and oval medallion on top drawer with urn, scrolled apron, French feet, turned mahogany pulls, some repairs, damage to veneer, top has been reworked, 43" w, 22" d, 39-1/2" h **3,500.00**

Country, refinished pine, red stain, solid bird's eye maple drawer fronts with natural finish, four dovetailed drawers, cut out feet and apron, old brass knobs, age cracks in front feet, 37-3/4" w, 35-3/4" h **1,100.00**

Louis Philippe, second quarter 19th C, walnut, later rect top, conforming case fitted with three drawers, shaped bracket feet, 47" w, 20" d, 31" h. **425.00**

Queen Anne, Southeastern New England, c1700, painted oak, cedar, and yellow pine, rect top with applied edge, case of four drawers each with molded fronts, separated by applied horizontal moldings, sides with two

recessed vertical molded panels above single horizontal panel, base with applied molding, four turned ball feet, old red paint, minor imperfections, 37-3/4" w, 20-1/2" w, 35" h . . **26,450.00**

Renaissance, Italian, walnut, composed of antique elements, fitted with three long drawers, foliate and shield shaped carved drawer pulls, paw feet, 36" w, 17" d, 37" h . . **2,450.00**

Sheraton

Curly and straight grain maple, pine secondary wood, one board top, four dovetailed drawers with replaced brass pulls, reeded stiles, high well turned legs, refinished, couple of age splits on side panels, minor chips on feet, 41-1/2" w, 18-1/2" d, 41-1/2" h **2,100.00**

Walnut, poplar and chestnut secondary woods, two board top, two small dovetailed drawers over four graduated dovetailed long drawers, inlaid diamond shaped escutcheons, orig brass pulls, paneled ends, scalloped aprons, high turned legs with small suppressed ball feet, refinished, one rear foot chipped, 40-3/4" w, 21" d, 54-1/2" h **1,650.00**

Hepplewhite, Pennsylvania, walnut, inlay, molded cornice, dovetailed case, eight dovetailed overlapping drawers, French feet, inlaid escutcheons, original oval brasses, 42" w, 66-1/2" h, $6,325. Photo courtesy of Garth's Auctions, Inc.

Victorian, American

Poplar, mahogany veneer facade, serpentine top drawer, two serpentine stepback drawers, five dovetailed drawers, applied beading, worn finish, 40" w, 19-3/4" d, 47" h **330.00**

Rosewood, ivory inlaid, rect top, four short and four long drawers, free standing reeded columns, inlaid base, turned feet, restoration on lower left base molding, 41-1/2" w, 20-1/4" d, 45" h **5,775.00**

William and Mary

American

Burl veneer, bachelor's, five dovetailed drawers, pull-out shelf, worn finish, veneer damage, replaced base molding, turned feet, and backboards, orig brasses, 30" w, 19" d, 35" h **1,980.00**

Oak, molded edge top, five dovetailed drawers, facade with applied moldings, bracket feet, old worn finish, orig engraved brasses, repairs, feet replaced, 36" w, 35-3/4" h **1,350.00**

Southern Massachusetts or Rhode Island, tiger maple, graduated drawer construction, two over four drawers, applied moldings to top and bottom, turned turnip feet, old grunge finish, three escutcheon plates present, rest of hardware missing, some repair, 36-1/4" w, 18-1/4" d, 48" h **2,950.00**

Chests of drawers, other

Bachelor, late George III, English, early 19th C, mahogany, rect top with molded edge, slide, four graduated cock-beaded drawers, bracket feet, veneer damage, restoration to feet, 37" l, 33-1/2" h **2,750.00**

Campaign, mahogany, pine secondary wood, brass trim, dovetailed case, int. with lift-out tray, one dovetailed drawer, some shrinkage to lid, 30-3/4" w, 18-1/4" d, 19" h **385.00**

Chamber, Federal, attributed to the Seymour Workshop, Boston, c1915, mahogany inlaid, rect top with inlaid edge overhangs case with single tripartite drawer above six smaller drawers flanking central cabinet on arched inlaid skirt, four turned reeded and tapering legs, similar arched side skirts, upper drawer with oval central stringing reserve, all drawers are outlined in ebonized inlay, missing dressing mirror from int. drawer, minor imperfections, 44-3/4" w, 19-1/2" d, 34-1/4" h **42,550.00**

Chest on chest

Chippendale, cherry, pine secondary wood, molded cornice, dovetailed cases, nine dovetailed overlapping drawers, scalloped apron, bracket feet, old mellow refinishing, interiors of drawers varnished, old brasses in orig holes, repairs, age cracks, 77-3/4" h **13,200.00**

George III, c1790, mahogany, upper section with dentil-molded cornice, fitted with two short over three long drawers, lower section fitted with three graduated long drawers, bracket feet, 43" w, 21" d, 67" h **7,000.00**

George III, third quarter 18th C, mahogany, upper section with two short over three long drawers, lower section with three long drawers, bracket feet, 47" w, 23" d, 70" h **1,265.00**

Queen Anne, Connecticut, c1780, carved cherry, molded and scrolled crest with carved urn finials, dentil molding, top section with three thumb-molded short drawers, central short drawer with pinwheel carving, four graduated long drawers, flanking engaged quarter columns; lower section: three graduated drawers, flanked by engaged quarter columns gadrooning below skirt with pinwheel carved pendant, four cabriole legs ending in pad feet, replaced brasses, restored, 37-1/2" w, 18-1/2" d, 48" h **9,200.00**

Chest on frame

Queen Anne, Connecticut, 1740-70, painted, flaring cornice with cove molding, case of thumb-molded drawers, arranged in two over four graduating pattern, frame with vigorously scrolling front and side skirts joined to cabriole legs with arris knees, arris disc feet, old red repaint, imperfections, 40" w, 23-1/4" d, 63-1/2" h **9,200.00**

Queen-Anne Style, English, walnut and burl veneer, mahogany secondary wood, case with four dovetailed drawers, brass teardrop pulls, cabriole legs, duck feet, 20th C, 19-1/4" x 33-1/2" base, 38-1/2" h **825.00**

Commode

Biedermeier, north Germany or Scandinavia, c1840, pearwood, stepped rect top, three drawers, shaped apron, 35" w, 20" d, 31" h **2,000.00**

Directorie, c1800, fruitwood, rect to, two long drawers, sq tapered legs, restored, 36-1/2" w, 32" h . . **2,500.00**

French Provincial, Neoclassical, early 19th C, gray and white mottled marble top, conforming case fitted with three drawers, sq tapered legs, 44" w, 21" d, 34-1/2" h **2,300.00**

Louis XV-Style, 20th C, gray and white veined marble top, bombe case fitted with three drawers, applied all over foliate and mask cast ormolu mounts, 45" w, 22-1/2" d, 34" h **3,450.00**

Credenza, attributed to Horner, New York, ebonized, marquetry inlaid, shaped inset marble top, ormolu bronze figural mounts, two drawers over two doors with concave sides, side panels inlay with flowers on green ground, front door panels inlay with baskets of flowers with bow tie ribbon, int. fitted with shelves, 67-1/2" w, 19-1/2" d, 41" h **8,000.00**

Highboy

Chippendale, associated with John Goddard and Job Townsend, Newport, RI, 1760-80, carved mahogany, enclosed scrolled pediment centering fluted plinth surrounded by urns and flame finials above two applied plaques over two short and three long graduated thumb molded drawers, set into lower case of one long and three short drawers above cyma curved skirt, centered carved shell, frontal cabriole legs ending in ball and claw feet, similar rear legs ending in pad feet, old replaced brasses, refinished, repairs, 39" w, 20-1/2" d, 84" h **36,550.00**

Queen Anne
America, mid-18th C upper section, curly maple, pine secondary wood, dovetailed top case, molded cornice and waist, dovetailed drawers with beaded edges, old replaced brasses, scalloped aprons, turned drops, cabriole legs, pad feet, refinished, restorations, 20th C base, 39-1/2" w, 20" d, 70-1/2" h **2,250.00**

Linden press, Chippendale, poplar, reeded quarter columns, top dental molding, two arched top drawers, secret compartment, base with three drawers over two drawers, replaced ogee bracket feet, 56" w, 23-1/4" d, 81" h, $4,125. Photo courtesy of Alderfer Auction Company, Inc.

America, mid-18th C upper section, cross-banded walnut, upper section with molded cornice over four long drawers, later base with three drawers, acanthus carved cabriole legs, 38-1/2" w, 22" d, 61" h **2,990.00**

Massachusetts, Salem area, 1750-80, carved tiger maple, upper section with flat molded cornice, case of five graduated thumb molded drawers, set into lower section of two long thumb molded drawers, lower with faux three drawer façade centering carved fan, scrolling skirt, four cabriole legs with arris knees, pad feet, orig brasses, refinished, minor imperfections, 36-1/2" w, 18-1/2" d, 77-1/4" h **43,125.00**

William and Mary-Style, 18th C, cross-banded walnut, upper section with two short over three long drawers, base with three drawers on trumpet turned legs, 40" w, 21" d, 69" h **1,850.00**

Liquor, England, late 18th C, oak, two handles, iron mounts, compartmented int. with 13 etched foliate dec bottles,

10 pressed brass and cork stoppers, 17-5/8" w, 12-3/8" d, 11-3/4" h .. **460.00**

Lowboy, Rhode Island, maple, pine secondary wood, case dovetailed at rear, pegged at sides, old replaced two-board curly maple top, four dovetailed drawers with beaded edges, batwing brasses, scalloped aprons, cabriole legs, slipper feet, refinished, small insect holes, restorations with some alterations, 32-1/2" w, 22-1/2" d, 30-1/4" h **1,760.00**

Mule chest, New England, pine, old dry red paint, one board top with shaped edge, wire hinges, bootjack ends with wooden peg construction, dovetailed drawer in base with molded edge, turned wooden pulls, slight warp to top, 38" w, 19-1/4" d, 35" h **1,350.00**

Spice, Pennsylvania, 1780-1800, walnut, dovetailed, cove-molded cornice, raised panel hinged door, opens to int. of eleven small drawers, brass pulls, molded base, old surface, 15-1/2" w, 11" d, 18-1/4" h ... **14,950.00**

Tall, Federal, New England, late 18th C, tiger maple, cove molded top, case with six thumb-molded drawers, central fan carved drop pendant flanked by high bracket feet, orig brasses, old refinish, repairs, 41" w, 54-5/8" h **8,625.00**

Wardrobe, Classical, mid Atlantic states, 1840, mahogany veneer, two recessed panel doors, similar sides, int. with veneered drawers, base with platform feet, small int. drawers added, 65" w, 26" d, 79-1/2" h **3,200.00**

Cradles

Chippendale-Style, birch, canted sides, scalloped headboard, turned posts and rails, refinished, 37-1/2" l **400.00**

Country

New England, 18th C, painted pine, arched hood continuing to shaped and carved dovetailed sides, rockers, old light green paint, old repairs, 40" l **300.00**

Pennsylvania, late 18th C, dovetailed, refinished curly maple, cut-out hearts, age cracks and shrinkage, 41" l **550.00**

Pennsylvania, 19th C, walnut, scrolled back and sides, shaped rockers, old refinish, repaired crest, 39" l, 18-1/4" d, 21" h **250.00**

Eastlake, 1875, walnut, paneled headboard, footboard, and sides, scrolling crest above short turned spindles, platform support, orig finish, dated............. **495.00**

Rustic, twig construction, rocker base, unsigned, 33" l, 22" d, 22" h **100.00**

Victorian, cast iron, painted black, wooden slat bottom, finial missing, 37" l, 21" d, 36" h **200.00**

Windsor, New England, c1800-20, bamboo turned spindles, worn finish **850.00**

Cupboards

Armoire

Arts & Crafts, English

Attributed to Liberty, Japanese style, overhanging top, three paneled cabinet doors over two drawers, hammered copper strap hardware, int. fitted with hooks and bars, unmarked, refinished, 84" w, 23" d, 72" h **5,175.00**

Single-door, overhanging top supported by corbels, mirror, emb copper panels of stylized flowers, unmarked, refinished, new back and shelves, one corbel missing, 40" w, 18" d, 75" h **1,050.00**

Classical, New York, c1835, mahogany, bold projecting molded Roman arch cornice, two paneled doors flanked by tapered veneered columns, ogee bracket feet, 74" w, 31" d, 94" h **3,200.00**

Empire-Style, French, late 19th C, oak, outstepped shaped cornice, ogee frieze, paneled sides, molded outline on doors, divided base drawers, shaped bracket feet, 63" w, 80" h **2,000.00**

Louis XV/XVI-style, transitional, 19th C, kingwood and parquetry, molded marble top with serpentine sides, pair of doors, each with two shaped and quarter-veneered flush panels, serpentine sides, coated stiles with gilt-brass chutes, sq-section cabriole legs joined by shaped skirt, stamped "Dubreuil," 44" w, 18-1/2" d, 59" h **950.00**

Restoration, New York, c1830, mahogany, flat top with cornice molding, two doors, birds' eye maple lined int., concealed drawer below, ribbed blocked feet, 56" w, 19-1/2" d, 90" h **2,800.00**

Victorian, American, c1840, walnut, bold double ogee molded cornice, two arched paneled doors, shelved int., plinth base, ogee bracket feet, 62" w, 24" d, 89" h **1,400.00**

Cupboard, Chippendale, mahogany, two doors over four graduating drawers, eagle brasses, bracket feet, $3,750. Photo courtesy of Garth's Auction, Inc.

Bee keeper's hutch, Canadian, pine, orig red and black painted top panel, paneled door on lower front, door on either end, drop front covers interior workshelf, hinged lid, pegged construction, lid marked "Patent Union, Bee Hive, W. Phelps Pat." 47" w, 19" d, 43-1/4" h **750.00**

Chifforobe, Art Deco, 1935, herringbone design waterfall veneer, arched center mirror, dropped center section, four deep drawers flanked by tall cupboard doors, shaped apron **450.00**

Chimney, decorated, poplar, pine shelves, ash backboards, orig dark red over lighter red dec, one door with four panes of glass at top over two raised panels, white mullions, white porcelain knob, surface wear, doors have restoration at hinges, price for pr **2,365.00**

Corner

Blind door, cherry, cove molded cornice, top doors with two panels each, three int. shelves, two door base with single int. shelf, ogee feet, molded base, restorations, replacements, 50-1/2" w, 21-1/2" d, 83-1/2" h.............. **1,925.00**

One piece, Chippendale, country, old dark brown painted dec simulates curly maple, small beveled cornice with applied trim, narrow beading around case with reeded pilasters on either side, two door top with two panels in each door, two paneled doors in base, ogee feet, molded base with relief carved fan drop at center, dark blue 20th C paint on int., old restorations, minor paint wear, 45-1/2" w, 20" d, 81-3/4" h **2,650.00**

One piece, Chippendale, Southern states, 1760s, pine, heavy projecting cornice molding above arched molded surround, flanking similarly shaped raised panel doors opening to two shelves above two additional fielded panel doors, flanked by fluted pilasters, opening to single serpentine shelf, refinished, hardware replaced, repairs, 64" w, 30" d, 93-3/4" h **7,475.00**

One piece, curly maple, pine secondary wood, molded cornice, two door top with six panes of glass each, molded mullions, raised panel doors on base, scalloped front apron, shaped feet, brass pulls, golden varnished finish, 20th C, 40" w, 19" d, 71-1/2" h **2,200.00**

One piece, paneled pine, New England, 19th C, flat ogee molded cornice, arched opening flanks three painted scalloped shelves, two fielded panel cupboard doors, single int. shelf, old refinish on ext., old red color on shelves, 50" w, 20" d, 88" h **4,255.00**

Two piece, curly maple mellow golden finish, pine secondary wood, cove molded cornice, two doors in top with molded mullions, six panes of glass each, molded center trim, center dovetailed drawer with batwing brass pull, two paneled base doors, bracket feet, 20th C, 46" w, 18" d, 75-1/4" h **1,980.00**

Hanging, New England, early 19th C, open, painted pine, three interior shelves, molded surround, backboard hanger possibly reshaped, 18" w, 9-1/2" d, 29-1/2" h **2,650.00**

Jelly, pine, old dark red over orange grained dec, one paneled front door, orig brass pull, turn buckle near top,

shaped bracket feet with cut-outs on ends of base, three int. shelves, top right end of top board and back splash missing, 37" w, 14" d, 53-1/2" h **550.00**

Kas, Long Island, NY, c1730-80, cherry, pine, and polar, architectural cornice molding, two raised panel thumb-molded doors flanked by reeded pilasters, applied moldings, single drawer, painted detachable disc and stretcher feet, replaced hardware, refinished, restored, 65-1/2" w, 26-1/4" d, 77-1/4" h **4,500.00**

Kitchen (Hoosier), American, early 20th C, oak, scalloped cornice over three cupboard doors, two glazed over two larger paneled doors, outset lower section with aluminum-lined work surface, over cupboard door flanked by three graduated drawers, 39-1/2" w, 28" d, 71-3/4" h **650.00**

Linen Press

Federal, Boston, 1820-25, mahogany veneer, three parts, veneered entablature with central rect outlined in stringing above veneered frieze, pair of recessed panel doors which open to five pull-out drawers with shaped sides, lower case with molding and three cock-beaded drawers, flaring high bracket feet, inlaid escutcheons, orig brasses, feet restored, surface imperfections, 48" w, 22-1/4" h, 83-1/2" h **6,900.00**

Regency, c1820, ebony and satinwood inlaid mahogany, molded overhanging cornice above two paneled doors opening to sliding shelves, lower case fitted with five short and two long drawers, bracket feet, 50" w, 22" d, 86" h **3,750.00**

Miniature, hanging, step-back, cherry and poplar, well executed step-down cornice, two paneled doors at top, divided interior, shaped shelves, paneled sides, molded base with five drawers, turned wooden pull on larger drawer to left of four stacked small drawers with brass pulls, all with applied border moldings, wire nail construction, minor base chips, 17-1/2" w, 11-1/4" d, 33" h **1,650.00**

Pewter, two part, top: cornice molding, two six-glass pane doors, two shelves, open pie shelf; base: two drawers over raised panel doors, one shelf int., short

turned feet, 56" w, 20" d, 87" h **2,250.00**

Pie Safe

Mixed hardwoods, pegged construction, scalloped crest, two doors with punched tin in each, punched tin on sides, tin punched in compass star surrounded by rings, scalloped borders, two dovetailed drawers, sq legs, replaced wooden pulls, refinished, 38-1/2" w, 18" d, 45" h ... **1,450.00**

Paint decorated, attributed to Shenandoah Valley, poplar, old worn blue paint on front, reddish-brown on sides, areas of earlier mustard paint, 12 punched tins, well-executed pots of flowers with scrolled handles, diagonal line punched borders, double doors, one drawer in base, high sq legs, few tins damaged, 38" w, 16-3/4" d, 54-1/2" h **2,300.00**

Cupboard, hanging, country, pine, old red, peaked top, one door with four panes of glass, 13-1/2" w, 6" d, 21-3/4" h, **$130.** *Photo courtesy of Garth's Auction, Inc.*

Poplar, 12 punched tins, three tins in each side, matching doors on front, punched stars surrounded by circles, three-line borders with corner fans, dovetailed drawer in base, turned wooden pulls, areas of pitting on some of the tins, old finish, front lightly cleaned, 41-1/2" w, 17-1/2" d, 57-1/4" h **1,000.00**

Southern, attributed to Washington County, VA, orig Rich Brothers punched tins, cherry, poplar and yellow pine secondary wood, double doors, tins with four pillars and arched on each door, intertwined foliage on each, eight rectangles with bowtie shaped designs and diamonds at top, dark red over earlier green paint on all tins, two dovetailed drawers at top, high turned legs, old dark finely alligatored varnish finish, 51" w, 17-3/4" d, 46-1/2" h **3,350.00**

Slant Back, New England, late 18th C, pine

Flat molded cornice above beaded canted front flanking shelves, projecting base with single raised panel door, old refinish, doors missing from top, imperfections, 37-1/2" w, 18" d, 73" h **2,300.00**

Flat overhanging cornice, cock-beaded front, three shelves, paneled door with wrought iron "H" and "L" hinges, old refinish, replaced door, 29-1/2" w, 12-3/4" d, 39" h **1,650.00**

Spice, northern Europe, last half 18th C, wall-type, painted, flat molded cornice, hinged cupboard door, molded recessed panel opening, compartmentalized int., molded base, old dark green paint bordered by red, int. drawers missing, imperfections, 16" w, 8" d, 17" h **1,500.00**

Step-back, wall

Pennsylvania, attributed to, one piece, curly maple, mellow golden color, two mortised and paneled doors on top, one int. shelf, two board top with high pie shelf, five dovetailed drawers in base in three-over-two configuration, turned legs with excellent figure, replaced brass pulls, one glued break on the lower corner of door, 44-1/2" w, 19-1/2" d, 60-1/4" h **8,525.00**

Pennsylvania or Ohio, attributed to, 1830-40, painted cherry, flaring cornice molding above fluted frieze, pair of glazed doors open to two shelf int., flanked by fluting above stepped out surface, two drawers over two recessed panel doors opening to single shelf int., recessed panel sides, four short

turned legs, all over red paint, brass pulls, imperfections, 50" w, 21-1/2" d, 88" h **18,400.00**

Wall

America, two piece, pine and walnut, old mustard paint and faint brown grain dec, traces of earlier red in some areas, brown sponging to three curved front drawers and on raised panels of lower doors, cove molded cornice, two-door top with six panes of glass in each door, vertical central panel with three panels, all top panes are tombstone shaped, chamfered corners, turned feet with applied half turned pilasters, blue painted int. with cut-outs for spoons, 61" w, 21" d, 85-3/4" h **5,500.00**

Canadian, Hepplewhite, two piece, pine, beveled and cove molded cornice, two doors in top section with two panes of glass each, two int. shelves with red and white paint, molded waist, five drawers in base with incised beading, turned wooden pulls, well scalloped base, high bracket feet, refinished, evidence of earlier red paint, edge chips, couple of glued splits to feet, 48" w, 23-1/2" d, 78-1/2" h **935.00**

Jacobean, oak and part painted, two part, upper section with pegs and shelves, projecting lower section with two doors, each with geometric and floral carving, 64" w, 20" d, 80" h **3,000.00**

New England, late 18th C, painted pine, molded cornice, two scalloped shelves, raised panel door, three-shelved interior, old blue paint, 33-3/4" w, 26-1/4" d, 75-1/2" h, minor imperfections **24,150.00**

New England, early 19th C, painted pine and cherry, rect case, single door with four recessed panels, scratch-beaded left edge, int. of 21 scratch-beaded drawers, seven compartments of assorted sizes, sides of case continuing to shaped cut-out feet, early red paint, minor imperfections, 27-3/4" w, 11-1/4" d, 59" h **4,370.00**

Wardrobe, Ohio

Phillip Falter II, Seneca County, poplar, orig dark red paint, old coat of over-varnish, cove molded cornice, double paneled door at top with beaded trim, small brass

pull, one dovetailed drawer in base, shaped feet, scalloped ends, 42" w, 17-1/4" d, 80" h . . . **2,200.00**

Unknown maker, curly maple, broad striped figure, walnut, maple, ash, and pine secondary woods, wooden peg and nail construction, broad cove molded cornice, two paneled doors, double end panels with chamfered edge detail, scalloped base aprons, two drawers in base, int. shelf near top, mellow brown refinish, orig architectural cupboard, back boards and cornice added later, 60" w, 21-3/4" d, 84" h . . . **2,100.00**

Desks

Aesthetic Movement, Herter Brothers, Washburn Commission, mahogany, fall front, top section: shelf with gallery top supported by turned and blocked posts, back panel with dec gold threaded material; middle section: slant lid, two supporting pull-out arms, central panel of marquetry inlaid with garland of flowers ending in bows, int. with two drawers, five cubbyholes, supported by two turned front legs, two bottom section with shelf and paneled back, missing orig writing surface, raised panel back, needs restoration, commissioned by Hon. William Drew Washburn for MN Greek Revival house, copy of orig bill of sale, 30" w, 20" w, 53-1/2" h **9,000.00**

Art Deco, Paul Frankl, Frankl Studios, New York, c1928, known as "Puzzle Desk," Chinese red lacquered body, four silver-leaf drawers with whimsical silver metal pulls, beveled mirrored top, fully restored, 40" w, 24" d, 28" h **16,000.00**

Arts & Crafts

Shop-of-the-Crafters, expressively grained wood, chalet, drop front, leaded glass cabinet doors, single drawer, lower shelf, flat cut-out flaring legs, replaced lower shelf and keyhole cover, new dark finish, unmarked, 41-1/2" w, 17-1/2" d, 45" h **1,150.00**

Stickley, Gustav, oak, chalet, gallery top, paneled drop-front door, chamfered back, keyed through-tenons, shoe feet, orig finish, restoration to foot, red decal, 24" w, 45-3/4" h **4,025.00**

Stickley, Gustav, postcard, gallery top, two drawers, tapered legs, orig finish, retail label, 38" w, 22" d, 38" h **1,150.00**

Chippendale

Connecticut, late 18th C, mahogany, block front, slant front lid, fitted tiered int. with nine dovetailed drawers, pigeonholes, two pull-out letter drawers with fluted columns, flame-carved finials and door with blocking and fan carving, dovetailed case, four dovetailed drawers, conforming apron, bracket feet, replaced brasses, old refinishing, feet replaced, repairs to case, 41-3/4" w, 21-1/2" d, 42-3/4" h **3,850.00**

Massachusetts, c1760-80, maple, slant front, two-stepped int., four balanced compartments, 14 drawers, case with four thumb-molded graduated drawers, bracket feet, old refinish, minor imperfections, 35" w, 19-3/4" d, 41-1/2" h **4,200.00**

Massachusetts, 18th C, carved mahogany, reverse serpentine, slant lid, two-stepped int. of valanced compartments and small drawers, case with four graduated scratch beaded serpentine drawers, conforming molded base with central drop, frontal ball and claw feet, shaped bracket rear feed, old refinish, repairs, 42" w, 22" d, 44-1/2" h **5,175.00**

New England, 18th C, slant lid, maple, pine secondary wood, dovetailed case, stepped interior with six drawers, blocked fronts, fan carving on top three, four pigeon holes, two dovetailed drawers on lower tier, four dovetailed drawers with molded trim, replaced batwing brasses and lock escutcheons, bracket feet with scalloped returns, molded base, refinished, some restorations, 36" w, 20" d, 41-1/4" h . . . **3,575.00**

New England, late 18th C, tiger maple, slat front, two-tiered int., valanced compartments, small drawers, carved central drawer flanked by document drawers with turned columns, four graduated drawers, replaced brasses, refinished, restoration, 36" w, 18" d, 39" h **2,550.00**

Rhode Island, late 18th C, cherry, slant front, stepped int. of small drawers, central one with shaping, case of beaded graduated drawers, ogee bracket feet, orig

brasses, old refinish, restoration, 39" w, 20" d, 43" h **3,800.00**

Eastlake, lady's, walnut, two part, top section sits on pegs, top: mirror with two columns supported shelves, fancy carving, pressed dec; base section: double hinged writing surface with dec floral carving, writing surface with two panels of green felt, lifts to reveal compartment desk int. with two drawers, one side fitted with two long drawers, gallery shelf in base, dec applied pieces, shoe foot base, metal asters, 31-1/2" w, 19" d, 57" h **1,150.00**

Edwardian, c1900, kneehole, mahogany, rect crossbanded top with central oval medallion, front canted corners, long frieze drawer, two banks of three drawers, center cupboard door, foliate marquetry dec, 37-1/2" w, 31" h **600.00**

Edwardian-Style, 20th C, marquetry inlaid mahogany, U-shaped superstructure fitted with drawers and doors, serpentine case fitted with drawers, sq tapered legs, 35" w, 24" d, 37" h. **2,645.00**

Desk, Empire, French, flame grain mahogany veneer, black marble top, thin long drawer, fall front, interior fitted with bird's eye maple veneer, leather writing surface, valanced shelf over eight drawers with line inlay, two-door base with three interior shelves, 32-1/2" w, 16" d, 57-1/2" h, $1,800. Photo courtesy of Sanford Alderfer Auction Co.

Empire, butler's, cherry and curly maple, poplar secondary wood, scrolled crest with turned rosettes, pull-out desk drawer with arched pigeon holes and three dovetailed drawers, three dovetailed drawers with applied edge beading, turned and carved pilasters, paneled ends, paw feet, old finish, some edge damage, 44-1/2" w, 23" d, 57-3/4" h . . . **1,925.00**

Federal

Massachusetts, attributed to Seymour Workshop, Boston, 1800, tambour, upper section with rect cornice, front edge inlaid with lunette design over two tambour doors interspersed with three inlaid pilasters, int. of six valanced compartments over four short drawers, all fitted into molded lower section with fold-out writing surface over three graduated long drawers with cross banding and inlaid ivory urn form escutcheons, flanked by panels defined by stringing, joined by straight skirt with applied molding on sq tapering legs with cuff inlays, imperfections, 36" w, 19" d, 43-1/4" h **18,400.00**

Massachusetts, central, early 19th C, lady's, mahogany inlaid, cove-molded top above three drawers with inlaid floral vines, checkered veneer banding opening to three-section int., end sections each with three drawers above openings flanking two central compartments over fold-out writing surface, cock-beaded bird's eye maple and mahogany veneer drawers flanked by colonettes above spiral carved engraved columns ending in turned feet, replaced brass, old surface, door inscribed "F. A. Butler, Deerfield, March 1864," legs pieced, other repairs, 40-3/4" w, 20-1/2" d, 54" h **4,325.00**

New England, early 19th C, mahogany and mahogany veneer inlaid, top section shaped gallery above flat molded cornice, two glazed doors enclosing compartments and drawer, flanking door and small drawer; projecting base with fold-out writing surface, two cock-beaded short drawers, two graduated long drawers, four sq tapering legs, inlaid cross-banding, old refinish, some restoration, inscribed "22 Geo. L.

Deblois Sept. 12th 1810,"
37-1/8" w, 20" d, 51-1/2" . . **3,000.00**

New Hampshire, early 19th C, slant lid, wavy birch, lid opens to two-stepped int. case of drawers with four cock-beaded surrounds, serpentine skirt, tall arched feet, orig brasses, old refinish, repairs, 37-1/2" w, 18-1/4" d, 45" h
. . . .**2,760.00**

New York State, early 19th C, mahogany veneer inlaid, slant lid and three graduated drawers outlined in stringing with ovolo corners, int. of veneer and outline stringing on drawers, valanced compartments, prospect door opening to inner compartments and drawers, flanking document drawers, orig brasses, old surface, veneer cracking loss and patching, other surface imperfections, 41-1/2" w, 21-1/2" d, 44" h
. . . .**2,550.00**

Pennsylvania, early 19th C, walnut inlaid, slant front, lid and cock-beaded drawers outlined in stringing, base with band of contrasting veneers, int. of small drawers above valanced compartments, scrolled dividers flanking prospect door which opens to two small drawers, three drawers, old refinish, repairs, 40" w, 20" d, 44-1/2" h **3,550.00**

George III, late, English, burl elmwood, slant front with rect crossbanding, fitted int. of pigeonholes and drawers, three graduated crossbanded drawers, serpentine apron, bracket feet, restorations, 30-1/2" w, 38" h . . **1,800.00**

George III-Style, partner's, third quarter, 19th C, burl elm, rect top, gold tooled green leather writing surface, molded edge, four crossbanded cock-beaded frieze drawers, two banks of three crossbanded cock-beaded and opposing cupboard doors, plinth base, 72" w, 31" h **2,875.00**

Hepplewhite

America, cherry, slant front, dovetailed case, four dovetailed drawers with edge beading, fitted int. with eight dovetailed drawers, two letter drawers and center door, scrolled apron, French feet, replaced brasses, old mellow refinishing, old pieced repairs, 41-1/2" w, 19" d, 35" h writing surface, 46" h **3,350.00**

Pennsylvania, early 19th C, walnut, rect top, thumb molded edge, string and quarter fan inlaid hinged slant front, fitted int., four line inlaid graduated long drawers, oval brass handles, shaped skirt with banded inlay, French feet, 42" w, 45" h **3,000.00**

Queen Anne

America, early 18th C, cross-banded walnut, slat front, fitted int. of wells and drawers, three frieze drawers, cabriole legs, pad feet . . **5,750.00**

Northern Maine, 19th C, maple, slant front, int. with valanced compartments above small drawers, end drawers separated by scrolled dividers, case of three thumb-molded drawers, molded bracket base with central drop pendant, old darkened surface, 35-1/2" w, 17-1/2" d, 40-1/4" h
. . . . **5,175.00**

Vermont, c1750, tiger maple and cherry, slant front, int. with central fan-carved drawer, two valanced compartments flanked by molded document drawers, four valanced compartments, three drawers, case with four thumb-molded graduated drawers, bracket feet, replaced brasses, old refinish, imperfections, and repairs, 36" w, 18" d, 41-1/2" h **3,220.00**

Renaissance Revival, English, partner's, carved oak, rect top with rounded corners, molded edge, front and back each carved with three frieze drawers, one pedestal with three drawers, other with paneled door opening int. with drawers and shelves, canted corners with figural pilasters, conforming molded plinth base, compressed bun feet, profusely carved with fruiting swags, grotesque masks, and heraldic devices, 72" w, 39-1/2" d, 30" h **5,500.00**

Sheraton

America, slant lid, birch and cherry, flame veneer, pine secondary wood, dovetailed case, four dovetailed drawers with applied beading and figured mahogany veneering, orig oval thistle brasses, scalloped apron with curly maple front apron with oval mahogany medallion inlay, ring turned feet, eight dovetailed int. drawers with brass knobs, 10 pigeon holes, some with scalloped tops, refinished, interior candle burns at back of writing surface, age splits

to case, lid hinges replaced, chips, restoration to beading, 39-1/2" w, 20" d, 47" h **1,320.00**

Country, slant lid, cherry, pine and poplar secondary wood, two dovetailed drawers behind slant lid, two large compartments, three dovetailed drawers in base, turned feet, orig oval brasses with emb pineapple in basket design, refinished, alternations, restored break on one back leg, 37" w, 19-1/4" d, 38-1/2" h **990.00**

Victorian

America, 19th C, mahogany, tooled brown leather writing surface, three frieze drawers, each pedestal fitted with three drawers, casters, 48" l, 36" d, 31" h **5,175.00**

America, second half 19th C, partner's, mahogany, gilt tooled leather writing surface, two frieze drawers on each side, pedestals fitted with four drawers opposed by cabinet doors, plinth base, 66", 54" d, 29" h **6,200.00**

William and Mary, attributed to CT, early 18th C, tulipwood and oak, fall-front lid with raised panel, int. of four compartments, three drawers, well with sliding closure, double arched molded front, base with long drawer, four turned legs, joined by valanced skirt, shaped flat cross stretchers, turned feet, replaced brasses, old refinish, minor imperfections, 24-3/4" w, 15" d, 42-1/2" h **17,250.00**

William and Mary-Style, American, 20th C, oak, seven dovetailed drawers, applied moldings, molded edge top, brass tear drop pulls, old finish, turned legs and stretchers, one piece of molding missing from drawer, 27-3/4" x 59" x 31" h **500.00**

Dry sinks

Curly maple, rect well, work surface on right with small drawer, two poplar wood cupboard doors, short bracket feet, hardwood edge stripes, minor repairs, refinished, 55" w, 34-1/2" h
. . . .**2,400.00**

Grain painted, New England, rect well with tin lining, rounded splashboard, two small drawers, two cupboard doors, shelf int., bracket feet, brown and yellow pine graining, 49" w, 38" h
. . . .**900.00**

Pine, three drawers on high back, sink with back-curved sides, paneled doors opening to self, stile feet, c1900, 43" w, 18-1/2" d, 33-1/2" h **900.00**

Pine and poplar, galleried well, one small dovetailed drawer, two paneled doors, cut-out feet, 46" w, 18-1/4" d, 37-3/4" h **600.00**

Poplar, painted, rect well above pair of paneled cupboard doors, scroll-cut apron continuing to low bracket feet, cast iron thumb latch replaced, layers of old worn green paint, 39-1/2" w, 16-13/4" d, 33" h **650.00**

Hall trees and hat racks
Bench
Gothic Revival, oak, composed of some antique elements, tall backrest inset with foliate and figural panels, lift seat and foliate carved lower panels, 34" w, 73" h **690.00**

Gothic-Style, late 19th C, oak, tall backrest fitted with three figural, foliate, and seraph carved panels, lift seat, chip-carved sq legs, 60" w, 66-1/2" h **1,855.00**

Chair
Arts & Crafts
Limbert, #79, hall chair, unique "bicycle" shape, orig leather back and shaped seat over slab leg with keyed construction, orig finish, branded and numbered, orig leather has been reinforced, 19" w, 20" d, 42" h **1,100.00**

Voysey, C. F. A., in the style of, c1895, five vertical back slats, paddle arms, tapering legs and back posts, tacked-on replaced burgundy leather seat, orig dark finish, accompanied by Nov 1899 issue of International Studio magazine where chair is pictured, 27" w, 20" d, 55" h **13,800.00**

Hall rack
Art Nouveau, France, early 20th C, mahogany, flaring mahogany panel, five brass curved coat hooks centered by mirror, umbrella stand below, 47" w, 85" h **1,200.00**

Arts & Crafts, attributed to Charles Rohls, early 20th C, oak, tall sq shaft, two tiers of four wooden hooks, each near the top, half buttresses running up from the cross base on all four sides, sq wafer feet, 64" h **1,100.00**

Colonial Revival, Baroque-Style, American, 1910, cherry, shell carved crest over cartouche and griffin carved panel back, lift seat, high arms, mask carved base, paw feet, 39-1/2" w, 21-1/2" d, 51" h **700.00**

Victorian, American, burl walnut, ball finials above paneled and shaped cornice, rect mirror flanked by turned garment holders, marble top drawer supported by turned legs, shaped base, painted metal plant holders, 29" w, 14" d, 93" h **1,400.00**

Hat rack
Arts & Crafts, wrought steel, hat and coat style, four sided, double hooks and spindles, unmarked, 21" w, 21" d, 75" h **865.00**

International Movement
Eames, Charles, hat rack, "Hang-It-All," manufactured by Tigrett Enterprises, c1953, white enameled metal frame, multicolored wooden balls, 20" w, 6" d, 16" h **800.00**

McArthur, Warren, coat rack, manufactured by Warren McArthur Industries, 1930s, anodized tubular aluminum frame with rubber "doughnut" feet, orig label, 24" d, 67" h **3,250.00**

Windsor, American, pine, bamboo turned, six knob like hooks, orig yellow varnish, black striping, 33-3/4" w **200.00**

Magazine stand, Arts & Crafts, L. & J. G. Stickley, slatted sides, arched apron, four shelves, original dark finish with overcoat. "The Work of..." decal, 42" x 21" x 12", **$1,355.** *Photo courtesy of David Rago Auctions.*

Stand
Arts & Crafts, coat and umbrella type, wrought steel, cut-out apron, spindles, brass hooks, unmarked, 27" w, 10-1/2" d, 73" h **850.00**

Blowing Rock, NC, c1920-25, root constructed stand, watch hutch, magazine rack, holders for writing accessories, old finish, 22-1/2" w, 11-1/2" d, 57" h **1,265.00**

Mirrors
Aesthetic Movement, America, c1880, overmantel, gilt, central cornice supported by two small columns over frieze dec with scene of snake attacking bird in tree, mirror plate highly dec with leaves, orig label of L. Utler, 47 Royal St., New Orleans, 64" w, 6" d, 84" h **3,600.00**

Art Deco, French, c1930, giltwood, frame closed at bottom and sides, carved chevrons, stylized sundials and Chinese scrolls, hung by gilt thread rope, tapered rect beveled mirror plate, 27" w, 37" h **1,500.00**

Arts & Crafts
Boston Society of Arts and Crafts, 1910, carved wood, rect, carved and gilded frame, ink mark, initials, orig paper label, 11-1/4" w, 18-1/2" h **700.00**

Limbert, oak, frame with geometric inlaid design over rect cane panel shoefoot base, recoated orig frame, orig glass, 20" w, 8" d, 22" h **600.00**

Baroque, Continental, second quarter 18th C, giltwood, fruit filled cartouche form resting, mirrored borders with grapevines and scrolls, foliate carved pendant, 63" h **5,750.00**

Biedermeier, c1830, walnut, ogee molded cresting, paneled sides, 26" w, 37" h **350.00**

Centennial, Queen Anne-style, American, late 19th C, mahogany faced, scalloped, shell pendant, 32" h **250.00**

Cheval, German, ebonized, swivel rect mirror, rounded ends, low sq mount, artist sgd, 70" h **425.00**

Chippendale, scroll
Mahogany, England, late 18th C, gilt stenciled star on crest over molded liner, orig finish, 12-1/4" w, 19-3/4" h **600.00**

Mahogany, old finish, molded frame, old replaced ears, some edge damage, replaced mirror, Philadelphia paper label in very poor condition, 16-1/2" w, 30" h **420.00**

Mahogany, orig finish, molded frame with gilded liner, composition eagle in crest with old gilding, orig mirror glass with minor wear to silvering, 19-3/4" w, 40-1/2" h......**3,575.00**

Refinished mahogany, molded frame, repairs, mirror replaced, 11-1/2" w, 19-3/4" h...... **225.00**

Walnut Veneer, England, late 18th C, walnut veneer, scrolled crest above four similar scrolled ears and drop pendant flank molded veneered mirror glass surround, old surface, old glass, minor imperfections, 21-1/2" w, 41" h........**4,315.00**

Chippendale-Style, mahogany, figured veneer, finely cut crest and base with molded liner with later gold paint, well carved pierced eagle crest, late 19th C, 23" w, 39-1/2" h............**1,155.00**

Mirror, Classical, convex, giltwood, surmounted by an eagle finial on rocky pedestal, convex mirror plate with ebonized slip and spherule-mounted border, leaf-carved pendant below, 18" d round mirror, 10" eagle finial, loss and restoration, $3,650. Photo courtesy of Sanford Alderfer Auction Co.

Classical

Dressing, America or England, 1810-20, carved mahogany and mahogany veneer, cylinder top opens to reveal four drawers, centering one door, ivory pulls, above single divided long drawer, restoration, 19" w, 10-5/8" d, 32" h **1,610.00**

Girandole, America or England, 1810-20 gilt gesso, crest with eagle flanked by acanthus leaves, convex glass, ebonized molded liner with affixed candle branches, foliate and floral pendant, imperfections, 23" w, 35" h **5,175.00**

Overmantel, New England, c1820-40, painted and giltwood, rect mirror frame with sq corner blocks, applied floral bosses joined by vase and ring turned split baluster columns, molded black liner, old gilt surface, replaced mirror glass, surface imperfections, 46" w, 23" h **920.00**

Wall, New York, 1830s, carved and eglomise, entablature overhangs veneered frieze, reverse painted land and waterscape flanked by leaf carved split balusters, orig eglomise and mirror glass, old refinish, minor losses and crazing, 38" h **460.00**

Courting, wooden frame, reverse painted glass inserts and crest with bird and flowers, orig mirror glass with worn silvering, penciled inscription on back with "restored 1914," touch-up to reverse painting, brass back corner braces, 10-7/8" w, 16-1/2" h **935.00**

Edwardian, late 19th C, overmantel, boxwood marquetry inlaid, arched cresting inlaid with musical still life and scrolling vines, shaped mirror plate flanked by cross-banded stiles, 60" w, 68" h **900.00**

Empire, flame mahogany veneer over pine, scalloped crest with scrolled ends, inset oval panel at top, applied half turned pilasters, ogee base, worn silvering, glue repairs at ends of crest, old alligatored varnish finish, 21" w, 51" h **770.00**

Federal

Architectural, two parts, old gold repaint, cove moldings top and bottom, reeded pilasters topped with gesso leaves, beveled mirror with worn silvering, top section divided into three sections, gold and black roses, tulips, and morning glories on white ground in center, silver and gold leaf designs on white, edge wear, 17-3/4" w, 32-1/2" h **450.00**

Architectural, two parts, pine, old alligatored white paint over orig gilding, stepped cornice with applied ball dec, molded pilasters on sides, applied corner blocks at

bottom, reverse dec with ribbons, silver, and black leaves on white ground, edge damage, 15-1/4" w, 24-1/4" h...............**450.00**

Girandole, America or England, 1810-20, gilt gesso carved, eagle with outstretched wings on rocky plinth, flanking foliate devices, circular frame with acanthus leaves, ebonized reeded liner with flanking candle sconces, foliate and floral drop pendant, regilding, 24" w, 43" h...........**5,475.00**

Over mantel, Boston, MA, c1820, gilt gesso, rect frame, central frieze of shell and grape vines in relief, mirror plate flanked by floral panes and mirrors, framed by spiral moldings, corner blocks with lions' heads, regilded, replaced mirrors, 56" w, 28" h...........**4,615.00**

Shaving mahogany veneer on pine, oval beveled mirror with scrolled posts, four dovetailed drawers, edge and veneer damage, one foot missing, 24-3/4" w, 9-1/4" d, 29-1/4" h...............**300.00**

Tabernacle, attributed to New York or Albany, 1795-1810, gilt gesso, molded cornice with pendant spherules over frieze with applied sunflower and wheat sheaf device, flanked by checkered panels over two part looking glass, flanked by applied double half columns, gilt surface, replaced glass tablet, 14" w, 30-1/2" h..........**865.00**

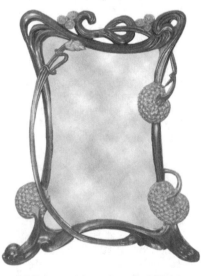

Art-Nouveau style, mahogany, old finish and gilding, age cracks, 47-1/2" h, 38" w, $175. Photo courtesy of Garth's Auctions, Inc.

Wall, giltwood, labeled "Parker and Clover Looking Glass and Picture Frame Makers 180 Fulton St. New York," molded cornice with applied spherules above eglomise table of girl in pasture landscape holding dove, mirror flanked by spiral carved pilasters, 13-3/4" w, 29-1/8" h **2,875.00**

Federal, late, attributed to New England, c1820-30, gilt gesso, molded cornice with acorn form drops over frieze centering carved leaf motif flanked by vine and leaf applied devices, two part mirror glass with grape and leaf designs, flanked by vase, ring, and spiral turned split balusters, old gilt surface, minor imperfections, including replaced mirror glass, 19" w, 37" h **700.00**

George II-Style, English, 19th C, carved gesso and giltwood, C-scroll and shell carved arched crest, serpentine and rect mirror plate, scrolled foliate corner pendants, C-scroll, shell, and acanthus carved shaped apron, 29" w, 65-1/2" h **1,800.00**

Hepplewhite, shaving, mahogany, inlay, two dovetailed drawers, feet, posts, and mirror are old replacements, 17-3/4" h **225.00**

Louis XV-Style, pier, 19th C, carved giltwood, large rect mirror topped by crest carved with leafy scrolls and rocaille, marble-topped ovolo 19-1/4" h shelf, flat leaf edge, gilt metal brackets, reeded scrolls with anthemion and female mask terminals, 33" w, 73" h **1,725.00**

Neoclassical, English, c1810-15, giltwood, flat molded cornice above eglomise tablet with center sailing vessel within a black oval, red and silver lattice panel bordered by black and white, mirror below flanked by reeded columns on sq plinths with rosettes, 18-1/8" w, 36" h **1,725.00**

Queen Anne, English

Mahogany, top carved round shell with gold highlights, scrolled crest, bottom with small shell carved circle, gold dec gesso liner, replaced beveled glass, 26" l **60.00**

Figured walnut veneer on pine, rubbed down finish, molded frame and scrolled crest, replaced glass, minor edge damage and some veneer repairs, 9" w, 15-3/4" h **770.00**

Oak, old finish, old glass with some wear to silvering, old replaced backboards, 13" w, 21-1/4" h **330.00**

Scroll, mahogany, old finish, molded frame, detailed scrolled crest, minor split in bottom edge of frame, 9" w, 16-1/4" h **550.00**

Walnut and parcel-gilt, scrolled crest, center pierced gilt gesso Prince of Wales device, gilt incised liner framing two-part beveled mirror, England, c1760, imperfections, 16" w, 40-1/4" h **1,955.00**

Walnut, scrolled cornice and pendant, molded liner framing mirror plate, England, 18th C, some imperfections and restoration, 18" w, 38-1/8" h **1,380.00**

Renaissance Revival, c1870, ebonized and parcel-gilt, elaborate pediment carved with cornucopia, dentil molding and foliage, arched mirror plate and anthemion carved borders, 50" w, 79" h **2,695.00**

Rococo, Continental, third quarter 18th C, giltwood, shaped mirror plate, arched top, frame carved with foliage and C-scrolls, 28" w, 54" h **4,025.00**

Sheraton, mahogany, spiral turned split columns and bottom rail, inlaid panels of mahogany, rosewood, and cherry, architectural top cornice, split mirror, 24-1/2" w, 47" h **300.00**

Rocker, Victorian, mahogany, carved lion heads on back rail, **$425.** *Photo courtesy of Joy Luke Auctions.*

Victorian, English

Cheval, baluster form cast iron stand, traces of red painted scrollwork, quatrefoil base, oval ebonized wood framed mirror, 51" l mirror, 44" h **400.00**

Pier, oak, late 19th C, rect, paneled cornice flanked by columns over marble shelf, turned feet, 25" w, 11" d, 96" h **600.00**

Rockers

Art Nouveau, American, c1900, oak, fumed finish, carved arms, saddle seat, three splats with floral-type capitals **400.00**

Arts & Crafts

American, oak, four vertical back slats, corbel supports under arms, recovered orig spring cushion, orig finish, 29" w, 34" d, 36" h . . . **200.00**

Limbert, #580, oak, T-back design, orig recovered drop-in cushion, recent finish, branded, 24" w, 29" d, 34" h **150.00**

Plail, oak, slatted barrel back, D-shaped recovered seat, refinished, unsigned, 26" w, 28" d, 31" h **2,500.00**

Stickley Brothers, oak, six vertical back slats, recovered orig spring cushion, worn orig finish, branded, 25" w, 27" d, 35" h **220.00**

Stickley, Charles, five slats under each arm, through-tenon construction, recovered cushions, minor wear to orig finish, remnant of decal, 34" w, 37" d, 41" h **1,400.00**

Stickley, L. & J. G., #831, Morris-type, adjustable back, open under arms, orig finish, sgd "The Work of...," back bar replaced, 30" w, 35" d, 38" h **1,500.00**

Boston, American, 19th C, maple, spindle back **200.00**

Colonial Revival, Windsor-style, Colonial Furniture Co., Grand Rapids, MI, comb back, birch, mahogany finish, turned legs, 21" w, 17" d, 27-1/2" h **200.00**

Decorated

America, orig black over red dec, gold stenciled urn of fruit and flowers on crest, shaped seat, scrolled arms, well turned legs, repaired damage to arms, 15" h seat, 40" h **220.00**

Pennsylvania, dark green, gold foliate on crest, slats, and seat, traces of red border with yellow line detail, turned legs, shaped medallion stretcher, scrolled arms, repaired break in one arm, 17" h seat, 42" h............ **220.00**

International Movement, Charles Eames, manufactured by Herman Miller, salmon fiberglass zenith shell, rope edge, black wire struts, birch runners, c1950, 25" w, 27" d, 27" h **1,400.00**

Ladderback, Portsmouth, NH area, late 18th C, turned finials above arched slats joined to down turned natural arms with carved Indian faces on terminals, old dark brown paint, imperfections, 16" h seat, 46-1/2" h........ **4,600.00**

Renaissance Revival, George Huntzinger, NY, 1876, walnut, ring turned armrests and stretchers, cloth wrapped wire seat and back, dated, 21" w, 33" h **400.00**

Wicker, painted white, sq back, basket weave pattern over openwork back, rect armrests with wrapped braces, openwork sides, braided edge on basketweave seat and skirt, X-form stretcher, 32" w, 33" h **200.00**

Windsor

American, c1850, grain painted, stencil dec, scrolled crest, tail spindle back, shaped seat, bamboo turned legs, box stretcher **450.00**

New Hampshire, upholstered, birch splayed legs, dark orig finish, pine base, coarsely woven light green fabric, rounded back, slightly rolled arms, few later rails added at tops of legs for support, 17-1/2" h seat, 43-1/2" h.............. **880.00**

Secretaries

Biedermeier-Style

Inlaid walnut, molded rect top, four drawers, top drawer with fall front, fitted int. with ebonized writing-surface, molded block feet, 50-1/4" w, 23-3/4" d, 35-1/2" h ...**1,000.00**

Walnut and parquetry, cavetto-molded cornice, front with frieze drawer, fall front opening to fitted int. with box-fronted cupboard and similar drawers, base of two door cupboard, flanked by convex stiles, molded plinth base, 42-1/2" w, 21-1/4" d, 67" h...... **2,300.00**

Centennial, inlay mahogany, two part: top with four drawers over six cubbyholes center, line inlay door opening to reveal two cubbyholes and large drawer, sliding tambour doors flanked by inlay panels with simulated columns; lower: fold-over line inlay lid,

two drawers with line inlay, diamond inlay on legs, some lifting to veneer, replaced cloth writing surface, 37-1/4" w, 19-3/4" d, 46" h..... **800.00**

Chippendale

Massachusetts, c1770-90, carved mahogany, scrolled and molded pediment above tympanum with projecting shell and arched raised panel doors flanked by fluted pilasters, candleslides, raised panel slant lid with blocked facade, molded conforming base, bracket feet, int. of upper bookcase divided into nine open compartments above four small drawers, int. of lower case with two fan-carved blocked drawers, similar prospect door, small blocked and plain drawers, scrolled compartment dividers, replaced brasses, old

Secretary, Chippendale, country, butternut, old dark red finish, dovetailed case, top with two doors with inset panels and scalloped crests, two dovetailed drawers, slant front, fitted int. of five dovetailed drawers with brass pulls, hidden drawer, eight pigeonholes, four dovetailed cock-beaded drawers, dovetailed bracket feet, H-hinges, some replaced brasses, scrolled brackets on pigeonholes replaced, found in Vermont, 37-1/4" w, 78-1/2" h, **$11,550.** *Photo courtesy of Garth's Auction, Inc.*

finish, restored, 39" w, 22" d, 93-1/2" h............ **19,550.00**

New England, c1780, cherry, two pieces, top section: flat cove molded cornice, two cupboard doors, molded recessed panels, projecting base with slant lid opening to int. of central prospect door flanked by three valanced compartments and drawers; lower section: case of four thumb-molded graduated drawers, bracket feet, replaced brasses, refinished, restored, 39-1/4" w, 20-1/8" d, 86" h........ **4,500.00**

Classical, Boston, 1820-25, secretaire a'abattant, carved mahogany and mahogany veneer, marble top above cove molding, mahogany veneer facade flanked by veneered columns topped by Corinthian capitals, terminating in ebonized ball feet, recessed panel sides, fall front opens to desk int. over two cupboard doors, old refinish, 35" w, 17-1/2" d, 57-1/2" h **16,100.00**

Colonial Revival, Colonial Desk Co., Rockford, IL, c1930, mahogany, broken arch pediment, center finial, two glazed mullioned doors, fluted columns, center prospect with acanthus carving flanked by columns, four graduated drawers, brass eagle, carved claw and ball feet, 41" w, 21" d, 87" h **1,000.00**

Eastlake, American, burl walnut and mahogany, shaped cornice, pair of glazed cabinet doors, cylinder front, writing surface, two doors in base, shaped apron, 27" w, 22" d, 66" h **1,500.00**

Empire-Style, late 19th C, gilt bronze mounted mahogany, rect top, fall front with fitted int., over pr of recessed cupboard doors, flanked by columns, paw feet, 44-1/4" w, 23-1/2" d, 49-1/4" h **1,955.00**

Federal

Massachusetts, Boston or North Shore, early 19th, mahogany inlaid, top section: central panel of bird's eye maple with cross-banded mahogany veneer border and stringing joined to the plinths by a curving gallery above flat molded cornice, glazed beaded doors with Gothic arches and bird's eye maple panels and mahogany cross-banding and stringing enclosing shelves, compartments, and drawers; lower: projecting section with fold-out surface inlaid with oval bird's eye maple panel set in mitered rect with cross-banded border and cock-beaded case, two drawers veneered with bird's eye maple panels bordered by mahogany cross-banding and stringing, flanked by inlaid panels continuing to sq double tapered legs, lower edge of case and leg cuffs with lunette inlaid banding, old finish, replaced brasses, imperfections, 41" w, 21-3/4" d, 74-1/2" h **9,775.00**

New Hampshire, paint decoration, two pieces, pine, old alligatored reddish-brown and yellow dec over earlier red, chamfered corners on dovetailed cases, molded cove cornice, tree dec on two paneled doors, slant front with tree dec, int. with 13 dovetailed drawers with central prospect door, four dovetailed drawers in base with applied beading, slightly shaped bracket feet with applied base molding, replaced wooden pulls, replaced H hinges, touch-up to top doors **7,425.00**

George III, English, early 19th C, japanned, swan neck pediment, rosette carved terminals, two glazed cupboard doors, fitted int. of compartments and small drawers, fall front writing surface with cubbyholes and drawers, four graduated drawers, shaped apron, bracket feet, gilt and polychrome warrior and figural landscape scenes, birds, and flowering trees, green ground, over painting and minor reconstruction, 40-1/4" w, 21-1/2" d, 96-1/2" h **5,000.00**

George III/Early Federal, America, third quarter 18th C, mahogany, two sections, upper: shaped architectural pediment with gilt-metal ball and spike finials, cavetto cornice over crossbanded frieze, chequer-banding, front with pair of thirteen-pane astragal doors, two adjustable shelves; base: outset fall-front opening, fitted int., four graduated cock-beaded oxbow-fronted drawers, conforming molded plinth base, molded and spurred bracket feet, 44-1/4" w, 24-1/4" d, 93-1/2" h **17,000.00**

Hepplewhite, two pieces, walnut and figured walnut veneer with inlay, pine and poplar secondary wood, top: removable cornice with high goosenecks, keystone and turned finials, double doors with adjustable shelves, stringing inlay with invected corners and inlay on cornice, base:

slant front lid, fitted int., with pigeon holes and 10 dovetailed drawers, center door, four dovetailed drawers with applied edge beading, bracket feet, old finish, period replaced brasses, pieced repairs, some edge damage, replaced finials, 39-5/8" w, 11" h x 42-1/4" cornice, 21" d x 40-1/2" w base, 90" h **20,900.00**

International Movement, Gilbert Rhode, manufactured by Herman Miller, upper bookcase with drop front desk over four doors, carved wooden pulls in burl and paldio veneers, refinished, c1940, 66" w, 15" d, 72" h **2,600.00**

Louis XV/XVI, c1860, tulipwood and kingwood parquetry, serpentine marble top, case fitted with three drawer sham fall front, fitted interior, four long drawers, foliate cast mounts, 24" w, 14" d, 50-1/2" h **1,035.00**

Renaissance Revival, American, c1865, walnut, two sections, upper: bookcase section, S-curved pediment with center applied grapes and foliage carving, two arched and molded glazed doors, shelved int., three small drawers with applied grapes and foliage carved pulls; lower: fold-out writing surface, two short drawers over two long drawers with oval molding and applied grapes and foliage carved pulls, matching ornamentation on skirt, 48" w, 21" d, 95" h **5,000.00**

Sheraton, New England, mahogany and mahogany flame veneer, cove molded cornice, three drawers across top with oval brasses, two paneled doors in top with fine flame veneer, three interior drawers, four pigeon holes with adjustable shelf, three dovetailed drawers with applied beading, figured book page veneer, reeded legs with ring turnings and molded surround at base of case, refinished, few repaired veneer splits, pierced repairs, stains in bottom, replaced brasses, 42" w, 20" d, 50-1/2" h **1,760.00**

Victorian, two pieces, walnut, top: crown molding cornice, two glazed doors with burl and walnut buttons; base: burl cylinder roll with two drawer walnut int., pigeon holes, slide-out writing surface, base: three long drawers with burl dec, tear drop pulls, refinished, 40" w, 23" d, 86" h . **1,850.00**

Settees
Art Deco, attributed to Warren McArthur, c1930, tubular aluminum frame, sheet aluminum seat and back supports, removable vinyl cushions, 68" l **5,750.00**

Arts & Crafts
Limbert, #939, oak, 11 back slats, corbels under arm, recovered orig drop-in cushion, branded, refinished, 75" w, 27" d, 40" h **800.00**

Stickley, L. & J. G., oak, drop-arm form, 12 vertical slats to back and drop-in orig spring cushion, recovered in brown leather, refinished, unsigned, 65" w, 25" d, 36" h **1,800.00**

Baroque Revival, Flemish, scroll, mahogany, old cane in back medallion, cane seat has been upholstered, old dark finish, 66" w, 50" h **750.00**

Biedermeier-Style, beechwood, curved open back, three vasiform splats, outcurved arms, caned seat raised on six sq-section sabre legs **650.00**

Classical, American, c1850, mahogany, serpentine front, carved crest, transitional rococo design elements, 82" l **600.00**

Colonial Revival, William and Mary style, American, c1930, loose cushions, turned baluster legs and stretcher, 48" l **750.00**

Empire-Style, late 19th/early 20th C
Gilt bronze mounted mahogany, settee, pair of side chairs, each with foliate and figural mounts, 80" l settee, price for three pieces **1,725.00**

Mahogany and parcel-gilt, two seat canapé, curved and padded back, reeded frame continuing into arms with swan-form supports, over-stuffed seat, sabre legs . . . **400.00**

Mahogany, two seats, curved backs, each armrest ending on ram's head, hoof-foot feet **2,100.00**

French Restauration, New York City, c1840, rosewood, arched upholstered back, scrolled arms outlined in satinwood terminating in volutes, rect seat frame with similar inlay, bracket feet, 80" l, 27" d, 33-1/2" h . . . **1,200.00**

George III, early 19th C, black lacquer and faux bamboo, settee, pair of arm chairs, price for three pieces . **1,265.00**

Gothic Revival, American, c1850, carved walnut, shaped crest rail surmounted by center carved finial, stiles with arched recessed panel and similarly carved finials, upholstered back and seat, open arms with padded armrests and scrolled handholds, carved seat rail, ring turned legs, ball feet, 67-1/2" w, 23-1/2" d, 49-3/4" h **800.00**

Louis XVI-Style, third quarter 19th C
Gilt bronze mounted ebonized maple, Leon Marcotte, New York City, c1860, 55-1/2" l, 25" d, 41-1/2" h **2,185.00**
Giltwood, settee, pr of arm chairs, each with rib band and foliate carving on circular fluted legs, 54" l settee, price for three pieces
. . . . **990.00**

Renaissance Revival, America, c1875, carved walnut, triple back, each having carved crest and ebonized plaque inlaid with musical instruments, red floral damask upholstery **1,200.00**

Rococo Revival
Attributed to John Henry Belter, c1885, 65" l settee, pair of lady's chairs, pair of side chairs, each with laminated rose and foliate carved cresting, grapevine openwork sides, cabriole legs, price for three pieces . . . **14,375.00**
Attributed to J. & J. Meeks, rosewood, laminated curved backs, Stanton Hall pattern, rose crest in scrolled foliage and vintage, tufted gold velvet brocade reupholstery, age cracks and some edge damage, 65-1/2" l . . . **5,500.0**

Victorian
Carved rosewood, c1870, shaped and padded back, two arched end sections joined by dipped section, each with pierced foliate crest, over upholstered serpentine front seat, flanked by scroll arms, conforming rail continue to cabriole legs, frame leaf carved **850.00**
Wrought and cast brass, lion finials on back posts, red and gold brocade seat cushions and upholstered back, 48-1/2" l
. . . . **825.00**

Wicker, tightly woven rect back, inverted triangle-dec, tightly woven arms, rect seat with woven diamond herringbone pattern, continuous braided edging from crest to front legs, turned spindle apron, 43" w, 36" h **500.00**

Sideboards

Art Nouveau, Louis Majorelle, 1900, oak and mahogany, rect, bowed front, inset marble top, two long drawers, undulating brass pulls cast with sheaves of wheat, two cupboard doors with large applied brass sheaves of wheat and undulating leaves, molded apron, four lug feet, 65" w, 39-1/8" h
. . . . **6,000.00**

Arts & Crafts
English, attributed to, with two "V" backsplashes, two drawers with ring pulls, bottom shelf, casters, orig finish, marked "S79FUM90," 42" l, 20" d, 45-1/4" h **1,150.00**
Limbert, Charles P., Grand Rapids, MI, c1910, oak, oblong top, mirrored back above case, three short drawers flanked by paneled cupboard doors over long drawer, cooper pulls and strap hinges, sq legs, chamfered tenons, branded mark, 49-1/2" w, 53-1/2" h . . **900.00**
Stickley, Gustav, plate rail, linen drawer over three drawers, two cabinet doors, orig finish, red decal, paper label, some veneer losses to door edges, 48" l, 18" d, 41-1/2" h **4,990.00**

British Colonial, early 19th C, bone and ebony inlaid padouk wood, top with slight concave ends, three drawers, turned pendants, sq tapered legs ending in spade feet, inlaid with stringing and foliage throughout, 51" w, 24" d, 31" h **9,775.00**

Centennial, Chippendale-Style, America, late 19th C, mahogany, block front with shell carving, four drawers, front cabinet doors, gadrooned apron, cabriole legs, claw and ball feet, 68" w, 24" d, 40" h **950.00**

Classical
Mid Atlantic States, 1840-45, carved mahogany and cherry veneer, rect top over mahogany veneered drawer, two recessed panel doors opening to one shelf int., flanked by veneered scrolled supports, veneered base, old refinish, hardware changes, splashboard missing, 40" w, 18-3/4" d, 40-1/8" h
. . . . **2,550.00**
New York, 1830s, carved mahogany veneer, splashboard with molded edge and four spiral carved and turned columns, topped by urn-shaped finials, rect top overhands recessed paneled case, cock-beaded drawers and cupboards outlined with crass banded mahogany veneer, two top drawers with dividers above short

Sideboard, Arts & Crafts, Stickley Brothers, tall mirrored backsplash with columns and shelf, three drawers and four paneled cabinet doors, copper hardware, good original medium finish, missing one bail, unmarked, 63-1/2" h, **$4,025.** *Photo courtesy of David Rago Auctions.*

drawers, bottle drawers flanked by end recessed panel doors, left one with single shelf int., right one with two shelf int., flanked by columnar leaf carved supports over frontal carved paw feet, rear feet are heavily turned and tapering, old refinish, imperfections, 60-1/4" w, 23-5/8" d, 56-3/4" h **2,760.00**

Empire, late, mahogany, three drawers over four drawers, mahogany veneer front on center drawer, two pull-out working surfaces above two smaller drawers, four mahogany turned front posts, four front hairy paw feet, two turned rear feet, glass pulls, 73" w, 24" d, 42" h **750.00**

English, late 19th century, two-piece, ornate dyed ivory marquetry inlay, beveled-edge mirrors, broken arch top over turned columns, spindled rails on top with single door, base with drawer over door over shelf on each side, center with domed door, French feet, 72-1/2" w, 23-1/2" d, 84-1/2" h, **$8,525.** *Photo courtesy of Alderfer Auction Company, Inc.*

Federal

Massachusetts, Boston, 1810-20, mahogany, maple, and rosewood veneer, two-tiered case, demilune superstructure, maple inlaid panels surrounded by cross-banded rosewood veneer above cock-beaded end drawers, small central drawer flanked by end cupboards, six ring turned tapering legs, case with concentric turnings, reeding, cockbeading, and scenic landscape jointed on underside of arched opening, old surface, replaced pulls, replaced leg, veneer loss, later landscape painting, 74-1/2" l, 24-1/2" d, 44-3/4" h **9,200.00**

Massachusetts, Boston, 1820-25, carved mahogany and mahogany veneer, molded rect top with convex and concave bowed front with sq corners, conforming case, one long cock-beaded drawer flanked by short drawers above central cupboard doors flanked by bottle drawers, reeded cupboard doors flanked by bottle drawers, reeded pilasters, beaded paneled drawers above beaded skirt, central fan carved pendant, six ring turned and reeded legs, carved hairy paw feet, old finish, imperfections, 71-3/4" w, 25-1/2" d, 42" h **25,300.00**

Massachusetts, c1810, mahogany inlaid, shaped top outlined in inlay, conforming case with central drawer with reserve, flanked by end drawers outlined in Greek key inlays, two central cupboard doors with beaded ovals, flanked by cupboard doors, legs with bellflower inlays on front of the upper and lower sections, replaced brasses, old surface, 71-1/2" w, 26-1/2" d, 42" h **21,850.00**

Middle Atlantic States, c1790, attributed to, mahogany and cherry inlaid, overhanging top with canted corners and serpentine front, central cock-beaded door inlaid with cherry panel with quarter fan inlays and mahogany mitered border, cock-beaded wine drawer with three-drawer facade at one end, three cock-beaded graduated drawers on other, ends with cherry veneered panels, four sq inlaid tapering legs ending in molded spade feet, lower edge of case with molding, old finish, minor imperfections, 48-1/2" w, 21-5/8" d, 37" h **19,950.00**

New England, c1790, mahogany and mahogany veneer, overhanging top with shaped front, conforming case, central pullout surface, bowed cock-beaded drawers, two cupboard doors flanked by concave drawers and

cupboard doors, six sq tapering legs, replaced brasses, old refinish, imperfections, 64" w, 20-1/8" d, 37-1/2" h **5,500.00**

Southern States, attributed to Francis Marion Kay 1816-87, cherry and other hardwoods, yellow pine secondary wood, replaced rest, three drawers over two doors, another drawer over prospect door at center, lower doors divided by half turned pilasters, six turned legs, one door is restored, hinges replaced, 60-1/4" w, 21-1/4" d, 49" h **3,410.00**

Southern States, huntboard, yellow pine, two board top, high tapered sq legs, single drawer with beveled edges, turned wooden pull, square nails, mortise and peg joints where legs meet apron, refinished, age splints, shallow chip on lower corner of drawer, 41-1/2" w, 23" d, 43" h **2,200.00**

Virginia, 1790-1810, walnut and yellow pine, molded rect top, cock-beaded case with end drawers, right drawer visually divided into two drawers, left with two working drawers, central cupboard cock-beaded door, four square tapering legs, old brass pulls, old refinish, repairs, inscription on drawer reads "Virginia Hunt Board, early 19th cent. from family of Admiral Todd, Naval Commander prior to and during the Civil War, Virginia," 56" w, 22" d, 39" h **5,520.00**

Federal-Style, Southern States, huntboard, yellow pine, overhanging rect top, case with three drawers, skirt with central shaping, four sq tapering legs, orig brasses, refinished, 21" w, 19-1/2" h **1,840.00**

George III, late 19th C, satinwood cross-banded mahogany, bow front, frieze drawer, two cupboard doors, sq tapered legs, spade feet, 60" w, 24" d, 37" h **4,600.00**

George III-Style, late 19th C

Inlaid mahogany, rect top, four drawers, reeded circular legs, 38-1/2" w, 21" d, 33-1/2" h
. . . .**2,530.00**

Mahogany, bowed front, three central drawers, flanked by short drawer over cupboard door, sq legs, 71" w, 24" d, 42" h . . **2,185.00**

Gothic, Kimbel & Cabus, New York, c1875, design no. 377, walnut, galleried top over two cupboard doors over open self over slant front over central drawer over open well flanked by two cupboard doors, galleried base shelf, bracket feet, 39-1/4" w, 17-3/4" d, 73" h **9,775.00**

Hepplewhite, mahogany and mahogany veneer with inlay, bowed center section with conforming doors and dovetailed drawer, two flat side doors, sq tapered legs, banding and stringing with bell flowers on legs, corner fans on doors and drawers, reworked, repairs, replaced brasses, 58-1/4" w, 18-1/2" d, 37-3/4" h **2,200.00**

Neoclassical, Boston, 1820-25, mahogany veneer, corner style, paneled and scrolled splashboard over top with veneered molded edge, curving front which overhangs conforming case of three veneered drawers over two recessed paneled doors, single shelved int., similar recessed panel sides above flattened ball feet with brass banding, replaced brass pulls, old surface with some imperfections, 60" w, 35" d, 42" h **55,200.00**

Regency-Style, 19th C, inlaid mahogany, two pedestals, central drawer, silver drawer, 58" w, 24" d, 36" h **1,610.00**

Renaissance Revival, America, cherry, curled mahogany drawer fronts, burled arched panel doors **900.00**

Sheraton, country, walnut and curly maple, beaded edge top, four dovetailed drawers, scalloped aprons, turned legs, line inlay around apron and drawer fronts, old varnish finish, replaced glass pulls, wear and edge damage, one heart inlay missing, large water stain on top, 69-1/2" w, 21-1/2" d, 43-1/2" h **5,500.00**

Victorian, American, late 19th C, pine, serpentine crest, rect top, four small drawers over two banks of four drawers, center cupboard, 65" w, 19" d, 51-1/2" h **750.00**

Sofas

Art Nouveau, Carlo Bugatti, 1900, ebonized wood, rect back, mechanical seat, slightly scrolling rect arms, parchment upholstery, painted swallows and leafy branches, hammered brass trim, four block form feet, 68-3/8" l **1,900.00**

Centennial, Chippendale-style, American, late 19th C, mahogany, shaped back, rolled arms, yellow velvet upholstered seat, gadrooned apron, cabriole legs with carved knees, claw and ball feet, 62" l **1,500.00**

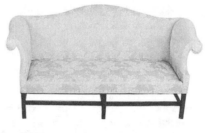

Chippendale style, camel back, scrolled arms, square legs, stretcher base, 74" l, 25" d, $2,290. Photo courtesy of Alderfer Auction Company, Inc.

Chippendale, country, step down back with step down arms, bowed front with large down filled cushions, eight molded carved legs, cup caster feet, reupholstered, 76" w, 32" d, 36" h **3,000.00**

Classical

Mid Atlantic States, 1805-20, carved mahogany and bird's eye-maple veneer, Grecian style, scrolled and reeded arm and foot, punctuated with brass rosettes, continuing to similar reeded seat rail with inlaid dies, reeded saber legs flanked by brass flowerettes, brass paw feet

on casters, old surface, 75" l, 14-1/2" h seat, 35" h **3,680.00**
New England, 1820-40, carved mahogany veneer, cylindrical crest ends, leaf carved volutes, upholstered seat and rolled veneer seat rail, leaf carved supports, carved paw feet, 92" w, 16-1/2" h seat, 34-3/4" h **1,650.00**

Empire

Mahogany and figured mahogany veneer frame, well-detailed carving with sea serpent front legs, turned back legs, lyre arms with relief carved flowers and cornucopia, rope turned crest rail, refinished, reupholstered in floral tapestry on ivory ground, bolster pillows, 107" l **3,850.00**
Mahogany veneer with carving, reupholstered in old rose and green floral brocade on beige ground, some damage to frame, 92" l **750.00**

Federal

America, carved mahogany, mahogany veer paneled top crest with scrolled sides, front carved with rosette and leaf dec, carved paw feet with front stylized wings, red flower dec upholstery, 96" w, 19-1/2" d, 32" h **1,000.00**
Massachusetts or New Hampshire, c1810, mahogany and bird's eye-maple veneer, raked veneered crest divided into three panels by cross banded mahogany inlay, flanked by reeded arms, similar

Sofa, federal, mahogany frame with carving attributed to McIntire, Salem, MA, acanthus and floral carved arms and crest with swags, arrows, floral medallions, punched background, turned arm posts, square tapered legs, 76-1/2" l, $9,350. Photo courtesy of Garth's Auctions.

supports terminating in down-scrolling terminals, ring turned baluster forms, slip seat, bird's eye maple veneered seat rail, four frontal reeded turned legs ending in casters, old refinish, minor re-veneering, 75-1/2" l, 32-1/2" h **6,900.00**
New Hampshire, c1815, carved mahogany, upholstered, straight crest continuing to shaped sides with carved arms on vase and ring reeded and swelled posts and cock-beaded panels, bowed seat rail, vase and ring-turned legs with cock-beaded rect inlaid dies, old finish, minor imperfections, 78" w, 24" d, 17" h seat, 34" h back **2,415.00**

George III-Style, English, carved oak, double arched upholstered high backrest, scrolled arms, loose cushion seat, acanthus carved legs, claw and ball feet, 58" l **1,200.00**

Louis XV-Style, 19th C, walnut, shaped, foliate carved crest rail, padded back, out-scrolled arms, foliate carved scrolled armrests, conforming molded seat rail, cabriole legs, pad feet, 85" l **800.00**

Neoclassical, Baltic, c1825, carved mahogany, paneled cresting, padded arms with lions heads and anthemia, upholstered seat and back, shaped feet, 68" l **2,185.00**

Rococo Revival, John B. Belter, carved rosewood, triple back, carved central rose and fruit on sides, scroll band underneath, carved segmented scroll, tufted back red silk upholstery, brass caster feet, old restoration to central crest, worn seat fabric, 62" w, 42" h **4,500.00**

Sheraton to Empire, transitional, carved mahogany, scrolled arms with molded detail, applied rosettes, relief carved leaf supports, brass caps on turned front legs, relief twist carvings, applied moldings on front panels, casters on base, dark refinish, glued break in one scroll, reupholstered, 70" w, 17-1/2" h seat, 34-1/2" h back **550.00**

Victorian, late, American, c1890, camel back, reupholstered, turned legs, 60" l **750.00**

Stands
Baker, wrought iron, 48" h, 14-1/2" d, 84" h **500.00**
Basin, Federal, attributed to Seymour Workshop, Boston, c1810-15,

mahogany and bird's eye-maple veneer, small round table with concentric incised circles around basin opening above three veneered and cock-beaded drawers, two of which are hinged, turned and reeded legs joined to the round incised platform, ending in brass paw feet, orig brasses, old refinish, 18-1/8" d, 28-1/4" h **36,800.00**

Bird cage, wicker, painted white, tightly woven quarter moon-shaped cage holder, wrapped pole standard, tightly woven conical base, 74" h **225.00**

Book, Gothic Revival, manufactured by Betjamann's, retailed by Tiffany & Co., Union Square, late 19th C, burlwood veneer, pointed arch uprights pierced with trefoils, beveled rect base, 13-1/2" l, 5-3/4" w **350.00**

Canterbury, Regency, early 19th C, mahogany, drawer with paper label for "G. Ibison Furniture Broker & Appraiser, Cumberland Place, Near the Elephant & Castle," restoration, 19-1/4" l, 14" d, 22-1/2" h **1,380.00**

Cellaret, George III, English, mid-19th C, mahogany, lozenge form, brass bands, twin loop carry handles, racked chamfered tapering legs, 24" w, 17-1/2" d, 27-1/2" h **7,500.00**

Chamber, Federal
New England, early 19th C, painted and dec, dec splashboard above wash stand top with round cut-out for basin, medial shelf with drawer below, orig yellow paint with green and gold stenciling and striping, paint wear, imperfections, 18-1/4" h, 1" d, 39-1/4" h . . . **350.00**
North Shore, MA, c1815-25, carved mahogany, shaped splashboard, veneered cabinet door flanked by ovolu corners, carved columns of leaves and grapes on punchwork ground, ring turned tapering legs, brass casters, old replaced brasses, old refinish, minor restoration, 21-1/2" w, 16" d, 35-5/8" h **2,300.00**
Portsmouth, NH, c1800, mahogany inlaid, shaped splashboard with center quarter round shelf, pierced top with bow front, square string inlaid supports continue to outward flaring legs with patterned inlays, medial shelf, satinwood skirt, small center drawer with patterned inlaid lower edge, shaped stretchers with inlaid paterae, old finish, minor imperfections, 23" w, 16-1/2" d, 41" h **5,750.00**

Stand, dumbwaiter, French, 19th C, mixed woods, retractable top divides into three parts, **$770.** *Photo courtesy of Sanford Alderfer Auction Co.*

Corner, Whatnot, Victorian, late 19th C, Chinoiserie, bamboo and lacquer, frame set with two diamond-shaped mirrors and shelves, 22" w, 13" d, 56" h
.... **250.00**

Dumbwaiter

George III style, 19th C, mahogany, three-tier, typical form, graduated dished tiers, baluster turned supports, tripod base, 43" h
.... **985.00**

Queen-Anne style, walnut, three circular shelves, splayed legs, pad feet, 21" d, 39" h......... **300.00**

Easel

Aesthetic Movement, attributed to Cincinnati furniture maker, cherry, intricate carved sunflowers and oak leaves, orig finish, 23" w, 36" d, 75" h **2,500.00**

Louis XVI-style, mahogany and parcel-gilt, picture support hung with berried laurel swags, trestle-end frame carved with acanthus, imbrications, and dolphins, 25" w, 23-1/2" d, 82" h
.... **950.00**

Stand, étagère, Victorian, walnut, beveled, arched top, central mirror, five shelves on each side, white marble top, cupboard in base, 43" w, 85" h, **$880.** *Photo courtesy of Joy Luke Auctions.*

Étagère

Classical, New England, 1860s, mahogany and mahogany veneer, spool turned gallery, ball finials, three shelves with similar supports, two recessed panel cupboard doors, single shelf int., ball turned feet, old refinish, imperfections, 35-1/4" w, 15-3/4" d, 66" h .. **990.00**

Regency, late, English, early 19th C, six tiers, corner, columnar supports, basal drawer, brass casters, 18" w, 14" d, 62" h
.... **3,000.00**

Victorian, late, English, bamboo and Japanese lacquer, three tiers, corner, scalloped form shelves, raised, colored and gilt Chinoiseries, 16-1/2" w, 45" h
.... **800.00**

Fernery, wicker, painted white, tightly woven, rect well, wrapped braced legs, X-form stretcher, 25-1/2" w, 18-1/2" d, 32" h **300.00**

Folding, Chippendale

New York State or Pennsylvania, 1755-775, cherry, dished top rotates and tilts, birdcage support, swelled and turned pedestal, cabriole tripod base, pad feet, old refinish, imperfections, 17-1/2" d, 26" h **3,220.00**

Pennsylvania, 1760-80, walnut, molded dish top, inscribed edge tilts, tapering pedestal with suppressed ball, cabriole legs ending in pad feet, imperfections, 22" d, 29" h **4,600.00**

Game board, New England, early 19th C, grain painted checkerboard top, single drawer, sq tapering legs, turned pull, paint imperfections, 17" w, 16" d, 29" h **700.00**

Magazine

Arts & Crafts

Stickley, Gustav, beveled overhanging top, three open shelves, good new finish, sgd under top, 15-1/4" w, 15-1/4" d, 53-1/4" h **2,070.00**

Stickley, L. & J. G., single broad slat on either side, arched toe board, new finish, "The Work of L. & J. G. Stickley" decal, 36" w, 12" d, 30" h **2,990.00**

Renaissance Revival, third quarter 19th C, mahogany, walnut, parcel-gilt, and ebonized gilt-metal, hanging, back plate with acanthus crest flanked by fleur-de-lis and bellflowers,

uprights mounted on top with gilt-metal bust roundels, central hinged magazine folio set with gilt composition oval bust of Mercury, gilt incised detailing, 19-3/4" w, 21-1/2" h............... **300.00**

Music, New England, c1840, painted ash and pine, adjustable, two canted sides, vertical slats on cylindrical shaft, chamfered rect post, chamfered cross legs, painted blue-green, 15-1/2" w, 14" w, 78" h **635.00**

Plant

Arts & Crafts, Limbert, ebon-oak line, overhanging top, four caned panels on each side, recent finish, branded signature, 14" w, 14" d, 34" h **2,100.00**

Folk Art, carved and painted root, America, polychrome painted animal heads radiating from entwined root base, inscribed "MAS 1897," 23" w, 38-1/2" h
.... **1,725.00**

Victorian, wirework, painted, late 19th C, demilune, three-tier, each tier with ornately curled rim, four slender legs heading by scrolled wire design, joined by single stretchers, X-bracing at back, casters, 45" l, 40" h **750.00**

Portfolio, William IV, English, c1830, carved rosewood, folding mechanism
.... **3,500.00**

Reading, Federal, Albany, NY, early 19th C, mahogany, reading stand above ring-turned tapering post on rect shaped canterbury, turned tapering spindles, casters, 22-1/4" w, 14" d, 47-1/2" h **3,200.00**

Sewing, Sheraton, country, black walnut, poplar secondary wood, lift top, fitted int. compartment with four int. dovetailed drawers and pigeon holes, single dovetailed drawer with figured front and incised beading, well-turned legs with ring turnings, replaced brass pull, pegged construction, lock missing, one leg with well-executed repair, 20" w, 19-1/2" d, 29" h .. **1,155.00**

Side

Empire, mixed hardwoods, flame mahogany veneer, one board top with drop leaves, two dovetailed drawers with pressed-glass pulls, flanked by half turned columns, apron with gadrooning at bottom, carved pineapple column, platform base with scrolled leaf returns to carved paw feet, 15-1/5" w, 16-3/4" d, 28" h **450.00**

Federal, New England, late 18th/early 19th C, cherry, oblong slightly overhanging top, four sq tapering legs joined by straight skirt with single drawer, old red washed surface, replaced pull, minor surface imperfections, 16-1/4" x 18-3/4" top, 29-1/2" h **1,350.00**

Federal, New England, early 19th C, tiger maple, overhanging sq top, conforming base, single drawer, four tapering sq legs joined by straight line inlaid skirt, replaced pull, refinished, restoration, 16-1/4" x 15" top, 27-1/2" h **1,265.00**

Federal, northern New England, early 19th C, overhanging sq top, conforming base, straight skirt, four vase and ring turned legs, flattened ball feet, all over faux bois paint simulating mahogany and bird's eye maple and string inlaid panels, minor surface and other imperfections, 19-3/4" x 20" top, 28-1/4" h **575.00**

Hepplewhite, solid curly maple and bird's eye, pine secondary wood, one board top, single dovetailed drawer, tapered legs, orig brass pull, refinished **1,550.00**

Sheraton, cherry, two board top with biscuit corners, dovetailed drawer, well defined ring-turned legs, orig brass pull, refinished, 19" w, 18-3/4" d, 26-1/2" h **990.00**

Sheraton, country, cherry, poplar secondary wood, single beaded dovetailed drawer, well executed rope twist carvings on legs, turned feet, orig brass pull, refinished, wear to finish on top, 15-3/4" w, 16" d, 26" h **715.00**

Sheraton, country, curly maple and cherry, poplar secondary wood, one board top, two dovetailed drawers with fine curl, internal lock on top one, turned walnut pulls, ring turned legs with paneled detail, refinished, 21" w, 17-3/4" d, 29" h **800.00**

Sheraton, country, curly maple, later top, dovetailed drawer, small brass pull with cast stars, turned legs with good figure, golden varnished finish, interior staining on aprons, top, and drawer, 17-3/4" w, 17-1/2" d, 27-3/4" h **880.00**

Sheraton, country, curly maple, two board top, dovetailed drawer fitted with turned wooden pull, well turned legs, golden refinish,

replacements, minor restoration, 21-3/8" w, 17-1/4" d, 28-3/4" h **935.00**

Sheraton, country, curly maple with good figure, poplar secondary wood, one board top, two dovetailed drawers with old replaced floral brass pulls, elaborate turnings on legs, refinished, 16-3/4" w, 18-3/4" d, 27" h **1,100.00**

Tilt-Top, Federal

New England, late 18th/early 19th C, mahogany, octagonal top, vase and ring turned post, tripod cabriole leg base, pad feet, refinished, imperfections, 21-1/2" x 15-1/2" top, 26-1/2" h **1,265.00**

Salem, MA, c1790-1805, mahogany, oval top, urn and ring-turned post, tripod cabriole legs, arris pad feet on platforms, refinished, repairs, 21-1/2" x 14-1/2" top, 27-1/2" h **2,300.00**

Wash

Empire, figured mahogany veneer, poplar secondary wood, dovetailed gallery fitted with narrow shelf, bowed top with cut-outs for wash bowl and two jars, serpentine front supports, turned rear posts, dovetailed drawer in base with brass pulls, high well turned legs, refinished, edge chips, 18" w, 16" d, 37-3/4 h **385.00**

Federal

American, mahogany and figured mahogany veneer, bow front with two small drawers, cutout for bowl, cutout sides, single dovetailed drawer in base, turned legs, worn finish, some water damage, replaced top and two small drawers, 20-1/4" w, 17-1/4" d, 30-1/4" h **275.00**

Rhode Island, c1790, mahogany veneer, top with four shaped corners, canted corners, engaged ring-turned columns ending in reeded legs flanking cock-beaded drawers outlined in cross-banded veneer, top two drawers with sections, replaced brasses, old refinish, imperfections, 20-3/4" w, 15-1/2" d, 28-1/2" h ... **4,025.00**

Hepplewhite, country, pine, worn brown paint over earlier red, dovetailed gallery on top, narrow shelf along back, sq legs, shaped two-board base shelf, 26-3/4" w, 18-1/2" d, 39-1/4" h....... **800.00**

Work

Hepplewhite, New England, c1810, cherry inlaid, sq top, outline stringing and quarter fan inlays on ovolo corners, line inlaid drawer and skirt, line inlaid sq tapering legs, crossbanded cuffs, brass drawer pull, refinished, 19" w, 19" d, 27" h **2,650.00**

Renaissance Revival, American, c1860, lift top opening to real satinwood interior fitted with compartments, narrow drawer above semi-circular bag drawer, pair of stylized lyre form ends jointed by arched stretcher surmounted by turned finial. **875.00**

Sheraton, New England, 1805-15, mahogany, veneered, outset rounded corners, shaped top, pull-out suspended fabric bag below single drawer, ring-turned and reeded round tapering legs ending in ring-turned tapering vasiform feet, old refinish, 16-1/2" w, 18-1/2" d, 28-1/4" h **3,500.00**

Steps

Bed, New England, early 19th C, pine and tulipwood, two steps, thumb-molded drawer below bottom one, flanked by shaped sides, demilune base, old color, repaired, 15-1/2" w, 10" d, 17-1/2" h................ **575.00**

Circus, America, early 20th C, painted white stringers, red, yellow, and blue treads, 25" w, 90" d, 27" h...... **435.00**

Library

George III, English, late 18th C, mahogany, rect molded hinged top, eight steps, 49-1/2" w, 53-1/2" h **2,500.00**

Regency, English, early 19th C, mahogany, three steps, inset green leather treads, scrolling banister, sq balusters, feet with brass casters, 46" w, 27" w, 56" h **2,400.00**

Stools

Cricket, Arts & Crafts, Limbert, #205-1/2", rect top covered with new leather, splayed sides, inverted heart cut-out, single stretcher with through-tenon, replaced keys, orig finish, branded, 20" w, 15" d, 18" h **950.00**

Foot

Arts & Crafts, oak

Barber Brothers, oak, nicely replaced leather seat, some color added to orig finish, paper label, 13" w, 13" d, 11" h **110.00**

Stool, foot, needlepoint top, three dogs decoration, $275. Photo courtesy of Joy Luke Auctions.

Limbert, cricket, #205-1/2, rect orig leather top and tacks, splayed sides with inverted heart cut-out having single stretcher with through-tenon construction, orig finish, branded and numbered, 20" w, 15" d, 19" h **2,000.00**

Orig leather and tacks, slightly arched rails, orig finish, 12" sq, 8" h. **90.00**

Worn orig drop-in leather cushion with four vertical slats to side, orig finish, 16" w, ·14" d, 14" h **260.00**

Queen Anne, 18th C, walnut, rect frieze, four cabriole legs each with shell carving on knees, pad feet, slip seat, 22-1/2" w, 17" d, 17" h **1,950.00**

Sheraton, curly and bird's eye maple, old finish, cane top, minor damage to top, 7-3/4" w, 13" l, 6-1/2" h. **440.00**

Victorian, late 19th C, carved walnut, short cabriole legs carved at knees with shells, shaped skirting carved with acanthus, velveteen upholstery, 12-3/4" w, 16" l, 11" h **175.00**

Windsor, attributed to Maine, early 19th C, rect top, four swelled legs joined by X-form stretchers, orig dark brown grain paint which resembles exotic wood, yellow line accents, paint imperfections, 12" w, 8" d, 7" h **625.00**

Joint

Early, oak, old finish, wear and age cracks, 11" w, 16-1/2" l, 17-3/4" h **990.00**

Jacobean-style, oak, rect plank top, shaped skirt, block and ring-turned legs joined by box stretcher, 18" w, 11-1/4" d, 21" h. **700.00**

Piano

Louis XVI-Style, late 19th C, carved beech, circular, adjustable, close-nailed over stuffed top, petal-carved frieze, leaf-capped turned, tapered, and fluted legs, wavy cross-stretcher **850.00**

Renaissance Revival, American, 1870, walnut, sq upholstered seat, acanthus carved baluster supports, four outswept legs, hoof feet **350.00**

Seat-type

Country, folk art, attributed to Fredericksburg, PA, late 19th/early 20th C, painted and dec, octagonal seat, chamfered edge, trimmed with border band of carved hearts, tall splayed and chamfered legs also trimmed with carved hearts and joined by slender rungs, overall polychrome **1,850.00**

George III, late 19th C, mahogany, gold floral satin upholstered rest seat, sq tapering supports, molded H-form stretchers, pr, 19-1/2" l, 17" h **1,650.00**

International Movement

Eames, Charles, manufactured by Herman Miller, Time-Life, walnut, concave seat, 13" d, 15" h **1,000.00**

Platner, Warren, manufactured by Knoll, bronze wire base, peach fabric upholstered seat, 17" d, 21" h **325.00**

Windsor, American, 19th C, oblong plant seat raised on three tall, turned and slightly swelled legs joined by T-stretcher, traces of old green paint, 15" w, 24-1/2" h **200.00**

Tables

Architect's, George III, English, late 19th C, mahogany, hinged tooled leather work surface above opposing hinged work surface, turned pedestal on three splayed legs, pad feet, some reconstruction, 29" w, 19-1/4" d, 29-1/2" h. **2,300.00**

Breakfast

Chippendale to Hepplewhite, transitional, walnut, one board top, beaded edge apron, sq legs with slight taper, molded corner, and inside chamfer, H stretcher, old finish, stains on top, 19" w, 29-1/4" l, 28-1/4" h **8,250.00**

Classical, New York, 1820-30

Carved mahogany inlaid, top with brass inlay in outline, stamped brass on edge of shaped leaves, one working and one faux drawers, flanked by drop pendants, four pillar curved platform support, leafage carved legs, carved paw feet, casters, replaced pulls, old finish, repairs, losses, 39" w, 24" d, 28" h **2,450.00**

Carved mahogany veneer, rect leaves with rounded ends, straight veneered skirt with panels and turned pendants, one end with working and one with faux drawer, fluted and turned four pillar veneer and shaped platform, four carved legs ending in carved paw feet and casters, old refinish, minor veneer imperfections, 22-1/2" w, 47-1/4" l extended, 30-1/4" h **2,300.00**

Federal

Massachusetts, central, c1810, inlaid cherry, rect hinged top with ovolo corners, base with straight skirt, edged with lunette inlay, flanked by sq tapering legs outlined in stringing, topped with icicle inlay, old refinish, 36" w, 17" d, 29" h **1,150.00**

New York City, c1815, carved mahogany veneer, rect top, shaped leaves, one working and one faux end drawers, cross-banded mahogany veneer, turned acanthus leaf carved pedestal, four acanthus leaf carved legs, brass hairy paw feet, old refinish, repairs, 25" w closed, 38-1/2" l, 30-1/4" h **1,725.00**

Card

Classical

Attributed to firm of Isaac Vine and Isaac Vine Jr., Boston, 1819-24, carved mahogany and mahogany veneer, rect top with beaded edges, skirt with recessed panel, C-scrolls and carved volutes over tapering pedestal accented by carved leafage above serpentine veneered platform with carved and scrolled feet on casters, old refinish, imperfections, 37" w, 17-1/2" d, 28-1/2" h . . . **1,840.00**

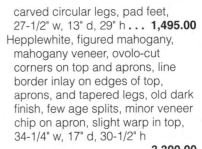

Attributed to Thomas Astens, New York City, 1822, carved mahogany and satinwood, rect swivel top with rounded ends, outlined in cross banded mahogany veneer, satinwood veneered skirt, faceted pineapple-like carving above acanthus leaf carving on pedestal, shaped legs, carved paw feet on casters, old refinish, imperfections, 36" w, 18-1/4" d, 28" h **3,335.00**

New York, 1820-30, carved mahogany, mahogany veneer rect swivel top with rounded front carved corners, leaf carved and shaped shaft, curving platform which joins four scrolling leaf caved legs ending in carved paw feet, refinished, minor imperfections, 36" w, 17-1/2" d, 30" h **1,495.00**

Federal

Fisk, Samuel, Roxbury or Boston, MA, c1800, mahogany and mahogany veneer, demilune folding top, conforming base,

four tapering sq legs, two of which swing, each imp "SF" at top, joined by straight beaded skirt, old refinish, minor imperfections, 33" w, 16" d, 29-1/4" h **3,220.00**

Newburyport, MA, c1800, mahogany veneer, elliptic shaped top with inlaid edge, overhangs divided skirt with panels of stringing and figured maple dies at top of sq tapering legs, outline stringing on legs with cuff inlays, old surface, veneer losses, 36" w, 17-5/8" d, 30" h **3,335.00**

Newburyport, MA, early 19th C, painted birch and pine, hinged top with molded edges, plain frieze with drawer, four sq tapering legs, orig dark mustard painted surface, orig brass pull, 39-1/2" w, 18-1/4" d, 29-1/2" h, imperfections **7,475.00**

Georgian-Style, late 19th C, carved mahogany, foliate carved top, polished playing surface, foliate

carved circular legs, pad feet, 27-1/2" w, 13" d, 29" h . . . **1,495.00**

Hepplewhite, figured mahogany, mahogany veneer, ovolo-cut corners on top and aprons, line border inlay on edges of top, aprons, and tapered legs, old dark finish, few age splits, minor veneer chip on apron, slight warp in top, 34-1/4" w, 17" d, 30-1/2" h **3,300.00**

Neoclassical, New York City, c1825, carved mahogany veneer, shaped swivel top with cross banded veneer in outline above inlaid edges and veneered skirt, central raised plaque above scrolled and waterleaf carved supports, fluted curving platform, similarly carved legs, carved paw feet on casters, old refinish, imperfections **4,600.00**

Sheraton, attributed to Salem, MA, faint signature on bottom "J. E. Skelton" (or Shelton), mahogany and mahogany veneers with banded inlay, figured top boards with ovolo corners, banded inlay around edges, half serpentine side aprons, serpentine front with banded inlay along bottom edges, figured satinwood panel on front with mahogany diamond, ring turned legs taper at base, reeded bands at centers, refinished, minor veneer loss, 36" w, 17-1/2" d, 29" h **5,500.00**

Center

Biedermeier, inlaid walnut, shaped rect top, molded frieze with drawer, canted, sq-section cabriole legs, 25" w, 37" l, 27-3/4" h **1,100.00**

Classical

Boston, c1840, carved mahogany veneer, circular top with rounded edge, conforming veneered apron with banded lower edge, carved and turned pedestal, shaped veneered platform above incised ball feet, 40-1/2" d top, 30-3/4" h **1,955.00**

Philadelphia, c1827, carved mahogany veneer, rect top with molded edge, cock-beaded frieze with single central working drawer flanked by faux drawers, turned and carved pedestal ending in gadrooning above stepped, curved pedestal, four belted ball feet, old surface, minor

*Table, drop leaf, Queen Anne, hardwood with old red, dovetailed apron scalloped ends, swing legs, cabriole legs, high duck feet and pads, wrought-iron butterfly hinges, 42-1/2" l, 15" d, 14-3/4" leaves, 28-1/4" h, **$28,600**. Photo courtesy of Garth's Auctions.*

imperfections, carving similar to work of Anthony G. Quervelle (1789-1856), Philadelphia, 45-1/4" w, 20" d, 34-3/4" h 2,550.00

George III-style, Irish, late 19th C, mahogany, 36" d, 21-1/2" d, 31-1/2" h 2,875.00

International Movement, Wienerwerkstatte, c1930, mahogany and brass, circular top with crossbanded edge, conforming frieze, sq-section support flanked by four further cylindrical supports, raised on truncated pyramidal base, 25-1/4" d, 30-1/2" h.......550.00

Louis XV-Style, 19th C, mahogany inlaid, ormolu mounted walnut, shaped rect top, one short drawer, opposite faux drawer, cabriole legs, cast sabots, 35" w, 22" d, 28" h 600.00

Renaissance Revival, American

c1875-80, burl walnut, top with rounded ends, turned pendants, trestle supports, carved stylized foliage and urns, 55" w, 31" d, 30" h...............1,610.00

c1880, walnut, shaped top with rounded ends, paneled frieze, circular legs joined by X-form stretcher, carved all over with angular foliage and Greek key bands, 39" w, 23" d, 29" h 1,100.00

Chair

American, late 18th C, cherry, three board top, hinged seat lid, scalloped edge sides, apron, shoe feet, black paint on underside of top, old refinishing on base, minor repairs, 45-1/2" d top, 28-1/2" h 9,350.00

New England, late 18th C, pine and birch, top tilts above plant seat flanked by sq tapering arm supports which continue to chamfered legs, four sq stretchers, old refinish, 40-1/2" w, 42" d, 28-3/4" h.............1,100.00

New England, 19th C, painted pine, rect cleated top, old red painted surface tilts above seat and shaped sides, 36" w, 43" d, 27-1/2" h.............3,220.00

Console

George III, c1790, japanned pine, serpentine top dec with black japanned scenes of Chinese landscapes, fluted frieze on fluted

sq legs, 34" w, 20" d, 32" h, price for pr 3,105.00

Regency, painted and parcel gilt-, rect marble top with outset corners, frieze carved with foliage, legs headed by masks and ending in hoof feet, plinth base, 44" w, 21" d, 31" h 1,955.00

Second Empire, French, second quarter 19th C, marble-top mahogany, rect speckled black marble top, frieze drawer, applied with wreaths, sq tapered legs headed by herm busts, plinth base, 37-1/2" w, 17" d, 34" h ...2,300.00

Dining

Arts & Crafts, Limbert, #403, cut-corner top over intricate base, slab supports with three spindles in an oval cut-out keyed stretchers connecting to a center leg, one leaf, orig finish, numbered, 50" w, 50" d, 30" h 2,500.00

Empire-Style, Continental, 19th C, walnut, quarter-veneered top with crossbanded border, conforming frieze, four canted scroll supports, rect platform stretcher with concave sides, gilt lion-paw feet, octagonal center support, one leaf, 46-1/4" w, 94-3/4" l extended, 31-1/4" h 2,300.00

Federal, New England, c1820-25, cherry and bird's eye maple, two part, two rect ends each with hinged drop-leaf, ring-turned tapering legs ending in ball feet, orig surface, minor surface mars, 82" w, 44-1/2" d, 28-3/4" h 1,725.00

Federal-Style, 20th C, mahogany, rect cross-banded top, two pedestal bases each with foliate carved posts on four downswept leaf carved legs, casters, three leaves, 72" l without leaves, 48" w, 29" h 3,220.00

George III-Style, mahogany, D-shaped top with rounded corners and reeded edge, twin pedestal bases of column raised on tripod base, downswept legs, brass toe caps and casters, 120" l, 44" w, 29-1/4" h 2,100.00

International Movement, Paul Evans, manufactured by Directional, sculptured bronzed metal abstract design base, plate-glass top, 72" w, 37" d, 29" h 2,300.00

Regency, Late, early 19th C, inlaid mahogany, three part, D-shaped ends, rect center section, all

cross-banded in satinwood, checker cross-banded frieze and sq tapered legs ending in spade feet, four leaves, 155 l, 54" w, 29" h 5,175.00

Regency-Style, late 19th C, mahogany, rect top, reeded edge, rounded corners, three ring turned pedestals, molded cabriole legs, casters, two leaves, 48" w, 177" l, 29" h...............17,250.00

Dressing

Empire, mahogany, small case top with drawer, dovetailed drawer in center, thin molding around lower apron, figured mahogany veneer over pine, high ring turned legs with relief rope twist carvings, small pieced restorations, 35-1/2" w, 17-3/4" d, 36-1/2" h......1,650.00

Federal, New York state, c1825, carved mahogany and mahogany veneer, brass inlaid, cock-beaded rect mirror, scrolled acanthus leaf carved supports with brass emb rosettes above three short drawers, projecting case of two short drawers, one long drawer joining four vase and ring-turned acanthus carved legs, casters, refinished, repaired, 36-1/4" w, 21-1/2" d, 55" h 1,725.00

Georgian, mid-18th C, mahogany, rect top above conforming case, fitted with one long drawer above six short drawers, central kneehole with recessed door, bracket feet, 36" w, 20" d, 32" h.......1,495.00

Painted and Decorated, New Hampshire or Massachusetts, early 19th C, shaped splashboard, table top with single drawer below, ring-turned legs, orig yellow ground, green and gold stencil dec, gold striping, replaced brasses, paint loss and wear, 34-1/4" w, 17-1/2" d, 37" h 1,150.00

Queen Anne, American, walnut, pine secondary wood, two board top with thumb-molded edge, mortised and pinned apron, two dovetailed overlapping drawers, round tapered legs, duck feet, old finish, edge damage to replaced top and drawer fronts, some damage to period brasses, 21-1/2" x 36" x 30-1/2" h.............7,700.00

Drop Leaf

Chippendale

Pennsylvania, late 18th C, walnut, shaped skirt, molded

Table, drop leaf, Hepplewhite, cherry, square tapered legs with stringing and bell flowers, banding at feet and apron, old refinishing, inlay added, top replaced, repair to one swing leg, 28-3/4" h, $650. Shown on top are three kugels with brass hangers, left: cranberry, 8" d, $990; center: blue, 10" d, $1,045; right: silver, (wear), 8" d, $150. Photo courtesy of Garth's Auction, Inc.

Marlborough legs, old surface, minor imperfections, 15-1/2" w, 46-3/4" l, 29" h........**550.00**

Rhode Island, c1780, carved mahogany, rect drop leaf top, four sq molded stop fluted legs joined by cut-out apron, repairs, 47-3/4" w, 38-1/4" d, 29" h **2,100.00**

Classical, New York, 1830s, mahogany, rect top with hinged shaped leaves, veneered straight skirts, leaf carved pedestal, four similarly carved legs, carved paw feet on casters, 38-3/4" l, 22-1/2" d, 29" h **650.00**

Federal, New England, early 19th C, tiger maple, rect leaves, straight skirt, sq tapering legs, old refinish, repairs, 46-1/2" w, 14" d, extends to 44-1/2", 26-3/4" h......**1,150.00**

Hepplewhite, cherry, one board top, finely tapered legs, old mellow finish, pieced restorations at rule joints, replaced hinges, 48-3/4" l, 15-1/4" d, 28" h **1,100.00**

Queen Anne, found in Newburg, NY, maple, oak, and pine secondary woods, old red paint, one board top, scalloped and shaped end

aprons, well shaped cabriole legs, pad feet, restorations, replacements, 48" l, 17-1/2" d, 28" h **990.00**

Sheraton, Country, birch, old red on one board top and leaves, later black on base, crisply turned legs pegged at aprons, crack in top of one leg, 36-1/4" w, 14" d, 10-7/8" l leaves, 28-3/4" h........ **495.00**

Folding, International Movement, Bruno Mathsson, manufactured by Carl Mathsson, walnut, refinished, 36" w, 10" d, 29" h **850.00**

Gallery, English, mahogany, turned column and round top and shelf with galleries, tripod base, old finish, wear and edge damage, some age cracks and repairs, late 19th C, 24" d, 30-3/4" h **330.00**

Game

Arts & Crafts, Miller Furniture Co., removable circular top, four plank legs inlaid with stylized floral design, paper label, felted gaming surface missing, overcoated top, 36" d, 31" h............**1,150.00**

Empire, tilt-top, mahogany and mahogany flame veneer, top with ogee aprons on sides, turned

drops, carved pineapple column, platform base with scrolled leaf returns to carved paw feet, one drawer on side, old dark finish, 40-1/2" w, 20" d, 30" h **450.00**

George III, c1790, cross banded mahogany, D-shaped, plain frieze, sq tapered and molded legs, 35" w, 17" d, 28" h **1,150.00**

George III, 18th C, mahogany, concertina-action, rect top, suede int., blind fret carved legs, 36" w, 17-1/2" d, 29" h **1,495.00**

Hepplewhite, American, 19th C, inlaid cherry, hinged demilune to, conforming apron, sq tapering legs **400.00**

Renaissance Revival, A. Cutler & Son, Buffalo, NY, c1874, ebonized and parcel-gilt, drop leaf, orig paper label, wear to base surface, 36" w, 13-3/4" d, 28-3/4" h..**700.00**

William and Mary style, with antique elements, seaweed marquetry inlaid walnut, D-shaped top with concave front, frieze similar shaped, frieze drawer, turned legs joined by stretchers, 32" w, 14" d, 30" h **2,875.00**

Harvest

New England, early 19th C, drop-leaf, pine, scrubbed top, hinged leaves, olive green painted base, ring turned tapering legs, early surface, 102-34" l, 18-1/4" d, 39-3/4" extended, 20-1/2" h **11,500.00**

New England, mid-19th C, drop-leaf, painted pine, rect hinged leaves with rounded corners flanking single drawer at each end, ring turned bulbous legs, orig olive-yellow surface, turned pulls, legs pierced, 72-1/2" l, 26-1/2" w, 26" w extended, 29-1/2" h **19,550.00**

Lamp, Arts & Crafts

Brooks, attributed to, four-sided top, flaring legs, floriform lower shelf, new finish, unmarked, seam separation on side, 20" w, 19-3/4" d, 29-3/4" h **2,300.00**

Stickley, Gustav, No. 644, circular top, arched cross-stretchers topped by finial, mortised legs, good new finish, replaced finial, Als Ik Kan brand, 29-1/2" d, 28-3/4" h **2,300.00**

Library

Arts & Crafts

English, overhanging top, arched apron, legs carved with stylized tulips, unmarked, refinished, seam separation to top, minor nicks and edge roughness at feet, 46" w, 27" d, 30" h
.... **1,955.00**

Stickley, L. and J. G., two drawer, corbels, flat medial stretcher, wrought copper pulls, old refinish to top, orig finish on base, Work of L. & J. G. Stickley, 48" l, 30" w, 29" h **2,530.00**

Georgian-Style, Morris and Co., late 19th/early 20th C, mahogany, tooled red leather top and gadrooned edge, two end drawers, boldly carved cabriole legs, claw and ball feet, 90" l, 53" d, 30" h
.... **3,450.00**

Renaissance Revival, third quarter 19th C, carved oak, rect top, two frieze drawers with mask form pulls, griffin form legs, shaped plinth, 54" w, 28" d, 30" h
.... **3,910.00**

Occasional

Arts & Crafts, Gustav Stickley, circular overhanging top, faceted finial over arched cross-stretchers, very good orig finish, red decal, 24" d, 29" h **2,185.00**

Biedermeier, early 19th C, birchwood, solid gallery top, inset petit point needlework panel, plain frieze, turned legs joined by stretchers, casters, inscription underneath reading "J. J. Werner, Paris," 21-1/2" w, 18-1/2" d, 29-3/4" h **2,760.00**

Parlor

Victorian, walnut, molded detail, white marble turtle top, carved dog on base shelf, old dark finish, old repairs, top cracked, 23" x 3" x 29" h **770.00**

Victorian, Gothic Revival, walnut, rosewood veneer apron, replaced top, 20" x 36" x 29-1/4" h .. **500.00**

Pedestal

Aesthetic Movement, French, c1875-80, brass and pottery, sq top with recessed tile, dec with foliage, pedestal with pottery cylinder, four angular legs, foliate dec, 14" w, 34" h **8,100.00**

Biedermeier-Style, cherry and burr poplar, circular top with crossbanded edge, conforming apron, hexagonal support rising from triangular platform base with concave sides, three scroll supports, 29-1/2" d, 27-1/2" h
.... **600.00**

Second Empire-Style, walnut, marquetry, and parcel-gilt, quarter-veneered circular top, polychrome floral marquetry, gilt-metal gadrooned edge, sq section tapered pedestal with concave sides and canted corners, gilt hairy-paw feet, 33-1/2" d, 28-1/4" h **1,000.00**

Pembroke

Chippendale, New England, late 18th C, mahogany, rect overhanging top, drop leaves, straight skirt, four sq tapering legs with inside chamfering, joined by "X" form sq stretchers, old refinish, imperfections, 29" w, 16" d, 30" extended, 27-3/4" h **1,840.00**

Federal, New England, 1795-1810, inlaid mahogany, oval top with outline stringing, conforming base with string inlaid drawer flanked by inlaid paterae in the dies, four sq tapering legs with stringing, pendant bellflowers, and inlaid cuffs, old refinish, minor imperfections, 32" w, 18-1/2" d, 27-1/2" h **10,925.00**

Sheraton, New York, mahogany, double drop shaped leaves, single end drawer, well proportioned tapering turned elongated legs fitted with brass ferrules and casters, inlaid mahogany tombstone panels beside drawer, fine reeding to legs, 43" w open, 21" closed, 35-1/2" d, 29" h
.... **6,500.00**

Pier, Classical, Boston, 1835-40, mahogany veneer, replaced carrara marble top, straight paneled veneered frieze above scrolled and carved frontal supports with flattened veneered columns flanking pier glass, old refinish, feet missing, some veneer loss, 41" w, 17-3/4" d, 36" h, price for matched pair **10,925.00**

Refectory, Continental, early 18th C, walnut, plank top, bold S-scrolled trestle ends joined by serpentine stretcher, 107" w, 27" d, 31" h **6,325.00**

Pembroke, Chippendale, American, 18th century, carved mahogany, 38" l, 27-1/2" h, **$2,750.**

Sawbuck, pine, two wide boards on top, tongue and groove joint at center (now separated), square nail construction, varnished finish, age splits, filled holes on base, 66" w, 34-1/4" d, 29-1/4" h **495.00**

Serving, George III, c1800

Mahogany, slightly bowed top, pair of drawers, sq tapering legs **1,725.00**

Satinwood and marquetry, demilune, later fitted with spring action drawers, restoration, 62-1/4" w, 23-1/2" d, 32-3/4" h **19,550.00**

Sewing

Federal

Boston, MA, c1805, mahogany veneer, mahogany top with outset corners above two veneered cock-beaded drawers, sliding bag frame, flanked by legs with colonettes above reeding, ending in turned tapering feet, old brass, old finish, 20-3/4" w, 15-3/4" d, 28-1/4" h **1,610.00**

New England, mahogany veneer, mahogany top with hinged drop leaves, reeded edge, flanking three veneered drawers, top fitted for writing, bottom with sliding sewing bag frame, ring-turned and spiral carved legs, casters, old refinish, replaced brasses, 18-1/2" w, 18-1/8" d, 29-1/4" h . . . **1,150.00**

Sheraton, mahogany, drop leaf, two drawers over one drawer, ring and spiral turned legs, brass cup and caster feet, 20-1/2" closed, 27-3/4" open, 18" d, 28-1/2" h . . . **1,200.00**

Side

Classical, New York, 1835-45, mahogany, rect marble top with rounded corners, conforming ogee molded skirt, pierced and scrolled supports, pillar and scroll bases, applied ripple molding joining scrolled medial shelf, casters, old finish, minor imperfections, 31" w, 18-1/2" d, 31" h **3,750.00**

Louis XV-Style, Provincial, 19th C, walnut, rect thumb-molded top, frieze drawer, shaped skirt, cabriole legs, 27" w, 21-1/2" d, 26-1/2" h **980.00**

Renaissance Revival, America, c1870, walnut, inset marble top, maidenhead carved frieze raised on angular legs, X-stretcher, 35" l, 22" d, 30-1/2" h **1,495.00**

Silver, George III, c1765, carved mahogany, galleried tray top, low relief carved everted lip, repeating border of C-scrolls and foliage, swirling scroll bordered apron, molded sq cabriole supports with trailing acanthus carving at knees, Spanish feet, alternations to top, repairs, 31-3/4" l, 28-3/4" h **2,000.00**

Sofa, Edwardian, c1895, painted satinwood, rounded drop leaves, two frieze drawers, trestle supports ending in brass paw casters, 36" w closed, 26-1/2" d, 28-1/2" h **8,100.00**

Tavern

Chippendale, Massachusetts or New Hampshire, late 18th/early 19th C, cherry top, thumb molded edge overhangs maple base with

straight molded skirt, sq tiger maple legs with beaded front edges, chamfered rear ones, early surface, minor surface stains, 34" w, 25" d, 27-5/8" h . . . **4,600.00**

Hepplewhite, two-board breadboard top, large overhang, one drawer base, tapered sq legs, grungy finish, 42-1/2" w, 29-3/4" d, 28" h **750.00**

Queen Anne, maple and pine, two board top with bread board ends, scalloped apron with molded trim across front, dovetailed drawer, wrought iron loop over remnants of another wooden pull, turned legs and feet, stretcher base, pegged construction, few rosehead nails, refinished, minor splits in top, feet

Table, Pembroke, Hepplewhite, refinished cherry, serpentine drop-leaf top, serpentine end aprons, conforming drawer, square tapered legs with inside chamber, stringing inlay on legs and aprons with fans and oval paterae, fretwork brackets, 35-3/8" w, 16-3/4" d, 8-3/4" leaves, 28" h, **$6,500.** *Photo courtesy of Garth's Auctions.*

ended out, other restorations, 47-3/4" w, 29" d, 27" h **1,980.00**

William and Mary, New England, 18th C, maple and pine, rect overhanging top, straight skirt with drawer, joining block base and ring turned legs, feet joined by square stretchers, old refinish, minor imperfections, 33" w, 21" d, 27" h **1,610.00**

Tea

Chippendale

America, cherry, tilt top, scalloped two board top, mortised block, tapered column with relief ring turnings, scalloped base, high cabriole legs with well shaped padded snake feet, refinished, replaced brass catch at top of block, 31" x 32" top, 28-1/4" h **1,450.00**

America, mahogany, round top, bird cage support, ring-turned column, well carved base, cabriole legs, padded snake feet, rosehead nails in iron brace, old dark refinish, splice added to top, restorations, 34-1/4" d, 2" h **1,265.00**

Pennsylvania, 18th C, cherry, dish top tilts on birdcage support, turned pedestal with belted ball, cabriole legs ending in pad feet on platforms, refinished, imperfections, 32-3/4" w, 28" h **2,990.00**

George III, third quarter 18th C, mahogany, tilt-top, circular top, turned standard, cabriole legs, pad feet, 39-1/2" d, 28" h **1,100.00**

Hepplewhite, tilt top, poplar one board top with cut corners, birch tripod base with spider legs, turned column, old refinishing with painted foliage border designs in shades of gold and black, top replaced, repairs, 15-1/2" w, 23-1/2" l, 28-3/4" h **440.00**

Queen Anne, curly maple, molded edge tray top, scrolled apron, cabriole legs, duck feet, refinished, top is old replacement, 20" w, 30-1/2" l, 27-1/4" h **3,025.00**

Tilt-Top

Federal, New England, mahogany inlaid, octagonal top with string inlay in outline, urn shaped pedestal, cabriole legs, arris pad feet on platforms, orig surface, very

minor imperfections, 22" w, 14-3/4" d, 29-1/2" h **3,750.00**

Georgian, late 18th C, mahogany, plain circular top over turned baluster standard, three cabriole legs ending in shaped pad feet, 32" d, 27-3/8" h **1,100.00**

Tray, Edwardian, c1900, satinwood and inlay, two oval tiers, removable wood and glass tray, slightly splayed sq tapering legs joined by stretcher, 36" w, 20-1/4" d, 32" h **1,150.00**

Vitrine, Louis XVI-Style, c1880, gilt bronze mounted mahogany, beveled glass panels and turned legs joined by stretchers, foliate cast bronze mounts, 26" w, 16" d, 30" h **3,450.00**

Work

Biedermeier-Style, cherry wood and burr popular, rect top, molded frieze with drawer, inverted, pierced, and lyre-form supports joined by pole stretcher, 22-1/2" l, 15-3/4" w, 25-1/4" h **650.00**

Classical, Boston, 1830, mahogany veneer, solid top, hinged rounded drop leaves with beaded edges, flank two convex veneered drawers, top one fitted for writing, lower with replaced fabric sewing fabric bag, turned tapering legs which flank shaped veneered platform, ebonized bun feet, orig stamped brass pulls, imperfections, minor warp in leaf, 19" w, 19" d, 28-3/4" h **980.00**

Hepplewhite, country, walnut and pine, wooden peg construction, one board top, tapered and splayed legs, later blue paint, thin coat of varnish, minor hairlines, split, minor insect damage on legs, 25" x 33" top, 29-1/2" h **650.00**

Hepplewhite, country, walnut, pegged construction, three board top, dovetailed drawer, turned wooden pull, tapered legs, old dark mellow finish, evidence of earlier blue paint, restoration and replacements, 55-3/4" w, 35-3/8" d, 27" h **450.00**

Queen Anne

Black walnut and pine, painted, PA, c1760-1800, removable blank three-board pine top, supported by cleats and four dowels, two thumb-molded drawers, straight skirt with breaded edge above straight

cabriole legs ending in pad feet, orig apple green paint, old replaced wooden pulls, surface imperfections, cracked foot, 48-1/2" w, 32" d, 27" h . **2,500.00**

Maple and pine, New England, late 18th C, scrubbed top, straight skirt with beaded edge, turned tapering legs ending in turned button feet, old surface, remnants of red on base, 28" w, 28-1/2" l, 27" h **2,530.00**

Painted Pine, New England, 18th C, overhanging oval scrubbed top, straight molded skirt, splayed ring-turned legs ending in turned feet, orig red paint on base, 35" w, 26-3/8" l, 26-1/4" h **14,950.00**

Pine and maple, two board pine bread board top with good old patina, mortised and pinned apron, turned tapered legs, button feet, maple base with traces of old paint, reddish brown finish, one corner of top has damage, 31-3/4" w, 64-1/2" l, 27-3/4" h **550.00**

Walnut, removable three-board top, two dovetailed overlapping drawers, mortised and pinned apron with edge beading, turned legs, weathered duck feet, old refinishing, period replaced brasses, pieced repairs to top, age cracks, 32" w, 49-1/2" l, 28" h . . **2,750.00**

Sheraton, mahogany and mahogany veneer, three dovetailed drawers, turned legs with ring turned detail, orig gilded lion head brasses, old finish, top drawer is fitted with tilt-up writing surface, age cracks in sides, some veneer damage to writing tablet, 16" w, 18" l, 27-3/4" h **1,430.00**

William and Mary-Style, walnut, ebonized trim, two board top, one dovetailed drawer, turned stretchers and legs, repairs and old replacements, 22-3/4" w, 34" d, 27-1/4" h **935.00**

Writing, Regency-style, 20th C, Carlton House, inlaid mahogany, demilune form, wrap-around gallery fitted with drawers and doors, desk fitted with one long and two short drawers, four sq tapered legs, 52" w, 27" d, 41" h **3,450.00**

GAME BOARDS

History: Wooden game boards have a long history and were some of the first toys early Americans enjoyed. Games such as checkers, chess, and others were easy to play and required only simple markers or playing pieces. Most were handmade, but some machine-made examples exist.

Game boards can be found in interesting color combinations. Some include small drawers to hold the playing pieces. Others have an interesting molding or frame. Look for signs of use from long hours of enjoyment.

Today, game boards are popular with game collectors, folk art collectors, and decorators because of their interesting forms.

Reproduction Alert.

Checkerboard

8-3/4" w, 10-1/4" h, painted pine, brown and white, sliding panel, compartment containing zinc checkers on reverse, 8-3/4" w, 10-1/4" h **2,760.00**

10-1/2" w, 19-1/2" h, painted green and yellow, late 19th C, paint imperfections **1,955.00**

12-1/2" w, 12-3/4" h, painted black and white, tan colored ground, sgd "F. Smith," PA, c1870 . . . . **1,955.00**

12-3/4" w, 20-5/8" h, painted bright red and green, line design, some wear to gallery edge **1,210.00**

13-7/8" w, 13-3/4" h, painted hunter green and iron red, black frame, yellow grain paint on reverse, America, 19th C, minor paint wear **1,380.00**

14" w, 20-1/4" h, oak and mahogany squares, galleried edge with two reserves on sides with sliding lid compartments to hold checkers, two sets of checkers, one round, one square, minor wear, light alligatoring to old black paint on lids and gallery **330.00**

14-1/4" sq, painted brown and yellow, obverse with checkerboard, reverse with caricature of President Zachary Taylor, America, c1849 . . . . . . **3,115.00**

15-1/4" sq, old repainted dec, green and brown checkerboard with red, blue, green, and burgundy borders, applied molding with worn black paint and chips, back inscribed "Lakland, Mar. 26, 1861. Presented to Hoover Hoenrey, By W. H. C." **770.00**

15-1/4" sq, painted black and salmon, New England, 19th C **2,300.00**

15-1/2" w, 15-3/4" h, painted red, pink, green, white, yellow and black, rose blossoms and leafy stems, applied border, America, 19th C **2,185.00**

16" sq, blue and white, yellowed varnish, New England, 19th C. **3,335.00**

16" w, 17-1/2" h, painted green, black, and mustard yellow, incised geometric designs on reverse, applied molded edge, New England, 19th C . . **2,645.00**

16" w, 17-1/2" h, painted red and white checkerboard, orig cherry frame, Newburyport, MA, c1850 . . . . . **980.00**

17" w, 16" h, painted green and white, unfinished, inscribed on reverse, late 19th/early 20th C **460.00**

17-1/4" w, 18" h, painted red field with black squares, yellow stars, bordered in yellow and black, Ohio, c1890 . . . . **2,415.00**

17-3/4" w, 17-5/8" h, painted salmon red with ochre and black checkerboard, indistinct pencil inscription on reverse, America, 19th C, scratches and minor paint wear **800.00**

18" w, 17" h, poplar, painted old black and green blocks, gray ground, orange on reverse, rounded molded edges, scratched signature "Joseph Bell, June 22, 1901" **550.00**

18" w, 21" h, painted red and black, yellow dec, Michigan, c1880 . . **2,415.00**

18-1/2" sq, painted yellow and black, green detailing, c1880 . . . . . . **5,465.00**

20" w, 18-3/4" h, painted and gilt dec, molded edge, reverse marked "Saco Lodge No. 2," Saco, Maine, 19th C **5,175.00**

22-1/8" w, 22-1/4" h, painted gold, red, crimson, and black, stamped "CA Brown 1852," minor paint wear **1,380.00**

25" w, 19" h, painted red and black, gilt trim, second half 19th C **2,300.00**

Double-sided

7-1/4" w, 7" h, painted pine, brown and black checkerboard on one side, painted brown Old Mill game inscribed on reverse, two sliding panel compartments, New York State, early 19th C **1,150.00**

12-1/4" w, 12" h, painted apple green, brown, and black, obverse with checkerboard, reverse with snake-motif game, America, mid-19th C . **36,800.00**

14" sq, painted salmon, green, and yellow, New England, 19th C, loss to frame **3,740.00**

14" w, 11-1/2" h, painted black, white, and green, initials "M. B.," America, early 19th C **1,725.00**

14-1/4" sq, painted black and red, obverse with checkerboard, reverse with Old Mill, applied molded edge, New England, c1850-70 . . . . . **4,890.00**

14-1/2" w, 14" h, painted green and yellow, New England, c1860 . **2,530.00**

The Owl, table-top type, Chicago, **$65.** *Photo courtesy of Joy Luke Auctions.*

14-7/8" w, 15-7/8" h, painted deep blue-green, red and black, checkerboard on obverse, backgammon on reverse, America, 19th C **2,530.00**

15" w, 16" h, painted mustard, red, and green, checkerboard on obverse, backgammon on reverse, America, 19th C **3,335.00**

17" w, 16-1/2" h, painted checkerboard on obverse, rose dec on reverse, America, c1890 . . . . **1,955.00**

17" sq, obverse with Parcheesi, painted red, teal, orange, and green, checkerboard on reverse with orange, black, and yellow paint, c1900, paint wear to obverse at edges **2,530.00**

18-1/2" w, 20" h, New Hampshire, Parcheesi game scribed and painted in eight colors, checkerboard on reverse, New Hampshire, 19th C, minor wear, crack **21,850.00**

20-1/2" w, 21" h, painted six-color Parcheesi game on one side, "Home" inscribed in center, fanciful red and yellow checkerboard on reverse with fleur-de-lis border dec, New York State, 19th C, wear, frame loss **2,875.00**

23" w, 17-1/4" h, painted apple green, black, and red, checkerboard on obverse, backgammon on reverse, game piece compartments, America, c1870-80 . . . . **3,750.00**

Folding

12-1/2" w, 31" h, painted avocado green, colorful raised segmented tracks, opens for storage, mid-20th C, wear **575.00**

Numbered, 14-1/2" w, 16-1/2" h, painted red and black, gold striping and numbers 1 through 32, New York, c1870 . . . . **4,350.00**

Parcheesi

17-3/4" sq, hunter and olive green, red, and yellow game, off-white ground, painted off-white on reverse, America, 19th C, minor paint loss, surface grime **1,725.00**

18" w, 17-3/4" h, folding, patriotic red, white, and blue stars and dec, New England, late 19th C **4,350.00**

18-1/2" sq, folding, painted American flag and spade, heart, diamond, and club motifs, MA, c1870, minor paint imperfections **46,000.00**

19" w, 20" h, painted red, yellow, orange, and green, late 19th C, paint wear **1,955.00**

19-1/2" sq, folding, painted green, white, black, and yellow, varied

geometric designs on game corners, America, 19th C **2,875.00**

22" w, 22" h, painted poplar, polychrome dec, center landscape, label on back "Parchesi board made approximately 1895 by a carriage striper, name of Pierce…," scratches **2,760.00**

25" w, 24-1/2" h, painted, center rosette, bull's eye corners, attributed to Maine, 19th C, wear **4,600.00**

27-1/2" w, 27" h, painted red, yellow, and green, New England, 1870-80 . . . . **5,750.00**

GAME PLATES

History: Game plates, popular between 1870 and 1915, are specially decorated plates used to serve fish and game. Sets originally included a platter, serving plates, and a sauce or gravy boat. Many sets have been divided. Today, individual plates are often used as wall hangings.

Birds

Plate

9-1/4" d, hp, set of 12 with different center scene of shore birds in natural setting, apple green edge, printed gold scrolled rim dec, artist sgd "B. Albert," Theodore Haviland & Co., France, early 20th C. **865.00**

9-1/2" d, bird, scalloped edge, mauve ground, gold trim, sgd "Vitet Limoges" **130.00**

9-1/2" d, duck, pastel pink, blue, and cream ground, duck flying up from water, yellow flowers and grasses, sgd "Laury," marked "Limoges," not pierced for hanging **120.00**

10" d, pheasant, Limoges, sgd "Max" **95.00**

10-1/2" d, game bird and two water spaniels, crimped gold rim, sgd "RK Beck" **95.00**

13-1/4" d, game bird and pheasant, heavy gold, scalloped emb rococo border, marked "Coronet Limoges, Bussilion" **250.00**

Platter

11" l, Limoges, artist sgd "Raly," marked "Coronet" with crown and "Limoges, France," script mark, gold trim, shows two ducks, pierced for hanging **410.00**

11" l, Limoges, artist sgd "S. Barbus," marked on back, gold trim, pierced for hanging . . . **450.00**

16" l, two handles, quail, hp gold trim, Limoges **150.00**

Set

Seven pcs, wild game birds, pastoral scene, molded edges, shell dec, Fazent Meheim, Bonn, Germany **250.00**

Twelve pcs, 10-1/2" d plates, game birds in natural habitat, sgd "I. Bubedi" **3,500.00**

Deer

Plate, 9" d, buck and doe, forest scene **60.00**

Set, 13 pcs, platter, 12 plates, deer, bear, and game birds, yellow ground, scalloped border, "Haviland China," sgd "MC Haywood" **3,200.00**

Fish, 10-3/4" x 23-3/4" platter, 12 9-1/2" d plates, gravy boat and under- plate, peach shading to ivory ground, gold trim, fish school decoration, unmarked, gravy boat damaged, flakes to some plates, **$550.** *Photo courtesy of Alderfer Auction Company, Inc.*

Fish

Plate

8" d, bass, scalloped edge, gray-green trim, fern on side of fish, Limoges **65.00**

8-1/2" d, colorful fish swimming on green shaded ground, scalloped border, gold trim, sgd "Lancy," "Bairritz, W. S. or S. W. Co. Limoges, France," pierced for hanging **50.00**

Platter

14" l, bass on lure, sgd "RK Beck" **125.00**

23" l, hp, Charoone, Haviland **200.00**

Set

Eight pcs, four plates, 24" l, platter, sauce boat with attached plate, cov tureen, Rosenthal **425.00**

Eleven pcs, 10 plates, serving platter, sgd "Limoges" **360.00**

Fifteen pcs, 12 9" plates, 24" platter, sauce boat with attached plate, cov tureen, hp, raised gold design edge, artist sgd, Limoges . **800.00**

GAMES

History: Board games have been commercially produced in this country since at least 1822, and card games since the 1780s. However, it was not until the 1840s that large numbers of games were produced that survive to this day. The W. & S. B. Ives Company produced many board and card games in the 1840s and 1950s. Milton Bradley and McLoughlin Brothers became major producers of games starting in the 1860s, followed by Parker Brothers in the 1880s. Other major producers of games in this period were Bliss, Chaffee and Selchow, Selchow and Righter, and Singer.

Today, most games from the 19th century are rare and highly collectible, primarily because of their spectacular lithography. McLoughlin and Bliss command a premium because of the rarity, quality of materials, and the extraordinary art that was created to grace the covers and boards of their games.

In the 20th century, Milton Bradley, Selchow and Righter, and Parker Brothers became the primary manufacturers of boxed games. They have all now been absorbed by toy giant Hasbro Corporation. Other noteworthy producers were All-Fair, Pressman, and Transogram, all of which are no longer in business. Today, the hottest part of the game collecting market is in rare character games from the 1960s. Parker Brothers and All-Fair games from the 1920s to 1940s also have some excellent lithography and are highly collectible.

References: *Board Games of the 50s, 60s & 70s with Prices*, L-W Books, 1994; Lee Dennis, *Warman's Antique American Games, 1840-1940*, Wallace-Homestead, Krause Publications, 1991; *Dexterity Games and Other Hand-Held Puzzles*, L-W Book Sales, 1995; Alex G. Malloy, *American Games Comprehensive Collector's Guide*, Antique Trader Books, 2000; Jack Matthews, *Toys Go to War*, Pictorial Histories Publishing, 1994; Rex Miller, *The Investor's Guide to Vintage Character Collectibles*, Krause Publications, 1999; Rick Polizzi, *Baby Boomer Games*, Collector Books, 1995; Rick Polizzi and Fred Schaefer, *Spin Again*, Chronicle Books, 1991; Desi Scarpone, *More Board Games*, Schiffer Publishing, 2000; Bruce Whitehill, *Games: American Boxed Games and Their Makers*, Wallace-Homestead, Krause Publications, 1992.

Periodicals and Internet Resources: *Gamers Alliance*, P.O. Box 197, East Meadow, NY 11554-0197, http://www.gamersalliance.com; *The Games Annual*, 5575 Arapahoe Road, Suite D, Boulder, CO 80303; *The Game Report*, 1920 N. 49th St., Seattle, WA, 98103, http://www.gamereport.com; *Toy Shop*, 700 E. State St., Iola, WI 54990.

Collectors' Clubs: American Game and Puzzle Collectors Association, PMB 321, 197M Boston Post Road West, Marlborough, MA 01752, http://www.agpc.org; Antique Toy Collectors of America, Inc., 2 Wall St., 13th Floor, New York, NY 10005; Cribbage Board Collectors Society, P.O. Box 170, Carolina, RI 28712-0170; Gamers Alliance, P.O. Box 197, East Meadow, NY 11554-0197, http://www.gamersalliance.com; Mah Jongg Collectors Club, 12 Van Every Circle, Kirkland, Quebec H9J 2P5 Canada.

Museums: International Checkers Hall of Fame, Petal, MS; Margaret Woodbury Strong Museum, Rochester, NY; Peabody Essex Museum, Salem, MA; University of Waterloo Museum & Archive of Games, Waterloo, Ontario, Canada; Washington Dolls' House and Toy Museum, Washington, D.C.

Additional Listings: See *Warman's Americana & Collectibles*.

Notes: While people collect games for many reasons, it is strong graphic images that bring the highest prices. Games collected because they are fun to play or for nostalgic reasons are still collectible, but will not bring high prices. Also, game collectors are not interested in common and "public domain" games such as checkers, tiddlywinks, Authors, Anagrams, Jackstraws, Rook, Pit, Flinch, and Peter Coodles. The game market today is characterized by fairly stable prices for ordinary items, increasing discrimination for grades of condition, and continually rising prices for rare material in excellent condition. Whether you are a dealer or collector, be careful to buy games in good condition. Avoid games with taped or split corners or other box damage. Games made after about 1950 are difficult to sell unless they are complete and in excellent condition. As games get older, there is a forgiveness factor for condition and completeness that increases with age.

These listings are for games that are complete and in excellent condition. Be sure the game you're looking to price is the same as the one described in the listing. The 19th century makers routinely published the same title on several different versions of the game, varying in size and graphics. Dimensions listed below are rounded to the nearest half inch.

Alley Oop, Stephen Sleisinger, 1937 . . . . **75.00**
Big Chief, Milton Bradley, 1938, 8" x 17" **125.00**
Big Trail Game, Parker Brothers, c1930, 13-1/2" x 17". **250.00**
Boy Hunter, The, shooting game, metal cork firing gun, 16" x 6" **185.00**
Bugs Bunny Adventure Game, Milton Bradley, c1961, 9-1/2" x 19" **35.00**
Bull in a China Shop, Milton Bradley, 1937. **100.00**
Bullwinkle and Rocky Role Playing Party Game, TSR, c1988 . . . . . . **20.00**
Chiromagia Game, McLoughlin, three answer sheets, two question discs, lid missing **100.00**
Clue, Parker Brothers, c1949, separate board and pieces box. **25.00**
Dixie Pollyana, Parker Brothers, c1952, 8" x 18", all wooden pcs, four orig dice and dicecups **100.00**
Eldorado, Parker Brothers, c1941, 15" x 24-1/2" **125.00**
Fish Pond, McLoughlin Bros., c1898, 8" x 18", children on cover. **125.00**
Fish Pond, Milton Bradley, c1910, 10" x 20", fisherman on cover. **75.00**

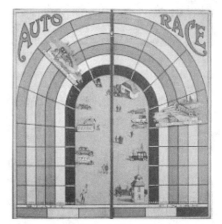

Auto Race, Alderman, Fairchild Co., Rochester, NY, patent date April 20, 1922, chromolithograph, six automobile playing pieces, 17-1/2" x 17-3/4", **$75.** Photo courtesy of Cowan Historic Americana Auctions.

Flap Jacks, Alderman-Fairchild, c1931, toss game, 15-1/2" x 12-1/2" **75.00**
Funny Sentences, A Party Game, AllFair, 5" x 7" **58.00**
Game of Battles or Fun For Boys, McLoughlin Bros., c1900, 23" x 23", cardboard soldiers and cannons **2,500.00**
Game of Billy Possum, c1910, 8" x 15" **600.00**
Game of Bo Peep, J. H. Singer, 8-1/2" x 14" **275.00**
Game of Dunce, The, W. H. Schaper, 1955 . . . . **25.00**
Game of Goose, by Mary D. Carrol, made by Charles Akerman, dated 1855, 20" w, opened. **230.00**
Game of Moon Tag, Parker Brothers, c1950, 10-1/2" x 20" **50.00**
Game of Oasis, Milton Bradley, c1937, 9-1/2" x 19-1/2". **150.00**
Game of Rival Policeman, McLoughlin Brothers, c1898, 12" x 21", comic-style cover art, lead figural playing pieces **4,000.00**
Game of the Wizard of Oz, The, Whitman, c1939, 7" x 13-1/2" . . . **300.00**
Gilligans Island Game, Game Gems, c1965, 9-1/2" x 18-1/2". **350.00**
Going to Jerusalem, Parker Brothers, c1955, 10-1/2" x 20" **75.00**
Hi Ho Silhouette Game, 1932. . . **30.00**
Hit That Line, The All American Football Game, La Rue Sales, Lynn, MA, 6" x 8" box, orig instructions **65.00**

Jolly Darkie Target Game, Milton Bradley, c1900, 10-1/2" x 19"... **750.00**

Jumpy Tinker, Toy Tinkers, 5" x 11" **70.00**

Limited Mail and Express Game, The, Parker Brothers, c1894, 14" x 21", metal train playing pieces.......... **250.00**

Mail Coach Game, Whitman, 13" x 13" **165.00**

Mansion of Happiness, The, W. & S. B. Ives, c1843 .... **950.00**

Mickey Mantle's Big League Baseball Game, Gardner Games....... **175.00**

Midget Auto Race, Samuel Lowe, 5" x 7" **70.00**

Monopoly, Parker Brothers, c1935, white box edition #9, metal playing pieces and embossed hotels .. **150.00**

Monopoly, Parker Brothers, 1946 Popular Edition, separate board and pieces box................. **25.00**

Motorcycle Game, Milton Bradley, c1905, 9" x 9"............... **250.00**

New Board Game of the American Revolution, Lorenzo Borge, 1844, colored scenes and events, 18-1/2" w opened **690.00**

One Two, Button Your Shoe, Master Toy Company, 11" x 12"....... **145.00**

Peter Coddles Trip to New York, Milton Bradley, orig instruction sheet, 6" x 8-1/2"..................... **65.00**

Pike's Peak or Bust, Parker Brothers, 1895, 7" x 7"............... **145.00**

Race To The Moon, All-Fair, c1932, early space target game, 10" x 19" **600.00**

Radio Amateur Hour Game, 10" x 13" **145.00**

Ralph Edwards This Is Your Life, Lowell, c1955, 13" x 19"....... **125.00**

Razzle Dazzle Football Game, Texantics, 1954, 10" x 17" **225.00**

Star Reporter, Parker Brothers, c1950, 10-1/2" x 20".................. **65.00**

Strange Game of Forbidden Fruit, Parker Brothers, c1900, 4" x 5-1/2" **35.00**

Tom Swift, Parker Brothers, c1966, 9-1/2" x 19-1/2" **250.00**

Truth or Consequences, Gabriel, c1955, 14" x 19-1/2"........... **75.00**

Whirlpool, McLoughlin Brothers, 1899, #408, 7-1/4" sq, instructions on cover **40.00**

Wonderful Game of Oz, The, Parker Brothers, 1921, 10" x 19"...... **275.00**

GAUDY DUTCH

History: Gaudy Dutch is an opaque, soft-paste ware made between 1790 and 1825 in England's Staffordshire district.

The wares first were hand decorated in an underglaze blue and fired, then additional decorations were added over the glaze. The over-glaze decoration is extensively worn on many of the antique pieces. Gaudy Dutch found a ready market in the Pennsylvania German community because it was inexpensive and extremely colorful. It had little appeal in England.

Museums: Henry Ford Museum, Dearborn, MI; Philadelphia Museum of Art, Philadelphia, PA; Reading Art Museum, Reading, PA.

Marks: Marks of various potters, including the impressed marks of Riley and Wood, have been found on some pieces, although most are unmarked.

References: Susan and Al Bagdade, *Warman's English & Continental Pottery & Porcelain*, 3rd Edition, Krause Publications, 1998; Eleanor and Edward Fox, *Gaudy Dutch*, published by author, 1970, out of print; John A. Shuman, III, *Collector's Encyclopedia of Gaudy Dutch & Welsh*, Collector Books, 1990, 1998 value update.

Collectors' Club: Gaudy Collector's Society, P.O. Box 274, Gates Mills, OH 44040.

Adviser: John D. Querry.

Reproduction Alert: Cup plates, bearing the impressed mark "CYBRIS," have been reproduced and are collectible in their own right. The Henry Ford Museum has issued pieces in the Single Rose pattern, although they are porcelain rather than soft paste.

Butterfly
Bowl, 11" d.............. **3,900.00**
Coffeepot, 11" h........ **9,500.00**
Cup and saucer, handleless, minor enamel flakes, chips on table ring **950.00**
Plate, 7-1/4" d **645.00**
Soup plate, 8-1/2" d, wear and scratches............. **1,275.00**
Sugar bowl, cov........... **900.00**
Teapot, 5" h, squat baluster form **2,400.00**

Carnation
Bowl, 6-1/4" d............. **925.00**
Creamer, 4-3/4" h.......... **700.00**
Pitcher, 6" h **675.00**
Plate, 8" d................ **950.00**
Plate, 9-3/4" d **1,265.00**
Saucer, cobalt blue, orange, green, and yellow, stains, hairline, minor flake on table ring, 5-1/2" d. **115.00**
Teapot, cov **2,200.00**
Toddy plate **975.00**
Waste bowl **675.00**

Dahlia
Bowl, 6-1/4" d **1,800.00**
Plate, 8" d **2,800.00**
Teabowl and saucer...... **8,000.00**

Coffeepot, Single Rose pattern, 12" h, chips on rim of lid and base, and spout, $4,100. Photo courtesy of Sanford Alderfer Auction Co.

Double Rose
Bowl, 6-1/4" d **545.00**
Creamer **650.00**
Gravy boat **950.00**
Plate, 8-1/4" d **675.00**
Plate, 10" d **935.00**
Sugar bowl, cov **750.00**
Teabowl and saucer....... **675.00**
Teapot, cov............. **1,900.00**
Toddy plate, 4-1/2" d **675.00**
Waste bowl, 6-1/2" d, 3" h... **850.00**

Dove
Creamer **675.00**
Plate, 8-1/8" d, very worn, scratches, stains **245.00**
Plate, 8-1/2" d **770.00**
Teabowl and saucer....... **500.00**
Waste bowl.............. **650.00**

Flower Basket, plate, 6-1/2" d . **375.00**

Grape
Bowl, 6-1/2" d, lustered rim . **475.00**
Plate, 8-1/4" d, cobalt blue, orange, green, and yellow, minor stains **450.00**
Sugar bowl, cov **675.00**
Teabowl and saucer....... **475.00**
Toddy plate, 5" d.......... **475.00**

Leaf, bowl, 11-1/2" d, shallow. **4,800.00**

No Name
Plate, 8-3/4" d **17,000.00**
Teapot, cov............. **16,000.00**

Plate, Oyster pattern, 9-1/2" d, **$575.**

Oyster
Bowl, 5-1/2" d	675.00
Coffeepot, cov, 12" h	10,000.00
Plate, 9-1/2" d	575.00
Plate, 10" d	1,550.00
Soup Plate, 8-1/2" d	550.00
Teabowl and Saucer	1,275.00
Toddy Plate, 5-1/2" d	475.00

Single Rose
Bowl, 6" d	650.00
Coffeepot, cov	8,500.00
Cup and saucer, handleless, minor wear and stains	330.00
Plate, 7-1/4" d	550.00
Plate, 8-1/4" d	650.00
Plate, 10" d	975.00
Quill holder, cov	2,500.00
Sugar bowl, cov	700.00
Teapot, cov	1,200.00
Toddy plate, 5-1/4" d	250.00
Waste bowl, 5-1/2" d, wear, hairlines, stains, flake on table rim, glaze rim flakes	365.00

Sunflower
Bowl, 6-1/2" d	900.00
Coffeepot, cov, 9-1/2" h	6,500.00
Creamer	850.00
Cup and saucer, handleless, wear, chips	575.00
Plate, 9-3/4" d	825.00

Urn
Creamer	475.00
Cup and saucer, handleless	550.00
Plate, 8-1/4" d	910.00
Plate, 9-7/8" d, very worn, scratches, stains, rim, chips	225.00
Sugar bowl, cov, 6-1/2" h, round, tip and base restored	295.00
Teapot	895.00

War Bonnet
Bowl, cov	225.00
Coffeepot, cov	9,500.00

Cup and saucer, handleless.	575.00
Plate, 8-1/8" d, pinpoint rim flake, minor wear	880.00
Teapot, cov	4,400.00
Toddy plate, 4-1/2" d	975.00
Zinna, soup plate, 10" d, impressed "Riley"	4,675.00

GAUDY IRONSTONE

History: Gaudy Ironstone was made in England around 1850. Ironstone is an opaque, heavy-bodied earthenware which contains large proportions of flint and slag. Gaudy Ironstone is decorated in patterns and colors similar to those of Gaudy Welsh.

Museums: Henry Ford Museum, Dearborn, MI; Philadelphia Museum of Art, Philadelphia, PA; Reading Art Museum, Reading, PA.

Marks: Most pieces are impressed "Ironstone" and bear a registry mark.

Bread plate, 10-1/4" l, 5-1/4" w, marked "Tunstall, England, by Enoch Wedgwood" ... 65.00

Coffeepot, cov, 10" h, Strawberry pattern ... 650.00

Compote, 8-1/4" d, 4" h, molded ironstone, floral designs, Gaudy floral dec, underglaze blue, red, green, and luster, minor wear and scratches ... 360.00

Creamer and sugar, 6-3/4" h, fruit finial, Blackberry pattern, underglaze blue, yellow, and orange enamel and luster, wear, small flakes, int. chip on sugar ... 990.00

Cup and saucer
Blackberry pattern, handleless, underglaze blue, yellow, and orange enamel and luster, imp

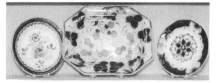

Left: plate, floral with eye, underglaze blue, red, and green enamel and luster, impressed "E. Walley, Niagara Shape," registry mark, wear and scratches, 8-1/2" g, **$120**; *center: Strawberry platter, underglaze blue with red, pink, and green enamel luster, wear, stains, some enamel flaking, 13-1/2" l,* **$770**; *right: plate, Pinwheel, underglaze blue with red and green enamel and luster, impressed "ironstone," minor wear, 8-3/8" d,* **$175.** *Photo courtesy of Garth's Auctions.*

label or registry mark with "E. Walley," price for set of 10 ... 1,375.00

Morning Glory pattern, underglaze blue, polychrome enamels . 170.00

Seeing Eye pattern ... 180.00

Jug, 7-1/2" h, yellow, red, white, and blue tulips on sides, light blue pebble ground, luster trim, rim outlined . 350.00

Pitcher, 11" h, six-color floral dec, blue, green, burgundy, mauve, black, and yellow, molded serpent handle, dec has been enhanced, then reglazed, spider ... 320.00

Plate
6-1/4" d, Morning Glories and Strawberries pattern, underglaze blue, polychrome enamel and luster trim ... 80.00

7-7/8" d, Urn pattern ... 70.00

Tea service, Strawberry pattern, includes teapot, sugar with lid, creamer, waste bowl, 10 handleless cups, 12 saucers, five 8-1/2" plates, six 9" plates, imperfections. **$2,125.** *Photo courtesy of Sanford Alderfer Auction Co.*

9-1/2" d, Blackberry pattern, underglaze blue, yellow, and orange enamel and luster, some wear, set of seven......1,320.00

Platter, 13-3/8" l, Gaudy blue and white floral dec, scalloped border, molded fish scale and feather design, minor wear.....................1,540.00

Soup plate, 9-7/8" d, Blackberry pattern, underglaze blue, yellow, and orange enamel and luster, one imp "Elsmore & Forster, Tunstall," price for set of three.................650.00

Sugar bowl, cov, 8-1/2" h, Strawberry pattern....................425.00

Toddy plate, 4-3/4" d, Urn pattern, underglaze blue, polychrome enamel and luster.................210.00

Vegetable, open, 8-3/4" d, Blackberry pattern, underglaze blue, yellow, and orange enamel and luster.....350.00

GAUDY WELSH

History: Gaudy Welsh is a translucent porcelain that was originally made in the Swansea area of England from 1830 to 1845. Although the designs resemble Gaudy Dutch, the body texture and weight differ. One of the characteristics is the gold luster on top of the glaze. In 1890, Allerton made a similar ware from heavier opaque porcelain.

Museums: Royal Institution of South Wales, Swansea Mills; St. Fagen's Welsh Folk Museum, Cardiff, Wales; Welsh National Museum, Cardiff, Wales.

Marks: Allerton pieces usually bear an export mark.

References: Susan and Al Bagdade, *Warman's English & Continental Pottery & Porcelain*, 3rd Edition, Krause Publications, 1998; John A. Shuman, III, *Collector's Encyclopedia of Gaudy Dutch and Welsh*, Collector Books, 1990, 1991 value update, out-of-print; Howard Y. Williams, *Gaudy Welsh China*, Wallace-Homestead, out-of-print.

Collectors' Club: Gaudy Collector's Society, P.O. Box 274, Gates Mills, OH 44040.

Cambrian Pot de Fleurs, spill vase, 4-1/2" d, 5" h 725.00

Carnation, 6-1/4" h 550.00

Chinoiserie, teapot, c1830-40 . 750.00

Cup and saucer, peppermint transfer, Shan We See, **$75.**

Platter, 13-1/2", Morning Glories, **$195.**

Columbine
Bowl, 10" d, 5-1/2" h, ftd, underglaze blue and polychrome enamel floral dec 400.00
Plate, 5-1/2" d 65.00
Tea set, c1810, 17-pc set ...625.00
Conwys, jug, 9" h...........750.00
Daisy and Chain
Creamer.................175.00
Cup and saucer...........95.00
Sugar, cov 195.00
Teapot, cov 225.00
Flower Basket
Bowl, 10-1/2" d..........190.00
Mug, 4" h 90.00
Plate.....................65.00
Sugar, cov, luster trim ...195.00
Grape
Bowl, 5-1/4" d............50.00
Cup and saucer...........75.00
Mug, 2-1/2" h 65.00
Plate, 5-1/4" d 65.00
Grapevine Variant, miniature pitcher and bowl, 4-1/4" h pitcher, 4-1/2" d bowl, cobalt blue, orange, green, and luster, scalloped edges 250.00
Oyster
Bowl, 6" d 80.00
Creamer, 3" h............100.00
Cup and saucer...........75.00
Jug, 5-3/4" h, c1820........85.00
Soup plate, 10" d, flange rim..85.00
Primrose, plate 8-1/4" d.......350.00
Strawberry
Creamer..................90.00
Cup and saucer...........75.00
Mug, 4 1/8" h 125.00
Plate, 8-1/4" d 150.00
Tulip
Bowl, 6-1/4" d.............50.00
Cake plate, 10" d, molded handles 120.00
Creamer, 5-1/4" h..........125.00
Plate, tea size 95.00
Sugar, cov, 6-3/4" h 140.00

Tea cup and saucer, slight crazing in cup.....................115.00
Teapot, 7-1/4" h.......... 225.00
Wagon Wheel
Cup and saucer 75.00
Mug, 2-1/2" h 95.00
Pitcher, 8-1/2" h........... 195.00
Plate, 8-3/4" d 85.00
Platter 125.00

GIRANDOLES AND MANTEL LUSTRES

History: A girandole is a very elaborate branched candleholder, often featuring cut glass prisms surrounding the mountings. A mantel lustre is a glass vase with attached cut glass prisms.

Girandoles and mantel lustres usually are found in pairs. It is not uncommon for girandoles to be part of a large garniture set. Girandoles and mantel lustres achieved their greatest popularity in the last half of the 19th century both in the United States and Europe.

Girandoles
9-7/8" w, 17" h, Longwy, Aesthetic Movement, third quarter 19th C, two-light, rect, central beveled mirror plate, surrounded by Islamic-inspired tiles in brass frame, scrolled candlearm with two acorn-shaped nozzles, removable bobeches 750.00

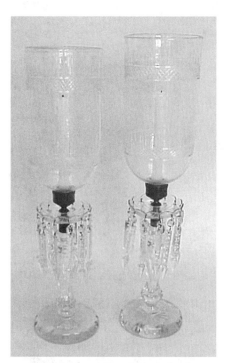

Mantel Lusters, cut crystal turned pedestal shafts supporting bobeche with prisms, and cut glass hurricane shade, 25" h, **$800.** *Photo courtesy of Sanford Alderfer Auction Co.*

Ruby glass, enamel forget-me-not decoration, original prisms, 14" h, **$450.**

16-3/4" h, Louis XIV-style, late 19th/early 20th C, three-light candelabra style, brass wirework lyre form standard, scrolled arms hung with colorless and amethyst glass drops, three short serpentine candlearms with tulip-shaped nozzles, offset with further drops, tripartite wirework base, price for pr **875.00**

17-3/4" h, 16-1/2" w, silver-plated figures of Indians and frontiersmen with three candle sockets, white marble base, back sgd "Cornelius, Pat. Dec 1848," some prisms missing **200.00**

18-1/4" h, 15-1/4" h, gilt metal figural centerpiece depicting capture of Major Andre, flanked by eagle, flag, shield, and arms, embellished with grapevines and crystal prisms, stepped marble bases, some prisms missing, chips on marble edges, America, mid-19th C, price for three-pc set **690.00**

18-1/2" w, 26" l, parcel gilt pale blue painted cartouche-shaped frame carved with rocaille and roses, applied gilt-metal two-light candlearms suspending short chain of faceted drops, Italian, late 19th/early 20th C, electrified, price for pr **980.00**

Mantel garnitures

10-1/4" h, urn form, two short scroll handles, incised on side with Japonesque florals in silver and gold coloration, trumpet foot further dec with Japonesque patterning and insects, sq section marble base, inset to front with mixed metal-style patinated plaque depicting drummer and dancer, Aesthetic Movement, third quarter 19th C, price for pr **690.00**

14" h, 12" h, three cov baluster jars and two vases, Hundred Antiques dec, in

famille rosé enamels, China, 19th C, price for five-pc set **2,185.00**

20-5/8" h, bronze and crystal, three-light candelabra, stylized lyre form garniture hung with cut and pressed glass prisms, above three scrolled candlearms, trefoil base, price for pr **980.00**

Mantel lusters

9" h, overlay glass, white cut to pink, enamel flowers, gilt accents, cut glass prisms, Bohemian, price for pr . **425.00**

12" h, ruby glass, overlay and enameled plaques, fluted, heavy gilt, cut glass prisms, France, 19th C, price for pr **2,645.00**

GOLDSCHEIDER

History: Friedrich Goldscheider founded a porcelain and faience factory in Vienna, Austria, in 1885. Upon his death, his widow carried on operations. In 1920, Walter and Marcell, Friedrich's sons, gained control. During the Art-Deco period, the firm commissioned several artists to create figural statues, among which were Pierrettes and sleek wolfhounds. During the 1930s, the company's products were mostly traditional.

In the early 1940s, the Goldscheiders fled to the United States and re-established operations in Trenton, New Jersey. The Goldscheider Everlast Corporation was listed in Trenton City directories between 1943 and 1950. Goldscheider Ceramics, located at 1441 Heath Avenue, Trenton, New Jersey, was listed in the *1952 Crockery and Glass Journal Directory*, but not listed in 1954.

Reference: Susan and Al Bagdade, *Warman's English & Continental Pottery & Porcelain*, 3rd Edition, Krause Publications, 1998.

Bust, 8-1/4" h, Indian Prince, turban, teal shirt **110.00**

Charger, 18-1/2" d, earthenware, riverscape scenes with cottages, one sgd "A. Keller," other sgd "A. Wagner," pr **1,200.00**

Clock, 28" x 15" x 5", pine branch, copper block face, Art Nouveau young Dutch girl blows opalescent bubbles, potted tulips at her feet, jeweled movement, sgd "Lenzkirch, Aug, 1 Million," also sgd "Frederick Goldscheider," incised number, artist sgd "Pecheur" **5,000.00**

Figure

    14" x 11" x 10", seated Gypsy dancer, resting feet on pillow, sgd "Kostral," incised number, 1923, small chip **1,850.00**

    14" x 18" x 6-1/2", Europa, paper label, sgd, incised number **4,300.00**

Dish, covered, multicolored bird, c1925, marked "Goldschneider Wein," 11" h, **$425.**

15" x 11-1/2" x 8-1/2", Minstrel Twins, artist sgd "Dakon," Goldschneider Austria stamp **7,500.00**

16" x 10-1/2" x 7", lady with borzoi, marked, few chips. **3,500.00**

18" x 8" x 6", Harem Girl, artist sgd "Lorenzl," Goldschneider Austria stamp, incised number . . **5,500.00**

19" x 16" x 6-1/2", Bat Girl, sgd "Lorenzal," stamped "Goldscheider," dated XXVII (1927) **4,750.00**

20" x 14" x 9", from Rose series, factory stamp, artist sgd, incised number **5,000.00**

21" x 10" x 6", topless nymph dancing, tree stump at her feet, artist sgd "Schmidt-Kestner," incised number **5,000.00**

21" x 17" x 11", Crystalnacht, paper label, sgd "Podany," and "D. L.," incised number **4,500.00**

Lamp base, 18" x 10" x 7", two figures dressed as Pierot, white costumes, trying to light cigarettes, pre-WW I mark, artist initials, incised number **3,500.00**

Plaque, 22" x 40" x 2", bas relief terra cotta, pseudo mosaic, young Dutch maiden carrying tray of fish, wind, clouds and windmills in background, sgd "Frederick Goldscheider," stamped "Reproduction Reserve, Brevete, S.G.D.G., D.R.G.M.," incised number, custom frame **8,500.00**

Vase, 8-7/8" h, thistle form, stylized leaf and heart motifs, blue and white glazes, black ground with orange banding **500.00**

Wall mask, 7-1/4" h, woman's face, dark brown hair, red lips, light beige face **295.00**

GONDER POTTERY

History: Lawton Gonder established Gonder Ceramic Arts, Inc., at Zanesville, Ohio, in 1941. He had gained experience while working for other factories in the area. Gonder experimented with glazes, including Chinese crackle, gold crackle, and flambé. Lamp bases were manufactured under the name "Eglee" at a second plant location. The company ceased operation in 1957.

Marks: Pieces are clearly marked with the word "Gonder" in various forms.

References: Susan and Al Bagdade, *Warman's American Pottery and Porcelain*, 2nd ed., Krause Publications, 2000; James R. Boshears and Carol Sumilas Boshears, *Gonder Ceramic Arts,* Schiffer Publishing, 2001.

Collectors' Club: Gonder Collectors Club, 917 Hurl Drive, Pittsburgh, PA 15236.

Museum: The Gonder Museum, Ayden, NC, http://www.happysemporium.com/gonderMuseum.html.

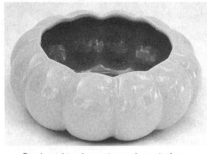

Bowl, melon shape, turquoise exterior, pink interior, impressed "E-12/Gonder/USA," 7" d, **$20.**

Bell, figural, Sovereign Bonnet Lady, Mold No. 800, 3-1/2" h **60.00**

Bowl, 8" d, gray, pink int., marked "H-29" **32.00**

Bulb bowl, 8-1/4" d, 3" h, melon ribbed, pale blue ext., pink int., imp "H-29 USA" **45.00**

Bust, 12" w, 8-1/2" d, 11" h, Chinese man, celadon green glaze, #541 . . . . **500.00**

Candlesticks, pr, 5" h, dolphins, blue glaze, #561, minor chips **100.00**

Console bowl, 15-1/2" l, 4-3/4" w, 7" h, #557, blue/green ext., pink int. . . **165.00**

Cookie jar, cov

Jar, Mold No. P-24, 8-1/2" h . . . **35.00**

Pirate, 8" h **225.00**

Sheriff, Mold No. 950, 12" h **1,100.00**

Cornucopia, 9" h, shaded green, brown, and pink, marked "Gonder USA H14" **60.00**

Ewer, 8" h, shaped angular handle, pink, gray, and purple glaze, marked "H-73" **75.00**

Figure, Chinese Water Bearer, woman, green, orig tag **45.00**

Lamp, cookie jar shape, Mold No. P-24, 8-1/2" h **30.00**

Pitcher, twist body, pale pink **65.00**

Planter, dolphin-type dec on sides, marked "Gonder 556" **65.00**

Swan, Mold #J-31, blue/green glaze, pink int., marked "J-31 Gonder USA" **65.00**

Urn, handles, gray, pink int., paper label on side, incised "H-49" **48.00**

Vase

8" h, shoulder handles, stylized rim, mottled peach and aqua, peach int., marked "Gonder USA," few pinpoints on rim **30.00**

12" h, 10" w, pale blue, pink int., feather motif **95.00**

12" h, 11" w, fan, white, K-15, small chip **110.00**

GOOFUS GLASS

History: Goofus glass, also known as Mexican ware, hooligan glass, and pickle glass, is a pressed glass with relief designs that were painted either on the back or front. The designs are usually in red and green with a metallic gold ground. It was popular from 1890 to 1920 and was used as a premium at carnivals.

It was produced by several companies: Crescent Glass Company, Wellsburg, West Virginia; Imperial Glass Corporation, Bellaire, Ohio; LaBelle Glass Works, Bridgeport, Ohio; and Northwood Glass Co., Indiana, Pennsylvania, Wheeling, West Virginia, and Bridgeport, Ohio.

Goofus glass lost its popularity when people found that the paint tarnished or scaled off after repeated washings and wear. No record of its manufacture has been found after 1920.

Marks: Goofus glass made by Northwood includes one of the following marks: "N," "N" in one circle, "N" in two circles, or one or two circles without the "N."

Periodical: *Goofus Glass Gazette*, 400 NE Martin Blvd, Kansas City, MO 64118.

Animal dish, cov, turkey, Westmoreland **125.00**

Ashtray, red rose dec, emb adv. **15.00**

Basket, 5" h, strawberry dec . . . **50.00**

Bonbon, 4" d, Strawberry pattern, gold, red, and green dec **40.00**

Bowl

6-1/2" d, Grape and Lattice pattern, red grapes, gold ground, ruffled rim **45.00**

7" d, Iris pattern, gold and red dec **35.00**

7" d, thistle and scrolling leaves, red dec, gold ground, ruffled rim **35.00**

8" d, 3-3/4" h, scalloped edge, gold leaves, cranberry flashed flowers **75.00**

9" d, 3" h, Narcissus, Indiana Glass, c1915-30, some paint loss . . **35.00**

10-1/2" d, 2-1/2" h, Cherries, gold leaves, red cherries **35.00**

Bread plate, 7" w, 11" l, Last Supper pattern, red and gold, grapes and foliage border **65.00**

Candy dish, 8-1/2" d, figure-eight design, serrated rim, dome foot . **60.00**

Charger, grape and leaves center **125.00**

Coaster, 3" d, red floral dec, gold ground **12.00**

Compote

4" d, Grape and Cable pattern **35.00**

6" d, Strawberry pattern, red and green strawberries and foliage, ruffled **40.00**

6-1/2" d, Poppy pattern, red flowers, gold foliage, green ground, sgd "Northwood" **40.00**

9-1/2" d, red and green floral and foliage dec, green ground, crimped and fluted rim, pedestal foot, sgd "Northwood" **40.00**

Decanter, orig stopper, La Belle Rose **50.00**

Dresser tray, 6" l, Cabbage Rose pattern, red roses dec, gold foliage, clear ground **35.00**

Jar, cov, butterflies, red and gold **35.00**

Jewel box, 4" d, 2" h, basketweave, rose dec **50.00**

Mug, Cabbage Rose pattern, gold ground **35.00**

Nappy, 6-1/2" d, Cherries pattern, red cherries, gold foliage, clear ground **35.00**

Perfume bottle, 3-1/2" h, pink tulips dec **20.00**

Oil lamp, raised floral design, yellow and red flowers, green highlights, gold background, $40.

Pickle jar, aqua, molded, gold, blue, and red painted floral design **50.00**
Pin dish, 6-1/2" l, oval, red and black florals **20.00**
Plate
6"d, Rose and Lattice pattern, relief molded **20.00**
6" d, Sunflower pattern, red dec center, relief molded **20.00**
7-3/4" d, Carnations pattern, red carnations, gold ground **20.00**
10-1/2" d, grapes dec, gold ground, irid pink edge **35.00**
11" d, Cherries, some paint worn off **35.00**
11" d, Dahlia pattern, red and gold **40.00**
Platter, 18" l, red rose dec, gold ground **65.00**
Powder jar, cov
3" d, puffy, rose dec, red and gold **40.00**
4-1/2" d, Cabbage Rose pattern, white cabbage rose, relief molded **35.00**
Salt and pepper shakers, pr, Grape and Leaf pattern **45.00**
Syrup, relief molded, red roses dec, lattice work ground, orig top.....**85.00**
Toothpick holder, red rose and foliage dec, gold ground **40.00**
Tray, 8-1/4" d, 11" d, red chrysanthemum dec, gold ground **45.00**
Tumbler, 6" h, red rose dec, gold ground **35.00**
Vase
6" h, Cabbage Rose pattern, red dec, gold ground.........**45.00**

6-1/2" h, Grape and Rose pattern, red and gold dec, crackle glass ground **35.00**
9" h, Poppies pattern, blue and red dec, gold ground **45.00**
10-1/2" h, Peacock pattern... **75.00**
12-3/4" h, Carnations, no paint, price for pr.................**150.00**

GOUDA POTTERY

History: Gouda and the surrounding areas of Holland have been principal Dutch pottery centers for centuries. Originally, the potteries produced a simple utilitarian tin-glazed Delft-type earthenware and the famous clay smoker's pipes.

When pipe making declined in the early 1900s, the Gouda potteries turned to art pottery. Influenced by the Art Nouveau and Art Deco movements, artists expressed themselves with free-form and stylized designs in bold colors.

References: Susan and Al Bagdade, *Warman's English & Continental Pottery & Porcelain*, 3rd ed., Krause Publications, 1998; Phyllis T. Ritvo, *The World of Gouda Pottery*, Font & Center Press, 1998.

Periodical: *Dutch Potter*, 47 London Terrace, New Rochelle, NY 10804.

Reproduction Alert: With the Art Nouveau and Art Deco revivals of recent years, modern reproductions of Gouda pottery currently are on the market. They are difficult to distinguish from the originals.

Chamberstick, matte green, yellow, blue, and cream dec, marked "1039 DAM III Holland," c1885, 6-1/2" d, 3" h, $115.

Bowl, 8-3/4" d, 6" h, stylized black, yellow, orange, green, beige, and blue, orig retailer's label **525.00**
Candlestick, Simona, marked "Simona, 1241, Gouda, Holland" **175.00**

Clock garniture, 20-1/2" h clock, 16-3/4" h pr candlesticks, circular clock mouth with painted ceramic face supported by four ceramic arms on baluster-shaped body and flared base, candlesticks of similar form, all dec with Art Nouveau-style flowers, glossy glaze pink, purple, blue, green, and tan, sgd "Zuid Holland" and imp house and "R" on base, repairs to candlesticks **2,875.00**
Charger, 12" d, multicolored flowers, rope border, black trim........**150.00**
Compote, 7 5/8", black ground, geometric design, multicolored scroll int........................**175.00**
Dish, handles, marked "Zuid Holland," c1908.....................**45.00**
Ewer, 12-1/4" h, Damascus III, matte glaze, deep rich colors, mottled green ground, green, blue, and gold patterned band with upright thistles and leaves, narrow band of cobalt blue dots on neck and lower base, c1917 ....**600.00**
Incense burner, 8" h, Roba, flowers and geometric designs, green ground **120.00**
Jug, 5-3/4" d, Rosalie, cream ground, green handle, turquoise interior, marked "Rosalie, #5155," and "Zuid-Holland, Gouda," c1930..............**195.00**
Pitcher
9" d, 13-1/2" h, Sammy **325.00**
9-3/8" h, Rosalie...........**200.00**
Plate, 8-1/4" d, Unique Metallique, scalloped edge, deep blue-green ground, irid copper luster dec ..**350.00**
Tobacco jar, cov, 5" h, Verona pattern **120.00**

Tobacco humidor, covered, Verona pattern, 5" h, $200.

Vase

7-3/4" h, raised rim, oval body tapering to base, central band with upside down stylized tulip blossoms in blue, green, and cream, green ground, painted marks include "Holland 091/1 R" **175.00**

10-1/4" d, Ivora, Juliana glaze, hp, cream colored ground, marked "Juliana Ivora Gouda 207," c1920, price for pr **1,200.00**

GRANITEWARE

History: Graniteware is the name commonly given to enamel-coated iron or steel kitchenware.

The first graniteware was made in Germany in the 1830s. Graniteware was not produced in the United States until the 1860s. At the start of World War I, when European companies turned to manufacturing war weapons, American producers took over the market.

Gray and white were the most common graniteware colors, although each company made its own special color in shades of blue, green, brown, violet, cream, or red.

Older graniteware is heavier than the new. Pieces with cast-iron handles date between 1870 to 1890; wood handles between 1900 to 1910. Other dating clues are seams, wooden knobs, and tin lids.

References: Helen Greguire, *Collector's Encyclopedia of Granite Ware: Colors, Shapes and Values*, Book 1 (1990, 1994 value update), Book 2 (1993, 2000 value update), Collector Books; David T. Pikul and Ellen M. Plante, *Collectible Enameled Ware: American & European,* Schiffer Publishing, 1998.

Collectors' Club: National Graniteware Society, P.O. Box 9248, Cedar Rapids, IA 52410, http://www.graniteware.org.

Reproduction Alert: Graniteware still is manufactured in many of the traditional forms and colors.

Additional Listings: See *Warman's Americana & Collectibles* for more examples.

Batter jug, 6" h, gray mottled, tin lid, tin spout cover, seamed body, wire handle with wood carrying grip **425.00**
Berry pail, cov, 7" d, 4-3/4" h, gray and black mottled **50.00**
Bowl, 11-3/4" d, 3-3/4" h, green and white **50.00**
Bread riser, cov, blue and white swirl, tin lid, large **175.00**
Cake pan, 7-1/2" d, robin's egg blue and white marbleized **45.00**
Child's feeding set, cup and dish, white, chickens dec, worn **35.00**
Coffee boiler, 11" h, Duchess Ware, blue, brown and white accents, wood knob and handle, white int. **745.00**

Berry pail, gray and black, 7" d, 4-3/4" h, **$40.**

Coffeepot, 10" h, gray, tin handle, spout, and lid **525.00**
Coffee roaster, 8-3/4" l, 5-1/4" w, black and white, screen drum, enamel worn **525.00**
Colander, 12" d, gray, pedestal base **30.00**
Cream can, Chrystolite, green **2,500.00**
Creamer, 5" h, turquoise swirl ... **18.00**
Cup, 2-3/4" h, blue and white medium swirl, black trim and handle **50.00**
Double boiler, red swirl **3,600.00**
Frying pan, 10-1/4" d, blue and white mottled, white int. **135.00**
Funnel, cobalt blue and white marbleized, large **50.00**
Grater, medium blue **115.00**
Hotplate, two burners, white graniteware, Hotpoint **165.00**
Kettle, cov, 9" h, 11-1/2" d, gray mottled **50.00**
Measure, one cup, gray **45.00**
Milk pan, blue and white **35.00**
Mixing bowls, red and white, nested set of four, 1930s **155.00**
Muffin pan, blue and white mottled, eight cups **250.00**
Pie pan, 6" d, cobalt blue and white marbleized **25.00**
Pitcher, 11" h, gray, ice lip **110.00**
Pudding pan, 8" d, cobalt blue and white swirl **40.00**
Refrigerator bowls, red swirl, four-pc set **585.00**
Roaster, emerald green swirl, large **250.00**

Skimmer, 10" l, gray mottled **25.00**
Spittoon, blue and white swirl . **325.00**
Teapot, 9-1/2" w, 5" h, enameled dec, small chips **525.00**
Tube pan, octagonal, gray mottled **45.00**
Utensil rack, 14-1/2" w, 22" h, shaded orange, gray bowls, matching ladle, skimmer, and tasting spoon ... **400.00**
Wash basin, 11-3/4" d, blue and white swirl, Blue Diamond Ware **150.00**
Water pail, lime green, brown, and white swirl, early 1900s **225.00**

GREENAWAY, KATE

History: Kate Greenaway, or "K.G.," as she initialed her famous drawings, was born in 1846 in London. Her father was a prominent wood engraver. Kate's natural talent for drawing soon was evident, and she began art classes at the age of 12. In 1868, she had her first public exhibition.

Her talents were used primarily in illustrating. The cards she decorated for Marcus Ward are largely unsigned. China and pottery companies soon had her drawings of children appearing on many of their wares. By the 1880s, she was one of the foremost children's book illustrators in England.

Reference: Ina Taylor, *Art of Kate Greenaway: A Nostalgic Portrait of Childhood*, Pelican Publishing, 1991.

Collectors' Club: Kate Greenaway Society, P.O. Box 8, Norwood, PA 19074.

Reproduction Alert: Some Greenaway buttons have been reproduced in Europe and sold in the United States.

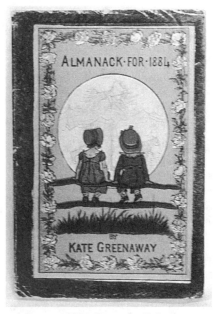

Almanac, 1884, George Routledge & Sons, **$85.**

Advertisement, 5" x 10" print, black and white, for Kate Greenaway fashions, two little girls dressed in Spanish Plaids **12.00**

Butter pat, transfer print of boy and girl **35.00**

Button, 3/4" d, girl with kitten on fence **12.00**

Calendar plate, 10" d, white ground, center scene with initials in lower left corner, back marked "For Sun Glo Studios, Hand-Colored Lithograph from an Original by Kate Greenaway, January" **25.00**

Calling card holder, 6-1/4" w, 6" h, silverplated, little girl holding puppy, marked "Rogers" **300.00**

Children's book, *That Pink and Blue Affair*, Ruth Campbell, illus by Hattie Longstreet Price, 1923 . . . .**60.00**

Figure
    5-3/4" h Emma, pink and white, Royal Doulton **375.00**
    6" h, Ruth, green and white, Royal Doulton **300.00**

Handkerchief, 11-1/2" sq, sunbonnet girl, "Love's gentle touch means so much," lace trim **5.00**

Inkwell, bronze, emb, two children **200.00**

Match safe, SP, emb children . . .**50.00**

Napkin ring, SS, girl feeding yearling **160.00**

Perfume bottle, 2" l, SS, low relief of girls, orig stopper **200.00**

Pie bird, bisque girl, 5" h, **$50.**

Picture frame, 10-7/8" w, 13-1/2" h, wood frame applied with stamped sheet of pewter, shepherdess and sheep, birds and flowering tree, easel back, England or America, early 20th C **150.00**

Salt and pepper shakers, pr, 2-3/4" h, incised "5103," wear to gold trim **95.00**

Tape measure, figural, girl holding muff **45.00**

Teaspoon, SS, figural, girl handle, bowl engraved with Lucy Locket verse **50.00**

Tile, each 6-3/8" d, transfer print, four seasons, one spacer, brown and white dec, blue border, stamped mark, produced by T & R Boote, 1881, framed, five-pc set **325.00**

Toothpick holder, 3-3/8" h, silverplated, girl with low-cut ball gown standing beside barrel holder, marked "2302/Derby Silver Co." **125.00**

GREENTOWN GLASS

History: The Indiana Tumbler and Goblet Co., Greentown, Indiana, produced its first clear, pressed glass table and bar wares in late 1894. Initial success led to a doubling of the plant size in 1895 and other subsequent expansions, one in 1897 to allow for the manufacture of colored glass. In 1899, the firm joined the combine known as the National Glass Company.

K.G.

In 1900, just before arriving in Greentown, Jacob Rosenthal developed an opaque brown glass, called "chocolate," which ranged in color from a dark, rich chocolate to a lighter coffee-with-cream hue. Production of chocolate glass saved the financially pressed Indiana Tumbler and Goblet Works. The Cactus and Leaf Bracket patterns were made almost exclusively in chocolate glass. Other popular chocolate patterns include Austrian, Dewey, Shuttle, and Teardrop and Tassel. In 1902, National Glass Company bought Rosenthal's chocolate glass formula so other plants in the combine could use the color.

In 1902, Rosenthal developed the Golden Agate and Rose Agate colors. All work ceased on June 13, 1903, when a fire of suspicious origin destroyed the Indiana Tumbler and Goblet Company Works.

After the fire, other companies, e.g., McKee and Brothers, produced chocolate glass in the same pattern designs used by Greentown. Later reproductions also have been made, with Cactus among the most heavily copied patterns.

Reference: James Measell, *Greentown Glass*, Grand Rapids Public Museum, 1979, 1992-93 value update, distributed by Antique Publications.

Collectors' Clubs: Collectors of Findlay Glass, P.O. Box 256, Findlay, OH 45839; National Greentown Glass Association, P.O. Box 107, Greentown, IN 46936.

Videotape: *Centennial Exhibit of Greentown Glass* and *Reproductions of Greentown Glass*, National

Greentown Glass Association, P.O. Box 107, Greentown, IN 46936.

Museums: Grand Rapids Public Museum, Ruth Herrick Greentown Glass Collection, Grand Rapids, MI; Greentown Glass Museum, Greentown, IN.

Additional Listings: Holly Amber and Pattern Glass.

Reproduction Alert.

Animal-covered dish
    Dolphin, chocolate, chip off tail **195.00**
    Rabbit, dome top, amber . . .**250.00**

Bowl, 7-1/4" d, Herringbone Buttress, green **135.00**

Butter, cov, Cupid, chocolate . .**575.00**

Celery vase, Beaded Panel, clear **100.00**

Compote, Teardrop and Tassel, clear, 5-1/4" d, 5-1/8" h **50.00**

Cordial, Austrian, canary **125.00**

Creamer
    Cactus, chocolate **85.00**
    Cupid, Nile green **400.00**
    Indian Head, opaque white . .**450.00**

Cruet, orig stopper, Leaf Bracket, chocolate **275.00**

Goblet
    Overall Lattice **40.00**
    Shuttle, chocolate **500.00**

Mug, Cactus, chocolate, 4-1/2" h, **$425.**

Mug, indoor drinking scene, chocolate, 6" w, 8" h **500.00**

Mustard, cov, Daisy, opaque white **75.00**

Nappy, Masonic, chocolate **85.00**

Paperweight, Buffalo, Nile green **600.00**

Pitcher, cov, Dewey, chocolate, 5-1/4" h, spout roughness **85.00**

Grueby Pottery

Plate, Serenade, chocolate **85.00**
Punch cup, Cord Drapery, clear. **20.00**
Relish, Leaf Bracket, 8" l, oval,
chocolate **75.00**
Salt and pepper shakers, pr, Cactus,
chocolate **150.00**
Sugar, cov, Dewey, cobalt blue. **145.00**

Syrup, Geneva pattern, chocolate glass, original tin top, **$615.**

Syrup, Cord Drapery, chocolate, plated lid, 6-3/4" h **350.00**
Toothpick holder
    Cactus, chocolate, hairlines . . **75.00**
    Hobnail and Shell, chocolate **185.00**
Tumbler
    Cactus, chocolate **60.00**
    Dewey, canary **65.00**
Vase, 8" h, Austrian **55.00**

GRUEBY POTTERY

History: William Grueby was active in the ceramic industry for several years before he developed his own method of producing matte-glazed pottery and founded the Grueby Faience Company in Boston, Massachusetts, in 1897.

The art pottery was hand thrown in natural shapes, hand molded, and hand tooled. A variety of colored glazes, singly or in combinations, were produced, but green was the most popular. In 1908, the firm was divided into the Grueby Pottery Company and the Grueby Faience and Tile Co. The Grueby Faience and

Tile Company made art tile until 1917, although its pottery production was phased out about 1910.

Minor damage is acceptable to most collectors of Grueby Pottery.

References: Paul Evans, *Art Pottery of the United States*, 2nd ed., Feingold & Lewis Publishing, 1987; Ralph and Terry Kovel, *Kovels' American Art Pottery*, Crown Publishers, 1993; Susan Montgomery, *The Ceramics of William H. Grueby*, Arts and Crafts Quarterly Press, 1993; David Rago, *American Art Pottery*, Knickerbocker Press, 1997.

Adviser: David Rago.

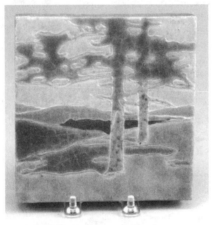

Tile, The Pines, cuenca decoration, green and blue landscape, unmarked, touch-ups to small chips on the four corners and light abrasion to surface. 6" square, **$3,450.** *Photo courtesy of David Rago Auctions.*

Lotus bowl, 7" d, 6" h, tooled and applied leaves, glossy green int. glaze, matte green ext., circular pottery mark/ER, rim glaze flake, couple of glaze misses **1,610.00**
Tile
    6" sq, cuenca dec, The Pines, green and blue landscape, unmarked, touch-ups to small chips on four corners, light abrasion to surface **3,450.00**
    7-3/4" x 8", cuerda seca dec, letter "G" in green framing polychrome Orientalist figure holding vase against matte sienna glaze, sgd "MK," design used as adv icon for Grueby Co., several small chips, couple of tight lines around edges **16,100.00**
Vase
    4" d, 5-1/2" h, ovoid, tooled and applied full height leaves, matte green glaze, circular pottery stamp, two small restored rim

Vase, 12" h, embossed upright leaves, one row ends at shoulder, other row extends to opening, **$20,000.** *Photo courtesy of David Rago Auctions, Inc.*

chips, kiln kiss on shoulder **2,300.00**
    5-1/2" d, 4-3/4" h, squatty, tooled and applied rows of leaves, fine leathery matte green glaze, stamped pottery mark, minute flecks on leave edges . . . **2,615.00**
    8-1/2" d, 17-3/4" h, tall neck, squat base, yellow trefoils around the neck, tooled and applied leaves around base alternating with long stems, leathery matte green glaze, by Wilhemina Post, pottery stamp/WP/188A **92,000.00**
    10" d, 15-1/4" h, bulbous, leathery ivory matte glaze, circular pottery mark, short line of bubbles and small glaze chips to base from grinding **2,415.00**
Vessel
    6" d, 3" h, squatty, by Marie Seaman, applied rounded leaves, fine matte green glaze, stamped Pottery mark/MS, few small nicks **4,875.00**
    7" d, 9-1/2" h, watermelon shape, tooled and applied leaves, curdled dark matte green glaze, orig price tag marked "No. 36A" . . . **5,750.00**

HAIR ORNAMENTS

History: Hair ornaments, among the first accessories developed by primitive man, were used to remove tangles and keep hair out of one's face. Remnants of early combs have been found in many archaeological excavations.

As fashion styles evolved through the centuries, hair ornaments kept pace with changes in design and usage. Hair combs and other hair ornaments are made in a wide variety of materials, e.g., precious metals, ivory, tortoiseshell, plastics, and wood.

Combs were first made in America during the Revolution when imports from England were restricted. Early American combs were made of horn and treasured as toiletry articles.

References: Mary Bachman, *Collector's Guide to Hair Combs, Identification and Values*, Collector Books, 1998; Evelyn Haetig, *Antique Combs and Purses*, Gallery Graphics Press, 1983.

Collectors' Club: Antique Comb Collectors Club International, 90 Highland Ave., #1204, Tarpon Springs, FL 34689-5351.

Museums: Leominster Historical Society, Field School Museum, Leominster, MA; Miller's Museum of Antique Combs, Homer, AK.

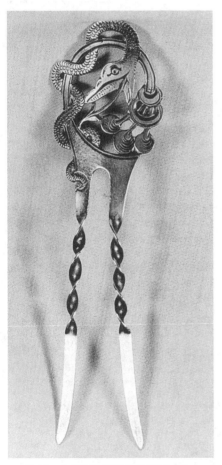

Comb, sterling serpent decoration, two prongs, 4" l, **$40.**

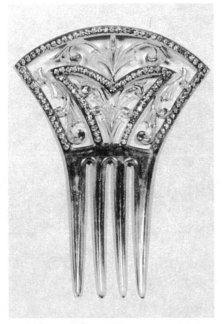

Comb, celluloid to imitate tortoiseshell, filigree ornamentation, set with blue rhinestones, 6-1/4" l, **$45.** *Photo courtesy of Julie Robinson.*

Barrette, 4" l, bar type, faux tortoiseshell with rhinestones ... **10.00**
Comb, baby type, sterling silver. **35.00**
Hair comb
   3-3/4" l, 2-3/8" w, rect, detailed design at top, hand painted. **75.00**
   4-1/2" l, 2-1/2" w, blue and black lacy plastic design, blue rhinestones, painted floral design **65.00**
   5" l, 2-1/2" w, tortoiseshell, 17 red rhinestones, openwork filigree design **95.00**
   5" l, 3" w, imitation tortoiseshell, clear rhinestone dec, modified horseshoe shape **70.00**
   7-1/4" l, 5" w, lacy curving design, imitation tortoiseshell **110.00**
   8-1/2" l, celluloid made to imitate tortoiseshell, central thistle pattern, Scottish............... **125.00**
Hairpin, 15 1/2" l, carved ivory, pierced and carved handle depicting two figures, Japanese **100.00**
Ornament
   4-1/2" l, plastic, simulated stones, c1935 .... **65.00**
   4-3/4" l, rhinestones and simulated pearls, c1925 .... **40.00**
Pompadour comb, Art Nouveau, faux tortoiseshell, gilt brass and turquoise glass accents, pr............ **80.00**

HALL CHINA COMPANY

History: Robert Hall founded the Hall China Company in 1903 in East Liverpool, Ohio. He died in 1904 and was succeeded by his son, Robert Taggart Hall. After years of experimentation, Robert T. Hall developed a leadless glaze in 1911, opening the way for production of glazed household products.

The Hall China Company made many types of kitchenware, refrigerator sets, and dinnerware in a wide variety of patterns. Some patterns were made exclusively for a particular retailer, such as Heather Rose for Sears.

One of the most popular patterns was Autumn Leaf, a premium designed by Arden Richards in 1933 for the exclusive use by the Jewel Tea Company. Still a Jewel Tea property, Autumn Leaf has not been listed in catalogs since 1978, but is produced on a replacement basis with the date stamped on the back.

References: Susan and Al Bagdade, *Warman's American Pottery and Porcelain*, 2nd ed., Krause Publications, 2000; Harvey Duke, *Hall China: Price Guide Update Two*, ELO Books, 1995; ——, *Official Price Guide to Pottery and Porcelain*, 8th ed., House of Collectibles, 1995; C. L. Miller, *Jewel Tea Grocery Products with Values*, Schiffer Publishing, 1996; ——, *Jewel Tea: Sales and Housewares Collectibles*, Schiffer Publishing, 1995; Jim and Lynn Salko, *Halls Autumn Leaf China and Jewel Tea Collectible*, published by authors (143 Topeg Dr., Severna Park, MD 21146); Margaret and Kenn Whitmyer, *Collector's Encyclopedia of Hall China*, 2nd ed., Collector Books, 1994, 1997 values update.

Periodicals and Internet Resources: http://www.hallchina.com.

Collectors' Clubs: Hall Collector's Club, P.O. Box 360488, Cleveland, OH 44136, http://www.chinaspecialities.com/hallnews.html; National Autumn Leaf Collectors Club, P.O. Box 900968, Palmdale, CA 93590-0968.

Additional Listings: See *Warman's Americana & Collectibles* for more examples.

Cookie jar, cov
Autumn Leaf, Tootsie **275.00**
Blue Blossom, Five-Band shape **300.00**
Blue Blossom, Sundial shape . **350.00**
Chinese Red, Five-Band shape **150.00**
Gold Dot, Zeisel............. **95.00**
Gold Lace, Flareware **65.00**
Grape, yellow, gold band....... **65.00**
Meadow Flower, Five-Band shape **260.00**
Owl, brown glaze........... **120.00**
Red Poppy.................. **50.00**

Kitchen ware
Bean pot, New England, #1, Orange Poppy.................... **100.00**
Casserole, cov, Chinese Red, Sundial, #4, 8" w.................. **125.00**

Coffeepot, Great American, Orange Poppy 65.00
Fork, Feather, experimental pattern, blue 200.00
Jug, Primrose, rayed 20.00
Reamer, lettuce green 450.00
Spoon, Feather, experimental pattern, yellow 300.00
Watering can, lilac 850.00

Autumn Leaf, teapot and coffee pot with filters, $50. Photo courtesy of Joy Luke Auctions.

Patterns
Autumn Leaf
Bean pot, cov 700.00
Bowl, 5-1/2" d 7.50
Bud vase, 5-3/4" h 300.00
Butter dish, cov, quarter-pound size 350.00
Butter dish, cov, one-pound size 500.00
Candy dish, pedestal, 4-5/8" h, 5-13/16" sq top 600.00
Coffeepot, electric 500.00
Creamer and sugar 10.00
Cup and saucer 18.00
Juice reamer 300.00
Plate, 8" d 15.00
Teapot, cov, automobile shape, 1993 . . . . 500.00
Tidbit tray, three tiers 125.00
Utensil holder, 7-1/4" h, marked "Utensils"" 275.00
Banded Indian Red, cookie jar. 100.00
Blue Bouquet
Creamer, Boston 25.00
Cup and saucer 28.00
French baker, round 35.00

Platter
13" l 35.00
15" l 40.00
Soup, flat 30.00
Spoon 100.00
Teapot, Aladdin infuser 200.00
Cactus, cookie jar, cov, five band 75.00
Cameo Rose
Bowl, 5-1/4" d 3.00
Butter dish, 3/4 lb 30.00
Casserole 25.00
Creamer and sugar 10.00
Cream soup, 6" d 7.00
Cup and saucer 9.00
Plate, 8" d 2.50
Teapot, cov, six cup 35.00
Tidbit, three tier 40.00
Fuji
Coffee server 40.00
Creamer and sugar 25.00
Gamebirds
Percolator, electric 140.00
Teapot, cov, two-cup size, ducks and pheasant 200.00
Little Red Riding Hood
Butter dish, cov, 6-3/4" w, 5-1/2" h 490.00
Mustard, cov, 3-1/2" w, 5-1/8" h, orig wood spoon 390.00
Mount Vernon
Coffeepot 125.00
Creamer 12.00
Cup 10.00
Fruit bowl 8.00
Gravy boat 20.00
Plate, 10" d 14.00
Saucer 4.00
Soup bowl, 8" d, flat 16.50
Vegetable bowl, 9-1/4" l, oval . 20.00
Red Poppy
Bowl, 5-1/2" d 5.00
Cake plate 17.50
Cake server 65.00
Casserole, cov 25.00
Coffeepot, cov 12.00
Creamer and sugar 15.00
Cup and saucer 8.00
French baker, fluted 15.00
Jug, Daniel, Radiance 28.00
Plate, 9" d 6.50
Salad bowl, 9" d 14.00
Teapot, New York 90.00
Silhouette
Bean pot 50.00
Bowl, 7-7/8" d 50.00
Coffeepot, cov 30.00
Mug 35.00
Pretzel jar 75.00
Trivet 125.00

Teapot, Philadelphia, pink, gold trim, Gold Label line, mid-1940s, five-cup, $40.

Tulip
Bowl, 10-1/4" l, oval 36.00
Coffee maker, drip, Kadota, all china 115.00
Condiment jar 165.00
Creamer 15.00
Cup and saucer 15.00
Fruit bowl, 5-1/2" d 10.00
Mixing bowl, 6" d 27.00
Plate, 9" d, luncheon 16.00
Platter, 13-1/4" l, oval 42.00
Shakers
Bulge-type, price for pr . . 110.00
Set, salt, pepper, flour, and sugar, handles 240.00
Sugar, cov 25.00

Teapots
Blue Blossom, airflow 950.00
Cadet, Radiance 350.00
Chinese Red, donut, 9-1/2" w, 7-1/2" h 600.00
Cleveland, turquoise and gold . 165.00
Los Angeles, cobalt blue 160.00
Orange Poppy, Bellvew, 6-1/2" w, 4" h 2,800.00
Radiance & Wheat 390.00

HAMPSHIRE POTTERY

History: In 1871, James S. Taft founded the Hampshire Pottery Company in Keene, New Hampshire. Production began with redwares and stonewares, followed by majolica in 1879. A semi-porcelain, with the recognizable matte glazes plus the Royal Worcester glaze, was introduced in 1883.

Until World War I, the factory made an extensive line of utilitarian and art wares including souvenir items. After the war, the firm resumed operations, but made only hotel dinnerware and tiles. The company was dissolved in 1923.

References: Susan and Al Bagdade, *Warman's American Pottery and Porcelain*, 2nd ed., Krause Publications, 2000; Ralph and Terry Kovel, *Kovels' American Art Pottery*, Crown Publishers, 1993.

Vase, flaring rim and two handles, covered in a fine dark green matte glaze, impressed "J.S.T. & Co./Keene NH," stamped "Hampshire Pottery, Keene, New Hampshire," 5-1/2" d, 15" h, $1,355. Photo courtesy of David Rago Auctions.

Bowl, 5-1/2" d, 2-1/2" h, matte green glaze over foliate-forms, imp "Hampshire, M.O." **320.00**

Candleholder, 6-1/2" h, shield back with handle, matte green glaze . **200.00**

Chocolate pot, 9-1/2" h, cream, holly dec **275.00**

Compote, 13-1/4" d, ftd, two handles, Ivory pattern, light green highlights, cream ground, red decal mark. . **175.00**

Inkwell, 4-1/8" d, 2-3/4" h, round, large center well, three pen holes **125.00**

Lamp base, 15" h, 9" d, tall cylindrical form, vertical leaves, stems, and flowers, matte green glaze . . . **2,185.00**

Stein, 7" h, 1/2 liter, transfer printed scene of Pine Grove Springs resort **110.00**

Tankard, 7" h, band of stylized dec, green matte glaze, imp "Hampshire" **100.00**

Vase
3-1/4" h, 4-1/4" d, squat, leathery matte green glaze, imp mark **375.00**

4-1/2" h, squat base, matte green glaze **295.00**

6-3/4" h, 4" w, raised tulip-style design, mottled blue glaze, sgd, artist sgd "Cadmon Robertson," ink numbers "636 64333" **895.00**

7" h, 4" d, cylindrical, flaring to base with two handles, feathered green matte glaze, imp marks "TO" **435.00**

Vase, molded full-length leaves alternating with buds, fine leathery matte teal-blue glaze, impressed mark, 6-3/4" h, 4" w, $600. Photo courtesy of David Rago Auctions, Inc.

7-1/2" h, 4" d, cylindrical, feathered matte blue glaze, imp mark "A.O." **520.00**

8-1/2" h, 6-1/2" d, bulbous, leathery matte green, blue, and brown dripping glaze, imp mark. **1,000.00**

11" h, green matte, squared off handles at shoulder **1,200.00**

HATPINS AND HATPIN HOLDERS

History: When oversized hats were in vogue, around 1850, hatpins became popular. Designers used a variety of materials to decorate the pin ends, including china, crystal, enamel, gem stones, precious metals, and shells. Decorative subjects ranged from commemorative designs to insects.

Hatpin holders, generally placed on a dresser, are porcelain containers which were designed specifically to hold these pins. The holders were produced by major manufacturers, among which were Meissen, Nippon, R. S. Germany, R. S. Prussia, and Wedgwood.

Reference: Lillian Baker, *Hatpins & Hatpin Holders: An Illustrated Value Guide*, Collector Books, 1983, 2000 value update.

Collectors' Clubs: American Hatpin Society, 20 Montecillo Drive, Rolling Hills Estates, CA 90274; Hatpin Society of Great Britain, P.O. Box 110, Cheadle, Cheshire Sk8 1GG U.K., http://www.hatpinsociety.org.uk; International Club for Collectors of Hatpins and Hatpin Holders, 1013 Medhurst Road, Columbus, OH 43220.

Museum: Los Angeles Art Museum, Costume Dept., Los Angeles, CA.

Hatpin
Brass
1-1/4" d, 9" l pin, Victorian Lady, cameo type profile, round, Victorian, orig finish **100.00**

1-1/4" x 1", 9" l pin, Indian with headdress, Victorian, orig finish **150.00**

1-1/2" x 1-3/4", 9" l pin, child with flowing hair, flanked by sunflowers, Victorian, orig finish. **125.00**

2" d, 9-1/2" l pin, military button **125.00**

2-1/4" l, oxidized, four citrine-colored stones in each of four panels, citrine-colored stones on 1/2" bezel **315.00**

Hand-painted china, violets, gold trim **35.00**

Left: green glass with silver deposit decoration, $72; right: sterling silver wreath, $70.

Glass
2" l faceted amber glass bead, 13-1/4" l japanned shaft . . .**125.00**

2-1/4" x 1-1/4" faceted rhomboid shape, black, 5-5/8" l **150.00**

Ivory, ball shape, carved design. **65.00**

Jet, 1-1/4" elongated oval knobby bead, 8" l pin **200.00**

Metal, 9-1/4" l, round disk, Art-Nouveau style lady with flowing hair **125.00**

Opalene Moonstone, blackened brass top, 8" l **90.00**

Satsuma, Geisha Girl dec **245.00**

Sterling silver

1-1/4" d, 11" l pin, Arts & Crafts motif of ivy leaf in circle, Charles Horner, hallmarks for Chester, England, 1911 . . . . **195.00**

6-1/2" l, elongated tear shape, marked "Horner" **95.00**

Hatpin holder, Belleek, African violets decoration, Willet mark, 5" h, $90.

Hatpin Holder

Belleek, 5-1/4" h, relief pink and maroon floral dec, green leaves, gold top, marked "Willets Belleek," dated 1911 . . . . **125.00**

Limoges, grapes, pink roses, matte finish, artist sgd **60.00**

Nippon, 4-7/8" d, hp blue daisy flowers, marked "E. O. China" **185.00**

Royal Bayreuth, tapestry, portrait of lady wearing hat, blue mark . . . **575.00**

R. S. Germany, 4-1/2" d, pink roses, green foliage, pink luster trim . . **315.00**

R. S. Prussia, 7" h, 3" d, peach flowers, green foliage **180.00**

HAVILAND CHINA

History: In 1842, American china importer David Haviland moved to

Limoges, France, where he began manufacturing and decorating china specifically for the U.S. market. Haviland is synonymous with fine, white, translucent porcelain, although early hand-painted patterns were

Dinner service, small pink roses decoration, 12 each: butter pats, cups, saucers, dessert bowls, small bowls, 9-1/2" dinner plates, salad plates, soup bowls; covered butter dish with drainer, gravy boat, two open vegetable bowls, two covered tureens, large soup tureen, creamer, covered sugar, covered teapot, waste bowl, small relish dish, four platters, price for 112 pieces, **$825.** *Photo courtesy of Joy Luke Auctions.*

generally larger and darker colored on heavier whiteware blanks than were later ones.

David revolutionized French china factories by both manufacturing the whiteware blank and decorating it at the same site. In addition, Haviland and Company pioneered the use of decals in decorating china.

David's sons, Charles Edward and Theodore, split the company in 1892. In 1936, Theodore opened an American division, which still operates today. In 1941, Theodore bought out Charles Edward's heirs and recombined both companies under the original name of H. and Co. The Haviland family sold the firm in 1981.

Charles Field Haviland, cousin of Charles Edward and Theodore, worked for and then, after his marriage in 1857, ran the Casseaux Works until 1882. Items continued to carry his name as decorator until 1941.

Thousands of Haviland patterns were made, but not consistently named until after 1926. The similarities in many of the patterns makes identification difficult. Numbers assigned by Arlene Schleiger and illustrated in her books have become the identification standard.

References: Susan and Al Bagdade, *Warman's American Pottery and Porcelain*, 2nd ed., Krause Publications, 2000; Mary Frank Gaston, *Haviland Collectibles & Art Objects*, Collector Books, 1984; Charles E. & Carol M. Ulrey, *Matching Services for Haviland China*, published by author, (P.O. Box 15815, San Diego, CA 92175); Arlene Schleiger, *Two Hundred Patterns of Haviland China*, Books I-V, published by author, 1950-1977; Nora Travis, *Haviland China*, Schiffer Publishing, 1997, 1998 value update; —, *Evolution of Haviland China Design*, Schiffer Publishing, 2000.

Collectors' Club: Haviland Collectors International Foundation, P.O. Box 802462, Santa Clarita, CA 91380.

Bone dish, 8-1/4" l, hp

Clam dec **60.00**
Crab dec **60.00**
Turtle dec **65.00**

Bouillon, underplate, Rajah pattern, marked "Theo Haviland" **25.00**

Bowl

6" d, scalloped edge, gold trim **18.00**

8" d, hp, yellow roses **35.00**

Butter dish, cov, Gold Band, marked "Theo Haviland" **45.00**

Butter pat, sq, rounded corners, gold trim **12.00**

Cake plate, 10" d, gold handles and border **35.00**

Celery dish, scalloped edge, green flowers, pale pink scroll **45.00**

Chocolate pot, cov, 10-1/2" l, Countess pattern, green mark, c1893 . . . . **475.00**

Cream soup, underplate, cranberry and blue scroll border **30.00**

Creamer and sugar, small pink flowers, scalloped, gold trim **65.00**

Cup and saucer, deep pink flowers, scalloped gold edge **30.00**

Demitasse cup and saucer, 1885 . . . . **30.00**

Dinner set, Gold Band, service for 12 . . . . **1,000.00**

Game plate, 9-1/4" d, hp, center scene of shore birds in natural setting, apple green edge, printed gold scrolled rim dec, artist sgd "B. Albert," Theodore Haviland & Co. blanks, early 20th C, price for set of 12 . . . . **865.00**

Gravy boat, attached underplate, Monteray **315.00**

Milk pitcher, 8" h, 4-3/4" d, pink flowers, green branches, underglaze green Haviland mark, red "Haviland & Co., Limoges for PDG, Indianapolis, Ind." **450.00**

Oyster plate, 9" d, blue and pink flowers, marked "Haviland & Co." **90.00**

Plate

6" d, Rajah pattern, marked "Theo Haviland" **16.00**

7-1/2" d, pink flowers, gold scalloped edge **20.00**

9" d, Fronteac. **135.00**

9-1/2" d, Princess. **35.00**

Platter

12" l, turquoise morning glories, gold scalloped edge **35.00**

14" l, Athena pattern **195.00**

Relish dish, blue and pink flowers
. . . . **25.00**

Sandwich plate, 11-1/2" d, Drop Rose pattern **275.00**

Teacup and saucer, small blue flowers, green leaves. **30.00**

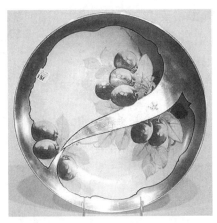

Charger, decorated with leaves and plums, signed "Osborne," 12-1/2" d, $195. Photo courtesy of Joy Luke Auctions.

Teapot, 7-1/2" h, 4-1/4" d, red flowers, green fern dec, gold highlights, marked "Theodore Haviland, Limoges, France," c1895 . . . . **245.00**

Tea set, 8-1/2" d, 8" h teapot, rope and anchor pattern, transfer-printed, hand tinted blossoms, stamped "Haviland-Limoges" mark, restoration to lids, price for three-pc set **200.00**

Tureen, cov, pink roses, green ivy, 12" l, 6-1/2" h **360.00**

Vase, 5-1/2" h, 3-5/8" d, tan, brown, pink, and rose, two oval scenes of lady in large hat, baskets and flower garlands, Charles Field Haviland and GDA Limoges mark **275.00**

Vegetable dish, cov, Rosalinde. **300.00**

Vegetable dish, open, Golden Quail, 9-1/2" x 7-1/2" **435.00**

HEISEY GLASS

1900–58

History: The A. H. Heisey Glass Co. began producing glasswares in April 1896, in Newark, Ohio. Heisey, the firm's founder, was not a newcomer to the field, having been associated with the craft since his youth.

Many blown and molded patterns were produced in crystal, colored, milk (opalescent), and Ivorina Verde (custard) glass. Decorative techniques of cutting, etching, and silver deposit were employed. Glass figurines were introduced in 1933 and continued in production until 1957 when the factory closed. All Heisey glass is notable for its clarity.

Marks: Not all pieces have the familiar H-within-a-diamond mark.

References: Neila Bredehoft, *Collector's Encyclopedia of Heisey Glass, 1925-1938*, Collector Books, 1986, 1999 value update; —; *Fifty Years of Collectible Glass, 1920-1970, Volume 1, Volume II*, Antique Trader Books, 2000; —; *Heisey Glass, 1896-1957*, Collector Books, 2001; Lyle Conder, *Collector's Guide to Heisey's Glassware for Your Table*, L-W Books, 1984, 1993-94 value update; Shirley Dunbar, *Heisey Glass, The Early Years, 1896-1924*, Krause Publications, 2000; Gene Florence, *Elegant Glassware of the Depression Era*, 8th ed., Collector Books, 1998; —, *Glass Candlesticks of the Depression Era*, Collector Books, 1999; Frank L. Hahn and Paul Kikeli, *Collector's Guide to Heisey and Heisey by Imperial Glass Animals*, Golden Era Publications, 1991, 1998 value update.

Collectors' Clubs: Bay State Heisey Collectors Club, 354 Washington St., East Walpole, MA 02032; Heisey Collectors of America, 169 W. Church St., Newark, OH, 43055, http://www.heiseymuseum.org; National Capital Heisey Collectors, P.O. Box 23, Clinton, MD 20735.

Videotape: Heisey Glass Collectors of America, Inc., *Legacy of American Craftsmanship: The National Heisey Glass Museum*, Heisey Collectors of America, Inc., 1994.

Museum: National Heisey Glass Museum, Newark, OH.

Reproduction Alert: Some Heisey molds were sold to Imperial Glass of Bellaire, Ohio, and certain items were reissued. These pieces may be mistaken for the original Heisey. Some of the reproductions were produced in colors never made by Heisey and have become collectible in their own right. Examples include: the Colt family in Crystal, Caramel Slag, Ultra Blue, and Horizon Blue; the mallard with wings up in Caramel Slag; Whirlpool (Provincial) in crystal and colors; and Waverly, a 7-inch, oval, footed compote in Caramel Slag.

Animal

Gazelle **1,450.00**

Plug horse, Oscar. **115.00**

Pony, kicking **175.00**

Pony, standing. **95.00**

Sealyham terrier **145.00**

Sparrow **150.00**

Ashtray

Old Sandwich, #1404, moongleam, individual size **67.50**

Ridgeleigh, #1469, club shape **10.00**

Rose **35.00**

Bitters bottle, #5003, tube **165.00**

Bowl

Empress, #1401, Alexandrite, dolphin foot, 10-7/8" w **735.00**

Orchid, ftd, 11" d, 5-3/4" h . . . **500.00**

Buffet plate, Lariat, #1540, 21" . . **70.00**

Butter dish, cov, Orchid **145.00**

Cake plate, Rose, 15" d, pedestal
. . . . **325.00**

Camellia bowl, Lariat, #1540, 9-1/2" d
. . . . **40.00**

Candelabra, crystal, 10" w, 16-1/2" h, price for pr **695.00**

Candlesticks, pr

Crystolite, three lite, #1503 . . . **75.00**

Lariat, two lite, #1150 . . . . **95.00**

Little Squatter, #99. . . . . **35.00**

Mercury, #122 . . . . **70.00**

New Era, #3877 . . . . **90.00**

Patrician, 7-1/2" h, cut pattern, hexagon shape **425.00**

Pinwheel, #121 . . . . **90.00**

Pluto, #114, hawthorne, pr . . **155.00**

Regency, two light, #1504. . . . **98.00**

Ridgeleigh, 2" sq, #1469. . . . . **80.00**

Thumbprint and Panel, #1433
. . . . **140.00**

Trophy, #126, flamingo **275.00**

Windsor, #22, 7-1/2" h **140.00**

Caramel, cov, Lariat, #1540, 7" . . **75.00**

Celery, Twist, #1252, flamingo, 13" l
. . . . **35.00**

Sherbet, Victorian pattern, footed, signed, $20.

Centerpiece bowl, Ridgeleigh, #1469, 11" d **225.00**

Champagne

Creole, Sahara, tall stem, price for set of seven **500.00**

Minuet. **30.00**

Rose Etch **30.00**

Tudor. **18.00**

Cheese dish, cov, Lariat, #1540, ftd **40.00**

Cheese plate, Twist, #1252, Kraft, moongleam **62.50**

Cigarette holder

Crystolite **25.00**

Orchid, ftd. **165.00**

Ridgeleigh **20.00**

Coaster

Colonial. **10.00**

Plantation **50.00**

Cocktail

Lariat, #1540, moonglo cut. . . **12.00**

Orchid Etch, 4 oz **40.00**

Rooster stem. **40.00**

Rose Etch **32.50**

Rosealie, 3 oz **10.00**

Cocktail shaker

Cobel, #4225, quart **55.00**

Orchid Etch, sterling foot . . . **200.00**

Cologne, #1489, cut stopper, 4 oz **155.00**

Compote, Rose, #1519, low, ftd, 6-1/2" **65.00**

Cordial

Carcassone, #390, Sahara. . **115.00**

Old Dominion, #3380, diamond optic, Sahara **145.00**

5th Avenue-Mitchell, #829 . . . **45.00**

Creamer, Ridgeleigh, #1469. . . . **20.00**

Creamer and sugar

Twist, #1252, oval, Sahara . . **165.00**

Waverly, #1519, orchid etch . . **75.00**

Cruet, Plantation, crystal, #1567 **155.00**

Cup and saucer

Empress, yellow, round. **40.00**

Twist, #1252, flamingo **55.00**

Custard cup, Pinwheel & Fan, moongleam **20.00**

Gardenia bowl, Crystolite, #1503, 12" d **175.00**

Goblet

Galaxy, #8005. . . . . **25.00**

Narrow Flute, #393 . . . . **28.50**

Old Dominion, #3380, marigold, 8-3/4" **55.00**

Provincial, #1506 . . . . **15.00**

Rose Etch, crystal. **40.00**

Sahara, tall stem, set of six, two with slight chips. **500.00**

Spanish, #3404, cobalt blue. **155.00**

Tudor. **12.00**

Honey, Plantation, #1567, ivy etch, 6-1/2" **80.00**

Hurricane lamp base, Lariat, #1540, pr **85.00**

Iced-tea tumbler, ftd, Plantation, #1567 . . . . **75.00**

Jelly, Ridgeleigh, #1469, handle, 6" **20.00**

Jug, Old Sandwich, #1404, Sahara, half gallon **225.00**

Mayonnaise ladle, #6, Alexandrite **245.00**

Muffin plate, Octagon #1229, 12" d, moongleam. **47.50**

Mustard, cov, Flat Panel, #352 . . **48.50**

Nut dish

Empress, #1401, individual, Alexandrite **175.00**

Narrow Flute, #393, moongleam **15.00**

Oyster cocktail, Pied Piper **15.00**

Paperweight, rabbit. **225.00**

Parfait glass, Orchid, 5-1/2" h, 2-7/8" d, price for set of eight **480.00**

Pickle tray, Twist, #1252, flamingo, 7" **20.00**

Pitcher, Orchid, tankard. **625.00**

Plate

Colonial, 4-3/4" d **4.75**

Empress, yellow

6" d, sherbet **13.00**

8" d, salad. **15.00**

Minuet, 8" d **19.75**

Orchid Etch, 7-1/4" d **18.00**

Ridgeleigh, #1469, 8" d **10.00**

Punch bowl set, Crystolite, punch bowl, 12 cups, ladle **400.00**

Relish

Empress, #1401, Minuet etch, three part **90.00**

Normandie etch, star, #1466. . **95.00**

Lariat, #1540, three part

10-1/2". **24.00**

12". **28.00**

Provincial, #1506, 12" **35.00**

Twist, #1252, flamingo, 13" l . . **40.00**

Waverly, #1519, 6-1/2", divided, three ft **25.00**

Rose bowl, Plateau, #3369, flamingo **65.00**

Salt shaker, Old Sandwich, #1404 . . . . **30.00**

Sandwich plate, Plantation, #1567, 14" d. **65.00**

Serving tray, center handle, Orchid Etch **150.00**

Sherbet

Orchid Etch, low **20.00**

Priscilla, 4 oz, high. **15.00**

Punch bowl, pedestal base, colorless, fluted design, scalloped edge, 15" d, 12-3/4" h, chips, roughness on bowl base, and rim of base, $100. Photo courtesy of Sanford Alderfer Auction Co..

Soda

Coronation, #4054, 10 oz **9.50**

Creole, #3381, 12 oz, ftd, diamond optic Alexandrite bowl, crystal foot **167.50**

Duquesne, #3389, 12 oz, ftd, tangerine **210.00**

Newton, #2351, 8 oz, Fronetnac etch **20.00**

Old Dominion, #3380, 12 oz, ftd, diamond optic Alexandrite. . **90.00**

Old Sandwich, #1404, 8 oz, moongleam **48.50**

Stanhope, #4083, 8 oz, ftd, zircon bowl and foot **155.00**

Strawberry dip plate, Narrow Flute, #393, with rim **195.00**

Tankard, Orchid, ice lip, 9-1/2" h, 7" w **480.00**

Toothpick holder

Fancy Loop, emerald, small base flake, wear to gold trim. . . . **120.00**

Waldorf Astoria, #333. . . . . . . **110.00**

Tumbler

Ridgeleigh, #1469, 8 oz **45.00**

Rose Etch, ftd, 12 oz **50.00**

Vase

Prison Stripe, #357, cupped, 5" **55.00**

Ridgeleigh, #1469, Sahara, cylinder, 8" h. **245.00**

Water bottle

Banded Flute, #150 . . . . **125.00**

Beaded Panel & Sunburst, #1235 . . . . **115.00**

Wine

Minuet. **65.00**

Orchid etch, 3 oz **75.00**

HOLLY AMBER

History: Holly Amber, originally called Golden Agate, was produced by the Indiana Tumbler and Goblet Works of the National Glass Co., Greentown, Indiana. Jacob Rosenthal created the color in 1902. Holly Amber is a gold-colored glass, with a marbleized onyx color on raised parts.

Holly (No. 450), a pattern created by Frank Jackson, was designed specifically for the Golden Agate color. Between January 1903 and June of that year, when the factory was destroyed by fire, more than 35 different forms were made in this pattern.

Reference: James Measell, *Greentown Glass, The Indiana Tumbler & Goblet Co.*, Grand Rapids Public Museum, 1979, 1992-93 value update.

Collectors' Club: National Greentown Glass Assoc., 19596 Glendale Ave., South Bend, IN 46637.

Museums: Grand Rapids Public Museum, Ruth Herrick Greentown Glass Collection, Grand Rapids, MI; Greentown Glass Museum, Greentown, IN.

Additional Listings: Greentown Glass.

Tumbler, 3-7/8" h, $350.

Berry bowl, 8-1/2" d 375.00
Butter, cov, 7-1/4" x 6-3/4" d . 1,200.00
Cake stand 2,000.00
Compote, cov, 8-1/2" d, 12" h 1,800.00
Creamer and sugar 1,550.00
Cruet, 6-1/2" h, orig stopper . 2,100.00
Jelly compote, 4-3/4" d 450.00
Match holder 400.00
Mug, 4-1/2" h 450.00
Nappy. 375.00
Parfait 575.00
Relish, oval 275.00
Salt and pepper shakers, pr. . .500.00
Sauce dish. 225.00
Spooner. 425.00

Syrup, 5-3/4" h, SP hinged lid **2,000.00**
Toothpick holder, 2-1/2" h, deep amber, fiery opalescence **695.00**
Tumbler. **350.00**

HORN

History: For centuries, horns from animals have been used for various items, e.g., drinking cups, spoons, powder horns, and small dishes. Some pieces of horn have designs scratched in them. Around 1880, furniture made from the horns of Texas longhorn steers was popular in Texas and the southwestern United States.

Additional Listings: Firearm Accessories.

Chair and stool, Texas Longhorn, chair made of 24 cattle horns, embossed leather panels, red imitation leather upholstery, secret compartment in footstool, covered in red velvet, four cattle horn feet, $575. Photo courtesy of Cowan Historic Americana Auctions.

Ale set, silver plate mounted cov 9-3/4" h jug, two 5-1/2" h beakers, fitted 17-3/4" l x 15" h plated frame with twisted gallery and upright handle, tripartite circular base with Greek Key border, raised on stepped block feet, English, early 20th C **850.00**
Arm chair, steer horn, leather upholstered seat, four pairs of matched horns form base, American, 20th C **575.00**
Calling card case, horn and ivory, floral design **48.00**
Comb case, 7-1/2" x 9", pocket type, diamond-shape mirror. **35.00**
Cup, 5" h, rhinoceros, carved as magnolia flower, base of branch and leaves, carved wood stand, 18th C or earlier, losses. **1,100.00**

Snuff mull (container)
 3" l, curved and carved dog's head, bone detailed eyes, gilt-metal neck rim etched with initials, Scottish, first half 19th C **520.00**
 3-1/4" l, short curved horn, brass fittings, hinge, and medallion on lid with engraved initials "W.D." and "I.L.," shallow chip on lid. . . **110.00**
Tea caddy, cov, 14-1/2" w, 9" d, 7-1/2" h, Ango-Indian, Vishapatnam, early 19th C, antler veneer, steer horn, ivory, int. cov compartments, etched scrolling vines, restorations **1,850.00**

Chair, various horns and antlers used in arms and back, wooden seat frame, carved animal legs with hoofs, old dark finish, seat reupholstered in brown moire silk, 36" h, pair, $825. Photo courtesy of Garth's Auctions, Inc.

Vinaigrette, Victorian, late 19th C, staghorn, 2-1/2" l rough-textured horn mounted with thistle-cast lid, quatrefoil neck band, horn with guilloche strapping, short link chain **350.00**

HULL POTTERY

History: In 1905, Addis E. Hull purchased the Acme Pottery Company, Crooksville, Ohio. In 1917, the A. E. Hull Pottery Company began making art pottery, novelties, stoneware, and kitchenware, later including the famous Little Red Riding Hood line. Most items had a matte finish, with shades of pink and blue or brown predominating.

After a disastrous flood and fire in 1950, J. Brandon Hull reopened the factory in 1952 as the Hull Pottery Company. New, more-modern-style pieces, mostly with glossy finish, were produced. The company added dinnerware patterns, and glossy finished pottery. The company closed its doors in 1986.

Marks: Hull pottery molds and patterns are easily identified. Pre-1950 vases are marked "Hull USA" or "Hull Art USA" on the bottom. Many also retain their paper labels. Post-1950 pieces are marked "Hull" in large script or "HULL" in block letters.

Each pattern has a distinctive letter or number, e.g., Wildflower has a "W" and a number; Waterlily, "L" and number; Poppy, numbers in the 600s; Orchid, in the 300s. Early stoneware pieces are marked with an "H."

References: Joan Hull, *Hull, The Heavenly Pottery*, 7th ed., published by author (1376 Nevada, Huron, SD 57350), 2000; —, *Hull, The Heavenly Pottery Shirt Pocket Price List*, 4th ed., published by author, 1999; Brenda Roberts, *The Ultimate Encyclopedia of Hull Pottery*, Collector Books, 1995, 1999 value update; Mark and Ellen Supnick, *Collecting Hull Pottery's Little Red Riding Hood, Revised Edition*, L-W Books, 1998.

Periodicals: *Hull Pottery Association*, 11023 Tunnel Hill NE, New Lexington, OH 43764.

Additional Listings: See *Warman's Americana & Collectibles* for more examples.

Adviser: Joan Hull.

Pre-1950 Matte
Bowknot
B-4 6-1/2" h vase 250.00
B-7 cornucopia. 325.00
B-11 10-1/2" h vase 500.00
B-12, 10-1/2" h basket 750.00
B-16 console bowl 325.00
B-17 candleholders, pr. 225.00

Calla Lily
500-32 bowl 200.00
520-33, 8" h vase 150.00

Dogwood (Wild Rose)
501, 8-1/2" h basket 300.00
508 10-1/2" window box 195.00
513, 6-1/2" h vase 125.00

Little Red Riding Hood, cookie jars, **$300 to $1,000 each.** *Photo courtesy of Joan Hull.*

Little Red Riding Hood
Creamer and sugar, side pour
. . . . 400.00
Dresser or cracker jar 800.00
Lamp 2,500.00
Matchbox for wooden matches
. . . . 900.00
Salt and pepper shakers, pr, small
. . . . 120.00
Teapot, cov 395.00
Wall pocket planter 620.00

Magnolia
3 8-1/2" h vase. 125.00
9 10-1/2" h vase. 200.00
14 4-3/4" h pitcher 75.00
20 15" floor vase 500.00

Open Rose/Camellia
106 13-1/2" h pitcher 650.00
114 8-1/2" h jardiniere 375.00
119 8-1/2" h vase. 175.00
127 4-3/4" h vase. 75.00

Orchid
301 4-3/4" h vase. 95.00
302 6" h vase. 175.00
303 8" h vase. 195.00
304 10-1/2" h vase. 350.00
310 9-1/2" jardiniere. 450.00

Poppy
601 9" h basket 800.00
607 10-1/2" h vase 450.00
610 13" pitcher. 900.00
613 6-1/2" h vase 200.00

Rosella
R-2 5" h vase 35.00
R-6 6-1/2" h vase 45.00
R-15 8-1/2" h vase 75.00

Tulip
101-33 9" h vase 245.00
103-33 6" h vase 250.00
107-33 6" h vase 125.00
109-33-8" pitcher. 235.00

Waterlily
L-14, 10-1/2" basket. 350.00
L-16, 12-1/2" vase 395.00

Wild Flower, No. Series
53 8-1/2" h vase. 295.00
61 6-1/2" h vase. 175.00
66 10-1/4" h basket 2,000.00
71 12" h vase. 450.00

Woodland
W9 8-3/4" h basket. 245.00
W11 5-1/2" flower pot and saucer
. . . . 175.00
W13 7-1/2" l wall pocket, shell
. . . . 195.00
W14 10-1/2" window box. . . . 200.00

Water Lily, creamer and sugar, pink florals, shaded white to green ground, **$35 each.**

Post 1950
Blossom Flite
T4 8-1/2" h basket. 125.00
T13 12-1/2" h pitcher 150.00

Butterfly
B9 9" h vase 55.00
B13 8" h basket 150.00
B15 13-1/2" h pitcher 200.00

Continental
C29 12" h vase 95.00
C55 12-1/2" basket. 150.00
C62 8-1/4" candy dish 45.00

Ebb Tide
E-1 7" h bud vase 75.00
E-8 ashtray with mermaid. . . 225.00
E-10 13" h pitcher. 275.00

Parchment and Pine
S-3 6" h basket 95.00
S-11 and S-12 tea set. 250.00
S-15 8" h coffeepot. 175.00

Serenade
S1 6" h vase 55.00
S-15 11-1/2" d fruit bowl, ftd. 125.00
S11 10-1/2" h vase 100.00
S17 teapot, creamer and sugar
. . . . 275.00

Sunglow
53 grease jar 60.00
82 wall pocket, whisk broom . 75.00
85 8-3/4" h vase, bird 60.00

Tokay/Tuscany
3 8" h pitcher 95.00
8 10" h vase 150.00
10 11" l cornucopia 65.00
12 12" h vase. 125.00

Tropicana
T53 8-1/2" h vase 550.00
T55, 12-3/4" h basket 750.00

Woodland (glossy)
W1 5-1/2" h vase. 45.00
W15 8-1/2" h vase, double . . . 75.00
W19 14" d console bowl. . . . 100.00

HUMMEL ITEMS

History: Hummel items are the original creations of Berta Hummel, who was born in 1909 in Massing, Bavaria, Germany. At age 18, she was enrolled in the Academy of Fine Arts in Munich to further her mastery of drawing and the palette. Berta entered the Convent of Siessen and became Sister Maria Innocentia in 1934. In this Franciscan cloister, she continued drawing and painting images of her childhood friends.

In 1935, W. Goebel Co. in Rodental, Germany, began producing Sister Maria Innocentia's sketches as three-dimensional bisque figurines. The Schmid Brothers of Randolph, Massachusetts, introduced the figurines to America and became Goebel's U.S. distributor.

In 1967, Goebel began distributing Hummel items in the U.S. A controversy developed between the two companies, the Hummel family, and the convent. Law suits and counter-suits ensued. The German courts finally effected a compromise: the convent held legal rights to all works produced by Sister Maria Innocentia from 1934 until her death in 1946 and licensed Goebel to reproduce these works; Schmid was to deal directly with the Hummel family for permission to reproduce any pre-convent art.

Marks: All authentic Hummel pieces bear both the signature "M. I. Hummel" and a Goebel trademark. Various trademarks were used to identify the year of production:

Crown Mark (trademark 1)	1935 through 1949
Full Bee (trademark 2)	1950-1959
Stylized Bee (trademark 3)	1957-1972
Three Line Mark (trademark 4)	1964-1972
Last Bee Mark (trademark 5)	1972-1979
Missing Bee Mark (trademark 6)	1979-1990
Current Mark or New Crown Mark (trademark 7)	1991 to the present

References: Ken Armke, *Hummel: An Illustrated History and Price Guide*, Wallace-Homestead, 1995; Carl F. Luckey, *Luckey's Hummel Figurines and Plates: A Collector's Identification and Value Guide*, 11th ed., Krause Publications, 1997; Robert L. Miller, *No. 1 Price Guide to M. I. Hummel: Figurines, Plates, More...*, 6th ed., —, *Hummels 1978-1998: 20 Years of "Miller on Hummel" Columns*, Collector News, 1998; Portfolio Press, 1995.

Collectors' Clubs: Hummel Collector's Club, Inc., 1261 University Dr., Yardley, PA 19067; M. I. Hummel Club, Goebel Plaza, Rte. 31, P.O. Box 11, Pennington, NJ 08534.

Museum: Hummel Museum, New Braunfels, TX.

Additional Listings: See *Warman's Americana & Collectibles* for more examples.

Bookends, pr
Chick Girl, #618, full bee, trademark-2 . . . . **320.00**
Playmates, #61A, full bee, trademark-2 . . . . **320.00**

Candleholder
Silent Night, #54, trademark 5 **175.00**
Watchful angel, #194, trademark 2 . . . . **400.00**

Candy box, cov
Happy Pastime, #III/169, trademark 4 . . . . **125.00**
Joyful, #III/53, trademark 4 . . . **115.00**

Christmas Angel
Boy, #117, trademark 3 . . . . . **45.00**
Girl, #116, fir tree, 3" h, trademark 3 . . . . **40.00**

Figure
Apple Tree Girl, #141, 6" h, stamped full bee, incised crown mark **425.00**
Band Leader, #129, trademark 5 . . . . **120.00**
Be Patient, #197/12/10, trademark 2 . . . . **125.00**
Chimney Sweep, #122/10, trademark 5 . . . . **70.00**
Congratulations, #17/0, 1971, MIB **150.00**
Culprits, orig paper label, #56/A, 6-1/4" H **425.00**
Daily News, #184, 5" h **400.00**
Farm Boy, #66, trademark 2, 1950-57, 5-3/4" h **375.00**
For Father, #87, stylized bee, 5-1/2" h **350.00**
Goose Girl, #47/0, trade mark 3, 4-3/4" h **425.00**
Happiness, #86, trademark 3 . **110.00**
Heavenly Angel, #21/0, trademark 3 . . . . **100.00**
Just Resting, #112/13/0, trademark 4 . . . . **90.00**
Kiss Me, #311, trademark 3 . **150.00**
Little Bookkeeper, #306, trademark 4 . . . . **220.00**
Little Tooter, #214/1, 3-1/4" x 5", trademark 4 . . . . **145.00**
Merry Wanderer, #11/0, trademark 2 . . . . **215.00**
Photographers, #178, trademark 4 . . . . **215.00**
Sensitive Hunter, #640, trademark 4 . . . . **150.00**
Strolling Along, #5, full bee mark, 5-3/4" h **550.00**
Umbrella Boy, #152, c1960-72, 8" h **500.00**
Wash Day, #3211, trademark 4 . . . . **100.00**
Wayside Harmony, #111/3/0, trademark 4 . . . . **100.00**

Harmony in Four Parts, #471, trademark 6, **$1,155.** *Photo courtesy of Jackson's Auctioneers & Appraisers.*

Font
Angel Cloud, #206, trademark 5 . . . . **45.00**
Child Jesus, #26/0, MK 4 . . . . **35.00**
Guardian angel, #248, trademark 4 . . . . **60.00**
Holy Family, #246, trademark 2 . . . . **85.00**
Seated Angel, #10/1, trademark 3 . . . . **420.00**

Lamp, table, Culprits, #44, 9-1/2" h, c1930 . . . . **475.00**

Nativity set, Virgin Mary, Carpenter, Wisemen, Shepherd and lamb, Baby Jesus in manger, stable, Robson, bee in V mark, 4-1/2" h figures, c1959-61 . . . . **795.00**

Plaque
Madonna, #48/0, trademark 7 . . . . **250.00**
Mail Coach, #140, trademark 5 . . . . **145.00**

Figures: Springcheer, #72, incised crown, full bee mark, 5-1/4" h, $90; Stormy Weather, #71, mark 3, 6" h, $135; Brother, #95, stamped "Made in US Zone, Germany," 5-1/4" h, $75; We Congratulate, full bee, mark 2, 3-1/2" h, $165; School Girl, #81-1/0, stylized bee, 4-1/2" h, $75; unmarked girl with basket (repaired), $10. Photo courtesy of Joy Luke Auctions.

IMARI

History: Imari derives its name from a Japanese port city. Although Imari ware was manufactured in the 17th century, the pieces most commonly encountered are those made between 1770 and 1900.

Early Imari was decorated simply, quite unlike the later heavily decorated brocade pattern commonly associated with Imari. Most of the decorative patterns are an underglaze blue and overglaze "seal wax" red complimented by turquoise and yellow.

The Chinese copied Imari ware. The Japanese examples can be identified by grayer clay, thicker glaze, runny and darker blue, and deep red opaque hues.

The pattern and colors of Imari inspired many English and European potteries, such as Derby and Meissen, to adopt a similar style of decoration for their wares.

Reference: Nancy N. Schiffer, *Imari, Satsuma, and Other Japanese Export Ceramics,* Schiffer Publishing, 1997.

Reproduction Alert: Reproductions abound, and many manufacturers continue to produce pieces in the traditional style.

Meat platter, 19-1/2" x 16", English, $450. Photo courtesy of Sanford Alderfer Auction Co.

Bowl
- 8-1/2" d, 3-1/4" h, red, blue, white, and gold dec **425.00**
- 10" d, 4" h, peach colored border, underglaze blue dec **875.00**
- 13-1/2" d, 5-1/2" h, blue and white, edge chips **715.00**
- 15" d, 5-3/4" h, blue and white, scalloped rim, early 20th C **220.00**

Charger
- 17-1/2" d, scalloped edge, 19th C **2,100.00**
- 17-3/4" d, blue and white dec, c1850 . . . . **1,100.00**
- 18" d, underglaze blue, enamel and gilt, central reserve of double gourds, fan-shaped panels with various scenes, Japan, 19th C **1,150.00**

Creamer and sugar, 5-1/2" h creamer, 5-7/8" cov sugar, ovoid, dragon form handles, gilt and bright enamels, shaped reserves, dragon-like beasts, stylized animal medallions, brocade ground, high dome lid, knob, cipher mark of Mount Fuji, Fukagama Studio marks, Meiji period **500.00**

Dish
- 8-3/8" d, central scene with fence and flowering tree dec, shaped cartouches enclosing flowers and hares on crackle blue ground at rim, gilt highlights, Meiji period, price for pr **650.00**
- 9-1/2" d, shaped rim, all over flowering vine dec, gilt highlights **150.00**

Food box, 6" h, three section, ext. and lid with phoenix and floral design, underglaze blue, iron-red, and gilt enamels, 19th C **400.00**

Jar, cov, ribbed, 19th C **725.00**

Jardiniere, 10" h, hexagonal, bulbous, short flared foot, alternating bijin figures and immortal symbols, stylized ground **250.00**

Planter and stand, 17" d, 43" h, lobed form, floral dec, brocade patterns, Japan, late 19th C **460.00**

Plate, 14-3/4" d, scalloped, floral dec, 16-1/2" h fitted wooden table form stand **375.00**

Platter, 18" d, alternating panels of figures and foliage, trellis work ground, Japanese, late 19th C **475.00**

Punch bowl, 12" d, rubbed, c1870 . . . . **1,650.00**

Teabowl and saucer, 5" d, floriform, floral spray dec, gilt highlights on saucer **200.00**

Umbrella stand, 24" h, iron-red and blue palette, bird and floral designs, Japan, late 19th C **690.00**

Urn, 21" h, gilt bronze mounts, deep bowl, red, blue, and gilt floral dec, everted pierced collar, S-scroll arms of leaves and cattails, mid band of plaited reeds, flaring porcelain base banded in bronze, pierced skirt interspersing four foliate clasps, pr **14,000.00**

Vase, 14-1/2" h, baluster, late Meiji period, c1900 . . . . **775.00**

IMPERIAL GLASS

History: Imperial Glass Co., Bellaire, Ohio, was organized in 1901. Its primary product was pattern

(pressed) glass. Soon other lines were added, including carnival glass, Nuart, Nucut, and Near Cut. In 1916, the company introduced Free-Hand, a lustered art glass line, and Imperial Jewels, an iridescent stretch glass that carried the Imperial cross trademark. In the 1930s, the company was reorganized into the Imperial Glass Corporation, and the firm is still producing a great variety of wares.

Imperial recently acquired the molds and equipment of several other glass companies—Central, Cambridge, and Heisey. Many of the retired molds of these companies are once again in use.

Marks: The Imperial reissues are marked to distinguish them from the originals.

References: Margaret and Douglas Archer, *Imperial Glass*, Collector Books, 1978, 1998 value update; Sean and Johanna S. Billings, *Peachblow Glass, Collector's Identification & Price Guide,* Krause Publications, 2000; Tom and Neila Bredehoft, *Fifty Years of Collectible Glass, 1920-1970, Volume 1, Volume II,* Antique Trader Books, 2000; Carl O. Burns, *Imperial Carnival Glass,* Collector Books, 1999; Gene Florence, *Elegant Glassware of the Depression Era,* 8th ed., Collector Books, 1998; Myrna and Bob Garrison, *Imperial's Boudoir, Etcetera,* 1996; National Imperial Glass Collectors Society, *Imperial Glass Encyclopedia: Volume I, A-Cane,* Antique Publications, 1995; ——, *Vol. II: Cape Code- L,* Antique Publications, 1998; ——, *Imperial Glass 1966 Catalog,* reprint, 1991 price guide, Antique Publications; Virginia R. Scott, *Collector's Guide to Imperial Candlewick,* published by author (275 Milledge Terrace, Athens, GA 30606); Mary M. Wetzel-Tomlka, *Candlewick: The Jewel of Imperial Books I and II,* published by author (P.O. Box 594, Notre Dame, IN 46556-0594); ——, *Candlewick The Jewel of Imperial, Personal Inventory & Record Book,* published by author, 1998; ——, *Candlewick The Jewel of Imperial, Price Guide 99 and More,* published by author, 1998.

Collectors' Clubs: National Candlewick Collector's Club, 17609 Falling Water Road, Strongsville, OH 44136, plus many regional clubs; National Imperial Glass Collectors Society, P.O. Box 534, Bellaire, OH 43906, http://www.imperialglass.org.

Periodical: *Glasszette,* National Imperial Glass Collector's Society, P.O. Box 534, Bellaire, OH 43528.

Videotapes: National Imperial Glass Collectors Society, *Candlewick: at Home, In Any Home, Vol. I: Imperial Beauty, Vol. II: Virginia and Mary,* RoCliff Communications, 1993; ——, *Glass of Yesteryears: The Renaissance of Slag Glass,* RoCliff Communications, 1994.

Additional Listings: See Carnival Glass, Pattern Glass, and *Warman's Americana & Collectibles* for more examples of Candlewick Pattern.

Engraved or hand cut

Bowl, 6-1/2" d, flower and leaf, molded star base **25.00**

Candlesticks, pr, 7" h, Amelia . . **35.00**

Celery vase, three-side stars, cut star base **25.00**

Pitcher, tankard, Design No. 110, flowers, foliage, and butterfly cutting **60.00**

Plate, 5-1/2" d, Design No. 12 . . **15.00**

Jewels

Bowl, 6-1/2" d, purple Pearl Green luster, marked **75.00**
Compote, 7-1/2" d, irid teal blue .**65.00**
Rose bowl, amethyst, green irid .**75.00**
Vase, 7-3/4" h, classic baluster, white body, mirror bright tray-blue surface, deep orange irid int. rim **320.00**

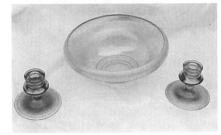

Console set, iridescent blue stretch glass, 10-1/4" d bowl, 3-1/4" h candle-sticks, price for set, $95.

Lustered (freehand)

Candlestick, 10" h, slender baluster, cushion foot, clear, white heart and vine dec, tall cylindrical irid dark blue socket, orig paper label **440.00**
Hat, 9" w, ruffled rim, cobalt blue, embedded irid white vines and leaves **120.00**
Ivy ball, 4" h, Spun, red, crystal foot **90.00**
Vase
7" h, opal white irid body, bright blue heart and vine dec, applied cobalt blue wrap, subtle orange lustered int. **800.00**
8-1/2" h, cylindrical, irid green heart and vine design, white ground, marigold lining, some wear .**385.00**
10" h, tall slender form, irid orange ext., deep orange throat . . .**195.00**

Nuart

Ashtray **20.00**
Lamp shade, marigold **50.00**
Vase, 7" h, bulbous, irid green . .**125.00**

Nucut

Berry bowl, 4-1/2" d, handles . . .**15.00**
Celery tray, 11" l **18.00**
Creamer **20.00**
Fern dish, 8" l, brass lining, ftd . .**30.00**
Orange bowl, 12" d, Rose Marie .**48.00**

Pressed

Bar bottle, Cape Cod **150.00**
Basket, Cape Cod, No. 160/73/0 . . . .**350.00**
Birthday cake plate, Cape Cod **325.00**

Rose bowl, Molly pattern, pink, short foot, four wide toes, eight scalloped top, light ribbed body, 4-1/2" h, 5-1/2" w, $25. Photo courtesy of Johanna Billings.

Bowl, Cape Cod, 11" l, oval **90.00**
Bowl, Windmill, amethyst, fluted, 8" d, 3" h **45.00**
Center bowl, Cape Cod, No. 160/751, ruffled edge **65.00**
Champagne, Cape Cod, azalea. **22.00**
Coaster, Cape Cod, No. 160/76 .**10.00**
Compote, Pillar Flutes, light blue **25.00**
Cruet, orig stopper, Cape Cod, No. 160/119, amber **28.00**
Decanter, orig stopper, Cape Cod, No. 160/163 . . . .**75.00**
Goblet, Cape Cod, No. 1602, Verde green **8.00**
Goblet, Monticello, crystal **12.00**
Mug, Cape Cod. **58.00**
Nappy, Quilted Diamond, marigold, ring handle **35.00**
Pitcher, Cape Cod, No. 160/19, ice lip **85.00**
Plate, Windmill, glossy, green slag, IG mark. **45.00**
Rose bowl, Molly, black, silver deposit floral dec, 5" h **45.00**
Salt and pepper shakers, Cape Cod, Verde green, orig tops. **40.00**
Toothpick holder, 2-1/2" h, carnival or milk white, IG mark **30.00**
Tumbler, Georgian, red. **18.00**
Whiskey set, Cape Cod, No. 160/280, metal rack, clear bottles, raised letters Bourbon, Rye, and Scotch **650.00**

INDIAN ARTIFACTS, AMERICAN

History: During the historic period, there were approximately 350 Indian tribes grouped into the following regions: Eskimo, Northeast and Woodland, Northwest Coast, Plains, and West and Southwest.

American Indian artifacts are quite popular. Currently, the market is stable following a rapid increase in prices during the 1970s.

References: C. J. Brafford and Laine Thom (comps.), *Dancing Colors: Paths of Native American Women*, Chronicle Books, 1992; Harold S. Colton, *Hopi Kachina Dolls*, revised ed., University of New Mexico Press, 1959, 1990 reprint; Lois Sherr Dubin, *North American Indian Jewelry and Adornment*, Harry N. Abrams, Inc., 1999; Gary L. Fogelman, *Identification and Price Guide for Indian Artifacts of the Northeast*, Fogelman Publishing, 1994; Lar Hothem, *Arrowheads & Projectile Points*, Collector Books, 1983, 1999 value update; —, *Collecting Indian Knives, Identification and Values*, 2nd ed., Krause Publications, 2000; —, *Collector's Guide to Indian Pipes*, Collector Books, 1999; —, *Indian Artifacts of the Midwest*, Book I (1992, 1996 value update), Book II (1995, 1999 value update), Book III (1997, 1999 value update), Book IV (2001), Collector Books; —, *Indian Axes & Related Stone Artifacts*, Collector Books, 1996; *North American Indian Artifacts*, 6th ed., Krause Publications, 1998; Preston E. Miller and Carolyn Corey, *The Four Winds Guide to Indian Trade Goods and Replicas*, Schiffer Publishing, 1998; Karen and Ralph Norris, *Northwest Carving Traditions*, Schiffer Publishing, 1999; Robert M. Overstreet, *Overstreet Indian Arrowheads Identification and Price Guide*, 6th edition, Avon Books, 1999; Lillian Peaster, *Pueblo Pottery Families*, Schiffer Publishing, 1997; Dawn E. Reno, *Native American Collectibles*, Avon Books, 1994; Nancy N. Schiffer, *Indian Dolls*, Schiffer Publishing, 1997; Peter N. Schiffer, *Indian Jewelry on the Market*, Schiffer Publishing, 1996; Lawrence N. Tully and Steven N. Tully, *Field Guide to Flint Arrowheads & Knives of North American Indians*, Collector Books, 1997, 2000 value update; Sarah Peabody Turnbaugh and William A. Turnbaugh, *Indian Baskets*, Schiffer Publishing, 1997; Barton Wright, *Hallmarks of the Southwest*, Schiffer Publishing, 2000.

Periodicals and Internet Resources: *American Indian Art Magazine*, 7314 E. Osborn Dr., Scottsdale, AZ 85251; *American Indian Basketry Magazine*, P.O. Box 66124, Portland, OR 97266; *Indian Artifact Magazine*, RD #1 Box 240, Turbotville, PA 17772, http://www.indian-artifacts.net; Longhouse Marketplace, http://www.indianbaskets.com; http://www.skookumgal.com; *The Indian Trader*, P.O. Box 1421, Gallup, NM 87305; *Whispering Wind Magazine*, P.O. Box 1390, Folsom, LA 70437, http://www.whisperingwind.com.

Collectors' Clubs: Antique Tribal Art Dealers Assoc., 215 Sierra SE, Albuquerque, NM 87108, http://www.atada.org; Genuine Indian Relic Society, 937 Eventide, Suite 2, San Antonio, TX 78209, http://www.artifactsetco.com/girs.htm; Indian Arts & Crafts Assoc., Suite B, 122 Laveta NE, Suite B, Albuquerque, NM 87108.

Museums: Amerind Foundation, Inc., Dragoon, AZ, http://www.amerind.org; The Heard Museum, Phoenix, AZ, http://www.heard.org; Colorado River Indian Tribes Museum, Parker, AZ; Favell Museum of Western Art & Indian Artifacts, Klamath Falls, OR, http://www.favellmuseum.com; Field Museum of Natural History, Chicago, IL, http://www.fieldmuseum.org; Grand Rapids Public

Museum, Grand Rapids, MI, http://www.grmuseum.org; Indian Center Museum, Wichita, KS; Institute of American Indian Arts Museum, Sante Fe, NM, http://www.iaiancad.org/museum; Inuit Art Centre, Ottawa, Ontario, Canada; Maryhill Museum of Art, Goldendale, WA, http://www.maryhillmuseum.org; Museum of New Mexico, Santa FE, NM, http://www.museumofnewmexico.org; Museum of the Cherokee Indian, Cherokee, NC, http://www.cherokeemuseum.org; National Museum of Natural History, Washington, DC, http://www.mnh.si.edu; National Museum of the American Indian, Washington, DC, http://www.si.edu/nmai; Navajo National Monument Museum, Tonalea, AZ, http://www.nps.gov/nava; Samuel K. Fox Museum, Dillingham, AK; Sheldon Jackson Museum, Sikta, AK; Southwest Museum, Los Angeles, CA, http://www.southwestmuseum.org; Totem Heritage Center, Ketchikan, AK; U.S. Dept. of the Interior Museum, Washington, DC, http://www.musuems.doi.gov/museum; Wheelwright Museum of the American Indian, Sante Fe, NM, http://www.wheelwright.org.

Adz, 8" l, Inuit, wood and ivory, wood handles, orig lashings, very dark patina **320.00**

Armband, 4-1/2" h, Northern Plains, possibly Crow, c1880, corrugated brass, partially legible orig tag "Crow Indian Armbands from 'Boy Chief of Crow,' Crow Agency, August 22, 1888," collected on Crow Reservation . **750.00**

Bag
8-1/2" l, Northern Plains, Crow, c1900, beaded hide, U-shaped, fringe at bottom, carrying strap, partially beaded on one side with classic Crow hourglass devices using typical Crow color seed beads **920.00**
14" l, Plains, Ute, c1870, rect buffalo hide, beaded on both sides, flap

with unusual Ute style linear geometric devices, bottom fringe **2,875.00**
16" x 9-1/2", Plateau, c1900, hide, rect form, beaded on front with warrior in profile, wearing feather headdress and necklace with heart-shaped medallion, various colored beads on light blue ground, contour overlay stitch, fringe at bottom, framed, not examined out of frame . . **1,725.00**

Bandolier bag, 40" l, Great Lakes, Ojibwa, c1900, wide shoulder strap beaded in meandering floral pattern, white ground, bag panel beaded with same motif, loom beaded tabs with yarn pompoms, backed in commercial cloth **1,495.00**

Basket
3-3/4" d, California, Pomo, late 19th C, gift, coiled, small compressed form, tightly woven with geometric devices, very fine feather tufts **1,265.00**
4-1/4" d, Northwest, Inuit, coiled baleen, tapered cylindrical form, woven in two shades of baleen, ivory disk base, ivory finial carved with pair of opposed seals, sgd "Eunice Hank" **1,380.00**
7" l, Northwest Coast, Tlingit, twined polychrome rattle top, lidded jar form, woven with bold false embroidered geometric devices using five colors **2,415.00**

Basketry bowl, coiled
3-1/4"h, Northern California, Hupa, early 20th C, globular form, two-color parallelograms, natural ground, old collection tag . . **550.00**
7" d, Western, Washo, c1900, slightly flared, simple stacked wedge devices **375.00**
21-1/2" d, California, Yokus, flaring, two bands of interlocking diamonds, minor stick loss, small rim break **2,990.00**

Basketry tray, 20-1/2" l, Northwest Coast, Tlingit, tightly twined oval, polychrome geometric devices, severe rim splits **350.00**

Belt, 23-1/2" l, Plains, c1900, hide, multicolored beadwork, early style barred design **350.00**

Belt pouch, 5" l, Plateau, c1900, beaded hide and cloth, fully beaded flap, simple multicolored floral device, pale blue ground, edge roll beaded, pouch with canvas facing **230.00**

Basket, Bridgeport tribe, woven decoration, two handles, shallow, **$300.**

Blanket, 2' 10" x 2' 10", Chimayo, hand woven, red, black, and white stripes and crillo design elements, gray ground, small holes **90.00**

Blanket strip, 58" l, Central Plains, Lakota, late 19th C, beaded hide, repeated cross roundel devices separated by barred zigzag devices, green, royal blue, white-center red, and metallic beads, white ground, water damage, bead loss **1,035.00**

Bottle, twined basketry cover
9-1/4" h, Northwest Coast, Tlingit, c1900, bands of repeated birds, simple fretz, openwork, glass decanter, minor fading **750.00**
11-1/4" h, Northern California, loosely wind form, simple geometric and two butterfly devices, glass bottle with broken top **175.00**

Bow, 47-1/2" l, Central Plains, last quarter 19th C, ash, tapered hand grip, double notch, twisted sinew string **750.00**

Bow case and quiver, 44" l, Southwest, Plains Apache, last quarter 19th C, hide bow case, red and yellow details, orig sinew-backed bow, well-worn quiver with eleven steel-tipped arrows, hide loss, stiffness to leather **2,415.00**

Bowl, pottery, Southwestern, Hopi, polychrome, red and dark brown slip, cream-colored ground
6" d, possibly Nampeyo, shallow, banded geometric devices, row of punctuate marks, sgd "Nampeyo" on bottom, two collection tags **750.00**
12" d, high rounded form, highly abstract avian devices, cross-hatching, two encircled stylized butterflies, corn logo at bottom **1,955.00**

Cane

31" l, Central Plains, probably Lakota, late 19th C, polychrome wood, carved as twined diamond-form snakes, traces of black and green pigments . **320.00**

36-1/2" l, Northwest Coast, late 19th C, carved totemic creatures, traces of pigment **1,380.00**

Club, Scull Cracker, Central Plains, probably Lakota, last quarter 19th C, rawhide wrapped wood handle

31" l, elliptical quartz head, roll beaded adornment attached to handle, traces of red pigment, head damaged **350.00**

33" l, elliptical stone head, beaded horsehair adornment attached go handle, red pigment on handle **375.00**

Cradle, 31" l, Plains, probably Cheyenne, c1880, buffalo hide form beaded with classic Cheyenne pattern, white-center red, green, and dark blue beads, white ground, hide board attachments remaining on back, orig tag reads "Crow Indian Baby cov from 'Spotted Tail' Crow Agency Montana, Ter. May 30th, 1888," collected on Crow Reservation. **1,500.00**

Cradleboard, 27" l, Central Plains, probably Cheyenne, beaded buffalo hide form attached to later boards, large stepped diamond devices, bottle green, greasy yellow, translucent rose, black, and white seed beads, bead loss **18,400.00**

Doll, female form

15" h, Northern Plains, c1900, muslin form, black trade cloth dress, yoke dec with dentilia shells, beaded belt, leggings, moccasins, facial features, some cloth **1,610.00**

15-1/2" h, Northern Plains, late 19th C, beaded cloth and hide, velvet and cloth dress, tubular beads at yoke, beaded leggings and moccasins, buckskin face with bead detailing, hair loss . **1,150.00**

18" h, Ute, late 19th C, floor length buckskin dress, multicolored beadwork detailing, face with bead and paint detailing, red cloth belt with orig tag "Ute Near Pine River Col." **3,115.00**

Doll, male form

15-1/2" h, Central Plains, probably Arapaho, late 19th C, muslin form, partially beaded and fringed buckskin shirt and leggings, hard

sole moccasins with Maltese cross devices, beaded eyes . . . **1,840.00**

15-1/2" h, Central Plains, c1900, partially beaded shirt and leggings, beaded belt, moccasins and facial details **1,150.00**

15-1/2" h, Southwest, late 19th C, partially beaded, beaded facial details, hide ears with dentilia shell ear pendants, fringe and hawkbell attachments on each hip, hair remnant, traces of orange-red pigment overall. **1,725.00**

Dress, child's, trade cloth, 30" l, Central Plains, late 19th C, blue, calico edged neck, six rows of dentilia shells sewn around collar, further dec with sequins, brass bells, and ribbon, minor loss **3,740.00**

Drum, 24" h, Southwest, possibly Taos, hollow cylindrical form, rawhide laced to each end, carved wood body painted earth red, two black stripes **1,610.00**

Fetish figure, carved stone, Southwest

5-1/2" l, probably Zia, c19th C, seated figure, relief carved legs and arms, head with broad nose, shallow round eyes possibly inlaid with mica, chest inlaid with irregular piece of turquoise, string necklace of early green turquoise beads with abalone pendant, smooth patina from handling **4,025.00**

6-1/2" l, probably Zuni, c late 19th C, bear form, hunched back . **575.00**

10" h, c19th C, volcanic stone, possibly representing snake, eyes inlaid with old turquoise beds, smaller stone piece tied to back with buckskin, traces of red pigment **520.00**

Half leggings, 19" l, Northern Plains, Crow, c1880, hide, lined with calico, partially beaded in multicolored Crow floral devices, traces of red ochre, collected on Crow Reservation in late 1880s. **920.00**

Handbag, 8-3/4" l, Plateau, late 19th C, beaded cloth and hide, rect canvas form, beaded on both sides, bold simple geometric devices, different color backgrounds, edged at opening, red trade cloth and buckskin . . **210.00**

Jar, pottery

8" h, Southwest, possibly Tesuque, bulbous form, black curvilinear devices, cream-colored slip, red bands painted on inside rim and below cream-colored slip. **1,380.00**

9" h, convex bottom, seed jar form, two bands of geometric devices, red pinstripe around neck and bottom. **920.00**

Kachina, Southwest, polychrome carved wood and cloth10-1/4" l, Hopi, first quarter 20th C, painted kilt, red and yellow body paint, large white case mask with protruding ears, snout, and Popeyes, black and red stepped devices connecting eyes and ears **2,070.00**

10-1/2" l, Hopi, early 20th C, cottonwood form, painted kilt and sash, traces of blue paint on upper torso and head, ears and part of one arm missing **865.00**

15" h, probably Zuni, c1940, cottonwood form, painted tablita, horsehair beard and hair, cloth clothing and sash, articulated arms **1,725.00**

Knife case, 11-1/4" l, Northern Plains, Crow, c1880s, beaded rawhide, knife shape, stained red on front and flap, partially beaded dark blue, green, light blue, greasy yellow, and white sawtooth pattern, two brass tacks remaining, orig tag reads "Indian Knife Sheath from Buffalo Calf, a Crow Indian, Crow Agency, Montana Ter. April 3rd, 1889," collected on Crow Reservation **3,450.00**

Mask, wood, painted

6-1/4" h, Inuit, northern Alaska, last half 19th C, hollow oval form, brow line in form of stylized whale fin, small round pierced eyes, pierced smiling mouth, traces of red pigment on upper lip, two small holes for attachment, minor wood loss **5,465.00**

10" l, Northwest, Iroquois, 20th C, hollow oval form, pierced eyes, large nose, pierced toothy grin, brown and red pigments. . . **490.00**

11-1/2" l, Cherokee, carved hollow tapered form, down turned pierced mouth, four top row teeth, prominent nose, pierced nostrils, pierced eyes, two short curved horns with intertwined rattlesnake, red and black pigments . **4,600.00**

14-1/2" l, Northwest Coast, early 20th C, hollow oval form crudely carved, pierced indented eyes, long nose, oval mouth, partially painted, black, blue, green, and red pigments **2,645.00**

Moccasins, pr, infant's, Woodlands, probably Micmac, mid-19th C, puckered tow soft hide, red cloth cuffs and vamps, beaded geometric and floral devices, multicolored small seed beads, silk ribbon ties **1,265.00**

Moccasins, pr, child's

4-1/4" l, Central Plains, Lakota, early 20th C, soft hide uppers sinew beaded with typical Lakota designs, orig tag "Sioux Indian Moccasins given N. B. Ward by Crazy Bull, grandson of Sitting Bull" **575.00**

5-1/2" l, Northern Plains, possibly Crow, c1880, soft sole side-seamed, beaded on vamps and along seam, multicolored linear devices, medium blue ground **1,100.00**

Moccasins, pr, man's, beaded hide, Central Plains, Lakota, 19th C

9-1/2" l, soft hide uppers beaded with simple geometric devices, damage to seams **320.00**

10" l, fully beaded uppers, dark blue buffalo tracks, polychrome geometric devices on white border, remnants of beaded tongues, buffalo rawhide soles **520.00**

10" l, fully beaded uppers, geometric and tipi devices, wine red, greasy yellow, and medium green beads **350.00**

10" l, soft hide uppers beaded with typical multicolored geometric designs, dark blue ground, hard soles, stiffness to hide **575.00**

Moccasins, pr, woman's

24" l, high-top, Southwest, Apache, first quarter 20th C, yellow stained tops and bottoms, rawhide soles with Cactus Kicker toes, beaded Maltese crosses on vamps, dark red, dark blue, and white seed beads **920.00**

Olla, pottery, Southwest

10" h, San Ildefonso, c1900, indented base, globular body, painted red and black, cream-colored clip, abstract floral devices on body, neck with band of tapered triangular devices, surface loss to lower body, rim crack **4,025.00**

10-1/2" h, Acoma, late 19th C, high rounded sides, tapering neck and concave base, orange, red, and dark brown slip, cream-colored ground, four large Acoma parrots, foliate, and rainbow devices, repaired neck section **8,625.00**

11" h, Santa Domingo, flared neck, black geometric bands, cream-colored ground, chips, repairs **3,740.00**

Paddle, 65-1/2" l, Northeast, carved wood, round shaft, stylized handgrip **375.00**

Parfleche case, Central Plains, Lakota, c1900, polychrome

11" l, small rect case lashed with buckskin, painted red, blue, yellow, and green pigment geometric and hourglass devices **920.00**

12-1/2" l, small tubular lidded case laced with hide over blue trade cloth, blue, red, green, and yellow stacked triangular motifs . . . **920.00**

Parfleche envelope, 25" l, Central Plains, c1900, front flaps painted with hourglass devices, blue, yellow, red, and green pigments **865.00**

Photograph, Standing Bear, Ponca Chief, Charles M. Bell, photographer, silver print, mounted on larger gray card-stock with Bell's Washington, DC blindstamp, $825. Photo courtesy of Cowan Historic Americana Auctions.

Pipe bag, beaded hide

18" l, Plains, Cheyenne, c1870, four-tab top edge beaded in white and white-center red seed beads, buckskin bag sinew sewn with three feather devices on each side, typical bar design pattern, white, dark bottle green, pumpkin, and Kiowa red, traces of yellow pigment on fringe and bag **6,900.00**

19" l, Central Plains, Lakota, late 19th C, buckskin bag roll beaded at top with three lanes of beadwork descending to lower panel beaded in multicolored geometric devices, white ground, horse track design, multicolored quilled slats and restored fringe hang below the panel, further beaded and quill attachments, traces of yellow pigment **1,955.00**

31" l, Northern Plains, Cree, c1880, six-tab top edge beaded in pink, panel beaded on both sides with multicolored bilateral floral devices, white ground, fringe with dark bugle bead attachments on top **1,725.00**

32" l, Central Plains, Lakota, late 19th C, native tanned hide bag, three rows of beadwork descending to central panel, split hourglass devices on both sides, bottom panel with quill wrapped slat, tin cone and feather danglers and fringe, beaded lizard fetish tied to one side of upper bags, tears to hide **1,265.00**

35" l, Central Plains, Lakota, last quarter 19th C, yellow stained buckskin bag, row of beadwork at top, three rows of lazy-stitch beadwork descending to a lower beaded panel, both sides beaded with typical Lakota dark blue, white centered, and green designs on white ground, below beaded panel are quill wrapped rawhide slats and long yellow stained fringe, "C. E. Dallin" printed on upper part **3,220.00**

Pictorial bag, 11" x 8-1/4", Plateau, early 20th C, beaded cloth, partially beaded on front, man and woman in full attire, each holding up black tipped feather in their right hand, framed, damage to cloth bag, not examined out of frame **2,530.00**

Pipe

8-1/2" l, Northwest Coast, Haida, 19th C, carved argillite, tubular stem, carved totemic creatures forming bowl, not pierced for smoking **2,875.00**

13" l, Plains, late 19th C, wood and stone, short rect polychrome stem, carved mouthpiece in form of bird's head, red pipe stone elbow-type bowl, cracked and repaired **150.00**

Pipe bag, 28" l, Central Plains, probably Lakota, c1900, buffalo upper with no dec, central panel beaded on both sides with typical polychrome geometric devices, white ground, lower panel on polychrome quill-wrapped slats and fringe. **865.00**

Pipe tomahawk, 21-1/2" l, Plains, hand forged head, ash stem pierced for smoking, file burned, incised with lightning device, pierced for suspension, further dec with 40 flat-top brass tacks, gasket replaced, collected in Colorado at end of 19th C, descended in family **14,950.00**

Pouch, beaded hide

4-1/2" l, Northern Plain, Crow, c1880, rect commercial hide, beaded on front in geometric devices, white-center red, dark and light blue, greasy yellow seed beads, tin cone danglers along bottom, orig tag "From the Crow Indian 'Alligator' Crow Agency Montana Ty April 27th 1888," collected on Crow Reservation **2,760.00**

5" l, Central Plains, probably Cheyenne, c1880, rect buffalo hide, beaded on front in typical Cheyenne pattern, white-center red, dark blue, and green, white ground, tin cones on flap and bottom, orig tag "Crow Indian Ration Ticket Case, from 'Shows A Fish' Crow Agency, Montana, April 9, 1889," collected on Crow Reservation **2,415.00**

5" l, Southwest, Apache, late 19th C, round, beaded flap, one side beaded with black and white center red geometric devices, white ground, tin cone danglers around edge **750.00**

6" l, Southwest, Apache, late 19th C, round, small flap beaded on one side with multicolored four-point devices, amber ground, tine cone danglers around edge. **920.00**

10-1/2" l, Northern Plains, Crow, c1870, sq buffalo hide pouch, long triangular flap beaded with classic Crow geometric devices, white-center red, green, dark blue, and white on medium blue ground, long unadorned belt, quill-wrapped fringes, orig tag "Sioux Indian Man's Ornament used by dancers Crow Agency Montana 1889," some bead loss, collected on Crow Reservation **14,950.00**

Rug, Navaho

2' 10" x 4' 7", Two Grey Hills, elongated sunrise design, spun and hand-carded wool, black, white, and gray, attached tag "Genuine Navaho Rug by Alfreda James Two Grey Hills" **275.00**

2' 10" x 5' 4-1/2", western regional, expanding serrate "X" design, gray, light brown, red, white, and black, fret border in light brown, white, and black **250.00**

3' 2-1/2" x 5' 8", Two Grey Hills, early, hand-carved wood, gray, natural, black, and tan, intricate stepped designs, each centered by stylized butterfly, some edge damage **225.00**

3' 9" x 4' 8", Ganado, stepped motif of two interlocking diamonds, deep red, dark brown, and cream, red ground, cream and brown stepped borders, c1930, minor stains **1,610.00**

3' 9" x 4' 5", red, dark brown, sienna, and cream geometric motifs, natural light brown ground, dark brown border, c1920 . . . . **1,855.00**

3' 11" x 6' 4", zigzag and broken lines, natural cream, light and dark brown, light brown ground, c1910 . . . . **1,840.00**

4' 2" x 5' 5", early Ganado area, finely hand-carded wool, black, white, tan, double dye red cross center, fret and geometric design . **700.00**

4' 6" x 7' 4", crystal regional weaving, spun and hand-carded wool, shaded gray/tan and natural white, minor wear, light stains, one end rebound **965.00**

Saddle blanket

Central Plains, Lakota, late 19th C, beaded hide, rect, extended corners, beaded multicolored geometric devices, white ground, severe hide stiffness, bead loss, 32" l. **815.00**

Navaho, red and orange stripes, corner blocks centered by geometric stylized butterflies, 2' 6" x 2' 6" **150.00**

Scepter, 33" l, Northeast, 19th C, carved wood, tapered form, profusely carved spiral, linear, and geometric devices, knobbed end carved with myriad devices, including snake, turtle, heart, and human face, dark patina **425.00**

Shot pouch, 27" l, Western Great Lakes, possibly Cree, mid-19th C, red cloth strap, black cloth inlay, olive worsted tape binding, partially beaded with liner and connecting diamond devices, white seed beads, U-shaped pouch with central bilateral floral device, edge of beaded triangular silk ribbon appliqué, beads in three shades of blue, green, red, clear, and greasy yellow, blue cloth pouch backing has been replaced **9,775.00**

Skirt, Northern California, probably Yurok, 19th C, back skirt an entire deerskin folded laterally, dec with thin strips wrapped with three colored maiden hair fern fibers, fringe dec with small white clam shells, large abalone plaques, and glass grade beads, smaller front apron of long buckskin fringe wrapped and braided with vegetal fibers, trimmed white olivella shells, minor damage to buckskin **36,800.00**

Snow snake, 92" l, Northwest, Iroquois, late 19th C, wood and metal, long rounded form, flattened belly, pointed end with pewter cap. **435.00**

Totem pole, Northwest Coast, carved wood

24" h, flat backed, bears and eagles, commercial paint details, first half 20th C **575.00**

31" h, openwork carved pole, frogs, birds, fish, and humans, whole cov with coat of commercial paint, "Sitka Alaska, July 1901" written on base, wood loss **2,415.00**

64" h, animal forms, avian, bear, and human, traces of pigment **2,070.00**

113", hollowed stem, raven, shaman eating frog, tribal chief eating frog, painted commercial pigments, collected in 1953, southeastern Alaska **5,750.00**

Vest, child's, Central Plains, Lakota, late 19th C, beaded hide, outside fully beaded with multicolored geometric designs on white ground, 15" h, severe water damage, bead loss **575.00**

Vest, child's, Central Plans, Lakota, late 19th C, front with geometric devices, back with two back-to-back flags and two facing elks, medium green, royal blue, faceted brass, white-center red beads on white ground, bead loss, heavy water damage **2,875.00**

Vest, man's, Central Plains, Lakota, late 19th C, fully beaded hide, geometric and tipi devices, typical Lakota colors,

white ground, damage, bead loss
. . . . **2,300.00**

War club, Central Plains, probably Lakota, last quarter 19th C, rawhide wrapped wood handle stained dark blue, ax-shaped white quartz head, quilled horsehair adornment attached to handle, 29-1/2" h **420.00**

Watch case, 7" l, Northern Plains, Crow, c1880, beaded cloth and hide, teardrop form, beaded front with multicolored geometric devices, back cov in calico, orig tag "Watch case made by Crow Indian half breed Martha Rumpard, Crow Agency, Mont., ty 1888," collected from Crow Reservation **1,265.00**

INK BOTTLES

History: Ink was sold in glass or pottery bottles in the early 1700s in England. Retailers mixed their own formula and bottled it. The commercial production of ink did not begin in England until the late 18th century and in America until the early 19th century.

Initially, ink was supplied in often poorly manufactured pint or quart bottles from which smaller bottles could be filled. By the mid-19th century, when writing implements had been improved, emphasis was placed on making an "untippable" bottle. Shapes ranging from umbrellas to turtles were tried. Since ink bottles were usually displayed, shaped or molded bottles were popular.

The advent of the fountain pen relegated the ink bottle to the back drawer. Bottles lost their decorative design and became merely functional items.

References: Ralph & Terry Kovel, *Kovels' Bottles Price List*, 11th ed., Three Rivers Press, 1999; John Odell, *Digger Odell's Official Antique Bottle and Glass Collector Magazine Price Guide Series*, Vol. 4, published by author (1910 Shawhan Road, Morrow, OH 45152), 1995.

Periodical: *Antique Bottle and Glass Collector*, P.O. Box 187, East Greenville, PA 18041.

Additional Listings: See *Warman's Americana & Collectibles* for more examples.

Cardinals ink, amber bottle, raised lettering, 1-3/4" d, 3-1/2" h **25.00**

Carter's

Cathedral, cobalt blue, emb lettering, orig cap, 3" d, 9" h
. . . . **250.00**

Permanent Blue-Black, orig paper label, some rusting to metal cap
. . . . **4.00**

Cylindrical, 5-5/8" h, America, 1840-60, "Harrison's Columbia Ink," cobalt blue, applied flared mouth, pontil scar, 3" crack, mouth roughness, C #764
. . . . **140.00**

Aqua, applied lip and collar, c1880, 3" h, **$12.**

Figural, America, 1860-90

2" h, house, domed offset neck for, emb architectural features of front door and four windows, colorless, sheared mouth, smooth base, Carter's Ink, some remaining int. ink residue, C #614 . . . . **650.00**

2" h, locomotive, aquamarine, ground mouth, smooth base, C #715 . . . . **800.00**

2-3/8" h, log cabin, rect, colorless, tooled sq collared mouth, smooth base, pinhead-sized hole in one base corner, some int. haze, C #680 . . . . **190.00**

2-5/8" h, house, 1 1/2-story cottage form, full label on reverse "Bank of Writing Fluid, Manuf by the Senate Ink Co Philadelphia," aquamarine, tooled sq collared mouth, smooth base, small area of label slightly faded, C# 682 . . . . **300.00**

Hexagonal, 9-7/8" h, America, 1900-20, "Carter," cathedral panels, colorless with pale yellow cast, machined mouth, smooth base, similar to C #820 . **700.00**

Inverted Concial

2-3/8" h, Stoddard, NH, 1846-1860, deep yellow-olive, sheared mouth, pontil scar, pinhead flake on mouth edge, C #15 . . . . **170.00**

2-1/2" h, America, 1840-60, medium cobalt blue, tooled mouth, tubular pontil scar, C #23 . . . . **800.00**

2-1/2" h, America, 1840-60, "Woods/Black Ink/Portland," aquamarine, inward rolled mouth, pontil scar, C #12, unearthed with some remaining stain **170.00**

Caw's Ink, New York, 1-7/8" square, 2-1/4" h, **$20.**

Octagonal

G. H. Gilbert Co., West Brookfield, MA, orig label **150.00**

Harrison's Colombian Ink, light green
. . . . **60.00**

Laughlin's And Bushfield Wheeling Va., 2-7/8" h, aquamarine, inward rolled mouth, pontil scar . . **300.00**

Sanford's, 2-1/4" h, 3-3/4" l, sterling silver stopper with flag and star dec
. . . . **125.00**

Sawyer's Crystal Blue Ink, 6-1/4" h
. . . . **10.00**

Umbrella, America, 1840-60

2-1/8" h, 12-sided, sapphire blue, inward rolled mouth, pontil, scar, C #182, professionally cleaned
. . . . **950.00**

2-1/4" h, New England, 1840-60, octagonal, golden amber, sheared mouth, C #145 . . . . **160.00**

2-3/8" h, octagonal, sapphire blue, inward rolled mouth, pontil, scar, C #141 . . . . **700.00**

2-5/8" h, octagonal, lime green, labeled "Williams/Black/Empire/Ink/ New York," tooled mouth, smooth base, label 95 percent intact, C #173 . . . . **160.00**

2-5/8" h, octagonal, sapphire blue, inward rolled mouth, pontil, scar, C #129 . . . . **950.00**

2-5/8" h, octagonal, yellow, inward rolled mouth, pontil, scar, C#129
. . . . **1,200**

Doll, Kammer & Reinhardt, 27" h, **$1,900**; early Steiff teddy bear, 12", **$950**. Photo courtesy of McMasters Doll Auction.

Doll, early Kestner, brown hair, brown paperweight eyes, feathered brows, closed mouth, marked "13," 19" l, **$2,200**. Photo courtesy of McMasters Doll Auction.

Baby buggy, ornate wicker, red velvet upholstery, **$425**. Photo courtesy of Joy Luke Auctions.

Art pottery, Frederick Rhead, University City, jardinière, incised with clusters of light blue trees, green field and yucca plants, ivory clouds, white semi-matte ground, incised HR/UC/1911/JUNE, some burst bubbles, 8-3/4" x 9-3/4", **$21,850**. Photo courtesy of David Rago Auctions.

T & G Limoges porcelain dresser tray decorated with portraits of George and Martha Washington, **$150**. Photo courtesy of Joy Luke Auctions.

Chintz teapot, James Kent, Rosalynde, **$350**. Photo courtesy of Susan Scott.

Chintz jam pot, Royal Winton, Royalty, **$250**. Photo courtesy of Susan Scott.

*Mulberry china, chamber pot with lid, Pelew pattern, made by Challinor, **$300**. Photo courtesy of Ellen King.*

*American hand-painted china jewelry, belt buckle brooch, 1-7/8" x 2-3/8" oval, decorated with bachelor buttons on a polychrome ground, irregular burnished gold border outlined in black, gold-plated bezel, 1900-1917, **$85**. Photo courtesy of Dorothy Kamm.*

*Pickard lemonade pitcher decorated with blackberries, signed Yeschek, 8-3/4" diameter, 1910-1912 mark, **$1,700**. Photo courtesy of Joy Luke Auctions.*

*Rookwood, vessel, Carved Matte, by William Hentschel, 1910, Glasgow roses under burgundy and teal blue glaze, flame mark/X/1110/WEH, 4" x 5 1/2", **$815**. Photo courtesy of David Rago Auctions.*

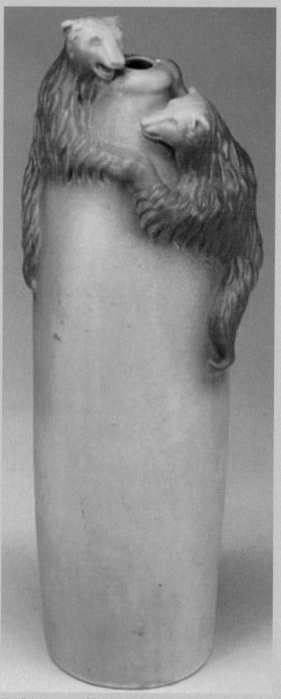

Nippon China, vase, two handles, Egyptian warship, scrolled gold moriage decoration, green M wreath mark, 11" h, **$935**. Photo courtesy of Jackson's Auction.

Van Briggle, vase, "Climbing for Honey," two bears hugging rim, blue and turquoise matte glaze, 1920s, marked "AA VAN BRIGGLE/USA," 5-1/2" d, 16" h, **$3,220**. Photo courtesy of David Rago Auctions.

Pickard China, vase, peacock on black ground, signed "Marker," 1925-30 mark, 8-1/4" h, **$600**. Photo courtesy of Joy Luke Auctions.

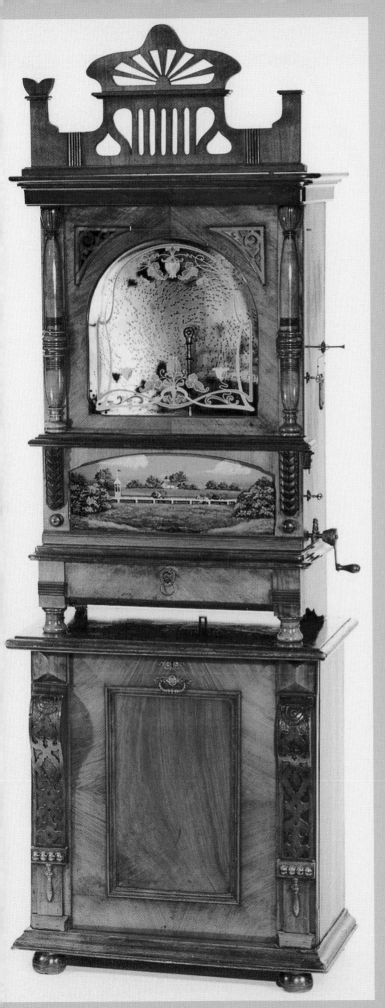

World War I Bond poster, designed by Charles Leydendecker, **$275**. Photo courtesy of David Rago Auctions.

Music box, Kalliope Panorama Automata, coin operated, German, c1905, rare horse game, **$24,100**. Photo courtesy of Auction Team Breker.

Handel, table lamp, bent caramel slag glass shade with applied metal and glass cattail decoration in russet and green, bronzed base, both shade and base stamped "Handel," 19-3/4" x 18", **$5,750**. Photo courtesy of David Rago Auctions.

Desk, Hepplewhite, New England, tiger maple, slant fall front, fitted interior, four-drawer dovetailed case, French bracket feet, shaped frieze, original hardware, 34" h writing surface, 42" h overall, **$9,100**. Photo courtesy of Sanford Alderfer Auction Co.

Indian basket, Northwest Coast, 9" h, **$700**. Photo courtesy of Jackson's Auction.

Cufflink box, hammered copper, embossed with quatrefoil and lined in leather, marked "KK," for Karl Kipp, old cleaning to patina, 2" x 6-1/2" x 3-1/4", **$2,550**. Photo courtesy of David Rago Auctions.

Crock, T. Harrington, Lyons, five gallon, large signature star-face decoration, professional restoration to full-length hairline on left side, c1850, 11-1/2" h, **$3,850**. Photo courtesy of Bruce and Vicki Waasdorp.

Silver, sterling chalice, **$5,750**. Photo courtesy of Jackson's Auction.

American hand-painted china, cup and saucer, decorated with conventional Celtic border design in celadon, light blue border, ivory center, cup bottom and interiors, burnished gold rims and handle, signed "L.E.S.," marked with crown in double circle, "Victoria, Austria," 1900-1920, **$30**. Photo courtesy of Dorothy Kamm.

Pitcher, blue and white spongeware, bulbous-shaped base, 9" h, **$385**. Photo courtesy of Bruce and Vicki Waasdorp.

Mexican Border Patrol grouping, Sgt. Orie Donley, two uniforms, three hats, cartridge belt, spats, two newspapers, and trunk, **$2,750**. Photo courtesy of Jackson's Auction.

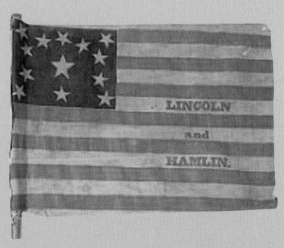

Flag, Lincoln & Hamlin, campaign, printed linen, unusual patterned canton, 12 small stars, one center larger star, canton rests on so-called "blood stripe" with names printed in white stripes in red, mounted with tacks to old wood shaft, linen slightly toned, two tears along border of red and white bars, modern shadow box frame with acid-free backing, **$11,825**. Photo courtesy of Cowan Historic Americana Auctions.

Newcomb College vase, by Corrine Marie Chalaron, 1923, ovoid, matte, decorated with broad leaves alternating with yellow and white stylized blossoms on denim blue ground, marked "NC/JM/MZ61/82/CMC," 8" x 4", **$4,320**. Photo courtesy of David Rago Auctions.

INKWELLS

History: Most of the commonly found inkwells were produced in the United States or Europe between the early 1800s and the 1930s. The most popular materials were glass and pottery because these substances resisted the corrosive effects of ink.

Inkwells were a sign of the office or wealth of an individual. The common man tended to dip his ink directly from the bottle. The years between 1870 and 1920 represent the golden age of inkwells when elaborate designs were produced.

References: Veldon Badders, *Collector's Guide to Inkwells: Identification and Values*, Book I (1995, 1998 value update), Book II, 1998, Collector Books; William E. Covill, Jr., *Inkbottles and Inkwells*, William S. Sullwold Publishing, out of print; Jean and Franklin Hunting, *The Collector's World of Inkwells*, Schiffer Publishing, 2000.

Collectors' Clubs: St. Louis Inkwell Collectors Society, P.O. Box 29396, St. Louis, MO 63126; The Society of Inkwell Collectors, 10 Meadow Drive, Spencerport, NY 14559, http://www.soic.com; Writing Equipment Society, 22 Strathmore Ave., Hull, HU6 7HJ UK.

Additional Listings: See *Warman's Americana & Collectibles* for more examples.

Figural, eagle with outstretched wings, supports for pen, silver, 6" h, $225. Photo courtesy of Joy Luke Auctions.

Brass

Embossed, double, two porcelain inserts, late 19th/early 20th C, 10-1/2" l, 6-1/2" w **150.00**

Engraved peaked cornice-form backplate cut with central trefoil and flowers, cabochon bloodstone surrounded by four cabochon red stones, rect base with engraved border, central cut glass well flanked by turned pen supports, Gothic Revival style, England, third quarter 19th C, 9-1/4" l, 5-7/8" h
. . . . **250.00**

Raised birds, cattails, flowers, sq base, ball feet, hinged lid with serpent finial, shell handles
. . . . **500.00**

Bronze

Central lidded baluster form inkwell, round dish raised on quadripartite leaf-form bronze base, dark green enamel ground, stylized foliate bands with gilt accents, faux jewelling, French, late 19th C, 8" d, 5-1/2" h **435.00**

Figural, woman, designed by George Bareau, stamped "Barbedienne" **5,000.00**

Gilt bronze, figure of recumbent Abyssinian-style lion, flanked by two inkwells with diagonal bands of paterae, flat leaf and acanthus borders, green marble ogee base with pen well, early 20th C, 14-1/2" l, 7" w **250.00**

Grapevine pattern, Tiffany, dark patina, green glass liner, orig insert, bakelite dipper, sgd
. . . . **975.00**

Freeblown glass, 1-3/4" h, attributed to America, 1840-60, sq, opaque electric blue, flared mouth, pontil scar. . **120.00**

Glass, crystal
Square, four molded rococo feet, 3-1/4" w, 3-1/2" h
. . . . **175.00**
Swirled design, brass collar . **225.00**

Gilt metal, 11" l, 4-1/2" h, double, Moorish pattern, cast brass, two hinged-top inkwells with hooks to hold pen, base imp "Tiffany & Co," foot restored, pen missing **345.00**

Grain-painted finish, stenciled dec, five quill holds, two orig inserts, bottom labeled "Silliman & Co, Chester, CT," 1820. . . . . **260.00**

Marble, 9-1/2" l, Sienna, modeled after sarcophagus of Lucius Seipio, Italian, 19th C **2,000.00**

Paperweight, 6-1/4" h, 4-1/2" d, multicolored concentric millefiore, base with 1848 date canes, Whitefriars
. . . . **175.00**

Porcelain, white ground, pink edge, gold floral decoration, German, $60.

Pearlware, 5-1/2" h, gilt highlights, imp "By F. Bridges, Phrenologist," and "EM" on base, England, 19th C, very minor chips, gilt wear **520.00**

Stoneware

Brushed cobalt blue on top, imp "C. Crolius.Manhattan-Wells, New York," 3-1/8" d, 1-5/8" h, few chips on base **3,200.00**

Incised oval stamp "C. Crolius Stone Ware Manufacturer Manhatten Wells, New York," flat cylindrical form, incised edges, upper one enhanced with cobalt blue slip, center well surrounded by three pen holders, 3-1/2" d, 1-1/4" h, three lower edge chips
. . . . **2,990.00**

Wood, Matthew Bolton, Birmingham, c1795, rect, emb silver mounts, gadroon and shell edge, two silver mounted cut glass inkwells in gardrooned holders, four scroll legs, paw feet, 14" l, 10" w **1,725.00**

IRONS

History: Ironing devices have been used for many centuries, with the earliest references dating from 1100. Irons from the medieval, Renaissance, and early industrial eras can be found in Europe, but are rare. Fine engraved brass irons and hand-wrought irons predominated prior to 1850. After 1850, the iron underwent a series of rapid evolutionary changes.

Between 1850 and 1910, irons were heated in four ways: 1) a hot metal slug was inserted into the body, 2) a burning solid, e.g., coal or charcoal, was placed in the body, 3) a liquid or gas, e.g., alcohol, gasoline, or natural gas, was fed from an external tank and burned in the body, or 4) conduction heat, usually drawing heat from a stove top.

Electric irons are just beginning to find favor among iron collectors.

References: Dave Irons, *Even More Irons by Irons*, published by author, (223 Covered Bridge Road, Northampton, PA 18067), 2000; ——, *Irons by Irons*, published by author 1994; ——, *More Irons by Irons*, published by author, 1997; ——, *Pressing Iron Patents*, published by author, 1994.

Collectors' Clubs: Club of the Friends of Ancient Smoothing Irons, P.O. Box 215, Carlsbad, CA 92008; Midwest Sad Iron Collectors Club, 24 Nob Hill Dr., St. Louis, MO 63138.

Web site: www.ironsantiques.com

Museums: Henry Ford Museum, Dearborn, MI; Shelburne Museum, Shelburne, VT; Sturbridge Village, Sturbridge, MA.

Additional Listings: See *Warman's Americana & Collectibles* for more examples.

Advisers: David and Sue Irons.

Slug, cast iron, turned and incised wood handle, cast iron slug, c1850, **$95.**

Charcoal, box

Brittany, cut work on sides, French
.... **200.00**
Dutch cut work, all brass...... **200.00**
Eclipse, patent Aug. 25, 1903.. **125.00**
Ne Plus Ultra, double chimney . **200.00**
Victorian Reg, turned chimney, English
.... **100.00**

Children's

Asbestos sadiron, two pieces, 1900
.... **50.00**
Charcoal, 3-1/2", tall chimney .. **300.00**
Detachable handle, 3-5/8"...... **65.00**
French cast iron, emb rooster, 4"
.... **170.00**
Ober, sleeve, 4-1/2".......... **150.00**
Sensible No. 0, two pieces, 4".. **120.00**
The Gem **180.00**
The Pearl **100.00**

Flat iron

Asbestos sadiron, two pieces ... **50.00**
All cast, anchor symbol........ **25.00**
Belgium, round back, "L" handle
.... **150.00**
Cast iron, slip-out handle...... **200.00**
Hoods Patent 1867, stone base **200.00**
Keystone symbol, double pointed
.... **150.00**
Le Gaiffa, No. 5, French **80.00**
Slant handle, two pieces...... **150.00**
Universal Thermo Cell, 1911, two
pieces **140.00**
Fluter, combination type, wire clip
closure, August 1870......... **140.00**

Fluter, machine type
Manville, cone shape **1,000.00**
The Original Knox **150.00**
Welcome, American Machine .. **130.00**

Fluter, rocker type
Geneva, 1866................ **85.00**
Lady Friend **150.00**
The Erie Fluter, Griswold, clip handle
.... **250.00**

Fluter, roller type
CW Whitfield................ **150.00**
Geneva, 3-1/2" **500.00**
Shepard Hardware Co........ **130.00**

Box, lift gate, wood handle, **$120.**

Goffering iron

Decorative cast base, single barrel
.... **400.00**
Handmade, monkey tail standard
.... **800.00**
Ribbon, 2" barrel, "S" wire **150.00**
S wire standard, round cast base **80.00**

Liquid fuel

Coleman, Model 4A, blue....... **80.00**
Comfort Iron **60.00**
German Alcohol, Feldmeyer type
.... **125.00**
Jubilee Iron................. **120.00**
Sun Mfg. Co................. **100.00**

Liquid fuel, natural gas
Acetylene Stove Mfg. Co........ **60.00**
Central Flat Iron Mfg. Go........ **60.00**
Uneedit Gas Iron **85.00**
Wright Patent 1911........... **120.00**

Mangle boards

Horse handle, geometric carved
designs.................... **600.00**
Plain handle, painted designs, dated
.... **175.00**

Miscellaneous

Advertising tip tray, Best Automatic
Electric Iron, by Dover........ **140.00**
Advertising trade card, featuring fluter
.... **35.00**
Candy mold.................. **35.00**
Patent model of iron **500.00**
Pin cushion, Victorian **150.00**
Pyramid heater, holds three irons
.... **150.00**
Suitcase iron, Iro case........ **200.00**
Toy, wind-up, ironing monkey .. **300.00**

Slug irons

Belgium, drop-in-the-back, slug, "L"
handle **200.00**
English, box, lift gate......... **100.00**
European, ox tongue type, brass
.... **250.00**
Magic, clip-off handle **350.00**
Portuguese, box, brass, cut work posts
.... **130.00**
Scottish, box, brass turned posts
.... **700.00**

Sleeve, Grand Union Tea Co., Scranton, Pa., c1870, removable bentwood handle, 4-1/2" h, 8" l, **$60.**

Special purpose

Ball iron, hand held **80.00**
Billiard table, rectangular **150.00**
Edge iron, scissors type **70.00**
French polisher, wavy bottom .. **200.00**
Glove form, brass **240.00**
Hat iron, brass.............. **120.00**
Hat iron, hotwater, English..... **240.00**
Hat iron, rotary, English **170.00**
Leaf iron, two pieces......... **125.00**
Mangle Machine, cast frame, wood
rollers..................... **200.00**
Plaiter, weights, clamps, etc.... **400.00**
Polisher, slip-out handle **250.00**
Polishing, Genoa, grid bottom .. **80.00**
Seam iron, narrow body **300.00**
Sleeve, Grand Union.......... **45.00**
Sleeve, Sensible No. 5, two pieces
.... **50.00**
Sleeve, Sherman's Improved .. **125.00**

IRONWARE

History: Iron, a metallic element that occurs abundantly in combined forms, has been known for centuries. Items made from iron range from the utilitarian to the decorative. Early hand-forged ironwares are of considerable interest to Americana collectors.

References: *Collectors Guide to Wagner Ware and Other Companies*, L-W Book Sales, 1994; Douglas Congdon-Martin, *Figurative Cast Iron*, Schiffer Publishing, 1994; *Griswold Cast Iron*, L-W Book Sales, 1997; Jon B. Haussler, *Griswold Muffin Pans*, Schiffer Publishing, 1997; Joan Kahr, *Edgar Brandt: Master of Art Deco Ironwork*, Harry N. Abrams, 1999; Kathryn McNerney, *Antique Iron Identification and Values*, Collector Books, 1984, 2001 value update; George C. Neumann, *Early American Antique Country Furnishings*, L-W Book Sales, 1984, 1993 reprint; David G. Smith and Chuck Wafford, *The Book of Griswold & Wagner,* 2nd ed., Schiffer Publishing, 2000.

Periodicals: *Cast Iron Cookware News*, 28 Angela Ave., San Anselmo, CA 94960; *Kettles 'n Cookware*, Drawer B, Perrysburg, NY 14129.

Collectors' Club: Griswold & Cast Iron Cookware Association, P.O. Drawer B, Perrysburg, NY 14129-0301.

Reproduction Alert: Use the following checklist to determine if a metal object is a period piece or modern reproduction. This checklist applies to all cast-metal items, from mechanical banks to trivets.

Period cast-iron pieces feature well-defined details, carefully fitted pieces, and carefully finished and smooth castings. Reproductions, especially those produced by making a new mold from a period piece, often lack detail in the casting (lines not well defined, surface details blurred) and parts have gaps at the seams and a rough surface. Reproductions from period pieces tend to be slightly smaller in size than the period piece from which they were copied.

Period paint mellows, i.e., softens in tone. Colors look flat. Beware of any cast-iron object whose paint is bright and fresh. Painted period pieces should show wear. Make certain the wear is in places it is supposed to be.

Period cast-iron pieces develop a surface patina that prevents rust. When rust is encountered on a period piece, it generally has a greasy feel and is dark in color. The rust on artificially aged reproductions is flaky and orange.

Additional Listings: Banks, Boot Jacks, Doorstops, Fireplace Equipment, Food Molds, Irons, Kitchen Collectibles, Lamps, and Tools.

Andirons, pr, 11" h, wrought, serpentine fronts with large buttons
........................**75.00**

Wrought iron utensil rack, ram's head detail, 26" w, 14-1/2" h, $1,980. Tools shown left to right: brass bowled dipper and skimmer with wrought iron handles, marked "F. B. S. Canton O.," $150; wrought iron double calipers, ring finial, stamped "J. R.," pitted surface, 17-1/2" l, $110; skimmer with 2-1/2" d brass bowl, simple tooled 13-1/2" l wrought iron handle, skimmer with 5-1/2" d brass bowl, 10-1/2" l wrought iron handle with eye hook, $150. Photo courtesy of Garth's Auction, Inc.

Apple roaster, 34-1/4" l, wrought, hinged apple support, pierced heat end on slightly twisted projecting handle, late 18th C **1,650.00**

Ashtray stand, 8-1/2" d, 27" h, wrought, Celtic repoussé pattern on base, copper liner, match holder, triangular Bradley & Hubbard mark **150.00**

Baker's lamp, 4-1/4" h, 8-1/2" l, cast iron, attached pan, hinged lid, bottom marked "No. 2 B. L.," pitted ... **250.00**

Bill holder, Atlantic Coast Line, cast, c1915, 4" h.................. **50.00**

Calipers, 12-3/4" w, 17" h, wrought, handle in form of coiling snake, continuing to shaft with four bifurcating riveted arms, attributed to Boston Foundry, late 18th C, surface corrosion, with stand **2,875.00**

Chopper, 15" l, 8" h, rect handle blade pivoting on female figural post, shaped wood block, old red paint, America, 19th C **490.00**

Cleaver

11-1/2" l, 4-1/2" h, figural-shaped blade with eagle's head, handle terminating in brass boot, 20th C,

stand, minor surface corrosion
.......................**490.00**

12-3/4" l, 7" h, incised blade in form of woman practicing calisthenics, leg continues to wood handle ending in brass foot, attributed to Northeast, c1880, stand, surface rust, minor nicks in blade **1,840.00**

Compote, 10" w, 7" h, cast, flower form bowl, shaped and molded star base, America, late 19th C, old rust surface
.........................**200.00**

Cookie mold, 5-1/4" l, oval, bird on branch, cast iron **335.00**

Door knocker, 5-1/2" l, cast, fox head, ring hangs from mouth.........**85.00**

Embossing wheel, 4" l, 1-3/4" w, 9-1/4" h, cast iron and bronze, scrolled foliate motif on wheel edge, imp maker's marks for M. W. Baldwin, Philadelphia, handle missing..............**460.00**

Figure

12" w, 23-1/2" h, relief sand-cast, male runner from Police Gazette Building, New York City, c1880, blackened surface, on stand
....................**1,035.00**

24-1/4" w, 39" h, cast, Lady Liberty, Mott Foundry, New York, c1850, holding goblet and torch with octagonal marble base, later white wood plinth **7,425.00**

Fireback, 21-1/2" w, 33" h, cast, late Regency-style, arch top flanked by dolphins, central polychrome scene of shepherd with his flock by fountain, beaded surround, scrolling leaf border
.........................**300.00**

Flint striker, 3-1/2" h, figural, child kneeling on scrolling sled, stand, found in Pennsylvania, late 18th/early 19th C, minor surface corrosion **1,265.00**

Christmas tree holder, painted green, holly decoration, 4" h, 7" square base, $60.

Herb grinder, 16-1/2" l, 4-1/2" w, 4" h, cast, footed trough form, 6" d round disk-shaped crusher with wooden handle through center, late 18th/early 19th C **980.00**

Loom light, 17-3/4" h, candle socket, sawtooth trammel, wrought iron **420.00**

Mold, 7-1/4" w, 8" d, 8" h, figural pumpkin, smiling man face, invented by John Czeszczicki, Ohio, 1930, used to grow pumpkins in human forms, surface corrosion, later stand . . **635.00**

Mortar and pestle, 10-1/2" d, 8-1/4" h, urn shape, cast iron, pitted **50.00**

Peel, 46" l, ram's horn handle, wrought, pitted **110.00**

Pipe tongs, 17-1/4" l, wrought iron, 18th C **1,150.00**

Shelf brackets, pr, 5-1/2" h, swivel **20.00**

Spittoon, cast iron, top hat, Standard Manuf Co., Pittsburgh, PA, painted black, glazed porcelain int. **415.00**

Trivet, 7-3/4" d, round, marked "The Griswold Mfg. Co., Eire, PA, USA/8/Trivet/206" **35.00**

Umbrella stand, 21" h, cast iron, heron, lily pads and fish in base, old polychrome repaint **275.00**

Utensil rack, 10-3/4" l, wrought iron, scrolled crest, five hooks with acorn terminals, minor brazed repair . **770.00**

Wafer iron, 5-1/4" d, 24" l, imp with seal of U.S., c1800, minor imperfections **550.00**

Wall frame, 8-1/2" h, 6" d, cast iron, gilt eagle crest, elaborately dec frame, C-scrolls and foliate devices, 19th C **575.00**

IVORY

History: Ivory, a yellowish white organic material, comes from the teeth or tusks of animals and lends itself to carving. Many cultures have used it for centuries to make artistic and utilitarian items.

A cross section of elephant ivory will have a reticulated crisscross pattern. Hippopotamus teeth, walrus tusks, whale teeth, narwhal tusks, and boar tusks also are forms of ivory. Vegetable ivory, bone, stag horn, and plastic are ivory substitutes, which often confuse collectors. Vegetable ivory is a term used to describe the nut of a South American palm, which is often carved. Look for a grain that is circular and dull in this softer-than-bone material.

References: Edgard O. Espinoza and Mary-Jacque Mann, *Identification for Ivory and Ivory Substitutes*, 2nd ed., World Wildlife Fund, 1992; Gloria and Robert Mascarelli, *Oriental Antiques*, Wallace-Homestead, out of print.

Periodical: *Netsuke & Ivory Carving Newsletter*, 3203 Adams Way, Ambler, PA 19002.

Collectors' Club: International Ivory Society, 11109 Nicholas Dr., Wheaton, MD 20902, http://www.ivoryinfo.com.

Note: Dealers and collectors should be familiar with The Endangered Species Act of 1973, amended in 1978, which limits the importation and sale of antique ivory and tortoiseshell items.

Bell, 6-3/8" h, figural Elizabethian lady, ivory clipper, Continental, early 20th C **825.00**

Box, 2-5/8" d, lid painted with profile busts of man and woman in 18th C dress, blue ground, gilt-metal mounts on lid and base, French, late 19th **450.00**

Bridge, 12" l, carved from hippopotamus tusk, various figures in palace setting. **175.00**

Brush pot, 4" h, carved, figures and pavilions, Chinese, c1885 . . . **1,000.00**

Bust and pedestal, 6-1/2" h, 6-3/8" h, one with Athena, other with Ajax, turned Ionic column pedestals, Continental, late 19th C, price for pr **1,150.00**

Carving

4" h, mountain scene with figures, rustic cottage, Japan, late 19th C **375.00**

11-1/2" h, Buddhist figures and dragons, hippopotamus tusk, Japan, 19th C **920.00**

Chess set, fully carved, red stained opposition, Chinese Export, later box, wear **750.00**

Cup, cov, foliate finial, oval body, carved frieze of putti with hound, mask and acanthus baluster stem, round foot, Continental, early 18th C. **1,200.00**

Fan, 11" l, sword form, anthemion-shaped fan, handle of fan with spiral reeding, kidskin case shaped as scabbard, ivory link chain and shield shaped belt clip with carved monogram, Continental, late 19th C **920.00**

Figure

Female dancer, sgd "Tomochika," Japan, 19th C, 8-1/2" h . . . **815.00**

Goddess Kuan Yin, China, 19th C, 12" h **230.00**

Hoi tie, carrying his bag of wealth surmounted by small child, Japan, 19th C, line to bag, 8" h . . . **520.00**

Immortal Lan Tsai Ho, basket of flowers, China, 19th C, 12" h **350.00**

Lion, Japan, 19th C, 4-1/2" l . **230.00**

Lohan with kharrhara and fly whisk, China, 19th C, 9-1/2" h **175.00**

Man and woman in erotic embrace, traces of pigment, Japan, late 19th C, 2-1/2" h **215.00**

Noh actor, Japan, Meiji period, 1868-1911, fan missing form one hand, 8-1/2" h **635.00**

Pekinese on Pillow, Continental, early 20th C, 1-5/8" w, 1-5/8" h **300.00**

Chess set, elaborately carved, 10" h kings, one pawn missing, **$8,500.** *Photo courtesy of Joy Luke Auctions.*

Poor Cleric, 6-1/2" h, standing male figure, tattered cloak, long crucifix, turned and carved ebonized wood socle, Continental, late 19th C **450.00**

Shukei dancing, holding sword and fan, China, 19th C, minor loss, 7-1/2" h **230.00**

St. George slaying dragon, wood base, Indian **400.00**

Icon, carved figural relief plaque, mixed metal filigree frame, red, green, and blue enameled decoration, 5-1/2" w, 9" h, **$3,600.**

Jagging wheel, 19th C

5-3/4" l, pierced carved, whalebone, minute losses **2,875.00**

6-1/4" l, open carved handle, minor cracks, minute chips **920.00**

7-1/8" l, figural, unicorn, inlaid eyes and nostrils, minor losses **4,600.00**

7-1/4" l, pistol handle, baleen spacer, cracks, old repair **230.00**

Measure, 14-7/8" l, whalebone, ivory, and exotic wood, American shield inlay, inscribed "WH," 19th C, minor imperfections. **195.00**

Miniature furniture, 4-1/2" h dressing table with two foliate pierced velvet-lined drawers, upright mirror, table with applied carved bottles, boxes, and basin, two miniature brushes and pen, glass dome, 5" l Regency-style scrolled settee with pierced outward scrolled arms, Continental, late 19th C **525.00**

Okimono, man giving grapes to child, Japanese, early 20th C **350.00**

Pickwick, 3-1/4" h, carved, 19th C, minor losses, repair. **210.00**

Plaque

3-3/8 x 2-1/8", rect carved ivory plaque, interior genre scene of man lighting pipe, framed, Continental **345.00**

7-1/2" x 4-1/2", Amida-Buddha on lotus flower arising from lotus pond flanked by two attendants, China, 19th C. **920.00**

Puzzle ball, 14" h, carved and pierced with dragons and flowers, China **320.00**

Rolling pin, 19th C, minor insect damage

13-5/8" l, exotic wood, baleen spacers, 19th C, cracks. . . **225.00**

15-3/4" l, walrus ivory and exotic wood, baleen spacers, red sealing wax inlaid scribe lines **375.00**

Sander, 2-1/4" h, miniature, walrus ivory, scribe line dec, 19th C, minor chips **320.00**

Seal, 3-7/8" l, intaglio, handle, 19th C, cracks **400.00**

Sewing bird, 4-1/8" l, four side-mounted spools, geometric and heart exotic wood inlay, 19th C, inlay loss and replacements **1,150.00**

Sewing egg, 2-1/2" l, walrus ivory, unscrews to reveal ivory spool, thimble, and needle case, 19th C **920.00**

Square, 10" l, whalebone and ivory inlaid walnut, diamond motif inlay, 19th C, cracks to ivory **1,095.00**

Stand, 7" h, pierced relief, pink and cream flowers, peony and lotus flowers, green stones **425.00**

Toy, 2-7/8" l, top, carved, sealing wax inlaid scribe lines, 19th C, minor cracks and chips **350.00**

Vase, 6-1/2" h, carved pavilions and figures in high relief, lion mask handles with jump rings, China **175.00**

Wrist rest, 10-1/4" h, carved in high relief with numerous figures in palace garden, China, 19th C **1,265.00**

Figure, Madonna and Child, Gothic style, 21" h, **$5,170.** *Photo courtesy of Jackson's Auctioneers & Appraisers.*

JADE

History: Jade is the generic name for two distinct minerals: nephrite and jadeite. Nephrite, an amphibole mineral from Central Asia that was used in pre-18th-century pieces, has a waxy surface and hues that range from white to an almost-black green. Jadeite, a pyroxene mineral found in Burma and used from 1700 to the present, has a glassy appearance and comes in various shades of white, green, yellow-brown, and violet.

Jade cannot be carved because of its hardness. Shapes are achieved by sawing and grinding with wet abrasives such as quartz, crushed garnets, and carborundum.

Prior to 1800, few items were signed or dated. Stylistic considerations are used to date pieces. The Ch'ien Lung period (1736-1795) is considered the golden age of jade.

Museum: Avery Brundage Collection, de Young Museum, San Francisco, CA.

Jewelry suite, necklace, bracelet, and ring, gold-filled settings, $100. Photo courtesy of Sanford Alderfer Auction Co.

Bangle bracelet, gray-green, gold mounts **115.00**
Box, 3-3/8" l, rect, silver mounted, early 20th C **320.00**
Bowl
  5" d, highly translucent stone of mottle green and black, China, 20th C **300.00**
  5-1/2" d, highly translucent stone with lavender tone, deeply infused with apple green, well-formed foot ring, China, 19th C **2,650.00**
Brush pot, 4-1/4" h, scrolling cloud pattern, Chinese, 19th C **320.00**
Candlesticks, pr, 12-7/8" h, dark green, carved low relief goose with out-spread wings, stands on tortoise, head supports three-tiered pricket, tripod bowl with int. carving, reticulated wood

base with carved key scroll motifs and floral scrolls **550.00**
Carving
  4" l, pair of crabs, celadon color, broad areas of russet **475.00**
  4" x 4", fisherman with basket in swirling waves with jumping fish, even celadon color with russet fissures, cloud-like inclusion, China, 19th C **325.00**
Dish, 5-3/4" d, brownish-celadon, carved in Mughal style, open chrysanthemum flower, China, 19th C **475.00**
Figure
  2-1/4" h, Buddha with monkey, white jade, Chinese **200.00**
  6-3/4" h, grotto, wrinkled elephant and attendant on ledge beneath rocky outcrop and pine trees on front, reverse with gnarled pine and sage on flight of stairs with climbing monkey, late 17th C **16,500.00**
  7-1/8" h, Meiren, standing, holding peach bough and hoe, mint green, China **2,000.00**
Flute, 22" l, light and dark colored cylinders of celadon green tone, wooden frame, India, early 20th C **75.00**
Inkstone, 3-5/8" l, oval, depression to one side, black and white mottling, incised rim band **200.00**
Letter opener, 10-3/4" l, carved interlocking C scrolls between keyfret bands handle, SS knife **250.00**
Libation cup, 5" l, celadon jade, incised dec, dragon head handles, Chinese, Qing dynasty, price for pr **425.00**
Plaque
  5-1/2" x 8", spinach-green, carved and pierced lattice pattern, squirrel with grapes, China, 20th C, price for pr **300.00**

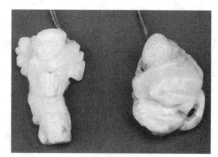

Pendants, type used in burial tombs, each, $125.

7" x 5", pale celadon, mountain pavilion, China, Ch'ien Lung period, 1735-1796, restruck oblong natural fissures in stones . . **350.00**
Snuff bottle
  Grayish-white, mottled russet skin on one side, rose quartz stopper **550.00**
  Greenish-white, sloping shoulder, oval foot, 1880-80, pr **650.00**
Urn, 8" h, ovoid, incised taotie mask dec, narrow neck, handles, domed lid with suspending carved chains, yoke-shape hanger **700.00**
Vase, 7" h, cov, celadon to gray jade, carved, two loose ring and fu dog head handles, foliate and stylized dec, fu dog finial, Chinese **250.00**

JASPERWARE

History: Jasperware is a hard, unglazed porcelain with a colored ground varying from the most common blues and greens to lavender, yellow, red, or black. The white designs, often classical in nature, are applied in relief. Jasperware was first produced at Wedgwood's Etruria Works in 1775. Josiah Wedgwood described it as "a fine terra-cotta of great beauty and delicacy proper for cameos."

In addition to Wedgwood, many other English potters produced jasperware. Two of the leaders were Adams and Copeland and Spode. Several Continental potters, e.g., Heubach, also produced the ware.

References: Susan and Al Bagdade, *Warman's English & Continental Pottery & Porcelain*, 3rd ed., Krause Publications, 1998; R. K. Henrywood, *Relief-Moulded Jugs*, 1820-1900, Antique Collectors' Club.

Museums: British Museum, London, England; Memorial Hall Museum, Philadelphia, PA; Museum of Fine Arts, Boston, MA; Victoria & Albert Museum, London, England.

Reproduction Alert: Jasperware still is made today, especially by Wedgwood.

Note: This category includes jasperware pieces made by companies other than Wedgwood. Wedgwood jasperware is found in the Wedgwood listing.

Cheese dish, cov
  7-1/2" h, light brown ground, white dec, cylindrical lid, flattened ball finial, pieced ventilation holes, round undertray, applied fox hunting scene, oak leaf banding, English, late 19th/early 20th C **170.00**
  8-1/2" d, 7" h, green ground, white dec, cylindrical lid, acorn final, applied anthemion and flat leaves, central bands of neoclassical maidens offset by attenuated flat

leaves, round undertray with acanthus and paterae band, England, late 19th C **150.00**

8-1/2" d, 8" h, cobalt blue, white classical figures, c1880.... **400.00**

10" d, 8" h, blue ground, white dec, cylindrical lid, acorn finial, applied anthemion and acanthus oak leaf band, central band of cherubs offset by attenuated flat leaves, round undertray with oak leaf band, England, late 19th C **300.00**

Clock, blue ground, white applied classical decoration, clock mechanism marked "Swiss Made," 6" h, $575.

Creamer, 2-1/2" h, sage green ground, pale pink frolicking Kewpies, sgd "O'Neill" **195.00**

Cup, 3-1/2" d, 2-1/2" h, green, white cherub, small feet, marked "3724.A" **45.00**

Hatpin, 4-1/2", star form, multi-faceted steel beading surrounded by blue jasper dip button, white floret in relief, England, late 18th C......... **450.00**

Jug, 4-7/8" h, 4-3/8" d, blue ground, white relief hunting scene with men on horses, dogs, and stag, white relief rim band, Copeland **85.00**

Pitcher, 3-3/4" d, 5-1/4" h, blue ground, white floral dec **65.00**

Tea set, 5-1/4" h teapot, creamer, cov sugar, ovoid, cerulean blue ground, white hunting scene dec, Spode, early 20th C.................... **200.00**

Tobacco jar, cov, 6-1/4" h, cylindrical, dark blue ground, white relief band around base, SP rim, bail handle, and cov, ivory finial, imp "Adams, Tunstall, England".................. **120.00**

Pitcher, brown ground, football motif, Copeland, marked "JMSD & S," Rg. 180288, 1895, 5-3/8" h, $250.

Vase

2-1/4" d, 5-3/4" h, light brown ground, white appliqué of tree **70.00**

2-3/4" d, 2-3/4" h, light blue ground, white appliqué of kissing children **75.00**

JEWEL BOXES

History: The evolution of jewelry was paralleled by the development of boxes in which to store it. Jewel-box design followed the fashion trends dictated by furniture styles. Many jewel boxes are lined.

Wood, double book shape, hinged cover, Victorian lady decoration, 5-1/4" l, 3-1/4" w, 2-7/8" h, $125.

3-7/8" w, 5-3/4" l, silver, Continental, probably German, late 19th/early 20th C, rect, lid and base with emb foliate bands, cast dog mounted to lid, four emb foliate feet, 17 troy oz **980.00**

4-1/2" x 2-1/2", malachite, veneer, rect, raised feet, satin lining, Russian, 19th C **250.00**

4-1/2" x 2-3/4", cranberry glass, enameled floral dec, silverplated rim **165.00**

4-5/8" h, 4-3/8" d, golden amber, inverted thumbprint, round, hinged, ormolu feet, sapphire blue serpent applied to lid, small enameled flowers and green leaves dec **235.00**

4-3/4" h, 4-3/8" d, egg shape, clear, cream-colored enamel scroll trim and edging, white enamel flower on top, fine sanded ground, gold trim, ormolu feet **185.00**

4-3/4" x 8-3/4", Russian Silver, rect, sky blue, deep red, and white enameled diapering patter, stylized flower heads, raised studded bands, swing handles on lid and sides, pale blue padded satin lining, four bun feet **2,500.00**

5-1/4" l, 2-5/8" d, 3-3/4" h, cranberry flashed glass, dome top box with scroll-engraved brass mounts, two round pendant handles, open C-scroll feet, Continental, late 19th C ... **750.00**

6" h, 10" w, 6-3/4" d, engraved whalebone, top polychrome dec of elegant ladies and child flanked by birds among trees, sides with reserves of birds among foliage, top lists to reveal a removable tray, four cov compartments and door, dec with snakes, fish, and foliate devices, shaped bracket feet, minor imperfections **5,660.00**

6-1/4" h, 10" d, 7" d, exotic woods, various geometric motifs, late 19th C, minor losses **320.00**

6-1/2" l, German Silver, heavily molded and bellied sides, winged dolphin form feet, early 19th C, 13 oz...... **850.00**

6-1/2" h, 11-1/4" w, 8" d, decoupage, cigar box construction, stamps dec, two drawers, America, early 20th C, minor imperfections **175.00**

7" x 6-1/2", Wave Crest, puffy egg crate mold, hp lid, child with bow and arrow, satin finish, ftd, orig lining ... **1,200.00**

8-1/8" l, 5-3/8" w, 2-7/8" h, mother-of-pearl and paper, rect box, mother-of-pearl plaques with floral etched banding on top and three sides, ormolu mounts cast with florals, husks, and beading throughout, sloped hinged lid set with painted paper floral spray under glass dome, four ball feet, faille-lined interior, French, Second Empire, c1870-80.......... **2,415.00**

9-1/2" h, 16" w, gilt bronze, elaborate Moorish design, semi precious stones, enamel dec **900.00**

German silver, footed, pink-velvet lining, raised figures of people and animals, 4-3/4" x 3" x 3-1/2", **$125.**

10" x 8" x 7", Art Nouveau, ormolu, raised figural and floral dec, plaque dated 1903 . . . . **245.00**

10" h, 11-1/2" w, 10-1/2" d, Victorian, painted and decoupage, lift top, pr of doors opening to small drawers, Chinese scenes on mustard yellow ground **815.00**

11-3/4" l, ebony, all over scrolling flowering foliage dec, inlaid ivory, 19th C **300.00**

12" h, 10" w, 10" d, painted papier-mâché, lit top, fitted int., two doors enclosing small drawers, Victorian, mid-19th, minor restorations **520.00**

13" x 5" x 4", sterling silver, repoussé sides, small petal-like beaded edges, fancy feet, red velvet lining, marked "Meriden" **160.00**

JEWELRY

History: Jewelry has been a part of every culture. It is a way of displaying wealth, power, or love of beauty. In the current antiques marketplace, it is easiest to find jewelry dating after 1830.

Jewelry items were treasured and handed down as heirlooms from generation to generation. In the United States, antique jewelry is any jewelry at least 100 years old, a definition linked to U.S. Customs law. Pieces that do not meet the antique criteria but are at least 25 years old are called "period" or "heirloom/estate" jewelry.

The names of historical periods are commonly used when describing jewelry. The following list indicates the approximate dates for each era.

Georgian	1714-1830
Victorian	1837-1901
Edwardian	1890-1920
Arts and Crafts	1890-1920
Art Nouveau	1895-1910
Art Deco	1920-1935
Retro Modern	1935-1945
Post-War Modern	1945-1965

References: Lillian Baker, *Art Nouveau & Art Deco Jewelry,* Collector Books, 1981, 1997 value update; ——, *Fifty Years of Collectible Fashion Jewelry, 1925-1975,* Collector Books, 1997 values; ——, *100 Years of Collectible Jewelry, 1850-1950,* Collector Books, 1978, 1999 value update; Joanne D. Ball, *Costume Jewelers: The Golden Age of Design,* 3rd ed., Schiffer Publishing, 2000; Joel A. Batech, *Kremlin Gold: 1000 Years of Russian Gems & Jewels,* Harry N. Abrams, 2000; Howard L. Bell, Jr., *Cuff Jewelry,* published by author (P.O. Box 11695, Raytown, MO 64138), 1994; C. Jeanenne Bell, *Answers to Questions about Old Jewelry,* 5th ed., Krause Publications, 1999; ——, *Collector's Encyclopedia of Hairwork Jewelry: Identification and Values,* Collector Books, 1998; France Borel, *Splendor of Ethnic Jewelry,* Harry N. Abrams, 1994; Marcia Brown, *Unsigned Beauties of Costume Jewelry,* Collector Books, 2000; Shirley Bury, *Jewellery 1789-1910,* Vols. I and II, Antique Collectors' Club, 1991; Deanna Farneti Cera, *Costume Jewellery,* Antique Collectors' Club, 1999; —— *The Jewels of Miriam Haskell,* Antique Collectors' Club, 1999; Monica Lynn Clements and Patricia Rosser Clements, *Cameos: A Pocket Guide,* Schiffer Publishing, 1999; Franco Cologni and Eric Nussbaum, *Platinum By Cartier, Triumphs of the Jewelers' Art,* Harry N. Abrams, 1996; Genevieve Cummins and Neryvalle Taunton, *Chatelaines,* Antique Collector's Club, 1994.

Ginny Redington Dawes and Corinne Davidov, *Victorian Jewelry,* Abbeville Press, 1991; Janet Drucker, *Georg Jensen, A Tradition of Splendid Silver,* Schiffer Publishing, 1997; Lois Sherr Dubin, *North American Indian Jewelry and Adornment,* Harry N. Abrams, Inc., 1999; Alastair Duncan, *Paris Salons 1895-1914,* Jewelry, two vols., Antique Collectors' Club, 1994; Martin Eidelberg, (ed.), *Messengers of Modernism, American Studio Jewelry 1940-1960,* Flammarion, 1996; Lodovica Rizzoli Eleuteri, *Twentieth-Century Jewelry,* Electa, Abbeville, 1994; Martha Gandy Fales, *Jewelry in America 1600-1900,* Antique Collectors' Club, 1999; Fritz Falk, *Lalique and His Circle,* Arnoldsche, distributed by Antique Collectors' Club, 1999; Charlotte Gere and Geoffrey Munn, *Pre-Raphaelite to Arts & Crafts Jewelry,* Antique Collectors' Club, 1999; Stephen Giles, *Jewelry, Miller's Antiques Checklist,* Reed International Books Ltd., 1997; Geza von Habsburg, *Fabergé in America,* Thomas and Hudson, 1996; S. Sylvia Henzel, *Collectible Costume Jewelry, Third Edition,* Krause Publications, 1997; Helmet Kahlert, Richard Mühe, Gisbert L. Brunner, *Wristwatches: History Of A Century's Development,* Schiffer Publishing, 1999;

Daniel Mascetti and Amanda Triossi, *Bulgari,* Abbeville Press, 1996; Daniel Mascetti and Amanda Triossi, *The Necklace, From Antiquity to the Present,* Harry N. Abrams, Inc., 1997; Antionette Matlins, *The Pearl Book,* GemStone Press, 1996; Patrick Mauries, *Jewelry by Chanel,* Bulfinch Press, 1993; Anna M. Miller, *Cameos Old and New,* Van Nostrand Reinhold, 1991; ——, *Illustrated Guide to Jewelry Appraising: Antique Period & Modern,* Chapman & Hall, 1990; Michael Poynder, *Jewelry, Reference & Price Guide,* Antique Collectors' Club, 1999; —— *Price Guide to Jewellery 3000 B.C.–1950 A.D.,* Antique Collectors' Club, 1990 reprint; Penny Proddow and Marion Fasel, *Diamonds, A Century of Spectacular Jewels,* Harry N. Abrams, 1996; Penny Proddow, Debra Healy, and

Marion Fasel, *Hollywood Jewels,* Harry L. Abrams, 1992; Dorothy T. Rainwater, *American Jewelry Manufacturers,* Schiffer Publishing, 1988; Christie Romero, *Warman's Jewelry,* 2nd ed., Krause Publications, 1998; Fred Rezazadeh, *Collectible Silver Jewelry,* Collector Books, 2000; ——, *Costume Jewelry,* Collector Books, 2000; Judy Rudoe, *Cartier 1900-1939,* Harry N. Abrams, 1997; Nancy N. Schiffer, *Silver Jewelry Designs,* Schiffer Publishing, 1996; ——, *The Best of Costume Jewelry,* 3rd ed., Schiffer Publishing, 1999; Sheryl Gross Shatz, *What's It Made Of? A Jewelry Materials Identification Guide,* 3rd ed., published by author (10931 Hunting Horn Dr., Santa Ana, CA 92705), 1991; Cherri Simonds, *Collectible Costume Jewelry,* Collector Books, 2000; Doris J. Snell, *Antique Jewelry with Prices, Second Edition,* Krause Publications, 1997; Ralph Turner, *Jewelry in Europe and America, New Times, New Thinking,* Thames and Hudson, 1995; Fred Ward, *Opals,* Gem Book Publishers, 1997; Janet Zapata, *Jewelry and Enamels of Louis Comfort Tiffany,* Harry N. Abrams, 1993.

Periodicals and Internet Resources: *All About Jewels, Illustrated Dictionary of Jewelry,* http://www.allaboutjewels.com; *Auction Market Resource for Gems & Jewelry,* P.O. Box 7683, Rego Park, NY 11374; *Estate Jeweler,* Estate Jewelers Assoc. of America, 608 Fifth Ave., Suite 410, New York, NY 10021, http://www.ejaa.net; *Gems & Gemology,* Gemological Institute of America, 5355 Armada Drive, Carlsbad, CA 92008; *Glittering Times,* P.O. Box 656675, Flushing, NY 11365; Tradelock.com, http://www.polygon.net; TradeShop, Inc., http://www.tradeshop.com/master/lobby.html.

Collectors' Clubs: American Society of Jewelry Historians, Box 103, 133A North Ave., New Rochelle, NY 10804, http://www.adornment.net; Assoc. for Collectors of Mourning Jewelry, P.O. Box 641, Burlington, WI 53105; Leaping Frog Antique Jewelry and Collectable Club, 4841 Martin Luther Blvd., Sacramento, CA 95820; Vintage Fashion & Costume Jewelry Club, P.O. Box 265, Glen Oaks, NY 11004-0265.

Videotapes: C. Jeanne Bell, "Antique and Collectible Jewelry Video Series," Vol. I: "Victorian Jewelry, Circa 1837-1901," Vol. II: "Edwardian, Art Nouveau & Art Deco Jewelry, Circa 1887-1930's," Antique Images; Leigh Leshner and Christie Romero, "Hidden Treasures," Venture Entertainment (P.O. Box 55113, Sherman Oaks, CA 91413).

Notes: The value of a piece of old jewelry is derived from several criteria, including craftsmanship, scarcity, and the current value of precious metals and gemstones. Note that antique and period pieces should be set with stones that were cut in the manner in use at the time the piece was made. Antique jewelry is not comparable to contemporary pieces set with modern-cut stones and should not be appraised with the same standards. Nor should old-mine, old-European, or rose-cut stones be replaced with modern brilliant cuts.

The pieces listed here are antique or period and represent fine jewelry (i.e., made from gemstones and/or precious metals). The list contains no new reproduction pieces. Inexpensive and mass-produced costume jewelry is covered in *Warman's Americana & Collectibles.*

Bar pin

Art Deco

Platinum and diamond, set with 17 transitional-cut 2.55 cts diamonds, engraved geometric gallery
.... **1,725.00**
Platinum and diamond, set with 105 old European and single-cut diamonds, filigree mount with millegrain accents, yellow gold pin stem................. **3,565.00**
Ruby, collet-set oval 5.5 x 4.7 x 3.5 mm ruby, flanked by four old European-cut diamonds, four mine-cut diamonds, platinum topped 14kt yellow gold mount with millegrain accents...... **1,265.00**
Edwardian, set with row of six old mine-cut diamonds, center suspending knife-edge bar with old min-cut diamond terminal, approx total 2.00 cts, French assay mark......... **1,150.00**
Etruscan Revival, 14kt gold, rose gold arched terminals, applied bead and wirework dec **260.00**
Victorian, tri-color pictorial scene with rose-cut diamond highlights, bar set with gold quartz, scallop, and gold bead dec **750.00**

Bracelet, Victorian-style, 14k yg, tassel ends, Helbros Co. watch, 1" w, approx 91.2 grams, 7-3/4" l bracelet, watch pin can be worn as pin or attached to bracelet, $1,650. Photo courtesy of Sanford Alderfer Auction Co.

Bracelet

Art Deco

18kt gold and jade, seven carved and pierced jade plaques of stylized birds and floral vines, joined by enamel and seed pearl engraved links, sgd "Tiffany & Co.," 7-1/2" l, cracks to jade ... **4,600.00**
Platinum and diamond, flexible, openwork, round and rect links set with approx 190 circular and single-cut diamonds, approx total 7.00 cts, French assay marks, 7" l
.... **7,765.00**
Platinum and diamond, flexible, slightly curved and shaped links set throughout with 120 transitional-cut diamonds, approx total 7.20 cts, 7" l **8,625.00**
Platinum and diamond, geometric design bead-set with old European and full-cut diamonds, 3.56 cts, calibre-cut emerald highlights, millegrain accents, 6-1/4" l, two extra links **4,500.00**
Platinum and diamond, line, 34 (approx total 3.40 cts) box-set circular-cut diamonds, two French-cut synthetic sapphire accents, engraved gallery, 6-1/2" l
.... **2,650.00**
Platinum and diamond, line, 35 box-set old European and

transitional cut diamonds, 6.50 cts, millegrain accents, 7" l .. **5,500.00**
Platinum and diamond, set throughout with approx 397 old European and transitional-cut diamonds, buckle closure, partially obliterated American hallmark, 7" l
.... **26,450.00**
Platinum, sapphire, and diamond, flexible design, center eight tapered plaques set with graduated oval sapphires alternating with old European-cut diamonds, integral diamond-set band, 3.44 cts, 7" l **4,725.00**
White gold, 18kt, seven flexible hinged plaques set with five 0.50 cts old European-cut diamonds alternating with triangular-cut blue stones completed by pierced rect box link bracelet, two extra links
.... **650.00**

Art Nouveau, amethyst and 14kt gold, round, faceted amethysts set within scrolled links, oval squares, 8" l, Sloan & Co. hallmark.............. **1,320.00**

Edwardian, portrait, three children within platinum topped 14kt gold and old European-cut diamond frames, joined by later platinum nautical links, 8" l..................... **2,300.00**

Victorian, Etruscan Revival, bangle, hinged
14kt gold, bead and wiretwist dec, 46.1 dwt, minor discoloration to gold, surface scratches, price for pr................... **2,530.00**
18kt gold, knot design with ball terminals, all over bead and wiretwist dec......... **2,415.00**

Victorian

Bangle, center rose-cut diamond flanked by oval yellow stones, framed by 14 rose-cuts, bead, and scroll motif rose gold hinged mount
.... **1,150.00**
Bangle, hinged, 14kt rose gold, surmounted by applied ovals and engraved buckles, seed pearl accent, Russian hallmarks, 2-1/4" dia, minor dents **350.00**
Bangle, hinged, garnet, oval design, four rows of faceted garnets, gilt metal mountings, price for pr, missing several garnets ... **750.00**
Link, 14kt gold and gem-set, textured expandable gold plaques accented by ruby, sapphire, and two old mine-cut diamonds
.... **1,035.00**

Slide, 14kt gold, flexible mesh design, shield form slide with applied plaque dec with seed pearls and black tracery enamel suspending foxtail fringe, similar fringe terminal, 28.0 dwt, minor enamel loss **465.00**

Brooch, Victorian, 18 kt gold, scalloped bezel, white gold crowned double eagle holding scepter and orb, set with 58 rose cut diamonds, one brown diamond, blue enamel ground, minor enamel chip, $1,200. Photo courtesy of Joy Luke Auctions.

Brooch

Art Deco

Platinum and diamond, bow, openwork mount set throughout with 118 single and transitional-cut diamonds, millegrain accents, yellow gold pin stem. **3,750.00**

Platinum and diamond, circle, 26 old European-cut and transitional-cut diamonds, millegrain accents, approx total 2.0 cts. **1,400.00**

Platinum and diamond, shaped rectangle, seven center collet-set old-European-cut diamonds, set throughout with old mine and European-cut diamonds in millegrain and pierced mount, approx total 5.60 cts. **3,565.00**

Platinum, center sugarloaf moonstone, flanked by square-cut sapphires, edged with rect moonstones, all channel-set, oval moonstone terminals, wiretwist filigree accents, yellow gold pin stem, sgd "Tiffany & Co.," 3" l **24,150.00**

Art Nouveau

Floral spray, white-cream translucent enamel lilies centered by cultured pearls, green enamel leaves, joined by gold coiled cord, 14kt polished gold stems. **750.00**

Four-leaf clover, light shading to dark green enameled leaves, old European-cut diamond center, polished gold stem, Crane & Theurer hallmark **1,380.00**

Krementz & Co., light green enamel scrolling leaves centering heart-shape peridot, three old European-cut diamond accents, hallmark. **1,150.00**

Orchid, light greenish-yellow and purple openwork leaves, baroque pearl and old European-cut diamond highlights, retractable bail, 14kt gold **1,265.00**

Orchid, light pink and mauve enamel leaves, old mine-cut diamond center, retractable bail . . **1,725.00**

Orchid, purple, pink, and green enamel leaves, old mine-cut diamond accent, minor chip to enamel. **1,610.00**

Pansy, yellow shading to purple enamel leaves edged by seed pearls, center old-European-cut diamond, retractable bail **1,495.00**

Scrolling elliptical form, center faceted citrine, 14kt gold, hallmark **490.00**

Trout, basse-taille greenish-blue fading to pinkish-white iridescent translucent enamel **850.00**

Edwardian

Amethyst, large oval faceted amethyst framed by pearls, 14kt gold mount, sgd Cartier, accompanied by copy of Cartier bill of sale **850.00**

Bow, plaited hair within platinum-topped yellow gold frame, rose diamond accents **460.00**

Circle, pearl and diamond, pierced and millegrain platinum frame surmounted by diamond set bow, inside circle set with row of seed pearls **950.00**

Flower basket, 100 bead-set diamonds, (approx total 2.50 cts), platinum-topped gold mount, minor lead solder **4,025.00**

Platinum and diamond, 1.50 cts old mine-cut diamond, lacy filigree mount set throughout with rose and single-cut diamonds, millegrain accents, French assay mark **7,475.00**

Platinum, diamond, and sapphire circle, four diamonds spaced by four sapphires, filigree mount, millegrain accents, yellow gold pin stem. **650.00**

Renaissance Revival, openwork circle set with amethyst, mother-of-pearl, and green stones, suspending three amethyst drops, enameled silver mount, hallmarks, losses to enamel . . . **350.00**

Retro

14kt bi-color flower spray, stylized polished gold bouquet set with faceted multi-colored stones, stems joined by head-set diamonds. **750.00**

14kt gold and chalcedony, spray of polished gold stems surmounted by chalcedony bead berries, stems joined by bead-set diamonds **450.00**

18kt gold, bow, set with groups of pear-shaped and circular jadeite jade, polished gold ribbon accent **375.00**

Victorian

Amethyst and seed pearl, oval 13.2 x 10.5 mm amethyst, 14kt gold frame set with concentric split seed pearls. **300.00**

Crescent, 21 oval-shaped rubies edged by old European-cut and mine-cut diamonds, silver-topped 14kt gold mount **2,300.00**

Moonstone, 14kt gold, oval split pearl frame centered by moonstone, flanked by textured leaves, later oval moonstone pendant terminal, solder to reverse **500.00**

Pertabgraph, India, 18kt gold, green transparent enamel plaque surmounted by openwork engraved floral and figural pattern cut from a thin sheet of gold, applied wiretwist and bead frame **650.00**

Buckle

Art Nouveau, sterling silver, two repoussé plaques of female faces with flowing hair and flower blossoms, hallmark for William B. Kerr & Co. **300.00**

Edwardian, rect openwork buckle edged with demantoid garnets spaced by old European-cut diamonds, silver-topped gold mount **1,380.00**

Cameo, Victorian, carved shell

Cupid and winged goddess, 14kt gold oval frame **425.00**

Owl and eagle surmounted by two classical females in profile, 18kt gold oval frame with ball and wiretwist dec, Italian hallmarks, boxed, hairlines **650.00**

Brooch/pin, sterling, C. 1935, round rectangular plaque, chased and repoussé cornucopia motif, marked "PEER SMED STERLING HAND CHASED," safety clasp, 2-1/2" w x 2", $750. Photo courtesy Janet Zapata.

Portrait bust of female in profile, 18kt gold and citrine frame with seed pearls, black enamel, and diamonds, chips to enamel **1,850.00**

Charm bracelet, Victorian, polished and chased curb links, suspending heart-shaped padlock, 9kt gold **250.00**

Chatelaine, Aesthetic Movement, late 19th C, silver plated, 6" l textured leaf clip set with tiny butterfly and lizard, suspending oval link chains with small Chinoiserie-style bell, flask engraved with fan, two European coins, miniature medallion flask, foliage covers for notepad, miniature painter's palette, longest drop 11-1/2" l **350.00**

Choker, Art Nouveau, eight pansy links in translucent yellow, green, and violet enamel shading, center motif suspending flexible pendant designed with collet-set diamond and two freshwater pearls, edged by fine trace link chain, accented by freshwater pearls, 13" l **2,990.00**

Clip
Art Deco
Platinum and diamond, two old European-cut diamonds, 35 old European-cut diamonds . **2,100.00**
Ruby and diamond, double clip, eight oval cabochon rubies, set throughout with bead-set circular-cut diamonds, 12 baguette diamond accents, approx total 2.85 cts, platinum mount **5,175.00**
Retro, pave and circular-cut diamond set caps surmounted by similarly set swag, suspending spray of 18 square-cut rubies and eight tapered baguette-cut ribbons, Austrian import assay marks, hallmark **4,715.00**

Cuff links, Art Deco, platinum, sq cut-corner design, set with horizontal line of single-cut diamonds and calibre-cut onyx **1,265.00**

Demi parure, Victorian
Coral, bracelet with brickwork links, coral bead flowerhead terminal, matching brooch, with chip on center drop, 6-1/2" l **475.00**
Gold and turquoise, engraved, scroll form pendant/brooch, surmounted by pavé turquoise and seed pearl dec, suspending gold drops, matching earrings (with later tops) **1,725.00**

Tiger's claw earrings, C. 1880, claw mounted on floral motif gf frame suspended by two chains from floral motif surmount, shepherd's hook earwires, 3/4" w x 2" tl, pair, $350. Photo courtesy of E. Foxe Harrell Jewelers, Clinton, IA.

Earrings
Art Deco, platinum and diamond, calibre-cut emerald tops, centering collet-set diamond, suspending line of bead and collet-set single-cut diamonds, diamond and calibre-cut emerald oval terminals, 18kt white gold findings with Dutch hallmarks, emeralds abraded **1,380.00**
Retro
Platinum and diamond, each set with 47 circular and baguette-cut diamonds, stamped "L. B." **4,025.00**
Ruby and diamond, pleated open discs accented by calibre-cut ruby and bead-set diamond arch, 14kt gold, one ruby missing **435.00**
Victorian
14kt, blue enamel links edged in trefoil design within oval frames, suspended gold bead **350.00**

Gold, engraved foliate tops suspending two gold balls . **920.00**

Lavaliere
Edwardian
Amethyst, 14kt gold, centered by oval amethyst within openwork scrolled frame surmounted by seed pearl trefoil, suspending similar drop, joined by trace link chain, 15" l **450.00**
Aquamarine, openwork foliate shield form, set with oval and pear-shape aquamarines, suspending five graduated gem-set drops, collet-set aquamarine gold trace link chain **1,850.00**
Peridot, openwork mount centered by collet-set peridot, framed by textured gold trefoils with pink stone highlights, flexibly-set pear-shape peridot drop, joined by trace link chain, 15" l **575.00**
Egyptian Revival, 14kt gold, centered by amethyst intaglio scarab within shaped lotus flower mount, baroque pearl drop terminal, stylized floral links, amethyst intaglio scarabs set at intervals, 16-1/2" l **1,380.00**

Locket
Art Nouveau, 18kt gold, portrait of a woman wearing diamond melee choker, 10.3 dwt **1,380.00**
Edwardian
Enamel, circular, grayish-blue guilloche enamel, surmounted by platinum and diamond openwork medallion **700.00**
Sapphire, diamond, and enamel, white guilloche enamel 14kt gold locket, surmounted by sapphire and rose-cut diamond sautoir motif set in silver, 14kt gold trace link chain, Russian hallmarks, minor enamel loss to edges **1,720.00**
Etruscan Revival, oval 10kt locket with bead, seed pearl, and wiretwist dec, verso with hinged compartment, suspended from woven 14kg gold chain **450.00**
Victorian
Agate cameo, profile of classical woman within etched green gold laurel leaf frame, fleur-de-lis pendant bail **250.00**
Gold and enamel, designed as hand holding moveable fan, oval frame with shell and foliate motifs, centered by red stones and pearl,

verso with glass compartment
. . . . **1,495.00**

Pietra Dura, rectangular gold frame, bead and wiretwist dec, surmounted by floral stone mosaic, reverse hinged locket, suspended from 14kt gold fancy 17-1/2" l link chain. **460.00**

Lorgnette

Art Nouveau, 14kt gold, repoussé iris handle, collet-set diamond highlight, verso monogrammed **990.00**

Edwardian, 18kt gold, engraved dec handle and eye piece, handle set with three bands of rose-cut diamonds, French assay marks **750.00**

Necklace, 14k yg, double woven link, marked "Cartier," 6/16" w, 15" l, 83.7 grams, $2,300. Photo courtesy of Sanford Alderfer Auction Co.

Necklace

Arts and Crafts, elliptical-shaped jade within conforming enamel scrolled links joined by trace link chains, similarly set pendant suspending three jade drops, 18kt gold, 18" l, sgd "Tiffany & Co.," some enamel loss **31,050.00**

Edwardian

Festoon, 9kt gold, amethyst, graduating collet-set oval, round, and pear-shape amethysts joined by double trace link chain, 17" l
. . . . **1,495.00**

Festoon, 14kt gold, centered by nine bezel-set amethysts joined by fine trace link chain, suspending five gold-capped amethyst briolettes, 13-1/4" l **850.00**

Fringe, platinum chain mounted with five (approx total 2.60 cts)

collet-set old European-cut diamonds joined by knife-edge bar links suspending similarly set diamond fringe, 15" l **4,025.00**

Etruscan Revival, barrel-shape links suspending stylized ivy leaf drops threaded through loop-in-loop chain, scarab clasp, 18kt gold, 16" l, accompanied by letter of provenance
. . . . **3,450.00**

Victorian

14kt gold and garnet, three floral engraved medallions surmounted by emerald-cut garnets set in ropetwist frames, reverse with plaited hair locket, suspended from 16-1/2" l snake chain **420.00**

14kt gold mesh, intricately woven flexible tubular chain, gold plunger clasp, 15.8 dwt, 15-1/2" l, minor dents **490.00**

Pearls, Edwardian, 47 graduated pearls, approx 4.8 x 5.3 mm to 6.6 x 7.2 mm, platinum-topped gold clasp set with old European-cut (approx 2.0 ct) diamond, crimped collet mounting, sgd "Tiffany & Co.," 18" l **5,750.00**

Pendant

Art Deco

Diamond, pierced shield shape set with two marquise and 85 (approx total 5.50 cts) old European-cut and transitional-cut diamonds, seven calibre-cut synthetic emeralds, fleur-de-lis bail, platinum mouth with millegrain accents, one emerald missing **3,125.00**

Enamel and onyx, navette-shape silver, ivory and black enamel plaque, center sugarloaf onyx, marcasite highlights, black cord, French hallmarks, sgd "Batik"
. . . . **875.00**

Platinum, diamond, and onyx, rect plaque set in geometric design with 34 diamonds and four buff-top onyx, millegrain accents, verso inscribed "V.I.H." **920.00**

Platinum, fancy cut aquamarine suspended from platinum-topped 14kt gold floral engraved box and rect link chain, Allsopp & Allsopp hallmark, 15-1/2" h. **3,800.00**

Art Nouveau

Enamel, pearl, and diamond, shaped anemone, highlighted by bezel-set circular 0.25 cts diamond, suspending flexibly-set baroque pearl pendant, 14kt gold hallmark, chips to enamel **1,840.00**

Opal and seed pearl, bezel-set opal and seed pearl openwork mounts, suspending a flexibly-set opal drop, 10kt gold, crack to opal
. . . . **375.00**

Plique-a-Jour Enamel, lavender and green irid enamel flowers, green, pink, and white plique-a-jour enamel leaves, rose-cut diamonds and pearl accents, 18kt gold mount with later faux pearl chain **1,265.00**

Edwardian

Demantoid garnet and diamond, openwork, 6.6 x 6.6 x 4.6 mm garnet, rose and old mine-cut diamonds, suspending pear-shape rose-cut diamond drop, fine platinum chains accented by rose-cut diamond trefoils . **6,100.00**

Enamel and diamond, center neo-classical painted porcelain plaque framed by single-cut diamonds, verso with blue guillouche and white enamel dec, opens to reveal two powder compartments, diamond-set bail, platinum topped yellow gold
. . . . **3,750.00**

Opal and diamond, oval-shaped opal set within navette-shape platinum mount, old European and single-cut diamonds, pierced gallery, millegrain accents, suspended from fine trace link chain **875.00**

Platinum, diamond, and enamel, quatrefoil form, cobalt blue guilloche enameled disk surmounted by diamond quatrefoil accent, rose and full-ct diamond filigree mount, fine trace link chain with pearl accent **3,500.00**

Portrait, young boy within round 18kt gold frame, delicate independent platinum frame highlighted with rose-cut diamond foliage swag
. . . . **700.00**

Victorian, pearl and turquoise, shield form set with pearls and buff-top turquoise, 18kt gold and silver mount, 18 kt gold snake chain **650.00**

Pendant watch, Edwardian

Platinum and diamond, C. H. Meylan, Brassus, round white porcelain dial with black Arabic numerals, Louis XIV hands, scroll and foliate motif case bead-set with rose, single, and full-cut diamonds, high grade jeweled nickel diamond slide and swivel clasp . . . **6,900.00**

Platinum and enamel, open-face engine-turned goldtone dial with black Arabic numerals, blue-steeled hands, blue-gray enamel guilloche case accented with collet and rose-cut diamonds, cabochon sapphire winder, rose-cut diamond bail and bow pendant, suspended from platinum chain **875.00**

Plaque de Cou, Art Deco, platinum and diamond, rect plaque set throughout with 43 old European-cut diamonds, flexible, hinged terminals, millegrain accents. **3,150.00**

Ring
Art Deco

Diamond, rect plaque set with 10 (approx total 1.52 cts) old European-cuts, pierced and engraved 18kt white gold mount, millegrain accents **1,275.00**

Platinum and diamond, bezel-set (approx total 0.45 cts) old European-cut diamond, closed pierced platinum mount, engraved gallery, millegrain accents. . **675.00**

Platinum and diamond, box-cut (approx total 0.75 cts) old European-cut diamond, within diamond-set stepped geometric mount, engraved shank . **1,850.00**

Platinum and diamond, 1.65 old European-cut diamond flanked by single and baguette-cut diamond shoulders. **5,290.00**

Platinum and diamond, center three collet-set diamonds, framed by 18 single and old European-cut diamonds, openwork mount with millegrain accents **1,265.00**

Platinum, diamond, and emerald, circular-cut 1.30 diamond, encircled by calibre-cut emeralds, 16 old mine and European-cut diamonds, diamond-set scrolled shoulders. **6,325.00**

Sapphire and diamond, center oval 7.1 x 5.4 x 5.6 mm sapphire, framed by circular-cut diamonds, pierced platinum mount, millegrain accents **1,265.00**

Sapphire and diamond, navette-shape, center circular cut diamond, three French-cut sapphires, highlighted by 18 single-cut diamonds, platinum mount **500.00**

Sapphire and diamond, three-stone, center (approx total 1.24 cts) old mine-cut diamond, flanked by pair of 5.2 x 4.5 x 3.4 mm oval

sapphires, engraved foliate platinum mount. **3,165.00**

Scarab, carved coral, three rose-cut diamonds, triangular onyx and rose-cut diamond shoulders, sgd "Koch" **2,185.00**

Edwardian

Diamond and pearl, four (approx total 0.88 cts) collet-set diamonds, framed by three pearls, old European-cut diamond trefoils, platinum topped 14kt gold mount **2,650.00**

Princess, three (approx total 1.82 cts) old European-cut diamonds, framed by 16 bezel-set diamonds, platinum topped 14kt gold mount **4,140.00**

Victorian, snake, tri-color gold engraved body, (approx total 0.45 cts) old European-cut diamond, stones missing from eyes **400.00**

Suite

Art Deco, gentleman's dress set, cuff links, four shirt studs, two collar studs, sq form with cut corners, diamond centers, platinum and 18kt yellow gold, Asprey fitted box **1,265.00**
Art Nouveau, brooch and earrings, 14kt gold, opaque light to dark pink enameled bleeding hearts, each bud accented with single-cut diamonds, translucent green enamel leaves, hallmark for Krementz & Co. . . **1,495.00**
Victorian, gold expandable fancy link bracelet with center enamel medallion portrait of young boy, matching bar pin **300.00**

Watch chain, Victorian, 14kt gold, curb link design, 30.5 dwt **300.00**
Watch fob, Victorian, 14kt gold, fleur-de-lis top suspending six trace link chains terminating in chased floral and vine motif, 3" l, 20 dwt **350.00**

Watch, wrist, lady's
See Watches, Wrist, for additional examples

Art Deco, platinum

Octagonal case, ivorytone with Roman numerals, platinum and 14kt yellow gold engraved bezel set with nine diamonds, cabochon blue stone winder, verso monogrammed, 6-3/4" l round woven gold band **300.00**
Octagonal white porcelain dial, rect bezel and lugs set with 84 single and old European cut-diamonds, 15 jewel movement by Cyma Tacy Watch Co., 6-3/4" l 18kt white gold integral mesh band **1,380.00**

Rectangular white dial, Arabic numerals, bezel, lugs, and band set with 108 single and baguette-cut diamonds, Niton Swiss 17 jewel movement, verso inscribed, 7" l **990.00**
Tonneau shape, ivory dial with Arabic numerals, blue-steeled hands, bezel and band set with 82 single-cut diamonds, verso monogrammed, 6-1/2" l, dial needs cleaning, crystal scratched. **750.00**

Retro, Perraux, 14kt gold, sq white metal dial with gold indicators, lugs set with modified bullet-shaped aquamarines, flanked by diamonds, 17 jewel movement, black cord band with deployment clasp. **635.00**

JUDAICA

History: Throughout history, Jews have expressed themselves artistically in both the religious and secular spheres. Most Jewish art objects were created as part of the concept of Hiddur Mitzva, i.e., adornment of implements used in performing rituals both in the synagogue and home.

For almost 2,000 years, since the destruction of the Jerusalem Temple in 70 A.D., Jews have lived in many lands. The widely differing environments gave traditional Jewish life and art a multifaceted character. Unlike Greek, Byzantine, or Roman art which have definite territorial and historical boundaries, Jewish art is found throughout Europe, the Middle East, North Africa, and other areas.

Ceremonial objects incorporated not only liturgical appurtenances, but also ethnographic artifacts such as amulets and ritual costumes. The style of each ceremonial object responded to the artistic and cultural milieu in which it was created. Although diverse stylistically, ceremonial objects, whether for Sabbath, holidays, or the life cycle, still possess a unity of purpose.

References: Anton Felton, *Jewish Carpets,* Antique Collectors' Club, 1999; Penny Forstner and Lael Bower, *Collecting Religious Artifacts (Christian and Judaic),* Books Americana, 1996; Eric and Myra Outwater, *Judaica,* Schiffer Publishing, 1999.

Collectors' Club: Judaica Collectors Society, P.O. Box 854, Van Nuys, CA 91408.

Museums: B'nai B'rith Klutznick Museum, Washington, DC, http://www.bnaibrith.org; Jewish Museum, New York, NY, http://www.jewishmuseum.org; Jewish Museum of Maryland, Baltimore, MD, http://www.jhsm.org; Judah L. Magnes Museum, Berkeley, CA; Museum of Jewish Heritage, Battery City Park, NY, http://www.mjhnyc.org; National Museum of American Jewish History, Philadelphia, PA; Sanford L. Ziff Jewish Museum of Florida, Miami Beach, FL, http://www.jewishmuseum.com; Sylvia Plotkin Judaica Museum of Temple Beth Israel, Scottsdale, AZ; United States Holocaust Memorial Museum, Washington, DC, http://www.ushmm.org; Yeshiva

University Museum at the Center for Jewish History, New York, NY.

Notes: Judaica has been crafted in all media, though silver is the most collectible.

Diecut, woman dressed in blue, white bodice, red and white striped skirt, holding key, opening gate to family of immigrants, copyright 1909 by Hebrew Pub. Co., 3-1/4" w, 4" h, **$15.**

Amulet, 2-3/4" h, Italian, 18th/19th C, silver and silver filigree, irregular outline, inscribed "Shadai," with pendant chain and fitted leather box **520.00**

Beaker, 2-3/4" h, silver, scale motif, German, c1800 . . . . **800.00**

Candlesticks, pr, 4" d, 8-3/4" h, sterling silver, raised letters, one with "Shabbat," other with "Kadosh," slightly flaring bobeche, European hallmarks **300.00**

Ceremonial ring, 3-1/4" h, sterling silver, top applied with pavilion, side pierced with door and windows, three semi-precious stones, chased Hebrew words **425.00**

Chalice, 13" h, Continental silver, Herman Lang, Augsburg, 17th C, 29 oz **2,400.00**

Charger, 23" d, Continental silver, repoussé floral and figural dec, c1780, 8 oz **1,650.00**

Charity container

3-3/4" h, silver, inverted-pear form, body engraved banding, and molding hinged lid with money slot and hasp, scroll handle, front inscribed "Zeduke für Arme kinder," German, late 19th/20th C **920.00**

5" d, cylindrical, sheet copper, German, 1800s **265.00**

Circumcision cup, 5" h, double, silver gilt, marked "Johanna Becker, Augsburg," 1855-57 . . . . . . **13,500.00**

Comb, 6" w, brass, Burial Society, Hungarian, 1881 . . . . **5,800.00**

Esther scroll, cased

9" l, parcel-gilt and filigree, Continental, 19th C, applied jewels, hand-form thumb pc, nicely written ink on vellum scroll, fitted box **9,200.00**

10-1/2" l, Austro-Hungarian silver, Vienna, c1846 . . . . **675.00**

Etrog box, 2-3/8" h, silver, Continental, late 19th/early 20th C, spherical, beaded rim set with semi-precious green stone, body with spiral reeded and beading, applied Hebrew letters, three ball feet, 3 oz **250.00**

Hanukah lamp

6" h, Russian bronze and enamel, late 19th C, arched backplate with rampant lions and servant lamp, bowed base with candleholders **420.00**

6-1/4 x 6-1/4", Israeli silver, shaped rect, back plate with Menorah flanked by figures below Hebrew inscription, fitted with eight oil candle sockets, four paw feet **800.00**

20-1/2" h, sterling silver, circular reeded base, applied grapevine rising to sq stem, eight branches, vasiform sconces with pierced covers, central flame finial, matching servant light and oil jug, hand hammered allover, 57 oz, 8 dwt **1,900.00**

Hanukah and Sabbath lamp, 6" h, Bezalel silver, c1930, detachable bar with eight candleholders, arched body, domed circular base, applied filigree dec, lacking servant light **920.00**

Invalid's home medal, 2-7/8" d, paperweight, bronze, Dutch, octagonal, titled "Vredige Levensavond," Star of David above bedridden patient, paper case **260.00**

Kiddish cup, sterling silver

3" h, George III, double barrel form, Charles Aldridge, London, 1791-92, inscribed with the seven benedictions of wedlock, pr **7,200.00**

5-1/2" h applied flowers, trellis and medallions, circular floral foot, 4 oz **150.00**

Swirled fluted lower body, applied foliage at intervals, upper body chased with scrolls and foliage, circular foliate and beaded foot, 4 oz, 4 dwt **425.00**

6" h, American Coin, second half 19th C, dedicatory inscription "Presented to Mark L. Hirsch by Solomon Hirsch Feb. 23rd 1863" **550.00**

6" h, repoussé, scrolls and foliage on stippled ground, conforming foot, gilt int., 4 oz, 8 dwt **450.00**

7" h, Wood & Hughes, late 19th C, contemporary enameling after Szyk **1,725.00**

Kiddush cup, Russia, silver, engraved decoration, hallmarked, c1888, 2-1/8" h, **$350.**

Light bulb, 3-3/4" l, Star of David **100.00**

Lithographs, portfolio of six, The Mishna, A. Raymond Katz, orig woodcuts based on six principals, as compiled by Rabbi Judah Nasi, titled Seeds, (Zeraim), Festivals, (Mo'ed) Women (Noshim), Damages (Nezikim), Holy Objects (Kodashim), and Purity (Tohorot), each 13" x 10" image on heavy paper, titled numbered, and sgd in pencil, published by Arthur Rothman Fine Arts, NYC, 1964, hard cover folio, commentary by Charles Angoff **575.00**

Menorah, 20" h, gilt bronze, after Salvador Dali, c1980, set on Jerusalem stone base **2,415.00**

Menorah wall sconce, 10-1/2" l, Continental silver, heraldic repoussé back shield, c1858, 18 oz . . . **2,900.00**

Mezuzah, 5-1/2" h, 14K yg, after Ilha Schor, emb and cut-out with figure of Moses, "shin" finial **920.00**

Paperweight, 3" d, Star of David, millefiori, Whitefriars, 1978, to commemorate 30th anniversary of Israel, orig box **395.00**

Passover plate, 14" d, pewter, Continental, c1800 . . . . **225.00**

Passover table cloth, 76" x 56", linen, rect with shaped edges, white background, multicolored embroidered Passover implements, some staining **920.00**

Pendant, 14K yg, enameled, high priest breast plate motif, 12 step-cut multicolored synthetic stones, Retro, 1-1/2" l, 7.4 dwt **70.00**

Prayer book, miniature

Seder U-Velechtekha Ba-derekh, Feival Monk, Warsaw, 1884, Ashkenazi rite, gilt-stamped calf, faux jewel insets, 60 x 40 mm **490.00**

Sidder Hadrat Zekenim, Y. M. Solomon, Jerusalem, 1845, contemporary roan gilt, 70 x 53 mm **230.00**

Rosewater bottle, 12" h, silver, South East Asian, late 19th/early 20th C, shaped as water bird swallowing fish swallowing acanthus bouquet, stepped pedestal base, emb and engraved dec, domed top pierced, approx 8 troy oz **225.00**

Sabbath candlesticks, pr, 16-1/4" h, Aaron Katz, London, 1894, Polish style **1,000.00**

Sabbath hanging lamp, 16" h, Continental, 18th/19th C, brass, eight pointed star-form oval section, plain and turned stem, ratchet suspension hook for adjustable height **375.00**

Sabbath platter, 10-1/2" l, tin washed copper, marked "Israel Made, Hakushut" orig sticker, die struck imprinted mark **150.00**

Seal, 5" h, Austrian, Baroque style, silver, for Bassevi von Treufeld, created 1622, formed as a rampant lion holding a shield, the crest three stars and two lion/leopards **1,840.00**

Soap dish, cov, insert, Star of David finial, cobalt blue, Etruscan majolica, hairline in base **3,025.00**

Spice box, silver, windmill form

3" h, flanked by house with pierced window and door, shaped rect base, 1 oz, 2 dwt **650.00**

5-1/2" h, applied with floral baskets and birds, sq base, four scroll and foliate feet, 7 oz, 4 dwt **875.00**

Spice tower, 10-3/4" h, Russian silver, sq base, four feet rising to knopped stem, two shaped sq sections, detachable spire, c1865, 13 oz **1,700.00**

Torah binder, printed linen, typical benediction of Torah, Hupah and Good Deeds, German, late 18th C, minor staining **300.00**

Torah pointer, Continental

6-1/2" l, silver mounted lapis lazuli, 19th C, fitted box **8,625.00**

11" l, gold-mounted coral, stem with scrolling vine design, gold hand, openwork knob, beryl finish, fitted box **1,725.00**

12-1/2" l, sterling silver, inscribed "Simcha ben Miriram vo Tova bat Esther," silver chain attached to handle, hallmarked "St. George (Moscow), 84," assayer's mark, 1865, maker's initials, oval enclosed double headed eagle **925.00**

Traveling menorah, 3-1/2" x 2-1/2", sterling silver, book form, pierced flowers, animals, center anukah lamp, int. fitted with dividers to form eight oil receptacles, 11 oz, 6 dwt **1,200.00**

Watch, 2-1/2" d, Near Eastern, 19th C, silver-gilt, enamel, and rock crystal, six-sided star, floral enamel work, Hebrew numbers, rock crystal bezel and backplate, minor damage, enamel losses **2,415.00**

JUGTOWN POTTERY

History: In 1920, Jacques and Julianna Busbee left their cosmopolitan environs and returned to North Carolina to revive the state's dying pottery-making craft. Jugtown Pottery, a colorful and somewhat off-beat operation, was located in Moore County, miles away from any large city and accessible only "if mud permits."

Ben Owens, a talented young potter, turned the wares. Jacques Busbee did most of the designing and glazing. Julianna handled promotion.

Utilitarian and decorative items were produced. Although many colorful glazes were used, orange predominated. A Chinese blue glaze that ranged from light blue to deep turquoise was a prized glaze reserved for the very finest pieces.

Jacques Busbee died in 1947. Julianna, with the help of Owens, ran the pottery until 1958 when it was closed. After long legal battles, the pottery was reopened in 1960. It now is owned by Country Roads, Inc., a nonprofit organization. The pottery still is operating and using the old mark.

Bowl, 2" h, 4-1/4" d, Chinese blue glaze, imp mark, pr **425.00**

Candlesticks, pr, 3" h, Chinese Translation, Chinese blue and red, marked **85.00**

Creamer, cov, 43/4" h, yellow **60.00**

Vase

3-3/4" h, 2-1/2" d, Chinese blue flambé glaze, imp mark . . . **325.00**

4" h, 2-3/4" d, Chinese blue glaze, imp mark **275.00**

6-3/4" h, 6" d, ovoid, thick white semi-matte glaze dripping over brown clay body, imp mark. **450.00**

7-1/2" h, 4-1/2" d, ovoid, Chinese blue glaze, tight line to rim, imp mark **850.00**

8-3/4" h, 6-1/2" d, stoneware, two small handles, top cov with matte mustard glaze, bottom with clear coating, imp mark **850.00**

11" h, 8-1/2" d, two small handles, Chinese blue mottled glaze, imp mark **3,200.00**

Vessel

7-1/4" h, 5" d, ovoid, white satin glaze, hairline to rim, stamped "Jugtown Ware" **300.00**

9" h, 6-1/4" d, four small handles, brown speckled luster glaze, red clay body, glaze flakes in making, imp mark **650.00**

Vase, bulbous, stoneware, incised with band of cobalt blue stripes, stamped circular mark, 8" x 5-1/2", **$365.** *Photo courtesy of David Rago Auctions.*

KPM

History: The "KPM" mark has been used separately and in conjunction with other symbols by many German porcelain manufacturers, among which are the Königliche Porzellan Manufactur in Meissen, 1720s; Königliche Porzellan Manufactur in Berlin, 1832-1847; and Krister Porzellan Manufactur in Waldenburg, mid-19th century.

Collectors now use the term KPM to refer to the high-quality porcelain produced in the Berlin area in the 18th and 19th centuries.

Cheese board, rose and leaf garland border, pierce for hanging, marked
. . . . **48.00**

Cup and saucer, hunting scene, filigree, 19th C **65.00**

Dinner service, partial, basketweave molded rim, enamel painted sepia-toned floral sprays, 10 6-3/4" d side plates, nine 9-1/2" d dinner plates, eight 8-3/8" d salad plates, 12" l oval platter, 13-5/8" l oval platter, 8" oblong dish, late 19th/early 20th C, price for 30-pc set **520.00**

Figure, 8-1/2" h, 3-1/2" d, young man with cocked hat, long coat, trousers, and boots, young lady in Empire-style dress, fancy hat and fan, white ground, brown details, gold trim, round base, blue underglaze KPM mark, price for pr
. . . . **350.00**

Perfume bottle, 3-5/8" l, rococo-cartouche form, sepia enamel dec of cherub in flight, floral bouquet, gilt detailing, gilt-metal and coral mounted stopper, late 19th C . . **230.00**

Platter, white, gold and black trim, 14" x 19-1/2", $200.

Plaque, painted porcelain

6-1/2" l plaque, oval, after painting "Titian Daughter," woman in Renaissance-style dress, velvet lined rect giltwood frame, 8-1/2" w, 10-5/8" h frame **1,100.00**

7-3/4" w, 12-7/8" h, Ruth holding sheaf of wheat, gray shift, after the painting by Bouguereau, imp mark, late 19th/early 20th C, unframed
. . . . **3,450.00**

7-3/4" w, 13" h, young Empress Louise descending staircase, sgd lower right "R. Dittrich," imp mark, giltwood frame, late 19th C
. . . . **5,175.00**

12-1/2" x 7-5/8" plaque, young brunette in plain cream gown, imp KPM mark, heavily scrolled gilt gesso frame, late 19th C . **3,740.00**

13" x 7-3/4" plaque, standing contemplative figure in Grecian-style gown and pink wrap, holding basket of roses, stately rose draped interior, scrolled giltwood frame, imp KPM mark, late 19th C **6,600.00**

13-3/4" dia. plaque, titled "Entflohen," two young beauties seated in windswept wood, diaphanous gowns, floral headbands, anthemion and quatrefoil border, irid teal ground, 22-1/4" d giltwood and gesso frame
. . . . **10,925.00**

Punch bowl, cov, 12" d, 14-1/2" h, domed lid, Dionysian putto figural finial, enamel dec on one side with 18th C wigged gentleman at a drunken meeting of punch society, similar scene of gentleman at table to one side, vignette of couple outside village on other, floral bouquets and sprigs, imp basketweave rim, gilt edging, underglaze blue mark, late 19th C **2,775.00**

Scent bottle, molded scrolls, multicolored painted bouquets of flowers, gilt trim, gilt metal C-scroll stopper, marked, mid-19th C . . . **175.00**

Serving bowl, 15" l, oval, enamel dec foliate design, gilt border **200.00**

Teapot, 6" h, oval, medallion with floral dec, gilt ground **95.00**

Vase, 8-1/2" h, baluster, two handles, hp multicolored florals, celery green ground **200.00**

KAUFFMANN, ANGELICA

History: Marie Angelique Catherine Kauffmann was a Swiss artist who lived from 1741 until 1807. Many artists who hand-decorated porcelain during the 19th century copied her paintings. The majority of the paintings are neoclassical in style.

References: Susan and Al Bagdade, *Warman's English & Continental Pottery & Porcelain*, 3rd ed.,

Krause Publications, 1998; Wendy Wassying Roworth (ed.), *Angelica Kauffmann*, Reaktion Books, 1993, distributed by University of Washington Press.

Box, cov, 2-3/4" x 4-1/2", lilac, two maidens and child in woods on cov, brass hinges **70.00**

Cake plate, 10" d, ftd, classical scene, two maidens and cupid, beehive mark
. . . . **90.00**

Compote, 8" d, classical scene, beehive mark, sgd **85.00**

Cup and saucer, classical scene, heavy gold trim, ftd **90.00**

Vase, two handles, transfer printed decoration with figures, marked "Kauffmann Transfer, #346," 14" h, price for pair, $225. Photo courtesy of Joy Luke Auctions.

Demitasse set, 8" h demitasse pot, creamer, sugar, three cups and saucers, extra saucers, all with country scene, marked "Conaty, Germany," sgd "Kauffmann" on scene, price for 13-pc set **150.00**

Dresser tray, 11-1/2" x 7-1/2", cherub center, marked "Carlsbad, Austria"
. . . . **75.00**

Inkwell, pink luster, classical lady **80.00**

Pitcher, 8-1/2" h, garden scene, ladies, children, and flowers, sgd **100.00**

Plate, 8" d, cobalt blue border, reticulated rim, classical scene with two figures **65.00**

Portrait plate, portrait with cherubs, dark green and cream ground, gold trim, sgd "Carlsbad, Austria, Kaufmann," four-pc set **495.00**

Tobacco jar, classical ladies and cupid, green ground, SP top, pipe as finial **415.00**

Vase, 10" h, baluster, small wing handles, cobalt blue ground, roundel with semi-nude painting, sgd "K," c1870, price for pr, damage to one handle **225.00**

KEW BLAS

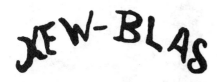

History: Amory and Francis Houghton established the Union Glass Company, Somerville, Massachusetts, in 1851. The company went bankrupt in 1860, but was reorganized. Between 1870 and 1885, the Union Glass Company made pressed glass and blanks for cut glass.

Art-glass production began in 1893 under the direction of William S. Blake and Julian de Cordova. Two styles were introduced: a Venetian style, which consisted of graceful shapes in colored glass, often flecked with gold; and an iridescent glass, called Kew Blas, made in plain and decorated forms. The pieces are similar in design and form to Quezel products, but lack the subtlety of Tiffany items.

The company ceased production in 1924.

Museum: Sandwich Glass Museum, Sandwich, MA.

Bowl, 14" d, pulled feather, red ground, sgd **1,400.00**

Candlesticks, pr, 8-1/2" h, irid gold, twisted stems **750.00**

Compote, 4-1/2" d, 3-1/2" d, gold irid, flared rim, applied pedestal foot with folded edge, inscribed "Kew Blas" on base **460.00**

Decanter, 14-1/2" h, 4-3/4" d base, gold irid, ribbed and painted stopper, purple-pink highlights, sgd on base **1,450.00**

Finger bowl and underplate, 5" d bowl, 6" d, plate, ribbed, scalloped border, metallic luster, gold and platinum highlights **475.00**

Pitcher, 4-1/2" h, green pulled feather pattern, deep gold irid int., applied swirl handle, sgd "Kew-Blas" **900.00**

Rose bowl, 4" d, scalloped rim, cased glass sphere, green vertical zipper stripes, orange irid int., inscribed "Kew Blas" on base **690.00**

Salt, irid gold **220.00**

Tumbler, 3-1/2" h, 3" d, irid gold, engraved signature within polished pontil **475.00**

Vase

6-1/2" h, 7" w, bulbous, oyster white ground, deep green hooked and pulled feathering, gold irid feathers, gold irid rim on neck, sgd **1,450.00**

12" h, poppy design at top, sgd in center of pontil **1,400.00**

KITCHEN COLLECTIBLES

History: The kitchen was the focal point in a family's environment until the 1960s. Many early kitchen utensils were handmade and prized by their owners. Next came a period of utilitarian products made of tin and other metals. When the housewife no longer wished to work in a sterile environment, enamel and plastic products added color, and their unique design served both aesthetic and functional purposes.

The advent of home electricity changed the type and style of kitchen products. Fads affected many items. High technology already has made inroads into the kitchen, and another revolution seems at hand.

References: Ellen Bercovici, Bobbie Zucker Bryson and Deborah Gillham, *Collectibles for the Kitchen, Bath and Beyond,* 2nd ed., Antique Trader Books, 2001; *Collector's Digest Price Guide to Griswold Mfg. Co. 1918 Catalog Reprint;* Edward C. Kvetko and Douglas Congdon-Martin, *Coffee Antiques,* Schiffer Publishing, 2000; Linda Fields, *Four & Twenty Blackbirds: A Pictorial Identification and Value Guide for Pie Birds,* published by author, 1998, (158 Bagsby Hill Lane, Dover, TN 37058); Gene Florence, *Kitchen Glassware of the Depression Years,* 5th ed., Collector Books, 1999; Linda Campbell Franklin, *300 Years of Housekeeping Collectibles,* Books Americana, 1992; ——, *300 Hundred Years of Kitchen Collectibles,* 4th ed., Krause Publications, 1997; Jon B. Haussler, *Griswold Muffin Pans,* Schiffer Publishing, 1997; *Griswold Cast Iron,* L-W Book Sales, 1997; Barbara Mauzy, *Bakelite in the Kitchen,* 2nd ed., Schiffer Publishing, 2001; ——, *The Complete Book of Kitchen Collecting,* Schiffer Publishing, 1997; Gary Miller and K. M. Mitchell, *Price Guide to Collectible Kitchen Appliances,* Wallace-Homestead, 1991; Jim Moffett, *American Corn Huskers,* Off Beat Books (1345 Poplar Ave., Sunnyvale, CA 94087), 1994; David T. Pikul and Ellen M. Plante, *Enameled Kitchenware American & European,* Schiffer Publishing, 2000; Don and Carol Raycraft, *Wallace-Homestead Price Guide to American Country Antiques,* 16th ed., Krause Publications, 1999; James Rollband, *American Nutcrackers,* Off Beat Books (1345 Poplar Ave., Sunnyvale, CA 94087), 1996; Don Thornton, *Apple Parers,* Off Beat Books, (1345 Poplar Ave., Sunnyvale, CA 94087) 1997; ——, *Beat This: The Eggbeater Chronicles,* Off Beat Books, 1994; ; ——, *The Eggbeater Chronicles,* 2nd ed., Thorton House, 1999.

Periodicals: *Cast Iron Marketplace,* P.O. Box 16466, St. Paul, MN 55116; *Cook Book Collector's Club Newsletter,* 4756 Terrace Dr., San Diego, CA 92116-2514; *Cook Book Gossip,* P.O. Box 56, St. James, MO 65559-0056; *Cookies Newsletter,* 9610 Greenview Lane, Manassas, VA 20109-3320, http://www.cookiesnewsletter.com; *Kettles 'n' Cookware,* P.O. Box B, Perrysburg, NY 14129; *Old Cookbook News & Views,* 4756 Terrace Dr., San Diego, CA 92116-2514.

Collectors' Clubs: Cook Book Collectors Club of America, P.O. Box 56, St. James, MO 65559-0056; Cookie Book Collector's Club, 4756 Terrace Dr., San Diego, CA 92116-2514; Cookie Cutter Collectors Club, 2763 310 St., Cannon Falls, MN 55009; Eggcup

Collectors' Corner, 67 Steven Ave., Old Bridge, NJ 08857; Griswold & Cast Iron Cookware Association, 3007 Plum St., Erie, PA 16508; International Society for Apple Parer Enthusiasts, 735 Cedarwood Terrace, Apt 735B, Rochester, NY 14609; Kollectors of Old Kitchen Stuff, 3038 E Woodland Dr., Hickory Corners, MI 49060; Mid-America Reamer Collectors, 2262 Clay St., Austinburg, OH 44010-9753; National Reamer Collectors Association, 47 Midline Court, Gaithersburg, MD 20878, http://www.reamers.org; Pie Bird Collectors Club, P.O. Box 192, Acworth, GA 30101-0192; Southwest Reamer Collectors Assoc., 2824 Willing, Fort Worth, TX 76110; Western Regional Reamer Collectors Assoc., 1478 W. Cypress Ave., Redlands, CA 92373-5613.

Museums: Birmingham Museum of Art, Birmingham, AL; Conrad N. Hilton Library at the Culinary Institute of America, Hyde Park, NY; Corning Glass Museum, Corning, NY; Johnson & Wales Culinary Archives & Museum, Providence, RI; Kern County Museum, Bakersfield, CA; Landis Valley Farm Museum, Lancaster, PA.

Additional Listings: Baskets, Brass, Butter Prints, Copper, Fruit Jars, Food Molds, Graniteware, Ironware, Tinware, and Woodenware. See *Warman's Americana & Collectibles* for more examples, including electrical appliances. See *Warman's Flea Market Price Guide* also.

Apple peeler, cast iron, Reading Hardware Co. **90.00**

Bread board, 24" x 18", tiger maple, shaped handle, short split where handles meets board, refinished with varnish on one side **150.00**

Broom holder, Little Polly Brooms, tin litho, image of little girl sweeping floor, 2-1/2" w, 6-1/4" h **425.00**

Butter churn, 49" h, old blue paint, America, 19th C, minor imperfections **345.00**

Butter paddle

6-1/4" l, maple, unusual carved handle resembling bird with open beak, small rim chip **125.00**

8-1/2" l, curly maple, good color and figure in simple hooked handle, old edge chip **110.00**

9-3/4" l, burl, dark patina, simple hooked handle **165.00**

Catalog

Buffalo Mfg. Co., Buffalo, NY, 20 pgs, makers of hot water, tea, coffee, and chocolate urns, cuts of 19 items **30.00**

Manning-Bowman & Co., Meriden, CT, c1920, 34 pgs, gas stoves, chafing dishes, accessories, some recipes **40.00**

Martin L. Hall & Co., Boston, MA, 1902, 20 pgs, *Grocers & Importers,* wholesale catalog **18.00**

Sidney Shepard & Co., Buffalo, NY, c1924, 32 pgs, kitchen specialists, cuts of steam cereal cooker, egg poacher, roaster, perfection tins, etc. **45.00**

Stransky & Co., New York, NY, 1901, 208 pgs, imported quadruple steel ware **175.00**

Cheese sieve, 10" d, 7" h, plus handle, hand-molded yellow clay, Albany glaze **320.00**

Cookbook, Ryzon Baking Book, Marion Harris Neil, 1916, 6-3/4" x 8-3/4", **$12.**

Cook book, distributed by manufacturers

Agate Iron Ware Mfg. Co., Boston, MA, 1890, 74 pgs, 4-1/2" x 6" **125.00**

A Lesson On Waffles & Griddle Cakes, H.H. Downing, Calumet Baking Powder Co., Chicago, IL, 16 pgs **10.00**

Birds Eye Brand Modern Foods for Modern Menus, General Foods Corp., New York, NY 1942, 36 pgs, miracle quick freezing facts, nutrition guide **10.00**

Certo, Sure Jell, Douglas-Pectin Corp., Rochester, NY, 1924, 14 pgs **8.00**

Good Things to Eat, Church & Dwight Co., New York, NY, 1924, 32 pgs, Arm & Hammer Bicarbonate of Soda recipes **10.00**

Majestic Manufacturing Co., St. Louis, MO, c1915, 96 pgs, 6" x 8-1/2" **20.00**

Metropolitan Life Cook Book, Metropolitan Life Insurance, New York, NY, 1957, 56 pgs, list of weights and measures, oven temperatures, recipes **10.00**

Secrets of Meat Curing & Sausage Making, B. Heller & Co., Chicago, IL, 1933, 302 pgs, how to cure hams, shoulders, bacon, corned beef, etc. **40.00**

The Granite Iron Ware Cook Book, St. Louis Stamping Co., St. Louis, MO, c1878 . . . . **75.00**

The Story of Cane Sugar, Pennsylvania Sugar Co., Philadelphia, PA, c1929, 16 pgs, 4" x 9", 16" x 18" color sheet folded as issued **15.00**

What Shall I Cook Today? Lever Brothers, Cambridge, MA, c1935, 50 pgs, 124 thrifty, healthful tested recipes from the makers of Spry shortening **12.00**

Wonderful Ways with Soups from Campbell's For You, Campbell Soup Co., Camden, NJ, 1958, 64 pgs **12.00**

Cookie mold

23-1/2" l, 5-1/4" w, people and rooster on one side, four animals and two birds on other, minor edge wear. **125.00**

25-1/2" l, 5" w, four people in European dress, two figures on each side, minor edge wear **125.00**

28" l, 3-3/8" w, carved woman at well, man and woman near potted plant, few worm holes **250.00**

Dough box, pine and turned poplar, PA, 19th C, rect removable top, tapering well, splayed ring-turned legs, ball feet, 38" w, 19-1/4" d, 29-1/2" h **425.00**

Egg beater, 10-1/2" l, Jacquette Scissor, marked "Jacquette, Phila, PA, Patented No. 3" **550.00**

Flatware, four 8-7/8" l knives and four forks, wooden handles, knife blades marked "J. Ward & Co., Riverside, Mass.," wear and some damage to orig box **90.00**

Flour sifter, 14" h, 12" w, Tilden's Universal, wood, partial intact paper label **335.00**

Food chopper, 7" w, wrought iron, scalloped edge blade, turned wood handle. **270.00**

Griddle, cast iron, Griswold, No. 10 . . . . **70.00**

Ice shaver, nickel-plated steel, marked "Enterprise," July 4, 1893 patent **. 45.00**

Funnel, wood, 7-1/4" h, 4-3/4" d, **$85.**

Instruction book, *The Tappan Owner's Guide with Instructions for Tappan Gas Range,* Tappan Stove Co., Mansfield, OH, 1955, 47 pgs, cooking charts, instructions, directions for canning, baking, broiler cooking **10.00**

Kettle, cast iron, Griswold No. 4. **85.00**

Kraut cutter, 25-5/8" l, 8" w, heart cut-out, maple, mellow patina . . **350.00**

Ladle, 15" l, wood, pot hook handle **50.00**

Lemon squeezer, iron, glass insert, marked "Williams" **50.00**

Nutmeg grater, 7" l, Champion, brass and wood **635.00**

Pantry box, cov, 11-1/2" d, 6-1/2" h, oak, bail handle. **175.00**

Pastry board, wood, three sided **32.00**

Pie crimper, 7" l, carved bone, unicorn with carved fish tail, ball-shaped hooves, front let glued, late replacement crimper, medium brown stain. **220.00**

Pie safe, hanging, 31" w, 19" d, 31" h, mortised pine case, old thin red wash, door, sides, and back with punched tins with geometric circles and stars, white porcelain door pull, two int. shelves, edge damage **990.00**

Potato masher, 9" l, turned maple **40.00**

Pot scraper, Sharples Tubular Separator, tin litho, graphic advertising on both sides, 3-1/8" x 2-1/4" . . **275.00**

Rack, 20" l, rect backplate with arched top, red and white enameled checkerboard pattern, narrow well, single rod suspending two strainer spoons. **250.00**

Rolling pin

15-3/4" l, blown glass, deep amber knopped handles, 19th C . **150.00**

16-1/2" l, curly maple, dark color, good patina **275.00**

22" l, milk glass, cylindrical, turned wood handles, marked "Imperial Mfg., Co. July 25, 1921". . . . **95.00**

Sausage stuffer, 17-1/2" l, turned wood plunger **30.00**

Skillet, cast iron, Griswold, No. 14 . . . . **165.00**

Spatula, 17-3/4" l, brass and wrought iron, polished **175.00**

Stove

Cast iron, chrome, nickel, colorful ceramic tile back **6,000.00**

Cast iron, enameled swirled pattern, white enamel knobs, black burner rings, separate oven and broiler, nameplate "The Champion Stove Co.," 46" w, 27" d, 49" h . . **5,750.00**

Taster, 7" l, brass and wrought iron, polished **150.00**

Ice box, oak, plaque marked "Sibera, Simmons Hardware, St. Louis, Mo," 32" w, 54" h, **$475.** *Photo courtesy of Joy Luke Auctions.*

Tin

Donovan's Baking Powder, Mt. Morris, NY, 1 lb, paper label, 5-1/4" h, 3" d **475.00**

Egg-O Brand Baking Powder, paper label, 2-3/4" h, 1-1/4" d **110.00**

Fulford Powder, multicolored . . **25.00**

Kavanaugh's Tea, 1 lb, little girl on porch in dress, talking to doll, mother sipping tea in window, cardboard sides, tin top and bottom, 6" h, 4-1/2" w, 4-1/2" d **500.00**

Maltby's Cocoaut, slip top **40.00**

Miller's Gold Medal Breakfast Cocoa, red and black, c1890, 2" h, 1-5/8" w, 1-1/8" d **250.00**

Opal Powdered Sugar, Hewitt & Sons, Des Moines, 8" h, 4-1/2" w, 3-1/4" d **180.00**

Parrot and Monkey Baking Powder, 4 oz, full, 3-1/4" h, 2-1/8" d . . **375.00**

Sunshine-Oxford Fruit Cake, early 1900s, sq corners **20.00**

Three Crow Brand Cream of Tartar, early, #1 . . . . **45.00**

Towle's Log Cabin Brand Maple Syrup, cabin shaped, woman and girl in doorway, 4" h, 3-3/4" l, 2-1/2" d **110.00**

Trivet, 12" l, lyre form, wrought iron frame and turned handle, brass top, replaced foot, stamped maker's mark **45.00**

Wafer iron, cast iron, octagonal, church with steeple and trees dec on one side, pinwheel with plants and star flowers on reverse, wrought iron handles **400.00**

KUTANI

History: Kutani originated in the mid-1600s in the Kaga province of Japan. Kutani comes in a variety of color patterns, one of the most popular being Ao Kutani, a green glaze with colors such as green, yellow, and purple enclosed in a black outline. Export wares made since the 1870s are enameled in a wide variety of colors and styles.

Beaker, 4-1/2" h, hp flowers and birds, red, orange, and gold, white ground, marked "Ao-Kutani" **95.00**

Biscuit jar, cov, Geisha Girl, c1890 . . . . **190.00**

Bowl, 6-3/8" d, gilt and bright enamel design, figural, animal, and floral reserves, kinrande ground, base inscribed "Kutani-sei," set of 10 . . . . **400.00**

Charger, 18-3/8" d, pomegranate tree, chrysanthemums, and two birds on int., birds and flowers between scrolling foliate bands, irregular floral and brocade border, 11-character inscription **600.00**

Chawan (tea bowl), 5" d, 3" h, sunflower design, orange and green, imp mark "RIJU" **100.00**

Chocolate pot, white ground, hp scenes of lake, three white cranes on shore, Mt. Fiji in distance, hills with wildflowers, white and pink chrysanthemums, two white cranes with black tails, lid painted with wild flowers on cliff, crane, gold bamboo branch, gold knob, cream colored handle, wear to knob **95.00**

Creamer and sugar, summer scene, two court ladies, red, blue, gray, and gold, red handle, spout, and feet with gold overlay, c1910 . . . . **95.00**

Dessert service, country life dec, gold cloud borders, eight plates, two compotes, 20th C **435.00**

Figure

12" h, Bodhidhama, standing, long red rope, flywisk in right hand **225.00**

14-1/4" h, Kannon, polychrome and gilt dec, standing, dragon mount, high coiffure, wind-swept rope, inscribed "Kutani-sei" **600.00**

Jar, cov, 20-1/2" h, ovoid, fan-shaped reserves of warriors, molded ribbon tied tasseled ring handles, shippo-tsunagi ground, multicolored brocade patterned dome lid, pr **1,400.00**

Sake cup, 2-3/16" h, 1-1/8" w, crane in red center, gold lacquer trim **35.00**

Tea caddy, 6" h, bulbous, hexagonal, Nishikide diapering, figural raised gold reserves of children, red script mark **195.00**

Teapot, cov, 8" h, white, trees and flowers, gold trim, marked "Hand Painted Craftsman China, Kutani 391 Japan" **45.00**

Tray, 14" l, polychrome and gilt dec, figural scene, red, orange, and gold border **350.00**

Vase

7-1/4" h, classic shape, white emb chrysanthemums on white ground, marked "Trade Mark Fujita Kutani, Made in Japan" **95.00**

12" h, baluster, dancing figures, symmetric floral designs, rusty-red, peach ground **95.00**

14" h, pear shape, Satsuma type dec of traveling scholar, Japan, late 19th/early 20th C **200.00**

Bowl, three men in red, 7-1/2" d, **$170.**

LACE AND LINENS

History: Lace, lacy linens, embroidery, and hand-decorated textiles are different from any other antique. They are valued both as a handmade substance and as the thing the substance is made into. Thread is manipulated into stitches, stitches are assembled into lace, and lace is made into handkerchiefs, edgings, tablecloths, and bedspreads. Things eventually go out of style or are damaged or worn, and just as the diamonds and rubies are taken from old jewelry and placed into new settings, fine stitchery of embroidery and lace is saved and reused. Lace from a handkerchief is used to decorate a blouse, fragments of a bridal veil are made into a scarf; shreds of old lace are remounted onto fine net and used again as a veil.

At each stage in the cycle, different people become interested. Some see fragments as bits and pieces of a collage, and seek raw materials for accent pieces. Others use Victorian whites and turn-of-the-century embroidered linens to complement a life style. Collectors value and admire the stitches themselves, and when those stitches are remarkable enough, they will pay hundreds of dollars for fragments a few inches square.

Until the 1940s, lace collecting was a highly respected avocation of the wealthy. The prosperity of the New World was a magnet for insolvent European royalty, who carried suitcases of old Hapsburg, Bourbon, Stuart, and Romanov laces to suites at New York's Waldorf hotel for dealers to select from. Even Napoleon's bed hangings of handmade Alencon lace, designed for Josephine and finished for Marie Louise, found their way here. In 1932, *Fortune* magazine profiled socially prominent collectors and lace dealers. For the entire first half of this century, New York City's Needle and Bobbin Club provided a forum for showing off acquisitions.

Until 1940, upscale department stores offered antique lace and lacy linens. Dealers specializing in antique lace and lacy linens had prominent upscale shops, and offered repair, restoration, remodeling, and cleaning services along with the antique linens. In addition to collecting major pieces—intact jabots from the French Ancient Regime, Napoleonic-era Alencon, huge mid-Victorian lace shawls, Georgian bed hangings appliquéd with 17th-century needle lace—collectors assembled study collections of postcard-size samples of each known style of antique lace.

When styles changed around the 1940s and 1950s and the market for antique lace and linens crashed, some of the best collections did go to museums; others just went into hiding. With renewed interest in a gracious, romantic lifestyle, turn-of-the-century lacy cloths from the linen closets of the barons of the industrial revolution are coming out of hiding. Collectors and wise dealers know that many of the small study pieces of irreplaceable stitchery—fragments collectors will pay ten to hundreds of dollars for—still emerge in rummage and estate sales.

Very large banquet-sized lace tablecloths, especially those with napkins, continue to be especially popular. Appenzell, a white-on-white embroidered lacework of 19th century Switzerland, has become one of the hottest collector's items. Strong interest continues in patterned silk ribbons, all cotton lace yardage, and other lacy materials for heirloom sewing and fashion.

The market for antique lace definitely is changing. Interest is still rising for elaborate lace for home decorating and entertaining, and interest in fine-quality lace collars is increasing. Large lace shawls and veils, especially for bridal wear, continue to be in demand. Internet auctions and chat groups make it possible for a dealer in Wyoming to link up with a collector in Louisiana, and find a home for an interesting piece. Those interested in fine-quality lace are realizing they need to start buying at market prices instead of waiting for that lucky find that they alone recognize. Current market prices, although rising, still are usually far below what the pieces would have cost when new, or during the early 20th century heyday of lace collecting.

As prices rise, buyers more often want an accurate identification: what is it, where was it made, and how old is it? What makes it worth the price? Word spreads quickly over the Internet when it is obvious a dealer has mislabeled something, especially labeling something as handmade that is obviously machine made. Lace has long been a sideline for most dealers, and they did not bother to learn to identify it. As long as they could turn it over quickly for a small markup, they were satisfied. That is changing. More sophisticated buyers won't put up with that.

The basic techniques are bobbin lace, needle lace, crochet, tatting, knitting, knotting, and needle weaving. Identifying how a piece was made is the easy part, and there is no excuse for a dealer not being able to separate crochet from bobbin lace. Anyone can identify the technique after just a weekend workshop, or by comparing a piece to pictures in a good textbook. The technique, plus the quality of the design and condition, provides nearly all the information anyone needs to decide what a piece is worth.

After identifying the technique, many like to apply a name to the style (Duchesse bobbin lace, Point de Gaze needle lace, Irish crochet). This serves as a useful shorthand in talking about lace, but adds nothing to the value of the piece. This is often the confusing part. Unlike most antiques, there is no uniformity in labeling styles of lace. Names changed at different points in time, different names were used for similar products made in different countries, and foreign names often were translated differently. Any dealer should be expected to be able to explain why they chose to use any specific style name.

The Internet offers a unique access to a wide variety of kinds of lace and lacy linens. The small pictures available on the Internet, however, rarely show enough detail to know just what you are buying. Insist on a return policy for any lace purchased sight unseen on the Internet. Even well-intentioned dealers may miss details that significantly affect the value of lace. Handmade meshes cannot be positively identified

without high-powered magnification. Repairs often go unnoticed and unreported. Color and texture make a great deal of difference in determining whether a piece of lace is attractive.

Whether purchasing fine quality collector's study samples, or boxes and bags of recyclable fragments for sewing, it is worth taking a close look at all the details. It is not uncommon to find good quality study samples that a collector will pay $10 to $100 for in the "rag bags."

Those who learn to recognize the artistry and value of old stitchery will not only enhance their lives with beauty, they may find a windfall.

References: Pat Earnshaw, *Identification of Lace*, Lubrecht and Cramer, 1989; Frances Johnson, *Collecting Antique Linens, Lace, and Needlework*, Wallace-Homestead, 1991; —, *Collecting More Household Linens*, Schiffer Publishing, 1997; Elizabeth Kurella, *Guide To Lace and Linens*, Antique Trader Books, 1998; —, *Secrets of Real Lace*, The Lace Merchant (P.O. Box 222, Plainwell, MI 49080), 1994; —, *Pocket Guide to Valuable Old Lace and Lacy Linens*, The Lace Merchant (P.O .Box 222, Plainwell, MI 49080), 1996; —, *The Complete Guide To Vintage Textiles*, Krause Publications, 1999; Marsha L. Manchester, *Vintage White Linens A to Z*, Schiffer Publishing, 1997; Roseanne Mihalick, *Collecting Handkerchiefs*, Schiffer Publishing, 2000; Emily Reigate, *An Illustrated Guide to Lace*, Antique Collectors' Club; Elizabeth Scofield and Peggy Zalamea, *Twentieth Century Linens and Lace*, Schiffer Publishing, 1997.

Collectors' Club: International Old Lacers, P.O. Box 554, Flanders, NJ 07836, http://members.aol.com/iolinc/ioli.html.

Museums: Chicago Art Institute, Chicago, IL; Cooper Hewitt (Smithsonian), New York, NY; Metropolitan Museum of Art, New York, NY; Museum of Early Southern Decorative Arts (MESDA), Winston-Salem, NC; Museum of Fine Arts, Boston, MA; Rockwood Museum, Wilmington, DE; Shelburne Museum, Shelburne, VT; Smithsonian Institution, Washington, DC.

Adviser: Elizabeth M. Kurella.

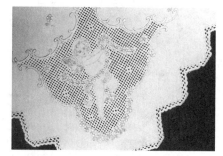

Table cloth, Swiss Appenzell, whitework, design of cherubs and lady, dressed in 18th-century costume, with parrot, eight matching napkins, 120" x 85", **$2,500.** *Photo courtesy of Elizabeth Kurella.*

Bedspread

Crochet, double size, filet crochet grid-style design, scrolling leaves design **85.00**

Embroidered, double size, white cloth with red "turkey work" embroidery, cartoon character designs, c1930 . . . . **150.00**

Princess Lace (machine tapes appliquéd to machine net) scrolling flower and leaves design . . **350.00**

Bridal veil

Point De Gaze needle lace in rose and leaf design with scrolls and medallions in 12" edge border on 7' long teardrop shape veil

. . . . **1,500.00**

Princess Lace, 65" x 48" oval, machine net decorated with floral and scroll design **325.00**

Bridge set, linen, embroidered in red and black motifs of playing-card suits, matching napkins **85.00**

Collar

Berthe-style, Brussels mixed lace, floral and scroll work of Duchesse bobbin lace with rose inserts of Point de Gauze, many exotic filling stitches of needle lace, 6" deep, 38" l **625.00**

Duchesse bobbin lace, c1870, roses, daisies, and scrollwork design, 5" at center back, 32" l
. . . . **125.00**

Point de Grace, 19th C Belgian needle lace, roses with shaded petals and leaves design, pr of 10" l labels, price for pr **75.00**

Curtains

Hand-embroidered machine net, c1900, iris, roses, and filigree elaborate designs, 48" x 96", pr
. . . . **50.00**

Machine lace, ecru, 36" x 72"
. . . . **75.00**

Doily

Crochet, roses, raised petals, 8" d round **10.00**

Flemish bobbin lace, c1900, goldfish design in Petit de Paris ground, 10" d round, 3" deep lace . . . **75.00**

Dresser scarf

Drawnwork, Victorian, white geometric design, 28" x 48" . **45.00**

White cotton, flower basket embroidered in bright colors, white crochet edging, c1930, 24" x 38"
. . . . **12.00**

Fragments of collector's lace

Gros Point de Venise, c1650, stylized scrolling floral design, motifs defined by raised and padded outlines dec with many styles of picots, 2" x 12" **285.00**

Tea cloth, white linen center, hem-stitched border, surrounded by intricate hand-crochet floral and mesh design, white, c1900, 54" square, $150.

Point de Neige, c1680, needle lace with minute stylized design and layers of raised picots, 10" x 18"
. . . . **285.00**

Point de Venise a Reseau, stylized floral design, Alencon mesh background, no cordonnet, 3" x 6" fragment of edging **185.00**

Handkerchief

Linen

Edged with colored crochet scallop design, 12" sq **2.00**

Edged with half inch of white tatting, 12" sq **6.00**

4" of Irish Youghal needle lace with stylized shamrocks design, background of stitched bars dec with picots, 16" sq . **375.00**

Whitework, French, 1870s, edged with embroidery, drawnwork, and needle-lace inserts **95.00**

Napkin

Cocktail, white, edge with single scallop of needle lace, 1" sq corner inserts of needle lace worked in stylized animal design, price for six-pc set **45.00**

Dinner, linen with needle-lace edging, corner insert, c1900, 24" sq, price for six-pc set **185.00**

Pillowcase

Cotton, embroidered multicolored flower-basket design, crochet edge, c1930, pr **15.00**

Linen, white, figural designs in needle-lace inserts, floral design in needle-lace edging, pr **125.00**

Maderia, white cotton, flower silhouetted in cutwork, embroidered with satin stitch, pr
. . . . **15.00**

Pillow cover, linen, white, dec with inserts of needle lace, scrolling floral designs, embroidered in satin stitch,

Cluny bobbin lace edging, 18" d round
. . . . **125.00**

Pincushion, white satin, top cov with sq of white Italian drawn work in heavy linen, embroidered raised flower and tendril design, corners dec with whimsical knotted tassels, 4" sq, 1" d **65.00**

Runner, Normandy work, patchwork of handmade Vaienciennes bobbin lace and other laces, mostly handmade, central motif of French embroidered whitework with birds and flowers, oval, 24" x 18" **145.00**

Tablecloth

Cotton, embroidered pussy willows and flowers design, tablecloth and six matching napkins, c1947
. . . . **75.00**

Crochet, round medallions design, 48" x 68" **75.00**

Cutwork

Floral and scrollwork satin-stitch embroidery, needle-lace inserts, 8" deep border of filet in figural designs, Italian, c1900, 42" sq
. . . . **175.00**

Floral designs in satin-stitch embroidery, inserts of needle lace with rose designs, 68" x 140", 12 matching napkins, price for set **975.00**

Filet, geometric design darned over knotted network, 48" x 72" . . **125.00**

Linen, natural color, Richelieu, all handmade cutwork and embroidery, floral and scroll motif, early 20th C, 68" x 100" **575.00**

Swiss Appenzell whitework, with designs of cherubs, and a lady with a parrot dressed in 18th C costume, 120" x 85", eight napkins, price for set **2,500.00**

LALIQUE

LALIQUE

A.LALIQUE

History: René Lalique (1860-1945) first gained prominence as a jewelry designer. Around 1900, he began experimenting with molded-glass brooches and pendants, often embellishing them with semiprecious stones. By 1905, he was devoting himself exclusively to the manufacture of glass articles.

In 1908, Lalique began designing packaging for the French cosmetic houses. He also produced many objects, especially vases, bowls, and figurines, in the Art Nouveau and Art Deco styles. The full scope of

Lalique's genius was seen at the 1925 Paris l'Exposition Internationale des Arts Décorative et Industriels Modernes.

Marks: The mark "R. LALIQUE FRANCE" in block letters is found on pressed articles, tableware, vases, paperweights, and automobile mascots. The script signature, with or without "France," is found on hand-blown objects. Occasionally, a design number is included. The word "France" in any form indicates a piece made after 1926.

The post-1945 mark is generally "Lalique France" without the "R," but there are exceptions.

References: Fritz Falk, *Lalique and His Circle*, Arnoldsche, distributed by Antique Collectors' Club, 1999; Kyle Husfloen, *Antique Trader's American & European Decorative and Art Glass Price Guide*, 2nd ed., Krause Publications, 2000.

Collectors' Club: Lalique Collectors Society, 400 Veterans Blvd., Carlstadt, NJ 07072, http://www.lalique.com/lcs.html.

Reproduction Alert: The Lalique signature has often been forged; the most common fake includes an "R" with the post-1945 mark.

Animal, hedgehog, 4-1/2" l, 2-1/2" h
.... **950.00**
Ashtray, 5-3/4" d, lion, molded gargoyle form rim, extended mane ridges, engraved script sgd **180.00**
Bonbon box, cov
  8-1/4" d, Boites Ronde Grande Libellulis, irid dragonfly, sgd "R. Lalique No. 51"........ **1,295.00**
  10-1/4" d, Lily of the Valley, marked "Claire d'Lune," block sgd . **695.00**
Bowl, 8-1/2" d, Honfleur, frosted lilypad leaves, script sgd, some scratches
.... **525.00**
Buttons, pr, coiled serpent over red backing, sgd "Lalique," converted into earrings **435.00**
Center bowl, 14" d, daisy, broad molded rim, clear, brown patina on floral border **465.00**
Champagne flute, 8-1/8" h, cylindrical bowls etched with angel's wings, top of stem with molded frosted face of angel, etched mark "Lalique ® France" on foot, price for eight-pc set **750.00**
Coupe, 9-3/8" d, 3-1/4" h, shallow bowl, Vases No. 1, colorless, repeating polished urn-forms alternating frosted stylized bouquets, center molded "R. Lalique" **230.00**
Decanter set, 11" h decanter with donut stopper, Highlands, four matching glasses, #13301 and #1333412................. **800.00**

Dresser jar, 3-1/2" h, Epines, domical stopper bottles, molded thorn bushes, strong blue patina, molded mark "R. Lalique," one stopper frozen, chip under edge, price for pr....... **230.00**
Dressing table mirror, 12" l, 6-1/2" d, Narcisse Couche, frosted glass frame and handle, molded foliate motif centering male nude above handle, orig gray patina in recesses, inscribed "R. Lalique, France" top rim, mirror slightly stained **980.00**
Figure, 10-1/4" h, Two Dancers, sgd in script, c1960.............. **1,475.00**
Medallion, 1-3/8" d, Dana les Fleurs, 1924 model, frosted low relief of nude female under blossoms, made for Fioret perfume box, marked "R. Lalique/Fioret/Paris" **520.00**

*Perfume bottle, Flausa, created for Roget & Gallet, 4-3/4" h, **$6,325**. Photo courtesy of Jackson's Auctioneers & Appraisers.*

Perfume bottle
  2-1/2" h, Imprudence, ridged bottle, silver trim, marked "R. Lalique France," orig Worth box ... **275.00**
  3-1/2" h, Chrysanthemum, 1950s, sgd **650.00**
Perfume flacon
  3-3/4" h, Salamandres, colorless flattened oval, polished roundels surrounded by curving lizards, gray-green patina in recesses, motif repeated on stopper, base

inscribed "L. Lalique, France"
.... **1,495.00**
  5-1/4" h, Ambre, polished sq bottle, molded draped women recessed at each corner, black sq stopper with floral motif, base mold mark "Lalique/Ambre D'Orsay," small chips inside top **1,380.00**
  5-1/2" h, Bouchon Mures, colorless barrel-shaped bottle, black ribbing, molded flawless matte black tiara stopper with berry clusters, molded "R. Lalique" on base **9,200.00**

*Plate, black, molded tree motif, 11-1/4" d, **$150**. Photo courtesy of Joy Luke Auctions.*

Plate, 7-1/4" d, black crystal, Algues, sgd "Catalogue Number 10421," price for set of eight **2,500.00**
Powder box, cov, sepia wash, two ladies, arms entwined, fancy scrolls and flowers on cov, sepia washed garlands of flowers on base, sgd "Coty" and "Lalique Depose," c1915.. **600.00**
Vase
  4-1/2" h, Eglantines, frosted oval, polished thorny branches and rose blossoms in relief, center base inscribed "R. Lalique" **400.00**
  5-1/2" d, 9-3/4" h, clear and frosted, ladies, garland of fruit and flowers, sgd "R. Lalique France".. **2,200.00**

LAMP SHADES

History: Lamp shades were made to diffuse the harsh light produced by early gas lighting fixtures. These early shades were made by popular Art Nouveau manufacturers including Durand, Quezal, Steuben, and Tiffany. Many shades are not marked.

Aladdin
  Cased, green **870.00**
  Satin, white, dogwood dec... **65.00**

Artichoke, 10" d
Green **1,000.00**
White **800.00**
Cased art glass, 5-1/2" h, 2-1/4" d fitter rim, cased gold, opal glass ruffled bell shade, green pulled feather motif, gold irid luster, price for four-pc set . . **435.00**
Ceiling shade, 22" d, 9-1/2" deep, 5" opening, hipped O' Brien dome, leaded green glass segments arranged in brickwork geometric progression, three orig int. bronze reinforcements, rim imp "Tiffany Studios, New York 1501"
. . . . **10,350.00**
Durand, 9-1/2" l, gold Egyptian crackle, blue and white overlay, bulbous, ruffed rim, sgd **225.00**
Fenton, 4" d, white opal hobnails, blue ground **90.00**
Fostoria, 5-1/2" d, Zipper pattern, green pulled dec, opal ground, gold lining **225.00**
Handel, 10" d, tam o'shanter, hand-painted green silhouette village scene with windmill and harbor, sgd "Handel 2862" **325.00**

Paneled green slag glass, brass frame, 21" d, $250. Photo courtesy of Joy Luke Auctions.

Imperial, NuArt, marigold **65.00**
Leaded glass, 17-1/2" d, 3" d opening, narrow topped umbrella-shape, dropped apron, four bright red starburst blossoms with yellow disks on green stems, green slag background segments, conforming motif on apron, some restoration to inside leading
. . . . **635.00**
Loetz, 8-1/2" d, irid green oil spotting, ribbon work, white glass int., c1900
. . . . **250.00**

Lutz type, 8" sq, 6-1/4" h, opaque white loopings, applied cranberry threading, ribbon edge **195.00**
Muller Freres, 6" h, frosted satin, white top, cobalt blue base, yellow highlights, three-pc set **400.00**
Opalescent and amber, optic, Coinspot pattern, c1880 . . . . . . **70.00**
Pairpoint, 7" h, puffy, flower basket, reverse painted pink and yellow poppies and roses **425.00**
Quezal, 5-1/2" d, dark green, platinum feathers, gold lining **650.00**
Rubena, 7-1/4" d, 3-7/8" d fitter ring, cranberry shading to clear, frosted and clear etched flowers and leaves, ruffled
. . . . **460.00**
Steuben, Aurene, irid brown, platinum applied border **425.00**
Tartan, 6" h, 3-1/4" fitter ring, gaslight, bands of white, yellow, and pink, sgd "Tartan Rd. No. 46498," registered by "Henry Gething Richardson, Wordsley Flint Glass Works, near Stourbridge, Feb 24, 1886" **285.00**
Tiffany, 51/4" d, bell shape, irid gold ground, four-pc set **1,200.00**
Verlys, 3-5/8" d, 5-3/4" h, raised birds and fish dec **285.00**

LAMPS AND LIGHTING

History: Lighting devices have evolved from simple stone-age oil lamps to the popular electrified models of today. Aimé Argand patented the first oil lamp in 1784. Around 1850, kerosene became a popular lamp-burning fluid, replacing whale oil and other fluids. In 1879, Thomas A. Edison invented the electric light, causing fluid lamps to lose favor and creating a new field for lamp manufacturers. Companies like Tiffany and Handel became skillful at manufacturing electric lamps, and their decorators produced beautiful bases and shades.

References: James Edward Black (ed.), *Electric Lighting of the 20s-30s* (1988, 1993 value update), *Volume 2 with Price Guide* (1990, 1993 value update), L-W Book Sales; John Campbell, *Fire & Light in the Home Pre 1820*, Antique Collectors' Club, 1999; J. W. Courter, *Aladdin Collectors Manual & Price Guide #19*, published by author (3935 Kelley Road, Kevil, KY 42053), 2000; —, *Aladdin, The Magic Name In Lamps, Revised Edition*, published by author, 1997; *Electric Lighting of the 20s-30s, Vol. 1* (1994, 1998 value update), *Vol. 2, (1994)*, L-W Book Sales, Carole Goldman Hibel, John Hibel, John Fontaine, *The Handel Lamps Book*, Fontaine Publishers, 1999; Donald B. Johnson and Leslie Pina, *1930s Lighting: Deco & Traditional by Chase*, Schiffer Publishing, 2000; Richard Miller and John Solverson, *Student Lamps of the Victorian Era*, Antique Publications, 1992, 1992-93 value guide; Herb Millman and John

Dwyer, *Art Deco Lighting*, Schiffer Publishing, 2001; Tom Santiso, *TV Lamps*, Collector Books, 1999; Jo Ann and Francis Thomas, *Early Twentieth Century Lighting Fixtures*, Collector Books, 1999; Jo Ann Thomas, *Early Twentieth Century Lighting Fixtures: Selections from the R. Williamson Lamp Catalog*, Collector Books, 1999; —, *Lighting Figures of the Depression Era*, Collector Books, 2000; Catherine M. V. Thuro, *Oil Lamps*, Wallace-Homestead, 1976, 1998 value update; —, *Oil Lamps II*, Collector Books, 1983, 2000 value update; John J. Wolfe, *Brandy, Balloons & Lamps: Ami Argand, 1750-1803*, South Illinois University Press, 1999; *Pairpoint Lamp Catalog: Shade Shapes Ambero through Panel*; *Pairpoint Lamp Catalog: Shade Shapes Papillon through Windsor & Related Material*, Schiffer Publishing, 2001.

Periodical and Internet Resources: *International Guild of Lamp Researchers,* http://www.dapllc.com/lampguild; *Light Revival*, 35 West Elm Ave., Quincy, MA 02170; http://www.aladdincollector.com; http://www.lavaworld.com; http://www.oillamp.com.

Collectors' Clubs: Aladdin Knights of the Mystic Light, 3935 Kelley Road, Kevil, KY 42053, http://www.aladdinknights.org; Historical Lighting Society of Canada, P.O. Box 561, Postal Station R, Toronto, Ontario M4G 4EI, Canada; Incandescent Lamp Collectors Association, Museum of Lighting, 717 Washington Place, Baltimore, MD 21201; International Coleman Collectors Club, 2282 W. Caley Ave., Littleton, CO 80120, http://www.colemancollectors.com; Night Light, 38619 Wakefield Ct., Northville, MI 48167; Rushlight Club, Inc., 260 Maryland Ave., NE, Washington, DC 20002, http://www.rushlight.org

Museums: American Sign Museum, Cincinnati, OH; Kerosene Lamp Museum, Winchester Center, CT; Pairpoint Lamp Museum, River Edge, NJ.

Reproduction Alert.

Astral

22-1/2" h, sq white marble base, ribbed then turned brass column, cut glass prisms, frosted shade with etched flowers and vintage dec, electrified
. . . . **250.00**

24" h, Cornelius & Co., Philadelphia, patent date April 18, 1845, marble base, later blue rimmed wheel cut and acid finish shade, electrified, gilt wear, minor base chips. **645.00**

24-5/8" h, grapevine etched colorless glass shade, gilt metal font, glass prisms, standard with Rococo bronze fittings, flared, ribbed, blue glass shaft with gilt highlights, white marble base, electrified, imperfections, America, 19th C **920.00**

Banquet, Bradley & Hubbard, brass font, frosted glass shade, **$275.** Photo courtesy of Joy Luke Auctions.

Banquet, Classical Revival, English, early 20th C, silver plate and cut glass, electrified

21-3/8" h, Goldsmiths Company, bowl form cut glass oil font, fluted Corinthian column, tapered sq section loaded base with flower filled urns connected by swags **800.00**

21-1/2" h, Mappin & Webb, bowl form cut glass oil font, stop reeded fluted columns, stepped gadrooned base **825.00**

Boudoir

Aladdin, 14-1/2" h, 8" d, reverse painted bell shade, pine border, floral molded polychromed metal base **225.00**

Cut glass, 9" h, mushroom shade, flared base, sunburst design . . . **400.00**

French, 11" d, 6" d, weighted brass base, crystal glass paneled insert, brass emb leaves and berries, rod curving upward holding night light, brass chains, and mounts, glass night light, holds candle **215.00**

Handel, 14" h, 7" d, gilt-finished spelter base, reverse painted etched glass shade with umber harbor scene, orange sky, shade stamped "Handel 6450," Handel Lamps cloth tag on base, chips to patina **1,150.00**

Obverse painted scenic, 13-1/2" h, closed top mushroom-cap glass shade with textured surface mounted on gilt metal handled lamp base, weighted foot, hand-painted silhouetted forested landscape scenes, rim marked "Patented April 29th, 1913" . . **1,150.00**

Van Erp, Dirk, 11" h, 10" d hammered copper bean pot base, single socket, conical four paneled mica shade, D'Arcy Gaw box mark with name removed, few shallow dents. **28,700.00**

Chandelier

Arts & Crafts, 27" h, 32" d six panel, red brass, replaced mica panels, three-light cluster, orig dark patina, period chain and ceiling cap . **2,300.00**

Empire-style, 31" l, 20th C, gilt metal and cut glass, six light, top with six outscrolled flat leaves hung with crystals, slender reeded standard with central cut glass orb, flat leaf ring supporting six short serpentine scrolled candle arms offset by pierced ribbon-tied laurel wreaths, strung throughout with crystal strands, end of standard with further crystals. **1,100.00**

Louis XV Style, late 19th C, cut crystal and gilt metal, six-light, top hung with large waisted teardrop shaped beveled lusters, each topped by flowerhead glass bosses, metal standard enclosed by ribbed molded glass balustroid segments, six serpentine luster hung candle arms and six further serpentine arms set with graduated faceted finials, arms hung with further teardrop crystals, standard ending in chain hung orb **4,025.00**

Desk

Handel

14-1/4" h, 7-1/4" w, arched pivoting arm ending in pivoting blossom-shaped shade with orig opalescent bent glass panels and

faux lead came, bronzed base, marked "HANDEL" **1,355.00**

22-1/4" h, 9-1/2" w, two caramel glass pyramidal shades with green and red geometric bands, bronzed base, new dark patina to base, shades stamped "HANDEL," cloth label on base **1,495.00**

Steuben, 20" h, 7" d, bronze, adjustable, irid hammered glass shade, orig patina, shade sgd "Steuben" **860.00**

Bradley & Hubbard, 13" h, 8-1/2" d adjustable tilt shade, narrow ribbed panels, reverse painted green, blue, and brown Arts and crafts border motif, single socket metal base **460.00**

Student

22" h, double, brass frame, electrified, cased green shades **605.00**

23-1/2" h, brass frame and adjustable arm, white glass shade, early 20th C **260.00**

Tiffany

13-1/2" h, 7" d swirl dec irid green ribbed dome Damascene shade cased to white, marked "L.C.T" on rim, swivel-socket bronze harp frame, rubbed cushion platform, five ball feet, imp "Tiffany Studios New York 419" **3,740.00**

17-1/2" h, 7" d swirl dec irid green cased dome Damascene shade, marked "L.C.T. Favrile," swivel-socket dark patina bronze harp frame with baluster shaft, ribbed cushion platform, five ball feet, imp "Tiffany Studios New York 7907" **4,025.00**

18" h, 10-1/2" d gold irid Steuben bell shade, swivel socket dark etched bronze wide harp frame, adjustable shaft above leaf and petal base, imp "Tiffany Studios New York 569" **1,100.00**

Early American

Betty lamp

3-1/2" h wrought iron lamp, stamped "M," 4-1/4" h redware stand with incised wavy lines, minor rim chips **440.00**

4-1/4" h, wrought iron, hanger, and pick **300.00**

Blown, colorless, 10" h, drop burners, pressed stepped base, chips on base, pr. **385.00**

Cage lamp, 6" d, wrought iron, spherical, self righting gyroscope font, two repaired spout burners. . . . **500.00**

Paneled green slag glass, brass frame, 21" d, $250. Photo courtesy of Joy Luke Auctions.

Candle holder, 19" h, wrought iron, hanging type, primitive twisted arms and conical socket 385.00

Candle stand, 57-1/4" h, 24-1/2" w, wrought iron, double arms, brass candleholders and drip pans, attributed to PA, 18th C, pitting, losses to drip pans 8,100.00

Dietz dainty, 12-1/2" h, brass, orig glass in doors, ring handles, slot for mounting bracket on either side, ruby glass inserts in backs, price for pr 225.00

Grease, 23" h, wrought and cast iron, circular base, rooster finial, bale top fitted with long hanger, brass ring, old dark pitted surface 450.00

Hour glass, 7" h, clear blown glass, pine and oak frame, whittled baluster posts, old brown finish, glued break in bottom plate 275.00

Loom light, 14-3/4" h, wrought iron, candle socket, trammel 500.00

Miner's lamp, 7-3/8" h, cast and wrought iron, chicken finial, replaced hanger 110.00

Peg, 2" d, 4-1/2" l, overlay glass, pink cut to white cut to clear, frosted peg attached with clear wafer, brass collar 450.00

Petticoat, 9" h, tin, round pan base, large ring handle applied to one side of column, small pick and chain attached to handle 260.00

Rush light holder
9" h, wrought iron, turned wooden base, pitted iron 225.00

9-1/2" h, wrought iron, candle socket counter weight, tripod base, penny feet, tooled brass disk at base of stem, simple tooling 470.00

Skater's lamp, 6-3/4 h, brass, clear glass globe marked "Perko Wonder Junior," polished, small splint in top of brass cap 160.00

Splint holder
9-1/2" h, wrought iron, candle socket counter weight, tripod base, diamond shaped feet 415.00

12-1/2" h, wrought iron, tripod base, penny feet, one leg brazed, later added candle socket 250.00

Taper jack, 5" h, Sheffield silver on copper, old repairs 195.00

Floor

Bradley and Hubbard, 56" h, 7" d, small domed leaded glass shade, green slag glass, gold key border, open framework adjustable standard, domed circular foot 400.00

Faries Mfg. Co., Decatur, IL, 65-1/4" h, 12" d, bright chrome torchere, flaring trumpet shade, diecast mark . . 150.00

Handel
56-1/2" h, 13-1/2" d hemispherical shade, all copper, bell shaped harp, some pitting to cleaned patina, unmarked 1,045.00

57-1/2" h, 13" d Steuben shade with irid band, patina loss on base, some dents, unmarked . . 3,105.00

61" h, 14" d, bronze, adjustable arm, four-sided shade with banded overlay, green and yellow slag glass panels, raised mark 1,840.00

64" h, 24" d yellow and amber opalescent bent glass paneled shade with faux lead came, green diamond details, five-light, patinated copper columnar base, scrolling feet, marked "HANDEL" on base 9,780.00

Tiffany/Aladdin, 50" h, 10" d spun bronze shade, reflective white int., marked "Tiffany Studios New York," adjustable bridge lamp base with Arabian Nights motif, orig dark bronze patina, elaborate platform base, stamped "Tiffany Studios New York 576" 2,990.00

Hanging

American, 19th C
18" h, patinated metal and cut glass, hall type, candle socket, Gothic arches, diamonds and flowerheads dec 1,380.00

23" h, clear blown glass, hall type, elaborate wheel cut dec of birds and deer in landscape, foliate devices, pressed brass mounts 2,415.00

Arts and Crafts, brass washed metal, four lanterns, hammered amber glass 1,000.00

Handel, 10" d, hall type, spherical form, acid cut, translucent white, brown, vase and foliate dec, ornate orig hardware 4,200.00

Perzel, 40-1/4" d, chrome, metal, and glass 1,225.00

Tiffany, 18" l, 15" d, attributed to Tiffany Glass and Decorating Co., late 19th C, square green and opalescent diamond-shaped glass jewels arranged as central pendant chandelier drop, twisted wire frame 2,990.00

Piano

Handel, 9" h, 22" l, 7" d conical leaded glass shade with straight apron of green slag and granite glass segments arranged in geometric design, mounted to adjustable socket, curved "dog's leg" shaft above weighed lappet dec base imp "Handel" 1,265.00

Tiffany, 6-3/4" h, 19" l tripartite gold amber glass turtleback shade, framed in bronze, three center gold irid turtleback tiles, single-socket swiveling "dog leg" shaft, shade and weighted base imp "Tiffany Studios New York" 4,025.00

Table

Bigelow Kennard, Boston, 26" h, 18" d domed leaded shade, opalescent white segments in geometric progression border, brilliant green leaf forms repeating motif, edge imp "Bigelow Kennard Boston/Bigelow Studios," three socket over Oriental-style bronze base cast with foo dog handles, Japonesque devices 2,875.00

Bradley & Hubbard, 15" sq octagon shade, 21-1/2" h, Prairie School, shade with geometric overlay on green and white slag glass panels with red squares, sgd on base and shade 1,150.00

Duffner and Kimberly, New York
24" h, 21" d conical leaded glass shade, amber slag background panels, three repeating intricate heraldic elements of lavender-amethyst glass superimposed on crimson red medial band, lower border glass in chevron motif, amber granite and

mauve ripple accent colors, three-socket bronzed shaft with cast foliate devices **4,600.00**

26" h, 24-1/2" d dome leaded glass shade with tuck-under irregular rim, multicolored blossoms with yellow centers, green leaves, long stemmed flowers extending to top on segmented white background, three socket bronze lobed shaft with quatraform shaped base **7,435.00**

Durand, 29-1/2" h, brass, blue glass standard, opaque white and clear feather pattern **300.00**

Handel

15-1/2" h, 11" d shade with cut-out panels of conforming motifs, over new mica panels, sterling silver bouquet overlay on bronze squatty base, orig verdigris patina, stamp mark **2,870.00**

19-3/4" h, 18" d bent caramel slag glass shade with applied metal and glass russet and green cattail dec, bronzed base, both stamped "HANDEL" **6,750.00**

22" h, 14" d chipped ice reverse painted shade with Virginia creeper dec, floriform bronzed base, orig vented cap, orig patina, both shade and base stamped "HANDEL," shade with patent and number 6299 . . . . **3,450.00**

Table, Pairpoint, #D3000, decorated with urn and flowers, reverse painted dome shade decorated with flowers, 18" d, 26-1/2" h, $3,525. Photo courtesy of Joy Luke Auctions.

Table, Handel, reverse painted dome shade with sunset landscape, tree and river, signed "Handel 7059," bronze base with Handel label, 14" d, 20" h, $2,400. Photo courtesy of Joy Luke Auctions.

Pairpoint, 20-1/2" h, 11-1/2" d domed closed top mushroom-cap glass shade, Vienna, coralene yellow int., painted stylized olive green leaves and red berries, gold outline on ext., ball-decorated ring supported by four arms, quatraform base molded with foliate devices, imp "Pairpoint Mfg Co., 3052" **2,070.00**

Pittsburgh, 22" h, 16" d, surface painted glass shade with sepia landscape, bronzed base, orig patina, unmarked, few small nicks around top inner ring of shade **1,725.00**

Suess Ornamental Glass Co., Chicago, 23" h, 22" d leaded glass shade with stylized yellow, orange, green, and white slag flowers and leaves, brass-washed base, unmarked **5,350.00**

Tiffany Studios

17" h, 11" d art glass flaring shade, white opalescent and green pulled feather design, three pendant fixtures, bronzed fluted base stamped "Tiffany Studios/New York" **3,220.00**

22-1/2" h, 12" d dome shade, irid swirl dec green Damascene shade cased to reflective white and amber, dark bronze three-arm spider and fluid unit, four-legged base, imp "S1089" on frame and font, also stamped "Tiffany Studios

New York" with TG&D Co. logo **5,175.00**

Van Erp, Dirk, 17-1/2" h, 13" d, hammered copper classical base, four paneled mica shade with vented cap, single socket, fine orig patina and mica, open box mark/San Francisco **9,200.00**

Williamson, Richard, & Co., Chicago, 25" h, 20" d peaked leaded glass dome, amber slag bordered by red tulips, pink and lavender-blue spring blossoms, green leaf stems, carved glass, mounted on four-socket integrated shaft with stylized tulip blossoms above leafy platform, imp "R. Williamson & Co./Washington & Jefferson Sts./Chicago, Ill," restored cap at top rim **3,220.00**

LANTERNS

History: A lantern is an enclosed, portable light source, hand carried or attached to a bracket or pole to illuminate an area. Many lanterns have a protected flame and can be used both indoors and outdoors. Light-producing materials used in early lanterns included candles, kerosene, whale oil, and coal oil, and, later, gasoline, natural gas, and batteries.

References: *Collectible Lanterns*, L-W Book Sales, 1997; Anthony Hobson, *Lanterns That Lit Our World*, Hiram Press, reprinted 1996; Neil S. Wood, *Collectible Dietz Lanterns*, L-W Book Sales, 1996.

Collectors' Club: Coleman Collectors Network, 1822 E. Fernwood, Wichita, KS 67216.

Brass, cast, Arts & Crafts, faceted, rustic branch pattern, original white frosted seedy glass panels, original patina, original chains, replaced ceiling plate, unmarked, 7" w, 9-1/2" h, price for pair, $630. Photo courtesy of David Rago Auctions.

Barn, 5-1/4" w, 5-3/4" d, 8-3/4" h, mortised wood frame, four panes of glass, bentwood handle, tin cover over top vent, twisted wire latch, old patina, discolored glass in door, minor damage, make-do repaired split on top **825.00**

Candle

3-1/2" x 3-1/2" x 8-1/2" h, four sided tin frame, panes of glass, peaked top with vents, ring handle, wire hanger, light rust **200.00**

10-1/4" w, 9-3/4" l, 16-1/2" h, old red painted pine, rect, pierced top, bentwood handle, four sides with three rect glazed and pierced panels, door with leather hinges opening to candle socket, New England, 19th C, door appears to be replacement, imperfections **2,415.00**

15-3/4" h, tin, stamped "Parker's Patent, 1855, Proctersville, VT," glass panels on all four sides with wire protectors, peaked top with star cut-outs, large ring handle **525.00**

Dark room, 17" h, orig black paint, white striping, tin kerosene font and burner "Carbutt's Dry Plate lantern, PA April 25th 1882" label **75.00**

Folding, 10" h, tin, glass sides, emb "Stonebridge 1908" **75.00**

Hall, 26" h, glass and polychrome, gold painted flat leaf top suspending cut glass drops, joined by curved scrolls, suspending ovoid shade formed by five curved colorless glass panels in metal framework topped by ribbon tied laurel branches, accented with faceted bead trim, bead and glass prism trefoils, Italian, late 19th C **2,100.00**

Wagon, 16-1/2" h, tin, "Ham's Cold Blast," original flue, C.T. Ham Co., Rochester, NY, $95.

Japanese, Patterson Bros., Lansing, MI, adv, panes with General U. S. Grant, puppies, young girl, and wilderness scene **195.00**

Miner's, 24-1/2" h, tin, orig black paint and kerosene burner, mercury reflector, stenciled label "C. T. Ham Mfg. Co.'s New No. 8 Tubular Square Lamp Label Registered 1886" **195.00**

Nautical, 23" h, 11" d, masthead, copper and brass, oil fired, orig burner, label reads "Ellerman, Wilson Line, Hull," mid-19th C **265.00**

Paul Revere Type, 16" h, punched tin, circular punching on door and body, cone top, round handle, light overall pitting **275.00**

Political rally, 67" h, gilded wrought iron, flat diamond shape with diamond shaped windows outlined with gilding, amber glass panels, "1842" in gilt, acorn finials, pine carrying staff, mounted on wood base **1,850.00**

Railroad, Pennsylvania Railroad, 5" h red globe, marked "Keystone Lantern Co., Philadelphia," wire ring base **445.00**

Skater's

11" h, brass, clear, bulbous globe, wire bail handle **135.00**

13-1/2" h, cast iron, lacy base, bulbous clear globe, pierced tin top and wire bail handle . . . **245.00**

Wood, 9-1/2" h, pine, old black over red paint, four sides glass, candle access from top, socket pulled by wire bale handle **690.00**

LEEDS CHINA

History: The Leeds Pottery in Yorkshire, England, began production about 1758. Among its products was creamware that was competitive with that of Wedgwood. The original factory closed in 1820, but various subsequent owners continued until 1880. They made exceptional cream-colored wares, either plain, salt glazed, or painted with colored enamels, and glazed and unglazed redware.

Marks: Early wares are unmarked. Later pieces are marked "Leeds Pottery," sometimes followed by "Hartley-Green and Co." or the letters "LP."

Reproduction Alert: Reproductions have the same marks as the antique pieces.

Bowl, ftd, 10-3/4" d, 4-3/4" h, blue, yellow, green, and brown polychrome dec on int. and ext., band of brown

vining below rim, professional restoration, hairlines **660.00**

Charger, 14-3/8" d, yellow urn with double handles and brown swag design holds cobalt blue, brown, and yellow flowers, green foliage, blue line detail surrounding dec, scalloped blue father edge, in-the-making separation along inner edge, minor glaze flakes **1,870.00**

Chop plate, 11-1/4" d, blue and yellow brown polychrome flowers, green foliage, white ground, blue scalloped feather edge, wear, old chip beneath rim **825.00**

Creamer, yellow, brown, and green tulip, umber and green sprig design on sides, dark brown stripe on rim and applied handle, flakes on table ring **800.00**

Cup and saucer, handleless

Blue, yellow, green, and goldenrod floral design, underglaze blue brushed crescent mark **220.00**

Brown rim stripes, blue, green, shades of gold, and yellow floral swag, flakes, chips on saucer table ring, stains on cup **150.00**

Egg cup, 2-3/4", creamware, reticulated **150.00**

Miniature

Creamer, yellow bands with green, orange, blue, and brown sprigs, flakes **250.00**

Creamer and sugar, blue flower, green and brown buds, tooled handle on 2-3/4" h creamer, minor flake on 2-1/2" h sugar **350.00**

Cup and saucer, handleless, pearlware

Blue, gold, and yellow peafowl sitting on brown and green tree branch, brown rim stripes, hairlines, saucer repaired **200.00**

Gold flower, green and brown leaves **275.00**

Grid design, green, orange dots, blue circles, short hairline in cup **220.00**

Strawberry, yellow, green, and brown, yellowed repairs . **220.00**

Yellow, blue, and green flowers, pinpoint flake, hairline in cup **275.00**

Teapot, cov, 4" h, yellow bands with green, orange, blue, and brown sprigs, flakes **450.00**

Mug, 5" h, multicolored polychrome floral dec **250.00**

Platter, blue feathered edge, relief feather design, 17" x 14", $325. Photo courtesy of Sanford Alderfer Auction Co.

Plate

7" d, Peafowl in tree, blue, gold, and yellow, green leaves, minor rim flakes **495.00**

9-1/2" d, Peacock sitting on tree branch, blue, yellow, and gold, black spots, green and brown branch, green feather edge **1,715.00**

10" d, Peafowl in tree, blue, gold, and yellow, green leaves .. **660.00**

Sauce tureen, undertray, ladle, 7-5/8" l, earthenware, green wavy edge, c1800, minor chips, staining **425.00**

Teapot, blue and white leafy decoration, impressed "L. Wood" in bottom, c1820, 7-1/2" h, 11" w, $425.

Teapot, cov, creamware

4-3/4" h, intertwined ribbed handle, molded floral ends and flower finial, polychrome enameled rose **$3,025.00**

5" h, molded spout, intertwined ribbed handle, polychrome enameled portraits of Prince of Orange, completely restored mismatched lid, some flakes, enamel wear **440.00**

Waste bowl

4-1/4" d, 3" h, blue band, green, gold, mustard, and black leaves, minor flakes on table ring .. **110.00**

6" d, 2-7/8" h, green and gold leaves with blue highlights, hairlines, some stains **110.00**

LEFTON CHINA

History: China, porcelain, and ceramic with that now familiar "Lefton" mark has been around since the early 1940s and is highly sought by collectors in the secondary marketplace today. The company was founded by George Zoltan Lefton, a Hungarian immigrant who arrived in the United States in 1939. In the 1930s, he was a sportswear designer and manufacturer, but his hobby of collecting fine china and porcelain led him to a new business venture.

After the bombing of Pearl Harbor in 1941, Lefton aided a Japanese-American friend by helping him to protect his property from anti-Japanese groups. As a result, Lefton came in contact with and began marketing pieces from a Japanese factory owned by Kowa Toki KK. At this time, he embarked on a new career and began shaping a business that sprang from his passion for collecting fine china and porcelains. Though his funds were very limited, his vision was to develop a source from which to obtain fine porcelains by reviving the postwar Japanese ceramic industry, which dated back to antiquity. As a trailblazer, George Zoltan Lefton soon earned the reputation of "The China King."

Figurines and animals, plus many of the whimsical pieces such as the Bluebirds, Dainty Miss, Miss Priss, Angels, Cabbage Cutie, Elf Head, Mr. Toodles, and the Dutch Girl, are popular with collectors. All types of dinnerware and tea-related items are eagerly acquired by collectors. As is true with any antique or collectibles, prices vary, depending on location, condition, and availability.

Marks: Until 1980, wares from the Japanese factory include a "KW."

References: Karen Barton, *Twentieth Century Lefton China and Collectibles*, Schiffer Publishing, 2001; Loretta DeLozier, *Collector's Encyclopedia of Lefton China*, Vol. 1 (1995), Vol. 2 (1997), Vol. 3 (1999), Collector Books; *1998 Lefton Price Guide*.

Collectors' Club: National Society of Lefton Collectors, 1101 Polk St., Bedford, IA 50833.

Animal

4-1/2" h, rabbit, marked "880," orig sticker, set of five **135.00**

5", squirrel, bisque **38.00**

8-1/4", bobcat and raccoon .. **120.00**

8-1/2", tiger, black, white with gold **65.00**

10", koala bear with club **180.00**

Bank, 7-1/4" h, Kewpie, orig foil label "Lefton Exclusives, Japan," stamped "145" **145.00**

Candy dish, three sections, Christmas Holly, green leaves, red berries, original box, $30.

Cake plate, 10" d, server, Hollyberry **45.00**

Candy bowl, 7" d, pastel green, pearlized bisque finish, fluted gold edge, cherub dec, #837 ...... **240.00**

Canister set, Americana pattern, 5-1/2" d, 8" h flour; 5" d, 7-1/4" sugar; 4-1/4" d, 6-3/8" h coffee; 3-7/8" d, 5-1/4" h tea, relief roses dec, all marked "946" with foil labels **250.00**

Cigarette set, Elegant Rose, five pcs **200.00**

Coffee set, 8-1/2" h coffeepot, creamer, cov sugar, 4" d coffee cups, 8" d scalloped plates, green and white background, deep pink roses, ornate gilt trim, price for 13-pc set.... **200.00**

Compote, 8-3/16" d, 3" h, Americana pattern, green mark "940" **125.00**

Cookie jar, cov

Holly, white, No. 6054 ....**115.00**

Lady with scarf, 7-1/4" h, pastels, marked "Geo. Z. Lefton, 1957, 040" **325.00**

Relief molded cookies, white, No. 102 .... **50.00**

Santa Claus, No. 2097, 7-1/4" h **115.00**

Cup and saucer

Christmas Cardinal **25.00**

Roses **45.00**

Demitasse cup and saucer, Rose Heirloom **25.00**

Figure

Flamingo mother watching young, wings wide spread, marked "Lefton's, Occupied Japan" **165.00**

Girl in White, white, sponge gold dec, #K8274, gold crown mark with

blue accent, "Lefton China" printed in arc over crown, "Hand Painted" script in semi-circular mark **. 120.00**
Pixie on mushroom watching frog, 4" h **20.00**
Rock A Bye Baby in the Treetop, 8" h **100.00**
Siamese Dancers, pr, 6-1/2" h **120.00**
Victorian lady, parasol with lace trim, violet blouse, pink lace trim, pink and white skirt with gold accent, #K8692, 8-3/8" h **135.00**

Head vase, 7" h, Kewpie, orig foil label "Lefton Exclusives, Japan," stamped "3631" **135.00**

Jam jar
Americana **65.00**
Dutch Girl. **95.00**

Miniature lamp, 3-5/8" d, 7-3/4" h, hp red flowers, green leaves, white ground, three gold dec feet, glass chimney with scalloped top, frosting on lower third, orig wick **15.00**

Mug
Hollyberry, 4" **10.00**
Green Holly **18.00**
Poinsettia, white ground **15.00**

Planter
Angel, on cloud, with stones . .**40.00**
Calico Donkey, 5-1/2". **32.00**

Plate
8" d, Berry Harvest, salad **28.00**
9" d, Magnolia **28.00**
9-1/4" d, To A Wild Rose **28.00**

Salt and pepper shakers, pr
Fruit Basket, 2-3/4". **24.00**
Rustic Daisy, 6-3/4" **24.00**
Thumblina **18.00**

Sugar, cov, Rose Chintz. **175.00**

Figure, #1103, There Was An Old Lady Who Lived In A Shoe, 5-1/2" x 6-1/2", $180. Photo courtesy of Loretta DeLozier.

Vase, #1544, Macaw decoration, white vase, multicolored bird and tree stump, 7-3/4" h, $85. Photo courtesy of Loretta DeLozier.

Tea cup and saucer, ftd, Elegant Rose 45.00

Teapot
Festival 145.00
Grape Line 85.00
Honey Bee 125.00

Wall plaque
Boy and Girl, oval, bisque, pr 120.00
Rose, black background, 5". . 24.00
Santa's Room, Memories of Home, 6-1/2" 30.00

LENOX CHINA

History: In 1889, Jonathan Cox and Walter Scott Lenox established The Ceramic Art Co. at Trenton, New Jersey. By 1906, Lenox formed his own company, Lenox, Inc. Using potters lured from Belleek, Lenox began making an American version of the famous Irish ware. The firm is still in business.

Marks: Older Lenox china has one of two marks: a green wreath or a palette. The palette mark appears on blanks supplied to amateurs who hand painted china as a hobby. The Lenox company currently uses a gold stamped mark.

References: Susan and Al Bagdade, *Warman's American Pottery and Porcelain*, 2nd ed., Krause Publications, 2000; Richard E. Morin, *Lenox Collectibles*, Sixty-Ninth Street Zoo, 1993.

Additional Listings: Belleek.

Bouillon cup and saucer, Detroit Yacht Club, palette mark 85.00
Bowl, two handles, etched gold trim, M-139, pre-1930. . . . . 45.00
Chocolate set, cov chocolate pot, six cups and saucers, Golden Wheat pattern, cobalt blue ground, 13-pc set 275.00
Cigarette box, white apple blossoms, green ground, wreath mark 40.00
Coffee set, Rhodora pattern, 8-1/8" h coffeepot, creamer, sugar, 17-1/2" l platter 675.00
Compote, 2" h, 5" d, brown rim, white ground, black hp insignia, pre-1930 . . . . 40.00
Cream soup, Tuxedo, green mark 40.00
Cup and saucer, Alden 25.00
Dinner set, Cattail, 40 pcs, eight-pc place settings, c1959. . . . . 520.00
Honey pot, 5" h, 6-1/4" d underplate, ivory beehive, gold bee and trim . 85.00
Jug, 4" h, hp, grapes and leaves, shaded brown ground, sgd "G. Morley" 250.00
Luncheon service, partial, burgundy red ground borders with gilt acanthus leaves, 14 10-1/2" d plates, 14 8-1/4" d plates, 12 8-3/8" soup plates, 12 6-1/4" plates, 24 cups and saucers, 20th C 750.00
Mug, 6-1/4" h, monk, smiling, holding up glass of wine, shaded brown ground, SS rim 160.00
Perfume lamp, 9" h, figural, Marie Antoinette, bisque finish, dated 1929 . . . . 650.00
Plate, Alden, dinner 20.00
Salt, 3" d, creamy ivory ground, molded seashells and coral, green wreath mark 35.00
Shoe, white, bow trim 190.00

Punch bowl, pedestal base, 11 matching cups, each painted with stylized purple grape clusters, green leaves, gilded rim, stamp mark, 15-1/2" d, 13" h, $575. Photo courtesy of David Rago Auctions.

Swan, salt, light coral body, green mark, 3" l, 2" h, $30.

Tea set, cov teapot, creamer, cov sugar, Hawthorne pattern, silver overlay **225.00**
Tea strainer, hp, small pink roses **70.00**
Vase
　6" h, pink and roses dec, green leaves, sgd "W. Morley" . . . **195.00**
　11-3/4" h, 4-1/2" d, corset shape, pink orchids dec by William Morley, green stamp mark, artist sgd **850.00**

LIBBEY GLASS

1896–1906

History: Edward Libbey established the Libbey Glass Company in Toledo, Ohio, in 1888 after the New England Glass Works of W. L. Libbey and Son closed in East Cambridge, Massachusetts. The new Libbey company produced quality cut glass, which today is considered to belong to the brilliant period.

In 1930, Libbey's interest in art-glass production was renewed, and A. Douglas Nash was employed as a designer in 1931.

The factory continues production today as Libbey Glass Co.

References: Tom and Neila Bredehoft, *Fifty Years of Collectible Glass, 1920-1970, Volume 1, Volume II,* Antique Trader Books, 2000; Bob Page and Dale Frederickson, *Collection of American Crystal,* Page-Frederickson Publishing, 1995; Kenneth Wilson, *American Glass 1760-1930,* 2 vols., Hudson Hills Press and The Toledo Museum of Art, 1994.

Additional Listings: Amberina Glass and Cut Glass.

Art glass
Bell, 5-3/4" h, colorless, acid etched dec "1893 World's Fair," circular logo surrounded by acid-etched florals and banners, shoulder int. molded "1893

World's Columbian Xposition" (sic), twisted frosted handle with star at top, metal clapper **25.00**
Bud vase, 12" h, amberina, shape 3004, c1917, sgd in polished pontil **1,400.00**
Celery vase, 6-1/2" h, 5" w, Maize, Pomona dec, amber kernels, blue leaves **395.00**
Compote, 10-1/2" w, 4" h, colorless, pink Nailsea-type loops, flaring top, sgd "Libbey" **595.00**
Creamer and sugar, 5-3/8" h creamer, 3-1/2" h, 4-3/4" d sugar, crystal, blue-green opaque dot trim, dark blue-green glass feet, polished pontil **475.00**
Rose bowl, 3-1/2" w, 2-1/2" h, melon ribbed bowl, beige ground, two pansies and leaves, white beads, sgd "Libbey Cut Glass" **550.00**
Sherbet, silhouette stem, black rabbit, sgd **145.00**
Vase
　4-1/4" h, ftd, red, vertical blue-gray dots form lines, swirled vertical ribs, unfinished pontil **775.00**
　5" d, 8" h, rose and opalescent, crystal foot **425.00**

Dish, shallow, opaque white, Santa Maria, pale blue sky, blue sea, sold by Libbey as souvenir of 1893 Colombian Exposition, $635. Photo courtesy of Clarence and Betty Maier.

Cut glass
Banana boat, 13" x 7" x 7", scalloped pedestal base, 24-point hobstar, hobstar, cane, vesica, and fan motifs, sgd **1,500.00**
Bowl
　8" d, hobstar, bands of strawberry diamond and fans, sgd **110.00**
　9" d, Somerset pattern, sgd . . **150.00**

Candy dish, cov, 7", divided, clover shape, hobstar and prism, sgd . . **90.00**
Charger, 14" d, hobstar, cane, and wreath motifs, sgd **300.00**
Miniature lamp, 2" sq base, 10-3/8" h, pinwheel design, sgd **425.00**
Tumble-up, star burst, hobstar, fern, and fan motifs, minor handle check **725.00**
Vase
　5" d, 10" h, sgd, c1910-20 . . **475.00**
　6" d, 14" h, c1906 . . . . **695.00**
　18" h, No. 982, Senora pattern, cut glass, ftd, hexed vesicas, deep miter cuts, three 24-point hobstars at top between crossed miter cuts, small stars and trellises, clear knob and stem, scalloped foot cut with extended single star, Libbey over saber mark, c1896-1906, some flaws **2,500.00**
Wine, Harvard pattern, faceted cut knob stems, sgd, 12-pc set . . . **350.00**

LIMITED EDITION COLLECTOR PLATES

History: Bing and Grondahl made the first collector plate in 1895. Royal Copenhagen issued its first Christmas plate in 1908.

In the late 1960s and early 1970s, several potteries, glass factories, mints, and artists began issuing plates commemorating people, animals, and events. Christmas plates were supplemented by Mother's Day plates and Easter plates. Speculation swept the field, fostered in part by flamboyant ads in newspapers and flashy direct-mail promotions.

References: Jay Brown, *The Complete Guide To Limited Edition Art Prints,* Krause Publications, 1999; *Collectors' Information Bureau Collectibles Market Guide & Price Index,* 18th ed., Krause Publications, 2000; Beth Dees, *Santa's Price Guide To Contemporary Christmas Collectibles,* Krause Publications, 1997; Carl Luckey, *Luckey's Hummel Figurines & Plates,* 11th ed., Krause Publications, 1997; Mary Sieber (ed.), *2002 Price Guide to Limited Edition Collectibles,* Krause Publications, 2001.

Periodicals: *Collector Editions,* 170 Fifth Ave., 12th Floor, New York, NY 10010; *Collectors Mart Magazine,* 700 E. State St., Iola, WI 54990; *Collectors News,* 506 Second St., P.O. Box 156, Grundy Center, IA 50638; *Insight on Collectibles,* 103 Lakeshore Road, Ste. 202, St. Catharines, Ontario L2N 2T6 Canada; *International Collectible Showcase,* One Westminster Place, Lake Forest, IL 60045; *Plate World,* 9200 N. Maryland Ave., Niles, IL 60648; *Toybox Magazine,* 8393 E. Holly Road, Holly, MI 48442.

Collectors' Clubs: Franklin Mint Collectors Society, US Route 1, Franklin Center, PA 19091; Hummel Collector's Club, Inc., P.O. Box 257, Yardley, PA 19067; International Plate Collectors Guild, P.O. Box

487, Artesia, CA 90702; M. I. Hummel Club, Goebel Plaza, Rte. 31, P.O. Box 11, Pennington, NJ 08534.

Museum: Bradford Museum of Collector's Plates, Niles, IL.

Additional Listings: See *Warman's Americana & Collectibles* for more examples of collector plates, plus many other limited edition collectibles.

Notes: The first plate issued in a series (FE) is often favored by collectors. Condition is a critical factor, and price is increased if the original box is available.

Limited edition collector plates, more than any other object in this guide, should be collected for design and pleasure and only secondarily as an investment.

Bing & Grondahl, July 1921, 7", $55.

Bing and Grondahl (Denmark)

Christmas plates, various artists, 7" d

1895 Behind the Frozen Window **3,400.00**
1896 New Moon Over Snow Covered Trees **1,875.00**
1897 Christmas Meal of the Sparrows **725.00**
1898 Christmas Roses and Christmas Star **700.00**
1899 The Crows Enjoying Christmas **900.00**
1900 Church Bells Chiming in Christmas **800.00**
1901 The Three Wise Men from the East **450.00**
1902 Interior of a Gothic Church **285.00**
1903 Happy Expectation of Children **150.00**
1904 View of Copenhagen from Frederiksberg Hill **125.00**
1905 Anxiety of the Coming Christmas Night **130.00**
1906 Sleighing to Church on Christmas Eve **95.00**
1907 The Little Match Girl . . . **125.00**
1908 St. Petri Church of Copenhagen **85.00**

1909 Happiness Over the Yule Tree **100.00**
1910 The Old Organist **90.00**
1911 First It Was Sung By Angels to Shepherds in the Fields **80.00**
1912 Going to Church on Christmas Eve **80.00**
1913 Bringing Home the Yule Tree **85.00**
1914 Royal Castle of Amalienborg, Copenhagen **75.00**
1915 Chained Dog Getting Double Meal on Christmas Eve . . . **120.00**
1916 Christmas Prayer of the Sparrows **85.00**
1917 Arrival of the Christmas Boat **75.00**
1918 Fishing Boat Returning Home for Christmas **85.00**
1919 Outside the Lighted Window **80.00**
1920 Hare in the Snow **70.00**
1921 Pigeons in the Castle Court **55.00**
1922 Star of Bethlehem **60.00**
1923 Royal Hunting Castle, The Hermitage **55.00**
1924 Lighthouse in Danish Waters **65.00**
1925 The Child's Christmas . . **70.00**
1926 Churchgoers on Christmas Day **65.00**
1927 Skating Couple **110.00**
1928 Eskimo Looking at Village Church in Greenland **60.00**
1929 Fox Outside Farm on Christmas Eve **75.00**
1930 Yule Tree in Town Hall Square of Copenhagen **85.00**
1931 Arrival of the Christmas Train **75.00**
1933 The Korsor-Nyborg Ferry **70.00**
1935 Lillebelt Bridge Connecting Funen with Jutland **65.00**
1937 Arrival of Christmas Guests **75.00**
1939 Ole Lock-Eye, The Sandman **150.00**
1941 Horses Enjoying Christmas Meal in Stable **345.00**
1943 The Ribe Cathedral . . . **155.00**
1945 The Old Water Mill **135.00**
1947 Dybbol Mill **70.00**
1949 Landsoldaten, 19th Century Danish Soldier **70.00**
1951 Jens Bang, New Passenger Boat Running Between Copenhagen and Aalborg . . **115.00**
1953 Royal Boat in Greenland Waters **95.00**
1955 Kalundborg Church **115.00**

1957 Christmas Candles **155.00**
1959 Christmas Eve **120.00**
1961 Winter Harmony **115.00**
1963 The Christmas Elf **120.00**
1965 Bringing Home the Christmas Tree **65.00**
1967 Sharing the Joy of Christmas **45.00**
1969 Arrival of Christmas Guests **30.00**
1971 Christmas at Home **20.00**
1973 Country Christmas **25.00**
1975 The Old Water Mill **25.00**
1977 Copenhagen Christmas . **25.00**
1979 White Christmas **30.00**
1981 Christmas Peace **50.00**
1983 Christmas in Old Town . . **55.00**
1985 Christmas Eve at the Farmhouse **55.00**
1987 The Snowman's Christmas Eve **55.00**
1989 Christmas Anchorage . . . **55.00**
1990 Changing of the Guards . **65.00**

Mother's Day plates, Henry Thelander, artist, 6" d

1969 Dog and Puppies **400.00**
1971 Cat and Kitten **20.00**
1973 Duck and Ducklings **20.00**
1975 Doe and Fawns **20.00**
1977 Squirrel and Young **25.00**
1979 Fox and Cubs **30.00**
1981 Hare and Young **40.00**
1983 Raccoon and Young **45.00**
1985 Bear and Cubs **40.00**
1987 Sheep with Lambs **40.00**
1989 Cow with Calf **45.00**
1990 Hen with Chicks **55.00**

Reed & Barton (United States)

Christmas Series, Damascene silver, 11" d through 1978, 8" d 1979 to present

1970 A Partridge in a Pear Tree, FE **200.00**
1971 We Three Kings of Orient Are **65.00**
1973 Adoration of the Kings . . **75.00**
1975 Adoration of the Kings . . **65.00**
1977 Decorating the Church . . **60.00**
1979 Merry Old Santa Claus . . **65.00**
1981 The Shopkeeper at Christmas **65.00**

Rosenthal (Germany)

Christmas plates, various artists, 8 1/2" d

1910 Winter Peace **550.00**
1911 The Three Wise Men . . . **325.00**
1912 Shooting Stars **250.00**
1913 Christmas Lights **235.00**
1915 Walking to Church **180.00**
1917 Angel of Peace **200.00**

1919 St. Christopher with the Christ
Child **225.00**
1921 Christmas in the Mountains
. . . . **200.00**
1923 Children in the Winter Wood
. . . . **200.00**
1925 The Three Wise Men . . **200.00**
1927 Station on the Way **200.00**
1929 Christmas in the Alps . . **225.00**
1931 Path of the Magi **225.00**
1933 Through the Night to Light
. . . . **190.00**
1935 Christmas by the Sea . . **185.00**
1937 Berchtesgaden **195.00**
1939 Schneekoppe Mountain **195.00**
1941 Strassburg Cathedral . . **250.00**
1943 Winter Idyll **300.00**
1945 Christmas Peace **400.00**
1947 The Dillingen Madonna **975.00**
1949 The Holy Family **185.00**
1951 Star of Bethlehem **450.00**
1953 The Holy Light **185.00**
1955 Christmas in a Village . **190.00**
1957 Christmas by the Sea . . **195.00**
1959 Midnight Mass **195.00**
1961 Solitary Christmas **225.00**
1963 Silent Night **185.00**
1965 Christmas in Munich . . **185.00**
1967 Christmas in Regensburg
. . . . **185.00**
1969 Christmas in Rothenburg
. . . . **220.00**
1971 Christmas in Garmisch . **90.00**
1973 Christmas in Lubeck-Holstein
. . . . **90.00**
1974 Christmas in Wurzburg . **90.00**

Royal Copenhagen (Denmark)

Christmas plates, various artists, 6" d
1908, 1909, 1910; 7" 1911 to present
1908 Madonna and Child . . **1,650.00**
1909 Danish Landscape . . . **150.00**
1910 The Magi **120.00**
1911 Danish Landscape . . . **135.00**
1912 Elderly Couple by Christmas
Tree **120.00**
1913 Spire of Frederik's Church,
Copenhagen **125.00**
1914 Sparrows in Tree at Church of
the Holy Spirit, Copenhagen
. . . . **100.00**
1915 Danish Landscape . . . **150.00**
1916 Shepherd in the Field on
Christmas Night **85.00**
1917 Tower of Our Savior's Church,
Copenhagen **90.00**
1918 Sheep and Shepherds . . **80.00**
1919 In the Park **80.00**
1920 Mary with the Child Jesus
. . . . **75.00**
1921 Aabenraa Marketplace . **75.00**
1922 Three Singing Angels . . **70.00**

*Royal Copenhagen, left: 1969, **$75**; right: 1995, **$70**. Photo courtesy of Joy Luke Auctions.*

1923 Danish Landscape **70.00**
1924 Christmas Star Over the Sea
and Sailing Ship **100.00**
1925 Street Scene from
Christianshavn, Copenhagen
. . . . **85.00**
1926 View of Christmas Canal,
Copenhagen **75.00**
1927 Ship's Boy at the Tiller on
Christmas Night **140.00**
1928 Vicar's Family on Way to
Church **75.00**
1929 Grundtvig Church,
Copenhagen **100.00**
1930 Fishing Boats on the Way to the
Harbor **80.00**
1931 Mother and Child **90.00**
1932 Frederiksberg Gardens with
Statue of Frederik VI **90.00**
1933 The Great Belt Ferry . . . **110.00**
1934 The Hermitage Castle . . **115.00**
1935 Fishing Boat off Kronborg
Castle **145.00**
1936 Roskilde Cathedral **130.00**
1937 Christmas Scene in Main
Street, Copenhagen **135.00**
1938 Round Church in Osterlars on
Bornholm **200.00**
1939 Expeditionary Ship in Pack-Ice
of Greenland **180.00**
1940 The Good Shepherd . . . **300.00**
1941 Danish Village Church . **250.00**
1943 Flight of Holy Family to Egypt
. . . . **425.00**
1945 A Peaceful Motif **325.00**
1947 The Good Shepherd . . . **200.00**
1949 Our Lady's Cathedral,
Copenhagen **165.00**
1951 Christmas Angel **300.00**
1953 Frederiksborg Castle . . **120.00**

1955 Fano Girl **185.00**
1957 The Good Shepherd . . . **115.00**
1959 Christmas Night **120.00**
1961 Training Ship Danmark **155.00**
1963 Hojsager Mill **80.00**
1965 Little Skaters **60.00**
1967 The Royal Oak **45.00**
1969 The Old Farmyard **35.00**
1971 Hare in Winter **80.00**
1973 Train Homeward Bound for
Christmas **85.00**
1975 Queen's Palace **85.00**
1977 Immervad Bridge **75.00**
1979 Choosing the Christmas Tree
. . . . **60.00**
1981 Admiring the Christmas Tree
. . . . **55.00**
1983 Merry Christmas **50.00**
1985 Snowman **50.00**
1987 Winter Birds **50.00**
1989 The Old Skating Pond . . **45.00**
1990 Christmas at Tivoli **65.00**

Mother's Day plates, various artists,
6 1/4" d
1971 American Mother **125.00**
1973 Danish Mother **60.00**
1975 Bird in Nest **50.00**
1977 The Twins **50.00**
1979 A Loving Mother **30.00**
1981 Reunion **40.00**

Wedgwood (Great Britain)

Christmas Series, jasper stoneware,
8" d
1969 Windsor Castle, FE . . . **225.00**
1970 Christmas in Trafalgar Square
. . . . **30.00**
1972 St. Paul's Cathedral **40.00**
1974 The Houses of Parliament
. . . . **40.00**
1976 Hampton Court **45.00**

1978 The Horse Guards 55.00
1980 St. James Palace 70.00
1982 Lambeth Palace 80.00
1984 Constitution Hill 80.00
1986 The Albert Memorial 80.00
1988 The Observatory Greenwich
. . . . 90.00
1989 Winchester Cathedral . . . 85.00

Mothers Series, jasper stoneware,
6 1/2" d
1971 Sportive Love, FE 25.00
1972 The Sewing Lesson 20.00
1974 Domestic Employment . . 30.00
1976 The Spinner 35.00
1978 Swan and Cygnets 35.00
1980 Birds 45.00
1982 Cherubs with Swing 55.00
1984 Musical Cupids 55.00
1986 Cupids Fishing 55.00
1988 Tiger Lily 45.00

LIMOGES

History: Limoges porcelain has been produced in Limoges, France, for more than a century by numerous factories, in addition to the famed Haviland.

Marks: One of the most frequently encountered marks is "T. & V. Limoges," on the wares made by Tressman and Vought. Other identifiable Limoges marks are "A. L." (A. Lanternier), "J. P. L." (J. Pouyat, Limoges), "M. R." (M. Reddon), "Elite," and "Coronet."

References: Susan and Al Bagdade, *Warman's English & Continental Pottery & Porcelain*, 3rd ed., Krause Publications, 1998; Debby DuBay, *Living with Limoges*, Schiffer Publishing, 2001; Mary Frank Gaston, *Collector's Encyclopedia of Limoges Porcelain*, 3rd ed., Collector Books, 2000; Raymonde Limoges, *American Limoges*, Collector Books, 1998; Faye Strumpf, *Limoges Boxes*, Krause Publications, 2000; Keith and Thomas Waterbrook-Clyde, *The Decorative Art of Limoges Porcelain and Boxes*, Schiffer Publishing, 1999.

Additional Listings: Haviland China.

Jardiniere, white ground, pink roses, gilded handles, pedestal base, marked "T. V. Limoges," 13" d, 9" h, crow's foot on side, $365. Photo courtesy of Joy Luke Auctions.

Berry set, 9-1/2" d, master bowl, eight 8" serving bowls, hp, purple berries on ext. white blossoms on int., marked "T & V" 265.00
Bowl, 4-1/2" h, ftd, hp, wild roses and leaves, sgd "J. E. Dodge, 1892" . 85.00
Box, cov, 4-1/4" sq, cobalt blue and white ground, cupids on lid, pate-sur-pate dec 195.00
Cache pot, 7-1/2" w, 9" h, male and female pheasants on front, mountain scene on obverse, gold handles and four ball feet 225.00
Cake plate, 11-1/2" d, ivory ground, brushed gold scalloped rim, gold medallion, marked "Limoges T & V" 75.00
Candy dish, 6-1/2" d, ftd, two handles, silver overlay, white ground, c1920 . . . . 95.00
Chocolate pot, 13" h, purple violets and green leaves, cream colored ground, gold handle, spout, and base, sgd "Kelly JPL/France" 350.00
Creamer and sugar, cov, 3-1/4" h, purple flowers, white ground, gold handle and trim 100.00
Cup and saucer, hp,. Flowers and leaves, gold trim, artist sgd 75.00
Dessert service, coffeepot, creamer, sugar, waste bowl, eight cups and saucers, 10 dessert plates, 12 lemon dishes, two 10" cake plates, hp gold florals, pale aqua shading to white ground, raised beading and scrollwork 450.00
Dresser set, pink flowers, pastel blue, green, and yellow ground, large tray, cov powder, cov rouge, pin tray, talc jar, pr candlesticks, seven-pc set . . 425.00
Figure, 25" h, 13" w, three girls, arms entwined, holding basket of flowers, books, and purse, marked "C & V" and "L & L" 460.00
Hair receiver, blue flowers and white butterflies, ivory ground, gold trim, marked "JPL" 80.00
Lemonade pitcher, matching tray, water lily dec, sgd "Vignard Limoges" 350.00
Mortar and pestle, 3-1/4" x 2" mortar, 3-1/2" l pestle, hp flowers gold trim, deep rose ground, marked "GL, Halga, Decor Main, Paris, France, Limoges" 95.00
Mug, corn motif, sgd "T & V Limoges France" 65.00
Nappy, 6" d, curved gold handle, gold scalloped edges, soft pink blossoms, blue-green ground 35.00

Oyster plate, 9-1/4" d, molded, scalloped edge, gilt rim, enamel dec of poppy sprays, raised gilt detailing, marked "A. Lanternier & Co., Limoges," early 20th C, price for set of eight 1,500.00
Panel, 4-1/2" x 3-3/8", enameled, Christ with crown of thorns, framed . . . 250.00
Pitcher, 6" h, 5-1/8" d, platinum handle, platinum mistletoe berries and leaves, gray and pink ground, Art Deco style, marked "J. P. Limoges, Pouyat" . 155.00
Plaque, 7-5/8" x 4-1/2", enameled, cavalier, after Meissonier, multicolored garb and banner, late 19th C . . . 460.00
Plate, 9" d, hp, pastel florals, Art Nouveau enameled gold dec, ornate gold scalloped rim 35.00
Punch bowl
13" d, 9-1/4" h, ornate floral dec, gold scrolling 2,350.00
15-1/8" d, 7-3/8" h, hp grapes dec, sgd "Henn, 1912," R. Denliniers Mark 3, c1894-1900 . . . . 1,700.00
Snuff box, cov, hp, wildflowers and gold tracery, pink ground, artist sgd, dated 1800 . . . . 200.00
Tankard set, 14" h tankard, four mugs, hp, grape dec, gold and green ground, five-pc set 450.00
Tea set, 9-1/2" h cov teapot, two 3" h cups, two 4-1/2" d saucers, 15" d tray, cream ground, floral dec, gold trim, red stamp "L. S. & S. Limoges France," green stamp "Limoges France" on two saucers, slight wear 500.00
Vase, 12" h, hand painted, light brown shading to butterscotch ground, mother of pearl center, two exotic birds perched on pine cones, marked "T & V," c1907 . . . . 525.00

LITHOPHANES

History: Lithophanes are highly translucent porcelain panels with impressed designs. The designs result from differences in the thickness of the plaque; thin parts transmit an abundance of light, while thicker parts represent shadows.

Lithophanes were first made by the Royal Berlin Porcelain Works in 1828. Other factories in Germany, France, and England later produced them. The majority of lithophanes on the market today were made between 1850 and 1900.

Collectors' Club: Lithophane Collectors Club, 2030 Robinwood Ave., P.O. Box 4557, Toledo, OH 43620.

Museum: Blair Museum of Lithophanes and Carved Waxes, Toledo, OH.

Candle shield, 9" h, panel with scene of two country boys playing with goat, castle in background 275.00

Hanging lamp, six sided, allegorical garden scenes, bordered by ruby glass upper and lower panels, brass mounts with Roman key and shield ornamentation, 12-1/2" h, loss to two finials, one panel repaired, $330. Photo courtesy of Sanford Alderfer Auction Co.

Cup and saucer, blue Oriental lady with nude lady **175.00**

Fairy lamp, 9" h, three panels, lady leaning out of tower, rural romantic scenes **1,250.00**

Lamp, 20-3/4" h, colored umbrella style shade, four panels of outdoor Victorian scenes, bronze and slate standard, German **675.00**

Plaque, windmill and ship, impressed "KPM/36S," c1860, 5-3/8" x 3-7/8", $190.

Night lamp, 5-1/4" h, sq, four scenes, irid green porcelain base, gold trim, electrified **650.00**
Panel
KPM
2-1/2" x 3-1/4", view from West Point **185.00**
3-7/8" x 5-1/4", lake setting, ship and windmill **165.00**
PPM
3-1/4" x 5-1/4", view of Paterson Falls **190.00**
4" x 6", woman and children with hay cart, incised "PPM. 553" **55.00**
PR Sickle, 4-1/4" x 5"
Cupid and girl fishing **160.00**
Scene of two women in doorway, dog, and two pigeons, sgd, #1320 . . . . **100.00**
Unmarked, 6" x 7-1/2", Madonna and Child **175.00**
Pitcher, puzzle type, Victorian scene, nude on bottom **175.00**
Stein, regimental, half liter **200.00**
Tea warmer, 5-7/8 h, one-pc cylindrical panel, four seasonal landscapes with children, copper frame, finger grip and molded base **250.00**

LIVERPOOL CHINA

History: Liverpool is the name given to products made at several potteries in Liverpool, England, between 1750 and 1840. Seth and James Pennington and Richard Chaffers were among the early potters who made tin-enameled earthenware.

By the 1780s, tin-glazed earthenware gave way to cream-colored wares decorated with cobalt blue, enameled colors, and blue or black transfers.

The Liverpool glaze is characterized by bubbles and frequent clouding under the foot rims. By 1800, about 80 potteries were working in the town producing not only creamware, but soft paste, soapstone, and bone porcelain.

References: Susan and Al Bagdade, *Warman's English & Continental Pottery & Porcelain*, 3rd ed., Krause Publications, 1998; Robert McCauley, *Liverpool Transfer Designs on Anglo-American Pottery*, Southworth-Anthoensen Press; Bernard M. Watney, *Liverpool Porcelain of the Eighteenth Century*, Antique Collectors' Club, Ltd., 1997.

Museums: City of Liverpool Museum, Liverpool, England; Henry Ford Museum, Dearborn, MI; Potsdam Public Museum, Potsdam, NY.

> **Reproduction Alert:** Reproduction Liverpool pieces were documented as early as 1942. One example is a black transfer-decorated jug made in the 1930s. The jugs vary in height from 8-1/2 to 11 inches. On one side is "The Shipwright's Arms"; on the other, the ship Caroline flying the American flag; and under the spout, a wreath with the words "James Leech."
>
> A transfer of the *Caroline* also was used on a Sunderland bowl about 1936 and reproduction mugs were made bearing the name "James Leech" and an eagle.
>
> The reproduction pieces have a crackled glaze and often age cracks have been artificially produced. When compared to genuine pieces, reproductions are thicker and heavier and have weaker transfers, grayish color (not as crisp and black), ecru or gray body color instead of cream, and crazing that does not spiral upward.

Cup and saucer, handleless, black transfer, bust of Washington and other gentleman on cup, "Washington, His Country's Father" on saucer, hairlines in cup **330.00**

Jug, creamware, transfer print
7-3/4" h, reserve of ships *L'Insurgent* and *Constellation,* reserve of ship yard, cracks, chips, minor losses, transfer imperfections . . . **1,265.00**

8-3/4" h, "The Greenwich Pensioner," text underneath, ship on reverse, repairs **460.00**

9-1/2" h, "Representation of the British defeat of the French Fleet of Brest by Earl Howe, 1794," reverse "The Flowing Cann," picture of drinking and dancing, descriptive text, minor glaze wear **815.00**

Jug, Commodore Prebler Squadron attacking City of Tripoli, Aug. 3, 1805, 6-5/8" h, $675.

9-1/2" h, Washington Monument, restored, new handle.... **2,200.00**

9-5/8" h, English hunting scenes "Jos Edge Caldon Grange" inscribed under spout, extensive repairs **345.00**

9-3/4" h, oval medallion portrait of John Adams, surrounded by Plenty, Justice, and Cupid, circular panel "Peace Plenty and Independence" on reverse flanked by Plenty and Peace destroying the implements of war, surmounted by spread eagle, chips, scratches, minor transfer wear..... **4,025.00**

9-3/4" h, reserves of Thomas Jefferson and James Monroe, misidentified as "Hancock," hp foliate gilt highlights, repairs, hairlines, minor chip, gilt, and enamel wear **20,700.00**

10" h, portrait of Thomas Jefferson, American eagle on reverse, chips, glaze wear to handle... **21,850.00**

Mug

3-3/4" h, dark brown transfer, Hope, allover luster trim, c1829-30 ....**200.00**

6" h, creamware, transfer printed three masted ship under sail, figure of Hope, "Jennett Lawson," hairline on base **750.00**

Tea cup and bowl saucer, 5-5/8" saucer, black transfer dec of English country scene, hairlines on both pieces **100.00**

Trinket pot, cov, 5-1/4" d, Delft, blue and white, two handles, chips and hairline in bottom **495.00**

Pitcher, American eagle on one side, poem "Oh Liberty Thou Goddess" on other, border of 15 states, base chip, 8-1/4" h, **$450.**

LOETZ

History: Loetz is a type of iridescent art glass that was made in Austria by J. Loetz Witwe in the late 1890s. The Loetz factory at Klostermule produced items with fine cameos on cased glass, good quality glassware for others to decorate, as well as the iridescent glasswares more commonly associated with the Loetz name.

Marks: Some pieces are signed "Loetz," "Loetz, Austria," or "Austria."

Reference: Robert and Deborah Truitt, *Collectible Bohemian Glass: 1880-1940*, R & D Glass, 1995.

Vase, flared rim, tapering to base, green, wave design, signed "Loetz/ Austria" on base, 9-3/4" h, **$1,320.** *Photo courtesy of Sanford Alderfer Auction Co.*

Bowl

5" d, 3" h, white, applied punties and rim **130.00**

7" d, 4" h, rolled rim, applied green tadpoles, highly irid, white ground **110.00**

Center bowl, 10" d, Onyx, dec **395.00**

Compote, 10-5/8" d, 5-1/4" h, bright orange int., deep black ext., white flaring circular rim, three ball feet, c1920.....................**310.00**

Inkwell, 3-1/2" h, amethyst, sq, irid, web design, bronze mouth **125.00**

Oil lamp, 19-1/2" h, 9-1/2" d, globular shade, bulbous base, all over irid oil-spot dec, orig brass fittings **3,000.00**

Pitcher, 8-1/2" h, cobalt blue ground, mauve, pink, blue, and turquoise highlight, crackle finish, gold painted

metal mount, cover with finial, curved metal handle...............**775.00**

Rose bowl, 6-1/2" d, ruffled purple irid raindrop dec................**265.00**

Sweetmeat jar, cov, 5" h, irid silver spider web dec, green ground, sgd **450.00**

Urn, 9-1/4" h, ovoid, irid, blue oil spot dec, inscribed "Loetz, Austria" **1,600.00**

Vase

5" h, bulbous, pulled dec, oil spots, lemon yellow ground, unmarked **800.00**

6-1/2" h, ruffled trefoil rim, ambergris body, symmetrical dec with three gold and silvery irid pulled feathers, base inscribed "Loetz Austria" **865.00**

6-1/2" h, tadpole neck, white irid ground, green rigaree..... **200.00**

7" h, trifoil top, black int., peacock feather-type irid, different shapes and sizes of glass pieces embedded in body, polished pontil **850.00**

7" h, 4-1/2" w, bulbous, three applied loop handles, silver overlay on handles and 2" top band, irid body **975.00**

7-1/2" h, 4-1/2" w, ovoid, purple and brown irid ground, large blue and purple pulled raindrops . **1,150.00**

8-3/4" h, Marmorierte, oval body, marbleized green, aubergine, and turquoise blue striations, cased to opal, lined in blue, dec with gilt enamel sunbursts, red glass "jewel" centers **460.00**

5" Loetz art glass vase with silver overlay, **$1,870.**

10-1/2" h, 6" w, bulbous swirl, applied shell handles, Rainbow, white lining, gold trim, cased in crystal, pink, yellow, and blue irid surface, pr **675.00**

15-1/4" h, 8-1/2" d, Papillion, lustered gold, purple, and green ... **750.00**

Wall sconce, three-light, brass, three bulbous opalescent shades with oil-spot pattern, green chain pattern, replaced brass parts, few minor nicks to top rim of one shade **690.00**

LUSTER WARE

History: Lustering on a piece of pottery creates a metallic, sometimes iridescent, appearance. Josiah Wedgwood experimented with the technique in the 1790s. Between 1805 and 1840, lustered earthenware pieces were created in England by makers such as Adams, Bailey and Batkin, Copeland and Garrett, Wedgwood, and Enoch Wood.

Luster decorations often were used in conjunction with enamels and transfers. Transfers used for luster decoration covered a wide range of public and domestic subjects. They frequently were accompanied by pious or sentimental doggerel, as well phrases which reflected on the humors of everyday life.

Copper luster was created by the addition of a copper compound to the glaze. It was very popular in America during the 19th century, and collecting it became a fad from the 1920s to the 1950s. Today it has a limited market.

Pink luster was made by using a gold mixture. Silver luster pieces were first covered completely with a thin coating of a "steel luster" mixture, containing a small quantity of platinum oxide. An additional coating of platinum, worked in water, was then applied before firing.

Sunderland is a coarse type of cream-colored earthenware with a marbled or spotted pink luster decoration, which shades from pink to purple. A solution of gold compound applied to the white body developed the many shades of pink.

The development of electroplating in 1840 created a sharp decline in the demands for metal-surfaced earthenware.

Reference: Michael Gibson, *19th Century Lustreware*, Antique Collectors' Club, 1999.

Reproduction Alert: The market for copper luster has been softened by reproductions, especially creamers and the "polka" jug, which fool many new buyers. Reproductions are heavier in appearance and weight than the earlier pieces.

Additional Listings: English Soft Paste.

Teapot, turquoise enamel decoration, copper luster body, 11-1/2" l, 7-1/2" h, $135.

Canary

Child's mug, 1-3/4" h, "A Present for Charles," pink luster trim, minor wear **625.00**

Miniature, creamer, 2-3/4" h, red and green flowers, pink luster accents and rim, pinpoint flake **850.00**

Pitcher, 6-1/2" h, enameled red, green, blue, and pink flowers, wear and crazing, hairline in spout **625.00**

Copper

Goblet, 3" d, 3-3/4" h, mauve and green colored band with floral dec around mid section, c1850 .... **85.00**

Pitcher

4" h, blue band with molded flower dec on both sides, copper luster bulbous base **50.00**

5-5/8" h, gold band with molded figures of men and women, orange, green, and purple enamel, in-the-making split in handle **65.00**

6-1/4" h, canary band with brown transfer scene of woman and two children, blue, yellow, and green enamel, hairline **70.00**

Planter, 4-1/4" d, 3-3/7" h, three ftd, kettle shape **25.00**

Tea cup and saucer, turquoise blue background, copper luster floral band **65.00**

Vase, 7-1/4" w, 6-1/2" h, two handles, stag scene **70.00**

Pink

Child's mug, 2" h, pink luster band, reddish hunter and dogs transfer, green highlighted foliate transfer **85.00**

Creamer, 4-3/8" h, stylized flower band, pink luster highlights and rim, ftd **75.00**

Cup and saucer, magenta transfers, Faith, Hope, and Charity, applied green enamel highlights, pink luster line borders **60.00**

Figure, 4-1/2" h, dogs, white, luster gilt collar, cobalt blue base with gilt trim, Staffordshire, pr............. **620.00**

Pitcher

5-1/2" h, House pattern, ornate pink luster dec.............. **120.00**

5-3/4" h, emb ribs, eagle, and flowers in pink and purple luster **150.00**

Plate

6-1/4" d, relief figures of dogs running on rim, highlighted with green, red, and pink luster, red, green, and blue stylized floral dec in center **55.00**

7-3/4" d, green transfer of "Employ time well," emb floral border with polychrome enamel and luster trim **75.00**

9-3/4" d, painted flowers and leaves, pink, purple, and yellow, green and red overglaze **45.00**

Plaque, 9-3/8" l, 8-3/8" h, rect, "The Great Eastern Steam Ship," black transfer with polychrome, pink luster shaped border **450.00**

Posset cup and saucer, tray, 5" h, wide luster bands flanked by two red bands, 19th C **295.00**

Teapot, 12" h, House pattern, Queen-Anne style, repaired finial on lid **285.00**

Toddy plate, 5-1/16" d, pink luster House pattern, emb floral sprigs border **45.00**

Waste bowl, 6" d, House pattern **125.00**

Silver

Coffee service, 7-3/8" h cov coffeepot, cov sugar bowl, six coffee cans and saucers, silver luster grape and leaves, rust enamel accents, yellow ground **450.00**

Creamer, 4" h, 5" w, ribbed loop base, incised band near top, shaped handle **85.00**

Cup and saucer, handleless, overall floral band on cup, scattered florals on saucer **45.00**

Figure, 11-7/8" l, standing lion, paw on globe, rect base, early 19th C, repaired **900.00**

Goblet, 4-3/8" h, silver luster grapes and vines, white ground, lustered foot **220.00**

Silver luster, bowl, footed, beaded rim, ribbed sides, copper luster interior, 5-1/8" d, 3" h, **$85.**

Jug

4-1/2" h, village scene **100.00**

5-1/2" h, blue printed hunting scene, border of flowers and leaves, luster ground, Staffordshire, c1815
. . . . **975.00**

6-1/2" h, shell detail, minor wear
. . . . **100.00**

Pitcher, 5-1/2" h, squatty body, wide lip, overall silver luster, 19th C **95.00**

Spill vase, 4-1/8" h, gray marbleized applied vines and fruits, silver luster accents, white int., pr **95.00**

Teapot, 5-1/4" h, reeded detail. . **140.00**

Sunderland

Bowl, 8-1/4" d, polychrome highlighted black transfers of ship and verse, pink marble luster, mid-18th C **265.00**

Creamer, 5" h, "The Sailor's Tear," outlined in florals, verse with sailing ship and "May Peace and Plenty…," luster trim **275.00**

Jug

7-1/2" h, transfer printed, painted polychrome enamels, Iron Bridge in Sunderland on one side, ship on reverse, chips, some wear . **300.00**

8-3/8" h, transfer printed, painted polychrome enamels, two marine rhymes, chips, some wear . **245.00**

Mug, 5" h, black transfer of compass on front, "The Sailor's Farewell" on reverse
. . . . **160.00**

Mustard pot, 4" h, loop handle . **150.00**

Pitcher, 7-1/8" h, hex panels, black transfers of John Wesley on one side, verse on other, pink marble luster, c1850. **150.00**

Plaque, 8-1/2" l, 7-1/2" w, "Thou God Seeist Me," luster trim, Dixon mark
. . . . **175.00**

Plate, 10" d, center transfer print of Pike and "Be always Ready to Die for your Country," pink luster and yellow banded border, c1820 . . . . **2,650.00**

Salt, master, Cloud pattern, ftd. . **50.00**

LUTZ-TYPE GLASS

History: Lutz-type glass is an art glass attributed to Nicholas Lutz. He made this type of glass while at the Boston and Sandwich Glass Co. from 1869 until 1888. Since Lutz-type glass was popular, copied by many capable glassmakers, and unsigned, it is nearly impossible to distinguish genuine Lutz products.

Lutz is believed to have made two distinct types of glass: striped and threaded. The striped glass was made by using threaded glass rods in the Venetian manner, and this style is often confused with authentic Venetian glass. Threaded glass was blown and decorated with winding threads of glass.

Barber bottle, 8" h, colorless ground, multicolored threaded latticino and opaque stripes **250.00**

Beverage set, 7-1/2" h tankard pitcher, four lemonade tumblers, four large tumblers, colorless ground, cranberry threading, engraved pattern of water plants and Great Blue Heron on pitcher
. . . . **650.00**

Bowl, latticino, blue ribbons, goldstone, clear bands, 4-1/4" d, 2" h, **$95.**

Bowl, 3-1/4" d, 3" h, colorless, white, amethyst, and yellow latticino, goldstone border **90.00**

Compote, 8-7/8" x 6-1/2", DQ, threaded, amberina, colorless hollow stem **500.00**

Epergne, 3 pcs, pink threads . . **275.00**

Finger bowl and underplate, 7" d, ruffled edge, amber swirls, amethyst latticino, gold metallic borders. . **165.00**

Lamp shade, 8" sq, 20-1/2" fitter ring, opaque white loopings, applied cranberry threading, ribbon edge
. . . . **180.00**

Punch cup, 3" x 2-5/8", cranberry threading, colorless ground, circular foot, applied colorless handle . . . **85.00**

Scent bottle, 2-1/8" l, blown, colorless, figural sea horse, opaque white spiral ribs, applied blue rigaree. **120.00**

Tumbler, 3-3/4" d, white and amethyst latticino goldstone highlights **75.00**

Vase, 7" h, cylindrical, cranberry threading **125.00**

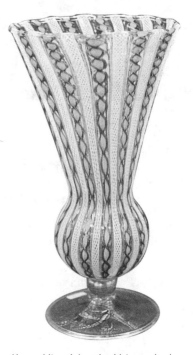

Vase, white, pink and goldstone edged lattice, flat base with gold highlights, 11-1/4" h, **$295.**

MAASTRICHT WARE

History: Petrus Regout founded the De Sphinx Pottery in 1836 in Maastricht, Holland. The firm specialized in transfer-printed earthenwares. Other factories also were established in the area, many employing English workmen and adopting their techniques. Maastricht china was exported to the United States in competition with English products.

Plate, Hong pattern, marked "Made in Holland," 9" d, $35.

Bowl

5-3/4" d, red, green, and blue agate pattern, "Petrous Regout, Maastricht" and lion mark... **35.00**

6" d, Sana pattern, black oriental transfer, orange wash, marked "Sana, Petrous Regout, Maastricht" **20.00**

8-1/4" d, ftd, windmill with people finishing, brown transfer.... **20.00**

Cup and saucer, Oriental pattern, 3-1/4" d, 2" h cup, c1929...... **22.00**

Pitcher, 5" h, rooster with iris and leaves, red transfer, marked "Regout & Co. Haan" **75.00**

Plate

7-1/2" d, rusty brown border, pink and yellow roses in center, Royal Sphinx mark, c1891 ...... **50.00**

8-1/4" d, Timor pattern **30.00**

8-1/2" d, Canton pattern, Geisha girls and man on walkway, marked "Canton, P. Regout Maastricht," c1836 .... **40.00**

10" d, Delft, blue and white windmill scene, Royal Sphinx mark .. **50.00**

Plate, multicolored Oriental-type scene, marked "Made in Holland/Society Ceramique Potiche," 7-3/4" d, $30.

Platter, 11-1/2" d, gaudy polychrome florals, red, yellow, and green white ground **70.00**

MAJOLICA

History: Majolica, an opaque, tin-glazed pottery, has been produced in many countries for centuries. It was named after the Spanish Island of Majorca, where figuline—a potter's clay—is found. Today, however, the term "majolica" denotes a type of pottery which was made during the last half of the 19th century in Europe and America.

Majolica frequently depicts elements of nature: leaves, flowers, birds, and fish. Designs were painted on the soft-clay body using vitreous colors and fired under a clear lead glaze to impart the rich color and brilliance characteristic of majolica.

Victorian decorative art philosophy dictated that the primary function of design was to attract the eye; usefulness was secondary. Majolica was a welcome and colorful change from the familiar blue and white wares, creamwares, and white ironstone of the day.

Marks: Wedgwood, George Jones, Holdcraft, and Minton were a few of the English majolica manufacturers who marked their wares. Most of their pieces can be identified through the English Registry mark and/or the potter-designer's mark. Sarreguemines in France and Villeroy and Boch in Baden, Germany, produced majolica that compared favorably with the finer English majolica. Most Continental pieces had an incised number on the base.

Although 600-plus American potteries produced majolica between 1850 and 1900, only a handful chose to identify their wares. Among these manufacturers were George Morely, Edwin Bennett, the Chesapeake Pottery Company, the New Milford-Wannoppee Pottery Company, and the firm of Griffen, Smith, and Hill. The others hoped their unmarked pieces would be taken for English examples.

References: Susan and Al Bagdade, *Warman's American Pottery and Porcelain*, 2nd ed., Krause

Publications, 2000; ——, *Warman's English & Continental Pottery & Porcelain*, 3rd ed., Krause Publications, 1998; Victoria Bergesen, *Majolica: British, Continental, and American Wares, 1851-1915*, Barrie & Jenkins, 1989; Leslie Bockol, *Victorian Majolica*, Schiffer Publishing, 1996; Helen Cunningham, *Majolica Figures*, Schiffer Publishing, 1997; Nicholas M. Dawes, *Majolica*, Crown, 1990; Marilyn G. Karmason and Joan B. Stacke, *Majolica, A Complete History and Illustrated Survey*, Abrams, 1989; Mariann Katz-Marks, *Collector's Encyclopedia of Majolica*, Collector Books, 1992, 2000 value update; Marshall P. Katz and Robert Lehr, *Palissy Ware: Nineteenth Century French Ceramics from Avisseau to Renoleau*, Athlone Press, 1996; *Price Guide to Majolica*, L-W Book Sales, 1997; Mike Schneider, *Majolica*, Schiffer Publishing, 1990, 1995 value update; Jeffrey B. Snyder and Leslie J. Bockol, *Majolica: European and American Wares*, Schiffer Publishing, 1994.

Collectors' Club: Majolica International Society, 1275 First Ave., Ste. 103, New York, NY 10021, http://www.majolicasociety.com; Pacific Northwest Majolica Club, 16302 34th St., N.E., Snohomish, WA 98290.

Adviser: Mary D. Harris.

Note: Prices listed below are for pieces with good color and in mint condition. For less-than-perfect pieces, decrease value proportionately according to the degree of damage or restoration.

Reproduction Alert: Majolica-style pieces are a favorite of today's interior decorators. Many exact copies of period pieces are being manufactured. In addition, fantasy pieces incorporating late Victorian-era design motifs have entered the market and confused many novice collectors.

Modern majolica reproductions differ from period pieces in these ways: (1) modern reproductions tend to be lighter in weight than their Victorian ancestors; (2) the glaze on newer pieces may not be as rich or deeply colored as on period pieces; (3) new pieces usually have a plain white bottom, period pieces almost always have colored or mottled bases; (4) a bisque finish either inside or on the bottom generally means the piece is new; and (5) if the design prevents the piece from being functional—e.g., a lip of a pitcher that does not allow proper pouring—it is a new piece made primarily for decorative purposes.

Some reproductions bear old marks. Period marks found on modern pieces include (a) "Etruscan Majolica" (the mark of Griffen, Smith and Hill) and (b) a British registry mark.

Bowl, low, Classical, white ground, green leaves, pink flowers, green center, Etruscan, 9-1/2" d, $200.

Advertising jar, cov, 8-1/2", "Avalon," Spaulding & Merrish, "Sunny Broth, Chicago" **300.00**

Basket, banks and thorley, basketweave and bamboo, yellow ground **325.00**

Bowl, 15" l, diamond shape, Oriental motif, turquoise ground **250.00**

Bread tray, 13" l
Eat Thy Bread With Thankfulness, wheat motif, mottled center . **285.00**
English, corn **475.00**
Pear and apple, brown ground, yellow fruit **300.00**

Bud vase, 4-3/4" h, triple, Wild Rose and Basket, cobalt blue and yellow **200.00**

Butter dish, cov, Shell and Cranes **250.00**

Butter pat
Blackberry and basketweave, yellow ground **125.00**
Copeland, pansy, brown and yellow **175.00**
Eureka, fan shape **125.00**

Cake stand, Etruscan, Morning Glory, white ground, green leaves, pink flowers **250.00**

Candleholders, pr, 5" h, Portuguese Palissy, serpent handles, shell tops **150.00**

Cheese keeper, cov
8-1/2", Holdcroft, Pond Lily, green and white **2,650.00**
9", George Jones, Cow, turquoise **5,000.00**
9" d, George Jones, Wild Rose and Tree Bark, brown ground, green leaves, white flower **3,500.00**

Compote, Etruscan
Cosmos, cobalt blue ground **350.00**
Maple Leaf, in basket **275.00**

Cup and saucer, Etruscan, Cauliflower **350.00**

Humidor, cov, figural head
5" h, Baby Face, green bonnet **200.00**
5" h, Black jockey **200.00**
5" h, Indian chief **150.00**
6" h, Clown **150.00**
7" h, Black man with fez and bowtie **275.00**

Match striker, Continental, monk with stein **200.00**

Mug
Etruscan, Oak Leaf **225.00**
Holdcroft, Water Lily, cobalt blue ground **225.00**
Wedgwood, Argenta, fan and prunus **150.00**

Pitcher, flying crane, green, blue, and gold band, brown handle, 7-1/2" h, $245.

Pitcher
4" h, shell shape, coral, creamy yellow and brown **275.00**
6" h, oak leaf and acorn picket fence **200.00**
7" h, Samuel Lear, water lily . **250.00**
8" h, Stork in Marsh pattern, Sharter & Sons, cobalt blue ground **250.00**
9-1/2" d, bird and bird next . . **300.00**
9-1/2" l, Sheaf of Wheat pattern, cobalt blue **275.00**

Plate
8-1/2" d, George Jones, Leaf and fern, turquoise ground **400.00**
8-1/2" d, Holdcroft, Crane in Flight, turquoise pebble ground . . **300.00**
8-3/4" d, Wedgwood, turquoise ground, leaf and snowberry design **350.00**

9" d, English, pineapple **275.00**
9" d, Etruscan, Oriental lady in frame, yellow **175.00**
9" d, Etruscan, Shell and Seaweed **300.00**
9" d, Wedgwood, shell border, turquoise center **250.00**
9-1/2" d, Fielding, parrot on branch, white ground, six sided **200.00**
9-1/2" d, Minton, cobalt blue and mottled **600.00**
10" d, fan shape plate, pink ground, prunus and dragonfly **275.00**

Plate in frame, Continental, small leaf plate, wire basket frame **175.00**

Platter
12-1/2" l, Holdcroft, Tobacco Leaf and Rosetto **225.00**
12-1/2" l, Wardle bird and fan, bamboo border **250.00**
14" l, begonia leaf on yellow basket **250.00**
25-1/2" l, Wedgwood, Ocean, Argenta **1,300.00**

Salt, Etruscan, Lily **175.00**

Sardine box, cov, George Jones, fish finial, turquoise ground **1,500.00**

Spittoon, Etruscan, Pineapple . **500.00**

Spooner, Samuel Lear, Water Lily **150.00**

Syrup, pewter top
3-1/4" h, Begonia Leaf, on basketweave **200.00**
6-3/4" h, Wild Rose, cobalt blue **300.00**

Teapot, cov
Figural elephant spout and handle, Oriental motif **350.00**
Flat sided, florals, rosebud lid, cobalt blue **300.00**
Tenuous Leaf, with bird's neck and head spout and handle **400.00**

Tea set, Strawberry and Bow, yellow, price for three pcs **450.00**

Tray
10" x 7", Parrot on Branch, pink ground **325.00**
12" l, leaves and fern, green, blue, oval **250.00**
13-3/4" l, fish shape **150.00**

Umbrella stand, 21-1/2" h, Holdcraft, Stork in Cattails with Fish, cobalt blue **3,000.00**

Vase, figural
5-1/2" h, Corn, yellow and green **250.00**
8" h, Art Nouveau lady, winged harp **350.00**
12" h, Continental, man and woman under a tree, price for pr . . . **300.00**

MAPS

History: Maps provide one of the best ways to study the growth of a country or region. From the 16th to the early 20th century, maps were both informative and decorative. Engravers provided ornamental detailing, such as ornate calligraphy and scrolling, especially on bird's-eye views and city maps. Many maps were hand colored to enhance their beauty.

Maps generally were published as plates in books. Many of the maps available today are simply single sheets from cut-apart books.

In the last quarter of the 19th century, representatives from firms in Philadelphia, Chicago, and elsewhere traveled the United States preparing county atlases, often with a sheet for each township and each major city or town.

References: *Antique Map Price Record & Handbook for 1996*, available from Spoon River Press (2319C W. Rohmann, Peoria, IL 61604), 1996; Melville C. Branch, *An Atlas of Rare City Maps: Comparative Urban Design, 1830-1842*, Princeton Architectural Press, 1997; Carl Morland and David Bannister, *Antique Maps*, Phaidon Press, 1993; K. A. Sheets, *American Maps 1795-1895*, available from Spoon River Press (2319C W. Rohmann, Peoria, IL 61604), 1995.

Periodicals and Internet Resources: http://www.mapforum.com; *Mercator's World*, 845 Williamette St., Eugene, OR 97401-2918, http://www.mercatormag.com.

Collectors' Clubs: Boston Map Society, Harvard College Library, Cambridge, MA, 02138, http://icg.harvard.edu/~maps/hpbms.html; California Map Society, 1109 Linda Glen Drive, Pasadena, CA 91105, http://www.raremaps.com/cms; Cartomania Plus, 8 Amherst Road, Pelham, MA 01002; Chicago Map Society, 60 W. Walton St., Chicago, IL 60610; International Map Collectors Society, 27 Landford Road, Putney, London SW15 1AQ UK, http://www.imcos~mapcollecting.org; Map Society of Wisconsin, P.O. Box 399, Milwaukee, WI 53201; North East Map Organization, 2504 Kerry Lane, Charlottesville, VA 22901; Northern Ohio Map Society, Map Department, Cleveland Public Library, 325 Superior Ave., Cleveland, OH 44111; Texas Map Society, c/o Dept. of History, University of Texas, P.O. Box 19529, Arlington, TX 76019-5029; Washington Map Society, 201 Huntington Ave., Alexandria, VA 22303-01547.

Museums: British Library Map Collection, London, UK; Harvard Map Collection, Harvard College Library, Cambridge, MA; Heritage Map Museum, Lititz, PA.

Notes: Although mass produced, county atlases are eagerly sought by collectors. Individual sheets sell for $45 to $95. The atlases themselves can usually be purchased in the $250 to $500 range. Individual sheets should be viewed solely as decorative and not as investment material.

SPECIAL AUCTION

Swann Galleries, Inc.
104 E. 25th St.
New York, NY 10010
(212) 254-4710

Alexandria, Braun and Hogenberg, Amsterdam, c1572, double page, engraved city map, Latin text on verso, hand colored, wide margins, 365 x 485 mm **575.00**

A Map of North America, Edward Wells, London, 1700, double page, engraved, wide margins, 355 x 480 mm **635.00**

A Map of the British Empire in America, from the Head of Hudson's Bay to the Southern bounds of Georgia, London, c1750, engraved, folding, hand colored and in outline, wide margins, 265 x 325 mm **260.00**

Americae Nova Tabula, Willem Blaeu, Amsterdam, 1633, double page, engraved, wide margins, 365 x 465 mm **2,990.00**

An Accurate Map of the West Indies, Emanuel Bowen, London, c1760, double-page, engraved, hand colored, wide margins, 355 x 425 mm . . . **290.00**

A New and Accurate Map of the World, John Overton, London, 1670, engraved, folding, double-hemispheric, margins trimmed, 390 x 515 mm **8,625.00**

A New and Accurate Map of the Islands of Newfoundland, Cape Breton, St. John and Anticosta, Emanuel Bowen, London, c1744, engraved, folding, hand colored, wide margins, 350 x 430 mm **140.00**

A New Chart of the Coast of New England, Nova Scotia, New France or Canada, Jacques Nicholas Bellin, Jeffreys, London, 1746, engraved, folding, hand colored in outline, no margins, 35 x 465 mm **165.00**

A New Map of America, John Cary, London, 1806, double page, engraved, hand colored, wide margins, browned along vertical fold, 465 x 525 mm **220.00**

A New Map of Nova Scotia, Thomas Jeffreys, London, 1750, double page, engraved, very wide margins, all edges tissue-backed on verso, 325 x 415 mm **220.00**

A Plan of the Town and Chart of the Harbour of Boston, London, February, 1775, engraved, folding, extracted from 1775 issue of *Gentleman's Magazine*, 290 x 350 mm **220.00**

Asia, Giovanni Botero, Rome, c1595, small double page, engraved, trimmed margins, 205 x 245 mm **300.00**

Bay of Seven Islands, J. F. Des Barries, London, 1779, double page,

engraved, hand colored, lower margin trimmed, 765 x 545 mm **115.00**

British Dominions in America agreeable to the Treaty of 1763, Thomas Kitchin, Dury, London, 1777, double page, engraved, hand colored in outline, wide margins, 445 x 540 mm **6,440.00**

Canada, titled, "This Map of Upper and Lower Canada and United States Contiguous Contracted from the Manuscript survey of P.F. Tardieu is Respectfully Inscribed by the Publics Most Obedient Servant Thomas Kensells," ribbon banner above this title cartouche reads "To The Officers of The Army of the Citizens of The United States," hand colored and drawn, mounted in modern black finished wood frame, 16" x 20", $880. Photo courtesy of Cowan Historic Americana Auctions.

Canada et Louisiane, George Louis Le Rouge, Paris, 1755, double page, engraved, wide margins, hand colored in outlined, 625 x 510 mm **375.00**

Chart of the Antarctic Polar Circle, Philippe Buache, London, 1763, engraved, folding, hand colored, margins trimmed, 200 x 230 mm **200.00**

Cruchley's New Plan of London, George Frederick Cruchley, London, 1836, engraved, 30-section map, hand colored, linen backed, orig board cover with publisher's label, 460 x 855 mm overall **175.00**

Custer's Battle-Field, Charles Becker, c1877, folding, lithographed, 420 x 475 mm **220.00**

Eastern Hemisphere, Western Hemisphere, Anthony Finley, Philadelphia, 1826, from *Finley's New General Atlas*, engraved, hand colored, wide margins, 315 x 250 mm, pr. **60.00**

Haemisphaerium Stellatum Astrale Antiquum, Andres Cellarius, Amsterdam, 1660, double page, engraved celestial map, hand colored, wide margins, clear tear at vertical fold at lower margin just extending into image, 440 x 515 mm **2,530.00**

Jamaica, John Thomson, Edinburgh, 1817, double page, engraved, two insets showing harbors of Bluefields and Kingston, wide margins, hand colored in outline, 440 x 630 mm **320.00**

Map of Arizona, 1876, Tunsion, hand colored, 14" x 11" **65.00**

Map of California, Nevada, Oregon, 1876, Tunsion, hand colored, 22" x 14" **85.00**

Map of Oregon and Upper California, John Charles Fremont, Washington, 1848, folding, lithographed, hand colored in outline, overall browning, 905 x 755 mm **2,185.00**

Map of the United States and Territories, Washington, 1866, litho, folding, hand colored in outline, some minor loss at folds, linen backed, 775 x 1,450 mm **550.00**

Marshfield, Massachusetts, litho on paper, John Ford Jr., Survenor, [sic] framed, 30" x 21-1/2" **345.00**

Nouveau Plan de Moscou, G. L. De Lavaur, Auguste Semen, Moscow, c1850, folding, lithographed, hand colored, early pencil notes, wide margins, 17 Moscow districts, text in French and Cyrillic, linen backed, 560 x 645 mm **345.00**

Ohio, A J. Johnson, New York, with view of capitol building in corner, from "*New Illustrated Family Atlas of the World 1864*," printed, hand colored, matted, unframed, 23" h, 29" w **75.00**

Plan de Longuvy, Guerin Cadet, Longuvy, 1686, manuscript map, detailed pen and ink drawing on left portion of map, 420 x 555 mm . . **345.00**

Survey Map, Jericho, New York or Vermont, showing lands owned by Henry Allen, several homesteads in the area, pen and ink, hand colored, 1794, imperfections, 28-1/2" x 30" **575.00**

The State of Ohio, Thomas Cowperthwalt and Company, Philadelphia, 1850, printed, hand colored, matted, unframed, 22" h, 19" w **55.00**

United States of America, W. and D. Lizars, London, c1810, engraved, folding, hand colored, margins trimmed, several folds closed at lower edge with archival tape, 395 x 460 mm **260.00**

MARBLEHEAD POTTERY

History: This hand-thrown pottery was first made in 1905 as part of a therapeutic program introduced by Dr. J. Hall for the patients confined to a sanitarium located in Marblehead, Massachusetts. In 1916, production was removed from the hospital to another site. The factory continued under the directorship of Arthur E. Baggs until it closed in 1936.

Most pieces found today are glazed with a smooth, porous, even finish in a single color. The most desirable pieces have a conventional design in one or more subordinate colors.

Reference: David Rago, *American Art Pottery*, Knickerbocker Press, 1997.

Vase, ovoid, by Hannah Tutt, matte painted stylized green, ochre, and blue trees, gray ground, stamped ship mark and "HT," 3-3/4" x 7", $5,175. Photo courtesy of David Rago Auctions, Inc.

Bowl, 5-1/2" d, deep blue, minor underglaze rim roughness **350.00**

Bulb bowl, 6" d, slate gray glaze, c1915. **160.00**

Centerpiece bowl, 3-3/4" h, 8-1/4" d, flaring, incised lotus leaf design on ext., dark blue matte glaze, imp ship mark **425.00**

Chamberstick, 4" h, 4-1/2" d, bright yellow matte glaze, imp ship mark **275.00**

Humidor, 5" h, 4-1/4" d, lightly modeled stylized dark blue flora, speckled sandy ground, rare large paper label, Arthur Baggs, marked "AEB and MHC/$5.00" **4,100.00**

Vase, stylized lillies, bands at neck and rim, impressed ship mark, 4-1/2" x 4", $4,500. Photo courtesy of David Rago Auctions, Inc.

Tile, 6" sq, cuerda seca, polychrome trees and house, matte gray ground, mounted in period frame, ship mark, remnant of paper label, restoration to Y-shaped crack **1,725.00**

Tile frieze, two 7-1/2" sq tiles, incised lake scene, matte yellow, browns, and greens, imp mark, paper label, orig price tag on each, orig frame retaining sticker marked "o. 2-64 tiles Poplars with Reflections, Dec by A. E. Baggs, Price $10.00," minor edge nicks, kiln pops, from estate of Dr. Hall, founder of Marblehead Pottery **21,850.00**

Trivet

6" sq, stylized flowers, matte blue, green, yellow, and red, imp mark, paper label, remnant of price label, from estate of Dr. Hall, founder of Marblehead Pottery. **865.00**

6-1/4" sq, red, blue, yellow, green, and orange floral basket, black ground, imp mark, paper label **435.00**

Vase

2-3/4" d, 4-1/4" h, cabinet, tapering, designed by Arthur Baggs, dec by Hannah Tutt, incised chevron pattern, two-tone mottled matte green glaze, imp ship mark, artist's cipher **5,350.00**

3-3/4" d, 4-1/2" h, cylindrical, incised stylized holly branches, green leaves, red berries, dark blue matte ground, imp ship mark . . **6,275.00**

3-3/4" d, 7" h, ovoid, matte painted with stylized trees, green, ochre, and blue, gray ground, by Hannah Tutt, stamped ship mark and "HT" **5,175.00**

4" d, 8-3/4" h, cylindrical, carved band of stylized palm fronds, gunmetal under speckled matte green ground, ship mark . **5,350.00**

4-1/4" d, 6-1/4" h, geometric, lightly tooled, stylized light brown trees, matte speckled sand-colored ground, imp ship mark . . . **4,750.00**

4-1/4" d, 7-1/4" h, organic dark brown flowers on tall stems, matte speckled green ground, imp ship mark and "H. T." (Hannah Tutt) **4,000.00**

5-1/4" d, 13-1/2" h, cylindrical, stylized trees, matte blue glaze over gray-green matte ground, incised ship mark **12,500.00**

6" d, 9" h, barrel shape, broad band of incised stylized flowers and leaves, amber, brown, and blue, matte mustard ground, by Hannah Tutt, ship mark and "HT" . **8,575.00**

8" d, 6-1/4" h, fan shape, matte blue glaze, imp mark, paper label **320.00**

Wall pocket, 5-1/4" w, 5" h, speckled gray ext., robin's egg blue int., unmarked **295.00**

MARY GREGORY TYPE GLASS

History: The use of enameled decoration on glass, an inexpensive way to imitate cameo glass, developed in Bohemia in the late 19th century. The Boston and Sandwich Glass Co. copied this process in the late 1880s.

Mary Gregory (1856-1908) was employed for two years at the Boston and Sandwich Glass factory when the enameled decorated glass was being manufactured. Some collectors argue that Gregory was inspired to paint her white enamel figures on glass by the work of Kate Greenaway and a desire to imitate pate-sur-pate. However, evidence for these assertions is very weak. Further, it has never been proven that Mary Gregory even decorated glass as part of her job at Sandwich. The result is that "Mary Gregory type" is a better term to describe this glass.

Reference: R. and D. Truitt, *Mary Gregory Glassware*, published by authors, 1992.

Museum: Sandwich Glass Museum, Sandwich, MA.

Reproduction Alert: Collectors should recognize that most examples of Mary Gregory type glass seen today are either European or modern reproductions.

Box, covered, amethyst ground, white enamel girl in garden setting, 5-1/2" d, $260.

Barber bottle, 7-1/8" h, deep sapphire blue, white enameled youngster playing tennis, cylindrical bulbous form, long neck, tooled mouth, pontil scar . **165.00**

Box, 2-7/8" d, 3-1/4" h, light sapphire blue, white enameled girl with apron and flowers, brass fittings and feet **395.00**

Cruet, 8-1/2" h, sapphire blue, sq dimpled sides, white enameled two girls facing each other, blue handle, orig stopper **495.00**

Decanter, 9-1/2" h, green, white enameled child marching, applied camphor glass handle, clear stopper **350.00**

Dresser set, pr 10-1/2" h perfume bottles, 7" cov dresser jar, deep cobalt blue, enameled young children and angels, sprays of flowers, crown tops **895.00**

Jewelry box, 2-1/4" x 4" x 5", dark amethyst, white enameled boy, hand extended toward bird in flight, silver fittings marked Middleton #34 **1,100.00**

Milk pitcher, 6" h, cranberry ground, white enameled girl, clear applied handle **50.00**

Miniature, pitcher, 1-3/4" h, cranberry ground, white enameled little girl blowing bubbles, clear glass handle with gold highlights **200.00**

Mug, 4-1/2" h, amber, ribbed, white enameled girl praying **65.00**

Paperweight, 2-1/2" w, 4" l, deep black ground, white enameled young boy and girl in garden setting **295.00**

Patch box, emerald green **295.00**

Pickle castor, 9-3/4" h, cranberry insert, white enameled boy, marked "Meriden B #304" **1,500.00**

Pitcher, sapphire blue, white enameled child, 10" h, $335.

Tumbler, 1-3/4" d, 2-1/2" h, cranberry, white enameled boy on one, girl on other, facing pr **100.00**

Syrup, cranberry, white enameled girl, SP top **275.00**

Vase

3" d, 6-3/4" h, pale amber, young girl in forest scene, reverse with spray of flowers and leaves, neck and shoulder with dec band . . . **225.00**

3-1/2" d, 8-1/4" h, amber, ruffled top, white enameled young girl . **185.00**

4" d, 10-5/8" h, cylinder shape, lime green, white enameled young girl carrying butterfly net **185.00**

4-3/4" d, 12-3/4" h, amethyst, white enameled angel reaching for branch **395.00**

6-1/4" h, cranberry, white enameled girl in garden, gold bands . **375.00**

MATCH HOLDERS

History: The friction match achieved popularity after 1850. The early matches were packaged and sold in sliding cardboard boxes. To facilitate storage and to eliminate the clumsiness of using the box, match holders were developed.

The first match holders were cast iron or tin, the latter often displaying advertisements. A patent for a wall-hanging match holder was issued in 1849. By 1880, match holders also were being made from glass and china. Match holders began to lose their popularity in the late 1930s, with the advent of gas and electric heat and ranges.

Reference: Denis B. Alsford, *Match Holders*, Schiffer Publishing, 1994.

Grading Condition. The following numbers represent the standard grading system used by dealers, collectors, and auctioneers:

C.10 = Mint
C. 9 = Near mint
C.8.5 = Outstanding
C.8 = Excellent
C.7.5 = Fine +
C.7 = Fine
C. 6.5 = Fine – (good)
C. 6 = Poor

Wall type, cast iron, embossed decoration, 4" l, 2-1/2" h, **$35.**

Advertising

Black Cat, 5-1/2" x 4-1/4", tin litho, hanging, Black Cat Shoe Dressing, Black Kitty Stove Enamel, trademark cat images and young black girl, C.8+ **1,600.00**

Cognac Richarpaulloud, celluloid covered tin clip, black and white with showgirl dancer wearing red feathered outfit on front and back, 1920s................... **65.00**

DeLaval Separator, emb litho tin, 6" h **130.00**

Dr. Shoop's Health Coffee, tin litho, hanging, 3-1/2" w, 5" l, C.8+ **275.00**

Ferris Seed Co., 6" h **30.00**

Honegger's Farms, 6" h **30.00**

Kelly & Springfield Tires, tin cover clip, black on buff celluloid insert, c1930 .... **40.00**

New Process Blue Flame Oil Stove, tin litho, hanging, red ground, blue image of stove, 2-1/2" w, 1" d, 3" h, C.8+ **275.00**

Bisque, 4" h, 3-5/8" d, natural-colored rooster with beige basket, two compartments, round base with pink band **135.00**

Brass

2" x 2-1/2", copper colored, hinged lid, Reading PA Fire Hall cello insert in lid, early 1900s **45.00**

3" h, bear chained to post, cast, orig gilt trim **225.00**

Bronze, 3" h, shoe, mouse in toe **125.00**

Cast iron, figural

Bird.................... **45.00**

High Button Shoe, 5-1/2" h, black paint, c1890 .... **50.00**

Glass, 3" h, 3-1/4" d, shaded rose to pink overlay satin, ball-shape, glossy off-white lining, ground pontil .. **155.00**

Roycroft, hammered copper, nested ashtray, 3-1/4" h, 3-1/4" d, **$290.**

Majolica

Bull dog, striker, large...... **440.00**

Dog, striker, Continental, rim chips and repair.............. **165.00**

Happy Hooligan with suitcase, striker, rim nick to hat **110.00**

Monk, striker, hairline in base **140.00**

Papier-mâché, 2-3/4" h, black lacquer, Oriental dec................. **25.00**

Porcelain, seated girl, feeding dog on table, sgd "Elbogen"........ **125.00**

Sterling silver, 1-3/4" x 2-1/2" , hinged lid, diecut striking area, cigar cutter on one corner, lid inscription "H. R." and diamond, inside lid inscribed "Made for Tiffany & Co./Pat 12, 09/Sterling" **95.00**

Tin, 2-3/8" h, top hat, hinged lid, orig green paint, black band........ **65.00**

Torquay pottery, 2" h, 3-1/8" d, ship scene, reads "A match for any Man, Shankin".................... **70.00**

MATCH SAFES

History: Pocket match safes are small containers used to safely carry matches in one's pocket. They were first used around the 1840s. Match safes can be found in various sizes and shapes, and were made from numerous materials such as sterling, nickel-plated brass, gold, brass, ivory, and vulcanite. Some of the most interesting and sought after ones are figurals in the shapes of people, animals, and anything else imaginable. Match safes were also a very popular advertising means from 1895-1910, and were used by both large and small businesses.

References: Deborah Shinn, *Matchsafes*, Scala Publishers in association with the Cooper-Hewitt Museum, 2001; W. Eugene Sanders Jr., and Christine C. Sanders, *Pocket Matchsafes, Reflections of Life & Art, 1840-1920*, Schiffer Publishing, 1997; Denis Alsford, *Match Holders, 100 Years of Ingenuity*, Schiffer Publishing, 1994; Audrey G. Sullivan, *History of Match Safes in the United States*, published by author, 1978; Roger Fresco-Corbu, *Vesta Boxes*, Lutterworth Press, 1983

Collector's Club: International Match Safe Association, P.O. Box 791, Malaga, NJ 08328-0791, www.matchsafe.org or IMSAoc@aol.com.

Reproduction Alert: Reproduction, copycat, and fantasy match safes abound. Reproductions include Art Nouveau styles, figural/novelty shapes, nudes, and many others. Fantasy and fakes include Jack Daniel's and Coca-Cola.

Many of the sterling match safes are marked "925" or "Sterling 925." Any match safe so marked requires careful inspection. Many period, American match safes have maker's marks, catalog numbers, 925/1000, or other markings. Period English safes have hallmarks. Beware of English reproduction match safes bearing the "DAB" marking. Always verify the date mark on English safes.

Check enameled safes closely. Today's technology allows for the economic faking of enamel motifs on old match safes. Carefully check condition of enameling for telltale clues.

Note: While not all match safes have a striking surface, this is one test, besides size, to distinguish a match safe from a calling card case or other small period boxes. Values are based on match safes being in excellent condition.

Alligator, figural, head forms lid, Souvenir St. Augustine, FL, brass, 2-1/2" x 1-1/2" **395.00**

Art Nouveau, flowers, sterline, 2-5/8" l, $65.

Alligator chasing Negro, Souvenir of Florida, insert type, by August Goertz, Co., plated brass, 2-3/4" x 1-1/2" **225.00**

Allsopp's India Ale bottle, brass, 2-3/8" x 3/4" **135.00**

American Brewing Co., red leather wrap with nickel-plated ends, 2-3/4" x 1-1/2" **75.00**

American Injector Co., by New Jersey Aluminum Co., aluminum, 3" x 1-1/2" **40.00**

Art Nouveau motif, lady's head, flowers, cattails, by E & J Bass, Empire silver, 2-3/8" x 1-5/8" **70.00**

Athena Riding Pegasus, by Wm. Kerr, cat. #19, 2-1/2" x 1-1/2" **295.00**

Banner Cigar adv., celluloid wrapped, by Whitehead & Hoag Co., 2-1/4" x 1-3/8" **150.00**

Barthlomay beer/winged logo, nickel-plated brass, 2-1/2" x 1-1/2" **85.00**

Bowling motif, by F. S. Gilbert, sterling, 2-5/8" x 1-3/8" **295.00**

Boxing glove, figural, sterling, 1-5/8" x 1 1/8" **550.00**

Bulldog motif, by R. Wallace & Sons, cat. #870, sterling, 2-5/8" x 1 3/4" **350.00**

Candle in box, domed lid, fold-out edge, candle, painted tin, 2-3/4" x 2-7/8" **125.00**

Cherurbs & wishbone motif, by Wm. Kerr, catalog #6, sterling, 2-5/8" x 1-1/2" **295.00**

Combo watch, sovereign holder and safe, by Wm. Neale, Birmingham, sterling, 3-3/8" x 1-3/8". **950.00**

Cupid in garden, by Gorham Mfg. Co., catalog #B1305, sterling, 2-5/8" x 1-3/4" **275.00**

Dog motif, enameled on sterling, by H. Johnston, Birmingham, 1-7/8" x 1-1/4" **395.00**

Dragon motif, Japanese, brass, 2-5/8" x 1-1/2". **95.00**

Eggplant with snail and insects, figural, Japanese, patinated brass, 2-1/2" x 1-5/8" **425.00**

Farm hut, figural, Japanese, patinated brass, 1-1/2" x 2-1/2" **535.00**

Firemen's Fund Insurance Co., 1905, by Shreeve & Co., hammered brass, sterling emblem, 2-1/2" x 1-3/4" . **450.00**

Flexible tube, figural, adv. U.S. Tubing Co., nickel plated, 1-3/4" x 1" . . . **130.00**

Friar drinking wine, sterling, 2-3/4" x 1-3/4" **325.00**

Frog, figural, by Gorham Mfg. Co., silver plate, 2" x 1-1/2" **395.00**

Gamewell Fire Alarm, by August Goertz Co., nickel-plated brass, 2-3/4" x 1-1/2" **395.00**

Gladstone, figural, flat back, plated brass, 1-7/8" x 1-1/2" **175.00**

Gold Dust Twins, by Wm. Schimper Co., plated brass, 3" x 1-5/8" . . . **275.00**

Goldstone, rectangular with rounded end, brass trim, 3" x 1-1/8" **125.00**

Golf motif, man hitting ball, sterling, 2-1/2" x 1-1/2" **450.00**

Gorham, mixed metals, cat. #176, sterling with copper, 2-3/4" x 1-1/4" **395.00**

Griffin motif, by Gorham Mfg. Co., hand wrought, sterling, 2-3/4" x 1-3/8" **175.00**

Hidden photo, "barrel" shaped, by Battin & Co., sterling, 2-1/2" x 1-5/8" **225.00**

Holly and berry motif, by Whiting, cat. #6209, 2-5/8" x 1-3/8" **165.00**

Home F & M Insurance, by Shreeve & Co., sterling, 2-1/2" x 1-3/8" **525.00**

Hot air balloon motif, by John Gammage, Birmingham, sterling and enamel, 2-5/8" x 1-1/8" **595.00**

Irish symbols-Iberian harp, shamrock, etc., book shaped, bog oak, 2" x 1-1/2" **85.00**

John Deere Plows adv., by Whitehead and Hoag, nickel-plated brass, 2-5/8" x 1-1/2" **750.00**

Knight in armor holding lance, castle background, sterling, 2-3/4" x 1-3/8" **175.00**

Liberty Fire Co. #5, Reading, PA, celluloid inserts, 2-3/4" x 1-1/2" . **175.00**

Lion motif, sterling, saw-tooth striker, 2-3/8" x 1-1/2" **200.00**

Lisk Company adv, multicolored celluloid inserts, nickel-plated brass, 2-3/4" x 1-1/2" **425.00**

Louisiana Purchase, 1803-1903, copyrighted by I.G.K., brass, 2-3/8" x 1-1/4" **95.00**

Maltese Cross & Baker Fabric Fire Hose, gutta percha, slip top, 2-3/4" x 1-1/8" **185.00**

Masonic emblem, enameled "G,", by August Goertz Co., nickel-plated brass ends and sides, inset type, 2-3/4" x 1-1/2" **75.00**

McKinley for President, nickel-plated brass, 2-7/8" x 1-1/2" **225.00**

Men fishing in stream, by James E. Blake Co., sterlinE, 2-3/8" x 1-5/8" **125.00**

Moreland Match enameled emblem on sterling, 2-1/4" x 1-5/8" **350.00**

Mythological devil, figural, by Gorham Mfg. Co., cat. #070, silver plated, 2-1/4" x 1-1/2" **395.00**

Nautical motif, book shaped, by Hamburg Rubber Works, vulcanite, 2" x 1-1/2" **145.00**

Never-slip horseshoes, celluloid wrapped, color graphics, by Whitehead & Hoag, 2-3/4" x 1-1/2" **150.00**

Order of Odd Fellows motif, insert type, nickel-plated brass, 2-3/4" x 1-1/2" **75.00**

Oriental motif, working compass, Japanese, patinated brass, 2-5/8" x 1-1/4". **225.00**

Owl, figural, Japanese, brass, 2-1/2" x 1-1/2" **425.00**

Padlock, sterling silver, English, c1882, 1-3/4" h, $285.

Pants/overalls, figural, pewter, 2-7/8" x 1-1/4" **125.00**

Privy, figural, man with top hat inside, nickel plated, 2" x 3/4" x 1/2" . . . **275.00**

Rabbit and badger motif, Japanese, brass, 2-1/2 x 1-3/8" **195.00**

Rattle snakes, intertwined, bold design, by Wm. Kerr, sterling, 2-3/4" x 1-5/8" **695.00**

Revolver, figural, plated brass with vulcanite handles, 2-3/8" x 3-3/4" **350.00**

Roman coin motif, pill-box type, by August Goertz Co., nickel-plated brass, 1-5/8" x 2-3/8" **45.00**

Royal Arcanum motif, insert type, by August Goertz Co., nickel-plated brass, 2-3/4" x 1-1/2" **85.00**

Saddle and polo mallet motif, quasi-figural, silver plate, 2-1/2" x 1-1/2" **165.00**

Samurai warrior, stamped "Kirin," Japanese, brass, 1-7/8" x 1-1/8". **395.00**

Scallop shell, figural, brass, 1-7/8" x 2-1/8" **95.00**

Scarab, figural, plated brass, 2-1/2" x 1-1/8" **375.00**

Schlitz Beer, double lid, stamp combo, by August Goertz Co., plated brass, 2-3/4" x 1-1/2" **85.00**

Scientific American newspaper, figural, by Enos Richardson & Co., sterling, enameled stamp, 2-3/8" x 1-1/8" **550.00**

Shoe, figural, hob-nailed type, 800 silver, 1-3/8" x 2-1/8" **300.00**

Skin-like motif, by Pairpoint, silver plated, 2-1/2" x 1-1/2" **85.00**

Skull, sunken eyes, figural, brass, hinged jaw, 1-3/4" x 1-1/2" **135.00**

Smoking motif, four faces, by R. Blackinton & Co., catalog #647, sterling, 2-5/8" x 1-3/4" **325.00**

Stein shaped, figural, embossed designs on sides, brass, 1-5/8" x 1" **125.00**

Syrene motif, by Unger Bros., concave back, sterling, 2-3/4" x 1-3/4" . . . **275.00**

Teddy bears dancing/advertising, insert type, by August Goertz Co., nickel-plated brass, 2-3/4" x 1-1/2" **225.00**

Tiger lady, by Gorham Mfg. Co., #B3612, sterling, 2-3/4" x 1-1/2" . **600.00**

Touring car, figural, brass, marked Made in Germany, 2" x 2-1/2" . . . **795.00**

United Mine Workers souvenir, Indianapolis, Jan. 21, 1903, by Whitehead & Hoag, brass, celluloid wrapped, 2-7/8" x 1-1/2" **150.00**

Unity, patented cigar cutter, by Horton Allday, sterling, 2" x 1-3/8" **165.00**

Turtle, crawling, tortoiseshell top, nickel-plated brass body, 2-3/8" l, $225.

Velocity oil/winged car, by August Goertz Co., insert type, nickel plated brass & metal, 2-3/4" x 1-1/2" . . **195.00**
Venus Rising, G. silver, 2-5/8" x 1-5/8" **70.00**
Washington/HMMBA by Gorham Mfg. Co., #MDS, sterling, 2-1/2" x 1-5/8" **225.00**
Work shoe, figural, nickel plated brass, 1-3/8" x 2-1/2" **135.00**

MCCOY POTTERY

History: The J. W. McCoy Pottery Co. was established in Roseville, Ohio, in September
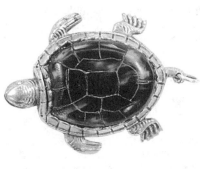
1899. The early McCoy company produced both stoneware and some art pottery lines, including Rosewood. In October 1911, three potteries merged, creating the Brush-McCoy Pottery Co. This firm continued to produce the original McCoy lines and added several new art lines. Much of the early pottery is not marked.

In 1910, Nelson McCoy and his father, J. W. McCoy, founded the Nelson McCoy Sanitary Stoneware Co. In 1925, the McCoy family sold their interest in the Brush-McCoy Pottery Co. and started to expand and improve the Nelson McCoy Co. The new company produced stoneware, earthenware specialties, and artware.

Marks: Most of the pottery marked "McCoy" was made by the Nelson McCoy Co.

References: Susan and Al Bagdade, *Warman's American Pottery and Porcelain*, 2nd ed., Krause Publications, 2000; Bob Hanson, Craig Nissen, and Margaret Hanson, *McCoy Pottery, Collector's Reference*, Collector Books, Vol. I, 1996, Vol. II, 1999; Sharon and Bob Huxford, *Collector's Encyclopedia of Brush-McCoy Pottery*, Collector Books, 1996; ——, *Collectors Encyclopedia of McCoy Pottery*, Collector Books, Vol. I, 1980, 1999 value update; Martha and Steve Sanford, *Sanfords' Guide to Brush-McCoy Pottery*, Book 2, Adelmore Press (230 Harrison Ave.,

Campbell, CA 95008), 1996; ——, *Sanfords' Guide to McCoy Pottery*, Adelmore Press, 1997; Jeffrey B. Snyder, *McCoy Pottery*, 2nd ed., Schiffer Publishing, 2001.

Periodicals: *NMXpress*, 8934 Brecksville Road, Suite 406, Brecksville, OH 44141-2318, http://www.members.aol.com/nmxpress./nmxpress.html.

Reproduction Alert: Unfortunately, Nelson McCoy never registered his McCoy trademark, a fact discovered by Roger Jensen of Tennessee. As a result, Jensen began using the McCoy mark on a series of ceramic reproductions made in the early 1990s. While the marks on these recently made pieces copy the original, Jensen made objects which were never produced by the Nelson McCoy Co. The best known example is the Red Riding Hood cookie jar, originally designed by Hull, and also made by Regal China.

The McCoy fakes are a perfect example of how a mark on a piece can be deceptive. A mark alone is not proof that a piece is period or old. Knowing the proper marks and what was made in respect to forms, shapes, and decorative motifs is critical in authenticating a pattern.

Additional Listings: See *Warman's Americana & Collectibles* for more examples.

Bean pot, cov, Suburbia Ware, brown, blue lid **48.00**
Coffee set, tall coffeepot, creamer, cov sugar, floral dec, green ground, gold trim, marked "24k gold" **125.00**

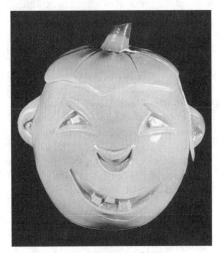

Cookie jar, Pumpkin Face, $375. Photo courtesy of House in the Woods Auction Gallery.

Cookie jar, cov
   Aunt Jemima **275.00**
   Basket of Fruit **65.00**
   Bean Pot **55.00**

Bobby Baker **55.00**
Boy on Baseball, 1978 . . . . . **310.00**
Bugs Bunny, cylinder, 1971-72
. . . . **185.00**
Burlap Sack **65.00**
Cauliflower Mammy **900.00**
Chairman of the Board, 10-1/2" h
. . . . **795.00**
Chef, "Cookies" on hat band . **75.00**
Chipmunk, c1960 . . . . **115.00**
Clown, bust, c1943 . . . . **95.00**
Clown in Barrel, marked "McCoy
USA," c1953-56, overall crazing
. . . . **145.00**
Coffee Grinder **65.00**
Covered Wagon, 1959 . . . . . **115.00**
Davy Crocket, 10" h, c1956 . **325.00**
Eagle Basket **45.00**
Elephant, seated, trunk towards
shoulder, c1943, wear to paint
. . . . **175.00**
Engine, black **175.00**
Friendship 7 . . . . **75.00**
Indian Head, 11" h, hairline in lid
. . . . **460.00**
Jack-O-Lantern, orange and green
. . . . **600.00**
Kangaroo with Joey, 12" h . . **525.00**
Kittens, basketweave base, 10-1/2" h
. . . . **1,285.00**
Little Red Riding Hood, 10-1/2" h
. . . . **650.00**
Panda, upside down, Avon label in
heart logo on paw **150.00**
Rooster, shades of brown, light tan
head, green highlights **225.00**
Squirrel **225.00**
Touring Car, 6-1/2" h, marked
"McCoy USA," c1962-64 . . **155.00**
W. C. Fields, marked "153 USA"
. . . . **200.00**
Creamer and sugar, Sunburst . **120.00**
Decanter set, Jupiter 60 Train, Central
Pacific locomotive, c1969 . . . . . **350.00**
Flower pot, saucer, hobnail and leaf
. . . . **40.00**
Frog, 8" l, naturalistically colored
. . . . **165.00**
Hanging basket, Pine Cone Rustic
. . . . **45.00**
Jardiniere pedestal, 16-1/4" h, Onyx
glaze, sgd "Cusick," c1909 . . . . **400.00**
Lamp base
14" h, cowboy boots, c1956
. . . . **150.00**
16-3/4" h figural whaling man, 32" h
overall, c1950 . . . . **400.00**
Mug
Corn **90.00**
Old Sleepy Eye, 4-1/2" d, 4-1/2" h
. . . . **260.00**

Pitcher, Hobnail, pastel blue, 48 oz
. . . . **120.00**
Planter
8" h, three large pink
chrysanthemums, marked
"McCoy" **155.00**
8-1/2" l, Driftwood, c1957 . . . . **40.00**
12" l, Hunting Dog, No Fishing on
sign **275.00**
Spoon rest, 8" l, yellow, foliage, 1940s,
overall crazing **145.00**
Strawberry jar, 12" h, stoneware
. . . . **150.00**
Tankard pitcher, 8-1/2" h, Buccaneer,
green **135.00**
Tea set, cov teapot, open creamer
and sugar
Daisy, c1940, hairline in sugar
. . . . **285.00**
Pinecone, c1946 . . . . **350.00**
Umbrella stand, 11" d, 22" h, maroon,
rose, and yellow glaze, c1915 . . **795.00**
Valet, eagle **75.00**

*Vase, white ground, pink flowers,
green leaves, brown twigs, 6-1/4" h,
$45.*

Vase
5" h, pillow, orange and yellow floral
dec, orange to brown ground, imp
"#400" **120.00**
6-1/2" h, Blossom Time **48.00**
7-1/4" h, cornucopia, green . . **125.00**
9-1/2" h, swan, white, gold trim
. . . . **350.00**
14-1/2" h, white ground, blue floral
dec, marked "McCoy, USA"
. . . . **235.00**
Wall pocket
Bellows **40.00**
Cuckoo Clock, brown, green, white,
yellow bird **225.00**
Fan, blue **45.00**

Post Box, green **50.00**
Sunflower, blue **40.00**
Woman in bonnet, bow, white, red
trim **50.00**
Window box, Pine Cone Rustic . **40.00**

McKee Glass

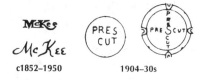

c1852–1950   1904–30s

History: The McKee Glass Co. was established in
1843 in Pittsburgh, Pennsylvania. In 1852, it opened a
factory to produce pattern glass. In 1888, the factory
was relocated to Jeannette, Pennsylvania, and began
to produce many types of glass kitchenwares,
including several patterns of Depression glass. The
factory continued until 1951, when it was sold to the
Thatcher Manufacturing Co.

McKee named its colors Chalaine Blue, Custard,
Seville Yellow, and Skokie Green. McKee glass may
also be found with painted patterns, e.g., dots and
ships. A few items were decaled. Many of the canisters
and shakers were lettered in black to show the purpose
for which they were intended.

References: Tom and Neila Bredehoft, *Fifty Years of
Collectible Glass, 1920-1970*, Volume 1, Volume II,
Antique Trader Books, 2000; Gene Florence, *Kitchen
Glassware of the Depression Years*, 7th ed., Collector
Books, 1995, values updated 1999; ——, *Very Rare
Glassware of the Depression Years*, 5th Series,
Collector Books, 1997.

Additional Listings: See *Warman's Americana &
Collectibles* for more examples.

*Children's dishes, custard, red trim,
10-piece set,* **$90.**

Batter bowl, 6-1/2" d, Skokie Green,
c1940 . . . . **45.00**
Berry set, Hobnail with Fan pattern,
blue, master berry and eight sauce
dishes **170.00**
Butter dish, cov, Wiltec pattern,
Pre-Cut Ware, frosted **70.00**

Candleholder, 6-3/4" w, 5-1/2" h, Rock Crystal, clear, double light **65.00**
Candy dish, cov, Rock Crystal, red, 4-1/2" w, 10-1/2" h **400.00**
Canister, cov, 5-1/2" h, white **85.00**
Cheese and cracker set, Rock Crystal, red **170.00**
Creamer, Aztec, purple carnival **125.00**
Egg beater bowl, spout, Skokie Green **32.00**
Egg cup, Custard **8.00**
Grill plate, custard, marked "McK" **25.00**
Hat, 4-1/4" h, straw hat type, light blue, c1940 . . . . **25.00**
Kitchen bowl, 7" d, spout, Skokie Green **75.00**
Measuring cup, 4-1/2" d, two cup, Skokie Green, sgd "McK" **80.00**
Mixing bowl, 11" d, 4-7/8" h, Chaline Blue **150.00**
Pitcher, 8" h, Wild Rose and Bowknot, frosted, gilt dec. **65.00**
Reamer, pointed top, Skokie Green **45.00**
Refrigerator dish, cov, Skokie Green, 4" x 5" **12.00**
Ring box, cov, Seville Yellow **20.00**
Salt shaker, 2-3/8" sq, 5" h, Skokie Green, orig label and top, inside rim chip **75.00**
Server, center handle, Rock Crystal, red **140.00**
Sugar bowl, Aztec, purple carnival **125.00**
Sugar shaker, 2-3/8" sq, 5" h, Skokie Green, orig label and top **115.00**

Bottoms Up Tumbler, opalescent, Pat. No. 77726, 3-1/4" h, **$325.**

Tom and Jerry punch bowl set, 11-1/2" d, 5" h punch bowl, eight 3-1/2" h mugs, white, black lettering and trim, three mugs with chips **125.00**
Tray, 13-1/2" l, 6-1/2" w, 2-1/2" h, Rock Crystal, red, rolled rim **150.00**
Tumbler, Bottoms Up, Skokie Green, 3-1/8" h, 2-3/4" d **100.00**
Water cooler, 21" h, spigot, vaseline, two pcs **325.00**
Wine, Rainbow pattern **40.00**

MEDICAL AND PHARMACEUTICAL ITEMS

History: Modern medicine and medical instruments are well documented. Some instruments are virtually unchanged since their invention; others have changed drastically.

The concept of sterilization phased out decorative handles. Handles on early instruments, which were often carved, were made of materials such as mother-of-pearl, ebony, and ivory. Today's sleek instruments are not as desirable to collectors.

Pharmaceutical items include those things commonly found in a drugstore and used to store or prepare medications.

References: A. Walker Bingham, *Snake-Oil Syndrome: Patent Medicine Advertising*, Christopher Publishing House, 1994; Patricia McDaniel, *Drugstore Collectibles*, Wallace-Homestead, 1994; J. William Rosenthal, *Spectacles and Other Vision Aids*, Norman Publishing (720 Market St., 3rd Fl., San Francisco, CA 94102), 1996; Keith Wilbur, *Antique Medical Instruments*: Revised 4th ed., Schiffer Publishing, 2000.

Periodical and Internet Resources:
Electrotherapy Museum, http://www.lvstrings.com/quack.html; http://www.medicalantiques.com; *Scientific, Medical & Mechanical Antiques*, P.O. Box 412 Taneytown, MD 21787-0412, http://americanartifacts.com/smma; U.S. National Library of Medicine, http://www.nlm.nih.gov.

Collectors' Clubs: Maryland Microscopical Society, 8621 Polk St., McLean, VA 22102; Medical Collectors Assoc., 1695-A Eastchester Road, #1695A, Bronx, NY 10461.

Museums: American Institute of the History of Pharmacy, University of Wisconsin, Madison, WI; Bakken Library & Museum, Minneapolis, MN; Country Doctor Museum, Bailey, NC; Dittrick Museum of Medical History, Cleveland, OH; Dr. Samuel D. Harris National Museum of Dentistry, Baltimore, MD; History of Pharmacy Museum, University of Arizona, Tucson, AZ; Hook's American Drugstore Museum, Indianapolis, IN; Hugh Mercer Apothecary Shop, Fredericksburg, VA; International Museum of Surgical Science & Hall of Fame, Chicago, IL; Lindan Historical Collection of Electrotherapeutic & Controversial Medical Devices, Cleveland, OH; McDowell House &

Apothecary Shop, Danville, KY; Museum of Questionable Medical Devices, Minneapolis, MN; Mutter Museum, College of Physicians of Philadelphia, Philadelphia, PA; National Museum of Health & Medicine, Walter Reed Medical Center, Washington, DC; National Museum of History and Technology, Smithsonian Institution, Washington, DC; Schmidt Apothecary Shop, New England Fire & History Museum, Brewster, MA; U.S. Army Medical Dept. Museum, Ft. Sam Houston, TX; Wellcome Library for the History & Understanding of Medicine, London, UK.

Microscope, J. Simons, London, 1780, brass, **$2,875.** *Photo courtesy of Auction Team Breker.*

Advertising

Match holder, wall type, Dr. Shoop's Health Coffee, tin litho, 3-1/2" w, 5" l, C-8+ **275.00**
Pocket mirror, Daniels Animal Medicines, multicolored celluloid, pretty lady in blue dress petting black dog, arm resting on brown horse, black text "For Dr. A. C. Daniels, Horse, Cattle, and Dog Medicine/Home Treatment for Dumb Animals," black text "Compliments of Mahlon Gary" **125.00**
Pot scraper, Ward's Remedies, Extracts, Toilet Articles, Ground Spices, 3-3/8" w, 2-7/8" h, tin litho diecut, red, gold, and white lettering **210.00**

Sign, C. F. Hussey Optometrist, zinc, double sided, polychrome and gilt dec, figural eyeglasses, name, and title in banner at base, late 19th C, 41" l, 12-1/2" h, imperfections **2,550.00**

Sign, Dr. Trovillion, Skin Diseases and Skin Cancer, gold letters, black galvanized metal ground, double sided, 14" w, 18" h, worn dec **85.00**

Sign, Glovers Dog Remedies, litho tin, bull dog, green ground, c1900, 13" d **1,210.00**

Tin, Dr. White's Cough Drops, tin litho, white ground, red lettering, 3-1/2" l, 2-1/4" w, 5/8" h, C-8+ **550.00**

Tin, SilverTex Deluxe, Killian Mfg. Co., 2-1/8" l, 1-5/8" w, 1/4" h, white ground, black lettering, red center stripe **130.00**

Advertisement/broadside

13" x 15", Dr. L. Roberts, New England, mid-19th C, proclaiming his ability to "insert teeth, cure toothaches," framed...... **230.00**

31" x 25", adv O. Howe's use of laughing gas, mounted on board, some loss to paper....... **215.00**

Apothecary cabinet/chest

13-1/4" w, 8" d, 10" h, mahogany, hinged lid opening to velvet lined interior, fitted with 17 colorless glass bottles, ceramic board, int. of lid with folio compartment, lower drawer fitted with compartments enclosing glass mortar and pestle, measure, two sterling spoons, and pan scale with weights, English, mid-19th C **700.00**

40" w, 16" d, 96" h, 46 drawers, each with brass label pulls, painted oak, some bottles and packages **1,610.00**

Bifocal spectacles, by McAllister, Philadelphia, silver frame, horseshoe-shaped lenses, sliding temples **375.00**

Book

Allergy in Adults, Med Clinics of N. America, 1974 .... **7.50**

Anatomy & Physiology, C. Gray, and D. Dimber, 1931, 8th ed., 629 pgs **25.00**

Diseases of the Blood, Roy R. Kracke, 1941, 2nd ed., 54 color plates, 46 illus, 692 pgs **25.00**

Harris' Principles and Practice of Dentistry, Ferdinand Gorges, D.D.S., Philadelphia, 1892,

10th ed., 1,222 pgs, ads and numerous illus **50.00**

Infectious Lung Diseases, Med Clinics of N. America, September 1978 .... **7.50**

Kennedy Case, The, Rita Dallas, 1973, Joseph Kennedy's nurse, Putnam, 344 pgs.......... **7.50**

Stedman's Medical Dictionary, Stedman, 1949, 17th rev edition, black leather cover **25.00**

Synopsis of Clinical Lab Methods, W. A. Bray, 1946, 93 illus, 20 color plates................... **20.00**

Textbook of Materia Medica, A. S. Blum, A. S. Garten, 1931, 5th printing, 623 pgs........... **15.00**

Davis-pattern coil, 9" w, twin contacts, rosewood base............. **260.00**

Dental cabinet

50" x 36", American Cabinet Co., Two Rivers, WI, two long over seven short drawers, two cupboards flanked by pillars, over two drawers, two doors **690.00**

55-3/4" h, 34" w, 12-1/8" h, mahogany, flat top surmounted at rear with long drop-front cabinet raised on stepped base, streamlined main cabinet fitted with tree banks of five stacked short drawers over two banks of two stacked short drawers, over three banks of assorted short drawers above central kneehole franked by two deep short drawers, molded colorless glass drawer pulls, some drawers with porcelain and white glass receptacles and liners, four sq tapering legs, old medium finish, America, early 20th C **1,035.00**

Dentist's chair, portable, 60" h extended, oak, adjustable height, back, and head rest, seat leather replaced, late 19th C **1,150.00**

Electro-medical induction coil, 10" h, T. Hall, Boston, silvered coil and switches, mahogany base, pair of later handles................. **1,150.00**

Electro-medical machine, 8-3/4" w, "Philadelphia," cell, coil, sponges, handles, and foot plate, mahogany case, instructions on lid **85.00**

Field surgeon's set, 10-1/2" w, Lentz & Sons, Philadelphia, all metal instruments, including Rust's pattern bone saw, Liston knife, trephine, bone forceps, etc., metal case with canvas cover case, both marked "2nd Reg. N.G.P." **350.00**

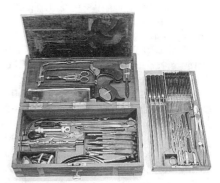

Surgeon's tools, orig wooden case, tracheotome, trocar and aspirator in original case, $1,800. Photo courtesy of Joy Luke Auctions.

Forceps tooth key, 7-1/2" l, removable bolster/claw, hatched handles, W & H Hutchinson, Sheffield, England, mid-19th C, restorations **690.00**

Hour glass, 9-1/2" h, Tartanware, McDuff pattern, half hour **175.00**

Jar, orig stopper, 10-1/2" h, Duff's Colic & Diarrhea Remedy, cylindrical glass, recessed reverse painted on glass label, ground stopper matches pattern at base, some minor staining .. **250.00**

Medicine chest, 13" w, 7-1/4" d, 11-3/4" h, mahogany and poplar, scrolled sides flank graduated shelves with round perforations above two small drawers, bottom of one inscribed "Grandmother Beal's Medicine Chest," New England, first half 19th C, old surface, minor staining and losses **460.00**

Optician's trial set, 21" w, Brown, Philadelphia, retailer's label, oak case, partial set.................. **175.00**

Optometrist's sample case, 20" w, mahogany, containing three trays of 20 spectacles each, chart in lid... **690.00**

Periodontal set, 16" l, 140 (out of 150) various scalers, fitted cream-colored painted wood case **60.00**

Phrenological bust, 9-1/2" h, plaster, Fowler, Wells & Co., Boston, labeled cranium, label on back, damaged **80.00**

Pill machine, 7-1/2" w, 15" l base, grooved wood top and base, brass construction, c1870.......... **225.00**

Plugger, 8" l, Goodman & Shurtler's Patent, mechanical gold foil, sprung, hinged mallet on ebonite body, interchangeable head........ **460.00**

Scarificator, brass, 16 blades, sgd "Kolb," European, early 19th C . **215.00**

*Surgical set, Baker, 244 Holborn, London, c1850, **$13,940.** Photo courtesy of Auction Team Breker.*

Spittoon, brass, Rochester Stamping Co. **90.00**

Tooth extractor, 6-3/4" l, W. R. Goulding, New York, marked "Baker & Riley patented 1845," removable claw/bolster, cross-hatched handles **1,380.00**

Tooth key

5" l, turned horn handle, cranked shaft, adjustable claw **150.00**
5-1/4" l, horn handle, turned shaft **175.00**
5-1/2" l, turned wood handle, straight shaft, kidney-shaped bolster, removable claw **150.00**
5-3/4" l, turned hardwood handle, cranked shaft, removable claw **90.00**
5-3/4" l, wrought-iron handle, cranked and curved octagonal shaft, circular bolster, 10 interchangeable claws, possibly French, 19th C. **635.00**
6" l, turned hardwood handle, cranked nickel shaft, removable claw **150.00**
6-1/2" l, turned and hatched removable rosewood handle, turned cranked shaft, adjustable circular bolster and claw, early 19th C **215.00**
7-1/2" l, turned ivory handle, turned shaft, adjustable claw **460.00**

Tooth key, combination, 5-1/2" h, adjustable claw, turned shaft and wood handle containing an elevator, English, late 18th/early 19th C **1,035.00**

Trepan, 10-1/4" l, burnished steel, sgd "Sir Henry a Paris," 18th C, arrowhead perforator, ivory pivot, ebony handle, five elevators **1,725.00**

Veterinary cabinet, 20" w, 10-1/4" d, 27-3/4" h, Humphrey's Remedies, tin front lists remedies, seven different

unopened orig remedies in cabinet, some damage **400.00**

MEDICINE BOTTLES

History: The local apothecary and his book of formulas played a major role in early America. In 1796, the first patent for a medicine was issued by the U.S. Patent Office. At that time, anyone could apply for a medicinal patent and as long as the dosage was not poisonous, the patent was granted.

Patent medicines were advertised in newspapers and magazines and sold through the general store and at "medicine" shows. In 1907, the Pure Food and Drug Act, requiring an accurate description of contents on a medicine container's label, put an end to the patent medicine industry. Not all medicines were patented.

Most medicines were sold in distinctive bottles, often with the name of the medicine and location of manufacture in relief. Many early bottles were made in the glass-manufacturing area of southern New Jersey. Later, companies in western Pennsylvania and Ohio manufactured bottles.

References: Joseph K. Baldwin, *Collector's Guide to Patent and Proprietary Medicine Bottles of the Nineteenth Century*, Thomas Nelson, 1973; Ralph and Terry Kovel, *Kovels' Bottles Price List*, 11th ed., Three Rivers Press, 1998; John Odell, *Digger Odell's Official Antique Bottle and Glass Collector Magazine Price Guide Series*, Vol. 5, published by author (1910 Shawhan Road, Morrow, OH 45152), 1995.

Periodical: *Antique Bottle and Glass Collector*, P.O. Box 187, East Greenville, PA 18041.

Collectors' Club: Federation of Historical Bottle Collectors, Inc., 88 Sweetbriar Branch, Longwood, FL 32750.

American Expectorant, America, 1840-60, octagonal, greenish aquamarine, outward rolled mouth, pontil scar, 5-7/8" h **425.00**

Arthurs Renovating Syrup, A. A., American, 1845-60, sq, narrow beveled corners, medium blue green, applied sloping collared mouth, iron pontil mark, 9" h **950.00**

Booth & Sedgwick's London Cordial Gin, American, 1845-60, sq, beveled corners, deep blue green, applied sloping collared mouth with ring, iron pontil mark, 9-3/4" h **375.00**

Brants Indian Balsam, America, 1840-60, octagonal, aquamarine, applied sloping collared mouth, pontil scar, 6-3/4" h **150.00**

C. Hemistreet & Co.

Troy, N.Y., America, 1840-60, octagonal, medium to deep sapphire blue, applied double collared mouth, pontil scar, 6-3/4" h, minor ext. haze. . . **180.00**
Troy, NY, tall octagonal shape, applied double collar mouth, open

J. R. Burdsell's Arnica Liniment, New York, aqua, open pontil, 5-3/8" h, **$35.**

pontil, c1845-55, medium sapphire blue, 7-1/8" h **335.00**

Davis & Miller Druggist, Baltimore, attributed to Baltimore Glass Works, Baltimore, MD, 1845-60, cylindrical, brilliant sapphire blue, applied sq collared mouth, iron pontil, mark, 3" d, 7-1/2" h **1,800.00**

Dr. Chas T. Price-67 William St., New York, Cure for Fits, oval, tooled mouth, smooth base, c1880-95, clear, 8-1/2" h **330.00**

Dr. Foster's Anti-Catarrh, eight-sided, tooled mouth, smooth base, c1890-1900, deep teal green, 3-3/4" l **150.00**

Dr. Ham's Aromatic Invigorating Spirit, cylindrical, applied mouth, smooth base, c1875-85, orange-amber, 8-1/2" h **65.00**

Dysentery Syrup, Graefenberg & Co., New York, rect, beveled corners, paneled sides, applied sloping collared mouth, open pontil, c1845-55, aqua, 6" h **80.00**

Duffy's Tower Mint Cure, Est. (castle mark) 184 Trade Mark, tall tapering building shape, applied mouth, smooth base, c1875-85, yellow-amber, 9" h **1,200.00**

E. A. Buckhout's Dutch Liniment, Prepared At Mechanicsville, Saratoga Co. NY, rect, beveled corners, figure of standing Dutch man, tooled mouth, pontil scar, 4-5/8" h **400.00**

From the Laboratory of G. W. Merchant, Chemist, Lockport, N. Y., attributed to Lockport Glass Works, Lockport, NY, 1840-60, rect, chamfered corners, deep yellowish green, applied sloping collard mouth, tubular pontil scar, 5-1/2" h **500.00**

Gargling Oil, Lockport, NY, rect, ABM lip, smooth base, orig paper label, c1910-15, cobalt blue, 5-1/8" h . **150.00**

Gleet Seven-Days Gonorrhea, rect, tooled mouth, "M. B.W. Millville" on smooth base, c1890-1910, deep cobalt blue, 5" h, some stains **800.00**

Gogings Wild Cherry Tonic, sq, beveled corners, tooled mouth, smooth base, c1890-1900, medium amber, 8-3/4" h **90.00**

Houcks Vegetable Pancea, Goodlestville, Tenn, rect, beveled corners, applied double-collar mouth, smooth base, c1855-60, deep blue-aqua, 7-1/8" h **700.00**

Iceland Balsam for Pulmonary Consumption, Iceland Balsam, America, 1830-50, rect, beveled corners, emb on three sides, yellow olive, short applied sloping collared mouth, pontil scar, 6-1/2" h, professionally cleaned, light emb lettering **5,500.00**

I. Newport's Panacea Purifier of the Blood, Nerwich, VT, attributed to Stoddard Glasshouse, Stoddard, NH, 1846-60, cylindrical, indented emb panels, yellow olive, applied sloping collared mouth with ring, iron pontil ring, 7-3/8 h, small chip on sloping collar **1,900.00**

J. L. Leavitt, Boston, attributed to Stoddard Glasshouse, Stoddard, NH, 1846-60, cylindrical, yellow olive, applied sloping collard mouth with ring, iron pontil mark, 8-1/8" h **275.00**

L. P. Dodge Rheumatic Liniment Newburg, America, 1840-60, rect, beveled corners, light golden amber, applied sloping collared mouth, pontil scar, 6" h, appears to have been cleaned **750.00**

Mother Putnam's Blackberry Cordial, Rheinstrom Bros. Proprietors, rect, paneled sides, applied mouth, tall ringed neck, smooth base, c1880-90, medium amber, 10-7/8" h **250.00**

NY Medical University, rect, tooled mouth, smooth base, orig paper label "Compound Fluid Extract of Cancer

Plant," c1885-95, deep cobalt blue, 7-3/8" h **800.00**

Orcuff's Sure Rheumatic Cure, rect, paneled sides, tooled lip, smooth base, c1885-95, deep cobalt blue, 6-1/2" h **635.00**

Pearl's White Glycerine, rect, sunken panel, tooled mouth, smooth base, c1890-90, deep cobalt blue, 6-3/8" h **145.00**

Sanford's Extract of Hamamelis (Witch Hazel), rect, tooled mouth, smooth base, orig paper label "Sanford's Radical Cure for Catarrh," c1870-80, deep cobalt blue, 7-5/8" h **175.00**

Shaker Family Pills, Dose 2 to 4, A. J. White, rect, paneled sides, sheared lip, smooth base, c1890-1900, medium amber, 2-1/4" h **95.00**

Sparks Perfect Health (trademark bust of man) For Kidney & Liver Diseases, Camden NJ, rect, beveled corners, tooled mouth, smooth base, c1880-95, medium amber, 9-1/2" h **275.00**

Swaim's Panacea, Philada, paneled cylinder, applied sloping double collar, open pontil, c1840-50, medium yellow-olive, 7-3/4" h **860.00**

Swift's Syphilitic Specific, flask form, applied mouth, smooth base, c1870-90, deep cobalt blue, 9-1/8" h, some roughness on orig strap edge . . **635.00**

Thorn's Hop & Burdock Tonic, yellow, 6-3/8" h **40.00**

Turner's Balsam, eight sided, aqua, 4-7/8" h **65.00**

Vaughn's Vegetable Lithontriptic Mixture, aqua, 8" h **125.00**

MERCURY GLASS

History: Mercury glass is a light-bodied, double-walled glass that was "silvered" by applying a solution of silver nitrate to the inside of the object through a hole in its base.

F. Hale Thomas of London patented the method in 1849. In 1855, the New England Glass Co. filed a patent for the same type of process. Other American glassmakers soon followed. The glass reached the height of its popularity in the early 20th century.

Bowl, 8" d, small plug in bottom, some wear **120.00**

Cake stand, 8" d, pedestal base, emb floral dec **80.00**

Candlestick, 10-1/2" h **110.00**

Cologne bottle, 4-1/4" x 7-1/2", bulbous, flashed amber panel, cut neck, etched grapes and leaves, corked metal stopper, c1840 . . . **160.00**

Salt, individual, silver, three applied clear glass feet, 1-3/4" d, 1-1/4" h, **$35.**

Creamer, 6-1/2" h, etched ferns, applied clear handle, attributed to Sandwich **140.00**

Curtain tiebacks, 3-1/8" d, 4-1/2" l, etched grape design, price for pr **140.00**

Door knob set, 2-1/4" d **80.00**

Goblet, 5" d, gold, white lily of the valley dec **40.00**

Pitcher, 5-1/2" x 9-3/4" h, bulbous, panel cut neck, engraved lacy florals and leaves, applied clear handle, c1840 . . . . **225.00**

Salt, 3" x 3", price for pr **100.00**

Sugar bowl, cov, 4-1/4" x 6-1/4", low foot, enameled white foliage dec, knob finial **65.00**

Vases, floral decoration, 10" h, pair, **$440.** *Photo courtesy of Jackson's Auctioneers & Appraisers.*

Vase, 9-3/4" h, cylindrical, raised circular foot, everted rim, bright enameled yellow, orange, and blue floral sprays and insects, pr **225.00**

METTLACH

History: In 1809, Jean Francis Boch established a pottery at Mettlach in Germany's Moselle Valley. His father had started a pottery at Septfontaines in 1767. Nicholas Villeroy began his pottery career at Wallerfanger in 1789.

In 1841, these three factories merged. They pioneered underglaze printing on earthenware, using transfers from copper plates, and also were among the first companies to use coal-fired kilns. Other factories were developed at Dresden, Wadgassen, and Danischburg. Mettlach decorations include relief and etched designs, prints under the glaze, and cameos.

Marks: The castle and Mercury emblems are the two chief marks, although secondary marks are known. The base of each piece also displays a shape mark and usually a decorator's mark.

References: Susan and Al Bagdade, *Warman's English & Continental Pottery & Porcelain*, 3rd ed., Krause Publications, 1998; Gary Kirsner, *Mettlach Book*, 3rd ed., Glentiques (P.O. Box 8807, Coral Springs, FL 33075), 1994.

Periodical: *Beer Stein Journal*, P.O. Box 8807, Coral Springs, FL 33075.

Collectors' Clubs: Stein Collectors International, 281 Shore Dr., Burr Ridge, IL 60521; Sun Steiners, P.O. Box 11782, Fort Lauderdale, FL 33339.

Additional Listings: Villeroy & Boch.

Note: Prices in this listing are for print-under-glaze pieces, unless otherwise specified.

Coaster, 4-7/8" d, PUG, drinking scene, marked "Mettlach, Villeroy & Boch" **150.00**
Jardiniere, 5-1/2" h, 8-3/4" x 10", green ground, off-white cameo figures of Grecian men and women riding in carriage, sitting at table and drinking, base imp "#7000" and "#17" . . . **425.00**
Lazy Susan, #1570, PUG, four compartments, handle in center, bird design, 1" side hairline, 11" d . . . **130.00**
Loving cup, 7-3/8" w, 6-3/4" h, three handles, musicians dec **185.00**
Plaque
#1044-1067, water wheel on side of building, sgd "F. Reiss," PUG, gold wear on edge, 17" d **495.00**
#1044-5171, Dutch scene, blue delft, 12" d **90.00**

#1108 enameled incised dec of castle, gilt rim, c1902, 17" d **230.00**
#1168, Cavalier, threading and glaze, sgd "Warth," chip on rear hanging rim, 16-1/2" d **465.00**
#2196, Stolzensels Castle on the Rhein, 17" d **1,100.00**
#2442, classical scene of Trojan warriors in ship, cameo, white high relief, blue-gray ground, artist sgd "J. Stahl," 18-1/4" d, some professional restoration . . **1,200.00**
#2443, classical scene of women and eight attendants, cameo, white high relief, blue-gray ground, artist sgd "J. Stahl," blue-gray ground, 18-1/4" d **1,550.00**
#7072, Phanolith, woman, 8" x 6" **415.00**

#284, 3/10 liter, two gnomes drinking, another playing lute, 1885-1930 mark, 7-3/4" h, **$275.** *Photo courtesy of Joy Luke Auctions.*

Stein
#1027, 1/2 liter, relief, beige, rust, green, inlaid lid, floral, and face **215.00**
#1526, transfer and enameled, Student Society, Amico Pectus Hosti Frontem, dated 1902, roster on either side of crest, pewter lid, slight discoloration to int. . . **465.00**
#1896, 1/4 liter, maiden on one side, cherub face on other, grape dec, pewter lift handle **350.00**
#2007, 1/2 liter, etched, black cat, inlaid lid **660.00**
#2018, 1/2 liter, character, pug dog, inlaid lid **1,100.00**

Stein, #2751, two men at wine table, inlaid lid, pewter fittings, 1907, impressed marks, 15-1/4" h, **$1,155.** *Photo courtesy of Garth's Auctions, Inc.*

#2028, 1/2 liter, etched, men in Gasthaus, inlaid lid **550.00**
#2057, 1/2 liter, etched, festive dancing scene, inlaid lid . . . **325.00**
#2093, 1/2 liter, etched and glazed, suit of cards, inlaid lid **700.00**
#2100, 1/3 liter, etched, Germans meeting Romans, inlaid lid, H. Schlitt **495.00**
#2204, 1/2 liter, etched and relief, Prussian eagle, inlaid lid . . . **780.00**
#2580, 1/2 liter, etched, Die Kannenburg, conical inlay lid, knight in castle **695.00**
#2755, 1/4 liter, cameo and etched, three scenes of people at table, Art Nouveau design between scenes, inlaid lid **560.00**
#2811, 1/2 liter, etched, Art Nouveau design, inlaid lid, slight int. discoloration **750.00**
#2922, 1/2 liter, etched, men around campfire, inlaid lid, shallow factory flake on top **400.00**
#2950, 1/2 liter, cameo, Bavarian crest, pewter lid with relief crest **825.00**
#5001, 4.6 liter, faience type, coat of arms, pewter lid **850.00**

Teapot, 3-1/2" h, #3051, etched, Art Deco repeating design, lid missing **95.00**

Vase, 6" d, 11" h, pale gray bisque, white pate sur pate flowers, cherub handles **500.00**

MILITARIA

History: Wars have occurred throughout recorded history. Until the mid-19th century, soldiers often had to provide for their own needs, including supplying their own weapons. Even in the 20th century, a soldier's uniform and some of his gear are viewed as his personal property, even though issued by a military agency.

Conquering armed forces made a habit of acquiring souvenirs from their vanquished foes. They also brought their own uniforms and accessories home as badges of triumph and service.

Saving militaria may be one of the oldest collecting traditions. Militaria collectors tend to have their own special shows and view themselves outside the normal antiques channels. However, they haunt small indoor shows and flea markets in hopes of finding additional materials.

References: Robert W. D. Ball, *Collector's Guide to British Army Campaign Medals*, Antique Trader Books, 1996; Thomas Berndt, *Standard Catalog of U.S. Military Vehicles*, Krause Publications, 1993; Ray A. Bows, *Vietnam Military Lore 1959-1973*, Bows & Sons, 1988; Nancy Britton, *A Splendid Little War: Collectibles and Commemoratives of the Spanish-American War*, Vol. I, published by author, 1998, (215 N. 8th, Batesville, AR 72501-3404); Max A. Collins, *For the Boys*, Collectors Press, 2001; W. K. Cross, *Charlton Standard Catalogue of First World War Canadian Corps Badges*, Charlton Press, 1995; ——, *Charlton Standard Catalogue of First World War Canadian Infantry Badges*, 2nd ed., Charlton Press, 1995; Robert Fisch, *Field Equipment of the Infantry 1914-1945*, Greenberg Publications, 1989; Gary Howard, *America's Finest: U.S. Airborne Uniforms, Equipment and Insignia of World War Two (ETO)*, Greenhill Books, Stackpole Books, 1994; Martin Jacobs, *World War II Homefront Collectibles*, Krause Publications, 2000; Ron Manion, *American Military Collectibles Price Guide*, Antique Trader Books, 1995; ——, *German Military Collectibles Price Guide*, Antique Trader Publications, 1995; Ron Menchine, *Propaganda Postcards of World War II*, Krause Publications, 2000; Marc Newman, *Civil War Knives*, Paladin Press, 1998.

Periodicals and Internet Resources: *Air War College Gateway to Military History*, http://www.au.af.mil/au/awc/awcgate/awc-hist.html; *American Militaria Sourcebook & Directory*, P.O. Box 245, Lyon Station, PA 19536-9986; *Antique & Collectible Firearms & Militaria Headquarters*, http://www.oldguns.net; *Antique Militaria & Collectibles Network*, http://www.collectorsnet.com; *Artilleryman*, 234 Monarch Hill Road, Tunbridge, VT 05077; *GI Journal*, http://www.militaria.com/gij.html; *Man at Arms*, P.O. Box 460, Lincoln, RI 02865; *MHQ: The Quarterly Journal of Military History*, 741 Miller Drive, SE, Suite 2, Leesburg, VA 20175; *Militaria International*, P.O. Box 43400, Minneapolis, MN 55443-0400; *Militaria Magazine*, P.O. Box 995, Southbury, CT 06488; *Military*, P.O. Box 189490, Sacramento, CA 95818; *Military Artifact*, 55 Abingdon Drive, Nepean, Ontario K2H 7M5, Canada; *Military Collectors Consortium*, http://www.lee-enfield.com; *Military Collector's Exchange*, http://www.tmcx.com; *Military Collector News*, P.O. Box 702073, Tulsa, OK 74170; *Military History*, 741 Miller Drive SE, Suite 2, Leesburg, VA 20175; *Military Trader*, P.O. Box 1050, Dubuque, IA 52004-1050; *Military Vehicles*, 700 E. State St., Iola, WI 54990; *Olive Drab*, http://www.olive-drab.com; *Regiment, Military Illustrated*, 1926 S. Pacific Coast Highway, Redondo Beach, CA 90277; *Revelance*, P.O. Box 4585, Stanford, CA 94309; *State of NY Division of Military & Naval Affairs*, http://www.dmna.state.ny.us/historic/histlink.html; *War of 1812 Consortium*, 844 E. Pratt St., Baltimore, MD 21202; *World War II*, 741 Miller Drive SE, Suite 2, Leesburg, VA 20175.

Collectors' Clubs: American Society of Military History, 1816 S. Figeroa, Los Angeles, CA 90015; American Society of Military Insignia Collectors, 526 Lafayette Ave., Palmerton, PA 18071; Assoc. of American Military Uniform Collectors, P.O. Box 1876, Elyria, OH 44036;California Inland Empire Military Vehicle Preservation Assoc., 455 N. Dahlia, Ontario, CA 91762; Civil War Collectors Society & The American Militaria Exchange, 5970 Toylor Ridge Dr., West Chester, OH 45069, http://www.civilwar-collectors.com; Company of Military Historians, North Main Street, Westbrook, CT, 06498; Imperial German Military Collectors Assoc., 82 Atlantic St., Keyport, NJ 07735; Indiana Chapter of the Military Vehicle Preservation Assoc., 2330 Crystal St., Anderson, IN 46012; Karabiner Collector's Network, P.O. Box 5773, High Point, NC 27262; Militaria Collectors Society of Florida, 140 NE. 55th St., Ft Lauderdale, FL 33334, http://www.militariacollectorssociety.com; Military Vehicle Preservation Assoc., P.O. Box 52037, Independence, MO 064052; Ontario Military Vehicle Assoc., 1248 Dartmoor St., Oshawa, Ontario L1K 2K2 Canada; Orders and Medals Society of America, P.O. Box 484, Glassboro, NJ 08028; Polish Military Collectors Assoc., 591 Humboldt St., Brooklyn, NY 11222; Red Ball Military Transport, 400 Ave. C, Stroudsburg, PA 18360; Sharkhunters International, Inc., P.O. Box 1539, Hernando, FL 33442; Society of East German Militaria Collectors, P.O. Box 2153, Reston, VA 20195-0153; The Great War Society, P.O. Box 4585, Stanford, CA 94309.

Museums: Allegheny Arms & Armor Museum, Inc., Custer City, PA; American Armored Foundation, Ronkonkoma, NY; American Society of Military History, El Monte, CA; Battlefield Military Museum, Gettysburg, PA; Donley's Wild West Town & Museum, Union, IL; Fort Ticonderoga Museum, Ticonderoga, NY; Historical Military Armor Museum, Anderson, IN; Liberty Memorial Museum of World War One, Kansas City, MO; Library of Congress, Washington, DC; Massachusetts National Guard Military Museum & Archives, Worcester, MA; Museum of Society & Industry, Chicago, IL; National Medal of Honor Museum of Military History, Chattanooga, TN; National Atomic Museum, Kirtland Air Force Base, Albuquerque, NM; Navy Historical Center, Washington, DC; National Infantry Museum of the National Infantry Assoc., Fort Benning, GA; Parris Island Museum, Beaufort, SC; Patton Museum of Cavalry & Armor, Fort Knox, KY; U.S. Air Force Museum, Dayton, OH; U.S. Army Center of Military History, Fort McNair, Washington, DC; U.S. Army Military Police Corps Regimental Museum, http://www.wood.army.mil/usamps/history/museum.html; U.S. Army Transportation Museum, Fort Eustis, VA; U.S. Army Women's Museum, Fort Lee, VA; U.S. Calvary Museum, Fort Riley, KS; U.S. Marine Corps Historical Center & Museum, Washington, DC; U.S. Military History Institute, Carlisle, PA; Virginia War Museum, Newport News, VA.

Reproduction Alert: Pay careful attention to Civil War and Nazi material.

Additional Listings: Firearms and Swords. See World War I and World War II in *Warman's Americana & Collectibles* for more examples.

Revolutionary War

Autograph

Document sgd, promotion of First Lieutenant, by Benjamin Harrison, 1783, paper seal, 6" x 8" .. **650.00**

Letter sgd, two pgs, Camp Springfield, June 1779, to Col. James Abale, orders supplies to be sent, mentions general Washington, by General Nathaneal Greene, sgd "Nath Greene Qmr," framed **1,600.00**

Pocket watch, key wound, orig key, inscribed "I Shelby 1802," watch movement by John J Wilmurt of NY, English silver case with paper label from GW Stewart, Lexington, KY watchmaker, hero Issac Shelby was first governor of KY **3,520.00**

Snuff box, cov, 2-7/8" d, gutta percha, round, relief scene of battle, ships, coastline, buildings, French inscription "Prise d'Yorck 1781 (Taking of Yorktown or Battle of Yorktown)" **750.00**

War of 1812

Broadside, Aug. 18, 1814, printed calvary orders for the 2nd Brigade 1st Visis, and 7th Reg 2nd Brig 1st Divis, Edmund Fitzgerland Lt. Col. 7th Reg & Cavalry, one sheet........... **375.00**

Cartridge Box, leather, white cloth strap, very worn, missing plate .. **70.00**

Flag, 60-1/2" x 110", 13 stars, Naval, hand sewn............... **1,100.00**

Military Drum, large eagle painted on sides, red, and blue stripes, one drum head, 22" h, 17" d **750.00**

Shoes, leather, pegged sole, brass buckle, stitching reads "H. S. Shawner, CT" **150.00**

Epaulettes, Civil War or pre-war, medical staff captain, gilded brass and thread, worn red silk and leather lining, signed "W. H. Horstman & Sons, Philadelphia," tole case with old black repaint, gold stenciled eagles and stars, worn brass tassels in center compartment, 9-3/4" l case, $1,320. Photo courtesy of Garth's Auction, Inc.

Civil War

Autograph album, GAR, 4-1/2" x 7", most pages signed at Milwaukee Reunion, Aug. 29, 1889, maroon velvet cover **110.00**

Belt and plate, black leather belt, brass loops, two-piece brass VA state plate, minor wear and splits **2,350.00**

Bond, Confederate States, Feb. 20, 1863, seven remaining coupons intact, framed, 15" x 13" **95.00**

Book

A Soldiers Recollections, Leaves from the Diary of a Young Confederate, McKimm, 1910, black leather, 362 pgs **45.00**

Battles for Chattanooga (Tennessee), The, The Shipwreck of Their Confederate Hopes, Cozzens **35.00**

Civil War Letters of Alfred Lacey Hough, 17th Pennsylvania Volunteers, Soldier in the West, 1957, University of PA Press, dj **65.00**

Confederate Navy in the Civil War, The, Soley and Ammen, 1899, two volumes **38.00**

Georgia Confederate Military Honor, Jos. T. Derry, CSA, 1898 .... **35.00**

Leslies History of the Civil War, maroon hardcover, gold detail, edge wear **95.00**

Life in the Confederate Army, Wm Watson, 1888, full black leather cover, 456 pgs **45.00**

Mississippi in the Confederacy: As Seen in Retrospect, James W. Silver, 1961, ex library copy. **25.00**

One of Stonewall Jackson's Foot Cavalry, J. Worsham, 1912, full black leather cover, 353 pgs **45.00**

Personal Recollections of a Cavalryman with Custer's Michigan Cavalry Brigade in the Civil War, J. Kidd, 1907, full black leather cover, 476 pgs, photos, maps **55.00**

Tennessee Confederate Military History, Porter, c1899 ...... **38.00**

Texas and Florida Confederate Military History, Col. O. M. Roberts, CSA and Col. J. J. Dickson, CSA, 1899, two volumes **38.00**

Canteen

7-5/8" d, bull's eye, orig woven cloth strap, pewter spout sgd "Hadden, Porter & Booth, Phila" **325.00**

8" d, worn blue cloth covering bull's eye design, orig tan cloth strap, pewter spout **550.00**

Cartridge box, cross belt and eagle plate, "Calhoune New York" maker's stamp on inner flap, tin liners, oval U.S. plate..................... **900.00**

Confederate notes, group of $500, $10, and $5, from Richmond, matted and framed, 21-1/2" x 17" **275.00**

Coat, Confederate Officer's, double breasted, blue-gray wool, low collar, blue piping along front, 12 large VA and NC buttons marked "Scovill Mfg. Waterbury," three small buttons with same markings, two have black velvet coverings, Captain's bars on collar, buttons and insignia removed for previous cleaning, minor moth damage to ext.................... **39,600.00**

Fife, 15-1/2" l, sgd "Firth, Pond & Co., Broadway, NY," large "C" below signature, brass ends, nickel silver and pewter mouth piece.......... **175.00**

Hat insignia, 2-1/2" x 3-3/4", Third Cavalry, black velvet covering bordered in gold wire, brass cross sabers, contemporary frame with riker mount back..................... **120.00**

Photograph, ambrotype

Calvary man, shell jacket, holding Colt revolver, another in his belt, sixth plate, uncased, light silver color, wear to emulsion ... **250.00**

Radio receiver, German Armed Forces, designed to top and determine enemy frequencies, 1944, $5,230. Photo courtesy of Auction Team Breker.

Two soldiers seated arm in arm, wearing kepis, one holding cocked Colt revolver, other with knife handle sticking out of his belt, bow ties and vests, sixth plate image, half case **770.00**

Virginia officer wearing coat, vest, watch fob, seated in Gothic chair, gutta-percha case with man in sailboat **225.00**

Photograph, tintype, cased

Cavalryman, wearing shell jacket with gilt detail on collar and buttons, lightly tinted blue pants, holding cavalry saber, Colt pistol in belt, forage cap with "D2," sixth plate **770.00**

Confederate, checked shirt, butternut colored coat, CDV mount **110.00**

Enlisted man, seated, elbow resting on table, wearing kepi, small flag on coat, sixth plate, half case **385.00**

Infantryman, waist-up portrait, holding Hardee hat with feather, "K," and bugle insignia, wearing epaulettes, cartridge box, holding musket with bayonet, ninth plate **550.00**

Ohio Infantrymen, two seated soldiers, legs crossed, wearing kepis, lightly tinted trousers, int. of case penciled "Co. G. 63rd Regt. O.V.I., Henry Heck our darling of the Co.-Retp.," quarter plate, case damaged at hinge **660.00**

Soldier, blue and gold tinting, holding burnside, wears burnside sling with belt, holster, cap box, hat with feather, gutta-percha case with geometric detail, ninth plate **1,100.00**

Soldiers in front of tent, very worn quarter plate tintype, gutta-percha case with relief scene of officers standing at table, scrolled border, minor edge chips **470.00**

Soldier, seated, forage cap, frock coat, vet, unusual liner with classical images, sixth plate **250.00**

Soldier wearing shell jacket, seated, slouch hat with feather, light pink tinting on cheeks, sixth plate, half case **250.00**

Two seated soldiers, cross-legged, wearing kepis and vets, one has stripe down side of pants, quarter plate, half case, minor bends **320.00**

Print, chromolithograph

Maj. General Wm. T. Sherman, Currier & Ives, gilt frame, margin stains, short tear, 20-1/4" x 16" **150.00**

Sheridan's Ride, Prang, copyright 1886, orig mount, margin stains, oak frame, 33" w, 26-1/2" h. **200.00**

Reunion cane, 36" l, relief carved openwork vining and acorns, rope with tassels, bird, crossed sabers, shaking hands, relief "G.A.R. and U.C.V." with "M. F. McDonald and J. J. D. Maker," whimsy ball top **3,960.00**

Spurs, pr, 4" h, brass, Confederate, Leech & Rigdon style **115.00**

Sword belt, officer's, rect brass eagle buckle, black leather belt, stitched designs, orig sword hangers, good patina. **660.00**

Indian War

Bayonet, Model 1873, 3-1/2" w blade **80.00**

Belt buckle, Naval officer, brass, stamped "Horstman, Phila" **120.00**

Broadside, Ohio massacre, No. 4, 1791, printed in Boston, 1792, foxed, water stained, modern frame . . **900.00**

Spanish American War

Hat badge, infantry, brass, crossed krag rifles, 2" l **55.00**

Cartridge box, U.S. Army **125.00**

Pin-back button, "Remember the *Maine*," battleship scene, patent 1896 . . . . **25.00**

Spy glass, pocket, brass, Naval, round holder, brown leather grip, 16" l . **110.00**

World War I

American flag, 6-1/4" x 10-1/4" sight, cloth, eight stars and five stripes, made by Prisoner of War, "Arlon Belgium Dec 11th, 1918" written on mat, framed, some losses, discoloration. **350.00**

Bayonet, British, MK II, No. 4, spike, scabbard **20.00**

Book, *Regimental History of the 316 Infantry* **25.00**

Buckle, U.S. Balloon Corps, emb hot air balloon. **75.00**

Compass, marked "Made in France" **45.00**

Dog tag stamping kit, orig wood box, complete. **250.00**

Flare pistol, Model 1918, French **100.00**

Gun sling, soft leather, 1917, for 03 Springfield **17.50**

Helmet, German, Pattern, 1916, painted gray/green. **80.00**

Map case, leather, strap, nine orig French tour maps **50.00**

Overcoat, U.S. Army officers, Melton, olive drab, wool, double breasted, 10 bone buttons **65.00**

Trench flashlight and note pad, German, black tin container, orig pad and pencil. **65.00**

Tunic and trousers, gabardine, pinback, Air Corps and U.S. discs **75.00**

Watch fob, Federal Seal, U.S. officer **15.00**

Japanese naval officer's cap, WW II, $275. Photo courtesy of Jackson's Auctioneers & Appraisers.

World War II

Armband, Japan, military police, red lettering, white cotton. **48.00**

Belt and buckle, German Luftwaffe, silver wash on brass, 1942. . . . . . **55.00**

Boots, U.S. Army, double buckle, brown leather, worn. **90.00**

Cane, 30-3/4" l, Civilian Conservation Corps, fully carved, U-shaped horse-head handle, one piece, carved low relief of trees, bathing beauty, alligator, name of carver's friends, "Middle Creek Camp F34 Co. 997," 1933, finish removed around later added date **125.00**

Cookbook, *Meat Reference Manual for Mess Sergeants and Cooks,* Prepared for the United States Army by the National Live Stock and Meat Board, March 1943, 36 pgs, soft cover . **18.00**

Flag, New Zealand PT boat, printed on blue cotton **55.00**

Flyers goggles, Japanese, boxed, gray fur lined cups, yellow lenses **35.00**

Gas mask, German, canister style, rubber mask, canvas straps, carrying container **80.00**

Helmet, Italian, steel, leather chip strap **100.00**

ID tag, U.S. Army, oval pattern, instruction envelope, chain **25.00**

Overcoat, German, enlisted, late war style, gray, wool, double breasted, 12 buttons **150.00**

Telescope, 14" l, Australian, MK 1, heavy leather case and carrying straps **45.00**

MILK GLASS

History: Opaque white glass attained its greatest popularity at the end of the 19th century. American glass manufacturers made opaque white tablewares as a substitute for costly European china and glass. Other opaque colors, e.g., blue and green, also were made. Production of milk-glass novelties came in with the Edwardian era.

The surge of popularity in milk glass subsided after World War I. However, milk glass continues to be made in the 20th century. Some modern products are reissues and reproductions of earlier forms. This presents a significant problem for collectors, although it is partially obviated by patent dates or company markings on the originals and by the telltale signs of age.

Collectors favor milk glass from the pre-World War I era, especially animal-covered dishes. The most prolific manufacturers of these animal covers were Atterbury, Challinor-Taylor, Flaccus, and McKee.

References: E. McCamley Belknap, *Milk Glass*, Crown Publishers, 1949, out of print; Frank Chiarienza and James Slater, *The Milk Glass Book*, Schiffer, 1998; Regis F. and Mary F. Ferson, *Today's Prices for Yesterday's Milk Glass*, published by authors, 1985; ——, *Yesterday's Milk Glass Today*, published by authors, 1981; Everett Grist, *Covered Animal Dishes*, Collector Books, 1988, 2000 value update; Lorraine Kovar, *Westmoreland Glass*, 2 vols.,

Antique Publications, 1991; S. T. Millard, *Opaque Glass*, 4th ed., Wallace Homestead, 1975, out of print; Betty and Bill Newbound, *Collector's Encyclopedia of Milk Glass*, Collector Books, 1995, 2000 value update.

Collectors' Club: National Milk Glass Collectors Society, 500 Union Cemetery Road, Greensburg, PA 15601, http://www.nmgcs.org.

Museum: Houston Antique Museum, Chattanooga, TN.

Notes: There are many so-called "McKee" animal-covered dishes. Caution must be exercised in evaluating pieces because some authentic covers were not signed. Furthermore, many factories have made, and many still are making, split-rib bases with McKee-like animal covers or with different animal covers. The prices below are for authentic McKee pieces with either the cover or base signed.

Numbers in listings prefixed with a letter refer to books listed in the references, wherein the letter identifies the first letter of the author's name.

Miniature lamp, Daisy and Button Variant pattern, original fittings and chimney, Smith #419, 7-3/8" h, $150.

Animal dish, cov

Bird, hand, blue glass stone ring, 5" x 8" x 5" 160.00

Dog, setter, white base, sgd "Flaccus," repair to lid 150.00

Fish, walking, divided horizontally, five central fins support body, detailed scales, red glass eyes (B167b) 195.00

Hen, marbleized, head turned to left, lacy base, white and deep blue, Atterbury (F8) 165.00

Plate, high relief bust portrait of McKinley and Dewey, 8-1/4" d, $95.

Bowl, 8-1/4" d, Daisy, all over leaves and flower design, open scalloped edge (F165) 85.00

Bust, 5-1/2" h, Admiral Dewey . 300.00

Butter dish, cov, 4-7/8" l, Roman Cross pattern, sq, ftd base curves outward toward top, cube-shape finial (F240) 75.00

Calling card receiver, bird, wings extended over fanned tail, head resting on leaf, detailed feather pattern (F669) 150.00

Celery vase, 6-5/8" h, Blackberry Pattern, scalloped rim, plain band above vertical surface, Hobbs Brockunier (F317) 110.00

Centerpiece bowl, 13" l, 11" w, lattice edge, Westmoreland 125.00

Compote

Atlas, lacy edge, blue 185.00

Cherry Thumbprint, Westmoreland, orig hang tag 265.00

Condiment set, 7" h, Teadrop, Fenton, four pc 150.00

Creamer and sugar, Trumpet Vine, fire painted dec, sgd "SV" 130.00

Egg cup, cov, 4-1/4" h, bird, round, fluted, Atterbury (F130) 135.00

Hat, Stars and Stripes, black rim 235.00

Lamp, 11" h, Goddess of Liberty, bust, three stepped hexagonal bases, clear and frosted font, brass screw connector, patent date, Atterbury (F329) 300.00

Milk pitcher, 8-3/4" h, Wild Iris, gilt trim, c1825 . . . . 125.00

Miniature lamp, Christmas Tree, gold trim 125.00

Mug

3" h, Ivy in Snow 40.00

3-1/4" , Medallion, c1870 . . . . 50.00

Plate, 6" d, two cats form upper edge, bracketed dog head, open work, swirling leaves, emb "He's all right" (B20d) 125.00

Spooner, 5-1/8" h, monkey, scalloped top (F275) 125.00

Syrup, 6" h, Bellflower pattern, single vine, dated, Collins & Wright (F155C0) 245.00

Tumbler, Royal Oak, orig fired paint, green band 50.00

Vanity box, cov, 7" l, 2" w, 2" h, hand painted enamel floral dec, gold trim, imp "16" on both lid and base . . 250.00

Wine, Feather pattern 40.00

MILLEFIORI

History: Millefiori (thousand flowers) is an ornamental glass composed of bundles of colored glass rods fused together into canes. The canes were pulled to the desired length while still ductile, sliced, arranged in a pattern, and fused together again. The Egyptians developed this technique in the first century B.C. It was revived in the 1880s.

Reproduction Alert: Millefiori items, such as paperweights, cruets, and toothpicks, are being made by many modern companies.

Miniature lamp, cobalt blue, orange and ochre canes, brass trim, electrified, 12" h, $625.

Beads, 16" l, multicolored millefiori beads, blue glass bead spacers. **55.00**

Bowl, 8" d, tricorn, scalloped, folded sides, amethyst and silver deposit **125.00**

Candy dish, 11-1/2" l, 9" w, light blue, various sized multicolored millefiori flowers, swirled shape, Murano, c1950 .... **85.00**

Creamer, 3" x 4-1/2", white and cobalt blue canes, yellow centers, satin finish **110.00**

Cruet, bulbous, multicolored canes, applied camphor handle, matching stopper **120.00**

Decanter, 12" h, deep black ground, all over multicolored flux and canes, including peachblow, and opal, enamel dec, Gundersen **1,450.00**

Demittase cup and saucer, red and white millefiori, angular applied pink handle, broken pontil scars, Italian **275.00**

Door knob, 2-1/2" d, paperweight, center cane dated 1852, New England Glass Co. **395.00**

Goblet, 7-1/2" h, multicolored canes, clear stem and base **150.00**

Lamp, 14-1/2" h, 8-1/2" d dome shade, glass base, electric **795.00**

Miniature vase, 3-3/4" w, 2-1/2" h, amber rigaree handles, red, white, blue, and yellow millefiori canes, Murano **150.00**

Pitcher, 6-1/2" h, multicolored canes, applied candy cane handle ... **195.00**

Slipper, 5" l, camphor ruffle and heal **125.00**

Sugar, cov, 4" x 4-1/2", white canes, yellow centers, satin finish..... **125.00**

Vase

Bulbous, cased, clear over emerald green, burnt orange int., scattered trailing millefiori dec, 8-1/4" h **375.00**

Bulbous, elongated flared crimped top, multicolored, broken pontil scar, Italian **475.00**

Flared, titled "Starry Night," small star-shaped white millefiori canes, cobalt blue ground, irid blue-gold int., sgd "Lundberg Studios" **175.00**

MINIATURE LAMPS

History: Miniature oil and kerosene lamps, often called "night lamps," are diminutive replicas of larger lamps. Simple and utilitarian in design, miniature lamps found a place in the parlor (as "courting" lamps), hallway, children's rooms, and sickrooms.

Miniature lamps are found in many glass types, from amberina to satin glass. Miniature lamps measure 2-1/2 to 12 inches in height, with the principle parts being the base, collar, burner, chimney, and shade. In 1877, both L. J. Atwood and L. H. Olmsted patented burners for miniature lamps. Their burners made the lamps into a popular household accessory.

References: Marjorie Hulsebus, *Miniature Victorian Lamps*, Schiffer Publishing, 1996; Frank R. and Ruth E. Smith, *Miniature Lamps* (1981), Book II (1982, rev 2nd ed., 2000) Schiffer Publishing; John F. Solverson, *Those Fascinating Little Lamps: Miniature Lamps and Their Values*, Antique Publications, 1988, includes prices for Smith numbers.

Collectors' Club: Night Light Miniature Lamp Club, 38619 Wakefield Ct, Northville, MI 48167-9060.

Reproduction Alert: Study a lamp carefully to make certain all parts are original; married pieces are common. Reproductions abound.

Note: The numbers given below refer to the figure numbers found in the Smith books.

China, blue Delft decoration, 6-1/8" h, **$180.**

Cobalt blue, raised egg band, Smith II-229, **$220.**

Amberina, 3-1/2" w, 9" h, pressed, deep red to yellow, several chips **175.00**

Consolidated, 10-1/4" h, milk glass, raised thumbprints **295.00**

Daisy and Button, blue, 3-3/4" w, 8-3/4" h, several small chips, electrified **190.00**

Fenton

Cranberry Coin Spot, 11" h, 4-1/2" d globe shade............ **600.00**

Cranberry Inverted Thumbprint, 7-1/2" h, orig chimney, 1950s **395.00**

Figural

Log Cabin, blue, handle... **1,200.00**

Santa Claus **2,750.00**

Shoe, amber, applied handle **1,100.00**

Libbey, cut glass, 10-3/4" h base, 2" sq base, sgd **425.00**

Milk glass

Angel dec, pink, Smith #325-I **165.00**

Apple Blossom, light pink band around top of base and shade, white mid-section with floral dec, green band at base, nutmeg burner, 7-1/4" h.......... **225.00**

Block and Dot pattern, 8-1/4" h **150.00**

Drape pattern, pink and white, Smith #231-I................... **75.00**

Embossed design, hp flowers, green shading on base, nutmeg burner, 8-3/4" h................. **225.00**

Maltese Cross, Smith #214-I **90.00**

Medallion, emb, Smith #211-I . **45.00**

Melon ribbed base with purple and green shading, marked "P & A Mfg Co.," 3-1/2" white globe shade, 10-1/2" h plus replaced clear chimney.............. **150.00**

Moon & Stars, L. G. Wright, white **295.00**

Plume pattern, pink ext., white int., gilt dec, nutmeg burner, 7-1/2" h **270.00**

Swan, Smith #327-II....... **250.00**

Opalescent, cranberry, Spanish Lace **750.00**

Pattern glass

Beaded Heart, clear, Smith #109-I **115.00**

Bull's Eye, clear, Smith, #110-1 **45.00**

Satin

Acanthus Leaf, red, 5" w, 9" h, c1890, replaced chimney .. **425.00**

MOP, Raindrop pattern, mother-of-pearl, yellow, applied frosted feet, nutmeg burner, no shade **180.00**

Unknown maker, Grecian Key, emb clear glass base, acorn burner, red cased to white shade, patent date Nov. 14, 1911 in glass around collar . **135.00**

MINIATURE PAINTINGS

History: Prior to the advent of the photograph, miniature portraits and silhouettes were the principal way of preserving a person's image. Miniaturists were plentiful, and they often made more than one copy of a drawing. The extras were distributed to family and friends.

Miniaturists worked in watercolors and oil and on surfaces such as paper, vellum, porcelain, and ivory. The miniature paintings were often inserted into jewelry or mounted inside or on the lids of snuff boxes. The artists often supplemented commission work by painting popular figures of the times and copying important works of art.

After careful study, miniature paintings have been divided into schools, and numerous artists are now being researched. Many fine examples may be found in today's antiques marketplace.

References: Daphne Foskett, *Miniatures: Dictionary and Guide,* Antique Collectors' Club, 1999; Dale T. Johnson, *American Portrait Miniatures in the Manney Collection,* The Metropolitan Museum of Art, 1990.

Museum: Colonial Williamsburg Foundation, Williamsburg, VA; Gibbes Museum of Art, Charleston, SC.

1-1/8" sight, on ivory, oval, gentleman in powdered wig, early 18th C, oval 3-3/4" giltwood frame **450.00**

Young blond woman, white dress, blue accessories, blue ground, brass frame with backing signed "Painted by Rd. Mills, Birmm, 1829," 3-3/4" w, 4-3/8" h, **$385.** *Photo courtesy of Garth's Auction, Inc.*

1-1/2" , on ivory, oval, woman in black dress, early 19th C, 3-3/4" l oval giltwood frame............. **250.00**

1-5/8" x 2", on ivory, oval, young brunette woman, white Empire-waisted gown, upswept hair, early 19th C, ebonized sq frame **200.00**

1-3/4" l, on ivory, round, gentleman with black wig, lace collar, 17th C, 4-1/4" l oval frame **300.00**

1-7/8" x 2-1/4", on ivory, Julia Clarke Brewster (1796-1826), attributed to John Brewster Jr., painted in the Columbia or Hampton, CT area, c1820, orig oval gilded copper locket case within orig red leather hinged case **4,600.00**

1-7/8" x 7-3/8", watercolor on ivory, gentleman, reverse labeled "F. M. Killam, Lois R. Killam, Father at 20 years," black lacquer frame, brass oak leaf hanger, paint losses, fading **290.00**

2", on ivory, oval, woman, sky background, early 19th C, 3-7/8" l oval frame.................... **250.00**

2-1/2" d, on ivory, oval, gentleman with wig, lower right sgd "Rocher," dated 1798, gilt surround, sq ebonized 5-1/8" w, 5-1/4" h frame, French...... **450.00**

2-1/2" d, on ivory, round, girl in white dress surrounded by clouds, sgd "Pet. Mar," dated 1832, gilt surround in sq ebonized 5-1/4" w, 5-1/2" h frame **450.00**

2-1/2" x 3", on ivory, gentleman, unsigned, American School, c1800, orig gilded copper case..... **2,875.00**

2-1/2" x 3-1/2", on paper, girl in blue, sgd "Ellsworth Painter," three-quarter length portrait of standing Elvira Warriner, gray, cloverleaf-shaped cloud over her head, mahogany veneer frame **11,500.00**

2-5/8" l, on ivory, young woman in white, early 19th C, 4-1/8" oval frame.. **200.00**

2-3/4" l, on ivory, young man, clothing left unfinished, first half 19th C, 4-1/4" l oval wood frame............. **150.00**

Admiral Dewey, signed "Vernet," on ivory, mounted in oval mount that is set in gilt 4-1/2" x 5-3/4" frame with brass label "Admiral Dewey, Hero of Cavite," **$990.** *Photo courtesy of Cowan Historic Americana Auctions.*

2-3/4" x 2-1/8", watercolor on ivory, gentleman, gilt metal pendant frame, central compartment containing fragment of fabric, sgd "A. J. Butler, 1836" on reverse, minor fading, damage to case............. **225.00**

2-3/4" x 2-1/8", watercolor on ivory, small girl with basket, American School, 19th C, period gilt metal frame **20,700.00**

2-3/4" x 2-1/4", on ivory, oval, stately woman, lace fichu and cap, English, late 18th C, framed.......... **260.00**

2-3/4" x 4-3/8", executed in pencil, oval, gentleman in powdered wig, gilt-metal surrounded topped by bale, reverse with label "Exhibited at the Victoria and Albert Museum 1914-1918," English, late 18th C **375.00**

*Czar Nicholas I, by Henry Benner, painted on porcelain panel, mounted in hinged lidded glass fronted box, 5-1/2" x 4", **$1,200.** Photo courtesy of Joy Luke Auctions.*

3" x 2-1/4", on ivory, oval, young woman with ermine wrap, gilt metal surround, red morocco case, English, early 19th C
.... **230.00**
3-1/8" x 2-3/16", watercolor on paper, waist length profile of young woman in black dress, white lace collar, framed, toning.................... **750.00**
3-1/8" x 2-3/8", watercolor on paper, profile of young man, identified on reverse "George Knowles Father when he was 23 years old," framed, general toning.................... **350.00**
3-5/8" x 2-7/8", on ivory, oval, man, black clothing, long white hair and beard, late 19th C, unframed .. **230.00**
4" x 3", on ivory, oval formal, young female saint with donkey and goat, Continental, 19th C, ebonized and gilt detailed frame.............. **490.00**
4-1/4" x 3-1/2", on ivory, woman in red dress, gold and pearl diadem, initialed on right "S. M.," English, late 19th C, ivory inlaid gilt-metal frame **230.00**
4-7/8" x 6-5/8", executed in pencil, square, profile of gentleman in top hat, England or France, early 19th C, ebonized frame with gilt meal surround
.... **250.00**
5-1/8" x 3-7/8", on ivory, woman in dark brown dress with lace collar and bonnet, seated on mahogany veneer classical sofa, boy standing at her side, wearing blue tunic, white trousers, poodle pull-toy, American School, early

19th C, eglomise mat, gilt frame, minor paint loss to column on one side
.... **4,890.00**
5-3/4" x 4-3/8", on ivory, Cupid with doves and puppy in bucolic setting, sgd lower left "Wm. Copper," dated 1839, English, giltwood frame ..**375.00**
5-7/8" w, 6-7/8" h, on ivory, young man identified as "Henry Ashfield Ellis 1800-1833," brown hair, blue eyes, dark blue frock coat, white vest, shirt, and collar, black neck tie, artist sgd "Mercier," gilt frame with rope twist detail...................... **660.00**

MINIATURES

History: There are three sizes of miniatures: dollhouse scale (ranging from 1/2 to 1 inch), sample size, and child's size. Since most early material is in museums or extremely expensive, the most common examples in the marketplace today are from the 20th century.

Many mediums were used for miniatures: silver, copper, tin, wood, glass, and ivory. Even books were printed in miniature. Price ranges are broad, influenced by scarcity and quality of workmanship.

The collecting of miniatures dates back to the 18th century. It remains one of the world's leading hobbies.

References: George M. Beylerian, *Chairmania*, Harry N. Abrams, 1994; Caroline Clifton-Mogg, *Dollhouse Sourcebook*, Abbeville Press, 1993; Nora Earnshaw, *Collecting Dolls' Houses and Miniatures*, Pincushion Press, 1993; Flora Gill Jacobs, *Dolls Houses in America*, Charles Scribner's Sons, 1974; ——, *History of Dolls Houses*, Charles Scribner's Sons; Constance Eileen King, *Dolls and Dolls Houses*, Hamlyn, 1989; Herbert F. Schiffer and Peter B. Schiffer, *Miniature Antique Furniture*, Schiffer Publishing, 1995.

Periodicals: *Doll Castle News*, P.O. Box 247, Washington, NJ 07882, http://www.dollcastlenews.com; *Dollhouse Miniatures*, P.O. Box 1612, Waukesha, WI 53187; *Dolls House World*, Avalon Court, Star Road, Partridge Green, West Sussex RH13 8RY UK, http://www.dollshouseworld.com; *Dolls & Miniatures*, 1040 Bentoak Lane, San Jose, CA 95129; *Miniature Collector*, Scott Publications, 30595 Eight Mile Road, Livonia, MI 48152.

Collectors' Clubs: International Guild Miniature Artisans, P.O. Box 629, Freedom, CA 95019-0629, http://www.igma.org; Miniature Enthusiasts Across Canada, 1133 Sixth Lane, Oakville, Ontario L6H 1W6 Canada, http://www.miniature.net; Miniature Industry Assoc. of America, P.O. Box 3388, Zanesville, OH 43702-3388m http://www.miaa.com; National Assoc. of Miniature Enthusiasts, P.O. Box 69, Carmel, IN 46032, http://www.miniatures.org.

Museums: Art Institute of Chicago, Chicago, IL; Colonial Williamsburg Foundation, Williamsburg, VA; Carole & Barry Kaye Museum of Miniatures, Los Angeles, CA, http://www.museumofminiatures.com; Denver Museum of Miniatures, Dolls & Toys, Denver, CO; Long Island Museum of American Art, Stony Brook, NY; Margaret Woodbury Strong Museum, Rochester, NY; Mildred Mahoney Jubilee Doll House Museum, Fort Erie, Canada; Toy and Miniature Museum of Delaware, Wilmington, DE; Toy and Miniature Museum of Kansas City, Kansas City, MO;

*Bed, five-drawer chest of drawers, dresser with beveled glass mirror, oak, **$1,450.** Photo courtesy of Joy Luke Auctions.*

Toy Museum of Atlanta, Atlanta, GA; Washington Dolls' House and Toy Museum, Washington, DC.

Additional Listings: See Dollhouse Furnishings in *Warman's Americana & Collectibles* for more examples.

Child or doll size

Blanket chest

10-1/4" w, 6-1/4" d, 5-1/4" h, pine, nail construction, mustard ground, front panel with red and green landscape, red and white house with multiple windows, dark green trees, red and black tulips on sides, black flower with petals and red and green leave on lid, wire staple hinges, tin hasp, dec by Jacob Weber, Lancaster County, PA, underside with pencil inscription "Peter S. Clark's box," mane has been removed from front panel, but date of "1851" remains, feet missing **18,400.00**

10-3/4" w, 5-3/4" d, 5-5/8" h, pine, nail construction, black ground, front panel with red, yellow, and green landscape, yellow-green trees, red and white house with multiple windows, marked "Catharina Porter 1847" in red script, sides with red and white tulips, yellow and green leaves, dec by Jacob Weber, Lancaster County, PA, lid well-dome replacement, till lid

missing, two feet repaired, wire staple hinges have added glue **2,750.00**

11-5/8" l, 5" d, 4-1/4" h, carved wood, dark stained finish, hinged lid, two openwork spindled flowerheads on front section, chip-carved and stippled stylized floral dec on sides, Normandy, early 20th C **300.00**

13" w, 7-1/2" d, 6-1/4" h, dovetailed case, old dark green paint, molded base and lid, int. till missing lid, hidden compartment in till, edge chips **495.00**

15" w, 8" d, 10" h, poplar, old black repaint, bracket feet with arched cut-outs on front and side aprons, applied beveled trim molding around lid, restorations to feet and hinge rail **440.00**

Buffet, 9" w, 4-3/4" d, 13-3/4" h, carved wood, dark stained finish, two spindled shelves, lower section with two chip carved front doors, carved and stippled stylized floral dec on sides, Normandy, early 20th C **235.00**

Bookcase, hp, scalloped cornice over four open shelves, base with three drawers, Peter Hunt dec **1,650.00**

Chair

Arm, Windsor, grain painted and parcel gilt, lowback, PA, first half

19th C, reserve scrolling concave crest continuing to downswept arms, six bulbous turned supports, plank seat, ring-turned tapering legs joined by stretchers, all over graining in brown and ochre, gilt highlights **850.00**

Side, 10-3/4" seat, 22" h, worn orig light green paint, black striping, gold stenciling, polychrome floral dec, pr **625.00**

Chest of drawers

Empire, late 19th C, mahogany, top drawer with brass pulls over two columns enclosing three drawers, 12" w, 8-3/4" d, 12" h **575.00**

Federal, CT, c1790, cherry, rect overhanging top with molded edge, case with four incised beaded graduated drawers, inlaid quarter fans and stringing, ogee bracket feet, old refinish, 38-3/4" w, 18" d, 34-1/4" h **6,900.00**

Sheraton, refinished walnut, scrolled crest, two dovetailed drawers with cockbeading, turned legs, 15-3/4" w, 9-1/4" d, 16-1/2" h **660.00**

Cook stove, black and white enameled steel, nickel steel fittings, working gas range, marked "Estate Fresh Air Oven," break in door frame, 15" l **2,420.00**

Dresser, 21" h, carved wood cornice, three small drawers next to mirror over three large drawers, glass pulls, cigar boxes used for drawers, mirror aged, checked finish **275.00**

Mantel luster, 3-1/4" d, 7" h, mint green Bristol glass, hp mauve and pink flowers, blue forget-me-nots, green leaves, ruffled edge, remnants of gold trim, polished pontil, c1890, 2" l crystal prisms **275.00**

Rocker, Empire style, mahogany, vase-shaped splat, rush seat, scrolled arms, 22" h **225.00**

Settee, 7-5/8" l, 7-5/8" w, 4-1/4" h, carved wood, dark stained finish, serpentine back, openwork spindled flowerheads and chip-carved and stippled stylized floral dec, hinged lid, Normandy, early 20th C **145.00**

Settle bench, 24" l, 6-1/2" w, 6-1/2" h seat, PA, orig gold, copper, and silver fruit dec along crest and back slats, mustard yellow ground with areas of wear and touch-up, scrolled arms, plank seat with incised borders, eight turned legs, restoration **825.00**

Spiral staircase, 17-5/8" w, 8-5/8" d, 22-1/8" h, mahogany, dark rosewood grained finials, rect base with demilune cut out in center, late 19th C . **1,500.00**

Blanket chest, Pennsylvania, decorated, reddish brown graining over yellow ground, pine, molded edge top, well-shaped bracket feet, 15-1/2" l, $5,610. Photo courtesy of Garth's Auctions, Inc.

Table, drop leaf, Sheraton, walnut, pine secondary wood, leaves with decoratively cut corners, one dovetailed drawer, turned legs, old finish, minor edge damage, hinges replaced, age crack on top, 23-1/2" l, 12-1/2" w, 10-3/4" l leaves, 19" h **1,100.00**

Tub, 5-5/8" d, 2-1/4" h, stave construction, metal bands, wire handles, orig blue paint, black bands **330.00**

Doll house accessories

Bird cage, brass, bird, stand, 7" h **65.00**

Candelabra, Petite Princess **25.00**

Carpet sweeper, gilt, Victorian .. **65.00**

Christmas tree, decorated..... **50.00**

Clock, metal **35.00**

Coffeepot, brass **25.00**

Crock, 2-5/8" h, 3-1/4" d, stoneware, two handles, cobalt blue dec, 19th C, minor chips, lid missing........ **115.00**

Cup and saucer, china, flower design, c1940..................... **10.00**

Decanter, two matching tumblers, Venetian, c1920.............. **35.00**

Fireplace, tin, Britannia metal fretwork, draped mantel, carved grate.... **85.00**

Iron, 2" h, pot metal, white ground, multicolored dec **6.00**

Miniature lamp, 2-1/2" h, pot metal, white ground, multicolored dec... **7.50**

Plate, 4-1/4" d, redware, slip dec, America, 19th C, minor rim chips, glaze wear..................... **805.00**

Radio, Strombecker, c1930 .... **35.00**

Refrigerator, Petite Princess.... **75.00**

Silhouettes, Tynietoy, c1930, pr. **25.00**

Telephone, wall, oak, speaker and bell, German, c1890 .... **40.00**

Towel stand, golden oak, turned post **45.00**

Umbrella stand, brass, ormolu, sq, emb palm fronds **60.00**

Urn, silver, handled, ornate.... **100.00**

Doll house furniture

Armoire, tin litho, purple and black **35.00**

Bathroom, wood, painted white, Strombecker **40.00**

Bedroom
French Provincial style, antique white, bed, dressing table, bench, pr night stands **195.00**
Victorian style, metal, veneer finish, bed, night stand, commode with faux marble tops, armoire and

mirror, cradle, Biedermeier clock, metal washstand **675.00**

Bench, wood, rush seat........ **25.00**

Blanket chest, 7-1/8" l, 4-3/4" h, painted wood, six-board, wallpaper lined int., open till, replaced hinges, lock missing, America, 19th C **2,990.00**

Buffet set, stenciled, three shelves, column supports, Biedermeier, 6" h **400.00**

Chair
Golden Oak, center splat, upholstered seat, German, c1875, pr...................... **75.00**
Ormolu, ornate, 3" h, c1900, pr **75.00**

Cradle, cast iron, painted green, 2" l **40.00**

Desk, Chippendale style, slant front, drawers open **60.00**

Dining room, Edwardian style, dark red stain, extension table, chairs, marble top cupboard, grandfather clock, chandelier, candelabra, 5" h bisque shoulder head maid doll, table service for six, Gebruder Schneerass, Waltershausen, Thuringa, c1915 .... **1,400.00**

Hall rack, walnut, carved fretwork, arched mirror back shelves, umbrella holder **450.00**

Kitchen set, litho tin, Modern Kitchen, all parts and pieces, animals, and related items, orig box, Louis Marx **250.00**

Living room
Empire style, sofa, fainting couch, two side chairs, upholstered tapestry, matching drapery **350.00**

Sofa, china, hand-painted pastel floral motif, gold trim, late 19th C, French or German, $120.

Victorian style, settee, two parlor chairs, footstool, two plant stands, two gilt filigree tables, three panel screen, upholstered red velvet, Gone with the Wind-style lamp **650.00**

Piano, grand, wood, 8 keys, 5" h **35.00**

Rocker, painted tin, lithographed tin seated child holding doll, compartment under seat concealed candy storage, Meier, Germany, 3" l **275.00**

Sewing table, golden oak, drawer, c1880 .... **100.00**

Table, tin, painted brown, white top, floral design, 1-1/2" x 3/4" h, ornate **30.00**

Tea cart, Petite Princess....... **25.00**

Vanity, Biedermeier **90.00**

MINTON CHINA

History: In 1793, Thomas Minton joined other men to form a partnership and build a small pottery at Stoke-on-Trent, Staffordshire, England. Production began in 1798 with blue-printed earthenware, mostly in the Willow pattern. In 1798, cream-colored earthenware and bone china were introduced.

A wide range of styles and wares was produced. Minton introduced porcelain figures in 1826, Parian wares in 1846, encaustic tiles in the late 1840s, and Majolica wares in 1850. Many famous designers and artists in the English pottery industry worked for Minton.

In 1883, the modern company was formed and called Mintons Limited. The "s" was dropped in 1968. Minton still produces bone-china tablewares and some ornamental pieces.

Marks: Many early pieces are unmarked or have a Sevres-type marking. The "ermine" mark was used in the early 19th century. Date codes can be found on tableware and majolica. The mark used between 1873 and 1911 was a small globe with a crown on top and the word "Minton."

References: Paul Atterbury and Maureen Batkin, *Dictionary of Minton*, Antique Collectors' Club, 1999; Susan and Al Bagdade, *Warman's English & Continental Pottery & Porcelain*, 3rd ed., Krause Publications, 1998; Joan Jones, *Minton: The First Two Hundred Years of Design and Production*, Swan Hill, 1993.

Museum: Minton Museum, Staffordshire, England; Victoria & Albert Museum, London, England.

Bowl, 12" x 10", oval, Palissy style, minor base chip **3,080.00**

Centerpiece, 16" l, elongated parian vessel, molded scroll handles and feet, pierced rim, two brown reserves, white pate-sur-pate amorini, gilding, dec, attributed to Lawrence Birks, marked "Minton," retailer's marks of Thomas Goode & Co., Ltd., London, c1889 .... **1,400.00**

Dinner plate, 10-3/8" d, white ground to center, cream rim, central band of anthemion urns and swags with gold jewelling, rim with gilt band of scrolls and demilune paterae, made for Spaulding & Co., Chicago, late 19th/early 20th C, price for set of 12 .... **2,100.00**

Dinner service, partial, Florentine pattern, earthenware, printed griffins and classical medallions, rust overglazing, 4-3/8" d demitasse saucer, nine 10-3/8" dinner plates, 9" d lunch plate, 17-5/8" l platter, 9-1/2" d soup plate, eight 10-3/8" soup plates, two 9" d soup bowls, 7-3/4" l sauce tureen, 9-5/8" tazza, price for 25 pcs ... **275.00**

Ewer, 21-1/4" h, majolica, heron and fish, after model by J. Protat, imp mark, 1869 date code **2,400.00**

Figure, 10-1/2" h, putti, yellow basket and grape vine, 1867, professional repair at rim of basket....... **2,750.00**

Floor urn, 35" h, 18" d, majolica, Neo-Classical, turquoise, massive foliage handles.......... **12,650.00**

Jardiniere, 7" h, molded wooden plants, white vines, lilac int., majolica, matching stands, pr **475.00**

Oyster plate, majolica
- Cobalt blue **1,650.00**
- Mottled.................. **935.00**
- Pink, minor rim nick **1,100.00**
- Turquoise............... **495.00**

Oyster server, four tiers, majolica, green and brown, white wells, turquoise finial, rim damage to six wells, mechanical turning mechanism missing **3,575.00**

Platter and covered tureen from partial dinner service, small pink and yellow flowers, blue border, $200. Photo courtesy of Joy Luke Auctions.

Plaque, 11-1/2" sq, painted scene of Dutch man reading document by row of books, initials "HH" lower right, date mark for 1883, framed........ **290.00**

Service plate, 10-5/8" d, raised gold dec, wide light blue ground banded borders, two sets of 12, one with floral dec, other with urn and scrolled leaf dec, printed marks, mid-20th C **3,450.00**

Soup tureen, cov, stand, 14-1/4" l, oval, enamel dec black transfer printed Oriental garden landscape, imp marks, c1882..................... **420.00**

Sweetmeat dish, 8" d, majolica, blue titmouse on branch, leaf-shaped dish, imp mark, 1888 .... **675.00**

Tower pitcher, 12-1/2" h, majolica, castle molded body with relief of dancing villagers in medieval dress, imp marks, c1873, chips to cov thumb rest, spout rim **1,035.00**

Vase, squeeze-bag decoration, ivory and green wreaths and stylized flowers, sang-de-boeuf ground, stamped "MINTON No.1," 6" d, 12-1/4" h, $750. Photo courtesy of David Rago Auctions.

Vase
5-1/2" d, 11-1/2" h, cuenca dec, peacocks, stenciled background, stamped "MINTON/21.88," small glaze flakes at base...... **425.00**

6" d, 12-1/4" h, squeezebag dec, ivory and green wreaths and stylized flowers, sang-de-bouef ground, stamped "Minton No. 1" **750.00**

Wash bowl, Gaudy English Imari pattern, blue transfer, red and yellow enameling, impressed mark, wear, crazing, and some possible hairlines, 15-1/2" d, 5" h, $165. Photo courtesy of Garth's Auctions, Inc.

MOCHA

History: Mocha decoration usually is found on utilitarian creamware and stoneware pieces and was produced through a simple chemical action. A color pigment of brown, blue, green, or black was made acidic by an infusion of tobacco or hops. When the acidic colorant was applied in blobs to an alkaline ground, it reacted by spreading in feathery designs resembling sea plants. This type of decoration usually was supplemented with bands of light-colored slip.

Types of decoration vary greatly, from those done in a combination of motifs, such as Cat's Eye and Earthworm, to a plain pink mug decorated with green ribbed bands. Most forms of mocha are hollow, e.g., mugs, jugs, bowls, and shakers.

English potters made the vast majority of the pieces. Collectors group the wares into three chronological periods: 1780-1820, 1820-1840, and 1840-1880.

Marks: Marked pieces are extremely rare.

References: Susan and Al Bagdade, *Warman's English & Continental Pottery & Porcelain*, 3rd ed., Krause Publications, 1998.

Reproduction Alert.

Bowl
4-3/4" d, 3-1/2" h, green band, canary yellow ground, yellow and black earthworm, partial imp mark "CL & - Mont-," chips and repairs **110.00**

6-1/2" d, band of earthworm dec,
late 19th C **235.00**

7-1/4" d, band of earthworm dec,
late 19th C **245.00**

Chamber pot

8-1/2" d, tan band, blue and black
stripes, blue, white, and black
earthworm, wear, repair, handle
replaced **110.00**

8-3/4" d, two-tone blue bands, black
stripes, black and white
earthworm, leaf handle, some wear
and edge flakes **125.00**

Creamer, 5-1/4" h, black and white
checkered band on shoulder, medium
blue glaze **215.00**

Cup, 2-7/8" h, imp border above brown
and white earthworm design, blue
ground, 19th C, imperfections . . **375.00**

Jar, cov, 5" h, pale blue band, black
stripes, white, black, and blue cat's eye
and earthworm dec, repairs and hairline
in lid **500.00**

Jug

6-1/8" h, blue and white raised
earthworm dec, two blue bands
. . . . **675.00**

8-1/2" h, two black and white
checkered bands, blue glaze,
foliate handle and spout . . . **345.00**

Measure, 5", 6", and 6-1/4" h, tankard,
blue, black and tan seaweed dec, one
with applied white label "Imperial Pint,"
other with resist label "Quart," minor
stains, wear, and crazing, three-pc set
. . . . **440.00**

Milk pitcher

4-5/8" h, dark bluish-gray band,
black stripes, emb band with green
and black seaweed, leaf handle,
wear and painted over spout flake
. . . . **440.00**

Cream pitcher, white ground, narrow
black bands, blue wide bands,
3-3/4" h, **$225.**

4-7/8" h, blue band, black and blue
stripes, brown, blue, and black,
earthworm dec, repairs **200.00**

Mug, tree design, wide blue band, black
ribbon bands, half pint, **$300.**

Mug

3-3/4" h, dark brown band and
stripes, blue, white, and tan
earthworm, leaf handle, hairlines
. . . . **550.00**

5-3/4" h, large band of pumpkin
seaweed dec, 19th C, large rim
chip **460.00**

Mustard pot, cov

3-3/4" h, tooled blue band, black
stripes, brown, black, white, and
blue earthworm design, leaf
molded handle, minor hairline,
flakes on lid **1,320.00**

3-3/4" h, wide brown band, black
stripes, seaweed dec, molded leaf
handle, rim flakes, minor enamel
wear **275.00**

Pitcher, 7-3/4" h, three bands of dark
brown seaweed on ochre ground,
alternating with imp dark brown shell
bands bordered with olive green
stripes, upper and lower imp chevron
bands on green ground, bordered with
olive green stripes, applied handle,
early 19th C, imperfections . . **3,750.00**

Salt, 3" d, 2-1/8" h, gray band, black
stripes, white wavy lines, stains in foot,
rim hairlines **330.00**

Shaker

4-1/8" h, tan bands, brown stripes,
black seaweed dec, chips . **220.00**

4-7/8" h, blue band, black stripe,
brown, black, and white earthworm
dec, blue top, repair **330.00**

Tea canister, 4" h, blue, black, and
white band on shoulder, white fluted
band on bottom, medium blue glaze
. . . . **125.00**

Teapot, 5-7/8" h, oval shape, medium
blue, fluted band on bottom, black and
white checkered band on top, acorn
finial **500.00**

Waste bowl

4-3/4" d, amber band, black
seaweed dec separated into five
segments by squiggly lines, green
molded lip band, stains and
hairlines **275.00**

5-5/8" d, 2-7/8" h, orange-tan band,
dark brown stripes, emb green
band with blue, white, and dark
brown earthworm, repairs . **550.00**

6-1/4" d, 3-1/4" h, tan band with
black stripes, seaweed dec,
repaired **55.00**

MONT JOYE GLASS

History: Mont Joye is a type of glass produced by
Saint-Hilaire, Touvier, de Varreaux & Company at their
glassworks in Pantin, France. Most pieces were lightly
acid etched to give them a frosted appearance and
were also decorated with enameled florals.

Vase, acid-etched, gilded chrysanthemums, lustered violet ground, etched
"Mont Joye L et Cie/3190," 3-1/2" d,
7-1/2" h, **$350.** Photo courtesy of
David Rago Auctions.

Jack in the pulpit vase, 14-1/2" h, amethyst shading to clear, enamel dec, gold sponged dec, polished pontil **995.00**

Pitcher, 10" h, amethyst, enameled flowers, aqua, blue, pink, and gold, sgd **350.00**

Rose bowl, 3-3/4" h, 4-1/4" d, pinched sides, acid etched, enameled purple violets, gold stems and dec **295.00**

Vase

4" h, pink enameled poppy and gold leaves, frosted textured ground, marked **275.00**

5-1/2" h, swirled shape, green, enameled flowers, c1890, sgd "Mont Joye" **445.00**

6" w, 16" h, colorless body, enameled purple iris on one side, white iris on other, green leaves, gold trim **2,200.00**

8" h, gourd shape, acid cut back, enamel floral dec, gilt trim, four applied handles **1,150.00**

9-1/2" h, gilded floral design, acid cut back frosty amethyst ground, gold wash highlights, polished pontil **1,100.00**

10" h, bulbous, narrow neck, clear to opalescent green, naturalistic thistle dec, gold highlights . **375.00**

18" h, green, enameled purple flowers, gold leaves, sgd . . **325.00**

Violet vase, 6" h, frosted etched surface, colorless glass, naturalistic enameled purple violet blossoms, gold highlights, base marked "Dimier Geneve" **260.00**

MOORCROFT

History: William Moorcroft was first employed as a potter by James Macintyre & Co., Ltd., of Burslem in 1897. He established the Moorcroft pottery in 1913.

The majority of the art pottery wares were hand thrown, resulting in a great variation among similarly styled pieces. Color and marks are keys to determining age.

Walker, William's son, continued the business upon his father's death and made wares in the same style.

References: Paul Atterbury, *Moorcroft: A Guide to Moorcroft Pottery 1897-1993*, rev. ed., Richard Dennis and Hugh Edwards, 1990; Susan and Al Bagdade, *Warman's English & Continental Pottery & Porcelain*, 3rd ed., Krause Publications, 1998; A. W. Coysh, *British Art Pottery, 1870-1940*, Charles E. Tuttle, 1976; Walter

Moorcroft, *Walter Moorcroft Memories of Life and Living*, Richard Dennis Publications, distributed by Antique Collectors' Club, 1999; Frances Salmon, *Collecting Moorcroft*, Francis-Joseph Books, 1994.

Collectors' Club: Moorcroft Collectors' Club, Lipert International Inc., 2922 M. St., NW, Washington, DC 20007.

Museums: Everson Museum of Art, Syracuse, NY; Moorcroft Museum, Stoke-on-Trent, England; Victoria & Albert Museum, London, England.

Marks: The company initially used an impressed mark, "Moorcroft, Burslem"; a signature mark, "W. Moorcroft" followed. Modern pieces are marked simply "Moorcroft," with export pieces also marked "Made in England."

Bowl, Florian Ware, blue tones, 7-5/8" h, 2-1/2" h, **$595.**

Bowl, 6-1/2" d, 3-1/4" h, Pomegranate pattern, stamped mark, 1918-29, restoration to rim chip **115.00**

Compote, 7-1/4" d, Lily motif, yellow and green ground **150.00**

Ginger jar, cov, 11-1/2" h, pomegranate dec **525.00**

Jar, cov

Cornflower, ivory ground, coat of arms of Kings College, Oxford, c1911 . . . . **1,450.00**

Poppy & Forget Me Not pattern, stippled ground, c1900, 5-3/4" d, 3-1/2" h **1,100.00**

Loving cup in the Pomegranate pattern, stamped, 1914-16, minor fleck to rim, 6" d, 5-1/2" h, **$1,150.** *Photo courtesy of David Rago Auctions.*

Lamp base, 6-1/4" d, 11-1/4" h, Anemone **920.00**

Loving cup, 6" d, 5-1/2" h, Pomegranate pattern, stamped mark, 1914-16, minor rim fleck**. 1,150.00**

Pitcher

6-1/4" h, Forget-Me-Not, c1902 . . . . **1,350.00**

6-1/2" h, Florian Ware, Tulip and Dianthus pattern, c1900 . **1,125.00**

Plate

7-1/4" d, toadstool, blue ground, imp "Moorcroft Claremont" **600.00**

8-1/2" d, Natural War, green and blue glaze, pr **250.00**

Vase

6" h, Freesia, c1930, sgd by William in blue, imp "Potter to HM The Queen" **975.00**

6-1/2" d, 15" h, Eventide pattern, ovoid, squeezebag green tall trees, cobalt blue ground, stamped "Moorcroft/Made in England" and signature, rim chip, 2" line **1,840.00**

7" h, Leaf & Berry, matte glaze, William's initials in blue . . **1,150.00**

9-1/2" h, Fish, c1930, sgd by William in brown, imp "Potter to HM The Queen" **2,700.00**

10" h, Clematis, blue Walter initials, imp mark **1,050.00**

10" h, Freesia, ochre ground, imp mark, full William signature **2,750.00**

10" h, Rachel Bishop's Swallow **1,050.00**

12" h, Orchid, flambé, sgd by William in blue, imp "Potter to HM The Queen" **4,350.00**

12" h, 7-3/4" d, Anemone, sgd **900.00**

MORGANTOWN GLASS WORKS

History: The Morgantown Glass Works, Morgantown, West Virginia, was founded in 1899 and began production in 1901. Reorganized in 1903, it operated as the Economy Tumbler Company for 20 years until, in 1923, the word "Tumbler" was dropped from the corporate title. The firm was then known as The Economy Glass Company until reversion to its original name, Morgantown Glass Works, Inc., in 1929, the name it kept until its first closing in 1937. In 1939, the factory was reopened under the aegis of a guild of glassworkers and operated as the Morgantown Glassware Guild from that time until its final closing. Purchased by Fostoria in 1965, the factory operated as a subsidiary of the Moundsville-based parent company until 1971, when

Fostoria opted to terminate production of glass at the Morgantown facility. Today, collectors use the generic term, "Morgantown Glass," to include all periods of production from 1901 to 1971.

Morgantown was a 1920s leader in the manufacture of colorful wares for table and ornamental use in American homes. The company pioneered the processes of iridization on glass, as well as gold and platinum encrustation of patterns. It enhanced Crystal offerings with contrasting handle and foot of India Black, Spanish Red (ruby), and Ritz Blue (cobalt blue), and other intense and pastel colors for which it is famous. The company conceived the use of contrasting shades of fired enamel to add color to its etchings. It was the only American company to use a chromatic silk-screen printing process on glass, its two most famous and collectible designs being Queen Louise and Manchester Pheasant.

The company is also known for ornamental "open stems" produced during the late 1920s. Open stems separate to form an open design midway between the bowl and foot, e.g., an open square, a "Y," or two diamond-shaped designs. Many of these open stems were purchased and decorated by Dorothy C. Thorpe in her California studio, and her signed open stems command high prices from today's collectors. Morgantown also produced figural stems for commercial clients such as Koscherak Brothers and Marks & Rosenfeld. Chanticleer (rooster) and Mai Tai (Polynesian bis) cocktails are two of the most popular figurals collected today.

Morgantown is best known for the diversity of design in its stemware patterns, as well as for its four patented optics: Festoon, Palm, Peacock, and Pineapple. These optics were used to embellish stems, jugs, bowls, liquor sets, guest sets, salvers, ivy and witch balls, vases, and smoking items.

Two well-known lines of Morgantown Glass are recognized by most glass collectors today: #758 Sunrise Medallion and #7643 Golf Ball Stem Line. When Economy introduced #758 in 1928, it was originally identified as "Nymph." By 1931, the Morgantown front office had renamed it Sunrise Medallion. Recent publications erred in labeling it "dancing girl." Upon careful study of the medallion, you can see the figure is poised on one tiptoe, musically saluting the dawn with her horn. The second well-known line, #7643 Golf Ball, was patented in 1928; production commenced immediately and continued until the company closed in 1971. More Golf Ball than any other Morgantown product is found on the market today.

References: Tom and Neila Bredehoft, *Fifty Years of Collectible Glass, 1920-1970*, Vol. 1, Vol. II, Antique Trader Books, 2000; Jerry Gallagher, *Handbook of Old Morgantown Glass*, Vol. I, published by author, 1995, values updated 2001; ——, *Old Morgantown, Catalogue of Glassware, 1931*, Morgantown Collectors of America Research Society, n.d.; Jeffrey B. Snyder, *Morgantown Glass From Depression Glass Through the 1960s*, Schiffer Publishing, 1998; Hazel Marie Weatherman, *Colored Glassware of the Depression Era*, Book 2 published by author, 1974, available in reprint; ——, *1984 Supplement & Price Trends for Colored Glassware of the Depression Era*, Book 1, published by author, 1984.

Collectors' Clubs: Old Morgantown Glass Collectors' Guild, P.O. Box 894, Morgantown, WV 26507, http://www.oldmorgantown.org.

Basket
Patrick, #19-4358, black, crystal twist handle, leaf form appliqués where handle joins basket, polished base, 10-1/4" w, 13-1/4" h **1,100.00**
Patrick, #19-4358, Ritz Blue, applied crystal twisted handle, mint leaf prunts, 5" d, 9-3/4" h **750.00**
Quilt, crystal, black/amethyst rope-twist handle, leaf form appliqués where handle joins basket, ground pontil ... **1,100.00**
Trindle, #4357, amethyst, applied crystal twisted reed handle, c1930, 9" **725.00**
Trindle, #4357, Stiegel Green, leaf applied to each end of handle, 10" d, 11-7/8" h **500.00**

Berry jug, Palm Optic, #37, pink, 8-1/2" w, 9-1/8" h **235.00**

Bowl
Fairlee, Glacier dec, #12, 12" d **595.00**
Fantassia, Bristol Blue, #67, 5-1/2" d **95.00**
Janice, #4355, Ritz Blue, 13" d **475.00**
Woodsfield, Genova Line, 12-1/2" d, #12-1/2 .... **565.00**

Brandy snifter, Golf Ball, #7643, red, crystal base, 4" w, 6-1/4" h **130.00**

Candleholders, pr
Golf Ball, #7643, Torch Candle, single, Ritz Blue, 6" h **300.00**
Hamilton, #87, Evergreen, 5" h **65.00**
Modern, #80, Moss Green, 7-1/2" h **90.00**
Monroe, #7690, Ritz Blue, 7" h **1,400.00**

Candy jar, cov
Mansfield, #200, burgundy matte, 12" h **200.00**
Palace, #9952, ruby, 6-1/2" h .. **75.00**
Rachael, crystal, Pandora cutting, 6" h **395.00**

Champagne
Athena, #7606-1/2", ebony, filament, #777 Baden etch.......... **90.00**
Golf Ball, #7643, Spanish Red, 5-1/2" oz **60.00**
Lawton, #7860, Azure, Festoon Optic, 5 oz............... **50.00**
Ruby Red Filament Stem, 3" d base, price for pr............... **90.00**

Cocktail
Golf Ball, #7643, Stiegel Green, 3-1/2 oz **48.00**
Top Hat, Copen Blue, 5-1/4" h, 3-1/8" d **95.00**

Venus, #7577, Anna Rose, Palm Optic, 3 oz **40.00**
Cocktail set, Deco, black, 7-3/4" h pitcher with weighted base, five 3" w, 3" h cocktail glasses **65.00**
Compote, Reverse Twist, #7654, aquamarine, 6-1/2" d, 6-3/4" h .. **225.00**
Console bowl, El Mexicana, #12933, Seaweed, 10" d............. **425.00**
Cordial, 1-1/2 oz
Brilliant, #7617, Spanish Red **140.00**
Golf Ball, #7643, Pastels **65.00**
Mikado, crystal **30.00**
Finger bowl, Art Moderne, #7640, Faun etch, crystal and black, 4-1/2" d, ftd **150.00**

Goblet, Yale, Spanish Red bowl, crystal stem and foot, 9-1/2 oz, $145.

Goblet
Art Moderne, #7640, Faun etch, crystal and black, 7-3/4" h . **125.00**
Courtney, #7637, DC Thorpe satin open stem **195.00**
Crinkle, #1962, ruby, 5-1/8" h, c1962, set of seven **95.00**
Golf Ball, #7643, cobalt blue, water **55.00**
Golf Ball, #7643, red, water .. **55.00**
Laura, #7665, Nasreen etch, topaz **115.00**
Paragon, #7624, ebony open stem, 10 oz **215.00**
Queen Louise, #7664, 3-1/2" d, 7-1/2" h............... **400.00**
Sunrise Medallion, 3-5/16" d, 7-7/8" h **70.00**
Guest set, Trudy, #23, Bristol Blue, 6-3/8" h **145.00**
Ice tub, El Mexicana, #1933, Seaweed, 6" d **225.00**

Jug

Kaufmann, #6, Doric star sand blast, 54 oz **295.00**

Melon, #20069, Alabaster, Ritz Blue trim **1,450.00**

Measuring cup, 3-1/8" d, 2-7/8" h, adv " Your Credit is Good Pickerings, Furnishings, 10th & Penn, Pittsburgh, clear **315.00**

Oyster cup, 2-3/8" d, Sunrise Medallion, blue **190.00**

Pilsner, Floret, etch #796, Lando, 12 oz **65.00**

Plate

Anna Rose, #734 American Beauty etch, 7" d **65.00**

Carlton Madrid, topaz, 6" d . . . **35.00**

Country Ladies Violets, 1982, orig box and certificate, 9" d **40.00**

Sherbet

Crinkle, #1962, pink, 6 oz **30.00**

Golf Ball, #7643, Stiegel Green **40.00**

Sophisticate, #7646, Picardy etch, 5-1/2 oz **55.00**

Tumbler, water

Belton, Primrose, vaseline, pillar optic, 9 oz **135.00**

Carlton, etch #778, ftd, 5-1/2" h **35.00**

Vase

Catherine, #26, Azure, #758 Sunrise Medallion etch, bud, 10" h . **265.00**

Daisy, #90, crystal, green and white wash, 9-1/2" w **475.00**

Palm Optic, meadow green body, jade green twist reed handles, 4-1/4" d jade green base, 9-3/4" h, 9" w handle to handle . . . **1,150.00**

Peacock Optic, tangerine, cylinder, c1958, 60-1/2" h **35.00**

Raindrop pattern, red/orange, yellow base, hobnail design on inside graduating in size down to base, 4-1/2" d, 10" h **35.00**

Wine

Art Moderne, Faun etch, crystal and black, 5-3/8" h **150.00**

Empress, #7680-1/2, Spanish Red, 3 oz **90.00**

Mikado, 3 oz, price for set of nine **225.00**

MOSER GLASS

History: Ludwig Moser (1833-1916) founded his polishing and engraving workshop in 1857 in Karlsbad (Karlovy Vary), Czechoslovakia. He employed many famous glass designers, e.g., Johann Hoffmann, Josef Urban, and Rudolf Miller. In 1900, Moser and his sons, Rudolf and Gustav, incorporated Ludwig Moser & Söhne.

Moser art glass included clear pieces with inserted blobs of colored glass, cut colored glass with classical scenes, cameo glass, and intaglio cut items. Many inexpensive enameled pieces also were made.

In 1922, Leo and Richard Moser bought Meyr's Neffe, their biggest Bohemian art glass rival. Moser executed many pieces for the Wiener Werkstätte in the 1920s. The Moser glass factory continues to produce new items.

References: Gary D. Baldwin, *Moser Artistic Glass, Edition Two,* Antique Publications, 1997; Gary Baldwin and Lee Carno, *Moser—Artistry in Glass,* Antique Publications, 1988; Mural K. Charon and John Mareska, *Ludvik Moser, King of Glass,* published by author, 1984.

Cruet, eight raised cabochon ruby gems, deep cut edges of burnished mold, clear body, eight alternating panels of brilliant gold squiggles and stylized leaves, six gold decorated panels each with ruby cabochon on stopper, 6" h, $585. Photo courtesy of Clarence and Betty Maier.

Basket, 5-1/2" h, green malachite, molded cherubs dec, pr **800.00**

Beverage set, 10-1/4" h, frosted and polished smoky topaz decanter, four cordials, molded nude women, five-pc set **265.00**

Bowl, 12-1/4" w, 3" h, cameo, cobalt blue, 18 elephants, nine palm trees, birds, large polished pontil, sgd in four places, minor int. scratching . . **3,000.00**

Centerpiece, 5" x 9", green, intaglio cut flowers **425.00**

Cologne bottle, 7-1/2" h, 3-1/2" d, amethyst shaded to clear, deep intaglio cut flowers and leaves, orig stopper, sgd **695.00**

Cup and saucer, amber, gold scrolls, multicolored enameled flowers . **295.00**

Demitasse cup and saucer, amber shading to white, enameled gilt flowers **100.00**

Ewer, 10-3/4" h, cranberry, gilt surface, applied acorns and clear jewels **2,000.00**

Goblet, 8" h, cranberry, Rhine-style, enameled oak leaves, applied acorns, four-pc set **1,800.00**

Loving cup, 6-3/4" h, three colorless handles, cranberry, gold enameled dec, polished pontil, marked "2773" **1275.00**

Perfume, 4-3/4" h, pink-lavender alexandrite, faceted panels, matching stopper, sgd in oval **275.00**

Pitcher, 6-3/4" h, amberina, IVT, four yellow, red, blue, and green applied glass beaded bunches of grapes, pinched in sides, three-dimensional bird beneath spout, all over enamel and gold leaves, vines, and tendrils **3,200.00**

Tankard, cranberry body with gold decoration, elaborate silver top, spout as face of old man, standing lion handle, inscribed mark, blue paper label, 14" h, 6-1/4" w, $495.

Portrait vase, 8-1/2" h, woman, gold leaves, light wear. **450.00**

Tray, 7-1/4" w, cranberry, crackle, hand enameled white and blue marsh scene with egret, polished edges . . . **2,500.00**

Urn, 15-3/4" h, cranberry, two gilt handles, studded with green, blue, clear, and red stones, highly enameled surface, multicolored and gilt Moorish dec **3,500.00**

Vase

6-1/2", cranberry, heavy applied dec of scrolls, abstract flowers, and butterflies, four ftd, #2208 . **950.00**

7" h, paneled amber baluster body, wide gold medial band of women warriors, base inscribed "Made in Czechoslovakia-Moser Karlsbad" **550.00**

8" h, floriform, pink and green, goliate dec, gilt trim **2,000.00**

9" h, cranberry, two gilt handles, medallion with hp roses, sgd **1,050.00**

10" h, heavy walled dark amethyst faceted body, etched and gilded medial scene of bear hunt, spear-armed men and dogs pursuing large bear **345.00**

12-1/2" h, trumpet, ruffled foot, pink ground, green at top, faceted int., gold and green arabesque design, pink and blue flowers, gold trim **1,500.00**

MOUNT WASHINGTON GLASS COMPANY

History: In 1837, Deming Jarves, founder of the Boston and Sandwich Glass Company, established for George D. Jarves, his son, the Mount Washington Glass Company in Boston, Massachusetts. In the following years, the leadership and the name of the company changed several times as George Jarves formed different associations.

In the 1860s, the company was owned and operated by Timothy Howe and William L. Libbey. In 1869, Libbey bought a new factory in New Bedford, Massachusetts. The Mount Washington Glass Company began operating there again under its original name. Henry Libbey became associated with the company early in 1871. He resigned in 1874 during the Depression, and the glassworks was closed. William Libbey had resigned in 1872, when he went to work for the New England Glass Company.

The Mount Washington Glass Company opened again in the fall of 1874 under the presidency of A. H. Seabury and the management of Frederick S. Shirley. In 1894, the glassworks became a part of the Pairpoint Manufacturing Company.

Throughout its history, the Mount Washington Glass Company made different types of glass including pressed, blown, art, lava, Napoli, cameo, cut, Albertine, and Verona.

References: Sean and Johanna S. Billings, *Peachblow Glass, Collector's Identification & Price Guide*, Krause Publications, 2000; Kyle Husfloen, contributing editor Louis O. St. Aubin Jr., *Antique Trader's American & European Decorative and Art Glass Price Guide*, 2nd ed., Krause Publications, 2000; Edward and Sheila Malakoff, *Pairpoint Lamps*, Schiffer Publishing, 1990; John A. Shuman III, *Collector's Encyclopedia of American Art Glass*, Collector Books, 1988, 1994 value update.

Collectors Club: Mount Washington Art Glass Society, P.O. Box 24094, Fort Worth, TX 76124-1094.

Museum: The New Bedford Glass Museum, New Bedford, MA.

Additional Listings: Burmese, Crown Milano, Peachblow, and Royal Flemish.

Adviser: Louis O. St. Aubin Jr.

Beverage set, satin, MOP

Coralene, yellow sea weed dec, glossy finish, 9" h, bulbous water pitcher, three spout top, applied reeded shell handle, three matching 4" h tumblers, two blisters on pitcher, three-pc set **750.00**

Herringbone, 9" h bulbous water pitcher, 7" w, applied frosted handle, deep rose to deep pink to pink, to off white, enameled and painted white wild roses, green, brown, and gold leaves, stems, branches, and thorns, four 3-3/4" h tumblers, damage to tumbler, five-pc set **1,750.00**

Biscuit jar, cov, 7" d, 7" h, melon rib, Smith Brothers enameled blue pansies dec, c1875-85 . . . . **795.00**

Bowl, 4-1/2" d, 2-3/4" h, Rose amber, fuchsia, blue swirl bands, bell tone flint **295.00**

Box, 4-1/2" h, 6-1/2" d, opalware, mint green ground, deep pink roses, small red cornflowers, gold trim, blown-out floral and ribbon design, #3212/20 . . . . **1,750.00**

Collars and cuffs box, opalware, shaped as two collars with big bow in front, cov dec with orange and pink Oriental poppies, silver poppy-shaped finial with gold trim, base with poppies, white ground, gold trim, bright blue bow, white polka dots, buckle on back, sgd "Patent applied for April 10, 1894," #2390/128. . . . . **950.00**

Cracker jar, 9-1/2" h, satin, pastel floral dec, SP top. **475.00**

Flower holder, 5-1/4" d, 3-1/2" h, mushroom shape, white ground, blue dot and oak leaf dec **425.00**

Fruit bowl, 10" d, 7-1/2" h, Napoli, solid dark green ground painted on clear glass, outside dec with pale pink and white pond lilies, green and pink leaves and blossoms, int. dec with gold highlight traceries, silver-plated base with pond lily design, two applied loop handles, four buds form feet, base sgd "Pairpoint Mfg. Co. B4704" . . . **2,200.00**

Humidor, 5-1/2" h, 4-1/2" d top, hinged silver-plated metalwork rim and edge, blown-out rococo scroll pattern, brilliant blue Delft windmills, ships, and landscape, Pairpoint **950.00**

Jar, cov, 6" w, 5-1/2" h, peachblow, rim of jar and rim of lid cased in gold metal with raised leaves **400.00**

Jewel box, 4-1/2" d top, 5-1/4" d base, 3-1/4" h, opalware, Monk drinking glass of red wine on lid, solid shaded green background on cover and base, fancy gold-washed, silver-plated rim and hinge, orig satin lining, artist sgd "Schindler" **550.00**

Jug, 6" h, 4" w, satin, Polka Dot, deep peachblow pink, white air traps, DQ, unlined, applied frosted loop handle **475.00**

Lamp, parlor, four dec glass oval insert panels, orig dec white opalware ball shade with deep red carnations, sgd "Pairpoint" base, c1890 . . . . . **1,750.00**

Lamp shade, 4-1/4" h, 5" d across top, 2" d fitter, rose amber, ruffled, fuschia shading to deep blue, DQ. **575.00**

Rose bowl, light heavenly blue satin top, fading to creamy white base, enameled gold daisies with red centers, painted foliage, nine soft crimps, gold highlights, shiny white int., polished pontil, marked "620," $395. Photo courtesy of Johanna Billings.

Miniature lamp, 17" h, 4-1/2" d shade, banquet style, milk glass, bright blue Delft dec of houses and trees, orig metal fittings, attributed to Frank Guba **795.00**

Mustard pot, 4-1/2" h, ribbed, bright yellow and pink background, painted white and magenta wild roses, orig silver-plated hardware **185.00**

Perfume bottle, 5-1/4" h, 3" d, opalware, dark green and brown glossy ground, red and yellow nasturtiums, green leaves, sprinkler top.....**375.00**

Pickle castor, 11" h, opalescent stripes with light and dark pink, Pairpoint #604 frame **850.00**

Pitcher, 6" h, 3" w, satin, DQ, MOP, large frosted camphor shell loop handle **325.00**

Rose bowl, 5" d, satin, blue shading to white base **45.00**

Salt shaker, 2-1/2" d, 1-3/4" h, melon rib, enameled floral dec, pewter top, salt shaker corroded on **245.00**

Sugar shaker, egg shape, pink and gold chrysanthemums, white shading to blue ground, orig top **385.00**

Tumbler, 4" h, satin, c1880

 Diamond Quilted, heavenly blue **165.00**

 Diamond Quilted, shaded yellow to white **165.00**

 Herringbone, shaded blue ..**165.00**

Vase, Verona, stylized florals outlined in gold and silver, pastel pink wash background, signed "Verona 918," 9" h, $1,250. Photo courtesy of Clarence and Betty Maier.

Vase

 3" w, 6-1/2" h, satin, Raindrop, Bridal White, MOP, applied frosted edge, pr **550.00**

 3-1/4" w, 6" h, bulbous stick, satin, flaring rim, apricot shading to white, DQ **375.00**

 4-1/2" d, 5-3/4" h, satin, flattened hobnail, MOP, deep raspberry shading to white base, rim divided into four in-folding curves, ground pontil..................**585.00**

 5" w, 8-1/4" h, satin, amberina coloration, MOP DQ, deep gold diamonds, white lining, slightly ruffled top.............**1,250.00**

 5-1/2" w, 6-1/4" h, satin, melon ribbed, MOP, Bridal White, muslin pattern, applied frosted edge, c1880 ....**425.00**

 5-1/2" d, 9" h, pink opalware, Delft windmill with person in front, gold trim top and base, Pairpoint **725.00**

 6" d, 6-1/2" h, satin, bulbous, DQ, deep rose shading to pink, two applied frosted "M" handles with thorns, cut edge, c1880...**750.00**

 7" d, 8" h, bulbous, satin, MOP, Alice Blue, Muslin pattern, applied frosted edge, three-petal top **675.00**

 8-3/8" h, Napoli, chicks standing in the rain dec **1,250.00**

 10" h, Neapolitan Ware, yellow, purple, rust, and gold spider mums, green leaves, gold spider webbing on ext., sgd "Napoli," #880 ....**1,450.00**

 11-1/4" h, gourd shape, 6" l flaring neck, satin, deep brown shading to gold, white lining, enameled seaweed design all over ..**550.00**

 11-7/8" h, bulbous stick, Colonial ware, glossy white, gold dec, all over vine and berry dec, two wreath and bow dec at top, sgd, #1010 ....**550.00**

 12-3/4" h, 5-1/2" w, Colonial ware, shaped like Persian water jug, loop handle on top, small spout, bulbous body, pedestal base, glossy white ground, pale pink and purple lilies, green leaves and stems, overlaid gold dec of leaves, stems, and daisies, sgd and #1022 ....**2,200.00**

 17-1/2" h, hp floral dec, white satin glass, swirl ribbed tall cylinder body..................**400.00**

MULBERRY CHINA

History: Mulberry china was made primarily in the Staffordshire district of England between 1830 and 1860. The ware often has a flowing effect similar to flow blue. It is the color of crushed mulberries, a dark purple, sometimes with a gray tinge or bordering almost on black. The potteries that manufactured flow blue also made Mulberry china and, in fact, frequently made some patterns in both types of wares. To date, there are no known reproductions.

References: Susan and Al Bagdade, *Warman's English & Continental Pottery & Porcelain*, 3rd ed., Krause Publications, 1998; Ellen R. Hill, *Mulberry Ironstone*, published by author, 1993; Petra Williams, *Flow Blue China and Mulberry Ware*, revised ed., Fountain House East, 1993.

Collectors' Club: Flow Blue International Collectors' Club, Inc., 9412 High Drive, Leawood, KS 66206.

Adviser: Ellen G. King.

Marble, child's wash bowl and pitcher, $350. Photo courtesy of Ellen King.

Bryonia, Utzschneider

 Butter dish, cov **235.00**
 Cake plate, 14" d, stemmed .**375.00**
 Creamer.................**120.00**
 Plate, 8" d **50.00**
 Teapot, cov **350.00**
 Vegetable bowl, open, 10" l, oval **135.00**

Corean, Podmore, Walker

 Mug....................**275.00**
 Pitcher.................**375.00**
 Plate, 9-3/4" d **85.00**
 Platter, 16" l **250.00**
 Punch cup...............**95.00**

Etruscan vase, Mayer & Elliot, platter, well and tree...............**225.00**

Genoa, Davenport

 Platter, 13-1/4" l **210.00**
 Teapot, cov **320.00**

Marble, sauce tureen, covered, tray, ladle, $475. Photo courtesy of Ellen King.

Washington Vase, teapot, covered, $250. Photo courtesy of Ellen King.

Heath's Flower, Heath
　Creamer and sugar bowl, cov
　. . . . . 250.00
　Platter, 13-3/8" l. 225.00
Ivy & Flowers, Mayer, tea set, cov
teapot, creamer, sugar bowl, cov, tray,
cups and saucers, plates, 14-pc set
. . . . 850.00
Jeddo, Adams, plate, 10" d. 90.00
Marble, unknown
　Mug, with frog. 275.00
　Plate, 9" d 60.00
　Sauce tureen, cov, base, tray, ladle
　. . . . . 475.00
　Wash set, child's, pitcher and wash
　bowl 350.00

Washington Vase, creamer, $225. Photo courtesy of Ellen King.

Pelew, Challinor
　Chamber pot, cov. 300.00
　Punch cup 55.00
　Sugar bowl, cov 195.00

Phantasia, Furnival, creamer and
sugar bowl, cov, cockscomb . . . **750.00**
Ranunculus, Wedgwood, sweetmeats
tazza, low **250.00**
Seaweed, Ridgway, plate, 9" d . . **65.00**
Tillenberg, Clementson, vegetable
tureen, cov **200.00**
Vincennes, Alcock, soap dish, cov,
base, liner. **275.00**
Washington Vase, Podmore, Walker
　Creamer. **225.00**
　Plate, 8" d. **60.00**
　Platter, 16" l **295.00**
　Tea cup and saucer, handleless cup
　. **110.00**
　Teapot, cov **250.00**
　Tea set, cov teapot, creamer, cov
　sugar bowl, waste bowl. . . . **575.00**

MUSICAL INSTRUMENTS

History: From the first beat of the prehistoric drum to the very latest in electronic music makers, musical instruments have been popular modes of communication and relaxation.

The most popular antique instruments are violins, flutes, oboes, and other instruments associated with the classical music period of 1650 to 1900. Many of the modern instruments, such as trumpets, guitars, and drums, have value on the "used," rather than antiques market.

Collecting musical instruments is in its infancy. The field is growing very rapidly. Investors and speculators have played a role since the 1930s, especially in early string instruments.

References: Tony Bacon (ed.), *Classic Guitars of the '50s*, Miller Freeman Books (6600 Silacci Way, Gilroy, CA 95020), 1996; S. P. Fjestad (ed.), *Blue Book of Guitar Values*, 2nd ed., Blue Book Publications, 1994; Alan Greenwood, *Vintage Guitar Magazine Price Guide*, 6th ed., Vintage Guitar Books, 1998; George Gruhn and Walter Carter, *Acoustic Guitars and Other Fretted Instruments*, GPI Books, 1993; ——, *Electric Guitars and Basses*, Miller Freeman Books, GPI Books, 1994; ——, *Gruhn's Guide to Vintage Guitars*, GPI Books, 1991; Philip F. Gura and James F. Bollman, *America's Instrument: The Banjo in the 19th Century*, Univ of North Carolina Press, 1999; Mike Longworth, *C. F. Martin & Co.*, 4 Maples Press, 1994; William G. Moseley, Jr., *Vintage Electric Guitars*, Schiffer Publishing, 2001; Paul Trynka (ed.), *Electric Guitar*, Chronicle Books, 1993; Michael Wright, *Guitar Stories, Vol. II*, Vintage Guitar Books, 2000.

Periodicals and Internet Resources: *Guitar Digest*, P.O. Box 66, Athens, OH 45701; *Jerry's Musical Newsletter*, 4624 W. Woodland Road, Minneapolis, MN 55424; *Midwest Musician's Hot Line*, P.O. Box 1052, Fort Dodge, IA 50501; *Piano & Keyboard*, P.O. Box 2626 San Anselmo, CA 94979; *Piano World*, http://www.pianoworld.com; *Piano Technician's Guild*, http://www.ptg.org; *PickNet*, http://wwwhome.att.net/~StevieLeavitt/index.html; *Player Piano & Mechanical Music Exchange*, http://www.mmd.foxtail.com; *Player Piano*, http://www.pianoworld.com; *Strings*, P.O. Box 151029, San Rafael, CA 94915, http://www.stringsmagazine.com; *Theatre Organ Home Page*, http://theatreorgans.com; *Twentieth Century Guitar*, 135 Oser Ave., Hauppauge, NY 11788, http://www.tcguitar.com; *Universal Guitar Pick Trader*, http://www.earthlink.net/~jeffwhite; *Vintage Guitar Classics*, P.O. Box 7301, Bismarck, ND 58507, http://www.vintageguitar.com; *Violink*, http://www.violink.com.

Collectors' Clubs: American Band Organ Assoc., 3766 Mann Road, Blacklick, OH 43004; American Musical Instrument Society, 495 St. Augustine Ave., Claremont, CA 91711, http://www.amis.org; Automatic Musical Instrument Collectors Assoc., 2150 Hastings Court, Santa Rosa, CA 95405, http://www.amica.org; Fretted Instrument Guild of America, 2344 S. Oakley Ave., Chicago, IL 60608; Harmonica Collectors International, 241 Cedar Field Court, Chesterfield, MO 63017; Musical Box Society International, 887 Orange Ave. E., St. Paul, MN 55106; Reed Organ Society, Inc., 3575 State Highway 258 East, Wichita Falls, TX 76310-7037; Society for the Preservation & Advancement of the Harmonica, P.O. Box 865, Troy, MI 48099-0865.

Museums: American Shrine to Music Museum, University of South Dakota, Vermillion, SD; C. F. Martin Guitar Museum, Nazareth, PA; International Piano Archives at Maryland, Neil Ratliff Music Library, College Park, MD; Kenneth G. Fiske Museum of the Claremont Colleges, Claremont, CA; Miles Musical Museum, Eureka Springs, AR; Museum of the American Piano, New York, NY; Museum of Musical Instruments, St. Paul, MN; Musical Museum, Deansboro, NY; Streitwieser Foundation Trumpet Museum, Pottstown, PA; University of Michigan, Stearns Collection of Musical Instruments, Ann Arbor, MI; Yale University Collection of Musical Instruments, New Haven, CT.

Banjo, five-string
　Morrison, James, nickel sheathed
　laminated wood pot, 24-bracket
　nickel-plated tension rim,

mahogany neck, 12-3/16" d head, labeled on dowel stick "Jas Morrison, Maker," on pot "James M. Morrison, 304 West 36th St., NY, Patent Applied For, No. 1"..**460.00**

Stewart, S. S., Philadelphia, labeled "Universal Favorite," 1905..**290.00**

Clarinet, English

Gerock & Wolf, London, 19th C, boxwood, six keys, ivory fittings, brass sq covered keys **230.00**

Meteler & Co., boxwood, eight round covered keys, brass fittings, loss to bell....................**220.00**

Clarinet, French, Buffet, Paris, ebony, nickel keys and fittings, with case **350.00**

Coronet, English, silver plated, stamped "F. Besson, Brevetee...," with case **320.00**

Fife, American

Meacham & Co., Albany, maple, brass fittings, case **320.00**

Pond & Co., Albany, 19th C, maple, carved, brass fittings.....**815.00**

Flute, American

Haynes, William S., Co., Boston, 1911, Grenadilla, open G key **1,100.00**

Hopkins, Asa, Litchfield, CT, 19th C, four keys, boxwood, ivory fittings, silver round covered keys, ivoroid repair to fittings **490.00**

Peloubet, C., five keys, rosewood, round key covers........**550.00**

Penzel & Muelkler, blackwood, nickel keys, case **460.00**

Coelophone Orchestra, French organette, cardboard music books, original table, c1900, **$3,925.** *Photo courtesy of Auction Team Breker.*

Phaff, John, Philadelphia, 19th C, faintly stamped "J. Phaff...," eight keys, rosewood, silver fittings, period case **1,265.00**

Flute, English

Binkes, L., 19th C, nine keys, rosewood, silver fittings and keys **750.00**

Cubitt, W. D., & Son, London, 19th C, blackwood, open and nickel covered case, case **690.00**

Monzani, London, 19th C, eight keys, head with turned reeding, silver fittings, round covered keys **200.00**

Rudall Carte & Co., London, silver, multiple stamps, hallmarks, case **750.00**

Wrede, H., London, c1840, four keys, stained boxwood, ivory fittings, silver round cover keys, case **320.00**

Guitar, archtop

D'Angelico, John, Model New York, irregular curl maple two-piece back, medium curl sides, medium grain with cross-bracing top, medium curl neck, bound peghead with inlaid pearl D'Angelico logo, bound ebony fingerboard with split-block pearl inlay, stamped internally "D'Angelico, New York, 1808," 21-7/16" l back, 18-1/2" w bottom bout, 1947 .....**13,800.00**

Gibson Inc., Model Super 300, labeled "Gibson Super Style '300,' Number ???? is hereby guaranteed, Gibson, Inc., Kalamazoo, Michigan, USA," c1950, with case **1, 380.00**

Gibson Inc., Model Super 400, irregular curl maple two-piece maple back, medium curl sides, spruce top with medium grain, light medium curl neck, inlaid pearl Gibson logo peghead with split-diamond design, bound fingerboard with split-block pearl inlay, natural finish, labeled "Gibson Super Style 400, Number EA-5309 is hereby guaranteed, Gibson Inc., Kalamazoo, Michigan, USA," 21-7/8" l back, 17-13/16" w lower bout, c1939, with orig hard shell case and cover ...**14,950.00**

Guitar, classical

Bazzolo, Thomas, three-piece rosewood back, similar sides, spruce top of fine grain fully bound, mahogany neck, ebony fingerboard, labeled "Thomas

Bazzolo, Luthier #65C24, 1994, Lebanon, Connecticut, USA," and sgd, 18-15/16" l back, 14-1/8" w lower bout, with case **750.00**

Chica, Manuel de la, two-piece Brazilian rosewood back, labeled "Manuel De La Chica, Constructore, De, Violines Y Guitarras, Placeta De La Silleria 8, Granada, Ano De 1966," 19-1/4" l back **1,725.00**

Martin, C. F., Style D-35, three-piece Indian rosewood back, similar sides, spruce top of fine to medium grain, mahogany neck with bound ebony fingerboard, inlaid pearl eyes, stamped internally "CF Martin & Co., Nazareth, PA, Made in USA, D-35," 1975 ....**1,475.00**

Fischesser, Leon, narrow curl two-piece back, similar ribs and scroll, fine grain top, red color varnish, labeled "Leon Fischesser Luthier D'Art, No. 47, 28 Faubuorg Poissonniere Paris L'Anno 1907," 14" l back, 356 mm, with case **2,760.00**

Nicolas, Didier, Mirecourt, narrow curl one-piece back, similar ribs and scroll, fine to medium grain top, red color varnish, stamped internally "A La Ville De Cremonne, Dn, D Nicholas Aime," 14-1/4" l back, 360 mm, with case and bow **1,955.00**

Violin, German, D'Amore, faint curl on one-piece back, irregular curl ribs, later carved scroll of narrow curl, fine grain top, brown color varnish, unlabeled, c 1780, 13-3/8" l back, 339 mm, case, ivory mounted period bow ...**4,150.00**

Violin, Hungarian, medium curl two-piece back, similar ribs, medium curl scroll, fine grain top, red color varnish, labeled "Janos Spiegel, Budapest, 1907," 14-1/16" l back, 358 mm, with case **6,620.00**

Violin, Italian

Attributed to Andrea Postacchini, narrow curl one-piece back, irregular curl ribs, faint curl scroll, fine grain top, golden brown color varnish, labeled "Andreas Postacchini Amieie Filius Fecit Firmi Anno 1819, Opus 11?," 14" l back, 356 mm, with case, accompanied by bill of sale **17,250.00**

Bisiach, Giacomo, and Leandro, medium curl two-piece back, similar ribs and scroll, fine grain

top, amber color varnish, labeled "Giacomo Leandro Bisiach, Fecero in Milano L'Anno 1961," sgd, 14" l back, 356 mm, with case
.... **12,650.00**

Bisiach, Leandro, strong medium curl two-piece back, strong narrow curl ribs and scroll, fine grain top, golden brown color varnish, labeled "Leandro Bisiach Da Milano, Fece L'Anno 1942," sgd, 14" l back, 356 mm, with case, undated numbered certificate
.... **18,400.00**

Oddone, Carlo, strong medium curl one-piece back, similar ribs, narrow curl scroll, fine to medium curl grain top, orange color varnish, labeled "Carlo Giuseppe Oddone, 235 Fece Torino A 1930," stamped "C. Oddone, Torino" at lower rib and upper and lower interior blocks, sgd on int. of top, 14-1/16" l back, 357 mm
.... **39,100.00**

Rovatti, Luigi, irregular narrow curl two-piece back, irregular curl ribs, narrow curl scroll, fine grain top, brown color varnish, labeled "Luigi Rovatti, Liutista, Buenos Aires-1922, ???, Kind 324," c1927, 14-1/16" l back, 357 mm, with case
.... **11,500.00**

Violin, Mittenwald, Klotz School, medium curl two-piece back, similar ribs and scroll, fine grain top, brown color varnish, unlabeled, c1780, 13-7/8" l back, 353 mm, with case
.... **2,415.00**

"Steinway & Sons Patent Grand, New York," worn ebonized finish, gilt label, turned and reeded legs, Eastlake carving, ebony and ivory keyboard, cracked soundboard, 1885, 54" w, 71" l, $1,100. Photo courtesy of Garth's Auctions, Inc.

Violin, Vienna, Thomas Zach, strong curl two-piece back, similar ribs, plain scroll, medium grain top, golden brown color varnish, labeled "Thomas Zach KK Priv, Geigen Macher Beb 1829T Z, Gemach ??? Wien 1887," 13-15/16" l back, 354 mm........... **4,025.00**

Violin bow, gold mounted

Ouchard, Emile, round stick stamped "Emile Ouchard" at butt, ebony frog with Parisian eye, plain gold adjuster, 63 grams . **4,025.00**

Seifert, Lothar, octagonal stick stamped "Lothar Seifert" at butt, ebony frog with Parisian eye, gold and ebony adjuster, 61 grams
.... **1,265.00**

Taylor, Malcolm, octagonal stick stamped "Malcolm M. Taylor" at butt, ebony frog with Parisian eye, gold and ebony adjuster, 61 grams
.... **1,035.00**

Unstamped, octagonal stick, later frog engraved "A. Vigneron A Paris 1886," 59 grams **1,485.00**

Violin bow, silver mounted

Hill, W. E., round stick stamped "W. E. Hill & Sons" at butt, ebony eye with Parisian eye, plain silver adjuster, 60 grams, baleen wrap
.... **2,530.00**

Morizot, Louis, French, round stick stamped "L. Morizot" at butt, ebony frog with Parisian eye, plain silver adjuster, 60.5 grams **2,300.00**

Nurnberger, Albert, octagonal stick stamped "Albert Nurnberger" at butt, "Saxony" under plain ebony frog, silver and ebony adjuster, 61 grams **1,265.00**

Peccatte, Charles, round stick stamped "Peccatte" at butt, ebony frog with Parisian eye, plain silver adjuster, 60.5 grams, with certificate from Kenneth Warren & Son, Chicago........ **18,400.00**

Pfretzchner Workshop, round stick stamped "H. R. Pfretzchner" at butt, stamped with maker's mark on the frog, plain ebony frog, silver and ebony adjuster, 57 grams
.... **2,100.00**

Unstamped, French, round stick, ebony frog with pearl eye, silver and ebony adjuster, 60 grams
.... **2,300.00**

Unstamped, French, Francois-Nicolas Voirin, c1860, round stick, ebony frog with pearl eye, later silver and ebony adjuster, 63 grams **4,890.00**

Weichold, Richard, octagonal stick stamped "R. Weichold A. Dresden" and "Imitation De Tourte" at butt, ebony frog with pearl eye, silver and ebony adjuster, 56 grams
.... **1,265.00**

Violoncello, America

Settin, Joseph, strong narrow curl two-piece back, similar ribs and scroll, fine to medium grain top, golden brown color varnish, labeled "Joseph Settin Venetus, Fecit Anno Domani 1953," 29-7/16" l back, 748 mm **8,100.00**

Violoncello, child's, plain one-piece back, similar ribs and scroll, medium curl top, brown color varnish, possibly Italian, 22-13/16" l back, 581 mm
.... **3,795.00**

Violoncello, Czech, two-piece medium curl back, similar ribs and scroll similar, medium curl top, red color varnish, labeled "CAK Dvorni, A Armadni Dodvatel, Preniceska Tovarna Nastrouju Na Morave, Joseflidil V Brne Zelny Irh 11," 30-3/16" l back, 767 mm . **3,795.00**

Violoncello, English, James and Henry Banks, narrow curl two-piece back, medium curl ribs, faint curl scroll, fine to medium grain top, red color varnish, sgd internally on table, "James and Henry Banks, Salisbury," c1800, 28-34" l back, 729 mm **18,400.00**

Violoncello, French

Brevetee, F. Breton, medium curl two-piece back, narrow curl ribs, plain scroll, medium grain top, amber color varnish, labeled "F. Breton Brevetee De Smg, Me La Duchesse D'Angouleme, A Mirecourt 1851 Breton, France," 29-15/16" l back, 760 mm
.... **2,760.00**

Gand, Francois Eugene, one-piece narrow curl back, similar ribs and scroll, medium grain top, red color varnish, labeled "Gand, Luthier De La Muisque Du Roi, E Du Conservatoire De Musique, Rue Croix De Petits Champs No. 24, Paris, 1845, 113," 14-1/16" l back, 357 mm, with case..... **13,800.00**

Thibouville-Lamy, Jerome, narrow curl two-piece back, similar ribs, medium curl scroll, medium to wide grain top, orange color varnish, labeled "Jerome Thibouville-Lamy, 70 Rue Reaumur, Paris, 1938," 29-3/4" l back, 756 mm, with case
.... **3,795.00**

Violoncello, German, irregular narrow curl two-piece back, similar ribs, narrow curl scroll, medium to wide grain top, orange color varnish, labeled "Erich Grunert, Penzberg Anno 1976," 29-3/4" l back, 756 mm, with case **1,150.00**

Violoncello bow, nickel plated, round stick stamped "L. Bausch, Leipzig," 81 grams **1,840.00**

MUSIC BOXES

History: Music boxes, invented in Switzerland around 1825, encompass a broad array of forms, from small boxes to huge circus calliopes.

A cylinder box consists of a comb with teeth which vibrate when striking a pin in the cylinder. The music these boxes produce ranges from light tunes to opera and overtures.

The first disc music box was invented by Paul Lochmann of Leipzig, Germany, in 1886. It used an interchangeable steel disc with pierced holes bent to a point which hit the star-wheel as the disc revolved, and thus produced the tune. Discs were easily stamped out of metal, allowing a single music box to play an endless variety of tunes. Disc boxes reached the height of their popularity from 1890 to 1910, when the phonograph replaced them.

Music boxes also were incorporated in many items, e.g., clocks, sewing and jewelry boxes, steins, plates, toys, perfume bottles, and furniture.

References: Gilbert Bahl, *Music Boxes*, Courage Books, Running Press, 1993; Arthur W. J. G. Ord-Hume, *Musical Box*, Schiffer Publishing, 1995.

Collectors' Clubs: Music Box Society of Great Britain, P.O. Box 299, Waterbeach, Cambridge CB4 4DJ England, http://www.mbsgb.org.uk; Musical Box Society International, P.O. Box 297, Marietta, OH 45750, http://www.mbsi.org.

Museum: Lockwood Matthews Mansion Museum, Norwalk, CT.

Additional Listings: See *Warman's Americana & Collectibles* for more examples.

Black Forest, 37" h, carved and inlaid walnut chair form, two air movement in seat, tune list **980.00**

Bremond, 23" w, No. 2630, 13" cylinder with bird strikers, nine bells, plays eight airs, veneered and inlaid case **3,680.00**

Cellesta, 8-1/4" disc, single-comb ratchet-wind mechanism, walnut case with bone inlaid top and color print in lid, 16 discs **980.00**

Eight-Air, 15" w, 4-1/2" nickeled cylinder and tune indicator, grained case **375.00**

Lecoulture, D., 17" l, 8-1/4" cylinder, plays four airs, plain case . . . **1,100.00**

Match striker, 9" h, gilt cast metal figure of man holding his chamber pot out

window, strike-plate activating two-air movement playing "Dixie" and "La Marsille". **635.00**

Mermod Freres

19-3/4" w, 7-1/2" cylinder, No. 67089, coin operated, plays two airs, tune card, Jacot safety check and coin mechanism, plain case . . . **980.00**

30" w, 13-1/2" cylinder, plays 12 airs, crank-wind motor, tune selector/indicator, grained case with veneered and inlaid front and lid, inner lid and divisions replaced **1,495.00**

Polyphon No. 102, 15-1/4" d metal discs, c1900, $3,450. Photo courtesy of Auction Team Breker.

Olympia

No. 2, 11-5/8" disc, single-comb movement and chromo print in lid, lacking discs and winding handle **815.00**

No. 6566, 20-1/2" upright disc, twin-comb mechanism, disengaged coin slide, manual control, two-piece mahogany cabinet, side disc storage, 32 discs, sounding boards replaced, 70" h **6,900.00**

Paillard, tune card

23" l, No. 29443, 13" cylinder, plays eight operatic and other airs, piccolo-zither, zither attachment,

grained case with veneered and inlaid front and lid **1,610.00**

23-1/2" l, No. 48375, 13" cylinder, plays 10 dance and other airs, tune indicator, tune card, grained case with inlaid lid **2,300.00**

29" l, No. 70288, 13" cylinder, plays 10 airs, nickeled movement double-spring machine, tune selector and indicator, piccolo-zither, zither attachment, grained case with inlaid lid, incomplete tune card, one tooth off, lacking interior lid **1,380.00**

34" l, No. 32378, Excelsior Interchangeable, three 9-1/4" cylinders, plays eight airs each, double-spring motor, tune indicator and zither attachment, grained case, torn tune card, veneered and inlaid front and lid, cylinder drawer in plinth **3,750.00**

36" w, 17" cylinder, No. 41738/39235, plays eight operatic airs by Verdi, Chopin, Rosetti, and others, double-spring motor, tune selector and indicator, grained case with inlaid lid, fitted Aesthetic Movement ebonized table with incised gilt dec **5,750.00**

Polychon, No. 27498, 15-1/2" disc, twin comb movement, coin slide, walnut case with bobbin turned corner columns, paneled and inlaid top, monochrome print in lid, disc storage drawer in plinth, 36 zinc disks, 24" w **460.00**

Regina

No. 13632, 15-1/2" disc, coin operated, twin-comb mechanism, coin slide, oak case with rope twist and egg and dart molding, instruction label, Murray, Sping & Co. Providence, RI, retailer's label, oak table with bobbin-turned legs, brass claw feet, 22 discks, 38" h **3,450.00**

No. 13286, 15-1/2" disc, twin-comb mechanism, oak case with rope twist molding, Myron J. Adams, Troy, NY, retailer's label, 12 discs **3,750.00**

No. 14225, 15-1/2" disc, twin-comb mechanism, mahogany case with paneled lid, rope twist molding, stand with two pull-out shelves, disc storage compartment enclosed by double doors, 100 zinc discs, print replaced, 42-1/2" h **5,465.00**

No. 55426, 15-1/2" disc, twin-comb movement, oak case with engaged corner columns, bone stringing, domed lid with monochrome print, 30 discs **5,175.00**

No. 67095, 12-1/4" disc, single-comb movement, mahogany case with orig price tag, monochrome print, domed lid, 32 discs, main spring defective **2,100.00**

Singing bird

3-3/4" w, blue enameled case, ivory beak, moving wings and perch, lid with Alpine scene and floral spray **2,645.00**

4" w, silver plated, serpentine front and sides, cast with views of country scenes, leather traveling case, bird detached and featherless **815.00**

10" h, tinplate, spinning bird, flapping wings, bellows operated song, German **215.00**

11" h, brass, moving head, circular base **420.00**

Unknown maker

5" w, 2-1/2" cylinder, No. 6215, plays two airs, rosewood case, brass, ivory, and kingwood inlaid lid **200.00**

5-3/8" w, 4" d, 6-5/8" h, morocco covered case formed as upright piano, plays march and air, hinged lid enclosing ivory and ebonized keys with starting latch, mirrored backplate, fitted with two glass perfume bottles, four-piece cut-steel manicure set, Continental, late 19th C **550.00**

8" l, automation, fabric covered cabbage, central white fur covered head of rabbit, glass eyes, plays one air as rabbit emerges from cabbage and moves ears, Continental, late 19th C **550.00**

14-1/4" w, 4-1/2" cylinder, No. 19560, plays six airs, two bells, tune card, inlaid lid **490.00**

21-1/2" w, 11" cylinder, six bells, plays eight airs, optional engine turned bells, veneered case **1,380.00**

Unknown Swiss maker

16" l, 10-1/4" d, 8-1/2" h, 6-1/4" cylinder, plays eight airs, drum with five strikers, tune card, rect case inlaid to hinged lid with central cartouche of drum and pipes, line banding throughout, bracket feet, late 19th C **2,425.00**

24-5/8" l, 12-3/8" w, 10-1/4" h, 15" cylinder, plays 12 airs, engine-turned bells, tune card, rect case inlaid to hinged lid with central brass and mother-of-pearl cartouche, bracket feet, late 19th C **2,645.00**

Swiss, by Charles Ullmann, c1880, orchestrion type, $3,925. Photo courtesy of Auction Team Breker.

NAILSEA-TYPE GLASS

History: Nailsea-type glass is characterized by swirls and loopings, usually white, on a clear or colored ground. One of the first areas where this glass was made was Nailsea, England, 1788-1873, hence the name. Several glass houses, including American factories, made this type of glass.

Fairy lamp, citron, shaped shade, bowl-shaped base, clear candle cup signed "S. Clarke Patent Trade Mark Fairy," 5-1/2" d, 5" h, $985. Photo courtesy of Clarence and Betty Maier.

Bell, 11-3/4" h, white, rose loopings **95.00**

Bottle, 8" h, gemel, flattened ovoid body, two necks, white casing, red, white, and blue loopings **400.00**

Candlestick, 10" h, colorless, white loopings, folded socket rim, hollow blown socket drawn out to a double knop, bulb shaped stem, two additional knops, inverted cone-shaped base, early 19th C **375.00**

Fairy lamp

   5-1/4" h, 6-1/4" d, frosted blue, opaque white loopings, colorless Clarke insert **695.00**

   6-1/2" h, red, sweeping white loops, dome-shaped shade, ruffled triangular base, colorless glass candle cup with ruffled edge, orig "Price's Royal Castle Night Light" candle **985.00**

Flask

   3-1/2" l, flattened ovoid, clear glass with red and white spirals, 19th C **300.00**

   7-1/4" h, broad oval form, ruby red ground, white herringbone-type

loopings, applied double-collared mouth, pontil scar. **400.00**

   7-3/4" h, pocket, elongated teardrop form, milk glass ground, blue and rose loopings, sheared mouth, pontil scar. **300.00**

   8-3/4" h, pocket, teardrop form, teal green, profuse white loopings, sheared mouth, pontil scar **240.00**

Lamp, 11-1/2" h, colorless ground, pink and white loopings on font and ruffled shade, applied colorless feet, berry prunt **2,500.00**

Pitcher, 6-1/2" h, 4" d, colorless ground, white loopings, ftd, solid applied base, triple ribbed solid handle with curled end, flaring formed mouth, attributed to South Jersey, c1840-60 . . . . . .**1,200.00**

Rolling pin, 13-3/4" l, freeblown, rose and white loopings, colorless ground, ground mouth, smooth base, 1850-80 . . . .**220.00**

Tumbler, white ground, blue loopings **120.00**

Vase, 8" h, 5" d, cylindrical, flared mouth and base, colorless, white loopings, plain sheared rim, pontil, attributed to South Jersey **195.00**

Witch ball, 4-3/8" d, white ground, pink and blue loopings **450.00**

NANKING

History: Nanking is a type of Chinese porcelain made in Canton, China, from the early 1800s into the 20th century. It was made for export to America and England.

Four elements help distinguish Nanking from Canton, two similar types of ware. Nanking has a spear-and-post border, as opposed to the scalloped-line style of Canton. Second, in the water's edge or Willow pattern, Canton usually has no figures; Nanking includes a standing figure with open umbrella on the bridge. In addition, the blues tend to be darker on the Nanking ware. Finally, Nanking wares often are embellished with gold; Canton is not.

Green and orange variations of Nanking survive, although they are scarce.

> **Reproduction Alert:** Copies of Nanking ware currently are being produced in China. They are of inferior quality and decorated in a lighter, rather than in the darker, blues.

Bowl, 10" d, shaped, 19th C . . .**880.00**

Candlesticks, pr, 9-1/2" h **775.00**

Cider jug, 10" h, gilt highlights, 19th C, pr **825.00**

Cup and saucer, handleless, 3-3/4" h cup, 5-3/4" d saucer, pagodas, man on bridge, c1780-1820 . . . .**235.00**

Platter, 11-1/2" x 14-1/2", $345.

Ewer, 11" h, small spout, blue and white, mid-19th C **300.00**

Pitcher, cov, 9-1/2" h, blue and white, Liverpool shape **550.00**

Plate, 9-1/2" d, water's edge scene, c1780-1800 . . . .**85.00**

Platter, 12-3/4" l, Chinese, 19th C, chips **415.00**

Posset pot, blue and white, intertwined handle, mismatched lid with gilded fruit finial **100.00**

Rice bowl, 19th C **100.00**

Salad bowl, 10" h, 19th C . . .**1,200.00**

Soup bowl, 9-1/2" d, pagodas, man on bridge, islands, and horse, c1840-60 . . . .**240.00**

Soup tureen, cov, 11-3/4" h, 19th C, imperfections **475.00**

Teapot, 6-1/2" h, globular, diaper border above watery pagoda landscape reserve **125.00**

Tray, 9-3/4" l, 19th C **500.00**

NAPKIN RINGS, FIGURAL

History: Gracious home dining during the Victorian era required a personal napkin ring for each household member. Figural napkin rings were first patented in 1869. During the remainder of the 19th century, most plating companies, including Cromwell, Eureka, Meriden, and Reed and Barton, manufactured figural rings, many copying and only slightly varying the designs of other companies.

Reference: Lillian Gottschalk and Sandra Whitson, *Figural Napkin Rings*, Collector Books, 1996.

Reproduction Alert: Quality reproductions do exist.

Additional Listings: See *Warman's Americana & Collectibles* for a listing of non-figural napkin rings.

Notes: Values are determined by the subject matter of the ring, the quality of the workmanship, and the condition.

Chick and egg, engraved "Best Wishes," Derby Silver, Birmingham, CT, 3-1/2" w, 2-1/4" h, **$190.**

Barrel on stand, 1-3/4" l, 3" h, silverplate **90.00**
Baby, seated, arms extended, Pairpoint #52, resilvered **650.00**
Bird, wings spread over nest of eggs **175.00**
Boy, sitting on bench, holding drumstick **200.00**
Brownie, climbing up side of ring, Palmer Cox **185.00**
Butterfly, perched on pair of fans **125.00**
Cat, glass eyes, ring on back . . **270.00**
Cherries, stems, leaf base, ball feet **90.00**
Cherub, sitting cross legged on base, candleholder and ring combination **195.00**
Chicken, nesting beside ring . . **150.00**

Child, crawling, ring on back . . . **300.00**
Dog, sitting next to barrel-shaped ring, sgd "Tufts, #1531" **125.00**
Double eagle, marked "Meriden" **85.00**
Double rifles, Meriden B. #235 . **850.00**
Dutch Boy, pulling on boots, resilvered **110.00**
Frog, holding drumstick, pushing drum-like ring **300.00**
Girl carrying basket, #734 . . . . **795.00**
Goat, pulling wheeled flower cart **250.00**
Horse, standing next to elaborate ring **185.00**
Kate Greenaway, girl with muff on one side, dog on other, Derby #514, resilvered **875.00**
Owl, sitting on leafy base, owls perched on upper limbs **250.00**
Parrot, on wheels, Simpson, Hall, Miller & Co. **185.00**
Rabbit, sitting alertly next to ring **175.00**
Ring on lotus flowers and pads, silverplate **100.00**
Sailor boy, anchor **220.00**
Schoolboy with books, feeding begging puppy **235.00**
Sphinx, Rogers & Bros. **750.00**
Square, monogrammed, marked "W" in oval, pierced by arrow **125.00**
Turtle, crawling, ornate ring on back **300.00**

NASH GLASS

History: Nash glass is a type of art glass attributed to Arthur John Nash and his sons, Leslie H. and A. Douglas. Arthur John Nash, originally employed by Webb in Stourbridge, England, came to America and was employed in 1889 by Tiffany Furnaces at its Corona, Long Island, plant.

While managing the plant for Tiffany, Nash designed and produced iridescent glass. In 1928, A. Douglas Nash purchased the facilities of Tiffany Furnaces. The A. Douglas Nash Corporation remained in operation until 1931.

Bowl, 7-3/4" x 2-1/2", Jewel pattern, gold phantom luster **285.00**
Candlestick, 4" h, Chintz , ruby and gray, sgd **450.00**
Compote, 7-1/2" d, 4-1/2" h, Chintz, transparent aquamarine, wide flat rim of red and gray-green controlled stripe dec, base inscribed "Nash RD89" **865.00**
Cordial, 5-1/2" h, Chintz, green and blue **95.00**

Dish, iridescent gold, blue-green, etched grape leaves and vines, marked "Nash 569 C-1," 5-3/8" d, 1/2" h, **$315.**

Creamer and sugar, 5-3/8" h creamer, 3-1/2" h sugar, blue-green opaque dots, dark blue-green base, creamer with polished pontil, sugar with waffle pontil **475.00**
Goblet, 6-3/4" h, feathered leaf motif, gilt dec, sgd **295.00**
Plate, 8" d, Chintz, green and blue **195.00**
Sherbet, bluish-gold texture, ftd, sgd, #417 . . . . **275.00**
Vase

5-1/2" h, Chintz, pastel, transparent oval, internally striped with pastel orange alternating with yellow chintz dec **275.00**

Monkey, dressed, standing next to ring, oval base, Derby Silver Co., #828, **$250.**

Vase, irid blue, marked "B526 Nash," 5-1/2" h, **$625.**

9" h, Polka Dot, deep opaque red oval, molded with prominent 16 ribs, dec by spaced white opal dots, base inscribed "Nash GD154" **1,100.00**

11" h, floriform trumpet, gold irid surface with light texture, blue, green, and pink highlights, sgd "Nash 538" in polished pontil **1,250.00**

NAUTICAL ITEMS

History: The seas have fascinated man since time began. The artifacts of sailors have been collected and treasured for years. Because of their environment, merchant and naval items, whether factory or handmade, must be of quality construction and long lasting. Many of these items are aesthetically appealing as well.

References: E. H. H. Archibald, *The Dictionary of Sea Painters of Europe and America,* Antique Collectors' Club, 1999; Donald F. Kuhlstrom, *Sunday Sailors: A Beginner's Guide to Pond Boats & Model Yachting Until the 1950s,* Turner Publications, 1998; J. Welles Henderson, *Marine Art & Antiques,* Antique Collectors' Club, 1999; David Joel, *Charles Brooking and the 18th Century British Marine Painters,* Antique Collectors' Club, 1999.

Periodicals and Internet Resources: *Lighthouse Digest,* P.O. Box 1690, Wells, ME 04090, http://www.lhdigest.com; *Mother of All Maritime Links,* http://www.boat-links.com; *Nautical Brass Online,* http://wwwhome.earthlink.net/~nbrass1/ezine.html; *Nautical Collector,* 1 Whale Oil Row, New London, CT 06320; *Nautical Research Guild,* http://www.naut-Res-Guild.org.

Collectors' Clubs: Air Horn & Steam Whistle Enthusiasts, 275 Windswept Dr., North East, PA 16428; Historical Diving Society USA, 3022 Cliff Dr., #405, Santa Barbara, CA 93109, http:/www.hds.org; Lighthouse Preservation Society, 4 Middle St., Newburyport, MA 01950, http://www.mayday.com/pls; National Maritime Historical Society, 5 John Walsh Blvd., Peekskill, NY 10566, http://www.seahistory.org; Nautical Research Guild, 71 Chestnut St., Wellsville, NY 14895, http://www.naut-Res-Guild.org; New England Lighthouse Foundation, P.O. Box 1690, Wells, ME 04090, http://www.lhdigest.com; Rocky Mountain Shipwrights, 8046 Lee Court, Arvada, CO 80005; Ships in Bottles Assoc. of America, P.O. Box 180550, Coronado, CA 92178; United States Lighthouse Society, 244 Kearney St., 5th Floor, San Francisco, CA 94108, http://www.maine.com/lights/uslhs.html.

Museums: Chesapeake Bay Maritime Museum, Saint Michaels, MD; Mariners' Museum, Newport News, VA; Maritime Museum of Monterey, Monterey, CA; Museum of Science and Industry, Chicago, IL; Mystic Seaport Museum, Mystic, CT; Peabody Museum of Salem, Salem, MA; San Francisco Maritime National Historical Park, San Francisco, CA; U.S. Naval Academy Museum, Naval Academy, MD.

Souvenir plank, book shape, carved "In Memory of the Eurydyce Sunk, March 24, 1878," 3-1/4" h, **$95.**

Account book, *Bark Arab,* showing purchases and sales from October 1853 to December 1856, 96 pgs, folio, New Bedford or Hawaii, label reads "purchased of John Kehew at his Navigation Store in New Bedford," Kehew's label mounted on front paste down, two volumes **1,955.00**

Account sheet, financial account for return of bark *Charles W. Morgan,* eight pgs, folio, New Bedford, 1880-93 . . . . **750.00**

Book

Allyn, Captain Gurdon L., *Old Sailor's Story, or a Short Account of the Life, Adventures, and Voyages, The,* Norwich, 1879, 111 pgs, 8vo, orig flexible cloth wrappers . **316.00**

Bennett, Frank M., *Steam Navy of the United States, The,* Pittsburgh, 1896, 8vo **195.00**

Bligh, William, *Dangerous Voyage of Captain Bligh, in an Open Boat, over 1200 Leagues of the Ocean, in the Year 1789,* Dublin, 1818, five full-page woodcut engraved illus, 180 pgs, small 12mo **345.00**

Dexter, Elisha, *Narrative of the Loss of the William and Joseph, of Martha's Vineyard,* Boston, 1842, five wood engraved plates, 54 pgs, 8vo **1,370.00**

Dix, William, *Wreck of the Glide, with an Account of Life and Manners in the Fiji Islands,* Boston, 1846, 122 pgs, 12 mo **290.00**

Little, Captain George, *American Cruiser's Own Book, The,* New York, 1846, carved wooden binding, ships, paddle-wheeler, and inscribed "Capt JC Pease Oswego 1874," price for eight volumes **920.00**

Flags of the Maritime Nations, Washington, 1870, second edition, 18 plates, gilt Morocco, rubbed **75.00**

Box, cov, 4-3/4" h, 12" l, 6-5/9" d, walnut, dovetailed, ropework handle, polyhedron carved terminals, attributed to New England sailor, early 19th C, one terminal missing **460.00**

Broadside, 415 x 335 mm, issued as circular to mariners at Table Bay, Robben Island, advising of berthing procedures, 1827 . . . . **345.00**

Canoe paddle, 60" l, painted deep red with black crescent moon and star, America, late 19th C, with stand **375.00**

Children's book

Adventures of Jack, or a Life on the Wave, The, Charles L. Newhall, Southbridge, 1859, 134 pgs, 12 mo **230.00**

On the Seas, a Book for Boys, Boston, c1875, plates, small 8vo **130.00**

Papa's Log or a Voyage to Rio de Janerio, Grant and Griffith, London, 1845, hand-colored illus, 28 pgs, small 4to **632.00**

Chronometer

7-1/2" h, 6-3/4" w, 6-3/4" d, "Morris Tobias, London, Maker to the Admiralty 31 Minories London," c1825, gimbal mounted in brass fitted rosewood case, brass bezel with silver wash dial **1,495.00**

8-1/2" h, 8-1/4" w, 8-1/4" d, "M.F. Dent, 33 Cockspur St. Chronometer Maker to the Queen, London," late 19th C, gimbal mounted in brass fitted mahogany case, brass bezel, silver wash dial, eight days **5,175.00**

Clock, 10-1/2" h, brass, Seth Thomas, one-day lever-striking movement, circular case, domed bell mounted below on wooden backboard, late 19th C. **520.00**

Compass, lifeboat, 8" sq, 7-1/4" h, boxed, 20th C. **175.00**

Crew list, partly printed, two languages, *Jireh Swift,* lists 13 additional Hawaiian crew members, Lahaina, March 29, 1865 . . . . **2,000.00**

Diorama, 32-1/2" w, 23" h, black, red, and green sailing ship, white sails, lighthouse and other sailing ships painted into background, gesso frame with old gold repaint **1,450.00**

Figurehead, 30" h, carved, Nantucket Island origin, c1830 . . . . **12,000.00**

Hooked rug, 43" sq, Mariner's Compass, center compass in black, white, pink, and blue, variegated ground, mounted on wooden stretcher, some edge loss, fading **575.00**

Hat, French officer's, black felt, silver thread and fabric, white feather plume, original travel case, c1812, 17" l, 11" h, $300.

Hourglass, 7" h, 19th C **550.00**

Inclinometer, 4-1/2" d, brass, cased, bubble type, Kelvin Bottomley & Baird Ltd. **65.00**

Journal, Daniel S. Emmerton of Salem, crewman serving on the *Horsburgh* from March 1852 to March 1853, 146 pgs, folio **1,610.00**

Ladle, 9-5/8" l, carved coconut shell, ivory handle, carved eagle, animals, ornaments, and foliate devices, 19th C, cracks **125.00**

Log book, two masted brig *Smyrna,* belonging to Ezra Weston of Duxbury, series of voyages between April 1848 and March 1854, kept by Captain Stephen Sprague, 290 pgs, folio, two volumes **635.00**

Masthead, 16" h, 9-1/2" d, copper and brass, oil fired, complete with burner, 360 degrees, late 19th C **200.00**

Model, painted wood
　16-1/2" h, 20-1/2" l, three-masted schooner, late 19th/20th C, shadowbox frame, repainted **575.00**
　21" h, 34" l, *Elia,* mounted in shadowbox frame, losses. **2,185.00**
　29-1/2" h, gig *Red Rover*. . . **2,185.00**
　37" h, 54" l, *Glory of the Seas,* full-rigged, 20th C, minor imperfections **1,725.00**

77-1/2" l, Chesapeake Bay Skip Jack *Carrie Price,* early 20th C, imperfections **3,795.00**

Navigational lesson book, 12" x 7-1/2", Benjamin Holt, Boston, 1834, watercolor illus of ships, architectural renderings, front papered board detached. . **865.00**

Oar, 57-1/2" l, curly maple, well carved, thin broad end, good figure **420.00**

Painting, watercolor, gouache, and graphite on paper, 9-7/8" x 13-1/4", steamer *Franconia,* A Bragg Commander, sgd "A. F. Olson" lower right, identified on pennant and in lower margin, framed, some tear in upper margin, staining, overall toning **2,760.00**

Print, lithograph on paper
　Bark Catalpa of New Bedford, 1876, The Forbes Lithograph Manufacturing Co., publishers, E. N. Russell, lithographer, identified in inscriptions in matrix, 10-3/4" x 16-3/4" image size, framed, overall toning **550.00**
　View of the Stone Fleet Which Sailed From New Bedford Nov. 16th, 1861, Louis Prang & Co., lithographer and publisher, after Benjamin Russell, identified in inscriptions in matrix, hand coloring, 16-1/2" x 25" image size, framed, repaired tears/punctures, creases, fox marks, toning . **865.00**

Quadrant, ebony, cased, marked "D Booth" and "New Zealand" **330.00**

Sailmaker's kit, 17" l, orig bag with various tools, ornate ropework ties, 19th C **350.00**

Sailor's valentine, 9-5/8" octagonal segmented case, various exotic shells, "For My Love," 19th C, very minor losses **750.00**

Sailor's whimsey, 7" h, carved wood, round nut pierced with diamond- and heart-shaped openings, surmounted by bird finial. **525.00**

Sea chest, 36" w, 19" d, 16-3/4" h, six-board dovetailed construction, painted red, canted sides, flat carved pink painted becket handles, Wiscasset, Maine, early 19th C . **980.00**

Shadow box, 48" l, 25-1/4" h, carved model of three masted ship *Big Bonanza,* painted black and white, tugboat painted black, white, red, and yellow, America, 19th C **1,610.00**

Ship in bottle, 12-1/2" l, 4-3/4" w, 4" h, carved and painted, paper label inscribed "Clipper Ship Flying Cloud record: 89 days New York-San Francisco," mounted on mahogany stand, bottle and stand dec with sailor's woven and painted rope work, America, 19th C **635.00**

Ship model, 31" l, 9-1/4" w, US Frigate *Constitution,* wood, America, 20th C **1,955.00**

Telescope, 32-3/4" l, silver plated, one draw, Troughton & Simms, London, mid-19th C, orig leather casing, inscription reads "Presented by the British Government, Captain Christopher Crowell, Master of the American Ship 'Highland Light' of Boston, in acknowledgment of his humanity and kindness to the Master and the Crew of the Barque 'Queen of Sheba' when he rescued from their waterlogged vessel, on the 16th, December 1861," damage to leather **980.00**

Vessel registration, *Jireh Swift,* certificate listing owners, specifying their shares, dimensions of the vessel, information on builder, one pg, folio, New Bedford, Sept. 1, 1862 . . **2,185.00**

NETSUKES

History: The traditional Japanese kimono has no pockets. Daily necessities, such as money and tobacco supplies, were carried in leather pouches, or inros, which hung from a cord with a netsuke toggle. The word netsuke comes from "ne"—to root—and "tsuke"—to fasten.

Netsukes originated in the 14th century and initially were favored by the middle class. By the mid-18th century, all levels of Japanese society used them. Some of the most famous artists, e.g., Shuzan and Yamada Hojitsu, worked in the netsuke form.

Netsukes average from 1 to 2 inches in length and are made from wood, ivory, bone, ceramics, metal, horn, nutshells, etc. The subject matter is broad based, but always portrayed in a lighthearted, humorous manner. A netsuke must have smooth edges and balance in order to hang correctly on the sash.

References: Raymond Bushell, *Introduction to Netsuke,* Charles E. Tuttle Co., 1971; George Lazarnick, *The Signature Book of Netsuke, Inro and Ojime Artists in Photographs,* first edition 1976, two-volume second edition 1981.

Periodicals: *Netsuke & Ivory Carving Newsletter,* 3203 Adams Way, Ambler, PA 19002; *Orientalia Journal,* P.O. Box 94, Flushing, NY 11363-0094, http://members.aol.com/Orientalia/index.html.

Collectors' Club: International Netsuke Society, P.O. Box 833272, Richardson, TX 75083-3272, http://www.netsuke.org/home.html.

Notes: Value depends on artist, region, material, and skill of craftsmanship. Western collectors favor katabori, pieces which represent an identifiable object.

Boxwood

Ashikaga and Tenaga seated **450.00**
Fisherman holding basket of fish, horn inlay, sgd "Akinide," Japan, 20th C **815.00**
Raiden, drum tied to his back, Japan, 19th C **265.00**
Rice mixer, ivory inlaid eyes, teeth, and rice, carved by Tokoku, 19th C **5,750.00**
Seated figure, tortoise, sgd with "kakihan," 18th/19th C. **435.00**
Shoki with demon, damage to sword **250.00**
Snail, crawling from shell, 19th C **495.00**
Study of Oni holding Shoki's sword, blowing trumpet, 19th C, chip to one toe, 3" l **1,495.00**
Turtle and snake, c1800, 2-3/8" l **10,120.00**

Horn

Lotus leaf, stag horn, 19th C . **100.00**
Shishi form, pressed, 19th C . . **50.00**

Carved ivory, ebony, and coral, mounted on carved ivory base of seashells and scrolling waves, 2" x 1-1/4", minor imperfections, $375. Photo courtesy of Sanford Alderfer Auction Co.

Ivory

Bell with dragon, sgd "Komei," 19th C **260.00**
Bowing samurai, stained details, sgd "Meigyokusai" **425.00**
Eggplant, carved and colored **195.00**
Fish on bed of reeds, naturalistically carved, stained, slight gold highlights, Japan, 19th C . . **750.00**

Frog and monkey, Japan, late 19th C **195.00**
Frogs with inlaid eyes, lotus plants, lightly colored details, 3-3/4" l **250.00**
Four children playing in tub . **250.00**
Gama Sennin, 18th/19th C, 2-1/4" l, repair to foot **290.00**
Hoe Tei being carried in a bag by children, sgd "Tadayasu," Japan, 19th C **700.00**
Juojin, small child, sgd "Meigyokusai" **415.00**
Monkey arm wrestling with Oni demon on lotus pad, Japan, 19th C **700.00**
Monkey training with small child, sgd "Gyokusho" **375.00**
Okami playing with kitten and ball of string, 19th C **125.00**
Oni with drum, 19th C, 1-3/4" h **200.00**
Ono no komachi seated on gate post, old can hat, 19th C . . **350.00**
Pair of chestnuts, carved and stained **125.00**
Parrot perched on branch, 19th C, 2-1/4" l **1,100.00**
Rooster, sgd "Chomei" **250.00**
Sennin holding staff, 18th/19th C, 3-1/4" l **250.00**
Skull with snake, 19th C **320.00**
Snail, 19th C **200.00**
Two sculptures working on dragon carp, cinnabar inlaid cartouche reading "Shizetomo," 19th C **350.00**
Ivory and wood, Oni demon in ivory, inside box with horn, coral, and gold inlay, sgd "Meigyokusai" **700.00**

Carved ivory, 19th C, $115.

Porcelain

Fruit and leaves, red, brown, and celadon, 19th C. **60.00**
Hotei, marked "Masakazu," 19th C **60.00**
Two puppies, 19th C **85.00**
Sandalwood, carved rustic retreat with pavilions, trees, mountains, and figures **635.00**

Wood

Geisha, seated, wearing flowing robe, holding tray, carved by Toshikazu, 19th C **245.00**
Karasu tengu, seated figure with beaked and fanged face, holding cucumber, carved by Jugyoko, 19th C **825.00**
Monkey, seated, clasping raised left knee, unsgd, first half 19th C **425.00**
Noblewoman, wretched beggar form, dying by roadside, carved by Ichihyo, first half 19th C . . **300.00**
Persimmon, stippled skin and leaves, unsgd, 19th C. **295.00**
Scribe, sitting, holding writing slip and brush, carved by Shinsai, 19th C **275.00**

NEWCOMB POTTERY

History: The Sophie Newcomb Memorial College, an adjunct of Tulane University in New Orleans, LA, was originated as a school to train local women in the decorative arts. While metalworking, painting, and embroidery were among the classes taught, the production of fine, hand-crafted art pottery remains its most popular and collectible pursuit.

Pottery was made by the Newcomb women for nearly 50 years, with earlier work being the rarest and most valuable. This is characterized by shiny finishes and broad, flat-painted and modeled designs. More common, though still quite valuable, are the matte glaze pieces, often depicting bayou scenes and native flora. All bear the impressed NC mark.

References: Ralph and Terry Kovel, *Kovels' American Art Pottery*, Crown Publishers, 1993; Jessie Poesch, *Newcomb Pottery: An Enterprise for Southern Women*, Schiffer Publishing, 1984; David Rago, *American Art Pottery*, Knickerbocker Press, 1997.

Collectors' Club: American Art Pottery Association, P.O. Box 1226, Westport, MA 02790.

Museum: Newcomb College, Tulane University, New Orleans, LA.

Adviser: David Rago.

Vase, carved by Sadie Irvine, 1914, tall pines covered in Spanish moss, marked "NC/SI/JM/184/B/GK11," remnant of paper label, minor chip to edge of foot ring, almost certainly from manufacture, 6-1/2" d, 8-1/4" h, $5,175. Photo courtesy of David Rago Auctions.

Bud vase, 9" h, 3-1/4" d, tapered, high glaze, carved yellow jonquils, tall green leaves, blue ground, by Anna Frances Simpson, 1908, marked "NC/Q/FS/CQ52/JM" **6,900.00**

Cabinet vase, 2" d, 4-1/2" h, by Anna F. Simpson, 1926, blue live oak and Spanish moss, gray ground, high glaze, marked "NC/JH/PP56/15/AFS" **3,335.00**

Jardiniere, 10" d, 8" h, yellow daffodils, blue-green leaves, ivory ground, by Harriet Joor, 1902, marked "NC/JM/R29/HJ," four lines to rim, shallow spider lines at base. **19,550.00**

Loving cup, 5" d, 4" h, by Katherine Kopman, 1902, painted white clover blossoms and green leaves, pale blue and white ground, "NC/KK/E18/X," 1" chip inside rim **2,615.00**

Print, woodblock, 5-1/2" w, 6" h sight, by Mary F. Baker, young girl dec vase, monogrammed "MFB" lower left, matted, framed........... **2,070.00**

Vase

3-1/2" d, 8-1/2" d, transitional, tapering, by Anna Simpson, 1912, stylized pale blue narcissus, green

and blue ground, marked "NC/M/B/AFS/EY82"..... **4,320.00**

3-3/4" d, 4-3/4" h, transitional, bulbous, by Anna F. Simpson, 1914, white orchids, green leaves, pale blue ground, marked "NC/JM/126/GO33/AFS" . **1,840.00**

4" d, 8" h, ovoid, by Corrine Marie Chalaron, 1923, broad leaves alternating with yellow and white stylized blossoms, denim blue ground, marked "NC/JM/MZ61/82/CMC".. **4,315.00**

4-1/2" d, 4-1/2" h, bulbous, live oaks and Spanish moss, by Anna Frances Simpson, 1929, orig paper label, "NC/RY17/JH/29/AFS" **2,875.00**

4-1/2" d, 5-1/2" h, bulbous, by Sadie Irvine, 1927, Espanol pattern, blue-green, pink, and white, dark denim blue ground, "NC/24/QH96/S"....... **4,025.00**

4-1/2" d, 6-1/2" h, carved matte, by Sadie Irvine, 1924, pink and red loquat fruit and leaves around undulating rim, marked "NC/SK/JM/I47/NP47," small chips to foot ring, short tight line to rim **1,150.00**

5" d, 9" h, bulbous, by Anna F. Simpson, 1921, carved wreath of pink trumpet vines, green leaves, denim blue ground, marked "NC/JM/LS97/179/A.F.S." . **3,220.00**

6-1/2" d, 8-1/4" h, transitional, by Sadie Irvine, 1914, tall pines cov in Spanish moss, marked "NC/SI/JM/184/B/GK11," remnant of paper label, minor chip on edge of foot ring **5,175.00**

Vessel

5-1/4" d, 3-1/4" h, squatty, transitional, by Sadie Irvine, 1914, carved light blue bell flowers, green leaves, dark blue ground, marked "NC/GN47/JM/257/SI" **2,300.00**

6-1/2" d, 4-1/2" h, matte, squatty, by Sadie Irvine, 1922, sharply carved pink Japanese iris, green stems, around undulating top conforming to shape of blossoms, purple and blue ground, marked "NC/SI/JM/213/MV17" ... **3,220.00**

7-1/2" d, 6" h, organically-shaped, by Marie De Hoa LeBlanc, c1905, three modeled ginkgo leaf handles, semi-matte olive green and gunmetal glaze, marked "NC/Q/JM/MHL," orig price tag **5,175.00**

Left, vase, deeply incised, green sheaves of wheat, dark blue ground, Henrietta Bailey, 1909, 9-1/2" h, $4,125; center, charger, incised white and yellow day lilies, green leaves, sky blue ground, Henrietta Bailey, glaze fleck, paper label, 13" d, $13,200; right, covered jar, incised blue dogwoods, yellow centers, light blue ground, Marie De Hoa LeBlanc, 1904, $12,000. Photo courtesy of David Rago Auctions, Inc.

NILOAK POTTERY, MISSION WARE

History: Niloak Pottery was made near Benton, Arkansas. Charles Dean Hyten experimented with native clay, trying to preserve its natural colors. By 1911, he perfected Mission Ware, a marbleized pottery in which the cream and brown colors predominate. The company name is the word "kaolin" spelled backward.

After a devastating fire, the pottery was rebuilt and named Eagle Pottery. This factory included enough space to add a novelty pottery line in 1929. Hyten left the pottery in 1941, and in 1946 operations ceased.

Marks: The early pieces were marked "Niloak." Eagle Pottery products usually were marked "Hywood-Niloak" until 1934, when the "Hywood" was dropped from the mark.

References: Susan and Al Bagdade, *Warman's American Pottery and Porcelain*, 2nd ed., Krause Publications, 2000; David Edwin Gifford, *Collector's Encyclopedia of Niloak*, 2nd ed., Collector Books, 2000.

Collectors' Club: Arkansas Pottery Collectors Society, P.O. Box 7617, Little Rock, AR 72217.

Additional Listings: See *Warman's Americana & Collectibles* for more examples, especially the novelty pieces.

Note: Prices listed below are for Mission Ware pieces.

Bowl, 4-1/2" d, marbleized swirls, blue, tan, and brown **65.00**
Candlesticks, pr, 8" h, marbleized swirls, blue, cream, terra-cotta, and brown **250.00**

Vase, corseted, Mission Ware, marbleized brown, blue and ivory clays, stamped mark, 4-1/2" d, 10" h, $230. Photo courtesy of David Rago Auctions.

Console set, pr 8-1/2" h candlesticks, 10" d bowl, marbleized swirls, marked **275.00**
Flower pot, ruffled rim, green matte glaze, c1930 . . . . **155.00**
Pot, 2-3/4" x 3-3/4", marbleized swirls, red, brown, and chocolate, early **125.00**
Toothpick holder, marbleized swirls, tan and blue **100.00**
Urn, 4-1/2" h, marbleized swirls, brown and blue **45.00**

Vase, Mission Ware, yellow, blue, and brown swirl, impressed mark, 5-1/4" h, $175.

Vase
    3" d, 5-1/2" d, blue, brown, and cream, second art mark, c1930 . . . . **175.00**
    4" h, second art mark **110.00**
    5-1/4" h, blue, brown, and cream, orig round blue and white label **220.00**
    5-1/2" h, corset cylinder, blue, brown, and cream **175.00**
    6" h, applied twisted handles, Ozark Dawn glaze, c1930 . . . . . . **120.00**
    6" h, broad rim, blue, brown, and cream **145.00**
    6-1/2" h, baluster, brown and cream **195.00**
    8-3/4" h, Ozark Dawn glaze, c1930 . . . . **140.00**
    10-1/2" h, swollen baluster with broad rim, brown, rose, blue, and cream, second art mark . . . **500.00**

NIPPON CHINA, 1891-1921

History: Nippon, Japanese hand-painted porcelain, was made for export between 1891 and 1921. In 1891, when the McKinley Tariff Act proclaimed that all items of foreign manufacture be stamped with their country of origin, Japan chose to use "Nippon." In 1921, the United States decided the word "Nippon" no longer was acceptable and required all Japanese wares to be marked "Japan," ending the Nippon era.

Marks: There are more than 220 recorded Nippon backstamps or marks; the three most popular are the wreath, maple leaf, and rising sun. Wares with variations of all three marks are being reproduced today. A knowledgeable collector can easily spot the reproductions by the mark variances.

The majority of the marks are found in three different colors: green, blue, or magenta. Colors indicate the quality of the porcelain used: green for first-grade porcelain, blue for second-grade, and magenta for third-grade. Marks were applied by two methods: decal stickers under glaze and imprinting directly on the porcelain.

References: Joan Van Patten, *Collector's Encyclopedia of Nippon Porcelain*, 1st Series (1979, 2000 value update), 2nd Series (1982, 1997 value update), 3rd Series (1986, 2000 value update), 4th Series, (1997), Collector Books; 5th Series (1998); 6th Series, 2000; Joan F. Van Patten and Linda Lou, *Nippon Dolls & Playthings*, Collector Books, 2000; Kathy Wojciechowski, *Wonderful World of Nippon Porcelain*, Schiffer Publishing, 1992.

Collectors' Clubs: International Nippon Collectors Club, 1521 Independence Ave., SE, Washington, DC 20003; Lakes & Plains Nippon Collectors Society, P.O. Box 230, Peotone, IL 60468-0230; New England Nippon Collectors Club, 64 Burt Road, Springfield, MA 01118; Sunshine State Nippon Collectors' Club, P.O. Box 425, Frostproof, FL 33843.

Additional Listings: See *Warman's Americana & Collectibles.*

Reproduction Alert

Distinguishing old marks from new:

A common old mark consisted of a central wreath open at the top with the letter M in the center. "Hand Painted" flowed around the top of the wreath; "NIPPO Box N" around the bottom. The modern fake mark reverses the wreath (it is open at the bottom) and places an hourglass form, not an "M," in its middle.

An old leaf mark, approximately one-quarter inch wide, has "Hand" with "Painted" below to the left of the stem and "NIPPO Box N" beneath. The newer mark has the identical lettering, but the size is now one-half, rather than one-quarter, inch.

An old mark consisted of "Hand Painted" arched above a solid rising sun logo with "NIPPO Box N" in a straight line beneath. The modern fake mark has the same lettering pattern, but the central logo looks like a mound with a jagged line enclosing a blank space above it.

Basket

7-1/4" h, rose dec, pale yellow ground, gilt accents, unmarked, flakes on base **265.00**

8-1/2" h, orchid design, gilt and green ground, green maple leaf mark **295.00**

Berry set, 10-1/4" d master bowl, four 5" d individual bowls, azalea dec, enameled and gilt floral borders, green M in wreath mark **90.00**

Bowl

6" d, 4" h, ftd, shaped edge, rose dec, gilt border and feet, blue maple leaf mark **210.00**

8-1/2" d, scalloped edge, rose dec, gilt borders, green and yellow ground, green maple leaf mark **110.00**

9-1/2" d, ftd, grape dec, gilt borders, green M in wreath mark ... **175.00**

9-1/2" d, octagonal, lavender coastal scene, green and gilt borders, blue maple leaf mark **295.00**

Cake plate, 10-1/2" d, lavender coastal scene, green and gilt borders, blue maple leaf mark **195.00**

Cake set, 10-1/4" d cake plate, six 6-1/2" d serving plates, two handles, scenic dec with swans, floral borders with gilt accents, green M in wreath mark..................... **330.00**

Chocolate set, chocolate pot, six cups and saucers, six dessert bowls, fuchsia flowers, dark green leaves, gilt borders, pale yellow and pink ground, unmarked, minor imperfections. **295.00**

Condensed milk jar, cov, underplate, pink roses, green leaves, gilt accents, unmarked **295.00**

Charger, hand-painted bulldog, 12" d, $450. Photo courtesy of Joy Luke Auctions.

Doll, 18-1/2" h, bisque socket head, brown glass eyes, closed pouty mouth, human hair wig, jointed wood and composition body, marked "FY/Nippon/304" on back of head, tiny chips at neck opening, body repainted with some flaking at joints **875.00**

Mayonnaise set, ftd bowl, matching underplate, ladle, delicate floral design, green M in wreath mark, blue mark on ladle **80.00**

Nut dish, 7-1/4" d, blown-out design, three ftd, green M in wreath mark **55.00**

Plate

7-1/2" d, rose dec, raspberry and gilt border, blue maple leaf mark **220.00**

9-3/4" d, floral dec, gilt borders, cobalt blue ground, blue maple leaf mark **350.00**

10" d, rose dec, gold ground, blue maple leaf mark.......... **135.00**

10" d, scalloped edge, rose dec, gilt dec, blue maple leaf mark . **250.00**

10-1/2" d, two handles, scalloped edge, floral design, gilt ground, Royal Kinran mark........ **250.00**

Punch set, bowl with double handles, claw foot base, six ftd cups, grape dec, green M in wreath mark **990.00**

Urn

8" h, painted sailboats on water, red and purple mottled ground, fading of gilt on handles and rim, price for pr..................... **250.00**

11-1/2" h, painted orange poppies, blue ground, Oriental bands at top and bottom, minor losses to squeezebag near base.... **250.00**

14-3/4" h, six-sided, hand painted, trees and lake scene, some fading of gilt on handles, rim, and base **400.00**

Vase

5" h, double handles, bulbous, mountainous landscape, gilt accents, blue maple leaf mark **600.00**

5-1/2" h, double-ring handles, squatty, portrait of woman, floral dec, gilt trim, blue maple leaf mark **330.00**

6" h, double handles, Moriage, gilt accents, blue enamel on green ground, blue maple leaf mark **600.00**

6-1/2" h, double handles, ruffled rim, multicolored flower dec, gilt accents, coralene dec, blue-green ground, Kinran U.S. Patent 912171 mark, price for pr....... **1,150.00**

Sugar bowl, covered, hand-painted scene, $40.

7" h, double-ring handles, rose dec, gilt accents, white enamel beading, blue maple leaf mark **495.00**

8" h, cylindrical, flared base, ruffled edge, pink, yellow, white, and green hollyhock dec, coralene dec, purple ground, Kinran U.S. Patent 912171 mark, restored rim. **500.00**

8-1/4" h, bulbous, some fading of gilt on handles and inside rim . **400.00**

8-1/2" h, apple blossom dec, enamel and gilt accents, blue maple leaf mark **250.00**

8-1/2" h, double serpent handles, depressed shoulders, rose dec, yellow, green, and gilt borders, blue maple leaf mark **250.00**

9" h, baluster, blown-out leaves dec, gilt accents, blue maple leaf mark **1,325.00**

9" h, double handles, cobalt blue ground, portrait of woman holding flowers, blue maple leaf mark **1,875.00**

9-1/2" h, cherry blossom and lattice design, flared rim, green M in wreath mark, base chip ... **200.00**

9-1/2" h, double handles, baluster form, landscape with large flowers, gilt Greek key borders, green M in wreath mark **265.00**

9-1/2" d, double-ring handles, ruffled rim, floral dec, gilt accents, blue maple leaf mark **330.00**

10" h, double handles, bulbous, mountainous landscape dec, gilt accents, green maple leaf mark **375.00**

10" h, double handles, purple and white flowers surrounded by heavy gilt beading, blue maple leaf mark **1,325.00**

10" h, double handles, rose dec, mulberry ground, gilt dec, Royal

Kinran mark, roughness on base
..................**120.00**
10-1/2" h, double handles, scenic
dec surrounded by gilt design,
white ground, blue maple leaf mark
..................**330.00**
10-1/2" h, double handles, white
flowers, brown and green ground,
blue maple leaf mark, flake on
base **335.00**
11" h, double handles, cylindrical,
azalea dec, maroon and gilt
borders, blue maple leaf mark
..................**275.00**
11" h, double-ring handles, scenic
design, grape and vine border,
matte finish, green M in wreath
mark **525.00**
11-1/2" h, double handles, Art
Nouveau form, lily dec, brown and
beige ground, gilt trim, blue M in
wreath mark..........**1,325.00**
12-1/4" h, double-twist handles, ftd,
panels of rose dec, large gilt areas
with beading, cobalt blue ground,
unmarked **495.00**
13-1/2" h, double handles,
cylindrical, iris, coralene dec, gilt
borders, Kinran U.S. Patent 912171
mark **2,200.00**
14" h, peony dec, geometric and
floral design, gilt borders, blue M in
wreath mark...........**825.00**

NODDERS

History: Nodders are figurines with heads and/or arms attached to the body with wires to enable movement. They are made in a variety of materials—bisque, celluloid, papier-mâché, porcelain, or wood.

Most nodders date from the late 19th century, with Germany being the principal source of supply. Among the American-made nodders, those of Disney and cartoon characters are most eagerly sought.

Reference: Hilma R. Irtz, *Figural Nodders*, Collector Books, 1997.

Collectors' Club: Bobbin' Head National Club, P.O. Box 9297, Lakeland, FL 32120.

Bisque

Buttercup, German **180.00**
Chinese man, 4-1/2" h, seated, legs
crossed, holding in hand, pink and
beige dec, beading.......**170.00**
Colonial woman, 7-1/2" h, bisque
..................**190.00**
Indian princess, 3-3/4" h, seated,
holding fan, pale blue, gold trim
..................**115.00**
Kayo, German **145.00**

Oriental figures, standing man and woman, porcelain, made by Mottahedeh, 14" and 15" h, $100. Photo courtesy of Joy Luke Auctions.

Little Orphan Annie, German .**115.00**
Monk, 5-3/4" h, standing, holding
wine pitcher, German.....**150.00**
Oriental couple, 8-3/4" h, pink robes,
seated before keyboard and music
book, gilt dec, Continental, 19th C
..................**500.00**
Policeman, Nassau, white hat and
jacket, black pants, minor loss to
paint.................**145.00**
Turkish girl, 6" h, white beading
..................**300.00**
Celluloid, goose, 3-1/2" l, paper label
"S. A. Reider & Co.," marked "BRGBA
DBGM © Made in Germany US Zone"
..................**65.00**
Ceramic
Cowboy, Japan...........**75.00**
Lady, 2-1/2" w, 6-1/2" h, green dress,
red trim, pink and blue hat, bank,
marked "Japan" **185.00**
Old Salt, 7" h sailor, white beard,
blue shirt, brown pants, black
boots **25.00**
Robin Hood, Japan........**85.00**
Siamese boy and girl, 4-1/2" h, salt
and pepper shakers, black,
orange, and gold outfits, orig box
mid "A Commodore Product,
Japan" **20.00**
Papier-mâché
Black boy, clockwork, felt and cotton
suit, 24" h, c1900 ....**1,265.00**
Japanese boy and girl, 5-1/2" h, pr
..................**50.00**
Mother Goose, red cape, black hat,
white goose **3,960.00**

Rabbit, 8" h, sitting, light brown
..................**90.00**
Shriner, 7" h **90.00**
Wood and papier-mâché
Comical man, 6-3/8" h, top hat, worn
orig polychrome **140.00**
Santa, clockwork, gray mittens,
cardboard and wood **900.00**
Santa, replaced red robe and beard
..................**920.00**

NORITAKE CHINA

History: Morimura Brothers founded Noritake China in 1904 in Nagoya, Japan. The company made high-quality chinaware for export to the United States and also produced a line of china blanks for hand painting. In 1910, the company perfected a technique for the production of high-quality dinnerware and introduced streamlined production.

During the 1920s, the Larkin Company of Buffalo, New York, was a prime distributor of Noritake China. Larkin offered Azalea, Briarcliff, Linden, Modjeska, Savory, Sheridan, and Tree in the Meadow patterns as part of its premium line.

The factory was heavily damaged during World War II, and production was reduced. Between 1946 and 1948, the company sold its china under the "Rose China" mark, since the quality of production did not match the earlier Noritake China. Expansion in 1948 brought about the resumption of quality production and the use of the Noritake name once again.

Marks: There are close to 100 different marks for Noritake, the careful study of which can determine the date of production. Most pieces are marked "Noritake" with a wreath, "M," "N," or "Nippon." The use of the letter N was registered in 1953.

References: Aimee Neff Alden, *Collector's Encyclopedia of Early Noritake*, Collector Books, 1995, 2000 value update; Walter Ayars, *Larkin China, Catalog Reprint*, Echo Publishing, 1990; Pat Murphy, *Noritake for Europe*, Schiffer Publishing, 2001; Joan Van Patten, *Collector's Encyclopedia of Noritake*, Collector Books, 1984, 2000 value update; David Spain, *Collecting Noritake, A to Z: Art Deco and More*, Schiffer Publishing, 1999.

Collectors' Club: Noritake Collectors' Society, 145 Andover Place, West Hempstead, NY 115532-1603.

Additional Listings: See *Warman's Americana & Collectibles* for Azalea pattern prices.

Berry set, Tree in the Meadow, master bowl with pierced handles, six sauce bowls **95.00**
Bowl, 10" l, oval, Rosewin #6584 pattern **30.00**
Cake set, 11" d cake plate, six 6-1/4" serving plates, desert scene with tent and man on camel, cobalt blue and gilt border, marked "Noritake/Made in Japan/Hand Painted" **770.00**
Candlesticks, pr, 8-1/4" h, gold flowers and bird, blue luster ground, wreath with "M" mark...............**125.00**

Dinner service, partial, Sorrento pattern, service for 12, serving pieces, total 95 pieces, $300. Photo courtesy of Joy Luke Auctions.

Dakota/Grand Forks, N.D./Made at School of Mines/N.D. Clay." Some early pieces are marked only "U.N.D." or "U.N.D./Grand Forks, N.D." Most pieces are numbered (they can be dated from University records) and signed by both the instructor and student. Cable-signed pieces are the most desirable.

References: Darlene Hurst Dommel, *Collector's Encyclopedia of the Dakota Potteries*, Collector Books, 1996.

Collectors' Club: North Dakota Pottery Collectors Society, P.O. Box 14, Beach, ND 58621.

Bowl, low, 6-3/4" d, 23/4" h, matte green, incised lines around rim, stamped mark, 1" bruise at rim . **210.00**
Figure, 4-1/2" h, 3-1/4" w, Bentonite cowboy, brick-red, black, and gold glaze, incised "JJ/13/UND," Julia Mattson, 1913 . . . . **650.00**

Creamer and sugar
　Art Deco, pink Japanese lanterns, cobalt blue ground, basket type handle on sugar, wreath with "M" mark **50.00**
　Tree in the Meadow, scalloped **85.00**
Cup and saucer, Florola, #83374 pattern **24.00**
Demitasse cup and saucer, Tree in the Meadow **45.00**
Dinner set, floral motif, gold rimmed, 115-pc set **375.00**
Gravy boat, Tree in the Meadow **50.00**
Hair receiver, 3-1/4" h, 3-1/2" w, Art Deco, geometric designs, gold luster, wreath with "M" mark **50.00**
Inkwell, owl, figural **125.00**
Jam jar, cov, basket style, handle, figural applied cherries on notched lid **55.00**
Marmalade, underplate, 5-1/2" h, poppy dec, double handled jar. **185.00**
Napkin ring, Art Deco man and woman, wreath with "M" mark, pr **60.00**
Place card holder, figural, bluebird with butterfly, gold luster, white stripes, wreath with "M" mark, pr **35.00**
Plate, two 8-1/2" d, seven 6-1/4" d, cranberry and pale blue rose motif dec, gilt borders, blue "RC Noritake Nippon Hand Painted" mark **175.00**
Platter, 11" l, Rosewin, #6584 . . . **25.00**
Punch bowl set, 12" h two-part punch bowl with three-ftd base, six 2-3/4" h cups
　Cottage landscape at dusk, swans in pond dec, cobalt blue and gilt borders, opalescent melon int **880.00**

Peacock design, cobalt blue and gilt borders, blue ground ext., melon and blue interior, "M" in wreath mark **600.00**
Salt, 3" l, swan, white, orange luster, pr **25.00**
Salt and pepper shakers, pr, Tree in the Meadow, marked "Made in Japan" **35.00**
Soup bowl, Florola **15.00**
Tea tile, Tree in the Meadow, 5" w, green mark **35.00**
Vegetable bowl, cov, 9" d, round, Rosewin **35.00**
Waffle set, handled serving plate, sugar shaker, Art Deco flowers, wreath with "M" mark **50.00**
Wall pocket, butterfly, wreath with "M" mark **75.00**

NORTH DAKOTA SCHOOL OF MINES

History: The North Dakota School of Mines was established in 1890. Earle J. Babcock, a chemistry instructor, was impressed with the high purity level of North Dakota potter's clay. In 1898, Babcock received funds to develop his finds. He tried to interest commercial potteries in the North Dakota clay, but had limited success.

In 1910, Babcock persuaded the school to establish a Ceramics Department. Margaret Cable, who studied under Charles Binns and Frederick H. Rhead, was appointed head. She remained until her retirement in 1949.

Decorative emphasis was placed on native themes, e.g., flowers and animals. Art Nouveau, Art Deco, and fairly plain pieces were made.

Marks: The pottery is marked with a cobalt blue underglaze circle of the words "University of North

Vase, squatty bulbous shape, white to light green ground, imp circular decoration separated by impressed leaf-shape decoration, stamp mark, "Huck" in circle, 4-1/2" d, 4" h, $1,125.

Vase
　3-1/2" d, 7" h, incised stylized turquoise blossoms, beige ground, stamped mark, illegible artist signature **1,300.00**
　4-1/2" d, 5" h, bulbous, emb prairie roses, mottled green crystalline glaze, circular ink mark, incised "Steen-Huck-1100," Huckfield and Steen **1,200.00**
　5" d, 3" h, conical, by Flora Huckfield and student, glossy celadon and brown glaze, circular ink stamp, incised "Huck" and "Le Masurier/2371" **230.00**
　5" d, 7-1/4" h, bulbous, emb cowboy scene, matte chocolate brown glaze, circular ink stamp, sgd "Flora Huckfield," titled "N. D. Rodeo" **1,500.00**

5" h, 9" d, carved mocha brown narcissus, dark brown ground, ink stamp, incised "E. Cunningham/12/6/50," E. Cunningham, 1950 . . . . . **1,000.00**

5-1/2" d, 7-1/2" h, bulbous, carved narcissus, brown and umber matte glaze, by Margaret Cable, stamped circular mark, incised "M. Cable/223" **1,840.00**

5-1/2" d, 8" h, carved daffodils, mahogany matte glaze, circular ink mark, incised "McCosh '48" **1,100.00**

5-1/2" d, 10" h, ovoid, carved sheaves of wheat, purple-brown matte glaze, ink stamped and incised "Huck 30/No. Dak. Wheat," F. Huckfield **1,300.00**

6-1/4" d, 4-3/4" h, sq tapering, repeating scenes of farmer and horse-drawn plow, green and brown matte glaze, circular ink mark, incised "The Plowman/Huck/119," F. Huckfield **1,200.00**

Vase, The Plowsman, carved field plowing scene, matte brown glaze, decorated by F. Huckfield, ink stamp, carved title and artist, 5" x 6-1/2", $1,700. Photo courtesy of David Rago Auctions, Inc.

Vessel

3-1/2" h, 3-1/2" d, beaker shape, matte brown glaze, stamped and incised marks, c1915, small rim chip **115.00**

6" d, 5-1/2" h, spherical, Prairie Rose, carved coral stylized flowers, green leaves, sand ground, circular ink stamp and "M. Cable/131-A/Prairie Rose," Margaret Cable **900.00**

7" d, 6" h, spherical, Covered Wagon, carved frieze of wagons and oxen, sandy brown matte glaze, circular ink mark, incised "M. Cable" and title, by Margaret Cable **1,400.00**

WALLACE NUTTING

History: Wallace Nutting (1861-1941) was America's most famous photographer of the early 20th century. A retired minister, Nutting took more than 50,000 pictures, keeping 10,000 of his best and destroying the rest. His popular and best-selling scenes included "Exterior Scenes," apple blossoms, country lanes, orchards, calm streams, and rural American countrysides; "Interior Scenes," usually featuring a colonial woman working near a hearth; and "Foreign Scenes," typically thatch-roofed cottages. Those pictures which were least popular in his day have become the rarest and most-highly collectible today and are classified as "Miscellaneous Unusual Scenes." This category encompasses such things as animals, architecturals, children, florals, men, seascapes, and snow scenes.

Nutting sold literally millions of his hand-colored platinotype pictures between 1900 and his death in 1941. Starting first in Southbury, Connecticut, and later moving his business to Framingham, Massachusetts, the peak of Wallace Nutting's picture production was 1915 to 1925. During this period, Nutting employed nearly 200 people, including colorists, darkroom staff, salesmen, and assorted office personnel. Wallace Nutting pictures proved to be a huge commercial success and hardly an American household was without one by 1925.

While attempting to seek out the finest and best early-American furniture as props for his colonial Interior Scenes, Nutting became an expert in American antiques. He published nearly 20 books in his lifetime, including his 10-volume State Beautiful series and various other books on furniture, photography, clocks, and his autobiography. He also contributed many photographs published in magazines and books other than his own.

Nutting also became widely known for his reproduction furniture. His furniture shop produced literally hundreds of different furniture forms: clocks, stools, chairs, settles, settees, tables, stands, desks, mirrors, beds, chests of drawers, cabinet pieces, and treenware.

The overall synergy of the Wallace Nutting name, pictures, books, and furniture, has made anything "Wallace Nutting" quite collectible.

Marks: Wallace Nutting furniture is clearly marked with his distinctive paper label, glued directly onto the piece, or with a block or script signature brand, which was literally branded into his furniture.

Note: "Process Prints" are 1930s' machine-produced reprints of 12 of Nutting's most popular pictures. These have minimal value and can be detected by using a magnifying glass.

References: Michael Ivankovich, *Alphabetical & Numerical Index to Wallace Nutting Pictures*, Diamond Press, 1988; ——, *Collector's Guide to Wallace Nutting Pictures*, Collector Books, 1997; ——, *Guide to Wallace Nutting Furniture*, Diamond Press, 1990; ——, *Wallace Nutting Expansible Catalog* (reprint of 1915 catalog), Diamond Press, 1987; Wallace Nutting, *Wallace Nutting: A Great American Idea* (reprint of 1922 catalog), Diamond Press, 1992; ——, *Wallace Nutting General Catalog* (reprint of 1930 catalog), Schiffer Publishing, 1977; ——, *Wallace Nutting's*

Windsors (reprint of 1918 catalog), Diamond Press, 1992.

Collectors' Club: Wallace Nutting Collectors Club, P.O. Box 2458, Doylestown, PA 18901.

Museum: Wadsworth Athenaeum, Hartford, CT.

Adviser: Michael Ivankovich.

Farm path winds through orchard's stone wall into blossoming apple orchard, Massachusetts, 9" x 15", $175. Photo courtesy of Michael Ivankovich Antiques & Auction Co., Inc.

Books

American Windsors **85.00**
Cruise of the 800, The **95.00**
England Beautiful, 1st ed. **125.00**
Furniture of the Pilgrim Century, 1st ed. **140.00**
Furniture Treasury, Vol. I **125.00**
Furniture Treasury, Vol. II **140.00**
Furniture Treasury, Vol. III **115.00**
Ireland Beautiful, 1st ed. **45.00**
Pathways of the Puritans **85.00**
Social Life In Old New England . . **75.00**
State Beautiful Series
Connecticut Beautiful, 1st ed. . . **75.00**
Maine Beautiful, 1st ed. **45.00**
Massachusetts Beautiful, 2nd ed. **45.00**
New Hampshire Beautiful, 1st ed. **75.00**
New York Beautiful, 1st ed. . . . **85.00**
Pennsylvania Beautiful, 1st ed. **48.00**
Vermont Beautiful, 2nd ed. . . . **40.00**
Virginia Beautiful, 1st ed. **60.00**
Catalog, Wallace Nutting's Original Studio **1,100.00**

Furniture

Candle stand, #17, Windsor **495.00**

Farm path runs through stone wall into large and very colorful orchard, signed and copyrighted on picture lower right, Massachusetts, 20" x 30", **$395.** *Photo courtesy of Michael Ivankovich Antiques & Auction Co., Inc.*

Chair
 #390, Ladderback, arm, script brand
 . . . . **300.00**
 #408, Windsor, bowback, arm, block
 brand **825.00**
 #440, Windsor, writing arm,
 Pennsylvania turnings, drawer
 beneath seat, block brand
 . . . . **2,145.00**
 #464, Carver, arm, script brand
 . . . . **550.00**
 #475, Flemish, arm, block brand
 . . . . **1,155.00**
Cupboard, #923, pine, scrolled
 . . . . **4,290.00**
High chair, liftable food tray, New England turnings, orig light maple finish, block branded signature
 . . . . **2,310.00**
Stool, #102, Windsor, script brand
 . . . . **220.00**
Table
 #619, crane bracket **685.00**
 #628b, Pembroke, mahogany
 . . . . **1,495.00**
Ironwork, potato cooker, imp mark on handle **2,145.00**

Girl works at drop-leaf table in formal parlor with detailed wallpaper, Connecticut, 11" x 17", **$350.** *Photo courtesy of Michael Ivankovich Antiques & Auction Co., Inc.*

Picture
A Gloucester Picture **1,870.00**
A Masque Picture **2,200.00**
A Perkiomen October, 9" x 11" . . **250.00**
Among the Ferns, 14" x 17" **165.00**
An Elaborate Dinner, 14" x 17" . . **200.00**
An Old Tune Revived **1,265.00**
A Pennsylvania Stream **770.00**
A Rug Pattern **690.00**
Better Than Mowing, 16" x 20" . . **490.00**
Between the Games **800.00**
Between the Spruces, 10" x 14" . **200.00**
Birch Hilltop, 15" x 22" **100.00**
By the Fireside, 9" x 13" **100.00**
California Hilltops, 11" x 14" **185.00**
Christmas Welcome Home . . . **1,100.00**
Colonial Days, Nantucket **1,128.00**
Dog-On-It, 7" x 11" **1,265.00**
Elizabeth Park Rose Garden . **1,210.00**
Elm Drapery, 15" x 22" **385.00**
Fleur-de-lis and Spirea, 13" x 16" **685.00**
Flume Falls, 12" x 15" **310.00**
Four O' Clock, cows **1,295.00**
Gloucester Cloister, 16" x 20" . **1,100.00**
Going for the Doctor, children **1,100.00**
Grandmother's Hollyhocks, 9" x 11"
 . . . . **400.00**
Helping Mother, 14" x 17" **410.00**
Hepatica **1,595.00**
Her First Proposal **1,240.00**
Lockside Cottage **745.00**
Parting at the Gate, 10" x 14" . . **550.00**
Pennsylvania Arches, 14" x 17" . **300.00**
Priscilla's Cottage, 14" x 17" . . . **360.00**
Rapid Transit, stagecoach scene
 . . . . **1,540.00**
Reflected Aspirations **1,705.00**
Roses and Larkspur **1,210.00**
Russet and Gold, 16" x 20" **315.00**
Shadowy Orchard Curves, 11" x 14"
 . . . . **85.00**
Stepping Stones to Bolton Abbey, 11" x 14" **330.00**
The Coming Out of Rosa **300.00**
The Delaware Canal Turn, PA . . **363.00**
The Donjon Chenaceau, French Castle
 . . . . **660.00**
The Isle in the Tiber **1,100.00**
The Meeting Place, horse and cows
 . . . . **2,420.00**
The Old Homestead **880.00**
To Meet the Rector **990.00**
Tranquillity Farm **880.00**
Village Spires, 10" x 12" **125.00**
Watching for Papa, 13" x 16" . . . **420.00**
Wilton Waters, 13" x 16" **155.00**
Wrencote **565.00**

Silhouette, girl arranges flower in tall spiral urn, **$45.** *Photo courtesy of Michael Ivankovich Antiques & Auction Co., Inc.*

Silhouettes
George and Martha Washington, 3" x 4"
 . . . . **90.00**
Girl at Vanity Desk, 4" x 4" **80.00**
Girl by Garden Urn, 4" x 4" **75.00**
Girl by Spider Web, 5" x 4" **50.00**
Scenes **40.00**

WALLACE NUTTING-LIKE PHOTOGRAPHERS

History: Although Wallace Nutting was widely recognized as the country's leading producer of hand-colored photographs during the early 20th century, he was by no means the only photographer selling this style of picture. Throughout the country, literally hundreds of regional photographers were selling hand-colored photographs from their home regions or travels. The subject matter of these photographers was comparable to Nutting's, including Interior, Exterior, Foreign, and Miscellaneous Unusual scenes.

Several photographers operated large businesses, and, although not as large or well known as Wallace Nutting, they sold a substantial volume of pictures which can still be readily found today. The vast majority of their work was photographed in their home regions and sold primarily to local residents or visiting tourists. It should come as little surprise that three of the major Wallace Nutting-like photographers—David Davidson, Fred Thompson, and the Sawyer Art Co.—each had ties to Wallace Nutting.

Hundreds of other smaller local and regional photographers attempted to market hand-colored pictures comparable to Wallace Nutting's during the period of 1900 to the 1930s. Although quite attractive, most were not as appealing to the general public as Wallace Nutting pictures. However, as the price of Wallace Nutting pictures has escalated, the work of these lesser-known Wallace Nutting-like photographers has become increasingly collectible.

A partial listing of some of these minor Wallace Nutting-like photographers includes: Babcock; J. C. Bicknell; Blair; Ralph Blood (Portland, Maine); Bragg; Brehmer; Brooks; Burrowes; Busch; Carlock; Pedro Cacciola; Croft; Currier; Depue Brothers; Derek; Dowly; Eddy; May Farini (hand-colored colonial lithographs); George Forest; Gandara; Gardner (Nantucket, Bermuda, Florida); Gibson; Gideon; Gunn; Bessie Pease Gutmann (hand-colored colonial lithographs); Edward Guy; Harris; C. Hazen; Knoffe; Haynes (Yellowstone Park); Margaret Hennesey; Hodges; Homer; Krabel; Kattleman; La Bushe; Lake; Lamson (Portland, Maine); M. Lightstrum; Machering; Rossiler Mackinae; Merrill; Meyers; William Moehring; Moran; Murrey; Lyman Nelson; J. Robinson Neville (New England); Patterson; Own Perry; Phelps; Phinney; Reynolds; F. Robbins; Royce; Frederick Scheetz (Philadelphia, Pennsylvania); Shelton, Standley (Colorado); Stott; Summers; Esther Svenson; Florence Thompson; Thomas Thompson; M. A. Trott; Sanford Tull; Underhill; Villar; Ward; Wilmot; Edith Wilson; and Wright.

References: Carol Begley Gray, *History of the Sawyer Pictures*, published by author, 1995 (available from Wallace Nutting Collector's Club, P.O. Box 2458, Doylestown, PA 18901); Michael Ivankovich, *Collector's Value Guide to Early Twentieth Century American Prints*, Collector Books, 1998; —, *Guide to Wallace-Nutting Like Photographers of the Early 20th Century*, Diamond Press, 1991.

Collectors' Club: Wallace Nutting Collector's Club, P.O. Box 2458, Doylestown, PA 18901.

Adviser: Michael Ivankovich.

Notes: The key determinants of value include the collectibility of the particular photographer, subject matter, condition, and size. Exterior Scenes are the most common.

Keep in mind that only the rarest pictures, in the best condition, will bring top prices. Discoloration and/or damage to the picture or matting can reduce value significantly.

David Davidson

Second to Nutting in overall production, Davidson worked primarily in the Rhode Island and southern Massachusetts areas. While a student at Brown University around 1900, Davidson learned the art of hand-colored photography from Wallace Nutting, who happened to be the minister at Davidson's church. After Nutting moved to Southbury in 1905, Davidson graduated from Brown and started a successful photography business in Providence, Rhode Island, which he operated until his death in 1967.

A Puritan Lady	70.00
A Real D.A.R.	150.00
Berkshire Sunset	80.00
Christmas Day	160.00
Driving Home the Cows	120.00
Heart's Desire	30.00
Her House in Order	75.00

David Davidson, Diadem Aisle, garden scene, narrow path winding between colorful flower garden and large park lake, 14" x 17", $150. Photo courtesy of Michael Ivankovich Antiques & Auction Co., Inc.

Neighbors	170.00
Old Ironsides	170.00
On A News Hunt	120.00
Plymouth Elm	20.00
Rosemary Club	40.00
Snowbound Brook	55.00
The Brook's Mirro	95.00
The Lamb's May Feast	130.00
The Seine Reel	190.00
The Silent Wave	35.00
Vanity	70.00

Sawyer

A father and son team, Charles H. Sawyer and Harold B. Sawyer, operated the very successful Sawyer Art Company from 1903 until the 1970s. Beginning in Maine, the Sawyer Art Company moved to Concord, New Hampshire, in 1920 to be closer to its primary market—New Hampshire's White Mountains. Charles H. Sawyer briefly worked for Nutting from 1902 to 1903 while living in southern Maine. Sawyer's production volume ranks third behind Wallace Nutting and David Davidson.

A February Morning	210.00
A New England Sugar Birth	300.00
At the Bend of the Road	35.00
Crystal Lake	65.00
Echo Lake, Franconia Notch	50.00
Indian Summer	35.00
Lake Morey	30.00
Lake Willoughby	50.00
Mt. Washington in October	55.00
Newfound Lake	73.00
Old Man of the Mountains	35.00
Original Dennison Plant	100.00
Silver Birches, Lake George	50.00
The Meadow Stream	80.00

Fred Thompson

Frederick H. Thompson and Frederick M. Thompson, another father and son team, operated the Thompson Art Company (TACO) from 1908 to 1923, working primarily in the Portland, Maine, area. We

know that Thompson and Nutting had collaborated because Thompson widely marketed an interior scene he had taken in Nutting's Southbury home. The production volume of the Thompson Art Company ranks fourth behind Nutting, Davidson, and Sawyer.

Apple Tree Road	45.00
Blossom Dale	75.00
Brook in Winter	190.00
Calm of Fall	50.00
Fernbank	35.00
Fireside Fancy Work	140.00
High and Dry	45.00
Knitting for the Boys	160.00
Lombardy Poplar	100.00
Nature's Carpet	50.00
Neath the Blossoms	95.00
Peace River	30.00
Portland Head	440.00
Six Master	100.00
Sunset on the Suwanee	45.00
The Gossips	80.00

Minor Wallace Nutting-Like Photographers

Generally speaking, prices for works by minor Wallace Nutting-like photographers would break down as follows: smaller pictures (5" x 7" to 10" x 12"), $10-$75; medium pictures (11" x 14" to 14" x 17"), $50-$200; larger pictures (larger than 14" x 17"), $75-$200+.

Baker, Florian A., Rushing Waters	50.00
Farini, In Her Boudoir	30.00
Gardiner, H. Marshall, The Rainbow Fleet, Nantucket	635.00
Gutmann, Bessie Pease Gutmann	
Lorelei	1,760.00
The Great Love	1,155.00
Haynes, Untitled Waterfalls	20.00
Higgins, Charles A., A Colonial Stairway	65.00
Payne, George S., Weekly Letter	25.00

Fred Thompson, Fireside Fancy Work, girl sews while sitting in settle beside Nuttinghame fire, interior scene taken in Wallace Nutting's Southbury, CT house, 7" x 9", $110. Photo courtesy of Michael Ivankovich Antiques & Auction Co., Inc.

OCCUPIED JAPAN

History: The Japanese economy was devastated when World War II ended. To secure necessary hard currency, the Japanese pottery industry produced thousands of figurines and other knickknacks for export. The variety of products is endless—ashtrays, dinnerware, lamps, planters, souvenir items, toys, vases, etc. Initially, the figurines attracted the largest number of collectors; today many collectors focus on other types of pieces.

Marks: From the beginning of the American occupation of Japan until April 28, 1952, objects made in that country were marked "Japan," "Made in Japan," "Occupied Japan," or "Made in Occupied Japan." Only pieces marked with the last two designations are of major interest to Occupied Japan collectors. The first two marks also were used during other time periods.

References: Florence Archambault, *Occupied Japan for the Home*, Schiffer Publishing, 2000; Gene Florence, *Price Guide to Collector's Encyclopedia of Occupied Japan*, Collector Books, 1999 (updated prices for five-book series *Collector's Encyclopedia of Occupied Japan*); Monica Lynn Clements and Patricia Rosser Clements, *Pocket Guide to Occupied Japan*, Schiffer Publishing, 1999.

Collectors' Club: The Occupied Japan Club, 29 Freeborn St., Newport, RI 02840-1821.

Additional Listings: See *Warman's Americana & Collectibles* for more examples.

Ashtray, 4-3/4" h, metal, spring-loaded head of young boy smoking cigar
.... **50.00**
Bowl, cov, Capo-di-Monte style, double handles, brightly colored enamel dec, winged cherubs in woodland scene, marked "Occupied Japan" **20.00**
Children's play dishes, play set, Blue Willow, 18-pc set **375.00**
Cigarette dispenser, mechanical, inlaid wood, spring-operated sliding drawer loads cigarettes into bird's beak
.... **55.00**
Clock, 10-1/2" h, bisque, double figure, colonial dancing couple, floral encrusted case **250.00**
Cornucopia, 7" x 8", chariot, rearing horse and two cherubs, multicolored beading, gold trim, unglazed bisque
.... **80.00**
Demitasse cup and saucer, 2" d cup, 4" d saucer, Dragonware, brown, green, and white enameled dragons, yellow and white ground, price for set of four cups and saucers **175.00**
Dinnerware, set of 12 place settings, serving pieces, marked "Made in Japan Royal Embassy China, Wheeling, Made in Occupied Japan," price for 55-pc set
.... **455.00**

Figure, man, blue turban, olive green jacket, rust pants, marked, 8-1/4" h, $60.

Figure

3-1/2" h, six musicians, one each playing bass, tambourine, fiddler, clarinet, horn, plus conductor, Tyrolean costumes **110.00**
5-1/2" h boy, 5-1/4" h girl, skiers, price for pr **80.00**
7" h, seated colonial couple, gentleman playing violin, lady reading, marked "Maruyama, Occupied Japan" **120.00**
7" h, standing colonial couple, facing pair **90.00**
Finger bowl, 5-3/4" h, porcelain, winged cherub and raspberries.. **30.00**
Fishing creel, wicker, 2-1/2" x 1-1/4" label with navy border includes patent number **750.00**
Flower frog, 6" h, figural, girl with bird on shoulder, pastel highlights, gold trim, bisque..................... **45.00**
Lamp, Colonial couple, gentleman with guitar, woman holding floral bouquet, floral emb base.............. **25.00**
Platter
12" l, oval, Blue Willow....... **95.00**
16" l, Courley pattern, heavy gold trim, marked "Meito Norleans China" **30.00**
Salt and pepper shakers, pr, coffeepots, cobalt blue glass, metal gray with red Bakelite handles, prig presentation box.............. **25.00**

Tape measure, 2-3/8" l, pig, stamped "Occupied Japan"........... **45.00**
Tea set, 4-3/4" h cov teapot, 4-1/2" d creamer, 5-1/4" d cov sugar, multicolored cottage style..... **125.00**
Toy, 14-1/2" h, celluloid, wind-up, twirls gradually to capture caged chick, mint in orig box **300.00**
Vase, 10" h, bisque, figural, young lady and scrolled cornucopia....... **65.00**
Wall pocket, flying geese, set of one large and three smaller pockets, four-pc set **25.00**

OHR POTTERY

G.E. OHR, BILOXI.

History: Ohr pottery was produced by George E. Ohr in Biloxi, Mississippi. There is a discrepancy as to when he actually established his pottery; some say 1878, but Ohr's autobiography indicates 1883. In 1884, Ohr exhibited 600 pieces of his work, suggesting that he had been a potter for some time.

Ohr's techniques included twisting, crushing, folding, denting, and crinkling thin-walled clay into odd, grotesque, and, sometimes, graceful forms. His later pieces were often left unglazed.

In 1906, Ohr closed the pottery and stored more than 6,000 pieces as a legacy to his family. He had hoped it would be purchased by the U.S. government, which never happened. The entire collection remained in storage until it was rediscovered in 1972.

Today Ohr is recognized as one of the leaders in the American art-pottery movement. Some greedy individuals have taken the later unglazed pieces and covered them with poor-quality glazes in hopes of making them more valuable. These pieces do not have stilt marks on the bottom.

Marks: Much of Ohr's early work was signed with an impressed stamp including his name and location in block letters. His later work was often marked with the flowing script designation "G. E. Ohr."

References: Susan and Al Bagdade, *Warman's American Pottery and Porcelain*, 2nd ed., Krause Publications, 2000; Garth Clark, Robert Ellison, Jr., and Eugene Hecht, *Mad Potter of Biloxi: The Art & Life of George Ohr*, Abbeville Press, 1989; Ralph and Terry Kovel, *Kovels' American Art Pottery*, Crown Publishers, 1993; David Rago, *American Art Pottery*, Knickerbocker Press, 1997.

Bank, 2" d, 4" h, acorn shape, lustered brown and mirror black glaze, int. rattle, stamped "G.E.OHR/Biloxi,Miss"
.... **1,100.00**
Candleholder, 6-1/2" h, 4" d, organic, pinched ribbon handle, in-body twist, ribbed base, yellow, green, and raspberry matte mottled glaze, small chip to base, script mark **3,300.00**

Creamer, slightly pinched spout, angular handle, $9,350. Photo courtesy of David Rago Auctions, Inc.

Chalice, 3-1/4" d, 6" h, ovoid cup, flaring base, lustered black and umber glaze, script signature, restoration to cup **805.00**

Demitasse cup, 2-1/2" h, 3-3/4" d, ext. with rare green, cobalt blue, and raspberry marbleized glaze, int. with sponged cobalt and raspberry volcanic glaze, die-stamped "G. E. Ohr, Biloxi, Miss" **1,500.00**

Jar, cov, 4-1/4" h, 5" d, spherical, gunmetal and green glaze dripping over mottled raspberry ground, shallow storage abrasion, die-stamped "G.E. OHR, Biloxi, Miss" **1,500.00**

Mustache cup, 2-3/4" h, 4" d, hand built as a shirt cuff, ribbon handle, sponged blue glaze, die-stamped "GEO. E. OHR/BILOXI, MISS" **2,000.00**

Pitcher, 4" h, 4-1/4" d, pinched handle, pink and green volcanic glaze, die-stamped "G. E. Ohr, Biloxi, Miss" **2,200.00**

Vase

2-3/4" d, 5-1/4" h, tapered, asymmetrically folded rim, gunmetal and yellow glaze ext., bright orange int., marked "G.E.OHR/Biloxi, miss," few minute rim flecks **4,875.00**

3" d, 8" h, bulbous, folded rim, top cov in speckled mahogany glaze, base in sponged green and amber, marked "G.E.OHR/Biloxi, Miss," couple of small nicks to rim, touch-up to kiln kiss on shoulder **10,450.00**

4-1/2" d, 4-1/2" h, bulbous, marbleized clay, clear glaze, stamped "G.E.OHR, Biloxi, Miss," restored rim **815.00**

7" h, three-sectioned bottle form, glossy olive glaze, top and bottom sponged dark blue, center purple metallic glaze, die-stamped "G. E. OHR/Biloxi, Miss" **1,200.00**

Vase, bulbous, folded rim, top covered in speckled mahogany glaze, the base in sponged green and amber, marked "G.E.OHR/Biloxi, Miss.," couple of small nicks to rim, touch-up to kiln-kiss on shoulder, 3" d, 8" h, $10,450. Photo courtesy of David Rago Auctions.

8-1/2" h, bottle shape, brown, green, and amber speckled lustered glaze, restoration to tiny rim chip, die-stamped "G. E. OHR, Biloxi, Miss" **1,200.00**

9-1/4" h, bottle shape, mottled raspberry, purple, cobalt blue, and green satin glaze, small abrasion ring around widest part from years of storage at production site, die-stamped "G. E. OHR/Biloxi, Miss" **2,500.00**

Vessel, 4-1/4" w, 2-1/2" h, squatty, torn rim, speckled brown semi-matte glaze, marked "GEO.E.OHR/BILOXI, MISS," minor touch-ups to rim and shoulder **865.00**

OLD IVORY CHINA

OLD IVORY
84

History: Old Ivory derives its name from the background color of the china. It was made in Silesia, Germany, during the second half of the 19th century.

Marks: Marked pieces usually have a pattern number (pattern names are not common), a crown, and the word "Silesia."

References: Susan and Al Bagdade, *Warman's English & Continental Pottery & Porcelain*, 3rd ed., Krause Publications, 1998; Alma Hillman, David Goldschmidt & Adam Szynkiewica, *Collector's Encyclopedia of Old Ivory China*, Collector Books, 1998.

Periodical: *The Elegance of Old Ivory*, 28101 SW Petes Mountain Road, West Lima, OR 97068-9357.

Collectors' Club: Society for Old Ivory & Ohme Porcelain, 5946 W. Morraine Ave., Littleton, CO 80128.

Berry bowl, individual
#29, three-pc set **65.00**
#40, three-pc set **75.00**
Biscuit jar, cov, #15 . . . . **350.00**
Bowl
6-1/2" d, #84 . . . . **65.00**
9-1/4" d, #200 . . . . **195.00**
Cake plate, #13, 10" d, open handles, roses around border, one in center
. . . . **125.00**
Chocolate set, #84, chocolate pot, six cups and saucers **850.00**
Creamer, #32 . . . . **50.00**

Cup and saucer, set of six sold for $300. Photo courtesy of Joy Luke Auctions.

Cup, #16, pr **38.00**
Demitasse pot, cov, #16 . . . . . . **395.00**
Mustard pot, cov, #16 . . . . **110.00**
Oyster bowl, #11 . . . . **195.00**
Place setting, cup, saucer, and 8" plate, Eglantine pattern **85.00**

Plate, floral decoration, marked "VIII," 9" d, $50.

Plate
7-3/4" d, #16, two-pc set **35.00**
8-3/4" d, #84, three-pc set **48.00**
Sugar bowl, cov, #75 . . . . **60.00**
Teapot, cov, #15 . . . . **395.00**
Toothpick holder, #16 . . . . **195.00**

OLD PARIS CHINA

History: Old Paris china is fine-quality porcelain made by various French factories located in and around Paris during the 18th and 19th centuries. Some pieces were marked, but most were not. In addition to its fine quality, this type of ware is characterized by beautiful decorations and gilding. Favored colors are dark maroon, deep cobalt blue, and a dark green.

Additional Listings: Continental China and Porcelain (General).

Vase, birds and flowers, 9-3/4" h, price for pair, **$150.** *Photo courtesy of Joy Luke Auctions.*

Basket, reticulated, gold and white dec, c1825 . . . .**1,400.00**
Cake stand, Honore style, green border, c1845 . . . . **220.00**
Charger, 13-1/2" d, hp portrait of young girl with feathered hat and ringlet curls, artist sgd "P. Amaury" **150.00**
Cup and saucer, 5-3/4" d saucer, ftd, floral dec **55.00**
Figure, 18-3/4" h, Napoleon, standing, one arm tucked behind back, other tucked into shirt, full military dress, gilt dec, low sq base, inscribed "Roussel-Bardell," late 19th C . . **700.00**
Luncheon set, light blue ground banding, gilt and iron-red cartouche and monogram, 28 9-1/4" d plates, 18 8-1/4" d plates, 11 6-5/8" d plates, 12 sauce dishes, 11 soup plates, oval 12-1/2" l serving bowl, oval 17-1/2" l platter, two circular cov vegetable tureens, cov sauce tureen, cov oval 12-1/4" tureen with underplate, cov jam jar with attached dish, chips, gilt wear **1,610.00**
Mantel vase, bell-like flowered handles, blue ground, paneled enamel portraits of lowers, gilt trim, minor flower damage, pr **350.00**
Plate, 9-1/2" d, dec by Boyer Feuillet Studio, cobalt blue and gold cobblestone border, hp flower arrangement in center, some wear to gilt, price for pr **250.00**

Urns, pair Italianate Village, handles with masks and foliage, deep rose ground, gold trim, 9-1/2" h, **$700.**

Tea set
5-3/4" h cov teapot, creamer, sugar, 8" d waste bowl, eight cups and saucers, gilt trim, floral design, enameled floral panels, 19th C, gilt wear, creamer handle broken **250.00**
8-5/8" h cov teapot, 7-3/4" h cream pitcher, 5-1/2" cov sugar bowl, gilt ground, enamel dec floral bouquets and banding, 19th C, sugar cov damaged **460.00**
Tray, 11" sq, shaped sides, hp floral dec, gold trim **225.00**
Vase, 7" w, 9" h, two nude women on sides, one draped with blue fabric, other with pink fabric, hp rose and peach flowers, wear to gilt trim **2,195.00**

OLD SLEEPY EYE

History: Sleepy Eye, a Sioux Indian chief who reportedly had a droopy eye, gave his name to Sleepy Eye, Minnesota, and one of its leading flour mills. In the early 1900s, Old Sleepy Eye Flour offered four Flemish-gray heavy stoneware premiums decorated in cobalt blue: a straight-sided butter crock, curved salt bowl, stein, and vase. The premiums were made by Weir Pottery Company, later to become Monmouth Pottery Company, and finally to emerge as the present-day Western Stoneware Company of Monmouth, Illinois.

Additional pottery and stoneware pieces also were issued. Forms included five sizes of pitchers (4, 5-1/2, 6-1/2, 8, and 9 inches), mugs, steins, sugar bowls, and tea tiles (hot plates). Most were cobalt blue on white, but other glaze hues, such as browns, golds, and greens, were used.

Old Sleepy Eye also issued many other items, including bakers' caps, lithographed barrel covers, beanies, fans, multicolored pillow tops, postcards, and trade cards. Regular production of Old Sleepy Eye stoneware ended in 1937.

In 1952, Western Stoneware Company made 22- and 40-ounce steins in chestnut brown glaze with a redesigned Indian's head. From 1961 to 1972, gift editions were made for the board of directors and others within the company. Beginning in 1973, Western Stoneware Company issued an annual limited edition stein for collectors.

Marks: The gift editions made in the 1960s and 1970s were dated and signed with a maple leaf mark. The annual limited edition steins are marked and dated.

References: Susan and Al Bagdade, *Warman's American Pottery and Porcelain*, 2nd ed., Krause Publications, 2000; Elinor Meugnoit, *Old Sleepy Eye*, published by author, 1979.

Collectors' Club: Old Sleepy Eye Collectors Club of America, P.O. Box 12, Monmouth, IL 61462, http://www.maplecity.com/~oseclub.

Reproduction Alert: Blue-and-white pitchers, crazed, weighted, and often with a stamp or the word "Ironstone" are the most common reproductions. The stein and salt bowl also have been made. Many reproductions come from Taiwan.

A line of fantasy items, new items which never existed as Old Sleepy Eye originals, includes an advertising pocket mirror with miniature flour-barrel label, small glass plates, fruit jars, toothpick holders, glass and pottery miniature pitchers, and salt and pepper shakers. One mill item has been made: a sack marked as though it were old, but of a size that could not possibly hold the amount of flour indicated.

Salt crock, 6-1/2" d, 5" h, **$270.** *Photo courtesy of Joy Luke Auctions.*

Mill items
Advertising premium cards, 5-1/2" x 9", full-color Indian lore illus, Old Sleepy Eye Indian character trademark, 10-pc set **875.00**
Cookbook, Sleepy Eye Milling Co., loaf of bread shape, portrait of chief **150.00**
Label, 9-1/4" x 11-1/2" d, egg crate, Sleepy Eye Brand, A. J. Pietrus & Sons Co., Sleepy Eye, MN, red, blue, and yellow **25.00**

Mug, Indian head on handle, Indian and village scenes, 7-1/2" h, $350.

Letter opener, bronze, Indian-head handle, marked "Sleepy Eye Milling Co., Sleepy Eye, MN" **750.00**
Pinback button, "Old Sleepy Eye for Me," bust portrait of chief **175.00**

Pottery and stoneware
Mug
> 3-1/2" d, 4-3/4" h, marked "WS Co. Monmouth, Ill" **395.00**
> 4-1/2" d, 4-1/2" h, attributed to Brush/McCoy **250.00**

Pitcher, 7-3/4" h, #4 . . . . **675.00**
Stein, 22 oz, chestnut brown, 1952 . . . . **275.00**
Tile, cobalt blue and white **950.00**

ONION MEISSEN

History: The blue onion or bulb pattern is of Chinese origin and depicts peaches and pomegranates, not onions. It was first made in the 18th century by Meissen, hence the name Onion Meissen.

Factories in Europe, Japan, and elsewhere copied the pattern. Many still have the pattern in production, including the Meissen factory in Germany.

Marks: Many pieces are marked with a company's logo; after 1891, the country of origin is indicated on imported pieces.

Reference: Robert E. Röntgen, *Book of Meissen*, revised ed., Schiffer Publishing, 1996.

Note: Prices given are for pieces produced between 1870 and 1930. Early Meissen examples bring a high premium.

Ashtray, 5" d, blue crossed swords mark **80.00**
Bowl, 8-1/2" d, reticulated, blue crossed swords mark, 19th C . . **395.00**
Box, cov, 4-1/2" d, round, rose finial **80.00**
Bread plate, 6-1/2" d **75.00**
Cake stand, 13-1/2" d, 4-1/2" h. **220.00**
Candlesticks, pr, 7" h **90.00**
Creamer and sugar, gold edge, c1900 . . . . **175.00**
Demitasse cup and saucer, c1890 . . . . **90.00**
Dish, 12" d, circular, divided . . . **175.00**
Fruit compote, 9" h, circular, openwork bowl, five oval floral medallions. **375.00**
Fruit knives, six-pc set **75.00**
Hot plate, handles **125.00**
Ladle, wooden handle **115.00**
Lamp, 22" h, oil, frosted glass globular form shade **475.00**
Plate, 10" d **100.00**

Platter, Meissen mark, impressed "11.27.00/128," 12-1/2" w x 25" l, $525

Platter
> 12-1/4" d **175.00**
> 13" x 10", crossed swords mark **295.00**

Pot de creme **65.00**
Serving dish, 9-1/4" w, 11" l, floral design on handle **200.00**
Tray, 17" l, cartouche shape, gilt edge **425.00**
Vegetable dish, cov, 10" w, sq . **150.00**

OPALESCENT GLASS

History: Opalescent glass, a clear or colored glass with milky white decorations, looks fiery or opalescent when held to light. This effect was achieved by applying bone ash chemicals to designated areas while a piece was still hot and then refiring it at extremely high temperatures.

There are three basic categories of opalescent glass: (1) blown (or mold blown) patterns, e.g., Daisy & Fern and Spanish Lace; (2) novelties, pressed glass patterns made in limited quantity and often in unusual shapes such as corn or a trough; and (3) traditional pattern (pressed) glass forms.

Opalescent glass was produced in England in the 1870s. Northwood began the American production in 1897 at its Indiana, Pennsylvania, plant. Jefferson, National Glass, Hobbs, and Fenton soon followed.

References: Gary Baker et al., *Wheeling Glass 1829-1939*, Oglebay Institute, 1994, distributed by Antique Publications; Bill Banks, *Complete Price Guide for Opalescent Glass*, 2nd ed., published by author, 1996; Bill Edwards and Mike Carwile, *Standard Encyclopedia of Opalescent Glass*, 3rd ed., Collector Books, 1999; William Heacock, *Encyclopedia of Victorian Colored Pattern Glass*, Book II, 2nd ed., Antique Publications, 1977; William Heacock and William Gamble, *Encyclopedia of Victorian Colored Pattern Glass*, Book 9, Antique Publications, 1987; William Heacock, James Measell, and Berry Wiggins, *Dugan/Diamond*, Antique Publications, 1993; ——, *Harry Northwood* (1990), Book 2 (1991) Antique Publications; Eric Reynolds, *The Glass of John Walsh*, Richard Dennis Publications, 1999.

Pump and trough, vaseline, $195.

Blown
Barber bottle, Raised Swirl, cranberry **295.00**
Berry bowl, master, Chrysanthemum Base Swirl, blue, satin **95.00**
Biscuit jar, cov, Spanish Lace, vaseline **275.00**
Bride's basket, Poinsettia, ruffled top **275.00**
Butter dish, cov, Hobbs Hobnail, vaseline **250.00**
Celery vase, Seaweed, cranberry **250.00**
Creamer
> Coin Dot, cranberry **190.00**
> Windows Swirl, cranberry . . . **500.00**

Cruet
> Chrysanthemum Base Swirl, white, satin **175.00**
> Ribbed Opal Lattice, white . . **135.00**

Finger bowl, Hobbs Hobnail, cranberry
. . . . **65.00**

Lamp, oil
　Inverted Thumbprint, white, amber
　　fan base **145.00**
　Snowflake, cranberry **800.00**

Mustard, cov, Reverse Swirl, vaseline
. . . . **65.00**

Pickle castor, Daisy and Fern, blue,
emb floral jar, DQ, resilvered frame
. . . . **650.00**

Pitcher
　Arabian Nights, white **450.00**
　Fern, blue **450.00**
　Hobbs Hobnail, cranberry . . **315.00**
　Seaweed, blue **525.00**

*Rose bowl, Opalescent Swirl, Fenton,
green, 5-1/2" h, 4-1/2" d, $90.*

Rose bowl, Opal Swirl, white . . . **40.00**
Salt shaker, orig top
　Consolidated Criss-Cross, cranberry
　. . . . . **85.00**
　Ribbed Opal Lattice, cranberry
　. . . . . **95.00**

Spooner, Reverse Swirl, cranberry
. . . . **165.00**

Sugar, cov, Reverse Swirl, cranberry
. . . . **350.00**

Sugar shaker
　Coin Spot, cranberry **275.00**
　Ribbed Opal Lattice, cranberry
　. . . . . **325.00**

Syrup, Coin Spot, cranberry . . . **175.00**

Tumbler
　Acanthus, blue **90.00**
　Christmas Snowflake, blue, ribbed
　. . . . . **125.00**
　Maze, swirling, green **95.00**
　Reverse Swirl, cranberry **65.00**

Waste bowl, Hobbs Hobnail, vaseline
. . . . **75.00**

Novelties
Back bar bottle, 12-1/4" h, robin's egg
blue ground, opalescent stripes swirled
to the right **100.00**

Barber bottle, 8" h, sq, diamond
pattern molded form, light cranberry,
white vertical stripes **275.00**

Bowl, Winter Cabbage, white . . . **45.00**

Bushel basket, blue **75.00**

Chalice, Maple Leaf, vaseline . . . **45.00**

Cruet, Stars and Stripes, cranberry
. . . . **575.00**

Hat, Opal Swirl, white **35.00**

Pressed
Berry bowl, master, Tokyo, green
. . . . **60.00**

Butter dish, cov, Water Lily and
Cattails, blue **300.00**

Card receiver, Fluted Scrolls, white
. . . . **40.00**

Cracker jar, cov, Wreath and Shell,
vaseline **750.00**

Creamer
　Inverted Fan and Feather, blue
　. . . . . **125.00**
　Swag with Brackets, green . . . **90.00**

Cruet, Fluted Scrolls, blue, clear
stopper **295.00**

Jelly compote, Intaglio, blue . . . **55.00**

Salt and pepper shakers, pr, Jewel
and Flower, canary yellow, orig tops
. . . . **250.00**

Sauce, Drapery, Northwood, dec, blue
. . . . **35.00**

Spooner, Swag with Brackets, blue
. . . . **50.00**

Toothpick holder, Ribbed Spiral, blue
. . . . **90.00**

Tumbler
　Drapery, blue **90.00**
　Jackson, green **50.00**
　Jeweled Heart, blue **85.00**

Vase, Northwood Diamond Point, blue
. . . . **75.00**

OPALINE GLASS

History: Opaline glass was a popular mid- to
late-19th century European glass. The glass has a
certain amount of translucency and often is found
decorated with enamel designs and trimmed in gold.

Biscuit jar, cov, white ground, hp,
florals and birds dec, brass lid and bail
handle. **165.00**

Bouquet holder, 7" h, blue opaline
cornucopia-shaped gilt dec flower
holders issuing from bronze stag
heads, Belgian black marble base,
English, Victorian, early 19th C, pr
. . . . **725.00**

*Mug, white opaque ground, cobalt blue
trim, French, 4" h, $95.*

Box, cov, 6" l, 4-3/4" d, 5" h, oblong,
green, serpentine scrolled ends,
gilt-metal mounts and escutcheon,
Continental, mid-19th C **920.00**

Candelabra, Louis XV style, late 19th C
　18-1/2" h, gilt bronze and blue
　　opaline, scrolled candle arms and
　　base, two-light **175.00**
　26-1/2" h, gilt metal and blue
　　opaline, five-light **400.00**

Chalice, white ground, Diamond Point
pattern **35.00**

Dresser jar, 5-1/2" d, egg shape, blue
ground, heavy gold dec **200.00**

Ewer, 13-1/4" h, white ground, Diamond
Point pattern **135.00**

Jardinieres, 5-1/4" h, gilt bronze and
blue opaline, sq, Empire style, tasseled
chains, paw feet, early 20th C, pr
. . . . **1,610.00**

Mantel lusters, 12-3/4" h, blue, gilt dec,
slender faceted prisms, Victorian,
c1880, damage, pr **250.00**

Oil lamp, 24" h, dolphin-form stepped
base, clear glass oil well, frosted glass
shade, late 19th C, converted to
electric, chips **460.00**

Oil lamp base, 22" h, blue, baluster
turned standard on circular foot, 20th C,
converted to electric, pr **635.00**

Perfume bottle, 4" h, baluster form,
blue opaline bottle, gilt metal floral
overlay, foot, and neck mounts, hinged
lid set with shell cameo of young man in
feathered cap, French, late 19th/early
20th C **200.00**

Salt, boat shaped, blue dec, white
enamel garland and scrolling . . . **75.00**

Water pitcher, 12-1/4" h, blue, high
looped handle, bulbous, early 20th C
. . . . **240.00**

ORIENTALIA

History: Orientalia is a term applied to objects made in the Orient, an area which encompasses the Far East, Asia, China, and Japan. The diversity of cultures produced a variety of objects and styles.

References: Sandra Andacht, *Collector's Guide to Oriental Decorative Arts*, Antique Trader Books, 1997; —, *Collector's Value Guide to Japanese Woodblock Prints*, Antique Trader Books, 1999; Carl L. Crossman, *The Decorative Arts of the China Trade*, Antique Collectors' Club, 1999; Christopher Dresser, *Traditional Arts and Crafts of Japan*, Dover Publications, 1994; R. L. Hobson and A L. Hetherington, *Art of the Chinese Potter*, Dover Publications, 1983; Duncan Macintosh, *Chinese Blue and White Porcelain*, Antique Collectors Club, 1994; Andrea and Lynde McCormick, *Chinese Country Antiques: Vernacular Furniture and Accessories, c1780-1920*, Schiffer Publishing, 2000; Nancy N. Schiffer, *Imari, Satsuma, and Other Japanese Export Ceramics*, Schiffer Publishing, 1997; C. A. S. Williams, *Chinese Symbolism and Art Motifs*, 3rd revised ed., Castle Books, 1974.

Periodical: *Orientalia Journal*, P.O. Box 94, Flushing, NY 11363-0094, http://members.aol.com/Orientalia/index.html.

Collectors' Clubs: China Student's Club, 59 Standish Road, Wellesley, MA 02181; Oriental Art Society of Chicago, 6122 N. Clark St., Chicago, IL 60660.

Museums: Arthur M. Sackler Gallery, Smithsonian Institution, Washington, DC; Art Institute of Chicago, Chicago, IL; Asian Art Museum of San Francisco, San Francisco, CA; George Walter Vincent Smith Art Museum, Springfield, MA; Morikami Museum & Japanese Gardens, Delray Beach, FL; Pacific Asia Museum, Pasadena, CA; University of Chicago's Oriental Institute Museum, Chicago, IL.

Additional Listings: Canton, Celadon, Cloisonné, Fitzhugh, Nanking, Netsukes, Rose Medallion, Japanese Prints, and other related categories.

Altar cloth, China, dragon, brown ground, 19th C **230.00**
Altar table, 58-1/2" x 34-1/4" x 16", China, chi chi mu or chicken wing wood, archaic-style spandrels, beaded borders, 18th C. **1,955.00**
Architectural capital, 30" l, Japan, cypress wood carved as shishi, peonies in their mouths, traces of pigment remaining, 18th/19th C, price for pr **1,150.00**
Box, Japan, mixed metal, presentation inscription inside, design of card made entirely of flowers, sgd, Taisho period, 1911-26 . . . . **490.00**
Bowl
7" d, China, blue and white, foliate form, exterior soufflé blue and gilt flowers, int. with floral medallion and peony borders, fan mark on

base, K'ang His period, 1662-1722, minor chips . . . **450.00**
7-3/4" d, China, Hundred Flowers, famille rose enamel, gilt ground, turquoise int., six-character mark on base, Chiang His Tzu Yu Kung Su, c1910 . . . . **290.00**
Bracelet, Japan, silver, Kashira or sword pommels of inlaid mixed metal work, inset in silver frame, 19th C **700.00**
Brocade panel, China, "Hundred Boys" motif, burgundy ground, 19th C **175.00**
Brush washer, 3-1/2" l, Japan, Hirado ware, pumpkin, blue and brown mice dec, 19th C, damage **435.00**
Buddha, 12" h, China, porcelain, celadon robes and throne, bisque hands, feet, and face, 19th C . . **250.00**
Chair, China
Elmwood, armchair, back splat carved with roundels of archaic dragons, 19th C, price for set of four **1,265.00**
Red lacquer, 17-1/2" w, 15" d, 34" h, 19th C, price for pr **1,050.00**
Cup, Chinese, porcelain, engraved dragons under egg yolk yellow color, six-character underglaze blue Kuang Hsu mark, 1874-1908, possibly of the period **200.00**

Cupboard, Shanki, Chinese, red lacquered façade, black and gilt scenes, black lacquered ends, two interior shelves, paneled construction, 47" w, 22" d, 72-3/4" h, **$2,000.** *Photo courtesy of Garth's Auction, Inc.*

Desk, 37" l, 20" d, 35" h, elmwood, two drawers, late 19th C **900.00**
Doctor's cabinet, 28" w, 16" d, 30" h, China, rosewood, mounted like picnic cabinet, int. fitted with numerous drawers, brass mounts, 19th C . **525.00**
Drum and stand, China, 25" d wooden drum, leather top held in place by iron tacks, wood frame with wrought iron attachments, 19th C **460.00**
Fan, folding, China, 19th C
Ivory, shaped stays with numerous figures in garden scenes, fan painted with harbor scene, other vignettes of idyllic village scenes, black lacquer box with gilt butterflies and flowers **490.00**
Wooden stays with black lacquer and gold dec, fan of paper dec with figures in silk and ivory, reverse magenta with three reserves of country scenes, gold and black lacquer case . . . **250.00**
Wooden stays with black lacquer and gold dec of figures in garden vignettes, fan of paper dec in silk and ivory, numerous figures, black and gold lacquered box, 10-1/2" l, very minor loss **230.00**
Fan, folding, Japan, 19th C
All ivory stays dec with shibayama inlay of gold lacquer and semi-precious inlay of birds and flowers, 11-1/2" l, orig box **4,025.00**
Carved ivory stays with shibayama inlay, one side dec with landscape, other with children watching fireworks **375.00**
Figure
3-1/2" h, China, woman, ivory head, lacquered hair, carved wood body, polychrome lacquer, 19th C **125.00**
6" x 5-1/2", horse, Japan, porcelain, Hirado ware, imp two character seal on underside, Meiji period, 1868-1911 . . . . **750.00**
7" h, Rakan with small boy and dragon, sgd "Gyokutomo, Japan, late 19th C, minor loss **230.00**
8-1/4" h, Japan, bisque, eagle, standing on pine tree, slight enameling, Meiji period, 1868-1911 . . . . **300.00**
10" h, Japan, porcelain, overall purple glaze, late 19th C, repair to ears **290.00**
14" h, bronze, standing cockerel, Japan, parcel gilt, silver and copper inlay, 19th C **350.00**

Postcard, Japanese Woman, H. Nakazauwa, **$150.** *Photo courtesy of Postcards International.*

14" h, Goddess Kuan Yin, two-part famille verte dec, China, late 19th C................... **750.00**

19-1/2" h, blanc de chine, Te Hua figure of Lan Tsai Ho, baskets of flowers, holding ling chich in other hand, sgd "Virtue extends even to Fisherman" in imp mark, carved hardwood stand, late 18th/early 19th C..............**7,200.00**

22" l, bronze, tiger, Japan, small signature on underside, burlwood base, Meiji period, 1868-1911 ....**1,150.00**

Ginger jar, 8-1/2" h, China, blue and white mythical animals and floral sprays, K'ang His mark on base, 19th C **250.00**

Incense burner, Japan

Porcelain, Hirado ware, basketweave design, underglaze blue floral sprays, late 19th C, 4-1/4" h **300.00**

Pottery, figure of elephant, urn on back, green, white, and purple enamel dec, 19th C, losses **520.00**

Jar, Japan

8" d, 6-1/2" h, Hirado ware, underglaze blue dragon and waves, dragon carved in the round applied to shoulder, 19th C, minor repairs **1,850.00**

8-1/2" h, Mizusahi, blue phoenixes and dragon, white ground, agate set wooden cov, 19th C ... **690.00**

Kang table, 55" l, 15" h, 19" h, China, elmwood, burgundy lacquer, side panels carved with archaic dragon roundels, 19th C............. **950.00**

Mirror, 11" h, China, base silver with enamel, inlaid jade, late 19th/early 20th C........................ **350.00**

Okimono, 3" l, ivory study of group of rats and lantern, horn inlay, 19th C **635.00**

Painting table, 69" l, 23" d, 34" h, China, Hung Mu, archaic-style spandrels, horse hoof feet, 18th/19th C **920.00**

Robe

Dragon, China, purple ground, brocade of dragons and Buddhist emblems, first quarter 20th C **550.00**

Winter, China, dark blue ground, roundels of Taoist motifs, rabbit fur lining, late 19th C **250.00**

Woman's, China, red silk, wan character frets in gold with blue chain stitch peonies, double sleeves, one with birds and flowers, others with "Hundred Antiques" in fine chain stitch on gold ground, 19th C **3,750.00**

Sake bottle, 11-1/4" h, Japan, Arita ware, Ko-imari dec, three friends pine, bamboo, and prunus, gray underglaze blue, crackled ground, 18th C .. **300.00**

Scholar's stone

21" x 13", yellow stone, elephant skin markings, fitted hardwood stand **250.00**

32" x 11", ling pi, well polished stone in form of sharp mountain peaks, fitted, hardwood stand.... **350.00**

Sculpture, bronze, Japan

10" x 7", Benkei, in armor, with studded club, stealing bell, dec with asparagus in relief, from Dodoji Temple, Meiji period, 1868-1911 .... **575.00**

11" h, standing young girl, Taisho period, 1911-26 .... **225.00**

Silk panel, 42" x 44", Imperial, yellow ground, brocade with five-claw dragon, peonies at corners, 18th C **690.00**

Table, 54" d, 18" h, Indo-Burmese, circular, rosewood ornately carved with foliage and animals......... **1,035.00**

Table screen, 48" l, 41" h, China, early 20th C, six-panel, lacquered wooden frame enclosing blue and white porcelain panels of landscapes and figures in garden scenes, early 20th C **350.00**

Tribute table, 41-1/2" l, 13" d, 32" h, China, Tich li mu, spandrels carved as archer dragons, 18th C, price for pr **2,100.00**

Umbrella stand, 24" h, Japan, Arita ware, blue sand white dec, relief dragon, Meiji period, 1868-1911 .... **700.00**

Vase, bronze

12" h, Japan, globular body, slightly trumpet form mouth, high relief fish dec, Meiji period, 1868-1911, mounted as lamp, repairs **460.00**

Screen, Coromandei, lacquer design on wood, white, black, gold, red, and blue flying cranes, 10 18" x 94" h sections, **$2,860.** *Photo courtesy of Garth's Auction, Inc.*

24" h. Japan, various archaic vessels dec, two character signature on base, Meiji period, 1868-1911 .... **635.00**

Vase, peachbloom, Chinese, 6-1/2" h, K'ang His six-character mark, 19th C, fitted wooden stand **350.00**

Vase, porcelain, Japan

8-1/2" h, greenish-gray glaze, slip flower, sgd "Makuso Kozan" in underglaze blue, Meiji period, 1868-1911 .... **350.00**

9-1/4" h, Japan, Sumida, relief rakan with incense burner, sgd, early 20th C **250.00**

11" h, blue bamboo design, white ground, sgd "Makuzo Kozan sei" within sq cartouche, Meiji period, 1868-1911 .... **1,725.00**

11" h, Japan, Sumida, relief figures in bisque with enamel dec, orange ground, glazed top, early 20th C, mounted as lamp **125.00**

11-1/2" h, relief carved, Fuji, cottages, and pines, charcoal gray glaze, two character marks in underglaze blue on base, early 20th C **1,495.00**

49" h, Japan, Arita, pear-shaped body, flared ribs, blue and white roundels of brocade patterns, fruit, birds, and flowers, 19th C, traces of lacquer remaining **460.00**

Vase and stand, 12" h, mixed metal, Japan, cherry branches handles, silver flowers, gold leaves, plate-like stand with fruiting apple branches, late 19th C **1,725.00**

Walking stick, Japan, carved ivory handle with bird, monkey, puppy, and crab, rosewood shaft, Meiji period, 1868-1911 .... **320.00**

Wine ewer, 6-1/4" h, Hirado ware, form of Hoi tea, bag of wealth, underglaze blue, yellow, pale green, tan, and black accents, 19th C, cover missing . **750.00**

Wine pot, 11" h, Japan, white glazed figure of balloon, Hirado ware, late 19th C, repair to spout, line across middle **415.00**

ORIENTAL RUGS

History: Oriental rugs or carpets date back to 3,000 B.C., but it was in the 16th century that they became prevalent. The rugs originated in the regions of Central Asia, Iran (Persia), Caucasus, and Anatolia. Early rugs can be classified into basic categories: Iranian, Caucasian, Turkoman, Turkish, and Chinese. Later India, Pakistan, and Iraq produced rugs in the Oriental style.

The pattern name is derived from the tribe which produced the rug, e.g., Iran is the source for Hamadan, Herez, Sarouk, and Tabriz.

References: J. R. Azizollahoff, *The Illustrated Buyer's Guide to Oriental Carpets*, Schiffer, 1998; Susan Gomersall, *Kilim Rugs: Tribal Tales in Wool*, Schiffer Publishing, 2000; Walter A. Hawley, *Oriental Rugs, Antique and Modern*, Dover Publications, 1970; Charles W. Jacobsen, *Check Points on How to Buy Oriental Rugs*, Charles E. Tuttle Co., 1981; Robert Pinner and Murray L. Eiland, Jr., *Between the Black Desert and the Red Turkmen Carpets from the Wiedersperg Collection*, Fine Arts Museum of San Francisco, Antique Collectors' Club, 1999; Pamela Thomas, *Oriental Rugs*, Smithmark, 1996.

Periodicals: *HALI*, P.O. Box 4312, Philadelphia, PA 19118; *Oriental Rug Review*, Sinclair Road, New Hampton, NH 03256, http://www.rugreview.com/orr.html; *Orientalia Journal*, P.O. Box 94, Flushing, NY 11363-0094, http://members.aol/com/Orientalia/index.html; *Rug News*, 90 John St., 5th Floor, New York, NY 10038; *Star News*, 2016 26th Ave. East, Seattle, WA 98112.

Collectors' Clubs: American Conference on Oriental Rugs, http://www.acor-rugs.org; Arizonia Oriental Rug/Textile Assoc., 3804 E. Calle DeSoto, Tucson, AZ 85716; Chicago Rug Society, 240 Market St., Rockford, IL 61107; International Hajji Baba Society, Inc. 6500 Pinecrest, Annadale, VA 22003; New Calgary Rug & Textile Club, #201, 618 Second Ave., NW, Calgary, Alberta, T2N 0#1 Canada; Rug Society of San Diego, 1010 Univ. Ave., PMB 241, San Diego, CA 92103; Seattle Textile & Rug Society, 2016 26th Ave. East, Seattle, WA 98112; South Florida Oriental Rug Club, 1633 NE 24th St., Fort Lauderdale, FL 33305-1402; Textile Group of Los Angeles, 894 S. Bronson Ave., Los Angeles, CA 90005; Textile Museum Assoc. of Southern California, P.O. Box 49160, Los Angeles, CA 90049; Triangle Rug Society, 3100 Cornwall Road, Durham, NC 27707.

Museum: Weaving Art Museum & Research Institute, http://www.weavingmuseum.org.

Reproduction Alert: Beware! There are repainted rugs on the market.

Notes: When evaluating an Oriental rug, age, design, color, weave, knots per square inch, and condition determine the final value. Silk rugs and prayer rugs bring higher prices than other types.

Afshar, South Persia, second quarter 20th C, 6' 4" x 5', five stepped polygons and two vases of flowers in midnight blue, navy blue, sky blue, gold, brown, and blue-green on terra-cotta red field, three narrow floral borders of similar coloration, small areas of minor wear, brown corrosion........... **1,035.00**

Agra, India, last quarter 19th C, 8' 6" x 6' 10", overall design of palmettes, rosettes, and flowering vines in rose, tan, light aubergine, ivory, olive, and blue-green on deep wine red field, wide blue-green border of similar design, small areas of wear, edges, and ends

very slightly reduced and machine reovercast............... **8,625.00**

Anatolian Yastik

2' 8" x 1' 10", last quarter 19th C, column of four hooked hexagonal medallions in navy blue, sky blue, red, gold, aubergine, apricot, and light blue-green, red spandrels, multicolored S-motif border, minor wear to center, slight moth damage **1,725.00**

3' x 1' 10", second half 19th C, three hooked diamond medallions flanked by triangles in red, royal blue, aubergine, gold, and blue-green on ivory field, aubergine rosette border, crease, moth damage, border slightly missing from both ends ... **980.00**

Armenian Karabagh, South Caucasus

8' 10" x 3' 9", dated 1911, three lightning medallions each inset with quatrefoil floral motifs, navy blue, royal blue, dark red, rose, camel, aubergine, and blue-green on midnight blue field, navy blue rosette border, small replied areas, corner repairs **1,265.00**

9' x 4' 9", dated 1890, large staggered palmette motifs surrounded by floral motifs in red, rose, brown, gold olive, and blue-green on dark brown field, flowering plant border of similar coloration, rewoven ends, slight brown corrosion **3,750.00**

Bahktiari, West Persia, second quarter 20th C, 7' x 4' 4", eight columns of star-in-octagonal motifs, red, rose, ice blue, slate blue, aubergine, gold, and blue-green on midnight blue field, red spandrels, slate blue floral meander border, slight end fraying **1,265.00**

Baluch, Northeast Persia

4' 4" x 2' 10", early 20th C, scattered geometric flowerheads, serrated lines, small animal motifs in red, aubergine-brown, navy blue, midnight blue on camel field, ivory meander border, slight even wear, minor moth damage, end fraying **1,265.00**

6' 9" x 4' 7", last quarter 19th C, hooked diamond medallion surrounded by small hexagons, deeply serrated leaves in dark red, coral, black, and light aubergine-brown on navy blue field, coral boat border, even wear, black and brown corrosion **1,150.00**

Beshir, West Turkestan, second half 19th C, 9' 6" x 5' 4", five circular medallions and overall lattice of boteh in red, navy blue, gold, apricot, brown, and blue-green border of similar design and coloration **6,325.00**

Bidjar, Northwest Persia, early 20th C, 12' 2" x 9' 4", overall Sfshan design in midnight blue, sky blue, rose, ivory, tan, camel, and light blue-green on abrashed terra-cotta red field, midnight blue palmette and leafy vine border **7,475.00**

Bidjov, prayer, Northeast Caucasus, second half 19th C, 3' 10" x 2' 9", central column of wing-like motifs and diamonds flanked by columns of mihrab motifs and ashik guls in red, royal blue, ivory, and gold on abrashed midnight blue and royal blue reciprocal trefoil border, small holes, end gouge, moth damage **1,955.00**

Ersari Ensi, West Turkestan, last quarter 19th C, 5' 8" x 4' 2", quartered rest-red garden pan field with plant motifs, midnight blue, ivory, apricot, and blue-green, rust-red cruciform hook motif border, dark brown flowering plant elem, small area of wear, small rewoven area, guard stripe missing from one end, end fraying **1,265.00**

Ersari Toroyal Blue, West Turkestan, last quarter 19th C, 5' 5" x 1' 9", two diamonds surrounded by serrated lines and half diamonds in midnight blue, rust-red, gold, ivory, and blue-green, wide multicolored compartmented diamond border, end fraying, small repair **650.00**

Fereghan-Sarouk, West Persia, late 19th C

6' 3" x 3' 10", large rosette medallion, matching spandrels and flowering vines, wine red, navy blue, brown, rose, dark tan-gold, and olive on ivory field, midnight blue flowerhead border, even wear to center, slight end fraying . **1,955.00**

6' 9" x 4' 8", lobed oval medallion, palmette pendants and blossoming vines, red, sky blue, camel, gold, apricot, dark brown, blue-green, on midnight blue field, large ivory spandrels, red palmette and paired arabesque leaf border . . . **5,465.00**

Gendje, South Central Caucasus, last quarter 19th C

9' x 4' 2", diagonal stripes of small hooked squares in red, navy blue, ivory, gold, and blue-green, multicolored diamond-in-

arrowhead motif border, small areas of wear, creases, end fraying **920.00**

9' 9" x 3' 9", diagonal stripes inset with leafy plants in midnight blue, sky blue, red, rust, rose, aubergine, gold, light blue-green, dark blue-green, ivory cruciform motif border, end gouge, small hole, some moth damage **920.00**

Hamadan, Northwest Persia, late 19th C, 13' x 10' 4", hexagonal lattice with stylized floral motifs in navy blue, sky blue, red, rose, gold, rust, and blue-green on camel field, gold turtle variant border, small areas of wear, creases **7,475.00**

Heriz, unusual design elements, red border and ground, dark blue spandrels, overall pile wear and damage, 10' 10" x 10' 13", **$12,925.** *Photo courtesy of Garth's Auction, Inc.*

Heriz, Northwest Persia, early 20th C

9' 6" x 6' 8", staggered rows of large flowerheads in royal blue, ice blue, red, rose, brown, gold, ivory, and blue-green on navy blue field, red cartouche border, small areas of wear. **2,645.00**

12' 4" x 9', large gabled square medallion with palmette pendants in midnight blue, sky blue, rose, gold, ivory, and blue-green on terra-cotta red field, sky blue spandrels, midnight blue turtle border, areas of wear . . . **1,725.00**

Karabagh, South Caucasus, last quarter 19th C, 7' 10" x 3' 10", three large lobed hexagonal medallions each inset with eight cloud band motifs in sky blue, ivory, gold, dark brown, and blue-green on red field, ivory crab variant border, small homes and corner gouges, end tear, brow corrosion **1,265.00**

Karachoph Kazak, Southwest Caucasus, last quarter 19th C, 8' x 6' 4", large octagonal medallion flanked by squares and four star-filled rectangles, ivory, royal blue, gold, rust, and blue-green on red field, royal blue quatrefoil arrowhead and serrated leaf border, moth damage, creases, end gouge, small holes and tear . . **9,200.00**

Karadja, Northwest Persia, early-mid 20th C, 6' 4" x 4' 6", three characteristic medallions surrounded by floral motifs in midnight blue, navy blue, sky blue, red, gold, ivory, rose, light blue-green, and dark blue-green on rust field, wide midnight blue flowering plant border, even center wear, guard stripe partially missing from one end **1,035.00**

Karagashili, Northeast Caucasus, late 19th C, 5' 6" x 3' 9", four sq medallions, red, royal blue, ivory, and camel on midnight blue field, red wine glass border, small areas of wear. . . **1,955.00**

Kashan, West Central Persia, second quarter 20th C, 12' 2" x 9' 2", lobed oval medallion, matching spandrels and blossoming vines in navy blue, sky blue, rose, camel, gray, brown, ivory, and light blue-green on red field, navy blue palmette, rosette, and leaf border, areas of wear, small burn mark **2,100.00**

Kazak, Southwest Caucasus

Prayer, third quarter 19th C, 3' 5" x 3' 3", star dec square prayer cartouche surrounded by hooked diamonds, navy blue, gold, ivory, and blue-green on abrashed red field, ivory star border, small areas of wear, guard stripe missing from one end, small crude repair **2,530.00**

Rug, 4' 6" x 2' 10", late 19th C, concentric gabled rect medallions and small boteh variant motifs in red, ivory, black, and red-brown on slate blue field, two red re-entry motifs, multicolored wine glass variant border, even wear to center, guard stripes partially missing from both ends, small rewoven areas **1,150.00**

Khamseh, Southwest Persia, late 19th/early 20th C, 9' 4" x 4' 3", staggered rows of boteh in midnight blue, navy blue, red, gold, and blue-green on ivory field, multicolored diagonal stripe border, even wear to center, small creases, end fraying, small repairs **2,100.00**

Khirghiz, Central Asia, mid-19th C, 9' 6" x 4' 4", diagonal rows of cruciform motifs, red, navy blue, and brown, red-brown and gold reciprocal border, areas of wear, small holes, border partially missing from both ends **1,150.00**

Kuba, Northeast Caucasus, last quarter 19th C

4' 6" x 3', three Lesghi stars in navy blue, sky blue, red, rose, gold, and blue-green on brown field, ivory, stylized flowerhead border, brown corrosion, small corner gouge, slight end graying **1,100.00**

5' x 3' 4", serrated hexagonal lattice of flowering plants in red, rose, sky blue, gold, ivory, and blue-green on dark brown field, ivory stylized flowerhead border, slight even wear, small rewoven area, brown corrosion **1,495.00**

Kurd, Northwest Persia

Bagface, early 20th C, 3' x 2' 7", three hooked concentric medallions in midnight blue and royal blue, red, apricot, aubergine, gold, and blue, green, midnight blue octagon border, slight wear to center, small repairs **865.00**

Rug, last quarter 19th C, 5' 10" x 3' 5", column of six irregular medallions flanked by two hexagons and numerous hook motifs in red, navy blue, ivory, and blue-green on mg field, blue-green floral meander border, rewoven areas **1,0335.00**

Rug, last quarter 19th C, 6' 6" x 4' 4", large hexagonal lattice with double palmette motifs, abrashed royal blue, red, rose, gold, red-brown, and blue-green on ivory field, red flowering plant border, moth damage, end fraying. **980.00**

Saddlebags, early 20th C, 4' 2" x 2' 2", columns of paired serrated leaves, ivory, red, navy blue, apricot, and aubergine on midnight blue field, ivory meander border, some moth damage, small repairs **575.00**

Kurd-Bidjar, Northwest Persia, last quarter 19th C

4' 10" x 3' 10", stepped hexagonal medallion with arrowhead pendants in midnight and sky blue, rose, red-brown, gold, and blue-green on terra-cotta red field, blue spandrels, ivory and dark brown reciprocal border, small areas of wear **2,070.00**

18' x 3' 8", staggered rows of rosettes surrounded by flowering dark red, rose, sky blue, gold, ivory, aubergine, and blue-green vines, midnight blue field, ivory boteh and vine border, slight even wear **2,300.00**

Marasali, East Caucasus, mid-19th C, prayer, 3' 10" x 3' 6", diamond lattice with boteh in navy blue, sky blue, red, ivory, brown, and blue-green on light gold field, narrow dark brown circle and triangle border, ends and one side rewoven, even wear, other small repairs **3,200.00**

Moghan, Southeast Caucasus, last quarter 19th C, 8' 8" x 3' 8", column of eight octagonal Memling guls in midnight blue, royal blue, ivory, gold, brown, and blue-green on red field, wide ivory endless knot motif border, small areas of minor wear, small corner gouge, edge repair, slight end fraying **3,335.00**

Northwest Persian, late 19th/early 20th C, 11' 2" x 8' 4", serrated diamond lattice with weeping willow motifs and flowering plants, midnight blue, royal blue, red, rose, gold, and blue-green on ivory field, midnight blue rosette and leaf border, rewoven areas . . **12,650.00**

Qashqai, Southwest Persia, late 19th C, 9' x 5' overall octagons, serrated leaves, hooked plant motifs, red, royal blue, ivory, gold, red-brown, light green, and dark blue-green on midnight blue field, ivory hooked octagon border **4,315.00**

Qashqai Soumak bag, Southwest Persia, early 20th C, 1' 2" x 1", three columns of hooked diamonds in red, sky blue, gold, ivory, camel, and dark green on midnight blue field, red diamond border, slight moth damage, small crude repair **750.00**

Sarouk, West Persia, early 20th C, 6' 5" x 4' 3", overall floral sprays, navy blue, red, camel, ivory, olive, and blue-green on wine red field, midnight blue palmette and floral spray border **1,610.00**

Sarouk, rust red border, midnight blue spandrels, ivory ground, 4' 3" x 6' 10", $3,575. Photo courtesy of Garth's Auctions, Inc.

Seichour, Northeast Caucasus, third quarter 19th C, 6' x 3' 7", three St. Andrew Cross motifs flanked by flowering vines, red, navy blue, rose, black, gold, and ivory, blue-green field, two navy blue and ivory Georgian borders, small areas of wear, small holes, crease, end fraying . . . **2,875.00**

Serab, Northwest Persia, early 20th C, 13' 8" x 3' 8", column of five hexagonal medallions flanked by stars and octagons in navy blue, ivory, red, gold, red-brown, and blue-green on camel field, ivory square motif and flowerhead border, small areas of wear, end fraying, black corrosion. **1,265.00**

Serapi, Northwest Persia, second half 19th C, 11' 4" x 10' 2", large concentric medallion flanked by serrated leaf motifs in midnight blue, sky blue, ivory, tan, rose, and blue-green on terra-cotta red field, turtle variant border of similar coloration, areas of wear, crease **7,200.00**

Shahsavan Soumak, Northwest Persia

Bagface, dated 1864, 1' 9" x 1' 7", staggered hooked diamonds, navy blue, sky blue, red, gold, and light blue-green on ivory field, navy blue hooked sq border, edges very

slightly reduced, small repairs
.....................**2,530.00**

Cargo bag, late 19th/early 20th C, 3' 6" x 1' 10" x 1' 5", four hooked diamonds, flanked by small triangle motifs in midnight blue, gold, blue-green, and white cotton on red field, multicolored serrated vine border, small home, slight corner wear **1,610.00**

Shirvan, East Caucasus

Kelim, early 20th C, 10' x 5' 3", diagonal rows of serrated diamonds, red, rust, royal blue, tan, gold, and black on ivory field, very narrow reciprocal border of similar coloration, slight wear ...**1,380.00**

Prayer, third quarter 19th C, 4' 4" x 2' 9", serrated hexagonal lattice of flowering plants, midnight blue, royal blue, red, light aubergine, and blue-green on gold field, red interrupted vine border, even wear, outer guard stripe missing all around, main border partially missing from both ends, slight moth damage..........**2,300.00**

Rug, last quarter 19th C, 4' x 3', large keyhole medallion insert with four octagons in royal blue, dark red, gold, ivory, and maroon multicolored hexagon border, even wear to center, slight moth damage and touch-up, black corrosion
.....................**1,265.00**

Soumak, Southwest Persia, early 20th C, salt bag, 1' 9" x 1' 5", square grid of indented diamonds, midnight blue, royal blue, red, rust, ivory, gold, and dark green, wide midnight blue boteh border, slight corner wear **1,380.00**

Tabriz, Northwest Persia

9' 10" x 7' 3", second quarter 20th C, diamond medallion surrounded by palmettes and leafy vines, midnight blue, royal blue, red, rose, brown, gold, olive, and pale green on ivory field, royal blue spandrels, red palmettes and diamond border, areas of minor war, slight touch-up
.....................**2,530.00**

11' 9" x 8' 7", early 20th C, overall harshang variant design, large palmettes in navy blue, sky blue, rose, gold, aubergine, camel, olive, light green, and dark green, on terra-cotta red field, multicolored paired half medallion border, areas of some wear, small replied areas at one end **9,200.00**

Talish, Southeast Caucasus, last quarter 19th C, 7' 9" x 3' 7", perimeter of gold arrowheads on empty navy blue field, ivory border of rosettes and square motifs in red, royal blue, gold, and blue-green, one end and other small areas rewoven........**7,475.00**

Tekke, West Turkestan

6' 6" x 4' 2", late 19th C, three columns of 10 main carpet guls in red, ivory, midnight blue, navy blue on rust field, rect motif border, pole tree elems of similar coloration, slight corner wear, small stains
....................**1,265.00**

7' 7" x 6', first half 19th C, five columns of 10 main carpet guls in midnight blue, light red, ivory, and blue-green, abrashed light rust field, ivory boat border, even wear, holes, crude repairs **4,025.00**

Ushak, West Anatolia, late 19th/early 20th C, 20' 8" x 13', lobed circular medallion surrounded by palmettes, cloud bands, vines in navy blue, red, rose, and tan on ivory field, rose rosette and paired leaf border, reduced in length, small areas of wear, some moth damage, small repairs **5,750.00**

Veramin, North Persia, early 20th C, 11' 2" x 4' 6", overall Mina Khani floral lattice in red, royal blue, ivory, gold, red-brown, and blue-green on midnight blue field, ivory diamond border, slight even wear, two small holes, small creases..................**1,610.00**

Yomud Chuval, West Turkestan, last quarter 19th C, 3' 9" x 2' 6", nin chuval guls in red, ivory, midnight blue, slate blue on aubergine field, red stepped polygon border, staggered flowering plant elem of similar coloration, small areas of minor wear, edges slightly reduced and re-overcast **980.00**

Zahatala, North Caucasus, last quarter 19th C, 6' 9" x 4' 4", large keyhole medallion insert with octagon and other geometric motifs in ivory, navy blue, red-brown, tan-gold, dark brown, and blue-green on wine red field, hooked rosette border of similar coloration, small areas of wear, rewoven and replied areas **5,475.00**

OVERSHOT GLASS

History: Overshot glass was developed in the mid-1800s. To produce overshot glass, a gather of molten glass was rolled over the marver, upon which had been placed crushed glass. The piece then was blown into the desired shape. The finished product appeared to be frosted or iced.

Early pieces were made mainly in clear glass. As the demand for colored glass increased, color was added to the base piece and occasionally to the crushed glass.

Pieces of overshot generally are attributed to the Boston and Sandwich Glass Co., although many other companies also made it as it grew in popularity.

Museum: Sandwich Glass Museum, Sandwich, MA.

Pitcher, amber, applied dark amber handle, Boston & Sandwich, 6-3/4" h, $325.

Basket, 7-1/4" h, 5" d, transparent green shading to colorless, ruffled swirled edge, sq thorn handle, melon-ribbed base with pineapple-like design, entire surface with overshot finish **285.00**

Bowl, 6" d, 3-7/8" h, pale blue opaque, applied amber rigaree around top, applied green leaves, white, pink, and blue applied flowers **235.00**

Celery vase, 6" h, 3-1/2" d, scalloped top, cranberry ground..........**90.00**

Cheese dish, dome cov, 8" d, 7" h, cranberry ground, enameled crane and cattails, applied colorless faceted finial
.........................**425.00**

Compote, 10" d, 10-1/4" h, cranberry ground, wide rounded bowl, scalloped crown gilt trimmed rim, compressed knop on cylindrical pedestal, wide flaring foot, late 19th C **300.00**

Fairy lamp, 4-1/4" h, 3" d, opalescent, figural, crown shape, colorless pressed "Clark" base **195.00**

Pitcher

8-1/4" h, green ground, amber shell handle, Sandwich, c1875, brown age line near lip **225.00**

9" h, tankard, cranberry ground, applied colorless reeded handle, hinged metal lid.........**195.00**

Vase, 5-1/2" h, pink ground, applied random amber threading **225.00**

OWENS POTTERY

History: J. B. Owens began making pottery in 1885 near Roseville, Ohio. In 1891, he built a plant in Zanesville and in 1897, began producing art pottery. After 1907, most of the firm's production centered on tiles.

Owens Pottery, employing many of the same artists and designs as its two cross-town rivals, Roseville and Weller, can appear very similar to that of its competitors, e.g., Utopian (brown glaze), Lotus (light glaze), and Aqua Verde (green glaze).

There were a few techniques used exclusively at Owens. These included Red Flame ware (slip decoration under a high red glaze) and Mission (over-glaze, slip decorations in mineral colors) depicting Spanish Missions. Other specialties included Opalesce (semi-gloss designs in lustered gold and orange) and Coralene (small beads affixed to the surface of the decorated vases).

References: Paul Evans, *Art Pottery of the United States*, 2nd ed., Feingold & Lewis Publishing, 1987; Frank Hahn, *Collector's Guide to Owens Pottery*, Golden Era Publications, 1996; Ralph and Terry Kovel, *Kovels' American Art Pottery*, Crown Publishers, 1993; Kristy and Rick McKibben and Jeanette and Martin Stofft, *Owens Pottery Unearthed*, published by authors (45 12th St., Tell City, IN 47586), 1996.

Bud vase
6-1/4" h, 2-1/2" w, standard glaze, yellow roses, marked "#804," initials for Harry Robinson ..**150.00**
9" h, molded body under metallic glaze, hairline to body.....**160.00**

Ewer, 10" h, brown high glaze, cherry design......................**200.00**

Jug, 8" w, 4-1/2" w, standard glaze, ear of corn dec, marked and sgd "Tot Steele" **230.00**

Lamp base, 5" d, 11-1/4" h, classic shape, painted yellow daffodils, unmarked, drilled, some glaze bubbles on back....................**365.00**

Mug, 7-1/2" h, standard glaze, cherries, marked "#830," sgd "Henry R. Robinson," hairlines to int. **110.00**

Pitcher, 8-1/2" h, dark brown to green, orange and brown flowers, green leaves, marked "JBO" intertwined, artist sgd "HK," crack in handle......**110.00**

Tankard
7" h, brown high glaze, Indian design, incised signature, restored **325.00**
12" h, brown glaze, artist sgd, imp mark..................**210.00**

Vase, Utopia, three handles, brown glaze, grape leaf decoration, artist signed "J. B. Owens, Utopia," 7" h, **$215.**

Vase
3-3/4" h, Utopia, dark brown, lighter brown, orange, and yellow floral dec, imp mark "#110," small base flake **100.00**
4" h, Lotus, bee flying above green blades of grass, ivory to blue ground, imp mark, artist initials **400.00**
4" h, Utopian, floral **135.00**
4" h, 4" w, yellow chick surrounded by thinly painted grass, four feet, artist sgd **300.00**
5-3/4" h, brown flowers, marked **100.00**
5-3/4" h, 3-3/4" w, brown clover, standard glaze, marked "#232" **100.00**
6-3/8" h, Utopian Ware, silver overlay, flared rim on tapered oviform,

glossy glaze, cream and brown rose blossoms and leaves, shaded brown ground, silver overlay imp "Utopian J. B. Owens 923" and "Phee F.N. Silver Co.," crazing, scratches, nicks **290.00**
7" h, fluted, Ida Steel, floral ..**625.00**
7-1/2" h, high glaze, orange, white, and green grapes, vines, and leaves, pink to green ground, imp "Owens #1260" **300.00**
8" h, Aqua Verdi, green matte, textured surface, incised geometrics, four handles around neck, unmarked **550.00**
8" h, 8-1/2" w, ftd pillow, dark to light brown with yellow ground, Indian portrait, cream and red vest, blue in hair, imp mark, repaired top **1,100.00**
8-1/2" h, standard glaze, yellow berry dec, green leaves, imp mark **100.00**
10" h, orange and yellow tulips, green leaves, brown ground, imp mark **250.00**
10" h, 5" w, standard glaze, marked "Owens #010"...........**210.00**
10-3/4" h, 5-3/4" d, sgraffito, orange and blue irises, dark brown ground, Henri Deux, unmarked, pea-sized burst bubble on shoulder ..**650.00**
11"h, Utopia, rose with green leaves, brown stems, orange and brown ground, marked, artist sgd .**260.00**
11-1/2" h, 5" w, Utopian, standard glaze, marked "Owens Utopian #1031," sgd "Sarah Timberlake" **375.00**
12" h, molded flowers and heads, green matte glaze, hairline .**160.00**
12-1/2" h, pink poppy, green stems and leaves, pink, ivory, and light blue ground, artist initialed, imp mark **600.00**
13-1/2" h, green, yellow, and brown leaves, swirling mahogany, yellow, and dark brown ground, artist initials "A. H.," incised bottom, sunburst "J. B. Owens"....**650.00**

PADEN CITY GLASS

History: Paden City Glass Manufacturing Co. was founded in 1916 in Paden City, West Virginia. David Fisher, formerly of the New Martinsville Glass Manufacturing Co., operated the company until his death in 1933, at which time his son, Samuel, became president. A management decision in 1949 to expand Paden City's production by acquiring American Glass Company, an automated manufacturer of bottles, ashtrays, and novelties, strained the company's finances, forcing it to close permanently in 1951.

Contrary to popular belief and previously incorrect printed references, the Paden City Glass Manufacturing Company had absolutely no connection with the Paden City Pottery Company, other than their identical locale.

Although Paden City glass is often lumped with mass-produced, machine-made wares into the Depression glass category, Paden City's wares were, until 1948, all handmade. Its products are better classified as "Elegant Glass" of the era, as it ranks in quality with the wares produced by contemporaries such as Fostoria, New Martinsville, and Morgantown.

Paden City kept a low profile, never advertising in consumer magazines of the day. It never marked its glass in any way because a large portion of its business consisted of sales to decorating companies, mounters, and fitters. The firm also supplied bars, restaurants, and soda fountains with glassware, as evidenced by the wide range of tumblers, ice cream dishes, and institutional products available in several Paden City patterns.

Paden City's decorating shop also etched, cut, hand painted, and applied silver overlay and gold encrustation. However, not every decoration found on Paden City shapes will necessarily have come from the factory. Cupid, Peacock and Rose, and several other etchings depicting birds are among the most sought-after decorations. Pieces with these etchings are commanding higher and higher prices even though they were apparently made in greater quantities than some of the etchings that are less known, but are just as beautiful.

Paden City is noted for its colors: opal (opaque white), ebony, mulberry (amethyst), Cheriglo (delicate pink), yellow, dark green (forest), crystal, amber, primrose (reddish-amber), blue, rose, and great quantities of ruby (red). The firm also produced transparent green in numerous shades, ranging from yellowish to a distinctive electric green that always alerts knowledgeable collectors to its Paden City origin.

Rising collector interest in Paden City glass has resulted in a sharp spike in prices on some patterns. Currently, pieces with Orchid or Cupid etch are bringing the highest prices. Several truly rare items in these etchings have recently topped the $1,000 mark. Advanced collectors seek out examples with unusual and/or undocumented etchings. Colored pieces, which sport an etching that is not usually found on that particular color, are especially sought after and bringing strong prices. In contrast, prices for common items with Peacock and Rose etch remain static, and the prices for dinnerware in ruby Penny Line and pink or green Party Line have inched up only slightly, due to its greater availability.

References: Jerry Barnett, *Paden City, the Color Company*, privately printed, 1979, out-of-print; Lee Garmon and Dick Spencer, *Glass Animals of the Depression Era*, Collector Books, 1993; Naomi L. Over, *Ruby Glass of the 20th Century*, The Glass Press, 1990, 1993-94 value update, Book II, 1999; Hazel Marie Weatherman, *Colored Glassware of the Depression Era 2*, Glassbooks, 1974; *Paden City Catalog Reprints from the 1920s*, The Glass Press, 2000.

Periodical: *Paden City Glass Collectors Guild*, 42 Aldine Road, Parsippany, NJ 07054.

Adviser: Michael Krumme.

Box, covered, Line #411, Mrs. B, Ardith etch on cover, base unetched, one interior diagonal divider, black, 7-1/2" w diagonally, 4" h, $150. Photo courtesy of Michael Krumme.

Color is crystal (clear) unless otherwise noted.

Animal, made by Paden City for Barth Art
Dragon Swan, light blue **495.00**
Squirrel **30.00**

Bowl, nappy
#412 Crow's Foot Square, 5", ruby **35.00**
#412 Crow's Foot Square, 7", Orchid etch, yellow **40.00**
9-1/2" oval, ruby............ **45.00**

Bowl, finger
#991 Penny Line, ruby....... **22.00**
#994 Popeye & Olive, with liner, royal blue **127.00**
#994 Popeye & Olive, ruby ... **34.00**

Bowl, console
#191 Party Line, rolled edge, light blue **45.00**
#210 Regina, 13" d, Black Forest etch, ebony **185.00**
#220 Largo, three-footed, cupped up, light blue **70.00**
#220 Largo, three-footed, flat rim, light blue, Garden Magic etch **127.00**
#300 Archaic, 11" d, Cheriglo, Cupid etch.................. **230.00**

#411 Mrs. B., Gothic Garden etch, yellow **50.00**
#412 Crow's Foot Square, rolled edge, cobalt blue......... **60.00**
#440 Nerva, 11" d, flat rim, light blue **50.00**
#881 Gadroon, Frost etch.... **65.00**
#888 12" low scalloped-edge bowl, Floral Medallion etch **59.00**

Bowl, two-handled serving
#210 Regina, Black Forest etch **110.00**
#210 Spire, Eden Rose etch.. **29.00**
#215 Glades, Spring Orchard etch **50.00**
#221 Maya, light blue....... **57.50**
#411 Mrs. B., Gothic Garden etch, yellow................. **135.00**
#411 Mrs. B., Ardith etch, pink **50.00**
#412 Crow's Foot Square, Orchid etch **68.00**
#412 Crow's Foot Square, silver overlay **60.00**
#440 Nerva, Fuchsia etch ... **52.00**

Cake salver, footed
#210 Regina, Black Forest etch **90.00**
#215 Glades, cutting **40.00**
#300 Archaic, Gothic Garden etch, topaz **99.00**
#300 Archaic, Peacock and Rose etch, Cheriglo............ **95.00**
#300 Archaic, Lela Bird etch, green **125.00**
#411 Mrs. B., Ardith etch, yellow **55.00**
#411 Mrs. B., Gothic Garden, green **50.00**
#412 Crow's Foot Square, Orchid etch, yellow **95.00**
#412 Crow's Foot Square, opal **50.00**
#895 Lucy, silver deposit **40.00**

Candy box, cov, flat
#411 Mrs. B., Ardith etch, green **150.00**
#411 Mrs. B., Orchid etch, pink **325.00**
#412 Crow's Foot Square, square shape, ebony with crystal lid **60.00**
#412 Crow's Foot Square, square shape, ruby **125.00**
#412 Crow's Foot Square, Orchid etch, ruby.............. **230.00**
#412-1/2 Crow's Foot Square, cloverleaf shape, cobalt blue **225.00**
#412-1/2 Crow's Foot Square, cloverleaf shape, ruby **96.00**

Candy dish, cov, footed
#191 Party Line, ftd, Black Forest etch **149.00**

#412-1/2 Crow's Foot Square cloverleaf shaped covered candy, cobalt blue **195.00**
#555, with beaded edge, ruby **67.00**
#890 Crow's Foot Round, amber **95.00**

Candleholders, pr
#191 Party Line, medium blue.**25.00**
#210 Regina, Black Forest etch **140.00**
#211 Spire, Spring Orchard etch **49.00**
#215 Glades, double, ruby . . .**75.00**
#220 Largo, crystal, satin finish, silver deposit. **30.00**
#300 Archaic, Cupid etch, pink **140.00**
#300 Archaic, Lela Bird etch, pink **135.00**
#412 Crow's Foot Square, 6-1/2" keyhole style, ruby **70.00**
#412 Crow's Foot Square, keyhole style, Orchid etch **125.00**
#444 Vale three-light with cutting **40.00**
#701 Triumph, Eden Rose etch, pink **90.00**
#890 Crow's Foot Round, ruby **107.00**
#2000 Mystic double candleholders, ruby, pair. **92.00**

Cheese and cracker set, #215 Glades, Spring Orchard etch. **35.00**

Cigarette box & lid, #220 Largo, ruby, very rare **240.00**

Cocktail shaker, #902, three-part with strainer and stopper, cut **50.00**

Compote, footed
#211 Spire, flared, Ardith etch.**85.00**
#300 Archaic, Cupid etch, pink **99.00**
#300 Archaic, Cupid etch, blue **450.00**
#411 Mrs. B., Ardith etch, yellow **75.00**
#411 Mrs. B, Gothic Garden etch, ebony, rolled edge **89.00**
#411 Mrs. B, Gothic Garden etch, yellow, flared **89.00**
#412 Crow's Foot Square, short stem, pink **25.00**
#412 Crow's Foot Square, tall stem, silver encrusted edge and floral etch, cobalt blue **200.00**
#412 Crow's Foot Square, 6-1/2", ruby. **70.00**
#412 Crow's Foot Square, 6-1/2", Orchid etch, ruby **120.00**
#412 Crow's Foot Square, 6-1/2", Orchid etch, cobalt blue . . .**135.00**

#412 Crow's Foot Square, 6-1/2", opal, silver overlay **180.00**
#412 Crow's Foot Round, 9", ruby **50.00**
#444 with ball stem, ruby **40.00**
Creamer, #90 Chevalier, ruby . . .**18.00**

Creamer and sugar
#191 Party Line, Cheriglo. . . .**24.00**
#210 Regina, Black Forest etch **75.00**
#210 Regina, green, Black Forest etch **115.00**
#300 Archaic, Cupid etch, green **295.00**
#411 Mrs. B Gothic Garden etch **45.00**
#412 Crow's Foot Square, mulberry **42.00**
#412 Crow's Foot Square, ruby **35.00**
#412 Crow's Foot Square, Orchid etch, ruby **265.00**
#503, no optic, pink **20.00**
#503, no optic, Cupid etch with gold-encrusted medallion, pink **495.00**
#555, Gazebo etch. **42.00**
#881 Gadroon, ruby **56.00**
#994 Popeye and Olive, ruby.**70.00**

Cream soup
#412 Crow's Foot Square, amber **10.00**
#412 Crow's Foot Square, ruby **25.00**

Cup and saucer, #211 Maya, ruby, $30. *Photo courtesy of Michael Krumme.*

Cup and saucer
#215 Glades, ruby **15.00**
#220 Largo, ruby **25.00**
#330 Cavendish, ruby **16.50**
#411 Mrs. B., Ardith etch, topaz **15.00**
#412 Crow's Foot Square, ruby **20.00**
#890 Crow's Foot Round, forest green **18.00**
#991 Penny Line cup only, Black Forest etch, ruby **100.00**
#991 Penny Line, ruby **12.00**
#994 Popeye & Olive ruby . . .**30.00**

Decanter
Georgian, cobalt blue, cobalt blue stopper **195.00**
Lobed-shape decanter, five Penny Line wines, Spring Orchard etch **80.00**
New Martinsville Radiance cordial decanter, Paden City's Trumpet Flower etching, with five plain cordials, unusual item. **250.00**

Epergne, three pieces, #888, Forest Green **175.00**

Ice bucket, metal bail
#902, Cupid etch, pink **225.00**
#902, Black Forest etch, pink **255.00**

Ice tub, tab handles#191 Party Line, green. **19.00**
#895 Lucy, Blue Willow etch .**129.00**

Marmalade with cover
#207 two-handled covered jam dish with ladle. **32.00**

Emeraldglo, metal lid, liner, and spoon **25.00**

Mayonnaise, bowl and underplate
#215 Glades, Spring Orchard etch **33.00**
#300 Archaic, Cupid, green, with orig ladle. **325.00**
#300 Archaic, Nora Bird etch, Cheriglo. **135.00**
#411 Mrs. B., Ardith etch, yellow, with orig ladle **157.00**
#411 Mrs. B., Ardith etch, with orig ladle **37.00**
#412 Crow's Foot Square, no underplate, opal **40.00**
#555 beaded edge and "wing" handles, Gazebo etch. **65.00**
#777 Comet, frosted rim, cut stars, with orig ladle **25.00**
#881 Gadroon, Black Forest etch, with ladle. **125.00**
#895 Lucy, Oriental Garden etch **58.00**

Napkin holder, #210 Regina, green **150.00**

Pitcher
#191 Party Line 74 oz with lid, green **95.00**
#210 Regina tall jug and four blown tumblers, Black Forest etch, green **1,825.00**
#994 Popeye & Olive, cobalt blue **395.00**

Plate
#210 Regina, Black Forest etch, 8" d **35.00**
#330 Cavendish, 10" dinner, ruby **30.00**

#412 Crow's Foot Square, 8-1/2", amber **7.00**
#412 Crow's Foot Square, 8-1/2", ruby **10.00**
#412 Crow's Foot Square, 11-1/2", ruby with gold-encrusted etch **90.00**
Platter, oval, #412 Crow's Foot Square, ruby **35.00**
Sugar bowl, #411 Mrs. B., Gothic Garden etch, green **45.00**
Sugar pourer
#94 "Bullet" style, threaded metal screw on base **125.00**
#154 Rena, swirl pattern, metal top, Cheriglo **125.00**
Syrup pitcher
#180 with glass lid, floral cutting, green **69.00**
#198 with glass lid, cutting . . . **35.00**
Tray, center handle
#210 Regina, Black Forest etch **78.00**
#215 Glades, Spring Orchard etch **35.00**
#220 Largo, ruby **95.00**
#411 Mrs. B., Ardith etch, yellow **58.00**
#412 Crow's Foot Square, Orchid etch, ruby **165.00**
#412 Crow's Foot Square, Delilah Bird etch, amber **95.00**
#412 Crow's Foot Square, opal, rare **350.00**
#555 . . . . **22.00**
#701 Triumph, aquamarine blue with cutting **18.00**
#701 Triumph, Delilah Bird etch **40.00**
#881 Gadroon, ruby **75.00**
#890 Crow's Foot Round, cupped up, floral etch **50.00**
#1504 swan-shaped handle, Gazebo etch **85.00**
#1504 swan-shaped handle, silver overlay **95.00**
Tray, two handled
#210 Regina, Black Forest etch, pink **95.00**
#411 Mrs. B., Gothic Garden, ebony **40.00**
#412 Crow's Foot Square, Sasha Bird etch **122.00**
Tumblers and stemware
#191 Party Line, tall footed soda, green **24.00**
#191 Party Line footed parfait, green **20.00**
#191 Party Line tumbler, medium blue **10.00**

#191 Party Line tumbler, Nora Bird etch, pink **129.00**
#210 Regina, goblet, tall stem, Black Forest etch, green **230.00**
#210 Regina, tumbler, 5-1/2", Black Forest etch, pink **80.00**
#215 Glades, 3-oz ftd cocktail tumbler, Spring Orchard etch **12.50**
#991 Penny Line, cordial, ruby with platinum rings **25.00**
#991 Penny Line, wine, ruby with platinum rings **22.00**
#991 Penny Line flat ice tea, ruby **22.50**
#991 Penny Line low-footed goblet, ruby **10.00**
#991 Penny Line footed goblet, mulberry **18.50**
#991 Penny Line low-footed sherbet, mulberry **12.50**
Blown tumbler, 5", Ardith etch, green **22.00**
Blown tumbler, 5-3/4" h, Black Forest etch, Cheriglo **75.00**
Vases
#11, 9", box shape, Utopia etch, ebony **270.00**
#182 8" elliptical, Cupid etch, Cheriglo **650.00**
#182 8" elliptical, Daisy etch, pink **142.50**
#182 8" elliptical, gold-encrusted Peacock and Rose etch, ebony **335.00**
#182 8" elliptical, Lela Bird etch, ebony **125.00**
#182 8" elliptical, Orchid etch, green **300.00**
#182 8" elliptical, Sunflower etch, green with gold trim **200.00**
#182-1/2 5" elliptical vase, Ardith etch, ormolu holder **75.00**
#184 10" bulbous-bottom, Lela Bird etch, ebony **150.00**
#184 10" bulbous-bottom, Utopia etch, ebony **195.00**
#184 10" bulbous-bottom, Peacock and Rose etch, Cheriglo . . . **165.00**
#184 10" bulbous-bottom, Rose Bouquet etch, green **158.00**
#184 10" bulbous-bottom, Lady with Grapes etch, Cheriglo **260.00**
#184, 10", Orchid etch, ruby . **330.00**
#184, 10", Utopia etch, ruby . **587.00**
#184 12" bulbous-bottom, Daisy etch, Cheriglo **170.00**
#184 12" bulbous-bottom, Eden Rose etch, ebony **142.00**
#184, 12", Leeuwen etch **155.00**
#184, 12", Gothic Garden etch, ruby **205.00**
#184, 12", Utopia etch, ruby . **205.00**

#184, 12", Cupid silver deposit **230.00**
#184, 12", Orchid etch, ebony **225.00**
#210 Regina 6-1/2", Harvesters etch, ebony **145.00**
#210 Regina 6-1/2", Black Forest etch, green **150.00**
#412 10" Crow's Foot Square, flared, ruby **96.00**
#412 10" Crow's Foot Square, Gothic Garden etch, ruby **430.00**
#412, 10", flared, Daisy etch, ruby **225.00**
#412, 12", cupped, Rose Bouquet etch **177.50**
Unknown #, small, bulbous, Orchid etch, ruby **465.00**
Unknown #, 12" cylindrical, Rose Bouquet etch, green **305.00**

PAIRPOINT

History: The Pairpoint Manufacturing Co. was organized in 1880 as a silver-plating firm in New Bedford, Massachusetts. The company merged with Mount Washington Glass Co. in 1894 and became the Pairpoint Corporation. The new company produced specialty glass items, often accented with metal frames.

Pairpoint Corp. was sold in 1938 and Robert Gunderson became manager. He operated it as the Gunderson Glass Works until his death in 1952. From 1952 until the plant closed in 1956, operations were maintained under the name Gunderson-Pairpoint. Robert Bryden reopened the glass manufacturing business in 1970, moving it back to the New Bedford area.

References: Sean and Johanna S. Billings, *Peachblow Glass, Collector's Identification & Price Guide*, Krause Publications, 2000; Marion and Sandra Frost, *The Essence of Pairpoint, Fine Glassware 1918-1938*, Schiffer Publishing, 2001; Kyle Husfloen, *Antique Trader's American & European Decorative and Art Glass Price Guide*, 2nd ed., Krause Publications, 2000; Edward and Sheila Malakoff, *Pairpoint Lamps*, Schiffer Publishing, 1990; John A. Shumann III, *Collector's Encyclopedia of American Art Glass*, Collector Books, 1988, 1996 value update; *Pairpoint Lamp Catalog: Shade Shapes Ambero through Panel*; *Pairpoint Lamp Catalog: Shade Shapes Papillon through Windsor & Related Material*, Schiffer Publishing, 2001.

Collectors' Clubs: Mount Washington Art Glass Society, P.O. Box 24094, Fort Worth, TX 76124-1094; Pairpoint Cup Plate Collectors, P.O. Box 890052, East Weymouth, MA 02189.

Museum: Pairpoint Museum, Sagamore, MA.

China

Box, cov, 5" l, 3-1/2" w, 2-1/2" h, raised gold rococo scrolls, reverse on lid with three Palmer Cox Brownies playing cards, Pairpoint-Limoges logo, numbered **750.00**

Dresser box, molded-in rococo swirls, gold single petal roses, pastel blue background, Wedgwood blue border, shiny gilt metal fittings, 7-1/2" d, 3" h, $785. Photo courtesy of Clarence and Betty Maier.

Chocolate pot, 10" h, cream ground, white floral dec, gold trim and scrolls, sgd "Pairpoint Limoges 2500 114" **675.00**

Gravy boat and underplate, fancy white china with scrolls, Dresden multicolored flowers, elaborate handle, Limoges, two pc **175.00**

Plate, 7-3/8" d, hp harbor scene, artist sgd "L. Tripp," fuchsia tinted rim, gold highlights, back sgd "Pairpoint Limoges" **550.00**

Vase, 7" h, 6-3/4" w, two handles, pink pond lily dec, soft beige ground, dark green trim on handles and ruffled top, sgd "P.M.C. 2004/261" **425.00**

Copper, trophy, 7" d, 8-1/2" h, copper, two fancy handles, feather design, plaque inscribed "New Bedford Yacht Club Ocean Race won by Nutmeg for the fastest time, Aug 5, 1909," base marked "Pairpoint Mfg Co.," "P" in diamond mark, numbered **400.00**

Glass

Box, 6" d, creamy ground, gold enamel and lavender trim, brass fittings.**695.00**

Candlesticks, pr, 9-1/2" h, Mt. Washington opalware glass, silver-plated overlay, deep pink painted ground, white peony dec, fancy Art Nouveau styled silver overlay base and socket, sgd "Pairpoint Mfg. Co" **1,250.00**

Compote, 6-3/4" d, 3-3/4" h, peachblow, hp florals, paper label **160.00**

Console set, three-pc set

12" d bowl, matching 3" h candlesticks, Tavern glass, bouquet of red, white, and green flowers **575.00**

12" d, bowl, matching mushroom candlesticks, Flambo Ware, tomato red, applied black glass foot, c1915 . . . .**1,950.00**

Cracker jar, cov

6-1/2" h, 6" d, 16 panels, gold/beige ground, white and deep pink roses, green leaves, cov sgd "Pairpoint-3932," base sgd "3932/222," fancy metal work **595.00**

6-3/4" h, 7-1/2" w, Mt. Washington opalware, pistachios green top and bottom, 3-1/2" w band of deep pink and red roses, green leaves, gold trim, fancy silver-plated cov, handle, and bail, cov sgd "Pairpoint -3912," base sgd "3912-268" **725.00**

Dish, fish shape, teal blue, controlled bubbles dec, late **275.00**

Salt shaker, white opaque body, yellow and pink flowers, green leaves, wreath, 12 panels, 3-1/4" h, 2-3/4" d, $55.

Lamp

27-1/2" h, 17" d Directorie scenic hexagonal heavy walled shade, reverse painted as six continuing panels, colorful landscaped ground with columned waterfront building, irid background coloring, paneled borders above and below, "The Pairpoint Corp.n" on border, gilt metal, onyx, and cut glass candle lamp form base, imp "Pairpoint Mfg. Co. E30001" **2,645.00**

Mushroom shape, cut glass, dome shade with orig prisms, cut Viscaria pattern, c1915 . . . .**1,850.00**

Perfume bottle, 6-3/4" h, amethyst, painted butterfly, teardrop stopper, "P" in diamond mark **375.00**

Pokal, cov, 14" h, Chrysopras, dark yellow-green, wheelcut grapes and leaves, finial wheelcut with eight-petaled flower **625.00**

Vase

5-1/2" h, 4-1/2" w, Tavern glass, bulbous, enameled floral dec of vase of flowers, base numbered **225.00**

6" h, Tavern glass, bulbous, enameled sailing galleon on wavy sea, sgd "D. 1507," c1900-38 . . . .**300.00**

14-1/2" h, flared colorless crystal trumpet form, bright -cut floral dec, gilt metal foliate molded weighted pedestal base, imp "Pairpoint C1509" **490.00**

PAPER EPHEMERA

History: Maurice Rickards, author of *Collecting Paper Ephemera*, suggests that ephemera are the "minor transient documents of everyday life," material destined for the wastebasket but never quite making it. This definition is more fitting than traditional dictionary definitions that emphasize time, e.g., "lasting a very short time." A driver's license, which is used for a year or longer, is as much a piece of ephemera as is a ticket to a sporting event or music concert. The transient nature of the object is the key.

Collecting ephemera has a long and distinguished history. Among the English pioneers were John Seldon (1584-1654), Samuel Pepys (1633-1703), and John Bagford (1650-1716). Large American collections can be found at historical societies and libraries across the country, and museums, e.g., Wadsworth Atheneaum, Hartford, CT, and the Museum of the City of New York.

When used by collectors, "ephemera" usually means paper objects, e.g., billheads and letterheads, bookplates, documents, labels, stocks and bonds, tickets, and valentines. However, more and more ephemera collectors are recognizing the transient nature of some three-dimensional material, e.g., advertising tins and pinback buttons. Today's specialized paper shows include dealers selling other types of ephemera in both two- and three-dimensional form.

References: Pamela E. Apkarian-Russell, *Postmarked Yesteryear*, Collectors Press, 2001; Edwin Barnes and Wayne Dunn, C*igar-Label Art Visual Encyclopedia with Index and Price Guide*, published by authors (P.O. Box 3, Lake Forest, CA 92630), 1995; Max A. Collins, *For the Boys*, Collectors Press, 2001; Robert Forbes and Terrence Mitchell, *American Tobacco Cards: Price Guide and Checklist*, Tuff Stuff Books, 1999; J. L. Mashburn, *Artist-Signed Postcard Price Guide*, Colonial House, 1993; ——, *Black Americana: A Century of History Preserved on Postcards*, Colonial House, 1996; ——, *Fantasy Postcards with Price Guide*, Colonial House, 1996; ——, *Postcard Price Guide*, 3rd ed., Colonial House, 1997; ——, *Super Rare Postcards of Harrison Fisher with Price Guide*, Colonial House, 1992; Ron Menchine, *Propaganda Postcards of World War II*, Krause Publications, 2000; Kenneth W. Rendell, *Forging History*, University of Oklahoma Press, 1994;

Paper Ephemera

Gene Utz, *Collecting Paper*, Books Americana, 1993; Jane Wood, *Collector's Guide to Post Cards*, L-W Book Sales, 1984, 2000 value update.

Periodicals and Internet Resources: *Antique Paper & Ephemera X-change*, http://www.apex-emphemera.com; *Back Issue Finder*, http://www.BackIssueFinder.com; *Illustrator Collector's News*, P.O. Box 1958, Sequim, WA 98382-1958, http://www.ollllypen.com/ticn; *Barr's Post Card News*, 70 S. 6th St., Lansing, IA 52151, http://www.bpcn.com; *Card Source*, http://www.thepostcard.com; *Collector Link*, http://www.collector-link.com; *Gloria's Corner*, P.O. Box 507, Denison, TX 75021; *Jim Mehrer's Postal History*, http://www.postal-history.com; *Paper & Advertising Collector*, P.O. Box 500, Mount Joy, PA 17552; *Paper Collectors' Marketplace*, P.O. Box 128, Scandinavia, WI 54977, http://www.pcmpaper.com; *Picture Postcard Monthly*, 15 Debdale Lane, Keyworth, Nottinghamshire, NG 12 5HT HK, http://www.argonet.co.uk/uers/reflections/index.html; *Postcard Collector*, P.O. Box 1050, Dubuque, IA 52004, http://www.collect.com/postcardcollector; *Postcard.Org*, http://www.postcard.org; *Postcard Collecting Worldwide*, http://deltiology.org; *Postcard Resources*, http://www.library.arizona.edu/users/mount/postcard.html; *Web-Pac Postcard Mall*, http://www.webpac.com/mall; Printed Ephemera Collection, Library of Congress, http://memory.loc.gov/ammem/rbpehtml/pehome.html.

Collectors' Clubs: *Barr's Post Card News* and *Postcard Collector* publishes lists of more than 50 regional clubs in the United States and Canada; Calendar Collector Society, American Resources, 18222 Flower Hill Way #299, Gaithersburg, MD 20879; Cigar Label Collectors International, P.O. Box 66, Sharon Center, OH 44274; Deltiologists of America, P.O. Box 8, Norwood, PA 19074; Ephemera Society of England, 8 Galveston Road, London, SW15 2SA UK, http://www.manacled.demon.co.uk/phaistos/ephsoc.html; Ephemera Society of America, Inc., P.O. Box 95, Cazenovia, NY 13035, http://ww.ephemerasociety.org; Gateway Post Card Club, P.O. Box 28941, St. Louis, MO 63132; Granite State Postcard Collectors Club, Rural Route #2, Box 3D, Parker Street, Canaan, NH 03741; Hawaii Postcard Club, P.O. Box 15273, Honolulu, HI 96830; International Federation of Postcard Dealers, Inc., P.O. Box 1765, Manassas, VA 20108; International Seal, Label & Cigar Band Society, 8915 E. Bellevue St., Tucson, AZ 85715; Monumental Postcard Club, 3013 St. Paul St., Baltimore, MD 21218; National Assoc. of Paper & Advertising Collectors, P.O. Box 500, Mount Joy, PA 17552; Postcard History Society, P.O. Box 1765, Manassas, VA 22110; Postcard Traders Assoc., Glanrhyd Station House, Marodeilo, Llandeilo, Dyfed SA19 7BP UK, http://www.postcard.co.uk; San Francisco Bay Area Post Card Club, P.O. Box 621 Penngrove, CA 94951; Society of Antique Label Collectors, P.O. Box 24811, Tampa, FL 33623; South Jersey Postcard Club, 11 S. Lafayette St., Cape May, NJ 08204-5301; The Ephemera Society of Canada, 36 Macauley Dr., Thornhill, Ontario L3T 5S5 Canada; Tucson Post Card Exchange Club, 820 Via Lucitas, Tucson, AZ 85718-1046; Wichita Postcard Club, P.O. Box 780282, Wichita, KS 67278-0282.

Museums: American Antiquarian Society, Worcester, MA; Crane Museum of Papermaking, Dalton, MA; Curt Teich Postcard Archives, Lake County Discovery Museum, Wauconda, IL, http://www.co.lake.il.us/forest/ctpa.html.

Additional Listings: See Advertising Trade Cards, Catalogs, Comic Books, Photographs, and Sports Cards. Also see Calendars, Catalogs, Magazines, Newspapers, Photographs, Postcards, and Sheet Music in *Warman's Americana & Collectibles*.

Bookmarks
Advertising
Austin Young & Co., Biscuits, multicolored, 2" x 7"........5.00
Bell Pianos, Art Nouveau woman, multicolored..............12.00
Eastman's Extract, silver gild, multicolored..............10.00
Palmer Violets Bloom Perfume, gold trim..................15.00
Youth's Companion, 1902, multicolored, 2-3/4" x 6".....8.00

Cross stitch on punched paper
Black Emancipation, black couple dancing, 1860s, 3-7/8" x 1-1/2"
....................40.00
Ever Constant-Ever True, young girl with basket of flowers, 2-5/8" x 7"
....................10.00
In God We Trust............10.00

Calendar
1882, Canada First, The Great Literary-Political Journal, broadside type, 8" x 12"................65.00
1893, Benton Hall Dry Goods, Palmyra, NY, 2-1/2"...................12.00
1894, C. I. Hood, Lowell, Mass, complete pad, titled "Sweet Sixteen"
....................140.00
1886, Middlesex Fire Insurance, Concord, MA, 11" x 5-1/2".....100.00
1899, C. I. Hood Co., Lowell, Mass, complete pad, titled "The American Girl"..................115.00
1901, Colgate, miniature, flower..20.00
1906, Hiawatha, multiple images of Indian scenes, monthly calendars placed throughout, metal band and grommet at top, metal band missing at bottom, 7-1/2" w, 36" h.......125.00
1909, Bank of Waupun, emb lady 32.00
1914, Youth's Companion, marching scene, easel back............10.00
1916, Putnam Dyes...........40.00
1918, Jan/Feb/March, Swifts Premium, soldier saying good-bye to his love, "The Girl I Leave Behind," illus by Haskell Coffin, 15" x 8-1/4".....100.00
1922, Warren National Bank, Norman Rockwell illus 300.00

1923, Winona, F. A. Rettke, Indian Princess on cliff overlooking body of water, full pad, 6-1/2" w, 21-1/2" l 50.00
1929, Clothesline.............65.00
1939, Rogers Statuary.........20.00
1940, Columbian Rope........40.00
1947, Petty, pin-up, 9" x 12"....155.00
1948, Esquire, pin-up, 9" x 12" . 135.00

Cigar label, La Flor de Erb, 10 cents, blue, yellow, and white letters, 13-1/2" l, 6" h, $28.

Cigar box label
Artoria, mounted and framed, 9-1/2" x 11-1/2"....................18.00
Chapman House, 10" x 6-1/2" .. 12.00
Club House, 8" x 6-1/2" 12.00
College Ribbon, marked "Title and Design Registered by El. F. C. Co.," printing off-center, 9" x 6-1/2" ... 10.00
Dan O'Brien, 6-3/4" x 8-1/2" 12.00
First Cabinet Cigars, 8" x 6" ... 10.00
King Alfred, 8-1/2" x 9".........8.00
Mutuel, black male enjoying cigar, 3-1/2" x 4-3/4" 60.00
Optimo, 8-1/2" x 6-1/2" 15.00
Perfecto Garcia & Bros., Perfecto Garcia Senators, Tampa, FL, diecut, 3-1/2" x 5-1/4" 4.00
Royal Hunter, 8-1/2" x 6-1/2" ... 15.00

Coloring books
Annie Oakley, Whitman, 11" x 14", 1955, unused 20.00
Blondie, Dell Publishing, 8-1/2" x 11", 1954, unused 24.00
Charlie Chaplin, Donohue & Co., 10" x 17", © 1917 .... 85.00
Dick Tracy, Saalfield, #2536, 8-1/4" x 11", © 1946 .... 30.00
Donald Duck, Whitman, 7-1/2" x 8-1/2", 1946, unused 25.00
Eve Arden, 1953, unused...... 30.00
Lone Ranger, Whitman, 8-1/2" x 11", Cheerios premium, 1956....... 75.00
Superman, Whitman, National Periodical Publications, © 1966, unused 25.00

Family record
13-9/16" x 10-1/2", polychrome watercolor on paper, John N. Mead,

born Nov. 12, 1791, Sally M. Recler, born Dec. 21, 1794, married Feb. 1, 1815, vital statistics for their 13 children, framed, water stains, foxing **. . 1,150.00**

14" x 11-1/2", polychrome watercolor on paper, Ensign Stover, born May 15, 1814, Barbara Snider, born Dec. 27, 1817, married Nov. 30, 1836, vital statistics for their children, framed, foxing and staining **. 4,600.00**

Greeting card
Birthday
Amos & Andy, brown portraits, message includes song title "Check and Double Check," inked birthday note, Rust Craft **. . . . 25.00**

Blondie, Dagwood illus, full color, Hallmark, © 1939 **. 18.00**

Snow White and the Seven Dwarfs, c1938 **. 42.00**

Space Patrol Man, diecut, full color, transparent green helmet, orig envelope **. 25.00**

Christmas, 4-3/4" x 6-1/2" closed, glossy stiff paper, choice color pop-up scene of Borden's Elsie and family retrieving Christmas tree trimmings from attic, greeting "From Elsie, Elmer, Beulah, Beauregard and all of us at Borden's," full-color Christmas tree and gift package art on front, copyright 1940s **. 45.00**

Get Well, Amos n' Andy, black and white photo, Hall Bros., © 1951 **. . 30.00**

Mother's Day, Cracker Jack, diecut puppy, full color, c1920 **. 18.00**

Invitations and programs
Eddie Cantor, "How To Make a Quack-Quack," program on back, portrait on cov, printed, black and white, four-part fold-out **. 15.00**

Grand Masquerade Ball, Marion House Co., NY, 1901, gold trim **. . 10.00**

Invitation and Program for Carnival in Honor of George Washington, Request at Opera House, 1893, multicolored cover **. 12.00**

Leap Year Party by Young Ladies, 1888, opens, dance program inside, printed black and white **. 10.00**

Richland Library Literary Society, Benefit Musical, opens, lists musical selections, poems to be read, black and white **. 5.00**

Sonja Henie Program, white cov, orig tissue cov, 1949 **. 12.00**

St. Patrick's Ball, Lusks Hall, Jacobs City, UT, 1878, red lettering, blue ground, emb, opens **. 15.00**

Menus
Banquet to the Western Michigan Press, Reed City, 1883, fold-over, Robison Engraving Co., 1882, printed, black and white **. 15.00**

Collation at Norombega Hall, Bangor, Wednesday, Oct. 18, 1871 to the President of the United States, the Governor-General of Canada...Upon the Formal Opening of the European & North America Railway, four pgs, decorative stick, 8" x 5-1/4" **. 95.00**

Francaise, Art Nouveau design, sgd "Mucha," dated 5 Janvier 1913, 5" x 9" **. 350.00**

Johnson Line. **. 15.00**

Metropolitan Hotel, four pgs, c1974 **. 35.00**

SS City of Omaha, Christmas, 1940 **. 10.00**

United States Hotel, Saratoga Springs, NY, 1892, 7" x 10" **. 15.00**

Postcard, artist signed Clarence Underwood, 1913, $20.

Postcards
Advertising
Case Stem Tractor, salesroom, Columbus, OH **. 60.00**

Champagne Rommeriz & Greno, French wines **. 30.00**

Planters Peanuts at Times Square, 1940s scene, unused **. 20.00**

Scottish Bagpipes, Swift's Premium Oleomargarine, ©1914, Swift's **. 50.00**

Victoria Quay, Guiness Brewery, Dublin **. 40.00**
Artist signed
Cady, Harrison, Happy Jack Squirrel **. 300.00**

Feilig, Hank, Sinner Liqueur, Elves Frog **. 50.00**

Fisher, Harrison, American Girl in England, framed **. 40.00**

Fisher, Harrison, Their New Love, couple with newborn, Charles Schribner Sons, NY, Reinthal and Newman Publisher, NY, glued to backing, framed **. 50.00**

Baseball, Palace of Fans Ballpark, Cincinnati, stamped "Sept. 18 1908" **. 125.00**

Dog
Borzoi, sgd "W. Klett," published in Switzerland, unused **. 30.00**

Dachshunds, one in doghouse, second one in front, comical verse, unused **. 25.00**

Scottish Terriers, sgd "M. Gear," published by Valentine & Sons, Ltd., Dundee and London, unused **. 30.00**

Hold to light
A Merry Christmas to You, unused **. 125.00**

Angel, A Merry Christmas, 1907, Belgium, used **. 100.00**

Art Nouveau couple dancing, used **. 35.00**

Cat and Mouse, kissing couple, used **. 15.00**

Cinderella, 1900, Belgium, used **. 85.00**

Girl with Umbrella, used **. 30.00**

Greetings from Antwerp, Netherlands, cathedral **. 60.00**

Happy New Year, 1910, windmill **. 85.00**

Kind Christmas Greetings, 1908, used **. 50.00**

US Treasury Building, Washington, DC, used **. 25.00**

Nazi
Humor, dated 1941 **. 15.00**

Portrait of Hitler, wearing formal attire **. 25.00**

Portrait of Hitler, wearing uniform, facsimile autograph, 3" x 5" **. . 30.00**

Real photo
Bakery interior **. 85.00**

Fabric store interior **. 100.00**

Shoe Maker, factory scene, workers at machines **. 40.00**

Steam roller **. 40.00**

Postcard, Mid-Pacific Carnival, Hawaii, 1910, $600. Photo courtesy of Postcards International.

Terry Ironing, Miss Ellen Tracy (actress) ironing, J. Beagles & Co., London **35.00**
Warner Bros. Studio, Jane Wyman, facsimile autograph, 1944 postmark, 3-1/4" x 5-1/2" . . . **20.00**

PAPERWEIGHTS

History: Although paperweights had their origin in ancient Egypt, it was in the mid-19th century that this art form reached its zenith. The finest paperweights were produced between 1834 and 1855 in France by the Clichy, Baccarat, and Saint Louis factories. Other weights made in England, Italy, and Bohemia during this period rarely match the quality of the French weights.

In the early 1850s, the New England Glass Co. in Cambridge, Massachusetts, and the Boston and Sandwich Glass Co. in Sandwich, Massachusetts, became the first American factories to make paperweights.

Popularity peaked during the classic period (1845-1855) and faded toward the end of the 19th century. Paperweight production was rediscovered nearly a century later in the mid-1900s. Contemporary weights still are made by Baccarat, Saint Louis, Perthshire, and many studio craftsmen in the U.S. and Europe.

References: Andrew H. Dohan, *The Dictionary of Paperweight Signature Canes: Identification and Dating,* Paperweight Press, 1997; Monika Flemming and Peter Pommerencke, *Paperweights of the World,* 3rd ed., Schiffer Publishing, 2000; Robert G. Hall,

World Paperweights, Millefiori and Lampwork, Schiffer Publishing, 2001; Paul Jokelson and Dena Tarshis, *Baccarat Paperweights and Related Glass,* Paperweight Press, 1990; Edith Mannoni, *Classic French Paperweights,* Paperweight Press, 1984; Bonnie Pruitt, *St. Clair Glass Collectors Guide,* published by author, 1992; Lawrence H. Selman, *All About Paperweights,* Paperweight Press, 1992; ——, *Art of the Paperweight,* Paperweight Press, 1988; ——, *Art of the Paperweight, Perthshire,* Paperweight Press, 1983; ——, *Art of the Paperweight, Saint Louis,* Paperweight Press, 1981 (all of the Paperweight Press books are distributed by Charles E. Tuttle Co., 1996); John Simmonds, *Paperweights from Great Britain,* Schiffer Publishing, 2000; Colin Terris, *The Charlton Standard Catalogue of Caithness Paperweights,* Charlton Press, 1999.

Collectors' Clubs: Caithness Collectors Club, 141 Lanza Ave., Building 12, Garfield, NJ 07026, http://www.caithnessglass.co.uk/caithness.htp; Cambridge Paperweight Circle, P.O. Box 941, Comberton, Cambridge, CB3 7GQ UK; Delaware Valley Chapter of Paperweight Collectors Assoc., 20 Chester County Commons, Malvern, PA 19355-1942; International Paperweight Society, 761 Chestnut St., Santa Cruz, CA 95060, http://www.paperweight.com; New England Paperweight Collectors, 15 Coleridge Road, Nashua, NH 03062, http://www.nepaperweights.org; Paperweight Collectors Assoc. Inc., P.O. Box 40, Barker, TX 77413-0040, http://www.paperweight.org; Paperweight Collectors Assoc. of Chicago, 535 Delkir Ct, Naperville, IL 60565; Paperweight Collectors Assoc. of Texas, 2900 Sussex Gardens Lane, Austin, TX 78748-2020, http://www.main.org/pcatx.

Museums: Bergstrom-Mahler Museum, Neenah, WI; Corning Museum of Glass, Corning, NY; Degenhart Paperweight & Glass Museum, Inc., Cambridge, OH; Museum of American Glass at Wheaton Village, Millville, NJ.

Antique

Baccarat, France, 19th C, Double Garland, double trefoil garland of red and white canes centered by ring of blue canes, pink white and green cane, 3" d, 2" h, minor wear **490.00**

Clichy, France, 19th C

Bottle, squat spherical body of colorless glass, dec internally with complex millefiori canes set concentrically on lace ground, 3-1/2" d, 3-1/2" h, stopper missing **2,185.00**
Chequer, complex millefiori canes centered by pink and green Clichy rose, all divided by white latticinio twists, 2-3/4" d, 2" h **1,265.00**
Millefiori, complex millefiori canes set in colorless crystal, 1-3/4" d, 1-3/8" h **375.00**
Millefiori on Lace, complex millefiori canes set concentrically on white lace ground, 2-1/2" d, 1-7/8" h, inclusions, minor wear **865.00**

Mushroom, close concentric design, large central pink and green rose surrounded by pin, white, cobalt blue, and cadmium green complex millefiori, middle row of canes with 10 green and white roses alternating with pink pastry mold canes, pin and white stems, 2-3/4" d **6,600.00**
Swirled, alternating purple and white pinwheels emanating from white, green, and pink pastry mold cane, minor bubbles, 2-5/8" d . . **2,200.00**

Degenhart, John, window, red crystal cube with yellow and orange upright center lily, one to window, four side windows, bubble in center of flower's stamens, 3-3/16" x 2-1/4" x 2-1/4" **1,225.00**

Gillinder, orange turtle with moving appendages in hollow center, pale orange ground, molded dome, 3-1/16" d **500.00**

Libbey

Frosted bust of woman, World's Fair 1893, 3" h **600.00**
Souvenir, showing Libbey Glass Company, 1893, 4" d **275.00**

Millville, umbrella pedestal, red, white, green, blue, and yellow int., bubble in sphere center, 3-1/8" d, 3-3/8" h **800.00**

Paul Ysart, dahlia, purple flower, circle of red and white canes, cobalt blue carpet, original paper label, signed "PY," $375.

New England Glass Co.

Crown, red, white, blue, and green twists interspersed with white latticinio emanating from a central pink, white, and green complex floret/cog cane, minor bubbles in glass, 2-3/4" d **2,400.00**

Pear, chartreuse with light blush color layering on colorless cooking glass base, 3" d, 2-1/4" h . . **690.00**

Pink Flower, striated pink five-petal flowers, millefiori cane center, pink bud on deep green leafy stem, white latticinio bed, 2-1/4" d, 1-3/4" h, minor wear **690.00**

Pinchbeck, pastoral dancing scene, couple dancing before grouped of onlookers, 3-3/16" d **650.00**

Sandwich Glass Co.

Dahlia, c1870, red petaled flower, millefiori cane center, bright green leafy stem, highlighted by trapped bubble dec, white latticino ground, 2-1/2" d, 1-3/4" h **650.00**

Poinsettia, double, red flower with double tier of petals, green and white Lutz rose, green stem and leaves, bubbles between petals, 3" d **1,200.00**

St. Louis

Fruit basket, red and green ripening fruits, latticino base basket, central base cane, 3" d, 2-1/2" h. **1,150.00**

Queen Victoria, c1840, sulfide portrait sgd "Victoria" in blue at base, 3-1/2" d, 2-1/2" h, few small inclusions **750.00**

Val St. Lambert, patterned millefiori, four red, white, blue, pistachio, and turquoise complex canes circlets spaced around central pink, turquoise and cadmium green canes circlet, canes set on stripes of lace encircled by spiraling red and blue torsade, minor blocking crease, 3-1/2" d **950.00**

Whitefriars, close concentric millefiori, pink, blue, purple, green, white, and yellow cog canes, 1948 date cane, minor bubble in dome, 3-5/8" d . **900.00**

Modern

Ayotte, Rick, yellow finch, perched on branch, faceted, sgd and dated, limited edition, 1979 . . . . **750.00**

Baccarat, Gridel pelican cane surrounded by five concentric rings of yellow, pink, green, and white complex canes, pink canes contain 18 Gridel silhouette canes, lace ground, 1973 date cane, signature cane, sgd and dated, limited ed. of 350, 3-1/16" d **850.00**

Banford, Bob

Cornflower, blue flower, yellow center, pink and white twisted torsade, "B" cane at stem, 3" d **550.00**

Zimmerman, free blown bubbles, crystal, signed, **$45.**

Flower bouquet, five red stemmed blossoms, "B" cane below, diamond cut recessed base, 3-1/4" d **475.00**

Iris and rose, purple, blue, and pink irises, center pink roe, recessed diamond-cut base, "B" cane at stem, 3" d **250.00**

Kaziun, Charles, concentric millefiori, heart, turtle silhouette, shamrocks, six-pointed stars, and floret canes encircled by purple and white torsade, turquoise ground flecked with goldstone, K signature cane, 2-1/16" d **1,200.00**

Kesey, Sunshine, Sunstone, multicolored abstract design, millefiori against background of multicolored leaves, sgd **75.00**

Lundberg, Art Nouveau design, irid orange, gray, and black flower, central millefiori star canes, irid dark green ground, sgd "Lundburg 73," 2-3/4" d **225.00**

Orient and Flume, red butterfly with blue and white accents, brown and green vines, white millefiori blossoms over dark ground, 3-1/2" d, dated 1977, orig sticker and box **235.00**

Parabelle

Five rows of concentrically arranged canes around larger center rose cane, closely packed white millefiori ground, signature/date cane, 2-3/8" d **425.00**

Small bouquet of four delicate flowers, green leaves and stem, closely packed white millefiori ground, signature and date cane, 2-13/16" d **425.00**

Tightly packed multicolored millefiori canes, dark blue ground, attributed to Gary and Doris Scrutton, signature and date cane, orig paper label, 2-3/4" d **575.00**

Perthshire

Miniature bouquet, yellow flowers, pink buds, basket of deep blue canes, green and pink millefiori canes cut to form base, orig box and certificate, 2-1/2" d **160.00**

Star of David, white stardust canes form star, encircled by millefiori garland, cobalt blue ground, 2-1/2" d, orig box **125.00**

Rosenfeld, Ken

Bouquet, red and lilac blossoms among white flowers and buds, green leafy stems, translucent blue ground, signature cane, inscribed "4/25 Ken Rosenfeld '93," 3-1/4" d, 2-3/4" h **500.00**

Spray of exotic lavender bellflowers, dark centered yellow flowers on leafy stems, "R" cane, sgd "Ken Rosenfeld '94" at side, 3-3/8" d **500.00**

Salazar, David, compound floral, lavender six-petal poinsettia star blossom, three-leaf stem over green and red wreath, white ground, inscribed "David Salazar/111405/Lundberg Studios 1991," 3-1/4" d **225.00**

Stankard, Paul, bouquet, yellow meadow wreath, blue forget-me-nots, red St. Anthony's fire, white bellflowers, and white chokeberry blossom and buds, 1977, 3" d **2,400.00**

Tarsitano, Debbie

Orange and purple bird of paradise flower on stalk, striped green leaves, star cut ground, DT signature cane, 2-15/16" d . **550.00**

Pansy, two central blue and yellow pansies flanked by three rose-pink blossoms, three yellow blossoms, green leafy stems, signature cane **475.00**

Whitefrairs, Star of David, five rows of tightly packed blue and white millefiori canes, 3" d **395.00**

Whittemore, Francis, two green and brown acorns on branch with three brown and yellow oak leaves, translucent cobalt blue ground, circular top facet five oval punties on sides, 20-3/8" d **300.00**

Ysart, Paul, green fish, yellow eye, yellow and white jasper ground encircled by pink, green, and white complex cane garland, PY signature cane **550.00**

PAPIER-MÂCHÉ

History: Papier-mâché is a mixture of wood pulp, glue, resin, and fine sand, which is subjected to great pressure and then dried. The finished product is tough, durable, and heat resistant. Various finishing treatments are used, such as enameling, japanning, lacquering, mother-of-pearl inlaying, and painting.

During the Victorian era, papier-mâché articles such as boxes, trays, and tables were in high fashion. Banks, candy containers, masks, toys, and other children's articles were also made of papier-mâché.

Candy container

5-1/2" h, turkey, polychrome dec **45.00**

10" h, angel, wax face, fur trim, German **575.00**

Cat, 4" h, black, Halloween type, head only **350.00**

Fan, 15-1/2" l, demilune, scalloped border, turned wooden handle, one side painted with variety of ferns on ochre ground, black japanning on other side, Victorian, late 19th C, price for pr **250.00**

Milliner's model, papier-mâché shoulder head, unmarked

8" h, painted brown eyes, closed mouth, molded and painted black hair with exposed ears, long side curls, braided bun in back, unjointed kid body with wooden lower arms and one wooden lower leg, orig white organdy dress, matching pants **225.00**

8-1/4" h, painted blue eyes, closed mouth, molded and painted hair with long side curls on shoulders, braided bun in back, kid body, wooden lower arms and legs, painted orange shoes, orig black silk dress with lace trim, orig underclothing **500.00**

Stereo viewer, gilt painted acanthus motif on one side, dog motif on lid, 19th C, 8-3/4" x 9-1/4" x 5", all-over crazing, hinge damage, $485. Photo courtesy of Sanford Alderfer Auction Co.

Nodder, 9-3/4" h, Easter Rabbit, oval cardboard base, orig polychrome paint **65.00**

Pip-squeak, 4-1/4" h, rooster, orig paint, yellow, orange, and black, recovered wooden bellows, faint squeak . . . **85.00**

Cup, gold ground, black base, red band at top, floral decoration, marked "Made in USSR," 2-1/2" h, $30.

Plate, 12" d, painted cat, marked "Patented August 8, 1880" **35.00**

Roly poly, 4-1/8" h, clown, orig white and blue polychrome paint, green ribbon around neck **65.00**

Snuff box, 3-7/8" d, round, lid painted with interior genre scene of family with baby, interior lid painted with title "Die Tanzpuppen," painted mark "StabwassersFabrik in Braunschweig," German, late 19th/early 20th C . **460.00**

Table, 16" d, 25-3/4" h, William VI, c1835, rosewood and papier-mâché, serpentine top dec with multicolored foliage and birds, leaf carved standard, three-sided base, price for pr **1,850.00**

Tray, 12" d, Victorian, English, mid-19th C, round, black ground, large central scene of Master of Hounds seated on bobtail bay in wooded setting, house in background, gold scroll painted rim **980.00**

Tray and stand, English

18-1/4" l, 14-1/8" w, rect, black ground, large central scene of white haired gentleman on bobtail chestnut, five hunting dogs in open field, border gold painted with egg and dart design, 7-3/4" w, 4-1/4" d, 9" h mahogany stand . . . **1,100.00**

30" l, 24" w tray, 11-1/4" w, oval, black ground, large central scene with two scarlet-coated huntsmen,

one standing, other seated on bobtail chestnut with black foal on a hill, border with gilt transfer printed guilloche border, Mark Knowles & Son maker, English Registry mark for 1864, burl hardwood 6-1/4" d, 18-3/4" h stand **1,250.00**

PARIAN WARE

History: Parian ware is a creamy white, translucent porcelain that resembles marble. It originated in England in 1842 and was first called "statuary porcelain." Minton and Copeland have been credited with its development; Wedgwood also made it. In America, parian ware objects were manufactured by Christopher Fenton in Bennington, Vermont.

At first, parian ware was used only for figures and figural groups. By the 1850s, it became so popular that a vast range of items was manufactured.

References: Paul Atterbury, ed., *The Parian Phenomenon*, Shepton Beauchamp, 1989; Susan and Al Bagdade, *Warman's English & Continental Pottery & Porcelain*, 3rd ed., Krause Publications, 1998; G. A. Godden, *Victorian Porcelain*, Herbert Jenkins, 1961; Kathy Hughes, *Collector's Guide to Nineteenth-Century Jugs* (1985, Routledge & Kegan Paul), Vol. II (1991, Taylor Publishing).

Museum: Victoria & Albert Museum, London, England.

Bust, lady with braided hair, four-strand pearl necklace, glazed porcelain base marked "Margaretha," signed "FC, 1857," 13" h, $495. Photo courtesy of Joy Luke Auctions.

Bust

9" h, Martha Washington, England, 19th C, very minor chips, firing blemishes **225.00**

10" h, Ulysses S. Grant, civilian dress, inscribed on back "Broome, Sculpt. 1876," and "Ott and Brewer Manufacturers, Trenton, New Jersey" **2,750.00**

12-3/4" h, Shakespeare, raised circular base, Robinson and Ledbetter mark, c1875, minor chip to hair **725.00**

15-1/2" h, Abraham Lincoln, raised circular base, English, c1860 . . . . **295.00**

Creamer, 5" h, Tulip pattern, relief dec **100.00**

Doll

18-1/2" h, Countess Dagmar, shoulder head, café au lait molded hair with side-swept wings to comb and curls in back, curls on forehead held by molded band, blue painted eyes, pierced ears, cloth body, brown leather arms, blue plaid wool dress, orig underwear, blue leather shoes, c1870 . . . . **250.00**

20" h, lady, bisque shoulder head, very pale coloring, center part blond hairstyle, 10 vertical curls, painted features, blue eyes, closed mouth, three sew holes, cloth body, kid arms, separate fingers, red cotton print jumper, white blouse with tucking and lace trim, leather slippers, Germany, c1870 . . **350.00**

20" h, lady, untinted bisque shoulder head, molded and painted café au lait hair with curls on back, painted blue eyes with red accent line, single stroke brows, closed mouth, gold beads, pink and white flowers, white leaves, molded blue and gold necklace, cloth body, untinted bisque lower arms, red and white striped lower legs with red leather boots as feet, antique white dotted Swiss outfit, areas of light kiln dust on bisque, chips off three flowers, aged and soiled body, new upper arms **875.00**

Figure

8-1/4" w, 12" h, Cupid, seated winged figure, quiver of arrows, ovoid base with imp Copeland mark, late 19th C **250.00**

11" h, Grecian goddess riding in carriage, pulled by five putti, c1890 . . . . **450.00**

11-3/4" h, Farmer, modeled seated on rocky freeform base, holding bagpipes, imp Copeland mark, c1875, pipes and fingers restored, small chips to sheaf of wheat **175.00**

15" h, Canova, imp title on circular base, imp Minton marks, c1863, chips to floral garland **750.00**

Pitcher, twig handle, raised foliage, grapes, Copeland, 4-1/2" h, $90.

Plaque, 6" d, relief, angels, brass frames, orig German labels, Boston retailers label, pr **275.00**

Sculpture, nude riding back of lion, early registry marks, c1860 . . . . **895.00**

Vase, 10" h, applied white monkey type figures, grape clusters at shoulders, blue ground, c1850, pr **265.00**

PATE-DE-VERRE

History: The term "pate-de-verre" can be translated simply as "glass paste." It is manufactured by grinding lead glass into a powder or crystal form, making it into a paste by adding a 2 percent or 3 percent solution of sodium silicate, molding, firing, and carving. The Egyptians discovered the process as early as 1500 B.C.

In the late 19th century, the process was rediscovered by a group of French glassmakers. Almaric Walter, Henri Cros, Georges Despret, and the Daum brothers were leading manufacturers.

Contemporary sculptors are creating a second renaissance, led by the technical research of Jacques Daum.

Bowl, pedestal, purple grape relief inside and out, signed "Gargy-Rousseau," 4" d, 1-5/8" h, $900.

Bookends, pr, 6-1/2" h, Buddha, yellow amber pressed molded design, seated in lotus position, inscribed "A Walter Nancy" **2,450.00**

Bowl, 4" d, 8-3/4" h, Almeric Walter, designed by Jules Cayette, molded blue green glass, yellow center, green around border, three brown scarab beetles with long black antennae, inscribed "A. Walter Nancy," and also "J. Cayette," "Made in France" on base **4,600.00**

Center bowl, 10-3/8" d, 3-3/4" h, blue, purple, and green press molded design, seven exotic long-legged birds, central multi-pearl blossom, repeating design on ext., raised pedestal foot, sgd "G. Argy-Rousseau" **6,750.00**

Clock, 4-1/2" sq, stars within pentagon and tapered sheaves motif, orange and black, molded sgd "G. Argy-Rousseau," clock by J. E. Caldwell **2,750.00**

Dagger, 12" l, frosted blade, relief design, green horse head handle, script sgd "Nancy France" . . . **1,200.00**

Jewelry

Earrings, pr, 2-3/4" l, teardrop for, molded violet and rose shaded tulip blossom, suspended from rose colored swirl molded circle **2,200.00**

Pendant, 1-1/4" d, molded amethyst portrait of Art Nouveau woman, flowing hair, gilt metal mount **400.00**

Paperweight, 3/4" w, 1-1/4" h, large beetle, green leaves, mottled blue ground, intaglio "AW" mark . . **6,800.00**

Sculpture, 9-5/8" l, crab in sea grasses, lemon yellow, chocolate brown, pale mauve, and sea green, sgd "A. Walter/Nancy" and "Berge/SC" **8,500.00**

Tray, 6" x 8", apple green, figural green and yellow duck with orange beak at one end, sgd "Walter, Nancy" . . **950.00**

Vase, 5-1/2" h, press molded and carved, mottled amethyst and frost ground, three black and green crabs, red eyes, naturalistic seaweed at rim, center imp "G. Argy-Rousseau," base imp "France" **5,500.00**
Veilleuse, 8-1/2" h, Gabriel Argy-Rousseau, press molded oval lamp shade, frosted mottled gray glass, elaborate purple arches with three teardrop-shaped windows of yellow, center teal-green stylized blossoms on black swirling stems, imp "G. Arty-Rousseau" at lower edge, wrought iron frame, three ball feet centering internal lamp socket, conforming iron cover **6,900.00**

PATE-SUR-PATE

History: Pate-sur-pate, paste-on-paste, is a 19th-century porcelain-decorating method featuring relief designs achieved by painting layers of thin pottery paste one on top of the other.

About 1880, Marc Solon and other Sevres artists, inspired by a Chinese celadon vase in the Ceramic Museum at Sevres, experimented with this process. Solon emigrated to England at the outbreak of the Franco-Prussian War and worked at Minton, where he perfected pate-sur-pate.

References: Paul Atterbury and Maureen Batkin, *Dictionary of Minton*, Antique Collectors Club, Ltd., 1996; Susan and Al Bagdade, *Warman's English & Continental Pottery & Porcelain*, 3rd ed., Krause Publications, 1998; Bernard Bumpers, *Pate-Sur-Pate*, Barrie & Jenkins, 1992; G. .A. Godden, *Victorian Porcelains*, Herbert Jenkins, 1961.

Museums: National Collection of Fine Arts, Smithsonian Institution, Washington, DC; Victoria & Albert Museum, London, England.

Box, cov, 5-3/4" d, round, white female portrait, blue ground, Limoges, France, late 19th C **690.00**
Centerpiece, 16" l, elongated parian vessel, molded scroll handles and feet, pierced rim, two brown reserves, white pate-sur-pate amorini, gilding, dec attributed to Lawrence Birks, marked "Minton," retailer's mark of Thomas Goode & Co., Ltd., London, c1889 . . . . **1,400.00**
Dresser jar, 3-3/4" d, ovoid, cobalt blue ground, lid with pate-sure-pate profile bust of classical woman, gilt banding, Meissen, Germany, early 20th C **1,955.00**
Lamp base, 16" h, cylindrical, pale green ground, pate-sur-pate dec of floral garland and insects, two scrolled paterae handles, Victorian scroll girdle, trumpet foot, gilt enamel accents, flat leaf base with concave corners, early 20th C **300.00**

Plaque, sowing scene, dark green ground, 4-3/8" h, 7-1/2" l, $325.

Plaque

5-1/4" x 11-1/4", Victoria Ware, Wedgwood, rust ground, gilt florets, applied white figure of Adam, imp mark, c1880, rim chip, framed **2,200.00**
7-5/8" d, one with maiden and cupid spinning web, other with maiden seated on bench with whip in one hand, sunflowers stalked with humanistic snail on other, artist sgd "Louis Solin," both marked on back, framed, pr **2,500.00**
11" x 16", mottled blue-gray ground, colored slips of partially clad female holding lantern, putt figure lights torch, titled "La Nouvelle Psyche," unsgd, attributed to Louis Solon **27,600.00**
15" l, demi-lune shape, green ground, white slip, central figure of Venus holding mirror in each hand, fending off two groups of putti with their reflections, artist sgd Louis Solin, rosewood frame. . . **9,200.00**
Plate, 9-1/8" d, deep brown ground, gilt trim, white dec of nude child behind net supported by two small trees, artist monogram sgd "Henry Saunders," printed and imp Moore Brothers factory marks, c1885 . . . . **750.00**
Portrait medallion, 3-7/8" d, circular, blue ground, white slip side self-portrait profile, artist sgd "Louis Solin," dated 1892 . . . . **1,265.00**
Urn, 8" h, double handles, pedestal base, portrait medallion, pale green ground, ivory trim, gilt accents. . **250.00**

Vase

6-1/2" h, cov, two handles, deep teal blue ground, gilt framed gray ground panel with white slip dec of reclining maiden, artist sgd Albione Birks, printed Minton factory marks, c1900, shallow restored chip on cov. **1,840.00**

Urn, double handles, pedestal, portrait medallion, pale green ground, ivory trim, gilt accents, 8" h, $250. Photo courtesy of Sanford Alderfer Auction Co.

6-7/8" h, two handles, blue ground, white female subjects within oval mauve ground cartouches, German printed marks, 20th C, pr **750.00**
7-1/4" h, 5-3/4" w, white flowers, green ground, gold serpent skin twisted handles, gold trim, pr **1,100.00**
13-3/4" h, cov, dark brown ground, white slip of partially draped female figure holding flowering branch, shaped tripod base, gilt dec at rim, artist sgd Louis Solon, printed and imp marks, 1898, rim cover damage, minor gilt wear . **2,300.00**
16-1/2" h, cov, deep green ground, circular panels dec in white slip, Psyche being carried heavenward by Mercury, maiden figures applied to shoulder, gilt trim, artist sgd Frederick Schenck, dated 1880, imp George Jones factory marks, cov damaged, hairlines to figures, light gilt wear **3,565.00**
37-1/2" h, blue ground, white clip depicting "Cupid's Tollgate," central frieze flanked by blue and green slip dec foliate designs, gold outlines, artist sgd Louis Solin, Minton factory marks, c1890 . . . . **55,200.00**

PATTERN GLASS

History: Pattern glass is clear or colored glass pressed into one of hundreds of patterns. Deming Jarves of the Boston and Sandwich Glass Co. invented one of the first successful pressing machines in 1828. By the 1860s, glass-pressing machinery had been improved, and mass production of good-quality matched tableware sets began. The idea of a matched glassware table service (including goblets, tumblers, creamers, sugars, compotes, cruets, etc.) quickly caught on in America. Many pattern glass table services had numerous accessory pieces such as banana stands, molasses cans, and water bottles.

Early pattern glass (flint) was made with a lead formula, giving many items a ringing sound when tapped. Lead became too valuable to be used in glass manufacturing during the Civil War, and in 1864, Hobbs, Brockunier & Co., West Virginia, developed a soda lime (non-flint) formula. Pattern glass also was produced in transparent colors, milk glass, opalescent glass, slag glass, and custard glass.

The hundreds of companies that produced pattern glass experienced periods of development, expansions, personnel problems, material and supply demands, fires, and mergers. In 1899, the National Glass Co. was formed as a combine of 19 glass companies in Pennsylvania, Ohio, Indiana, West Virginia, and Maryland. U.S. Glass, another consortium, was founded in 1891. These combines resulted from attempts to save small companies by pooling talents, resources, and patterns. Because of this pooling, the same pattern often can be attributed to several companies.

U.S. Glass created the States series by using state names for various patterns, several of which were new issues while others were former patterns renamed. Other glass companies named their patterns after states also, but not all 50 states have patterns named after them. For this edition of *Warman's*, the States series and other states have been used as an example of the current pattern-glass market.

References: Bill Edwards and Mike Carwile, *Standard Encyclopedia of Pressed Glass, 1860-1930*, 2nd ed., Collector Books, 2000; William Heacock, *Encyclopedia of Victorian Colored Pattern Glass: Book 1: Toothpick Holders from A to Z*, 2nd ed. (1976, 1992 value update) *Book 5: U. S. Glass from A to Z* (1980), *Book 7: Ruby Stained Glass from A To Z* (1986), *Book 8: More Ruby Stained Glass* (1987), Antique Publications; ——, *Old Pattern Glass*, Antique Publications, 1981; ——, *1000 Toothpick Holders*, Antique Publications, 1977; ——, *Rare and Unlisted Toothpick Holders*, Antique Publications, 1984; Kyle Husfloen, *Antique Trader's American Pressed Glass & Bottles Price Guide*, 2nd ed., Krause Publications, 2000; ——, *Collector's Guide to American Pressed Glass*, Wallace-Homestead, 1992; Bill Jenks and Jerry Luna, *Early American Pattern Glass—1850 to 1910*, Wallace-Homestead, 1990; Bill Jenks, Jerry Luna, and Darryl Reilly, *Identifying Pattern Glass Reproductions*, Wallace-Homestead, 1993; William J. Jenks and Darryl Reilly, *American Price Guide to Unitt's Canadian & American Goblets Volumes I & II*, Author! Author! Books (P.O. Box 1964, Kingston, PA 18704), 1996.

Minnie Watson Kamm, *Pattern Glass Pitchers*, Books 1 through 8, published by author, 1970, 4th printing; Ruth Webb Lee, *Early American Pressed Glass*, 36th ed., Lee Publications, 1966; ——, *Victorian Glass*, 13th ed., Lee Publications, 1944; Mollie H. McCain, *Field Guide to Pattern Glass*, Collector Books, 2000; Alice Hulett Metz, *Early American Pattern Glass*, published by author, 1958 (reprinted by Collector Books, 2000, with revisions); ——, *Much More Early American Pattern Glass*, published by author, 1965 (reprinted by Collector Books, 2000, with revisions); S. T. Millard, *Goblets I* (1938), *Goblets II* (1940), privately printed, reprinted Wallace-Homestead, 1975; Ellen T. Schroy, *Warman's Pattern Glass*, 2nd ed., Krause Publications, 2000; Doris and Peter Unitt, *American and Canadian Goblets*, Clock House, 1970, reprinted by The Love of Glass Publishing (Box 629, Arthur, Ontario, Canada NOG 1A0), 1996.

Collectors' Clubs: Early American Pattern Glass Society, P.O. Box 266, Colesburg, IA 52035, http://www.eapgs.org; The National Early American Glass Club, P.O. Box 8489, Silver Spring, MD 20907.

Museums: Corning Museum of Glass, Corning, NY; Jones Museum of Glass and Ceramics, Sebago, ME; National Museum of Man, Ottawa, Ontario, Canada; Sandwich Glass Museum, Sandwich, MA; Schminck Memorial Museum, Lakeview, OR.

Reproduction Alert: Pattern glass has been widely reproduced. Items in the listing marked with an φ are those for which reproductions are known to exist. Care should be exercised when purchasing such pieces.

Additional Listings: Bread Plates, Children's Toy Dishes, Cruets, Custard Glass, Milk Glass, Sugar Shakers, Toothpicks, and specific companies.

Advisers: John and Alice Ahlfeld.

Abbreviations:

ah	applied handle
GUTDODB	Give Us This Day Our Daily Bread
hs	high standard
ind	individual
ls	low standard
os	original stopper

ALABAMA

Beaded Bull's Eye and Drape, U.S. Glass Pattern Line No. 15,062

Made by United States Glass Company, c1898, this pattern is known as one of the States series patterns. Made in non-flint clear and ruby stained. Several pieces have been found in emerald green and their value would be 150 percent. Very rare ruby and amber-stained pieces would be valued at 300 percent.

Items	Clear	Ruby stained	Items	Clear	Ruby stained
Berry bowl, master, open, flat, 8" d	70.00	—	Dish, rectangular	20.00	—
Bowl, rectangular	30.00	—	Honey dish, cov, flat	65.00	—
Butter dish, cov	50.00	150.00	Jelly compote, open, 5" d	35.00	—
Cake stand, hs	65.00	—	Mustard pot, cov, notched lid	100.00	—
Castor set, four bottles, glass frame	125.00	—	Pickle dish	15.00	—
Celery tray	55.00	—	Pitcher, water	72.00	—
Celery vase	35.00	110.00	Relish, rectangular	24.00	35.00
Child's butter dish, cov	225.00	—	Salt and pepper shakers, pr	65.00	—
Child's creamer	65.00	—	Sauce, flat, 4" d	18.00	—
Child's spooner	65.00	—	Sauce, footed, 4" d	18.00	
Child's sugar bowl, cov	90.00	—	Spooner	30.00	—
Compote, cov, 7" d	100.00	—	Sugar bowl, covered	48.00	—
Compote, cov, 8" d	125.00	—	Syrup, orig top	125.00	250.00
Creamer, individual size	20.00	35.00	Toothpick holder	60.00	150.00
Creamer, table size	45.00	60.00	Tumbler	45.00	—
Cruet, os	65.00	—	Water tray, 10-1/2" d	50.00	—

ALASKA
Lion's Leg

Manufactured by Northwood Glass Co., 1897-1910. The forms of this pattern are square, except for the cruet, salt and pepper shakers, and tumblers. Made in a non-flint opalescent glass and some clear colors, including emerald green, clear, and blue. Some pieces have enamel decoration, which adds 75 percent to the clear value shown below. Sauces can be found in clear ($30); the creamer ($110) and spooner ($95) are known in clear blue.

Items	Clear Emerald Green	Blue Opalescent	Vaseline Opalescent	White Opalescent
Banana boat	85.00	250.00	250.00	125.00
Berry bowl, ftd	65.00	100.00	95.00	45.00
Butter dish, cov	150.00	280.00	275.00	100.00
Celery tray	45.00	125.00	120.00	85.00
Creamer	40.00	75.00	65.00	40.00
Cruet, os	225.00	250.00	265.00	135.00
Pitcher, water	75.00	385.00	275.00	175.00
Salt shaker, decorated	—	50.00	55.00	45.00
Sauce	30.00	45.00	40.00	25.00
Spooner	55.00	85.00	55.00	50.00
Sugar bowl, covered	65.00	150.00	130.00	100.00
Tumbler	45.00	75.00	65.00	55.00

CALIFORNIA
Beaded Grape, Beaded Grape and Vine, Grape and Vine

Manufactured by United States Glass Company, Pittsburgh, PA, c1890, as one of its States series. Also attributed to Burlington Glass Works, Hamilton, Ontario, Canada, and Syndenham Glass Company, Wallaceburg, Ontario, Canada, c1910. Made in clear and emerald green. Some pieces found with gilt trim.

Reproductions: A variety of clear, milk glass, and several colors forms have been made by various companies, including Westmoreland Glass Co. A goblet with three beaded ovals and grape clusters on a stippled base have been made. Some are found with an amber stained or cranberry stained rims. The reproductions tend to be of heavier non-flint and the stippling is usually coarse and uneven.

Items	Clear	Emerald Green	Items	Clear	Emerald Green
Bowl, rect, 5-1/2" x 8"	30.00	36.00	Cruet, os	66.00	130.00
Bowl, round, 8" d	210.00	42.00	Goblet φ	42.00	60.00
Bowl, square, 5-1/2" w	17.50	24.00	Jelly compote, open, hs	55.00	66.00
Bowl, square, 6" w	24.00	30.00	Olive, handle	24.00	42.00
Bowl, square, 7-1/2" w	30.00	42.00	Pickle	24.00	36.00
Bread plate	30.00	55.00	Pitcher, milk	75.00	110.00
Butter dish, cov	66.00	85.00	Pitcher, water	85.00	124.00
Cake stand, 9" d	66.00	85.00	Plate, sq, 8-1/4" w	210.00	48.00
Celery tray	36.00	55.00	Salt and pepper shakers, pr	55.00	66.00
Celery vase	48.00	72.00	Sauce, 4" d φ	18.00	24.00
Compote, cov, hs, 7" d φ	75.00	85.00	Spooner	30.00	55.00
Compote, cov, hs, 8" d φ	95.00	110.00	Sugar bowl, cov, large, ftd, Australian	72.00	75.00
Compote, cov, hs, 9" d φ	120.00	135.00	Sugar bowl, cov, regular	55.00	55.00
Compote, open, hs, 5" w, sq	55.00	75.00	Sugar shaker	75.00	85.00
Compote, open, hs, 7" d	55.00	66.00	Toothpick holder	48.00	66.00
Compote, open, hs, 8" d	55.00	85.00	Tumbler φ	30.00	48.00
Compote, open, hs, 9" d	66.00	75.00	Vase, 6" h	30.00	55.00
Creamer	48.00	60.00	Wine φ	42.00	66.00

CAROLINA

Inverness, Mayflower

Manufactured by Bryce Brothers, Pittsburgh, PA, c1890, and later by United States Glass Company, Pittsburgh, as part of the States series, c1900. Made in clear and ruby stained. Some ruby-stained pieces are engraved as souvenirs. Other pieces have been found with gilt or purple stain.

Item	Clear	Ruby Stained	Item	Clear	Ruby Stained
Berry bowl	15.00	—	Compote, open, hs, deep bowl, 8" d	40.00	—
Bowl, oval, beaded rim, deep or shallow, 5" d or 6" d	10.00	—	Compote, open, hs, saucer bowl, 8" d	20.00	—
			Compote, open, hs, saucer bowl, 9" d	25.00	—
Bowl, oval, beaded rim, deep or shallow, 7" d, 8" d, or 9" d	15.00	—	Compote, open, hs, saucer bowl, 10" d	30.00	—
Bread tray, handles	40.00	—	Compote, open, ls, 5" d	20.00	—
Butter dish, cov	35.00	—	Compote, open, ls, 6" d	20.00	—
Cake stand, hs, 9-1/2" d	35.00	—	Compote, open, ls, 7" d	20.00	—
Cake stand, hs, 10-1/2" d	40.00	—	Compote, open, ls, 8" d	25.00	—
Cake stand, hs, 11" d	40.00		Creamer, pint, tankard	20.00	—
Compote, cov, hs, 5" d	55.00	—	Creamer, pint, table	20.00	—
Compote, cov, hs, 6" d	55.00	—	Cruet, os	45.00	—
Compote, cov, hs, 7" d	60.00	—	Goblet	25.00	45.00
Compote, cov, hs, 8" d	60.00	—	Jelly compote, open	10.00	—
Compote, cov, ls, 5" d	35.00	—	Mug	20.00	35.00
Compote, cov, ls, 6" d	35.00	—	Pitcher, milk, quart	45.00	—
Compote, cov, ls, 7" d	35.00	—	Pitcher, water, half gallon		
Compote, cov, ls, 8" d	40.00	—	Plate, 7" d or 7-1/2" d	10.00	—
Compote, open, hs, crimped bowl, 6" d	20.00	—	Relish tray	10.00	25.00
Compote, open, hs, crimped bowl, 7" d	20.00	—	Salt and pepper shakers, pr	30.00	65.00
Compote, open, hs, crimped bowl, 8" d	20.00	—	Sauce, flat, 4" d or 4-1/2" d	8.00	—
Compote, open, hs, crimped bowl, 9" d	25.00	—	Sauce, footed, 4" d or 4-1/2" d	10.00	—
Compote, open, hs, deep bowl, 5" d	15.00	—	Spooner	20.00	—
Compote, open, hs, deep bowl, 6" d	20.00	—	Sugar bowl, cov	25.00	—
Compote, open, hs, deep bowl, 7" d	25.00	—	Syrup, orig top, orig top	40.00	—
			Tumbler	10.00	—
			Wine	20.00	35.00

COLORADO

Lacy Medallion

Manufactured by United States Glass Company, Pittsburgh, PA, c1898 to 1920, as one of its States series. Made in non-flint, Dewey blue, clear, and green. The green is sometimes found with copper-wheel engraving. Also made in amethyst stained, ruby stained, and opaque white with enamel floral trim, all of which are scarce compared to the solid colors. Some pieces are found with ornate silver frames or feet. Purists consider these two separate patterns, with the Lacy Medallion restricted to souvenir pieces.

Reproductions: Many reproductions exist. The Summit Art Glass Company, Mogadore/Rootstown, OH, made a toothpick holder in clear and other original colors.

Item	Dewey Blue	Clear	Green
Banana stand	65.00	35.00	50.00
Bowl, crimped, 5" d	30.00	20.00	25.00
Bowl, crimped, 6" d	35.00	25.00	30.00
Bowl, crimped, 7" d	40.00	30.00	35.00
Bowl, crimped, 8" d	45.00	35.00	40.00
Bowl, flared, 5" d	35.00	25.00	30.00
Bowl, flared, 6" d	40.00	30.00	35.00
Bowl, flared, 7" d	45.00	35.00	40.00
Bowl, flared, 8" d	50.00	40.00	45.00
Bowl, ftd, 5" d	35.00	20.00	30.00
Bowl, ftd, 6" d	40.00	30.00	35.00

COLORADO (cont.)

Item	Dewey Blue	Clear	Green
Bowl, ftd, 7" d	45.00	35.00	40.00
Bowl, ftd, 7-1/2" d	40.00	25.00	35.00
Bowl, ftd, 8" d	45.00	35.00	40.00
Bowl, ftd, 8-1/4" d	65.00	45.00	60.00
Butter dish, cov	200.00	60.00	125.00
Cake stand	75.00	55.00	65.00
Calling card tray	45.00	25.00	35.00
Celery vase	65.00	35.00	75.00
Compote, open, ls, 5" d	35.00	20.00	30.00
Compote, open, ls, 6" d	45.00	20.00	45.00
Compote, open, ls, 9-1/2" d	95.00	35.00	65.00
Cracker jar, cov	125.00	50.00	100.00
Creamer, individual, bulbous	45.00	30.00	40.00
Creamer, individual, tankard	45.00	30.00	40.00
Creamer, regular	95.00	40.00	70.00
Custard cup, ah, ftd, large	30.00	20.00	25.00
Custard cup, ah, ftd, small	30.00	20.00	25.00
Dresser tray	45.00	25.00	35.00
Mug	40.00	20.00	30.00
Nappy	40.00	20.00	35.00
Olive dish	40.00	20.00	30.00
Pickle dish	40.00	20.00	30.00
Pitcher, milk, ah, quart	250.00	—	100.00
Pitcher, water, ah, half gallon	375.00	95.00	185.00
Plate, 6" d	50.00	18.00	45.00
Plate, 8" d	65.00	20.00	60.00
Punch cup	30.00	18.00	25.00
Salt shaker	65.00	30.00	40.00
Sauce, ftd, ruffled, or flared rim, 4" d	30.00	15.00	25.00
Sherbet, large or small	50.00	25.00	45.00
Spooner	65.00	40.00	60.00
Sugar bowl, cov, table	75.00	60.00	75.00
Sugar bowl, open, individual, handles	35.00	25.00	30.00
Sugar bowl, open, individual, without handles	35.00	25.00	30.00
Toothpick holder φ	60.00	30.00	45.00
Tumbler	35.00	18.00	30.00
Vase, 12" h	85.00	35.00	60.00
Violet bowl	60.00	—	—
Wine	—	25.00	40.00

CONNECTICUT

Manufactured by United States Glass Company, c1900, as one of its States series. Made in non-flint, clear, plain and engraved. Two varieties of ruby-stained toothpick holders have been identified and are currently valued at $125.

Item	Clear	Item	Clear	Item	Clear
Basket	50.00	Compote, open, hs, scalloped, 7-1/2" d	30.00	Pickle jar, cov	35.00
Biscuit jar	25.00			Pitcher, milk, quart, tankard	35.00
Bowl, 4" d	10.00	Compote, open, hs, scalloped, 8-1/2" d	35.00	Pitcher, water, half gallon, bulbous	40.00
Bowl, 6" d, pattern on rim or base	15.00			Pitcher, water, half gallon, tankard	45.00
Bowl, 8" d, pattern on rim or base	15.00	Compote, open, hs, scalloped, 9-1/2" d	40.00	Relish	12.00
Butter dish, cov	35.00	Compote, open, ls, 7"	25.00	Salt and pepper shakers, pr	35.00
Cake stand, hs, 10" d	40.00	Creamer	30.00	Sauce, flat, belled, patterned base, 4" d or 4-1/2" d	10.00
Celery tray	20.00	Cruet, os	25.00		
Celery vase	35.00	Custard cup	5.00	Sauce, flat, straight sided, patterned base, 4" d or 4-1/2" d	10.00
Cheese, cov, plate	50.00	Dish, oblong, 8" l	20.00		
Compote, cov, hs, 5" d	25.00	Goblet	20.00	Sherbet	5.00
Compote, cov, hs, 5-1/2" d	25.00	Lamp, oil, orig burner and chimney	85.00	Spooner	25.00
Compote, cov, hs, 6" d	30.00	Lemonade, handle	20.00	Sugar bowl, cov	35.00
Compote, cov, hs, 7" d	35.00	Marmalade jar, cov	40.00	Toothpick holder	55.00
Compote, cov, hs, 8" d	40.00			Tumbler	18.00
Compote, open, hs, scalloped, 6" d	45.00			Wine	35.00

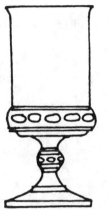

DAKOTA
Baby Thumbprint, Thumbprint Band

Manufactured by Ripley and Company, Pittsburgh, PA, in the late 1880s and early 1890s. It was later reissued by United States Glass Company, Pittsburgh, PA, at Factory "F," as one of the States series patterns. Made in non-flint, clear, clear etched, and ruby stained. One of the most popular etchings was named "Fern and Berry." Prices listed as "etched" below are for that etching. Another etching was known as "Fern" and has no berry. "Oak Leaf" and "Grape" etching are scarcer. Other etchings include fish, swan, peacock, bird, and insect, bird and flowers, ivy and berry, stag, spider and insect, buzzard on dead tree, and crane catching fish. Ruby stained may have the same etchings as found on clear pieces.

Reproductions: Only the tankard water pitcher has been known to be reproduced.

Items	Clear, Etched	Clear, Plain	Ruby Stained, Plain
Basket, metal handle, 10" x 2"	240.00	190.00	240.00
Berry bowl, master	55.00	42.00	—
Bottle, 5-1/2" h	75.00	85.00	—
Butter dish, cov, hotel size	85.00	410.00	180.00
Butter dish, cov, table size	65.00	48.00	130.00
Cake cover, high dome, 8" d	360.00	240.00	—
Cake cover, high dome, 9" d	32500	270.00	—
Cake cover, high dome, 10" d	360.00	300.00	—
Cake cover, high dome, 11" d	375.00	275.00	—
Cake stand, hs, 8" d	60.00	42.00	—
Cake stand, hs, 9" d	55.00	48.00	—
Cake stand, hs, 9-1/2" d	72.00	55.00	—
Cake stand, hs, 10" d	65.00	60.00	—
Cake stand, hs, 10-1/2" d	65.00	60.00	—
Celery tray	42.00	30.00	—
Celery vase, hotel size	48.00	36.00	—
Celery vase, table size	55.00	42.00	—
Cologne bottle, os	85.00	65.00	—
Compote, cov, hs, 5" d	72.00	60.00	—
Compote, cov, hs, 6" d	65.00	55.00	—
Compote, cov, hs, 7" d	85.00	72.00	—
Compote, cov, hs, 8" d	75.00	65.00	—
Compote, cov, hs, 9" d	95.00	85.00	—
Compote, cov, hs, 10" d	110.00	95.00	—
Compote, cov, hs, 12" d	120.00	110.00	—
Compote, open, hs, 5" d	48.00	36.00	—
Compote, open, hs, 6" d	55.00	42.00	—
Compote, open, hs, 7" d	55.00	42.00	—
Compote, open, hs, 8" d	60.00	48.00	—
Compote, open, hs, 9" d	55.00	55.00	—
Compote, open, hs, 10" d	72.00	60.00	—
Compote, open, ls, 7" d	55.00	48.00	—
Condiment tray	—	75.00	—
Creamer, hotel size	75.00	42.00	65.00
Creamer, table size	55.00	36.00	72.00
Cruet, os	110.00	55.00	142.00
Dish, flat, oblong, 8" l	48.00	55.00	60.00
Dish, flat, oblong, 9" l	55.00	72.00	55.00
Dish, flat, oblong, 10" l	60.00	65.00	72.00
Goblet	42.00	30.00	75.00
Honey dish, flat or footed	24.00	30.00	36.00
Mug, ah	55.00	55.00	65.00
Pepper sauce bottle, os	75.00	85.00	—
Pitcher, milk, ah, jug, pint	120.00	95.00	190.00
Pitcher, milk, ah, jug, quart	120.00	95.00	190.00
Pitcher, milk, ah, tankard, pint	115.00	75.00	165.00
Pitcher, milk, ah, tankard, quart	115.00	75.00	165.00
Pitcher, water, ah, jug, half gallon	85.00	75.00	195.00
Pitcher, water, ah, tankard, half gallon φ	130.00	85.00	270.00
Plate, 10" d	95.00	85.00	—
Plate, 12" d	85.00	75.00	—

DAKOTA (cont.)

Items	Clear, Etched	Clear, Plain	Ruby Stained, Plain
Relish tray	48.00	55.00	—
Salt shaker	65.00	110.00	130.00
Sauce, flat, 4" d or 5" d	24.00	18.00	30.00
Sauce, footed, 4" d or 5" d	30.00	24.00	36.00
Spooner, hotel size	42.00	36.00	95.00
Spooner, table size	36.00	30.00	65.00
Sugar bowl, cov, hotel size	75.00	85.00	115.00
Sugar bowl, cov, table size	65.00	75.00	85.00
Tumbler	42.00	36.00	55.00
Waste bowl	85.00	110.00	75.00
Water tray, hotel size	120.00	75.00	
Water tray, table size, 13" d	120.00	75.00	—
Wine	36.00	24.00	55.00
Wine tray, 10-1/2" d	115.00	85.00	—

DELAWARE

American Beauty, Four Petal Flower

Manufactured by United States Glass Company, Pittsburgh, PA, c1889-1909. Also made by Diamond Glass Company, Montreal, Quebec, Canada, c1902. Made in non-flint, clear, green with gold trim, rose with gold trim. Rare examples are found in amethyst, clear with rose stain, custard, and milk glass.

Reproductions: Reproductions of this popular pattern are limited to a butter dish, creamer, and sugar bowl. Reproductions are found in cobalt blue (with gold trim), green, and pink. The reproductions tend to be much thicker and tend to have coarse stippling. The reproductions are marked only with paper labels reading "Made in Taiwan."

Items	Clear	Green with Gold	Rose with Gold
Banana bowl	48.00	55.00	65.00
Bowl, 8" d	36.00	48.00	60.00
Bowl, 9" d	30.00	42.00	55.00
Bottle, os	95.00	180.00	225.00
Bride's basket, silver plate frame	75.00	118.00	165.00
Butter dish, cov φ	95.00	118.00	180.00
Claret jug, tankard shape	135.00	1115.00	240.00
Celery vase, flat	75.00	110.00	115.00
Creamer, individual	55.00	65.00	85.00
Creamer, table size φ	55.00	65.00	85.00
Cruet, os	110.00	240.00	300.00
Finger bowl	30.00	60.00	75.00
Fruit bowl, oval, 11-1/2" l	30.00	55.00	55.00
Fruit bowl, round, 11" d	42.00	60.00	72.00
Lamp shade, electric	85.00	—	130.00
Pin tray	36.00	55.00	115.00
Pitcher, water	65.00	180.00	130.00
Pomade box, jeweled	120.00	300.00	360.00
Puff box, bulbous, jeweled	120.00	240.00	318.00
Punch cup	30.00	24.00	42.00
Salt shaker, orig top	75.00	130.00	180.00
Sauce, flat, boat shape, 5-1/2" d	18.00	42.00	36.00
Sauce, flat, round, 4" d	18.00	30.00	36.00
Spooner	55.00	60.00	55.00
Sugar bowl, cov, individual	42.00	60.00	72.00
Sugar bowl, cov, table size φ	65.00	85.00	120.00
Toothpick holder	42.00	130.00	180.00
Tumbler	24.00	48.00	55.00
Vase, 6" h	30.00	55.00	75.00
Vase, 8" h	30.00	55.00	75.00
Vase, 9-1/2" h	48.00	95.00	85.00

FLORIDA

Emerald Green Herringbone, Paneled Herringbone, Prism and Herringbone, U.S. Glass Pattern Line No. 15,056

Manufactured by United States Glass Company, Pittsburgh, PA, in the 1890s, as one of the States series patterns. Made in non-flint, clear, and emerald green. A sapphire blue water pitcher is known and valued at $175.

Reproductions: The goblet has been reproduced in amber, amethyst, blue, emerald green, and ruby red.

Items	Clear	Emerald Green	Items	Clear	Emerald Green
Berry set	75.00	135.00	Nappy	18.00	30.00
Bowl, cov, 4" d	30.00	48.00	Pickle dish, oval	30.00	55.00
Bowl, open, 7-1/4" d	12.00	18.00	Pitcher, water	60.00	75.00
Bowl, open, 9" d	18.00	24.00	Plate, 7-1/2" d	15.00	25.00
Butter dish, cov	60.00	85.00	Plate, 9-1/4" d	18.00	30.00
Cake stand, large	72.00	75.00	Relish, square, 6" w	12.00	18.00
Cake stand, small	36.00	48.00	Relish, square, 8-1/2" w	18.00	25.00
Celery vase	36.00	42.00	Salt shaker	30.00	60.00
Compote, cov, hs, sq, 6-1/2" w	48.00	60.00	Sauce, round, sq top, handle	10.00	15.00
Compote, open, hs, sq, 6-1/2" w	36.00	48.00	Sauce, round, sq top, no handle	6.00	12.00
Cordial	30.00	42.00	Spooner	24.00	42.00
Creamer	36.00	55.00	Sugar bowl, cov	42.00	60.00
Cruet, os	48.00	65.00	Syrup, orig top	72.00	190.00
Goblet φ	30.00	48.00	Tumbler	24.00	36.00
Mustard pot, cov, attached underplate	30.00	55.00	Wine	30.00	60.00

GEORGIA

Peacock Feather

Manufactured by Richards & Hartley, Tarentum, PA, and reissued by United States Glass Company, Pittsburgh, PA, in 1902, as part of its States series. Made in non-flint clear. Rare examples are known in blue (lamp, chamber, $275). No goblet is known in this pattern.

Items	Clear	Items	Clear	Items	Clear
Bonbon, ftd	30.00	Compote, cov, hs, 6" d	48.00	Lamp, chamber, pedestal	85.00
Bowl, 5" d, 6" d, or 7" d	24.00	Compote, cov, hs, 7"	55.00	Lamp, hand, oil, 7" h	95.00
Bowl, 8" d	36.00	Compote, cov, hs, 8" d	60.00	Mug	30.00
Butter dish, cov, quarter pound	55.00	Compote, open, hs, 5" d	24.00	Nappy	30.00
Butter dish, cov, table size	55.00	Compote, open, hs, 6" d	30.00	Pitcher, water	85.00
Cake stand, hs, 9-1/2" d	48.00	Compote, open, hs, 7" d	36.00	Plate, 5-1/4" d	18.00
Cake stand, hs, 9" d	55.00	Compote, open, hs, 8" d	42.00	Preserve dish, 8" l	12.00
Cake stand, hs, 10" d	60.00	Compote, open, hs, 9" d	48.00	Relish tray	18.00
Cake stand, hs, 11" d	55.00	Compote, open, hs, 10" d	55.00	Salt shaker	48.00
Castor set, two bottles	72.00	Condiment set, tray, oil cruet, salt & pepper	75.00	Sauce, flat, 4" d or 4-1/2" d	12.00
Celery tray, 11-3/4" l	42.00	Creamer	42.00	Spooner	42.00
Celery vase	48.00	Cruet, os	55.00	Sugar bowl, cov	55.00
Child's cake stand	42.00	Decanter, os	85.00	Syrup, orig top, metal lid	65.00
Child's creamer	42.00			Tumbler	42.00
Compote, cov, hs, 5" d	42.00				

ILLINOIS

Clarissa, Star of the East, U.S. Glass Pattern Line No. 15,052

Manufactured by United States Glass Company, Pittsburgh, PA, c1897, as one of the States series. Made in clear, emerald green, and some ruby-stained pieces, including salt ($60) and lidless straw holder ($105). Most forms are square.

Reproductions: The butter dish and celery vase have been reproduced by L. E. Smith Glass Company, Mt. Pleasant, PA.

Item	Clear	Emerald Green	Item	Clear	Emerald Green
Almond stand, hs, 5" d	60.00	—	Pitcher, milk, round,		
Basket, ah, 11-1/2" h	120.00	—	silver plate rim	190.00	—
Bonbon, hs, 5" d	60.00	—	Pitcher, milk, square	80.00	—
Bonbon, hs, 6" d	72.00	—	Pitcher, water, square	80.00	—
Bonbon, hs, 7" d	85.00	—	Pitcher, water, tankard,		
Bowl, round, 5" d	24.00	—	round, silver plate rim	90.00	142.00
Bowl, round, 8" d	30.00	—	Plate, square or round, 7" w	30.00	—
Bowl, sq, 6" d	30.00	—	Puff box, cov	55.00	—
Bowl, sq, 8" w	36.00	—	Relish, 7-1/2" x 4"	110.00	48.00
Bowl, sq, 9" w	42.00	—	Relish, 8-1/2" x 3"	110.00	—
Butter dish, cov φ	72.00	—	Relish, 9" x 3", canoe	48.00	—
Butter pat, sq	30.00	—	Salt, individual	18.00	—
Cake stand, hs, 11" d	80.00	—	Salt, master	30.00	—
Candlesticks, pr	115.00	—	Salt and pepper shakers, pr	48.00	—
Celery tray, 11" l	48.00	—	Sauce, flat, 4" d or 4-1/2" d	18.00	—
Celery vase φ	60.00	—	Spooner, hotel size	48.00	—
Cheese dish, cov	90.00	—	Spooner, table size	42.00	—
Compote, open, hs, sq, 5" d	48.00	—	Spoon tray, rect, 8-1/4" l	65.00	—
Compote, open, hs, sq, 9" d	72.00	—	Straw holder, cov	190.00	480.00
Creamer, individual	36.00	—	Sugar bowl, cov, table	65.00	—
Creamer, table	48.00	—	Sugar bowl, open, hotel size	55.00	—
Cruet, os	80.00	—	Sugar bowl, open, individual	36.00	—
Finger bowl	30.00	—	Sugar shaker, orig pewter		
Ice cream dish, rect, 5" l	42.00	—	or silver plate top	90.00	—
Ice cream tray, rect, 12" l	60.00	—	Syrup, orig top, pewter top	115.00	—
Lamp, banquet, two sizes	760.00	—	Toothpick holder, adv emb in base	55.00	—
Marmalade jar, cov	142.00	—	Toothpick holder, plain	36.00	—
Olive dish	110.00	—	Tray, 12" x 8", turned up sides	60.00	—
Pickle dish, rect, 7-1/4" l	24.00	—	Tumbler	36.00	48.00
Pickle jar, cov, sq	65.00	—	Vase, 6" h, sq	42.00	55.00
			Vase, 9-1/2" h	—	130.00

INDIANA

Doric, Prison Windows, U.S. Glass Pattern Line No. 15,029

Manufactured by United States Glass Company, c1897, at Factory "U," Glass City, IN. Made in non-flint, clear, and rarely in ruby stained.

Items	Clear	Items	Clear	Items	Clear
Bowl, scalloped rim, 5" d, 6" d, or 7" d	18.00	Cruet, os, matching undertray	60.00	Salt shaker	24.00
Bowl, scalloped rim, 8" d or 9" d	24.00	Dish, oval, 7" l, 8" l, or 9" l	18.00	Sauce, flat, 4" d or 4-1/2" d	18.00
Butter dish, cov	55.00	Finger bowl	30.00	Spooner	42.00
Catsup bottle	80.00	Ice tub	90.00	Sugar bowl, cov	55.00
Celery tray	30.00	Jelly compote, open, hs	36.00	Syrup, orig top	60.00
Celery vase	36.00	Perfume bottle	72.00	Tray, oblong	60.00
Creamer	42.00	Pitcher, water, tankard	80.00	Tumbler	42.00
				Water bottle	72.00

IOWA
Paneled Zipper, U.S. Glass Pattern Line No. 15,069

Manufactured by United States Glass Company, Pittsburgh, PA, c1902, as part of the States series. Made in non-flint and clear. Also found in clear glass with gilt trim (add 20 percent) and ruby or cranberry stained. Also found in amber (goblet, $85,) green, canary, and blue. Add 50 percent to 100 percent for color.

Items	Clear	Items	Clear	Items	Clear
Berry bowl, master	15.00	Cruet, os	36.00	Sauce, 4-1/2" d	6.50
Bread plate, motto	95.00	Cup	18.00	Spooner	36.00
Butter dish, cov	48.00	Decanter, 1-1/2 pints	48.00	Sugar bowl, cov	42.00
Cake stand, hs	42.00	Goblet	210.00	Toothpick holder	24.00
Carafe	42.00	Lamp, oil	130.00	Tumbler	30.00
Compote, cov, hs, 8" d	48.00	Olive tray, handle	18.00	Vase, 6" h	18.00
Corn liquor jug, os	72.00	Pitcher, water, tankard	60.00	Vase, 8" h	24.00
Creamer	36.00	Punch cup	18.00	Vase, 10" h	30.00
		Salt shaker, single, large or small	30.00	Wine	36.00

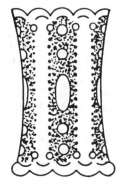

KANSAS
Jewel and Dewdrop, Jewel with Dewdrop, U.S. Glass Pattern Line No. 15,072

Manufactured by the Co-Operative Flint Glass Company, Beaver Falls, PA. Later produced as part of the States series patterns by United States Glass Company, Pittsburgh, PA, in 1901, Kokomo Glass Manufacturing Company, Kokomo, IN, c1903, Federal Glass Company, Columbus, OH, c1914, and by Jenkins Glass Company, c1915-25. Made in non-flint, clear. Also known with jewels stained in pink or gold.

Reproductions: Mugs have been reproduced in vaseline, amber, and blue. They tend to be smaller and of inferior quality.

Items	Clear	Items	Clear	Items	Clear
Banana stand	90.00	Celery vase	45.00	Compote, open, ls, scalloped rim, 5" d	25.00
Bowl, oval, 7" l	35.00	Compote, cov, hs, beading on pedestal, 7" d	65.00	Cordial	40.00
Bowl, round, scalloped rim, 6" d or 6-1/2" d	25.00			Creamer	40.00
		Compote, cov, hs, beading on pedestal, 8" d	85.00	Cup, handle	15.00
Bowl, round, scalloped rim, 7" or 7-1/2" d	30.00	Compote, cov, hs, notched lid, 6" d	55.00	Goblet	55.00
				Jelly compote, 5" d	50.00
Bowl, round, scalloped rim, 8" d	40.00	Compote, cov, hs, solid lid, 5" d	45.00	Mug, regular	45.00
Bread plate, ODB	45.00	Compote, cov, hs, solid lid, 6" d	50.00	Mug, tall	25.00
Butter dish, cov, flanged, attached under plate	65.00	Compote, open, hs, beading on pedestal, 6" d	30.00	Pitcher, milk, quart	50.00
				Pitcher, water, half gallon	60.00
Butter dish, round, no under plate	55.00	Compote, open, hs, beading on pedestal, 7" d	35.00	Preserve dish, 6-1/2" w, 8-1/2" l	20.00
Butter dish, notched lid	75.00	Compote, open, hs, beading on pedestal, 8" d	45.00	Relish, oval, 8-1/2" l	20.00
Cake plate	65.00			Salt shaker	50.00
Cake stand, hs, 7-5/8" d	45.00	Compote, open, ls, saucer bowl, scalloped rim, 7-1/2" d	35.00	Sauce, flat, scalloped rim, 4" d	12.00
Cake stand, hs, 9" d	75.00			Sugar bowl, cov	65.00
Cake stand, hs, 10" d	85.00	Compote, open, ls, saucer bowl, scalloped rim, 8-1/2" d	40.00	Syrup, orig top	125.00
Cake stand, ls, 8" d	50.00			Toothpick holder	65.00
Cake stand, ls, 9" d	55.00	Compote, open, ls, saucer bowl, scalloped rim, 9-1/2" d	45.00	Tumbler, flat	45.00
Cake stand, ls, 10" d	60.00			Whiskey	15.00
				Wine	65.00

KENTUCKY

U.S. Glass Pattern Line No. 150,051

Manufactured by United States Glass Company, Pittsburgh, PA, c1897, as part of the States series. Made in non-flint, clear, and emerald green. The goblet is found in ruby stained ($50). A footed, square sauce, ($30) is known in cobalt blue with gold. A toothpick holder is also known in ruby stained ($150).

Items	Clear	Emerald Green	Items	Clear	Emerald Green
Bowl, 7" d	20.00	—	Dish, oblong, flat, 7" or 8" l	15.00	—
Bowl, 8" d	20.00	—	Goblet	20.00	50.00
Butter dish, cov	50.00	—	Nappy	10.00	15.00
Cake stand, hs, 9-1/2" d	40.00	—	Olive, handle	25.00	—
Cake stand, hs, 10-1/2" d	45.00	—	Pitcher, water	55.00	—
Celery tray, large	30.00	—	Plate, sq, 7" w	15.00	—
Celery tray, small	30.00	—	Plate, sq, 9" w	15.00	—
Celery vase	35.00	—	Punch cup	10.00	15.00
Compote, cov, hs, 5" d	35.00	—	Salt shaker, orig top	10.00	—
Compote, cov, hs, 6" d	40.00	—	Sauce, flat, sq, 4" w or 4-1/2" w	8.00	10.00
Compote, cov, hs, 7" d	45.00	—	Sauce, ftd, sq, 4" w or 4-1/2" w	10.00	12.00
Compote, cov, hs, 8" d	50.00	—	Spooner	35.00	—
Compote, open, hs, 5" d	25.00	—	Sugar bowl, cov	30.00	—
Compote, open, hs, 6" d	25.00	—	Syrup, orig top	65.00	—
Compote, open, hs, 7" d	30.00	—	Toothpick holder, sq	35.00	85.00
Compote, open, hs, 8" d	30.00	—	Tumbler	20.00	30.00
Creamer	25.00	—	Wine	28.00	38.00
Cruet, os	45.00	—			
Custard cup	10.00	20.00			

LOUISIANA

Sharp Oval and Diamond, Granby, U.S. Glass Pattern Line No. 15,053

Manufactured by Bryce Brothers, Pittsburgh, PA, in the 1870s. Reissued by the United States Glass Company, Pittsburgh, PA, c1898, as part of the States series. Made in clear, some forms frosted. Also found with gilt trim.

Items	Clear	Items	Clear	Items	Clear
Berry bowl, 9" d	24.00	Celery vase	36.00	Match holder	42.00
Bowl, cov, flat, 6" d	30.00	Compote, cov, hs, 6" d	65.00	Mug, handle	30.00
Bowl, cov, flat, 7" d	36.00	Compote, cov, hs, 7" d	75.00	Mustard, cov, matching patterned	
Bowl, cov, flat, 8" d	42.00	Compote, cov, hs, 8" d	90.00	under plate	48.00
Bowl, open, round, 6" d	18.00	Compote, open, hs, deep bowl, 6" d	18.00	Pickle, boat shape	48.00
Bowl, open, round, 7" d	24.00	Compote, open, hs, deep bowl, 7" d	24.00	Nappy, cov, 4" d	36.00
Bowl, open, round, 8" d	30.00	Compote, open, hs, deep bowl, 8" d	30.00	Pitcher, milk, ph	60.00
Bowl, open, square, 6" w	24.00	Compote, open, hs, flared bowl, 6" d	24.00	Pitcher, water, ph	75.00
Bowl, open, square, 7" w	24.00	Compote, open, hs, saucer bowl, 8" d	30.00	Relish tray	18.00
Bowl, open, square, 8" w	30.00	Compote, open, hs, saucer bowl, 10" d	55.00	Salt shaker	30.00
Bowl, open, square, 9" w	30.00	Creamer	36.00	Sauce, flat, round, 4" d or 4-1/2" d	12.00
Butter dish, cov	75.00	Dish, cov, 6" d	30.00	Sauce, flat, square, 4" d or 4-1/2" d	12.00
Cake stand, hs, 7" d	55.00	Dish, open, flat, 6" d	24.00	Spooner	36.00
Cake stand, hs, 9" d	65.00	Goblet	36.00	Sugar bowl, cov	55.00
Cake stand, hs, 10" d	75.00	Jelly compote, open, hs, 5" d	48.00	Tumbler	30.00
				Wine	42.00

MAINE

Paneled Stippled Flower, Stippled Primrose, Stippled Paneled Flower

Manufactured by United States Glass Company, Pittsburgh, PA, c1899, as part of its States series. Researchers dispute if goblet was made originally. Made in non-flint, clear, and emerald green. Sometimes found with enamel trim or overall turquoise stain.

Items	Clear	Emerald Green	Items	Clear	Emerald Green
Bowl, cov, round, flared, 8" d	55.00	—	Compote, open, ls, 9" d	36.00	75.00
Bowl, oval, 8" l, 6" w	30.00	—	Creamer	36.00	—
Bowl, round, 6" d	24.00	12.00	Cruet	95.00	—
Bowl, round, 7" d	30.00	18.00	Goblet	115.00	—
Bowl, round, 8" d	36.00	48.00	Jelly compote, cov	60.00	90.00
Bread plate, oval, 10" l, 7-3/4" w	36.00	—	Mug	42.00	—
Butter dish, cov	410.00	—	Pickle tray, 8" l	18.00	36.00
Cake stand, hs, 8" d	48.00	72.00	Pitcher, milk, quart	75.00	100.00
Cake stand, hs, 9" d	55.00	75.00	Pitcher, water, half gallon	60.00	130.00
Cake stand, hs, 10" d	65.00	85.00	Plate, 10" d	42.00	—
Cake stand, hs, 11" d	72.00	90.00	Relish	18.00	—
Celery vase	60.00	—	Salt shaker, single	36.00	—
Compote, open, hs, 5" d	24.00	55.00	Sauce, flat, 4" d	18.00	—
Compote, open, hs, 6" d	24.00	55.00	Spooner	30.00	48.00
Compote, open, hs, 7" d	24.00	55.00	Sugar bowl, cov	55.00	90.00
Compote, open, hs, flared bowl, 8" d	42.00	72.00	Syrup	90.00	230.00
Compote, open, hs, flared bowl, 9" d	48.00	75.00	Toothpick holder	130.00	—
Compote, open, hs, flared bowl, 10" d	55.00	85.00	Tumbler, flat	36.00	55.00
Compote, open, ls, 8" d	310.00	65.00	Wine	60.00	90.00

MARYLAND

Inverted Loop and Fan, Loop and Diamond, U.S. Glass Pattern Line No. 15,049

Manufactured originally by Bryce Bros., Pittsburgh, PA. Continued by United States Glass Company, Pittsburgh, PA, as one of its States series patterns. Made in non-flint, clear, clear with gilt trim, and ruby stained.

Items	Clear, Gilt Trim	Ruby Stained	Items	Clear, Gilt Trim	Ruby Stained
Banana dish	42.00	100.00	Custard cup	24.00	—
Berry bowl, master, 8" d	18.00	42.00	Goblet	36.00	410.00
Bowl, 6" d	18.00	42.00	Honey dish, flat, 3" d	36.00	72.00
Bowl, 7" d	18.00	—	Jelly compote, open	30.00	55.00
Bread plate	30.00	—	Olive, handle	18.00	—
Butter dish, cov	75.00	115.00	Pickle, oval, flat, handle	24.00	42.00
Cake stand, hs, 8"	48.00	—	Pitcher, milk, quart	55.00	142.00
Cake stand, hs, 9" d	55.00	—	Pitcher, water, half gallon	60.00	120.00
Cake stand, hs, 10" d	60.00	—	Plate, 7" d	30.00	—
Celery tray	24.00	42.00	Preserve dish, 8" d	24.00	—
Celery vase	210.00	75.00	Relish, oval	18.00	65.00
Compote, cov, hs, 6" d	55.00	—	Salt shaker, single	36.00	—
Compote, cov, hs, 7" d	65.00	—	Sauce, flat	12.00	18.00
Compote, cov, hs, 8" d	75.00	120.00	Spooner	36.00	65.00
Compote, open, deep, 6" d	24.00	65.00	Sugar bowl, cov	55.00	72.00
Compote, open, deep, 7" d	30.00	72.00	Sweetmeat, cov, 7" d	48.00	—
Compote, open, deep, 8" d	36.00	75.00	Toothpick holder	130.00	190.00
Compote, open, saucer bowl, 7" d	30.00	—	Tumbler, flat	30.00	60.00
Compote, open, saucer bowl, 8" d	36.00	—	Wine	48.00	90.00
Creamer	30.00	65.00			

MASSACHUSETTS

Arched Diamond Points, Cane Variant, Geneva #2, MR-131, Star and Diamonds

Manufactured in the 1880s by an unknown maker. Reissued in 1898 by United States Glass Company, Pittsburgh, PA, as one of the States series. Made in non-flint, clear. A vase ($55) and wine ($55) are known in emerald green. Some pieces have been reported in cobalt blue and marigold carnival glass.

Reproductions: Reproduced butter dish in clear and colors.

Items	Clear	Items	Clear	Items	Clear
Almond dish, flat, 5" l	24.00	Cruet, os	55.00	Rum jug, large	110.00
Bar bottle, metal shot glass for cover	90.00	Custard cup	18.00	Rum jug, medium	110.00
Basket, 4-1/2", ah	60.00	Decanter, os	65.00	Rum jug, small	110.00
Bonbon, flat, 5" d	60.00	Goblet	55.00	Salt shaker, large, square	30.00
Bowl, sq, folded or pointed sides, 6" w	18.00	Gravy boat	36.00	Salt shaker, small, bulbous	30.00
Bowl, sq, folded or straight sides, 9" w	24.00	Hot whiskey, stem	42.00	Salt shaker, tall, round	30.00
Bowl, sq, pointed or straight sides, 7" w	18.00	Juice tumbler	30.00	Sauce, oval or square, 4"	18.00
Bowl, sq, pointed sides, 8" w	24.00	Lamp, oil, orig globe, burner, and chimney, banquet size	760.00	Sherry	48.00
Brandy bottle	55.00			Shot glass	18.00
Butter dish, cov φ	60.00	Lamp, oil, orig globe, burner, and chimney, table size	950.00	Spooner, two handles	24.00
Candy dish, flat, 8" l or 9" l	24.00	Lemonade tumbler, flared rim or straight sides	42.00	Spoon tray, rolled sides	30.00
Celery tray	36.00			Sugar bowl, cov, individual	30.00
Celery vase	36.00	Mayonnaise, handle, flat	24.00	Sugar bowl, cov, table	48.00
Champagne	42.00	Mug, handle, large	30.00	Syrup	75.00
Claret	42.00	Mug, handle, small	24.00	Tabasco sauce	55.00
Cocktail	42.00	Mustard Jar, cov	42.00	Toast tray	30.00
Cologne bottle, os	37.50	Olive, 6" l	8.50	Toothpick holder	48.00
Compote, open, ls, cupped bowl	42.00	Olive, 8-1/2" l	15.00	Tumbler, soda or pony beer, flared rim, or straight sides	42.00
Condiment set, cruet, mustard, salt shaker, tray	130.00	Orange tray, 9" l	42.00	Tumbler, water, round or square	48.00
		Pin tray, 5" sq	30.00	Vase, trumpet, 6-1/2" h	30.00
Cordial	65.00	Pitcher, water, half gallon, squatty	75.00	Vase, trumpet, 7" h	30.00
Creamer, individual	24.00	Pitcher, water, half gallon, tankard	90.00	Vase, trumpet, 9" h	42.00
Creamer, medium	30.00	Plate, sq, 8" w	40.00	Water bottle	42.00
Creamer, table	36.00	Punch cup	18.00	Whiskey	30.00
		Relish tray, 4-1/2" l, 2-3/4" w	18.00	Wine, round or square bowl	48.00
		Relish tray, 5-1/2" l, 3-3/4" w	24.00	Wine bottle	75.00

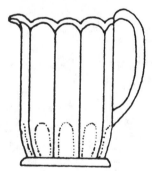

MICHIGAN

Loop and Pillar, Paneled Jewel, U.S. Glass Pattern Line No. 15,072

Manufactured by United States Glass Company, Pittsburgh, PA, c1902, as one of the States series patterns. Made in non-flint, clear, and rose stained. The 10-1/4" bowl ($45) and punch cup ($15) are found with yellow or blue stain and also with painted carnations. Other colors include "Sunrise," gold, and ruby stained.

Reproductions: The toothpick holder has been reproduced by the Degenhart Glass Company, Cambridge, OH. It created a new mold and used new colors.

Items	Clear	Rose Stained	Items	Clear	Rose Stained
Bowl, deep, 6" d	12.00	30.00	Butter dish, cov, quarter pound	75.00	—
Bowl, deep, 7" d	18.00	36.00	Butter dish, cov, table size	72.00	130.00
Bowl, deep, 8-1/2" d	24.00	42.00	Candlestick	90.00	—
Bowl, flared rim, shallow, 5" d	12.00	30.00	Celery vase	48.00	100.00
Bowl, flared rim, shallow, 7-1/2" d	18.00	36.00	Child's butter dish, cov	180.00	325.00
Bowl, flared rim, shallow, 8-1/2" d	24.00	42.00	Child's creamer	72.00	120.00
Bowl, flared rim, shallow, 10" d	30.00	48.00	Child's nappy, handle	36.00	—
Bowl, straight sided, shallow, 6" d	12.00	30.00	Child's pitcher, water	75.00	118.00
Bowl, straight sided, shallow, 7" d	18.00	36.00	Child's spooner	72.00	120.00
Bride's basket, silver plated holder	72.00	130.00	Child's stein, 2-3/4" h	55.00	—

MICHIGAN (cont.)

Items	Clear	Rose Stained
Child's sugar bowl, cov	130.00	260.00
Child's tumbler	24.00	—
Compote, cov, hs, deep bowl, 5" d	60.00	100.00
Compote, open, hs, deep bowl, straight sided, 6" d	30.00	48.00
Compote, open, hs, deep bowl, straight sided, 7" d	36.00	55.00
Compote, open, hs, deep bowl, straight sided, 8" d	42.00	60.00
Compote, open, hs, flared bowl, shallow, 7-1/2" d	65.00	90.00
Compote, open, hs, flared bowl, shallow, 8-1/2" d	72.00	95.00
Compote, open, hs, flared bowl, shallow, 9-1/4" d	75.00	100.00
Creamer, individual, 6 oz, tankard	24.00	75.00
Creamer, table	36.00	60.00
Cruet, os	72.00	230.00
Crushed fruit bowl	90.00	—
Custard cup	18.00	—
Dish, flat, oval, 7-1/2" l	18.00	—
Dish, flat, oval, 9-1/2" l	24.00	—
Dish, flat, oval, 10-1/2" l	30.00	—
Dish, flat, oval, 12-1/2" l	30.00	—
Finger bowl	18.00	—
Goblet	42.00	75.00
Honey dish	12.00	—
Jelly compote, 4-1/2" d	55.00	90.00
Lemonade mug	30.00	48.00
Nappy, Gainsborough handle	42.00	—
Olive, two handles	12.00	30.00

Items	Clear	Rose Stained
Pickle dish, oval, two handles	15.00	24.00
Pitcher, milk, quart, 8" h	60.00	—
Pitcher, water, three pints, helmet shape	72.00	—
Pitcher, water, half gallon, tankard, 12" h	85.00	180.00
Plate, 5-1/2" d	18.00	—
Punch bowl, 8" d	60.00	—
Punch cup	10.00	—
Relish tray	24.00	42.00
Salt shaker, single, three types	24.00	36.00
Sauce, flat, flared or straight sided, 4" d or 4-1/2" d	15.00	25.00
Sauce, footed, 4" d or 4-1/2" d	18.00	30.00
Sherbet cup, handled	18.00	24.00
Spooner	60.00	90.00
Sugar bowl, cov, table	60.00	90.00
Sugar bowl, open, individual	18.00	—
Syrup	115.00	190.00
Toothpick holder φ	55.00	120.00
Tumbler	36.00	48.00
Vase, bud, 8" h	42.00	48.00
Vase, bud, 12" h	42.00	48.00
Vase, bud, 16" h	48.00	—
Vase, bud, 17" h	48.00	—
Vase, ftd, 6" h	48.00	—
Vase, ftd, 8" h	55.00	—
Wine	42.00	60.00

MINNESOTA

Muchness, U.S. Glass Pattern Line No. 15,055

Manufactured by the United States Glass Company, Pittsburgh, PA, in the late 1890s, at Factory "F" and Factory "G." It is one of the States series patterns. Made in non-flint, clear, and ruby stained. Some pieces have gilt trim. A two-piece flower frog has been found in emerald green ($50).

Items	Clear	Ruby Stained
Almond dish, oblong, pointed ends	18.00	—
Banana stand	75.00	—
Basket, ah	75.00	—
Biscuit jar, cov	65.00	180.00
Bonbon, 5" l	18.00	—
Bowl, boat shape, pointed ends, 5" l	18.00	—
Bowl, boat shape, pointed ends, 6" l	24.00	—
Bowl, boat shape, pointed ends, 7" l	30.00	—
Bowl, boat shape, pointed ends, 8" l	30.00	—
Bowl, flared, round, 6" d	18.00	—
Bowl, flared, round, 7" d	24.00	—
Bowl, flared, round, 8-1/2" d	36.00	120.00
Bowl, oval, 9-1/2" d	30.00	—
Bowl, oval, 10" d	30.00	—
Bowl, square, 6" w	18.00	—
Bowl, square, 7" w	24.00	—
Bowl, square, 8" w	30.00	—
Bread tray, 13" l	42.00	—
Butter dish, cov	60.00	—
Candy dish, cov, scalloped sides, pointed ends, 7" l or 8" l	24.00	

Items	Clear	Ruby Stained
Carafe	42.00	—
Celery tray, oblong, 13" l	30.00	—
Celery tray, square, 10" w	30.00	—
Cheese plate, 7" d, turned up serrated sides	18.00	
Compote, open, hs, deep, flared bowl, 7-1/2" d	55.00	—
Compote, open, hs, deep, flared bowl, 8-1/2" d	60.00	—
Compote, open, hs, deep, flared bowl, 9-1/2 " d	65.00	—
Compote, open, hs, deep, flared bowl, 10" d	72.00	—
Compote, open, hs, straight-sided bowl, 6" d	42.00	—
Compote, open, hs, straight-sided bowl, 7" d	48.00	—
Compote, open, hs, straight-sided bowl, 8" d	55.00	—
Compote, open, hs, square, deep bowl, 6" d	42.00	—

MINNESOTA (cont.)

Items	Clear	Ruby Stained
Compote, open, hs, square, deep bowl, 7" d	48.00	—
Compote, open, hs, square, deep bowl, 8" d	55.00	—
Compote, open, hs, square, shallow bowl, folded sides, 8" d	55.00	—
Compote, open, hs, square, shallow bowl, folded sides, 9" d	60.00	—
Compote, open, hs, square, shallow bowl, folded sides, 10" d	65.00	—
Compote, open, ls, square, 6" w	30.00	—
Compote, open, ls, square, 7" w	36.00	—
Compote, open, ls, square, 8" w	42.00	—
Compote, open, ls, square, 9" w	65.00	—
Compote, open, ls, square, 10" d	65.00	—
Condiment set, cruet, salt and pepper shakers, tray	90.00	—
Confection dish, cov, scalloped sides, pointed ends, 5" l	24.00	
Cracker jar, cov	100.00	—
Creamer, individual	24.00	
Creamer, table	36.00	—
Cruet, os	42.00	—
Crushed fruit jar, cov	100.00	
Custard cup	110.00	—
Fruit plate, 8" d, serrated rim	24.00	
Goblet	42.00	60.00
Hair receiver	36.00	—
Humidor, jeweled silver plate lid	180.00	
Juice glass	24.00	—

Items	Clear	Ruby Stained
Lemonade mug, ph	18.00	—
Match safe	30.00	—
Mint tray, 6" d	18.00	—
Mug	30.00	—
Olive dish, 5" l or 6" l	18.00	30.00
Orange tray, 10" l	55.00	—
Pickle dish, 7-1/2" l	18.00	
Pitcher, water, ah, bulbous, half gallon	120.00	—
Pitcher, water, ah, bulbous, three-quarter gallon	118.00	—
Pitcher, water, ah, tankard	100.00	240.00
Plate, 5" d, turned up edges	30.00	—
Plate, 7-3/8" d	18.00	—
Pomade jar, cov	42.00	—
Preserve dish, rect, 9" l	24.00	
Relish tray	24.00	—
Salt shaker	30.00	—
Sauce, boat shape, flared, square, or straight sided	12.00	30.00
Spooner	30.00	—
Spoon tray, 8" l, folded sides	24.00	—
Sugar bowl, cov	42.00	—
Sweetmeat, hs, 7-1/2" d	55.00	—
Syrup	75.00	—
Toothpick holder, three handles	36.00	180.00
Tray, 8" l	18.00	—
Tumbler	24.00	—
Water tray	55.00	—
Wine	48.00	—

MISSOURI

Palm and Scroll, Palm Leaf and Scroll, U.S. Glass Pattern Line No. 15,058

Manufactured by the United States Glass Company, Pittsburgh, PA, c1898, as one of the States series patterns. Made in non-flint, clear, and emerald green. Also made in amethyst, blue, and canary.

Items	Clear	Emerald Green
Bowl, cov, 6" d	42.00	—
Bowl, cov, 7" d	55.00	—
Bowl, cov, 8" d	60.00	—
Bowl, open, 6" d	18.00	36.00
Bowl, open, 7" d	18.00	42.00
Bowl, open, 8" d	36.00	48.00
Butter dish, cov	55.00	75.00
Cake stand, hs, 8" d	48.00	60.00
Cake stand, hs, 9" d	55.00	65.00
Cake stand, hs, 10" d	60.00	72.00
Cake stand, hs, 11" d	65.00	75.00
Celery vase	36.00	—
Compote, cov, hs, 5" d	42.00	—
Compote, cov, hs, 6" d	48.00	—
Compote, cov, hs, 7" d	55.00	—
Compote, cov, hs, 8" d	60.00	—
Compote, open, hs, deep bowl, 5" d	30.00	—
Compote, open, hs, deep bowl, 6" d	36.00	—
Compote, open, hs, deep bowl, 7" d	48.00	—
Compote, open, hs, deep bowl, 8" d	55.00	—
Compote, open, hs, saucer bowl, 8" d	55.00	—
Compote, open, hs, saucer bowl, 9" d	60.00	—

Items	Clear	Emerald Green
Compote, open, hs, saucer bowl, 10" d	72.00	—
Cordial	42.00	72.00
Creamer	30.00	48.00
Cruet, os	65.00	136.00
Dish, cov, 6" d	75.00	75.00
Doughnut stand, hs, 6" d	48.00	65.00
Goblet	60.00	72.00
Jelly compote, cov, hs, 5" d, notched or plain lid	42.00	65.00
Mug	42.00	55.00
Olive dish	18.00	30.00
Pickle dish, rect	18.00	30.00
Pitcher, milk	48.00	100.00
Pitcher, water	90.00	100.00
Relish dish	12.00	12.50
Salt shaker, single	42.00	55.00
Sauce, flat, 4" d	12.00	20.00
Spooner	30.00	410.00
Sugar bowl, cov	60.00	75.00
Syrup	100.00	190.00
Tumbler	36.00	48.00
Wine	48.00	55.00

NEW HAMPSHIRE

Bent Buckle, Maiden's Blush, Modiste, Red Loop and Fine Cut, U.S. Glass Pattern No. 15,084

Manufactured by United States Glass Company, Pittsburgh, PA, c1903, as one of the States series patterns. Made in non-flint, clear, clear with gilt trim, rose stained, and ruby stained.

Items	Clear w/Gilt Trim	Rose Stained	Ruby Stained
Biscuit jar, cov	90.00	—	—
Bowl, flared, 5-1/2" d	12.00	—	30.00
Bowl, flared, 6-1/2" d	18.00	42.00	—
Bowl, flared, 7-1/2" d	24.00	48.00	—
Bowl, flared, 8-1/2" d	18.00	30.00	—
Bowl, straight-sides, 6-1/2" d	18.00	42.00	—
Bowl, straight-sides, 7-1/2" d	24.00	48.00	—
Bowl, straight sides, 9-1/2" d	30.00	55.00	—
Bowl, square, 6-1/2" w	18.00	42.00	—
Bowl, square, 7-1/2" w	24.00	36.00	—
Bowl, square, 8-1/2" w	30.00	55.00	—
Butter dish, cov	55.00	85.00	—
Cake stand, hs, 8-1/4" d	36.00	—	—
Carafe	72.00	—	—
Celery vase	42.00	60.00	—
Compote, cov, hs, 5" d	60.00	—	—
Compote, cov, hs, 6" d	72.00	—	—
Compote, cov, hs, 7" d	75.00	—	—
Compote, cov, hs, 8" d	90.00	—	—
Compote, open, flared rim, 7" d	42.00	60.00	—
Compote, open, flared rim, 8" d	48.00	65.00	—
Compote, open, flared rim, 9" d	55.00	72.00	—
Creamer, breakfast	24.00	36.00	—
Creamer, individual	24.00	36.00	—
Creamer, table	36.00	55.00	—
Cruet, os	65.00	142.00	—
Custard cup	12.00	18.00	—
Goblet	30.00	55.00	—
Jug, ph, three pints	100.00	—	—
Lemonade mug	18.00	24.00	—
Mug, large	24.00	55.00	60.00
Olive dish, diamond shape, 6-3/4" l	24.00	42.00	—
Olive dish, oblong	24.00	42.00	—
Pickle dish, flat, oval, 7-1/2" l	18.00	36.00	—
Pitcher, water, bulbous, ah	110.00	—	—
Pitcher, water, tankard, molded handle	72.00	110.00	—
Plate, 8" d	30.00	42.00	—
Relish	110.00	—	—
Salt and pepper shakers, pr, hotel size	42.00	48.00	—
Salt and pepper shakers, pr, small	42.00	48.00	—
Salt and pepper shakers, pr, table	42.00	48.00	—
Sauce, round or square, 4"	12.00	—	—
Sugar bowl, cov, breakfast	36.00	48.00	—
Sugar bowl, cov, table	55.00	72.00	—
Sugar bowl, open, individual, two handles	24.00	30.00	—
Syrup, orig top	90.00	—	60.00
Toothpick holder	30.00	48.00	48.00
Tumbler	24.00	42.00	48.00
Vase, 6" h	42.00	60.00	—
Vase, 8" h	42.00	60.00	—
Vase, 9" h	42.00	60.00	—
Wine, flared bowl	36.00	60.00	—
Wine, straight-sided bowl	36.00	60.00	—

NEW JERSEY
Loops and Drops

Manufactured by United States Glass Company, Pittsburgh, PA, c1900-08, as one of the States series patterns. Made in non-flint, clear, clear with gilt trim, and ruby stained. Items with perfect gilt trim (gold) are worth more than those with worn gold. An emerald green 11" vase is known (value $90).

Items	Clear w/Gilt Trim	Ruby Stained
Bowl, deep or flared bowl, 6" d	24.00	48.00
Bowl, deep or flared bowl, 7" d	30.00	60.00
Bowl, deep or flared bowl, 8" d	30.00	60.00
Bowl, oval, plain or pointed ends, 8" d	30.00	60.00
Bowl, oval, plain or pointed ends, 9" d	36.00	72.00
Bowl, oval, plain or pointed ends, 10" l	36.00	90.00
Bowl, saucer, 9" d	32.50	75.00
Bread plate	36.00	
Butter dish, cov, flat	90.00	120.00
Butter dish, cov, footed	130.00	—
Cake stand, hs, 8" d	75.00	—
Carafe	72.00	—
Celery tray, rect	30.00	48.00
Compote, cov, hs, 6" d	55.00	85.00
Compote, cov, hs, 7" d	65.00	95.00
Compote, cov, hs, 8" d	75.00	110.00
Compote, open, hs, 6" d	36.00	72.00
Compote, open, hs, 7" d	42.00	75.00
Compote, open, hs, 8" d	72.00	90.00
Compote, open, hs, shallow bowl, 10-1/2" d	75.00	—
Creamer	42.00	72.00
Cruet, os	60.00	—
Dish, oval, scalloped rim, 6" l	18.00	—
Dish, oval, scalloped rim, 8" l	24.00	—
Dish, oval, scalloped rim, 10" l	30.00	60.00

Items	Clear w/Gilt Trim	Ruby Stained
Fruit bowl, hs, 12-1/2" d	65.00	135.00
Fruit plate, 9-1/2" d	24.00	—
Fruit plate, 10-1/2" d	30.00	—
Fruit plate, 12" d	36.00	—
Goblet	48.00	75.00
Jelly compote, cov, hs, 5" d	55.00	65.00
Molasses can	110.00	—
Olive dish, pointed ends	18.00	—
Pickle dish, rect	18.00	—
Pitcher, milk, ah	90.00	175.00
Pitcher, water, ah, bulbous	95.00	212.00
Pitcher, water, ph, straight sides	60.00	200.00
Plate, 8" d	36.00	55.00
Salt and pepper shakers, pr, hotel	60.00	118.00
Salt and pepper shakers, pr, small	42.00	65.00
Sauce, flat, 4" d	12.00	36.00
Spooner	35.00	90.00
Sugar bowl, cov	72.00	95.00
Sweetmeat, cov, 8" d	75.00	110.00
Syrup, orig top	110.00	—
Toothpick holder	65.00	230.00
Tumbler	36.00	60.00
Water bottle	55.00	110.00
Wine, flared bowl	48.00	72.00
Wine, straight bowl	48.00	72.00

NEW MEXICO
Aztec

Manufactured by McKee & Brothers, Jeannette, PA, c1894 to 1915. It is considered to be a late imitation cut-glass pattern. Pieces are often found marked "PRES-CUT" in a circle on the base. This extensive pattern contains about 75 different forms. Made in clear and some milk white pieces.

Reproductions: Tiffin Glass Company, Tiffin, OH, produced a punch bowl set, c1955. This non-flint version does have the Pres-Cut trademark. The punch cups have a less-flared shape. The Jeannette Glass Company, Jeannette, PA, issued two punch bowl sets, c1966. This punch bowl set also is reputed to be from the original molds. L E. Smith, Mt. Pleasant, PA, reproduced the punch bowl from an original mold, but removed the Pres-Cut trademark, c1981. The Fenton Art Glass Company, Williamstown, WV, reproduced the toothpick from the original McKee mold in 1987. It was created as a limited edition for the Fenton Art Glass Collectors of America for its annual convention. The Fenton logo has replaced the McKee trademark. Also, John E. Kemple Glass Works, East Palestine, OH, and Kenova, WV, and the Summit Art Glass Co., Mogadore, OH, have reproduced items, renaming their pattern "Whirling Star."

Items	Clear
Berry bowl	15.00
Bonbon, ftd, 7" d	15.00
Bowl, deep, flared, scalloped, 9" d	20.00
Bowl, deep, flared, scalloped, 10-1/2" d	20.00
Bowl, deep, scalloped, 7" d	15.00
Bowl, deep, scalloped, 8" d	15.00
Bowl, deep, triangular, scalloped, 7" d	20.00

Items	Clear
Bowl, deep, triangular, scalloped, 8" d	20.00
Bowl, shallow, scalloped, 7" d	15.00
Bowl, shallow, scalloped, 8" d	15.00
Bowl, shallow, scalloped, 10-1/2" d	15.00
Butter dish, cov, round or sq scalloped base φ	40.00
Cake plate, tri-lobed	20.00
Cake stand	30.00

Items	Clear
Candlestick	30.00
Carafe, water	40.00
Celery tray, 11" l	15.00
Celery vase, 5-1/4" h	18.00
Champagne	25.00
Cologne bottle, globular	25.00
Cologne bottle, tall	30.00
Compote, open, hs	30.00
Condensed milk jar, notched lid	20.00

NEW MEXICO (cont.)

Items	Clear	Items	Clear	Items	Clear
Cordial, 3/4 or 1 ounce	20.00	Lemon bowl, two parts, pedestal		Sauce, heart shape, scalloped	15.00
Cracker jar, cov	50.00	base, two quart, 10-1/2" d	25.00	Sauce, triangular, deep, 4-1/2" d	10.00
Creamer, individual	15.00	Marmalade jar, cov, ftd	20.00	Sherbet, ftd	25.00
Creamer, regular φ	25.00	Olive tray	15.00	Soda fountain accessory,	
Creamer, tankard	30.00	Pickle jar	20.00	crushed fruit jar	55.00
Cruet, os	35.00	Pickle tray	15.00	Soda fountain accessory,	
Crushed fruit bowl, cov, 8-1/2" d	75.00	Pitcher, water, ah, half gallon	35.00	straw holder, glass lid	65.00
Custard cup	8.00	Pitcher, water, ph, tankard,		Spooner	15.00
Decanter, cut stopper	32.50	half gallon	35.00	Sugar bowl, cov, scalloped	
Dish, flat, handle, round, 5" d	15.00	Plate	20.00	or smooth rim	25.00
Dish, flat, handle, sq, 5" d	15.00	Punch bowl φ	75.00	Sugar bowl, open, scalloped rim,	
Dish, flat, handle, triangular, 5" d	15.00	Punch cup φ	5.00	handle	25.00
Egg nog bowl, two parts,		Punch set, bowl, stand, 12 cups	125.00	Syrup, orig nickel or silver	
flat base, two quarts, 10-1/2" d	25.00	Relish tray	15.00	plated top	50.00
Finger bowl, underplate	20.00	Rose bowl, 4-1/2" d	15.00	Toothpick holder φ	24.00
Goblet	25.00	Rose bowl, 7" d	20.00	Tumbler, water	20.00
Iced tea tumbler	22.00	Rose jar	25.00	Vase, 10" h, scalloped rim	20.00
Jug, ah, squatty, half gallon	35.00	Salt and pepper shakers, pr,		Whiskey	12.00
Jug, ah, tall, half gallon	35.00	bulbous or tall	35.00	Whiskey jug, os, handle	25.00
Lamp, 18-1/4" h	75.00	Sauce, flat, round, scalloped, 4" d	10.00	Wine, two or three ounce	15.00
Lemonade pitcher, half gallon	35.00	Sauce, flat, round, scalloped,			
		4-1/2" d	10.00		

OREGON #1

Beaded Loop, U.S. Glass Pattern Line No. 15,073

Manufactured by United States Glass Company, Pittsburgh, PA. It was reissued after the 1891 merger as one of the States series patterns. Made in clear.

Reproductions: Reproductions have been made by Imperial Glass in clear and colors.

Items	Clear	Items	Clear	Items	Clear
Berry bowl, cov, 9" d	30.00	Celery vase	36.00	Pickle dish, boat shape	18.00
Berry set, master, six sauces	75.00	Compote, cov, hs, 6" d	60.00	Pitcher, milk	48.00
Bowl, 3-1/2" d	12.00	Compote, cov, hs, 7" d	72.00	Pitcher, water	72.00
Bowl, 4" d	12.00	Compote, cov, hs, 8" d	66.00	Relish	18.00
Bowl, 6" d	15.00	Compote, open, hs, 5" d	30.00	Salt and pepper shakers, pr	48.00
Bowl, 7" d	18.00	Compote, open, hs, 6" d	36.00	Salt, master	24.00
Bowl, 8" d	18.00	Compote, open, hs, 7" d	42.00	Sauce, flat, 3-1/2" to 4" d	6.00
Bread plate	42.00	Compote, open, hs, 8" d	48.00	Sauce, footed	12.00
Butter dish, cov, English	66.00	Creamer, flat	36.00	Spooner, flat	30.00
Butter dish, cov, flanged	60.00	Creamer, footed	42.00	Spooner, footed	210.00
Butter dish, cov, flat	48.00	Cruet	60.00	Sugar bowl, cov, flat φ	30.00
Cake stand, 8" d	48.00	Goblet φ	42.00	Sugar bowl, cov, footed	36.00
Cake stand, 9" d	55.00	Honey dish	12.00	Syrup, orig top	55.00
Cake stand, 10" d	60.00	Jelly compote, cov, hs, 5" d	55.00	Toothpick holder	55.00
Carafe, water	42.00	Mug	42.00	Tumbler	30.00
				Wine	60.00

PENNSYLVANIA

Balder, Hand, and Kamoni, U.S. Glass Pattern Line No. 15,048

Manufactured by United States Glass Company, Pittsburgh, PA, in 1898, at Factory "O" and Factory "GP." Made in non-flint, clear, and emerald green. Also known in ruby stained. A ruffled jelly compote documented in orange carnival.

Reproductions: Reproduction spooners were made in the mid-1980s.

PENNSYLVANIA (cont.)

Items	Clear w/Gold	Emerald Green	Items	Clear w/Gold	Emerald Green
Biscuit jar, cov	90.00	130.00	Jelly compote, open, hs, ruffled	60.00	—
Bowl, eight-pointed, 6" d or 7" d	18.00	—	Juice tumbler	30.00	60.00
Bowl, eight-pointed, 8" d	35.00	—	Molasses can	90.00	—
Bowl, scalloped, shallow, 5" d	18.00	36.00	Olive dish, scalloped rim	18.00	—
Bowl, scalloped, shallow, 7" d or 8" d	35.00	48.00	Pickle dish, scalloped rim	35.00	—
Bowl, square, 6" or 7" w	18.00	36.00	Pickle jar, cov	55.00	—
Bowl, square, 8" w	35.00	48.00	Pitcher, water, bulbous	72.00	—
Butter dish, cov, hotel size	72.00	100.00	Pitcher, water, tankard	75.00	
Butter dish, cov, table size	60.00	90.00	Plate, 8" d	42.00	
Carafe	55.00	—	Punch bowl	190.00	—
Celery tray	36.00	—	Punch cup	12.00	—
Celery vase	55.00	—	Salt, individual	35.00	—
Champagne	30.00	60.00	Salt, master	36.00	—
Cheese dish, cov	75.00	—	Salt shaker, bulbous, three sizes	18.00	
Child's butter dish, cov	65.00	—	Salt shaker, straight-sided	12.00	
Child's creamer	75.00	—	Sauce, flat, eight-pointed, scalloped,		
Child's spooner	60.00	—	square, or straight-sided bowl, 4" d	12.00	—
Child's sugar bowl	75.00	—	Spooner ϕ	30.00	42.00
Claret	42.00	—	Sugar bowl, cov	48.00	65.00
Claret jug, os, handle	100.00	—	Syrup, orig top, tapered	60.00	—
Creamer, individual	30.00	60.00	Toothpick holder	42.00	110.00
Creamer, table	42.00	72.00	Tumbler	210.00	48.00
Cruet, os	55.00	—	Whiskey	35.00	42.00
Decanter, os, handle	120.00	—	Wine	18.00	48.00
Goblet	30.00	—			
Ice tub	55.00	—			

TENNESSEE

Jewel and Crescent, Jeweled Rosette

Manufactured by King, Son & Company, Pittsburgh, PA, and continued by United States Glass Company, Pittsburgh, PA, in 1899, as a part of the States series. Made in non-flint, clear, and clear with colored jewels.

Items	Clear	Colored Jewels	Items	Clear	Colored Jewels
Berry bowl, master	24.00	36.00	Compote, open, hs, 8" d	48.00	—
Bowl, cov, 6" d	45.00	—	Compote, open, hs, 9" d	60.00	—
Bowl, cov, 7" d	48.00	—	Compote, open, hs, 10" d	75.00	—
Bowl, cov, 8" d	60.00	—	Compote, open, ls, 7" d	45.00	—
Bowl, open, 8" d	45.00	48.00	Creamer	36.00	—
Bread plate	48.00	90.00	Cruet, os	75.00	—
Butter dish, cov	65.00	—	Goblet	48.00	—
Cake stand, hs, 8" d	45.00	—	Mug	48.00	—
Cake stand, hs, 9-1/2" d	42.00	—	Pitcher, milk	65.00	—
Cake stand, hs, 10-1/2" d	55.00	—	Pitcher, water	75.00	—
Celery vase	45.00	—	Relish	24.00	—
Compote, cov, hs, 5" d	48.00	65.00	Salt shaker	36.00	—
Compote, cov, hs, 6" d	55.00	—	Sauce, flat	18.00	24.00
Compote, cov, hs, 7" d	60.00	—	Spooner	45.00	—
Compote, cov, hs, 8" d	72.00	—	Sugar bowl, cov	55.00	—
Compote, open, hs, 5" d	30.00	—	Syrup, orig top	110.00	—
Compote, open, hs, 6" d	36.00	—	Toothpick	90.00	100.00
Compote, open, hs, 7" d	45.00	—	Tumbler	45.00	—
			Wine	75.00	100.00

TEXAS

Loop with Stippled Panels, U.S. Glass Pattern Line No. 15,067

Manufactured by United States Glass Company, Pittsburgh, PA, c1900, as one of the States series patterns. Made in non-flint, clear, clear with gold, and rose stained. Occasionally pieces are found in ruby stained.

Reproductions: Reproduced in solid colors by Crystal Art Glass Company, Cambridge, OH, and Boyd Glass Company, Cambridge, OH.

Items	Clear w/Gold	Rose Stained	Items	Clear w/Gold	Rose Stained
Bowl, cov, 6" d	90.00	120.00	Cruet, os	72.00	175.00
Bowl, cov, 7" d	100.00	124.00	Goblet	115.00	112.00
Bowl, cov, 8" d	115.00	148.00	Horseradish, cov	60.00	—
Bowl, open, flared, scalloped, 7-1/2" d or 8-1/2" d	36.00	55.00	Jelly compote, 5" d	55.00	110.00
			Olive dish, scalloped rim	24.00	55.00
Bowl, open, flared, scalloped, 9-1/2" d	45.00	60.00	Pickle, 8-1/2" l	30.00	60.00
			Pitcher, water, ah, bulbous	260.00	600.00
Bowl, open, flared, smooth rim, 7-1/2" d, 8-1/2" d, or 9-1/2" d	45.00	60.00	Pitcher, water, ph, tankard	130.00	480.00
Bowl, open, straight-sided, 6" d	18.00	45.00	Plate, 9" d	45.00	72.00
Bowl, open, straight-sided, 7" d	24.00	48.00	Relish tray	30.00	55.00
Bowl, open, straight-sided, 8" d	30.00	55.00	Salt, master, ftd	60.00	100.00
Bread tray	45.00	100.00	Salt Shaker, tall or squatty	90.00	160.00
Butter dish, cov	90.00	130.00	Sauce, flat, round, flared rim, 4-1/2" d	18.00	30.00
Cake stand, hs, 9" d	75.00	130.00	Sauce, flat, straight-sides, scalloped or smooth rim, 4" d	12.00	24.00
Cake stand, hs, 9-1/2" d	75.00	130.00			
Cake stand, hs, 10" d	90.00	145.00	Sauce, footed, round, smooth rim, 4" d	24.00	30.00
Cake stand, hs, 10-1/2" d	90.00	145.00			
Cake stand, hs, 11" d	100.00	155.00	Sauce, footed, round, straight-sides, flared rim, 5" d	24.00	30.00
Celery tray	36.00	60.00	Spooner	45.00	95.00
Celery vase	48.00	100.00	Sugar bowl, cov, individual φ	55.00	—
Compote, cov, hs, 6" d	72.00	130.00	Sugar bowl, table, cov	90.00	130.00
Compote, cov, hs, 7" d	85.00	160.00	Syrup, orig top	90.00	190.00
Compote, cov, hs, 8" d	90.00	190.00	Toothpick holder	30.00	115.00
Compote, open, hs, 5" d	55.00	90.00	Tumbler	48.00	120.00
Compote, open, hs, 7-1/2" d	55.00	100.00	Vase, 6-1/2" h	30.00	—
Compote, open, hs, 8-1/2" d	65.00	115.00	Vase, 8" h	36.00	—
Compote, open, hs, 9-1/2" d	75.00	120.00	Vase, 9" h	45.00	—
Creamer, individual φ	24.00	55.00	Vase, 10" h	48.00	—
Creamer, table	55.00	100.00	Water bottle	100.00	160.00
			Wine φ	90.00	148.00

THE STATES

Cane and Star Medallion, U.S. Glass Pattern Line No. 15,093

Manufactured by United States Glass Company Pittsburgh, PA, in 1905. Made in non-flint, clear, and clear with gold trim. Many forms also found in emerald green (add 50 percent).

Items	Clear w/Gold Trim	Items	Clear w/Gold Trim	Items	Clear w/Gold Trim
Bowl, 7" d, three handles	30.00	Creamer, ph, regular, round	36.00	Sauce, flat, tub shape, 4" d	18.00
Bowl, 9-1/4" d	36.00	Goblet	45.00	Spooner	30.00
Butter dish, cov	75.00	Jelly dish, flat	18.00	Sugar bowl, cov, regular	48.00
Celery tray	24.00	Pickle tray	18.00	Sugar bowl, open, individual	18.00
Celery vase	24.00	Pitcher, water, ph, half gallon	55.00	Syrup, orig top	75.00
Cocktail	30.00	Plate, 10" d	30.00	Toothpick holder, flat, rectangular, curled lip	55.00
Compote, open, hs, 7" d	36.00	Punch bowl, 13"d	90.00		
Compote, open, hs, 9" d	48.00	Punch cup	10.00	Tray, 7-1/4" l, 5-1/2" w	20.00
Creamer, ph, individual, oval	24.00	Relish, diamond shape	45.00	Tumbler	24.00
		Salt and pepper shakers, pr	48.00	Wine	36.00

UTAH
Frost Flower, Twinkle Star

Manufactured by United States Glass Company, Pittsburgh, PA, and Gas City, IN, in 1901 as one of the States series patterns. Made in non-flint, clear, and clear with frosting. Add 25 percent for frosting.

Items	Clear	Items	Clear	Items	Clear
Bowl, cov, 6" d	30.00	Castor set, two bottles	55.00	Creamer	42.00
Bowl, cov, 7" d	30.00	Celery vase	30.00	Cruet, os	55.00
Bowl, cov, 8" d	30.00	Compote, cov, hs, 5" d	55.00	Goblet	35.00
Bowl, open, 6" d	25.00	Compote, cov, hs, 6" d	65.00	Pickle tray	20.00
Bowl, open, 7" d	25.00	Compote, cov, hs, 7" d	75.00	Pitcher, water, three pints	65.00
Bowl, open, 8" d	20.00	Compote, open, hs, 6" d	30.00	Pitcher, water, half gallon	65.00
Butter dish, cov, large	45.00	Compote, open, hs, 7" d	35.00	Salt shaker, orig top	30.00
Butter dish, cov, small	42.00	Compote, open, hs, 7-1/2" d	35.00	Sauce, flat, 4" d	10.00
Cake plate, 9" d	30.00	Compote, open, hs, 8" d	42.00	Spooner	25.00
Cake stand, hs, 7" d	45.00	Compote, open, hs, 9" d	45.00	Sugar bowl, cov	45.00
Cake stand, hs, 8" d	30.00	Compote, open, hs, 10" d	55.00	Syrup, orig top	75.00
Cake stand, hs, 10" d	42.00	Condiment set,		Tumbler	25.00
		salt and pepper shakers, holder	65.00	Wine	35.00

VERMONT
Honeycomb with Flower Rim, Inverted Thumbprint with Daisy Band, US Glass Pattern Line No. 15,060

Manufactured by United States Glass Company, Pittsburgh, PA, 1899-1903, as part of its States series. Made in non-flint, clear, and green. Both clear and green are found with gold trim. Rare examples are found in blue, clear with amber stain, clear with ruby stain, and clear with green stain. Very rare in custard (usually decorated), milk glass, and blue.

Reproductions: Toothpick holders have been reproduced by Cambridge, OH, companies Crystal Art Glass, Mosser Glass, and Degenhart Glass, which marks its colored line.

Items	Clear w/Gold	Green w/Gold	Items	Clear w/Gold	Green w/Gold
Basket, handle	42.00	65.00	Finger bowl	35.00	65.00
Berry bowl	35.00	65.00	Goblet	55.00	75.00
Butter dish, cov	55.00	110.00	Pickle tray	30.00	42.00
Card tray, large	30.00	45.00	Pitcher, water	75.00	135.00
Card tray, medium	30.00	42.00	Salt shaker	30.00	45.00
Card tray, small	25.00	35.00	Sauce, footed	25.00	30.00
Celery tray	42.00	45.00	Spooner	35.00	110.00
Compote, cov, hs	80.00	135.00	Sugar bowl, cov	45.00	115.00
Compote, open, hs	45.00	90.00	Toothpick holder φ	42.00	75.00
Creamer, ph, 4-1/4" h	42.00	80.00	Tumbler, footed	30.00	55.00
			Vase	30.00	65.00

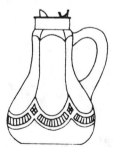

VIRGINIA
Galloway Mirror Plate, U.S. Mirror, Woodrow

Manufactured by United States Glass Company, Pittsburgh, PA, c1904 to 1918. Jefferson Glass Company, Toronto, Canada, produced it from 1900 to 1925. Made in non-flint, clear with or without gold trim, rose stain, and ruby stain.

Reproductions: United States Glass Company, Tiffin, OH, reissued the punch bowl set in 1955. The toothpick holder has also been reproduced and can be found in amber, amethyst, blue, green, and orange.

VIRGINIA (cont.)

Items	Clear w/Gold	Rose Stained	Items	Clear w/Gold	Rose Stained
Basket, ah	75.00	130.00	Dish, oval, plain rim, 9-1/2" l	36.00	55.00
Bowl, belled, 5-1/2" d or 6-1/2" d	24.00	42.00	Dish, oval, plain rim, 10" l	42.00	72.00
Bowl, belled, 7-1/2" d	30.00	48.00	Egg cup	48.00	72.00
Bowl, belled, 8-1/2" d	36.00	55.00	Finger bowl	48.00	65.00
Bowl, belled, 10" d	42.00	60.00	Goblet	75.00	115.00
Bowl, oval, 8" l or 8-1/2" l	42.00	55.00	Lemonade, handle	42.00	55.00
Bowl, rect, 6" l	30.00	48.00	Mug	48.00	60.00
Bowl, rect, 9" l	36.00	55.00	Nappy, tricorn	30.00	60.00
Bowl, round, 5-1/2" d or 6-1/2" d	24.00	36.00	Olive, 6" l	24.00	36.00
Bowl, round, 7-1/2" d	30.00	42.00	Pickle castor, silver plate holder and lid	65.00	240.00
Bowl, round, 8-1/2" d	36.00	55.00	Pickle dish, crimped rim,		
Bowl, round, 9-1/2" d	42.00	60.00	8-1/2" l, 2-1/2" h	30.00	65.00
Bowl, round, 11" d	55.00	65.00	Pickle jar, open	42.00	55.00
Butter dish, cov, hotel size	65.00	130.00	Pitcher, ice jug, ah, two quarts	75.00	130.00
Butter dish, cov, quarter pound	60.00	120.00	Pitcher, milk, one quart	72.00	95.00
Butter dish, cov, table size	65.00	130.00	Pitcher, tankard, large	75.00	130.00
Cake stand, hs, 8-1/2" d	65.00	110.00	Pitcher, tankard, medium	85.00	124.00
Cake stand, hs, 9" d	85.00	115.00	Pitcher, tankard, small	65.00	118.00
Cake stand, hs, 10" d	75.00	120.00	Pitcher, water, ice lip	65.00	190.00
Carafe, water	55.00	85.00	Plate, 4" d	36.00	48.00
Celery vase	42.00	75.00	Plate, 5" d or 6" d	42.00	55.00
Champagne	72.00	190.00	Plate, 8" d	48.00	65.00
Child's pitcher, water, 4-1/4" h	36.00	55.00	Punch bowl, ftd φ	172.00	270.00
Child's tumbler	12.00	24.00	Punch bowl plate, 20" d φ	95.00	130.00
Compote, cov, hs, 6" d	110.00	130.00	Punch cup φ	12.00	18.00
Compote, cov, hs, 7" d	115.00	135.00	Relish tray	24.00	36.00
Compote, cov, hs, 8" d	120.00	142.00	Rose bowl	30.00	72.00
Compote, open, hs, deep bowl, 5-1/2" d	30.00	60.00	Salt, individual, flat, oblong	30.00	48.00
Compote, open, hs, deep bowl, 6-1/2" d	36.00	55.00	Salt, master, oblong or round, flat	42.00	72.00
Compote, open, hs, deep bowl, 7-1/2" d	42.00	72.00	Salt and pepper shakers, pr, squatty or tall	48.00	75.00
Compote, open, hs, deep bowl, 8" d	48.00	65.00	Sauce, flat, flared,		
Compote, open, hs, deep bowl, 8-1/2" d	55.00	60.00	or straight-sided, 4" d or 4-1/2" d	12.00	24.00
Compote, open, hs, deep bowl, 9" d	60.00	65.00	Sherbet, ftd, 4-1/2" d	30.00	36.00
Compote, open, hs, deep bowl, 10" d	55.00	85.00	Spooner, hotel size	36.00	95.00
Compote, open, hs,			Spooner, table size	42.00	85.00
deep bowl, 10-1/2" d	72.00	75.00	Sugar bowl, cov, hotel size	55.00	75.00
Compote, open, hs, scalloped, 10" d	55.00	75.00	Sugar bowl, cov, table size	72.00	95.00
Cracker jar, cov,			Sugar bowl, open, individual, oval, flat	60.00	85.00
orig Brittannia or patterned glass lid	180.00	270.00	Sugar shaker	48.00	120.00
Creamer, hotel size	36.00	60.00	Syrup, orig top, two sizes	65.00	142.00
Creamer, individual size	24.00	48.00	Toothpick holder φ	36.00	55.00
Creamer, table size, tankard	42.00	55.00	Tumbler, hotel size	42.00	55.00
Cruet, os	55.00	130.00	Tumbler, water	36.00	48.00
Dish, oblong, 8" l	30.00	55.00	Vase, cylindrical, pulled rim, 11" h	36.00	60.00
Dish, oblong, 9" l	36.00	60.00	Vase, straight sides, 5-1/2" h	30.00	55.00
Dish, oblong, 10" l	42.00	55.00	Vase, straight sides, 18" h	42.00	55.00
Dish, oblong, 11" l	48.00	72.00	Waste bowl	48.00	65.00
Dish, oval, crimped rim, 6-1/2" l	24.00	42.00	Water bottle	48.00	85.00
Dish, oval, crimped rim, 8-1/2" l	30.00	48.00	Water tray, 8-1/2" d	75.00	135.00
Dish, oval, plain rim, 5-1/4" l	24.00	42.00	Water tray, 10" d	85.00	124.00
Dish, oval, plain rim, 8-1/2" l	30.00	60.00	Wine	55.00	65.00

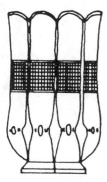

VIRGINIA #1

Banded Portland, Maiden's Blush

Manufactured originally as Virginia by Portland Glass Company, Portland, ME. It was considered to be one of the States Series. Made in clear and clear with painted decoration in fired-on green, yellow, blue, and possibly pink, ruby stained, and rose stained. Glass researcher Ruth Webb Lee refers to the rose staining as Maiden's Blush. Double flashed refers to color above and below the center band. Single flashed refers to color above or below the band only.

VIRGINIA #1 (cont.)

Items	Clear	Color Flashed	Maiden's Blush
Bonbon, oval, flared, pointed ends, 5-1/2" l	24.00	—	36.00
Bowl, cov, 6" d	48.00	—	55.00
Bowl, cov, 7" d	55.00	—	72.00
Bowl, cov, 8" d	60.00	—	75.00
Bowl, open, shallow, 7-1/2" d	36.00	—	55.00
Bowl, open, shallow, 8-1/2" d	36.00	—	55.00
Bowl, open, shallow, 9-1/2" d	42.00	—	72.00
Bowl, open, straight sides, 6" d	30.00	—	55.00
Bowl, open, straight sides, 7" d	36.00	—	60.00
Bowl, open, straight sides, 8" d	42.00	—	55.00
Butter dish, cov	60.00	165.00	85.00
Cake stand, hs	55.00	—	110.00
Candlesticks, pr	95.00	—	130.00
Carafe	95.00	—	110.00
Celery tray	30.00	—	48.00
Celery vase	42.00	—	55.00
Cologne bottle, large	60.00	66.00	85.00
Cologne bottle, small, 4 oz	48.00	—	75.00
Compote, cov, hs, 7" d	85.00	—	130.00
Compote, cov, hs, 8" d	75.00	—	118.00
Compote, open, hs, scalloped, flared, 6" d	30.00	—	48.00
Compote, open, hs, scalloped, flared, 7" d	36.00	—	55.00
Compote, open, hs, scalloped, flared, 8" d	42.00	—	60.00
Compote, open, hs, straight sided, 6" d	30.00	—	48.00
Compote, open, hs, straight sided, 7" d	36.00	—	55.00
Compote, open, hs, straight sided, 8" d	48.00	—	60.00
Creamer, individual, oval	30.00	42.00	48.00
Creamer, individual, tankard	30.00	—	48.00
Creamer, table, 6 oz	42.00	55.00	60.00
Cruet, os	55.00	55.00	66.00
Decanter, handle	72.00	110.00	130.00
Dresser tray	60.00	—	120.00
Goblet	48.00	55.00	66.00
Jelly compote, cov, 6" d	48.00	66.00	110.00
Lamp, oil, flat	55.00	—	—
Lamp, oil, tall	60.00	—	—
Marmalade, orig notched cover, ftd, 4-1/2" d	48.00	—	55.00
Match holder	48.00	—	55.00
Nappy, sq	18.00	55.00	66.00
Olive	110.00	—	42.00
Pin tray	110.00	—	30.00
Pitcher, water, half gallon, tankard	75.00	115.00	248.00
Pomade jar, cov	42.00	55.00	85.00
Puff box, orig glass cover	48.00	—	55.00
Punch bowl, hs	135.00	—	360.00
Punch cup	24.00	—	36.00
Relish, 6-1/2" l	30.00	36.00	24.00
Relish, 8-1/4" l	24.00	42.00	48.00
Ring holder	75.00	—	130.00
Salt and pepper shakers, pr	55.00	75.00	75.00
Sardine box, cov	55.00	—	110.00
Sauce, oval, round, or square, flat, 4" d or 4-1/2" d	12.00	—	24.00
Spooner	210.00	—	55.00
Sugar bowl, cov, table size	410.00	75.00	75.00
Sugar bowl, open, individual size	30.00	—	48.00
Sugar shaker, orig top	55.00	—	85.00
Sweetmeat compote, cov, hs, 7" d	85.00	—	124.00
Syrup, orig top	60.00	—	142.00
Toothpick holder	48.00	55.00	55.00
Vase, 6" h	24.00	—	310.00
Vase, 9" h	42.00	—	60.00
Wine	42.00	—	75.00

WASHINGTON

Manufactured by United States Glass Company, Pittsburgh, PA, as part of its States series. Made in clear, frosted with colored floral decoration (add 25 percent), and ruby stained (add 40 percent). Rare in custard and milk glass. A very rare covered sugar is known in emerald green, valued at $120.

Items	Clear	Items	Clear	Items	Clear
Bowl, flat, oblong, 6" l	35.00	Compote, cov, ls, 7" d	80.00	Jelly compote, open, hs, 4-1/2" d	45.00
Bowl, flat, oblong, 8" l	45.00	Compote, cov, ls, 8" d	90.00	Lemonade cup	25.00
Bowl, flat, oblong, 10" l	75.00	Compote, open, hs, 5" d	45.00	Oil bottle	75.00
Bowl, round, 3" d	25.00	Compote, open, hs, 6" d	45.00	Olive dish, oval	42.00
Bowl, round, 3-1/2" d	25.00	Compote, open, hs, 7" d	55.00	Pickle dish, oval	42.00
Bowl, round, 4" d	30.00	Compote, open, hs, 8" d	65.00	Pitcher, milk, tankard, quart	90.00
Bowl, round, 4-1/2" d	30.00	Compote, open, ls, 3-1/2" d	25.00	Pitcher, milk, tankard, three pints	110.00
Bowl, round, 5" d	30.00	Compote, open, ls, 5" d	30.00	Pitcher, milk, tankard, half gallon	110.00
Bowl, round, 6" d	35.00	Compote, open, ls 6" d	35.00	Pitcher, water, tankard, quart	90.00
Bowl, round, 7" d	35.00	Compote, open, ls, 7" d	35.00	Pitcher, water, tankard, three pints	450.00
Bowl, round, 8" d	42.00	Compote, open, ls, 8" d	42.00	Pitcher, water, tankard, half gallon	500.00
Butter dish, cov	85.00	Cordial	75.00	Powdered sugar, cov	120.00
Cake stand, hs, 10" d	75.00	Creamer, individual	65.00	Salt, individual	35.00
Celery tray	65.00	Creamer, table	65.00	Salt, master	35.00
Champagne	42.00	Creamer, tankard, pint	65.00	Salt shaker	65.00
Claret	42.00	Custard cup	25.00	Spooner	65.00
Compote, cov, hs, 5" d	80.00	Fruit bowl, hs, 7-1/2" d	55.00	Sugar, cov, table	85.00
Compote. cov, hs, 6" d	80.00	Fruit bowl, hs, 8-1/2"d	65.00	Sugar, open, individual	45.00
Compote, cov, hs, 7" d	85.00	Fruit bowl, hs, 9-1/2" d	75.00	Toothpick holder	45.00
Compote, cov, hs, 8" d	90.00	Goblet, small	45.00	Tumbler	45.00
Compote, cov, ls, 5" d	65.00	Goblet, large	45.00	Wine	45.00
Compote, cov, ls, 6" d	75.00	Jelly compote, cov, hs, 4-1/2" d	80.00		

WISCONSIN

Beaded Dewdrop, U.S. Glass Pattern Line No. 15,079

Manufactured by United States Glass Company, Pittsburgh, PA, at Factory "U," (Gas City, IN) in 1903. One of the States series patterns. Made in non-flint and clear.

Reproductions: The toothpick holder has been reproduced in colors by Crystal Art Glass Company, Cambridge, OH, and also by Degenhart Glass, Cambridge, OH. Degenhart's reproductions are marked with a "D" within a heart mark. After Degenhart's death, the company was purchased by Boyd's Crystal Art Glass Inc., and it continued production, changing to a "B" within a diamond mark. Guernsey Glass Company, also of Cambridge, OH, created toothpick holders in many colors.

Items	Clear	Items	Clear	Items	Clear
Banana stand	110.00	Cake stand, hs, 9-1/2" d	80.00	Condiment set, individual size creamer, cov sugar, salt and pepper shakers, tray	125.00
Bonbon, cov	35.00	Cake stand, hs, 11-1/2" d	85.00		
Bowl, cov, oval, handle, 6" l	55.00	Celery tray	55.00		
Bowl, oval, 7-1/2" l, 4-1/2" w	30.00	Celery vase, pedestal	65.00	Condiment set, salt and pepper shakers, mustard, horseradish, tray	150.00
Bowl, round, 6" d	45.00	Compote, cov, hs, 5" d	65.00		
Bowl, round, 7" d	55.00	Compote, cov, hs, 6" d	75.00	Creamer, individual	45.00
Bowl, round, 8" d	65.00	Compote, cov, hs, 7" d	85.00	Creamer, table	75.00
Butter dish, cov, quarter pound, flange	90.00	Compote, cov, hs, 8" d	110.00	Cruet, os	115.00
		Compote, open, hs, 5" d	42.00	Cup and saucer	75.00
Butter dish, cov, table size, double handles	110.00	Compote, open, hs, 6" d	45.00	Custard cup	15.00
		Compote, open, hs, 7" d	55.00	Dish, cov, oval, handle, 6" l	75.00
Butter dish, cov, table size, flat, flange	110.00	Compote, open, hs, 8" d	75.00	Dish, open, round, 7" d	85.00
		Compote, open, hs, 9" d	85.00	Goblet	90.00
Butter dish, open, table size, double handles	85.00	Compote, open, hs, 10" d	110.00	Marmalade jar, straight sides, glass lid	135.00
Cake stand, hs, 6-1/2" d	55.00	Compote, open, ls, 5" d	42.00		
Cake stand, hs, 8-1/2" d	65.00	Compote, open, ls, 7" d	45.00	Mug	45.00

WISCONSIN (cont.)

Items	Clear	Items	Clear	Items	Clear
Mustard jar, cov, bulbous	65.00	Preserve, oblong, 8" l	60.00	Sugar bowl, open, individual	42.00
Olive, handle, 5-1/2" d	45.00	Punch cup	20.00	Sugar shaker, orig top	125.00
Pickle dish, rect	30.00	Relish	35.00	Sweetmeat, cov, ftd, 5" d	55.00
Pickle jar, cov	125.00	Salt shaker, orig top, bulbous or tapered	42.00	Syrup, orig top	150.00
Pitcher, milk, ph, footed, quart	80.00	Sauce, flat, 4" d	15.00	Toothpick holder, kettle ϕ	80.00
Pitcher, water, ph, footed, half gallon	100.00	Sherbet cup	20.00	Tumbler	55.00
Plate, square, 6-3/4" w	35.00	Spooner	42.00	Vase, 6" h	45.00
		Sugar bowl, cov, table	80.00	Wine	110.00

WYOMING

Bull's Eye, Enigma, U.S. Glass Pattern Line 15,081

Manufactured by United States Glass Company, Pittsburgh, PA, at Factory "U" (Gas City, IN) and Factory "E" (Tarentum, PA), c1903, as one of the States series patterns.

Items	Clear	Items	Clear	Items	Clear
Bowl, flat, scalloped rim, 6" d	25.00	Compote, open, hs, deep bowl, 8" d	55.00	Pickle dish, oval, handles	30.00
Bowl, flat, scalloped rim, 7" d	30.00	Compote, open, hs, saucer bowl, 8" d	85.00	Pitcher, milk, ph, quart	90.00
Bowl, flat, scalloped rim, 8" d	35.00	Compote, open, hs, saucer bowl, 9" d	90.00	Pitcher, water, ph, three pints	110.00
Butter dish, cov	75.00			Preserve dish, oval, 8" l	30.00
Cake plate	80.00	Compote, open, hs, saucer bowl, 11" d	110.00	Relish tray	25.00
Cake stand, 9" d, 10" d, or 11" d	100.00	Creamer, cov, individual, tankard	75.00	Salt and pepper shakers, pr	65.00
Compote, cov, hs, 6" d	85.00	Creamer, open, individual, tankard	45.00	Sauce, flat, 4" d	15.00
Compote, cov, hs, 7" d	110.00	Creamer, open, table	55.00	Spooner, pedestal	42.00
Compote, cov, hs, 8" d	110.00	Goblet	90.00	Sugar bowl, cov	65.00
Compote, open, hs, deep bowl, 6" d	42.00	Mug	65.00	Syrup, glass cov, small	90.00
Compote, open, hs, deep bowl, 7" d	45.00			Tumbler	80.00
				Wine	110.00

PAUL REVERE POTTERY

History: Paul Revere Pottery, Boston, Massachusetts, was an outgrowth of a club known as The Saturday Evening Girls. The S.E.G. was composed of young female immigrants who met on Saturday nights to read and participate in craft projects, such as ceramics.

Regular pottery production began in 1908, and the name "Paul Revere" was adopted because the pottery was located near the Old North Church. In 1915, the firm moved to Brighton, Massachusetts. Known as the "Bowl Shop," the pottery grew steadily. In spite of popular acceptance and technical advancements, the pottery required continual subsidies. It finally closed in January 1942.

Items produced range from plain and decorated vases to tablewares to illustrated tiles. Many decorated wares were incised and glazed either in an Art Nouveau matte finish or an occasional high glaze.

Marks: In addition to an impressed mark, paper "Bowl Shop" labels were used prior to 1915. Pieces also can be found with a date and "P.R.P." or "S.E.G." painted on the base.

References: Susan and Al Bagdade, *Warman's American Pottery and Porcelain*, 2nd ed., Krause Publications, 2000; Paul Evans, *Art Pottery of the United States*, 2nd ed., Feingold & Lewis Publishing, 1987; Ralph and Terry Kovel, *Kovels' American Art Pottery*, Crown Publishers, 1993; David Rago, *American Art Pottery*, Knickerbocker Press, 1977.

Collectors' Club: American Art Pottery Assoc., P.O. Box 1226, Westport, MA 02790.

Bookends, pr, 4" h, 5" w, night scene of owls, 1921, ink marked "S.E.G./11-21," flat chip to one base........ **1,300.00**

Bowl

4-1/4" d, 2-1/4" h, yellow and black band of walking ducks, marked "S.E.G. 6-21, B.L." **520.00**

5-1/4" d, tree bands with black outline scene, blue sky, green trees, marked "S.E.G. 4/15, I.G." **275.00**

8-1/4" d, 2-3/4" h, flaring, dripping blue-gray satin glaze, marked "P. R.P./Lewis/2nd Firing" **275.00**

8-1/2" d, tree bands with black outline scene, blue sky, green trees, marked "S.E.G. 20/3.15, I.G.," hairline **225.00**

Cake set, Tree pattern, black outline scene, blue sky, green trees, 10" d cake plate, six 8-1/2" d serving plates, each marked "J.G., S.E.G.," three dated 7/15, three dated 1/4/15, one dated 3/15, price for seven-pc set **1,840.00**

Cereal set, 8" d bowl, matching 7-1/2" d plate, set of three, dec with "Mildred, Blanche, Our Guest" in cuerda seca on blue ground, sgd "SEG," slight chips and hairlines, price for six-pc set **1,380.00**

Humidor, cov, 6-1/4" h, 5-3/4" d, spherical, blue matte glaze, pink int., minute int. rim nick, sgd in slip "P.R.P. 3/36" **400.00**

Lamp base, 16" h. 9" d, cuerda seca dec, white Queen Anne's lace, green foliage, white, blue, and green ground, hairline to base comes up side, bruise and short hairline to top rim, ink mark "S.E.G." **15,000.00**

Plate

6-1/2" d, incised white mice, celadon and brown band, ink mark "Dorothy Hopkins/Her Plate," 1911 ....**1,300.00**

7-1/2" d, blue and white band, center medallion of blue scene, yellow sky and dock, initials "J.I.T.," marked "S.E.G. F.L. 7/19" and "S.E.G., F.L. 8/15," price for pr **520.00**

8" d, cuerda seca dec, white and blue geese and water lilies, green matte ground, marked "S.E.G./6-17/AM".......**1,380.00**

Ring tray, 4" d, circular, blue-gray and green band of trees, blue-gray ground, marked "S.E.G./J.G." **275.00**

Teapot, 4-1/2" h, 9" d, brown and white wavy band of sailboats, yellow sky, 1918, restored **700.00**

Plate, cuerda seca decoration, white and blue geese and water lilies, green matte ground, marked "S.E.G./6-17/AM," 1917, 8" d, **$1,380.** *Photo courtesy of David Rago Auctions.*

Luncheon set, coffeepot, 7" h teapot, sugar pot, six 10" d luncheon plates, five teacups, five saucers, semi-matte cobalt glaze with sponged-on yellow, 1926, circular stamp mark, artist's initials and 6/26, missing sugar lid, several pieces with hairlines, **$980.** *Photo courtesy of David Rago Auctions.*

Tile, 3-3/4" sq, Washington Street, blue, white, green, and brown, marked ""H.S. S4 9/1/10," edge chips **420.00**

Trivet

4-1/4" d, medallion of house against setting sun, blue-gray ground, 1924, imp P.R.P. mark. **425.00**

5-1/2" d, medallion of goose standing on hill, dark blue ground, 1924, imp P.R.P. mark. **550.00**

5-1/2" d, medallion of poplar trees in landscape, blue-green ground, 1925, imp P.R.P. mark. **600.00**

Vase

4-1/4" h, 3" d, bottle shape, glossy orange and matte brown glaze, ink P.R.P. mark **225.00**

6-1/4" h, 3-1/2" d, ovoid, band of green trees, satin blue-gray ground, small glaze bubble on body, imp circular P.R.P. mark, 1924 . . . . **1,300.00**

7" h, 5-1/4" d, baluster shape, band of orange lotus blossoms, frothy green ground, green base, imp P. R. mark **1,300.00**

10-1/2" h, 5-3/4" h, satin green glaze, ink "S.E.G." mark **250.00**

PEACHBLOW

History: Peachblow, an art glass which derives its name from a fine Chinese glazed porcelain, resembles a peach or crushed strawberries in color. Three American glass manufacturers and two English firms produced peachblow glass in the late 1880s. A fourth American company resumed the process in the 1950s. The glass from each firm has its own identifying characteristics.

Hobbs, Brockunier & Co., Wheeling peachblow: Opalescent glass, plated or cased with a transparent amber glass; shading from yellow at the base to a deep red at top; glossy or satin finish.

Mt. Washington "Peach Blow": A homogeneous glass, shading from a pale gray-blue to a soft rose color; some pieces enhanced with glass appliqués, enameling, and gilding.

New England Glass Works, New England peachblow (advertised as Wild Rose, but called Peach Blow at the plant): Translucent, shading from rose to white; acid or glossy finish; some pieces enameled and gilded.

Thomas Webb & Sons and Stevens and Williams (English firms): Peachblow-style cased art glass, shading from yellow to red; some pieces with cameo-type relief designs.

Gunderson Glass Co.: Produced peachblow-type art glass to order during the 1950s; shades from an opaque faint tint of pink, which is almost white, to a deep rose.

Marks: Pieces made in England are marked "Peach Blow" or "Peach Bloom."

References: Sean and Johanna S. Billings, *Peachblow Glass, Collector's Identification & Price Guide*, Krause Publications, 2000; Kyle Husfloen, *Antique Trader's American & European Decorative and Art Glass Price Guide*, 2nd ed., Krause Publications, 2000; James Measell, *New Martinsville Glass*, Antique Publications, 1994; John A. Shuman III, *Collector's Encyclopedia of American Glass*, Collector Books, 1988, 1994 value update; Kenneth Wilson, *American Glass 1760-1930*, 2 vols., Hudson Hills Press and The Toledo Museum of Art, 1994.

Bowl, iridescent gold interior, 28 molded-in ribs, crimped edge, New Martinsville, 5" d, 2" h, $165. Photo courtesy of Clarence and Betty Maier.

Gundersen

Bottle, 2-1/2" d, 6" h, shaded pink to white **110.00**

Cruet, 8" h, 3-1/2" w, matte finish, ribbed shell handle, matching stopper with good color. **875.00**

Cup and saucer. **275.00**

Decanter, 10" h, 5" w, Pilgrim Canteen form, acid finish, deep raspberry to white, applied peachblow ribbed handle, deep raspberry stopper **950.00**

Goblet, 701/4" h, 4" d top, glossy finish, deep color, applied Burmese glass base **285.00**

Jug, 4-1/2" h, 4" w, bulbous, applied loop handle, acid finish **450.00**

Pitcher, 5-1/2" h, Hobnail, matte finish, white with hint of pink on int., orig label **550.00**

Plate, 8" d, luncheon, deep raspberry to pale pink, matte finish **375.00**

Punch cup, acid finish. **275.00**

Tumbler, 3-3/4" h, matte finish . . **275.00**

Urn, 8-1/2" h, 4-1/2" w, two applied "M" handles, sq cut base, matte finish **550.00**

Vase

4-1/4" h, 3" d, acid finish **225.00**

5" h, 6" w, ruffled top, pinched-in base **525.00**

9" h, 3-1/4" w, Tappan, acid finish **425.00**

Wine glass, 5" h, glossy finish . . **175.00**

Mount Washington

Bowl, 3" x 4", shading from deep rose to bluish-white, MOP satin int. . . **150.00**

Bride's basket, shades of pink, replated Meriden frame. **650.00**

Milk pitcher, 7" w handle to spout, 5-3/4" h, thin walls, gray handle **3,950.00**

Vase, 8-1/4" h, lily form, satin finish **1,850.00**

New England

Celery vase, 7" h, 4" w, sq top, deep raspberry with purple highlights shading to white **785.00**

Cruet, 6-3/4" h, 4" d at base, petticoat form, applied white handle and stopper, three lip top, acid finish. **1,950.00**

Pitcher, 6-3/4" h, 7-1/2" w, 3-1/4" w at top, bulbous, sq top, applied frosted handle, 10 rows of hobs, Sandwich **550.00**

Spooner, sq top, acid finish . . . **825.00**

Tumbler

3-3/4" h, shiny finish, deep color upper third, middle fading to creamy white bottom, thin walls **445.00**

3-3/4" h, velvety satin finish, deep raspberry red extends 2/3 down, faces to 1/2" pure white band **400.00**

Vase

3-1/4" h, 2-1/2" d, bulbous bottom, ring around neck, flaring top, matte finish. **550.00**

5-1/2" h, satin finish, bulbous **485.00**

6-1/2" h, 3" w at top, lily, glossy finish, deep pink shading to white **650.00**

7" h, lily, satin finish, wafer base **945.00**

7-3/4" h, lily, glossy, shading from near white to dark pink rim. **875.00**

10-1/2" h, 5" w at base, bulbous, tapering neck, cup top, deep color, orig glossy finish **1,250.00**

10-1/2" h, 5" w at base, bulbous gourd shape, deep raspberry with fuchsia highlights to white, coloring extends two-thirds way down, four dimpled sides **1,450.00**

Webb

Cologne, 5" h, bulbous, raised gold floral branches, silver hallmarked dome top. **900.00**

Creamer, satin finish, coralene dec, rolled rim, flat base **650.00**

Finger bowl, 4-1/2" d, cased . . **195.00**

Rose bowl, gold Jules Barbe enameled floral decoration on front, gold enamel butterfly on back, eight soft crimps, lined with gold enamel, creamy white lining, polished pontil, 3" h, 3" w, $550. Photo courtesy of Johanna Billings.

Vase, 11-1/4" h, 6-1/2" d, pine needles, boughs, and trailing prunus blossoms, buds, and branches, two butterflies in flight, deep cherry red shading to pink-peach, creamy white lining, gold trim at top and base, dec by Jules Barbe **750.00**

Wheeling

Cruet, 6-3/4" h, Hobbs, Brockunier & Co., teardrop shape, mahogany spout, neck, and shoulder changes to butter yellow, amber applied handle and faceted stopper **1,085.00**

Ewer, 6-3/4" h, 4" w, glossy finish, duck bill top, applied amber loop handle **3,500.00**

Morgan vase, 8" h, shiny finish, mahogany neck and shoulder, butterscotch on one side, other side with darker butterscotch with red overtones **585.00**

Morgan vase with stand, 10" h, Hobbs, Brockunier & Co., satin finish, deep blush at neck and shoulders shades to buttery cream, satin Griffin holder with small flake **1,750.00**

Mustard, SP cov and handle . . . **475.00**

Pear, hollow blown
  4-3/4" w, 3" w base, matte finish, bright red and yellow, white lining, very tip of stem gone **900.00**
  5-1/2" h, 3" w base, glossy finish, tip of stem gone **800.00**

Punch cup, 2-1/2" h, Hobbs, Brockunier **535.00**

Tumbler, shiny finish, deep colored upper third shades to creamy base **385.00**

Vase
  9-1/4" h, ball shaped body, 5" slender neck, shape #11 . . **735.00**
  11-1/2" h, creamy int., enameled dogwood branches **750.00**

PEKING GLASS

History: Peking glass is a type of cameo glass of Chinese origin. Its production began in the 1700s and continued well into the 19th century. The background color of Peking glass may be a delicate shade of yellow, green, or white. One style of white background is so transparent that it often is referred to as the "snowflake" ground. The overlay colors include a rich garnet red, deep blue, and emerald green.

Bowl, green overlay, white ground, carved prunus branches, flowers, and butterfly, late Ching dynasty . . . **375.00**

Cup, 2-1/2" h, deep form, gently flaring rim, ring foot, continual band of overlapping dragons, cloud collar border, lappet border, red overlay, Snowflake **2,185.00**

Dish, 11-3/4" l, flattened round form, bright yellow, 19th C **850.00**

Ginger jar, cov, 9-1/4" h, three different scenes on white grounds, coral-colored ground **750.00**

Snuff bottle, green over white, floral design, attached spoon, carved ivory top **400.00**

Vase, blue and white, honeycomb cut overlay, 9-1/2" h, $395.

Vase
  7" h, high shouldered form, ducks swimming among tall lotus plants, green overlay, white ground, pr **500.00**
  7-1/2" h, ovoid, elongated neck, red overlay, Snowflake pattern, body with two dragons and two phoenix, neck with dragon and phoenix, Qianlong period, pr **4,600.00**
  8-3/4" h, carved green over white lotus design, small rim chip **900.00**
  9-1/4" h, ovoid, opaque raised yellow flowers, translucent yellow ground, 19th C **525.00**

PELOTON

History: Wilhelm Kralik of Bohemia patented Peloton art glass in 1880. Later it was also patented in America and England.

Peloton glass is found with both transparent and opaque grounds, although opaque is more common. Opaque colored glass filaments (strings) are applied by dipping or rolling the hot glass. Generally, the filaments (threads) are pink, blue, yellow, and white (rainbow colors) or a single color. Items also may have a satin finish and enamel decorations.

Biscuit jar, 7" h, 6-1/2" d, powder blue body, white, yellow, blue, and vivid pink filaments, 48 molded-in vertical ribs, silverplated fittings, barn swallow emb on lid **785.00**

Bowl, 6-1/2" d, 6" h, white ground, brown and yellow filaments, all over ribbed surface, three applied crystal thorn feet, eight-point star top . . **325.00**

Finger bowl, colorless, multicolored filaments **75.00**

Pitcher
  5-1/2" h, colorless ground, multicolored threads, applied clear ribbed handle **450.00**
  7-1/2" h, aqua blue ground, multicolored threads, enameled floral dec, polished pontil, applied clear ribbed handle **485.00**

Punch cup, turquoise ground, multicolored filaments, enameled florals, set of six **325.00**

Rose bowl
  4" h, 4" w, ftd, four pulled edges, sq shape, applied crystal edge, six shell feet, glossy finish shaded blue ground, yellow, pink, white, blue, and red filaments **395.00**
  6" h, 5-1/2" w, ftd, eight-point star shaped top, white lining, ribbed and swirled, brown shaded filaments **325.00**

Toothpick holder, 3" h, colorless, white filaments **145.00**
Tumbler, 3-3/4" h, colorless ground, yellow, pink, red, light blue, and white filaments **125.00**

Vase, bulbous, cranberry red filaments, 7" h, **$270.**

Vase

3-1/2" h, 3 x 3-7/8" d, orchid pink cased body, emb ribs, pink, blue, and yellow filaments, pinched together in center **195.00**

4" h, 4-3/4" d, bulbous base, folded over tricorn shape top, white ribbed cased body, pink, yellow, blue, and white applied filaments **290.00**

6" h, 5" w, ribbed, bright pink ground, yellow, blue, white, red, pink, and purple filaments, white lining, two applied ribbed handles **450.00**

PERFUME, COLOGNE, AND SCENT BOTTLES

History: The second half of the 19th century was the golden age for decorative bottles made to hold scents. These bottles were made in a variety of shapes and sizes.

An atomizer is a perfume bottle with a spray mechanism. Cologne bottles usually are larger and have stoppers which also may be used as applicators. A perfume bottle has a stopper that often is elongated and designed to be an applicator.

Scent bottles are small bottles used to hold a scent or smelling salts. A vinaigrette is an ornamental box or bottle that has a perforated top and is used to hold aromatic vinegar or smelling salts. Fashionable women of the late 18th and 19th centuries carried them in purses or slipped them into gloves in case of a sudden fainting spell.

References: Roselyn Gerson, *The Estée Lauder Solid Perfume Compact Collection,* 1967 to 2001, Collector Books, 2001; Jacquelyne Jones-North, *Commercial Perfume Bottles,* 3rd ed., Schiffer Publishing, 1996; —, *Perfume, Cologne and Scent Bottles,* 3rd ed., Schiffer Publishing, 1999; Jacquelyne Y. Jones-North, et. al., *Czechoslovakian Perfume Bottles and Boudoir Accessories,* revised ed., Antique Publications, 1999; L-W Book Sales, *Diamond I Perfume Bottles Price Guide and other Drugstore Wares,* L-W Book Sales, 2000; Monsen and Baer, *A Century of Perfume: The Perfumes of François Coty,* published by authors, 2000; —, *Beauty of Perfume,* published by authors (Box 529, Vienna, VA 22183), 1996; —, *Legacies of Perfume,* published by authors, 1997; —, *Memories of Perfume,* published by authors, 1998.

Periodicals and Internet Resources: *Art & Fragrances Perfume Presentation,* FDR Station, P.O. Box 5200, New York, NY 10150-5200; *Montage,* http://www.cicat.com/montage; *Passion for Perfume,* http://passionforperfume.com.

Collectors' Clubs: International Perfume Bottle Assoc., 3314 Shamrock Road, Tampa, FL 33629, http://www.perfumebottles.org; Miniature Perfume Bottle Collectors, 28227 Paseo El Siena, Laguna Niguel, CA 92677; Parfum Plus Collections, 1590 Louis-Carrier Ste. 502, Montreal Quebec H4N 2Z1 Canada.

Atomizer, colorless and amber panels, SP top, silver cord, 7-1/2" h, **$150.**

Atomizer

Cambridge, 6-1/4" h, stippled gold, opaque jade, orig silk lined box . **140.00**
Cameo, Gallé, 8" h, lavender flowers and foliage, shaded yellow and frosted ground **1,250.00**

Moser, 4-1/2" h, sapphire blue, gold florals, leaves, and swirls, melon ribbed body, orig gold top and bulb. . . **275.00**

Cologne

Art glass, 11" h, transparent green bottle, delicate floral design, colorless pedestal foot, faceted teardrop stopper **175.00**
Baccarat, 5-7/8" h, colorless, panel cut, matching stopper **75.00**
Cut glass, 7" h, cranberry cut to colorless, cane cut, matching stopper **250.00**
Paperweight, 7" h, 5" d, , double overlay, crimson red over white over colorless squatty bottle, five oval facet windows reveal concentric millefiore cane int., matching stopper . . . **460.00**
Vaseline, 4-1/2" h, vaseline, attributed to New England Glass Co., flint, orig stopper **225.00**

Perfume

Enamel, Continental

2-1/8" l, tapered colorless glass bottle encl in rect enamel case with hinged lid, pink ground, green ground roundels with white birds and flowers, crenellated surrounds, late 18th/early 19th C **115.00**

3-1/4" l, pear shape, silvered metal lid with bale, green ground, two central cartouches of courting couples, late 18th/early 19th C **215.00**

Glass

3-3/4" l, Continental, late 19th C, pink and white overlay, cut to clear, waisted ovoid form, gilt-metal repoussé lid enclosing glass stopper **150.00**

3-7/8" l, Continental, early 19th C, latticino, tapered ovoid, clear, white, and yellow strands, ext. of bottle with horizontal ribbing, silver gilt floral engraved hinged lid, enclosing glass stopper . . . **425.00**

4" h, French, late 19th/early 20th C, baluster form, blue opaline bottle, gilt metal floral overlay, foot, and neck mounts, hinged lid set with shell cameo of young man in feathered cap **200.00**

4-1/2" h, New England Glass Co., Cambridge, MA, c1865, colorless six sided body, petal base, orig stopper **150.00**

5-1/4" h, French, late 19th C, double, ruby glass, tapered cylindrical body with floral and garter engraved silver mounts, one end with round hinged lid opening to glass stopper, other end with round lid hinged silver mount at center, opening to vinaigrette grille, ends mounted with link chain. . . . **575.00**

Glass and silver, Victorian, London, 1885, fish-form flask, 6-1/4" l, green and metallic flecked blown glass body, gilt over enamel detailing of scales and eyes, engraved silver tail, retailed by W.Thornill & Co., fitted velvet lined case **1,500.00**

Porcelain

2-1/2" l, Continental, late 19th C, underglaze blue crossed swords mark, leg-form, garter and pale blue shoe, flat metal lid **230.00**

2-1/2" l, Meissen, Germany, late 19th C, courting couple, ivy covered tree trunk, enamel and gilt detailing, orig stopper **635.00**

2-7/8" l, Samson & Co., France, late 19th C, boy with vessel seated on dolphin, enamel detailing, boy's head as stopper **230.00**

3-1/4" l, Continental, late 18th/19th C, swaddled infant shape, enamel detailing, silvertone domed lid, tapered base. **325.00**

3-1/2" l, Brenner & Liebmann, Eduard Liebmann Porcelain Factory, Germany, late 19th C, oblong, Blue Onion style underglaze dec, red overpainted detailing, silver gilt neck and stopper mount **290.00**

Silver gilt, 1-3/4" l, shield shaped, collet-set heart-shaped opal applied to front, surrounded by applied ropetwist, green and yellow enamel dec, back engraved with leafy scrolls, conical screw-in stopper, Hungarian, 20th C **115.00**

Silver plate, Victorian, London, 1885, 2-3/4" l, bud shape, engraved rim, all over repoussé reeding, glass int. **190.00**

Sterling silver

2-1/4" l, Anglo Indian, late 19th/early 20th C, circular, cylindrical lid with emb foliates, body with vignettes of animals, 1 troy oz **115.00**

2-3/4" l, Victorian, London, 1885, bud shape, engraved rim, body with all over repoussé reeding, glass int. **175.00**

3-1/4" l, Birmingham, England, 1897, hinged heart-shaped case, domed lid, emb angel dec, gilt int. with heart-shaped green glass bottle, monogrammed, 2 troy oz . . **230.00**

Sterling silver and champleve enamel, Gorham, everted oblong flask with diapered champleve centered by stars on cobalt blue enamel ground, small silver screw-in lid, late 19th/early 20th C **290.00**

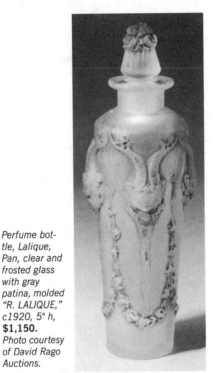

Perfume bottle, Lalique, Pan, clear and frosted glass with gray patina, molded "R. LALIQUE," c1920, 5" h, $1,150. Photo courtesy of David Rago Auctions.

Scent

Agate, 3" h, flattened globe form, silver hinged rim and screw cap, marked "Black, Starr, & Frost" **260.00**

Early American glass

2-1/2" h, amethyst, teardrop shape, emb sunburst design **225.00**

4-1/8" h, blown, colorless, cranberry and white stripes, white and gold metallic twist **95.00**

Ivory, 3-3/4" h, figural, woman holding basket of flowers in one hand, fan in other, polychrome dec, Japan. . . **90.00**

Pattern glass, Rose In Snow, blue, orig stopper **45.00**

Porcelain

3" h, egg shape, Germany or Russia, late 19th C, dec with scene of pedestrians in front of building and monument, gilt border, reserves of gilt foliate scrolls, corn and brass stopper **1,955.00**

3-1/4" h, figural, modeled as male and female, each holding dog, removable heads, Germany, 19th C, pr **435.00**

Satin glass

3-3/4" h, bridal white, Peacock Eye, MOP, orig glass stopper, push-on silverplated lid with monogram "C" **435.00**

4" d, bridal white, 24 white vertical stripes, 12 silk ribbons alternating with 12 muted satin ribbons, sterling silver flip top cap, collar stamped "CS, FS, STd, SILr," engraved name. **400.00**

Silver, Japanese, late 19th/early 20th C, 3-5/8" l, tear shape, molded dragon dec on stippled ground, attached silver chains, approx 1 troy oz **450.00**

Set

Perfume and etui, 3-3/4" l, France, late 18th/early 19th C, enameled pear shape, white ground, enamel dec with floral sprays, opening at center to storage box base, lid mounted with bird-form perfume stopper **490.00**

Perfume and vinaigrette, 3-1/2" l, paneled cylindrical segmented clear glass bottle, mounted on one end with engine turned gold lid, with lappet neck, top set with central seed pearl surrounded by band of calibre cut turquoises, other end of bottle set with flat monogrammed lid with lappet band, opening to grille for vinaigrette, fitted Tiffany & Co. red morocco case, third quarter 18th C **1,840.00**

Perfume bottles, three 3-3/8" h square bottles mounted with gilt-metal quatrefoil neck bands, gilt-metal rope twist-edged lids set with painted miniatures on ivory under glass, each depicting European city scene, enclosed in 6" l, 2-3/4" w, 3-3/8" h leather carrying case, mounted with mother-of-pearl bands accented by gilt metal flowerheads, Continental, late 19th C. **575.00**

Vinaigrette

Cranberry glass, 2-1/4" x 1", rect, all over cutting, enameled tiny pink roses, green leaves, gold dec, hinged lid, stopper, finger chain **185.00**

Cut glass, 3-7/8" l, cobalt blue, yellow flashing, sterling silver overlay, emb sterling silver cap. **125.00**

English, silver

7/8" l, tooled purse shape, gilded int., John Turner, Birmingham hallmarks, 1792. . . . . **250.00**

1" w, 1-1/2" l, marker's mark "JT," Birmingham, c1845, rect, foliate engraved lid, base with molded

scroll rims, gilt interior with pierced and engraved dec, approx 1 troy oz **290.00**
1-1/4" l, tooled purse shape, gilded int., S. Pemberton, Birmingham hallmarks, 1790 . . . . **220.00**

European, silver, late 19th/early 20th C, 3" shaped as three squashes on vine, engine-turned textured dec, threaded bases, largest with pierced grate to interior, 1 troy oz **350.00**

Victorian, late 19th C, staghorn, 2-1/2" l rough-textured horn mounted with thistle-cast lid, quatrefoil neck band, horn with guilloche strapping, short link chain **350.00**

PETERS AND REED POTTERY

History: J. D. Peters and Adam Reed founded their pottery company in South Zanesville, Ohio, in 1900. Common flowerpots, jardinieres, and cooking wares comprised the majority of their early output. Occasionally, art pottery was attempted, but it was not until 1912 that their Moss Aztec line was introduced and widely accepted. Other art wares include Chromal, Landsun, Montene, Pereco, and Persian.

Peters retired in 1921 and Reed changed the name of the firm to Zane Pottery Company.

Marks: Marked pieces of Peters and Reed Pottery are unknown.

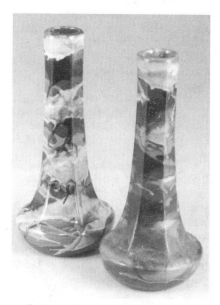

Bud vase, faceted, one blue, one orange, covered in yellow and black marbleized glaze, unmarked, 1" glaze chip to body of orange, **$150.** *Photo courtesy of David Rago Auctions.*

Bowl, 10" d, Landsun, shades of blue **90.00**
Creamer, Sprig Dawn, unmarked **95.00**
Doorstop, cat, yellow. **375.00**
Ewer, 11" h ,orange and yellow raised grapes dec, brown ground **50.00**
Jardiniere, 9-1/2" d, 9" h, Moss Aztec, c1925, unmarked, few small chips to dec **200.00**
Mug, blended glaze **40.00**
Pitcher, 4" h, green and yellow raised fern leaves, gloss dark brown ground **65.00**

Vase, pine cones and needles decoration, **$125.** *Photo courtesy of David Rago Auctions.*

Vase
4-1/4" d, 10-1/2" h, Moss Aztec, corseted, stylized flowers and leaves, unmarked **230.00**
10-1/2" h, squatty base, one in yellow, blue, and black dripping glaze, other in orange, yellow and black dripping glaze, unmarked, price for pr. **225.00**

Vessel, 5-1/4" h, Sprig Dawn, unmarked **95.00**

PEWTER

History: Pewter is a metal alloy consisting mostly of tin with small amounts of lead, copper, antimony, and bismuth added to make the shaping of products easier and to increase the hardness of the material. The metal can be cast, formed around a mold, spun, easily cut, and soldered to form a wide variety of utilitarian articles.

Pewter was known to the ancient Chinese, Egyptians, and Romans. England was the primary source of pewter for the American colonies for nearly 150 years until the American Revolution ended the embargo on raw tin, allowing the small American pewter industry to flourish until the Civil War.

References: Marilyn E. Dragowick (ed.), *Metalwares Price Guide*, Antique Trader Books, 1995; Donald M. Herr, *Pewter in Pennsylvania German Churches*, Vol. XXIX, The Pennsylvania German Society, 1995; Henry J. Kauffman, *American Pewterer*, Astragal Press, 1994.

Collectors' Clubs: Pewter Collectors Club of America, 504 W. Lafayette St., West Chester, PA 19380-2210, http://www.members.aol.com/pewterpcca; The Pewter Society, Llanannt Farm, Penalt, Monmouth, NP25 4AP UK, http://www.pewtersociety.org.

Museum: The Currier Gallery of Art, Manchester, NH.

Note: The listings concentrate on the American and English pewter forms most often encountered by the collector.

Baptismal bowl, 9" d, Boardman, Hartford, CT, stamped "BX," marked "Jacobs," 19th C **950.00**

Basin
6-5/8" d, 1-1/2" h, Blakeslee, Philadelphia, PA, partial eagle touch, wear and battering . **175.00**
7-3/4" d, 1-7/8" h, Gershom Jones, Providence, RI, eagle touch, dents, wear, and scratches. **375.00**
8" d, 2" h, Thomas Compton, English **220.00**

Beaker, 5-1/8" h
Thomas D. and Sherman Boardman, Hartford, CT, marked "Laughlin," c1810-30 . . . . **650.00**
Timothy Boardman and Co., NY, marked "Laughlin," c1825 . **630.00**

Bud vase, 5" d, 10-1/2" h, Secessionist style, orig green glass insert, peacock feather emb, stamped "WMF". . **865.00**

Candlesticks, pr
8-3/4" h, marked "Jacobs," 1822-71 . . . . **950.00**
9-3/4" h, unmarked American, attributed to CT, with bobeches **275.00**

Charger
12-1/2" d, faint angel touch on back, engraved "C. K." along rim, tooled rim around edge, knife marks, minor dents **200.00**
13-1/4" d, touchmarks for Thomas Danford II, knife scratches and areas of pitting **660.00**

Coffeepot, cov
7" h, Israel Trask, Beverly, MA, lighthouse, bright cut engraving **350.00**
10-5/8" h, Freeman Porter, Westbrook, ME. **470.00**
11" h, R. Dunham **275.00**

13" h, James Dixon, England
. . . . **250.00**
13-1/2" h, Reed and Barton, marked
"Leonard Reed & Barton 3500"
. . . . **250.00**

Communion chalice, 6-1/4" h,
unmarked American, handles removed,
pr **200.00**

Creamer, 5-7/8" h, unmarked American,
teapot shape **250.00**

Deep dish, 13-1/8" d, Stephen Barnes
eagle touch, Middletown or Wallingford,
CT, minor scratches and wear . . **415.00**

Flagon
9-1/2" h, thumb piece, engraved
floral and amorous couple on
bench design, German inscription
and "F C S 1809," soldered repair
. . . . **165.00**
12-1/2" h, attributed to Israel Trask,
Beverly, MA, 1807-56, minor dents
. . . . **300.00**
14" h, Thomas D. and Sherman
Boardman, Hartford, CT, marked
"Laughlin," 1810-30 . . . . . **3,750.00**

Inkstand, 3-1/2" h, 5-1/2" w, 9-1/2" l,
unmarked, ftd **175.00**

*Left: lamp, marked "Yale & Curtis, NY,"
whale oil burner, 8-1/4" h, $220; cen-
ter: tall pot, marked "G. Richardson"
(Boston), 10-1/2" h, shaped wood handle, $335; right: lamp, unmarked
American, repair on base, fluid burner
with brass tubes, pewter snuffer caps
and chain, 7-3/4" h, $250. Photo cour-
tesy of Garth's Auctions, Inc.*

Lamp
5-3/4" h plus brass and tin whale oil
burner, Putnam touch, James
Putnam, Madison, MA, some splits
in rim of base **315.00**
7" h plus fluid burner, unmarked
American, attributed to Meriden,
reeded detail on base, ear handle,
light pitting **110.00**
8-1/2" h plus burner, Yale and Curtis,
NY 1 touch, matching fluid burner
missing, snuffers and one brass
tube loose **190.00**

Measure
2-3/8" to 8" h, assembled set, bellied,
English, minor damage **550.00**

5-3/4" h, John Warne, English, brass
rim, battered, old repair, quart
. . . . **100.00**

Mug, quart
4" h, Thomas Danforth Boardman,
Hartford, CT, tankard, partial
"T.D.B." touch, some battering,
soldered repairs **500.00**
5-7/8" h, Samuel Hamlin, Hartford,
Middletown, CT, and Providence
RI, dent at base **625.00**

Pitcher
6" h, Freeman Porter, Westbrook,
ME, two quart **225.00**
6-1/2" h, Continental, swirl design,
hinged lid, angel touch **85.00**

Plate
7-1/2" d, Richard Austin, Boston, MA,
1792-1817, surface scratches
. . . . **415.00**
7-3/4" d, Blakslee Barns,
Philadelphia, PA, 1812-17, surface
scratches **400.00**
7-7/8" d, Asbil Griswold, Meriden,
CT, eagle touch some battering
and knife scratches **160.00**
7-7/8" d, B. Barns, Philada and
"B.B." eagle touch, wear and dents
. . . . **200.00**
7-7/8" d, Joseph Danforth lion touch,
minor wear **330.00**
8" d, rampant lion touch, Edward
Danford, Middletown and Hartford,
CT, minor wear and scratches
. . . . **200.00**
8-3/8" d, David Melville, Newport, RI,
1776-94, marked on base, knife
marks, minor pitting **500.00**

Platter, 28-3/4" l, Townsend and
Compton, London, pierced insert,
marked "Cotterell" **2,400.00**

Porringer
3-7/8" d, cast handle, marked "TD &
SB" touch (Thomas Danford
Boardman, et al, Hartford) . **220.00**
4-3/4" d, cast crown handle, marked
"I.G.," Boston area, pitting, pinpoint
hole **140.00**
5-1/2" d, unmarked American, cast
flowered handle **150.00**

Soup plate, 8-7/8" d, unmarked
Continental, angel touch **75.00**

Sugar bowl, 6" h, Ashril Griswold,
Meriden, CT, eagle touch **490.00**

Syrup pitcher, 4-1/2" h, hinged lid,
unmarked, American **220.00**

Tablespoon, rattail handle, heart on
back of bowl, marked "L. B.," (Luther
Boardman, MA and CT). set of six
. . . . **330.00**

*Stein, German, engraved pot-
ted flowers and trees, hinged
lid, 10" h, $100. Photo
courtesy of Sanford Alderfer
Auction Co.*

Tea caddy, 3-3/4" h, B G S & Co,
American, 1825-30, almond shape,
bright cut designs, touch mark, wear,
pitted **200.00**

Teapot
6-3/4" h, Roswell Gleason,
Dorchester, MA, eagle touch
. . . . **495.00**
6-3/4" h, Ashbil Griswold, Meriden,
CT, eagle touch, some battering
and repairs **200.00**
7" h, Eben Smith, Beverly, MA,
1813-56, minor pitting and
scratches **375.00**
7-1/2" h, L. Boardman, Warranted
touch, (Luther Boardman, South
Reading, MA,) repairs, spout
replaced **200.00**
7-5/8" h, Putnam touch (James H.
Putnam, Walden, MA,) repairs
. . . . **150.00**
7-3/4" h, Smith & Co touch, (Albany,
NY,) some battering and damage
. . . . **175.00**
8-1/8" h, A. Griswold eagle touch,
(Ashbil Griswold, Meriden, CT),
some battering and repair, splits to
bottom **200.00**
8-1/2" h, Continental, pear shaped,
old soldered repair **160.00**

Tobacco box, 4-3/8" h, Thomas
Stanford, cast eagle feet, engraved
label with scroll work "Thomas Stanford,
Gospel Hill, 1838," wear, final and one
foot soldered **125.00**

Tumbler, 2-3/4" h, Thomas Danforth Boardman, Hartford, CT, partial eagle touch **175.00**

Warming platter, 19" l, hot water type, tree and well, marked "Dixon & Sons," English, repairs **250.00**

PHOENIX GLASS

History: Phoenix Glass Company, Beaver, Pennsylvania, was established in 1880. Known primarily for commercial glassware, the firm also produced a molded, sculptured, cameo-type line from the 1930s until the 1950s.

References: Tom and Neila Bredehoft, *Fifty Years of Collectible Glass, 1920-1970*, Volume 1, Volume II, Antique Trader Books, 2000; Jack D. Wilson, *Phoenix & Consolidated Art Glass*, Antique Publications, 1989.

Collectors' Club: Phoenix & Consolidated Glass Collectors Club, 41 River View Drive, Essex Junction, VT 05452, http://www.collectoron-line.com/club-PCGCC-wp.html.

Lamp, white ground, red berries, green leaves, brown stems, bronze plated base, 22" h, $145.

Ashtray, Phlox, large, white, frosted **80.00**

Bowl, 14" d, nude diving girl, white **495.00**

Creamer and sugar, Catalonia, light green **45.00**

Floor vase, 9" d, 18" h, emb blackberries and leaves, lavender, unmarked, minute grinding chips at rim **750.00**

Lamp shade, ceiling type, 12" d, pale pink, emb floral dec **115.00**

Umbrella stand, 18" h, Thistle, pearlized blue ground **450.00**

Vase

4-3/4" d, 4-3/4" h, Jewel, brown over milk glass **200.00**

6" w, 7" h, white ferns, blue ground **130.00**

6-1/2" w at top, 3-1/2" d base, 7-1/2" h, blue, white floral dec, orig sticker, two chips on inside rim **190.00**

7" h, Bluebell, brown **125.00**

8" h, Daisy, pearlized daisies, light green ground, orig label . . . **360.00**

8-1/8" d, 11-3/4" h, Nude Scarf Dancers, light brown ground, cream figures, orig label . . . **650.00**

10" h, Wild Geese, pearlized white birds, light green ground . . . **225.00**

10-3/4" h, Dogwood, green and white **600.00**

11" h, Wild rose, blown out, pearlized dec, dark rose ground, orig label **275.00**

14" h, Philodendron, blue, ormolu mounts **400.00**

PHONOGRAPHS

History: Early phonographs were commonly called "talking machines." Thomas A. Edison invented the first successful phonograph in 1877; other manufacturers followed with their variations.

References: Timothy C. Fabrizio and George F. Paul, *Antique Phonograph Gadgets, Gizmos, and Gimmicks*, Schiffer Publishing, 1999; —, *Discovering Antique Phonographs, 1877-1929*, Schiffer Publishing, 2000; —, *The Talking Machine: An Illustrated Compendium, 1877-1929*, Schiffer Publishing, 1997; Neil Maker, *Hand-Cranked Phonographs*, Promar Publishing, 1993; Arnold Schwartzman, *Phono-Graphics*, Chronicle Books, 1993; Eric L. Reiss, *The Compleat Talking Machine*, 3rd ed., Sanoran Publishing, 1998.

Periodicals and Internet Resources: *Antique Phonograph Gallery Online*, http://www.inkyfingers.com/Record.html; *Jerry's Musical Newsletter*, 4624 W. Woodland Road, Minneapolis, MN 55424; *Nipperland Antique Phonographs*, http://www.nipperhead.com; http://www.oldcrank.com; *RadioGallery.com*, http://www.radiogallery.com; *The Electronic Collector*, P.O. Box 1193, Mabank, TX 75147.

Collectors' Clubs: Antique Phonograph Collectors Club, 502 E. 17th St., Brooklyn, NY 11226-6606; Buckeye Radio & Phonograph Club, 4572 Mark Trail, Copley, OH 44321; California Antique Phonograph Society, 18242 Timberline Drive, Yorba Linda, CA 92686-5345; Canadian Antique Phonograph Society, 122 Major St., Toronto, Ontario M5S 2L2 Canada; City of London Phonograph & Gramophone Society, 51 Brockhurst Road, Chesham, UK; Federation of Recorded Music Societies, 67 Galleys Bank

Kidsgrove, Staffordshire, ST7 4DE, UK; Hudson Valley Antique Radio & Phonograph Society, P.O. Box 207, Campbell Hall, NY 10916; Michigan Antique Phonograph Society, Inc., 60 Central St., Battle Creek, MI 49027; Vintage Radio & Phonograph Society, Inc., P.O. Box 165345, Irving, TX 75016; Wolverine Antique Music Society, 252 Mill St., Silverton, OR 97381.

Museums: Edison National Historic Site, West Orange, NJ; Johnson Victrola Museum, Dover, DE; Seven Acres Antique Village & Museum, Union, IL.

Adviser: Lewis S. Walters.

Grobes Luxus-Trichter Grammophon, Maestrophone, giant brass horn, $4,700. Photo courtesy of Auction Team Breker.

Columbia

HG cylinder player **2,400.00**

BQ cylinder player **1,200.00**

BN disc player **1,000.00**

Decca, Junior, portable, leather case and handle **150.00**

Edison

Excelsior, coin op **2,500.00**

Gem, maroon, 2- to 4-minute reproducer **1,700.00**

Opera, has moving mandrel and fixed reproducer **2,500.00**

Standard, Model A, oak case with metal horn **550.00**

Triumph, with cygnet horn, mahogany case **2,500.00**

S-19 Diamond Disc, floor model, oak case **400.00**

Amberola 30 . . . . **400.00**

Fireside, with original horn . . **900.00**

Army-Navy, WWI **1,200.00**

Diamond Disc VV-19, William and Mary **500.00**

Edison, oak case, domed top, old varnished finish, original horn and crank, sold with 60 cylinders, needs new belt, 12-1/4" x 16" x 8-3/4", **$415.** *Photo courtesy of Garth's Auctions, Inc.*

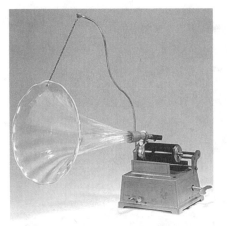

Pathé Le Gaulois, original glass horn, 1900-1903, **$5,230.** *Photo courtesy of Auction Team Breker.*

Graphone

12.5 oak case, metal horn, retailer's mark, cylinder **450.00**

15.0 oak case with columns on corners, nickel-plated platform, metal horn, stenciled cast-iron parts **725.00**

Home Grand, oak case, nickel-plated works, #6 spring motor **1,300.00**

Harvard, trumpet style horn **300.00**

Kalamazoo, Duplex, reproducer, original horns with decals, pat. date 1904 . . . . **3,300.00**

Odeon Talking Machine Co., table model, crank wind, brass horn, straight tone arm **500.00**

RCA-Victor, "45" Bakelite Record Player **65.00**

Silvertone (Sears), two reproducers **500.00**

Sonora

Gothic Deluxe, walnut case, triple spring, gold-plated parts, automatic stop and storage **400.00**

Luzerne, renaissance-style case with storage **200.00**

Talk-O-Phone, Brooke, table model, oak case rope decorations, steel horn **200.00**

Victor

Credenza, crank **1,100.00**

Monarch, table model, corner columns, brass bell horn **1,500.00**

Victor I, mahogany case, corner columns, bell horn **1,500.00**

Victor II, oak case, black bell horn **1,200.00**

Victor II, oak case, smooth oak horn **5,500.00**

Victor III, papier-mâché horn **1,400.00**

Victor V, oak case, corner columns, no horn **1,500.00**

Victor VI, oak case, no horn **4,000.00**

School House **2,500.00**

PHOTOGRAPHS

History: A vintage print is a positive image developed from the original negative by the photographer or under the photographer's supervision at the time the negative is made. A non-vintage print is a print made from an original negative at a later date. It is quite common for a photographer to make prints from the same negative over several decades. Changes between the original and subsequent prints usually can be identified. Limited edition prints must be clearly labeled.

References: Diane VanSkiver Gagel, *Ohio Photographers, 1839-1900: A History and Directory*, Carl Mautz Publishing, 1998; O. Henry Mace, *Collector's Guide to Early Photographs*, 2nd ed., Krause Publications, 1999; Craig A. Tuttle, *An Ounce of Preservation, A Guide to Care of Papers and Photographs*, Rainbow Books, 1995.

Periodicals and Internet Resources: *Art On Paper*, 39 E. 78th St., #601, New York, NY 10021; *Daguerreotype Collection*, Library of Congress, http://memory.loc.gov/ammen/daghtml/daghome.htm l; *History of Photography*, Rankine Road, Basingstoke, Hants RG24 8PR UK; *Journal of the Print World*, P.O. Box 978, Meredith, NH 03253-0978; *Mathew Brady's Portraits*, National Portrait Gallery, Smithsonian Institution, http://www.ngp.si.edu/exh/brady; *Military Images*, P.O. Box 2391, Southeastern, PA 19399; *Photograph Collector*, 301 Hill Ave., Suite 2, Langhorne, PA 18047.

Collectors' Clubs: American Photographic Historical Society, Inc., 1150 Avenue of the Americas, New York, NY 10036; Assoc. of International Photography Art Dealers, 1609 Connecticut Ave. NW #200, Washington, DC 20009; Daguerrean Society, 3045 W. Liberty Ave., Ste 9, Pittsburgh, PA 15226; Michigan Photographic Historical Society, P.O. Box 2278, Birmingham, MI 48012-2278; Photographic Collectors of Great Britain, 5 Buntingford Road, Hadon Bridge, Hexham, Northumberland SG11 1RT, UK; Photographic Historical Society, Inc., P.O. Box 39563, Rochester, NY 14604; Photographic Historical Society of Canada, P.O. Box 54620, Toronto, Ontario M5M 4N5 Canada; Photographic Historical Society of New England, P.O. Box 65189, Newton, MA 02165; Photographic Society of America, 3000 United Founders Blvd., Suite 103, Oklahoma City, OK 73112-3940; Western Photographic Collectors Assoc., Inc., 8500 La Entrada, Whittier, CA 90605.

Museums: American Museum of Photography, Huntington Woods, MI; Center for Creative Photography, Tucson, AZ; International Center of Photography, New York, NY; International Museum of Photography at George Eastman House, Rochester, NY; International Photographic Historical Association, San Francisco, CA; National Archives & Records Administration, Still Picture Branch, College Park, MD; National Museum of Photography, Film & Television, UK, http://www.nmsi.ac.uk/nmpft; National Portrait Gallery, Washington, DC.

Additional Listings: See *Warman's Americana & Collectibles* for more examples.

Album

"A Souvenir of the Harriman Alaska Expedition, volumes I and II," 251 photographs, more than 100 by Edward Curtin, additional images by Edward H. Harriman, C. Hart Merriam, G. K. Gilbert, D. G. Inverarity, and others, silver prints, various sizes to 6" x 7-1/2", several with handwritten credit and date in negative, others with copyright, album disbound and defective, title pages and map laid in, prints generally in excellent condition, 1899, pr. **21,850.00**

"Kodak," 104 photographs of Eastern and Midwestern U. S. by Wm Hoblitzell, prints document his train ride across country from MD to Missoula, MT, unposed glimpses of trains and local stations, Missoulan bicyclists and Native-Americans on horseback, handwritten captions and/or dates on mount rectos, mounted four per page recto and verso, oblong 4to, gilt-lettered morocco, spine and edges worn, pgs loose, photographer's handstamp on front and rear pastdowns, ties missing, 1890-91 . . . . **575.00**

Two daguerreotype images of standing Civil War soldiers, identified as "Mr. Chas. S. Pryer, taken at Louisville, age when taken 21 years, enlisted Aug 1862, 88th Reg. For term of service three years, Price $5.50, written April 21th 1872, by W. N. Lowery, Farmer City, Ill, Dewitt Co.," and "Mr. Ira Pryer, Brother," hinged gutta-percha case, $850. Photo courtesy of Joy Luke Auctions.

Albumen print

Lincoln's conspirators having hoods and nooses adjusted, mounted, sgd by Alexander Gardner
. . . . **7,700.00**
View of the Oswego Harbor, arched top, 13" x 16-1/2", title, photographer, and date printed on label affixed below image, 1869
. . . . **1,380.00**

Ambrotype, William Gannaway Brownlow, known as Parson Brownlow, the fightin' preacher, half plate **3,190.00**

Cabinet card

Buffalo Bill, albumen photograph
. . . . **357.50**
Chief Thunder, posed holding ceremonial pipe, D. F. Barry and printed title on label affixed to mount recto, Barry's West Superior, Wis., imprint on mount verse, 1891
. . . . **1,265.00**
Oakley, Annie, mounted albumen photograph, facsimile signature
. . . . **2,860.00**
Sitting Bull, D. F. Barry, titled, copyrighted, dated, and Barry's imprint on recto, Bismarck D. T. imprint on mount verso, 1885, 7" x 5" **1,495.00**
Wilde, Oscar, age 32, Alfred Ellis & Wallery imprint on mounts recto and verso, period German inscription handwritten on mount verso, 1892, 5" x 4" **1,100.00**

CDV, carte de visite

Davis, Jefferson, President of Confederacy **80.00**
Emancipation Proclamation . . . **80.00**
Lincoln, Abraham, taken by Matthew Brady, 1864 . . . . **1,045.00**
Mrs. Lincoln, portrait with spirit of Abe behind her, Wm Mumler's Boston imprint on mount verso, c1869 . . . . **1,725.00**

Daguerreotype

Folk Art painting showing two children in profile facing each other, six-plate, slight tarnish halo, sealed in damaged leatherette case, late 1840s **1,210.00**
Gentleman, leatherette half case, unsigned, attributed to work of the Prior Hamilton School, minor imperfections, 3-3/4" x 3-1/4"
. . . . **1,610.00**
Husband and wife in single case, minor hallo, remains sealed, liner flakes **130.00**

Magic lantern slides, group of 320 photographic images from 1920s and 1930s, Atlantic City views and events, yachting, fireboats, Mohonk (NY), Duluth (MN), etc. housed in four individual carrying cases, several slides cracked **230.00**

Photograph

Aspens, New Mexico, 1958, by Ansel Adams, sgd "Ansel Adams" in ink on mount, identified on label from Boston gallery on reverse, 19-1/2" x 15-1/2", framed
. . . . **6,325.00**
Mother and Child in a Barn, unsigned, Julia Margaret Cameron, 8" x 4-1/2", framed **490.00**
Portrait of Albert Einstein, c1938, by Lotte Jacobi, sgd "Lotte Jacobi" in pencil lower right, 9-3/4" x 7", framed **1,265.00**

Clearing Winter Storm by Ansel Adams (1902-1984), 15" x 19", $11,787. Photo courtesy of Jackson's Auctioneers & Appraisers.

Portrait of Kathe Kollwitz with a Camera, by Lotte Jacobi, sgd "Lotte Jacobi" in pencil lower right, 9" x 6-1/4", framed........**415.00**

Portrait of Lotte Lenya, c1930, by Lotte Jacobi, sgd "Lotte Jacobi" in pencil lower right, 7-1/2" x 9-1/2", framed.............**1,035.00**

Portrait of Marc Chagall and His Daughter in His Studio, by Lotte Jacobi, sgd "Lotte Jacobi" in pencil lower right, 6-3/4" x 5-1/2", framed **300.00**

Silver print, Chief Hairy Chin, dressed as Uncle Sam, photographer's (D. F. Barry) blindstamp on recto, 1889, printed c1900, 6-1/4" x 4".....**825.00**

Tintype

Family, identified on mat "Marshall Kimpton," man wearing military coat, wife wearing elaborate hat, huge bow, daughter stands behind, ninth plate, cased, minor bends, case hinge has old taped repair.................**150.00**

Young woman, swatch of twill from jacket, 1-5/8" gold filled engraved locket case **85.00**

PICKARD CHINA

History: The Pickard China Company was founded by Wilder Pickard in Chicago, Illinois, in 1897. Originally the company imported European china blanks, principally from the Havilands at Limoges, which were then hand painted. The firm presently is located in Antioch, Illinois.

References: Susan and Al Bagdade, *Warman's American Pottery and Porcelain*, 2nd ed., Krause Publications, 2000; Alan B. Reed, *Collector's Encyclopedia of Pickard China with Additional Sections on Other Chicago China Studios*, Collector Books, 1996, 2000 values update.

Collectors' Club: Pickard Collectors Club, 300 E. Grove St., Bloomington, IL 61701.

Bowl

6" d, Autumn Blackberries, sgd "O. Goess" (Otto Goess), 1905-10 mark **200.00**

8-1/2" d, shallow, fish dec, sgd "Motzfeldt" (Andrew Motzfeldt), 1903-05 mark...........**500.00**

9-1/2" d, 4-1/2" h, ftd, strawberries, white blossoms, and gooseberries dec, sgd "E. Challinor" (Edward Challinor), 1905-10 mark ..**300.00**

10" d, pink and blue flowers, gilding, unsigned, 1912-18 mark ...**70.00**

10" d, Rose and Daisy pattern, central scenic panel with bird, sgd "E. Challinor" (Edward Challinor), 1919-22 mark..........**250.00**

Celery set, two-handled oval dish, five matching salts, allover gold dec, 1925-30 mark **125.00**

Chocolate pot, white poppies, gilded band, sgd "Menges" (Edward Mentges), 1905-10 mark......**350.00**

Claret set, claret jug, five tumblers, 11-1/2" d tray, Deserted Garden pattern, sgd "J. Nessy" (John Nessy), 1912-18 mark **2,600.00**

Coffee set

Aura Argenta Linear, coffee pot, creamer, sugar, six demitasse cups and saucers, two salt shakers, sgd "Hess" (Robert Hessler), 1910-12 marks **1,300.00**

Modern Conventional pattern, coffee pot sgd "Hessler" (Robert Hessler), 1910-12 mark, eight cups and saucers sgd "Hess & RH" (Robert Hessler), 1912-18 mark ..**1,450.00**

Creamer

4-3/4" h, red and yellow currants, green leaves, unsigned, 1905-10 mark.................**165.00**

5-1/4" h, Tulip Conventional, sgd "Tomash" (Rudolph Tomascheko), 1903-05 mark..........**400.00**

Creamer and sugar

Deserted Garden pattern, sgd "J. Nessy" (John Nessy), 1912-18 mark.................**200.00**

Violets dec, sgd "Z. Mac" (Zuie McCorkie), 1903-05 mark...**110.00**

White Poppies & Daisy, sgd, 1912-18 mark.................**250.00**

Demitasse cup and saucer

Gold Tracery Rose & Daisy pattern, green band, 1925-30 mark .**40.00**

Poppy pattern, sgd "LOH" (John Loh), 1910-12, price for pr.**325.00**

Lemonade pitcher

Encrusted Honeysuckle pattern, 1919-22 mark..........**100.00**

Schoner Lemon pattern, sgd "Schoner" (Otto Schoner), 1903-05 mark.................**1,700.00**

Three Pickard plates, all hand painted, gold trimmed, and artist signed, from left: red cherries and shaded green leaves, $115; orchids decoration, white and purple flowers, $125; three color roses and leaves, heavy gold border, $120. Photo courtesy of Joy Luke Auctions.

Match holder, Rose & Daisy pattern, all over gold, 1925-30............**40.00**

Pin dish, violets dec **40.00**

Plate

8-1/4" d, gooseberries dec, sgd "P. G." (Paul Gasper), 1912-18 mark **45.00**

8-1/4" d, scenic, unsigned, 1912-18 mark **120.00**

8-1/2" d, blackberries and leaves, sgd "Beitler" (Joseph Beitler), 1903-15 ....**90.00**

8-1/2" d, Calla Lily pattern, sgd "Marker" (Curtis H. Marker), 1905-10 mark **225.00**

8-1/2" d, chestnuts dec, 1903-05 mark **70.00**

8-1/2" d, Gibson Narcissus pattern, sgd "E. Gibson" (Edward Gibson), 1903-05 mark **300.00**

8-1/2" d, Lilium Ornatum pattern, sgd "Beulet" (F. Beulet), 1910-12 mark **100.00**

8-3/4" d, Florida Moonlight, sgd "E. Challinor" (Edward Challinor), 1912-18 mark **2,300.00**

8-3/4" d, orange flowers, sgd "James" (Florence James), 1905-10 mark **100.00**

9" d, Yeschek Currants in Gold pattern, sgd "Blaha" (Joseph Blaha), 1905-10 mark **110.00**

Tankard, 16" h, hexagonal, Chrysanthemums, Lustre & Matte Red pattern, sgd "Rean" (Maxwell Rean Klipphahn), 1905-10 mark **950.00**

Tea set, cov teapot, creamer, cov sugar, Carnation Garden pattern, each sgd "Yeschek" (Joseph T. Yeschek), 1903-05 marks **2,600.00**

Vase

5-1/4" h, three ftd, flying geese, sgd "E. Challinor" (Edward Challinor), 1938-present mark **550.00**

Vase, scenic, decorated with trees and lake, signed "E. Challinor," 1912-18 mark, 10" h, $1,100. Photo courtesy of Joy Luke Auctions.

8" h, Golden Pheasant pattern, sgd "E. Challinor" (Edward Challinor), 1919-22 mark **500.00**

8-1/4" h, scenic, sgd "E. Challinor" (Edward Challinor), 1912-18 mark **425.00**

11" h, Calla Lily pattern, sgd "Marker" (Curtis H. Marker), 1905-10 mark **550.00**

13-3/4" h, two handles, scenic, birch trees, gilding, sgd "E. Challinor" (Edward Challinor), 1912-18 mark **1,900.00**

16" h, Cherokee Rose, sgd "Walt" (Frederick Walters), 1910-12 mark **2,100.00**

PICKLE CASTORS

History: A pickle castor is a table accessory used to serve pickles. It generally consists of a silver-plated frame fitted with a glass insert, matching silver-plated lid, and matching tongs. Pickle castors were very popular during the Victorian era. Inserts are found in pattern glass and colored art glass.

Amberina, melon ribbed IVT insert, SP lid, ftd frame, lid, tongs, c1875-95 . . . . **700.00**

Bluebird, enameled, resilvered frame **725.00**

Colorless, 11-3/4" h, acid etched insert, floral dec with bird medallion, octagonal SP frame, marked "Meriden Co. 182" **200.00**

Cranberry

IVT insert, enameled blue and white florals, green leaves, shelf on frame dec with peacocks and other birds **325.00**

Paneled Spring insert, SP frame, c1875-95 . . . . **450.00**

Double

Colorless inserts, emb fans and flowers, matching cov, fancy tulip finials, Viking head ftd oval handled frame, sgd "Meriden" **275.00**

Vaseline, pickle leaves and pieces, resilvered frame **800.00**

Pattern glass, Daisy and Button pattern, amber, silver plated Tufts frame, original tongs, $220.

Mt. Washington, 11" h, 6" d, decorated satin glass insert, blue enamel and painted yellow roses, green leaves, orange and yellow blossoms, silver-plated Rogers stand and tongs **875.00**

Opalescent

Daisy & Fern, blue, emb DQ floral jar, resilvered frame **450.00**

Vertical white stripes, colorless ground, resilvered angel frame, elephant's head and trunk feet **625.00**

Pink, shiny pink Florette pattern insert, white int., bowed out frame **325.00**

PIGEON BLOOD GLASS

History: Pigeon blood refers to the deep orange-red-colored glassware produced around the turn of the century. Do not confuse it with the many other red glasswares of that period. Pigeon blood has a very definite orange glow.

Biscuit jar, ribbed body, silver plated fittings, 8-1/2" h, $250.

Berry bowl, master, Torquay . . **195.00**

Berry bowl, individual size, Torquay **50.00**

Butter dish, cov, Torquay **595.00**

Celery vase, Torquay **200.00**

Condiment set, Torquay **1,150.00**

Cracker jar, cov, Quilted Phlox, Consolidated Glass Co, resilvered hardware **325.00**

Creamer, Venecia, enameled dec **125.00**

Cruet, Torquay **900.00**

Decanter, 9-1/2" h, orig stopper **145.00**

Hand cooler, 5" l, cut panels, two compartments, SS fittings **145.00**

Pickle castor, cov, Torquay . . . **895.00**

Pitcher, 9-1/2" h, Bulging Loops, applied clear handle, ground pontil **225.00**

Salt and pepper shakers, pr, Bulging Loops, orig top **150.00**

Spooner, Torquay **125.00**

Syrup pitcher, squatty, Torquay **450.00**

Syrup pitcher, tall, Torquay . . **1,200.00**

Sweetmeat, Torquay **125.00**

Tobacco jar, cov, Torquay **450.00**

Tumbler, 3-1/4" h, alternating panel and rib **85.00**

Water carafe, Torquay **395.00**

PINK SLAG

History: True pink slag is found only in the molded Inverted Fan and Feather pattern. Quality pieces shade from pink at the top to white at the bottom.

Reproduction Alert: Recently, pieces of pink slag made from molds of the now-defunct Cambridge Glass Company have been found in the Inverted Strawberry and Inverted Thistle patterns. This is not considered true pink slag and brings only a fraction of the price of the Inverted Fan and Feather pieces.

Jelly compote, Inverted Fan & Feather, 5" h, **$600.** *Photo courtesy of Clarence and Betty Maier.*

Tumbler, Inverted Fan and Feather pattern, 4" h, **$450.**

Berry bowl, 10" d **750.00**
Creamer **465.00**
Cruet, 6-1/2" h, orig stopper . . **1,300.00**
Jelly compote, 5" h, 4-1/2" d, scalloped top **375.00**
Marmalade jar, cov **875.00**
Pitcher, water **775.00**
Punch cup, 2-1/2" h, ftd **275.00**
Salt shaker **300.00**
Sauce dish, 4-1/4" d, 2-1/2" h, ball feet **225.00**
Spooner **350.00**
Sugar bowl, cov **550.00**
Toothpick holder **825.00**
Tumbler, 4-1/2" h **475.00**

PIPES

History: Pipe making can be traced as far back as 1575. Pipes were made of almost all types of natural and manmade materials, including amber, base metals, clay, cloisonné, glass, horn, ivory, jade, meerschaum, parian, porcelain, pottery, precious metals, precious stones, semiprecious stones, and assorted woods. Some of these materials retain smoke and some do not. Chronologically, the four most popular materials and their generally accepted introduction dates are: clay, c1575; wood, c1700; porcelain, c1710; and meerschaum, c1725.

Pipe styles reflect nationalities all around the world, wherever tobacco smoking is custom or habit. Pipes represent a broad range of themes and messages, e.g., figurals, important personages, commemoration of historical events, mythological characters, erotic and pornographic subjects, the bucolic, the bizarre, the grotesque, and the graceful.

Pipe collecting began in the mid-1880s; William Bragge, F.S.A., Birmingham, England, was an early collector. Although firmly established through the efforts of freelance writers, auction houses, and museums, but not the tobacco industry, the collecting of antique pipes is an amorphous, maligned, and misunderstood hobby. It is amorphous because there are no defined collecting bounds, maligned because it is perceived as an extension of pipe smoking, and now misunderstood because smoking has become socially unacceptable—even though many pipe collectors are avid non-smokers.

References: Ben Rapaport, *Collecting Antique Meerschaum Pipes: Miniature to Majestic Sculpture*, Schiffer Publishing, 1999; R. Fresco-Corbu, *European Pipes*, Lutterworth Press, 1982; Benjamin Rapaport, *Complete Guide to Collecting Antique Pipes*, Schiffer Publishing, 1979.

Periodicals: *Agricultural and Mechanical Gazette*, P.O. Box 930401, Wixom, MI 48939, http://www.digiscape.com/a&mgazette/BriarPipes.html; *Pipes & Tobaccos*, 3000 Highwoods Blvd., Suite 300, Raleigh, NC 27604-1029, http://www.pt-magazine.com.

Collectors' Clubs: Chicagoland Pipe Collectors Club, 540 South Westmore, Lombard, IL 60148-3028; International Assoc. of Pipe Smokers' Clubs, 647 S. Saginaw St., Flint, MI 48502; New York Pipe Club,

440 East 81, Apt 1C, New York, NY 10028; North American Society of Pipe Collectors, P.O. Box 9642, Columbus, OH 43209-9642, http://www.naspc.org; Pipe Collectors Club of America, P.O. Box 5179, Woodbridge, VA 22194, http://www.pipesmoke.com; Pipe Club of London, 40 Crescent Drive, Petts Word, Orpington, Kent BR5 1BD. Society for Clay Pipe Research, 30 Ongrils Close, Pershore, Worcestshire WR10 1QE.

Museums: Museum of Tobacco Art and History, Nashville, TN; National Tobacco-Textile Museum, Danville, VA; Pipe Smoker's Hall of Fame, Galveston, IN; U.S. Tobacco Museum, Greenwich, CT.

Clay, Leblanc, Ardennes, 9-1/2" l, **$30.**

Burl, 3-1/2" w, 7-1/4" h, carved tiered archways and staircase, animal and human faces, traces of old dark paint, America, late 19th/early 20th C, minor repair **115.00**
Clay, 6-5/8" l, red clay, 18 incised presentation signatures, unglazed, chips **55.00**
Glass, large ovoid bowl, long shaped stem, red and ivory dec **90.00**

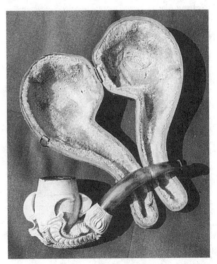

Meerschaum, original leather case, **$90.**

Meerschaum
  3-1/2" l, two carved dogs on top, cracked amber mouthpiece, orig leather case with velvet and satin lining **125.00**
  4-3/4" l, 2" h, horses and barking dog, orig case **345.00**
  6-1/2" l, 1-1/2" h, face of black boy, carved elephant on stem, marked "Made in Tranzania" **165.00**

Porcelain

9" l, Graf Zeppelin, marked "P.O.B" **125.00**

12" l, floral, relief dec **125.00**

19" l, drunken man lying under barrel, small porcelain animal on bowl lid **280.00**

29" l, hunter, sleeping **135.00**

Pottery, monk, post war **50.00**

Regimental, 41" l, porcelain bowl, 112 Infantry, Sohlettstadt 1888, named to Res. Huck., two scenes, helmet cover, new spike and hairline in bowl, minor repair on flexible cord **225.00**

Tortoiseshell, 5-1/2" l, woman's, 1" w octagonal bowl with clear and colored rhinestones, six clear rhinestones on stem, early 1900s **100.00**

Wood, carved

7-1/2" l, hand carved bears crawling on stump, 3-5/8" l celluloid stem **250.00**

8-1/4" l, bearded man's head above deer's head, stem with carved dog's head, America, 19th C, stand **700.00**

POCKET KNIVES

History: Alcas, Case, Colonial, Ka-Bar, Queen, and Schrade are the best of the modern pocket-knife manufacturers, with top positions enjoyed by Case and Ka-Bar. Knives by Remington and Winchester, firms no longer in production, are eagerly sought.

References: Jerry and Elaine Heuring, *Collector's Guide to E. C. Simmons, Keen Kutter Cutlery Tools*, Collector Books, 1999; Jacob N. Jarrett, *Price Guide to Pocket Knives*, L-W Books, 1993, 1998 value update; Joe Kertzman, *Knives* 2001, 21st ed., Krause Publications, 2000, and *Knives 2002*, 22nd ed., Krause Publications, 2001; Bernard R. Levine, *Levine's Guide to Knives and Their Values*, 5th ed., Krause Publications, 2000; Jack Lewis and Roger Combs, *The Gun Digest Book of Knives*, 5th ed., Krause Publications, 1997; Jim Sargent, *American Premium Guide to Pocket Knives & Razors*, 5th ed., Krause Publications, 1999; Ron Stewart and Roy Ritchie, *Big Book of Pocket Knives*, Collector Books, 2000; ——, *Cattaraugus Cutlery Co.*, Collector Books, 2000; ——, *Standard Knife Collector's Guide*, 3rd ed., Collector Books, 1993, 1999 value update; J. Bruce Voyles, *International Blade Collectors Association's Price Guide to Antique Knives*, Krause Publications, 1995; Richard D. White, *Advertising Cutlery*, Schiffer Publishing, 1999.

Periodicals: *Blade*, 700 E. State St., Iola, WI 54990; *Knife World*, P.O. Box 3395, Knoxville, TN 37927.

Collectors' Clubs: American Blade Collectors, P.O. Box 22007, Chattanooga, TN 37422; Canadian Knife Collectors Club, Route 1, Milton, Ontario L9T 2X5 Canada; National Knife Collectors Association, P.O. Box 21070, Chattanooga, TN 37421.

Museum: National Knife Collectors Museum, Chattanooga, TN.

Additional Listings: See *Warman's Americana & Collectibles* for more examples.

Notes: Form is a critical collecting element. The most desirable forms are folding hunters (one or two blades), trappers, peanuts, Barlows, elephant toes, canoes, Texas toothpicks, Coke bottles, gun stocks, and Daddy Barlows. The decorative aspect also heavily influences prices.

Case

Case uses a numbering code for its knives. The first number (1-9) is the handle material; the second number (1-5) designates the number of blades; the third and fourth numbers (0-99) the knife pattern, stage (5), pearl (8 or 9) and bone (6) are the most sought handle materials. The most desirable patterns are 5165—folding hunters, 6185—doctors, 6445, scout, muskrat—marked muskrat with no number, and 6254—trappers. In the Case XX series, a symbol and dot code are used to designate a year.

Case, Nantaucket whaling scene, scrimshaw handle, **$160.**

3254, yellow composition, 4-1/8", stamped "XX," 1940-65 .... **150.00**

4200, white composition, 5-1/2", serrated master blade, melon tester, stamped "USA," 1965-70 ..... **125.00**

5265, stag, 5-1/4", saber ground, stamped "USA," 1965-70 ...... **100.00**

6265, 5-1/4", flat blade, stamped "Tested XX," green bone, 1920-40 .... **300.00**

8271, genuine pearl, 3-1/4", long pull, stamped "XX," 1940-65 ..... **450.00**

9265, imitation pearl, 5-1/4", flat blade, stamped "Tested XX," 1920-40 . **450.00**

420657, white composition, 3-3/8", "Office Knife" marked on handle, 1940-56 .... **100.00**

Ka-Bar (Union Cut. Co., Olean, NY)

The company was founded by Wallace Brown at Tidiote, PA, in 1892. It was relocated to Orlean, NY, in 1912. The products have many stampings, including Union (inside shield); UOR co.; Tidoute (variations); Union Cutlery Co. Olean, NY; Aklcut Olean, NY; Kenwell, Olean, NY, and Ka-Bar. The larger knives with a profile of a dog's head on the handle are the most desirable. Pattern numbers rarely appear on a knife prior to the 1940s.

6191L **600.00**

6260KF **120.00**

31187, two blades **185.00**

61161, light celluloid handle ... **130.00**

61187, Daddy Barlow **175.00**

Figural, English, lying dog, **$90.**

Keen Kutter (Simons Hardware, St. Louis, MO)

K1881, Barlow **85.00**

K1920 .... **300.00**

6354, Scout **125.00**

Remington

R293, Field and Stream Bullet, bone, long pull **1,800.00**

R953, toothpick, bone **250.00**

R3273, Cattle, brown bone, equal end **275.00**

Winchester

1621, Budding, 4-3/4", ebony .. **150.00**

2337, Senator, 3-1/4", pearl **125.00**

2703, Barlow, 3-1/2", brown bone **160.00**

3944, Whittler, 3-1/4", bone **225.00**

POISON BOTTLES

History: The design of poison bottles was meant to serve as a warning in order to prevent accidental intake or misuse of their poisonous contents. Their unique details were especially helpful in the dark. Poison bottles generally were made of colored glass, embossed with "Poison" or a skull and crossbones, and sometimes were coffin-shaped.

John H. B. Howell of Newton, New Jersey, designed the first safety closure in 1866. The idea did not become popular until the 1930s, when bottle designs became simpler and the user had to read the label to identify the contents.

Bowker's Pyrox Poison, colorless **30.00**

Chloroform, 5-3/4" h, green, ribbed, label, 1900 .... **80.00**

Vase, scenic, decorated with trees and lake, signed "E. Challinor," 1912-18 mark, 10" h, $1,100. Photo courtesy of Joy Luke Auctions.

Coffin, 3-1/2" h, cobalt blue, emb, 1890 . . . . **100.00**

Cylindrical, crosshatch dec, cobalt blue, flared mouth with stopper, smooth base, 6-1/4" h **250.00**

Diamond Antiseptics, 10-3/4" h, triangular shape, golden amber, emb **385.00**

Figural, skull, America, 1880-1900, cobalt blue, tooled mouth, smooth base, 2-7/8" h **500.00**

Imperial Fluid Co. Poison, one gallon, colorless **95.00**

Lysol, 3-1/4" h, cylindrical, amber, emb "Not To Be Taken" **12.00**

Mercury Bichloride, 2-11/16" h, rect, amber **18.00**

Not To Be Taken, dark amber, $15.

Norwich Coffin, 3-3/8" h, amber, emb, tooled lip **95.00**

Owl Drug Co., 3-3/8" h, cobalt blue, owl sitting on mortar **70.00**

Plumber Drug Co., 7-1/2" h, cobalt blue, lattice and diamond pattern **90.00**

Poison, 3-1/2" h, hexagonal, ribbed, cobalt blue **20.00**

Tinct Iodine, 3" h, amber, skull and crossbones **45.00**

POLITICAL ITEMS

History: Since 1800, the American presidency has been a contest between two or more candidates. Initially, souvenirs were issued to celebrate victories. Items issued during a campaign to show support for a candidate were actively being distributed in the William Henry Harrison election of 1840.

There is a wide variety of campaign items—buttons, bandannas, tokens, pins, etc. The only limiting factor has been the promoter's imagination. The advent of television campaigning has reduced the quantity of individual items, and modern campaigns do not seem to have the variety of materials that were issued earlier.

References: Herbert Collins, *Threads of History*, Smithsonian Institution Press, 1979; Theodore L. Hake, *Encyclopedia of Political Buttons, United States, 1896-1972* (1974), *Book II, 1920-1976* (1977), *Book III, 1789-1916* (1978), revised prices for all three books (1998) Americana & Collectibles Press, (P.O. Box 1444, York, PA 17405); ——, *Hake's Guide to Presidential Campaign Collectibles*, Wallace-Homestead, 1992; Margaret Brown Klapthor, *Official White House China: 1789 to the Present,* 2nd edition, Harry N. Abrams, Inc., 1999; Edward Krohn (ed.), *National Political Convention Tickets and Other Convention Ephemera*, David G. Phillips Publishing (P.O. Box 611388, N. Miami, FL 33161), 1996; Keith Melder, *Hail to the Candidate*, Smithsonian Institution Press, 1992; James W. Milgram, *Presidential Campaign Illustrated Envelopes and Letter Paper 1840-1872*, David G. Phillips Publishing (P.O. Box 611388, N. Miami, FL 33161), 1996; Edmund B. Sullivan, *American Political Badges and Medalets, 1789-1892*, Quarterman Publications, 1981; ——, *Collecting Political Americana*, Christopher Publishing House, 1991; Mark Warda, *100 Years of Political Campaign Collectibles*, Sphinx Publishing (P.O. Box 25, Clearwater, FL 34617), 1996; ——, *Political Campaign Stamps*, Krause Publications, 1998.

Periodicals: *Political Bandwagon*, P.O. Box 348, Leola, PA 17540; *Political Collector*, P.O. Box 5171, York, PA 17405.

Collectors' Clubs: American Political Items Collectors, P.O. Box 340339, San Antonio, TX 78234; Ford Political Items Collectors, 18222 Flower Hill Way #299, Gaithersburg, MD 20879; NIXCO, Nixon Collectors Organization, 975 Maunawili Cr, Kailua, HI 96734; Third Party & Hopefuls, 503 Kings Canyon Blvd., Galesburg, IL 61401.

Museums: National Museum of American History, Smithsonian Institution, Washington, DC; Western Reserve Historical Society, Cleveland, OH.

Additional Listings: See *Warman's Americana & Collectibles* for more examples.

Adviser: Theodore L. Hake.

Clothing button, Blaine and Logan, 3/4" d, brass, domed front with detail image of knight in armor, plumes on helmet, symbolizing Blaine's nickname "The Plumed Knight" **32.00**

Badge, William McKinley, 1896-1900, $75.

Cuff link, McKinley, real photo, brass frame, clear celluloid over sepia portrait, c1896 . . . . **18.00**

Earrings, Stevenson, silver luster metal, showing Adlai shoe sole . . **15.00**

Jugate, Hoover, black and white oval photos below brown eagle, red, white, and blue background, 1-1/4" d, $600. Photo courtesy of Hake's Americana & Collectibles.

Flicker, pin back

I Like Ike, blue and white, silver metal reverse **24.00**

Kennedy for President/He Will Win, black and white photo and slogan panels, dark blue metal reverse **28.00**

LBJ For The USA, multicolored picture on one panel, wording on other, encased in blue metal, bar pin on reverse. **8.00**

Framed photo, Cleveland, 1-1/4" h, emb brass frame, full luster, eagle and flag dec, sepia cardboard photo, stickpin reverse, c1888, similar to Hake #3200, but different pose **165.00**

Golf tee, Eisenhower, 1-1/2" x 2" red, white, and blue pack of three Ike golf tees **18.00**

Jugate

Ford-Reagan, black and white photos, white background, red top lettering, blue bottom lettering, red stars, pre-convention, 1976 . **35.00**

Goldwater/Miller, black and white photos in center, white background, red, white, and blue lettering **5.00**

Johnson-Humphrey, bluetone photos, red, white, and blue background, blue stars **8.00**

Let's Back Ike & Dick, 1-1/8" h, bluetone photo, red and white inscription, rare size, 1952 . **125.00**

McKinley and Roosevelt, 1-1/4", dark blue background, image of black and white working man's lunch pail, "A Full Dinner Bucket/Employment for Labor," background around

photos is dark, back paper with few light spots **110.00**

Parker & Davis, 13/16" d, red, white, and blue flag motif rim surrounding sepia photos, covered back . **70.00**

Reagan-Bush, Inauguration Day, black and white, large bluetone jugate center photo **18.00**

Lapel stud

Eisenhower, 3/4" h, brass, blue enamel background, "I Like Ike," needle post and clutch fastener **5.00**

Goldbug, 3/4" h white porcelain, "Sound Money" below bright gold image of bug accented by small green head, black legs, antenna **75.00**

Harrison, 1/18", white and blue enamel flag, white enamel background, blue enamel ribbon design with brass letters "R.L.U.S.," c1888 . . . . **12.00**

Hughes, red, white, and blue enamel shield on brass, fixed to brass lapel stud backing **18.00**

McKinley, diecut, white metal, black finish, cut-out circle surrounding portrait, c1896 . . . . **10.00**

McKinley/Hobart, Protection/Sound Money, center jugate photos, white background, red lettering, vertical center mark, 1896 . . . . **12.00**

Nixon-Lodge, 1-1/4" d, black and white photos outlined in gold shield, two red, white, and blue stripes, made by Pennsylvania Badge, used in PA, 1960 . . . **95.00**

Talked to Death, black, white, and light red, showing man in coffin, 1896 McKinley/Bryan campaign era **8.00**

Willkie, small brass stud, red, white, and blue enamel paint **4.00**

Matchbook

Humphrey For President, black and white photo of Humphrey on front, red, white blue HHH-Humphrey on back, full pack. **8.00**

Nixon's The One, red lettering, white background, unused. **5.00**

Mechanical flag, 1" x 1" brass flag, red, white, and blue enamel, flag front pulls open on spring, 1/2" celluloid cov real photo of T. Roosevelt **160.00**

Mechanical pin, Taft Presidential Chair, 2" h, vertical stickpin on reverse, slogan on mint brass luster chair back, mint brass luster legs, seat area in silver luster reads "Who Shall Occupy It," small tab at bottom seat edge pulls and

seat flies open to reveal sepia real photo, 1908 . . . . **235.00**

Medalet

Grant Memorial, brass hanger with eagle perched on crossed cannons, cannonballs below, white metal, portrait name, reverse with wreath surrounding dates of birth and 1885 death, some fading to silver luster **18.00**

Harrison, 1-1/2", white metal, name, portrait, and date of birth on front, reverse shows log cabin, flag, and cider barrel, inscription "The Peoples Choice/The Hero of Tippecanoe," small brass loop in rim hole, DeWitt #1840-13 . . **80.00**

Medallion

Humphrey, HHH-Humphrey, 3" d cream colored plastic, 9" l red, white, and blue fabric necklace **12.00**

"Wilson, The Man Of The Hour," 1" d silver luster medallion, loop at top, profile and name on front, slogan on reverse **38.00**

Perpetual calendar, Cleveland, 1-1/8" d, bright nickel-plated finish, 1884, metal loop at rim, Hendricks depicted in reverse, both men surrounded by tiny letters representing days of the week on an inner dial, inner dial now frozen in place **80.00**

Pin, Kennedy, 1-1/4" h, donkey, rhinestones, white metal, bright gold luster, emerald green rhinestones for ears, name in diecut letters below feet **24.00**

Pinback button

Bush 1992, 2" sq, center multicolored photo of Bush, red, white, and blue flag in background, red and blue lettering and stars on outer white background **12.00**

Carter Inauguration, black and white photos, red, white, and blue background **8.00**

Clinton-Gore, '92 Leadership For A Change, 2" x 3" multicolored, photo inserts of candidates in foreground of Capitol **6.00**

Coolidge and Dawes, 7/8" d, red, white, and blue blanket on white elephant, dark blue background **15.00**

Cox and Roosevelt, 5/8" d, white litho, Cox in dark red printed over "And Roosevelt" in dark blue **42.00**

Dewey, 1-5/8" d, God Bless America, 1944-1948, litho, red rim, black and white photo on pale gray . . . **24.00**

Dick Nixon for President, 7/8" d, litho, bluetone center photo, red, white, and blue stripe background, blue stars..........**5.00**

Draft Eisenhower for President, 1-1/4" d, red, white, and blue, bluetone photo, 1948 ......**12.00**

Goldwater for President, 1-1/8" litho, blue and white, bluetone photo, red slogan "A Choice For A Change" **8.00**

Harding, 5/8" d, browntone photo, white letters on blue rim **12.00**

Harding Coolidge GOP, 3/4", gold and blue, gray elephant in enter keystone **15.00**

Hoover, Speed Recovery, Re-Elect Hoover, 5/8" d, white letters, medium blue background...**10.00**

Hughes, 7/8" d, black and white photo surrounded by gold oval accent line, red, white, and blue flag, green wreath, red berries **38.00**

Johnson, 1-1/4" d, black and white photo, white background, blue and white lettering **4.00**

Kennedy for President, 7/8" d, black and white illus, red, white, and blue background, litho **8.00**

Landon/Knox, 7/8" d, yellow, brown, litho, yellow felt petal attachment **4.00**

McKinley, black and white photo, gold scrolls, red, white, and blue rim **24.00**

Our 35th President, John F. Kennedy, 1-3/4" d, red, white, and blue, black and white photo, issued for inauguration **22.00**

The Hatters McKinley & Hobart League, 3/4" d, gold lettering, red, white, and blue flag, cream background..........**18.00**

Roosevelt, FD, 2-1/2" d, full color illus, white circle background, c1944 ....**24.00**

Roosevelt, FD, 7/8" d, Rally Around Roosevelt, red, white, and blue, repeating letters "RRR" in center **35.00**

Roosevelt, Theodore, 7/8" d, black and white photos, multicolored flag, eagle, and gold star, from series from Baltimore Badge, 1904, scarce size **120.00**

Roosevelt, Theodore, Roosevelt Memorial Association, 7/8" d, white, dark brown, c1920 ....**20.00**

Smith, Alfred E. For President, 13/18" d, brown on white

background, brown rim edge, white lettering **10.00**

Vets for Ike, 1-1/8" d, dark blue background, white lettering ..**3.00**

Victory for Reagan, 2-1/4" d, multicolored dog on gray-blue background, black lettering..**8.00**

Willkie, 7/8", black and white real photo **14.00**

Wilson, For Me and Mine, 5/8" black and white, white letters on dark blue rim **18.00**

Postcard, Teddy Roosevelt and Asians, newspaper headline reads "Protestional, Californienne," satire, **$300.** *Photo courtesy of Postcards International.*

Press badge, 2" x 3", NBC News 72, red, white, and blue flag, white lettering on black background, cardboard reverse with clasp for attaching to pocket **12.00**

Ring, flicker, I'm For Barry, dark blue plastic, flicker top, blue slogan, bluetone photo **38.00**

Stickpin

Hoover, 1-3/4" x 2" red, white, and blue cloth covered, 1-1/4" w bar, pencil notation on back "60 Cts. Doz" **24.00**

McKinley, 3/4" finely detailed emb brass shell goldbug, 1" vertical stickpin, 1896..........**18.00**

McKinley, 1-7/8" h, cardboard photo, emb brass shell depicts five point star, 3/4" center cardboard photo of

McKinley, vertical stickpin on reverse **95.00**

Roosevelt, FD, 1-1/8" h white plastic shield, mounted black and white real photo **8.00**

Tab, unbent

Nixon, 1-1/2" h, yellow and dark blue, 1962 Governor........**8.00**

Roosevelt, FD, 7/8" d, red, white, and blue..........**4.00**

Wilkie, silver foil, red and blue metallic backgrounds, emb lettering "Watch Wilkie Win" ..**5.00**

Telephone dialer, Nixon-Lodge, 3" bar, deep blue plastic, rounded end, bright gold lettering **20.00**

Thimble, Sew It Up For Nixon-Lodge/ Experience Counts, 1" h, white plastic, red and blue lettering..........**8.00**

Tie bar

Agnew, 2-1/4" l, highly polished gold colored tie bar, spring clasp on reverse, white enamel circle on front inscribed "Vice President of the Unites States" surrounding VP seal in brass luster **20.00**

Landon, 2-1/2" l, silvered brass, enameled yellow and tan enamel sunflower mounted in center.**18.00**

Ronald Reagan, brass bar, facsimile signature in black presidential seal in full color..........**35.00**

Tie tac

John Kennedy, 2" l diecut white metal name, bright gold luster, reverse with tie tac and clutch **18.00**

Stevenson, 1" h sterling shoe sole with hole, needle post and clutch fastener..........**20.00**

Sheet music, "Taft March," full portrait of President Taft, crossed American flags, F. K. Root & Co. publishers, **$15.**

Watch chain charm, McKinley, 5/8" sq by 1/2" thick, glass cube, band surrounding side edge, small loop for fastening, front with black and white illus under glass, reverse with red, white, and blue flag design under glass, 1896 .... 75.00

Watch fob

Good Luck Taft, Our Choice Taft & Sherman, 1-5/8", emb metal, black finish, silver luster highlights, horseshoe design surrounds jugate high relief images......... 28.00

Roosevelt and Fairbanks 1904 Washington, 1-3/4" h, diecut brass, incised lettered accented in black 25.00

Teddy Roosevelt, 1-7/8", emb brass, high relief center portrait, orig luster, few tiny dark varnish dots around shoulder area...... 48.00

Young Democratic Clubs of America/First National Convention Kansas City, 1933, brass, raised lettering 10.00

POMONA GLASS

History: Pomona glass, produced only by the New England Glass Works and named for the Roman goddess of fruit and trees, was patented in 1885 by Joseph Locke. It is a delicate lead, blown art glass which has a pale, soft beige ground and a top one-inch band of honey amber.

There are two distinct types of backgrounds. First ground, made only from late 1884 to June 1886, was produced by making fine cuttings through a wax coating followed by an acid bath. Second ground was made by rolling the piece in acid-resisting particles and acid etching. Second ground was made in Cambridge until 1888 and until the early 1900s in Toledo, where Libbey moved the firm after purchasing New England Glass works. Both methods produced a soft frosted appearance, but fine curlicue lines are more visible on first-ground pieces. Some pieces have designs which were etched and then stained with a color. The most familiar design is blue cornflowers.

Do not confuse Pomona with Midwestern Pomona, a pressed glass with a frosted body and amber band.

References: Joseph and Jane Locke, *Locke Art Glass*, Dover Publications, 1987; Kenneth Wilson, *American Glass 1760-1930*, 2 vols., Hudson Hills Press and The Toledo Museum of Art, 1994.

Bowl, 4-1/2" d, 3" h, first ground, rich deep amber staining 275.00

Butter dish, cov, 4-1/2" h, 8" d underplate, first ground, gold stained acacia leaf dec, reeded curlicue handle 1,275.00

Celery vase, 6-1/8" h, 4-1/2" d, first ground, acacia leaf dec 550.00

Pitcher, Cornflower, first grind, light amber collar, 4-1/2" h, $490.

Champagne, 5" h, stemmed, second ground, amber staining 245.00

Creamer, second ground, Daisy and Butterfly, applied colorless handle, three applied colorless feet 275.00

Cruet, 7-1/4" h, first ground, orig ball stopper.................... 365.00

Finger bowl, first ground....... 75.00

Goblet, 6" h, first ground, little amber stain remains 115.00

Pitcher, 5-1/2" h, first ground, applied unstained handle, sq mouth.... 490.00

Punch cup

Cornflower, first ground, blue staining 145.00

Cornflower, second ground.. 110.00

Inverted Thumbprint, first ground, amber staining 85.00

Sauce boat, 6-3/8" l, 2-3/4" h, first grind, irid gold embellishments 285.00

Tankard pitcher, 6-3/4" h, first ground, optic diamond quilted body, gold stain on clear glass handle and upper border 385.00

Toothpick holder, triangular rim, amber stain at top 135.00

Tumbler

3-3/4" h, 2-5/8" d, Cornflower, second ground, DQ glass, honey amber stain top and bottom, rich blue stained flowers 145.00

4" h, Cornflower, second ground, blue tinted dec, gold tint rim, price for set of four............ 245.00

Vase

3" h, 6" w, fan, first ground, Cornflower, blue stained flower dec and violet spray.......... 250.00

6" h, first ground, rigaree around ruffled top and neck ring, etched waisted body, first ground, faded amber stain 215.00

PORTRAIT WARE

History: Plates, vases, and other articles with portraits on them were popular in the second half of the 19th century. Although male subjects, such as Napoleon or Louis XVI, were used, the ware usually depicts a beautiful, and often unidentified, woman.

A large number of English and Continental china manufacturers made portrait ware. Because most was hand painted, an artist's signature often is found.

Charger, 14" d, Marie Antoinette, sgd "Johner," dark green border, gilt scrolled and leaf dec, blue Austrian beehive mark.............. 275.00

Medallion

3-1/2" d, Gitana, sgd "Wagner," woman in drape, red cap, jeweled gilt bronze frame 925.00

3-1/2" d, Le Pensee, sgd "Wagner," jeweled gilt bronze frame.. 975.00

Plaque

2-3/4" d, round, profile bust of young woman in red scarf, sgd lower right "Leroux," French, early 20th C, 6-1/2" w, 8-5/8" h gilt metal mounted Empire Revival frame with crown above ribbon, columns, acanthus surround, topped by cornucopia in flat leaf wreath flanked by pairs of further cornucopia............. 850.00

6" x 4", La Poeme nach Coomans, portrait of women, one seated with scroll, other looking on, gilt highlights on jewelry, German 950.00

Plate, Wiener Frowen Schonhert, woman with fan and pearl necklace, surrounded by banded gilt decoration, rim decorated with gilt, blue enamel on cranberry ground, signed "H. Roldas," Austrian beehive mark, 9-1/2" d, gilt loss, $400. Photo courtesy of Sanford Alderfer Auction Co.

6" x 4", woman in white gown, pink drape, outstretched hand with flowers, gilt bronze frame, putti and garlands, minor scratches **725.00**

Left: plate, classically robed maiden in five lobed gilt cartouche, gilt flowers on burgundy field, signed "Wagner," Royal Vienna, late 19th C, 9-9/16" d, $1,050; right: portrait of Daphne, signed "Wagner," Royal Vienna, early 20th C, 8" d, $800. Photo courtesy of Freeman\Fine Arts of Philadelphia, Inc.

Plate

9-1/4" d, Lamballe, sgd "Wagner," woman with roses in her hair, floral gilt dec border, white ground, red Austrian beehive mark .. **1,165.00**

9-1/4" d, Parabere, sgd "Wagner," woman with flowers, floral and animal gilt dec border, blue-green ground, red Austrian beehive mark, wear to ground and gilt, repair to rim **825.00**

9-1/2" d, Anmuth, sgd "Greiner," woman in blue drape, floral and animal gilt dec panels, pink and burgundy ground, blue Austria beehive mark............**575.00**

9-1/2" d, Elisabeth-Konigin von England, sgd "Wagner," borders of Roman key, green garlands, red berries, white ground **600.00**

9-1/2" d, Lohengrin's Abschied, medial lovers, swan dec, gilt border, cobalt ground, incised Carlsbad mark, minor gilt loss **790.00**

9-1/2" d, Nach dem Ball, sgd "Wagner," borders of Roman key, green garlands, red berries, white ground................**785.00**

9-1/2" d, Napoleon I, sgd "Wagner," cobalt blue and pale blue band, cornucopia and urn ornamentation, inscribed "Made for Mrs. John Doyle" verso, minor gilt loss **970.00**

9-1/2" d, Traumerci, sgd "Wagner," young woman seated on trunk, boughs of flowers, heavily gilt border with urns and garlands, pale green ground, blue Austrian beehive mark, hairline, gilt loss **790.00**

9-1/2" d, white dog with ivory top cane, scalloped border, paneled blue band, gilt dec birds and medallions, Brownfield, craquelure in band, surface wear **285.00**

9-1/2" d, Wiener Frowen Schonhert, sgd "H. Roldas," woman with fan, pearl necklace, banded gilt dec, rim dec with gilt and blue enamel on cranberry ground, blue Austrian beehive mark, gilt loss **425.00**

9-1/2" d, woman with sheath of wheat, gilt dec floral band, pale green ground, scalloped edge, marked "RK" with crown .. **600.00**

10" d, Abend, sgd "F. Koller," mythological figures floating in clouds with bat, gilt and enameled border on cobalt ground .. **495.00**

10" d, Reflexion, sgd "Wagner," woman in red drape, scalloped reticulated border, heavy gilt Art Nouveau design, light blue jewels on cobalt blue ground, blue Dresden mark.........**1,210.00**

Punch bowl, 14-1/4" d, 8-3/4" h, Napoleonic scenes on outside and int., peacock blue borders, gilt leaves dec, four ftd claw base, marked "Bataille de Friedland, Combat de Heilsburg, Bataille d'Iena," imp "TK 2 41 06," gold crown over "N," base marked "Vienna, Austria," 3-1/2" hairline on edge of bowl **500.00**

Soup bowl, 9-1/2" d, Rinaldo & Armida, lovers in garden, soldiers looking on, paneled border, sections of animals and floral dec, pink and violet grounds, blue Austria beehive mark, gilt loss **275.00**

Tray, 9-1/2" sq, Napolean I, standing, looking left, left hand behind back exposing dress sword and medals, background of fine furniture and papers, gilt garland border, dark blue-green ground, fitted frame, sgd "Reseh," marked "Vienna, FD, Austria" **1,320.00**

Urn, cov, 15-1/2" h, double handles, "Mme de Montesson," central portrait of French woman wearing white wig, floral designs, reverse with floral dec, marked "2912, S-2," illegible ring mark, restored lid.......................**275.00**

Vase

4-3/4" h, bulbous, titled "Ariadne," sgd "Wagner," maroon ground, gilt floral dec, Austrian beehive mark **850.00**

6" h, portrait of woman, sgd "Erbluht," ivory ground, gilt medallions, pale blue enameled jewels, hairline, chip **525.00**

6-3/4" h, titled "Ruth," white ground, gilt dec, blue and pink enameling, obscured Dresden mark, restoration on base.......**245.00**

7" h, double handles, central portrait of woman, titled "Solitude," sgd "Wagner," brown opalescent ground, gilt dec, Austrian beehive mark **1,200.00**

8-1/2" h, Clementine, sgd "N. Kiesel," Art Nouveau form, green-brown mirrored ground, heavily gilt acanthus leaves and vines, bearing mark of Richard Klemm...............**1,690.00**

9" h, portrait of woman with conch shell to ear and flower, Art Nouveau form, blue ground fading to violet, gilt dec, enamel jewelling, mark of Erdmann Schlegelmilch, early 1900s, loss to jewels, wear to background............**485.00**

12" h, woman holding yellow roses, opalescent ground in shades of green and purple, gilt floral design, Dresden, wear to gilding **1,570.00**

13-1/8" h, French, Aesthetic Movement, third quarter 19th C, earthenware, portraits of ladies in exotic costumes, one sgd lower right "Leonard" in gilt border, reverse painted with landscape scenes, sides with royal blue stars outlined in gold on cobalt blue ground, two short gilt handles, ovoid foot, price for pr... **2,300.00**

POSTERS

History: Posters were a critical and extremely effective method of mass communication, especially in the period before 1920. Enormous quantities were produced, helped in part by the propaganda role posters played in World War I.

Print runs of two million were not unknown. Posters were not meant to be saved; they usually were destroyed once they had served their purpose. The paradox of high production and low survival is one of the fascinating aspects of poster history.

The posters of the late 19th and early 20th centuries represent the pinnacle of American lithography. The advertising posters of firms such as

Strobridge or Courier are true classics. Philadelphia was one center for the poster industry.

Europeans pioneered posters with high artistic and aesthetic content, and poster art still plays a key role in Europe. Many major artists of the 20th century designed posters.

References: George Theofiles, *American Posters of World War I*, Dafram House Publishers; Susan Theran (ed.), *Leonard's Annual Price Index of Posters & Photographs*, Auction Index (30 Valentine Park, Newton, MA 02165), 1995; Jon R. Warren, *Collecting Hollywood*, 3rd ed., American Collector's Exchange, 1994; Bruce Lanier Wright, *Yesterday's Tomorrow*, Taylor Publishing, 1993.

Periodicals and Internet Resources: *Plakat Journal*, Oskar-Winter Str. 3 D30160 Hannover, Germany; *Poster Guide*, http://www.posterguide.com.

Museum: Museé de la Publicité, 107 Rue de Rivoli, Paris, France.

Additional Listings: See *Warman's Americana & Collectibles* for more examples.

Adviser: George Theofiles.

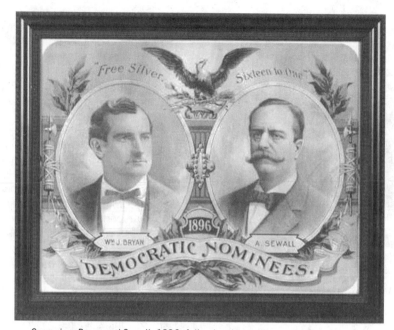

Campaign, Bryan and Sewell, 1896, full-color chromolithograph, oval black and white bust portraits of candidates, spread winged bald eagle sitting atop U.S. shield and arrows, and "Free Silver Sixteen to One" above laurel wreath and ribbon banner with ""Democratic Nominees" and "1896" below, light blue background, red band across center, 20-1/4" x 26-1/4" poster, mounted on acid free backing and framed, light even toning, $3,100. Photo courtesy of Cowan Historic Americana Auctions.

Advertising

Do It Electrically, "Comfort, Convenience, Efficiency in the Home...Save Fuel, Food, Time, Money -By Wire," image of angel holding electric motor, period electrical appliances, full color, blue background, expert restoration to edges, c1915, 27" x 35" **600.00**

Ediswan Electric Home Iron, full color, showing 1930s electric iron, c1935, 11" x 18" **60.00**

Ferry's Seeds, full-color image of pretty young lass amid towering hollyhocks, light fold lines, restoration to edges, thin tears, 1925, 21" x 28" **325.00**

Fire! Fire! Fire!, "Chicago Lost But J. Dearman of Knoxville, Penna. Continues to Roll Up, Bundle Up, and Box Up As Many Goods As Ever!" red and black, some replacement to border, Oct. 15, 1871, 22" x 27" **225.00**

Granite Iron Ware, paper, woman carrying milking pail, cow, "For Kitchen and Table Use," 12-1/2" x 28" . . . **75.00**

Lady Esther Face Cream, printed on board, beautiful young woman in oval vignette, "A Skin Food-An Astringent," c1920, 23 x 36" **325.00**

Kix Cereal, Lone Ranger 6-shooter ring, General Mills premium, "Only 15 cents plus Kix box top," c1948. 17" x 22" **225.00**

Popcorn Starch, packages and little girl, color litho, c1900, 10" x 13" . **200.00**

Richfield Gasoline, race driver in car, c1930, 39" x 53" **1,100.00**

Royal Portable Typewriter, dark green detailed manual portable typewriter against leafed red and green ground, c1940, 24" x 36" **285.00**

Waterman's Ideal Fountain Pen, paper, Uncle Sam at Treaty of Portsmouth, early 1900s, 41-1/2" x 19-1/2" **950.00**

Circus, Shows, and Acts

Barnum and Bailey Circus, Strobridge Litho, Co., "Jockey Races,"" 1908, 19" x 28" **900.00**

Downey Bros. Big 3 Ring Circus, "Leaps-Revival of that Astounding and Sensational exhibition," group of elephants, camels, and horses in line, aerial artist leaping overhead, audience background, c1925, 41" x 27" . . **125.00**

Hollywood Peep Show, burlesque strip revue, c1950, 27" x 41" . . . **150.00**

Hot From Harlem, black burlesque show, color, Anon, c1947, 22" x 28" **250.00**

Ringling Bros. Barnum & Bailey Liberty Bandwagon, color litho, ornate wagon with Merue Evans portrait, 1943, 30" x 19" **225.00**

Tim McCoy's Wild West, circle of riders around red circle, on canvas, 1938, 54" x 41" **900.00**

Magic

Buddha and Heartstone, Polish magician performing tricks, English and Polish text, c1914, 14" x 26" . . . **100.00**

Carter the Great-A Baffling Chinese Mystery—The Elongated Maiden, Otis Litho, "A pretty Chinese girl tied to a torture rack without seeming discomfort..," life-sized Chinese nobleman looking down on vignettes of complicated rack, stretched maiden, banshees, imps, devils, in color, c1920, 41" x 81" **650.00**

Friedlander Stock Magic, Adolph Friedlander #6966, smiling devil holds card-like vignettes of magic acts in one hand, wand in other, yellow ground, c1919, 14" x 19" **150.00**

Kar-Mi Swallows a Loaded gun Barrel, National, "Shoots a cracker from a man's head," Kar-Mi with gun in mouth blasts away at blindfolded assistant, crowd of turbaned Indians, 1914, 42" x 28" **350.00**

Movie

"African Queen," French release of classic Bogart and Hepburn film, color portraits of both above steamy jungle setting, c1960, 22" x 31" **150.00**

"Alias Boston Blackie," Columbia Pictures, Chester Morris, full color, 1942, 27" x 41" **100.00**

"Amazing Transparent Man," Miller Consolidated, D. Kennedy, Marguerite Chapman, sci-fi silhouette against blue, 1959, 27" x 41" **125.00**

"Anatomy of a Murder," Columbia, Saul Bass design, 1959, 27" x 41" **125.00**

"Atlantic City," Republic, Constance Moore, Jerry Colonna in drag, by James Montgomery Flagg, 1941, 14" x 36" **200.00**

"Blondie in the Dough," Columbia Pictures, Penny Singleton, Chick Young's Blondie cartoon film, full color, 1947, 27" x 41" **95.00**

"Bad Boy," James Dunn and Louise Fazenda, Fox, 1934, 27" x 41" . . **150.00**

"Buck Privates," Relart re-release, Bud Abbott, Lou Costello, the Andrews Sisters, full-color montage, 1953, 27" x 41" **95.00**

"Cheaters At Play," Thomas Meighan and Charlotte Greenwood, Fox, 1931, 27" x 41" **275.00**

"Double Danger," Preston Foster and Whitney Bourne, RKO, 1938, 27" x 41" **110.00**

"Dr. No," United Artist, Sean Connery, Ursula Andress, 1962, 27" x 41" . **325.00**

"False Paradise," Hopalong Cassidy, United Artists, 1947, 27" x 41" . . **125.00**

"Farmer's Daughter," RKO, Loretta Young, Joseph Cotton, Ethel Barrymore, Cotton kneeling to pick up blond Young in maid's outfit, 1947, 27" x 41" . . **125.00**

"Flipper," MGM, Chuck Connors, 1963 . . . . **20.00**

"Goodbye Mr. Chips," Robert Donat and Greer Garson, MGM, 1939, 27" x 41" **450.00**

"I'll Be Seeing You," Ginger Rogers, Joseph Cotton, and Shirley Temple, United Artists 1945, 27" x 41" . . . **150.00**

"Love Takes Flight," Bruce Cabot and Beatrice Roberts, Grand National, 1937, 22" x 28" **135.00**

"Mule Train," Columbia Pictures, Gene Autry, Champion, full-color portraits, 1950, 27" x 41" **150.00**

"New York, New York," United Artists, Robert Diniro, Liza Minnelli, 1977 **35.00**

"One-Eyed Jacks," Paramount, Marlon Brando, Karl Malden, full color, 1959, 27" x 41" **85.00**

"Pursuit of the Graf Spee," John Gregson and Anthony Quayle, Rank, c1955, 22" x 28" **150.00**

"Smoldering Fires," Pauline Frederick and Laura La Plante, Universal, 1925, 14" x 22" **125.00**

Political and patriotic

America Lets Us Worship As We Wish—Attend The Church Of Your Choice, for American Legion sponsored "Americanism Appreciation Month," full-color image of praying Uncle Sam, family at dinner table behind him, c1945, 20" x 26" **225.00**

Bridge of Peace, Venette Willard Shearer, anti-war poster from American Friends Service Committee, National Council to Prevent War, in color, children of all nations play beneath text of song of peace, c1936, 16" x 22" **125.00**

Carry On With Franklin D. Roosevelt, portrait in gravure, black letters against white ground, framed, 1936, 9" x 11" **15.00**

Let's Go! US Marines, by J. A. Thomason, 1942, 29" x 41", $275. Photo courtesy of George Theofiles.

Confidence, large color portrait of Roosevelt over yacht at sea, "Election Day was our salvation/Franklin Roosevelt is the man/Our ship will reach her destination/Under his command… Bring this depression to an end…," c1933, 18" x 25" **250.00**

United Nations Day, blue and white U.N. banner waves over airbrushed stylized brown and yellow globe, minor edge crumple, 1947, 22" x 23" . . **250.00**

Theater

Black Dwarf, Beck & Pauli Litho, Milwaukee, detailed stage set with nine strutting players, cat-like character, a knight, ladies, etc., folio fold, expert restoration to upper cream border, c1870, 28" x 21" **325.00**

Bringing Up Father, McManus, "Jiggs, Maggie, Dinty Moore-George McManus's cartoon comedy with music," early newspaper cartoon characters against New York skyline, c1915, 41" x 81" **425.00**

Claudine Clerice Fr, Collette Willy opera, full color, French, 1910, 26" x 35" **275.00**

Dangers of a Great City, National show Print, Chicago, play by Oliver North, men fighting in an office, gleaming stock ticker, "Give me the papers or I'll…," c1900, 21" x 28" **150.00**

Irene Vanbrugh, Ernest Hamlin Baker, stage actress dressed in purple, grays, yellow, green, and orange hat, fur-collared coat, c1910, 20" x 28" **350.00**

No No Nanette, Tony Gibbons, Theatre Mogador, Paris, European production of American musical, c1925, 15" x 22" **375.00**

Transportation

Air France—North Africa, Villemot, stylized imagery of mosques and minarets, lavenders, yellow, and blues against sky blue background, plane and Pegasus logo, c1950, 24" x 39" **225.00**

Motorlobene-Fano, Alfred Olsen, Danish auto race, car raising cloud of dust, 1922, 24" x 35" **1,250.00**

Royal Mail Atlantis, Padden, tourists in Royal mail motor launch approaching harbor village, mountains in background, c1923, 25" x 38" . . **675.00**

SS France, Bob Peak, launching of French ocean liner, champagne and confection in front of huge, night-lit bow of ship, 1961, 30" x 46" **450.00**

SS Michelangelo* and *SS Raffaello, Astor, detailed cutaway of Italian ocean liners, designed for use in travel office, printed on plasticized stock, metal frame, 1964, 54" x 22" **300.00**

SS Rex, P Klodic, advertisement for Italian ocean liner, designed for use in travel office, framed, c1936, 40" x 29" **750.00**

Travel

Arizona—Fly TWA, Austin Briggs, full-color western lass in 1950s style, c1955, 25" x 40" **300.00**

Boston—New Haven Railroad, Nason, full color, stylized montage of Historic Boston by day and night, faint folio folds, c1938, 28" x 42" **275.00**

Britain in Winter, Terence Cuneo, color rendering of horseman, hunters, and tourists outside rustic inn, 1948, 19" x 29" **125.00**

Come to Ulster, Norman Wilkinson, sailboats and fishermen in front of lighthouse, full color, c1935, 50" x 40" **450.00**

Hawaii—United Air Lines, Feher, stylized wahini, island behind her, full color, c1948, 25" x 40" **650.00**

Palace Hotel Wengen, Klara Borter, hotel in foothills of Alps, 1928, 27" x 40" **800.00**

Paris, Paul Colin, doves floating above stylized Eiffel tower and Arc de Triumph, 1946, 24" x 39" **600.00**

World War I

Call to Duty—Join the Army for Home and Country, Cammilli, recruiting image of Army bugler in front of unfurled banner, 1917, 30" x 40" **325.00**

Clear the Way!, Howard chandler Christy, Columbia points the way for Naval gun crew, c1918, 20" x 30" **250.00**

Follow the Flag—Enlist in the Navy, James Daugherty, sailor plants flag on shore, 1917, 27" x 41" **450.00**

Man the Ships, Enroll Here for the Merchant Marines, bald eagle flying towards sunset over fleet of ships, artwork by James Daugherty, 30" x 20", slight fold weakness **135.00**

Treat 'Em Rough—Jon The Tanks, A. Hutaf, window card, electric blue-black cat leaping over tanks in fiery battle, white border, c1917, 14" x 22" . . **900.00**

You Wireless Fans—Help The Navy Get A Hun Submarine—A Thousand Radio Men Wanted, C. B. Falls, wireless operator reaching up to grab lightening bolt, starry night background, blue, green, red, and white, 1918, 27" x 44" **550.00**

Which? Soldier Or Mechanic, L.H., "Enlist in the 57th Engineers (Inlaid Waterways) and Be Both…Camp Laurel, Maryland," 1918, 18" x 23" **200.00**

Will You Supply Eyes For The Navy? Gordon Grant, "Navy Ships Need Binoculars and Spy-Glasses…Tag Each Article with Your Name and Address, Mail to Hon. Franklin D. Roosevelt, Asst. Sec'y of Navy,…" image of Naval captain ready with blindfold on stormy deck, gun crew at ready behind him, 1918, 21" x 29" **625.00**

POT LIDS

History: Pot lids are the lids from pots or small containers which originally held ointments, pomades, or soap. Although some collectors want both the pot and its lid, lids alone are more often collected. The lids frequently are decorated with multicolored underglaze transfers of rural and domestic scenes, portraits, florals, and landmarks.

The majority of the containers with lids were made between 1845 and 1920 by F. & R. Pratt, Fenton, Staffordshire, England. In 1920, F. & R. Pratt merged with Cauldon Ltd. Several lids were reissued by the firm using the original copper engraving plates. They were used for decoration and never served as actual lids. Reissues by Kirkhams Pottery, England, generally have two holes for hanging. Cauldon, Coalport, and Wedgwood were other firms making reissues.

Marks: Kirkhams Pottery reissues are often marked as such.

References: Susan and Al Bagdade, *Warman's English & Continental Pottery & Porcelain*, 3rd ed., Krause Publications, 1998; A. Ball, *Price Guide to Pot-Lids and Other Underglaze Multicolor Prints on Ware*, 2nd ed., Antique Collectors' Club, 1991 value update.

Note: Sizes given are for actual pot lids; size of any framing not included.

Arctic Expedition, T. J. & J. Mayer, multicolored, 3" d, rim chip **320.00**

Bale's Mushroom Savoury, white glaze, brown and black transfer, 3-1/8" d, orig base **95.00**

Bloater Paste, black label, white ironstone, 4-1/2" d, marked "England" **45.00**

Burgess's Genuine Anchovy Paste, white glaze, brown and black transfer, 3-1/4" d, shallow chips on reverse **50.00**

Cold Cream, white glaze, brown and black transfer, 2-1/2" d **40.00**

Dr. Hassall's Hair Restorer, 1-3/4" d **250.00**

Dublin Industrial Exhibition, multicolored, 3-3/4" d **65.00**

Embarking For The East, Pratt, multicolored, 4-1/8" d, orig jar . . **125.00**

Golden Eye Ointment, white glaze, brown and black transfer, 1-3/4" d **50.00**

Hazard, Hazard & Co., Violet Cold Cream, 1150 Broadway New York, white glaze, brown transfer, 2-3/4" d . **210.00**

Jules Hauel, Saponaeceous Shaving Compound, 120 Chestnut St., Philadelphia, white glaze, red transfer, 4" d, minor staining, orig base . **190.00**

Hide and Seek, multicolored, 4" d, minor chips on reverse **75.00**

Morris's Imperial Eye Ointment **200.00**

Mrs. Ellen Hale's Celebrated Heal All Ointment, black on white, 4" d . **350.00**

Persuasion, multicolored, 4-1/8" d **160.00**

Queen Victoria on Balcony, T. J. & J. Mayer, large. **275.00**

Roussels's Premium Shaving Cream Philadelphia, white glaze, gray transfer, 3" d, minor age line in rim of lid, orig base **220.00**

The Late Prince Consort, 4-1/8" d, $250.

The Sportsman, multicolored, 4-1/8" d, $90.

Tam O' Sahnger and Souter Johnny, 4" d, framed **275.00**

The Rivals, multicolored, 4" d, minor chips on reverse **85.00**

View of Windsor Castle, Pratt, 6-1/2" d **170.00**

Walmer Castle, Kent, Tatnell & Son, 4-1/2" d **215.00**

PRATT WARE

PRATT

PRATT
FENTON

History: The earliest Pratt earthenware was made in the late 18th century by William Pratt, Lane Delph, Staffordshire, England. From 1810 to 1818, Felix and Robert Pratt, William's sons, ran their own firm, F. & R. Pratt, in Fenton in the Staffordshire district. Potters in Yorkshire, Liverpool, Sunderland, Tyneside, and Scotland copied the products.

The wares consisted of relief-molded jugs, commercial pots and tablewares with transfer decoration, commemorative pieces, and figures and figural groups of both people and animals.

Marks: Much of the early ware is unmarked. The mid-19th century wares bear several different marks in conjunction with the name Pratt, including "& Co."

References: Susan and Al Bagdade, *Warman's English & Continental Pottery & Porcelain*, 3rd ed., Krause Publications, 1998; John and Griselda Lewis, *Pratt Ware 1780-1840*, Antique Collectors' Club, 1984.

Museums: City Museum & Art Gallery, Stoke-On-Trent, England; Fitzwilliam Museum, Cambridge, England; Potsdam Public Museum, Potsdam, NY; Royal Pavilion Art Gallert & Museum, Brighton, England; Royal Scottish Museum, Edinburgh, Scotland; Victoria & Albert Museum, London, England; William Rockhill Nelson Gallery of Art, Kansas City, MO.

Additional Listings: Pot Lids.

Creamer, 5-1/4" h, cow and milkmaid, yellow and black sponged cow, underglaze enamels, translucent green stepped rect base, horns chipped **450.00**

Cup plate, 3-1/8" d, Dalmatian, white, black spots **95.00**

Figure, 5-1/2" h, Summer, pearlware, green, brown, and yellow ochre, chip on base **385.00**

Jar, 7-3/4" h, molded oval panels of peacocks in landscapes, blue, brown, green, and ochre, lower section with vertical leaves, band of foliage on rim, c1790 . . . . **620.00**

Jug

7-3/4" h, large oval molded reserve, exotic barnyard fowl, still leaf-tip band at edge of reverse, molded rim band with flowering branches, base with long stiff leaves alternating with slender flowering branches, polychrome enamel highlights, c1800 . . . . **1,450.00**

8" h, molded leaves at neck and base, raised and polychrome painted hunting scene on colored ground, c1800 . . . . **750.00**

Miniature, 4-3/4" l, dish, center molded with spring of two ochre plums, green leaf, brown stem, feather molded rim, underglaze blue edging, small rim chip, c1800 . . . . **350.00**

Mug, 4" h, colorful tavern scene transfer **95.00**

Mustard jar, cov, dark blue hunt scene, tan ground **75.00**

Pitcher, molded form, green, yellow, orange, and brown enamel decoration, 5-7/8" h, $375.

Pitcher

5-5/8" h, molded figures on sides, leaves at rim and base, one side with Toby Philpots, other with classical warrior, green, gold, dark brown, and cobalt blue, flakes on base and handle, short hairline on spout **675.00**

6-1/8" h, molded hunt scene with riders and dogs chasing rabbit, cobalt blue, dark brown, green, and gold, molded oak leaves and acorns at rim and shoulder, leaves on base, blue feather edge spout and handle **935.00**

Plaque, 6-1/4" x 7-1/4", Louis XVI portrait, oval form, beaded border, polychrome enamels, c1793, rim nicks, glaze wear **900.00**

Plate, 9" d, Haddon Hall, classical figure border **120.00**

Tea caddy, 6-1/4" h, rect, raised figural panels front and back, fluted and yellow trimmed lid, blue, yellow, orange, and green dec **350.00**

PRINTS

History: Prints serve many purposes. They can be a reproduction of an artist's paintings, drawings, or designs, but often are an original art form. Finally, prints can be developed for mass appeal rather than primarily for aesthetic fulfillment. Much of the production of Currier & Ives fits this latter category. Currier & Ives concentrated on genre, urban, patriotic, and nostalgic scenes.

References: Jay Brown, *The Complete Guide To Limited Edition Art Prints*, Krause Publications, 1999; William P. Carl, *Currier's Price Guide to American and European Prints at Auction*, 3rd ed., Currier Publications, 1994; Karen Choppa, *Bessie Peace Gutmann*, Schiffer Publishing, 1998; Karen Choppa and Paul Humphrey, *Maud Humphrey*, Schiffer Publishing, 1993; Max Allen Collins and Drake Elvgren, *Elvgren: His Life & Art*, Collectors Press, 1998; Erwin Flacks, *Maxfield Parrish Identification & Price Guide*, 3rd ed., Collectors Press, 1998; Patricia L. Gibson, *R. Atkinson Fox & William M. Thompson Identification & Price Guide*, Collectors Press, 1994; Michael J. Goldberg, *Maxfield Parrish Vignettes*, Collectors Press, 1998; William R. Holland, Clifford P. Catania, and Nathan D. Isen, *Louis Icart*, Schiffer Publishing, 1994; William R. Holland and Douglas L. Congdon-Martin, *Collectible Maxfield Parrish*, Schiffer Publishing, 1993; Robert Kipp, *Currier's Price Guide to Currier & Ives Prints*, 3rd ed., Currier Publications, 1994; Stephanie Lane, *Maxfield Parrish*, L-W Book Sales, 1993; Coy Ludwig, *Maxfield Parrish*, 2nd ed., Schiffer Publishing, 2000; Ian Mackenzie, *British Prints*, Antique Collectors' Club; Rita C. Mortenson, *R. Atkinson Fox, His Life and Work*, Vol. 1 (1991, 1994 value update), Vol. 2 (1992), L-W Book Sales; Norman I. Platnick, *Coles Philips*, published by author (50 Brentwood Road., Bay Shore, NY 11706); Tina Skinner, *Harrison Fisher: Defining the American Beauty*, Schiffer Publishing, 1999; Kent Steine and Frederick B. Taraba, *J. C. Leyendecker Collection*, Collectors Press, 1996; Susan Theran and Katheryn Acerbo (eds.), *Leonard's Annual Price Index of Prints, Posters & Photographs*, Auction Index, published annually; Naomi Welch, *The Complete Works of Harrison Fisher Illustrator*, Images of the Past, 1999.

Periodicals: *Art On Paper*, 39 E. 78th St., #601, New York, NY 10021; *Dali Collectors Quarterly*, 153232 Antioch St., Suite 108, Pacific Palisades, CA 90272; *Illustrator Collector's News*, P.O. Box 1958, Sequim, WA 98382; *Journal of the Print World*, P.O. Box 978, Meredith, NH 03253, http://www.journaloftheprintworld.com; *Print Collector's Newsletter*, 119 East 79th St., New York, NY 10021.

Collectors' Clubs: American Antique Graphics Society, 5185 Windfall Road, Medina, OH 44256; American Historical Print Collectors Society, P.O. Box 201, Fairfield, CT 06430, http://www.ahpcs.org; Gutmann Collector Club, P.O. Box 4743, Lancaster, PA 17604; Prang-Mark Society, P.O. Box 306, Watkins Glen, NY 14891; Print Club of Albany, P.O. Box 6578, Albany, NY 12206-0578.

Museums: American Museum of Natural History, New York, NY; Audubon Wildlife Sanctuary, Audubon, PA; John James Audubon State Park and Museum, Henderson, KY; Museum of the City of New York, NY; National Portrait Gallery, Washington, DC; Salvador Dali Museum, St. Petersburg, FL.

Reproduction Alert: The reproduction of Maxfield Parrish prints is a continuing process. New reproductions look new, i.e., their surfaces are shiny and the paper crisp and often pure white. The color on older prints develops a mellowing patina. The paper often develops a light brown to dark brown tone, especially if it is acid based or was placed against wooden boards in the back of a frame.

Size is one of the keys to spotting later reproductions. Learn the correct size for the earliest forms. Be alert to earlier examples that have been trimmed to fit into a frame. Check the dimensions before buying any print.

Carefully examine the edges within the print. Any fuzziness indicates a later copy. Also look at the print through a magnifying glass. If the colors separate into dots, this indicates a later version.

Apply the same principles described above for authenticating all prints, especially those attributed to Currier & Ives. Remember, many prints were copied soon after their period introduction. As a result, reproductions can have many of the same aging characteristics as period prints.

Additional Listings: See Wallace Nutting.

Appel, Karel, Nu, color litho on paper, sgd "Appel" in pencil lower right numbered "44/50" in pencil lower left, 30" x 22-1/4", framed **520.00**

Arms, John Taylor, Rodez/The Tower of Notre Dame, etching on paper, edition of 120 plus six trial proofs, sgd and dated "John Taylor Arms-1927" in pencil lower right, inscribed "Arms 1926" and "Rodez 1926" in the plate, 11-7/8" x 4-7/8", framed **230.00**

Currier & Ives, Home Sweet Home, carved walnut frame, 26" x 34", **$465.** *Photo courtesy of Joy Luke Auctions.*

Baldridge, Cyrus LeRoy, Grand Canyon, etching on paper, 1938, sgd, dated, and dedicated in pencil lower right, titled in pencil lower left, 15-3/4" x 11-3/4" plate size, framed **350.00**

Beal, Gifford, Rowboats, Central Park, etching on paper, sgd "Gifford Beal" in pencil lower right, indistinctly inscribed in pencil lower left, 7-3/4" x 9-7/8" plate size, framed **375.00**

Benson, Frank Weston

Geese Alighting, drypoint on paper, 1916, second of two published states, sgd "Frank W. Benson" in pencil lower left, dated in the plate lower left, numbered "44" in pencil lower right, 9-3/4" x 8" plate size, framed **1,035.00**

Marshes at Evening, etching on paper, 1918, published edition of 150, sgd "Frank W. Benson" in pencil lower left, numbered "57" in pencil lower right, identified from Philadelphia gallery label on reverse, 8-3/4" x 10-7/8" plate size, framed **815.00**

Benton, Thomas Hart, lithograph on paper, sgd "Benton" in pencil and in matrix, published by Associated American Artists, identified from AAA label affixed to mat

Edge of Town, 1938, edition of 250, 8-7/8" x 10-3/4", full sheet with deckled edges, framed
. . . . **1,670.00**

Homestead, 1938, edition of 250, 10-1/4" x 13", matted **980.00**

Rainy Day, 1938, edition of 250, 8-3/4" x 13-1/4", full sheet with deckled edges, framed . . **1,100.00**

Chagall, Marc, The Cello, color litho on wove paper, sgd "Marc Chagall" in pencil lower right, numbered "38/50" in pencil ll., 13-1/2" x 9-3/4", framed
. . . . **5,750.00**

Chase, W. Corwin, color woodcut on paper, sgd and dated "W. Corwin Chase 27" lower right, titled lower left, identified on label "Summerland" on mat, 12-1/2 x 8-1/2" image size, 1/4" or more margins, matted **920.00**

Currier & Ives, hand-colored lithograph

A Crack Team at a Smashing Gait, C#1282, set of carriage horses breaking through toll gate, glued on, minor surface wear, stains, some edge damage, 27-1/2" w, 20-1/43" h, contemporary 32-1/4" w, 25" h frame **770.00**

American Country Life May Morning, C#121, two horseback riders

passing mansion, light staining, 28" w, 21-13/16" h, matted, contemporary 32-1/2" w, 26-5/8" gilt frame **1,100.00**

American Fruit Piece, C#161, large folio, gray tinted background, bright colors, some edge damage and stains, 30" w, 22" h, matted, contemporary 36" w, 29" h frame
. . . . **1,210.00**

American Homestead Summer, C#171, edge tears, damage to sky area, 15-3/8" w, 11-1/8" h, matted and framed, 19-1/2" w, 16-3/4" gold repainted frame with some repair
. . . . **110.00**

American Homestead Winter, C#172, stains, margins trimmed to 9" x 12", repainted old molded frame, 10-1/2" x 13-5/8" **75.00**

Siege of Vera Cruz March 1947, C#5512, partially colored in blue, green, and yellow, minor stains and edge damage, matted and framed, 21" w, 17-1/2" h **425.00**

Skating Scene-Moonlight, C#556, couples on large moonlit lake, margins trimmed, minor edge damage, two tears at top into image, 14" w, 10-1/4" h, matted, contemporary 20-3/4" w, 17" h frame **660.00**

The Great West, C#2658, cropped at edge of image, glued to backing paper, title and signature lines added, 16-15/16" w, 10-3/4" h, contemporary 20-3/4" w, 16-3/4" h frame **220.00**

The Home of Evangeline, C#2863, panoramic view, margins trimmed, 27-5/8" w, 21-13-16" h, matted with 31-3/4" w, 26-3/8" h wormy chestnut frame **880.00**

The Old Farm House, C#4557, winter scene, man riding in horse drawn sleigh, 10-3/8" x 14", added bottom margin, new title, 16-3/4" x 20-3/4" Victorian walnut molded frame
. . . . **220.00**

Curry, John Steuart, John Brown, litho on paper, 1939, edition of 250, published by Associated American Artists, sgd "John Steuart Curry" in pencil lower right, initialed and dated in the matrix, titled in pencil lower left, 13-3/4" x 11", framed **2,760.00**

Endicott & Co, Hambletonian, 1865, identified within matrix, chromolithograph on paper, 20-1/2" x 26", framed **230.00**

Gearhart, Frances Hammel, color woodcut on paper, sgd "Frances H. Gearhart" in pencil lower right, titled or numbered in pencil lower left, identified on label on mat

A Tatoosh Vista, 10-1/4" x 7-1/2" image size, 1/2" or more margins, matted **1,495.00**

Geraniums, 8" x 4-1/4" image size, 1/4" or more margins, matted **575.00**

The Peach Orchard, 9" x 10" image size, 1/2" or more margins, matted **2,070.00**

The Wave, 7-3/4" x 4-3/4" image size, 1/4" or more margins, matted **690.00**

Hall, Edith Emma Dorothea, Still Life/Vegetables, color woodcut on paper, sgd and dated "Emma Hall '54" in pencil lower right, 9-1/4" x 7-1/2", matted **115.00**

Hundertwasser, Friedensreich, Pacific Steamer, color woodcut on paper, 1986, dated, numbered and inscribed "989/999 ©...868A Auckland 3 March 1986" in ink lower left, sgd with various chops lower right, 20-1/2" x 15-3/4" image size, framed, deckled edges **2,875.00**

Hyde, Helen, Moon Bridge at Kameido, color woodcut on paper, sgd "Helen Hyde" in pencil lower right, monogram and clover seals lower left, numbered "67" in pencil lower left, inscribed "Copyright, 1914, by Helen Hyde" in the block lower left, 13-1/4" x 8-7/8", framed **460.00**

Icart, Louis, color etching with aqua tint and hand coloring on paper, identified within the plate, subtle toning

Coursing, III, 1929, sgd "Louis Icart" in pencil lower right, artist's drystamp lower left, 15-3/4" x 25-3/4" plate size, framed **1,840.00**

La Belle au Bois Dormant, 1927, sgd "Louis Icart" in pencil lower right, artist's drystamp lower left, oval format, 15-1/4" x 18-3/4" . **1,035.00**

La Robe De Chine, 1926, sgd "Louis Icart" in pencil lower right, inscribed "Ep d'A" in pencil lower left, artist's dry stamp lower left, 15-3/4" x 19-1/4" plate size, framed **1,265.00**

L'Attende, 1927, sgd "Louis Icart" in pencil lower right, inscribed "E. 156" in pencil lower left, artist's dry stamp lower left, oval format,

14-3/4" x 19-1/2" plate size, framed **1,035.00**

L'Oiseau Preferere, 1925, sgd "Louis Icart" in pencil lower right, inscribed "253" in pencil lower left, oval format, 14-1/2" x 19" plate size, framed, unobtrusive mat stain **920.00**

Petite Prisonniere, 1924, sgd "Louis Icart" in pencil lower right, inscribed "229" in pencil lower left, oval format, 15-1/2" x 19-1/4" plate size, framed **1,265.00**

Kellogg, The Farmer's Pet, girl in pink dress, holding yellow, blue, and red rooster, light stains, margin damage, 12-1/4" w, 16" h, period paint dec frame **415.00**

Kirmse, Marguerite, And Who Are You, etching and drypoint on paper, sgd "Marguerite Kirmse" in pencil lower right, titled in pencil lower left, 8-1/4 x 11-1/4", framed **420.00**

Kent, Rockwell, Hero, litho on paper, sgd "Rockwell Kent" in pencil lower right, 12-1/8" x 9", framed **345.00**

Landeck, Armin, Shadow, litho on paper, 1932, sgd "Landeck" in pencil lower right, numbered "1/10" in pencil lower left, annotated along lower margin, 10-7/8" x 9-1/8", framed **1,100.00**

Lewis, Martin, drypoint on laid paper

Chance Meeting, 1940/41, sgd "Martn Lewis" in pencil lower right, initialed in the plate lower left, inscribed with title in pencil lower left, 10-1/2" x 7-1/2", matted **4,370.00**

Down to the Sea at Night, 1929, sgd "Martin Lewis-imp" in pencil lower right, sgd in the plate lower left, inscribed with title in pencil lower left, several partial watermarks, 7-7/8" x 12-7/8", matted . . **3,115.00**

Marin, John, La Cathedral de Meaux, 1907, etching on Arches wove paper with watermark, sgd "...de J. Marin" in pencil lower center, sgd and dated within the plate, 8-1/2" x 6-1/8" plate size, matted, deckled edges on two sides **350.00**

Marsh, Reginald, Old Paris Night Street with Two Girls, litho on chine collé, sgd "Reginald Marsh" in pencil lower right, sgd and dated within the matrix, inscribed "30 proofs" in pencil lower left, 12-3/4" x 8-7/8" image size, framed **1,150.00**

Miller, Lilian May, Rain Blossoms, Japan, 1928, color woodcut on paper,

sgd, titled, and dated "Lilian Miller/1928..." in ink lower left, inscribed "(Edition A)" in ink lower right, monogrammed in the block lower left, 9-3/4" x 14-1/2", matted **815.00**

Pissarro, Camille, "Marche aux Legumes, a Pontoise," 1891, etching with squat int printed in brown on paper, second state, stamped initials below the plate, numbered "30/46" in pencil lower right, 10" x 7-7/8" plate size, deckled edges, subtle mat toning and soiling **1,840.00**

Riggs, Robert, lithograph on wove paper, sgd "Robert Riggs," in pencil lower right and within the matrix, titled in pencil lower left

Clown Acrobats, 1934, dedicated in pencil lower center, 14-3/8" x 19", matted **400.00**

On the Lot, c1934, 12-1/4" x 17-3/4", matted **750.00**

Ripley, Aiden Lassell, Flight Woodcock, etching on paper, sgd "A. Lassell Ripley" in pencil lower right, titled with copyright mark in pencil lower left, 8-7/8" x 12" plate size, framed **1,610.00**

Roth, Ernest David, Florentine Roofs, Florentine, etching on laid paper with "G" watermark, sgd and dated "Ernest D. Roth 1912" in pencil lower center, titled dated and inscribed "Trial Proof" in pencil lower left, 10-1/2" x 10-3/8", matted, soiling, breaks to hinges **315.00**

Sachse, View of Washington City, Capitol building in foreground, Washington monument in back, colored lithograph, marked "Lith. & Print by E. Sacshe & Co., Baltimore, MD," stains and edge tears, 36" w, 28" h . . . **700.00**

Sloan, John, Washington Arch, etching on paper, sgd "John Sloan" in pencil lower right, sgd and dated within the plate lower right, titled in pencil lower left, 7-3/4" x 4-3/4", framed. . . **1,265.00**

Sterner, Albert Edward, The Reveil, etching with drypoint on wove paper with watermark, sgd "Albert Sterner" in pencil lower right, numbered "Ed. 250" in pencil lower left, annotated within lower margin, 8-7/8" x 7" plate size, matted **325.00**

Prang & Mayer, publishers, J. F.A. Cole, delineator and lithographer, "New Bedford, Massachusetts," identified in inscriptions in the matrix, hand coloring, 16" x 32" image size, framed, repaired tears and punctures, scattered fox marks, staining, light toning **865.00**

Vogt, C H., View of the City of New Bedford, Massachusetts, 1876, identified in inscriptions in the matrix, 22" x 33" image size, framed, tear at left margin, scattered fox marks, overall toning **525.00**

Welliver, Neil G., Shadow from Zeke's, color screen print on paper, sgd "Welliver" in pencil lower right, numbered "116/144" lower left, identified on label on reverse, 36" x 36-1/4", framed **920.00**

Wengenroth, Stow, Great Horned Owl, litho on paper, 1960, sgd "Stow Wengenroth" in pencil lower right, numbered "Ed./50" in pencil lower left, titled and annotated lower left, 15-1/4" x 11-3/4", matted, deckled edges on two sides, mat and other toning. . . . **575.00**

Whistler, James Abbott McNeill

Billingstate, c1859, etching with drypoint on paper, sgd and identified within the plate, 6" x 9" plate size, framed, rippling, minor creases **1,035.00**

Fumette, c1858, etching on paper, sgd and identified within the plate, identified on label from Frederick Keppel, NY, on reverse, 6-1/2" x 4-1/4", framed, rippling . . . **1,495.00**

Grant Wood, Seed Time & Harvest, signed, 1937, $325.

Wood, Grant, published by Associated American Artists

Tree Planting Group, litho on paper, sgd "Grant Wood-1937" in pencil lower right, 8-3/8" x 10-7/8", matted **4,025.00**

Vegetables, 1938, litho with hand coloring on paper, sgd "Grant Wood" in pencil lower right, identified on label from AAA on reverse, 7" x 9-1/2", framed **550.00**

PRINTS, JAPANESE

History: Buying Japanese woodblock prints requires attention to detail and abundant knowledge of the subject. The quality of the impression (good, moderate, or weak), the color, and condition are critical. Various states and strikes of the same print cause prices to fluctuate. Knowing the proper publisher's and censor's seals is helpful in identifying an original print.

Most prints were copied and issued in popular versions. These represent the vast majority of the prints found in the marketplace today. These popular versions should be viewed solely as decorative since they have little monetary value.

A novice buyer should seek expert advice before buying. Talk with a specialized dealer, museum curator, or auction division head.

The following terms are used to describe sizes: chuban, 7-1/2 x 10 inches; hosoban, 6 x 12 inches; and oban, 10 x 15 inches. Tat-e is a vertical print; yoko-e a horizontal one.

Reference: Sandra Andacht, *Collector's Value Guide to Japanese Woodblock Prints*, Krause Publications, 2000.

Collectors' Club: Ukiyo-E Society of America, Inc., FDR Station, P.O. Box 665, New York, NY 10150, http://www.ukiyo-e.org.

Periodical: Orientalia Journal, P.O. Box 94, Flushing, NY 11363-0094, http://members.aol.com/Orientalia/index.html.

Museum: Honolulu Academy of Fine Arts, Honolulu, HI.

Note: The listings include the large amount of detail necessary to determine value. Condition and impression are good unless indicated otherwise.

A Beauty, toned impression, **$40.**
Photo courtesy of Joy Luke Auctions.

Album

Toyokuni III, Kuniyoshi, Hiroshige, mostly from series *Ogura Imitations of the One Hundred Poets* and *Keniyshi Genji* **2,645.00**

Utamaro, Tokoyuni, Koyomine, Eizan, and Kuniyosu, 18 prints of women, trimmed, toned, some stains and wear **2,300.00**

Chikanobu, framed triptych of women by lake, c1890, good impression, somewhat faded **125.00**

Eishi, four courtesans in elaborate kimonos, 1790s, framed, good impression, somewhat faded . . **345.00**

Eizan

Courtesan at her mirror, c1810, framed, good impression and color **290.00**

Courtesan in elaborate kimono with her kamuro, c1810, framed, good impression and color **290.00**

Harunobu, pillar print of woman carrying bucket, framed, very good impression, horizontal creases and tears **345.00**

Hasui

Evening Snow, Mukojima, boats and buildings by lake covered in snow, good impression, framed . . **435.00**

Single figure with umbrella before pagoda in snow, Watanbe circular seal lower right, good impression **475.00**

Hiroshige

Sakanoshita, from *The Hoeido Tokaido*, good impression, faded, coil trimmed, framed **300.00**

The Ferry on the Tenryn River near Mitsuke, from *Upright Tokaido*, Meiji printing, framed, good color **90.00**

The Outer Bay at Choshi Beach in Simosa Province, from *Sixty Odd Provinces* series, good impression and color, some stains **230.00**

Triptych of three women, each with umbrella in snowy landscape, c1850, framed **750.00**

Hiroshige II, Mimeguiri Embankment and the Sumida River, from "Toto Meisho," 1862, good impression, fine color **350.00**

Hiroshi Yoshida

Fuji san from Yamanka, good impression, juzuri seal, good color, slight soil to margins **375.00**

Market of Mukden, people in market place before temple gate, good

impression, juzuri seal, framed
.....................**525.00**
The Little Temple Gate, juzuri seal,
very good impression, framed
.....................**475.00**
Hokusai, In The Totomi Mountains, from
Thirty-Six Views of Fuji, aizuri printing
with blue outline, modern impression,
wrinkled, torn, stains........**1,610.00**
Jacoulet, Joaquina et su Mere, young
woman and mother, good impression,
faded, framed..............**290.00**
Junichiro Sekino, portrait of actor
Kichiemon, "il ne etat," printed
signature and seal lower right within the
image, pencil sgd, 13/50 in lower
margin, 22" x 18"............**920.00**
Kawamishi, the Water Lily Season, sgd
and titled in pencil, dated, numbered,
framed **425.00**
Kuitsu, landscape of moonlight bay
with sailboats, Watanabe circular seal
lower left..................**200.00**

*Kunisada, Utgawa, 1786-1868, 13-1/2"
x 9-1/2", $125.*

Kunihisa, portrait of actor carrying
bucket and broom over his shoulder,
c1800 ....**425.00**
Kunisada, courtesan and two kamuro,
landscape in background, printed in
blue, c1830, good impression and color
.........................**215.00**
Kuniyoshi
From *Hundred Poets* series, woman,
infant, and child by stream, good
impression, faded........**200.00**
From *Tokaido* series, Yoshitsune and
Benkei, c1842, very good
impression, slight fading...**200.00**

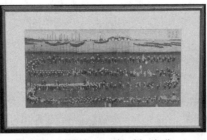

*Yoshitora triptych, parade with winding
lines of figures near harbor with boats,
19th C, 13-3/4 x 28,"* **$725.** *Photo
courtesy of Sanford Alderfer Auction Co.*

Half length portrait of samurai, arms
crossed, gray ground, c1842, good
impression and color **750.00**
Man and woman sharing wine cup,
very good impression and color,
slight soil **260.00**
Portrait of woman carrying wash
bucket within a circle, red
carnations border circle, very good
impression, good color, slight soil
.....................**415.00**
Tripytch, lord and his retainers in an
int., good impression and color,
1840s backed, some damage
.....................**230.00**
Tripytch, 19 seated warriors, against
yellow ground, names above each,
c1842, very good impression,
good color, backed and joined,
some soil **435.00**
Woman shielding herself from falling
snow, dog behind her, 1842, good
impression, framed **350.00**
Okiie Hashimoto, Village in the
Evening, sgd in pencil in margin, dated,
Hashi seal, good impression, framed,
17" x 21-1/2"...............**250.00**
Sekino, bridge in snow, sgd in image,
seal, good impression, 18" x 12-1/2"
.........................**200.00**
Shigenobu, surimono of courtesan in
an interior, make-up table and mirror to
left, fine impression and color..**634.00**
Toyokuni, perspective print of busy
shopping area and temple grounds,
1790s, framed, good impression, faded
.........................**260.00**
Toyokuni II, Kakemono-e portrait of
monk peering under blanket on his
head, bamboo flute in land, framed,
very good impression, somewhat faded
.........................**230.00**
Toyokuni III
Pentaptcyh of people in boat feeding
goldfish, iris garden, framed, very
good impression, missing leaf,
somewhat faded.........**230.00**

Two actors in roles, framed, very
good impression and color, slight
damage to bottom........**115.00**
Utamaro II, three women in an interior,
c1811, good impression, faded, soiled
.........................**175.00**
Yoshitoshi, early triptych of naval
battle, fierce warriors in combat about
ship, c1860s, sgd in gourd cartouche
with pawlonia seal, framed, good
impression, very good color....**475.00**

PURPLE SLAG (MARBLE GLASS)

History: Challinor, Taylor & Co., Tarantum,
Pennsylvania, c1870s-1880s, was the largest
producer of purple slag in the United States. Since the
quality of pieces varies considerably, there is no doubt
other American firms made it as well.

Purple slag also was made in England. English
pieces are marked with British Registry marks.

Other slag colors, such as blue, green, and
orange, were used, but examples are rare.

Reference: Ruth Grizel, *American Slag Glass,*
Collector Books, 1998.

Additional Listings: Greentown Glass (chocolate
slag) and Pink Slag.

Reproduction Alert: Purple slag has been heavily
reproduced over the years and still is reproduced at
present.

Animal
Bunny, Fenton, purple, 3" l, 2" w,
3-1/2" h **115.00**
Swan, Imperial, deep purple, 9-5/8" l,
5-1/4" w, 5-1/8" h **125.00**
Bowl, 9" d, Rose, caramel slag,
Imperial IG mark..............**50.00**
Cake stand, Flute, purple **75.00**
Compote, cov, Eagle, Imperial, orig
sticker, dark purple, 6-1/4" l, 5-1/4" d,
8-3/4" h...................**150.00**
Creamer, Flower and Panel, purple
.........................**85.00**
Goblet, Flute, purple **40.00**
Jar, cov, figural, owl, glossy, green slag,
Imperial IG mark..............**60.00**
Match holder, Daisy and Button, green
.........................**30.00**
Miniature lamp, Imperial, orig sticker,
white shade, purple and white swirled
base, 4-1/2" w, 8" h..........**225.00**
Mug, rabbit, purple **65.00**
Pickle castor, 12" h, emb pickles and
leaves on dark purple insert, resilvered
frame, marked "Tufts #2361" . **1,100.00**
Pitcher, Windmill, glossy, purple slag,
Imperial IG mark..............**45.00**

Fluted Rib pattern, Challinor, celery vase, 8-1/4" h, 4-1/4" d, $95.

Plate, 10-1/2"d, closed lattice edge, purple **75.00**
Platter, oval, notched rim, wildflowers dec, purple, nick **20.00**
Spooner, Majestic, dark purple, 3-3/4" w, 5-1/2" h **125.00**
Sugar bowl, cov, Flute, purple . **190.00**
Toothpick holder, Scroll and Acanthus, Northwood, blue and purple, 1902 . . . . **165.00**

PUZZLES

History: The jigsaw puzzle originated in the mid-18th century in Europe. John Spilsbury, a London map maker, was selling dissected-map jigsaw puzzles by the early 1760s. The first jigsaw puzzles in America were English and European imports aimed primarily at children.

Prior to the Civil War, several manufacturers, e.g., Samuel L. Hill, W. and S. B. Ives, and McLoughlin Brothers, included puzzles in their lines. However, it was the post-Civil War period that saw the jigsaw puzzle gain a strong foothold among the children of America.

In the late 1890s, puzzles designed specifically for adults first appeared. Both forms—adult and child—have existed side by side ever since.

Prior to the mid-1920s, the vast majority of jigsaw puzzles were cut out of wood for the adult market and composition material for the children's market. In the 1920s, the die-cut, cardboard jigsaw puzzle evolved and was the dominant medium in the 1930s.

Interest in jigsaw puzzles has cycled between peaks and valleys several times since 1933. Mini-revivals occurred during World War II and in the mid-1960s, when Springbok entered the American market. Internet auction sites are impacting the pricing of puzzles, raising some (Pars, Pastimes, U-Nits, figure pieces), but holding the line or even reducing others (Straus, Victory, strip cut). As with all auctions, final prices tend to vary depending upon the time of year and the activity of at least two interested bidders.

References: *Dexterity Games and Other Hand-Held Puzzles*, L-W Book Sales, 1995; Jack Matthews, *Toys Go to War*, Pictorial Histories Publishing, 1994; Chris McCann, *Master Pieces, The Art History of Jigsaw Puzzles*, The Collectors Press, 1998.

Collectors' Club: American Game and Puzzle Collectors Association, PMB 321, 197M Boston Post Road West, Marlborough, MA 01752, http://www.agpc.org.

Adviser: Bob Armstrong.

Note: Prices listed here are for puzzles which are complete or restored, and in good condition. Most puzzles found in attics do not meet these standards. If evaluating an old puzzle, a discount of 50 percent should be calculated for moderate damage (one to two missing pieces, three to four broken knobs), with greater discounts for major damage or missing original box.

Children's

Northwoods Workshop, 1950s, Koala Babies Stay Close To Their Mothers, plywood, 10" x 12", 50 pcs, large curve knob, interlocking, Jacob Bates Abbott artist **15.00**
Tuco, 1950-60, Hold On Gramps, cardboard, 7" x 10-1/2", 60 pcs, diecut, round knob strip, interlocking, orig box **6.00**

Parker Brothers, Pastime, plywood, orig box
Clown and the Dancer, The, 6" x 11", 155 pcs, one replaced, curl knob, interlocking, 18 figures **75.00**
Colonel's Story, The, 15-3/4" x 11-3/4", 302 pcs, round knob, jagged, color line cutting, interlocking, 35 figures, V. Ward artist **150.00**
Glory of Autumn, 16" x 12", 300 pcs, bulb knob, jagged, color line cutting, interlocking, 37 figures, G. Wiegand artist **150.00**
Gothic Bridge, 1930-40, 19-1/2" x 15-1/4", 407 pcs, one replaced, color line cutting, interlocking, 49 figures **200.00**
Home by the River, The, 14-3/4" x 7-3/4", 150 pcs, long angular, color line cutting, interlocking, four figures, M. Lowell artist **70.00**
Indian Lovers, 5-3/4" x 7-3/4" h, 73 pcs, curve knob, color line cutting, interlocking, nine figures, Walter Demaris artist **35.00**
Old Dutch Mill, The, 23" x 16-3/4", 530 pcs, random, color line cutting, semi-interlocking, 60 figures . . . **250.00**
Riva and the Italian Alps, 23-3/4" x 11-1/2", 400 pcs, long angular knob, color line cutting, semi-interlocking, 60 figures **200.00**
Village in Brittany, 23-1/2" x 19", 600 pcs, two replaced, 72 figures . . . **220.00**

Par Puzzles Ltd.
New York, NY, 1930-40, Debate, 16th C court scene, plywood, 24-1/4" x 15-1/2", 750 pcs, earlet, jagged, semi-color line cutting, orig box, 12 figures . . . **800.00**

Joseph K. Straus, plywood, orig box
Cottage By the River, 1930s, 19-3/4" x 16", 500 pcs, curve knob variable strip, interlocking **60.00**
French Winter Scene, 1940-50, 27-3/4" x 22", 1,000 pcs, long round, interlocking, 24 figures, C. Pissarro artist **160.00**
Getting Into Port, 1950-60, 23-3/4" x 7-3/4", 750 pcs, curved knob strip, interlocking **100.00**
Guardian Angel, The, 11-3/4" x 15-3/4", 300 pcs, two replaced, jagged knob, interlocking, orig box, seven figures **75.00**
Hunt is On, 1940-50, 12" x 8-3/4", 175 pcs, one replaced, curve knob strip, interlocking **20.00**
Painted Peaks, 1950-60, 20" x 16", 500 pcs, one replaced, round knob strip, interlocking **60.00**
Yosemite National Park, 1950-60, 19-3/4" x 15-3/4", 500 pcs, rd kr variable strip, interlocking **60.00**

Wood and/or hand-cut puzzles, pre-1930
Ayer, Isabel, 1920s, Picture Puzzle Exchange, A Pair of Workers (horses), plywood, 9" x 7", 91 pcs, push-fit, color line cutting, orig box **50.00**
Mason, Pauline, c1909, Assistant to Santa Claus, solidwood, 12" x 8", 200 pcs, push-fit, color line cutting, orig box **80.00**
Noyes, Helen, c1909, The First Crossing, 1492 Galleons, plywood, 12-3/4" x 6-3/4", 146 pcs, push-fit, color line cutting, orig box, one figural piece, J. L. G. Ferris artist **60.00**
Parker Bros., 1910s, Tea Time, plywood, 10-1/2" x 7-3/4", 126 pcs, crooked line, semi-strip, replaced box **35.00**
Richardson, Margaret, Perplexity Puzzles, c1909, peaceful countryside scene, solidwood, 9-1/2" x 13-1/4", 275 pcs, five replaced, long push-fit, color line cutting, replaced box **100.00**
Unknown maker
For Love and the Colonies, solidwood, 19-3/4" x 13-1/4", 450 pgs, three replaced, push-fit, color line cutting, orig box **180.00**

Homeward Bound, nighttime clipper ship scene, solidwood, 12" x 14-3/4", 153 pcs, push-fit, orig box **20.00**

Valley of Roses, plywood, 8" x 5", 61 pcs, push-fit, orig box **20.00**

Wood and/or hand-cut puzzles, 1930s-40s, plywood

A-1 Puzzle Club, Bloomfield, 1930s, Whose for the Road Today? 14-1/2" x 9-1/2", 267 pcs, four replaced, round knob, color line cutting, semi-interlocking, replaced box . .**75.00**

Bay State Puzzle, 1930s, The Fishing Fleet, 9" x 12", 120 pcs, round knob strip, interlocking, orig box **15.00**

Clark, Edward Leggett, 1930s, untitled, man fishing, 22" x 16", 850 pcs, seven replaced, long round, semi-color line cutting, interlocking, orig box **200.00**

Gold Seal Toy Co., Locktite, 1930s, Bootjack and his Dog, 12" x 9", 100 pcs, random, interlocking, orig box . . .**18.00**

Hamlen, H. E., Little Cut-Up, 1930s, untitled, woman with scenery, 10" x 8", 104 pcs, four replaced, fantasy knob, color line cutting, interlocking, replaced box **30.00**

Hammond, Leisure Hour, 1930s, Friendly Greetings, 16" x 14", 500 pcs, curl, round knob, interlocking, orig box **140.00**

Happy Hour Picture Puzzles, 1930s, Romance, courtship, 16" x 12", 321 pcs, 1-by-1 round knob, interlocking, orig box, eight figures, Vladimir Pavlosky artist **100.00**

Hassett, W., Pine Tree, 1930s, The Whale Fishery, 13-1/2" x 8-1/2", 269 pcs, one replaced, round knob stripe, interlocking, orig box, Currier & Ives scene **60.00**

Hayter, Victory, Poplar, 1940/50, Houses of Parliament, 10-1/2" x 6-3/4", 125 pcs, two replaced, round knob strip, interlocking, orig box, Max Hofler artist **20.00**

Jacobs, D. S., 1930s, Peaceful Mount Vernon, 22" x 11", 424 pcs, sq knob, semi-color line cutting, interlocking, orig box, 20 figures, Brownscomb artist **150.00**

Jewel Picture Co., 1930s, Fishermen's Return, 9" x 12", 170 pcs, long curl, interlocking, orig box, four figures .**50.00**

Lending Library, 1930s, The Bride, 6-3/4" x 20-1/4", 331 pcs, one replaced, long, knobby, interlocking, orig box **110.00**

MacDonald, H. C., 1920/30, Fishing Fleet at Sunset, 16" x 12", 419 pcs, round knob, semi-color line cutting, interlocking, orig box, five figures, G. Maroniez artist **125.00**

Macy's, 1932, Washington Arms, 11-3/4" x 8-3/4", 200 pcs, curl knob, color line cutting, interlocking, orig box, 18 figures **80.00**

Madmar, Interlox

Holland Flower Market, 15-3/4" x 12", 374 pcs, one replaced, long curve knob, semi-interlocking, orig box **100.00**

Old Meeting House at Twilight, 5" x 7", 80 pcs, one replaced, long knobby, interlocking, orig box **25.00**

Pied Piper, fairytale scene, 9-3/4" x 7-1/4", 150 pcs, long round knobs, interlocking, orig box, Carrie Solomon artist **30.00**

Milton Bradley, Premier, 1930s

At The White Horse Tavern, 11-1/2" x 8-3/4", 158 pcs, one replaced, long jagged knobs, semi-color line cutting, interlocking, orig box, 12 figures **50.00**

Covered Wagon, 8" x 7-1/4", 74 pcs, long jagged knob, interlocking, orig box, five figures **25.00**

New Book Libraries, 1930s, Call to Contest, 12" x 10", 259 pcs, 1-by-1 curve knob, color line cutting, interlocking, orig box, Phillip R. Goodwin artist **75.00**

Parker Bros., Picture Puzzle Mart, 1930s, Waiting at the Pier, 12-1/4" x 16-1/4", 252 pcs, round knob, jagged, color line cutting, interlocking, orig box, 31 figures, cut special for Josephine Flood by Pastime cutters **125.00**

Per-Plex Puzzle Co., 1930s, Over Field and Fence, 9" x 12", 153 pcs, 1-by-1 round knob, interlocking, orig box, J. S. Sanderson artist **25.00**

Ponda, 1930s, The Landlord's Brew, 23-1/2" x 17-1/2", 1,000 pcs, round knob strip, interlocking, orig box, M. Dovaston artist **120.00**

Rialto Mfg, Moderne, 1930s, Progress of Democracy, 10-3/4" x 8", 221 pcs, two replaced, random, semi-interlocking, orig box, four figures **85.00**

Russell, Charles, 1930-40, Bright As Day, 24" x 17", 561 pcs, one replaced, one sq, color line cutting, interlocking, orig box, 53 figures **175.00**

Schreiner, Clarence, Du Lux, 1940s, Beauty of Countryside, 19-3/4" x

15-3/4", 590 pcs, one replaced, sq knob, interlocking, orig box, 32 figures **150.00**

Schwartz, Special Cut, 1940-50, Excitement on the Range, 15-3/4" x 12", 300 pcs, curve knob, angular, interlocking, orig box, 14 figures, Hinton, cut by Straus **70.00**

Scranton's, Easy Library, 1930s, Hooked But Not Caught, 13-1/4" x 9-1/4", 200 pcs, two replaced, curl knob, interlocking, orig box, 23 figures, Frank Stick artist **70.00**

Stoughton Stud, Tiz-A-Teezer, 1930s, Rugged Grandeur, 5-3/4" x 7-3/4", 62 pcs, round knob, angular, interlocking, orig box, W. W. Thompson artist .**12.00**

Tuck, Zag-Zaw, 1930s, Mioton & Marion Delorme, 29" x 21-1/4", 1,250 pcs, six replaced, earlet, interlocking, orig box, 130 figures, Bruzk artist **400.00**

Unknown maker, 1930s

Blossom Time, 10" x 8", 185 pcs, random, color line cutting, interlocking, replaced box, 12 figures **70.00**

Morning on the Mohawk, 22" x 15-1/4", 518 pcs, one replaced, 1-by-1 round knob, interlocking, replaced box **125.00**

Valley of the Oise, 12" x 9", 130 pcs, 1 replaced, sq knob strip, interlocking, orig box **15.00**

Winsor, Allen P., 1937, Good Luck Everybody, 10" x 6-3/4", 152 pcs, push-fit, color line cutting, orig box **60.00**

Wood and/or hand-cut puzzles, post-1950, plywood

Atlantic, Kingsbridge, untitled, bouquet of flowers, 10-1/2" x 8-1/4", 182 pcs, one replaced, round knob strip, interlocking, orig canister, label missing. **18.00**

Browning, James, U-Nit, Montmarte, 23-1/2" x 19-3/4", 790 pcs, four replaced, random knob, japed, interlocking, orig box, 122 figures, Maurice Utrillo artist **350.00**

Guiles/Glencraft/Shape-Cut, The Lone Sailor, 19" x 14" 517 pcs, 1-by-1 earlet, interlocking, orig box, 14 figures, Y. E. Soderberg artist **130.00**

Hayter, Victory, Fruit and Flowers, 16" x 12", 350 pcs, round knob strip, interlocking, orig box **40.00**

Unknown, Old Ironstone on a Lee Shore, 16-1/4" x 12-3/4", 306 pcs, two replaced, round knob strip, interlocking, replaced box **40.00**

QUEZAL

Quezal

History: The Quezal Art Glass Decorating Company, named for the quetzal—a bird with brilliantly colored feathers—was organized in 1901 in Brooklyn, New York, by Martin Bach and Thomas Johnson, two disgruntled Tiffany workers. They soon hired Percy Britton and William Wiedebine, two more Tiffany employees.

The first products, which are unmarked, were exact Tiffany imitations. Quezal pieces differ from Tiffany pieces in that they are more defined and the decorations are more visible and brighter. No new techniques were developed by Quezal.

Johnson left in 1905. T. Conrad Vahlsing, Bach's son-in-law, joined the firm in 1918, but left with Paul Frank in 1920 to form Lustre Art Glass Company, which copied Quezal pieces. Martin Bach died in 1924 and by 1925, Quezal had ceased operations.

Marks: The "Quezal" trademark was first used in 1902 and placed on the base of vases and bowls and the rims of shades. The acid-etched or engraved letters vary in size and may be found in amber, black, or gold. A printed label which includes an illustration of a quezal was used briefly in 1907.

Chandelier, five ruffled shades in pulled-feather design, signed, **$2,100.** *Photo courtesy of James D. Julia.*

Bowl, 9-1/2" d, irid gold Calcite ground, stretch rim, pedestal foot, sgd "Quezal" **800.00**

Cabinet vase, 1-3/4" h, 4-1/4" dec, squatty, 16 ribs, undulating flared rim, irid blue-gold, strong red highlights, polished pontil mkd "Quezal D685" **550.00**

Candlesticks, pr, 7-3/4" h, irid blue, sgd **575.00**

Chandelier, gilt metal
14" h, four elaborated scroll arms, closed teardrop gold, green, and opal shades, inscribed "Quezal" at collet rim, very minor roughness at rim edge **2,000.00**
16" h, three shouldered flared opal shades, rib molded design, gold irid int., collet rim inscribed "Quezal," classic shaped socket, wheel with chain drop **450.00**
Cologne bottle, 7-1/2" h, irid gold ground, Art Deco design, sgd "Q" and "Melba" **250.00**

Lamp, desk, 14-1/2" h, irid gold shade with green and white pulled feather dec, inscribed "Quezal" at rim, gilt metal adjustable crook-neck lamp **575.00**

Quezal lamp shade, iridescent glass with pulled-feather design in white, with applied threading, etch signed on inner rim "Quezal," 6 1/2" tall, very minor loss to applied threading, **$300.** *Photo courtesy of Sanford Alderfer Auction Co.*

Lamp shade, 4" h, 4" flared opening, 2" fitter ring, Calcite, irid, bulbous, two minor flakes on fitter rim **185.00**
Salt, open, 2-1/2" w, 1-1/4" h, irid, sgd **375.00**
Toothpick holder, 2-1/4" h, melon ribbed, pinched sides, irid blue, green, purple and gold, sgd **200.00**
Vase
7-1/4" h, bottle shape, irid gold shades to bluish-red at rim, sgd "Quezal" in polished pontil, small scratch on side **965.00**

4-1/2" d, 7-3/8" h, flared rim, irid gold, blue-green coiled dec, polished pontil mkd "Quezal" **2,500.00**
8-1/4" h, three pulled and folded loop handles, irid gold, strong red and blue highlights, polished pontil, unsigned **1,350.00**
Whiskey taster, 2-3/4" h, oval, irid gold, four pinched dimples, sgd "Quezal" on base **200.00**

QUILTS

History: Quilts have been passed down as family heirlooms for many generations. Each one is unique. The same pattern may have hundreds of variations in both color and design.

The advent of the sewing machine increased, not decreased, the number of quilts made. Quilts are still being sewn today.

References: Cuesta Benberry, *Always There: The African-American Presence in American Quilts*, Kentucky Quilt Project, 1992; Roberta Benvin, *Antique Quilting Designs*, American Quilter's Society; Barbara Breckman, *Encyclopedia of Pieced Quilt Patterns*, American Quilter's Society; Linda Emery, *A Treasure of Quilting Designs*, American Quilter's Society; Deborah Harding, *Red & White: American Redwork Quilts and Patterns*, Rizzoli, 2000; Patricia T. Herr, *Quilting Traditions*, Schiffer Publishing, 2000; Carter Houck, *Quilt Encyclopedia Illustrated*, Harry N. Abrams and Museum of American Folk Art, 1991; Eileen Jahnke-Trestain, *Dating Fabrics: A Color Guide, 1800-1960*, American Quilter's Society; Donald B. Kraybill, Patricia T. Herr, Jonathon Holstein, *A Quiet Spirit: Amish Quilts from the Collection of Cindy Tietze & Stuart Hodosh*, UCLA Fowler Museum of Cultural History (405 Hilgard Ave., Los Angeles, CA 90024); Elizabeth Kurella, *The Complete Guide To Vintage Textiles*, Krause Publications, 1999; Patricia J. Morris and Jeannette T. Nuir, *Heirloom Quilts from Old Tops*, Krause Publications, 2001; —, *Worth Doing Twice*, Krause Publications, 1999; Nancy and Donald Roan, *Lest I Shall be Forgotten*, Goschenhoppen Historians, Inc. (P.O. Box 476, Green Lane, PA 18054), 1993; Shelly Zegart, *American Quilt Collections/Antique Quilt Masterpieces*, Nihon Vogue Ltd., 1996; *Protecting Your Quilts*, rev. 2nd ed., American Quilter's Society.

Periodicals: *American Quilter*, American Quilter's Society, P.O. Box 3290, Paducah, KY 42001, http://www.aqsquilt.com; *Quilters Newsletter Magazine*, 741 Corporate Circle, Suite A, Golden, CO 80401.

Collectors' Clubs: American Quilt Study Group, P.O. Box 4737, Lincoln, NE 68504-0737; American Quilter's Society, P.O. Box 3290, Paducah, KY 42001, http://www.aqsquilt.com; Crazy Quilt Society, P.O. Box 19452, Omaha, NE 68119, http://www.crazyquilt.com; National Quilting Assoc., Inc., P.O. Box 393, Ellicott City, MD 21043, http://www.napquilts.org.

Museums: American Museum of Quilts & Textiles of San Jose, San Jose, CA; Colonial Williamsburg

Foundation, Colonial Williamsburg, VA; Doll & Quilts Barn, Rocky Ridge, MD; Museum of the American Quilter's Society, Paducah, KY; National Museum of American History, Washington, DC; New England Quilt Museum, Lowell, MA; Quilter's Hall of Fame, Marion, IN; Shelburne Museum, Shelburne, VT; Virginia Quilt Museum, Harrisonburg, VA.

Notes: The key considerations for price are age, condition, aesthetic appeal, and design. Prices are now level, although the very finest examples continue to bring record prices.

Appliqué, album, 30 squares with floral and bird appliqués, red, green, yellow, and gold calico, some blue/green floral chintz, red and green calico border, cotton homespun ground, five squares with quilted initials, descended through Saint Mary's County, Maryland family, 77" x 91", $4,950. Photo courtesy of Garth's Auction, Inc.

Appliqué

Flower Basket, red, green, and yellow calico, white ground, toning, minor staining, fabric wear, 77-1/2" x 67" **885.00**

Floral Medallions, pastel pink, green, and yellow, swag border, minor stains, 82" x 90" **415.00**

Four floral medallions with scattered flowers, red, green, and goldenrod, hand stitched, diamond quilting, stains, small area of edge damage, 84" sq **1,210.00**

Grape vine border and medallions with green leaves, light brown puffed grapes, hand stitched, diagonal quilting, cross stitched initials, light stains and wear, 90" x 102" ... **1,200.00**

Roses and buds, dark red, yellow centers, bluish-gray leaves, hand stitched, diagonal quilting, some fading and stains, 77" x 100" **250.00**

Rose Wreath Variant, red and green roses and leaves, meandering vine border, white ground, red banding, America, mid-19th C, fading, minor staining, 79" x 68" **500.00**

Tree of Life, Brodene Perse, 19th C, staining, 112" x 114" **4,600.00**

Pieced and appliqué, calico and chintz, cotton homespun ground, large central star, chintz border, appliqué chintz birds, butterflies, and flowers, flower and foliage quilted design, wear, age stains, some wear to chintz border, attributed to New York state, 115" x 142", $4,400. Photo courtesy of Garth's Auction, Inc.

Appliqué and pieced

Album, red plaid separates squares with appliquéd polychrome prints, most are floral, some have deer or birds, two have Eastern scenes with camels and elephants, inked signatures, dates in the 1850s, stains, 64" sq **1,870.00**

Nine floral medallions, red, yellow, and green, red and green sawtooth edging, hand quilted, feathering between medallions, scroll work along border, stains, 82" x 83" **1,430.00**

Tulips, pink, purple, and orange, green leaves and borders, hand quilted with flowers, feathering, and diamonds, dark black and blue pencil lines, light green edging, 70" x 82" **770.00**

Chintz

Printed overall design of exotic birds drinking from urns hanging from trees, brown on white, printed gold, blue, green, and reddish-brown, brown floral baking, light stains, 94" x 116" . **1,450.00**

Crazy

Pieced, multicolored embroidery of animals, girls, sgd "Lottie Seely," burgundy velvet border, reddish-brown velvet baking, minor war and stains, 62" sq. **715.00**

Pieced velvet, black, burgundy, purple, red, gold, gray, green, and brown solid and printed shaped patches, arranged in 16 squares, colorful velvet border, late 19th C, 72" x 74" **885.00**

Pieced

Basket, light brown, white squares alternating with red squares, triple border, hand stitched, 76" x 88" . **800.00**

Bow Tie, dark maroon and floral chintz squares alternating with multicolored bow tie squares, brown border with yellow stars, hand stitched, stains, 92" x 96" **1,320.00**

Bow Tie, small green and red triangles, red zig zag border with green sawtooth edging, hand stitched four petal flower quilting, red edging, slight wear and facing, 74" sq **1,575.00**

Broken Star, orange, yellow, green, red, brown, blue, and white printed calico patches, red and white calico Flying Geese border, PA, 19th C, 80" x 76" **460.00**

Chinese Lanterns, green, red, blue, yellow, and white printed calico and solid patches, blue and white ground, red border, diamond and rope quilting, PA, late 19th C, minor staining, 82" x 84" **1,495.00**

Courthouse Steps, various silk colors, black border, highlighted by decorative embroidery, late 19th C, minor wear, 20" x 26-1/2" **260.00**

Flower Garden, red, white, and brown print, deep gray-green ground, red back, 83" x 86" **175.00**

Flying Geese, multicolored silk bands of triangles alternating with blue bands and border, light blue cotton backing, late 19th/early 20th C, 86" x 85" . **350.00**

Log Cabin

Black, purple, gray, blue, brown, ivory, red, and green, striped flannel backing, Mennonite, 71" x 84" **350.00**

Made from jockey silks, red, blue, yellow, orange, purple, brown, and black, yarn tied to brown silk back, found in KY, 91" x 100" **715.00**

Sunshine and shadow pattern, blue, red, pink, and two shades of gray, hand stitched by Marie Trumbly, Chazy, New York by the Canadian border, 71" x 72" **495.00**

Lone Star, pink, blue, lavender, and salmon, blue ground, quilted with horses, flowers, etc., Mennonite, minor stains, 76" x 79" **660.00**

Four large stylized floral medallions, red and khaki with goldenrod star centers, border stripes, well quilted, several dark stains, some light overall stains, 83" x 85", $385. Photo courtesy of Garth's Auctions, Inc.

Nine Patch, various colors, red grid, hand and machine stitched, backed and bound with red and white printed fabric, late 19th/early 20th C, minor fading, 79" x 71"............ **230.00**

Nine Patch variant

Chintz squares edged with triangles, floral printed border, hand stitched, diamond and floral quilting, orig pencil marks, some stains, 82" x 83" **1,540.00**

Multicolored squares alternating with off-white, arranged diagonally in block and surrounded by red grid, sawtooth border, backed with white, red binding, minor imperfections, 81-1/2" x 75" **460.00**

Philadelphia Pavements, blue, red, orange, and white square printed and solid patches, orange and red banded borders with feather and floral fine quilting, PA, late 19th/early 20th C, 84" x 80" **825.00**

Pinwheel Squares, green and pink alternating with red squares, pink and green double border, plaid backing, hand stitched, fish-scale quilting, 92" x 93" **400.00**

Rolling Stones, pink, green, blue, and white patches, banded borders, Mennonite, PA, late 19th/early 20th C, 82" x 84"................... **425.00**

Roman Wall, multicolored and black silk and satin triangles, embroidered signature "Jessie Mull 1897," minor imperfections, 75" x 68"....... **460.00**

Serrated Square, corresponding border, pink and green calico, shell and diamond quilting, 82" x 84" **320.00**

Spider Web, pink, red, blue, purple green, peach, and brown printed calico patches, wide purple calico border, diagonal line quilting, Mennonite, PA, late 19th C, some staining, 82" x 80" **825.00**

Star of Bethlehem, purple, green, red, blue, and pink calico, white ground, early 20th C, toning, minor staining, fabric wear, 82" x 73-1/2" **650.00**

Grid, red, white, and blue, some overall wear and small stains, 82" x 91", $225. Photo courtesy of Garth's Auctions, Inc.

Stars, 30 red stars, white cotton ground, divided by feather wreath quilting, pencil marks, some stains, 83-1/2" x 72-1/2" **690.00**

Sunburst in squares, burgundy alternating with green and dark blue-gray, burgundy flannel gathered bordered, plaid backing, yellow and white stitching, Mennonite, 52" x 84" **200.00**

Tulips in Square, red, green, and yellow printed calico patches, broad brown, red, green, and white coronation chintz and rosevine border, PA, 19th C, 94" x 91" **920.00**

Windmill, yellow, red, green, and blue printed calico patches, wide red calico with swag quilting, PA, late 19th C, 86" x 76"........................ **690.00**

Trapunto, white on white, feather wreaths alternating with wavy lines, wear and stains, 72" x 46" **495.00**

QUIMPER

History: Quimper faience, dating back to the 17th century, is named for Quimper, a French town where numerous potteries were located. Several mergers resulted in the evolution of two major houses—the Jules Henriot and Hubaudière-Bousquet factories.

The peasant design first appeared in the 1860s, and many variations exist. Florals and geometrics, equally popular, also were produced in large quantities. During the 1920s, the Hubaudière-Bousquet factory introduced the Odetta line which utilized a stone body and Art Deco decorations.

The two major houses merged in 1968, the products retaining the individual characteristics and marks of the originals. The concern suffered from labor problems in the 1980s and was purchased by an American group.

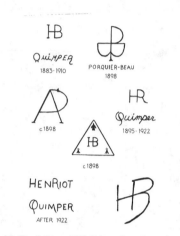

Marks: The "HR" and "HR Quimper" marks are found on Henriot pieces prior to 1922. The "Henriot Quimper" mark was used after 1922. The "HB" mark covers a long time span. Numbers or dots and dashes were added for inventory purposes and are found on later pieces. Most marks are in blue or black. Pieces ordered by department stores, such as Macy's and Carson Pirie Scott, carry the store mark along with the factory mark, making them less desirable to collectors. A comprehensive list of marks is found in Bondhus book.

References: Susan and Al Bagdade, *Warman's English & Continental Pottery & Porcelain*, 3rd ed., Krause, 1998; Sandra V. Bondhus, *Quimper Pottery: A French Folk Art Faience,* printed by author, 1981, revised edition, 1995; Millicent Mali, *French Faience,* United Printing, 1986; Millicent Mali, *Quimper Faience,* Airon, Inc., 1979; Adela Meadows, *Quimper Pottery, A Guide to Origins, Styles, and Values,* Schiffer Publishing, 1998; Ann Marie O'Neill, *Quimper Pottery, 2nd Edition,* Schiffer Publishing, 1998; Marjatta Taburet, *La Faience de Quimper,* Editions Sous le Vent, 1979, (French text).

Collectors' Club: USA Quimper Club, 2519 Kansas Ave., Suite 108, Santa Monica, CA 90404.

Museums: Musee des Faiences de Quimper, Quimper, France; Musee Departemental Breton, Quimper, France; Victoria and Albert Museum, French Ceramic Dept., London, England.

Advisers: Susan and Al Bagdade.

Additional Terms:

A la touche border decor—single brush stroke to create floral

Breton Broderie decor—stylized blue and gold pattern inspired by a popular embroidery pattern often used on Breton costumes, dates from the Art Deco era.

Croisille—criss-cross pattern

Decor Riche border—acanthus leaves in two colors

Fleur de lys—the symbol of France

Ivoire Corbeille pattern—red dots circled in sponged blue with red touches forming half a floral blossom, all over a tan ground

Quintal—five-fingered vase.

Plate, left: male peasant, right: female peasant, blue and pale green costumes, red, blue, yellow, and green vertical florals, light green and red single stroke designs on border, blue outlined shaped rim, "HR Quimper" on front, 9-1/2" d, price for pair, $300. All Quimper photos courtesy of Susan and Al Bagdade.

Apothecary jar, cov, 10" h, paneled, frontal view of peasant woman holding water jug in landscape on front, flower burst on reverse with four blue dot designs, blue acanthus bands on base, neck and cov border with orange bands, blue knob, "HB Quimper" mark **385.00**

Basket, 5-1/4" sq, lobed body, male peasant on int. with red dot flowerheads and green leaves, scattered florals on ext., overhead four strap handle with yellow-orange flowerhead knobs, "HR Quimper" mark **425.00**

Biberon, 7-7/8" h, Ivoire Corbeille, side panel with bust of female peasant in green dress, high coif, reverse with large red half stylized flowerhead, yellow band on shoulder, band of red dots in green circles, blue sponged border, spout, side, and overhead handle, "HenRiot Quimper" mark **100.00**

Bowl

4-1/2" sq, male peasant holding pipe, red, and green florals on inner body, ermine tails on corners, indented sides, blue outlined rim, pierced for hanging, "HR Quimper France" mark **125.00**

6-1/2" d, peasant blowing horn, green shirt, red trimmed jacket, orange pantaloons, red, blue, and green floral border chain on int. and ext., indented rim, blue

sponged rope handles, yellow ground, pierced for hanging, "HenRiot Quimper France" mark, chip on rim **70.00**

Butter dish, cov, attached underplate, 6-3/4" d, male peasant on cov, red, blue, and green floral spray, molded shell knob, ribbed body with band of red, green, and blue florals, blue half circle band on base, "HenRiot Quimper France" mark **160.00**

Chamberstick, 6-1/2" l, leaf shape, female peasant on base, red and green floral sprays on leaf tips, black ermine tails, yellow four dot design, yellow lined handle and dots, "HB" mark **350.00**

Clock, 9-1/2" h, rococo shape, raised blue, green, or orange-yellow border swirls, standing male peasant holding walking stick, butterfly on top, florals on sides of clock face, floral branches and four blue dot design sides, "HB Quimper" mark **1,350.00**

Cup and saucer

Hex shape, male peasant on panel, orange jacket, blue pantaloons, scattered red and blue florals, blue outlined rims, gold outlined wishbone handle with blue dashes, "HenRiot Quimper France" marks **50.00**

Trefoil shape, scattered blue sprigs and four dot design, "HB" mark **125.00**

Dish, 10-5/8" l, fan shape, molded rays, male peasant, dark blue coat, red pantaloons, red and green vertical florals, blue sponged wavy rim, "HB Quimper France" mark **50.00**

Doll dish, 3" d, dark blue and gold star-shaped geometric design, dark blue banded rim, "HenRiot Quimper" mark **50.00**

Egg cup, 4" l, 2" h, figural baby chick, blue dots and feathers, yellow accents, blue and yellow banded shaped rim on attached underplate, "HenRiot Quimper France" mark **55.00**

Figure

3-3/4" h, standing female peasant, green blouse, basket over arm, gold lined base with "Loisik" on front and blue double "V" designs on sides, "HenRiot Quimper" mark, chip on base **220.00**

8-3/4" h, standing Mary holding infant Jesus, blue striped robe, orange trim, sponged base, unmarked **330.00**

10-1/4" h, standing boy, hand in pocket, orchid shirt, dark blue jacket, yellow vest with red buttons, pale green trousers, yellow and red banded black hat, light brown sq base with dark brown and green splashes, "BERTHE SAVIGNY" on side, "HP Quimper" mark . .**350.00**

Fish platter, male peasant, blue jacket, orange pants, female peasant in blue dress, maroon apron, pale blue, red, and yellow florals, red and orange outlined rim, pierced for hanging, "HenRiot Quimper" mark, 19" l, 1,100.

Fish plate, 10-1/2" l, figural fish, red and blue head, blue fins, red and blue striped tail, red male on one, female peasant on other, red, blue, and green foliates at sides, "HenRiot Quimper France" mark, price for pr **100.00**

Fish platter, 19" l, male peasant, blue jacket, orange pants, female peasant in blue dress, maroon apron, pale blue, red, and yellow florals, red and orange outlined rim, pierced for hanging, "HenRiot Quimper" mark **1,100.00**

Holy water font, 6-1/4" h, ermine tail shape, little peasant girl kneeling before gold cross, scattered red and green florals, raised crest of Brittany on bowl, blue outlined rim with blue dashes, pierced for hanging, "HR Quimper" mark **357.00**

Hors d'oeuvre serving dish, 15" w, seated male peasant with yellow jacket, blue trousers, walking female peasant carrying buckets, profile of female peasant in each of three sections, border of sprigs of bleeding hearts, blue rick-rack, and dots, "HB Quimper" on front **440.00**

Jardiniere, 10" handle to handle, male and female peasants on front, stick fence and butterflies on reverse, scattered blue and red bushes and trees, blue dot flowers with yellow clusters, four molded animal feet on base, blue outlined flowing rim, blue sponged ring handles, pastel palette, "HB Quimper" on int. **425.00**

Menu, 6-1/2" h, female peasant holding distaff, pink blossoms next to "Menu," yellow, green, and blue molded swirl border, seashell feet, "HR Quimper" mark. **425.00**

Oyster plate, 9" d, center well with blue shaded fleur-de-lys and HR Quimper, band of tassel and dot design and gold rim, six wells, male or female peasant in two wells, green, red, and blue vertical florals in other four wells, raised shell and four blue dots between wells **1,000.00**

Pitcher

4" h, stoneware, white top, blue vertical stripes on lower half, blue handle, "HB Odetta" mark . . **75.00**

7" h, bulbous shape, male peasant on front, red and green floral sprays and four blue dot designs, blue banded borders, blue dash handle, "HB Quimper France" mark **100.00**

8-1/2" h, male peasant on side, horizontal band of red, green, blue, and yellow florals, wide yellow band with blue stripes on base and neck, blue zigzag and dot handles with yellow bands, "HenRiot Quimper France" on shoulder **125.00**

Plate

6" d, large red single stroke flower with half blue single stroke flower in center, single stroke red and green florals and leaves, orange sponged rim, "HenRiot Quimper France 104" mark **55.00**

6-3/4" d, yellow and blue target center, red stylized flower buds and green leaves, blue dashes between, red squiggles, three blue line border, yellow banded rim, "HR Quimper" mark **125.00**

8-1/2" d, male peasant holding pipe, red, blue, and green florals at side, border with three blue stripes and red stripe, yellow rim, "HR Quimper" mark **100.00**

9" d, male peasant, yellow striped bag over shoulder, dark blue jacket, light blue pantaloons, border of green and red florals, four blue dots between, "HB Quimper" on front **250.00**

9-1/2" d, male or female peasant, blue and pale green costumes, red, blue, yellow, and green vertical florals, light green and red

single stroke designs on border, blue outlined shaped rim, "HR Quimper" on front, price for pr **300.00**

10-1/4" d, frontal view of male peasant in center, forest background, inner chain border, red and blue crisscross border panels alternating with yellow stylized flowerhead panels, blue outlined lobed and serrated rim, "HenRiot Quimper" mark . . . **200.00**

Platter

13" l, oval, female peasant, pointed coif, holding flower bouquet, red, green, blue, and yellow vertical flowers, border band of red and green florals, four blue dot designs, blue outlined shaped rim, unmarked **500.00**

15-5/8" l, rect, cut corners, center with four peasant women at well, two male peasant musicians, gold inner border with band of red curlicues, dark blue décor riche border, gold and blue outlined rim, "HB Quimper" on front . . **1,150.00**

Porringer, 6-1/4" handle to handle, male or female peasant, blue, green, and red vertical flowers, three blue stripes and yellow band on inner border, blue sponged handles, "HR Quimper" marks **100.00**

Quintal, 5-7/8" h, orange outlined lobed cartouche of seated female peasant, blue bordered center band of red and blue zigzags, scattered florals, and four blue dots, orange and blue outlined openings, "HenRiot Quimper France"" mark **275.00**

Salt, 4-5/8" h, blue hat, green shirt, orange trousers, green and orange flower on base, blue zigzag on border, blue dash rim, "HenRiot Quimper France" mark **250.00**

Snuff bottle, 3" l, book shape, blue and red floral spray, reverse with peasant man, pipe, yellow page edges, cobalt blue spine, "HB Quimper" mark **210.00**

Tray, 12-1/4" l x 5-1/2" w, rect, cut corners, large red, blue, or yellow single stroke flowerheads in center, red and green foliage, blue outlined rim, "HB Quimper" mark **125.00**

Trivet, 6" sq, four small feet, male peasant, blue jacket, red pantaloons, border band of red, green, and blue flowers, blue lined rim, green sponged edge, "HenRiot Quimper France 485" mark **150.00**

Salt, 4-5/8" h, blue hat, green shirt, orange trousers, green and orange flower on base, blue zigzag on border, blue dash rim, "HenRiot Quimper France" mark, 4-5/8" h, **$250.**

Tulipiere, 10" h, shield shape, spread foot, seated female peasant and jug in yellow cartouche, red dots, reverse with male peasant playing bagpipes, blue décor riche scrolling border, 10 tubes with blue décor riche design and yellow banding, Porquier-Beau **2,500.00**

Tureen, cov, 10-1/2" h, 11" handle to handle, male peasant on base with vertical florals, blue striped base, yellow banded rim, two blue sponged handles, band of red, blue, and green florals and foliage on cover, blue and yellow striped rim, blue sponged turnip knob, "Heroic Quimper France" mark. **650.00**

Wall pocket

7-1/4" h, bellows shape, front view of peasant, blue coat, yellow pantaloons, red, green, and blue florals at sides, blue dash border, black ermine tail on spout, sides with blue lattice, green dots, and red "X's," blue sponged handle, "HR Quimper" mark **500.00**

9-1/2" h, overlapped cone shape, standing male peasant blowing horn, blue jacket, orange pantaloons, vertical red, blue, and green florals, blue outlined margins, "HenRiot Quimper" mark **250.00**

10-1/2" h, figural fleur-de-lys, frontal view of female peasant, medium blue jacket, red striped shirt, light blue apron, red, green, and blue scattered flowers, blue chain at center, blue ermine tails and four dot designs on border and backplate, "HB Quimper" mark **425.00**

RADIOS

History: The radio was invented more than 100 years ago. Marconi was the first to assemble and employ the transmission and reception instruments that permitted the sending of electric messages without the use of direct connections. Between 1905 and the end of World War I, many technical advances affected the "wireless," including the invention of the vacuum tube by DeForest. Technology continued its progress, and radios filled the entertainment needs of the average family in the 1920s.

Changes in design, style, and technology brought the radio from the black boxes of the 1920s to the stylish furniture pieces and console models of the 1930s and 1940s, to midget models of the 1950s, and finally to the high-tech radios of the 1980s.

References: Robert Breed and Marty Bunis, *Collector's Guide to Novelty Radios, Book II,* Collector Books, 1999; Marty and Sue Bunis, *Collector's Guide to Transistor Radios,* Collector Books, 1994, 1996 values; Marty Bunis and Robert Breed, *Collector's Guide to Novelty Radios,* Collector Books, 1995; Harold Cones, and John Bryant, *Zenith Radio: The Early Years, 1919-1935,* Schiffer Publishing, 1997; Chuck Dachis, *Radios by Hallicrafters,* 3rd ed., Schiffer Publishing, 1999; Alan Douglas, *Radio Manufacturers of the 1920s,* Vol. 1 (1988), Vol. 2 (1989), Vol. 3 (1991), Vestal Press; John Slusser, *Collector's Guide to Antique Radios,* 5th ed., Collector Books, 2001; Mark Stein, *Machine Age to Jet Age, Radiomania's Guide to Tabletop Radios—1933-1959,* published by author (2109 Carterdale Road, Baltimore, MD 21209).

Periodicals and Internet Resources: *Antique Radio Classified,* P.O. Box 2, Carlisle, MA, 01741, http://www.antiqueradio.com; *Antique Radio Collector,* http://members.aol.com/wrldradio; *Antique Radio Page,* http://members.aol.com/djadamson/arp.html; *Hallicrafters Collectors Assoc.,* http://www.hallicrafters.org; *Nostalgia Air,* http://www.nostalgiaair.org; *Radio Gallery,* http://www.radiogallery.com; *Phil's Old Radios,* http://www.antiqueradio.org; *Radio Netherlands' Antique & Old Time Radio Page,* http://www.rnwl.nl/realradio/html/antiqueradio.html; *The Electronic Collector,* P.O. Box 1193, Mabank, TX 75147; *Transistor Network,* RR1, Box 36, Bradford, NH 03221; http://web2.airmail.net/vanew (Atwater Kent).

Collectors' Clubs: Alabama Historical Radio Society, P.O. Box 26452, Birmingham, AL 35226; Antique Radio Club of America, 81 Steeplechase Road, Devon, PA 19333; Antique Radio Club of Illinois, 1025 Erie St., Oak Park, IL 60302; Antique Radio Collectors & Historians, 8141 Stratford Drive, St. Louis, MO 63105-3707; Antique Radio Collectors of Ohio, 2929 Hazelwood Ave., Dayton, OH 45419; Antique Wireless Assoc., Box E, Breesport, NY 14816, http://www.antiquewireless.org; Arizona Antique Radio Club, Inc., 2025 E. LaJolla Drive, Tempe, AZ 85251-5910; British Vintage Wireless Society, 23 Rosendale Road, West Dulwich, London SE21 8DS UK; Buckeye Radio & Phonograph Club, 4572 Mark Trail, Akron, OH 44321-1462; California Historical Radio Society, P.O. Box 31659, San Francisco, CA 94131-0659; California Historical Radio Society,

North Valley Chapter, P.O. Box 31658, San Francisco, CA 94131; Canadian Vintage Radio Society, 4895 Mahood Drive, Richmond, British Columbia V4N 3V8, Canada; Carolina Chapter, AWA, P.O. Box 3015, Matthews, NC 28106-3015; Central Ohio Antique Radio Assoc., 3782 Millstream Drive, Hilliard, OH 43026; Colorado Radio Collectors, 5270 E. Nassau Circle, Englewood, CO 80110; Connecticut Vintage Radio Collectors Club, 563 W. Avon Road, Avon, CT 06001; Delaware Valley Historic Radio Club, P.O. Box 847, Havertown, PA 19803; Florida Antique Wireless Group, 660-A Clay St., Winter Park, FL 32789; Greater New York Vintage Wireless Assoc., 52 Uranus Road, Rocky Point, NY 11778-8842; Houston Vintage Radio Assoc., P.O. Box 31276, Houston, TX 77231-1276; Indiana Historical Radio Society, 245 N. Oaklane Ave., Indianapolis, IN 46201-3360; International Antique Radio Club, P.O. Box 5367, Old Bridge, NJ 08857; London Vintage Radio Club, 42 Clamatis Road, London, Ontario M2J 4X 2 Canada; Michigan Antique Radio Club, 22400 Nowlin, Dearborn, MI 48124; Mid-America Antique Radio Club, 10332 Mowhawk Lane, Shawnee Mission, KS 66206-2525; Mid-Atlantic Antique Radio Club, P.O. Box 352, Washington, VA 22747-0352; Nebraska Antique Radio Collectors Club, 905 W. First, North Platte, NE 69101; New England Antique Radio Club, P.O. Box 201, Spofford, NH 03462; New Jersey Antique Radio Club, 125 Warf Road, Egg Harbor Twp, NJ 08234-8501; New Mexico Radio Collectors Club, 39 Chaco Loop, Sandia Park, NM 87047; Niagara Frontier Wireless Assoc., 135 Autumnwood, Cheetowaga, NY 14227; Northland Antique Radio Club, P.O. Box 18362, Minneapolis, MN 55418; Northwest Vintage Radio Society, P.O. Box 82379, Portland, OR 97282-0379; Oklahoma Vintage Radio Collectors, P.O. Box 50625, Midwest City, OK 73140-5625; Pittsburgh Antique Radio Society, 407 Woodside Road, Pittsburgh, PA 15221; Pugent Sound Antique Radio Assoc., P.O. Box 2092, Snohomish, WA 98291-2095; Radio History Society, Inc., 13 Bitterroot Court, Rockville, MD 20853; Sacramento Historical Radio Society, P.O. Box 162612, Sacramento, CA 95816-9998; Society for the Preservation of Antique Radio Knowledge, P.O. Box 482, Dayton, OH 45449; Society of Wireless Pioneers, Inc., P.O. Box 86, Geyserville, CA 95441-0086; Southern California Antique Radio Society, 24803 Pitcaris Way, Torrance, CA 90505-6614; Southern Vintage Wireless Assoc., 1901 Spanish Oaks, Huntsville, AL 35803-0068; Tube Collectors Assoc., P.O. Box 1181, Medford, OR 97501; Vintage Radio & Phonograph Society, Inc., P.O. Box 165345, Irving, TX 75016; Western Wisconsin Antique Radio Collectors Club, 1611 Redfield St., LaCrosse, WI 54601.

Museums: Antique Radio Museum, St. Louis, MO; Antique Wireless Museum, Bloomfield, NY; Antique Wireless Assoc.'s Electronic Communication Museum, Breesport, NY; Bellingham Antique Radio Museum, Bellingham, WA; Indiana Historic Radio Museum, Ligonier, IN; Museum of Radio & Technology, Inc., Huntington, WV; Museum of Television & Radio, New York, NY; Museum of Television & Radio, Beverly Hills, CA; New England Wireless and Steam Museum, Inc., East Greenwich, RI; Pavek Museum of Broadcasting, Minneapolis, MN; Vintage Radio & Communication Museum of CT, East Hartford, CT 06108; Virginia City Radio Museum, Virginia City, NV; Voice of the Twenties, Orient, NY.

Additional Listings: See *Warman's Americana & Collectibles* for more examples.

Adviser: Lewis S. Walters.

Admiral
Portable, #33-35-37	**30.00**
Portable, #218, leatherette	**40.00**
Portable, #909, All World	**85.00**
Y-2127, Imperial 8, c1959	**45.00**

Air King, tombstone, Art Deco **3,000.00**

Arvin
Mightymite #40	**30.00**
Rhythm Baby #417	**275.00**
Hoppy with lariatenna	**575.00**
Table, #444	**65.00**
Table, #522A	**30.00**
Tombstone, #617 Rhythm Maid	**215.00**

Atwater Kent Type TA, 1924, **$1,465.** *Photo courtesy of Auction Team Breker.*

Atwater Kent
Breadboard style, Model 9A	**550.00**
Breadboard style, Model 10, with orig tags	**1,300.00**
Breadboard style, Model 10C	**1,100.00**
Breadboard style, Model 12	**1,250.00**
Cathedral, 80, c1931	**200.00**
Table, #55 Keil	**225.00**
Table, #318, radio-dome	**115.00**
Tombstone, #854	**155.00**
Type R Horn	**200.00**

Bulova, clock radio
#100	**30.00**
# 110	**25.00**
#120	**30.00**

Colonial "New World Radio" . **1,000.00**
Columbia, table radio, oak **125.00**

Crosley
ACE V	**170.00**
Bandbox, #600, 1927	**80.00**
Dashboard	**100.00**
Gemchest, #609	**425.00**
Litfella, 1N, cathedral	**175.00**
Pup, with box	**575.00**
Sheraton, cathedral	**290.00**

Showbox, #706 .... **100.00**
Sleigh **140.00**
Super Buddy Boy **125.00**
#4-28 battery operated..... **130.00**
#10-135 .... **55.00**
Dumont, RA346, table, scroll work,
1938 .... **110.00**
Emerson
AU-190 Catalin Tombstone . **1,600.00**
BT-245 .... **1,300.00**
Patriot **900.00**
Porcelain Dealer Sign **150.00**
#274 brown Bakelite **165.00**
#400 Aristocrat **525.00**
#409 Mickey **1,400.00**
#411 Mickey **1,400.00**
#411 Snow White **1,200.00**
#570 Memento **110.00**
#640 Portable **30.00**
#888 Vanguard **80.00**
Fada
#43 .... **240.00**
#53X **200.00**
#60W **75.00**
#115 bullet shape **1,000.00**
#136 .... **1,000.00**
#252 .... **575.00**
#625 rounded end, slide rule dial
.... **700.00**
#1000 red/organe bullet ... **1,200.00**
#L56 Maroon and White ... **2,600.00**
Federal
#58DX **500.00**
#110 .... **550.00**
General Electric
#81, c1934 .... **200.00**
#400, 410, 411, 414 .... **30.00**
#515, 517 clock radio **25.00**
K-126 .... **150.00**
Tombstone **250.00**
Grebe
CR-8 .... **500.00**
CR-9 .... **400.00**
CR-12 .... **600.00**
MU-1 .... **250.00**
Service Manual **50.00**
Halicrafters
TW-600 .... **100.00**
TW-200 .... **125.00**
Majestic
Charlie McCarthy **1,000.00**
#59, wooden Tombstone ... **375.00**
#92 .... **125.00**
#381 .... **225.00**
Treasure Chest **125.00**
Metrodyne Super 7, 1925..... **265.00**
Motorola
#68X11Q Art Deco **75.00**
Jet Plane **55.00**
Jewel Box **80.00**
M logo **25.00**
Pixie **45.00**

Tombstone, 1934, walnut, front round airplane dial, upper grill cloth, Art Deco cut outs, four knobs, AC, **$120.**

Ranger, portable **60.00**
Ranger #700 .... **30.00**
Table, plastic **35.00**
Olympic, radio with phonograph. **60.00**
Paragon
DA, two table **475.00**
RD, five table **600.00**
Philco
T-7, 126 transistor **65.00**
T1000 clock radio **80.00**
#17, 20, 38 Cathedral **250.00**
#20 Cathedral **200.00**
#37, 62 table, two tone **60.00**
#37, 84 Cathedral, 1937 .... **175.00**
#40, 180 console wood **150.00**
#46, 132 table **20.00**
#49, 506 Transitone **35.00**
#52, 544 Transitone **40.00**
#49, 501 Boomerang **475.00**
#60, Cathedral **125.00**
#551, 1928 .... **175.00**
Radiobar, with glasses and decanters
.... **1,700.00**
Radio Corporation of America–RCA
LaSiesta **550.00**
Radiola
#17 .... **120.00**
#18, with speaker **125.00**
#20 .... **165.00**
#24 .... **170.00**
#28 console **200.00**
#33 .... **60.00**
#6X7 table, plastic **25.00**
8BT-7LE portable **35.00**
40X56 World's Fair **1,000.00**
Silvertone-Sears
#1 table **75.00**
#1582 Cathedral, wood..... **225.00**

#1955 Tombstone **135.00**
#9205 plastic transistor **45.00**
Clock radio, plastic **15.00**
Sony, transistor
TFM-151, 1960 .... **50.00**
TR-63, 1958 .... **145.00**
Sparton
#506 Blue Bird, Art Deco .. **3,300.00**
#5218 .... **95.00**
Stewart-Warner, table, slant... **175.00**
Stromberg Carlson, #636A console
.... **125.00**
Westinghouse, Model WR-602 . **50.00**
Zenith
#500 transistor, owl eye **75.00**
#500D transistor **55.00**
#750L transistor, leather case **40.00**
#6D2615 table, boomerang dial
.... **95.00**
Trans-Oceanic **90.00**
Zephyr, multiband **95.00**

RAILROAD ITEMS

History: Railroad collectors have existed for decades. The merger of the rail systems and the end of passenger service made many objects available to private collectors. The Pennsylvania Railroad sold its archives at public sale.

References: Stanley L. Baker, *Railroad Collectibles*, 4th ed., Collector Books, 1990, 1999 value update; Richard C. Barrett, *Illustrated Encyclopedia of Railroad Lighting*, Vol. 1 (1994); Vol. 2 (1999), Railroad Research Publications; Barbara J. Conroy, *Restaurant China: Restaurant, Airline, Ship & Railroad Dinnerware,* Collector Books, Vol. 1 (1998), Vol. 2 (1999); Don Stewart, *Railroad Switch Keys & Padlocks*, 2nd ed., Key Collectors International, 1993; Joe Welsh, et. al., *The American Railroad*, MBI Publishing, 1999.

Periodicals and Internet Resources: *Central Pacific Railroad Photographic History Museum*, http://www.cprr.org; *Key, Lock and Lantern*, 35 Nordholl Place, Englewood, NJ 07631; *Railroad Web Ring*, http://webring.rrdepot.com; *Railfan & Railroad Magazine*, P.O. Box 700, Newton, NJ 07860-0700; *Railroad & Tourist Rail Magazine*, P.O. Box 1089, Mt. Pleasant, NC 28124-1089; *Railway Collector's Journal*, 7 Ascot Road, Moseley, Birmingham, West Midlands, B13 9#N UK; *Ribbon Rail Productions*, http://www.rrhistorical.com; *Trains*, P.O. Box 1612, Waukesha, WI 53187, http://www2.trains.com/trains.

Collectors' Clubs: American Assoc. of Private Railroad Car Owners, 421 New Jersey Ave., SE, Washington, DC 20000; American Southwestern Railway Assoc., P.O. Box 39846, Los Angeles, CA 90039, http://www.mcscom.com/asra; Canadian Railroad Historical Assoc., 99 Atlantic Ave., Unit #220, Toronto, Ontario, M6K 3J7 Canada; Chesapeake & Ohio Historical Society, Inc., P.O. Box 79, Clifton Forge, VA 24422; Key, Lock & Lantern, Inc., 35 Nordholl Place, Englewood, NJ 07631; National Railway Historical Society, P.O. Box 58547, Philadelphia, PA 19102-8547, http://www.nrhs.com;

New York Central System Historical Society, Inc., P.O. Box 58994, Philadelphia, PA 19102-8994; Railroadiana Collectors Assoc., 550 Vernonica Place, Escondido, CA 92027, http://www. railroadcollectors.org; Railway and Locomotive Historical Society, P.O. Box 292927, Sacramento, CA 95829-2927; Tourist Railway Assoc., Inc., P.O. Box 1245, Chama, NM 87520-1245, http://www.train.org.

Museums: Baltimore and Ohio Railroad, Baltimore, MD; California State Railroad Museum, Sacramento, CA; Frisco Railroad Museum, Van Buren, AR; Museum of Transportation, Brookline, MA; National Railroad Museum, Green Bay, WI; New York Museum of Transportation, West Henrietta, NY; Old Depot Railroad Museum, Dassel, MN; Santa Fe Dept. Railroad & Heritage Museum, Temple, AZ.

Additional Listings: See *Warman's Americana & Collectibles* for more examples.

Notes: Railroad enthusiasts have organized into regional and local clubs. Join one if you're interested in this collectible field; your local hobby store can probably point you to the right person. The best pieces pass between collectors and rarely enter the general market.

Ashtray, Soo Line, ceramic, track and car design border, "Denver Wright Co." backstamp, 7" d **25.00**

Book

From San Francisco to Salt Lake City Along the Western Pacific Railroad, c1920, orig mailer **60.00**

Katy Railroad and the Last Frontier, The, V. V. Masterson, Univ. of Oklahoma, Norman, 1952, 1st ed., 328 pgs, illus, maps, index . . **55.00**

1900 Chicago Rock Island & Pacific History, Biographical Publishing Co., 756 pages, CRIP and representative employees, beautiful tooled and gilt engine dec cover, gilt edges, center signatures are loose **260.00**

Brake gauge, Westinghouse, brass, two dial indicators, 140 lbs, 6-1/2" d **35.00**

Broadside, Chicago, Rock Island & Pacific, c1870, full-color lithograph, int. of dining and restaurant cars on Rock Island route, black waiters, verso with hand-written family tree in black and red ink describing 76 generations of the Fowler family beginning with William Fowler (1637-1660), first magistrate of New Haven, CT, Cameron, Amberg & Co. Railroad Printers, Lake St. Chicago, glazed front and back, minor losses, 14" x 22" **4,255.00**

Builders plate

American Locomotive Co. #68777 Schenectady Works, cast iron, dated January 1937, 14" x 7-1/2" **115.00**

Broadside, "Cheap Holiday Excursion, West Shore Route of New York, West Shore, and Buffalo Railway for Christmas and New Years 1883/4, graphics of Santa in sleigh being pulled by engine from NY, WS & B Railroad, titled "Old Chris Kringle Adopts Modern Locomotive and Takes the NY, WS, and B Ry," map of railways routes, black, white, and red, some separation at folds, staining, edge chipping, 36" x 16", **$775.** *Photo courtesy of Sanford Alderfer Auction Co.*

Baldwin-Lima, cast iron, dated 1952, emb letters, for diesel electric locomotive const. #75180, model AS616, hp 1600, red enamel paint. 14-1/2" x 7-1/2" **85.00**

Corps of Engineers U.S. Army 45-ton Diesel Electric Locomotive Manufactured by Vulcan Iron Works, cast bronze, dated 1941, 11" x 6" **85.00**

Fairbanks-Morse, stainless steel, etched letters on enamel ground, 1955, serial #166-972, 17" x 8" **115.00**

Calendar

Missouri Pacific Lines, Route of the Eagles, Engine #7003, color litho

on tin, removable date cards, 19" x 13" **75.00**

Missouri Pacific Lines, steam engine #6615, color litho on tin, green ground, removable date cards, 19" x 13" **130.00**

New York Central, 1922, illustration depicting travel in 1830 and 1920, timetables for various lines in margins, some minor losses, period oak frame, 18" x 30" . **265.00**

Soo Line, 1930, illus, Lake Louise Alberta by R. Atkinson Fox, later oak frame and mat, overall 34" x 29" **230.00**

Calendar plate, Pennsylvania Lines, 1949, after a painting by Grif Teller, framed, 30" x 23" **35.00**

Cap

Agent, Soo Line, pill box style, embroidered "Agent" and "Soo Line," labeled "Marshall Field & Co. Chicago," size 7" **50.00**

Brakeman's, open-weave crown, missing name plate, labeled "A. G. Meier & Co. Chicago," size 6-3/4" **35.00**

Railroad Conductors, labeled "A.G. Meier & Co. Chicago," size 7-1/4" **95.00**

Chimes, dining car, wood case, four tone bars, orig striker, 10-1/2" l . . **150.00**

China

Chocolate pot, Pullman Porcelain, green glaze, gilt pin striping & "Pullman" lettering, Hall China back stamp, 6" h **345.00**

Plate, Chesapeake & Ohio Railroad, Olde Ivory, Buffalo China, Gilbert Stuart George Washington portrait in center, 2-1/4" w 24 kt emb border, 10-3/4" d **575.00**

Crimper, railroad seal, nickel plate, dies marked "CNS & M. R. R. Co.," handle emb "Porter Safety Seal Co.," 7" l **115.00**

Cabinet card, The Shenandoah Valley Excursion of 1885, price for group of 17 cards, **$1,155.** *Photo courtesy of Jackson's Auctioneers & Appraisers.*

Cuspidor

Missouri Pacific Railroad, white porcelain on metal, black "MOPAC" lettering, minor loss, 7-1/2" d **150.00**

St. Louis & Southwestern Railroad, brass, handle, removable collar, emb "STL.S.W.RY.CO" & "S.G.Adams-St.Louis," 9" l . **130.00**

Texas & Pacific Railroad, white porcelain on metal, blue lettering, minor loss, 8" d **260.00**

Date stamp, Atlantic Coast Line Railroad, c1940, Defiance Stamp Co., 4" h **35.00**

Depot clock, electric, patent date 1908, oak case, hinged face, marked "Property of the Ball RR Time Service St. Paul, Minn," 21" sq **210.00**

Depot sign, Rock Island System, reverse painted and mother of pearl, c1890, Chicago, Rock Island & Pacific 4-4-0 locomotive #476 pulling 11 cars, against tree-lined Midwest route, orig oak ogee frame with gilt liner, overall 50" x 22" **23,000.00**

Directory, *Soo Line Shippers Directory, Vol. III,* 1918-19, soft cover, 644 pgs, gilt, ads, illus, two-pg Soo Line map, four color maps of MI, MN, ND, WI **60.00**

Fire bucket, Missouri, Kansas & Texas Railroad, orig red paint, stenciled "Fire," emb "MK&T," 12" h **60.00**

Flare and flag box, Gulf Mobile & Ohio, tin, stenciled letters, contains flag and fuses, 30" l **20.00**

Conductor's hat, Milwaukee RR, Carlson & Co., Chicago, IL, **$45.**

Hat

Chicago & Illinois Valley, celluloid name tag with "#1," size 7" . . **60.00**

Soo Line, brakeman's, open weave crown, silver nameplate, labeled "Carlson & Co. Chicago," size 7-1/4" **185.00**

Hollowware

Coffee pot, silver plate, "Dixie" engraved on front, ornate emb handle and lid, insulated zinc lining, copper bottom, 19th C, lid detached, some damage and losses, 11" h **60.00**

Coffee pot, silver plate, Chicago & Eastern Illinois, 10-oz size, marked "Reed & Barton 086-H, C&E.I.RY.CO" on base, 7" h **265.00**

Coffee pot, silvered, Union Pacific, 32 oz, side stamped "The Challenger," figural wing finial on lid, backstamped "International Silver 05085, 32 oz. U.P.R.R." **115.00**

Coffee server, silvered, Nashville, Chattanooga & St. Louis, applied emb "N.C.& St. L" logo on front, gooseneck spout, long wood handle, backstamped "Reed & Barton 482-32 oz, N.C. & St. L" **520.00**

Sauce tureen, silvered, Chicago Great Western Railway, two handles, lid. backstamped "C.G.W.R.R.–Reed & Barton," 8" l **125.00**

Sugar bowl, silvered, New York Central, imp "NYC" on hinged lid, 3-3/4" h **50.00**

Tea pot, silvered, Missouri Pacific & Iron Mountain, 10-oz size, front engraved "M.P.I.Mt.RY," backstamped "Missouri Pacific & Iron Mountain R. Wallace 03295," 4-1/2" h **230.00**

Water bottle, Pullman, by Stanley, front imp "Pullman," 11" h . . . **35.00**

Illustration, Great Northern Railway, orig illus for cover of travel brochure, scenic marvel of America, Glacier National Park, c1920, full-color gouache on paper, detailed study, 9-1/2" x 14", 1/2" margins **315.00**

Jug, Baltimore & Ohio, stoneware, brown cone top, one gal, 11-1/2" **210.00**

Kerosene can, Chicago & Northwestern, one gal, oxidized finish, emb "C&NRR," 13" h **25.00**

Lantern

Boston & Albany, 1865, fixed globe etched "B& A," 13" h **165.00**

Boston & Worchester, emb "B&W RR," fixed globe, 13" h **665.00**

PRR, etched 5" red globe and dome, marked "Keystone Lantern Co., Phila, PA, USA," wire ring bail **445.00**

Lantern globe, clear, emb letters, by CNS, 5-1/2" h

Burlington Route **70.00**

Long Island RR **70.00**

Pennsylvania RR, logo **60.00**

Pere Marquette **90.00**

Pittsburgh & Lake Erie RR . . . **60.00**

Letter opener, Southern Pacific, orig case, 7-3/4" l **30.00**

Locomotive nose plate, Frisco, black, heavy 1/8" stainless steel, 28" l **1,150.00**

Map

Chicago, Iowa, and Nebraska Railroad, color litho, published by J. Sage & Sons, Buffalo, NY, 1859, some discoloration and losses, mounted on linen, 26" x 23" **450.00**

Soo Line, Minneapolis, St. Paul, and Sault Ste. Marie RY, printed by Matthews, Northrup & Co. Buffalo, NY, c1890, 39" x 16" **130.00**

Williams Telegraph and Railroad Map of the New England States, dated 1852, by Alexander Williams, published by Redding & Co. Boston, printed table of construction costs for area railroads, hand-colored state borders, separated folds with later linen backing, some toning, 32" x 30" **60.00**

Name plate, Soo Line, cast aluminum, mounted on walnut back board, 24" l **95.00**

Paperweight

Adlake Centennial, 1857-1957, extruded aluminum, 5" l **40.00**

Atlantic Coast Line, emb brass, ACL logo and "Safety Always," remnants of enameling, 3-3/4" d **25.00**

Platform, International & Great Northern, cast iron with diamond pattern, letters "I&GN RR," date "1894," quarter round leading edge, 32" x 16" **115.00**

Photo

Chicago, Rock Island & Pacific, Rocky Mountains, c1910, orig frame, 7" mat, 53" x 23" . . . **920.00**

Denver & Rio Grande Railroad Depot, Canyon of the Rio Las Animas, Colo, hand colored black and white print, printed logo and title, "Copyright 1900 by Detroit Photographic Co.," orig oak frame, stains in margin, overall 33-1/2" x 27-1/2" **2,645.00**

Lima Locomotive Works Builders of Soo Line 4-8-4 engine #5000, black and white silver gelatin print, orig double mat and frame, applied Lima logo on mat, framers label on verso for "Schell's Book Store, Lima Ohio" missing glass, overall 22" x 9" **415.00**

Machinist Apprentices of the Chicago & Alton R.R., dated Sept. 5th 1908, depicting 34 apprentices posed on C & A R.R. locomotive #605, Stafford B. Cable photo, Bloomington, IL, orig frame and mat, 17" x 11" image size . .**490.00**

Soo Line, Lake Louise early 20th C, hand-colored black and white print, orig titled mat with Soo Line logo, orig oak frame, overall 25" x 21" **50.00**

Poster, Howard Chandler Christy Rail Safety Poster, colorful, Assoc. of American Railroads, 1936, some smudges, 14" x 22" **345.00**

Press Proof, Great Northern Railway for "The New Oriental Limited" travel brochure c1923, framed, 12" x 9" **70.00**

Print, Union Pacific Railroad, c1910, "The Mail and Express" crossing the famous Dale Creek embankment, black and white heliotype, printed title and logos in margin, orig oak frame, brass plaque, minor stains in margin, 31-1/2" x 27-1/2" **1,265.00**

Steam whistle, brass

3" h, single chime, lever control, Sherburne Co., Boston, Massachusetts, Patent 1890212 . . . .**115.00**

3" d, 8" h, single chime, lever control **200.00**

5-1/2" d, 12" h, triple chime, manufactured by Crosby Steam, Gage & Valve Company, Boston, Pat. Jan. 30, 1877 . . . .**720.00**

Step ladder, ST.L.K& N-W Railroad, folding, wooden, four steps, stenciled "St.L.K&N-W" and "Mail Car 103" **270.00**

Step stool

Denver & Rio Grande Western RR, rubber no-skid top, 9" h. . . .**260.00**

NYC & HR, wood with metal corners, 9" h **100.00**

Switch plate, iron, emb "US&S CO," patented 1914, attached brass impedance plate, 16-1/2" x 12-1/2" **35.00**

Ticket cabinet, Soo Line, c1914, oak, locking tambour slant front, divided

compartments for tickets, timetables, one drawer, stenciled "M.ST.P. & S.S.M.RY" on back, 21"x 35"x16" **460.00**

Ticket window

24" x 35", wood frame, reverse painted window "Ticket Office" in red and black on cream ground, double hung window frame, minor losses, late Soo Line placard with hours attached **415.00**

28" x 33-1/2", Baltimore & Ohio, clear emb glass, B&O logo on diamond point textured field, later walnut frame **600.00**

Tobacco tin, Fast Mail Tobacco, Bagley & Co., tin litho, flat pocket type, detailed image of early train, some darkening to gold highlights, 3-5/8" l, 2-3/8" w, 5/8" h **1,000.00**

Tray, Soo Line, Montana Success, map of Soo Line Route, tin litho, 10-1/2" x 15" **200.00**

Wax sealer

American Exchange Co., El Paso, III, brass die with wood handle, 3" l **150.00**

American Railway Express Co., Maple Lake, Minn, one-piece brass die and handle, 2-1/2" l . . .**150.00**

Illinois Central Railroad, Agent-Minonk, brass die, wood handle, 4" l **375.00**

S.W. & B.V. RR, Agent-Bryan, Texas, one-piece brass die and handle, 2-1/2" l **550.00**

Toledo, Peoria & Western, Agent-El Paso, III, brass die, wood handle, 4" l **525.00**

Window, 44-3/4" h, Smoke Room, etched glass, reverse tinted gray and yellow. **1,125.00**

RAZORS

History: Razors date back several thousand years. Early man used sharpened stones; the Egyptians, Greeks, and Romans had metal razors.

Razors made prior to 1800 generally were crudely stamped "Warranted" or "Cast Steel," with the maker's mark on the tang. Until 1870, razors were handmade and almost all razors for the American market were manufactured in Sheffield, England. Most blades were wedge shaped; many were etched with slogans or scenes. Handles were made of natural materials: horn, tortoiseshell, bone, ivory, stag, silver, or pearl.

After 1870, razors were machine made with hollow ground blades and synthetic handle materials. Razors of this period usually were manufactured in Germany (Solingen) or in American cutlery factories. Hundreds of molded-celluloid handle patterns were produced.

Cutlery firms produced boxed sets of two, four, and seven razors. Complete and undamaged sets are

very desirable. The most popular ones are the seven-day sets in which each razor is etched with a day of the week.

References: Ronald S. Barlow, *Vanishing American Barber Shop*, Windmill Publishing, 1993; *Safety Razors: A Price Guide*, L-W Book Sales, 1995; Roy Ritchie and Ron Stewart, *Standard Guide to Razors*, 2nd ed., Collector Books, 1999 value update; Jim Sargent, *American Premium Guide to Pocket Knives & Razors*, 5th ed., Krause Publications, 1999.

Periodical: *Blade Magazine*, P.O. Box 22007, Chattanooga, TN 37422.

Additional Listings: See *Warman's Americana & Collectibles* for more examples.

Notes: The fancier the handle or more intricately etched the blade, the higher the price. Rarest handle materials are pearl, stag, sterling silver, pressed horn, and carved ivory. Rarest blades are those with scenes etched across the entire front. Value is increased by the presence of certain manufacturers' names, e.g., H. Boker, Case, M. Price, Joseph Rogers, Simmons Hardware, Will & Finck, Winchester, and George Wostenholm.

Ideal Safety Razor, patented Sept. 21, 1868, June 12, 1900, and March 5, 1906, leather like case, 9-1/2" l, **$20.**

American blades

Case Bros., Tested XX, Little Valley, NY, hollow point, slick black handles, MOP inlaid tang. **400.00**

Cattaraugus Cutlery Co., Little Valley, NY, sq point, blue handles with white liners. **35.00**

Crandall Cutlery Co., Bradford, PA, sq point, blade etched "I. Must Kut," cream-colored handles with beaded border. **70.00**

Kane Cutlery Co., Kane, PA, hollow point, cream and rust twisted rope handles, c1884. . . . .**45.00**

Southington Cutlery Co., Southington, CT, Crescent Safety Razor, razor in orig 1-1/4" x 2-1/8" x 1/2" tin. **1,050.00**

Standard Knife Co., Little Valley, NY, arc mark, round point, yellow mottled handles with beaded borders, 1901-03 . . . .**150.00**

Union Cutlery Co., Olean, NY, AJ Case Shoo-Fly, tiger-eye handle, c1912 . . . .**125.00**

English blades, Sheffield

George Wostenholme, etched adv on blade, emb ivory handle **40.00**

Joseph Rodgers & Sons, wedge blade, stag handle with inlaid rect escutcheon plate............ **125.00**

F. J. Elwell, Rockdale, NY, 1900, images of political figures, $250.

German blades

Cosmos Mfg. Co., hollow ground blade, ivory handle, raised nude picking purple grapes, green leaves **125.00**

F. A. Koch & Co., ivory handle, colored scene with deer, branches, and oak leaves **50.00**

Imperial Razor, blade etched with U.S. Battleship Oregon scene, dark blue celluloid handle **45.00**

Wadsworth Razor Co., semi-wedge blade, carved bone handle, c1870 .... **60.00**

Sets of razors

Crown & Sword, seven-day set, blades etched "The Crown & Sword Razor Extra Hollow Ground," black handles with raised "Crown and Sword," homemade wood case with felt lining, emb "RAZORS," plaque on top.. **85.00**

G. W. Ruff's Peerless, two, hollow ground blade, ivory handles, leather over wood case with "Gentlemen's Companion Containing 2 Razors Special Hollow Ground," red lining **70.00**

Wilkinson Sword, seven days, safety, 5" l, 2-1/2" d, 1-5/8" h orig box.. **125.00**

RECORDS

History: With the advent of the more sophisticated recording materials, such as 33-1/3 RPM long-playing records, 8-track tapes, cassettes, and compact discs, earlier phonograph records became collectors' items. Most have little value. The higher-priced items are rare (limited-production) recordings. Condition is critical.

References: Mark Allen Baker, *Goldmine Price Guide to Rock 'n' Roll Memorabilia*, Krause Publications, 1997; Mark Brown, Thomas Conner, and John Wooley, *Forever Lounge*, Antique Trader Books, 1999; John Clemente, *Girl Groups, Fabulous Females That Rocked the World*, Krause Publications, 2000; Les Docks, *American Premium Record Guide, 1900-1965*, 5th ed., Krause Publications, 1997; Goldmine Magazine, *Goldmine's 1997 Annual*, Krause Publications, 1996; ——, *Goldmine Roots of Rock Digest*, Krause Publications, 1999; Ron Lofman, *Goldmine's Celebrity Vocals*, Krause Publications, 1994; Chuck Miller, *Warman's American Records*, Krause Publications, 2001; William M. Miller, *How to Buy & Sell Used Record Albums*, Loran Publishing, 1994; Tim Neely, *Goldmine Christmas Record Price Guide*, Krause Publications, 1997; ——, *Goldmine's Country & Western Record Price Guide*, 2nd ed., Krause Publications, 2000; ——, *Goldmine's Jazz Album Price Guide*, Krause Publications, 2000; ——, *Goldmine's Price Guide to Alternative Records*, Krause Publications, 1996; ——, *Goldmine's Price Guide to 45 RPM Records*, Krause Publications, 1996; ——, *Goldmine Standard Catalog of American Records 1950-1975*, 2nd ed., Krause Publications, 2000; Tim Neely and Dave Thompson, *Goldmine British Invasion Record Price Guide*, Krause Publications, 1997; Jerry Osborne (comp.) *Rockin' Records, 1998 Ed.*, Antique Trader Books, 1997; Charles Szabala, *Goldmine 45 RPM Picture Sleeve Price Guide*, Krause Publications, 1998; Neal Umphred, *Goldmine's Price Guide to Collectible Jazz Albums*, 1949-1969, 2nd ed., Krause Publications, 1994; ——, *Goldmine's Price Guide to Collectible Record Albums*, 5th ed., Krause Publications, 1996; ——, *Goldmine's Rock 'n' Roll 45 RPM Record Price Guide*, 3rd ed., Krause Publications, 1994.

Periodicals and Internet Resources: *Cadence*, Cadence Building, Redwood, NY 13679; *DISCoveries Magazine*, P.O. Box 1050, Dubuque, IA 52004-1050; *Film Source Monthly*, 8503 Washington Blvd., Culver City, CA 90232; *Goldmine*, 700 E. State St., Iola, WI 54990, http://www.krause.com; *Jazz Beat Magazine*, 61 French Market Place, New Orleans, LA 70116; *Joslin's Jazz Journal*, P.O. Box 213, Parsons, KS 67357; *New Amberola Graphic*, 37 Caledonia St., St. Johnsbury, VT 05819; *Records Universe*, http://www.collectors.com; *78 Quarterly*, P.O. Box 283, Key West, FL 33041.

Collectors' Clubs: Assoc. of Independent Record Collectors, P.O. Box 222, Northford, CT 06472-0222; Canadian Antique Phonograph Society, 122 Major St., Toronto, Ontario M5S 2L2 Canada; International Assoc. of Jazz Record Collectors, 12366 Quinlan Ave., Port Charlotte, FL 33981; *Record Collectors Guild*, http://thercguild.tripod.com.

Additional Listings: See *Warman's Americana & Collectibles* for more examples.

Note: Most records, especially popular recordings, have a value of less than $3 per disc. The records listed here are classic recordings of their type and are in demand by collectors.

Children's

Dumbo, Disneyland, record and book, 1968, some wear **7.60**

Higitus Figitus, Walt Disney Productions, Little Golden Record, 1938 .... **8.00**

Star Wars, 24-page read-along book, 33-1/3 rpm record, Buena Vista .. **5.00**

Strawberry Shortcake, 1980, LP **20.00**

The Night Before Christmas, Golden Record, R33, 78 RPM, as told by Peter Donald, full orchestra directed by Mitchell Miller, c1950, some scratches and wear **5.00**

3 in 1 Golden Record, nursery school songs, some wear **5.00**

3 in 1 Golden Record, This Little Pig, Wee Willie Winkle, Pussy Cat, some wear....................... **5.00**

Country, LP

Glen Campbell, Christmas with Glen Campbell, Capitol, SL 6699, black label with pink colorband............ **8.00**

Glen Campbell, Gentle on My Mind, Capitol, ST 2809, black label with rainbow border **12.00**

Danny Davis & Nashville Brass, Movin On, RCA, LSP 4232, orange label, 1969.................. **8.00**

Jerry Lee Lewis, All Country, 1969 .... **10.00**

Roger Miller, SMASH Mercury, SRS 67123, red label **12.00**

Jim Reeves, The Intimate Jim Reeves, RCA Victor, LSP-2216, black label with dog at top **22.00**

Statler Brothers, The Big Hits, Columbia, CS 9519, red label... **18.00**

Kitty Wells, Country Music Time, Decca DL 74554, black label with rainbow band through center **8.00**

Lounge, LP

Fred Astaire, Another Evening with Fred Astaire, Chrysler 1088 .... **12.00**

Charles Ross Taggart, Victor, 78 rpm, black label, 12" d, $7.50.

Teresa Brewer's Greatest Hits, Phillips, PHS 600-062, black label with rainbow band through center, 1960s **16.00**

Perry Como, Merry Christmas Music, Pickwick, Camden, CAS-660, black label with rainbow letter "P" in center, 1961 . . . .**10.00**

Ray Conniff & Johnny Mathis, Something Special, four-album boxed set, Columbia Special Products, C4 10303, red labels **18.00**

Bing Crosby, Jerome Kern Songs, Decca, 5001 . . . .**20.00**

Bob Crosby & His Orchestra, The Bob Cats Ball, Coral Records CRL 57705, some wear to jacket **13.00**

Martin Denny, Hawaii Tattoo, Liberty LST-7394 . . . .**10.00**

Doris Day Wonderful Day, Columbia Records XTV 82022, 1960s **8.00**

Duke Ellington, Masterpieces by Ellington, Columbia, 4418 . . . . . .**30.00**

Pete Fountain, Those Were The Days, Coral, CRL 757505, black label with multicolored band through center **15.00**

Tom Jones, Tom, Parrot, XPAS 71037, black label with green and yellow parrot **18.00**

Brenda Lee, 10 Golden Years, Decca, DL 74757, black label with rainbow band through center **22.00**

Mantovani Today, London, PS 572, blue label **8.00**

Dean Martin's Greatest Hits, Vol. 1, Reprise, RS 6301, gold/orange label **12.00**

Mills Brothers, The, Fortuosity, Dot, DLP 25809, black label, c1959 . .**12.00**

Buddy Morrow, Impact, RCA LPM-2042 . . . .**10.00**

Frank Sinatra, Cycles, Reprise, 1027, gold/orange label with picture of Frank **8.00**

Mel Torme, California Suite, Capital P-200 . . . .**30.00**

Paul Weston, Columbia Record Club Giveaway, CB-6 . . . .**9.00**

Andy Williams, Honey, Columbia, CS 9662, red label **8.00**

Rock

Asylum Choir, Asylum Choir II, Shelber, SW-8910, LP, orig insert .**10.00**

Beatles, Old Brown Shoe, Apple EPEM-10540, Mexican pcs, 45 rpm **18.00**

David Bowie, Man Who Sang, Mercury SR-61325, LP **18.00**

Fat Mattress, Atco SD 33-309, Noel Redding, LP **10.00**

Golden Earring, Greatest Hits, Polydor 236228, Dutch imp, LP **10.00**

John Lennon, Roots, Adam Vii-A-80180, orig, LP **200.00**

Liverpool Five, Out of Sight, RCA LSP-33682, German imp, LP **8.00**

Pretty Things, Rainin In My Heart, Fontana TE-17422, UK pose **30.00**

REDWARE

History: The availability of clay, the same used to make bricks and roof tiles, accounted for the great production of red earthenware pottery in the American colonies. Redware pieces are mainly utilitarian—bowls, crocks, jugs, etc.

Lead-glazed redware retained its reddish color, but a variety of colored glazes were obtained by the addition of metals to the basic glaze. Streaks and mottled splotches in redware items resulted from impurities in the clay and/or uneven firing temperatures.

Slipware is the term used to describe redwares decorated by the application of slip, a semi-liquid paste made of clay. Slipwares were made in England, Germany, and elsewhere in Europe for decades before becoming popular in the Pennsylvania German region and other areas in colonial America.

References: Susan and Al Bagdade, *Warman's American Pottery and Porcelain*, 2nd ed., Krause Publications, 2000; William C. Ketchum, Jr., *American Pottery and Porcelain*, Avon Books, 1994.

Bowl, 8" d, 3-1/2" h, **$240.**

Bank, 3-1/4" h, apple shape, red and yellow paint **160.00**
Bottle, 5-3/4" h, pinched sides and tooling, green glaze, brown flecks, green striping, incised label, "Made by I. S. Stahl, 11-1-1939" **70.00**
Bowl, 4-1/4" d, 2-1/8" h, cream, dark green and brown running glaze, two round applied handle buttons on each side, Shenandoah, crazing and minor glaze flakes **550.00**
Bowl with spout, 6" d, 3-3/4" h, tea-cup shape, applied ribbed handle on side,

incised line, brown mottled glaze **220.00**
Canning jar, 4-1/2" d, 6-1/4" h, mottled dark brown stripes, incised line around middle, bottom inscribed "Medinger," attributed to Jacob Medinger, c1880-1900, Montgomery County, PA **495.00**
Charger, 13" d, molded bust of Washington, star ringed medallion, coggled rim, brown fleck glaze .**475.00**
Cooler, 18" h, ovoid, glaze flaking, mounted as lamp **75.00**
Creamer, 4-1/2" h, burnt orange glaze, running light green highlights, glazed over separation at handle, rim flakes **200.00**
Crock, 7-1/4" h, brown glaze, ivory running splotches, incised lines, roughness at rim **1,595.00**
Cup, 3-3/4" h, flared lip, applied handle, clear glaze with mottled amber, minor wear and glaze flakes **90.00**
Cuspidor, 8" x 4-1/4", tooled bands, brown and green running glaze, brown dashes, some wear and edge chips **265.00**
Dish
4" d, 4-3/4" l, hand modeled as goose, few incised feathers, pinched scalloped rim, black running glaze with faint green tinge, minor edge damage to tail **1,115.00**
5-1/4" d, coggled edge, yellow clip dec, three wavy lines, small rim flake. **990.00**
Figure
3-1/2" h, seated cat, molded with white glaze, brown sponging, green daubs, hairlines, edge damage. **220.00**
7" h, dog, seated, incised collar and chain, sgd "Van Vorhis," glazed over repair. **250.00**
Flower pot, attached saucer base, 5-1/2" d, 5" h, imp "John W. Bell Waynesboro," Rockingham type brown mottled glaze **880.00**
Food mold, miniature, 4-1/4" d, 1-1/2" h, raised beaded edge, black mottling around rim **295.00**
Grease lamp, 4-1/2" h, single pinch spout, strap handle, and saucer base, dark Albany glaze, black grease stains **725.00**
Jar, 5-1/4" d, 5-1/2" h, slightly ovoid, raised rim, imp "John Bell," tiny black spots in glaze, few rim chips . . .**330.00**

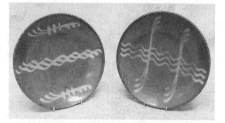

Plates, left: triple wavy line design intersected by two S-curved lines, crimped edge, flake on rim, 9" d; right: three sets of wavy lines, crimped edge, small flakes on rim, large chip, price for pr, $1,650. Photo courtesy of Sanford Alderfer Auction Co.

Jug

7" h, bulbous, applied handle, wheel thrown, dark brown slip . . . **110.00**

9" h, ovoid, strap handle, clear glaze, black splotches, small chip on lip, glaze flakes **110.00**

Milk bowl

8" d, rim spout. **150.00**

9" d, white slip dec, greenish-amber glaze, surface chips. **250.00**

Pie plate, coggled rim

8" d, yellow slip dec of wavy lines and flourishes, shallow rim flakes
. . . . **990.00**

8" d, yellow slip dec, wavy lines and flourishes, crazing and chips
. . . . **420.00**

9-7/8" d, yellow and green slip dec of double loops and wavy lines
. . . . **7,590.00**

10" d, yellow slip dec of three wavy lines, flag-like shapes, rim flake, minor stains **1,045.00**

10-1/4" d, yellow slip dec of wavy lines and series of dots, rim chip and two hairlines **385.00**

10-3/4" d, yellow slip dec, three sets of wavy lines, few edge flakes
. . . . **615.00**

11-1/4" d, yellow slip dec, three sets of wavy lines. **935.00**

Pitcher

7-1/2" h, wheel thrown, applied handle, coggled top edge and band at top of handle, slip colored with copper oxide (green) at top working down to iron oxide (rust) mottled with manganese (dark brown), attributed to Jacob Medinger, c1900-20 . . . . . . **600.00**

10-3/4" h, Albany slip, sgraffito "Independence Pottery Dilts & McKibben, Messenger Office, My Country" surrounded by foliate, finger marks of potter in glaze on

either side of base, hairline, rim chips **1,375.00**

Turk's Head Hold, 8-3/4" d, 4", mottled brown glaze, imp "John Bell Waynesboro," minor roughness, rim flake **715.00**

RED WING POTTERY

History: The Red Wing pottery category includes several potteries from Red Wing, Minnesota. In 1868, David Hallem started Red Wing Stoneware Co., the first pottery with stoneware as its primary product. The Minnesota Stoneware Co. started in 1883. The North Star Stoneware Co. was in business from 1892 to 1896.

The Red Wing Stoneware Co. and the Minnesota Stoneware Co. merged in 1892. The new company, the Red Wing Union Stoneware Co., made stoneware until 1920 when it introduced a pottery line which it continued until the 1940s. In 1936, the name was changed to Red Wing Potteries, Inc. During the 1930s, this firm introduced several popular patterns of hand-painted dinnerware which were distributed through department stores, mail-order catalogs, and gift-stamp centers. Dinnerware production declined in the 1950s and was replaced with hotel and restaurant china in the early 1960s. The plant closed in 1967.

Marks: Red Wing Stoneware Co. was the first firm to mark pieces with a red wing stamped under the glaze. The North Star Stoneware Co. used a raised star and the words "Red Wing" as its mark.

References: Dan and Gail DePasquale and Larry Peterson, *Red Wing Collectibles*, Collector Books, 1985, 1997 value update; —, *Red Wing Stoneware*, Collector Books, 1983, 2000 value update; B. L. Dollen, *Red Wing Art Pottery*, Collector Books, 1997; B. L. and R. L. Dollen, *Collector's Encyclopedia of Red Wing Art Pottery*, Collector Books, 2000; —, *Red Wing Art Pottery Book II*, Collector Books, 1998; Ray Reiss, *Red Wing Art Pottery Including Pottery Made for Rum Rill*, published by author (2144 N. Leavitt, Chicago, IL 60647), 1996; —, *Red Wing Dinnerware*, published by author, 1997.

Collectors' Clubs: Red Wing Collectors Society, Inc., P.O. Box 50, Red Wing, MN 55066; RumRill Society, P.O. Box 2161, Hudson, OH 44236.

Additional Listings: See *Warman's Americana & Collectibles* for more examples.

Basket, #1275 . . . . **45.00**

Bean pot, cov, stoneware, adv . . **85.00**

Beater jar, stoneware, half gallon, "Stanhope, Ia" adv **95.00**

Bookends, pr, fan and scroll, green
. . . . **20.00**

Bowl, stoneware

7" d, blue, rust, and cream sponging
. . . . **75.00**

9-3/4" d, brown and blue sponging, marked "Red Wing Saffron Ware"
. . . . **35.00**

Dinnerware, fruit decoration, 64-piece set consisting of eight dinner plates, eight salad plates, eight bread plates, seven cups, eight saucers, two oval platters, butter dish, water pitcher, lidded sugar, creamer, oval lidded tureen, gravy boat, two salt shakers, pepper shaker, oval divided dish, nine custard bowls, two soup bowls and two cereal bowls, some chips, $170 for set, not all shown. Photo courtesy of Joy Luke Auctions.

Butter crock, 20#, large wing, tight hairline. **550.00**

Buttermilk feeder, stoneware. . . **75.00**

Casserole, cov, 8" d, sponge band, chip on handle **165.00**

Cookie jar, cov

Bob White. **95.00**

French Chef, blue glaze. . . . **250.00**

Grapes, yellow, marked "Red Wing USA," 10" h. **85.00**

Rooster, green glaze, #249, 9-1/4" l
. . . . **150.00**

Creamer and sugar, #1376 . . . . **20.00**

Crock, stoneware, one gallon, large wing. **400.00**

Figure

Cowboy, rust. **175.00**

Cowgirl, #B1414, white. **175.00**

Giraffe, 1995 convention commemorative **95.00**

Jug, five gallon, shoulder, large wing, "California White Wine" stencil . **135.00**

Mason jar, 7" h, stoneware, screw top metal lid, marked ""Stone Mason Fruit Jar, Union Stoneware Co., Red Wing, Minn". **330.00**

Mixing bowl, 7" d, stoneware, "Cap," blue sponge dec, white ground **100.00**

Pitcher, 9" h, stoneware, brown glazed grape dec, rick-rack border, waffle ground, "Red Wing North Star Stoneware" mark. **90.00**

Planter

Canoe. **25.00**

Puppy. **20.00**

Salt and pepper shakers, pr, Town and Country, dark green. **65.00**

Teapot, cov, yellow rooster, gold trim
. . . . **65.00**

Vase, tapered cylinder, straight neck, relief floral design, red matte glaze, stamped "Red Wing/Union/Stone-ware/Co./Red Wing/Minn," 8-1/4" h, **$75.**

Vase

6-1/2" h, bulbous, leaf design, molded ring handles, shiny jade green glaze, marked "Red Wing Art Pottery" **80.00**

8" h
#1103 . . . . **35.00**
#1357 . . . . **35.00**
11-1/2" h, handles, #1376 . . . . **45.00**

Water cooler

Five gallons, small wing, no lid, small hairline **275.00**
Six gallons, small wing, no lid
. . . . **385.00**

RELIGIOUS ITEMS

History: Objects used in worship or as expressions of man's belief in a superhuman power are collected by many people for many reasons.

This category includes icons, since they are religious mementos, usually paintings with a brass encasement. Collecting icons dates from the earliest period of Christianity. Most antique icons in today's market were made in the late 19th century.

Reference: Penny Forstner and Lael Bower, *Collecting Religious Artifacts (Christian and Judaic)*, Books Americana, 1995.

Internet Resources: *Bible Cards*, http://www.antiques-oronoco.com; *Ecclesiological Society*, http://www.ecclsoc.org; *Resurrection Art*, http://www.geocities.com/Athens/Parthenon/1501; *Saints Unlimited*, http://members.xoom.com/bjdevitt.

Collectors' Clubs: Foundation International for Restorers of Religious Medals, P.O. Box 2652, Worcester, MA 01608; Psalm Card Collectors &

Traders, 10802 Greenscreek Drive, Suite 203, Houston, TX 77070-5365.

Museum: American Bible Society, New York, NY; Don Brown Rosary Collection, Skamania Interpretive Center, Stevenson, WA; National Christmas Center, Paradise, PA.

Reproduction Alert: Icons are frequently reproduced.

Additional Listings: Judaic, Russian Items.

Needlepoint panel, Holy Family, rose-wood frame, 54" w, 63" h, **$825.** *Photo courtesy of Joy Luke Auctions.*

Altar cross, 10" x 6", polished brass, two-pc construction, Russian . . **550.00**

Altar gospels, 12" x 14-3/4", silvered and gilded repoussé and chased metal, front cover with repoussé image of the Resurrection & Descent into Hades in center, corners with Old Testament Prophets, back cover with repoussé and chased image of Crucifixion, corners with the four Evangelists, matching clasps with double-headed eagles, limited edition of the divine and holy Gospel in English. **675.00**

Altar niche, 41" w, 22" d, 42" h, carved wood, fluted columns, fancy work, polychrome and gilding, 19th C **880.00**

Altar shrine, circumference 80", 41" h, Gothic-style wood, ext. with applied cherub heads and four side-mounted votive stands, int. rotates to reveal shine, when closed it exhibits a carved-in relief Eucharistic Lamp beneath grapes and wheat, 19th C **935.00**

Angel, 21" and 21-1/4" h, carved, pale green finish, standing, one at prayer, other in repose, sq block base, inscribed on back "Fera Demetz,

Ortisei," Italian, early 20th C, price for pr **2,185.00**

Bible, 3-3/8" w, 4-1/8" h, German, late 19th/early 20th C, .800 silver cover with emb openwork genre scenes within scroll border, 1882 text, approx 4 troy oz **290.00**

Bible cover, 10-1/2" x 7-1/2", vellum cover, front overlaid with massive gilded bronze and silvered plaque with champlevé enamel, depicting crucifixion with the four Evangelists, back cover with gilded bronze Romanesque-style angel and polished stone feet held in gilded and enamel frames, spine imp "Santa Biblia," matching bronze clasps. **1,100.00**

Book

A Religious History of the American People, Sidney Ahlstrom, Yale University Press, 1973, 1,158 pgs, dj **20.00**
In the Steps of St. Paul, H. V. Morton, Dodd, Mead & Co., c1936, 13th printing **8.00**
Survey of American Church Records, E. Kay Kirkam, Deseret Book Co., Salt Lake City, 1959, 217 pgs **12.50**

Buddha

China, Ming dynasty, 1368-1644, bronze, seated on detachable lotus throne, traces of lacquered surface, 16-1/2" h **500.00**
China, possibly Yuan period, 1279-1368, wooden, seated on lotus throne, gilt and polychrome dec, 13-1/2" h **300.00**
Japan, 27" h, carved wood, figure of Amida with halo, seated on red lotus supported by vajra, 19th C **900.00**
Japan, seated, 19th C or earlier **1,725.00**
Tibetan, 18th C, primordial Buddha, Vajradhara, thunderbolt and bell, lapis lazuli, turquoise, coral, and pearl inlay, 9" h **1,150.00**
Thailand, Sukhothai period, 16th C, bronze, 12" h **400.00**

Candlesticks, pr

15" h, Sabbath, brass, classical and floral design, Polish, minor wear, repair, dents **245.00**
28" h, bronze, Gothic style . . **935.00**

Crucifix pendant, 5-3/8" l, 44" l gold-plated rope chain, Ecclesiastic, central enameled depiction of Christ on the cross, gilt-metal surround, border of white metal crimped collet-set faceted colorless pastes, similar tripartite spandrels set with central green-faceted stone, ends of cross set with red stones, base with C-scroll suspending oval prong set green pates surrounded by colorless pastes, topped by red and green stone, crown-form bail, Continental, early 20th C . . **575.00**

Figure, 12-1/2" h, St. John the Baptist, wood, gesso, standing nude figure with naturalistic painting, holding silver metal cross set with faceted red stone, silver metal halo set with faceted pink stone, Continental, late 19th/early 20th C **635.00**

Figure in bottle, 5" d, 13-1/2" h, carved and painted figure of Crucifixion of Christ, various carved symbolic items, such as a book, rooster, ax, bell, and spear, polychrome dec, gold leaf and foil, PA, c1910 . . . . **865.00**

Gospel cover, 13-1/4" x 15", gilded bronze and champlevé enamel, one-pc solid wood spine and back cover, hinged wood front with massive plaque, applied border dec, central gilded bronze and enamel Christ, corners with symbols of the four Evangelists, back cov with gilded bronze and enamel clover-shaped medallions of an arch angel, matching bronze clasps . **880.00**

Icon, Greek

19" x 15", The Mother of God of the Life Bearing Font, tempera on wood panel **1,250.00**

Icon, Christ Enthroned, Russian, 17th C, 35" x 45", $14,950. Photo courtesy of Jackson's Auctioneers & Appraisers.

Icon, Russian, tempera on wood panel, 19th C

8-3/4" x 10-1/2", Baptism of Christ **1,155.00**

14" x 12", double-sided processional, the Holy Village and Baptism of Christ, attributed to Palekh **3,025.00**

16" x 30", The Prophet Elijah with Life Scenes, gold leaf, Elijah in the desert in center, fiery ascension at top, surrounded by life scenes, overlaid with gilded metal riza **4,125.00**

Miniature icon pendant, painted porcelain, gilt metal surround topped by bale, each corner mounted with collet-set faceted red stones, icon depicting bishop saint flanked by small figures of Mary and Jesus, eastern European, 19th C **460.00**

Painting

9-3/8" x 7", oil on copper, unsigned Continental School, 19th C, inscribed "Faith, daughter of...Anna Piatto Florentini 1732" on reverse, framed, scattered losses and retouch, surface grim . . **950.00**

Madonna, carved wood, 16" h, $575. Photo courtesy of Jackson's Auction.

10-1/2" x 13-3/4", oil on canvas, Madonna and Child, unsigned, German School, 19th C, scattered punctures, damage to tacking edges, surface grim, craquelure, 17th C frame **1,610.00**

Plaque

4-3/4" w, 6-5/8" h, painted porcelain, Virgin Mary, demure pose, white gown, blue cloak, heavily scrolled gilt gesso frame, Germany, late 19th C **750.00**

12" w, 2" d, 13-1/2" h, relief-carved pine, Samson and the Lion, attributed to Ulysses Davis (1914-92, Savannah, GA), blue-green painted border **5,750.00**

19" l, painting on porcelain, Christ at foot of the cross, "Des aendimiento de la sus XIII," oak frame . . **225.00**

Processional cross, 27" x 12", silvered and polished bronze, applied corpus, reverse with Mary Magdalene, receptacle base **715.00**

Reliquary cross, 10" x 15", tempera, gold leaf, porcelain on wood cross, reverse with old Slavonic inscription denoting that cross was blessed on Mt. Athos at the Russian Monastery of St. Panteleimon, relic inset on reverse is old square wood fragment, Russian, 19th C **1,650.00**

Retablo, Mexican, painted on tin, late 19th C

9-1/2" x 13-3/4", Our Lady of Sorrows **250.00**

9-3/4" x 13-1/2", Our Lady Refuge of Sinners, black flat iron frame **235.00**

Santos, Philippine, carved and painted wood

13" h, carved winged angel playing lute **200.00**

14" h, The Christ Child **120.00**

15" h, Saint Martin **110.00**

19" h, Mary **150.00**

Shrine

10" w, 10" d, 20" h, carved and turned rosewood, pavilion form, China, late 19th/early 20th C **150.00**

41" h, central figure of Amida standing on double lotus throne, black lacquer case, gilt interior painted with apsaras, Japan, 18th C **3,600.00**

Traveling shrine, 9" h, black lacquer case, int. of gold lacquer with figure of Nyorai seated on lotus throne, Japan, early 20th C **250.00**

REVERSE PAINTING ON GLASS

History: The earliest examples of reverse painting on glass were produced in 13th-century Italy. By the 17th century, the technique had spread to central and eastern Europe. It spread westward as the center of the glassmaking industry moved to Germany in the late 17th century.

The Alsace and Black Forest regions developed a unique portraiture style. The half and three-quarter portraits often were titled below the portrait. Women tend to have generic names, while most males are likenesses of famous men.

The English used a mezzotint, rather than free-style, method to create their reverse paintings. Landscapes and allegorical figures were popular. The Chinese began working in the medium in the 17th century, eventually favoring marine and patriotic scenes.

Most American reverse painting was done by folk artists and is unsigned. Portraits, patriotic and mourning scenes, floral compositions, landscapes, and buildings are the favorite subjects. Known American artists include Benjamin Greenleaf, A. Cranfield, and Rowley Jacobs.

In the late 19th century, commercially produced reverse paintings, often decorated with mother-of-pearl, became popular. Themes included the Statue of Liberty, the capitol in Washington, D.C., and various world's fairs and expositions.

Today craftsmen are reviving this art, using some vintage-looking designs, but usually with brighter colors than their antique counterparts.

Sign, Drugs and Soda, trapezoidal, crinkle background, original copper frame, 29" x 10-1/2", $725. Photo courtesy of James D. Julia, Inc.

Portraits

Fredericke, orig frame, 13-1/2" x 10-5/8" **385.00**
Geisha, facing pr, geisha seated next to table, vase with flower, bamboo dec, mirrored ground, Chinese Export, 19th C, framed, losses, 16" h, 11-1/2" w, pr **625.00**
Lincoln, Abraham, framed, 21-1/2" h, 18" w **425.00**
Rosinia, polychrome, dark green ground, orig frame, 9-1/8" h, 6-1/2" w **450.00**
Van Buren, Martin, marked "M. V. Buren," northern Europe, c1840, for American market, period frame, 7-3/4" w, 9-3/4" h **750.00**
Washington, George, silhouette, intricately painted border maple veneer frame, gilded liner with minor damage, 12-3/4" h, 11" w **250.00**

Scenes

Country house in winter, gold painted frame, 10-1/2" h, 12-1/2" w **75.00**
Perry's Lake Erie Victory, Sept. 10, 1813, naval battle scene, multicolored, 7" x 9" **250.00**
Roundel, 2" d reverse painted roundel with scene of Continental buildings and figures, beaded gilt metal surrounds, set in 13-1/4" h diamond-shaped giltwood shadowbox frames, early 20th C, price for pr **100.00**
Ship, *Ohio*, side wheeler steamship, poplar frame, 10-1/2" h, 12-1/2" w **175.00**
Statue of Liberty, mica accents, oval frame **175.00**
The Oxford and London Coach, screened silhouette of English coaching scene, black, red, blue, and green, gilt title, eglomise mat, bird's eye maple frame, 17-5/8" w, 12-5/8" h **150.00**

RIDGWAY

History: Throughout the 19th century, the Ridgway family, through a series of partnerships, held a position of importance in the ceramics industry in Shelton and Hanley, Staffordshire, England. The connection began with Job and George, two brothers, and Job's two sons, John and William. In 1830, John and William dissolved their partnership; John retained the Cauldon Place factory and William the Bell Works.

By 1862, the porcelain division of Cauldon was carried on by Coalport China Ltd. William and his heirs continued at the Bell Works and the Church (Hanley) and Bedford (Shelton) works until the end of the 19th century.

Marks: Many early pieces are unmarked. Later marks include the initials of the many different partnerships.

References: Susan and Al Bagdade, *Warman's English & Continental Pottery & Porcelain*, 3rd ed., Krause Publications, 1998; G. A. Godden, *Ridgway Porcelains*, Antique Collectors' Club, 1985.

Museums: Cincinnati Art Museum, Cincinnati, OH; Potsdam Public Museum, Potsdam, NY.

Additional Listings: Staffordshire, Historical; and Staffordshire, Romantic.

Cheese dish, cover, light brown, floral transfer, 8-1/2" x 10", $65.

Beverage set, 9-1/2" h pitcher, six 4" h mugs, 12-1/2" d tray, Coaching Days, black coaching scenes, caramel ground, silver luster trim **325.00**
Bowl, 9-1/2" d, Coaching Days and Ways, "Henry VII and the Abbot,"" black and caramel brown **45.00**
Cup and saucer, boy fishing on lake **30.00**
Dinner service, partial, Hanley, Staffordshire, late 19th C, all over blue transfer printed Chinoiserie and Middle Eastern-style scenic cartouches, 11 teacups, nine saucers, nine 9" d dinner plates, eight 7-3/8" d soup bowls, eight 7-3/4" dessert bowls, seven 5" d fruit bowls, seven 7-3/4" d luncheon plates, 12-7/8" l platter, teapot, creamer, cov sugar bowl and underplate, trivet, cov 9-3/4" l tureen, price for 65 pcs . **950.00**
Ice pail, cov, 13" h, horizontal band of gilt edged orange feathery scrollwork reserved on pale yellow ground, above acanthus leaf molding, rope twist handles with trailing vine leaf terminals, cov with finials modeled as rhytons brimming with fruit, finial repaired, c1840, iron-red number **3,500.00**
Mug, 4" h, Boating Days, New Haven and Eton, brown body, silver luster trim **45.00**

Left: Burslem Ware, tureen, cover, two handles, Willow pattern, blue and white, square, 10" w, $100; right: Ridgways, tureen, cover, borders with flowers and leaves, molded handles outlined in gold trim, blue and white, $80. Photo courtesy of Joy Luke Auctions.

Pitcher, 4-1/4" h, red transfers of family scenes on cream ground in roundels, reserved on cobalt blue ground, c1890, "Humphrey's Clock and William Ridgway" mark **225.00**

Plate, 8-1/2" d, rose, rust, and purple Oriental-type florals with yellow centers, gray-green branches, raised, ribbed, scalloped edge, white ground, c1830, No. 2004 . . . . **65.00**

Sauce tureen, cov, underplate, 6-3/4" h squat body, leaf handles, peaked lid, annulated steam with shaped foot, peach border, floral sprays, gilding, 8" l ovoid underplate with short handles, third quarter 19th C, price for pr **475.00**

Teapot, cov, 6" h, 6" l, brown and white whooping cranes and foliage, emb leaves, dated 1877, marked . . . **125.00**

Tray, 9-1/2" l, 7-1/2" w, Pickwick design, silver luster trim, scalloped rim, open handles **60.00**

RING TREES

History: A ring tree is a small, generally saucer-shaped object made of glass, porcelain, metal, or wood with a center post in the shape of a hand, branches, or cylinder. It is a convenient object for holding finger rings.

Glass

Black, 3-7/8" d, 4" h, all over dec on saucer and post, lacy gold vines and green enamel leaves, light blue, white, orange, and cream flowers **95.00**

Bristol, 3" h, 3-1/4" d, turquoise blue, lacy yellow leaves and large gold leaves dec **85.00**

Cameo, 3-1/4" h, 4" d, acid cut, red flowers, leaves, and stems, leaf ground, St. Louis **160.00**

Clear, 3" h, 3-3/4" d, cut floral dec, black enameled bands **65.00**

Cranberry, 3-1/4" h, 3-1/2" d, hp, multicolored flowers, gold leaves **115.00**

Porcelain, tree trunk standard, forest scene with road and pasture, 3" h, $30.

Opalescent, 2-1/2" h, 3-1/2" d, vaseline, striped **65.00**

Waterford, crystal **35.00**

Porcelain

Austria, hp pink and green floral dec, gold trim, marked "M. Z. Austria" . **70.00**

Limoges, multicolored blossoms, white ground, marked "T. & V. Limoges" **40.00**

Minton, 3" h, pastel flowers, gold trim, marked "Minton England" **45.00**

Nippon, gold hand, rim dec **35.00**

Noritake, 3-1/2" d, 3" h, white hand, painted blue and pink flowers . . . **35.00**

Royal Worcester, 2-3/4" h, 4-1/2" l, oval dish, three-pronged holder, hp pink and yellow flowers, beige ground, c1898 . . . . **150.00**

R. S. Germany, 2-3/4" h, 5-1/2" l, hp, pink flowers, green leaves, told tree, sgd "E. Wolff" **50.00**

Sterling silver, saucer base, repoussé, three wire ring holders, marked "RW & S," 3" d base, 2" h, $145.

Wedgwood, 2-3/4" h, jasperware, center post, white cameos of classical ladies, floral border, blue ground, marked **150.00**

Silver

Tiffany & Co., angel shape . . . **450.00**

Wilcox, open hand, saucer base, engraved edge, sgd **60.00**

ROCKINGHAM AND ROCKINGHAM BROWN-GLAZED WARES

History: Rockingham ware can be divided into two categories. The first consists of the fine china and porcelain pieces made between 1826 and 1842 by the Rockingham Company of Swinton, Yorkshire, England, and its predecessor firms: Swinton, Bingley, Don, Leeds, and Brameld. The Bramelds developed the cadogan, a lidless teapot. Between 1826 and 1842, a quality soft-paste product with a warm, silky feel was developed by the Bramelds. Elaborate specialty pieces were made. By 1830, the company employed 600 workers and listed 400 designs for dessert sets and 1,000 designs for tea and coffee services in its catalog. Unable to meet its payroll, the company closed in 1842.

The second category of Rockingham ware includes pieces produced in the famous Rockingham brown glaze that became an intense and vivid purple-brown when fired. It had a dark, tortoiseshell appearance. The glaze was copied by many English and American potteries. American manufacturers which used Rockingham glaze include D. & J. Henderson of Jersey City, New Jersey; United States Pottery in Bennington, Vermont; potteries in East Liverpool, Ohio; and several potteries in Indiana and Illinois.

References: Susan and Al Bagdade, *Warman's American Pottery and Porcelain*, 2nd ed., Krause Publications, 2000; Susan and Al Bagdade, *Warman's English & Continental Pottery & Porcelain*, 3rd ed., Krause Publications, 1998; Mary Brewer, *Collector's Guide to Rockingham*, Collector Books, 1996.

Museum: Bennington Museum, Bennington, VT.

Additional Listings: Bennington and Bennington-Type Pottery.

Bedpan, 15" l, Rockingham glaze, chip **40.00**

Bowl
9-1/2" d, 3-1/4" h **65.00**
10-1/2" d, 4-3/4" h, molded ext. ribs, scalloped band **50.00**

Casserole, cov, 12" l, 10-1/4" h, oval, fruit finial, applied handles **275.00**

Bowl, mocha and gold decoration, 7-3/8" d, 3-1/4" h, **$70.**

Creamer, 6-3/4" h, cow-form, 19th C, minor chips **260.00**
Cuspidor, 6-5/8", 4" h, four sides, molded eagles, dark brown Rockingham glaze **330.00**
Dish, 11-1/2" l, octagonal, spotted Rockingham glaze **170.00**
Figure, 10-5/8" h, dog, open front legs, seated on scalloped base, molded features, dark brown Rockingham glaze, few edge chips **330.00**
Flask, 8" h, molded floral dec, band **45.00**
Flower pot, 10-1/4" h, emb acanthus leaves, matching saucer **45.00**
Inkwell, 4-1/8" l, shoe shape **60.00**
Mixing bowl, nested set of three, emb design **95.00**
Pie plate, Rockingham glaze
8-3/8" d **65.00**
10" d **80.00**

Pitcher, mocha, gold, floral decoration, unmarked, 6-1/2" h, **$135.**

Pitcher, Rockingham glaze
4-3/8" l, squatty, C scroll handle **75.00**
6-3/8" h, molded Gothic Art design **65.00**
8" h, molded peacocks, rim chips **90.00**

Plate
9" d, painted center with exotic bird in landscape, raised C-scroll border with gilt and painting, puce griffin and green number marks **650.00**
9-1/4" d, painted vase of flowers overflowing onto marble table, medium blue ground, gilt line band, shark's tooth and S-scroll border, c1831-42 . . . . **875.00**
Potpourri vase, 4-3/8" h, waisted rect shape, painted front and reverse with river landscape between gilt formal borders, four paw feet, pierced cov with acorn knob, double handles, c1826, iron-red griffin mark **950.00**
Scent bottle, 6" h, onion shape, applied garden flowers, gilt line rims, c1831-40, printed puce griffin mark **465.00**
Tray, 8-1/2" x 11", scalloped rim **100.00**
Vase
4-3/8" h, flared, painted view of Larington Yorkshire, figures and sheep, wide gilt border, dark blue ground, restored, c1826-30, iron-red griffin and painted title **420.00**
6-1/2" h, flared hexagon, painted sprays of colored garden flowers alternating with blue panels, gilt scrolls, c1831-42, puce griffin mark **800.00**
Washboard, 24-1/4" h, 19th C, imperfections **350.00**

ROCK 'N' ROLL

History: Rock music can be traced back to early rhythm and blues. It progressed until it reached its golden age in the 1950s and 1960s. Most of the memorabilia issued during that period focused on individual singers and groups. The largest quantity of collectible material is connected to Elvis Presley and The Beatles.

In the 1980s, two areas—clothing and guitars—associated with key rock 'n' roll personalities received special collector attention. Sotheby's and Christie's East regularly feature rock 'n' roll memorabilia as part of their collectibles sales. At the moment, the market is highly speculative and driven by nostalgia.

It is important to identify memorabilia issued during the lifetime of an artist or performing group, as opposed to material issued after they died or disbanded. Objects of the latter type are identified as "fantasy" items and will never achieve the same degree of collectibility as period counterparts.

References: Jeff Augsburger, Marty Eck, and Rick Rann, *The Beatles Memorabilia Price Guide*, Antique Trader Books; Mark A. Baker, *Goldmine Price Guide to Rock N' Roll Memorabilia*, Krause Publications, 1997; John Clemente, *Girl Groups, Fabulous Females That*

Rocked the World, Krause Publications, 2000; Goldmine Magazine eds., *Goldmine Roots of Rock Digest*, Krause Publications, 1999; ——, *The Beatles Digest*, Krause Publications, 2000; Marty Eck, *The Monkees Collectibles Price Guide*, Antique Trader Books, 1998; Dr. Anthony J. Gribin and Dr. Matthew M. Schiff, *The Complete Book of Doo-Wop*, Krause Publications, 2000; Joe Hilton and Greg Moore, *Rock-N-Roll Treasures*, Collector Books, 1999; David Loehr and Joe Bills, *The James Dean Collectors Guide*, L-W Book Sales, 1999; Chuck Miller, *Warman's Records*, Krause Publications, 2001.

Periodicals: *Beatlefan*, P.O. Box 33515, Decatur, GA 30033; *Good Day Sunshine*, 397 Edgewood Ave., New Haven, CT 06511.

Collectors' Clubs: Beatles Connection, P.O. Box 1066, Pinellas Park, FL 34665; Elvis Forever TCB Fan Club, P.O. Box 1066, Pinellas Park, FL 34665; Liverpool Productions Monkees Buttonmania Club, 315 Derby Ave., Orange, CT 06477; Working Class Hero Club, 3311 Niagara St., Pittsburgh, PA 15213.

> **Reproduction Alert:** Records, picture sleeves, and album jackets, especially for The Beatles, have been counterfeited. When compared to the original, sound may be inferior, as may be the printing on labels and picture jackets. Many pieces of memorabilia also have been reproduced, often with some change in size, color, and design.

Additional Listings: See The Beatles, Elvis Presley, and Rock 'n' Roll in *Warman's Americana & Collectibles* and *Warman's Flea Market Price Guide*.

Autograph, photo
Greg Allman **40.00**
Chuck Berry **75.00**
Jon Bon Jovi **40.00**

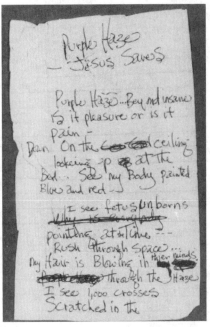

Signed document, Jimi Hendrix, hand-written lyrics, "Purple Haze," **$18,000.**

Michael Jackson **195.00**
Mick Jagger **135.00**
Madonna **195.00**
Paul McCartney **275.00**
Bruce Springsteen **150.00**

Backstage pass, cloth
Aerosmith, Pump Tour '89, afternoon
. . . . **10.00**
Black Sabbath, working personnel
. . . . **9.00**
Bon Jovi, NJ Guest **7.00**
KISS, 10th anniversary, after show,
unused **7.00**
Cindi Lauper, Crew '86-87 . . . . **6.00**
Pink Floyd, Mixer '94 . . . . **9.00**
Rolling Stones, American Tour '81
. . . . **15.00**

Book
Beatlebook of Recorded Hits, No. 2,
copyright 1964, pullout photo
section, official fan club
membership application form,
slight wear to cover **95.00**
Elvis Presley, 1994, 240 pgs . . **24.00**

Bubble gum cards, complete set,
issued by Boxcar Enterprises, 1978
. . . . **135.00**

Comic book
Frank Zappa, #32, 1991 . . . . . **20.00**
Queensryche I, #19 . . . . **20.00**

Cookie jar, Elvis Presley, 15" h . **275.00**

Counter display, Rolling Stones,
"Made In The Shade," 1976, 21" x 19",
3-D cardboard, bowed diecut, with four
previous LP covers at left and "Rolling
Stones & Tongue" logo on silver at top
right **250.00**

Divider card, Yardbirds, LP bin type,
Epic, 1988, 12" x 14" plastic, purple
names and logos emb at top . . . **200.00**

Drumsticks
Alice in Chains **25.00**
Black Crows, concerned used, logo
. . . . **20.00**
Randy Castillo, Ozzy Osbourne
. . . . **35.00**
Iron Maiden, 1985 . . . . **50.00**
Steve Riley, WASP **20.00**

Flyer, concert
Aerosmith, 1988, 8" x 6", two sided,
Whitesnake and Def Leppard on
back **45.00**
Led Zeppelin, Tarrant County
Convention Center, Ft. Worth, TX,
8/22/70, 8-1/2" x 11-1/2" **60.00**

Jacket, Billy Joel, promo, black leather,
aviator style, detachable sleeves,
keyboard, wings logo embroidered on
left breast pocket, five outer pockets,
size large **325.00**

*Drawing, Psychedelic, Jimi
Hendrix, 1969,* **$6,875.**

Label sticker, Deep Purple, promo LP
label made for Come Taste The Band
. . . . **25.00**

Magazine, *Life,* Oct. 24, 1968, Beatles
on cover, feature article **40.00**

Menu, Elvis Presley, Las Vegas Hilton
Hotel, 8-1/2" x 11" **1,000.00**

Merchandising kit, Queen, Night At the
Opera, Elektra, 1985, 24" x 24"
cardboard and tin paper poster with LP
cover, two 15" x 24" two-sided thin
cardboard "Hanging Arrow" displays,
two 9" x 10" oval posters with LP cover
art **200.00**

Pennant, 29-1/2" l, We Love Lil Richard,
felt, white, red design and border, orig
30" l wood stick, 1950s **50.00**

Plaque, Bon Jovi, Anytime, Anywhere,
with unused tickets from Belgium, Italy,
and Istanbul, gold CD, only 45
produced **250.00**

Portrait, Elvis Presley, by Ivan Jesse
Curtain, wooden frame, 1960s . . **125.00**

Postcard, Beatles, wearing gray suits,
made in Germany **35.00**

Press kit, KISS, Casablanca, 1976,
custom folder, three-page bio,
one-page press clipping, five 8" x 10"
black and white photos, orig mailing
envelope with no writing or postage
. . . . **500.00**

Print, Chuck Berry, by Red Grooms,
color screenprint on paper, 1978,
edition of 150, published by
Marlborough Graphics, NY, sgd "Red
Grooms" in pencil lower right,

numbered "77/150" in pencil lower left,
24-1/2" x 18-1/2" **345.00**

Promotional standee, Elvis Presley,
"Aloha From Hawaii," RA, 1973, 34" x
56" **175.00**

Record
Elvis Presley, The Memphis Record,
RCA Victor, RCA 6222-1-1-R,
two-record set, 1987 . . . . . . **15.00**

Record award
Beatles, "20 Greatest Hits," orig
RIAA Gold strip plate award, gold
wood frame **795.00**
Billy Joel, "Songs from the Attic,"
RIAA Platinum Strip plate, orig
silver wood frame **450.00**
Eagles, "The Long Run," RIAA
Platinum for four million sales
. . . . **600.00**
Hootie & the Blowfish, "Fairweather
Johnson," RIAA Gold LP . . **600.00**
KISS, "Alive," Casablanca, in-house
Platinum floater **595.00**

Scarf, Beatles, glossy fabric, half
corner design, marked "The
Beatles/Copyright by Ramat & Co.,
Ltd./London, ECI," 25" sq, c1964
. . . . **160.00**

*Pinback button, Elvis Presley
National Fan Club Member, black
and white, c1956, 15/16" d,* **$175.**
*Photo courtesy of Hake's Americana
& Collectibles.*

Ticket
Aerosmith, Pacific, 1989 . . . . . **5.00**
Bruce Springsteen, LA Sports, 1988
. . . . **5.00**
Elvis, 9/88 . . . . **75.00**
Yardbirds/Doors, 1967 . . . . . . **50.00**

Tour book
Depeche Mode, Devotional Tour
1993/94 . . . . **10.00**
KISS, 10th anniversary, Vinnie V in
makeup **125.00**

T-shirt

Bob Dylan, XL, True Confession, worn....................**10.00**

Bon Jovi, L, Slippery When..., never worn....................**25.00**

Deep Purple, L, Perfect Str...'85, never worn................**25.00**

Rolling Stones, XL, Steel Wheels, never worn................**20.00**

Wallet, Beatles, red and white, imprinted autographs and photo on front, clasp missing **95.00**

ROCKWELL, NORMAN

History: Norman Rockwell (February 3, 1894-November 1978) was a famous American artist and illustrator. During the time he painted, from age 18 until his death, he created more than 2,000 works.

His first professional efforts were illustrations for a children's book; his next projects were done for *Boy's Life*, the Boy Scout magazine. His most famous works are those that appeared as cover illustrations on the *Saturday Evening Post*.

Norman Rockwell painted everyday people in everyday situations, mixing a little humor with sentiment. His paintings and illustrations are treasured because of this sensitive approach. Rockwell painted people he knew and places with which he was familiar. New England landscapes are found in many of his illustrations.

References: Denis C. Jackson, *Norman Rockwell Identification and Value Guide to: Magazines, Posters, Calendars, Books*, 2nd ed., published by author, 1985; Karal Ann Marling, *Norman Rockwell*, Harry N. Abrams, 1997.

Collectors' Club: Rockwell Society of America, 597 Saw Mill River Road, Ardsley, NY 10502.

Museums: Museum of Norman Rockwell Art, Reedsburg, WI; Norman Rockwell Museum, Northbrook, IL; Norman Rockwell Museum, Philadelphia, PA; Norman Rockwell Museum, Stockbridge, MA.

> **Reproduction Alert:** Because of the popularity of his works, images have been reproduced on many objects. These new collectibles, which should not be confused with original artwork and illustrations, provide a wide range of collectibles and prices.

Additional Listings: See *Warman's Americana & Collectibles* for more examples.

Historic

Autograph, typed letter sgd, one page, 8vo, Stockbridge, April 24, 1973, answering questions relating to his work
..........................**450.00**

Book

My Adventures as an Illustrator, Rockwell, 1960 ....**25.00**

Tom Sawyer, Heritage Press, 1936
......................**20.00**

Calendar, 1941, boy and dog illus, Hercules Powder Co. adv, 13" x 30-1/2"
......................**175.00**

Magazine, cover illus, *Life*, Aug. 14, 1964, Lyndon B. Johnson **12.00**

Magazine cover, Saturday Evening Post, September 1958, Checkup, 11" x 14", $40.

Magazine, cover illus, *Saturday Evening Post*

Aug. 27, 1960, men's club ...**18.00**

December 1975 ....**25.00**

Oct. 29, 1960, John F. Kennedy
......................**30.00**

Nov. 5, 1960, Richard Nixon..**30.00**

Jan/Feb 1979, In Loving Memory of Norman Rockwell.........**15.00**

Magazine tear sheet, Jell-O adv, *Country Gentleman*, 1922, matted
......................**40.00**

Poster

Freedom of Speech, WWII, 1943
......................**60.00**

Maxwell House Coffee adv, 1932
......................**350.00**

Modern

Coin, Ford Motor Co., 50th Anniversary
..........................**40.00**

Dealer's sign, 5-1/4" h, hand-painted porcelain, 1980 ....**125.00**

Figure

Gorham Fine China, Four Seasons, Childhood, 1973, set of four
......................**500.00**

Grossman Designs, Inc., Tom Sawyer, Series No. 1, 1976 .**95.00**

Plate

Christmas, 1981, Rockwell Museum, MIB **80.00**

Scotty Gets His Tree, Christmas Series, Rockwell Society of America, 1974...........**175.00**

Summer-The Mysterious Malady, 1971, MIB **95.00**

Fall-Pride of Parenthood, 1971, MIB
......................**95.00**

Print

Gilding the Eagle, Eleanor Ettinger, Inc., litho, 21" x 25-1/2" ..**3,500.00**

Music Hath Charms, Circle Fine Arts, sgd and numbered **3,000.00**

People Praying, color offset litho, sgd in pencil lower right, numbered, 28-1/4" x 22" ...**900.00**

ROGERS AND SIMILAR STATUARY

History: John Rogers, born in America in 1829, studied sculpture in Europe and produced his first plaster-of-paris statue, "The Checker Players," in 1859. It was followed by "The Slave Auction" in 1860.

His works were popular parlor pieces in the Victorian era. He produced at least 80 different statues, and the total number of groups made from the originals is estimated to be more than 100,000.

Casper Hennecke, one of Rogers' contemporaries, operated C. Hennecke & Company from 1881 until 1896 in Milwaukee, Wisconsin. His statuary often is confused with Rogers' work, since both are very similar.

References: Paul and Meta Bieier, *John Rogers' Groups of Statuary*, published by author, 1971; Betty C. Haverly, *Hennecke's Florentine Statuary*, published by author, 1972; David H. Wallace, *John Rogers*, Wesleyan University, 1976.

Periodical: *Rogers Group*, 4932 Prince George Ave., Beltsville, MD 20705.

Museums: John Rogers Studio & Museum of the New Canaan Historical Society, New Canaan CT; Lightner Museum, Saint Augustine, FL.

Notes: It is difficult to find a statue in undamaged condition and with original paint. Use the following conversions: 10 percent off for minor flaking; 10 percent, chips; 10 to 20 percent, piece or pieces broken and reglued; 20 percent, flaking; 50 percent, repainting.

Checkers Up At the Farm......**525.00**

Coming to the Parson's **375.00**

Council of War **1,300.00**

Faust and Margeurite Leaving the Garden..................**1,300.00**

Going for the Cows **450.00**

Ha, I Like Not That **550.00**

It is So Nominated in the Bond..**650.00**

Parting Promise **400.00**

Checkers at the Farm, c1875, 20" h, $525.

Picket Guard **825.00**
Rip Van Winkle at Home, damage
. . . . **275.00**
Speak for Yourself John. **550.00**
Taking the Oath **650.00**
Union Refugee, broken gun . . . **325.00**
We Boys. **475.00**
Weighing the Baby, damage. . . **575.00**

ROOKWOOD POTTERY

History: Mrs. Marie Longworth Nicholas Storer, Cincinnati, Ohio, founded Rookwood Pottery in 1880. The name of this outstanding American art pottery came from her family estate, "Rookwood," named for the rooks (crows) which inhabited the wooded grounds.

Though the Rookwood pottery filed for bankruptcy in 1941, it was soon reorganized under new management. Efforts at maintaining the pottery proved futile, and it was sold in 1956 and again in 1959. The pottery was moved to Starkville, Mississippi, in conjunction with the Herschede Clock Co. It finally ceased operating in 1967.

Rookwood wares changed with the times. The variety is endless, in part because of the creativity of the many talented artists responsible for great variations in glazes and designs.

Marks: There are five elements to the Rookwood marking system—the clay or body mark, the size mark, the decorator mark, the date mark, and the factory mark. The best way to date Rookwood art pottery is from factory marks.

From 1880 to 1882, the factory mark was the name "Rookwood" incised or painted on the base. Between 1881 and 1886, the firm name, address, and year appeared in an oval frame. Beginning in 1886, the impressed "RP" monogram appeared and a flame mark was added for each year until 1900. After 1900, a Roman numeral, indicating the last two digits of the year of production, was added at the bottom of the "RP" flame mark. This last mark is the one most often seen on Rookwood pieces in the antiques marketplace.

References: Anita J. Ellis, *Rookwood Pottery*, Schiffer Publishing, 1995; Herbert Peck, *Book of Rookwood Pottery*, Crown Publishers, 1968; ——, *Second Book of Rookwood Pottery*, published by author, 1985; David Rago, *American Art Pottery*, Knickerbocker Press, 1997.

Internet Resource:
http://www.mimurphy.home.mindspring.com/information/index.html.

Collectors' Club: American Art Pottery Assoc., P.O. Box 834, Westport, MA 02790-0697, http://www.amartpot.org.

Plaque, vellum glaze, landscape, titled "Sunset," by Sara Sax, original frame and backing, c1910-15, 4-3/4" x 9", $4,000. Photo courtesy of Freeman\Fine Arts of Philadelphia, Inc.

Architectural tile, 17-1/2" sq, cuenca, tree landscape, blue, green, and tan matte glazes, mounted in Arts & Crafts frame, imp "Rookwood Faience"
. . . . **3,450.00**
Bookend, 6-1/4" w, 5-3/4" h, elephant, semi-matte ivory glaze, production,
1920, flame mark/XX/244C, firing line to back, X'd for glaze drip. **145.00**
Bowl, 6" d, 1-1/4" h, Standard Glaze, almond husk shape, by Grace Young, 1899, incised golden flowers, brown ground, flame mark/279A-Y/G.M.Y., crack and several nicks **100.00**
Cabinet vase, 3" d, 3" h, Tiger Eye, flame mark obscured by glaze, two very minor grinding base chips **350.00**
Candlestick, 4" d, 10" h, Cameo Ware, by Harriet Wilcox, 1887, painted translucent white flowers, shaded blue-gray ground, gilded details, flame mark/238C/W7/H.E.W., light wear to gilding near rim **690.00**
Charger, 12-1/2" d, mauve and ochre galleon center, light blue splashed border, John Wareham, dated 1905
. . . . **1,500.00**
Chocolate pot, 10" h, standard glaze, oak leaves and across dec, shape #722, Lenore Ashbury, 1904. . . **700.00**
Ewer
4" d, 5-1/2" h, by Josephine E. Zettel, 1891, standard glaze, orchids on shaded ground, Gorham silver floral overlay, flame mark/509/W/artist's cipher, Gorham stamp on overlay **2,300.00**
5-1/2" d, 7" h, by Albert Valentien, 1885, tiger eye, painted in Limoges style, swallows and branches, gilded highlights, imp "ROOKWOOD/1885/45" and artist's cipher, few shallow scratches **980.00**
Figure, 7-1/2" d, 8" h, woman's head, matte white glaze, 1924, flame mark/XXIV/2026. . . . . **365.00**
Flower boat, 16" l, standard glaze, pansies dec, shape #3745, Matt A. Daly, 1890 . . . . **900.00**
Flower frog, #2251, 1915. . . . . **325.00**
Humidor, 6" h, standard glaze, carved and dec salmon pansies, 1889, crazing
. . . . **500.00**
Jug, 3-1/2" d, 5-1/4" h, by Albert Humphrys, 1882, Limoges style, geese flying over bamboo thicket, stamped "ROOKWOOD 1882 A.H." with anchor
. . . . **490.00**
Mug, 5" d, 5-1/2" h, emb owl on oak branch, matte green glaze, 1906, flame mark/VI/X, X'd for small glaze blister on owl's toe, peppering **230.00**
Paperweight, 3-1/2" d, elephant, 1928
. . . . **250.00**

Pitcher

4-3/4" h, 6" w, tri-cornered, incised oak leaves, blue ground, Albert Pons, 1900, flame mark/753/D/artist's cipher **. . 425.00**

7-1/2" d, 6-1/2" h, oviform, incised palm leaves, gold and blue highlights, imp "Rookwood, 1883, small kiln, 'Y' 13" **. 230.00**

Planter, 8-3/4" h, 8-1/2" d, incised stylized leaves, frothy brown-green matte glaze, c12910, flame mark/XI/180C **. 500.00**

Trivet, 6-1/4" d, production, star shape, purple flowers, green heart shaped leaves, ivory ground, flame mark/x'd **. 200.00**

Urn, 3-1/2" d, 4-3/4" h, Standard Glaze, baluster, by Edith Felten, 1899, hibiscus dec, flame mark **. 400.00**

Vase, wax matte, classical, by Jens Jensen, 1929, stylized yellow, red, and purple flowers on pink ground, flame mark/XXIX/2303/artist's cipher. 9-1/2" x 6", $1,610. Photo courtesy of David Rago Auctions.

Vase, carved matte

2-3/4" d, 10" h, by Charles Todd, 1914, ovoid, blue grape clusters and leaves, mottled green and red matte ground, flame mark/XIV/1844/C.S.T. **. 980.00**

7" d, 12" h, by Rose Fechheimer, 1905, purple cala lilies, leaves, light green ground, flame mark/V/943B/V/RF, X'd for in-the-firing glaze bubbles on shoulder **. 1,725.00**

Vase, Iris Glaze, 4-3/4" d, 11-1/2" h, by Lenore Ashbury, 1904, white water lilies, green leaves, shaded pink and green ground, flame mark/IV/320/LA, seconded mark, glaze miss, in-making flaw **. 690.00**

Vase, Jewel Porcelain, 7" d, 7-1/2" h, by Jens Jensen, 1926, bulbous, cobalt blue and blue nudes and flowers, shaded taupe ground, flame mark/XXVI/2969/artist's cipher **. 4,875.00**

Vase, scenic vellum

3" d, 7-1/2" h, by Carl Schmidt, 1922, marine, shaded pink to blue ground, flame mark/XXII/904E/V/artist's cipher, light overall crazing **. 2,415.00**

3-1/4" d, 7" h, by Edward Diers, 1921, landscape vista of tall trees, flame mark/XXI/2102/V/ED, uncrazed **. 2,070.00**

3-1/2" d, 8-1/2" h, by Carl Schmidt, tapering, white and lavender lady slipper orchids, green leaves, shaded pink to green ground, flame mark/V/960D/V/CS, fine crazing **. 4,025.00**

3-1/2" d, 9" h, by Lorinda Epply, 1914, blue and ivory trees, flame mark/XIV/588E/V/LE, uncrazed **. 1,725.00**

4-1/4" d, 10" h, by Sallie Coyne, 1915, misty tall trees landscape, pastels, flame mark/XV/2032D/artist's cipher, small bruise to base **. 920.00**

Vase, Squeezebag, 5" d, 6-1/4" h, by Jens Jensen, 1928, brown and blue-gray stylized leaves, yellow ground, flame mark/XXVII/1781/artist cipher **. 1,150.00**

Vase, standard glaze

4-1/2" d, 6-1/2" h, by A. M. Valentien, 1891, oak leaves and acorns, light glaze, flame mark/346B/W/A.M.V **. 750.00**

4-1/2" d, 7" h, by C. F. Bonsall, 1903, two handles, auburn maple leaves, flame mark/III/604D/C.F.B. **. 575.00**

4-3/4" d, 9" h, by Kataro Shirayamadani, 1900, floating draped skeleton bearing lamp, silver-washed copper overlaid rim and handle emb with half moon, wind-swept clouds, and incense from skeleton's burner, flame mark/564D/artist's cipher, tight line to base goes on inch up side, short

tight lines below metal rim **. 3,450.00**

Vase, Vellum

3-1/4" d, 7-3/4" h, by Mary Grace Denzler, 1915, band of Art Deco roses around rim, flame mark XV/2032E/V/MGD, some peppering around rim **. 980.00**

4" d, 9-1/2" h, by Lenor Asbury, 1913, pink and white apple blossoms, shaded teal, ivory, and pink ground, flame mark/XII/2060D/V/L.A., fine overall crazing **. 815.00**

4-1/2" d, 7" h, by Ed Diers, 1911, pink roses, shaded celadon, teal, and pink ground, flame mark/XI/136E/V/ED, fine overall crazing **. 575.00**

Vase, Wax Matte

2-3/4" d, 6-1/4" h, by Margaret Helen McDonald, 1935, fine yellow glaze, white snowdrops, uncrazed, flame mark/XXXV/S/MHM **. 980.00**

3-1/4" d, 6-1/4" h, by Caroline Steinle, 1918, band of cherry blossoms, semi-matte green glaze, flame mark/XVIII/924/CS **. 750.00**

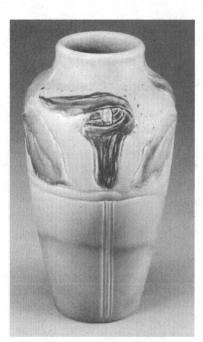

Vase, carved matte, by Rose Fechheimer, 1905, with purple calla lilies and leaves on light green matte ground, flame mark V/943B/V/R.F, X'ed for glaze bubbles to shoulder, in the firing, 12" x 7", $1,725. Photo courtesy of David Rago Auctions.

4-1/2" d, 9-1/2" h, by Janet Harris, 1929, shouldered, mauve and white daffodils and leaves, orchid matte ground, flame mark/XXIX/1920/JH. **1,150.00**

6" d, 9-1/2" h, by Jens Jensen, 1929, stylized yellow, red, and purple flowers, pink ground, flame mark/XXIX/2303/artist's cipher **1,610.00**

Vessel

5-1/2" w, 4" h, carved matte, squatty, by William Hentschel, 1910, Glasgow roses, burgundy and teal blue glaze, flame mark/X/1110/WEH **815.00**

8" w, 3" h, production, squat, cut-out ferns, matte green and brown glaze, flame mark/IX/1888/V, 1909 . . . . **575.00**

9" w, 6-1/2" h, vellum, by Lenore Ashbury, 1920, squatty, golden dandelions, green leaves, blue and mauve ground, flame mark/XX/1375/V/L.A. **1,380.00**

ROSE BOWLS

History: A rose bowl is a decorative open bowl with a crimped, pinched, or petal top which turns in at the top, but does not then turn up or back out again. Rose bowls held fragrant rose petals or potpourri, which served as an air freshener in the late Victorian period. Practically every glass manufacturer made rose bowls in virtually every glass type, pattern, and style, including fine art glass.

Reference: Johanna S. Billings with Sean Billings, *Collectible Rose Bowls*, Antique Trader Books, 1999.

Internet Resource: Stuhorn@voicenet.com.

Reproduction Alert: Rose bowls have been widely reproduced. Be especially careful of Italian copies of satin, Mother of Pearl satin, peachblow, and Burmese, and recent Czechoslovakian ones with applied flowers.

Additional Listings: See specific glass categories.

Bohemian

2" h, 2-1/4" w, transparent amethyst with enameled flowers, polished bottom, six crimps **225.00**

3-1/4" h, 3-3/4" w, cranberry, faint vertical ribbing in glass, enameled female figure and gold outlined background, six crimps with light gold edging, engraved mark on bottom which looks similar to a scripted E, possibly Rossler **125.00**

Dugan, 4" h, 4" w, Japanese line, light yellowish green, three crimps, three indentations on side, decorated with vertical rows of frit, collar base, c1907 . . . . **45.00**

Czechoslovakia, gold textured stucco-type design, smooth gold Vs and vertical gold stripes within the Vs, creamy interior, iridescent finish, eight crimps, bottom marked with green frown and "TK Czechoslovaia" and signed "H Ludeman '23 to Mother," $85. Photo courtesy of Johanna Billings.

Fenton

3-1/4" h, 3-1/2" w, Beaded Melon, white with yellow interior, eight crimps, collar base **45.00**

4-1/2" h, 4-1/2" w, vaseline opalescent hobnail, eight crimps, collar base. **125.00**

Mt. Joye, acid etched, enameled purple violets, gold stems, gold dec, pinched sides, 4-1/4" d, 3-3/4" h, $190.

Mt. Washington

3" h, 3-1/2" w, mother-of pearl satin, blue, counter clockwise swirl pattern, soft white interior, nine crimps, polished base. **300.00**

3-1/4" h, 4-1/4" w, lustreless (white satin), well-done cottage decorated dogwood blossoms in mint condition, nine soft crimps, polished bottom **75.00**

Murano

3" h, 3" w, millefiore, glossy white opaque background with individual

millefiore scattered throughout the glass, nine uneven crimps, semi-ground bottom, c1960. **45.00**

3-3/8" h, 4-1/4" w, transparent Caribbean blue, diamond optic pattern in glass, applied clear rigaree around base, eight crimps, rough pontil, 1960s **75.00**

Porcelain, 2-3/4" h, 3-3/4" w, shaded light heavenly blue to creamy yellow with small bouquet of blue flowers on front, greenish brown stems circling the piece with two smaller bouquets in back, these highlighted with pink flowers, all with green leaves, off-white interior, eight soft crimps with gold edges, marked on bottom with wreath and the words "Q. & E. G. ROYAL Austria" **45.00**

Satin

2-3/4" d, baby blue, MOP, ground pontil, attributed to Webb . **385.00**

3" h, 3-1/2" w, shaded pink to white, soft white interior, undecorated, eight crimps, ground pontil . **45.00**

3" h, 4" w, shaded yellow to white, soft white interior, cherub decal decoration, eight crimps, polished pontil **175.00**

3-1/4" h, 3-3/4" w, light green, embossed apple blossoms in glass, eight crimps, ground pontil **150.00**

3-7/8" h, 3-3/4" w, apricot, soft white interior, enameled with purple and white violets, gold foliage and scrollwork, eight crimps, ground pontil **175.00**

4-3/4" h, 5-3/4" w, Embossed Shell & Seaweed pattern, shaded purple to lavender, white interior, eight crimps, rough pontil, Consolidated Lamp & Glass Co., c1894 . **125.00**

Stevens & Williams, Jewell glass, Zipper pattern, light sapphire blue, six box pleats, polished pontil, Rd. #55693, 4" h, 5" w, $125. Photo courtesy of Johanna Billings.

Stevens & Williams, 2-1/8" h, 2-3/4" w, jeweled

Cranberry red, threaded in "zipper" pattern, 12 tiny crimps, engraved registry number Rd 55693 on polished bottom **140.00**

Sapphire blue, threaded with raindrop effect, 12 tiny crimps, engraved registry number Rd 81051 on polished pontil...**160.00**

ROSE CANTON, ROSE MANDARIN, AND ROSE MEDALLION

History: The pink rose color has given its name to three related groups of Chinese export porcelain: Rose Mandarin, Rose Medallion, and Rose Canton.

Rose Mandarin, produced from the late 18th century to approximately 1840, derives its name from the Mandarin figure(s) found in garden scenes with women and children. The women often have gold decorations in their hair. Polychrome enamels and birds separate the scenes.

Rose Medallion, which originated in the early 19th century and was made through the early 20th century, has alternating panels of figures and birds and flowers. The elements are four in number, separated evenly around the center medallion. Peonies and foliage fill voids.

Rose Canton, introduced somewhat later than Rose Mandarin and produced through the first half of the 19th century, is similar to Rose Medallion except the figural panels are replaced by flowers. People are present only if the medallion partitions are absent. Some patterns have been named, e.g., Butterfly and Cabbage and Rooster. Rose Canton actually is a catchall term for any pink enamel ware not fitting into the first two groups.

Periodical: *Orientalia Journal*, P.O. Box 94, Flushing, NY 11363-0094, http://members.aol.com/Orientalia/index.html.

Reproduction Alert: Rose Medallion is still made, although the quality does not match the earlier examples.

Rose Canton

Brush pot, 4-1/2" h, scenic, ladies, reticulated, gilt trim...........**275.00**

Charger, 13" d, floral panels, 19th C **215.00**

Platter, 16-1/2" l, 19th C, enamel and gilt wear **200.00**

Puzzle teapot, 6" h, Cadogan, painted birds and foliage, light blue ground, late 19th C, minor chips **150.00**

Umbrella jar, 24-1/4" h, 19th C, minor chips......................**805.00**

Rose Mandarin, platter with insert, armorial crests, fish, monogram, and "Avise La Fin," 17-3/8" l, **$3,250.** *Photo courtesy of Garth's Auctions, Inc.*

Urn, cov, 19-1/4" h, minor chips, cracks, gilt wear, pr **2,990.00**

Vase, 14" h, 19th C, chips, minor cracks, pr **1,265.00**

Rose Mandarin

Bowl, 9-1/2" d, scalloped edge **300.00**

Charger, 16-1/4" d...........**440.00**

Creamer, 3-5/8" h, three feet, plain handle **50.00**

Cup and saucer, scalloped edge rim, chips, price for pr **60.00**

Dish, 11" d, kidney shape.....**440.00**

Plate

6-1/2" d, mandarin scene ... **200.00**

8-1/2" d, fluted rim, scalloped edge, colored-in flake, small hairline **50.00**

Platter, 16-1/4" l, chip **250.00**

Rice bowl, 4-5/8" d, scalloped rim, four-pc set.....................**110.00**

Sauce boat, 8-1/4" l, intertwined handle **110.00**

Serving dish, 9-7/8" d, 19th C, minor chips, enamel wear........**460.00**

Soup plate, 9-3/4" d, three with chips, six-pc set....................**55.00**

Sugar bowl, cov, 4-7/8" h, intertwined handles, fruit finial, minor enamel flaking **50.00**

Teapot, cov, 8-1/2" h, domed lid **660.00**

Tureen, 13-3/4" l, 11-1/4" h, gilded handles and finial **1,100.00**

Umbrella stand, 24" h, wrapped bamboo form, 19th C, star cracks, gilt and enamel wear..........**1,495.00**

Vase, 10" h, beaker, figural cartouche, chicken skin ground, Qianlong, c1775, price for pr................**1,900.00**

Vegetable dish, cov, 11-1/2" d, almond shaped, fruit finial, minor flakes. **200.00**

Rose Medallion charger, wooden stand, 24-1/2" d, **$1,100.** *Photo courtesy of Joy Luke Auctions.*

Rose Medallion

Basket and undertray, 9-3/4" l, 7-1/4" w, 3-3/4" h, two handles, reticulated, China, 19th C, chips **325.00**

Bowl

9" x 10-1/4", 4" h, reticulated high sides, flared rim, Mandarin scenes, red, blue, pink, and yellow, orange peel glaze, tiny rim flakes .. **450.00**

10-1/4" d, celadon, scalloped rim, imperfections **350.00**

Platter

13-5/8" l, 10-1/2" w, Mandarin scenes with figures, gold accents in their hair **825.00**

16-1/2" l, 13" w, oval, well and tree, celadon, mid-19th C **650.00**

Serving dish, 10-3/4" l, 9-1/4" w, 1-3/4" h, oval, shaped rim, celadon, mid-19th C **400.00**

Vase

13-3/4" h, Moon, gilt Kylin handles, 19th C **1,610.00**

25" h, extended flared rim, tapered oval body, foo dog handles, China, 19th C, gilt wear **865.00**

36" h, baluster form, foo dog handles, dragon appliqués, numerous figures in garden vignettes, mid-19th C, minor imperfections **1,890.00**

Vegetable dish, cov, 9-1/2" l, 9" w, 5-1/2" h, celadon, pinecone knop, mid-19th C, imperfection **450.00**

Wall cone, 13-1/2" h, 19th C ... **865.00**

ROSENTHAL

History: Rosenthal Porcelain Manufactory began operating at Selb, Bavaria, in 1880. Specialties were tablewares and figurines. The firm is still in operation.

Reference: Dieter Struss, *Rosenthal*, Schiffer Publishing, 1997.

Box, cov, Studio Line, sgd "Peynet" **175.00**

Cake plate, 12" w, grape dec, scalloped ruffled edge, ruffled handles **75.00**

Candlestick, 9-1/2" h, Art Deco woman holding candlestick **275.00**

Chocolate set, San Souci pattern, six cups and saucers, cov pot, creamer and sugar, marked "Selb Bavaria," c1880, 15-pc set **425.00**

Creamer and sugar, pate-sur-pate type blue cherries dec **115.00**

Cup and saucer, San Souci pattern, white **20.00**

Demitasse cup and saucer, Marie pattern **25.00**

Design page, 6" w, 9-1/2" h, hand rendered, each page showing transfer printed and hand-tinted designs, most numbered or named, some on graph paper, 10 pages **230.00**

Dinner service, Donatello pattern, cherries decoration, three luncheon plates, 10 dessert plates, five bread plates, 12 cups and saucers, teapot, coffeepot, covered sugar, price for 45 pieces, $165. Photo courtesy of Joy Luke Auctions.

Figure

6" h, clown **225.00**
9" h, ram, mottled gray **200.00**
10-1/2" h, Fairy Queen, sgd "L. Friedrich-Granau" **325.00**
14" h, kneeling nude, sgd "Klimsch" **775.00**

Plaque, 9" x 7-1/2", titled "Die Falknerin," sgd "Hans Makart" **1,100.00**

Plate

8" d, Moss Rose pattern, six-pc set **90.00**
10" d, girl and lamb dec, multicolored **40.00**

Portrait plate, 9-7/8" d, bust portrait of lady, pale yellow and white ground, faux green, turquoise, blue, and red hardstone jewels **350.00**

Vase

7" h, modeled owls on branch **165.00**
7-1/4" h, violet cameo, Greek god, cream ground, gold bead trim, c1930, pr **140.00**
9-7/8" h, vertical ribs, banded top and base, polychrome floral bouquet in center, marked "Rosenthal" **65.00**
11" h, hp, multicolored roses **125.00**

ROSEVILLE POTTERY

Roseville U.S.A.

History: In the late 1880s, a group of investors purchased the J. B. Owens Pottery in Roseville, Ohio, and made utilitarian stoneware items. In 1892, the firm was incorporated and joined by George F. Young who became general manager. Four generations of Youngs controlled Roseville until the early 1950s.

A series of acquisitions began: Midland Pottery of Roseville in 1898, Clark Stoneware Plant in Zanesville (formerly used by Peters and Reed), and Muskingum Stoneware (Mosaic Tile Company) in Zanesville. In 1898, the offices also moved from Roseville to Zanesville.

In 1900, Roseville introduced Rozane, an art pottery. Rozane became a trade name to cover a large series of lines. The art lines were made in limited amounts after 1919.

The success of Roseville depended on its commercial lines, first developed by John J. Herald and Frederick Rhead in the first decades of the 1900s. In 1918, Frank Ferrell became art director and developed more than 80 lines of pottery. The economic Depression of the 1930s brought more lines, including Pine Cone.

In the 1940s, a series of high-gloss glazes were tried in an attempt to revive certain lines. In 1952, Raymor dinnerware was produced. None of these changes brought economic success and in November 1954, Roseville was bought by the Mosaic Tile Company.

References: Mark Bassett, *Bassetts Roseville Prices*, 2nd ed., Schiffer Publishing, 2001; John and Nancy Bomm, *Roseville In All Its Splendor*, L-W Book Sales, 1998; Virginia Hillway Buxton, *Roseville Pottery for Love or Money*, updated ed., Tymbre Hill Publishing Co. (P.O. Box 615, Jonesborough, TN

37659), 1996; John W. Humphries, *Roseville Pottery by the Numbers*, published by author, 1999; Sharon and Bob Huxford, *Collectors Encyclopedia of Roseville Pottery*, 1st Series (1976, 2001 value update), 2nd Series (1980, 2001 value update), Collector Books; ——, *The Roseville Pottery Price Guide, #12*, Collector Books, 1997; James S. Jenkins, Jr., *Roseville Art Pottery, 1998-1/2 Price Guide, Volume II*, Clinical Pharmacology Consultants, 1998; Gloria Mollring, *1999 Roseville Price Guide, 5th ed.*, published by author (P.O. Box 22754, Sacramento, CA 95822); Randall B. Monsen, *Collectors' Compendium of Roseville Pottery*, Monsen and Baer (Box 529, Vienna, VA 22183), 1995, ——, *Collectors' Compendium of Roseville Pottery, Volume II*, Monsen and Baer, 1997; David Rago, *American Art Pottery*, Knickerbocker Press, 1997; Betty Ward and Nancy Schiffer, *Weller, Roseville, and Related Zanesville Art Pottery and Tiles*, Schiffer Publishing, 2000.

Collectors' Clubs: American Art Pottery Assoc., P.O. Box 834, Westport, MA 02790-0697, http://www.amartpot.org; Roseville Historical Society, 91 Main St., Roseville, OH 43777; Valley of the Sun Roseville Collectors Club, 4681 N. 84th Way, Scottsdale, AZ 85251-1864.

Additional Listings: See *Warman's Americana & Collectibles* for more examples.

Basket

Blackberry, unmarked, 6" d, 7-1/2" h, very small nick to one berry **1,355.00**
Columbine, brown, raised mark, No. 365-7" **290.00**
Fuchsia, attached flower frog, brown, imp mark, No. 350-8" **365.00**
Gardenia, green, raised mark, No. 618-15" **490.00**
Jonquil, pillow, unmarked, 10-1/2" d, 7-1/2" h **750.00**
Mock Orange, No. 908-6, white blossoms, green leaves, rose ground, 6" h **200.00**
Mock Orange, No. 911-10, white blossoms, green leaves, green ground, 10" h **180.00**
Poppy, green, raised mark, No. 347-10" **350.00**
Thorn Apple, conical, brown, imp mark, No. 342-10" **415.00**
Vista, unmarked, 4-3/4" d, 6-3/4" h **575.00**

Basket planter

Apple Blossom, green, asymmetrical rim, raised mark, No. 311-12" **490.00**
Cosmos, ftd, green, raised mark, No. 358-12" **460.00**
Iris, spherical, pink, imp mark, No. 354-8" **365.00**

Bookends, pr

Burmese, green, raised marks,
4-3/4" w, 6-3/4" h **255.00**
Dawn, pink, imp mark, 4-1/4" w,
4-1/2" d, 5-1/4" h **575.00**
Iris, book shape, blue, raised mark,
No. 5, 5-1/4" w, 5-1/4" h **290.00**

Bowl

Ferella, flaring, brown, black paper
label, 8-1/2" d, 5" h, restoration to
rim chip **5,175.00**
Ferella, flaring, red, attached flower
frog, unmarked, 9-1/4" d, 4-1/4" h
. . . . **1,150.00**
Futura, 12-1/2" d, 3-3/4" h, flaring,
flower frog, mottled blue, green,
and orange glaze, unmarked
. . . . **490.00**
Rosecraft Panel, rolled rim, orange
floral dec, brown ground, c1920,
8" d, 2-3/8" h **140.00**

Bud vase

Panel, double, green, emb
sunflowers, RV ink mark, 7-1/2" w,
5-1/4" h, fleck to rim **145.00**
Pine Cone, blue, raised mark, 5" d,
7-1/2" h, minute flake on base
. . . . **400.00**

Dealer's sign, pink, 7-1/2" h, **$1,925.**
*Photo courtesy of Jackson's Auctioneers
& Appraisers.*

Candlesticks, pr

Blackberry, gold foil label, 4" d,
4-1/2" h **690.00**
Ferella, red, unmarked, 3-1/4" d, 4" h
. . . . **750.00**
Moderne, ivory, triple, incised mark,
No. 1112, 5-1/4" d, 6-1/4" h
. . . . **490.00**
Sunflower, black paper label,
3-3/4" d, 4-1/4" h **800.00**
Wisteria, brown, unmarked, 4-3/4" d,
4-3/4" h **460.00**

Coffee set, cov coffeepot, cov teapot, creamer, cov sugar

Mock Orange, green, raised marks,
10-3/4" h coffeepot, minor spider
lines to spout **490.00**

Wincraft, blue, raised marks, 9-3/4" h
coffeepot, minor fleck to spout
. . . . **490.00**

Console bowl

Cremona, oval, pink, unmarked,
11" d, 2-1/4" h **95.00**
Ferella, ovoid, brown, black paper
label, 13" l, 5-3/4" h **815.00**
Moderne, semi-matte ivory glaze,
incised mark, No. 301-10" . **230.00**

Console set

Fuchsia, brown, imp marks, No.
1133-5 and No. 350-8" **490.00**
Iris, pink, No. 360-10" oval
centerbowl, pair of No. 1135-4-1/2"
candlesticks, imp marks . . **375.00**
Thorn Apple, pink, low center bowl
No. 307-6", pair of No. 1111
candlesticks, imp marks . . **290.00**

Cookie jar, cov

Clematis, No. 3-8, blue ground
. . . . **400.00**
Clematis, No. 3-8, brown ground
. . . . **430.00**
Clematis, No. 3-8, green ground
. . . . **550.00**
Freesia, No. 4-8, blue ground
. . . . **550.00**
Freesia, No. 4-8, terra cotta ground
. . . . **440.00**
Magnolia, No. 2-8, blue ground
. . . . **425.00**
Magnolia, No. 2-8, tan ground
. . . . **450.00**
Water Lily, No. 1-8, blended blue
ground **400.00**
Water Lily, No. 1-8, gold shading to
brown ground **555.00**
Zephr Lily, No. 5-8, blue ground
. . . . **360.00**

Cornucopia

Mock Orange, No. 922-8, white
blossoms, green leaves, green
ground, 8" h **110.00**
White Rose, double, raised mark No.
145-8", one pink, other blue, price
for pair **215.00**

Ewer

Apple Blossom, green, raised mark,
NO. 318-15, minute fleck to body
. . . . **630.00**
Carnelian I, pink and gray glaze, RV
ink mark, 7" d, 12-1/4" h . . . **345.00**
Freesia, green, raised mark, No.
21-15", two base chips **290.00**
Gardenia, brown, raised mark, No.
618-15" **490.00**
Mock Orange, No. 918-16, white
blossoms, green leaves, pink
ground, 16" h **310.00**

Pine Cone, brown, raised mark, No.
909-10" **690.00**
Teasel, blue, imp mark, No. 890-18"
. . . . **630.00**

Floor vase

Fuchsia, brown, raised mark, No.
905-18" **750.00**
Pine Cone, brown, incised mark, No.
913-18", repair to rim and base
. . . . **815.00**
Vista, bulbous, 18" h, unmarked,
several bruises and chips . . **860.00**
Water Lily, green, raised mark,
No.85-18" **630.00**
White Rose, pink, raised mark, No.
994-18" **630.00**

Flower pot and underplate

Iris, blue, raised marks, No. 648-5",
1" bruise to rim **365.00**
Pine Cone, blue, raised mark, No.
633-5", minute fleck to handle
. . . . **435.00**

Hanging basket, Mock Orange, white

blossoms, green leaves **375.00**

Jardiniere

Bleeding Heart, blue, 651-10", raised
mark, two tight rim lines . . . **460.00**
Fuchsia, bulbous, blue, imp mark,
No. 645-8" **350.00**
Jonquil, spherical, unmarked, 9" d,
6" h, small stilt-pull chips. **2,300.00**
Mostique, unmarked, 8-3/4" d,
7-1/2" h **230.00**

Jardiniere and pedestal

Apple Blossom, raised marks, No.
302-8, No. 305-8 . . . . **800.00**
Columbine, brown, raised mark
. . . . **980.00**

Lamp base, Pine Cone, brown,

unmarked, 7-3/4" d, 10-1/4" h, small
base chips **1,955.00**

Low bowl

Blackberry, unmarked, 7-3/4" d,
3-1/4" h, minor glaze bubbles
. . . . **345.00**
Sunflower, low shoulder, unmarked,
7-1/4" d, 4" h, burst bubble on one
leaf **535.00**

Mug, Pine Cone, blue, imp mark, No.

960-4", price for pr **700.00**

Pedestal

Art Craft, unmarked, 11-1/2" d,
16-1/2" h, 1" rim chip **575.00**
Freesia, brown, marked "U.S.A.,"
11" d, 16-3/4" h, base chip . **175.00**

Pitcher

Fuchsia, brown, imp mark, 8-1/2" d,
8" h, peppering to body . . . **400.00**
Pine Cone, blue, imp mark, 7-1/2" h
. . . . **920.00**

Rozane Mongol, orange crystalline glaze, marked "Rozane/Mongol," 4-1/4" d, 6" h **860.00**

Rozane Olympic, Ulysees at the Table of Circe, signed and titled, 8-1/2" d, 7" h, restoration to 5" spider lines **1,495.00**

White Rose, pink, raised mark, No. 1324, 8" d, 7" h, glaze drip around rim **275.00**

Planter, Dahlrose, rectangular unmarked, 6-1/4" x 13", $600. Photo courtesy of David Rago Auctions.

Planter

Blackberry, faceted, unmarked, 9-3/4" d, 3-1/2" h **435.00**

Florentine, brown, rect, 11-1/4" l, 5-1/4" h, few base chips . . . **290.00**

Matte Green, bulbous, four buttresses, unmarked, 5-3/4" h **400.00**

Morning Glory, oblong, green, unmarked, 11" l, 4-3/4" h . . **520.00**

Pine Cone, coupe shape, blue, imp mark, No. 124, 5" h **350.00**

Primrose, bulbous, pink, incised mark, No. 634-6", flecks to flowers and one handle **85.00**

Sunflower, four-sided, unmarked, 11" l, 3-3/4" h **1,380.00**

Planter bookends, pr, Columbine, blue, raised mark, 5" w, 5" d, 5-1/4" h **260.00**

Sand jar, Primrose, blue, 15-3/4" h, base chip and hairline **575.00**

Teapot, cov, Rozanne Della Robbia, hearts, cups, saucers, and Japanese fans dec, brown and celadon, Rozane Ware wafer, small lid nicks, 1" clay burst at rim **1,355.00**

Tea set, cov teapot, creamer, cov sugar

Clematis, green, raised marks, burst bubble on spout, other flaws **230.00**

Freesia, blue, raised marks . **415.00**

Peony, yellow, raised marks . **415.00**

Snowberry, blue, raised marks **750.00**

Snowberry, pink, raised marks, clay burst on creamer handle in firing **365.00**

White Rose, pink raised marks **490.00**

Wincraft, brown, raised marks, minor flaws **200.00**

Zephyr Lily, brown, raised marks, small burst bubble **435.00**

Umbrella stand

Florentine, white, raised mark, No. 298-18", 10" d, 18-3/4" h, minor burst to body, two small flecks inside rim **435.00**

Pine Cone, brown, raised mark, No. 777-20", minor scaling area at handle, 1" rim bruise **2,070.00**

Urn

Baneda, bulbous, pink, black foil label, 7-3/4" d, 10-1/2" h . **1,355.00**

Blackberry, bulbous, collared rim, unmarked, 8-1/4" d, 12-1/4" h, minute rim fleck **1,150.00**

Carnelian I, pink and gray glaze, RV ink mark, 8-1/4" d, 9-1/2" h . **375.00**

Carnelian II, squatty, mottled lavender, pink, and green glaze, unmarked, 7-1/2" d, 5" h . . . **365.00**

Iris, bulbous, pink, imp mark, No. 928-12" **460.00**

Moss, bulbous, buttressed base, incised mark, restorations to base and rim **200.00**

Pine Cone, blue, imp mark, No. 912-15", restoration to rim chip **2,185.00**

Teasel, flaring, blue, imp mark, No. 888-12" **435.00**

Thorn Apple, ftd, pink, imp mark, No. 822-10" **290.00**

Vase

Baneda, flaring, pink, foil label, 4-1/4" d, 7-1/2" h **630.00**

Vase, Wisteria, blue, bottle-shape, two handles, unmarked, 9-1/4" x 6", $1,600. Photo courtesy of David Rago Auctions.

Baneda, spherical, green, unmarked, 6-1/2" d, 5-1/2" h **920.00**

Blackberry, tapering, unmarked, 4-1/4" d, 5" h **490.00**

Cremona, bulbous, two handles, green, unmarked, 6" d, 10-1/4" l **370.00**

Dahlrose, bulbous, black paper label, 5" d, 8-1/4" h **290.00**

Earlham, bulbous, green, unmarked, 6-3/4" d, 5-1/2" h **290.00**

Earlham, pillow, mottled pink, orange, and purple glazes, unmarked, 10-1/4" w, 6-1/4" h, small glaze miss to one side **490.00**

Falline, flaring, blue, unmarked, 6" d, 8-1/2" h **1,045.00**

Ferella, beehive shale, two handles, brown, unmarked, 6-1/4" d, 5-3/4" h, restoration to one handle **460.00**

Ferella, oil lamp shape, red, unmarked, 6" h **815.00**

Futura, pillow, buttressed handles, emb geometric pattern, pink and gold glossy glaze, unmarked, 61/4" w, 8-1/2" h, very minor overglaze fleck at base . . . **860.00**

Gardenia, gray, raised mark, No. 689-14" **320.00**

Hexagon, flaring rim, green, RV ink mark, 3-1/2" d, 5-1/2" h, very minor flat base flakes **460.00**

Imperial I, bulbous, unmarked, 8" d, 10" h **290.00**

Jonquil, bulbous, silver foil label, 6-1/4" d, 4-1/2" h **350.00**

Morning Glory, flaring pillow, green, silver foil label, 4-1/4" w, 7-1/2" h **690.00**

Morning Glory, pear shape, white, foil label, 7" d, 10-1/4" h, base grinding chips **495.00**

Rosecraft Panel, No. 293-8," bulbous, round shoulder, orange vines, leaves, and fruit dec, brown ground, c1920, 8" h **360.00**

Roxana Chloron, two handles, squatty, emb arabesques, matte green glaze, ink stamped "Chloron/TRPCO," 8" d, 4" h **690.00**

Rozane Aztec, bulbous shoulder, tapering body, white, yellow, and blue stylized flowers and swags, blue-gray ground, unmarked, 4-1/2" d, 11" h, burst bubbles, couple of minor nicks **435.00**

Vase, Blackberry, 5" h, $440. Photo courtesy of Jackson's Auctioneers & Appraisers.

Rozane, classical shape, by Walter Myers, sailboat on water, dark brown ground, stamped, numbered, artist's initials, 3-1/4" d, 6" h, touch-up to small rim chip, base chip **815.00**

Rozane Royal Dark, tapering, by Hester Pillsbury, painted yellow wild roses, Roxane Ware wafer, 7" d, 8-3/4" h, overglaze crackling **435.00**

Rozane Woodland, corseted, enamel dec, white blossoms, green leaves, Rozane Ware/Woodland wafer, 3" d, 10" h, restoration to base chip **535.00**

Sunflower, bulbous, 7" d, 6-3/4" h, unmarked **1,150.00**

Velmoss, flaring, broad leaves dec, unmarked, 5" d, 11-1/2" h, four rim chips **435.00**

Vista, bulbous, unmarked, 7-1/2" d, 17-1/2" h **1,890.00**

Wisteria, bottle shape, two handles, brown, unmarked, 5-3/4" d, 9-1/4" h **630.00**

Wisteria, bulbous, blue, 7-1/2"d, 15" h, unmarked, rim bruise **2,530.00**

Vessel

Baneda, bulbous, collared rim, green, black paper label, 5" l, 9-1/2" h **1,600.00**

Chloron, tapering, two handles, scalloped rim, body emb with cherries, stamped "Chloron/T.R.P. Co.," 7" d, 6-1/2" h **1,380.00**

Jonquil, squatty, pinched and scalloped rim, unmarked, 7" l, 5" h **495.00**

Rozane Egypto, scalloped rim, emb broad leaves, unmarked, 5" l, 5-1/4" h **500.00**

Savona, covered, yellow, black paper label, 8" l, 4" h **980.00**

White Rose, spherical, blue, raised mark, NO. 388-7", 1" firing bruise to inner rim **230.00**

Wall pocket

Blackberry, flaring, unmarked, 7-3/4" l **1,610.00**

Cosmos, double, blue, unmarked, silver foil label **630.00**

Earlham, unmarked, 6-1/2" l . **920.00**

Foxglove, pink, unmarked, 8-1/2" l **460.00**

Jonquil, flaring, silver foil tag, 8" l **860.00**

Moss, bucket, pink, unmarked, 10" l, 1/2" chip, small edge nick . **520.00**

Panel, green, emb nude, RV ink mark, 7-1/4" h **520.00**

Pine Cone, triple, blue, raised mark, 9" l **1,725.00**

Rosecraft Vintage, RV ink mark, small tip chip, 8-1/2" l **265.00**

Savona, blue, unmarked, 8-1/4" l **630.00**

Silhouette, pink, ivy leaves, raised mark No. 766-8" **290.00**

Wall shelf

Iris, blue, imp mark, No. 2, minute and shallow bruise to one side **5,175.00**

Pine Cone, green, unmarked, 5" w, 8" h **490.00**

ROYAL BAYREUTH

History: In 1794, the Royal Bayreuth factory was founded in Tettau, Bavaria. Royal Bayreuth introduced its figural patterns in 1885. Designs of animals, people, fruits, and vegetables decorated a wide array of tablewares and inexpensive souvenir items.

Tapestry wares, in rose and other patterns, were made in the late 19th century. The surface of the piece feels and looks like woven cloth. Tapestry ware was made by covering the porcelain with a piece of fabric tightly stretched over the surface, decorating the fabric, glazing the piece, and firing.

Royal Bayreuth still manufactures dinnerware. It has not maintained production of earlier wares, particularly the figural items. Since thorough records are unavailable, it is difficult to verify the chronology of production.

Marks: The Royal Bayreuth crest used to mark the wares varied in design and color.

References: Susan and Al Bagdade, *Warman's English & Continental Pottery & Porcelain*, 3rd ed., Krause Publications, 1998; Mary J. McCaslin, *Royal Bayreuth*, Antique Publications, 1994.

Collectors' Club: Royal Bayreuth Collectors Club, 926 Essex Circle, Kalamazoo, MI 49008; Royal Bayreuth International Collectors' Society, P.O. Box 325, Orrville, OH 44667-0325.

Creamer, Sun Bonnet Babies, laundry day, blue mark, 3-3/8" h, $180.

Ashtray, elk **225.00**

Bell

Musicians scene, man playing cello and mandolin **300.00**

Peacock dec, 2-1/2" d, 3" h . . **275.00**

Creamer

Apple **195.00**

Bird of Paradise **225.00**

Bull, gray **225.00**

Cat, black and orange **200.00**

Clown, red **275.00**

Crow, brown bill **200.00**

Duck **200.00**

Eagle **300.00**

Frog, green **225.00**

Lamplighter, green **250.00**

Pear **295.00**

Robin **195.00**

Water Buffalo, black and orange **225.00**

Cup and saucer, yellow and gold, purple and red flowers, green leaves, white ground, green mark **80.00**

Hatpin holder, courting couple, cutout base with gold dec, blue mark . . **400.00**

Milk pitcher

Alligator **450.00**

Butterfly **1,200.00**

Owl **550.00**

Miniature, pitcher, portrait **95.00**

Plate, 6-1/4" d, musicians **65.00**

Ring box, cov, pheasant scene, glossy finish **85.00**

Salt and pepper shakers, pr, Elk **165.00**

Vase, 3-1/2" h, peasant ladies and sheep scene, silver rim, three handles, blue mark **60.00**

Patterns
Conch Shell
Creamer, green, lobster handles **125.00**
Match holder, hanging **225.00**
Mustard, orig spoon **85.00**
Sugar, cov, small flake **85.00**

Corinthian
Chamberstick, 4-1/2" h, enameled Grecian figures, black ground **60.00**
Creamer and sugar, classical figures, black ground **85.00**
Pitcher, 12" h, red ground, pinched spout **225.00**
Vase, 8-1/2" h, conical, black, blue mark **225.00**

Devil and Cards
Ashtray **650.00**
Creamer, 3-3/4" h **195.00**
Mug, large **295.00**
Salt, master **325.00**

Lobster pattern, mustard, covered, leaf spoon, **$85.**

Lobster
Ashtray, claw **145.00**
Candy dish **140.00**
Celery tray, 12-1/2" l, figural, blue mark **245.00**
Pitcher, 7-3/4" h, figural, orange-red, green handle **175.00**
Salt and pepper shakers, pr. **150.00**

Nursery Rhyme
Bell, Jack and the Beanstalk **425.00**
Bell, Little Bo Peep **375.00**
Planter, Jack and the Beanstalk, round, orig liner **225.00**
Plate, Little Jack Horner **125.00**
Plate, Little Miss Muffet **100.00**

Snow Babies
Bowl, 6" d **325.00**
Creamer, gold trim **110.00**
Jewelry box, cov **275.00**
Milk pitcher, corset shape . . **185.00**
Tea tile, 6" sq, blue mark **100.00**

Sunbonnet Babies
Bell, babies sewing, unmarked **425.00**
Cake plate, 10-1/4" d, babies washing **400.00**
Cup and saucer, babies fishing **225.00**
Dish, 8" d, babies ironing, ruffled edge, blue mark **175.00**
Fruit bowl, 9-3/4" d, babies washing and hanging wash **95.00**
Mustard pot, cov, babies sweeping, blue mark **395.00**
Plate, babies ironing **100.00**

Tomato
Celery tray **95.00**
Creamer and sugar, blue mark **190.00**
Milk pitcher **165.00**
Mustard, cov **125.00**
Salt and pepper shakers, pr . . **85.00**

Rose tapestry
Basket, 5" h, reticulated **400.00**
Bell
American Beauty Rose, pink, 3" h **500.00**
Three-color roses, gold loop handle, 3-1/4" h **400.00**
Boot **550.00**
Bowl, 10-1/2" d, pink and yellow roses **675.00**
Cache pot, 2-3/4" h, 3-12/4" d, ruffled top, gold handles **200.00**
Creamer **250.00**
Dresser tray **395.00**
Hairpin box, pink and white . . . **245.00**
Nut dish, 3-1/4" d, 1-3/4" h, three color roses, gold feet, green mark . . . **175.00**
Pin tray, three color roses **195.00**
Plate, 6" d, three color roses, blue mark **150.00**
Salt and pepper shakers, pr, pink roses **375.00**
Shoe
Roses **550.00**
Roses and figures dec **550.00**

Tapestry, miscellaneous
Bowl, 9-1/2" d, scenic, wheat, girl, and chickens **395.00**
Box, 3-3/4" l, 2" w, courting couple, multicolored, blue mark **245.00**
Charger, 13" d, scenic, boy and donkeys **300.00**
Dresser tray, goose girl **495.00**

Hatpin holder, swimming swans and sunset, saucer base, blue mark **250.00**
Tumbler, 4" h, barrel shape, gazebo, deer standing in stream, blue mark **200.00**

ROYAL BONN

History: In 1836, Franz Anton Mehlem founded a Rhineland factory that produced earthenware and porcelain, including household, decorative, technical, and sanitary items.

The firm reproduced Hochst figures between 1887 and 1903. These figures, in both porcelain and earthenware, were made from the original molds from the defunct Prince-Electoral Mayence Manufactory in Hochst. The factory was purchased by Villeroy and Boch in 1921 and closed in 1931.

Marks: In 1890, the word "Royal" was added to the mark. All items made after 1890 include the "Royal Bonn" mark.

Cake plate, 10-1/4" d, dark blue floral transfer **35.00**
Cheese dish, cov, multicolored floral dec, cream ground, gold trim . . . **90.00**
Cup and saucer, relief luster bands, marked **40.00**

Clock, cobalt blue case, flowers decoration, Flowers le Clede pattern, Ansonia clock, 10-1/2" h, **$490.** *Photo courtesy of Joy Luke Auctions.*

Plaque, blue and white cows decoration, 7-3/4" x 12-3/4", $365. Photo courtesy of Joy Luke Auctions.

Ewer, 10-1/8" h, red and pink flowers, raised gold, fancy handle. **75.00**
Plate, 8-1/2" d, red and white roses, green leaves, earthtone ground, crazing, c1900 . . . .**20.00**
Portrait vase, 8-1/4" h, central female portrait, floral landscape, printed mark, c1900 . . . .**575.00**
Tea tile, 7" d, hp, pink, yellow, and purple pansies, white ground, green border, marked "Bonn-Rhein" . . .**35.00**
Urn, cov, 13" h, hp, multicolored flowers, green, and yellow ground, two gold handles, artist sgd **120.00**
Vase
   8" h, pink and lavender orchids, outlined in gold **110.00**
   18-3/4" h, blue ground, gilt and enameled floral designs, scrolled handles, printed and imp marks, late 19th C. **400.00**
   20" h, 5" d, hp multicolored floral spray with raised gold dec, link handles, ftd **240.00**

ROYAL
COPENHAGEN

History:
Franz Mueller established a porcelain factory at Copenhagen in 1775. When bankruptcy threatened in 1779, the Danish king acquired ownership, appointing Mueller manager and selecting the name "Royal Copenhagen." The crown sold its interest in 1867; the company remains privately owned today.

Blue Fluted, Royal Copenhagen's most famous pattern, was created in 1780. It is of Chinese origin

and comes in three styles: smooth edge, closed lace edge, and perforated lace edge (full lace). Many other factories copied it.

Flora Danica, named for a famous botanical work, was introduced in 1789 and remained exclusive to Royal Copenhagen. It is identified by its freehand illustrations of plants and its hand-cut edges and perforations.

Reference: Nick and Caroline Pope, *A Comprehensive Guide to Royal Copenhagen Porcelain*, Schiffer Publishing, 2001.

Marks: Royal Copenhagen porcelain is marked with three wavy lines, which signify ancient waterways, and a crown, added in 1889. Stoneware does not have the crown mark.

Additional Listings: Limited Edition Collector Plates.

Figure, Little Mermaid, 8-1/2" h, $100. Photo courtesy of Joy Luke Auctions.

Bowl, reticulated blue and white
   Round. **125.00**
   Shell shaped. **150.00**
Butter pat, Symphony pattern, six-pc set **35.00**
Candlesticks, pr, 9" h, blue floral design, white ground, bisque lion heads, floral garlands **160.00**
Cream soup, #1812 . . . .**75.00**
Cup and saucer, 2-1/2" h cylindrical cup with angular handle, 5-1/2" d saucer with molded and gilded rim, hp floral specimen, 20th C **575.00**
Dish, reticulated blue and white **175.00**
Figure
   4" h, young girl, traditional dress, holding garland, No. 12418
   . . . .**250.00**

   4-1/2" x 4-1/2", wire haired fox terrier, #3165 . . . .**150.00**
   5-3/4" h, young, native dress, kneeling and holding floral garland, No. 21413, No. 12414, pr . .**550.00**
   6-3/4" h, girl knitting, No. 1314
   . . . .**350.00**
   11-1/2" h, snowy egret, standing bird enclosed in reticulated water grasses, 20th C. **300.00**
   15-1/4" h, nude female nymph with timid satyr kneeling at feet, naturalistic ovoid base, 20th C
   . . . .**1,100.00**
Fish plate, 10" d, different fish swimming among marine plants, molded and gilt border, light green highlights, gilt dentil edge, crown circular mark, 10-pc set **8,250.00**
Inkwell, Blue Fluted pattern, matching tray **150.00**
Pickle tray, 9" l, Half Lace pattern, blue triple wave mark. **70.00**
Plates, two 7-5/8" d, six 10" d, each with gilt serrated rim and central hp floral specimen, price for eight-pc set
   . . . .**2,990.00**
Platter, 14-1/2" l, #1556 . . . .**140.00**
Salad bowl, 9-7/8" d, Flora Danica, botanical specimen, molded gilt border, dentil edge, pink highlights, blue triple wave and green crown mark . . .**825.00**
Soup tureen, cov, stand, 14-1/2" l, Flora Danica, oval, enamel painted botanical specimens, twin handles, finial, factory marks, botanical identification, modern
   . . . .**5,750.00**
Tray, 10" l, Blue Fluted pattern . . .**65.00**

Vase, dogwood spray, butterflies, marked "1584-271," 4-1/2" h, $170.

Underplate for Cream Soup, #1626
.... **75.00**
Vase, 7" h, sage green and gray
crackled glaze............. **150.00**
Vegetable bowl, #1622, sq **110.00**

ROYAL CROWN DERBY

History: Derby Crown Porcelain Co., established in 1875 in Derby, England, had no connection with earlier Derby factories which operated in the late 18th and early 19th centuries. In 1890, the company was appointed "Manufacturers of Porcelain to Her Majesty" (Queen Victoria) and since that date has been known as "Royal Crown Derby."

Most of these porcelains, both tableware and figural, were hand decorated. A variety of printing processes were used for additional adornment. Today, Royal Crown Derby is a part of Royal Doulton Tableware, Ltd.

References: Susan and Al Bagdade, *Warman's English & Continental Pottery & Porcelain*, 3rd ed., Krause Publications, 1998; John Twitchett, *Dictionary of Derby Porcelain 1748-1848*, Antique Collectors' Club; John Twitchett and Betty Bailey, *Royal Crown Derby*, Antique Collectors' Club, 1988.

Museums: Cincinnati Art Museum, Cincinnati, OH; Gardiner Museum of Ceramic Art, Toronto, Canada; Royal Crown Derby Museum, Osmaston Road, Derby; Derby Museums & Art Gallery, The Strand, Derby; Victoria & Albert Museum, London, England.

Marks: Derby porcelains from 1878 to 1890 carry only the standard crown printed mark. After 1891, the mark includes the "Royal Crown Derby" wording. In the 20th century, "Made in England" and "English Bone China" were added to the mark.

Cup and saucer, 5" d saucer, Imari pattern, 20th C............. **65.00**
Dinner set, partial, Imari pattern
  34 pcs, c1909, retailed by James Creen & Nephew, London, 12 8-3/4" plates, 10 10" d plates, six 10" d soup plates, six 8" l kidney-shaped dishes, gilt detailing **2,650.00**
  84 pcs, first quarter 20th C, 18 7" d plates, 12 2-1/2" h coffee cups, nine 2-3/8" h shaped tea cups, six 2" h tea cups, 12 5-1/2" d saucers, 10 5-1/2" d molded edge saucers, five 5-3/4" d molded edge saucer, 8" l oblong ftd serving dish, 11-3/4" l oblong ftd serving dish, 3-1/4" h cylindrical creamer, 5" l creamer, 5-1/2" l creamer, 6" l cov sugar, 7" l cov sugar, 4-3/4" h jug (lacking lid), 5-1/2" h teapot, 12-3/4" l cov tureen, 9" d round platter, 10-3/4" sq platter.. **3,500.00**

Mug, satyr's face, multicolored, marked, **$90.**

Ewer
  7-1/2" h, cobalt blue, profuse gold gilt and floral dec, sgd **200.00**
  12-1/2" h, mottled blue ground, raised gilt and iron-red dec bird and foliate design, pierced handle, shape #409, printed mark, c1888 .... **690.00**
Jug, Imari palette, pink round, gold trim, c1885, pr **750.00**
Mug, grapes and vines dec, blue and gold **125.00**
Plate, 8" d, Daisy pattern, blue transfer print, gilt details, late 19th/early 20th C, price for set of 11 .... **260.00**
Soup plate, 9-7/8" d, inner band of gold jewelling with wide rim of gilt quatrefoils, grapevine, and leaf sprays, some leaves accented with bronze tone, shaped beaded edge, retailed by Tiffany & Co., early 20th C, price for set of 18 .... **5,750.00**
Tea set, Imari pattern, oval 9-1/4" h teapot, 3-1/4" creamer, 6" l cov sugar, c1883, rim repairs, gilt wear.... **260.00**
Urn, 12" h, squatty, double reticulated handles and finials, birds, butterfly, and floral designs, ivory ground, gilt accents, marked "Bailey, Banks, and Biddle," dripped for lamp, finials replaced, restoration to one handle, price for pr **1,325.00**
Vase
  6" h, cylindrical, flared rim, blue, iron-red, and green, gilt accents **365.00**
  11-1/2" h, double reticulated handles, pale yellow ground, maroon banding, gilt floral dec, crown mark over "Davis Collamore & C. E".............. **1,100.00**

12-1/2" h, Imari pattern, baluster, double-serpent handles, gilt loss **1,690.00**

ROYAL DOULTON

History: Doulton pottery began in 1815 under the direction of John Doulton at the Doulton & Watts pottery in Lambeth, England. Early output was limited to salt-glazed industrial stoneware. After John Watts retired in 1854, the firm became Doulton and Company, and production was expanded to include hand-decorated stoneware such as figurines, vases, dinnerware, and flasks.

In 1878, John's son, Sir Henry Doulton, purchased Pinder Bourne & Co. in Burslem. The companies became Doulton & Co., Ltd. in 1882. Decorated porcelain was added to Doulton's earthenware production in 1884.

Most Doulton figurines were produced at the Burslem plants, where they were made continuously from 1890 until 1978. After a short interruption, a new line of Doulton figurines was introduced in 1979.

Dickens ware, in earthenware and porcelain, was introduced in 1908. The pieces were decorated with characters from Dickens's novels. Most of the line was withdrawn in the 1940s, except for plates which continued to be made until 1974.

Character jugs, a 20th-century revival of early Toby models, were designed by Charles J. Noke for Doulton in the 1930s. Character jugs are limited to bust portraits, while Royal Doulton toby jugs are full figured. The character jugs come in four sizes and feature fictional characters from Dickens, Shakespeare, and other English and American novelists, as well as historical heroes. Marks on both character and toby jugs must be carefully identified to determine dates and values.

Doulton's Rouge Flambé (Veined Sung) is a high-glazed, strong-colored ware noted primarily for the fine modeling and exquisite colorings, especially in the animal items. The process used to produce the vibrant colors is a Doulton secret.

Production of stoneware at Lambeth ceased in 1956; production of porcelain continues today at Burslem.

Marks: Beginning in 1872, the "Royal Doulton" mark was used on all types of wares produced by the company.

Beginning in 1913, an "HN" number was assigned to each new Doulton figurine design. The "HN" numbers, which referred originally to Harry Nixon, a Doulton artist, were chronological until 1940, after which blocks of numbers were assigned to each modeler. From 1928 until 1954, a small number was placed to the right of the crown mark; this number added to 1927 gives the year of manufacture.

References: Susan and Al Bagdade, *Warman's English & Continental Pottery & Porcelain*, 3rd ed., Krause Publications, 1998; Diana and John Callow and Marilyn and Peter Sweet, *Charlton Price Guide to*

Beswick Animals, 2nd ed., Charlton Press, 1995; Jean Dale, *Charlton Standard Catalogue of Royal Doulton Animals*, 2nd ed., Charlton Press, 1998; ——, *Charlton Standard Catalogue of Royal Doulton Beswick Figurines*, 6th ed., Charlton Press, 1998; ——, *Charlton Standard Catalogue of Royal Doulton Beswick Jugs*, 5th ed., Charlton Press, 1999; ——, *Charlton Standard Catalogue of Royal Doulton Beswick Storybook Figurines*, 6th ed., Charlton Press, 2000; ——, *Charlton Standard Catalogue of Royal Doulton Figurines*, 7th ed., Charlton Press, 2000; ——, *Charlton Standard Catalogue of Royal Doulton Jugs*, Charlton Press, 1991; Jean Dale and Louise Irvine, *Charlton Standard Catalogue of Royal Doulton Bunnykins*, Charlton Press, 1999; Doug Pinchin, *Doulton Figure Collectors Handbook*, 4th ed., Francis-Joseph Books, 1996.

Periodicals: *Collecting Doulton*, BBR Publishing, 2 Strattford Ave., Elsecar, Nr Barnsley, S. Yorkshire, S74 8AA, England; *Doulton Divvy*, P.O. Box 2434, Joliet, IL 60434.

Collectors' Clubs: Heartland Doulton Collectors, P.O. Box 2434, Joliet, IL 60434; Mid-America Doulton Collectors, P.O. Box 483, McHenry, IL 60050; Royal Doulton International Collectors Club, 700 Cottontail Lane, Somerset, NJ 08873; Royal Doulton International Collectors Club, 850 Progress Ave., Scarborough Ontario M1H 3C4 Canada.

Animal

Alsatian, HN117 . . . . **175.00**
Bonzo dog, model 883, blue glaze, brown and black detailing, 2" h
. . . . **1,320.00**
Bull terrier, K14 . . . . **325.00**
Dalmatian, HN114 . . . . **250.00**
English bulldog, HN1074 . . . . **175.00**
English setter, HN1050 . . . . . **150.00**
French poodle, HN2631 . . . . **150.00**
Irish setter, HN1055 . . . . **150.00**
Salmon, 12" h, flambé, printed mark
. . . . **435.00**
Scottish terrier, K18 . . . . **165.00**
Tiger, 14" l, flambé, printed mark
. . . . **375.00**
Winnie the Pooh set, Pooh, Kanga, Piglet, Eeyore, Owl, Rabbit, and Tigger, Beswick, boxed set . **650.00**
Bowl, 7-3/8" d, stoneware, incised and glazed enamel florals, titled "H. Gibbs 20th Jan 1939," artist sgd, modeled by Vera Huggis, imp marks **175.00**
Candlesticks, pr, 6-1/2" h, Walton Ware, Battle of Hastings, cream color earthenware ground, stamped mark, c1910, small base chip on one . **290.00**
Chamberstick, 2" h, Walton Ware, fishermen dec, ivory earthenware ground, stamped mark, c1910, one of pair damaged **400.00**
Character jug, large
Cardinal **150.00**
Poacher, D6781 . . . . **350.00**
Veteran Motorist **125.00**

Character jug, miniature
Blacksmith **50.00**
Pickwick **65.00**
Character jug, small
Pearly King **35.00**
Pirate, no beard, 1967 . . . . . **960.00**
Toby Philpots **85.00**
Charger, 12-5/8" d, hp, all over incised leaf, berry, and vine border, central fruits and leaves, attributed to Frank Bragwyn, printed mark, c1930 . **245.00**
Clock case, King's Ware, night watchman, c1905 . . . . **450.00**
Cuspidor, 7" h, Isaac Walton Ware, polychrome dec, transfer printed, fisherman on ext., verses on int. lip, printed mark **325.00**
Dinner plate, Walton Ware, fisherman dec, ivory earthenware ground, stamped mark, c1910, price for seven-pc set **750.00**

Capt. Ahab, copyright 1958, D6506, 4" h, **$65.**

Figure

Carolyn, HN 2112, 71/4" h, 3-1/2" d
. . . . **335.00**
Fair Lady, coral pink, HN2835
. . . . **225.00**
Girl Saying Grace, green floral gown and hair net, HN 62, 1916-38
. . . . **4,480.00**
Jester, brown and black, black cap, 1929, two bells missing from cap
. . . . **3,840.00**
Lady Charmain, HN1949 . . . **225.00**
King Charles I, dark brown gloves, black flora at boots, imp date 1919
. . . . **1,312.00**
Michelle, HN2234 . . . . **225.00**
Nicola, HN2839 . . . . **350.00**
Orange Lady, HN1758 . . . . . **245.00**
Queen Mother's 80th Birthday, HN464, 1980 . . . . **720.00**

Priscilla, pantaloons showing beneath crinoline, HN1380, 1920-40 . . . . **288.00**
Sandra, HN2275 . . . . **200.00**
The Leisure Hour, HN2055 . . **400.00**
Top of the Hill, HN1833 . . . . . **225.00**
Victorian Lady, HN1208, 1926-38
. . . . **355.00**
Yardley's Old English Lavender seller, c1925 . . . . **400.00**
Fish plate, 9" d, swimming fish centers, pale yellow ground, gold bands and rims, sgd "J. Hallmark," 10-pc set
. . . . **700.00**
Flask
6-1/2" h, triangular, printed, Sydney Harbour, Dewars on reverse, c1914
. . . . **575.00**
7-1/2" h, King's Ware, Admiral Lord Nelson, Dewars on reverse, c1914
. . . . **550.00**
Humidor, 7-1/2" h, Walton Ware, Battle of Hastings, cream color earthenware ground, stamped mark, c1910 . . **365.00**
Inkstand, 3" h, stoneware, tapered cylindrical form molded with floral sprays, blue, ochre, and brown glazes, silver mounts, Doulton Lambeth, hallmarked London, 1901 . . . . . **215.00**

Jardiniere, children decoration, 9" d, 7" h, **$250.** *Photo courtesy of Joy Luke Auctions.*

Jardiniere, 4-1/2" h, Walton Ware, Battle of Hastings, cream color earthenware ground, stamped mark, c1910 . . . . **350.00**
Jug, 10-1/2" h, Regency Coach, limited edition, printed marks, 20th C . . **930.00**
Loving cup
9-3/4" h, Three Musketeers, limited edition, sgd "Noke, H. Fenton," orig certificate, 20th C **920.00**
10-1/4" d, King George V and Queen Mary, 25-year reign anniversary, c1935 . . . . **750.00**

Mug

4" h, gladiator, #D6553 .... **300.00**
6-1/2" h, cardinal, A mark ... **100.00**
8-1/4" h, St. John Falstaff **95.00**

Pitcher

12-1/2" h, Coaching Days series, continuous scene, dark green rim **265.00**
12-1/2" h, Walton Ware, fishermen dec, ivory earthenware ground, stamped mark, c1910, price for pr, one with bruise and restoration **400.00**

Plate, 10-1/2" d, Gibson Girl, black transfer, each with different titled scene from orig Charles D. Gibson drawings, reserve center, transfer printed cobalt blue stylized foliage border, printed lion and crown mark, c1901, 24-pc set **1,650.00**

Platter, 12-1/2" l, three handles, Walton Ware, fishermen dec, ivory earthenware ground, stamped mark, c1910, restoration to one handle...... **460.00**

Service plate, 10-5/8" d, cream-colored ground, interior band of gilt anthemia, rim with gilt scrollwork over cream-colored ground, apple green reserves, gilt-shaped rim, mold date mark 1910, price for 18-pc set **5,465.00**

Spirits barrel, 7" l, King's Ware, double, silver trim rings and cov, oak stand, c1909.................... **1,200.00**

Tankard, 9-1/2" h, hinged pewter lid, incised frieze of herons among reeds, blue slip enamel, imp mark, sgd, c1875 .... **1,600.00**

Teacup and saucer, cobalt blue, heavy gold dec **120.00**

Tea set, Walton Ware, cov teapot with underplate, creamer, sugar bowl, Battle of Hastings, cream-colored earthenware ground, stamped mark, chip on spout, hairline on sugar lid **365.00**

Tobacco jar, 8" h, incised frieze of cattle, goats, and donkeys, imp mark, sgd, worn SP rim, handle and cover, dated 1880 .... **995.00**

Toby jug

Beefeater, #D6206, 6" h **85.00**
Winston Churchill, #8360 .... **95.00**

Toothpick holder, Walton Ware, Battle of Hastings, cream-color earthenware ground, stamped mark, c1910, set of six **535.00**

Umbrella stand, 23-1/2" h, stoneware, enamel dec, applied floral medallions within diamond formed panels, framed by button motifs, imp mark, glaze crazing, c1910 .... **550.00**

Vase

4-1/2" d, 8-1/4" h, hand painted by Margaret Walker, Art Nouveau-style winged fairies, purple ground, stamped "Doulton/Lambeth/ England," marked "MW/A113," price for pr........... **1,495.00**
5" d, 11" h, Flambe Sung, ovoid, painted foxes, grapes, and vine scroll, stamped mark, "Sung/702058E/Noke"... **1,380.00**
10" h, Walton Ware, fisherman dec, ivory earthenware ground, handle, stamped mark, c1910, base chips, price for pr.............. **535.00**

ROYAL DUX

History: Royal Dux porcelain was made in Dux, Bohemia (now the Czech Republic), by E. Eichler at the Duxer Porzellan-Manufaktur, established in 1860. Many items were exported to the United States. By the turn of the century, Royal Dux figurines, vases, and accessories, especially those featuring Art-Nouveau designs, were captivating consumers.

Marks: A raised triangle with an acorn and the letter "E" plus "Dux, Bohemia" was used as a mark between 1900 and 1914.

Figure, man on camel, boy with baskets, bisque, 18" h, **$250.** *Photo courtesy of Joy Luke Auctions.*

Bowl, 17-1/2" l, modeled as female tending a fishing net, oval shell-form bowl, imp mark, early 20th C .. **490.00**

Bust, 14" h, female portrait, raised leaves and berries on base, Czechoslovakia, early 20th C, unmarked, chips **290.00**

Compote, figural

14-1/2" l, modeled as female atop shell-form bowl, another figure within the wave modeled freeform base, imp mark, early 20th C **750.00**
20-1/4" h, leaf and floral molded bowl mounted to central free-form support, surrounded by three females, imp and printed marks, 20th C................ **635.00**

Figure, dog, pink triangle mark, 11-3/4" l, **$290.**

Figure

9" x 11" x 5", lady with two frolicking cats, "E" triangle mark **950.00**
15" x 9-1/2" x 4-1/2", flamenco dancer, cobalt blue and white glaze, gold trim, pink triangle mark, stamped, numbered **1,250.00**
17" x 13" x 6", semi-nude harem dancer, cobalt pantaloons, gold-trim slippers....... **2,000.00**
18" x 11" x 6", Pierrrot serenading lover, perched on harvest moon, pre-war "E" mark, price for facing pair.................. **3,500.00**
19" x 10" x 8", nude woman seated on small draped table, hands folded................ **3,000.00**
21" x 11", mother and child, roses, partial pink triangle mark . **2,250.00**

Tazza, 19-1/2" h, figural, putti and classically draped woman supporting shell, price for pr, one with hairline in base **880.00**

Vase

11" h, Grecian, "E" mark.... **595.00**
19-1/4" h, bisque, Art Nouveau-style female to one side of leaf and floral molded body, imp mark, early 20th C.................... **290.00**

ROYAL FLEMISH

1892

History: Royal Flemish was produced by the Mount Washington Glass Co., New Bedford, Massachusetts. The process was patented by Albert Steffin in 1894.

Royal Flemish is a frosted transparent glass with heavy raised gold enamel lines. These lines form sections—often colored in russet tones—giving the appearance of stained-glass windows with elaborate floral or coin medallions.

Collectors' Club: Mount Washington Art Glass Society, 60 President Ave., Providence, RI 02906.

Advisers: Clarence and Betty Maier.

Biscuit jar, cov, 8" h, ovoid, large Roman coins on stained panels, divided by heavy gold lines, ornate SP cov, rim, and bail handle, orig paper label "Mt. W. G. Co. Royal Flemish" **1,750.00**
Box, cov, 5-1/2" d, 3-3/4" h, swirled border, gold outlined swirls, gold tracery blossoms, enameled blossom with jeweled center on lid. . . . **1,500.00**

Ewer, sepia colored body, eight vertical panels framed in heavy raised gold, four panels tinted pink mauve, raised gold tendril dec, entrusted gold and tinted autumn leaves, 12" h, $7,500. Photo courtesy of Clarence and Betty Maier.

Ewer, 10-1/2" h, 9" w, 5" d, circular semi-transparent panel on front with youth thrusting spear into chest of winged creature, reverse panel shows mythical fish created with tail changed into stylized florals, raised gold dec, outlines, and scrolls, rust, purple, and gold curlicues, twisted rope handle with brushed gold encircles neck, hp minute gold florals on neck, burnished gold stripes on rim spout and panels **4,950.00**
Jar, 8" h, classical Roman coin medallion dec, simulated stained glass panels, SP rim, bail, and cov, paper label "Mt. W. G. Co. Royal Flemish" **1,650.00**

Vase, Guba duck decoration, attributed to Frank Guba, raised gold sun, lead mallard, 10 other ducks encircle perimeter, irregular panels of pastel tan and frosted clear, mauve, and gold embellishments on upper 3" of crown-like top, 15-3/4" h, $7,200.

Vase, 6" d, 6-1/2" h, stylized scrolls of pastel violet sweep down two tiny handles and across body, realistically tinged sprays of violets randomly strewn around frosted clear glass body, gold lines define violet nosegays and frame scrolls, gold accents daubed here and there, sgd with Royal Flemish logo and "0583" **2,200.00**

ROYAL RUDOLSTADT

GERMANY
RW
RUDOLSTADT

History: Johann Fredrich von Schwarzburg-Rudolstadt was the patron of a faience factory located in Rudolstadt, Thuringen, Germany, from 1720 to c1790.

In 1854, Ernst Bohne established a factory in Rudolstadt.

The "Royal Rudolstadt" designation originated with wares which Lewis Straus and Sons (later Nathan Straus and Sons) of New York imported from the New York and Rudolstadt Pottery between 1887 and 1918. The factory manufactured several of the Rose O'Neill (Kewpie) items.

Marks: The first mark of the original pottery was a hayfork; later, crossed two-prong hayforks were used in imitation of the Meissen mark.

"EB" was the mark used by Ernst Bohne. A crown over a diamond enclosing the initials "RW" is the mark used by the New York and Rudolstadt Pottery.

Box, cov, 4-1/2" w, 5" d, 5-1/2" h, relief dec panels of nude allegorical garden scene, bronze trim and hinge, mark of crowned N, Ernst Bohne Sons, early 1900s. **425.00**
Bust, 15" h, classical figure, glazed to simulate marble. **165.00**

Cake plate, 12" d, pink, white roses, gold handles and trim **75.00**
Ewer, 10" h, ivory, floral dec, gold handle and trim **125.00**
Figure, 8-1/4", muse Euterpe, wearing classical garb, flowers in hair, lute at her feet, holding scroll of poetry and flute **225.00**
Hatpin holder, lavender and roses **45.00**
Nut set, master bowl, six small bowls, white and green roses, fluted, ftd, "B" under crown mark **265.00**
Plate, 8-1/2" d, pink, white, and yellow roses, gold molded piecrust rim . **35.00**
Teapot, cov, 5-1/2" h, hp, ivory, pink, lavender, and green floral dec . . . **95.00**
Urn, 10" h, mythological scene, Hector and Andro crowning maiden, cobalt blue ground, gold handles, artist sgd, stand **145.00**
Vase, 4" h, floral dec, elephant handles **90.00**

ROYAL VIENNA

1749 - 1864

History: Production of hard-paste porcelain in Vienna began in 1720 with Claude Innocentius du Paquier, a runaway employee from the Meissen factory. In 1744, Empress Maria Theresa brought the factory under royal patronage; subsequently, the ware became known as Royal Vienna. The firm went through many administrative changes until it closed in 1864, but the quality of its workmanship was always maintained.

Marks: Several other Austrian and German firms copied the Royal Vienna products, including the use of the "Beehive" mark. Many of the pieces on today's market are from these firms.

Cabinet vase, 3-1/2" h, children of four seasons, blue beehive mark . . . **350.00**
Chocolate pot, cov, 10" h, large reserve with artist dec vase, woman looking on, cream ground, gilt handles and trim, Knoeller **350.00**
Cup and saucer, 2-3/4" h, 5" d saucer, floral design, pink, lavender, yellow, and melon grounds, gilt borders, set of four **475.00**
Ferner, 7-3/4" w, 4" h, portrait of lady one side, portrait of different lady on other, burgundy, green , and gold, beaded, scalloped edges, ftd, marked "Royal Vienna, Austria," artist sgd **425.00**

Cake plate, two handles, girl holding basket of flowers deck, 9-3/4" l, $50. Photo courtesy of Joy Luke Auctions.

Portrait plate, 9-1/2" d, titled "Vergissmeinicht," portrait of girl holding flowers, landscape background, sgd "Dittrich," paneled gilt border in pink, blue, green, maroon, gilt geometric designs, blue beehive mark **500.00**

Snuff box, 3" w, 2-1/2" d, 2-1/8" h, quatrefoil, landscape on lid, floral dec sides, blue beehive mark **250.00**

Stein, quarter liter, hp, copy of early Meissen Chinese scene, elaborate battle surmounted by gold border, four flowers painted in rear, similar scene of harbor of top of lid, floral design painted on underside of lid, eagle thumb lift, beehive mark **2,310.00**

Urn, cov

11-1/2" h, hp, elaborate scene of man, women, and cherub, cobalt blue ground, gold trim, beehive mark **1,200.00**

30" h, gilt intertwined serpent handles, gilt scroll dec and band, classical figures on cobalt blue ground, sq plinth painted with figural reserves on two sides, repaired, c1900 . . . . **4,000.00**

Vase

10-1/2" h, baluster, portrait of Welda, hp, flowing hair, sgd "Wagner," opalescent ground with gilt floral dec, marked "Royal Vienna/Welda/ Dec 241," imp "523" **2,450.00**

10-1/2" h, facing female portrait medallions, banded ground of medium green, pale green, and pink, gilt filigree, floral panels, blue beehive mark, gilt wear, price for pr **1,890.00**

ROYAL WORCESTER

History: In 1751, the Worcester Porcelain Company, led by Dr. John Wall and William Davis, acquired the Bristol pottery of Benjamin Lund and moved it to Worcester. The first wares were painted blue under the glaze; soon thereafter decorating was accomplished by painting on the glaze in enamel colors. Among the most-famous 18th-century decorators were James Giles and Jefferys Hamet O'Neale. Transfer-print decoration was developed by the 1760s.

A series of partnerships took place after Davis' death in 1783: Flight (1783-1793); Flight & Barr (1793-1807); Barr, Flight, & Barr (1807-1813); and Flight, Barr, & Barr (1813-1840). In 1840, the factory was moved to Chamberlain & Co. in Diglis. Decorative wares were discontinued. In 1852, W. H. Kerr and R. W. Binns formed a new company and revived the production of ornamental wares.

In 1862, the firm became the Royal Worcester Porcelain Co. Among the key modelers of the late 19th century were James Hadley, his three sons, and George Owen, an expert with pierced clay pieces. Royal Worcester absorbed the Grainger factory in 1889 and the James Hadley factory in 1905. Modern designers include Dorothy Doughty and Doris Lindner.

References: Susan and Al Bagdade, *Warman's English & Continental Pottery & Porcelain*, 3rd ed., Krause Publications, 1998; Anthony Cast and John Edwards, *Charlton Price Guide to Royal Worcester Figurines*, Millenium Ed., Charlton Press, 2000; John Edwards, *The Charlton Standard Catalogue of Royal Worcester Animals*, Charlton Press, 2001; G. A. Godden, *Victorian Porcelain*, Herbert Jenkins, 1961; Stanley W. Fisher, *Worcester Porcelain*, Ward Lock & Co., Ltd., 1968; David, John, and Henry Sandon, *Sandon Guide to Royal Worcester Figures*, Alderman Press, 1987; Henry Sandon, *Flight & Barr Worcester*, Antique Collectors' Club, 1992; Henry Sandon and John Sandon, *Dictionary of Worcester Porcelain*, Vol. II, Antique Collectors' Club, 1995; ——, *Grainger's Worcester Porcelain*, Barrie & Jenkins, 1990; John Sandon, *The Dictionary of Worcester Porcelain*, Vol. I, Antique Collectors' Club, 1993.

Museums: Charles William Dyson Perrins Museum, Worcester, England; Roberson Center for the Arts and Sciences, Binghamton, NY.

Basket, 8-1/2" d, flaring pierced sides mounted with floral heads, pine cone and floral cluster int., blue and white transfer dec, first period, mid-18th C **550.00**

Biscuit jar, cov, 7-1/4" h, fluted body, raised spear head borders surrounding enamel floral design **550.00**

Bowl, 10" d, scalloped border, shell molded boy, fruit and floral spray, blue and white transfer dec, first period, mid-18th C **320.00**

Butter tub, cov, 4-1/4" d, 3-1/4" h, cylindrical, fully sculpted finial, painted floral sprays below geometric borders, first period, c1765 . . . . **450.00**

Centerpiece, 6-1/4" h, oval, ftd, Royal Lily pattern, first period, c1800, repaired **125.00**

Dish, 8" l, leaf form, molded body, underglaze blue floral sprays, branch handle, first period, c1765 . . . . **500.00**

Ewer

12-1/2" h, gilt and enamel floral dec, late-19th C **210.00**

15-3/4" h, scrolled foliate handle, raised gilt and red enamel leaf and floral designs, light gilt wear, 1896 . . . . **1,495.00**

Figure

5-1/4" h, politician, white glaze, late-19th C, staining, hat rim chip restored **290.00**

6-1/2" h, Welsh girl, shot enamel porcelain, sgd "Hadley," late-19th C **690.00**

7-3/4" h and 8-1/4" h, lady and gentleman, George III costumes, sgd "Hadley," pr **1,100.00**

8-3/4" h, Cairo water carrier, 1895 . . . . **635.00**

Fish plates, 9-1/4" d, bone china, hp fish, gilt lattice and foliage border, sgd "Harry Ayrton," printed marks, c1930, 13-pc set **2,300.00**

Fruit cooler, 6-1/4" h, cylindrical, Royal Lily pattern, stylized floral reserve, stepped circular foot, first period, c1800 . . . . **225.00**

Plate, cattle decoration, signed "o," 10" d, $1,540. Photo courtesy of Jackson's Auctioneers & Appraisers.

Lamp base, 13-3/4" h, baluster vase form, slender gilt neck, two short Moorish-style gilt handles, hand-painted scene of gilt shipwreck on shore by lighthouse, reverse with small scenic roundel, gilt guilloche foot, electrified **325.00**

Mustard pot, 4" h, cylindrical, blue and white transfer, floral clusters, floral finial, first period, mid-18th C. **325.00**

Plate

7" w, octagonal, landscape fan form reserves, cobalt blue ground, first period, 18th C, pr **350.00**

7-3/4" d, Blind Earl pattern, raised rose spray, polychrome floral sprays, scalloped border, first period, mid-18th C **1,100.00**

8" d, diaper pattern border surrounding floral spray, blue and white transfer dec, first period, mid-19th C. **220.00**

10-3/4" d, Tewkesbury, natural colors, gold edge, artist sgd "Nickolis," 1953 mark **190.00**

Sauce boat, 41/4" h, geometric band above foliate molded body, painted floral sprays, oval foot, first period, c1765, pr **275.00**

Sweetmeat, 6" l, leaf form, blue and white transfer chinoiserie landscapes, first period, mid-18th C. **325.00**

Tankard, 6" h, cylindrical, blue and white transfer dec of parrot among fruit, first period, mid-18th C. **325.00**

Teabowl and saucer, painted chinoisiere vignette, blue border, first period, c1865 . . . .**185.00**

Teapot, cov, 6-1/2" h, globular form body, fully sculpted blossom finial, domed top, painted floral sprays, first period, c1765 . . . .**375.00**

Urn, cov, 11-1/2" h, pierced dome top, globular body, painted floral sprays, basketweave molded base, early 20th C **195.00**

Vase, 5" w, 4" h, hexagonal, mottled tan ground, sterling silver overlay in floral design, silver marked "The Metcalf Co." and "Solid Silver," vase marked "Royal Worcester England Patent Rd. NO. 374993 2176," hand marked in glaze "2176" **335.00**

ROYCROFT

History: Elbert Hubbard founded the Roycrofters in East Aurora, New York, at the turn of the century. Considered a genius in his day, he was an author, lecturer, manufacturer, salesman, and philosopher.

Hubbard established a campus which included a printing plant where he published *The Philistine, The Fra,* and *The Roycrofter.* His most-famous book was *A Message to Garcia,* published in 1899. His "community" also included a furniture manufacturing plant, a metal shop, and a leather shop.

References: Kevin McConnell, *Roycroft Art Metal,* 2nd ed., Schiffer Publishing, 1994; The Roycrofters, *Roycroft Furniture Catalog, 1906,* Dover, 1994; Paul Royka, *Mission Furniture ,from the American Arts & Crafts Movement,* Schiffer Publishing, 1997; Marie Via and Marjorie B. Searl, *Head, Heart and Hand,* University of Rochester Press (34 Administration Bldg, University of Rochester, Rochester, NY 14627), 1994.

Collectors' Clubs: Foundation for the Study of Arts & Crafts Movement, Roycroft Campus, 31 S. Grove St., East Aurora, NY 14052; Roycrofters-at-Large Assoc., P.O. Box 417, East Aurora, NY 14052.

Museum: Elbert Hubbard Library-Museum, East Aurora, NY.

Additional Listings: Arts and Crafts Movement; Copper.

Ali Baba bench, 42-1/2" l, 11" w, 20" h, half-log top, flaring plank legs, keyed through tenon stretcher, carved orb and cross mark, minor loss to bark, orig finish. **16,500.00**

Bookcase, slab sides with keyed tenon construction, plate rail top, orig iron hardware, orb mark, refinished, 46" w, 16" d, 71" h. **9,775.00**

Bookends, pr

5-1/2" w, 3-1/4" h, line work at edges, ornamental crimping, orig patina, early mark **245.00**

6-1/2" w, 4-1/4" h, open style, applied strap, riveted construction, middle mark **215.00**

Bowl, 10-1/4" d, 4-1/8" h, hammered copper, rolled rim, shouldered bowl, three point feet, red patina, imp mark, traces of brass wash **450.00**

Vase, white hand holding green vase, white auctioneer's label, 6" h, **$220.** *Photo courtesy of Joy Luke Auctions.*

Ali Baba bench, half-log top, flaring plank legs with keyed through-tenon stretcher, Carved orb & cross mark, excellent original finish and condition, minor loss to bark, 20" x 42-1/2" x 11", **$16,500.** *Photo courtesy of David Rago Auctions.*

Candle lamp, blue art glass, baluster form, flaring foot, stamped "Roycroft," electrified **175.00**

Candle sconce, 3-1/2" w, 10" h, hammered copper, riveted strap holder, imp backplate, orig dark brown patina, orb and cross mark, few scratches, price for pr **630.00**

Candlestick

3-1/4" d, 7-3/4" h, hammered copper, Princess style, double stems, faceted bases, stamped orb and cross mark, orig patina, price for pr **980.00**

5" d, 12-3/4" h, hammered copper, twisted stem, circular base, fine orig patina, orb and cross mark, price for pr **980.00**

Chamberstick, 1-1/2" d, 3" h, hammered copper, stamped orb and cross mark, normal wear to orig patina, price for pr **460.00**

Chandelier, from Roycroft Inn, 14-1/2" w, 10-3/4" h, copper, triangular strap support base with cut-out hearts and three pendant fixtures, each with enameled amber glass shade dec in stylized floral motif, triangular ceiling plate, hanging chains, orb and cross mark **1,955.00**

Desk lamp, 14-3/4" h, 7" d Steuben blown glass lustered glass shade, hammered copper, shaft of four curled and riveted bands, stamped orb and cross mark **5,750.00**

Desk set, hammered copper, paper knife, pen tray, stationery holding, perpetual desk calendar, pr of bookends, flower holder, match holder with nested ashtray, c1915 . . . . **550.00**

Frame

15" w, 20-1/2" h, orig print, orig finish **450.00**

16-1/4" w, 13-1/2" h, orig watercolor landscape by J. L. Judson, painting sgd **450.00**

Goody box, 23" l, 13" d, 10" h, mahogany, wrought cooper strap hardware, monogrammed "H," orig finish, carved orb and cross on top **630.00**

Humidor, 4-3/4" w, 5-3/4" h, hammered copper, covered in brass wash, Trillium pattern, stamped orb and cross mark, minor wear to patina **690.00**

Lamp base, 7" d, 20" h, hammered copper, tall tapering form, flaring base, riveted bands, articulated handles, three-light fixture, orb and cross mark **2,760.00**

Humidor, covered, hammered copper, Trillium pattern, covered in brass wash, stamped orb and cross mark, minor wear to patina, 5-3/4" x 4-3/4", $690. Photo courtesy of David Rago Auctions.

Mirror, 23-1/2" w, 41-1/2" h, rect, beveled, orig medium finish, lap joint construction, unmarked **1,265.00**

Nut set, hammered copper, ftd bowl, spoon, six plates, six picks, all picks marked with orb and cross, orig patina, price for 14-pc set **4,890.00**

Plaque, motto, 5-1/4" h, 9-1/4" l, carved oak, "Be Yourself," orig dark finish, carved orb and cross mark . . **3,400.00**

Presentation bowl, 11" d, 3" h, squat-form, broad shoulder engraved "To Boardie from the Squash Crowd 1928," orig dark patina, imp mark **200.00**

Sconce, 7-1/4" l, 5" w, 7" h, copper, from Roycroft Inn, spiral mount on shaped base, pressed glass shades, one replaced shade, price for pr . . . **690.00**

Tray

18" d, hammered copper, circular, two riveted handles, stamped orb and cross mark, normal wear to orig reddish patina **690.00**

22" l, 9-1/2" w, oval, brass washed hammered copper, simple chased design, two handles, orig patina, orb and cross mark **415.00**

Vase, 3" d, 6" h, hammered copper, cylindrical, applied German silver band in Secessionist pattern, orig patina, stamped orb and cross mark . **1,380.00**

RUBENA GLASS

History: Rubena crystal is a transparent blown glass which shades from clear to red. It also is found as the background for frosted and overshot glass. It was made in the late 1800s by several glass companies, including Northwood, and Hobbs, Brockunier & Co. of Wheeling, West Virginia.

Rubena was used for several patterns of pattern glass including Royal Ivy and Royal Oak.

Bowl, 4-1/2" d, Daisy and Scroll . **65.00**

Butter dish, cov, Royal Oak, fluted **250.00**

Compote, 14" h, 9" d, rubena overshot bowl, white metal bronze finished figural standard **170.00**

Cracker jar, cov

Aurora, inverted rib, Northwood **325.00**

Cut fan and strawberry design, fancy sterling silver cov, 7" h, 6" w **1,150.00**

Creamer and sugar bowl, cov, Royal Ivy **250.00**

Decanter, 9" h, bulbous body, narrow neck, applied clear handle **170.00**

Finger bowl, Royal Ivy **65.00**

Pickle castor, enameled daisy dec, ornate sgd frame with two handles, pickle fork in front **245.00**

Pitcher, enameled apple blossom motif, 7-1/2" h, $495.

Salt shaker, Coquette **150.00**

Sauce dish, Royal Ivy **35.00**

Sugar shaker, Royal Ivy **250.00**

Toothpick holder, Optic **150.00**

Tumbler, Medallion Sprig **100.00**

Tumble-Up, tumbler and carafe, Baccarat Swirl **175.00**

Vase, 10" h, ruffled rim, hp enameled flowers, gold trim, Hobbs, Brockunier & Co. **175.00**

Water pitcher

Opal Swirl, Northwood **275.00**

Royal Ivy, frosted **295.00**

RUBENA VERDE GLASS

History: Rubena Verde, a transparent glass that shades from red in the upper section to yellow-green in the lower, was made by Hobbs, Brockunier & Co., Wheeling, West Virginia, in the late 1880s. It often is found in the Inverted Thumbprint (IVT) pattern, called "Polka Dot" by Hobbs.

Tumbler, Inverted Thumbprint pattern, 3-7/8" h, $125.

Bowl, 9-1/2" d, IVT, ruffled **175.00**
Butter dish, cov, Daisy and Button
. . . .**250.00**
Celery vase, 6-1/4" h, IVT **225.00**
Creamer and sugar bowl, cov, Hobnail, bulbous, applied handle
. . . .**550.00**
Cruet, 7" h, IVT, teepee shape, trefoil spout, vaseline handle and faceted stopper, Hobbs, Brockunier **550.00**
Finger bowl, IVT **95.00**
Jack in the Pulpit Vase, 8" h . . . **250.00**
Pickle castor, Hobb's Hobnail, SP frame, cov, and tongs. **500.00**
Pitcher, 4-1/2" h, applied handle and feet **125.00**
Salt and pepper shakers, pr, IVT
. . . .**210.00**
Tumbler, IVT. **125.00**
Vase, 9-1/4" h, paneled body, enameled daises dec. **85.00**
Water pitcher, Hobb's Hobnail .**395.00**

RUSSIAN ITEMS

History: During the late 19th and early 20th centuries, craftsmen skilled in lacquer, silver, and enamel wares worked in Russia. During the Czarist era (1880-1917), Fabergé, known for his exquisite enamel pieces, led a group of master craftsmen located primarily in Moscow. Fabergé also had an establishment in St. Petersburg and enjoyed the patronage of the Russian Imperial family and royalty and nobility throughout Europe.

Almost all enameling was done on silver. Pieces are signed by the artist and the government assayer.

ВРАТЬЕВЪ
Baterin's factory
1812-1820

КОРНИЛОВЫХЪ
Korniloff's factory
c1835

The Russian Revolution in 1917 brought an abrupt end to the century of Russian craftsmanship. The modern Soviet government has exported some inferior enamel and lacquer work, usually lacking in artistic merit. Modern pieces are not collectible.

References: Joel A. Batech, *Kremlin Gold: 1000 Years of Russian Gems & Jewels*, Harry N. Abrams, 2000; Martin J. Goodman, *Lenin's Legacy*, Schiffer Publishing, 2000; Vladimir Guliayev, *Fine Art of Russian Lacquered Miniatures*, Chronicle Books, 1993; P. Hare, *The Art & Artists of Russia*, Methuen & Co., 1965; L. Nikiforova, compiler, *Russian Porcelain in the Hermitage Collection*, Aurora Art Publications, 1973; Marvin Ross, *Russian Porcelains*, University of Oklahoma Press, 1968; A. Kenneth Snowman, *Fabergé*, Harry N. Abrams, 1993; John Traina, *The Fabergé Case: From the Private Collection of John Traina*, Harry N. Abrams, 1998; Ian Wardropper, et. al., *Soviet Porcelain*, The Art Institute of Chicago, 1992.

Museums: Cleveland Museum of Art, Cleveland, OH; Forbes Magazine Collection, New York, NY; Hermitage, Leningrade, Russia; Hillwood, The Marjorie Merriweather Post Collection, Washington, DC; Russian Museum, Leningrad, Russia; Virginia Museum of Fine Arts, Lillian Thomas Pratt Collection, Richmond, VA; Walters Art Gallery, Baltimore, MD.

Bowl, silver-gilt and enamel, by Imperial Russian silver maker Fyodor Ruckert, 8", $9,490. Photo courtesy of Jackson's Auctioneers & Appraisers.

Enamels
Cigarette case, 3-1/2" l, 2-1/4" w, 84 standard, silver gilt, robin's egg blue enamel, feathered guillouche ground, opaque white enamel borders, diamond chips on clasp, gilt in., Ivan Britzin, St. Petersburg, 1908-17, small losses and chips to enamel. **1,200.00**

Cup, champleve enamel, marked "84" in circle and "BA" in square, 5" l, 2-3/4" h, $3,650.

Coffee spoon, blue dot border in bowl, stylized polychrome enamel foliage, gilt stippled ground, twisted gilt stem, crown finial, G Tokmakov, c1890
. . . .**300.00**
Egg, silver gilt and shaded enamel ware, two-pc construction, cabochon stone, maker's mark obliterated, 20th C
3" h, ftd **700.00**
4" h, separate base **800.00**
Kovsh, 3" l, silver gilt, Art Nouveau-style enameling, pointed prow, hooked handle, Maria Semenaova, Moscow, c1900 . **1,900.00**
Letter opener, 10-1/2" l, cylindrical handle, enameled translucent green guillouche ground, overlaid gilt trellis dec, horse head finial, red cabochon eyes, seed pearl border, agate glade
. . . .**925.00**
Napkin ring, 1-3/4" x 1" x 1-1/2", enameled green, blue, pink, brown, white, light blue and maroon, Maria Semenova, Moscow, c1890 . . . . **700.00**
Teaspoon, turquoise ground, filigree cloisonné, white enamel dot border, red and white enamel flower in center of bowl, red flower on handle, gilt stern, V Akhimov, 1896 . . . . **300.00**

Icon
10-1/4" w, 12-1/4" h, Virgin Kazanskaya, brass riza pressed with guilloche border, late 19th/early 20th C. . . **250.00**
10-1/4" w, 12-3/8" h, Christ the Pantokrator, chased and emb silvered brass riza with stylized relief halo, early 19th C. **460.00**
12" x 10", Conversational, late-18th C, visitation of Mary to Sexton Yuri, tempera on wood panel, overlaid with silver gilt riza with indistinguishable maker's mark, cloth covering on reverse inscribed "With God's Blessing to Duke and Duchess Alexandar Ivanovich Devletkideyew and their daughter

Anastasyia from Alandra Michaliovana Drobovaya" **1,375.00**

12" x 10", St. Nicholas, 19th C, tempera on wood panel, overlaid with silver riza **1,375.00**

12-1/8" w, 14-1/8" h, Virgin Kazanskaya, faces painted in Byzantine style, wide rect border, mid-19th C **350.00**

14" w, 17" h, scenes from life of Christ, large center scene, surrounded by smaller scenes, figure of saint on each corner, mid-19th C **575.00**

Icon, celebrating Romanov Tercentenary, c1914, 12-1/4" x 10-1/4", $6,040. Photo courtesy of Jackson's Auctioneers & Appraisers.

Metal

Basket, 11" l, silver, oval, foliate border, bail handle 18 oz **295.00**

Belt, 29" l, turquoise links spaced with silver gilt links, large turquoise clasp, hallmarks **185.00**

Bonbonniere, 3-3/8" d, 2-3/16" h, orchid guillouche enamel on silver, cylindrical, cast silver bas-relief applied dec on cov and back, applied relief, monogram of Nicholas II set with precious stones, Henrik Wigstrom, workmaster, St. Petersburg, 1908-17, slight damage. **4,225.00**

Figure, 14-1/2" h, 12" l, bronze, equestrian group, officer and lady riding astride horse, dark brown patina, sgd, 20th C. **865.00**

Safe, 3" l, patinated, applied plaque with Russian characters **125.00**

Samovar, 18" h, brass, bowl and tray **275.00**

Serving spoon, silver, dated 1857, 4 oz, 4 dwt. **200.00**

Tabernacle, 23" h, silver gilt, multiple piece, hallmarked Moscow, dated 1893, Cyrillic maker's mark "I.A."
. . . . **3,300.00**

Tray, 16-1/4" l, silver, pierced border, reeded rim, two reeded handles, marked "Marvei Kostorv, Moscow, 1806," 26 oz, 4 dwt. **2,000.00**

Miscellaneous

Stool, 13-1/2" w, 9-1/4" d, 8-7/8" h, painted, top with geometric strapwork dec, turned tapered legs, early 20th C
. . . . **125.00**

Porcelain

Cabinet plate, 9" d, cobalt blue, green, and red central rosette, gilt ground
. . . . **275.00**

Cup and saucer, 4-1/2" h, blue glazed, honoring coronation of Nicholas II, 1878, M. S. Kuznetsov **250.00**

Dessert plate, floral rim, magenta ground, Islamic script, printed mark, I. E. Kuznetsov, 19th C, set of six . **265.00**

Egg, 4-1/2" l, floral and foliate polychrome dec, gilt highlights. . **50.00**

Plate

> 6-1/4" d, central scene of women peasants in landscape, shaped flower-filled panel rim, gilt highlights, Kustentzoff, price for pr
> **175.00**

> 9" d, bucolic scene, sepia, A. G. Popov, Moscow, 19th C, minor wear, chips, 10-pc set **690.00**

Portrait plate, 8" d, Empress Elizabeth, Safronov, early 19th C, hairline . **315.00**

Tankard, 8" h, figural, Turk's head, marked "F. Gardner, Moscow," 19th C, restored **1,210.00**

Urn, 10-3/4" h, baluster, medallion handles, panel with Arab and maiden, polychrome dec, puce ground . **425.00**

Vase, 8" h, one green with medallion of Olga, other puce with medallion of Vladimir, allover gilt foliate dec, Gardner, 19th C, drilled, price for pr
. . . . **250.00**

Silver

Box, 2-3/4" d, 2-1/8" h, cylindrical, enameled blue, green, white, and coral, star design on lid, panels of bird and scroll designs on sides, gilt int., marked "?84" and double-headed bird, crazing in white enamel band on lid . . . **600.00**

Cordial set, 7-3/4" h, maker's mark "BC," early 20th C, stoppered ewer, six footed cordials, circular tray, engraved foliates and stylized houses, approx 15 troy oz **260.00**

Teaspoon, child's, 5-5/8" l, handle in form of standing teddy bear, beige and brown enameling, turquoise and white plinth, 20th C, 1 troy oz **175.00**

SALOPIAN WARE

ℂ 𝒮 SALOPIAN

History: Salopian ware was made at Caughley Pot Works, Salop, Shropshire, England, in the 18th century by Thomas Turner. At one time, the product was classified "Polychrome Transfer" because of the method of decoration, but the ware is better known by the more popular name "Salopian." Much of the output was sold through Turner's Salopian warehouse in London

Marks: Pieces are impressed or painted under the glaze with an "S" or the word "Salopian."

Plate, brown transfer decoration, stag in landscape, floral border, blue, green and yellow over glaze accents, 7" d, $250. Photo courtesy of Sanford Alderfer Auction Co.

Bowl
  6-1/2" d, 3-1/2" h, bright yellow, green, and blue, rural scene of milk maid, cow, cottage, and church steeple in background, colorful flower border, professionally repaired **575.00**
  7-3/4" d, milkmaid milking cow in meadow scene, panels of men at work separated by florals, brown-black transfer with polychromed enamels **250.00**
Creamer, 6" h, black transfer of maiden with urn, yellow and burnt orange accents, black and white frieze, black, white, orange, and yellow florals around rim border, c1790 . . . . **225.00**
Cup and saucer
  Chinoiserie pattern **350.00**
  Deer pattern, blue, black, yellow, and green transfer, chip on rim **250.00**
  Elephant pattern, chips on the foot rim of the saucer, handle repaired **195.00**

Oriental scene, light green, dark blue enamel edge, hairline in cup **210.00**
Pastoral scene, thatched roof cottage, stream, water wheel, grazing sheep, 3-1/2" d cup, 5-1/2" d saucer **225.00**
Scene of man and woman along river watching workers gathering reeds, blue crescent mark . **225.00**
Plate
  7-1/4" d, hand painted, yellow, blue, and orange floral design, blue edge trim, geometric border, blue glaze, pearlware **475.00**
  7-1/4" d, white stag center, floral border, black transfer with polychrome enamels **115.00**
Posset pot, 4" h, brown transfer of large and small flowers highlighted by light blue, orange, yellow, and green **350.00**
Sugar bowl, cov, pastoral scene, shepherd with sheep, thatched roof cottage, bright yellow, blue, and green, blue glaze **350.00**
Teabowl and saucer, brown transfer of farm scene **150.00**
Tea caddy, 4" h, black transfer of deer and cottage, pink and yellow accents **275.00**

Teapot, blue transfer of boy carrying lamb, c1790, 8-1/4" l, 4" h, $495.

Teapot
  Elaborate classical scene, black and white transfer, dark blue enamel trim, minor roughness at spout **375.00**
  Scene of man and woman along river watching workers gathering reeds, blue crescent mark, some roughness at spout **1,240.00**
Waste bowl, classical cartouches in brown transfers with three maidens, cobalt blue, yellow, green, and ochre flowers, int. with brown transfer of florals **200.00**

SALT AND PEPPER SHAKERS

History: Collecting salt and pepper shakers, whether late 19th-century glass forms or the contemporary figural and souvenir types, is becoming more and more popular. The supply and variety is practically unlimited; the price for most sets is within the budget of cost-conscious collectors. In addition, their size offers an opportunity to display a large collection in a relatively small space.

Specialty collections can be by type, form, or maker. Great glass artisans, such as Joseph Locke and Nicholas Kopp, designed salt and pepper shakers in the normal course of their work.

References: Larry Carey and Sylvia Tompkins, *1003 Salt & Pepper Shakers*, Schiffer Publishing, 1997; —; *1004 Salt & Pepper Shakers*, Schiffer Publishing, 1998; —; *1006 Salt & Pepper Shakers*, Schiffer Publishing, 2000; Melva Davern, *Collector's Encyclopedia of Figural & Novelty Salt and Pepper Shakers*, Collector Books, First and Second Series, 2000 value updates; Helene Guarnaccia, *Salt & Pepper Shakers*, Vol. I (1985, 1999 value update), Vol. II (1989, 1998 value update), Vol. III (1991, 1998 value update), Vol. IV (1993, 2001 value update), Collector Books; Mildred and Ralph Lechner, *World of Salt Shakers*, 2nd ed., Collector Books, 1992, 1998 value update; Arthur G. Peterson, *Glass Salt Shakers*, Wallace-Homestead, 1970, out of print; Sylvia Tompkins and Irene Thornburg, *America's Salt and Pepper Shakers*, Schiffer, 2000.

Collectors' Clubs: Antique and Art Glass Salt Shaker Collectors Society, 1775 Lakeview Drive, Zeeland, MI 49464, http://www.cbantiques.com/ssc; British Novelty Salt & Pepper Collectors Club, Coleshill, Clayton Road, Mold, Flintshire CH7 1SX UK; Novelty Salt & Pepper Shakers Club, P.O. Box 677388, Orlando, FL 32867-7388.

Museum: Judith Basin Museum, Stanford, MT.

Additional Listings: See *Warman's Americana & Collectibles* and *Warman's Flea Market* for more examples.

Art glass (priced individually)
Burmese, 4" h, branches and leaves dec, metal top, Mt. Washington . . **85.00**
Cobalt Blue, 4" h, deep color, sterling push-on lid with English hallmarks "E.E.," "HH," and a lion facing left, sterling collar marked "E.E.," anchor, and lion facing left **285.00**
Cranberry, Inverted Thumbprint, sphere **175.00**
Fig, enameled pansy dec, satin, orig prong top, Mt. Washington **120.00**
Hobnail, sapphire blue, Hobbs, Brockunier & Co., one orig metal top, 2-3/4" h **95.00**
Scrollware, blue scrolling **170.00**
Wave Crest, Erie Twist body, hp flowers, 2-1/2" h **185.00**

Opaque white ground, yellow and orange flowers, green leaves, St. Paul in gold letters, egg shape, original tops, 2" h, pair, $215.

Figural and souvenir types
(priced by set)

Black cat, mother and baby, nodders, yellow and red collars, marked "Patent TN" and "Made in Japan," 4" h . **425.00**

Bride and groom, pigs, nodders, marked "Made in Japan," c1950 .... **325.00**

Cardinal Tuck, holding book, marked "Goebel, W. Germany" bee inside V mark, paper label **325.00**

Christmas, barrel shape

Amber.................... **80.00**

Amethyst................. **145.00**

Ducks, 2-1/2" h, sitting, glass, clear bodies, blue heads, sgd "Czechoslovakia" **45.00**

Elsie the Cow, Beulah and Beauregard, marked "Made in Japan," 5" h..................... **295.00**

Egg shape

Opaque white body, holly dec, 23 red raised enameled berries, Mt. Washington............. **185.00**

Pastel tint, pink enameled blossoms, lid loose **65.00**

Goofy and car, Goofy riding in yellow, red, and green car, orig souvenir label "Souvenir Burlington Iowa," marked "Japan," 4" l, 4-1/4" h........ **295.00**

Mammy and broom, orig "Norcrest Fine China Japan" foil labels, numbered H424, 4-1/4" h **395.00**

Matador and bull, nodders, marked "Made in Japan," c1940-50.... **295.00**

Strawberries, flashed amberina glass strawberry-shaped shakers, white metal leaf caps, suspended from emb white metal fancy holder, 2-3/4" h strawberries, 5" h stand, sgd "Japan," c1921-41 .... **285.00**

Opalescent glass
(priced individually)

Argonaut Shell, blue.......... **65.00**

Fluted Scrolls, vaseline....... **65.00**

Jewel and Flower, blue, (164-J), replaced top.................. **45.00**

Seaweed, Hobbs, cranberry **60.00**

Windows, Hobbs, blue, pewter top **50.00**

Opaque glass (priced individually)

Bulge Bottom, blue........... **20.00**

Cathedral Panel, blue **20.00**

Creased Bale, pink **20.00**

Fanband, white **20.00**

Fleur de Lis Scrolling, custard.. **20.00**

Heart, blue **25.00**

Leaf Clover, blue **20.00**

Little Shrimp

Blue **25.00**

White **20.00**

Rib Pointed, blue............ **25.00**

Spider Web, pink............ **25.00**

Swirl Wide Diagonal, white.... **20.00**

Torch Wreath, white **20.00**

Pattern glass, Daisy & Cube, light blue, original top, $30.

Pattern glass (priced individually)

Actress, pewter top.......... **45.00**

Beautiful Lady, colorless, 1905.. **25.00**

Block and Fan, colorless, 1891.. **20.00**

Crown Jewel, c1880, etched ... **35.00**

Four Square, Billows......... **100.00**

Franesware, Hobbs, Brockunier Co., c1880, hobnail, frosted, amber stained **45.00**

Leaf Umbrella, old tops...... **350.00**

Lobe, squatty............... **120.00**

Tulip..................... **100.00**

Twelve Panel, scrolled pink.... **130.00**

SALT-GLAZED WARES

History: Salt-glazed wares have a distinctive pitted surface texture made by throwing salt into the hot kiln during the final firing process. The salt vapors produce sodium oxide and hydrochloric acid which react on the glaze.

Many Staffordshire potters produced large quantities of this type of ware during the 18th and 19th centuries. A relatively small amount was produced in the United States. Salt-glazed wares still are made today.

References: Susan and Al Bagdade, *Warman's English & Continental Pottery & Porcelain*, 3rd ed., Krause Publications, 1998; A. & N. Harding, *Victorian Staffordshire Figures, 1835-1875*, Book Three, Schiffer Publishing, 2000; Arnold R. Mountford, *The Illustrated Guide to Staffordshire Salt-Glazed Stoneware*, Barrie & Jenkins, 1971; Louis T. Stanley, *Collecting Staffordshire Pottery*, Doubleday & Co., 1963.

Museums: American Antiquarian Society, Worcester, MA; City Museum, Stoke-On-Trent, England; British Museum, London, England, Colonial Williamsburg Foundation, Williamsburg, VA; Fitzwilliam Museum, Cambridge, England; Museum of Art, Rhode Island School of Design, Providence, RI; Victoria & Albert Museum, London, England; William Rockhill Nelson Gallery of Art, Kansas City, MO.

Pitcher, bamboo design, rope banding, gray, marked "Ridgway & Co., England," 9" h, $115.

Bottle, 7-1/2" h, flat form, Albany glaze int., c1810 .... **210.00**

Bowl, 11-1/2" l, oval, matching undertray, reticulated, edge wear and hairlines................... **1,320.00**

Canister, 7-1/4" h, one gallon, relief oak leaf design, blue and navy blue accents, orig matching lid and bale handle, relief diamond pattern all around..................... **220.00**

Canteen, 7-1/2" h, relief and blue accented tavern scene on front, relief and blue accented leaf design around rim, orig bale handle........ **495.00**

Cheese jar, 4-1/2" h, blue accent bands, diamond point design, imp and blue accented "Bayle's Cheeses St. Louis, MO," nicely fitted replacement wooden lid, int. surface chip on back **110.00**

Cream pitcher, 6-1/4" h, relief daffodil dec on front and back, heavy blue accents at floral designs and on handle **110.00**

Dish, 9" d, circular, scroll and latticino dec **325.00**

Figure, 4-1/2" l, 3-1/4" h, seated ram, molded stoneware, blue accents at eyes and end of protruding horns, attributed to mold maker George Hehr, Red Wing Stoneware Co., c1896, piece broken off one horn, museum inventory code number inked on bottom . . **825.00**

Humidor, cov

   5-1/4" h, matching stoneware lid, relief and blue accented design of woman milking cow, blue accents **165.00**

   6-1/2" h, matching lid, relief and blue accented hunting dog on front, blue accent band at rim, overall diamond relief pattern **250.00**

Mug

   4" h, bulbous, two blue accent bands, imp and blue accented "Granby CT 1896," blue accents at handle, Albany glaze int., short hairline extending from rim . **440.00**

   4-1/4" h, two blue accent bands, hand-tooled diamond design pattern top and bottom, imp "2" above star on front, Albany glazed int., c1870 . . . . **275.00**

   4-1/2" h, incised and blue accented drinking elves design, blue accent bands top and bottom with blue accents at handle **55.00**

   5-1/2" h, blue accents at handle, blue bands top and bottom, imp and blue accented "The Indian King/Haddonfield, NJ, 1850-1910," imp Indian profile in circle below name, base imp "C. W. & Bro.," surface chip, short rim hairline **360.00**

   5-1/2" h, blue and gray, Windy City, base imp "The Robinson Clay Products Co., Akron, Ohio" . . **55.00**

Mustard pot, 4" h, relief and blue accented grape vine design on front, blue accent band at rim and knob of orig lid, turned wooden spoon . . **220.00**

Pilsner glass

   7" h, imp and blue accented tooled lines top and bottom, center imp "Crystal Springs Lager" . . . **330.00**

   7" h, imp and blue accented tooled lines top and bottom, center imp "Haberle's Lager" **330.00**

Pitcher

   8" h, bark, relief design of bearded man on one side, man with key on opposite side, relief vines and roses on both sides, cobalt blue, brown accents, few short rim hairlines that occurred in the making **110.00**

   8-1/2" h, blue and white, salt glaze, stenciled Dutch Boy and Girl scene on front and back **275.00**

   9" h, applied and blue accented female figure designs on each side, relief and blue accented banner incised "1889," blue accent and tooled relief designs top and bottom, attributed to Whites **330.00**

   9" h, relief and blue accented tooled bands top and bottom, accented and incised design of man drinking, incised "Prosit," incised and blue accented keg hanging in a ribbon on one side, opposite side with ribbon and beer stein, early Whites Utica mark, couple short hairlines from rim **110.00**

   9" h, relief and imp tooled design, four lines of cobalt accents, Whites, clay separation at handle occurred in making, professional restoration to surface chip at rim **110.00**

Plate, shaped reticulated rim

   8-1/4" d, emb border **600.00**

   9-3/4" d, emb diaper border . **375.00**

Platter, 16-3/4" d, molded diaper-work panels, scalloped rim, 18th C . . **250.00**

Salt, helmet shape, latticino star and lion, bird and shell dec, claw feet, c18th C **880.00**

Sauce boat, 3-1/8" l, oval, relief-molded diaper, ozier, and scrolling panels, loop handle **425.00**

Stein, 8" h, orig pewter lid, relief and blue accented Longfellow on one side, framed German verse on opposite, blue accents on designs and handle, minor glaze flakes at base **110.00**

Syrup pitcher, 6-1/2" h, cylinder shape, relief and blue accented grape-vine design **90.00**

Tea caddy, 4-1/4" h, pear shape, latticino dec, knob finial, 18th C **375.00**

Syrup, celadon hue, classical decoration, pewter lid, 7" h, $150.

Teapot, cov, 7" h, ball shape, raised branch dec, bird finial on lid, 18th C **2,850.00**

Tray, 7-3/4" l, oval, latticino dec, scalloped rim **350.00**

Water pitcher, 12-1/2" h, bulbous, incised fleck marks on body, hinged pewter lid **425.00**

SALTS, OPEN

History: When salt was first mined, the supply was limited and expensive. The necessity for a receptacle in which to serve the salt resulted in the first open salt, a crude, hand-carved, wooden trencher.

As time passed, salt receptacles were refined in style and materials. In the 1500s, both master and individual salts existed. By the 1700s, firms such as Meissen, Waterford, and Wedgwood were making glass, china, and porcelain salts. Leading glass manufacturers in the 1800s included Libbey, Mount Washington, New England, Smith Bros., Vallerysthal, Wave Crest, and Webb. Many outstanding silversmiths in England, France, and Germany also produced this form.

Open salts were the only means of serving salt until the appearance of the shaker in the late 1800s. The ease of procuring salt from a shaker greatly reduced the use of and need for the open salts.

References: Mr. and Mrs. A. E. Coddington, *Old Salts*, privately printed, 1940 (available in reprint from *Salty Comments*, 401 Nottingham Road, Newark, DE 19711); William Heacock and Patricia Johnson, *5,000 Open Salts*, Richardson Printing Corporation, 1982, 1986 value update; Allan B. and Helen B. Smith have authored and published 10 books on open salts beginning with *One Thousand Individual Open Salts Illustrated* (1972) and ending with *1,334 Open Salts Illustrated: The Tenth Book* (1984). Daniel Snyder did the master salt sections in volumes 8 and 9. In 1987, Mimi Rudnick compiled a revised price list for the 10 Smith Books; George and Carolyn Tompkins, *Gorham*

Silver Salts, privately printed; Kenneth Wilson, *American Glass 1760-1930*, two vols., Hudson Hills Press and The Toledo Museum of Art, 1994.

Periodical: *Salty Comments*, 401 Nottingham Road, Newark, DE 19711.

Collectors' Clubs: Central Mid-West Open Salt Society, 10386 Fox River Drive, Walnut Springs, Newark, IL 60541; Mid-West Open Salt Society, 9123 S. Linden Road, Swartz Creek, MI 48473-9125; New England Society of Open Salt Collectors, P.O. Box 177, Sudbury, MA 01776-0177; Open Salt Collectors of the Atlantic Region, 71 Clearview Lane, Biglerville, PA 17307-9407; Open Salt Seekers of the West (Northern Chapter), 84 Margaret Drive, Walnut Creek, CA 94596; Open Salt Seekers of the West (Southern Chapter), 2525 East Vassar Drive, Visalia, CA 93292; Salt Collector's South East, 1405 N. Amanda Circle, Atlanta, GA 30329-3317.

Note: The numbers in parentheses refer to plate numbers in the Smiths' books.

Master salt, lacy type pattern, cobalt blue, **$325.**

Condiment sets with open salts

German silver, two castors, two salts, two salt spoons, Renaissance style with swan supports, c1900, marked ".800 fine" **800.00**
Limoges, double salt and mustard, sgd "J. M. Limoges" (388) **80.00**
Metal, coolie pulling rickshaw, salt, pepper, and mustard, blown glass liners, Oriental (461) **360.00**
Quimper, double salt and mustard, white, blue, and green floral dec, sgd "Quimper" (388) **120.00**

Early American glass

2-3/8" h, 2-3/4" d, pressed vaseline, emb rib, SP ftd holder **55.00**
2-5/8" l, colorless, variant, Neal MN3, chips **315.00**
3" h, cobalt blue, paneled with diamond foot. **125.00**
3" h, colorless, blown, expanded diamond bowl, applied petal foot **145.00**
3" l, colorless, lacy, eagle, Neal EE1, chips **200.00**
3-1/8" l, cobalt blue, Neal CN 1a, two feet replaced, small chips **200.00**

3-1/8" l, fiery opalescent, 3-1/8" l, Neal BS2, chips **275.00**
3-1/4" l, fiery opalescent, eagles, Neal EE3b, chips **500.00**
3-3/8" h, cobalt blue, facet cut, fan rim, sq foot, edges ground **125.00**
3-5/8" l, sapphire blue, Neal BT 2, very minor flakes **1,075.00**

Figurals

Basket, 3" h, 2-3/4" d, coral colored glass, SP basket frame, salt with cut polished facets. **55.00**
Boat, lacy, colorless, New England, Neal BT-9, slight rim roughness . **160.00**
Bucket, 2-1/2" d, 1-5/8" h, Bristol glass, turquoise, white, green, and brown enameled bird, butterfly and trees, SP rim and handle **75.00**
Sea horse, Belleek, brilliant turquoise, white base, supports shell salt, first black mark (458) **350.00**

Individual

Cambridge, Decagon pattern, amber (468) **40.00**
Cameo, Galle, green pedestal, enamel dec, sgd (205) **295.00**
Cut glass, 2" d, 1-1/2" h, cut ruby ovals, all-over dainty white enameled scrolls, clear ground, gold trim, scalloped top **60.00**
German silver, dolphin feet, 1890-1910 (353) **100.00**
Moser, cobalt blue, pedestal, gold bands, applied flowers sgd (380) **70.00**
Mount Washington, blue Johnny Jump-ups, cream ground, raised gold dots on rim **135.00**
Pattern glass
    Crystal Wedding **25.00**
    Fine Rib, flint **35.00**
    Hawaiian Lei, (477) **35.00**
    Pineapple and Fan **25.00**
    Three Face. **40.00**
Purple slag, 3" d, 1-1/4" h, emb shell pattern **50.00**
Royal Bayreuth, lobster claw (87) **80.00**
Russian, 1-1/4" h, 1-3/4" d, colorless glass liner, gold finished metal, red and white enamel scallop design, Russian hallmarks, c1940 . . . . **110.00**
Sterling silver, Georg Jensen, Denmark, porringer (238). **200.00**

Intaglios

Niagara Falls, scene (368) **75.00**
Tree, six intaglios, Venus and Cupid (423). **115.00**

Lusterware, 3" d, 2-1/4" h, **$65.**

Masters

Coin silver, made by Gorham for retailer Seth E. Brown, Boston, ftd, gold washed int., monogrammed, pair in fitted case, two coin silver spoons by Jones, Ball & Poor, pr, approx 4 troy oz **375.00**
Cranberry, 3" d, 1-3/4" h, emb ribs, applied crystal ruffed rim, SP holder with emb lions heads **160.00**
Cut glass, 2" d, 2" h, green cut to clear, SP holder. **115.00**
Green, light, dark green ruffled top, open pontil (449). **90.00**
Mocha, seaweed band, yellow ware ground, 2" h. **250.00**
Pattern glass
    Bakewell Pears. **30.00**
    Barberry, pedestal **40.00**
    Basketweave, sleigh (397) . . **100.00**
    Diamond Point, cov **75.00**
    Excelsior. **30.00**
    Portland, branches handle. . . **110.00**
    Snail, ruby stained **75.00**
    Sunflower, pedestal **40.00**
Pewter, pedestal, cobalt blue liner (349) **65.00**
Sterling silver, 1-3/4" h, Stieff Co., early 20th C, chased and emb allover floral pattern, applied floral rim, three scrolled shell feet, pr, 6 troy oz **260.00**
Vaseline, 3" d, 2-1/4" h, applied crystal trim around middle, SP stand . . **125.00**

SAMPLERS

History: Samplers served many purposes. For a young child, they were a practice exercise and permanent reminder of stitches and patterns. For a young woman, they were a means to demonstrate skills in a "gentle" art and a way to record family genealogy. For the mature woman, they were a useful occupation and method of creating gifts or remembrances, e.g., mourning pieces.

Schools for young ladies of the early 19th century prided themselves on the needlework skills they taught. The Westtown School in Chester County, Pennsylvania, and the Young Ladies Seminary in Bethlehem, Pennsylvania, were two institutions. These schools changed their teaching as styles changed. Berlin work was introduced by the mid-19th century.

Examples of samplers date back to the 1700s. The earliest ones were long and narrow, usually done only with the alphabet and numerals. Later examples were square. At the end of the 19th century, the shape tended to be rectangular.

The same motifs were used throughout the country. The name of the person who stitched the piece is a key factor in determining the region.

References: Ethel Stanwood Bolton and Eva Johnston Coe, *American Samplers*, Dover, 1987; Elizabeth Kurella, *The Complete Guide to Vintage Textiles*, Krause Publications, 1999; Glee Krueger, *Gallery of American Samplers*, Bonanza Books, 1984; Jack L. Lindsey, *Worldly Goods, The Arts of Early Pennsylvania, 1680-1758*, Pennsylvania Museum of Art, distributed by Antique Collectors' Club, 1999; Betty Ring, *American Needlework Treasures*, E. P. Dutton, 1987; Anne Sebba, *Samplers*, Thames and Hudson, 1979.

Museums: Cooper-Hewitt Museum, National Museum of Design, New York, NY; Smithsonian Institution, Washington, DC.

Note: Samplers are assumed to be on linen, unless otherwise indicated.

1770, petit point needlework, linen, shades of ivory, blue, green, tan, yellow, and black, alphabets, peacocks, cottages, running animals, Adam and Eve, apple tree, serpent, two men carrying bunch of grapes, well, Crucifixion, Lady Justice, chair, candlestick, armorial eagle or dragon, wreaths with crowns and initials "MSB," partial date 1768 near Adam and Eve, date 1770 in wreath, framed, light stains, several small holes, 20-7/8" w, 14-1/4" h **2,100.00**

1777, finely woven linen, silk thread in shades of ivory, gold, some green, and brown, alphabet, numbers, and vase, birds in fruit trees, vining strawberries, flowers, hearts, and crowns, "Mary Black Aged 10 Years 1777," old gilt frame with gold touch-up, linen aged considerably, 16" w, 21" h. **990.00**

1788, cross stitch, linen, faded silk threads of green, gold, pink, and brown, geometric and vining strawberry borders, two verses, one "An Address to Young Ladies," other "On Youth," flowers, crown, and stylized boats, by "Mary Harrop, Bury Novr 5th 1788," minor stains, professionally framed in

old carved frame with black paint, 19-1/4" w, 19" h **935.00**

1796, Elizabeth Stone, linen ground, pink, green, and cream silk threads, rows of alphabets, zigzag border, trees, figures, "Elizabeth Stone was born in Danvers Janury (sic) 30th worked this in the 10th year of her age 1796," 7-1/2" w, 11-1/2" h **3,400.00**

1806, Sarah Hodge, bands of alphabet letters separated by various stitches, two large flowering plants surrounding "Sarah Hodge/1806," top and bottom floral borders, 11-3/4" x 9-1/2", unframed **1,025.00**

1811, Elizabeth Hatton's work aged 8 years New York, geometric floral border, building, moths, and trees, verse titled "The Rose," "Child of summer, lovely rose, In thee what blushing beauty glows! But ere to-morrow's setting sun Thy beauty fades, thy form is gone. Yet though no grace thy buds retain, Thy pleasing odours still remain. Ye fair betimes the moral prize, tis lasting beauty to be wise," 15" x 13-1/4", minor loss **1,225.00**

1815, E. Butler, silk on finely woven homespun, vining strawberry border, stylized flowers, bids, and houses, sgd "E. Butler, 1915," green, tan, black, and cream, war and holes, framed . **300.00**

1818, alphabets and inspirational verse, worked in black thread, "Miranda J. Sweet born in Georgetown May 18, 1818," framed, 7-3/4" w, 17-1/4" h, all over toning **460.00**

1819, cross stitch, homespun, shades of blue, brown, green, ivory, yellow, and black, vining strawberry border, house surrounded by trees, bar, and out building, octagonal medallion has alphabets, verse, "Elisa Walker's Samplar (sic) made 1819," few red stitches appear to be added later, framed, 18-5/8" w, 16-1/2" h . . **2,475.00**

1821, Mary Ward, Adam and Eve in the Garden of Eden, adorned with potted plants, dogs, peacocks, various birds, flowers, hearts, and bird house designs, embroidered cartouche in upper center that reads "Mary Ward/Jan' 12 1821," surrounded by geometric border, shades of green, brown, ivory, and blue, 9" x 12-1/2", framed, minor damage **1,800.00**

1823, silk floss in 3-D, shades of ivory, blue, green, and pale yellow, wide strawberry border around panel with poem, basket of fruit and flowers, tabby cat, rooster, butterfly, arbor, bird in

cage, two trees, assorted animals, spotted dogs chasing deer, "Louise Bickleys Work Done in the 13th year of her Age Dect. 5th 1823," framed, 17-5/8" w, 21-3/4" h, dark brown floss has run and stained **1,100.00**

1825, alphabets above inspirational verse above Federal house flanked by trees and birds, surrounded by stylized flowering vine border, "Amelia Green, wrought in the 12 year of her age," framed, general scattered staining and fading, accompanied by written genealogy of Amelia **1,100.00**

1825, linen, satin stitched silk floss, shades of dark green, ivory, dark blues, pale pink, yellow, green, and blue, butterflies, baskets of flowers, roses, bird in tree, two white rabbits, verse and "Ann Murphey Anno Domini 1825," framed, minor stains, small stitched hole, 18-5/8" w, 18-7/8" h **2,100.00**

1825, panels of alphabets and numerals, band of geometric flowers above "Charlotte G. Richardson Aged 13 yrs Lancaster 1825," (Massachusetts), two baskets of flowers and hearts below stylized floral border, framed, 16-1/2" sq, imperfections **1,495.00**

1831, Magdalen F. Parry, mixed floral borders surrounding designs of potted plants, birds, flowers, wreath, and text which reads "Extract Religions sacred lamp alone, Unering pointe the way, Where happiness forever shines, with unpoluted ray, Magdalen F. Parry, 1831," 16" x 17", unframed. . . **2,450.00**

1839, "Catherine Dickerman, aged 12 years, under the instructions of Miss Beda Dickerman," three sets of alphabets, numeral band, flower, and tree, four different borders, framed, $650.

1831, "Margaret Swayer was born April 29th, 1817, Her Sampler, Margaret Swayer came here May 13th 1931, Pl, 23rd 1844," rows of alphabets, brown, red, blue, pale, green, and yellow, matted, framed, 17" w, 15-1/2" h, minor stains, vertical tear with some stitched repair **715.00**

1832, Susannah Funks, center floral arrangement in basket, flanked by other floral and bird designs, floral and ivy top and side borders, lower landscape of trees, stag, goose, other animals, "Susannah Funks Work done in the year of our lord 1832," 16-1/4" x 20-1/2" framed **2,450.00**

1836, English, cross-stitched, rows of practice motifs including floral bases, peacocks, animals, trees, and human figures, sgd in band at bottom "Caroline Brown," flowering strawberry vine border, framed, matted, 16" w, 17" h **980.00**

1836, finely stitched, shades of green, brown, pink, blue, yellow, and ivory, deer, birds, flowers, house, butterflies, and floral border, verse on friendship, "Mary Ann Nicholls Aged 12 Years 1836," age and date numerals are done in two shades of thread by different hand, holes, some repair, eglomise mat, maple frame with some bird's eye figure, 19-1/4" w, 22-1/4" h. **990.00**

1836, "Martha L. Bruner's sampler wrought at Sister France's School at the age of 10 years South Manor, July 30, 1836," alphabet and numbers in various stitches, building, tree, and birds beneath verse "Jesus Permit thy gracious name to stand as the first effort of an infant hand and while her fingers oer this canvas engage her tender heart to seek thy love with thy dear children let her share," 16" x 17-1/4", minor loss **1,995.00**

1837, Mary V. Throckmorton, aged 13 years and 8 months, April 7, verse "A Solemn march we take towards the silent grave a lodging all must quickly take and carnel pleasures leave," alphabet border, int. sq border surrounding center panel with verse circled in floral garland, American eagle with shield, birds, potted plants, fruit basket, house, and cypress trees, 17" x 17" **5,250.00**

1839, alphabets above memorial scene, manor house, urn, and trees, stylized geometric border, "Ann Augusta Plummer, Aged 10 Years East Cambridge Female School, 1839,"

framed, linen loss, old repair, scattered staining, toning, and foxing, 16-1/2" x 16-3/4" **635.00**

1845, hand embroidered, "Stitched by Catharine Roshong, May 1, 1845 at 8 years of age," accompanied by two signed documents for Catharine, a church membership and marriage certificate from 1856, $495. Photo courtesy of Joy Luke Auctions.

1840, wool thread worked in floral border with floral garland surrounding verse, bunch of grapes, cherries, various berries in basket, inscribed "Respectfully presented to John and Christine Kandle by their affectionate daughter Elizabeth Kandle done in the 13th year of her age AD 1840," 22" x 21-1/2", minor loss **36,300.00**

1873, Jane A. Padbury, October 3rd 1873, Aged 13 Years, large brick building flanked by flowering trees, surrounded by animal, floral, and foliate devices, geometric border, fading and toning, 12-1/4" x 12-1/4" **980.00**

Undated

Homespun, silk threads, shades of gold, blue, green, and brown, peacock with strawberry in its mouth, vining strawberry border, birch tree, butterfly, some stains, old reeded frame with gilt liner, 13-3/8" w, 10-1/2" h **990.00**

Linen, floral border, partial verse "See the bee as from flower to flower be?" over panel of flowers with bees, Louisa Beihmauer, 16-1/2" x 20-1/2", fading, light staining **495.00**

Linen, Jenne Bumand, aged eight years, simple border with alphabet over basket of fruit, crowns, verse panel, panel with flowers and pine trees, losses **350.00**

Linen, rows of alphabets, house, urn of flowers, heart flower, small dog, shades of green, blues, gold, and browns, "Betsey M. Burrows" and "AF," unframed, 15-1/2" x 16", some stains **450.00**

Wool, alphabet letters in pink, dark blue, red, and green wool, various stitching and letter styles, birds, potted flowers at base, initials "D.S.," c1850, 21" x 21-1/2", minor loss, folded over to fit into frame **350.00**

SANDWICH GLASS

History: In 1818, Deming Jarves was listed in the Boston Directory as a glass factor. That same year, he was appointed general manager of the newly formed New England Glass Company. In 1824, Jarves toured the glassmaking factories in Pittsburgh, left New England Glass Company, and founded a glass factory in Sandwich.

Originally called the Sandwich Manufacturing Company, it was incorporated in April 1826 as the Boston & Sandwich Glass Company. From 1826 to 1858, Jarves served as general manager. The Boston & Sandwich Glass Company produced a wide variety of wares in differing levels of quality. The factory used the free-blown, blown three mold, and pressed glass manufacturing techniques. Both clear and colored glass were used.

Competition in the American glass industry in the mid-1850s resulted in lower-quality products. Jarves left the Boston & Sandwich company in 1858, founded the Cape Cod Glass Company, and tried to duplicate the high quality of the earlier glass. Meanwhile, at the Boston & Sandwich Glass Company, emphasis was placed on mass production. The development of a lime glass (non-flint) led to lower costs for pressed glass. Some free-blown and blown-and-molded pieces, mostly in color, were made. Most of this Victorian-era glass was enameled, painted, or acid etched.

By the 1880s, the Boston & Sandwich Glass Company was operating at a loss. Labor difficulties finally resulted in the closing of the factory on January 1, 1888.

References: Raymond E. Barlow and Joan E. Kaiser, *Glass Industry in Sandwich*, Vol. 1 (1993), Vol. 2 (1989), Vol. 3 (1987), Vol. 4 (1983), and Vol. 5 (1999), distributed by Schiffer Publishing; ——, *A Guide to Sandwich Glass: Cut Ware, A General Assortment and Bottles*, Schiffer Publishing, 1999; ——, *Price Guide for the Glass Industry in Sandwich Vols. 1-4*, Schiffer Publishing, 1993; Ruth Webb Lee, *Sandwich Glass Handbook*, Charles E. Tuttle, 1966; ——, *Sandwich Glass*, Charles E. Tuttle, 1966; George S. and Helen McKearin, *American Glass*, Random House, 1979; Catherine M. V. Thuro, *Oil Lamps II*, Collector Books, 1994 value update; Kenneth Wilson, *American Glass 1760-1930*, 2 vols., Hudson Hills Press and The Toledo Museum of Art, 1994.

Museum: Sandwich Glass Museum, Sandwich, MA, http://www.sandwichglassmuseum.org.

Additional Listings: Blown Three Mold and Cup Plates.

Bowl, 7-1/2" d, pressed, lacy, Tulip and Acanthus pattern **45.00**

Butter dish, cov, colorless, flint, Gothic pattern **195.00**

Candlesticks, pr

7" h, canary, pressed, loop base, Barlow #3047, very minor chips, gauffering marks **375.00**

7-1/2" h, hexagonal base, purple-blue petal socket, translucent white **575.00**

10-1/4" h, canary, dolphin, flint, one flake under petal, minor base roughness **850.00**

Champagne, Sandwich Star . . . **850.00**

Compote, 10-1/2" w, 4-3/4" h, cranberry overlay, oval cuts, enameled birds and flowers on inner surface, c1890 . . . . **495.00**

Creamer and sugar, colorless, flint, Gothic pattern. **125.00**

Cup plate, lacy

Blue, ship. **125.00**

Violet Blue, heart **325.00**

Decanter, 6-3/4" h, cobalt blue, ribbed, tam o'shanter stopper. **195.00**

Toilet bottle, colorless, c1820, 5-1/4" h, $70.

Goblet, colorless, flint, Gothic pattern, 12-pc set **650.00**

Inkwell, 2-9/16", cylindrical-domed form, colorless, pink and white stripes, sheared mouth, applied pewter collar and cap, smooth base **2,300.00**

Lamp

8-1/2" h, Waffle pattern, opaque blue and white, camphene burner, whale oil **950.00**

11-3/4" h, colorless blown font, sq scrolled pressed base, lion head dec, paw feet, very minor chips and cracks **290.00**

12-1/2" h, pressed blue glass fonts, clambroth column and stepped base, minor base chips and cracks, pr. **1,840.00**

Paperweight, 3-1/2" w, 1-1/4" h, colorless and frosted, portraits of Queen Victoria and Prince Consort, 1851. **220.00**

Pitcher, 10" h

Amberina Verde, fluted top. . **325.00**

Electric Blue, enameled floral dec, fluted top, threaded handle **425.00**

Reverse Amberina, fluted top **400.00**

Plate

6" d, lacy, Shell pattern. **165.00**

7" d, Rayed Peacock Eye . . . **125.00**

Pomade, cov, figural, bear, imp retailer's name

3-3/4" h, clambroth, imp "F. B. Strouse, N.Y.," chips. **525.00**

4-1/2" h, blue, base imp "X. Bazin, Philada," chips **300.00**

Salt, 2" h, 3-1/8" d, blue, pressed, floral, Barlow 1460, minor chips, mold imperfections. **690.00**

Spooner, colorless, flint, Gothic pattern **85.00**

Sugar, cov, translucent blue, Lacy Gothic pattern **1,300.00**

Toddy, 5-3/8" d, brilliant dark amethyst, lacy, Roman Rosette, edge chips **330.00**

Undertray, Heart, lacy, flint. . . . **400.00**

Vase

9-1/4" h, amethyst, Three Printie Block pattern, trumpet shape, gauffered rim, triple ring turned connector, pressed colorless base, hairlines to base. **2,900.00**

10" h, dark amethyst, pressed, tulip, octagonal base, few chips to underside of base, pr. . . . **2,500.00**

11-1/4" h, trumpet, brilliant cobalt blue, ruffled rim, panel and arch bowl, hexagonal waterfall base, small flakes on base. **1,650.00**

Whiskey taster, cobalt blue, nine panels **185.00**

SARREGUEMINES CHINA

SARREGUE MINES

History: Sarreguemines ware is a faience porcelain, i.e., tin-glazed earthenware. The factory which made it was established in Lorraine, France, in 1770, under the supervision of Utzschneider and Fabry. The factory was regarded as one of the three most prominent manufacturers of French faience. Most of the wares found today were made in the 19th century.

Marks: Later wares are impressed "Sarreguemines" and "Germany" as a result of changes in international boundaries.

Basket, 9" h, quilted, green, heavy leopard skin crystallization. **250.00**

Centerpiece, 14-3/4" h, 14-3/4" d, bowl with pierced ringlets to sides, supported by center stem flanked by sea nymphs either side, mounted atop circular base on four scrolled feet, polychrome dec, imp marks, chips, restorations, c1875. . . . . **900.00**

Cup and saucer, Orange, majolica, crack to one cup, nicks, set of four **200.00**

Dinnerware service, white china, multicolored scenes, six luncheon plates, six bread and butter plates, six demitasse cups, six porringers, two platters, divided dish **150.00**

Face jug, majolica

Danish woman, bonnet, minor nick **880.00**

Suspicious Eyes, #3320 . . . . **550.00**

Upward Eyes, #3257, hairline **220.00**

Lamp, crystalline glaze, tan, impressed mark, 21-1/2" h, $190.

Garniture, Art Nouveau faience, 10-3/4" h pr of vases, shouldered trumpet form, shaped oval centerpiece bowl, each with wide gilt band of foliage within diamond borders centered by decorative medallion, verte ground **350.00**

Humidor
  Man with top hat, majolica .. **165.00**
  Pig, 6" h, #481, ear repair, no lid **220.00**

Plate, 7-1/2" d, dec with music and characters from French children's songs, 12-pc set **375.00**

Tankard, cov, 11" h, stoneware, continuous country scene of dancing and celebrating villagers, branch handle, pewter lid with porcelain medallion and painted polychrome coat of arms, dated 1869 .... **325.00**

Urn, 31-1/4" h, gilt metal mounted majolica, baluster form, cobalt blue glazed, mounted with the figure of a crowned lion holding sword, lion and mask handled sides, pierced foliate rim, raised on four scrolling foliate cast feet, imp "Majolica Sarreguemines," second half 19th C **1,800.00**

SARSAPARILLA BOTTLES

History: Sarsaparilla refers to the fragrant roots of a number of tropical American, spiny, woody vines of the lily family. An extract was obtained from these dried roots and used for medicinal purposes. The first containers, which date from the 1840s, were stoneware; glass bottles were used later.

Carbonated water often was added to sarsaparilla to make a soft drink or to make consuming it more pleasurable. For this reason, sarsaparilla and soda became synonymous even though they originally were two different concoctions.

References: Ralph and Terry Kovel, *Kovels' Bottles Price List*, 11th ed., Three Rivers Press 1998; Carlo and Dot Sellari, *Standard Old Bottle Price Guide*, Collector Books, 1989.

Periodical: *Antique Bottle and Glass Collector*, P.O. Box 187, East Greenville, PA 18041.

Additional Listings: See *Warman's Americana & Collectibles* for a list of soda bottles.

Bristols Extract of Sarsaparilla, aqua, open pontil, 5-1/2" h **70.00**
Bull's Extract of Sarsaparilla, beveled corners, 7" l **400.00**
Carl's Sarsaparilla & Celery Compound, aqua, 7-3/8" h **70.00**
Compound Extract of Sarsaparilla, amber, gallon **140.00**

Dr. Ira Belding's, Honduras Sarsaparilla, colorless, 10-1/2" h . **30.00**
Dr. Townsend's Sarsaparilla, olive green, pontil **85.00**
Foley's Sarsaparilla, light amber **40.00**
Genuine Sands' Sarsaparilla, aquamarine, rect, beveled corners, applied double collared mouth, pontil scar....................... **215.00**
Guysott's Yellow Dock & Sarsaparilla **40.00**
Lancaster Glassworks, barrel, golden amber..................... **125.00**
Old Dr. J. Townsend's Sarsaparilla, light bluish-green, sq, beveled corners, applied sloping collared mouth, iron pontil, 9-1/2" h.............. **250.00**
Radway's Sarsaparilla Resolvent **25.00**
Skoda's Sarsaparilla, amber ... **25.00**
Walker's, aqua.............. **130.00**
Warren Allen's Sarsaparilla Beer, tan, pottery **125.00**

SATIN GLASS

History: Satin glass, produced in the late 19th century, is an opaque art glass with a velvety matte (satin) finish achieved through treatment with hydrofluoric acid. A large majority of the pieces were cased or had a white lining.

While working at the Phoenix Glass Company, Beaver, Pennsylvania, Joseph Webb perfected mother-of-pearl (MOP) satin glass in 1885. Similar to plain satin glass in respect to casing, MOP satin glass has a distinctive surface finish and an integral or indented design, the most well known being diamond quilted (DQ).

The most common colors are yellow, rose, or blue. Rainbow coloring is considered choice.

Additional Listings: Cruets, Fairy Lamps, Miniature Lamps, and Rose Bowls.

Reproduction Alert: Satin glass, in both the plain and mother-of-pearl varieties, has been widely reproduced.

Left: jar, covered, diamond quilted, rose exterior, white interior, 6" h; right: rose bowl, rose exterior, white interior, 4-1/2" h, each $95.

Bowl, 6-1/2" d, 4-3/4" h, shaded blue, MOP, DQ, frosted thorny base feet extend to open crimped top ... **395.00**
Bride's basket, 15-1/2" h, deep rose, enamel swan and floral dec, heavy bronze holder with birds perched at top **450.00**
Compote, 8" h, pink ruffled bowl, gilt edge, enameled floral dec, three ftd SP floral dec base **250.00**
Creamer, 3-1/4" h, 3-1/4" d, globular, blue MOP, ruffled top, white lining, applied frosted handle **325.00**
Cup and saucer, Raindrop MOP, pink to white, 3" h cup, 5" d saucer.. **385.00**
Epergne, 13-3/4" h, 10" d, pink and white, hobnail bowl, resilvered base and lily vase holder **395.00**
Finger bowl, 4-1/4" d, 2-3/4" h, pink, MOP, IVT, ruffled top **165.00**
Lamp, 17-1/8" h, 9" d, deep pink shading to lighter MOP, DG, ruffled, silverplated base emb designs of cupids, etc., white int........ **895.00**

Lamp shade, Tartan pattern, octagonal, pinched base, rippled edge, 8-1/2" d, 4" d fitter ring, $685.

Mustard pot, 2-1/2" h, bright yellow, gold prunus dec, SP top, Webb **450.00**
Salt shaker, 3-1/4" h, rose shaded to white, MOP, DQ, tapered barrel, orig two-pc lid................. **550.00**
Scent bottle, 7-1/2" h, 4-1/2" d, Peacock Eye, MOP, creamy yellow, hallmarked sterling crown like cap (with dent), collar with sterling chain . **650.00**
Sugar shaker, 6-1/4" h, blue, Raindrop, MOP, SP top **425.00**
Tumbler, 3-1/2" h, Rainbow, DQ, enameled floral dec, pr....... **375.00**
Vase
  4-1/4" h, opaque white, stork standing in midst of marsh clutching eel in upraised beak, Joseph Locke, several minor flakes off base edge.......... **745.00**

4-1/2" d, 7" h, Federzeichnung MOP, chocolate, gold tracery, pearlescent sheen, folded quadric-form top, gold enamel signature on pontil "Pat 9159" **2,500.00**

6-1/4" h, pistachio yellow to lime cream, cased int., ground pontil **85.00**

Vase holder, Griffin, for a Morgan Vase, slight damage. **250.00**

SATSUMA

History: Satsuma, named for a war lord who brought skilled Korean potters to Japan in the early 1600s, is a hand-crafted Japanese faience (tin-glazed) pottery. It is finely crackled, has a cream, yellow-cream, or gray-cream color, and is decorated with raised enamels in floral, geometric, and figural motifs.

Figural satsuma was made specifically for export in the 19th century. Later satsuma, referred to as satsuma-style ware, is a Japanese porcelain also hand decorated in raised enamels. From 1912 to the present, satsuma-style ware has been mass produced. Much of the ware on today's market is of this later period.

Reference: Nancy N. Schiffer, *Imari, Satsuma, and Other Japanese Export Ceramics*, Schiffer Publishing, 1997.

Periodical: *Orientalia Journal*, P.O. Box 94, Flushing, NY 11363-0094, http://members.aol.com/Orientalia/index.html.

Charger, four samurai warriors by water-fall, floral decoration on reverse, nine character mark, 18" d, $440. Photo courtesy of Sanford Alderfer Auction Co.

Box, cov, 10" d, pottery, form of stylized chrysanthemum, various figures and brocade pattern, four-character signature in red Kinkozan sei, Japan,

Meiji period, 1868-1911, one flake to enamel. **3,750.00**
Cache pot, 6-1/2" h, figural and landscape scene. **120.00**
Censor

3-1/2" h, ovoid, three cabriole legs, two shaped handles rising from shoulder, lid with large shishi seated on top, continual river landscape scene, patterned lappet border above, key fret border below, base sealed "Yabu Meizan," minor loss to one ear on shishi **2,990.00**

10-1/4" h, tapering rect form, lobed base, two squared handles, pierced domed lid, all-over dec or Arhats, Meiji period **635.00**
Cup and saucer, bird and floral motif, cobalt blue border, Kinkozan, Japanese **115.00**
Dish, 14" d, male and female figures gathered around a goddess, all in landscape, patterned border, Meiji period **115.00**
Jar, cov, 8-1/2" h, cylindrical, paneled sides, bird and floral motif, phoenix on patterned border, sgd "Made in Kyoto, Japan," 19th C, discoloration . **3,200.00**
Koro, pierced lid

2-3/4" h, ovoid, three short feet, continual scene of festival with men, women, and children playing games, eating, playing music, brocade shoulder border, 19th C **635.00**

3" h, hexagonal, six bracket feet, each side with flowers blooming behind garden fences, domed lid, sgd with Shimazu mon . . . **2,185.00**
Miniature cup, 2" d, interior painted with Bishamon and Hoi tei, ext. with dancing children, mille fleur borders, sgd with paulownia crest in gold, Japan, Meiji period, 1868-1911. **980.00**
Seal paste box, 5" d, cobalt blue, gilt trim, reserve of children flying kites, sgd "Kozan," Japan, Meiji period, 1868-1911, minor int. chip. **320.00**
Tea bowl, 4-3/4" d, dec with butterflies, powdered gold ground, sgd "Kinkozan," Japan, Meiji period, 1868-1911 . . . . **350.00**
Tea cup and saucer, 1-3/4" h cup, 4-3/4" d saucer, colorful groups of flowerheads with scrolling gilt vines, minor gilt wear, sgd "Yabu Meizan" **900.00**
Tea set, 6-1/2" h teapot, creamer, sugar, six cups and saucers, six 7-1/4" d

plates, paneled designs of courtesans in courtyard settings, c1900. . . . **290.00**
Tray, 6-1/2" x 9-3/8", rect, scalloped corners, garden setting with women playing game, fan border, sgd "Ryozan," 19th C **1,400.00**
Urn, 37-1/2" h, dragon handles, geishas in landscape. **295.00**

Vases, pair, mountain, river, foliage, and peasant scene, original velvet-lined case, Meiji period (1867-1912), 4-3/4" h, $700.

Vase

3-1/2" h, rounded square form, insects on gold-splashed ground, sgd "Yasudo," Japan, Meiji period, 1868-1911, repaired mouth chip **460.00**

5" h, bottle form, figures in an interior, sgd "Gyokuzan," early 20th C **125.00**

5-3/4" h, form of green shishi carrying vase on it's back, Japan, Meiji period, 1868-1911 . . . **320.00**

6-1/4" h, mille fleur borders enclosing view of Fuji and pavilions in landscape, sgd "Unzan" in gold, Japan, Meiji period, 1868-1911 . . . . **2,645.00**

7" h, form of shishi carrying vase on it's back, "100 Rakan" pattern, sgd on underside, Japan, Meiji period, 1868-1911 . . . . **350.00**

7-1/2" h, cobalt blue, gilt trim, reserves of courtiers, sgd "Kozan," Japan, late 19th/early 20th C **300.00**

9-1/2" h, tied back form, ornate brocade patterns, floral reserve, Japan, Meiji period, 1868-1911, chip **635.00**

16" h, reserves of people in garden vignettes, cobalt blue ground, gilt trim, sgd "Kinkozan," Japan, Meiji period, 1868-1911, drilled for lamp **1,495.00**

25" h, globular, tall cannon-mouthed neck flanked by two gate posts with entwined dragons, one side with sun goddess and various Buddhist divinities, other side with woman in garden scene, neck dec with Tokugawa mons and various brocade patterns, sgd "Kinkozan" in brown-colored seal characters within sq on base, Japan, Meiji period, 1868-1911, minor rubbing to gilt, small repair to dragon on one side **6,900.00**

SCALES

History: Prior to 1900, the simple balance scale was commonly used for measuring weights. Since then, scales have become more sophisticated in design and more accurate. There are a wide variety of styles and types, including beam, platform, postal, and pharmaceutical.

Reference: Bill and Jan Berning, *Scales: A Collector's Guide,* Schiffer Publishing, 1999.

Collectors' Club: International Society of Antique Scale Collectors, 300 W. Adams St., Suite 821, Chicago, IL 60606.

4-1/2" h, postal, Nolan Scale Co., Boston, nickel plated, sq pan, dial graduated 0-7, 1889 patent date, desk clamp..................... **175.00**

4-1/2" h, 6-3/4" l, postal, S. Mordan & Co., England, 19th C, plates with blue and white Wedgwood jasper neoclassical roundels in ropetwist surround, rect base with three weights **350.00**

5-1/2" w, pocket balance, steel, silvered pans, silver mounted shagreen case, engraved plaque, velvet-lined interior, two fitted circular weights and various others **575.00**

6" x 14" x 10", store, Hanson Weightmaster, cast iron, gold case with ground, black lettering and indicator **45.00**

7-3/4" h, postal, candlestick-style, gilt metal, British, 1840s, for American market, circular pan with scrolled foliate borders, red enameled stem, trellis work and C-scrolls, rate table with eagle dec, circular foot modeled in high relief with locomotive, steam clipper and farm

implements interspersed with cornucopia **275.00**

9" l, Allender's Gold Scale, I. Wilson, New London, CT, cast brass rocker balance, slots and platforms for $1, 2-1/2, 5, 10, and 20, additional weight and instructions in shaped paper box, mid-19th C **490.00**

11" l, Chonodrometer (grain scale), brass, Fairbanks, arm graduated for "lbs per bush," "lb & oz," and "% of lb," sliding weight, bucket, and suspension ring **350.00**

14" l, balance, cast iron, orig red paint with black and yellow trim, nickel plated brass pans, marked "Henry Troemner, Phila. No. 5B, Baker's" **120.00**

15-1/4" h, 17-1/2" w, merchant's type, "Computing Scale Co., Dayton, Ohio" **225.00**

16-1/2" l, analytical beam balance, Whitall, Tatum & Co., glazed mahogany case **175.00**

18" w, analytical beam balance, lacquered brass fittings, glazed mahogany case, set of weights .**175.00**

19-1/2" l, 15-3/4" h, apothecary, walnut, fitted ivory dec **250.00**

23" l, counter top, Toledo Scale Co., c1920, Style 621D, slight weight for 1-51 lbs, glazed display and pouring pan, repainted **175.00**

26" h, balance, J. L. Brown & Co., 83 Fulton St., New York, circular pans, baluster turned cast iron stand .**690.00**

63" h, platform, Peerless Junior, Peerless Weighing Machine Co., porcelainized steel, tiled platform, gold lettering.....................**350.00**

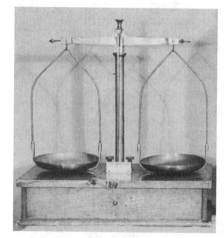

Balance, H. Kohlbusch, NY, brass column, brackets and pans, wood base with drawer, old Kohlbusch label in drawer, 20-1/2" x 20-1/4" x 10-1/2", **$165.** *Photo courtesy of Garth's Auctions, Inc.*

SCHLEGELMILCH PORCELAINS

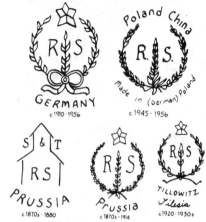

History: Erdmann Schlegelmilch founded his porcelain factory in Suhl in the Thuringia region in 1861. Reinhold, his brother, established a porcelain factory at Tillowitz in Upper Silesia in 1869. In the 1860s, Prussia controlled Thuringia and Upper Silesia, both rich in the natural ingredients needed for porcelain.

By the late 19th century, an active export business was conducted with the United States and Canada due to a large supply of porcelain at reasonable costs achieved through industrialization and cheap labor.

The Suhl factory ceased production in 1920, unable to recover from the effects of World War I. The Tillowitz plant, located in an area of changing international boundaries, finally came under Polish socialist government control in 1956.

Marks: Both brothers marked their pieces with the "RSP" mark, a designation honoring Rudolph Schlegelmilch, their father. More than 30 mark variations have been discovered.

References: Susan and Al Bagdade, *Warman's English & Continental Pottery & Porcelain,* 3rd ed., Krause Publications, 1998; R. H. Capers, *Capers' Notes on the Marks of Prussia,* Alphabet Printing (667 E. 6th St., El Paso, IL 61738), 1996; Mary Frank Gaston, *Collector's Encyclopedia of R. S. Prussia and Other R. S. and E. S. Porcelain,* 1st Series (1982, 1993 value update), 2nd Series (1986, 1994 value update), 3rd Series (1994), 4th Series (1997, 2001 value update), Collector Books; —, *R. S. Prussia Popular Lines,* Collector Books, 1999; Leland and Carol Marple, *R. S. Prussia: The Art Nouveau Years,* Schiffer, 1998; —, *R. S. Prussia: The Early Years,* Schiffer Publishing, 1997; —, *R. S. Prussia: The Wreath and Star,* Schiffer Publishing, 2000.

Collectors' Club: International Association of R. S. Prussia Collectors Inc., 212 Wooded Falls Road, Louisville, KY 40243.

Reproduction Alert: Many "fake" Schlegelmilch pieces are appearing on the market. These reproductions have new decal marks, transfers, or recently hand-painted animals on old, authentic R. S. Prussia pieces.

Reproduction Alert: Dorothy Hammond in her 1979 book, *Confusing Collectibles*, illustrates an R. S. Prussia decal which was available from a china-decorating supply company for $14 a sheet. This was the first of several fake R. S. Prussia reproduction marks that have caused confusion among collectors. Acquaint yourself with some of the subtle distinctions between fake and authentic marks as described in the following.

The period mark consists of a wreath that is open at the top. A five-pointed star sits in the opening. An "R" and an "S" flank a wreath twig in the center. The word "Prussia" is located beneath. In the period mark, the leg of the letter "P" extends down past the letter "r." In the reproduction mark, it does not. In the period mark, the letter "I" is dotted. It is dotted in some fake marks, but not in others.

The "R" and the "S" in the period mark are in a serif face and uniform in width. One fake mark uses a lettering style that utilizes a thin/thick letter body. The period mark has a period after the word "Prussia." Some fake marks fail to include it. Several fake marks do not include the word "Prussia" at all.

The period mark has a fine center line within each leaf of the wreath. Several fake marks do not.

Vases, blue ground, multicolored floral decoration, gold trim, 11-1/4" h, price for pair, **$850.**

R.S. Germany

Biscuit jar, cov, 6" h, loop handles, roses dec, satin finish, gold knob. **95.00**
Bonbon dish, 7-3/4" l, 4-1/2" w, pink carnations, gold dec, silver-gray ground, looped inside handle ... **40.00**
Bread plate, iris variant edge mold, blue and white, gold outlined petals and rim, multicolored center flowers, steeple mark............... **115.00**
Bride's bowl, floral center, ornate ftd stand....................**95.00**
Cake plate, deep yellow, two parrots on hanging leaf vine, open handles, green mark....................**235.00**

Celery tray, 11" l, 5-3/4" w, lily dec, gold rim, open handles, blue label .. **120.00**
Chocolate pot, white rose florals, blue mark..................... **95.00**
Cup and saucer, plain mold, swan, blue water, mountain and brown castle background, RM **225.00**
Demitasse cup and saucer, 3" h, pink roses, gold stenciled dec, satin finish, blue mark.................... **90.00**
Dessert plate, 6-1/2" d, yellow and cream roses, green and rich brown shaded ground, six-pc set **135.00**
Ewer, 7" h, four portrait panels of women in 19th C gowns, brown ground, heavy gilding, minor imperfections **475.00**
Hatpin holder, floral dec....... **95.00**
Napkin ring, green, pink roses, white snowballs.................. **55.00**
Nut bowl, 5-1/4" d, 2-3/4" h, cream, yellow, roses, green scalloped edge **65.00**
Pitcher, 5-3/4" h, light blue, chrysanthemums, pink roses, gold trim **85.00**
Plate, 9-3/4" d, white flowers, gold leaves, gilded edge, green ground, marked "RS Germany" in dark green, script sgd "Reinhold Schlegelmilch/ Tillowitz/Germany" in red....... **45.00**
Powder box, cov, green poppies, green mark **50.00**
Punch bowl, 17-1/4" d, 8" h, mahogany shading to pink, polychrome enameled flowers with gilt, imp fleur-de-lis mark with "J. S. Germany" **275.00**
Sauce dish, underplate, green, yellow roses, blue mark **45.00**
Tea tile, peach and tan, greenish white snowballs, RM over faint blue mark **165.00**
Vase, 6" h, crystalline glaze, orange and white.................. **45.00**

R. S. Poland

Berry bowl, 4-1/2" sq, white and pale orange floral design, green leaves, small orange-gold border flowers, marked **45.00**
Creamer, soft green, chain of violets, applied fleur-de-lis feet, RM **110.00**
Dresser set, glossy, pink roses, pr 6-1/4" h candlesticks, 5" h hatpin holder, 13" x 9" tray **425.00**
Flower holder, pheasants, brass frog insert **675.00**
Vase
  8-1/2" h, 4-3/4" d, large white and tan roses, shaded brown and green ground **195.00**

10" h, cottage scene, woman with sheep in foreground, ornate handles, gold trim........ **650.00**
12" h, 6-1/4" d, white poppies, cream shaded to brown ground, pr
.... **750.00**

Compote, low standard, white ground, pink and green floral decoration, gold decoration, scalloped edge, 7" d, 4-1/2" h, **$275.**

R. S. Prussia
Bowl
  10" d, Hidden Images, portrait of woman, hair in bun, additional molded florals, pastel green ground................ **240.00**
  10-1/2" d, carnation mold, white, peach shading, Tiffany carnations, pink roses dec, satin finish, RM
.... **595.00**
  10-1/2" d, Iris mold, pink poppies and daisies, green ground, RM
.... **300.00**
Butter dish, cov, porcelain insert, cream and gold shading, pink roses, raised enamel, RM.......... **715.00**
Cake set, 9-1/2" d plate, six 7" d plates, carnation mold, pale greens, Tiffany carnations, pink and white rose dec, RM **995.00**
Celery tray
  9" l, carnation mold, white, peach shading, Tiffany carnations, pink roses dec, RM.......... **375.00**
  9" l, gold and lavender, roses, bar mark **350.00**
Chocolate pot, 9-1/2" h, Melon Boy scene, jeweled accents, gilt loss
.... **2,650.00**
Creamer, floral **225.00**
Demitasse cup and saucer, dainty flowers **100.00**
Ferner, 7" d, mold 876, florals on purple and green ground, unsgd **165.00**

Hair receiver, green lilies of the valley, white ground, RM **95.00**
Milk pitcher, 5" h, Morning Glory mold, pink carnations dec.......... **200.00**
Mustard pot, white, light blue and multicolored tiny roses........ **150.00**
Plate, 11" d, Carnation mold, white, peach shading, Tiffany carnations, satin finish, slight wear to gilt........ **250.00**
Portrait vase, 9" h, double handles, mottled pink and blue ground, gilt flowers, portrait medallion of young lady with falling snow, red mark, wear **2,235.00**
Relish dish, 9" d, blown-out mold, lavender and pink gloss finish, pink and white roses, two handles, RM ... **95.00**
Spoon holder, 14" l, pink and white roses **200.00**
Syrup, Melon boy with dog, underplate **990.00**
Tankard, 11" h, Carnation mold, white, all-over pink poppies, Tiffany carnations, satin finish, RM ...**1,100.00**
Toothpick holder, green shadows, pink and white roses, jeweled, six feet, RM **250.00**
Urn, cov, Melon boy with dog dec, jeweled accents, regilt handles, gilt loss **2,250.00**
Vase, 4-3/8" h, 2-5/8" d, Pheasant scene, handle, Mold 918...... **500.00**

R. S. Suhl, dish, light green ext., green ground, white, pink, and yellow classical maidens, 8" l, 4-5/8" w, $490.

R. S. Suhl

Coffee set, 9" h, coffeepot, creamer, sugar, six cups and saucers, figural scenes dec, some marked "Angelica Kauffmann" **1,750.00**
Pin tray, 4-1/2" d, round, Nightwatch **375.00**
Plate
  6-3/4" d, cherubs dec....... **90.00**
  8-1/2" d, windmill scene and water, green mark **125.00**
Powder dish, cov, Nightwatch, green shading **425.00**
Vase, 8" h, four pheasants, green mark **275.00**

Relish dish, flower garland decoration, marked "R. S. Tillowitz," oval, 9-1/2" l, $45.

R. S. Tillowitz

Bowl, 7-3/4" d, slanted sides, open handles, four leaf-shaped feet, matte finish, pale green ground, roses and violets, gold flowered rim, marked **125.00**
Creamer and sugar, soft yellow and salmon roses **65.00**
Plate, 6-1/2" d, mixed floral spray, gold beading, emb rim, brown wing mark **120.00**
Relish tray, 8" l, oval, hp, shaded green, white roses, green leaves, center handle, blue mark............ **45.00**
Tea set, stacking teapot, creamer, and sugar, yellow, rust, and blue flowers, gold trim, ivory ground, marked "Royal Silesia," green mark in wreath ... **95.00**
Vase, 10" h, pheasants, brown and yellow, two curved handles **125.00**

SCHNEIDER GLASS

Schneider   *Schneider*

History: Brothers Ernest and Charles Schneider founded a glassworks at Epiney-sur-Seine, France, in 1913. Charles, the artistic designer, previously had worked for Daum and Gallé. Robert, son of Charles, assumed art direction in 1948. Schneider moved to Loris in 1962.

Although Schneider made tablewares, stained glass, and lighting fixtures, its best-known product is art glass which exhibits simplicity of design and often has bubbles and streaking in larger pieces. Other styles include cameo-cut and hydrofluoric-acid-etched designs.

Marks: Schneider glass was signed with a variety of script and block signatures, "Le Verre Francais," or "Charder."

Bowl, 4-1/2" d, 2-1/2" h, mottled, slightly cupped.................... **195.00**
Ewer, 10-3/4" h, elongated spout, mottled purples, pink, yellow, and orange splashes, applied purple handle, bulbed disk foot, acid stamp "France" on base, c1925 ...... **450.00**

Dish, orange shading to dark blue, amethyst with white ribbing base, etched signature, 13-1/2" d, 5-1/2" h, $295.

Finger bowl and underplate, 4-1/2" d bowl, 7-1/4" d underplate, mottled red, burnt umber and clear, stamped mark **350.00**
Tazza, 7-5/8" h, shallow white bowl rising to mottled amethyst and blue inverted rim, amethyst double-bulbed stem, disk foot, sgd "Schneider," c1920 .... **865.00**
Vase

  7" h, bulbous, cylindrical neck, yellow and pink mottled ground, brown casing, two applied crimped orange handles, engraved "Schneider" and logo, slightly ground top **450.00**
  13-3/4" h, baluster, smoky topaz, dec at shoulder with acid etched band of overlaid leaves, two applied floral cluster prunts, sgd "Schneider" near base, c1925 .... **980.00**
  14" h, tapering cylindrical, baluster neck, orange overlay, five clusters of pendant grapes, geometric pattern cut foot over yellow mottled ground, inset cane at base **650.00**

SCHOENHUT TOYS

History: Albert Schoenhut, son of a toy maker, was born in Germany in 1849. In 1866, he ventured to America where he worked as a toy-piano repairman for Wanamaker's in Philadelphia, Pennsylvania. Finding the glass sounding bars inadequate, he perfected a toy piano with metal sounding bars. His piano was an instant success, and the A. Schoenhut Company had its beginning.

From that point on, toys seemed to flow out of the factory. Each of his six sons entered the business, and it prospered until 1934, when misfortune forced the company into bankruptcy. In 1935, Otto and George Schoenhut contracted to produce the Pinn Family Dolls.

The Schoenhut Manufacturing Company was formed by two other Schoenhuts. Both companies operated under a partnership agreement that eventually led to O. Schoenhut, Inc., which continues today.

Some dates of interest:

1872	toy piano invented
1903	Humpty Dumpty Circus patented
1911-1924	wooden doll production
1928-1934	composition dolls made.

References: E. Ackerman and F. Keller, *Under the Big Top with Schoenhut's Humpty Dumpty Circus*, published by author (P.O. Box 217, Culver City, CA 90230), 1997; Carol Corson, *Schoenhut Dolls*, Hobby House Press, 1993; Elizabeth Stephan (ed.,) *O'Brien's Collecting Toys*, 9th ed., Krause Publications, 1999.

Collectors' Clubs: Schoenhut Collectors Club, 1003 W. Huron St., Ann Arbor, MI 48103; Schoenhut Toy Collectors, 1916 Cleveland St., Evanston, IL 60202.

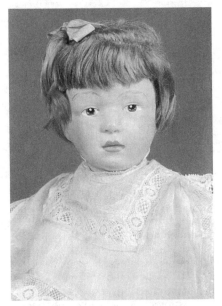

Doll, girl, #16/301, wood head, painted facial features, original wig, 16" h, $1,900. Photo courtesy of McMasters.

Animal, wood, jointed

Cow, 5-1/4" h, 8-1/2" l, painted eyes, leather ears and horns, jointed at neck and hips, twine tail, small metal bell on old red ribbon, orig wood 2-1/2" x 2-1/4" x 3-1/4" wood manger **315.00**

Dromedary camel, 8-3/4" l, painted eyes, leather ears, woven cotton tail, minor chipping to orig paint, some wear. **300.00**

Goat, 8-1/4" l, black and white, painted eyes, leather horns and tail, leatherette ears, paint very good, minor chipping, ears damaged. **175.00**

Gorilla, 8" h, two-part head, composition-type face, painted

features, leather ears, long arms with pink palms, some wear to paint, unmarked **3,400.00**

Hyena, 4" h, 6-3/4" l, glass eyes, leather ears, jointed at neck, shoulders, and hips, cord tail, orig paint flaking somewhat, left ear missing, unmarked. **3,550.00**

Monkey, 8" h, painted features, molded ears, cord tail, dressed in orig red felt costume and hat with gold trim, unmarked. **375.00**

Character figure

Felix the Cat, 3-3/4" h, c1920, worn ears **175.00**

Felix the Cat, 8-1/2" h, label on foot, stringing loose, paint wear. **215.00**

Maggie and Jiggs, 7" h Jiggs, 9" h Maggie, c1920, orig lunch bucket and rolling pin, minor flaking **750.00**

Circus box, set No. 20/36, wooden sides, illus circus, animals, and people performing tricks on top, marked "Schoenhut's Humpty-Dumpty Circus, Made in the U.S.A., The Toy Wonder, 10,001 New Tricks, Unbreakable," hinges slightly loose **350.00**

Circus character, 8" h, jointed wood

Hobo, jointed shoulders and hips, orig red and white shirt, brown felt coat and hat, brown tweed pants, leatherette belt **200.00**

Negro Dude, painted features, leather ears, two-part head with face molded as separate piece from head, orig red and white print shirt, white vest, black felt jacket, plaid pants, black felt hat, some crazing to face, unmarked. **425.00**

Ringmaster and Lady Circus Rider, painted features, molded and painted hair, jointed, orig paint, ringmaster wearing orig white shirt and pants, yellow felt vest, red felt jacket, white top hat; lady circus rider with replaced gold body suit, orig skirt, some paint flaking, price for pair **165.00**

Circus set, reduced size, 4-1/2" h horse, 5-1/2" h giraffe, 4-1/2" h donkey, 4-1/2" h elephant, 6-1/2" h ringmaster, 6-1/2" h clown, 8-1/2" h ladders, 2-1/2" h barrel, 4-1/2" h chair, all with painted eyes, orig painted body, general wear and flaking. **350.00**

Circus tent, 18" x 24" wood base, blue painted sides, bottom painted to resemble sand with red wood ring, wood support in back holds up canvas tent with red curtained door, wire

supports have trapeze and metal rings over ring on base, triangular flags of all nations on front with "Humpty-Dumpty Circus," marked "Humpty-Dumpty Circus, Reg. U. S. Pat. Off" on label on front and both sides of base, tent aged and discolored, normal wear . . . **500.00**

Doll, boy, pouty expression, wood, spring jointed body, marked "75," $495.

Doll

14" h, boy, wooden socket head, blue intaglio eyes, worn brows, closed pouty mouth, carved and painted hair, spring-jointed body, jointed at shoulders, elbows, wrists, hips, knees, and ankles, well re-dressed, marked "2" on back of head, "Schoenhut Doll, Pat. Jan 17, '11 USA & Foreign Countries" **675.00**

14" h, girl, #14/105, wooden socket head, blue intaglio eyes, feathered brows, closed mouth, carved and painted hair with blue band, spring-jointed wooden body jointed at shoulders, elbows, wrists, hips, knees and ankles. Dressed in antique white dress, slip, knit union suit, cotton socks, antique white shoes, marked "Schoenhut Doll/Pat. Jan. 17. '11, U.S.A./&

Foreign Countries," repaint on face below eyes, repaint on blue ribbon, general wear on hair, body shows general wear, most of paint flaked off right arm and left lower arm, right hand partially repainted, wear on legs and edges of feet . **625.00**

16" h, girl, #16/300. wooden socket head, brown intaglio eyes, closed pouty mouth, replaced human hair wig, spring jointed wooden body jointed at shoulders, elbows, wrists, hips, knees and ankles, redressed in old cotton red dress, knit union suit, replaced socks and shoes, marked "Schoenhut Doll/Pat. Jan 17, '11 U.S.A./& Foreign Countries," facial coloring rather faded, brows missing, craze lines on forehead, nose, upper lip and chin **300.00**

21" h, girl, #21/308, wooden socket head, brown intaglio eyes, feathered brows, closed pouty mouth, replaced mohair wig, spring-jointed wooden body with joints at shoulders, elbows, wrists, hip, knees and ankles, Schoenhut-style dress made of old fabric, antique underclothing, new socks and shoes, marked "Schoenhut Doll/Pat. Jan. 17, '11 U.S.A./& Foreign Countries," finish flaking off arms and legs, joints worn to bare wood **600.00**

Dollhouse

19" h, wood, white "stucco" covering, working front door, working door at second story balcony, two windows on each end and two in front, removable red roof, back opens to four rooms with orig litho floor covering, plain yellow walls, marked "Schoenhut Doll House. Made in U.S.A." on label on side of base, part of orig label missing, light wear. . **1,150.00**

27-5/8" h, 25-1/2" w, 23-5/8" d, Daggle, No. 5/50, 1923, wood and fiberboard, two-story, emb faux gray stone siding, emb faux green tile roof, off-white window and door trim, wooden front steps and chimney, eight int. rooms plus attic, litho paper int., some wood, fiber, and paint damage **2,415.00**

Roly poly, papier-mâché head

9-7/8" h, red head, yellow, green, and light blue suit, separation in seam around middle **115.00**

10" h, Buster Brown, painted blue eyes, single stroke brows, accent around eyes, closed mouth, molded and painted hair, one-piece papier-mâché body with arms molded to body, painted clothing, some paint flaking and wear. **590.00**

14" h, painted large eyes, feathered brows, open-closed smiling mouth with six painted teeth, molded and painted hair and yellow faux straw hat, papier-mâché round unjointed body, weight in base, molded and painted clothing, marked "Schoenhut Rolly Dolly, Patented Dec 15, 1908, Other Patents Pending" on round label on base, some surface cracks on neck and edges of hat, light wear to finish **800.00**

SCIENTIFIC INSTRUMENTS

History: Chemists, doctors, geologists, navigators, and surveyors used precision instruments as tools of their trade. Such objects were well designed and beautifully crafted. They are primarily made of brass; fancy hardwood cases also are common.

The 1990s have seen a keen interest in scientific instruments, both in the auction market and at antique shows. The number of collectors of this mechanical wonders is increasing as more and more interesting examples are being offered.

References: Florian Cajori, *History of the Logarithmic Slide Rule and Allied Instruments*, Astragal Press, 1994; Gloria Clifton, *Directory of British Scientific Instrument Makers 1550-1851*, P. Wilson Publishers, 1994; William H. Skerritt, *Catalog of the Charles E. Smart Collection: Antique Surveying Instruments*, published by author, (12 Locust Ave., Troy, NY 12180), 1996; Gerard L. E. Turner, *Scientific Instruments 1500-1900: An Introduction*, University of California Press, 1998.

Periodicals: *Tesseract*, P.O. Box 151, Hastings-on-Hudson, NY 10706; *Scientific, Medical & Mechanical Antiques*, P.O. Box 412, Taneytown, MD 21787, http://americanartifacts.com/smma.

Collectors' Clubs: International Calculator Collectors Club, 14561 Livingston St., Tustin, CA 92680; Maryland Microscopical Society, 8261 Polk St., McLean VA, 22102; The Oughtred Society, 2160 Middlefield Road, Palo Alto, CA 94301; Zeiss Historical Society, P.O. Box 631, Clifton, NJ 07012.

Museum: National Museum of American History, Smithsonian Institution, Washington, DC.

Binocular microscope, C. Collins, London, c1875, $1,325. Photo courtesy of Auction Team Breker.

Barograph, 12" w case, Wilson, Warden & Co., London, No. 4707/44, lacquered brass mechanism, clockwork motor, glazed mahogany case . **215.00**
Celestial globe, 17-1/2" h, Loring, 10", Boston, 1854, colored gores, illustrated constellations, brass meridian circle, walnut stand, printed horizon ring, four baluster turned legs, one (of two) cross-stretcher, cracks to globe, paper loss to horizon **2,990.00**
Circumferentor, 5-1/4" h, 9" d outside dia., 4-1/8" compass in center, attached to rotating sight vane/vernier arm, inset vial, silvered dial and outer ring, engraved with eight point star, two outer fixed sight vanes, brass, marked "Dollond London," c1825 . . . . **1,955.00**
Educational globe, Holbrook's Apparatus Mfg Co., Westerfield, CT, c1860, 3", hinged sphere, colored gores on ext., world maps on int. of Western and Eastern hemispheres, varnish wear, interior lifting . . . **2,100.00**
Microscope, compound monocular 12" h, 8-1/4" l, 1-1/8" d tube with one obj, fine focus on arm, 3-1/2" d stage with condenser and diaphragm, double mirror on calibrated rotating arm, japanned and lacquered brass, case, extra obj., marked "3373," c1885
. . . . **575.00**

12" h, 8-1/2" l, 1-1/8" d, tube with one obj, fine focus on arm, rect stage, five-hole diaphragm, double mirror on rotating arm, extra eyepiece, orig case, japanned and lacquered brass, sgd "Wm. H. Armstrong & Co., Indianapolis, Ind.," #11737, c1893 . . . . **635.00**

13-1/4" h, 9" l, 1-1/2" d single nosepiece tube with 3-1/2" d stage, condenser and double mirror revolve on arms centered on stage, against graduated vertical circular silvered dial, four obj. and three eyepieces, lacquered brass, case, marked "14668, Pat. Oct 13, 1885" **1,840.00**

15-1/2" h, 10-1/2" l, 1-1/4" d tube with single nosepiece, fine focus on front of tube, 4-1/2" d stage, two sub-stage condenses, double mirror, detachable parabolic mirror, extra 8" l, 1-1/8" d draw tube, detachable stand condenser lens with "B" holder, prism eyepiece, two obj., two eyepieces, lacquered brass, orig case, marked "Tolles Boston, 272," c1875 . . . . **2,275.00**

Octant, 10-7/8", Riggs & Bro., Philadelphia, ebony, ivory inlaid signature panel, scale with brass trim **550.00**

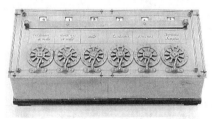

Replica of first mechanical calculator, by Blaise Pascal, Paris, 1652, **$11,500.** *Photo courtesy of Auction Team Breker.*

Palmer's computing scale, 8-1/2" d computing wheel on 11-1/4" sq outer scale, instructions on reverse, one fixed and one rotating logarithmic scale, values and gauge points numbered and noted, red, yellow, gold, and black, marked "Aaron Palmer, 1843 patent" **550.00**

Patent revolving interest table, 7-3/4" sq, C. M. Riley, Cincinnati, Ohio, twin revolving discs for calculating interest on prices, card folder with marbled cover, inscribed "1839 Cost $1.00" **575.00**

Recording device, 9" d, sgd "La Ledoise, Lede," circular nickeled case,

twin recording dish, fitted mahogany case. **150.00**

Refractometer, 13" h, Zeiss, No. 4255, arc, vernier, and rack-and-pinion adjustment, mahogany case. . . **260.00**

Sextant, nautical

8-3/4" h, brass, black paint, two eye pieces, seven colored lenses, wooden handle, engraved "N. Beck Pedersen, Arendal," minor wear **495.00**

9-1/2" h, brass, eye piece, six colored lenses, ebonized wood handle, small piece broken off **110.00**

11" h, ebonized wood, brass fittings, ivory label and measurements, pinhole eye piece, five colored lenses, "D. McGregor & Co., Glasgow & Greenock" **440.00**

Sketching case, 10-1/2" l, 7" w, 4-1/2" x 6-1/8" plotting surface, 5" d graduated plotting scale, 2" l rotating trough compass, two paper rollers, varnished hardwood and lacquered brass, marked "W. & L. E. Gurley, Troy, N.Y., patented Sept 28, 1897" **750.00**

Solar time piece, 23" h, Timby's, by L. H. Whiting, Saratoga Springs, New York, No. 236, 6" terrestrial globe by Gilman Joslin, Boston, 1860, 24-hour ring divided 1-12-1-12, single train movement, upright architectural walnut case, torn instruction sheet in transit case, lacking finial. **4,890.00**

Spectrascope, 9" h, by Heele, Berlin, lacquered brass body tubes, cast iron stand **245.00**

Telescope

5-7/8" l open, 1-3/4" d, brass mounts, shagreen, embossed scrolling foliage on leather draw, E. Nairne, London, first quarter 19th C **550.00**

20-1/4" l, brass and leather, one draw, engraved "G. Young & Co. London Day & Night," England, 19th C, replaced leather . . . **400.00**

21" l, brass and mahogany, one draw, 19th C **320.00**

Terrestrial globe 14" h, Hammond, 8", oxidized tripod stand, paw feet **375.00**

18-1/2" h, Hammond, 9", brass meridian circle, printed horizon ring, oxidized brass tripod stand **320.00**

29" h, Leipzig, by Pavel Rath and Professor A. Krause, 13" d, Empire-style ebonized stand with gilt Greek key border, early 20th C **750.00**

SCRIMSHAW

History: Norman Flayderman defined scrimshaw as "the art of carving or otherwise fashioning useful or decorative articles as practiced primarily by whalemen, sailors, or others associated with nautical pursuits." Many collectors expand this to include the

Left: Magnifying glass, cherry frame, turned base, 22-5/8" h, **$385;** *center: F. A. Hardy Opthalmoscope, iron base, cast detail, some wear, electric powered, 22-1/2" x 25",* **$165;** *right: Spencer Lens, Buffalo, NY, microscope, mostly brass, lacquered finish, enameled brass, orig case and booklet, 14" h,* **$200.** *Photo courtesy of Garth's Auctions, Inc.*

work of Eskimos and French POWs from the War of 1812.

References: Stuard M. Frank, *Dictionary of Scrimshaw Artists*, Mystic Seaport Museum, 1991; Nina Hellman and Norman Brouwer, *Mariner's Fancy*, South Street Seaport Museum, Balsam Press, and the University of Washington Press, 1992; Martha Lawrence, *Scrimshaw*, Schiffer Publishing, 1993.

Museums: Cold Spring Whaling Harbor Museum, Cold Spring Harbor, NY; Kendall Whaling Museum, Sharon, MA; Mystic Seaport Museum, Mystic, CT; National Maritime Museum, San Francisco, CA; New Bedford Whaling Museum, New Bedford, MA; Pacific Whaling Museum, Waimanalo, HI; Sag Harbor Whaling & Historical Museum, Sag Harbor, NY; San Francisco Maritime National Historical Park, San Francisco, CA; South Street Seaport Museum, New York, NY; Whaling Museum, Nantucket, MA.

Reproduction Alert: The biggest problem in the field is fakes, although there are some clues to spotting them. A very hot needle will penetrate the common plastics used in reproductions but not the authentic material. Ivory will not generate static electricity when rubbed, plastic will. Patina is not a good indicator; it has been faked by applying tea or tobacco juice, burying in raw rabbit hide, and in other ingenious ways. Usually the depth of cutting in an old design will not be consistent since the ship rocked and tools dulled; however, skilled forgers have even copied this characteristic.

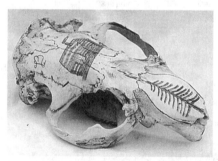

Beaver skull, log cabin, pine tree, and other decoration, upstate New York, c1910, 5-1/2" l, $160.

Box, 2-1/4" d, 2" h, circular, engraved and stained, whaling scene, large whale surrounded by compass positions, late 19th C **225.00**

Busk
11-7/8" l, whalebone, polychrome dec, memorial, foliate and geometric devices, 19th C, cracks **320.00**
12-3/8" l, bone, scratch carved eagle, pinwheels, vining foliage, compass stars, and heart at top, black coloring with red in eagle's

shield and one flower, small chip at top **550.00**
13-7/8" l, wood, dec with eagle, shield, lovebirds, and ship under sail, heart and foliate devices, inscribed "GC & EW," dated 1840 . . . . **345.00**

Cribbage board
18" l, engraved and inked, pictorial, top with caribou, game board, sides with sled dog team and caribou in landscape, back with bears approaching walrus ice float, Inuit carved, early 20th C . . **750.00**
19" l, engraved ivory, pictorial, tusk form, playing board flanks relief carved scene of pinniped head, pictorial style engraving, horse pulling sled, sea monster threatening hunter, canine in leg-hold trap, hunter getting close look at underside of caribou, attached pinniped form emerging from ice, sgd "A. LAMKA," loss to pegs and support **1,100.00**

Domino box, 6-7/8" l, bone and wood, shoe form, pierced carved slide top with star and heart dec, domino playing pcs, Prisoner of War, 19th C, cracks, minor insect damage **520.00**

Game box, 5-3/4" x 6-1/2", bone, pierced carved box with geometric dec, three slide tops, compartmented int., backgammon and other playing pcs, traces of paint dec, Prisoner of War, 19th C, repair, warping to tops, very minor loses **690.00**

Jagging wheel, 7-1/4" l, dec with building flying American flag, berried vines, 19th C, very minor losses. **520.00**

Obelisk, 13-3/8" h, inlaid mahogany, inlaid with various exotic woods, abalone and ivory in geometric and star motifs, 19th C, minor losses, minute cracks **815.00**

Paperweight, 3-1/8" l, carved block, inked caribou, salmon, and insect motifs, Intuit **325.00**

Salt horn, 5-1/2" l, engraved "John Snow March...1780 by S. H.," crosshatched borders enclosing reserve of ship, geometric, and foliate devices, insect damage **460.00**

Seam rubber, 4" l, whalebone, geometric designs on handle, traces of orig paint, 19th C **850.00**

Snuff box, 5" l, horn, architectural and marine motifs, dated "AD 1853" and "William Sandilands Plumber," English **950.00**

Whale tooth, sailor with British flag with red highlights, schooner Phoebe, 3-3/4" h, $225.

Walrus tusk
12-1/2" l, polychrome engraving of whales, eagles, displays of arms, ships under sail, figure on horseback, 19th C, restoration, losses, pr **1,265.00**
17-3/4" h, reserves of animals, courting couples, ships under sail, memorials, sailors and armaments, later engraved brass presentation caps, "Presented by George M. Chase to Ike B. Dunlap Jan. 25th 1908," cracks, one restored, pr **2,530.00**
18-7/8" l, walrus, dec with two eagles, lady, Indian, and vulture, age cracks, 19th C **1,840.00**

Watch hutch, 11-7/8" h, bone, pierce carved floral and figural dec, brass backing, polychrome foliate highlights, Prisoner of War, 19th C, custom-made case, minor cracks, losses, repairs **750.00**

Whale's tooth, 19th C
4-3/8" l, dec with ship, woman resting on anchor holding flag, two potted plants, chips, minor cracks, 19th C **690.00**
5" h, courting couple on one side, Victorian building on other, geometric and foliate swag border, minor cracks **690.00**
5-1/4" h, young couple and two elegant ladies, cracks **460.00**
6-1/4" h, dec with three-masted ship "Cyane" and memorial . . . **2,300.00**
6-1/2" h, four-masted shaping ship "Clipper Chip Great Republic Built E. Boston 1853" **550.00**

6-5/8" h, historic landmarks, dec on both sides, very minor cracks and chips **865.00**

6-7/8" h, various ships under sail and young lady, cracks **1,380.00**

Whimsey, 5-3/4" h, carved bone, French soldier sharpening his sword on grinding wheel, Prisoner of War, 19th C, minor paint wear.......... **4,715.00**

SEVRES

History: The principal patron of the French porcelain industry in early 18th-century France was Jeanne Antoinette Poisson, Marquise de Pompadour. She supported the Vincennes factory of Gilles and Robert Dubois and their successors in their attempt to make soft-paste porcelain in the 1740s. In 1753, she moved the porcelain operations to Sevres, near her home, Chateau de Bellevue.

The Sevres soft-paste formula used sand from Fontainebleau, salt, saltpeter, soda of alicante, powdered alabaster, clay, and soap. Many famous colors were developed, including a cobalt blue. The wonderful scenic designs on the ware were painted by such famous decorators as Watteau, La Tour, and Boucher. In the 18th century, Sevres porcelain was the world's foremost diplomatic gift.

In 1769, kaolin was discovered in France, and a hard-paste formula was developed. The baroque gave way to rococo, a style favored by Jeanne du Barry, Louis XV's next mistress. Louis XVI took little interest in Sevres, and many factories began to turn out counterfeits. In 1876, the factory was moved to St. Cloud and was eventually nationalized.

References: Susan and Al Bagdade, *Warman's English & Continental Pottery & Porcelain*, 3rd ed., Krause Publications, 1998; Carl Christian Dauterman, *Sevres Porcelain, Makers and Marks of the Eighteenth Century*, Metropolitan Museum of Art, 1986; Linda Humphries, *Sevres Porcelain from the Sevres Museum 1740 to the Present*, Hund Humphries, 1997; George Savage, *Seventeenth & Eighteenth Century French Porcelain*, Hamlyn Publishing Co., Ltd., 1969.

Museums: Art Institute of Chicago, Chicago, IL; British Museum, London, England; Frick Collection, New York, NY; Gardiner Museum of Ceramic Art Museum, Toronto, Canada; J. Paul Getty Museum, Los Angeles, CA; Metropolitan Museum of Art, New York, NY; Musee de Louvre, Paris, France, Musee National e Ceramique, Sevres, France; Victoria & Albert Museum, London, England; Wadsworth Atheneum, Harford, CT.

Marks: Louis XV allowed the firm to use the "double L" in its marks.

Reproduction Alert.

Box, cov
2-1/2" l, 1-1/4" w, 1-1/2" h, oval, cobalt blue ground, panels of putti dec, sgd "JB," chip on base **425.00**

3-1/4" l, 2" w, 2" h, genre dec top panel, landscape face panel, turquoise blue ground, gilt floral ornamentation, bun feet, entwined "L" mark, date mark "L," wear to gilt **180.00**

5-1/2" x 3-1/2" x 2-1/2", figural clam shell form, floral panels on blue ground, gilt accents, int. dec with flowers, entwined "L" mark with dated mark "S".......... **400.00**

Bud vase, 6" h, gilt ground, enamel Art Nouveau stylized leaf and flower design, printed mark **635.00**

Bust, 13" h, Marie Antoinette, bisque bust, gilt highlights, cobalt blue ground, molded porcelain socle with central garland and monogram, 19th C **650.00**

Café au lait cup and saucer, 6" h, ftd cup, cobalt blue enameled ground, gilt eagle roundel and torcheres, corresponding molded saucer, early 20th C **200.00**

Candelabra, pr, 30" h, porcelain urn, figure in landscape, fruit-filled cartouches, blue ground, candle nozzles and flowers, two handles cast with putti and floral dec, bronze mounts, worn gilt trim **5,250.00**

Centerpiece, 20-1/4" h, four youths in procession, each supporting basket, mounted on freeform base, white biscuit, imp mark, early 20th C . **320.00**

Cup and saucer, bird in landscape, trellis and florals in cartouche on wide border, 18th C, **$250.**

Chandelier, 26" 2, 36" l, baluster and urn shaft with portrait panels, eight arms with electric candlestick sockets **1,320.00**

Clock and garniture, painted porcelain and ormolu, 21" h Louis XVI-style clock, two-train half-strike movement, dial enamel dec with swags, shaped case, front painted with scene of Cupid and Venus, lower left sgd "Petit," pair of 21" h associated five-light candelabra, rocaille scrolled candle arms, central nozzle with rocaille finial, baluster stem, shaped foot painted to front with Cupid, early 20th C **2,990.00**

Figure
14-1/4" and 16-1/4" h, standing soldiers, one titled "En Sentinelle," other "La Petite en Danger," gilt accents, late 19th/early 20th C, price for pr **440.00**

18" h, bisque, Diana stands with attendants and dogs, ormolu base with cast rosette and circlet border, four acanthus feet, imp mark, second half 19th C **3,000.00**

Ginger jar, 12" h, blue flambé, ormolu mounts, pr **2,000.00**

Lamp base, electrified
28" h, cov urn, pink ground, body painted with central cartouche depicting old woman teaching a little girl to dance, lower right sgd "F. Yogt" in gilt surround, further all over gilt rococo scrollwork, late 19th C **5,175.00**

32-1/2" h, body painted with continuous scene of Russian troika drawn by three horses being chased by wolves through winter landscape at sunset, lower right sgd "Kowalsky," gilt banding, burgundy ground, gilt-metal flower-form foot, early 20th C **9,200.00**

Patch box, cov, 3-1/4" l, shaped ovoid, green ground, hinged lid with hand painted scene of Napoleon on horseback, sgd lower right "Morin" **250.00**

Plaque, 10-1/2" l, 9-5/8" w oval format, Marie Antoinette, mauve gown, blue celeste border with gilt scrollwork, 10-3/4" x 13-5/8" giltwood and crème painted frame, late 19th C **550.00**

Portrait plate, 9" d
Lobelia portrait, surrounded by wreath, cobalt blue band border with gilt dec including Napoleonic crest and crowns, mounted in shadow box frame, gilt loss **150.00**

Plates, left: portrait, signed "d G. Perier," blue border with panels of flowers, marked "Roi de Rome," 9" d, $110; right: man and woman decoration, pink border, floral panels and gilt trim, metal stand, 9-1/2" d, $275. Photo courtesy of Joy Luke Auctions.

Mme Duchatelet portrait, sgd "G. Perlex," cobalt blue border with floral panels and gilt accents, scalloped rim, entwined "L" mark, dated "BB" **125.00**

Tazza, 11-1/2" d, blue flambé, ormolu mounts **350.00**

Tray, 18-1/2" x 13", six-sided oblong form, French allegorical park scene, ladies with parasols, Florentine gilt border, sgd "Bertien" **525.00**

Urn

10" h, white ground, gilt lattice and floral sprays, allegorical garden scene, gilt bronze ormolu mounts, sgd "P. Rorhe," entwined L's mark, initial "V" **675.00**

18" h, allegorical garden scenes with male and female figures, landscape dec on reverse, accented with bands of red, gilt ornamentation, acanthus leaf and ring handles, ormolu mounts, sgd "E. Grisard," entwined "L" mark, dated "S," price for pr . . . **2,200.00**

39" h, baluster form, French figural dec on front panel, landscape dec on reverse, ivory and gilt ground, cobalt blue base and neck, gilt ornamentation, sgd "E. Parot," restoration **1,650.00**

Vase

6-3/8" h, hexagonal, light blue ground, central painted roundel of 18th C gentleman making elegant leg, signed lower right, heavily applied gilt scroll handles, gilt quatrefoil reserves, gilt line detailing, French, early 20th C **115.00**

11" h, pink ground, oval cartouches with figural landscapes and ornaments, metal mount, pr **1,380.00**

Wine cooler, 10-1/4" h, Louis XVI style, circular tapering form, top section with gilded ram's heads over reeded band, base dec with ribboned garlands and entwined laurel, multicolored, white ground **2,300.00**

SEWING ITEMS

History: As recently as 50 years ago, a wide variety of sewing items were found in almost every home in America. Women of every economic and social status were skilled in sewing and dressmaking.

Iron or brass sewing birds, one of the interesting convenience items which developed, were used to hold cloth (in the bird's beak) while sewing. They could be attached to a table or shelf with a screw-type fixture. Later models included a pincushion.

References: *Advertising & Figural Tape Measures,* L-W Book Sales, 1995; by New Leaf Publishers); Elizabeth Hughes and Marion Lester, *The Big Book of Buttons,* 1981 (reprint by New Leaf Publishers); Averil Mathis, *Antique & Collectible Thimbles and Accessories,* Collector Books, 1997; Bridget McConnel, *The Story of Antique Needlework Tools,* Schiffer Publishing, 1999; Wayne Muller, *Darn It!,* L-W Book Sales, 1995; Florence Zacharie Nicholls, *Button Handbook, with three supplements, 1943-1949,* (reprints by New Leaf Publishers); Helen Lester Thompson, *Sewing Tools & Trinkets,* Collector Books, 2000; Estelle Zalkin, *Zalkin's Handbook of Thimbles & Sewing Implements,* Warman Publishing Co., 1988, distributed by Krause Publications, http://www.krause.com.

Collectors' Clubs: Birchcroft Thimble Collectors Club, http://www.thimble.net; International Sewing Machine Collectors Society, 158 Hampton Road, Chingford, London E1 9UB UK, http://ismacs.net; National Button Society, 2733 Juno Place, Apt. 4, Akron, OH 44313-4137; Thimble Collectors International, 7409 Millbrook Road, Norfolk, VA 23505, http://www.thimblecollectors.com; Thimble Guild, P.O. Box 381807, Duncanville, TX 75138-1807.

Periodicals and Internet Resources: *Antique Treasures,* http://www.antiquetreasures.com; *Button Bytes,* http://www.tias.com/articles/buttons; *Campbell's Guide to Toy Sewing Machines,* http://users.erols.com/quilts/index.html; *Online Antique Sewing Machine Resource,* http://yahoo.geocities.com/claw.geo; *Rosie's Needle Book Museum,* http://www.geocities.com/rosierider; *Sewing Machine Collector,* http://www.dincum.com; *Tangled Threads,* http://kbs.net/tt/faq; *That Darn Newsletter,* 461 Brown Briar Circle, Horsham, PA 19044; *Thimbletter,* 93 Walnut Hill Road, Newton Highlands, MA 02161-1836.

Museums: Antique Sewing Machine Museum, Oakland, CA; Button Bytes, http://www.tias.com/museum/clothingbuttons.html; Fabric Hall, Historic Deerfield, Deerfield, MA; Frank Smith's Sewing Machine Museum, Arlington, TX, http://rampages.onramp.net/~arlprosv/museum.html; Museum of American History, Smithsonian Institution, Washington, DC; Shelburne Museum, Shelburne, VT.

Additional Listings: *Warman's Americana & Collectibles* for more examples.

Sewing machine, toy, tin, threads and needles in wooden box, $275. Photo courtesy of Joy Luke Auctions.

Bodkins, whalebone and ivory, sealing wax inlaid scribe lines, 19th C, minor losses, nine-pc set **400.00**

Book, *Fleisher's Knitting & Crocheting Manual,* S. B. & B. W. Fleisher, Inc., Philadelphia, PA, 1924, 112 pgs, 7" x 9-1/2", 21st edition **15.00**

Catalog, E. Butterick & Co., New York, NY, 1878, 32 pgs, 7-1/2" x 10", Catalog for Fall of Women's Clothing Patterns **38.00**

Folder, 8-3/4" x 14-1/4", Wm. R. Moore Dry Goods Co., Memphis, TN, three pgs, c1937, heavy weight, "Guaranteed Fast Color No. 10 Batfast Suitings," 10 tipped-in blue Batfast Suiting swatches, 19-1/4" x 2" colored swatches tipped in **28.00**

Etui, 3-1/2" l, tapered ovoid agate case, ormolu mounts, hinged lid, fitted interior with scissors, knife, pen, ruler, needle, pincers, and spoon, Continental, late 18th/early 19th C **700.00**

Hand book, Davis Sewing Machine Co., Watertown, NY, *Centennial Hand Book Presented at the Great Exhibition,* 12 pgs, directions to get around at Exhibition, info. on sewing machine, cabinets, etc. **65.00**

Instruction book, *Singer Sewing Machines No. 99,* c1910, 32 pgs, 3-1/2" x 5-1/4" **16.00**

Magazine

Home Needlework Magazine, Florence Publishing Co., Florence,

MA, 176 pgs, 1899, Vol. 1, No. 2, April **20.00**

Star Needlework Journal, American Thread Co., 1922, Vol. 7, No. 2, published quarterly **20.00**

The Ladies Standard Magazine, Standard Fashion Co., August 1893 . . . . **20.00**

Needle book

Rocket Gold Tipped Needles, cov illus of man and woman riding needle shaped like rocket, night time sky background, marked "Made in Japan," 1940s **10.00**

With Oil Heat, the weather is always wonderful indoors, child playing with Raggedy Ann on cover . . **8.00**

Needle case, tri-color 18kt gold, chase and engraved geometric and floral motifs, European hallmark **320.00**

Pin cushion

Half Doll, cotton skirt, marked "Germany," c1920 . . . . **40.00**

Strawberry, 5-1/2" l, red fabric, green and brown shaded velvet top, minor wear **85.00**

Sewing box

5-1/2" w, 3-1/2" d, 3-1/4" h, inlaid hearts, arrows, diamonds, and circles, one dovetailed drawer, turned pull, worn pin cushion top, minor edge damage at corner **275.00**

5-3/4" l, figured mahogany veneer on pine, inlay, table clamp, dovetailed drawer, pincushion, wear and edge damage, thumb screw missing **220.00**

6-3/4" l, 5" w, 7" h, mahogany, lift off lid with pin cushion, single drawer, cathedral style **330.00**

11-1/8" l, 9-1/8" w, 6" h, Tunbridge, serpentine front, hinged lid and sides inlaid with florals, int. lid with inlay border surrounding pleated satin, center inlaid roundel, int. fitted with removable upper compartment, four inlaid flattened ball feet, England, late 19th C **260.00**

Sewing machine, child's, Betsy Ross, green metal machine, leather-looking case, 1949 . . . . **95.00**

Tape measure, figural

Cozy Kittens, Holt Howard, ceramic **45.00**

Owl, metal, German **45.00**

Thimble, brass, fancy band design **15.00**

Thimble holder

3" h, fox with baton and open book leads a dog and cat in song, two thimble holders in front, oval base, marked "Waters & Thorr New York" **350.00**

Tape measure, chariot and rider, celluloid made to imitate bronze, 1-3/4" h, $225. Photo courtesy of Julie Robinson.

5-3/4" h, fisherman holding large rod, beautifully detailed large fish on ground, bucket by fish, post in front of fisherman, rect base, marked "Miller Silver Co. Silver Plate" **350.00**

Thread cabinet

Clarks, white lettering, four drawers, some damage to case **100.00**

Dexter Fine Yarn, oak, four drawers, 18-3/4" h, 18-5/8' w, 16" d . . **650.00**

Merrick's Spool Cotton, oak, cylindrical, curved glass, 18" d, 22" h **725.00**

Willimantic, four drawers, ornate Eastlake style case, 14-1/4" h **550.00**

Transfer book, H. Heminway & Sons Silk, 1896, 24 artistic designs, 23 color plates with text on verso **40.00**

SHAKER

History: The Shakers, so named because of a dance they used in worship, are one of the oldest communal organizations in the United States. This religious group was founded by Mother Ann Lee, who emigrated from England and established the first Shaker community near Albany, New York, in 1784. The Shakers reached their peak in 1850, when there were 6,000 members.

Shakers lived celibate and self-sufficient lives. Their philosophy stressed cleanliness, order, simplicity, and economy. Highly inventive and motivated, the Shakers created many utilitarian household forms and objects. Their furniture reflected a striving for quality and purity in design.

In the early 19th century, the Shakers produced many items for commercial purposes. Chairmaking and the packaged herb and seed business thrived. In every endeavor and enterprise, the members followed

Spool dispenser, counter top, Merrick's, curved glass sides, $1,980. Photo courtesy of Jackson's Auctioneers & Appraisers.

Mother Ann's advice: "Put your hands to work and give your heart to God."

References: Edward Deming Andrews and Faith Andrews, *Masterpieces of Shaker Furniture,* Dover Publications, 1999; Christian Becksvoort, *The Shaker Legacy: Perspectives on an Enduring Furniture Style,* The Taunton Press, 1998; Michael Horsham, *Art of the Shakers,* Apple Press, 1989; John T. Kirk, *The Shaker World: Art, Life, Belief,* Harry N. Abrams, 1997; Charles R. Muller and Timothy D. Rieman, *The Shaker Chair,* Canal Press, 1984; June Sprigg and Jim Johnson, *Shaker Woodenware,* Berkshire House, 1991; June Sprigg and David Larkin, *Shaker Life, Work, and Art,* Stewart, Tabori & Chang, 1987; Timothy D. Rieman, *Shaker: The Art of Craftsmanship,* Art Services International, 1995; Timothy D. Rieman and Jean M. Burks, *Complete Book of Shaker Furniture,* Harry N. Abrams, 1993.

Collectors' Clubs: Shaker Heritage Society, 875 Watervliet-Shaker Road, Albany, NY 12211-1051, http://www.crisny.org/not-for-profit/shakerwv; Western Shaker Study Group, 1700 Pentbrooke Trail, Dayton, OH 45459; http://www.shakerwssg.org.

Museums: Canterbury Shaker Village, Canterbury, NH; Hancock Shaker Village, Pittsfield, MA; Shaker Historical Museum, Cleveland, OH; Shaker Museum and Library, Old Chatham, NY; Shaker Museum at South Union, South Union, KY; Shaker Village of Pleasant Hill, Harrodsburg, KY 40330.

Book, two copies of Volume I A Holy, Sacred and Divine Roll and Book; From The Lord God of Heaven, To The Inhabitants of Earth, United Society [of Shakers] Canterbury, N.H., 1843, 12mo, full calf, some damp staining in places, minor foxing and very light even toning, minor chips on spines, 402 pages plus, $400. Photo courtesy of Cowan Historic Americana Auctions.

Apothecary cabinet, 66" x 14", stained wood, rect, front fitted with 12 small drawers, molded white glazed porcelain handles, identification labels, drawer sides inscribed with various content titles, New England, 19th C **450.00**

Basket, 12" x 12" x 4-3/8" h, finely woven splint, sq shape, two delicate bentwood handles, minor damage, traces of old red stain **360.00**

Blanket chest, 40-1/2" w, 18-1/2" d, 36" h, New Lebanon, NY, 1830-40, hinged rect breadboard lift top, nail construction well, two long scratchbeaded drawers, tapering cut-out feet, all over later grain paint to simulate exotic wood, old replaced pulls, surface imperfections .. **1,265.00**

Bonnet, dark brown palm and straw, black ribbons, 9" flounce, KY ... **395.00**

Book, *How the Shakers Cook & the Noted Cooks of the Country, Feature the Chefs and Their Cooking Recipes,* A. J. White, New York, NY, 1889, 50 pgs, 3-3/8" x 6-1/8', bust of men illus, dusted, chips....................... **15.00**

Bottle, 9" h, aqua, emb "Shaker Pickles," base labeled "Portland, Maine, E.D.P. & Co."........... **90.00**

Butter churn, old red paint, strap hinges, $380.

Box, cov, bentwood

4-1/2" w, 3-1/8" d, 1-5/8" h, finger construction, two fingers on base, one finger on lid, copper tacks, cherry stain on lid, rim, and base, varnish with yellow tinge ... **150.00**

5-1/2" w, 3-1/2" d, 2-1/8" h, finger construction, two fingers on base, one finger on lid, copper tacks, old green repaint, some wear on lid **850.00**

6-1/8" w, 4" w, 2" h, finger construction, two fingers on base, one finger on lid, brass tacks, old green (black) repaint over traces of earlier green, minor wear .. **690.00**

7-1/4" w, 4-5/8" d, 2-7/8" h, finger construction, two fingers on base, one finger on lid, copper tacks, natural patina, some wear on lid, base with minor edge damage at tack **110.00**

7-1/2" w, 5-1/8" d, 2-1/2" h, finger construction, two fingers on base, one finger on lid, copper tacks, reddish stain **320.00**

7-5/8" w, 5-3/4" d, 3-1/4" h, oval, Harvard lap, copper tacks, mellow natural finish............ **330.00**

9-1/2" w, 7" d, 3-3/4" h, finger construction, two fingers on base, one finger on lid, copper tacks, old blue paint, some wear ... **1,400.00**

12" w, 8-3/8" d, 4-3/4" h, oval, Harvard lap, copper tacks, mellow natural finish, remnants of paper label on one end **440.00**

Box, cov, domed lid, 25-1/2" w, 15-1/2" d, 15-1/4" h, attributed to Hancock community, pine, divided interior, dovetailed drawer, compartment at both ends of lid with sliding covers, old age splits in lid, refinished.................. **550.00**

Carrier, 6-3/8" x 9", 2-7/8" h plus bentwood swing handle, bentwood, oval, four fingers, copper tacks, varnished finish, four sets of drilled holes to secure lining, stamped "Shaker Goods Alfred ME Trademark" .. **250.00**

Chair, 15" h seat, 40" h back, side, Harvard, MA, third quarter 19th C, three slightly arched slats joining turned stiles, tall pommels, splint seat, turned legs joined by double turned stretcher, repainted red, paint wear, underside of seat dated "1830" in green paint **420.00**

Chest of drawers, 63" w, 17-1/2" d, 39-1/2" h, pine, eight graduated dovetailed drawers arranged in two banks of four, turned pulls, six high feet with semi-curved cut-outs, old mellow refinish, replaced back boards, some pulls replaced **14,300.00**

Child's rocker, Mount Lebanon, NY

8-1/2" h seat, 25" h back, No. 0, imp "0" on reverse of top slat, decal on a rocker, cherry, arms, old gold velvet seat, orig varnished surface **1,955.00**

12" h seat, 28" h back, No. 1, imp "#1" on top slat, "Shaker's Mt. Lebanon" label on bottom slat, orig dark finish, woven paper rush seat, tapering rear posts with turned finials **495.00**

Correspondence, five letters written from Boston and Dorchester to Shaker Village, Pittsfield, MA, and Pawtucket, RI, to Cogswell family, c1846-47, containing family and neighborhood news, mention of Mexican-American War, Ship Fever, pen and pink on paper, postmarks, remnants of wax seals
...........................**115.00**

Dough scraper, 4-1/2" l, wrought iron
...........................**40.00**

Flax wheel, 33-1/2" h, various hardwoods, old dark brown finish, stamped "SR. AL," (Deacon Samuel Ring of Alfred, Maine 1784-1848), two pieces of distaff replaced......**330.00**

Grain measure, 7-1/2" d, bentwood, stencil label "Shaker Society, Sabbathday Lake, Me," minor edge damage **160.00**

Hanger, 24" w, bentwood, chestnut
...........................**65.00**

Recipe book, Laura Sarle, Canterbury, Shaker Village, New Hampshire, 1883-87, inscribed by author, recipes, brief autobiography, short play, housekeeping, records, knitting instructions, pen and ink on paper, mottled orange cardboard cover with black binding, wear to cover, few random annotations by later hand
.......................**5,520.00**

Rocking chair, Mount Lebanon, #0, turned arm posts, shaped arms, mushroom caps, three slats, turned finials, replaced green, beige, and black woven tape seat, old refinishing, **$770.** *Photo courtesy of Garth's Auctions, Inc.*

Rocker, 15" h seat, 33-1/2" h, unmarked, Mt. Lebanon, orig dark surface, turned posts with shaped arms, mushroom cap handholds, small turned finials on rear posts, woven olive green and red striped tape seat and back in historically accurate manner, glued crack near back of one arm
...........................**325.00**

Sewing box, 14-3/4" l, 10-1/8" w, 5" h, late 19th C, dovetailed and pegged construction, rect, hinged lid, brass handle, lift-out tray with three compartments, ivory and whalebone sewing, crochet, and knitting implements **750.00**

Sewing carrier, cov, 9-1/2" l, 6-1/4" w, 7" h, attributed to Mount Lebanon, NY, c1930, maple and cherry, oval, body with three lapped fingers, swing handle, pink silk lining, seven sweetgrass baskets, five thimbles in various shapes and sizes, velvet pincushion, silk pincushion, two needle sharpeners, thread wax, thread, large number of ivory and whalebone knitting and sewing implements **490.00**

Table, 34-3/4" x 35-1/2" x 28", maple, drop leaf, rect top, hinged rect leaves, single drawer, sq tapering legs, first half 19th C **6,500.00**

Table swift, 29-3/4" d extended, 25" h, maple, 19th C **230.00**

Wash tub, 24" d, 16-1/2" h, New England, late 19th C, stave and lap fingered hoop construction, two handles, old red paint, imperfections
...........................**460.00**

SHAVING MUGS

c1908

History: Shaving mugs, which hold the soap, brush, and hot water used to prepare a beard for shaving, come in a variety of materials including tin, silver, glass, and pottery. One style, which has separate compartments for water and soap, is the scuttle, so called because of its coal-scuttle shape.

Personalized shaving mugs were made exclusively for use in barber shops in the United Sates. They began being produced shortly after the Civil War and continued to be made into the 1930s.

Unlike shaving mugs that were used at home, these mugs were personalized with the owner's name, usually in gilt. The mug was kept in a rack at the barber shop, and it was used only when the owner came in for a shave. This was done for hygienic purposes, to keep from spreading a type of eczema known as barber's itch.

The mugs were usually made on European porcelain blanks that often contained the mark of "Germany," "France," or "Austria" on the bottom. In later years, a few were made on American-made semi-vitreous blanks. The artwork on mugs was done by decorators who worked for major barber supply houses. Occasionally the mark of the barber supply house is also stamped on the bottom of the mug.

After a short time, the mugs became more decorative, including hand-painted floral decorations, as well as birds, butterflies, and a wide variety of nature scenes, etc. These are classified today as "decorative" mugs.

Another category, "fraternal mugs," soon developed. These included the emblem of an organization the owner belonged to, along with his name emblazoned in gold above or below the illustration.

"Occupational mugs" were also very popular. These are mugs which contained a painting of something that illustrated the owner's occupation, such as a butcher, a bartender, or a plumber. The illustration might be a man working at his job, or perhaps the tools of his trade, or a product which he made or sold.

Of all these mugs, occupationals are the most prized. Their worth is determined by several factors: rarity (some occupations are rarer than others), size of mug, and size of illustration (the bigger the better), quality of artwork, and condition—although rare mugs with cracks or chips can still be valuable if the damage does not affect the artwork on the mug. Generally speaking, a mug showing a man at work at his job is usually valued higher than that same occupation illustrated with only the tools or finished product.

The invention of the safety razor by King C. Gillette, issued to three and one-half million servicemen during World War I, brought about changes in personal grooming—men began to shave on their own, rather than visiting the barber shop to be shaved. As a result, the need for personalized shaving mugs declined.

References: Susan and Al Bagdade, *Warman's English & Continental Pottery & Porcelain*, 3rd ed., Krause Publications, 1998; Ronald S. Barlow, *Vanishing American Barber Shop*, Windmill Publishing, 1993; Keith E. Estep, *Shaving Mug & Barber Bottle Book*, Schiffer Publishing, 1995.

Museums: Atwater Kent History Museum, Philadelphia, PA; Barber Museum, Canal Winchester, OH; Lightner Museum, Saint Augustine, FL; National Shaving & Barbershop Museum, Meriden, CT.

Note: Prices shown are for typical mugs which have no damage and show only moderate wear on the gilt name and decoration.

Fraternal

B.L.E.E., Brotherhood of Locomotive Eng., "BLE" monogram **95.00**

B.P.O.E., Elks, double emblem, Dr. title
.......................**300.00**

F. of A., gilt deer's head, two crossed American flags, floral designs, gilt dec, fuchsia rim, marked "Germany"..**35.00**

Indian, hand painted, base marked "Daddy from Junior, Xmas, 1915," green mark "Hutschenreuther Selb Bavaria," $200.

F.O.E., Fraternal Order of Eagles, eagle holding F.O.E. plaque **260.00**

IB of PM, International Brotherhood of Paper Makers, paper-making machine, clasped hands. **275.00**

I.O.M., International Order of Mechanics, ark ladder. **270.00**

Loyal Knights of America, eagle, flags, six-pointed star **275.00**

Loyal Order of the Moose, gold circle with gray moose head, purple and green floral dec, gilt rim and base, marked "Germany" **220.00**

United Mine Workers, clasped hands emblem flanked by crossed picks and shovels, floral dec, rose garland around top, marked "Germany". **125.00**

Bartender, gold trim, **$295.**

Occupational

Baker, detailed hand-painted image of two bakers working at brick oven, automated mixing, kneading, etc. machinery, image worn, name and gold

trim very worn, chip on back, 3-7/8 d", 4" h **170.00**

Bicycle, detailed hand-painted image of man on bicycle, light wear to gold lettering and trim, small base chip, 3-5/8" d, 3-1/2" h. **700.00**

Electrician, hand-painted image of electrician wiring inside of electrical box, T & V Limoges, France, wear to gold lettering and trim, 3-5/8" d, 3-5/8" h **2,500.00**

Fabric store, colorful hp shop int., owner waiting on well-dressed woman, gold trim and name, 3-5/8" x 4-1/2" **700.00**

General store, pork, flour, and whiskey barrels, Limoges, 4" x 4-3/4". . . . **650.00**

Hotel clerk, clerk at desk, guest signing register. **375.00**

House painter, detailed hand-painted image of man painting side of building, marked "Fred Dole" on bottom, light crack mark around top of handle, wear to gold lettering and trim, 3-1/2" d, 3-1/2" h **350.00**

Magician, detailed hand-painted image of man in suit holding top hat while flying through cloud-filled moon-lit sky, light wear to gold lettering and trim, 3-7/8" d, 3-7/8" h. **275.00**

Mover, detailed hand-painted image of two men in moving van, gold name and trim, Royal China Int'l, 3-7/8" d, 3-5/8" **1,400.00**

Photographer, detailed hand-colored image of portrait photographer, marked "Webb Bros" in gold, wear to gold lettering and trim, 3-5/8" d, 3-1/2" h **700.00**

Railroad, detailed hand-painted image of two railway workers on hand car, wear to gold lettering and trim, 3-1/2" d, 3-5/8" h **650.00**

Shoemaker, hp, scene of shoemaker in shop, gilt foot and swags around name **195.00**

Trainman, red plank caboose, gilt dec, marked "H. & B. T RR" **185.00**

Trolley repair wagon, horse drawn, scaffolding **1,250.00**

Tugboat, boat in water, crew and captain **750.00**

Writer, black desk inkwell with sander, pen, and brass handle **350.00**

Other

Bicycle racer, pink and yellow flowers, gilt banner with "Bicycle Racers Madison Square Garden," trophy with inscription. **550.00**

Coronation of H M King Edward VII, 18th May 1937, British seal with monarch, flags on reverse, scuttle **40.00**

Drape and flowers, purple drape, pot of flowers, gold name **85.00**

Fish shape, scuttle, green and brown **75.00**

Horses in storm, white and black horses, copied from painting . . **100.00**

Skull, white, gray, black, and cream, scuttle, marked "Bavaria" **135.00**

SHAWNEE POTTERY

History: The Shawnee Pottery Co. was founded in 1937 in Zanesville, Ohio. The company acquired a 650,000-square-foot plant that had previously housed the American Encaustic Tiling Company. Shawnee produced as many as 100,000 pieces of pottery a day until 1961, when the plant closed.

Shawnee limited its production to kitchenware, decorative art pottery, and dinnerware. Distribution was primarily through jobbers and chain stores.

Marks: Shawnee can be marked "Shawnee," "Shawnee U.S.A.," "USA #——," "Kenwood," or with character names, e.g., "Pat. Smiley" and "Pat. Winnie."

References: Jim and Bev Mangus, *Shawnee Pottery*, Collector Books, 1994, 2000 value update; Mark Supnick, *Collecting Shawnee Pottery*, L-W Book Sales, 2000; Duane and Janice Vanderbilt, *Collector's Guide to Shawnee Pottery*, Collector Books, 1992, 1998 value update.

Collectors' Club: Shawnee Pottery Collectors Club, P.O. Box 713, New Smyrna Beach, FL 32170.

Ashtray, Monte Carlo **38.00**
Bank, bulldog **50.00**
Basket, 9" l, 5-1/2" h at handle, turquoise glaze, relief flowers and leaves, USA 688 . . . . **45.00**
Batter pitcher, Fern **65.00**
Casserole, cov, Corn Queen, large **40.00**

Casserole, covered, Basket of Fruit, banana, peach, grapes, apples, and pears, yellow basket weave base, marked "Shawnee USA 83," 7-5/8" d, **$50.**

Cookie jar, cov

Cinderella, unmarked **125.00**
Cottage, marked "USA 6," 7" h
. . . .**900.00**
Drum major, marked "USA 10," 10" h
. . . .**295.00**
Dutch Boy, striped pants, under
glaze dec, marked "USA," 11" h
. . . .**150.00**
Dutch Girl, under glaze dec, marked
"USA," 11-1/2" h **150.00**
Great Northern Boy, marked "Great
Northern USA 1025," 9-3/4" h
. . . .**375.00**
Jo-Jo the Clown, marked "Shawnee
USA, 12," 9" h **300.00**
Little Chef. **75.00**
Muggsy Dog, blue bow, gold trim
and decals, marked "Patented
Muggsy U.S.A.," 11-3/4" h . . **900.00**
Owl. **110.00**
Smiley Pig, clover blossom dec,
marked "Patented Smiley USA,"
11-1/2" h **550.00**
Winnie Pig, clover blossom dec,
marked "Patented Winnie USA,"
12" h **575.00**

Creamer

Elephant. **25.00**
Puss n' Boots, green and yellow
. . . .**65.00**
Smiley Pig, clover bud. **165.00**

Figure

Bear **45.00**
Gazelle. **45.00**
Puppy **50.00**
Squirrel. **30.00**
Rabbit **40.00**

Fruit bowl, Corn Queen. **25.00**

Mug, Corn King **35.00**

Paperweight, Muggsy **65.00**

Pitcher

Bo Peep, blue bonnet, yellow dress
. . . .**125.00**
Chanticleer **75.00**

Planter

Canopy bed, #734. . . . . **95.00**
Donkey with basket, #722 . . . . **35.00**
Gazelle. **25.00**
Horse with hat and cart **25.00**
Locomotive, black **65.00**
Mouse and cheese, pink and yellow
. . . .**25.00**
Rocking horse, blue. **32.00**
Wheelbarrow **20.00**

Salt and pepper shakers, pr

Chanticleer, large, orig label . . **45.00**
Dutch Boy and Girl, large **55.00**
Milk cans **20.00**
Mugsey, small **65.00**

*Sugar bowl, covered, Corn pattern,
5-1/4" h,* **$35.**

Puss n' Boots, small **30.00**
Smiley, small **30.00**
Watering cans. **27.50**

Teapot

Granny Ann, peach apron . . .**115.00**
Horseshoe, blue **45.00**
Tom Tom, blue, red, and yellow
. . . .**125.00**

Utility jar, Corn King **50.00**

Wall pocket

Bird House **25.00**
Fern **35.00**

SILHOUETTES

History: Silhouettes (shades) are shadow profiles produced by hollow cutting, mechanical tracing, or painting. They were popular in the 18th and 19th centuries.

The name came from Etienne de Silhouette, a French Minister of Finance, who cut "shades" as a pastime. In America, the Peale family was well known for the silhouettes they made.

Silhouette portraiture lost popularity with the introduction of the daguerreotype prior to the Civil War. In the 1920s and 1930s, a brief revival occurred when tourists to Atlantic City and Paris had their profiles cut as souvenirs.

Marks: An impressed stamp marked "PEALE" or "Peale Museum" identifies pieces made by the Peale family.

Museums: Peabody Essex Institute, Salem, MA; National Portrait Gallery, Washington, DC.

3-1/2" h, 2-1/2" w, woman, hair up in bun, green dress with large ruffled sleeves, lace collar, gold pin, antique black molded frame **600.00**
4" h, 4" w, gentleman, reverse painted glass with dec oval in gold surrounded by black, gold highlights, antique black molded frame, pencil inscription on back "Parker Emerson," some damage to reverse painting **90.00**
4-3/4" h, 3-3/4" w, man and woman, oval portraits, Hat & Thomas Newell, mounted in lemon gold molded frame **150.00**
5-1/4" h, 3-3/4" w, cut-out portrait of matronly woman wearing bonnet, penciled eyelash, reeded frame with black paint and punched brass rosettes, minor edge damage to frame **220.00**
5-1/2" h, 4-1/2" w, hollow cut, gentleman, stenciled frock coat, eglomise glass mat with yellow painted designs, black velvet backing, black painted frame with traces of yellow on outer edge **475.00**
5-3/4" h, 4-3/8" w, hollow cut, portrait of boy under leafy branch, very faint name underneath, worn gilt frame, fold lines with minor damage. **85.00**
5-3/4" h, 4-3/4" w, hollow cut, portrait of boy, cut-out eyelash, stains, faint ghost image of earlier mat, alligatored brown paint on frame **110.00**
5-3/4" h, 4-7/8" w, hollow cut, bust, lady with ornate hat, back marked "Mrs. Norman" and "Mrs. Norman, Henley on Thames," black lacquered case with gilded fittings, wear and stain . . **200.00**
5-3/4" h, 4-7/8" w, portrait of gentleman in black ink, coat details in glossy black, gold inked hair, alligatored brown paint on frame **275.00**
6" h, 5-1/4" w, hollow cut, man and woman, man with high collar, woman with hair comb, black cloth backing, molded gold frame, some foxing of paper, price for pair **440.00**
6-1/4" h, 5" w, gentleman, hollow cut, old label "G. Saufer, Passe-Portouts, Philadelphia," framed, tears and repair **90.00**
6-3/8" h, 5-3/8" w, young man, old frame, stains and tears. **100.00**
6-3/8" h, 5-3/8" w, young woman, hollow cut, cut detail at collar, pencil inscription "Sarah Sage," stains. **200.00**
6-1/2" h, 10" w, man and woman, hollow cut, ink and watercolor details, framed together, sgd "Doyle," eglomise glass mat with two ovals, gilded frame **425.00**
6-5/8" h, 5-1/2" w, man and wife, hollow cut, ink details, rosewood veneer frames, pr. **580.00**
6-3/4" h, 6" w, gentleman, black lacquer frame with gilded brass liner, minor stains **90.00**

Painted, Daniel Kemper, Revolutionary Wary clothier, 12" x 8" ink silhouette on heavy red textured cardstock, titled in ink "Col. Daniel Kemper. Aug 28-1749-Aug 6 1847 New Brunswick N.J. Bishop Jackson Kemper father," bird's eye maple frame, $475. Photo courtesy of Cowan Historic Americana Auctions.

7-5/8" h, 9-1/2" w, boy and girl, full length, standing facing each other, hollow cut, gilt detail, bird's eye veneer ogee frame **725.00**

8" h, 7" w, husband, wife, baby on knee, grandparents, two children, hollow cut, watercolor and pencil details, black cloth backing, paper professionally cleaned, orig bird's eye maple frames, turned dark wood buttons on corner blocks, five-pc set **9,975.00**

8-1/8" h, 5-1/8" w, hollow cut, full length, man in top hat, old molded pine frame **175.00**

9-3/4" x 7", full length, young gentleman, Augt. Edouart, fecit Saratoga Springs, Aug. 1844, sgd and dated lower left, cut and laid down on lithographed background, matted and framed, tears, minor stain, toning **520.00**

14-3/4" h, 11-7/8" w, full-length cut portrait, gentleman in top hat, frock coat, holding cane, signed in ink "Augst Edouart, fecit 1841," lithographed background has walkway with Romanesaque ruins, matted with gilt frame, some surface wear **1,450.00**

SILVER

History: The natural beauty of silver lends itself to the designs of artists and craftsmen. It has been mined and worked into an endless variety of useful and decorative items. Pure silver is too soft to be fashioned into strong, durable, and serviceable utensils. Therefore, a way was found to give silver the required degree of hardness by adding alloys of copper and nickel.

Silversmithing in America goes back to the early 17th century in Boston and New York and the early 18th century in Philadelphia. Boston artisans were influenced by the English styles, New Yorkers by the Dutch.

References: Louise Belden, *Marks of American Silversmiths in the Ineson-Bissell Collection*, University of Virginia Press, 1980; Frances M. Bones and Lee Roy Fisher, *Standard Encyclopedia of American Silverplate*, Collector Books, 1998; Frederick Bradbury, *Bradbury's Book of Hallmarks*, J. W. Northend, 1987; Stephen G. C. Ensko, *American Silversmiths and Their Marks*, Dover Publications, 1983; Rachael Feild, *Macdonald Guide to Buying Antique Silver and Sheffield Plate*, Macdonald & Co., 1988; Tere Hagan, *Silverplated Flatware*, 4th ed., Collector Books, 1990, 1999 value update; —, *Sterling Flatware*, L-W Book Sales, 1999; Stephen J. Helliwell, *Understanding Antique Silver Plate, Reference and Price Guide*, Antique Collectors' Club; William P. Hood Jr., *Tiffany Silver Flatware, 1845-1905, When Dining Was An Art*, Antique Collectors' Club, 1999; Kenneth Crisp Jones (ed.), *Silversmiths of Birmingham and Their Marks*, N.A.G. Press, 1981, distributed by Antique Collectors Club; Henry J. Kaufman, *Colonial Silversmith*, Astragal Press, 1995; Ralph and Terry Kovel, *Kovels' American Silver Marks*, Crown Publishers, 1989; Daniel Low and Co., *Gold and Silversmiths Catalogue*, 1901, reprinted by Bridgham Antiques, 1998; (Box 28204, San Diego, CA 92198); Everett L. Maffett, *Silver Banquet II*, Silver Press, 1990; Penny C. Morrill and Carole A. Berk, *Mexican Silver: 20th Century Handwrought Jewelry and Metalwork*, 3rd ed., Schiffer Publishing, 2001; Harold Newman, *An Illustrated Dictionary of Silverware*, Thames & Hudson, 2000; Richard Osterberg, *Silver Hollowware for Dining Elegance*, Schiffer Publishing, 1996; —, *Yesterday's Silver Flatware for Today's Table*, Schiffer Publishing, 2001; Ian Pickford, *Jackson's Silver and Gold Marks of England, Scotland & Ireland*, Antique Collectors' Club; —, *Silver Flatware, 1660-1980*, Antique Collectors' Club; Dorothy T. Rainwater, *Encyclopedia of American Silver Manufacturers*, Revised 4th ed., Schiffer Publishing, 1998; Dorothy T. Rainwater and Donna Feiger, *American Silverplate*, 3rd ed., Schiffer Publishing, 2000; *Sterling Silver, Silverplate, and Souvenir Spoons*, revised ed., L-W Book Sales, 1987, 1994 value update; Charles Venable, *Silver in America 1840-1940*, Harry Abrams, 1994; Seymour B. Wyler, *Book Of Old Silver*, Crown Publishers, 1937 (available in reprint).

Periodicals and Internet Resources: *Silver Edition*, 2005 Locust St., Philadelphia, PA 19103-5606; *Silver & Gold Report*, P.O. Box 109665, West Palm Beach, FL 33410, http://www.wessinc.com; *Silver Magazine*, P.O. Box 9690, Rancho Santa Fe, CA 92067, http://www.silvermag.com; *Silver Update* and *Sterling Silver Hollowware Update*, P.O. Box 2157, Ellicott City, MD 21041-2157; *Spratlnig Silver*, http://www.spratlingsilver.com; http://www.smpub.com.

Collectors' Clubs: International Assoc. of Silver Art Collectors, P.O. Box 28415, Seattle, WA 98118-8415; Society of American Silversmiths, P.O. Box 704, Chepatchet, RI 02814, http://www.silversmithing.com.

Museums: Bayou Bend Collection, Houston, TX; Boston Museum of Fine Arts, Boston, MA; Colonial Williamsburg Foundation, Williamsburg, VA; Currier Gallery of Art, Manchester, NH; Dallas Museum of Art, Dallas, TX; Yale University Art Gallery, New Haven, CT; Wadsworth Antheneum, Hartford, CT.

Additional Listings: See Silver Flatware in *Warman's Americana & Collectibles* for more examples.

American, 1790-1840
Mostly coin

Coin silver is slightly less pure than sterling silver. Coin silver has 900 parts silver to 100 parts alloy. Sterling silver has 925 parts silver. American silversmiths followed the coin standards. Coin silver is also called Pure Coin, Dollar, Standard, or Premium.

American, hot water urn, Gorham, cupid finial, putti handle, twin square "C" handles with satyr masks, four raised bust medallions on rim, four flaring feet, original burner, 18-1/4" h, 105 troy oz., $7,850.

Beaker, 3" h, 3" d, top and bottom molded rims, engraved, minor dents, Anthony Rasch, Philadelphia, 1807, 4 troy oz **490.00**

Cake server, 9-1/8" l, George C. Shreve, late 19th C, mark partially rubbed, shaped blade engraved with harbor scene within foliate cartouche, unfurling flag, engine-turned ground, fitted case, 3 troy oz **200.00**

Coffee spoon, John David Jr., Philadelphia, PA, 1795-99, made for Cooch family, monogrammed, one with damage, dents, wear, 5-1/4" l, price for set of eight, 4 troy oz **1,035.00**

Creamer and sugar, 7-3/4" h unmarked creamer, 9-1/2" h sugar with two handles and cover, repoussé dec with vintage pattern, fine form finial and handles, engraved, minor dents, Allcock & Allen, New York City, c1820, 35 troy oz **980.00**

Cream jug, 4-3/4" h, oval form, applied rim, molded base and strap handle, engraved on bottom, minor dents, Joseph Foster, 1760-1839, 8 troy oz **490.00**

Dessert spoon, William Hollingshead, Philadelphia, PA, 1754-85, marked "WH" in shaped stamp, twice on each handle, engraved "KIS," wear to bowls, imperfections, price for set of five, 9 troy oz **490.00**

Ewer

7-5/8" h, Gorham, third quarter 19th C, chased and emb florals and foliage, plain central roundel with serpentine handle topped by flat leaf, low stem, stepped foot, 15 troy oz **435.00**

12" h, ftd, repoussé vintage dec, vine form handle extending round shoulder and around base of both pieces, engraved, minor dents, William F. Ladd, New York City, 1828-45 . . . . **1,200.00**

Ewer and tray, 9-1/4" h ewer, 11-1/4" d tray, Jones, Ball & Poor, Boston, c1845, bulbous ewer with molded rim, neck band, body vertically reeded, stepped circular foot, circular tray with molded rim, face with engraved foliates, modified, both monogrammed . . **550.00**

Forks, 7-3/4" l, stem with applied medallion profile roundel of young woman, engraved details, 11 troy oz, eight-pc set **690.00**

Goblet, 6-1/2" h and 6-3/4" h, Simon Chaudron, Philadelphia, PA, 1812-15, marked "Chaundron" in banner, floriform, raised flutes at base of bowls, applied foliate band on bases, price for pr, 16 troy oz **3,750.00**

Jug, 7" h, J. B. Jones & Co. makers, 2nd quarter 19th C, inverted pear-shaped body, scroll handle and stepped neck, round stepped foot, name engraved under spout, 12 troy oz **700.00**

Knives, 8-1/8" l, third quarter 19th C, medallion profile roundel to end of handle, engraved handle and blade, monogrammed on reverse, 14 troy oz, nine-pc set **920.00**

Mug, 4" h, John L. Westervelt, Newburgh, NY maker, mid-19th C, cylindrical, fine beading to foot and rim, scroll handle, central cartouche engraved with name and dated 1863, engraved Greek key border, all over engine turned ground, 6 troy oz . **200.00**

Pitcher, 8" h, mid-19th C, bulbous, molded rim above engraved band, body with all over repoussé strawberries and vines, weighted circular foot with emb dec, inscription on front and foot **290.00**

Salt, 1-1/2" x 3-1/2", oval form, four hoofed feet, repoussé floral and wreath dec at knees, gold wash bowls, minor dents, Ball, Black & Co., New York City, 1851-76, 7 troy oz, pr **290.00**

Snuff box, stamped "PP," flattened ovoid form, bottom inscribed "I trust this triffle in thy mind will favor find, 1791," imperfections, 1-1/2" x 3-1/2" x 2-5/8", 2 troy oz **1,100.00**

Soup ladle, Simon Chaudron, Philadelphia, PA, 1812-15, marked "Chaundron" in banner, English crest dec, 14-1/2" l, 10 troy oz **920.00**

Sugar bowl, cov, 8" h, Gorham, mid-19th C, squat baluster, stepped foot, wide band of engine-turning, one plain and one engraved cartouche, two serpentine handles, domed lid with flower form finial, 17 troy oz, minor dents **175.00**

Tablespoon, 8" l, front tips, back engraved, bowl with emb scallop shell below short drop handle, minor dents, wear, Samuel Edwards, Boston, 1705-62, 2 troy oz **635.00**

Tea and coffee set, William B. Hever, New York City, 1776-1828, 11" h coffeepot, teapot, cov sugar, creamer, and waste bowl, graduated finial, rect gadrooned body, pedestal with four ball feet, die stamped band on shoulder with rural scenery, single narrow band of anthemion leaves on the finial, upper and lower rims, minor dents, five pcs, 110 troy oz **3,565.00**

American, 1840-1920
Mostly sterling

There are two possible sources for the origin of the word *sterling*. The first is that it is a corruption of the name Easterling. Easterlings were German silversmiths who came to England in the Middle Ages. The second is that it is named for the sterling (little star) used to mark much of the early English silver.

Sterling is 92.5 percent per silver. Copper comprises most of the remaining alloy. American manufacturers began to switch to the sterling standard about the time of the Civil War.

Basket, 9" d, 3" h, Whiting Mfg Co., late 19th C, reticulated, sides with scrolls and diapering, scroll rim, three scroll feet, fluted base, monogrammed, 11 troy oz **460.00**

Bowl

8" d, 2-1/2" h, Black, Starr & Frost, late 19th C, repoussé, chased and emb with flowers and scrolling leaves, applied C-scroll rim, low base, monogrammed, gold washed int., 15 troy oz **350.00**

10-7/8" d, 4-1/2" h, International Silver, early 20th C, fluted bowl, vitruvian scroll band at top, domed base with low concave foot, 28 troy oz **600.00**

11-1/2" d, circular, broad border repoussé with flowers and leaves on fine stippled ground, scroll and foliate border, marked "S. Kirk & Son Sterling, #227," 1903-1925, 18 oz **650.00**

Castor, S. Kirk & Sons, Baltimore, Egyptian Revival, 1861-1868, 5-3/4" h, urn form, domed lid with repoussé leaves, bud form finial, body with three cast loop handles, all over repoussé foliates, three cast sphinx feet, monogram, 4 troy oz **690.00**

Center bowl, 14-1/2" d, Frank W Smith Silver Co., Inc., late 19th C, retailed by Bigelow, Kennard & Co., ovoid, engraved with quilted style pattern, edges reticulated with engraved leafy scrolls, edge with wide cast border of rocaille shells and C-scrolls, monogrammed center, 31 troy oz **1,840.00**

Coffee set, nesting, 7" h, Lebkuecher and Co., Newark, NY, 1896-1909, single serving, three-part set, cov sugar, creamer, pot, two angled wood handles, cylindrical form, bulbous base, flared circular foot, imp maker's mark "Sterling, 02741 5 12 oz," 12 troy oz, repair to handle **375.00**

Compote, 8-3/4" d, 4-1/2" h, Bigelow, Kennard & Co., late 19th C, Etruscan-style, bowl with central roundel of classical man holding grapes, seated woman with baby, dog, beaded surround, engraved anthemion and flowerheads, short stem with single rib to center, trumpet foot, plain flattened loop handles, applied Greek key rim, 22 troy oz **700.00**

Dish, cov, 5-1/2" h, Ball, Tompkins, & Black, New York, 1939, repoussé, ovoid, shaped edge, four scroll and shell feet, domed lid with engraved mottoed crest and initials, ribbed mushroom finial, 19 troy oz **500.00**

Dresser set, International Silver Co., Meriden, CT, early 20th C, cut glass powder jar, hair receiver, three dresser jars, all with sterling lids, pair of cut glass perfume bottles with silver mounted stoppers, hair brush, two clothes brushes, mirror, nail buffer, shoehorn, and nail file, all with engraved and banded rims, monograms **920.00**

Fish Knives, Gorham, Providence, Aesthetic Movement, late 19th C, blades with ornate monograms and bright cut foliates, mixed metal Japanese-style Kozuka handles with molded dec, price for set of 12 . . . . **2,300.00**

Fruit bowl, 12-1/2" d, Dominick & Haff, late 19th/early 20th C, retailed by Shreve, Crump & Low, fluted int., wide reticulated edge with realistically modeled chrysanthemums and daisies, 21 troy oz **1,150.00**

Ice cream slice

10" l, George W. Shiebler & Co., late 19th C, hammered finish, handle with Roman style male medallion on end, engraved bands of classical style designs, gold washed blade with further classical style engraving, medallion to lower right, central horizontal band of further small medallions, monogrammed on back of handle, 6 troy oz **4,025.00**

12-1/4" l, Dominick & Haff, late 19th C, Rococo pattern, retailed by Bigelow, Kennard & Co. monogrammed on back, 6 troy oz **320.00**

Jug, Lewis E. Jenks, Boston, c1875, 10" h, vasiform, shaped lid with cast bird finial, lid and body with all over repoussé foliates, central monogrammed cartouche, spreading circular foot, 17 troy oz **635.00**

American, tea set, Reed and Barton, 11" h teapot, cream pitcher, open sugar, 16" x 10" tray, baluster shape, scroll work cartouches flanked by repoussé floral decoration, applied double scroll handles, $825. Photo courtesy of Alderfer Auction Company, Inc.

Kettle-on-stand

13" h, bombe repoussé all over with flowers and leaves on fine stippled ground, hinged cover with similar dec, floral finial, fixed handle, circular base with conforming dec on four paw feet issuing from foliage, marked "S. Kirk & So., #101," c1903-24, burner marked "JI sterling silver," 56 oz . **2,500.00**

15" h, Ball, Thompkins & Black, third quarter 19th C, bulbous baluster kettle with two horizontal bands of foliate heart-shaped motifs, scroll spout, hinged upright handle, domed lid with squatty ball finial, engraved with mottoed heraldic crest, scroll legs, four rocaille shell feet, 52 troy oz **1,150.00**

Mustard pot, 4-1/2" d, S. Kirk & Son, Baltimore, mid 19th C, vegetal finial, glass liner, 7 troy oz **150.00**

Perfume flask, Dominick & Haff, 9" l, tapered cylindrical, floral chased and emb at lid, neck, and base, wide band of horizontal fluting at center, monogrammed, 5 troy oz **490.00**

Platter, Dominick & Haff, oval, border repoussé with flowers and leaves on fine matted ground, monogrammed, 16 oz **475.00**

Punch bowl and ladle, 14-3/4" d, 8-3/4" h, Gorham, bowl dated 1908, squat ovoid bowl, shaped edge, waterlilies dec, gold-washed int., domed foot, applied water lily dec, engraved with double monogram, names engraved on underside, 15" l ladle with fruiting berry vines, also

monogrammed and dated, 92 troy oz **5,175.00**

Punch ladle, 9-1/2" l, terminal applied with scrolling foliage, monogrammed **100.00**

Roast platter, 20-5/8" l, 14-1/8" w, Gorham, early 20th C, Greek key border **750.00**

Salad serving set, spoon and fork

9" l, Chambord pattern, Reed & Barton, monogrammed, 5 oz, 6 dwt **200.00**

11" l, Love Disarmed pattern, Reed & Barton, 14 oz, 2 dwt **650.00**

Salt, open

3-1/4" l, 1-3/4" h, Black, Starr & Frost, late 19th C, Classical Revival style, ovoid body, hoof feet terminating in lion's heads, red glass liner, 8 troy oz, four-pc set **450.00**

3-3/4" d, 1-1/2" h, Gorham, third quarter 19th C, bucket-shape, three bands of horizontal reeding, two reeded drop handles suspended from flowerhead roundels, small butterflies, frosted glass liner, pr, 6 troy oz . . . **425.00**

Salver, 7-1/4" x 7-1/8", Theodore B. Starr, late 19th C, sq, shaped edge reticulated with scrolls offset with small rocaille shells, pr, 14 troy oz . . . **385.00**

Sauce ladle, Wood & Hughes, New York, second half 19th C, 6-3/4" l, scalloped bowl, beaded handle with portrait medallion of classical warrior, monogrammed on reverse, 1 troy oz **320.00**

Serving dish, cov, Thomas Kirkpatrick, NY, third quarter 19th C, 8-7/8" w, 11-5/8" l, oval, domed lid with beaded band, cast stag finial, emb key pattern and beading on underside of rim, base with similar dec, some loses, 59 troy oz **1,035.00**

Tazza, 7-1/8" d, 2-1/2" h, Howard & Co., dated 1898, vessel with wide reticulated band and applied scroll rim, center monogram, applied scroll base, reticulated foot, pr, 19 troy oz . . **700.00**

Tea and coffee service, S. Kirk & Son, Baltimore, 1880-90, teapot, coffeepot, creamer, cov sugar, waste bowl, kettle on stand, raised repoussé lids with foliage finials, angular handles with ram head mounts, bodies with all over repoussé foliates on stippled ground, knopped stems and circular bases, kettle with cast Asian figure finial and four foliate legs with rose knees, monogrammed, 163 troy oz . . **7,475.00**

Teapot, cov, 9" h, attributed to William Williams, London, 1742, George II, Rococo-style, domed lid with pineapple finial, body with all over repoussé foliates and scrolls, engraved crest on each side, bone scroll handle, molded circular foot, 23 troy oz **2,300.00**

Tea service

Ball, Black & Co., third quarter 19th C, tapered ovoid teapot, cov sugar, helmet-shaped open creamer, each with applied profile medallion and anthemion engraving, pendant handles, monogrammed, 36 troy oz **2,185.00**

Gorham, retailed by Bigelow, Kennard & Co., early 20th C, 5-1/4" h teapot, cov sugar, open creamer, ovoid with reeding, angular handle, reeded lids, monogrammed, 36 troy oz . **575.00**

Shreve, Stanwood & Co., 1860, 16" h hot water urn on stand, creamer, cov sugar, open sugar, and 9" h teapot, ovoid, beaded detailing, lids with swan finials, domed stepped foot, urn with presentation inscription on side, burner and one sugar lid missing, 35 troy oz **2,185.00**

Tea tray, Gorham, Providence, 1912, 17-7/8" w, 25-3/4" l, shaped molded rim, beaded band, pierced handles, monogrammed, 114 troy oz . . **1,725.00**

Tete-a-tete, Gorham, Providence, 1880, 4" h teapot, creamer, open sugar, cone shape, ball finial, reeded handles, banded necks, gilt interiors, monogrammed, 16 troy oz **320.00**

Travel clock, 3-5/8" l, 3-1/8" w, Wm Kerr & Co., late 19th C, plain rect case with rounded corners, eight-day movement, oct goldtone engine-turned face, black Roman numerals, silver surround with engine turning, engraved scrolls and floral sprays, monogrammed cover **200.00**

Tray, Reed & Barton, Taunton, MA, late 19th/early 20th C, 10-1/4" w, 14-1/4" l, rect, shaped molded rim with openwork and engraved band, monogrammed center, 24 troy oz **350.00**

Trophy pitcher, Whiting, New York, Harvard University, c1892, cylindrical, inverted rim, waisted body with inscription on front, circular base with molded scroll dec, 33 troy oz . **1,380.00**

Vase

11-1/4" h, I. N. Deitsch, early 20th C, reticulated tapered body, engraved flowers and leaves, trumpet foot, glass liner **690.00**

13-7/8" h, 6-3/4" d, Bailey, Banks, and Biddle, early 20th C, cylindrical body flaring outward at top, engraved husk swags and flowerheads, monogrammed roundel on one side, engraved inscription on other, slightly everted rim, domed base, 31 troy oz **635.00**

15-3/4" h, J. E. Caldwell & Co., late 19th/early 20th C, tapered baluster form with engraved laurel wreath on each side, one with monogram, everted rim with engraved band of lines and circles, trumpet foot with similarly engraved band, 34 troy oz **750.00**

Vegetable dish, cov, 11" l, Gorham, 1894, shaped oval, wide edge embellished with scrolls and rocaille shells, shallow lid with scroll edge and flat leaf handle, lid monogrammed, 25 troy oz **575.00**

Water pitcher

Dominick & Haff, New York, 20th C, 9" h, vasiform, molded rim, "S" scroll handle, molded base, 22 troy oz **375.00**

Gorham, Providence, 1885, 9-1/4" h, paneled vasiform, rim and base with beaded bands, handle with cast acanthus dec, octagonal molded base, monogrammed, 26 troy oz **635.00**

International Silver Co., Meriden, CT, early 20th C, 6-3/4" h, bulbous, molded rim, "C" scroll handle, monogram, 13 troy oz **250.00**

Arts & Crafts

Hand-crafted silver from the Arts & Crafts period is one of the most sought after types of silver. Wonderful examples can be found, usually with a hammered finish, and proudly displaying maker's marks, etc. Because much research has been done, individual makers in the various studios and shops are known to collectors.

Most pieces have impressed marks. Because the Arts & Crafts movement was international, guilds were located in the United States, Great Britain, Germany, and Austria, creating many forms.

Bowl

4-1/8" d, 2" h, Katherine Pratt, hammered finish, floriform, five petal-like panels, scalloped rim, stepped circular base, engraved initials on one panel, date on base, imp "Pratt, Sterling" **200.00**

7-1/8" d, 1-7/8" h, Kalo Shops, hammered finish, floriform, five petal-like panels, rolled rim, imp "Hand Wrought At The Kalo Shops Chicago and New York, Sterling, 18" **400.00**

8-1/4" d, 3-1/8" h, Arthur Stone, executed by Herbert A. Taylor, 1910-38, circular form, central tooled flower, dot, and engraved line border, circular stepped foot, makers mark "Stone, Sterling," and "T," 18 troy oz, scratches and spotting **1,150.00**

8-7/8" d, 2" h, Kalo, Chicago, circular, seven-sided rolled rim, circular flared ftd base, hammered finish, imp "Sterling Kalo 57" **350.00**

9-1/2" d, 3" h, J. O. R. Randall, hammered, floriform, stamped "J.O.R. Randall/Sterling/Hand-wrought" **500.00**

9-3/4" d, 1-3/4" h, Kalo Shop, Chicago, shallow circular five petaled form, inverted rim, inscribed presentation, base imp "Sterling Kalo M323" **425.00**

Candy dish, 5-1/2" d, 5-3/4" h, Kalo Shop, hammered finish, trumpet base, stamped "Kalo Shops/Park Ridge Ills/Serling" **900.00**

Demitasse spoon, Liberty, set of six, orig leather case, spoons hallmarked, cast stamped "Liberty" **200.00**

Arts & Crafts, pitcher, Kalo, hammered sterling silver, embossed sections, monogrammed, stamped mark, 10-1/2" x 8", $2,600. Photo courtesy of David Rago Auctions, Inc.

Ladle, 8-1/8" h, Kalo Shop, Chicago, hammered finish, notched handle, entwined raised "KP" monogram, imp "Sterling Kalo 8597" **260.00**

Martini pitcher, 9-1/2" h, 7" d, LeBolt, hammered finish, strainer spout, angular handle, die-stamped mark and "LeBolt/Hand Beaten/Sterling 801" **600.00**

Martini spoon, 13-1/2" h, Kalo Shop, Chicago, hammered finish, stamped "Sterling Kalo 243" **200.00**

Pitcher

9" h, 6-1/2" d, Kalo, hammered, sterling, ovoid, stamped "Kalo Sterling/Chicago/New York" **2,415.00**

9-1/8" h, Hamilton, bulbous, beaded rim, neck waisted, twisted ear handle, circular cast foot with beaded rim, applied stylized buds, monogram, 32 troy oz . . . **1,380.00**

Plate, 9-3/4" d, Handicraft Shop, Boston, style of Mary Knight, circular, pinched and emb scrolling floral and leaf design around extended and rolled rim, imp Handicraft Shop mark, "Sterling, 1904" **435.00**

Salt and pepper shakers, pr, Stone Associates, c1937, flattened baluster form, initials engraved on side, imp "Stone" with lower case "h" in shield, "Sterling" and "H" on base, 8 troy oz **460.00**

Serving spoon, 9" l, Th. Marthinsen, Norway, hammered finish bowl, squirrel and acorn motif handle, imp marks, "830S" **375.00**

Tea set, Arthur Stone, Gardner, MA, c1918, teapot, creamer, cov sugar, waste bowl, ivory finials and insulators, leaf detail on spout, bulbous body, initialed "H" for Arthur L. Hartwell, Master Craftsman, engraved with presentees initials and date, 44 troy oz **3,000.00**

Continental

Generations have enjoyed silver created by Continental silversmiths. Expect to find well-executed forms with interesting elements. Most Continental silver is well marked.

Austria-Hungary

Beaker, 3-1/4" h, late 19th C, base with thin beaded rim, engraved with diapering centered by flowerheads with central cartouche with coat of arms **175.00**

Candlesticks, pr, 12-1/2" h, Rococo-style, late 19th C, paneled baluster stem and socket, scrolled

weighted base, removable bobeche, lacquered **690.00**

Casket, mid/late 19th C, 3-3/8" w, 5-1/4" l, rect, lid with cast pear form finial, molded rim and foot, waisted body with silver mount on lock, 14 troy oz **575.00**

Continental

Asparagus server, 11-1/4" l, late 19th C, reticulated handles topped by crowned lion's head, flowerheads and scrolls, standing figure, ending in cherub face above floral basket flanked by cherub herms over reticulation, blades reticulated with C-scrolls and engraved with flowers and further scrolls, monogrammed, 9 troy oz . . **230.00**

Box, cov, 7-1/2" d, 2-3/4" h, late 19th/early 20th C, squatty ovoid, repoussé foliate and scroll banding, hinged lid with floral roundel, 14 troy oz **345.00**

Candelabra, 21-1/2" h, three-light, shaped sq lobed foot with scroll and floral rim rising to fluted stem applied with similar dec, two scrolling foliate branches, central fixed sconce, detachable bobeches, convertible to candlestick, engraved with monogram below crown, weighted base **900.00**

Condiment jar, 4-3/4" h, late 19th/early 20th C, formed as sedan chair, stamped with scrolls and cartouches of dancing couples, hinged lid with quadripartite finial, cobalt blue glass liner, restorations, 5 troy oz **375.00**

Creamer, 5-1/2" l, 4-1/4" h, figural, horned cow, fly hinged lid, 19th C **800.00**

Danish

Child's fork and spoon, 5-7/8" l, each with tapering handle, openwork finials formed as soldier fleeing peasant woman, 2 troy oz . . . **65.00**

Tea and coffee service, Georg Jensen, Johan Rohde, c1915, 45C pattern teapot, 10-1/2" h coffeepot, creamer, cov sugar, 45D pattern milk jug, 45 pattern tea strainer and stand, domed tops with ball finials, reeded handles with beaded terminals, reeded bases, 96 troy oz **13,800.00**

Water pitcher, 9-3/4" h, 20th C, tapered egg-shaped body, flared stem with beading to top, stepped foot, spout with curved reeding to

underside, wooden handle with stylized floral terminal to top **750.00**

Wine coaster, F. Hingelberg, 20th C, 4-3/4" d, molded rim, twisted wire sides, composition base, price for pr **490.00**

Dutch

Bowl, 14-1/4" l, 3" h, 19th C, .833 fine, Dutch export mark, repoussé, lobed, reserves with chased and emb country scenes, two pierced handles with putto to top, central flowers flanked by putto riding dolphins, 15 troy oz **460.00**

Box, late 19th C, .833 silver, 2-5/8" w, 5-1/2" l, rect, shaped lid with engraved nativity scene within foliates, base with two biblical scenes, banded sides with engraved foliates, 8 troy oz **960.00**

Chatelaine, c1890, 12-1/8" l, cast brooch with scene of putti with goddess, medallion mounted chains supporting two boxes, cylindrical container, pair of scissors, stylized crown, 9 troy oz **600.00**

Coffeepot, 8" h, late 19th C, .833 fine, baluster form pot with all over scroll and foliage repoussé, windmill vignette on one side, scroll cartouche topped by crown flanked by putto on other side, legs topped by crowned human masks, four ball and claw feet, turned wood handle set at right angle to ram-horned grotesque spout, flattened lid with vertical ribbing, rampant lion finial, 11 troy oz **800.00**

Pitcher, 5-1/2" h, late 19th C, .833 line, baluster form, neck with band of fluting, repoussé to lower section of foliage, birds and putti, domed foot with vertical ribbing, spout with putto, beaded serpentine handle, lid with vertical reeding, repoussé and vegetal finial, base engraved "Esther Cleveland," 6 troy oz, descended in family of Grover Cleveland **260.00**

French, .950 fine

Coffeepot, 8-1/2" h, Louis XVI, Bourdeaux, late 18th C, pear-shaped, scroll legs ending in plain cartouches, three hoof feet, turned wood handle in silver socket set at right angle to short fluted spout, domed hinged lid with scroll thumbpiece and flower finial, monogrammed, 22 troy oz **1,725.00**

Coffeepot, 9-1/4" h, third quarter 19th C, pear-shaped, cast quadripartite scroll embellished serpentine spout and handle, heat stops, domed lid with flower form finial, 22 troy oz **460.00**

Dish, cov, undertray, Paris, 1819-38, "C. P." maker's mark, cylindrical body with acanthus and flat leaf handles, rim with beading and flat leaf band, base with band of flat leaves, foot with band of laurel, lid with beaded edge, removable circular handle formed as cornucopia on leaf and flower base, fitted leather case, 30 troy oz **2,615.00**

Fish serving platter, 27-3/4" l, 11-1/2" w, oval, reeded rim, monogrammed, 66 troy oz **1,265.00**

Serving dish, 11-3/4" l, 2-1/4" h, third quarter 19th C, oval, two shell handles, vertical reeded border, 17 troy oz **490.00**

Sweetmeat dish, 5-1/2" l, 5" h, Odiot, Paris, maker, late 19th/20th C, shell form vessel drawn by sea creatures, reins held by two putti, flanking central standing putto poised as Neptune, holding trident-form fork, shaped rect base cast as water, 65 troy oz, pr **2,100.00**

Tray, 17-3/8" l, 13" w oval, late 19th C, partially obscured maker's mark, beaded edge, engraved initial in center, 34 troy oz **575.00**

Tureen, cov, 12-3/4" l, 10-1/2" h, third/fourth quarter 19th C, sprays of acorns and oak leaves to top, reeded rim, lid with flat leaf rim, stem with reeded shoulder, oval foot, flat leaf band, angular handles with flat leaf to bottom, stylized corn finial about flat leaf and lotus ground **1,840.00**

Wine taster, late 19th C, .950 fine, inset with crest to handle ... **125.00**

German, .800 fine

Basket, 14" l, shaped oval, paneled sides pierced with flowers, garlands, and scrolling foliage centering four vacant cartouches, center repoussé with flowers, foliage, and three putti at play, 15 oz, 8 dwt **200.00**

Beaker and underplate, 2-1/2" h cup, 5-7/8" d underplate, cylindrical cup stamped with cartouches of courting couples, everted rim, gold-washed int., plates with foliage and scroll rim, well for cup, monogrammed, 14 troy oz, pr **375.00**

Box, 3-3/8" w, 4-1/4" l, 20th C, rect, hinged lid, sides and lid emb with foliates and scrolls, lid mounted with cast saddled horse, gilt int., 9 troy oz, some loss to gilt ... **690.00**

Compote, 7-3/8" l, 6" h, late 19th C, four putto perm flanked by husk swags supporting ovoid reticulated body with winged putto, scrolls, swags, and foliate baskets, ovoid base with band of stamped scrolls and shells, monogrammed cartouche, clear glass liner, 34 troy oz, pr **1,850.00**

Kettle-on-stand, 16" h, compressed circular with lobed sides, four hoof feet, detachable cover with wooden finial, central swing partial wooden handle, multi-scroll stand with border, 48 oz, 8 dwt .. **325.00**

Sauceboat, late 19th/early 20th C, 10-3/4" l, shape of open-mouthed fish, emb and engraved scales, open back with molded rim, tail shape handle, supported by cast fins, glass eyes, 13 troy oz **1,495.00**

Serving dish, 12" d, 3-1/2" h, Wilhelm T. Binder, c1900, rounded trefoil shape, three handles, repoussé leaf bud and line dec, scalloped, ribbed glass insert, imp "WTB, 800 fine" **1,150.00**

Wedding cup, 9" h, figural, beaded figure with chased and emb skirt, cup chased and emb with scrolls and grotesques, 15 troy oz **1,955.00**

Italian

Asparagus tongs, F. Broggi, Milan 20th C, 5-1/4" l, individual, plain, tapered form, set of six, 6 troy oz **115.00**

Punch bowl, 12-5/8" d, 10-1/2" h, late 19th/early 20th C, repoussé, bowl with band of flat leaves to base below further continuous hunt scene of men attacking various animals, domed foot with band of flat leaves below continuous hunt scene, removable liner, 146 troy oz **4,025.00**

Portuguese, .833 silver

Bowl, Oporto, 20th C, 11-3/4" d, molded scroll and shell rim, band of chased dec, molded circular foot, 14 troy oz **230.00**

Chalice, 12-1/2" h, domed lid with applied openwork foliate band, engraved bands and cruciform finial, bowl with engraved band with Latin inscription, applied gothic style openwork mounts, stem with beaded and engraved knop, stepped circular base, int. gilt, 31 troy oz **690.00**

Ewer, maker's mark "S&P," late 19th/early 20th C, 11-3/4" h, bulbous, molded shaped rim, body with chased stippled dec, emb foliate, scroll, and shell band, cast scroll handle, molded circular foot with emb dec, 33 troy oz ... **815.00**

Kettle-on-stand, maker's mark effaced, second half 19th C, 14-1/4" h, inverted pear form, domed lid with cased foliates and wood urn finial, upright handle with cast silver acanthus mounts, body with all over chased and engraved foliates and scrolls, circular stand with four scroll legs and shell feet, chased and engraved burner with turned wood handle, 54 troy oz **920.00**

Salver, 11-5/8" d, molded openwork scroll and foliate rim, bright cut foliate dec on face, three cast legs with shell feet, 25 troy oz ... **350.00**

Tongs, Oporto, late 19th/early 20th C, 12-1/4" l, one openwork and one shovel form pincer, cast scroll handles, 7 troy oz **290.00**

Tray, maker's mark "GP," 20th C, 13-1/2" w, 22-5/8" l, rect, openwork raised rim with molded grape dec, cast foliate handles, face with engraved dec, 85 troy oz **1,265.00**

Viennese, cane handle, 4-3/4" l, Franz Hiess & Son, late 19th C, eagle form, realistically modeled as head of eagle, glass eyes, tapering to rocaille scroll handle, monogrammed **500.00**

English

From the 17th century to the mid-19th century, English silversmiths set the styles which inspired the rest of the world. The work from this period exhibits the highest degree of craftsmanship. English silver is actively collected in the American antiques marketplace.

Basket

6" d, 3-1/2" h, J. R. Hennell maker, London, 1884, Victorian, reticulated foliate pattern, circular banding, shaped edge with bead and flat leaf rim, four scroll and cylinder feet with husk swags, glass liner, 21 troy oz, pr **1,725.00**

10" d, 7-3/4" h, maker's mark partially rubbed, London, 1911, applied scroll and floral rim, trumpet-form basket with similar reticulation, spreading base reticulated with scrolls, reticulated swing handle, 25 troy oz **1,610.00**

Berry spoon, George III, marks partially obscured, later engraving, chasing and embossing, pr. . . . **200.00**

Bowl, 5-1/4" d, 1-1/2" h, W. Comyns & Sons maker, London, 1902, Edward VII, shallow bowl emb with shield-shaped panels, hand-hammered surface, low flower form foot, 7 troy oz **435.00**

Candelabra, pr, 12-1/2" h, maker attributed to Stephen Smith, London, 1875, Victorian, Renaissance Revival-style, convertible, two foliage scroll and foliate candle arms each with flat leaf nozzle, foliate and acorn finial between arms, stem and foot with stamped foliage, masks, and herms, applied openwork scroll detailing to stem, round foot raised on three scroll feet, small engraved device on foot, 59 troy oz, pr. **4,600.00**

Castor

Attributed to Jabez Daniel, London, 1750, George II, pear shape, pierced domed lid, should banded, spreading circular foot, 2 troy oz, 4" h, restorations. **230.00**

Hester Bateman, London, 1788, George III, urn form, engraved pierced lid with cast urn finial, engraved bands at shoulder, waist, and spreading circular foot, 2 troy oz, 5-3/4" h **690.00**

Caudle cup

4-3/4" h, makers mark "LG," also marked "Lamber Coventry St.," London, 1894, cylindrical, lower body repoussé with alternating leaves, two scroll handles, gilt int., 9 oz. **250.00**

6" h, 10-1/2" l, Samuel Wastell maker, London, 1704, William III, Brittania Standard, tapered cylindrical body with single applied molded band, cast ear-shaped handles, spreading domed foot, engraved on one side, heraldic device in rococo-style cartouche, 26 troy oz **2,990.00**

English, teapot, repoussé, all over flowers and scrolls, maker "ICWR," hallmarked, 1823, $625. Photo courtesy of Joy Luke Auctions.

Center bowl, 17" l, 5-1/2" h, Robert Garrard, London, 1811, George III, lobed ovoid body, two short scroll and acanthus handles, gadroon and shell border offset with two scroll details to each side, four cast paw feet topped by group of scrolls, 51 troy oz. . . **4,325.00**

Chamberstick, 4" l, 1-3/4" h, W. Comyns maker, London, 1888, Victorian, chased and emb with flowers and scrolls, removable bobeche, handle with monogrammed thumb-piece, 2 troy oz **115.00**

Charger, 11-3/4" d, Rebecca Emes and Edward Barnard, London, 1826, George IV, shaped edge, applied gadroon and shell border, engraved gartered heraldic device on rim, 29 troy oz **1,380.00**

Chop tongs, maker's mark "WE," George III, 4 troy oz, 9-1/2" l . . . **350.00**

Coaster, 4-3/8" d, Edward VII, Birmingham, 1904, "W.H.H." maker's mark, round, inset to center with George III Irish 10-pence bank tokens dated 1905, 4 troy oz, pr **115.00**

Coffeepot

11-1/2" l, 8-7/8" h, Robert Hennell maker, London, 1806, George III, partially reeded oblong body, fruitwood loop handle, oval trumpet foot, partially reeded lid, replaced finial, 35 troy oz **750.00**

14-1/2" h, William Grundy maker, London, 1767, George III, baluster, spreading foot, scroll handle with ivory heat stops, serpentine spout with rocaille shell to base, flat leaf to spout, engraved monogram within foliate rococo-style cartouche, domed hinged lid with spiral reeded egg-shaped finial, 60 troy oz **5,750.00**

Compote, 12-1/2" d, 7" h, Benjamin Smith maker, London, 1845, Victorian, bowl with shaped edge and vertical ribbing, everted rim with applied grapevine dec, tree-trunk form base with twining grapevine, 36 troy oz **1,150.00**

Creamer, 2-7/8" h, Paul Storr, London, 1831, William IV, tapered cylindrical, short spout, scroll handle with shell terminal, applied stepped base, monogrammed, side marked "Storr & Mortimer". **200.00**

English, candlesticks, William Café, London hallmarks for 1758-59, each engraved on underside of base "The Gift of Eliz. Sauvaire to her grandson Thos. De Jersey 1759," 8-1/4" h, pair, $5,950. Photo courtesy of Garth's Auctions, Inc.

Cream jug, 5-1/4" h, Hester Bateman, London, 1782, George III, vasiform, chased beaded rim, body with repoussé farm scenes surrounding central cartouche, trumpet foot with spreading rim, 3 troy oz, restoration **225.00**

Cup, 5-5/8" h, Samuel Godbeheve, Edward Wigan and J. Bolt makers, London, 1800, George III, baluster form, two handles, four drill holes in base, 11 troy oz **490.00**

Demitasse spoon, 5" l, John Wren maker, London, 1791, George III, bright cut engraved stem, fluted bowl, 3 troy oz, set of six **260.00**

Dish cross, 12" l, "BD" maker's mark, (Burrage Davenport), London, 1772, George III, pierced shell form feet and plate supports, burner with gadrooned rim, 15 troy oz **1,265.00**

Egg cup frame, Henry Nutting maker, London, 1800, George III, reeded central handle, four ball feet, six associated Sheffield egg cups, five associated demitasse spoons, 18 troy oz **550.00**

Entree dish, cov, 12-1/8" l, 5-3/4" h, "BS" makers mark, London, 1820, George IV, lid modified with later band of foliate repoussé and engraved with heraldic crest and monograms, base with gadroon and shell rim, removable leaf and shell handle, 67 troy oz **1,725.00**

Epergne, 10-1/2" l, 11-3/4" h, "GJ DF" maker's mark, London, 1913, George V, central stem below navette-shaped reticulated basket with applied border, flanked by smaller removable baskets on scrolled arms, ovoid reticulated base with applied scroll and shell border, four scroll feet, 76 troy oz **6,325.00**

Fish server, 11-1/4" l, attributed to John Neville, London, 1770, George III, reticulated blade with scrolling foliage, stem end with shell, handle, engraved with gadrooned edge, central heraldic device, 4 troy oz **1,100.00**

Goblet
   6-1/2" h, maker's mark partially obscured (attributed to Henry Greenway), London, 1775, George II, beaded collar, tapered round funnel bowl, beaded trumpet foot, engraved coat of arms in roundel, 16 troy oz, pr **1,955.00**
   7" h, Daniel Pontifex maker, London, 1801, George III, tapered ovoid bowl stamped with flat leaves to

lower section, octagonal panel shaping above, plain wide rim, tapered stem with collar, ribbed trumpet foot, octagonal base, gilt washed int., 21 troy oz, pr **1,150.00**

Hot water kettle on stand, 12" h, John Emes maker, London, 1807, George III, lid partially reeded with wood finial, pot with ovoid body partially reeded with gadrooned edging, on tapered circular foot, fluted tap, upright silver and wood handle, stand with gadrooned rim with burner and cover, flat leaf legs, four hairy paw feet with wooden ball supports, pot engraved with mottoed coat of arms, small heraldic device on pot lid, burner lid, and burner, 83 troy oz **2,100.00**

Jug, cov, 7-3/4" h, "C. W." maker's mark, London, 1769, George III, later Victorian adaptations, stamped bands flanking convex band at rim, ovoid body with twisted reeding and fluting to lower section, central cartouche flanked by C-scrolls, serpentine handle, domed foot, short spout, domed hinged lid with Victorian hallmarks, twisted reeding, fluting on urn finial, 18 troy oz .. **400.00**

Meat skewer, 13" l, William Chawner, London, 1829, George IV, King's pattern, molded dec, engraved crest, 4 troy oz **230.00**

Mirror, 14-1/4" h, 10" d, "JR SJ" makers, London, 1887, Victorian, rect, curved top, reticulated with scrolls and flowers, mask center at base, grotesque beasts on either corner, beveled edge mirror, easel stand on back **980.00**

Muffineer
   6-3/4" h, Charles Stuart Harris maker, Brittania standard marks, London, 1894, lid with three-tiered finial, cylindrical body with twisted banding, domed foot, 7 troy oz **290.00**
   8-1/2" h, Charles Stuart Harris maker, Brittania standard marks, London, 1899, tapered paneled lid with engraving, baluster form finial, paneled baluster form, tiered foot, 14 troy oz **800.00**

Mug, Richard Beale, London, 1731, George II, cylindrical, cast "S" scroll handle, molded circular foot, engraved crest, 6 troy oz, 3-3/4" h **980.00**

Mustard pot, attributed to William Barrett II, 1827, George III, circular, disk finial, reeded rim and base, reticulated sides with engraved foliates and urns,

associated glass insert, 3 troy oz, 2-1/2" h **290.00**

Salt, open
   2-1/4" d, circular, London, 1787, Georgian, molded banded rim, three pad feet, monogrammed, cobalt blue glass liner, 4 troy oz, price for set of four **375.00**
   2-3/4" d, circular, Georgian, emb foliate dec, three legs, scalloped rim, pad feet, marks rubbed **100.00**

Salver
   9-3/4" l, 7" w, John Crouch & Thomas Hannan, London, 1813, George III, oval, banded molded rim, face with engraved band, central engraved coat of arms, four molded feet, 12 troy oz **915.00**
   11" d, Thomas Hannan & John Crouch, London, 1766, George III, lobed circular, molded rim with gadrooned edge, three scroll legs with paw feet, engraved coat of arms in center, 24 troy oz **1,380.00**
   12-1/4" d, attributed to Ebenezer Coker, London, 1762, George III, shaped molded edge with reeded scroll and shell border, engraved center monogram within scroll and shell cartouche, three hairy ball and claw feet, each entwined with lion's tail, 30 troy oz..... **2,070.00**
   12-3/8" d, John Tuite maker, London, 1783, George II, shaped molded rim offset with shells, central engraved coat of arms in rococo cartouche, four scrolled leaf feet, 32 troy oz **2,185.00**
   16-1/4" d, John Cotton & Thomas Head maker, London, 1813, George III, beaded and ribbed border, four beaded and ribbed feet, center engraved with mottoed coat of arms, 64 troy oz . **3,750.00**
   17-1/4" d, Mappin & Webb makers, London, 1946, shaped edge with bead shell border, four scrolled feet, 60 troy oz **1,610.00**
   22-7/8" h, Robert Abercomby maker, London, 1750, George II, shaped edge, engraved with wide band of florals, fruits, shells, scrolls, and diapered cartouches, four paw feet topped by shells, engraved central Chinoiserie-style coat of arms, 156 troy oz **4,320.00**

Sauce boat, 7-3/8" l, 5" h, George III, London, 1763, no maker's mark, shaped edge, flying scroll handle, engraved initials on one side, three hoof

feet topped by shells, 11 troy oz
. . . . **550.00**

Sauce tureen, cov, 9-1/4" l, 5-1/2" h, George Smith and Thomas Hayter makers, London, 1804, George III, domed lid with urn finial, boat shaped body with ribbed rim, loop handles, pedestal foot, lid and body monogrammed, 33 troy oz, pr
. . . . **2,760.00**

Serving spoon, 11-3/4" l, William Eley and William Fearn, London, 1818, George III, engraved crest, 3 oz, 6 dwt
. . . . **175.00**

Soup tureen, cov, 14-1/2" l, 10-1/4" h, William Elliott maker, London, 1819, George III, gadrooned rim, acanthus handles, four paw feet terminating in shell and acanthus leaves, lid with two bands of gadrooning and ribbed removable handle, engraved coat of arms on body and lid, 136 troy oz
. . . . **7,475.00**

Standish, 11-3/8" l, 7-1/2" w, J. C. Vickery maker, London, 1906, Edward VII, rect, reeded border, two horizontal pen wells, two tapered inkwells with canted corners and hinged lids, central ovoid covered well, hinged lid fitted with eight-day clock, four ball and claw feet, some restoration needed, 32 troy oz
. . . . **2,100.00**

Sugar basket, 5-1/2" l, 3-1/2" w, Peter & Ann Bateman, London, 1798, George III, navette shape, molded banded rim and swing handle, engraved body with reticulated bands, banded oval foot, monogrammed, cobalt glass insert, 3 troy oz **920.00**

Sugar bowl, 6" l, 5-3/8" h, Georgian, marks rubbed, beaded rim, ovoid body with ribbon-tied floral sprays and swags, roundels on each side, heraldic device, spiraled loop handles, trumpet foot with bands of bright cut engraving, 5 troy oz **350.00**

Sugar tongs, Georgian, cast with shell, foliage, scrolls engraved with flowers, center vacant cartouche, 1 oz, 2 dwt
. . . . **95.00**

Sweetmeat dish, 9-1/8" l, 5-5/8" w, 2-1/4" h, R & S Garrard maker, London, 1879, ovoid, flanked by male and female figure, auricular scroll and stylized shell handle, four periwinkle shell feet, 13 troy oz **1,495.00**

Tablespoon, 8-3/4" l, William Eley, London, 1826, George IV, fiddle pattern, monogrammed, pr, 6 troy oz
. . . . **200.00**

Tankard, 7-3/4" h, John Longlands I maker, Newcastle, 1769, George III, tapered cylindrical form, plain body with engraved cartouche, serpentine handle with reticulated thumb-piece, gadrooned foot rim, slightly domed lid with gadrooned rim, engraved presentation inscription, lacquered, 26 troy oz **1,265.00**

Tapersticks, pr, 4-1/4" h, Jas. Gould maker, London, 1737, George II, flattened knop, paneled step with ribbed shoulder, plain sconce, shaped stepped base, nozzles not present, 7 troy oz **1,035.00**

Tazza, 7-3/4" d, 3-1/4" h, Charles Stuart Harris maker, London, 1902, Edward VII, body with gadrooned rim and stamped border of faces and Chinoiserie-style motifs, tapered stem, domed foot stamped with band of foliage dec, center monogrammed, 14 troy oz **385.00**

Teapot

5" h, attributed to Augustus Le Sage, London, 1771, George III, cylindrical, disc finial, wood ear handle, engraved antelope crest on lid and side, 13 troy oz
. . . . **1,100.00**

5-1/2" h, Andrew Fogelberg, London, 1796, George III, ovoid, domed lid with wood finial, body with engraved foliate bands, wood ear handle, 16 troy oz, restorations
. . . . **550.00**

6-1/4" h, George Smith & Thomas Hayter, London, 1796, George III, fluted ovoid, engraved domed lid, bone mushroom finial and handle, engraved foliates and central crest, 15 troy oz, restorations **525.00**

Teapot stand, 7" l, Robert & David Hennell, London, 1795, Georgian, oval with beveled corners, molded rim engraved, face with engraved and bright cut foliate bands, central cartouche, four feet, 5 troy oz, 4-7/8" w
. . . . **435.00**

Tea and coffee service, Rebecca Eames & Edward Barnard, London, 1814-15, George III, 8-3/4" h coffeepot with gadrooned pedestal, teapot, creamer, open sugar, sq bulbous form, emb lids with cast foliate finials, molded gadrooned rims, bodies with bands of spiral reeding, four ball feet, 73 troy oz
. . . . **2,300.00**

Tea service

7-3/4" h teapot, Peter, Ann, and William Bateman makers, London,

1800, George III, ovoid teapot, helmet shaped cov creamer with angular handle, cov sugar with angular handles, all with partial vertical lobing, bands of bright cut engraving and engraved heraldic device, wooden pineapple finials, 33 troy oz **1,495.00**

9" h coffeepot, 16" h kettle on stand, Crichton Bros. makers, London, 1930, George V, coffee and teapots, kettle on stand, creamer, open sugar, cov sugar, all with ovoid body, arcaded and ribbed banding, teapot and coffeepot with wooden handles topped with silver flat leaves, lion's head roundels, reamer and sugar with curved handles terminating in lion's head roundels, 174 troy oz **2,990.00**

Tea urn, 15" h, maker's mark "I. R.," London, 1778, lid with tapered egg-shaped finial, beaded tape with ivory handle, beaded loop handles, four ball feet with stepped rect base and beaded edge, bright cut engraving throughout with husks, cartouches, and floral swags, 37 troy oz **2,100.00**

Tray

25" l, 16-1/4" w, "EB" makers mark, London, 1822, George IV, rect, gadrooned border, handles with shells and leaves, four paw feet flanked by floral roundels and stylized wings, engraved allover pattern of flowers and leaves, center with mottoed crest and later monogram, 120 troy oz . . **2,760.00**

25-1/2" l, 15-5/8" w, "IM" makers mark, London, 1817, George III, rect, gadrooned edge, handles terminating in stylized feathers, four gadrooned feet, engraved with wide band of florals, fruits, scrolls, and diapered cartouches, center with mottoed coat of arms, 104 troy oz, restoration **2,415.00**

Waxjack, 6-1/2" h, attributed to Augustus Le Sage, London, third quarter 18th C, George III, cast handles, attached snuffer, spindle with spirally reeded bud form finial, domed base with beaded rim, supported by three cast claw and ball feet, inscription on base, 4 troy oz **980.00**

Wine coaster, 5-3/4" d, 2-3/4" h, Joseph and John Angel makers, London, 1846, Victorian, applied scroll and shell rim, reticulated sides, engraved to base with scrolls, shells, and central heraldic crest, pr **5,465.00**

Irish

Fine examples of Irish silver are becoming popular with collectors.

Candlesticks, pr, George III/IV, Dublin, attributed to John Laughlin, Jr., larger gadrooned knob over gadrooned knob below partially vertically reeded stem with single horizontal beaded band, well with applied stylized wheat or grass fronds, domed gadrooned base, vertically reeded sconce, removable nozzle with gadrooned rim, small heraldic crest engraved on foot and nozzle, 49 troy oz **7,475.00**

Caudle cup, cov, 7-1/4" h, Dublin, mid-18th C, marked for John Hamilton, domed lid topped by ovoid finial, body with single molded band, crabstock handles, lobed spreading foot, no date mark, 37 troy oz, pr. **5,175.00**

Cup, 4-7/8" h, mid-18th C, marked for John Letabliere, tapered cylindrical body with leaf cut card work, band of foliate engraving, domed spreading foot, scroll handles topped with flat leaves, engraved on one side with cartouche, no date marks, 44 troy oz, pr **5,465.00**

Salver, 6-1/2" l, George II/III, Dublin, William Townsend maker, shaped molded border, engraved center with heraldic crest in rococo cartouche, three pad feet with scroll legs, 8 troy oz **1,100.00**

Snuffer tray, George III, Dublin, 1798, William Doyle maker, octagonal boat shape, base with bright-cut engraved husk drops, heraldic crest within roundel flanked by leaves, sides reticulated with arcading, paterae, 4 troy oz. **700.00**

Soup ladle, 13" l, John Power, Dublin, 1791, reeded bowl, engraved lozenge handle, 5 troy oz. **435.00**

Scottish

Not to be outdone by their Irish and English neighbors, Scottish silversmiths also created fine objects.

Berry spoon, Edinburgh, 1820, George Fenwick maker **75.00**

Punch ladle 13-1/2" l, Edinburgh, 1789, maker's mark "CD," 6 troy oz **300.00**

14-1/2" l, Edinburgh, 1820, maker's mark "AH," ovoid bowl, twisted baleen handle, silver end cap **150.00**

Sheffield, English

Sheffield silver, or Old Sheffield Plate, has a fusion method of silver-plating that was used from the mid-18th century until the mid-1880s, when the process of electroplating silver was introduced.

Sheffield plating was discovered in 1743, when Thomas Boulsover of Sheffield, England, accidentally fused silver and copper. The process consisted of sandwiching a heavy sheet of copper between two thin sheets of silver. The result was a plated sheet of silver, which could be pressed or rolled to a desired thickness. All Sheffield articles are worked from these plated sheets.

Most of the silver-plated items found today marked "Sheffield" are not early Sheffield plate. They are later wares made in Sheffield, England.

Basket, 7-3/4" w, 13-3/4" l, S. Smith & Son, England, second half 19th C, oval, molded foliate rim, emb and reticulated sides, cast foliage handles, oval reticulated and engraved base, cobalt blue glass liner **460.00**

Carving set, 16-1/2" l, fork, knife, and steel, engraved image of Windsor Castle on knife blade, horn handles, silver plated crown finials, leathered case, late 19th C **350.00**

Claret jug, 11" h, cut glass body mounted at neck, hinged cover, baluster finial, multi-scroll foliate handle, c1943S. **500.00**

Domed lid, 22" h, 11" l, engraved armorial whippet, oval handle, early 19th C **575.00**

Sheffield, teapot, warming stand, **$625.** *Photo courtesy of Joy Luke Auctions.*

Flatware service, Hanover pattern, William Hutton & Sons, England, late 19th C, service for six plus ladle, carving set, stuffing spoon, brass mounted wood case. **550.00**

Plate, 9-3/4" d, circular, gadrooned rim, engraved Carlill crest, George III, price for pr. **175.00**

Platter and meat cover, 26" l oval tree platter, four ball feet, two wooden handles, gadrooned rim, armorials on both sides, dome cover with gadrooned rim, reeded handles, engraved armorials. **2,750.00**

Serving dish, cov, England, first half 19th C, rect, gadrooned rim and lid, cast branch and maple leaf handle, engraved coat of arms, 11-1/2" l, 8-5/8" w. **230.00**

Tantalus, England, late 19th/early 20th C, central casket with two engraved hinged lids below handle, sides supporting two cut and pressed glass decanters, pedestal base supported by four column legs, 5-3/4" w, 15" l . **490.00**

Vegetable dish, cov, 13" l, plated, shaped rect, applied grapevine, scroll, and foliage handle, monogrammed **250.00**

Wax jack bougie box, 3-1/2" h, cylindrical, pierced dec, flat detachable top, reeded loop handle, snuffer attached by chain **300.00**

Wine bottle holder, 16" l, wooden base, vintage detail, ivory casters **275.00**

Silver, plated

Englishmen G. R. and H. Elkington are given credit for being the first to use the electrolytic method of plating silver in 1838.

An electroplated-silver article is completely shaped and formed from a base metal and then coated with a thin layer of silver. In the late 19th century, the base metal was Britannia, an alloy of tin, copper, and antimony. Other bases are copper and brass. Today, the base is nickel silver.

In 1847, Rogers Bros. of Hartford, Connecticut, introduced the electroplating process in America. By 1855, a number of firms were using the method to produce silver-plated items in large quantities.

The quality of the plating is important. Extensive polishing can cause the base metal to show through. The prices for plated-silver items are low, making them popular items with younger collectors.

Bun warmer, 12-1/2" l, oval, cover chased with flowers and foliage, beaded rim, paw feet, liner, two reeded handles. **275.00**

Candelabra, pr, 12" h, Continental, three-light, tapering stem issuing central urn-form candle-cup and two scrolling branches supporting wax pan and conforming candle-cup, oval foot with reeded border, vertical flutes
. . . . **150.00**

Candlesticks, pr

7-1/2" h, Wurtembergishe Metallwarenfabrik, sq base applied with bow-tie garlands and foliage, rim with stylized leaves and beads rising to Corinthian column stems, detachable bobeches with beaded rims. **375.00**

14" h, English Regency-style, late 19th C, flat leaf socket, fluted standard, three monopodia supports offset with anthemion
. . . . **550.00**

Claret jug

9-1/2" h, eagle-form, textured cranberry glass body with realistic silver plate head and feet, set with glass eyes, hinged at neck, clear draw handle, Continental, early 20th C. **460.00**

14" h, Elkington & Co., Birmingham, England, late 19th C, tapered cylindrical body, domed lid with emb cherubs and foliate finial, neck with emb classical horseman, cut glass body with all over cut stars, silver plate foot with key pattern band. **425.00**

Coffee urn

Continental, 19-1/2" h, vase form, body and lid fluted in sections, acanthus-capped handles, reeded spigot, sq pedestal base with ball feet **375.00**

Victorian, 16" h, baluster shape, repoussé grapevines centering two vacant cartouches, two handles in form of branch applied with similar dec, circular base pierced with scrolls at internals on four scroll, foliate, and beaded supports, detachable cover, grapevine finial
. . . . **125.00**

Egg cup, 2-3/4" h, England, early 20th C, stems formed as cast kangaroos resting in circular underplates, price for pr **100.00**

Epergne

8-1/8" h, England, late 19th/early 20th C, tripartite base with central ring supporting bulbous bowl with ruffled rim, three serpentine arms with ball terminals supporting bud

vases with similar ruffled rims
. . . . **165.00**

16-1/2" h, English or America, second half 19th C, four branches with cut glass bowls surrounding central large bowl, all over emb and cast acanthus leaf and foliate dec, stem with petal shape knops, cruciform pedestal base supported by four acanthus feet, minor losses
. . . . **2,100.00**

21-1/2" h, English, late 19th/early 20th C, central trumpet form vase with banded rim and shell motifs, three smaller vases, gilt tripartite shell-shaped dish, three cast dolphin feet **750.00**

Fish set, English, late 19th C, six forks, six knives with engraved blades, mother-of-pearl handles, wood case
. . . . **320.00**

Flatware service, Marly pattern, Christofle, France, 20th C, service for 12 . . . . **990.00**

Game platter, 16" h, 26-1/2" l, English, late 19th C, well and three-platter base with attached hot water pan, raised on four medallion-capped feet, associated domed cov with beaded bands and engraved wide border of entwined circlets, applied open handle surrounded by conforming engraved dec, body with engraved griffin
. . . . **700.00**

Garniture, 6-1/4" h ftd compote with repoussé floral and foliate bands, each side pc with conforming dec, Tiffany & Co. **350.00**

Inkwell, 11-1/2" h, England or America, 20th C, fence form, central fence supporting two urn form candle sconces, ends with three stakes bearing square cut glass inkwells with silver plated lids **195.00**

Monteith cooler, attributed to England, late 19th C, oval, shaped rims and cast loop handles, 7-3/4" w, 13" l, price for pr
. . . . **815.00**

Punch cup, Lavigne, 1881 Rogers
. . . . **25.00**

Sandwich box, 5-3/4" h, 4-1/8" h, English, early 20th C, rect, loop handle, hinged lid monogrammed, gilt int., leather carrying case **80.00**

Snuff box, 2-3/4" l, English, late 19th C, foliate scroll engraved lid, set with central faceted purple stone, cowry shell body. **300.00**

Teapot, presentation type, 7" d, Mackay Cunningham & Co., Edinburgh, late 19th C, realistically modeled as curling

stone, lid with bone and faux ivory handle, engraved reeded band on sides, engraved inscription, tapered circular silver plated stand **375.00**

Toast rack, 7" l, 2-5/8" w, England, late 19th/early 20th C, oval, central ring handle above cast cricket ball, rack formed as crossed cricket bats, four ball feet **90.00**

Tray, 32" l, Victorian, oval, field engraved with floral and diaper medallions flanked by foliage with foliate garlands at intervals, beaded and geometrical design border and handles **350.00**

Sheffield, plated

Englishmen G. R. Elkington and H. Elkington are given credit for being the first to use the electrolytic method of plating silver in 1838.

Plated, vase, white irid glass vase, silver plated holder with three-dimensional French Revolutionary War couple, square base, made by Derby, c1880, 8-5/8" h, $160.

Candlesticks, pr

9" h, telescopic, circular base, gadrooned band rising to tapered cylindrical stem, vasiform scones, detachable bobeche with gadrooned rim, c1800 . . . . **475.00**

24" h, ornate columns with composite capitals, pale blue blown glass hurricane shades with cut floral designs **425.00**

Entree dish

11" x 8", shaped rect, gadrooned rim, detachable handle with gadroon dec **75.00**

14-1/2" l, shaped oval, grapevines applied at rim and cover, detachable branch form handle **100.00**

Hot water urn, 22-3/4" h, early 19th C, Philip Ashberry & Sons makers, urn-form body with flat leaf engraving at base, wide central band of engraved anthemion, round domed base with beaded rim, trumpet foot with band of guillouche centered by flowerheads and accented with husks, angular handles terminating in flat leaves, anthemion handle on top, domed lid with flat leaf engraving and foliage baluster finial, inner sleeve **750.00**

Sauceboat with underplate, rim applied with grapevines **95.00**

Soup tureen, 16" l, 10-3/4" h, early 19th C, ovoid body with applied gadroon and shell border, two fluted handles with leaf terminals, four scroll and flat leaf feet, domed lid with reeded band, leaf-form finial, body and lid with let-in engraved heraldic device, fitted drop-in liner, restorations, rosing. **1,725.00**

Tankard, 5" h, Hy Wilkinson & Co. makers, tapered cylindrical form, plain ear handle, gold washed int., fitted leather case, 10 troy oz **235.00**

Tea and coffee service, baluster shaped coffeepot, 12-1/4" h kettle-on-stand, teapot, creamer, two handled open sugar, waste bowl, oval with canted corners, angular handles **425.00**

SILVER DEPOSIT GLASS

History: Silver deposit glass was popular at the turn of the century. A simple electrical process was used to deposit a thin coating of silver on glass products. After the glass and a piece of silver were placed in a solution, an electric current was introduced which caused the silver to decompose, pass through the solution, and remain on those parts of the glass on which a pattern had been outlined.

Bowl, 10-1/2" d, cobalt blue ground, flowers and foliage, silver scalloped edge **85.00**

Cologne bottle, 3-3/8" h, clear ground, bulbous, floral and flowing leaf motif **165.00**

Creamer, 2-3/4" h, clear ground, scrolling silver design. **15.00**

Vase, green body, Art Nouveau silver decoration, c1920, 16" h, $250.

Decanter, 13-1/4" h, clear ground, Continental silver mounts, grape clusters, and leaves, dec, orig stopper **90.00**

Ice tub, clear ground, floral and foliage dec, closed tab handles, matching sterling silver ice tongs **125.00**

Perfume bottle, 4-1/2" h, clear ground, vine and grape leaf dec **60.00**

Sugar shaker, clear ground, vine and grape leaf dec, SP top **65.00**

SILVER OVERLAY

History: Silver overlay is silver applied directly to a finished glass or porcelain object. The overlay is cut and decorated, usually by engraving, prior to being molded around the object.

Glass usually is of high quality and is either crystal or colored. Lenox used silver overlay on some porcelain pieces. Most designs are from the Art Nouveau and Art Deco periods.

Reference: Lillian F. Potter, *Re-Introduction to Silver Overlay on Glass and Ceramics*, published by author, 1992.

Basket, 5-1/2" l, 6" h, deep cranberry body, all-over floral and lattice design, sterling handle. **600.00**

Decanter, 11-1/2" h, molded, pinched oval bottle, surface bamboo dec overall, base disk imp "Yuan Shun/Sterling," faceted crystal hollow stopper **375.00**

Flask, 5" h, clear bottle shaped body, scrolling hallmarked silver, hinged cov **275.00**

Inkwell, 3-3/4" x 3", bright green ground, rose, scroll, and lattice overlay, matching cov, monogram **650.00**

Jug, 9" h, colorless glass, tapered baluster form, star-cut base, silver cased applied draw handle, overlay of twining grapes and grape vines, plain cartouche beneath spout, stylized cobweb overlay below, Alvin Mfg Co., late 19th/early 20th C **1,380.00**

Perfume bottle

4" h, bulbous, dark green glass, ornate silver overlay, floral and scroll dec, cased dec, monogrammed "CSE," pr . . **395.00**

4-1/4" h, squat baluster, colorless glass, large flowers and foliage overlay, central vacant cartouche **275.00**

5" h, baluster, elongated neck, colorless glass, scrolling foliage overlay, central monogrammed cartouche **225.00**

Tea set, 8-3/4" h, Lenox porcelain body, Reed & Barton silver overlay, three-pc set. **325.00**

Vase

5" d, 12-1/4" h, bronze, sterling silver overlay of trees, verdigris patina, Heintz **850.00**

6" w, 10" h, baluster, mulberry glazed pottery, stylized tulip design applied in silver, marked "Spahr/800". **495.00**

Decanter, scrolling Art Nouveau type silver overlay with trellis-type decoration on neck, $375.

8-1/4" h, colorless glass cylinder, flared to rim and foot, ruffled top edge, overlay of two large engraved roses, reticulated lozenge, Matthews Co., Newark, early 20th C **865.00**

9-1/2" h, 3-1/2" d, bronze, cylindrical, overlaid sterling cyclamen, orig bronzed patina, stamped "HAMS" and "Patent," Heintz, shallow dent at rim an base **400.00**

10" h, cylindrical, silver overall band at neck pierced with leaf swags, applied pink tone to int. of band, body of vase etched with horizontal beaded bands enclosing floral sprays, flanked by vertical pinstripe cuts, Edwardian, early 20th C. **275.00**

SMITH BROS. GLASS

History: After establishing a decorating department at the Mount Washington Glass Works in 1871, Alfred and Harry Smith struck out on their own in 1875. Their New Bedford, Massachusetts, firm soon became known worldwide for its fine opalescent decorated wares, similar in style to those of Mount Washington.

Marks: Smith Bros. glass often is marked on the base with a red shield enclosing a rampant lion and the word "Trademark."

References: Kenneth Wilson, *American Glass 1760-1930*, 2 vols., Hudson Hills Press and The Toledo Museum of Art, 1994.

Reproduction Alert: Beware of examples marked "Smith Bros."

Biscuit jar

6-1/2" d, 9" h, realistic stalks of bearded wheat with raised gold highlights, cream body, melon ribbed body, metal fittings, lid sgd "S B 4402" **575.00**

7" d, 7" h, melon rib, yellow shoulders shading to white ground, enameled pansies dec **795.00**

7" d, 8-1/2" h, green and pastel brown tendrils of ivy wind around melon ribbed body, gold plated fittings, sgd "405" **885.00**

Bowl

3" d, lobed, pale pink ground, daisies dec, red rampant lion mark **150.00**

6" d, 2-3/4" h, melon ribbed, two shades of gold prunus dec, beaded white rim **375.00**

8" d, melon ribbed, creamy beige ext., white int., delicate acorns and leaves dec. **575.00**

9" d, 4" h, melon ribbed, beige ground, pink Moss Rose dec, blue flowers, green leaves, white beaded rim **675.00**

Bride's bowl, 9-1/2" d, 3" h bowl, 16" h overall, opal glass bowl, painted ground, 2" band dec with cranes, fans, vases, and flowers, white and gray dec, fancy silver-plated holder sgd and numbered 2117 . . . . **1,450.00**

Creamer and sugar, 4" d, 3-3/4" h, shaded blue and beige ground, multicolored violet and leaves dec, fancy silverplated metalware . . . **750.00**

Humidor, 6-1/2" h, 4" d, cream ground, eight blue pansies, melon-ribbed cov **850.00**

Juice tumbler, blue, stork dec . . **50.00**

Mustard jar, cov, 2" h, ribbed, gold prunus dec, white ground **300.00**

Plate, 7-3/4" d, Santa Maria, beige, brown, and pale orange ship . . . **635.00**

Rose bowl

2-1/4" h, 3" d, cream ground, jeweled gold prunus dec, gold beaded top, sgd **285.00**

4-1/4" h, 4" d, enameled pansy blossoms, row of raised dots on rim **385.00**

Salt and pepper shakers, silverplate napkin ring center on platform base, white shakers with blue floral trim, marked "Rockford #29" **750.00**

Salt, open, 2-1/2" d, 1-1/4" h, white ground, amber dec, sgd with trademark and lion shield **225.00**

Biscuit jar, cream ground, pink and green floral decoration, silver plated lid and bail handle, 8-1/2" h, $270.

Sugar shaker

5-3/4" h, pillar ribbed, white ground, pink wild rose and pale blue leaves, blue beaded top, orig cov fair **495.00**

6" h, 2-1/2" d, cylindrical, vertical ribs, opaque white body, stylized dec of pink, blue, and gray summer blossoms, wispy stalks, pewter top **575.00**

Toothpick holder

2" h, ribbed blank, purple and blue violets, beaded top **285.00**

2-1/4" h, barrel shape, opaque white body, swag of single petaled blossoms **265.00**

2-1/4" h, pillar ribbed, white ground, pink wild rose and pale blue leaves, blue beaded top . . **250.00**

2-1/2" h Little Lobe, pale blue body, single petaled rose blossoms, raised blue dots on rim . . . **245.00**

Vase

5-1/4" h, 3-1/2" d, pinched-in, apricot ground, white wisteria dec, gold highlights, sgd **375.00**

5-1/4" h, 4" d, triangular shape, pale yellow ground, white daisy-like flowers, sgd **425.00**

5-1/2" h, petticoat shape, flared base, pink ground, multicolored foliage and herons, stamped mark on base, "Smith brothers-New Bedford, MA," pr **850.00**

7" h, soft pink ground, inverted dec of white pond lily, blue-green and black leaves, brown stems, maroon trim, c1870, pr **375.00**

7-1/4" h, 8" d, double canteen, pink rose sprays centered in three decorative reserves, lime-yellow ground, two restored enameled dots, small int. chip **325.00**

8" h, conical shape, pink, white blossoms and hummingbird dec, script sgd, pr **225.00**

8-1/2" h, double bulbed form, opal glass, repeating molded foliate panel at top, hp chrysanthemum blossoms and leaves, yellow, pink, brown, and green, cream ground, gold enamel highlights, wear to gilt, mold imperfection under neck
. . . . **460.00**

8-1/2" h, double bulbed form, repeating molded foliate and panel motifs at top, hp chrysanthemum blossoms and leaves, cream and green ground, stamped "Smith Brothers" trademark in red on base
. . . . **1,150.00**

10" h, 6" d, pillow, soft ground, purple wisteria, green, and gold leaves, slight roughage on base
. . . . **925.00**

10" h, 8" w, shaded rust, brown, yellow and gold ground, white apple blossoms, green leaves and branches, painted beige int.
. . . . **595.00**

12-1/2" h, Verona, colorless ground, deep purple and white irises, gold trim, green leaves and stems, int. vertical ribs **550.00**

SNOW BABIES

History: Snow babies, small bisque figurines spattered with ground porcelain that resembles snow, were made originally in Germany and marketed in the early 1900s. One theory about their origin is that German doll makers copied the designs from the traditional Christmas candies. While sales were modest at first, demand increased after the birth of Admiral Peary's daughter in Greenland in 1893 and her subsequent popularity as the "Snow Baby," so-named by the Eskimos.

Hertwig and Company, a German manufacturer of china doll heads and bisque figurines, was the first to make these small figures dressed in hooded snowsuits and posed in a variety of positions. They reached their greatest popularity between 1906 and 1910, when they were manufactured by a variety of German firms and imported by many American companies.

Reference: Mary Morrison, *Snow Babies, Santas, and Elves: Collecting Christmas Bisque Figures,* Schiffer Publishing, 1993.

Reproduction Alert: During the 1940s and as late as the 1970s, many inferior Japanese-made snow babies entered the market, some marked with an impressed "Japan," others with a paper label. Their crudely painted features, awkward poses, and coarser "snow" make them easy to distinguish from the original German examples. Since 1977, Dept. 56® has been marketing a line of products called The Original Snow Village.

Baby, sitting, 1-1/8" h, $85.

Baby

In sleigh, sitting, both arms raised, reindeer in front **150.00**

Playing drum, marked "U. S. Zone, Germany," 2" h **75.00**

Riding bear, red, white, and maroon, 2-7/8" h **150.00**

Sitting, 2" **175.00**

Sledding, single baby pulled by huskies, 2-3/4" h **100.00**

Sledding, three seated babies, bisque sled **165.00**

Standing, holding tennis racket, stamped "Germany" **115.00**

Standing, laying banjo, stamped "Germany" **135.00**

Standing, waving, 1-1/4" h . . . **95.00**

Bear

On four paws **100.00**

Standing, 2-1/2" h **115.00**

Elf, 1-1/2" h **70.00**

Girl, seated on snowball, red skirt, arms raised **125.00**

Ice skaters, 2" h, boy and girl, pr
. . . . **250.00**

Sheep, 2" h **75.00**

Snowman **65.00**

SNUFF BOTTLES

History: Tobacco usage spread from America to Europe to China during the 17th century. Europeans and Chinese preferred to grind the dried leaves into a powder and sniff it into their nostrils. The elegant Europeans carried their boxes and took a pinch with their finger tips. The Chinese upper class, because of their lengthy fingernails, found this inconvenient and devised a bottle with a fitted stopper and attached spoon. These utilitarian objects soon became objets d'art.

Snuff bottles were fashioned from precious and semi-precious stones, glass, porcelain and pottery, wood, metals, and ivory. Glass and transparent-stone bottles often were enhanced further with delicate hand paintings, some done on the interior of the bottle.

Collectors' Club: International Chinese Snuff Bottle Society, 2601 N. Charles St., Baltimore, MD 21218; http://www.snuffbottle.org.

Internet Resource: *The Snuff Bottle Store,* http://www.snuffbottlestore.com.

Agate, Chinese

Baluster, blue, carved and incised birds amid flowering branches, conforming stopper with floral finial, 3" h **175.00**

Cameo, carved running horse. **80.00**

Carved, man rowing boat and pine trees **175.00**

Ovoid, brown relief figure, honey ground, rose quartz stopper, 3" h
. . . . **175.00**

Amber, landscape and figures, caramel inclusions, conforming id, Chinese, late 19th C, 4" l **1,265.00**

Celadon

Light jade, flattened ovoid short neck, 2-1/4" h **185.00**

Mottled jade, gray and brown inclusions, dog mask and ring form handles, Qing dynasty, Chinese
. . . . **400.00**

Chrysoprase, flattened ovoid, light green, conforming stopper, 3" h. **215.00**

Cinnabar lacquer, ovoid, continual scene of scholars and boys in a pavilion landscape, dark red, conforming stopper, 3-1/4" h **230.00**

Cloisonné, auspicious symbols among clouds, yellow ground, lappet base border, ruyi head neck border, conforming stopper with chrysanthemum design, Qianlong four-character mark **185.00**

Coral, cylindrical, carved kylin, Chinese, 2-1/2" h **175.00**

Enameled glass, each side dec with deer beneath flowing trees, seal mark in red on base, 2-3/8" h **920.00**

Cloisonné, floral motif on one side, forest scene with deer on other, wood base, 3-3/8" h, **$245.**

Famille rose, porcelain, floral and scrolling foliate dec, blue ground, Qing dynasty, Chinese **80.00**

Ivory, 3-3/4" l, curved ivory carved with bulrushes and crocodiles, flatleaf cap with ball finial, pebbled gilt-metal lid with glass-inset neck, mounted with short neck chain, Indian, late 19th/early 20th C **300.00**

Jade
Apple-green and celadon, silver mounted, Chinese **750.00**
Black, flattened rect form, relief carved mountains, applied white jade figural grouping on one side, rose quartz stopper, wood base, 2-1/2" h **255.00**
Blue-gray jade, bands of black, well-hollowed, relief carved dragon rising from waves above tiger, China, mid-19th C **5,750.00**
White jade, golden skin, D-shaped body, well hollowed, silver stopper mounted with amethyst, 19th C **300.00**

Lapis lazuli, ovoid, relief carved, figures beneath tree, Chinese, 4" h **115.00**

Malachite, carved, gourd, Chinese, 3" h **75.00**

Opal, carved sage seated before gourd, Ch'ing Dynasty, 3" h **125.00**

Overlay glass, seven colors, one side with floral designs in two archaic-form vases, reverse with immortal attending

a crane and deer, bats flying above, each side with animal mask and ring handles, green, blue, mauve, coral, brown, and yellow, on white ground, 19th C **520.00**

Peking glass, Snowflake
Blue overlay, each side with prancing deer, head turned with a lingchi branch in mouth, 19th C, 2-1/2" h **490.00**
Red overlay, flattened ovoid, one side with serpent and tortoise, other with frog sitting under lily pad, 2-1/4" h **1,265.00**

Porcelain, Chinese, blue and white, floral dec, wood stand, Qianlong mark **450.00**

Porcelain, Famille rose dec, deer with lingchi, pair of magpies, reverse with books, bees, and monkey, red Tao Kuang mark, c1821-48, glue adhering to foot rim **125.00**

Rose quartz, flattened ovoid, relief carved leaves and vines, Chinese, 3" h **45.00**

Stag horn, flattened ovoid, one side with inset ivory panel with two laughing figures, reserve with inset panel with gold archaic script, 2-1/8" h **175.00**

Turquoise, flattened body, high shoulder, relief carved auspicious symbol, agate stopper, wood stand, 2-3/8" h **165.00**

SOAPSTONE

History: The mineral steatite, known as soapstone because of its greasy feel, has been used for carving figural groups and designs by the Chinese and others. Utilitarian pieces also were made. Soapstone pieces were very popular during the Victorian era.

Reference: *Soapstone*, L-W Book Sales, 1995.

Bookends, pr, 5" h, carved, block form, fu lion resting on top, Chinese . . **300.00**

Candlesticks, pr, 5-1/8" h, red tones, flowers and foliage **85.00**

Carving
3" h, even white color, servant kneeling before woman holding fan, China, 19th C **115.00**
4" w, 4-1/2" d, 3-1/2" h, dog's head, old darkened color, America, 19th C, chips, with stand **420.00**
6-3/4" h, bird in flowering tree . **50.00**
7" h, 7-1/2" w, seated Buddha **125.00**
8-1/2" h, loon, green, sgd "Pauloosie" **315.00**

Hot plate, 16" l, 8-1/2" w **75.00**

Vase, tan and brown, carved rodent, 2-1/2" h, **$85.**

Plaque, 9-1/2" h, birds, trees, flowers, and rocks **125.00**

Sculpture, 10-1/4" h, 4-1/2" w, kneeling nude young woman, Canadian . . **95.00**

Sealing stamp, carved dec
5" h, 1" d, curved scroll **95.00**
5-3/4" h, 2" d, fu dog on pediment, Oriental, c1900 . . . . **110.00**

Toothpick holder, two containers with carved birds, animals, and leaves **85.00**

SOUVENIR AND COMMEMORATIVE CHINA AND GLASS

History: Souvenir, commemorative, and historical china and glass includes those items produced to celebrate special events, places, and people.

China plates made by Rowland and Marcellus and Wedgwood are particularly favored by collectors. Rowland and Marcellus, Staffordshire, England, made a series of blue-and-white historic plates with a wide rolled edge. Scenes from the Philadelphia Centennial in 1876 through the 1939 New York World's Fair are depicted. In 1910, Wedgwood collaborated with Jones, McDuffee, and Stratton to produce a series of historic dessert-sized plates showing scenes of places throughout the United States.

Many localities issued plates, mugs, glasses, etc., for anniversary celebrations or to honor a local historical event. These items seem to have greater value when sold in the region in which they originated.

Commemorative glass includes several patterns of pressed glass which celebrate persons or events. Historical glass includes campaign and memorial items.

References: Pamel E. Apkarian-Russell, *A Collector's Guide to Salem Witchcraft & Souvenirs*, Schiffer Publishing, 1998; Monica Lynn Clements and Patricia Rosser Clements, *Popular Souvenir Plates*, Schiffer Publications, 1998; Barbara J. Conroy,

Restaurant China, Volume 2, Collector Books, 2000; Bessie M. Lindsey, *American Historical Glass,* Charles E. Tuttle Company, 1967; David Weingarten and Margaret Majua, *Monumental Miniatures,* Antique Trader Books, 1998; Lawrence W. Williams, *Collector's Guide To Souvenir China,* Collector Books, 1998.

Periodicals: *Antique Souvenir Collectors News,* Box 562, Great Barrington, MA 01230; *Souvenir Building Collectors Society,* P.O. Box 70, Nellysford, VA 22958-0070.

Collectors' Clubs: Souvenir Building Collectors Society, P.O. Box 70, Nellysford, VA 22958; Statue of Liberty Collectors' Club, 26601 Bernwood Road, Cleveland, OH 44122.

Additional Listings: Cup Plates, Pressed Glass, Political Items, and Staffordshire, Historical. Also see *Warman's Americana & Collectibles* for more examples.

Ashtray, Cazenoia Lake, NY, white ground, multicolored decal transfer center, stamped "Hampshire, Keene, New Hampshire" on back, 5" w, $35.

Bust, Gillinder
Lincoln, frosted **325.00**
Napoleon, frosted and clear . **295.00**
Shakespeare, frosted. **150.00**

Creamer
New Academy, Truro, multicolored image on white medallion, cobalt blue ground, gold and white dec
. . . .**30.00**
Wadsworth Atheneum, Hartford, CT, multicolored image on white medallion, lustered ground, 2" h, marked "Wheelock China, Austria"
. . . .**18.00**

Cup, Entrance to Soldier's Home, Leavenworth, Kansas, multicolored, beaded dec, 2-1/2" h, marked "Germany," slight wear to gold dec
. . . .**18.00**

Cup and saucer
Niagara Falls, cobalt blue ground, gold trim, 1-1/4" h x 1-3/4" d, 3-1/2" d saucer, scene of falls on

saucer, marked "Made in Japan," matching wooden display stand
. . . .**20.00**
Souvenir of Edina, Missouri, white ground, rose dec, gold trim, 2-1/2" h x 3-3/4" w cup, 5-1/2" w cup, marked "Japan" **20.00**
Souvenir of Rock City, Lookout Mountain, TN, 1-3/4" h x 1-3/4" w cup, 3-3/4" d saucer, marked "Made in Japan". **12.00**
Washington and Lafayette, transfer print portraits on cup of George Washington and Lafayette, saucer with portrait titled "Washington His Country's Father," 1-3/4" h, creamware, England, early 19th C
. . . .**490.00**

Demitasse cup and saucer
My Old Kentucky Home, 2" h x 2" w cup, 4" d saucer, marked "Handpainted, Made in Japan, NICO". **15.00**
Souvenir of Chicago, Ill, Victorian man and woman on inside of cup, 2" h x 2-1/2" w cup, gold trim, marked "Crest O Gold, Sabin, Warranted 22K" **17.50**

Dish
Beauvoir House, Jefferson Davis House, Biloxi, MS, 3-1/4" d, marked "Made by Adams, England for the Jefferson Davis Shrine" **20.00**
DeShong Memorial Art Gallery, Lester, PA, yellow luster ground, 3-3/4" x 3-1/4", marked "Made in Germany," wear to lettering and gold trim. **12.00**
Dish, cov, Remember the *Maine,* green opaque glass. **135.00**

Goblet
G.A.R., 1887, 21st Encampment
. . . .**100.00**
Mother, Ruby Thumbprint pattern
. . . .**35.00**

Mug
Market Place and Town Hall, Preston, photos on front and back, pink luster ground, dated 1894, 3-1/2" h. **35.00**
Ross Castle, Killarney, Ireland, orange luster ground, dec handle, 2-1/2" h, marked "G. H. O., Austria"
. . . .**25.00**

Paperweight
Moses in Bulrushes, frosted center
. . . .**145.00**
Plymouth Rock, clear **95.00**
Ruth the Cleaner, frosted . . .**125.00**
Washington, George, round, frosted center. **295.00**

Water pitcher, pattern glass, colorless, "Gridley You May Fire When Ready," 9-1/4" h, $200. Photo courtesy of Joy Luke Auctions.

Pitcher, 10-1/2" h, Trans-Atlantic Cable, ironstone, cable form inscribed "To God in the highest, on earth peace, good will towards men, Europe and America are united by telegraph," England, 19th C, cracks and chips to base. **345.00**

Plate
Atlantic City, NJ, Rowland and Marcellus, 10-1/2" d **50.00**
Florida, Saint Augustine, Vernon Kilns, marked "Designed exclusively for J. Carver Harris"
. . . .**20.00**
Hogg, James Stephen, first native born governor of Texas, brown print, Vernon Kilns, marked "Designed for Daughters of the Republic of Texas" **25.00**
Idaho, state seal, Vernon Kilns **20.00**
Marietta College 125th Anniversary, 1960, Wedgwood **25.00**
Nebraska, University of Nebraska, Vernon Kilns **30.00**
Oklahoma, Agricultural and Mechanical College, Vernon Kilns, marked "Designed especially for Creech's Stillwater, Oklahoma"
. . . .**32.00**
Oklahoma, Heart of the Great Southwest, state seal, Vernon Kilns
. . . .**20.00**
President Nixon **15.00**
Sulphur Springs, Delaware, OH, light blue and black transfer, Staffordshire, NY retailer's label, 10-1/2" d, chip on table ring
. . . .**200.00**
Texas, Southwest Methodist University, Dallas, Vernon Kilns,

marked "Made exclusively for
Titche-Goettinger Co." **35.00**
University of Chicago **20.00**
Washington, Bellingham, green print,
Vernon Kilns **50.00**
Tile, 4" d, Detroit Women's League,
multicolored irid glass **135.00**
Tumbler, etched
Lord's Prayer. **15.00**
Niagara Falls, Prospect Point, gold
rim **20.00**
Whittier birthplace, waisted, tall
. . . . **60.00**

SOUVENIR AND COMMEMORATIVE SPOONS

History: Souvenir and commemorative spoons have
been issued for hundreds of years. Early American
silversmiths engraved presentation spoons to honor
historical personages or mark key events.

In 1881, Myron Kinsley patented a Niagara Falls
spoon, and in 1884, Michael Gibney patented a new
flatware design. M. W. Galt, Washington, D.C., issued
commemorative spoons for George and Martha
Washington in 1889. From these beginnings, a
collecting craze for souvenir and commemorative
spoons developed in the late 19th and early 20th
centuries.

References: Wayne Bednersch, *Collectible Souvenir
Spoons*, 2nd ed., Collector Books, 2000; George B.
James, *Souvenir Spoons (1891)*, reprinted with 1996
price guide by Bill Boyd (7408 Englewood Lane,
Raytown, MO 64133), 1996; Dorothy T. Rainwater and
Donna H. Fegler, *American Spoons*, Schiffer
Publishing, 1990; ——, *Spoons from Around the
World*, Schiffer Publishing, 1992; *Sterling Silver,
Silverplate, and Souvenir Spoons with Prices*, revised
ed., L-W Book Sales, 1987, 1994 value update.

Collectors' Clubs: American Spoon Collectors,
7408 Englewood Lane, Raytown, MO 64133; Silver
Spoon Club of Great Britain, Glenleigh Park, Sticker,
St. Austell, Cornwall PL26 7JD UK,
http://www.silver-spoon.com; Spoon Club of
Southern California, 6032 Triangle Drive, City of
Commerce, CA 90040; Washington State Spoon
Collectors, 1992 S. Elger Bay Road, Box 151,
Stanwood, WA 98292.

Internet Resources: *American Souvenir Spoons*,
http://www.souvenirspoons.com; *Souvenir Spoons
Museum*, http://www.geocities.com/souvenirspoons.

Additional Listings: See *Warman's Americana &
Collectibles* for more examples.

Bingham Canyon, Utah, copper mine,
marked "Klephs Arts Copper Mine,"
copper, 5" l **12.00**
Boulder, CO, name in bowl, Indian
head handle **40.00**
B. P. O. E. Elks #896, marked "Reed &
Barton Klitzner RI," silverplate, 4-1/2" l
. . . . **15.00**
Cawston Ostrich Farms, marked
"Sterling," 3-1/4" l **15.00**
Denver, CO, sterling, gold washed
bowl, acid etched pack mule, stem-end
topped with winch with handle that
turns, applied pick and shovel, stem
entwined with rope, ending in bucket,
opposed by modeled rock, 1 troy oz,
late 19th C **85.00**
Dodge City, KS, Boot Hill, marked
"Sterling," 4-1/4" l **17.50**
Fort Dearborn, 1803-1857, marked
"Sterling, Hyman Berg," 6" l **20.00**
Golden Gate Bridge, San Francisco,
CA, marked "Holland 90" and hallmark,
5" l **15.00**
Grand Army of the Republic,
engraved bowl **70.00**
King Cotton **45.00**
Memorial Arch, Brooklyn, NY, round
oak stove **40.00**
Palm Springs, Aerial Tramway, SP,
John Brown, marked "Antico" . . **100.00**
Philadelphia, Independence Hall in
bowl, SS **45.00**
Portland, OR, SS **40.00**
Prophet, veiled **135.00**
Richmond, MO, SS **30.00**
Royal Canadian Mounted Police,
"Victoria, British Columbia" in bowl,
marked "Made in Holland," 4-1/2" l
. . . . **30.00**
Salem, MA, witch handle **45.00**

Seattle World's Fair, marked "Sterling,
1961, Century 21 Exposition, Inc.," 6" l
. . . . **42.00**
SS Momus, Westfield Pattern, Meridan
Britannia, 1903, back engraved "L. P.
Co.," 6" l **10.00**
St. Paul, The Tower, Houses of
Parliament, West Minister, each marked
"L. E. P. A1" on back, set of four in orig
box **42.00**
Thousand Islands, fish handle,
engraved bowl, SS, Watson **45.00**
Timberline Lodge, OR, marked
"Sterling," 5-1/2" l **32.00**
Vista House, Columbia River, OR,
detailed handle, marked "Sterling"
. . . . **32.00**
Windmill, detailed curved handle,
movable blades on figural windmill,
hallmarked. **38.00**

SPANGLED GLASS

History: Spangled glass is a blown or blown-molded
variegated art glass, similar to spatter glass, with the
addition of flakes of mica or metallic aventurine. Many
pieces are cased with a white or clear layer of glass.
Spangled glass was developed in the late 19th century
and still is being manufactured.

Originally, spangled glass was attributed only to
the Vasa Murrhina Art Glass Company of Hartford,
Connecticut, which distributed the glass for Dr. Flower
of the Cape Cod Glassworks, Sandwich,
Massachusetts. However, research has shown that
many companies in Europe, England, and the United
States made spangled glass, and attributing a piece to
a specific source is very difficult.

Basket
7" h, 6" l, ruffled edge, white int.,
deep apricot with spangled gold,
applied crystal loop handle, slight
flake **225.00**
9" h, lobed body, pink shading to
white, mica flecks, applied clear
handle **175.00**
Beverage set, bulbous pitcher, six
matching tumblers, rubena, opalescent
mottling, silver flecks, attributed to
Sandwich, c1850-60 . . . . **250.00**
Bride's bowl, 10-3/8" d, multicolored,
ruby, cranberry, and green, ivory-yellow
ground, silver flecks **120.00**
Candlesticks, pr, 8-1/8" h, pink and
whit spatter, green aventurine flecks,
cased white int. **115.00**
Creamer, 3-1/4" d, 4-3/4" h, bulbous,
molded swirled ribs, cylindrical neck,
pinched spout, blue ground, swirled
mica flecks, applied clear reeded
handle **225.00**

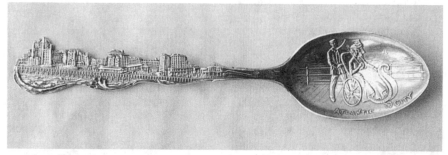

Atlantic City, skyline on handle, ocean scenes on back, push cart on bowl, sterling silver, 6" l, **$60.**

Vase, egg shape, eight crimp top, shaded yellow to white base, gold mica flecks, 4" h, 3-1/2" w, $65.

Cruet, Leaf Mold pattern, cranberry, mica flakes, white casing, Northwood
. . . . **450.00**

Ewer, 9-1/2" h, raspberry pink ext., white int., mica flecks, twisted applied handle, rough pontil **250.00**

Jack-in-the-pulpit vase, 6-1/4" h, oxblood, green, and white spatter, mica flakes, c1900 . . . . **125.00**

Pitcher, 8-1/2" h, white, and amber cased to clear, mica flakes, applied amber reeded handle **550.00**

Rose bowl, 3-3/8" d, 3-1/2" h, eight-crimp top, cased deep rose, heavy mica coral like dec, white int.
. . . . **115.00**

Salt shaker, cranberry, cased white int., molded leaf design, Hobbs, c1890
. . . . **125.00**

Sugar shaker, cranberry, mica flakes, white casing, Northwood **115.00**

Toothpick holder, butterscotch, gold mica flecks, white lining **175.00**

Tumbler, 3-3/4" h, pink, gold, and brown spatter, mica flecks, white lining
. . . . **90.00**

Vase, 4-3/4" h, 4" d, amethyst ground, collared scalloped top, goldstone flakes around body **145.00**

SPATTER GLASS

History: Spatter glass is a variegated blown or blown-molded art glass. It originally was called "end-of-day" glass, based on the assumption that it was made from batches of glass leftover at the end of the day. However, spatter glass was found to be a standard production item for many glass factories.

Spatter glass was developed at the end of the 19th century and is still being produced in the United States and Europe.

Reference: William Heacock, James Measell, and Berry Wiggins, *Harry Northwood*, Antique Publications, 1990.

Reproduction Alert: Many modern examples come from the area previously called Czechoslovakia.

Fairy lamp, satin finish, cased, white, green, and blue, white interior, 3-3/4" d, 4-5/8" h, $195.

Basket

6-1/2" h, 6-1/4" l, 5" w, rect, maroon, brown, yellow, blue, red, green spatter, white int. lining, clear thorn loop handle, tightly crimped edge with two rows of hobnails . . **250.00**

7-1/2" h, 6" l, brown and jade green spatter, white ground, thorn handle, ruffled star shaped edge, c1890
. . . . **275.00**

Berry set, master bowl and two sauces, Leaf Mold, cranberry vaseline
. . . . **300.00**

Bowl, 10" d, deep red and white spatter, gold enamel dec, pedestal base, sgd and numbered "97412 LZ '75" **475.00**

Box, cov, cranberry ground, white spatter, clear knob finial **200.00**

Candlestick, 7-1/2" h, yellow, red, and white streaks, clear overlay, vertical swirled molding, smooth base, flanged socket **60.00**

Cologne bottle, 5-1/2" h, white spatter, enamel dec, orig stopper applicator, marked "Made in Czechoslovakia," price for pr. **115.00**

Creamer, Leaf Mold, cranberry vaseline
. . . . **250.00**

Darning egg, multicolored, attributed to Sandwich Glass **125.00**

Ewer
Cranberry ground, white spatter, applied clear handle **65.00**
Yellow ground, white spatter, tri-fold spout, flared applied clear handle, sharp pontil, 8-3/4" h **85.00**

Finger bowl and underplate, 6" d, 3-1/4" d, tortoiseshell, ruffled . . . **275.00**

Jack-in-the-pulpit, 5" h, 3-1/2" d, Vasa Murrhina, deep pink int., clear ruffled top **115.00**

Pitcher, 6-1/2" d, 8" h, burgundy and white spatter, cased in clear, ground pontil, clear reeded handle **395.00**

Miniature lamp, Beaded Swirl pattern, brown and green spatter, 8-7/8" h, $275.

Rose bowl
Leaf Mold, cranberry ground, vaseline spatter **250.00**
Mt. Washington, pink, blue, and white spatter on colorless ground, white opalescent scalloped top
. . . . **135.00**

Salt, 3" l, maroon and pink, white spatter, applied clear feet and handle
. . . . **125.00**

Sugar shaker, Leaf Umbrella pattern, cranberry **495.00**

Tumbler, 3-3/4"h, emb Swirl pattern, white, maroon, pink, yellow, and green, white int. **65.00**

Vase

4" h, yellow ground, white spatter, floral dec **95.00**

7" h, 4-1/2" d, golden yellow and white, enameled bird and flowers, applied clear handles, colored enamel dec **180.00**

11" h, 6-1/2" d, sapphire blue ground, blue spatter, ruffled top with colorless edging, pr . . **450.00**

Watch holder, 3-3/4" x 4-1/4" dish, ruffled rim, blue spatter, 7" h ormolu metal watch holder **175.00**

Water set, Leaf Mold, cranberry vaseline **1,495.00**

SPATTERWARE

History: Spatterware generally was made of common earthenware, although occasionally creamware was used. The earliest English examples were made about 1780. The peak period of production was from 1810 to 1840. Firms known to have made spatterware are Adams, Barlow, and Harvey and Cotton.

The amount of spatter decoration varies from piece to piece. Some objects simply have decorated borders. These often were decorated with a brush, requiring several hundred touches per square inch to achieve the spatter effect. Other pieces have the entire surface covered with spatter.

Marks: Marked pieces are rare.

References: Susan and Al Bagdade, *Warman's English & Continental Pottery & Porcelain*, 3rd ed., Krause Publications, 1998; Kevin McConnell, *Spongeware and Spatterware*, Schiffer Publishing, 1990.

Museum: Henry Ford Museum, Dearborn, MI.

Reproduction Alert: Cybis spatter is an increasingly collectible ware in its own right. The pieces, made by the Polishman Boleslaw Cybis in the 1940s, have an Adams-type peafowl design. Many contemporary craftsmen also are reproducing spatterware.

Notes: Collectors today focus on the patterns—Cannon, Castle, Fort, Peafowl, Rainbow, Rose, Thistle, Schoolhouse, etc. The decoration on flatware is in the center of the piece; on hollow ware, it occurs on both sides.

Aesthetics and the color of spatter are key to determining value. Blue and red are the most common colors; green, purple, and brown are in a middle group; black and yellow are scarce.

Like any soft paste, spatterware is easily broken or chipped. Prices in this listing are for pieces in very good to mint condition.

Bowl, 5-1/2" d, Morning Glory flowers, red spatter, purple flowers, light overall crazing, small table rim chip **65.00**

Charger, 12" d, Persian Ware, marked "Allerton, Persian Ware, England," imp "10" **135.00**

Creamer

3-1/2" h, red and green rose, brown and black spatter, rim flake . **650.00**

3-3/4" h, Morning Glory, blue and green flower, red spatter . **2,750.00**

4" h, Rainbow Thumbprint, red, yellow, and blue peafowl, red, blue, and green spatter, damage and restoration **1,650.00**

4-1/2" h, red and green tulip variant, blue spatter, stains and repairs, hairline on base **890.00**

5" h, red and green cockscomb design, blue spatter, paneled, stains on foot, minor flakes . **860.00**

5-5/8" h, Peafowl, red, green, and blue, paneled, unusual squiggly branches, minor enamel flake in blue **770.00**

Cup, blue stick spatter looping pattern, red, green, and blue long tulip . . . **75.00**

Cup and saucer, handleless, green and red design, 2-3/4" d, $120.

Cup and saucer, handleless

Dark blue, green, and red pomegranate, yellow dots, blue spatter, light stains, crazed saucer **800.00**

Light brown spatter, red and blue spray with green leaves, hairlines **385.00**

Peafowl, red, yellow, and blue, blue spatter, minor wear spot on tail **325.00**

Rainbow, Drape pattern, red, yellow, and green, small rim repair on cup, minor stains on saucer . . **3,080.00**

Red and green Christmas ball dec, light stains on cup **3,960.00**

Red, mustard, and green six-pointed star, stains on cup, foot chip **925.00**

Red, yellow, and green tulip dec, blue spatter, colors on cop are darker than on saucer **200.00**

Red, yellow, green, and blue tulip dec, blue spatter, cup has stained area, filled-in flakes, hairline **110.00**

Miniature, cup and saucer, handleless

Peafowl, light red, yellow, and blue, sitting on green spatter tree branch **330.00**

Peafowl, red, yellow, and dark blue, dark green sponged tree branches, short hairline on saucer, flake **220.00**

Tulip, red and green, yellow spatter, hairline, flake on saucer . . **1,760.00**

Pitcher

4-3/4" h, blue drape with bands on shoulder, rim, and handle, hairlines, some stains, in-the-making separation at handle **460.00**

7-3/8" h, red rose, green leaves, paneled, molded spout, repaired handle with hairline **1,430.00**

7-7/8" h, Rainbow, blue and reddish-purple, paneled sides, molded spout, handle with slight wear, repaired spout **1,715.00**

8-1/2" h, Acorns, yellow and teal green, green and dark brown leaves, purple spatter, paneled, bubbles in brown and yellow, stains, rim repair **3,650.00**

Plate, Tulip pattern, yellow rim, wear, knife marks, 8-1/2" d, $265.

Plate

7-1/2" d, Peafowl, red, yellow, and green, blue spatter border, rim chips **110.00**

8-1/4" d, red, green, and yellow primrose, blue spatter border, 10-sided, crow's foot **75.00**

8-3/8" d, blue border, blue, red, and green dahlia pattern **350.00**

8-1/2" d, blue border, center red and green flower, light stains . . **150.00**

8-1/2" d, Peafowl, dark blue, green, and dark brown, long tail, red spatter, short hairline, in-the-making chip on table ring **715.00**

8-1/2" d, Rainbow, light red, blue, and yellow border, rim flake **3,300.00**

8-1/2" d, Rainbow, red and blue border, criss-cross center, minor stains **770.00**

8-5/8" d, Rainbow, red, yellow, and blue spatter, few minor knife scratches **3,250.00**

8-3/4" d, green double loops on border, red stripes, center purple and yellow viola, surface has been scoured, some additional wear, colors good **50.00**

8-3/4" d, red border, red, blue, and green flowers, minor enamel imperfections, minor stains . **110.00**

9-1/8" d, Rainbow, blue and yellow rainbow border, faded red and blue tulip with green leaves, hairlines, stains, filled in rim chip . . **4,400.00**

9-1/4" d, white center shield with blue stripes, red stars, blue spatter, back imp "Pekin China, T & Booth" **1,155.00**

9-1/2" d, Peafowl, red, yellow, and green, long tail extending into blue borer, three rim flakes, small burst bubbles **770.00**

10-1/2" d, Rainbow, red, blue, and green border, scalloped edge, imp "Adams," filled-in rim chip . . **385.00**

10-3/4" d, blue flowers, red and blue flowers green leaves **150.00**

Platter

8-1/4" x 10-3/4", Peafowl, red, blue, and dark brown, appears to have been scoured, two hairlines, and flake on rim underside **615.00**

10-1/2" x 13-3/4", red and green rainbow border, large red and blue tulip with green and black foliage, imp anchor mark, restorations, hairline **4,510.00**

12-3/8" d, 15-7/8" w, light blue borders, rect white center panel, oblong, scalloped corners, minor rim flakes **220.00**

13-3/4" x 17-1/2", dark brown eagle and shield transfer center, blue spatter border, octagonal, stains and hairline **295.00**

Soup plate

8-3/4" d, blue border, red, green, and yellow stripes, floral center . **165.00**

8-3/4" d, blue flowers, red open roses, green leaves, imp "...Malkin...," light crazing and stains **65.00**

Sugar bowl, cov

5" d, 5" h, blue, green, and red designs, blue stripes, minor roughness on inside flange **250.00**

5-3/4" h plus lid, paneled, red school house, green spatter trees and grass, blue spatter, small crow's foot, restored handles, lid blue transfer replacement **715.00**

Teapot

5" h, Rainbow, green and yellow with purple loops, black spots, stains, filled-in rim chip, restoration to handle, spout, and lid . . .**5,060.00**

7-5/8" h, Cockscomb, red and green design, blue spatter, hairlines in base, restored replaced lid **550.00**

9" h, Peafowl, red spatter, panel sides with arched panels, scrolled handle, domed lid, small chips on spout **1,980.00**

Tea set, 10-1/2" h cov teapot, 9" h cov sugar, 6" h creamer, blue on white, red roses, green foliage on both sides, ear-shaped handles with scalloped detail, old restorations to finials, repaired chip on teapot lid, minor handle chips **1,760.00**

Waste bowl, 6-1/4" d, 3-1/2" h, brown, red, and black Fort pattern, blue spatter, hairline **200.00**

SPONGEWARE

History: Spongeware is a specific type of decoration, not a type of pottery or glaze.

Spongeware decoration is found on many kinds of pottery bodies—ironstone, redware, stoneware, yellowware, etc. It was made in both England and the United States. Pieces were marked after 1815, and production extended into the 1880s.

Decoration is varied. On some pieces, the sponging is minimal with the white underglaze dominant. Other pieces appear to be solidly sponged on both sides. Pieces made between 1840 and 1860 have circular or horizontally streaked sponging.

Blue and white are the most common colors, but browns, greens, ochres, and a greenish blue also were used. The greenish blue results from blue sponging with a pale yellow overglaze. A red overglaze produces a black or navy color. Blue and red were used on English creamware and American earthenware of the 1880s. Other spongeware colors include gray, grayish green, red, dark green on stark white, dark green on mellow yellow, and purple.

References: Susan and Al Bagdade, *Warman's American Pottery and Porcelain*, 2nd ed., Krause Publications, 2000; ——, *Warman's English &*

Continental Pottery & Porcelain, 3rd ed., Krause Publications, 1998; William C. Ketchum, Jr., *American Pottery and Porcelain*, Avon Books, 1994; Kevin McConnell, *Spongeware and Spatterware*, Schiffer Publishing, 1990.

Coffeepot, blue and white, c1830, unmarked, **$295.**

Bank, 5-1/2" l, figural, piggy, blue and cream, pierced coin slot on top . **155.00**

Bowl, 7" d, fluted, brown and blue sponge, cream ground **60.00**

Butter crock

4-5/8" d, 3" h, blue and white, back labeled "Village Farm Dairy," chips, hairlines, crazing **300.00**

9" d, 6" h, blue and white **300.00**

Carpet ball, 3-1/4" d

Brown **85.00**

Green **75.00**

Red and white plaid **90.00**

Creamer, 3" h, green, blue and cream **100.00**

Cup and saucer, blue flower dec on cup **60.00**

Dish, 6-1/2" x 8-1/2", blue and white, serpentine rim **200.00**

Marble, 2" d, gray, blue sponge, late 19th C **220.00**

Milk pitcher, 7-1/2" h, black sponge, white ground **185.00**

Miniature

Bottle, 3-1/2" h, Bristol glaze, handle, red sponge dec, c1910 . . . . **40.00**

Bowl, 2" x 4-1/2", blue and white **125.00**

Pitcher, 3" h, cabin, teepee and bust of Harrison, two-tone gray-white and blue dec **300.00**

Sugar bowl, 4-7/8" h, blue and white, paneled body, crazing, stains, mismatched lid **95.00**

Teapot, 4-1/8" h, blue and white dec, minor chips. **850.00**

Mush cup and saucer, blue and white, worn gilt trim, slight hairline in cup base **85.00**

Pitcher, blue and white, 8-1/2" h, **$250.** *Photo courtesy of Bruce & Vicki Waasdorp.*

Pitcher

6-1/2" h, blue and white, blue accent around rim, professional restoration to surface chip at spout, two short hairlines **155.00**

7-3/8" h, blue and white dec, minor chips on spout and rim. . . . **110.00**

7-7/8" h, green and faded purple grapes, blue sponge dec, molded leaf spout, chips, handle glued **615.00**

8-1/4" h, blue and white dec, blue stripes. **225.00**

9" h, navy blue and white, bulbous-shaped base **385.00**

10" h, barrel shape, green, gold, and brown sponge **110.00**

Plate

8-3/4" d, red, yellow, and green tulip center, blue sponged border, imp "Cotton and Barlow," stains, filled-in rim chip, area of flaked glaze. **85.00**

9-1/2" d, red, green, and black central flower dec, red and green sponged border **190.00**

Platter, 13-1/4" l, octagonal, central red and blue foliate chain, blue band border, cream ground, imp factory mark, Elsmore & Foster, Tunstall, 19th C **115.00**

Spittoon, 5" h, blue sponge, linear dec on white glazed ground, late 19th C **90.00**

Sugar bowl, cov, 4" h, floral reserve, brown sponge, English, 19th C . . **95.00**

Umbrella stand, 21" h, American, 19th C **600.00**

Wash bowl and pitcher, blue sponge underglaze dec, ironstone, 9" h pitcher, 12" d, 4" h bowl. **415.00**

Whimsey, 5-1/2" l, figural cowboy hat, dark blue sponging, c1900, some glaze crazing **35.00**

SPORTS CARDS

History: Baseball cards were first printed in the late 19th century. By 1900, the most common cards, known as "T" cards, were those made by tobacco companies such as American Tobacco Co. The majority of the tobacco-related cards were produced between 1909 and 1915. During the 1920s, American Caramel, National Caramel, and York Caramel candy companies issued cards identified in lists as "E" cards.

During the 1930s, Goudey Gum Co. of Boston (from 1933 to 1941) and Gum Inc. (in 1939) were prime producers of baseball cards. Following World War II, Bowman Gum of Philadelphia (B.G.H.L.I.), the successor to Gum, Inc., led the way. Topps, Inc. (T.C.G.) of Brooklyn, New York, followed. Topps bought Bowman in 1956 and enjoyed almost a monopoly in card production until 1981.

In 1981, Topps was challenged by Fleer of Philadelphia and Donruss of Memphis. All three companies annually produce sets numbering 600 cards or more.

Football cards have been printed since the 1890s. However, it was not until 1933 that the first bubble gum football card appeared in the Goudey Sport Kings set. In 1935, National Chickle of Cambridge, Massachusetts, produced the first full set of gum cards devoted exclusively to football.

Both Leaf Gum of Chicago and Bowman Gum of Philadelphia produced sets of football cards in 1948. Leaf discontinued production after its 1949 issue; Bowman continued until 1955.

Topps Chewing Gum entered the market in 1950 with its college-stars set. Topps became a fixture in the football card market with its 1955 All-American set. From 1956 thorough 1963, Topps printed card sets of National Football League players, combining them with the American Football League players in 1961.

Topps produced sets with only American Football League players from 1964 to 1967. The Philadelphia Gum Company made National Football League card sets during this period. Beginning in 1968 and continuing to the present, Topps has produced sets of National Football League cards, the name adopted after the merger of the two leagues.

References: *All Sports Alphabetical Price Guide*, Krause Publications, 1995; Mark Allen Baker, *All-Sport Autograph Guide*, Krause Publications, 1995; —, *Collector's Guide to Celebrity Autographs*, 2nd ed., Krause Publications, 2000; Tol Broome, *From Ruth to Ryan*, Krause Publications, 1994; *Charlton Standard Catalogue of Canadian Baseball & Football Cards*, 4th ed., The Charlton Press, 1995; Jeff Kurowski and Tony Prudom, *Sports Collectors Digest*

Pre-War Baseball Card Price Guide, Krause Publications, 1993; Mark Larson, *Complete Guide to Baseball Memorabilia*, 3rd ed., Krause Publications, 1996; —, *Complete Guide to Football, Basketball & Hockey Memorabilia*, Krause Publications, 1995; —, *Sports Collectors Digest Minor League Baseball Card Price Guide*, Krause Publications, 1993; Mark Larson (ed.), *Sports Card Explosion*, Krause Publications, 1993; Bob Lemke, ed., *2001 Standard Catalog of Baseball Cards*, 10th ed., Krause Publications, 2000; Bob Lemke and Sally Grace, *Sportscard Counterfeit Detector*, 3rd ed., Krause Publications, 1994; Michael McKeever, *Collecting Sports Cards*, Alliance Publishing, 1996; Tom Mortenson, *Standard Catalog of Sports Autographs*, Krause Publications, 2000; Alan Rosen, *True Mint*, Krause Publications, 1994; Sports Collectors Digest, *Baseball Card Price Guide*, 14th ed., Krause Publications, 2000; —, *Baseball's Top 500 Card Checklist & Price Guide*, Krause Publications, 1999; —, *Premium Insert Sports Cards*, Krause Publications, 1995; —, *2001 Standard Catalog of Basketball Cards*, 4th ed., Krause Publications, 2000; —, *2001 Standard Catalog of Football Cards*, 4th ed., Krause Publications, 2000; —, *Standard Catalog of Football, Basketball, & Hockey Cards*, 2nd ed., Krause Publications, 1996, http://www.krause.com.

Periodicals: *Allan Kaye's Sports Cards News & Price Guides*, 10300 Watson Road, St. Louis, MO 63127; *Baseball Update*, Suite 284, 220 Sunrise Hwy, Rockville Centre, NY 11570; *Beckett Baseball Card Monthly*, 15850 Dallas Pkwy, Dallas, TX 75248; *Beckett Baseball Card Magazine*, 15850 Dallas Pkwy, Dallas, TX 75248; *Beckett Basketball Card Magazine*, 15850 Dallas Pkwy, Dallas, TX 75248; *Beckett Football Card Magazine*, 15850 Dallas Pkwy, Dallas, TX 75248; *Canadian Sportscard Collector*, P.O. Box 1299, Lewiston, NY 14092; *The Old Judge*, P.O. Box 137, Centerbeach, NY 11720; *Sport Card Economizer*, RFD 1 Box 350, Winthrop, ME 04364; *Sports Cards Magazine & Price Guide*, 700 E. State St., Iola, WI 54490; *Sports Card Trader*, P.O. Box 443, Mt. Morris, IL 61054; *Sports Collectors Digest*, 700 E. State St., Iola, WI 54990; *Tuff Stuff*, P.O. Box 1637, Glen Allen, VA 23060; *Your Season Ticket*, 106 Liberty Road, Woodsboro, MD 21798.

Baseball
American Caramel

E90-1, 1909-11, Keeler, throwing, even corner wear. **695.00**

0, Cobb, red, 1911, T-206, PSA Grade 3 . . . . **1,500.00**

87, Jackson, 1916 M101-4 SN, PSA Grade 4 . . . . **5,500.00**

Bowman
1948

1, Eliot, PSA Grade 8. . . . **325.00**

8, Rizzuto, PSA Grade 8 . **750.00**

14, Reynolds, PSA Grade 7 . . . . **100.00**

24, Leonard, PSA Grade 8 **75.00**

1949

36, Reese, PSA Grade 7 . . . . **2,750.00**

50, Robinson, PSA Grade 8
. . . . **2,000.00**
84, Campanella, PSA Grade 8
. . . . **1,500.00**
131, Lather, PSA Grade 8 . . **35.00**
186, Kerr, PSA Grade 7. . . . **75.00**
208, Trout, PSA Grade 8 . . **175.00**

1950

98, Williams, PSA Grade 5 **500.00**
157, Roe, PSA Grade 8. . . **150.00**
194, Cox, PSA Grade 8. . . **125.00**
215, Looat, PSA Grade 8 . **125.00**

1951

1, Ford, PSA Grade 7 . . . . **850.00**
3, Roberts, PSA Grade 8 . **325.00**
26, Rizzuto, PSA Grade 8. **475.00**
56, Branca, PSA Grade 7 . **125.00**
152, Abrams, PSA 8 . . . . . **100.00**
203, Law, PSA 8 . . . . **100.00**
253, Mantle, PSA 7 . . . . **8,500.00**
259, Dressen, PSA 8. . . . . **200.00**

1952

4, Roberts, PSA Grade 8 . **275.00**
33, McDougald, PSA Grade 7
. . . . **100.00**
43, Feller, PSA Grade 8. . . **500.00**
101, Mantel, PSA Grade 7
. . . . **2,500.00**
217, Stengel, PSA Grade 8
. . . . **425.00**
232, Slaughter, PSA Grade 7
. . . . **200.00**

1953, color

6, Ginsburg, PSA Grade 7 . **50.00**
9, Rizzuto, PSA Grade 7 . . **275.00**
18, Fox, PSA Grade 7 . . . . **200.00**
19, Dark, PSA Grade 8 . . . **125.00**
32, Musial, PSA Grade 7 **1,000.00**
33, Reese, PSA Grade 6. . **675.00**
46, Campanella, PSA Grade 7
. . . . **525.00**
59, Mantle, PSA Grade 4
. . . . **1,250.00**
68, Reynolds, PSA Grade 7
. . . . **125.00**
74, Mueller, PSA Grade 7 . . **65.00**

1954

19, Shantz. **12.00**
98, Kinder **17.00**
171, Bernier **17.00**
201, Thomson **10.00**

Cracker Jack, 30, Ty Cobb, 1914, PSA
8, framed **24,950.00**
Diamond Star, Ott, 50, 1935, PSA
Grade 5 . . . . **875.00**
Fleer, complete sets1959, near mint
. . . . **1,750.00**
1960, good to excellent **200.00**
1961, excellent/mint. **400.00**

1963, good to excellent, marked
. . . . **750.00**
1982, near mint. **70.00**
1984, near mint. **100.00**
1986, near mint. **90.00**

Goudey

75, Kamm, 1933, PSA Grade 7
. . . . **125.00**
87, O'Rouke, 1933, PSA Grade 5
. . . . **75.00**
91, Zachary, 1933, PSA Grade 6
. . . . **100.00**
92, Gehrig, 1933, PSA Grade 6
. . . . **3,000.00**
93, Welsh, 1933, PSA Grade 5
. . . . **65.00**
101, Coffman, 1933, PSA Grade 5
. . . . **65.00**
144, Ruth, 1933, PSA Grade 3
. . . . **1,750.00**
Sheet, uncut, 1933, printed backs,
framed **6,995.00**

Leaf

1, DiMaggio, PSA Grade 4 . **1,000.00**
4, Musial, PSA Grade 6 . . . . **750.00**
76, Williams, PSA Grade 6 . . **750.00**

Playball

14, Williams, 1941, PSA Grade 5
. . . . **1,750.00**
27, DiMaggio, 1939, PSA Grade 7
. . . . **2,500.00**
27, DiMaggio, 1940, PSA Grade 7
. . . . **2,500.00**
71, DiMaggio, 1941, PSA Grade 5
. . . . **2,000.00**
92, Williams, 1939, PSA Grade 8
. . . . **4,500.00**
103, Berg, 1939, PSA Grade 3
. . . . **300.00**

Topps

1951

3, Ashburn, PSA Grade 8 **325.00**
20, Branca, PSA Grade 9 **250.00**
50, Mize, PSA Grade 8 . . **250.00**
52, Chapman, PSA Grade 8
. . . . **175.00**

1952

37, Snider, PSA Grade 7 . **425.00**
44, Dempsey, PSA Grade 8
. . . . **100.00**
88, Feller, PSA Grade 7 . . **325.00**
124, Kennedy, PSA Grade 8
. . . . **100.00**
195, Minoso, PSA Grade 8
. . . . **250.00**
356, Atwell, PSA Grade 7 **275.00**
384, Crosetti, PSA Grade 6
. . . . **375.00**
392, Wilhelm, PSA Grade 7
. . . . **900.00**

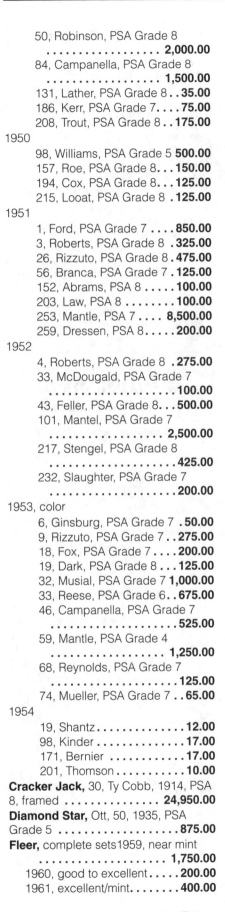

Topps #311, Mickey Mantle, rookie card, regular back, 1952, **$24,150.**

1953

1, Robinson, PSA Grade 7
. . . . **750.00**
4, Wade, PSA Grade 7 . . . . **75.00**

1954

11, Smith **15.00**
22, Greengrass **24.00**
65, Swift. **24.00**
94, Banks. **250.00**

W. W. Gum

55, Gehrig, 1933, PSA Grade 4
. . . . **2,500.00**
78, Ruth, 1935, PSA Grade 5
. . . . **3,250.00**
80, Ruth, 1933, PSA Grade 5
. . . . **5,000.00**

Basketball
Bowman

1948

2, Hamilton **18.00**
3, Bishop. **18.00**
19, Ehliers. **45.00**
20, Vance **35.00**
27, Norlander **18.00**
31, Gilmur **35.00**

Topps

1957

1, Cufton **90.00**
2, Yardley **20.00**
4, Braun **15.00**
5, Sharman **60.00**
12, Martin **50.00**
19, Heinsohn. **105.00**
20, Thieben. **25.00**
21, Meineke **25.00**

52, Spoelstra **25.00**
58, Colin **15.00**
77, Russel **675.00**

1974-75
1, Jabbar **25.00**
10, Maravich **18.00**
39, Walton **50.00**
200, Irving **40.00**

Football
Bowman, 1950
80, Wildung **30.00**
81, Rote **30.00**

Fleer
1961
30, Unitas **18.00**
197, Otto **25.00**
204, Burford **4.00**
1963
1, Garron **18.00**
6, Long **95.00**
36, Blanda **30.00**
59, Powell **12.00**
72, Alworth **175.00**

Topps
1955, All Americans
4, Pinkert **5.00**
12, Graham **75.00**
22, Muller **12.00**
65, Donchess **15.00**
1959
44, Johnson **3.00**
118, Cardinal team **6.00**
126, Rams Pennant **4.00**
161, Brown Team **6.00**
1960
1, Unitas **27.00**
4, Berry **10.00**
23, Brown **120.00**
31, Starr **23.00**
60, Packer team **5.00**
62, Ryan **7.00**
1961, 166, Kemp **95.00**
1964, 30, Kemp **110.00**
1966, 96, Namath **60.00**

Hockey
Topps
1966, 73, Beliveau **40.00**
1966, 109, Howe **190.00**
1971, 100, Orr **45.00**
1973, 17, Dionne **10.00**
1973, 88, Gilbert **5.00**

SPORTS
COLLECTIBLES

History: People have been saving sports-related equipment since the inception of sports. Some was passed down from generation to generation for reuse;

the rest was stored in dark spaces in closets, attics, and basements.

In the 1980s, two key trends brought collectors' attention to sports collectibles. First, decorators began using old sports items, especially in restaurant decor. Second, card collectors began to discover the thrill of owning the "real" thing. By the beginning of the 1990s, all sport categories were collectible, with baseball items paramount and golf and football running close behind.

References: Ted and David Bacyk, *The Encyclopedia of Shotgun Shell Boxes*, SoldUSA, 2000; Mark Allen Baker, *Sports Collectors Digest Complete Guide to Boxing Collectibles*, Krause Publications, 1995; David Bushing, *Guide to Spaulding Bats 1908–1938*, published by author; ——, *Sports Equipment Price Guide*, Krause Publications, 1995; Arlan Carter, *19th Century Fishing Lures*, Collector Books, 2000; Chuck Furjanic, *Antique Golf Collectibles, A Price and Reference Guide*, 2nd ed., Krause Publications, 2000; Carl Luckey, *Old Fishing Lures and Tackle*, 6th ed., Krause Publications, 2002; Kevin McGimpsey and David Neach, *Golf Memorabilia*, Philip Wilson Publishers, distributed by Antique Collectors' Club, 1999; Tim Mortenson, *2000 Standard Catalog of Sports Memorabilia*, Krause Publications, 1999; Dudley Murphy and Rick Edmisten, *Fishing Lure Collectibles*, 1995, 2000 value update, Collector Books.

Periodicals: *Baseball Hobby News*, 4540 Kearney Villa Road, San Diego, CA 92123; Beckett Focus on Future Stars, 15850 Dallas Pkwy, Dallas, TX 75248; *Boxing Collectors News*, 7541 Raleigh Lane, Jonesboro, GA 30236; Boxing Collectors Newsletter, 59 Boston St., Revere, MA 02151; *Coykendall's Sporting Collectibles Newsletter*, P.O. Box 29, East Dorset, VT 05253-0029; *Diamond Angle*, P.O. Box 409, Kaunakakai, HI 97648; *Diamond Duds*, P.O. Box 10153, Silver Spring, MD 20904; Fantasy Baseball, 700 E. State St., Iola, WI 54990; Golfiana Magazine, P.O. Box 688, Edwardsville, IL 62025; *Hunting & Fishing Collectibles Magazine*, P.O. Box 40, Lawsonville, NC 27022; *Old Tyme Baseball News*, P.O. Box 833, Petroskey, MI 49770; *Sports Collectors Digest*, 700 E. State St., Iola, WI 54990; *Trapper and Predator Caller*, 700 E. State St., Iola, WI 54990, http://www.krause.com; *Tuff Stuff*, P.O. Box 1637, Glen Allen, VA 23060; *U.S. Golf Classics*, 5407 Pennock Point Road, Jupiter, FL 33458.

Collectors' Clubs: Boxiana & Pugilistica Collectors International, P.O. Box 83135, Portland, OR 97203-0135; Call & Whistle Collectors Assoc., 2839 E. 26th Place, Tulsa, OK, 74114-4309; Callmakers & Collectors Assoc. of America, 518 Heather Place, Nashville, TN 37204, http://www.quackin.com/ccaa; Glove Collector Club, 14057 Rolling Hills Lane, Dallas, TX 75240-3807; Professional Bowhunters Society, P.O. Box 246, Terrell, NC 28682, http://www.bowsite.com/pbs; Tennis Collectors Society, Guildhall Orchard, Mary Lane North, Great Bromley Colchester, Essex C07 7TU.

Museums: Aiken Thoroughbred Racing Hall of Fame & Museum, Aiken, SC; Colorado Ski Museum, Vail, CO; Hockey Hall of Fame, Toronto, Ontario, Canada; International Boxing Hall of Fame, Canastota, NY; Kentucky Derby Museum, Louisville, KY; Metropolitan Museum of Art, The Jefferson Burdich Collection, New

York, NY; Naismith Memorial Basketball Hall of Fame, Springfield, MA; National Baseball Hall of Fame & Museum, Inc., Cooperstown, NY; National Bowling Hall of Fame & Museum, St. Louis, MO; National Soccer Hall of Fame, Oneonta, NY; New England Ski Museum, Franconia, NH; New England Sports Museum, Boston, MA; PGA/World Golf Hall of Fame, Pinehurst, NC; Tuner's Curling Museum, Weyburn, Saskatchewan, Canada; University of New Haven National Art Museum of Sport, W Haven, CT; US Hockey Hall of Fame, Eveleth, MN; U.S. Lacrosse Museum & National Hall of Fame, Baltimore, MD; U.S. National Ski Hall of Fame & Museum, Ishpeming, MI.

RECORD PRICE Shoeless Joe Jackson's favorite bat, affectionately referred to as "Black Betsy," was auctioned in August 2001 for $525,100. The historically significant bat, used for 13 seasons by Jackson, was auctioned by eBay for Real Legends. The hand-carved hickory bat had its one leather carrying case and is engraved with the Spaulding logo and the words "Old Hickory No. 150." The bat was kept in the Jackson family since Jackson's death in 1951.

SPECIAL AUCTIONS

Dixie Sporting Collectibles
1206 Rama Road
Charlotte, NC 28211
(704) 364-2900

Lang's
30 Hamlin Road
Falmouth, ME 04105
(207) 797-2311

Baseball
Baseball, autographed, sgd by members of team
American League All-Star Team, 1937, Foxx, Gehrig, DiMaggio
. . . . **7,000.00**
Boston, 1964, Herman, Yastrzemski
. . . . **250.00**
Los Angeles, 1983, Sax, Valenzuela, Welch, Stewart **150.00**
Milwaukee, 1979, Molitor, Young
. . . . **200.00**
National League All-Star Team, 1955, Musial **600.00**
New York, 1960, Stengel, Kubek, Maris, Howard, Berra, Ford **700.00**
Oakland, 1981, Martin, Henderson
. . . . **200.00**
Baseball cap, autographed, game used
Bench, Johnny, 1970s Cincinnati Reds **450.00**
Jackson, Bo, 1994 California Angels
. . . . **85.00**
Walker, Larry, 1995 Colorado Rockies **165.00**

Baseball glove
Ashburn, Richie **45.00**
Berra, Yogi **100.00**
Reese, Pee Wee **65.00**
Bat
Mostil, Johnny, signed by Shoeless
Joe Jackson **55,200.00**
Jackson, Shoeless Joe, Black Betsy
. . . . **525,100.00**
Calendar, Kist Soda, 1951, illus as
Medcalf's Hall of Fame painting of
young ball payer with Lou Gehrig
watching from sky, full pad, 16" w, 33" l
. . . . **230.00**
Jersey, game used
1955, Ken Griffey **2,800.00**
1987, Reggie Jackson **700.00**
1988, Mark McQwire **1,500.00**
Magazine, *Baseball,* December 1926,
cover with Ruby and Hornsby shaking
hands during 1926 World Series
. . . . **295.00**
Pennant, felt
Brooklyn Dodgers, Ebbert Field,
blue, 1940s **190.00**
Cooperstown, blue, multicolored
Braves style Indian head, 1940s
. . . . **75.00**
Minnesota Twins A. L. Champs
World Series, photo, 1965 . . **125.00**
New York Yankees, photo "M&M
Boys Last Year Together!," 1966
. . . . **95.00**
Photograph, Brandon Mill Braves,
shows team and Shoeless Joe Jackson
. . . . **3,800.00**
Presentation bat, 34" l, red painted
bat, polychrome Odd Fellows symbols,
incised in gold "West Lynn 15-3
Kearsarge West Lynn 23 East Lynn 5
Presented by H. W. Eastham, July 21,
1900, Aug. 18, 1900," (MA), with stand
. . . . **4,025.00**
Program
All Star, Philadelphia, 1943 . . **495.00**
All Star, St. Louis, 1948 . . . . **325.00**
New York Yankees, 1937 . . . . **195.00**
New York Yankees, 1951 . . . . **195.00**
World Series, 1950, at Philadelphia
. . . . **250.00**
Roster sheet, Pirates, 1927 . . . . **175.00**

Basketball
Autograph, basketball
Archibald, Nate **100.00**
Bing, Dave **100.00**
Bird, Larry **200.00**
Bradley, Bill **150.00**
DeBusschere, Dave **125.00**
O'Brien, Larry **125.00**
Thompson, John **100.00**

Autograph, photograph, 8" x 10"
McGuire, Dick **20.00**
Phillip, Andy **20.00**
Thurmond, Nate **24.00**
Bumper sticker, Kentucky Colonels, 4"
x 15", ABA ball, team logo, name in blue
and white, unused, 1974-75 . . . . **20.00**
Magazine, *Sports Illustrated,* Feb.
1949, Ralph Beard, Kentucky cover
. . . . **95.00**
Pin, Chicago Americans Tournament
Championship, brass, 1935 . . . . **75.00**
Program
Basketball Hall of Fame
Commemoration Day Program, orig
invitation, 1961 . . . . **75.00**
NCAA Final Four Championship,
Louisville, KY, 1967 . . . . . . **175.00**
World Series of Basketball, 1951,
Harlem Globetrotters and College
All-Americans **55.00**
Shoes, pr, game used, autographed
Drexler, Clyde, Avais **225.00**
Sikma, Jack, Converse **100.00**
Webber, Chris, Nikes **550.00**
Souvenir book, *Los Angeles Lakers,*
with two records, Jerry West and Elgin
Baylor on action cover **75.00**
Ticket
NBA Finals Boston Celtics at Los
Angeles Lakers, 1963 . . . . . **95.00**
San Antonio Spurs ABA Phantom
Playoff, 1975, unused **15.00**
St. Louis Hawks at San Francisco
Warriors, Dec. 17, 1963 . . . . **50.00**
Yearbook
1961-62, Boston Celtics **150.00**
1965-66, Boston Celtics **85.00**
1969-70, Milwaukee Bucks . . . **40.00**

Boxing
Autograph, photo, sgd
Max Baer, 8" x 10" **180.00**
Mike Tyson **60.00**
Badge, 4" d, Larry Holmes, black and
white photo, red and black inscriptions,
1979 copyright Don King Productions
. . . . **25.00**
Boxing gloves, 35 readable
autographs **380.00**
Cabinet card, 4" x 6"
Corbett, James F., dressed in suit
. . . . **375.00**
Ryan, Paddy, full boxing post, dark
brown border **395.00**
Sullivan, John L., dark brown border,
"John L. Sullivan, Champion of the
World" **495.00**
Figure, 8" w, 20-1/4" h, carved
fruitwood, fully carved figure throwing

right jab, standing on continuation of
trunk with tree bark intact, attributed to
New Hampshire, c1900 . . . . . **1,955.00**
Plaque, 12-1/2" w, 16-3/4" h, carved
pine, polychrome, figure of John L.
Sullivan carved in relief against
landscape in horseshoe-form, inscribed
at base "J. L. Sullivan," old darkened
crackled painted surface, New York,
late 19th C **2,185.00**

*Postcard, Jim Jeffries vs. Jack
Johnson, Heavyweights, $200.
Photo courtesy of Postcards
International.*

Fishing
Book, *McClane's Standard Fishing
Encyclopedia and International Angling
Guide,* A. J. McClaine, Holt, Rinehart,
Winston, 1965, 2nd printing, 1,057 pgs,
color and black and white illus by R.
Younger, dj **22.00**
Catalog
Garcia Fishing Equipment &
Supplies, Garcia Corp., Teaneck,
NY, c1955, eight pcs, 7-1/2" x
11-1/4", accordian fold large
11-1/4" x 30" sheet **20.00**
Montague Rod & Reel Co.,
Montague City, MA, c1949, 16 pgs,
8-1/2" x 11", Catalog No. 49-M
. . . . **55.00**
Penn Fishing Tackle Mfg.,
Philadelphia, PA, 1952, 32 pgs,
8-1/4" x 10-3/4", Catalog No. 17 of
Penn Reels **32.00**
Shakespeare Co., Kalamazoo, MI,
44 pgs, 1951, 8-1/4" x 11", Catalog

Reel, brass P. A. Altmaire, Harrisburg, PA, Pat. Nov. 9, 1869, $2,145. Photo courtesy of Lang's Sporting Collectables, Inc.

of Fine Wonerod Fishing Tackles
.... 32.00
Weber Lifelike Fly Co., Stevens
Point, WI, 1941, 112 pgs, 6-1/4" x
9-1/4", Catalog No. 22, Flies & Fly
Tackle 70.00
White, E. M. & Co., Old Town, ME,
c1922, 4 pgs, 4-5/8" x 7", E. M.
White Builders of White Canoes
.... 40.00

Creel, 12" w, 6" d, 8-1/2" h, painted splint, carved wooden wire-hinged top, forest green, America, early 19th C
.... 920.00

Sign, "The Flatfish, World's largest selling fishing plug," Helen Tackle Co., Detroit, metal framed glass, 8" x 16"
.... 350.00

Tobacco tin, Forest & Stream, pocket size, 4-1/4" x 3" x 7/8" 600.00

Football
Autograph, football
Bergey, Bill 70.00
Ditka, Mike 125.00

Pin, Lehigh University, brown and gold ribbon, 4-1/2" l celluloid football player, c1950, $40. Photo courtesy of Julie Robinson.

Flaherty, Ray 150.00
Green, Roy............... 70.00
Long, Howie.............. 75.00
Autograph, helmet
Aikman, Troy, Dallas Cowboys
.... 265.00
Dawson, Len, Kansas City Chiefs
.... 250.00
Elway, John, Denver Broncos 275.00
Autograph, photograph, 8" x 10"
Bradshaw, Terry........... 40.00
Brown, Jim............... 30.00
Thomas, Thurman 25.00
Game, Tom Hamilton's Navy Football Game, 1940s 45.00
Pennant, felt, A.F.L.
Boston Patriots, white on red, multicolored Patriot 75.00
Buffalo Bills, white on blue, pink buffaloes 95.00
Houston Oilers, white on light blue
.... 75.00
Pinback button, 1-1/4" d, Philadelphia Eagles, logo, football dangle, early 1950s 45.00
Playoff guide, 1965 NFL, Green Bay Packers vs. St. Louis Cardinals .. 40.00
Program
Army vs. Duke, at the Polo Grounds, 1946 .... 40.00
Army vs. Navy, Michie Stadium, 1952 .... 25.00
Green Bay Packers, 1960 .... 30.00
Heisman Trophy, 1957, John David Crow 30.00
Rose Bowl, 1974, USC vs. Ohio State 40.00

Golf
Autograph, photo, sgd, Tiger Woods
.... 60.00
Book
George Fullerton Carnegie, *Golfiana: or Niceties Connected with the Game of Golf*, Edinburgh, 1833, 18 pgs of poetry........ 21,850.00
The Architectural Side of Golf, London, 1925 .... 14,950.00

Magazine, *American Golfer*, June 1932
.... 10.00
Noisemaker, 2-3/4" d, 6-1/2" l, litho tin, full-color image of male golfer, marked "Germany" on handle, 1930s ... 35.00
Print, Charles Crombie, *The Rules of Golf Illustrated*, 24 humorous lithographs of golfers in medieval clothes, London, 1905....... 1,265.00
Program, Fort Worth Open Golf Championship, Glen Garden Country Club, Ft Worth, TX, 1945 ...... 100.00

Hockey
Autograph
Orr, Bobby, photograph, 8" x 10"
.... 50.00
Smith, Clint, photograph, 8" x 10"
.... 12.00
Thompson, Tiny, puck 50.00
Watson, Harry, puck....... 55.00
Worsley, Gump, sgd 1968-69 Topps card 15.00
Hockey stick, game used, autographed
Beliveau, Jean, 1960s CCM, cracked 700.00
Cashman, Wayne, Sher-wood, uncracked 175.00
LeBlanc, J. B., Koho, cracked 50.00
Jersey, game used, Wayne Gretzky, Rangers, autographed 415.00
Magazine, *Sport Revue*, Quebec publication, Feb 1956, Bert Olmstead, Hall of Fame cov 15.00
Program, Boston Bruins, Sports News, 1937-38................... 250.00
Stick, game used, autographed
Bondra, Peter, Sherwood 90.00
Lindros, Eric, Bauer Supreme
.... 295.00
Tobacco tin, Puck Tobacco, Canadian, tin litho, detailed image of two hockey players on both sides, 4" d, 3-1/4" h
.... 190.00

Hunting
Badge, Western Cartridge Co., plant type, emb metal, pin back, 1-3/4" x 1-3/8" 100.00
Book, *The World of the White-Tailed Deer*, Leonard Lee Rue III, J. B. Lippencott, 1962, 134 pgs, black and white illus, dj 15.00
Box, Peters High Velocity, two-pc cardboard shot gun shells, multicolored graphics, 25 16-gauge shells .. 250.00
Calendar top, Winchester, paper, man atop rock ledge, hunting rams, artist sgd "Philip R. Goodwin," metal top rim, 20" x 14"................... 125.00

Sign

Paul Jones Whiskey, game-hunting scene, orig gold gilt frame, 43" x 57" **750.00**

Remington UMC, diecut cardboard

15" x 14", oversized shell next to box of ammunition **200.00**

15-1/2" x 9", Nitro Club Shells, English Setter atop pile of Remington Shotgun Shells **100.00**

L. C. Smith Guns, paper, two setters pointing to prey, 14" x 14-3/4" **1,200.00**

Winchester, diecut, cardboard, stand-up, Indian Chief with Winchester shotgun in one hand, additional barrels in other hand, 24" x 60" **200.00**

Trophy, 10-1/2" h, silverplate teapot, engraved in German "2nd Prize of the First Shooting Festival in Cincinnati held the 29th and 30th of September 1867 and won by Julius Lang," Eastlake style, some denting **295.00**

Watch fob, Savage Revolver, figural, metal. **110.00**

STAFFORDSHIRE, HISTORICAL

History: The Staffordshire district of England is the center of the English pottery industry. There were 80 different potteries operating there in 1786, with the number increasing to 179 by 1802. The district includes Burslem, Cobridge, Etruria, Fenton, Foley, Hanley, Lane, Lane End, Longport, Shelton, Stoke, and Tunstall. Among the many famous potters were Adams, Davenport, Spode, Stevenson, Wedgwood, and Wood.

References: David and Linda Arman, *Historical Staffordshire* (1974), 1st Supplement (1977), published by authors, out of print; Susan and Al Bagdade, *Warman's English & Continental Pottery & Porcelain*, 3rd ed., Krause Publications, 1998; A. W. Coysh and R. K. Henrywood, *Dictionary of Blue and White Printed Pottery* (1982), Vol. II (1989), Antique Collectors' Club; Mary J. Finegan, *Johnson Brothers Dinnerware*, published by author, 1993; N. Hudson Moore, *The Old China Book,* Charles E. Tuttle, Co., second printing, 1980; Jeffrey B. Snyder, *Historical Staffordshire American Patriots and Views*, 2nd ed., Schiffer Publishing, 2000.

Museums: American Antiquarian Society, Worcester, MA; Cincinnati Art Museum, Cincinnati, OH; City Museum & Art Gallery, Stoke-on-Trent, England; Colonial Williamsburg Foundation, Williamsburg, VA; Elverson Museum of Art, Syracuse, NY; Henry Ford Museum, Dearborn, MI; Hershey Museum, Hershey, PA; Metropolitan Museum of Art, New York, NY; The National Museum of History & Technology, Washington, DC; The Henry Francis DuPont

Winterthur Museum, Winterthur, DE; William Rockhill Nelson Gallery of Art, Kansas City, MO; Yale University Gallery of Fine Arts, New Haven, CT.

Notes: The view is the most critical element when establishing the value of historical Staffordshire; American collectors pay much less for non-American views. Dark blue pieces are favored; light views continue to remain under-priced. Among the forms, soup tureens have shown the largest price increases.

Prices listed below are for mint examples. Reduce prices by 20 percent for a hidden chip, a faint hairline, or an invisible professional repair; by 35 percent for knife marks through the glaze and a visible professional repair; by 50 percent for worn glaze and major repairs.

The numbers in parentheses refer to items in the Armans' books, which constitute the most detailed list of American historical views and their forms.

Adams

W. ADAMS & SONS   ADAMS

The Adams family has been associated with ceramics since the mid-17th century. In 1802, William Adams of Stoke-on-Trent produced American views.

In 1819, a fourth William Adams, son of William of Stoke, became a partner with his father and was later joined by his three brothers. The firm became William Adams & Sons. The father died in 1829 and William, the eldest son, became manager.

The company operated four potteries at Stoke and one at Tunstall. American views were produced at Tunstall in black, light blue, sepia, pink, and green in the 1830-40 period. William Adams died in 1865. All operations were moved to Tunstall. The firm continues today under the name of Wm. Adams & Sons, Ltd.

Bowl, 11" d, 2-1/2" h, English scenes with ruins, dark blue transfer, yellowed repair on back **155.00**

Creamer, 5-3/8" d, English scene, imp "Adams," dark blue **175.00**

Pitcher, 7-1/2" h, Seal of the United States, dark blue (443) **1,200.00**

Adams, plate, Mitchell & Freemans China & Glass Warehouse, Chatham Street, Boston, dark blue transfer, c1804-10, marked, 10-1/4" d, **$715.**

Plate, 10-1/4" d, Mitchell & Freeman's China & Glass Warehouse, Chatham Street, Boston, imp "Adams," dark blue **715.00**

Teapot, Log Cabin, medallions of Gen. Harrison on border, pink (458) . . **450.00**

Clews

From sketchy historical accounts that are available, it appears that James Clews took over the closed plant of A. Stevenson in 1819. His brother Ralph entered the business later. The firm continued until about 1836, when James Clews came to America to enter the pottery business at Troy, Indiana. The venture was a failure because of the lack of skilled workmen and the proper type of clay. He returned to England, but did not re-enter the pottery business.

Plate, America and Independence, central landscape surrounded by George Washington, Justice and Liberty, border listings states of NY, DE, VA, NH, MA, RI, CT, NC, SC, GA, VY, KY, NJ, PA, MD, marked "Clews Warranted Staffordshire," 10-1/2" d, **$440.** *Photo courtesy of Joy Luke Auctions.*

Bowl, Landing of Lafayette, 9" d, ext. floral design, rim repair **410.00**

Cup plate, Landing of Lafayette at Castle Garden, dark blue. **400.00**

Plate

7-7/8" d, Welcome Lafayette the Nations Guest and Our Country's Glory, molded rim with blue edge, imp "Clews," dark blue . . **1,155.00**

8-3/4" d, America and Independence, dark blue transfer, states border, imp mark, wear, stains, crazing, minor scratches **275.00**

10" d, Landing of General Lafayette, imp "Clews," dark blue, very minor wear **350.00**

10-1/4" d, Peace, Plenty, dark blue transfer, imp mark, chip on table ring **495.00**

10-5/8" d, States series, America and Independence, fisherman with net, imp "Clews," dark blue, small rim flake **440.00**

Platter, 17" d, Landing of Lafayette, imp "Clews," dark blue, scratches and wear **1,100.00**

Soup plate

10-3/8" d, Winter View of Pittsfield, Mass, imp "Clews," dark blue **440.00**

10-1/2" d, Picturesque Views, Hudson, Hudson River, imp "Clews," black transfer **165.00**

10-1/2" d, Picturesque Views, Pittsburgh, PA, imp "Clews," steam ships with "Home, Nile, Larch," black transfer, chips on table ring **330.00**

Saucer, Landing of Gen. Lafayette, dark blue transfer, imp "Clews Warranted Staffordshire" **275.00**

J. & J. Jackson

J.&J. JACKSON

Job and John Jackson began operations at the Churchyard Works, Burslem, about 1830. The works formerly were owned by the Wedgwood family. The firm produced transfer scenes in a variety of colors, such as black, light blue, pink, sepia, green, maroon, and mulberry. More than 40 different American views of Connecticut, Massachusetts, Pennsylvania, New York, and Ohio were issued. The firm is believed to have closed about 1844.

Deep dish, American Beauty Series, Yale College (493) **125.00**

Plate, 10-3/8" d, The President's House, Washington, purple transfer . . . **275.00**

Platter, American Beauty Series 12" l, Iron Works at Saugerties (478) **275.00**

17-1/2" l, View of Newburgh, black transfer (463) **575.00**

Soup plate, 10" d, American Beauty Series, Hartford, CT, black transfer (476) **150.00**

Thomas Mayer

In 1829, Thomas Mayer and his brothers, John and Joshua, purchased Stubbs' Dale Hall Works of Burslem. They continued to produce a superior grade of ceramics.

Wash bowl and pitcher, Abbey, 1790, George Jones & Sons, England, medium blue transfer, 16" d, 12" h, **$440.** *Photo courtesy of Sanford Alderfer Auction Co.*

Cream pitcher, 4" h, Lafayette at Franklin's Tomb, dark blue **550.00**

Gravy tureen, Arms of the American States, CT, dark blue (498) . . . **3,800.00**

Plate, 8-1/2" d, Arms of the American States, RI, dark blue (507) **800.00**

Platter

8-1/4" l, Lafayette at Franklin's Tomb, dark blue **525.00**

19" l, Arms of the American States, NJ, dark blue (503) **7,200.00**

Sugar bowl, cov, Lafayette at Franklin's Tomb, dark blue (510) **850.00**

Mellor, Veneables & Co.

Little information is recorded on Mellor, Veneables & Co., except that it was listed as potters in Burslem in 1843. The company's Scenic Views with the Arms of the States Border does include the arms for New Hampshire. This state is missing from the Mayer series.

Plate, 7-1/2" d, Tomb of Washington, Mt. Vernon, Arms of States border **125.00**

Platter, 15" l, Scenic Views, Arms of States border, Albany, light blue (516) **265.00**

Sugar bowl, cov, Arms of States, PA, dark blue **350.00**

Teapot, 9-1/2" h, Windsor pattern, dark blue **200.00**

J. & W. Ridgway and William Ridgway & Co.

John and William Ridgway, sons of Job Ridgway and nephews of George Ridgway, who owned Bell Bank Works and Cauldon Place Works, produced the popular Beauties of America series at the Cauldon plant. The partnership between the two brothers was dissolved in 1830. John remained at Cauldon.

William managed the Bell Bank Works until 1854. Two additional series were produced based upon the

J.W.R.

Stone China

W. RIDGWAY

etchings of Bartlett's American Scenery. The first series had various borders including narrow lace. The second series is known as Catskill Moss.

Beauties of America is in dark blue. The other series are found in light transfer colors of blue, pink, brown, black, and green.

Plate

6" d, Catskill Moss, Anthony's Nose (925) **85.00**

7" d, American Scenery, Valley of the Shenandoah from Jefferson's Rock, brown (289) **120.00**

10" h, Beauties of America, City Hall, NY, dark blue (260) **225.00**

10-1/4" h, Columbian Star, Harrison's Log Cabin, side view, green (277) **250.00**

Platter, 19" l, Catskill Moss, Boston and Bunker's Hill, imp "William Ridgway Son & Co," medium blue, dated 1844, minor chips, knife marks, edge wear . **525.00**

Soup plate, 9-7/8" d, Octagon Church Boston, imp "Ridgway," dark medium blue **330.00**

Vegetable dish, 1-" l, open, American Scenery, Peekskill Landing, Hudson River, purple (287) **195.00**

Wash bowl, American Scenery, Albany (279) **325.00**

Rogers

John Rogers and his brother George

ROGERS

established a pottery near Longport in 1782. After George's death in 1815, John's son Spencer became a partner, and the firm operated under the name of John Rogers & Sons. John died in 1916. His son continued the use of the name until he dissolved the pottery in 1842.

Cup and saucer, Boston Harbor, dark blue (441) **650.00**

Cup plate, Boston Harbor, dark blue (441) **1,400.00**

Plate, 9-5/8" d, The Canal at Buffalo, lace border, purple transfer, int. hairline **55.00**

Platter, 16-5/8" l, Boston State House, medium dark blue (442) **1,000.00**

Waste bowl, Boston Harbor, dark blue (441) **850.00**

Stevenson

As early as the 17th century, the name Stevenson has been associated with the pottery industry. Andrew Stevenson of Cobridge introduced American scenes with the flower and scroll border. Ralph Stevenson, also of Cobridge, used a vine and leaf border on his dark blue historical views and a lace border on his series in light transfers.

The initials R. S. & W. indicate Ralph Stevenson and Williams are associated with the acorn and leaf border. It has been reported that Williams was Ralph's New York agent and the wares were produced by Ralph alone.

Cup and saucer, New Orleans, floral and scroll border **95.00**
Jug, 8-1/4" h, dark blue print . . . **750.00**
Plate
6-1/2" d, Catholic Cathedral, NY, floral and scroll border, dark blue (395) **1,650.00**
6-7/8" d, Battery, NY, vine border (367) **800.00**
7-1/2" d, Columbia College, NY, acorn and oak leaves border, dark blue (350) **450.00**
Soup plate, 10" d, Erie Canal at Buffalo, lace border (386) **95.00**
Wash bowl, Riceborough, GA, lace border (388) **375.00**

Stubbs

In 1790, Stubbs established a pottery works at Burslem, England. He operated it until 1829, when he retired and sold the pottery to the Mayer brothers. He probably produced his American views about 1825. Many of his scenes were from Boston, New York, New Jersey, and Philadelphia.

Pitcher, 6-1/2" h, Boston State House and New York City Hall, rose border, dark blue (335) **1,100.00**
Plate, Bank of the United States, Philadelphia, Joseph Stubbs, spread eagle among flowers and scrolls border **655.00**
Platter, 14-1/2" l, State House, Boston, spread eagle border, dark blue (331) **750.00**
Salt shaker, Hoboken in NJ, spread eagle border, dark blue (326) . . **700.00**

Unknown makers
Bowl, 11-1/8" d, 3-1/4" d, Franklin, scene of Ben flying kite, red transfer, minor wear **495.00**
Pitcher
6-7/8" h, America, Independence, mansion with winding drive, dark blue transfer, chips and hairline **660.00**

7-3/8" h, Seal of the United States with eagle, dark blue transfer, wear and stains **1,320.00**
Plate
7" d, Junction of the Sacandaga & Hudson River, black transfer, small rim glaze defect **95.00**
7-3/4" d, Near Fishkill, small chip on table ring **100.00**
8" d, View from Coenties-slip, scene of Great Fire, City New York, light blue transfer, wear, small edge flakes **385.00**
8-1/2" d, Boston State House, dark blue transfer, unmarked, minor wear **200.00**
8-3/4" d, Nahant Hotel near Boston, dark blue transfer, wear, chips on table ring **200.00**
9" d, "The Residence of the late Richard Jordon, New Jersey," brown, minor wear and stains **250.00**
9-3/4" d, British Views, dark blue, minor wear and pinpoints . . **215.00**
9-3/4" d, City Hall, New York, dark blue transfer, minor wear . . . **275.00**
10-1/8" d, The Baltimore & Ohio Railroad, dark blue transfer, wear, stains **965.00**
Platter, 16-5/8" l, Sandusky, dark blue, very minor scratches **8,525.00**
Saucer, 5-7/8" d, scene of early railroad, engine and one car, floral border, dark blue **275.00**
Soup plate, 10-1/4" d, ---burgs, Yorkshire, medium blue **220.00**
Teapot, 8-1/4" h, The Residence of the Late Richard Jordon, New Jersey, brown transfer, small chip, stain and repair to lid **715.00**

Wood
Enoch Wood, sometimes referred to as the father of English pottery, began operating a pottery at Fountain Place, Burslem, in 1783. A cousin, Ralph Wood, was associated with him. In 1790, James Caldwell became a partner and the firm was known as Wood and Caldwell. In 1819, Wood and his sons took full control.

Enoch died in 1840. His sons continued under the name of Enoch Wood & Sons. The American views were first made in the mid-1820s and continued through the 1840s.

It is reported that the pottery produced more signed historical views than any other Staffordshire firm. Many of the views attributed to unknown makers probably came from the Woods.

*Stevenson, left: soup plate, View of Governor's Island, dark blue transfer, impressed mark, minor wear and small flakes, 10-3/8" d, **$2,475**; right: plate, New York from Brooklyn Heights, dark blue transfer, impressed mark, minor wear, chip on table ring, 10-1/4" d, **$1,485**. Photo courtesy of Garth's Auctions, Inc.*

Marks vary, although always include the name Wood. The establishment was sold to Messrs. Pinder, Bourne & Hope in 1846.

Creamer, 5-3/4" h, horse drawn sleigh, imp "Wood," dark blue, minor hairline in base...................... **550.00**

Cup and saucer, handleless

Commodore MacDonnough's Victory, imp "Wood & Sons," dark blue, pinpoints on cup table ring **355.00**

Ship with American flag, Chancellor Livingston, imp "Wood & Sons" **770.00**

Wood, plate, Erie Canal Aqueduct Bridge at Rochester, dark blue transfer, 7-5/8" d, $145.

Plate

6-1/2" d, Catskill House, Hudson, imp "Wood & Sons," dark blue, white spot near center, pinpoint rim flake **495.00**

7-5/8" d, The Capitol Washington, shell border, imp "Wood & Sons," dark blue **935.00**

8-3/8" d, Chief Justice Marshall, Troy, imp "Wood & Sons," dark blue, small chip.............. **600.00**

9-1/4" d, The Baltimore & Ohio Railroad, (incline), imp "Enoch Wood," dark blue **770.00**

10-1/8" d, Commodore MacDonnough's Victory, dark blue transfer, imp mark, wear, stains, crazing **385.00**

10-1/4" d, Boston State House, imp "Wood & Sons," medium blue **165.00**

10-1/4" d, The Baltimore & Ohio Railroad, (straight), imp "Wood," dark blue, minor scratches. **825.00**

10-3/8" d, Constitution and Guerriere, imp "Wood," dark blue minor scratches **1,760.00**

Platter

16-5/8" l, London Views, St. George's Chapel, Regents Street, imp "Wood," dark blue, minor wear, scratches, pinpoint flakes .. **660.00**

18-1/2" l, Castle Garden Battery New York, dark blue transfer, imp mark, minor wear, shallow glaze flakes, stains............... **3,100.00**

Toddy plate

5-3/4" d, ship scene, shell border, scene not identified, imp "Wood," dark blue.............. **330.00**

6-1/2" d, dark blue transfer, Catskill House, Hudson, imp "Wood," minor wear and stains......... **525.00**

STAFFORDSHIRE ITEMS

History: A wide variety of ornamental pottery items originated in England's Staffordshire district, beginning in the 17th century and still continuing today. The height of production took place from 1820 to 1890.

These naive pieces are considered folk art by many collectors. Most items were not made carefully; some even were made and decorated by children.

The types of objects are varied, e.g., animals, cottages, and figurines (chimney ornaments).

Reproduction Alert: Early Staffordshire figurines and hollowware forms were molded. Later examples were made using a slip-casting process. Slip casting leaves telltale signs that are easy to spot. Look in the interior. Hand molding created a smooth interior surface. Slip casting produces indentations that conform to the exterior design. Holes occur where handles meet the body of slip-cast pieces. There is no hole in a hand-molded piece.

A checkpoint on figurines is the firing or vent hole, which is a necessary feature on these forms. Early figurines had small holes; modern reproductions feature large holes often the size of a dime or quarter. Vent holes are found on the sides or hidden among the decoration in early Staffordshire figurines; most modern reproductions have them in the base.

These same tips can be used to spot modern reproductions of Flow Blue, Majolica, Old Sleepy Eye, Stoneware, Willow, and other ceramic pieces.

References: Susan and Al Bagdade, *Warman's English & Continental Pottery & Porcelain*, 3rd ed., Krause Publications, 1998; A. and H. Harding, *Victorian Staffordshire Figures 1835-1875*, Book Three, Schiffer Publishing, 2000; Adele Kenny, *Staffordshire Spaniels*, Schiffer Publishing, 1997; Griselda Lewis, *A Collector's History of English Pottery*, 5th ed., Antique Collectors' Club, 1999; Arnold R. Mountford, *The Illustrated Guide to Staffordshire Salt-Glazed Stoneware*, Barrie & Jenkins, 1971; Clive Mason Pope, *A-Z of Staffordshire Dogs*, Antique Collectors' Club, Ltd., 1996; P. D. Gordon Pugh, *Staffordshire Portrait Figures of the Victorian Era*, Antique Collectors' Club, 1987; Dennis G. Rice, *English Porcelain Animals of the 19th Century*, Antique Collectors' Club, 1989; Louis T. Stanley, *Collecting Staffordshire Pottery*, Doubleday & Co., 1963.

Museums: American Antiquarian Society, Worcester, MA; Brighton Museum, England; British Museum, London, England; City Museum and Art Gallery, Stoke-on-Trent, England; The Detroit Museum of Arts, Detroit, MI; Fitzwilliam Museum, Cambridge, England; Victoria & Albert Museum, London, England.

Note: The key to price is age and condition. As a general rule, the older the piece, the higher the price.

Figural group, man and woman seated under arbor, 14-1/4" h, $275. Photo courtesy of Joy Luke Auctions.

Bank, 5-1/4" h, cottage shape, repairs **195.00**

Bowl and underplate, 12" x 8-1/2" x 3-3/8" h reticulated bowl, 12" x 8-1/2" underplate, molded leaf handles, transfer label "R. Hall's Select Views, Luscombe, Devonshire," minor edge wear, flake on table ring of bowl **1,650.00**

Cake stand, blue and white transfer, Wild Rose pattern, crazing, 12" d, 2-1/2" h **400.00**

Cheese dish, cov, 9-3/4" l, 7-1/2" h, figural, cow head, enamel and pink luster detailing, shaped undertray **265.00**

Child's plate, 4-1/2" d, molded dressed goose, green, brown, and black enamel **55.00**

Cup and saucer, handleless, Gaudy floral design, blue, dark green, and gold, saucer imp "Clews Warranted Staffordshire," small rim flake on cup **250.00**

Figure

3-3/8" h, barefoot girl in wingback chair, red plaid dress, yellow edging on chair, green base, some roughness on base **420.00**

4" h, dogs, seated, white, polychrome, orange pots in mouth, one with hairlines and chip to base, pr **400.00**

4-1/4" h, Spring, pearlware, brown and green glaze, small flakes, old repair **220.00**

4-5/8" h, Winter, canary, minor wear, small flakes **660.00**

5-1/2" h, 3-1/2" l, boy and girl under tree canopy, sheep and dog, oval base, two small nicks **90.00**

6-1/2" h, 3-1/4" d, lad up in tree, bird in hand, nest nearby, girl seated below, oval base, repairs . . . **65.00**

7" h, squirrel, sitting upright holding nut, naturalistic stump base, ear repaired **125.00**

13" h, King Charles Spaniel, pr **440.00**

Dogs, seated King Charles Spaniels, white, gilt decoration, brown glass eyes, 13" h, some crazing to glaze, price for pair, **$440.** *Photo courtesy of Sanford Alderfer Auction Co.*

Hen on nest, 10-1/2" l, polychrome, good color, minor edge wear and chips on inner flange of base **715.00**

Jar, cov, 3-1/4" h, melon shape, alternating yellow and green stripes, cov with molded leaf, lead glaze, 18th C, hairline to cover, finial and rim chips **4,315.00**

Mantel ornament, 9" h, cottage, Potash Farm, hairlines **175.00**

Miniature, tea set, Gaudy pink and green rose dec, 4-1/4" h teapot, creamer, sugar, waste bowl, two cups and saucers, few flakes, repairs **425.00**

Pitcher, 4-7/8" h, mask, pink luster rim, glaze wear, hairline to spout **175.00**

Plate, 10" d, feather edge, blue, emb rim design **55.00**

Platter

11-3/4" x 15", dark blue transfer, Conway Castle, acanthus leaf edges with fruit surrounding castle medallion center, marked "R. Halls Select Views, Conway castle," rim chip **440.00**

14-1/2" x 18-3/4", Church of St. Charles Polytechnic School, Vienna, Germany, blue and white transfer, blue printed maker's mark and pattern mark, scratches, wear **1,035.00**

16-1/2" x 20-1/2", The Girl Musician, country landscape scene, floral border, blue and white transfer, printed maker's mark for John and Richard Riley, Burslem, 1914-28 . . . . **980.00**

Sauce boat, 7-7/8" l, fruit and flowers, molded feet and handle, dark blue, rim chips **330.00**

Sauce tureen, 7-1/2" l, blue transfer, pastoral scene, chips **345.00**

Teapot, 6-1/2" h, blue transfer, central dec of bird's nest with eggs . . . **460.00**

Waste bowl, 5-5/8" d, Forget Me Not, red transfer, edge roughness . . . **60.00**

STAFFORDSHIRE, ROMANTIC

History: In the 1830s, two factors transformed the blue-and-white printed wares of the Staffordshire potters into what is now called "Romantic Staffordshire." Technical innovations expanded the range of transfer-printed colors to light blue, pink, purple, black, green, and brown. There was also a shift from historical to imaginary scenes with less printed detail and more white space, adding to the pastel effect.

Shapes from the 1830s are predominately rococo with rounded forms, scrolled handles, and floral finials. Over time, patterns and shapes became simpler and the earthenware bodies coarser. The late 1840s and 1850s saw angular gothic shapes and pieces with the weight and texture of ironstone.

The most dramatic post-1870 change was the impact of the craze for all things Japanese. Staffordshire designs adopted zigzag border elements and motifs such as bamboo, fans, and cranes. Brown printing dominated this style, sometimes with polychrome enamel highlights.

Marks: Wares are often marked with pattern or potter's names, but marking was inconsistent and many authentic, unmarked examples exist. The addition of "England" as a country of origin mark in 1891 helps to distinguish 20th-century wares made in the romantic style.

References: Susan and Al Bagdade, *Warman's English & Continental Pottery & Porcelain*, 3rd ed., Krause Publications, 1998; Jeffrey B. Snyder, *Romantic Staffordshire Ceramics,* Schiffer Publishing, 1997; Petra Williams, *Staffordshire: Romantic Transfer Patterns* (1978), *Staffordshire II* (1986), *Staffordshire III* (1996), Fountain House East (PO Box 99298, Jeffersontown, KY 40269).

Museums: City Museum & Art Gallery, Stoke-on-Trent, England; Henry Ford Museum, Dearborn, MI.

Caledonia, Williams Adams, 1830s

Plate, 9-1/2" d, purple transfer, imp "Adams" **60.00**

Platter, 17" l **500.00**

Soup plate, two colors **175.00**

Canova, Thomas Mayer, c1835; G. Phillips, c1840

Plate, 10-1/2" d **95.00**

Pudding bowl, two colors . . . **200.00**

Vegetable, cov **325.00**

Cheshire pattern, Burleigh Ware, cheese dish, cov, 9-1/4" l, 5" h, rect, sloped lid, underglaze blue ovoid finial, rect undertray, transfer printed green and blue, scenes of milkmaids and cheesemakers, aesthetic movement floral motifs, gilt accents, third quarter 19th C **115.00**

Columbia, W. Adams & Sons, 1850

Creamer **115.00**

Cup and saucer **65.00**

Cup plate **65.00**

Plate, 10" d **60.00**

Relish **65.00**

Cup and saucer, Venus pattern, Podmore, Walker & Co., pink, **$48.**

Dado, Ridgways, 1880s

Creamer, brown **75.00**

Cup and saucer, polychrome . **80.00**

Plate, 7-1/2" d, brown **35.00**

Delzoni, plate, 8-3/4" d, brown transfer **60.00**

India, plate, 9" d, red transfer scene, floral border **65.00**

Japonica, creamer and sugar . . **275.00**

Marmora, William Ridgway & Co., 1830s

Platter, 16-1/2" l **325.00**

Sauce tureen, matching tray . **350.00**

Soup plate **100.00**

Millenium, Ralph Stevenson & Son, 1830s, plate, 10-1/2" d **145.00**

Palestine, William Adams, 1836
Creamer and sugar **265.00**
Cup and saucer, two colors . **135.00**
Cup plate **75.00**
Plate, 7" d **60.00**
Platter, 13" l **325.00**
Vegetable, open, 12" l **200.00**

Quadrupeds, John Hall, 1814-32
Plate, 10" d, central medallion with lion, printed maker's mark for John Hall, 1814-32, pattern mark in crown, price for pr **865.00**
Platter, 14-3/4" x 19", Quadrupeds pattern, central cartouche of elephant, printed maker's mark for John Hall 1914-32, pattern mark in crown, minor surface imperfections **4,315.00**

Union, William Ridgway Son & Co., 1840s
Plate, 10-1/2" d **70.00**
Platter, 15" l **165.00**

Venus, Podmore, Walker & Co., 1850s, plate, 7-1/2" d **50.00**

STAINED AND/OR LEADED GLASS PANELS

History: American architects in the second half of the 19th century and the early 20th century used stained- and leaded-glass panels as a chief decorative element. Skilled glass craftsmen assembled the designs, the best known being Louis C. Tiffany.

The panels are held together with soft lead cames or copper wraps. When purchasing a panel, protect your investment by checking the lead and making any necessary repairs.

Reference: Web Wilson, *Great Glass in American Architecture*, E. P. Dutton, New York, 1986.

Periodicals: *Glass Art Magazine*, P.O. Box 260377, Highlands Ranch, CO 80126; *Glass Patterns Quarterly*, P.O. Box 69, Westport, NY 40077.

Collectors' Club: Stained Glass Association of America, 4450 Fenton Road, Hartland, MI 48353.

Museum: Corning Museum of Glass, Corning, NY.

Leaded

Firescreen, 48-1/2" w, 32" h, three panels, clear glass top half, hammered white glass lower half, central applied Art Nouveau floral design, green bull's eye highlights **2,750.00**

Panel, 96" h, 20" w, rect, rippled, and opaque glass, turquoise, white, and avocado, clear glass ground, stylized

flowering plant motif, c1910, six panels **6,000.00**

Sketch for leaded glass window
Charcoal on paper, The Crucifixion, 26" d, America, c1920 ..... **170.00**
Charcoal on paper, The Temptation, 26" d, America, c1920 ..... **150.00**
Watercolor, garden scene, mother and child before Christ figure, sgd on mat "Louis Comfort Tiffany," 6-3/4" x 4-1/2" **1,725.00**

Triptych, 34-3/4" h, 17-3/4" w, twining grapevines and grape clusters, green slag, textured purple and brown glass, amber border segments, textured colorless glass background, wood frame, cracks **1,380.00**

Window
23" h, 25-1/2" w, Prairie School, copper caming, textured clear and green glass, stylized floral pattern **1,000.00**
29-1/2" h, 18" w, attributed to Belcher Mosaic Glass Co., passion flower, pink ribbon, and rose bud against variegated amber ground, opalescent roundels, sea green and reddish umber frame of mosaic glass, unsigned . **2,400.00**
36" h, 16-1/4" d, Prairie School, zinc caming, clear, white, green, and violet slag glass, stylized lilies and tulips, set of five, few minor cracks in glass **4,250.00**

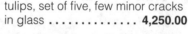

*Stained and leaded window, red petaled flowers, brown and gold background, opalescent jewel centers, slight bowing to stained glass, several cracks in glass, 30" x 45", **$450**. Photo courtesy of James D. Julia, Inc.*

Stained

Panel
24" x 14", red, white, green, pink, and blue floral design, two layers of striated and fractured glass, green patinated bronze frame, stamped "Tiffany Studios New York" pr **2,400.00**
26" x 21", Richard the Lion-Hearted on horseback, 1883 ...... **675.00**

Transom window, 59" x 17", arched form, amber, green, and red, later walnut frame, brass plaque "Illinois Traction System Car Number 523" **260.00**

Window
35-1/8" w, 15-1/2" h, rect, arched top, brown glass border, gold glass panels, central stain pained medallion of bush of classical male, sgd "Louis Shuys," scrolled leaf surround, late 19th/early 20th C. **425.00**
61-1/2" h, 61" l, over entry door type, blue and orange shield and geometric design, c1920 .. **490.00**

STANGL POTTERY BIRDS

History: Stangl ceramic birds were produced from 1940 until the Stangl factory closed in 1978. The birds were produced at Stangl's Trenton plant and either decorated there or shipped to its Flemington, New Jersey, outlet for hand painting.

During World War II, the demand for these birds, and other types of Stangl pottery as well, was so great that 40 to 60 decorators could not keep up with the demand. Orders were contracted out to be decorated by individuals in their own homes. These orders then were returned for firing and finishing. Colors used to decorate these birds varied according to the artist.

Marks: As many as 10 different trademarks were used. Almost every bird is numbered; many are artist signed. However, the signatures are used only for dating purposes and add very little to the value of the birds.

References: Harvey Duke, *Stangl Pottery*, Wallace-Homestead, 1992; Robert C. Runge, Jr., *The Collector's Encyclopedia of Stangl Dinnerware*, 1998, 2000 value update; Mike Schneider, *Stangl and Pennsbury Birds*, Schiffer Publishing, 1994.

Collectors' Clubs: American Art Pottery Association, P.O. Box 834, Westport, MA 02790-0697, http://www.amartpot.org; Stangl/Fulper Collectors Club, P.O. Box 538, Flemington, NJ 08822.

Website: www.stanglfulper.com

Additional Listings: See *Warman's Americana & Collectibles* for more examples.

Adviser: Bob Perzel.

Note: Several birds were reissued between 1972 and 1977. These reissues are dated on the bottom and are worth approximately the same as older birds, if well decorated.

3250, gazing duck, Antique Gold 50.00
3250, preening duck 125.00
3273, rooster, 5-3/4" h. 1,000.00
3274, penguin 500.00
3275, turkey 425.00
3276, bluebird 90.00
3281, mother duck 580.00
3285, rooster, 4-1/2" h, early blue green base .100.00
3286, hen, 4-1/2" h, late lime green base 50.00
3285, 3286, rooster and hen shakers, late, pr .80.00
3400, lovebird, old, wavy base. . 100.00
3400, lovebird, revised leaf base .60.00
3402, pair of orioles, revised . . .125.00
3402, pair of orioles, old. 275.00
3404, pair of lovebirds, old. 400.00
3404, pair of lovebirds, revised .100.00
3405, pair of cockatoos, revised, open base .135.00
3406, pair of kingfishers, blue . .165.00
3407, owl 300.00
3430, duck, 22". 5,000.00
3431, duck, standing 850.00
3432, rooster, 16" h. 3,000.00
3443, flying duck, teal 300.00
3444, cardinal, pink, glossy 90.00
3445, rooster, yellow. 185.00
3446, hen, gray 300.00
3449, paroquet. 160.00
3450, passenger pigeon 1,700.00
3451, William Ptarmigan. 3,500.00
3453, mountain bluebird. 1,100.00
3454, Key West quail dove, single wing up 275.00
3454, Key West quail dove, both wings up 1,800.00
3455, shoveler duck. 1,400.00
3457, walking pheasant 2,600.00
3458, quail 1,500.00
3459, falcon/fish hawk/osprey 6,000.00
3490, pair of redstarts 200.00
3492, cock pheasant 225.00
3518, pair of white-headed pigeons 950.00
3580, cockatoo, medium 110.00
3580, cockatoo, medium, white .450.00
3581, group of chickadees. 200.00
3581, group of chickadees, black and white. .300.00
3582, pair of green parakeets . .250.00
3582, pair of blue parakeets . . .220.00
3584, cockatoo, large. 275.00

3584, cockatoo, large, matte white 1,075.00
3590, chat 165.00
3591, Brewers blackbird 160.00
3595, Bobolink. 150.00
3596, gray cardinal 70.00
3597, Wilson warbler, yellow 55.00
3599, pair of hummingbirds . . . 325.00
3625, Bird of Paradise, large, 13-1/2" h 2,300.00
3627, Rivoli hummingbird, with pink flower. 175.00
3634, Allen hummingbird 90.00
3635, group of goldfinches 215.00
3715, blue jay with peanut 650.00
3717, pair of blue jays. 2,800.00
3746, canary, rose flower 250.00
3749, scarlet tanager 460.00
3750, pair of western tanagers . 500.00
3751, red-headed woodpecker, pink glossy 250.00
3752, pair of red-headed woodpeckers, red matte 500.00
3754, single white-winged crossbill 5,000.00
3754, pair of white-winged crossbills, pink glossy 425.00
3755, audubon warbler. 475.00
3756, pair of audubon warblers 500.00
3757, scissor-tailed flycatcher. 1,100.00
3758, magpie jay. 1,400.00
3810, blackpoll warber 185.00
3811, chestnut chickadee. 145.00
3812, chestnut-sided warbler . . 180.00
3813, evening grosbeak 150.00
3814, blackthroated green warbler 165.00
3815, western bluebird 440.00
3848, golden crowned kinglet. . 125.00
3850, yellow warbler 135.00
3852, cliff swallow 170.00
3853, group of golden crowned kingfishers 780.00
3868, summer tanager 700.00
3921, yellow-headed verdin . . 1,700.00
3922, European finch 1,100.00
3923, vermillian flycatcher . . .2,100.00
3924, yellow-throated warbler. . 680.00
Bird sign. 1,700.00

STATUES

History: Beginning with primitive cultures, man created statues in the shape of people and animals. During the Middle Ages, most works were religious and symbolic in character and form. During the Renaissance, the human and secular forms were preferred.

During the 18th and 19th centuries, it was fashionable to have statues in the home. Many famous works were copied for use by the general public.

Reference: H. Nicholas B. Clark, *A Marble Quarry: The James H. Ricau Collection of Sculpture at the Chrysler Museum of Art*, Hudson Hills Press, 1997.

Carved wood, female saint, Continental, 18th C, **$6,050.** *Photo courtesy of Jackson's Auctioneers & Appraisers.*

5-1/2" h, bronze, old man leaning on fence, hat on post, grassy base, sgd "Au Diable Les Lecons". 125.00
6" h, gilt bronze, Pan, seated, flute, mounted on dark green marble base, sgd "Rolano" 165.00
12" h, nude boy, seated on pillow incised with foliate designs, white marble, Continental, 19th C 635.00
12-1/2" h, Indian, sandstone, sgd "D. Fulton, 1981," kneeling in front of log, removable bone knife. 220.00
14-1/2" h, The Eternal Woman, Ernst Hegenbarth, nude female, arms crossed over her chest, sits

triumphantly atop her male victims, bronze, green brown patina, inscribed "ER Hegenbarth 1908," Wiener Gesell Schaft, Vienna foundry **1,200.00**
20" h, bronze, Mercury, sgd "M. Amodie, Napoli" **750.00**
24" h, bronze, female seated on rock with cattail, titled "Le Fil de la Veirge," sgd "Emile Hebert" **1,320.00**
28-3/4" h, La Nature Se Devoilant Devant La Science (Nature Revealing Herself Before Science), Louis Ernest Barrias, standing partially nude female emerging from under wraps, inscribed "E. Barrias," dated "20 Mars 1902," stamped "Susse Fres Edition" foundry seal, bronze and silvered bronze figure, gold, green, and silver patina
.... **13,000.00**
30" h, Master of the Hounds, Hippolyte Moreau, sgd in case, "Hippolyte Moreau, Lecourtier," dark brown patina
.... **4,500.00**
33" h, Madonna Nursing Child, carved stone, unknown 18th C German artist, some remaining polychrome paint
.... **2,000.00**
47-3/4" h, Stehender Torso, Herman Hubacher, sgd "Hubacher," dated "24," stamped foundry mark, "M. Pastori, cire perdue, Geneva," bronze lost wax process, greenish-black patina
.... **3,750.00**
53" h, Young Neptune, marble, sgd, located, and dated "Pio fede, Sculp, Firenze, 1859," restorations...**2,500.00**
58" h, 45" l, Nude Woman, bronze, ballet pose, large green marble base, figure sgd "V. Salmones 88 B-20 PA"
.... **3,300.00**
63-1/2" h, Three Graces, marble, Continental, artist unknown, after the antique.................. **2,500.00**

STEIFF

History: Margarete Steiff, GmbH, established in Germany in 1880, is known for very fine-quality stuffed animals and dolls, as well as other beautifully made collectible toys. It is still in business, and its products are highly respected.

The company's first products were wool-felt elephants made by Margaret Steiff. In a few years, the animal line was expanded to include a donkey, horse, pig, and camel.

By 1903, the company also was producing a jointed mohair teddy bear, whose production dramatically increased to more than 970,000 units in 1907. Margarete's nephews took over the company at this point.

Newly designed animals were added: Molly and Bully, the dogs, and Fluffy, the cat. Pull toys and kites

also were produced, as well as larger animals on which children could ride or play.

Marks: The bear's-head label became the symbol for the firm in about 1907, and the famous "Button in the Ear" round, metal trademark was added.

References: Peter Consalvi, Sr., *2nd Collector Steiff Values*, Hobby House Press, 1996; Margaret and Gerry Grey, *Teddy Bears*, Running Press, Courage Books, 1994; Dee Hockenberry, *Steiff Bears and Other Playthings Past and Present*, Schiffer Publishing, 2000; Margaret Fox Mandel, *Teddy Bears and Steiff Animals*, 1st Series (1984, 2000 value update), 2nd Series (1987, 2000 value update), 3rd Series (2000), Collector Books; —, *Teddy Bears, Annalee Animals & Steiff Animals*, 3rd Series, Collector Books, 1990, 1996 value update; Dee Hockenberry, *Big Bear Book*, Schiffer Publishing, 1996; Linda Mullins, *Teddy Bear & Friends Price Guide*, 4th ed., Hobby House Press, 1993; Ken Yenke, *Teddy Bear Treasury*, Collector Books, 2000.

Collectors' Clubs: Steiff Club USA, 31 E. 28th St., 9th Floor, New York, NY 10016, http://www.steiff-club.com; Steiff Collectors Club, 5001 Monroe St., Toledo, OH 43623, http://www.toystorenet.com.

Additional Listings: Teddy Bears. See also Stuffed Toys in *Warman's Americana & Collectibles* for more examples.

Notes: Become familiar with genuine Steiff products before purchasing an antique stuffed animal. Plush in old Steiff animals was mohair; trimmings usually were felt or velvet. Unscrupulous individuals have attached the familiar Steiff metal button to animals that are not Steiff.

Bear

3-1/2" h, honey blond mohair, black bead eyes, embroidered nose and mouth, fully jointed, padless style, c1950 .... **100.00**

5" h, blond mohair, black shoe button eyes, ear button, fully jointed, lacking mouth and nose embroidery, overall wear, hole in left arms, right leg, no pad style, c1910 .... **375.00**
5" h, blond mohair, rattle, no button, black shoe button eyes, fully jointed, embroidered nose and mouth, overall wear, stains, rip on arm, working rattle, excelsior stuffing, no pad style, c1910
.... **415.00**
5-1/2" h, blond mohair, glass eyes, embroidered nose and mouth, no pad style, dressed in pink print dress with pink checked collar, yellow knit overalls, green corduroy jacket, red scarf, black felt hat and a bell around his neck, c1930
.... **345.00**
8-1/2" h, golden mohair, shoe button eyes, embroidered nose, mouth, and claws, fully jointed, excelsior stuffing, no pad arms, c1915, moth damage to foot pads **1,380.00**
12-1/2" h, light apricot, ear button, fully jointed, shoe button eyes, embroidered nose, mouth, and claws, excelsior stuffing, felt pads, c1905, fur loss, lower back and back of legs, slight moth damage on pads **1,610.00**
13" h, blond mohair, glass eyes, ear button, brown embroidered nose, mouth and claws, excelsior stuffed, felt pads, c1930........ **150.00**

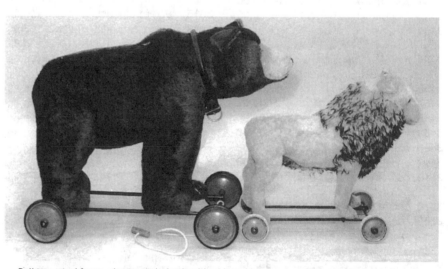

Pull toys, steel frame, sheet metal wheels with white rubber treads, left: bear, brown mohair coat, glass eyes, ear button with ribbon, ring pull voice box, added leather collar and rope pull, 31" l, 24" h, $2,100; right: lion, worn gold mohair coat, glass eyes, worn streaked mane, tail missing, ring pull voice box, 21" l, 18" h, $495. Photo courtesy of Garth's Auction, Inc.

14" h, golden mohair, ear button, black embroidered nose and claws, mouth missing, black shoe button eyes, squeaker, fully jointed body, excelsior stuffing, original felt pads, c1905, one-inch fabric tear right front arm joint, very minor fur loss, overall soil **1,955.00**

14" h, blond mohair, underscored ear button, black shoe button eyes, black embroidered nose, mouth and claws, fully jointed, tan felt pads, excelsior stuffing, shaved muzzle, c1905, 14 in. . . . **2,070.00**

14" h, light golden mohair, underscored ear button, black shoe button eyes, center seam, black embroidered nose, mouth, and claws, fully jointed, tan felt pads, c1905, holes in hand pads **4,890.00**

17" h, One Hundredth Anniversary Bear, ear button, gold mohair, fully jointed, plastic eyes, black embroidered nose, mouth, and claws, peach felt pads, excelsior stuffing, certificate no. 3934, orig box **230.00**

19" h, tan mohair, shaved muzzle, ear button, glass eyes, embroidered nose, fully jointed, synthetic plush pads, excelsior stuffing, c1950-60 . . . . **175.00**

20" h, golden long mohair, shoe button eyes, embroidered nose, mouth and claws, fully jointed, excelsior stuffing, c1905 . **8,920.00**

21" h, Zotty, long curly beige mohair, apricot chest, ear button, fully jointed glass eyes, airbrushed mouth, embroidered nose, peach felt pads, 1950s-60s **175.00**

30" h, blond mohair, script ear button, glass eyes, embroidered nose, mouth, claws excelsior stuffed, fully jointed, mid-19th C, felt feet pads have scattered moth holes, break at sides **1,955.00**

Beaver, 6" l, Nagy, mohair, chest tag, post WWII **95.00**

Bison, 9-1/2" l, mohair, ear button, chest tag, post WWII **200.00**

Boxer, 16-1/2" l, 15-1/2" h, beige mohair coat, black trim, glass eyes, leather collar marked "Steiff," head turns, minor wear, straw stuffing **165.00**

Boxer puppy, 4-1/4" h, paper label "Daly" **135.00**

Cat

7" h, beige velvet, black paint, faded red ribbon, pink hand warmer, ear button, wear, tail sewn back **550.00**

14" l, pull top, white mohair coat, gray stripes, glass eyes, worn pink ribbon with bell, pink felt ear linings, button, cast iron wheels **1,980.00**

Cocker spaniel, 5-3/4" h, sitting, glass eyes, ear button, chest tag, post WWII **125.00**

Cocker spaniel puppy, 4-3/4" h, button **90.00**

Dalmatian puppy, 4-1/4" h, paper label "Sarras" **145.00**

Dog, 15-1/2" l, 14" h, pull toy, orange and white mohair coat, glass eyes, steel frame, cast iron wheels, one ear missing, button in remaining ear, voice box does not work **280.00**

Frog, 3-3/4" l, velveteen, glass eyes, green, sitting, button and chest tag **125.00**

Goat, 6-1/2" h, ear button **150.00**

Gussy, 6-1/2" l, white and black kitten, glass eyes, ear button, chest tag, post WWII **125.00**

Horse on wheels, 21" l, 17" h, ear button, glass eyes, white and brown, wear and breaks to fabric, on solid metal wheels, non-functioning pull-ring, c1930 . . . . **215.00**

Kangaroo and joey, 20-3/4" h mother, mohair, jointed head and arms, glass eyes, black embroidered nose and mouth, ear button and tag, 4" h velveteen baby with glass eyes, embroidered nose and mouth, ear button and tag missing **375.00**

Koala, 7-1/2" h, glass eyes, ear button, chest tag, post WWII **135.00**

Lion

21" l, 18" h, pull toy, worn gold mohair coat, glass eyes, worn streaked mane incomplete, no tail, ring pull voice box, steel frame, sheet metal wheels with white rubber treads marked "Steiff" **500.00**

26" l, recumbent, glass eyes, embroidered nose, mouth, and claws, post WWII, ears and button missing, spotty fur loss **55.00**

Lizard, 12" l, Lizzy, velveteen, yellow and green, black steel eyes, chest tag **200.00**

Llama, 10" h, glass eyes, ear button, chest tag, post WWII **125.00**

Monkey, 5" h, Coco, glass eyes, ear button, chest tag, post WWII . . . **125.00**

Owl, 4-1/2" h, Wittie, glass eyes, ear button, chest tag, post WWII **95.00**

Palomino colt, 11" h, ear button, wear **330.00**

Panda, 6" h, black and white mohair, fully jointed, glass eyes, excelsior stuffing, felt open mouth and pads, c1950, some fur loss, moth damage on pads, button and tag missing . . **260.00**

Parakeet, 6-1/2" h, Hansi, bright lime green and yellow, airbrushed black details, plastic eyes, button tag, chest tag, plastic beak and feet **115.00**

Penguin, 5-1/2" h, Peggy, glass eyes, ear button, chest tag, post WWII . **95.00**

Pig, 15" l, pull top, blond mohair, button eyes, ear button, cast iron wheels, repairs, very worn mohair **330.00**

Rabbit, 9-1/2" h, unmarked, wear **220.00**

Seal, riding, button on tail flipper, steel frame, rubber tread wheels, worn ivory colored mohair and salmon colored embroidered nose and mouth, nylon filament whiskers, eyes missing, straw stuffing, 28" l, $200. Photo courtesy of Garth's Auctions, Inc.

Sheep, 12-1/2" l, pull toy, woolly mohair coat, felt legs and face, button eyes, worn ribbon with bell, head turns, cast iron wheels, one ear incomplete, button missing **935.00**

Soldier, 14" h, c1913, slight moth damage, hat and equipment missing **460.00**

Squirrel, 6" h, unmarked **75.00**

Tiger

5-3/4" h, glass eyes, minor fading, not marked **50.00**

31" l, recumbent, unjointed, pink embroidered nose, black mouth and claws, ear button, post WWII, some damage **115.00**

Turtle, 7" l, Slo, plastic shell, glass eyes, ear button, chest tag, post WWII **85.00**

Walrus, 6-1/2" l, Paddy, plastic tusk, glass eyes, ear button, chest tag, post WWII **145.00**

STEIN, LEA

History: Lea Stein, a French-trained artist born in Paris in 1931, began making her whimsical pieces of jewelry in 1969, after her husband, Fernand Steinberger, came up with a process of laminating layers of rhodoid (cellulose acetate) sheets with interesting textures and colors. The layers were baked overnight with a secret component of his creation and then cut into shapes for various designs of pins, bracelets, earrings, and shaped decorative objects. From the side, in some pieces, as many as 20 layers of cellulose have been bonded together to make these pieces.

The most easily recognizable Lea Stein pin is the 3-D fox, produced in a myriad of colors and designs. Often, lace or metal layers were incorporated into the celluloid, which produced an astounding number of unique textures. The 3-D fox's tail is looped from one piece of celluloid.

Many different styles of cats, dogs, bugs, bunnies, birds, ducks, and other creatures were introduced, as well as Art Deco-styled women, mod-styled children, flowers, cars, hats, purses, gold-encased and rhinestone encrusted designs, and lots of little "things," such as stars, hearts, rainbows, and even pins resembling John Travolta and Elvis Presley. In addition, collectors can find many bangles, rings, cuffs, earrings, barrettes, and rarer boxes, mirrors, and cigarette cases. The designs seem endless and to a Lea Stein collector, the ability to collect one of everything is almost impossible, because so many pieces were one of a kind. One particularly elusive piece is called "Joan Crawford" in the U.S. and "Carmen" in France. This piece was made in limited quantity and always hard to find, but, lo and behold, a new cache has recently hit the market.

These "vintage" pieces of jewelry were made from 1969 until 1981 and are identified by a V-shaped pin back, which is heat mounted to the back of each piece, as are the pin backs on her newer pieces. While some early pieces may not be marked, the majority of pieces will always be marked "Lea Stein Paris." Early pieces are also marked with a small oval paper tag, which reads "Made in France." Some of the later issues have riveted backs, but all of them are marked in the same way. At one time, the age of a pin could be determined by the pin back, but because of many newly released pieces in the past few years, that no longer is always the case.

Stein's workshop is still producing jewelry. While some of the vintage pieces are rare, it is virtually impossible to tell the difference between old and new releases, except with the knowledge of which designs were created at what time in Stein's career. Whether old or new, Lea Stein's jewelry is quite collectible and very much wearable.

Many different stories about the history of Lea Stein's jewelry have been circulated, but here are the facts, some of which are in direct discrepancy with many of the well-known jewelry collecting books.

In 1957, Lea Stein started her own company, and from 1957 to 1965 was in the textile business. From 1965 to 1967, she made buttons. In 1967, she began making buttons in rhodoid, the cellulose acetate associated with her jewelry. Her skills at making rhodoid buttons were put to use in her first jewelry collection, which she began producing in 1969.

The vintage period of Lea Stein's jewelry was really a very short period of 12 years, from 1969 to 1981, when her company, which by that time employed 50 workers and was mass-producing jewelry, failed due to the influx of Asian competition.

Reports in different books describing Stein's jewelry vary the time period of her "golden years" as anywhere from the 1930s to the 1960s. This is untrue, as she would have been but a schoolgirl in the 1930s. Part of this speculation is due to the fact that Lea Stein's work is heavily influenced by the Art-Deco period and that rhodoid strongly resembles Bakelite and some older plastics, such as galalith.

After the failure of her company in 1981, an American dealer in New York bought a big part of her remaining stock and began selling her jewelry in the U.S. It was not until after 1981 that the trademark Lea Stein pieces began to be well known in the U.S. It was somewhat ironic that Stein became known as a famous designer of French jewelry only after the failure of her business.

In the late 1980s, after running a computer business, Lea Stein returned to the profession which she liked best—creating and making plastic jewelry. Every year since 1988, she has created a new piece for her collection. These new designs include: Buba (owl), Bacchus (cat's head), Gomina (sleeping cat), Attila (standing cat), the tortoise, and Ric the dog. Her newest designs are the Porcupine and Goupil in 2000 and the Penguin, Cicada, and Christmas Tree in 2001. There are no first and second editions of these pieces, since they did not exist in the 1970s and early 1980s.

Some of Stein's designs are once again being produced in Paris. New releases are still being made, both from the older and newer patterns, making it more difficult to differentiate between old and new pieces. Dealers in France still unearth old stock from time to time.

References: Lillian Baker, *Twentieth Century Fashionable Plastic Jewelry*, Collector Books, out of print; Judith Just, *Lea Stein Jewelry*, Schiffer Publishing, 2001; Ginger Moro, *European Designer Jewelry*, Schiffer Publishing, 1995.

Internet Resource:
http://www.baubles-and-bibelots.com

Adviser: Judy Smith.

Bracelet, bangle, dark green and red peppermint stick swirls **75.00**

Earrings, pr, clip, bright green swirls on pearly white, stamped on back, 1-3/8" d
. . . . **75.00**

Pin, all with signature Lea Stein-Paris V-shaped pin back

Bacchus, cat, pearly silver and black, 2-3/8" w, 1-1/8" h **65.00**

Bee, transparent wings with gold edge, faux ivory body and head, topaz colored glass edge eye, 2-3/8" wingspan **70.00**

Blueberries, peach lace, 2-7/8" l
. . . . **65.00**

Mistigri, cat, mottled caramel color, faux ivory ears and eyes, signature V-shaped Lea Stein-Paris safety clasp, 4" w, 1-7/8" h, **$65.** *Photo courtesy of Judy Smith.*

Cat, standing, magenta lace, faux-mother-of-pearl ears and eyes, 3-3/4" l, 1-3/4" h **75.00**

Cicada, irid red wings, striped body and head, 3-3/8" l, 1-1/4" w . **75.00**

Double Totie, left in white lace, dark blue bow around neck with bright blue nose, right is magenta lace, black neck bow and nose, 2-1/4" w, 1-5/8" h **95.00**

Edelweiss, coral flowers, white and marbled green stem, 3-3/8" h
. . . . **65.00**

Flamingo, pink, 1-7/8" w, 2-3/8" h
. . . . **55.00**

Flower pot, two flowers, one aqua lacy turquoise, other purple lacy, dark blue leaves, turquoise lacy pot, 1-1/2" w, 2-1/2" h **65.00**

Fox, red tones **100.00**

Goldenberries, shades of plum, gold, and white, 2-3/8" w, 1-5/8" h
. . . . **65.00**

Golden Raptor, translucent blue body, golden overlay, topaz colored glass bed eye, 2-1/8" w, 2-1/4" h **80.00**

Gomina, cat, shiny black body, accented with waves of silver and blue, dark pearly blue ears and eyes, 3" w, 1-7/8" h **85.00**

Joan Crawford **125.00**

Mistigri Kitty, caramel, 4" w, 3-7/8" h
. . . . **70.00**

Oriental girl, shades of blue and white, transparent light blue hat, faux-ivory face, transparent light blue eye, 2" w, 2-1/8" h **90.00**

Goldenberries, shades of yellow, gold and white, striped translucent berries, signature Lea Stein-Paris V-shaped clasp, 2-3/4" w, 1-5/8" h, $75. Photo courtesy of Judy Smith.

Panther, pearly ivory harlequin, medium faux tortoiseshell, 4-1/4" l, 1-3/4" h **65.00**

Panther, shades of brown, irid faux tortoiseshell, 4-1/4" l, 1-3/4" h **65.00**

Panther, silvery moiré, 4-1/4" l, 1-3/4" h **65.00**

Penguin, dark red brocade body and head, yellow lace beak, eye, neck, and feet, pearly harquelin lace body, 1-3/4" w, 3-1/8" h .**70.00**

Porcupine, irid gold and dark red body with black accents, black face and paws, dark red eye and nose, 3" w **80.00**

Flowerpot, turquoise lace flower with red lacy center and a purple lace flower with a light blue lace center, flanked by shiny dark, dark blue leaves, lacy turquoise flowerpot, signed V-shaped clasp, 1-1/2" w, 2-1/2" h, $75. Photo courtesy of Judy Smith.

Ric, pearly ivory harlequin pattern, shiny black ears, nose, eye and collar. **65.00**

Sailor, faux ivory face, neck, hands and feet, pearly purple suit and cap, pearly gray collar, 1-5/8" w, 2-3/8" h **80.00**

Swallow, pink and white lace wings, 2-3/4" w, 1-3/8" h. **60.00**

Three ducks, orange lace bodies, dark royal blue heads, dark blue wings, 1" w, 2-1/4" h **75.00**

STEINS

1892-1921

History: Steins, mugs especially made to hold beer or ale, range in size from the smaller 3/10 and 1/4 liter to the larger 1, 1-1/2, 2, 3, 4, and 5 liters, and in rare cases to 8 liters. A liter is 1.05 liquid quarts.

Master steins or pouring steins hold 3 to 5 liters and are called krugs. Most steins are fitted with a metal hinged lid with thumb lift. The earthenware character-type steins usually are German in origin.

References: Susan and Al Bagdade, *Warman's English & Continental Pottery & Porcelain*, 3rd ed., Krause Publications, 1998; Gary Kirsner, *German Military Steins*, 2nd ed., Glentiques (P.O. Box 8807, Coral Springs, FL 33075), 1996; ——, *Mettlach Book*, 3rd ed., 1994; Gary Kirsner and Jim Gruhl, *The Stein Book, A 400-Year History*, Glentiques, 1990.

Periodicals: *Regimental Quarterly*, P.O. Box 793, Frederick, MD 21705; *The Beer Stein Journal*, P.O. Box 8807, Coral Springs, FL 33075.

Collectors' Clubs: Stein Collectors International, P.O. Box 5005, Laurel, MD 20726-5005; Sun Steiners, P.O. Box 11782, Fort Lauderdale, FL 33339.

Museum: Milwaukee Art Center, Milwaukee, WI.

Character

Beethoven, half liter, porcelain, lire on side of body and on porcelain inlaid lid, E. Bohne & Sohn **570.00**

Frederick III, in uniform, 1/2 liter, porcelain, porcelain lid, Schierholz, chips on lid repaired, int. color yellowing **1,735.00**

Indian, 1/4 liter, porcelain, inlaid lid, E. Bohne & Sohn **440.00**

L.A.W. high-wheel bicycle, half liter, porcelain, lithophane of man falling onto woman, inlaid lid, Schierholz. . . **440.00**

Monk, 1/3 liter, design by Frank Ringer, marked "J. Reinemann, Munchen" on underside of base, inlaid lid, 5" h **580.00**

Singing pig, 1/2 liter, porcelain, Schierholz, inlaid lid **580.00**

Skull, 1/3 liter, porcelain, large jaw, inlaid lid, E. Bohne & Sohn, pewter slightly bent **550.00**

Faience

Thuringen, 1 liter, 9-1/2" h, hp, floral design on front, purple trees on sides, pewter top rim and lid, pewter base ring, 18th C, tight hairline on side **1,155.00**

Glass

9-1/2" h, 1 liter, blown, wedding type, hp floral design and verse, pewter lid with earlier date of 1779, pewter brass ring, c1850. . . . .**925.00**

15-1/4" h, 6-1/2" d, amber, encased in fancy French pewter frame, ram's heads around stein, hinged top lid **495.00**

Ivory, hand carved, c1850-70 11-1/2" h, elaborate battle scene with approx. 100 figures, carving around entire body, silver top with figural knight finial, cherub bases and fruit in repousse o lid, figural handle of man in armor, silver base with touch marks, discoloration to ivory **6,700.00**

High glaze, panoramic view of city of Munich, city seal, highly glazed lion on cover, 19" h, $600.

13-1/2" h, elaborate hunting scene, four men on horseback, 15 dogs, ivory lid with various animals carved around border, 3-1/2" h finial of man blowing trumpet with dog, figural handle of bare breasted woman with crown, dog head thumb lift, left arm and trumpet missing
.........................**11,550.00**

Porcelain

Delft, 1/2 liter, elaborate scene of two people playing lawn tennis, porcelain inlaid lid of sail boat, marked "Delft, Germany" **1,390.00**
Meissen, 1 liter, 7" h, hp, scene of three people in forest, floral design around sides, porcelain lid with berry finial and painted flowers, closed hinge, cross swords and "S" mark, c1820, strap repoured **3,100.00**
Schierholz, Musterchultz, Sad Radish
.........................**295.00**

Pottery

1/4 liter, transfer and enameled, color, Ulmer Splatz!, The Bird from the City of Ulm, pewter lid.............**115.00**
1/2 liter, relief, tan, brown, and green, chicken with egg body design, relief pewter lid with bust of Bismarck, repaired tear in pewter, 2" hairline on body **130.00**

Regimental, 1/2 liter, porcelain
2 Schwer. Reit. Regt. Erzh. Fz, Ferd u. Osterr-Este Esk Landshut 1899-02, named to Friederich Schmidt, two side scenes, lion thumb lift, old tear on lid repaired, minor scruffs, 11-1/2" h**675.00**
11 Armee Corps, Mainz 1899, names to Res. Doring, two side scenes, plain thumb lift, strap tear repaired, lines in lithophane, 10" h **485.00**
30 Field Artillery, Rastatt 1897-99, named to Freund Hilfstromp, two side scenes, roster, thumb lift missing
.........................**375.00**
61 Field Artillery, Dartmstadt 1910-12, named to Kanonier Boxheimer, four side sides, roster worn, lion thumb lift
.........................**415.00**
120 Infantry, Ulm 1899-01, named to Tambour Wurst, two side scenes, Wurttemberg thumb lift, 10-1/2" h
.........................**520.00**
123 Grenadier, Ulm 1908-10, named to Grenadier Schindler, four side scenes, roster, bird thumb lift, open blister on int. base, finial missing **550.00**
127 Infantry, Ulm 1910-12, named to Musketier Vollm, four side scenes, roster, bird thumb lift, 11-1/2" h . **475.00**

Half liter, playing cards, #1255A, pewter lid, $450. Photo courtesy of Joy Luke Auctions.

Wood and pewter, Daubenkrug
1/2 liter, 6-1/2" h, pewter scene of deer, vines and leaves on sides, pewter handle and lid, c1820, some separations to pewter.........**925.00**
1/3 liter, 5-1/2" h, floral design on sides, oval with crown on front, pewter handle and lid, 18th C, splints in pewter and wood....................**1,270.00**

STEUBEN GLASS

History: Frederick Carder, an Englishman, and Thomas G. Hawkes of Corning, New York, established the Steuben Glass Works in 1904. In 1918, the Corning Glass Company purchased the Steuben company. Carder remained with the firm and designed many of the pieces bearing the Steuben mark. Probably the most widely recognized wares are Aurene, Verre De Soie, and Rosaline, but many other types were produced.

The firm is still operating, producing glass of exceptional quality.

1903-32

References: Thomas P. Dimitroff, Charles R. Hajdamach, Jane Shadel Spillman, and Robert F. Rockwell III, *Frederick Carder and Steuben Glass: American Classic,* Schiffer Publishing, 1998; Paul Gardner, *Glass of Frederick Carder,* Schiffer Publishing, 2001; Kyle Husfloen, *Antique Trader's American & European Decorative and Art Glass Price Guide,* 2nd ed., Krause Publications, 2000; Paul Perrot, Paul Gardner, and James S. Plaut, *Steuben,* Praeger Publishers, 1974; Kenneth Wilson, *American Glass 1760-1930,* 2 vols., Hudson Hills Press and The Toledo Museum of Art, 1994.

Museums: Corning Museum of Glass, Corning, NY; Rockwell Museum, Corning, NY.

Aurene

Bowl, 6" d, blue, irid surface... **275.00**
Bud vase, 3" d base, 10" h, blue, gold highlights, sgd "Steuben Aurene 2556"
.........................**700.00**
Cabinet vase, 2-9/16" d, 2-3/8" h, gold, ruffled rim, sgd "Aurene 2649," also sgd "F. Carder" across ground pontil **725.00**
Candlesticks, pr, 10-1/8" h, catalog #686, amber, twist stems on applied disc foot, strong gold luster, sgd "Aurene 686," c1920........**1,100.00**
Darner, 5-1/2" l, 2-1/4" d, gold, some nicks and scratches from use.. **850.00**
Lamp shade, 4-3/8" h, shape #2320, ribbed, bell shape, obscure silver fleur-de-lis paint stamp, pr **400.00**

Perfume

4-1/4" h, tapered and paneled body, raised neck, floral molded stopper, strong blue irid with green and purple highlights, pontil sgd "Aurene 2758," c1920, light surface scratches **865.00**
4-3/4" h, catalog #1455, melon ribbed, gold, ball top stopper with applied gold bead, base sgd "Aurene 1455" within polished pontil, c1910, stopper possible replacement........... **635.00**

Planter, 12" d, blue, inverted rim, three applied prunt feet, engraved "Aurene 2586".....................**775.00**

Vase

4-3/4" h, catalog #209, green pulled loops, gold irid, inscribed "Aurene 209" **1,035.00**
5-1/2" h, gold, dimples, ruffled rim, polished pontil, sgd "Aurene 145"
....................**1,200.00**
8-1/2" h, catalog #2697, blue, flattened cone, raised pedestal foot, white vines and gold Aurene hearts, base engraved "Steuben Aurene 2697".........**2,000.00**

Celeste Blue

Candlesticks, brilliant blue, applied foliate form bobeche and cups, bulbed shafts, c1920-33, set of four .. **2,300.00**
Center bowl, 16-1/4" d, 4-1/4" h, catalog #112, swirled optic ribbed broad bowl, rolled rim, applied fluted foot, partially polished pontil, c1925
.........................**400.00**

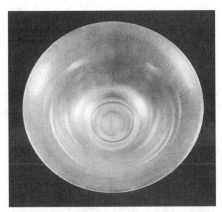

Verre de Soie, bowl, unsigned, 8" d, 3-1/4" h, $140.

Finger bowl, underplate, catalog #2889, 5" d flared bowl, 6-1/2" underplate, swirled ribbed design, c1925, set of 12, some chips . . . **600.00**

Iced tea goblet, 6-1/2" h, catalog #5192, blue, flared, light ribbon, c1918-32, set of eight **400.00**

Juice glass, 4-1/2" h, catalog #5192, blue, flared, light ribbon, c1918-32, set of eight **375.00**

Luncheon plate, 8-1/2" d, molded blue body, Kensington pattern variant, engraved border of leaves and dots, c1918-32, set of 12 . . . . **550.00**

Vase, 10" d, 12-1/4" h, clear glass handles **1,700.00**

Cluthra

Lamp base, 12-1/2" h, ovoid, creamy white cluthra acid-etched Art-Deco flowers, acid-etched fleur-de-lis mark near base, orig gilded foliate bronze lamp fittings, c1925 . . . . **2,070.00**

Vase, 8" h, catalog #2683, rose, acid stamp script mark **2,600.00**

Wall pocket, 15-1/2" w, 8" h, half round flared bowl, black and white cluthra, cut and mounted to foliate gilt metal framework, polished pontil, c1930, slight corrosion to metal **490.00**

Crystal

Bud vase, 6-3/4" h, elongated neck on swollen base, applied ball and scroll dec, base inscribed "Steuben," designed by Don Wier, 1947, Madigan catalog #7947, light staining . . . **200.00**

Cocktail set, 15" h cocktail shaker, six matching 2-1/2" h glasses, two applied red cherries, wheel-cut leaves, and stems on shaker, ruby stopper, same dec on glasses, some with fleur-de-lis marks, slight damage to stopper **3,700.00**

Goblet, 7-1/16" h, flared cylindrical vessel, knobbed stem, sq base, small "S" inscribed on base, designed by Arthur A. Houghton, Jr., 1938, Madigan catalog #7846, set of six, two with small chips **260.00**

Vase
7-3/8" h, catalog #SP919, flared wing form, pedestal base, inscribed "Steuben" on base **330.00**
10-1/2" h, catalog #7500, oviform, disk base, engraved grasses and stars, design by Walter Teague, acid stamp mark on pontil . **575.00**

Grotesque

Bowl, 11-1/2" l, 6-1/4" h, blue jade, Frederick Carder design, minor int. surface wear, fleur-de-lis mark **3,850.00**

Vase, 9-1/4" h, amethyst, catalog #7090, pillar molded floriform body, ruffled rim shaded to colorless crystal at applied disk foot, acid script "Steuben" mark in polished pontil, c1930 . **525.00**

Jade

Bowl, 8" d, 6" h, two-line pillar, ftd, alabaster int., fleur-de-lis acid stamp mark **800.00**

Candlesticks, pr, 10" h, No. 2956, jade candle cup and base, alabaster shaft, gold foil labels **550.00**

Compote, 10" h, yellow, ftd . . . **1,450.00**

Lamp base
10-1/4" h, green jade bulbous base, long flared neck, rolled rim, applied spiral of alabaster glass ending with rosettes, silvered metal lamp fittings, c1925 . . . . **900.00**
12" h, catalog #7001, urn form, plum jade, intricately etched in Belgrade pattern, gilt-metal lamp fittings, c1925, chips to rim under mounting **2,415.00**
13" h flared double gourd shaped dark amethyst body cased to alabaster int., overlaid with amethyst, cameo etched in Chinese pattern, double etched with scrolling design, gilt metal fittings with three scroll arms, shallow chip under fixture **1,850.00**

Parfait, 6" h, applied alabaster foot **350.00**

Rose bowl, 7" d, 7" h, spherical, smooth jade crystal **350.00**

Vase
3-1/2" d base, 8" h, catalog #1169, alabaster int., floral design **2,450.00**

Vase, acid cut back, jade green, sculptured chrysanthemums, 9-1/2" h, $800. Photo courtesy of Garth's Auctions, Inc.

8" d, 7" h, spherical, acid cut back Matsu pattern, alabaster int. **1,750.00**
9" h, catalog #7316, flared rim, swirled ribs, flattened hollow green jade ball joins vase to alabaster foot, broken pontil mark, unsgd **800.00**
10" d, 13" h, alabaster int., acid cut lattice design, fleur de lis mark, small rim chip **1,295.00**

Miscellaneous

Bowl, 6-1/2" h, Old Ivory, catalog #7307, pillar ftd, applied raised foot, c1930 . . . . **435.00**

Candlesticks, pr, 11-3/4" h, catalog #2956, amber glass baluster shaped stems, wide disk foot, c1925 . . . **690.00**

Compote, 8" d, 8" h, Selenium Red, swirled ribs and foot, wheel cut grape and vine pattern on stem, fleur-de-lis mark **800.00**

Exhibition sculpture, 18" h, Salmon Run, designed by James Houston, engraved by George Thompson, number 14 in series of 20, orig red leather and velvet box **13,500.00**

Lamp base
10-1/4" h, catalog #8023, urn form, swirled purple, blue, and red moss agate, gilt-metal lamp fittings, acanthus leaf dec, purple glass jewel at top, needs rewiring **2,415.00**
14" h, catalog #8006, bulbous, long flared neck, alabaster, etched

Grape pattern, silvered metal lamp fittings, c1925 . . . . **1,150.00**

Paperweight, Excalibur, designed by James Houston, 1963, catalog #1000, faceted hand-polished solid crystal embedded with removable sterling silver sword, 18kt gold scabbard, base inscribed "Steuben" **1,955.00**

Parfait and underplate, 4-1/2" h, 5-1/4" d underplate, Calcite, gold, partial paper label **625.00**

Pitcher, 9" h, catalog #6665, Spanish Green, slightly ribbed oval, flared mouth, applied angled handle, raised disk foot, acid fleur-de-lis mark . **460.00**

Serving plate, 14-1/4" d, 2" h, catalog #3579, Bristol Yellow, board convex and folded rim, slight optic ribbing, wear scratches **200.00**

Vase

6" h, Oriental Poppy, shape #6501 . . . . **3,200.00**

12-1/2" h, 9-1/4" d, catalog #7389, Strawberry Mansion, flared bulb form, colorless, sq plinth base, two applied "M" handles, designed by Frederick Carder, 1934, nick at base **1,035.00**

Rosaline

Bowl, 8" l, 7" w, 3-1/4" h, one end folded in, other pinched spout, inscribed "F. Carder Steuben 723" on edge of polished pontil **350.00**

Compote, 4" h, ruffled, alabaster stem and foot **275.00**

Goblet, crystal foot **90.00**

Perfume, 5-3/8" h, catalog #6412, teardrop shape, cloudy pink, applied alabaster glass foot, c1925, pr . **435.00**

Verre De Soie

Bonbon, 6" h, compote form, overall irid surface, swirled celeste blue finial, twisted stem **850.00**

Perfume, 4-1/2" h, catalog #1455, ribbed body, celeste blue flame stopper, c1915 . . . . **400.00**

Vase, 10" h, classic form, notched rim, all over floral motif **450.00**

STEVENGRAPHS

History: Thomas Stevens of Coventry, England, first manufactured woven silk designs in 1854. His first bookmark was produced in 1862, followed by the first Stevengraphs, perhaps in 1874, but definitely by 1879 when they were shown at the York Exhibition. The first portrait Stevengraphs (of Disraeli and Gladstone) were produced in 1886, and the first postcards incorporating the woven silk panels in 1904. Stevens offered many other items with silk panels, including valentines, fans, pincushions, and needle cases.

Stevengraphs are miniature silk pictures, matted in cardboard, and usually having a trade announcement or label affixed to the reverse. Other companies, notably W. H. Grant of Coventry, copied Stevens's technique. Their efforts should not be confused with Stevengraphs.

Collectors in the U.S. favor the Stevengraphs with American-related views, such as "Signing of the Declaration of Independence," "Columbus Leaving Spain," and "Landing of Columbus." Sports-related Stevengraphs such as "The First Innings" (baseball), and "The First Set" (tennis) are also popular, as well as portraits of Buffalo Bill, President and Mrs. Cleveland, George Washington, and President Harrison.

Postcards with very fancy embossing around the aperture in the mount almost always have Stevens' name printed on them. The two most popular embossed postcard series in the U.S. are "Ships" and "Hands across the Sea." The latter set incorporates two crossed flags and two hands shaking. Seventeen flag combinations have been found, but only seven are common. These series generally are not printed with Stevens' name. Stevens also produced silks that were used in cards made by the Alpha Publishing Co.

Stevens' bookmarks are longer than they are wide, have mitered corners at the bottom, and are finished with a tassel. Many times his silks were used as the top or bottom half of regular bookmarks.

Marks: Thomas Stevens' name appears on the mat of the early Stevengraphs, directly under the silk panel. Many of the later portraits and the larger silks (produced initially for calendars) have no identification on the front of the mat other than the phrase "woven in pure silk" and have no label on the back.

Bookmarks originally had Stevens' name woven into the foldover at the top of the silk, but soon the identification was woven into the fold-under mitered corners. Almost every Stevens' bookmark has such identification, except the ones woven at the World's Columbian Exposition in Chicago, 1892 to 1893.

References: Geoffrey A. Godden, *Stevengraphs and Other Victorian Silk Pictures*, Associated University Presses, 1971; Chris Radley, *Woven Silk Postcard*, privately printed, 1978; Austin Sprake, *Price Guide to Stevengraphs*, Antique Collectors' Club, 1972.

Collectors' Club: Stevengraph Collectors' Assoc., 2829 Arbutus Road, #2103, Victoria, British Columbia, V8N 5X5, Canada.

Museums: Herbert Art Gallery and Museum, Coventry, England; Paterson Museum, Paterson, NJ.

Note: Prices are for pieces in mint or close-to-mint condition.

Bookmarks

Assassination, Abraham Lincoln **395.00**

Centennial, USA, 1776-1876, General George Washington, The Father of Our Country, The First in Peace, The First in War, The First in the Hearts of Our Countrymen!, few small stains . . **125.00**

Forget-Me-Not, Godden #441 . . **350.00**

Das Ende, horse race, orig mat, German label on back, $150.

I Wish You a Merry Christmas and a Happy New Year **65.00**

Lord Have Mercy **400.00**

Mail Coach **225.00**

Mother and Child, evening prayers, 10-1/2" l, 2" w, 1-1/2" silk tassel . **400.00**

Mourning, Blessed Are They Who Mourn, 9-1/2" l, 2" w, 2" silk tassel **450.00**

My Dear Father, red, green, white, and purple **200.00**

Old Armchair **150.00**

Prayer Book Set, five orig markers attached with small ivory button, cream-colored tape fastened to orig frame, Communion, Collect, Lesson I, Lesson II, Psalms, gold lettering, gold silk tassels, orig mount, c1880-85 . . . . **3,400.00**

The Old Arm Chair, chair, full text, musical score, four color, 2" w, 11" l **95.00**

The Star Spangled Banner, U.S. flag, full text and musical score of song, red tassel, seven color, no maker's mark, 2-1/2" w, 11" l **85.00**

To One I Love, Love me little, love me long is the burden of my song, Love that is too hot and strong, burneth soon to waste, Still I would not have thee cold, not too backward or too bold; Love that lasteth till this old fadeth not in haste **75.00**

Postcard

RMS *Arabic*, Hands Across the Sea **465.00**

RMS *Elmina* **225.00**

RMS *Franconia* **175.00**

RMS *Iverina* **165.00**

USMS *Philadelphia* **185.00**

Stevengraph

Betsy Making the First United States Flag, Anderson Bros., Paterson, NJ, 5" x 8-1/2" **60.00**

Buffalo Bill, Nate Salsbury, Indian Chief, orig mat and frame, 8" x 7" **500.00**

Chateau Frontenac Hotel, Quebec, silver filigree frame **75.00**

Coventry, 7-1/4" x 13", framed . . **100.00**

Death of Nelson, 7-1/4" x 2-1/2" . **200.00**

Declaration of Independence . **375.00**

Dick Turpin's last ride on his Bonnie Black Bess **175.00**

For Life or Death, fire engine rushing to burning house, orig mat and frame **350.00**

Good Old Days, Royal Mail Coach, 5-3/4" h, 8-1/2" l, orig frame **200.00**

God Speed the Plow **175.00**

H. M. Stanley, famous explorer . **300.00**

Jeyhanne d'Arc, F. Lematte, 12-1/2" x 6-1/2" w **50.00**

Kenilworth Castle, 7-1/4" x 13" framed **100.00**

Landing of Columbus **350.00**

President Cleveland **365.00**

Oxford, Cambridge, Are You Ready, 5-3/4" h, 8-1/2" l, orig frame **300.00**

The Water Jump **195.00**

Untitled, life-saving boat **175.00**

STEVENS AND WILLIAMS

19th C

History: In 1824, Joseph Silvers and Joseph Stevens leased the Moor Lane Glass House at Briar Lea Hill (Brierley Hill), England, from the Honey-Borne family. In 1847, William Stevens and Samuel Cox Williams took over, giving the firm its present name. In 1870, the company moved to its Stourbridge plant. In the 1880s, the firm employed such renowned glass artisans as Frederick C. Carder, John Northwood, other Northwood family members, James Hill, and Joshua Hodgetts.

Stevens and Williams made cameo glass. Hodgetts developed a more commercial version using thinner-walled blanks, acid etching, and the engraving wheel. Hodgetts, an amateur botanist, was noted for his brilliant floral designs.

Other glass products and designs manufactured by Stevens and Williams include intaglio ware, Peach Bloom (a form of peachblow), moss agate, threaded ware, "jewell" ware, tapestry ware, and Silveria. Stevens and Williams made glass pieces covering the full range of late Victorian fashion.

After World War I, the firm concentrated on refining the production of lead crystal and achieving new glass colors. In 1932, Keith Murray came to

Stevens and Williams as a designer. His work stressed the pure nature of the glass form. Murray stayed with Stevens and Williams until World War II and later followed a career in architecture.

Reference: Sean and Johanna S. Billings, *Peachblow Glass, Collector's Identification & Price Guide*, Krause Publications, 2000.

Additional Listings: Cameo Glass.

Biscuit jar, cov, 7-1/2" h, 5-1/2" d, cream opaque, large amber and green applied ruffled leaves, rich pink int., SP rim, lid, and handle **300.00**

Bowl, 6" d, 3" h, Matsu No Ke, creamy yellow satin bowl, applied dec twisted, knurled, and thorny frosted clear branch winds around perimeter, 36 florets, inscribed registry number "Rd 15353," chip to one floret **985.00**

Box, cov, 4-1/2" d, 2-1/2" h, hinged, aventurine, green and red spatter, green metallic flakes, white lining, polished pontil **250.00**

Calling card receiver, 10" l, applied amber handle, rolled edge, translucent opalescent ground, three applied berries, blossoms, and green leaves, three applied amber feet **750.00**

Ewer, 8-1/2" h, 5" w, Pompeiian Swirl, deep rose shading to yellow, off white lining, frosted loop handle, all over gold enameled wild roses, ferns, and butterfly **1,500.00**

Jardiniere, 6-1/2" d, 10" h, pink opalescent, cut back, two spatter flowers and sunflowers, three applied opalescent thorn feet, leaves, and stems, minor damage **350.00**

Vase, bulbous, crimped undulating tricorn top, applied white opaque flowers and clear leaves, white ground, pink int., 7-1/2" h, **$415.**

Perfume, 4-3/4" h, spherical, heat reactive dark amber shaded to green satin, spiraled air-trap switch, hallmarked and chased silver cap, c1890 . . . . **635.00**

Pitcher, 7" h, 4-1/2" d, mint green ext., robin's egg blue lining, three white and pink blossoms, amber leaves, twisting clear amber glass tendril which twists to form handle, end of handle ground smooth **385.00**

Rose bowl, 4-1/2" d, 3-1/2" h, Cottage Ware, sea shell scalloped pattern, multicolored spatter over white lining, colorless ext. layer **150.00**

Vase

6-1/2" h, bulbous base, slender neck, white cased to rose pink ext., deeper pink spatter **95.00**

6-1/2" h, cylindrical, white cased to rose pink ext., acid etched floral spray, c1880 . . . . **325.00**

7-1/8" h, gourd shape, spiraled air-trap swirls, bronze satin shaded to light blue cased to yellow int., polished pontil, c1885 . . . . . **350.00**

10" h, pale rose pink cased to transparent green, wheel cut intaglio foliate panels, horizontal stepped flared rim **1,850.00**

10-1/2" h, ovoid body, elongated and bulbed neck, deep red overlaid in white, cameo etched and engraved grosbeak on flowering branch with two butterflies, central stylized floral border, c1890, chip on base border **2,185.00**

STICKLEYS

History: There were five Stickley brothers: Albert, Gustav, Leopold, George, and John George. Gustav often is credited with creating the Mission style, a variant of the Arts and Crafts style. Gustav headed Craftsman Furniture, a New York firm, much of whose actual production took place near Syracuse. A characteristic of Gustav's furniture is exposed tenon ends. Gustav published *The Craftsman*, a magazine espousing his antipathy to machines.

Originally, Leopold and Gustav worked together. In 1902, Leopold and John George formed the L. and J. G. Stickley Furniture Company. This firm made Mission-style furniture and cherry and maple early American style pieces.

George and Albert organized the Stickley Brothers Company, located in Grand Rapids, Michigan.

References: David Cathers, *Furniture of the American Arts and Crafts Movement: Revised Edition*, Turn of the Century Editions, 1996; —, *Stickley Style: Arts and Crafts Homes in the Craftsman Tradition*, Simon & Schuster, 1999; Donald A. Davidoff and Stephen Gray, *Innovation and Derivation: The*

Contribution of L. & J. G. Stickley to the Arts and Crafts Movement, Craftsman Farms Foundation, (2352 Route 10-W, Box 5, Morris Plains, NJ 07950), 1996; Donald A. Davidoff and Robert L. Zarrow, *Early L. & J. G. Stickley Furniture*, Dover Publications, 1992; *Furniture of the Arts & Crafts Period*, L-W Book Sales, 1992, 1995 value update; Thomas K. Maher, *The Kaufmann Collection: The Early Furniture of Gustav Stickley*, Treadway Gallery (2029 Madison Road, Cincinnati, OH 45208), 1996; Paul Royka, *Mission Furniture, from the American Arts & Crafts Movement*, Schiffer Publishing, 1997.

Periodical: Style 1900, 333 Main St., Lambertville, NJ 08530.

Collectors' Club: Foundation for the Study of Arts & Crafts Movement, Roycroft Campus, 31 S. Grove St., East Aurora, NY 14052.

Museum: Craftsman Farms Foundation, Inc., Morris Plains, NJ.

Combination bookcase and table, L. and J. G. Stickley, square overhanging top, two divided shelves, vertical slats, original finish and condition, unmarked, minor wear to top with staining, chip to top edge, 27" x 27" x 29-1/4", **$11,150.** Photo courtesy of David Rago Auctions.

Bed, 80-1/2" l, 56-1/2" w, 30" h, headboard with narrow vertical slats and panels, tapered feet, orig side rails, orig finish, minor scratches, stenciled "9001-1/2," attributed to Stickley Bros. **1,355.00**

Bookcase, quarter sawn oak
29-3/4" w, 12" d, 55-1/4" h, single door, 16 mullioned panes, gallery top, keyed through tenons, refinished, hardware replaced, L & J. G. Stickley Handcraft label **4,875.00**
35-1/2" w, 12" d, 50" h, double door, slatted gallery top, single panes of glass, orig medium finish, brass Stickley Bros tag. **4,875.00**

49" w, 12" d, 54-1/2" h, double door, 12 panes per door, gallery top, three shelves, keyed through-tenons on sides, orig medium finish, "The Work of L. & J. G. Stickley" decal, stain on top **6,275.00**
54" w, 13" d, 55" h, double door, 12 panes per door, gallery top, brass V-pulls, mortised top, paper Gustav label, refinished, warp in right door, stripped hardware. **5,175.00**

Chair, arm
24-1/2" w, 21" d, 38-1/2" h, spindled back, open arms, corbels, seat recovered in leather, refinished, unmarked L. & J. G. **690.00**
27" w, 20-1/2" d, 37" h, V-back, vertical back slats, replaced leather seat, orig faceted tacks, good orig finish, red Gustav decal **1,045.00**
32-1/2" w, 33" d, 41" h, fixed back, drop arm, slats to seat, corbels, replaced drop-in green leather spring seat and back cushion, waxed finish, L & J. G. Stickley Handcraft label **5,750.00**

Chair, dining
37" h, ladder-back, four slats, cloud-lift aprons, drop-in seats recovered in leather, overcoat finish, roughness to edges, some with red Gustav decal, set of eight **6,300.00**
37-1/2" h, 17" w, arched vertical back slats, drop-in spring seat, covered in new green leather, good new finish, L. & J. G. Handcraft labels, price for set of four. **3,335.00**

Chamber stick, 7" d, 9" h, hammered copper, riveted handle, orig patina, Als ik kan Gustav stamp **520.00**

Chest of drawers
36" w, 20" d, 42-1/4" h, back splash, five drawers, hammered copper pulls, paneled sides, orig finish,

Dresser, L & J. G. Stickley, two small drawers over three graduated long drawers, V backsplash, chamfered sides, original dark finish, **$14,300.** Photo courtesy of David Rago Auctions, Inc.

bails slightly bent, branded Gustav mark **5,750.00**

38" w, 21" d, 40" h, two small drawers over four long drawers, backsplash, arched toe board, sq brass pulls, refinished, brass Stickley Bros tag **2,870.00**

China cabinet, 36" w, 15" d, 60" h, No. 803, Harvey Ellis design, overhanging top, one pane glass door with hammered copper V-pull, three shelves, orig finish, orig Gustav Stickley key, Craftsman label, branded mark **11,500.00**

Desk

24" w, 45-3/4" h, chalet, gallery top, paneled drop-front door, chamfered back, keyed through-tenons, shoe feet, orig finish, restoration to foot, red Gustav decal **4,025.00**

32" w, 13" d, 47-1/4" h, fall front, gallery top, cut-out and mortised sides, fitted int., three drawers over one shelf, riveted curvilinear patinated hardware, orig finish, unmarked Stickley Bros. . **2,530.00**

32" w, 14-3/4" d, 43" h, fall front, gallery top, two short drawers over two long drawers, mortised through sides, full gallery int. with drawers and cubicles, Gustav branded mark, good new finish, veneer replaced on outside of lid, lock missing on inside of cabinet door **1,725.00**

Drink stand

18" d, 27-3/4" h, circular top copper-covered overhanging top, flaring legs, arched aprons, orig finish, Stickley Bros. Quaint metal tag **3,000.00**

18" d, 28" h, circular copper-covered overhanging top, circular apron, cross stretchers, orig finish, conjoined L & J. G. label, replaced z-clamps under top, repairs **2,760.00**

Hall chair, 16" w, 14-1/4" d, 38-1/2" h, tall tapering back, vertical slats, saddle seat, refinished, unmarked Stickley Bros. **690.00**

Lamp base, 7" d, 22" h, hammered copper, bulbous, orig dark patina, stamped Als ik kan Gustav mark, replaced sockets, minor dent. **2,760.00**

Lamp, table, 16" h, 10" d orig wicker shade with replaced silk lining, faceted oak base, orig acorn chain pull, unmarked Gustav **1,150.00**

Lamp table, No. 644, circular top, arched cross-stretchers topped by finial, mortised legs, good new finish, replaced finial, Gustav Als Ik Kan brand, 29-1/2" d, 28-3/4" h . . . **2,300.00**

Lantern, hanging, 5-1/2" sq, 10" h, hammered copper, four-sided top overhanging frame with grid and yellow hammered glass, orig wall mount, orig verdigris patina, stamped Gustav circular mark **4,600.00**

Library table

36" l, 24" d, 29" h, No. 652, single drawer, iron "V" pull, overhanging top, one shelf, top refinished, orig finish on base, some separation at top, red Gustav decal . . . **2,415.00**

42" l, 29-1/2" d, 30" h, two drawers, oval iron pulls, long corbels, broad lower shelf mortised through stretchers, orig finish, Gustav paper label, wear and few stains to top, seam separation **1,840.00**

48" l, 30" w, 29" h, trestle, orig tacked-on leather top, double keyed through tenon lower shelf, red Gustav decal, Robert Mitchell Furniture Co. label, wear to orig finish, abrasion to edge of lower shelf **3,450.00**

60-1/4" l, 35-1/2" d, 30" h, overhanging top, three drawers, riveted patinated brass hardware, through tenons, new finish, Stickley Bros paper label. **1,610.00**

Magazine stand

13" w, 13" d, 43" h, Tree of Life, four shelves, corbels under sq top, carved tapering sides with tree motif, tacked-on leather trim, Gustav **1,100.00**

13-3/4" w, 10" d, 40-1/4" h, half moon cut-out handles over three shelves, thick over coat, unsigned Gustav **1,045.00**

15-1/4" w, 15-1/4" d, 53-1/4" h, Gustav, beveled overhanging top, three open shelves, good new finish, sgd under top **2,070.00**

21" w, 12" d, 42" h, slatted sides, arched apron, four shelves, orig dark finish with overcoat, "The Work of L. & J. G. Stickley" decal **1,955.00**

Mirror, 24" w, 21" h, mortised construction, replaced beveled glass, refinished, unmarked, attributed to Stickley Bros. **630.00**

Morris chair

30" l, 32-1/2" w, 39" h, open arm, trapezoidal arms, corbels, new

leather drop-in cushion, wooden slat foundation, good orig finish, Gustav Eastwood label, some nicks to legs **2,870.00**

30" l, 36" w, 40" h, spindled sides to floor, long corbels under flat arms, new green leather cushions, new finish, unmarked Gustav, front stretcher cap repaired and split **5,175.00**

31" w, 40" d, 41" h, No. 332, slats to the floor under flat arms, drop-in spring seat with replaced leather, unmarked Gustave, refinished, replaced pins, replaced chip to back leg **5,350.00**

31-1/2" l, 35-1/4" w, 41" h, flat arm, orig finish on base, tops of arms refinished, L & J. G. Stickley Handcraft label **2,300.00**

32" l, 35" w, 43" h, vertical slats under arms, corbels, new brown leather tufted cushion, orig finish, stencil L & G Stickley and George Flint label, presentation plaque to "Brother James H. Clark by Washington F & A M. Eliza NJ Oct 2, 1908," accompanied by sepia photo of orig owner **2,415.00**

Pedestal, 14-1/2" d top, 17" d base, 36" h, narrow circular top, four long legs, crossed shoe feet, orig dark finish, remnant of paper label, attributed to Gustav **2,530.00**

Plant stand, Stickley Brothers, square overhanging top, apron, vertical side slats, and stretchers mortised through legs, very good original finish, Quaint metal tag, 17" square, 34-1/2" h, $1,610. Photo courtesy of David Rago Auctions.

Plant stand, 34-1/2" h, 17" sq overhanging top, apron, vertical side slats, stretchers mortised through legs, very good orig finish, Stickley Bros. Quaint metal tag **1,610.00**

Sconce, 7-1/2" w, 6-1/2" h, hammered copper, double ribbon frame ending in curls, fine orig patina, early circular Gustav stamp with Als Ik Kan, electrified, price for pr **1,855.00**

Server, 44-1/8" l, 18-1/4" d, 45" h, backsplash, three short drawers over one long drawer over one shelf, hammered copper pulls, The Work of L. & J. G. Stickley brand, fair orig finish, stains and finish loss on top, some looseness **2,870.00**

Settle

50" l, 22-1/2" d, 33" h, cube, vertical slats, orig drop-in seat covered in new green leather, excellent orig finish, stenciled number, Stickley Bros. **2,530.00**

53" l, 26" w, 36" h, open arm, cloud lift top rail, horizontal backslat and corbels, new tan leather upholstered seat cushion, new finish, The Work of L & J. G. Stickley label, some looseness **1,650.00**

59-3/4" l, 31" d, 29-1/4" h, No. 225, single board horizontal back panel, vertical side slats, recovered brown leather drop-in seat, over-coated orig finish, unmarked Gustav **7,475.00**

72" l, 27" w, 28" h, cube, border vertical panels on back and under each arm, brown leather cushion, orig condition and finish, orig upholstery, "The Work of L. and J. G. Stickley" label **3,450.00**

76-1/2" l, 32" d, 29-1/4" h, No. 208, even arm, vertical slats all around, top rail mortised through legs, drop-in spring seat covered in new green leather, red Gustav decal, light standing, some color added to orig finish **6,900.00**

Sideboard

54" l, 24" d, 48-1/4" h, plate rail, two doors, hammered copper strap hinges and pulls, four drawers, linen drawer, refinished, L. and J. G. Handcraft decal **6,275.00**

69-1/2" l, 25" w, 49" h, chamfered plate rack, four drawers, two doors, eight legs, hammered copper hardware, refinished, replaced bottom on top drawer, new bales

on pulls, unmarked Gustav **10,925.00**

72" l, 25" d, 63-1/2" h, tall mirrored backsplash with columns and shelf, three drawers, four paneled cabinet doors, copper hardware, orig medium finish, unmarked Stickley Bros., missing one bail **4,025.00**

Table, dining, 54" d, 30" h, circular top, split pedestal, four leaves, orig finish to base, branded Gustav mark . **5,175.00**

Table, director's, 96" l, 48-1/4" w, 29-1/4" h, No. 631, overhanging rect top, trestle base, pegged construction, new finish, separations to top, unmarked Gustav **11,500.00**

Tabouret, 15" sq clip corner octagonal top, 17" h, legs mortised through top, arched cross-stretchers, remnant of L. & J. G. decal, new finish **750.00**

Tea cart, 29" l, 16-3/4" d, 28-1/4" h, glass tray top, orig finish, stenciled "80," Stickley Bros., needs glueing **690.00**

Telephone stand, 14" sq top, 32" h, two lower shelves, refinished, metal Stickley Bros. tag **410.00**

Vanity, 44" l, 20" d, 55" h, No. 9035, paneled sides and back, five drawers, round wooden pulls, triple mirror, orig finish, Stickley Bros. Quaint decal, staining on top **2,185.00**

Vase, 6" d, 10-1/2" h, hammered copper, flaring, rolled rim, orig dark patina, Als ik kan Gustav stamp **2,415.00**

STIEGEL-TYPE GLASS

History: Baron Henry Stiegel founded America's first flint-glass factory at Manheim, Pennsylvania, in the 1760s. Although clear glass was the most common color made, amethyst, blue (cobalt), and fiery opalescent pieces also are found. Products included bottles, creamers, flasks, flips, perfumes, salts, tumblers, and whiskeys. Prosperity was short-lived; Stiegel's extravagant lifestyle forced the factory to close.

It is very difficult to identify a Stiegel-made item. As a result, the term "Stiegel-type" is used to identify glass made during the time period of Stiegel's firm and in the same shapes and colors as used by that company.

Enamel-decorated ware also is attributed to Stiegel. True Stiegel pieces are rare; an overwhelming majority is of European origin.

References: Frederick W. Hunter, *Stiegel Glass*, 1950, available in Dover reprint; Kenneth Wilson,

American Glass 1760-1930, 2 vols., Hudson Hills Press and The Toledo Museum of Art, 1994.

Reproduction Alert: Beware of modern reproductions, especially in enamel wares.

Bottle, blown

4-3/4" h, amethyst, daisy-in-diamond pattern, tiny interior pot stones **4,750.00**

5-3/8" h, brilliant deep peacock green, 15 diamonds, pot stone in neck **440.00**

5-5/8" h, octagonal, colorless, red, yellow, white, blue, and pale green floral designs and scrollwork, pewter collar **365.00**

5-7/8" h, hexagonal, colorless, enameled white dove, red rose, scroll work, red, blue, yellow, and white floral designs, flared lip **175.00**

7" h, octagonal, colorless, enameled yellow, white, blue, and red flowers on side, white doves in yellow circles front and back, pewter threaded neck, hairline at neck **110.00**

Mug, enameled, center shield with carpenter's and blacksmith's tools, floral decoration on sides, "Das ihre bare Huff" and "Wassen/Schmidt Hand Werck 1790," 6-1/2" h, $325.

Flip glass, colorless, sheared rim, pontil scar, form similar to McKearin plate 22, #2

3-1/2" h, handle, engraved repeating swag motif around rim, lower body emb with graduated panels **210.00**

6-1/4" h, engraved floral motif and sunflower **300.00**

7" h, engraved bird in heart dec within sunburst motif **400.00**

7-7/8" h, engraved pair of birds perched on heart within sunburst motif. **475.00**

8" h, engraved large flower and floral motif. **325.00**

Flask

4-3/4" h, amethyst diamond and daisy **495.00**

5" h, amethyst, globular, 20 molded ribs, minute rim chip **1,380.00**

Jar, cov, 10-1/2" h, colorless, engraved sunflower and floral motifs, repeating dot and vine dec on cov, applied finial, sheared rim, pontil scar, form similar to McKearin plate 35, #2 and #3 . . **750.00**

Miniature, flip glass, 3" h, colorless, engraved bird within sunburst motif, seared mouth, pontil scar. **325.00**

Tankard, handle, cylindrical, applied solid reeded handle, flared foot, sheared rim, pontil scar, form similar to McKearin plate 22, #4

5-1/2" h, milk glass, red, yellow, blue, and green enameled dec of house on mountain with floral motif, old meandering fissure around body of vessel **150.00**

5-3/4" h, colorless, engraved with bird in elaborate sunburst motif **500.00**

Tumbler, 2-7/8" h, colorless, paneled, polychrome enameled flowers . . **220.00**

STONEWARE

History: Made from dense kaolin and commonly salt-glazed, stonewares were hand-thrown and high-fired to produce a simple, bold, vitreous pottery. Stoneware crocks, jugs, and jars were made to store products and fill other utilitarian needs. These intended purposes dictated shape and design—solid, thick-walled forms with heavy rims, necks, and handles and with little or no embellishment. Any decorations were simple: brushed cobalt oxide, incised, slip trailed, stamped, or tooled.

Stoneware has been made for centuries. Early American settlers imported stoneware items at first. As English and European potters refined their earthenware, colonists began to produce their own wares. Two major North American traditions emerged based only on location or type of clay. North Jersey and parts of New York comprise the first area; the second was eastern Pennsylvania spreading westward and into Maryland, Virginia, and West Virginia. These two distinct geographical boundaries, style of decoration, and shape are discernible factors in classifying and dating early stoneware.

By the late 18th century, stoneware was manufactured in all sections of the country. This vigorous industry flourished during the 19th century until glass fruit jars appeared and the use of

refrigeration became widespread. By 1910, commercial production of salt-glazed stoneware came to an end.

References: Susan and Al Bagdade, *Warman's American Pottery and Porcelain*, 2nd ed., Krause Publications, 2000; Jim Martin and Bette Cooper, *Monmouth-Western Stoneware*, published by authors, 1983, 1993 value update; Don and Carol Raycraft, *Collector's Guide to Country Stoneware & Pottery*, 1st Series (1985, 1995 value update), 2nd Series (1990, 1996 value update), Collector Books; ——, *Stoneware*, Wallace-Homestead, 1995, ——, *Wallace-Homestead Price Guide to American Country Antiques*, 16th ed., Krause Publications, 1999; Terry G. Taylor and Terry and Kay Lowrance, *Collector's Encyclopedia of Salt Glaze Stoneware*, Collector Books, 1996, 2001 value update.

Collectors' Clubs: American Stoneware Association, 208 Crescent Ct, Mars, PA 16066; Federation of Historical Bottle Collectors, Inc., 1485 Buck Hill Drive, Southampton, PA 18966.

Museum: Museum of Ceramics at East Liverpool, East Liverpool, OH.

Advertising jug, Ottman Bros. & Co., Ft. Edward, NY, two gallon, blue script on front "A. Schell, 380 Broadway Albany," c1870, 13" h, minor glaze flake and staining at spout, **$250.** Photo courtesy of Bruce & Vicki Waasdorp.

Advertising jug

13" h, E. W. Farrington, Elmira, NY, two gallons, blue script "E. E. S. Harvey/226 Pearl St./Buffalo, NY," nicely carved wooden stopper, c1870, cinnamon cast to clay in the making, glaze burn on left side, large surface chip on spout in front **180.00**

14" h, unsigned, two gallons, thick blue gallon designation and initials "E. B's" imp and blue accented at shoulder, "Fuchs Brother's/ Importers of/Wines, Brandies, Cegars, Etc., 390 Main St./Buffalo, NY," c1860, overall staining, minor glaze flake spot on back. . . **415.00**

Batter pail

8" h, White & Co., Binghamton, four quarts, large brushed blue accents at ears, spout, name, and lug handle on back, orig bale handle, c1860 . . . . **495.00**

8-1/2" h, unsigned, New York State origin, one gallon, orig bale handle, brush blue tulip design below spout, c1870, some very minor int. surface chipping at rim, minor staining from use. **315.00**

Bottle

9-1/2" h, imp and blue accented "C. F. Washburn," minor crow's foot at shoulder **35.00**

9-1/2" h, imp and blue accented "1851, Rice & Plummer" at shoulder, chip at base in back **110.00**

10" h, imp and blue accented "B. F. Haley California Pop Beer 1889," glaze drip at shoulder to right of imp name **135.00**

Cake crock

6" x 9-1/2", unsigned, decorated lid, flowers and vines repeated front and back, squiggle accent line under ears, c1850, lid not orig but good match. **550.00**

6-1/4" h, unsigned, PA origin, attributed to Remmey factory, flowers and vines all around, blue accents at handle, deep blue matching design on orig stoneware lid, imp "I" under applied ear, c1850, two nickel-sized surface chips at rim, dime size stone ping **715.00**

7-1/2" h, J. & E. Bennington, VT, brilliant blue thistle design, c1855, very minor glaze flaking at base on back **715.00**

9-1/2" h, Ottman Bros & Co., Fort Edward, NY, facing left bird perched on twig, c1870, professional restoration to some glaze flaking **600.00**

Canning jar, 9-1/2" h, unsigned, one gallon, four wide accent stripes across front, c1850, stack mark, glaze burns on left side **110.00**

Crock, unsigned, attributed to Clark-son Crolius, New York City, one gallon, ovoid, incised budding flower design, deeply imp design motif repeated on back, cobalt blue accents at applied looped handles and in design, c1800, 9-1/4" h, $2,420. Photo courtesy of Bruce & Vicki Waasdorp.

Chicken waterer, 11" h, unsigned, probably PA origin, one gallon, imp "I" at shoulder, brushed blue accents at button top and inner and out rim of watering hole, c1840 . . . . **415.00**

Churn

13" h, unsigned, two gallons, table top type, fitted carved wooden guide, brushed double plume design repeated front and back, c1870 . . . . **275.00**

17" h, Hart Bros, Fulton, NY, four gallons, floral and plume dec, brush and slip application, c1880, some surface chipping to orig dasher guide **440.00**

17" h, J. Burger, Jr., Rochester, NY, four gallons, stoneware guide, dotted quail and jack in the pulpit flower, c1885 . . . . **5,500.00**

17" h, Whites Utica, NY, five gallons, signature orchid design, orig stoneware dasher guide, c1865, some overglazing in the making, two minor stone pings, surface side rim chip **660.00**

19" h, J. Fisher & Co., Lyons, NY, six gallons, orig dasher and dasher guide, brushed double flower designs and "6" in blue, accents at ears and factory name, c1880, very tight long line through either side of design, third line on back, piece sold as stable **690.00**

20" h, J. Burger Jr., Rochester, NY, six gallons, stoneware guide, profusely applied cobalt blue, striped and dotted standing lion, c1885, extensive damage restored to museum quality display condition **8,250.00**

Cream pot

8" h, I. Seymour, Troy, three gallons, ovoid, blue accents at name, large slip blue gallon designation, c1830, very tight crows foot through line at base on back, some int. lime staining **180.00**

9-1/2" h, G. Haidle & Co., Union Pottery, Newark, NJ, two gallons, ovoid, brushed blue "2.G." surrounds imp name, brushed blue swimming swan sits above script "Old Scotch," other brushed blue floral dec, c1871, very tight 6" hairline extending from rim to right of design, minor surface wear and lime staining on int. **1,265.00**

12" h, J. & E. Norton, Bennington, VT, three gallons, ovoid, bright blue dotted sunburst floral dec, c1855, few grease stain spots on back, glaze spider, stone ping at base in front **615.00**

Crock

7-1/2" h, N. A. White & Son, Utica, NY, 1-1/2" gallon, blue paddle tail running bird, looking backward, c1870, tight freeze line around base **360.00**

8" h, "Hamilton & Jones, Greensboro, PA, 2," stenciled scroll dec on both sides, freehand lines, double handles, raised rim, hairlines **250.00**

8" h, unsigned, attributed to W. H. Wheaton, Danicisonville, CT, stenciled standing horse, brushed blue accents, horse outlined and blue filled, brushed blue accent at imp "6," c1870 . . . . **2,640.00**

8-1/4" h, partial mark for "N. Clark Jr. Athens N," short, ovoid, double handles, cobalt dec, faint spider on side, shallow rim chips **635.00**

9" h, imp signature for "S. B. Bosworth, Hartford, CT, 2," double handles with incised line detail, raised rim, cobalt blue flower design, in-the-making imperfections on rim, minor flake on handle **110.00**

9" h, John Burger, Rochester, two gallons, unusual accents around gallon designation, c1855 . . **315.00**

9" h, J. Burger, Jr., Rochester, two gallons, blue slip floral, ribbed leaves, c1885, very tight freeze line across base, minor glaze spider on back **250.00**

9" h, unsigned, Albany, NY, two gallons, vase of flowers on front, c1860, two very tight hairlines on front extending from rim through design **220.00**

10" h, unsigned, two gallons, cobalt blue stencil "From F. H. Behrens, Grocer, Center, Wheeling," tapered sides, raised rim **1,100.00**

10" h, imp signature for "Haxton Ottman & Co., Ft. Edwards, N.Y. 2," cobalt blue floral dec, applied double handles, shallow base chip, edge chips on one handle . **425.00**

10" h, partial maker's mark and "Fort Edward, N. Y." signature, deep blue stylized floral dec, double handles **330.00**

10" h, unsigned, potted, heart-shaped vine floral surrounding "Grover Cleveland 1884" in blue script, attributed to Whites Utica factory, c1884, short clay separation line at rim occurred in the making **3,960.00**

10" h, unsigned, three gallons, intense blue dec, tornado, plumes, and squiggles, c1870 . . . . **360.00**

11" h, John Burger Jr., Rochester, NY, four gallons, blue slip double flowers, c1880, two very minor surface chips at right ear . **1,155.00**

11" h, partial Woodroff mark "Cortland," cobalt blue tulip dec, double handles, flared rim, hairline **275.00**

11-1/4" h, imp mark for "John Burger, Rochester," cobalt blue wreath surrounding "2," double handles with flared rim, base hairlines **110.00**

11-1/2" h, T. Harrington, Lyons, five gallons, large signature starface dec, eight-point star covers front, c1850, professional restoration to full length hairline on left side **3,850.00**

12" h, W. Roberts, Binghamton, NY, five gallons, ovoid, large snowball flower, c1860, two hairlines on back, both appear stable . . **190.00**

12-3/8" h, 14-1/2" d, lug handles, cobalt blue peafowl perched on floral spray, imp "Whites Utica" near rim, brownish discoloration **2,990.00**

12-1/2" h, imp label with cobalt blue highlights "J. A. & C. Underwood, Fort Edward, N.Y. 3," brushed cobalt blue bird perched on stump, glued crack around circumference, flakes.................**360.00**

13" h, Burger & Co., Rochester, NY, five gallons, large triple fern dec, c1877, few minor surface chips from use................**525.00**

14" h, stenciled dec "David Morgan, New York," incised cobalt blue hearts and swags, imperfections **2,760.00**

14" h, stenciled dec "R. T. Williams, New Geneva, PA, 3," floral and line detail, double handles.....**175.00**

14-1/2" h, stenciled dec, cobalt roses above and below signature "_ Hi-eneix, New Geneva, PA, 4," applied double handles, raised rim, good contrast with some wear, int. lime deposits........**330.00**

15" h, John Burger, Rochester, six gallons, top to bottom slip design of double flowers, c1855, very tight hairline on back......**10,175.00**

16" h, J. Fisher, Lyons, NY, 10 gallons, brushed tulips cover entire front, brushed blue accent under applied ears, cobalt blue gallon designation, c1880, professional restoration to three full-length through lines...........**470.00**

16-1/2" h, sgd "J. T. Hosdgens, Merchant, Portland Station" in cobalt blue stencil, freehand vine dec, applied double handles, shallow chip on one handle **330.00**

25-1/4" h, stenciled signature "C. L. Williams and Company, Best Blue Stoneware, New Geneva, PA, 20," some freehand line dec, double handles, flared rim, cracks.**495.00**

Flask, 6-1/2" h, unsigned, brushed blue tree dec, design repeated on both sides, incised reeded accents at neck, c1810, minor surface wear at base, stack mark..............**2,630.00**

Jar

7" h, quart, double handles, raised rim, cobalt blue tulip dec, imp "L. H. Yeager & Co., Allentown, PA," damage................**250.00**

11" h, unsigned, two gallons, ovoid, flying bird over tulip design, c1870 ....**750.00**

11-1/2" h, N. Clark & Co., Lyons, two gallons, ovoid, stoneware lid, double tulip dec, dots and lines

accentuate vines, blue accents at ears and factory name, c1840, couple of surface chips at rim **800.00**

12-1/4" h, ovoid, applied handles, raised rim, cobalt blue highlights on incised bird, hairline crack in side...................**990.00**

15" h, unsigned, attributed to Frederick Carpenter, three gallons, light ochre accents at shoulder and handles, deep incised accent lines at shoulder and rim, c1800, some surface chipping and staining from use...................**495.00**

Jug, Whites Utica, two gallon, large bird with long tail on plume, filled wing, c1865, 13-1/2" h, $1,320. Photo courtesy of Bruce & Vicki Waasdorp.

Jug

7-1/4" h, ovoid, applied handle, incised lines around neck, incised "BLK 1802" with brushed cobalt blue highlights, paper label on front "George S. McKearin Collector of American Pottery No. 1258," some bruises and imperfections **8,690.00**

9-1/2" h, unsigned, one gallon, brushed blue flower, overall staining, make-do repair to replace broken handle, c1850 ....**125.00**

9-7/8" h, ovoid, imp signature "Orcutt H-miston & Co. Troy," (New York), deep cobalt blue leaf dec, applied

double handles, shallow rim chips **385.00**

10-3/4" h, ovoid, imp signature of "T. Reed," large cobalt blue tulip on one side, raised rings around spout, applied strap handle, shallow base chip........**770.00**

11" h, J. S. Taft & Co, Keene, NH, one gallon, large bird on twig, c1875, stone ping on side, clay separation line in the handle, some staining **360.00**

11" h, unsigned, one gallon, ovoid, cobalt blue grapevine design, blue accents at handle, incised in sgraffito "Henry Frederick" at shoulder, c1830, overall staining to dark earthenware clay color, dry glaze in the making.......**470.00**

11-1/2" h, E. & L. P. Norton, Bennington, VT, one gallon, stylized dotted plume dec, c1880 ....**250.00**

11-1/2" h, imp "Rich" on shoulder, (Roscoe, Muskingham County, Ohio,) ovoid, applied handle, flared spout...................**200.00**

11-1/2" h, imp "Whites Utica," cobalt blue bird dec, shallow chips on handle.................**440.00**

12" h, Binghamton, NY, one gallon, pine tree design, c1870, few glaze flakes at spout...........**275.00**

12" h, John B. Caire & Co., two gallons, ovoid, squat, cobalt blue gallon designation, blue accents at name and ribbed vine at shoulder, also blue at handle, c1850.**420.00**

12" h, Lehman & Rudinger, Poughkeepsie, N.Y. 2, imp in small block letters, some letters missing, cobalt blue floral dec, ovoid, applied strap handle, shallow base chips.................**525.00**

12-1/2" h, T. Reed, (Ohio), cobalt blue brushmarks over signature and top of handle, lip chips, short hairline................**275.00**

13-1/2" h, Harrington & Burger, Rochester, two gallons, large cobalt blue floral dec.....**650.00**

14" h, G. Lent, Troy, two gallons, detailed incised large fish at shoulder, entire design shaded in blue cobalt wash, blue accents at handle, c1820, glaze drip on side **10,450.00**

14" h, J. & E. Norton, Bennington, VT, two gallons, blue dotted stylized floral design, c1855....**1,020.00**

14" h, Jordan, two gallons, striking double flowers over gallon designation, strong cobalt blue dec, c1850, staining at shoulder
. . . . **470.00**

14" h, N. Clark Jr., Athens, NY, two gallons, unusual sunburst dec, c1850, few stone pings . . . **525.00**

14" h, unsigned, attributed to Fulper Bros, New Jersey, two gallons, applied Bristol glaze, singing bird on twig dec, c1880 . . . . . . **330.00**

14" h, unsigned, two gallons, three brushed flowers at shoulder, eight very deep incised accent lines at shoulder, blue accents on handle, deeply mottled tan clay color, c1790, stone pings and kiln burns, minor rim chip, some staining
. . . . **330.00**

15-1/2" h, I. Seymour, Troy, three gallons, light brush blue plume design at shoulder, c1830, stack mark at center of design, two stone pings at side, all occurred in making **275.00**

19" h, J. Burger, Jr., Rochester, NY, 4-1/2 gallon, floral design, vintage wooden stopper, c1885, very minor surface chipping at spout . **440.00**

Milk pitcher, 17" h, unsigned, Shenandoah Valley origin, attributed to Remmey factory, three gallons, brushed blue floral design fills entire front, c1850, professional restoration to handle, partially replaced **1,210.00**

Mug, 3-1/4" d, 4-3/4" h, applied handle, two brushed cobalt bands with incised edging **250.00**

Pitcher, Whites Binghamton, one gallon, slip blue dotted poppy design, bulbous, c1860, 9-1/2" h, $1,045. Photo courtesy of Bruce & Vicki Waasdorp.

Pitcher

7" h, ovoid, applied handle, brushed cobalt blue flower with long leaves, three flourishes around rim at handle, interior with grown glaze, hairline at base **675.00**

7-1/4" h, brushed cobalt blue three-petaled flowers, incised lines at rim and shoulder, applied strap handle **1,455.00**

9-1/2" h, Whites Binghamton, one gallon, slip blue dotted poppy design, bulbous, c1860 . **1,045.00**

10" h, Lyons, one gallon, brushed tulip, blue imp name, c1860, minor kiln burns at top occurred in making, professional restoration to chip at spout **550.00**

10" h, unsigned, PA origin, one gallon, top to bottom floral dec, blue accents at handle, brushed designs on either side of spout, imp "I" at shoulder, c1860 . . . **1,815.00**

10" h, Whites Binghamton, incised line around middle, raised rim, cobalt blue polka dot floral dec
. . . . **615.00**

10-1/2" h, unsigned, attributed to Lyons, NY, factory, one gallon, wreath surrounding floral design, blue accent at handle, cobalt blue has bled because of heavy application by potter, c1860, surface chip at spout may be in the making. **330.00**

11" h, J. Burger, Rochester, NY, one gallon, blue accents at handle and imp name, bow tie dec, c1880
. . . . **605.00**

Preserve jar

10" h, Fulper Bros, Flemington, NJ, 1-1/2 gallon, fitted stoneware lid, chicken pecking corn dec, c1885, hairlines extending from rim, stone ping, glaze drip in front at base, overall dry glaze in the making
. . . . **800.00**

10" h, Little West, 12th St. N. Pottery Works, 1-1/2 gallons, double dropping flower design, c1870, two short clay separation lines at rim probably occurred in making
. . . . **495.00**

10-1/2" h, E. & L. P. Norton, 1-1/2 gallons, stylized dotted floral design, c1880, very minor stone ping on side **275.00**

10-1/2" h, John Burger, Rochester, two gallons, blooming daffodil dec, c1855, long crow's foot spide on side, some staining on back
. . . . **220.00**

10-1/2" h, Lyons, two gallons, triple flower dec with double "2s," and blue accents at ears, stoneware lid, c1860, spider line to right of design
. . . . **440.00**

11" h, J. Heiser, Buffalo, NY, two gallons, lid, brushed double flower dec, blue at name, c1852 . **220.00**

11" h, Lyons, two gallons, brushed blue dec with double "2s" and accents at ears, stoneware lid, c1860, separation line at one handle that probably occurred in the making **605.00**

11" h, S. Hart, Fulton, two gallons, vine/floral design above brushed blue gallon designation, c1875, some staining and surface chipping from use **250.00**

11" h, Whites, Utica, two gallons, long tailed bird on twig, c1865, stack mark/kiln burns at base, large grease stain spot on side and back **360.00**

11-1/2" h, John Burger, Rochester, two gallons, orig stoneware lid, triple fern design surrounds large "2," c1865, minor crow's foot glaze spider on side **580.00**

11-1/2" d, N. Clark & Co., Rochester, NY, two gallons, stoneware lid, finely executed floral design, c1850, int. lime staining, couple of surface chips at rim, stone ping on side **1,760.00**

11-1/2" h, New York Stoneware Co., Fort Edward, NY, two gallons, signature bird design, c1880, professional restoration to surface chip at rim **690.00**

12" h, Brady & Ryan, Ellenville, NY, two gallons, fitted stoneware lid, bushy tailed bird on dotted plume dec in bright blue, c1885, surface chip on lid, mottled clay color in the making **470.00**

12" h, Cortland, three gallons, brushed plume design, blue accent at name, c1850, minor surface chips from use . . . **165.00**

Water cooler

11" h, Gates City, six quarts, stoneware lid, orig spigot, cobalt blue bird dec, patented May 25, 1886 . . . . **935.00**

15" h, W. H. Farrar & Co., Geddes, NY, five gallons, ovoid, triple detailed flower, dotted tornadoes on either side, profuse use of dots, c1850, professional restoration to three hairlines. **1,020.00**

Water cooler, Gates City, patented May 25, 1886, six quart, stoneware lid, original spigot, cobalt blue bird decoration, c1886, 11" h, $935. Photo courtesy of Bruce & Vicki Waasdorp.

19" h, Satterlee & Mory, Fort Edward, NY, six gallons, double handle, stylized plume dec in bold cobalt blue, c1870 . . . . **1,210.00**

STRETCH GLASS

History: Stretch glass was produced by many glass manufacturers in the United States between 1915 to 1935. The most prominent makers were Cambridge, Fenton (which probably manufactured more stretch glass than any of the others), Imperial, Northwood, and Steuben. Stretch glass is pressed or blown-molded glass, with little or no pattern, that is sprayed with a metallic salt mix while hot, creating a iridescent, onionskin-like effect, that may be velvety or shiny in luster. Look for mold marks. Imported pieces are blown and show a pontil mark.

References: John Madeley and Dave Stetlar, *American Iridescent Stretch Glass*, Collector Books, 1998; Berry Wiggins, *Stretch Glass*, Antique Publications, 1972, 1987 value update.

Collectors' Club: Stretch Glass Society, 508 Turnberry Lane, St. Augustine, FL 32080.

Bowl, 10" d, Double Dolphin, #1602, Fenton, crimped edge, ice green, iridescence **215.00**
Candlesticks, pr, 8-3/4" h, #657, Northwood, vaseline **150.00**
Candy jar, cov, #636, Northwood, vaseline, one-pound size **85.00**
Compote, Interior Paneled, ice green, sides pulled up on two sides . . . **160.00**
Console bowl, 9-1/2" d, stretch, dark marigold, Imperial iron cross mark **90.00**

Vase, fluted top, white irid body, 5" h, $345.

Cornucopia candlesticks, pr, Fenton, white **65.00**
Creamer and sugar, Rings pattern, tangerine **75.00**
Hat, 4" h, purple, Imperial **60.00**
Ice cream bowl, 8-1/2" d, Wide Panel, Imperial, deep **225.00**
Nappy, 7" w, Fenton, vaseline . . . **35.00**
Plate, 8" d, Wide Panel, Imperial, red **85.00**
Punch bowl base, Fenton, red . **900.00**
Sandwich server, sq, green, center handle **35.00**
Vase
  4-3/4" h, Smooth Panels, Imperial, squatty, red to amberina . . **400.00**
  10" h, Smooth Panels, Imperial, swung, red **350.00**
  11-1/2" h, #1531, Fenton, aquamarine, ruffled rim . . . **235.00**

STRING HOLDERS

History: The string holder developed as a useful tool to assist the merchant or manufacturer who needed tangle-free string or twine to tie packages. The early holders were made of cast iron, with some patents dating to the 1860s.

When the string holder moved into the household, lighter and more attractive forms developed, many made of chalkware. The string holder remained a key kitchen element until the early 1950s.

Reference: Sharon Ray Jacobs, *Collector's Guide to Stringholders*, L-W Book Sales, 1996.

Advertising

Chase & Sanborn's Coffee, tin, 13-3/4" x 10-1/4" sign, 4" d wire basket string holder insert, hanging chain. **825.00**

Reproduction Alert: As a result of the growing collector interest in string holders, some unscrupulous individuals are hollowing out the backs of 1950s figural-head wall plaques, drilling a hole through the mouth, and passing them off as string holders. A chef, Chinese man, Chinese woman, Indian, masked man, masked woman, and Siamese face are altered forms already found on the market.

Figural wall lamps from the 1950s and 1960s also are being altered. When the lamp hardware is removed, the base can be easily altered. Two forms that have been discovered are a pineapple face and an apple face, both lamp-base conversions.

Dutch Boy Paints, diecut tin, Dutch Boy painting door frame, hanging bucket string holder, American Art Sign Co., 13-3/4" x 30" . . **2,000.00**
Es-Ki-Mo Rubbers, tin, cutout center holds string spool, hanging boot moves up and down on sign, 17" x 19-3/4" h **2,500.00**
Heinz, diecut tin, pickle, hanging, "57 Varieties," 17" x 14" . . **1,650.00**
Figural
Ball of string, cast iron, figural, hinged, 6-1/2" x 5" h **100.00**
Black boy, 8-1/2" h, cardboard head and arms, fabric body holds string, felt feet **50.00**
Black man and woman, chalkware, matched pair **275.00**
Boy, top hat and pipe, chalkware, 9" h **125.00**
Bride, ceramic, marked "Made in Japan," 6-1/4" h **145.00**
Carrots, chalkware, 10" h **225.00**
Cat, ball of twine and bow, black cat, white face, green bow, chalkware, 6-1/2" h **100.00**
Chef, white, chalkware, 7-1/4" h **145.00**

Cast iron, beehive, 6-1/2" d, base, $40.

Plaster, man in top hat, 8-3/4" h, $25.

Milk glass, hand-painted flowers, original top, 5-1/2" h, $35.

Chipmunk, ceramic, 5-1/8" h **135.00**
Dutch girl, chalkware, 7" h **. . 100.00**
Gourd, green, chalkware, 7-1/2" h
. . . . **135.00**
Jester, chalkware, 7-1/4" h **. . 195.00**
Mammy, chalkware, scissors in
pocket, 6-1/2" h **385.00**
Parrot, chalkware, 9-1/4" h . . **185.00**
Pear, chalkware, 7-3/4" h **90.00**
Pineapple, face, chalkware, 7" h
. . . . **165.00**
Senorita, chalkware, 8" h . . . **275.00**
Shirley Temple, chalkware, 6-1/4" w,
6-3/4" h **395.00**
Strawberry, chalkware, 6-1/2" h
. . . . **115.00**
Terrier, chalkware, gray and white,
8-1/2" h **195.00**
Woody Woodpecker, chalkware,
copyright Walter Lantz, 9-1/2" h
. . . . **345.00**

SUGAR SHAKERS

History: Sugar shakers, sugar castors, or muffineers all served the same purpose: to "sugar" muffins, scones, or toast. They are larger than salt and pepper shakers, were produced in a variety of materials, and were in vogue in the late Victorian era.

Reference: William Heacock, *Encyclopedia of Victorian Colored Pattern Glass*, Book III, Antique Publications, 1976, 1991-92 value update.

China

Nippon, white, gold beading **. . . 60.00**
R. S. Prussia, Schlegelmilch, 5" h,
scalloped base, pearl finish, shaded
roses, green leaves, red mark **. . 250.00**
Wedgwood, jasperware, white classical
design, dark blue ground **50.00**

Glass

Bristol, 6-1/4" h, tall tapering cylinder,
pink, blue flowers and green leaves dec
. . . . **75.00**

Cranberry, Parian Swirl **185.00**
Crown Milano, melon shape, ribbed,
dec, Mt. Washington two-pc top
. . . . **395.00**
Custard, Paneled Teardrop **110.00**
Cut glass, Russian pattern alternating
with clear panels, orig SS top. . . **375.00**
Depression glass, Early American
Sandwich pattern, Duncan & Miller,
clear, orig top **95.00**
Fig, 3-3/4" h, opaque cream ground,
pale pink at creases, base, and rim,
pale pink blossoms **1,950.00**
Green opaque, Parian Swirl, dec
. . . . **110.00**

Opalescent
  Beatty Rib, blue **250.00**
  Bubble Lattice, blue, bulbous ring
    neck, orig top **225.00**
  Coin Spot, blue, orig top **195.00**
  Daisy and Fern, Parian Swirl mold,
    cranberry **385.00**
  Leaf Umbrella, orig top, Northwood
. . . . **295.00**

Milk glass, Waffle pattern, metal top, bottom embossed "Pat'd Appl. For," 7" h, $45.

Ribbed Lattice, cranberry, orig top
. . . . **135.00**

Spanish Lace, cranberry, orig top
. . . . **150.00**
Satin, Leaf Mold, cased blue, orig top,
Northwood. **285.00**
Smith Bros., Ribbed Pillar, dec
. . . . **375.00**

SURVEYORS' INSTRUMENTS

History: From the very beginning of civilized cultures, people have wanted to have a way to clearly delineate what lands they owned. Surveying instruments and equipment of all kinds were developed to help in this important task. The ancients learned to use the sun and other astronomical bodies as their guides. Early statesmen like Washington and Jefferson used brass and ebony instruments as they surveyed the young America. A surveyor must know how to measure lines and angles of a piece of land, using the principles of geometry and trigonometry.

To accomplish this often complicated mathematics, instruments of all types were invented and often patented. Accuracy is important, so many are made with precision components. A surveyor's level is an instrument which consists of a revolving telescope mounted on a tripod and fitted with cross hairs and a spirit level. It is designed to allow surveyors to find points of identical elevation. A transit is used to measure horizontal angles and consists of a telescope mounted at right angles to a horizontal east-west axis. English mathematician, Leonard Digges, invented an instrument called a "theodolite," used to measure vertical and horizontal angles. From a simple compass to high-tech transits, today's collectors are finding these devices interesting. Fine examples of early instruments are coming into the antiques and collectibles marketplace as modern day surveyors now use sophisticated lasers and computers.

References: Florian Cajori, *History of the Logarithmic Slide Rule and Allied Instruments*, Astragal Press, 1994; Gloria Clifton, *Directory of British Scientific Instrument Makers 1550-1851*, P. Wilson Publishers, 1994; William H. Skerritt, *Catalog of the Charles E. Smart Collection: Antique Surveying Instruments*, published by author, (12 Locust Ave., Troy, NY 12180), 1996; Gerard L. E. Turner, *Scientific Instruments 1500-1900: An Introduction*, University of California Press, 1998.

Periodicals: *Rittenhouse*, P.O. Box 151, Hastings-on-Hudson, NY 10706; *Scientific, Medical & Mechanical Antiques*, P.O. Box 412, Taneytown, MD 21787.

Collectors' Clubs: International Calculator Collectors Club, 14561 Livingston St., Tustin, CA 92680; The Oughtred Society, 2160 Middlefield Road, Palo Alto, CA 94301; Zeiss Historical Society, P.O. Box 631, Clifton, NJ 07012.

Museum: National Museum of American History, Smithsonian Institution, Washington, DC.

Alidade, cased, 11" l, W. & L. E. Gurley, Troy, NY, orig leather covered case, minor spots to lacquered finish . **440.00**

Anemometer, six register, eight blades, 2-5/8" d, fan drives 2-1/4" d silvered dial, brass, mounting bracket, softwood case, c1875 .... **345.00**

Astronomical Theodolite, 15-1/2" h, 10-1/2" l telescope, 5-1/2" d, two vernier vertical circle, 6", two vernier 20" horiz. circle, telescope and plate vials, microscope vernier readers, detachable alcohol lamp, detachable four-screw leveling base, trough compass on telescope, orig dovetailed mahogany box with accessories, marked "Stanley, Great Turnstile, Holborn, London, 7534," c1890, Heller & Brightly label mahogany ext. leg tripod **2,185.00**

Astronomical Transit, 20" h, 8-1/2" w, 15-3/4" telescope with rt. Angle prism eyepiece with removable strider level, 7" d double frame, two vernier, vertical circle with indexing vial and circle control, 6" d, two vernier, 15", silver horizontal scale, plate vial with ivory scale, tribrach leveling base, bright brass finish, pine case, marked "Blunt, New York," c1860 .... **7,500.00**

Replica of world's first working calculating machine for all four basic arithmetical operations, by German Philipp Matthäus Hahn, 1774, $25,100. Photo courtesy of Auction Team Breker.

Circumferentor, 5-1/4" h, 9" d outside dia., 4-1/8" compass in center, attached to rotating sight vane/vernier arm, inset vial, silvered dial and outer ring, engraved with eight-point star, two outer fixed sight vanes, brass, marked "Dollond London," c1825 .... **1,955.00**

Drawing instruments, French, cased set, brass and steel instruments, wood scale, brass protractor, rosewood veneered case with warped lid . **220.00**

Flat plate transit, Edmund Draper, Philadelphia, #259, 13-1/2" h, 7-3/4" w, 10" telescope, 5" d vert. circle, 4-1/2" compass, 6" d single vernier, silver horiz. scale, two plate vials, four screw leveling, darkened brass finish, pine case, c1850............... **1,725.00**

Nonius compass, 6 inch
  15-1/8" x 6-7/8" x 7-1/8" h, 5-1/4" l detachable sight vanes, top designed to hold 7/8" d telescope, plate vials, silvered dial and edge engraved outer ring, unique 5' vernier moves the south sight vane by means of worn gear, mahogany case, marked "J. Hanks," Troy, NY, c1825 .... **1,725.00**
  15-78" x 6-7/8" x 9-1/2" h, 7-1/4" l detachable sight vanes, 4-3/4" rad., 20°, 1' outside vernier ring, also edge graduated, staff adapter, lacquered brass, marked "Phelps & Gurley, Troy, N.Y.," c1850 .... **2,530.00**

Octant, 10-7/8", Riggs & Bro., Philadelphia, ebony, ivory inlaid signature panel, scale with brass trim **550.00**

Pocket compass
  1-1/2 inch, 2-1/4" x 2-1/4" mahogany case with hinged cov, 1-1/2" needle floats over engraved finely detailed mariner's star inside 2° increment quadrant outer ring, marked "T. T. Rowe, Lockport, N.Y.," c1825 .... **230.00**
  2 inch, 2-5/8" d, brass, worn silvered dial, full circle, 180° cliometer scale, marked "Breiothaupt in Cassel," c1800......... **565.00**

Reconnaissance transit
  Buff & Buff Mfg. Co., Boston, 12007, 10-1/2" h, 5-1/4" w, 8 3/4" l telescope with rt. Angle solar eyep., 3-1/2" vial, 4" d vert. circle, crossed vials, 3" compass 4-1/2" d, two vernier, 1', silver horiz. scale, four-screw leveling, black leather finished brass, mahogany box, c1918 .... **920.00**

Keuffel & Esser Co., New York, 37037, 10" h, 7-3/4" l telescope, 3-1/2" d vert. circle, 3-1/2" compass, 5" d horiz. circle, telescope and plate vials, four-screw leveling, orig box with plummet and accessories, c1918 .... **800.00**

Saegmuller solar attachment, Fauth & Co., Washington, DC, Saegmuller's pat May 2, 81, 6-1/2" l, 4" h, brass and aluminum construction, level vial, sun lens, horiz. motion, c1885 .... **920.00**

Solar transit, 17" h, Burt Solar Attachment, hour circle, 6.45" engineer's transit, 11" telescope, 3" rad vert. arc., 5" compass, telescope and plate vials, four-screw leveling, brass construction, rubbed bronze finish, detailed mahogany case, label, brass plummet, accessories, "W. & L. E. Gurley, Troy, NY," c1890 ..... **3,335.00**

Surveying/astronomical theodite, 15-1/2" h, 10-1/2" l telescope, 5-1/2" d, two vernier vertical circle, 6", two vernier 20" horiz. circle, telescope and plate vials, microscope vernier readers, detachable alcohol lamp, detachable four-screw leveling base, trough compass on telescope, orig. dovetailed mahogany box with accessories, Heller & Brightly label, mahogany ext., leg tripod, "Stanley, Great Turnstile, Holborn, London, 7535," c1890 .... **2,185.00**

Surveyor's compass
  Davenport, Wm, Phila, 5" engraved face with tripod mount, plum bob, small magnifying glass, ivory scale, 14" l cherry case stenciled "A. C. Farrington" in gold and white **1,155.00**
  Patten, Richard, NY, 6" compass with engraved face, walnut case with litho label of eagle, ship, and signature, minor age cracks in lid, resoldered rim on brass cover, early tripod **990.00**

Surveyors' and engineers' transit
  Buff & Burger, Boston, #2149, 11" telescope wit vial, vert. arc., 6-1/4", 30" horiz. circle with inlaid silver scales, plate vials, four-screw leveling, green leather finish, orig dovetailed mahogany box with labels, c1890........... **920.00**
  Paten, Richard, & Son, 6" d lens, 13-1/2" l, 8-5/8" h, brass, glass lens and level compass labeled "Richard Paten & Son, Baltimore," no tripod base.......... **385.00**

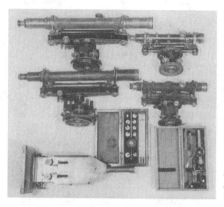

Top left: Bausch, Lomb and Saegmuller level, brass and enameled brass, some wear, rings for tube have engine turnings, mahogany case, 8-3/8" x 21", **$330**; top right: W. & L. E. Gurley level, orig carrying case and tripod, 6-3/8" x 11-1/4", **$300**; middle row: left, Wm. Ainsworth & Sons, Denver, CO, level, enameled brass, some wear, dovetailed mahogany case with leather strap, **$300**; middle right: unidentified maker, level, tripod, and carrying case, with wear, 6-3/4" x 11-1/4", **$275**; bottom row: left: (scientific instrument) J. Dubosco & P. Pelin, Paris, colorimeter, brass, steel base, label "Arthur Thomas, Phila," minor surface rust, 15-1/2", **$385**; center: Sikes Hydrometer, inlaid mahogany case with label "Re-adjusted by W. R. Loftus Ltd. London," plate missing from ext. lid, 2" x 8" x 4", **$110**; left: small microscope, mahogany case, 3" x 8-3/4" x 3-1/2", $140. Photo courtesy of Garth's Auctions, Inc.

Pike, B. & Sons, 166 Broadway (N.Y.), 10-1/2" h, 8-3/8" w, 9-1/4" l telescope with vertical circle, 5" compass, 6-1/2" d horiz. scale (single vernier), telescope vial, plate vials, lacquered brass, orig mahogany case with Gurley label, dated 11/11/1873 . . . . **980.00**

Surveyors' vernier transit compass, 13-1/2" h, 11" telescope with vial, 3-1/2" d vert. circle, 5-3/4" compass, 4" rad. Declination vernier, two plate vials, cross sights, four-screw detachable leveling base, staff adaptor, stiff leg tripod, brass plumb bob, orig case with labels, bronzed brass, marked "W. & L. E. Gurley, Troy, NY," c1874 . . . . **1,840.00**

Theodolite

Stackpole & Brother, New York, 147, city, 8-3/4" h, 6-3/4" w, 14" l telescope with 6" l vial, telescope reversible in yokes, crossed vials, 3-1/4" compass, 6" d, 2 vernier, 20" beveled, silver horiz. scale, four-screw leveling, sgd "Moody 1886," and "P. Leustn/France Richeau," darkened brass, tripod, c1865 . . . . **1,150.00**

Tackpole & Brother, New York, 1559, miniature, 8-1/2" h, 4-1/8" w, 7-1/8" l telescope with vial, 3-1/4" d, 1' vert. circle, 2" compass, 3-1/2" d, 2 vernier, 1' vert. circle, 2" compass, 3-1/2" d, two vernier, 1' silver horiz. scale, tribrach leveling base, black and brass finish, orig box, extension leg tripod, c1870 . . . . **1,495.00**

Theodolite/Level, one-minute type, Wm Wurdemann, Washington, DC, 10" l telescope, 5-1/2" h, labeled "Gr. No. 5," 4" d, 1' vernier, silver metal horiz. scale,

bull's eye-level vial, telescope motion screw, three-screw leveling base, telescope reversible in its yokes, c1860 . . . . **635.00**

Theodolite with compass, Wm Wurdemann, Washington, DC, No. 155, 10-1/2" reversible telescope, 12-3/4" h, 6" d silver metal horiz. scale, two microscope read verniers, 4" compass, single-plate vial, telescope vial, three-screw leveling base and truss frame, c1865 . . . . **1,725.00**

Vernier compass

Gurley, W. & L. E., Troy, NY, 13-1/4" h, 11" telescope, 6" compass with outside declination vernier, crossed plate vials, detachable four-screw leveling base, leveling adapter, sunshade, orig mahogany box with label, bronzed finish brass, c1865 . . . . **2,300.00**

Helffricht. Wm, Maker Philadelphia, 14-7/8" l, 6-1/2" w, 9-5/8" h, 7-1/4" l detachable sight vanes, crossed level vials, 16-count outkeeper, 25° 5' vernier, silvered dial and outer ring, brass cover, 6" l, adapter, dovetailed mahogany box with 20-1/2" x 3-1/2" Helffricht label, sgd "C. S. Woolman," c1850 . **1,150.00**

Young, Wm. J, Maker 3694 Philadelphia, 13-3/4" l, 6-1/8" w, 9-1/4" h, detachable sight vanes, bull's eye vial (empty), outkeeper, non-reflecting dial and silver ring, 25° 5' vernier, brass cover and 6-1/8" l adapter, darkened brass, case and Jacob staff **1,725.00**

Wye Level, 8-1/4" h, 4" w, 16-1/4" l, 1-3/8" d reversible telescope with 6-3/4" l, 4 screw leveling base, horiz. motion clamp and screw, eyepiece attachment, marked "Kuebler &

Seelhorst Makers Philada, 597, Oct. 1, 1867 Patent" **500.00**

SWANSEA

History: This superb pottery and porcelain was made at Swansea (Glamorganshire, Wales) as early as the 1760s, with production continuing until 1870.

Marks: Marks on Swansea vary. The earliest marks were "Swansea" impressed under glaze and "Dillwan" under glaze after 1805. "Cambrian Pottery" was stamped in red under glaze from 1803 to 1805. Many fine examples, including the botanical series in pearlware, are not marked but may have the name of the botanical species stamped underglaze.

References: Susan and Al Bagdade, *Warman's English & Continental Pottery & Porcelain*, 3rd ed., Krause Publications, 1998; W. D. John, *Swansea Porcelain*, Ceramic Book Co., 1958.

Museums: Art Institute of Chicago, Chicago, IL; Glynn Vivian Art Gallery, Swansea.

> **Reproduction Alert:** Swansea porcelain has been copied for many decades in Europe and England. Marks should be studied carefully.

Note: Fine examples of Swansea often may show imperfections such as firing cracks. These pieces are considered mint because they left the factory in this condition.

Bowl, 6-3/8" d, gilt cartouches with idyllic landscape scenes, gilt line borders, William Billingsley, c1815, red Swansea mark **750.00**

Cup and saucer, ribbed, gold fluted border and handle, white int., c1820 . . . . **175.00**

Plate, wild rose and trailing blue flowers, elaborate gilt diaper and foliage well, molded flower wreath and C-scroll border, reserved with gilt green berried foliage, gilt line rim, William Pollard, red stencil mark, c1820 **990.00**

Tureen, 6-5/8" h, multicolored floral sprays, gilt scrolling and borders, double handles, gilt triple ram's head finial, c1820 . . . . **1,550.00**

Vase, 6-3/4" h, floral band, gilt borders, flared base with painted flowers, applied bee handles, imp "Swansea" and triden mark, c1815-20, restored, pr **4,750.00**

SWORDS

History: The first swords used in America came from Europe. The chief cities for sword manufacturing were Solingen in Germany, Klingenthal in France, and Hounslow and Shotley Bridge in England. Among the American importers of these foreign blades was

Horstmann, whose name is found on many military weapons.

New England and Philadelphia were the early centers for American sword manufacturing. By the Franco-Prussian War, the Ames Manufacturing Company of Chicopee, Massachusetts, was exporting American swords to Europe.

Sword collectors concentrate on a variety of styles: commissioned vs. non-commissioned officers' swords, presentation swords, naval weapons, and swords from a specific military branch, such as cavalry or infantry. The type of sword helped identify a person's military rank and, depending on how he had it customized, his personality as well.

Following the invention of repeating firearms in the mid-19th century, the sword lost its functional importance as a combat weapon and became a military dress accessory.

References: *Swords and Hilt Weapons*, Barnes & Noble Books, 1993; Gerald Welond, *Collector's Guide to Swords, Daggers & Cutlasses*, Chartwell Books, 1991.

Collectors' Clubs: Assoc. of American Sword Collectors, P.O. Box 288, Parsonburg, MD 21849-0288; Wilkinson Collectors Society, 19-21 Brunel Road, London, W3 7UH UK.

Museum: Fort Ticonderoga Museum, Ticonderoga, NY.

Note: Condition is key to determining value.

Sword

Artillery, 25" l, Ames, 18-3/4" blade stamped with faint signature, U. S. and inspectors' markings, brass hilt with fish scale design, relief eagle **440.00**

Artillery officer's saber, 33" l, 27-1/2" l curved blade, wide fuller, eagle head pommel and hilt show most of orig fire gilding, replaced wooden handle, early 19th C **330.00**

Calvary saber

41" l, 35-1/2" l import blade with later date stamp of 1851, brass three branch hilt missing leather and wire wrapping, with scabbard . . **220.00**

42" l, Ames, Model 1860, 35" blade stamped "U.S. 1862," with scabbard **675.00**

42-3/4", Model 1860, Emerson & Silver, Trenton, NJ, signature on ricasso, inspector's initials and 1863 on other side, brass three branch hilt with good patina, dark leather wrapped handle missing its wire, browned steel scabbard **825.00**

43" l, 1840, stamped "U. S. 1862," brass three branch hilt with leather and wire wrapped handle, steel scabbard **660.00**

Foot officer

Cast brass helmet shaped pommel with single branch hilt, openwork detail on front of guard, leather and wire wrapped handle, 32" blade with "Clauberg," browned steel scabbard, nickel silver ring at entry, areas of orig etching on blade, some pitting, 41-1/2" l **330.00**

Model 1850, etched signature for "Emerson & Silver, Trenton, NJ," blade maker's stamp "Clauberg, Soligen" on ricasso, 32" blade with faint etching "U.S." on one side, eagle on other cast openwork brass hilt with floral detail, shark skin grip, wire wrap, 37-1/2" l **220.00**

Infantry officer, Model 1850, Ames, 30-1/4" l etched and engraved blade with "Chicopee, Mass" address, cast hilt wash with open work, leather scabbard with brass bands and drag, engraved "Lt. Geo. Trembley, 174th N.Y.S.I.," 36-1/4" l **1,980.00**

Light artillery, 1842 pattern, moderately curved blade, 1-3/8" at ricasso, single wide fuller, left ricasso marked with early Ames logo, and right "1862," surcharged "Conn," handle leather wrapped with braided brass wire, large oval plain pommel cap, single D-guard with ball quillion, plain nickel plated scabbard with two hangers, 33" l **450.00**

Naval officer, Model 1850 naval officer's, non-regulation, double fuller blade marked "W./CLAUBERG/ SOLINGEN" surrounding standing knight in armor, etching on one side of blade of eagle and fouled anchor, other side etched with fouled anchor "U.S.N." and "IRON/PROOF," plated brass guard with spread wing eagle over "US" cut to metal, iron scabbard with copper mounts, 29-1/2" l **700.00**

Officer saber, U.S. War of 1812, curved blade marked "PORTER" in dec on left side, "P" guard dec with ovals and globes, bone handle engraved with line and chevrons, simple brass throat carrying ring and drag on leather scabbard, 75 percent bright blue with scattered areas light to medium pitting, grip cracked full length, 31" l . . . **550.00**

Staff and field officer, Model 1850, emb letter within two circles on ricasso "S. H.," etched and engraved 31" blade with stand of flags, eagle, "E. Pluribus Unum," scrolled foliage with "U.S," orig wire wrap with section of orig sword knot, blued steel scabbard with brass bands and drag, descended in family of Col. Edward Scovel, stationed at Johnson Island, some surface rust, 37" l **1,265.00**

Saber, American, unmarked, cast brass eagle pommel, simple knuckle-bow, quillon, spiral ribbed bone grip, somewhat pitted 26-1/2" single-edged blade with 3/4 length fuller, black leather scabbard, brass throat having frog stud and carrying ring, simple clipped tip brass 3-1/2" long tip, 31-3/4" total length, **$1,150.** *Photo courtesy of Cowan Historic Americana Auctions.*

TEA CADDIES

History: Tea once was a precious commodity and stored in special boxes or caddies. These containers were made to accommodate different teas and included a special cup for blending.

Around 1700, silver caddies appeared in England. Other materials, such as Sheffield plate, tin, wood, china, and pottery, also were used. Some tea caddies are very ornate.

Pewter and green glass, Liberty/Tudric, rim embossed with stylized leaves, the finial top with three foil-glass cabochons, unmarked, 6" x 5", $1,100. Photo courtesy of David Rago Auctions.

Ivory tusk, 4-1/4" w, 5" h, formed as section of tusk, silver-plated mountings, flat hinged top with foliate finial, engraved scrolls, beaded and waved rim bands, 19th C **460.00**

Papier-mâché, 9-1/4" l, 6-3/4" d, 6" h, Regency Chinoiserie-style, rect case with canted corners, ornately dec with figural reserves within flower blossoms bordered by wide bands of gilding, conforming hinged lid opening to int. fitted with two removable pewter tea canisters with dec chasing **950.00**

Quillwork, 8-3/8" l, 4-3/4" d, 5-1/4" h, hexagonal, inlaid mahogany frames, blue and gilt quillwork panels covered with glass, floral vintage and leaf designs with crown and "MC 1804," two int. lidded compartments, replaced foil lining, English **2,750.00**

Silver
5" h, tapered ovoid form, chased and emb with reeding below foliate scrolls and cartouches, lid with beaded edge, rising to foliate finial, monogrammed, early 20th C, 6 troy oz **325.00**

7" h, lobed hexagonal form, lobed lid with filigree finial, all over Eastern style bird and foliate enamel dec, mounted with semi-precious stones, gilt int., approx 17 troy oz, Europe, late 19th/early 20th C **500.00**

Whieldon, Cauliflower pattern, beige and green, oval base, 4" h, $725.

Wood
Burl walnut veneer, 9" l, 4-3/4" d, 4-5/8" h, dome top hinged lid with metal strapwork, centered by decorative quatrefoil mounted with ivory plaque, front with similar metal and ivory escutcheon, int. with two wells with grades of foil, mahogany lids, mid-19th C **250.00**
Burl walnut veneer, 12-1/2" l, 6" d, 7-1/2" h, George III, rect case, hinged stepped domed lid, well fitted int. with two conforming veneered compartments, each opening to lead lined interiors, center section for mixing bowl, associated glass bowl..... **650.00**
Cherry, 10" l, Chippendale, mahogany cross banding, ogee feet, base and lid edge moldings, old finish, three int. compartments, orig brass escutcheon and bale with tooling, minor repairs **2,750.00**
Cherry veneer, 4-3/4" w, 3-3/8" d, 4-3/4" h, octagonal, banding inlay on lid and front panel, imitation fluting on corner panels, front with flower in oval medallion, conch shell inlay and oval medallion on lid, brass hinges and incomplete lock, brass keyhole escutcheon, age cracks and minor veneer damage................. **715.00**

Figured mahogany, 10-7/8" w, 6" d, 6-1/2" h, dark narrow band inlay around all edges, diamond-shaped lock escutcheon inlay, divide int. with three cov tin liners, line inlay beneath lid, orig brass bale handle, refinished, minor corner chip and hairline **440.00**
Rosewood veneer, 12" l, 6-1/4" d, 7-3/8" h, Federal, inlay, brass ring handles with cornucopia escutcheons and batwing keyhole escutcheon, int. with two lidded compartments and clear cut glass mixing bowl **990.00**

TEA LEAF IRONSTONE CHINA

History: Tea Leaf ironstone flowed into America from England in great quantities from 1860 to 1910 and graced the tables of working-class America. It traveled to California and Texas in wagons and down the Mississippi River by boat to Kentucky and Missouri. It was too plain for the rich homes; its simplicity and durability appealed to wives forced to watch pennies. Tea Leaf found its way into the kitchen of Lincoln's Springfield home; sailors ate from it aboard the *Star of India*, now moored in San Diego and still displaying Tea Leaf.

Contrary to popular belief, Tea Leaf was not manufactured exclusively by English potters in Staffordshire. Although there were more than 35 English potters producing Tea Leaf, at least 26 American potters helped satisfy the demand.

Anthony Shaw (1850-1900) is credited with introducing Tea Leaf. The most prolific Tea Leaf makers were Anthony Shaw and Alfred Meakin (1875-present), Johnson Bros. (1883-present), Henry Burgess (1864-1892), Enoch Wedgwood, and Arthur J. Wilkinson (1897-present), all of whom shipped much of their ware to America.

Although most of the English Tea Leaf is copper luster, Powell and Bishop (1868-1878) and their successors, Bishop and Stonier (1891-1936), worked primarily in gold luster. Beautiful examples of gold luster were also made by H. Burgess; Mellor, Taylor & Co. (1880-1904) used it on children's tea sets. Other English potters also were known to use gold luster, including W. & E. Corn, Thomas Elsmore, and Thomas Hughes, companies which have been recently identified as makers of this type of ware.

J. & E. Mayer, Beaver Falls, Pennsylvania, founded by English potters who immigrated to America, produced a large amount of copper luster Tea Leaf. The majority of the American potters decorated with gold luster that had no brown underglaze beneath the copper luster.

East Liverpool, Ohio, potters such as Cartwright Bros. (1864-1924), East End Pottery (1894-1909) and Knowles, Taylor & Knowles (1870-1934) decorated only in gold luster. This also is true of Trenton, New Jersey, potters, such as Glasgow Pottery, American Crockery Co., and Fell & Thropp Co. Since no underglazing was used with the gold, much of it has been washed away.

By the 1900s, Tea Leaf's popularity had waned. The sturdy ironstone did not disappear; it was stored in barns and relegated to attics and basements. While the manufacture of Tea Leaf did experience a brief resurgence from the late 1950s through the 1970s, copper lustre Tea Leaf didn't recapture the hearts of the American consumer as it had a generation before.

Tea Leaf collectors recognize a number of "variant" decorative motifs as belonging to the Tea Leaf family: Teaberry, Morning Glory, Coral, Cinquefoil, Rose, Pre-Tea Leaf, Tobacco Leaf, Pepper Leaf, Pinwheel, Pomegranate, and Thistle & Berry, as well as white ironstone decorated with copper lustre bands and floral and geometric motifs. Once considered the stepchildren of Tea Leaf, these variants are now prized by collectors and generally bring strong prices.

Today's collectors eagerly seek out Tea Leaf and all of its variant motifs, and copper-lustre decorated white ironstone has once again become prized for its durability, beauty, simplicity, craft, and style.

References: Annise Doring Heaivilin, *Grandma's Tea Leaf Ironstone*, Wallace-Homestead, 1981, 1996 reprint distributed by L-W Book Sales; Jean Wetherbee, *White Ironstone, A Collector's Guide*, Tea Leaf Club International (324 Powderhorn Dr., Houghton Lake, MI 48629), 1996.

Collectors' Club: Tea Leaf Club International, 324 Powderhorn Dr., Houghton Lake, MI 48629.

Museums: Lincoln Home, Springfield, IL; Ox Barn Museum, Aurora, OR; Sherman Davidson House, Newark OH.

Adviser: Dale Abrams.

Notes: Tea Leaf values have increased steadily for the last decade, but there are some general rules of thumb for the knowledgeable collector. English Tea Leaf is still more collectible than American, except for rare pieces. The earlier the Tea Leaf production (1850s-1860s), the harder it is to find pieces and, therefore, the more expensive they are. Children's pieces are highly collectible, especially those with copper lustre decorative motifs. Hard-to-find Tea Leaf pieces include mustache cups, eggcups, covered syrup pitchers, ladles, oversized serving pieces, and pieces with significant embossing. Common pieces (plates, platters) of later production (1880-1900) need to be in excellent condition or should be priced accordingly, as they are not that difficult to find.

Bone dish

Meakin, crescent shape
. . . . .55.00
Shaw, fluted edge 60.00

Bowl, Alfred Meakin, 8-1/2" sq, 2-7/8" h
. . . . .40.00

Brush vase

Burgess, Pagoda. 215.00
Meakin, Fishhook. 200.00
Shaw, plain round, drain hole **225.00**

Butter dish, three pcs, base, cover, liner

Meakin, Fishhook. 185.00
Wedgwood, simple square . .185.00

Butter dish liner, sq **25.00**

Butter pat, Meakin

Square 15.00
Round, Chelsea 25.00

Cake plate

Edwards, Peerless (Feather), sq, handles. 185.00
Meakin, Bamboo, 8-3/4" with handles. 85.00
Wilkinson, Senate shape, oval
. . . . 150.00

Chamber pot, Meakin

Bamboo, two pcs 265.00
Scroll, two pcs 285.00

Children's dishes

Mug, child's, Shaw 375.00
Tea set, Knowles, Taylor & Knowles, four cups and saucers, teapot, creamer and sugar. 850.00
Tea set, Mellor-Taylor, round bottom, gold luster, six cups and saucers, six plates, teapot, creamer, sugar, waste bowl 1,850.00

Coffeepot, cov

Furnival, Gentle Square (Rooster)
. . . . 325.00
Meakin, Chelsea. 300.00
Shaw, Lily-of-the-Valley. 475.00

Compote

Mellor Taylor, sq, ridged 325.00
Red Cliff, simple square, 1960s
. . . . 150.00
Shaw, plain, round 310.00
Unmarked, unusually deep bowl, 8" d, 5" h 435.00

Creamer

Edwards, Peerless (Feather) 285.00
Meakin, Bamboo. 185.00
Red Cliff, Chinese shape, 1960s
. . . . 80.00
Shaw, Cable 250.00

Cup and saucer

Adams, Empress shape, 1950s
. . . . 30.00
Meakin 65.00
Shaw, Lily-of-the-Valley. 125.00

Egg cup

Meakin, Boston Egg Cup, 4" d, 1-3/4" h 395.00
Unmarked, 3-1/2" h 325.00

Gravy boat

Johnson Bros., Acanthus, with stand
. . . . 160.00
Mayer, American. 90.00
Meakin, Bamboo. 85.00
Shaw, basketweave, with stand
. . . . 185.00
Wedgwood, simple square. . . 65.00

Mug

Meakin, Scroll. 195.00

Shaw, Lily-of-the-Valley 350.00

Mush bowl, Meakin 85.00

Nappy

Meakin, Fishhook, 4-1/4" sq . . 20.00
Wedgwood, 4-1/4" sq, scalloped edge 24.00

Pitcher and bowl set

Furnival, Cable 495.00
Meakin, Fishhook. 285.00
Shaw, Cable 525.00

Pitcher/jug

Meakin, Chelsea 375.00
Shaw, Chinese shape, 7-1/2". 500.00

Plate

Furnival, plain, round, 8-1/4" . . 12.00
Johnson Bros., Acanthus, 9" d
. . . . 22.00
Meakin, plain, round, 8-7/8" d, chip on table rim 15.00
Shaw, plain, round, 10" d. 25.00
Wedgwood, 8-5/8" d, some discoloration 15.00

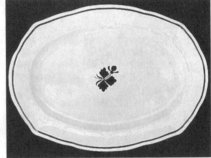

Platter, Alfred Meakin, England, Royal Ironstone China, oval, scalloped edges, single center Tea Leaf, 12-1/2" l, $55.

Platter

Meakin, Chelsea, 10" x 14", oval
. . . . 65.00
Royal Ironstone, W. H. Grindley & Sons, England. 70.00
Shaw, Lily-of-the-Valley, 13". 150.00

Punch bowl, Shaw, Cable. 525.00

Relish dish, Shaw, Chinese shape
. . . . 265.00

Sauce tureen

Furnival, Cable, three pcs . . . 185.00
Meakin, Bamboo, four pcs, including ladle 425.00
Red Cliff, four pcs, including ladle
. . . . 175.00

Serving bowl, open

Grindley, round, scalloped edge
. . . . 135.00
Meakin, sq, scalloped edge, 6" sq
. . . . 45.00

Soap dish, cov

Grindley, Bamboo, three pcs, liner, rect **225.00**

Shaw, Cable, three pcs, liner, oval **300.00**

Soup bowl, Meakin, 7" d **18.00**

Soup plate, Meakin, plain, round, 10" d **50.00**

Soup tureen, Meakin, Bamboo, four pcs with ladle **1,500.00**

Sugar bowl, cov

Meakin, fishhook **85.00**

Shaw, cable shape **145.00**

Vanity box, cov, Furnival, Cable, horizontal **325.00**

Vegetable, cov

Meakin, Bamboo **165.00**

Powell & Bishop, c1866-78 . . **200.00**

Shaw, basketweave **325.00**

Wilkinson, Maidenhair Fern . **275.00**

Waste bowl

Meakin, plain, round **110.00**

Shaw, Niagara Fan **120.00**

TEAPOTS

History: The origins of the teapot have been traced to China in the late 16th century. Early Yixing teapots were no bigger than the tiny cups previously used for drinking tea. By the 17th century, tea had spread to civilized nations of the world. The first recorded advertisement for tea in London is dated 1658 and called a "China drink...call Tcha, by other Nations Tay, alias Tee..." Although coffee houses were already established, they began to add tea to their selections.

While the Chinese had long been producing teapots and other tea items, the English were receiving these wares along with shipments of tea. By the early 1700s, British china and stoneware producers were manufacturing teapots. It was in 1706 that Thomas Twining bought his own coffee house and thwarted the competition of the many other such establishments by offering a variety of quality tea. Coffee houses were exclusively for males; thus, women would wait outside, sending their footmen inside for purchases. For the majority of the 1700s, teapots were Oriental imports. British factories continued experimenting with the right combination of materials which would make a teapot durable enough to withstand the daily rigors of boiling water. Chinese Export Porcelain was an inspiration to the British and by the end of the 1700s, many companies found the necessary combinations of china clay and stone, fired at high temperature, which could withstand boiling water needed to brew precious pots of tea.

From the very first teapots, figural shapes have always been a favorite with tea drinkers. The Victorian era saw a change from more utilitarian teapots toward beautiful, floral, and Rococo designs, yet figural pots continued to be manufactured.

Early American manufacturers mimicked Oriental and British designs. While the new land demanded sturdy teapots in the unsettled land, potteries were established steadily in the Eastern states. Rockingham teapots were produced by many companies, deriving this term from British companies manufacturing a strong, shiny brown glaze on heavy pottery. The best known are from the Bennington, Vermont, potteries.

By the 1800s and the turn-of-the-century, many pottery companies were well established in the U. S., producing a lighter dinnerware and china including teapots. Figural teapots from this era are highly desired by collectors, while others concentrate on collecting all known patterns produced by a company.

The last 20 years has seen a renewed interest in teapots and collectors desire not only older examples, but high-priced, specialty manufactured teapots such as those from the Lomonosov factory in Russia or individual artist creations commanding hundreds of dollars.

References: Edward Bramah, *Novelty Teapots,* Quiller Press, London, 1992; Tina M. Carter, *Teapots,* Running Press, 1995; —, *Collectible Teapots, Reference and Price Guide,* Krause Publications, 2000; Robin Emmerson, *British Teapots & Tea Drinking,* HMSO, London, 1992.

Periodicals: *Tea, A Magazine,* P.O. Box 348, Scotland, CT 06264; *Tea Talk,* P.O. Box 860, Sausalito, CA 94966; *Tea Time Gazette,* P.O. Box 40276, St. Paul, MN 55104.

Collectors' Club: Cardew Collectors' Club, 200 S. 31st St., Paducah, KY 42001.

Reproduction Alert: Teapots and other ware with a blurry mark of a shield and two animals, ironstone, celadon-colored body background, and a design made to look like flow blue, are new products, possibly from China. Yixing teapots have been reproduced or made in similar styles for centuries; study this type of teapot to help determine the old from the new.

Adviser: Tina M. Carter.

Royal Doulton, Dickensware, Little Nell, **$195.** *Photo courtesy of Joy Luke Auctions.*

Belleek, sea urchin and coral, Echinus Tea Ware, Ireland, first black mark **850.00**

Cadogan, brown Rockingham-style pottery, no mark, possibly made in England, late 1800s **195.00**

Cloisonné, panel with butterflies and flowers, Chinese, late 19th C . . . **450.00**

Copper, spun, E. W. Allen, 1940s **550.00**

Flow blue, Scinde pattern, Alcock, octagonal, 8 1/2" h **950.00**

Graniteware, large teapot with pewter handle, lid and spout, Manning Bowman & Co. Manufacturers, called Perfection Granite Ironware, West Meriden, Connecticut **325.00**

Ironstone, Mason's Ironstone, Vista pattern, red and white scenic dec, matching trivet **165.00**

Lenox, Art Deco, applied sterling silver dec, c1930, three-pc set **400.00**

Majolica, fish, multicolored, Minton, no mark, late 1800s **2,000.00**

Old Worcester, first period, Old Japan Star, 1765-70 . . . . **5,250.00**

Parian ware, Brownfield, Mistletoe pattern **450.00**

Porcelain, pink and gray luster swirls, Surf Ballet, by California artist, Sascha Brastoff, c1953 . . . . **265.00**

Rockingham style, triple-spouted teapot, brown pottery, relief design, late 1800s, early 1900s **2,000.00**

Silver, 5-3/4" h, Hester Bateman, London, 1786, oval, domed lid with beaded rim, engraved bands, body with engraved bands and central cartouche, wood ear handle and finial, approx 13 troy oz **3,450.00**

Wedgwood

Earthenware, cabbage, lettuce, melon, various designs . . . **650.00**

Jasperware, unglazed porcelain with decoration in white relief, modern set includes creamer and sugar, mark, Wedgwood, England, set **295.00**

Yixing

Bamboo handle, Chinese "chop mark" or signature, c1880 . **450.00**

Padded storage box, fixed handle, all over Chinese writing, imported by Midwest Importers, made in China, orig pamphlet explaining centuries old tradition, modern **75.00**

TEDDY BEARS

History: Originally thought of as "Teddy's Bears," in reference to President Theodore Roosevelt, these stuffed toys are believed to have originated in Germany. The first ones to be made in the United States were produced about 1902.

Most of the earliest teddy bears had humps on their backs, elongated muzzles, and jointed limbs. The fabric used was generally mohair; the eyes were either glass with pin backs or black shoe buttons. The stuffing was usually excelsior. Kapok (for softer bears)

and wood-wool (for firmer bears) also were used as stuffing materials.

Quality older bears often have elongated limbs, sometimes with curved arms, oversized feet, and felt paws. Noses and mouths are black and embroidered onto the fabric.

The earliest teddy bears are believed to have been made by the original Ideal Toy Corporation in America and by a German company, Margarete Steiff, GmbH. Bears made in the early 1900s by other companies can be difficult to identify because they were all similar in appearance and most identifying tags or labels were lost during childhood play.

References: Shawn Brecka, *Big Book of Little Bears,* Antique Trader Books, 1999; Dee Hockenberry, *Steiff Bears and Other Playthings Past and Present,* Schiffer Publishing, 2000; Constance King, *The Century of the Teddy Bear,* Antique Collectors' Club, 1999; Margaret Fox Mandel, *Teddy Bears and Steiff Animals,* 1st Series (1984, 2000 value update), 2nd Series (1987, 2000 value update), 3rd Series (2000), Collector Books; —, *Teddy Bears, Annalee Animals & Steiff Animals,* 3rd Series, Collector Books, 1990, 1996 value update; Carol J. Smith, *Identification & Price Guide to Winnie the Pooh Collectibles,* Hobby House Press, 1994; Ken Yenke, *Bing Bears and Toys,* Schiffer Publishing, 2000; —, *Teddy Bear Treasury, Identification & Values,* Collector Books, 2000.

Periodicals: *Antique & Collectables,* P.O. Box 12589, El Cajon, CA 92022, http://www.collect.com/antiqueandcollectables; *Beans & Bears!* P.O. Box 3070, Richmond, VA 23228, http://www.beansmagazine.com; *National Doll & Teddy Bear Collector,* P.O. Box 4032, Portland, OR 97208; *Teddy Bear & Friends,* 741 Miller Drive, SE, Suite D2, Harrisburg, PA 20175; http://www.cowles.com/maglist.html; *Teddy Bear Review,* 170 Fifth Ave., 12th Floor, New York, NY 10010; *Teddy Bear Times,* Avalon Court, Star Road, Partridge Green, West Sussex RH13 8RY, http://www.teddybeartimes.com.

Collectors' Clubs: Good Bears of the World, P.O. Box 13097, Toledo, OH 43613, http://www.goodbearsoftheworld.org; Hugglets Teddy Bear Assoc., P.O. Box 290, Brighton, East Sussex, BN2 IDR UK; http://www.hugglets.com; My Favorite Bear: Collectors Club for Classic Winnie the Pooh, 468 W. Alpine #10, Upland, CA 91786; Steiff Club USA, 31 E. 28th St., 9th Floor, New York, NY 10016, http://www.steiff-club.com; Teddy Bear Boosters Club, 19750 SW. Peavine Mountain Road, McMinnville, OR 97128.

Museums: Teddy Bear Museum of Naples, Naples, FL; The Bear Museum, Petersfield, Hampshire, UK.

Additional Listings: See Steiff.

Notes: Teddy bears are rapidly increasing as collectibles and their prices are rising proportionately. As in other fields, desirability should depend upon appeal, quality, uniqueness, and condition. One modern bear already has been firmly accepted as a valuable collectible among its antique counterparts: the Steiff teddy put out in 1980 for the company's 100th anniversary. This is a reproduction of that company's first teddy and has a special box, signed certificate, and numbered ear tag; 11,000 of these were sold worldwide.

Mohair, brown, 20" h, **$1,025**, Hertel, Schwab & Co. #152 baby doll, 12" h, **$400.** *Photo courtesy of McMasters Auctions.*

3-3/8" h, Schuco, golden mohair perfume bear, black steel eyes, embroidered nose and mouth, jointed at shoulders and hips, overall fur loss, soil, c1920 . . . . **150.00**

10" h, blond mohair, fully jointed, black steel eyes, excelsior stuffing, c1906, traces of fur, nose, mouth, and claws re-embroidered, replaced pads **175.00**

10" h, ginger mohair, fully jointed, black steel eyes, black embroidered nose, mouth, and claws, felt pads, Steiff, blank ear button, spotty fur loss **1,150.00**

10" h, light yellow short mohair pile, fully jointed, excelsior stuffing, black steel eyes, embroidered nose, mouth, and claws, felt pads, Ideal, c1905, spotty fur and fiber loss, pr **920.00**

10-1/2" l, pull toy, brown wool, on all fours, glass eyes, leatherette muzzle, metal traces and wheels, early 20th C, some loss to wheels, fur loss . . . **200.00**

11" h, blond mohair, fully jointed, excelsior stuffing, black steel eyes, open composition mouth with full set of teeth, c1908, fiber wear around mouth and nose, some fur wear at seams . . **750.00**

11-1/2" h, gold mohair, fully jointed, glass eyes, excelsior stuffing, Steiff, button missing, remnants of embroidered nose, mouth, and claws, spotty fur loss, extensive moth damage to pads **200.00**

12" h, yellow mohair, fully jointed, glass eyes, embroidered nose and mouth,

excelsior stuffing, felt pads, Schuco, early 1920s, moth damage, spotty fur loss **350.00**

13-1/2" h, saffron rayon plush, fully jointed, excelsior stuffing, glass eyes, embroidered nose, mouth, and claws, felt pads, some fur loss, and fiber damage, c1930 . . . . **115.00**

15" h, mohair, gold plush, swivel head, brown glass eyes, shaved muzzle, black floss nose and mouth, excelsior stuffing, jointed at shoulders and hips, gold felt pads on paws and feet, unmarked, right paw pad damaged **150.00**

16" h, ginger mohair, fully jointed, excelsior stuffing, glass eyes, long arms, shaved muzzle, vertically stitched nose, felt pads, arrow ear button, Bing, c1907, very slight fur loss, head disk broken through front of neck . **2,300.00**

16" h, golden mohair, shoe button eyes, very long snout, black embroidered nose and (new) mouth, barely furred, left ear and three pads replaced, probably American, c1920 . . . . . **200.00**

16" h, golden yellow mohair, fully jointed, glass eyes, brown still nose, embroidered mouth, excelsior stuffed, light fur loss, felt pads damaged, probably American, c1920 . . . . . **260.00**

16-1/2" h, ginger mohair, fully jointed, black steel eyes, black embroidered nose, mouth, and claws, beige felt pads, excelsior stuffing, American, c1919, patchy fur loss, felt damage **800.00**

17" h, gray mohair, brown glass eyes, embroidered features, mouth redone, fully jointed, velveteen pads, some wear to lush pads, American, c1920 . **150.00**

18" h, possibly Ideal, worn and patched, replaced shoe button eyes, retains one glass eye, which may be original, c1915, accompanied by photo of orig child owner **175.00**

19" h, brown tint gold mohair, fully jointed, glass eyes, shaved muzzle, black embroidered nose and mouth, excelsior stuffing, clipped mohair pads, Hermann, 1940s, fur slightly matted in spots **250.00**

20-1/2" h, greenish-gold mohair, articulated body, glass eyes, ivory felt paw pads, worn coat **200.00**

21" h, brown-tipped blond long mohair, brown glass eyes, embroidered nose, mouth, claws shaved muzzle, and inner ears, crier, fully jointed, felt pads, mid-20th C **175.00**

21-1/2" h, light yellow mohair, fully jointed, glass eyes, excelsior stuffing, embroidered nose and claws, replaced pads, some fur loss, fiber damage to left foot, 1930s-40s **90.00**
22" h, aqua rayon mohair, fully jointed, glass eyes, embroidered nose and mouth, excelsior stuffing, cotton pads, 1920s, some soiling, fading, and matting. **115.00**
24" h, black mohair, brown glass eyes, embroidered nose and mouthy, fully jointed, worn velveteen pads, America, c1920. . . . .**1,610.00**
24" h, golden brown mohair, fully jointed, glass eyes, embroidered nose and mouth, kapok and excelsior stuffing, felt pads, wearing dress, bonnet, and glasses, 1920s, spotty fur loss and felt damage. **350.00**
25" h, gold mohair, articulated body, glass eyes, ivory felt paw pads are worn, one replaced, wear **525.00**
25" h, yellow mohair, fully jointed, glass eyes, black embroidered nose, mouth, and claws, felt pads, excelsior stuffing, Ideal, 1920s, slight fur loss and matting **635.00**
26" h, brown mohair, articulated body, glass eyes, ivory felt paw pads **. 360.00**
26" h, light gold mohair, articulated body, glass eyes, very worn ivory felt paw pads, one paw repaired . . **250.00**
26-1/2" h, gold mohair, articulated body, glass eyes, pink felt paw pads, some wear and repair **550.00**
27" l, light gold mohair, articulated body, glass eyes, very worn ivory felt paw pads, squeak voice box **360.00**
29" l, beige curly mohair, fully jointed, glass eyes, brown embroidered nose, mouth, and claws, excelsior stuffing, felt pads, Steiff, post WWII, ear button, some pad damage, wearing train engineer's outfit **575.00**
32" l, curly gold mohair, fully jointed, glass eyes, shaved muzzle, open rose felt mouth, tan embroidered nose, cream felt pads, excelsior stuffing, Richard Cramer, Germany, 1930s, some spotty fur loss, moth damage to pads and mouth **1,955.00**

TEPLITZ CHINA

History: Around 1900, there were 26 ceramic manufacturers located in Teplitz, a town in the Bohemian province of what was then known as Czechoslovakia. Other potteries were located in the nearby town of Turn. Wares from these factories were molded, cast, and hand decorated. Most are in the Art Nouveau and Art Deco styles.

Marks: The majority of pieces do not carry a specific manufacturer's mark; they are simply marked "Teplitz," "Turn-Teplitz," or "Turn."

Bust, 22-1/2" h, young woman, elaborate dress, fan, flowers, and hat with reticulated border, putto on shoulders, Ernest Wahliss, c1900, repaired **1,700.00**
Candlestick, 13" h, applied flowers, gold trim **90.00**
Creamer, hp, scene of bird in flight, gold trim **195.00**
Ewer, 10-5/8" h, gilt trimmed ivory ground, enameled birds in paneled sides, c1900. . . . .**345.00**

Figure, Arab warrior and horse, marked "Amphora Teplitz," base, impressed mark, 10" h, 9-3/4" l oval, **$400.**

Figure
8" h, 8-1/2" l, two children, young boy in hat with pink ribbon, pushing young girl carrying umbrella and basket, soft beige ground, pink and blue highlights, sgd "Teplitz Bohemia," imp "4007" **450.00**
8-1/2" w, 17" h, nymph, standing on base with plants, muted greens, gold highlights, sgd "Whaliss" **2,500.00**
20" x 21" x 7", child, woman with amphora on head, riding black bull, sgd "Stellmacher, Teplitz," repair to foot **7,500.00**
21" h, gentlemen, 18th century style dress **675.00**

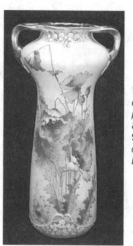

Vase, two handles, orange poppies decoration, 8-1/2" w, 16" h, $880. Photo courtesy of Joy Luke Auctions.

Jar, 8-1/4" w, 6-1/2" h, hp, parcel gilt, molded dragon handles, marked "Alfred Shellmacher Teplitz" . . . **850.00**
Pitcher, 12" h, cylindrical, bulbous base, leaf-shaped handle, reticulated rim, ivory ground, iris and foliate dec, Ernst Wahliss Alexandra Porcelain Works, early 20th C, crown and shield mark on underside, hairline and crack at handle **110.00**
Urn, 14" h, ovoid, two delicate handles, textured neck, handles, and base, ivory and pale green, gilding, hp floral center, marked "Turn-Teplitz-Bohemia" in circle around vase mark, also marked "RS + K Made in Austria" **295.00**
Vase

3-1/2" d, 8" h, rose pattern . . **320.00**
5-3/4" d, 7" h, gourd shape, four handles, band of white and gold Glasgow roses, green leaves, gold details, gray-green leathering ground, stamped "Teplitz/Made in Austria/1174/18" **460.00**
10" w, 12" h, double handles, Art Nouveau floral design, burgundy ground, sgd "Julius Dresser, Teplitz" **750.00**
11-1/2" h, stylized blue and green scene of sun through trees, lower band with ivory and blue insect and blue floral dec, gold accents, stamped "Turn-Teplitz-Bohemia/ RS+K/Made in Austria" . . . **490.00**
12" h, lustered central panel with Art-Nouveau style female portrait, c1900 . . . . **575.00**
17" h, 12-1/2" d, tear shape, two handles, slip dec, yellow flowers, black stems, olive ground, stamped "Austria" **350.00**
24" h, pierced foliate dec handles, floral dec, late 19th C **175.00**

TERRA-COTTA WARE

History: Terra-cotta is ware made of hard, semi-fired ceramic. The color of the pottery ranges from a light orange-brown to a deep brownish red. It is usually unglazed, but some pieces are partially glazed and have incised, carved, or slip designs. Utilitarian objects, as well as statuettes and large architectural pieces, were made. Fine early Chinese terra-cotta pieces recently have sold for substantial prices.

Collectors' Club: Friends of Terra Cotta, 771 West End Ave., #10E, New York, NY 10025-5539.

Architectural fragment, 38" l, lintel supports, from Solomon Blumenfield Flats, 1884, pr.. . . . .**550.00**
Bowl, 6" d, 2" h, glazed **30.00**
Bust, 22" h, young woman, Chas Eugene Breton, 1916 . . . .**665.00**
Casino chip, 1-1/2" d, Club Forest, inlaid address, crest, 18 encrusted stars **25.00**
Figure
　7-1/2" h, Aphrodite, dressed in tunic, open back, South Italian, third century B.C. **345.00**
　11" h, St. Joseph, wearing long loose robes, black hat, polychrome dec, Spanish, 19th C. **600.00**
　18-1/4" l, nude reclining on naturalistic base, gazing to left, both hands on head, French, 20th C **650.00**
　18-3/4" l, reclining male figure with dog, inscribed "Claude Janin" **400.00**
　20" h, bulldog, Continental **1,850.00**
Pedestal, 7" sq top, 24" h, price for pr **400.00**

Planter
　10-1/4" h, garland and mask motif **100.00**
　Rectangular, Italian. **70.00**
Plaque, 7" x 8-1/4", girl in bonnet, marked "Czechslovakia," numbers, and maker's mark, some crazing to glaze **150.00**
Statue, 55" h, Minera, woman in draped toga, grape and cable head dress, holding wine cup. **2,000.00**
Tray, 9" x 7", hp, pilgrims resting, gilt dec, 1920 . . . . **85.00**
Urn, 29-1/2" h, molded putti and foliage dec, green glaze, waisted neck, two handles, circular base. **395.00**
Water pitcher, 13" h, c1810, base chip **325.00**

TEXTILES

History: Textiles is the generic term for cloth or fabric items, especially anything woven or knitted. Antique textiles that have survived are usually those that were considered the "best" by their original owners, since these were the objects that were used and stored carefully by the housewife.

　Textiles are collected for many reasons—to study fabrics, to understand the elegance of a historical period, for decorative purposes, or to use as was originally intended. The renewed interest in antique clothing has sparked a revived interest in period textiles of all forms.

References: Dilys E. Blum, *The Fine Art of Textiles: The Collection of the Philadelphia Museum of Art*, Philadelphia Museum of Art, 1997; M. Dupont-Auberville, *Full-Color Historic Textile Designs*, Dover Publications, 1996; Loretta Smith Fehling, *Terrific Tablecloths from the '40s and '50s*, Schiffer, 1998; Frances Johnson, *Collecting Household Linens*, Schiffer Publishing, 1997; Elizabeth Kurella, *The Complete Guide To Vintage Textiles*, Krause Publications, 1999; Sheila Paine, *Embroidered Textiles: Traditional Patterns from Five Continents, With a Worldwide Guide To Identification*, Thames & Hudson, 1997; Mildred Cole Peladeau, *Art Underfoot: The Story of Waldoboro Hooked Rugs*, American Textile History Museum, 1999; Raffaella Serena, *Embroideries and Patterns from 19th Century Vienna*, Antique Collectors' Club Ltd., 1998; Jessie A. Turbayne, *Hooked Rug Treasury*, Schiffer Publishing, 1997.

Periodicals: *HALI*, P.O. Box 4312, Philadelphia, PA 19118; *International Old Lacers Bulletin*, P.O. Box 554, Flanders, NJ 07836; *Textile Museum Newsletter*, The Textile Museum, 2320 S St NW, Washington, DC 20008.

Collectors' Clubs: American Needlepoint Guild, Inc., P.O. Box 1027, Cordova, TN 38088-1027, http://www.needlepoint.org; Colonial Coverlet Guide of America, 5617 Blackstone, La Grante, IL 60525-3420; Costume Society of America, P.O. Box 73, Earleville, MD 21919, http://www.costumesocietyamerica.com; Embroiders Guild of America, 335 W. Broadway, Suite 100, Louisville, KY 40202, http://www.egausa.org; Knitting Guild of America, http://www.tkga.org; Stumpwork Society, 55 Ferncrest Ave., Cranston, RI 02905-3510; International Old Lacers, Inc., P.O. Box 554, Flanders, NJ 07836, Rug & Textile Society of Indiana, 8940 Sassafras Court, Indianapolis, IN 46260; Textile Group of Los Angeles, Inc., 894 S. Bronson Ave., Los Angeles CA 9005-3605.

Museums: American Textile History Museum, Lowell, MA; Cooper-Hewitt Museum, New York, NY; Lace Museum, Sunnyvale, CA; Mayhill Museum of Art, Goldendale, WA; Museum for Textiles, Toronto, Ontario, Canada; Museum of American Textile History, North Andover, MA; Museum of Art, Rhode Island School of Design, Providence, RI; Philadelphia College of Textiles & Science, Philadelphia, PA; Shelburne Museum, Shelburne, VT; Textile Museum, Washington, DC; Valentine Museum, Richmond, VA.

Additional Listings: See Clothing, Lace and Linens, Quilts, and Samplers.

Chair pad, 14" sq, hooked, polychrome rooster, yellow tail, worn edge . . . **40.00**
Coverlet, jacquard, two pieces
　69" x 75", double weave, navy blue and natural white, octagonal floral medallions, floral border, corner blocks, dated "1856," some damage. **450.00**
　71" x 92", floral medallions with vining tulip border, red, navy, light olive, and natural white, "Issac Sheaffer Coverlet Weaver Jackson Township Stark C. Ohio 1842," some stains, small holes, fringe loss **440.00**
　73" x 90", summer/winter, natural white, navy blue, red, and gold stripes, floral design, star and vining berry borders, corner blocks

Coverlets, two-piece single-weave jacquards, bottom right: floral medallions and star flowers with vintage and fruit borders, eagle corners, labeled "Jacob Garver, Salt Creek Township, Picaway, Co., Ohio, 1848," navy blue and natural white, 74" x 84", $935; top: floral, star flower and star medallions with bird and tree borders, hoses and birds on bottom border, corners labeled "Somerset, Ohio 1846, L. Hesse, Weaver," navy blue, tomato red, green, and natural white, 74" x 90," minor moth damage, $770; bottom left: floral medallions, vintage border, corners labeled "W. in Mt. Vernon, Knox County, Ohio, by Jacob and Michael Archer, 1855," navy blue, salmon red, pale gold, and natural white, 74" x 82", wear, some edge damage, fringe loss, $550. Photo courtesy of Garth's Auction, Inc.

with turned squares and "1859" **200.00**

74" x 82", summer/winter, natural white, red, and gray stripes, central medallion with fruit, roses, and feather scroll borders, "Umbros Miller Blair Co.," (PA), some color fading **150.00**

74" x 86", summer/winter, natural white, navy, tomato red, and olive, floral grid pattern with diamond border on two sides, floral and column border on others, "J. Keagy Globe Factory Morrisons Cove Bedford County, Penna," stains **495.00**

74" x 94", summer/winter, blue and white, small blocks of five squares, geometric borders, staining on white side, top rebound . . . **220.00**

75" x 81", summer/winter, natural white, red, green, and navy blue stripes and fringe on three sides, central medallion on fish scale ground, capitol buildings, birds in borders, corners with portraits of George Washington with steamboats, horses, eagles and "Washington, Hail 1869," along sides "Made by Philip Schum Lancaster, PA," minor fringe loss **550.00**

76" x 84", natural white, navy blue, tomato red, and green, central medallion, vintage border, eagles with shields in corners, few stains **250.00**

78" x 88", double weave, navy and natural white, floral medallions with two types of borders, one with building and eagles and "E. Pluribus Unum," other with deer chased by dogs and hunter on horseback, "The Deer Hunt, Woven at the Ithaca Carpet Factory by Archd. Davidson, 1838," some stains, worn areas, mostly on summer side, two ends bound **825.00**

80" x 86", summer winter, natural white, red, green, and blue stripes and fringe, floral medallion and borders, quail in corners, 80" x 86" **500.00**

82" x 90", double weave, geometric, navy and white, pine tree border, some fringe loss, small hole **350.00**

84" sq, double weave, floral medallions with eagle and flower border, navy and natural, light stains **425.00**

86" x 83", summer/winter, blue and white, central medallion of stylized pineapples, flowers, and foliage, border of foliate devices, sgd in border "Anna C. Smith, January 1, 1850" **500.00**

90" x 80", summer/winter, blue and tomato red, alternating stripes with circles and blocks, fringed edges **450.00**

102" x 78-1/2", red, dark blue, medium green, and light olive green on natural ground, central starburst, foliate, floral, and small diamond patterns, border sgd "Henry Dannert, Allentown, PA," minor imperfections **350.00**

102" x 81", red, navy, and green on natural ground, central leafy medallion, small geometric devices, side borders, floral border on bottom edge, corner block sgd "made by J. Haag in Emaus for (blank) 1850," minor imperfections **350.00**

Coverlet, overshot, two pieces

72" x 92", optical pattern, natural white and pale gold **125.00**

101" x 86", block and nine patch pattern, rust and white **200.00**

Draperies, Fortuny, early 20th C, four 19-1/4" w by 54" l panels, three 40" l by 54" l panels, large green fleur-de-lis patterns on taupe ground **2,990.00**

Coverlet, jacquard, two-piece, double weave, four rose medallions and stars, floral border, corners labeled "Wove at Newark, Ohio, by G. Stich 1846," blue/black and white, some wear and small holes, 74" x 86", price for pair, $1,100. Photo courtesy of Garth's Auctions, Inc.

Family register, 19-3/4" x 15-5/8" sight, needlework of Emily Knox, Berwick, Maine, dated 1826, documenting John Knox, his wife Sally and their 10 children, walnut frame, spotty fiber loss, toning, and foxing **2,530.00**

Hooked rug

29" l, 22" h, brick Federal house in Townsend, MA, late 19th C, red, green, gray, brown, blue, and cream-colored, photograph of house in carved oak frame accompanies rug **980.00**

31-1/2" l, 41-1/2" h, map of Newfoundland, partial coastline of Labrador, scattered houses, spouting whale, ships, shades of brown, green, blue, black, white, and yellow, woven maker's tag on reverse reads "Grenfell Labrador Industries, Newfoundland and Labrador," early 20th C . . **2,990.00**

36" l, 27-1/2" h, central reserve with eight black and gray chickens surrounded by red and pink flower blossoms on top sides, brown and black horse below, stretched on wooden frame, fading, wear **690.00**

37" l, 19-1/2" h, oblong central panel with dog, surrounded by line and floral borders, dark orange, tan, dark purple, red, green, and blue-gray, Frost, minor edge wear **275.00**

42-1/2" l, 23" w, colorful baskets of flowers, black, dark brown, and gray ground, large flower and leaves in each corner divided by multicolored borders, light overall wear **990.00**

43-3/4" l, 31" w, pictorial, blue horses and tree, abstract landscape, mounted, America, c1900 . . . . **2,990.00**

44" l, 23" w, raised and clipped wool on burlap, central bowl of flowers surrounded by scrolling foliage, Waldeboro, Maine, c1875 **6,900.00**

45-1/2" l, 26" h, pink, white, mauve, light purple, and yellow water lily, red, blue, and black ground **450.00**

46" l, 26" w, bright red, mauve, black, brown, gray, and light blue geometric designs, triangle borders, semicircles in each corner, rect center with chevron design, mounted on frame. **330.00**

48" l, 27" w, symbols of the Daughters of Pythias, fire department motifs, America, c1880, mounted on cloth backing and stretchers **1,265.00**

53-1/2" l, 24-1/2" w, Waldoboro, Maine, c1880, bouquet centered by garland of roses **875.00**

59" l, 35-1/2" w, black ground, 15 panels separated by ivory lines, each panel with picture in soft shades of ivory, green, purple, and brown, most are fruit, one horse carriage, another grinding stone **150.00**

70" l, 39" w, Old New England Coachline pattern, by Ralph W. Burnham, Ipswich, MA, c1935, carriage drawn by four horses in landscape setting, initials "C.B.C.M." in lower right corner, minor wear **980.00**

Needlepoint map, 18-1/2" d, Britain, dated 1796, round format, counties of England and Wales, stitched on cotton with multicolored silk threads, sgd "Susanna Murphy, Mr. Melick Boarding School," dated 1796 lower left, guilloche border, mahogany veneered and inlaid circular frame **1,150.00**

Needlework memorial, 16-1/2" x 20-5/8" sight size, silk threads and watercolor on silk, urn topped memorials flanking pointed section with verse, kneeling woman to side, willow tree behind monuments, sailing vessels in background, left memorial in memory of Paul Mandell Esq. 1809, right memorial in memory of Mrs. Susannah, consort of Mr. Paul Mandell 1812, MA, c1812, framed, some foxing and staining, tears, stabilized in middle of monument **980.00**

Pillow, Arts & Crafts, stylized gold and red floral motif, beige ground, 20" x 20" $365. Photo courtesy of David Rago Auctions.

Pillow, 15" h, 14" l, beadwork, central demi-lune beaded panel, white, gray, pink, and blue floral scene, gray velvet ground, blue, gray, and maroon silk trim, late 19th C **200.00**

Rug, yarn sewn wool

12-1/2" w, 26" h, undulating leafy vines and sprays of flowers, New England, c1820 . . . . . . **63,000.00**

64-1/2" w, 30" h, floral, clipped on linen, pinks, mauves, browns, on tan ground, gold border, Maine, early 19th C **6,900.00**

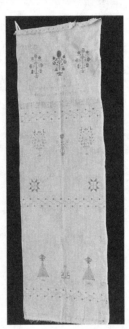

Show towel, faded red embroidery, 16-1/2" w, 50-1/2" l, $225.

Show towel

14-1/2" w, 40" l, strong blue and dark pink cross-stitch geometric design, "Susanna Johnson 1839" . . **200.00**

15-3/4" w, 54" l, homespun, pink and two shades of blue cross-stitch needlework, urns of flowers, one with birds, hearts, diamond, and fretwork lines, "Elisabeth Schli 1810," fringed, few small holes, some repaired **440.00**

19" w, 62" l, homespun, dark brown finely stitched urns of flowers, one urn is heart shaped, "Betz Huhn 1808," woven decorative bands with pulled work and fringe at end, one end is bound **250.00**

19-1/2" w, 58" l, red, pale blue, pink, and yellow yarn crewel work flowers, potted tree, dark blue cross-stitched "ER 1840," decorative woven bands, wear to yarn border, stitch loss, very minor stains, added fringe **385.00**

Table cloth, 58" x 70", overshot linen, hand-tied fringe, some stains . . . **100.00**

Table mat, 41" x 53", pieced, red, green, black, white, and light blue wool, scalloped edges with diamond borders, star in each corner, large red and black checkered blocks within center panel surrounded by another band of diamonds, tacked blocks at each corner, smaller checkerboard blocks surround panel, black cloth backing and stretcher, minor damage and stains **1,155.00**

Table rug

20" w, 42" l, appliqué, penny, mostly orange, blue, light green, and mauve wool, oblong with "tongue" border, round blue cut-outs, light purple background, some stains **250.00**

24-1/2" w, 15" h, wool yarn, two flowering plants, pink and beige blossoms, olive ground, New England, early 19th C, some losses **2,875.00**

THIMBLES

History: Thimbles often are thought of as common household sewing tools. Many are. However, others are miniature works of art, souvenirs of places, people, and events, or gadgets—thimbles with expanded uses such as attached threaders, cutters, or magnets.

There were many thimble manufacturers in the United States prior to 1930. Before we became a "throw-away" society, hand sewing was a never-ending chore for the housewife. Garments were mended and altered. When they were beyond repair, pieces were salvaged to make a patchwork quilt. Thimble manufacturers continuously tried to create new thimbles to convince home sewers that "one was not enough."

By the early 1930s, only one manufacturer of gold and silver thimbles remained in business in the United States—the Simons Brothers Company of Philadelphia, which was founded by George Washington Simons in 1839. Simons Brothers' thimbles from the 1904 St. Louis World's Fair and the 1893 Colombian Exposition are prized acquisitions for any collector. The thimble in the shape of the Liberty Bell is one of the most novel.

Today, the company is owned by Nelson Keyser and continues to produce silver and gold thimbles. The Simons Brothers Company designed a special thimble for Nancy Reagan as a gift for diplomats' wives who visited the White House. This thimble has a picture of the White House and the initials "N. D. R."

Thimbles have been produced in a variety of materials: gold, silver, steel, aluminum, brass, china, glass, vegetable ivory, ivory, bone, celluloid, plastics, leather, hard rubber, and silk. Common-metal thimbles usually are bought by the intended user, who makes sure the size is a comfortable fit. Precious-metal thimbles often were received as gifts.

Threaded Glass

Many of these do not show signs of wear, probably because either they did not fit the recipient or were considered too elegant to use for mundane work.

During the 20th century, thimbles were used as advertising giveaways. It is not unusual to find a thimble that says "You'll Never Get Stuck Using Our Product" or a political promotion stating "Sew It Up—Vote for John Doe for Senator."

References: Averil Mathis, *Antique and Collectible Thimbles and Accessories*, Collector Books, 1986, 1997 value update; Bridget McConnel, *Collector's Guide to Thimbles*, Wellfleet Press, 1990; Estelle Zalkin, *Zalkin's Handbook of Thimbles & Sewing Implements*, Warman Publishing, 1988, distributed by Krause Publications.

Periodical: *Thimbletter*, 93 Walnut Hill Road, Newton Highlands, MA 02161-1836.

Collectors' Clubs: Birchcroft Thimble Collectors Club, http://www.thimble.net; Thimble Collectors International, 7409 Millbrook Road, Norfolk, VA 23505, http://www.thimblecollectors.com; Thimble Guild, P.O. Box 381807, Duncanville, TX 75138-1807.

> **Reproduction Alert:** Reproductions can be the result of restrikes from an original die or can be casts from a mold made from an antique thimble. Many reproductions are sold as such and priced accordingly. Among the reproduced thimbles are a pre-revolution Russian enamel thimble and the Salem Witch thimble (the reproduction has no cap and the seam is visible).

Gold

Applied arches border, blue enamel highlights, small diamond in each arch, English, late 19th C . . **450.00**
Applied cherubs holding garlands of flowers, foliate cartouche engraved with initial, Simons Bros., early 20th C **230.00**
Applied contrasting color gold flowers and foliage, vacant shaped cartouche, matted ground, cast floral and foliate rim, French, late 19th C **450.00**
Applied engraved scrollwork dec interspersed with turquoise, vacant shield-shaped cartouche, matted ground, wavy rim, conforming border, English, late 19th C **235.00**
Applied two-color gold foliage and flowers, each flower set with emerald, matted ground, vacant shield shaped cartouche, engraved rim, English, mid-19th C **555.00**
Heavily cut friezes, blue enameled geometric highlights, English, late 19th C **415.00**
Parcel-gilt, dropped rim type, holly leaves and berries, ruby set cartouche,

Ketcham & McDougall, early 20th C **130.00**
Porcelain
Border of flowers and foliate, worn gilt rim, squatty, American Belleek, late 19th C **245.00**
Border painted with roses, forget-me-nots, and foliage, gilt rim, American Belleek, late 19th C **925.00**
Hand painted, Meissen, c1950 . . . . **25.00**
Scrimshaw, whalebone **95.00**
Silver
Applied enameled pink flowers and green foliage, moonstone top, apex engraved with registration umber, Norwegian, 1904 . . . . **525.00**
Chased flowerheads and scrolled foliage, scalloped rim, Indian, late 19th C **410.00**
Cupid and garlands, Simons . . **95.00**
Cupid in high relief, c1900-40 . . . . **120.00**
Engraved, two birds on branch **35.00**
Flowers, high relief **45.00**

THREADED GLASS

History: Threaded glass is glass decorated with applied threads of glass. Before the English invention of a glass-threading machine in 1876, threads were applied by hand. After this invention, threaded glass was produced in quantity by practically every major glass factory.

Threaded glass was revived by the art glass manufacturers such as Durand and Steuben, and it is still made today.

Vase, green threading, colorless body, 5" h, $65.

Biscuit jar, cov, 7" h, vaseline glass, black threading, SP rim, lid, and handle **190.00**
Champagne, 5-1/2" h, yellow, black threading, sgd "Steuben" **200.00**
Creamer, 4-3/4" h, colorless, threaded neck and lip, applied ribbed handle, slight blue tint, Pittsburgh **175.00**
Epergne, blue ground, blue threading **225.00**
Lamp shade, 11-3/8" d rim, 13-3/8" d, 7" h, broad mushroom shape, amber mottled glass, internal random red-maroon threading, all over irid, Austrian **550.00**
Pitcher
6-3/4" h, aqua, threaded neck, applied handle **425.00**
7" h, aqua, lily pad, threaded neck, applied tooled foot and handle **5,500.00**
Rose bowl, cranberry ground, cranberry threading, attributed to Mount Washington **100.00**
Tumbler, 3-7/8" h, Favrile, Flemish design, gold irid, shades of blue and rose, sgd "1294 L. C. T. Favrile," tiny flake off threading **775.00**
Vase
5-1/2" h, baluster, colorless ground, blue threading, fire polished pontil, Pallme Koenig **250.00**
6" d, 6" h, irid green ground, lighter green threading, attributed to Loetz **825.00**
6-1/2" d, 12" d, wide ruffled form, green ground, ext. dec with green threading, int. with slight irid luster, polished pontil, attributed to Loetz, Austria, minor thread loss . **450.00**
7" h, creamy yellow, green, and rose, white int., Czechoslovakia . **160.00**
8" h, 5" d, gourd shape, light blue satin ground, allover applied colorless threading, MOP herringbone **450.00**
14-1/4" h, spiral ribbed form, extended neck, bulbous base, olive green, all over random threading in manner of Pallme-Konig, Bohemia, lightly irid surface, polished pontil, repair, crack **500.00**

TIFFANY

History: Louis Comfort Tiffany (1849-1934) established a glass house in 1878 primarily to make stained glass windows. In 1890, in order to utilize surplus materials at the plant, Tiffany began to design and produce "small glass," such as iridescent glass lamp shades, vases, stemware, and tableware in the Art Nouveau manner. Commercial production began in 1896.

Tiffany developed a unique type of colored iridescent glass called Favrile, which differs from other art glass in that it was a composition of colored glass worked together while hot. The essential characteristic is that the ornamentation is found within the glass; Favrile was never further decorated. Different effects were achieved by varying the amount and position of colors.

Louis Tiffany and the artists in his studio also are well known for their fine work in other areas—bronzes, pottery, jewelry, silver, and enamels.

Marks: Most Tiffany wares are signed with the name "L. C. Tiffany" or the initials "L.C.T." Some pieces also are marked "Favrile," along with a number. A variety of other marks can be found, e.g., "Tiffany Studios" and "Louis C. Tiffany Furnaces."

References: Victor Arwas, *Glass, Art Nouveau and Art Deco*, Rizzoli International Publications, 1977; Alastair Duncan, *Louis Comfort Tiffany*, Harry N. Abrams, 1992; William P. Hood Jr., *Tiffany Silver Flatware, 1845-1905, When Dining Was An Art*, Antique Collectors' Club, 1999; Robert Koch, *Louis C. Tiffany*, Schiffer Publishing, 2001; David Rago, *American Art Pottery*, Knickerbocker Press, 1997; John A. Shuman III, *Collector's Encyclopedia of American Art Glass*, Collector Books, 1988, 1996 value update.

Museums: Chrysler Museum, Norfolk, VA; Corning Glass Museum, Corning, NY; University of Connecticut, The William Benton Museum of Art, Storrs, CT.

Reproduction Alert: A large number of brass belt buckles and badges bearing Tiffany markings were imported into the United States and sold at flea markets and auctions in the late 1960s. The most common marking is "Tiffany Studios, New York." Now, more than 25 years later, many of these items are resurfacing and deceiving collectors and dealers.

A partial list of belt buckles includes the Wells Fargo guard dog, Wells Fargo & Company mining stage, Coca-Cola Bottling, Southern Comfort Whiskey, Currier and Ives express train, and U.S. Mail. Beware of examples that have been enhanced through color enameling.

An Indian police shield is among the fake Tiffany badges. The badge features an intertwined "U" and "S" at the top and a bow and arrow motif separating "INDIAN" and "POLICE."

Bisque
Pitcher, 5" d, 12-1/4" h, emb, tall leaves and cattails, speckled glossy green int., incised "LCT," short tight firing rim lines **1,955.00**

Vessel
5-1/4" d, 6" h, artichoke shape, speckled green int., incised "LCT," tip of one leaf missing, several rim hairlines **1,355.00**
7" d, 4" h, squatty emb seaweed and fish, smooth green glaze int., incised "LCT," several short tight rim lines **2,070.00**

Bronze
Ashtray, 4" d, 7/8" h, circular, two linear etched loop handles, imp "Tiffany Studios New York 1711," c1910, int. wear to patina **400.00**
Bookends, set of four, 4-5/8" w, 5-1/4" l, 6" h, Zodiac pattern, dark patina, imp "Tiffany Studios New York 1091" **690.00**
Box, cov, 4-1/2" l, 3-1/2" w, 2" h, Zodiac pattern, imp "Tiffany Studios, New York 106" **920.00**
Candlestick, 9-3/4" h, stylized plant form base, three legs supporting urn-form Favrile glass cup set with seven green and gold iridized glass jewels, brown and green patina, base stamped "Tiffany Studios, New York, 7158" **1,610.00**

Cigar box, 6-1/2" l, 6" d, 2-1/2" h, rect hinged box, Zodiac pattern, multicolored enameling to each medallion, partial cedar liner, base stamped "Tiffany Studios New York 1655" **1,610.00**
Cigarette box, 6-1/4" l, 3-3/4" w, 2-1/8" h, etched finish, rect cedar lined hinged box, enameled blue and green dec, imp "Louis C. Tiffany Furnaces Inc., Favrile 130" **750.00**
Desk set, Zodiac pattern, #1009 and #10044 two-tiered letter holder, #1072 rocker blotter, pr #996 blotter corners, #414 stamp box, small tray, dark brownish-green patina, imp marks, six pcs **1,495.00**
Frame, gilt, easel back
10-1/4" w, 12" h, cast Heraldic pattern, lower recessed finished in patinated brown, imp mark "Louis C. Tiffany Furnaces Inc. 61" **1,035.00**
8" w, 10" h, etched, repeating freeform zigzag border in relief, recesses finished with patinated brown, imp Tiffany Furnaces mark, "Louis C. Tiffany Furnaces, Inc., Favrile 66" **750.00**
Glove box, 13-1/2" l, 4-1/2" d, 3-1/8" h, Grapevine pattern, striated green slag glass inserts, ball feet, imp "Tiffany Studios, New York" **980.00**

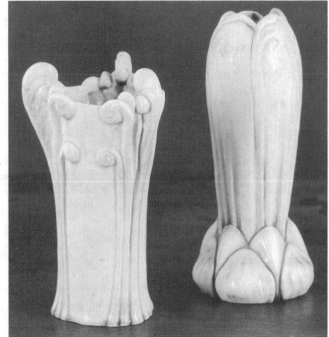

Pottery, vases, left: **$13,200;** *right:* **$1,650.** *Photo courtesy of David Rago Auctions, Inc.*

Inkstand, 4" h, 7" l, No. 849, pierced bronze and blown opaque green glass, orig glass insert, stamped "Tiffany Studios/New York/25055," c1900 . . . .**2,500.00**

Letter holder, 5" h, Grape & Leaf, bronze and slag, two tiers **700.00**

Letter opener, 8-1/2" l, orig dark patina, scroll dec handle, imp "Tiffany Studios New York," c1910 . . . . **125.00**

Paperweight, 1-1/2" h, 2-1/4" l, sphinx, orig patina, some gilt, stamped "Tiffany Studios New York" **275.00**

Thermometer, 8-3/4" h, Grapevine pattern, beaded border, green patina, green slag glass, easel stand, imp "Tiffany Studios New York" on reverse, minor corrosion **1,495.00**

Tray

9-7/8" d, circular with extended rim and handles, etched, enameled blue, pink, and green floral cloisonné dec on handles, imp "Louis C. Tiffany Furnaces Inc., Favrile 512" under handle . **460.00**

14-3/4" d, circular, rolled rim, fire-polished random design, sgd with Tiffany Glass & Decorating monogram and "Tiffany Studios New York/8/9064" **995.00**

Twine holder, 3" h, Bookmark pattern, hexagonal form, hinged lid, reddish patina in lower recesses, imp "Tiffany Studios New York 905," minor spotting **1,035.00**

Glass, all Favrile

Bowl

6-1/4" d, 2-3/4" h, ribbed, crimped edge, gold engraved leaf and vine border, marked "L. C. Tiffany Favrile" **635.00**

7" d, 2-3/4" h, shallow, ribbed ext., scalloped everted rim, irid blue, purple and green highlights, sgd "L. C. T., Favrile" **650.00**

Bud vase, 13" h, 3-1/4" d, gold body, enameled green and gold circular base, stamped "Louis C. Tiffany Furnaces Inc" **900.00**

Candlestick, 22-3/4" h, patinated bronze and favrile, ribbed floriform amber glass shade with shaded violet irid, fitted on circular knop, seven irid dark blue, purple, green, red, and amber irid turtle back cabochons, slender stem base, wide circular foot, imp "Tiffany Studios/New York/1213," shade inscribed "L.C.T." **9,750.00**

Carafe, 11" h, pinched ovoid body, elongated neck, topped with pinched

and beaded stopper, ambergris, overall strong gold irid, polished pontil, base sgd "L. C. Tiffany Favrile 430," slight wear to rim **1,035.00**

Center bowl and flower frog, 10-1/2" d, 1-3/4" h, irid gold, beveled edge, center dec with green leaves and vine, sgd "L. C. Tiffany Favrile, #9354L" **1,950.00**

Compote

2-1/2" h, 6" d, opalescent pink, scalloped, 10 gentle curves, squatty stem connects bowl to milky-clear base with band of white around rim, sgd "1954 L. C. Tiffany Favrile" **1,795.00**

6-1/2" h, 8" x 6-1/4" bowl, 4-3/8" d foot, gold, scalloped oval, wheel cut leaf and vine pattern, marked "L. C. Tiffany Favrille 1911" on polished pontil **4,900.00**

Finger bowl and underplate, 5-3/4" d bowl, 7" d underplate, eight-ruffled bowl, conforming underplate, fine gold stretched irid, both inscribed "L. C. T." **490.00**

Flower bowl, 12-1/2" d, circular, colorless body, brilliant gold irid vines and leaves, base inscribed "L. C. Tiffany Favrile 4034K" **980.00**

Jack-in-the-pulpit, lustrous amber gold irid body, flared and ruffled rim with stretched irid to edge, pink optic ribbed throat tapering to slender stem supported by bulbous base, inscribed "L. C. T. Y5472," paper label on button pontil, c1905 . . . . **14,950.00**

Nut dish, 4-1/8" d, 1-1/4" h, eight ribs and ruffled rim, irid gold, base inscribed "L. C. T." **375.00**

Rose bowl, 3-3/4" h, 10-ribbed form, ruffled rim, cobalt blue, overall blue irid luster, polished pontil sgd "L. C. Tiffany Favrile 1103-7725K," some scratches **865.00**

Salt, 2-1/8" d, broad shouldered vessel, eight pulled prunts, strong blue irid, base inscribed "L. C. T. FavrileX620" **800.00**

Toothpick holder, irid glass, dimpled sides, etched "LCT" on base . . . **175.00**

Vase

3" d, 4" h, millefiori, gold, green hearts and vines, millefiori inclusions, marked "7890B L. C. Tiffany-Favrile" **5,000.00**

3-1/2" d, 6-1/2" h, blue, white centered green leaves on darker blue leaves, base marked "6576K L. C. Tiffany Favrile" around polished pontil **3,600.00**

Vase, Favrile, iridescent olive green, wavy line decoration, marked "LCT #4135," $1,150.

4-3/4" h, ovoid, colorless body internally dec with pale mauve on cream morning glory blossoms, variegated green leaf vines, int. golden irid rising to cream at neck, base sgd "L. C. T. Y5626," c1905, base drilled, rust spotting to int. irid surface **3,450.00**

4-3/4" h, 10 ribbed form, wide pinched shoulders, raised ruffled rim, deep blue luster rising to lighter blue at top, polished pontil, sgd "L. C. Tiffany Favrile 1071-2666K," c1915, internal staining **1,035.00**

5" h, flared amber Favrile glass oval body, 25 tiny white cane blossoms among emerald green leaf leaves, amber stems, overall irid luster, inscribed "LCT Tiffany Favrile 2889C" around button pontil **2,415.00**

5" h, ovoid, reactive ground of cream and cloudy blue at base shading to deep red, striated ochre, red, and light green trailing ivy leaves, base sgd "L. C. T. Y4812," c1905, button pontil **6,900.00**

5-1/2" h, floriform, bulbous body, cobalt blue ground, wide flaring and ruffled rim, stretch irid to rim, strong blue luster, short stem, applied disk foot, inscribed "L. C. Tiffany, Favrile 9041E" **980.00**

6" h, floriform, blue, white and green hearts and vines dec, foot marked

"5090 L. C. Tiffany Favrile" **4,800.00**

7" h, gold, high rounded shoulders with irid opal dec, marked "L. C. T. O1105" **3,250.00**

7-1/4" h, ovoid, pale aqua ground, internally dec with yellow, red, and black millefiori flowers among dark green trailing heart leaves and vines, ochre swirls, base inscribed "L. C. Tiffany-Favrile 3527 P," partial paper label on button pontil, c1920 .... **6,900.00**

9" h, swollen body tapering to bulbed stem, amber, dec with trailing vines and heart leaves, applied dark foot, sgd "L. C. Tiffany - Favrile 5603G," bubbles below surface **1,840.00**

9" h, 10 ribbed, bulbed, flared rim, applied ribbed base, strong blue irid, sgd "L. C. Tiffany Favrile 1524-3333 P" **2,415.00**

9-1/2" h, pale transparent amber crystal stem, peach-opal petal blossom, applied irid folded foot, marked "L. C. T. M1142," two folded blossom ribs..... **1,955.00**

10-1/4" h, 10-ribbed gourd form, flared and ruffled rim above bulbed top, round disk foot, blue irid, inscribed "L. C. Tiffany Favrile 1089-68201" **1,495.00**

13-1/2" h, cylindrical, amber gold irid glass, long green leaves, base marked "L. C. T.," inserted into elaborate dark and gold dore bronze holder stamped "Tiffany Studios New York 717" .. **1,495.00**

16" h, bud, slender cylinder of gold irid glass, six elongated green leaves rising from base, inscribed "L. C. T.," inserted into elaborate open scrolled bronze mount, stamped "Tiffany Studios New York 714" **1,035.00**

20-1/4" h, double bulbed form, elongated neck of ambergris grass, dec with blue irid pulled feathers rising to red and gold luster at top, base sgd "L. C. T. E550," paper label in polished pontil, c1895, rust colored blemish to irid on neck, inclusion on neck **2,760.00**

Lamps

Boudoir, 15-1/2" h, dome shade, restored oviform base, irid gold glass dec with intricate intaglio carved green leaves, trailing budded vines, both sgd

"L. C. Tiffany Favrile," shade also marked "5594L"........... **9,775.00**

Candle lamp, 12-3/4" h, swirled gold irid candlestick base, with strong blue luster at base, white glass stem insert with five puled green leaves, ruffled gold to blue irid shade, both inscribed "L. C. T.," bases with paper labels, c1900, burst bubble in bobeche, needs rewiring **1,265.00**

Floor, 55" h, 10" d spun bronze shade, reflective white int., swing socket, shaft with stylized leaf motif, scroll foot circular base, base stamped "Tiffany Studios New York 425," pr.... **7,475.00**

Mantel lamp, 8" h, slight octagonal form, cream colored glass rising to bulbed top, caramel and gold pulled petal design, fitted gilt bronze and wood base............... **1,150.00**

Table lamp, bronze, fluted base, three pendant fixtures, each with flaring white opalescent and green pulled feather art glass shade, base stamped "Tiffany Studios/New York," 17" x 11" $3,220. Photo courtesy of David Rago Auctions.

Table

22" w, 15-1/2" h, bronze, double branch, each branch with three irid glass shades, central bronze stem hollowed to one side to accept separate candle snuffer (missing), base imp "Tiffany Studios 10456" on each glass shade, sgd "LCT" minor roughness on base of shades **12,500.00**

24" h, 14-1/2" d linen-fold shade, 12-sided Favrile fabric golden amber glass arranged in panel configuration, dark gold dore finish on leading and cap, matching gold dore three-socket paneled lamp base, shade and base imp "Tiffany Studios New York," pr .. **24,150.00**

28" h, 18" d leaded geometric blue and green slag glass shade, tree-shaped bronze base with six sockets, orig patina, shade stamped "Tiffany Studios/New York" **21,000.00**

28-1/2" h, 22-1/2" d leaded glass globe shade, mottled green geometric slag glass segments progressively arranged, stamped "Tiffany Studios" on rim, four socket bronze standard, domed, stepped, circular base, stamped "Tiffany Studios New York 532" on base **19,550.00**

Silver
Bowl

5-3/4" d, 3" h, incised banding, everted rim, low domed foot, c1907-38, 11 troy oz...... **200.00**

9-1/4" h, 3-5/8" h, stylized floral band flanked by vertical incised lines, low base, c1938-47, 28 troy oz **1,380.00**

9-1/4" h, 4-1/4" h, ftd, shaped edge with applied flowerhead and fern rim, stylized pad and paw feet with scrolled legs topped by acanthus leaves, center monogram, 1891-1902, 24 troy oz ... **1,610.00**

11-1/8" d, 5-3/8" h, tapered ovoid bowl, outward flaring rim, engraved date on base, low foot, c1907-38, 41 troy oz **1,150.00**

Bread basket, 7" w, 10-3/4" l, oval, molded rim, center monogram, 1925-47, approx 12 troy oz **215.00**

Cake plate, 13-1/4" d, circular, shaped rim with molded foliate edge, face with reticulated and engraved bands, domed circular foot with engraved and reticulated dec, center monogram, c1908-1947, approx 47 troy oz **1,955.00**

Candelabra, 12-1/4" h, three-light, cornucopia shoulder and central sconce, flanked by reeded scroll candle arms and further cornucopia sconces, plain columnar stem, foliate cornucopia and shell edge, round floral repoussé foot, removable beaded

nozzles, sq base, 1902-07, 26 troy oz
. . . . **1,150.00**

Cigarette case, 3-3/8" x 2-1/4", rect, rounded corners, gold-washed ovoid push button clasp, gold-washed interior, engraved on front with name and date, suspended from silver link chain, c1907-38, 4 troy oz **90.00**

Cocktail set, 6-3/8" h cocktail shaker, six 4-1/8" cordial glasses, tapered ovoid shaker with hammered surface, engraved initials and date in base, glasses with conical bowl, baluster stem, plaint foot, monogrammed, c1875-91, 26 troy oz **865.00**

Compote, 15" w, 10" d, 5" h, wheat handles, engraved monogram
. . . . **2,800.00**

Dresser set, 10 pcs, three brushes, comb, covered jar, receiving jar, hand mirror, shoe horn button hook, rect box, floral and scroll acid etched dec, gold-washed int. on jars and boxes, monogrammed, c1907-38, 23 troy oz
. . . . **1,850.00**

Flask, 5-1/4" l, c1860-70, glass body, silver ball stopper, plain cap, monogrammed **175.00**

Flower basket, flattened bell shape, flared sides, engraved husk drops and floral swags, reticulated to rim in guillouche pattern, overhead handle engraved with further husks, oval foot, 1907-38, pr, 26 troy oz **2,645.00**

Fruit bowl, 8-7/8" d, Eastern-style, circular, all over emb and engraved foliate dec, stippled ground, four central cartouches with Eastern European religious figures, four empty cartouches, banded spreading foot, gilt interior, 1907-47, approx 27 troy oz
. . . . **1,725.00**

Kettle on stand, 11-1/2" h, bulbous, domed lid, reeded bud finial, cast upright handle with leather mount, body with engraved band, circular stand with openwork skirt, three cast scroll legs with shell feet, 1916-47, 59 troy oz
. . . . **1,495.00**

Ladle, 10-1/2" l, Renaissance pattern, lobed ovoid bowl, handle monogrammed, 1902-07, 7 troy oz
. . . . **920.00**

Muffiner, 7-1/2" h, 1891-1902, urn form body with bat's wing fluting below applied stylized leaf banding, spiral reeded stem, sq base, screw-in domed lid with paneled ball finial,12 troy oz
. . . . **635.00**

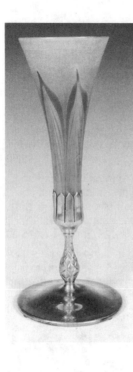

Trumpet vase, "Pulled Feather," with bronze stand, 12", $2,310. Photo courtesy of Jackson's.

Pie server, 11-1/4" l, strawberry handle, gold-washed blade, early 20th C, 4 troy oz **920.00**

Pitcher, 8-1/2" h, repoussé, waisted baluster form, ear handle, short spout, chased and emb all over with flowers and leaves, 1891-1902, 32 troy oz
. . . . **3,220.00**

Serving dish
11-1/8" l, 5-1/2" h , crenelated banding, lid with ovoid handle flanked by anthemion, c1854-70, 41 troy oz **1,150.00**
11-1/4" l, oval, divided into two wells, applied incised edge, 20th C, 22 oz. **435.00**

Strawberry set, 11 strawberry forks, one sugar sifter, all gilt, twisted openwork handles and strawberry finials, early 20th C **1,800.00**

Stuffing spoon, 12-1/2" l, Chrysanthemum pattern, monogrammed, 8 troy oz **750.00**

Tea and coffee service, 8-1/2" h coffeepot, teapot, cov sugar, and creamer, all with Classical Revival-style embossing, paneled baluster coffeepot, angular handles, flattened urn finials, monogrammed, c1907-38, 69 troy oz
. . . . **3,750.00**

Tea service, Aesthetic Movement, 1895-91, 4-1/2" h teapot, creamer, cov sugar, three-molded cylindrical form, engraved Chinoiserie-style flowers, birds, and insects, rim border of stamped band of lozenges and

flowerheads, teapot with short spout, foliate angular handle and ball finial, three foliate angular handles on sugar, engraved with Chinese-style letter monogram, 19 troy oz **2,875.00**

Travel clock, 2-5/8" w, 3" l, rect, rounded corners, hand hammered surface, Arabic numerals, 20th C
. . . . **490.00**

Tray, 12-5/8" d, octagonal, ftd, molded guilloche rim, body with molded and engraved foliate scrolls with geometric panels, molded octagonal foot, monogrammed center, 1914-47, 35 troy oz. **1,495.00**

TIFFIN GLASS

c1960

History: A. J. Beatty & Sons built a glass manufacturing plant in Tiffin, Ohio, in 1888. On January 1, 1892, the firm joined the U. S. Glass Co. and was known as factory R. Fine-quality Depression-era items were made at this high-production factory.

From 1923 to 1936, Tiffin produced a line of black glassware called Black Satin. The company discontinued operation in 1980.

Marks: Beginning in 1916, wares were marked with a paper label.

References: Fred Bickenheuser, *Tiffin Glassmasters*, Book I (1979, 1994-95 value update), Book II (1981, 1994-95 value update), Book III (1985), Glassmasters Publications; Tom and Neila Bredehoft, *Fifty Years of Collectible Glass, 1920-1970, Volume 1, Volume II*, Antique Trader Books, 2000; Gene Florence, *Glass Candlesticks of the Depression Era*, Collector Books, 1999; Ruth Hemminger, Ed Goshe, and Leslie Pina, *Tiffin Glass 1940-1980*, Schiffer Publishing, 2001.

Collectors' Clubs: Tiffin Glass Collectors, 950 Pierce St., San Francisco, CA 94115, http://clubs.yahoo.com/clubs/tiffinglasscollectors; Tiffin Glass Collectors' Club, P.O. Box 554, Tiffin, OH 44883, http://tiffinglass.org.

Museum: Tiffin Glass Museum, Tiffin, OH, http://www.tiffinglass.org/glassmuseum.html.

Bowl, 10" l, 6-1/4" w, 4" h, Twilight, sq, ftd **290.00**
Bud vase, Fuchsia, crystal, 11" h
. . . . **100.00**
Celery, Flanders, pink. **140.00**
Champagne
Cherokee Rose, crystal **20.00**
Flanders, pink. **45.00**
Cocktail
Byzantine, crystal **18.00**
Byzantine, yellow **15.00**
Fuchsia, crystal **20.00**
June Night, crystal **20.00**

Compote, cov, #17523, Wisteria, crystal Cellini foot, two minute rim nicks ...**395.00**

Console bowl, Fuchsia, crystal, flared, 12-5/8" d ...**135.00**

Cordial
Cordelia, crystal...**10.00**
Flanders, pink ...**150.00**
Fuchsia, crystal ...**40.00**
Nude woman, basket of grapes on her head, semi-draped, clusters of grapes draped across front, back, and sides, frosted stem...**200.00**
Persian Pheasant, crystal ...**45.00**

Vase, black ground, red coralene flowers, 6-1/2" h, **$80.**

Cornucopia, Copen Blue, 8-1/4" .**90.00**

Creamer, Flanders, pink, flat ...**230.00**

Cup and saucer, Flanders, yellow ...**100.00**

Decanter, Byzantine, crystal ...**600.00**

Goblet
Cerise, crystal ...**25.00**
Cherokee Rose, crystal ...**28.00**
Flanders, crystal ...**88.00**
Fuchsia, crystal ...**25.00**

Iced tea tumbler, Flanders, pink, ftd ...**70.00**

Juice tumbler, ftd, Byzantine, crystal ...**18.00**

Lamp, 8-1/2" h, 5" d, owl, detailed coloring, rewired...**500.00**

Martini glass, 4-1/2" d, 3" h, Shawl Dancer, set of four ...**150.00**

Perfume bottle, 4" h, parrot, slate gray painted finish, enamel dec, orig label ...**125.00**

Plate, Byzantine, yellow, 7-1/2" d.**15.00**

Rose bowl, 5-1/2" x 5", Swedish Optic, citron green, c1960, mold #17430 ...**145.00**

Sherbet, Byzantine, crystal, low .**12.00**

Sherry
June Night, crystal...**30.00**
Shawl Dancer, crystal ...**55.00**

Sugar
Cerice, crystal ...**25.00**
La Fleure, yellow...**40.00**

Vase
5-1/2" d, 7" h, Twilight, few air bubbles ...**125.00**
7-3/8" d, 14" h, crystal, artist sgd ...**400.00**
8" h, Dahlia, cupped, Reflex Green, allover silver overlay...**225.00**
8-3/4" h, dark amethyst satin, poppy like flowers ...**200.00**

Wall pocket, 9" l, 3-1/4" w, ruby **175.00**

Water set, cov 12" h pitcher, Classic etch, Nile green handle, lid and foot, 11 8" h goblets with Nile green stem and foot, etched cameos of dancing girl ...**1,750.00**

Wine
Byzantine, crystal ...**18.00**
Flanders, pink...**90.00**
Fuchsia, crystal ...**35.00**

TILES

History: The use of decorated tiles peaked during the latter part of the 19th century. More than 100 companies in England alone were producing tiles by 1880. By 1890, companies had opened in Belgium, France, Australia, Germany, and the United States.

Tiles were not used only as fireplace adornments. Many were installed into furniture, such as washstands, hall stands, and folding screens. Since tiles were easily cleaned and, hence, hygienic, they were installed on the floors and walls of entry halls, hospitals, butcher shops, or any place where sanitation was a concern. Many public buildings and subways also employed tiles to add interest and beauty.

References: Susan and Al Bagdade, *Warman's American Pottery and Porcelain*, 2nd ed., Krause Publications, 2000; ——, *Warman's English & Continental Pottery & Porcelain*, 3rd ed., Krause Publications, 1998; Norman Karlson, *American Art Tile, 1876-1941*, Rizzoli Publications, 1998; Ralph and Terry Kovel, *Kovels' American Art Pottery*, Crown Publishers, 1993; Richard and Hilary Myers, *William Morris Tiles*, Richard Dennis (distributed by Antique Collectors' Club), 1996; David Rago, *American Art Pottery*, Knickerbocker Press, 1997; Betty Ward and Nancy Schiffer, *Weller, Roseville, and Related Zanesville Art Pottery and Tiles*, Schiffer Publishing, 2000.

Periodical and Internet Resource: *Flash Point*, P.O. Box 1850, Healdsburg, CA 95448, http://www.aimnet.com/~toolson/pages/tileorgs.thfinfo.html; *Tiles on the Web*, http://www.tiles.org.

Collectors' Clubs: Tiles & Architectural Ceramics Society, 36 Friars Ave., Stone, Staffordshire ST15 0AF UK, http://www.tilesoc.org.uk.

Museums: Boymans-van Beuningen Museum, Rotterdam, Holland; City Museum, Stoke-on-Trent, England; Iron Bridge Gorge Museum, Teford, England Lambert Van Meerten Museum, Delft, Holland; Malibu Lagoon Museum, Malibu, CA; Mercer Museum & Tile Works, Doylestown, PA; Victoria & Albert Museum London, England.

Notes: Condition is an important factor in determining price. A cracked, badly scuffed and scratched, or heavily chipped tile has very little value. Slight chipping around the outer edges of a tile is, at times, considered acceptable by collectors, especially if these chips can be covered by a frame.

It is not uncommon for the highly glazed surface of some tiles to have become crazed. Crazing is not considered detrimental as long as it does not detract from the overall appearance of the tile.

Art pottery
6" h, 12" w, landscape with birds and moose in foreground, dark green high gloss glaze ...**175.00**
6" h, 12" w, landscape with moose, dark green high gloss glaze ...**175.00**

Arts & Crafts, 10" x 5-1/2", framed, scene of salt marsh landscape, blues, greens, and white, c1907...**2,100.00**

Batchelder, 6" h, 18" l, beige bisque clay with blue engobe, stamped "Batchelder/Los Angeles"
Bouquet of flowers and birds, slight abrasion to surface...**375.00**
California desert landscape, abrasion to a few spots...**850.00**
Peacocks, chips and abrasion, pr ...**1,000.00**

California Art, 8" h, 12" l scene of California court yard with fountain, restored color and varnish, imp mark, mounted in Arts & Crafts frame ...**1,600.00**

Cambridge Art Tile, Covington, KY, 6" x 18"
Goddess and Cherub, amber, pr ...**250.00**
Night and Morning, pr ...**500.00**

Claycraft
6" x 12", horizontal, English thatched roof cottage next to foot bridge, semi-matte polychrome, mounted in period ebonized Arts and Crafts frame, covered stamp mark ...**1,610.00**
7-3/4" x 4", molded lone tree rising over ocean, matte polychrome glazes, stamped "Claycraft," mounted in new Arts & Crafts frame ...**815.00**
13-1/4" h, 35" l, five tile faience panel, molded landscape of Mediterranean houses by sea, marks hidden by contemporary Arts & Crafts frame ...**2,400.00**

Grueby Pottery, cuenca decoration, bright yellow and green, 6" square, $1,980. Photo courtesy of David Rago Auctions, Inc.

Grueby, 6-1/4" sq, mottled matte green glaze, mustard yellow blossom, ftd copper frame, raised indecipherable mark on base............**1,100.00**

J. & J. G. Low, Chelsea, MA

4-1/4" sq, putti carrying grapes, blue, pr................ **75.00**

6" d, circular, yellow, minor edge nicks and glaze wear...... **35.00**

6" sq, woman wearing hood, brown **95.00**

6-1/8" x 4-1/2", rect, blue-green, woman, titled "Autumn" **90.00**

KPM, 5-3/4" x 3-3/8", portrait of monk, titled "Hieronymous of Ferrara sends this image to the prophet to God," small nicks to corners............ **245.00**

Marblehead, 4-5/8" sq, ships, blue and white, pr.................. **125.00**

Minton China Works

6" sq, Aesops Fables, Fox and Crow, black and white.......... **75.00**

6" sq, Cows crossing stream, brown and cream.............. **85.00**

6" x 12", wild roses, polychrome slip dec.................... **50.00**

8" sq, Rob Roy, Waverly Tales, brown and cream.............. **95.00**

Minton Hollins & Co.

6" sq, urn and floral relief, green ground **45.00**

8" sq, Morning, blue and white **100.00**

Moravian

10" x 7-1/4", Tempus, Father Time, blue and ivory glaze, red clay showing through, unmarked, small glaze flake on one edge **1,150.00**

Moravian, "Tempus," depicting Father Time, covered in blue and ivory glaze, red clay showing through, unmarked, small glaze flake to one edge, 10" x 7-1/4", $1,150. Photo courtesy of David Rago Auctions.

18" d, 1-1/2" h, Autumn, young man picking apples, basket at his feet, stamped "MR," made for Old Wicker Art School, Detroit, MI, 1920s, custom made wrought iron museum stand........ **5,750.00**

Mosaic Tile Co., Zanesville, OH

6" sq, Fortune and the Boy, polychrome.............**80.00**

8" sq, Delft windmill, blue and white, framed..................**55.00**

Pardee, C.

4-1/4" sq, chick and griffin, blue-green matte........**175.00**

6" sq, portrait of Grover Cleveland, gray-lavender **125.00**

Providential Tile Works, Trenton, NJ, round, stove type, hold in center, flowered **20.00**

Rookwood Faience, 8" h, emb pink, ochre, and green geometric floral pattern, Arts & Crafts frame, stamped "RP," chips to corners.........**325.00**

Sherwin & Cotton

6" sq, dog head, brown, artist sgd **100.00**

6" x 12", Quiltmaker and Ledger, orange, pr **145.00**

Trent, 6" sq, head of Michelangelo, sea green glaze, sgd by Isaac Broome, imp mark **115.00**

U. S. Encaustic Tile Works, Indianapolis, IN

6" sq, wreath, flowered, emb, light green.................**20.00**

6" x 18", panel, Dawn, green, framed **150.00**

Wedgwood, England

6" sq, Red Riding Hood, black and white...................**110.00**

6" sq, calendar, November, boy at seashore, peacock blue ... **95.00**

8" sq, Tally Ho, man riding horse, blue and white **85.00**

TINWARE

History: Beginning in the 1700s, many utilitarian household objects were made of tin. Because it is nontoxic, rust resistant, and fairly durable, tin can be used for storing food; and because it was cheap, tinware and tin-plated wares were in the price range of most people. It often was plated to iron to provide strength.

An early center of tinware manufacture in the United States was Berlin, Connecticut, but almost every small town and hamlet had its own tinsmith, tinner, or whitesmith. Tinsmiths used patterns to cut out the pieces, hammered and shaped them, and soldered the parts. If a piece was to be used with heat, a copper bottom was added because of the low melting point of tin. The industrial revolution brought about machine-made, mass-produced tinware pieces. The handmade era had ended by the late 19th century.

References: Dover Stamping Co., *1869 Illustrated Catalog*, Astragal Press, 1994 reprint; Marilyn E. Dragowick (ed.), *Metalwares Price Guide*, Antique Trader Books, 1995; John Player, *Origins and Craft of Antique Tin & Tole*, Norwood Publishing, 1995 (available from Christie & Christie Association, P.O. Box 392, Cookstown, Ontario, Canada LOL 1LO).

Museum: Cooper-Hewitt Museum, New York, NY.

Additional Listings: See Advertising, Kitchen Collectibles, Lanterns, Lamps and Lighting, and Tinware, Decorated.

Anniversary top hat, 11" d, 5-3/4" h, 19th C **1,150.00**

Book box, 9-1/4" l, remnants of painted design.....................**125.00**

Candle box, 14-1/2" h, cylindrical, hanging, some battering...... **220.00**

Candle mold

12-1/2" l, 11-1/8" h, 24 tin tubes, double handles **350.00**

14" w, 3-3/4" d, 10-1/2" h, 12 tin tubes, sq nail construction pine frame, orig dark finish ...**1,210.00**

17" w, 60 tubes, applied ear handles, minor corner break on base, couple spots resoldered .. **495.00**

Candle sconces, pr, 12-7/8" h, semicircular, candle socket and tall back with crimped crest, later white and green flowers, yellowed varnish, price for pr **250.00**

Cheese sieve, 6" h, heart shape, resoldered hanging ring **360.00**

Candle mold, four candles, handle, 10" h, 3-3/4" w, $70.

Coffee pot, polychrome paint dec, America, mid-19th C, minor paint loss

8-3/4" h, straight spout, strap handle, green, yellow, and red floral dec, yellow flourishes at top and lid **865.00**

9" h, straight spout, strap handle, green, red, and yellow stylized floral dec, yellow flourishes at to and lid **1,380.00**

10" h, goose neck spout, stylized floral dec front and back, embellishment on bottom ..**575.00**

Creamer, 4" h, polychrome spray of yellow, green, and red flowers beneath spout, attributed to New York, mid-19th C, minor paint loss **200.00**

Bread bin, Home Comfort Bread and Cake Cabinet, $100. Photo courtesy of Joy Luke Auctions.

Foot warmer, 7" x 9" x 5-1/2" h, punched tin panels with circles and hearts, mortised wood frame with turned posts, wire bale handle, wear, some edge damage **250.00**

Lamp

Grease, 1-5/8" h, colorful glaze **165.00**

Petticoat, 4" h, orig whale oil burner, orig black paint **65.00**

Skater's, 6-3/8" h, light teal-green globe **225.00**

Lantern, 17-1/2" h, hanging, old dark green repaint, rococo detail, six panes of glass with reverse painted dec, candle socket in base, attributed to Ohio, one pane with corner missing **420.00**

Quilt template

4-5/8" d, star **30.00**

7" d, flower **35.00**

Tea bin, 8-3/4" w, 8" d, 10" h, painted red, litho portrait of pretty young lady, stenciled gold dec, America, 19th C, minor paint loss, price for pr ...**750.00**

Teapot, 6-1/2" d, spout resoldered **150.00**

Wall pocket, 6-3/4" w, 11-3/4" l, two tiers, extended round top back, punched hanging hole, America, 19th C, minor corrosion............**115.00**

Wall sconce, 13-1/2" h, scalloped shaped hood, mid-19th C, minor corrosion **350.00**

TINWARE, DECORATED

History: The art of decorating sheet iron, tin, and tin-coated sheet iron dates back to the mid-18th century. The Welsh called the practice pontypool; the French, töle peinte. In America, the center for tin-decorated ware in the late 1700s was Berlin, Connecticut.

Several styles of decorating techniques were used: painting, japanning, and stenciling. Designs were done by both professionals and itinerants. English and Oriental motifs strongly influenced both form and design.

A special type of decoration was the punch work on unpainted tin practiced by the Pennsylvania tinsmiths. Forms included coffeepots, spice boxes, and grease lamps.

Reference: Marilyn E. Dragowick (ed), *Metalwares Price Guide*, Antique Trader Books, 1995.

Box, cov

6-3/8" l, dark brown japanning, gold and orange stenciled floral dec, "Friendship," some wear and soldered repair at hinges ...**55.00**

7" d, 6-1/2" h, cylindrical, orig dark brown japanning, red, white, yellow, green, and black floral dec, white band, hinged lid **750.00**

Bread tray, 12-1/2" x 8-1/4", red, green, and yellow floral dec, yellow swag border, red edge, black ground, minor paint loss **345.00**

Canister, cylindrical

6-1/4" h, 6" h, red cherries, green leaves, white border, yellow stylized leaves and swag borders, lid centered with leaf dec, red japanned ground, minor scratches **400.00**

8-1/2" d, 8-1/2" h, red cherries, green leaves, white border, red flowers, yellow stylized leaves, starburst at ring handle, black ground, minor paint loss...............**290.00**

Coffeepot, red, yellow, and green floral design, banded decoration, 10" h, loss to ground, $470. Photo courtesy of Sanford Alderfer Auction Co.

Coffeepot, cov, goose neck spout, dome top

9-1/2" h, red, green, yellow, and white floral dec, black ground, crusty surface with some touch-up, rust on int., some battering .**825.00**

10-1/2" h, red, green, brown, blue, and yellow floral dec, dark brown japanning, wear and old touch-up repaint, repairs **495.00**

10-1/2" h, red and yellow flowers, stylized leaves, black ground, paint loss **490.00**

10-1/2" h, yellow birds, red pomegranates, yellow stylized leaves, black ground, minor paint loss, lid unattached, repair to finial **1,100.00**

Creamer, hinged lid, 4-1/4" h, dark brown japanning, yellow, green, red, and white floral dec, some wear
..... **525.00**

Deed box, dome top

6-3/4" w, 3-1/8" d, 3-5/8" h, orig dark brown japanning, white band on front panel, green leaves, red cherries, yellow border dec, wire bale handle, tin latch, slight wear
..... **660.00**

7-7/8" w, 3-7/8" d, 4-1/8" h, japanned ground, yellow star flowers and flourishes on lid and sides, yellow and ivory band on front with red acorns and green oak leaves, red, green, and ivory drapery, wire bale handle, tin hasp, minor wear, mostly to lid edges **660.00**

8" w, 4" d, 4-3/4" h, black ground, yellow swags and lines, front with fruit, yellow, and green foliate, wire bale handle, tin hasp, minor wear, mostly to lid edges **250.00**

Document box, 11-1/2" w, 5" d, 6-1/4" h, dome top, brown japanning, red raped swags, yellow leaves, wavy lines, tin hasp, brass bale handle, int. lined with remnants of glue-on leaves, minor touch-up on front of lid and some edges, some wear **990.00**

Milk can, 8-1/2" h, black japanning, stenciled red and gold stylized floral design **200.00**

Spice box, 7-1/4" d, round, seven int. containers, worn orig brown japanning, gold stenciled labels **175.00**

Milk can, black ground, original red and gold stenciled flowers and border, 8-1/2" h, $200.

Sugar bowl, 3-1/2" h, worn orig red paint, brown and yellow comma type foliage, foot slightly battered **190.00**

Tea caddy, 8-1/4" l, dark ground, worn stenciled bronze powder dec, int. lift-out tray fits over two lidded compartments, orig emb brass handle, minor damage **220.00**

Tray

17-1/2" d, later 18-1/2" maple bamboo stand, Victorian, c1860, openwork edge, painted central scene of ruins, green ground **375.00**

25-1/2" l, 19-1/2" w, painted Chinoiserie dec, three pagodas in wooded landscape, red ground, 19th C **350.00**

Urn, cov

13-1/4" h, slender stem, ovoid foot, gilt florals, birds, and butterflies, 19th C, pr **1,725.00**

Two handles, acorn finials, dec with floral sprays and birds, scalloped floral and repeating gilt leaf borders, weighted base, French, 19th C, some paint loss, minor dents, pr **575.00**

TOBACCO CUTTERS

History: Before pre-packaging, tobacco was delivered to merchants in bulk form. Tobacco cutters were used to cut the tobacco into desired sizes.

Arrow Cupples Co., 19" l, 6-3/4" h **125.00**
Brown's Mule, iron, counter top . **70.00**
Brunhoff Mfg. Co., Cincinnati, orig black paint, floral design around base, 15-1/2" l, slight rust **115.00**
Climax, 17" l **60.00**
Cupples, Arrow & Superb **50.00**
Drummond Tobacco Co. **75.00**
Enterprise Mfg. Co., Philadelphia, patent April 13, 1875 ..... **195.00**
John Finzer & Brothers, Louisville, KY, Five Bro's Tobacco W'ks, 18" l, 6-3/4" h **175.00**
Griffin Goodnow Grocer Co., Tulsa, OK, 12-3/4" l, 4-1/4" w, 8-1/2" h. . **195.00**
Griswold Tobacco Cutter, Erie, PA **70.00**
Keen Kutter, E. C. Simmons ... **225.00**
Lorillards Chew Climax Plus, brass, Penn Hardware Co., Reading, PA **100.00**
Sprague Warner & Co. **75.00**
Star Tobacco Plug, 19" l **75.00**

Red Tin Tag, Lorillards Chew Climax Plug, brass, made by Penn Hardware Co., Reading, PA, 17-1/4" l, $115.

T. C. Johnson Co., Quincy, IL, Pat Dec. 1, 1914, orig black paint, part of base missing **40.00**
Unmarked, graduated 6-1/4" to 7-1/2" w, 10-/12" l, cast iron cutter, wood base **45.00**

TOBACCO JARS

History: A tobacco jar is a container for storing tobacco. Tobacco humidors were made of various materials and in many shapes, including figurals. The earliest jars date to the early 17th century; however, most examples seen in the antiques market today were made in the late 19th or early 20th centuries.

Reference: Joseph Horowitz, *Figural Humidors, Mostly Victorian,* published by author, 1997 (FTJ Publications, 3011 Fallstaff Road, Baltimore, MD 21209).

Collectors' Club: Society of Tobacco Jar Collectors, 3011 Fallstaff Road, Baltimore, MD 21209-2960.

Bisque, seated black lady holding pug dog, 8" h, $575. Photo courtesy of Joy Luke Auctions.

Bear with beehive, 6-1/2" h, majolica, Continental **770.00**
Blackamoor, 6" h, majolica, marked "DEP" in circle, c1900, some restoration **330.00**
Black boy, red hat with tassel, majolica, repainted, nicks **275.00**

Bull dog, porcelain, German . . . **275.00**
Creamware, 9" h, 6" d, plum colored transfers on side, one titled "Success to the British Fleet," striped orange, blue, and yellow molding, domed lid . **900.00**
Crystal, 7" h, hammered copper top, Roman coin dec, , sgd "Benedict Studios" **250.00**
Dog's head, with pipe and green hat and collar, majolica **375.00**
Dwarf in sack, 8" h, terra cotta, multicolor dec, marked "JM3478," chips, wear **255.00**
Girl on side, pipe on lid, majolica, Continental **75.00**
Indian, 5-1/2" h, black, majolica. **330.00**
Jasperware, raised white Indian chief on cov, Indian regalia on front, green ground **195.00**
Majolica, 6" h, barrel shape, cobalt blue, green, gold, and brown, Doulton, Lambeth, England, #8481, artist's initials **225.00**
Mandarin, papier-mâché **95.00**
Man with pipe, large bow tie, with match holder and striker, rim chips, hairline **165.00**

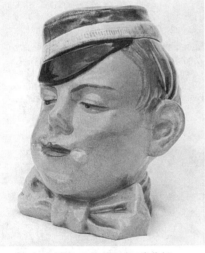

Student, blue cap, yellow band, light green bow tie, high glaze, marked "6597/71," 4-7/8" h, $90.

Man with top hat, majolica, Sarreguemines, hairline in base. **165.00**
Moose, porcelain, Austrian **200.00**
Owl, 11" h, majolica, brown, yellow glass eyes **825.00**
Rosewood, 12" l, 7-1/2" h, rect, four compressed bun feet, hinged lid, central compartment for mixing bowl flanked by two compartments for tobacco storage, removable lids, Continental, early 20th C **225.00**

Royal Winton, hp relief scene, marked "Royal Winton, England" **195.00**
Salt glazed stoneware, matching lid, 6-1/2" h, relief and blue accented hunting dog on front, blue accent band at rim, overall diamond relief pattern **250.00**
Toby type, Shorter and Sons . . . **55.00**
Wave Crest, 5" sq, white opaque body, SP fittings **450.00**
Winking Scotch man, 6" h, porcelain, blue beret with plaid band and orange tuft, green collar **200.00**

TOBY JUGS

History: Toby jugs are drinking vessels that usually depict a full-figured, robust, genial drinking man. They originated in England in the late 18th century. The term "Toby" probably is related to the character Uncle Toby from Tristram Shandy by Laurence Sterne.

References: Susan and Al Bagdade, *Warman's English & Continental Pottery & Porcelain*, 3rd ed., Krause Publications, 1998; Vic Schuler, *Collecting British Toby Jugs*, 2nd ed., Kevin Francis Publishing Ltd., 1987.

Museums: American Toby Jug Museum, Evanston, IL; City Museum & Art Gallery, Stoke-on-Trent, England; Victoria & Albert Museum, London, England.

Additional Listings: Royal Doulton.

> **Reproduction Alert:** During the last 100 years or more, tobies have been copiously reproduced by many potteries in the United States and England.

Bennington type, 9-1/2" h, standing **175.00**
Delft, 11-1/4" h, man seated on barrel, green hat, green and black sponged coat, blue and yellow pants, old cork stopper, c19th C **365.00**
Luster ware, 6-1/2" h, blue coat, spotted vest, 19th C **175.00**
Majolica, 8-3/4" h, monk **165.00**
Minton, 11-1/4" h, majolica, Quaker man and woman, polychrome dec, imp mark, pr **4,600.00**
Portobello pottery, 10" h, standing, spatter enamel dec, orig cov, c1840 . . . . **275.00**
Pratt
  9-1/4" h, pearlware glaze, typical blue, brown, and ochre palette, hat inset, small chips **425.00**
  10-3/4" h, Hearty Good Fellow, blue jacket, yellow-green vest, blue and yellow striped pants, blue and ochre sponged base and handle, stopper missing, slight glaze wear, c1770-80 . . . . **1,500.00**

Hearty Good Fellow, red coat, yellow breeches, 11-1/2" h, $200.

Royal Doulton
  2-3/4" h, The Fortune Teller . . **500.00**
  4-1/2" h, Sam Weller, #d6265, "A" mark **190.00**
  4-1/2" h, 4" d, "The Best is Not Too Good," style 2, c1939-60 . . **500.00**
  6-1/4" h, Field Marshall Montgomery, mark and large "A" **135.00**
  6-1/2" h, stoneware, blue coat, double XX, Harry Simson . . **395.00**
  8-1/2" h, Falstaff, designed by Charles Noke, D6062, 1939-91 . . . . **175.00**

Pratt type, brown hat, olive green jacket, rust breeches, 6" h, $2,400.

8-1/2" h, Happy John, designed by Harry Fenton, D6031, 1939-91 .... **175.00**

9" h, Winston Churchill, DT6171 .... **175.00**

Shorter Son, Ltd., England, Long John Silver, 9-3/4" h **375.00**

Staffordshire

5-1/4" h, 4-1/4" h, seated, holding jug in one hand, glass in other, cobalt blue jacket, plaid vest, orange trousers, yellow hat, c1850. **235.00**

9" h, pearlware, seated figure, sponged blue jacket, ochre buttons, ochre and lavender speckled vest and trousers, brown hair and hat, green glazed base, shallow flake inside hat rim, attributed to Ralph Wood, c1770-80 .... **1,950.00**

9-1/4" h, Martha Gunn, translucent brown and ochre glazes, pearl body, brim repaired at hairline **1,265.00**

9-1/4" h, Thin Man, full chair, green, blue and brown, holding pipe and foaming mug, attributed to Ralph Wood, c1765-75 .... **5,000.00**

9-3/4" h, mottled and translucent glazes, cream-colored body, small foot rim chips **460.00**

10-1/2" h, King Charles Spaniel, enamel dec, restored hat, late 19th C **275.00**

10-3/4" h, cat, enameled dec, holding letter, restored hat, late 19th C **300.00**

11-3/4" h, Rodent's Sailor, black hat, green coat, white trousers with blue stripes, imp "65" on base, Ralph Wood, lid missing., c1765-75 .... **5,900.00**

Whieldon, 9-1/2" h, pearlware, seated figure, yellow greatcoat, green vest, blue trousers, holding brown jug in left hand, raises foaming glass of ale towards mouth, lid missing, c1770-80 .... **1,600.00**

Wilkinson

10" h, Marshall Joffre, modeled by Sir Francis Carruthers Gould, titled "75mm Ce que joffre," printed mark, c1918, hat brim restored **345.00**

10-3/4" h, Field Marshall Haig, modeled by Sir Francis Carruthers Gould, titled "Push and Go," printed marks, c1917 ..... **460.00**

11-3/4" h, Marshall Foch, modeled by Sir Francis Carruthers Gould,

titled "Au Diable Le Kaiser," printed marks, c1918............ **345.00**

11-3/4" h, Winston Churchill, multicolored, designed by Clarice Cliff, black printed marks, number and facsimile signature, c1940 .... **825.00**

Yorkshire-Type, 7-3/4" h, caryatid form handle, Pratt palette dec, sponged base and hat brim int. **750.00**

TOOLS

History: Before the advent of the assembly line and mass production, practically everything required for living was handmade at home or by a local tradesman or craftsman. The cooper, the blacksmith, the cabinet maker, and the carpenter all had their special tools.

Early examples of these hand tools are collected for their workmanship, ingenuity, place of manufacture, or design. Modern-day craftsman often search out and use old hand tools in order to authentically recreate the manufacture of an object.

References: Ronald S. Barlow, *Antique Tool Collector's Guide to Value,* L-W Book Sales, 1999; Kenneth L. Cope, *American Machinist's Tools,* Astragal Press, 1993; Martin J. Donnelly, *Catalogue of Antique Tools,* published by author (31 Rumsey St., Bath, NY 14810), 1998; Garrett Hack, *The Handplane Book,* Taunton Press, 1997; Jerry and Elaine Heuring, *Collector's Guide to E. C. Simmons, Keen Kutter Cutlery Tools,* Collector Books, 1999; Herbert P. Kean and Emil S. Pollak, *Price Guide to Antique Tools,* Astragal Press, 1992; ——, *Collecting Antique Tools,* Astragal Press, 1990; Kathryn McNerney, *Antique Tools, Our American Heritage,* Collector Books, 1979, 2000 value update; Emil and Martyl Pollak, *Guide to American Wooden Planes and Their Makers,* 3rd ed., The Astragal Press, 1994; ——, *Prices Realized on Rare Imprinted American Wood Planes, 1979-1992,* Astragal Press, 1993; John Walter, *Antique & Collectible Stanley Tools, Guide to Identity & Value,* 2nd ed.., The Tool Merchant, 1996; C. H. Wendel, *Encyclopedia of American Farm Implements & Antiques,* Krause Publications, 1997; John M. Whelan, *The Wooden Plane,* Astragal Press, 1993; Jack Wood, *Early 20th Century Stanley Tools,* L-W Book Sales, 2000; ——, *Town-Country Old Tools,* 6th ed., L-W Book Sales, 1997, 1999 value update.

Periodicals and Internet Resources: *Fine Tool Journal,* 27 Fickett Road, Pownal, ME 04069, http://www.FineToolJ.com; *Plumb Line,* 10023 St. Clair's Retreat, Fort Wayne, IN 46825; *Stanley Tool Collector News,* 208 Front St., P.O. Box 227, Marietta, OH 45750, http://www.thetoolmerchant.com; *The Electronic Neanderthal,* http://www.cs.cmu.edu/~alf/en.en.html; *Tool Ads,* P.O. Box 33, Hamilton, MT 59840-0033.

Collectors' Clubs: American Barbed Wire Collectors Society, 1023 Baldwin Road, Bakersfield, CA 93304-4203; Blow Torch Collectors Club, 3328 258th Ave. SE, Issaquah, WA 98027-9173, http://www.indy.net/~toper/BTCA; Collectors of Rare & Familiar Tools Society, 38 Colony Ct, Murray Hill, NJ 07974, http//www.craftsofnj.org; Collectors of Rare

& Familiar Tools Society of New Jersey, 38 Colony St., New Providence, NJ 07974-2332, http://www.craftsofnj; Early American Industries Assoc., 167 Bakersville Road, South Dartmouth, MA 02748-4198, http://www.eaiainfo.org; Early American Industries-West, 8476 West Way Dr., La Jolla, CA 92038; Long Island Antique Tool Collector's Assoc., 31 Wildwood Drive, Smithwotn, NY 11787-3452; Mid-West Tool Collectors Assoc., P.O. Box 8016, Berkley, CA 94707-8016; New England Tool Collectors Assoc., 836 N. King St., Northampton, MA 01060-1127; Ohio Tool Collectors Assoc., P.O. Box 261, London, OH 43140-0261; Pacific Northwest Tool Collectors, 12780 SW 231st Place, Hillsboro, OR 97123, http://www.tooltimer.com/PNTC.htm; Preserving Arts & Skills of the Trades, 2535 Grambling Way, Riverside, CA 9250y, http://www.tooltalk.org; Potomac Antique Tools & Industries Assoc., 6802 Newbitt Pl, McLean, VA 22101; Richmond Antique Tool Society, 2208 Lochwood Court, Richmond, VA 23233; Rocky Mountain Tool Collectors, 1435 S. Urban Way, Lakewood, CO 80028; Society of Workers in Early Arts & Trades, 606 Lake Lena Blvd., Auburndale, FL 33823; Southwest Tool Collectors Assoc., 712 S. Lincoln Lane Court, Mustang, OK 73069-4141, http://www.swtca.org; Three Rivers Tool Collectors, 310 Old Airport Road, Greensburg, PA 15601-5816; Tool & Trades History Society, Seanton Lodg, Swanton, St., Bredgar, Sittingbourne, UK; Tool Group of Canada, 7 Tottenham Road, Ontario MC3 2J3 Canada, http://www.thetoolgroupofcanada.com; Western New York Antique Tool Collector's Assoc., 3162 Avon Road, Genesco, NY 14454, http://physics.sci.genesco.edu/WNYATCA/info.html.

Museums: American Precision Museum Assoc., Windsor, VT; Barbed Wire Museum, La Crosse, KS; Living History Farms, Urbandale, IA; Mercer Museum, Doylestown, PA; National Agricultural Center & Hall of Fame, Bonner Springs, KS; Post Rock Museum, La Crosse, KS; Shelburne Museum, Shelburne, VT; Winchester Mystery House, San Jose, CA; World of Tools Museum, Waverly, TN.

Anvil, hand forged, 8"........ **60.00**

Archimedian drill, bit, c1915... **50.00**

Awl, bone, 5" l.............. **25.00**

Bench press, Sherman, solid brass, 12 lbs, 9-1/2" x 6" **65.00**

Clamp, wood, jaws, 13-1/2" l, pr **115.00**

Broad ax, hand forged, early 1900s, 12-1/4" w blade, $85.

Chisel, blade stamped "E. Connor," 22-1/2" l 45.00
Cooper's howel, L. & I. J. White, Buffalo, NY, No. 20, beechwood, 15" l
. . . . .225.00
Drill
 Bow, ivory, brass, rosewood, Erlandsen type, 13" l 845.00
 Hand, Goodel and Pratt, brass ferrules 28.00
File, half round, 20" l 15.00
Hammer, claw type
 Iron, wood handle, c180 . . . . .35.00
 Winchester 55.00
Key hole saw, British, 15-1/2" l . .30.00
Level, wood and brass
 Davis & Cook, patent "Dec, 1886"
. . . . .45.00
 Goodell-Pratt, brass bound mahogany, orig decal, 24" l
. . . . .225.00

Stanley, rosewood, patent 1896, 30" l
. . . . 150.00
Line level, W & LE Curley Troy, NY, brass, orig wood box with makers label, printed "M.S. STE M & A. RY", 20" l
. . . . 575.00
Mallet, burl, hickory handle, 34" l
. . . . 200.00
Marking gauge, Stanley, Williams' Patent, patented May 26, 1857, 7" l
. . . . 445.00
Mitre box, laminated maple, birch, and oak, graduated quadrant, Stanley 45.00
Plane
 Keen Kutter, K110 . . . . 45.00
 Ohio Tool Co., walnut, inscribed with carpenter's name, 9-1/2" l . . 25.00
 Pond, W. H., New Haven, CT, carriage maker's molding planes, 1840s, 7" l, four-pc set 595.00
 Sandusky, 7/8" dado molding, No. 62, 9-1/2" l 115.00
 Stanley, #10-1/2 . . . . 120.00
 Varvill & Son, York, England, boxed bead molding planes, 9-1/2" l, 10-pc set 595.00
 Winchester Repeating Arms Co. No. 3208, smoothing, metallic, mahogany handles, 9" l . . . 185.00
Pruning knife, hand forged iron blade, wood handle, c1800 . . . . 35.00
Router, Stanley, #71-1/2", patent date 1901 . . . . 40.00
Rule, Stanley, #32, two-fold, 12" l, caliper 120.00

Saw
 Band, mortised and pinned wood frame, orig red paint with blue and white striping, laminated cherry and maple top, 76" 300.00
 Buck, wood, worn varnish finish, marked "W. T. Banres," 30" . .45.00
 Dovetail, Hague, Clegg & Barton, brass back, 9" l 95.00
 Turning, W. Johnson, Newark, NJ, Richardson blade, 21" l 165.00
Screwdriver, flat wood handle, round sides, 9" blade 35.00
Scribe, curly maple adjustable fence and arm, 21" l 75.00
Shoot board, Stanley, No. 51/52, orig decal, 14" l 1,295.00
Square, cherry, iron, brass bound blade, marked "Set Tray" 50.00
Sugar auger, New England, 19th C, dual turned wooden handle, corkscrew-shaped wrought iron implement, black metal stand, 9-1/2" w, 15" h 230.00
Wagon wrench 30.00
Wheel measure, wrought iron, 14-1/2" l
. . . . .45.00

TOOTHPICK HOLDERS

History: Toothpick holders, indispensable table accessories of the Victorian era, are small containers made specifically to hold toothpicks.

They were made in a wide range of materials: china (bisque and porcelain), glass (art, blown, cut, opalescent, pattern, etc.), and metals, especially silver plate. Makers include both American and European firms.

By applying a decal or transfer, a toothpick holder became a souvenir item; by changing the decal or transfer, the same blank could become a memento for any number of locations.

References: Neila and Tom Bredehoft and Jo and Bob Sanford, *Glass Toothpick Holders,* Collector Books, 1999; William Heacock, *Encyclopedia of Victorian Colored Pattern Glass,* Book I, 2nd ed., Antique Publications, 1976, 1992 value update; ——, *1,000 Toothpick Holders,* Antique Publications, 1977; ——, *Rare & Unlisted Toothpick Holders,* Antique Publications, 1984; National Toothpick Holders Collectors Society, *Toothpick Holders,* Antique Publications, 1992.

Collectors' Club: National Toothpick Holder Collectors, P.O. Box 852, Archer City, TX 76351, http://www.collectoronline.com/clubNTHCS.html.

Additional Listings: See *Warman's Americana & Collectibles* for more examples.

Bisque, skull, blue anchor-shape mark
. . . . .65.00
Burmese, 2-1/2" h, shiny, soft peach blush fading to buttery-yellow, eggshell-thin body 435.00

Carpenter's chest, 38" l, 25" h, $700. Photo courtesy of Joy Luke Auctions.

Left to right: amber frog with jar; amber tree trunk; blue tree trunk with three monkeys; blue saddle, price for lot of four, $100. Photo courtesy of Joy Luke Auctions.

China

Royal Bayreuth, elk........ 120.00
Royal Doulton, Santa scene, green handles................. 75.00
R. S. Germany, Schlegelmilch, MOP luster.................. 40.00

Glass

Amberina, DQ, sq top...... 350.00
Cameo, Daum Nancy, winter scene, sgd................... 750.00
Cranberry, coralene beaded flowers 285.00
Cut, pedestal, chain of hobstars 145.00
Libbey, Little Lobe, hp violets, blue beading around top 250.00
Milk, Parrot and Top Hat, c1895 .... 45.00
Opalescent, Reverse Swirl, blue 85.00

Pattern glass

Arched Fleur-De-Lis 45.00
Carnation, Northwood....... 75.00
Daisy and Button, blue...... 75.00
Delaware, rose stain, gold dec 175.00
Fandango, Heisey 55.00
Hartford, Fostoria 85.00
Florida, ruby amber 265.00
Jewel with Dewdrop 55.00

Peachblow, New England, 2-1/4" h, $425.

Kansas.................. 45.00
Kentucky, green, gold trim... 125.00
Michigan, clear, yellow stain . 175.00
Paneled 44, Reverse, platinum stain 75.00
Spearpoint Band, ruby stained 195.00
Texas, gold trim 50.00
Truncated Cube, ruby stained . 75.00
Vaseline, two children holding up barrel, on pedestal 35.00

TORTOISESHELL ITEMS

History: For many years, amber and mottled tortoiseshell has been used in the manufacture of small items such as boxes, combs, dresser sets, and trinkets.

Note: Anyone dealing in the sale of tortoiseshell objects should be familiar with the Endangered Species Act and Amendment in its entirety. As of November 1978, antique tortoiseshell objects can be legally imported and sold with some restrictions.

Also see *Celluloid* for imitation tortoiseshell items.

Bellows, 20-1/8" l, 8" w, Continental, late 19th C, coromandel backing, front with premier part Renaissance-style scroll inlay, woven leather panel over brass tip 575.00
Box, cov, 2-1/2" d, 1" h, enamel insert on lid surrounded by gold band, hp enamel with seated woman in garden looking into mirror held by putti, French, loss to tortoise shell 450.00
Casket, 7" l, 2" h, shaped oval, tortoiseshell hinged lid, pique inlay of scrolling foliage suspending floral swag, silver case with floral and foliate feet, Birmingham, 1916 .... 750.00
Cigar case
5-1/2" l, rect, case inlaid with three-color gold, reserve with vacant silver cartouche, hinged, pink silk lined int., fitted, expandable, Victorian, 19th C 450.00
5-5/8" x 2-7/8", rect, silver inlaid crane and foliate stalks, brass border with clasp, silk lined int., monogrammed, Continental, late 19th C 550.00
Cigarette case, 4-1/4" l, domed oval, applied central carved monogram, Continental, late 19th/early 20th C 325.00
Clock, mantel
4-3/8" w, 3-1/2" d, 9-1/8" h, George III-style, early 20th C, balloon

shape, enamel dial with Roman numerals, silver plated banding on front, four plated ball feet.. 950.00
4-5/8" w, 3-3/4" d, 8-5/8" h, Regency-style, attributed to Birmingham, 1907, handle on top of rect case, sloped cornice, round bezel, enamel dial with Roman numerals, silver banding to front, four flattened ball feet, retailer's label for Pearce & Sons, Leeds 950.00
Clock, travel, 4-3/8" l, 3-3/4" w case, 3-3/4" l watch, London, c1910, rect black morocco case with tortoiseshell panel on front in silver surround, enclosing nickel-cased watch with eight day movement.............. 290.00
Comb and hairpin, gold lacquer dec, Japan 230.00

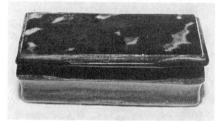

Box, hinged lid, 1-1/2" x 3-1/2", $145.

Diary

3-3/4" x 2-5/8", silver inlaid floral bouquet and bird, silk lined int. fitted with pencil, monogrammed, French, late 19th C....... 400.00
4-1/2" x 3-1/8", front inlaid with silver and gold fleur-de-lis suspending floral swag, gold clasp, silk lined int., French, late 19th C ... 425.00

Display case, 21" w, 11-1/2" d, 19-1/2" h, veneer and ebonized, pieced gallery with finials over single door, conforming base, ebonized compressed bun feet, Dutch . 1,080.00
Dresser box, 4" l, 3-1/2" w, 2-1/8" h, Birmingham, England, 1901, maker's mark "L. & S.," heart shape, hinged lid with tortoiseshell inlaid with silver harp and ribbon tied husk swags, husk surround, velvet-lined interior, three short ball and claw feet....... 575.00
Dressing table mirror, 7" w, 5-1/4" d, 8-1/4" h, Regency-style, mid-19th C, oval mirror plate in ivory surround, round ivory standards on tortoiseshell columns, ormolu finial, breakfronted with tortoiseshell and ivory base, four ormolu female herm supports . 1,265.00

Etui, 1-7/8" w, 1-1/2" d, 3-1/2" h, French, mid-19th C, tapered rect form, hinged lid with sloping sides, scalloped silver mounts at edges, fitted int. with four utensils, glass perfume bottle **. .550.00**

Letter box, 11-1/2" w, 5-1/2" d, 8" h, William Comyns, London, 1896, bombé morocco case mounted to front with tortoiseshell, silver rococo cartouche with foliate spandrels in center, shell shaped escutcheon, C-scroll and foliage edge mounts, moiré-lined interior. **1,465.00**

Longnette, 3-1/2" l closed, silver border with floral details, applied tortoiseshell over engine-turned ground, lever action, maker's mark rubbed, Continental, late 19th C **150.00**

Miniature, mandolin, 5-1/4" l, tortoiseshell, ivory, and mother-of-pearl, Continental **175.00**

Scent box, 2-1/4" h, trapezoid, blond tortoiseshell veneer, divided int. compartments, late Regency, c1825, scent bottles missing **375.00**

Snuff box, 3-3/8" l, 1-7/8" w, 1-1/8" d, book form, realistically modeled, tortoiseshell on front and back, cover set with oval silver plate formal miniature of 18th C boy and girl, sgd lower left "D. Drouris(?)" **350.00**

Tea caddy, 5-3/4" w, 4-1/4" d, 5-3/8" h, Regency-style, England, late 19th C, bombé sarcophagus shape, silver plate cartouche on lid, stringing, escutcheon, opening to velvet-lined lid, two lidded compartments with foil lining, ivory banding at rim, four celluloid ball feet **1,495.00**

TOYS

History: The first cast-iron toys began to appear in America shortly after the Civil War. Leading 19th-century manufacturers include Hubley, Dent, Kenton, and Schoenhut. In the first decades of the 20th century, Arcade, Buddy L, Marx, and Tootsie Toy joined these earlier firms. Wooden toys were made by George Brown and other manufacturers who did not sign or label their work.

Nuremberg, Germany, was the European center for the toy industry from the late 18th through the mid-20th centuries. Companies such as Lehman and Marklin produced high-quality toys.

References: Linda Baker, *Modern Toys, American Toys*, Collector Books, 1985, 1993 value update; Ronald S. Barlow (ed.) *The Great American Antique Toy Bazaar, 1879-1945: 5,000 Old Engravings from Original Trade Catalogs*, Windmill Publishing, 1998; Larry Bloemker, Robert Genat, and Ed Weirick, *Pedal Cars*, MBI Publishing, 1999; Jim Bunte, Dave Hallman and Heinz Mueller, *Vintage Toys: Robots and Space Toys*, Krause Publications, 2000; Steve Butler, *Hubley Toy Vehicles, 1946-1965*, Schiffer Publishing, 2001; Brad Cassity, *Fisher-Price Toys*, Collector Books, 1999; Jurgen and Marianne Cieslik, *Lehmann Toys*, New Cavendish Books, 1982; Greg Davis and Bill Morgan, *Collector's Guide to TV Toys and Memorabilia*, 2nd ed., Collector Books, 1999; Judith Anderson Drawe and Kathleen Bridge Greenstein, *Lithographed Paper Toys, Books, and Games, 1880-1915*, Schiffer Publishing, 2000; Edward Force, *Corgi Toys*, Schiffer Publishing, 1984, 1997 value update; —, *Dinky Toys*, 5th ed., Schiffer Publishing, 2001; —, *Lledo Toys*, Schiffer Publishing, 1996; —, *Solido toys*, Schiffer Publishing, 1993; Jurgin Franzke, *Tinplate Toys: From Schuco, Bing & Other Companies*, Schiffer Publishing, 2000; Tom Frey, *Toy Bop: Kid Classics of the '50s & '60s*, Fuzzy Dice Productions, 1994;

William Gallagher, *Japanese Toys*, Schiffer Publishing, 2000; Kurt Guile, Mike Willyard and Gary Konow, *Wyandotte Toys Are Good and Safe*, Wyandotte Toys Publishing, 1996; Ted Hake, *Hake's Price Guide To Character Toys*, 3rd ed., Gemstone Publishing, 2000; Tom Heaton, *The Encyclopedia of Marx Action Figures*, Krause Publications, 1999; Sharon and Bob Huxford (eds.,) *Schroeder's Collectible Toys*, 7th ed., Collector Books, 2000; Don Hultzman, *Collector's Guide to Battery Toys*, Collector Books, 1998; Dana Johnson, *Matchbox Toys 1947-1996*, 3rd ed., Collector Books, 1999; Sharon Korbeck and Elizabeth Stephan, *Toys & Prices, 2001*, 8th ed., Krause Publications, 2000;

David Longest, *Antique & Collectible Toys 1870-1950*, Collector Books, 1994; —, *Character Toys and Collectibles* (1984, 1992 value update), 2nd Series (1987), Collector Books; —, *Toys*, Collector Books, 1990, 1994 value update; Rex Miller, *The Investor's Guide to Vintage Character Collectibles*, Krause Publications, 1999; Richard O'Brien, *Collecting American Made Toy Soldiers*, Krause Publications, 1997; —, *Collecting Foreign-Made Toy Soldiers*, Krause Publications, 1997; Bob Parker, *Hot Wheels*, 4th ed., Schiffer Publishing, 2000; —, *Marx Toys*, Schiffer Publishing, 1996.

Mark Rich, *Toys A to Z*, Krause Publications, 2001; Michelle Smith, *Marx Toys Sampler, Playthings from an Ohio Valley Legend*, Krause Publications, 2000; Elizabeth Stephan, ed., *O'Brien's Collecting Toys, Ninth Ed.*, Krause Publications, 1999; —, *Collecting Toy Cars & Trucks*, 3rd ed., Krause Publications, 2000; —, *Today's Hottest Die-Cast Vehicles*, Krause Publications, 2000; —, *Toy Shop's Action Figure Price Guide*, Krause Publications, 2000; Craig Strange, *Collector's Guide to Tinker Toys*, Collector Books, 1996; Stuart W. Wells, III, *Science Fiction Collectibles: Identification & Price Guide*, Krause Publications, 1999; Harry A. and Joyce A. Whitworth, *G-Men and FBI Toys and Collectibles*, Collector Books, 1998; Neil S. Wood, *Evolution of the Pedal Car, Volume 4*, L-W Book Sales, 2000; Myra Yellin and Eric B. Outwater, *Cast Iron Automotive Toys*, Schiffer Publishing, 2000.

Periodicals and Internet Resources: *About.com Hobbies*, http://www.home.about.com/hobbies; *Action Figure Times*, http://www.primenet.com/~btn/aft.html; *AntiqueTOY.com*, http://www.antiquetoy.com; *Antique Toy World*, P.O. Box 34509, Chicago, IL 60634; *Big Red Toybox Toy Encyclopedia*, http://www.bigredtoybox.com; *Canadian Toy Mania*, P.O. Box 489, Rocanville, Saskatchewan S0A 3L0 Canada; *Collectible Action Figure*, http://www.exit109.com/~lmelogra/cafg.html; *HotWheels.com Collector's Center*, http://www.hotwheelsclub.com; *Hot Wheels Newsletter*, 26 Madera Ave., San Carlos, CA 94070-2937; *Magical World of Fisher-Price*, http://www.mwfp.com; *Master Collector*, 225 Cattle Barron Parc Drive, Fort Worth, TX 76108; *Mr Potato Head Collectors' Page*, http://www.fun1st.com/collectors.html; *Pressed Steel Toys*, P.O. Box 1289, McAfee, NJ 07428-1289; *SpecTacular News*, P.O. Box 368, Dyersville, IA 52040-0368; http://www.speccast.com; *Tinplate Temptations*, http://www.sable.co.uk/tinplate; *Toy Cars & Vehicles*, 700 East State St., Iola, WI 54990, http://www.krause.com; *Toy Farmer*, 7496 106th Ave. SES, Lamoure, ND 584458-9404; *Toy Ray Guns*, http://www.toyraygun.com; *Toy Shop*, 700 East State St., Iola, WI 54990, http://www.krause.com; *Toy Tractor Times*, P.O. Box 156, Osage, IA 50461; *Traders Horn*, 1903 Schoettler Valley Road, Chesterfield, MO 63017-5203; *Yo-Yo Net*, http://www.Yo-Yos.net; *Yo-Yo Times*, 627 163rd St. South, Spanaway, WA 98387.

Collectors' Clubs: A. C. Gilbert Heritage Society, 1440 Whalley, Suite 252, New Haven, CT 06515, http://www.acghs.org; Action Toy Organization of Michigan, 2884 Hawks, Ann Arbor, MI 48018, http://www.atomgroup.com; American Flyer Collectors Club, P.O. Box 13269, Pittsburgh, PA 1524300269; American-International Match Collectors & Exchange Club, 532 Chestnut St., Lynn, MA 01904-2717; Anchor Block Foundation, 1670 Hawkwood Court, Charlottesville, VA 22901; Antique Engine, Tractor & Toy Club, Inc., 5731 Paradise Road, Slatington, PA 18080; Antique Toy Collectors of America, 13th Floor, Two Wall St., New York, NY 10005; Assoc. of Game & Puzzle Collectors, PMB 321, 197M Boston Post Road West, Marlborough, MA 01752, http://www.agca.com; Blues City Hot Wheels Club, 4807 Walden Glen, Memphis, TN 38128; Canadian Toy Collectors Society, 91 Rylander Blvd., Unit 7, Suite 245, Scarborough, Ontario M1B 5M5, Canada, http://www.ctcs.on.ca; Corgi Official Collector Club, P.O. Box 323, Seansesa, SAI 1BJ UK; Ertl Collectors Club, P.O. Box 500 Dyersville, IA 52040-0500; Etch-A-Sketch Club, P.O. Box 111, Bryan, OH 43506-0111; Figure Collectors Club, 10120 Main St., Clarence, NY 14031-2049; Fisher-Price Collectors Club, 1442 N. Ogden, Mesa, AZ 85205; Girder & Panel Collectors Club, P.O. Box 494, Bolton, MA 01740-0494; Heartland Hot Wheelers Club, P.O. Box 6572, Omaha, NE 68106-0372; Hot Wheelin, 1428 E. Maple Ave., El Segundo, CA 90245; Kentucky Hot Wheels Assoc., 119 Etna St., Russell, KY 41169; Matchbox Collectors Club, P.O. Box 977, Newfield, NJ 08344-0977; Matchbox USA, 62 Saw Mill Road, Durham, CT 06422-2602; Northern California Hot Wheels Collectors Club, P.O. Box 18023, San Jose, CA 95158; Ohio Art Collectors Club, 18203 Kristi Road, West, Liberty, MO 64068; San Francisco Bay Brooklin Club, P.O. Box 61018, Palo Alto, CA 94306; Schoenhut Collectors Club, 1003 W Huron St, Ann Arbor, MI 48103-4217; Society of

Obsessive Female Toy Traders, http://www.geocities.com/Wellesley/5031; Southern California Meccano & Erector Club, P.O. Box 7653, Porter Ranch Station, Northridge, CA 91327-7653; Texas Action Figure Ring, http://www.angelfire.com/tx/afring; Tonnerville Trolley Collectors, 6045 Camelot Court, Montgomery, AL 36117-2555; Toy Car Collectors Assoc., P.O. Box 1824, Bend, OR 97701-1824; http://www.toynutz.com/TCGA.html; Wheels of Fire-Hot Wheels Club of Arizona, P.O. Box 86431, Phoenix, AZ 85080-6431.

Museums: American Museum of Automobile Miniatures, Andover, MA; Bethnal Green Museum of Childhood, London, UK; Binney & Smith, Inc., Crayola Hall of Fame, Easton, PA; Denver Museum of Miniatures, Dolls, & Toys, Denver, CO; Eli Whitney Museum, Hamden, CT; Eugene Field House & Toy Museum, St. Louis, MO; Evanston Historical Society, Evanston, IL 60201; Fawcett's Antique Toy Museum, Waldeboro, ME; Forbes Magazine Collection, New York, NY; Hobby City Doll & Toy Museum, Anaheim, CA; Howie's Toy Museum, Lisbon, NH; Margaret Woodbury Strong Museum, Rochester, NY; Matchbox & Lesney Toy Museum, Durham, CT; Matchbox Road Museum, Newfield, NJ; Museum of the City of New York, New York, NY; Smithsonian Institution,

Washington, DC; National Farm Toy Museum, Dyersville, IA; Spinning Top Exploratory Museum, Burlington, WI; Toy & Miniature Museum of Delaware, Wilmington, DE; Toy & Miniature Museum of Kansas City, Kansas City, MO; Toy Museum of Atlanta, Atlanta, GA; Washington Dolls' House & Toy Museum, Washington, DC; Western Reserve Historical Society, Cleveland, OH.

Additional Listings: Characters, Disneyana, Dolls, and Schoenhut. Also see *Warman's Americana & Collectibles* and *Warman's Flea Market* for more examples.

Notes: Every toy is collectible; the key is condition. Good working order is important when considering mechanical toys. Examples in this listing are considered to be at least in good condition, if not better, unless otherwise specified.

Arcade, Greyhound bus, Century of Progress, Chicago, 1933, cast iron, painted white and white, original label, rubber tires, 11-1/2" l, **$425.**

Arcade, USA

Airplane, cast iron, Air France Fighter, 1941, painted blue fuselage, yellow pressed steel wings, nickeled propeller, 10" wingspan **250.00**

Auto, cast iron

Chevrolet, coupe, 1928, painted gray and black, classic styling, full running boards, nickeled wheels, spare mounted on trunk, 8-1/4" l **1,320.00**

Desoto, sedan, painted gray, nickeled grill and bumper, decal on trunk reads "Sundial Shoes," rubber tires, 4" l **130.00**

Runabout, open seat touring car, wood, pressed steel seat, painted blue, red cast iron spoke wheels, seated driver, 9" l **500.00**

Sedan and Red Cap Trailer, sedan painted red, pulling small Mullens Red Cap trailer, lift-up hood, 8-3/4" l **220.00**

Touring Coupe, Model T, painted black, spoke wheels, 5" l . . . **470.00**

Bread truck, cast iron, painted black and white, side panel decals with children, side doors contain International decals, Hathaway's, replaced tires **1,650.00**

Arcade, Farmall tractor, driver, disc, cast metal, **$740.** *Photo courtesy of Joy Luke Auctions.*

Car carrier, Austin, cast-iron truck, painted green, pulling red sheet metal flat bed containing three Austin coupes, 14" l, some replaced tires **460.00**

Car hauler

Cast iron tractor, painted green, pulling two tiers, pressed steel body, four cast iron vehicles, 1939, large size, 15-3/8" l **440.00**

Cast iron truck, cast headlights, painted green, pulling red pressed steel flat bed trailer, three cast iron couples, 19" l, replaced trailer, repaired cars **360.00**

Chester Gump car, cast iron, pulled by single horse, red spoke wheels, 7-1/2" l, repainted **200.00**

City ambulance, cast iron, painted white, red cross, emb on sides, black rubber tires, 5-7/8" l, over painted **240.00**

Dump truck, cast iron, International Harvester, painted green, red chassis, yellow pressed steel dump body, 11-1/4" l **275.00**

Fire trailer truck, red, blue fireman, detachable trailer, hose reel and ladder turntable, 16" l, ladders missing, paint loss **325.00**

Ice truck, cast iron, Mack, railed open bed body, rear platform, rubber tires, emb sides, painted blue, 6-7/8" l **275.00**

Milk truck, cast iron, Borden's, painted green, classic milk bottle design, rubber tires **1,430.00**

Pick-up truck, cast iron, "International"" decals on door, painted bright yellow, black rubber tires, 9-1/4" l, some rust on left side **330.00**

Racer, Bullet, cast iron, classic bullet-shaped body, painted red, nickeled driver and mechanic, side pipes, and disc wheels, emb "#9" on side **550.00**

Tank, cast iron, camouflage painting, large metal wheels, 7-1/4" l **330.00**

Taxi, cast iron, painted blue, black trim, emb luggage rack, seated driver and passenger, rubber tires, 8-1/4" l . **660.00**

Thresher, McCormick-Deering, gray and cream wheels, red lining, chromed chute and stacker, 12" l **320.00**

Touring car, cast iron, 1923 Ford, painted black, spoke wheels, 6-1/2" l **320.00**

Tractor, cast iron, partial green and yellow paint, 3-1/2" l **70.00**

Trolley, Greyhound, New York World's Fair, blue and orange, nickel driver, decals, three cars with tinplate canopies, black tires, 16" l, some chipping and scratching **635.00**

Wrecker, cast iron, Ford, red cab and body, green Weaver crane, nickeled driver, wheels, and hoist parts, crane stenciled "Weaver" on side, 8" l . **660.00**

Arnold, USA

Cycle, turquoise, no longer sparks **650.00**

Ocean liner, twin funnels, white superstructure, black and red hull, tinplate, clockwork motor, lg. 13 in. **460.00**

Bing, Gebruder, Germany

Auto, tin, clockwork, center door model, black, seated driver, radiator cap ornament, spare tire on rear, 6-1/4" l **385.00**

Garage, litho tin, double doors, extensive graphics, houses sedan and roadster **550.00**

Limousine, litho tin windup, red, maroon and orange striping, orig driver, c1910, 5-1/4" l **690.00**

Open tourer, four seater, litho tinplate, gray-green, black and yellow lining, red button seats, black wings, front steering, orange and gray wheels, twin lamps, windscreen frame, hand-brake operated clockwork motor, c1915, 12-1/2" l, chauffeur missing, lamps detached **2,400.00**

Touring car, driver, tinplate, clockwork motor, front steering, 6-1/2" l **230.00**

Union ferry boat, hand-painted tin, clockwork, red hull, brown open deck, white deck housing, railing on side, window cut-outs on both sides, stack on roof, 12" l **1,200.00**

Borgfeldt, George, NY

Pluto the Pup, articulated wood, orig maker's box, 6" l **920.00**

Buddy L, steam shovel, pressed steel, $285.

Buddy L, USA

Army truck, pressed steel, painted army green, cloth covered bodies, rubber tires, marked "Army" on canopy, 31" l **145.00**

Bucket loader, pressed steel, gray, black loading buckets, cast iron, wheels, all chain driver, side cranks, 16-1/2" l **200.00**

Dump truck, black, red chassis and wheels, open cab, front steering, decal under dashboard, hinged tailgate, 25" l, lacks chain to wheels, some scratches **1,150.00**

Electric Emergency Unit wrecker, white pressed steel, rear hoist, 16-1/2" l, paint wear and staining **215.00**

Express Line delivery truck, black pressed-steel, front steering and rear doors, 24" l **750.00**

Fire truck, extension ladder, red pressed steel, white ladder, 29" l **150.00**

Greyhound bus, pressed steel, clockwork, bright blue and white, "Greyhound Lines" on sides, rubber tires, 16" l **275.00**

Outdoor railroad, No. 1000 4-6-2 locomotive and tender, No. 1001 caboose, No. 1003 tank, No. 1004 stock, No. 1005 coal cars (one with orig decal), 121-1/2" l, repainted . . **1,840.00**

Parcel delivery truck, pressed steel, brown and beige, large slat back body, rear doors, decals on sides, solid rubber wheels, 24" l, rooftop missing **275.00**

Railway Express delivery truck, green, Baby Ruth and Butterfinger adv, 22" l **575.00**

Shell Oil, 1938, Bud Krause restoration **3,850.00**

Steam shovel, No. 220, black, red corrugated roof and base, cast wheels, boiler, decal and winch, 14" h, surface rust, paint crazing on roof **115.00**

Telephone maintenance truck, No. 450, two-tone green, ladder, two poles, orig maker's box **350.00**

Wrecker, orig condition **3,950.00**

Buffalo Toys

See-Saw, litho tin, boy and girl seated at each end of plank, 14" l **275.00**

Carette, Germany

Lighthouse, hand-painted tin, clockwork, central lighthouse, railed deck on each side hovers over tin water basin where boat with seated driver circles, 11" h, 10" d **715.00**

Cast iron, unknown American makers

Dump truck, green Mack style front, C-cab, red bed with spring lever, spoked nickel wheels, 7-3/4" l . . **490.00**

Gasoline truck, blue, Mack-style front, C-cab, rubber tires, one tire missing, 7" l **200.00**

Milk wagon, black cast-iron horse, gilt harness, yellow wheels, blue steel wagon body, 6-3/4" l **150.00**

Stake truck, Ford Model A, red, 7" l **200.00**

Champion

Auto, cast iron, coupe, painted red, nickeled grill and headlights, rumble seat, rubber tires, spare mounted on trunk, 7" l, repainted **250.00**

Gasoline truck, cast iron, painted red, Mack "C" cab, tanker body, emb on sides, rubber tires, 8-1/8" l **385.00**

Panel truck, cast iron, enclosed panel van, cast spare tires and headlights, traces of orig blue paint, spoked metal wheels, 7-1/2" l, poor condition . **180.00**

Racer, cast iron, painted red, silver trim, wind deflector on rear, separately cast driver painted blue, nickeled disc wheels, 8-1/2" l **1,815.00**

Stake truck, cast iron, painted red, Mack "C" cab, stake side body, nickeled spoke wheels, 7" l **660.00**

Truck, cast iron, "C" Mack cab, blue body, 7-3/4" l, replaced wheels . **195.00**

Wrecker, cast iron, red C-cab with crane, nickel plated crank and barrel, rubber tires, 8-1/4" l **330.00**

J. Chein & Co., World War I Lorry, $80.

Chein

Barnacle Bill, tinplate, red hat, clockwork walking mechanism, 6-1/4" h
.... **290.00**

Disneyland ferris wheel, clockwork motor, bell, six gondolas, litho Disney characters and fairgrounds scenes, 16-3/4" h, distortion and paint loss
.... **350.00**

Easter Bunny, tinplate, pulling basket, multicolored, 10" l **145.00**

Hercules ferris wheel, clockwork motor, bell, six gondolas, litho children and fairground scenes, 16-1/2" l **325.00**

Wagon, horse-drawn, "Fine Groceries," tinplate, 12" l **290.00**

Chromolithograph paper on wood, unknown maker

Bagatelle game, two clowns with cup hats, patent date "March 7, 1895," 15" l
.... **290.00**

Battleship *Texas*, sides printed with anchor, guns, and gangway, deck with two wood cannons, funnel, mast, one flag pole, second one detached, red flag, attached manuscript Christmas tag, 14" l.................. **490.00**

Brownie Ten Pins, set of 10 different Palmer Cox Brownie figures, each with printed poem on reverse about their character, © Palmer Cox 1892, two mallets and three balls, wood box
.... **1,150.00**

Noah's Ark, incised and applied dec, hinged roof, four carved humans, 40 animals, 19" l hull........... **750.00**

Trinity Chimes, eight chimes, cathedral scenes, upright case, 18" h
.... **150.00**

Citroen, France

Aviation fuel truck, pressed steel, clockwork, painted red, enclosed cab with opening driver's door, tanker body with filler cap and brass drain valve, electric headlights, rear decal "AVIA," 18" l.....................**1,350.00**

5CV, open tourer, two-seat, blue boat tail body, black wings and wheels, gray tires, front steering and clockwork motor, orig maker's box, 12" l.. **2,070.00**

Fire engine, painted tin, clockwork, red, open bench seats, removable hose reel, ladders mount on rear body, disc wheels, rubber tires, orig box, 18" l
...........................**2,900.00**

Race car, pressed steel, clockwork, blue, molded seated figure with hand painted composition head, rubber tires, decal "Petite Rosalie," 12-1/4" l. **450.00**

Converse, USA

Heffield Farms delivery wagon, articulated horse, 21-1/2" l, considerable wear and paint loss
..............................**320.00**

Klondike Ice Co. delivery wagon, tinplate on wood, two litho horses, 17" l, paint poor...................**175.00**

Trolley, open sides, pressed steel, blue and mustard, stenciled dec, marked "City Hall Park 175" on both ends, reversible benches, large clockwork motor, 16" l, paint poor, destination boards missing..............**260.00**

Cor-Cor

Automobile, Graham, 1936, 20" l, pressed steel

Brown and beige, full running boards, black rooftop, electric headlights, spare disc wheels, emb "Cor-Cor Toys," chromed grill and rubber tires, restored.....**935.00**

Green, electric headlights, switch on side, rubber tires, metal wheels, chromed grill, restored **660.00**

Bus, sheet metal construction, green, orange wheels, "Inter City" decals on side, bench seats diecut from window wells, 23-1/2" l..............**990.00**

Dump truck, black body, orange bed and wheels, pressed steel, 23-1/2" l
..............................**260.00**

Stake truck, sheet-metal construction, black, brown stake body and rear platform, rubber tires, emb "Cor-Cor" on sides.....................**770.00**

Truck, sheet-metal construction, enclosed black cab, green van body, rear platform, large painted metal wheels, 23" l.................**825.00**

Cragston

Robot, 10-1/2" h, battery-operated tinplate, silver-gray body, red arms and chest, domed clear-plastic head with visible mechanism, orig maker's box
...........................**1,725.00**

Shuttling freight train, locomotive, two wagons, accessories, orig box and wrapping **90.00**

Dayton Friction Co.

Patrol wagon, pressed metal and wood, friction driven, painted red, stenciled "Police Patrol" on front panel, seated driver on open bench seat, spoke wheels. 10" l..........**200.00**

Touring car, pressed metal, painted red, gold spoke wheels, open sides, friction driver, 12" l..........**470.00**

Dent, USA

Auto, sedan, 1930, cast iron, painted blue, partial black paint on roof, nickeled wheels, spare on rear, 7-1/2" l, repainted...................**330.00**

Contractor's truck, cast iron, Mack, painted red, dual dump gondolas, open frame, nickeled disc wheels, painted centers, emb on sides, 7-1/2" l **1,050.00**

Dump truck, cast iron, green-gray, Mack-style front, C-cab, driver, red spoked wheels, spring-operated bed, swinging tailgate, 7" l, paint loss
..............................**320.00**

Fire patrol, cast iron, open-seat truck, rail sided open-bed body, rear platform, disc wheels, 5-3/4" l.........**220.00**

Ice cream can, cast iron, painted yellow, "Breyers Ice Cream" emb on side, three removable ice cream doors on other side, 1921, old store stock, 8-1/2" l, repainted **275.00**

Taxi, cast iron, painted orange and black

Repainted seated driver, replaced painted disc wheels......**315.00**

Seated figure, painted disc wheels, spare disc wheel on rear, 7-1/2" l
.....................**385.00**

Transfer wagon, cast iron, open seat, wagon painted orange, flared sides, seated driver on full width bench set and splash board sides, marked "Transfer," yellow spoked wheels, pulled by three horses, 18" l .. **1,100.00**

Doepke, aerial ladder fire truck, original box, $600. Photo courtesy of Joy Luke Auctions.

Fisher Price, USA

American Airlines plane, paper litho over wood, bright orange and blue, extensive graphics, two propellers, 20" wingspan...................**500.00**

Mickey Mouse, No. 748, articulated paper on wood, pull-toy, xylophone, 9" l
..............................**350.00**

French, unknown maker

Clown, articulated, playing cymbals, papier-mâché head, blue and red costume, wood body, push-toy action, c1900, 8" h **460.00**

Soldier Pins, unopened set, five pins, knit-covered ball, c1900 . . . . **325.00**

Gibbs

See-saw, yellow tower, hand-painted boy and girl, 14-1/2" h **140.00**

Girard/Woods

Coupe, Pierce Arrow, pressed steel, pink and maroon, clockwork motor, battery operated lights, rubber tires and bell, 14" l, one headlight missing, scratches **1,200.00**

Man pushing wheelbarrow, red plaid jacket, yellow trousers, green cart with orange wheels, 5-3/4" l **150.00**

Gong Bell

Columbus bell, cast iron, Columbus standing, men rowing ornate ship mounted to spoke wheels, bell rings, emb on side "Landing of Columbus," 7-1/4" l, replaced figure **420.00**

See saw, pull type, cast iron, figures of black man on one end, clown on other end, spoked wheel platform, central bell rings when figures articulate, 6-1/2" l **660.00**

Herolin, Germany

Farm yard set, No. 744/2, pressed card, chromolithograph, house, family, animals, and trees, maker's box with label, early 20th C, 12-3/4" w, some damage to box **175.00**

Hess, Germany

Ambulance, early litho, penny toy, brightly colored, seated driver, disc wheels, 4" l **290.00**

Hubley, Lancaster, PA

Airplane, cast iron

Bremen, painted green, nickeled wheels, propeller, and figure, 7" l, repainted **330.00**

Lindy Glider, painted red, yellow wings, driver seated on front, emb wings, 6-1/2" l **1,210.00**

Auto, cast iron

Airflow, painted blue, nickeled grill, bumper and running boards, spare on trunk, rubber tires, 6-1/4" l **250.00**

Lincoln Zephyr and trailer, painted green, nickeled grill and bumper, 13-1/2" l **825.00**

Sedan and trailer, painted red sedan, trailer panted silver and red, rubber tires, factory sample tag, 9-1/2" l **715.00**

Studebaker, roadster, painted red, nickeled front grill with headlights, front and rear bumpers, side running boards, rubber tires, trunk mounted spare, 6-3/4" l . . . **640.00**

Bell telephone, cast iron

8-1/4" l, painted green, silver sides, emb company name, Mack "C" cab, nickeled ladders, long handled shovels, pole carrier, spoked wheels, repainted . **250.00**

9-1/4" l, painted green, winch, auger, nickel water barrel on side, ladders, and pole carrier, fatigued rubber tires **660.00**

Boat, cast iron, painted red, emb "Static" on sides, sleet form, seated driver, hand on throttle of attached motor, chromed air cleaner, painted orange, three tires, clicker, 9-1/2" l, over painted **1,650.00**

Cement mixer truck, cast iron, red and green, nickel tank, rubber wheels, Mack, 8" l, restored **1,760.00**

Fire wagon, painted cast iron, hook and ladder wagon, articulated triple team, two drivers, four ladders, red ground, yellow hitch and wheels, early 20th C, 31" l **1,650.00**

Gasoline truck, cast iron, painted silver, red spoked wheels, cast figure, round tank body, rear facets, c1920, 6" l **495.00**

Milk truck, cast iron, painted white, emb "Borden's" on side panel, rear opening door, nickeled grill, headlights, and spoke wheels, 7-1/2" l, repaired headlights **1,980.00**

Motorcycle and side car, Indian, cast iron, cast aluminum handlebars, rubber tires, sprung steel noise-maker, some paint and decal loss, one tire damaged **865.00**

Panama steam shovel, cast iron, painted rd and green, large scale, nickeled shovel, cast people on trailer, dual rubbers on rear, 12" l **935.00**

Pull toy, Old Dutch Girl, cast iron, white and blue dress, holding yellow can of cleanser, rubber tires, c1932, 9" l, repaired stick, orig checker floor **4,100.00**

Racer, cast iron

Painted blue, painted red articulated pistons, seated driver, black tires, spoked wheels, 10-1/2" l . **1,760.00**

Painted green, red emb "5" on sides, hood opens on both sides to show extensively cast engine, disc wheels, seated driver, replaced hood doors, 9-1/2" l **1,100.00**

Painted red, seated driver, emb "#1" on sides, rubber tires, 7-3/4" l **385.00**

Road roller, Huber, cast iron, painted green, large fancy spoke wheels painted red, figure stands on rear platform, 7-1/2" l **1,320.00**

Stake truck, cast iron, two piece mold, chassis and hood painted red, stake body and cab painted blue, six rubber tires, 6-1/2" l **375.00**

Steam shovel truck, cast iron, painted green and red, nickeled shovel, fatigued rubber tires, 8-1/4" l . . . **385.00**

Take apart wrecker, cast iron, painted red and yellow, low hook and rubber tires, 6-1/4" l, fatigued tires **220.00**

Taxi cab, painted orange and black, separate driver chassis and luggage rack, rubber tires, yellow cab stencil on rear doors, 8-1/4" l, professionally restored **470.00**

Ives, Bridgeport, CT

Cuzner trotter, red tinplate carriage marked "Pat'd March 7, 1871," black spoked wheels, white horse with articulated legs, driver with striped trousers, black hat, brass clockwork motor, 11-1/2" l, some chipping **2,590.00**

Steamer, *King*, clockwork motor, black and red hull, brown superstructure with single funnel, 10-1/2" l, some wear **345.00**

Japanese

Haji, 8" l, car with boat trailer, friction powered, blue Ford convertible, red and cream Speedo motor boat with friction-powered motor, red trailer, orig packing and maker's box **400.00**

San, tugboat, 12-1/2" l, battery operated tinplate, red, cream, yellow, and blue, smoking mechanism, orig maker's box **200.00**

T.N.

Dump Truck, 11" l, friction powered tinplate, red and cream, automatic side dump action, orig maker's box **150.00**

Great Swanee Paddle Wheeler, 10-1/4" l, friction powered tinplate, whistle mechanism, orig maker's box **175.00**

Space Patrol Car, 9-1/2" l, battery operated, litho, blue, cream, and silver, red astronaut, green laser, spinning antenna, orig maker's ox **1,265.00**

Y.H./Daiwa, car with sailboat, 6-1/4" l, friction powered tinplate, thunderbird style car, red body, black roof, red and cream sailboat with blue trailer . **435.00**

JEP Voisin

Saloon car, No. 7392, tin, red body, black roof and wings, litho running boards, brass finished radiator, horn, battery-operated spotlight, front steering, clockwork motor, black disc wheels with gray tires, maker's and Paris retailer's labels, 14-1/2" l, one wing loose, one headlight front missing
.... **1,380.00**

Kelmet Corp., New York

Dump truck, sheet metal, orig black and red paint, marked "White Big Boy, Kelmet Corp. New York, NY," minor wear, headlights missing, dump mechanism incomplete, 26" l. . . **990.00**

Kenton, road scraper, #151, cast iron, green body, nickel plated blade, rubber tires, $150.

Kenton, Kenton, OH

Bus, Nile Coach, cast iron **750.00**
Elephant and clown chariot, remnants of silver paint and red blanket, yellow spoked wheels, detachable clown, 6-1/4" l, considerable paint wear and chips **130.00**
Farm wagon, cast iron, orig driver, one upright broken off, good paint, 11-1/2" l
.... **165.00**
Fire pumper, cast iron, painted red, gold boiler top and lamps, driver, white tires, 10-1/4" l, some chipping . . **230.00**
Hose reel, cast iron, three white horses, white carriage and reel, driver, hose, and spoked wheels, 13-3/4" l, horses repainted, other paint poor **435.00**
Overland circus, cage wagon, red, yellow wheels, white horses, driver, and outrider, 14" l **425.00**
Sulky and driver, nickeled cast iron, red spoked wheels, 5" l **115.00**
Tractor trailer set, all cast iron, tractor painted red, orange tanker, two speed stake trailers, nickeled disc wheels, 22" l **1,210.00**
Touring car, cast iron, painted white spoke wheels, cast headlamps and

lanterns, 7-3/4" l, replaced figures
.... **250.00**
Yellow cab, cast iron, painted orange and black, white disc wheels, orange centers, 6-1/2" l **495.00**

Left, Buck's Junior cast iron stove, $1,150; Stitchwells child's sewing machine, $550; Kenton Novelty cast iron stove, $550. Photo courtesy of Jackson's Auctioneers & Appraisers.

Keystone Mfg. Co., Boston

Fighter plane, "Ride 'Em," silver pressed-steel, red wings, propeller and seat, 25" l **520.00**
Flat-bed truck, pressed steel, winch, over-painted, 26" l **175.00**
Packard ride-on water tower, tower, nozzle, tank, and seat, lg. 32" l
.... **1,035.00**
U. S. Mail truck, Packard, black cab, green body, red chassis, 26" l, rear doors missing **800.00**

Kilgore, Canada

Airplane, cast iron, Seagull, painted red, nickeled wheels and wing mounted propeller, 7-3/4" l **880.00**
Auto, open roadster, 1928, cast iron, painted blue, nickeled wheels and driver, decal reads "Kilgore, Made in Canada," 6-1/8" l **825.00**
Delivery truck, cast iron, Toy Town, painted red, emb on side panels, gold highlights, silver disc wheels, 6-1/8" l, repainted **360.00**
Dump truck, cast iron, painted blue enclosed cab, red dump body, lever to lift, nickeled disc wheels, 8-1/2" l
.... **330.00**
Ice cream truck, cast iron, enclosed cab painted blue, orange body, emb "Arctic Ice Cream" on sides, disc wheels, 8" l **420.00**

Kingsbury Toys, USA

Blue Bird racer, black details, U.S. and U.K. flags, 20" l **4,140.00**
Dump truck **200.00**
Streetcar, orange, black bumpers
    No. 781, 9-1/4" l, scratching and chipping **200.00**
    No. 784, clockwork motor, fixed turning and bell, 14" l, paint chipped **150.00**

Lehmann, Germany

Autin, coil-spring motor, wood grain litho cart, blue jacketed box, 3-3/4" l
.... **290.00**
Beetle, spring motor, crawling movement, flapping wings, maker's box, one leg detached, but present, early Adam trademark **230.00**
Kadi, flywheel movement **290.00**
Na-Ob, red and yellow cart, blue eccentric wheels, gray donkey, marked "Lehmann Ehe & Co.," 6" l, front wheel missing **145.00**
Oh-My Alabama coon jigger, lithograph tinplate, clockwork motor, 10" h **460.00**
Truck, tinplate, cream, red, and yellow, blue driver, fixed steering, clockwork motor, marked "Lehmann Ehe & Co.," 6-3/4" l **435.00**
Tut Tut motor car, white suited driver, horn, front steering, bellows, coil springs, paint loss, rust spotting, 6-1/2" l
.... **635.00**
Walking Down Broadway, rack and pinion flywheel drive, litho couple, pug dog, orig lady's handbag, paint loss, 6-1/4" h **1,840.00**

Linemar, Japan

Donald Duck, Huey, Louey, and Dewey Marching Soldiers, clockwork motor, rubber titles, 11-1/4" l, scratches
.... **375.00**
Gym toy, Donald Duck, clockwork motor, celluloid figure, red bar, doing acrobatics, 4-1/2" h **245.00**
Mickey Mouse with xylophone, litho, clockwork motor, black, red, and yellow, foliate dec on xylophone, orig box lid, 7" h, chips, tears to lid **750.00**
Popeye, rowboat, battery-operated tinplate, orig controller and maker's box
.... **9,200.00**

Lineol, Germany

Armored car, litho tin clockwork, camouflage colors, revolving turret with gun, opening doors, spring lever for gun, wire guard covers vehicle, rubber

tires, 10" l, symbols repainted, minor paint loss **935.00**
Cannon, 88MM, litho tin, camouflage colors, stabilizer arms, elevation cranks, four-tire open frame, tow hook, 14-1/2" l.....................**935.00**
Motorcycle with side car, composition figures, tin fenders, disc wheels, 4-1/2" l **300.00**

Lionel
Mickey Mouse hand car, composition Mickey and Minnie figures and track **290.00**

Marklin, Goppingen, Germany
Field cannon, 13" l, cast iron, olive finish, firing mechanism, adjustable barrel **115.00**

Marx, litho tin wind-up, car, **$95.**

Marx, Louis & Co., NY
Big Parade, moving soldiers, cannon, ambulance, clockwork motor, stationary buildings, 24" l, airplane missing, faded **200.00**
Buck Rogers rocket ship, for Daisey, lithograph tinplate, clockwork motor, maker's box, lg. 12 in........ **1,495.00**
Bulldozer/tractor, gold body, rubber treads, plow and farmer driver, blue and red stake wagons, hitch, two discs, plow, corn planter, harvester ...**230.00**
Bus, Royal Bus Line, orange, red, and green, driver, clockwork motor, 9-3/4" l **400.00**
Charlie McCarthy benzine buggy, litho, black, cream, and red, clockwork motor, erratic action, 7" l, scratches and wear **375.00**
Dick Tracy squad car, battery operated motor and light, litho, green, characters in windows, 11-1/4" l, dent to roof, some scratches **175.00**
G-Man pursuit car, pressed steel and tinplate, red and blue, armed agent, clockwork motor, 14-1/4" l, scratches **750.00**
Honeymoon Express, clockwork motor, circular base **100.00**

Lumar wrecker service truck, multicolored pressed steel, rear winch, 16" l, scratches and staining ... **200.00**
Lumber contractor's truck, steel, red and yellow, 20" l.............**115.00**
Machinery equipment service moving truck, pressed steel, black, red, yellow, and silver, traversing crane, plastic motor, two wooden crates, maker's box, 22" l, truck rust and discoloration, box taped and water stained **175.00**
Merrymakers Band, tinplate, one dancer missing **575.00**
Popeye and parrots, tinplate, clockwork motor, 8-1/4" h **350.00**
Railway Express Agency delivery truck, green, yellow details, silver roof, cream, red, and blue logos, operating tailgate, Wyandotte tires and accessories including dolly and miniature packages, 1950s, 20" l, few scratches and scuffs........ **375.00**
Siren fire chief car, red pressed-steel, clockwork motor, and electric lights, lg. 14 in. **460.00**
U. S. Army division tank, No. 392, green, detailing, recoiling gun barrel, clockwork motor with start/stop action, 9-1/2" l **60.00**
Zippo the climbing monkey, multicolored litho tinplate, pull-string mechanism, 10" l............. **60.00**

Meier, Germany
Ambulance, horse drawn, litho tin, two horses, spoke wheels, 4-1/2" l.. **260.00**
Cart and canon, litho tin, two horses pulling cart with seated soldier, trailing cannon, 6" l **175.00**
Field bakery truck, litho tin, open driver's seat, boiler style field bakery body, tall stack, spoke wheels, 4-1/4" l **210.00**
Field kitchen truck, litho tin, open bench seat, spoke wheels, replaced stack, 4" l **125.00**

Metalcraft
Coca-Cola delivery truck, pressed steel, red and yellow, bottles, decals, 10-1/2" l, scratches **490.00**

Paris Mfg. Co., South Paris, ME
Peerless No. 400 wagon, pine body, stenciled and painted dec, handle, red disc wheels with solid rubber tires, 36" l wagon **175.00**

Plank, Ernst
Airship, shaded mustard-colored superstructure and tubular fins, twin-bladed celluloid propeller, each

emb with E. P. trademark, steel-blue colored gondola with captain holding telescope, airman standing by engine, ventilator, rudder and tinplate forward propeller, cloth covered suspension wire and cast metal winding key, 11" l, excelsior filled maker's carton with chromolithograph label of Jules Verne-style character riding rocket over German town, catalog no. label 962/1, torn triangular label with indistinct trademark, some damage and chipping **23,000.00**

Pratt & Letchworth
Dray wagon, cast iron, open bed wagon, single slat slides, wooden floor, standing figure, red spoke wheels, one horse, 10-1/4" l.............. **175.00**
Hook and ladder truck, cast iron, horse drawn, one red and one white horse, black frame with red detailing, spoked wheels, seated front driver, seated rear steerer, two wood ladders and bell, 23" l **460.00**
Surrey, cast iron, open carriage, low splash board, two full width seams with arm and back rests, emb upholstering mounted on two prs of spoked wheels, pulled by one horse, c1900, 14" l **990.00**

Schuco, trademark of Schreyer and Co., Germany
Acrobat bear, yellow mohair, glass eyes, embroidered nose and mouth, turns somersaults when wound, orig key, 1950s, 5" h **575.00**
Hopsta dancing monkey, red and yellow, baby mouse, clockwork motor, 4-1/2" h.................... **175.00**
Monkey bellhops, Yes/No monkey with painted metal face, metal eyes, ginger mohair head and tail, red and black felt outfit and hands, Acrobatic monkey with painted metal face, metal eyes, ginger mohair head, red and black felt outfit and hands, winds by rotating arms, oak Mission style settee, 1930s, 8-1/2" h, moth damage on both . **435.00**
Porsche microracer, No. 1037, red, key missing **55.00**
Teddy bear on roller skates, wind-up, beige mohair head, glass eyes, embroidered nose and mouth, cloth and metal body and legs, cotton shirt, felt overalls, hands, and boots, rubber wheels, marked "Schuco, U. S. Zone, Germany," clothes faded, key not orig **490.00**
Teddy bear on scooter, friction auction, yellow mohair bear, black steel

eyes, embroidered nose and mouth, black felt pants, blue litho scooter, 1920s, 5-3/4" h **1,035.00**
Tumbling monkey **100.00**

Skoglund & Olson, Sweden
Coupe, cast iron, painted gray, spare tire mounted on rear, rubber tires, red disc wheels, 8" l, repainted **550.00**
Farm tractor, cast iron, painted blue, red traction wheel, seated nickel driver, replaced steering wheel **1,100.00**
Gasoline truck, cast iron, painted red, enclosed cab, two cast fill caps on tank body, rubber tires, blue disc wheels, 10" l, repainted **615.00**
Ladder truck, cast iron, painted red, black cast side boxes, nickeled supports, rubber tires, removable house reel on open frame, one tin ladder, 16" l, repainted **715.00**
Pick-up truck, cast iron, painted yellow, enclosed cab, low side body, removable tailgate, rubber tires, red disc wheels, 10-3/4" l, repaired . **950.00**
Sedan and ramp, cast iron, green touring sedan with spare tire, resting in gray car ramp, 7-1/4" to 14-1/4" l, overpainted **1,870.00**
Wrecker, cast iron, painted white, red winch and crane on open body, rubber tires, painted red disc wheels, sides emb "Central-Garage," 11-3/4" l **1,540.00**

Steelcraft
Pedal car, City Fire Department, Mack front, poor condition, 40" l **435.00**

Stevens & Brown
Girl on velocipede, cast-iron frame, brass clockwork motor, stencil dec red tinplate cover, red jacket and striped pantaloons, 11" l, steering rod missing **2,070.00**

Strauss, Ferdinard, Corp., New York City
Flying graf zeppelin, aluminum, clockwork mechanism, maker's box, 16" l, some tabs broken **290.00**
Jazzbo Jim, clockwork litho tinplate, banjo player, plaid jacket, cabin dec with caricatures, maker's box, hole in lid, 10-1/4" h **500.00**
Red cap porter, bulldog popping out of trunk, lid missing, uniform faded **230.00**
Santee Claus, lithograph tinplate with two reindeer and clockwork motor, arms missing **375.00**
Trolley car, litho tin wind-up, 6-1/2" l **210.00**

Sturditoy Construction Co.
Dump truck, pressed steel, rack lifting mechanism, 27" l, repainted, orig decals visible **635.00**

Structo
Cement mixer truck, 18-1/2" l, 9" h **150.00**
Fire truck, hydraulic hook and ladder, pressed steel, red, 3" l **175.00**

Technofix
Cable car, clockwork motor, shaped tinplate base, litho Alpine scenes, maker's box, some tape on box, 18-1/2" w **130.00**

Tinplate, unknown makers
Clown violinist, stilt-legs, striped trousers, clockwork motor, 9" h, poor condition **60.00**
Delivery carriage, litho, black, red, yellow, and pink, flywheel drive, 4-1/4" l **150.00**
Horse-drawn omnibus, attributed to Francis, Field and Francis, Philadelphia, 1850s, two white horses, black painted harnesses, wheel operated trotting, dark green roof with black fleur-de-lis and lining, emb gilt foliate surround, emb rear steps, door surround, driver's rear rest, emb window frames with painted curtains, red front, rear upper section, lower half with hand-painted polychrome floral and foliate dec, over blue-gray, ochre int. with ochre vis-a-vis bench seating along sides, wheels, 23" l, overall paint flaking, wheels detached, one window frame partially detached . . . **48,300.00**
Locomotive, attributed to Fallows, clockwork motor, cast wheels, high wings, cow catcher and bell, old repaint, 10" l **460.00**
Locomotive, Victory, red boiler, bell, black and gilt stack, red and blue cab with green roof, silver stenciled windows, yellow chassis, spoked wheels, 4-3/4" l, one wheel damaged, scratches and paint loss **990.00**
Porter and trolley, clockwork motor in hinged trunk, blue uniform, red and orange electric-type trolley, 4-1/2" l **145.00**
Steamer, three funnels, hand painted, red, cream, and gray hull, cream superstructure, 10" l **350.00**
Two-seater tourer, litho, red, yellow, and cream, driver, fly-wheel drive, 3" l **400.00**

Turner
Lincoln sedan, pressed steel, gray body, black roof and lines, green int., red wheels and rubber tires, 26-1/2" l, paint loss and surface rust . . . **1,840.00**

Unique Art, Li'l Abner Band, litho tin wind-up, **$550.**

Unique Art, Newark, NJ
Hee Haw, litho tinplate milk cart, clockwork motor, milk cans, donkey, and hillbilly, 10" l **350.00**
Kiddy cyclist, clockwork motor . **90.00**
Jazzbo Jim, dancing figure, checkered jacket and trousers, log cabin dec with caricature figures, coil-spring motor, 9-1/2" h, some rust spotting and fading **260.00**

Wilkins
Ladder truck, pressed steel chassis, cast driver and operator, red spoked wheels, clockwork motor and ladder, 13-1/4" l, old repainting **230.00**
Steam pumper, cast iron, two black and one white horse, yellow frame, red wheels, nickeled boiler, 21" l . . . **690.00**

Wolverine Supply & Mfg. Co.
Car and trailer, press-and-go motor, litho tin, blue and orange 1940s style four-door sedan, four-wheel blue, white, and orange trailer, some scratches, dent in auto roof, 27-1/2" l **200.00**
Panama pile driver, gravity toy, falling ball-operated driver, patent date December 1905, seven clay balls, 15-1/2" h, paint flaking **230.00**
Zilotone, wind-up, figure plays tunes on xylophone, three interchangeable discs, repaired orig box lid, some paint chips **650.00**

Wyandotte, USA
Airplane carousel, multicolored tinplate, four planes, canopy and rack mechanism, 6-3/4" h **90.00**

Ambulance, painted pressed steel, nickeled grill, operating rear door, minor scratches, 11" l **150.00**
Car and trailer, painted pressed steel, red, streamlined auto and travel trailer with operating rear door, replaced white rubber tires, paint worn, chips, and scratches, 25" l **215.00**
Humphrey mobile, litho tinplate, fixed steering, clockwork motor, rear door, moving hat and arm, 9" l, some scratching **350.00**
Pan Am clipper, painted pressed steel, red and white, brass engines, nickeled propellers, 9" l **275.00**

TRAINS, TOY

History: Railroading has always been an important part of childhood, largely because of the romance associated with the railroad and the prominence of toy trains.

The first toy trains were cast iron and tin; wind-up motors added movement. The golden age of toy trains was 1920 to 1955, when electric-powered units and high-quality rolling stock were available and names such as Ives, American Flyer, and Lionel were household words. The advent of plastic in the late 1950s resulted in considerably lower quality.

Toy trains are designated by a model scale or gauge. The most popular are HO, N, O and standard. Narrow gauge was a response to the modern capacity to miniaturize. Its popularity has decreased in the last few years.

References: Paul V. Ambrose, *Greenberg's Guide to Lionel Trains, 1945-1969*, Vol. III, Greenberg Publishing, 1990; Paul V. Ambrose and Joseph P. Algozzini, *Greenberg's Guide to Lionel Trains 1945-1969*, Vol. IV, Uncatalogued Sets (1992), Vol. V, Rare and Unusual (1993), Greenberg Publishing; Tom Blaisdell and Ed Urmston, St., *Standard Guide to Athearn Model Trains*, Krause Publications, 1998; John O. Bradshaw, *Greenberg's Guide to Kusan Trains*, Greenberg Publishing, 1987; Pierce Carlson, *Collecting Toy Trains*, Pincushion Press, 1993; W. G. Claytor, Jr., P. Doyle, and C. McKenney, *Greenberg's Guide to Early American Toy Trains*, Greenberg Publishing, 1993; Joe Deger, *Greenberg's Guide to American Flyer S Gauge*, Vol. I, 4th ed. (1991), Vol. II (1991), Vol. III (1992), Greenberg Publishing; Cindy Lee Floyd (comp.), *Greenberg's Marx Train Catalogues*, Greenberg Publishing, 1993; John Glaab, *Brown Book of Brass Locomotives*, 3rd ed., Chilton, 1993; John Grams, *Toy Train Collecting and Operating*, Kalmbach Publishing, 1999;

Bruce Greenberg, *Greenberg's Guide to Ives Trains*, Vol. I (1991), Vol. II (1992), Greenberg Publishing; —— (Christian F. Rohlfing, ed.), *Greenberg's Guide to Lionel Trains: 1901-1942*, Vol. 1 (1988), Vol. 2 (1988), Greenberg Publishing; ——, *Greenberg's Guide To Lionel Trains: 1945-1969*, Vol. 1, 8th ed. (1992), Vol. 2, 2nd ed. (1993), Greenberg Publishing; *Greenberg's Lionel Catalogues*, Vol. V, Greenberg Publishing, 1992; *Greenberg's Marx Train Catalogues*, Greenberg Publishing, 1992; *Greenberg's*

Pocket Price Guide, American Flyer S Gauge, , Kalmbach Publishing, 1998; *Greenberg's Pocket Price Guide, LGB, 1969-1996*, 3rd ed., Kalmbach Publishing, 1996; *Greenberg's Pocket Price Guide, Lionel Trains, 1901-1999*, Kalmbach Publishing, 1998; *Greenberg's Pocket Price Guide, Marx Trains*, 7th ed., Kalmbach Publishing, 1999; Ron Hollander, *All Aboard-The Story of Joshua Lionel Cowen and His Lionel Train Company*, Workman Publishing, 2000; George Horan, *Greenberg's Guide to Lionel HO*, Vol. II, Greenberg Publishing, 1993; George Horan and Vincent Rosa, *Greenberg's Guide to Lionel HO*, Vol. I, 2nd ed., Greenberg Publishing, 1993; John Hubbard, *Story of Williams Electric Trains*, Greenberg Publishing, 1987; Steven H. Kimball, *Greenberg's Guide to American Flyer Prewar O Gauge*, Greenberg Publishing, 1987; Roland La Voie, *Greenberg's Guide to Lionel Trains, 1970-1991*, Vol. I (1991), Vol. II (1992), Greenberg Publishing.

Lionel Book Committee, *Lionel Trains: Standard of the World, 1900-1943*, Train Collectors Association, 1989; Dallas J. Mallerich III, *Greenberg's American Toy Trains: From 1900 with Current Values*, Greenberg Publishing, 1990; ——, *Greenberg's Guide to Athearn Trains*, Greenberg Publishing, 1987; Eric J. Matzke, *Greenberg's Guide to Marx Trains*, Vol. 1 (1989), Vol. II (1990), Greenberg Publishing; Robert P. Monaghan, *Greenberg's Guide to Marklin OO/HO*, Greenberg Publishing, 1989; John R. Ottley, *Greenberg's Guide to LGB Trains*, Greenberg Publishing, 1989; Peter H. Riddle, *America's Standard Gauge Electric Trains*, Antique Trader Books, 1998; Robert Schleicher, *Fun with Toy Trains*, Krause Publications, 1999; ——, *N Scale Model Railroading*, Krause Publications, 2000; Alan R. Schuweiler, *Greenberg's Guide to American Flyer, Wide Gauge*, Greenberg Publishing, 1989; Gerry & Janet Souter, *The American Toy Train*, MBI Publishing, 1999; John D. Spanagel, *Greenberg's Guide to Varney Trains*, Greenberg Publishing, 1991; Elizabeth A. Stephan, *O'Brien's Collecting Toy Trains*, 5th ed., Krause Publications, 1999; Robert C. Whitacre, *Greenberg's Guide to Marx Trains Sets*, Vol. III, Greenberg Publishing, 1992.

Periodicals and Internet Resources: *Classic Toy Trains*, 21027 Crossroads Circle, P.O. Box 1612, Waukesha, WI 53187, http://www2.classtrain.com; http://www.webring.redepot.com; *Garden Railways*, P.O. Box 1612, Waukesha, WI 53187; *LGB Telegram*, P.O. Box 332, Hershey, PA 17033; *Model Railroader*, P.O. Box 1612, Waukesha, WI 53187; *N Scale Collector*, 31 Homsteader Lane, West Haven, CT 06516; *O Gauge Railroading*, P.O. Box 239, Nazareth, PA 18064, http://www.ogaugerr.com; *S Gaugian*, 7236 W. Madison Ave., Forest Park, IL 60130-1765; *Trains, Trains & Railroading*, http://www.notry.com/trains.html; *Trains.com*; http://www.trains.com.

Collectors' Clubs: A. C. Gilbert Heritage Society, 1440 Whalley, Suite 252, New Haven, CT 06515, http://www.acghs.org; American Flyer Collectors Club, P.O. Box 13269, Pittsburgh, PA 15234; Hornby Railway Collectors Assoc., 2 Ravensmore Road, Sherwood, Nottingham, NG5 2AH UK; Ives Train Society, 21 Academy St., Forestville, NY 14052; LaCrosse & Three Rivers Railroad Club, 624 Jackson St., La Crosse, WI 54601-5374; LGB Model Railroad Club, 1854 Erin Drive, Altoona, PA 16602; Lionel Collectors Club of America, P.O. Box 479, LaSalle, IL 61301; Lionel Operating Train Society, 6376 W. Fork

Road, Cincinnati, OH 45247-5704; Lionel Railroader Club, 26750 23-Mile Road, Chesterfield, MI 48051; Marklin Club-North America, P.O. Box 510559, New Berlin, WI 53151; Marklin Digital Special Interest Group, P.O. Box 510559, New Berlin, WI 53151; National Assoc. of S Gaugers, 220 Swedesboro Road, Gibbstown, NJ 08027-1504; National Model Railroad Assoc., 4121 Cromwell Road, Chattanooga, TN 37421, http://www.nmra.org; Toy Train Collectors Society, 109 Howedale Drive, Rochester, NY 14616-1534; Toy Train Operating Society, Inc., Suite 308, 25 West Walnut St., Pasadena, CA 91103; Train Collectors Assoc., P.O. Box 248, Strasburg, PA 17579, http://www.traincollectors.org.

Museums: Delaware Train and Miniature Museum, Wilmington, DE; Raysville Model Train Museum, Monticello, IL; Toy Train Museum of the Train Collectors Association, Strasburg, PA.

Additional Listings: See *Warman's Americana & Collectibles* for more examples.

Notes: Condition of trains is critical when establishing price. Items in fair condition and below (scratched, chipped, dented, rusted, or warped) generally have little value to a collector. Accurate restoration is accepted and may enhance the price by one or two grades. Prices listed below are for trains in very good to mint condition, unless otherwise noted.

American Flyer
Boxcar, #33514, HO gauge, Silver Meteor, brown **45.00**
Caboose
#935, S gauge, 1957, brown . . **60.00**
#33515, HO gauge, C&O, lighted, yellow, center cupola **75.00**

Crane car, #944, S gauge, 1952-57, Industrial Brown hoist **30.00**

Flat car

#936, S gauge, 1953-54, Erie, depressed center, spool load **38.00**

#24558, S gauge, 1959-60, Canadian Pacific, Christmas tree load **145.00**

Gondola

#941, S gauge, 1953-57, Frisco **10.00**

#33507, HO gauge, D&H, brown, canister load............. **60.00**

Locomotive

#342, S gauge, steam, 1946, nickel plate, switcher, 0-8-0, tender marked "Nickel Plate Road" **750.00**

#345, S gauge, steam, 1954, Silver Bullet, Pacific, 4-6-2 ...... **200.00**

#426, HO gauge, B&O, blue and gray **150.00**

#3020, O gauge, electric, 4-4-4, c1922-25 .... **375.00**

Set, O gauge

Freight, #476 gondola, #478 boxcar, #480 tank car, #484 caboose **130.00**

Passenger, Railway Post Office car, Paul Revere coach, Lexington observation, orange **115.00**

Set, standard gauge, passenger

#4331, #4331, #4332 ...... **300.00**

#4340, #4341, two-tone red, brass trim.................... **290.00**

#4390, #4391, #4392, #4393, two-tone blue, President's Special **1,035.00**

#4653 electric locomotive, two Bunker Hill coaches, Yorktown observation car, orange, pre-war **865.00**

Bing, German

Locomotive, O gauge, pre-war

Clockwork, cast iron, no tender, headlight missing **70.00**

Live steam, 0-4-0, minor fire damage, no tender........ **815.00**

Set, O gauge, passenger, litho, #2395 combine, Winnegago coach, Lakewood observation, green with brown roofs **130.00**

Set, #1 gauge, passenger, litho, dark maroon, lettered "Pennsylvania Lines," combine #1250, coach #1207.. **435.00**

Bub, Karl, German

Set, O gauge, litho, clockwork steam locomotive, tender, two boxcars, gondola, crane, some parts missing **130.00**

Buddy L

Industrial, set, #51 locomotive, #52, #53, #54, #55, #55, #56, 25 sections of track, c1929-31 .... **1,150.00**

Dorfan

Set, O gauge, passenger, #52 locomotive, #492 Railway Express, #493 Seattle coat, #494 observation, c1924-33 .... **750.00**

Set, standard gauge, passenger, #789, #790, yellow **220.00**

Ives

Baggage car

#50, 1908-09, O gauge, four wheels, red litho frame, striped steps, white/silver body, sides marked "Limited Vestibule Express, United States Mail Baggage Co." and "Express Service No. 50," three doors on both sides, one on each end, black roof with celestory **150.00**

#70, 1923-25, O gauge, eight wheels, red litho body, simulates steel, tin roof with celestory stripe, sliding center door, marked "The Ives Railway Lines, Express Baggage Service, 60, U. S. Mail" **30.00**

Caboose, #67, 1918, O gauge, eight wheels, red litho body, sliding door on each side, gray painted tin roof with red cupola, "The Ives Railway Lines". **45.00**

Gravel car, #63, 1913-14, O gauge, eight wheels, gray litho, rounded truss rods, marked "63" on sides **35.00**

Livestock car, #65, c1918, O gauge, eight wheels, orange-yellow litho body, type D trucks, gray painted roof with catwalk, sides marked "Livestock Transportation, Ives RR"........ **27.50**

Locomotive

#11, 1910-13, O gauge, 0-4-0, black boiler and cab, litho plates beneath arched cab windows, cast iron wheels, L. V. E. No. 11 tender **165.00**

#19, 1917-25, O gauge, 0-4-0, black cast iron boiler and cab, two arched windows and "IVES No. 19" beneath, cast-iron wheels, NYC & HR No. 17 tender....... **225.00**

#25, 1906-07, O gauge, 4-4-2, black body, boiler tapers towards front, four separate boiler bands, three square windows on both sides of cab, gold frames and stripes, tin pony wheels, four-wheel L.V.E. No. 25 tender **275.00**

#3200, 1911, O gauge, 0-4-0, cast iron S-type electric center cab, green body, gold trim, cast iron six-spoke wheels, center door flanked by two windows, raised lettering "Ives" and "3200" below windows **250.00**

#3236, 1928, Standard gauge, 0-4-0, electric box cab, tan tin body, stamped steel frame, diecast wheels, operating headlight, three windows per side, brass plates "The Ives Railway Lines" and "Motor 3236" **265.00**

Parlor car

#62, 1924-30, O gauge, eight wheels, tin litho steel, red-brown, one-pc roof with clerestory stripe, five windows, two doors on each side, marked "The Ives Railway Lines" above windows **75.00**

#72, 1910-15, one gauge, eight wheels, white tin body, litho to simulate wood, tin roof with

Marklin, steam locomotive, rare green version, 1935, **$3,555.** *Photo courtesy of Auction Team Breker.*

clerestory stripe, four double windows, three small windows, door at each end, marked "Twentieth Century Limited Express, No. 72, Chicago" . **490.00**

Set, O gauge, litho, freight, #3 cast iron stem locomotive, #1 tender, three #54 gravel cars, #56 caboose, c1910-14 . . . . **700.00**

Set, standard gauge, #170, #171, #172, tan, c1924-25 . . . . **70.00**

Tank car, #66, 1921-35, O gauge, eight wheels, gray painted body, black dome **25.00**

Tender, #25, 1928-30, O gauge, diecast body, coal load, two four-wheel trucks **150.00**

Lionel

Baggage car, #2602, O gauge, 1938, red body and roof **100.00**

Boxcar
#00-44, OO gauge, 1939 . . . . . **45.00**
#HO-874, HO gauge, 1964, NYC **25.00**

Caboose
#217, Standard gauge, 1926-40, orange and maroon **150.00**
#2682, O27 gauge, 1938, red . **12.00**
#HO-841, HO gauge, 1961, NYC **10.00**

Cattle car, #213, Standard gauge, 1926-40, cream body, maroon roof **450.00**

Hopper car, #216, Standard gauge, 1926-40, silver, Sunoco decal . . **350.00**

Locomotive
#5, standard gauge, 0-4-0, steam, c1910-18, missing cow catcher, no tender **415.00**
#10E, standard gauge, electric **70.00**

#156, O gauge, electric, 4-4-4, dark green, c1917-23 . . . . **265.00**

Observation car
#322, Standard gauge, 1924 . **95.00**
#754, O gauge, 1934, streamliner **70.00**
#2436, O27 gauge, 1954, Mooseheart **45.00**

Pullman
#35, Standard gauge, c1915, orange **65.00**
#420, Standard gauge, 1930, Blue Comet, light blue body, dark blue roof, marked "Faye" **450.00**
#607, O gauge, 1926 . . . . . . **45.00**
#2533, O gauge, 1952, marked "Silver Cloud" **85.00**

Refrigerator car, #214R, Standard gauge, 1929-40, ivory body, peacock roof **400.00**

Set, O gauge
Passenger, #252 electric locomotive, #529 coach, #530 observation, olive green, c1926 . . . . . . **175.00**
Passenger, Lionel Lines tender, two #1690 passenger cars, #1691 passenger car, Lionel Junior, c1933 . . . . **70.00**
Passenger, Union Pacific, #752E power unit, #753 coach, #754 observation, silver, c1934 . **350.00**

Set, standard gauge, freight
#11, #12, #14, #15, c1906-26 **175.00**
#12, #17, #17, c1909-23 . . . . . **70.00**
#12, #12 with crane, #13, #14, c1909-23, missing one pair of trucks **95.00**
#13, #16, #17, c1903-23 . . . . **200.00**
#511, #512, #514R, #517, c1927-29 . . . . **140.00**
#513, #516, #517, c1926-32 . **290.00**

Set, standard gauge, passenger
#18, #19, #190, dark olive green, c1906-10 . . . . **230.00**
#10 electric locomotive, two #337 passenger cars, #338, c1925-29 . . . . **350.00**
#33 electric locomotive, #35, #36 cars, dark olive green, c1913-23, locomotive missing some parts **70.00**
#309, #310, #312, c1924-29 . **260.00**
#337, #337, #338, c1925 . . . . **150.00**

Trolley and motor car, #2, lettered "Electric-Rapid Transit #2," red body, cream windows, 1906-15 . . . . **4,025.00**

TRAMP ART

History: Tramp art was an internationally practiced craft, brought to the United States by European immigrants. Its span of popularity was between the late 1860s to the 1940s. Made with simple tools—usually a pocketknife, and from scrap woods—non-reusable cigar box wood, and crate wood, this folk-art form can be seen in small boxes to large pieces of furniture. Usually identifiable by the composition of thin-layered pieces of wood with chip-carved edges assembled in built-up pyramids, circles, hearts, stars, etc. At times, pieces included velvet, porcelain buttons, brass tacks, glass knobs, shards of china, etc., that the craftsmen used to embellish his work. The pieces were predominantly stained or painted.

Collected as folk art, most of the work was attributed to anonymous makers. A premium is placed on the more whimsical artistic forms, pieces in original painted surfaces, or pieces verified to be from an identified maker.

References: Helaine Fendelman and Jonathan Taylor, *Tramp Art: A Folk Art Phenomenon*, Stewart, Tabori, and Chang, 1999; Clifford A. Wallach and Michael Cornish, *Tramp Art, One Notch At A Time*, Wallach-Irons Publishing, 1998.

Adviser: Clifford Wallach.

Lionel, set, Norfolk & Western, steam engine, 4-8-4, tender, #6-8100, seven Norfolk & Western passenger cars, #6-9562, 6-9563, 6-9564, 6-9565, 6-9566, 6-9567, 6-19108, all in original boxes, **$575.** Photo courtesy of Joy Luke Auctions.

Box, hinged, 13" w, 9" h, **$110.** Photo courtesy of Joy Luke Fine Art Brokers and Auctioneers.

Bank, 6" h x 4" w x 4" d, secret access to coins **335.00**

Bird cage, 28" h x 22" w x 13-1/2" d, house with two compartments. . **775.00**

Box, cov

4-1/4" w, 3" d, 1-3/4" h, hinged cover, dove, heart, and anchor dec
. . . . **200.00**

9" w, 7" d, 11" h, rect, chip-carved paneled sides, conforming base, white-washed, c1900 . . . . . **260.00**

14" l, 7-1/8" d, 8-1/4" h, hinged top, cast brass pull, mounted pincushion on base, two concealed short drawers, painted blue and gold, c1890-1910
. . . . **815.00**

Cabinet, 44" h x 22-1/2" w x 14" d, scratch built cabinet, embellished with pyramids, floral pattern on blue doors, crest and secret compartment
. . . . **6,500.00**

Chest of drawers, 40" h x 29" w x 20" d, scratch built from crates with four drawers, 10 layers deep **2,400.00**

Christmas tree, 25-1/2" h, carved wood, branching sections, painted cross finial, stepped polychrome base, sgd "D. Hafner," c1900 . . . . . . **2,070.00**

Clock, table, curlique outline, light and dark woods, 13" h x 15" w, x 4" d, $475. Photo courtesy of Clifford Wallach.

Clock, mantel, 22" h x 14" w x 7" d, red stain with drawers at base. **475.00**

Comb case, 27" h x 17" w x 4" d, adorned with horseshoes, hearts, birds, two drawers and mirrors **700.00**

Crucifix, 16" h x 7" w x 4-1/2" d, wooden pedestal base, wooden carved figure
. . . . **185.00**

Document box, 14" h x 9-1/2" w x 9" d, diamond designs, sgd and date
. . . . **375.00**

Desk accessory box, decorated with sea shells, initialed "K. H.," 7" h, 18" w, 6" d, $750. Photo courtesy of Clifford Wallach.

Doll furniture

Chair, 10" h, 7" w, 12" d, dec with brass tacks **450.00**

Bureau, 14" h x 12" w x 9" d, drawers and mirror **650.00**

Frame

9" h, 6-3/4" w, photograph of maker, signed and dated "1906" . . **275.00**

13" h x 12" w, horseshoe shape, light and dark wood **465.00**

14" x 12", hearts and diamonds, painted gold **255.00**

14" h x 24" w, double opening frame with oval opening for photos
. . . . **325.00**

16" h x 18" w x 4-3/4" d, crown of thorns, multiple opening frame with minor losses, dark stain . . . **495.00**

16" h, 22" w, block corner style, with painted hearts, pair of frames by same maker. **225.00**

25" h, 22" w, 13-1/2" x 15-1/2" opening five layers, hearts in each corner, orig gold and red speckled paint, minor wear. **715.00**

26" h x 24" w, velvet panels and sq corners **350.00**

Grotto, 12" w, 8" d, 29" h, carved and painted, carved cross steep on bell tower above grotto, applied floral, foliate, and geometric motifs, int. fitted with platform and drawer, two standing floral devices, painted red and green, cream-white ground, found in Ohio, late 19th/early 20th C **420.00**

Jewelry box

6" h x 11" w x 6" d, covered with hearts painted silver over gold, velvet lined **595.00**

6-3/4" h x 11-1/2" w x 7" d, hinged jewelry box with velvet top and sides **175.00**

8" h x 11" w x 7" d, hinged, pedestal, dark stain. **175.00**

9" h x 11-1/2" w x 7" d, large, dated "1898," metal lion pulls . . . **300.00**

16" h x 14" w x 10" d , shallow drawers and carved finial on top
. . . . **395.00**

Lamp

24" h, 10" w, 10" d, table, double socket. **550.00**

68" h, 17" w, 17" d, floor, heavy pedestal base, no shade . **1,200.00**

Match safe, 9" h x 2" w x 2" d, strike surface, open holder for matches **75.00**

Medicine cabinet, 22" h x 18" w x 10" d, light and dark woods. **675.00**

Miniature

Chair, 8" h x 6" w x 5-1/2" d, crown of thorns **245.00**

Chest of drawers, 14" h x 5" w x 4" d, made of cigar boxes **375.00**

Music box, 3" h x 7" w x 6" d, velvet sides **425.00**

Night stand, 37" h x 22" w x 14" d, dark stain, drawer on top and cabinet on bottom, no losses **1,600.00**

Pedestal

6 1-2" h x 10" w x 7" d, lift off lid, velvet lined. **225.00**

14 1-2" h x 12" w x 8" d, multi-level, six draws **675.00**

16" h x 7" w x 4-1/2" d, polychromed in green and black paint . . **950.00**

Pedestal box

8-1/4" h x 9" w x 6-1/2" d, double, bar connecting top pyramids, velvet lined, precise notching . . . **325.00**

29-1/2" h x 16" w x 15" d, light and dark stained, made from fruit crates **1,850.00**

Plant stand, 22" h x 11" w x 11" d, painted gold, heavily layered . . **675.00**

Pocket watch holder, 9" h x 6-1/2" w x 5-1/2" d, ftd **375.00**

Radio cabinet, 50" h x 33" w x 16" d, box type radio encased behind doors, ornate **3,600.00**

Sewing box

8-1/2" h x 11-1/2" w x 8-1/2" d, velvet pin cushion on top **265.00**

9" h x 16-1/2" w x 8" d, painted red, white and blue sewing box, Uncle Sam cigar label under lid . **1,600.00**

Sewing cabinet, 27" h x 16" w x 9" d, lift top and three drawers made from crate wood **1,400.00**

Side by side, bookcase/desk, 49" h x 29" w x 20" d, glass cabinet door with shelves on one side, other side is drop front desk **3,200.00**

Vanity mirror, 26" h, 14" d, 10" d, table top, heart on top and drawer . . **375.00**

Wall pocket

7" h x 9" w x 4" d, open work and porcelain buttons **95.00**

8-1/2" h x 16" w x 4-3/4" d, shelf and diamonds for design **125.00**

14" h x 11" w x 7" d, painted with hearts and stars, pr **700.00**

20" h x 18" w x 5-1/2" d, carved leaves and acorns surrounding mirror **1,400.00**

TRANSPORTATION MEMORABILIA

History: Most of the income for the first airlines in the United States came from government mail-carrying subsidies. The first non-Post Office Department flight to carry mail was in 1926 between Detroit and Chicago. By 1930, there were 38 domestic and five international airlines operating in the United States. A typical passenger load was 10. After World War II, four-engine planes with a capacity of 100 or more passengers were introduced.

The jet age was launched in the 1950s. In 1955, Capitol Airlines used British-made turboprop airliners for domestic service. In 1958, National Airlines began domestic jet passenger service. The giant Boeing 747 went into operation in 1970 as part of the Pan American fleet. The Civil Aeronautics Board, which regulates the airline industry, ended control of routes in 1982 and fares in 1983.

Transoceanic travel falls into two distinct periods—the era of the great clipper ships and the era of the diesel-powered ocean liners. The golden age of the later craft took place between 1900 and 1940.

An ocean liner is a city unto itself. Many have their own printing rooms to produce a wealth of daily memorabilia. Companies such as Cunard, Holland-America, and others encouraged passengers to acquire souvenirs with the company logo and ship name.

Certain ships acquired a unique mystic. The *Queen Elizabeth, Queen Mary,* and *United States* became symbols of elegance and style. Today the cruise ship dominates the world of the ocean liner.

References: Barbara J. Conroy, *Restaurant China: Identification & Value Guide For Restaurant, Airline, Ship & Railroad Dinnerware,* Collector Books, Volume 1 (1998), Volume 2 (1999); Joshua Stoff, *Transatlantic Flight: A Picture History, 1873-1939,* Dover Publications, 2000.

Collectors' Clubs: Bus History Assoc., 965 McEwan, Windsor Ontario N9B 2G1 Canada; International Bus Collectors Club, 12 Gunnels St., Goose Creek, SC 29445; Lighter-Than-Air-Society, 1436 Triplett Blvd., Akron, OH 44306; National Assoc. of Timetable Collectors, 125 American Inn Road, Villa Ridge, MO 63089, http://www.rrhistorical.com/naotc; Transport Ticket Society, 4 Gladridge Close, Earley, Reading Berks RG6 2DL England, http://www.binternet.com/~transport.ticket; World Airline Historical Society, P.O. Box 660583, Miami Springs, FL 33266.

Museums: Cole Land Transportation Museum, Bangor, ME; Forney Transportation Museum, Denver, CO; Henry Ford Museum, Dearborn, MI; Museum of Bus Transportation, Lemoyne, PA; Navy Lakehurst Historical Society, Lakehurst, NJ; Owls Head Transportation Museum, Owls Head, ME; Pacific Bus Museum, San Anselmo, CA; Pate Museum of Transportation, Pate, TX; South Street Seaport Museum, New York, NY, Western Reserve Historical Society, Cleveland, OH.

Additional Listings: See Automobilia and Railroad Items. See also Aviation Collectibles, Ocean Liner Collectibles, and Railroad Items in *Warman's Americana & Collectibles.*

Postcard, R.M.S. Titanic, pre-sinking, $850. Photo courtesy of Postcards International.

Ashtray, cast iron, Art-Nouveau form, woman with fan, adv S. G. Gray, Carriages & Buggies, Ottawa, Ill, 6-1/2" l **230.00**

Baggage label, 4-1/4" x 6", full-color paper, *Graf Zeppelin,* German lettering for South Atlantic flight, c1929, unused **60.00**

Bicycle, 58" l, oak frame, steel wheels, hard rubber tires, leather seat, 19th C **575.00**

Blotter, 3" x 5-1/4", Firestone Bicycle Tires, black, white, orange and blue, unused, 1920s **20.00**

Booklet, *St. Lawrence Route to Europe,* Canadian Pacific, 1930, 16 pgs, 8" x 11" **25.00**

Brochure, *USS Henderson,* ship's ball, 6-1/4" x 9-1/2" blue softcover 24-page brochure, Shenghai, China, March 4, 1934 . . . . **10.00**

Can, Ronson Motor Oil, Wynne Oil Co., Philadelphia, 4" d, 5-1/2" h, white ground, blue streamlined image of speeding car, plane, and train, yellow trim, full, unopened, C.8+ **600.00**

Cap badge, Pacific Greyhound Bus Line, chrome, blue and green cloisonné enameling, 2-1/2" x 2" **325.00**

Coaster wagon, 33" l, Kelly Karwood, iron frame, hard rubber wheels, made

by Burnham Mfg. Co., Charles City, IA **185.00**

Date stamp, 4" l, Seaboard Airline Railroad, "Received-Agent, Clinton, S.C.," hard rubber handle **25.00**

Deck plan, *S. S. Hamburg,* fold out, 1930 . . . . **35.00**

Game, 13" x 14-1/2", United Air Lines Skyways, cardboard folder opens to 14-1/2" x 26" playing board, 1937 copyright, "Approved by United Air Lines," distributed by Levi & Gade, Chicago, Mainliner, two-engine plane on cov **70.00**

Identification fob, 1-3/4" d, celluloid mounted on black cardboard watch fob slotted disk, red and green inscriptions, reverse grommetted to hold inner diecut paper identification tag, Commercial Travelers, Boston benefit association, unused **35.00**

Lighter, *R..M.S. Queen Elizabeth,* 1/2" x 1-3/4" x 2" h, chrome, metal disk official insignia on one side with red, blue, and copper enamel accents, 1950s . . **35.00**

Paperweight, 2-1/2" d, dark luster lead, "Aero Club of America," raised image of eagle soaring beneath sun rays above world globe nestled in cloud banks, also inscribed "13th Annual Banquet Feb. 19, 1919, Waldorf-Astoria" . . **20.00**

Pin

1-3/8" h, Reliance Yacht, dark charcoal luster, detailed replica of racing yacht, America's Cup Competition, c1900 . . . . **15.00**

1-1/2 h, Laughing Indian Motorcycle, diecut thin brass, pewter-like silver luster, reverse marked "Indian Motocycles," locking bar pin, 1920s **65.00**

Pinback button

Anderson Carriage Co., Detroit, High School Line, black and white portrait of stylish young lady, white background, maroon lettering, early 1900s **40.00**

Banner Buggies, 2-1/8" d, celluloid, black, white, and red banner over gray and black circular belt strap, early 1900s **75.00**

Cleveland Orphans Automobile Outing Day, Aug. 24, 1908, multicolored art of parade horse carriage dec in blue flowers, adult and children passengers . . . **75.00**

Easthampton Boat Club, blue and white, pennant symbol inset by small white triangle, late 1890s **10.00**

Excursion Boat *Arrow*, sepia real
photo of paddlewheel boat,
inscribed "All Aboard For
Put-In-Bay," Ohio-Lake Erie, inked
date Saturday, Aug. 31, 1901
. . . . **18.00**
Fly to Dayton, orange and blue
aircraft against pale blue sky, dark
blue silhouette of city spires, 1929
copyright, Dayton Ohio Chamber
of Commerce **35.00**
Indian Motorcycles, Hendee Mfg
Co., Springfield, Mass,
multicolored trademark grinning
Indian, red lettering, c1920 . **75.00**
International Auto Sight Seeing
Transit Co., Touring Interior Public
Buildings, black and white center
image of Washington primitive
motor tour bus in front of Capitol
dome, early 1900s **30.00**
Lusitania-Mauertania Hand
Baggage, 1" d, multicolored. **65.00**
Rotary Yacht Contest, silver and blue
design, center white boat sails,
c1920 . . . . **8.00**
Wembley Speedway Supporters
Club, diecut brass, alternating
white, cranberry porcelain enamel,
griffin-like lion symbol, reverse
names London maker, bar pin
fastener **35.00**
Print, 26" x 22", Empress of Britain,
Canadian steamship, orig titled mat and
frame, c1950 . . . . **25.00**
Scooter, 31" l, wooden, orig finish
. . . . **115.00**
Sign, Cunard Line, tin, ocean liner in
New York Bay, Statue of Liberty in
background, *Berengaria*, sgd on lower
right corner "Bishop 1924," 43-1/2" x
34" **320.00**
Stickpin
Anchor Buggy Co., miniature naval
anchor symbol, brass. **15.00**
BSA Motorcycle, small brass rect,
dark green porcelain enamel, sack
of three crossed rifles above
England, 1930s **30.00**
Cutting Motor Car, diecut thin brass
cursive lettering, brass stickpin,
c1910-12 . . . . **45.00**
Zeppelin Flight Commemorative,
silvered metal pin, blue porcelain
enamel highlights, dark silver
profile of airship, German
inscription "Auch im Zeppelin/Mut
Der Hapag," 1920s. **75.00**
Stock certificate, Brooklyn Rapid
Transit Co., engraved, rear of street car
vignette, c1910 . . . . : **35.00**

Stud
Crescent Bicycles, black text,
orange crescent moon, white
ground. **6.00**
Gendron Bicycle, white text, black
star **8.00**

Tobacco tin, Hi-Plane Smooth Cut
Tobacco, four-engine plane, red ground,
vertical pocket type, **$600**. Photo cour-
tesy of Bear Pen Auction.

Hoffman Bicycles/Triangular
Reinforced Frames, purple and
white **10.00**
Keating Bicycles, multicolored
celluloid on metal **12.00**
Tribune/The Cyclodial Sprocket, red
and blue text, white ground . . **8.00**
Yellow Fellow, Journal Examiner
Trans-Continental Relay Souvenir,
bicycle race sponsored by Hearst
newspapers. **35.00**
Tape measure, Souvenir of Florida,
multicolored celluloid canister, silvered
tin perimeter wall, each side with choice
color image of ripe orange, white buds,
green leaves, blue ground, cloth tape,
c1930 . . . . **5.00**
Ticket, 3-1/4" x 5-1/2", passenger,
Hindenburg, U.S. to Germany flight in
connection with Transatlantic Airship
Demonstration, 1936, inked name,
unused **125.00**
Tie clasp, 2-1/2" w, silvered brass
spring clip suspending matching chain
holding miniature 1/2" h dark pewter
luster Indian head pendant, wearing
feathered war bonnet, for Indian Cycle
Co., c1930 . . . . **45.00**

Trade label, 9-1/2" x 10-3/4", Atlantic
Sugar Corn, gouache, watercolor, and
graphite on paper, two funnel steamer
Atlantic in full sail, "Packed by Atlantic
Canning Company, Atlantic, Iowa" in
lower margin, repaired losses and
tears, scattered retouch, hinged and
partly taped to mat, minor flaking
. . . . **920.00**
Vase, 10-1/2" h, *Normandie*, silvered
metal, trumpet form, sq base with
beaded foot, Compagnie generale
Translantique monogram, imp "E.
Brandt" and "G. Bastard" **1,200.00**

TRUNKS

History: Trunks are portable containers that clasp
shut and are used for the storage or transportation of
personal possessions. Normally "trunk" means the
ribbed flat- or domed-top models of the second half of
the 19th century.

References: Roseann Ettinger, *Trunks, Traveling
Bags and Satchels,* Schiffer, 1998; Helenka Gulshan,
Vintage Luggage, Phillip Wilson Publishers, 1998;
Martin and Maryann Labuda, *Price & Identification
Guide to Antique Trunks,* published by authors, 1980;
Jacquelyn Peake, *How to Recognize and Refinish
Antiques for Pleasure and Profit,* 3rd ed., Globe
Pequot Press (P.O. Box 833, Old Saybrook, CT
06475), 1995.

Notes: Unrestored trunks sell for between $50 and
$150. Refinished and relined, the price rises to $200
to $400, with decorators being a principal market.

Early trunks frequently were painted, stenciled,
grained, or covered with wallpaper. These are collected
for their folk-art qualities and, as such, demand high
prices.

Chinese, brass bound camphor wood,
19th C, minor imperfections
16" h, 36" w, 18" d, polychrome
foliate dec on top, nailhead trim
. . . . **1,035.00**
16-1/2" h, 36-1/4" w, 18-1/4" d,
nailhead dec, monogrammed
brass plaque **865.00**
Dome top
11" h, 24" w, 13" d, paint dec, poplar,
top with central floral device within
yellow and green painted oval
bordered by green, tan, and black,
front initialed "PG" within foliate
painted escutcheon rimmed by
painted oval, light tan background,
New England, early 19th C
. . . . **1,035.00**
11-1/2" h, 28" w, 14" d, paint dec,
black painted ground, central
vined pinwheel bordered by
meandering floral and arched
vines, front with tassel and drape

border, central MA, early 19th C **1,035.00**

19" l, fabric on wood, worn painted dec in ivory and green, red border designs and flowers, interior lined with green marbleized paper, worn **425.00**

28" w, 14" d, 12" h, grain painted, ext. covered with yellow and burnt sienna fanciful graining with green and yellow bordering simulating inlay, orig surface, some hardware missing, New England, early 19th C **260.00**

32-1/2" w, 20" d, 20" h, orig red grained paint with small yellow initial "R" at center, dovetailed pine, molded base, canted sides, interior till and lock with domed lid, iron handles on either end, minor insect

holes in base, small areas of touch-up **385.00**

33-1/4" w, 16-1/4" d, 18-3/4" h, black japanned brass mounts, gilt Chinoisiere dec of figures in garden landscape, side handles, late 18th/early 19th C, restoration **750.00**

44-1/2" w, 22-3/4" d, 19-1/2" h, hinged top, dovetailed box, white painted vine, floral and leaf dec over black painted ground, int. papered with early 19th C Boston area broadsides, attributed to MA, 19th C, some later paint . . **1,035.00**

Flat top

14" x 8", Chinese, pigskin, red, painted Oriental maidens and landscapes within quatrefoils, brass loop handles and lock, 19th C **125.00**

15-1/4" l, tooled leather on pine, iron straps, brass buttons and lock, lined with worn newspaper dated 1871, hinged replaced, some edge damage **385.00**

29-1/4" x 15-1/2" x 16-1/4", tin over wood, brass banded ends, wood rim, int. shelf missing **100.00**

Military, 21-3/4" w, 17" d, 12-1/2" h, brass bound camphor wood, hinged rect top, storage well, brass bail handles, English, second half 19th C **200.00**

Steamer

21-3/4" h, 45" w, 21-1/2" d, Louis Vuitton, early 20th C, pigskin lining **2,100.00**

40-3/4" w, 22" d, 13" h, brass bound, Louis Vuitton, "LV" device, late 19th/early 20th C **1,380.00**

Flat top, wood rim, brass banding on ends, 16-1/4" x 29-1/4" x 15-1/2", $120. Photo courtesy of Joy Luke Auctions.

Camel back, blue, wooden strapping. $150. Photo courtesy of Joy Luke Auctions.

VAL ST.-LAMBERT

History: Val St.-Lambert, a 12th-century Cistercian abbey, was located during different historical periods in France, Netherlands, and Belgium (1930 to present). In 1822, Francois Kemlin and Auguste Lelievre, along with a group of financiers, bought the abbey and opened a glassworks. In 1846, Val St.-Lambert merged with the Socété Anonyme des Manufactures de Glaces, Verres à Vitre, Cristaux et Gobeletaries. The company bought many other glassworks.

Val St.-Lambert developed a reputation for technological progress in the glass industry. In 1879, Val St.-Lambert became an independent company employing 4,000 workers. The firm concentrated on the export market, making table glass, cut, engraved, etched, and molded pieces, and chandeliers. Some pieces were finished in other countries, e.g., silver mounts were added in the United States.

Val St.-Lambert executed many special commissions for the artists of the Art Nouveau and Art Deco periods. The tradition continues. The company also made cameo-etched vases, covered boxes, and bowls. The firm celebrated its 150th anniversary in 1975.

Ashtray, 6" w, hexagon, colorless crystal **35.00**
Candlesticks, pr, 9-1/2" h, colorless crystal, orig paper labels **250.00**
Compote, 3-1/2" d, amberina, ruby rim, mottled glass bow, applied amber foot and handles **175.00**

Atomizer, cut glass, green, bulb missing, marked "Val St. Lambert for Saks," 6" h, $165.

Epergne, 19-1/4" h, 17" w, colorless crystal, marked "Val St Lambert Belgique," plated pot metal base
. . . . **550.00**
Figure
   3-1/4" h, soccer ball on pedestal, colorless crystal, sgd "Val St. Lambert" **125.00**
   3-1/2" d base, 7-1/4" h, parrot perched on bell, light cranberry, sgd "Val St Lambert, Belgique"
. . . . **275.00**
   4" l, 2" w, 2" h, cat, black, acid script signature, artist's name, orig paper label **110.00**
   6" l, 3-1/4" w, 3-1/4" h, cat, colorless crystal, acid script signature, artist's name, orig paper label
. . . . **150.00**
Paperweight
   4" h, apple, colorless crystal, acid etched script signature **85.00**
   5-1/2" h, pear, colorless crystal, acid etched script signature **85.00**
Vase
   6-1/2" d, 7-3/4" h, free-form cylindrical shape, exterior moldings twisted around stylized foliate motif, colorless crystal with very slight yellow cast, orig paper label, acid etched script signature
. . . . **175.00**
   8-3/4" d, 12" h, emerald and colorless crystal **550.00**

VALENTINES

History: Early cards were handmade, often containing both handwritten verses and hand-drawn pictures. Many cards also were hand colored and contained cutwork.

Mass production of machine-made cards featuring chromolithography began after 1840. In 1847, Esther Howland of Worcester, Massachusetts, established a company to make valentines which were hand decorated with paper lace and other materials imported from England. They had a small "H" stamped in red in the top left corner. Howland's company eventually became the New England Valentine Company (N.E.V. Co.).

The company George C. Whitney and his brother founded after the Civil War dominated the market from the 1870s through the first decades of the 20th century. They bought out several competitors, one of which was the New England Valentine Company.

Lace paper was invented in 1834. The golden age of lacy cards took place between 1835 and 1860.

Embossed paper was used in England after 1800. Embossed lithographs and woodcuts developed between 1825 and 1840, and early examples were hand colored.

There was a big revival in the 1920s by large companies, like R. Tuck in England, which did lots of

beautiful cards for its 75th Diamond Jubilee; 1925 saw changes in card production, especially for children with paper toys of all sorts, all very collectible now. Little girls were in short dresses, boys in short pants, which helps date that era of valentines. There was an endless variety of toy types of paper items, many companies created similar items and many stayed in production until World War II paper shortages stopped production both here and abroad.

References: Robert Brenner, *Valentine Treasury*, Schiffer Publishing, 1997; Dan & Pauline Campanelli, *Romantic Valentines*, L-W Book Sales, 1996; Roberta B. Etter, *Tokens of Love*, Abbeville Press, 1990; Katherine Kreider, *One Hundred Years of Valentines*, Schiffer, 1999.

Collectors' Club: National Valentine Collectors Association, P.O. Box 1404, Santa Ana, CA 92702.

Adviser: Evalene Pulati.

Embossed, c1860-70, 7" l, 5-1/4" h, **$30.**

Animated, large
   Felix, half tone, German **25.00**
   Jumping Jack, Tuck, 1900 . . . **65.00**
Bank True Love note, England, 1865
. . . . **75.00**
Bank of Love note, Nister, 1914 **38.00**
Charm string
   Brundage, three pcs **45.00**
   Four hearts, ribbon **45.00**
Comic
   Sheet, 8" x 10", Park, London . **25.00**
   Sheet, 9" x 14", McLoughlin Co., USA, 1915 . . . . **20.00**
   Woodcut, Strong, USA, 1845 . **25.00**
Diecut foldout
   Brundage, flat, cardboard . . . **25.00**
   Cherubs, two pcs **40.00**
   Clapsaddle, 1911 . . . . **60.00**
Documentary
   Passport, love, 1910 . . . . **45.00**
   Wedding certificate, 1914 . . . **45.00**
English Fancy, from "Unrequited Love Series"
   8" x 10", aquatint, couple, wedding
. . . . **135.00**
   8" x 10", aquatint, girl and grandmother **95.00**

German,
diecut
stand-up,
6-3/4" x
3-3/4"
$20.

Engraved
5" x 7", American, verse......**35.00**
8" x 10" sheet, English, emb, pg
.....................**65.00**
8" x 10" sheet, English, hand colored
.....................**45.00**

Handmade
Calligraphy, envelope, 1885 .**135.00**
Cutwork, hearts, 6" x 6", 1855
.....................**250.00**
Fraktur, cutwork, 1800......**950.00**
Pen and ink loveknot, 1820 ..**275.00**
Puzzle, purse, 14" x 14", 1855
.....................**450.00**
Theorem, 9" x 14", c1885....**325.00**
Woven heart, hand, 1840 ....**55.00**

Honeycomb
American, kids, tunnel of love .**48.00**
American, wide-eyed kids, 9" .**40.00**
German, 1914, white and pink, 11"
.....................**75.00**
Simple, 1920, Beistle, 8" **18.00**

Lace paper
American, B & J Cameo Style
Large.................**75.00**
Small, 1865.............**45.00**
American, layered, McLoughlin Co.,
c1880 ....**35.00**
Cobweb center, c1855 .....**250.00**
English, fancy
3" x 5", 1865 ....**35.00**
5" x 7", 1855 ....**75.00**
8" x 10", 1840 ....**135.00**
Hand Layered, scraps, 1855..**65.00**
Layered, in orig box 1875, Howland
.....................**75.00**
1910, McLoughlin Co.....**45.00**
Orig box, c1890...........**55.00**
Simple, small pc, 1875 .....**22.50**

Tiny mirror center, 4" x 6" **75.00**
Whitney, 1875, 5" x 7" **35.00**
Novelty, American Fancy, c1900,
originally sold in a box
5" x 7-1/2", mat, fancy corners,
parchment, orig box.....**32.50**
7-1/2" x 10", rect, panel with silk,
celluloid, orig box........**45.00**
10-1/2" x 10", star shape, silk
rusching, orig box **55.00**
16" x 10-1/2", oblong, satin, celluloid,
orig box **65.00**
Pulldown, German
Airplane, 1914, 8" x 14"....**175.00**
Auto, 1910, 8" x 11" x 4" **150.00**
Car and kids, 1920s **35.00**
Dollhouse, large, 1935 ......**45.00**
Rowboat, small, honeycomb paper
puff **65.00**
Seaplane, 1934, 8" x 9".....**75.00**
Tall Ship, 8" x 16"..........**175.00**
Silk fringed
Prang, double sided, 3" x 5".. **24.00**
Triple layers, orig box **38.00**
Standup novelty
Cupid, orig box............**45.00**
Hands, heart, without orig box **35.00**
Parchment
Banjo, small, with ribbon
.....................**65.00**
Violin, large, boxed **125.00**

VALLERYSTHAL GLASS

History: Vallerysthal
(Lorraine), France, has
been a
glass-producing center
for centuries. In 1872,
two major factories,
Vallerysthal
glassworks and
Portieux glassworks,
merged and produced art glass until 1898. Later,
pressed glass animal-covered dishes were introduced.
The factory continues to operate today.

Animal dish, cov
Hen on nest, opaque aqua, sgd
.....................**75.00**
Rabbit, white, frosted **65.00**
Swan, blue opaque glass... **100.00**
Box, cov, 5" x 3", cameo, dark green,
applied and cut dec, sgd **950.00**
Butter dish, cov, turtle, opaque white,
snail finial.................**100.00**
Candlesticks, pr, Baroque pattern,
amber **75.00**
Compote, 6-1/4" sq, blue opaque glass
.....................**75.00**

Dish, cov, figural, lemon, opaque white,
sgd........................**70.00**
Mustard, cov, swirled ribs, scalloped
blue opaque, matching cover with slot
for spoon **35.00**
Plate, 6" d, Thistle pattern, green **65.00**

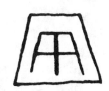

*Salt, cobalt blue, ram's head, three feet,
2-1/2" d, 1-1/2" h, marked,* **$45.**

Salt, cov, hen on nest, white opal
.........................**65.00**
Sugar, cov, 5" h, Strawberry pattern,
opaque white, gold trim, salamander
finial **85.00**
Toothpick holder, hand holding ribbed
vessel, opaque blue...........**30.00**
Tumbler, 4" h, blue............**40.00**
Vase, 8" h, flared folded burgundy red
rim, oval pale green body, matching red
enamel berry bush on front, inscribed
"Vallerysthal" on base **490.00**

VAN BRIGGLE POTTERY

History: Artus Van
Briggle, born in 1869, was a talented Ohio artist. He
joined Rookwood in 1887 and studied in Paris under
Rookwood's sponsorship from 1893 until 1896. In
1899, he moved to Colorado for his health and
established his own pottery in Colorado Springs in
1901.
Van Briggle's work was heavily influenced by the
Art Nouveau schools he had seen in France. He
produced a great variety of matte-glazed wares in this
style. Colors varied.
Artus died in 1904. Anne Van Briggle continued
the pottery until 1912.

Marks: The "AA" mark, a date, and "Van Briggle"
were incised on all pieces prior to 1907 and on some
pieces into the 1920s. After 1920, "Colorado Springs,
Colorado" or an abbreviation was added. Dated pieces
are the most desirable.

References: Richard Sasicki and Josie Fania,
Collector's Encyclopedia of Van Briggle Art Pottery,

Collector Books, 1993, 2000 value update; David Rago, *American Art Pottery*, Knickerbocker Press, 1997.

Collectors' Clubs: American Art Pottery Assoc., 125 E. Rose Ave., St. Louis, MO 63119; Van Briggle Collectors Society, 600 S. 21st St., Colorado Springs, CO 80901, http://www.vanbriggle.com.

Museum: Pioneer Museum, Colorado Springs, CO.

Reproduction Alert: Van Briggle pottery still is made today. These modern pieces often are mistaken for older examples. Among the glazes used are Moonglo (off white), Turquoise Ming, Russet, and Midnight (black).

Bowl

4-1/2" d, 3-1/4" h, fine leathery robin's egg blue and charcoal glaze, incised mark, 1905 . . . . . . **690.00**

6-1/4" d, 3-1/4" h, No, 735, flaring shoulder, interlocking and repeating rig and X raised in relief on body, tapering to cylindrical foot, dark blue mottled matte glaze, incised mark **390.00**

Chamberstick, 5-1/2" h, molded-leaf shape, hood over candle socket, green glaze **115.00**

Figure, 7" h, female nude holding shell, matte Persian blue glaze, incised "Van Briggle" **250.00**

Left and right: boudoir lamps, maroon, original shades, $250 for pair, center: vases, turquoise, 9" h, late, $70 for pair. Photo courtesy of Joy Luke Auctions.

Night light, 8-1/2" h, figural, stylized owl, bulb cavity, light refracting glass eyes, turquoise blue matte glaze, unsgd **425.00**

Sconce, owl

3" d, 6" h, matte green glaze, incised mark, 1916, fittings missing, glaze scaling **435.00**

3-3/4" d, 9-1/2" h, Persian Rose glaze, incised mark, rewired **400.00**

Vase, embossed poppies, turquoise matte glaze, incised "AA/1916," 7-1/2" h, 4" d, $850. Photo courtesy of David Rago Auctions, Inc.

Tile, 18" x 12", six tile frieze, cuenca with stylized trees against blue sky, framed **250.00**

Vase

4-1/4" d, 9-1/2" h, Lorelie, Persian Rose glaze, incised mark, c1920, very small base chip **860.00**

5-1/2" d, 16" h, Climbing for Honey, two bears hugging rim, blue and turquoise matte glaze, 1920s, marked "AA VAN BRIGGLE/USA" **3,220.00**

7-1/4" d, 9-1/2" h, bulbous, Persian Rose glaze, band of flowers around rim, incised mark **460.00**

8-1/2" d, 16-1/2" h, emb with iris and broad leaves, turquoise, green, and blue matte glaze, buff clay body showing through, incised "AA/VAN BRIGGLE/Colo. Spgs/723," c1908-11 . . . **7,475.00**

9-1/4" h, Lorelei, woman wrapped around rim, cadmium yellow matte glaze, restoration to small base chip, incised "AA/VAN BRIGGLE/ COLO. SPRINGS" **3,000.00**

Vessel, squatty, modeled with poppy pods, fine burgundy matte glaze, 1906, incised "AA/Van Briggle/1906," 3-1/2" x 6", $1,150. Photo courtesy of David Rago Auctions.

10" h, corset, shape No. 671, emb stylized iris, smooth microcrystalline French blue matte glaze, clay showing through, incised "AA/Van Briggle/ Colo.Spgs.671," c1908-11 . **850.00**

Vessel, 6" d, 3-1/2" h, squatty, modeled with poppy pods, fine burgundy matte glaze, incised "AA/Van Briggle/1906" **1,150.00**

VENETIAN GLASS

History: Venetian glass has been made on the island of Murano, near Venice, since the 13th century. Most of the wares are thin walled. Many types of decoration have been used: embedded gold dust, lace work, and applied fruits or flowers.

Reference: Sheldon Barr, *Venetian Glass, Confections in Glass, 1855-1914,* Harry N. Abrams, Inc., 1998.

Periodical: *Verti: Italian Glass News,* P.O. Box 191, Fort Lee, NJ 07024.

Reproduction Alert: Venetian glass continues to be made today.

Beverage set, 10-1/2" h, pitcher, applied striped handle, eight flared tumblers, six spherical glasses, each striped with opaque orange, transparent yellow-amber, and clear crystal, design attributed to Fulvio Bianconi, 15-pc set **1,950.00**

Paperweight, blue and gold-stone decoration, millefiori accents, crystal base, 13" h, $215.

Bowl, 7-1/2" w, 6-1/8" w, deep quatraform bowl, applied quatraform rim, blue, clear internal dec, trapped air bubble square, circles, and gold inclusions, c1950 . . . . **360.00**

Candlesticks, pr, 8-3/8" h, white and black glass, formed as coat on twisted stem coat rack on tripod base, black domed foot, 20th C **275.00**

Centerpiece set, two 8-1/2" baluster ftd ewers, 78-1/2" ftd compote, red and white latticino stripes with gold flecks, applied clear handles and feet, three-pc set **150.00**

Decanter, 13" h, figural clown, bright red, yellow, black, and white, aventurine swirls, orig stopper **250.00**

Goblet, 7" h, etched, enameled biblical scenes **200.00**

Sherbet, 4" d, 4-1/2" h, ruby bowl, clear stem, gold knob **195.00**

Sherry, amber swirled bowls, blue beaded stems, eight-pc set **495.00**

Table garniture, two 14-1/4" h clear glass dolphins on white diagonally fluted short pedestals, six 5-3/4" h to 7-3/4" h clear glass turtle, bird, seahorse, dolphin, two bunches of fruit in bowls, figures on similar white pedestals, including 20th C **550.00**

Vase, 8" h, handkerchief shape, pale green and white pulled stripe, applied clear rope base, attributed to Barovier, 1930s **65.00**

Wine goblet, 8" h, amber conical bowl, bifurcate ribbed stem topped by pierced bird, flattened pincered knob, spreading foot, early 20th C **60.00**

VILLEROY & BOCH

History: Pierre Joseph Boch established a pottery near Luxembourg, Germany, in 1767. Jean Francis, his son, introduced the first coal-fired kiln in Europe and perfected a water-power-driven potter's wheel.

Pierre's grandson, Eugene Boch, managed a pottery at Mettlach; Nicholas Villeroy also had a pottery nearby.

In 1841, the three potteries merged into the firm of Villeroy & Boch. Early production included a hard-paste earthenware comparable to English ironstone. The factory continues to use this hard-paste formula for its modern tablewares.

References: Susan and Al Bagdade, *Warman's English & Continental Pottery & Porcelain*, 3rd ed., Krause Publications, 1998; Gary Kirsner, *Mettlach Book*, 3rd ed., Glentiques (P.O. Box 8807, Coral Springs, FL 33075), 1994.

Additional Listings: Mettlach.

Beaker, 1/4 liter, figural decoration, price for pair, **$100.** *Photo courtesy of Joy Luke Auctions.*

Beaker, quarter liter, couple at feast, multicolored, printed underglaze **115.00**

Bowl, 8" d, 3-3/4" h, gaudy floral dec, blue, red, green, purple, and yellow, marked "Villeroy & Boch," minor wear and stains **50.00**

Charger, 15-1/2" d, gentleman on horseback, sgd "Stocke" **600.00**

Dish, cov, triangular, orange and black dec, marked "Villeroy & Boch, Mettlach," and "Made in Saar-Basin," molded "3865," c1880-1900 . . . **125.00**

Ewer, 17-3/4" h, central frieze of festive beer hall, band playing white couples dance and drink, neck and foot with formal panels between leaf molded borders, subdued tones, c1884, imp shape number, production number and date codes **900.00**

Figure, 53" h, Venus, scantily clad seated figure, ribbon tied headdress, left arm raised across chest, resting on rock, inscribed "Villeroy & Boch," damage to foot and base **1,900.00**

Charger, village scene, marked "Villeroy & Boch/Mettlach/Gesehutzt, Remagen Dec 158" impressed "1044," 12-3/4" l, **$275**

Jardiniere, 13" d, 12-1/2" h, maidens in field scene, marked "Villeroy & Boch" and Mettlach castle mark, early 1900s **895.00**

Platter

9-1/4" l, 8" w, white basketweave ground, blue fish and aquatic plants dec, marked "Villeroy & Boch, Delphin, Mettlach, Ceschutzt" **110.00**

12-3/4" d, Burgenland, dark pink transfer, white ground **165.00**

Stein, #2942, liter pewter lid, brown ground, beige earthenware cartouche "Braun ist meine Maid, Schaumt uber jeder-zeit," Jewish Star of David on reverse, marked "Villery & Boch/Mettlach, 7 02" **275.00**

Tray, 11-1/4" d, metal gallery with geometric cut-outs, ceramic base with border and stylized geometric pattern, white ground, soft gray high gloss glaze, blue accents, base marked **200.00**

Tureen, cov, 11" w, Burgenland, dark pink transfer, white ground, marked "Mettlach, Made by Villeroy & Boch" **195.00**

Vase, 15" h, bulbous, cylindrical, deep cobalt blue glaze, splashes of drizzled white, three handled SP mount cast with leaves, berries, and blossoms, molded, pierced foot, vase imp "V" & "B," "S" monogram, numbered, c1900, price for pr **2,750.00**

WARWICK

History: Warwick China Manufacturing Co., Wheeling, West Virginia, was incorporated in 1887 and remained in business until 1951. The company was one of the first manufacturers of vitreous glazed wares in the United States. Production was extensive and included tableware, garden ornaments, and decorative and utilitarian items.

Pieces were hand painted or decorated with decals. Collectors seek portrait items and fraternal pieces from groups such as the Elks, Eagles, and Knights of Pythias.

Some experimental, eggshell-type porcelain was made before 1887. A few examples are found in the antiques market.

Reference: John R. Rader, Sr., *Warwick China*, Schiffer Publishing, 2000.

Bowl, swirled edge, painted violet and blue flowers, cream ground, raised gold branches and accents, crossed swords mark. **35.00**

Bread and butter plate, Silver Poppy **12.00**

Chocolate pot, cov, 7-1/2" h, cherries design **65.00**

Cup and saucer
   Chateau pattern **10.00**
   NPM1 . . . . **9.00**

Dinner plate
   Garlands of pink roses, gold trim, 9" d, c1900 . . . . **20.00**
   NPM1 . . . . **12.00**
   Regency, rim wear **14.00**
   Silver Moon **18.00**
   Vienna **15.00**

Dresser tray, 10" l, 6" w, fluted, small blue and yellow flowers, pale blue and yellow ground, marked "Warwick China" **35.00**

Pitcher, white ground, pink and yellow roses, green leaves, gold trim, **$75.**

Fruit bowl
   NPM1 . . . . **8.00**
   Silver Poppy **8.00**
Gravy boat, Silver Moon **25.00**
Pitcher, 9-1/2" h, poppies, IOGA mark **120.00**

Plate
   8-1/4" d, swimming fish decal . **50.00**
   10" d, coach scene, yellow and gold bands **95.00**
Platter, 15" l, raised matte gold ribbed border design, scalloped trim, green helmet mark **45.00**
Portrait plate, 9-1/2" d, Chief Grant Richards, green IOGA mark with knight and crossed swords mark **85.00**
Salad plate, 7-1/4" d, palm trees with red flowers, red border, marked "Warwick China, Made in USA, 1940" **24.00**

Soup bowl
   Restaurant Ware, brown wave-like border, c1948 . . . . **8.00**
   Silver Moon **12.00**
   Silver Poppy **10.00**

Urn, roses decoration, brown ground, two handles, marked "IOGA," 10" h, **$125.**

Spirit jug, 6" h, Dickens character with guitar, shaded brown ground **95.00**
Tankard, monk filling tankard from keg, Warwick IOGA backstamp with helmet and crossed swords, chip on back **50.00**
Tray, 11-1/4" l, scattered bunches of pink and red roses, gold rim, open handles **25.00**
Vase
   9-1/2" h, bulbous oval base, narrow neck, flared rim with gold outline, two tapered loop handles, open

red flower, green leaves, shaded brown ground, IOGA mark. **155.00**
   10-1/2" h, red roses, blue-green ground **95.00**
Wash pitcher, 12-1/2" h, transfer print, hand tinted blue, yellow, green and brown transparent glaze, spout and handle with emb gold leaves . . **200.00**

WATCHES, POCKET

History: Pocket watches can be found in many places—from flea markets to the specialized jewelry auctions. Condition of movement is the first priority; design and detailing of the case is second.

Descriptions of pocket watches may include the size (16/0 to 20), number of jewels in the movement, whether the face is open or closed (hunter), and the composition (gold, gold filled, or some other metal). The movement is the critical element, since cases often were switched. However, an elaborate case, especially if gold, adds significantly to value.

Pocket watches designed to railroad specifications are desirable. They are between 16 and 18 in size, have a minimum of 17 jewels, adjust to at least five positions, and conform to many other specifications. All are open faced.

Study the field thoroughly before buying. There is a vast amount of literature, including books and newsletters from clubs and collectors.

References: T. P. Camerer Cuss, *Antique Watches*, Antique Collectors' Club, 1999; Roy Ehrhardt, *European Pocket Watches*, Book 2, Heart of America Press, 1993; Roy Ehrhardt and Joe Demsey, *Cartier Wrist & Pocket Watches*, Clocks, Heart of America Press, 1992; ——, *Patek Phillipe*, Heart of America Press, 1992; ——, *American Pocket Watch Serial Number Grade Book*, Heart of America Press, 1993; Alan Sherman, *Pocket Watches of the 19th and 20th Century*, Antique Collectors' Club, 1999; Cooksey Shugart and Richard E. Gilbert, *Complete Price Guide to Watches*, No. 20, Collector Books, 2000.

Periodicals: *International Wristwatch*, 89 Parkway, Regent's Park, Stamford, CT NW1 7PP UK; *The Premium Watch Watch*, 24 San Rafael Drive, Rochester, NY 14618; *Vintage Wrist Watch Report*, P.O. Box 74, Evansville, WI 53536; *Watch & Clock Review*, 2403 Champa St., Denver, CO 80205.

Collectors' Clubs: American Watchmakers-Clockmakers Institute, 701 Enterprise Drive, Harrison, OH 45030-1696, http://www.awi-net.org; American Watchmakers Institute Chapter #102, P.O. Box 933, Hilton, NY 14468; British Watch & Clock Collectors Assoc., 5 Cathedral Lane, Truro, Cornwall TR1 2SQ UK, http://www.timecap.co.uk; Early American Watch Club Chapter #149, P.O. Box 5499, Beverly Hills, CA 90210; National Assoc. of Watch & Clock Collectors, 514 Poplar St., Columbia, PA 17512, http://www.nawcc.org; Pocket Horology, Chapter #174, http://www.pocketwatch.org.

Museums: American Clock & Watch Museum, Bristol, CT; Hoffman Clock Museum, Newark, NY; National Assoc. of Watch and Clock Collectors

Museum, Columbia, PA; Timexpo Museum, Waterbury, CT.

Abbreviations:

gf gold filled
j jewels
S size
yg yellow gold

Lady's, gold filled case, **$190.**

Lapel, lady's

Unknown maker, 18kt gold and enamel, cream porcelain dial with Roman numerals, gold fancy scroll hands, jeweled gilt movement, cylinder escapement, back cover with cobalt blue enamel and gold fleur-de-lis, woven watch chain with enamel and seed pearl barrel-shape slides, onyx fob and key, back cover detached
. . . . **450.00**

Pendant, lady's

Edwardian, octagonal-shaped pendant, one side with classical female framed in rose-cut diamonds, other side with goldtone dial with black Arabic numerals, all over green and white enamel dec, some enamel loss
. . . . **1,380.00**

Eterna, 18k yg, rushed gold, rect form, black line indicators, hallmark, 23.10 dwt. **230.00**

Figural, insect, 18k yg, rose-cut diamond accents, blue enamel hinged wings opening to reveal white dial, Roman numerals, flat 23-1/2" trace link chain **4,500.00**

Pocket, gentleman's

Audemars, 18 kt gold, hunting case, white enamel dial with Arabic numerals, Louis XIV hands, jeweled nickel movement, monogrammed case, 16 size **980.00**

Baree, Neuchatel, No. 18332, 14k yg, repeater, Roman numerals, subsidiary dial for seconds, hairline to dial **500.00**

Bautte, Jq Fd. Geneve, 18k yg, white dial, Roman numerals, chased case with bi-color floral bouquet on one side, mixed meal and enamel dec on other, scalloped edges, enamel damage
. . . . **260.00**

Bijou Watch Co., lady's label, 14k yg, dec dial with ornate hands, subsidiary seconds hand and dial, diamond-set engraved crescent moon and star on case, 14k yg ribbon shaped watch pin, c1900. . . . . **390.00**

Bourquin, Ami, Locle, #30993, 18 kt yg, key wind, white porcelain dial, black Roman numerals, subsidiary seconds dial, engraved case with black and blue enamel, accented with rose-cut diamonds, fitted wooden box with inlaid dec **1,100.00**

Boutte, #277389, 14k yg, 10 rubies, white dial, black Roman numerals, chased case with red and blue enamel star dec, Russian hallmarks, 29" l ropetwist chain, enamel loss. . . **300.00**

Caldwell, J. E., & Co., openface, 18 kt gold, white enamel dial, black Roman numerals, subsidiary seconds dial, Vacheron and Constantin jeweled movement, cavette dated June 5, 1900, verso monogrammed, 16 size. . **900.00**

Champney, S. P., Worcester, MA, 18k yg, openface, gilt movement, #8063, key wind, white dial, Roman numerals, subsidiary seconds dial, hallmarks, orig

key, c1850, dial cracked, nicks to crystal. **250.00**

Elgin, 14kt gold, hunting case, white porcelain dial, black Arabic numerals, blue-steeled hands, subsidiary seconds dial, 15 jewel nickel movement, monogrammed, 16 size, suspended from 14kt gold curb link watch chain **300.00**

Howard, E., & Co., Boston, 18kt gold, hunting case, white enamel dial, black Roman numerals, blue-steeled scroll hands, subsidiary seconds dial, dust cover inscribed and dated June 6, 1872, monogrammed, 16 size . . **980.00**

Hampden, hunting case, lever set, gold fill, **$195.**

Jacot, Charles E., 18k yg hunter case, nickel jeweled movement, #9562, numbered on dust cov, case and movement, white porcelain dial, Roman numerals, subsidiary dial for seconds, monogrammed case, orig wood case with extra spring, 14k yg chain . **750.00**

Jurgensen, J. Alfred, Copenhagen, #784, 18k yg hunter case, highly jeweled movement, patent 1865, white porcelain dial, subsidiary dial for seconds, fancy hands, elaborate monogram **3,300.00**

L'Epine, Paris, openface, white enamel dial, key wind, tri-color gold engraved case, 8 size, hand missing, chips to dial
. . . . **375.00**

Meylan, C. H., Brassus, openface, 18kt gold, white enamel dial, Arabic numerals, scrolled hands, subsidiary seconds dial, 19 jewel movement, 10 size. **635.00**

Patek Philippe & Co., Geneve, 18k yg, open face, movement and case No. 161442, white dial, Roman numerals, bail missing **575.00**

Pocket, lady's

Meylan, C. H., 18kt gold and enamel, openface, white enamel dial with black Arabic numerals, fancy scrolled hands, gray guilloche enamel bezel, cover enameled with gold flowers set with diamonds, suspended from platinum and purple guilloche enamel baton link chain, crystal replaced, minor enamel loss **850.00**

Unknown maker, retro, pink gold, hinged rect cover surmounted by rubies and diamonds, similarly set scroll and geometric shoulders, snake link bracelet, 6-1/4" l **750.00**

Vacheron & Constantin, 18kt gold, hunting case, white enamel dial, Roman numerals, gilt bar movement, cylinder escapement, sgd on cuvette, engraved case, 10 size **350.00**

WATCHES, WRIST

History: The definition of a wristwatch is simply "a small watch that is attached to a bracelet or strap and is worn around the wrist." However, a watch on a bracelet is not necessarily a wristwatch. The key is the ability to read the time. A true wristwatch allows you to read the time at a glance, without making any other motions. Early watches on an arm bracelet had the axis of their dials, from 6 to 12, perpendicular to the band. Reading them required some extensive arm movements.

The first true wristwatch appeared about 1850. However, the key date is 1880 when the stylish, decorative wristwatch appeared and almost universal acceptance occurred. The technology to create the wristwatch existed in the early 19th century with Brequet's shock-absorbing "Parachute System" for automatic watches and Ardien Philipe's winding stem.

The wristwatch was a response to the needs of the entrepreneurial age with its emphasis on punctuality and planned free time. Sometime around 1930, the sales of wristwatches surpassed that of pocket watches. Swiss and German manufacturers were quickly joined by American makers.

The wristwatch has undergone many technical advances during the 20th century including self-winding (automatic), shock-resistance, and electric movements.

References: Hy Brown and Nancy Thomas, *Comic Character Timepieces*, Schiffer Publishing, 1992; Gisbert L. Brunner and Christian Pfeiffer-Belli, *Wristwatches, A Handbook and Price Guide*, Schiffer Publishing, 1997; James M. Dowling and Jeffrey P. Hess, *The Best of Time: Rolex Wristwatches, An Unauthorized History*, 2nd ed., Schiffer Publishing, 2001; Roy Ehrhardt and Joe Demsey, *Cartier Wrist & Pocket Watches, Clocks*, Heart of America Press, 1992; —, *Patek Phillipe*, Heart of America Press, 1992; —, *Rolex Identification and Price Guide*, Heart of America Press, 1993; Sherry and Roy Ehrhardt and Joe Demesy, *Vintage American & European Wrist Watch Price Guide*, Book 6, Heart of America Press, 1993; Edward Faber and Stewart Unger, *American Wristwatches*, revised ed., Schiffer Publishing, 1997; Heinz Hampel, *Automatic Wristwatches from Switzerland*, Schiffer Publishing, 1997; Helmet Kahlert, Richard Mühe, Gisbert L. Brunner, *Wristwatches: History of a Century's Development*, 4th ed., Schiffer Publishing, 1999; Anton Kreuzer, *Omega Wristwatches*, Schiffer Publishing, 1996; Fritz von

Osterhausen, *Movado History*, Schiffer Publishing, 1996; —, *Wristwatch Chronometers*, Schiffer Publishing, 1997; Benno Richter, *Breitling Timepieces*, Schiffer Publishing, 2000; Cooksey Shugart and Richard E. Gilbert, *Complete Price Guide to Watches*, No. 19, Collector Books, 1999.

Periodical: *International Wrist Watch*, 242 West Ave., Darien, CT 06820.

Collectors' Clubs: International Wrist Watch Collectors Chapter 146, 5901C Westheimer, Houston, TX 77057; National Association of Watch & Clock Collectors, 514 Poplar St., Columbia, PA 17512; The Swatch Collectors Club, P.O. Box 7400, Melville, NY 11747.

Museums: American Clock & Watch Museum, Bristol, CT; Hoffman Clock Museum, Newark, NY; National Association of Watch and Clock Collectors Museum, Columbia, PA; The Time Museum, Rockford, IL.

Gentleman's

Borel, cocktail, 14k yg, 17 jewels, black dial with kaleidoscope like center, goldtone Arabic numerals, abstract indicators, leather Borel strap .. **400.00**

Boucheron, dress tank, A250565, white gold, reeded bezel and dial, invisible clasp, black leather Boucheron strap, French hallmarks, orig leather pouch **2,150.00**

Buccellati, Gianmaria, dress, 18k yg, fancy engrave dial, black tracery enamel, black leather strap, 18k yg clasp, Italian hallmarks **6,900.00**

Cartier, 18k hg, rect convex white dial, black Roman numerals, round gold bezel, black leather strap.... **1,380.00**

Concord, Delirium, 18kt gold, round goldtone dial without indicators, flat rect bezel, quartz movement, Swiss hallmarks, 9" l orig crocodile band **1,265.00**

Garsons, 14kt gold, sq goldtone dial with simulated jewel indicators, 17-jewel nickel movement, subsidiary seconds dial, 8-1/4" l integrated mesh band **345.00**

Jurgensen, Jules, dress, 14k white gold, Swiss movement, silvertone brushed dial, abstract indicators, diamond-set bevel, black faux alligator strap **290.00**

Le Coultre, Futurematic, goldtone dial, subsidiary seconds dial, power reserve indicator, 10k yg-filled mount, lizard strap, 1950s **435.00**

Movado, 14k yg, tank, stepped lugs, slightly bowed sides, goldtone dial, Roman numerals and abstract indicators, subsidiary seconds dial, worn leather strap, crystal loose **230.00**

Gruen Tank, 14K yg, 17 jewel, $65.

Nardin, Ulysse, 14k yg, chronometer, goldtone dial, luminescent quarter sections, applied abstract and Arabic numeral indicators, subsidiary seconds dial, lugs with scroll accents, leather strap, discoloration and scratches to dial. **290.00**

Omega, 18k yg, round cream dial, goldtone Arabic numeral and abstract indicators

Heavy mesh bracelet, mild soil to dial, 44.80 dwt **460.00**
Subsidiary seconds dial.... **225.00**

Philippe, Patek, 18kt white gold, rect, silvertone dial, raised Arabic numerals, 18-jewel nickel movement, eight adjustments, subsidiary seconds dial, triple signed, leather band, c1930 .... **6,900.00**

Rolex, Oyster Perpetual

14k yg, goldtone dial, abstract indicators, sweep second hand, ostrich strap, slight spotting to dial **850.00**

Stainless steel, Air King, silvertone dial, applied abstract indicators, sweep second hand, oyster bracelet with deployant clasp, discoloration to dial, scratches to crystal. **575.00**

Tiffany & Co., 18k yg, lapis lazuli color dial, stepped bezel, black crocodile strap **635.00**

Universal, Geneve, Uni-Compax, 18K yg, two-dial chronograph, silver-tone dial, sweep seconds hand, black lizard strap **980.00**

Vacheron & Constantin, 18kt gold, white round dial, abstract numeral indicators, 17-jewel nickel movements, 7-1/4" l associated 18kt gold brickwork band **1,495.00**

Lady's

Bueche Girod, 18k yg, elongated oval goldtone dial, rect bezel with stylized hinge lucks, satin band, c1970 **. 980.00**

Bucherer, 18k yg, Swiss movement, 17 jewels, designed as double-hinged engraved bangle, center covered watch, cream dial, applied goldtone Arabic and abstract indicators, Swiss hallmarks **165.00**

Cartier, 18kt gold, Pathere, sq goldtone dial with diamond bezel, quartz movement, case and deployment buckle sgd "Cartier," flat rect link band **4,025.00**

Chopard, Geneva, 18kt gold and diamond

Clipped corner rect case, goldtone dial, diamond-set bezel and shoulders, 7-1/4" l flexible flat horizontal link band **850.00**

Oval goldtone dial within larger oval crystal with seven floating collet-set diamonds, diamond-set dial, crystal, and shoulders, 8" l maroon leather band **2,760.00**

Elgin, lady's, 14k yg, MOP dial, black abstract and Arabic numeral indicators, hinged freeform cover with diamonds and cultured pearl accent, tapering link bracelet with mesh edges, 33.80 dwt **500.00**

Hamilton, lady's, 17 jewels, model 750, #72052A, 14K white gold decorated case framed with 17 single cut diamonds, white gold band decorated with 38 single-cut diamonds, replaced clasp, one stone missing, 10.6dwt., $260. Photo courtesy of Sanford Alderfer Auction Co.

Glycine Watch Co., Art Deco, platinum, rect cream-tone dial with black Arabic numerals, bezel, lugs and integral hexagon-link band set with 208 single and full-cut diamonds, sgd 17-jewel movement, 7-1/2" l . . **3,450.00**

Hamilton Watch Co., lady's

Art Deco, bezel and shoulders set with round and baguette diamonds, platinum mount, black chord strap, white gold-filled clasp, minor discoloration to dial **. 460.00**

Dress, silvertone rect dial, applied Arabic numerals, flanked by four graduating collet set diamonds, diamond-set platinum bracelet, 2.16 cts. **2,300.00**

Herna, lady's, 14k yg, 17 jewels, sq cream dial, applied gold indicators, heavy mesh bracelet, 22.70 dwt **320.00**

Le Coultre, Jaeger, 14kt gold, Reverso, silvertone dial with black Arabic numeral indicators, blue-steeled hands, case flips to reveal polished gold monogrammed cover, case sgd and numbered, 8" l tan ostrich leather strap **1,380.00**

Lehman, lady's, Retro, Uti movement, 18k yg, round goldtone dial with ruby indicators, one half framed in graduated calibre-cut channel-set rubies, snake like bracelet, French hallmarks, slight discoloration to dial **1,495.00**

Lucien Piccard, lady's, Retro, 14k yg, MOP dial, Arabic numeral and abstract indicators, framed in channel-set rubies, bracelet of circular links centered by gold discs framed in rubies, orig box **980.00**

Movado, 14kt gold, round, silvertone dial, diamond bezel and lugs, jeweled movement, black suede band**. . 325.00**

Philippe, Patek, 18kt

Gold covered, sq, ivorytone dial with abstract indicators, 20-jewel nickel movement, 6-1/2" l integral mesh band, boxed **1,150.00**

Gold, round, white porcelain dial with black Roman numerals, quartz movement, 7" l integral gold mesh band, orig certificate and box **3,565.00**

White gold, sq silvertone dial with baton indicators, 7-3/4" l black crocodile band, orig Patek Philippe suede pouch **1,955.00**

Rolex, Oyster Perpetual, stainless steel

Crenelated bezel, silvertone dial, abstract indicators, sweep second

hand, magnifying glass on date aperture, jubilee bracelet **1,035.00**

Precision, cream dial, abstract indicators with phosphorescent, subsidiary seconds dial, slight discoloration to dial. **1,380.00**

Swiss, 18k yg, Swiss movement, manual wind, domed bezel, goldtone dial, black Roman numerals, hallmark, leather strap **920.00**

Tiffany & Co., 14kt gold, oval white dial with black Roman numerals, diamond-set bezel, 6-3/4" l flexible flat rect link band **1,150.00**

Tilden and Thurber, 14kt yellow gold, Swiss movement by E. Huguenin, 14kt band with two horse head intaglios with small buckle links, first half 20th C **460.00**

Uti, Paris, Spritzer and Furhmann, lady's, 18k yg, silvertone dial, applied goldtone indicators, leather strap with keyhole form closure, hallmarks, wear to strap **575.00**

WATERFORD

History: Waterford crystal is high-quality flint glass commonly decorated with cuttings. The original factory was established at Waterford, Ireland, in 1729. Glass made before 1830 is darker than the brilliantly clear glass of later production. The factory closed in 1852. One hundred years later it reopened and continues in production today.

Bowl, 9-3/4" d, Kileen pattern . . **260.00**

Cake plate, 10" d, 5-1/4" h, sunburst center, geometric design **85.00**

Cake server, cut-glass handle, orig box **80.00**

Champagne flute, 6" h, Coleen pattern, 12-pc set **450.00**

Christmas ornament, Twelve Days of Christmas Series, crystal, orig box, dated bag, orig sticker, brochure

1982, Partridge in Pear Tree **. 450.00**

1985, second, two turtle doves **250.00**

1986, three French hens **225.00**

1987, four calling birds **200.00**

Claret, Colleen, set of six, orig box **480.00**

Compote, 4-1/4" h, 4-7/8" d, $165.

Compote, 5-1/2" h, all over diamond cutting above double wafer stem, pr
.... **400.00**

Creamer and sugar, 4" h creamer, 3-3/4" d sugar, Tralee pattern ... **85.00**

Decanter, orig stopper
10" h, ship's, diamond cutting
.... **200.00**
12-3/4" h, all over diamond cutting, monogram, pr.......... **300.00**

Honey jar, cov.............. **70.00**

Lamp, 23" h, 13" d umbrella shade, blunt diamond cutting, Pattern L-1122
.... **450.00**

Napkin ring, 2" h, 12-pc set ... **225.00**

Old fashioned tumbler, 3-1/2" h, Comeragh pattern, pr **70.00**

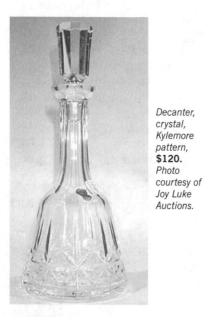

Decanter, crystal, Kylemore pattern, $120. Photo courtesy of Joy Luke Auctions.

Ring dish, 5" d, colorless, cut glass, price for three-pc set **110.00**
Sherry, Colleen, set of six, orig box
.... **360.00**
Tumbler, Colleen, set of six, orig box
.... **400.00**
Vase
6" h, diamond pattern, wreath around center, sgd **195.00**
8" h, crosshatch pattern, sgd
.... **175.00**

WAVE CREST

WAVE CREST WARE

c1892

History: The C. F. Monroe Company of Meriden, Connecticut, produced the opal glassware known as Wave Crest from 1898 until World War I. The company bought the opaque, blown-molded glass blanks from the Pairpoint Manufacturing Co. of New Bedford, Massachusetts, and other glassmakers, including European factories. The Monroe company then decorated the blanks, usually with floral patterns. Trade names used were "Wave Crest Ware," "Kelva," and "Nakara."

References: Wilfred R. Cohen, *Wave Crest*, Collector Books, out-of-print; Elsa H. Grimmer, *Wave Crest Ware*, Wallace-Homestead, out-of-print; Kyle Husfloen, *Antique Trader's American & European Decorative and Art Glass Price Guide*, 2nd ed., Krause Publications, 2000; Carrol Lyle and Whitney Newland, *The C. F. Monroe Co. Catalogue No. 11, 1906-1907*, L & N Associates (P.O. Box 2013, Santa Barbara, CA 93120.)

Collectors' Club: Wave Crest Collectors Club, P.O. Box 2013, Santa Barbara, CA 93120.

Biscuit jar, cov, unmarked
5-1/2" d, 5-1/2" h, pink and white background, melon ribbed, hp flowers................. **250.00**
8" h, blue and white ground, swirled, cherry blossoms dec, lid with handle................. **150.00**
8" h, white ground, fern dec . **200.00**

Bonbon, 7" h, 6" w, Venetian scene, multicolored landscape, dec rim, satin lining missing **1,200.00**

Box, cov
5-1/2" w, man on bended knee proposing to lady, roses, rococo swirls, orig lining **1,300.00**
5-1/2" w, 4-3/4" h, white daisies, green leaves, earth tone details, unmarked **675.00**

7" w, pink florals, fancy ormolu fittings................. **800.00**
7" w, yellow hp ground, blue and lavender daisies, orig lining
.... **1,795.00**
7-1/4" d, 3-3/34" h, Baroque Shell, Moorish Fantasy design, raised pink-gold rococo scrolls, fancy Arabic designs of pale turquoise and natural opaque white, lace-like network of raised white enamel beads, satin lining missing
.... **1,250.00**
7-1/4" d, 3-3/4" h, Moorish Fantasy design, opaque white ground, center geometric design, raised pink-gold rococo scrolls, fancy Arabic turquoise designs, white enamel beads, bright ormolu fittings, satin lining missing
.... **1,250.00**

Cigar humidor, 8-3/4" h, blue body, single-petaled pink rose, pink "Cigar" signature, pewter collar, bail, and lid, flame-shaped finial, sgd "Kelva" **685.00**

Cracker jar, 5-1/4" d, 10-1/2" h, blue and white hp florals, green and brown leaves, white Johnny jump-ups, puffy egg crate mold **700.00**

Dresser box, 5" d, Helmschmied Swirl, tiny flowers dec, unmarked.... **500.00**

Ewer, pink and white ground, multicolored floral decoration, gilt trim, signed, metal spout and base, 15-1/2" h, $550.

Decanter, crystal, Kylemore pattern, $120. Photo courtesy of Joy Luke Auctions.

Ewer, lavender, figural woman on handle, ornate base **225.00**
Ferner, 7-1/2" w, hp white florals, pink tint opalware ground, rococo swirls, brass colored ormolu fittings . . . **650.00**
Jewel stand, 4" d, 3" h, green and white ground, scroll design, pink floral dec, unmarked **90.00**
Mustard jar, cov, spoon, green ground, floral dec, unmarked **140.00**
Pickle castor, 5-1/2" h, white ground, floral dec, fork holder on both sides of SP holder, unmarked **150.00**
Pin dish, open
  3-1/2" d, 1-1/2" h, pink and white, swirled, floral dec, unmarked
  . . . . **35.00**
  4-1/4" d, 2" h, pink and white, eggcrate mold, blue violets dec, marked **80.00**
  5" d, 1-1/2" h, white, scrolls, pink floral dec, marked **80.00**
Plate, 7" d, reticulated border, pond lily dec, shaded pale blue ground. . **750.00**
Salt and pepper shakers, pr
  Swirled, light yellow ground, floral dec, unmarked **75.00**
  Tulip, brown and white ground, birds and floral dec **70.00**
Sugar shaker, 3-1/2" d, 5-1/4" h, Helmschmied Swirl, enameled pink florals, gray and brown foliage. . **575.00**
Syrup pitcher, Helmschmied Swirl, ivory-colored body, blue and white floral dec, smoky-gray leafy branches, SP lid and collar **485.00**
Trinket dish, 1-1/2" x 5", blue and red flowers **175.00**

Vase, 10" h, pale pink accents on white, pink and orange chrysanthemums, enameled foliage, beaded white top
. . . . **600.00**

WEATHER VANES

History: A weather vane indicates wind direction. The earliest known examples were found on late 17th-century structures in the Boston area. The vanes were handcrafted of wood, copper, or tin. By the last half of the 19th century, weather vanes adorned farms and houses throughout the nation. Mass-produced vanes of cast iron, copper, and sheet metal were sold through mail-order catalogs or at country stores.

The champion vane is the rooster—in fact, the name weathercock is synonymous with weather vane—but the styles and patterns are endless. Weathering can affect the same vane differently; for this reason, patina is a critical element in collectible vanes.

Whirligigs are a variation of the weather vane. Constructed of wood and metal, often by the unskilled, whirligigs indicate the direction of the wind and its velocity. Watching their unique movements also provides entertainment.

References: Robert Bishop and Patricia Coblentz, *Gallery of American Weathervanes and Whirligigs*, E. P. Dutton, 1981; Ken Fitzgerald, *Weathervanes and Whirligigs*, Clarkson N. Potter, 1967; A. B. & W. T. Westervelt, *American Antique Weathervanes* (1883 catalog reprint), Dover Publications, 1982.

Reproduction Alert: Reproductions of early models exist, are being aged, and then sold as originals.

Arrow

  32" l, 19" h, acorn and baluster form finial, cast iron arrow top, corrugated sheet copper feathers, verdigris surface, black metal stand, imperfections **920.00**
  37" l, 9-1/4" h, cast-iron arrow point on shaft, sheet copper scrolled ornament, corrugated copper tail, verdigris surface, traces of gilt, with stand, losses, separations
  . . . . **1,035.00**
  39" l, iron, old green repaint on tip and feathers, traces of earlier gilt beneath, contemporary enameled steel base. **935.00**

Bannerette

  25" w, 20" h, gilt copper, initial "G" in banner, frame with flowers, spheres, and scroll, traces of gilt and yellow paint, verdigris surface, attributed to J. W. Fiske, New York, late 19th C, minor imperfections
  . . . . **2,185.00**
  25-1/2" w, 26" h, copper and zinc, old verdigris finish over earlier gilt, pierced geometric designs with an "F" and corner fan at front, four

small applied flowers on stems near top, attributed to Harris, Boston, contemporary black enameled stand, minor dents, small split in tube just below banner. **2,860.00**
Bird and fish, 18-1/2" w, 19" h, molded metal, full bodied, bird flies with aid of propellers above fish, marble eyes, unpainted weathered gray surface, Illinois, early 20th C, tall stand
. . . . **1,150.00**
Eagle, 14-1/2" l, 23-1/2" w, 19" h, molded copper, full bodied, perched on sphere, verdigris finish, America, 19th C, stand, loss, seam separations, dents
. . . . **1,100.00**
Fish
  12-3/4" l, 3-1/4" h, carved wood, full bodied, tail wrapped with lead sheeting, tacked button eyes, Midwestern U.S., late 19th C, remnant of post, minor losses, with stand **2,645.00**
  26" l, 6-1/2" h, white painted carved wood and sheet metal, America, mid-20th C, tall stand . . . **1,495.00**
  27" l, 6" h, carved and painted wood, salmon orange, chamfered edge, tin reinforced carved bracket, Wakefield, MA, 19th C, inscribed "this set on a cedar tree near our farm before the Civil War," with stand **1,150.00**
Heart and feather, 76-3/4" l, 13-1/4" h, sheet iron, found in New York state, late 18th C, fine rust and overall pitting, with stand **4,900.00**
Horse, flying, molded copper, verdigris and partial gilt surface, late 19th C, bullet holes, 24-1/2" l, 19" h . . **1,850.00**
Horse, running, 23" l, 17" h, copper, full bodied, verdigris patina. **1,650.00**

Horse, cast iron, flat, attributed to Massachusetts, c1830, 32" l, $1,500.

Horse, trotting, 26-1/2" l, 16-1/2" h, copper, full bodied, verdigris surface, black metal stand, America, late 19th C, minor dents **4,325.00**

Man on horseback, 20-1/2" w, 19" h, figural sheet steel, areas of old silver paint, pitted surface, arm raised, wide brim hat, contemporary enameled steel stand **1,480.00**

Mink, 24" l, 18-3/4" h, sheet iron, America, 19th C, metal stand, imperfections **4,890.00**

Pig, 32" l, 20-1/4" h, molded copper, weathered dark verdigris surface, traces of gilt, stand, late 19th C, imperfections **32,300.00**

Rooster, 11-3/4" w, 15" h, painted sheet metal, yellow over gilt, America, c1900, imperfections and loss, with stand
. . . . **1,840.00**

Seahorse, 20" l, 10" h, painted sheet metal, cut-out eyes and snout, stand, America, 19th C, corrosion, paint and metal losses **4,325.00**

Whirligig

Band leader, 9" w, 2-1/2" d, 20" h, polychrome carved pine, copper hat, bowtie and buttons, glass eyes, attributed to WI, late 19th C, stand, some paint wear **10,925.00**

Bicycle rider, 19" l, 4-1/2" d, 21" h, painted wood and sheet metal, man with metal wide brimmed hat, red body, high wheel green bicycle activated by blades in wheel, America, early 20th C
. . . . **3,450.00**

Cottage birdhouse, propeller on front, arrow tail in rear, painted cream, green and yellow trim, late 19th/early 20th C, 18" l, 8" w, 13" h **250.00**

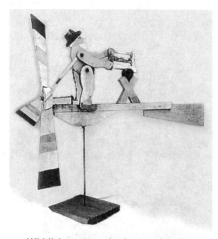

Whirligig, man sawing log, wood, red, white, and blue, c1930, 25-1/4" l, 24-3/4" h, **$150.**

Whirligig, Dutch mill, wood, gray and black paint, weathered surface, 16-1/2" h, **$175.**

Fish and men, 21-3/4" l, 10" d, 13" h, carved and painted tin, propeller activates two men in long coats mounted on silver, black, and red painted fish with tin fins, America, early 20th C, with stand **1,265.00**

Flying fish

17" l, 13-1/2" d, 5-1/2" h, carved and silver painted fish decoy, added tin wings and tail fin, rubber wheels, weathered surface, attributed to Minnesota, mid-20th C, with stand
. . . . **250.00**

25" l, 11" d, 6" h, painted wood and metal, painted blue-green, glass marble eyes, cut-out sheet metal fins and teeth, America, c1940, tall stand, weathered surface, eye missing **575.00**

Hessian soldier, 32-1/4" h, carved wood, c1870-90, paint imperfections, stand. **4,890.00**

Military officer, 12-3/8" h, finely carved figure, Rhode Island, 19th C, traces of paint, hands, and feet damaged, part of metal strap missing **4,025.00**

Policeman, 10" w, 18-1/8" h, polychrome carved pine and tin, mustache and beard, arms constructed with tin at elbows, orig painted surface, America, late 19th C, paddles missing
. . . . **11,500.00**

Trotting horse, tin propeller, horse with articulated legs, painted white, weathered surface, metal stand, 28-1/2" l, 21-1/2" w, 28-1/4" h **375.00**

Uniformed man, 21-1/2" h, carved and painted wood, America, c1870, some paint wear, stand **2,990.00**

WEBB, THOMAS & SONS

History: Thomas Webb & Sons was established in 1837 in Stourbridge, England. The company probably is best known for its very beautiful English cameo glass. However, many other types of colored art glass were produced, including enameled, iridescent, heavily ornamented, and cased.

References: Sean and Johanna S. Billings, *Peachblow Glass, Collector's Identification & Price Guide,* Krause Publications, 2000; Charles R. Hajdamach, *British Glass, 1800-1914,* Antique Collectors' Club, 1991.

Additional Listings: Burmese, Cameo, and Peachblow.

Bowl

5-1/2" w, 5" h, Rainbow MOP satin, triangular, deep pink, yellow, blue, and white, applied thorn feet, raspberry prunt, sgd "Patent"
. . . . **1,500.00**

5-3/4" d, 4-1/2" h, avocado green, sapphire blue stripes, mica flakes, crystal applied fancy drippings on sides, applied crystal rigaree around top edge, applied clear feet, clear berry pontil **235.00**

Fairy lamp, Burmese, garland of stylized purple blossoms, green leaves, gold highlights, interior signed "S. Clarke's Fairy Pyramid Patent Trade Mark," bottom of base with Tunnicliffe mark and 1444A, 6" d base, 4-3/4" h, **$1,250.** *Photo courtesy of Clarence and Betty Maier.*

12" d, 3" h, ruffled, blue ext., cased white int., sgd "Thomas Webb & Sons" **350.00**

Cologne bottle, 6" h, cameo, spherical, clear frosted body, overlaid white and red, carved blossoms, buds, leafy stems, and butterfly, linear pattern, hallmarked silver dec, molded and chased blossoms dec **3,200.00**

Cream pitcher

3-1/4" h, sepia to pale tan ground, heavy gold burnished prunus blossoms, butterfly on back, gold rim and base, clear glass handle with brushed gold **385.00**

3-3/4" h, 2-1/2" d, bulbous, round mouth, brown satin, cream lining, applied frosted handle **210.00**

Ewer, 9" h, 4" d, satin, deep green shading to off-white, gold enameled leaves and branches, three naturalistic applies, applied ivory handle, long spout, numbered base.......**425.00**

Perfume bottle, 4-1/4" h, undulating body, yellow overlaid in white, cut and carved as swimming dolphin, inscribed registry mark, "Rd. 18100," rim and cap missing **4,950.00**

Vase

3-1/2" h, 5-1/2" w, pocket type, Flower and Acorn pattern, MOP satin, bridal white, gold flowers and leaves **650.00**

3-3/4" h, Queensware Burmese, sgd "Thomas Webb & Sons," registry number **750.00**

Vase, cameo, white morning glories, citron ground, marked, 5-1/8" h, **$1,650.** *Photo courtesy of Garth's Auctions, Inc.*

4" h, 4" w, Larch pattern, designed by Jules Barbe, pink and white **900.00**

5" h, cameo, white florals and tendrils dec, citron green ground **600.00**

5" h, 6" w, 18" circumference, shaded blue, sky blue to pale white cream, applied crystal edge, enameled gold and yellow dec of flowers, leaves, and buds, full butterfly, entire surface acid-cut in basketweave design **425.00**

5-1/4" h, 3-1/2" d, opaque ivory, cut leaves and berries, brown staining, circular cameo mark on base "Simulated Ivory English Cameo Glass," hallmarked silver rim and frosted ball feet **625.00**

7" h, gourd-shaped body, butterscotch yellow shaded to turquoise blue, cased to opal white, outer layer etched and carved as five-petaled rose on front, ornamental grasses on back, linear borders above and below **1,955.00**

7" hg, 4" d, satin, robin's egg blue, leaves, berries, and vines dec, flowing gold and scroll design, white lining **450.00**

7" h, 5" w, satin, basketweave mother of pearl, bulbous base shading from deep blue to pale blue, creamy lining **750.00**

7-1/4" h, 4" w at shoulder, Rainbow MOP satin, pink, yellow, blue, and white, DQ, flaring top, broad shoulder, tapered body, glossy white int., sgd "Patent"...**1,250.00**

7-1/4" h, Japonesque, pale oval heat reactive body, white Burmese to pink at top, overall delicate oriental sepia scenes **345.00**

7-1/2" h, 5-5/8" d, shaded orange overlay, off-white lining, gold flowers and fern-like leaves, gold butterfly on back, applied bronze-colored glass handles **255.00**

8" h, 4" w, satin, pink and white stripes, fancy frilly top, bulbous base, unlined **425.00**

10" h, 4" w, satin, pulled down edges, deep rose shading to pink, creamy lining, ruffled top, dome foot, pr **550.00**

10-1/2" h, gourd shape, satin, bright yellow shading to pale yellow, creamy white lining, bleed-through in pontil................**285.00**

Vase, peachblow, multicolored decoration, unmarked, 6-1/4" h, **$300.**

10-1/2" h, 4" w, bulbous, gold floral prunus blossoms, leaves, branches, pine needles, and insect, satin ground shaded brown to gold, creamy white lining, Jules Barbe dec..............**450.00**

10-3/4" h, 6" w bulbous base, slender stick neck, pink, yellow, and amber, solid white neck, small flake on side **125.00**

11-1/2" h, peachblow, creamy int., enameled dogwood and branches dec **750.00**

20" h, 7" w, banjo shape, bright yellow-green ground, pink and white azalea dec, green and white leaves, gold highlights, all over small enameled flowers on neck, painted and enameled collar, dome foot, two applied thorn handles, slight roughness to handles **895.00**

WEDGWOOD

History: In 1754, Josiah Wedgwood and Thomas Whieldon of Fenton Vivian, Staffordshire, England, became partners in a pottery enterprise. Their products included marbled, agate, tortoiseshell, green glaze, and Egyptian black wares. In 1759, Wedgwood opened his own pottery at the Ivy House works, Burslem. In 1764, he moved to the Brick House (Bell Works) at Burslem. The pottery concentrated on utilitarian pieces.

Between 1766 and 1769, Wedgwood built the famous works at Etruria. Among the most-renowned products of this plant were the Empress Catherina of Russia dinner service (1774) and the Portland Vase (1790s). The firm also made caneware, unglazed earthenwares (drabwares), piecrust wares, variegated and marbled wares, black basalt (developed in 1768), Queen's or creamware, and Jasperware (perfected in 1774).

Bone china was produced under the direction of Josiah Wedgwood II between 1812 and 1822 and revived in 1878. Moonlight luster was made from 1805 to 1815. Fairyland luster began in 1920. All luster production ended in 1932.

A museum was established at the Etruria pottery in 1906. When Wedgwood moved to its modern plant at Barlaston, North Staffordshire, the museum was expanded.

References: Susan and Al Bagdade, *Warman's English & Continental Pottery & Porcelain*, 3rd ed., Krause Publications, 1998; Diana Edwards, *Black Basalt*, Antique Collectors Club, 1994; Robin Reilly, *The New Illustrated Dictionary of Wedgwood*, Antique Collectors' Club Ltd., 1995; —, *Wedgwood Jasper*, Thomas Hudson, 1994.

Periodical: *ARS Ceramica*, 5 Dogwood Court, Glen Head, NY 11545.

Collectors' Clubs: Wedgwood International Seminar, 22 DeSavry Crescent, Toronto, Ontario M4S 212 Canada, http://www.www-l-s.org; Wedgwood Society of Boston, Inc., P.O. Box 215, Dedham, MA 02027-0215, http://www.angelfire.com/ma/wsb; Wedgwood Society of Great Britain, P.O. Box 5921, Bishop's Stortford, Herts CM22 7EP, UK; Wedgwood Society of New York, 5 Dogwood Court, Glen Head, NY 11545, http://www.wsny.org; Wedgwood Society of Washington, DC, 3505 Stringfellow Ct, Fairfax, VA 22033.

Museums: Birmingham Museum of Art, Birmingham, AL; Brooklyn Museum, Brooklyn, NY; Victoria & Albert Museum, London, England; Wadsworth Atheneum, Hartford, CT; Wedgwood Museum, Barlaston, Stoke-on-Trent, England.

Agate ware

Candleholder, 6-1/2" h, surface agate, applied creamware drapery swags, black basalt base, wafer Wedgwood & Bentley mark, c1775, restored chip to socle **1,495.00**

Vase, cov, 9-1/2" h, solid agate, creamware sibyl finials, traces of gilding, black basalt base, imp wafer Wedgwood & Bentley marks, c1770, gilt rim wear, covers with rim chips, nicks to bases, pr **7,500.00**

Basalt, teapot, 8-1/2" h, **$320.**

Basalt

Bowl, ball feet, marked "Wedgwood Made in England 8" **600.00**
Bust
  7" h, Byron **630.00**
  7-3/4" h, Locke, raised base, imp title and mark, c1865 . . . . **525.00**
  18" h, Minerva, imp mark and title, imp as lamp, chips restored to nose. **1,610.00**
Crater urn, 11-1/2" d, pierced disc cover, inset lid, polychrome enamel floral designs, iron-red trim, imp mark, restored rim chips **1,265.00**
Crocus pot and tray, 9-3/4" l, hedgehog shape, imp marks, c1800, repaired chips **920.00**
Figure
  5-1/8" h, reclining baby, after Della Robbia, imp mark, mid-19th C, foot rim chips **690.00**
  5-1/4" h, Toucan group, two birds with glass eyes, freeform circular base, modeled by Ernest Light, c1913, imp marks **1,380.00**
  7-1/2" h, Cupid and Psyche, seated figures, oval base, imp mark and title. **1,380.00**
Incense burner, 5-1/2" h, pierced cover seated on bowl supported by three dolphins, triangular base, imp "Josiah Wedgwood Feb 2, 1805," cov chips restored **1,610.00**
Orange bowl, 8-3/4" d, short wide flaring round pedestal, scrollwork and basketweave bands and festoons, imp mark, late 19th C **1,065.00**

Pitcher, 6-1/2" h, Club, enameled floral dec, imp mark, c1860 . . . . **345.00**
Plaque, 10-3/4" x 19-1/4", black, "Death of a Roman Warrior," high relief, warrior figures carrying body of Meleanger, imp mark, small restored chips . . . **2,875.00**
Vase
  9-3/4" h, engine turned, fixed lid, applied bacchus head handles and drapery swags, Wedgwood & Bentley wafer mark, handles restored **1,200.00**
  12-1/2" h, two handles, iron-red, black, and white classical figures on one side, stylized palmette design on reverse, gadroon and dot, palmette, laurel, and dot, and spearhead and dot borders, imp mark, c1800 . . . . **4,325.00**
  14" h, cov, serpent handles terminating to satyr masks, relief of Venus and Cupid, engine turning to base, shoulders, neck and cover, imp Wedgwood & Bentley wafer mark, c1775 . . . . **1,725.00**
Wine and water ewers, 15-1/2" h, water ewer with triton seated on shoulders and head of marine monster below the spout, wine with bacchus seated on shoulders, ram's head below spout, imp marks, mid-19th C, base restored to water ewer, pr **1,955.00**

Bone china, First period, c1820
Celery dish, gilt diamond border, printed mark, foot rim, light gilt war **175.00**
Tea set, 11" cov teapot, 51/2" l creamer, 5-1/2" cup and saucer, 6-1/2" cov sugar, 5-1/2" d waste bowl, blue transfer printed Chinese figural landscape, printed marks, slight damage, five pcs **435.00**
Tureen, cov, underplate, 7-1/8" l, oval, polychrome floral dec, printed mark, rim chip to cov. **346.00**

Caneware, teapot, basketweave body, sheaf of wheat finial, 3-1/2", **$225.**

Caneware

Game pie, 7" l, oval, liner, molded, rabbit finial, imp mark, 1865, liner cracked **435.00**

Pie dish, 12" l, oval, liner, leaf molded cover, imp marks, 1863 . . . . **920.00**

Potpourri basket, 4-1/4" h, black basalt fruiting grapevine relief, imp mark, rim staining **575.00**

Teapot, cov, 7" l, white fruiting grapevine relief, imp mark, c1830, base rim chip **175.00**

Cream Ware

Bowl, 8-1/8" l, reticulated, molded fiddleback ladle, imp "Wedgwood," stains, edge chip **160.00**

Plate, 9-1/8" d, scenic, little girl and mother buying buns from the Bun Man, back titled "Buns!, Buns!, Buns!," 1863 mark and artist sgd "Lessore" . . **335.00**

Vase, 6" h, molded grape vines and foliage, painted band of strawberries, mid-19th C, minor damage **90.00**

Jasper

Barber bottle, 11" h, three colors, green ground, white relief and lilac ground medallions, bacchus head reliefs to shoulder, imp mark, mid-19th C, cover insert damaged **2,100.00**

Bowl, 5" d, solid light blue, white foliate relief, polished int., imp mark, c1800
. . . . **550.00**

Door knobs, 1-7/8" x 2-5/8" oval, solid light blue, white relief classical subject, 19th C, pr **400.00**

Jasper, biscuit jar, white classic cameos, black ground, silver plated mountings and lid, impressed mark, **$465.**

Jardiniere, 4-1/2" h, black, white classical figures, imp marks, early 20th C **435.00**

Letter box, 8-1/4" l, 5" d, 6" h, seven blue jasper plaques with white classical reliefs, ormolu mounts **1,955.00**

Medallion, 3-1/2" x 4-1/4", light green dip, oval, portrait of Admiral Richard Howe, imp title and mark, ... **260.00**

Oenochoe jug, 7-1/2" h, solid light blue, white ring mounts to neck and socle, bacchus mask relief to handle terminal, imp mark, 19th C, handle repairs **575.00**

Perfume bottle, 4-3/4" h, oval, green jasper dip, white classical relief, SP screw top **690.00**

Plaque, 14-1/2" l, 6" h, black ground, applied white relief dec of groups of boys after designs by Lady Diana Beauclerk, imp marks, set in ebonized wood frames, 19th C, losses, price for pr **3,450.00**

Pot, cov, 3-1/2" h, light green jasper dip, white classical and foliate relief, imp mark, late 19th C **425.00**

Vase

8-3/4" h, cov, "Apollo," light blue, white jasper relief and raised Latin verse, "CC Posnatum Conditorem Anno Viget Ars Eturiae Redilnegrata," designed by John Goodwin to commemorate 200th anniversary of birth of Joseph Wedgwood, limited edition of 50, mounted on ebonized wood base, imp marks, 1930, cover restored
. . . . **1,100.00**

9-1/2" h, black, white relief, satyr mask handles, classical subjects, foliate borders, imp mark, 19th C
. . . . **1,100.00**

10-1/2" h, solid black, white classical relief, base with half-length figure wearing Phrygian cap, imp "T. Lovatt," factory mark, c1877
. . . . **1,955.00**

15-3/4" h, solid pale blue, white relief of children playing Blind Man's Bluff, mounted to white marble base set with oval Wedgwood pale blue jasper medallion with white relief of children playing, modern cov, imp mark, late 18th C, minor damage **1,850.00**

Lusters

Bowl, Daisy Makeig Jones marks, c1923

4-3/4" d, Butterfly, Z5063 . . . **675.00**

7-1/4" d, Fish, Z4826 . . . . **950.00**

7-1/2" d, Butterfly, Z4827 . . **1,200.00**

10" d, Dragon, Z4692 . . . . **1,650.00**

13-1/4" d, Butterfly, Z4830 . **1,950.00**

Coffeepot, cov, 5-1/2" h, Moonlight, imp mark, c1810, small chips to spout and cover **690.00**

Cup, 2" h, three handles, Dragon, blue ext., gilt reptiles, eggshell int. with central dragon, printed mark, c1920
. . . . **275.00**

Dish, 4-3/4" d, Dragon, Daisy Makeig Jones marks, Z4831, c1914-31 . **675.00**

Malfrey pot, cov, 8-1/8" h, Fairyland, black, Candlemas design, printed mark, cov restored **2,300.00**

Punch bowl, 11" d, Fairyland, Firbolgs, ruby ext., MOP Thumbelina int., printed mark and no., c1920 . . . . **3,600.00**

Teapot, cov, 3" h, Moonlight, drum form, imp mark, c1810, rim chips restored, nicks to spout rim **575.00**

Vase, 9-3/4" h, Fairyland, black, trumpet, shape 2810, Z4968, Butterfly Women, printed marks, c1920, pr
. . . . **4,000.00**

Wall pocket, 10" l, Moonlight, nautilus shell, c1810, restorations, pr . . . **575.00**

Majolica, plate, brown rim, yellow trim, green center portrait, impressed mark, c1878, 8-3/4" d, **$195.**

Majolica

Bowl, 11" d, cauliflower, multicolored, cobalt blue, rim nick on back . . . **495.00**

Caterer jug **770.00**

Compote, 8-1/2" d, 8-1/2" h, cherub, cattails and flowers **770.00**

Dessert plate, Argenta, 5-3/4" d
. . . . **250.00**

Floor urn, 26" h, cobalt blue, ladies seated at top of bulbous vase, drapes of laurel wreaths and ladies head at base, turquoise, yellow, white, brown, green, and pink, repair to one base, minor nicks and repair to feet of ladies, pr **5,500.00**

Fruit plate, 6-1/2" d, turquoise basketweave **250.00**

Jug, 8-1/2" h, cobalt blue, green ivy and grapes, brown ground, hinged silver top, handle re-attached **715.00**

Oyster plate, brown basketweave and shell **1,210.00**

Pitcher, 7" h, sunflower and urn, turquoise **770.00**

Plate

8-3/4" d, mottled, reticulated. **165.00**

9" d, Argenta, bird and fan, rim wear, slight hairline **110.00**

9" d, crane **690.00**

9" d, wicker, minor rim nicks on back **200.00**

Sugar, Argenta, bird and fan, repair to lid, hairline in base **125.00**

Umbrella stand, 24" h, Argenta Fan, hairlines **1,760.00**

Miscellaneous

Mortar and pestle, 6" h, 3-1/8" d, "Vitreous Stoneware," wood handle, imp marks, mid-19th C **225.00**

Pitcher, 6-1/4" h, Etruria, horse and hound hunting scene, hound handle **175.00**

Plate, luncheon, hunt scene, copper luster border, Etruria, six-pc set. **600.00**

Wine cooler, 10" h, redware, fruiting vine molded body, raised mask handles, imp mark, early 19th C **550.00**

Pearlware

Display teapot, cov, 18-1/2" h, gray enhanced gilt dec, leaf design to spout, banded borders, central knot emblems, imp mark and "pearl," c1850, finial restored at join, handle restored, slight gilt wear **1,380.00**

Platter, well and tree, gaudy cobalt blue and rust Chrysanthemum pattern, c1800, repaired **595.00**

Potpourri vase, pierced cov, blue ground, white relief floral swags, band above engine-turned fluting, imp mark, c1800, body restoration, married cover **230.00**

Queen's Ware

Basket, 9" l, oval, undertray, basketweave molded bodies, pierced galleries, green and black enamel oak leaves and trim lines, imp mark, early 19th C **290.00**

Panel, brown glazed, relief profile of young girl, date marked for March 1888 12-1/2" x 8", $225. Photo courtesy of Joy Luke Auctions.

Bidet, 21-1/2" l, fitted mahogany stand with cov, imp mark **425.00**

Orange bowl, cov, 9-1/2" h, low pedestal foot, wide lobe-fluted flaring rim, high domed pieced cover with long tapering ovals framed by molded scroll lattice and floral designs, imp mark, 20th C **635.00**

Plate, 9" d, octagonal, raised oak leaf border, central enameled dec figural landscape, artist sgd "Emile Lessore," imp mark, c1872 . . . . **320.00**

Platter, 15-3/4" x 20-3/8", oval, polychrome bird and floral dec in Chelsea style, imp mark, 1871 . . . . **375.00**

Veilleuse, 3-3/8" h, cover and stand, iron-red and blue enamel banding, imp mark, early 19th C, staining, rim wear **460.00**

Rosso Antico

Bust, 7-1/4" h, Matthew Prior, mounted on raised circular base, imp mark and title, restorations **420.00**

Crater potpourri, pierced disc cover and insert lid, black basalt vine relief, imp mark, early 19th C, foot rim and insert flakes **1,150.00**

Inkstand, 4" h, applied black basalt leaf and berry border on stand, supported by three dolphin feet, central pot insert, imp mark, early 19th C, foot rim restored **550.00**

Sugar bowl, cov, 4-1/2" h, classical black basalt relief between foliate panels, widow finial, imp mark, c1820 . . . . **450.00**

Vase, 6-1/2" h, modeled as open mouth fish, enamel and gilt dec squid designs, imp marks and date letters, c1870, rim chips, restoration, pr **1,900.00**

WELLER POTTERY

History: In 1872, Samuel A. Weller opened a small factory in Fultonham, near Zanesville, Ohio. There he produced utilitarian stoneware, such as milk pans and sewer tile. In 1882, he moved his facilities to Zanesville. Then in 1890 Weller built a new plant in the Putnam section of Zanesville along the tracks of the Cincinnati and Muskingum Railway. Additions followed in 1892 and 1894.

In 1894, Weller entered into an agreement with William A. Long to purchase the Lonhuda Faience Company, which had developed an art pottery line under the guidance of Laura A. Fry, formerly of Rookwood. Long left in 1895, but Weller continued to produce Lonhuda under the new name "Louwelsa." Replacing Long as art director was Charles Babcock Upjohn. He, along with Jacques Sicard, Frederick Hurten Rhead, and Gazo Fudji, developed Weller's art pottery lines.

At the end of World War I, many prestige lines were discontinued and Weller concentrated on commercial wares. Rudolph Lorber joined the staff and designed lines such as Roma, Forest, and Knifewood. In 1920, Weller purchased the plant of the Zanesville Art Pottery and claimed to produce more pottery than anyone else in the country.

Art pottery enjoyed a revival when the Hudson Line was introduced in the early 1920s. The 1930s saw Coppertone and Graystone Garden ware added. However, the Depression forced the closing of the Putnam plant and one on Marietta Street in Zanesville. After World War II, inexpensive Japanese imports took over Weller's market. In 1947, Essex Wire Company of Detroit bought the controlling stock, but early in 1948, operations ceased.

References: Sharon and Bob Huxford, *Collectors Encyclopedia of Weller Pottery*, Collector Books, 1979, 1999 value update; Betty Ward and Nancy Schiffer, *Weller, Roseville, and Related Zanesville Art Pottery and Tiles*, Schiffer Publishing, 2000.

Internet Resource: http://www.weller.com.

Collectors' Club: American Art Pottery Assoc., P.O. Box 834, Westport, MA 02790-0697, http://www.amartpot.org.

Additional Listings: See *Warman's Americana & Collectibles* for more examples.

Bookends, pr, 3-1/2" w, 9" h, Kappa, semi-matte sky blue glaze, marked "KKT," minor glaze miss to tip of one ear, couple of minor flakes on base **1,355.00**

Candlesticks, pr, Glendale **165.00**

Compote, Bonito, 4" h **65.00**

Console bowl, Sydonia, 17" x 6" . **90.00**

Console set, Glendale, 15-1/2" d flaring center bowl, flower frog, pair of low candlesticks, bruise to flower frog, kiln mark **1,100.00**

Cookie jar, Mammy, bow on head, chip on back, two hairlines....... **1,100.00**

Cornucopia

Lido, mauve **55.00**
Wild Rose, peach and green.. **45.00**

Ewer, Barcelona Ware, orig label **250.00**

Flower frog, Marvo, blue **55.00**

Fountain frog, 5-1/2" h, 6-1/2" w, Coppertone, bright green and brown glaze, hole in base and mouth for tube, marked "12," glaze thinning at base **635.00**

Jardiniere, 7" h, 7-3/4" d, architectural form, four buttresses and four squares on each panel, eggplant glaze with green highlights, marked "Weller" **435.00**

Jardiniere with pedestal, 12" d, 10-3/4" h, 9" d, 18" h pedestal, Forest, pedestal marked "XJY" at base, 9" crack from rim of jardinière, glaze flaking to body **575.00**

Lamp base

5" d, 11-1/4" h, Forest, unmarked, 2" chip next to hole at base... **460.00**

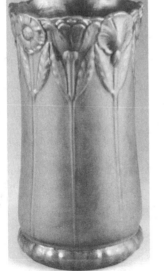

Umbrella stand, embossed with tall tulips, covered in matte green glaze, 11" d, 20" h, $690. Photo courtesy of David Rago Auctions.

10" d, 13-1/4" h, Louwelsa, by Hattie Mitchell, gourd shape, painted yellow cherry blossoms, stamped "Weller Louwelsa," sgd "H. Mitchell" on body **460.00**

Mug, Dickensware, dolphin handle and band, sgraffito ducks **250.00**

Pitcher, Louwelsa, 14" h, artist sgd, #750. .... **600.00**

Planter, Forest Tub, 4"........ **135.00**

Salad plate, Zona, 7-1/2" d..... **40.00**

Tub, Flemish **85.00**

Vase

3" d, 5" h, triangular form, foliate dec, irid glaze, sgd "Weller, Sicard" **490.00**

3" d, 6" h, Glendale, ovoid, birds and cattails, unmarked **690.00**

3-1/4" d, 10-1/2" h, ovoid, modeled, etched, white rose, orange ground, unmarked, restored 2" area at base **490.00**

3-3/4" d, 9-1/4" h, cylindrical, Hudson, by McLaughlin, seascape with sailboats and rocks, artist sgd, incised, 3-1/2" area of thinner glaze, short dark crazing lines to rim **2,415.00**

3-3/4" d, 10" h, cylindrical, Dickenware II, by L. J. Burgess, incised portrait of Chief Blackheart, shaded brown and green ground, stamped "Weller Dickensware," restoration to two rim chips **920.00**

4" d, 9-1/2" h, Hudson, white, blue, and green blooming iris, blue ground, sgd "Walch, Weller Pottery"................ **550.00**

Vase, Lasa, 16" h, $2,070. Photo courtesy of Jackson's Auctioneers & Appraisers.

4-1/4" d, 9" h, cylinder, tapering outward to base, irid glaze, stylized peacock feathers, sgd "Weller, Sicard" **1,035.00**

4-1/2" d, 8-1/4" h, Glendale, ovoid, birds and flowers, unmarked **1,150.00**

6" d, 12" h, Coppertone, flaring, four frogs at base, kiln mark.. **2,760.00**

6-1/2" d, 7-1/2" h, Faience, oviform, white and green birds wearing hats on one foot, tobacco brown glaze, sgd "Rhead, Weller, Faience, V509"................ **1,840.00**

7" d, 15-1/4" h, Etna, cupped rim, pink chrysanthemums, shaded gray ground, stamped "Weller/Etna," imp "Weller" on body **860.00**

13" d, 24-1/2" h, Aurelian, oviform, flaring rim, four blossoming irises, high gloss glaze, sgd "L. J. Dibowski," base marked "Weller, Aurelian No. 52," minor glaze nicks **1,955.00**

Wall pocket, Pearl, 8-1/2" l **150.00**

WHALING

History: Whaling items are a specialized part of nautical collecting. Provenance is of prime importance since collectors want assurances that their pieces are from a whaling voyage. Since ship's equipment seldom carries the ship's identification, some individuals have falsely attributed a whaling provenance to general nautical items. Know the dealer, auction house, or collector from whom you buy.

Special tools, e.g., knives, harpoons, lances, and spades, do not overlap the general nautical line. Makers' marks and condition determine value for these items.

References: Nina Hellman and Norman Brouwer, *Mariner's Fancy*, South Street Seaport Museum, Balsam Press, and University of Washington Press, 1992; Martha Lawrence, *Scrimshaw*, Schiffer Publishing, 1993.

Museums: Cold Spring Harbor Whaling Museum, Cold Spring Harbor, NY; Kendall Whaling Museum, Sharon, MA; Mystic Seaport Museum, Mystic, CT; National Maritime Museum Library, San Francisco, CA; New Bedford Whaling Museum, New Bedford, MA; Pacific Whaling Museum, Waimanalo, HI; Sag Harbor Whaling & Historical Museum, Sag Harbor, NY; San Francisco Maritime National Historical Park, San Francisco, CA; South Street Seaport Museum, New York, NY.

Additional Listings: Nautical Items and Scrimshaw.

Alphabet Game set, whalebone and ivory, slide top box, 19th C, minor imperfections **195.00**

Billet head, 18-1/4" l, carved and painted wood, scrolling design, 19th C
. . . . **920.00**

Block, carved whalebone, 19th C, pr
2-1/2" l **575.00**
3-1/4" l **1,095.00**

Blubber knife, 67" l, sheath, minor losses **550.00**

Book

Andrews, Roy C., *Whale Hunting with Gun and Camera*, NY, 1925, 8vo, cloth **90.00**

Ashley, Clifford W., *The Yankee Whaler*, Boston, 1938, illus, gilt buckram, minor rubbing . . . **125.00**

Beale, Thomas, *The Natural History of the Sperm Whale*, London, 1838, 393 pgs, three plates, illus, 12 mo
. . . . **690.00**

Bennett, Frederick Debell, *Narrative of a Whaling Voyage round the Globe, from the Year 1833 to 1836*, London, 1840, folding map, two plates, two volumes, 8vo . **1,620.00**

Brown, John Ross, *Etchings of a Whaling Cruise, with Notes of a Sojourn on the Island of Zanzibar*, NY, 1846, plates and illus, 8vo
. . . . **815.00**

Stern, Edward, Sketch of the Old New Bedford Whaling Bark "Stafford," Philadelphia, c1892, 30 pgs, 8vo, orig pictorial wrappers
. . . . **420.00**

Broadside

255 x 175 mm, *Land of the West, Greenland Whale Fishery*, 12-stanza poem, London, second half 19th C **110.00**

490 x 580 mm, *List of Shipping Owned in the District of New Bedford, Jan 1, 1832, Employed in the Whale Fishery and Foreign Trade*, lists vessels, tonnage, managing owners, New Bedford, 1832 . . . . **575.00**

Dipper, sperm whale tooth handle carved as seal, incised decoration on coconut shell dipper, 8" w, $395.

Chart square, 29-7/8", brass and wood, inscribed "MST," 19th C **200.00**

Club, 11-7/8" l, whalebone, 19th C
. . . . **950.00**

Dipper, 9-1/4" l, turned mahogany handle, ivory attachment, coconut shell bowl with incised rosette, chain, and liner dec **550.00**

Ditty box, 5-7/8" l, whalebone, oval, single finger construction, 19th C
. . . . **1,150.00**

Domino set, whalebone and baleen, sliding top box, 19th C, minor imperfections **190.00**

Duster, 15-1/2" l, whalebone and carved wood, 19th C **415.00**

Fid, 16" l, whalebone, 19th C, minor cracks **490.00**

Figure, 16-3/8" l, carved baleen, whale, whalebone inlaid eye, 19th C, repair to tail **865.00**

Game board, 9-1/4" sq, whalebone and mahogany, 19th C, minor edge roughness **1,035.00**

Harpoon

39" l, double flue, inscribed "Alpha," 19th C, pitting, minor corrosion
. . . . **290.00**

60" l, double-tined, cracks, loss to pole **285.00**

99-1/2" l, toggle, mounted on pole, 19th C **1,265.00**

Horn book, 3-7/8" l, whalebone, miniature **175.00**

Ladle, 14" l, whalebone, coconut, and copper, 19th C **345.00**

Lance, 103-1/2" l, minor corrosion
. . . . **600.00**

Lantern, 10-1/2" h, whalebone, pierced arched copper top, pierced base, ball feet, 19th C, replaced glass, minor loss
. . . . **1,380.00**

Marking gauge, 9-1/8" l, whalebone, 19th C **1,035.00**

Miniature, stool, 4-3/4" h, engraved whalebone, compass star and heart motif, top with lightly inscribed names, dates, and initials, baleen inlaid exotic wood, turned legs, 19th C, repair
. . . . **1,150.00**

Pan bone, 2-1/4" x 3-1/4", double sided engravings of three-masted ships under sail, 19th C, crack, gouges **375.00**

Parceling tool, 5-7/8" l, whale ivory, crossbanded design, engraved "N. D. 1829," repair **175.00**

Pickwick, 3-3/4" h, whale ivory, green and red sealing wax inlaid scribe line dec, 19th C, minute chip to finial
. . . . **1,495.00**

Picture frame, 6-1/4" h, 4" w, whalebone, pierce carved bird, star, and heart motif, 19th C, minute chip
. . . . **4,600.00**

Pie crimper, 6-3/8" h, carved and engraved whale's tooth, figural, woman in Empire gown, emerging from scrolling foliage, crimper pierced with trefoil devices, stand **8,625.00**

Pin cushion table clamp, 6-3/4" h, mahogany and whalebone **200.00**

Print, lithograph with hand coloring

16" x 32-1/4", Sperm Whaling with Its Varieties, J. H. Bufford, lithographer and publisher, after Benjamin Russell, framed, minor abrasions, foxing, toning **690.00**

21-1/2" x 32", Private Signals of the Whaling Vessels Belonging to the Port of New Bedford, Charles Taber & Co., identified in inscriptions in center of sheet, laid down on canvas, losses, tears, overall toning, scattered stains . . **1,380.00**

Rattle and whistle, 5-3/4" l, whalebone and whale ivory, 19th C, minor cracks
. . . . **575.00**

Rubber, whalebone, 19th C . . . **425.00**

Scribe, 8" l, whalebone, 19th C
. . . . **1,150.00**

Sewing carrier, 6-7/8" h, 7" l, reticulated whalebone and pine, 19th C, repair, minor cracks **1,150.00**

Shadow box, carved and painted three-masted ship with detailed rigging, painted red, gray, black, and gold, watercolor background of early 19th C dockside scene, America, late 19th C
. . . . **1,610.00**

Ship log book, 13-1/2" h, 8-1/2" w, Bark *Mercury*, New Bedford, outlining trip to North Pacific, entries from December 1876 to May 1878, staining, toning
. . . . **2,415.00**

Spool stand, three tiers, ftd, 19th C

6-3/8" h, whale ivory and exotic wood, cup finial above three graduated circular tiers, five bun feet, 19th C, minor cracks
. . . . **575.00**

7-1/8" h, whalebone, ivory, and wood, doughnut shaped ivory thimble holder above three graduated scalloped tiers, sealing wax inlaid scribe lines, tripod base, traces of blue pigment, missing three spool holders, very minor losses, minor cracks **750.00**

Swift, 19th C

22-5/8"l, whalebone and ivory, red and black sealing wax inlaid scribe lines, cup finial, barrel form clasp, cracks, minor losses **920.00**

23" l, whalebone, ivory, and wood, ball final, clamp carved with crosshatched diamond motif, minor losses, old repair **460.00**

Trade sign, 30" l, carved folk art, figural whale, old dry red paint over earlier white, sq head nail eyes, wrought iron hangers, possible tail restoration, dark stain touch-up at mouth **935.00**

Watch hutch

7-1/2" h, 5" w, 3-3/4" d, hanging, whalebone, arched crest pierce carved with star and crescent motifs, backed with painted cloth, 19th C, minor cracks, minute losses **8,625.00**

9-1/8" h, whalebone and cherry, scrolled crest above ring turned posts, kidney-shaped base, scribed bun feet, 19th C, minor cracks **690.00**

13-3/4" h, tall case clock form, baleen and ivory inlaid walnut, star and heart motif, 19th C, very minor losses **4,025.00**

Whip, 24-1/4" l, whalebone handle, 19th C, losses to leather **175.00**

Yardstick, 35-7/8" l, whalebone, 19th C **490.00**

WHIELDON

WHIELDON

History: Thomas Whieldon, a Staffordshire potter, established his shop in 1740. He is best known for his mottled ware, molded in the shapes of vegetables, fruits, and leaves. Josiah Spode and Josiah Wedgwood, in different capacities, had connections with Whieldon.

Whieldon ware is a generic term. His wares were never marked, and other potters made similar items. Whieldon ware is agate-tortoiseshell earthenware, in limited shades of green, brown, blue and yellow. Most pieces are utilitarian items, e.g., dinnerware and plates, but figurines and other decorative pieces also were made.

Coffeepot, cov, 7-1/2" h, molded spout and strap handle, brown tortoise shell glaze, blue and green, mismatched lid, old professional repair **475.00**

Creamer, 4-1/4" h, Cauliflower, molded design green and clear laze, applied handle, old yellowed repair on spout, wear, stains, minor edge damage **385.00**

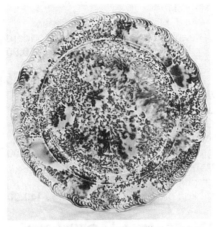

Plate, brown glaze, emb scroll at border, **$250.**

Figure, horse, mottled manganese drip, mottled green and manganese, flat pad base, professionally repaired **6,800.00**

Pitcher, 4-3/4" h **350.00**

Plate

8-1/2" d, octagonal, flow blue, marked "Whieldon Ware, Corona, F. Winkle & ? England," c1890. **40.00**

9" d, shaped, late 18th C, hairlines, pr **290.00**

9-1/4" d, majolica **165.00**

9-3/8" d, tortoise shell, brown sponging, blue and green spots in center, bands on rim, in-the-making hairline and glaze imperfections **495.00**

9-3/4" d, mottled, rim nick . . . **250.00**

Platter, 17-1/2" l, 14" w, shaped oval, molded edge, tortoiseshell gray, brown, yellow, and green glaze, brown and white ext., 19th C, imperfections **650.00**

Sugar, cov, 4-3/8" d, 3-5/8" h, cauliflower, molded design, green and clear glaze, wear, stains, edge chips **3,245.00**

Tea caddy, 4-1/4" h, Cauliflower, molded design, green and clear glaze, lid missing, wear, light stains. . . **550.00**

Teapot, cov, 3-3/4" h, creamware body, Cauliflower, cream-glazed florets, green glazed leaves, 18th C, restorations **475.00**

WHIMSIES, GLASS

History: During lunch or after completing their regular work schedule, glassworkers occasionally spent time creating unusual glass objects known as whimsies, e.g. candy-striped canes, darners, hats, paperweights, pipes, and witch balls. Whimsies were taken home and given as gifts to family and friends.

Because of their uniqueness and infinite variety, whimsies can rarely be attributed to a specific glass house or glassworker. Whimsies were created wherever glass was made, from New Jersey to Ohio and westward. Some have suggested that style and color can be used to pinpoint region or factory, but no one has yet developed an identification key that is adequate.

Glass canes are among the most collectible types of whimsies. These range in length from very short (under one foot) to 10 feet or more. They come in both hollow and solid form. Hollow canes can have a bulb-type handle or the rarer C- or L-shaped handle. Canes are found in many fascinating colors, with the candy striped being a regular favorite with collectors. Many canes are also filled with various colored powders, gold and white being the most common and silver being harder to find. Sometimes they were even used as candy containers.

References: Gary Baker et al., *Wheeling Glass 1829-939*, Oglebay Institute, 1994, distributed by Antique Publications; Joyce E. Blake, *Glasshouse Whimsies*, published by author, 1984; Joyce E. Blake and Dale Murschell, *Glasshouse Whimsies: An Enhanced Reference*, published by authors, 1989; Wayne Muller, *Darn It*, published by author (P.O. Box 903, Pacific Palisades, CA 90272.)

Collectors' Club: Whimsey Club, 2 Hessler Court, Dansville, NY 14437, http://www.whimsey.org.

Bracelet

2" to 3" d, Lutz type, clear, multicolored twists and spirals, gold **85.00**

3" d, solid glass, varied colored stripes **65.00**

Buttonhook

5" to 10" l, plain

Bottle green **35.00**

Colorless **25.00**

7" h, bottle green, elaborately twisted body, amber ends **75.00**

Cane, solid

46-1/2" l, aqua, spiraled, mid-19th C **175.00**

48" l, cobalt blue, shepherd's crook handle **265.00**

60" l, bottle green, finely twisted, curved handle **150.00**

Darner

5" l, amber head, applied colorless handle **200.00**

6" l, Aurene, gold, Steuben . . **300.00**

7" l, white ground, blue Nailsea loopings **165.00**

Egg, hollow, milk glass, various colored splotches

2" h **65.00**

4-1/2" h **85.00**

Hat, 6" l, 4" h, amber, blown, slight sickness **110.00**

Horn

8-1/2" l, French horn type, candy
stripes. **300.00**
20" l, trumpet type, red, white, yellow,
purple, and green candy stripes
. . . . **175.00**

Ladle, 10" l, hollow, gold powder filled,
colored splotches, curved handles
. . . . **70.00**

Pen

Elaborate, green, finely twisted
applied bird finial **85.00**
Simple design, amber, colorless nib,
7" l. **35.00**

Pipe

20" l, spatter, large bowl, English
. . . . **250.00**
36" l, long twisted stem, small hollow
bowl, aqua, America, c1900
. . . . **120.00**

Potichomanie ball, 12" d, blown, aqua,
paper cut-outs of flowers, etc.,
matching 24" h stand, attributed to
Lancaster NY. **600.00**

*Witch ball and goblet, pink, white, and
gold lattice, 7" h goblet, 4" d witch ball,
$400.*

Rolling pin

14" l, black or deep olive green,
white dec, early Keene or Stoddard
. . . . **150.00**
15" l, Nailsea type, cobalt blue
ground, white loopings **165.00**

Witch ball, 3-1/2" d, freeblown,
attributed to Boston and Sandwich
Glass Works,1850-80, rose and green
loops on white milk glass background,
ground moth, smooth base **375.00**

Witch ball holder, 3-1/2" d, 6" h, dark
amber, blown, sickness with small
broken blister **440.00**

WHISKEY BOTTLES, EARLY

History: The earliest American whiskey bottles were generic in shape and blown by pioneer glass makers in the 18th century. The Biningers (1820-1880s) were the first bottles specifically designed for whiskey. After the 1860s, distillers favored the cylindrical "fifth" design.

The first embossed brand-name bottle was the amber E. G. Booz Old Cabin Whiskey bottle which was issued in 1860. Many stories have been told about this classic bottle; unfortunately, most are not true. Research has proven that "booze" was a corruption of the words "bouse" and "boosy" from the 16th and 17th centuries. It was only a coincidence that the Philadelphia distributor also was named "Booz." This bottle has been reproduced extensively.

Prohibition (1920-1933) brought the legal whiskey industry to a standstill. Whiskey was marked "medicinal purposes only" and distributed by private distillers in unmarked or paper-labeled bottles.

The size and shape of whiskey bottles are standard. Colors are limited to amber, amethyst, clear, green, and cobalt blue (rare). Corks were the common closure in the early period, with the inside screw top being used between 1880 and 1910.

Bottles made prior to 1880 are the most desirable. When purchasing a bottle with a label, condition of that label is a critical factor. In the 1950s, distillers began to issue collectors' special-edition bottles to help increase sales.

References: Ralph & Terry Kovel, *Kovels' Bottles Price List*, 11th ed., Three Rivers Press, 1998; John Odell, *Digger Odell's Official Antique Bottle and Glass Collector Magazine Price Guide Series*, Vol. 8, published by author (1910 Shawhan Road, Morrow, OH 45152), 1995 Carlo and Dorothy Sellari, *Standard Old Bottle Price Guide*, Collector Books, 1989.

Periodicals: *Antique Bottle and Glass Collector*, P.O. Box 187, East Greenville, PA 18041; *Bottles & Extras*, P.O. Box 154, Happy Camp, CA 96039.

Museum: The Seagram Museum, Waterloo, Ontario, Canada.

Additional Listings: See *Warman's Americana & Collectibles* for a listing of Collectors' Special Edition Whiskey Bottles.

Bininger's Regular, 19 Broad St., New York, 1840-50, clock shape, deep gold amber, applied double-collared mouth, pontil scar, 5-7/8" h **300.00**

Bininger's Travelers Guide, A. M. Bininger & Co., No. 19 Broad St., NY, 1860-80, teardrop form, golden amber, applied double collared mouth, smooth base, 6-3/4" h **200.00**

C. A. Richards & Co., 99 Washington St., Boston, Mass, 1860-80, sq with beveled corners, yellow green, applied sloping collared mouth, smooth base, 9-1/2" h, 3/8" potstone. **550.00**

Caspers Whiskey, Made by Honest North Carolina People, 1870-90, cylindrical, paneled shoulder, cobalt blue, tooled sloping collared mouth with ring, smooth base, 11-3/4" h . . . **325.00**

Chestnut Grove Whiskey, 1840-60, flattened chestnut form, applied handle, golden amber, applied mouth with ring, pontil scar, 9" h **110.00**

Freeblown jug, applied handle, America, 1840-60

6-1/8" h, pear form, red amber, applied sloping collared mouth, pontil scar **220.00**
8" h, cylindrical corseted form, golden amber, applied double collared mouth, pontil scar **350.00**
8" h, flattened chestnut, golden amber, applied mouth with ring, pontil scar, 8" h. **475.00**

Spruance Stanley & Co., San Francisco, CA, 1869, amber, 6-1/2" h, $30.

Griffith Hyatt & Co., Baltimore, 1840-80, globular, flattened label panels, applied handle, golden amber with olive tone, applied sq collared mouth, pontil scar, 7" h **375.00**

Lancaster Glassworks, Lancaster, NY, 1860-80, barrel, puce amber, applied double collared mouth, smooth base, 9-5/8" h **180.00**

Old Continental Whiskey, yellow amber, 9-1/4" h **650.00**

Weeks Glass Works, Stoddard, NH, 1860-70, emb base, cylindrical, yellow amber with olive tone, applied sloping collared mouth with ring, smooth base, 11-1/2" h, retains cork and some int. residue **200.00**

WHITE-PATTERNED IRONSTONE

History: White-patterned ironstone is a heavy earthenware, first patented under the name "Patent Ironstone China" in 1813 by Charles Mason, Staffordshire, England. Other English potters soon began copying this opaque, feldspathic, white china.

All-white ironstone dishes first became available in the American market in the early 1840s. The first patterns had simple Gothic lines similar to the shapes used in transfer wares. Pattern shapes, such as New York, Union, and Atlantic, were designed to appeal to the American housewife. Motifs, such as wheat, corn, oats, and poppies, were embossed on the pieces as the American prairie influenced design. Eventually, more than 200 shapes and patterns, with variations on finials and handles, were made.

White-patterned ironstone is identified by shape names and pattern names. Many potters only identified the shape in their catalogs. Pattern names usually refer to the decorative motif.

References: Annise Doring Heaivilin, *Grandma's Tea Leaf Ironstone*, Updated Price Guide, L-W Book Sales, 1996; Dawn Stolzfus & Jeffrey B. Snyder, *White Ironstone, A Survey of its Many Forms, Undecorated, Flow Blue, Mulberry, Copper Lustre*, Schiffer Publishing, 1997; Jean Wetherbee, *White Ironstone*, Antique Trader Books, 1996.

Collectors' Clubs: Mason's Ironstone Collectors' Club, 2011 East Main St., Medford, OH 97504; White Ironstone China Association, RD #1, Box 23, Howes Cave, NY 12092.

Butter dish, cov, Athens, Podmore Walker, c1857 . . . . **85.00**

Cake plate, 9" d, Brocade, Mason, handled **140.00**

Chamber pot, cov, emb Fleur-De-Lis & Daisy o handle, 1883-1913, marked "Johnson Bros." **135.00**

Coffeepot, cov
  Livesley Powell & Co. **195.00**
  Wheat and Blackberry, Clementson Bros. **120.00**
Compote, ftd, Taylor & Davis, 10" d, 6" h **220.00**
Creamer
  Fig, Davenport **65.00**
  Wheat in the Meadow, Powell & Bishop, 1870 . . . . **45.00**
Cup and saucer
  Acorn and Tiny Oak, Parkhurst **35.00**
  Grape and Medallion, Challinor **40.00**
Ewer, Scalloped Decagon, Wedgwood **150.00**
Gravy boat
  Bordered Fuchsia, Anthony Shaw **45.00**
  Wheat & Blackberry, Meakin . **35.00**
Milk pitcher, Leaf, marked "Royal Ironstone China, Alfred Meakin, England," 9" h, discolored chip on base **145.00**
Nappy, Prairie Flowers, Livesley & Powell **20.00**
Pancake server, octagonal, Botte, 1851. **40.00**
Pitcher
  Berlin Swirl, Mayer & Elliot . . **120.00**
  Japan, Mason, c1915 . . . . . . **275.00**
  Syndenhaum, T. & R. Boote . **195.00**
  Thomas Furnival, 9" w, 9-1/2" h **100.00**
  Wheat, W. E. Corn. **85.00**
Plate
  Ceres, Elsmore & Forster, 8-1/2" d **15.00**
  Corn, Davenport, 10-1/2" d. . . **20.00**
  Fluted Pearl, Wedgwood, 9-1/2" d **15.00**
  Gothic, Adams, 9-1/2" d **20.00**
  Prairie, Clemenston, Hanley, 6-5/8" d **12.00**
  Wheat and Clover, Turner & Tomkinson **18.00**
Platter
  Columbia, 20" x 15". **125.00**
  Wheat, Meakin, 20-3/4" x 15-3/4" **75.00**
Punch bowl
  Berry Cluster, J. Furnival. . . . **175.00**
  Rosettes, handles, Thomas Furnival & Sons, c1851-90, 9-1/2" 3, 6" h **315.00**
Relish
  Ceres, Elsmore & Forster, 1960 . . . . **40.00**
  Wheat, W. E. corn **30.00**

Sauce tureen, cov
  Columbia, underplate, Joseph Goodwin, 1855 . . . . **115.00**
  Prize Bloom, T.J. & J. Mayer, Dale Hall Pottery **220.00**
  Wheat & Blackberry, Clementson Bros. **175.00**
Soap dish, Bordered Hyacinth, cov, insert, W. Baker & Co., 1860s . . **150.00**
Soup plate, Fig, Davenport, 9-1/2" d **25.00**
Sugar bowl, cov
  Hyacinth, Wedgwood **45.00**
  Fuchsia, Meakin **40.00**
  Livesley Powell & Co., registry mark, 6-1/2" handle to handle, 8" h **195.00**
Teapot, cov, T & R Boote, Burslem, registry mark for Nov. 26, 1879, 9-1/2" h **140.00**
Toothbrush holder
  Bell Flower, Burgess **50.00**
  Cable and Ring, Cockson & Seddon **40.00**
Vegetable, cov
  Blackberry **75.00**
  Prairie Flowers, Livesley & Powell **85.00**

WILLOW PATTERN CHINA

History: Josiah Spode developed the first "traditional" willow pattern in 1810. The components, all motifs taken from Chinese export china, are a willow tree, "apple" tree, two pagodas, fence, two birds, and three figures crossing a bridge. The legend, in its many versions, is an English invention based on this scenic design.

By 1830, there were more than 200 makers of willow pattern china in England. The pattern has remained in continuous production. Some of the English firms that still produce it are Burleigh, Johnson Bros. (Wedgwood Group), Royal Doulton (continuing production of the Booths' pattern), and Wedgwood.

By the end of the 19th century, production of this pattern spread to France, Germany, Holland, Ireland, Sweden, and the United States. Buffalo Pottery made the first willow pattern in the United States beginning in 1902. Many other companies followed, developing willow variants using rubber-stamp simplified patterns, as well as overglaze decals. The largest American manufacturers of the traditional willow pattern were Royal China and Homer Laughlin, usually preferred because it is dated. Shenango pieces are the most desirable among restaurant-quality wares.

Japan began producing large quantities of willow pattern china in the early 20th century. Noritake began about 1902. Most Japanese pieces are porous earthenware with a dark blue pattern using the traditional willow design, usually with no inner border. Noritake did put the pattern on china bodies. Unusual forms include salt and pepper shakers, one-quarter pound butter dishes, and canisters. The most desirable Japanese willow is the fine quality NKT Co. ironstone with a copy of the old Booths pattern. Recent Japanese willow is a paler shade of blue on a porcelain body.

The most common dinnerware color is blue. However, pieces can also be found in black (with clear glaze or mustard-colored glaze by Royal Doulton), brown, green, mulberry, pink (red), and polychrome.

The popularity of the willow design has resulted in a large variety of willow-decorated products: candles, fabric, glass, graniteware, linens, needlepoint, plastic, tinware, stationery, watches, and wall coverings. All this material has collectible value.

Marks: Early pieces of Noritake have a Nippon "Royal Sometuke" mark. "Occupied Japan" may add a small percentage to the value of common table wares. Pieces marked "Maruta" or "Moriyama" are especially valued.

References: Leslie Bockol, *Willow Ware: Ceramics in the Chinese Tradition,* Schiffer Publishing, 1995; Robert Copeland, *Spode's Willow Pattern and Other Designs after the Chinese,* Studio Vista, 1980, 1990 reprint; Mary Frank Gaston, *Blue Willow,* 2nd ed., Collector Books, 1990, 2000 value update; Jennifer A. Lindbeck, *A Collector's Guide to Willow Ware,* Schiffer Publishing, 2000.

Periodical: *The Willow Review,* P.O. Box 41312, Nashville, TN 37204.

Collectors' Club: International Willow Collectors, 503 Chestnut St., Perkasie, PA 18944, http://www.willowcollectors.org.

Reproduction Alert: The Scio Pottery, Scio, Ohio, currently manufactures a willow pattern set sold in variety stores. The pieces have no marks or backstamps, and the transfer is of poor quality. The plates are flatter in shape than those of other manufacturers.

Note: Although colors other than blue are hard to find, there is less demand; thus, prices may not necessarily be higher priced.

Berry bowl, small
   Blue, Homer Laughlin Co. **6.50**
   Pink, marked "Japan" **5.00**
Bowl, 9" d, Mason **45.00**
Bread and butter plate, 6-3/8" d, Royal China Co. **4.00**
Butter dish, cov, 1/4 lb, Royal China Co. **30.00**
Cake plate, Newport Pottery Ltd., England, SP base, c1920 . . . . . **300.00**
Cereal bowl, 6-1/4" d, Royal China Co. **12.00**
Charger, 13" d **35.00**
Child size
   Teapot, 4-1/8" h, minor flake on lid rim **165.00**

Berry bowl, oval, Buffalo China mark, 6-1/2" l, oval, **$28.00**

Tea Set, 2-1/4" h teapot, 1" h creamer, 1-1/2" h cov sugar, two 1" h tea cups, two 2-1/8" d plates, red pattern, each marked "Japan," orig box marked "Made in Japan, Toy China Tea Set, Service for 2" **150.00**
Coffeepot, cov, 10" h, 3" h warmer stand. **165.00**
Creamer, round handle, Royal China Co. **10.00**
Cup and saucer
   Booths **30.00**
   Buffalo Pottery **25.00**
   Homer Laughlin **10.00**
   Japanese, decal inside cup, pink **25.00**
   Shenango **15.00**
Dinner plate
   Allerton, 10" d **25.00**
   Buffalo Pottery, 9" d **20.00**
   Johnson Bros., 10" d **15.00**
   Royal China Co. **4.00**
Gravy boat, 5" x 6-1/2", Royal China Co. **15.00**
Pie plate, 10" d. **50.00**
Platter, 19" x 14-1/2", marked "Copeland, Made in England," c1940 . . . . **195.00**
Snack plate, with cup, 9-1/8" d, Royal China Co. **50.00**
Soup bowl, Royal China Co. **10.00**
Sugar, cov
   Allerton **65.00**
   Royal China Co., handleless . . **30.00**
Tea cup and saucer, scalloped, Allerton **45.00**
Tea service, partial, earthenware, underglaze transfer printed dec, 2-1/2" h cream jug, 10 2-5/8" d teacups, 11 5-1/8" d saucers, 2" h sugar bowl, English, early 19th C, price for 23-pc set. **115.00**
Toby jug, 6" d, overall crazing . . **930.00**

Platter, impressed crown mark, 15-1/2" l, 12-1/2" w, **$150.**

Vegetable bowl, 9" d, Royal China Co. **20.00**
Wash bowl and pitcher, 7-1/2" h pitcher, 12" d bowl, Adderlys Ltd., Staffordshire, c1906, age crack in pitcher **375.00**
Water set, 9" h pitcher, six 3-5/8" h tumblers, c1940-50 . . . . **195.00**

WINDMILL WEIGHTS

History: Cast-iron windmill weights were an important part of any windmill. There are four types of windmill weights. The biggest is a "counter-balance weight" or tail weight. A "counter-balance weight" is used to balance the weight of the wheel upon the tower bearing. The second type is known as a "governor weight." This type of weight is used to control the action of the wheel if the wind speed increased. The third type is a "spoke weight" and as the name implies, it was put directly on the spoke of a wheel. The fourth type is the "regulator weight" and is found bolted to the regulator pump or bolted to the tower. Most collectors seek the "counter weight" type since it usually is the largest and most decorative.

Windmills were a very important part of the American landscape. After heavy use, some windmills wore out; others were destroyed by weather. However, the cast-iron weights were often saved. They would take on other uses around the farm, from doorstops to yard art. Because they often took on a second life, most were repainted. Skillful repairs generally do not detract from the value of a vintage windmill weight.

Today, windmill weight collectors often compete with the folk art collector who appreciates the style and whimsical nature of some of the designs.

References: Rick Nidey and Don Lawrence, *Windmill Weights,* printed by author, (Box 1141 Boise City, OK 73933); Milt Simpson, Bob Krist, *Windmill Weights,* Johnson & Simpson, 1985.

Periodical: *Windmillers' Gazette,* P.O. Box 507, Rio Vista, TX 76093-0507.

Museum: Dalley Windmill Collection, Portales, NM.

Reproduction Alert: Reproduction windmill weights are available. Look for signs of use, well-seasoned cast iron, or weathered rust. Bright new paint is often a sign that the windmill weight is new.

Bull, flat, attributed to Fairbury Windmill Co., Fairbury, NE, early 20th C, no lettering, orig factory base, one with traces of silver and green paint, other with black paint, surface imperfections, 18-1/2" x 24-1/2", 17-3/4" x 9-7/8" base, price for pr **1,610.00**

Bull, full bodied, cast iron

Dempster Manuf Co., Des Moines, IA, early 20th C, "Boss," raised lettering, painted black, tan highlights, 13" x 13-1/4" x 4"
. . . . **1,495.00**

Fairbury Windmill Co., Fairbury, NE, attributed to, early 20th C, no lettering, painted red, white highlights, surface imperfections, 18-1/4" x 24-1/2" **865.00**

Fairbury Windmill Co., Fairbury, NE, attributed to, early 20th C, raised lettering, painted red, mounted to orig base, minor imperfections, 18-1/2" x 24-1/2", 17-3/4" x 9-7/8" base **1,150.00**

Simpson Windmill and Machine Co., Fairbury, NE, early 20th C, no lettering, traces of red paint, imperfections, 12-3/4" x 13-1/2" x 10-1/2" including crossmount bracket **1,035.00**

Horse, bob-tail, flat, Dempster Mill Manuf Co., Beatrice, NE, early 20th C, cast iron, raised mane, casting mark "58G," 16-5/8" x 17-1/4"

Painted green **650.00**
Painted white **600.00**
Unpainted **500.00**

Horse, crescent-tail, flat, Dempster Mill Manuf Co., Beatrice, NE, early 20th C, cast iron, unpainted, 15" x 16" . . **815.00**

Horse, long-tail, flat, Dempster Mill Manuf Co., Beatrice, NE, early 20th C, cast iron

Silver paint, mounted on short base, surface imperfections, 18-1/2" x 17-1/2", 3-1/4" x 12" x 2-1/4" base **920.00**

Traces of black paint, mounted on orig crossmount, surface imperfections, 19-1/4" x 17-1/4" **1,380.00**

Horseshoe, unknown maker, late 19th/early 20th C, cast iron, unpainted, 10-1/4" x 8-3/4" x 2-1/2" **920.00**

Rooster, Elgin Wind Power and Pump Co., Elgin, IL, early 20th C, cast iron

No lettering, painted white, red and yellow details, integral C-shaped base, surface imperfections, 19-1/2" x 18", 3-1/2" x 8-1/2" x 3-1/2" base, price for pr **2,990.00**

No lettering, painted white, red details, integral C-shaped base, surface imperfections, 16" x 16-1/2", 3-1/2" x 8-1/2" x 3-1/2" base **1,150.00**

Raised numbers on tail "10ft N. 2," painted silver, red details, rect integral base, surface imperfections, 16" x 16-1/2", 3-3/4" x 9-3/4" x 4-1/2" base **1,495.00**

Rooster, barnacle-eye, Elgin Wind Power and Pump Co., Elgin, IL, early 20th C, cast iron, painted white, red and yellow details, no base, surface imperfections, 18-1/2" x 17-3/4", price for pr **2,990.00**

Rooster, Hummer, Elgin Wind Power and Pump Co., Elgin, IL, early 20th C, cast iron, long stem, raised lettering on tail

Mounted on rect integral base, traces of red paint, 17-1/2" x 16", 5-1/4" x 13-1/2" x 4-1/2" base **1,150.00**

Numbered "E184," traces of white and red paint, 13-1/4" x 10" **865.00**

Rooster, Mogul, Elgin Wind Power and Pump Co., Elgin, IL, late 19th C, cast iron, painted white, red details, surface imperfections, 18" x 20-1/2" . . . **5,175.00**

Rooster, rainbow tail, attributed to Elgin Wind Power and Pump Co., Elgin, IL, early 20th C, cast iron

Traces of white paint, red details, mounted on green base, 19-1/4" x 18-1/2" **5,750.00**

White paint, yellow and red details, mounted on black base, surface imperfections, 17-1/2" x 18"
. . . . **2,100.00**

Squirrel, Elgin Wind Power and Pump Co., Elgin, IL, early 20th C, cast iron, squirrel perched on rect integral base, brown, gold, and green paint, 19-1/2" x 13-1/2" x 3", 5-1/8" x 9-5/8" x 3" base **3,750.00**

Star

Flint and Waling Co., Kendallville, IN, early 20th C, cast iron, raised five-point star on each end of cylinder, raised numbers "RR2," 7-1/2" d, 3-1/2" w **920.00**

U. S. Wind Engine and Pump Co., Batavia, IL, late 19th/early 20th C, cast iron, referred to as "Halladay Standard," one with silver paint, 15" x 15", price for pr **2,530.00**

"W," Althouse Wheeler Co., Waupun, WI, early 20th C, cast iron, 9" x 16-1/2" x 11", on stand **980.00**

Warship, *Monitor*, Baker Manuf Co., Evansville, WI, early 20th C, cast iron and concrete, painted blue, 7-1/2" x 28-1/2" x 12" **1,955.00**

WOODENWARE

History: Many utilitarian household objects and farm implements were made of wood. Although they were subjected to heavy use, these implements were made of the strongest woods and well cared for by their owners.

References: Arene Burgess, *19th Century Wooden Boxes,* Schiffer Publishing, 1997; Jonathon Levi and Robert Young, *Treen for the Table,* John Campbell, *Fire & Light in the Home Pre 1820,* Antique Collectors' Club, 1999; George C. Neumann, *Early American Antique Country Furnishing,* L-W Book Sales, 1984, 1993 reprint.

Collectors' Club: International Wood Collectors Society, 2300 W. Rangeline Road, Greencastle, IN 46135-7875, http://www.woodcollectors.org.

Additional Listings: See *Warman's Americana & Collectibles* for more examples.

Bag stamp, 5" h, pine, relief carved tulip in heart-dec urn, PA, c1750 . . . . **2,100.00**

Bank, 4-1/2" w, 3-13/16" d, 3-5/8" h, rect, carved gardenia blossoms and leaves on top and sides, dark blue painted ground **525.00**

Bas relief carving

5" w, 6-3/4" h, woman holding bird, found in Iowa **525.00**

6-1/8" l, 4-1/8" h, basket of fruit, repaired **435.00**

Bowl, carved

5" d, 1-1/2" h, burl, good figure, dark patina, int. with few scorch marks **880.00**

6-1/4" w, 2-1/2" d, 4" h, double carved horse heads, incised eyes, carved ears, mouths, and forelocks, wear from use . . . **450.00**

8-1/2" w, 17" l, 2-1/2" h, double molded rim, inscribed and dated "Kenai Indian Alaska, 1886" **1,150.00**

11-1/2" d, 4" h, burl, ash, very good figure, old scrubbed surface, incised ring detail around base, ext. with raised rim, rim split **880.00**

12" d, 4-1/4" h, burl, banded rim tapering to base, old surface, America, 19th C **635.00**

13-3/8" d, 4-1/4" d, burl, very good figure, dark brown patina, thinly turned, turned foot, raised rim ring, couple of old minor splits **1,210.00**

14-11/16" d, 8" h, burl, deep oval form, handled, ftd, 18th C **5,750.00**

17" d, 13-1/2" d, 7" h, burl, vestiges of handles, red paint, Eastern Woodlands, New England, early 19th C. **1,100.00**

19" d, 4-3/4" h, ash burl, very good figure, thinly turned, scrubbed surface, low sides, turned foot, incised rings, slanted groove treatment along outer rim, slightly misshaped, small areas of filler on ext. **1,650.00**

19-1/2" w, 15-1/4" d, 5" h, ash burl, good figure, old mellow brown surface, oval, beveled handles at ends, old rim split, natural defects **750.00**

21" d, 8-1/2" h, burl, turned, America, late 18th/early 19th C **2,415.00**

Box, cov

5-1/4" d, 3-3/8" h, oval, bentwood, single finger construction with opposite directions on lid and base, iron tacks, old dark green paint shows lighter under lid, minor wear to paint. **2,420.00**

5-3/4" w, 4" d, 1-3/4" h, book shape, spruce, inland bands, star, crescent boon, hearts, and leaves, one end with sliding lid, minor alligatoring to varnish, short age cracks. **200.00**

6-3/8" w, 3" d, 1-7/8" h, book shape, Frisian carved, made from solid piece of wood, sliding lid, overall geometric carving, matching patterns on front and back, hearts and pinwheel on spine, good patina, int. with ivory paint, yellowed varnish, minor edge damage, few worm holes. . **220.00**

8-1/4" w, 6-1/4" d, 4-1/4" h, oval, bentwood, single finger on lid, overlapping seams on base, steel tacks, old medium blue paint, wear to lid **495.00**

12" w, 6-1/4" d, 5-3/4" h, pine and poplar, orig red paint, applied molding on lid, dovetailed case, molded base, int. slotted for divider (missing). **550.00**

Bucket, cov, tongue and groove stave construction

4-3/4" d, 3-7/8" h, old gray paint, brass bands, wood and wire bale handle, base imp "Washington Mfg Co. Troy, NY" **220.00**

8-3/4" d, 8-1/2" h, faded orig red paint below center band, black iron bands and finial, slightly tapered sides, fittings for bale handle stamped "Pat. Oct. 27, 85" . **220.00**

Bucket, open, 11-1/2" d, 12-1/4" h, stave construction, wood bands, bentwood swing handle, layers of old red paint, some water damage on bottom **550.00**

Busk, 12" h, carved maple, engraved with Indian smoking pipe, chip-carved geometric compass designs, attributed to New England, early 19th C, stand **980.00**

Canoe cup, 5-3/4" l, 2-1/4" h, cup with elongated bowl, carved beaver, New England, 19th C, with stand **520.00**

Charger, 21-3/4" d, treenware, scribed dec, late 18th/early 19th C, minor imperfections **1,035.00**

Churn, 49-1/2" h, stave construction, refinished pine, lollipop handle, tapered sides, turned lid with dasher, replaced copper bands. **165.00**

Flax wheel, 45" h, upright type, mixed hardwoods, four turned legs, single treadle, double flyers with bobbins, single wheel at top with turned spokes, few replacements. **250.00**

Lawn bowling ball, Thomas Taylor, Scotland, late 19th C, inlaid ivory personalized medallions, imp marks, wear, price for set of six **300.00**

Measuring device, carved and inlaid shoe-form, carved head of gentleman, ivory inlaid eyes, inlaid metal buckle, two ivory inlaid panels each dec with two engraved shoes, Holland, late 18th C, minor losses, wear, crack . . . **920.00**

Mortar and pestle, 6-1/4" d, 18-1/4" h, turned maple, acorn-shaped knop, three incised lines on cylindrical pestle, mortar with molded base, 19th C, cracks. **90.00**

Sugar bucket, marked "C. S. Hersey," 9-1/2" c, 9" h, **$295.**

Pantry box, 12" d, 8-1/4" h, bentwood, old deep red painted surface, iron tacks **690.00**

Pencil box, 8" l, rect, heart finial, compass star on slide cover, attributed to New Hampshire, c1800. . . . **1,265.00**

Picture frame

13-3/8" w, 15-1/2" h, stenciled and painted, rect, gold floral dec on black ground, remnants of paper label on reverse **375.00**

13-3/4" w, 17-5/8" h, painted pine, black half round frame, meandering fruited vine and plant border, 19th C, finish alligatored **520.00**

19-5/16" w, 22" h, rect, reticulated scalloped edge, compass star corner rosettes, painted black, 19th C, finish alligatored . . **550.00**

Saffron container, 2-1/2" d, 4-5/8" h, Lehnware, turned wood, knob on lid, salmon ground, white, red, and green flowers around base, strawberries on lid, minor edge chip on base . **1,980.00**

Scoop, 9-3/4" l, carved, America, 19th C **210.00**

Sugar bowl, cov, 8" d, 7-1/2" h, turned maple, acorn finial on flaring domed lid, bulbous body, flaring foot, old refinish, loss to inside rim **690.00**

Sugar bucket, cov

13-1/2" h, orig dark green paint, faint signature "C. Wilder & Son, So. Hingham, Mass" on lid, tapering sides, lapped staves, copper tacks, arched bentwood handle, minor edge chips. **550.00**

15" h, orig blue paint, old hand plane marks, copper and steel tacks, arched bentwood handle, stenciled "E. F." on bottom, chips . . . **450.00**

Trivet, 4-1/4" x 7-7/8" x 4-3/8" h, pine, wire nails, cutout feet and ends on apron, old robin's egg blue with red stripes, hand painted decoupaged print of Mt. Vernon on top, minor flaking, multiple nail holes in one area. . **350.00**

Tub, 3-5/8" d, 2-1/2" h, Treenware, chip carved edge, two handles, heart cut-outs, dark green (black) ext., yellowed ivory paint int., split . **1,375.00**

Ventriloquist's head, mounted on later stand

5" w, 6" d, 8" h, carved pine, natural surface, America, c1930, eyes missing. **375.00**

5-1/2" w, 5" d, 8-1/2" h, carved yellow pine, fixed eyes, spring-activated mouth with pull string, old patina, attributed to southern U.S., last quarter 19th C **1,150.00**

5-1/2" w, 6-1/2" d, 9-1/2" h, carved, polychrome features, America, c1930, eyes and some paint missing **350.00**

Wall shelf, 38-1/2" l, 6-1/2" d, 16" h, bird's eye maple, carved, shaped and slightly bowed top shelf with incised front on pierced, shaped, scrolling supports, each with three circular bosses joined by incised medial bar, lower shaped shelf, old finish, New England, mid-19th C, minor imperfections **920.00**

Wand, 21-5/8" h, carved wood, upright hand, traces of red paint, attributed to Penitente, American Southeast, c1890 . . . . **1,265.00**

Wash tub, 23-3/4" d, 16-1/2" h, painted pine, circular, pierced handle, stave and metal band construction, old red paint, America, late 19th C, wear, loose bands **260.00**

Watch hutch, Hepplewhite, cherry, inlaid banding, star-burst, and paterae, old finish, minor edge damage and veneer loss, 11-1/4" h, $3,575. Photo courtesy of Garth's Auction, Inc.

WORLD'S FAIRS AND EXPOSITIONS

History: The Great Exhibition of 1851 in London marked the beginning of the World's Fair and Exposition movement. The fairs generally featured exhibitions from nations around the world displaying the best of their industrial and scientific achievements.

Many important technological advances have been introduced at world's fairs, including the airplane, telephone, and electric lights. Ice cream cones, hot dogs, and iced tea were first sold by vendors at fairs. Art movements often were closely connected to fairs, with the Paris Exhibition of 1900 generally considered to have assembled the best of the works of the Art Nouveau artists.

References: *Crystal Palace Exhibition Illustrated Catalogue* (London, 1851), Dover Publications, n.d.; Robert L. Hendershott, *1904 St. Louis World's Fair Mementos and Memorabilia*, Kurt R. Krueger Publishing (160 N. Washington, Iola, WI 54945), 1994; Joyce Grant, *NY World's Fair Collectibles: 1964-1965*, Schiffer Publishing, 1999; Frederick and Mary Megson, *American Exposition Postcards*, The Postcard Lovers, 1992; Howard M. Rossen, *World's Fair Collectibles: Chicago, 1933 and New York 1939*, Schiffer Publishing, 1998.

Collectors' Clubs: 1904 World's Fair Society, 12934 Windy Hill Drive, St. Louis, MO 63128, http://www.inlink.com/~terryl; World's Fair Collectors' Society, Inc., P.O. Box 20806, Sarasota, FL 34276.

Museums: Atwater Kent Museum, Philadelphia, PA; Buffalo & Erie County Historical Society, Buffalo, NY; California State University, Madden Library, Fresno, CA; 1893 Chicago World's Fair Colombian Exposition Museum, Columbus, WI; Museum of Science & Industry, Chicago, IL; The Queens Museum, Flushing, NY.

Crystal Palace, 1851

Pipe, white clay Pipe, 6" l, Crystal Palace on bowl **100.00**

Pot lid, Pratt, 5" d **200.00**

Crystal Palace, NY, 1853

Dollar, so called, 1-3/4" d, shows seated Liberty and Crystal Palace **75.00**

Print, Currier and Ives, Crystal Palace **400.00**

Centennial, 1876

Bank, still, cast iron, Independence Hall, 9" h x 7" w **350.00**

Glass slipper, Gillinder

Clear **35.00**

Frosted **40.00**

Medal, wooden, Main Building, 3" d **60.00**

Scarf, 19 x 34", Memorial Hall, Art Gallery colorful **100.00**

Bookmark, woven, "Souvenir of the World's Columbian Exposition, Chicago, 1893," and framed woven silk panel "Women's Pavilion International Exhibition, 1876," price for two-piece lot, **$135.** *Photo courtesy of Joy Luke Auctions.*

Colombian Exposition, 1893

Album, 5-3/4" x 9", hardcover, gold emb "World's Fair Album of Chicago 1893" **50.00**

Book, *History of the World's Fair Being A Complete Description of the World's Colombian Exposition from Inception*, Major Ben C. Truman, illus, 592 pgs **60.00**

Creamer and sugar, peachblow, made by Libbey **985.00**

Mug, 4-3/4" h, salt glazed stoneware, imp, blue accents "World's Fair Chicago 1893" **165.00**

Plate, Wedgwood, dark blue and white, Administration Building in middle **45.00**

Sheet music, "World's Colombian Expo March" **75.00**

Watch case opener, Keystone Watch Case Co. **15.00**

Trans-Mississippi, 1898

Change purse, leather and mother of pearl, showing fair name on side **45.00**

Pan American, 1901

Cigar case, hinged aluminum 2-1/2" x 5-1/2" **35.00**

Frying pan, pictures North and South America, 6" long **75.00**

Plate, frosted glass, three cats painted on dec, 7-1/2" d **35.00**

Chicago, change purse, white metal top, nautical and patriotic motifs, leather body, 2-3/4" x 1-7/8", $65.

St. Louis, 1904

Match safe and cigar cutter, 2-3/4" w, 1-1/2" h, detailed drawing of Palace of Varied Industries on one side, picture of Gardens and Terraces of States on other, tarnished **150.00**

Medal, silvered brass, 2-3/4" d . . **60.00**

Pocket mirror, multicolored map of Alameda County, showing San Francisco, Oakland, Alameda, adjoining harbors and bays, two orange poppy flowers **115.00**

Stamp holder, aluminum, 1-1/8" x 1-3/8" **35.00**

Souvenir mug, bronze, emb scene of Palace of Electricity, 6" h **115.00**

Souvenir plate, 7" d, Festival Hall, Cascade Gardens **55.00**

Tumbler, 4" high, copper plated base, metal, shows Louisiana Purchase Monument, Cascades, Union Station and Liberal Arts Bldg **35.00**

Alaska-Yukon, 1909

Watch fob, three pcs, State Building, Totem Pole, Fair Logo in Center, 4" l **75.00**

Hudson-Fulton, 1909

Pin back, color pictures profiles of Hudson and Fulton, 1-1/4" d **25.00**

Panama-Pacific, 1915

Pocket watch, official, silver plated, 2" d **300.00**

Postcard **5.00**

Century of Progress, Chicago, 1933

Booklet, Cracker Jack, 1-1/2" x 2-1/2" premium, 12 pgs, red, white, and blue Cracker Jack box, full-color illus of fair sites **120.00**

Change purse, 2-3/4" **30.00**

Playing cards, full deck, showing views of the fair, all different, black and white **45.00**

Poker chip, red, white, or blue, 1-1/2" d **15.00**

Ring, silver plated, blue and white, comet and star, adjustable **20.00**

Souvenir key, Trowel, orig box . . **70.00**

Tape measure, silver, blue, and white official logo, other side with black and white photo of Paris replica village exhibit **32.00**

Toy wagon, red, white wheels, decal of Transportation Bldg in middle approx 3-1/2" l **175.00**

Great Lakes, 1936

Pin back, Florida, with state flag on the face, 1-1/2" d **18.00**

Texas Centennial, 1936

Playing cards, colorful with Texas state flag on back, boxed **40.00**

Golden Gate, 1939

Bookmark, typical view, 4" l **20.00**

Match book, orig matches, pictures Pacifica **10.00**

Token, shows Sun Tower and Bridge, 1-1/8" d **15.00**

New York, 1939

Candy tin, miniature, by Bagatele, very colorful, 4-1/4" x 6-1/2" **65.00**

Cigarette holder, Lenox, pink, yellow, blue, green, white, 2-1/2" h **350.00**

Folder, 6-1/4" x 12", printed paper, blue, white, and orange, one side with three images of Borden's Elsie, Trylon, and Perisphere, reverse with blue and white printing, pictorial family endorsement, recipe, and text relating to Borden's Chateau cheese, August 1939 publication date **20.00**

Pinback button, General Motors, blue and white "I Have Seen The Future," back paper identification for General Motors exhibit, c1940 . . . . **12.00**

Pipe, when standing on bowl looks like Trylon and Perisphere, 5-1/2" l . . **125.00**

Postcard, photo type **6.00**

Souvenir spoon, 7" l, Theme Building on front, "Pat. Pend., Wm Rogers Mfg. Co." **25.00**

Tapestry, 17" sq, edges worn . . . **45.00**

Brussels, 1958

Paperweight, Atomaton, chrome plated on marble base, 4-1/2" x 4-1/2" x 4-1/2" **75.00**

New York, 1964

Dime, circular plastic case with 1946 Eisenhower dime in center, reads "NY World's Fair, 1964-1965 Neutron Irradiated Dime," back reads "Atomic Energy Commission, United States of America," 2" d **40.00**

Fork and spoon display, 11" l, mounted on wooden plaque, Unisphere decals on handles **45.00**

Hat, black felt, Unisphere emblem, white cord trim, feather, name "Richard" embroidered on front **25.00**

Lodge medallion, bronze luster finish, image of Unisphere and two exhibit buildings, brass hanger loop, inscribed "The Grand Lodge I.O.O.F. of the State of New York" **15.00**

Paperweight, panoramic scenes **40.00**

Postcard, 10 miniature pictures, 20 natural color reproductions, unused **20.00**

Puzzle, jigsaw, 2" x 10" x 11", Milton Bradley, 750 pcs, unopened **20.00**

Salt and pepper shakers, pr, Unisphere, figural, ceramic **50.00**

Souvenir book, *Official Souvenir Book of the New York World's Fair*, 1965 . . . . **25.00**

Boot, Centennial Exposition, clear glass, metal top, 3-1/2" h, 2" w, $45.

YARD-LONG PRINTS

History: In the early 1900s, many yard-long prints could be had for a few cents postage and a given number of wrappers or box tops. Others were premiums for renewing a subscription to a magazine or newspaper. A large number were advertising items created for a store or company and had calendars on the front or back. Many people believe that the only true yard-long print is 36 inches long and titled "A Yard of Kittens," etc. But lately collectors feel that any long and narrow print, horizontal or vertical, can be included in this category. It is a matter of personal opinion.

Values are listed for full-length prints in near-mint condition, nicely framed, and with original glass.

References: C. G. and J. M. Rhoden and W. D. and M. J. Keagy, *Those Wonderful Yard-Long Prints and More*, Book 1 (1989), Book 2 (1992), Book 3 (1995), published by authors (605 No. Main, Georgetown, IL 61846).

Reproduction Alert: Some prints are being reproduced. Know your dealer.

Advisers: Charles G. and Joan M. Rhoden, and W. D. and M. J. Keagy.

Note: Numbers in parentheses below indicate the Rhoden and Keagy book number and page on which the item is illustrated, e.g. (3-52) refers to Book 3, page 52.

Animals

A Happy Family, #1037, copyright 1904, third in series, nine monkeys playing and relaxing (Bk 3-24) . . **400.00**

At the North Pole, copyright 1904, Jos. Hoover & Son, Philadelphia (Bk 2-29) **350.00**

Four kittens climbing tree, Helena Maguire (Bk 3-23) **350.00**

In Sunny Africa, #1038, copyright 1904, Jos. Hoover & Son, Philadelphia (Bk 3-28) **450.00**

Kittens with mother, eight kittens, one reading book, one playing with spool (Bk 2-25) **275.00**

Yard of Dogs, copyright 1903, eight dogs, one with bird in mouth, one with bandage on head covering eye (Bk 2-21) **300.00**

Calendar

1906, Pabst Extract, Indian, by C. W. Henning, "Hiawatha's Wooing" poem on back of print (Bk 2-101) **500.00**

1909, Pabst Malt Extract, Rose Girl, calendar at bottom (Bk 3-57) . . . **400.00**

1910, Clay, Robinson & Co., American Beauty Souvenir, adv and calendar on front, (Bk 3-44) **450.00**

1914, Pabst, American Girl, lady in full-length gown, muted shades of tangerine, yellow, and green (Bk 1-17) **400.00**

Sweet Peas, Book 1-52, **$250.** *Photo courtesy of Joy Luke Auctions.*

1915, Pompeian, lovely lady with handsome young man, grandfather clock in background (Bk 1-23) . **325.00**

1916, Pompeian, by Forbes, sgd "Sincerely, Mary Pickford," Mary in pale blue dress, seated, holding daisy in her hands (Bk 1-25) **400.00**

1918, American Farming Magazine, sgd "W. H. Lister," lady in light gray and pale yellow dress, parasol, carrying basket of flowers (Bk 1-9) **400.00**

1929, Seiz Good Shoes, sgd "Earl Chambers," calendar at bottom (Bk 2-85) **350.00**

Children

A Shower of Roses, copyright 1893, child at top spilling roses to child at bottom catching them in her apron (Bk 3-99) **400.00**

A Yard of Kids, black and white, 11 stages of "hatching" (Bk 3-121) **300.00**

Cupid's Festival, copyright by Art Interchange Co. of New York (Bk 3-109) **375.00**

Easter Greetings, copyright 1894 by Knopp Co., Paul DeLongpre (Bk 3-107) **425.00**

Morning Glories, copyright 1892 by Mast, Crowell & Kirkpatrick, Springfield, Ohio, Maud Humphrey (Bk 2-105) **400.00**

Flowers and fruits

A Yard of Baby's Breath & Roses (Bk 1-52) **275.00**

A Yard of Chrysanthemums, Maud Stumm (Bk 2-33) **250.00**

Carnations, Grace Barton Allen (Bk 2-30) **250.00**

Chrysanthemums, C. Klein (Bk 2-34) **250.00**

Dogwood and Violets, Paul DeLongpre (Bk 3-28) **300.00**

Yard of Cherries and Flowers, LeRoy (Bk 2-70) **250.00**

Yard of Roses, V. Janus, copyright by Perry Mason & Co. (Bk 2-51) . . **250.00**

Long ladies

Clay, Robinson & Co., Live stock Commission by R. Ford Harper, 1914, beautiful lady in sailor outfit, holding blue trimmed straw hat (Bk 3-47) **375.00**

Lady in wide brim hat, seated with dog at her knees, 1916, sgd "H. Dirch," The Clay Robinson & Co. Army of Employees shown on back (Bk 2-91) **350.00**

Lady on balcony, facing moon lit waters, flowers in her hand (Bk 2-89) **300.00**

Lovely lady in long pale blue dress, seated, holding fan in her gloved hand, roses at her feet (Bk 3-96) **500.00**

Lovely lady in red dress, seated in chair, carved lion's heads on chair arms, several roses at her feet (Bk 2-87) **350.00**

Pompeian Art Panel, titled "Irresistable," by Clement Donshea, dated 1930, lovely blond lady, handsome young man, rose garden (Bk 3-63) **350.00**

Stockman Bride, for National Stockman and Farmer magazine, dated 1911, beautiful dark haired lady in floor length white gown, holding long stem red roses (Bk 3-53) **450.00**

The Girl with the Laughing Eyes, copyright 1910 by F. Carlyle, lady in long off-shoulder gown, holding paper lantern (Bk 2-92) **300.00**

Walk-Over Shoe Co., pretty girl dressed in cowgirl outfit, standing behind tree where she has carved "Walk-Over" (Bk 1-47) **450.00**

YELLOWWARE

History: Yellowware is a heavy earthenware which varies in color from a rich pumpkin to lighter shades, which are more tan than yellow. The weight and strength varies from piece to piece. Although plates, nappies, and custard cups are found, kitchen bowls and other cooking utensils are most prevalent.

The first American yellowware was produced at Bennington, Vermont. English yellowware has additional ingredients which make its body much harder. Derbyshire and Sharp's were foremost among the English manufacturers.

References: Susan and Al Bagdade, *Warman's American Pottery and Porcelain*, 2nd ed., Krause Publications, 2000; William C. Ketchum, Jr., *American Pottery and Porcelain*, Avon Books, 1994; Joan Leibowitz, *Yellow Ware*, Schiffer Publishing, 1985, 1993 value update; Lisa S. McAllister, *Collector's Guide to Yellow Ware*, Collector Books, 1996, 2000 value update; Lisa S. McAllister and John L. Michael, *Collecting Yellow Ware*, Collector Books, 1993.

Bank, 3-5/8" h, house shape, molded detail highlighted in black, roof marked "For My Dear Girl," firing crack at chimney **660.00**

Bean pot, cov, 6-1/2" h, three white slip accent bands, bands repeated on orig matching lid, relief lines on both, Watt pottery logo on base, orig lid has been broken and reglued, bowl has some staining from use **165.00**

Bowl, 13" d, 6" h, two wide white accent bands **165.00**

Canister, 7" d, 9-3/4" d, barrel shape, raised rings, running blue, green, and brown glaze, white label with "Meal," no lid, hairline **140.00**

Creamer

3-7/8" h, black stripes, white band, green seaweed dec, hairline at base of handle **165.00**

4-3/4" h, brown stripes, white band, blue seaweed dec, shallow flake on inside edge of table ring **440.00**

Figure, 12" h, seated spaniel, open front feet design, attributed to Bennington factory, Rockingham glaze, c1850, few minor glaze flakes on base **275.00**

Flask, 11" x 6", fish shape . . . **1,000.00**

Food mold

3-3/4" d, 1-1/4" h, miniature, Yellow Rock, Phila mark **185.00**

7-1/2" d, 2-3/4" h, turk's head. **145.00**

Jar, 3-1/2" h, three blue band accent bands, "Spices" in relief on front, reeded relief design around base, imp mold mark #118 on bottom, stained from use **190.00**

Measure, 5-3/4" h, 6-1/2" d, Spearpoint & Trellis **300.00**

Mug, 3" h, flared sides, white slip dec **150.00**

Nappy

9-1/2" d, 2-3/4" h, applied copper luster design in Pennsylvania-style floral design, c1860, very light 1" hairline extending from rim, overall wear to copper luster at int. rim **275.00**

10" d, Jeffords blue diamond mark **225.00**

Pepper pot, 4-1/2" h, blue seaweed dec, band dec **475.00**

Pie funnel, 2-1/2" h, unmarked . **125.00**

Pitcher, decorated with three panels of black transfer depicting Faith, Hope, and Charity, silver luster banding, 6-1/2" h, $785. Photo courtesy of Sanford Alderfer Auction Co.

Pie plate, 10" d, unmarked **90.00**

Rolling pin, wood handles, adv **125.00**

Spittoon, 8" d, Rockingham glaze, overall relief vine pattern **30.00**

Syllabub cub, 3" h **125.00**

Teapot, 5" h, applied brown/green sponged glaze, orig lid, small glaze flake **110.00**

Wash board, 5" w, 12" l, mottled Rockingham glaze, c1880, wooden frame with dry worn surface . . . **615.00**

Wash bowl and pitcher, 9-1/2" d bowl, 7-3/4" h pitcher, brown and blue sponged dec, brown stripe on pitcher **335.00**

ZANE POTTERY

History: In 1921, Adam Reed and Harry McClelland bought the Peters and Reed Pottery in Zanesville, Ohio. The firm continued production of garden wares and introduced several new art lines: Sheen, Powder Blue, Crystalline, and Drip. The factory was sold in 1941 to Lawton Gonder.

Reference: Jeffrey, Sherrie, and Barry Hersone, *Peters and Reed and Zane Pottery Experience*, published by authors, 1990.

Additional Listings: Gonder, and Peters and Reed.

Jardiniere and pedestal base, green matte glaze, artist signed "Frank Ferreau," 34" h, $375.

Bowl

5" d, brown and blue **45.00**
6-1/2" d, blue, marked "Zanesware"
. . . . **35.00**
Figure, 10-1/8" h, cat, black, green eyes **500.00**
Jardiniere, 34" h, green matte glaze, matching pedestal, artist sgd "Frank Ferreu" **375.00**
Vase

5" h, green, cobalt blue drip glaze
. . . . **30.00**
7" h, flowing medium green over dark forest green ground . . . **85.00**
8" h, ivory glaze, emb flowers and leaves **75.00**

ZANESVILLE POTTERY

LA MORO

History: Zanesville Art Pottery, one of several potteries located in Zanesville, Ohio, began

production in 1900. At first, a line of utilitarian products was made; art pottery was introduced shortly thereafter. The major line was La Moro, which was hand painted and decorated under glaze. The firm was bought by S. A. Weller in 1920 and became known as Weller Plant No. 3.

Marks: The impressed block-print mark "La Moro" appears on the high-glazed and matte-glazed decorated ware.

References: Louise and Evan Purviance and Norris F. Schneider, *Zanesville Art Pottery in Color*, Mid-America Book Company, 1968; Evan and Louise Purviance, *Zanesville Art Tile in Color*, Wallace-Homestead, 1972, out-of-print.

Bowl, 6-1/2" d, fluted edge, mottled blue glaze **45.00**
Jardiniere

7-1/8" h, 8-1/2" d, waisted cylindrical form, landscape scene, blue, green, and maroon matte glaze, c1908 . . . . **175.00**
8-1/4" h, ruffled rim, cream to light amber peony blossoms, shaded brown ground **75.00**
Plate, 4-1/2" d, applied floral dec **25.00**
Vase

8" h, mottled green matte glaze
. . . . **150.00**
8-3/4" h, cone shaped top, bulbous base, La Morro, marked "2/802/4"
. . . . **350.00**
10-1/4" h, light gray horse portrait, light olive green to blue-green ground, matte ext., glossy brown int., sgd "R. G. Turner" **825.00**

ZSOLNAY POTTERY

History: Vilmos Zsolnay (1828-1900) assumed control of his brother's factory in Pécs, Hungary, in the mid-19th century. In 1899, Miklos, Vilmos's son, became manager. The firm still produces ceramic ware.

The early wares are highly ornamental, glazed, and have a cream-colored ground. Eosin glaze, a deep rich play of colors reminiscent of Tiffany's iridescent wares, received a gold medal at the 1900 Paris exhibition. Zsolnay Art Nouveau pieces show great creativity.

Reference: Susan and Al Bagdade, *Warman's English & Continental Pottery & Porcelain*, 3rd ed., Krause Publications, 1998; Federico Santi and John Gacher, *Zsolnay Ceramics: Collecting a Culture*, Schiffer Publishing, 1998.

Internet Resource: *The Online Zsolnay Tile Museum*, http://www.drawrm.com.

Marks: Originally, no trademark was used; but in 1878 the company began to use a blue mark depicting the five towers of the cathedral at Pécs. The initials "TJM" represent the names of Miklos's three children.

Note: Zsolnay's recent series of iridescent-glazed figurines, which initially were inexpensive, now are being sought by collectors and steadily increasing in value.

Vase, La Moro, bulbous, cone top and neck, two handles, marked, 8-3/4" h, $315.

Bowl, 6-1/2" l, 2-1/2" h, sea shell shape, hp florals, gold highlights and edging, blue mark "Zsolnay Pecs," castle mark, "Patent," imp factory mark and numbers
. . . . **160.00**

Cache pot, 13" d, young girls dance holding hands around stylized tree form, blue, pale silver, and pale lilac glazes. **4,250.00**

Chalice, 6" h, four flower stems as handles attached to upper body, flowers and berries in relief as terminals, green and blue Eosin glazes, red int., form #5668, c1899, millennium factory mark, ext. rim chip repaired
. . . . **1,650.00**

Coffee set, 8-1/2" h cov coffeepot, creamer, sugar, cake plate, six cups, saucers, and dessert plates, cobalt blue and gold trim, white ground
. . . . **600.00**

Figure, iridescent green-gold, marked "Made in Hungry, Zsolnay," and castle mark, 6-1/4" h, $250.

Compote, 11" d, ribbed, four caryatids molded as angels supports, blue-green irid glaze **1,100.00**

Creamer, 6-1/2" l, fierce dragon handle, repair to handle **185.00**

Ewer, 8" d, 8-1/4" h, c1920, minor repair at base of handle **295.00**

Figure

Bears, pair, emerald green glaze, 7-1/2" l, 5" h **695.00**

Mallard ducks, 7" l, 7" h **195.00**

Nude, curled position, irid glaze, stamped "Zsolnay," incised #8, 10" l, 6" h **375.00**

Spaniel, artist sgd, 5" h **95.00**

Garden seat, 18-1/2" h, form #1105, c1882, wear to top surface, repairs to applied dec **1,850.00**

Jardiniere, 16" l, ovoid, multicolored florals, protruding pierced roundels, cream ground, blue steep mark. **450.00**

Jug, 10-1/2" h, yellow glaze, worn gilt highlights, form #109, c1882 . . . **500.00**

Pitcher, 7-1/2" h, form #5064, red/maroon metallic Eosin ground, cream and pale brown flower dec, c1898, millennium factory mark . **750.00**

Puzzle jug, 6-1/2" h, pierced roundels, irid dec, cream ground, castle mark, imp "Zsolnay" **195.00**

Vase

3-3/4" h, all over hp flower and leaf design, red, cream and gold-green metallic Eosin glazes, sgd "Flora Nici," dated Nov. 14, 1923
. . . . **1,200.00**

4-1/4" h, form #2289, hand-drawn factory mark and name, c1882
. . . . **1,500.00**

8" h, four squared off handles, light blue glaze with speckled red glaze, painted gold designs on handles with yellow and turquoise elements, round raised mark, form #820, c1899-1920 . . . . **600.00**

9" h, tapering reeded baluster, gold and cobalt blue irid finish. . **225.00**

Wine flask, 6-1/2" h, relief dec, putty ground, c1902. . . . . **450.00**

Vessel, two-headed dragon, four legs, green, brown, gold, impressed mark, 7-3/4" h, 11-1/2" w, $225.

INDEX